Achieve for *Scientific American: Lifespan Development*: Setting the New Standard for Teaching and Learning

LearningCurve Adaptive Quizzing

Based on extensive learning and memory research, and proven effective for hundreds of thousands of students, LearningCurve focuses on the core concepts in every chapter, providing individualized question sets and feedback for correct and incorrect responses. The system adapts to each student's level of understanding, with follow-up quizzes targeting areas where the student needs improvement. Each question is tied to a learning objective and linked to the appropriate section of the e-book to encourage students to discover the right answer for themselves. LearningCurve has consistently been rated the #1 resource by instructors and students alike.

- LearningCurve's game-like quizzing promotes retrieval practice through its unique delivery of questions and its point system.

- Students with a firm grasp on the material get plenty of practice but proceed through the activity relatively quickly.

- Unprepared students are given more questions, therefore requiring that they do what they should be doing anyway if they're unprepared—practice some more.

- Instructors can monitor results for each student and the class as a whole, to identify areas that may need more coverage in lectures and assignments.

E-book

Macmillan Learning's e-book is an interactive version of the textbook that offers highlighting, bookmarking, and note-taking. Built-in, low-stakes self-assessments allow students to test their level of understanding along the way, and learn even more in the process thanks to the *testing effect*. Students can download the e-book to read offline, or to have it read aloud to them. Achieve allows instructors to assign chapter sections as homework.

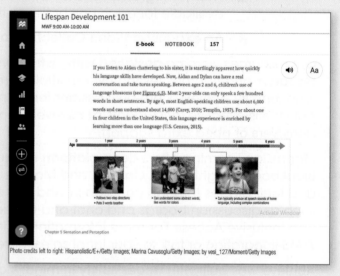

Test Bank

The Test Bank for *Scientific American: Lifespan Development* offers thousands of questions, all meticulously reviewed. Instructors can assign out-of-the-box exams or create their own by:

- Choosing from thousands of questions in our database.
- Filtering questions by type, topic, difficulty, and Bloom's level.
- Customizing multiple-choice questions.
- Integrating their own questions into the exam.

Exam/Quiz results report to a Gradebook that lets instructors monitor student progress individually and classwide.

Practice Quizzes

Practice Quizzes mirror the experience of a quiz or test, with questions that are similar but distinct from those in the test bank. Instructors can use the quizzes as is or create their own, selecting questions by question type, topic, difficulty, and Bloom's level.

Achieve for *Scientific American: Lifespan Development*:	Engaging Every Student

Achieve is designed to support and encourage active learning by connecting familiar activities and practices out of class with some of the most effective and approachable in-class activities, curated from a variety of active learning sources.

Scientific American Profile

Meet Kevin

Scientific American Profiles

These short video clips, central to this project, take readers into the homes of the children, families, and elders they meet in every chapter. In addition to providing context for the major concepts, these videos foster an emotional connection to the material that will stick with students.

Video Collection for Developmental Psychology

Development comes to life when you see babies taking their first steps or preschoolers participating in Piaget's conservation-of-mass task. This expansive collection is a broad curation of news clips, documentary footage, interviews with leading researchers, and more.

Accompanying assessment makes these videos assignable, with results reporting to the Achieve Gradebook. Our faculty and student consultants were instrumental in helping us create this diverse and engaging set of clips. All videos are closed-captioned and found only in **Achieve**.

Spotlight on Science

These interactive activities focus on high-interest studies, such as the effects of the media on body image in adolescence and the effect of social media on depression in late adulthood. They reinforce students' understanding of the steps of the scientific method, walking students through each study, honing critical thinking and scientific literacy skills by posing questions. Students view and interact with data, study stimuli, and are scaffolded through a discussion of the research approach, limitations, and conclusions.

Chapter 4: Physical and Cognitive Development in Infancy and Toddlerhood

Spotlight on Science

Using the Experimental Method to Fight Allergies

Learning Goals

- You will follow the steps of the experimental research design, from hypothesis through random assignment, treatment and control conditions.

Begin Activity

Jose Luis Pelaez Inc/Getty Images

Concept Practice Tutorials

Achieve includes dozens of these dynamic, interactive mini-tutorials that teach and reinforce the course's foundational ideas. Each of these brief activities (only 5 minutes to complete) addresses one or two key concepts, in a consistent format—review, practice, quiz, and conclusion.

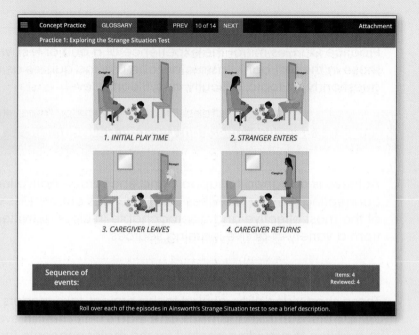

Instructor Activity Guides

Instructor Activity Guides provide instructors with a structured plan for using Achieve's active learning opportunities in both face-to-face and remote learning courses. Each guide offers step-by-step instructions—from pre-class reflection to in-class engagement to post-class follow-up. The guides include suggestions for discussion questions, group work, presentations, and simulations, with estimated class time, implementation effort, and Bloom's taxonomy level for each activity.

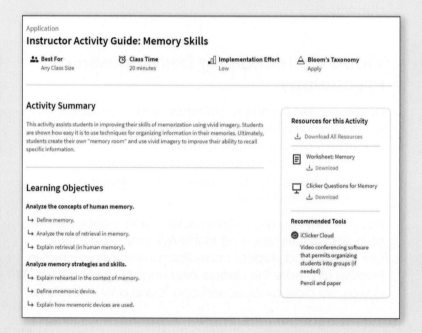

Developing Lives

Developing Lives provides a robust interactive experience in which users "raise" their own child from conception to adolescence. As the child grows, the student responds to events both planned and unforeseen, making important decisions (nutrition choices, doctor visits, sleeping location) and facing uncertain moments (illness, divorce, a new baby), with each choice affecting how the child grows. Each stage of development is accompanied by a quiz to help students apply the main concepts of the course to their experience as a virtual parent.

iClicker Classroom Response System

Achieve seamlessly integrates iClicker, Macmillan Learning's highly acclaimed classroom response system. iClicker can help make any classroom—in-person or virtual—more lively, engaging, and productive. Access to iClicker is included with Achieve at no additional cost.

- iClicker's attendance feature helps make sure students are actually attending in-person classes.
- Instructors can choose from flexible polling and quizzing options to engage students, check their understanding, and get their feedback in real time.
- iClicker allows students to participate using laptops, mobile devices, or in-class remotes.
- iClicker easily integrates instructors' existing slides and polling questions—there is no need to re-enter them.
- Instructors can take advantage of the questions in our Instructor Activity Guides and our book-specific questions within Achieve to improve the opportunities for all students to be active in class.

Achieve for *Scientific American: Lifespan Psychology*:   **Supporting Every Instructor**

Learning Objectives, Reports, and Insights

Content in Achieve is tagged to specific Learning Objectives, aligning the coursework with the textbook and with the APA Learning Goals and Outcomes. Reporting within Achieve helps students see how they are performing against objectives, and it helps instructors determine if any student, group of students, or the class as a whole needs extra help in specific areas. This enables more efficient and effective instructor interventions.

Achieve provides reports on student activities, assignments, and assessments at the course level, unit level, subunit level, and individual student level, so instructors can identify trouble spots and adjust their efforts accordingly. Within Reports, the Insights section offers snapshots with high-level data on student performance and behavior, to answer such questions as:

- What are the top Learning Objectives to review in this unit?
- What are the top assignments to review?
- What's the range of performance on a particular assignment?
- How many students aren't logging in?

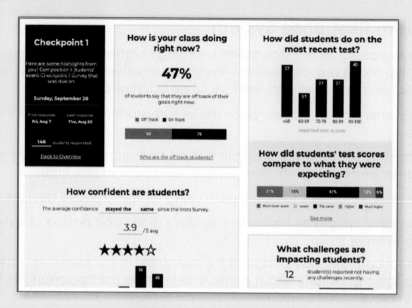

Achieve's **Innovation Lab** offers surveys that help students self-direct, and develop confidence in, their own learning:

- The **Intro Survey** asks students to consider their goals for the class and how they plan to manage their time and learning strategies.

- **Checkpoint surveys** ask students to reflect on what's been working and where they need to make changes.

- **Each completed survey generates a report** that reveals how each student is doing, beyond the course grade.

These tools help instructors engage their students in a discussion on soft skills, such as metacognition, effective learning and time management strategies, and other noncognitive skills that impact student success.

Additional Instructor Resources in Achieve: All Within One Place

Image Slides and Tables

Presentation slides feature chapter illustrations and tables and can be used as is or customized to fit an instructor's needs. Alt text for images is available upon request via WebAccessibility@Macmillan.com

Lecture Slides

Accessible, downloadable presentation slides provide support for key concepts and themes from the text, and can be used as is or customized to fit an instructor's needs.

Customer Support

Our Achieve Client Success Team—dedicated platform experts—provides collaboration, software expertise, and consulting to tailor each course to fit your instructional goals and student needs. Start with a demo at a time that works for you to learn more about how to set up your customized course. Talk to your sales representative or visit www.MacmillanLearning.com/College/US/Contact-Us /Training-and-Demos for more information.

Pricing and bundling options are available at the Macmillan Student Store: Store.MacmillanLearning.com

Scientific American:
LIFESPAN DEVELOPMENT

Executive Vice President and General Manager, Content Strategy: Charles Linsmeier
Vice President, Social Sciences & High School: Shani Fisher
Executive Program Manager: Daniel DeBonis
Senior Development Editor: Andrea Musick Page
Associate Development Editor: Nick Rizzuti
Assistant Editor: Allison Curley
Executive Marketing Manager: Katherine Nurre
Marketing Assistant: Claudia Cruz
Senior Market Development Manager: Stephanie Ellis
Executive Media Editor: Laura Burden
Executive Director, Digital Workflow Strategy: Noel Hohnstine
Assistant Media Editor: Clarah Grossman
Senior Director, Content Management Enhancement: Tracey Kuehn
Senior Managing Editor: Lisa Kinne
Senior Content Project Manager: Peter Jacoby
Lead Media Project Manager: Joseph Tomasso
Senior Workflow Supervisor: Jennifer Wetzel
Senior Photo Editor: Sheena Goldstein
Photo Researcher: Jennifer Atkins
Director of Design, Content Management: Diana Blume
Senior Design Services Manager: Natasha A. S. Wolfe
Senior Cover Designer: John Callahan
Interior Design: Studio Montage and Lumina Datamatics, Inc.
Art Manager: Matthew McAdams
Illustrations: Lumina Datamatics, Inc., Eli Ensor, Matthew McAdams
Composition: Lumina Datamatics, Inc.
Printing and Binding: Lakeside Book Company
Icon Credits: aslann/Shutterstock, johavel/Shutterstock, Ermin13/Shutterstock, Pro Symbols/Shutterstock,
    Kirill Mlayshev/Shutterstock
Brief Contents and Contents photos: © Macmillan, Photo by Sidford House

Library of Congress Control Number: 2022932034
ISBN-13: 978-1-319-06244-6
ISBN-10: 1-319-06244-X

Printed in the United States of America
1   2   3   4   5   6   27   26   25   24   23   22

Worth Publishers
120 Broadway
New York, NY 10271
www.macmillanlearning.com

ABOUT THE AUTHORS

Scientific American: Lifespan Development has united experienced classroom teachers and highly respected researchers Allison Sidle Fuligni and Andrew J. Fuligni with writer and producer Jessica Bayne. As developmental scientists with a deep love for the nitty-gritty of research and theory, Andrew and Allison share a deep desire to make sure that this science makes it out into the world to improve lives.

Allison is a professor in the Department of Child and Family Studies at California State University, Los Angeles, and teaches development every semester. She has spent much of her research career focused on understanding and improving the environments where young children develop, at the Columbia University National Center for Children and Families, the UCLA Center for Improving Child Care Quality, and at California State University, Los Angeles. She was involved with several longitudinal studies of children's development, including the Los Angeles Exploring Children's Early Learning Settings and the National Early Head Start Research and Evaluation Project. Allison received her Ph.D. from the University of Michigan.

Andrew is a professor in the Departments of Psychiatry and Biobehavioral Sciences and Psychology at University of California, Los Angeles, where he teaches courses on child and adolescent development. He also directs the Adolescent Development Lab at UCLA and is co-executive director of the UCLA Center for the Developing Adolescent, which is dedicated to improving the health and well-being of young people through the translation and dissemination of developmental science. He has published extensively on the sociocultural experience and biobehavioral development during adolescence and young adulthood, with a focus on young people from Latin American, Asian, European, and immigrant backgrounds. Andrew has received numerous awards for his teaching and research and is a former associate editor of the journal *Child Development*. Like Allison, he received his Ph.D. at the University of Michigan.

Jessica is a writer, editor, and producer who has been creating videos and media content for college courses for more than 20 years. She has collaborated with leading researchers and educators and led the development of a wide array of products for higher education. Jessica's approach is grounded in her own experiences working in nursing homes, coaching theater, and raising four children.

Anwar Torres

Anwar Torres

Ella Ryan

BRIEF CONTENTS

CONTENTS

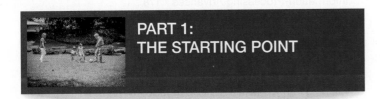
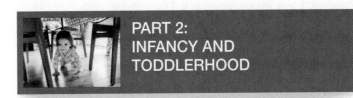

**PART 3:
EARLY CHILDHOOD**

**PART 4:
MIDDLE CHILDHOOD**

**PART 5:
ADOLESCENCE**

PART 6:
EARLY ADULTHOOD

PART 7:
MIDDLE ADULTHOOD

PART 8:
LATE ADULTHOOD

Chapter 16 Physical and Cognitive Development in Late Adulthood 461

Chapter 17 Social and Emotional Development in Late Adulthood 496

Epilogue:
The End of Life

PREFACE

Welcome! This project is inspired by the idea that developmental science can change lives for the better. Sometimes information can provide inspiration: changing how we work, investigate phenomena on our own, or advocate for others in our community. At other times, science provides us with reassurance: Maybe it is relieving to know that, yes, most 4-year-olds are full of energy and enjoy jumping on the couch. Or, that many parents wonder whether they are doing enough for their children and many adults complain about their partner's cell phones. Or, that most everyday forgetfulness is not a sign of impending cognitive impairment.

At its heart, developmental science combines a long tradition of rigorous scientific research with advocacy designed to support well-being. We know from our own teaching experience (and our own learning experiences when we were in college) that this class can change lives, and empirical research supports this: The classes we take in school can indeed make us kinder and more prosocial adults (Harrell-Levy & Kerpelman, 2015). This course also enables us to explain how science itself works. Understanding science better can help us think critically about research, evaluate empirical evidence for claims, and understand how what we know changes over time.

Developmental science is a subject we love to teach and share with others, whether in the classroom or through conversations around our own dinner table. One of the reasons we love teaching this course is that developmental science is relevant to everyone. In this project, we take full advantage of this inherent relatability by sharing the science that addresses our curiosity about the world. Why is learning to move so hard, yet so important, for infants? What are skills that can help young adults land a job? Do children who experience early trauma carry emotional scars for a lifetime? Is your personality set at birth? Is there a secret to living to 100? Psychologists find that making the material relevant does not just keep the conversation going after class is over: It helps everyone think more deeply and retain the material.

This is an exciting time in developmental science, with new innovations that strengthen communities and bolster our resilience. Scientists are now able to connect understanding of the brain and the biology of development with our social and cultural

Interventions That Work Throughout this book, you will see examples of ways that developmental science helps build on people's strengths. For example, these parents benefited from a group prenatal health program, Centering Pregnancy, that helps leverage the power of social bonds to improve pregnancy outcomes. They enjoyed the program so much they returned to introduce their babies after they were born.

Meet Some of the Family You will meet Olivia (*left*), learning yoga as she adjusts to pre-K in Chapter 6. Doug and Stephanie (*right*) will share the unvarnished truth about middle age in Chapter 15 (hint: it is not for the faint of heart).

context in new ways. Applications of developmental knowledge in child care, schools, and health care, among other arenas, demonstrate that science can make an impact. Developmental science can transform how we work, care for each other, and grow, which is what inspired us to write a textbook that brings all of this into the classroom.

Developmental science is not just about facts and scholarly research: It is also about people. To tell its story, our team has traveled around the United States to find the 17 children, adolescents, and adults (and their families) who have shared their lives with us. We tracked down professionals in fields from architecture to art, library science to literacy promotion, who describe how developmental science has changed how they work. As a result, each chapter includes a profile of a family both in text and on video and a professional in the field in our *Science in Practice* features.

Over the years, our work has given us the honor of getting to know a variety of families. We have been privileged to share the birth of Alizah and Spencer's first child, Courage, and to cheer for Telele as she learns to say her first words in Inupiaq and in English. We have rooted for Jesús as he finishes yet another mural as well as the eleventh grade. We have shared the joy (if not the sweat) of a midlife mini-marathon with Sandra. And we have shed tears with Bart as he plans for life with a diagnosis of Alzheimer disease. The stories that appear in every chapter, along with the photographs and videos, come from communities across the United States, from Alaska to Florida, and are one way that we have tried to make developmental science memorable.

Key Approaches

In this project, we employ five major strategies for sharing content: (1) stories of real people; (2) inclusive coverage of individuals and families; (3) accessible treatment of current science; (4) a strengths-based perspective; and (5) a focus on skills that will help students in their future careers and personal lives.

Storytelling You Will Remember

Scientific American: Lifespan Development presents students with vivid stories of individuals and families. Within our own classes, we talk about real people each day. We talk about our families in class (and even feature them in clicker questions). We bring in guest speakers, from neuroscientists to clinicians who work hands-on with families. When we run into former students or read their course evaluations, we find that those personal stories stick with them.

Contemporary learning science supports our anecdotal experiences: When students have a personal, emotional connection to what they learn, they remember it better and have an easier time applying it (Landrum et al., 2019). Stories even help us relate better to the scientists and theorists who have shaped the field. Drawing on the science of teaching and learning, we know that people relate more to stories of famous people when we emphasize their personal stories, how their successes were not inevitable, and how they surmounted obstacles of their own on their way to being prominent names in a textbook (Lin-Siegler et al., 2016). Therefore, you will learn not just that John Watson is credited with popularizing the science of behaviorism, but also that he was in trouble with the law in high school and needed quarts of Coca-Cola to get through his exams (Moore, 2017).

As we have described, each chapter of this book tells the story of a child or adult and their family in the text and in the accompanying online videos. These include 10-year-old Amara from Los Angeles, who has already helped to write a number of songs and a book, and 24-year-old Hiroki, who was adjusting to marriage and her job as a school counselor in Connecticut during the COVID-19 pandemic. These stories and video profiles help students see the challenges and opportunities of each life stage: We think we remember what it was like to be 10, but the video of Amara reminds us what it is *really* like, for someone whose life experience is different from our own.

In addition, in our *Science in Practice* sections, you will be introduced to 17 professionals who share their personal experiences of how developmental science has made a difference in their lives. You will learn about Nicolle Gonzalez, C.N.M., a midwife, who incorporates Indigenous traditions into pregnancy and postpartum care for women near the Diné reservation in New Mexico and Justine Ann Fonte, a teacher who works with children to help them understand and talk about sexuality and gender.

Inclusive Coverage to Represent the Broad Contexts That Impact Development

Like many instructors, we have often struggled to explain to our students why their textbooks do not reflect their lives or families and describe a world that they often cannot relate to. Textbooks do not always reflect the broad variety of experiences that make up human development. We have always seen this course as a way of connecting people to the experiences of other human beings: Whether we are looking at the impact of urbanization on families in China or the stress of remote schooling for families in Chicago, understanding the impact of context to development is important. Throughout this book, you will find research from Ghana to Geneva and stories from families from Lhasa to Los Angeles.

Building from our experiences, this book casts a broad net over what *diversity* means. We set out to write a book that would better represent the diverse legacy of the science itself, the individuals and families we interview, and the current issues we discuss. We cover complex family structures, intersectional identities, and challenges faced by those who are affluent and those who are less well-off. One challenge for students is relating to people older than themselves: We find that our students quickly lose focus when talking about older adults. Our coverage of adulthood and aging provides a fresh perspective of the recent science on this dynamic part of the lifespan. We include topics that will inform and engage today's students, such as older-adult romance in the digital age and the benefits of an aging population to the environment and the community.

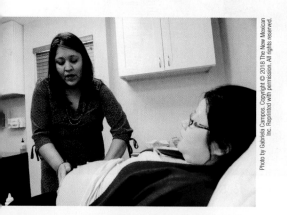

Science at Work Developmental science is not knowledge that stays in the classroom. It is information that enriches careers and lives outside of class. Portraits of professionals like Nicolle Gonzales (*top*), a midwife in New Mexico, and Heather Kosakowski, a researcher in neuroscience in Boston (*bottom*), appear in each chapter.

Developmental Science Changes Lives Whether it is an intervention to understand the strengths of Yazidi refugees (*left*) or to help migrant children adjust to life in the United States (*right*), developmental science can help identify effective practices to make things better.

This book includes the stories of people from diverse cultures, family configurations, health and abilities, and access to resources. In this way, we connect to students' own diverse experiences as well as enable them to stand in someone else's shoes. Students will be able to see themselves reflected in these pages, and also learn about populations that they may interact with one day, whether in the supermarket or on the job. Much of this coverage is not just abstract, but also practical: We try to model how to talk about differences and diversity throughout the book. For instance, there is in-depth discussion about what it means to talk about culture, race, and identity labels in Chapter 1. In Chapter 10, we talk about the impact of labels on body size and weight-related stigma. In Chapter 16, we present research about how to talk about age without being ageist.

We know from learning science that this is not just the right thing to do, but also an effective way of building student motivation (Byrd, 2016). However, we also know that we need to apply the principles of cultural humility to our own efforts (Abbott et al., 2019). Working closely with our colleagues at Macmillan Learning, we engaged with many expert reviewers and instructors to ensure that all students would feel represented in this text. Sensitivity reviewers read the manuscript word by word to ensure we were up to date on the most current ways to communicate inclusively. As a result of these efforts, we have written for a broad audience but acknowledge that we may not always get it quite right. Our aim is to make sure that people of all backgrounds and identities feel that this is a course where they belong.

Engaging and Current Science

We teach this course and chose to author this book because we find scientific research exciting and interesting. One of the biggest challenges we faced while writing each chapter was in deciding which concepts and topics to omit, many of which we thought students would love to know: Could we have more on glia? Could we squeeze in another example of adolescent activism? What about more theoretical coverage of cultural variations in the acceptance of diversity? What about post-pandemic mental health? We have tried to limit ourselves to what students can realistically get through in a semester, while continuing to share our enthusiasm.

One of our goals is to make developmental science engaging and accessible, as well as to explain the value of science as a discipline. In the spirit of *Scientific American* magazine, this brings the excitement of important breakthroughs in science using language that anyone can understand. You will find the latest science on

Joy of Science Developmental scientists studied the effects of early education on children's lives in Brazil: helping build evidence that children, like this little girl, benefit from early opportunities.

glia's role in brain maturation in Chapter 16 and the benefits of young people's community involvement in Chapter 11. You will see our excitement about science in the visual program, as well: in the infographics about brain development (see Brain Development in Early Childhood on page 165) and about the impact of context on development (see Contexts of Early Adulthood on page 397). Brief descriptions of current research that inspires us appears in marginal *Share It!* features, designed to encourage students to look beyond the text and delve into the research themselves. Online *Spotlight on Science* activities walk students through current and classic scientific work, from Harlow's research on attachment to empirical tests of intervention research in late life. Throughout, we share our curiosity about developmental research. From epigenetics to executive function, you will find cutting-edge science on every page.

A Strengths-Based Perspective

We teach and do research in developmental science because we believe that science is a tool to support well-being in development and break barriers that may limit our growth. Although the world is full of challenges, we want students to view developmental science as a source of solutions that help and empower people throughout all stages of life. Throughout the book, we highlight how to boost resilience and promote positive developmental practices.

A focus on the unique strengths and resilience found in all communities enhances our discussions of challenges and disparities. We incorporate the most current research so that students have the tools they need to make the world a better place for themselves and for others. You will find many major sections that include examples of empirical interventions, from home visiting to tutoring for college students, that have been shown to improve lives. We focus on applications as well as abstraction. For instance, you can read about an intervention that supports early language development on page 131 or that identifies risk factors for suicide on page 340 or that highlights jobs of the future on page 430.

Building Skills

In addition to making developmental science accessible and relevant, as educators we aim to build lasting skills people can use in the real world. Among the most important are critical thinking and scientific literacy to help everyone navigate a world full of information. Many development textbooks introduce the scientific method in the introductory chapters and then never address it again.

We revisit the design and conduct of research in the text, in figures that highlight specific results and in special features. In Chapters 9 and 17, for instance, we examine issues of experimental versus correlational studies. In Chapter 15, we explore sample bias in research about the midlife crisis. In Chapter 16, we acknowledge where research is still incomplete in our understanding of how to prevent cognitive decline.

We also demonstrate how to interpret multiple claims and news stories that we encounter every day. Scientific literacy involves learning how to read and interpret graphs, tables, and figures—skills that are addressed throughout the book. Scientific literacy also means being able to communicate about science, which means being able to use appropriate terms to talk about everything from social categories to age stages.

Part of thinking like a scientist means confronting ideas that may run counter to our own upbringing or experience, whether that is research about how to feed a baby or what types of support help children learning to read. One of the joys of developmental science is that it covers topics that are personal and often connected to our lived experiences, so prepare to disagree! Scientific thinking also demands that we master a great deal of vocabulary in order to communicate effectively. Some of these terms

Paul J. Richards/AFP via Getty Images

Persevering for the Win The girls' robotics team from Afghanistan impressed the world in 2018 with their strong showing in international competition. Years later, they have been trying to solve new problems: Some have developed cost-effective ventilators and sanitizing devices to help during the COVID-19 pandemic. Others have left Afghanistan and are adjusting to a new life in Mexico and Qatar.

may be new and unfamiliar, and, although we have tried to make it accessible, some specialized terminology may be difficult. For people who are new to these concepts, please stick with it. We hear from most of our students that after the first few weeks of the course, things get easier, more concrete, and more relevant to everyday life and your future career. Thinking about your goals and knowing how typical it is for course material to seem rigorous, can help you persist (Binning et al., 2020).

Integrated Features

We have integrated a set of highlighted sections into this project to spotlight key aspects of developmental science and build critical-thinking skills.

- *Can You Believe It?* features embedded in every chapter present a controversial topic or common myth in the field and ask readers to unpack the evidence. Each section examines study designs, identifies author biases, and searches for outsized claims in the context of high-interest topics, such as whether mobile apps have changed dating (page 388), or whether knowing your time is limited makes you more aware of what is important (page 506).
- *Making a Difference* features present the important work and interventions from developmental science that promote well-being in the lives of children, adolescents, and adults. For example, we cover how science is changing attitudes about spanking (page 212), how research on the long-term effects of concussions is making sports safer in high school (page 305), and how culturally appropriate interventions support marriage (page 445).
- *Science in Practice* features profile people from a variety of professions who use developmental science at work, such as pre-K teacher Johnathon Hines from Atlanta, Georgia (page 44), who applies the charisma that once helped him on the basketball court to teach phonics. Or robotics engineer Randi Williams from Cambridge, Massachusetts (page 174), who applies lessons from Piaget to designing interactive machines for children. These profiles introduce a variety of potential careers and help explain how research informs the world of work in diverse professions including teaching, nursing, medicine, criminal justice, case work, child care, and neuroscience.

Developmental Science in the Real World Johnathan Hines (*left*) is an award-winning pre-K teacher in Georgia: and a role model. Randi Williams (*right*) studies how children interact with technology to help design robots.

The World Is Changing Whether it is war in Ukraine or a global pandemic, lives are constantly in flux. Highlighting strength-based interventions helps identify ways we can all develop more resilience to adjust to the constancy of change.

- ***Learn It Together*** are interactive group activities that appear in every chapter (including this preface). One of many lessons from the pandemic is that it can be beneficial to learn in a group; sometimes there is no better way to learn than with others. From asking students to role play parent–adolescent conflict or parenting style, to assignments that analyze ageism in the media, these engaging activities will help students take their learning to the next level.

- ***Share It!*** callouts in the margins address practical and high-interest topics to hook students into the more abstract material, but also to provide information useful for their own lives and careers. They answer some of the practical questions students have on topics such as health and wellness. For example, what does science tell us about how to soothe an inconsolable baby? What are ways developmental scientists have helped young adults find a job with meaning—and a good salary?

- **Innovative figures and photographs that teach** We employ the latest approaches to visualizing data that *Scientific American* uses to make science clear and accessible to a popular audience. Every chapter also integrates infographics that are designed to visually reinforce the material in the text itself. Graphics review the chronology of major events in development (see Figure 7.8 on page 220) and integrate various theories of development (see Infographic 2.1 on page 48). We know that brain and biological development is often challenging to visualize, so infographics bring together what we know about brain development in every age stage. Context is also important to development, so each age stage includes a diagram showing the factors that promote resilience and risk, including special coverage of the impact technology and the environment have on development around the world.

Interactive Features

We take full advantage of online learning tools to enhance the learning process and give students real-time feedback. We have worked closely with a group of video producers, visionary content providers, and the capable team at Macmillan Learning to pull together materials for you to use in your course that we have used in our own teaching.

- ***Scientific American Profiles*** are the short video clips that are so central to this project. These videos reflect the families that we talk about in every chapter: They take readers into the homes of the children and adults. In addition to providing context for the major concepts, these videos foster an emotional connection to the material that will stick with students.

- ***Spotlight on Science*** activities focus on studies we found particularly interesting and wanted to take more time with. We wrote these activities to walk students through scientific studies, focusing on the nitty-gritty of research and highlighting its methodology. Students will examine and interpret data, reinforce scientific concepts, and make meaningful connections to chapter content, whether the topic relates to an in-depth discussion of the impact of age on happiness in Chapter 1 or an analysis of the experimental method as used to understand childhood allergies for Chapter 4.

- For the first time, the popular *Concept Practice* **tutorials** by Thomas Ludwig (Hope College) are available for lifespan development. These short activities enable students to practice their understanding of more than 50 important concepts in less than 5 minutes each.
- The *Video Collection for Human Development* is an extensive archive of over 200 video clips that covers the full range of the course and includes classic experiments, research footage, interviews, news clips, and more. This collection is newly updated with recent videos on cyberbullying, food insecurity, online dating, talking about race, body image, gender neutral parenting, and the effects of the COVID-19 pandemic on mental health and learning. Assign a video along with a short quiz with a few clicks or show the video in class. All Macmillan Learning videos are closed captioned and accompanied by a transcript to accommodate all learners.
- *Scientific American Library*. We have chosen more than 25 classic and contemporary *Scientific American* articles to supplement the book. Students can read Jean Piaget, Stella Thomas, and Alexander Chess in their own words: bringing science to live in a different way. Each article is accompanied by scaffolding and with a brief assessment.
- *Developing Lives* provides a robust interactive experience in which users "raise" their own child from conception to adolescence. As the child grows, the student responds to events both planned and unforeseen, making important decisions (nutrition choices, doctor visits, sleeping location) and facing uncertain moments (illness, divorce, a new baby), with each choice affecting how the child grows. The entire product has been revised and features new scenarios, including celebrating baby's first birthday, discovering cultural practices around losing baby teeth, and exploring rites of passage.

ACHIEVE for *Scientific American: Lifespan Development*

Achieve for *Scientific American: Lifespan Development* is a comprehensive online learning platform that makes it easy to integrate assessments, activities, and analytics into your teaching. Built from the ground up for today's learners, it includes an interactive e-book, LearningCurve adaptive quizzing, and all of the interactive features of *Scientific American: Lifespan Development*. Achieve can be integrated with all major LMS providers and meets a high level of web accessibility standards. See the very front of the text for more information about these engaging digital resources.

Additional Instructor Resources in Achieve: All in One Place

- The test bank was written specifically to match the content and learning outcomes of *Scientific American: Lifespan Development*. Authors Lora Garrison (Rogers State University), Carmon Weaver Hicks (Ivy Tech Community College), and Christine Park (California State University, Los Angeles) worked in consultation with the authors to craft an assessment package as carefully constructed as the book and media. In total, it comprises over 3,000 multiple-choice and essay items written at several levels of Bloom's taxonomy and tagged to the text's learning outcomes, the book page, the chapter section, and guidelines of the APA, NAEYC, and NCLEX.
- The Lecture Slides reimagine the content of the text for in-class presentation with abundant images, a concise presentation of the major points, and questions for discussion. Each presentation is also annotated with tips for teaching and other instructor resources to help build effective and engaging classroom experiences.

Also Available: Achieve Read & Practice

Achieve Read & Practice marries Macmillan Learning's mobile-accessible e-book with the acclaimed LearningCurve adaptive quizzing. Instructors can assign reading and quizzing easily, students can complete assignments on any device, and the cost is significantly less than that of a printed book. Find out more at http://macmillanlearning.com/readandpractice.

Thanks

Creating this project has taken many years and help from many, many instructors and students who shared with us what worked for them in the classroom. We are very appreciative for the candid feedback we have received from so many people who care about this course and getting accessible developmental science out into the world. These include:

Jacobose Victor Ammons, I., Kansas City Kansas Community College

Cheryl Anagnopoulos, Black Hills State University

Darlene Earley Andrews, Southern Union State Community College

Mary Ann Massoglia, Howard Community College

Sheryl Attig, Tri County Technical College

Karen Beck, Rio Hondo College

Or'Shaundra Benson, College of Dupage

Cassendra M. Bergstrom, University of Northern Colorado

Shannon Bert, University of Oklahoma Norman Campus

Jennifer A. Bradley, Northampton Community College — Monroe

Pamela Cole Bradley, Sandhills Community College

Catherine Brown, University of Nebraska-Lincoln

Laura Byers, Grand Rapids Community College

Kristine A. Camacho, Northwestern Connecticut Community College

L. Grant Canipe III, University of North Carolina — Chapel Hill

Lucy Capuano, Ventura College

Brandy S. Carter, Anne Arundel Community College

Deborah Caudell, Indiana University Bloomington

Erik Cheries, University of Massachusetts Amherst

Katie E. Cherry, Louisiana State University and Agricultural & Mechanical College

Chrystal Christman-Hennel, University of Cincinnati — Blue Ash

Alli Cipra, Governors State University

Lisa Daniel, East Texas Baptist University

Lauren Denver-Potter, Texas A & M University — Corpus Christi

Timothy W. Derifield, East Central College

Rebecca DesRoches, Regis College

Adebimpe Diji, Century Community and Technical College

Alicia Domack, Milwaukee School of Engineering

Jennifer Domila-McAvoy, University of South Carolina Lancaster

Kelley L. Drayer, University of South Alabama

Tracey M. Duck, Gwinnett Technical College

Mary Dwinnells, Kent State University at Trumbull

Milushka Elbulok-Charcape, Cuny Brooklyn College

Rebecca Escoto, North Lake College

Kerry Evans, Onondaga Community College

Robert B. Faux, Ulster County Community College

Diane Feibel, University of Cincinnati — Blue Ash

Victoria M. Ferrara, Mercy College and Marist College

Michael J. Figuccio, Farmingdale State College

Ross Flom, Southern Utah University

Kristin C. Flora, Franklin College

Claire Ford, Bridgewater State University

Allen Alexander Franchino, Essex County College

Darrell Frost, Northern Oklahoma College

Amanda Gabriele, Forsyth Technical Community College

Alice Ganzel, Cornell College

Tina Garrett, Holmes Community College — Grenada

John Geiger, Cameron University

Nathan R. George, Adelphi University

Jonathan Gibson, South Dakota School of Mines and Technology

Jerry Green, Tarrant County College NW

Gladys S. Green, State College of Florida Manatee Sarasota

James Guinee, University of Central Arkansas

Christina Halawa, Kankakee Community College

Amber J. Hammons, California State University Fresno

Julie B. Hanauer, Suffolk County Community College Ammerman

Jennifer Headrick, Augusta University

Lisa K. Hill, Rappahannock Community College

Brooke Hindman, Greenville Technical College

Elizabeth Hood, Nash Community College

Jessica Houser, West Shore Community College

Rachel Howard, East Central College

Kesong Hu, Lake Superior State University

Aimee Huard, Great Bay Community College

Anika Z. Hunter, Prince George's Community College

Sabra P. Jacobs, Holyoke Community College

Colette Jacquot, The University of Texas at Arlington

Aaron Jasso, Cerritos College

Kimberly Jayne, Portland State University

Benjamin Jeppsen, Augustana College

Wendi L. Johnson, Texas Woman's University

Rex Johnson, Delaware County Community College

Maegan E. Jones, Saint Cloud State University

David R. Jones, Holmes Community College

Deepti Karkhanis, Bellevue College

Linda Kieffer, Delgado Community College

Sonya Kitsko, Robert Morris University

Jennifer Knapp, Baton Rouge Community College

Rebekah Knight-Baughman, Colorado Christian University

Larry Kollman, North Iowa Area Community College

Dylan Kriescher, University of Northern Colorado

Michelle Kwok, Texas A&M University

Cindy J. Lahar, University of South Carolina Beaufort

Rachel Laimon, Mott Community College

Betsy Langness, Jefferson Community & Tech — Downtown

Candace Lapan, Wingate University

Julie Lazzara, Paradise Valley Community College

Marc D. Lee Sr., Prince George's Community College

Philip Lemaster, Concordia College at Moorhead

Noelle Lopez, Diablo Valley College

Megan G. Lorenz, Augustana College

Rebecca A. Lundwall, Brigham Young University — Provo

Lisa Maag, East Carolina University

Ivan L. Mancinelli-Franconi, Clackamas Community College

Carrie M. Margolin, The Evergreen State College

Tesia Marshik, University of Wisconsin La Crosse

Amanda L. Martens, Simpson College

Catherine Matson, Harper College

James R. May, Tulsa Community College SE

Kellie McCants-Price, Anne Arundel Community College

Steven M. McCloud, Cuny Borough of Manhattan Community College

Kristin McCombs, Wheeling Jesuit University

Jason McCoy, Cape Fear Community College

Donna Marie McElroy, Atlantic Cape Community College

R. M. McHugh, University of Pittsburgh Bradford

James McManus, Fulton Montgomery Community College

Amanda McPherson, Pima Community College

Alan Meca, Old Dominion University

A. Mehta, Providence College

Nan Metzger, Mount Mary College

Kristi Moore, Angelo State University

Suzanne Morrow, Old Dominion University

Elizabeth Moseley, Cleveland State Community College

Elizabeth A. Mosser, Harford Community College

Kristen Mudge, Jackson Community College

Ranell Mueller, Saint Francis University

Tonya Nascimento, University of West Florida

Laima Nauckunaite-Duru, University of Rhode Island

Teak Nelson, Truman State University

Angela Newbill, College of Dupage

Elina Newman, Southeast Community College Area

Diane Newsham, Central Piedmont Community College

Kristina Nguyen, Cerritos College

P. M. Nix, Lander University

Laura A. Oramas, Georgia Gwinnett College

Natasha Otto, Morgan State University

Cara A. Palmer, Montana State University

Maribeth Palmer-King, Suny Broome Community College

Eirini Papafratzeskakou, Mercer County Community College

Dax-Andrew Parcells, Palm Beach State College — Lake Worth

Jacqueline Parke, Vanguard University of Southern California

Kathy R. Phillippi-Immel, University of Wisconsin — Fox Valley

Pete Phipps, Dutchess Community College

Debbie Phythian, Assiniboine Community College

Jamie Piercy, The University of British Columbia — Okanagan Campus

Pamela Porter, Ashland Community and Technical College

Melanie Prasad-Dehaney, Gwinnett Technical College

Courtney Ray, Cuny Brooklyn College

Elif Angel Raynor, Palm Beach State College Boca Raton

William Reboli III, Wayne Community College

Kara M. Recker, Coe College

Maria Reid, Florida International University — Biscayne Bay Campus

Dawn Rodgers, Grace Bible College

Qu'Nesha Sawyer, California State University San Jose

Mary Schindler, California State University Sonoma

Tamara Schnepel, Kirkwood Community College

Derek Schorsch, Valencia College

H. Russell Searight, Lake Superior State University

Carla Mae Sewer, Texas Woman's University

Shubam Sharma, University of Florida

JoAnne Shayne, Southern New Hampshire University

Meghan M. Sinton Miller, College of William and Mary

Kari L. Sisk, Alderson Broaddus College

Peggy Skinner, South Plains College

Patrick K. Smith, Thomas Nelson Community College

Albert F. Smith, Cleveland State University

Ray Soh, Miami University Middletown

Richard Mark States, Gannon University

Nan Rosen Statton, Union County College

Cari Stevenson, Kankakee Community College

Gary Stoner, University of Rhode Island

Katie Swart, College of Charleston

Laura S. Talcott, Indiana University South Bend

Rachelle Tannenbaum, Anne Arundel Community College

Julie Taylor-Massey, Colorado State University Fort Collins

Andi J. Thacker, Dallas Theological Seminary

Deirdre Thompson, Prince George's Community College

Diane Ashe Thompson, Valencia College—West Campus

Brad Thurmond, Ivy Tech Community College Bloomington

Janet C. Titus, Heartland Community College

Kristina Todorovic, University of Toledo

Margot Underwood, College of DuPage

Bethany Bustamante Van Vleet, Arizona State University

Arturo Vazquez Jr., Elgin Community College

Daniel Velisek, College of Dupage

Bettina Viereck, University of Hartford

Naomi Wagner, California State University San Jose

Jill Walker, Greenville Technical College

Kathleen Walker, Paradise Valley Community College

Dana Marie Weachter, Bucks County Community College

Carmon Weaver Hicks, Ivy Tech Community College Central Indiana

Lisa Weisman-Davlantes, California State University Fullerton

Heather M. Whaley, Carson Newman University

Vicki Whiteman, Harcum College

Michele Wolff, Saddleback College

Michelle F. Wright, College of Dupage

Yingying (Jennifer) Yang, Montclair State University

Monica C. Yndo, Concordia University—Austin

Valerie Young-Gutierrez, Central Oregon Community College

Antonio Zamoralez, Brazosport College

This project is much more than a text. The words created by the dedicated team of Test Bank and LearningCurve authors will be some of the ones our students will pay the most attention to. We are grateful to Lora Garrison, Carmon Weaver Hicks, and Christine Park for accompanying us on this journey. Writing assessment questions is not for the faint of heart: It takes tremendous creativity, empathy, and dogged persistence. We are so fortunate to have this team of instructors to share their energies to help students get the most out of the course.

We are particularly grateful to the team at Macmillan Learning who have worked with us over the years. We have been so fortunate to work on this project with the expert guidance of Dan DeBonis and Andrea Musick Page, who cared about us, the instructors they work with, and the science as much as we did, dreaming and thinking about this project on what was supposed to be their off time. Thank you to the management team at Macmillan Learning, including Charles Linsmeier, Shani Fisher, and Christine Brune, for giving us the support we needed. Over the years, we have also been fortunate to work with other thoughtful editors and publishers, including Rachel Losh, Kevin Feyen, Dan McDonough, Matthew Wright, and Mimi Melek. A first-edition project like this takes a village of people who are inspired, ambitious, and a little obsessive.

We have been lucky to work with a team of people who are also caring and fun. Assistant editor Allison Curley kept track of the many, many details and shared her insights with preternatural good humor. Associate development editor Nick Rizzuti has worked with us for nearly four years and, throughout her work on the manuscript and on the media activities, has always been a smart, reliable, and creative support. Executive media editor Laura Burden has shared her enthusiasm and expert vision for making this project a truly interactive student experience. Art manager Matthew McAdams helped us make our words into pictures and connected us with the amazingly talented illustrator and designer Eli Ensor, who knows brain anatomy, design, and how to make things beautiful. We are grateful for Eli's time and creativity in helping us make the infographics and figures on these pages. John Callahan created a cover that helps to share the stories and the people that are at the heart of the book.

Jennifer Atkins e-mailed strangers and spent many months helping us find the beautiful photographs that appear in this project, with expert assistance from Sheena Goldstein and Jennifer MacMillan. Our production and copyediting team of Peter Jacoby, Deborah Heimann, Cheryl Adam, and the team at Lumina Datamatics were flexible, careful, and insightful in making sure the details were right. Daria Kaczorowska, Olivia Madigan, Joyce Clannon, and Elizabeth Blach-Crystal helped with researching and keeping track of references over the years. We appreciate the team from Writing Diversely, including Renee Harleston, Isabelle Felix, and Sossity Chiricuzio, who shared their expertise and lived experience in helping us write to a broad group of readers with empathy.

Jessica would like to send a note of thanks for the patience of her family, including Emily, Brianna, Ella, and Zach; her sisters, Liz, Robin, and Zoe, for their stories of development; and her parents: Lea, for always saying something nice with emoji, her father, for reading every word (and sending in references), and her mother and Gary, for painting her house so she could spend more time at work. She would also like to particularly thank Allison and Andrew for embarking on this journey with her, for giving her a chance to share their enthusiasm about science and openness to learning new things, and, even in the grueling bits of this adventure, for being optimistic and kind.

Allison and Andrew would also like to thank their families for their love and support throughout this project, for always asking "how's the textbook going?" and never asking "why is it taking so long?" They are grateful to Ben and Gabe, for putting up with endless discussions about textbook details that continued at the dinner table, and to Jessica, for her incredible creativity, vision, and determination — they could not have had a better partner on this adventure. They thank each other for mutual support through yet another collaboration beyond marriage, home, and parenting.

Enormous appreciation to Kate Super and her team, including Joe Gamez and Jim Arounness, at Sidford House production, for coordinating with the profiled families and creating beautiful, moving footage.

We produced this book during the height of the COVID-19 pandemic and would like to give special thanks for the families of everyone on our team, particularly Josephine, Caroline, Cece, Frances, Helen, Emma, and Zach, who shared their parents with this project while they worked at home: Thank you for putting up with our odd hours, our unfunny Zoom calls, and the time and effort your parents put into this project while also supervising school and snacks.

Most of all, thank you to the families, the professionals, and the children who shared their stories and homes with us: trusting us to share your stories, your children's first steps, and your own challenges, hopes, and dreams. Thank you for making the story of development come to life.

Allison S. Fuligni   *Andrew J. Fuligni*   *Jessica Bayne*

1 The Science of Human Development

© Macmillan, Photo by Sidford House

Development Is a Science

1.1 Define scientific thinking.

1.2 Define developmental science.

The History of Developmental Science

1.3 Describe the historical origins of developmental science.

Themes of Developmental Science

1.4 Analyze four key themes addressed by developmental science.

1.5 Explain the contexts of family, community, country, and historical moment in shaping development.

1.6 Describe the complexity of understanding culture and development.

1.7 Explain the ways in which developmentalists describe human growth and change.

Selected Resources from

Activities

Spotlight on Science: Understanding the Impact of Culture on Development

Scientific American Library: "How to Overcome Anti-Scientific Thinking"

Assessments

LearningCurve

Practice Quiz

Videos

Scientific American Profiles

Thinking Critically in a "Post-Truth" World

Michelle always had a plan. She focused on the values her parents taught her: Strive for the best and be kind. As a child, this helped her start over many times because of her father's career in the Air Force, making new friends in several cities in Germany and the United States. Her plan helped her stay connected with family around the world, including her extended family in Spain and Argentina and her close family in Florida. It enabled her move to Norway in her 20s and start a new job in a new language. Now in her 40s, she is poised, organized, likeable, and fluent in Spanish, Norwegian, and English — all qualities that benefit her career in public relations.

After the birth of her second baby, Nina, it may have looked as if Michelle had the perfect life. She had a good job, a loving husband, Patricio, a beautiful toddler, Lucia, and an easy newborn. Her parents lived nearby to help.

Then she got a call at work in the middle of the day. It was Patricio, her athletic husband who loved to ride his bike and who played soccer every weekend. The person who always kept her going with his optimism. The information came quickly: He had cancer that had metastasized and spread to his lymph nodes. The statistics were not good. Michelle was terrified. She was afraid she would lose her husband. That she would have to raise her girls on her own.

Just 15 years ago, Patricio's cancer would have been considered incurable (Weiss et al., 2019). But by 2011, scientists had learned how to harness the power of the body's own immune cells to fight off the invasive disease. For Patricio, getting better wasn't easy. There were setbacks. He couldn't exercise. Even picking

1

up his girls was difficult. But a year later, his scans came back clear, indicating that the treatments were working. Michelle and Patricio credit science for saving his life.

Things look different for Michelle and her family now: Nina, their newborn, is now 2. Lucia is in preschool and excited about a *Little Mermaid*–themed birthday party. They are confident that Patricio will be there to blow out the candles with her. Michelle feels like she's changed: She is grateful and believes the best is yet to come. She even had the courage to start her own public relations business.

Michelle's family story is exceptional, but it illustrates some universal questions about human development that fascinate scientists, and the rest of us, such as:

- What makes us able to adapt to our environment, as Michelle did when she learned to fit in in schools around the world?
- How can we develop **resilience**, or the ability to bounce back and recover despite difficult life circumstances?
- Will the treatments that helped Patricio survive cancer impact how he ages?
- How does Michelle's cultural background help her?

As you will learn, human development is complex — dependent on different factors and elements mixed together over time. Its study is focused on learning how, when, and why development happens — for Michelle and her family and for humanity as a whole (Lerner, 2021; Raeff, 2016). Michelle and her family exemplify the amazing potential of human beings to grow and adapt despite challenges. They also remind us of the power of science, one reason why Michelle and her family, despite their scary year, have been able to thrive.

Scientific American Profile

Meet Michelle and Her Family

Development Is a Science

Learning Objectives

1.1 Define scientific thinking.

1.2 Define developmental science.

Michelle's family was helped by **science**, the process of gathering and organizing knowledge about the world in a way that is testable and reliable. Science is based on the idea that there are universal, objective truths that can be studied *empirically*, which is to say they can be verified by systematic study. Science is not a set of facts, but a way of learning that is based on rigorously questioning what you know, testing that information, and relying on other people to cross check what you discover.

Scientific breakthroughs helped Patricio make it to his daughter's second birthday. Such breakthroughs have also made people around the globe healthier and enabled more of us to live longer, happier lives than ever before in human history (Aburto et al., 2021; Catillon et al., 2018).

Nearly everyone has ideas about how human beings develop. You probably have your own hunches about the right ways to raise a child, how best to get through middle life, and how people should act when they get older. Science is different from opinion, or even your own individual experiences, because it can be supported (or disproven) by evidence.

Science can be surprising: Did you know that getting enough sleep is one of the best ways teenagers can improve their mental health (Urrila et al., 2017)? Or that newborns can recognize their parents on the day they are born (Lee & Kisilevsky, 2014)? That sex and romance get better for most people after age 50 (Forbes et al., 2017; Syme et al., 2019)? Or that being bilingual helps older adults avoid cognitive decline (Borsa et al., 2018)?

resilience The ability to bounce back and recover despite difficult life circumstances.

science A process of gathering and organizing knowledge about the world in a way that is testable and reliable.

What Is Development?

Lifespan development refers to the changes that happen between birth and death. It is also the study of what in the environment and in our genes make each of us unique. Worldwide, there are major differences between adults' and children's ability to think, manage their feelings, and survive independently. No one believes that children are simply "short adults": Everyone recognizes that *something* changes between birth and adulthood beyond just getting taller (Garbarino & Bruyere, 2013, p. 259). Development is the study of what exactly that something is.

Similarly, we recognize that there are differences between people in their 20s and people in their 80s. Adults continue to grow and develop in some predictable ways after they reach maturity. Life events, like having a baby, falling in love, and going to work, all change you (Costa et al., 2019). But how we change and the pace at which we age differs dramatically depending on what we experience (Sharifian et al., 2022). Much of the growth in adulthood helps to make us more satisfied. Indeed, many older people in the United States report that they are the happiest they have ever been (Carstensen et al., 2020).

All living beings, from amoebas to elephants, change as they grow. But only humans have such a long period between birth and adulthood (Hrdy & Burkart, 2020; Stearns, 2017). The two decades that it takes humans to mature enable children and adolescents to learn how to thrive in a social world, including how to communicate with language and manage their feelings in groups (Gopnik et al., 2020). This has allowed human beings to develop the complex relationships and skills that lead to the cultural and technological innovations that characterize the modern world (Caspari & Lee, 2004).

Like some other animals and our early humanoid ancestors, human beings are social animals: We live in groups, nurture our children over many years, and take care of members of the community who need help (Bribiescas, 2020; Kessler, 2020). Scientists believe that the long period of human late adulthood has been biologically programmed to allow us to live long enough to lend a helping hand to others, often as grandparents (Hawkes, 2020; Hilbrand et al., 2017).

Across time, cultures and communities have distinguished childhood from adulthood and later life. Some of this categorization is informed by biology, as with the milestones of birth, the beginning of adolescence in puberty, the end of fertility in middle life, and the gradual physical weakening of late life. But culture helps determine what biological milestones are important and even when we meet them. Community practices influence the timing and the pace of these milestones: What you eat and how you live, for instance, affect how quickly you age or reach puberty (Brix et al., 2019).

Cultures also have different ways of distinguishing stages of the lifespan, like whether you start school at 6 or 9, or whether you are expected to retire from work at 60 or 72. As you will learn, for many people in our era, developmental milestones are more flexible than ever: You can go to college in your 70s or your 20s, have a baby in your teens or your 50s, or fall in love in your 30s or your 80s.

Despite the flexibility of many key events in today's world, most developmental scientists divide the lifespan into nine major sections, as you see in **Figure 1.1**.

This categorization of development is neither precise nor universal. Diversity is an essential part of development. For instance, a baby does not stop being a toddler on the day they turn 2½, a child does not transform into an adolescent on their twelfth birthday, and an adult doesn't recognize themselves as an older person when they turn 65. Many children develop quickly—learning to walk before they turn 1 or reaching puberty before they are 10. Others take extra time. Some adults around the world age quickly, worn out by hard work and daily strain, while others are fortunate to feel young at 75. But regardless of the variations, describing children and adults

Old Enough to Help Scientists divide the lifespan into stages, but no matter what age they are, people feel a sense of obligation to contribute, however challenging their circumstances. This young woman is just 17 and has been working in North Carolina tobacco fields since she was 13. She is using a plastic trash bag to protect herself from the pesticides used on the farm.

lifespan development The pattern of changes and stability in individuals that happens between birth and death. It is also the study of what in the environment and in our genes make each of us unique.

The prenatal period
The period before birth, which plays an important role in later development, influencing health and psychological development.

Early childhood
The years between about 2½ and 6, when children begin to manage their own behavior and emotions.

Adolescence
The stage that begins with the biological changes of puberty, at about 11 or 12, and lasts until young people take on adult roles.

Middle adulthood
The longest stage of the lifespan, lasting from your 30s to your 60s. It begins when you establish an independent identity and ends when you recognize yourself as being older.

Death and grief may come at any age. Grieving the death of a loved one and preparing for your own passing have their own developmental sequence. Hopefully this comes after a long and full life, but for many it comes too early.

Age   0 2.5 6   12   18   30   60   80

The infant and toddler years
The first two and a half years, when many typical children begin to move and communicate on their own.

Middle childhood
The period from about age 6 until about age 12, which is the time for making friends and exceling in school.

Early adulthood
A period with unclear boundaries, from about age 18 to 30, when young people have taken on some adult roles and are in their peak years of fertility, yet are not done growing and often are still dependent on their families. (Sometimes called *emerging adulthood*.)

Late adulthood
The period that begins when you recognize yourself as older, which may be in your early 60s or early 80s, depending on where you live, and ends with death. For some, this may be one of the longest periods of the lifespan. Today, babies born in wealthy communities are expected to live until age 104.

FIGURE 1.1 **Major Periods of Lifespan Development** Many distinctions between periods in development are based on cultural expectations. Most developmental scientists recognize nine major periods as we develop. Dying, the final stage, may happen at any time in the lifespan. We may think of the stages in childhood and adolescence in terms of where children go to school: preschool (between ages 3 and 5); elementary school (between 6 to 10); middle school (between 11 and 13); and high school ages (14 to 18).

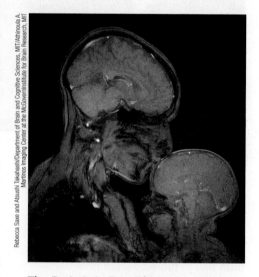

The Brain Is in Everything . . . Even in a parent's love for her child. How did a neuroscientist show her attachment to her baby? She lay down with him in an MRI scanner. There is no single area in the brain of neuroscientist Rebecca Saxe or her 4-month-old son that represents love in this scan. However, you can see signs of attachment in the way she kisses his head and in the fact that she wanted to make this image as a reminder of their bond.

developmental science The systematic study of how humans grow and the underlying processes that create change and stability over time.

who are about the same age—and how the pace of change sometimes differs between them—is one of the major projects of developmental science.

What Is Developmental Science?

Developmental science is the systematic study of how humans grow and the underlying processes that create change over time. The goal of developmental science is to both explain and improve the lives of children and adults. Developmental researchers are diverse, but they share a common vocabulary, agree on some basic facts about development, and use common methods for studying how people change. They also share values, such as a commitment to accurate science, an appreciation for all kinds of human beings, and empathy for the people they study.

Development is complex and takes place in multiple interconnected circumstances. Michelle's growth, for instance, was affected by her genes, her family, her culture, and her community. Developmental scientists often divide development into *domains*, or broad areas of study, including physical, cognitive, social, and emotional development, areas that often overlap (see **Figure 1.2**). For instance, although brain development, part of the physical domain, is separate from other areas, your brain and its maturation play a crucial role in everything from how you learn language to how you make decisions about fairness in late life. Similarly, it is impossible to consider any of these domains separately from the cultural context. Across the lifespan, culture affects how people grow, express their emotions, and even think (Marks & García Coll, 2018; Rogoff et al., 2017).

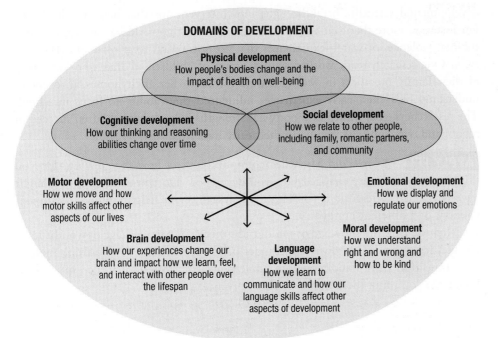

DOMAINS OF DEVELOPMENT

Physical development
How people's bodies change and the impact of health on well-being

Cognitive development
How our thinking and reasoning abilities change over time

Social development
How we relate to other people, including family, romantic partners, and community

Motor development
How we move and how motor skills affect other aspects of our lives

Emotional development
How we display and regulate our emotions

Brain development
How our experiences change our brain and impact how we learn, feel, and interact with other people over the lifespan

Language development
How we learn to communicate and how our language skills affect other aspects of development

Moral development
How we understand right and wrong and how to be kind

FIGURE 1.2 Domains of Human Development When developmental scientists analyze how we grow, they often separate our behaviors into broad areas of study, called domains, that overlap and intersect.

Developmental science is both interdisciplinary and international. Many researchers come from psychology, but others come from anthropology, neuroscience, pediatrics, sociology, economics, nursing, biology, education, and even engineering. Some specialize in human development or in **gerontology**, the study of aging. Like other scientists, developmentalists around the world hold each other accountable, review each other's work, and collaborate to create breakthroughs in how we understand people and how they grow. These researchers are located in all seven continents: Understanding what about human development is unique to one community and what is universal is an essential part of developmental science.

Most developmental scientists have advanced degrees, which typically require more than 10 years of studying development after high school. They often have years or even decades of hands-on experience working with people and conducting research, which involves testing new ideas. This education helps them learn the specialized vocabulary, standards, and techniques for contributing to developmental knowledge.

Developmental scientists use a variety of *methods*, or ways of studying development over the lifespan, which will be described in more depth in Chapter 2. Many scientists invite children or adults to participate in laboratory experiments. Others study participants' brains with high-tech scanning devices, and still others may work with people in more naturalistic settings, observing children in schools or interviewing families in their homes. Developmental researchers also have differing areas of *focus*. For instance, some researchers may focus on close relationships, others on the development of thinking, and others on creating policy or advocating for social justice. However, as trained developmental scientists, they all agree on some broad outlines of human development.

Developmental science provides a framework for professionals working with children and adults, such as nurses, teachers, social workers, lawyers, probation officers, doctors, coaches, clergy, and many others. These professionals are often able to adapt

How Do You Become a Developmental Scientist? For Dr. Deborah Rivas-Drake, it started with majoring in psychology and going on to receive her master's and Ph.D. degrees. She is now a professor at the University of Michigan, where she teaches and directs the Contexts of Academic + Socioemotional Adjustment (CASA) Lab. Dr. Rivas-Drake collaborates with a team of undergraduate, graduate, and postdoctoral students to understand how schools, families, peers, and communities can promote the development of youth of color. She publishes research papers, gives lectures across the country, consults with non-profit groups (including the makers of Sesame Street), and co-wrote an award-winning book. What does Dr. Rivas-Drake seek in her work? "To amplify the ways youth and their families feel empowered by their identities, their narratives, and their roots, so that they may realize a world that is free, in ways beyond what we can imagine ourselves."

gerontology The study of aging.

Zaid Al-Obeidi/AFP via Getty Images

Building Strengths with Friends Around the world, more than 20 million children have been forced from their homes as a result of war or natural disaster. Developmental scientists work with children and their families to help them become resilient. These children are playing table football in Sinjar, Iraq. This game is far from the mountainous villages where their families lived until 2014, when the Islamic State forced them, along with other members of the Yazidi community, from their land.

Learning Objective

1.3 Describe the historical origins of developmental science.

developmental scientific breakthroughs into interventions that help people thrive. For instance, more than one in four children around the world has survived serious trauma, violence, or war—experiences that do not always wear off (McLaughlin et al., 2020). One research team worked with a group of children in Iraq who lost many of their family members in war, and were forced to flee their homes, in order to understand how their early experiences influenced their ability to focus in school. The researchers' goal was to find out what strengths helped these children succeed in school and overcome the trauma in their early lives (Pellizzoni et al., 2019).

APPLY IT! **1.1** How did Michelle's community affect how she grew up? Do you think your community changed how you developed? Do you think that you might have developed differently if you had lived in a different neighborhood, a different country, or a different family?
1.2 Michelle is in the life stage of middle adulthood. What age stage do you fit into? Do you feel your age, or do you feel older or younger? What do you think marked your transition from childhood into adolescence, or from adolescence into adulthood? Do you think these transitions are universal?

The History of Developmental Science

People have tried to understand how to nurture development since the beginnings of human life. Some of the oldest archeological discoveries are miniature tools that were designed to teach children (Crawford et al., 2018; Sánchez Romero, 2018). In the earliest written records, dating back more than 2,000 years, thinkers from the Middle East, China, and Europe sought to better understand development by learning how embryos develop in the uterus and theorizing about how adults should spend their retirement (Kinney, 1995; Stearns, 2017; Troyansky, 2015).

Throughout history, as in the present, life has been difficult for many children. Some wealthy young people were educated—whether in elementary schools in China or by private tutors in ancient Egypt, but most lives were short and filled with hard work (Kinney, 1995; Stearns, 2016). Until about 1900, about one in three children in the United States would die before their fifth birthday because of illness, starvation, or complications of birth itself (Coontz, 2016; Mintz, 2004). Adults' lives were not much easier. Disease was common, women died in childbirth, and people of all ages died before their time due to war, slavery, or dangerous work. But despite the poor odds, some adults survived into late adulthood (Gurven & Kaplan, 2008).

Archeologists believe *longevity*, or the ability to live until later life, is one reason human culture became more sophisticated around 30,000 years ago. More older adults in their 60s and 70s meant more people who were able to create new technologies and cultural achievements (Caspari & Lee, 2004). Even though many adults died young, even 2,500 years ago ancient thinkers were nonetheless making plans for their 100 years on Earth: years that were spent building community (Panikkar, 1994).

Despite widespread inequality and the recent global pandemic, improvements in health and human rights make today the best time to be alive for many. For instance, babies born today are twice as likely to live into adulthood as they were 30 years ago (UNICEF, 2020). Before the pandemic, more than 9 in 10 children attended school (Winthrop & McGivney, 2015). Most children in need are cared for by family members or in foster families—and fewer than 6 million worldwide are now housed in institutions like orphanages (Desmond et al., 2020). Although the global pandemic made COVID-19 the leading cause of death for older adults worldwide in 2020, adults

How Do We Support Each Other? Communities often share a commitment to take care of each other, but that does not mean that everyone is treated with dignity or respect. In the past and in the present, some people have been neglected. One of these photographs shows the small, coffinlike accommodations that were provided to men who needed a place to sleep overnight in the city of London, England, around 1900. The other photograph shows children and adolescents who were separated from their parents after seeking refuge in the United States. They are shown here waiting in caged rooms in McLaren, Texas, in 2018.

are living longer and are in better health than at any other time in history (Aburto et al., 2021).

The Origins of Modern Developmental Science

While human beings have always had ideas about how people mature over the lifespan, developmental science is a recent invention. It combines scientific methodology with a commitment to the human rights and well-being of all people.

European philosophers from the 1600s and 1700s helped to develop a vocabulary for thinking about development. These philosophers had big ideas about how people developed, but they did not base them in empirical study or observation. However, their thoughts about the core nature of human beings continue to be a reference point today. For instance, the English doctor John Locke (1632–1704) believed that children were born "blank slates" to be written upon by life experiences (Locke, 1690/1847). The Swiss philosopher Jean Jacques Rousseau (1712–1778) argued that children were born good until they were corrupted by the world around them (Rousseau, 2010).

Modern science, with an emphasis on empirical observation and testable ideas, began with the advent of the **scientific method** in the late 1500s. Researchers owe a debt of gratitude to Iraqi neuroscientist Ibn al-Haytham, who lived in the 1100s (Di Ventra, 2018). His idea that building knowledge required rigorous experimental study was adapted by European scientists into the scientific method in the late 1500s, as you will learn in Chapter 2. The scientific method became a shared set of rules and assumptions that helped scientists around the world, who spoke dozens of languages and were often trained quite differently, build on each other's work and create a common body of knowledge.

By the mid-1800s, science began to look much as it does today. Researchers worked in laboratories, published their writing, and challenged each other in scholarly articles (Dear, 2008). Over the next 75 years, the foundations for modern disciplines like psychology, economics, and biology took hold (Poskett, 2019). Important breakthroughs established how we learn, challenged prevailing beliefs, and established that early experiences can shape our adult personalities.

scientific method A way of learning about the world that involves making observations, developing theories or hypotheses about those observations, and then testing them.

■ Major
   Developmental
■ Theories

■ Early Advocacy
   and Social
● Welfare
   Movement
   (1870–1950)

■ Modern Hallmarks
   that Advanced the
■ Rights of Children
   and Vulnerable
   People of All Ages
   (1947–present)

■ Discoveries in
   Genetics and
● Brain Science

Rebecca Lee Crumpler (1831–1895)
A pediatrician and advocate for improving the health of Black Americans. Wrote an early textbook on the care of mothers and children.

Mary Tape (1857–1934)
An advocate for Chinese American rights who sued to desegregate elementary schools in California so her daughter could attend the same schools as her friends.

Jane Addams (1860–1935)
An early social worker and sociologist who worked to establish safer living conditions for low-income people in U.S. cities.

Solomon Fuller (1872–1953)
A pioneering brain scientist and grandson of enslaved people. Produced the first U.S. studies of Alzheimer's disease.

Zitkála-Šá (1876-1938)
A Dakota teacher and writer who organized opposition to boarding schools that stripped Native American children of their culture.

Mary McLeod Bethune (1875–1955)
An advocate for Black equality who founded schools and colleges throughout the American South.

Abraham Epstein (1892–1942)
An immigrant to the United States who advocated for a national system of late-life financial support that became Social Security.

Marjory Warren (1897–1960)
An English physician who advocated to provide rehabilitation and specialized medical care, creating the field of geriatric medicine.

UNICEF
The largest international organization that advocates for the rights of children, founded in 1946.

Menendez v. Westminster
Legal case that abolished the exclusion of Mexican American children from California schools.

1860   1880   1900   1920   1940

Evolutionary Perspective
Charles Darwin (1809–1882), an English biologist and scientist, was an early contributor to the evolutionary perspective, the idea that human behavior is an adaptation to our environment.

Cultural and Context Perspective
Anthropologists, including Franz Boas and Margaret Mead, began to challenge ideas that development is driven only by biology and showed that culture plays an important role.

Santiago Ramón y Cajal (1852–1934),
a Spanish neuroscientist, pioneered research into how neurons work.

Growing in Stages
James Mark Baldwin (1861–1934), a U.S. psychologist, studied children's development and argued that people usually develop in stages.

Learning Theories Perspective
Popularized by U.S. psychologist John Watson (1878–1958), it focused on how we learn and behaviors that can be observed.

Psychodynamic Perspective
Sigmund Freud (1856-1939), an Austrian physician and psychoanalyst, popularized the idea that our early emotional experiences can influence our adult personalities and mental well-being.

Maturational Perspective
U.S. researchers, including Arnold Gesell (1880–1961), believed that human growth was driven by innate characteristics.

Influence of Nurture
Pioneering scientist Myrtle McGraw (1899–1988) gave babies extra attention, and even roller skates as a way of demonstrating that practice helped children grow.

Cognitive Perspective
Jean Piaget (1896–1970), a Swiss psychologist, argued that children's thinking develops in stages.

Developmental Science: A Legacy of Theory, Research and Advocacy People have always had ideas about how we grow and how best to protect children and other vulnerable people. Developmental science is a recent invention that combines modern scientific methodology, classic theories, and a commitment to human rights and the protection of all people across the lifespan.

Early Concerns for Social Welfare

From ancient times, governments and religious organizations often intervened in peoples' lives—passing laws to regulate child labor, set ages for marriage, or establish rest homes for older people (Popple, 2018; Wagner, 2005). But as communities became larger and more complex, institutions took a more active role. By the 1900s, many cities around the world had established rudimentary social services, like schools, hospitals, and homes and public health services for older adults (Oakley, 2018).

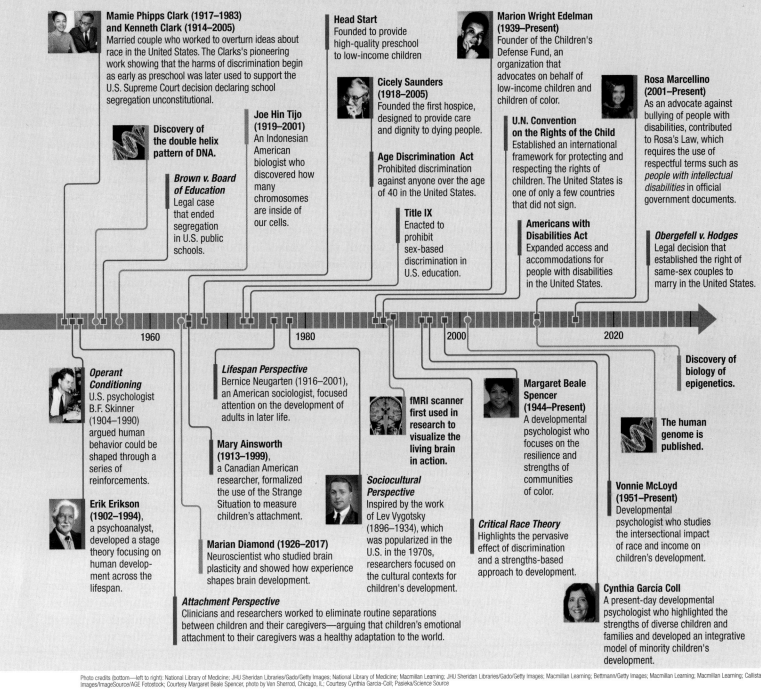

Mamie Phipps Clark (1917–1983) and Kenneth Clark (1914–2005)
Married couple who worked to overturn ideas about race in the United States. The Clarks's pioneering work showing that the harms of discrimination begin as early as preschool was later used to support the U.S. Supreme Court decision declaring school segregation unconstitutional.

Discovery of the double helix pattern of DNA.

Brown v. Board of Education
Legal case that ended segregation in U.S. public schools.

Joe Hin Tijo (1919–2001)
An Indonesian American biologist who discovered how many chromosomes are inside of our cells.

Head Start
Founded to provide high-quality preschool to low-income children

Cicely Saunders (1918–2005)
Founded the first hospice, designed to provide care and dignity to dying people.

Age Discrimination Act
Prohibited discrimination against anyone over the age of 40 in the United States.

Title IX
Enacted to prohibit sex-based discrimination in U.S. education.

Marion Wright Edelman (1939–Present)
Founder of the Children's Defense Fund, an organization that advocates on behalf of low-income children and children of color.

U.N. Convention on the Rights of the Child
Established an international framework for protecting and respecting the rights of children. The United States is one of only a few countries that did not sign.

Americans with Disabilities Act
Expanded access and accommodations for people with disabilities in the United States.

Rosa Marcellino (2001–Present)
As an advocate against bullying of people with disabilities, contributed to Rosa's Law, which requires the use of respectful terms such as *people with intellectual disabilities* in official government documents.

Obergefell v. Hodges
Legal decision that established the right of same-sex couples to marry in the United States.

1960   1980   2000   2020

Operant Conditioning
U.S. psychologist B.F. Skinner (1904–1990) argued human behavior could be shaped through a series of reinforcements.

Erik Erikson (1902–1994), a psychoanalyst, developed a stage theory focusing on human development across the lifespan.

Lifespan Perspective
Bernice Neugarten (1916–2001), an American sociologist, focused attention on the development of adults in later life.

Mary Ainsworth (1913–1999), a Canadian American researcher, formalized the use of the Strange Situation to measure children's attachment.

Marian Diamond (1926–2017)
Neuroscientist who studied brain plasticity and showed how experience shapes brain development.

Attachment Perspective
Clinicians and researchers worked to eliminate routine separations between children and their caregivers—arguing that children's emotional attachment to their caregivers was a healthy adaptation to the world.

fMRI scanner first used in research to visualize the living brain in action.

Sociocultural Perspective
Inspired by the work of Lev Vygotsky (1896–1934), which was popularized in the U.S. in the 1970s, researchers focused on the cultural contexts for children's development.

Critical Race Theory
Highlights the pervasive effect of discrimination and a strengths-based approach to development.

Margaret Beale Spencer (1944–Present)
A developmental psychologist who focuses on the resilience and strengths of communities of color.

Discovery of biology of epigenetics.

The human genome is published.

Vonnie McLoyd (1951–Present)
Developmental psychologist who studies the intersectional impact of race and income on children's development.

Cynthia García Coll
A present-day developmental psychologist who highlighted the strengths of diverse children and families and developed an integrative model of minority children's development.

Many of these institutions were not equally open to all. They were often harsh and imposed rigid ideas about what kind of behavior was "right." For instance, Indigenous children in the United States, Canada, and Australia were often taken from their families and put into boarding schools where they were forced to become "proper" English-speaking citizens (Lomawaima et al., 2018). Older adults were rejected from late-life care if they were immigrants or unfairly deemed of "low moral character" (Tice, 2020). But many early social workers and public health workers were deeply committed to human well-being.

In a time when American and European culture was dominated by White men, advocating for the health of children and older people was an area of public service that was more open to women, immigrants, and people of color, as you can see in **Infographic 1.1** (Oakley, 2018).

Early Developmental Science

By the early 1900s, university scientists were writing popular books about the "science" of parenting and the right way to age. One best seller was a book that claimed the good life began at 40! (Pitkin, 1932). Much of this work was inspired by efforts to make social progress and reform the world. By 1940, many major organizations were founded, such as the Society for Research in Child Development, the American Association of Pediatrics, and the Gerontological Society of America, all of which still exist today to promote scientific work that advocates for children and older adults.

Early advocates and scientists often had disturbing ideas about children, older adults, gender, and race. Many, including those who wrote for *Scientific American*, and those who worked for leading organizations in developmental science, embraced inhumane, racist, and sexist beliefs (Hopkins, 1921; Nutall, 1911). For instance, G. Stanley Hall (1846–1924), the first U.S. man to receive a Ph.D. in psychology, a university president, and author of a popular book about parenting, suggested in one of his top-selling books that women were "weaker in body and mind" than men and that people of color were "naturally impulsive and undeveloped" (Arnett, 2006; Fasteland, 2019; Hall, 1904). Sigmund Freud believed that anyone over 40 was too old and inflexible to benefit from therapy (Freud, 1905/1953). Unfortunately, these offensive ideas were common. However, even then, many developmental scientists rejected those beliefs, and today's scholars are at the forefront of advancing social justice and equality across the lifespan (Killen et al., 2011; National Council on Aging, 2020).

Early developmental scientists were eager to use their scientific knowledge to help people thrive — and to change popular misconceptions about development. They demonstrated that learning, and not just inevitable maturation, helped children grow (McGraw, 1943). They showed that cognitive loss in some older people was the result of serious brain malformations and not bad character (Fuller, 1912; Mohammed, 2021). They worked to end routine separations between children and their caregivers and improved medical care for older adults (Bowlby, 2008; Spitz, 1945; Warren, 1948). Developmental scientists even helped change laws in the United States and contributed to ending legal segregation in schools (Clark & Clark, 1940; Kluger, 2011).

Modern Developmental Science

The racist genocide of more than 11 million Jewish people and members of other groups during World War II had a profound effect on the world and on developmental science. As a result, many more scientists and scientific organizations rejected racism and the idea that personality or behavior is genetic. Scholars turned their attention to focus on the basics about how people grow — and on testing their ideas more rigorously in the laboratory (Hagen et al., 2020). As you will learn in Chapter 2, the influential theories of child development were established after World War II, in the last half of the 1900s. Prominent developmental thinkers explored how learning takes place, the role of relationships in development, and how maturation and cultural contexts influence development.

Technological breakthroughs in the late 1900s also changed how scientists thought about the biology of human development (Boddice, 2019; Kandel, 2012). Scientists were able to use computers and scanning devices to look at the living brain. Genetics research made it possible to analyze human genes — and look for patterns associated with how they are activated over time (Hesson & Pritchard, 2019). An international group of researchers, including Zing-Yang Kuo (1898–1970) in Hong Kong and Gilbert Gottlieb (1929–2006) in the United States, discovered experimental and theoretical evidence pointing to the importance of **epigenetics**, or the role of experience in activating genetic information in human maturation (Gottlieb, 2007; Qian et al., 2020).

In Love and Changing the World Mamie Phipps Clark and Kenneth Clark were pioneering psychologists and advocates for civil rights (and a married couple for 46 years). In the 1940s, the Clarks studied preschoolers and showed that even 3-year-olds understood racial labels, and that racism was affecting their self-esteem and ability to succeed. Their work was crucial to the landmark 1954 U.S. Supreme Court case, *Brown v. Board of Education*, which established racial integration in public schools.

epigenetics The role of experience in activating genetic information in human growth.

Today, developmental science is still an international, multidisciplinary enterprise spurred by scientists trying to understand how people grow and how to help them thrive. The field balances basic scientific discoveries—such as measuring how many neural connections we develop every year—with more practical research—such as studying why children have trouble learning fractions or how to build interventions to help adults fight loneliness (National Academies of Sciences, 2020; Siegler et al., 2020). Appreciating the importance of culture and community to development continues to spur the field to ensure that the benefits of science are relevant to all people around the world.

 CAN YOU BELIEVE IT?

Why Should You Trust Science If Scientists Do Not Agree?

One thing you will learn in this book is that scientists do not always agree. You know this if you follow the news. You may have read reports proposing that breastfeeding boosts intelligence, that video games cause aggression, that a midlife crisis is inevitable, or that there is an epidemic of loneliness in older people (Gavin, 2020; Oster, 2019; Rothman, 2018). Or you may have read the exact opposite. You just read in these pages that over the years, developmental scientists have made radical changes in what they think about human development. With these changing and sometimes contradictory pieces of information, you may wonder if science really has any answers. Can you trust what you are reading? Developmental scientists would say yes: Science builds over time, and diversity of opinion makes for better science that you can trust *more*. Remember two things:

First: When you see a claim in the news, know that it may not be the full story. If you read beyond the brief descriptions, you may find that scientists actually agree much more than they disagree. The headlines may be exaggerated or made more dramatic so that you click to read further (Jellison et al., 2020).

When you read about science in the media, it is often because one team of researchers is excited to share what they have discovered in their laboratory. But it usually takes more than one single discovery to build agreement. After scientists have repeatedly discovered the same thing, uncertainty fades and *scientific consensus* builds (Fischhoff, 2013). Scientific consensus means that researchers from a variety of backgrounds agree on a set of facts or observations. This doesn't mean every researcher is on board, but that a wide majority agree. In this book we present research conclusions that are accepted by most scientists and we point out where research is still ongoing.

Second: Diversity of ideas and points of view makes science better. When you read about disagreements between experts, it is a sign that science is healthy. Disagreements and contradictions are a crucial part of the research process, because they motivate investigators to test and evaluate their work. Scientific evaluation relies on **critical thinking**, which is the ability to thoughtfully question what you believe or what other people believe (Halonen, 2008). In science, critical thinking means that you evaluate everything carefully against what is accepted and check to make sure that proper procedures have been followed. Scientific disagreements help build new consensus.

In developmental science, strong disagreements have helped to build new consensus. Consensus now exists on a wide variety of subjects. For instance, researchers agree that spanking is unhealthy for children, that separating babies from their families is harmful, and that older people should be actively engaged in their communities (Bouza et al., 2018; Butler & Katona, 2019; Sege et al., 2018). Exciting investigations continue in other areas. For instance, how can we help children learn to focus more easily, encourage

CONNECTIONS

Are you wondering which of these claims is true? You will find your answers in the Can You Believe It? sections in Chapters 4, 7, and 16. You will find Can You Believe It? sections throughout this book, designed to help build scientific and critical-thinking skills.

critical thinking The ability to thoughtfully question what you believe or what other people believe.

teenagers to stay in school, or help people stay happy in their romantic partnerships? Learning about the science of development will arm you with some new ways of understanding what is behind the headlines. You will become skilled in the vocabulary of developmental science. And you will learn about what theories, methods, and cultural biases impact scientific discovery so you can think critically about them yourself. 🧑

APPLY IT!   **1.3** Early developmental advocates wanted to help improve lives and address inequities they saw in the world around them. Do you see things in your world you would like to change?

1.4 Michelle's partner, Patricio, benefited from a new treatment for cancer that didn't exist 15 years ago. How did scientific change, discovery, and consensus help him?

1.5 Developmental scientists are looking for answers to help guide our understanding of why we grow and change. Michelle asked us what a developmental scientist would say about the impact of her husband's illness on her young children. What questions do you have about how we develop?

Themes of Developmental Science

Learning Objectives

1.4 Analyze four key themes addressed by developmental science.

1.5 Explain the contexts of family, community, country, and historical moments in shaping development.

1.6 Describe the complexity of understanding culture and development.

1.7 Explain the ways in which developmentalists describe human growth and change.

Some fields of study are fairly narrow. For instance, doctors may focus on health and educators on learning. But developmental science is a broad field, focusing on health and learning and everything in between and finding patterns in the many factors that influence development.

Four major themes pervade developmental science:

1. Each person's development is a complex interaction between them and the world.
2. The process of development is universal but also unique to each person.
3. Culture and community context are critical.
4. Change is constant, but some elements of ourselves remain the same.

Although these concepts may seem abstract, the goal of developmental science is very concrete: to improve the lives of children and adults (Lerner & Murray, 2016).

Beyond Nature Versus Nurture

How did Michelle have the courage to start her own business in her 40s, after overcoming years of worry as her husband fought cancer? Many of us may offer a simple answer: Maybe Michelle was just born strong. Or maybe her husband's endless optimism made her brave. Developmental scientists might call this a trick question. Growth arises from a mind-boggling combination of factors that interact to create who we are. So, a scientist might not give you a simple answer about what made Michelle take a risk. Instead, they may draw you a chart of the intersecting and overlapping factors that all contribute to her ability to make a fresh start.

This complexity of development offers hope: It allows for change to happen at any point and for a great diversity of possible outcomes. The many factors that impact development are interconnected in a complex, interrelated system (Lerner, 2021; Overton, 2015; Witherington & Boom, 2019). This means, for instance, that it is very unusual that one risk factor in development always leads universally and predictably to another—multiple factors are always in play as people grow (Sameroff, 2020). Small things can add up: Repeated experiences of discrimination at work or multiple lucky breaks can change a life for better or worse (Hicken et al., 2018; Jackson, 2011).

Outside of developmental science, people often simplify human development as resulting from someone's genetics or from what they've experienced. Researchers often refer to the influence of genetics on development as **nature** and to the influence of

nature The influence of genetics on development.

experience on development as **nurture**, calling this the question of nature versus nurture. For instance, if you said that Michelle's resilience was something she was born with or inherited from her parents, like a gene for trying new things, you would be attributing her talents to her *nature*. On the other hand, if you said that Michelle's resilience was something she learned from her family, you would be attributing it to her *nurture*.

Developmental scientists have learned that it isn't accurate to label development as either nature *or* nurture (Lerner, 2021). In fact, as you will learn in Chapter 3, even your genetic code is influenced by your environment. Your genes also change your environment. For instance, researchers have found that newborns who have genetically driven characteristics like being very fussy are more likely to evoke irritable responses from their careworn families than those who are more mellow, leading to a cascade of changes for those babies and their families (Quist et al., 2019). Researchers have found that your genes and the environment around you interact and mutually influence each other in a complex and ever-changing dance that occurs over your entire lifespan (Overton, 2013).

It is also common for people to wonder whether the brain drives behavior. Does something in Michelle's brain explain her resilience? Developmental scientists believe that complex traits, like perseverance, will never be identified as coming from one place inside your skull. Researchers also caution that even if they could prove that Michelle's brain is a little different from someone else's, that doesn't necessarily prove anything. Those differences may be *caused* by her resilient activities—rather than her resilient activities being caused by her brain. Just as your genes interact with the environment (and vice versa), your brain interacts with the world.

Scientific American Profile

Changing Together

Development Is Both Universal and Unique

There are about 8 billion people on the Earth right now, each one of them unique (UN, 2019). Even identical twins are, as described in Chapter 3, actually different—right from the beginning (Jonsson et al., 2021). These 8 billion people live in more than 195 countries and 24 time zones, and they speak more than 7,000 different languages (Ethnologue, 2021). You may wonder how, with so much diversity and variation, we can possibly tell a universal story about human development.

Developmental science explains typical patterns in human development and explores why there are variations. For instance, as people grow, some predictable age-related differences occur: Most children walk around their first birthday, most 9-year-olds have a best friend, many 14-year-olds are capable of acing algebra, many 45-year-olds are working, and most 75-year-olds have four grandchildren (AARP, 2019). This doesn't mean all of this is true for everyone. However, understanding these common patterns helps those who work with people across the lifespan to know what to expect at different ages.

For instance, although Michelle is unique (not all 43-year-olds have raised two children while facing their partner's life-threatening cancer diagnosis), she is still subject to some universal patterns of development. In other words, a 43-year-old is still a 43-year-old. Knowing the typical challenges of adulthood can help Michelle be prepared for the emotional, social, and even physical changes she might experience as she ages. Michelle might, for instance, feel less alone if she knew that she wasn't the only person in their middle years who feels frazzled by the challenge of raising a family, maintaining a romantic relationship, and working full time (Blanchflower & Graham, 2020).

Understanding typical patterns also helps researchers make sense of variations. For instance, scientists now understand that culture influences how babies learn how

Universal and Unique David Mas Masumoto's life has been shaped by the land in the Central Valley of California that he has farmed for more than 40 years. His commitment to his peaches and nectarines may be unique, but his development is also shaped by some universal factors. Like many middle-aged adults, he has been changed by his experiences as a parent, a romantic partner, and a son.

context The term used by developmental scientists to describe the broad external factors that surround and influence each individual.

culture The ideas, beliefs, and social practices that a group of people shares.

What Is Your Microsystem? For some, family includes our parents, who may have time to play with blocks on the rug. Other children may be lucky enough to grow up with attention from parents, grandparents, and even great-grandparents.

to move: Infants whose families encourage them to be active tend to learn how to walk months earlier than other babies (Adolph & Hoch, 2019). As humans, we all share many unifying characteristics, and as individuals, we exhibit our uniqueness in many areas, such as in our appearance and personality. All of these are part of the complex process of development.

Context Shapes Growth

As scientists study and document the variations and the similarities between people, it becomes abundantly clear that a person's environment has an enormous impact on how they grow. Developmental scientists use the term **context** in referring to the broad external factors that surround each of us, which includes where in *time* you live. This would be important if you were comparing the development of Michelle, for instance, with that of a girl born 100 years earlier when women were not allowed to vote, and Spanish speakers might not have been allowed to attend the same schools as English speakers (Strum, 2014). Context also includes your **culture**, or the ideas, beliefs, and social practices that a group of people shares (García Coll et al., 2018; Cole & Packer, 2016). For instance, Michelle grew up in a culture that believed *all* children should contribute to their families and work hard in school — even if they were girls.

Context is such a complex factor in development that theorists and researchers have developed models to keep all the bits and pieces in mind. These *contextual models* include Uri Bronfenbrenner's *bioecological model*, Cynthia García Coll's *integrative model*, and Tara Yosso's *Community Cultural Wealth model*, as well as more focused investigations of the developmental impacts of money, historical moments, and culture.

Bronfenbrenner's Bioecological Model The bioecological model describes the environments that affect development as being organized into a series of nested systems, like the layers of an onion, that interact with each other (Bronfenbrenner, 1977, 2005). This model was developed by the U.S. psychologist Uri Bronfenbrenner (1917–2005), a theorist and researcher who also played an important role in founding Head Start, the early-childhood program designed to help low-income children succeed in school (Fox, 2005).

Although depiction of the bioecological model in **Infographic 1.2** might suggest that you are passively trapped in the center of these overlapping spheres, developmental scientists believe that people are not entirely helpless nor powerless. People, even children, make choices, and may have an influence on what happens to them (Lerner, 2021). In addition, their unique biology — genetic makeup and health — also plays an important part in their development. The layers in this model don't rank the importance of each factor; they separate them to make them easier to analyze.

In the center of this model is the *person* who interacts with the environment in their own, unique way. Around this person is a series of layers that represent the parts of their context.

Surrounding the individual is the *microsystem*, which includes the most immediate relationships and physical settings, including family, friends, school, and work. For most around the world, family includes a wide variety of people — sometimes including biological parents, friends, romantic partners, their caregivers' partners, their grandparents, grandchildren, half- and step-siblings, and their own children and stepchildren. The microsystem affects development through direct interaction.

The *mesosystem* is made up of all of the microsystems that the person interacts with and that interact with each other, like the family, school, sports programs, workplaces, and places of worship. For instance, family–school connections may affect children's experiences in both of those microsystems, or stresses at work may influence family life. While a child may not even be sure where their parent works, their

Developmental scientists agree that culture and context play an important role in development, but they have different ways of describing and modeling how this works. Scientists use figures to make these models more concrete and to communicate how people interact with various parts of their environment as they grow.

Bioecological Model of Human Development

Bronfenbrenner's bioecological model is a classic model of social context. The nested circles demonstrate how there are multiple levels of the social environment that interact with each other to influence development. Researchers such as Cynthia García Coll point out that although culture is represented in the outermost level, it permeates all the layers of the system. In addition, people are not just passive recipients of the context: They influence and change their environment.

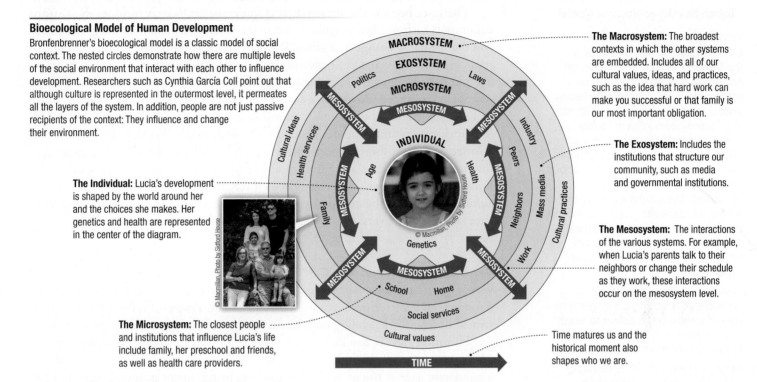

The Macrosystem: The broadest contexts in which the other systems are embedded. Includes all of our cultural values, ideas, and practices, such as the idea that hard work can make you successful or that family is our most important obligation.

The Exosystem: Includes the institutions that structure our community, such as media and governmental institutions.

The Mesosystem: The interactions of the various systems. For example, when Lucia's parents talk to their neighbors or change their schedule as they work, these interactions occur on the mesosystem level.

The Individual: Lucia's development is shaped by the world around her and the choices she makes. Her genetics and health are represented in the center of the diagram.

The Microsystem: The closest people and institutions that influence Lucia's life include family, her preschool and friends, as well as health care providers.

Time matures us and the historical moment also shapes who we are.

Integrative Model of Human Development

The integrative model, originally developed by Cynthia García Coll and others, highlights how social position helps determine how people are affected by context and culture. Privileges are not divided equitably. Adaptive culture can help people thrive.

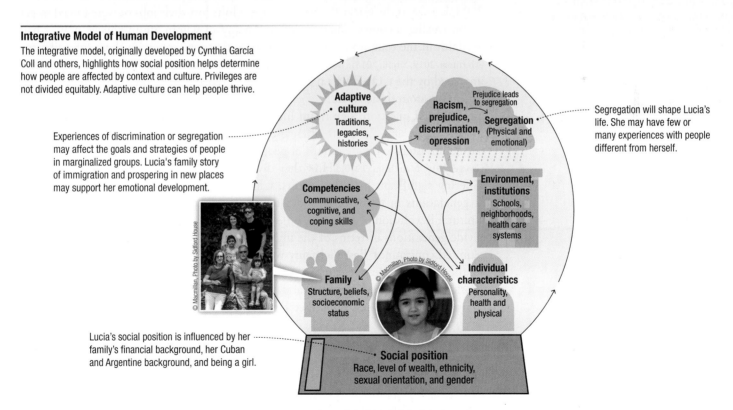

Experiences of discrimination or segregation may affect the goals and strategies of people in marginalized groups. Lucia's family story of immigration and prospering in new places may support her emotional development.

Segregation will shape Lucia's life. She may have few or many experiences with people different from herself.

Lucia's social position is influenced by her family's financial background, her Cuban and Argentine background, and being a girl.

Learn It Together

Teach the Bioecological Model

Plan Review the layers of the bioecological model. Write down the features of your own individual ecological system including your microsystem (your immediate family, school, and others). Can you identify any mesosystem influences (do any of your microsystems interact with each other)? What exosystems impact your environment (think about local policies and organizational structures, like school systems and religious organizations)? Describe the macrosystem you live in and think about the historical moment and what impacts these have on your experiences.

Engage Divide into groups and compare your ecological systems to design a slide presentation to teach your peers how people's ecological systems may affect their development.

Reflect How does understanding your own bioecological system help you see the similarities and differences in others' systems?

job may have important effects on the child. A raise may allow parents to pay for an afterschool program, or an irregular work schedule may make it difficult for a parent to find consistent child care.

The layer beyond the mesosystem is the *exosystem*, which includes the person's community—from their neighborhood to the local, state, and national governments and the media. A change in a school district's policies will be felt in the child's classroom experience. A change in government policy might affect an adult's ability to get a job or their likelihood of finding medical care.

Surrounding the exosystem is a more abstract level, called the *macrosystem*, which includes the culture, beliefs, and customs of a community (Bronfenbrenner, 1977). This level includes cultural attitudes about people, such as whether they are privileged in a society (as when they are born into a wealthy family) or whether they experience discrimination (perhaps as a result of a disability or the language they speak). This layer doesn't just hover on the outside, as it might seem to in a diagram: Beliefs and cultural practices of the macrosystem will pervade everyday life experiences and influence all the other layers, as you see in Infographic 1.2 (Rivas-Drake & Umaña-Taylor, 2019; Spencer, 2017; Vélez-Agosto et al., 2017).

Generational Change: You Can't Beat Time Development occurs over time and within a particular historical period. Your age is important—whether you are a baby, a toddler, an adolescent, an adult, or a centenarian. People of different ages may be treated differently depending on where they live and the culture they grow up in.

Historical time is also important. What you live through and how old you were when you experienced it will change you—whether a terrorist attack, a tornado, or a pandemic (Elder & George, 2016). For instance, in the major economic downturn of 2008, known as the Great Recession, many adults lost their jobs or were forced to get by on smaller incomes. Their children—many of whom are in college now—had less faith in the economic system, an attitude that may stay with them for a lifetime (Mortimer, 2019; Sironi, 2018). Newer research will tell us how people of different ages were impacted by the COVID-19 pandemic and its repercussions on health, finances, and education around the world.

Without question, significant historical events mark how young people develop (Elder & George, 2016). Experts often use major events like wars, economic crises, or natural disasters to divide groups of people into generations, or **birth cohorts** (Elder & George, 2016; Mannheim, 1970). How they divide groups often depends on communities' differing significant historical events. Chinese researchers, for instance, might look at generations in terms of how old they were when they experienced the Chinese Cultural Revolution of 1966–1976 (Jennings & Zhang, 2005). German researchers tend to divide generations in terms of the impact of the fall of the Berlin Wall in 1989 that reunited communist East Germany with democratic West Germany (Liepmann, 2018). In the United States, researchers tend to divide generations by major wars—like World War II and the Vietnam War (Dimock, 2019). These generations are often referred to by nicknames (Twenge, 2020). (See **Figure 1.3**.)

Social Status: Money Isn't Everything Many aspects of context relate to a family's, a community's, or a country's finances. It turns out that money matters a great deal in human development. For instance, in the microsystem of the family, severe poverty, such as struggling to pay the bills and avoid eviction, can add to stress and limit the ability to provide nurturing care (Yu et al., 2020). And at the macrosystem level, if a nation is unable to provide enough food for all its people, some people are more likely to die early, like the more than 1 in 26 children around the world who die before their fifth birthday (UNICEF, 2020).

birth cohorts The categories that experts use to group people from different generations.

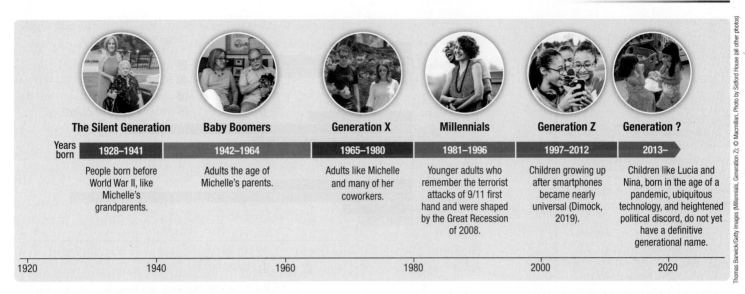

	The Silent Generation	Baby Boomers	Generation X	Millennials	Generation Z	Generation ?
Years born	1928–1941	1942–1964	1965–1980	1981–1996	1997–2012	2013–
	People born before World War II, like Michelle's grandparents.	Adults the age of Michelle's parents.	Adults like Michelle and many of her coworkers.	Younger adults who remember the terrorist attacks of 9/11 first hand and were shaped by the Great Recession of 2008.	Children growing up after smartphones became nearly universal (Dimock, 2019).	Children like Lucia and Nina, born in the age of a pandemic, ubiquitous technology, and heightened political discord, do not yet have a definitive generational name.

1920   1940   1960   1980   2000   2020

FIGURE 1.3 What Makes a Generation? The historical events that you experience, whether a natural disaster, a technological innovation, or a global pandemic, will shape your development. In the United States, major wars have often defined the generations, but these are not the only important historical markers. Other cultural and social changes, such as a lawsuit challenging segregated schools or a change in immigration policy, are also important events that can change lives (Vélez-Agosto et al., 2017).

There are several ways of analyzing how money can influence development. Some scientists look at associations between families' income or bank balance and their development. As you might have guessed, your income is related to many measures of well-being (Jebb et al., 2018). High-income people are likely to be healthier and happier throughout the lifespan (D'Ambrosio et al., 2020; Kim & Kim, 2018). This is not because money magically erases all challenges, but because people with higher incomes usually have other advantages that lower-income people do not. Higher-income families often experience less financial stress, less environmental pollution, fewer experiences of discrimination, and less neighborhood violence (Puterman et al., 2020; van Raalte et al., 2018).

Around the world, wealth is linked to health, and a family's economic advantages and disadvantages persist across generations. For instance, in low-income countries, children from wealthy, urban families are 30 percent more likely to live until adulthood than their rural peers (Gaigbe-Togbe, 2015). In the United States, adults who grew up in low-income families in the United States are likely to die more than 10 years before adults who grew up in high-income families (Chetty et al., 2016). Even in a relatively wealthy country like the United States, where a child starts financially is very predictive of where they end up in adulthood: More than 9 in 10 children who are born into low-income families remain low-income in adulthood (Chetty, 2021).

In the United States, experts often evaluate family income in terms such as *upper-*, *middle-*, and *lower-income* and above or below the *poverty line* (Bennett et al., 2020). In the United States, about one in six children, one in nine adults, and one in ten older adults live below the federal poverty line of $25,500 for a family of four (Semega et al., 2020). (See **Figure 1.4**.)

The size of your bank account is not always the most accurate way to measure the impact of economic hardship. Some experts focus instead on whether material needs are being met: If you have enough to eat, a stable place to live, and access to affordable health care. During childhood and adolescence, researchers have found that measuring material deprivation in addition to income may provide a more accurate understanding of a family's circumstances (Schenck-Fontaine et al., 2020). During late adulthood, researchers have measures of poverty that take into account the unreimbursed costs

What Will This Generation Be Remembered For? For many, it may be linked to efforts to combat climate change. These young adults are protesting in Washington, D.C., to raise awareness of environmental justice.

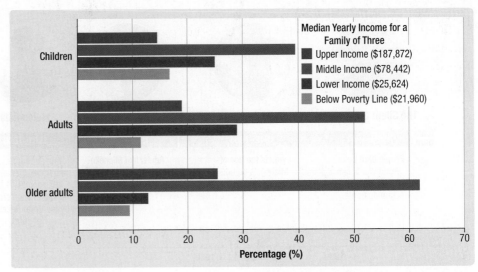

Data from Kochhar, 2018, Semega et al., 2020, and Burtless, 2019.

FIGURE 1.4 Income in the United States by Age Social scientists assess income categories by dividing them into three groups: upper, middle, and lower. The poverty line is an income threshold determined each year by the federal government and is based on current prices and household size. Notice that older adults, who benefit from income supports from Social Security, are less likely to be low-income. Children are more likely to be poor.

Looking for New Home: Must Love Dogs. One of the costs of economic insecurity is losing your home. This young girl is leaving with her pet as her family is evicted from their apartment near Phoenix, Arizona, during the COVID-19 pandemic.

socioeconomic status (SES) A key measure of a family or individual's income and social capital.

Community Cultural Wealth The areas of strength and resilience identified by developmental scientists and educators that help people, particularly those who are marginalized or are people of color, succeed in a discriminatory world.

of health care, which often force one in seven older adults to choose between paying for necessities like groceries or paying for home health care or prescriptions (Carr, 2019; Mutchler et al., 2020).

Scientists also look at the nonfinancial assets a person may have. For instance, a family might have a lot of *social capital*, or a strong network of relationships and contacts that may make it easier to find the right school system, an internship, a job, or a volunteer opportunity after retirement (Hanifan, 1916; Holland et al., 2007; Putnam, 2000). A key measure of a family's income and social capital is called **socioeconomic status (SES)** (Entwisle & Astone, 1994).

Scientists have different measures of SES that combine a family's social status with their income. Some analyze adults' education level, reasoning that someone with an advanced degree probably has more social capital than someone with a high school degree. Others look at the prestige of jobs by ranking, for instance, a supervisor or a manager above someone who is a clerk in a retail store (Duncan et al., 2015). Many researchers have found that measuring a household's SES in addition to their material income results in a more accurate understanding of differences. As you will learn, measuring SES may be helpful, but it is far from the only factor that can impact your life.

 MAKING A DIFFERENCE
Cultural Wealth Builds Resilience

Money and social connections are not the only thing that helps people be happy and successful. Tara Yosso described the strength that can help us persevere in systems that can be hostile and discriminatory as **Community Cultural Wealth** (Yosso, 2006, 2020; Yosso & Solórzano, 2005).

Yosso is part of a new generation of developmental scientists and educators who identify the areas of strength and resilience that help people, particularly those who are marginalized or people of color, succeed in a discriminatory world. In the words of

Icon credit: johavel/Shutterstock

researcher Kris Gutiérrez, cultural values create a "grammar of hope, possibility, and resilience" in a world where being different often means you are treated as if you were deficient (Gutiérrez, 2016, p. 188). According to the Community Cultural Wealth model (Yosso, 2005, 2006), there are six forms of cultural strength that contribute to resilience:

1. *Aspirational capital* is the ability to maintain hopes and dreams, even in the face of barriers and challenges. Researchers have found that communities with high expectations and encouragement for their children's success, as with many in the Latino community, help inspire their children to persevere in school (Enriquez, 2011).

2. *Linguistic capital* refers to communication skills, often in the form of family stories or oral histories. Some researchers have suggested that the language skills developed by children and adults who are bilingual help build cognitive strengths that last a lifetime (van den Noort et al., 2019).

3. *Familial capital* includes a sense of togetherness, caring, and connection, bringing together a community's memories and cultural knowledge. This strong sense of kinship can be protective throughout the lifespan. For instance, African American family caregivers may be somewhat protected from burnout because of the strong community support they receive for their work (Pristavec, 2019).

4. *Social capital* includes networks of peers and other social contacts that provide support for navigating society. Community groups, faith communities, and cultural centers can help develop and sustain a sense of identity. For instance, some scientists found that first-generation college students who had stronger support from their friends were more likely to persevere through college than their peers (Mishra, 2020).

5. *Navigational capital* includes skills for maneuvering through social institutions that were not typically created for diverse communities or have a history of structural exclusion. Many Deaf college students need to build navigational capital in order to understand how to get the most out of their education (Listman & Dingus-Eason, 2018).

6. *Resistant capital* includes knowledge and skills developed in practices that challenge inequality and subordination. People who are marginalized have always had to step up to protect themselves and their families. Some of Yosso's current work focuses on rediscovering the stories of Mexican American families who worked to desegregate California schools (García & Yosso, 2020).

Researchers suggest that it is easy for people to fall into the *deficit model* viewpoint, in which people are considered to simply be a collection of problems, rather than a complex combination of challenges and strengths. In the United States, this is particularly relevant for people of color, who have experienced multiple forms of historical and current discrimination, and whose family, community, and cultural contexts may differ from the patterns of the privileged, typically White society. Focusing on strengths helps practitioners and scholars support positive outcomes.

Understanding Culture

Culture is a source of strength and a critical variable in the contexts in which we develop. In developmental science, culture refers to the ideas, beliefs, and social practices that a group of people share (Cole & Packer, 2016). Culture is a critical way that human beings learn from each other and get along (Tomasello, 2016; Whiten, 2017). Sharing culture creates an easy shorthand for social interactions and helps people feel that they belong. As you will learn throughout this book, culture influences all aspects of development (Goodnow & Lawrence, 2015). It may determine what a parent eats during pregnancy, when a child starts school for the first time, or even when a person starts to feel old. Culture changes our bodies, brains, how we think, and how we feel.

Scientists look at culture on multiple levels, from characterizing cultures that cross continents to cultures that extend only to a small group (Jahoda, 2012). Sometimes,

Share It!

Cultural strengths can help you learn how to collaborate with other people, even with your siblings.

(Alcalá et al., 2018)

Scientific American: Lifespan Development

Scott Olson/Getty Images

Nurturing Farming Culture and Community For many families, connection to the environment and the land is part of their culture. In Marengo, Iowa, one tradition is to crown a Poultry Princess at the County Fair. Kameryn won the honors in 2018.

intersectionality A term that refers to the fact that we all have multiple, intersecting identities relating to age, gender, ability, ethnicity, nationality, romantic preferences, and so forth.

cultural humility An openness to cultural diversity and a self-awareness of your own cultural background that helps to create respectful relationships in which everyone learns from each other and no one feels superior.

culture refers to your country or community background, as when you define yourself as Egyptian American or Turkish German, also referred to as *ethnicity*. At other times, culture refers to a smaller subgroup, or a *microculture*, like the cultural community of online gamers who play *World of Warcraft*, people who identify as *neurodiverse*, or even a single family (Faherty & Mitra, 2020; Oyserman, 2017).

Cultural distinctions often overlap with other ways you categorize yourself, like the language you speak at home, your ethnic background, your racial identity, your religion, your gender, your physical and cognitive abilities, your romantic preferences, and even your neighborhood. All of us are part of many cultures, evident in the holidays we observe, the languages and slang that come easily, and the ways we greet each other. Scientists emphasize that it is our interpretation of these differences, rather than something essential in them, that is most important. **Intersectionality** refers to the fact that we all have multiple, intersecting cultural identities (Crenshaw, 1989; Ghavami et al., 2016). Like Michelle, we may identify as Latina, as Cuban American, as a woman, as a parent, and as an entrepreneur.

How to Talk About Culture Culture may be so fundamental that it is invisible: You may not always see its impact in your own life. This may be particularly true for people who belong to the dominant or majority culture. Your culture may be something you take for granted. As one writer put it, when a young fish was once asked how he liked the water, he responded by asking, "What the hell is water?" (Wallace, 2009).

In development, understanding culture is essential to understanding the great diversity of contexts in which people can thrive. It can also help identify when people may experience cultural discrimination and it may protect them (Rivas-Drake & Umaña-Taylor, 2019). Stereotypes and assumptions about our potential begin at birth. For many, like Michelle, the discrimination they may encounter is intersectional: The bias they confront can be based on ethnicity, gender, family income, and physical ability, among others.

From the beginning of life to its end, discrimination based on racial and cultural differences pervades people's lives (Umaña-Taylor, 2016). For instance, in the United States, Asian American and White European babies are more likely to be born at more highly funded hospitals. But African American or Latino babies tend to be born in hospitals that serve low-income communities and typically have less access to life-saving and life-preserving treatments. In addition, even if African American or Latino babies are born at the best hospitals, they tend to receive less intensive treatment, perhaps because as one expert noted, "biases make their way in" to medical care, putting them at twice the risk for dying in the first month of life (Horbar et al., 2019; Profit et al., 2017).

The goal of learning about culture is not necessarily to become familiar with all the cultures of the world. With more than 350 languages and more than 900 different ethnic groups in the United States alone, that would never be possible within one lifetime (US Census Bureau, 2015). Becoming *culturally competent* means you are familiar with and sensitive to the diversity in cultures, a goal that may be out of reach (Choi et al., 2018).

Another important objective is to develop **cultural humility** (Tervalon & Murray-Garcia, 1998), openness to cultural diversity and a self-awareness of your own cultural background with the goal of creating respectful relationships in which everyone learns from each other and no one feels superior (Foronda et al., 2016). Cultural humility not only helps us make friends and strengthens our relationships; it also is a job skill. Cultural understanding is a core competency for many professions, from health care to education to police work.

Many of us feel awkward when talking about culture and cultural differences. In fact, we may go to great lengths to avoid talking about differences—whether religious, ethnic, or racial. This begins in childhood. In one experiment, researchers asked a diverse group of children to sort photographs of people. All of the children avoided using skin color to sort the paper figures, even if it made the process more time-consuming and confusing (Pauker et al., 2015).

People often believe it is impolite to talk directly, particularly to children, about differences—from gender to ability to language spoken—that may result in discrimination or stereotypes (Hilliard & Liben, 2019). Developmental science, however, tells us that talking about variations is essential to understanding their impact on people's lives and helps guard against discrimination (Fasoli & Raeff, 2021). Even more, differences can be celebrated as a source of pride.

What Does Race Tell Us? Around the world, physical and cultural differences alike have been used to categorize and divide people. Some communities separate people by ability, appearance, skin color, religion, language, or ethnicity, and being part of one or more of these groups often leads to stereotyping, bias, discrimination, and uneven opportunities.

In the United States, researchers often look at the impact of *race* and *ethnicity* on development. When scholars talk about **race**, they refer to a system of categorizing people based on their physical characteristics (Goodman et al., 2012). Racial categories include those you may have checked off on a form, such as "Asian," "Native American," "White," or "Black." These physical differences are often assumed to overlap with people's geographical origins, but this is not always true. **Ethnicity** refers to groups that are based on their geographic origins and often cultural heritage, like Mexican Americans or Polish Americans.

Historically, racial categories were based on appearance, like your skin color or the shape of your facial features. Although these details result from genetics—you look like your biological parents—categorizing people into groups based on appearance has no basis in biology. Genes may cause differences in skin color but are not linked to differences between groups in other, more meaningful characteristics such as personality, health, or intelligence (Nelson, 2017; Yudell et al., 2016).

Scientists have found that 99.9 percent of human genes are shared, regardless of race, ethnicity, or skin color. There are no significant genetic differences between people based on their historical geographic origins (Panofsky & Bliss, 2017; Yudell et al., 2016). When researchers look at the genes of people from different geographic origins or with different skin colors, they find that the genetic differences *within* one group are vastly larger than those *between* two groups, as you can see in **Figure 1.5** (Hunley et al., 2016). In fact, the genetic variations among the people who now live in Africa are significantly greater than those of the people who live in every other part of the world combined (Williams et al., 2021).

Furthermore, the idea that our biological differences are based on where we come from is profoundly flawed: None of us live where we originated. Humans have been migrating and partnering with each other since the beginning of humanity. Being multiracial and multiethnic is a long-standing part of what it means to be human (Reich, 2018).

So, what is race? It was a historical invention, developed in the 1800s by people who adopted scientific-sounding words to justify White European domination over other people (McMahon, 2018). Indeed, racial categories have been adopted and adapted around the globe to help one group oppress another. For instance, in Romania, people from the Roma ethnic group, who many Americans would consider light-skinned White people, are considered "Black" (Grill, 2018). Racial distinctions are arbitrary and

race A system of categorizing people based on their physical characteristics. These physical differences are often assumed to overlap with people's genes or geographical origins, but this is not accurate.

ethnicity A way of referring to groups by their geographic origins and often their cultural heritage.

Thomas Nybo/UNICEF/Redux

Still Looking for Home Exclusion and discrimination can happen because of many factors, including what we look like or our cultural identity. Rohingya Muslims were driven out of Myanmar by the majority Buddhist government in 2017. Minara, shown here at age 7, was sheltering under a plastic tent when her Rohingya family fled their home in Myanmar after they were attacked during the genocide. Many are still living, like Minara, in refugee camps and are unable to return home safely.

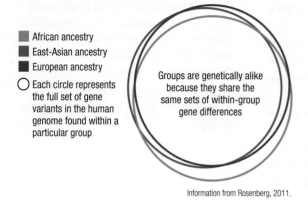

■ African ancestry
■ East-Asian ancestry
■ European ancestry
○ Each circle represents the full set of gene variants in the human genome found within a particular group

Groups are genetically alike because they share the same sets of within-group gene differences

Information from Rosenberg, 2011.

FIGURE 1.5 How Much Do Our Geographical Origins Contribute to Our Differences? When scientists measure our genes, they find that we are all 99.9 percent the same. If researchers compare the tiny 0.1 percent that accounts for all human differences, they find that the vast majority, or 95.7 percent, of these variations occur between people with similar geographical origins, and a mere 4.3 percent overlap between people of different geographical origins. In other words, the overwhelming majority of what makes us unique has nothing to do with where our ancestors came from.

people of color An inclusive term for people who identify as multiracial and for people who are Black, Latino, Asian American, or Native American and who have a feeling of solidarity and shared experience of marginalization.

based on local history and customs (Reich, 2018). Race is a social category, not a biological reality, but nevertheless, racial group membership shapes our experiences throughout the lifespan.

In many places around the world, discriminatory categories are based on skin color (Dixon & Telles, 2017). Your skin color is based on a complicated mix of genes (Martin et al., 2017; Tang & Barsh, 2017). Darker skin and lighter skin both offer biological advantages. Darker skin protects against the dangers of too much sun exposure. Lighter skin helps people get more vitamin D from sunlight (Goodman et al., 2012). People with dark- or light-colored skin live all over the world, and where they live has changed over human history (Goodman et al., 2012; Quillen et al., 2019). For instance, until at least 8,000 years ago, many Europeans were dark-skinned (Brace et al., 2018).

But despite the complexity of skin color, in many places around the world, bias and discrimination based on color, known as *colorism*, is prevalent. Light-colored skin is often seen as a sign of wealth and success (Dixon & Telles, 2017). In the United States, color often complicates race and ethnicity-based discrimination. Discrimination based on skin color often increases the experiences of bias against darker-skinned members of Black, Latino, Native American, and Asian American communities (Brown et al., 2018; Hargrove, 2019; Lee & Thai, 2015).

If race is not based in biology, does this mean you should ignore it? Quite the opposite. Race, ethnicity, colorism, culture, and the experience of discrimination all play an important part in human development (Tatum, 2017). Many people around the world, particularly those from privileged groups, still endorse incorrect, racist beliefs. In fact, one in five Americans who are not Black believes that biologically based racial differences are the reason why Black Americans tend to have lower income than White Americans (Morning et al., 2019).

Race- and culture-based bias and discrimination affect how you feel about yourself, what kind of schools you have access to, what kind of job you get, how much money you earn, and even your health, as you can see in **Figure 1.6** (Cobbinah & Lewis, 2018). Discrimination occurs in institutions, in everyday interactions between people, and in people's own beliefs. Its everyday toll begins before a baby is born and extends into the end of life (Trent et al., 2019). More positive race- and culture-based pride and *positive identity* can help people thrive, serving as a protection against the harms of discrimination (Yip et al., 2019).

The United States is increasingly a nation of people of color: More than half of children, and more than 4 in 10 adults, identify as Latino, Black, Native American, or Asian American (Schneider, 2020). **People of color** and *Black, Indigenous, and people of color (BIPOC)* are inclusive terms for people who identify as multiracial as well as for those who are Black, Latino, Asian American, and Native American and who have a feeling of solidarity and shared experience of marginalization (Perez, 2020). As you will see, creating a positive identity often begins with the freedom to select your own label or group identity, whether that means calling yourself a person of color or another term of your choosing.

What's in a Name? Your name and how you refer to your own identity are important to how you present yourself to the world. In the United States, people identify themselves many different ways, including by their cultural origins, gender identity, immigration status, and where they live. Families may identify as having one identity, multiple intersecting identities, or a mixed identity. Or, in the words of one college student, they may just "not want to label themselves" at all (qtd. in Saulny, 2011).

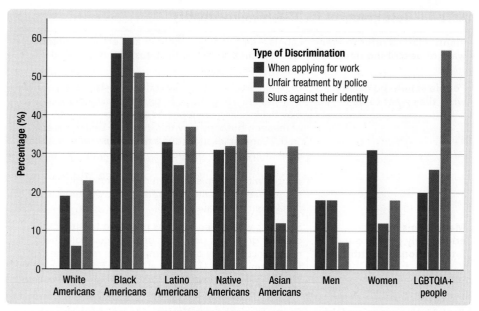

Data from NPR, Robert Wood Johnson Foundation, and Harvard T.H. Chan School of Public Health, 2018.

FIGURE 1.6 Discrimination in Many Settings Discrimination occurs on a number of levels. Institutional discrimination can include bias in hiring or policing. Interpersonal discrimination can include social exclusion, rejection, or humiliation, including being harassed or called names. This graph shows results from a survey of people's experiences of discrimination based on gender, ethnic and racial identity, and LGBTQIA+ identity—only a few of the ways that we can be subjected to exclusion and bias.

Variations abound. For people who work directly with children and families, the principles of cultural humility demand you call each individual what they want to be called—and check in from time to time to make sure that you are still getting it right. (See **Table 1.1**.) As high school student Kiarra Spottsville, who identifies as Diné (a Navajo Native American group) and African American, explained, "It is out of respect to call us how we want to be called...; it shows you care" (Blackhorse, 2015). Developmental scientists tell us that people who feel affirmed and supported in their identities tend to be happier and more creative (Austin & Pisano, 2017).

Institutions and government agencies contribute data to developmental science but often lag behind in adopting labels. For instance, the U.S. government often refers to people with Spanish-language heritage as *Hispanic*. Similarly, U.S. government data often refer to specific ethnic and racial categories, which ask people to identify themselves and their families as *American Indian*, *Asian*, *Black*, or *White*, and these terms appear in sources adapted from the U.S. Census (Brown, 2020). Professional organizations also establish standards and guidelines for group labels that further influence the terminology used in developmental science (APA, 2020; SRCD, 2021). However, within this complexity, some things are clear: Including the experiences of a wide variety of people and respecting their identities is critical to the study of development. As you will learn, studying the variations in development among different communities makes it more likely that all of us can thrive.

Celebrating New Beginnings Liam and Raquelle were together for years before they decided the time was right to start a family. They are both transgender but stopped transitioning in order to conceive. Liam was able to get pregnant, and now their daughter, Aspen, is celebrating her first birthday.

Dan Koeck/The New York Times/Redux

Culture Can Be Something You Eat.
For many of us, cultural identity comes down to food. The comfort foods of home help define who we are. Chef Sean Sherman, who identifies as Oglala Lakota, has made it his mission to restore the awareness of authentic indigenous foods. He grew up in Pine Ridge, North Dakota, and now advocates for and teaches about eating healthy ingredients, like the sunflower and bergamot petals shown here, in all communities around the world.

TABLE 1.1 Best Practices for Referring to Identity

Identity labels refer to many ways of describing people.	Labels refer not only to gender and ethnic or cultural identity, but also to health status, ability, physical appearance, and age.
People should be called what they want to be called.	Understand common, respectful variations and confirm that you are using the right one. For instance, you may think calling someone as an "elder" is a sign of respect, but they may think you are calling them "old." Sometimes individuals reappropriate labels that have been used to define them, turning their labels into identity-first points of pride. For instance, some people with autism spectrum disorder proudly refer to themselves as Autistic, whereas others prefer people-first labeling (Callahan, 2018).
Many labels do not adequately convey our intersectional identities.	Scientific work often requires grouping together the data for groups of people in order to compare their experiences. Many of the terms do not match the terms families use (Taylor et al., 2012). For instance, some families choose more precise labels—like calling themselves Syrian rather than Arab American.
Broad inclusive group labels do not always match research labels.	Group labels that are designed to be affirming and inclusive, such as BIPOC (Black, Indigenous, and people of color) and LGBTQIA+ (lesbian, gay, bisexual, transgender, questioning or queer, intersex, and agender, asexual, and/or ally), are not always consistent with the designations used in research (Baker & Harris, 2020). When we report research, we are limited to the data that we have. We cannot generalize, for instance, research findings about transgender people to the LGBTQIA+ community or about Mexican Americans to the BIPOC community.
Group labels often obscure important differences within groups.	Common designations like Latino include people from many possible countries. Similarly, terms like Asian American, African American, European American, and Native American obscure important differences within these groups. Some may include recent immigrants with different cultural identities than those who have lived in the United States for generations or even millennia (Blitvich, 2018). Some people may not identify with group labels that lump them with European Americans, such as those from the Middle East.
The terms that groups prefer are dynamic.	Community leaders may not agree on the best term to use. For instance, some Latino people, particularly those involved in research and advocacy, prefer the term Latinx as a gender-neutral alternative to Latino or Latina (Salinas, 2020). Many in the African American community prefer the term Black (Eligon, 2020). And in the Native American community, some members refer to themselves as American Indian or Indigenous (Blackhorse, 2015). Some Americans identify with their religious rather than their geographic or cultural identity, as with some Muslim or Jewish Americans.

Are There Cultural Differences? When should an infant start walking? Is a second-grader old enough to babysit? Should teenagers be able to get married? Should older people retire? Rethink your assumptions: Not everyone in the world agrees with you. While all communities share the challenge of raising children who will grow into adults with fulfilling, happy lives, there are distinctions among cultural communities in what families expect, how they raise children, and how people grow to see and interact with the world (Greenfield et al., 2003; Vélez Agosto et al., 2017).

Culture influences people in ways that are specific to each individual and determined by their everyday experiences (Harkness & Super, 2021; Rogoff et al., 2018). Each of us grows up in a specific **developmental niche**, or cultural environment, subject to the specific cultural practices, material setting, and beliefs of our families (Super & Harkness, 1994). Customs, or *cultural practices*, are sometimes easy to see, like what you wear or what holidays you celebrate, but often are less obvious, like how loud you talk or how often you smile (Keller, 2020). One practice with many cultural variations is what to do with a crying baby. Should you always rush to pick up your baby, as caregivers do in the Efe community of the Congo (Morelli et al., 2017)? Should babies learn to soothe themselves, as many do in the United States?

The *material setting*, or physical place where you grow up, will also influence how you grow. For instance, if you grow up with brothers and sisters on a farm in rural Iowa, your development may be different from that of an only child growing up in urban Chicago. What your family believes about how people grow will also play an important role in how they raise you. Does your family think that people can be easily spoiled? Or that they should be creative? Experts often call parents' ideas or beliefs about people's development **ethnotheories** (Harkness & Super, 2021).

Developmental scientists go beyond just listing variations in how children are raised or differences between cultures. They try to find patterns in those variations and describe their effect on people as they grow. One common variation is how much families value independence in thinking and their obligations to other people (Kagitcibasi, 2017; Keller, 2020; Miyamoto et al., 2018). Are adults and children encouraged to express their own individuality? Or are they deeply entwined with the lives of their family and loved ones? (See **Figure 1.7**.)

In developmental science, researchers use the term *independence*, or *autonomy*, to refer to how strongly a community values individual rights (Raeff et al., 2000). Communities with an **independent** orientation might allow children to have temper tantrums out of respect for their feelings, permit school-age children to refuse to do chores, and let adults question whether they should help their parents as they age, but they also encourage individuality and personal choices (LeVine & LeVine, 2016). Communities that have strong traditions of valuing independence are often said to be **individualistic**, because they tend to value the individual over larger groups, communities, or families. Families with individualistic ethnotheories may have smaller families, enabling them to focus their attention on a few children who they hope will be able to thrive in a competitive, global world (Doepke & Zilibotti, 2019; Lareau, 2015).

In contrast, **collectivist** communities place more value on relatedness and closeness and want children to rely on other people—and to be reliable in turn (Strand et al., 2018). These communities tend to value the family or the group over the individual. Children raised in collectivist families may help out around the house, even at young ages, and are expected to take care of their siblings and even their parents without being pestered (LeVine & LeVine, 2016). Experts also call collectivist families *interdependent*, because these families value the relationships between people and the group over the individual. Interdependence is often more common in communities where families rely on children to help—whether in urban communities where children need to watch their siblings while their parents work, or in rural farming communities where children may be working in the fields (Keller, 2020).

developmental niche A person's cultural environment, which is subject to the specific cultural practices, material setting, and beliefs of their family.

ethnotheories Parents' ideas or beliefs about children's development.

independent Communities that value individual rights. (Also known as *autonomy*.)

individualistic Communities that have strong traditions of valuing the individual over larger groups, communities, or families.

collectivist Communities that place more value on relatedness and closeness and tend to value the family or the group over the individual.

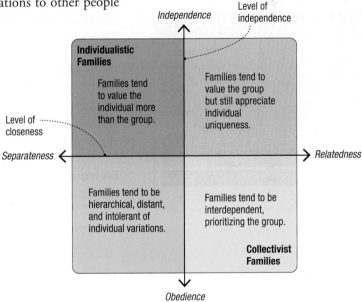

Information from Kağıtçıbaşı, 2005.

FIGURE 1.7 Dimensions of Cultural Variation Many contemporary developmental scientists look at cultures in terms of their levels of independence and relatedness. For instance, measures of individualism might indicate how much a community values following group norms or how much a community accepts uniqueness. Measures of relatedness might indicate how much you value relating to the world as part of your group, or whether you value being on your own. This schematic diagram shows where individualistic and collectivist groups might fit on these dimensions.

maturation The genetically programmed growth that drives many aspects of development.

Share It!

Families can help their children feel proud of their cultural identity in a process known as *ethnic (or racial) socialization*.

(Wang et al., 2020)

Scientific American: Lifespan Development

Scientific American Profile

Culture and Family

However, researchers agree that, in every community and country, there is a mix of ethnotheories about human relationships. Ideas about how best to raise children do not apply universally (Oyserman et al., 2002; Suizzo, 2020). The differences between individual families are typically greater within a community than between cultures. Although the United States is a relatively wealthy nation, not all Americans stress independent, autonomous values in raising their children, particularly if they are from immigrant or less affluent backgrounds (Markus, 2017).

Many families are *bicultural* or *multicultural* or may have cultural values that mix autonomy, obedience, independence, and interdependence (Markus, 2017; Park & Lau, 2016). For instance, while individualistic values are at work in Michelle's family, as with her concern that her daughters develop their own unique talents and identities, many collectivist values are also evident, like a commitment to their extended family in Argentina and the United States and to sticking it out together, no matter what the cost. While researchers often describe general patterns in cultural variations, individual families do not always match the statistics (Keller, 2017). Despite the diversity across communities all over the world, the most important goals that families have are strikingly similar (Lansford et al., 2021). More than anything, families want to raise children who become healthy and happy adults.

How Does Change Happen?

People change in many ways as they develop from wiggly newborns into social adults. They can learn to talk, make friends, and eventually may have children, grandchildren, and great-grandchildren of their own. Developmental researchers focus on *how* we change over time, investigating whether change is slow and steady or more rapid and irregular. They also look at what causes developmental change, examining whether it is something inevitable or caused by something in the environment. Researchers also study what stays the same in an individual as they grow, like whether an easygoing baby is likely to be a mellow grandparent.

Biological and Environmental Triggers Biology and the environment interact to help set the pace of maturation and aging. In the prenatal period and in much of childhood and adolescence, many aspects of development are driven by genetically programmed growth, or what developmentalists would call **maturation** (Gesell, 1928; Thelen & Adolph, 1994). As you see in **Figure 1.8**, the passage of time results in

FIGURE 1.8 How Do We Change As We Grow? Developmental scientists study how we change over time, along with how the pace of change contributes to the great diversity in our communities. This series of photographs documents the life of a family over nearly 25 years. Every year on the same day, photographer Zed Miller took pictures of his friends near their home in London, England, documenting their lives as their son grew into adulthood and they slowly aged. For the young boy, now a grown man studying engineering, the photographs remind him how much he's changed over the years. For his father, they are a memory of how short childhood is (Davies, 2010).

predictable developmental changes. Aging is also managed by your genes, but it is more heavily regulated by the environment than early maturation (Dato et al., 2018). As you get older, some changes are inevitable: Stresses from the environment trigger changes in your genes that lead to the vulnerability and declining health that often characterize later life (Horvath, 2013; Jones et al., 2015).

Throughout the lifespan, the environment can accelerate or slow down your growth. For instance, inadequate nutrition during prenatal development and the first year of life can accelerate infants' early growth and make them more vulnerable to heart disease later in life (Barker, 2004). But warm, nurturing relationships in middle life can help slow down the pace of aging (Klijs et al., 2017). Environmental toxins also play a role in how we mature. Physician Mona Hanna-Attisha sees the impact of this on the families she works with every day.

SCIENCE IN PRACTICE
Mona Hanna-Attisha, M.D.

One of the hallmarks of developmental science is a commitment to advocating for safer environments to help all people mature in the healthiest way possible. Dr. Mona Hanna-Attisha, a pediatrician, researcher, and public health advocate in Flint, Michigan, embodies this commitment. She was one of the first people to alert the public that families in Flint were suffering from high levels of lead in their drinking water, which was so polluted that it was damaging car parts at a nearby automotive plant. Her work helped expose a public health disaster (Hanna-Attisha, 2019; Hanna-Attisha et al., 2016).

The families who Dr. Hanna-Attisha served in Flint were facing challlenges even before they were exposed to lead. Poverty and health challenges meant that life expectancy in Flint was nearly 15 years shorter than it was in more affluent towns nearby (Hanna-Attisha, 2019). Discrimination and racism also played a part: Nearly 60 percent of the population of Flint is Black (Hammer, 2019).

Families in Michigan are not the only ones whose growth and development are harmed by environmental pollution. More than one in four deaths around the world is caused by toxins in the environment—from respiratory infections caused by air pollution to gastrointestinal diseases caused by unsafe drinking water or dangerous chemicals in food (Prüss-Üstün et al., 2016). And marginalized communities worldwide tend to have more toxic air and water than more affluent ones (Apergis et al., 2020).

Dr. Hanna-Attisha's study of the levels of lead in Flint began with nights spent poring over spreadsheets. She needed to confirm that changes in Flint's water supply were linked to increases in children's lead levels. Any amount of lead can be toxic to the growing brain. The injuries do not stop in childhood: Lead leads to more rapid cognitive aging in adults and a 40-percent higher risk of early death in later life (Lanphear et al., 2018).

Dr. Hanna-Attisha's data showed that the average lead levels of children in Flint nearly doubled after government officials failed to install corrosion control in their water system. After Dr. Hanna-Attisha published her findings and began advocating for cleaner water, she was attacked in the media and told that she was overreacting (Hanna-Attisha, 2019).

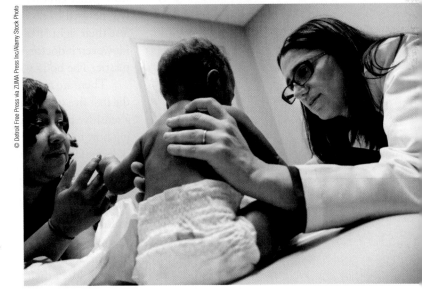

Just Another Check-up Dr. Mona Hanna-Attisha has been all over the country spreading the word about the dangers of lead pollution. But most days, she is still in her office, checking babies and talking to families, as she is here, helping make sure Courtney's daughter, Isabella, is doing well.

Dr. Hanna-Attisha was prepared. Her activism began when she was a teenager in Michigan, protesting a trash incinerator that was linked to higher levels of asthma (Hanna-Attisha, 2019). Her parents, who were immigrants from Iraq, had instilled in her a commitment to science and to giving back.

Despite the attacks that Dr. Hanna-Attisha received when she first published her work, her advocacy worked. The residents of Flint now have new pipes and clean water. Families with high blood lead levels are receiving extra services to help manage their symptoms. Dr. Hanna-Attisha is still in Flint, working in her small office on the second floor of a farmer's market to make sure that all families in Flint have access to fresh fruit and vegetables. She still feels fortunate to be able to work with children, but more than ever, she is also certain that she needs to fight injustice. 🔆

Plasticity and Its Limits　The brain and body are vulnerable to the effects of lead and other toxins throughout the lifespan because of **plasticity**, which means that you can be molded, like plastic, by your experiences. Plasticity helps us adapt to the environment we live in, which means we are vulnerable to negative experiences, like toxins, but also to positive experiences in the environment. People can have agency and change in order to thrive in their surroundings by learning the skills their cultures value, whether it is riding horses in Mongolia, playing Roblox in Los Angeles, or doing gymnastics in Singapore.

Scholars have found that there are certain developmental periods when change is more likely to occur, when our bodies, brains, and behaviors are more plastic and more easily shaped by the environment. These are **sensitive periods**, times when growth is particularly responsive to input from the world.

Scientists believe sensitive periods begin before birth and extend through adolescence (Blakemore & Mills, 2014; Frankenhuis & Walasek, 2019). For instance, if infants don't see anything at all because of an untreated eye disease, their brains will develop differently from other children: Brain regions typically devoted to processing visual information will be used to do other things, like process language (Lewis & Maurer, 2005). People who lose their sight later in life have different patterns of brain development (Pant et al., 2020). However, if doctors are able to reverse the visual impairment, the brain is still relatively plastic: The body will adapt, the brain will change, and people can develop new sight.

There are more sensitive periods early in development, particularly prenatally and in the first five years of life (Frankenhuis & Walasek, 2019; Zeanah et al., 2011). But adolescence is also a sensitive period. During the teenage years, children are particularly responsive to learning how to fit in with their community, a flexibility that allows them to learn new social skills and take on adult roles specific to what their culture values (Fuhrmann et al., 2015).

While scientists believe that there is tremendous potential for people to be plastic and resilient, sensitive periods make some kinds of change more difficult than others (Nelson et al., 2020; Van IJzendoorn et al., 2007). One way that scientists learned this was to study children who have endured serious adversity, such as being abandoned in orphanages. They found that many children who were housed in institutions experienced delays in their development: They were physically smaller and more prone to sickness than other children their age. Even if they were taken away from the orphanages and placed in nurturing homes, these children often had more difficulties with learning and with establishing strong relationships with their caregivers (Wade et al., 2020).

Children who had lived in abusive orphanages often recovered substantially and experienced some catch-up growth once they were in a safe place, but the researchers in this study also found that there were limits to this plasticity. While some children thrived after they were adopted into loving homes, most did not completely recover

plasticity　The idea that human development is moldable, like plastic, by experiences.

sensitive periods　The times in the lifespan when growth is particularly responsive to input from the world.

Courtesy Ionica Adriana

Ionica: Then and Now Ionica spent the first months of her life in an overcrowded orphanage in Romania where food was in short supply and human attention rare. (She is the baby on the left.) She was adopted into a loving family in England as a toddler and is now a thriving young actor who also works to promote adoption around the world. Although Ionica was able to adapt and thrive despite her early challenges, not all children who have experienced similar adversity have her good fortune.

(Humphreys et al., 2020; Sonuga-Barke et al., 2017). Children who were removed from the abusive or neglectful situations very early in their lives, before they were 3 to 6 months old, recovered much more fully than those who were older.

These findings tell us that people are more plastic earlier in life: It becomes more difficult to recover from stress as the years add on. Although people can build resilience over the lifespan, it is more difficult for an older adult, for instance, to recover from stress than it is for a young child (Sampedro-Piquero et al., 2018).

Can Science Predict the Future? If you look at a photograph of Michelle's daughter Nina, you may wonder if scientists can predict what will happen to her. Is there a way to tell how the rest of her life will play out? Will Michelle turn into a doting grandparent like her father? Will fussy babies grow up to be unhappy adults? Will early walkers turn out to be athletes? Developmental science does help explain how people's pasts predict their future, but development is complex. Plenty of challenging babies grow into contented children, and inactive young adults may turn into marathon runners in their later years.

Experts describe two models of change: continuous and discontinuous growth. **Continuous** growth is relatively constant and stable. In this type of growth, "slow and steady wins the race": Bodies get bigger and skills get better, without major shifts in the type of change. Language development typically builds slowly over time until it peaks in late adulthood.

Another model for how people change over time is called **discontinuous** growth. As you might guess, discontinuous growth is more irregular and unstable, happening in sprints and pauses. For instance, scientists measuring children's height found that they grow in bursts—sometimes as much as two-thirds of an inch (1.62 cm) in one day! (Lampl & Schoen, 2017).

Discontinuous growth can happen in discrete **stages**, or periods, where development changes dramatically. As we acquire a new cognitive skill, there is often an

continuous A model of change that is relatively constant and stable.

discontinuous A model of change that is more irregular and unstable, happening in sprints and pauses.

stage A period in which development changes dramatically.

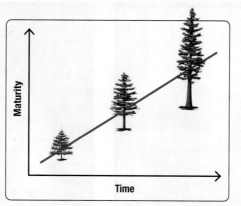 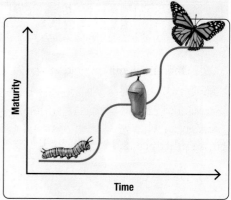

FIGURE 1.9 How Do We Change Over Time? Is change *discontinuous* and stagelike, like the separate stages in the life of a Monarch butterfly who grows from a tiny caterpillar into a beautiful butterfly? Or do humans grow more *continuously* like a redwood tree, gradually growing bigger every year little by little? Developmental scientists suggest it may be a little of both.

"Aha!" moment when everything becomes clear. For instance, some children walk for the first time and then never return to pulling themselves around on the furniture (Adolph et al., 2012). Many classic theories of development describe growth in terms of stagelike progressions.

Some types of development, like how you acquire language, is both continuous and discontinuous. For instance, vocabulary development is continuous (it keeps getting bigger as you age) even though the rate varies. But the acquisition of *grammar*, or how you use language to communicate, is more stagelike, with qualitatively different periods as children move from cooing to babbling to eventually being able to talk back.

Many moments in development appear to be dramatic, but sudden changes have been preceded by many small developments that allowed that change to happen. Children learn to walk, for instance, after taking more than 17 falls per hour—and most continue to use their tried and true methods of moving around, like crawling, for a few days after they take their first steps (Adolph et al., 2012). In thinking, too, it is typical for development not to happen in a straight line: Learning a new way of counting or reasoning doesn't mean we will always use it all the time (see **Figure 1.9**). Children's development may be divided into stages, but these stages may overlap, like waves, as children grow (Siegler & Ellis, 1996).

Throughout the lifespan, people go through many predictable changes as their bodies and brains mature, and their social experiences expand from their family relationships into a complex social, educational, and occupational world. Experiences can be unpredictable, too, as Michelle learned firsthand when Patricio was diagnosed. But people build on their past and adapt to new events.

APPLY IT! **1.6** If you had to choose just five words, how would you identify yourself? How has your identity changed over the years?

1.7 How has your context, such as your community, your culture, or your family, changed who you are?

Wrapping It Up ⬭

LO 1.1 Define scientific thinking. (p. 2)

Science is the process of gathering knowledge in a way that is testable and reliable. Scientific thinking is based on rigorously questioning what you know, testing that information, and relying on other people to cross check what you have discovered.

LO 1.2 Define developmental science. (p. 2)

Developmental science is the systematic study of how humans grow and the underlying processes that create change over time. The goal of developmental science is to both explain and improve the lives of children and adults. It combines scientific methodology with a commitment to the well-being of people of all ages.

LO 1.3 Describe the historical origins of developmental science. (p. 6)

People have tried to understand how to nurture development since the beginnings of humanity. Modern developmental science arose from the combination of scientific methods with new advocacy for the rights of children, older adults, and vulnerable people of all ages.

LO 1.4 Analyze four key themes addressed by developmental science. (p. 12)

There are four major themes that pervade developmental science: How is development created by the interaction between each unique person and their context? How is development universal and individual? How do culture and community impact how we grow? How do we both change and stay the same?

LO 1.5 Explain the contexts of family, community, country, and historical moment in shaping development. (p. 12)

A person's environment has an enormous impact on how they grow. Context includes the time period when we live, our culture, our physical environment and financial status, and our health. Models of context include Bronfenbrenner's bio-ecological model, García Coll's integrative model, and Yosso's Community Cultural Wealth model.

LO 1.6 Describe the complexity of understanding culture and development. (p. 12)

Culture is the ideas, beliefs, and social practices that a group of people share. Cultural practices shape how we grow over a lifespan.

LO 1.7 Explain the ways in which developmentalists describe human growth and change. (p. 12)

People can change over their lifespan, but how plastic we are depends on our context. Some types of development are continuous and others are more discontinuous, or stagelike.

KEY TERMS

birth cohorts (p. 16)
collectivist (p. 25)
Community Cultural Wealth (p. 18)
context (p. 14)
continuous (p. 29)
critical thinking (p. 11)
cultural humility (p. 20)
culture (p. 14)
developmental niche (p. 25)
developmental science (p. 4)
discontinuous (p. 29)
epigenetics (p. 10)
ethnicity (p. 21)
ethnotheories (p. 25)
gerontology (p. 5)
independent (p. 25)
individualistic (p. 25)
intersectionality (p. 20)
lifespan development (p. 3)
maturation (p. 26)
nature (p. 12)
nurture (p. 13)
people of color (p. 22)
plasticity (p. 28)
race (p. 21)
resilience (p. 2)
science (p. 2)
scientific method (p. 7)
socioeconomic status (SES) (p. 18)
sensitive periods (p. 28)
stage (p. 29)

CHECK YOUR LEARNING

1. At 4 months, Michelle began to put Nina to bed in her own crib and let her cry for a while before she fell asleep, to help her learn to soothe herself. The belief that learning to sleep independently will keep babies from becoming spoiled and dependent is an example of a(n):
   a) mesosystem.
   b) developmental niche.
   c) ethnotheory.
   d) birth cohort.

2. Which of the following is NOT an example of a developmental context?
   a) Parenting styles
   b) Birth cohort
   c) Culture
   d) Scientific method

3. Some experiences trigger genes to be expressed or not expressed during development. This is known as:
   a) exosystem.
   b) epigenetics.
   c) gerontology.
   d) resilience.

4. Which major period of development begins with the biological changes of puberty?
   a) Early childhood
   b) Early adulthood
   c) The prenatal period
   d) Adolescence

5. Which domain of development addresses how thinking and learning changes over time?

   a) Motor development
   b) Cognitive development
   c) Emotional development
   d) Physical development

6. The scientific study of aging is known as:

   a) gerontology.
   b) psychology.
   c) anthropology.
   d) nursing.

7. The scientific method:

   a) is impossible to define.
   b) is based on the opinions of researchers.
   c) involves testing hypotheses using systematic observations.
   d) only became common in the past 50 years.

8. As scientists compare their findings and identify commonalities across multiple studies, they arrive at:

   a) diverging views.
   b) scientific consensus.
   c) scientific overload.
   d) absolute truth.

9. Which of the following is an important implication of Bronfenbrenner's bioecological model?

   a) Interventions to improve people's life can be targeted at many different levels of their environment.
   b) Different microsystems operate independently and do not influence each other.
   c) The macrosystem is more influential than the microsystem.
   d) Biology doesn't matter in development.

10. Michelle and Lucia are members of different birth cohorts: Michelle lived through the 2008 recession, and Lucia was 4 years old during the COVID-19 pandemic. How might the historical events they have experienced have influenced their development?

11. What are some indicators of the socioeconomic status of Michelle and her family?

Theories and Methods of Human Development

© Macmillan, Photo by Sidford House

Theories of Developmental Science

2.1 Identify why developmental scientists use theory to guide their work.

2.2 Explain how the biological perspective links the brain and body to developmental change.

2.3 Explain how the psychodynamic perspective links early experiences to personality development.

2.4 Explain how the behaviorist perspective focuses on how people learn.

2.5 Describe how the cognitive perspective focuses on how thinking changes as we mature.

2.6 Explain how the cultural perspective focuses on how culture shapes development.

How to Study Development

2.7 Define the steps and guiding principles of the scientific method.

2.8 Describe the ethical standards governing science and practice.

Selected Resources from

Achieve

Activities

Spotlight on Science: Understanding Resilience

Concept Practice: Psychology's Research Methods

Assessments

LearningCurve

Practice Quiz

Videos

Scientific American Profiles

Imprinting

Natural Experiments in Psychology

Hugo is a 70-year-old grandfather with warm eyes, good posture, and big hugs who lives outside of Miami, Florida. He spent 43 years working for the U.S. government, 26 of them for the Air Force in more than a dozen locations around the world. Now, he is retired and, along with his wife of more than 40 years, Marta, specializes in naptime and preschool pickups. His granddaughters, Nina and Lucia, adore him. It is no surprise that Hugo has been called the ultimate overachiever: He is a super grandpa just as he was once a super Air Force officer.

It was not always this easy. When he came to the United States as a second-grader, Hugo didn't speak English and was terrified of failure. He and his mother were on their own, worried about money and starting a new life after leaving his father and their extended family behind in Cuba in the wake of the 1961 revolution. He was afraid that he might not make it. That he might not get through school. That they wouldn't be able to keep the lights on.

But beginning again was his heritage. He knew his grandparents had started their lives over, long before he was born, and that this ability was what his family expected of him. "You have to be prepared to start from scratch," he explained. And he did. He says he learned that the material things don't matter: It is your knowledge, your faith, and your family that will stay with you. Hugo worried about making it through each grade, but he did more than just get through school. He graduated high school and went to college on scholarship and graduate school in the Air Force. He devoted himself to his career and to his family — Marta, his two children, and now his grandchildren.

What does developmental science tell us about how Hugo came to be who he is? Scientists often use the term *resilience* to describe the ability to bounce back, and they might attribute Hugo's ability to thrive to his close relationships with the people who believed in him: his parents and grandparents who encouraged him to stay in school and start again. Hugo benefited from caring people who made him feel like he mattered.

Developmental scientists might also be curious about how Hugo has both changed and stayed the same with age. What parts of Hugo have stayed the same, as he grew from a frightened 8-year-old boy in a new country to a confident Air Force officer? What parts have changed, as that high-achieving student learned to crawl around on his hands and knees after his granddaughters? How did his relationship with Marta change who he is?

In this chapter, we will look at what questions scientists might ask about Hugo and how theorists might explain his resilience and his maturation. We will see what is unique about Hugo as well as what is universal about his family's journey through the lifespan.

Developmental theorists and scientists understand that development involves a complex interplay of genes, contexts, cultures, and history. Theories help to organize these ideas to create predictions about development, and the scientific method guides researchers as they build what they know. We now present major developmental theories with the goal of helping you apply your analytical skills, your ability to question what you see, and your skill in contrasting different perspectives.

Scientific American Profile

Meet Hugo

Theories of Developmental Science

Learning Objectives

2.1 Identify why developmental scientists use theory to guide their work.

2.2 Explain how the biological perspective links the brain and body to developmental change.

2.3 Explain how the psychodynamic perspective links early experiences to personality development.

2.4 Explain how the behaviorist perspective focuses on how people learn.

2.5 Explain how the cognitive perspective focuses on how thinking changes as we mature.

2.6 Explain how the cultural perspective focuses on how culture shapes development.

theory An organized set of ideas that helps scientists think critically about what they observe.

Ideas about what drives human development have been around since human beings first sought to understand why people do what they do every day. Do you already have a hunch about why Hugo found happiness in his adult life, despite the transitions and challenges he encountered as a young person? If so, you have formed a **theory**, which is how scientists organize their ideas and think critically about how to investigate what they observe. In developmental science, theories are explanations for how people change based on what can be observed or tested in real life. They provide a link between ideas and scientific findings by helping to generate hypotheses as well as give a lens for interpreting evidence.

Theories help direct the questions that scientists ask. For instance, researchers who adopt the biological perspective on human development might ask how Hugo's lifetime of good health impacts his life and his ability to bounce back from difficulties. Theories help researchers refine their research questions and choose what to study.

Theories Lead to Critical Thinking

As you will soon learn, contemporary developmental science includes a diversity of theories and ideas about what drives development. We have highlighted five theoretical perspectives (biological, psychodynamic, behaviorist, cognitive, and cultural) and more than 12 named theories. Why so many? First, knowing these theories will help you build expertise in developmental science and make you more comfortable interpreting the research you read about in this book and later on in your life.

Second, understanding different theories of development gives you practice in critical thinking. Contrasting and comparing diverse ideas helps scientists — and all of us — think more deeply and get closer to the truth. Taking someone else's point of view helps you learn more about what you think. Being challenged by someone who disagrees with you makes it less likely that you will make a mistake.

Third, each theory and perspective gives you a different way of looking at the world around you. They are designed to help you think carefully: This is at the heart of science. So, do not expect any one theory to tell the whole story. Understanding different perspectives helps us look at development from many angles.

Theories are influenced by the personalities, the history, and the beliefs of the community that created them. Many of the classic theories of developmental science were conceived of more than a hundred years ago by scholars who held values that are abhorrent to modern scientists. The first recognized theorists of developmental science were mostly White men. Many had views that were racist, sexist, ableist, and elitist: beliefs that were shared with many, but not all, of the people of their era (Allen, 2011; Yakushko, 2019). Modern developmental scientists have worked to preserve the universal and insightful aspects of their theories, while rejecting their bias, prejudice, and discrimination.

As you read about the theorists and see their old photographs, you might assume that they were solitary geniuses whose ideas sprang into being spontaneously (Oreskes, 2019; Shermer, 1990). This is incorrect: When the story of science is simplified, often one person gets the credit for ideas that were conceived by a team (Higgitt, 2017; Lin-Siegler et al., 2016; MacLeod, 2009). Just as they do today, scientists in the past worked with collaborators, romantic partners, students, and assistants. They were influenced by people outside the academic world, by their travels around the globe, and by their interactions with children and adults who did not share their elite, White backgrounds (King, 2019; Syed & Fish, 2018). Many of these people who inspired and collaborated on the classic theories of development remain invisible, but researchers today are eager to put them back into the narrative (García & Yosso, 2020).

The Biological Perspective

Developmentalists who take a **biological perspective** emphasize that psychological and behavioral development begin with roots in our brain, our genes, and innate or inborn instincts. Scientists who take a biological perspective might ask how development is changed by the genes we were born with and how those genes are changed by our environment. They might look at the brain to see whether there are signs that our brain development has affected who we are.

Evolutionary Theory The evolutionary perspective is, as you might guess, based on the theory of **evolution**, the idea that all life on Earth develops and changes to adapt to its environment over successive generations. Evolutionary theorists explain that over time, traits that help living beings survive are passed on to their offspring. This process, known as *natural selection*, allows some successful genes, traits, or behaviors to be replicated in the next generation (Darwin, 1872/2009). Thus, specific ways of growing or behaving were *adaptive* in allowing people to thrive—in the present and in the ancient past (Bjorklund, 2020; Ellis & Del Giudice, 2019). Developmental scientists might look at Hugo's life and ask how resilience helped human beings adapt to changing and often challenging circumstances over the millennia, or how human biology and maturation support resilience (Feldman, 2020; Masten, 2019)?

If you wonder whether evolution is compatible with your religious beliefs, you are not alone (Dunk et al., 2019; Hawley & Sinatra, 2019). Even the man whose name is most closely connected with the theory of evolution, Charles Darwin, worried about whether his ideas contradicted his faith (Heiligman, 2009). Like some other religious scientists, Darwin became confident that evolutionary ideas were compatible with his faith (Collins, 2006).

Evolutionary theory continues to inspire new discoveries about how human beings have adapted to the challenges of life on Earth (Legare et al., 2018; Meehan &

biological perspective An emphasis on how psychological and behavioral development begins with roots in our brain, our genes, and innate or inborn instincts.

evolution The idea that life on Earth develops and changes to adapt to the environment over successive generations.

Happiness Is in the Young. Charles Darwin and his wife, Emma, had 10 children. He is shown here with his oldest son, William. He doted on his children, telling a friend that he "cared more for them than for anything in this world" (Darwin, 1856).

ethology The theory that some human behaviors are universal and innate despite the wide diversity in human beings around the world.

epigenetics An area of study within the biological perspective that examines how physical and inborn characteristics, including gene activation, are changed by a person's environment.

Crittenden, 2016). Evolutionary scholars use innovative methods, visiting people in remote communities to look for hints about the earliest human interactions as well as comparing human behavior to that of primates like chimpanzees or bonobos (de Waal, 2019). No matter where they work, developmentalists with an evolutionary approach ask provocative questions about how human behavior evolved, such as why bullying persists through the generations and why women stop being fertile in the middle of their lives (Hawkes, 2020; Hawley, 2016).

The evolutionary perspective has its critics. Some researchers caution that the theory is speculative—since it is impossible to go back in time and see how humans really developed (Downes, 2015). Others note that some of the early work in this area was hampered by gender stereotypes (Buss & von Hippel, 2018). Nevertheless, the idea that our behavioral traits are an adaptation to the environment helps scientists appreciate the wide diversity in how people develop and thrive in many environments.

Ethological Theory The theory that some human behaviors are universal and innate despite the wild diversity among humans is known as **ethology**. For instance, healthy people learn to communicate, move, and relate to the world (Bateson, 2017). Ethologists look for traits that are universal within a species, suggesting that these are part of their genetic makeup. Ethologists are trained to observe animals and human beings and might look at orangutans or birds for insights into human behavior.

Some animal behaviors appear without ever being taught—kittens do not need to be shown how to scratch litter, and birds will learn how to fly even if they are raised in cages. Among some animals, even the close bond between the young and their caregivers is triggered by biology. For instance, some ducklings and goslings *imprint*, or establish a strong attachment, to the first object with eyes they see when they are a few days old—be that a parent, a human, or even a stuffed animal (Gottlieb, 2002; Lorenz, 1981).

Human beings are not ducklings: Our complex behaviors require back-and-forth social interaction in order to develop. For instance, a baby will not learn to talk or relate to other people without human contact (Bateson, 2015). But scientists believe our complexities are supported by inborn tendencies linked to our genes.

Jessica Meir, Scripps Institute of Oceanography at UCSD

Are You My Parent? Researcher Jessica Meir allowed a brood of baby geese to imprint on her so she could develop a close relationship with them and, eventually, learn how they fly. Humans also bond when they are young, but they do not imprint like birds.

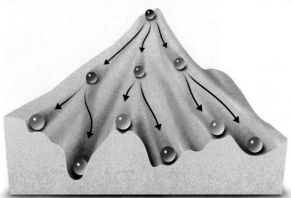

FIGURE 2.1 The Epigenetic Landscape of Development Human behavior may begin with genes, but genetic expression takes many pathways as we develop. Researchers use the analogy of a marble running down a mountain to express the many pathways we have available to use. Some of these paths, or channels, may be deeper than others (and more protected from environmental interference), and others may be the path less taken.

Epigenetic Theory Epigenetics builds on the biological perspective by examining how our physical and inborn characteristics, including how our genes operate, are changed by our environment (Waddington, 1952). Epigenetic researchers focus on how our everyday experiences, from what we eat to how we are loved, have a cascading effect on our development (Jovanovic et al., 2017). They recognize the complicated, bidirectional interaction between our inborn tendencies and the environment (Lickliter & Witherington, 2017).

Some epigenetic theorists compare development to a series of paths taken by a marble rolling down a mountain, as you can see in **Figure 2.1**. The marble begins its journey on top of the mountain with a fixed genetic route. As it continues down the mountainside, the environment leads it to follow one of many different possible paths. Some routes are deeper and therefore more likely to be taken, making the marbles more difficult to push off course (these are the paths that have a stronger inborn component). Other paths, or variations, are also possible (Van Speybroeck, 2002; Waddington, 1952).

Epigenetic theories have inspired exciting discoveries:

• Why do some children seem to bounce back from adversity more easily than others, as Hugo did? Researchers have found that not all children have the same sensitivity to the environment. In a theory known as *differential susceptibility*, researchers have found that some children have dispositions that are more easily changed by their life experiences. These children might be more easily changed by a positive, or negative, experience than other children (Belsky et al., 2021).

- Are your life experiences ever passed on to the next generation? It turns out that some extreme experiences, like living through a famine, will make biological changes in your genes, those of your children, and even your grandchildren (Bošković & Rando, 2018).

MAKING A DIFFERENCE
What Do We Really Need?

What do we really need to be happy? If you are like most people, you probably expect you would be happier if you had more money, more time, and stronger relationships (Luhmann et al., 2014).

More than 80 years ago, psychologist Abraham Maslow developed a list of what motivates us, often called the *hierarchy of human needs*, that has enduring appeal (Bland & DeRobertis, 2020). Maslow suggested that we have five categories of needs: (1) *physiological needs*, like the need for food, water, and the ability to breathe; (2) the need for *safety*, like knowing that you have a place to live and the resources you need to survive and not be hurt; (3) the need for *belonging* and connection to others; (4) the need for *esteem*, or respect from those around you; and finally (5) your need to be *self-actualized*, or engaged in the creative, moral, or unique work that you feel drawn to do.

Maslow suggested that most of us struggle with balancing and satisfying our needs throughout our lives, and very few are ever able to achieve self-actualization (Maslow, 1943, 1970). Maslow was not a specialist in lifespan development, and his ideas were based on a study of just 18 people from his own culture who he considered to be self-actualized. He was also inspired by his time spent among the Blackfoot people of Alberta, which exposed him to the idea of a hierarchy of being from lowly fungi to the sparkling stars (Brown, 2014; Heavy Head, 2007).

In the United States, Maslow's hierarchy has become core to patient assessment in health care and to human resources management in the business world (Beccaria et al., 2018; Kaufman, 2019). Developmental researchers have criticized Maslow's hierarchy, suggesting that it is based on a single cultural perspective rather than solid research (Morrison et al., 2011). A huge study of life satisfaction, based on global surveys of more than 800,000 people, found that material wealth was actually more important to people from affluent countries than it was to people who were struggling to survive (Tay et al., 2014). In many communities, including the Blackfoot nation, the goal of human development is not just one person's success but the well-being of the group, the culture, or the world (Maware et al., 2016; Winston, 2016).

Hands-on research has found that, contrary to what Maslow's hierarchy might suggest, human connection is essential for health across the lifespan (Holt Lunstad, 2017). Even if they have enough food, babies require human connection to thrive (Wade et al., 2019). And at the end of life, many adults will gladly give up some of their basic needs, and forgo medical procedures, to have more time to be creative, to connect with others, and to feel that they are living with dignity (Gawande, 2015). The psychodynamic theorists, who we turn to next, are one reason developmentalists understand that human connection is more than "nice to have"; it is essential for growth.

The Psychodynamic Perspective

The **psychodynamic perspective** considers how human behaviors are based on satisfying innate, biological needs for connection, protection, and love (Fonagy et al., 2016). According to psychodynamic theory, much of your personality, including how you

psychodynamic perspective An emphasis on how human behaviors are based on satisfying innate and often subconscious, biological needs for connection, protection, and love.

psychosexual stages The five stages of Freud's psychodynamic theory in which children learn how to manage different sensual and sexual energies.

manage stress and relate to others, results from patterns that were set when you were a tiny baby (Groh et al., 2017). Psychodynamic theorists might ask how Hugo's earliest relationships with his family helped turn him into the positive person he is today.

Freud's Psychosexual Theory Psychodynamic theory began with the writings of Sigmund Freud (1856–1939), who himself was inspired by other late-nineteenth-century scientists and philosophers who examined the role of the unconscious in human development (Gay, 1998; Grayling, 2010). Like the biological theorists, Freud believed that human behavior often results from unconscious urges that arose early in human evolution to help the human species survive.

Freud was a medical doctor and researcher from Vienna, Austria, who became famous for his radical theories and his talk therapy (Gay, 1996). He was born into poverty, threatened by anti-Jewish prejudice, and used cocaine (Crews, 2017). But, with his vivid writing style and his frank discussions of human sexuality, Freud became an international celebrity (Grayling, 2010). One of his most enduring contributions came from his belief that mental illness could be treated. Freud concluded that many psychological problems stemmed from unresolved childhood issues, such as traumatic experiences with weaning, toilet-training, or being abandoned or hurt by caregivers (Gay, 1996).

Freud thought that development involved five **psychosexual stages**, in which children learned how to manage a different sensual energy, as you can see in **Table 2.1** (Freud, 2018).

Many of the terms used in Freud's stages remain alive in popular culture today, like the idea of an *oral fixation* or an *anal personality*. However, most of his theory has been discredited because it lacks empirical evidence and was built based on his limited clinical work (Grayling, 2010). Developmental scientists have also critiqued many of the degrading assumptions Freud had about girls, women, and people outside of Europe and North America (Frosh, 2013; Stoute, 2020; Tate, 1996). Despite his disparaging beliefs, Freud's emphasis on the link between the first years of life and later emotional development influenced other theorists.

Erikson's Psychosocial Theory One of the many theorists influenced by Freud was the psychoanalyst Erik Erikson (1902–1994). After high school, Erikson traveled around Europe, teaching art and searching for his life's mission. He ended up teaching at a Montessori school in Vienna, Austria, where Freud had established his first training institute in psychoanalysis. Freud's daughter, Anna, turned Erikson into a psychoanalyst and supported him in identifying his calling: helping people. Although he never graduated from college, Erikson became a prolific writer and one of the first psychoanalytic therapists for children in the United States (Friedman, 2000).

TABLE 2.1 Freud's Stages of Psychosexual Development

Stage	Age	Characteristics
Oral	Birth to age 1	Babies learn how to manage the urge to feed and stimulate their mouth. They experience the satisfaction of being fed or sucking a pacifier, or they must cope with the disappointment of hunger or of being unable to suck.
Anal	About ages 1 to 3	Toddlers learn to balance the pleasure and challenge of controlling their elimination during toilet training.
Phallic	About ages 3 to 6	Children learn that they can derive pleasure from their genitals and adjust to society's gender roles. (Although this stage refers to the penis, Freud believed that all children have this experience.)
Latency	About ages 6 to 12	Children's sexual drives are temporarily quiet as they transfer that energy into learning and education until puberty.
Genital	About ages 12+	Adolescents can satisfy their sexual desires with romantic partners and take on adult responsibilities at work and in loving relationships.

Like Freud, Erikson focused on the role early experiences and social interaction plays in our lives and created a stage theory of *psychosocial development*. Erikson's stages are based on resolving a series of eight psychological crises triggered by physical maturation and society's expectations, as you can see in **Table 2.2** (Erikson, 1993; Erikson & Erikson, 1998). Erikson had the optimistic belief that psychological development continued across the lifespan.

Many of Erikson's contributions to developmental science still resonate. He embraced the complicated social context of development, describing personal growth that occurs within the family and the community (McAdams & Zapata-Gietl, 2015). In this way, Erikson's work is in line with contemporary sociocultural researchers who look at the impact of the wider world, or the *mesosystem*, on children's development (Syed & Fish, 2018).

Erikson's focus on identity development and the importance of generativity and giving back also continue to inspire researchers (Côté, 2019). However, many point out that creating a fulfilling life may not be as linear or as orderly as Erikson's stages make it seem, particularly for those who are not elite (Jordan & Tseris, 2018). Now more than ever, developmental scientists and policy makers believe that the first few years of life can create patterns of relating that last a lifetime, and that giving back to others, across the lifetime, is a necessary ingredient for satisfaction (Becchetti & Bellucci, 2020; Shonkoff et al., 2021).

Attachment Theory Many experts in the past knew that the early years were critical to children's development, but this did not mean that children were always nurtured and cared for warmly. Sometimes experts advised just the opposite: that babies didn't have emotional needs, that parents shouldn't pick up their children when they cried, and that separating infants from their families would not harm them (van der Horst & van der Veer, 2010). As a result, until the mid-1900s, babies who were hospitalized were sometimes placed in glass cages and not held. During World War II, some infants were even taken away from their families and put in overnight residential nurseries to enable their parents to keep working to contribute to the war effort (Midgley, 2007). Many argued that as long as babies were kept clean, fed, and safe, they could be resilient.

Share It!

Is watching children more important than college? Although he taught at Harvard, Erikson never graduated from college. Erikson said he learned more from children than he did in school and that watching a child play was like watching an artist paint.

("Eric Erikson," 1994)

Scientific American: Lifespan Development

TABLE 2.2 Erikson's Stages of Psychosocial Development

Stage	Age	Characteristics
Trust versus mistrust	Birth to about 18 months	The infant's conflict concerns whether or not the world feels safe. Infants with responsive caregivers learn that the world is a reliable place where they are likely to be cared for.
Autonomy versus shame and doubt	About 18 months to age 3	Toddlers strive to be independent, or *autonomous*, as they learn to walk, talk, and feed themselves. They may doubt themselves when they fail or cannot accept necessary limits on their behavior.
Initiative versus guilt	About ages 3 to 8	Preschoolers are eager to try new things and to be "big." Since they are unable to get everything right, they must manage their guilt at their missteps.
Industry versus inferiority	About ages 8 to 12	By middle childhood, children are ready to work at what their culture values. Children build a sense of their own industriousness and may struggle if they feel they are not meeting their community's expectations.
Identity versus confusion	About ages 12 to 19	Adolescents' central task is to actively discover their own identity. If they are too timid in that quest, they may be lost, confused, and unfulfilled.
Intimacy versus isolation	About ages 20 to 39	After the focus on the self of adolescence, young adults begin a search for intimacy. They learn to share their lives with others or struggle with loneliness.
Generativity versus stagnation	About ages 39 to 60	In middle adulthood, the focus moves to becoming *generative*, or productive. Adults learn to contribute by raising children or through work or creative efforts.
Ego integrity versus despair	About age 60 until the end of life	Older adults reflect on their lives and evaluate their successes and failures, making sense of themselves and achieving a feeling of wholeness.

manonallard/E+/Getty Images

Time Together Brought to You By Science Developmental scientists helped make this moment possible by establishing that young children benefit from close contact with people who care about them. As a result, this man and his son, in a hospital in Quebec, are able to spend time together, which scientists believe will help them both adjust as they grow.

Not all scientists agreed. Many believed that lack of emotional contact could be destructive. Doctors noticed that infants who were separated from their caregivers tended to become listless and were more likely to die (Spitz, 1945). Some even studied how isolation and separation hurt animals as well as human babies (Harlow, 1958).

It took a new theory and new scientific methods to change the practice of separating babies from their loved ones. A pioneering English medical doctor, John Bowlby (1907–1990), publicized his theory, later called **attachment theory**, maintaining that children's bonds to their caregivers are essential to their development. Like other ethological and evolutionary scholars, Bowlby believed that humans have a biological need to be attached and cared for in early life (Sroufe, 2016). Children who do not experience loving care are more likely to have difficulties forming adult relationships and could develop emotional and behavioral problems as a result (Bowlby, 2012).

Bowlby's theory gained more scientific approval after he met a Canadian psychologist, Mary Ainsworth (1913–1999), who also believed in the importance of strong early relationships (Bretherton, 1992, 2003; van Rosmalen et al., 2016). Mary Ainsworth traveled all over the world studying children—moving from Toronto, Canada, to London, England, to Kampala, Uganda, and later settling in Baltimore, Maryland. During her travels, she developed rigorous methods for assessing early relationships through real-life observation and laboratory experiments (Van Rosmalen et al., 2015). Together, Ainsworth and Bowlby developed and elaborated on attachment theory, which would help scientists understand and measure children's earliest relationships— and their effects throughout the lifespan.

Attachment theorists found that having healthy, close bonds in toddlerhood helps you to have healthy close partnerships in adulthood (Sroufe, 2021). Like psychoanalytic theorists, attachment researchers believe that early bonds create a pattern for future relationships and personality development (Mesman, 2021). Contemporary scientists agree: The value of close relationships does not end: Until the end of your life, having responsive, sensitive relationships helps predict your health, your happiness, and even how long you live (Ehrlich & Cassidy, 2021).

The Behaviorist Perspective

The biological and psychodynamic perspectives tend to focus on how people feel—on their emotions, their instincts, and their early relationships. *Behaviorist* scientists point out that there is more to people than feelings and instincts: Humans discover planets, do math, figure out how to get home on the bus, and how to build elaborate worlds in *Minecraft*. **Behaviorism**, or the behaviorist perspective, is a branch of psychology that is focused on things that are measurable, such as what a person *does* rather than what they think or feel (Watson, 1913). Classic forms of behaviorism focused on how human beings learn. One form, *social learning theory*, emphasized the role of social relationships in shaping behaviors.

The Theory of Behaviorism How do we learn and develop? The early behaviorists would say you should not ask someone what their motivations are, speculate on their unconscious drives, or wonder how they are feeling. Instead you should carefully observe the events that trigger their behaviors and watch what they actually do. To a behaviorist, feelings, thoughts, and unconscious motivations are unscientific, vague, and unmeasurable.

The man who did the most to popularize behaviorism was a U.S. researcher named John Watson (1878–1958) (Harris, 2011). Watson had a troubled young life: He was a bully who was arrested twice in high school for threatening his neighbors. College did not help very much: Although he crammed for his exams, powered by cocaine-laced Coca Cola, he graduated at the bottom of his class (Buckley, 1989). Nevertheless, Watson gets credit for bringing modern scientific methods to psychology and was one of the most famous researchers of his generation.

attachment theory The theory pioneered that maintains that children's emotional bonds to their caregivers are an essential part of their development.

behaviorism A branch of psychology that is focused on things that are measurable and suggests that we learn through pairing causes and effects.

Although Watson personally liked the ideas of psychodynamic theory, he was frustrated by the claim that inborn biology drove all human activity (Malone, 2017). In an era when many psychologists believed individual differences were based on genetics, Watson argued that they were the result of experience. He believed that all babies were born equally capable and that children learned everything they knew (Malone, 2014; Watson, 1913).

Classical Conditioning Watson believed that you learn everything—how to talk, how to walk, and even how to relate to other people—through a process called **classical conditioning**. According to this model, learning is a process of linking a *stimulus* (or experience) to a *response* (or behavior). The process of classical conditioning builds from existing automatic reflexes and works in animals (even snails) as well as in more complicated organisms like people. The principle of classical conditioning was first observed by Russian scientist Ivan Pavlov (1849–1939), who showed that dogs could "learn" to drool in response to a bell ringing, if they had practice hearing the bell while being served dinner (Gewirtz, 2001). Watson, like other scientists, believed that human beings also learned this way and was one of the first to demonstrate that children could be conditioned like animals.

Watson believed that classical conditioning might be a way to cure debilitating anxiety and fear, like the anxiety (now known as *posttraumatic stress disorder [PTSD]*) suffered by war veterans (Powell et al., 2014). But in order to demonstrate that conditioning could cure people's fear, Watson and his team needed to show that fear itself could be conditioned. They decided to train an infant to be afraid, and they found a baby boy in a nearby hospital who became known as "Little Albert" for their experiment (Digdon, 2020).

The team was successful: By making a loud noise that terrified the baby at the same time that he saw a white rat, they conditioned Little Albert to fear white rats and other white, fluffy things, even without the loud noise. The experiment was so effective that Watson suggested that Little Albert even became terrified of Santa Claus's white beard. Little Albert had shown that human beings could learn through conditioning just like animals (Powell & Schmaltz, 2020).

Most agree that the treatment of Little Albert was unethical. But fortunately, according to many historians, Albert lived to old age and never complained about what had happened to him in childhood (Digdon, 2020). Later research by other behaviorists, including Mary Cover Jones, made use of Little Albert's contributions by showing that classical conditioning could also be used to *remove* fears and help people recover from trauma by pairing the fearful stimulus with a positive, comforting one (Cover Jones, 1924).

Classical conditioning is used today to toilet-train newborns (see **Figure 2.2**), to help children get over their fear of dogs, and to help teenagers and adults recover from trauma (Fullana et al., 2020).

Operant Conditioning Have you ever given yourself a well-earned reward after an hour of studying or working out? Or were you told as a child that you would not get dessert if you kept misbehaving? These are behavioral principles and a form of learning described by American psychologist B. F. Skinner as **operant conditioning** (Skinner, 1938). The idea is that a behavior will be more likely to happen if it is rewarded—and less likely to occur if it is ignored or punished. In operant conditioning, rewards and punishments are used to shape behaviors.

Researchers like B. F. Skinner looked at animals as a model for how human beings learn, and they suggested that children, like animals, learn everything they know by a complex system of **reinforcements** and **punishments** (Skinner, 2011). A reinforcement is anything that strengthens a behavior and makes it more likely to happen. It can be a

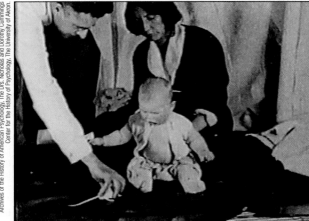

Learning to Be Afraid In this video still, the baby known as Little Albert seems to react with childish curiosity as researcher John Watson shows him a rat. John Watson showed that this curiosity could be turned into terror through classical conditioning.

classical conditioning A model of learning in which a *stimulus* (or experience) is linked to a *response* (or behavior).

operant conditioning A process of learning in which rewards and punishments are used to shape behaviors.

reinforcement Anything that strengthens a behavior, making it more likely to happen.

punishment Anything that weakens a behavior, making it less likely to happen.

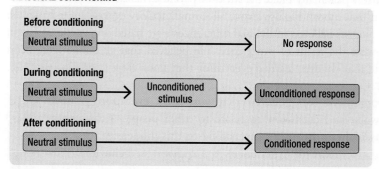

CLASSICAL CONDITIONING

Before conditioning

| Neutral stimulus | → | No response |

During conditioning

| Neutral stimulus | → | Unconditioned stimulus | → | Unconditioned response |

After conditioning

| Neutral stimulus | → | Conditioned response |

POTTY TRAINING WITH CLASSICAL CONDITIONING

Typically during an infant's first 3 months, parents who use this method begin to pair whistling (or another neutral stimulus) with the infant's urination, placing the baby on a potty at the same time. This links the unconditioned neutral stimulus (whistling), the reflexive feeling of elimination, and the act of eliminating in the toilet. After conditioning, babies are able to eliminate in the toilet after hearing the whistling prompt.

Before classically conditioning potty training

| Whistling (Neutral stimulus) | → | No response |

During classically conditioning potty training

| Whistling (Neutral stimulus) | → | Eliminating (Unconditioned reflex/ Unconditioned stimulus) | → | Eliminating in the toilet |

After classically conditioning potty training

| Whistling (Neutral stimulus) | → | Eliminating in the toilet |

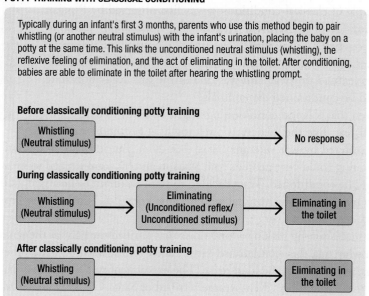

FIGURE 2.2 A Recipe for Classical Conditioning In the process of classical conditioning, a neutral stimulus (like whistling or bell ringing) is paired with an involuntary, reflexive response (like drooling in hunger or going to the bathroom) when it happens naturally. But gradually, after the neutral stimulus happens at the same time as the reflexive response, the stimulus alone will trigger the response. For instance, if a caregiver whistles every time a baby goes to the bathroom, the baby will eventually be triggered to go to the bathroom every time they hear the whistle.

Working Toward a Goal Some adults might use bullet journals, or nudges. This little girl is using a sticker chart to mark how far she's gone toward her goals.

reward, like a treat after finishing a hard run or a smile from a teacher. A punishment, as you might imagine, is the opposite of a reinforcement and is anything that makes an activity *less* likely to happen, such as when an instructor takes away a student's cell phone as a consequence of their distraction.

Why shouldn't you give a screaming toddler that candy bar they are reaching for in the checkout line at the grocery store? Remember operant conditioning: If you give in this one time, you are reinforcing their behavior and they are likely to scream again next time. This is why the principles of operant conditioning are widely used in everything from training animals to health care.

Operant conditioning helps researchers understand how adolescents reinforce each other's bad behavior by laughing when a friend breaks the rules (Patterson, 2016). It is also at work in education: Skinner felt passionately that learning should be customized, responsive, and give students immediate feedback—ideas that are incorporated into many technologies today, such as the "like" button on Instagram (Skinner, 1989). Behavioral techniques also form the core of applied behavioral analysis therapies, which are used by many families to help their children with autism spectrum disorder (Hyman et al., 2020; Lovaas, 1987).

Although modern scientists agree that operant conditioning is an important part of how children learn, few agree it is the only way. Other scientists have demonstrated that children also learn just from watching other people—with no reinforcement or punishment necessary.

Social Learning Theory According to **social learning theory**, learning occurs through observing and imitating others. Social learning theorists suggest that learning involves thinking and reasoning. People who are respected, like your parents or your admired friends, are more likely to be imitated. Reinforcement may shape your learning, but it does not have to be direct. If children see someone else being rewarded or punished, that will affect their decision whether or not to imitate their behavior.

Real-life examples of social learning can be sweet—as when a 3-year-old puts on their mother's uniform and pretends to go to work—or less so, as when your younger brother repeats the swear-words he heard you say. Researchers who take a social learning approach point out that the most important part of how people learn is often other people. Humans are social—and from birth, we are highly attuned to the facial expressions and behaviors of other people—which helps us learn from each other (Dunbar, 2020; Tomassello, 2020).

Albert Bandura (1925–2021) focused on the mechanics of how people learn in a social world (Bandura, 1999, 2018). He found that people *model* behavior—whether it is how to stand inside the elevator or how to sit while they are waiting for class to start. Learners pick up new behaviors through *observation*, or watching a model—as when we study a dance on TikTok before trying it. We also learn from *imitation*, or by echoing or repeating something we have observed—as when a child in the back seat mimics a hand gesture they saw in the front seat. Social learning theorists demonstrated that we can learn without direct experience, as with watching something on Zoom, watching someone else experience something, or even hearing about it third-hand (Maccoby, 1992).

Social learning theories have guided decades of scientific investigations. Research suggests that imitation starts early: Newborns might imitate a facial expression of someone nearby, and toddlers will quickly learn how to play with a toy from someone they have just met in the laboratory (Meltzoff & Marshall, 2018; Tomasello, 2019). Studies of the impact of technology on human behavior investigate whether violent videos games might teach us to be violent in real life and whether television programs can be beneficial, discouraging substance use disorder and forced marriage (Anderson et al., 2017; Bandura, 2019). Social learning theory has also inspired some people to take up jobs in the classroom.

social learning theory The theory that learning occurs through observing and imitating others.

Courtesy Albert Bandura Trust

The TV Made Me Do It. In the early years of television, Albert Bandura and his team showed that children were more likely to whack an inflatable toy called a Bobo doll if they had seen another child or adult do the same thing—even if they only saw it on television. Bandura also observed that children were more likely to imitate what they saw other children get rewarded for. Imitating what you see on TV is not always harmful: Programs like Sesame Street harness children's tendency to imitate to help them learn.

cognitive development theory The theory that growth in thinking and understanding happens as a result of active exploration of the world.

Role Model and Award Winner Johnathon Hines is an award-winning pre-K teacher at Barack Obama Elementary School in Atlanta, Georgia, and a role model for students who want to grow up to teach and help others.

SCIENCE IN PRACTICE
Johnathon Hines, Pre-K Teacher

Johnathon Hines may not be what most families expect when they sign up their children for his pre-kindergarten class. He's tall. He's Black. And he is a man. Hines did not expect to become a teacher, either. Like many other teenagers, he dreamed of being a basketball player. Social learning theory is why he became an award-winning pre-K teacher at Barack H. Obama Elementary Magnet School of Technology in Atlanta. Social learning theory explains that role models help us set goals, help us see what is possible, and inspire our work (Morgenroth et al., 2015).

Hines wanted to be a role model: He wanted to inspire young children and show them that being a happy, successful person could mean nurturing students and caring about school. He knew that in the United States, fewer than one in four elementary school teachers is male, and even fewer are Black (U.S. Department of Education, 2021). He wanted to show children that Black men could be successful off the basketball court and in the classroom. As he puts it, he wanted to be a "hero" by showing young people how much school matters.

Empirical research supports Hines' belief: Culturally diverse teachers help students of all backgrounds succeed by reducing their biases and making them more comfortable in a diverse world (Perry, 2019). Black students who have Black teachers tend to do better in school and stay in school longer (Egalite & Kisida, 2018). One study found that Black students who had an elementary school teacher who looked like them were more than 10 percent more likely to go to college (Gershenson et al., 2018).

For Hines, being a role model is more fun than he imagined, even when it means hosting show-and-tell on Zoom during the COVID-19 pandemic. He teaches phonics and encourages kids to wait their turn, but he enjoys his students' enthusiasm, their energy, and their love of learning.

The Cognitive Perspective

Scientists who focus on cognitive development try to understand how learning shapes development—and how thinking changes through the lifespan. There are several theories about how thinking develops, including those of Jean Piaget and the information-processing researchers. Along with the behaviorists, cognitive researchers brought careful laboratory techniques and observation to their work—and they made developmental science more rigorous (Anderson, 1956).

Piaget's Theory of Cognitive Development Most behavioral theories explain that learning happens in the same way for babies as it does for adults. **Cognitive development theory** takes another view: The thinking of a baby is categorically different from that of a toddler, a school-age child, and an adult (Flavell, 1996). In contrast to the behaviorists and social learning theorists, the revolutionary Swiss psychologist Jean Piaget (1896–1980) argued that growth happens as a result of our active exploration of the world. Children's thinking matures as they actively construct and build what they know (Piaget & Inhelder, 2019). Piaget became the most famous developmentalist of his time as he empathized with children trying to learn about the world—how to grab, suck, and talk. He believed that their thinking develops in distinct stages; that they are not capable of reasoning like adults, nor should they be expected to. But according to Piaget, their unique ways of reasoning are creative and adaptive (Miller, 2011).

A Scientist and an Inventor Jean Piaget was not just good at making theories. He also made his own baby carriers, so he could take his son, Laurent, and his other children hiking in the mountains near his home in Geneva, Switzerland.

Piaget had a difficult childhood and a rocky early career as a shellfish researcher before he began studying children's development. He turned the careful observation skills he had used for categorizing marine creatures to the task of studying children. While he and his wife Valentine (also a trained psychologist) carefully observed their three children, Piaget was formulating a new theory of how children's thinking develops through breakthroughs in understanding (Fischer & Hencke, 1996; Kohler, 2014).

Piaget developed a specialized vocabulary to describe mental activities: The word **schema** refers to each bit of knowledge a person develops (Piaget, 2013). A schema can be a skill, like grabbing a rattle, or a concept, like understanding that the category of "dogs" includes your dog and others you see in the neighborhood or in a picture book. Schemas grow and become more sophisticated with development and practice, through processes of *assimilation* and *accommodation*.

Piaget's concept of **assimilation** is the expansion of an existing schema with new knowledge or experience. For instance, infants are good at sucking—they can suck a bottle or a pacifier just fine. And this sucking ability can be adapted to something else entirely, like Daddy's phone. The baby has assimilated this new, hard beeping object into their existing sucking schema that had previously just been used for soft things. As they get older, their assimilation may become more sophisticated: They may assimilate cougars into their schema for giant cats or add kale to their schema for foods.

Sometimes children's existing schemas need to be changed because new information just does not work with the old schema. **Accommodation** is the process of reorganizing knowledge when that happens. For instance, a sucking baby may realize that they cannot suck the dog (without a mouthful of fur). A toddler may realize that beach sand is not as tasty as it appears. Their schemas need to be altered to accommodate knowledge that dogs and sand are not objects to suck.

Piaget's stage theory of development described four discrete periods, or **stages**, in cognitive development, as you see in **Table 2.3**. While some other psychologists speculate that more realms of thought exist beyond this stage, Piaget himself believed that formal operational thought included all the cognitive tools that most adults would use throughout their lives (Labouvie-Vief, 1985; Piaget, 2013; Sinnott et al., 2020).

Piaget's revolutionary contributions to developmental science include not just what he discovered about how children think, but how he did his work: He talked to

schema The word for each bit of knowledge a person develops.

assimilation The expansion of an existing schema with new knowledge or experience.

accommodation The process of reorganizing knowledge based on new experiences.

Piaget's stage theory of development The five periods of cognitive development described by Jean Piaget, in which children's thinking proceeds through qualitatively different ways of understanding the world.

stages Distinct time periods when development changes dramatically.

TABLE 2.3 Piaget's Stages of Cognitive Development

Stage	Age	Characteristics
Sensorimotor	Birth to about age 2	Infants use their senses and physical abilities to explore the world. This stage begins with involuntary movements, such as reflexes, and ends with independent movement, language, and imagination. Babies and toddlers gradually learn that there is more to the world than what they can feel or manipulate with their bodies. As they grow, they can mentally represent ideas and think about them before they happen, an achievement that marks the end of the sensorimotor period.
Preoperational	About ages 2 to 6 or 7	Young children can communicate with language, use their imagination, and think symbolically, but they cannot yet think logically and are easily tricked by appearances. A young child might believe that a costume turns someone into Captain Marvel and will have difficulty imagining things from someone else's perspective. This period is called *preoperational* because children are not yet able to perform mental operations or think through events.
Concrete operational	About ages 6 or 7 to 11 or 12	This stage is all about logic. Children can now reason through problems and examine situations from differing perspectives, as long as they are not too abstract. They can categorize things and put them in order. However, thinking is more reliable when it is linked to what can be seen, heard, or touched.
Formal operational	About age 11 through adulthood	This stage involves grasping abstract or hypothetical ideas, concepts, and scenarios. Teenagers and adults can ponder the idea of a world without money or the meaning of the word *justice*. This will enable adolescents and adults to create amazing things like new vaccines or more efficient cars—as well as more everyday insights like how to get through math class.

All the Cognition He Needs to Help Others Piaget's stage theory of cognitive development suggests that we develop all the cognitive skills we need by the time we are adolescents. By eighth grade, Shubham was able to design an inexpensive machine to print Braille for people with visual impairments. It is based on an early model he made with Lego blocks for his school science fair.

children directly and sympathetically. When a boy told him that dreams came from his blanket, Piaget did not correct him—he just asked more questions. Piaget's description of children's thinking helped to create a whole new field of developmental science devoted to children's cognition (Flavell, 1996). His belief that children did not need to be rushed from one stage to another and that their thinking is creative within each stage continues to influence how educators work with children (Zigler & Gilman, 1991). And unsurprisingly, Piaget's stance as a curious and empathetic observer remains a model for teachers, child-care workers, and developmental scientists alike (Waite-Stupiansky, 2017).

While Piaget's stages remain a touchstone in developmental science, many have questioned how accurate they are (Carey et al., 2015). In many studies, children's cognitive development does not proceed neatly in precise periods and often depends on how much enrichment and formal schooling they receive (Busch et al., 2020; Siegler & Ellis, 1996). Babies actually display more logical thinking and more inborn abilities than Piaget observed when he first formulated his theories (Baillargeon et al., 2016). And while Piaget was not very impressed with the cognitive maturation of adults, subsequent scientists have pointed out that thinking changes in adulthood, in ways Piaget did not predict (Salthouse, 2019). Nevertheless, Piaget's stages of cognitive development remain a shared vocabulary within developmental science for describing cognitive growth.

Information-Processing Theory While Piaget was becoming the most prominent developmental scientist of his generation, another group of researchers was looking at the development of thinking from a perspective known as **information processing**. They studied the individual components of how you process what you perceive: how you pay attention, remember, and react to the world (Lachman et al., 1979). Inspired by computer technology, information-processing theory describes thinking and learning using the metaphor of a computer, exploring *inputs* (such as your sensation, perception, and ability to pay attention), *processing* (such as thinking and learning), *storage* and *retrieval* (memory), and *output* (your behavioral responses). (See **Figure 2.3**.)

Information-processing scientists also look at more complex thinking processes, like *executive function*, or your ability to actively regulate your thinking and behavior to accomplish a goal. Unlike Piaget, information-processing theorists do not believe that development occurs in stages, although they have observed substantial changes in people's cognitive abilities from infancy to late life (Salthouse, 2019).

The information-processing approach to development has led to important discoveries about what very young babies are capable of, how older children learn,

information processing An approach that studies the development of thinking and understanding by describing how a person pays attention, remembers, and reacts to the world, similar to how a computer processes information.

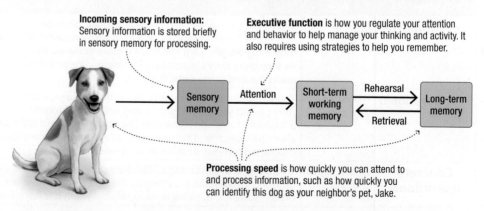

Incoming sensory information: Sensory information is stored briefly in sensory memory for processing.

Executive function is how you regulate your attention and behavior to help manage your thinking and activity. It also requires using strategies to help you remember.

Sensory memory → Attention → Short-term working memory → Rehearsal → Long-term memory → Retrieval

Processing speed is how quickly you can attend to and process information, such as how quickly you can identify this dog as your neighbor's pet, Jake.

FIGURE 2.3 How Do You Process "Dog"? Information-processing theorists look at the individual components of our thinking, including how we process incoming sensory information, store it in memory, and make decisions about how to regulate our attention.

and how aging changes your thinking. For instance, researchers watching infants' eye movements found that at just 4 months of age, infants expect an object that has disappeared to reappear, suggesting an early understanding of object permanence (von Hofsten & Rosander, 2018). Scientists have studied how babies use statistics to find patterns in the speech they hear, helping them learn what to focus on in language learning (Saffran, 2020). Information-processing research has also shown that adults continue to learn over the lifespan, although the speed at which they react to new stimuli tends to slow down in later life (Ackerman & Kanfer, 2020).

The Cultural Perspective

Developmental scientists' commitments to recognize the value of all people, embrace diversity, and advocate for increased tolerance and an end to discrimination means that the *cultural perspective* is one of the most prominent theories in research today (Brown et al., 2019; García Coll et al., 2018). The **cultural perspective** explains how culture is integrated into all of development and how cultural variations and strengths can help everyone thrive. Cultural theorists ask questions about the impact of culture on development, including how culture gives us strength and how discrimination can challenge us. A scientist with a cultural perspective might examine how Hugo's cultural values contributed to his resilience. Other scholars might want to learn about the impact of intersectional discrimination on Hugo as he grew up in a world that is often prejudiced against immigrants and people who are bilingual.

Sociocultural Theory Sociocultural theory observes that culture plays a role in every part of human development (Packer & Cole, 2020). Cultural theorists emphasize how children's learning is based on interactions with other people in a cultural context (Rogoff et al., 2017). Even how you see, how you remember, and how your brain develops are influenced by culture (Wang, 2016). Rather than describing culture as the outside, or the macrosystem, of human development, sociocultural theorists see culture as embedded inside each part of how we grow (Vélez-Agosto et al., 2017).

Russian psychologist and educator Lev Vygotsky (1896–1934) was one of the first to observe how deeply culture affects how we grow. Vygotsky worked in the 1920s and 1930s, and his research was forgotten to a large extent after his early death at age 37. But in the late 1970s, it was rediscovered and retranslated into English (Vygotsky & Cole, 1978; Yasnitsky & van der Veer, 2015). Vygostky had many passions—from writing about Shakespeare to studying law—but teaching is what profoundly changed his thinking (Yasnitsky, 2018). While sick with the lung disease that later took his life, Vygotsky began to teach children with major disabilities and children who had never been exposed to the written word (Gindis, 1999). Unlike many others, Vygotsky did not overlook or dismiss the fact that these children were capable and he argued that their differences could be strengths.

Sociocultural theorists working in his tradition now have three major approaches to studying culture in developmental science:

1. *Interpreting what you observe through the lens of culture helps you see more accurately.* For instance, what do you think when you see a child in the fields, as in this photograph? Is Nikbakt too young to be helping out? Or does she feel proud of her contribution? Researchers point out that unless you understand the cultural meaning that the child and their community attach to what she is doing, you will not understand it accurately (White & Mistry, 2016). Work can be helpful or harmful to children depending on their cultural beliefs and context.

cultural perspective Explains how culture is integrated into all of development and how cultural variations and strengths can help everyone thrive.

sociocultural theory The theory that culture plays a role in every part of human development.

Gone Too Early Lev Vygotsky was a teacher, scholar, and advocate for children and people with disabilities. Without the benefits of modern science, he died at just 37, leaving behind his wife and their two young children.

Is She Working, Doing Homework, or Just Checking for Likes? The sheep will never know. Nikbakt is watching over her family's sheep while doing homework in the mountains near her home in Afghanistan. Even though she lives in a remote area, her high school still manages to send most of their graduates to the top universities in their region. Scientists suggest that understanding the impact of chores means understanding their context.

Developmental scientists use theoretical models to think about and study the complex ways culture and context influence human development. How might each theoretical approach explain how Hugo changed and grew from an anxious second-grader to a confident and affectionate grandparent?

Major Questions	What is the pattern of change?	How do people change or grow?	How does this explain Hugo's growth?

THE BIOLOGICAL PERSPECTIVE

 How is development triggered by our brain, our genes, and our innate or inborn instincts? How does our body influence how we grow?

Evolutionary Theory	Human behavior gradually adapts and changes over millennia through natural selection to better align with the environment.	Individual variations and diversity demonstrate how human beings can successfully adapt to their environment. Some of our variety, however, may not be a perfect adaptation to our current situation.	Some evolutionary theorists suggest that humans live into late adulthood to become grandparents, one of the ways our species provides for its young.
Ethological Theory	Many human behaviors are universal and innate despite the diversity in human beings around the world.	Change is driven by inborn programming.	An ethologist might suggest that Hugo had an innate capability to bond with young Nina and Lucia.
Epigenetic Theory	Inborn characteristics, including your genes, have been shaped and changed by your environment.	Each of our paths can change, but at some times our inborn tendencies or the environment can make change easier or harder than at other times.	Hugo was shaped by his inborn temperament and also by the cascade of his life events, from his close relationship to his mother to his marriage. These events helped create a doting, caring grandfather.

THE PSYCHODYNAMIC PERSPECTIVE

 How are human behaviors driven by our innate, biological needs for connection, protection, and love? How do our earliest experiences in our families and communities shape our developing personality?

Freud's Psychosexual Theory	We develop through five psychosexual stages, in which we learn how to manage a different sensual and sexual energy.	With positive early experiences, we address our unconscious longings and are able to live a fulfilling life.	Hugo's healthy early experiences satisfied his need for love, enabling him to develop close relationships with his grandchildren.
Erikson's Psychosocial Theory	We develop through eight psychological crises triggered by physical maturation and society's expectations. Ideally, these establish our ability to trust and relate to others.	We address and resolve crises to feel whole, trusting, and generative.	Hugo is experiencing generativity in later life: He is giving back to the world through grandparenting.
Attachment Theory	Our earliest bonds shape our future relationships with other people and with the world around us. Adult life is shaped by the pattern of relating set in early infancy.	Through supportive early attachments, we learn to trust others to love us, and to see ourselves as worthy of love.	Hugo is a supportive attachment figure as a caregiver for his granddaughters.

2. *Cross-cultural research focuses on comparing human maturation around the world* (Greenfield, 2018). Understanding variations in how we grow helps researchers appreciate human beings' ability to adapt to different contexts and can broaden what we think of as "typical" milestones and pathways for development (Keller, 2017; Rogoff, 1990). For instance, the age when babies typically learn to sit on their own is not universal. Many babies in Cameroon sit at about 4 months—but it takes babies in the United States about two more months to reach this milestone (Karasik et al.,

THE BEHAVIORIST PERSPECTIVE

? *How does learning result from an interaction between people and their environment? How can we measure who people are and how they behave, rather than simply guessing?*

Behaviorist Theory	Development is a gradual, continuous process as we learn from birth until later life via classical and operant conditioning.	Learning changes us: All development is a process of linking a stimulus (or experience) with a response (or behavior). Behaviors that are reinforced happen more frequently.	Hugo learned to be a grandparent by gradually accumulating skills over his lifespan. His caring for others was reinforced, so he did it more.
Social Learning Theory	We learn through observing and imitating others. We continue to learn over the lifespan but our early role models and habits often persist.	We are likely to imitate people we admire and respect. Our role models and our community cause us to grow.	Hugo had family role models who inspired him to be an active, doting grandparent.

THE COGNITIVE PERSPECTIVE

? *How does our thinking shape our development? How does our thinking change as we get older?*

Piaget's Constructivist Theory	Children and adolescents go through four discrete stages of development as their thinking matures.	Development is driven by inborn biological maturation and by active exploration of the world as you construct and build what you know.	Hugo is in the stage of postformal thought, so he can think about big social concepts like kindness and generosity.
Information-Processing Theory	Development is a continuous process of maturation in our information-processing systems, including attention, memory, processing, and reacting to the world around you.	Many of the individual components of how we think and process information mature and age at different rates, driven by experience and biological maturation.	Hugo developed strong executive function early in his life, enabling him to do well in school, thrive in the Air Force, and now juggle all the duties of being a hands-on grandparent.

THE CULTURAL PERSPECTIVE

? *How does culture impact every part of development, shaping how we grow, think, and relate to one another?*

Sociocultural Theory	Growth occurs continuously over the lifespan as we mature in a specific cultural environment.	Change, growth, and learning happen through interactions with other people who pass on knowledge and skills in a cultural context.	Hugo's cultural community values close family relationships, and he seeks to pass on his cultural traditions to the next generation.
Theories of Social Justice	Growth and maturation happen continuously over the lifespan and are shaped by our social status. Cultural strengths and community can help us thrive.	Change results from our interactions and our individual identity in relation with other people embedded in a hierarchical community.	Hugo has experienced both privilege and marginalization, giving him a unique identity as a Cuban American man living in Florida. Grandparenting little Latina girls gives him a new social position.

2010). Common variations in development are often based on factors like whether people live in rural or urban communities or whether they live in industrialized or agricultural economies (Packer & Cole, 2020). But culture does not always mean differences—it can also mean similarities (Wang et al., 2017). All cultures recognize that children need responsive, loving relationships in order to thrive (Keller, 2021).

3. *Cultural research identifies variations within communities.* For instance, children experience different cultures and have different experiences depending on their

B. & C. Alexander/Science Source

Enjoyment of Good Friends Is Universal. Cross-cultural researchers often study the similarities and differences between communities around the world. These men from the Sami community in Northern Norway are drinking coffee as they take a break from watching their reindeer.

social status, often based on their race, ethnicity, or income (Spencer, 2017). Researchers have even found that variations in culture can happen in different afterschool classrooms. For instance, a program held in a library developed a distinctive culture when researchers compared it to one held in a Boys-and-Girls club (and, yes, it was quieter!) (Cole, 2017).

Theories of Social Justice Scholars who focus on social justice, including those who identify as *critical race theorists*, evaluate how social inequality and discrimination affect us and how cultural identity can help us thrive (Brown et al., 2019). They point out that societies around the world have varying levels of inequality, oppression, and discrimination based on gender identity, race, age, physical and cognitive ability, sexual orientation, health, color, or culture. These communities include indigenous Maori in New Zealand, Muslim Uighurs in China, same-sex couples in Uganda, and low-income people and people of color in the United States. In the United States, critical race theorists have pointed out that discrimination based on race has been a part of government, cultural, and legal systems since early colonization (Delgado et al., 1995).

Discrimination is often *intersectional*, meaning it involves overlapping systems of mistreatment based on ethnicity, immigration status, gender identity, religion, physical ability, income level, age, body size or appearance, and sexual orientation (Crenshaw, 1989; Ghavami et al., 2016; Velez & Spencer, 1995). People experience discrimination through systemic discrimination, everyday microaggressions, and targeted aggression and bullying (Syed, 2021). Everyday discrimination can build up and contribute to poor health, lower academic achievement, and shorter lifespans (Paradies et al., 2017). But cultural identity can be protective, connecting people to their communities and giving them a feeling of meaning and belonging, and it can help people to live longer, happier lives (Anderson & Stevenson, 2019; Park et al., 2018).

Social justice scholars have a number of research approaches:

1. *Make disparities visible.* Throughout the lifespan, prejudice and inequality based on our identities contribute to stress and poor health. Quantifying and studying how and when discrimination makes an impact can lead to interventions to protect people of all ages.

2. *Document the development of group identity and group prejudice over the lifespan.* Researchers are trying to understand when prejudice and bias begin in the toddler years and whether people become fairer over the lifespan (Elenbaas et al., 2020). Other scholars focus on how cultural identity changes over the lifespan, from when babies learn that they are part of one group to how identity changes in late life (García Coll et al., 2018).

3. *Fix systems.* Rather than expecting individual people to display resilience so that they better fit into a system that does not treat them fairly, focus on interventions that change institutions so that they serve all people (Duchesneau, 2020).

4. *Look to strengths.* What developmental competencies do people develop as a result of living in an unequal system? From experience in advocating for yourself to enhanced executive function as a result of code switching, many people adapt to an unequal system and develop strengths that help them cope (Cabrera & Tamis-LeMonda, 2013; Cavanaugh et al., 2018; Rogoff et al., 2017; Yosso, 2005).

No matter what aspect of development they focus on, social justice theorists inspire questions and investigation designed to make the world fairer and more compassionate to all of us.

APPLY IT! **2.1** Erikson's theory of psychosocial development would predict that Hugo is in the stage of *ego integrity versus despair*. What signs do you see that Hugo is integrating his life story and evaluating successes and failures? How would you evaluate your own limitations and victories?

2.2 How would a behavioral theorist, a social learning theorist, and a sociocultural theorist explain how Hugo has adapted to his role as a doting grandfather? How would you describe the roles you have taken on in your family or friend group? Was it something you learned, imitated, or adapted through observation?

How to Study Development

Theories help us define questions and predictions about development. The next step is to put these questions to the test carefully and methodically.

When scientists wanted to know, for instance, what factors made people, like Hugo and many others, resilient, one group of researchers met with a group of children and their families for over 60 years to pinpoint the circumstances and traits that supported positive development and those that put people at risk (Werner, 1995). The scientists found that for many children, like Hugo, particular protective factors helped them overcome some of the adversity they experienced. The most important element? Finding at least one adult who supported and understood them when they were small.

The Scientific Method

Science begins with the simple idea that everything needs to be tested. And tested again. And analyzed critically. The **scientific method** is a multistep process in which scientists evaluate their ideas and find out if they are accurate. As you will see in **Figure 2.4**, this process has five steps: *observation, hypothesis, data collection, analysis,* and *sharing.*

1. *Make an observation:* Science begins with curiosity, and researchers are curious people who want to know why and how come. Maybe you want to find out how some young people were able to develop resilience during the COVID-19 pandemic. Maybe you noticed that some people you know who stuck to a routine during lockdown did better than others. That might be your first observation.

2. *Form a hypothesis:* A **hypothesis** is a prediction about what researchers expect to find from the data. Many hypotheses are inspired by one or more theoretical perspectives. For instance, you may have wondered whether young people developed resilience more easily if they had a strong structure, like the routine of staying in school. Your hypothesis might be: Adolescents who attended in-person school throughout the pandemic had less depression and more resilience.

3. *Collect the data:* Gathering data is the hallmark of empirical inquiry. Scientists don't rely on their personal experiences, their friends' opinions, or stories that have been passed down. They make multiple measurements of the phenomena they are studying. Collecting data can take many forms: Researchers may conduct experiments, observe people over time, look at their brains in a scanner, sample their genes, do an in-depth case study—or all of the above. For instance, to study the resilience of teenagers during the COVID-19 pandemic, one group of researchers assessed data on the mental health of an international group of more than 1,300 adolescents before and after the outbreak that began in March 2020 (Barendse et al., 2021).

4. *Analyze the data:* Making sense of data can involve formulating statistical analyses to compare how people did on tests, using powerful computers to evaluate

Learning Objectives

2.7 Define the steps and guiding principles of the scientific method.

2.8 Describe the ethical standards governing science and practice.

scientific method A multistep process in which scientists evaluate their ideas and find out if they are accurate through collecting and analyzing data.

hypothesis A prediction about what a researcher expects to find from the data.

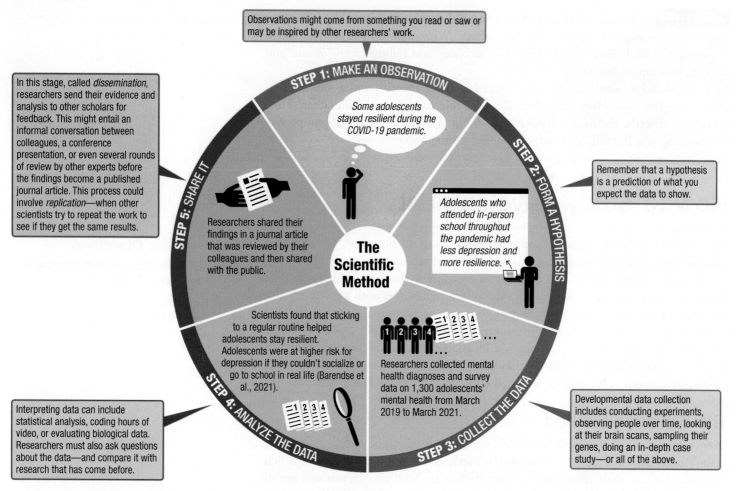

FIGURE 2.4 The Steps of the Scientific Method Developmental researchers use the scientific method to evaluate their ideas and make sure they are accurate. This process has five steps: *observation*, *hypothesis*, *data collection*, *analysis*, and *sharing*.

brain imagery, or watching hours of video to code behavior. It also involves asking questions about the data—and comparing it with research that has come before. In the end, scientists need to conclude whether their hypothesis was supported by the data. When the researchers looking at adolescent mental health during the pandemic looked at their data, they found that sticking to a routine and going to school helped adolescents stay resilient. Adolescents were at higher risk for depression during the pandemic, particularly if they were under lockdown restrictions that limited in-person schooling (Barendse et al., 2021).

5. *Share it:* The last step in the scientific process is to send your work out into the world. This is formally called *dissemination*. In this stage, researchers send their evidence and their analysis to other scientists for feedback. This step might include an informal conversation between colleagues, a conference presentation, or even several rounds of review from other experts before taking the form of a published journal article. Part of this process might involve *replication*—when other scientists test what has been done by repeating it on their own to see if they get the same results. Often this leads to new questions and new studies—and back to the beginning of the scientific process.

Although the steps in the scientific method are common to many sciences, many of the methods that developmental scientists use are unique—because the population they study is a bit different: people of different ages. See **Infographic 2.2** to learn more about reading scientific data.

Research Design

If you want to find out what personal strengths helped adolescents be resilient during the pandemic, you need to decide *how* you are going to test your ideas and learn more. You have to design a research study. There are a lot of options. In developmental science, common research designs include experiments, correlational studies, and descriptive research. All of these methods can be used to study people of the same age—or can be used to study changes over time.

Experimental Research In developmental science, an experiment helps to determine *why* something happens. An **experiment** tests a hypothesis that one factor is caused by another. The factors that are studied are known as **variables**, which must be measured and must vary, or differ, among different participants in the research study. Researchers check to see how one factor, called the **independent variable**, causes change in another, called the **dependent variable**. The independent variable is something that the researcher can change.

Let's describe a hypothetical experiment to make things clearer: Say you wanted to measure how adolescents' involvement in a hypothetical Zoom-based mental health project called Resilience Boosters affected their resilience. In this case, whether teenagers were randomly selected to attend the program or not would be the independent variable and mental health would be the dependent variable. If resilience is significantly higher among those who were part of the program, you will be able to conclude that the program worked. The change in the dependent variable reveals the outcome of your experiment—like whether your program worked.

In an ideal experiment, scientists are able to control all aspects of the procedure so that they can be sure their conclusions are accurate. In the case of our experiment, part of this process involves making sure that we compare adolescents who were involved in the program, also known as the *experimental group*, with another group that did not attend Resilience Boosters, called the *control group*. Both groups should be as similar as possible—so that you know it was Resilience Boosters and not something else that caused the changes you are looking for.

Ideally, you want to *randomly assign* the children to the different groups in your experiment. This means that both your experimental group and your control group are made up of the same types of children—you will not want to have all boys in one group or all girls in the other, or just tenth-graders in one group and all twelfth-graders in the other. It is important to keep as many distracting factors as you can out of the way. For instance, it would confuse the results if the teenagers in your control group all happened to be in another program on mindfulness. In a well-controlled experiment, the primary difference between the groups should be that one group was in the program and one group was not.

As you will see in **Figure 2.5**, in the hypothetical Resilience Boosters experiment, researchers randomized 100 students to either attend the program or a control group. As Infographic 2.2 shows, the program seemed to have positive effects. The students who attended the program had less depression than those who did not attend the program.

In some cases, scientists want to study something that would be impossible or unethical to study in a controlled experiment—like the effect of a natural disaster, poverty, war, or famine. However, sometimes they are able to collect data in the midst of life-changing events that are out of their control. Scientists call these *natural experiments*. In these studies, researchers compare a group of people who experienced, say, an ice storm or a hurricane or a pandemic with a group of their agemates who were not exposed—allowing the scientists to discover that natural disasters can have

experiment The act of testing a hypothesis that one factor is caused by another.

variables The factors that are studied in an experiment.

independent variable A factor that is tested to see if it causes change in another variable. An independent variable is something that the researcher can change.

dependent variable The factor that is measured during an experiment to determine the effect of the independent variable.

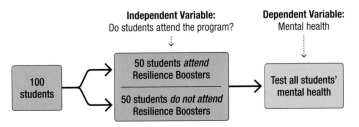

FIGURE 2.5 In the hypothetical Resilience Boosters experiments, 100 students were randomly assigned to either attend the intervention program or to attend another program. This intervention was the independent variable. The outcome was a measurement of students' mental health after the program concluded. The students' mental health was the dependent variable.

Developmental science has its own vocabulary for describing human development that includes both words and pictures. The way scientists display data has its own conventions. Learning how researchers display their results visually helps you understand the strength of their evidence. A hypothetical study of a "Resilience Boosters" intervention is used to illustrate these conventions.

HOW SCIENTISTS SHARE DATA

Bar graphs show a comparison between two groups. The groups are separated into individual bars and measured along the same continuum.

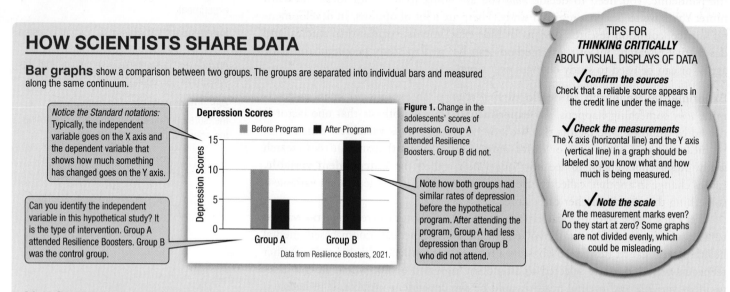

Notice the Standard notations: Typically, the independent variable goes on the X axis and the dependent variable that shows how much something has changed goes on the Y axis.

Can you identify the independent variable in this hypothetical study? It is the type of intervention. Group A attended Resilience Boosters. Group B was the control group.

Data from Resilience Boosters, 2021.

Figure 1. Change in the adolescents' scores of depression. Group A attended Resilience Boosters. Group B did not.

Note how both groups had similar rates of depression before the hypothetical program. After attending the program, Group A had less depression than Group B who did not attend.

TIPS FOR THINKING CRITICALLY ABOUT VISUAL DISPLAYS OF DATA

✓ **Confirm the sources**
Check that a reliable source appears in the credit line under the image.

✓ **Check the measurements**
The X axis (horizontal line) and the Y axis (vertical line) in a graph should be labeled so you know what and how much is being measured.

✓ **Note the scale**
Are the measurement marks even? Do they start at zero? Some graphs are not divided evenly, which could be misleading.

Line Graphs describe the relationship between two types of variables that are changing at the same time. This graph shows the relationship between participants' scores of depression and resilience in our hypothetical intervention.

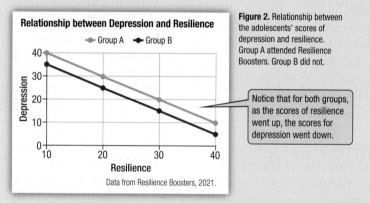

Data from Resilience Boosters, 2021.

Figure 2. Relationship between the adolescents' scores of depression and resilience. Group A attended Resilience Boosters. Group B did not.

Notice that for both groups, as the scores of resilience went up, the scores for depression went down.

Pie Charts describe the variation in a group of people. This pie chart illustrates how many participants were in groups A and B and how many did not complete the study. Pie charts work best when the data do not represent amounts or values, which are better displayed on a numeric graph.

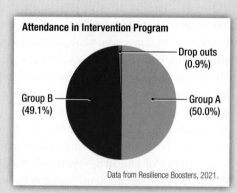

Data from Resilience Boosters, 2021.

Figure 3. Participation in the intervention program. Group A attended Resilience Boosters. Group B did not. One person dropped out of the program before it was completed.

ALTERNATIVE DATA DISPLAYS

In addition to traditional charts and graphs, scientists sometimes use maps, word clouds, and biological images to explain their data.

Maps are used to visually represent the relationship of geography to data. For instance, if you wanted to explain how the effect of Resilience Boosters differed by country after it had been implemented around the world, you might display it on a map.

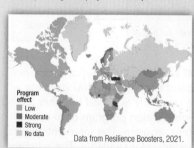

Data from Resilience Boosters, 2021.

Figure 4. Strength of effects of the intervention program. After Resilience Boosters was offered to adolescents worldwide, the strength of the effect was compared. The key indicates the strength of the reduction in adolescent depression around the world.

Word Clouds are used to describe the relative value of words, like the frequency that they appear in documents. For instance, if you interviewed the participants in Resilience Boosters program about the value of their experience, you might display their feedback in a word cloud.

Biological Figures are used to describe changes that are happening in the body. For instance, if MRI brain scans were taken of the participants in our study, their results might look like the image below.

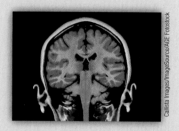

Callista Images/ImageSource/AGE Fotostock

an impact on development (Jones et al., 2019). Sometimes natural experiments focus on the good. In one study, researchers found that families who were unexpectedly lifted out of poverty (as a result of earnings distributed to them from a local casino) had much lower rates of significant psychological illnesses than those who remained poor (Akee et al., 2018). This natural experiment helped to establish that raising family's incomes can help protect children from psychological illnesses.

Correlational Research Doing an experiment may not always be possible or even provide an accurate description of the phenomena scientists are studying. Say, for instance, researchers want to understand more about the economic benefits of a college education. Hypothetically, it would be possible to conduct an experiment. You might be able to convince some high school graduates to go to college and convince others to go right to work, and then compare the salaries years later. But this may be unethical, expensive, and take a long time. You might want to try another approach. A correlational study is your answer.

In a **correlational study**, a researcher gathers data and looks for relationships between variables but does not actually manipulate them. A *correlation* refers to the statistical relationship between two variables in a study. For instance, researchers conducted a correlational study of people who had attended college and those who had not, comparing their salaries. They looked for the correlation between college attendance and salary. (A correlation is *positive* if both variables tend to increase together or decrease together, *negative* if one variable tends to increase while the other decreases, or *zero* if no connection is evident.)

Unsurprisingly, the correlation between college attendance and annual salary is *very large and positive*, as you will see in **Figure 2.6** (Ma et al., 2016). But studies don't always find positive correlations—sometimes they are negative. For instance, adults who are sexually active are less likely to experience cognitive decline as they get older—sexual activity is *negatively* correlated with low scores of intellectual functioning (Wright et al., 2019). And some variables are not consistently related, such as whether homework is correlated with higher academic achievement (De Bruyckere et al., 2020; Fan et al., 2017).

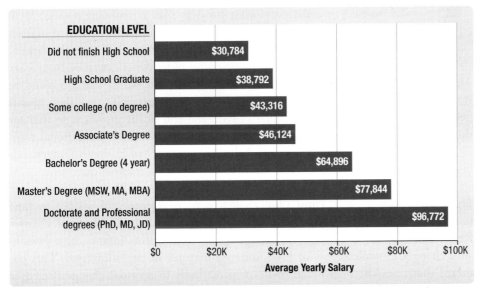

FIGURE 2.6 **What Are the Financial Benefits of College?** The number of years you stay in school correlates with your average yearly salary. So, on average, someone with a professional degree, such as a physician or a lawyer, makes more than three times as much as someone who did not complete high school.

Information from Bureau of Labor Statistics, 2020

 Learn It Together

Experimental and Correlational Studies

Plan Design a study to test the hypothesis: Children's behavior is affected by eating sweets.

Engage Divide into groups. Have one group design a correlational study to evaluate this hypothesis. Have another group design an experiment to test the effect of eating sugar. What methods and measures might you use?

Reflect Compare your research plans either as a slide presentation or as a discussion. What are the strengths and weaknesses of each design?

correlational study A study in which a researcher gathers data and looks for relationships between variables but does not actually manipulate them.

Enjoying School in Monte Alegre, Brazil Scientists often use case studies to establish how interventions work in different contexts. One research team measured the impact of early-childhood education on children's development by watching it in action in schools in Brazil.

What Is It Really Like? Ethnographers might interview this chef to find out the nitty gritty of what it is like to work in a busy restaurant kitchen.

case study An in-depth analysis of one person, family, or institution's experience.

ethnography A longer, richly detailed investigation of everyday life.

longitudinal research The study of the same group of people over time.

Correlational studies are powerful tools for understanding how we grow, but like experiments, they also come with a caution. Just because two variables have a relationship, does not mean variable caused the other. Experts remind us: *Correlation is not causation*. Without conducting an actual controlled experiment, we can never rule out the possibility that there is a mystery variable that links them. For instance, do popsicles cause gun violence? Statistics show that there is a positive correlation between popsicle sales and gun violence (Harper, 2013). But nothing in frozen treats leads people to become violent. The missing variable is summer: More time outside seems to be related to more opportunities for conflict—and the hot weather also leads to more popsicle sales. The false associations (and the surprisingly legitimate associations) between correlation and causation mean interpretation must be done carefully.

Case Study and Ethnographic Research In experiments and correlational studies, scientists need to study a great number of people—and often this means that they cannot spend a lot of time with any one person. Big studies provide information about groups—but not about individuals. Scientists have some alternatives when they want to understand people in depth.

A **case study** is an in-depth analysis of one person, family, or institution's experience. If you spent a few weeks with Hugo, interviewing his family and his friends, you might be able to put together a case study about him. Scientists often use case studies to explore the development of specific people to understand, for instance, the impact of brain injury on one person's development or to describe how someone has been able to recover from abuse. Much of the work of psychodynamic theorists was based on case studies. Case studies are also used to describe an institution's experiences—as in a case study about Brazilian preschools that implemented a successful program to help support children's executive function (Dias & Seabra, 2015).

An **ethnography** is a longer investigation of everyday life. Ethnography was originally used in anthropology and sociology but now is used in developmental science more broadly (Abebe, 2018). Some ethnographers spent time with children in a nonprofessional role, after their teachers explained they shouldn't be thought of as typical grownups but as adults who wanted to experience what life was like as children (Corsaro, 2017). Others embedded on the field with athletes who had spinal cord injuries (Sparkes et al., 2018). One researcher did fieldwork with home health workers, mostly from Ghana, who were caring for older Americans (Coe, 2019, 2020). The researcher's ethnography found highs and lows in care work: The job could be stifling and demeaning. But health workers had special expertise that their clients needed: They had developed a familiarity with the end of life and how to manage the emotional and practical aspects of a person's last days in a transformational way.

Case studies and ethnographies can help give scientists an in-depth understanding of one particular experience and can help generate new research questions.

Studying Change over Time One challenge in developmental science is how to capture time. At its heart, much developmental science is the study of change. Researchers want to understand how language develops during infancy, how personality changes in adolescence, or how romance matures in late adulthood. This has meant that researchers have had to develop methods to measure change itself (see **Figure 2.7**).

Longitudinal research involves studying the same group of people over time. This can be a short period of time, as when researchers track babies from birth until they learn to talk or schoolchildren during one school year. Or it may be a marathon: Some notable research studies around the world track children from birth until the

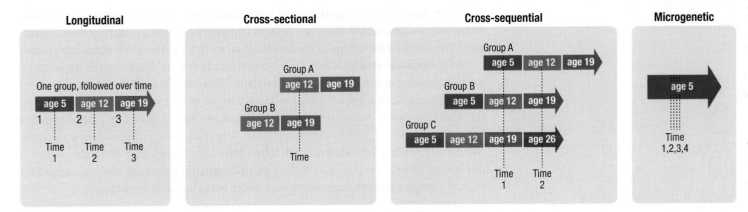

FIGURE 2.7 Age As a Variable Researchers have several ways to consider the impact of time itself on people's development. A longitudinal design requires multiple time points of data collection (noted as Time 1, 2, and 3 above) to document individuals' change over time. In a cross-sectional design, only one time point of data collection is required, as groups of people of different ages are compared. A cross-sequential design combines both aspects, conducting multiple times of study with groups of different ages. A microgenetic study engages in multiple frequent measurements, to capture the moment of developmental change when it occurs.

end of life. A longitudinal researcher might be interested in how Hugo, for instance, changed throughout his life: How did he transform from a timid second-grader into an authoritative Air Force officer in his middle life? Collecting data on the same people over a long period of time allows researchers to find correlations between different experiences throughout life.

Longitudinal research can be a powerful tool to observe what happens over time, but it has some limitations. One of these is logistics. It is expensive and time-consuming for researchers to keep track of their research participants and convince them to stay in touch. When participants "drop out" of a longitudinal study, the results are not as strong, since researchers cannot be sure that the findings would be the same for the people who left the study as it was for the people who stayed. Time is also a limitation in longitudinal studies: What happens when historical events change the lives of your participants? Economic downturns, natural disasters, and even climate change can impact the lives of those who participate in research studies—and these big-picture changes can make interpreting data complicated (Miller, 2017).

Researchers who want a sprint rather than a marathon may try a **cross-sectional study**, which compares development in two or more groups of different ages at one point in time. For example, researchers used a cross-sectional approach to study the development of sharing behavior by comparing groups of 2- and 3-year-olds. They found that while the 2-year-olds had a sense that they should share, they very rarely shared equally. On the other hand, the 3-year-olds, with a stronger ability to divide things evenly and more experience with social situations, shared things equally nearly all the time (Tomasello, 2018). This demonstrates the advantage of cross-sectional research: Scientists can compare the behavior of children of different ages without waiting for those children to grow up. However, it is often difficult to prove that age alone causes the difference between the two age group's reactions since the groups are not precisely the same.

Another method of looking at how change happens over time is called the **cross-sequential study**. Cross-sequential studies follow two or more different age groups over time in a combination of cross-sectional and longitudinal designs. For instance, one group of researchers was curious about how the brain changes as you age (Pfefferbaum & Sullivan, 2015). They collected a series of brain scans over a period of about eight years from 200 people aged 20 to 70. This enabled them to compare not just 20-year-olds with 70-year-olds but also to examine the rate of change within each group. Thus, they found that brain aging does not happen in a smooth, constant way, but accelerates

Scientific American Profile

Change over Time

cross-sectional study A study that compares development in two or more groups of different ages at one point in time.

cross-sequential study A study that follows two or more different age groups over time in a combination of cross-sectional and longitudinal designs.

at certain ages, like at around age 50 and around age 70 (Fjell et al., 2013). The cross-sequential design enabled them not only to compare how change happened in individuals over time (the advantage of the longitudinal study) but also to compare age groups.

Microgenetic research focuses on understanding how development happens by studying change as it happens (Siegler, 2006, 2016). Researchers used this type of study to discover what factors helped children learn how to trick someone else, by observing the children closely over 10 days. These scientists found that some developments happened relatively quickly: Although most 3-year-olds didn't know how to deceive someone in a game of hide-and-seek when the study began, they were able figure it out within three days (Ding et al., 2018). The microgenetic approach allowed researchers to study longitudinal change over a very short period of development.

Gathering the Evidence

Once scientists have decided who they are going to study and when they are going to study it, they turn to the question of *how*. Gathering data comes next. Scientists' mission is to collect *empirical information*, or information that is provable or verifiable.

Quantitative research uses numbers to measure the topics being studied and to analyze the outcome. Scientists might interview children, observe families, or conduct experiments—but they use numbers to record and analyze their data.

Qualitative research involves in-depth analysis, observation, and description. Scientists may observe families, conduct focus groups, or spend years living with people to better understand them. Some of the most famous theorists in developmental science, like Jean Piaget and Erik Erikson, conducted qualitative research involving close observation and interviews with children and adults (Erikson, 1969; Piaget, 1952).

Qualitative research is often used to explore questions about *why* and *how* people do what they do or to understand the cultural meaning that we have for our behavior. In many types of developmental science, qualitative and quantitative methods are combined together in what is called *mixed-methods research* (Rojas et al., 2020; Weisner, 2020).

Observation Research often involves **observation**. Observational research occurs when scientists closely watch and record what people are doing—either in real life or in the laboratory. Scientists can record what they see on video or watch what happens live and take written notes. They can do their work behind one-way mirrors when they are not seen at all, or go undercover in the classroom. The key to observation is that it involves finding ways to record, count, or quantify behaviors. This can be done in the form of *naturalistic observation*, when researchers record behaviors in everyday life, or it can be more experimental, as when participants interact with research stimuli in a laboratory setting. Observational research can also allow researchers to get at the cultural meanings behind behaviors—by capturing the context that surrounds them (Barata & Yoshikawa, 2014).

For instance, one group of researchers in California used observation to watch what happened at parent–teacher conferences where children translated for their families. They were curious about how accurate children's translations were: Would they skip the bad parts? It took observation to find out that, in most cases, children skipped the *good* parts. Children tended not to tell their parents the nice things their teachers said about them—focusing on the areas of challenge rather than the areas of strength (Orellana & Phoenix, 2017).

However, observation has its disadvantages: In many cases, the mere act of being watched can change how people behave—people tend to be on their best behavior,

Carsten Goerling/Getty Images

What Are They Talking About? Researchers used qualitative research methods to find out what adolescent boys felt about their friendships.

microgenetic research Research that focuses on understanding how development happens by studying change as it happens.

quantitative research Research that uses numbers to measure the topics being studied and to analyze the outcome of a study.

qualitative research Research that involves in-depth analysis, observation, and investigation.

observation When scientists closely watch and record what people are doing—either in real life or in the laboratory.

at least in the beginning, when they know they are being observed. Researchers may be biased in what they record or remember. Observation also takes time and lots of effort, including training observers to be reliable. Finally, there are certain things you just can't see as an observer—like a person's past or what they believe.

Surveys and Interviews In developmental research, surveys and interviews can be a fairly quick and efficient way to get information. Surveys can be powerful tools for research because they often rapidly build a large data set, providing a rich source for data analysis and hypothesis testing.

In today's interconnected, mobile age, developmental scientists can ask research participants to answer survey questions at any time of day or night on their phones (van Berkel et al., 2019). This may enable people to be more honest about what they are doing—and more accurately report how they are feeling or who they are with (Myin-Germeys et al., 2018).

When a group of researchers decided to do a study on adversity in young families, called the Fragile Families and Child Wellbeing Study (FFCWS), they began with a carefully structured interview—that they gave to more than 5,000 new parents (Brooks-Gunn et al., 2003). They even asked every new parent about their romantic relationships—even getting into details like how often they went on dates. As they tracked these families over time, they continued to use surveys and structured interviews. By the time the children were in fourth grade, they and their families had been interviewed or surveyed more than five times. What researchers learned from these surveys and interviews has now produced nearly 1,000 published articles, working papers, and books (FFCWS, 2021). One recent finding is that when fathers can take time off from work after their children are born, they are likely to have stronger relationships—not just with their children but with their partner—boosting the entire family's well-being for years to come (Petts et al., 2020).

Despite the many strengths of surveys and interviews as data collection tools, they also can come with some drawbacks. One of these is that babies are not very good at filling out forms. For young children, researchers need to rely on the reports of family members. Also, it is hard to tell whether someone is being completely truthful. As a result, researchers often supplement survey and interview data with other forms of observation (FFCWS, 2021).

Testing Some types of variables are measured through **assessment**—the use of a standardized tool or test. Assessments allow researchers to compare people's development—whether it is measuring how tall they are, how large their vocabulary is, or how well they get along with others.

Developmental scientists use a variety of assessments. Sometimes they use standardized tests. At other times, they develop their own tests that are designed to represent challenges people might face in real life. For instance, researchers developed the Snack Delay Task to measure how long children can wait before eating a piece of candy. Being able to wait a long time shows that preschoolers have developed self-control and are not just impulsively grabbing a Twix bar in order to gratify their impulses (Ravindran et al., 2019). Another group of researchers created fake websites to measure what makes adults susceptible to online scams (Gavett et al., 2018).

Testing allows scientists to compare their data with that of other researchers. If two researchers, for instance, are using the same assessment for evaluating self-control, they can compare their research findings more directly.

Biological Assessment Developmental assessment can also be used to measure what is going on in the body. When they were studying the 5,000 young adults in the

Helen H. Richardson/The Denver Post via Getty Images

How Do You Keep Track of How Many Words a Baby Hears? Brian and Lisa signed up to be one of the early testers of a tiny recording device that records everything. They tucked the recorder into their son Matthew's pocket and learned that he was often hearing more than 20,000 words each day.

assessment The use of a standardized tool or test.

Fragile Families study, researchers sampled DNA along with conducting their family visits and interviews. When they were 22, the participants even had their brains scanned (FFCWS, 2021).

Biological assessment has a long history in developmental science. Since ancient times, researchers have measured how tall babies are in an attempt to assess their health (Weaver, 2010). Nowadays, researchers can quickly assess a person's stress level by measuring hormones from a sample of their saliva. They can send a DNA sample off to a lab to see whether it shows signs of premature aging. Or they can measure the electrical impulses in your brain while you are playing a game in an MRI scanner (see **Figure 2.8**).

Biological assessment comes with its own challenges. It is often expensive—which means that researchers are often limited to doing these assessments on a small group, who may not represent a broader range of development (Cantlon, 2020; Dahl, 2017). The nature of children, in particular, can make biological assessment difficult. For instance, most brain scans must be done on an absolutely still head. Typically, babies can be scanned while sleeping, and older children and adults are better at controlling their bodies, but getting an accurate picture of a 4-year-old's brain is a challenge, unless they are watching a movie (Greene et al., 2018).

Is It Accurate?

After researchers have conducted observations, interviews, or testing, they need to make sure that their data are accurate. Critical thinking is an essential part of the scientific process, since every step requires reflection and interpretation against existing scientific knowledge. This often comes down to three key criteria: Is it valid, reliable, and replicable?

- *Validity* means that a measure or an assessment actually measures what it claims to measure. For instance, if a researcher investigating health habits in elementary school children asks 8-year-olds to provide a list of everything they snacked on in the past week, their reports are unlikely to be very accurate. The second-grader will probably forget what they ate (Laursen et al., 2012). The survey is not likely to be valid.
- *Reliability* means that a particular assessment stays consistent with multiple measurements. A ruler used correctly will always give the same measurement of the width of your textbook, so it is a reliable measure. In developmental science, reliable measurements often depend on the skills and training of the researchers. Some

DTI	fMRI	EEG	CT
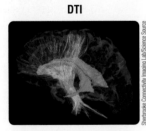	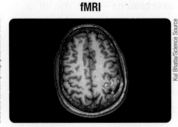		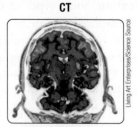
DTI, or diffusion tensor imaging, uses an MRI scanner to create a 3-D image of the white matter connections by looking at the water molecules in the brain. These scans show how the brain is interconnected.	fMRI, or functional magnetic resonance imaging, is a form of MRI that uses magnetic and radio waves to measure the amount of oxygen used by the brain in a series of images over a period of time. Because participants must stay very still, fMRI scans are difficult to use with small children. fMRI tells researchers which regions of the brain are activated during a particular activity.	EEG, or electroencephalogram, records the electrical activity in the brain from electrodes on the scalp. Researchers use a special hat that contains sensors that record electrical signals. It doesn't take very long and you can move around while it is being performed. EEG is often used to study sleep.	CT stands for computerized tomography. CT scans use X-rays to show the density of brain structures. These scans can show the size of different brain structures, but because they expose participants to radiation they are rarely used in research.

FIGURE 2.8 Biological Assessment New technologies have allowed scientists to look at bodies, genes, and brains in a way that they were unable to in the past. This has led to increased understanding of how connected our bodies and brains are as we grow.

measures, like those used to measure the quality of caregiving for older adults, require days of training to make sure that all observers are rating the programs in a similar way (Berthelsen & Kristensson, 2015).

- *Replicability* means that the results of your study can be confirmed or clarified by repeating it with another group of participants. Replication can reveal complexity and even contradict a study's findings. For instance, researchers in Europe and the United States were once sure that it was universally true that babies became afraid of strangers at about 8 months (Keller, 2018). That was, until other scientists tried to replicate their findings. It turns out that babies who are accustomed to interacting with new people and who are encouraged not to be fussy do not display this "universal" behavior at all (Otto et al., 2014). In this case, the *failure to replicate* explained something important: The way children express emotions is affected by their experiences. Not even fear is universal. Replication is particularly difficult in developmental science—particularly when families are affected by cultural and historical change (Greenfield, 2018).

The Importance of Inclusive Research In developmental science today, researchers make efforts to be inclusive. But too many studies are still focused on the development of relatively affluent people from White European backgrounds and are conducted by researchers from similar backgrounds (Barbot et al., 2020; Sternberg, 2017; Syed et al., 2018). This challenge is not unique to developmental science: In some medical studies, more than 98 percent of research participants are White (Hamel et al., 2016).

This focus on wealthy White people is sometimes referred to (in an attempt at being amusing) as emphasizing *Western, Educated, Industrialized, Rich, and Democratic (WEIRD)* cultures rather than the majority of the globe (Schulz et al., 2018). Only about 12 percent of people worldwide are *WEIRD*, so focusing just on them will not give a universal or accurate picture of how most of the world develops. For instance, about 30 percent of children in the world live in rural farming communities (Keller, 2020). Looking at the majority of the world, who are often low-income, sometimes rural, and often from Asia, Africa, or South America, helps scientists understand the wide diversity in human development and how culture shapes us. **Cross-cultural research** focuses specifically on comparing the development of people from diverse cultural communities (Broesch et al., 2020).

Protecting People and Science

The goal of developmental science is to improve the lives of people across the lifespan. Protecting people also happens when developmental scientists are doing their everyday jobs—when scientists conduct research, they need to make sure that they are safeguarding participants' interests. Scientists are bound by **ethical standards**, or moral guidelines, that provide principles for how to protect the public's interests and how to make sure their scientific work is honest.

Keeping Research Safe Developmental scientists are responsible for keeping research participants safe and making sure that their rights are respected when they participate in research (Fisher et al., 2015; Miller et al., 2015; Powell et al., 2012). Although developmental scientists work around the globe, most are bound by similar ethical principles, based on guidelines from professional organizations including the American Psychological Association, the Society for Research in Child Development, and even the United Nations (APA, 2018; Berman et al., 2016; Graham et al., 2013; SRCD Governing Council, 2021).

One frequently used approach to keeping research consistent with safety guidelines is to bring in more voices to help researchers decide the right thing to do. Around the globe, most researchers have the benefit of an **Institutional Review Board (IRB)**,

 Share It!

Diversity in science helps drive change and innovation. Ideas once considered out of the mainstream often help push science forward.

(Dietze et al., 2019)

Scientific American: Lifespan Development

 Share It!

Communities include many cultures and subcultures. Cultures are complex and do not always align with national borders.

(Oyserman, 2017)

Scientific American: Lifespan Development

cross-cultural research Research that compares people from two or more different cultural communities.

ethical standards Moral guidelines for protecting the interests of research participants and making sure scientific work is as honest as it can be.

Institutional Review Board (IRB) A committee that is designed to review scientific research and ensure that it is safe and adequately protects participants.

a committee that is designed to review scientific research and help make sure it is adequately protecting participants. The IRB follows several basic principles.

1. *Participants should not be harmed.* This may seem obvious, but in real life it is often more complex. How do you define harm? Is it unfair to scare a child if you are doing a research experiment to understand how children develop fear? Is it inappropriate to ask a teenager to give a public presentation in front of strangers just to measure their level of stress? Most scientists would agree that a little bit of distress may be an acceptable part of research, particularly because being scared or having to talk in front of a group is typical of everyday life. Researchers must identify both risks and benefits to justify their plans, which is not always easy. For instance, researchers who were interviewing young people in Tanzania and Zimbabwe who had recently lost a parent to HIV/AIDS found that the participants frequently cried. Was asking about their experiences "cruel"? Or was the distress worth the insight that would be gained from understanding their shared experiences (Robson & Evans, 2013)? There are no easy answers. In this study, researchers asked the participants what they thought. They reported that they wanted to share their stories, despite the tears.

2. *Participants need to be informed.* Scientists must get permission from participants before research begins. Formally this is known as *informed consent*. Young children are considered too young to understand what it means to participate in a research study, so their parents are responsible for giving permission. Adolescents, depending on their age and on local regulations, may be legally able to consent to participate in a research study on their own. Regardless of age, all participants need to be able to opt out of a research study. Getting informed consent may be difficult when researchers are studying some groups, such as adolescents and people with cognitive impairment (Biros, 2018).

3. *Participants should not be pressured to participate.* Adults, children, and their families often receive stickers, T-shirts, rides to the laboratory, or even dinners out as part of research projects, but scientists shouldn't entice people to participate in research for the money. Some populations need extra protection from coercion. For instance, college students are often invited to participate in research conducted on campus, but they should not be required to participate in exchange for a grade. Similarly, people who are incarcerated should have the fully protected right to refuse to participate in research, without any consequences.

4. *Participants' personal information needs to stay private.* When researchers are conducting studies, they may have access to test scores, dating profiles, genetic information, and even pictures of a person's brain. All this information must stay confidential. But what if researchers come across information that may point to a problem? For instance, in nearly one out of every eight brain scans, scientists find an unusual brain structure—which could be entirely typical or a sign of disease—and in these cases, scientists are required to inform the participant or their family (Li et al., 2021). Similarly, many researchers are also legally *mandated reporters*, who must report suspected abuse to local protection agencies.

Protecting the Integrity of Science Researchers are not just required to keep people safe—they are also responsible for making sure that their science is trustworthy. More than 20 years ago, one medical researcher damaged the reputation of science and put millions of lives at risk. In 1998, Andrew Wakefield, an English surgeon, published a research paper that claimed the measles vaccine caused autism spectrum disorder (*The Lancet*, 2010; Wakefield et al., 1998; Ziv & Hotam, 2015). Wakefield became a world-traveling anti-vaccine advocate, triggering a decline in vaccination rates around the world that has accelerated after the COVID-19 pandemic (Callaghan et al.,

2021). The problem: His research was a fraud. He ultimately admitted that he had used false data. Wakefield lost his medical license; his published paper was removed, or retracted, from the journal where it was printed; and he was sued (Deer, 2020). Why? He had violated multiple standards of research ethics.

Researchers are required to follow some basic ethical guidelines:

1. *Data cannot be falsified.* Scientists cannot just make things up. This is exactly what Wakefield did in his study: He said that he interviewed and reviewed medical records for 12 children who developed autism after receiving the measles vaccine. But it was not true. Only one child developed autism after receiving the measles vaccines. Eight had other developmental illnesses before receiving the vaccine, and three were healthy (Deer, 2011). Furthermore, simply developing autism soon after a vaccination does not suggest that the vaccination was the cause. An abundance of experimental research using experimental and control groups has shown there is no link between vaccines and autism (Hviid et al., 2019).

2. *Bias needs to be avoided.* Scientists, like other people, have hunches and ideas they hope are true. Wakefield recruited children to participate in his study by working with an anti-vaccine campaign, rather than finding a representative sample (Deer, 2020).

3. *Research must be shared for replication and verification.* Researchers are encouraged to share their research data with other scientists and reviewers to help verify their claims. Wakefield was reluctant to share his sources with reviewers. He did not even share his data with the people who coauthored his paper.

4. *Possible conflicts should be reported.* Researchers are required to identify how they are funded and their possible conflicts of interest. For instance, a researcher doing experiments about the effects of video games on children would need to disclose if they were receiving payments from the makers of *World of Warcraft*. Wakefield did not disclose that his research was funded by a law firm that was suing the manufacturers of the measles vaccine. He also failed to mention that he had patented his own vaccine (Deer, 2011).

Ethical breaches as extreme as Andrew Wakefield's are extremely rare. The majority of scientists, share the goal of learning the truth. Layers of review, critical thinking, and data sharing make it nearly impossible for a wholesale fabrication like Wakefield's to occur. More common is the misinterpretation of research findings, such as overstating the strength of the results. Critical thinking is necessary for us as consumers of research as well—the next time you see a shocking headline on your social media feed, explore more deeply.

CAN YOU BELIEVE IT?
How Do You Spot Fake Science?

How do you spot fake science? It is not always easy. Most people in the United States trust science, but we are still vulnerable to falling for something that is overhyped, particularly if it is in a field that is new to us (Funk et al., 2019). Here are three steps to help you pick out what's real from a story that might be trying to scare you, sell you something, or play to your existing biases.

1. *Learn more.* In developmental science, or any other complex field, it is hard to pick out the overhyped pseudoscience from the real breakthroughs if you are not sure what the existing science is. For instance, by the time you finish this book you will know which of these claims refers to a real scientific discovery: (1) Newborns can count; (2) online media has made teenagers more selfish; or (3) the rate of

sexually transmitted infections is rising more quickly in older people than in any other age group. Knowing the basics will help you pick out the real science from the clickbait.

As you will learn, scientists have indeed found that infants are born with an innate sense of number: They know the difference between three and one of something. To say they can count is an exaggeration, because they cannot talk or hold up their fingers to indicate number, but this headline is based on a plausible scientific discovery (see Chapter 4; Butterworth et al., 2018). Did you guess that adolescents have become more selfish since the advent of Snapchat filters? Scientists have actually found the opposite: All that online socializing happens because teenagers are intensely interested in other people (James et al., 2017). Did you guess that older adults are at higher risk for sexually transmitted infections? They aren't aware of their own risks, and health care providers are often too embarrassed and ageist to have frank conversations with them (Smith et al., 2020). If you guessed incorrectly, research may have played into one of your biases, which brings us to tip #2.

2. *Be aware of your own biases.* Many times, fake science news or pseudoscience is appealing because it supports what we think we already know, what we feel in our "gut," or what we think "intuitively" (Kenrick et al., 2017; Tangherlini et al., 2020). For instance, the idea that teenagers are self-centered and difficult is a common cultural bias. Similarly, many people don't think older adults are sexually active. So, when you read that teenagers are selfish, you are more likely to think it is true. Or if you read that older people are having more sex, you might disbelieve it. All of us are more likely to believe information that confirms what we already think, whether or not it is true.

3. *Be comfortable with complexity.* One sign of fake science is when someone tells you that they have found the answer to everything. When social scientists compare conspiracy theories to actual science, they find that conspiracies are simpler than the real thing, because reality is often uncomfortably complex (Tangherlini et al., 2020). Pseudoscience often gives people a chance to become an expert immediately, without getting an advanced degree or even reading a book. As you have probably already realized, developmental science experts are comfortable with detail and inconsistencies. A high level of detail helps them make sure they are making the right choices when they turn science into practice and develop interventions to improve lives. 🌐

APPLY IT! **2.3** How would you apply the scientific method to a study of Hugo's life? You need to make an observation, form a hypothesis, collect some data (maybe by watching his video again), analyze what you've learned, and share it with others. You might notice that Hugo credits his family values for his resilience. What has contributed to your ability to bounce back in your life?

2.4 Evaluating research is a key element of scientific thinking. How would you evaluate the validity, reliability, and replicability of your observations about Hugo? Would you want to do another case study? Sharing your findings is an important way of checking your work. Can you share your own hypotheses and observations about your own resilience and see how the feedback you receive helps you refine your own ideas?

Wrapping It Up

LO 2.1 Identify why scientists use theory to guide their work. (p. 34)

In developmental science, theories provide a link between ideas and scientific findings to help explain how people change or stay the same based on what can be observed or tested. Theories generate *hypotheses* and give researchers a perspective with which to interpret evidence. Contrasting theories help scientists think critically about what they observe or believe.

LO 2.2 Explain how the biological perspective links the brain and body to developmental change. (p. 35)

Scholars who adopt the biological perspective include those who apply evolutionary theory to development. Evolutionary theorists suggest that human life, and even some human behaviors, have developed over time to help us adapt and survive. Ethology theory suggests that some human behaviors are inborn, and many ethologists study animals to look for insight into human behaviors. Epigenetic theory argues that our environment shapes how our genes are expressed and describe how some changes are easier to make than others.

LO 2.3 Explain how the psychodynamic perspective links early experiences to personality development. (p. 37)

Psychodynamic theory suggests that human beings have inborn needs for connection and safety and that early experiences help shape our personality development. Freud was an early psychodynamic thinker who theorized that we advance through five psychosexual stages as we master our unconscious physical urges. Erikson was a psychodynamic thinker who developed an eight-stage theory of psychosocial development. He emphasized that children need a sense of safety and acceptance of their limitations and that adults need to feel generative. Attachment theory suggests that close emotional bonds between infants and their caregivers shape our relationships and way of approaching the world throughout the lifespan.

LO 2.4 Explain how the behaviorist perspective focuses on how people learn. (p. 40)

Behaviorist theorists focus on what scientists can measure, like behavior, rather than what people think or feel, which is difficult to measure. Classical conditioning is a process of human and animal learning that links a stimulus and a response. Watson demonstrated classical conditioning in children by conditioning Little Albert to fear of white fuzzy objects. Operant conditioning is a theory of learning that explains a behavior will be more likely to happen if it is rewarded—and less likely to occur if it is ignored or punished. Social learning theory suggests that learning involves our thinking and feeling and occurs through observing and imitating others.

LO 2.5 Describe how the cognitive perspective focuses on how thinking changes as we mature. (p. 44)

Piaget's theory of cognitive development suggests that thinking matures as children actively explore the world until they reach intellectual maturity in adolescence. Piaget argued that there are four major stages of cognitive development children go through as they use their bodies and their developing thinking skills to explore the world. Information-processing theorists look at the individual components of thinking like memory, processing speed, and executive function and how they change.

LO 2.6 Explain how the cultural perspective focuses on how culture shapes development. (p. 47)

Cultural theorists explain that culture is integrated into all of development from our relationships and thinking to our biology. Sociocultural theory is inspired by the work of Vygotsky, who argued that how we think and develop is shaped by our social relationships and cultural practices. Theories of social justice look at the impact of structural inequality and discrimination on development and seek to identify strengths and systemic changes that could help all people thrive.

LO 2.7 Define the steps and guiding principles of the scientific method. (p. 51)

The scientific method is a process of testing what you know to make sure it is true and consists of five steps: observation, hypothesis, data collection, analysis, and sharing. Developmental scientists have many ways of designing their research projects, including experiments, correlational studies, or descriptive research. Change over time can be measured using a longitudinal, cross-sectional, cross-sequential, or microgenetic research design. Data can be gathered using quantitative or qualitative research methods, which could include observation, biological assessment, surveys, or formal tests. Scientists test accuracy by making sure their data is valid, reliable, and replicable.

LO 2.8 Discuss the ethical standards governing science and practice. (p. 61)

Ethical standards are designed to protect people who are participating in research and to make sure scientific research is trustworthy. Scientists are required to be honest, avoid bias, declare their possible conflicts, and share their research.

KEY TERMS

theory (p. 34)
biological perspective (p. 35)
evolution (p. 35)
ethology (p. 36)
epigenetics (p. 36)
psychodynamic perspective (p. 37)
psychosexual stages (p. 38)
attachment theory (p. 40)
behaviorism (p. 40)
classical conditioning (p. 41)
operant conditioning (p. 41)
reinforcement (p. 41)

punishment (p. 41)
social learning theory (p. 43)
cognitive development theory (p. 44)
schema (p. 45)
assimilation (p. 45)
accommodation (p. 45)
Piaget's stage theory of development (p. 45)
stage (p. 45)
information processing (p. 46)
cultural perspective (p. 47)

sociocultural theory (p. 47)
scientific method (p. 51)
hypothesis (p. 51)
experiment (p. 53)
variables (p. 53)
independent variable (p. 53)
dependent variable (p. 53)
correlational study (p. 55)
case study (p. 56)
ethnography (p. 56)
longitudinal research (p. 56)

cross-sectional study (p. 57)
cross-sequential study (p. 57)
microgenetic research (p. 58)
quantitative research (p. 58)
qualitative research (p. 58)
observation (p. 58)
assessment (p. 59)
cross-cultural research (p. 61)
ethical standards (p. 61)
Institutional Review Board (IRB) (p. 61)

CHECK YOUR LEARNING

1. The biological perspective on development focuses on the impact of genetics and physical growth on development. Which of the following theoretical approaches is NOT an example of the biological perspective?
   a) Epigenetic theory
   b) Behaviorist theory
   c) Ethological theory
   d) Evolutionary theory

2. Three-year-old Nina holds a baby doll up to her chest after watching her mother nurse her baby sister. Which theory would describe this behavior in terms of *modeling* and *imitation*?
   a) Erikson's psychosocial theory
   b) Piaget's constructivist theory
   c) Information-processing theory
   d) Social learning theory

3. Theories of social justice focus on:
   a) operant and classical conditioning.
   b) the impacts of discrimination on development.
   c) considering thinking in terms of the actions of a computer.
   d) assimilation and accommodation.

4. Which of the following theories describes development in terms of discrete stages?
   a) Sociocultural theory
   b) Piaget's constructivist theory
   c) Erikson's psychosocial theory
   d) Freud's psychosexual theory

5. Celina is a developmental scientist interested in the experiences of migrant children who do agricultural work in the United States. She spent three weeks among the workers, picking fruit with them, talking about their lives, and taking extensive notes on the children's daily routines, their interactions, and the culture of the farmworker community. This type of research is known as:
   a) ethnographic research.
   b) biological assessment.
   c) experimental research.
   d) cross-sectional research.

6. Of the following steps in the scientific method, which one typically would come first?
   a) Collect data.
   b) Form a hypothesis.
   c) Analyze data.
   d) Disseminate results.

7. Which of the following is an example of a *cross-sectional* study?
   a) A study that compares sleep patterns of four groups: 12-year-olds, 16-year-olds, 25-year-olds, and 40-year-olds
   b) A study that measures the correlation between sleep and anxiety
   c) A study that tracks sleep patterns of 200 participants over a 10-year period, from age 50 to age 60
   d) A study testing the effects of a new sleep drug on the sleep patterns of older adults

8. To test the effects of exercise on memory, Dr. Dolan selected 50 adults to participate in a three-week exercise class, and another 50 to join a cooking class. After the classes, she gave memory tests to all 100 adults and compared the scores of the exercise group to the scores of the cooking group. This is an example of a(n):
   a) case study.
   b) correlational study.
   c) experimental study.
   d) cross-cultural study.

Genetics, Prenatal Development, and Birth

© Macmillan, Photo by Sidford House

Understanding the Genome

3.1 Define key components of human genetics.

3.2 Explain basic principles of genetic transmission of traits.

3.3 Explain how the environment can affect gene expression through the epigenome.

Prenatal Development

3.4 Describe the key stages of prenatal development.

3.5 Describe the principles of prenatal risk and resilience.

Birth and the Newborn

3.6 Explain the process of vaginal childbirth and its common risks and protective factors.

3.7 Describe how newborns' senses and capabilities help them thrive.

Alizah always wanted to have a baby. She believed that when the time was right, it would happen. She was sure 2020 was going to be "the year": She was tending to her health, seeing a doctor, and taking medicine for her thyroid condition; she had a great job as a teacher in Los Angeles; and she was an active member of a creative community, mentoring students in an afterschool program on yoga, music, and social justice. So, she hoped, wished, and asked her friends to pray for her.

Alizah's partner, Spencer, was equally sure that the time was right to have a child and that Alizah was "the one." With all the challenges in the world, Spencer felt like his and Alizah's baby could make the world a brighter place. Alizah and Spencer were crazy about each other.

Not everything in Alizah and Spencer's lives was as perfect as their relationship and the lovely nursery they created for their baby. 2020 turned out to be Alizah and Spencer's year to have a baby, but it was also tumultuous — the year of the COVID-19 pandemic. Alizah was pregnant in the middle of a crisis, complicating many of her plans for her pregnancy and birth. Spencer couldn't come to her doctor's appointments. Alizah's mother in Louisiana couldn't get on a plane to help. But there were unexpected benefits: Alizah and Spencer got to spend more time together, and Alizah no longer had to commute to her job.

Most importantly, Alizah and Spencer stayed healthy and avoided COVID-19, and so did their growing fetus. They picked a name: Courage, after the strength they hoped he would have to thrive in a difficult world. They worried about the effects of isolation during the pandemic, about getting medical care and staying safe while the baby was born. Alizah even worried about the effect of all that worry on her growing fetus. But both mother and baby were healthy, and Alizah was ready to show her newborn to her students on Zoom after he was born.

When Alizah's pregnancy test told her that Courage was on the way, he was just a 32-celled creature, scarcely bigger than the period at the end of this sentence. Those tiny cells contained the genetic information that would guide Courage's development. His genes shape how he grows and develops, but the environment also plays a major role. For most of us, genes are not destiny. Your genome contributes to who you are, but who you are also changes your genome.

The months fetuses spend inside the uterus also play an important role in creating who they are. Some babies are born smaller than others. Some fetuses, like Courage, have advantages that others do not. But no matter how newborns arrive, they are already remarkably capable. Like Courage, they are born ready to learn about the world and form relationships that will guide them for a lifetime.

Scientific American Profile

▶ Meet Alizah and Spencer

Understanding the Genome

Learning Objectives

3.1 Define key components of human genetics.

3.2 Explain basic principles of genetic transmission of traits.

3.3 Explain how the environment can affect gene expression through the epigenome.

genome The unique set of instructions that includes everything a cell might need for creating your body parts and maintaining them over the lifespan.

chromosomes The 23 pairs of long molecules of DNA containing genetic information and found in the nucleus of human cells.

deoxyribonucleic acid (DNA) A spiral-, or helix-, shaped structure made up of paired chemicals that carries the genetic code.

mitosis A type of cell division that creates two, new identical cells.

genes Sections of DNA that create particular proteins.

alleles Genes that have different forms.

You often hear about genetics, perhaps as an explanation for the traits you inherited. People might tell you that you have your grandfather's smile. Or you might see a news story that tells you that a genetic test can predict the risk for breast cancer. When scientists use the term *genetics*, they mean that some of your observable characteristics are inherited and have been triggered by the genetic sequence inside your cells.

If you could take a microscope and look inside yourself, you would see that each bit of you is made up of cells. What they do is directed by the **genome**, the unique set of instructions that includes everything a cell might need for creating all of your body parts, maintaining them over the lifespan, and even telling your body, one day, how to die.

These instructions are packed in 46 **chromosomes** located inside the nucleus of each cell. Most of the time, they look like a tangled bunch of yarn, as you will see in **Infographic 3.1** (Collombet et al., 2020). But inside this crumpled mass is a precise organizational structure. Each tiny chromosome is lined up into one of 23 pairs. Inside each chromosome is a spiral, or *helix*, that can stretch out to more than two inches long and is made up of four chemicals arranged like a ladder. These chemicals are part of a molecule called **deoxyribonucleic acid**, better known as **DNA**.

The ladder-like structure of DNA allows the genetic information in each cell to be duplicated every time a new cell is created. New cells are created as people grow from a single-celled *zygote* into a 30 trillion-celled adult. In addition, the body continuously creates new cells throughout the lifespan to replace those that have worn out. DNA replicates itself each time through a mechanism known as **mitosis**. In this process, the ladder of DNA rips down the middle. Each half of the ladder rebuilds to create two new identical strands of DNA, copying genetic information into each new cell.

Genes are sections of DNA that create particular proteins. Human beings have about 22,000 genes, and each one tells the cell how to create a specific protein (Abascal et al., 2018). Not everyone has exactly the same version of each gene. Genes have different forms that are known as **alleles**.

The particular alleles you inherit can affect your individual characteristics, as well as your risks for disease. For instance, millions of people have *sickle-cell disease*, the

Every bit of the human body grows, matures, and changes because of directions from their genome. Inside every cell are genetic instructions that tell the cell when to duplicate itself, what proteins to create, and even when to die. Some aspects of our genome are set at conception, but the way our genes are expressed over our lifespan is determined, in part, by the environment. Changes to our gene expression are made through *epigenetic marks,* chemical messengers that help turn specific genes on and off. Your own genome is known as your *genotype,* and it contributes to your unique *phenotype.*

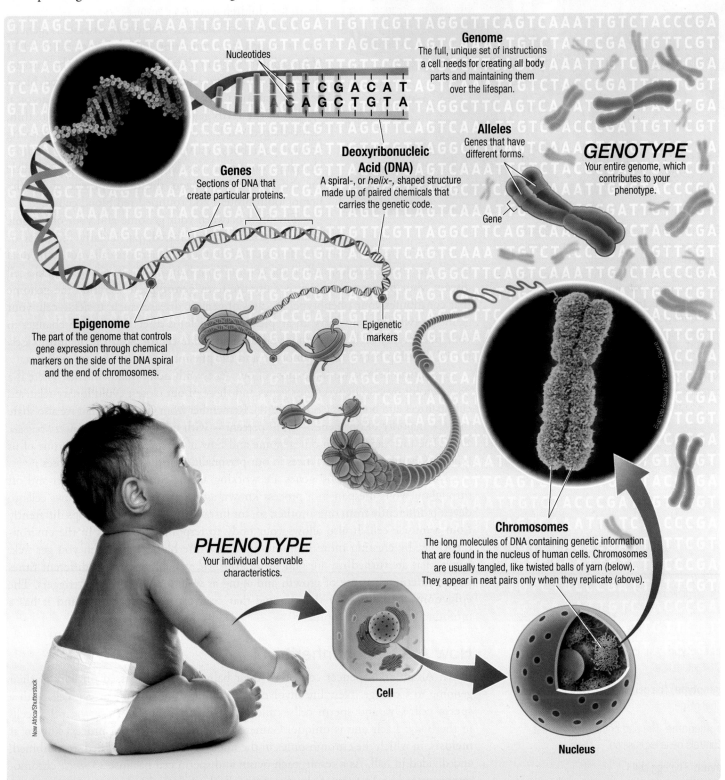

Nucleotides

Genome
The full, unique set of instructions a cell needs for creating all body parts and maintaining them over the lifespan.

Alleles
Genes that have different forms.

GENOTYPE
Your entire genome, which contributes to your phenotype.

Genes
Sections of DNA that create particular proteins.

Deoxyribonucleic Acid (DNA)
A spiral-, or *helix-,* shaped structure made up of paired chemicals that carries the genetic code.

Gene

Epigenome
The part of the genome that controls gene expression through chemical markers on the side of the DNA spiral and the end of chromosomes.

Epigenetic markers

PHENOTYPE
Your individual observable characteristics.

Chromosomes
The long molecules of DNA containing genetic information that are found in the nucleus of human cells. Chromosomes are usually tangled, like twisted balls of yarn (below). They appear in neat pairs only when they replicate (above).

Cell

Nucleus

New Africa/Shutterstock

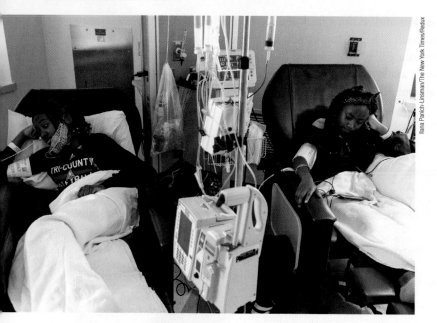

Ilana Panich-Linsman/The New York Times/Redux

Sisters in Sickness and Health. Sickle-cell disease is the most common single-gene disorder in the world. Kami and Kyra's parents were both carriers of sickle cell, and both girls have had serious complications from the disease. Here, the teenagers receive blood transfusions in the hospital near their home in San Antonio, Texas, to help with the pain associated with the disease while they wait for gene therapy, a more permanent treatment.

phenotype Your individual observable characteristics.

genotype The genome that contributes your phenotype.

epigenome The part of the genome that controls gene expression.

ovum The egg cell.

sperm The reproductive cell from a male.

meiosis A special form of cell division that creates the gametes, or sperm and ova cells.

most common single-gene disorder in the world (Kato et al., 2018). Sickle-cell disease can keep the body from getting enough oxygen—leading to painful sickle-cell crises and even death if people can't receive treatment. As a result, globally, sickle-cell disease remains a leading cause of death for children (Oron et al., 2020).

Unlike most diseases, sickle-cell disease is genetic and is caused by a mutation in one gene, called HBB (*H*emoglobin su*B*unit *B*eta). HBB contains the instructions for *hemoglobin*, the protein that allows red blood cells to transport oxygen around the body. The atypical version of the HBB gene causes your body to create thin, sickle-shaped red blood cells that have difficulty moving around your body, starving it of oxygen and sometimes clogging your blood vessels. In contrast, the typical allele for the HBB gene triggers the development of healthy hemoglobin protein and rounded red blood cells.

The links between your genome and your observable characteristics are complicated, particularly for traits or diseases that are more complex than sickle-cell disease. Scientists call your individual observable characteristics, such as the color of your hair or the symptoms of sickle-cell disease, your **phenotype**. Scientists use the term **genotype** to describe the genome that contributes your phenotype. In cases of genetic diseases such as sickle-cell, your genotype (whether you carry an atypical HBB allele) is directly linked to changes in your phenotype, such as whether you develop sickle-cell disease. But in most cases, the relationship between the genotype and the phenotype is much more complex.

As human beings, we share most of our genes with nonhuman animals. There is a 98.7 percent overlap between our genes and those of our closest evolutionary relatives, chimpanzees and bonobos (Staes et al., 2019). Remember from Chapter 1 that we also share the vast majority of our genes—99.9 percent—with other humans (Collins & Mansoura, 2001). The tiny variations in our genome and how it is expressed make each one of us unique, whether that is differences in our personalities or the shape of our noses.

Not all of your 22,000 genes are working all the time. Genes turn on and off throughout your lifespan in a process known as *gene regulation*. This allows cells to develop differently from one another, so, for instance, a blood cell develops differently from a muscle cell. It also allows your body to respond to changes in the environment, say, by creating more immune-fighting white blood cells when you get sick. Genes that are turned on are said to be *expressed*, which happens at different times in your lifetime because of growth and aging as well as environmental triggers. The **epigenome** is the part of the genome that controls gene expression, and it has a profound effect on development.

How Are Genes Inherited?

When Alizah and Spencer conceived their baby, they each passed on part of their genome to Courage. New life involves the joining of an **ovum**, or egg cell, with a **sperm** cell. Ova and sperm cells, called *gametes*, are different from the other cells in the body: Each one is unique. Gametes are created through a process known as **meiosis**, in which the chromosomes in the nucleus of a cell are shuffled, recombined, and divided in half. As a result, each ovum and sperm cell has just 23 *single* chromosomes instead of 23 *pairs* of chromosomes. Each of these 23 chromosomes has been randomly selected from the 23 pairs of chromosomes in the parent's cells.

When an ovum and sperm meet in the moment of conception, the 23 chromosomes from the ovum match up with 23 chromosomes from the sperm cell. This creates a new human cell with 46 chromosomes in 23 pairs, known as a **zygote**. In each of the zygote's 23 pairs of chromosomes, one chromosome is inherited from the ovum, and the other is inherited from the sperm. When you account for the random selection of chromosomes in the creation of gametes with the random selection of chromosomes in conception, the chromosomes in one zygote could be combined in one of more than 8 million possible combinations, each with half of the parent cell's genetic information! Each baby is truly one of 8 million possible siblings two biological parents could create (Bell et al., 2020).

The Genetics of Sex

In human cells, the 23rd pair of chromosomes is unique. This pair is known as the **sex chromosomes**, which are referred to by their shape as X or Y chromosomes. Most people who identify as men have one Y chromosome and one X chromosome, and most who identify as women have two X chromosomes. When gametes are formed, each one will have only one chromosome in the 23rd position. So, each ovum contains a single X, and each sperm cell will have either a single X or a single Y. Most genetically female babies inherit an X chromosome from each parent, so that their 23rd pair of chromosomes is XX, and genetically male babies inherit an X from their mother and a Y from their father, making their 23rd chromosome pair XY.

Scientists use the term **sex** to refer to the biology that relates to being female (primarily XX) and male (primarily XY) and the spectrum of variation beyond these binary labels. Sex can refer to your genotype and also your phenotype, which includes observable characteristics like reproductive organs and genitals. The broader term, **gender**, is used to describe the social and cultural distinctions that are linked to ideas about being male, female, and other labels, including nonbinary or genderless identities. Gender ideas often change over time. (Did you know that until the 1940s, American boys wore pink and girls wore blue? Or that nonbinary genders are not new? Ancient cultures often celebrated gender variation [Helle, 2018; Paoletti, 2012].) The term **gender identity** refers to your sense of yourself as a man, woman, or as someone who is not within the lines of these binary labels. **Gender expression** describes how you express your gender in daily life, such as with makeup, hairstyle, or clothing.

Scientists think that almost 1 in 100 people are of a sex that is less binary than a simple distinction between XX and XY (Arboleda et al., 2014; Ernst et al., 2018). These people may be *intersex,* describe themselves as having a gender variance or *difference of sex development (DSD),* the term medical professionals use (Ernst et al., 2020). Many people with DSD feel comfortable in the gender they were assigned at birth, even if it does not match the XX or XY in their genotype (Lee et al., 2016). Usually, the best gauge of someone's gender is not in their chromosomes, but in what they feel.

Maria José Martínez-Patiño learned about the complexity of biological sex from experience. The fastest hurdler in Spain, she was expected to compete in the 1988 Olympics. However, a blood test given to all female athletes at the time revealed that Maria José had an X and a Y chromosome. She was told to quietly withdraw from competition but refused. With many scientists' support, she argued that there was more to sex and gender than X and Y, and that she couldn't drop out and "pretend to be a man" (Martínez-Patiño, 2005). She fought for four years to rejoin the national team.

Maria José had *androgen insensitivity*, a condition that prevents people with XY chromosomes from developing male genitals. Most people with androgen insensitivity identify as women: They have breasts and vaginas but may lack interior reproductive organs like ovaries. At that time, the Olympic Committee considered sex to be binary and based on chromosomes alone. In the years since Maria José missed her chance at an Olympic medal, other athletes whose bodies do not conform to a narrow understanding of sex and gender have faced similar discrimination (Rogol & Pieper, 2018).

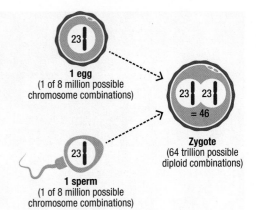

1 egg
(1 of 8 million possible chromosome combinations)

1 sperm
(1 of 8 million possible chromosome combinations)

Zygote
(64 trillion possible diploid combinations)

FIGURE 3.1 The Diversity of New Life When new life is formed, the 23 chromosomes from the ovum match up with 23 chromosomes from the sperm cell. This creates a new human cell with 46 chromosomes in 23 pairs, known as a zygote. When you account for the random selection of chromosomes in the creation of gametes with the random selection of chromosomes in conception, the chromosomes in one zygote could be combined in one of more than 8 million possible combinations.

CONNECTIONS

Differences of sex development, such as being intersex, are different from being transgender or nonbinary. As you will learn in Chapter 7, children who identify as transgender or who are gender diverse do not feel comfortable with the gender they were assigned at birth.

zygote A new human cell with 46 chromosomes in 23 pairs.

sex chromosomes The 23rd pair of chromosomes.

sex The physical and genetic characteristics usually associated with being male, female, or a mixture.

gender The term for the social and cultural distinctions describing binary and less binary distinctions between men and women.

gender identity The term for your sense of yourself as a man, woman, or someone not as exclusively within the lines of these binary labels.

gender expression The term for how you express your gender in daily life, such as how you wear makeup, style your hair, or what clothing you like.

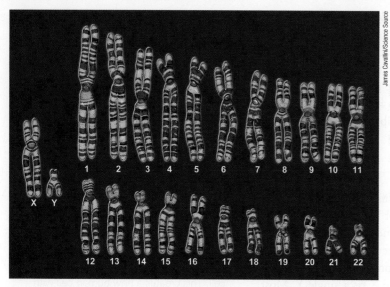

James Cavallini/Science Source

One of These Is Not Like the Others. One of these chromosomes is shown as a pair: an X and a Y. The others are shown unpaired in their duplicated form, ready for cell division. In order to visualize the chromosomes, they were chemically stained, separated, and arranged by size, to make them easier to look at. This is a photograph taken through a microscope that has been enlarged about 4,000 times.

recessive inheritance pattern A type of genetic inheritance for single-gene conditions. In order to develop a recessive condition, you must have two of the disease-carrying alleles.

Single-Gene Inheritance Patterns

Some traits and conditions, like sickle-cell disease, are called *single-gene disorders* because they are linked to a single gene. In these cases, it may be possible to predict and even prevent the transmission of the disease if the gene has been found.

Sickle-cell disease has a **recessive inheritance pattern**. Remember that a zygote includes half of the chromosomes from the ovum and half from the sperm. The resulting child will have two versions of each gene, called *alleles*. In recessive disorders, two copies of the disease-carrying allele must be inherited, one from each of their parents, for the disorder to be expressed. Such conditions are called "recessive" because healthy versions of the gene are *dominant*, or more likely to be expressed, so the disease tends to *recess*, or not appear, when the dominant form of the gene is present.

In the example of sickle-cell disease, healthy hemoglobin genes are dominant, so a child must inherit disease-carrying alleles from *both* parents to have the disease. A genetic *carrier* is someone who has inherited one allele for a disease or trait, and does not express the disorder but can pass it on to their children. If two parents are carriers for sickle-cell disease, each of their children has a 50 percent chance of inheriting *one* disease-carrying allele and will be carriers, with one typical allele and one sickle-cell allele. As you can see in **Figure 3.2**, each child has a 25 percent chance of inheriting two typical

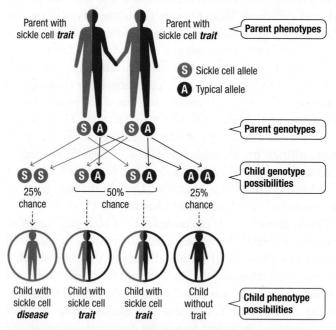

FIGURE 3.2 Recessive Inheritance Patterns: Transmission of Sickle-Cell Disease If both parents are carriers of the recessive sickle-cell disease allele, each of their children will have a 25 percent chance of inheriting the sickle-cell allele from both parents and getting sickle-cell disease. Each child will have a 50 percent chance of inheriting one diseased allele and being a carrier, like their parents, and a 25 percent chance of inheriting a set of typical alleles.

alleles and a 25 percent chance of inheriting two disease-carrying alleles and developing sickle-cell disorder.

Other disorders that follow a recessive inheritance pattern include *thalassemia*, a blood disorder; *cystic fibrosis*, a lung and digestive disease; and *Tay Sachs disease*, a fatal neurological syndrome. While single-gene disorders are rare, they are more common in groups that are isolated or where intermarriage within tightly knit communities is common. For instance, families from European Jewish, South Asian, and Finnish backgrounds tend to have higher rates of single-gene disorders (Nakatsuka et al., 2017).

Some single-gene disorders only require one copy of the disease-carrying allele. In these cases, even if you inherit one healthy allele and one disease-carrying allele, you will still develop the illness. These diseases are based on **dominant inheritance**, because the disease is expressed even if a single copy of the diseased allele is inherited. These diseases include *Huntington disease*, a fatal neurological illness that strikes in middle life, and *Marfan syndrome*, a chronic and sometimes fatal connective tissue disease. For dominant inheritance pattern diseases, each child born to a parent with the condition has a 50 percent chance of inheriting the affected gene and the disorder, as you can see in **Figure 3.3**.

A special form of single-gene transmission, known as *sex-linked transmission*, occurs when disorders are transmitted on the sex chromosomes. For example, *hemophilia*, a now-treatable disease that makes it difficult for blood to clot, is caused by one recessive gene located on the X chromosome (Batty & Lillicrap, 2019). As a result, nearly all people with hemophilia are men, or people with only one X chromosome. Most women have two X chromosomes, and are much more likely to inherit at least one dominant allele, but when they inherit the allele for hemophilia, most of the time they are protected by the healthy variant on the other chromosome (Shah et al., 2017). Having a double copy of the X chromosome serves to protect people from the worst effects of a number of diseases, as it does with hemophilia: In these cases, the disease-carrying gene may be silenced or inactivated by the healthy one from the other X chromosome (Galupa & Heard, 2018).

The X chromosome can also carry genes for other conditions, although transmission of these disorders tends to be more complex. These conditions include male-pattern baldness and some forms of color blindness (Hunt & Carvalho, 2016; Yap et al., 2018). Damage to the X chromosome can lead to the development of *Turner syndrome*, which can cause infertility and other conditions in women (Gravholt et al., 2019). It can also trigger *fragile X syndrome*, which is linked to some intellectual disabilities and forms of autism spectrum disorder (Salcedo-Arellano et al., 2020). The tiny Y chromosome carries only a few disorders, most notably a risk for male infertility, but disruptions in the Y chromosomes may be one reason men are predisposed to some conditions, including Parkinson disease and high blood pressure (Lau, 2020; Signore et al., 2020).

Marfan Syndrome Maya Brown-Zimmerman has Marfan syndrome, a single-gene disorder that is passed on through an autosomal dominant pattern. Marfan syndrome is a multi-system connective tissue disorder that can be painful, sometimes debilitating, and life-threatening. Maya and her husband, Mark, have four children. Her younger son, Julian, has Marfan syndrome like his mother. She says that people criticized her decision to have children. Maya says ". . . having a perfect body is not the most important thing. Even though my body is not perfect, there's a lot that I can add to the world around me. I felt that our kids would be able to do the same, even if they inherited Marfan syndrome" (Brown-Zimmerman, 2012).

Multiple Genes, Many Factors

Most conditions or traits, from Spencer's brown eyes to Alizah's curls, are influenced by multiple genes, which require a trigger or specific influence from the environment in order to be expressed. These traits and diseases are called **polygenic**. They are carried by a number of alleles, in a number of locations on different chromosomes, that need to be inherited and triggered at one particular time to spark the development of particular traits, or conditions.

dominant inheritance pattern A type of genetic inheritance for single-gene disorders. A person with a dominant condition may have just one of the disease-carrying alleles.

polygenic Genetic characteristics that require a trigger or specific influence from the environment in order to be expressed.

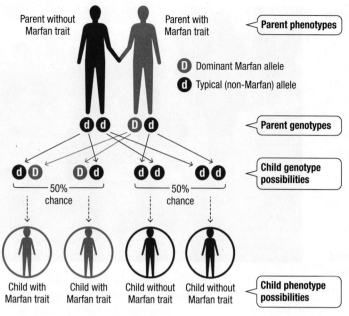

Parent without Marfan trait

Parent with Marfan trait

Parent phenotypes

D Dominant Marfan allele

d Typical (non-Marfan) allele

Parent genotypes

Child genotype possibilities

50% chance   50% chance

Child phenotype possibilities

Child with Marfan trait   Child with Marfan trait   Child without Marfan trait   Child without Marfan trait

FIGURE 3.3 Dominant Inheritance Patterns: Transmission of Marfan Syndrome If one parent is a carrier of the dominant Marfan syndrome allele, each of their children will have a 50 percent chance of inheriting the gene for the trait and developing the disorder.

Consider eye color. In the past, many scientists thought it could be easily predicted using the rules of single-gene inheritance, but they turned out to be wrong. There are at least 16 individual genes that control whether you end up with deep brown eyes or icy blue ones (Ludwig et al., 2016). Most of the time, babies end up with brown eyes, perhaps because extra melanin in dark eyes protects you from the dangerous effects of UV light (Jablonski, 2018). The genetic complexity of eye color means that not even a geneticist can predict what color your baby's eyes will be.

In most cases, developing a disease or a particular trait requires you to inherit multiple genes, and also to be exposed to particular environmental influences. Scientists call these diseases or traits **multifactorial** because there are multiple variables that influence them (Donovan et al., 2021). For example, in order to develop a severe psychological disorder such as schizophrenia, a child who is born with multiple genes that put them at risk for the disease would also need to experience specific environmental events, which might include prenatal exposure to a virus or smoking marijuana in adolescence (Richetto & Meyer, 2021).

Researchers suggest that there are some consistent principles that guide how genes act:

1. *Your genetic map usually gives you a continuum of traits.* Most traits and disease risks aren't something you either have or you don't. They exist on a continuum (Katsanis, 2016). Skin color, for instance, is one of a rainbow of possible colors. Your personality traits are also on a spectrum, as is your genetic risk for a neurocognitive disorder, such as Parkinson disease or Alzheimer disease, as you get older (Baldacci et al., 2020).

2. *The environment can change how genes are expressed.* Your epigenome helps regulate gene expression. Environmental factors, from prenatal exposure to toxins to living through childhood trauma, can trigger gene expression (Marini et al., 2020).

3. *Your genes influence your environment.* Your individual relationship with your environment can support or change your gene expression. For instance, so-called "easy" babies are often much more likely to elicit smiles from their families than babies with less flexible or interactive personalities. On the flip side, so-called "fussy" babies may stress their families, leading to more irritable responses, contributing to an ongoing cycle of stress (Austerberry & Fearon, 2021).

4. *Genes help determine how changeable you are.* The environment plays a critical role in how everyone develops. Scientists have discovered that some genes can make you more sensitive (or *plastic*) to what is around you in what is known as *differential susceptibility* (van IJzendoorn & Bakermans-Kranenburg, 2012). People with some genetic variations are more likely to be changed by life events—whether traumatic or beneficial—than others.

5. *We're all different.* With trillions of possible combinations of DNA and environments, we all have different combinations of strengths and weaknesses, risks and benefits. For instance, someone may have genes that predispose them to being sensitive to stress, but at the same time, they may also have genes that predispose them to be quick learners. As a result, creating a life that is healthy and satisfying may require something different for each genetically distinct individual. Researchers take this tremendous complexity into account when designing interventions (van IJzendoorn et al., 2020).

multifactorial Traits that are influenced by multiple variables.

Chromosomal Differences

You just read about patterns of genetic inheritance, when a child's genes are passed on from their parents. However, not all genetic conditions are inherited. Sometimes, differences in DNA arise spontaneously as a result of errors in replication during mitosis or meiosis, known as *mutations*. Many of these anomalies are harmless, but at other times they may lead to serious challenges.

The most common form of DNA anomaly occurs before conception, during the maturation of ova and sperm. In about 3 out of every 10 ova, and in 2 in every 100 sperm cells, gametes contain an extra chromosome (Wartosch et al., 2021). When these cells combine, zygotes have too many chromosomes, and most do not survive. However, if the extra chromosome appears in the very small 21st chromosome, many will live.

This extra 21st chromosome causes **Down syndrome**, or *trisomy-21*. Children with Down syndrome have differences in brain development and, sometimes, muscle tone and cardiovascular development. Compared to typically developing children, the *cortex*, or the part of the brain linked to logical thought, memory, and controlling your behavior, is much smaller in children with Down syndrome. But other areas of the brain, like the subcortical structures involved in memory and emotional processing, are unaffected (Baburamani et al., 2019). As a result, children with Down syndrome have challenges with language and learning that can make independent living more difficult and worsen with age. By age 40, nearly all people with Down syndrome show signs of neurocognitive decline, similar to those seen in Alzheimer disease (Lott & Head, 2019). Researchers are now making strides in understanding the complex genetics of Down syndrome and even addressing some of the symptoms prenatally (Antonarakis et al., 2020).

A blood test can now detect Down syndrome in the 12th week of pregnancy to allow families time to prepare for the needs of their babies (Bull, 2020). The risk for Down syndrome is strongly connected to the age of the ovum: Young adolescents (under 15) and older parents (above 35) are at much greater risk for having ova with extra chromosomes (Wartosch et al., 2021). This means that a woman in her 40s is 20 times more likely to have a baby with Down syndrome than a woman in her 20s (Mikwar et al., 2020). Emerging evidence links age with genetic anomalies in sperm, but these are less frequently attributed to Down syndrome (Denomme et al., 2020; Thompson, 2019). Age may increase some genetic risks to the developing fetus, but older parents also tend to have many advantages, including more financial stability (Barbuscia et al., 2020).

"My Life Is Worth Living." Frank Stephens is an advocate for people with Down syndrome, as well as an actor and accomplished equestrian. Here, he testifies in Congress for more research into Down syndrome, explaining why his life was not only worthy of research, but also worth living.

The Epigenome

Genes are an important part of the genome, but they make up only 2 percent of it (Pertea et al., 2018). What is the rest? Scientists have more questions than answers, but they suspect that much of the rest of the genome is devoted to turning genes on and off and helping DNA copy itself. Remember from Infographic 3.1 that the *epigenome* is the area of the genome that is devoted to gene regulation. The epigenome controls which genes are expressed by changing the chemicals around the double helix of DNA, which are called *epigenetic marks* (O'Donnell & Meaney, 2020). Some epigenetic marks are inherited, others are created during prenatal development, and others are formed later on in the lifespan (Collins & Roth, 2021).

Dozens of factors, from parenting to nutrition, impact the epigenome (Collins & Roth, 2021). For instance, children exposed to trauma show epigenetic changes associated with stress compared to children who haven't experienced trauma

Down syndrome A condition caused by an extra 21st chromosome that results in anomalies in brain development and may also impair muscle tone and cardiovascular development.

Chromosome Pairs
3-year-old twins vs.
50-year-old twins

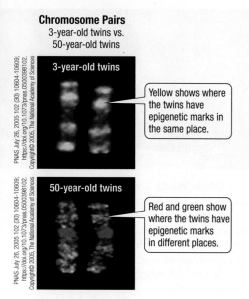

PNAS July 26, 2005 102 (30) 10604–10609;
https://doi.org/10.1073/pnas.0500398102.
Copyright© 2005, The National Academy of Sciences

3-year-old twins

Yellow shows where the twins have epigenetic marks in the same place.

50-year-old twins

Red and green show where the twins have epigenetic marks in different places.

PNAS July 26, 2005 102 (30) 10604–10609;
https://doi.org/10.1073/pnas.0500398102.
Copyright© 2005, The National Academy of Sciences

FIGURE 3.4 Epigenetic Changes over the Lifespan As you see here, at age 3, monozygotic twins have very similar genomes, shown in the yellow markers on the third chromosome. When the twins are young, most of their epigenetic marks overlap and are shown as yellow. As they grow, epigenetic changes multiply. By age 50, there are many differences (Fraga et al., 2005).

CONNECTIONS

Remember from Chapter 2 that the evolutionary perspective focuses on the adaptive value of genetic change. Genetic flexibility and variety allow organisms to adapt to the environment. Natural selection means that traits that allow an individual to survive and reproduce will be passed on to future generations and become more common in the population.

monozygotic Twins with nearly identical DNA because they start off as a single zygote that separates into two in the first days after fertilization.

dizygotic Twins that develop when two (or more) ova are fertilized by separate sperm.

(Katrinli et al., 2020). As you can see in **Figure 3.4**, epigenetic changes continue as we mature and even follow a so-called *epigenetic clock* that keeps track of the pace of aging (Li et al., 2020).

Epigenetic changes can be transmitted to future generations through alterations in meiosis, when egg and sperm cells are formed. For instance, the children and grandchildren of adults who survived massive famines, like those in Holland during World War II and China in the 1950s, have higher rates of physical and emotional illnesses because of damage to their parents' or grandparents' sperm and egg cells (Lassi & Teperino, 2020; Wu et al., 2017). Epigenetic changes in ova or sperm cells can also result from everyday behaviors and stresses, such as smoking cigarettes or having a poor diet (Wang et al., 2019). The effects of healthy behaviors can be passed on as well. For instance, fathers who exercise regularly may pass on epigenetic changes to their children that lower their risk for diseases like Parkinson disease or schizophrenia (Donkin & Barrès, 2018).

Epigenetic research is leading to more understanding and treatment of the environmental triggers for many disorders, from depression to Alzheimer disease (Cavalli & Heard, 2019). It is also helping scientists understand how epigenetic changes can be reversed: The impact of chronic stress in infants born preterm, for instance, can be overcome with the help of nurturing relationships (Kommers et al., 2016).

Evolutionary theorists point out that our flexible genome offers some benefits. For instance, having one copy of the sickle-cell allele (being a carrier) is protective against *malaria*, a mosquito-borne disease common in many parts of the world, including sub-Saharan Africa and parts of Asia and South America. As a result, carriers of the sickle-cell allele are less likely to die of malaria, particularly in infancy (Kariuki & Williams, 2020). Similar patterns are seen in other genetic conditions: Carriers of the neurological disorder Tay Sachs are protected against tuberculosis. The gene for cystic fibrosis is protective against typhoid and cholera (Ewald & Swain Ewald, 2019). So, generations ago, before modern medicine, some of these genetic traits may have helped us survive. Today, millions affected by these diseases are grateful for effective treatments and early intervention.

The Genetics of Twins

Sometimes, soon after ovum and sperm combine, the zygote splits in two, or more than one zygote is created. **Monozygotic** twins (or, more rarely, monozygotic triplets, quadruplets, and so on) have nearly identical DNA because they start off as a single zygote that separates into two in the first 13 days after fertilization (Jonsson et al., 2021). Because the resulting zygotes started as a single cell, they share that original set of genes, until epigenetic changes and random mutations begin to occur.

Dizygotic twins develop when two (or more) ova are released and fertilized by separate sperm. Since they typically have the same parents, like any set of siblings, they share about half of their genetic information. It is possible for the ova to be fertilized by two different sets of sperm if a woman has different partners (Segal et al., 2020). But most of the time, when twins look very different, do not assume they have different parents. There is often a lot of natural variety between siblings or twins.

Subtle differences in the prenatal environment and the complexity of cell division mean that even monozygotic twins are never truly identical. Sometimes this results in subtle phenotypic distinctions, such as different hair or fingerprints, but others may be more profound (Jonsson et al., 2021). For example, some

Which Are Monozygotic? Twins do not always look exactly alike, whether they are born from one zygote or two. Teenagers Maria and Lucy are dizygotic twins: They developed from two separate ova fertilized by two different sperm cells. They are as alike as any set of siblings. Toddlers Amelia and Jasmine do not look exactly alike, either: They are monozygotic twins, so they developed from one ova fertilized by one sperm cell, that split early in development. However, early developmental changes helped make the girls look a little different from each other.

monozygotic twins have different eye colors because of epigenetic changes during early development or from small differences in early cell replication (Butler et al., 2016; Somers, 2016).

For some families, getting pregnant with two babies or more is a gift. But this joy may come with danger. Twins and other multiples have a higher risk of serious complications for both the babies and their families. Multiples are more likely to be born prematurely, have low birthweight, or even die before or soon after birth (Hack et al., 2018). Even healthy multiple babies can stress families, because parents must divide their attention and energy (Ronkin & Tone, 2020). Nevertheless, many of us are curious about twins, perhaps because, as one twin researcher points out, we secretly wish "to have someone just like us" (Nancy Segal, quoted in Muhlenkamp, 2012).

Researchers have studied twins for centuries to better understand how environment and genetics interact to make each of us unique (Turner et al., 2020). Many studies have found that monozygotic twins are significantly more alike than dizygotic twins (Turkheimer, 2019). But modern research has also revealed that there are many genetic differences between monozygotic twins caused by epigenetic changes and random variations as cells duplicate over the lifespan (Ouwens et al., 2018). Indeed, studies of twins have helped researchers understand the impact of the environment on our mental and physical health and appreciate the complexity in the unpredictable interactions between our genotype and our phenotype (Lam et al., 2019).

Testing the Genome

Have you had your DNA tested? About 1 in every 25 people has, as genomic testing has become increasingly affordable and accessible (Lawton & Ifama, 2018). Genetic testing promises enormous benefits, but the science is complex, as are the possible ethical issues and concerns about gene-based discrimination (Joly et al., 2020). No tests are without risks: Getting your genetic test results creates stress and can change how you take care of your health (Turnwald et al., 2018). There are more than 50,000 distinct genetic tests that can be performed by more than 500 different laboratories to test for more than 16,000 different conditions (Regalado, 2018). What can they tell us?

Most experts and professionals do not advise getting your genome tested at home to assess your risk for a disease. Home genetic tests are not always reliable and do not usually provide the medical counseling needed to make sense of the results (Horton et al., 2019). Medical professionals and genetic counselors recommend genetic testing only when it is both *reliable* and *actionable* (Green et al., 2013). This means that a test needs to reliably and consistently diagnose the risk for a genetic disease and help you act on this information. So, for example, genetic counselors would advise getting tested for a single-gene disorder like sickle-cell disease that has clear treatments and a possible cure, particularly if you have a family history of risk (Oron et al., 2020). Similarly, genetic counselors might recommend being screened if you have a family history of breast, ovarian, or pancreatic cancer (Daly et al., 2020).

Most genetic counselors would caution against testing a child or a fetus for a disease or disorder if the results are not actionable during early childhood. For instance, knowing that your fetus or child carries some genes that may increase their risk for developing a neurocognitive disorder like Alzheimer disease may only cause unnecessary worry early in life, since the relationship between these conditions and genetics is far less direct (Eid et al., 2019; NSGC, 2019).

Alizah and Spencer, like many other families, had some genetic testing, a process they remember as stressful and confusing (Parens & Applebaum, 2019). Researchers have found that this is common. Facing the prospect that your fetus or child might have a serious genetic disease involves families' deepest-held beliefs about what makes life worthwhile. A skilled genetic counselor can help but is not always available (Clarke & Wallgren Pettersson, 2019). Culture is also relevant: Health care providers and counselors working with families who speak another language or have a different cultural background need to use cultural humility to connect with and support their clients (Ault et al., 2019; Warren, 2020).

Some forms of genetic testing promise to link you with your ancestors. Scientists advise you to take these genealogical results with a healthy dose of skepticism: They are rarely consistent when checked against those of different providers (Blell & Hunter, 2019; Grayson, 2018). In addition, most of these tests compare your DNA patterns to those of people living in other nations around the globe, but since people have moved over time, the results may never be able to tell you accurately where your ancestors lived 50 or even 200 years ago (Fullwiley, 2021; Saey, 2018). In addition, test results often oversimplify ancestry and can reinforce the idea that our genome defines who we are (Roth et al., 2020).

For many, ancestry testing brings up questions of identity (Roth & Ivemark, 2018). However, the science doesn't quite match up with the advertising copy and our expectations (Walajahi et al., 2019). Knowing that you are Native American, for instance, requires much more than just a genetic test match; it requires understanding a shared history and relationships within a community (Carey, 2019). Black Americans looking to pinpoint their origins in Africa often find that there are not enough data to determine where exactly they are from (Lawton et al., 2018; Padawer, 2016). More than anything, ancestry testing reminds us that identity is not biology. Memories and relationships are what link people together, regardless of the genes within us.

APPLY IT! **3.1** Spencer and Alizah want baby Courage to inherit some of their traits, like Spencer's laugh and Alizah's flexibility. What would you tell them about the likelihood that these characteristics are passed on through their genome?

3.2 There is much diversity in our genome and many parts of our genetic expression can be altered by the context we grow up in. How do developmental scientists explain the benefits of a complex and flexible genome?

Prenatal Development

Learning Objectives

3.4 Describe the key stages of prenatal development.

3.5 Describe the principles of prenatal risk and resilience.

Before Courage was born, Alizah and Spencer couldn't see the developing fetus: They just viewed him on one fleeting ultrasound and felt his impressive kicks. In the space of 38 weeks, a bundle of cells smaller than this "o" transform into a squalling newborn. Scientists have a better view of what goes on inside the uterus: They use cameras and magnetic resonance imaging (MRI) to observe fetuses in the womb. They have found that learning and psychological development start before birth (Manczak & Gotlib, 2019).

Scientists divide prenatal development into three stages (see **Infographic 3.2**). During the **germinal stage**, the single-celled zygote divides and implants into the uterus. In the **embryonic stage**, in weeks 2 through 8, the embryo develops the major parts of its body—from legs to brain. In the **fetal stage**, the fetus finally looks like a baby and adds pounds and the organs and brain structures that will allow it to survive on its own.

Conception

Did you know that you actually started out inside your mother's mother? Each of us began as one of 6 million ova created inside our mother's body when she was still a fetus developing inside of her mother's uterus. Each ovum is 10 times the size of most other cells and almost big enough to see without a magnifying glass (Alberts et al., 2002). Each includes not only the genetic code necessary to grow a new being, but also enough energy to sustain the zygote in the first days after conception.

An ovum cannot make a baby on its own: It needs sperm. Starting at puberty, sperm are created every day. Sperm are not very big: It would take about 30 of them to be the size of one ovum. Sperm's claim to fame is their flexibility not their size. If they were human-size, they would be pulled toward the ovum nearly a hundred miles an hour. (See **Figure 3.5**.)

A pregnancy can only occur after a mature ovum has been released from one of the ovaries and vacuumed up by one of the fallopian tubes. The sperm meets the ovum after it has been ushered in through the vagina, cervix, uterus, and into the fallopian tube. After the sperm is drawn inside the ovum, *fertilization* happens, as the 23 chromosomes from the sperm and 23 chromosomes from the ovum fuse to form the full complement of 46 chromosomes necessary for life. Less than 24 hours after the sperm is absorbed into the egg, the two are now a zygote, a single cell that contains genetic information from both parents (Molè et al., 2020).

Diverse Beginnings In many families, as in Courage's family, parents' gender identities are male and female. However, there is much diversity in families and in how parents describe their gender (Carone et al., 2020). The language of pregnancy and childbirth often assumes a gender-binary other-sex married couple, which can alienate gender-diverse, LGBTQ+ families and unmarried and single parents. These families often struggle to find culturally competent care, feeling rejected by labels that refer to pregnant people as women and childbirth centers as "mothers' places" (Besse et al., 2020; Duckett & Ruud, 2019). For instance, transgender men who are pregnant may not always identify as women or as mothers (Besse et al., 2020). In our discussion of pregnancy and childbirth, we have tried to use inclusive terms to refer to people who are pregnant and experiencing childbirth: The goal is to help all people identify with the joys and challenges of parenting and pregnancy, regardless of their gender identity (Moseson et al., 2020).

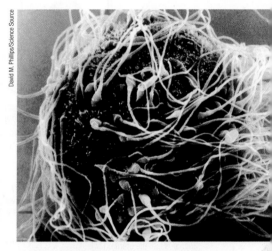

FIGURE 3.5 The Moment of Conception Hundreds of sperm have been pulled toward the ovum through the fallopian tubes and now surround the ovum, as shown in this photograph that has been colorized and magnified more than 1,000 times.

germinal stage The first stage of prenatal development, in which the single-celled zygote divides and implants into the uterus in the first week of development.

embryonic stage The second stage of prenatal development, in weeks 2 through 8, in which the embryo develops the major parts of its body—from legs to brain.

fetal stage The third stage of prenatal development, weeks 9 through birth, in which the fetus begins to look like a baby and adds pounds and the organs and brain structures that will allow it to survive on its own.

Whether you measure it in stages or trimesters, prenatal development is the fastest period of growth of the lifespan, as the zygote transforms into a fetus capable of living outside of the uterus.

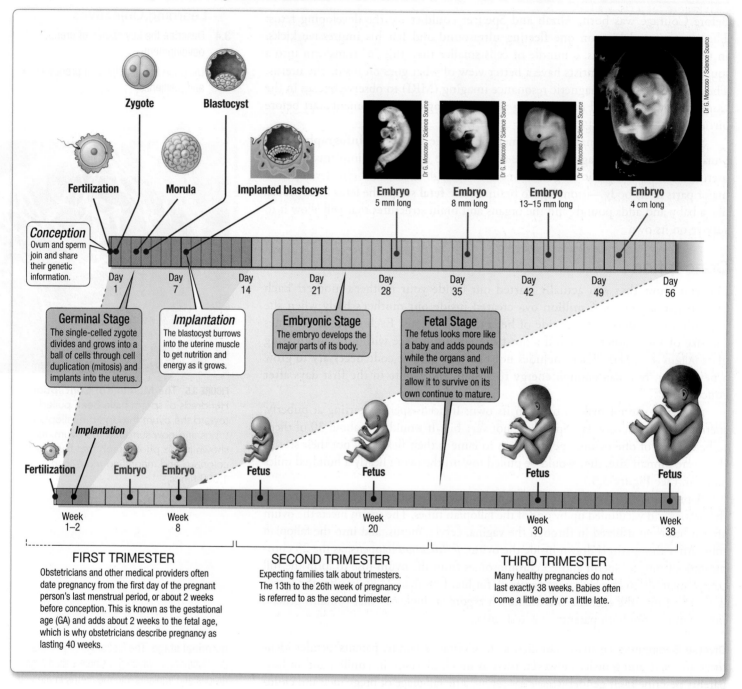

Zygote

Blastocyst

Fertilization

Morula

Implanted blastocyst

Embryo
5 mm long

Embryo
8 mm long

Embryo
13–15 mm long

Embryo
4 cm long

Dr. G. Moscoso / Science Source

Conception
Ovum and sperm join and share their genetic information.

Day 1 · Day 7 · Day 14 · Day 21 · Day 28 · Day 35 · Day 42 · Day 49 · Day 56

Germinal Stage
The single-celled zygote divides and grows into a ball of cells through cell duplication (mitosis) and implants into the uterus.

Implantation
The blastocyst burrows into the uterine muscle to get nutrition and energy as it grows.

Embryonic Stage
The embryo develops the major parts of its body.

Fetal Stage
The fetus looks more like a baby and adds pounds while the organs and brain structures that will allow it to survive on its own continue to mature.

Implantation

Fertilization

Embryo

Embryo

Fetus

Fetus

Fetus

Fetus

Week 1–2 · Week 8 · Week 20 · Week 30 · Week 38

FIRST TRIMESTER
Obstetricians and other medical providers often date pregnancy from the first day of the pregnant person's last menstrual period, or about 2 weeks before conception. This is known as the gestational age (GA) and adds about 2 weeks to the fetal age, which is why obstetricians describe pregnancy as lasting 40 weeks.

SECOND TRIMESTER
Expecting families talk about trimesters. The 13th to the 26th week of pregnancy is referred to as the second trimester.

THIRD TRIMESTER
Many healthy pregnancies do not last exactly 38 weeks. Babies often come a little early or a little late.

in vitro fertilization (IVF) A procedure in which doctors combine egg and sperm outside the body in a hospital laboratory and then place the resulting zygotes in the uterus, where they can implant and develop into a baby (or babies).

Millions of families around the world have been formed with the help of *assisted reproductive technology*, or *ART*. Modern medical techniques include *gestational surrogacy*, in which someone nurtures a fetus in their uterus for another family; *intrauterine insemination (IUI)*, in which a sperm is directly inserted into the uterus; and the use of donor eggs and sperm.

In the United States and around the world, many ART procedures include **in vitro fertilization**, or **IVF** (Sunderam, 2020). In IVF, doctors combine eggs and sperm outside the body in a laboratory. Physicians then place the resulting zygotes into the uterus, where they can implant and develop into a healthy baby (or babies). In some cases, if parents are carriers for a genetic disorder, gene technology can be used to test each zygote for a risky allele.

Among those who use IVF to conceive are same-sex couples, single parents, couples with a history of genetic diseases, and couples who have been diagnosed with *infertility*, meaning that they have been trying to get pregnant for at least 12 months without success. More than one in eight U.S. couples reports that they have trouble conceiving (Kelley et al., 2019). Rates of infertility are even higher elsewhere. In many low-income communities around the world where health care is hard to access, nearly 3 out of 10 people have difficulty getting pregnant or helping their partners get pregnant (Sun et al., 2019).

Fertility treatments can have risks. Primary among these is having more than one baby (Sunderam, 2020). Another is a slightly higher risk of having babies who are born small, too early, or with a disability (Luke et al., 2021). One of the biggest risks, however, is that the process will not work at all. More than one in three prospective parents who start fertility treatments are not able to have biological children (Troude et al., 2016). Many cannot afford to pursue treatment (Kelley et al., 2019). Some choose adoption in order to build a family.

CONNECTIONS

You will read more about the impact of infertility on adults in Chapter 14.

Gifts from Technology Four-month-old twins, Marina Belle and Jason, Jr., were conceived through IVF. Their father, Jason, was injured during his military service and needed IVF in order to have children. Jason and his wife, Rachel, helped advocate to make fertility and adoption services available to more veteran families like theirs.

The Germinal Stage

Whether a zygote originates in a laboratory and is transferred into the body or is fertilized inside the fallopian tube, it will rapidly begin to divide and then implant into the uterus. This first stage in prenatal development, from zygote to implantation, is known as the germinal stage.

Shortly after fertilization, the single-cell zygote begins to replicate. Just three days after fertilization, this single cell has turned into a tightly packed ball of 32 cells, now called a *morula*, and has made its way down the fallopian tubes toward the uterus, where it will implant (Moore et al., 2020). By the time it is five days old, the ball of cells has become much larger and has separated into an outer layer and an inner mass, and is more than 150 cells. It is now called a **blastocyst**. As you can tell by looking closely at **Figure 3.6**, it is no longer filled with identical cells.

In the first few days of development, the zygote contains cells that are exactly the same. But as early as two days after fertilization, genes activated in the nucleus of each cell began to direct them to specialize in a process known as *differentiation* (Straussman et al., 2009). By the fourth day after fertilization, the outer layer of cells in the blastocyst have separated from the inner mass, which will become the embryo. This outer layer will form the fetus's support system: the *placenta* and the *umbilical cord*, and the inner mass will develop into the embryo.

Differentiation helps the blastocyst through its first major transition: *implantation*. This turning point in the life of the blastocyst depends on perfect timing. There are only four days in every monthly cycle when the uterus is receptive to implantation. When a blastocyst arrives at the right time, about 10 days after fertilization, it burrows deep into the fleshy inside of the uterine muscle, looking for blood vessels that will bring it nutrition and energy as it grows (Ochoa-Bernal & Fazleabas, 2020).

The Embryonic Stage

After implantation, the blastocyst begins to transform. During the *embryonic stage*, which lasts from implantation until eight weeks, cell growth accelerates. Arms and legs will appear, and the embryo begins to move. The entire body is organized around the developing nervous system, which is the embryo's first distinguishing feature.

blastocyst The ball of cells during the germinal stage of prenatal development that becomes larger and then separates into an outer layer and an inner mass, replicating until it is more than 150 cells.

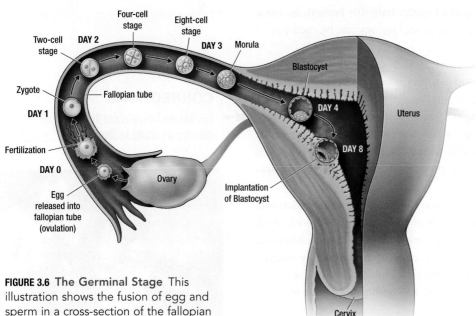

FIGURE 3.6 The Germinal Stage This illustration shows the fusion of egg and sperm in a cross-section of the fallopian tube and movement of the zygote down the fallopian tubes toward the uterus for implantation. Note that the zygotes and blastocysts are shown cut in half to show what they look like on the inside, since from the outside they look like a ball.

placenta An organ that allows energy and waste to be transferred between the parent's body and the developing embryo through the umbilical cord.

neurons Nerve cells.

Professional Fine Tuning Michael Zangari is a professional wheelchair technician who works to keep athletes' wheelchairs in their best condition. He also uses a wheelchair himself, because he was born with the neural tube defect *spina bifida*.

As the blastocyst settles into the uterus, its cells begin to differentiate further into cells that will become part of the skin, brain, intestines, or the muscles. The location of cells in the blastocyst—in the middle or on the outer edge—will determine whether they end up as hair cells, heart cells, or brain cells (Moore et al., 2020).

At two weeks after fertilization, the embryo now has a support team and these supportive structures are larger than the embryo itself. A tough, fluid-filled transparent membrane called the *amniotic sac* gives the embryo an extra layer of protection, like bubble wrap, as it bounces around inside the uterus. The **placenta** is an organ that allows energy and waste to be transferred between the parent's body and the developing embryo through the *umbilical cord*. The developing embryo cannot eat, breathe, or excrete while it is in the uterus, so the placenta takes care of these tasks. The health of the placenta plays a critical role in the healthy development of the embryo (Bové et al., 2019).

At three weeks after fertilization, the embryo is less than a quarter of an inch long (5 millimeters) and resembles a shrimp. The embryo now has so many cells that a heart is necessary to move oxygen and nutrition around the growing body, and a heartbeat is detectable. The most important system, however, is the growing brain.

Brain development begins in the third week after fertilization. Nerve cells, called **neurons**, begin to cluster into what looks like a flat plate. In the fourth week, this plate rolls up to become the *neural tube*, which will become the brain and the spinal cord.

Anomalies in the formation of the nervous system can cause physical differences called *neural tube defects*. Some embryos diagnosed with these differences can be operated on inside the uterus, before birth (Sacco et al., 2020). Where early medical care is not available, neural tube defects can lead to severe complications. Around the world, more than 300,000 children are born every year with neural tube defects, such as spina bifida, and almost one in three dies (Blencowe et al., 2018). People living with neural tube defects may have trouble moving independently but are often able to adapt to their challenges (Avagliano et al., 2019).

By the fourth week, the embryo's neural tube has turned into a factory for neurons. The pace at which neurons are produced during this period is breathtaking. More than 200,000 neurons are being created every minute!

As the embryo's brain is developing, so is the rest of its body. The embryo slowly transitions into looking like a little human. Arms appear in the third week, and fingers two weeks later. Legs begin to grow during the fourth week and toes two weeks later. By the end of week 8, the embryo is still just about one inch (27 mm) long, but can be seen moving on an ultrasound.

The Fetal Period

The fetal period begins around week 9 and lasts until birth. During the next 29 weeks, the fetus will grow at an incredible rate—growing about 19 inches and putting on more than 7 pounds. The fetus will develop the ability to survive on its own. This requires maturation not only in the fetus's body—but also in its brain.

From week 9 until week 17, the fetus's organ systems are maturing rapidly. The intestines mature, although until birth, the fetus will continue to send fecal waste back into the mother's bloodstream through the umbilical cord. By 12 weeks, the kidneys have begun to work, excreting urine into the amniotic cavity. By 17 weeks, the pace of growth begins to slow as the fetus builds the fat and muscle it will need to support itself outside the uterus. However, major organ systems are not finished developing. One of the last organ systems to mature is the lungs, which are not ready to breathe air until about 26 weeks. This is one of the challenges for babies who are born early.

The reproductive organs are another slow-growing system. Male and female organs are very similar early in development: Not until around 9 to 12 weeks can a fetus's genitals be seen on an ultrasound. Fetal testes and ovaries release hormones that cause the genital and reproductive organs to mature. By around 16 weeks, the ovaries begin to fill with immature ova. It will take until 30 weeks (and sometimes later) before the testes mature enough to leave the pelvic cavity, and it will be many years before they produce sperm.

If you have ever looked at an ultrasound image of a fetus, you probably noticed that its head was overly large, almost the same size as the rest of its body. Inside, millions of neurons are being created and rapidly building the brain. Many will form the *cortex*, or the outer layer of the brain, which is activated when thinking, language, and learning take place. As neurons multiply, the cortex gets bigger and more wrinkled (see **Infographic 3.3**). The *subcortical structures* under the cortex are also maturing. These areas are involved in memory and emotion but are also critical for the control of life-sustaining behaviors, like breathing, that will allow the fetus to survive outside the uterus. At the same time, pathways built of fast neural connections, called *white matter*, begin to speed communication across the brain, enabling some babies who are born early to survive (Edde et al., 2021).

The older and larger fetuses are, the more likely they are to survive premature birth. For instance, even with the best medical care, it is very unusual, although not impossible, for newborns to survive if they are born at less than a pound (400 g) or younger than 22 weeks (Brumbaugh et al., 2019). For babies who are born at 22 weeks, their chance of survival depends greatly on what kind of medical treatment they receive (Mercurio & Carter, 2020). With the most advanced treatment, about half will live and many will grow up without major impairment (Söderström et al., 2021).

In the United States, babies born between 20 and 25 weeks are known as *periviable infants*, and how much medical treatment they receive depends not just on how old they are but also on how big and mature they are and the wishes of their families (Rysavy et al., 2020). However, any baby born after 23 weeks in the United States is generally given medical treatment. This date is known as the *age of viability*, because it refers to the age at which most newborn might have a reasonable chance to survive (Stefano et al., 2020).

What Can a Fetus Do?

From the outside, it is difficult to know exactly what a fetus is doing. Alizah felt Courage moving when she was about four months along. A few months later, his poking elbows

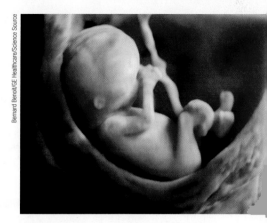

Curled Up to Grow This fetus was photographed with a 3D ultrasound at about 10 weeks after fertilization. Some of the support structures that help it to grow are visible, including the umbilical cord that attaches it to its parent and the amniotic sac that cushions it inside the body. But the largest structure is the fetus's head.

What Does a 24-Week-Old Fetus Look Like? A lot like this little baby. This child's skin looks red because it is so thin that veins are visible. The newborn has fingernails, but lung development is still not complete.

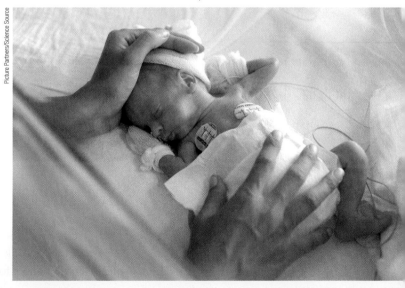

During the prenatal period, the structures of the brain form, and communication across brain structures and between the brain and body begins.

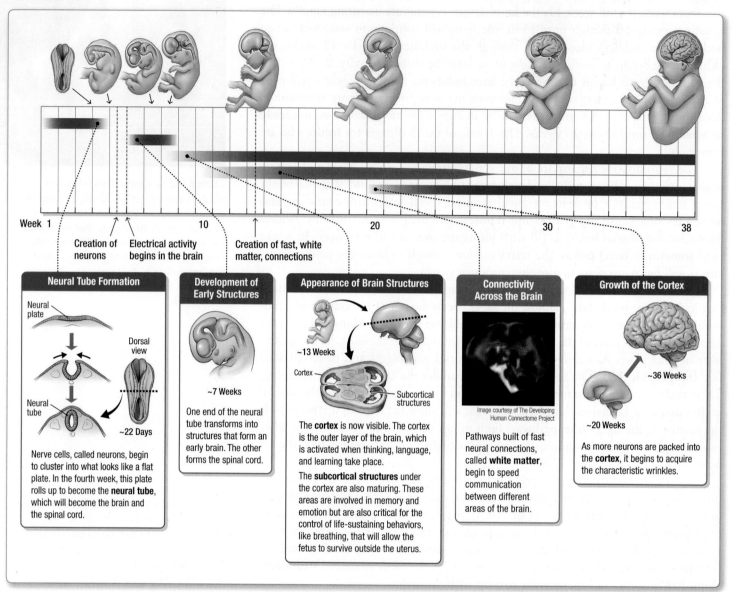

Neural Tube Formation

Neural plate

Dorsal view

Neural tube

~22 Days

Nerve cells, called neurons, begin to cluster into what looks like a flat plate. In the fourth week, this plate rolls up to become the **neural tube**, which will become the brain and the spinal cord.

Development of Early Structures

~7 Weeks

One end of the neural tube transforms into structures that form an early brain. The other forms the spinal cord.

Appearance of Brain Structures

~13 Weeks

Cortex

Subcortical structures

The **cortex** is now visible. The cortex is the outer layer of the brain, which is activated when thinking, language, and learning take place.

The **subcortical structures** under the cortex are also maturing. These areas are involved in memory and emotion but are also critical for the control of life-sustaining behaviors, like breathing, that will allow the fetus to survive outside the uterus.

Connectivity Across the Brain

Image courtesy of The Developing Human Connectome Project

Pathways built of fast neural connections, called **white matter**, begin to speed communication between different areas of the brain.

Growth of the Cortex

~36 Weeks

~20 Weeks

As more neurons are packed into the **cortex**, it begins to acquire the characteristic wrinkles.

Week 1   10   20   30   38

Creation of neurons

Electrical activity begins in the brain

Creation of fast, white matter, connections

and knees often protruded far enough to be visible, and for Spencer to be impressed with his high karate kicks. Scientists have used technology such as MRI scanners, ultrasound wands, and even microphones to look inside the abdomens of pregnant people to see what fetuses are capable of (Dunn & Reid, 2020).

In the uterus, fetuses practice skills that will allow them to thrive after they are born. The prenatal environment influences everything, from the languages babies are ready to learn to the foods they will recognize after they are born (Hepper, 2015).

Moving Movement typically begins just as soon as the developing embryo has a body to wiggle. Embryos begin to bend at 5 weeks (Hadders-Algra, 2018). At 16 weeks, fetuses can be observed with ultrasound or MRI sucking their fingers and even making faces (Reissland et al., 2016). Fetal movements peak at around 30 weeks and become harder for a parent to feel as the growing fetus becomes increasingly

TABLE 3.1 Prenatal Development of the Senses

Vision	It is dark inside the uterus, but starting at about 24 weeks, a fetus will move more quickly if a bright light is shone outside the abdomen. What fetuses see is very dim, lacking color and detail, but this light exposure helps set sleep schedules.
Touch and Pain	The sense of touch develops early in the embryonic period. From about 20 weeks on, fetuses move when the outside of their pregnant parent's abdomen is touched. Although researchers believe that fetuses can feel pain, many suggest that they process pain differently from full-term babies because of immature brain connectivity.
Hearing	The noise of a pregnant parent's stomach and heartbeat means that the sound level in the uterus is about 90 decibels, similar to a school cafeteria or a subway train. Nevertheless, beginning at about 25 weeks, fetuses react to loud sounds with activation in their brain stem. A few weeks later, fetuses recognize sounds they hear frequently, like their parents' voices.
Smell and Taste	By 26 weeks, a fetus can smell and taste, including their parent's breakfast! The taste and the smell of what their parent eats enters amniotic fluid, allowing the growing fetus to taste and smell a bit of that morning bagel.

Information from Clark-Gambelunghe & Clark, 2015; Derbyshire & Bockmann, 2020; Draganova et al., 2018; Hepper, 2015; Lee & Kisilevsky, 2014; Logan & McClung, 2019; Marx & Nagy, 2017.

cramped (Verbruggen et al., 2018). Early activity helps muscles and bones mature and develop the connections in the brain that will allow newborns to control their bodies (Borsani et al., 2019).

Responding to Stress Fetuses are also learning how to respond emotionally to the world and how to regulate their physical reactions. For instance, a fetus's heart rate is in sync with their parent's (DiPietro et al., 2015). As a result, pregnant parents whose heart rates mirror disorders like anxiety or depression are more likely to have babies who share their stress response patterns (O'Sullivan & Monk, 2020). Fetuses and newborns differ in how intensely they respond to stressful situations and how quickly they recover from a scare, upset, or disappointment. These differences, established prenatally, can be one of the factors that lead a child to be fussy or easy to soothe (Manczak & Gotlib, 2019).

Sensing Although you may think of fetuses as isolated from the outside world, they experience sounds, light, smells, and even tastes (see **Table 3.1**). This early experience stimulates fetuses to develop the senses they will need after birth.

 CAN YOU BELIEVE IT?
Does Learning Happen Before Birth?

Some families-to-be recite books and sing songs to their fetuses long before birth, hoping to make their babies more capable. Is there any evidence that this helps? While there isn't any evidence that families *should* be educating their fetuses before birth, there is ample evidence that even without special efforts, fetuses are developing their cognitive skills long before birth.

Scientists have been testing learning in fetuses for more than 100 years. In the past, researchers observed that fetuses jerked after someone blew a car horn near the pregnant parent's abdomen (Dirix et al., 2009). But after the scientists blew the horn a few times, the fetuses stopped responding. Researchers observed that

Scientific American Profile

Preparing for Baby

fetuses had become *habituated*, or used to, the sound, and as a result, they didn't startle when they heard it again. Today, researchers test what fetuses remember and what they learn by examining their heart rate, brain activity, and movement (Reid & Dunn, 2021).

Scientists also assess prenatal learning by testing newborns to see if they remembered what they were exposed to before they were born (DeCasper & Fifer, 1980; Reissland & Kisilevsky, 2016). Researchers exposed fetuses to various sounds and noises, from nursery rhymes to jazz standards, and found that newborns reacted differently to sounds they heard in the uterus than to new sounds. Newborns appear to have habituated to the sounds they heard before, reacting more powerfully to the new sounds (Partanen & Virtala, 2017).

Using these techniques, scientists discovered, for instance, that one area of the fetus's brain is activated when a fetus hears their parents' voice, but that another is activated when they hear an unfamiliar voice (Carvalho et al., 2019). Fetuses can distinguish the tones of different languages, and the language they hear before birth even affects the way newborns cry when they are born (Manfredi et al., 2019). Researchers shining lights at a fetus have even shown that fetuses can recognize patterns before they are born, and even seem to prefer face shapes (Donovan et al., 2020; Reid et al., 2017).

Does this research mean that families need to stimulate their fetuses' brains before birth? No. However, an understanding of what fetuses learn before birth has had enormous benefits for babies born prematurely. For instance, interventions that provide new babies with extra exposure to the sounds of their parents' voices can help them learn and soothe their pain (Filippa et al., 2020). 👶

Protective and Risky Factors During Prenatal Development

Although scientists do not think that fetuses need to be read to in order to develop well, contemporary research has found that stress, disease, and environmental hazards faced by families *do* have an impact on the health of a fetus and the person it will become (Camerota & Willoughby, 2021). Research based on the theory of *fetal programming* investigates the impact of prenatal experience on lifelong health (Barker, 1995). For instance, scientists have observed that fetal malnutrition can lead to greater risk for high blood pressure and heart disease in adulthood (Crump & Howell, 2020). Parents who experience severe trauma during pregnancy may transmit risk to their children through changes in their brain development, hormones, and epigenetic marks (Carroll et al., 2020). However, most researchers agree that although prenatal experiences may increase risks, there are ample opportunities after birth for change (Camerota & Willoughby, 2021). Pregnancy offers opportunities to build resilience and good health (Davis & Narayan, 2020).

Prenatal Care For many families, pregnancy motivates them to get healthy. Alizah says she's never eaten so many greens. She and Spencer experienced some unexpected stresses during the pregnancy, like the global pandemic, but they also enjoyed some of the key ingredients for good health during pregnancy: early prenatal care and supportive family relationships.

Around the world, medical providers are the first line of intervention for expectant parents and their fetuses. Medical care is critical. For instance, prenatal care around the world was disrupted by the COVID-19 pandemic, leading, experts suggest, to a near 50 percent jump in *stillbirths*, or newborns who die during delivery or after the 20th week of pregnancy (Chmielewska et al., 2021; Watson, 2020).

In the United States, *traditional prenatal care* involves regular one-on-one checkups with a medical doctor or midwife (Peahl & Howell, 2021). Around the globe, most expectant parents receive some prenatal care, but only three in five receive the minimum of four visits, which makes childbirth more dangerous for infants and expectant parents around the world (UNICEF, 2021). No matter where they live, younger, less affluent parents and those from groups that face discrimination are particularly at risk for inadequate prenatal care (Barfield, 2021; Slaughter-Acey et al., 2019).

Innovative methods of prenatal care encourages expectant families to create supportive relationships both in person and through virtual visits. In *group prenatal care* such as the Centering Pregnancy program, pregnant families provide support to each other while also receiving their regular health assessments. Group care has been found to be more effective than traditional one-on-one prenatal care, leading to fewer preterm births and more satisfied parents, particularly for those at risk of premature delivery or delivering babies with low birthweight (Buultjens et al., 2020; Mazzoni & Carter, 2017).

Other alternatives to traditional prenatal care include *home visiting*, where nurses check in on pregnant parents at home. In successful programs such as the Nurse–Family Partnership, nurses visit expectant families and build long-term relationships. Visiting nurses educate new families about healthy lifestyle choices and supportive parenting and give practical advice about education and career development. Home visiting, which you will read more about in Chapter 4, has also had success in preventing premature birth in at-risk families (Anthony et al., 2021).

Social and Family Support Whether they pester you to exercise, hold your hand during an early ultrasound, or pick up groceries after work, other people are a critical source of support during pregnancy.

The vast majority of pregnant people, like Alizah, are in a romantic relationship when they get pregnant, and more than 90 percent will have a partner when they give birth (CPS, 2021). In general, people who are in supportive relationships tend to experience less anxiety and stress during pregnancy and have lower rates of premature birth and babies with low birthweight (Shapiro et al., 2018).

Emotional support doesn't have to come from a partner: It can also come from extended social networks such as parents, siblings, coworkers, or community groups. Pregnant people who feel connected to others and have someone to rely on have lower levels of stress hormones (Cheadle et al., 2020). Pregnant parents who lack close personal connections or who can't access community resources are particularly at risk for complications during pregnancy.

Risks During Prenatal Development Despite the hope and excitement of bringing a new life into the world, not all babies are born healthy, and, around the world, pregnancy and childbirth are a leading cause of death in young parents and newborns (Ahn et al., 2020; Douthard et al., 2021). Some of the difficulties infants might face will be obvious on the day that they are born. Others may not appear for years, as with learning disabilities caused by prenatal alcohol exposure.

Almost 6 out of every 100 babies born around the world arrive with a major abnormality in their body or brain. These abnormalities are often called **birth defects** (WHO, 2019). While this is the term used by the medical and public health communities, it is considered demeaning by many families and adults with disabilities because it focuses on limitations (Elliott & Evans, 2015; NCDJ, n.d.). Advocates encourage the use of terminology such as *differences,* or simply naming the specific condition.

Despite advances in fetal medicine and developmental science, doctors can only find a cause for a few major prenatal abnormalities. Some are genetic, such as sickle-cell disease (Hassan Toufaily et al., 2018). Others, are caused by **teratogens**, or factors in a parent's body or the environment that damage the fetus (Hales et al., 2018). Teratogens can include diseases like the coronavirus (COVID-19) and substances in

Still Friends Centering Pregnancy is a group-based program of prenatal care. It gives expectant parents a chance to build social relationships with other expectant families, establishing friendships and support that help make pregnancy easier. These families in New York liked the experience so much they came back for a reunion after their babies were born.

birth defects Major abnormalities in the body or brain functioning present at birth.

teratogens Factors in a parent's body or the environment that damage the fetus.

Learn It Together

Assess the Risks of Teratogens

Alma is pregnant and planning to attend her best friend's wedding. She wonders if it is safe to have a glass of wine at the reception. Using the concepts of timing and dosage, what advice would you give her?

Plan Review the concepts of teratogens, including the importance of timing and dosage, and the timeline of prenatal development.

Engage In a small group of classmates, imagine Alma's scenario above and add some important details: Determine how far along she is in her pregnancy and how much she might drink at the wedding. How do the timing and dosage (amount of alcohol) affect your advice to her?

Reflect What was it like trying to think about applying scientific knowledge to a real-life scenario? What factors might complicate a person's decision to follow scientific advice?

the environment, such as lead paint or car exhaust (Taruscio et al., 2017; Woodworth et al., 2020). They also include medications or prescriptions, whether over-the-counter or prescribed, legal or illegal. Even factors like a parent's age, level of stress, depression, or anxiety can be classified as teratogens.

Scientists have discovered several underlying principles about prenatal risk:

1. *Timing is important.* If an embryo is exposed to a teratogen in the first eight weeks of pregnancy, the embryo may be so compromised that pregnancy loss, sometimes referred to as *spontaneous abortion* or *miscarriage*, may occur. Some weeks or even days are *critical periods* for the development of specific organ systems. For instance, a toxin might damage an embryo's arms if exposure occurs in the third week of development, or its legs if exposure is in the fourth week (see **Figure 3.7**) (Hales et al., 2018). Other organ systems, like the brain, have longer critical periods, called *sensitive periods*. The brain can be damaged at any time during development.

2. *Dosage matters.* Exposure to a large amount of a teratogen can have more of an effect than exposure to a small amount. For instance, if a fetus is malnourished for a few days while its parent suffers from a terrible bout of morning sickness, the outcome is much less severe than if its parent suffers from significant malnutrition throughout the pregnancy (Inselman & Slikker, 2018).

3. *Individual variations make predictions difficult.* Sometimes fetuses or parents have genetic differences that may alter the power of a teratogen (Cardenas et al., 2017). For instance, some fetuses may be more sensitive to alcohol exposure than others. Dizygotic twins (who share only about half of their genes), exposed to the same environment in the parent's uterus, do not always develop the same developmental and neurological problems because of their parent's alcohol use (Lambert, 2016).

4. *Both parents' health matters.* While the pregnant parent's health is particularly critical during the prenatal period, the biological father's health, substance use, or exposure to environmental toxins can damage sperm in ways that can be passed on to children. The psychological health of the partner is a crucial part of the pregnant parent's emotional support system (Day et al., 2016; Daniele et al., 2021).

5. *Teratogens interact in unexpected ways.* Many fetuses are exposed to multiple teratogens, which may multiply risks. For instance, a recent study of the effects of air pollution on fetal development showed that the danger caused by a pregnant parent's exposure was magnified if they had other stressors, such as living far away from social support (Liu et al., 2018).

Sources of Danger Around the world, some of the most common dangers for fetuses and pregnant parents come from diseases and environmental pollutants. Infectious diseases like malaria and HIV are a major cause of early birth and low birthweight around the world, with malaria the biggest cause of newborn mortality (Romero et al., 2014). Immune system changes during pregnancy make pregnant people particularly susceptible to diseases, like the coronavirus, that can then be passed on to their fetuses (Rasmussen & Jamieson, 2021).

Environmental toxins in food, air, and water can harm the developing fetus and lead to miscarriage, developmental delays, or diseases. Contaminated drinking water everywhere, from Bangladesh to Appalachia, and toxic fertilizers in Florida and Ecuador, invisibly poison developing embryos (Gómez-Roig et al., 2021).

Chronic and often unavoidable health conditions also may harm the health of a fetus and their parent. In many wealthy countries, researchers believe that unhealthy weight is a leading contributor to preterm birth and prenatal difficulties (Marchi et al., 2015). Scientists believe that too much weight can trigger inflammation and

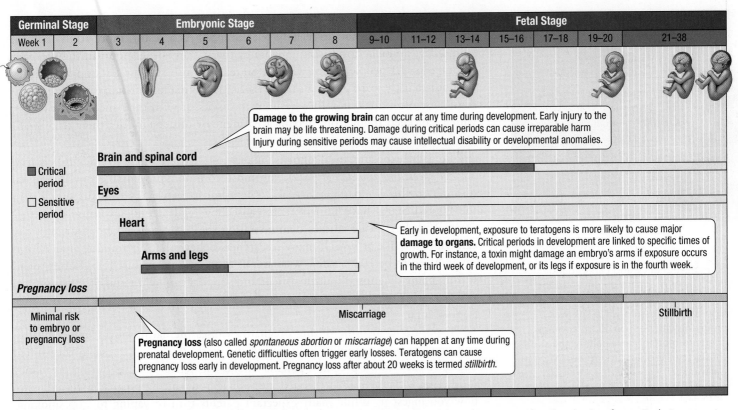

Germinal Stage	Embryonic Stage						Fetal Stage						
Week 1	2	3	4	5	6	7	8	9–10	11–12	13–14	15–16	17–18	19–20	21–38

Damage to the growing brain can occur at any time during development. Early injury to the brain may be life threatening. Damage during critical periods can cause irreparable harm Injury during sensitive periods may cause intellectual disability or developmental anomalies.

Brain and spinal cord

■ Critical period

□ Sensitive period

Eyes

Heart

Arms and legs

Early in development, exposure to teratogens is more likely to cause major **damage to organs**. Critical periods in development are linked to specific times of growth. For instance, a toxin might damage an embryo's arms if exposure occurs in the third week of development, or its legs if exposure is in the fourth week.

Pregnancy loss

Minimal risk to embryo or pregnancy loss

Miscarriage

Stillbirth

Pregnancy loss (also called *spontaneous abortion* or *miscarriage*) can happen at any time during prenatal development. Genetic difficulties often trigger early losses. Teratogens can cause pregnancy loss early in development. Pregnancy loss after about 20 weeks is termed *stillbirth*.

FIGURE 3.7 Timing Matters. Risks in early development can lead to pregnancy loss or to damage to the developing fetus. Early in development, critical periods are times when damage may not be reversible. Sensitive periods are times when development is particularly affected by the environment.

difficulties with processing sugar, which prevent the placenta from functioning as well as it should. In the end, this can lead to a higher risk for early birth and health problems later in life for the fetus. Weight is also linked to increased risk for the pregnant parent's own health, potentially doubling the risk of death during pregnancy (Catalano & Shankar, 2017; Simon et al., 2020; Saucedo et al., 2021). Other health concerns, such as high blood pressure and diabetes, are also linked to health complications for the pregnant parent and increase risk of developmental disabilities, prematurity, and high birthweight in the newborn (Sanchez et al., 2018).

Unhealthy weight is stigmatized, particularly during pregnancy (Hill & Rodriguez, 2020). As a result, conversations about weight can be awkward, even shaming and hurtful (Nikolopoulos et al., 2017; Christenson et al., 2019). Conversations about pregnancy risk often devolve into "blaming" parents, when many of these problems are linked to systemic issues like discrimination, unequal access to resources, and social status, rather than individual choices (Richardson et al., 2014; Scott et al., 2019). In addition, healthy weight is difficult to measure during pregnancy: Scientists are developing interventions to address the risks caused by discrimination related to weight to help pregnant people protect their health, and help health care providers treat some of the risky conditions associated with weight (Incollingo Rodriguez et al., 2019; Hill, 2021; Saucedo et al., 2020).

Alcohol and Substances Developmental scientists have known for generations that many medications and substances, including alcohol, marijuana, nicotine, and other psychoactive drugs, can be dangerous for fetal development. Pregnant parents are advised to consult with their health care providers about any

Share It!

Talk about risks during pregnancy without blaming parents. Expectant parents often explain that they want to hear the science, but providers need to be careful to provide humility, empathy, and respect.

(Christenson et al., 2019)

Scientific American: Lifespan Development

Thriving After Pregnancy High blood pressure is a common complication during pregnancy and can endanger the lives of pregnant parents and their fetuses. Lara developed dangerously high blood pressure while she was pregnant with her son, Zion, and now needs to monitor her health while she's chasing her toddler around her home in California.

prescription and over-the-counter medication they consume, and to stop using any recreational substances (Pinheiro & Stika, 2020). As a result, more adults abstain from drugs and alcohol during pregnancy than at any other point in the lifespan. About 8 in 10 people in the United States who use substances stop when they find out that they are pregnant (Kar et al., 2021). Stigma and criminalization of substance use often make families hesitant to discuss it with their medical providers, which can keep them from getting treatment or understanding their risks (Frazer et al., 2019).

Prenatal exposure to alcohol is linked to a cluster of disabilities called *fetal alcohol spectrum disorder (FASD)*, the most common preventable developmental disorder in the world (McQuire et al., 2020). Almost 5 in every 100 first-graders in the United States have impairments caused by fetal alcohol exposure (May et al., 2018). With large-scale studies demonstrating that even one alcoholic drink a day can triple the risk of FASD, many researchers believe that no amount of alcohol is "guaranteed to be 100% safe" (Williams et al., 2015). Stigma against FASD often keeps it from being diagnosed, but treatment and support can help reduce the symptoms, which can include learning difficulties, speech delays, and impulsive behavior (Popova et al., 2017).

Exposure to nicotine during pregnancy causes premature births, infant deaths, and prenatal birth complications around the world (Lange et al., 2018). In the United States, about 1 in 14 pregnant parents smokes cigarettes or vapes during pregnancy (Azagba et al., 2020; Liu et al., 2021). Nicotine is dangerous during pregnancy regardless of how you ingest it. While many expectant parents turn to vaping to stop smoking, vape pens can be nearly as dangerous to a developing fetus as a pack of cigarettes (Taylor et al., 2021).

About 1 in 20 parents use recreational drugs while pregnant. Like many prescription medications, recreational drugs are not safe during pregnancy, and they can cause complications in pregnancy and long-term challenges in newborns. Even if babies exposed to substances prenatally look healthy at birth, they are more likely to develop psychological or learning disorders later in life (Corsi et al., 2020). About 5 percent of parents in the United States report that they have used marijuana during their pregnancy to soothe anxiety or to manage morning sickness (Ko et al., 2020). Researchers have connected the use of marijuana to stillbirth, preterm birth, and long-term neurological and emotional problems, including difficulties with learning and attention (Kharbanda et al., 2020; Paul et al., 2021).

Sadness and Worry Most families seem to manage the daily hassles and report that they are happy during their pregnancies (DiPietro et al., 2015). But, about one in four pregnant people reports feeling depressed, anxious, or overwhelmed by stress (van den Bergh et al., 2018). Expectant parents who are depressed or anxious may not be taking care of themselves, adding emotional difficulties to poor nutrition, lack of physical activity, and limited social support. As a result, researchers have found that depression or anxiety can increase the likelihood of having a baby who is low birthweight, is born prematurely, or has a higher risk of emotional problems in childhood (Borchers et al., 2021; Ghimire et al., 2021).

Love Helps. Getting help for substance abuse can be difficult during pregnancy. With support from her family, Jennifer was able to find treatment in St. Louis, Missouri, that helped her deliver a healthy baby girl, Rikki Lynn, and continue her recovery.

Partners also experience mental health problems that can impact their ability to provide emotional support and adjust to parenting. As many as one in four partners is also anxious or depressed during their partner's pregnancy (Darwin et al., 2021). If one partner has depression or anxiety, it makes it hard to support their pregnant partner, making the transition to parenthood more difficult (Pinto et al., 2020). Nevertheless, partners are often left out of the screening and intervention processes (Mayers et al., 2020).

Most studies of the mental health of families during pregnancy have focused on expectant women and their male partners rather than on same-sex, gender-diverse, or transgender couples, but the studies that have investigated same-sex couples during pregnancy have found that, like other couples, they sometimes have emotional problems. However, on top of the typical pregnancy-related stresses, gender-diverse and other-sex couples must also manage additional stigma and discrimination because of their gender identity (Pollitt et al., 2020).

Stress is the feeling of being overwhelmed and comes in two forms. *Chronic stress* is nonstop and occurs over a long time, such as the worry about not having enough money to pay the bills. *Episodic stress* is typically caused by a single event, as in the trauma of a death, natural disaster, or an act of violence. Like many expecting parents, Alizah and Spencer juggled multiple sources of stress during pregnancy, from worries about the pandemic to hassles with work. They even stressed about the effects of stress on the developing fetus.

Pregnant people tend to be more stressed during pregnancy because of the social and emotional changes that come with a new role, and because their bodies are particularly sensitive to stress hormones while they are carrying a fetus. The placenta creates extra stress hormones that enter the parent's body and may increase feelings of being overwhelmed (Cheadle et al., 2020).

A fetus exposed to *too much* stress in the uterus has a higher risk for developing problems with attention and impulsivity (Entringer, 2020; Van den Bergh et al., 2018). On the other hand, researchers believe that *moderate* amounts of stress may actually be good for the developing brain. Moderate stress is part of a healthy, active lifestyle and will help the fetus develop a mature stress-response system to adjust to a world with everyday annoyances (DiPietro, 2015). No one can tell for sure what impact Alizah's long days teaching on Zoom had on her pregnancy: For her baby's sake, she hopes that they were manageable enough.

Chronic stressors like financial insecurity, family conflict, and racism take a much greater toll on pregnant people. Researchers link them to higher rates of preterm birth and lower birthweight (Davis, 2019). Scientists speculate that the long-term effects of racial discrimination may be a significant factor in why people who suffer discrimination, like Black American women, have a 50 percent higher rate of premature birth than White women (Jackson et al., 2020). As you'll read, this is one reason for significant income and ethnic disparities in the numbers of newborns who are born prematurely or die after birth in the United States.

A Shared Stress Millions of families experienced the uncertainty and stress of pregnancy during a global pandemic, including this woman in Hong Kong. While exposure to viruses, including COVID-19, can be dangerous to pregnant people and their fetuses, social support can help build resilience.

Support Works. One way of helping families cope with pregnancy and childbirth is to provide them with extra support. Claire Littleton (*center*) benefited from the presence and expertise of her doula, Clara Sharpe (*left*), as she prepared for the birth of her baby.

 MAKING A DIFFERENCE
Protecting Pregnant Parents from Prejudice

Kim didn't think she had any risk factors for premature birth or birth complications when she was pregnant. She had taken care of herself during her pregnancy. She was a successful lawyer working on a case she wanted to wrap up before going on leave. But her daughter had other plans: Kim went into labor unexpectedly three months before her due date. Danielle arrived weighing just two pounds (Adelman, 2008).

stress The feeling of being overwhelmed.

Missing a Brother Chrissy and her husband were expecting twins, but one of them was stillborn at just 25 weeks. Their surviving son, Cassius, was born prematurely but is now thriving. Chrissy and her husband worry that racism played a part in her health care, preventing her from getting the attention she needed to save the son he lost, whom she named Apollo. Black infants face a higher likelihood of being stillborn or arriving prematurely: Black mothers also are more likely to lose their lives during pregnancy.

Kim had only one risk factor for pregnancy complications, but it was an important one: racism. Scientists have found that the ongoing stress of discrimination experienced by pregnant Black parents like Kim increases their risk for complications and premature birth, regardless of their education or income (Johnson et al., 2020; Slaughter-Acey et al., 2019). There are similarly high risks for other groups, including Native Americans, who experience prejudice (Janevic et al., 2017).

As Samantha, a Black mother who lost two children to premature birth, explained: "Stress leads to labor. And African-American women lead a more stressful life, and so we hit preterm birth at an alarming rate" (Chatterjee & Davis, 2017). Researchers are trying to better understand how to prevent preterm births in Black parents and other at-risk groups. Currently, experts recommend that parents at risk get appropriate prenatal medical care and lots of social support, such as that provided by prenatal groups or culturally appropriate doula care (Byerley & Haas, 2017; Kozhimannil et al., 2016; Mazzoni & Carter, 2017). Advocates and health care providers are working to reduce systemic racism and inequity in the medical system to ensure that all parents receive the best medical care they can (Scott et al., 2019). Kim hopes that her own daughter, who attended medical school, will have a chance to experience birth without the risks she endured (California Newsreel, 2008). 🌐

APPLY IT! **3.3** Alizah and Spencer, like many expecting parents, were emotionally attached to their fetus even before birth. They gave it a pet name, and Spencer sang to it. How does prenatal experience help fetuses prepare for life after birth?

3.4 Alizah learned that she was pregnant about four weeks after conception. What can you tell Spencer and Alizah about how large the embryo was?

3.5 Alizah and Spencer worry that talking about all the things that could go wrong during a pregnancy leads parents to blame themselves and feel guilty before their baby is even born. This is a common concern. What could you tell expectant parents about the protective factors that can help make fetuses more resilient?

Birth and the Newborn

Learning Objectives

3.6 Explain the process of vaginal childbirth and its common risks and protective factors.

3.7 Explain how newborns' senses and capabilities help them thrive.

Birth is a major social and biological transition for fetuses and their families. For Alizah and Spencer, childbirth started with a remarkable sunset, a check-in with the midwife and the obstetrician and a night of contractions and pushing. Whether it happens vaginally or surgically, delivering a baby is called *labor*, in recognition of the hard, physical work that must happen before the baby is born.

The Stages of Vaginal Childbirth

Vaginal childbirth starts when a chemical signal released by the mature fetus's lungs signals the body to begin contractions (Menon, 2019). Labor is not over when the baby is delivered. The final stage occurs *after* birth, with the delivery of the placenta that has been helping to support the fetus. How long does labor take? After reviewing the normal progress of labor in thousands of women from Japan, China, Nigeria, Uganda, and the United States, researchers found that a healthy labor may progress very slowly—as long as 20 or even 30 hours (Oladapo et al., 2018).

Contractions are painful for the pregnant parent, but the fetus's journey is also dramatic. As you can see in the MRI images, fetuses' brains are compressed during a vaginal delivery as they squeeze through the cervix (Ami et al., 2019). Fetuses are shocked by a rush of hormones that mature their lungs and immune system to prepare the baby to breathe independently (Morton & Brodsky, 2016).

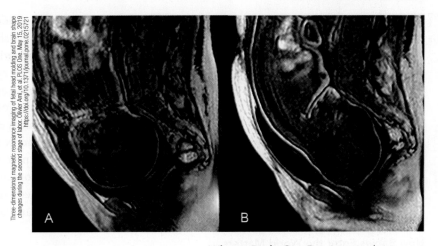

Three-dimensional magnetic resonance imaging of fetal head molding and brain shape changes during the second stage of labor. Olivier Ami, et al. PLOS One. May 15, 2019 https://doi.org/10.1371/journal.pone.0215721

Cultural and Social Support During Childbirth

Childbirth is an important social and cultural event. For first-time parents, it marks the beginning of parenthood. For the baby, it marks the beginning of relationships with family and community. Many cultures designate childbirth as a special, even spiritual event. In the past, when babies weren't delivered in medical facilities, some communities created a secluded, private place for childbirth. Whether a room or a hut, separate spaces gave laboring families a break from normal activities and a chance to focus on birth and recovery without the distractions of other responsibilities (DiTomasso, 2019; Sharma et al., 2016).

Around the world, as childbirth has become safer, it has become more medicalized. But cultural beliefs about what is appropriate during childbirth remain powerful. Families often want to bring their children into the world in a way that respects their traditions (Benza & Liamoputtong, 2014). Within the United States, there are many cultural variations in what families expect, how they understand labor pain, and what kind of pain relief they receive (Kozhimanil et al., 2013; Lange et al., 2017; Scrimshaw et al., 2020).

One critical part of supporting and respecting parents during labor is allowing them to have someone with them as they labor. *Continuous support* may be provided by a partner, a family member, or a paid *doula*, or birthing assistant, all of whom provide comfort and encouragement. This leads to improved health outcomes, including shortened delivery times, improvements to the newborn's health, and reduced rates of cesarean sections by as much as 20 percent (Bohren et al., 2015; WHO, 2020). Among the challenges of the COVID-19 pandemic were limitations on partners and family members accompanying laboring people in the hospital, which made labor and delivery more stressful for many families (Davis-Floyd et al., 2020).

What a Body Can Do Amazingly, a pregnant French woman agreed to give birth in an MRI scanner. This allowed researchers to observe the transition of childbirth, including the impressive, and temporary, way the skull and brain is distorted during the final stages of childbirth.

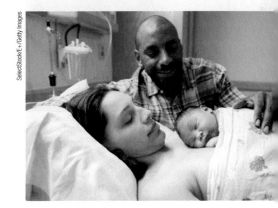

SelectStock/E+/Getty Images

Well-Earned Rest What does a newborn look like? A lot like this little one, resting after the journey along with their mother.

SCIENCE IN PRACTICE
Nicolle Gonzales, Certified Nurse Midwife

Nicolle Gonzales grew up on and near the Diné (also known as the Navajo) reservation in New Mexico, where she now delivers babies as a midwife. The landscape that has nurtured Nicolle since she was born is beautiful, but it hides a great deal of pain. The legacy of discrimination and inequality means that Native American women are over 200 percent less likely than White American women to get prenatal care and twice as likely to die after childbirth (CDC, 2021; Petersen et al., 2019).

Nicolle knows firsthand why many Diné women might not feel at home in a traditional medical environment. Nicolle experienced difficulties herself during her first childbirth, which she describes as "traumatic": Her provider wouldn't answer her questions, and she was afraid she was going to die of blood loss (van Gelder, 2017).

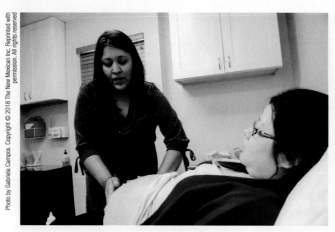

How Babies Enter the World Matters.
Nicolle Gonzalez tries to provide expectant families with connections and support that will help them have healthier deliveries, babies, and lives.

Labor in Her Mother's Arms Maria Florencia was lucky enough to go through childbirth with the help of her mother in the soothing, warm water of a birthing pool at her home in Veracruz, Mexico.

cesarean section A surgical procedure that involves making a small cut into the uterus and removing the baby. (Also called *c-section*.)

premature Birth that occurs less than 35 weeks after fertilization.

low birthweight (LBW) Babies born weighing less than 2,500 grams (about 5½ pounds).

small for gestational age (SGA) Babies born smaller than expected for their level of development.

CONNECTIONS

You will learn more about how families cope with the loss of a child in the Epilogue.

As a result of her experiences, Nicolle has a unique connection with her clients. As she explains, "I feel like when I visit with them one-on-one in midwifery, there's this connection because I do understand where they are coming from" (Gupta, 2015).

Nicolle wants Native American women to have a role in their own prenatal care and childbirth. So, she has researched Diné birthing practices and ceremonies and helps to empower indigenous women. She is now working to open the first Native American birthing center in the United States, fulfilling her vision to help birthing women feel comfortable and supported, and to get the care they need to start their families with joy and with the familiar customs that mark the beginning of life. ⊙

Medical Support During Childbirth

Medical interventions during childbirth can help save the lives of laboring people and their newborns and alleviate the discomfort from hours of contractions. More than 800 women and 2,700 newborns die each day during childbirth (UN IGME, 2020; WHO, 2020). Medical help can manage expectant parents' risk of infection, bleeding, and stroke and prevent the risk that a baby will die during delivery or as a result of being born sick or preterm (UNICEF, 2019; WHO, 2019).

Like many parents around the world, Alizah was able to give birth vaginally with the assistance of an experienced midwife, and with her mother and partner by her side. Not all mothers give birth this way. Many need to give birth by **cesarean section**, or *c-section*. One of the oldest kinds of surgery, a cesarean section involves removing the baby from the body through a small cut in the uterus. In many cases, a cesarean section saves the life of an expectant parent or newborn. Nonetheless, medical professionals are concerned that it may be performed too often (Molina et al., 2015; Ye et al., 2014). Parents have a lengthier recovery time after a cesarean and a higher risk of infection and re-hospitalization.

Labor is often extremely painful, and some medical options for pain relief are highly effective (Anim-Somuah et al., 2018; DiTomasso, 2019). Laboring people may also get relief from nonmedical approaches such as warm showers and gentle exercise (Henrique et al., 2018). In low-income countries around the world, many labor without medication, often without other measures to assuage their discomfort, like a partner or other support person (Bohren et al., 2015; Karn et al., 2016). Alizah was grateful that she not only delivered a healthy baby, she also benefited from the coaching of her mother, Spencer, and her midwife, as well as a warm bath during her four hours of hard pushing. Courage was born at about 5:30 AM.

Vulnerable Newborns

A baby's birth day is the most dangerous day in its life. More than 2 million babies around the world and more than 13,000 each year in the United States are born dead, or *stillborn*, either because they do not survive childbirth or because they perished before labor began (Hoyert & Gregory, 2020; Peven et al., 2021). In the United States, about 15,000 newborns die every year (Ely & Driscoll, 2020).

More than 13 million babies are born **premature**, or less than 35 weeks after fertilization (Chawanpaiboon et al., 2019). Many of these babies, and others who are born after 35 weeks, are among the 20 million who are **low birthweight** (**LBW**), or below 2,500 grams (about 5½ pounds) (Lee et al., 2019). Some babies, whether they are born at full term or prematurely, are considered **small for gestational age** (**SGA**), or smaller than expected for their level of development (Finken et al., 2018).

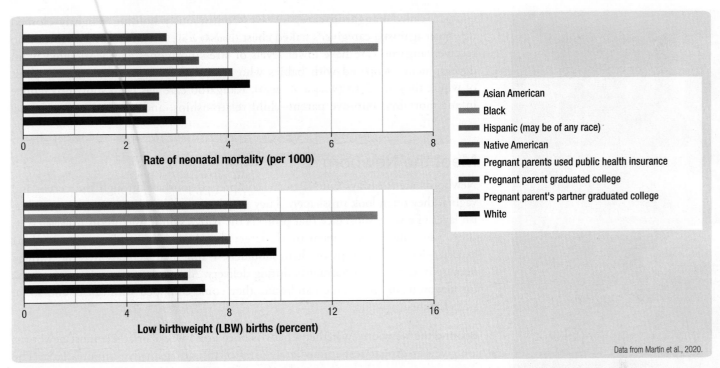

FIGURE 3.8 Inequity in Loss Losing a baby or worrying about one born with LBW are concerns that are not shared equally. This chart shows the rate of early newborn death (in the first 28 days) from LBW in the United States for every 1,000 babies born. Risks are higher for groups that experience discrimination and lower for those whose families benefit from status, including college education.

Prematurity, LBW, and being SGA can cause immediate and long-term health crises for newborns.

Risk Factors Around the world, most babies are at risk for being premature, LBW, or SGA because their parent developed an infectious disease or has other health conditions (Chawanpaiboon et al., 2019). Some babies face challenges associated with difficulties such as a lack of oxygen, or *anoxia*, during labor (Gillam-Krakauer & Gowen, 2020). All of these risks are more common in low-income families, who tend to have poorer health due to limited access to medical care, segregated and inadequate housing and nutrition, and other unmet needs (Beck et al., 2020). (See **Figure 3.8**.)

The vast majority, or 9 out of 10, of babies born premature or LBW catch up to their peers. But some infants, particularly if they are born *very* early or *very* small, often experience long-lasting effects if they survive, including difficulties with physical coordination, learning, hearing, and vision (Wolke et al., 2019). Researchers suspect that a combination of genetic vulnerability plus the stresses of early birth puts these children at risk (Thomason et al., 2017).

Researchers have developed innovative treatments to help preterm and LBW babies survive. However, these lifesaving processes are often painful and stressful, with infants subjected to frequent blood draws, disrupted sleep, and separation from their families (Nist et al., 2019). Interventions designed to limit these infants' stress have helped improve their outcomes. One model program integrates families into the day-to-day care of their fragile infants by letting parents hold, soothe, and breastfeed them whenever possible (Franck & O'Brien, 2019). These practices result in immediate improvements, including increased brain maturation (Volpe, 2019).

Although babies around the world do not always have access to high-quality care, they can all benefit from a low-tech intervention that improves LBW babies' chances of survival by more than a third. A particular form of skin-to-skin

Guillermo Legaria/AFP via Getty Images

A Father's Heart Sometimes low-technology solutions are the most effective. In a hospital in Colombia, Cesar holds his son, who was born prematurely, against his naked chest, providing him with warmth and calming them both as they adjust to life together.

kangaroo care A form of skin-to-skin contact that involves holding a lightly clothed newborn against a caregiver's chest.

Apgar test A quick medical evaluation of breathing, activity, responsiveness, and heart rate that assesses which newborns need immediate medical care.

contact, called **kangaroo care**, involves continuously holding a lightly clothed newborn against a caregiver's naked chest (Boundy et al., 2016). Premature babies who receive kangaroo care have lower levels of stress hormones and accelerated brain development compared with babies who are cared for in incubators, regardless of where they are born (Wang et al., 2021). Kangaroo care has been shown to reduce infant mortality, improve parent–child relationships, and accelerate growth (Gill et al., 2021).

Meet the Newborn

Newborns aren't always cute. After a compressed journey through the cervix and vagina, they often look misshapen. They may be covered with *vernix caseosa*, a whitish layer of a waxy substance that protects the baby's skin in the uterus (Nishijima et al., 2019). Their head might seem overly large; they have hair in places you wouldn't expect—like on the tops of their shoulders—and their genitals may be swollen because of exposure to hormones during delivery. Although it may take a few weeks for newborns to grow more handsome, they come equipped with senses and social skills for their new life.

Scoring the Newborn Whether a baby is born at 23 weeks or at 41, most newborns are given an **Apgar test** immediately after birth and again five minutes later. The Apgar test is a quick medical evaluation of a newborn's breathing, activity, responsiveness, and heart rate that assesses which babies need immediate medical care (Rüdiger & Rozycki, 2020). Most healthy babies score 7 or higher. Babies with scores of 5 or lower are at higher risk for medical complications and may need intensive interventions.

Sensing and Moving Courage, like all babies, was born with several skills that helped him survive and thrive in the outside world. Some of these are *reflexes*, or automatic responses to stimulation out of his control, like breathing or eye blinking. Others are patterns of moving and sensing the environment. Remember that fetuses are developing all of their senses in the uterus, though they haven't practiced using them in the real world. But their senses are developed enough to help them recognize and create connections with their caregivers.

The development of fetal eye structures ends at birth, but their brains are still developing. Typical newborn vision is usually a blurry 20/400; what they see at about 20 feet away is as hazy as what an adult with good vision would see 400 feet away (Goldstein & Cacciamani, 2021). At birth, anything farther than about 10 inches is blurry to a typical newborn (Clark-Gambelunghe & Clark, 2015). Nevertheless, 10 inches is the right distance for a newborn to make out a caregiver's face, which means that despite their blurry vision, newborns can recognize that something is a face. In fact, they prefer to look at faces more than anything else (Buiatti et al., 2019). By the end of his first day of life, Courage could see his mother, grandmother, and his father and tell them apart.

Similarly, although the world becomes much quieter as newborns leave the uterus, they can already recognize the familiar voices of their caregivers as well as the characteristic sounds of the languages they speak (Moon, 2017). Alizah and Spencer are sure Courage recognized the songs they sang to him before he was born. Newborns also recognize the scent of their parents' breasts, which may smell like the amniotic fluid that they remember from inside the uterus. Scientists believe that this may help newborns orient themselves so they can nurse (Hym et al., 2021). Babies' sense of taste is closely linked to smell. Newborns recognize the flavors of breast milk and amniotic fluid, which stimulates their appetite (Muelbert et al., 2021).

If you have ever watched an infant get their first shots, you likely agree that newborns feel pain. Newborns are more sensitive to pain and to other bodily sensations like skin-to-skin contact or massage than adults or older children are (Perry et al., 2018). Brief painful experiences like a shot do not seem to have any ill effects. However, researchers worry about the long-term effect of pain on newborns, such as premature babies who must undergo multiple uncomfortable procedures (Walker, 2019).

Many early movements are not under the baby's control. Most fetuses develop **reflexes**, automatic motor responses to stimuli to help them adjust to the world. These are processed in the parts of the nervous system that are the earliest to develop—the spinal cord and subcortical brain structures (Futagi et al., 2012). (Developmental reflexes are different from deep tendon reflexes, like the one in your knee, that exist lifelong.) Most developmental reflexes gradually disappear as brain maturation enables infants to have more control over their body.

Medical providers often evaluate a newborn's reflexes to make sure that their nervous system is developing as expected (see **Table 3.2**) (Salandy et al., 2019). Some reflexes help a newborn learn to nurse. In the *rooting reflex*, the baby automatically turns toward a touch on the cheek, like the brush of a hand or a nipple, and opens their mouth. Others seem designed to help the baby grab on to a caregiver. In the *Moro reflex*, a baby will move their arms forward when they feel that they are falling, as if they are trying to keep from tumbling down. In the *grasping reflex*, a baby's toes or hands will curl in to automatically grab anything close to them.

Building New Relationships As you just read, newborns are responsive to the people around them. The bodies of newborns and their parents are designed to make it easier to form new relationships and even, as Spencer described it, "to be so full of gratitude for him."

After birth, babies are undergoing brain and hormonal changes that enable bonding. Though newborns have elevated levels of stress hormones after the birth experience, the hormone *vasopressin* helps them manage the stress of birth and also bond

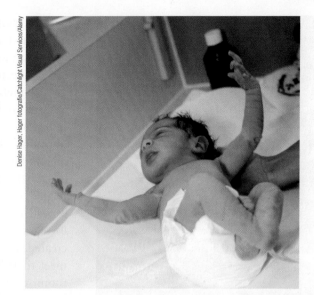

Designed to Thrive from the Beginning In the first minutes of life, infants demonstrate developmental reflexes such as the Moro reflex, in which arms swing out, and the rooting reflex, in which a baby spontaneously turns and sucks something (like their own hand) that touches their cheek.

TABLE 3.2 **Developmental Reflexes**

Rooting reflex	If a newborn's cheek is touched, they will turn their head and open their mouth in preparation for nursing. Disappears by 2–3 months.
Moro reflex	If a newborn feels as if they are falling, their arms will swing in and out suddenly. Disappears by 5–6 months.
Palmar grasp	If you press a newborn's palm, their fingers will curl in. Disappears by 5–6 months.
Plantar grasp	If you press the sole of a newborn's foot, their toes will curl in. Disappears by 9–10 months.
Babinski reflex	If you run your finger along the sole of a newborn's foot, their toes will fan out. Disappears by 12–24 months.

reflexes Automatic motor responses to stimuli that help babies adjust to the world.

Joanne Rathe/The Boston Globe via Getty Images

New Beginnings Families do not always begin in the hospital. For this family, legal recognition started in a Massachusetts courtroom, when a judge declared little Alexandra to officially be her parents' daughter.

adoption When parents become legal caregivers to a baby or child who is born to another biological parent.

©Macmillan, Photo by Sidford House

Scientific American Profile

Becoming a Family

with their families (Evers & Wellmann, 2016). *Oxytocin* is another hormone that increases in infants during the birth process and is critical in forming social relationships, making them feel connected and loved (Kingsbury & Bilbo, 2019).

Women who are biological parents also experience a surge in oxytocin during and after birth (Olza-Fernández et al., 2014). Men who are biological parents experience hormonal changes as well, including a decline in testosterone and an increase in oxytocin (Diaz-Rojas et al., 2021; Gettler et al., 2021). Other caregivers, whether they are biologically related or not, as in adoptive or same-sex families, also experience elevated oxytocin levels (Abraham & Feldman, 2018; Bakermans-Kranenburg et al., 2019). More than 1 in 10 families is created through **adoption**. Even if adoptive parents do not meet their babies until after they appeared in the delivery room, they experience some of the same hormonal and brain changes of biological parenthood (Goldberg et al., 2013; Kreider & Lofquist, 2014).

Caregivers' brains continue to adapt after they have a newborn: They show stronger connections in brain areas connected to empathy and understanding others (Shimon-Raz et al., 2021). These connections help parents regulate their emotions as they face the new stresses of parenthood (Rutherford et al., 2020). As many as one in five new parents experiences depression, anxiety, or another *perinatal emotional disorder* after having a newborn, which can impact their functioning (Howard & Khalifeh, 2020; Philpott et al., 2020). Interventions such as family psychotherapy or medication help new parents adjust (O'Hara & Engeldinger, 2018).

Newborns arrive in the world after remarkable growth guided by the genes they inherited and their experiences in the womb. They are now ready to learn about the world and form relationships that will guide them through their lifetime.

APPLY IT! **3.6** Alizah and Spencer were afraid of being separated during the birth because of restrictions imposed by the COVID-19 pandemic. Their midwife made sure that they could stay together, safely, during labor and delivery. Explain how social support gives laboring families the extra strength they need to be resilient through the biological transition of birth.

3.7 Much of the science of childbirth concerns worries about what might go wrong. Can you list three practices that help things go right?

Wrapping It Up ⊙⊙

LO 3.1 Define key components of human genetics. (p. 68)

The genome includes every instruction a cell might need to create and maintain your body. These instructions are located in 46 chromosomes, each of which is made up of a helix-shaped ladder of chemicals called deoxyribonucleic acid (DNA). Genes are sections of DNA that create particular proteins and have different forms, called alleles. Genes are expressed at different times because of maturation, aging, and environmental triggers. The epigenome controls genetic expression.

LO 3.2 Explain basic principles of genetic transmission of traits. (p. 68)

Some traits and diseases can be inherited. A few disorders and traits are single-gene disorders. Some are recessive disorders, when a child must inherit the two copies of the disease-carrying allele for the disorder to be expressed. Most traits and genes are polygenetic and multifactorial and are linked to numerous individual genes and environmental factors. The genome establishes a continuum of traits, but the environment can change how genes are expressed. Your genetic makeup also influences how susceptible you are to being changed by the context.

LO 3.3 Explain how the environment can affect gene expression through the epigenome. (p. 68)

The epigenome controls which genes are expressed by changing epigenetic marks. Some epigenetic marks are inherited; others are created later in the lifespan. Twins are an illustration of the impact of epigenetics on development. Monozygotic twins have nearly identical DNA, but epigenetic changes make their genetic expression different. Dizygotic twins develop when two (or more) ova are released, and they are fertilized by separate sperm. Dizygotic twins typically share only about half of their genome.

LO 3.4 Describe the key stages of prenatal development. (p. 79)

New life involves the joining of an ovum, or egg cell, with a sperm cell. This creates a new human cell with 46 chromosomes in 23 pairs, known as a zygote. During the germinal stage, the single-celled zygote divides and implants into the uterus in the first week of development. Support structures include the amniotic sac, the placenta, and the umbilical cord. In the embryonic stage, the major organ systems and limbs, including the brain, begin to develop. In the fetal stage, the fetus adds pounds and matures the organs and brain structures that will allow it to survive on its own. Fetuses are surprisingly capable before they are born. The prenatal period allows the fetus to practice skills, including sensing and moving, that will allow them to adapt to the world.

LO 3.5 Describe the principles of prenatal risk and resilience. (p. 79)

The context of prenatal development, including experiences of stress, disease, and environmental hazards, has an impact on fetal health. Supportive factors include prenatal care and social support. Risk factors, often called teratogens, can lead to atypical birth outcomes. Teratogens can include diseases; substances including medications, alcohol, or recreational drugs; and health conditions such as high blood pressure. Stress and depression in expectant parents can also affect the development of the fetus.

LO 3.6 Explain the process of vaginal childbirth and its common risks and protective factors. (p. 92)

Birth is a major social and biological transition. A healthy labor could take 20 hours or even 30 and can happen vaginally or through a cesarean section. Medical interventions can save the lives of pregnant people and their newborns. Some babies are born premature, or less than 35 weeks after fertilization. Some are also low birthweight (LBW), or below 2,500 grams (about 5½ pounds). Others are considered small for gestational age (SGA). Risk factors include poor health during pregnancy and trauma during childbirth itself.

LO 3.7 Describe how newborns' senses and capabilities help them thrive. (p. 92)

Newborns arrive with senses and reflexes that help them adjust to the world. They can see just as far as the face of the person holding them. They are especially attuned to faces and can hear and identify familiar voices. At birth, babies have limited control over their movement and rely on reflexes. Both new babies and their caregivers experience a rush of hormones that help them bond with each other.

KEY TERMS

genome (p. 68)
chromosomes (p. 68)
deoxyribonucleic acid (DNA) (p. 68)
mitosis (p. 68)
genes (p. 68)
alleles (p. 68)
phenotype (p. 70)
genotype (p. 70)
epigenome (p. 70)
ovum (p. 70)
sperm (p. 70)
meiosis (p. 70)

zygote (p. 71)
sex chromosomes (p. 71)
sex (p. 71)
gender (p. 71)
gender identity (p. 71)
gender expression (p. 71)
recessive inheritance pattern (p. 72)
dominant inheritance pattern (p. 73)
polygenic (p. 73)
multifactorial (p. 74)

Down syndrome (p. 75)
monozygotic (p. 76)
dizygotic (p. 76)
germinal stage (p. 79)
embryonic stage (p. 79)
fetal stage (p. 79)
in vitro fertilization (IVF) (p. 80)
blastocyst (p. 81)
placenta (p. 82)
neurons (p. 82)

birth defects (p. 87)
teratogens (p. 87)
stress (p. 91)
cesarean section (p. 94)
premature (p. 94)
low birthweight (LBW) (p. 94)
small for gestational age (SGA) (p. 94)
kangaroo care (p. 96)
Apgar test (p. 96)
reflexes (p. 97)
adoption (p. 98)

CHECK YOUR LEARNING

1. The structure of DNA is often compared to a(n):
   a) skyscraper.
   b) twisted ladder.
   c) almond.
   d) checkerboard.

2. Which of the following statements about the genetic origins of twins is TRUE?
   a) Monozygotic twins are generally conceived from two sperm joining with one ovum.
   b) Dizygotic twins occur after a single sperm and single ovum join into a zygote, which later divides into two distinct balls of cells.
   c) Monozygotic twins occur after a single sperm and single ovum join into a zygote, which later divides into two distinct balls of cells.
   d) Dizygotic twins are the result of two ova merging together before conception.

3. Langston has sickle-cell disease, but both his parents are healthy. Which of the following explanations is BEST?
   a) His mother is a carrier, but his father is not.
   b) His father is a carrier, but his mother is not.
   c) Neither of his parents are carriers.
   d) Both of his parents are carriers.

4. Which of the following may contribute to a person's gender?
   a) The pattern of sex chromosomes (X and or Y) inherited from their biological parents
   b) Their body's sensitivity to hormones during prenatal development
   c) Their feelings about their identity
   d) All of the above

5. The chemicals in the epigenome that guide lasting impacts of environmental experiences on gene expression and regulation are known as:
   a) gametes.
   b) epigenetic marks.
   c) chromosomes.
   d) nuclei.

6. What milestone marks the end of the germinal stage in prenatal development?
   a) The blastocyst implants in the wall of the uterus.
   b) The contractions of labor begin the process of childbirth.
   c) The fetal heartbeat is present.
   d) The brain and spinal cord are fully developed.

7. Which of the following statements regarding the senses of a developing fetus is TRUE?
   a) During the third trimester, a fetus is responsive to light, touch, sound, smell, and taste.
   b) Prior to birth, a fetus has no exposure to sounds.
   c) Prior to birth, a fetus has no responsivity to visual stimulation.
   d) Fetuses cannot feel pain.

8. Supportive prenatal care may include all of the following EXCEPT:
   a) social support, like a family member helping out with errands.
   b) a support group, where expectant parents share their experiences with others in their communities.
   c) a strict diet to prevent weight gain.
   d) regular visits with a medical professional to assess the growth of the fetus and health of the mother.

9. A harmful substance or experience that may impact fetal development is known as a(n):
   a) teratogen.
   b) fetal anomaly.
   c) epidural.
   d) fertilization.

10. A newborn's condition is assessed in the moments after birth in an assessment of their breathing, heart rate, and responsiveness known as the:
    a) newborn IQ.
    b) Apgar.
    c) CPR.
    d) c-section.

4 Physical and Cognitive Development in Infancy and Toddlerhood

© Macmillan, Photo by Sidford House

Growing

4.1 Explain factors promoting healthy patterns of growth and development during the first two years.

The Changing Brain

4.2 Explain the role of neurons and synapses in brain function during the first two years.

Sensing and Moving

4.3 Describe vision and hearing development in infancy.

4.4 Explain how the typical maturation of movement changes a baby's experience of the world.

Cognitive Development and Learning

4.5 Explain maturation in sensorimotor thinking, attention, and memory during infancy and toddlerhood.

4.6 Describe the factors influencing learning during the first two years.

Language Development

4.7 Describe the typical pattern of language development in the first two years.

Selected Resources from

 Achieve

Activities

Spotlight on Science: Using the Experimental Method to Fight Allergies

Concept Practice: Sequence of Motor Development

Assessments

LearningCurve

Practice Quiz

Videos

Scientific American Profiles

Observing Development: Language Development in Infancy and Toddlerhood

Marjorie and Dewey were excited to be parents. Before their daughter Telele arrived, they went to dozens of doctor's visits, read baby books, and picked a pediatrician. They wanted to make sure that their daughter had the best beginning possible.

Marjorie and Dewey knew that learning is important even in the first few years of life. As members of their Iñupiaq and Denaakk'e Alaskan communities, they wanted Telele to know from the beginning that she was linked to her people and their land. They wanted to welcome their daughter with the beauty of their culture: Marjorie even had Iñupiaq symbols tattooed on her legs so that they were the first images Telele saw as she was born. And the first words Telele heard were in Iñupiaq and Denaakk'e: "We love you baby. Welcome, welcome."

Marjorie and Dewey fell in love through a shared commitment to their Indigenous community, speaking their native languages and living close to the land. When they met, Dewey was teaching Denaakk'e at a Head Start center, and Marjorie was in graduate school and working as an artist. Marjorie, whose background is Iñupiaq and Kiowa, had been speaking Iñupiaq since she was a teenager. Dewey became passionate about learning and teaching Denaakk'e after he finished college.

Like many caregivers, Marjorie and Dewey have big dreams for their child. They want Telele to identify as a proud, Indigenous adult and to feel connected to their communities. They want to teach her to fish for salmon, collect berries, and bead intricate designs like her great-grandmothers. They also want to ensure that Telele is healthy and can make her way in an English-speaking world. Therefore,

101

Scientific American Profile

▶ Meet Telele

© Macmillan, Photo by Sidford House

Telele is learning not only Denaakk'e and Iñupiaq but also English and a little sign language. Like one in five American children, Telele will be *multilingual*, a speaker of more than one language (ACS, 2015).

In the nearly two years since her birth, Telele has grown from a newborn small enough to hold with one arm to a toddler who is nearly too heavy to carry. She has learned how to move, eat pancakes and blueberries, and (most of the time) sleep through the night, as well as how to talk and understand her surroundings. Telele's brain has gotten bigger, too, more than doubling in size and sending signals up to 100 times faster (Johnson & deHaan, 2015; Zhang et al., 2019). Telele is now a *toddler*, a term that refers to the wobbly toddling movements of 1- to 3-year-olds.

Like Telele, infants and toddlers are flexible in how they adapt, whether it is speaking one language or three, sleeping through the night or waking up to cuddle, or eating chili peppers or chocolate, depending on the expectations of their families and communities. The first years of life set the foundation for health and cognitive development later on. As you will learn, there are a variety of ways to support babies as they develop the healthy bodies and curious minds they will need to thrive.

Growing

Learning Objective

4.1 Explain factors promoting healthy patterns of growth and development during the first two years.

malnutrition When someone does not have adequate nutrients to support their growth.

wasting When a child is so seriously malnourished that they are below the 5th percentile in the ratio of weight to height, or lighter for their height than 95 percent of children their age and height.

percentile A way of statistically comparing an individual to a group.

stunting When a child's growth has slowed so much that they are significantly shorter than they should be for their age.

Telele had a lot of doctor's visits in her first years of life. Pediatricians recommend infants and toddlers get weighed and measured frequently, because babies grow more rapidly than at any other point in the lifespan, and their health is more fragile (BrightFutures, 2021).

By their second birthday, babies nearly triple their birthweight and grow about a foot taller. When she was a month old, Telele weighed 8½ pounds (3.6 kg). A year later she weighed 20 pounds, and by age 2, she had added another 7 pounds (3.2 kg), a typical trajectory for babies as they quickly grow muscle, bone, and brain tissue. Their body shape changes, too. It takes a few weeks for newborns to take on the soft, round shape we think of as babyish. Infants get lankier and leaner again around 12 months as they begin moving around (Brown et al., 2016).

Babies grow up to be adults of different heights, but they are remarkably similar in size for the first two years of life (de Onis, 2017). Genes play a long-term role in height, but they don't make a major difference for infants' size. This is why health workers around the world use the same *growth charts* that track the optimal increase in babies' height and weight (see **Figure 4.1**). If babies are growing too quickly or not quickly enough, usually something in their environment or an illness is the culprit.

Around the globe, more than one in five infants experience **malnutrition**, or do not get enough food or nutrients to support their growth. That number is expected to increase in coming years as a result of disruptions caused by the COVID-19 pandemic (Headey et al., 2020). Before the pandemic, researchers found that about 7 percent of children worldwide were so seriously malnourished that they experienced **wasting** (UNICEF/WHO/World Bank Group, 2020). Children who have growth wasting are below the 5th **percentile** in the ratio of weight to height, or lighter than 95 percent of other children their age and height.

Children can experience growth wasting when they do not have enough food or develop a serious illness. For instance, Telele was a typical 23 pounds (10.5 kg) at 16 months. A child with growth wasting would weigh less than 18½ pounds (8.5kg). If babies are malnourished for a long period, they may also experience **stunting**, which means that their growth has slowed so much that they are significantly shorter

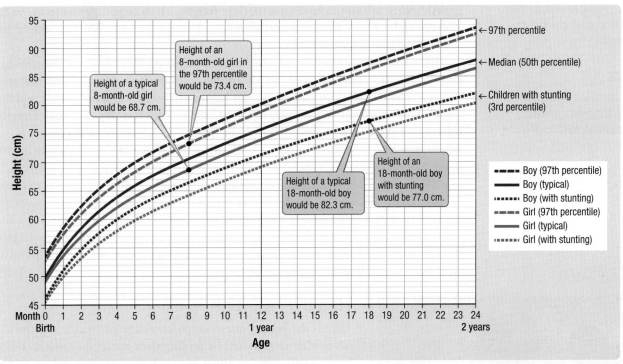

Height of a typical 8-month-old girl would be 68.7 cm.

Height of an 8-month-old girl in the 97th percentile would be 73.4 cm.

Height of a typical 18-month-old boy would be 82.3 cm.

Height of an 18-month-old boy with stunting would be 77.0 cm.

← 97th percentile

← Median (50th percentile)

← Children with stunting (3rd percentile)

- - - - Boy (97th percentile)
—— Boy (typical)
••••• Boy (with stunting)
- - - - Girl (97th percentile)
—— Girl (typical)
••••• Girl (with stunting)

Data from World Health Organization, 2006.

FIGURE 4.1 Understanding the Growth Curve Growth charts help health professionals track individual growth. For instance, a child in 35th or 70th percentile would likely track around that same level at each checkup. Diverging from the percentile might indicate a problem, such as when an infant suddenly drops into the 25th percentile from the 70th percentile.

than they should be for their age, or smaller than 98 percent of all other children (de Onis et al., 2019). For instance, at age 2, Telele was 31 inches (79 cm) tall, but a toddler with stunting might be just 27 inches (69 cm) tall. Around the world, more than one in five children show signs of stunting (UNICEF/WHO/World Bank Group, 2020). In the United States, as in other affluent countries, very few children—fewer than 3 in every 100—develop stunting (Fryar et al., 2020a).

Malnutrition affects the brain as well as the body and is likely to lead to learning challenges (McCormick et al., 2020). Prevention begins with improving nutrition during pregnancy and breastfeeding, as well as making sure babies are well-nourished and avoid chronic infections early in life (Bhutta et al., 2020). Public health **interventions**—evidence-based programs or services designed to improve health, psychological well-being, or behavior—have dramatically improved the rate of malnutrition and helped children recover. Interventions may happen at the population level, as when an entire community benefits from extra nutrients in milk, or at the individual level, as when one family is offered supplemental vitamins. A generation ago, twice as many children around the world had stunted growth. Today, more children are growing to their full potential (Vaivada et al., 2020).

In the United States and many other communities around the world, being too large is more common than being too light (Fryar et al., 2020b). Infants who are heavier for their age and height than most other children, or above the 85th percentile on

Benedicte Kurzen/NOOR /Redux

Checking the Garden In rural Senegal, access to fresh water for drinking and growing has made it easier for families to grow healthy food.

interventions Evidence-based programs or services designed to improve health, psychological well-being, or behavior.

overweight When a child is heavier for their age and height than most other children, or above the 85th percentile.

CONNECTIONS

We will look more in depth into controversies about measuring size and health, and the stigma against larger bodies, in Chapter 6.

growth charts, are said to have an unhealthy weight, which medical providers refer to as **overweight**. In the United States, about one in eight 2-year-olds has an unhealthy weight (Fryar et al., 2020b).

Babies with an unhealthy weight have an increased likelihood for poor health later in life, including a higher rate of asthma, cardiovascular disease, and diabetes (Deal et al., 2020). This is particularly true for babies who were born prematurely and for those who gain weight very quickly in the first six months (Ou-Yang et al., 2021). Experts believe that these early months program an infant's metabolism (Fall & Kumaran, 2019). Babies who gain weight too rapidly are less likely to stay at a healthy weight in adulthood (Zheng et al., 2018).

Even when it comes to infants, talking about weight is difficult (Pesch et al., 2021). Larger bodies are stigmatized in communities around the world (Puhl et al., 2021). Medical providers must explain that weight is one of many factors influencing children's health without shaming families. Conversations about weight often trigger feelings of parental guilt, which make it more difficult for families to build positive attitudes about eating (Hagerman et al., 2020).

Healthy Nutrition

One of the biggest questions parents have for health care providers is what they should be feeding their babies (Lavigne et al., 2017). Early foods vary. In some places, babies are not fed at all for the first days of life. In others, infants may be given special tea, honey, or formula (Chea & Asefa, 2018; O'Neil et al., 2017). Regardless of where they live, all infants must be fed frequently because their small bodies can handle only tiny servings, and they need extra nutrients to fuel their rapid growth.

Human Milk Experts agree that babies should ideally be fed only human milk from birth until they are about 6 months old. From about 6 months to 2 years, or longer, babies may continue to drink human milk but also begin to eat other foods (Meek et al., 2020).

Human milk is a complex and living concoction of stem cells, immune-boosting antibodies, immune cells, and disease-fighting proteins (Boquien, 2018). But producing milk is not always easy. More than 8 in 10 nursing parents in high-income countries report difficulties with expressing milk, including breast infections and intense nipple pain (Lucas et al., 2019). Difficulties are more common for adoptive or transgender parents, who *may* be able to express human milk and nurse but often lack the medical and social support to get started (Paynter, 2019; Trautner et al., 2020). You do not need to identify as a woman in order to create human milk: With hormonal support, early reports suggest that breast tissue in many people can support infant development. Some people feel uncomfortable with the gender labels for expressing milk, and may prefer the more neutral term *chestfeeding* to breastfeeding (MacDonald et al., 2019).

Nursing Can Be Hard for Parents... But it is fascinating for big brother. Song Dan helps make nursing easier on parents (and babies) as a professional lactation consultant near her home in Beijing, China.

📱 Share It!

For people who are used to getting milk from the refrigerator, human milk can be surprising. The yellowish paste that is first expressed, known as *colostrum*, is supercharged with nutrients and beneficial bacteria.

(Bardanzellu et al., 2017)

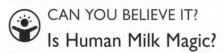
Scientific American: Lifespan Development

🧒 CAN YOU BELIEVE IT?
Is Human Milk Magic?

You have probably heard many claims about the benefits of human milk—that it makes children smarter or reduces their risk of developing an unhealthy weight. For many caregivers, especially those who do not identify as women, those who work, and those who have certain physical conditions expressing milk can be challenging or impossible. Some families may feel judged for not feeding their infants human milk (Penniston et al., 2021). What is the evidence for the benefits of human milk in this sometimes sensationalized discussion (Jackson et al., 2021)?

Scientists have investigated the benefits of human milk through large observational studies of families, comparing babies who received human milk with those who did not. As you may remember from Chapter 2, these are *correlational studies*, because they look at the correlation, or the relationship, between babies' health and what and how they are fed (Azad et al., 2018).

Correlational studies have found that babies who receive human milk are less likely to die early in life or develop diarrheal and infectious diseases (Christensen et al., 2020; Victora et al., 2016). Some studies have found that benefits continue after infancy: Babies who received human milk are at lower risk for unhealthy weight, diabetes, and cardiovascular disease when they are older (Güngör et al., 2019; Rzehak et al., 2017). Some research even suggests that babies who receive human milk score slightly higher on intelligence tests later in life and may have an easier time regulating their emotions (Horta et al., 2018; Weaver et al., 2018). There are benefits for people who express milk, too, including lower risks for cardiovascular disease, cancer, and depression (Sattari et al., 2019).

Some of the associations between human milk and children's outcomes are very strong; others are weaker. For instance, babies in low-income countries are about 14 times more likely to survive to their first birthday if they receive human milk instead of formula, which is a strong association (Horta, 2019). However, babies who receive human milk have intelligence test scores that are only two-tenths of a percentage point higher than formula-fed babies, a much smaller association (Oster, 2019).

Stronger evidence also comes when there is a testable explanation for *why* the relationships occur. Some studies have found observable differences in the process of nursing and in human milk itself that make it beneficial. Human milk is lower in protein than formula, contains different fats, and conveys microbes that help develop intestinal bacteria: This may account for some of the health benefits (Deoni et al., 2018; Horta, 2019). Behaviors matter, too: Families tend to interact with babies differently when they are nursing than during bottle-feeding. There is more skin-to-skin contact and back-and-forth interaction, and infants have more control. These distinctions may contribute to later differences in babies' emotion regulation, appetite, and cognitive development (Hodges et al., 2020).

Remember from Chapter 2 that experiments are a gold standard for research because they seek to identify a *causal relationship* between variables. Experiments conducted in Belarus, an Eastern European country, compared the outcomes of babies who were randomly assigned to receive either human milk or formula (Singhal et al., 2004). The researchers established that babies who received human milk were healthier than those who did not receive human milk and scored slightly higher on intelligence tests, although these differences decreased over time (Yang et al., 2018).

As a result of decades of research, scientific consensus is that there are strong benefits for human milk, particularly when it is delivered through nursing and particularly for families who live in low-resource settings with limited health care (Azad et al., 2018; National Academy, 2020). However, in communities like the United States, human milk is not a cure-all. Nutrition is complex: Dramatic effects due to a single variable are rarely seen in developmental science. While human milk is certainly helpful, babies can thrive without it. Relationships are more central to how infants grow than micronutrients are, and relationships are not built on *what* babies drink but on *how* they are fed (Hairston et al., 2019). 😊

Around the world, fewer than half of families are able to feed their babies human milk exclusively for the first six months of life (UNICEF, 2020). In affluent countries

Westend61/Getty Images

Sharing a Moment Bottle-feeding takes patience, attention, and time. Feeding a newborn gives parents and babies time to get to know each other.

📱 **Share It!**

Small children are vulnerable to exposure to environmental toxins. Recent studies have found that many U.S. commercial foods for infants and toddlers include potentially dangerous amounts of heavy metals, including cadmium, arsenic, and lead.

(Mousavi Khaneghah et al., 2020; Radwan, 2019)

📖 **Scientific American: Lifespan Development**

like the United States, income and cultural differences influence how families feed their children (Beauregard et al., 2019). Parents who are female and have immigrated to the United States or identify as Latina are also more likely to nurse their babies than Black or White parents. This may be because they are more likely to have family support, particularly from mothers or grandmothers who also nursed their babies (Dennis et al., 2019). In addition, higher-income families with more years of education are more likely to provide human milk to their infants, perhaps because they can afford to stay home or have jobs that offer them more flexibility (Victora et al., 2016).

Around the world, parents who work often have difficulty sustaining nursing because they do not have adequate breaks or a place to pump. This is problematic whether they work as doctors or wait tables (Kavle et al., 2017; Melnitchouk et al., 2018). As one parent working in retail explained, "I couldn't just leave the register to pump when I needed. At first I was leaking everywhere, and then my milk supply dropped and I had to start formula" (Spencer et al., 2015, p. 979). Less than half of nursing parents report that their employer accommodates nursing (Johnson et al., 2015).

Alternatives to Human Milk Babies who are not fed human milk exclusively drink commercial formulas containing a mix of cow's milk, soy or corn proteins, and a mix of nutrients. In Canada, the European Union, and the United States, all infant formulas are regulated and include the same nutrients (Harris & Pomerantz, 2020). Infant formula provides complete nutrition for babies and is convenient for multiple care-givers and those without access to human milk. Like nursing, formula-feeding comes with logistical challenges. One of these is cost: Many families struggle to pay for it (Frank, 2020).

As with nursing, the mechanics of formula-feeding are not always intuitive (Kotowski et al., 2021). Pediatricians recommend holding babies while they are feeding and allowing babies to decide when they're done, practices that ensure bottle-fed babies experience social interaction and learn to regulate their appetite (Kotowski et al., 2020). Babies who are bottle-propped do not get that interaction and may be at risk for overeating or suffocation. Nevertheless, 40 percent of U.S. parents put their babies to bed with a bottle, and about a quarter use a pillow or stuffed animal to prop a bottle in an infant's mouth (Perrin et al., 2014).

Moving to Solid Food Marjorie and Dewey intended to start Telele out with a traditional food like blueberries, she has been known to taste French fries. As babies become more mobile, solid food becomes interesting. Between about 4 and 6 months, pediatricians recommend offering soft versions of a fully balanced diet, and letting babies take the lead in discovering the joys of eating (Ahluwalia, 2020; NAS, 2020).

Solid food sets the stage for a lifetime of eating habits, and learning to eat involves many of baby's new skills. It takes social awareness and close attention to watch what other people are eating. And it takes fine motor skills to pick up those peas. Eating offers toddlers an opportunity to build responsive relationships, letting caregivers know what they like and do not like, and to learn to regulate their own feelings of hunger (Nix et al., 2021).

Many families are not able to provide the fruits, vegetables, and proteins their infant needs. In the United States, more than one in five babies does not eat fruits or vegetables every day, and more than one in three regularly has sweetened drinks (Roess et al., 2018). Experts speculate that caregivers' food choices are often influenced by marketing and the convenience of packaged foods that do not provide ideal nutrition (Harrison et al., 2017; Spyreli et al., 2021). Biology is working against families, as well: Infants are born with a strong preference for sweet and salty foods (Mennella et al., 2018). If given the choice, babies will always prefer cookies to kale.

Babies' focus on other people also helps them develop a preference for French fries. If babies see other people enjoying a food, they are more likely to try it (Liberman et al., 2021). Simply being exposed to foods will help babies learn to enjoy them, and these preferences will stick: Whether it is mouthed, eaten, or rubbed into the hair, early food experiences will help determine baby's tastes for the rest of their life (Switkowski et al., 2020).

Staying Healthy

Despite the best efforts of caregivers and health care providers, babies and toddlers in the United States typically get sick 8 to 14 times a year (Vissing et al., 2018). During the recent pandemic, many came down with COVID-19, but their immune systems, primed to fight new diseases, often prevented them from developing the most severe physical responses to the virus (Suwanwongse & Shabarek, 2020).

Babies who are in child care tend to get sick twice as frequently as other infants, because they are exposed to a broader variety of viruses. However, by the time these toddlers reach school age, they will be ill less frequently (Ansari & Gottfried, 2020).

Disease and Mortality Around the world, nearly 4 out of every 100 babies die before their fifth birthday. Many of them die shortly after birth as a result of birth trauma, genetic disorders, prematurity, or low birthweight (UN IGME, 2020). Older babies tend to die from diseases such as malaria and pneumonia, which are often made worse by environmental pollution and malnutrition (Heft-Neal et al., 2020; WHO, 2020). While rates of infant and toddler mortality had been improving prior to the COVID-19 pandemic, experts expect that the global disruption to health services will lead to a sharp increase in deaths during those years (Roberton et al., 2020). ◄

Even in a technologically advanced nation like the United States, 2 out of every 1,000 children die before their third birthday. Many of those babies die accidentally (CDC, NCHS, 2021). Babies are particularly vulnerable to everyday hazards like falls and car accidents and are too small and fragile to recover if they experience violence or abuse. Others die of sleep-related injuries (Ely & Driscoll, 2020).

Babies at higher risk tend to be from low-income families and often live in rural areas (Ehrenthal et al., 2020; Mohamoud et al., 2021). This is not unique to the United States. In New Zealand, Indigenous Māori people, who tend to have lower incomes and experience discrimination, also have higher rates of unexplained infant death (Rutter & Walker, 2021). Many of these babies were at higher risk before they were born, perhaps because they were premature or had LBW. Inequitable access to health care and the pervasive effects of discrimination contribute to such disparities (Owens-Young & Bell, 2020).

One successful intervention for preventing early mortality is to provide families with home visits by nurses, social workers, or community health workers after a baby is born (le Roux et al., 2020; Supplee & Duggan, 2019). These visits give caregivers extra social support, including advice for soothing babies, encouragement for responsive feeding, and consultations about safe sleep. Decades of research on home visiting has demonstrated its significant success (Goodman et al., 2021). One randomized study in Memphis, Tennessee, had dramatic results: Home visits reduced the mortality rate for children and their mothers by half, with benefits that stuck with children through adolescence (Kitzman et al., 2019; Olds et al., 2014).

CONNECTIONS

Remember from Chapter 3 that there are striking disparities in birth outcomes by income and racial background. Babies from Black and Native American families are more than five times as likely as Asian or White infants to die before they are a month old.

Extra Support Helps Families Thrive. Adjusting to life with a newborn can be easier with someone to talk to and an extra set of hands. Lorrie Arnt is a nurse with the Nurse–Family Partnership, who came to Shelby and Rafael's house in Reading, Massachusetts, to help them with their new baby, Jaden.

Immunizations Shots, vaccinations, jabs—no matter what you call them, routine vaccinations are one of the biggest scientific success stories of all time, saving the lives of millions every year (Okowo-Bele, 2015). **Immunizations** protect against diseases by introducing a tiny part of an infectious virus into the body to teach it to defend itself. If you encounter the virus later, you are much less likely to get sick because your body's immune system is prepared to protect you. More than 9 in 10 U.S. toddlers have received basic vaccines, but they often skip their annual flu shots (Hill et al., 2020).

Despite generations of research indicating that vaccines are safe, worries are common around the world (Puri et al., 2020). Families who are hesitant about vaccination are often distrustful of the scientific community and government institutions (Salmon et al., 2015). Others are concerned, despite evidence to the contrary, that vaccines may cause developmental disorders, or that they may be unnecessary (Kempe et al., 2020).

In many countries, families who chose not to vaccinate their children have contributed to outbreaks of preventable infectious diseases, such as whooping cough and measles (Dubé et al., 2021; Phadke et al., 2020). A recent outbreak in the Pacific nation of Samoa resulted in more than 80 measles deaths, most of them in children under 5 (Graig et al., 2020). Immunizations have been extensively tested for safety and are one of the most important ways of reducing infant mortality around the world.

Sleep

Like all babies, Telele spent almost half of her first two years fast asleep. In infancy, sleep is essential to rebuilding energy, growing, and recovering from disease. Babies who do not get enough tend to be more irritable and have poorer health (Meltzer et al., 2021). Experts suggest that between 4 and 12 months, babies should be getting 12–16 hours of sleep per day, and from 12 months to 2 years, they should be getting between 11 and 14 hours (Paruthi et al., 2016).

While infants sleep, the brain is building networks that help them remember what they have learned (Konrad & Seehagen, 2020). Even a brief nap can help babies retain information. For instance, in one study, researchers taught 15-month-olds new words, and the ones who slept after they learned the words remembered them better when tested later than did babies who skipped the nap (Werchan et al., 2021).

At around 4 months, a baby's **circadian rhythm** matures (Barry, 2021). Circadian rhythm is your internal clock for the daily cycle of rest, wake, and sleep. It is highly influenced by the activity levels and light babies are exposed to; bright lights, movement, and noise help them learn when it is time to be awake (Yates, 2018).

Researchers who observe infants while they are sleeping have seen what most caregivers do not: Babies never "sleep through the night" (Adams et al., 2020; St James-Roberts et al., 2015). Neither do adults—we all have periods of wakefulness, even if we may not remember them in the morning. This short period of waking or drowsiness happens each time we transition from one cycle to another. The milestone caregivers are really hoping for is that babies will settle themselves back to sleep without needing help.

Many babies can go five hours without needing a caregiver's attention by about 4 months (Barry, 2021). To scientists, this means they have achieved the milestone of sleeping through the night. But there is tremendous variability in when babies go eight hours without needing care. While many do so by 6 months, what a baby does on one night may not happen the next (Pennestri et al., 2018, 2020). By age 2, however, babies typically can make it eight hours with only one awakening (Paavonen et al., 2020). Three factors lead to this milestone: (1) babies are big enough not to need to eat overnight; (2) experience with the outside world has led to the development of strong circadian rhythms; and (3) infants have learned how to settle themselves after waking.

Managing Sleep When caregivers do not get enough sleep or feel that their babies are not sleeping enough, they have difficulties functioning and are at increased risk for

immunization A means of protection against diseases that introduces a tiny amount of an infectious virus into the body to teach it to defend itself against that virus. If the immunized person encounters the virus later, they are less likely to get sick, because their immune system is prepared.

circadian rhythm Your internal clock for the daily cycle of rest, wake, and sleep.

depression (Bai et al., 2020; Wilson et al., 2019). However, the ideal sleep schedule varies from family to family (Pennestri et al., 2018). In the United States, bedtime is typically around 8 P.M., but in Korea, Brazil, and Italy, infants regularly go to bed around 10 P.M. (Netsi et al., 2017). How often infants are expected to wake up during the night also varies. Babies in the United States are typically only expected to wake up once nightly after 6 months, whereas babies in China, India, Finland, and Vietnam are usually expected to wake up at least twice (Lin et al., 2019; Mindell et al., 2010).

Every year in the United States, about 3,500 babies die while they are sleeping (Bombard et al., 2018). When otherwise healthy infants pass away, their deaths are termed **sudden unexpected infant deaths (SUID)**. If investigators determine that sleep practices caused the death, as with being smothered, the death is called a *sleep-related suffocation*: These account for most of the SUID deaths in the United States (Parks et al., 2021).

Children who die while they are asleep often have three intersecting risk factors. First, the babies are very young, typically under 6 months. Second, even though they may appear healthy, they tend to have medical vulnerabilities, such as heart irregularities, brain abnormalities, or complications from being born prematurely (Cummings & Leiter, 2019; Kinney et al., 2018; Ostfeld et al., 2017). Third, they are often exposed to environmental risks, such as drugs or alcohol in their prenatal environment; exposure to nicotine, cigarette smoke, or other pollutants after they are born; an unsafe sleeping arrangement; or a minor illness like a cold (Anderson et al., 2019; Vivekanandarajah et al., 2021).

Managing sleep is often part of firmly held cultural practices. For instance, some caregivers in the Ivory Coast wake up their babies when they have visitors (Gottlieb, 2004). In other places, families prepare a separate room where their baby will sleep. Particularly in Asia and Africa, many caregivers *bed-share* or *cosleep* with their babies (Rudzik & Ball, 2021). This is also true for more than half of parents in the United States (Bombard et al., 2018; Ordway et al., 2020).

Compared to other affluent countries, pediatricians in the United States have the strictest policies about sleep safety and sternly admonish against co-sleeping (Doering et al., 2019). Some researchers suggest that these policies may communicate cultural insensitivity and even frighten families from getting advice about safe sleep (Mandlik & Kamat, 2020). Caregivers can reduce risk when they are co-sleeping (see **Table 4.1** for a list of ways to make sleep safer; Erck Lambert et al., 2019). Successful public health initiatives are often designed to bridge traditional practices with science, including the New Zealand program of providing traditional *wahakura*

Sleeping Like a Baby Public health officials in New Zealand adopted traditional woven wahakura baskets to promote safe-sleep practice. Notice that New Zealand experts allow caregivers to tuck infants in with sheets and blankets. There is limited international consensus on this practice: U.S. experts advise keeping blankets out of babies' beds.

TABLE 4.1 Safe Sleep Recommendations

- Put babies to sleep on their backs, where they are less likely to suffocate, until age 1.
- Babies should sleep on a firm mattress in an approved surface, with no bottles, blankets, bedding, bumpers, pillows, or stuffed animals.
- Babies should not sleep on couches or recliners, or in car seats or playpens.
- Pacifiers help babies sleep and prevent sleep-related injuries.
- Families should not smoke during pregnancy and should avoid exposing babies to secondhand smoke.
- Babies should share a room (but not a bed) with their caregiver until 6 months.
- Falling asleep while feeding or soothing a baby in the middle of the night is common. It is safer to feed a baby in bed than on a recliner or a couch if the caregiver is concerned about falling asleep.
- Parents who have been drinking, using drugs or sedatives, or are extremely tired should have someone else watch the baby.
- Be extra cautious when there is a change of caregivers, sleep patterns, or sleep situations.
- Monitor babies closely at night when they are sick or have an underlying medical problem, as they may be more prone to suffocation.

Information from Mölloborg et al., 2015; Moon et al., 2016.

sudden unexpected infant deaths (SUID) When an otherwise healthy infant dies. SUIDs can include *sleep-related suffocation*.

bassinets that can be used in the bed to protect babies from suffocation (Tipene-Leach & Abel, 2019).

APPLY IT!   **4.1** Dewey and Marjorie encourage 18-month-old Telele to eat with them and feed herself. What might Telele be learning from these experiences?
4.2 All families want to keep their babies safe in the first years when their health is fragile. How would you use principles of cultural humility to communicate the benefits of safe sleep, vaccination, and responsive feeding to new families?

The Changing Brain

Learning Objective

4.2 Explain the role of neurons and synapses in brain function during the first two years.

The first two years are a time of major milestones: first steps, first words, first teeth. Telele is learning to scribble, negotiate for more ice cream, and navigate the playground. Her growing brain powers all these capabilities. The experiences Telele encounters, including the hundreds of words she hears each day and the thousands of times she wiggles her fingers, shape how her brain grows.

Scientists use brain imaging to see exactly what is changing in a baby's brain in the first two years, but you can guess what is happening without an MRI machine. As you will see in **Infographic 4.1**, the brain grows dramatically in the first year. Skull size in adulthood is predictive of nothing but hat size, but an infant's expanding skull actually is important. (This is why health providers measure it at every visit.) By 2 years, the brain has doubled in volume (Thompson et al., 2020).

Remember from Chapter 3 that babies are born with just about all the *neurons*, or brain cells, that they will have in their life. Explosive growth is not caused by new neurons, but by new, faster connections between them (Gilmore et al., 2018). These connections help Telele learn how to control her body and also how to talk and connect with other people.

During infancy, the brain becomes customized to what babies' experience, an individualization that can also have a downside. If growing infants don't have certain experiences in the first few years, like hearing language or seeing through both eyes, it may be more difficult for them to recover their skills. The young brain is particularly vulnerable, and early injuries and deprivation can have lifetime consequences (Gabard-Durnam & McLaughlin, 2020).

More Connections Make a Larger Brain

Brain growth is so critical in infancy that infants expend more calories growing the brain than growing the body (Kuzawa et al., 2014; Vasung et al., 2019). In newborns, the brain grows by 1 percent every day (Holland et al., 2014).

The fastest growing area of the infant brain? The area devoted to movement and language. As Telele learned to control her body, sit without toppling over, and pull herself up, the part of her brain known as the *cerebellum* grew and expanded most quickly (Sathyanesan et al., 2019). Also fast-growing are the *subcortical structures*, which are involved in emotional processing and relationships and will help Telele learn to connect with her parents and manage her feelings (Gilmore et al., 2018). The regions of the brain that drive her communication skills grow quickly as well: The *cortex*, the outer, wrinkled part of the brain, gets thicker as Telele grasps more words and grammar (Gilmore et al., 2020).

More Connections The expansion of the brain is caused by changes you could only see with a high-powered microscope. Individual neurons are connecting and sending information to one another, which accounts for the extra pounds of brain Telele is carrying around (Thompson et al., 2020).

THE BRAIN INCREASES DRAMATICALLY IN SIZE

Birth | 3 months

Photo courtesy of Dominic Holland, University of California, San Diego School of Medicine. Structural Growth Trajectories and Rates of Change in the First 3 Months of Infant Brain Development. Dominic Holland, et al. JAMA Neurol. 2014;7(10).

The brain doubles in size between birth and age two. Most of this explosive growth happens in the first months of life. These brain scans were taken just 90 days apart.

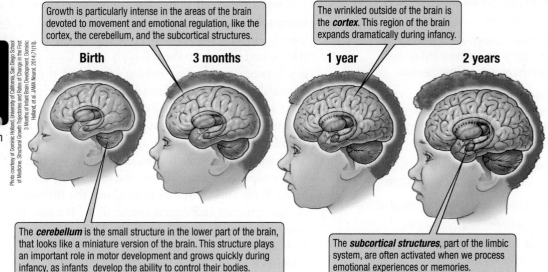

Growth is particularly intense in the areas of the brain devoted to movement and emotional regulation, like the cortex, the cerebellum, and the subcortical structures.

The wrinkled outside of the brain is the *cortex*. This region of the brain expands dramatically during infancy.

Birth | 3 months | 1 year | 2 years

The *cerebellum* is the small structure in the lower part of the brain, that looks like a miniature version of the brain. This structure plays an important role in motor development and grows quickly during infancy, as infants develop the ability to control their bodies.

The *subcortical structures*, part of the limbic system, are often activated when we process emotional experiences or memories.

NEURONS AND CONNECTIONS GROW VIBRANTLY

Experiences shape the creation of new synapses and neural connections. The brain creates millions of new connections every second, and the network of neurons in the brain becomes denser over time.

Synaptogenesis

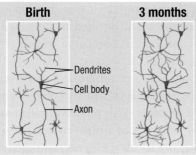  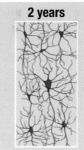

Birth | 3 months | 1 year | 2 years

Dendrites
Cell body
Axon

These drawings illustrate what a thin section of brain tissue might look like showing neurons connecting with each other.

Anatomy of a neuron

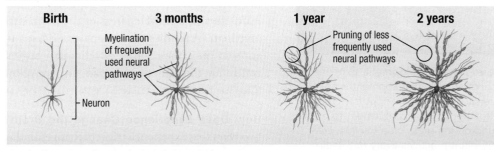

Axon: The long tail-like structure that sends information from one cell to another.

Cell body

Dendrites: The outgrowths from the body of the neuron transmit information received from other cells at synapses

Myelin: The cholesterol filled outer covering of an axon that helps speed messages from one neuron to another.

Synapse: Neurons communicate with other neurons through electrical impulses and chemical messages passed at synapses. Synapses can occur between dendrites, axons and cell bodies.

EXPERIENCE SHAPES THE BRAIN THROUGH MYELINATION AND PRUNING

Neural connections that are used frequently are more likely to be myelinated. These connections become stronger and faster. They are known as white matter. Connections that are used less frequently are likely to be pruned away.

Neuron maturation

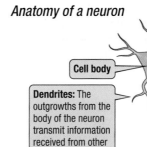

Birth | 3 months | 1 year | 2 years

Myelination of frequently used neural pathways

Neuron

Pruning of less frequently used neural pathways

axon The long, tail-like structure attached to the cell body that transmits a chemical signal to other neurons.

dendrite A branch-like appendage that grows out of the cell body and receives communication from other neurons.

synaptogenesis The process of creating new synapses between neurons, which begins before birth and continues throughout the lifespan.

synaptic pruning The process in which the brain cuts back on underused synapses.

myelination The lifelong process of adding myelin to axons.

myelin Layers of cholesterol-rich fat that insulate the axon, helping to speed up communication.

experience-expectant brain development Brain maturation that relies on nearly universal environmental inputs.

Nice-to-Have Development Experience-dependent brain development is not universal and relies on input from the environment. Not all babies get to push around on the grass on a toy lion, but if this infant practices every day, their brain will respond to this experience by myelinating the connections that respond to the movement.

Neurons make connections through their **axon**, the long, tail-like structure attached to the cell body that transmits a chemical signal to other neurons (see Infographic 4.1). This communication is received by other neurons' **dendrites**, branch-like appendages that grow out of the cell body. Sometimes the message is transmitted directly to the cell body itself. Communication occurs in the *synapse*, the gap between the sending neuron's axon and the receiving neuron's dendrite, where chemical packets carry information from one neuron to another.

Each neuron's axon may connect to multiple dendrites from many different neurons (Han et al., 2018). Neurons connect to as many as 7,000 other neurons, with some including as many as 30,000 synapses (Mohan et al., 2015). Each axon may be very long: The longest axons stretch from the brain way down to the bottom of the spinal cord.

Synaptogenesis, or the process of creating new synapses between neurons, begins before birth and continues throughout the lifespan. Experiences shape the creation of new synapses and neural connections. Because the brain creates millions of new connections every second, by age 2, Telele will have more synaptic connections than there are grains of sand on a beach (Stiles & Jernigan, 2015). She will have 80 percent more synapses than she did at birth and far more than she will have as an adult (Sakai, 2020).

Creating Efficient Connections As babies grow, their neural connections change. The strength and density of synapses correspond to experience: The more a synapse is used, the stronger it gets. For instance, if an infant hears a lot of language, the part of the brain devoted to language will be larger as a result of increasing synaptic connections, compared to babies who don't hear as much language (Merz et al., 2019).

New connections are created every second and get stronger with experience, and the brain manages this complexity and creates efficiency by cutting back on underused synapses. This process is called **synaptic pruning**, named for the practice of pruning branches of a plant to make it stronger. Synaptic connections operate on a "use it or lose it" idea: Connections that are used are strengthened, and those that aren't die off (Cheadle et al., 2020). This increases speed in the brain, because neural signals travel more quickly along thicker, more robust connections.

Synaptic pruning, as with the process of creating new synapses, begins before birth and continues throughout the lifespan. It peaks between about 18 months and 2 years (Huttenlocher & Dabholkar, 1997).

Making Faster Connections The process of **myelination** also helps Telele's brain process information more quickly. Some axons in the brain are covered with **myelin**, layers of cholesterol-rich fat that insulate the axon. Just like the plastic covering an electrical line, myelin speeds communication by up to 100 times (Kanda, 2019).

Myelination is controlled by both genes and experience. Axons that are used more frequently are more likely to be myelinated than those used less frequently (Rosenke et al., 2021). Individual experiences matter, as well. For instance, as a toddler learns to ride a tricycle, areas of the brain that control movement of the pedals will myelinate. A toddler who has never ridden a tricycle, however, will not show myelination in the same regions. Myelination begins prenatally, peaks during infancy, and continues through the lifespan until myelin itself begins to degrade in later life (Chapman & Hill, 2020; Dai et al., 2019).

How Does Experience Change the Brain? Neuroscientists distinguish between two ways that experience triggers changes in the brain: *experience-expectant development* and *experience-dependent development*. **Experience-expectant brain development** is brain maturation that relies on nearly universal environmental inputs (Greenough et al., 1987). These processes affect a broad range of functions, from the senses to emotional, language, and cognitive development. Experience-expectant brain development is triggered by typical, basic inputs in the environment, including nutrition, sensory stimulation, and caregiving, that are required in order for the neural circuits in the brain to develop.

Remember from Chapter 1 that *sensitive periods* are times in development when the body or brain is particularly sensitive to the environment. Infancy is a sensitive period for a few forms of experience-expectant development (Frankenhuis & Walasek, 2020). If necessary experiences do not happen at all, or at the expected time, a baby may never develop typical functioning. For instance, since brain development requires adequate nutrition, even short periods of deprivation in infancy can have lifelong effects. This was demonstrated in Israel, where, for a few weeks, some babies drank formula that lacked *thiamine*, a B vitamin, due to a manufacturing error. Since the brain requires thiamine to trigger language development, these babies' language abilities were permanently altered. Despite intensive interventions, they never caught up with their peers who received healthy formula (Harel et al., 2017).

Unlike experience-expectant brain development, **experience-dependent brain development** is not universal; it includes features that are "nice to have" but not required. These processes rely on the quantity or quality of environmental input and, like all learning, continue throughout the lifespan (Fandakova & Hartley, 2020; Rosenzweig & Bennett, 1996). For instance, the ability to produce and understand language is an experience-expectant process, but the *quality* of a baby's language skills and which languages they speak are experience-dependent. Experience-dependent processes may make life richer, as with learning to play patty-cake or fasten Velcro, but these experiences don't necessarily need to happen at a specific time or during a sensitive period.

CONNECTIONS

As explained in Chapter 3, critical periods are a special type of sensitive period. Maturation that happens during a critical period operates on a "now or never" principle: If it does not happen at that time, there is no workaround. Scientists believe that critical periods happen only during prenatal development: After birth, most maturation is more flexible.

Principles of Early Brain Development

Over the past 30 years, scientists have observed some principles that explain the significance of changes in the brain (Nelson et al., 2019).

1. *Brain development is a long process that allows personalization.* Brain development begins in the embryo, but the brain isn't mature until early adulthood. It continues to change until the end of life (Walhovd & Lovden, 2020). Slow brain development allows the brain to be shaped to experience. As a result, each baby's brain is as unique as their fingerprints.

2. *Brain development is affected by genes* and *the environment.* Instructions in the genome direct brain development, but genes need to be epigenetically triggered by the environment (Frith, 2019). For instance, monozygotic twins share similar genetic instructions and may even share some of the same prenatal conditions, but their experiences vary, and as a result, their brains are never the same (McEwen & Bulloch, 2019).

3. *There are limits to the brain's* plasticity, *or ability to adjust to the environment.* The brain is always changing, as new synapses are being created and myelinated, but development requires some experience-expectant experiences to happen at particular times. As the foundational structures of the brain are being built, trauma and deprivation can cause damage that will be challenging, and perhaps impossible, to overcome (Wade et al., 2020).

APPLY IT! **4.3** How does myelination and the creation of new synapses support Telele's ability to learn new skills, like how to draw with a crayon?

4.4 Why do scientists think the first years of life are so important to brain development?

experience-dependent brain development
Brain maturation that relies on the quantity or the quality of environmental input and, like all learning, continues throughout the lifespan.

Sensing and Moving

Learning Objectives

4.3 Describe vision and hearing development in infancy.

4.4 Explain how the typical maturation of movement changes a baby's experience of the world.

CONNECTIONS

Remember from Chapter 3 that a baby's senses begin to develop while they are still in the uterus. At birth, newborns have remarkable abilities to see, hear, smell, taste, and feel the world around them. These early senses are shaped by prenatal experiences and help them make connections with the people in their world.

When you are picking out mangos at the grocery store, you might take for granted your ability to smell, see, and feel the mango and to hear the phone buzzing in your pocket. But you weren't born with all these skills working the way they do today and there are many individual differences in how our senses work and develop. As infants develop, real-world experience builds the connection between body and brain that helps their senses change and mature (see **Figure 4.2**). Here we focus on the typical development of two critical senses that help infants learn and connect to the world: vision and hearing.

Seeing

Dewey remembers how intensely newborn Telele looked into his face. Young babies are drawn to faces, people, and animals moving around them, and their preference for people helps propel their impressive learning abilities (Grossman, 2017; Kelly et al., 2019). In the first two years, babies' vision typically improves quickly, along with their ability to move their focus from one object to another. By 3 or 4 months, infants can see a full spectrum of colors and may even have a favorite (researchers have found that

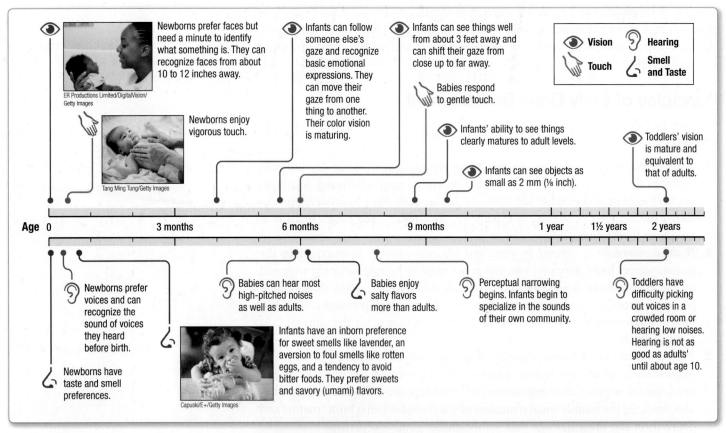

Newborns prefer faces but need a minute to identify what something is. They can recognize faces from about 10 to 12 inches away.

ER Productions Limited/DigitalVision/Getty Images

Newborns enjoy vigorous touch.

Tang Ming Tung/Getty Images

Infants can follow someone else's gaze and recognize basic emotional expressions. They can move their gaze from one thing to another. Their color vision is maturing.

Infants can see things well from about 3 feet away and can shift their gaze from close up to far away.

Babies respond to gentle touch.

Infants' ability to see things clearly matures to adult levels.

Infants can see objects as small as 2 mm (⅛ inch).

Toddlers' vision is mature and equivalent to that of adults.

Vision   Hearing   Touch   Smell and Taste

Age 0   3 months   6 months   9 months   1 year   1½ years   2 years

Newborns prefer voices and can recognize the sound of voices they heard before birth.

Newborns have taste and smell preferences.

Babies can hear most high-pitched noises as well as adults.

Infants have an inborn preference for sweet smells like lavender, an aversion to foul smells like rotten eggs, and a tendency to avoid bitter foods. They prefer sweets and savory (umami) flavors.

Capuski/E+/Getty Images

Babies enjoy salty flavors more than adults.

Perceptual narrowing begins. Infants begin to specialize in the sounds of their own community.

Toddlers have difficulty picking out voices in a crowded room or hearing low noises. Hearing is not as good as adults' until about age 10.

FIGURE 4.2 Highlights of Sensory Development Typically, infants are born with some sensory abilities, like the ability to recognize their caregivers close up, and some of the sounds and tastes they may have experienced before birth. But their senses are not fully developed until they are much older. Many senses show evidence of *perceptual narrowing* before a baby's first birthday, as an infant's perception begins to specialize in the sights and sounds they experience most frequently.

most babies prefer yellow to blue) (Skelton & Franklin, 2020). Their ability to see details improves rapidly between 6 and 9 months (Goldstein & Brockmole, 2017). When Telele saw the candle on her first birthday cupcake, she could see as well as her parents, including all the colors of the decorations.

Scientists use the **preferential looking technique** to measure what babies perceive and to identify their favorite color. In this procedure, researchers harness babies' intrinsic interest in new things. Babies turn their heads to look at what they are interested in and naturally look longer at an object they haven't seen before. They also look longer at an image that interests them, such as a picture of a face as opposed to an abstract image.

What Do Babies Look At? Babies move from looking at faces to looking at hands as they develop the ability to move their own hands and get around the house. Miles is 14 months old and wears a camera over his eye to track what he is looking at. Researchers use eye-tracking to better understand exactly how children see the world.

Hearing

When Telele was a newborn, Marjorie and Dewey tried not to speak too loudly, even if she was in the other room. However, this may have been unnecessary (Werner, 2017). In the first few months, typically-developing babies can hear normal conversations but not whispers (Litovsky, 2015). Infants (and other young children) also have a hard time ignoring background noises or distinguishing speech from background noise (Leibold & Buss, 2019). Despite these limitations, babies are particularly attuned to speech, especially the voices of people they know (McDonald et al., 2019; Newman et al., 2013). What do they hear best? The sound of their caregivers calling their name.

Hearing improves quickly due to maturation in the ear canal, the tube that runs from the eardrum to the outside of the ear. As it grows, it works like an amplifier to make sounds louder (Werner, 2017). Hearing doesn't just happen in the ears: Sound is processed in the brain as you make sense of what you hear. In infancy, neural circuits are building between the ear, the brainstem, and the cortex, which helps the brain process sensory information. As these circuits mature and change over the lifespan, people can continue to develop their hearing, including the ability to perceive musical notes, rhythms, or new languages (Reetzke et al., 2018). About 2 in every 1,000 babies has some type of hearing impairment: early identification helps these infants get the support they need (Bussé et al., 2020).

The Specialization of the Senses

Could you tell the difference between two monkeys? Unlike most adults, a 6-month-old can. However, by 9 months, babies have lost the ability (Pascalis et al., 2002; Simion & Di Giorgio, 2015). Similar changes happen in babies' hearing. In the first months of life, babies can perceive a wide variety of tones and language sounds. A few months later, they lose this skill. For instance, English-speaking adults have difficulty perceiving sounds that only appear in other languages, like consonants unique to in Czech or Kikuyu, or tones that appear in Thai. Infants do not: They can perceive the sounds of all the languages of the world (Maurer & Werker, 2014). However, by age 1, their ability to hear sounds is more limited, and they no longer respond to sounds that do not occur in their own languages (Kuhl et al., 2014).

Researchers call this phenomenon **perceptual narrowing**. At birth, infants are sensitive to a wide variety of sensory input whether that is monkey faces or the sounds of languages, but they become *less* sensitive during their first year: Babies' brains have begun to specialize. Developmental processes including neural pruning and myelination make this possible; frequently used connections become faster and more efficient, and unused connections fade. As a result, babies who grow up hearing Mandarin will be good at hearing tonal differences in Mandarin. Babies who are raised among people will learn to distinguish between different people's faces and lose the ability tell the differences between monkeys (Barry-Anwar et al., 2018).

preferential looking technique A procedure that measures what babies perceive in which researchers harness babies' intrinsic interest in new things.

perceptual narrowing The process by which infants become less sensitive to sensory input as they grow and begin to specialize in the sights and sounds to which they are exposed more often.

motor development The development of body coordination.

gross motor development The development of bigger movements like walking, jumping, or skipping.

fine motor development The development of small movements requiring precise coordination, like picking up little objects, swallowing, or pointing.

FIGURE 4.3 What Can Babies Do with Their Bodies? No baby's development matches the precise order on a chart, but researchers have observed a common sequence for many infants and toddlers. The timing of development depends on individual and cultural factors. You will see some average ranges for typically developing children indicated in parentheses. Learning to move will change infants' thinking, relationships, and ways of responding to the world.

Moving

For many families, one of the highlights of early development is movement. Babies, too, seem enthralled by their ability to control their environment, whether that means dropping a spoon from the highchair or running to catch up to an older friend. Learning to control the body not only changes how babies see the world and relate to other people, but it also changes their brains (Adolph & Hoch, 2020). Although babies can move in the uterus, learning to move independently after they are born takes a long time.

The development of body coordination is called **motor development**. Scientists analyze the development of bigger movements like walking, jumping, or skipping, called **gross motor development** (*gross* here means "large"). They also study the development of small movements requiring precise coordination, like picking up little objects, swallowing, or pointing, called **fine motor development** (*fine* here means "tiny"). (See **Figure 4.3**.)

Large Movements

At 5 months, Telele dropped a ball, and it tumbled out of her reach. She leaned forward gingerly to avoid toppling over while grabbing it, but she could not make it quite far enough. She had a face of complete frustration as she cried out for help.

We should be sympathetic. Almost a quarter of babies' weight is in their large head, and they need tremendous muscle strength to manage the 2-pound weight (Bayley, 1956; Salzmann, 1943). Stabilizing the head is just the first step in the ability to move. As Telele found, controlling the body begins in the core. Without enough control to keep from tipping or swaying, babies cannot move much else (Rachwani et al., 2019).

As Telele gets older, her body proportions will change and her growth will slow down, making movement easier. A 2-year-old's head is still about one-fifth the size of their body, but they aren't growing as quickly as they were as an infant (Huelke, 1998). Their bodies are also narrower, with less fat and more muscle. These new proportions make it easier to control movement.

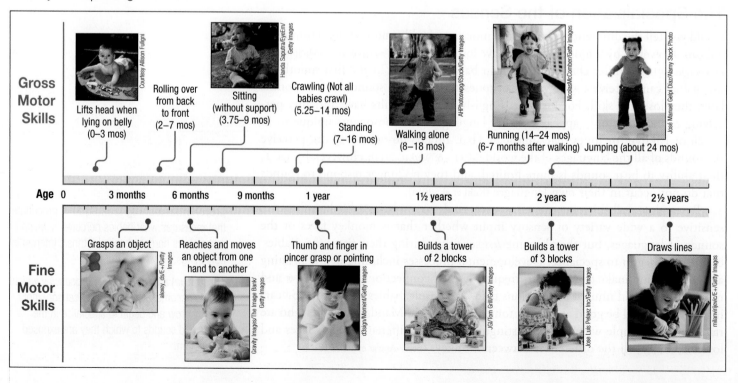

Gross Motor Skills

Lifts head when lying on belly (0–3 mos) · Rolling over from back to front (2–7 mos) · Sitting (without support) (3.75–9 mos) · Crawling (Not all babies crawl) (5.25–14 mos) · Standing (7–16 mos) · Walking alone (8–18 mos) · Running (14–24 mos) (6-7 months after walking) · Jumping (about 24 mos)

Age 0 · 3 months · 6 months · 9 months · 1 year · 1½ years · 2 years · 2½ years

Fine Motor Skills

Grasps an object · Reaches and moves an object from one hand to another · Thumb and finger in pincer grasp or pointing · Builds a tower of 2 blocks · Builds a tower of 3 blocks · Draws lines

Babies learn to control their bodies in a **cephalocaudal**, or head-downward, pattern, beginning with the ability to support their heavy heads. By about 6 weeks, babies can hold their heads up consistently, allowing them to look at what they are interested in (Adolph & Franchak, 2017). At around 4 months, being able to roll from their back to their front or vice versa means they can now tumble off couches and are no longer safe even lying in the middle of a bed (Shoaibi et al., 2019). Sitting, which typically happens around 6 months, is another critical development. Now infants can keep themselves from toppling over and also see their hands to pick up toys and explore more of their world (Franchak, 2019).

Babies typically walk on their own at about 1 year because of practice, faster neural connections, and stronger muscles, which give them more power (Adolph, 2019). As the brain develops, connections are myelinated between the muscles, the spine, and the brain, and within areas of the cortex, making walking easier (Marrus et al., 2018). But faster neural connections don't make it effortless: A typical 1-year-old baby might take more than 2,400 steps an hour and fall more than 12 times (Adolph, 2019; Han & Adolph, 2020).

The development of gross motor skills does not end with walking. By age 2, babies can typically jump and even begin to climb steps and scramble up ladders or into boats, depending on where they live. As with walking and crawling, the development of more coordinated skills like jumping or hopping takes practice (Veldman et al., 2018).

Controlling the Hands

While caregivers may focus on their infants' walking ability, babies are also learning how to make smaller movements. Fine motor skills require infants to coordinate many abilities: perceiving what is around them (where the Cheerio is on the table); making a plan (I want to pick up that last Cheerio); and manipulating their bodies to do their bidding (thumb and forefinger at the ready) (Adolph & Franchak, 2017).

It is difficult to reach for and grab an object if your torso is swaying back and forth. Thus, babies must be able to balance their core and torso before they can control their arms and hands. This pattern of physical development, where control of movement begins in the core and expands outward, is called the **proximodistal principle**.

Babies also need to learn how to manage their strength. At birth, newborns have a powerful whole-hand grasp, called the *palmar grasp*, that would crush a blueberry. They learn to be gentler: At around 10 months, they develop their *pincer grasp*, coordinating the thumb and fingers to hold small objects (Gonzalez et al., 2018). This makes it easier to eat blueberries, and also to grab little, potentially dangerous objects such as pills or batteries. By age 1, as a result of practice and brain maturation, babies are able to point, reach, and grasp small objects (Karl et al., 2019).

Fine motor dexterity also means that by age 1, babies can use basic tools such as such as spoons or markers, buttons or chopsticks (Rachwani et al., 2020). In many families, these tools also include tablets and other electronic devices, despite pediatricians' cautions against media use (Souto et al., 2020).

Culture and Motor Development

Across time and place, there are significant variations in how and when typical babies learn to move. *Ethnotheories*, or caregivers' beliefs about how children should be raised, are critical. For instance, some caregivers believe that children shouldn't be pushed to walk before they are "ready," but others may encourage babies to walk so that they can be more independent (Harkness et al., 2013; Mendonça et al., 2016).

Many communities around the world encourage children's mobility, beginning with infant massages and practice (Adolph & Hoch, 2020). Babies who get this exercise

cephalocaudal Development that occurs in a head-downward pattern, beginning with a baby's ability to support their heavy head.

proximodistal principle A pattern of physical development in which control of movement begins in the core and expands outward.

 Share It!

Can babies learn when parents text? Researchers watched as parents tried to teach infants a new skill while being interrupted by a text on their phones. Their babies tended to fuss while their parents were distracted but were still able to learn the new skill. Texting may not be ideal, but it does not make learning impossible.

(Konrad et al., 2021)

Scientific American: Lifespan Development

affordance The term for what people can learn from objects in the world around them.

learn to control their bodies earlier than others. For instance, babies in Cameroon typically sit on their own at 4 months, two months earlier than babies in the United States. On the other extreme, infants in Norway, where parents are often reluctant to "push children to perform," cannot walk with assistance until about 10½ months (Karasik et al., 2018; WHO, 2006). There are many ways that babies may learn to walk, and *when* babies learn to walk depends on their experience. But whether they spend a lot of time sitting still or get lots of practice, most typical babies develop all the motor skills necessary for their culture (Adolph & Hoch, 2019).

Learning from Moving

Telele's face lights up when she scoots across the room for the first (and second, and third, and eighteenth) time. Learning to move independently, whether crawling, walking, or pushing a toy, changes how infants experience the world (Franchak, 2020; Gibson, 1988). Moving also changes how other people relate to babies. A walking and running child is treated much differently from an immobile infant. Movement launches a cascade of development across different parts of a baby's life.

Movement helps babies learn more about the many possibilities in the physical world. For instance, a phone may be good for sucking, for tapping on, or even for throwing off a highchair. Researchers have a term for what people can make from objects in the world around them: **affordance** (Gibson, 1979, 1988). One of the basic affordances infants make about the environment is whether it is safe. For instance, what will happen if they head down the stairs?

Over the years, researchers have put babies into dozens of situations to learn how they understand what is safe. They have thrown things toward babies' heads to see if they would duck (the flying objects would never actually hit them) and found that even very small children can accurately gauge how fast a ball is moving and when to move away. They have observed how babies walk or crawl on a jiggly waterbed or over a gap in the floor. Researchers famously tested babies' willingness to take risks by watching to see if they would crawl right

Hugh Scott, Sooner Magazine

How Does Movement Change the Brain? Professor Thubi Kolobe studies how infants learn to wriggle, crawl, and walk. She has also invented devices to help give extra support to babies who cannot move easily on their own, reinforcing their inborn drive to move.

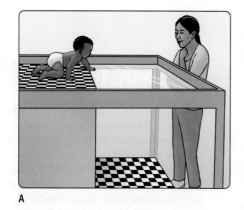

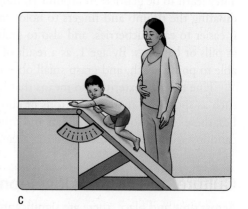

FIGURE 4.4 Learning from Experience Researchers study how infants think about decisions in the laboratory by watching how they move. In panel A, you can see how a baby investigates the visual cliff, a piece of plexiglass that appears transparent. This baby seems to be an inexperienced crawler and is making a risky choice, which might result in a tumble in real life. In panel B, a new walker is taking a chance by going head-first down a sleep slope. Without practice, they are likely to fall. In panel C, a more experienced walker takes the safer route and goes down the steep slope on their belly.

off a ledge, using a device called a **visual cliff** (Anderson et al., 2013; Gibson, 1988; LoBue & Adolph, 2019). Originally designed to test babies' visual depth perception (Gibson & Walk, 1960), the visual cliff is a 2½-foot gap covered with plexiglass that, if properly lit, appears to be an empty gap.

This research demonstrated that it takes weeks of experience before babies learn what is safe. Experienced walkers or crawlers will stop before the edge of a dangerous situation, whether that is a big gap or a steep slope, but babies who have just learned to crawl or walk tend to make mistakes (Han & Adolph, 2020). The practical note is that babies are in more danger of making mistakes right after they have learned a new skill. They will fall off beds and tumble down stairs or slopes. Babies need time to integrate the new movements with the sensory information they receive from the environment (Adolph, 2019).

APPLY IT! **4.5** Health providers often check infants' hearing as part of their developmental screening. Why is hearing so important to babies' development?
4.6 Practice and experience change what we can perceive. How does this support Marjorie and Dewey's decision to expose Telele to multiple languages early in development?
4.7 Babies are at risk for accidents as they learn new skills. What should families be careful of as their babies learn to move independently?
4.8 How do infants' new motor skills change how people respond to them?

Cognitive Development and Learning

The first two years of life involve huge amounts of learning. Telele came into the world with eyes blinking, hardly able to see her surroundings. By her second birthday, she was confident enough in her understanding of the world that she could count both of her birthday candles and gently put her stuffed moose to sleep by singing an Iñupiaq lullaby. There is certainly a lot of development in Telele's ability to reason and understand the world, in her memory, and in her ability to pay attention and learn.

Piaget's Theory of Cognitive Development

Remember from Chapter 2 that Jean Piaget changed attitudes about infant's minds, helping researchers realize that even infants are curious and inventive in their approach to understanding the world. Piaget saw young infants' early cognitive activity as a combination of their senses and their motor activities (Piaget, 1952). Piaget described the first 18 months of a baby's life as the **sensorimotor** period because of the focus on learning through sensation and movement. He divided this stage into six substages (see **Table 4.2**).

In stage 1, called *reflexes*, from birth to about 1 month, newborns are a bundle of reflexes, as you read in Chapter 3 (Piaget, 1968). Newborns are not limited to reflexes for very long. They may begin by indiscriminately sucking anything that comes close to their mouths, like a finger or even a button, but this teaches them that they can't suck everything as they do with a breast or a bottle. Infants begin to recognize and develop *schemas* about what can be sucked. This is a major accomplishment: They are remembering and developing concepts about how the world works.

In stage 2, called **primary circular reactions**, from about 1 to 4 months, babies begin to adapt their reflexes to new uses and show more creative behaviors (Piaget, 1952). The term "primary circular reaction" refers to an experience the baby repeats with their own body (primary), and that is repeated on purpose again and again (circular). Piaget believed babies' first adaptation to the world is to apply their basic reflexes, like sucking and grasping, to new purposes. Piaget observed

Learning Objectives

4.5 Explain maturation in sensorimotor thinking, attention, and memory during infancy and toddlerhood.

4.6 Describe the factors influencing learning during the first two years.

visual cliff A means of assessing what risks babies will take while crawling, in which a 2½-foot gap is covered with plexiglass that, if properly lit, appears to be an empty gap.

sensorimotor Piaget's term for the cognitive stage that spans the first 18 months of a baby's life and focuses on learning through sensation and movement.

primary circular reactions The second stage of the sensorimotor period, from about 1 to 4 months, in which babies begin to adapt their reflexes to new uses and show more creative behavior.

TABLE 4.2 Piaget's Sensorimotor Stage of Cognitive Development

Stage	Key Events	
Stage 1 **Reflexes** (birth to 4–6 weeks)	Babies cannot consciously control much of their bodies, but they can move nonetheless. Their hands reflexively grasp and suck whatever approaches their mouths. In this stage, they begin to assimilate new behaviors, like sucking their thumb, onto existing reflexes.	 Thirawatana Phaisalratana/Getty Images
Stage 2 **Primary Circular Reactions: Adaptation of Reflexes** (1–4 months)	Infants can now adapt their movements and newborn reflexes to the world around them. They can suck a pacifier differently than a stuffed animal. They can grasp a finger differently than a rattle. In primary circular reactions, they can repeat adapted reflexes again and again.	 LiuSol/iStock/Getty Images
Stage 3 **Secondary Circular Reactions: Making Fun Last** (4–8 months)	Infants can manipulate their bodies as well as other people or things. They enjoy not only their own movement but also the effect of this movement on something in the world. They can watch as a toy on a mobile jiggles again and again as they shake it.	 Dorling Kindersley ltd/Alamy Stock Photo
Stage 4 **Coordination of Secondary Reactions: Making a Plan for Action** (8 months–1 year)	Babies can begin to make a plan and carry it out. They can anticipate what is going to happen next, like giggling with happiness as they try to put on a hat to go out into the snow.	 Seth Hill/Getty Images
Stage 5 **Tertiary Circular Reactions: Little Scientists Running Experiments** (1 year–18 months)	Toddlers can manipulate their world to explore through trial-and-error: "What happens if I drop this toy off of my highchair?" or "What happens if I squeeze all the diaper cream out of the tube into a pile?"	 Dorling Kindersley ltd/Alamy Stock Photo
Stage 6 **Mental Combinations: Thinking before Doing** (about 1 ½–2 years)	Toddlers can make a plan in their mind without taking action. They can also use symbols, like language, to get what they want. They can call for their father for help or indicate that they have lost their sock.	 Cavan Images/Getty Images

this stage in his own children as they learned to suck their fingers for the joy of it (Piaget, 1952).

In stage 3, called **secondary circular reactions**, from about 4 to 8 months, babies learn to extend their activities to manipulate the world around them. Infants discover that they can use their bodies to act on an external object, which could be a toy, a person, or a pet, to get a reaction. Babies in this stage are happily interactive. Piaget described his daughter, Jacqueline, gently shaking a doll hanging from her bassinet. She clearly enjoyed her new power and, in Piaget's words, the glory of "making interesting sights last" (Piaget, 1952). She understood what the shaking would do, and when she was later lying in her bassinet for a nap, she remembered the action that led to the shaking doll and did it again.

In stage 4, *coordination of secondary circular reactions*, from about 8 to 12 months, babies can make a plan and combine separate schemas to accomplish their goals. At this age, Piaget observed that babies have discovered **object permanence**, the understanding that objects continue to exist even when they are out of sight (Piaget, 1954). Rather than appearing to ignore a hidden object, a baby who has achieved object permanence will search for it, looking around and lifting items to look underneath. This ability to keep the idea of an object in mind after it disappears from sight is an important milestone in infants' thinking. This means that Dewey could no longer trick Telele by hiding his keys out of her sight in the diaper bag.

In stage 5, *tertiary circular reactions*, between 12 and 18 months, Telele was even more clever. Sometimes, as when she discovered the joy of smearing shaving cream on a bathroom floor, this is a messy stage. Piaget called children this age *active experimenters* and *little scientists*. They demonstrate **tertiary circular reactions**, or the ability to deliberately vary their actions to see the results. Like scientists, babies are trying to learn more about the world and the results of their actions (Piaget, 1952).

In stage 6, *mental combinations*, from about 18 to 24 months, babies can think through their plans and experiments *before* they take action. For instance, right before she turned 2, Telele revealed just how highly motivated she was to eat cookies. She moved quietly into the kitchen, pushed a chair toward the counter, and began "mixing" ingredients into a bowl. She remembered what she had done before and had a plan for getting her cookies. Even though she made a mess, she was showing evidence of **mental representation**—the ability to think things through using internal images rather than needing to act on the environment and the first sign of true intelligence.

Piaget's theory is nearly 100 years old, and research over the decades has refined some of his ideas. Researchers now believe that babies are much more capable than Piaget gave them credit for: that they understand object permanence, for instance, much earlier than he thought (Carey et al., 2015; Rochat, 2018). In addition, Piaget did not write much about the influence of culture and the social world on babies' development (Davis et al., 2021). Now, through observation of babies in different contexts, researchers know that emotional and social cues are critically important for babies' cognitive development. A baby raised in a structured environment and carried much of the time, for instance, will be less of a "little scientist" than one allowed ample unstructured time and the space to practice dropping Cheerios on the floor.

Information Processing

In the decades since Piaget first wrote about children's thinking, many modern researchers have taken an *information-processing approach* to understand how children and adults think. Remember from Chapter 2 that this approach focuses on the

secondary circular reactions The third stage of the sensorimotor period, from about 4 to 8 months, in which babies learn to extend their activities to manipulate the world around them.

object permanence Piaget's term for the understanding that objects continue to exist even when they are out of sight.

tertiary circular reactions Babies' ability to deliberately vary their actions to see the results.

mental representation The ability to think things through using internal images rather than needing to act on the environment.

Building Mental Representation with Grandpa This little girl is learning to love reading and building her mental representations for what books mean with her grandfather at home in New Jersey.

individual components of thought and intelligence as they develop over time. These include *attention*, the process of focusing on the information we take in through our senses; *memory*, how we save this information for later use; and *processing speed*, how quickly we are able to retrieve and use this information.

Paying Attention If you watch a newborn for a few minutes, you might wonder if they ever really pay attention. Over the course of a few minutes, a newborn might look out into space, yawn, cry, and then nurse. Researchers watching how infants suck and where they look have discovered that although newborns' attention may look haphazard, they actually can focus (Hendry et al., 2019). Over their first year, babies get better at paying attention, whether on a toy they are playing with or on the face of someone singing them a lullaby (Abney et al., 2020).

When babies are first born, they struggle to move from looking at one thing to another. Researchers call this *sticky fixation*. Once they start looking at one thing—say, the gently swaying mobile above their crib—it is hard for them to move their attention to something else (Rosander, 2020). By 4 months, as their sight improves, so does their ability to shift their attention. They become able to scan what is in front of them—which makes it easier to, say, pick out a particular toy from a pile. By 9 months, they start to look at things that are interesting, rather than just fixating on whatever is in front of them (Papageorgiou et al., 2014).

One way that babies learn to focus is through coordinated or *joint attention*, the process of focusing on something with someone else (Amso & Lynn, 2017; McQuillan et al., 2020). Joint attention is at work when Dewey shares a book with Telele and they look at the pictures together: Caregivers model and motivate babies to focus by telling a story, pointing to and explaining a new toy, or singing a silly song. This early attention training later helps children focus in school (Blankenship et al., 2019).

 MAKING A DIFFERENCE
Early Screening and Intervention

Just a generation ago, health care professionals often took a "wait and see" approach when families were concerned about differences in their babies' early cognitive development. They suggested that children would "grow out of" any developmental delays and that early interventions would not help (Raspa et al., 2015). But developmental scientists changed that. In the past decade, researchers have shown that dramatic growth happens in infants' thinking and learning in the first years. Health care providers and scientists are now able to identify differences in cognitive development—and intervene early to help when the brain is highly sensitive to environmental input (Zwaigenbaum et al., 2015). Screening for cognitive milestones is now part of standard well-child visits in the United States (Lipkin et al., 2020).

Intervention and screening have particularly benefited children with an increased likelihood of having **autism spectrum disorder (ASD)**, a cognitive and communication disorder that is diagnosed in about 1 in every 54 U.S. children (Maenner et al., 2020; White et al., 2020). Some of the early signs of ASD include lack of eye contact, joint attention, and difficulties engaging in responsive back-and-forth communication, including pointing or talking (APA, 2022; Hyman et al., 2020). Young children with increased likelihood of developing ASD also may be especially reactive to sounds, lights, taste, or touch and may have passionate interests in one type of activity or toy (Smith et al., 2020). Early screening has helped reliably identify children as young as 12 months who may need support (Zwaigenbaum et al., 2021).

Scientific American Profile

How Caregiving Builds Cognitive Skills

© Macmillan. Photo by Sidford House

autism spectrum disorder (ASD) A cognitive and communication disorder characterized by difficulties with communication and social interaction.

Experts believe ASD is linked to genetic and brain anomalies. It is a *spectrum* disorder, which means that children with ASD have variable levels of skills and challenges. Some may require significant support: About 3 in 10 children diagnosed with ASD cannot talk, and about half have intellectual disabilities (Hyman et al., 2020). Others may have more subtle symptoms but also benefit from support, particularly in building relationships and resilience to stigma (Kapp, 2018).

Children and adults with ASD often face challenges in a world that is not open to people who are different and must grapple with inaccurate stereotypes about the disorder (White et al., 2020). Early identification enables children with ASD to receive intervention earlier, boosting their communication skills (Rogers et al., 2019). Interventions also encourage responsive caregiving, acceptance of children's distinctive abilities, and an understanding of the benefits of a neurodiverse world. The goal is not to eliminate the differences between children diagnosed with ASD and their peers, but to help children develop the skills—particularly communication—that will allow them to advocate for themselves and live meaningful lives (Bottema-Beutel et al., 2021; Kapp, 2018). 🌐

Memory Babies may not be able to explain what happened to them last week, but they remember more than you might think. Marjorie tells us that at just 6 months, Telele remembered the pediatrician's office (she cried as soon as she recognized the mobile hanging from the ceiling). It is very likely that she was right.

How do we know what babies remember? First, we react differently to things we remember. Recall from Chapter 3 that **habituation** is a basic form of learning in which you become bored with something if you experience it repeatedly. Researchers use it to observe whether babies notice differences between experiences or objects, called *stimuli*. If babies habituate to one object, they will ignore it and look away. Given a choice of two objects, one they have seen many times and one that is new, they prefer the new one. In this way, researchers can tell whether babies notice the difference between the two. Researchers also examine how long it takes babies to become habituated. Whereas newborns typically need to look at a new stimulus, like the dots in **Figure 4.5**, a few times before they can remember it, 1-year-olds only need to look for 10 seconds before they remember it (Hayne et al., 2015).

Changes in Memory Infants are born with some unique memory strengths: They are very good at remembering people, which helps them learn new skills and processes from their caregivers, from picking up a cup to taking off their diaper. The memory for these skills and processes and the ability to habituate are referred to as **implicit memory**, which is nearly mature by 3 months (Rovee-Collier & Giles, 2010; Vohringer et al., 2018). At the same time, they are lacking in **explicit memory**, which is the memory for names, dates, or details (Amso & Kirkham, 2021).

Some ground-breaking studies have helped researchers understand the strength of babies' early implicit memory and the fragility of their long-term memory (Cuevas & Sheya, 2019; Schneider & Ornstein, 2019). Babies as young as 2 months were introduced to a crib mobile with a ribbon hanging down from it (see **Figure 4.6**). Then researchers tied one of the baby's legs to the mobile so that the baby could move the mobile by moving their leg. After the baby realized the association between the movement of their leg and the movement of the mobile, the researchers untied the ribbon. If the baby continued to try to move the mobile by kicking their leg, the researchers concluded

habituation A basic form of learning in which you become bored with something if you experience it repeatedly.

implicit memory Memory of new skills and processes and ability to habituate.

explicit memory Memory of names, dates, and details.

FIGURE 4.5 Which Dots Speak to You? A researcher in Grenoble, France, watches to see where this newborn is looking. Will they recognize the difference between the shapes shown on the right and the left? This experimental design can help scientists understand how long it will take babies to habituate to a stimuli and what they prefer to look at.

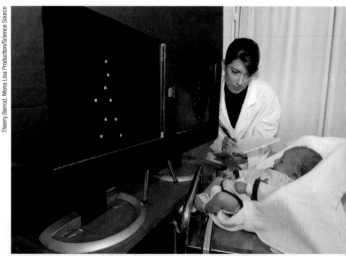

Thierry Berrod, Mona Lisa Production/Science Source

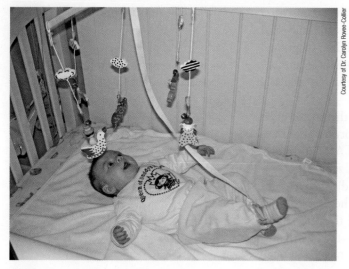

FIGURE 4.6 Scientific Experiments Can Be Fun. Researcher Carolyn Rovee-Collier noticed that her son was happy when he could jiggle the mobile above his crib (as seems to be the case with this baby), allowing her some time to work. She turned this observation into groundbreaking research, demonstrating that babies, like this little girl, have strong procedural memory very early in their lives.

that the baby remembered the procedure. If the baby didn't move their leg at all, researchers concluded that they had forgotten.

The babies studied in this experiment, even those just a few months old, had a tremendous memory for this experience. However, infants' memories were fragile. If something changed in the environment, for example, if the crib was decorated differently or if the room had an unusual smell, babies were likely to forget to kick altogether (Rovee-Collier & Cuevas, 2009).

What Do Babies Know Already?

You might not think that Telele knew very much as a newborn, but some researchers argue that babies are born with a wide range of innate knowledge about how the world works. This **nativist** (or *core knowledge*) **approach** represents the "nature" side of the nature/nurture continuum. For instance, Telele knows that three objects cannot magically become two and that there is a difference between a living being, such as an animal, and an inanimate object, such as a coffee cup (Smith et al., 2020; Tardiff et al., 2020). Using habituation methodologies to observe how babies respond to different possible and "impossible" scenarios, scientists have demonstrated that even newborns understand some basic processes, including:

- *Basic physics.* Not only do babies understand the principle of gravity, that unsupported objects should fall, but they also understand that two objects can't take up the same physical space (Lin et al., 2021).
- *Basic math.* Even newborns seem to have an innate sense that counting can refer to the number of things in a row, and they know when one item disappears from that row (Spelke, 2017).
- *Basic biology.* Babies have some simple ideas about what makes an animal different from an inanimate object; for example, it can move on its own and it is not hollow inside (Tardiff et al., 2020).
- *Basic psychology.* Even infants have a sense that people are more likely to help other people they know or who are part of their same group (Ting et al., 2020). They also assume that in a conflict, bigger players will win over smaller players (Thomsen, 2020).

Does this mean that core knowledge researchers think that babies are ready for college? Not at all. Instead, these scientists ask us to appreciate the tremendous capabilities that infants are born with. Awareness of what babies are born knowing can be used to design interventions that help young children learn (Dillon et al., 2017).

Born to Imitate

Nativist or core knowledge theorists aren't the only developmental scientists who recognize newborn babies' innate genius. More than 40 years ago, when one researcher sat in front of a newborn and stuck out his tongue, he found that, with enough time and patience, the newborn will often respond with a similar facial expression in return (Meltzoff, 2020; Meltzoff & Moore, 1977).

Imitation is another tool that helps infants learn and adjust to the world. Learning how to talk, for example, is much easier if a baby can watch a caregiver's mouth and mimic the same shapes with their own mouth. Understanding that someone else's body is similar to one's own is an essential part of early imitation (Nagy et al., 2020). Although babies may continue to imitate and learn (think about

nativist approach A theoretical perspective that maintains that babies are born knowing a great deal about how the world works. (Also called the *core knowledge approach*.)

how easily a toddler can pick up a "bad" gesture they have seen just once), automatic imitation tends to fade in favor of more active imitation games later in life (Yu & Kushnir, 2020). How strong and robust early imitation is remains controversial, but scientists agree that copying is a crucial part of how children learn (Davis et al., 2021; Slaughter, 2021).

Culture, Context, and Early Cognition

Developmental scientists who study the impact of culture address how much early development is determined by culture and context, rather than by a universal genetic blueprint. They are interested in the "nurture" part of the nature/nurture continuum: Does how a baby is cared for impact how their thinking develops? Many cognitive abilities, like the abilities to learn, talk, imitate, and remember, are experience-expectant: They develop in all children who are given care, nutrition, and stimulation. However, context is also critical. Many early cognitive skills, from how children learn to their attention and memory, are experience-dependent, contingent on the cultural context around them (Arauz et al., 2019; Legare, 2019).

Do As I Do. Newborn babies sometimes imitate caregivers' facial expressions. The drive to copy helps propel infants' early learning.

Even as young as 1 month, babies in some cultures have longer memories and greater attention spans than those in others (Clearfield & Jedd, 2012; Werchan et al., 2019). All babies will learn to pretend and to find hidden objects, but some will do so as much as 18 months earlier than others (Callaghan, 2020; Callaghan et al., 2011). Many of these skills seem to be experience-dependent: Babies receive a lot of early practice in skills valued by their communities and, as a result, perform better at these skills. For instance, toddlers who spend a lot of time talking about the past tend to remember their early experiences longer than other children. This enriched experience builds memory (Hayne et al., 2015).

CONNECTIONS

Remember from Chapter 1 that many theorists, including Lev Vygotsky, emphasize the critical role of culture in how children learn.

How babies learn also depends on what families expect from children. Inspired by Vygotsky, researchers have observed that in many cultures, adults don't spend much time explicitly teaching babies one-on-one (Shneidman et al., 2016a, 2016b). Babies in these cultures learn primarily from watching, overhearing, and even helping with what is going on, called *learning through observation and pitching in* (Rosado-May et al., 2020). Developmentalists have found that babies who live in communities where observational learning is encouraged are better at learning from this teaching style than other children are. Thus, babies learn how to learn in a way that fits their culture (see **Infographic 4.2**.) (Shneidman et al., 2016a).

Early Learning

At age 2, Telele has already learned a great deal. Like many babies, she benefits from lots of enrichment: Telele has been read to and sung to, and is learning four languages. She has doting parents and an extended family who are thrilled to be helping to raise the next generation.

It is challenging for researchers to measure early cognitive skills in babies. A missed nap or a growth spurt can make it difficult to know whether a baby has fallen behind or is just having a bad day (LoBue et al., 2020). However, researchers who have tracked babies' development over time begin to see strengths and challenges in

Learning Through Observation and Pitching In Alondra is helping out her family and learning how to safely peel a mango. Her sister, Susy, is close by, as they prepare a snack at their home in Valladolid, Mexico. Watching what bigger people do is an important way small children learn about the world around them.

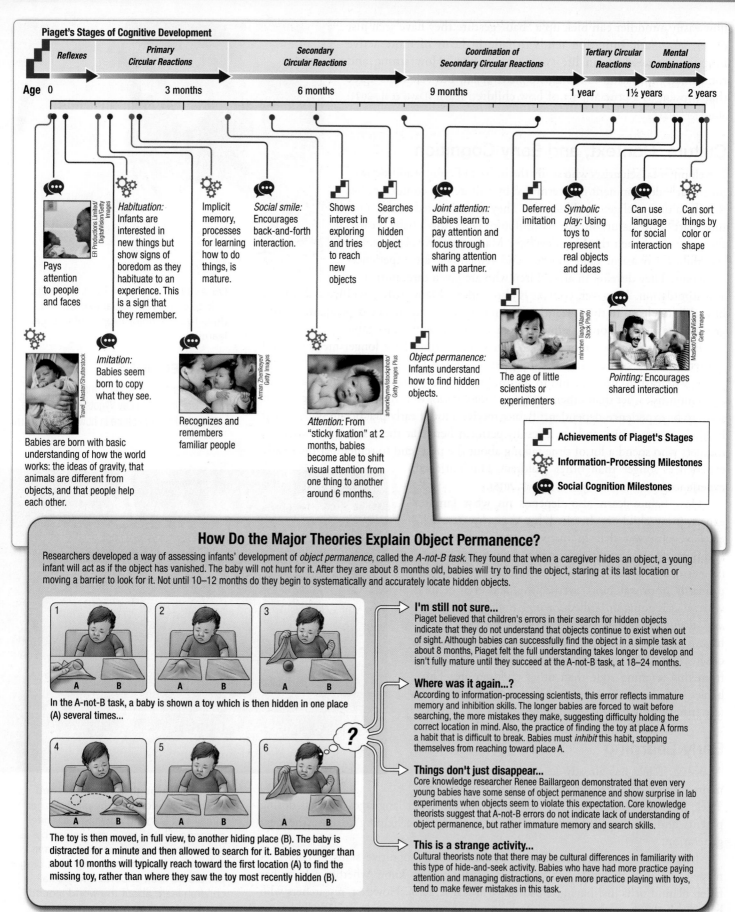

Piaget's Stages of Cognitive Development

Reflexes	Primary Circular Reactions	Secondary Circular Reactions	Coordination of Secondary Circular Reactions	Tertiary Circular Reactions	Mental Combinations

Age: 0 — 3 months — 6 months — 9 months — 1 year — 1½ years — 2 years

Pays attention to people and faces

Babies are born with basic understanding of how the world works: the ideas of gravity, that animals are different from objects, and that people help each other.

Imitation: Babies seem born to copy what they see.

Habituation: Infants are interested in new things but show signs of boredom as they habituate to an experience. This is a sign that they remember.

Implicit memory, processes for learning how to do things, is mature.

Recognizes and remembers familiar people

Social smile: Encourages back-and-forth interaction.

Shows interest in exploring and tries to reach new objects

Attention: From "sticky fixation" at 2 months, babies become able to shift visual attention from one thing to another around 6 months.

Searches for a hidden object

Joint attention: Babies learn to pay attention and focus through sharing attention with a partner.

Object permanence: Infants understand how to find hidden objects.

Deferred imitation

Symbolic play: Using toys to represent real objects and ideas

The age of little scientists or experimenters

Can use language for social interaction

Can sort things by color or shape

Pointing: Encourages shared interaction

Legend:
- ▧ Achievements of Piaget's Stages
- ⚙ Information-Processing Milestones
- 💬 Social Cognition Milestones

How Do the Major Theories Explain Object Permanence?

Researchers developed a way of assessing infants' development of *object permanence*, called the *A-not-B task*. They found that when a caregiver hides an object, a young infant will act as if the object has vanished. The baby will not hunt for it. After they are about 8 months old, babies will try to find the object, staring at its last location or moving a barrier to look for it. Not until 10–12 months do they begin to systematically and accurately locate hidden objects.

In the A-not-B task, a baby is shown a toy which is then hidden in one place (A) several times...

The toy is then moved, in full view, to another hiding place (B). The baby is distracted for a minute and then allowed to search for it. Babies younger than about 10 months will typically reach toward the first location (A) to find the missing toy, rather than where they saw the toy most recently hidden (B).

I'm still not sure...
Piaget believed that children's errors in their search for hidden objects indicate that they do not understand that objects continue to exist when out of sight. Although babies can successfully find the object in a simple task at about 8 months, Piaget felt the full understanding takes longer to develop and isn't fully mature until they succeed at the A-not-B task, at 18–24 months.

Where was it again...?
According to information-processing scientists, this error reflects immature memory and inhibition skills. The longer babies are forced to wait before searching, the more mistakes they make, suggesting difficulty holding the correct location in mind. Also, the practice of finding the toy at place A forms a habit that is difficult to break. Babies must *inhibit* this habit, stopping themselves from reaching toward place A.

Things don't just disappear...
Core knowledge researcher Renee Baillargeon demonstrated that even very young babies have some sense of object permanence and show surprise in lab experiments when objects seem to violate this expectation. Core knowledge theorists suggest that A-not-B errors do not indicate lack of understanding of object permanence, but rather immature memory and search skills.

This is a strange activity...
Cultural theorists note that there may be cultural differences in familiarity with this type of hide-and-seek activity. Babies who have had more practice paying attention and managing distractions, or even more practice playing with toys, tend to make fewer mistakes in this task.

Information from Baillargeon, 1987; Brace et al., 2006; Diamond, 1985; Lipina et al., 2005; Marcovitch et al., 2016; Marcovitch & Zelazo, 1999; Piaget, 1954.

infants' cognitive skills even before they turn 2 (Betancourt et al., 2016; Johnson et al., 2016). What builds a baby's cognitive skills?

- *Good health.* As already explained, adequate nutrition before and after birth is essential for early brain development. Lack of iron or exposure to toxins, even in babies with good health, can cause delays and challenges in cognitive development (Georgieff et al., 2018; Valentine, 2020).
- *Attention.* Babies benefit from shared, joint attention from caregivers. Whether Telele is pointing at a bird on the feeder, watching her mother unpeel a banana, or drawing with her parents, eye contact and shared attention help babies learn to focus (Brandes-Aitken et al., 2019; Suarez-Rivera et al., 2019).
- *Responsive caregiving.* Caregivers who respond to vocalizations, movements, and gazes are encouraging their babies to explore, communicate, and learn from them. Back-and-forth, or *contingent*, interactions, where babies and caregivers share a toy, a conversation, or a clapping game, are critical to early cognitive development (King et al., 2019; McCormick et al., 2020; Rosen et al., 2020).

Around the world, nearly one in three children is at risk for cognitive delays or disabilities that begin in infancy (McCann et al., 2020). The major cause is poor health, often due to malnutrition or chronic diseases like malaria (Black et al., 2020; French et al., 2020). In affluent countries like the United States, cognitive challenges are more frequently caused by neglect and adversity. Researchers have various measures for the number of *adverse experiences* a family faces during infancy, like the loss of a primary caregiver, violence, living with a family member with a serious mental health or substance use disorder, discrimination, or food or housing insecurity (Felitti et al., 1998; Hodel, 2018). The more adverse experiences an infant's family faces without enough support, the more likely the baby is to have cognitive consequences (Luby et al., 2020).

In the United States, about one in three young children has experienced at least one adverse experience, and one in five lives in a family with low income (ACS, 2020; Crouch et al., 2019). Caregivers who are stressed may have less time to give infants the attention they need. Exposure to too many stress hormones can disrupt brain development, and neglect, leading to a lack of early stimulation, can cause critical neural pathways to be pruned instead of grown (Amso & Lynn, 2017). Early difficulties often stem from systemic issues in the community, rather than problems in an individual family (Shonkoff et al., 2021). Adversity is a risk factor, not a prediction: Millions of babies whose families experience poverty, trauma, or stress do not have cognitive delays (Noble & Giebler, 2020).

Approaches to Boost Cognitive Development

Around the world, many early interventions to promote children's development focus on taking care of families' basic needs and well-being, such as making sure adults have access to parental leave, health care, and basic financial resources (Clark et al., 2020; Richter et al., 2017). Programs also focus on enhancing caregiving, so that parents, grandparents, and even older siblings can have responsive interactions with babies (Cuartas et al., 2020). Home-visiting programs, such as the Nurse–Family Partnership and ChildFirst, have shown to be effective in fostering children's early cognitive development and caregivers' well-being (Heckman et al., 2017; Molloy et al., 2021).

Another way of supporting and advancing cognitive development in young children is to make sure that they receive high-quality care outside of the home (Burchinal & Farran, 2020). High-quality child care typically has a lower ratio of children to caregivers, who have an academic background in child development and

How Does It Work? Exploring a toy in this child care center in Tupelo, Mississippi, involves trial-and-error and engaging conversation. A caregiver's responsive, back-and-forth interactions with these toddlers will help them grow.

provide responsive, developmentally appropriate care. Early Head Start and Educare, a public-private partnership program, have both been shown to provide high-quality, center-based child care (Yazejian et al., 2017).

Unfortunately, these programs are not accessible to all families: For example, Early Head Start serves fewer than half of all eligible children due to inadequate funding (NASEM, 2018). During the COVID-19 pandemic, even fewer toddlers were able to access quality out-of-home care, as many programs shut down around the world (Gilliam et al., 2021). One sign of poor-quality early child care is if babies and toddlers spend time in front of a screen or if caregivers are particularly stressed (Blasberg et al., 2019; Hewitt et al., 2018; Reid et al., 2021).

SCIENCE IN PRACTICE
Shoneice Sconyers, BSW, MS, Family Resource Partner

Shoneice describes herself as a "connector," someone who brings people together. She uses these skills and her graduate degree in social work to get help for children and families in need. One of the things that hurts young children's developing cognitive skills is trauma, which can result from homelessness, having a caregiver with a mental illness, or having a serious illness of their own. Trauma can keep families from back-and-forth communication with children, and young children's language and cognitive development may suffer as a result.

Shoneice has years of training and coursework but she describes her job is to be a "fairy godmother" who keeps connections strong. If parents, grandparents, or community have let a child down, her job is to help them pick themselves back up. Filling in the gaps was often difficult in the middle of a global pandemic that turned home visits into video calls, but she knows what she does is important. It is more difficult for caregivers to function if they are under strain, and programs like Shoneice's have been shown to encourage more back-and-forth between toddlers and their caregivers, which continues even after the intervention services are over (LoRe et al., 2018). Shoneice says she loves the work which "lights her up on the inside."

Keeping Screens Out of Strollers

Screens are popular with families of small children, but pediatricians and developmental scientists have found that babies do not benefit from and may even be harmed by too much exposure to screen media (AAP, 2016; WHO, 2019). For instance, the American Academy of Pediatrics (AAP) advises that babies not watch any video or screens at all until 18 months of age, and that older babies be limited to an hour a day viewed with an adult.

Developmental scientists suggest that time spent in front of a screen is time when babies are not doing things that are proven to help them develop. Infants and toddlers on screens are not engaging in responsive interaction, playing, or sleeping—activities that spur their social, cognitive, and emotional development (Madigan et al., 2020; Willumsen & Bull, 2020).

Despite these recommendations, many babies are exposed to more than six hours of background television and are actively watching screens for more than three hours a day (Barr et al., 2020; Chen & Adler, 2019; NSCH, 2021). The amount of screen time for babies increased dramatically during the recent pandemic (Monteiro et al., 2021). Caregivers often use media to keep children occupied, allowing them to play a smartphone game or watch a video while a parent is on a Zoom call or washing dishes (Chen & Adler, 2019;

Rideout, 2013). Babies are quieter and less disruptive when they are in front of a screen, but that helps the caregivers, not the infant.

Many caregivers, perhaps influenced by claims of the educational value of videos or apps, believe that media can accelerate cognitive development. Researchers have come to the opposite conclusion: Screens do not offer the critical back-and-forth, contingent interaction that babies need in order to learn (Li et al., 2017). However, babies interacting with real people through real-time video, such as a Zoom or Face-Time call, *do* pick up new words and information. As a result, developmentalists and pediatricians conclude that there is some benefit to infants who engage in video chats because they involve a responsive give-and-take (Strouse et al., 2018).

APPLY IT! **4.9** How would Piaget explain why Telele methodically drops pieces of pear from her highchair and watches them fall?

4.10 How does Telele's memory help her learn how to pet a dog, beat a drum, and eat with a spoon, but make it difficult to memorize the alphabet?

4.11 How does the development of object permanence explain why Telele got better at searching for lost toys when she entered toddlerhood?

4.12 Telele's parents are planning to send her to early child care. What qualities would you suggest they look for in a caregiver or child-care center?

4.13 What would you tell Dewey and Marjorie about the relationship between screen media and toddlers' cognitive development?

Language Development

At age 2, Telele can now point, talk, and complain. She can ask for pears instead of cheese with dinner at 13 months and tattle on her cousin at 24 months. By age 2, babies are able to understand language at about 150 words per minute and respond in a conversation in about 200 milliseconds (Chater et al., 2016). Language is not only the words you say or read; it is a complex, rule-based system for using symbols to communicate. These symbols include spoken words, gestures, shrugs, facial expressions, finger signs, and even emojis.

Learning Objective

4.7 Describe the typical pattern of language development in the first two years.

Steps to Talking and Understanding

Babies communicate from the moment they are born, beginning with the cry that reassures everyone in the room that they survived childbirth. They soon begin to make other noises, such as grunts, growls, and squeals. These noises begin to get happier over the first few months, with laughter appearing at about 3 months, and become easier to interpret as contented or fussy expressions (Oller et al., 2019).

At the same time, babies are listening. Infants can understand language long before they are able to produce it, perhaps because they get more practice listening than they do speaking (Chater et al., 2016). By 5 months, they can recognize a few words, such as their name (Holzen & Nazzi, 2020). At about 6 months, they can associate words with a wide variety of things (see **Figure 4.7**).

One challenge from a baby's perspective is that there are so many words and so many things they could refer to. Researchers tracking babies' eyes have observed that they use cues such as gesture, shared attention, eye gaze, and even intonation to learn what people are talking about (Smith et al., 2018). Babies even use statistics: They notice combinations of sounds that are common. Statistics also help them figure out which parts of words are frequently repeated, like endings (*-ed*, *-ing*, or *-s* in English) and function words (*of*, *to*, and *that* in English) (Saffran, 2020).

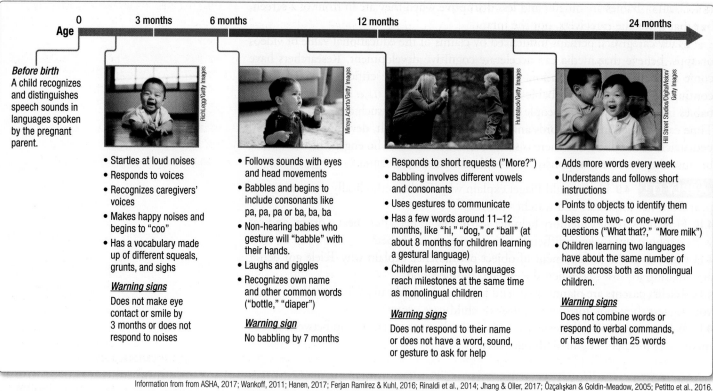

Age	0	3 months	6 months	12 months	24 months

Before birth
A child recognizes and distinguishes speech sounds in languages spoken by the pregnant parent.

- Startles at loud noises
- Responds to voices
- Recognizes caregivers' voices
- Makes happy noises and begins to "coo"
- Has a vocabulary made up of different squeals, grunts, and sighs

Warning signs
Does not make eye contact or smile by 3 months or does not respond to noises

- Follows sounds with eyes and head movements
- Babbles and begins to include consonants like pa, pa, pa or ba, ba, ba
- Non-hearing babies who gesture will "babble" with their hands.
- Laughs and giggles
- Recognizes own name and other common words ("bottle," "diaper")

Warning sign
No babbling by 7 months

- Responds to short requests ("More?")
- Babbling involves different vowels and consonants
- Uses gestures to communicate
- Has a few words around 11–12 months, like "hi," "dog," or "ball" (at about 8 months for children learning a gestural language)
- Children learning two languages reach milestones at the same time as monolingual children

Warning signs
Does not respond to their name or does not have a word, sound, or gesture to ask for help

- Adds more words every week
- Understands and follows short instructions
- Points to objects to identify them
- Uses some two- or one-word questions ("What that?," "More milk")
- Children learning two languages have about the same number of words across both as monolingual children.

Warning signs
Does not combine words or respond to verbal commands, or has fewer than 25 words

Information from from ASHA, 2017; Wankoff, 2011; Hanen, 2017; Ferjan Ramírez & Kuhl, 2016; Rinaldi et al., 2014; Jhang & Oller, 2017; Özçalışkan & Goldin-Meadow, 2005; Petitto et al., 2016.

FIGURE 4.7 Highlights of Language Development Language skills help infants learn and build relationships. There are many variations in how children learn to understand and produce language, but most children follow a predicable sequence. Children whose development is not quite typical may need some extra support.

The World from a Baby's Perspective
How does this baby know that his caregiver is talking about the oatmeal in the bowl? Researchers believe that babies use social cues, shared attention, and statistics. Frequently used words are more likely to be associated with frequently used objects. For instance, in this photo, "spoon" more likely refers to what the baby is grabbing.

babbling Short, repetitive, syllable sounds, like ba-ba-ba or pa-pa-pa (in English), that begin at about 4 months and become more speechlike by 7 months.

fast-mapping A child's ability to quickly learn new words.

At about 5 months, infants can predictably produce sounds. In the next few months, they begin to experiment with short sounds that sound more like language (Cychosz et al., 2020). These short, repetitive, syllable sounds, like ba-ba-ba or pa-pa-pa (in English), are called **babbling**. Babbling begins at about 4 months and becomes more and more speechlike by 7 months, as combinations of consonants and vowels are produced and reproduced. Babies around the world typically babble regardless of whether they are raised by talkative families or in quieter homes, whether they are babbling in speech or in gestural languages, like American Sign Language (Flaherty et al., 2021; Petitto & Marentette, 1991).

No matter where they are born, babies usually begin to produce their first words around the time of their first birthdays (MacWhinney, 2017). Babies who use gestural languages sign their first words a few months earlier (Ozcaliskan & Goldin-Meadow, 2005). Around the world, caregivers report that babies' first words are about them: words like *Mama* (in English and Spanish) or *Baba* (*father* in Arabic and Marathi) (Ferguson, 1964). *Mama* and *Dada* are usually followed by other early words like *hi*, *bye*, *more*, and *no*, reminding us that toddlers use words socially (Frank et al., 2021). Telele's first word was *bath*.

While babies' vocabularies are building, their language acquisition varies dramatically (Dick et al., 2016). Some babies will show a vocabulary "burst," but others may show a slow-and-steady rise with many typical variations (Werker, 2018). By age 2, children typically produce between 75 and 225 words but understand many more (Rescorla, 2019).

By 18 months, they can learn new words almost instantaneously. For instance, if you offer a toddler a kumquat, saying: "Here, try a kumquat," they will immediately understand that the word "kumquat" refers to the tiny orange fruit in your hand (Weatherhead et al., 2021). This ability to quickly learn new words is called **fast-mapping**

(Byers-Heinlein et al., 2018; Carey, 1978, 2010). Fast-mapping increases babies' vocabularies exponentially, which is why people who spend a lot of time with small children must watch what words they are using. Babies can just as easily fast-map that word you used to describe a bad driver as the name for a zoo animal.

This rapid vocabulary development can mean being overly rigid about what words refer to, in errors of **overextension** or **underextension**. A toddler who is overextending might assume that a specific term relates to a larger category, such as insisting that all birds are called pigeons. A toddler who is underextending might insist that the word *cat* only applies to their pet and never to the neighbors' cat. These errors will generally be corrected naturally as children use them in give-and-take conversations with others.

What Helps Babies Learn to Talk?

Babies all over the world learn to communicate in one or more of 6,000 languages. How many words they learn and how fluently they use them depends on how much early language they practice. Just like learning to walk or ride a bike, learning to talk takes work. Babies who hear and use a lot of language develop larger vocabularies, which seems to help children do well later in school (Ramírez et al., 2020).

Many adults use high-pitched, sing-songy tones and simple sentences when they talk to infants, which scholars call **infant-directed speech (IDS)**. Infant-directed speech helps babies pick out a single word in a mass of sounds and helps them focus (Byers-Heinlein et al., 2021). IDS does not have to be high-pitched baby talk; its key characteristic is a responsive give-and-take, even if the child may not respond in full sentences or can only coo (Masek et al., 2021).

In many communities, adults don't speak directly to babies and toddlers very often. For instance, adults in Polynesia and Samoa believe that small children shouldn't be spoken to until they begin to speak. The idea, as one scientist explains, is that the "child has to adapt . . . rather than the other way around" (Stoll & Lieven, 2014, p. 26). Rather than talking, families may rock, touch, or bounce their infants to entertain them. Despite this lack of early language exposure, babies in these cultures learn to talk at about the same age as babies in other places (Shneidman & Goldin-Meadow, 2012). However, the more babies are directly spoken to, the larger their vocabularies (Lopez et al., 2020; Madigan et al., 2019). The more responsive caregivers are to their babies' attempts to communicate, often called "bids" for attention, the more verbal their babies will become (Anderson et al., 2021).

Within the United States, the amount of talk babies hear—and how verbally responsive their caregivers are—varies dramatically. Research that uses voice-activated recorders has shown that some families speak to their children as much as 20 times more than others (Bergelson et al., 2019; Hart & Risley, 1995). The more language a baby hears, the larger their vocabulary, language understanding, and even their scores on cognitive development tests (Madigan et al., 2019). Does this mean that caregivers are to blame if their children do not meet the expectations for language development? Some have suggested that identifying the differences in language exposure may stigmatize toddlers who have limited vocabulary (Adair et al., 2017; Williams, 2020). Others point out that families' interactions with their babies may reflect systemic marginalization and stress rather than cultural choices (Golinkoff et al., 2019).

Theories of Language Development

For many researchers, understanding how language develops comes down to a question of the environment, or nurture, versus genes, or nature (Chomsky, 1957; Friederici et al., 2017). On one side of the debate are scholars who

overextension An error in which a child assumes that a specific term relates to a larger category.

underextension An error in which a child insists that a word only applies to a specific member of the group, rather than the whole group itself.

infant-directed speech (IDS) Adults' use of high-pitched, sing-songy tones and simple sentences when they talk to infants.

📱 Share It!

Did masks affect language development? Some researchers found that babies were able to learn new words from people who wore traditional, opaque masks but had trouble learning from people who wore clear masks. Researchers suspected that the relatively unusual clear masks made it hard for babies to focus.

(Singh et al., 2021)

📰 Scientific American: Lifespan Development

Do They Mean to Be Rude? Babies learn about the world by pointing, interacting, and playing peek-a-boo with Dad.

CONNECTIONS

Remember from Chapter 2 that behaviorism focuses on measuring what we do. Behaviorist researchers like B. F. Skinner explained that language development was shaped through operant conditioning. Social learning theorists suggest learning comes from observing and imitation.

Scientific American Profile

How Multilingualism Boosts Cognition

 Learn It Together

Reflect on Multilingual Development

Plan Analyze the benefits of multilingual language development.

Engage Divide into groups and share personal experiences or reflections from Telele's story about the cultural and cognitive benefits and potential challenges of multilingual development.

Practice Connect personal experience with research on multilingual development. Practice your skills in scientific communication.

Reflect How does your personal experience help support or challenge what you've learned about the research on multilingual development?

universal grammar A child's inborn ability to recognize and use grammar.

emergentist Scholars who argue that humans' drive to communicate and imitate and ability to recognize patterns, rather than brain processes specifically devoted to language, created the uniquely human ability to use language. (Also called *constructivist.*)

believe that all humans are genetically programmed to develop language (Berwick & Chomsky, 2017). In particular, these researchers point to babies' unique ability to recognize grammatical rules without being taught them (Pinker, 1984). These *nativist* scholars, who follow the theoretical approach we discussed earlier in this chapter, call this inborn ability **universal grammar** (MacWhinney, 2017). They note that all world languages have grammar and argue that the infant brain is programmed to pay attention to grammar in the language they hear.

In the other camp are those who suggest that language is not a unique cognitive process but rather is another skill that emerged as the human brain developed to allow us to think and relate to others (Bohn et al., 2019). These **emergentist**, or *constructivist*, scholars argue that human abilities to recognize patterns and the drive to communicate and imitate, rather than brain processes specifically devoted to language, created the uniquely human ability to use language. Similarly, learning theories like *behaviorism* and *social learning theory* apply their basic concepts of conditioning and imitation to language development. These theorists would argue that infants' early vocalizations are rewarded with praise and attention, and that children observe and imitate the language models around them.

As brain and behavioral research has expanded, most developmental scientists today adopt something close to the emergentist position. They recognize that language has both genetic *and* environmental influences. Most focus on the connections between language and other types of learning and communication. Although the complexity of language is different from other cognitive skills, it builds on many other forms of communication and thinking that toddlers demonstrate, such as their ability to imitate, think symbolically, and remember.

The Multilingual Advantage

Growing up speaking more than one language is the norm for most people around the world (Ramírez & Kuhl, 2016). In the United States, about one in five children speaks a second language (ACS, 2018).

Children raised in multilingual homes have a host of benefits. Switching from one language to another can improve attention and communication skills and builds executive function (Antoniou, 2019). For instance, babies exposed to two languages have to remember whether Grandma says "cat" or "gato" like Mom, so they must use their attention and perspective-taking skills a little more every day. These benefits can last a lifetime (Bialystok, 2020).

Multilingual infants reach their early language development milestones, like babbling and first words, at about the same time as children exposed to only one language (Petitto et al., 2001). However, they tend to lag behind monolingual children in developing vocabularies and more sophisticated grammar in each individual language (Höhle et al., 2020). Children who are learning two or more languages are typically exposed to fewer words in each language, so although their combined vocabulary in both languages may be the same as that of monolingual children, their vocabulary in each separate language tends to be smaller (Lauro et al., 2020). Multilingual children may not catch up to monolingual children until they are about 10 (Hoff & Core, 2015).

What does this mean for Telele? Being fluent in multiple languages is not her only advantage. Like all multilingual children, she will likely demonstrate more advanced executive function than monolingual children her age. In addition, it will create a sense of identity and belonging to her community (Lynch, 2018). Language helps connect Telele and her parents to their ancestors, their land, and the sacred knowledge of their community. As Dewey and Marjorie explain, every word they teach Telele reminds them that language is "a connection to culture and a guidebook to survival," a way to "give Telele strength and a sense of who she is."

APPLY IT! **4.14** A friend of Marjorie's is worried that her 18-month-old makes mistakes when she speaks. For instance, she sometimes calls cats in their neighborhood "Twinkles"—the name of her pet cat. What should Marjorie say to reassure her about her daughter's development?

4.15 Telele already speaks four languages at home with her family. What would you tell her parents about the strengths and possible challenges for multilingual toddlers?

Wrapping It Up ⦾⦾

LO 4.1 Explain factors promoting healthy patterns of growth and development during the first two years. (p. 102)

Infants grow more rapidly than at any other point in the life-span, and their health is more fragile. Infant mortality remains high around the world and is distributed inequitably. Healthy nutrition, ideally including human milk, helps set the stage for a lifetime of health. Adequate sleep, access to health care, and vaccination also help babies thrive.

LO 4.2 Explain the role of neurons and synapses in brain function during the first two years. (p. 110)

The brain doubles in volume and adds *synapses*, or connections between neurons, during the first two years. Communication in the brain is faster as a result of myelination. Pruning of underused neural connections helps make brain circuits more efficient. The brain develops in response to experience, adding synapses and myelin to regions of the brain that are frequently activated. The brain is *plastic*, or flexible, in responding to the environment, but there are limits to its ability to bounce back from traumas.

LO 4.3 Describe vision and hearing development in infancy. (p. 114)

Infants are born with a preference for faces, and their vision develops rapidly in the first years, allowing them to shift their focus and perceive details. Babies' hearing is also improving but is attuned to voices and speech. Perceptual narrowing describes how babies' senses gradually specialize in the sights and sounds they are exposed to most frequently.

LO 4.4 Explain how the typical maturation of movement changes a baby's experience of the world. (p. 114)

Babies develop independent control of their gross and fine motor systems. They tend to learn to move their bodies in a *cephalocaudal*, or head-downward pattern, as they develop the ability to move their heads. They also learn to control their core first, in what is called *proximodistal development*. It takes practice for babies to learn how to move, and it often requires readjustment of how they see the world.

LO 4.5 Explain maturation in sensorimotor thinking, attention, and memory during infancy and toddlerhood. (p. 119)

Piaget called infancy and toddlerhood the sensorimotor period, which is divided into six stages: reflexes, primary circular reactions, secondary circular reactions, coordination of secondary circular reactions, tertiary circular reactions, and mental combinations. Infants develop object permanence and can mentally represent the results of their actions. Information-processing researchers look at the components of cognition, such as attention and memory. Babies learn from others through joint attention. Babies have strong implicit memory (memory for how to do something), but weaker explicit memory (memory for facts). Core knowledge, or nativist, theorists focus on the knowledge babies are born with. Cultural theorists study how cultural expectations and caregiving change how babies think and learn.

LO 4.6 Describe the factors influencing learning during the first two years. (p. 119)

The first two years are a time of rapidly building skills. Learning depends on good health, attention from caregivers, and responsive back-and-forth stimulation. Interventions can help families build stronger, responsive relationships. Experts agree that screens and apps do not help babies learn in the first few years and take time away from more important interactions.

LO 4.7 Describe the typical pattern of language development in the first two years. (p. 129)

Babies are born attuned to language, which can include spoken words, gestures, and facial expressions. Communication typically develops through stages, from babbling, to telegraphic speech, to complex speech. Toddlers typically learn words quickly through fast-mapping and usually speak 200 words by age 2, but they understand many more. Nativist theorists suggest that language development is a unique human ability distinguished by a universal grammar. Emergentist scholars suggest that language development is more closely connected to other cognitive skills. Responsive caregiving and infant-directed speech (IDS), help build language skills. Multilingual and bilingual children tend to have stronger executive function and self-control but take longer to build their vocabularies.

KEY TERMS

malnutrition (p. 102)
wasting (p. 102)
percentile (p. 102)
stunting (p. 102)
intervention (p. 103)
overweight (p. 104)
immunization (p. 108)
circadian rhythm (p. 108)
sudden unexpected infant
    deaths (SUID) (p. 109)
axon (p. 112)
dendrite (p. 112)
synaptogenesis (p. 112)
synaptic pruning (p. 112)

myelination (p. 112)
myelin (p. 112)
experience-expectant brain
    development (p. 112)
experience-dependent
    brain development (p. 113)
preferential looking
    technique (p. 115)
perceptual narrowing,
    (p. 115)
motor development (p. 116)
gross motor development
    (p. 116)
fine motor development
    (p. 116)

cephalocaudal (p. 117)
proximodistal principle
    (p. 117)
affordance (p. 118)
visual cliff (p. 119)
sensorimotor (p. 119)
primary circular reactions
    (p. 119)
secondary circular reactions
    (p. 121)
object permanence (p. 121)
tertiary circular reactions
    (p. 121)
mental representation
    (p. 121)

autism spectrum disorder
    (ASD) (p. 122)
habituation (p. 123)
implicit memory (p. 123)
explicit memory (p. 123)
nativist approach (p. 124)
babbling (p. 130)
fast-mapping (p. 130)
overextension (p. 131)
underextension (p. 131)
infant-directed speech (IDS)
    (p. 131)
universal grammar (p. 132)
emergentist (p. 132)

CHECK YOUR LEARNING

1. Why is it important to identify which babies may be at risk for malnutrition in early life?
   a) To check for early evidence of eating disorders
   b) To make sure their bodies are getting the nutrition they need to build their brain
   c) To see if they are eating too much
   d) To evaluate their appetite

2. What is the major cause of infant mortality in the United States and around the globe?
   a) Complications from birth and prenatal development
   b) HIV/AIDS
   c) Malnutrition
   d) Sleep injury

3. How is infant sleep different from adult sleep?
   a) Infants' brain development and memory consolidation happen at night.
   b) Infants require assistance to get back to sleep.
   c) Infants often wake up between sleep cycles.
   d) Missing sleep affects infants' mood.

4. Which of these processes is unique to infancy?
   a) The volume of the brain increases dramatically.
   b) Myelin helps to speed neural communication.
   c) Synapses that are unused are pruned away.
   d) New synaptic connections are created.

5. How does practice change babies' progress with motor development?
   a) More practice usually helps infants learn more quickly.
   b) The timing of motor milestones is entirely genetic, so practice does not matter.
   c) Practice is overwhelming to infants and is not safe.
   d) Practice destroys babies' motivation to move.

6. How does responding to infants or interacting with them influence their cognitive development?
   a) Infants do best without too much outside stimulation.
   b) Infants benefit from regular stimulation in most contexts.
   c) Infants' cognitive development is entirely genetic.
   d) Infants are easily stressed by extra attention.

7. When do infants begin to respond to language and communication?
   a) At 12 months
   b) At 3 months
   c) At birth
   d) At 6 months

8. Piaget developed his theories based on close observation of his three children. This is the case study method. How did this method help Piaget develop his breakthrough ideas? Can you explain some of the limitations of this method?

9. How might culture impact toddlers' thinking? Use examples from language development and information processing.

10. Some isolated children with profound hearing impairment in Nicaragua developed their own sign language when they were grouped together in a school with no other way to communicate. Scholars rushed to Nicaragua to study the children, communicate with them, and learn their language. Can you explain what nativist or universal grammar theorists would expect to find in these children?

Social and Emotional Development in Infancy and Toddlerhood

©Macmillan, Photo by Sidford House

Theories of Early Emotional, Personality, and Social Development

5.1 Compare and contrast the traditional theories of emotional development.

5.2 Assess the roles of culture and context in emotional development.

Emotional Development

5.3 Describe infants' and toddlers' emotional maturation.

Personality and Temperament in the Early Years

5.4 Explain how babies begin to develop unique personalities.

Family Relationships

5.5 Describe how caregiving impacts emotional development.

5.6 Explain common variations in caregiver–child attachment relationships.

Child Care and Media in Infancy

5.7 Explain the impact of experiences outside the family on infants' emotional development.

Selected Resources from

Activities

Concept Practice: Attachment

Spotlight on Science: How Did Animals Help Scientists Learn About Attachment?

Assessments

LearningCurve

Practice Quiz

Videos

Scientific American Profiles

Ainsworth and the Strange Situation

Still-Face Experiment with Edward Tronick

Makena started out as a calm and quiet baby. She didn't cry; she just squeaked. Her parents, Stephanie and Jen, thought that meant she was going to be shy, the opposite of her older sister, Maya, an outgoing 3-year-old. Stephanie and Jen didn't mind the quiet: They were balancing two jobs and two children, so an easy baby was a bonus.

Stephanie and Jen's two girls started out differently: Both were adopted, but while Maya's biological mother was outgoing and resolved about adoption, Makena's biological mother was heartbroken and conflicted about placing her daughter for adoption. Makena was quiet. Maya was loud.

But six months later, something had changed in Makena: That quiet infant had become a spunky, enthusiastic toddler. Makena is now a curious, adventurous explorer, happy to take on her sister in a tussle over sharing blocks or to dance and scream at the top of her lungs. She is capable of loud, high-energy romps around the house and also of kindness: If one of her mothers looks sad, Makena is the first to rush over with an empathetic hug and a close inspection of how she is really feeling.

As Makena grows up, Stephanie and Jen wonder which parts of her will be linked to her biological parents, prenatal experiences, and first stressful days of life, and which parts will be linked to their family. Was Makena quiet as a newborn because her biological mother was sad and worried? Would she be protected by her new parents' warm and consistent parenting? Did Makena turn out loud and mischievous because, as Jen suggests, it was the only way she could get noticed

Scientific American Profile

▶

Meet Makena

around her outgoing sister, Maya? Or is it typical for children to become more outgoing as they grow?

In this chapter, you will read that the important achievements during the first years of life go beyond walking and talking. Emotional development, which includes learning to manage strong feelings and to trust other people, is also crucial. You will also see how infants' first relationships and inborn tendencies shape their personality and emotion regulation, and how developmental science helps explain Makena's new exuberance as well as her kindness. It can be hard to tell what a young child is feeling, but developmental science helps us understand those squeals of joy—and the bouts of tears—a little better.

Theories of Early Emotional, Personality, and Social Development

Learning Objectives

5.1 Compare and contrast the traditional theories of emotional development.

5.2 Assess the roles of culture and context in emotional development.

When Jen and Stephanie talk about how they raised Makena and how she has developed, their experiences are shaped by their own upbringings and by Jen's expertise as a social worker. Informed by their own *ethnotheories* about the importance of close early bonding to development, they spent hours holding newborn Makena after they first met her in the hospital. They moved together as a family ("like a herd of sheep") from room to room.

Adults around the world have different ideas about what drives the early social and emotional development of babies. Many, like Jen and Stephanie, believe that babies do best when they are showered with attention. Others might believe that toddlers are more like "stubborn mules" who should be dealt with strictly, because they will be spoiled if adults are too responsive (Pearl & Pearl, 2015).

Developmental science is strongly influenced by classic theories, such as those of Erikson and Freud, which established that the first years lay a critical framework for the life that follows. Contemporary approaches, influenced by breakthroughs in genetics and neuroscience, remind us that the impact of the first years is not the same for every infant. Some babies may be especially vulnerable, or they may be particularly resilient like Makena, who is thriving.

Traditional Theories

More than a hundred years ago, popular U.S. parenting experts advised caregivers to be strict with their children (Magai & McFadden, 1995). They recommended that babies not be held, because too much touch would turn them into "little tyrants" (Fullerton, 1911, p. 189). Other experts, like behavioral psychologist John Watson, suggested that adults "never hug and kiss" their little ones (Watson, 1928, p. 81). Psychodynamic theorists, like Sigmund Freud and, later, Erik Erikson, helped upend these traditions. They argued that children were different from adults. They also believed that the social relationships formed in a baby's first years help set the stage for their future relationships and personality.

The Legacy of Freud Sigmund Freud raised his six children in the emotionally frigid way recommended by the experts of his community. When the family met, Freud did not greet anyone with affection. As his granddaughter later recalled, "You did not hug" (Sophie Freud qtd. in Grubin, 2002). Ironically, this old-fashioned father radically changed people's cold child-rearing traditions and views.

Freud believed that many psychological challenges in adulthood stemmed from unresolved childhood issues, such as weaning or toilet training (Freud, 1977).

TABLE 5.1 Erikson's Stages of Psychosocial Development in Infancy and Toddlerhood

Stage	Age	Characteristics
Trust versus mistrust	Birth to 18 months	In their first year, children who have responsive caregivers learn to trust the world around them. Those who have unresponsive caregivers start to doubt that their needs will be met.
Autonomy versus shame and doubt	18 months to 3 years	At this age, children are more capable and begin to assert their *autonomy*. If caregivers respond sensitively to their attempts at independence, children develop an awareness that they can take care of themselves. If caregivers cast doubt on those attempts, children may feel ashamed and lack self-control and confidence in their ability to care for themselves.

Remember from Chapter 2 that he believed that development progressed through stages related to the mastery of a basic biological urge. During early development, babies pass through the *oral stage* and the *anal stage*. They learn how to manage the pleasure they receive from sucking, and also self-control from learning how to control their bladder and anus.

Most of Freud's stage theory has been discredited: Contemporary scholars no longer connect toilet training to later personality development (Crews, 2018). Remember from Chapter 2 that scholars also question Freud's methods of studying children, which were primarily based on his observations of adults who were remembering their childhoods. However, Freud's ideas influenced Erik Erikson, who designed his own stage theory of development that remains relevant for many who work with children today.

Erikson's Stages Erikson's developmental theory is based on the idea that all human beings develop through a series of psychological crises (see Chapter 2). In contrast to Freud, who observed stages based on biological maturation, Erikson believed that both biology and cultural expectations shape the crises in each stage.

According to Erikson, the first major crisis of development, **trust versus mistrust**, occurs during the first 18 months of life. In a successful resolution of this stage, babies learn that the world is safe and reliable. This happens when babies are nurtured responsively, and they know that they will be cared for. This trust helps babies grow into adults who feel safe in their place in the world (Erikson, 1993, 1994).

The next crisis, **autonomy versus shame and doubt**, occurs during the toddler years. Erikson keenly appreciated the reality of young children who are not always able, or motivated, to follow the rules of the world. Young children frequently change their minds, demand to "do it themselves," and defy limits, which is why he called raising toddlers "guerrilla warfare" (Erikson, 1959, p. 66). Toddlers are building the skills to direct their own behaviors: to move around or reach for a favorite toy. Erikson believed that caregivers must sensitively manage children's early attempts at independence (autonomy), like allowing their messy attempts to feed themselves, or they will feel a sense of shame and doubt that could last a lifetime (Erikson, 1993). Erikson predicted that children who can accept the limits of the adult world without feeling ashamed of their own failures will grow up healthiest (see **Table 5.1**).

The Impact of Culture

The basic emotions of distress, happiness, fear, and anger are universal, but the expressions of emotions and their developmental progression vary depending on cultural practices and expectations (see **Figure 5.1**). Even the timing of a baby's smiles, tantrums, and helping behaviors are not the same around the world (Keller, 2020). From the very beginning, caregivers raise their babies in ways that align with their cultural values (Lansford & Bornstein, 2020).

trust versus mistrust The first crisis in Erikson's stage theory of development in which infants learn that the world is reliable.

autonomy versus shame and doubt The second crisis in Erikson's stage theory of development in which toddlers learn to balance their desire to be independent with their limitations and frequent missteps.

How Do Ethnotheories Explain How Caregivers Get Babies to Eat Their Carrots? In Japan, parents often want to instill a strong sense of empathy. This can even be seen at the dinner table, as some researchers have observed that parents try to convince children to eat all their vegetables by begging, pleading, and asking their little ones to eat them all to please the carrot as well as the carrot farmers.

FIGURE 5.1 Culture Shapes Emotional Development. Parents' ethnotheories about development vary around the world. Soothing and cuddling babies is universal, but how caregivers talk about and label babies' behavior is not always the same. In this study, researchers asked parents in various communities in Fiji, Kenya, and the United States when they thought babies were capable of smiling, feeling pain and pleasure, and thinking. The parents' expectations remind us that how we label babies' development may not be universal at all.

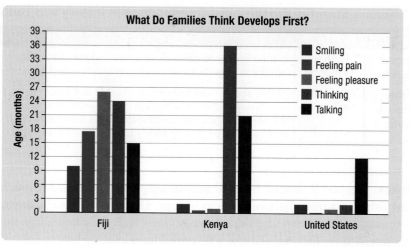

Data from Broesch et al., 2016.

CONNECTIONS

You read in Chapter 1 that ethnotheories are a family's shared cultural beliefs about how to care for children and why children do what they do.

CONNECTIONS

Remember from Chapter 1 that communities that encourage and value independence in their children are called individualistic cultures. In collectivist cultures, the individual's needs are balanced with those of family and community.

proximal Caregiving practices that include physical closeness but not necessarily face-to-face contact.

distal Caregiving practices that are physically distant but may include joint attention and face-to-face contact.

Culture affects caregivers' *ethnotheories* about what is best for their children (Harkness & Super, 2021). All families hope their children will be successful and happy, but they often believe that success comes from different sources. For instance, German parents often tell researchers that they hope that their children will learn to express their own ideas and develop their own unique talents. Rural Cameroonian parents frequently tell scientists they hope their children will learn to respect their elders and do what they are told (Keller & Otto, 2009). Many U.S. families report that they believe their babies will be successful if they are smart and independent (Feng et al., 2020).

One way of looking at the impact of culture on development is to measure families' levels of *collectivism* or *individualism*. Babies in collectivist cultures are often seen as important members of a community, who are connected to others through strong ties of respect and obligation. For instance, in Beng families in Côte d'Ivoire, this starts at birth, when newborns are expected to politely grunt in greeting to their visitors (Gottlieb, 2019). Collectivist practices encourage interdependence or relatedness (Amir & McAuliffe, 2020). Rather than encouraging a toddler's independent exploration, families who value interdependence might encourage good manners.

In collectivist cultures, families tend to use **proximal** practices, which are characterized by physical closeness. For example, caregivers in rural Kenya have been observed to hold their babies four times as much as parents in the United States (LeVine & LeVine, 2016). Families in collectivist cultures tend to soothe babies with touch and frequent nursing.

Individualistic communities and families, like many in the United States and other wealthy urban communities around the world, tend to have caregiving practices that include lots of face-to-face contact, playing with toys, and infant-directed talk (Aschemeyer et al., 2021; Little et al., 2019). These practices are termed **distal**, meaning that the caregiver and child are physically distant. Many distal caregiving practices involve joint attention, rather than physical closeness. For instance, when Makena plays on a blanket in the middle of the living room while Stephanie is making dinner, Stephanie can reassure Makena by calling across the room when she drops a favorite toy.

Around the world, more educated and affluent families tend to use individualistic parenting styles designed to build independence (Otto et al., 2017; Park & Lau, 2016). Rural, agricultural families tend to use more relational parenting styles focused on

Close in Different Ways Proximal and distal parenting both are ways of raising children. When parents use proximal practices, they are often physically close but not engaging in face-to-face contact, as when this father in Richmond, Virginia, uses a baby carrier while he moves the laundry. Distal parenting often involves face-to-face contact with less physical closeness, but for this family in Kazakhstan, cuddling includes aspects of both distal and proximal care.

raising calm, cooperative children. However, while it may seem easy to divide the world into those who emphasize independence and those who do not, the reality is much more complex. Many immigrant communities and communities in transition mix the values of independence and interdependence in parenting. Caregivers often use both proximal and distal practices, but the balance varies. Abstract values do not easily predict what happens in real life (Röttger-Rössler, 2020).

MAKING A DIFFERENCE
How Understanding Culture Helps Soothe Babies

Some amount of distress—whether from immunizations, diaper rash, or a splash of bathwater—is inevitable in a baby's life. As a result, babies everywhere cry, but how much they cry varies dramatically depending on how caregivers manage it. Caregivers who have difficulty coping with their infant's upsets are at higher risk for depression and even child abuse, and their babies are also at higher risk for depression and behavior problems (Garratt et al., 2019).

No one likes to hear a baby cry, but parents have different ideas about what to do about it. Some cultures value emotional restraint and believe that crying should be limited. For instance, in rural Nso communities in Cameroon, caregivers expect their babies to be calm and may tell their little ones "we do not cry here" (Keller & Otto, 2009, p. 1003). In other places, however, families might report that crying is inevitable or a sign of an individual baby's difficult personality (Super et al., 2020).

In one classic study, scientists compared how often babies cried in rural villages in Botswana with babies in more urban areas in the Netherlands. Babies in both communities got upset about the same number of times every day, but infants in Botswana were soothed much more quickly. It took about seven minutes for a caregiver in Holland to settle their 3-month-old, compared to about three minutes in Botswana (Barr et al., 1991). Over the course of a typical day, this meant that babies in the Netherlands were crying twice as long as babies in Botswana.

What caused the difference? Families in Botswana used proximal parenting techniques. They responded immediately when their babies cried, and their babies were

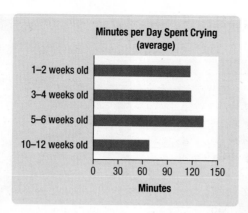

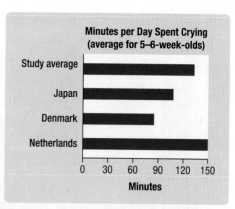

FIGURE 5.2 How Much Do Babies Cry Around the World? Most babies cry more at about 6 to 8 weeks than they do at other times in development, but how much they cry is shaped by how they are cared for. Babies who experience more proximal parenting practices tend to cry less. Parenting practices, particularly how often babies are held, are critically important in how much time babies spend distressed.

Displacement Can Be Frightening, Despite a Mother's Love. This mother is carrying her child in temporary housing in Gaza, Palestinian Territories, after they were displaced from their ancestral homes near Beersheva in Southern Israel. Researchers who studied traditionally nomadic Bedouin families, like hers, before they were forced to leave their homes in the Negev desert, found that their children were becoming anxious around strangers, perhaps because of the looming threat of war, even though their parents hoped they would be friendly and outgoing.

held, carried, or breast-fed almost all the time (Devore & Konner, 2019). These results have been replicated: Babies whose caregivers use proximal techniques have shorter bouts of crying, spending half as much time upset as babies who receive distal parenting (Wolke et al., 2017). (See **Figure 5.2**.)

In multiple studies, educating new families about typical crying behavior and proximal techniques for managing it has helped caregivers better cope with their babies' distress (St James-Roberts et al., 2019). These interventions help parents avoid depression, stress, and dangerous responses to crying, like shouting or shaking (Gilkerson et al., 2020; Wolfe & Kelly, 2019). 🌐

Current Approaches to Emotion Development

Breakthroughs in the understanding of genes and the brain have added three important insights about babies' emotional development: (1) The first years of life shape brain development and genomic expression; (2) not every infant responds in the same way to the environment; and (3) biological and genomic changes can often be reversed (Beijers et al., 2020).

Remember that scientists have explained that one way early experiences shape us is through the brain and the genome. The environment can change the genome by changing the chemistry of the epigenetic marks that surround DNA, causing some genes to be expressed and others to be repressed. The genome, like the brain, is particularly sensitive during the first few years of life so that infants can adapt to their surroundings (Krol et al., 2019a; Montirosso et al., 2021).

Researchers studying children who have endured difficult experiences, such as being raised in an institution or by caregivers who are overwhelmed or unresponsive, have found signs of biological changes in their bodies. These include epigenetic changes to their genome, alterations to how their bodies manage stress and release hormones, and changes to how their brains develop (Naumova et al., 2019; Nelson et al., 2019; Shakiba et al., 2020). Does this mean that children who have grown up with adversity will not be able to have happy, meaningful lives? Not at all. As you will see, early adversity does not affect all children in the same way, and not all adversity is equal.

For instance, fear, neglect, and illness may have different effects, all of which, in turn, are dependent on when they happen and how children perceive them (Milojevich et al., 2020; Smith & Pollak, 2021). As a result, some children may have difficulties that are the result of early adversity (Colich et al., 2020). Some may develop resilience and recover from trauma, and others may even develop new strengths (Ellis et al., 2020). But adversity sometimes harms children irreversibly, which is why developmental scientists are working to develop effective interventions to help keep children safe.

Differential Susceptibility Researchers remind us that not all children react to adversity or to their environments in the same way (Zhang et al., 2021). While children's lives are mostly improving over time due to public health achievements, as you can see from **Infographic 5.1**, the number of babies exposed to trauma and chronic stress is mind-boggling (Finkelhor et al., 2020). Around the world, more than 140 million children grow up without families because of war or poverty (Nelson et al., 2019). In the United States, about one in eight children has been exposed to a parent's substance abuse, and 1 in 12 has been physically abused by a caregiver (Biglan et al., 2020; Simon et al., 2018). More than 420,000 children in the United States are now living in foster care after being removed from their homes (USDHHS, 2020).

The theory of **differential susceptibility** explains that some children, because of their specific genotype, are more reactive to the environment than others. A harmful environment can cause a more negative outcome for children with this plasticity genotype than it does for a typical child (see **Figure 5.3**). However, for these children, a positive environment can have even more beneficial outcomes (van IJzendoorn et al., 2020; Zhang & Belsky, 2020).

SCIENCE IN PRACTICE
Heather Kosakowski

Heather Kosakowski faced more than her share of adversity in childhood: She was raised by seven different foster families. Nevertheless, after serving in the Marines for five years, Heather earned an associate's and then a bachelor's degree, and is now in graduate school studying developmental science and raising a child of her own.

How does Heather Kosakowski utilize what she knows about development every day? She uses her firsthand knowledge of babies to make silly faces and find lost pacifiers in order to keep infants still in an fMRI scanner. She also uses everything she learned about babies in her development courses. She knows why a baby's brain looks darker than an adult brain in a scanner (more myelin makes an adult brain lighter and brighter), and she knows some parts of babies' brains activate when they look at faces and other parts activate when they look at landscapes.

Heather does not think that science will ever identify which part of her brain gave her persistence. She credits her resilience to her faith and to Parris Island, where she went through Marine boot camp. As she remembers, although her love for babies began when she was a child herself, it was the Marine Corps that "instilled in me a greater sense of discipline . . . [and] a greater appreciation and understanding about the world" (Wellesley College, 2013).

Resilience Experiences in infancy can have lifelong effects, but contemporary developmental science also highlights the ability for change. Scientists are developing intensive therapies, parenting interventions, exercises, and even medication to help children and adults recover from the effects of early trauma (Hays-Grudo et al., 2021).

Children's capacity for change and adaptation to challenges is often called *resilience*, as you may recall from Chapter 1. In a classic study, researchers studied more than 70 babies who had experienced chronic early life stress and who were adopted by families in Minnesota. As expected, these children were more likely than other children to have stress-related difficulties, higher rates of disorders like ADHD, and even social problems like trouble making friends. Not all of the children in this study, however, had these difficulties.

differential susceptibility Individual differences in how sensitive people are to environmental effects.

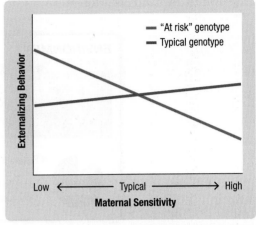

Information from Bakermans-Kranenburg & van IJzendoorn, 2015.

FIGURE 5.3 Life Changes Children Differently Research on the effects of parenting on children with different gene variants found that some children with a particular genotype were very sensitive to the effects of parenting. Among children with the "risky" genotype, those with "sensitive" mothers had much lower rates of acting-out behaviors at 18 months, whereas those who experienced less-sensitive parenting had higher rates of aggressive behavior at 18 months. These findings suggest that some children may be more strongly influenced by parenting experiences than others.

Caitlin Cunningham, McGovern Institute for Brain Research at MIT

Developmental Science in Action Heather Kosakowski studies brain development in small babies, which involves hands-on work making sure infants stay still in a scanner and also understanding how their neurons mature.

Every year, 140 million babies are born worldwide. Each will be shaped by the complex systems that surround them, as well as by their own individual strengths. Each baby's social structures and physical environment reflect vast inequalities and wide diversity in our capacity to thrive. Caregivers are a major source of resilience for small children, as they gradually develop the ability to regulate their own feelings and behavior.

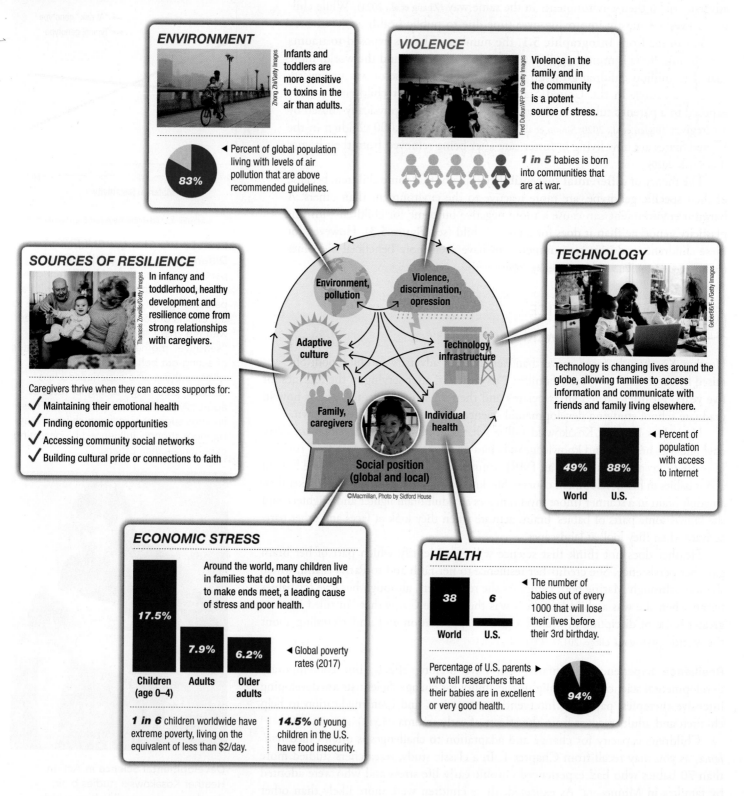

ENVIRONMENT

Infants and toddlers are more sensitive to toxins in the air than adults.

◄ Percent of global population living with levels of air pollution that are above recommended guidelines.
83%

Zhong Zhu/Getty Images

VIOLENCE

Violence in the family and in the community is a potent source of stress.

1 in 5 babies is born into communities that are at war.

Fred Dufour/AFP via Getty Images

SOURCES OF RESILIENCE

In infancy and toddlerhood, healthy development and resilience come from strong relationships with caregivers.

Caregivers thrive when they can access supports for:
✓ Maintaining their emotional health
✓ Finding economic opportunities
✓ Accessing community social networks
✓ Building cultural pride or connections to faith

Thanasis Zovoilis/Getty Images

TECHNOLOGY

Technology is changing lives around the globe, allowing families to access information and communicate with friends and family living elsewhere.

◄ Percent of population with access to internet
49% World **88%** U.S.

Geber86/E+/Getty Images

Environment, pollution

Violence, discrimination, opression

Adaptive culture

Technology, infrastructure

Family, caregivers

Individual health

Social position (global and local)

©Macmillan, Photo by Sidford House

ECONOMIC STRESS

Around the world, many children live in families that do not have enough to make ends meet, a leading cause of stress and poor health.

◄ Global poverty rates (2017)

17.5% Children (age 0–4)
7.9% Adults
6.2% Older adults

1 in 6 children worldwide have extreme poverty, living on the equivalent of less than $2/day.

14.5% of young children in the U.S. have food insecurity.

HEALTH

38 World **6** U.S.

◄ The number of babies out of every 1000 that will lose their lives before their 3rd birthday.

Percentage of U.S. parents ► who tell researchers that their babies are in excellent or very good health.
94%

Two groups showed resilience. Some children, particularly those who were adopted when they were infants, had lower rates of psychological disorders. The other group had received exceptional caregiving, "supercharged" parenting that was unusually positive and emotionally supportive. Children raised by supercharged caregivers were able to make friends and avoid emotional problems; they were in many ways indistinguishable from children who had never lived in orphanages (Pitula et al., 2019).

This finding reminds us that although early challenges can have lasting effects, they are not insurmountable. Early intervention can modify and even reverse some early difficulties, and, as you will learn in Chapter 10, adolescence offers another important opportunity to recalibrate early social and emotional challenges (Gunnar et al., 2019). We know that Jen and Stephanie worry about Makena's risk of inheriting some of her biological mother's difficulties, since her biological mother has been diagnosed with depression, but their supercharged parenting may have helped Makena be happy and well-adjusted nevertheless.

APPLY IT! **5.1** Jen and Stephanie want to encourage Makena's *resilience*, or her ability to bounce back from stress. How do early relationships help babies such as Makena manage stress?

5.2 At age 2, Makena wants to "do it herself," whether that means getting dressed on her own or pouring water. How would Erikson's theory of psychosocial development explain this drive?

5.3 After Jen and Stephanie adopted Makena, they spent a lot of time holding her and in skin-to-skin contact. Explain how researchers think this type of proximal parenting practice might shape infants' development.

Emotional Development

At just 6 months, it was clear that Makena already had feelings. Much of the time she was filled with giggles, bringing so much laughter to her sister and her parents. At other times, like when she was trying to reach for a toy that had fallen out of reach, she was clearly frustrated.

Babies gradually move from reacting automatically to having some control over their emotions. Young infants begin the process of managing the disappointments and unexpected events in the world, such as the annoyance of being strapped into a car seat or the joy of seeing their father again after a nap.

Learning Objective

5.3 Describe the progress of infants' and toddlers' emotional maturation.

Happiness from the Very Beginning The fleeting smiles of a newborn are often random and not in their control, but by the time a baby is a year old, smiles and laughter are easy to identify. By the time a toddler is 2, they know how to grin and pose for the camera.

Measuring What Babies Are Feeling

A major challenge in understanding babies is figuring out what they are feeling. How do you know what someone is feeling if they cannot use words?

Facial expressions are not very helpful. Because they lack the motor control to make all the facial expressions adults can, young babies are good at sad faces but have a lot of difficulty smiling (Adolph & Franchak, 2017). Newborns can control their mouths in order to suck but cannot use their lips to smile on purpose (Shultz et al., 2018). It takes weeks before babies master the mouth movements necessary for a smile. Not until age 3 or so do toddlers' emotional expressions approach the sophistication of adults', and even these vary by culture and are not always a precise presentation of how they are really feeling (Barrett et al., 2019; Holodynski & Seeger, 2019).

Similarly, it will take months before infants' cries communicate more than just distress. While some parents claim that they can tell a newborn's "pain cry" from a "hunger cry," researchers have found that young infants cannot control their voices enough to communicate these nuances. Scientists have found that even experts cannot predict why a very young infant is crying from the sounds they make (Zefman & St James-Roberts, 2017).

So, how do experts measure a baby's feelings? It is not easy, but technology helps. Scientists look into the baby's eyes, and they measure their hearts and their neural activity. It turns out that even at just 1 month, infants' pupils will get bigger if they are looking at something they like, such as a picture of their mother (Geangu et al., 2011). Researchers also connect babies to electrodes to measure how quickly their hearts respond or how their brain activity changes. This has helped experts understand that some babies are more reactive to emotional stimuli than others, even if they are too young to show it or talk about it (Ostlund et al., 2019).

The Basic Emotions

You can probably list a dozen emotions easily, but defining them is more difficult. **Emotions** involve your *body* (the racing heartbeat when you get scared), your *thoughts* (your awareness that you are scared), and your *behaviors* (scrambling away from a loud noise at the window). However, everyday experiences of emotion do not always include all three parts of this definition (Pollak et al., 2019). For instance, babies may not think about their pain in a logical way, but they still experience it. Adults may feel disappointment when a bad grade lands on their desk in front of a bunch of college classmates but cover it up with a fake smile.

Which emotions do infants have? Traditional Chinese and Korean scholars believed greed and hate were core emotions (Lim, 2016). In the Philippines, families who speak Tagalog have a word for over-the-top adorableness, *gigil*, that does not exist in any other language (Cachero et al., 2017). Today, most developmentalists agree that only a few basic emotions are shared by infants (and adults) around the world. Distress, happiness, fear, and anger are the first feelings to emerge in infancy. As babies mature, more complex emotions like empathy, pride, and embarrassment begin to appear (see **Figure 5.4**).

Distress Infants often feel hungry, cold, and tired, unfamiliar and unpleasant feelings for newborns adjusting to new, intense sensory input and physical sensations that they did not experience in the uterus. For the first four months of life, sadness, pain, and anger are intertwined in one general expression of *distress* (Holodynski & Seeger, 2019). At about 6 weeks, most infants cry less and become easier to soothe. At 3 months, most babies in affluent countries are fussy for less than an hour a day, typically even less in communities that practice proximal caregiving (St James-Roberts, 2012).

Happiness Newborns can show contentment, perhaps as they share eye contact or stare at a rotating fan. However, it is hard to see if they feel joy because they cannot

emotions Reactions to your thoughts or your environment that involve your body, your thoughts, and your behaviors.

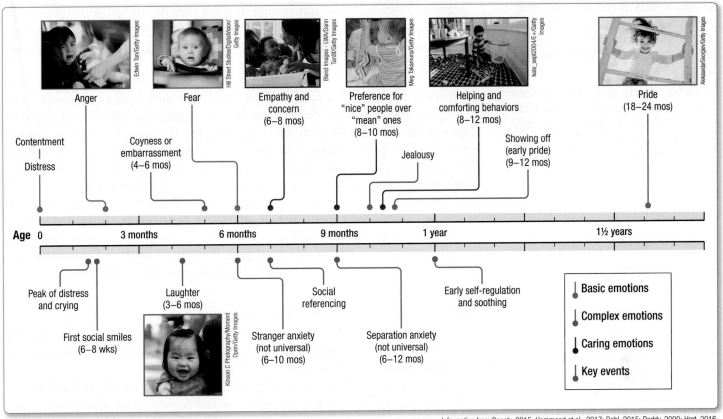

FIGURE 5.4 Highlights in the Development of Emotions As infants turn into toddlers, they have more ability to express what they are feeling and more complex reactions to the world around them.

smile in reaction to anything caregivers do. In their first few weeks, babies' first spontaneous smiles occur mostly during sleep, but researchers think they happen just to give facial muscles practice (Kawakami et al., 2017). At around 6 or 8 weeks, however, babies' smiles are no longer random (Camras, 2019). Babies can lock eyes and grin. This is the **social smile**, which is in reaction to the sight or sound of someone a baby likes, like a parent or a sibling.

Social smiles emerge at about the same time around the world, and in babies with typical development as well as those who may have visual, physical, or intellectual disabilities (Lewis, 2017). How often young babies smile depends on their caregivers. The babies of caregivers who smile a lot and who have a lot of face-to-face interactions with their babies tend to smile more (Lavelli et al., 2019).

Many European and U.S. parents tend to encourage positive, outgoing social behavior in their infants. As a result, babies in the United States tend to smile more than babies in most other places. In many cultures, parents may not focus on face-to-face interaction or outgoing emotions. Such caregivers may not expect their babies to share social smiling until around 6 months (Wörmann et al., 2014). In Fiji, for instance, parents do not anticipate that their babies will share a smile with them until about 10 months (Broesch et al., 2016).

Smiling is quickly followed by laughing, giggling, and other signs of joy. Most infants in the United States begin to laugh before 3 months (Jhang & Oller, 2017). Babies understand simple humor, clowning, and some jokes between 3 and 5 months (Mireault et al., 2018; Reddy, 2019a).

Anger You may not think of anger as an emotional accomplishment, but it is a sign of maturity. A newborn can be upset, but it takes a few months until they can express

Do It Again! As babies grow, smiles and laughter become more interactive and responsive. Babies who experience more face-to-face, expressive interaction tend to be more outgoing, like this little girl.

social smile A smile in reaction to the sight or sound of someone an infant is connected to. These smiles may appear as early as 6 weeks, but their development is influenced by caregiving practices.

stranger anxiety Babies' demonstration of caution around new people, which emerges by about 8 months. This phenomenon is not culturally universal but is influenced by caregiving practices.

separation anxiety By about 6 months and continuing into toddlerhood, infants are upset and worried if their caregivers go away. This phenomenon is not universal but is influenced by cultural practices.

anger. By 8 weeks, babies can become angry if they do not get what they expect. Researchers are experts at measuring this using just a car seat and a toy. Strapping a baby into a car seat or taking away a toy that they had been enjoying is nearly guaranteed to produce anger (Ekas et al., 2018; Liu et al., 2018).

Like other emotions, anger is often in the eyes of the beholder. Culture plays an important role in whether families think their babies should get angry (Raval & Walker, 2019). For instance, some Nepalese families encourage their children to stay calm even in the face of frustration (Cole et al., 2006). On the other hand, many German and American parents expect their babies to express their feelings and show anger at 5 months (Jaramillo et al., 2017; Keller & Otto, 2009). However, U.S. parents typically find their babies' anger embarrassing, particularly in front of strangers (Keller, 2019).

By the toddler years, anger and aggression become more common (Lorber et al., 2018). In U.S. toddlers, ages 1 to 3 are among the most violent years of the lifespan. Toddlers hit, pull hair, and grab more than older children (and certainly more than adults) (Hay, 2017). Most of this aggression, however, is random or uncoordinated rather than deliberately hurtful, like pulling a sibling's braid out of curiosity or patting a dog too hard (Dahl, 2019).

Fear Newborns can be startled, but they do not remember what has frightened them long enough to show fear (Rousseau et al., 2017). As a result, babies do not show true fear until about 6 months, when their brains mature enough to remember dangers and anticipate them (Thomas et al., 2019).

Fear appears at about the same age in infants around the world. Evolutionary theorists suggest that as babies become more mobile, as they are able to sit on their own, perhaps even crawl and grab objects (some of which could hurt them), they become more sensitive to danger (Bjorklund et al., 2015). Being able to quickly learn that they should be afraid—whether it is of growling dogs or angry people—helps to keep babies safe (Frankenhuis, 2019).

Some things are scarier than others to babies. Slithering snakes, spiders, and sharp-toothed lions and tigers are at the top of the list (Bertels et al., 2020; Hoehl et al., 2017). Dangerous animals aren't the only things that babies are prepared to fear. Infants are particularly attentive to fearful and angry faces. Just as snakes can sometimes be dangerous, so can people and poisonous plants (Aktar et al., 2018; Safar & Moulson, 2020; Zhang et al., 2019).

In many cultures, by 8 months, babies have learned to be cautious around new people, a phenomenon called **stranger anxiety**. This can be embarrassing for families: A photograph with the Easter Bunny or an unfamiliar relative results in shrieks and terror as soon as they hand the baby over. Scholars call this growing unhappiness at being away from the people they care about **separation anxiety**. In many cultures, this behavior is typical for babies between around 6 and 12 months and can be a sign of their developing *attachment*, as you will learn later in this chapter. At 4 months, babies may have been happy to be handed off to a visiting cousin, but a few months later, they may fuss. These anxieties peak by 12 months but may continue until age 3 (Brand et al., 2020; Van Hulle et al., 2017).

Many researchers believe the increase in babies' anxiety is a symptom of their strong preference for their usual caregivers, the people who they rely on and have come to trust. However, uneasiness around new people is far from universal (Gottlieb, 2019). In many communities, babies continue to be friendly to strangers and do not develop stranger or separation anxiety. In these places, separation anxiety may even be seen as a form of rudeness (Keller, 2018). As a Bedouin mother living in Israel explained to a researcher, "It is desirable that the baby

Not Yet Afraid No one is born afraid of snakes, but by 4 months, babies pay more attention to snakes (and spiders) than other creatures and may more readily develop a fear of them. This baby seems fascinated, rather than terrified, of the python displayed at a festival in Lisbon, Portugal.

PATRICIA DE MELO MOREIRA/AFP via Getty Images

has relationships with many people" so "people will love him and agree to keep him when I'm not around" (Marey-Sarwan et al., 2016, p. 326).

By about 7 months, caregivers may notice that their babies check in with them when they see something new or unusual (Rochat, 2018). As Jen and Stephanie explained, raising a baby during the pandemic made this tendency even worse. For six months, as they raised their girls in the New York City region that was the epicenter of the first wave, Makena did not see anyone outside her immediate family. She responded by clinging to her mothers' legs when she first went out in public and looking closely to make sure everything was okay. This careful attention to caregivers' feelings, called **social referencing**, helps babies learn about danger. For instance, if an infant's caregiver is afraid of something, whether it is a suspicious stranger or a thunderstorm, being attentive to that teaches babies about dangers (Elsner & Wertz, 2019).

Angela Georges/Getty Images

More Complex Emotions

Now that Makena is a toddler, she seems to show many complex emotions: anger, sadness, joy, and fear, as well as jealousy and even embarrassment. As babies become more interactive, as Makena is, they begin to display more social emotions like embarrassment and concern (Davidov et al., 2021; Reddy, 2019b).

Self-Awareness Do babies know that they are separate beings? This is one of the philosophical questions that developmental scientists grapple with. Researchers define **self-awareness** as the understanding that you have a self that is separate from the world. Until recently, many researchers believed that babies weren't capable of this (Lewis & Brooks-Gunn, 1979; Mahler, 1974; Rochat, 2018).

Scientists have provided a fresh analysis of a classic (and cute) measure of self-awareness called the *mirror self-recognition test* (Gallup, 1970). The experiment is simple: Without attracting any attention, researchers place a red dot on an infant's nose. Then the baby is placed in front of a mirror. If the baby shows an understanding that there is a red dot on their own nose, say, by touching or rubbing it, they are said to have self-awareness, because they recognize the image in the mirror as themselves. If babies ignore the dot, they are said to lack self-awareness.

More than 40 years ago, some pioneering psychologists found that by 18 months, most of the babies they sampled in urban and suburban North America could recognize themselves in a mirror (Amsterdam, 1972; Brooks-Gunn & Lewis, 1975). However, later researchers found that the experiment didn't work for babies outside of affluent, urban nations. In some rural communities in Kenya, Peru, and Fiji, children as old as 4 froze and stared at the mirror after a mark was placed on their faces. They didn't point to the dot on their noses or try to wipe it off (Ross et al., 2017). However, these children exhibited more advanced emotions and self-awareness than other children, like empathy and caring. The profound cultural variations in babies' responses led scientists to question the usefulness of the mirror self-recognition test and develop new ways of assessing toddlers' emotional maturation (Broesch et al., 2020).

Other research suggests that infants show elements of self-awareness long before they can recognize themselves in a mirror (Lou et al., 2020). For instance, scientists using *functional near-infrared spectroscopy (FNIRS)*, which utilizes light to measure blood flow in the brain, showed that babies can distinguish themselves from other people. Different regions of their brains were activated when infants touched themselves as compared to when someone else touched them (Padilla & Lagercrantz, 2020). Also, long before they recognize themselves in the mirror, babies respond to their names, interact with others, and show social emotions like jealousy, embarrassment, and concern (Davidov et al., 2021; Grossmann & Dela Cruz, 2021; Hart, 2020).

What's That? Some researchers use the mirror self-recognition test to see if babies have self-awareness. If a baby recognizes that they have a spot on their nose, they are said to have self-awareness. Other researchers believe that this test may better assess mirror awareness or messy awareness than actual self-awareness: They suggest that babies' have self-awareness from birth.

social referencing The use of someone else's emotional response as a guide before expressing your own reaction to a new place, person or object.

self-awareness The understanding that you have a self that is separate from others.

emotional contagion The tendency to mimic feelings we observe in others.

empathy The ability to identify with someone else's feelings.

prosocial Behaviors that are helpful or caring toward someone else.

Embarrassment What is embarrassment? You may experience it as your cheeks flush when you do something in front of others you wish you hadn't, or when you unexpectedly become the center of attention (Nikolić et al., 2018). Before 6 months, babies show signs of self-conscious embarrassment, like turning their heads or looking away when they get too much attention (Colonnesi et al., 2020). After 6 months, babies begin to show embarrassment when they make a mistake, like spilling cereal. Embarrassment may be uncomfortable at any age, but showing regret for something you have done or discomfort with being the center of attention signals that you care what other people think (Grossmann, 2020). This concern helps create close relationships.

By 18 months, nearly 9 in 10 babies show signs of embarrassment if they are overpraised. What triggers this embarrassment? Researchers told toddlers that they were going to share their photos so their "friends can see how cute [they] are!" (Eggum-Wilkens et al., 2015).

Concern for Others From the time they are born, infants show some awareness of the feelings of others. For instance, in a hospital nursery, newborns will begin to cry after they hear another baby's wail, which researchers call **emotional contagion** (Palagi et al., 2020; Ruffman et al., 2017). (You have experienced this if you have ever felt the urge to yawn after seeing someone else do it.)

Babies are born with the capacity for **empathy**, the ability to identify with someone else's feelings (Tomasello, 2020). As one researcher explained, typically developing babies have a "basic tendency to be nice" (Sebastián-Enesco et al., 2013, p. 186). Scientists believe that they even prefer to look at kind, helpful people than those who are unfair (Margoni & Surian, 2018). As they grow, they become more capable of behaving **prosocially**, or helpfully, acting in ways that help other people, such as sharing or cooperating.

A critical part of empathy is the ability to sense what others are feeling. Although newborns can sense big upsets, like screaming, they cannot pick up on more subtle cues (Decety & Steinbeis, 2020). But by the time they are a few months old, babies respond to adults' emotional expressions and tend to mirror what they observe (Lavelli et al., 2019). In other words, infants are likely to smile when their caregiver is smiling or frown when their caregiver is upset (Wass et al., 2019; Waters et al., 2017).

A few months later, babies start trying to be helpful. This is their first prosocial achievement. By 6 or 8 months, babies will pat someone who is upset (Davidov et al., 2021). If they see someone trying to grab an object that is out of reach, they will push it toward them (Tomasello, 2021). By age 2, many toddlers are even willing to give up a favorite toy to comfort someone else (Cowell & Decety, 2015).

Babies may begin helping out around the house, perhaps by putting their toys away, before age 1 (Dahl & Brownell, 2019). Many communities expect toddlers to pitch in by doing small tasks, such as carrying food to the table. As you might expect, in places where this behavior is expected of children, babies tend to be helpful at earlier ages (Köster & Kärtner, 2019). In urban families in the United States, babies who are not quite 1 often help out in everyday activities, especially with encouragement from parents (Dahl, 2019). Even if babies do not have chores, they can help their caregivers change their diaper or put on their hat. Babies can be cooperative, but they are not very reliable. Toddlers tend to be unreliable as when they are asked to put away their toys or put on their shirt, until they are about 2½ (Hammond & Brownell, 2018; Kärtner et al., 2021).

Does an early capacity to be nice mean that toddlers share eagerly? Far from it (Waugh & Brownell, 2017). The most difficult prosocial behavior for toddlers is sharing, and the difficulty persists until about age 4 (Poelker & Gibbons, 2019). Toddlers may be willing to share a cookie, but most will not give up the toy they were playing with. However, just because sharing is difficult for toddlers does not mean that caregivers should stop encouraging it. Caregivers who encourage sharing are

Born to Be Nice. Some researchers suggest that babies are born with a basic tendency to be kind. Six-month-olds will try and comfort someone who is upset, and older children, like these girls, are often willing to share with a friend.

helping toddlers learn to get along with other children and allowing them to experience the good feelings that come from generosity (Song et al., 2020).

Managing Emotions

When Makena fussed when she was 6 months old, Jen and Stephanie did not mind. That behavior is quite different in a 2-year-old. As infants grow into toddlers and then into little kids, adults increasingly expect them to manage their emotions. As they gain experience in the world and as their brains develop, babies can better control their feelings and emotional responses. But this process does not always go smoothly.

Emotion regulation is the ability to manage emotions in a way that is appropriate for the cultural context. In many cases, this means that caregivers expect children to calm themselves down or minimize the expression of negative emotions like frustration or sadness. Emotion regulation also involves positive feelings. For instance, at a birthday party, Jen and Stephanie hope that Makena will be able to smile, clap, and sing along with other guests as a cake is brought in, but not be too loud.

Infants are not capable of calming themselves and depend on caregivers to help soothe them. As babies mature, they develop behaviors and brain connections that help them avoid emotional extremes without as much help. Scientists believe that infancy is a sensitive period for infants to develop emotion regulation and learn about what feelings are acceptable in their unique cultural and family context (Gee, 2020).

The *still-face procedure* is one way that researchers have measured infants' ability to manage their feelings (Tronick et al., 1978). This short test is designed to upset a baby and then measure how easily they can be soothed. What is guaranteed to upset a baby? Being ignored. In this procedure, a caregiver is asked to be unresponsive and keep a "still face."

Researchers using this procedure and others have found that over the first two years, babies develop the ability to tolerate upsetting events and to calm themselves (Gago Galvagno et al., 2019). By age 1, infants anticipate that a caregiver will help them feel better, and so the sound of an approaching caregiver will quiet a wailing baby (Brownell et al., 2015). Toddlers also learn independent ways of coping with their feelings: They may pick up a distracting toy, look away, or suck their thumb (Bozicevic et al., 2021; Planalp & Braungart-Rieker, 2015).

Although most toddlers have fewer ups-and-downs than younger babies, they are far from even-tempered. In many communities around the world, families struggle with a new form of dysregulation as babies become toddlers—the *meltdown*, or temper tantrum. A meltdown is typically a moment of upset that begins as anger and transitions into hysterical sadness. Toddlers may collapse, kick, scream, or even hold their breath. More than 9 in 10 2-year-olds in U.S. communities have one meltdown every week (Manning et al., 2019). What triggers a meltdown? New limits and expectations. Toddlers' new abilities, such as talking and walking, often lead to higher adult expectations. In addition, many families have difficulty soothing upset toddlers. They no longer use the calming methods, like nursing or rocking, that worked for younger children, and verbal methods that work for older children, like logical reasoning, are often ineffective (Deichmann & Ahnert, 2021; Kopp, 1989).

APPLY IT! 5.4 Makena starts to look sad and cry when Stephanie picks up her phone, but Makena recovers in a minute. How is this experience similar to the still-face procedure?

5.5 Families with young children often have different ethnotheories about sharing. How might you explain the science of sharing and caring to Jen and Stephanie, who wonder whether they should expect Makena to share with Maya?

emotion regulation The ability to manage your feelings in a way that is appropriate to your community circumstances.

Lovett Stories + Strategies

Not the Still Face Again! In the still-face procedure, caregivers are asked to maintain a neutral expression for just two minutes. In this video still from Dr. Edward Tronick's laboratory at the University of Massachusetts, a baby reacts with characteristic upset while their parent tries to remain unreactive. Don't worry: The baby was easily consoled after the procedure, which mimics what might happen when a caregiver is temporarily distracted or unavailable in real life.

 **Share It!**

Wait until my executive function kicks in! Executive function helps reduce tantrums and explosive behavior: Babies with strong executive function are less likely to melt down than those whose executive function is slower to develop.

(Hughes et al., 2020)

Scientific American: Lifespan Development

Personality and Temperament in the Early Years

Learning Objective

5.4   Explain how babies begin to develop unique personalities.

Jen and Stephanie thought Makena was going to be a shy, quiet person when she was a newborn. She was a subdued baby. But as she grew, she became an outgoing, goofy, loud, and affectionate toddler. Like Makena, some babies are a little hesitant about new people, while others have an easy smile for strangers in the checkout line. Even the intensity of babies' responses to the world varies. Some seem to have mild responses, whether to an immunization or a new person. Others are more intense. Are Jen and Stephanie right to think that Makena's outgoing attitude to the world is something she learned from her equally exuberant big sister, Maya? How have Jen and Stephanie's parenting and Makena's own biology influenced her personality?

Researchers are fascinated by these questions. They are trying to understand **personality**, or the individual differences in emotions, thinking, and behaviors that make each of us unique. Early patterns of feelings and reactions in infants and toddlers are known as **temperament**, a precursor to personality (Shiner, 2017).

What Are the Dimensions of Temperament?

In the 1950s, pioneering child psychiatrists Alexander Thomas and Stella Chess developed a way of analyzing temperament in small children. They wanted to understand why babies were so different and why some were out of sync with their caregivers (Chess et al., 1963; Thomas & Chess, 1957). Thomas and Chess identified three basic temperamental categories: **easy**, **slow-to-warm-up**, and **difficult** (Thomas & Chess, 1977). Easy babies, about 40 percent of the sample in Thomas and Chess's work, were flexible in new situations and usually happier than other babies. Slow-to-warm-up babies, about 15 percent of the group, were shyer than other children and slower to adjust to new circumstances, but they were not intense in their reactions. The 10 percent of children classified as difficult were easily frustrated, slow to adapt to change, and tended to react intensely.

Did you notice that those percentages do not add up to 100 percent? Thomas and Chess were aware of this, too: Their classification system was not designed to exactly match the complexity of all children (Thomas et al., 1970). In the years since Thomas and Chess's groundbreaking work, many researchers have moved empirically beyond those temperamental categories. For instance, many now suggest that Thomas and Chess's terminology, including the word *difficult* stigmatizes babies. Whereas Thomas and Chess were quite candid about the challenges of intense and explosive behavior in babies, many contemporary researchers prefer more neutral and person-first terms, referring to such behavior as "undercontrolled" or "challenging" (Super et al., 2020).

Instead of fitting all babies into three basic categories, many contemporary researchers think of early temperament as a set of traits that are displayed on a continuum of intensity (Putnam et al., 2019). Researchers focus on three major elements of early personality: *effortful control*, *negative affect*, and *extraversion*. The ability to focus attention and control behavior is called effortful control. Some babies are always looking for something new and have trouble controlling their focus for a long time. Babies who are higher in effortful control may be content to play with one toy for a long time.

The second major factor in personality is how often and how strongly babies display their negative feelings, often called negative affect. Some babies are just more irritable than others, easily scared by new things, or more likely to be frustrated when lunch is late or a nap has been missed. Others, like Makena, are more flexible.

The third element is the baby's level of extraversion, or how outgoing they are. In babies, being physically active and approaching new things happily is often seen as a sign of extraversion. An active explorer like Makena is considered high in extraversion.

personality Habits of emotionally relating and responding to people and events in our lives.

temperament An early pattern of personality in infants and toddlers.

easy In Thomas and Chess's dimensional approach to temperament, babies who are flexible and usually content.

slow-to-warm-up In Thomas and Chess's dimensional approach to temperament, these babies tend to be shy and slower to adjust to new circumstances, but not intense in their responses.

difficult In Thomas and Chess's dimensional approach to temperament, babies who are easily frustrated, are slow to adapt to change, and react intensely. This term is no longer preferred, outside of scholarly research.

Other scientists have described additional elements of personality beyond these three categories (Planalp & Goldsmith, 2020). Some focus on a baby's level of fear or shyness in new situations, often called *inhibition* (Kagan, 2018). Others look at a baby's level of *agreeableness*, or their level of openness to new experiences (Cloninger et al., 2019). No matter what researchers focus on, they find that the early years are critical in laying the foundation for personality.

CAN YOU BELIEVE IT?
Is Personality Something You Are Born With?

Is your personality something set in your DNA? Or is it something you learn as you grow? Many families attribute babies' early temperament to genes. They may blame an intense mother for an aggressive toddler's behavior or attribute an easygoing baby's personality to being "just like their dad" (Stover et al., 2015). Researchers suggest that this thinking might be misguided: Makena's development, it turns out, is not completely shaped by the tendencies she inherited from her biological parents, her prenatal experience, or the hours she's spent running around the house with her spunky big sister. Personality, like so much of development, is complicated, and genes do not hold all the answers.

Personality development is an example of how the environment and genetics work together epigenetically (Shiner, 2017). It is also an example of how children's characteristics can shape their environment just as the environment shapes them. Genes play a role in what kind of person babies become, but they are far from the only answer (Beam & Turkheimer, 2017; Kandler et al., 2021).

The first few years of life are a time when early personality is molded by the environment: More genes related to personality are activated during the first three years than at any other point in the lifespan (Conradt, 2017). What causes these genes to be activated or not? The environment, including prenatal exposure to hormones, early health, and, perhaps most importantly, early parenting (Gartstein & Skinner, 2018; Jones & Sloan, 2018; Miguel et al., 2019). Caregivers influence their baby's ability to manage strong feelings and to focus, as well as how positive they are. For instance, babies whose parents are depressed, stressed, or have a mental illness are more likely to be emotionally reactive than those whose caregivers are more stable (Brooker et al., 2020; Martinez-Torteya et al., 2018). Supportive parenting can help moderate challenging personality characteristics, such as extreme shyness or high energy (Augustine & Stiller, 2019; Planalp & Goldsmith, 2020).

Blaming (or crediting) the environment for babies' personalities does not give a complete picture of who we are. It turns out that caregiving is also influenced by a baby's temperament (Ayoub et al., 2019). Infants who are difficult to soothe and frequently upset are more challenging for parents than other babies; their behavior stresses the relationship, and as a result, they may receive less-sensitive caretaking (Freund et al., 2019).

Personality development doesn't end in toddlerhood. Personality can change. A baby who seems overly irritable or easily frustrated is more likely to become even-tempered two years later than at any other time during the lifespan (Parade et al., 2018). And personality continues to develop: A new school, new job, divorce, or hurricane are all events that can change personality over the lifespan (Turkheimer et al., 2014).

Managing Early Personality

Thomas and Chess coined the term **goodness of fit** to highlight the fact that everyone, particularly small children, benefits from caregivers who meet the needs of their unique personalities (Chess & Thomas, 1991). For instance, babies who tend to be anxious may have more difficulty adjusting to new circumstances and may need a few days of gentle adjustment when being dropped off at a new child-care center. As Chess

goodness of fit The idea that babies benefit from a good match between their personalities and their caregivers.

and Thomas pointed out, this does not mean anything is *wrong* with these children; being anxious is just a variation. Chess and Thomas advised that caregivers, parents, teachers, and health care providers should use their understanding of early personality to adjust their expectations of babies' needs (Chess & Thomas, 1996).

Over the past decades, researchers studying infant–caregiver interactions have generally supported Thomas and Chess's conclusions. All children benefit from strong relationships. Children with more challenging temperaments, typically those who have a lot of energy, lack effortful control, or who are particularly fearful, show more intense benefits from strong, understanding connections with caregivers (Gartstein et al., 2018; Wittig & Rodriguez, 2019).

The Impact of Culture

Jen and Stephanie are smitten with Makena's laughter and the energetic way she chases her sister around the house, but other adults might be horrified. Culture plays an important role in how we understand babies' behavior, and these expectations, as researchers have found, can shape an infant's early temperament. Parents in Italy, for instance, tend to prize the flexibility of babies who easily adapt to different social settings, but caregivers in Holland tend to place more value on cheerfulness (Chen, 2018). Babies in Finland tend to smile more than babies in the United States. Chinese babies tend to be shyer (Slobodskaya et al., 2018). (See **Figure 5.5**.)

Researchers have found that U.S. parents, on average, prefer their babies to be outgoing and energetic, and babies in the United States typically are rated accordingly (Sung et al., 2015). This extraversion seems to arise because U.S. parents tend to encourage their children to be bold and outgoing and discourage fear or anger (Gartstein & Putnam, 2018). Some scientists suggest that children are more likely to be outgoing in communities that are individualistic, like those in the United States, where children must

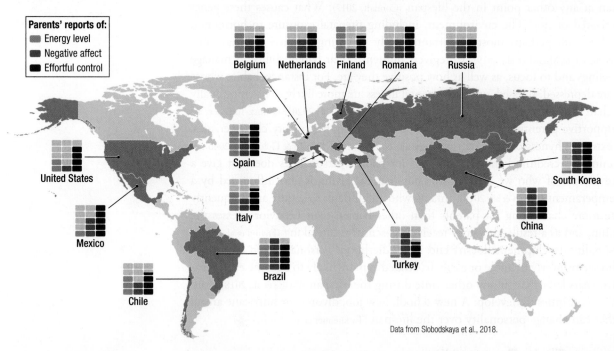

Data from Slobodskaya et al., 2018.

FIGURE 5.5 Where Are the Happiest Babies in the World? Researchers in 14 countries asked families to describe their babies' temperaments and found that families often described their toddlers in ways that reflected their cultural values. These scientists used temperamental categories to look at their data: Babies with high energy are said to be energetic and outgoing and have lots of positive emotions. Those with high scores for negative affect have families that report that they are more likely to be distressed, perhaps reflecting ethnotheories that are more accepting of fussiness. Those with high effortful control are said to be flexible and better able to control their behavior to match expectations. If you were looking for babies who were rarely distressed and showed outgoing, positive emotions, you might find them in Finland.

advocate for themselves in a competitive world. In contrast, in cultures that are more collectivist, families tend to encourage children to control their impulses, and to be less outgoing and more reserved so they will get along better with others (Chen, 2018).

It is important to point out that these are general patterns and not predictions of what will be true in any given family. The United States, like other countries, represents many cultural traditions. For instance, the expectation that families in less individualistic cultures are more likely to appreciate shyness in their children does not necessarily predict how one family will feel about their reserved toddler (Chen, 2019). Parents raising their children in a diverse community may worry about how their shy child will succeed in a dominant culture that values extraversion. Understanding the impact of culture on early personality is important, and very complex.

APPLY IT! **5.6** Stephanie and Jen worry that Makena's experience growing up during a global pandemic might increase her risk for emotional difficulties later in life. What does developmental science say about risk in early development and the power of caregiving?

5.7 Based on what you know about Makena, a good sleeper who had mild reactions to most everyday experiences as a baby, what temperament do you think she has?

Family Relationships

Even during a global pandemic, Jen and Stephanie worked hard to stay close to family, which meant trying to explain to Makena that the people in the screen could not be touched. They wanted their daughters to remain in touch with their cousins, grandparents, and birth mothers, who still connect with Makena and her sister online. Dozens of people make up Makena's family, created by bonds of love. Developmental scientists believe that a child's relationships with close caregivers in the first years of life create patterns of relating to others that last a lifetime.

What Makes a Family?

Consider the family members on Jen's FaceTime list or in your "favorites" on your phone. What defines family varies from person to person (Cavanagh & Fomby, 2019). In the United States, about 9 in 10 babies come home from the hospital with their birth parent and their partner, but by the time they are toddlers, about 1 in 12 has experienced a family transition, like a divorce, remarriage, or repartnering (Declercq et al., 2013). Families in the United States are often complex, comprised of parents and their married or unmarried partners, along with other siblings, who may or may not be biologically related. Around the world, babies are often raised by their biological parents, but siblings, grandparents, and neighbors also play a critical role. The idea that one or even two adults provide all the care a baby needs is not typical of most communities across the world (Abraham & Feldman, 2018; Sear, 2021).

Close relationships between an infant and a caregiver can be formed regardless of the biological or legal relationship or the identity of the caregiver. Parents with any gender identity or intimate relationship status, adoptive parents, and caregiving siblings or grandparents can all help babies thrive (Golombok, 2017). Research on caregiving in developmental science has historically tended to focus on female caregivers and often neglected both male caregivers and children's extended family; however, many suggest that the basic principles of sensitive parenting are similar (Cabrera et al., 2018; Gettler et al., 2020; Schoppe-Sullivan & Fagan, 2020). As you will see, it is the specific caregiving practices and the quality of the relationship, rather than the caregiver themselves, that are important.

Learning Objectives

5.5 Describe how caregiving impacts emotional development.

5.6 Explain common variations in caregiver–child attachment relationships.

Caregiving Comes in Different Sizes. Sometimes love, and help with a runny nose, comes from a big brother and not an adult. Siblings often provide caregiving in families around the world.

responsiveness The idea that a caregiver should acknowledge and react to an infant's bids for attention.

Scientific American Profile

▶

Supportive Parenting and Responsiveness

Measuring Caregiving in Infancy and Toddlerhood

Much of what caregivers do with babies is unique to each family or community. Parents have different values about caregiving and how they want their children to turn out (Harkness & Super, 2021). Across cultures, however, caregivers who are responsive and supportive with their babies seem to have better-adjusted children, even though specific parenting practices may differ.

Supportive Parenting Despite cultural variations, all caregivers engage in some of the same practices. They all tend to their upset babies, teach them to communicate and move, and keep them clean. When researchers ask parents around the world what makes an ideal parent, they agree on some core ideas: responsiveness, sensitivity, and positivity (Lansford et al., 2021).

Responsiveness is the idea that a caregiver should promptly respond to a baby's signals, whether they are cries of distress or giggles of happiness (Bornstein, 1989, 2019). There are many cultural variations in how adults respond. For example, when Stephanie hears Makena fussing, she sometimes turns on a video to keep her occupied. In other families, adults may attend to fussy babies by nursing them, patting them, or picking them up. The critical element in responsiveness is establishing the back-and-forth relationship between caregiver and child (Mesman et al., 2018). Responsiveness helps babies learn their caregivers are reliable and helps infants regulate their feelings (see **Figure 5.6**).

Supportive caregiving can also be characterized as *sensitive*. Sensitive caregivers accurately interpret their child's signals (Mesman, 2021). When Jen expertly redirects Makena after the baby puts her hands in Jen's eyes, she understands that Makena is just trying to be close. She is interested in Makena's point of view but still manages to convince her to keep her fingers out of her eye sockets. When researchers examine these kinds of back-and-forth interactions, they often see their movements, facial expressions, and even sounds aligning. Scientists call this close coordination of responses *synchrony* (DePasquale, 2020). Caregivers and infants who are in sync share energy levels, patterns of brain activity, heart rates, and may even show a boost in *oxytocin*, the hormone associated with close attachments (Azhari et al., 2019; Levy et al., 2021).

Another aspect of supportive caregiving is that it is *positive*. Stephanie and Jen clearly enjoy being with Makena, even when she is challenging. Caregiving is undoubtedly hard, and families are frequently forced to impose limits on curious toddlers. However, parents who enjoy being with their children and who can communicate affection develop more positive relationships and foster their children's emotion regulation more easily (Planalp et al., 2017).

Babies who do not experience supportive parenting are at risk. Sometimes parents are stressed, depressed, or perhaps just unaware of how critical it is to be responsive to their child. Less commonly, infants may live in institutions where caregivers are

Families Around the World Ranked What Caregivers Should and Should Not Do:

Caregivers should...	Caregivers should not...
1. Demonstrate they care by touch.	1. Act negatively or critically to the child.
2. Show that the child makes them happy.	2. Ignore and be unresponsive to the child.
3. Share praise with the child.	3. Behave as if the child is inanimate or inhuman.
4. Encourage the child to try new things.	4. Get annoyed if the child wants to sit close to them.
5. Be happy around the child.	5. Ignore the infant's smiles or sounds.

Information from Mesman et al., 2016.

FIGURE 5.6 Sensitive Parenting Around the World Is the job of a caregiver to keep a baby safe, to show them love, or to teach them? You will notice that being physically close seems to be a universal behavior.

too busy to be attentive (Humphreys et al., 2018). Two styles of caregiving are particularly harmful in the early years: *detachment*, when a caregiver is unresponsive and inattentive, and *harshness*, when a caregiver is consistently negative, angry, or frightening. Infants who lack supportive parenting may later have trouble making friends and establishing close relationships and have learning, behavioral, or emotional problems (Crouch et al., 2017; Wu & Feng, 2020).

Attachment

Stephanie gets misty-eyed when she talks about Makena: "She's just brought so much joy to our family." Both Jen and Stephanie admit to worrying initially about bonding with their adopted babies, but they found that their love for their girls came naturally and bountifully. Jen and Stephanie may refer to their relationship with Makena as "love," but developmental scientists call this bond **attachment**. Attachment is a close, ongoing relationship between a child and their caregiver.

Jen, Stephanie, and Makena have built a relationship that makes Makena feel safe but also allows her to grow and explore. In times of stress, whether that is a new person in the room or just naptime, babies seek out their attachment figures. Researchers call this **proximity seeking**. Babies may seek attachment by climbing into an adult's lap or by clinging to their arms. Animals show this behavior as well, as demonstrated in the research of Harry Harlow: Monkeys raised in a laboratory with inanimate caregivers would seek comfort from these figures if they were soft and cuddly, even if they did not provide physical nourishment (Harlow, 1958).

Attachment figures also help children investigate the world by providing a **secure base**, or a safe haven for them to return to when they feel nervous or worried. For instance, when a new babysitter comes to the house, Makena checks in with her parents, but it doesn't take long for her to scoot over to meet them. Her parents act as a secure base for her exploration, allowing her to make new friends.

The patterns set in their first relationships will be taken into babies' future relationships. Researchers call this memory an **internal working model** (Bowlby, 1980; Bretherton & Munholland, 2016). Internal working models are not all positive: Attachment happens regardless of the quality of the bond. Babies can be attached to caregivers who are supportive but also to those who are neglectful or abusive (Perry et al., 2017). However, infants who have positive and responsive early relationships are more likely to develop internal working models that help them form better and stronger friendships (Sroufe, 2021).

The first years of life is a sensitive period for the development of attachment (Groh et al., 2017; Roisman & Groh, 2021). Attachment does not end in infancy; adults are attached, too, to romantic partners, friends, and their own parents. Even in adulthood, we continue to rely on our attachment figures for comfort. (Perhaps you have been known to call your parents when times get tough.)

Measuring Attachment Remember from Chapter 2 that it was a young doctor, John Bowlby, who helped develop attachment theory (Bowlby, 1951; Bowlby et al., 1952). At that time, many experts believed it was safer for sick babies to be cared for in a sterile hospital ward without their families, but Bowlby believed that children could not thrive in such isolation (Bowlby, 1969). He was one of many scientists who emphasized the importance of early relationships in creating emotional resilience across the lifespan and who looked to animals as a model for human behavior (Harlow, 1958). This approach remains at the forefront of developmental science today (Mikulincer & Shaver, 2019; Schuengel et al., 2021).

Bowlby's colleague, Canadian scientist Mary Ainsworth, explored individual differences in attachment and developed a categorization of attachment styles that continues to be influential today (Ainsworth & Bowlby, 1991; Bretherton, 1992). After studying children from Uganda, Canada, England, and the United States, Ainsworth created a test to assess

attachment An emotional bond in a close relationship. Attachment begins with the relationship between infants and their caregivers and may not always be positive.

proximity seeking The tendency for children (and adults) to seek comfort by being physically close to someone they are attached to.

secure base In attachment theory, a safe haven for children to return to when they may feel anxious.

internal working model In attachment theory, the idea that our early habits of relating to our caregivers create a pattern of relating that we will use later on in our lives.

Strange Situation An empirical method for evaluating the attachment status of toddlers developed by Mary Ainsworth.

secure attachment In attachment theory, children who have a sense of trust in their caregivers that allows them to explore their environment.

insecure attachment In attachment theory, children who have not established a sense of trust in their caregivers to soothe them when they are upset.

insecure-resistant attachment In attachment theory, a form of insecure attachment characterized babies' angry and hostile responses to their caregiver who they perceive as inconsistent and unreliable.

insecure-avoidant attachment In attachment theory, a form of insecure attachment characterized by babies' emotional distance from their caregivers who they perceive as being unable to soothe them.

disorganized attachment In attachment theory, children who have unusual responses in the Strange Situation procedure and who may be afraid of their caregivers.

Are You My Mommy? The Strange Situation is designed to temporarily stress toddlers to assess how they react to their caregivers and how they regulate their emotions in a new situation. In this video still, a baby adjusts to a new caregiver (the Stranger) after their parent has left the room.

how children investigated the world around them and how they responded in times of stress. Ainsworth discovered that briefly separating and reuniting babies with their caregivers could measure attachment behaviors (Ainsworth et al., 2015). Her experimental procedure became known as the **Strange Situation**, because it tested how toddlers reacted when separated from their caregivers in an unfamiliar place. In a span of 20 minutes, a toddler between 12 and 20 months was separated from their caregiver, watched by a friendly stranger, briefly left alone, and then reunited with their caregiver.

Types of Attachment Researchers who study toddlers' reactions in the Strange Situation find that they fall into four different types, called attachment styles or statuses. In **secure attachments**, toddlers feel comfortable exploring the laboratory and playing on their own but might show some distress when separated from their caregiver. They are also happy to see their caregivers when they return and are comforted by their caregivers when they are upset. Securely attached babies trust that their caregivers will be there when they need them; this gives them confidence and security to explore the world (Ainsworth et al., 2015). Warm, sensitive relationships between parents and children produce secure attachments.

Most studies of families around the world estimate that about 60 percent of toddlers are securely attached (Mesman et al., 2016). This means that about 40 percent of children are not. Ainsworth called these children **insecurely attached** and theorized that such toddlers have not developed trust in someone to take care of them when they are upset (Ainsworth et al., 2015).

Ainsworth and subsequent researchers described three varieties of insecure attachment. During the Strange Situation, toddlers who have an **insecure-resistant attachment** are upset when their caregivers leave and return, but they react with mixed or angry feelings and are difficult to calm (Ainsworth et al., 2015). These children feel insecure about separation and do not trust that their caregivers will return. They may not feel comfortable exploring the environment even when their caregiver is present and may be clingy. Researchers believe this pattern of attachment stems from an inconsistent parenting style (Leerkes & Zhou, 2018). In many communities, about 15 percent of babies exhibit this type of attachment (Mesman et al., 2016).

Children who display **insecure-avoidant attachment** do not appear to react when their caregivers leave the room. Instead, they tend to focus on objects in the room. When their caregivers return, they do not attempt to reconnect (Ainsworth et al., 2015). Researchers believe that these children may actually be upset by the Strange Situation but hide their feelings because they do not expect to be soothed. Children with insecure-avoidant attachment styles tend to have caregivers who are less attentive, so they learn to adapt by no longer expecting to be nurtured (Szepsenwol & Simpson, 2021). About 15 percent of toddlers in the United States are classified as insecure-avoidant. This type of attachment is much less common in communities where infants are not often separated from their caregivers, as some studies from South Korea and Israel have found (Jin et al., 2011; Zreik et al., 2017).

Children with the last type of insecure attachment, **disorganized attachment**, exhibit unusual behaviors in the Strange Situation (Main & Solomon, 1986). They might freeze, stare off into space, or seem afraid of their caregiver. These reactions are more frequently seen in children who have experienced serious trauma or whose caregivers are frightening. In many communities around the world, about 10 to 15 percent of children fall into this category (Granqvist et al., 2017).

After studying children in the Strange Situation, researchers determined that children with different attachment styles tended to have different life experiences when they grew up. No matter what type of early personality children had, those who showed secure attachment in

Shortcuts TV/BoClips

the Strange Situation were more likely to get along with their peers and develop good friendships, perhaps because they had learned successful ways of relating to others in infancy. On the other hand, children with insecure or disorganized attachment types were more likely to have difficulty making friends. Children who had developed an insecure-avoidant or a disorganized attachment style were also more likely to have emotional problems, such as a lack of emotion regulation (Groh et al., 2017).

Critiques of the Strange Situation Researchers generally agree that attachment is a universal human need, but they also remind us that attachment looks different in different cultures. The Strange Situation in particular has been often criticized, even by Ainsworth herself, for oversimplifying the complexities of real life (Ainsworth & Marvin, 1995; Keller, 2018; Vicedo, 2017).

In some cases, attachment theory has been used in legal settings that theorists never intended. Elements of the Strange Situation itself, meant to be a research assessment, have been used to measure caregiving in divorce and child welfare proceedings, and even to justify removing children from their families (Forslund et al., 2021). Indigenous families in North America, Australia, and New Zealand have been particularly concerned about misuse of attachment theory to justify the separation of children from their ancestral communities (Choate et al., 2019, 2020).

One concern about attachment theory is that in most families, babies have attachments to multiple caregivers and may show different patterns of relating to them (Keller, 2018). For instance, in the Central African Republic, researchers observed that babies in one close-knit village were attached to six people on average (Meehan & Hawks, 2013). The Strange Situation focuses on a single relationship, which may not provide an accurate measure of how a baby will relate to others or how sensitive any one caregiver is. Researchers have found that combining the patterns of babies' attachment to all of their caregivers may be more accurate than just focusing on one relationship (Dagan & Sagi-Schwartz, 2018).

In addition, the Strange Situation test does not take cultural variations into account. In some communities where babies are very unused to being cared for by new people, the procedure was extremely stressful. In others, it was not stressful at all. For instance, in some experiments with German families in the 1980s, about half of the babies were classified as having an insecure-avoidant attachment status, nearly double what researchers expected. What happened? The German babies had been raised to be very independent, to soothe themselves, and to expect less comfort when they were stressed (Grossmann et al., 1985; LeVine & LeVine, 2016). On the other hand, in South Korea and Japan, researchers observed that very few babies had developed the independence and the ability to explore that would lead to a designation of secure attachment (Jin et al., 2011). These babies were not used to being separated from their families at all, and the situation itself was too stressful for them. Many researchers now use measures of caregiving quality that avoid the stresses of the Strange Situation (Mesman, 2021).

Although the Strange Situation is not a perfect measure, few researchers question the importance of early relationships. While it remains difficult to accurately measure the bond between caregivers and children, experts agree that forming strong, enduring relationships is critical to healthy development (Keller, 2018).

The Biology of Early Family Relationships

Whereas Ainsworth tried to measure attachment using observation, some contemporary developmental scientists use brain-imaging technology and hormone tests to assess the biological bases of early relationships. Scientists have found that early caregiving programs babies' hormonal stress systems and brain connectivity (Gee, 2020; Nelson et al., 2019).

Scientific American Profile

▶ Building New Attachments

Bonding Helps You Cross the Street. Strong attachments may not always be easy to measure, but they help when you are making your way home from soccer practice. Elan's bond with his father, Dennis, helps them walk to their home in New York City.

These researchers believe that since caregivers soothe and suppress babies' responses to acute stress in cases of trauma, sensitive caregiving protects them from the long-term effects of too much exposure to stress hormones like cortisol (Gunnar, 2020).

For babies without supportive caregiving, early stress may epigenetically program the stress system to respond with more or less powerful stress responses in the future. For instance, less-attentive parenting seems to cause higher levels of stress hormones in babies, which may suppress their stress responses later in life (Moore, 2017). Infants under more acute stress experience a more extreme phenomenon: Babies and toddlers who receive neglectful care, like those in institutions or orphanages, can become unresponsive to normal stressors, which prevents them from responding flexibly to their environment (Gunnar, 2020).

Cortisol is not the only hormone that is affected by early caregiving; oxytocin plays an important role as well (Krol et al., 2019b). Caregivers with higher levels of oxytocin tend to be more attentive to their newborns and exhibit higher levels of synchrony (Feldman & Bakermans-Kranenburg, 2017). Caregivers with depression, on the other hand, often have lower levels of oxytocin (Ellis et al., 2021). Much of this biological research has focused on the relationship between babies and their female caregivers. However, researchers have also found that men's hormone levels change as they parent: Men, too, have higher levels of oxytocin when they do hands-on caregiving (Bakermans-Kranenburg et al., 2019; Dijk et al., 2020; Li et al., 2017).

Neuroscientists theorize that early baby–caregiver relationships do not just change hormones—they actually shape the neural networks in the brains of caregivers and babies. As you may remember, the circuits connecting the subcortical structures that process emotion, such as the amygdala, and the prefrontal cortex, where more thinking and planning take place, help babies control and manage their feelings. Supportive caregiving *delays* the development of these brain networks. Babies with caregivers who soothe them and reduce their stress rely on their caregivers to manage their strong feelings while their brains are still maturing (Gunnar, 2020).

In contrast, these circuits mature early in babies who are neglected (Tottenham, 2020). You might think that accelerated development is a good thing, but in this case, early maturation brings challenges. These babies' brains adapted to help them survive in neglectful environments, making it difficult for them to adapt to a world in which they need to develop healthy relationships and learn social skills. Children who have been neglected often have difficulties managing their feelings and accurately responding to the feelings of those around them.

Does this mean that babies should never experience any stress? Actually, researchers say mild stresses help train the brain to handle everyday stresses in the future. What you experience in infancy gives you practice and training for life to come: Some stress is actually a good thing (Gee, 2020; Gunnar, 2020). Concerns arise not with mild everyday stressors, but with acute trauma and long-term neglect.

Challenges in Early Parenting

Not everyone's experience with early parenting is easy. One young parent in Vancouver, British Columbia, experienced depression when her daughters were newborns. She remembered "falling apart" in the aisles of Costco, struggling to smile back at her daughter, and not knowing what to say when her toddler asked, "Mommy, are you happy?" (Goyette, 2016). She was diagnosed with depression, like almost one in five new mothers and one in eight new fathers around the world (Da Costa et al., 2019; Granat et al., 2017). Depression is not the only challenge faced by new parents. Nearly one in two U.S. families with infants and toddlers struggles financially, with more than one in six experiencing food insecurity (Coleman-Jensen et al., 2019; Jiang et al., 2015).

Early treatment for mental health challenges is critical. Depression or overwhelming stress can make it difficult to give children the responsive back-and-forth that is essential for infants as they develop emotion regulation and social skills (Granat et al.,

2017). Depression in women has gotten the most attention from researchers and health care providers, but all parents, including men and people who are nonbinary, are also susceptible (Charter et al., 2021). Depressed partners not only have difficulty responding to their babies, but their depression is also more likely to strain their relationship with the other parent (Da Costa et al., 2019). Relationship conflicts, from bickering to breakups, can also stress young families (Zhou et al., 2017).

Nearly 1 in 7 U.S. families with an infant includes a caregiver who uses alcohol or other substances in an unhealthy way, or has substance use disorder (SUD): a rate that has been increasing in recent decades (Clemans-Cope et al., 2019; Finkelhor, 2020; Kuppens et al., 2020). Babies in families marked by SUD are more likely to be fussy, irritable, and at higher risk for neglect and abuse and for developing emotional and behavioral problems later in life (Kuppens et al., 2020).

Infants and toddlers who have parents with SUD are also more likely to end up in the foster-care system, as a result of the criminalization of substance use disorder in many communities (Meinhofer & Angleró-Díaz, 2019). Interventions often take a family-focused approach, treating the caregivers' mental health issues while coaching them to be more responsive, supportive, and patient with their children (Barlow et al., 2019; Smith et al., 2016).

APPLY IT! **5.8** When Makena met the babysitter for the first time, she initially clung to Stephanie before venturing out to meet the new person. How is this an example of using her parent as a secure base?

5.9 Infants are often attached to their caregivers, even if they are subjected to neglect and abuse. How does attachment theory explain this?

Staying Close No Matter What
Christine and her two-month-old daughter, Isabelle, are allowed to stay together even though Christine is temporarily incarcerated in a correctional center in Illinois. They have benefited from a program that helps new parents maintain custody of their infants while they are incarcerated.

Child Care and Media in Infancy

Around the globe, babies spend time in child care. Even when they are cared for at home, many babies spend time in front of screens and on devices, contrary to the advice of experts. Both child care and screen time can have profound effects on babies' developing social and emotional skills.

Learning Objective

5.7 Explain the impact of experiences outside the family on infants' emotional development.

How Does Media Affect Emotional Development?

Like many caregivers, Jen and Stephanie's screen time rules changed during the COVID-19 pandemic. Without a video, they could not return phone calls and get work done. As you may recall from Chapter 4, experts recommend that babies avoid screens, except for video calls, until about 18 months, at which point their screen use should be limited to less than an hour a day (AAP, 2016). However, like Jen and Stephanie, many caregivers use media to entertain their children, and the amount of time small children spent on screens skyrocketed during the COVID-19 pandemic (Parents Together, 2020). Many caregivers feel, as Jen and Stephanie do, that the recommendations about screen use are simply unworkable and unrealistic: Screens are often on, and every caregiver has a cell phone (Barr et al., 2020; Radesky, 2019).

Some parents also spend too much time on screens, often while taking care of their children. New parents report that they are distracted by their phones or by the television at least 30 percent of the time that they are feeding their infants (Ventura et al., 2019). Caregivers who use media in this way tend to have fewer back-and-forth interactions with their children and are less attentive (Stockdale et al., 2020; Wan et al., 2021). Some early evidence indicates that toddlers whose parents are often distracted by technology may have higher rates of emotional disorders (McDaniel & Radesky, 2018).

Early Care in a Language They Know Zoe and Pelle are attending state-subsidized early education in Germany, provided in their heritage language, Danish. In their community in Flensburg, families often speak both German and Danish.

 Learn It Together

The Transition to Child Care

Plan Imagine your cousin has been a stay-at-home father to his 9-month-old since the baby's birth, and they have a warm emotional relationship. Now, he is thinking about going back to work, but is worried about how this will affect his relationship with the baby, and whether being with a child-care provider will be stressful for his daughter. Using your understanding of attachment theory and sensitive caregiving, give him your expert advice. Review information about attachment security, including factors that help promote secure attachment and information about attachment to multiple caregivers.

Engage Working with a few classmates, discuss the factors to consider relating to infant care. How does the baby's age, at 9 months, impact how she might respond to a new caregiver? What features should your cousin look for in a child-care provider? What features should he avoid? Should he be worried about his own relationship with his daughter?

Reflect Do you have any personal experience with this issue? Do you know anyone who has recently made a decision regarding infant care? Has learning about attachment security changed how you think about child care in the early years?

What about when babies use media by themselves? Babies exposed to technology for long periods of time are at greater risk for emotional problems or for falling behind in their physical or cognitive development, but it is difficult to determine whether it is their family circumstances or the media exposure that is the culprit (Lin et al., 2020; McHarg et al., 2020; Supanitayanon et al., 2020). In addition, because mobile and online media use in infants and toddlers is relatively new, researchers have not had time to study its effects in children over time.

Scientists have found that parents of infants and toddlers who see their children as difficult expose them to more media (McDaniel & Radesky, 2020; Munzer et al., 2018). However, it is not clear why this happens: Do parents of challenging children put them in front of a television or mobile device so they can get a break? Or do parents with limited skills in managing their children allow too much screen time, which exacerbates their children's difficult behavior? There is evidence for both theories. In either case, parents who rely on media to quiet their children may benefit from professional help to learn how to better manage their children's behavior and how to have responsive, back-and-forth interactions that will help their children flourish.

Early Child Care

Like many other working parents, Jen and Stephanie struggled to balance caring for two young children with jobs that had been changed by the pandemic. Maya's child-care center was closed, and Jen's parents only had so much time and availability to watch the children while she and Stephanie worked. They eventually found someone who would brave the pandemic to watch the girls so that they could work a few hours a day simultaneously.

Around the world, working parents rely on help from family members and from paid caregivers to balance their jobs and the needs of their young children. However, finding high-quality and affordable infant and toddler care is difficult (Malik et al., 2020). This is one of the reasons many parents take a leave from work when they have small children (Dotti Sani & Scherer, 2018). But in some places, affordable child care is subsidized by the community. For instance, quality child care is one of the reasons families in Denmark are able to continue to work after their children are born. The local government pays more than three-quarters of child care costs (BBC, 2016). In other countries, including the United States, infant child care is expensive and difficult to find (Banghart et al., 2020; OECD, 2020).

In the United States, infants and toddlers are not likely to attend a child-care center. More than 97 percent of child care in the United States is provided in private homes, and most child-care providers for infants and toddlers are informal and unpaid (Paschall & Tout, 2018). Many of these home-based child-care providers are friends or neighbors who have agreed to watch the baby as a favor (National Survey of Early Care and Education, 2016). Others are more formal arrangements. Parents tend to choose child care based on advice from family members and friends and look for a provider who can work with their budget and their schedule and who understands their culture (Forry, 2015; Forry et al., 2013; Gordon et al., 2008).

Recall from Chapter 4 that research has shown that early child care can provide many cognitive benefits. Being able to work also relieves families from economic strain. In addition, mothers who work are less likely to experience depression, in part because work offers important social support (Lewis et al., 2017). Babies and toddlers benefit from developing supportive relationships with their care providers (Ereky-Stevens et al., 2018).

High-quality infant-care programs nurture the attachment between babies and caregivers in a supportive environment (McMullen, 2018). Programs that foster warm relationships share three key features:

1. They provide continuity of care—a consistent relationship between one caregiver and an infant, rather than a changing roster of caregivers (Bratsch-Hines et al., 2020).

2. They have low infant-to-caregiver ratios, which enable caregivers to individually attend to infants' needs. Most experts advise that one provider be responsible for fewer than four infants under 15 months old and fewer than six toddlers (NAEYC, 2018).

3. They hire caregivers who understand typical infant development, are positive, and do not feel overwhelmed by spending all day with babies (NAEYC, 2019).

Unfortunately, much infant and toddler care in the United States does not meet these standards (Burchinal, 2018). Like parents, many child-care providers are overstressed, exhausted, and depressed (Kwon et al., 2019). Caregivers tend to be underpaid and underprepared for their challenging work (Kwon et al., 2020). Many programs are unable to provide continuity of care and move babies between providers every six months or every year (Ruprecht et al., 2016). What does this mean for babies? Some reports suggest that babies who spend a lot of time in poor-quality child care may be at risk for emotional or behavioral problems (Brownell & Drummond, 2020; Donoghue et al., 2017). Babies who have access to high-quality care do well; Jen and Stephanie count their daughters among the lucky ones.

APPLY IT! **5.10** Jen and Stephanie, like many parents, are worried about the recommendations for small children and screen media. What advice can you give them about managing their children's media exposure?

5.11 Jen and Stephanie want to find a new child-care situation for their daughters. What should they look for?

Share It!

It happens fast: Even when child-care providers are nurturing multiple children, being able to respond quickly helps create a secure bond. Scientists have found that some caregivers were able to respond in as little as 3 to 7 seconds.

(Ahnert, 2021)

Scientific American: Lifespan Development

Wrapping It Up

LO 5.1 Compare and contrast the traditional theories of emotional development. (p. 136)

Classic theories of emotional development, including those of Erikson and Freud, established that the social relationships formed in a baby's first years help set the stage for their future relationships and personality. There are two major crises of development in Erikson's theory of psychosocial development: trust versus mistrust and autonomy versus shame and doubt. Erikson believed children need to learn to trust and develop confidence in their ability to take care of themselves.

LO 5.2 Assess the roles of culture and context in emotional development. (p. 136)

Emotional maturation is shaped by cultural expectations and practices. The timing and expression of basic emotions varies around the world. Families may adopt proximal or distal parenting practices, or a mix of the two. Families' ethnotheories may emphasize collectivist or individualistic values. Contemporary research emphasizes the negative impact of early adversity on infants' development and their differential susceptibility to trauma and stress.

LO 5.3 Describe infants' and toddlers' emotional maturation. (p. 143)

Babies gradually develop some control over their emotions. Measuring infants' emotions is difficult: Their facial expressions, vocalizations, and physiology all give researchers clues about how they

might be feeling. Small infants are capable of contentment and distress but as they grow older, more complex emotions appear, depending on cultural expectations, including anger, fear, and empathy. Even babies are capable of *prosocial*, or helpful, behaviors.

LO 5.4 Explain how babies begin to develop unique personalities. (p. 150)

Early patterns of reactions in infants and toddlers are known as *temperament*, a precursor to personality. Thomas and Chess described infant temperament in three broad categories: easy, slow-to-warm-up, and difficult. Other researchers examine babies' effortful control, agreeableness, or level of shyness. Children's personalities are a result of genetics, early prenatal experience, and early caregiving. Cultures vary in the personality traits they appreciate but all children benefit from *goodness of fit*, a mutually supportive match between caregivers and their babies.

LO 5.5 Describe how caregiving impacts emotional development. (p. 153)

Babies can thrive in a variety of family configurations. Developmental scientists believe that a child's relationships with close caregivers in the first years of life create patterns of relating to others that last a lifetime. Across cultures, caregivers who are responsive and supportive with their babies seem to have better-adjusted children, even though specific parenting practices may differ.

LO 5.6 Explain common variations in caregiver–child attachment relationships. (p. 153)

The theory of attachment describes how caregivers can act as a secure base for the infants, allowing them to explore their environment. Based on the theoretical and empirical work of Bowlby and Ainsworth, some researchers describe four attachment styles: secure, insecure-resistant, insecure-avoidant, and disorganized attachment. Attachment can be measured through the Strange Situation. Scientists concur on the value of close relationships between caregivers and babies but do not always agree on how to measure it.

LO 5.7 Explain the impact of experiences outside the family on infants' emotional development. (p. 159)

Early child care can benefit infant and toddlers' development if it is of high quality. High-quality early child care supports early relationships. Many families have difficulty finding high-quality early child care. Many infants and toddlers are exposed to media in their early years, which can interrupt the development of responsive relationships.

KEY TERMS

trust versus mistrust (p. 137)
autonomy versus shame and doubt (p. 137)
proximal (p. 138)
distal (p. 138)
differential susceptibility (p. 141)
emotions (p. 144)
social smile (p. 145)
stranger anxiety (p. 146)

separation anxiety (p. 146)
social referencing (p. 147)
self-awareness (p. 147)
emotional contagion (p. 148)
empathy (p. 148)
prosocial (p. 148)
emotion regulation (p. 149)
personality (p. 150)
temperament (p. 150)

easy (p. 150)
slow-to-warm-up (p. 150)
difficult (p. 150)
goodness of fit (p. 151)
responsiveness (p. 154)
attachment (p. 155)
proximity seeking (p. 155)
secure base (p. 155)
internal working model (p. 155)

Strange Situation (p. 156)
secure attachments (p. 156)
insecure attachment (p. 156)
insecure-resistant attachment (p. 156)
insecure-avoidant attachment (p. 156)
disorganized attachment (p. 156)

CHECK YOUR LEARNING

1. At 18 months, Makena wanted to hold her own spoon when eating cereal. Most of the cereal and milk went onto her lap, on the table, and in her hair. Thinking about Erikson's stage of autonomy versus shame and doubt, what advice would you give her parents?

   a) Her attempts should be encouraged, even though she isn't very coordinated yet.

   b) She should be taught that it is not okay to make a mess.

   c) Her parents should take over the feeding to save time and show her the proper way to use a spoon.

   d) She may have a developmental disorder.

2. Cultural differences in adults' expectations for their infants' emotional expressions are known as:

   a) collectivism.

   b) ethnotheories.

   c) social exclusion.

   d) attachment.

3. Which of the following is an example of a proximal parenting practice?

   a) Providing a variety of toys for the baby to play with on a blanket

   b) Holding an infant in a carrier strapped to the parent's body while folding laundry

   c) Playing music and singing songs with the baby

   d) Allowing the baby to practice putting on her own hat

4. Although early experiences of stress and trauma can negatively impact infants' brain development, some children have more severe reactions than others due to their particular genotype. This variation is known as:

   a) hyperplasticity.

   b) nonreactivity.

   c) head-sparing.

   d) differential susceptibility.

5. Which of the following emotions is typically NOT expressed by a 7-month old?

   a) Pride

   b) Distress

   c) Happiness

   d) Fear

6. The still-face procedure is designed to demonstrate infants' emotional reactions to a violation of their expectations by:

   a) forcing babies to keep their own faces motionless.

   b) instructing caregivers to look unresponsively at their infants.

   c) showing babies pictures of clown faces.

   d) teaching babies a simple form of "freeze-tag."

7. Individual differences in babies' patterns of emotional responsiveness that seem to be present soon after birth are known as:

   a) temperament.

   b) resilience.

   c) personality disorder.

   d) meltdowns.

8. Supportive parenting includes all of the following EXCEPT:

   a) sensitivity.

   b) discipline.

   c) responsiveness.

   d) positivity.

9. How is a securely attached 14-month-old likely to react when her grandmother drops her off with a new babysitter?

   a) She may cry when Grandma leaves and will look for a reassuring cuddle with Grandma when she returns.

   b) She will feel confident to explore the new space and will not cry when Grandma leaves.

   c) She will cry when Grandma leaves and continue to feel angry after Grandma returns.

   d) She will react with anger when Grandma returns and cling to the babysitter for comfort.

10. How can the concept of *goodness of fit* be applied to advice for a parent coping with an irritable infant?

11. Why are patterns of secure and insecure attachment using the Strange Situation assessment different in countries like South Korea when compared to countries like Germany? What are some cultural explanations for these variations?

6 Physical and Cognitive Development in Early Childhood

© Macmillan, Photo by Sidford House

Changing Body and Brain

6.1 Describe typical growth in the body and brain from age 2½ to 6.

6.2 Explain the connection between the development of motor skills and children's feelings of competence.

Staying Healthy

6.3 Describe common health challenges during early childhood.

Cognitive Development

6.4 Identify the key features of Piaget's preoperational stage.

6.5 Apply Vygotsky's theory of development to young children's thinking.

6.6 Describe advances in information-processing skills during early childhood.

Developing Language in Early Childhood

6.7 Discuss vocabulary and grammar development during early childhood.

Supporting Early Learning

6.8 Explain developmentally appropriate early education.

Selected Activities from

Activities

Spotlight on Science: The Long-Term Impact of Preschool

Concept Practice: Developing a Theory of Mind

Assessments

LearningCurve

Practice Quiz

Videos

Scientific American Profiles

Early-Childhood Education

They call Aidan the mayor. His city: the playground near his apartment in New York City. Aidan knows everyone's name, even the names his father can't remember, and he greets everyone. He only just turned 5 but excels at the monkey bars and, unlike many children his age, can ride any kind of bike on his own. What he cannot do on the playground is catch his big sister, Dylan. At age 7, she is too fast for him. Play is Aidan's favorite thing to do: outside in the park, blanket forts, Spider-Man and Star Wars with Dylan, or games on the tablet.

Like many parents, Alex and Sinead want to make sure Aidan is ready for kindergarten. He has attended preschool for years, which he loves: His favorite part is serving pretend drinks to his classmates from the play kitchen. However, Aidan's parents imagine that kindergarten will be more serious and are not sure he is looking forward to it. Although he can already count, write his name, and read simple words, sitting down to do schoolwork is not so fun.

Like many young children, Aidan would rather run around, pretend, or draw than do a worksheet or flashcards. He procrastinates when his parents set aside time for him to do academic work. Sometimes he even complains that he is "having a breakdown" and tries to negotiate his way out of it. His parents worry that this may be unusual immaturity and that he is getting into the habit of procrastinating hard work. According to developmental science, Aidan is not immature for his age at all: He is just not grown up yet.

Scientific American Profile

▶

Meet Aidan

Early childhood is the period between about ages 2½ to 6. It typically begins as toddlers develop the language and movement skills that drive their independent exploration. It ends as preschoolers develop more abstract thinking and independent living skills and, in many communities, start formal schooling. Early childhood is an important period for the development of many abilities that children will draw on later in life, including early math and reading skills as well as social and emotional understanding. This does not mean that children like Aidan are ready to sit still at a desk. Young children are eager to learn, but most of that learning comes easiest if it is integrated with the social and physical activities that children enjoy — like play.

From this glimpse of Aidan's life and his accomplishments, like counting to 100, you will learn about the physical and cognitive markers of early childhood. You will read about the importance for young children to get enough to eat and opportunities to be active, play, and learn. You will also learn about the many interventions that have improved the lives of young children around the world.

Changing Body and Brain

Learning Objectives

6.1 Describe typical growth in the body and brain from age 2½ to 6.

6.2 Explain the connection between the development of motor skills and children's feelings of competence.

Aidan is like many 5-year-olds: He sometimes spills, and he fusses at school drop-off. But, as he himself acknowledges, he is closer to being a "big kid": His growing body and brain enable him to learn more about the world. Children in other families may be learning gardening or gymnastics rather than bike riding, but young children everywhere are developing the ability to master new skills, powered by their bigger bodies and brains.

Changing Body

Over the years of early childhood, Aidan grew about 9 inches (23 cm) and gained about 20 pounds (9 kg). He turned from a chubby-cheeked toddler into a longer and leaner little boy. At around age 5, children typically have the least amount of body fat of the lifespan, giving them a more grown-up appearance (Gallagher et al., 2020). Aidan's growing body will enable more challenging physical activities, but it will also lead adults to expect more mature behavior.

Monitoring physical growth continues to be a measure of children's health. If illness or malnutrition slows growth, brain development may suffer (Galler et al., 2021). Children around the world have similar patterns of maturation in early childhood: Most are roughly similar in height until around age 5 (Karra et al., 2017). As you might recall from Chapter 4, some children who were profoundly malnourished in their first few years of life have growth that is *stunted* and are shorter for their age. While these children may get heavier, most will continue to be smaller than their peers (Leroy et al., 2020).

After their fifth birthday, as children's long bones begin to grow, inborn genetic differences begin to show (Lampl & Schoen, 2017). Some children, particularly those with tall parents, will begin to grow noticeably taller than their preschool classmates. Others may stay relatively petite. When children are given the necessary nutrition, their physical growth reflects the genetic predispositions they were born with.

What's Happening in the Brain?

early childhood The period between ages 2½ and 6. It typically begins as toddlers develop language and movement skills and ends as they develop more abstract thinking and independent living skills and, in many communities, start formal schooling.

The brain continues to grow during early childhood, but at a slower pace than in infancy. By age 6, Aidan's brain will be about 95 percent of adult size (Gilmore et al., 2018). Whereas overall brain size stays about the same, the number of connections between neurons and the complexity of the *cortex* (the surface area on the outside of the brain) increase. There are about a quadrillion synapses in the brain during early childhood (that is 15 zeros!) (Zelazo & Lee, 2010).

INCREASING CONNECTIVITY

During early childhood, the body spends most of its energy building the brain. Much of this is creating new connections between neurons and myelinating them to make them faster and more efficient. Images of a cross-section of the brain taken with MRI scans show it becoming progressively whiter, a sign of the buildup of white matter.

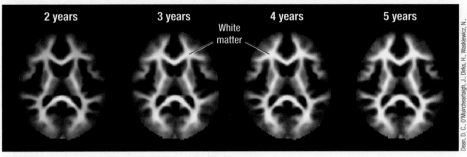

2 years   3 years   4 years   5 years

White matter

Dean, D. C., O'Muircheartaigh, J., Dirks, H., Waskiewicz, N., Walker, L., Doernberg, E., Piryatinsky, I., & Deoni, S. C. L. (2015). Characterizing longitudinal white matter development during early childhood. Brain Structure and Function, 220(4), 1921–1933. https://doi.org/10.1007/s00429-014-0763-3

MATURATION IN THE CORTEX

There are different ways to look at the growing brain: from the outside, from the top, or use a scanning device to visualize a slice through the middle. Each way allows researchers to see different structures. During early childhood, maturation in the cortex helps young children control their behavior and learn new skills.

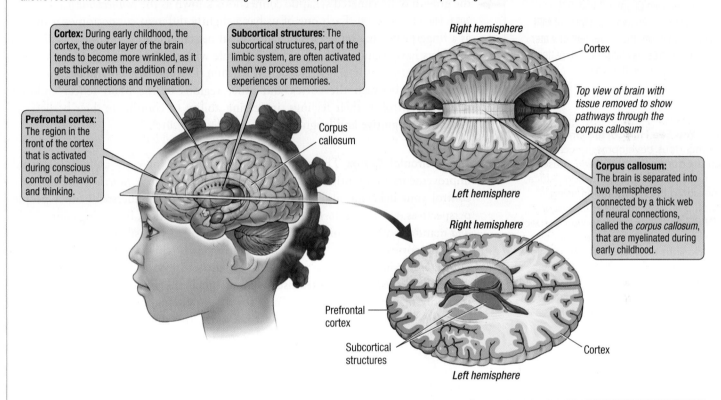

Cortex: During early childhood, the cortex, the outer layer of the brain tends to become more wrinkled, as it gets thicker with the addition of new neural connections and myelination.

Subcortical structures: The subcortical structures, part of the limbic system, are often activated when we process emotional experiences or memories.

Prefrontal cortex: The region in the front of the cortex that is activated during conscious control of behavior and thinking.

Corpus callosum

Right hemisphere

Cortex

Top view of brain with tissue removed to show pathways through the corpus callosum

Left hemisphere

Corpus callosum: The brain is separated into two hemispheres connected by a thick web of neural connections, called the *corpus callosum*, that are myelinated during early childhood.

Right hemisphere

Prefrontal cortex

Subcortical structures

Cortex

Left hemisphere

Individualized Connectome

There are some universal patterns in brain development, but life experiences give each child a slightly different network of white matter connections reflecting ongoing myelination. Each one of us has a slightly different connectome, as distinct as a fingerprint, that represents our individual neural circuitry. This is a DTI image showing the pattern of white matter development in the brain of one 4½-year-old girl who was able to sit very still in an MRI.

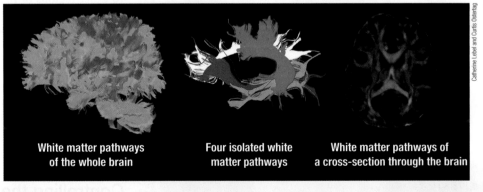

The individual connectome of one 4-year-old

White matter pathways of the whole brain

Four isolated white matter pathways

White matter pathways of a cross-section through the brain

Catherine Lebel and Curtis Ostertag

prefrontal cortex The area at the front of the brain beneath the forehead that is critical to logical thinking and controlling behavior.

CONNECTIONS

Remember from Chapter 2 that *DTI*, or *diffusion tensor imaging*, is a form of MRI scanning in which the movement of water in the brain creates images of the pattern of myelinated axons in the brain.

Can You See Her Cortex Growing? Tremendous development occurs in cortex during the early years. Researchers in Keneba, Gambia, in western Africa, measured brain maturation using *functional near infared spectroscopy (fNIRS)*. In fNIRS, children wear a special head covering that enables scientists to use light to measure the blood flow and oxygen levels in the cortex. An advantage of fNIRS is that once children have put the cap on, they can move naturally, allowing scientists to visualize their brain in action.

Early childhood is a period of intensive growth of the connections that link different parts of the brain, a process that will continue throughout childhood and adolescence. In addition, the cortex continues to mature in early childhood, particularly the **prefrontal cortex**, an area at the front of the brain beneath the forehead that is critical to logical thinking and controlling behavior.

Increasing Connectivity During early childhood, neurons in the brain continue to add myelin, the fatty insulating layer that helps speed communication between them (Lebel & Deoni, 2018). The biggest tract of myelin covers a large set of neural connections called the *corpus callosum*, which connects the right and left hemispheres of the brain (Danielsen et al., 2020). This bridge helps young children coordinate their movements and will contribute to more complex thinking.

Breakthroughs in DTI brain scanning technology have helped scientists visualize the growth of myelinated synaptic connections known as the *connectome* (Ciarrusta et al., 2021; Howell et al., 2019). Each one of us has a slightly different connectome, as distinct as a fingerprint, that represents our individual neural circuitry. Despite this diversity, scientists have found shared patterns in people with psychological disorders or environmental stressors (Cao et al., 2017; Kim et al., 2019). During early childhood, increasing connections between the cortex and other regions of the brain reflect children's stronger control of their feelings, increasing ability to coordinate their bodies, and expanding cognitive and language skills (Reynolds et al., 2019).

The Prefrontal Cortex The major cognitive advances of early childhood include improvements in attention and memory as well as *executive function*, the ability to control your behavior, and *theory of mind*, the ability to understand other people's perspectives (Blair et al., 2016; Fiske & Holmboe, 2019). Myelination, increasing connectivity, *and* maturation in the cortex make these cognitive gains possible.

The cortex increases and thickens during early childhood, resulting in more prominent wrinkles as these new dendrites squeeze into the skull (Long et al., 2017). A preschool-aged child's cortex uses twice as much energy as an adult's cortex, as it is rapidly maturing (Dienel, 2019). This growth allows children to better control their behavior, improve their memory, and think more logically.

The prefrontal cortex is activated during logical thought and planning. It allows children to think about what they are doing and, as it matures, to better plan ahead and consider the consequences of their actions. During early childhood, the prefrontal cortex typically becomes more active, as it increasingly connects to other regions of the brain (Buss & Spencer, 2018).

The rapid growth of the cortex and the proliferation of the connections linking to the prefrontal cortex is one reason why early childhood is a sensitive period for the development of many skills, such as executive function, attention, and language (OECD, 2017). The brain is shaped particularly easily by the environment as it grows. Scientists have found that experiences such as being read to, spending time on screens, and being exposed to environmental toxins all contribute to patterns of brain maturation (Grohs et al., 2019; Hutton et al., 2020a, 2020b).

Controlling the Body

Aidan is so coordinated that he can ride a bike and even let go of the handlebars from time to time (much to his parents' dismay). Thus, it may not surprise his parents that researchers say that 4-year-olds display the same level of coordination and balance as adults (Gabel & Scheller, 2013).

Aidan has done more than excel at *gross motor skills* such as pulling himself up on the monkey bars—he has also developed some *fine motor skills*. He can sit still to write his name, and he also knows how to use a tablet and his parents' phones. At the same time, Aidan clearly needs help with some motor skills: It takes a village of caregivers to help all the children on his soccer team put on cleats and shin guards correctly.

Motor-skill development does not happen automatically as children mature; it requires practice (Haga et al., 2018). Children around the world learn the motor skills important to their culture, from writing their names, to threading a loom, to tap dancing. Unlike many of the motor achievements of infancy and toddlerhood, the motor advances of early childhood and beyond are far from universal.

Motor skills give children a feeling of competence that can help them to better interact with friends and do schoolwork (Cameron et al., 2016; Robinson et al., 2015). Practicing physical skills strengthens children's brains as well as their bodies: This practice improves their executive function and their ability to control their behavior (McClelland & Cameron, 2019).

Gross Motor Skills In early childhood and throughout the lifespan, motor development is influenced by opportunity as well as biological maturation (Feitoza et al., 2018). Even within a single country, differences in children's environments may affect when they develop typical skills. For example, researchers in Myanmar found that 5-year-olds from rural areas are more likely to hop and leap than those who grew up in cities, perhaps because they had more open space to play in. On the other hand, children from urban areas were better at playing with a ball (kicking, throwing, catching), probably because they had more instruction in and time to play organized games (Aye et al., 2017). In communities around the world, the environment is critical to which motor skills children develop (Tomaz et al., 2019).

Understanding community expectations for motor-skill development can help educators and health care providers identify children who may need extra help meeting those expectations (Hulteen et al., 2020). Since motor skills take practice, more participation in physical activity generally leads to more advanced skills (Wick et al., 2017) (see **Figure 6.1**).

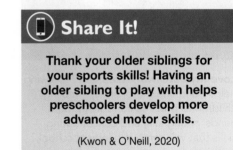

Share It!

Thank your older siblings for your sports skills! Having an older sibling to play with helps preschoolers develop more advanced motor skills.

(Kwon & O'Neill, 2020)

Scientific American: Lifespan Development

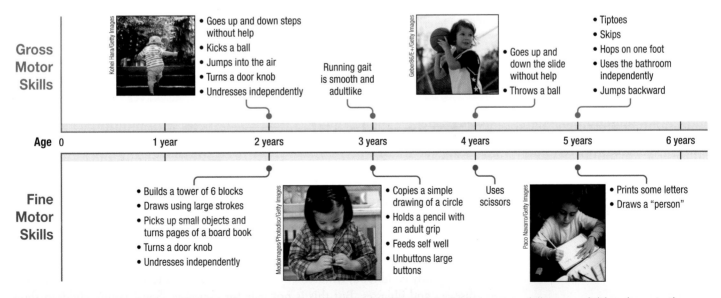

Gross Motor Skills

- Goes up and down steps without help
- Kicks a ball
- Jumps into the air
- Turns a door knob
- Undresses independently

Running gait is smooth and adultlike

- Goes up and down the slide without help
- Throws a ball

- Tiptoes
- Skips
- Hops on one foot
- Uses the bathroom independently
- Jumps backward

Age 0   1 year   2 years   3 years   4 years   5 years   6 years

Fine Motor Skills

- Builds a tower of 6 blocks
- Draws using large strokes
- Picks up small objects and turns pages of a board book
- Turns a door knob
- Undresses independently

- Copies a simple drawing of a circle
- Holds a pencil with an adult grip
- Feeds self well
- Unbuttons large buttons

Uses scissors

- Prints some letters
- Draws a "person"

FIGURE 6.1 Progression of Motor-Skill Development in Early Childhood These are some common skills many children learn in the United States. They are based on cultural norms, rather than physical or neurological development: If children are never allowed to use scissors, they will not automatically learn how to use them at age 4. Similarly, many children can ride a tricycle at age 3, but if they do not have a tricycle or access to a slide, or if they are not allowed to walk up stairs on their own, they will not develop these capabilities.

Love My Patchwork Elephant? Drawing helps build fine motor skills, enabling children to practice controlling their hands, sitting still, and concentrating—skills that will come in handy at school.

It may not be as fun as learning to play soccer or tap dance, but toilet training, like dressing and undressing, is essential to children's growing independence (de Carvalho Mrad et al., 2021). In many affluent countries, children typically begin toilet training before they are enrolled in pre-kindergarten. However, more than 1 in 10 still have toileting accidents when they enter kindergarten at age 5 (Jackson et al., 2020). Pediatricians in the United States usually recommend against toilet training until children show interest in using the bathroom and awareness of their own elimination, which can occur anytime between age 18 months and 4 years (Wolraich & American Academy of Pediatrics, 2016). In many countries, including China, Nigeria, and Vietnam, children are trained much earlier, often before their first birthdays (Rouse et al., 2017; Solarin et al., 2017).

Successful toilet training requires the coordination of body awareness, the language to talk about it, the ability to plan when to get to the bathroom, and the motor skills to get dressed and undressed (Baird et al., 2019). Children who are trained very early, before these skills have fully developed, require extra adult support and flexibility (Bender & She, 2017). However, children who start later may be less interested in learning to use the bathroom and less flexible about trying new routines (Van Aggelpoel et al., 2019).

Fine Motor Skills In early childhood, young children develop more control over their hands, enabled by increasing connections in the brain. By kindergarten, they are expected to be able to draw a person and write their name with a marker. How well children control their hands in preschool often predicts how they will do in kindergarten and even in elementary school (Cadoret et al., 2018; Macdonald et al., 2018). This is because 4-year-olds who have developed strong fine motor skills are likely able to focus, sit still, and control their behavior.

Indeed, many children with strong fine motor skills also have more mature executive function (Hudson et al., 2020; McClelland & Cameron, 2019). The brain networks activated when young children are controlling themselves are very similar to those that they use when practicing fine motor skills (Kim et al., 2018).

APPLY IT! **6.1** Alex and Sinead worry that people expect more of Aidan now that he looks more like a little boy than a toddler. How should they explain why Aidan's brain is still not like an adult's?

6.2 Describe two aspects of brain maturation that support Aidan's learning during early childhood.

6.3 Aidan has terrific coordination on the playground. How might his ability to control his body help him adjust to kindergarten?

Staying Healthy

Learning Objective

6.3 Describe common health challenges during early childhood.

Although preschoolers are developing minds of their own and their ability to articulate details like why they dislike the mushy texture of plantains, they are still dependent on the adults around them to keep them healthy. The things children do every day—moving, eating, and getting rest—foster healthy bodies, brains, and relationships. The habits that adults teach children, from trying plantains to enjoying running on the playground, can last a lifetime.

In early childhood, children's bodies are sturdier and less vulnerable to infectious diseases and illnesses. But this is not true for everyone: Some young children show signs of chronic conditions that may take a toll on their health later in the lifespan. During early childhood, children are susceptible to the dangers of pollution and toxins in their environment, and also to injury as they explore their world more independently and sometimes fearlessly.

Sleep in Early Childhood

Sinead and Alex are serious about sleep. At 7:30 P.M., Aidan and Dylan are in their room, lights out, with the sound machine on and a command to stop the giggling. Sinead and Alex believe that sleep is important to their children's happiness, and scientists agree. Getting enough sleep is essential for brain development; without it, preschoolers can have difficulties with emotion regulation and learning (Hoyniak et al., 2019; Williams et al., 2019).

Most preschoolers get the recommended 10–13 hours of sleep, but about one in four families struggles with managing sleep (Newton et al., 2020; Paruthi et al., 2016). Families with consistent routines have an easier time getting their children to bed (Covington et al., 2019). Consistency is not the only answer, however. Children who are on screens or watch television as part of their bedtime routine may have trouble sleeping through the night (Janssen et al., 2020).

One major transition for families in the United States is giving up the afternoon nap. However, in many countries, including Australia, Japan, and China, children continue to nap into the school years (Jeon et al., 2021; Staton et al., 2020). Children in the United States generally stop napping by age 5, most likely because U.S. families tend to find it difficult to schedule and are eager to consolidate sleep (Staton et al., 2020). However, many 3- and 4-year-olds are not ready to go all day without a rest, and naps continue to have emotional and cognitive benefits for older children (Horváth & Plunkett, 2018). Children outgrow naptime at different ages, leaving parents to guess and child-care centers to manage a classroom of children with variable napping needs (Thorpe et al., 2020).

Naptime in Kabul An after-lunch rest is common in day-care centers around the world. These children are napping at a child-care center in Afghanistan. Sleep is essential for brain development and emotion regulation in early childhood.

Staying Active

Early childhood is one of the most physically active periods of the lifespan. If you visit a preschool, you will see children racing around the playground and dashing down the corridors. In early childhood, this physical activity is often called *gross motor play*, or *big body play* (Carlson, 2011).

The Best Playground in the World? It is probably the one you are playing in. Whether children are enjoying water play in a public playground in Singapore or climbing on monkey bars in Mumbai, they are getting the physical activity they need to stay healthy.

Some of the benefits of active play are not surprising. Preschoolers who are very physically active are more likely to stay healthy and develop strong muscles and better coordination (Wiersma et al., 2020). Other benefits may be less obvious: Active children have an easier time planning and controlling their behavior (Cook et al., 2019). Physically active children may also be less likely to act out or be depressed (Dale et al., 2019; McNeill et al., 2018). Scientists suggest that being stuck inside was one reason young children's mental health deteriorated during the early months of the COVID-19 pandemic (Li et al., 2021).

Experts recommend that preschool-age children get about three hours of physical activity a day (USDHHS, 2018; WHO, 2019). Unfortunately, not all U.S. children get that much (Tulchin-Francis et al., 2021; Webster et al., 2019). Researchers have identified several reasons why children stay still. First, some preschools emphasize academic skills rather than play, so children may not have enough time on the playground (Ellis et al., 2017). Even when children *do* have time to play at preschool, teachers may worry that outdoor play is unsafe, too hot, or too cold (Sandseter et al., 2021).

Furthermore, when at home, many children spend more time in *sedentary*, or seated, activities, such as watching television or playing with tablets or phones, instead of running around (Madigan et al., 2020; Wadsworth et al., 2020). Parents are often too busy to make sure their children are active, and some also worry about safety when children play outside (Tandon et al., 2017; Yoon & Lee, 2019). Rural children may live too far from playmates or from a safe playground (Wende et al., 2020). Urban children may live close to other children but stay home because adults fear broken playground equipment or lack the time to supervise their children (Finkelstein et al., 2017; Hoyos-Quintero & García-Perdomo, 2019).

Eating for Health

Like all active 4-year-olds, Aidan needs sufficient calories to make it through the day. Sinead and Alex try to make sure that he eats a balanced diet with lots of vegetables, but like many of us, he wants his share of sweets.

During early childhood, families can help young children establish eating patterns that reduce health risks (Nix et al., 2021). Experts believe that diets heavy on sugar contribute to unhealthy weight among young children. But compared to other age groups, preschoolers eat more fruits and vegetables (Hoy et al., 2020). The average preschooler in the United States eats more healthily than most teenagers (Kim et al., 2014).

Selective Eating Like many young children, Aidan sometimes has some curious eating habits: He always separates his food from other food on the plate so that it doesn't touch. Half of preschoolers around the world are *picky* or *selective eaters* like Aidan (Chao, 2018; Fernandez et al., 2020). Researchers have an evolutionary explanation for this vexing behavior: Children generally become more selective at about the same time that they can find food on their own (Ahlstrom et al., 2017). Pickiness may have protected our ancestors from eating unsafe foods, like poisonous berries or rotten meat, and may have been adaptive when children were able to forage on their own. Today, selective eating is challenging for preschool teachers who are trying to serve cantaloupe to a group of disgusted 4-year-olds and for caregivers who want to support their children but also get through dinnertime without tears (Schuster et al., 2019; Taylor & Emmett, 2019).

The Impact of Body Size Young children are not only observant about what their food looks like: They are already absorbing messages about their body size (Stanford & Kyle, 2018). Scientists have found that children as young as 3 respond to stigma about what they look like. As a result, experts recommend talking with sensitivity about

CONNECTIONS

Remember from Chapters 3 and 4 that during the prenatal period and the first two years, taste preferences develop that will last a lifetime. Babies who gain weight too quickly establish metabolic and immune responses that may make a healthy weight harder to maintain later on.

📱 Share It!

Give it another chance! Researchers have found that it takes multiple exposures, sometimes more than 10 tries before children will happily eat a new food.

(Appleton et al., 2018)

📰 **Scientific American: Lifespan Development**

children's bodies (Pont et al., 2017). Language matters: Using terms like *unhealthy weight* to refer to a person's size is preferred to terms like *overweight* and *obesity*, even though medical terms are still used in research (Rubino et al., 2020; Smith et al., 2020).

Determining healthy weight is not a simple calculation: Individual variations, like a family history of diabetes, high blood pressure, bone mass, or a lot of physical activity, make it difficult to predict exactly how big one child should be (Strings, 2019; Vanderwall et al., 2018). Children, like the rest of us, come in a variety of healthy shapes and sizes. However, there is a scientific consensus that some types of heavier bodies are associated with health risks in later life: For instance, children whose weight is higher than the 97.5th percentile on a standardized growth chart are considered to have *obesity*. They may not experience any immediate health consequences but are likely to remain larger, which may increase their risk of complications later on (Yan et al., 2019).

In the United States, about one in seven preschool children has obesity, a rate similar to other high-income countries (de Bont et al., 2020; Fryar et al., 2020). Around the world, more children and adults develop an unhealthy weight because of what researchers call a *nutrition transition*, and in many countries, weights that many doctors consider unhealthy have become typical (Ronto et al., 2018). Families are transitioning from a diet filled with traditional fruits and vegetables to more processed, convenient, high-calorie foods that have more sugar and salt and fewer nutrients (Jaacks et al., 2019).

Children who are bigger than their peers may be targets for bullying or exclusion, even in preschool: They may need adults to stand up for them (Donkor et al., 2021; Rex-Lear et al., 2019). Caregivers and other adults can model kindness and inclusion of all children to help prevent the harms that can come from peers and other adults.

A major risk factor for health is low income: Good nutrition is expensive. Young children are often wasteful, either through pickiness or clumsiness. In addition, they are likely to demand the convenient and tasty foods marketed to them (Cornwell et al., 2020). About one in seven U.S. families with young children is *food insecure*, meaning that they may be skipping meals or running out of groceries because of the cost (Coleman-Jensen et al., 2020). Children whose families worry about affording food are more likely to have an unhealthy weight, particularly as they grow older (Ontai et al., 2019). Researchers suspect that financial stress and limited availability of nutritious food contribute to unhealthy weight (Na et al., 2021; Vargas et al., 2017).

Interventions to Improve Nutrition Helping families with nutritional problems, whether caused by food insecurity or by other factors, often means addressing the needs not just of the children, but of the entire group (Smith et al., 2020). Any intervention must reduce the stigma around weight, normalize the challenge of maintaining a healthy weight when the environment makes it hard to do so, and support a family's strengths. Interventions designed to improve children's nutrition are not always successful: Some even increase poor body image and stigma (Dietz, 2019; Richmond et al., 2021).

Families play a critical role in managing taste preferences and establishing healthy eating patterns. The most powerful predictor of what a child eats is the food adults offer them: If caregivers do not provide sugary drinks or high-calorie snacks, children will not eat them (Rex et al., 2021). Also critical to nutrition is whether adults model and encourage healthy choices (Gibson, Androutsos, et al., 2020). This does not mean being excessively restrictive: Caregivers with too many rules about food may see them backfire (Adams et al., 2020). Furthermore, families who can eat together at home tend to have healthier diets than those who eat on the run, or who feed children separately (Glanz et al., 2021).

CONNECTIONS

Remember from Chapter 4 that health professionals often use a standardized growth chart or the body mass index (BMI) to evaluate a weight. These measures are imperfect but continue to be used as a convenient starting point for evaluating children's health (Cole, 2012; Gallagher et al., 2020).

Do It Yourself. One way to improve nutrition and provide food security is to grow your own. This little girl is showing the squashes she has grown in her family's garden in Jinotega, Nicaragua.

Swimming Is Fun and Keeps You Safe. Drowning is a leading cause of death in young children around the world, particularly in communities with open water, rivers, and pools. These young children are learning to swim in a pond in Bangladesh.

Common Hazards

Like the rest of us, children are susceptible to colds and the occasional gastrointestinal illness. During the recent COVID-19 pandemic, however, they typically benefited from a strong immune system in combating the virus (Pierce et al., 2020; Weisberg et al., 2021). As a result, young children were less likely to develop serious COVID-related complications, even though, like other common viruses, it traveled widely through child-care centers and preschools (Bhopal et al., 2021; Kim et al., 2021).

Young children may have been spared the worst of the pandemic, but they feel the effects of other infectious diseases (Dawood et al., 2020; WHO, 2020). The easiest way to prevent many of these illnesses is by doing something you have probably been told a million times: Wash your hands. Scientists have found that doing so can reduce gastrointestinal infections in early-childhood centers by about 30 percent and respiratory infections by 20 percent (van Beeck et al., 2016).

In the United States, young children who go to day care are sick enough to stay home at least four times every year (National Health Interview Survey, 2015). Even a minor illness can be a substantial strain on families, particularly when parents cannot take time off from work or lack backup care to take care of a sick child (CS Mott Children's Hospital, 2017).

Dangers in the Environment Children can also be sickened by their environment. Around the world, more than one in four deaths in children under age 5 is caused by pollution, from respiratory infections caused by air pollution to gastrointestinal diseases caused by unsafe drinking water or dangerous chemicals or toxins in food (Prüss-Üstün et al., 2016). Young children are particularly sensitive to environmental toxins, because doses of chemicals or pollutants that would not hurt an adult can cause immediate or long-term consequences in their tiny bodies, including disorders of cognitive development and even death (Costa et al., 2020; Landrigan et al., 2019).

In the United States and around the world, the toll of environmental pollution often falls heavily on marginalized, low-income communities (Nigra, 2020). Rural children and children of color are more than twice as likely to be exposed to lead as their city-dwelling, more affluent peers, frequently due to poor-quality water in rural homes (Gibson, Fisher, et al., 2020).

Accidents and Injuries Young children are healthier than babies, but they face a new danger: accidental injury, a leading cause of death for preschoolers around the world (NCHS, 2021; WHO, 2020). Such deaths are tragic: preschoolers struck by cars while in strollers, drowned in swimming pools, or consumed by house fires. Accidents are also a leading cause of nonfatal injury: In the United States, one in eight preschoolers each year goes to the emergency room because of an accidental injury (Albert & McCaig, 2014).

Children are particularly vulnerable during early childhood because their developing motor skills may lead them to take physical risks they are not ready for (Damashek & Kuhn, 2014). Young children act quickly and often unexpectedly, which leads to accidents. While researchers estimate that more than 90 percent of injuries can be prevented by safer environments and more supervision, they caution that children should be allowed to explore, even if it means climbing a tree or to the top of the play set (Morrongiello, 2018).

The rate of accidental injury in the United States is twice that of other high-income countries (Morrongiello, 2018). The culprit? Unequal access to safe living environments (Thakrar et al., 2018). The number of children in hazardous living conditions, such as housing with overloaded electrical systems, scalding hot water, or windows without safety guards, is double that of other affluent countries (Pressman, 2017; Slemaker et al., 2017; Tilburg, 2017). These children may live in neighborhoods lacking streetlights and crosswalks to protect pedestrians, or without fences around pools and ponds to prevent drownings (Frank et al., 2019).

APPLY IT! **6.4** Families are responsible for encouraging healthy habits in early childhood, but they may have different ethnotheories about safety. How would you apply the principle of cultural humility when talking to a family about establishing healthy routines with their preschooler?

6.5 Aidan's family is proud of his physical skills. How would you explain the benefits of physical activity to Alex and Sinead? Which types of accidental injuries should they worry about?

Cognitive Development

Despite Aidan's hard work in learning his numbers and letters, aspects of his thinking are still characteristic of early childhood. He has a lot to say, and his ideas are wide ranging. Aidan has ideas about the past and the future: putting wings on superheroes and supervising a matchup between Green Lantern and Batman. How is Aidan's thinking different from both an infant and a more mature first-grader?

Developmental scientists like Jean Piaget developed theories to explain the characteristics of thought that make early childhood unique. Other researchers, like Lev Vygotsky, explained how children learn and how the way they learn shapes their cognitive skills. Young children's advances—pretending, talking, and learning—are powered by brain maturation and a better ability to pay attention, remember, and process information. Their research clarifies some of the interesting inconsistencies in children's thinking in early childhood, such as why Aidan still believes in the Tooth Fairy and why it may be impossible to teach him algebra at this age.

Learning Objectives

6.4 Identify the key features of Piaget's preoperational stage.

6.5 Apply Vygotsky's theory of development to young children's thinking.

6.6 Describe advances in information-processing skills during early childhood.

Piaget's Theory of Preoperational Thought

When Aidan insists that he is Spider-Man, he is being a typical 5-year-old. Piaget's classic research drew attention to the inventiveness of children's thinking during early childhood, suggesting that Aidan's magical ideas indicate a special kind of intelligence.

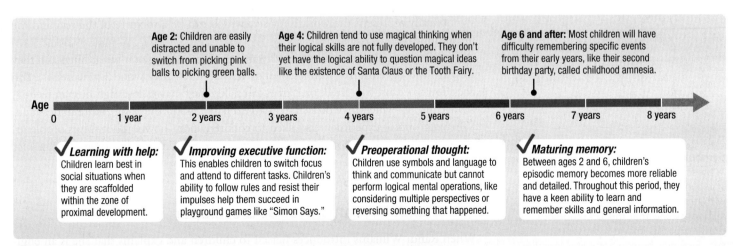

FIGURE 6.2 Highlights of Cognitive Development in Early Childhood Researchers use insights from Piaget, Vygotsky, and information-processing theorists to describe the maturation of children's thinking as they grow.

preoperational thought The second stage in children's cognitive development spanning about ages 2 to 7, in which young children are capable of symbolic, but not quite logical, thought.

animism The tendency to describe nonliving things as if they are alive and have human feelings or motives.

TABLE 6.1 Characteristics of Piaget's Period of Preoperational Thought

Symbolic thought	Children use objects to stand in for, or symbolize, another object. A block can become a rocket ship; the space under the table can be a house.	
Intuitive thought	This is the stage of "why?" Children begin to have a more logical sense of how the world works but still display some limitations.	
Centration	Children focus on one feature of a problem (like how wide a glass is) to the exclusion of other features.	
Magical thinking	Children often come up with illogical or magical explanations for events they do not fully understand.	

CONNECTIONS

In Chapter 2, you read that Piaget developed a classic stage theory of development. His theory is often called *constructivist*, because he believed children construct their own knowledge as they mature and interact with the world around them. In Chapter 4, you read about the period of *sensorimotor development*.

Symbolic Thinking in Two Dimensions A preschool-aged child drew this picture. The sun doesn't really look like a circle with rays coming out from it, but we all understand that this preschooler's drawing of this image represents the sun. Similarly, human arms and legs are thicker than the single lines used here to represent arms and legs, but we understand that this figure is a child.

Preoperational thought is the second stage in children's thinking and spans ages 2 to 7. Young children in the preoperational stage are capable of *symbolic*, but not quite logical, thought (see **Table 6.1**). For instance, children can use language and their imaginative ideas to talk about things they cannot see and to play make-believe. However, children are still "preoperational" since they cannot perform logical mental operations, like reversing or undoing something that just happened or considering multiple perspectives on a problem. During early childhood, preschoolers even struggle with basic logical ideas like "more than" or "less than."

Symbolic Thought One of the hallmarks of the preoperational stage is the imagination that Aidan shows while he throws spider webs out of his fingertips. During early childhood, children show more symbolic thinking. Remember that during the sensorimotor period, toddlers begin to demonstrate *some* symbolic thought, as they learn to use words as symbols to represent objects that are not there. Preschoolers take symbolic play further. They can play with others and adopt adult roles, becoming a "chef" in a play kitchen or Mr. Incredible on the swings. They even use drawings to symbolically represent the world they see, which can be a mixture of the real and the metaphorical (Piaget & Inhelder, 1969).

Many preschool-age children display **animism**, describing nonliving things as if they are alive and have human feelings or motives. Children may wonder whether the sun goes down because it is tired, or if trees can talk. They may even assign human feelings to machines—which may be a strategy to explain a world they don't quite understand. When a group of experimenters talked to children about how a robot solves problems, younger children were more likely to explain that a robot had feelings (Druga et al., 2018).

SCIENCE IN PRACTICE
Randi Williams, Robot Developer

When Randi Williams introduces herself to children and explains that she is an engineer, she is often asked what kind of train she drives. (Many children think engineers drive steam engines.) Randi, however, develops robots for young children. And, she knows that many people fear the impact that robots and "smart" devices like Alexa,

Science in Action Randi Williams studies how children interact with robots to understand how children think and how to use robots to help them learn.

Google Home, or Siri may have on small children (Madrigal, 2017). Williams does not share this fear. In fact, she designs robots that will help young children learn to program on their own. She hopes this will help them develop a critical understanding of robots and also inspire a new generation of engineers.

Williams has discovered that, as Piaget might have predicted, young children have animistic beliefs about robots. According to most children, you should be nice to Alexa or Siri lest their feelings get hurt (Druga et al., 2017, 2018). Her studies have shown that children ask robots concrete questions to test how real they are, such as "What is your favorite color?" and "How old are you?" One favorite: "Can I eat you?" (Druga et al., 2017). In Williams's work technology inspires children's creativity and gives children and researchers insights into how these smart devices actually work (Williams et al., 2019).

Limitations of Logic in Early Childhood A 4-year-old is likely to believe in magic (Subbotsky, 2014). As children grow older, however, fewer resort to fantastical explanations. Thus, without exceptional intervention, fewer 6-year-olds than 3-year-olds will believe in Santa Claus or the Tooth Fairy (Kapitány et al., 2020).

Young children's creative thinking and reliance on magical explanations often conceal their limited understanding of cause and effect and the logic of the world around them. Preschool-age children tend to be focused on their perceptions of their surroundings, rather than looking at a problem from different perspectives to think it through logically. Piaget called children's focus on their own perspective *egocentrism*, a perspective that can keep children from seeing the big picture or even someone else's point of view (Piaget, 1968).

For instance, young children often have difficulty with the idea of *reversibility*. This is part of what makes masks so scary for preschoolers: They are truly afraid that the act of putting on a mask is permanent and cannot be reversed. In a classic study, a researcher brought her very patient cat into a preschool and put a rabbit mask on it. She was able to convince a group of 3- and 4-year-olds that the cat had magically turned into a rabbit (de Vries, 1969). Researchers interpret children's inability to conceive that actions may be reversible as a sign of their inability to perform mental operations.

Piaget created a number of hands-on tasks to measure how preschooler's logical thinking develops. One classic series of measures are known as the **conservation tasks** (Piaget, 1952). Each involves asking children what has happened to an object or a set of objects that is rearranged or manipulated to look different right in front of them. For instance, one ball of clay may be squished down while the other is rolled into a long form. Are children able to mentally reverse this operation and understand that the amount of the clay has not changed? Preschoolers struggle to logically complete the conservation tasks, but over time, their abilities improve.

Share It!

Preoperational thought can make medical procedures frightening for children, but play can help. Children who watched a doll go through a difficult medical procedure (having a cast removed) were less anxious than those who did not get to play.

(Wong et al., 2018)

🐦 Scientific American: Lifespan Development

conservation tasks Piaget's hands-on tasks that measure how preschoolers' logical thinking develops. Each involves asking children what has happened to an object or a set of objects that is rearranged or manipulated in front of them to look different. Preschoolers struggle to logically complete the conservation tasks, but over time, their abilities improve.

three mountains task Piaget's test of how well children can imagine how someone else would see the world.

egocentrism In the Piagetian sense, children's inability to see the world from other people's point of view.

Conservation Task	Original Presentation	Transformation
Number	Are the same number of pennies in each row?	Now, are the same number of pennies in each row, or does one row have more?
Liquid	Is there the same amount of water in each glass?	Now, is there the same amount of water in each glass, or does one have more?
Mass	Is there the same amount of clay in each ball?	Now does each piece have the same amount of clay, or does one have more?

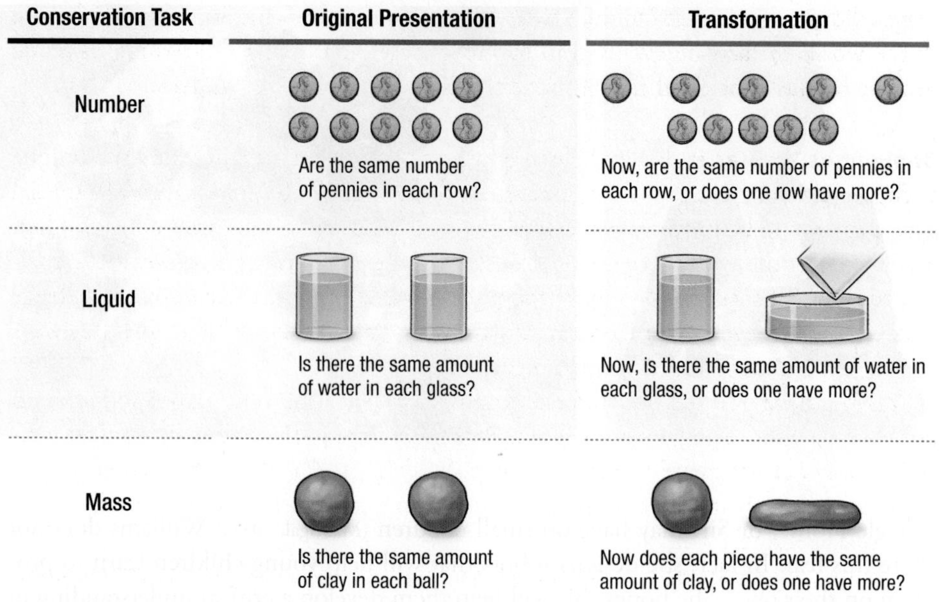

FIGURE 6.3 Piaget's Conservation Tasks: Mass, Number, and Liquid As they get older, children develop experiences and strategies that enable them to understand that number, liquid, and mass are conserved. Children in the preoperational stage are easily confused and typically fail these tasks, because they focus on one feature of the problem rather than the whole. For instance, a preschooler might argue that there are more objects in a longer row of pennies than a shorter one or more play dough in a flat shape than in a round one.

In the classic conservation-of-liquid task, an experimenter pours liquid into two identical glasses. Next, the experimenter pours one glass of liquid into a container of a different shape, either taller and thinner or shorter and wider. The child is then asked which container has "more" of the liquid. Preschool-age children focus on the height of the glasses rather than the amount of liquid, an error known as *centration*, or they believe that the amount has magically changed (Piaget & Inhelder, 1969). (See **Figure 6.3**.)

Most children develop a sense of conservation over time, achieving it in these tasks by about age 8 (Lozada & Carro, 2016). Practice and experience can contribute to typical variations. Children who spend a lot of time playing with clay, for instance, will have a sense of the conservation of mass earlier than those without hands-on experience with clay (Price-Williams et al., 1969). Children who are allowed to pour the water themselves are often better able to display logical reasoning than are those who are passive observers (Lozada & Carro, 2016).

Egocentrism In addition to the conservation tasks, Piaget devised ways to assess whether children can consider someone else's point of view. Piaget's **three mountains task** tests how well children can imagine how someone else would see the world. In this problem, Piaget and his team constructed a diorama of three mountains. This three-dimensional model included alpine peaks of different shapes and sizes and other landmarks nestled among the hills (see **Figure 6.4**). Piaget and his colleagues asked children what objects a doll across the room would see (Piaget & Inhelder, 1956). Children had great difficulty consistently predicting what someone else would see until they were about 8. Younger children consistently guessed that someone else would see the scene as they did, an error Piaget called **egocentrism**.

When used in the Piagetian sense, egocentrism means that children are unable to see the world from other people's point of view. However,

FIGURE 6.4 What Do You See? In Piaget's three mountains task, children are asked to imagine a scene from someone else's point of view: What would the doll see if she looked at this mountain scene? Would the little girl be able to understand that they saw things differently?

Piaget did not mean that children were self-centered in the emotional or social sense of the word. In fact, he even began to move away from using the term *egocentrism* because he was concerned that it made children seem selfish (Piaget, 1968).

Challenges to Piaget Piaget helped educators and scientists appreciate the unique strengths of young children's thinking. He believed that early childhood was a special time that should be protected, and that play was an essential way that young children make sense of the world (Piaget & Inhelder, 1969). Other researchers, however, have challenged many of the details of his theory. For instance, scientists have found evidence that children's development of conservation and perspective-taking do not always happen according to Piaget's timetables (Dasen, 1994; Gelman, 1973).

Critics have pointed out that children who have not been to school and who do not have experience playing with objects like those used in the conservation tasks generally show delayed development on the tasks. However, if these children are tested with tools from their own communities, they pass the conservation tasks earlier (Cole, 1990; Greenfield, 2012; Piaget, 1970).

Many contemporary researchers believe that some children fail the conservation tasks because logical reasoning does not develop all at once. Children, just like adults, use strategies of logical reasoning at some times but not others (Siegler, 1999). Many scientists now believe that development occurs not in strict stages, but in starts and stops, more like overlapping waves than discrete steps. Despite these critiques, developmental science remains indebted to Piaget for valuing the thinking that children display before they master logic.

Vygotsky's Theory of Children's Learning

Like Piaget, the Russian developmental theorist Lev Vygotsky appreciated the creativity and playfulness of preschool children's thinking (Vygotsky, 1933/2016). Unlike Piaget, Vygotsky did not believe cognitive development occurred in universal stages. Instead, he felt that social and cultural factors were critical to cognitive development. Remember from Chapter 2 that Vygotsky believed that cognitive maturation is the result of a complex, social interaction between children and their environment that begins on the day that they are born (Vygotsky & Cole, 1978).

Learning in the Zone When you think about learning, you probably picture sitting at a desk in school or reading a textbook like this. Vygotsky believed that learning also happens outside of school. Children learn important skills, like turn-taking or language skills, through play, whether they are pretending a stick is a galloping horse or building a river in the sandbox (Vygotsky & Cole, 1978).

Vygotsky believed that teaching happens in a variety of contexts, but that it works best when a sensitive partner individually targets a child's capabilities. Do you ever have trouble focusing in class? Perhaps that is because you just don't find what you're learning to be meaningful (Hulleman et al., 2016). According to Vygotsky and researchers inspired by his work, children are motivated by sensitive teaching that engages them by considering their interests and individual abilities (Vygotsky & Cole, 1978). This teaching can be done by formal teachers, but also by friends, peers, or family members. Researchers term this sensitive, one-on-one, guidance **scaffolding** (Wood et al., 1976).

Vygotsky used the term **zone of proximal development (ZPD)** to describe the range of what students can learn with help (Vygotsky & Cole, 1978). Your zone of proximal development is not what you know right now, but what you are capable of if you are scaffolded. Many educators describe tasks that are in the ZPD as having a "perfect balance" between being too boring and too hard. Children in the ZPD feel both challenged and engaged at the same time.

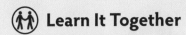 **Learn It Together**

Classic Conservation Tasks

In this activity, you will observe a young child engaging in a classic task that is commonly used to illustrate thinking during early childhood.

Plan Review some of the key characteristics of preoperational thinking, such as egocentrism, centration, and irreversibility. Then search Achieve or other internet sources for a video of one of the following:

- Conservation task
- Three mountains task
- False-belief task

Engage In a small group, review the video and analyze the task:

- What did the child have to do?
- What cognitive ability was being demonstrated?

Reflect Analyze the child's performance:

- What was the child's response?
- Did the child provide the expected age-typical response?
- What does this task and the child's reaction to it illustrate about thinking during early childhood?

scaffolding Vygotsky's term for teaching, whether by formal teachers, friends, peers, or family members, that engages children by considering their interests and individual abilities.

zone of proximal development (ZPD) Vygotsky's term for the range of what students can learn with adult help.

Cooking with Help Following a recipe is one way young children can learn math in the real world. If parents engage their children's interest in counting and math during a simple cooking activity, their children will do better at counting and basic addition than children who are not actively engaged in cooking.

Reading in the Zone Sometimes the Zone of Proximal Development happens when you get a chance to share a book with a friend, as Ricki reads to her friend Destiny in a child care center in Ontario, Canada.

private speech Vygotsky's term for the language children use when they talk to themselves.

For instance, a sensitive gymnastic coach might start Aidan out on a balance beam close to the ground, hovering over him a bit. The low beam is in his ZPD, whereas the high beam and a flipped dismount are beyond his capability. Not all coaches know Vygotsky by name, but as expert teachers, they know to keep instruction within the ZPD.

Vygotsky was a hands-on educator who worked with many different children, some with serious disabilities and others living in extreme poverty. He knew that formal assessments could not give an accurate reading on these children's potential or intelligence. Children's ability to learn when sensitively scaffolded was a better measure of their capabilities than a traditional test. For example, if a teacher tests preschoolers to see if they can count to 10, one 4-year-old may not be capable of keeping their numbers straight. If the same 4-year-old is sensitively scaffolded, with prompting or pointing, they may be able to count to 10 or even 100 (Beller et al., 2018).

Vygotsky's insights about how to help children learn have tremendous results in the classroom. Collaborative and sensitive scaffolding can change children's feelings about school and make early education more successful (Rogoff, 1990). Scaffolding need not come from an adult: Children, including siblings and friends, are capable of teaching (Howe et al., 2016).

Learning comes with different expectations depending on families' cultural backgrounds. In many communities around the world, children learn basic tasks like laundry, cooking, and cleaning by observing and helping the adults around them. Remember from Chapter 2 that the phrase *learning by observing and pitching in* describes this process (Rogoff, 2016; Rogoff et al., 2016). When children are integrated into family work, they are not explicitly taught how to fold napkins, for instance, but instead learn while doing.

In contrast, in other families, children are explicitly taught by being verbally instructed and even rewarded. In these families, children's focus and motivation are managed by adults (Paradise et al., 2014). For instance, in Indigenous cultures, scaffolding may include storytelling and direct experience with the land. One study found that rural Turkana children in Kenya learned the concepts of the national science curriculum through observational and hands-on scaffolding from parents and the narratives of their elders (Ng'asike, 2011).

Vygotsky also theorized that thinking is made up of various mental tools or strategies. One key tool is language. Vygotsky called the language children use when they talk to themselves **private speech** (Vygotsky, 1962). You may hear preschoolers using private speech to coach themselves when they get upset or face a challenging task. Private speech can also help preschool-age children scaffold their own learning. Over time, children internalize private speech as *inner speech*, or silent thinking.

Information-Processing Advances

Adults expect preschoolers to develop the maturity to sit still long enough to scrawl their names, get dressed on their own, and explain what happened during their day. How does a 5-year-old become capable of taking the bus to school and telling long stories about a day at kindergarten? Remember that the information-processing approach looks at the components of thinking and provides new insights about how children mature. During this period, children's memory and attention advance, as do their executive function skills that will enable them to sit still at school.

Developing Stronger Memory Skills

A key part of children's cognitive growth involves improvements in the ability to remember. In preschool, children learn to remember the letters in their name and the rules for circle time. At the same time, children may sometimes struggle to keep track of what they are supposed to do, and even to recall what happened during the day.

Episodic Memory One type of memory involves your long-term memory, such as your memory of your fifth birthday party or a first date. Scientists call this long-term memory for specific events **episodic memory**. Episodic memory allows you to remember the who, what, and when of something that happened in the past, like the cupcakes, piñata, and sudden fire alarm at your fifth birthday party.

By preschool, children are only just beginning to develop episodic memories. Episodic memory improves rapidly due to improving language skills, practice with telling stories, and maturity in the parts of the brain that process memory, like the *hippocampus*, a set of seahorse-shaped brain structures located under the cortex (Ngo et al., 2017; Riggins et al., 2018). Children's memory improves as new connections between the hippocampus and the cortex form and strengthen.

By kindergarten, if properly motivated, children generally will be able to provide a detailed description of their day. Talking about past events helps children learn how to remember and retain their memories (Fivush, 2014). The preschoolers with the best memories in the world are said to be from Maori families in New Zealand, which have a rich storytelling tradition. Maori families often reminisce in great detail with their small children about the past (Reese & Neha, 2015).

It is unusual for adults to remember their first day of kindergarten in detail. Children, however, are able to remember significant events from infancy, even from as early as 6 months, although these memories are usually forgotten as they get older (Mullally & Maguire, 2014). It isn't until between ages 7 and 9 that children will have the same ability to store and retain their memories as adults (Bauer & Larkina, 2014).

Although children's memory improves, they are not yet ready to memorize their multiplication tables. Remembering facts, lists, and dates of unrelated information, or *semantic memory*, is difficult for young children. Children need years of practice before they can remember bits of information well, particularly if this information isn't personally relevant (Bauer, 2015).

Working Memory One type of short-term memory that does not last long but is essential to learning and to controlling behavior is called **working memory**. Children's episodic memory gradually reaches adult levels by middle childhood, but working memory isn't mature until adolescence. Whereas episodic memory is dependent on the hippocampus and neural circuits that run to it, working memory depends on circuits in the late-developing cortex (Bathelt et al., 2018).

Working memory is crucial for developing the academic skills children will need in kindergarten (Jones et al., 2020). It enables children to remember parts of a basic math problem (Purpura et al., 2017). For instance, in order to calculate the answer to "2+3," children need to be able to keep the 2 and the 3 in mind. Children learning how to read must hold letter sounds in working memory to decode even simple words. Over the preschool years, children's working memory becomes more efficient and reliable, allowing them to remember more complicated instructions and even begin to learn basic academic skills (Perlman et al., 2016).

davidf/E+/Getty Images

Tell Me Another! This little girl from the Maori community in New Zealand is whispering into her father's ear. Telling stories helps children build their long-term memory, and Maori children have some of the most impressive memories in the world.

episodic memory Long-term memory for specific events.

working memory A type of short-term memory that is essential to learning and to problem solving.

Hands-on Learning Can Happen Anywhere. Children's cognitive development is shaped by their environment. These preschool children spend every school morning in the middle of a forest near their home in rural Marsac, France, learning from and observing nature (and friendly dogs).

Share It!

What would a superhero do? Sometimes children can quickly boost their executive function by imagining what someone else would do in the same situation.

(White & Carlson, 2016)

Scientific American: Lifespan Development

executive function A group of thinking skills that allow you to control your behavior, suppress impulsive actions and implement long-term plans.

Attention and Executive Function

If you observe a story hour at the library, you will find that most preschoolers have difficulty sitting still. They whisper. They may stare into the distance or at the ceiling. The librarian may say "eyes on me," but within a minute, most eyes will drift away. This is all typical for preschoolers.

Young children are slowly developing the ability to pay attention and control their behavior, but this does not mean they can happily sit for hours to take tests or attend Zoom-based preschool, as many families learned during the pandemic (Ristic & Enns, 2015). Remember from Chapter 4 that *attention* allows you to focus, shut out distractions, and keep your mind from wandering. **Executive function** refers to a group of thinking skills that allow you to suppress impulsive actions and implement long-term plans. Both skills are works in progress during early childhood, as the prefrontal cortex matures and strengthens connections with other parts of the brain.

Children who have stronger executive function skills are better prepared to learn and succeed in school (Moriguchi et al., 2016). They can manage their impulses most of the time and focus when they need to, making it easier to listen to a friend's ideas or to a teacher explaining how to write a perfect number 5. Scientists see dramatic maturation in attention skills during early childhood. A 5-year-old's focus is much more reliable than that of a toddler. Children's other executive function skills, such as planning, take much longer to develop and will not be fully mature until late adolescence (Doebel, 2020). Many first-graders forget to bring their coats to school, and many fourth-graders may forget their coats on the bus, both age-typical behaviors.

You can see children's fast-developing executive function skills at work in the game Simon Says. Preschool-age children have great difficulty controlling their impulses, which is precisely why Simon Says is so exciting for them but easy and thus boring for older children. Scientists created the "head-toes-knees-shoulders" task, a game that is similar to Simon Says, in which children must first imitate and then do the opposite of what an adult tells them to do. Accomplishing this task requires children to stop themselves from imitating what the adult says and does, remember the rules, and focus their attention. The game is challenging for 3-year-olds; half of them cannot follow the directions at all (Ponitz et al., 2008). Children's performance is three times as accurate by the time they are in first grade (von Suchodoletz et al., 2013).

A number of factors influence whether young children will use their attention or executive function at any given time (Zelazo, 2020). Too much excitement may make it difficult for children to focus, and what motivates one child may bore another. For instance, in one experiment, preschool boys tended to perform better on some tests of executive function because they were less excited than the girls about the reward they would receive for participating: glittery stickers (Garon et al., 2012). Emotional involvement can also sometimes help children focus. As experienced teachers will remind you, effective learning means that children are emotionally engaged in what they are learning, like listening to stories they enjoy rather than those that bore them (Lennox, 2013).

The development of self-control and attention is partially driven by brain maturation. Remember that the prefrontal cortex, the region linked to logical thought, matures and becomes more connected to other parts of the brain during the preschool years, allowing children to better control their behavior (Posner et al., 2016). The development of executive function is also shaped by experience and practice. Early childhood is a critical period for children to learn these skills (Diamond & Ling, 2016).

Early-intervention programs and formal school can help children who have difficulties with executive function (Zhang et al., 2019). Some teach them mindfulness and prompt them to reflect on their behaviors (Semenov et al., 2020). Others encourage executive function through physical activities like tae kwon do or basketball. Some programs boost focus within relationships both at home and at school.

In an intervention called Tools of the Mind, children work on self-control through group play and make-believe. The focus is on helping children be intentional and reflective, by encouraging them to make "play plans" before engaging in an activity. Based on Vygotsky's theory of learning, activities are designed to engage children where they are in their learning, in their zone of proximal development. At home, parents encourage impulse control and the ability to follow directions. In one evaluation of this program, children with executive function delays were able to catch up with their peers after just one year (Diamond & Ling, 2016).

Checking Her Plan In interventions like Tools of the Mind, children are encouraged to plan their play, building their planning skills, fine motor skills, and executive function while having fun in the process.

Challenges to Attention and Self-Control Preschoolers are full of energy. However, this worries some families: Nearly half of all parents believe that their preschool children have trouble with attention (Fiks et al., 2016; Jacobson et al., 2018).

In the United States, about 1 out of every 10 children has been diagnosed with **attention-deficit/hyperactivity disorder (ADHD)**, which is characterized by consistent inattention, hyperactivity, or impulsity that prevents them from fully functioning at school and at home (APA, 2022; Wong & Landes, 2021). Effective treatments are available for ADHD (Wolraich et al., 2019). Some scientists have found that if preschoolers who are at risk receive behavioral and family therapy, including advice about establishing regular routines and supportive disciplinary practices, one in five will no longer meet the criteria for the diagnosis as they grow up (Murray et al., 2021; Sudre et al., 2018). The most common and effective intervention for children with ADHD is medication, such as Ritalin or Adderall (Harstad et al., 2021).

Diagnoses of ADHD can be controversial. Some suggest that the disorder might be misdiagnosed or overdiagnosed in some children (Kazda et al., 2021). Others worry that schools and teachers might be too intolerant of children's age-typical levels of energy and exuberance. These researchers point out that every child has a hard time sitting still once in a while, and that diagnoses rise when the demands of school are mismatched with children's age-typical maturity (Caye et al., 2020; Hinshaw, 2018). Still others are concerned that ADHD may be *underdiagnosed* in children who have neurocognitive differences but are treated as if they have a discipline problem (Simoni, 2021).

There are significant gender and ethnic differences in the diagnoses of ADHD. Teachers tend to be more likely to identify Black children's behavior as ADHD than similar behavior in a White child (Accavitti & Williford, 2020; Kang & Harvey, 2020). Affluent families tend to be more comfortable with a medical explanation for their children's behavior than less-affluent families, resulting in fewer ADHD diagnoses in low-income children (Owens, 2021; Simoni, 2021). Preschoolers who identify as girls tend to differ from those who identify as boys in their patterns of ADHD, such as being overly talkative rather than having difficulty sitting still (DuPaul et al., 2020).

Even with treatment, children with ADHD still face difficulties: They are more likely to be expelled from preschools and pre-K programs than their peers (Zeng et al., 2021). One challenge is that teachers and other adults often stigmatize children with ADHD *and* their families, blaming the children and their parents instead of differences in their brain functioning (Metzger & Hamilton, 2021; Nguyen & Hinshaw, 2020).

attention-deficit/hyperactivity disorder (ADHD) A disorder in which children have high energy levels and problems with focusing or controlling themselves, that interfere with school and/or home life.

Waiting for a Treat In the original studies, Mischel did not just use marshmallows. Some kids were lucky enough to be tested with Oreos, and a few only got pretzels. We used gummy bears to assess Aidan's ability to wait.

Scientific American Profile

Delaying Gratification

CAN YOU BELIEVE IT?
Does Waiting to Eat a Marshmallow Mean You'll Be Successful?

Whether experts call it grit, perseverance, or self-control, there is a substantial body of research and popular media attention devoted to helping children (and adults) exert more self-control (Claro et al., 2016; Duckworth & Seligman, 2017). In early childhood, self-control means being able to listen in school and pay attention, even when the day seems long.

Researchers have devised multiple ways to measure children's developing self-control, including what is informally known as the "marshmallow test" (Mischel, 2015; Mischel et al., 1989). This task focuses on the *delay of gratification*, or how long children can wait to get something they want, which is a skill that helps us throughout the lifespan.

Noted social psychologist Walter Mischel developed the marshmallow test in the 1960s in an affluent preschool on the campus of Stanford University (Mischel, 2015; Mischel & Ebbesen, 1970). Children were asked to sit facing a plate with one marshmallow on it and told that they could eat it immediately, or they could wait a little while and get to eat *two* marshmallows. Then, the researchers left the room, telling the children they would be back in a bit and that they could ring a bell if they couldn't wait any longer. Some children were able to wait longer than 17 minutes before ringing the bell. Others grabbed the marshmallow even before the researcher was out of the room. Most waited about six minutes (Mischel, 2015).

Years later, Mischel and his colleagues followed up with the children and found that the children who were able to postpone gratification and wait for two marshmallows were more socially and academically successful when they grew up. Children who were unable to wait very long did not do as well as their peers: They were more likely to develop a substance use disorder and less likely to finish college (Mischel, 2015; Shoda et al., 1990). Of course, these results were only a correlation; many factors could have contributed to these long-term results.

In fact, while some researchers and policy makers inspired by Mischel's research went on to design interventions to help children ace the marshmallow test and develop more self-control, other scientists raised some serious questions about the marshmallow task (Mischel, 2015). They replicated the test with different groups and questioned how accurately it predicted the children's future. They found:

- A lack of self-control is not the only reason children might reach for the marshmallow right away. If children saw the experimenter treat another adult unkindly or did not trust the experimenter for some other reason, they were more likely to eat the marshmallow quickly: They may not have thought they could trust the experimenter to keep their word (Michaelson & Munakata, 2020).
- When Mischel's study was repeated with a more diverse group of children, the results were not as conclusive, particularly over time. In these samples, being able to exert self-control alone wasn't predictive of better academic or social outcomes. Among these children, self-control mattered to their success, but it was less important than their performance on cognitive tests or their behavior in school (Watts et al., 2018).

To sum it up, researchers agree that self-control is important, but the difficulties contemporary researchers faced in replicating Mischel's work remind us that measuring development is complex. As Vygotsky suggested nearly a century ago, one test cannot represent all of what any preschooler (or adult) can do (Vygotsky & Cole, 1978). And the best test of science and scientific interventions designed to help children is to make sure they are replicated.

Theory of Mind

Preschool-aged children are beginning to understand that not everyone thinks quite the same way they do. They know that Daddy's favorite color is green and that their sister's favorite color is purple. These developments are a sign of preschoolers' growing **theory of mind**, which is the ability to understand that other people have different beliefs, ideas, and desires (Astington et al., 1988; Peterson & Welman, 2019).

Researchers test theory of mind with elaborate tricks. In one classic test, they presented children with what appeared to be a box of candy. The child was excited to open it up, only to find that the experimenter had replaced the candies with pencils. The interesting part of the experiment was not that the 3-year-old was disappointed; it was that the 3-year-old was sure that their friend would not be tricked by the box of "candy." Like most 3-year-olds in the experiment, they assumed that everyone else knew what they now knew—that there were pencils in the box (Astington & Gopnik, 1988; Wimmer & Perner, 1983).

What Is Inside That Box? What do you think this 4-year-old will say is inside the crayon box? After he finds out that this box is filled with M&Ms, will he think his mother, who was in the other room, will know that the box is filled with M&Ms? Children who have developed a "theory of mind" will be able to understand that not everyone knows what they know: and that their mother will not guess that a treat hides inside the crayon box.

Children quickly grow out of this limitation: By age 4 or 5, children have developed a much more robust understanding of other people's minds (Wellman, 2018). They will happily tell an experimenter that someone else would also be tricked by the pencils-in-the-box experiment. They no longer assume that everyone else can read their minds, and they understand that other people often have different perceptions than they do.

Theory of mind opens up a new world for children. Once they understand that other people can have different beliefs than they do, they can lie. This is why a 2-year-old is unlikely to fib about eating the last cookie, but a 5-year-old would do so easily (Lavoie et al., 2017a, 2017b).

Not all children develop a theory of mind at age 4 or 5. Those who develop it a bit early tend to have more social skills, perhaps because they understand other people better, that others think differently than they do (Hughes & Devine, 2015; Slaughter et al., 2015). Children who are bilingual, and children who have a lot of social interaction with other people (for instance, they have siblings or friends at school), tend to develop a theory of mind earlier (Hughes et al., 2018). Children who have limited early conversational experience, as with babies born with hearing impairment to hearing parents who have not yet learned alternative forms of communication, tend to be delayed in developing theory of mind (Peterson & Wellman, 2019).

In many communities around the world, children generally pass theory of mind tasks between ages 4 and 5, although there are some differences. Children who do not start school until age 6, as in Japan and Italy, tend to develop theory of mind a little later (Hughes et al., 2014). Children who are seldom tested by outsiders, as with children from the remote South Pacific nation of Vanuatu, are often unable to pass the task until early adolescence (Dixson et al., 2018).

Children with *autism spectrum disorder (ASD)* also have difficulty with executive function and theory of mind (Jones et al., 2018). In one recent study, only 4 percent of children with ASD had typical responses to assessments of theory of mind (Peterson et al., 2016). Inability to understand other people's motivations makes it difficult for young people with autism to learn from other people—or engage in imaginary play (Kang et al., 2016). Typically, theory of mind develops through experiences with others who have different understandings or beliefs, as occurs in early childhood during interactive play, storytelling, and problem solving (White & Carlson, 2021).

theory of mind The ability to understand that other people have different beliefs, ideas, and desires.

APPLY IT!   **6.6** Like many preschoolers, Aidan is easily confused by the classic cognitive tasks of early childhood. He can sit still, follow directions, and talk about the conservation of liquid, but he may not be able to explain that the amount of Gatorade remains the same, whether it is in a tall, thin glass or a shorter, squatter one. What logical capabilities would Piaget say Aidan is missing?

6.7 How would you explain to the family of a preschooler the cognitive strengths of early childhood according to Piaget, Vygotsky, and information-processing theorists?

Developing Language in Early Childhood

Learning Objective

6.7 Discuss vocabulary and grammar development during early childhood.

If you listen to Aidan chattering to his sister, it is startlingly apparent how quickly his language skills have developed. Now, Aidan and Dylan can have a real conversation and take turns speaking. Between ages 2 and 6, children's use of language blossoms (see **Figure 6.5**). Most 2-year-olds can only speak a few hundred words in short sentences. By age 6, most English-speaking children use about 6,000 words and can understand about 14,000 (Carey, 2010; Templin, 1957). For about one in four children in the United States, this language experience is enriched by learning more than one language (U.S. Census, 2015).

Growth in Vocabulary and Complexity

Children use a number of strategies to build their vocabularies. Most preschoolers only need to hear a new word once before they remember it for weeks or months (Carey & Bartlett, 1978; Kan, 2014). Remember from Chapter 4 that children continue to use their *fast-mapping* skills to quickly learn new words. Attention and social skills help preschoolers observe what other people are looking at when they hear new terms (Baldwin & Meyer, 2007).

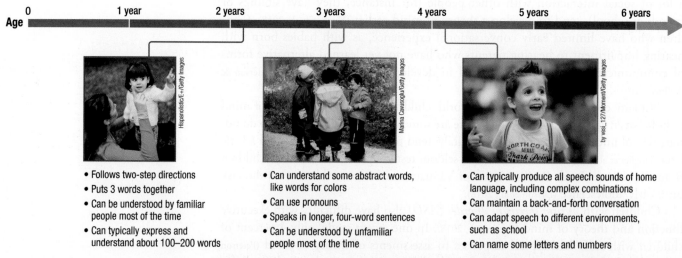

| Age | 0 | 1 year | 2 years | 3 years | 4 years | 5 years | 6 years |

- Follows two-step directions
- Puts 3 words together
- Can be understood by familiar people most of the time
- Can typically express and understand about 100–200 words

- Can understand some abstract words, like words for colors
- Can use pronouns
- Speaks in longer, four-word sentences
- Can be understood by unfamiliar people most of the time

- Can typically produce all speech sounds of home language, including complex combinations
- Can maintain a back-and-forth conversation
- Can adapt speech to different environments, such as school
- Can name some letters and numbers

FIGURE 6.5 Achievements in Language Development During Early Childhood Language development allows young children to better communicate and express themselves and forms a foundation for success in school. Understanding typical development helps identify children who need extra support.

Children's mastery of grammar is evident as they slowly move from short two-word combinations ("more cookie") into more complicated, sophisticated forms by age 6. Developing more complex language skills often leads to errors. In languages with irregular verb forms, such as English, children often confuse unfamiliar forms, saying "I drinked it" rather than "I drank it." But more familiar irregular forms, such as "ran" rather than "runned," tend to be mastered more quickly (Ambridge et al., 2015).

Communicating with other people helps children build their grammar, vocabulary, and articulation skills (Masek et al., 2021a). But the quantity of children's language exposure is not the only important piece: Quality also matters (Masek et al., 2021b). If a preschooler is surrounded by an endless monologue or is just overhearing conversation, they may struggle to acquire new words or more sophisticated grammar. Preschoolers learn more if they are engaged by adults who ask questions such as "why," "when," or "how" (Rowe et al., 2017). Children learn to talk by talking and responding, not just by listening (Ribot et al., 2018).

Families and teachers can help expand children's language skills by extending conversations and gently recasting errors or mispronunciations (Alper et al., 2021). Many conversations with children miss opportunities to engage and extend the content and sophistication of their talk (Cabell et al., 2015). This is partly because talking to children takes time. Children can take almost 10 times as long as adults to answer a question, as they work out what to say (Casillas et al., 2016). The quality of language skills, such as vocabulary size and level of sophistication, is critical to children's success in school and in their social relationships (Golinkoff et al., 2019; Suggate et al., 2018).

About 1 in 10 kindergarteners has trouble with communication, including difficulty with speech articulation or with expressing or understanding language, that may be diagnosed as a *speech-language disorder* (Norbury et al., 2017). Global communication disorders, such as difficulty understanding and expressing language, tend to be more persistent than problems with articulation, such as mispronouncing your "r"s (Fernald & Marchman, 2012; Määttä et al., 2014). Speech-language interventions during early childhood are aimed at addressing these issues before they become entrenched (Norbury & Sonuga-Barke, 2017).

Multilingual Language Development

Most children around the world grow up learning more than one language, which gives them cognitive advantages in addition to the joy of being able to talk to more people (Barac et al., 2014). Early childhood is a critical period for multilanguage learners. For children who have never learned a second language, this is the ideal time to begin learning one.

Young children typically have stronger language skills in their home language than in their second language, simply because they have more opportunities for practice (Unsworth, 2016). In Belgium, for instance, where Flemish and French are both spoken, many children's language abilities are weaker in their second language than in their home language (De Houwer, 2020). Similarly, in the United States, many *dual language learners (DLLs)* have stronger language skills in their home language, like Spanish, Mandarin, or Tagalog, than they do in English when they enter preschool, even if they have learned both (Barrow & Markman-Pithers, 2016).

In the United States, many DLLs tend to have more limited language development in *both* their home and their second language (Hoff, 2018; Lewis et al., 2016). This may make the transition to kindergarten difficult, but bilingualism itself is not the reason. Many DLLs also have other experiences associated with academic

CONNECTIONS

Remember from Chapter 4 that people who grow up speaking more than one language are building higher levels of executive function. Often called *dual language learners (DLLs)*, children who speak multiple languages are not just learning language skills, they are also maintaining an important cultural connection.

TABLE 6.2 Supporting Language Development in Early Childhood

Talk *and* listen.	Children build language by using it; they need to practice speaking and listening.
Be responsive.	When a child makes a bid for attention or reaches out (even if you cannot quite understand), try to respond to encourage their efforts.
Read, sing and tell stories.	Reading aloud, singing, and telling stories builds vocabulary and attention and introduces children to more complex words and grammar than they might hear in everyday conversation.
Go on longer.	Aim for conversations with multiple back-and-forths or turns.
Use the language that comes easily.	Speak to the children in the language you are most comfortable with, whether that is the majority language or your heritage language.
Complexity is helpful.	Do not be afraid to use complicated language or grammar when speaking to children. There is no reason to oversimplify: They will learn to keep up.
Talk about things that are not in the here-and-now.	Engage children by asking questions and using language to talk about the past, the future, and even to speculate on why things are the way they are. Language is useful for building thinking skills as well as vocabulary.
Expect mistakes and language mixing.	Children make errors and, if they are raised in a multilingual environment, will mix up their languages from time to time. This is a typical part of being multilingual.

Roslan Rahman/AFP via Getty Images

Sounding It Out in a New Language Tommy is working on his reading in a preschool in Singapore, where most preschools are bilingual or multilingual in the official languages of Singapore: English, Chinese, Malay, and Tamil.

difficulties, like limited opportunities to practice language skills, living in low-income neighborhoods, or lack of access to high-quality early-childhood education (Ansari & Crosnoe, 2018). In other countries, being bilingual is linked to higher academic achievement. For instance, in Singapore, most children enter kindergarten speaking English and a home language such as Mandarin Chinese, and these children score better than their monolingual peers (Sun & Yin, 2020).

Quality early education can help narrow the gap for low-income DLLs. When early education is provided in children's home language, it supports language development in both the home language and the second language and contributes to later academic success (Park et al., 2017). Preschool education in children's home language may be ideal, but high-quality preschool in any language can help DLLs become more successful academically later on (Yazenjian et al., 2015) (see **Table 6.2**).

APPLY IT! 6.8 Aidan's parents are considering sending him to a dual-language kindergarten. What would you tell them about the advantages of learning more than one language in the early years?

6.9 Like most 5-year-olds, Aidan talks differently than many adults. What advice would you give to his pre-K teacher in facilitating responsive conversation with him?

Supporting Early Learning

Learning Objective

6.8 Explain developmentally appropriate early education.

In an apartment building in Accra, Ghana, 5-year-old Herbert practices his reading with his father, reviewing flashcards and going over his letters before bedtime. His father, Herman, is also focused on making sure that Herbert starts kindergarten ready to learn, so that Herbert can grow up to do "whatever he wants to do" (Aizenman & Warner, 2018). Many longitudinal studies of children's academic performance support Herman's goals. Preschool can build a foundation for children's developing academic skills (OECD, 2017).

Early-Childhood Education

Like Herbert and Aidan, most children around the world begin formal schooling at the end of early childhood, at about age 6 (see **Figure 6.6**). However, the majority are cared for outside of the home at a much earlier age in informal preschools, child-care centers, or kindergartens (Crosnoe et al., 2016). In the United States, where most communities do not have public preschool or pre-kindergarten programs, children who attend preschool are from relatively affluent families (NIEER, 2019). In other places in the world where child care and preschool are well supported by the government, such as Finland and Italy, more children attend preschool, and early child care is considered a human right (OECD, 2017). Aidan benefited from going to a community preschool for much of his early childhood and then transitioned to the pre-K program at a nearby public school in New York City.

In most communities, early-childhood education was disrupted by the recent COVID-19 pandemic (Pramling Samuelsson et al., 2020). Preschool is difficult to move online. Although some schools attempted to engage young children in remote learning, concerns arose about the quality and the equity of the educational materials that were provided (Hashikawa et al., 2020; Timmons et al., 2021).

Learning Through Play Around the world, educators engage young children through relationships and fun. In Ghana, in western Africa, this kindergarten has implemented a play-based curriculum that prepares children for learning by boosting their academic and social skills through responsive, playful interactions.

Boosting Skills

Many preschoolers arrive at school filled with a love of learning and desire to master skills they think are "fun" (Eccles & Wigfield, 2020). Preschoolers tend to have abundant **intrinsic motivation** to learn. Intrinsic motivation refers to the drive to do something because it is its own reward, whereas **extrinsic motivation** refers to doing something for a tangible reward, for example, more time on the tablet in exchange for setting the table. In early childhood, intrinsic motivation is critical in helping children succeed in school, because children need to be able to motivate themselves to master reading, writing, and math (Wigfield et al., 2015a, 2015b). Research shows that many preschoolers are enthusiastic. They love school. Intrinsic motivation is more powerful at driving children's learning than extrinsic rewards are (Alvarez & Booth, 2014).

Around the world, research has shown that high-quality preschool experiences boost children's academic skills (Gray-Lobe et al., 2021; OECD, 2017). Early education can help develop *emergent literacy*, or the early reading skills that help children learn how to decode text and write stories. Learning how to read begins with *phonemic awareness*, or being aware of the individual sounds that make up words (Castles et al., 2018). However, literacy goes beyond memorizing sounds and the letters of the alphabet: One big predictor of children's later reading skills is how much time they spend with books and practicing reading and writing. This practice includes being read to, writing letters, or simply flipping through the pages of a board book (Carroll et al., 2019; Grolig et al., 2020).

Also critical to later school success are early math skills, which involve a basic awareness of numbers (see **Table 6.3**). For instance, children should have a sense of *ordinality*, or counting in order, like first, second, third, fourth, and so on. Over time they will also develop the concept of *seriation*, or the ability to order things, such as by size. When children in a preschool classroom order blocks by size, or meticulously count popsicle sticks, they are not just playing, they are actually working on their math concepts.

Many families read to their children, but few practice math. Parents often explain that they are often anxious about incorporating math into everyday life (Berkowitz et al., 2015).

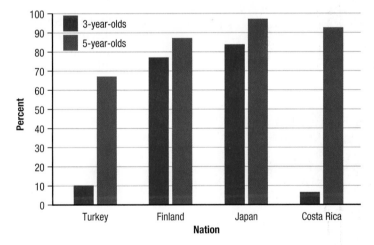

FIGURE 6.6 Who Goes to Preschool? About 6 out of 10 preschool-age children in the United States attend some preschool, most commonly a year of pre-K before starting kindergarten at age 5. Parents with more education and higher incomes are much more likely to enroll their children in preschool. Fewer children in the United States attend preschool than in other affluent countries, but the rate of preschool attendance is rising dramatically around the world.

intrinsic motivation The drive to do something because it is its own reward and just doing it feels rewarding.

extrinsic motivation The drive to do something because you are hoping for a reward.

TABLE 6.3 What Does It Take to Be Ready for School?

Self-regulation skills	Can you follow simple instructions? Can you keep working on a task until it is done? Can you settle down after being upset or overexcited?
Social and emotional skills	Are you able to recover from frustration or disappointment most of the time? Can you be caring and empathetic to other people? Can you make a friend? Can you play with other children?
Health	Do you receive any needed health care and other supports to be able to go to school and attend regularly?
Early academic skills	Do you recognize the letters of the alphabet? Can you link sounds to letters? Can you name common shapes and colors? Can you count to 20?

Information from Paschall et al., 2020.

Scientific American Profile

Creativity and Intrinsic Motivation

Asking children to count the number of plates at the table or socks in the hamper can help build math concepts (Hanner et al., 2019). This enables preschoolers to meet the higher expectations many kindergarten teachers have for their students. Many of these teachers tell researchers that they expect their students to be able to count to 100 and write a sentence (Mader, 2020).

Preschool has particular advantages for children whose parents are less affluent or less educated or do not speak the majority language; however, these children are often less likely to be enrolled in school (Cui & Natzke, 2021; Gupta & Simonsen, 2016; Yazejian et al., 2015). For instance, a year in Head Start, a federal early-education program in the United States that serves low-income families, accelerates children's language skills by an extra six months and their general cognitive skills by three months (Yoshikawa et al., 2016).

Quality Practices

On a playground in San Antonio, Texas, 4-year-olds build castles and cottages in a Lego construction contest (McNeel, 2018). These children are part of San Antonio's ambitious pre-K program that builds their attention, executive function, and social skills through hands-on learning, creative play, and collaboration, rather than an

Early Learning Around the World Outdoor time and tricycles are part of universal pre-K in San Antonio, Texas, where Samantha and her older sister, Addison (*left*), enjoy the playground. In London, England (*right*), learning is hands- and goggles-on. Hands-on work is a characteristic of Montessori education, as in this classroom: Hammering helps build fine motor skills and concentration.

emphasis on reading. The children spend a lot of time outside, growing their own food and stomping in mud puddles (Lieberman, 2019). The effort has paid off: Even though they do not focus on testing, children in the program tend to outperform those from other pre-K programs.

Three thousand miles away, in a classroom in London, England, the scene is calm and orderly. Working by herself, a little girl carefully pours water from one pitcher into another. Another child painstakingly hammers a nail into a tree trunk. These children are part of a preschool program based on the work of Maria Montessori, an Italian physician and teacher who believed children learn best through independent exploration and hands-on practice. Montessori classrooms encourage children to work on their own using specially prepared materials, such as counting beads and wooden blocks, designed to build fine motor, cognitive, and language skills (Lillard, 2016).

The London and San Antonio programs look very different, but they demonstrate some elements common to successful preschools. Experts describe these universal features as *developmentally appropriate practices* (Bredekamp, 1992; NAEYC, 2020). They include:

1. Building warm communities. Children are social learners, so preschools need to build supportive relationships in a safe environment. These responsive bonds are formed not only between teachers and children, but also between children and their peers.
2. Individualized guidance. Children have unique ways of learning, so teaching should be customized to meet their needs.
3. Establishing goals. While successful schools may have different curricula or theories about learning, they all have explicit objectives that guide learning and aspire to build children's skills.
4. Assessment. Keeping track of how children are learning and developing helps educators evaluate the effectiveness of their programs.
5. Supporting families. Preschool programs need to work with families to support their children's learning, whether that means ensuring that caregivers feel that they belong or helping them get extra community support when needed.

Most high-quality preschools harness children's intrinsic motivation and playfulness, rather than drilling them with facts. Experts agree that flashcards and memorization are not developmentally appropriate for 4-year-olds, whose bodies and brains are best prepared to learn when they can move their bodies and manipulate objects to learn about them. In fact, much research indicates that children learn more when they engage in *child-directed*, rather than *teacher-directed*, activities or direct instruction (McCoy & Wolf, 2018). One research study in Accra, Ghana, where Herbert went to preschool, showed that programs that encourage hands-on learning in which children have some choice or autonomy in what they do, like "cooking" in a pretend kitchen, actually develop more academic skills than programs that emphasize memorization and lecture (McCoy & Wolf, 2018). Programs that balance child-directed work with some structured, teacher-directed activity tend to lead to stronger language and cognitive outcomes (Fuligni et al., 2012).

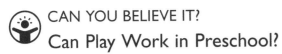

CAN YOU BELIEVE IT?
Can Play Work in Preschool?

Many families will tell you that children should work hard in preschool (Kabay et al., 2017). They are often surprised to hear that drills, and workbooks are not the most effective ways to help young children learn (McCoy & Wolf, 2018). Educators also often worry about balancing learning and play in preschool (Rentzou et al., 2019). However, researchers have found when children play, they are learning (Hirsh-Pasek, 2021).

One of the experiences children missed out on most during the recent COVID-19 pandemic was social play. Isolated at home, children had few opportunities for play. Even if children could go to school, teachers worried about the risks of virus transmission and often curtailed play (O'Keeffe & McNally, 2021).

Piaget and Vygotsky valued pretend play in early childhood because it helps children develop cognitive skills such as theory of mind and abstract thinking (Piaget, 1952; Vygotsky, 2016). Make-believe allows children to practice their emotion regulation skills by pretending to be afraid or angry (Slot et al., 2017). Dressing up and working together in a play kitchen on an imaginary spaceship can be so engaging that children are unaware they are building their social, language, and executive function skills (Thibodeau et al., 2016).

Dressing up as Spider-Man or serving pretend pancakes does not overtly teach children reading or math. Experts have found that *teacher-guided play*, in which a teacher works within the framework of children's play to build academic skills, is more effective than direct instruction (Weisberg et al., 2016). Guided play incorporates children's creativity, imagination, and motivation with guidance from an adult to connect it to learning. For instance, in one classroom a teacher writes down students' creative stories and has them act them out. This helps the children build language skills while having fun pretending to be monsters (Nicolopoulou et al., 2015). This teacher is meeting children at their developmental level and using creative play to help them grow academically. 🎭

Encouraging Learning at Home

Children who do not attend a preschool program can still prepare for formal schooling. Parents can help by reading with their children, engaging them in conversation, and doing simple math problems (Loeb, 2016; York et al., 2019). They can also encourage play that builds executive function and fine motor skills, from dress-up to arts and crafts (LaForett & Mendez, 2017). Families can cultivate their children's social and emotional skills by adopting positive disciplinary practices and maintaining high expectations (MacPhee et al., 2018).

Children from high-income families tend to develop academic skills earlier than children from lower-income families. However, thanks to increasing enrollment in preschool, these gaps are narrowing (Bassok et al., 2016). Researchers believe the gaps occur because high-income families have more financial resources to spend on cultural or educational activities and more time for intensive, one-on-one play and instruction (Reardon & Portilla, 2016). Systemic challenges are the primary cause. However, while developmental scientists advocate for institutional changes to help boost the academic readiness for young children, they also point to ways individual families can help their children succeed. These include encouraging parents to believe they can shape their children's cognitive development through back-and-forth responsive communication, time for open-ended play, and regular routines (Alper et al., 2021; Doebel, 2020; Moore et al., 2020).

Researchers have found that resilient families have particular social and emotional strengths, such as knowing when and how to take care of themselves: Caregivers who are depressed or stressed have more difficulty providing children with cognitive stimulation (Pratt et al., 2016). Relationships also matter. Even in families who experience

A Little Math Before Bed Responsive communication is important to young children's development and can even include a little counting practice, as this father tries with his little one at home Slovakia.

Halfpoint/iStock/Getty Images

adversity, strong parent–child relationships promote resilience and school success (Anderson, 2018).

APPLY IT! **6.10** During the initial months of the COVID-19 pandemic, Aidan's preschool was closed, and he was at home with his family. What activities or practices would you have recommended to his family to encourage his cognitive growth at home?

6.11 Aidan's family is not sure what to look for in a quality after-school program. What would you recommend they look for?

Wrapping It Up

LO 6.1 Describe typical growth in the body and brain from age 2½ to 6. (p. 164)

During early childhood, children typically begin with the softer, rounder body of a toddler and grow longer and leaner, with more adult body proportions. The brain continues to grow, but at a slower pace than in infancy. This is a period of intensive growth of the faster, myelinated connections that link different parts of the brain, called the connectome. In addition, the cortex continues to mature in early childhood, particularly the prefrontal cortex, an area at the front of the brain that is critical to logical thinking and controlling behavior.

LO 6.2 Discuss connections between the development of motor skills and self-control and children's feelings of competence. (p. 164)

Motor-skill development in early childhood requires practice. Children learn the skills that their communities and cultures support, whether tricycle riding or ballet dancing. Motor skills help children feel competent and build executive function skills and self-control. During early childhood, if not before, most children learn to manage their own toileting and develop fine motor skills, allowing them to be more independent and adjust to formal school.

LO 6.3 Discuss common challenges in health during early childhood. (p. 168)

Sleep continues to be important to health in early childhood. In many communities in the United States, children give up daytime napping at this age. Many children have sleep difficulties, which may be connected to media use. Physical activity and nutritious foods are important to health, but many children do not get enough. Even in preschool, children are aware of the stigma around body size, so adults must be careful about how they talk about weight. Although most young children were protected from the worst effects of the COVID-19 pandemic, infectious diseases still take a toll on preschoolers around the world. Children are particularly susceptible to environmental dangers, like lead. Accidents are a leading cause of death and injury as children are better able to explore but have trouble making safe choices.

LO 6.4 Identify the key features of Piaget's preoperational stage. (p. 173)

Piaget's stage of preoperational thought spans the period of about ages 2 to 7. Young children's thinking is now symbolic but not quite logical. Most children can use language and their imagination to talk about things they cannot see, but they cannot perform logical mental operations, like mentally reversing or undoing something that just happened or considering multiple perspectives on a problem. Classic Piagetian tasks, like the conservation and three mountains tasks, illuminate the gaps in children's thinking.

LO 6.5 Apply Vygotsky's theory of development to young children's thinking. (p. 173)

Vygotsky believed that children's cognitive maturation results from social interaction and is best when customized to the needs of the individual learner. Vygotskian researchers suggest that children learn best with sensitive guidance, or scaffolding, in the zone of proximal development (ZPD). Children may talk to themselves, or use private speech, to help direct their own thinking or activity.

LO 6.6 Describe advances in information processing skills, including memory, attention, executive function, and theory of mind, during early childhood. (p. 173)

During early childhood, memory and attention advance, as well as the executive function that will enable children to sit still at school. Episodic memory improves dramatically due to brain maturation and practice, but semantic memory remains immature.

Improvements in working memory help children learn to read, count, and follow directions. Their attention and executive function are still developing, but they are increasingly able to focus and regulate their own behavior. Children at this age are also developing *theory of mind*, the ability to see things from other people's perspective.

LO 6.7 Discuss vocabulary and grammar development during early childhood. (p. 184)

Children's language grows dramatically between ages 2 and 6. By age 6, most English-speaking children use about 6,000 words and can understand about 14,000 words. Many children speak more than one language. Children's grammar becomes more sophisticated. Language growth happens through high-quality,

responsive conversations. Most children typically have stronger language skills in their home language than in their second language, because they have more opportunities for practice.

LO 6.8 Explain developmentally appropriate early education. (p. 186)

Early education, in preschool or at home, develops children's early academic skills. Quality preschools come in many different forms, but they all nurture strong relationships and harness children's intrinsic motivation to learn. Play can help children learn in and out of school. Building children's executive function and cognitive skills can also happen at home or at school, through arts and crafts, pretend play, or engaging conversations.

KEY TERMS

early childhood (p. 164)
prefrontal cortex (p. 166)
preoperational thought (p. 174)
animism (p. 174)
conservation tasks (p. 175)

three mountains task (p. 176)
egocentrism (p. 176)
scaffolding (p. 177)
zone of proximal development (ZPD) (p. 177)
private speech (p. 178)

episodic memory (p. 179)
working memory (p. 179)
executive function (p. 180)
attention-deficit/ hyperactivity disorder (ADHD) (p. 181)

theory of mind (p. 183)
intrinsic motivation (p. 187)
extrinsic motivation (p. 187)

CHECK YOUR LEARNING

1. During early childhood, the band of neurons connecting the brain's two hemispheres becomes increasingly myelinated. This connective brain structure is known as:
   a) gray matter.
   b) the cell nucleus.
   c) the corpus callosum.
   d) synaptic pruning.

2. Which of the following is an example of a gross motor skill that may develop during early childhood?
   a) Jumping
   b) Folding origami
   c) Eye blinking
   d) Using chopsticks

3. During early childhood, which of the following issues may affect eating and nutrition?
   a) High risk of developing food allergies
   b) Selective eating
   c) Greatly increased appetite
   d) Inability to distinguish sweet and salty flavors

4. According to the constructivist theory of Jean Piaget, which stage of cognitive development in early childhood includes symbolic thought but limitations to logic?
   a) Concrete operations
   b) Sensorimotor
   c) Preoperational
   d) Formal operations

5. Which of the following helps explain the risks of accidental injury in early childhood?
   a) Preschoolers' lack the physical coordination and the ability to think through the possible consequences of their actions.
   b) Preschoolers cannot feel pain, so they do not mind falling off the monkey bars.
   c) Young children cannot learn from their experiences, so they tend to repeat dangerous behaviors.
   d) Young children need some painful experiences in order to learn how to be safe in the world.

6. When applied to the thinking of early childhood, *egocentrism* means that:
   a) young children do not care about other people.
   b) young children have difficulty seeing the world from others' point of view.
   c) young children want all the attention to be on them at all times.
   d) young children's brains are growing from the center outward.

7. Which skill is developed as young children's executive function improves?
   a) Excelling at the game Simon Says
   b) Being able to climb a ladder
   c) Long-distance vision
   d) Speaking four-word sentences

8. Which statement about learning and speaking more than one language in early childhood is FALSE?

   a) A majority of children around the world learn more than one language.

   b) Children are likely to become confused if learning more than one language at the same time.

   c) Children learning two languages may show smaller vocabulary in each language during the early-childhood years.

   d) Children learning two languages show some stronger executive function skills than children learning only one language.

9. A preschool child who is practicing skills like building a block tower in a specific order and learning to pour liquids may be in which type of preschool program?

   a) Developmentally inappropriate

   b) Academically focused

   c) Vygotskyian

   d) Montessori

10. Describe the role of culture in motor development. Are the gross motor skills and fine motor skills developed during early-childhood universal?

11. What are some key features of Vygotsky's sociocultural theory, and how can they be applied to providing developmentally appropriate practices in preschool classrooms?

7 Social and Emotional Development in Early Childhood

Development of Self

7.1 Analyze the advances in emotional expression and regulation during Erikson's stage of initiative versus guilt.

7.2 Describe features of young children's understanding of their identity or self-concept.

Creating an Identity

7.3 Discuss the major theoretical viewpoints on gender development in early childhood.

7.4 Describe the development of stereotypes in early childhood.

Family Relationships in Early Childhood

7.5 Describe variations in parenting practices and styles and their impact on development.

Getting Along with Peers

7.6 Describe the features of play and their role in learning and development.

Getting Along in the World: Moral Development

7.7 Describe aggressive and prosocial behaviors in early childhood.

Selected Resources from

 Achieve

Activities

Concept Practice: Caregiving in Early Childhood

Spotlight on Science: Measuring the Impact of Fathers on Early Development

Assessments

LearningCurve

Practice Quiz

Videos

Scientific American Profiles

Racial Preferences in Preschoolers

Types of Play

© Macmillan, Photo by Sidford House

Four-year-old Olivia has a ready smile and dances to any song she hears (even if she is unsure of the words). She was a miracle baby, born prematurely and weighing just 3 pounds after her mother, Brionnah, developed dangerously high blood pressure midway through her pregnancy. Fortunately, Brionnah's health improved after Olivia was born, and Olivia was an "easy baby": Her mother recalls that even in the hospital, she was quiet and content. But as she has grown, Olivia has become an outgoing, empathetic child who can always make her mother laugh. She is sweet to other children, always the first to congratulate a friend for getting something right or to hug someone who is having a bad day.

Olivia is not just learning about other people's feelings and how to be kind, she is also learning about her own emotions and ideas. Olivia's parents have encouraged this, respecting Olivia's emerging ability to say what she wants. They even set up their apartment so Olivia can reach the snacks she wants and find the toys she loves on lower shelves. As developmental theorists would suggest, Olivia is filled with the capability and initiative of early childhood, ready to explore the world.

Like many children, Olivia transitioned from a cozy life at home with her mother, father, and the occasional friend to babysit, to life at preschool. There, Olivia faced a new routine of required morning circle time, assigned cubbies, lining up for recess, and waiting until she was called upon. Preschool is not always a perfect fit for the exuberant initiative characteristic of children this age. Olivia's parents and her good-natured teacher, Jennifer, sometimes worried about Olivia's adjustment. Four-year-olds have no shortage of creative ideas and dance routines, but they are not always ready for the more controlled behavior expected by teachers managing a classroom of children.

Many children have to work hard to control their strong feelings when things do not go their way. Emotions can be overwhelming in early childhood, and meltdowns are sometimes unavoidable. Developmental scientists point out that many adults, even parents and teachers, often overestimate the capabilities of young children, who may be able to talk and walk and play but are not yet experts in self-control. Understanding caregiving, like the warmth and empathy shown by Olivia's parents, and consistent expectations, make the adjustment easier.

In this chapter, you will read about the hallmarks of social and emotional development during early childhood. Preschoolers' emotion regulation and self-control are more mature than in the toddler years, but these are still peak years for hitting, crying, and melting down. Young children make mistakes, messes, and even enemies on the playground. Nevertheless, with guidance, they can learn to be kind and develop an early sense of identity.

For Olivia, life at school got easier. She got used to the routine, and her mother observes that she now feels even more competent and confident. Both Olivia and her family are excited about the future.

Scientific American Profile

Meet Olivia

Development of Self

A typical 2-year-old knows their name and may be able to tell you about their big brother or baby sister. By the time that toddler turns 6, they will be able to describe what they are good at (almost everything) and manage feelings that may have reduced them to tears (or tantrums) when they were younger. In early childhood, children develop emotion regulation and a sense of who they are that will help them succeed in the years to come (Robson et al., 2020). Developing these skills is not something that happens magically: It takes practice and patience.

Erikson's Theory of Early Childhood Development

If you watch preschoolers on the playground, you might be impressed by their willingness to try new things. Most of the time, young children are confident enough to "go for it," jumping off the monkey bars even if they might scratch a knee. Erik Erikson describes this enthusiasm as *initiative*. Remember from Chapter 2 that each of Erikson's eight stages of human development involves a unique psychological crisis. The third stage, which occurs between ages 3 and 5, is known as **initiative versus guilt** (Erikson, 1950/1993; see **Table 7.1**).

Learning Objectives

7.1 Analyze the advances in emotional expression and regulation during Erikson's stage of initiative versus guilt.

7.2 Describe features of young children's understanding of their identity or self-concept.

TABLE 7.1 Erikson's Stage of Initiative Versus Guilt

Stage	Age	Characteristics
Initiative versus guilt	3–5 years	Children have abundant *initiative*, or enthusiasm, to try new things and do them independently. They also often experience disappointment when they do things incorrectly. Some *guilt*, or remorse about getting things wrong, ensures that children learn to be careful with other people's feelings and to get things right. Healthy development requires children to preserve their initiative without feeling too much guilt about making mistakes.

initiative versus guilt Erikson's third stage of development, which occurs between ages 3 and 5 and involves the conflict between children's enthusiasm to try new things independently and their remorse when they get things wrong.

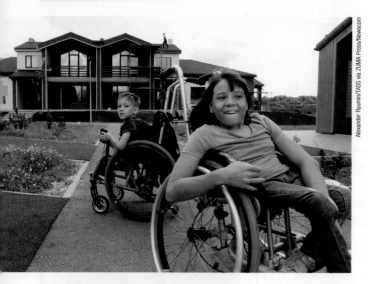

Sometimes Initiative Means Having Your Own Wheels. Young children are often eager to try things themselves. Wheelchairs and lots of space to go fast make that possible for Kiril and Yana, who are playing near their home in the village of Bogoslovska, in Russia.

CONNECTIONS

Remember from Chapter 5 that *emotion regulation* refers to the ability to manage emotions appropriately to the situation.

Initiative is abundant in preschoolers' play. They are anxious to be like "big kids" and grownups, whether that means buckling their car seat by themselves or pretending to be a parent while doing make believe. This drive is accompanied by the risk of failure. In early childhood, milk is spilled. It is hard to settle down when it is bedtime or when a teacher says it is time to stop playing and join circle time. Feelings of guilt emerge as preschoolers recognize these shortcomings, which can become amplified when someone responds insensitively.

Erikson's insight was that healthy development requires a balance between preschoolers' initiative and guilt. Shame or guilt may arise if adults respond with too much anger or frustration over children's mistakes. This might lead to a hesitancy to take healthy risks later in life. On the other hand, if children are not given limits and protections, they may never learn to take responsibility and follow the rules. In Erikson's view, caregivers and teachers can help children successfully navigate the crisis of early childhood by protecting them with limits, while allowing them to preserve their imaginative dreams.

For Olivia, both her preschool and family tried to respect her enthusiasm by combining predictable structure with choices for Olivia to make on her own. When Olivia gets home from school, she knows she can choose between reading a story or doing some art, and she knows where to find the markers and paper that are just for her. Her family is supporting Olivia's initiative while decreasing the likelihood that Olivia will be frustrated because she cannot watch TV all afternoon.

Emotion Regulation in Early Childhood

As toddlers grow into preschoolers, adults expect them to control their behavior and their feelings. Children who are successful in developing *emotion regulation* have an easier time adjusting to the world as they grow (Denham, 2019; Harrington et al., 2020). Brain maturation and cognitive development help preschoolers learn to control their emotions. Emotional maturation also happens in a social context: Children learn different ways of managing their feelings from their communities, differences which in turn will shape how their brain and bodies respond to the world around them (Kitayama & Salvador, 2017).

Advances in Self-Regulation During early childhood, children become more *self-regulated* when it comes to managing their feelings, rather than depending on others to help calm them down. Toddlers may cling and wail when dropped off at day care, but children who are Olivia's age are expected to arrive at school and say goodbye without too much upset, although that does not always happen. Preschoolers are even expected to modulate their positive feelings: When Olivia is excited about getting to play outside during recess, her teachers remind her to use her "inside voice."

There are cultural and individual differences in families' expectations for their children, such as whether children are expected to be happy and friendly in public, or whether an occasional bout of jealousy is acceptable or hidden (Ding et al., 2021). However, preschoolers around the world are expected to grow more independent and more capable of managing their feelings. This does not mean that 3-year-olds do this as well as adults: Preschoolers have many ups and downs and meltdowns. Younger children are particularly prone to bouts of upset, tantrums, and separation anxiety, which resolve but do not completely disappear as they get older (Battaglia et al., 2017; Wakschlag et al., 2018).

Caregivers often have unrealistic expectations of their preschoolers' capabilities (Zero to Three, 2016c). For instance, most think that preschool-aged children should be

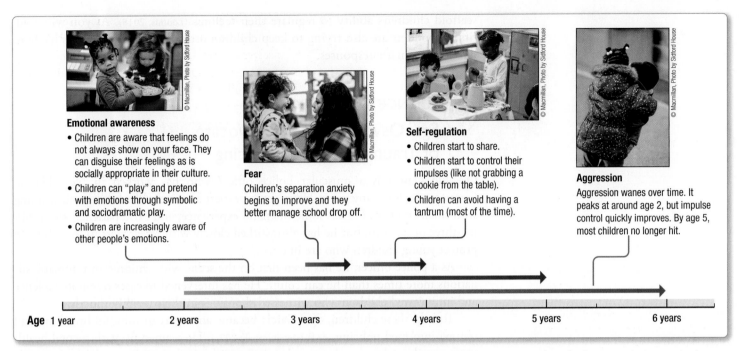

Emotional awareness
- Children are aware that feelings do not always show on your face. They can disguise their feelings as is socially appropriate in their culture.
- Children can "play" and pretend with emotions through symbolic and sociodramatic play.
- Children are increasingly aware of other people's emotions.

Fear
Children's separation anxiety begins to improve and they better manage school drop off.

Self-regulation
- Children start to share.
- Children start to control their impulses (like not grabbing a cookie from the table).
- Children can avoid having a tantrum (most of the time).

Aggression
Aggression wanes over time. It peaks at around age 2, but impulse control quickly improves. By age 5, most children no longer hit.

Age 1 year   2 years   3 years   4 years   5 years   6 years

FIGURE 7.1 Emotion Regulation in Early Childhood As children grow, they are better able to manage their feelings on their own in the ways that their communities expect. During early childhood, children still need help and encouragement to manage big feelings, but meltdowns become less frequent.

able to share and avoid tantrums when they are just 2½. However, most developmental scientists do not think most children are capable of these accomplishments until at least age 4, and even then they should not be expected to control themselves consistently (see **Figure 7.1**).

Difficulties with Emotion Regulation Some young children struggle more than others with emotion regulation. **Psychological disorders** can occur when disruptions in children's feelings, thinking, or behavior interfere with their ability to function in everyday life. It is estimated that if all preschoolers were screened, one in five would meet the diagnosis for a psychological disorder: a number that increased during the COVID-19 pandemic (Panchal et al., 2021; Whalen et al., 2017). Such children might get excessively upset at being separated from their families or experience atypical fears or phobias (Mian & Gray, 2019). Some acquire skills to manage these challenges, but those who continue to have emotional difficulties benefit from treatment (Finsaas et al., 2020).

Developmental scientists have identified some red flags for emotion regulation challenges that are not age-typical. For instance, children who get upset very quickly and frequently, or who hurt people or damage property when they are distraught, may not outgrow their difficulties without intervention (Wakschlag et al., 2018). Children whose anxiety does not improve may also need extra help (Battaglia et al., 2017). Preschoolers who have trouble managing their feelings need encouragement, modeling, and reinforcement (Dunst & Espe-Sherwindt, 2017).

Some children have trouble regulating their emotions because of early trauma, such as witnessing family or community violence or being seriously injured (Bartlett, 2021). More than one in four children will experience early trauma and are at higher risk to develop long-term psychological disorders such as PTSD, anxiety, and depression (Copeland et al., 2018). Family therapy can build resilience by fostering and reinforcing strong relationships. Teachers help by providing *trauma-informed care*, in which consistent, warm relationships nurture strong attachments and

psychological disorders Disruptions in feelings, thinking, or behavior that interfere with a person's ability to function in everyday life.

CONNECTIONS
Recall from Chapter 6 that as many as 1 in 10 children in the United States will be diagnosed with ADHD.

scaffold children's ability to regulate their feelings (Loomis, 2018). As you will read, first responders are also trying to keep children protected, so they are less likely to develop traumatic responses.

SCIENCE IN PRACTICE
Sgt. Osvoldo Garcia, Advocate of Trauma-Informed Policing

Osvoldo Garcia is a muscular police officer who has worked in New Haven, Connecticut, for many years. He is also an expert at mindful breathing and working with small children. He has some firsthand experience, and extra patience, from raising three of his own, but he has also worked closely with researchers to learn how to protect young children who are in crisis.

As a police officer, he has been first on the scene with children in traumatic situations more times than he can count: He has intervened in cases of family violence and interviewed children who witnessed shootings in their neighborhoods.

To help these children, Sgt. Garcia became an expert in mindful breathing and trauma-informed policing (de la Fontaine et al., 2021). He teamed up with mental health professionals and spent days in the classroom trying to understand how to apply developmental science to his police work. He has even become a trainer, explaining to fellow officers how important it is to protect children in times of crisis.

Sgt. Garcia has learned that experiencing trauma will change children. He explains that these situations will change their daily lives and that their minds may constantly replay what has happened. He understands that children under stress might respond in any number of ways that are age appropriate: They might giggle, stare off into space, or just cry and be clingy, even to a parent who has just been violent (Marans & Hahn, 2017).

Parents and other adults might not want to accept that children have experienced a crisis: They might believe that children slept through it or were distracted by the TV. Sgt. Garcia tells them the truth: that children pick up on more than adults realize, and in addition to the other stresses people in crisis need to manage, caregivers must address children's reactions to difficult experiences.

Sgt. Garcia is aware that interacting with police can often be a source of trauma itself: Many children are afraid of the police. His job is to avoid exposing children to trauma whenever possible: avoiding making arrests in front of children and ensuring that they always have someone safe to take care of them. Since Sgt. Garcia is often the first person a child sees after something horrible has happened, he must be honest, reassure them that he is there to protect them, and address their worries, even if that means checking under the bed and in closets.

He also offers these children some techniques to cope with stress, because even preschoolers can calm themselves down. He teaches them to breathe quietly, to do something with their hands to distract themselves, like color, and to make sure they have a safety plan and a safety person in case something scary happens again. The dream is that making children feel safe will help them do a little better in the future.

Brain Maturation for Self-Regulation Brain development and new cognitive strategies help young children better manage their feelings. Olivia is developing her own strategies, including deep breaths, yoga poses, using her words to talk about her frustration, and distracting herself by thinking about something she likes (like snack!).

Young children, as well as the rest of us, process emotions through networks connecting the *subcortical* parts of the brain with the more logical prefrontal

Trauma Care on the Front Lines
Osvoldo Garcia is a police officer in New Haven and also an expert in trauma-informed care for children. Like other officers, he is often the first on the scene when children experience a crisis, and he tries to make them feel safe amidst difficult circumstances.

Christopher Peak/New Haven Independent

cortex. These circuits mature over a long time, beginning before birth and continuing into early adulthood. That long period of maturation allows experiences and environment to shape development (Tottenham, 2020). Emotion-regulating networks become more robust around age 4 or 5, at which point the prefrontal cortex can help children to control impulsive actions and to calm upset feelings (Gee, 2016; Zelazo, 2020).

However, these networks do not develop identically in all children. Major adversity can alter them, resulting in problems with emotion regulation (VanTieghem et al., 2021). These networks need to be "just right": Difficulties in early caregiving or too much stress may make subcortical structures too sensitive or not sensitive enough. For instance, children who have difficulty regulating emotions may be overly sensitive and may overreact to new or scary events. On the other hand, children who are not sensitive enough may be unimpressed by a teacher's command to stop and listen. Just because children *can* control their behavior does not mean that they will always be able to do so; they may not know that it is necessary or may be tired, hungry, or overexcited.

One way scientists study children's growing emotional maturity is to ask them what they would do if they received a disappointing gift, in what is called the *disappointing gift task* (Saarni, 1984). By age 6, most children can mask their true feelings with a polite smile or other appropriate behavior (Cole & Jacobs, 2018; Ip et al., 2021). They may be able to use their developing cognitive skills, like their theory of mind or perspective-taking ability, to control how they display their feelings. Remember, children can lie by this age, and they may use this new cognitive skill to avoid hurting the gift giver's feelings (Demedardi et al., 2021). This is a sign of emotional maturity and a form of kindness. How many times have you told someone their new haircut looked great?

Culture and Socializing Emotions *Emotional socialization* is the process of learning how to express feelings in a way that is appropriate for your culture (Eisenberg, 2020). Sometimes children are explicitly taught how to express emotions, such as when Olivia's teacher, Jennifer, tells Olivia to talk about what she feels instead of crying. At other times, children learn by watching others express their emotions. Families' *ethnotheories*, or beliefs about why emotions happen and how to display them, are a crucial part of emotional socialization (García Coll et al., 1996; Liu et al., 2020).

How children display their feelings is far from universal. For instance, many communities, including some in the United States, value being emotionally expressive. In these families, intense emotional behavior, like tantrums or howls of joy, may be expected and even appreciated (Perez Rivera & Dunsmore, 2011; Raval & Walker, 2019). In some U.S. studies, families who identified as Black or White were more likely to believe that "kids will be kids" and tend to have more acceptance of their children's expressions of their feelings and even their misbehavior (Labella, 2018; Parker et al., 2012).

Other communities' ethnotheories value more emotional restraint. For instance, in the United States, Mexican American mothers are less likely to talk about emotions with their preschoolers than European American mothers (Eisenberg, 1999; Lugo-Candalas et al., 2015). Preschoolers in nations like India, Japan, Korea, and China tend to be less emotionally expressive and more self-controlled (Grabell et al., 2015; Yang & Wang, 2019). Emotional restraint even extends to picture books (Ding et al., 2021). Researchers found that in U.S. picture books, children were often shown with big, outgoing smiles. In Taiwanese books, however, the smiles were calmer and less exaggerated (Tsai et al., 2007).

Families' emotion-regulation strategies often reflect cultural values (Halberstadt et al., 2020). Many U.S. families value independence and expect that even young children will learn to manage their strong feelings on their own (Corapci et al., 2018). (See **Figure 7.2.**)

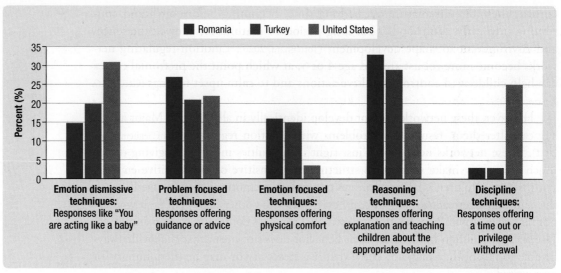

Data from Corapci et al., 2018.

FIGURE 7.2 How Do Families Respond If a Preschooler Has a Tantrum? Practices for managing emotion regulation vary around the world. Researchers asked families in three different countries—Romania, Turkey, and the United States—how they might manage a preschooler's meltdowns. U.S. parents were much less likely to use emotion-focused comforting techniques, like holding or hugging a child, than those from Romania or Turkey. They were also more likely to use emotionally dismissive techniques and to manage outbursts with time-outs.

Despite the variations in emotion socialization, some practices have been found to foster preschoolers' emotion regulation across diverse communities. *Emotion-coaching* involves adults strategizing or problem solving with their children about how to manage feelings while setting limits (Gottman, 2011; Katz et al., 2020). Other supportive techniques include empathic listening or physical comfort, like hugs (Bergnehr & Cekaite, 2018). Talking about feelings also tends to help build stronger emotion regulation skills (Curtis et al., 2020). Some practices, such as responding with dismissiveness, disdain, or anger, are associated with long-term developmental challenges (Hooper et al., 2018; Marçal, 2021).

Developing a Sense of Self

If you talk to a group of 4-year-olds, they will tell you that they are going to be celebrities, inventors, presidents, and NBA stars. This is because, as Erikson predicted, young children display a great deal of initiative and confidence as they develop a sense of who they are, called a *self-concept* (Harter, 2015). Preschoolers' self-concept is more positive than at any other time during the lifespan (Dweck, 2002; Wigfield & Eccles, 2020).

As children grow, their understanding of who they are becomes more complex. In early childhood, self-concept is initially limited by children's concrete thinking and tends to be based on very tangible characteristics, such as "I like pizza" or "I have red hair" (Pesu et al., 2016). As they grow, children are building an early physical self-concept, or *body image* (Rodgers et al., 2017). Even in preschool, children may have a sense of how they do in school, an early *academic self-concept* (Compagnoni & Losenno, 2020). By age 4 or 5, children can articulate a self-concept that is more abstract (Cimpian et al., 2017). This is closely tied to *self-esteem*, or how they feel about themselves generally (Harter, 1993; Rosenberg, 1963).

Preschoolers' self-esteem tends to stick: Young children who think they are capable tend to do better in school and are more motivated to succeed (Marsh et al., 2019;

Orth et al., 2018). Children who feel negatively about themselves are at higher risk of experiencing difficulties in school and with friends and developing emotional disorders like depression (Keane & Loades, 2017).

Community expectations differ in terms of how young children should express their self-concepts. In Olivia's classroom, her teacher Jennifer enthusiastically cheers when a child does something good, like staying seated during circle time. Her encouragement of positive self-concept and appreciation of pride is neither unusual nor universal (Raval & Walker, 2019). When researchers watched how preschoolers in Japan and the United States reacted to success on a game, they noticed that U.S. children expressed pride when they had been successful. Japanese preschoolers were much less likely to express pride at their successes and much more likely to express embarrassment at their failures (Lewis et al., 2010).

Scientific American Profile

Social-Emotional Learning in Early Childhood

CAN YOU BELIEVE IT?
Is Praise Poison?

If you spend time in a preschool classroom, you will likely hear "Great job!" or "You're the best!" many times throughout the day. Does telling a 5-year-old that they did a great job actually help them work harder? Researchers have found that it may hurt rather than help (Cimpian et al., 2007; Zentall & Morris, 2010). Praise can have unintended consequences, like reducing children's self-esteem and even discouraging them from working hard (Brummelman et al., 2016; Brummelman & Dweck, 2020).

First, preschoolers' self-concept and self-esteem are more sensitive than many of us realize. As young children begin school and face new social situations and pressure to perform, their self-concepts become more fragile (Cimpian, 2017). Their concrete thinking may lead them to misconstrue a comment about something specific, like how they wrote their name, to be an overall commentary on them as a person (Muenks et al., 2018).

Second, decades of research have revealed that certain types of praise seem to backfire, sapping children's motivation, discouraging them from trying their hardest, and actually making them feel worse about themselves. Shockingly, these effects can last for years. In a classic study, scientists tested 4-year-olds to see how they would react to hearing different types of praise. Half of the children received generic praise that focused on their personal characteristics, such as "You are a good artist." The other group was given praise that focused on the process, rather than ability: They were told that they "did a good job drawing."

These slight differences in wording made a big difference. If children had trouble making a drawing, the children who received generic praise were more likely to react emotionally. In fact, they told experimenters that they might just walk away after making a mistake. On the other hand, children who received process-oriented praise had an easier time recovering from mistakes (Cimpian et al., 2007). Over the years, studies with older children and different types of praise have reinforced this finding: Warm encouragement—like a high five—boosts motivation, but telling children they are smart does not (Morris & Zentall, 2014). Too much praise that emphasizes personal characteristics tends to lead to struggles when children encounter inevitable setbacks.

Praise affects children's achievement as well as their motivation. Process-oriented praise helps them to understand that social and academic success happen through hard work and dedication, rather than inborn talent. Indeed, children who receive process-oriented praise seem to be more dedicated to their studies and score higher in tests of reading and math (Gunderson et al., 2018).

So, does this mean that adults need to stop being positive? No. But praising the process keeps the focus on effort. Kind words about a preschooler's hard work will enable them to fail gracefully and learn from their mistakes, as they continue to grow.

APPLY IT!   **7.1** Olivia wants to "do it by herself." How would Erikson explain her drive to be independent?

7.2 Olivia's teacher encourages her students to talk about their feelings and manage them with yoga and mindfulness. How might these approaches be shaped by culture and community expectations?

Creating an Identity

Learning Objectives

7.3 Discuss the major theoretical viewpoints on gender development in early childhood.

7.4 Describe the development of stereotypes in early childhood.

CONNECTIONS

A number of terms describe sex, gender, and gender identity (see Chapter 3). *Sex* refers to the biological markers that relate to reproductive characteristics. *Gender* refers to cultural and social ideas about men, women, and less binary distinctions. *Gender identity* refers to your sense of yourself as male, female, or something less binary. *Gender expression* describes how people display their gender in terms of their name, pronouns, or characteristics such as hair style.

Preschoolers may still sit in car seats, but they have already developed complex ways of comparing themselves to other people. Young children are quickly learning, imitating, and even overimitating the adults and peers in their lives (Hoehl et al., 2019). Children at this age tend to be more inflexible about labels than people are at other times of life. For instance, young children may rigidly assert that only boys can be firemen or only girls can dance (Poulin-Dubois et al., 2002). Preschoolers' ideas about gender, ethnicity, and other social categories develop along with other aspects of cognition (Wang et al., 2021). While most of these ideas become more flexible with time, some biases may persist (Baron & Banaji, 2006; Rhodes & Baron, 2019).

Gender Development

Gender is an important part of how many children and adults define themselves. In early childhood, children are beginning to develop their *gender identity*, or their sense of themselves as boys, girls, or another less binary or more fluid label (Diamond, 2020). Culture, family, and biology play important parts in helping children understand these social roles.

In early childhood, and across the lifespan, there is diversity in how people express their gender. Many communities are moving away from rigid stereotypes about social roles (Charlesworth & Banaji, 2021). For instance, in some schools in Sweden, teachers and children actively avoid gender labels, revising nursery rhymes to avoid stereotypes and even using gender-neutral pronouns for all children (Shutts et al., 2017). But many families remain more enthusiastic about gender stereotypes (Halim et al., 2018; Parker et al., 2017).

Perspectives on Gender Development Across human history, people have observed that gender distinctions go beyond the binary division of "boys' toys" and "girls' toys" that you will find in the aisles of a big box store. For instance, ancient Chinese medicine taught that all beings included a balance of male and female energy (Furth, 1988). Traditional cultures around the world often incorporated ideas about people who belonged to less binary genders, like the *kitesha* of the Bala people in Zaire, the *bakla* in the Philippines, or the gender-bending Greek god Dionysus (David & Cruz, 2018; Merriam, 1971).

The repercussions of gender stereotypes go far beyond whether parents buy a pink glitter tutu or a football jersey for their 4-year-old. Gender roles are linked to power and social status. For instance, in some communities in India, preschool girls are more likely to get sick than preschool boys, in part because they are less likely to receive vaccinations (Chaudhuri, 2015). On the other hand, in the United States, many families tend to prefer to have girls, and if they have a daughter they will not continue to try for a son (Blau et al., 2020). In many U.S. and European communities, children who do not conform to gender stereotypes, and particularly those who tend to be more feminine, are at higher risk for bullying and may need protection from social rejection (Sullivan et al., 2018; Warren et al., 2019).

Room for Everyone in the Kitchen At this preschool in Stockholm, Sweden, children are encouraged to play together in diverse groups, regardless of their gender identity. Teachers try to avoid stereotypes and make sure everyone has a turn at the play stove.

Andrea Bruce/The New York Times/Redux

Social Learning Theories of Gender In developmental science, the discussion of gender often goes back to Sigmund Freud. Like many thinkers of his time, Freud had some shocking ideas about gender, including a profound belief in women's inferiority (Freud, 1927, 1968a, 1968b; Sauerteig, 2012). But while his more outlandish ideas have been rejected, some of his theoretical ideas continue to be influential (Bell, 2018; Zakin, 2011).

Freud argued that gender is something that children learn as they grow, rather than something they are born with (Freud, 1917/1989). He also believed that children develop a gender identity through *identification*, or modeling their own identity on their same-sex parent (Freud, 1899/1964). Most developmental psychologists still agree that gender roles are learned: Researchers who adopt a *social learning theory* describe the process of learning about gender as occurring through *modeling* and *reinforcement* (Bussey & Bandura, 1999; Mischel, 1966).

From the color of their bedding, to the books they are read, to the toys they play with, children are surrounded by gender messages (MacPhee & Prendergast, 2019). How many of us have seen T-shirts for toddlers printed with gender stereotypes like "Does this diaper make my butt look big?" or "Lock up your daughters" (Barbara, 2019). In families worldwide, gender changes how people treat children. Boys tend to be taken to play outside more than girls, and they also receive harsher, more physical punishment (Bornstein et al., 2016).

Researchers call the embedding of gender stereotypes in children's environments—and even their personalities—*gender-typing* (Kollmayer et al., 2018). Children are expected to adhere to a binary distinction between boys and girls. Boys are expected to be strong, aggressive, and often naughty, whereas girls are assumed to be nurturing, beautiful, and obedient (Halim et al., 2017). Adults may not be aware of their own stereotypes, but they often unconsciously display them. They may frown with disapproval if their son picks up a Barbie or discourage their daughter from dressing as a ninja (Bussey & Bandura, 1999; Endendijk et al., 2019).

Adults and children are much more open to girls who break gender stereotypes than they are to boys. For instance, girls who play sports are often seen as "strong" or "independent," but boys who do ballet are received less warmly (Parker et al., 2017). Boys who do not adhere to stereotypes often face social ostracism and bullying (Leaper & Brown, 2018). Many adults believe boys who are less masculine are gay, and homophobic prejudices amplify the pressure on boys to conform (Skočajić et al., 2020; Sullivan et al., 2018).

Adults and children also *model* ideas about gender (Bussey & Bandura, 1999). **Gender roles** refer to social and cultural ideas about appropriate behaviors or roles of people often based on binary ideas about gender. For instance, in many other-sex, two-parent families, people who identify as women are more likely to be the primary caregivers for children and to do more household chores like cooking and cleaning (Saguy et al., 2021). People who identify as men are more likely to work outside the home full time and do household chores like outdoor work and home repairs.

Young children pick up on ideas about gender by observing the adults in their families and communities (Halpern & Perry-Jenkins, 2016; Sinno et al., 2017). Children who grow up in families where men do more hands-on caregiving tend to have fewer gender stereotypes (Dawson et al., 2015). Some studies have found that, in families with gay and lesbian parents, children often have more flexible stereotypes about gender but tend not to differ from their peers in their sense of their own gender identity (Carone et al., 2020; Farr et al., 2018; Sumontha et al., 2017).

Cognitive Theories of Gender Remember from Chapter 6 that preschoolers are rapidly developing the ability to think and assimilate new information but often struggle with logic. These cognitive strengths and limitations are reflected in their thinking about gender categories (Ruble et al., 2007).

 Share It!

Even Happy Meals are gendered. And the messages they send may not be equal. One researcher found that Happy Meals designed for boys encouraged them to be more active than girls.

(Hourigan, 2021)

Scientific American: Lifespan Development

gender roles The social and cultural ideas a person holds about appropriate behaviors or roles of people based on their gender.

Jessica Nelson/Getty Images

Stereotypes Versus the Weather
Sometimes the power of stereotypes can defy the weather report. It is not unusual for young children to fall in love with clothes that are inappropriate for the forecast. Children are particularly rigid about categories during the preschool years, which can make them more likely to choose clothing that expresses a strong gender stereotype, even if it means getting cold.

CONNECTIONS

Remember from Chapter 2 that developmental psychologists like Piaget use the term *schema* to describe how you sort and categorize information as you learn new things.

CONNECTIONS

The biology of sex begins in your genome (see Chapter 3). Zygotes typically have either two X chromosomes (XX) and female reproductive anatomy or an X and a Y chromosome (XY) and male reproductive anatomy. Remember that the biology of gender may be more complex than a simple X and Y. *Gender identity*, or the gender people feel they are, is often less binary than the distinction between boys and girls.

gender schema A framework for understanding the world in terms of cultural expectations related to gender identity.

In communities around the world, children become aware of social ideas and categories about gender very early in development. For instance, even as toddlers, children identify themselves using gendered labels (Campbell et al., 2002). But between ages 3 and 5, children begin to develop *gender stereotypes*, with the most rigid ones appearing at around age 5 (Martinez et al., 2019). Most preschool-age children, whether they are transgender or identify with their gender assigned at birth, tend to have very fixed and often binary ideas about gender (Gülgöz et al., 2021). This is the age children may clamor for gender-typed clothing.

Young children are often unclear about the relationship between anatomical distinctions and the social categories that refer to gender. One researcher, Sandra Bem, who encouraged flexibility about social roles in her own children, recalled the reaction her son received when he wore barrettes to school (Golden & McHugh, 2017). One child suggested that barrettes would turn him, perhaps permanently, into a girl. Another, perhaps demonstrating the egocentrism Piaget might have predicted in a preschooler, along with a characteristic rigidity about gender categories insisted, "Everybody has a penis; only girls wear barrettes" (Bem, 1989, p. 662).

Cognitive theorists suggest that rigid social categories about gender develop as a result of children's use of **gender schemas** (Bem, 1981; Martin & Halverson, 1981). By the time they are toddlers, children organize their world by gender, becoming "gender detectives" to figure out what applies to which gender (Halim et al., 2017). For instance, a 3-year-old girl may look at a screwdriver and think "not for me" and at a pair of sparkly shoes and think "for me." Preschoolers are integrating a vast amount of new information about the world. Although schemas help them assimilate and adapt much of this information quickly, they make children vulnerable to stereotyping of all kinds (Cimpian, 2016).

During early childhood, children typically show an awareness of social groups, and a preference for the gender they identify with (Martin & Ruble, 2010). As a result, social divisions may appear on the playground that reflect the adult social roles children see (Lew-Levy et al., 2020). Children who identify as boys and girls often split off and play separately, in what is called *gender segregation* (Maccoby & Jacklin, 1987). As they approach kindergarten age, children become more flexible in their understanding of social categories. This will help them try new things and play with children who are different from themselves (Halim, 2016).

Biological Research on Gender Many people assume that biology, rather than culture, helps to create gender identity in children: This idea is often linked to an insistence that gender is binary and unchangeable (Saguy et al., 2021). Many scientists, as you have seen, point to culture and social expectations, rather than biology, as the main drivers of gender development. Most scientific consensus rejects the idea that there are unchangeable, binary distinctions between genders. In fact, scientists point out that there is no "boy" brain and no "girl" brain: Brains, like the rest of gender, exist on a continuum rather than a binary divide (Zhang et al., 2021). Additionally, neuroscientists are not sure whether any of the minute differences, estimated at just 1 percent, found between the brains of various groups are a function of social experiences or innate distinctions (Eliot et al., 2021; Rippon et al., 2021).

Researchers have found that even though the differences in the brain may be small, biology still plays a role in children's gender development. Biology can change how sensitive children are to social messages about gender (Hines, 2020). Prenatal experience may make children more flexible about stereotypes than their peers. For instance, some researchers found that preschoolers who identified as girls and who were exposed to more testosterone prenatally were more likely to play with toys typically oriented toward another gender than other girls, perhaps because they were less sensitive to social stereotypes that told them what they "ought" to do than their peers (Spencer et al., 2021).

However, while biology and life experience both contribute to shaping identity, even in these studies, the absolute differences in ability and brain development between children who identify as boys, girls, or other gender labels are very small (Forger, 2018; Rouse & Hamilton, 2021).

The Influence of the Media on Gender in Early Childhood The people children know in real life are not the only influence on their ideas about gender. Spider-Man, Doc McStuffins, and Barbie may be even more important. Despite recommendations from experts, young children spend nearly three hours on media every day—much of it spent absorbing stereotypes about gender (Chen & Adler, 2019; Rideout & Robb, 2020).

Researchers have found that the more time girls spend watching princess movies, the more likely they are to be drawn to feminine toys. They are also more likely to believe that being beautiful is important and that working hard is not feminine (Coyne et al., 2016). Similarly, boys who spend more time watching superhero movies are more likely to engage in more masculine play like play-fighting than boys who watch more neutral shows do (Coyne et al., 2014). Other research suggests that media also communicates messages about power and gender (Golden & Jacoby, 2018; Walsh & Leaper, 2020; Ward & Grower, 2020). Many shows feature active, powerful male characters and passive female characters. As a result, the more television children watch, the more likely they are to believe that boys are more powerful and capable than girls, a belief that may stick with children for a lifetime (Halim et al., 2013).

Sometimes Changing the World Requires Strings. In 2017, puppeteer Mansoora Sherzad showed children a puppet from the Afghan version of Sesame Street. The puppet, a 6-year-old girl named Zari, is spunky and energetic and loves school. The show's producers hoped that their program would encourage young girls to go to school in a time when schools in Afghanistan were open to all.

Gender Questioning and Conformity As children grow, most integrate stereotypically male and female interests and characteristics into who they are. Many stay flexible about gender roles, which can be a good thing. Children who are more flexible in terms of interests and stereotypes, and who have more positive attitudes about children who are different from them tend to get along with others better than their peers do (Xiao et al., 2021).

At some time or another, about one in four preschool-age children feels unhappy with the gender they have been assigned: many are simply dissatisfied with the gender stereotypes or systems they are surrounded by (Halim et al., 2013). Other children may have gender expression that is *nonconforming*, or outside the binary gender stereotypes, but may not identify as *transgender* (Rae et al., 2019). According to most experts, about 1 in 100 children is transgender (Fast & Olson, 2018; Rafferty et al., 2018). Children who identify as **transgender** consistently feel that their gender identity does not match the sex they were assigned at birth. Preschoolers usually begin to verbalize their feelings about their preferred gender between the ages of 2 and 5 (Gülgöz et al., 2019).

For transgender children, the feeling of being in the wrong body is neither a "phase" nor the result of willfulness or unusual parenting. Transgender children's dissatisfaction with the sex assigned to them at birth is very different from the feeling many children report of wanting to break free of gender stereotypes. Experts advise that children's expressed gender identity should be supported (Rafferty et al., 2018). Researchers who have studied children who have transitioned or been affirmed in their new gender find them well adjusted and with stable gender identities similar to those of other children (Fast & Olson, 2018).

Tyler, the Way He Wants to Be. Tyler began to insist he was a boy when he was in preschool. With his family's support, he transitioned to a new name and a chosen gender identity when he started kindergarten. Like many children his age, he loves soccer, Spider-Man, and riding his bike.

transgender A person who consistently feels that their gender identity does not match the sex they were assigned at birth.

The Impact of Ethnicity

Young children do not just observe and form stereotypes about gender: They are also keenly observant of other social categories, such as age, beauty, and wealth (Perszyk et al., 2019; Shutts, 2015; Vermeir & Van de Sompel, 2017). By early childhood, children begin to articulate preferences and prejudices about ethnicity and are more aware of discrimination (Banerjee & Eccles, 2019). Without intervention, the effects of these stereotypes can persist (Qian et al., 2017).

Many preschoolers have developed ethnic preferences, frequently favoring their own group but often favoring another, more socially dominant group. Children may internalize the prejudice they experience. In the 1930s, pioneering Black psychologists Mamie and Kenneth Clark asked Black preschoolers if they would rather play with a dark-skinned doll or a light-skinned doll (Clark & Clark, 1939, 1940). The children chose the light-skinned doll and said that the dark-skinned doll was probably bad. In the 1950s, the Clarks' research was pivotal in the famous U.S. Supreme Court case, *Brown v. Board of Education*, which helped to overturn legal segregated public schools in the United States. The Supreme Court agreed with the Clarks that segregation had made Black children feel inferior and that desegregating schools was one way to help repair their self-esteem.

Some scientists have replicated the Clarks' results with children raised in more contemporary communities. For instance, in one study, researchers asked preschool children to plan a birthday party for a group of dolls. White girls preferred to invite White dolls, and so did Black girls (Kurtz-Costes et al., 2011). However, other studies have found that Black children no longer seem to prefer light-skinned dolls (Davis, 2005; Hraba & Grant, 1970; Jarrett, 2016; Spencer, 2010).

Preschoolers' ethnic preferences and exposure to discrimination occur in communities around the world: In multiethnic societies, as in the United States, it is not unusual for children to prefer a higher status or the majority ethnic group over the others, even at the expense of their own group (Newheiser et al., 2014; Setoh et al., 2019). It is also not unusual for adults, even teachers who care for children, to harbor discriminatory attitudes (see **Figure 7.3**) (Gilliam et al., 2016).

Children pick up on the prejudices around them, and their innate sense of categorization helps perpetuate this phenomenon. Preschoolers automatically categorize people, as they do objects, and they tend to prefer things they see frequently, such as familiar faces (Qian et al., 2021; Skinner & Meltzoff, 2019). Many children grow out of their ethnic preferences as they do their rigid ideas about gender, but some do not (Lee et al., 2017). Children who are exposed to diverse types of people are less likely to dislike new or different people. In one research study, children from China who had limited exposure to people who were not Han Chinese learned to differentiate and accept people from other ethnic groups once they were exposed to them (Qian et al., 2019). Similarly, in the United States, children who were exposed to a diverse group of children in preschool had lower racial bias later in life and developed more diverse friendships (Gaias et al., 2018; Qian et al., 2017).

In the United States, many preschool teachers and White parents feel that preschoolers are too young to talk to openly about ethnicity or prejudice (Farago et al., 2019). Scientists suggest the opposite: Helping children develop a sense of pride in their background can build resilience in a prejudicial world (Dunbar et al., 2017; Wang et al., 2020). White American families rarely talk with their kindergartners about their cultural heritage, but these conversations are common among Black, Latino, and Asian American, and other multiethnic families (Vittrup, 2018). One Black mother explained that she felt that her 3-year-old was not too young to learn about her background: "She needs to understand her heritage, where she comes from and how society is going to react to her as a strong Black female" (Suizzo et al., 2008, p. 298).

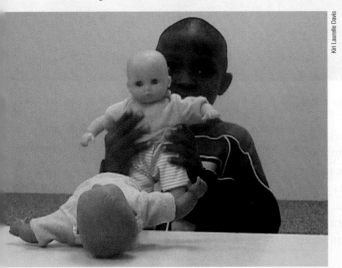

Why Is She Nice? Documentary filmmaker Kiri Laurelle Davis replicated Mamie and Kenneth Clark's famous 1930s doll test while studying Brown v. Board of Education during high school. She showed 4- and 5-year-old children in New York City Black and White baby dolls and asked them to show her the "nice doll." This little boy (like 15 out of the 21 other children) picked up the White doll. "And why is that the nice doll?," Davis then asked. "Because she's White." More than 70 years after the Clarks' pioneering work, this film demonstrated that young children still showed signs of internalized bias.

Kiri Laurelle Davis

FIGURE 7.3 Bias in Preschool Which child is acting up? When scientists asked teachers to look at a photograph similar to this one and identify which children were causing trouble, 43 percent identified a Black child. In reality, none of the children was doing anything wrong. How do you combat this conscious or unconscious prejudice in the classroom? Some scientists suggest educating teachers about bias, combatting teachers' classroom stress, training to identify true behavioral challenges, and alternative methods for managing disruptions (Gilliam et al., 2016).

APPLY IT! **7.3** Olivia says she wants to grow up to be "just like Mommy." Freud would describe this comment as an example of what kind of process?

7.4 A preschool teacher with a diverse classroom wonders whether his students are too young to understand social categories and ethnic differences. What would you explain about the current research about children's understanding of social categories?

Family Relationships in Early Childhood

Spend any amount of time with a parent of a preschooler and you will likely hear the mix of joy, optimism, and a little guilt, we heard from Olivia's parents. As Brionnah explained to us, she finds "so much joy" in being Olivia's mother. Olivia's big grin can make Brionnah's day. Nevertheless, Brionnah still sometimes worries about the future—about kindergarten and whether she is preparing Olivia for what she will face next. Indeed, developmental scientists argue that although family is critical in early childhood, many factors in development are not within a family's control (Lansford & Bornstein, 2020; Teti et al., 2017). For instance, Brionnah's challenges getting through college as a working parent and finding an affordable apartment have much more to do with systemic societal issues than her parenting skills.

Parental Beliefs

During early childhood, families build on the foundation set in infancy to create habits of relating that can impact children's development for a lifetime (Groh et al., 2017; Sroufe, 2016). However, parenting preschool-age children is often difficult. The years between 2 and 4 are some of the most stressful for parents as their children demand time, patience, and attention (Olson et al., 2017; Weaver et al., 2015). Caregivers who feel competent and capable and who have positive beliefs about their preschoolers have an easier time navigating this often-challenging time (Bornstein, 2015). Brionnah, for instance, takes a lot of responsibility for her daughter's behavior.

Learning Objective

7.5 Describe variations in parenting practices and styles and how they affect children's development.

Each young child is shaped by both the complex systems surrounding them and their individual strengths. The social structures and physical environment children grow up in illustrate the vast inequalities around the world, as well as the great diversity in our capacity for resilience. In early childhood, resilience develops through relationships with caregivers inside and outside the home.

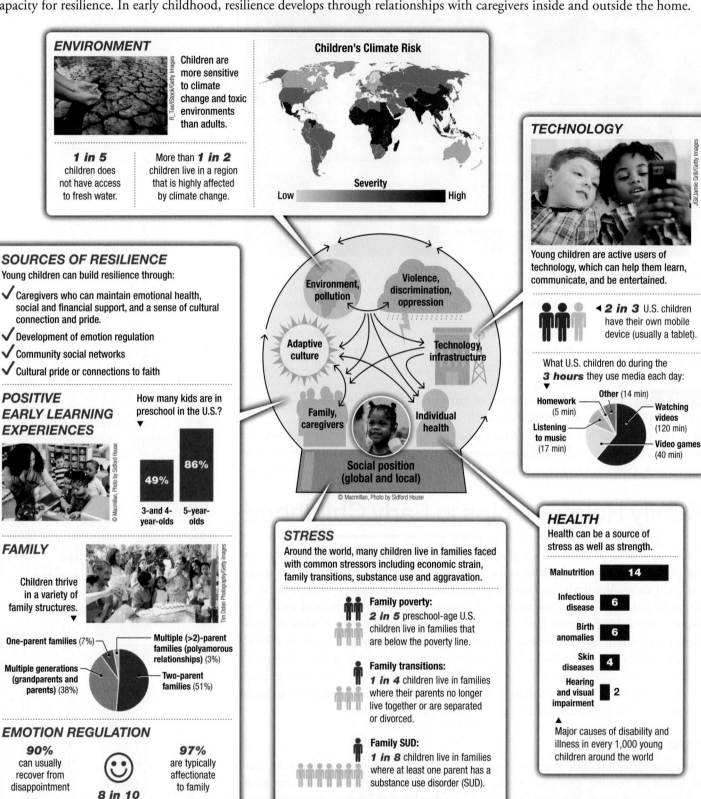

ENVIRONMENT

Children are more sensitive to climate change and toxic environments than adults.

1 in 5 children does not have access to fresh water.

More than *1 in 2* children live in a region that is highly affected by climate change.

Children's Climate Risk

Severity
Low — High

TECHNOLOGY

Young children are active users of technology, which can help them learn, communicate, and be entertained.

◄ *2 in 3* U.S. children have their own mobile device (usually a tablet).

What U.S. children do during the *3 hours* they use media each day:

Homework (5 min)
Listening to music (17 min)
Other (14 min)
Watching videos (120 min)
Video games (40 min)

SOURCES OF RESILIENCE

Young children can build resilience through:

✓ Caregivers who can maintain emotional health, social and financial support, and a sense of cultural connection and pride.
✓ Development of emotion regulation
✓ Community social networks
✓ Cultural pride or connections to faith

Environment, pollution
Violence, discrimination, oppression
Adaptive culture
Technology, infrastructure
Family, caregivers
Individual health
Social position (global and local)

© Macmillan, Photo by Sidford House

POSITIVE EARLY LEARNING EXPERIENCES

How many kids are in preschool in the U.S.?

49% — 3-and 4-year-olds
86% — 5-year-olds

FAMILY

Children thrive in a variety of family structures.

One-parent families (7%)
Multiple (>2)-parent families (polyamorous relationships) (3%)
Multiple generations (grandparents and parents) (38%)
Two-parent families (51%)

EMOTION REGULATION

90% can usually recover from disappointment

97% are typically affectionate to family

8 in 10 young children show emotional strengths

96% are usually curious

99% are usually smiling

STRESS

Around the world, many children live in families faced with common stressors including economic strain, family transitions, substance use and aggravation.

Family poverty:
2 in 5 preschool-age U.S. children live in families that are below the poverty line.

Family transitions:
1 in 4 children live in families where their parents no longer live together or are separated or divorced.

Family SUD:
1 in 8 children live in families where at least one parent has a substance use disorder (SUD).

Family aggravation:
1 in 9 children live in families where a caregiver sees them as difficult.

HEALTH

Health can be a source of stress as well as strength.

Malnutrition — 14
Infectious disease — 6
Birth anomalies — 6
Skin diseases — 4
Hearing and visual impairment — 2

▲ Major causes of disability and illness in every 1,000 young children around the world

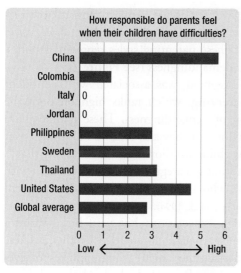

How responsible do parents feel when their children have difficulties?

China
Colombia
Italy 0
Jordan 0
Philippines
Sweden
Thailand
United States
Global average

0 1 2 3 4 5 6
Low ⟷ High

Data from Bornstein et al., 2011.

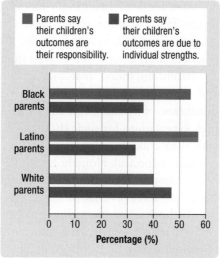

■ Parents say their children's outcomes are their responsibility. ■ Parents say their children's outcomes are due to individual strengths.

Black parents
Latino parents
White parents

0 10 20 30 40 50 60
Percentage (%)

Data from Parker & Horowitz., 2015.

parenting styles Dimensional descriptions of caregiving relationships during childhood.

FIGURE 7.4 Parental Beliefs How important is parenting to children's development? Researchers believe that the work parents do to nurture their children is critical to healthy development, but parents are not always sure that their caregiving will have an impact.

Like Brionnah, caregivers from Black and Latino backgrounds are more likely to agree that their children's successes or struggles are due to parenting. This can be a good thing: Parents who feel that they have a lot of control over their children's outcomes are more likely to invest in their children and, like Brionnah, to offer more effective, supportive caregiving (Bornstein et al., 2011). However, not all families agree that their children's success depends on the quality of their parenting: Only about half of U.S. caregivers believe that their children's successes are due to their parenting skills, rather than their child's inborn strengths (Parker & Horowitz, 2015; see **Figure 7.4**).

Families around the world overestimate what preschoolers are capable of (Durrant et al., 2017). Realistic expectations help parents react more warmly to their children's behavior (NASEM, 2016). When parents attribute hostility or willfulness to young children's behavior, they are more likely to treat their children harshly (Milner & Crouch, 2013). Misunderstanding behaviors, such as assuming that a child wakes up in the night because they are spoiled, or that a child has dumped everything out of the kitchen cabinet just to annoy you, can lead to overreaction or even abuse (Beckerman et al., 2018; Durrant et al., 2017). On the other hand, positive beliefs about parenting help build closer relationships and better outcomes (Bornstein et al., 2018).

Parenting Styles

Researchers often analyze caregiving practices by looking at **parenting styles**. For more than 50 years, psychologist Diana Baumrind's dimensional approach to parenting styles has been the standard for describing caregiving relationships during childhood. To develop her measures, Baumrind conducted a longitudinal study with a group of preschoolers and families in Northern California. She measured the degree of *warmth* and *demandingness* in parents' daily interactions with their children and then observed them over time (Baumrind, 1971, 2013; Baumrind & Black, 1967). The level of warmth in Baumrind's typology refers to how sensitive, responsive, and supportive caregivers are. The level of demandingness, or control, refers to the type of expectations families have for children's behavior.

Scientific American Profile

Parental Aspirations for Their Children

Sometimes Caregivers Are Grandparents. Family often means more than just parents: many children around the globe, including this little boy in Shanghai, China, are cared for by their extended family.

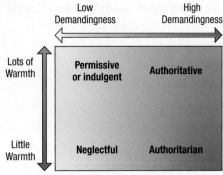

FIGURE 7.5 **Parenting Styles** In Baumrind's classic dimensional approach to parenting styles, caregiving relationships are analyzed in terms of how warm or demanding they are. Four categories—permissive, authoritative, authoritarian, and neglectful—represent common variations.

authoritative parenting A type of caregiving associated with confident and successful children in which caregivers have high expectations for their children's behavior, but they also are warm and communicative.

authoritarian parenting A type of caregiving in which caregivers have high expectations for their children's behavior but very little warmth. Authoritarian parents make rules and expect their children to obey them.

permissive parenting Caregiving without rules. Permissive parents have low expectations for children's behavior but a high degree of affection.

neglectful parenting Caregiving without warmth or expectations. Children from neglectful families are at high risk for emotional and behavioral difficulties as they grow up.

As a result of Baumrind's pioneering work, developmental scientists now recognize four parenting styles: *authoritative, authoritarian, permissive,* and *neglectful* (Baumrind, 1989, 1991; Maccoby & Martin, 1983). These parenting styles represent families' practices along dimensions of warmth and demandingness (see **Figure 7.5**).

Baumrind found that one type of caregiving was associated with confident and successful children: **authoritative parenting**, which ranks high on both the dimension of warmth and the dimension of demandingness. These families have high expectations for their children's behavior, but they also tend to talk things over with their children. They expect that their children follow the rules in a way that is mutually respectful. Households with authoritative caregivers tend have children with better emotion regulation and self-control, who are happier and more independent (Baumrind et al., 2010; Pinquart & Kauser, 2018; Steinberg et al., 1994).

Authoritarian parenting involves high expectations but very little warmth. Authoritarian parents make rules and expect their children to obey them. These households are orderly, but cold: They may lack the laughter, hugs, and responsiveness of an authoritative household. Over time, Baumrind observed that children raised with authoritarian caregiving did reasonably well in the classroom but did not handle stress well and were less friendly with other children. As a result, children from authoritarian families are more likely to have emotional problems like depression, acting out, and lack of academic motivation (Braza et al., 2015; Pinquart & Kauser, 2018).

Permissive parenting is caregiving without rules. Permissive parents, sometimes known as indulgent parents, have low expectations for children's behavior but a high degree of affection. In permissive households, children do what they want, and the parents are not completely in charge. Because permissive parents expect very little, their children typically lack self-control and maturity. However, research on the outcomes of permissive parenting have been inconsistent: Children raised by permissive parents tend to have strong social skills but may have difficulty following directions (Baumrind et al., 2010; Steinberg et al., 1994).

Neglectful parenting is caregiving without warmth or expectations (Baumrind, 1989, 1991; Maccoby & Martin, 1983). Neglectful parents do not focus much on their children, perhaps because they are occupied with their own challenges and, as a result, may fail to keep children safe. Children from neglectful families are at high risk for emotional and behavioral difficulties as they grow up, from serious disciplinary problems in school to academic struggles and substance abuse (Pinquart, 2017; Steinberg et al., 1994).

In the many years since Baumrind originally made her observations, scientists have continued to find that the combination of caring and control characteristic of the authoritative parenting style is linked to more successful and emotionally healthy children in a variety of circumstances, families, and cultures around the world (Pinquart & Kauser, 2018; Smetena, 2017). Children whose caregivers are harsh and use emotionally manipulative techniques to manage their children's behavior—like shame, embarrassment, or rejection—are more likely to act out in school and to develop other emotional problems. Children whose caregivers are warm and who manage their children's behavior while respecting their developing independence have stronger social relationships and lower risks for emotional disorders or academic challenges (Pinquart, 2017; Smetena, 2017).

Despite the influence of Baumrind's dimensional parenting styles on developmental science, parts of her work remain controversial. Contemporary researchers have argued that Baumrind's parenting styles do not give enough weight to the roles culture, the external environment, and children themselves play in caregiving (Wittig & Rodriguez, 2019; Zamir et al., 2020).

Evaluating parenting styles can be challenging, particularly when comparing families from different cultures and ethnotheories (Pinquart & Kauser, 2018; Sorkhabi & Mandara, 2013). Warmth and control may be expressed in different ways in different communities across the globe, since the specific parenting practices families adopt are often vastly different. For instance, in Japan, preschoolers often sleep with their parents, but in the United States, experts recommend that children sleep independently (LeVine & LeVine, 2016). Does this mean that Japanese parents are permissive? Many scholars would say no. Researchers suggest using the principle of *cultural humility* when comparing parenting practices across communities, recognizing that behaviors are shaped by cultural contexts and remaining open to learning from different cultures (Williams et al., 2019).

Over the years, researchers and parents have taken exception with the rule that authoritative parenting works, but those claims rarely pan out. For instance, one Chinese American parent argued that cold "tiger parenting" was essential for Chinese American children to be successful (Chua, 2011). Researchers (and other Chinese American families) objected to this, stating that there is little truth in the assertion that being tough leads to happier or more successful children (Chuang et al., 2018). To the contrary, studies in the United States and in China have found that preschool children who have authoritative parents have fewer emotional problems and are more successful in school than those with authoritarian ones (Doan et al., 2017; Pomerantz & Wang, 2009).

In the past, some scholars argued that Black families were also an exception to the recommendation for authoritative caregiving. Researchers suggested that a harsher parenting style might be adaptive for families who are in situations of high stress, like poverty and systematic racism (Baumrind, 1972). Scientists working with one group of Black families from rural southeastern United States found that some families who were stricter than typical authoritative parents had children who were more successful on some measures than those raised in traditionally authoritative families. These families were not quite authoritarian: They were slightly stricter than typical authoritative families but just as warm, so they were given a new label: *no-nonsense* parents (Brody & Flor, 1998).

Subsequent researchers studying other families found that this style of parenting did not always translate to other contexts. In fact, researchers have found that the strictness of no-nonsense parenting can create additional risks for children in many communities (Anton et al., 2015; Querido et al., 2002). Most researchers have found that despite the context, parenting that balances warmth and high expectations without harshness works best for most children around the world.

You Can't Go Wrong with Warmth. Families communicate affection in different ways depending on their cultural ethnotheories. Some may prefer hugs and kisses, as in this family in Canada. Others may be more reserved, but young children thrive no matter how care is communicated.

Discipline: Helping Children to Get Along

While parenting styles describe the overall pattern of how parents interact with their children on a day-to-day basis, the specific practices parents use to shape children's behavior come down to **discipline**, which is any strategy used to teach children how to behave by setting rules, encouraging good behavior, and discouraging missteps (Grusec et al., 2017). (See **Figure 7.6**.)

More than half of all parents in the United States admit that they struggle with finding effective ways to manage their preschoolers' behavior (Zero to Three, 2016c). As a mother in Chicago explained, "Lately, I've been so frustrated I'm screaming like a banshee most of the time . . . [then] I will hear them playing, and then my daughter . . . will be screaming at her brother in exactly the same tone of voice" (Zero to Three, 2016b). As this mother discovered, some forms of discipline have negative consequences.

Developmental scientists divide disciplinary practices into *power assertive* and *inductive reasoning* techniques (Lansford, 2017). Strategies that rely on parents' control are called **power-assertive techniques** and have a number of benefits (Baumrind, 2012). Power assertion is often immediately effective, as with immediately picking up a

discipline Caregiving practices or strategies used to teach children how to behave by setting rules, encouraging good behavior, and discouraging missteps.

power-assertive techniques Disciplinary strategies that rely on parents' control.

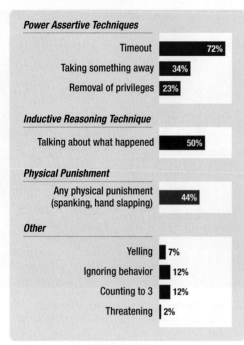

Power Assertive Techniques

Timeout	72%
Taking something away	34%
Removal of privileges	23%

Inductive Reasoning Technique

Talking about what happened	50%

Physical Punishment

Any physical punishment (spanking, hand slapping)	44%

Other

Yelling	7%
Ignoring behavior	12%
Counting to 3	12%
Threatening	2%

Data from Thompson et al., 2017.

FIGURE 7.6 Common Disciplinary Practices There may be no easy answer: Warmth and high expectations work in the long run, but in practice, parents often struggle with finding methods to help children manage their emotions and behave appropriately. Common forms of discipline in the United States include power-assertive and inductive discipline. Harsh and rejecting practices are destructive and harmful. Growing up takes time and patience for both caregivers and children.

inductive reasoning A disciplinary approach that relies on motivating children to change their behavior through talk.

3-year-old who is running into traffic rather than having a long discussion about the dangers it poses. Other common forms of power assertion include the *time-out*, counting to three, rewards for good behavior, and removing privileges (like taking away a video game). Research indicates that these forms of discipline are effective if used consistently and positively (Kazdin et al., 2018).

However, as researchers and Brionnah have found, talking things out often fosters better long-term relationships and better behavior (Grusec et al., 2017; Lansford et al., 2018). Brionnah explains that disciplining Olivia by slowing things down and taking time to talk about why Olivia is upset, no matter what the cause, makes things easier. This approach to discipline, called **inductive reasoning**, relies on motivating children to change their behavior through talk. Caregivers who use inductive reasoning explain their reasoning and listen to the child's perspective (Hoffman, 1977). Children in families that use this approach are more likely to develop strong self-regulation skills and to behave kindly and prosocially (Eisenberg et al., 2015). They are less likely to act out and more likely to be socially successful later in life (Choe et al., 2013).

Some practices, such as physical punishment and shaming, are destructive (Sege et al., 2018). Children who experience them are more likely to act out and have emotional disorders like depression (Lansford et al., 2021). Emotional rejection, like when a parent tells a child, "I can't believe I have to put up with such a brat," is harmful. Physical punishment also has unintended long-term consequences, as you will learn (Sege et al., 2018).

MAKING A DIFFERENCE
The Science Against Spanking

What happens when children push the limits too far? In about two in three families in the United States, the consequence is spanking (Thompson et al., 2017). Nearly 8 in 10 U.S. adults believe that physical punishment is sometimes necessary to get children to behave (Lansford et al., 2015; Perrin et al., 2017). Nineteen states allow spanking in public preschool and pre-kindergarten programs (Gershoff et al., 2019).

However, beliefs about spanking are changing. Scientific consensus supports the finding that physical punishment is not effective and can hurt children in the long run (Gershoff & Grogan-Kaylor, 2016). Parents are using physical discipline less than they used to, even when they are under stress (Finkelhor et al., 2019). In recent years, developmental scientists and pediatricians in the United States have joined those from around the world to advocate against physical punishment (Sege et al., 2018).

Parents often explain that they spank because their children were not doing what they were told to do. When researchers track what children were doing before a spanking, many of them were making fairly minor mistakes: eating improperly or getting out of a chair without permission. They were not hurting someone or willfully destroying something. According to observational reports, families turn to spanking just 30 seconds after a child has misbehaved (Holden et al., 2014).

No matter what sparks a spanking, it simply does not work. In the short term, children who are spanked are no more likely to sit still, eat their carrots, or stop talking back. In fact, when researchers recorded what happened when parents disciplined their preschoolers, they observed that, within 10 minutes of a spanking, most children repeated the behavior (Holden et al., 2014). As Laura, a mother in Illinois put it, "We gave him a spanking and then he just laughs in our face" (Zero to Three, 2016a).

Scientists have also found that children who are spanked have more, rather than fewer, conflicts with their caregivers (Alampay et al., 2017). They tend to act out more after parents start spanking (Gershoff et al., 2019). Families who use physical discipline are also more likely to escalate their interactions with their children into something more aggressive and abusive (Sege et al., 2018). As a result, pediatricians and scientists now caution against spanking in all cases.

Maltreatment and Violence in the Family

Around the world, more than three in four children are regularly exposed to violence in their homes (UNICEF, 2020). In the United States, about one in five families reports that they are currently experiencing the effects of family violence and abuse (Brieding, 2014). Children may not just see violence: They may be its victim. In the United States, more than 15 in 1,000 preschoolers are the victims of abuse (USDHHS, 2021).

Scientists use the words *maltreatment, abuse,* and *neglect* to describe the wide range of harm that can come to children. While these terms are often used interchangeably, they also have precise legal definitions that vary regionally (Stoltenborgh et al., 2015). **Maltreatment** is the general term scholars use to describe the many types of abuse and neglect of children by adults who are responsible for them. In the United States, **abuse** is the legal term used to describe the most serious types of harm to children (Child Welfare Information Gateway, 2019).

Maltreatment may involve *physical abuse,* which involves harm to a child's body, as when a child is beaten or bruised. It can also include *emotional abuse,* when a child's emotional well-being is chronically threatened, as when a child is repeatedly belittled, rejected, or frightened (English et al., 2015). *Sexual abuse* involves any intimate activity affecting a child, including sexual touch between an adult and a child, child pornography, and human trafficking. *Neglect* occurs when adults fail to take care of the basic physical, emotional, educational, and medical needs of children for whom they are responsible (Children's Bureau, 2019). Neglect may not be intentional, and can be caused by poverty, by substance abuse within the family, or by a decision not to access the medical or educational resources available in a community. (See **Figure 7.7.**)

No Nonsense About Spanking Stacey Patton is a historian, journalist, and child advocate working to change beliefs about parenting and discipline. Dr. Patton aims to change attitudes about harsh physical violence, including appearing on television and radio shows. As she argues, "disciplining children shouldn't hurt."

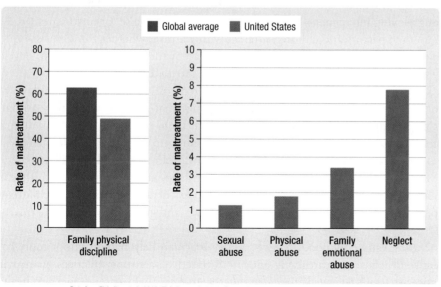

Data from Finkelhor et al., 2013; Finkelhor et al., 2019; Gewirtz-Meydan & Finkelhor, 2020; UNICEF, 2017; Vanderminden et al., 2019.

FIGURE 7.7 Rates of Maltreatment in the United States and Around the World Maltreatment and family violence are difficult to measure. Community expectations help define what abuse is, and it is often hidden or described as punishment. When researchers survey families, parents are much more likely to volunteer information about harsh physical discipline than abuse. The extent of children's exposure to violence is not clear, particularly for children who are too young to explain what has happened to them.

maltreatment The general term scholars use to describe the many types of abuse and neglect of children by adults who are responsible for them.

abuse The legal term used to describe the most serious types of harm to children, which can be physical, emotional, sexual, or neglectful.

During early childhood, many instances of physical and emotional abuse arise from overreaction to typical preschooler behaviors, like separation anxiety, slip-ups when learning to use the bathroom, or unwillingness to follow directions (Christian & Committee on Child Abuse and Neglect, 2015; Flaherty et al., 2010). As one mother explained, "Our beating is out of love. We can't help carrying out beating for the child's good" (Qiao & Xie, 2017, p. 214). Children who act out, who have high energy, and who have developmental disabilities face increased risk for maltreatment (Christian & Committee on Child Abuse and Neglect, 2015).

Some parents do not think it is wrong to use physical violence, but developmental scientists and pediatricians disagree (Lansford et al., 2018; Sege et al., 2018). Children may feel the consequences of maltreatment for the rest of their lives, with higher rates of emotional disorders, substance abuse, and physical problems like diabetes and heart disease. Like other forms of trauma, maltreatment changes the brain, causing structural and functional changes that may be difficult to alter (Teicher & Samson, 2016). In kindergarten, children who have experienced trauma and abuse have a harder time controlling themselves and focusing, which affects their classroom performance (Jimenez et al., 2016).

Supporting Positive Relationships

Maintaining positive, supportive relationships during early childhood is critical to children's emotional health, teaches them right from wrong, and helps them learn to relate to others (Kochanska et al., 2019). Scientists have observed that positive relationships in early childhood are characterized by closeness, warmth, and positivity (Esposito et al., 2017; Pastorelli et al., 2016).

Caregivers' ability to regulate their own emotions is critical to healthy relationships (Belsky, 1984). Adults need to be able to stay positive and consistent in the face of preschoolers' often-challenging behavior (Hajal et al., 2015; Morris et al., 2017). Parents with poor emotion regulation are also more likely to be harsh, demeaning, or negative with their children, making it more likely that their children will have trouble making friends or develop externalizing disorders (Smith et al., 2014).

Caregivers' goal is to communicate affection and warmth. This is usually done through loving interchanges, like cuddling or hugging, praise, or nicknames (Lee et al., 2013). When parents and children interact with warmth, whether through fist-bumps or a crazy dance, children are more likely to accept their parents' direction, develop self-regulation skills, and get along with others (Kochanska et al., 2019).

One goal of families is to convince children to do what they are told. In the laboratory, researchers measure this by watching what happens when they ask families to pick up toys after they have played with them (Matas et al., 1978). Children are typically capable of being compliant and cleaning up as young toddlers (Kochanska, 2002; Kochanska et al., 2019). However, this does not mean that children will actually do it. Many children in U.S. studies will refuse to help, at least initially, until they are about 7 (Huang & Lamb, 2014). Parents who are successful at convincing their children to help out are teaching them to control themselves and get along with others (Eisenberg et al., 2015).

During early childhood, *parent-training programs* help parents adopt more constructive beliefs about caregiving and more effective parenting practices. Caregiving practices that are reviewed in *evidence-based programs* help parents increase healthy interactions with their children, avoid harsh patterns, and understand developmental norms. A few weeks of classes can help caregivers better manage their stress and be more responsive (Barlow et al., 2014; Mingebach et al., 2018). Helping parents helps children: Children are less likely to act out after their parents have participated in a parenting program (Nystrand et al., 2019).

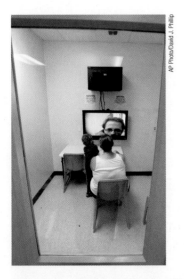

AP Photo/David J. Phillip

Sometimes Daddy Is Just on Screen. About 8 in every 100 children have a parent who is incarcerated, but families still manage to maintain bonds, even if they only happen virtually. Here Edna tries to make sure her 4-year-old son keeps in touch with his father while he is in jail through video visitation near their home in Texas.

Sibling Relationships

One thing Brionnah has not given Olivia, despite her hints, is a little brother or sister. For now, Olivia is an only child, as is true for about 1 in 10 children in the United States (Kotecki, 2018). For many families, early childhood is the time when a new baby arrives, typically when the first child is about 3 or 4 (Copen et al., 2015). Siblings can help children learn how to share, be helpful, and care for someone else (Hughes et al., 2018).

Many people believe that the birth of a sibling creates a crisis for the older child, but current research indicates that this is not necessarily the case (Volling, 2012). The first few weeks of having a new baby in the house are typically filled with jealousy, readjustment, and excitement, but not trauma (Volling et al., 2014). How children react to a new baby depends on existing relationships, individual personalities, and how parents manage the transition (Yaremych & Volling, 2020). For instance, in families where first children were securely attached before their sibling was born, most adjust positively. However, if children have an insecure attachment style, their relationships with their parents and the new baby could be more conflictual (Volling et al., 2014).

The sibling relationship plays an important role in how children will interact not just with brothers and sisters, but also with peers. Relationships between siblings are often filled with conflict, but this does not mean that bullying in families is healthy (Dirks et al., 2019). In one survey, siblings fought once every 10 minutes during the preschool years (Dirks et al., 2015). About 4 in 10 sibling pairs have a difficult relationship, which can escalate into bullying (Dantchev & Wolke, 2019; Oh et al., 2015). But families can encourage their children to solve their conflicts with less aggression and with more warmth. These skills provide good training for building friendships outside the family that will sustain children as they grow.

Sibling Love Learning to care for a brother or sister can help create a model for future relationships. Supportive, warm bonds between siblings can be a source of strength across the lifespan.

APPLY IT! **7.5** Olivia's parents have adopted regular routines and show her lots of affection. Which parenting styles and ethnotheories does this reflect?
7.6 Parenting styles do not just apply to families. Some researchers use them to evaluate caregiving at school. How might a preschool teacher show characteristics of warmth and demandingness?

Getting Along with Peers

Learning to get along with other children is a central challenge in early childhood. Most of the time, it is also a time of joyful play. If you watch children on the playground pretending to be Black Panther and Wolverine, or selling each other "ice cream," or endlessly chasing around the swings, it may be hard to imagine that for some children, this part of development does not come easily. Learning how to socialize taps into — and helps build — children's rapidly growing emotional and cognitive skills.

Learning Objective

7.6 Describe the features of play and their role in learning and development.

Play

In Olivia's preschool, like many in the United States, children can choose to spend time at a number of stations, including a pretend kitchen, a block area, and a dress-up

parallel play When children play physically close together but are not working on a shared project.

cooperative play Playing together on a joint project.

functional play Play that has a goal or achievement orientation, such as art, puzzles, rule-based games, and physical skills such as hopping, climbing, etc.

sociodramatic play Play that involves pretending to be something you are not and requires symbolic thought and theory of mind.

Getting Ready for School Sociodramatic, or pretend, play can help children practice skills they may need in real life, like getting ready for school and wearing masks in the classroom.

corner filled with firefighter's hats and sparkly tiaras. Olivia's school made space for play because it helps children learn skills in self-regulation, executive function, and forming social relationships (Howe & Leach, 2018; Rubin et al., 2015).

Early childhood is a peak time for play. Between the ages of 2½ and 5, children spend more time playing than they ever will again (Weisberg, 2015). Play is certainly fun, but it also involves a lot of learning about language, symbolic thinking, and problem solving (Lillard, 2017). When children are playing, they typically show more maturity, focus, and creativity than they do in their everyday life (Gray, 2017). As Vygotsky explained, "In play a child is always above his average age, above his daily behavior; in play it is as though he were a head taller than himself" (Vygotsky, 2016, p. 102).

Scientists define play as an enjoyable activity that children choose to do for its own sake (Burghardt, 2010). Children twirling pretending to be fairies while waiting in line to go to the cafeteria for lunch, are playing, but children waiting patiently, staring into space, are not. Play takes different forms depending on children's level of maturity and the constraints of the environment around them.

Social and Cognitive Components of Play Developmental scientists analyze play based on the level of social and cognitive sophistication it reveals. As children grow, their play becomes more social, but the development of play is not a progression from one stage to another (Coplan et al., 2006; Parten, 1932). Toddlers begin playing by themselves in what is known as *solitary play*, for example, acting out a scene with stuffed animals or building a block tower. They may also engage in *onlooker play*, where a preschooler observes other children playing but is not engaged in it. For example, one child may watch intently from the sidelines, reluctant to join in, as a group of children plays with trains.

When children play physically close together but are not working on a shared project, they are engaged in **parallel play**. For instance, two children may be sitting together at a table working with play dough and may even look up from time to time to see what their friend is doing or share tools, but they are not playing together. Truly **cooperative play**, or playing together on a joint project, takes a while for preschoolers to grasp; it may not be until they are 4 or 5 before they can play well together. Consider all the skills it takes for a group of preschoolers to play superhero chase on the playground, taking turns being Spider-Man and analyzing each other's web-throwing skills: They are taking turns, listening to each other's ideas, and sharing a vision of what Spider-Man and web-throwing looks and sounds like.

Types of Play Play becomes more cognitively complex as children grow. Babies engage in a lot of **functional play**, repeating an action over and over again just for the joy of it. Toddlers and preschoolers also enjoy functional play, which defines most types of gross motor play. Swinging on the swing, hopping, or yelling in the bathroom to hear the echo of your voice against the tiles are all forms of functional play.

As children grow older, functional play is likely to become more complex and turn into *games with rules*, like hopscotch, Simon Says, hide-and-seek, or something of their own invention. Games with rules become more popular as children get older and can focus their attention for longer periods of time (Rubin et al., 2015). *Constructive play* includes all forms of creativity, from making a fort out of couch pillows to cutting shapes out of construction paper. **Sociodramatic play** involves pretending to be something you are not and requires symbolic thought and theory of mind. In this type of play, children need to keep track of what everyone knows about the game they are playing, whether it is pretending to take a pet to the vet's office or playing "house" (Lillard, 2017).

One of the hallmarks of early childhood, sociodramatic play helps children build cognitive and social skills (Lillard et al., 2013; Weisberg, 2015). Some families provide children with dress-up materials, read them fairy tales, and show them movies that provide fodder for the imagination (Haight, 2006). In other communities, families discourage pretend play because of religious reasons or because they prefer their children focus on other skills, like getting ready for school or helping out around the house (Roopnarine & Davidson, 2015; Weisberg, 2015). Sociodramatic play is particularly popular in the United States, where many families value building social skills and encouraging imagination (Singer et al., 2009).

Another common but sometimes controversial form of play is **rough-and-tumble play**, or the physically active play where children chase, play fight, and wrestle (Howe & Leach, 2018). This type of play is also common in other young animals from kittens to orangutans (Lillard, 2017; Pellegrini & Smith, 1998). Rough-and-tumble play can sometimes look violent or involve play swords, superheroes, and fire-breathing zombies, but most researchers agree that it is helpful (Hart & Tannock, 2019; Levin & Carlsson-Page, 2005). In fact, when play guns or violent fantasy play is forbidden, it often "goes underground," as children turn blocks into weapons and juice box straws into shooters (Yanik & Yasar, 2018).

Friendship

As children play together, they develop close relationships and learn how to be friends. Even children as young as age 3 want to have friends and are aware of who has social status within the group. Children who make friends easily tend to be those with stronger social and language skills who can navigate their way around the playground. However, this is not always easy.

Even in preschool, children are anxious about finding friends and keeping them. "You didn't sit next to me," Pinar, a little girl in a Turkish preschool said to her friend. "You're [still] my friend, aren't you?" (Yanik & Yasar, 2018, p. 492). Throughout childhood, the ability to make friends and be accepted by the group are important measures of social success. Children who have friends are better at managing relationships of all kinds and tend to be better at managing conflict and communicating, and more likely to be generous. Building friendships gives children practice in resolving problems and taking turns but also gives them the delight of sharing interests (Hartup, 1996).

In early childhood, friendships tend to be built around shared interests and activities (Selman, 1980). Children are aware of social distinctions such as income level and ethnicity, and they tend to associate with children who they see as "like them" (Rubin et al., 2015). These early friendships are generally long-lasting; more than two in three preschoolers can maintain a friendship for more than six months (Gottman & Graziano, 1983).

About one in eight children has a hard time making friends. Some of these children struggle with emotion regulation and aggression; others are anxious or shy and may have difficulties interacting and learning to play with others. Some children may experience rejection from others based on differences in race, ability, or other characteristics. In general, children with strong, securely attached relationships with their parents and who are better at managing their emotions have an easier time finding friends (Rubin et al., 2015).

Peer Pressure in Preschool Preschoolers are cute, but they are not always kind: Preschool is not too soon for peer pressure and bullying. Children, like all of us, are acutely sensitive to what their friends and peers think of them (Haun & Tomasello, 2011). It is not unusual for preschool children to exclude and reject other children (Swit & Slater, 2021). Since they are still developing an understanding of the world and learning

rough-and-tumble play Physically active play where children chase, play fight, and wrestle.

 Learn It Together

Play in Early Childhood

Your classmate is looking for a preschool for her 4-year-old child. She visited the neighborhood child development center, but was concerned because when she visited, "the children were just playing all day." Given what you have learned about physical, cognitive, and social development during early childhood, what advice can you give her about the role of play in early childhood development?

Prepare: Review the key features of development for typical 4-year-olds. Consider cognitive and language development, physical and motor development, and what you have learned in this chapter about Erikson's stage of initiative versus guilt, the development of self-regulation, play, and relationships.

Engage: In a small group of classmates, discuss how play during early childhood may play a role in each domain of development described above. Develop a set of "talking points" you could use to explain how play in the preschool setting may influence development.

Reflect: Consider the connections you have made between different domains of development. Did this activity help you to see ways that the growing brain and body are involved in advancing cognitive, language, and social development?

about categories and identity, preschoolers can be even *more* rigid about categories than older children. This makes them more likely than older children to exclude others who are not following the social rules (Köymen et al., 2014; Toppe, 2020).

When one group of researchers observed preschool children on the playground, they found that social exclusion happened about every 6.5 seconds. One 4-year-old approaching a group in the sandbox heard: "Go away! You're not our friend." Another group of children schemed: "I'm not inviting her to my birthday" (Fanger et al., 2012). Experiencing repeated exclusion is particularly damaging early in life and may set the stage for later victimization (Godleski et al., 2015). Even if young children are not the direct victims of rejection or aggression, ostracism can poison the school climate for all (Marinović & Träuble, 2021). Teachers and other caregivers can help try to create a more welcoming and inclusive classroom by identifying potential biases, recognizing unkind behavior when it happens, and encouraging children to defend and comfort their friends who have been ostracized (Allen et al., 2021; Smith-Bonahue et al., 2015).

APPLY IT! **7.7** A parent asks why preschools allow children to spend so much time playing. How would you explain the value of play in early childhood?

7.8 Despite her teacher's best efforts, Olivia has witnessed some rejecting behaviors in her classroom. Is she too young to understand what is going on? How would you explain bullying to a preschooler?

Getting Along in the World: Moral Development

Learning Objective

7.7 Describe aggressive and prosocial behaviors in early childhood.

During early childhood, children learn how to maintain relationships, understand the difference between right and wrong, and figure out how to put these ideas into practice. This is not always easy. For the most part, young children get along, but they are also learning new ways to hurt each other. During early childhood, preschoolers acquire a sense of *morality*, or an understanding of how people should treat one another (Dahl & Killen, 2018). They also become more able to behave in a kind, or *prosocial*, way.

Children's social emotions, such as empathy and guilt, encourage them to be kind. These emotions take advantage of children's perspective-taking and theory-of-mind skills, which make it more painful to hurt someone and, after the fact, create a potent memory of how badly it felt (Davidov et al., 2016; Malti & Dys, 2018). Sometimes, however, feelings can be overwhelming. For instance, a child could be so distressed by their friend's tears that they are unable to get help or even give a hug. Or, a child could be so overwhelmed by guilt after breaking something that they may not be able to apologize or help repair it (Vaish & Hepach, 2020). As children are better able to regulate their emotions, they are more likely to be responsive to others.

Getting along with others not only helps children make friends in preschool; it will also help them get along with others later in life (Scrimgeour et al., 2016). Acting out is common in early childhood, but becoming kind and managing aggression are aspects of the self-regulation children need as they grow up. Longitudinal research reveals that the social skills that children have when they enter kindergarten often influence how successful they are later on in school (Jones et al., 2015).

Hurting Others

New cognitive and social skills make it possible for young children to hurt each other in new ways—through words and relationships. Many researchers describe the toddler years and early childhood as the most violent time of the lifespan (Côté et al., 2006;

Lorber et al., 2018). But physical violence decreases quickly as children learn to control their bodies and replace kicks with criticisms.

Developmental science has many ways of describing how children hurt each other (Sukhodolsky et al., 2016). Preschoolers can be *physically aggressive*, for example, when an angry 3-year-old throws a toy across the room. They can also be **relationally aggressive**, or use their words and relationships to hurt another person socially or emotionally (Crick & Grotpeter, 1996).

Both physical and relational aggression can be *reactive* or *proactive*. **Reactive aggression** is a hostile action out of frustration or anger in an immediate reaction to something that has just happened. **Proactive aggression**, sometimes called *instrumental aggression*, is aggression that is planned and executed on purpose to gain personal advantage (Rieffe et al., 2016). This may include knocking another child down to grab candy out of their hand or tattling on another child to gain social status in the classroom.

As children develop the ability to control themselves, the ways they hurt each other change. Two-year-olds kick, shove, pull hair, and grab toys out of other children's hands at a shocking rate (Alink et al., 2008). For instance, about 7 in 10 2-year-olds have hit someone in the last week, but by age 4, only about one in five have (NICHD, 2004). However, many young children do not hit out of a desire to harm (Dahl, 2016; Hay, 2017; Hay et al., 2021). In fact, for many young children, hitting may be a mishandled attempt to engage in rough-and-tumble play. For children who struggle with controlling their aggression, acting out that continues after preschool can trigger a cascade of problems, from stresses in the family to troubles in school that can last throughout childhood and adolescence (Hay et al., 2021; Olson et al., 2017).

Physical aggression tends to decline, but relational aggression increases. Children who employ relational aggression often have poorer social skills than their classmates and lack empathy (Camodeca & Coppola, 2016). The victims of bullying may be children who also lack social skills, or they may be chosen at random (Huitsing & Monks, 2018). Some children are able to defend their peers against bullies. These defenders often have stronger social skills than their peers and keen abilities to understand and empathize with other people's emotions.

Becoming Kind

When many parents in the United States think about kindness in children, they think about manners. They tell interviewers that they want children who can say "please" and "thank you." They see these skills as more important than more abstract concepts like developing empathy (Sesame Workshop, 2016). Developmental scientists point out that having good manners does not always mean that children are kind. They suggest that prosocial behavior can go beyond politeness: Prosocial behavior is what Olivia shows when she hugs a classmate who bursts into tears, reassures her mother that everything will be okay when they are running late, or helps out by putting her socks into the hamper.

When children are just 2 or 3, they already prefer kind people to those who are cruel or unfair (Cowell et al., 2017; Dahl & Killen, 2018). For instance, in research studies, 3-year-olds will complain about someone who tears up someone's drawing and are less likely to help an adult who has been unhelpful (Vaish & Hepach, 2020). Young children can also distinguish between breaking the rules and being truly unkind: for example, being "naughty" by making a mess as opposed to being "mean" by kicking a friend (Dahl & Kim, 2014).

Children's increased emotional and cognitive maturity helps them think and talk about moral issues in a more sophisticated way in early childhood (see **Figure 7.8**),

relationally aggressive Using words and relationships to hurt another person socially or emotionally.

reactive aggression A hostile action out of frustration or anger in an immediate reaction to something that has just happened.

proactive aggression Aggression that is planned and executed on purpose to gain personal advantage (sometimes called *instrumental aggression*).

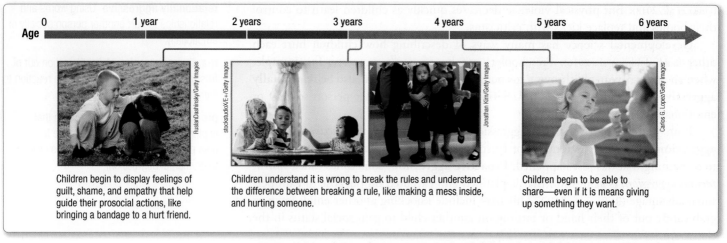

Age   0   1 year   2 years   3 years   4 years   5 years   6 years

Children begin to display feelings of guilt, shame, and empathy that help guide their prosocial actions, like bringing a bandage to a hurt friend.

Children understand it is wrong to break the rules and understand the difference between breaking a rule, like making a mess inside, and hurting someone.

Children begin to be able to share—even if it is means giving up something they want.

FIGURE 7.8 Moral Development in Early Childhood As children grow, their ability to control their behavior and understand both the expectations of their community and the feelings of other people help them behave more prosocially. Researchers believe that even toddlers are capable of empathy and care, but mistakes still happen: Sharing and kindness are difficult skills to learn.

however they are not always able to do the right thing in the heat of the moment. Conflicts over toys, treats, and trinkets are common (Smetana, 2015). In fact, when researchers asked 4-year-olds how they would feel after stealing a toy from a friend, some admitted knowing that it was wrong, but many said that they would probably feel happy about it (Arsenio, 2014). Children have difficulty balancing their understanding of their own anticipated happiness at getting a toy in their hands with their ability to understand their friend's perspective. This makes it easier for children to forgive their own mistakes than someone else's (Smetana, 2015). However, as they get older, children begin to anticipate the guilt they would feel from doing wrong, which helps prevent them from swiping a friend's toy.

Preschoolers face similar challenges with sharing. They are very sensitive to being treated unfairly and can explain that a dozen pieces of candy should be equally shared between two hypothetical children (Malti & Dys, 2018; Rochat et al., 2009). In real life, however, they often give themselves a little extra (Smith et al., 2013). They are also more likely to share fairly with people they are friendly with than with people they do not like or know very well (Smetana, 2015). Expectations about sharing differ in communities around the world. For instance, many U.S. and Chinese children are taught that sharing equally is an important form of kindness at an early age, but there is less emphasis on sharing in some other communities, such as those in Turkey and South Africa (Cowell et al., 2017).

Family and community expectations certainly play an important part in helping children share (House, 2018). If children are not encouraged to do it, they are less likely to do so (Cowell et al., 2017; Huppert et al., 2019). Sharing is often overwhelming for children, pitting their desires against their still developing self-control, theory of mind, empathy, and counting ability (Chernyak et al., 2020). In addition, children often have social preferences and beliefs about who to share with and when that may make handing over a favorite truck difficult (Smetana, 2015).

Despite these challenges, experts recommend that adults keep on encouraging children to be kind. Does it matter if someone says they are sorry? Researchers have found that 4-year-olds report that they think people who apologize are nicer than those who do not, and they understand that saying sorry can make people feel better. While only about half of all preschoolers' apologies are unprompted by an adult, practicing can help children learn to be kind (Smith et al., 2017).

Families who develop warm, supportive relationships are more likely to have children who are kind (Davidov et al., 2016; Kochanska et al., 2015). While practice helps, simply

📱 Share It!

Adversity might have a (small) upside: It may make children kinder, at least temporarily. Researchers studying sharing in Sichuan, China, found that experiencing an earthquake firsthand made children more likely to be generous.

(Li et al., 2013)

Scientific American: Lifespan Development

TABLE 7.2 Best Practices for Prosocial Development

Be a coach. Acknowledge, name, and help to problem-solve big feelings. This can help children learn to calm down and learn to be kinder in the heat of the moment.
Talk about it. Discussing feelings can model empathy and concern. Remind children that how we feel when we are upset is often different than how we feel when we have calmed down. Ask them to think big in tough situations: What would a grownup or a superhero do in the same situation?
Start early. Do not shy away from talking about moral choices. Young children often want to talk about "good guys" and "bad guys." Do not be afraid to talk about the moral choices that they face every day, such as how to share fairly or who to include in play.
Talk about differences. Children are aware enough to know that not everyone is the same, and it is not too early to talk about prejudice, racism, and exclusion. Make sure they know it is wrong to exclude.
Expect kindness. If you want children to combat unkindness, do not just tell them not to do it: give them a job to do. Remind children that they can stand up for each other, defend each other, and comfort people who are hurt.
Help repair mistakes. Everyone makes mistakes and hurts people from time to time. Work with children to go beyond saying "I'm sorry" and help them make amends.

being told what to do will not help children develop the internal conscience that helps them do the right thing (see **Table 7.2**). Preschoolers fare better when they follow an adult's example and suggestions, rather than when caregivers use power assertion to impose kindness (Killen & Smetana, 2015).

Talking is another way to promote kindness. Children who talk a lot with their families—about right and wrong, "bad guys" and "good guys", being nice and being mean—have better social and prosocial skills (Conte et al., 2018; Salmon & Reese, 2016). Preschoolers who acquire better communication skills can use words to figure out solutions to their social challenges. These skills will help children as they move on to their next adventure: middle childhood and a world of more opportunities and responsibility as they enter formal school.

APPLY IT! **7.9** Unkind behavior is common in preschoolers. How would you explain to a caregiver why this typical behavior should not be ignored?

7.10 Brionnah often talks to Olivia about the importance of "doing the right thing" even when sharing or saying sorry might feel awkward. How does her practice reflect the research finding that at learning kindness takes both practice and good examples who also show caring, thoughtful behaviors?

Practicing Kindness Being generous and caring to other people is a skill preschoolers are learning. Some families encourage children to be expressive (and work on their handwriting) by giving handmade gifts.

Wrapping It Up

LO 7.1 Analyze the advances in emotional expression and regulation during Erikson's stage of initiative versus guilt. (p. 195)

Erikson believed the crisis of the third stage, between ages 3 and 5, was a conflict between initiative and guilt. Children have enthusiasm to try new things and do them independently but are often unable to do things quite right. Some remorse over mistakes ensures that children become careful about other people's feelings and learn to work hard to accomplish tasks. During early childhood, children are expected to develop more emotion regulation. Brain development and cognitive maturity help young children have an easier time managing their feelings. Emotional maturation also happens in a social and cultural context: Children learn different ways of managing their feelings from their communities. Caregivers often expect children to be able to control their big feelings, but this is unrealistic.

LO 7.2 Describe features of young children's understanding of their identity or self-concept. (p. 195)

Your sense of who you are in the world is known as your self-concept. Your general feelings about yourself are known as your self-esteem. Preschoolers tend to have a more positive self-concept than older children, but it tends to be very concrete and built on visible characteristics. They are beginning to build a sense of their body image and academic self-concept. Feeling good about themselves helps children's adjustment but not all communities encourage boasting about successes. Praise and overinflated flattery can backfire and make children feel confused or even badly about themselves.

LO 7.3 Discuss the major theoretical viewpoints on gender development in early childhood. (p. 202)

In early childhood, children develop their *gender identity*, or their sense of themselves as boys, girls, or another less binary gender label. Young children tend to be rigid and overly concrete about categories and stereotypes, including those of gender. Children who do not conform to gender stereotypes can be vulnerable to bullying. Freud argued children learned gender through identification with their parents. Social learning theorists believe that gender is learned through a process of modeling and reinforcement. Cognitive theorists point out that children's thinking about gender, like other forms of logical thought, is often limited. Biological research suggests that all children, regardless of their gender identity, are very similar. Media plays a role in enforcing gender stereotypes. Some emerging research suggests that biology may play a role in making children more or less sensitive to social stereotypes. Scientific consensus supports affirming children's expressed gender identity.

LO 7.4 Describe the development of stereotypes in early childhood. (p. 202)

Young children are aware of many social categories, including those relating to ethnicity. They have preferences and prejudices about ethnicity and are more aware of discrimination. Many children have preferences for higher-status social groups. Talking to children about social categories is a helpful way of building pride and protecting them from some of the effects of discrimination.

LO 7.5 Describe variations in parenting practices and styles and how they affect children's development. (p. 207)

Families' relationships build on the foundation set in infancy to create habits of relating that can impact children for a lifetime. They are affected by the context, like cultural issues and economic conditions, and by individual factors, like a parent's personality. Parenting during early childhood is often challenging for parents. Families may not have accurate understanding of what small children are capable of. Parenting styles, including authoritative, authoritarian, permissive, and neglectful, describe caregiving based on levels of warmth and demandingness. Caregiving practices that help shape children's behavior are called discipline. There are variations in parenting practices around the world, but children everywhere thrive when their caregivers express warmth and have consistent expectations. Scientific consensus opposes physical punishment and spanking. Neglectful, abusive, and shaming parenting harms children. Interventions can help improve caregiving.

LO 7.6 Describe the features of play and their role in learning and development. (p. 215)

Children play more during early childhood than they will again. Play gives children an opportunity to learn about relationships and build language and cognitive skills. Researchers describe different types of play, including solitary and onlooker play, parallel play, cooperative play, functional play, constructive play, sociodramatic play, and rough-and-tumble play. Communities vary in how much they encourage some forms of play.

LO 7.7 Describe aggressive and prosocial behaviors in early childhood. (p. 218)

In early childhood, children become more aware of morality, or right and wrong, and have more ability to behave prosocially. Their feelings, like empathy and guilt, influence how they treat other people. During early childhood, children begin to develop a sense of morality, but they can also hurt other children, either through physical aggression or through relational aggression. Aggression can be planned or impulsive and reactive. Children may not always behave prosocially and may have difficulty sharing, but adult encouragement helps.

KEY TERMS

initiative versus guilt (p. 195)
psychological disorders (p. 197)
gender roles (p. 203)
gender schema (p. 204)
transgender (p. 205)
parenting styles (p. 209)

authoritative parenting (p. 210)
authoritarian parenting (p. 210)
permissive parenting (p. 210)
neglectful parenting (p. 210)
discipline (p. 211)

power-assertive techniques (p. 211)
inductive reasoning (p. 212)
maltreatment (p. 213)
abuse (p. 213)
parallel play (p. 216)
cooperative play (p. 216)

functional play (p. 216)
sociodramatic play (p. 216)
rough-and-tumble play (p. 217)
relationally aggressive (p. 219)
reactive aggression (p. 219)
proactive aggression (p. 219)

CHECK YOUR LEARNING

1. When 5-year-old Capri grabbed her classmate Jacob's crayons, Jacob cried for a minute, but soon recovered. This developing ability to control emotional reactions is known as:
   a) trauma.
   c) a subcortical structure.
   b) emotion regulation.
   d) self-concept.

2. According to Erikson's psychosocial stage theory, the period of early childhood involves a conflict of:
   a) trust versus mistrust.
   b) autonomy versus shame.
   c) initiative versus guilt.
   d) industry versus inferiority.

3. A 4-year-old's self-concept may include which of the following?
   a) I have two dogs, and I like soccer.
   b) I am not very good at writing my name.
   c) I am trustworthy and patient.
   d) I am optimistic.

4. The authoritative parenting style described by developmental scientist Diana Baumrind is characterized by:
   a) high warmth and high demandingness.
   b) high permissiveness.
   c) high warmth and low demandingness.
   d) low warmth and low communication.

5. Tara adores her three children. She thinks it is funny when they jump on the sofa and rarely asks them to put away their toys. Which parenting style BEST describes Tara?
   a) Authoritative
   c) Dismissive
   b) Authoritarian
   d) Permissive

6. Which discipline technique is most likely to help children develop their own self-regulation?
   a) Power assertion
   c) Inductive discipline
   b) Spanking
   d) No-nonsense parenting

7. What do most developmental experts recommend regarding the use of spanking?
   a) It is okay before the age of 7.
   b) It can be effective at immediately stopping a behavior but may lead to more misbehavior later.
   c) It is illegal.
   d) It is okay after the age of 7.

8. Which of the following is NOT a possible outcome of children's experiences of trauma or maltreatment?
   a) Altered stress responses to traumatic events
   b) Difficulty with self-regulation
   c) Advanced executive function
   d) Difficulty focusing attention

9. Which of the following examples represents sociodramatic play commonly seen in early childhood?
   a) A group of children playing a made-up game of "superheroes and dragons"
   b) A group of children playing Simon Says
   c) A child playing alone with a jigsaw puzzle
   d) Two children riding tricycles

10. Which of the following statements about young children's exposure to media and television is TRUE?
    a) Many shows depict gender stereotypes.
    b) Watching screens is harmful for developing vision.
    c) Children cannot understand what they see on television.
    d) Most children do not watch enough television or other media.

11. Alisha and Kamal are preschool classmates. While building a block tower together, Kamal got frustrated and knocked down the tower. Alisha responded by throwing a block at Kamal. Alisha's behavior could be described as:
    a) proactive aggression.
    c) instrumental aggression.
    b) reactive aggression.
    d) bullying aggression.

8 Physical and Cognitive Development in Middle Childhood

Growth in Body and Brain

8.1 Describe variations in growth and motor development and developmental changes in the brain during middle childhood.

Managing Health

8.2 Identify common health challenges and protective habits in middle childhood.

Cognitive Development

8.3 Explain the key features of Piaget's concrete operational stage and why Vygotsky believed that learning comes from social interaction.

8.4 Describe the typical cognitive improvements during middle childhood.

Language Development

8.5 Explain how language advances support children's learning.

Learning In and Out of School

8.6 Explain how schools influence achievement during middle childhood.

Selected Resources from

 Achieve

Activities

Concept Practice: Memory and Learning

Spotlight on Science: Are Children Smarter Than Adults?

Assessments

LearningCurve

Practice Quiz

Videos

Scientific American Profiles

Brain Development Animation—Process of Myelination

Education in Middle Childhood

© Macmillan, Photo by Sidford House

Things can change quickly when you are 10. For many families around the world, the global pandemic changed everything. Life changed for Logan, too, but in many ways, remote learning was something he was already used to. While many children had difficulty adjusting to virtual school, Logan had been homeschooling for a while and enjoyed having time to focus on what he loves: spending time with his aging dog and playing on the beach. For him, fourth grade ended up being a wonderful experience. One of the best parts: more time online, meeting new friends who also loved to play chess, playing video games, and planning his future career as a Twitch creator and YouTube influencer.

Logan's chess coach, Tom, and Logan's family helped him find solace in chess and learning even during a global pandemic. Chess helps Logan relax, helps him focus, and gives him something predictable and memorizable: the gambit, the French defense, the challenge of trying to predict what another player will do. Logan dreams about chess, visualizes it to calm himself down, and memorizes opening moves in his spare time. And during the pandemic, he has Tom's guidance over Zoom as he does it. Coach Tom is understanding, kind, and funny: He "gets" Logan and inspires him to show up and compete under pressure.

Not everything is as easy as chess for Logan: He still falls apart from time to time. He recently lost his video game privileges. But chess is something he can fall back on. It enables him to practice the skills that will help him in other parts of his life: accepting losses, preparing himself for new situations and competitors, and showing up to work hard.

Like Logan, most children have tremendous capacity for growth and change during **middle childhood**, the years from about 6 to 11. This stage begins as children develop the independence and self-regulation to take on new responsibilities, such as starting elementary school, doing chores, and watching younger siblings (Rogoff et al., 1975). Middle childhood ends as children begin adolescence, a period marked by the outward signs of the physical maturation of puberty. The skills Logan is mastering, from pickleball to emptying the dishwasher, may be unique to his culture and his family, but children everywhere are learning to take care of themselves (Grove & Lancy, 2018).

This chapter covers the hallmarks of physical and cognitive development during middle childhood. You will learn how health and cognitive development are intertwined: Children who are healthy are more likely to go to school, and physical activity can give children a sense of competence and helps build their identity.

You will read about several approaches to understanding thinking during childhood, including Piaget's theory of children's reasoning, Vygotsky's emphasis on the sociocultural context, and research that focuses on information processing and executive functioning. You will also learn how scientists investigate how children can connect with learning in school: Part of Logan's pandemic success occurred when his curious, adventurous thinking was linked with a game that inspired him to work harder than he ever had before.

middle childhood The period spanning ages 6 to 11 that begins as children develop the independence and self-regulation to take on new responsibilities.

Scientific American Profile

Meet Logan

Growth in Body and Brain

In middle childhood, children's physical growth slows from the frantic pace of early childhood, as much of their energy is diverted from body development to brain development (Bogin, 1997). They are focused on learning, whether playing chess, programming robots, adding and subtracting, or making new friends (Kuzawa & Blair, 2019). This learning leads to the reshaping of children's *cortex*, the outer layer of the brain that helps children better control their behavior and think more efficiently (Hong et al., 2021).

Learning Objective

8.1 Describe variations in growth and motor development and developmental changes in the brain during middle childhood.

Physical Growth

In the United States, children typically gain about 5 pounds (2 kilograms) and more than 2 inches (5 centimeters) each year during middle childhood (Section on Endocrinology, 2014). Typically, 6-year-olds are about 45 pounds (20 kilograms) and 45 inches (110 centimeters) tall; by age 12, they are nearly 85 pounds (45 kilograms) and 5 feet (145 centimeters) tall (Kuczmarski et al., 2000). Children are slowly growing stronger, putting on the muscle that will allow them to throw a ball through a basketball hoop or carry a heavy backpack (Yamato et al., 2018).

Because of hormonal changes, most children start to add more body fat and muscle mass and begin a rapid *growth spurt* at the end of middle childhood. For most girls, this growth spurt typically begins at around age 10, and for boys, it begins about two years later (Sanders et al., 2017). As a result, by the end of elementary school, girls often tower over boys.

During middle childhood, differences in size become more apparent, which can affect a child's developing body image and even lead to social exclusion (De Coen et al., 2021; Nabors et al., 2019). Some children are taller or heavier than others. For well-nourished children, height is highly

FIGURE 8.1 Rate of Growth in Middle Childhood During middle childhood, the pace of growth tends to slow, until the rapid growth spurt that is an early sign of puberty.

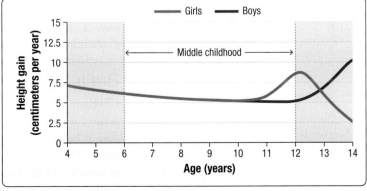

Data from Bogin, 1997.

influenced by genes, which also dictate the timing of their growth spurts. However, in many communities around the globe where children experience chronic infections, malnutrition, or disease, size is more closely related to children's health than to their genome (Jelenkovic et al., 2020).

Motor Skill Development

In middle childhood, children can perform complex physical activities: Many can hit a ball with a bat or write a neat paragraph. Their bodies are still not as strong or fast as adults', even adjusting for their smaller size, but anyone who has chased a 7-year-old around the playground knows that children have more energy than many adults. In fact, when experts measure children's aerobic capacity and ability to recover from exertion, they find that the average child rivals a trained triathlete (Bontemps et al., 2019).

During middle childhood, children typically acquire the motor skills that will foster independence, academic success, and a sense of competence among their friends. At this age, they are generally expected to be self-sufficient in everyday self-care: Most 7-year-olds are able to dress themselves and stay dry through the night (Vaziri Flais et al., 2018). Children at this age also need fine motor skills in order to succeed academically: Difficulty with writing often leads to academic difficulties later on (Gaul & Issartel, 2016).

Learning to Sit Still One of the hallmarks of middle childhood is an increased ability to control the body. In this classroom in Canada, this includes practicing sitting still and doing yoga.

Many physical education experts hope that children also develop gross motor skills such as doing sit-ups, throwing and catching a ball, or walking on a balance beam. Logan's family agrees: They make sure he practices his jiu-jitsu and has time to boogie board at the beach with his younger brother. However, formal athletic skills like these require practice and opportunity—putting them out of reach of many children around the world who do not have the resources Logan benefits from (Barnett et al., 2016; Bruininks & Bruininks, 2005; Logan et al., 2015). Whatever physical activities a community values, feeling physically competent increases the likelihood that children will do better in school and stay physically active later in life (Barnett et al., 2020).

Much of what children do in school involves fine motor skills, whether that means clicking on a chat box in a Zoom class, writing numbers clearly, or constructing a beautiful diorama about bats. As many as one in four children around the world struggle with fine motor skills like handwriting (Coker & Kim, 2018; Rosenblum, 2018). Messy or slow writing may seem like an old-fashioned concern, particularly in an era of keyboards and smartphones, but children who have trouble with the motor coordination involved in writing also tend to have difficulties with getting their ideas down clearly (Limpo & Graham, 2020). The solution that works for most? More practice. Handwriting requires integrating visual perception, motor coordination, and planning skills, which, for many children, just take more practice to develop (McClelland & Cameron, 2019; Ose Askvik et al., 2020). Once children can write by hand, they can put more of their energy into deeper thinking.

Brain Development

Children's brains are maturing during middle childhood, which gives them greater control over their thoughts, emotions, and bodies. This is why Logan can keep smiling even if he loses the final match and can remember how to spell "friend" (most of the time). These changes are supported by two major developments in the brain: First, maturation in the cortex speed up children's thinking, improving skills such as reading, math, and planning ahead (Butterworth & Walsh, 2011; Ronan et al., 2020; Thiebaut de Schotten et al., 2014). Second, increasing connectivity in the brain helps children learn to manage their

FatCamera/E+/Getty Images

emotions, master new social relationships, and develop individual personalities and ways of responding to the world (Kopala-Sibley et al., 2020; Tottenham & Gabard-Durnam, 2017).

Faster Connections and Pruning in the Cortex As described in Chapter 6, your brain develops according to a use-it-or-lose-it principle. Synaptic connections that are used frequently get stronger; those used less frequently tend to fade away. This is particularly true during middle childhood, when children are learning a great deal—building new synaptic connections and automatizing the skills they have acquired. Remember from Chapter 4 that the neurons involved in pathways that are used more often become *myelinated*, or insulated with a substance called myelin, which speeds up transmission and turns the cells into *white matter*. During middle childhood, myelination occurs throughout the cortex, building *white matter* (Natu et al., 2019).

Remember that myelinated white matter connections are the fast, long-range synaptic connections that create what neuroscientists refer to as the *connectome*, or the network that links regions of the brain (Kim et al., 2019). These improved connections enhance the motor coordination, executive function, attention, and memory skills that children need in order to control their behavior, do long division, and remember their login passwords (Piccolo et al., 2019).

As frequently used synaptic connections become myelinated, synapses and dendrites which are not used are gradually *pruned*, or fade away. As you may remember, unmyelinated connections are referred to as *gray matter*. During middle childhood, pruning continues in the cortex, and gray matter is pruned so much that the cortex itself becomes thinner as unnecessary connections disappear (Tamnes & Mills, 2020; Walhovd et al., 2017). This thinner, smaller cortex has more longer, faster myelinated connections, or *white matter*, that also changes shape over time: The surface of the cortex continues to fold in on itself, deepening the characteristic wrinkles and whorls, known as *sulci* and *gyri*, visible on the outside (Garcia et al., 2018).

Variations in the pace of cortical thinning are common during middle childhood, when the cortex is particularly plastic because of the experiences that are constantly shaping children's brains (Tooley et al., 2021). Remember that children's bodies and brains often show accelerated development as a response to stress in the environment or prenatal injuries. This is believed to be the case with cortical thinning (Alnæs et al., 2020). Children who have significant cognitive gains build more synapses in the cortex, leading to a slower rate of cortical thinning or even to cortical thickening (Estrada et al., 2019).

This is not always true of children who are exposed to significant adversity: Children who are frequently afraid, feel unsafe, or lack opportunities for learning may have a different, faster rate of cortical thinning and accelerated maturation of neural circuits (Colich et al., 2021; Smith & Pollak, 2021). Fewer opportunities for cognitive stimulation and more exposure to stress hormones may shape how children's memory and attention skills adapt to their circumstances. This can actually lead to some unique strengths, like enhanced ability to pick up on new information in the environment (Chad-Friedman et al., 2021; Ellis et al., 2017).

Connections for Emotion Learning Children learn a great deal during middle childhood, whether out with friends or at home during the pandemic like Logan, but some of their most important learning involves managing their feelings. Researchers are particularly interested in how brain development reflects children's emotional maturity (Kopala-Sibley et al., 2020).

Remember from Chapter 6 that emotions are processed deep in the brain's subcortical structures, particularly in the *amygdala*. During middle childhood, the fast, long-range synaptic connections between the subcortical structures and the *prefrontal cortex* (*PFC*), the hub of decision making and conscious thought, are strengthened. These connections shape children's personalities, their emotion regulation, and their

CONNECTIONS

Remember the principles of brain development (see Chapter 4): Experiences create new synaptic connections; connections that are used become faster through myelination; and, as children grow, shorter, localized connections are replaced with more efficient, long-range connections across regions of the brain.

 **Share It!**

Could there be benefits to stress? Children adapt to stressful circumstances. Some researchers suggest that this may give them unique strengths: better procedural memory (which helps them learn new skills) and a greater ability to perceive changes in their environment.

(Frankenhuis & Nettle, 2020)

Scientific American: Lifespan Development

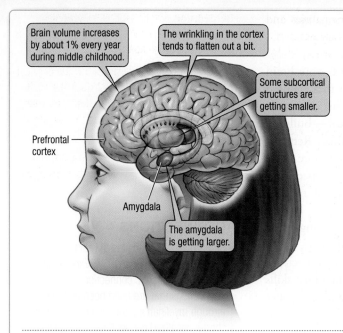

Brain volume increases by about 1% every year during middle childhood.

The wrinkling in the cortex tends to flatten out a bit.

Some subcortical structures are getting smaller.

Prefrontal cortex

Amygdala

The amygdala is getting larger.

CONNECTIONS FOR EMOTIONAL LEARNING

During middle childhood, the fast, long-range synaptic connections between the subcortical structures including the amygdala, and the prefrontal cortex (PFC), the hub of decision making and conscious thought, are strengthened. These connections are stronger in one direction in middle childhood—more from the subcortical structures to the PFC than from the PFC to the subcortical structures.

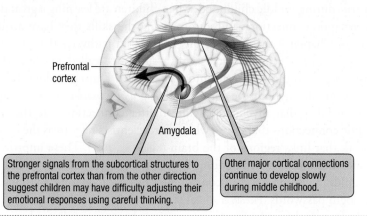

Prefrontal cortex

Amygdala

Stronger signals from the subcortical structures to the prefrontal cortex than from the other direction suggest children may have difficulty adjusting their emotional responses using careful thinking.

Other major cortical connections continue to develop slowly during middle childhood.

THINNING OF THE CORTEX

As frequently used neural pathways become myelinated, unused synapses and dendrites are gradually pruned, leading to thinning of the cortex. Scientists believe this is connected to increasing efficiency in neural communication and, as a result, faster thinking and learning.

GRAY MATTER DECREASE AND WHITE MATTER INCREASE

Increasing myelination along with continued pruning increases the volume of white matter and decreases the volume of gray matter. This helps propel children's learning and ability to control their behavior.

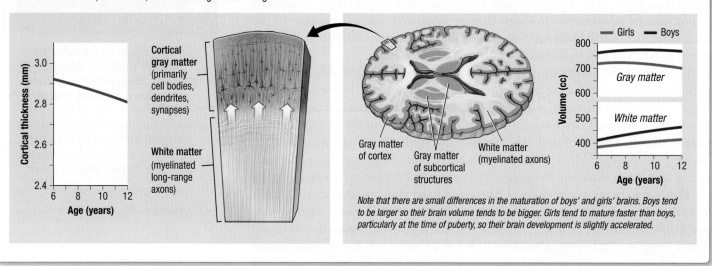

Cortical gray matter (primarily cell bodies, dendrites, synapses)

White matter (myelinated long-range axons)

Gray matter of cortex

Gray matter of subcortical structures

White matter (myelinated axons)

Note that there are small differences in the maturation of boys' and girls' brains. Boys tend to be larger so their brain volume tends to be bigger. Girls tend to mature faster than boys, particularly at the time of puberty, so their brain development is slightly accelerated.

ways of relating (Callaghan & Tottenham, 2016). These connections are stronger in one direction in middle childhood—more from the amygdala to the PFC than from the PFC to the amygdala. They are stronger in the opposite direction during adolescence and adulthood, when the PFC starts to manage and inhibit input from the amygdala (Cohodes et al., 2021). In essence, during middle childhood, children's emotional experiences shape how they think and make decisions (Tottenham, 2020).

The neural changes just described help explain the typical challenges children have with emotion regulation. Although they are much less prone to tantrums than preschoolers, school-age children are still less emotionally mature than teenagers. They still rely on their caregivers for comfort and have an easier time tackling new challenges—like starting at a new school or getting a flu shot—if family members come along (Tan et al., 2020). Their brains do not yet have strong connections between the PFC (the "thinking" part) and the amygdala (the "fear" part), so they cannot use thinking to change how they feel. Therefore, children need to use other methods to manage their feelings, like reaching out for support or avoiding upsetting situations altogether. Whereas children might cover their eyes or hide during the scary parts of a movie, adults can remind themselves that it's "just a movie" (Silvers & Guassi Moreira, 2019).

Early Signs of Puberty

If you look at the group of elementary school students who attend Logan's chess matches or play pickleball, you might not believe that any of them are experiencing hormonal activity. They seem far from adolescence. However, inside their bodies, new hormones are triggering maturation (Rosenfield, 2021). Most of this happens because the *adrenal glands,* two thumb-sized structures on the top of your kidneys, begin to secrete higher levels of hormones such as dehydroepiandrosterone (DHEA) between the ages of 5 and 9 (Goddings et al., 2021; Keestra et al., 2021). This stage, which prepares the body for puberty and initiates physical maturation, is called **adrenarche**.

Adrenarche triggers the appearance of some **secondary sex characteristics**, the physical markers that are associated with adult appearance, including pubic hair, facial hair, the Adam's apple, and breasts. (**Primary sex characteristics** are the reproductive organs that babies are typically born with, like genitals.) Adrenarche triggers the maturation of some secondary sex characteristics, such as pubic hair and a more adult smell. By age 8, one in five typical girls may have some pubic hair (Kaplowitz et al., 2016; Stein et al., 2019). By age 10, children may need deodorant and have acne breakouts. Children at this age often begin to have romantic or sexual desires, like crushes, although their sexual identity often takes a few more years to develop (Bishop et al., 2021; Fortenberry, 2014).

As you will read in Chapter 10, puberty is triggered by a different set of hormones than adrenarche. Ovarian hormones trigger some early signs of puberty, including the

adrenarche The first hormonal changes preparing the body for puberty, typically occurring between ages 5 and 9.

secondary sex characteristics The physical markers of what makes people look like adult males or females after puberty. Secondary sex characteristics include pubic hair, facial hair, the Adam's apple and breasts.

primary sex characteristics The physical markers that babies are typically born with, like genitals.

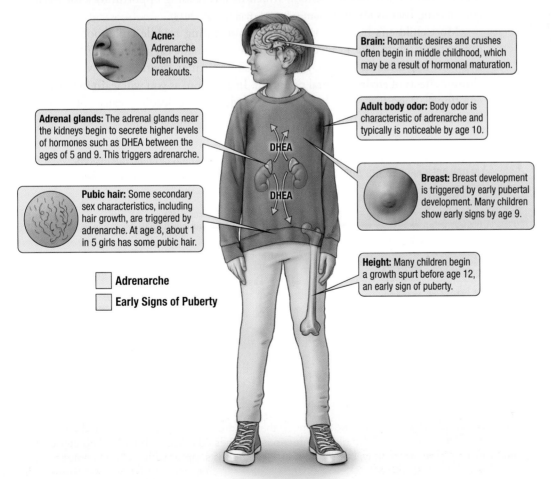

Acne: Adrenarche often brings breakouts.

Brain: Romantic desires and crushes often begin in middle childhood, which may be a result of hormonal maturation.

Adrenal glands: The adrenal glands near the kidneys begin to secrete higher levels of hormones such as DHEA between the ages of 5 and 9. This triggers adrenarche.

Adult body odor: Body odor is characteristic of adrenarche and typically is noticeable by age 10.

Breast: Breast development is triggered by early pubertal development. Many children show early signs by age 9.

Pubic hair: Some secondary sex characteristics, including hair growth, are triggered by adrenarche. At age 8, about 1 in 5 girls has some pubic hair.

Height: Many children begin a growth spurt before age 12, an early sign of puberty.

☐ Adrenarche
☐ Early Signs of Puberty

FIGURE 8.2 The Changes of Adrenarche Typically between ages 5 and 9, hormonal changes triggered by the adrenal glands mark the beginning of adrenarche. Adrenarche leads to the development of some secondary sex characteristics, including changes in smell, skin, and hair growth.

beginnings of breast development, at around age 9 (Greenspan, 2017; Kaplowitz et al., 2016). Changes triggered by puberty begin a few years later for children with testes, but they may begin to put on weight in advance of a growth spurt that begins around age 12 (Sanders et al., 2017). Children who are transgender or identify as nonbinary may need to prepare for some of these physical changes: Their families may consider beginning hormone treatments to postpone maturation before the teenage years (Shumer & Araya, 2019). But for all children, understanding adrenarche and the early signs of puberty can reassure children that there is nothing unusual about what they are going through.

APPLY IT!   **8.1** Logan's family has encouraged him to learn some specialized physical skills, including jiu-jitsu and pickleball, not just chasing his dog and his brother on the local beach. How does the development of culturally valued motor skills benefit Logan and other young children?

8.2 Logan has never heard of adrenarche. What are the three things he might want to be prepared for before he turns 11?

Managing Health

Learning Objective

8.2 Identify common health challenges and protective habits in middle childhood.

Share It!

Healthy teeth are more than a pretty smile: They also mean you are more likely to be in school. Cavities and tooth decay hurt, and pain keeps children out of school.

(Rebelo et al., 2019)

Scientific American: Lifespan Development

Like Logan, most children in the United States are thriving during middle childhood. In recent surveys, nearly 98 percent of U.S. families reported that their children's health was good or excellent (NCHS, 2021). However, if you look at the health statistics in detail, the overall picture is not quite as rosy. Like other periods in the lifespan, the school years come with health risks. Poor health not only impacts children's bodies; it also has cognitive and social consequences (Allison et al., 2019). If children are not well, they are more likely to miss school, which means missing opportunities for learning and making friends (Ansari & Gottfried, 2021; Bundy et al., 2018).

Most children's health troubles are minor during middle childhood. But some can be more severe, like a cancer diagnosis or a traumatic car accident. Other children live with impairments that may be less visible, such as cavities, poor vision, or the chronic effects of environmental pollution. In addition, as you will learn in Chapter 9, emotional, cognitive, and behavioral disorders are a leading cause of children's disability around the world (Patel et al., 2018; Whitney & Peterson, 2019).

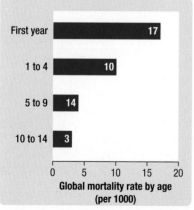

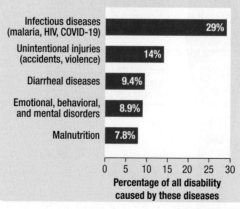

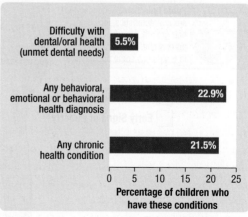

FIGURE 8.3 How Healthy Are Children Around the World? Bigger, studier bodies mean that children are healthier during middle childhood than they are during earlier periods in the lifespan. Around the globe, infectious diseases continue to be a leading cause of illness in young children. In the United States, most children are healthy, but more than 1 in 5 needs support with a chronic emotional, behavioral, or health condition.

Childhood Illnesses

In the United States, about one in five children has a chronic physical health condition, like asthma or diabetes, that impacts their everyday life (Blackwell et al., 2019). In low-income countries, middle childhood is more perilous: About 6 of every 1,000 children lose their lives as a result of chronic disease or malnutrition (Bundy et al., 2017; UN IGME, 2020). In such places, infectious diseases continue to be the leading cause of death in young children.

As noted in Chapter 6, children's active immune systems protected most children from the worst effects of COVID-19, although they could still pass the virus on to other people (Bhopal et al., 2021). Children who already had a serious condition, like HIV or malnutrition, were more likely to lose their lives to the disease (WHO, 2020). But even amidst the COVID-19 pandemic, in affluent countries, the death of a young child is an extraordinarily rare event, usually caused by an accident (Cunningham et al., 2018; Dorney et al., 2020).

Children become healthier as they get older and are better able to handle the stresses of common illnesses, but between ages 5 and 9, they are still vulnerable. Not until after age 10 are children strong enough to reliably recover from these diseases (Bundy et al., 2017; see **Figure 8.3**). As you will learn, caring for children who are ill or have a disability requires families and health care providers to be imaginative and sensitive to their developmental needs (Law et al., 2019).

Share It!

Keep them securely stored: Children are naturally inquisitive. Guns are involved in one in four accidental deaths in children in the United States.

(Cohen et al., 2021)

Scientific American: Lifespan Development

 SCIENCE IN PRACTICE
Camille Frasier, Child Life Specialist

Camille Fraser doesn't remember the name of the woman who changed her life. Diagnosed with cancer as a teenager, Camille was terrified of needles but needed a tube inserted in her chest to allow physicians to administer her medication and take blood. When Camille felt too panicked to allow them close to her, a Child Life Specialist showed her exactly what the doctors were going to do, soothing Camille and helping her get through the procedure. This kindness led Camille to a mission: After recovering from cancer, Camille decided to become a Child Life Specialist in order to help children who were experiencing similar difficulties. She now works at a hospital near her home in Nashville, Tennessee.

Child Life Specialists are health care providers with a background in child development, including an undergraduate and sometimes a master's degree, who undergo intensive hands-on training to support children with various conditions and their families. They work in hospitals to prepare children for invasive procedures or to help reduce the pain or anxiety they may have about their illnesses.

Camille spent weeks in the hospital over the course of her treatment, but she left committed to turning her experience into an opportunity to help other children. Thirteen years later, Camille became certified as a Child Life Specialist, a job she loves. From her own experience as a patient, she remembers "what it feels like to be stuck in your room for long periods of time. . . . I know what it means to be a part of a family that is dealing with a very difficult diagnosis," she explains (Echegaray, 2017). Now she works with children with heart disease, sometimes pulling out her puppet friend, Hank, who makes young children smile as he "explains" the details of a complicated medical procedure.

Children may not understand why they are at the hospital or what is wrong with them. Child Life Specialists explain what is happening and help children who may be coping with loneliness or separation from family, sometimes for the first time. Camille has been known to pull out candy and marshmallows to explain leukemia. She explains that IV fluids will be cold and that the alcohol used to clean children's

Slime Helps. Child Life Specialists understand that although they may be sick, children are still children even in the hospital. Here, a specialist at Vanderbilt University Medical Center helps explain science and brings a little joy by making slime in a hospital bed.

skin may have a strong smell. She can coax a child to watch a movie on an iPad to keep them still for an MRI.

Children who have worked with Child Life Specialists recover more quickly from serious illnesses and short procedures like IV placement or a trip to the emergency room, with less pain and less emotional upset (Committee on Hospital Care, 2014; Pillai, 2020; Romito et al., 2021). For Camille, it is a dream job. She feels honored to make a difference and return the empathy that helped her in her own recovery. ⊚

Ongoing Conditions

In affluent countries, deadly illnesses and accidents are rare, but chronic conditions and illnesses are not (Pulcini et al., 2017). They are often linked to structural and environmental conditions that are beyond the control of children and their families. In the United States, as many as one in five children has been diagnosed with a condition like asthma, allergies, or dental issues that interferes with school and increases their likelihood for health complications later in life (Ullah & Kaelber, 2021).

An increasing number of children in affluent countries have challenges linked to diet and weight that may affect their physical development and health in later years (Sahota et al., 2020; Tagi & Chiarelli, 2020; Wühl, 2019). Public health experts suggest about one in five children around the globe may be too heavy and that, for some children, this weight may trigger changes in their metabolism and cardiovascular system that result in diabetes, liver disease, and heart disease (Caprio et al., 2020; Smith et al., 2020; UNICEF, 2021). Stigma and bias against children who are heavy may also be linked to their increased risk for metabolic and cardiovascular complications. In communities that allow children and adults to exclude others based on their appearance, children who are bigger than their peers are more likely to experience bullying, poor body image, and depression, an additional stress that can undermine their health (Killedar et al., 2020; Morales et al., 2019).

Systems beyond children's control make it difficult to maintain a healthy weight: Genetics, early metabolic programming, and biology lead school-age children to prefer sweets and salty snacks to fruits and vegetables (Beckerman et al., 2017; Kansra et al., 2020). In many nations around the world, processed foods are less expensive than fresh fruits and vegetables, and families are often overwhelmed by marketing that promotes unhealthy diets (Fischer et al., 2021; Headey & Alderman, 2019).

Environmental Impacts on Health

More than 90 percent of the world's children breathe toxic air every day, the result of traffic, industry, or of burning fuels like wood and kerosene for cooking (WHO, 2018). Children's developing bodies and brains are particularly sensitive to pollution and stresses caused by natural disasters (Helldén et al., 2021). Air pollution causes respiratory infections in children and can lead to cognitive difficulties and cancer (Brumberg et al., 2021; Landrigan et al., 2019).

Children are also vulnerable to the effects of climate change, which has led to an increase in global temperatures and extreme weather. Climate change is expected to increase air pollution, transmission of infectious diseases, and serious weather events such as hurricanes, droughts, and winter storms (Helldén et al., 2021). Children are more easily impacted by environmental stresses, from the overpopulation of disease-bearing ticks to heat-stroke from high temperatures (Stanberry et al., 2018).

Even a few days of hot weather can have unexpected effects. For instance, students in schools without air conditioning have difficulty concentrating when the weather gets hot. In one study of children in New York City, students who took their exams in a classroom with no air conditioning on a hot day scored 15 points lower than those who sat for exams on a cooler day (Heal & Park, 2015). Most children

Share It!

Bias happens even in the hospital. Unconscious bias often leads health care providers to discount pain experienced by Black and Latino children, who are less likely to receive opiate relief when they break a bone or have appendicitis.

(Goyal et al., 2020)

Scientific American: Lifespan Development

Jake May/The Flint Journal via AP

Children Making Change Children are more sensitive than adults to toxins in the air and water. Mari Copeny tried to do something about it: She raised thousands of dollars to provide free, safe water to her neighbors in Flint, Michigan. Here, Mari and her cousin, Ivory Moon, help load vehicles with water donations.

can tolerate a few days of heat, but for the children around the world who already experience daily adversity, the effects of climate change may be more stressful and, ultimately, more deadly (Clark et al., 2020).

Building Health

How can families and communities foster health in young children amidst a host of challenges, including the COVID-19 pandemic, the allure of TikTok, and easy access to sweets? Experts recommend four behavioral practices to build physical resilience in children: getting sufficient sleep, activity, nutrition, and play.

Sleep Remember that sleep is essential for brain development, helping children consolidate their learning and better control their behavior (Cheng et al., 2020). Experts recommend that children aged 6–12 get between 9 and 12 hours of sleep a night, but many children fall short of this goal (Paruthi et al., 2016). Parents report that as many as 3 in 10 children have sleep-related difficulties, from resistance to bedtime to chronic daytime sleepiness (Bathory & Tomopoulos, 2017).

Bedtime battles may have their origins in biology. Natural circadian rhythms cause all of us to have a period of alertness in the evening, or a "second wind," and for children this often occurs before bedtime, making it particularly difficult to settle down (Bruni & Novelli, 2010). Another challenge comes from technology: Children who are on phones or play video games before bed often have difficulty falling asleep. The excitement of playing combined with the brain-stimulating blue light emitted by screens interfere with children's sleep (LeBourgeois et al., 2017; Przybylski et al., 2019).

Eating for Health A nutritious diet is essential to good health in children (and adults). Undernutrition and food insecurity can make it difficult for children to learn. Eating too much or missing out on essential nutrients like iron and zinc also harm brain development (Black et al., 2020).

You may not have fond memories of your school lunches, but whether it is green bean casserole in the United States, polenta and beans in Zimbabwe, or sushi in Japan, cafeteria lunches provide nearly half of a child's daily calories and sustain more than 368 million children around the world (Cohee et al., 2021). In affluent countries, most children get their midday meals at school, enabling them to have a meal in the middle of the day without having to pack a sandwich. In low-income countries, school lunch programs are more limited but are important in fighting malnutrition (Downs & Demmler, 2020).

Snacks with Friends School lunches are a public health success story, providing healthy nutrition to children. Yadier and Samantha *(left)* are digging into lunch in Old Havana, Cuba, including chicken, taro, and pea soup. During the height of the COVID-19 pandemic, children in Shanghai *(right)* ate rice, too, but separated by plastic partitions to protect them from disease.

Children's diets at home are also crucial for getting the healthy nutrition they need. Poor nutrition is more common among families in low-income communities, which are more likely to be *food deserts* (neighborhoods without supermarkets), or *food swamps* (neighborhoods with an overabundance of fast-food restaurants) (Bell et al., 2019). Limited access to food—whether it is unaffordable or just not locally available—reflects widespread social inequalities. Low-income families have less access to healthy food (Lacko et al., 2021; Monsivais et al., 2021). Prepared foods, sugary drinks, and high-calorie snacks often fill the void, because they cost less, last for a long time, and immediately satisfy hungry children (Moran et al., 2019).

Staying Active Some parents invest in exercise trackers to see how much their children are moving each day. Logan's parents have not gone that far: Most experts advise that detailed tracking is not helpful. Like Logan, most children are motivated by the fun of running on the beach, not by a reminder to get their steps in, and they tend to be more active than adults. (Experts recommend children his age get between 12,000 and 16,000 steps each day; most adults get only 5,000 [Tudor-Locke et al., 2011]).

Moving the body builds strong bones and prevents cardiovascular disease (Physical Activity Guidelines Advisory Committee, 2018). Regular physical activity even improves cognition (Álvarez-Bueno et al., 2020; Ishihara et al., 2018). Exercise often requires children to practice executive function skills, which stimulates the creation of neurons, strengthens myelinated connections in the brain, and supports the growth of brain structures that facilitate memory and thinking (Meijer et al., 2020; Valkenborghs et al., 2019). Researchers agree that, in the words of one neuroscientist, "exercise is like Miracle-Gro for your brain" (Ratey & Hageman, 2013).

During middle childhood, children need just about an hour a day of physical activity (Physical Activity Guidelines Advisory Committee, 2018). However, in the United States and in Europe before the global pandemic, fewer than 3 in 10 children met guidelines for exercise recommended by experts (Coppinger et al., 2020; NPAPA, 2018). The COVID-19 pandemic canceled soccer games and dance classes across the world: Missing out on organized sports made it even less likely that children stayed active (Tulchin-Francis et al., 2021).

One key reason children do not get enough physical activity is that they are in school. Once children begin kindergarten, they spend much of their time sitting. Children may have breaks for recess or gym, but most of their time is what researchers call *sedentary*: sitting or standing still in a classroom. During the COVID-19 pandemic, sedentary time increased for many children as they sat in front of screens to attend school, rather than running across the play yard (Dunton et al., 2020).

Children who get enough physical activity tend to exercise outside of school. They may walk to school or the bus, or practice poses in jiu-jitsu, as Logan does. Many play organized sports, which has its own benefits: Participating in sports can encourage children to be more outgoing, more persistent, and less reactive, and sometimes it can decrease the likelihood of depression (Conley et al., 2020; Gorham & Barch, 2020; Logan et al., 2019). Athletic activities also help children learn new motor skills and develop new relationships and a social identity that can persist into adulthood (Aumètre & Poulin, 2018).

Participation in sports is not always equitable: Equipment, private clubs, and transportation are expensive. As a result, children from low-income families are less likely to be involved in sports. Children with disabilities may be left out altogether (NPAPA, 2018). Physical activity has many benefits, but what may be most important is that it is enjoyable (Logan et al., 2019). Children, and adults, are more likely to stick

Jose Cabezas/AFP via Getty Images

A Dose of Sunshine Before School Silvia, Henry, and Rosario are walking to school in Metalio, El Salvador, with their mother, Nuya. In the United States, only 1 in 10 children walks or bikes to school. Around the world, it is common for children to walk to school, providing sunshine and physical activity before school begins.

📱 **Share It!**

Screens are not the only problem: Screen time is often blamed for children's sedentary behavior, but many non-screen ways of passing time, from Legos to reading, also involve sitting.

(Hoffmann et al., 2019)

Scientific American: Lifespan Development

with something because they love it than because it is good for them: Activity needs to be fun (Dietz et al., 2019).

During middle childhood, children increasingly focus on screens rather than on active play when they are not at school, doing an adult-supervised activity or homework. Screens give children who are unable to socialize with other children after school the opportunity to do so remotely or to catch up on games everyone talks about at school. However, this screen time often takes away from more beneficial in-person activities (McArthur et al., 2021). In the United States, most children spend nearly than five hours a day using their screens for entertainment (Rideout & Robb, 2019). During the COVID-19 pandemic, screen time increased. Early reports indicated that children's recreational screen time with Roblox and TikTok increased, on top of the time spent in online school (Fischer et al., 2021).

Finding Joy on the Ice Jade, a fourth-grader, excels at figure skating in an after-school program near her home in New York City. She has not only learned how to do a difficult spiral; she has also built up her self-confidence, made new friends, and feels a sense of freedom and joy when she spins on the ice.

![] MAKING A DIFFERENCE
Children Need More Freedom to Play

It is true that technology, the cost of organized sports, and school keep children from being active, but there is another major factor: Many children simply have much less unsupervised free time than their parents or grandparents did (Hofferth, 2009; Lee et al., 2021). They are not outside playing tag or street hockey, or climbing trees. Children spend at least 25 percent less time playing than they did 20 years ago (Gray, 2020; Loebach & Gilliland, 2019; Mullan, 2019). Some estimates indicate that children spend as few as seven minutes a day in free play (Sobchuk et al., 2019).

Play has been curtailed for a variety of reasons. Some families keep their children indoors and in supervised activities because they worry their children will be injured or become the victims of a crime (Rixon et al., 2019). Changes in neighborhood dynamics and in work schedules have meant many families are less connected to their neighbors, and fewer adults are available to keep an eye out for children (Ross et al., 2020). Other families feel pressure to engage their children in activities that will help them in school (Pynn et al., 2019). Much of this reflects a parenting strategy, often called *intensive parenting* or *concerted cultivation*, that is focused on achievement and adult supervision (Lareau, 2011; Weininger et al., 2015).

Outdoor Play Free play can take place in adventure playgrounds, like this one in London, or in more traditional ones, like this one in Jordan. In an adventure playground, children are allowed to build their own structures using hammers and nails, encouraging physical activity, independent play, and problem solving, despite the occasional bruised thumb.

Developmental scientists are confident that children benefit from unstructured play, in which they can make their own choices about what to do and how to do it (Nijhof et al., 2018). It helps children develop social skills and relationships, encourages evaluating acceptable physical risks, and spurs creativity (Farmer et al., 2017; Louv, 2008; Sobchuk et al., 2019). Free play builds cognition: Children who engage in self-directed play, like fort building or a spontaneous round of capture the flag, have stronger executive function (Barker et al., 2014).

Developmental scientists suggest that children need opportunities to guide their own play and do some problem solving on their own, with adults available to help only when needed. 🌐

APPLY IT! **8.3** One of the best things that happened to Logan during the pandemic was when he finally got to play in the park with his friends after a long period of isolation. How would you explain the benefits of free, active play to adults who might not remember how fun it was?

8.4 During 2020, Logan says he looked forward to meals, craving homemade tomato basil soup. How does nutrition help children grow?

Cognitive Development

Learning Objectives

8.3 Explain the key features of Piaget's concrete operational stage and why Vygotsky believed that learning comes from social interaction.

8.4 Describe the typical cognitive improvements during middle childhood.

When Logan was asked what makes someone good at chess, instead of listing great memory skills or even the ability to think ahead, he said it came down to focus and imagination. These are talents that Logan has in abundance (he even has "chess dreams"). Most children's core cognitive skills blossom during middle childhood, including their reasoning ability, executive function, and problem solving. Two qualities reflect the unique thinking of children: curiosity and flexibility.

The Benefits of Thinking Like a Child

If you talk with a school-age child, even a very capable one like Logan, you may notice how much they do not know. So much is new to them. Developmental scientists, however, point out that children have a number of cognitive strengths and that their thinking can be even more creative than adults' (Gopnik, 2020; Schulz et al., 2019).

In a transition some developmental scientists term the *5 to 7 shift*, children's ability to manage their own thinking and behavior improves dramatically as children begin school (Sameroff & Haith, 1996). Around the world, children begin to take on new responsibilities at about age 6. Families expect that by this age children have developed the skills to control themselves (Burrage et al., 2008; Lancy, 2021). Wiggling and distracted kindergartners develop into self-regulated first-graders who can focus long enough to sound out words and write down the date (Morrison et al., 2019).

This burst of reasoning ability is a result of brain maturation triggered by experience. One group of neuroscientists conducted a clever study to show how a year of first grade makes a difference in how children use their brain (see **Figure 8.4**) (Brod et al., 2017). Researchers compared two groups of children very close in age. One group included children who were just old enough to start first grade, and the other group was slightly younger. They found that children who completed the first grade used their brains differently than children who stayed in kindergarten.

When the children were asked to perform executive function tasks, like pressing a button for "dog" and not "cat," the prefrontal cortex (PFC) was activated in both the kindergartners and first-graders. (Remember that the PFC is the area of the brain activated during logical thought and planning.) However, there was a difference in

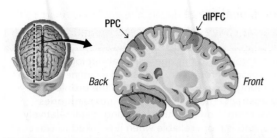

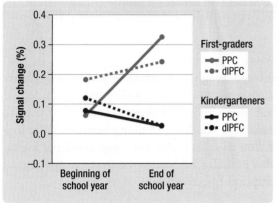

Data from Brod et al., 2017.

FIGURE 8.4 Practice in First Grade Creates Changes in the Brain. Researchers compared fMRI scans of children who had been through a year of first grade (*green lines*) with children who did not make the birthday cutoff for first grade (*blue lines*). When the two groups of children were asked to perform tests of executive function, fMRI scans showed that they used their brains differently. Children who had been through first grade showed more activation in their prefrontal cortex related to executive functioning, like the regions known as the posterior parietal cortex (PPC) and the dorsilateral prefrontal cortex (dlPFC). In contrast, the children who had not been to first grade used broader, less specialized regions of their cortex. The researchers' explanation was that those children had more practice using their executive function skills. A year's experience in first grade taught them to focus and follow directions. As a result, their brains were activated more efficiently: These skills no longer required as much prefrontal cortex activation and conscious control.

how the two groups used their PFC. Many *more* areas of the PFC were activated in kindergartners than in first-graders. The more limited activation in the first-graders' brains, primarily in two regions connected to executive function, indicated that these tasks no longer required as much effort. In effect, the first-graders' brains had become more efficient, developing brain regions that specialized in following directions and boosted executive function (Brod et al., 2017). Similar studies have replicated this finding: Formal schooling, whether it starts in kindergarten or first grade, shapes children's functioning (Kim et al., 2021).

Scholars consistently observe a similar phenomenon across middle childhood: As children develop, the brain becomes more efficient. Throughout development, the PFC is activated when children need to use lots of conscious effort, focus, and thinking. In early childhood, the PFC is activated much of the time when children need to control their behavior or do something that requires conscious thought. As children grow and acquire new tasks, the entire PFC no longer needs to be as involved. Following basic directions or remembering to raise their hand in class, or playing a G on the violin, no longer requires as much activation. Instead, more specialized areas of the brain manage these jobs (Putkinen & Saarikivi, 2018).

During middle childhood, advances in executive function combined with children's inexperience in the world make them amazing learners. School-age children are hungry for learning and are more flexible, creative, and curious in their thinking than younger children or adults (Schulz et al., 2019). Indeed, children's inexperience often spurs them to create innovative and interesting solutions. When scientists test children and adults in the laboratory, they find that children are not afraid to come up with new solutions. Adults tend to target their efforts, but children attend to everything, which gives them a broader awareness and more creativity (Blanco & Sloutsky, 2019).

Piaget's Stage of Concrete Operations

Remember that developmental theorist Jean Piaget devised practical, hands-on ways of testing children to investigate what they understood and thought about the world. Piaget called middle childhood the stage of **concrete operations** (Piaget & Inhelder, 1969). He believed that children's logical thinking abilities gradually improve throughout

Children's Curiosity Can Spark Science. With support from their school, a visiting scientist, and a devoted teacher, a group of children in Blackawton, England, published a peer-reviewed paper on bees. The children did not know how to present a scientific study, but they had other strengths: They were able to come up with new ideas. They discovered that bees use both color and space to choose which flowers to pollinate, and they concluded that "science is cool and fun because you get to do stuff that no one has ever done before" (Blackawton et al., 2011, p. 1).

concrete operations Piaget's stage of cognitive development occurring in middle childhood in which children's logical thinking abilities gradually improve as they begin to understand problems of greater complexity.

Scientific American Profile

Thinking Things Through

TABLE 8.1 Piaget's Concrete Operational Stage

Stage	Age	Characteristics
Concrete operational	About age 6 to 12	The breakthroughs at this age are all about logic. Children can now reason through problems and examine situations from differing perspectives, as long as the problem is not too abstract. They can put things into categories and order them. However, their thinking is still relatively concrete, and is more reliable when it is linked to what can be seen, heard, or touched.

middle childhood, as they work their way through understanding problems of greater complexity. The term *concrete operations* refers to children's ability to perform logical operations, or transformations, in their minds and apply them to concrete or real-life situations. In the concrete operational stage, children's thinking becomes more logical and flexible, enabling them to follow more complex rules and avoid the logical mistakes common in the *preoperational* period. Children in the concrete operational stage can look at problems from multiple perspectives (Piaget, 1971).

CONNECTIONS

Remember from Chapter 6 that early childhood is Piaget's period of preoperational thought in which children are able to think symbolically (and do make-believe) but struggle with logical operations.

The Logic of Concrete Operations With age, children begin to consider multiple aspects of a simple problem and are less susceptible to being tricked by appearances, as demonstrated by the conservation task described in Chapter 6. By age 8, most children are able to explain that there is no magic involved when you pour liquid from one container to another. Children in the concrete operational stage are more flexible thinkers; they can reverse events in their minds and shift their focus (Houdé et al., 2011). They are also able to activate networks in the brain that inhibit instinctive and emotional responses to produce more logical decisions. These breakthroughs occur because of brain maturation as well as practice answering questions and focusing in school (Inhelder & Piaget, 1964).

Children's developing flexible thinking allows them to apply categories more accurately and logically. They can now more reliably complete **classification** tasks, in which they must categorize objects and group them according to multiple dimensions (Inhelder & Piaget, 1964). (See **Figure 8.5.**) For instance, in one classic Piagetian task, children are presented with a row of flowers that includes eight roses and two daffodils and are asked: "Are there more roses or more flowers?" In order to correctly answer this question, they need to remember that roses and daffodils are flowers and that something can belong to more than one category at once. Being able to attend to multiple categories is a powerful cognitive tool that enables Logan to organize Lego bricks by color and by shape.

FIGURE 8.5 The Classification Task Are there more red beads or more wooden beads? In order to correctly answer this question, children must attend to multiple categories, like what color the beads are and what they are made of.

Children's ability to think about categories also allows them to organize objects in a series according to an abstract rule, which Piaget referred to as **seriation**. For instance, school-age children can order a group of rods in order of size or put a collection of blocks in rainbow order (Inhelder & Piaget, 1964).

Piaget believed that children's reasoning in middle childhood has major strengths, but that it was not fully mature. He pointed out that it was most accurate when applied to concrete objects. As children get older, they can apply their logical thinking skills to more abstract ideas, from geometric proofs and algebraic equations to ideas about war and peace.

classification The categorization and grouping of objects according to multiple dimensions.

seriation The ordering of objects in a series according to an abstract rule.

Lessons from Piaget Contemporary researchers agree that children's thinking changes dramatically between ages 5 and 7, but they have refined Piaget's observations. They point out that children tend to be unpredictable, and their development doesn't always move forward in a straight line.

Remember from Chapter 1 that there is an ongoing debate in developmental science about whether maturation is continuous or stagelike. Many researchers argue that children's development is based on specific improvements in discrete areas that add up over time, rather than on an overarching, global jump in skills (Siegler & Ellis, 1996). They may take a skills-based look at children's thinking, focusing on children's maturity in specific areas of thinking like executive function, memory, or spatial skills (Carey et al., 2015; Viarouge et al., 2019).

Piaget believed that children do not display concrete reasoning until between ages 6 and 8, but later researchers identified signs of logical thought much earlier. Children may even show signs of their reasoning ability before they are able to articulate it in words, for example, by showing with gestures that they know which one is "more" even if they are not verbalizing it (Goldin-Meadow, 2015). Nevertheless, Piaget's theory remains extremely popular with many educators. A skilled observer of children, Piaget was captivated by and respectful of children's creative thinking. His argument that it should be motivated by curiosity and not be hurried along continues to inspire (Flavell, 1996; Ponticorvo et al., 2020).

Hands-On Science These third-graders from Bridgeport, Connecticut, are collecting ocean data through Project Oceanology in New York's Long Island sound. They are taking samples to measure the ocean water's temperature and saltiness. When they are off the boat, they learn how to sort their findings and even display their data graphically according to multiple dimensions.

Vygotsky and the Sociocultural Approach to Children's Thinking

Whereas Piaget's ideas about children's thinking changed developmental science in the 1970s and 1980s, Lev Vygotsky's ideas revolutionized the science of education in the 1990s and early 2000s (Davydov, 1995; Gauvain, 2020).

Vygtosky and the sociocultural theorists inspired by his work established that children's cognitive skills build on their relationships and the cultural activities they do every day (Gauvain & Nicolaides, 2015; Rogoff, 2003; Vygotsky, 1962; Vygotsky & Cole, 1978). They argue that there is no universal "right way" of thinking (Greenfield, 1997). Instead, they recognize that children often develop different cognitive strengths because of the diversity in cultures and communities around the world (Qi & Roberts, 2019; Saxe & de Kirby, 2014). For instance, researchers found that children from Indigenous communities in Australia develop strong spatial reasoning skills from their daily activities that help them to solve arithmetic problems (Kearins, 1981). Similarly, children who buy and sell items, whether in a farmer's market or on the street, develop sophisticated understanding of ratios in order to compute their profit (Saxe, 1988).

Vygotsky argued that children's thinking is most apparent not in their results on standardized tests, but when they are working with another person in their ZPD (Gauvain & Perez, 2015; Vygotsky & Cole, 1978). Targeting learning at children's individual ZPD rather than generically teaching a group, classroom, or reading level helps children learn more quickly and effectively (Connor et al., 2013).

Vygotsky's impact on educational psychology and on classrooms around the world cannot be overstated (Davydov, 1995; Moll, 2013). How many times have you been encouraged to work in a group? Have you engaged in hands-on active learning? Have you ever had to verbalize your reasoning? Vygotsky is one of the theorists you have to thank for these educational innovations (Moll, 2013). His optimistic belief that "there is no right way to think," his argument that social interactions build thinking, and his advocacy for diversity and an end to inequity echo throughout current scholarship on how to improve school.

CONNECTIONS

Unlike Piaget, Vygotsky believed that children's thinking is shaped by social interactions (see Chapter 2). Piaget believed that children's thinking progresses through a sequence of stages, but Vygotsky believed children's development was continuous.

CONNECTIONS

Remember from Chapter 8 that the *zone of proximal development (ZPD)* refers to the range of children's capabilities that includes what children can do on their own and what they can do with help.

What You Do Every Day Changes Your Thinking. Selling eggs at this farmer's market in Santa Barbara might have a benefit beyond just dollars. Researchers have found that making change and figuring out how to earn a profit build cognitive skills that help with formal math.

CONNECTIONS

Remember that executive function refers to the ability to control attention and thinking in the short and long term through planning, focus, and memory.

Learning with Others Motivation for Ricky Rodriguez has meant playing Scrabble. Appreciating his love for words has enabled Ricky to build new relationships with other Scrabble players, like his friend Pat Griffith.

Improvements in Information Processing

When Logan meets with a group for a chess match, there are moments of laughter and other moments of quiet punctuated with the clicking of pieces. This level of effort would have been impossible a few years before, when they were distractible kindergartners. In middle childhood, children develop an impressive array of thinking skills that help them excel at chess and manage school's increasing demands. Remember from Chapter 6 that researchers who take an *information-processing perspective* look at the components of thinking, including executive function, memory, and the ability to think about and use these new cognitive strategies. These advances are supported by brain maturation and new environmental demands, such as school.

Executive Function Throughout middle childhood, children refine their executive function skills, which helps them to succeed in school (Zelazo & Carlson, 2020). Executive function is particularly important in the early grades, as children learn skills such as reading, writing, and basic math that serve as a base for their academic performance later in school (Ahmed et al., 2019). During the COVID-19 pandemic, executive function proved particularly crucial as many children were forced to take on more independent responsibility for their academic activities: managing their own Zoom work and learning to regulate their behavior in a new format (Lake & Olson, 2020).

As children grow, the components of executive function, like working memory, selective attention, inhibition, and planning, become easier to measure and evaluate (Zelazo & Carlson, 2020). Children's *working memory*, or the mental workspace that allows them to remember things in the short term, develops incrementally (Fiske & Holmboe, 2019). If children are tested to see how many numbers they can repeat back immediately, most will struggle to remember all 7 or 10 numbers in a typical phone number and will only be able to remember about 5 numbers, a few less than the typical adult (Dehn, 2011). Even if not fully developed, working memory allows children to learn to sound out words as they learn how to read, as well as remember which numbers they are carrying as they practice arithmetic (Diamond, 2013; Downes et al., 2017).

Children's *selective attention*, or their ability to control their focus, improves dramatically over middle childhood, but it is still not at adult levels (Turoman et al., 2021). Scientists estimate that children are asked to focus for long periods of time in school for about 17 minutes at a stretch, and most are not paying attention at least 25 percent of the time (Godwin et al., 2016, 2021). Young children are often easily distracted by visually enticing classroom displays, animations, or something happening in another window. Many children have difficulties focusing when there is a lot of background noise, whether a friend tapping their pen or a sibling doing Zoom in the other room (Fisher et al., 2014).

Working in school also requires controlling or inhibiting impulses. Sometimes this means switching from multiplication to addition on the same worksheet or not blurting out the first thing that comes to mind without raising your hand first. Researchers measure *inhibition* by giving children tasks that require them to repress their initial impulses, like saying "day" when shown a picture of a moon or "night" when shown a picture of the sun (De Haan, 2015). Practice and brain maturation help children inhibit their impulses throughout middle childhood.

Executive function helps children to remember to get on the correct bus after school and to do their homework (Moffett & Morrison, 2020). Planning for both short- and long-term goals becomes more important, as children take on more responsibility with their own learning and with tasks at home, like doing chores and even watching younger siblings. Planning builds on children's skills in memory, inhibition, and attention (Gauvain et al., 2018). Scientists test children's planning skills by asking them to solve puzzles, such as the pyramid puzzle (see **Figure 8.6**).

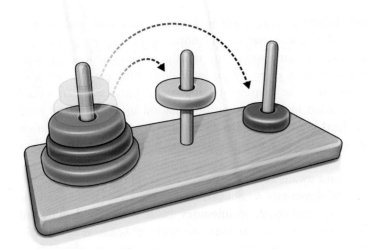

FIGURE 8.6 Pyramid Puzzle Can you solve this puzzle? The goal is to move the tower of discs from one tower to another by moving only one disc at a time and never placing a larger disc on a smaller one. In a three-disc game, you should be able to solve the puzzle in just seven moves.

Memory Young children are capable of amazing feats of memory. For instance, every year, hundreds of elementary school children participate in international Qur'an competitions held in major cities like Cairo, Egypt, and Doha, Qatar. All of them have memorized the entire *Qur'an*, the Muslim holy book, which takes more than 15 hours to recite. One young girl, Rifdah Rasheed, won third prize in the competition at age 10 after spending three years memorizing. She returned home to the Maldives with enough money to buy her family a new house. Ordinary children as well as elite memorizers, like those who participate in Qur'an competitions, spelling bees, and memory Olympiads, are capable of impressive recall (Black et al., 2020).

When children are reciting the Qur'an or solving 6 × 7, they use a specific form of explicit memory known as **semantic memory**, or the mental store for facts and information. When children tell their families about their field trip or remember how they felt when their dog died, they are using their *autobiographical memory*, or their memory about their own past. Both semantic and autobiographical memory mature during middle childhood and are essential for developing a sense of self and for learning about the world.

Children's new memory skills develop because of maturation of the *hippocampus*, the brain structure central to memory storage, and the PFC, which both mature slowly during childhood and adolescence. The leisurely pace of the development of the hippocampus means that, even in middle childhood, children are best at remembering the general overview of a situation or a concept and at looking for repeating patterns rather than focusing on the details (Keresztes et al., 2017).

Expert memorizers like Rifdah may appear to be born with a special talent, but actually, what makes Rifdah different from the rest of us is practice. It takes years of practice to learn to remember bits of information, particularly if it isn't personally meaningful (Stenson et al., 2019). Around the world, children acquire and remember semantic information, although their memory skills may differ depending on what their community values. Some communities, like Rifdah's, may value memorizing religious texts while others value memorizing the multiplication tables (Rogoff & Mistry, 1985).

Memorization skills are critical to school success, and focusing in school helps build memory skills (Blankenship et al., 2018; Peng & Kievit, 2020). Even in the era of being able to look everything up online, children who have strong understanding of math and reading facts are more successful in school. Learning information so well that it becomes *automatized*, or reflexively remembered, helps children tackle complex tasks more easily (Magallón et al., 2016).

Andrew H. Walker/Getty Images

Amazing Feats of Memory Rifdah Rasheed came in third in the International Qur'an Competition held in Cairo, Egypt, impressing the audience with her style and beautiful voice. She is from an island in the Maldives, in the Indian Ocean, where she had the support of her parents in memorizing and reciting the Qur'an.

semantic memory The mental store for facts and information.

Strategies to encode information into memory include rehearsal, elaboration, organization, and visualization. **Rehearsal** is a memorizing technique that involves repetition. This could mean repeating something multiple times out loud, in your head, or in front of someone else, or even just writing it down multiple times. Rifdah called another strategy she used the "sentimental approach," but researchers would call it **elaboration**. Elaboration involves adding information to the facts you need to remember so that the facts become more detailed and easier to recall. Elaboration builds on the fact that it is easier to remember things that you find meaningful or emotional.

Many children have some awareness of the process of keeping track of information by the time they are in elementary school (Simons et al., 2020). Researchers call the awareness of the process of remembering **metamemory** (Flavell, 1979). Children do not always have a strong sense of the accuracy of their memories (Fandakova et al., 2018). In school, children often overestimate how well they will remember something, from lines in a play to their spelling words (Karably & Zabrucky, 2009).

Improvements in memory help children develop a sense of their own personal history as their *autobiographical memory* improves (Fivush, 2019; Nelson, 2018). As children grow, it will become easier for them to remember and keep track of details about their lives (Bauer & Larkina, 2019). By the time children are about 7, their hippocampus, the brain structure involved in memory, has matured enough so that they are no longer subject to *childhood amnesia*, or the forgetting of childhood experiences (Riggins et al., 2020). Children begin to build memories that may stick with them for a lifetime, although children's memories, like adults', can still erode and become less reliable over time (Brubacher et al., 2019).

Around the world, children are sometimes the only witnesses in serious criminal cases, including war crimes and abuse, and prosecutors rely on them to deliver justice (Amani & Khalfaoui, 2019; Pantell et al., 2017). But are children's memories reliable? Like adults, children can be *suggestible*, or vulnerable to having their memories influenced (Ceci & Bruck, 1993). Some studies have shown that because children are respectful of adults and authority figures, they can be more suggestible than adults and more likely to form false memories (Otgaar et al., 2018). Unlike adults, children often do not know what is expected of them and do not necessarily have preconceived biases about what adults want to hear. As a result, they are *less* likely than adults to form spontaneous false memories and are more likely to accurately report their memories (Otgaar et al., 2018).

Thinking About Thinking When asked how he memorizes new chess strategies or spelling words, Logan has trouble explaining exactly how the magic happens. Talking about thinking can be a little awkward. But Logan knows when he is doing focused or creative work, and he pays attention to when he feels "brain tired" and needs a break (or a chess game to refresh his thinking). Developmental scientists call this **metacognition**, or awareness of how you are thinking and reflecting on it, which can maximize your learning and productivity (Bayard et al., 2021; Flavell, 1979).

Children do not usually learn how to think about thinking on their own. They benefit when teachers and other adults help scaffold and strategize with them about how to build awareness of their thinking (Simons et al., 2020). One metacognitive technique is just the awareness of how hard you are working. Children are often aware if they are expending what researchers call *cognitive effort*, or hard mental work, on a project (Chevalier, 2018).

Motivation plays a major role in whether children can regulate their own thinking. Metacognitive strategies often come more easily to children who are already doing well in school and who have had some success. Metacognition helps such children jump even further ahead of their peers (Connor, 2016).

rehearsal A memorization technique that involves repetition, either out loud, in your head, in front of someone else, or on paper.

elaboration Adding information to the facts you need to remember so that they become more detailed and easier to recall.

metamemory The awareness of the process of remembering.

metacognition Awareness of how you are thinking and reflecting on it.

The Quest to Measure Intelligence

What makes someone "smart"? For many, the idea of **intelligence** is often complicated by stereotypes and cultural expectations. When developmental scientists use the term "intelligence," they are referring to the ability to learn and apply what has been learned (Niu, 2020). However, how these abilities are measured depends on who is doing the measuring (Greenfield, 1998).

Understanding Differences Scholars and policy makers around the world have been trying to define who is smart for millennia, whether it was to pick priests in ancient Egypt or find capable civil servants in China (Higgins & Xiang, 2009; Van der Horst, 1987). In the United States and Europe, intelligence testing began in earnest in the 1800s as researchers tried to use science to predict who would be successful in school and at work (White, 2006).

French scientists created the first intelligence test that reliably recorded differences in children's cognitive capabilities. They wanted to identify which children needed help so they could be given extra support. The researchers believed that an objective test would eliminate biases from teachers, parents, and school administrators who might be motivated to exaggerate or minimize children's talents or difficulties (Siegler, 1992). The early test was adapted in 1916 at Stanford University in California and took the name *Stanford-Binet*. This test still exists today, although it has been adapted greatly over the years. The Stanford-Binet was followed by a U.S. test developed for children by David Wechsler in the 1940s. Weschler's test is now known as the *WISC*, or the *Wechsler Intelligence Scale for Children* (Weschler, 2014).

One feature of intelligence tests is that they provide scores on a standardized scale that is easy to understand. The scores on these tests are known as the **IQ**, or *intelligence quotient*. The "typical" or average range on the test is between 85 and 115, meaning that more than two in three people score in that range. Most people who take the test score in the "typical range" with relatively fewer in the extremes. People who fall in the extremely high end of the spectrum are said to have exceptional abilities, while those in the lower end are likely to have *intellectual disabilities*. If you plot these scores graphically, you will see that they fall into a bell shape (see **Figure 8.7**). This type of statistical distribution, with most people falling into the middle and with relatively fewer at the extremes, is often called a *bell curve.*

Early intelligence tests designed to identify children with learning disabilities were soon put to a more sinister purpose (Stough, 2015). Many early scientists used

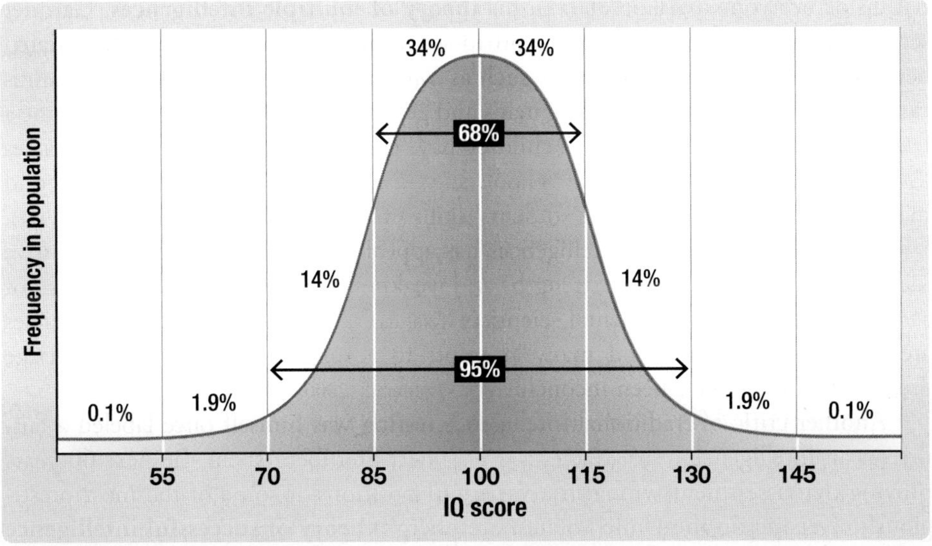

intelligence The ability to learn and apply what has been learned.

IQ A person's score on a standardized intelligence test which, for most people, is between 85 and 115.

FIGURE 8.7 The Range of Intelligence
This is a graphical depiction, known as a *bell curve*, of how people score on intelligence tests. Most people score in the average range, or in the big hump in the middle of the bell. Fewer fall in the extremely high or low ends of the spectrum. People who fall at the extremely low end of the distribution are likely to have an intellectual disability. Those at the extremely high end of the distribution may benefit from specialized education.

intelligence tests to promote the idea that some people are inherently superior to others—an incorrect belief that informed *eugenics*, which was a popular social movement in many parts of the world (Bashford & Levine, 2010). Eugenicists thought that they could improve society by preventing those they deemed less intelligent from having children or getting an education. By lavishing resources on those they thought were capable, eugenicists believed they could increase the overall "intelligence" of the population (Galton, 1883; Stoskopf, 2012; Terman, 1916).

Many early intelligence tests were biased: Elite and educated people often scored high, but less educated, lower-income people often received lower scores. Intelligence testing was used to discriminate against people by keeping them out of school, sterilizing them, and even institutionalizing them (Reddy, 2007; Terman, 1916). After the horrors of racial and ethnic hatred during World War II, support for eugenics decreased in the scientific community in the United States, although discrimination and stigma still persist. Intelligence tests have been revised to reduce bias (Black, 2012; Stern, 2015; Wechsler, 2014).

Group differences remain in intelligence test scores. Typically, children whose parents are more educated and have higher income score higher on the tests (Kaufman et al., 2015). Traditional intelligence tests are not the most reliable predictor of academic success; children's ability to control themselves and their motivation is more influential (Braaten & Norman, 2006). Intelligence tests, however, are a helpful way to screen children for learning disabilities, brain injuries, and exceptional abilities (Giofrè et al., 2017). They must be administered in a child's first language by a professional who understands the child's background and culture (Chen & Lindo, 2018).

Test results around the world have revealed that as communities become healthier and more affluent, and as more children attend school for longer periods of time, the general population tends to score higher on intelligence tests (Bratsberg & Rogeberg, 2018). This trend for population's average IQ test scores to rise over time is termed the *Flynn effect*, after the researcher from New Zealand who first documented it (Flynn, 2020).

Other Models of Intelligence Traditional intelligence assessments have many critics. Many argue that they do not predict success in the way some of their adherents promised (Sternberg, 2021). Others believe that that the tests measure the wrong kind of intelligence, that being smart is a broader set of talents than traditional tests measure (Gardner, 2011; Sternberg, 2021).

Howard Gardner, a neuroscientist who loves the arts and plays the piano, was one such critic. He never felt that traditional IQ tests recognized the bigger potential inside everyone (Gardner, 2011). In his **theory of multiple intelligences**, Gardner set out his idea that intelligence is a broad set of discrete abilities. He differentiated between different types of thinking, such as *linguistic skills* (language and communicating), *spatial skills* (understanding maps and geometry), and *musical skills*, to name a few. Gardner has suggested that all children have components of all these intelligences (Gardner, 1999). He has argued that schools should nurture and build abilities beyond math and verbal skills and assess students' skills in less traditional ways (Gardner, 2011).

The theory of multiple intelligences has appeal because it validates the intuitive idea that we all have different strengths and weaknesses. This theory, however, is not as popular among developmental scientists (Kaufman et al., 2015). Multiple intelligences are difficult to evaluate, and many attempts to accurately identify them in large groups of children have been inconclusive (Visser et al., 2006).

Another critic of traditional intelligence testing was himself once labeled a failure on an intelligence test (Sternberg, 2015). Robert Sternberg spent the next 60 years proving that assessment wrong in a variety of positions at some of the most prestigious universities in the United States. Sternberg's **theory of successful intelligence**

theory of multiple intelligences Gardner's idea that intelligence is a broad set of discrete abilities and that all children have components of all these intelligences.

theory of successful intelligence Sternberg's idea that intelligence can best be measured by how you create a successful life through three types of intelligence.

(formerly known as the *triarchic theory of intelligence*) argues that intelligence can best be measured by how you create a successful life through three types of intelligence (Sternberg, 1985, 2018a). *Analytic intelligence* involves thinking abstractly and solving problems. *Creative intelligence* involves the generation of new ideas. *Practical intelligence* involves applying ideas to real life, or common sense (Sternberg, 1997, 2018b). In addition to these components, Sternberg has suggested that people who are high in successful intelligence also have wisdom, moral understanding, and the ability to change (Sternberg, 2015, 2021).

Myths About Intelligence   Despite the value of measuring intelligence, particularly for children with learning disabilities or brain injuries, myths abound. Let's look critically at some of these myths:

- *Is intelligence your destiny?* Many studies support the idea that children who perform well on intelligence tests are more successful later in life. They do better in school, are more likely to be promoted at work, and live longer (Halpern-Manners et al., 2020). However, scholars caution that this may be a *correlation*, not an indication of a causal relationship between testing well and doing well. Intelligence test scores are not the best or only predictor of success. According to developmental scientists, other factors may better predict lifetime achievement: physical and mental health, strong relationship skills and attachment, metacognition, personality, and cognitive traits such as self-control and conscientiousness (Dixson et al., 2016; Ohtani & Hisasaka, 2018).
- *Is intelligence fixed for life?* Scores on intelligence tests are more changeable early in life, but change is possible across the lifespan. (IQ scores can be affected by prenatal and early life factors, such as the health of the pregnant parent, stress, early education, and nutrition [Nisbett et al., 2012; Protzko, 2017].) During middle childhood, good health, a balanced diet, training in executive function, and playing a musical instrument have all been identified as ways to boost intelligence test scores (Protzko, 2017). Educational interventions are also effective for children with low IQ scores (Colbert et al., 2018).
- *Is intelligence only genetic?* Some developmental scientists argue that genetics plays an important role in how we think (Plomin & von Stumm, 2018), but no single gene or group of genes has been identified as responsible for intelligence test scores (Kong et al., 2018). Scientists believe that some aspects of cognitive function are influenced by genes, but the relationship is complex, epigenetic, and highly influenced by the environment (Kong et al., 2018). For instance, in some studies children's intelligence test scores are more closely tied to those of their adopted families than their biological ones, indicating the importance of environment to cognitive development (Nisbett et al., 2012).

APPLY IT!   **8.5** Logan told us that he has several strategies for remembering, like writing down his spelling words and reciting his multiplication tables. How might his use of these strategies help him in school?

8.6 Logan says he learns best when he can focus on what he is interested in with other people at hand to coach him. How does this idea support Vygotsky's view of how children learn?

Language Development

During middle childhood, children's use of language continues to expand, sometimes dramatically, and they develop the more complex ways of communicating that they will use at school. Children's vocabulary and grammar become more advanced. For most children around the world, this means using more than one language both at school and at home. Language acquisition—of one or many—is a skill that will help children succeed at school and in their relationships (Lee, 2010; Westrupp et al., 2020).

Learning Objective

8.5   Explain how language advances support children's learning.

pragmatics Knowing how to talk with other people including, what is appropriate to talk about, and how to interpret tone of voice, gestures, and other cues.

Reading with Family Although reading aloud may seem like something children outgrow, like footed pajamas, shared reading continues to help children build vocabulary and abstract thinking skills even after they have started school.

 Learn It Together

Supporting English Learners in School

Your neighborhood elementary school is interested in learning more about the best practices for supporting their students whose home language is not English. They have asked your class for some expert advice.

Prepare: Review information about language development, bilingual development, and learning in elementary school. What are some of the strengths and challenges for students whose home language doesn't match the majority language at school?

Engage: Have a conversation with a few of your classmates about personal experiences with learning English. Did everyone in your group learn English at home? If not, when did you begin to learn English, and what was your schooling experience like? Apply the information from the textbook to identify the key messages you would want to communicate to the elementary school principal.

Reflect: As you thought about the best, science-based approaches to support English Learners in elementary school, did you think of any barriers? What might make it difficult for schools to follow your recommendations, and how could you address them?

More Words

Children's vocabularies increase as they enter school. These new words are linked to school success, allowing children to communicate and write with more precision and accuracy. Some children learn 3,000 new words every year, and others pick up nearly 5,000 (Anderson & Nagy, 1993). Scholars believe that some schools and teachers are more effective at teaching vocabulary—a challenging undertaking—than others (Marulis & Neuman, 2010). It is often a lower priority than phonics and math skills (Snow & Matthews, 2016). Some promising interventions come from play-oriented classrooms that build vocabulary through acting out stories (Flint, 2020).

Individual differences also affect the speed at which children's vocabularies grow. Children with larger vocabularies learn more words more quickly than those with smaller vocabularies, and these differences increase as children begin to read (Stanley et al., 2018; Suggate et al., 2018). As children progress through elementary school, one of the biggest predictors of the size of their vocabulary is how much they read, especially printed books (Sullivan & Brown, 2015; Torppa et al., 2020). Environmental factors such as family stress and the parents' educational achievement continue to influence children's language development (Song et al., 2015).

Using Language to Communicate

Children use language not only to ace tests or write book reports, but also to gossip, taunt each other, and make each other laugh. In addition to using his vocabulary to plan chess moves and write poetry, Logan uses language to socialize. Scholars call this ability to shift language styles **pragmatics**, which involves knowing how to talk with other people, what is appropriate to talk about, and how to interpret tone of voice, gestures, and other cues to keep a conversation going (Toe et al., 2020).

As children get older, there are greater demands for them to use language appropriately as they make friends and develop relationships with adults outside their families (Fujiki & Brinton, 2017). Younger children may have just grasped the difference between indoor voices and outdoor voices, but older children must understand when to change the subject when talking to a friend about a sensitive subject (Locke & Bogin, 2006).

Culture profoundly influences the pragmatics of language (DeCapua & Wintergerst, 2016). Children who act as *language brokers*, or informal translators, for their families or friends, often develop sophisticated and detailed understanding of social pragmatics, which benefits them into adulthood (Garcia-Sanchez, 2018; Guan et al., 2014). Logan adjusts his pragmatics as he interacts with adults, speaking much more casually with his brother than he does with his teachers and parents. In many languages, children even use a formal pronoun, like *usted* in Spanish, to respectfully address their elders.

Acquiring Multiple Languages

In the United States, about one in six elementary school children is an *English learner (EL)*, the term most schools use to refer to someone who is learning English in addition to another language or languages. Remember from Chapter 6 that speaking more than one language has cognitive benefits, such as improved executive function, and substantial economic benefits, including higher income and greater employability in adulthood (Bialystock & Barac, 2012; Gándara, 2018).

As a group, ELs bring important strengths to their school experience: They are typically emotionally well-adjusted and more socially competent than their peers (Gándara, 2017). Nevertheless, they often score poorly on achievement tests and have other academic difficulties (Takanishi & Le Menestrel, 2017). One reason is that many ELs are from low-income families who must navigate a U.S. education system that gives lackluster support to new immigrants (Ansari & Crosnoe, 2018; Sorensen Duncan & Paradis, 2020). Another reason is that they are learning core academic subjects in a language that they do not yet understand (Barrow & Markman-Pithers, 2016; Collier & Thomas, 2017; MacSwan et al., 2017). Finally, ELs are more likely to attend under-resourced schools and less likely to feel accepted by their school community (Bialystock, 2018; Echevarria et al., 2015).

Policy makers, parents, and educators often disagree about how best to help ELs succeed. Developmental scientists studying the outcomes of thousands of children have found repeatedly that those who enter school without strong English skills benefit from being taught core academic subjects in their home languages, while also learning English (MacSwan et al., 2017; Committee on Fostering School Success 2017). They suggest that learning core skills is nearly impossible if children do not understand the language of instruction. In addition, when schools support children's home language, children benefit from being dual- or multiple-language speakers, including improved executive function, strong self-esteem, and a sense of connection with their families and cultural identity. In fact, children who remain connected to their heritage and their home language may be protected from some risks, such as leaving school early (López et al., 2021).

APPLY IT! **8.7** Logan speaks differently depending on whether he is hanging out with his family or responding to a teacher online. Why is learning pragmatics important in middle childhood?

8.8 What are benefits of speaking a second (or third) language in middle childhood?

Learning In and Out of School

Prior to the pandemic, more children were attending school around the world than ever before, with higher literacy levels than at any other time in history (UNICEF, 2021). The COVID-19 pandemic changed education everywhere and exacerbated educational inequalities: Many children still do not have basic internet access (UNESCO, 2020; Yorke et al., 2021). Developmental scientists hope that, in the long term, children will recover from the educational changes of the pandemic. In fact, educators are hopeful that the pandemic allowed schools to "reset" and emerge with new commitment to help children develop the skills they need to participate in a modern, knowledge-based, global economy (Darling-Hammond & Hyler, 2020).

Variations in Schools

Around the world, school not only improves children's lives, it also saves them. Particularly in low-income countries, going to school means children have access to health care and nutrition, saving more than 7 million lives in recent years (Pradhan et al., 2017).

Learning Objective

8.6 Explain how schools influence achievement during middle childhood.

Learning at Home Ayinde (*right*) was being homeschooled in Washington, D.C., long before Zoom became a household word. Other children around the world, like 6-year-old Kaya in Sydney, Australia (*left*), had to start homeschooling in the middle of a global pandemic. Learning at home, as so many families have learned, takes flexibility and dedication.

Most young people attend school, but what school looks like and how children learn differ around the world. In some countries, like Ireland, children may attend elementary schools run by religious institutions. In others, like Chile, most children attend private schools. In Finland, all children follow a rigorous, standardized curriculum, and the vast majority attends public schools (García et al., 2021). The United States has a strong tradition of local control over schools and respect for parental choice in making educational decisions. As a result, U.S. schools vary dramatically depending on the community (Thompson & Thompson, 2018). Although inequality in schools is common in low-income countries, the United States stands out among affluent countries for its level of inequity (Chzhen et al., 2018).

Where U.S. children go to school is usually determined by where families live (Owens, 2018; see **Figure 8.8**). This results in schools that are vastly different. Children in high-poverty neighborhoods are more likely to have crowded classrooms and enjoy fewer after-school programs than those in more affluent neighborhoods (Jang & Reardon, 2019). The wealthiest districts in the United States, most of them suburban and mostly White, spend nearly three times as much per student as those in the poorest districts (Kelly, 2020). However, these statistics do not tell the entire story. Schools are made up of people, and many teachers have an impact beyond what funding levels might predict.

Variations in Achievement

One measure that researchers use to compare schools around the world and within the United States is *achievement test scores.* Unlike intelligence tests, which are designed to measure how children think, achievement tests are standardized tests that measure what children have learned, including reading comprehension and math and science skills. The United States often ranks in the lower tier of affluent countries on these assessments, which many researchers blame on high rates of poverty (Yu & Cantor, 2016). However, prior to the COVID-19 pandemic, the achievement gap between high- and low-income U.S. students had been closing because of new investments in early education (Hanushek et al., 2019).

In countries with long histories of discrimination like the United States, children from marginalized communities often fall behind in school because of unequal access to resources (Meek et al., 2020). Many U.S. children live in neighborhoods that are

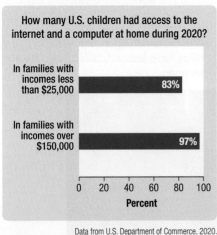

INEQUITABLE ACCESS

How many U.S. children had access to the internet and a computer at home during 2020?

In families with incomes less than $25,000: 83%

In families with incomes over $150,000: 97%

Percent

Data from U.S. Department of Commerce, 2020.

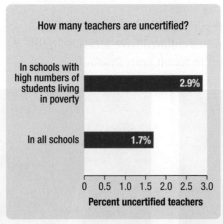

INEQUITY IN TEACHER PREPARATION

How many teachers are uncertified?

In schools with high numbers of students living in poverty: 2.9%

In all schools: 1.7%

Percent uncertified teachers

Data from U.S. Department of Education, 2016.

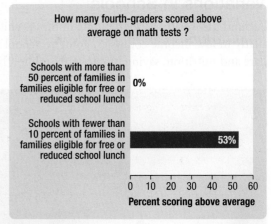

INEQUITY IN LEARNING OUTCOMES

How many fourth-graders scored above average on math tests ?

Schools with more than 50 percent of families in families eligible for free or reduced school lunch: 0%

Schools with fewer than 10 percent of families in families eligible for free or reduced school lunch: 53%

Percent scoring above average

Data from TIMSS, 2019.

FIGURE 8.8 Inequity in Education in the United States In the United States, schools are managed locally, which often means low-income neighborhoods cannot offer the access to resources like computers, internet access, or highly qualified teachers that more affluent neighborhoods can. The inequities are often linked to learning outcomes: students who attend more highly resourced schools are more likely to score above average on tests.

segregated by race or ethnicity. Since funding for schools is highly localized, children of color, whose families are typically less affluent, are more likely than White children to attend schools in districts with lower levels of funding for books, teacher salaries, and art supplies (Reardon et al., 2019).

Additionally, children from marginalized groups are often stigmatized and discriminated against by their peers and even their teachers (Gillen-O'Neel et al., 2011; Johnston-Goodstar & VeLure Roholt, 2017; Priest et al., 2014). This increases anxiety, saps motivation, and makes it harder to learn (Killen, 2019; Verkuyten et al., 2019). In the United States, immigrant children as well as Black, Native American, and Latino children often feel disconnected from their schools and may not consider themselves high achievers. A sense of belonging can be strongly protective, leading to higher achievement (DeNicolo et al., 2017; Gillen-O'Neel & Fuligni, 2013). Ethnic pride is also protective, increasing self-esteem and, in turn, academic performance (Hernández et al., 2017; Rivas-Drake et al., 2014).

Strategy, Creativity, Achievement Chess uses many of children's cognitive skills. Here James is just relaxing with a game of chess in the park near his home in Brooklyn, New York, but at school, he led his team to the win the national Junior High School Chess championships.

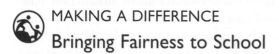 MAKING A DIFFERENCE
Bringing Fairness to School

All children have moments when they misbehave in school. Sometimes sitting in your seat, staying in line on the way to lunch, or being quiet during snack is difficult. But sometimes misbehavior is more serious, as when children skip school, get in a playground fight, or lash out at an adult.

For some, the punishment for acting out is being handcuffed, confined in a locked box, paddled, or even sent to jail overnight. For one 11-year-old, kicking a trash can in the school lunchroom in Virginia led to juvenile court (Ferriss, 2015). For more than 150,000 children in the United States, getting in trouble has led to physical punishment, such as being spanked or hit by their teachers (Gershoff et al., 2019). About one in three children faces high-stakes discipline, like expulsion, suspension, or in-school detention, during the course of their school career (Rosenbaum, 2020).

Children who are suspended in their first few years of school are likely be suspended again, initiating an escalating pattern of challenges that some call the *school-to-prison pipeline* (Gilliam, 2016; Rosenbaum, 2020; Yang et al., 2018). This type of harsh discipline falls disproportionately on children with disabilities and children from Black, Native American, and Latino backgrounds. Children from these groups are disciplined two to three times more often than their peers (Ahranjani, 2020; Gershoff & Font, 2016; Mallett, 2016; Welsh & Little, 2018; Whitaker & Losen, 2019).

Why are such children at risk? Experimental and correlational research has found that educators often stereotype children's behavior. For instance, teachers are more likely to recommend discipline for Black boys who act up than for White boys who act up (Okonofua & Eberhardt, 2015; Okonofua et al., 2016). And because Black boys and girls are often perceived to be older than their classmates, they are perceived as more threatening if they misbehave and are often held to higher standards (Epstein et al., 2017; Goff et al., 2014). Children with behavioral disabilities like ADHD are often thought to be intentionally disruptive, sometimes triggering harsh responses from teachers eager to keep classrooms calm (Miller & Meyers, 2015; Ramey, 2015). However, no child benefits from harsh discipline.

The solution? First, educators and families must learn about various disabilities and conditions, acknowledge their own biases, and have more empathy for their students (Gregory & Fergus, 2017; Meek et al., 2020). Second, families and educators can reduce factors that lead to disciplinary problems by boosting the children's social and emotional regulation and making sure they have access to mental health resources, particularly those designed to treat trauma (Dutil, 2020). Restorative, relationship-based interventions help teachers, children, and communities get along better and keep schools safer for everyone (Ahranjani, 2020; Darling-Hammond et al., 2020). 🌐

literacy Reading and writing skills.

numeracy The ability to manipulate numbers and do arithmetic.

phonics-based instruction Instruction that builds children's reading skills by reinforcing the links between letters and their sounds.

whole-language approach Instruction that is based on the idea that children will learn how to read more effectively in an environment that weaves literacy into everything they do.

Scientific American Profile

Advancing Language Skills

Reading Is Her Superpower. In Georgia, Cicely Lewis, a school librarian, builds children's motivation to read through her program "Read Woke."

Skills for School

Unlike walking and talking, learning to read and write are not skills that children naturally develop without being taught. Scholars call reading and writing skills **literacy** and the ability to manipulate numbers and do arithmetic **numeracy**. Building literacy and numeracy takes lots of practice and leads to brain development as the skills are acquired (Bathelt et al., 2018; Hyde, 2021).

Building Literacy Learning to read builds on children's existing language skills but also requires new ones. Children need to build their *phonemic awareness*, the ability to identify the sounds in words. Then they need practice sounding out words and to understand what they are reading in order to build their reading comprehension (Christopher et al., 2015). Learning how to read builds new neural connections between brain areas that relate to processing visual information and language (Chyl et al., 2021).

The best practices for teaching children to read can be a controversial research area with passionate advocates on both sides. **Phonics-based instruction** builds reading skills by reinforcing the links between letters and their sounds. Phonics-based instruction is designed to build phonemic awareness and is considered by researchers to be the most effective way to teach early reading (Castles et al., 2018). However, some teachers worry that phonics takes the joy out of reading and saps students' motivation with its focus on repetition and memorization and, as a result, are often unprepared to teach phonics (Drake & Walsh, 2020). In addition, applying science to the classroom is often complex in practice (Seidenberg et al., 2020; Shanahan, 2020).

Much reading instruction in the United States relies on the **whole-language approach**, which is based on the idea that children will learn how to read naturally in an environment that weaves literacy into everything they do (Gunderson, 2013; Krashen, 1999). In a whole-language classroom, books and written words are visible everywhere, and children are encouraged to tell stories and practice "writing" even before they learn all the rules of print and spelling. Despite the popularity of the whole-language approach, researchers believe that more phonics instruction would reduce the number of children who struggle with reading by two-thirds (Putnam & Walsh, 2021).

However, whole-language approaches can build students' love of reading, which may be more important now than in the past. Elementary schoolchildren around the world are reading less than they did in previous generations (Parsons et al., 2018). Many are less motivated to read, and when they do read, they choose less-challenging books. What can reverse this trend? Allowing children to choose their own books and develop their own interests, perhaps with the help of an expert school librarian (Wigfield et al., 2016).

Building Numeracy Most Americans understand the importance of teaching children to read well, but a surprising number believe that math is no longer necessary (Budd, 2015). However, even in an era of smartphones with built-in calculators, numeracy is essential to help children and adults think critically about the numbers that surround them. At a higher level, mathematical knowledge is important for building a career in the sciences, for evaluating evidence, and even for everyday life skills. How much math children know in second grade is a good predictor of how successful they will be at work 30 years later, regardless of their affluence, reading scores, or IQ (Ritchie & Bates, 2013; Zacharopoulos et al., 2021).

The goal of most elementary school teachers is to build a sense of numbers and their magnitude, place value, and basic arithmetic functions, such as addition and subtraction (Aunio & Räsänen, 2016). Many children struggle with early skills like counting and understanding the relative size of numbers: for example, whether 571 is bigger than 517 (Clark et al., 2013).

As children build their math skills, they use strategies for solving and understanding math problems such as counting with their bodies, which makes computation easier by reducing the demands on working memory (Friso-van den Bos et al., 2018; Siegler & Braithwaite, 2017). Most children use their fingers to keep track of numbers until at least age 8 (de Chambrier & Zesiger, 2018). As children become more experienced with numbers, basic skills become automated, and they rely less on their bodies (Butterworth & Varma, 2013).

Improving Learning in School

From Coach Tom's chess tutoring to project-based learning, there are thousands of ideas for improving student learning in schools. Interventions based on developmental science apply theories of development to classroom practices.

Relationships matter. The responsive relationships that children cultivate in early-education programs help them in elementary school. However, once children enter elementary school, many teachers focus more on learning than on building connections (Rucinski et al., 2018). When students and teachers get to know each other, children develop a stronger sense of belonging in school, which can lead to higher test scores (Walton & Brady, 2020; Wang et al., 2020). This can be particularly important for students of color, who may not feel connected and understood in a classroom with White teachers (Gehlbach et al., 2016; Gray et al., 2018).

Building a growth mindset. Researchers refer to children's beliefs about learning as their *mindsets*. They distinguish between students with a *growth mindset*, who believe that their abilities can change over time, and those with a *fixed mindset*, who believe that talents and intelligence are set and cannot be changed. Scientists have shown that it is possible to change children's mindsets so that they understand that working hard is essential to learning (Dweck & Yeager, 2019; Paunesku et al., 2015).

Building motivation. What makes Logan stay focused on his chess game for hours? Some developmental scientists would call it *motivation*. As children move through elementary school, their motivation and excitement about school typically diminishes (Scherrer & Preckel, 2019; Wigfield et al., 2015). School becomes "boring" and "irrelevant" at the same time it often becomes harder. Harnessing students' intrinsic motivation can start with encouraging them to work on things they are interested in, thereby respecting their growing independence and need for autonomy over their learning (Guthrie et al., 2006).

Other scholars study how motivation is sparked by a sense of **self-efficacy**, or the belief in one's own ability to make a change or have an impact (Bandura, 1999, 2019). Students with a stronger sense of self-efficacy use self-regulation to focus harder, plan out their work, and increase awareness of what they need to do. Building self-efficacy can come from repeated small successes and from working collaboratively with peers (Høigaard et al., 2015; Schunk & DiBenedetto, 2016).

Some researchers have suggested that a key factor in school success is self-control, or a closely related concept called *grit* (Duckworth & Gross, 2014; Mischel, 2014). **Grit** refers to the ability to persevere in order to achieve a long term-goal. Impulse control, like putting off watching a movie to study for a science test or turning off your phone to read a book, is often part of becoming successful.

However, critics caution that children need more than characteristics of self-efficacy, motivation, and grit to succeed (Generett & Olson, 2020; Gorski, 2016; Schreiner, 2017). As you will learn, this is particularly true for children with learning differences who especially benefit from expert support.

Fingers Help. Counting on your fingers can make things easier as children learn math.

self-efficacy The belief in one's ability to make a change or have an impact.

grit The ability to persevere in order to achieve a long-term goal.

CONNECTIONS

Remember from Chapter 6 that there are two types of motivation. *Intrinsic motivation* is the joy you get from learning about something you care about or that is meaningful to you. *Extrinsic motivation* is when you are working to earn a reward, such as a paycheck or a grade.

Project-Based Learning Can Boost Students' Motivation These children in Michigan worked with their second-grade teacher to investigate safety problems at a local park. Here they work on the poster they presented to a local city councilperson. The children learned an important civics lesson and helped improve their community; their motivation was credited with helping them do better on achievement tests (Barshay, 2018).

specific learning disabilities Difficulties with language development, reading, or arithmetic that lead to problems functioning in school or at home.

intellectual disabilities Difficulties with academics, practical skills, or social relationships.

Love Has No Label. Bonnie has intellectual disabilities and her daughter, Myra, is in gifted education. Myra says that her mom is a "good parent and just because [she is] disabled doesn't mean [she does] anything less for me."

Reaching All Learners

In any classroom, some children may struggle while learning comes easily to others. Myra Brown is one of those children for whom things came easily: She has been in gifted-and-talented classes since elementary school (Simon, 2013). But she knows firsthand that not everyone has this experience. Her mother, Bonnie, who has an intellectual disability, raised Myra as a single parent. Like Myra and Bonnie, there are many children in classrooms around the world who learn differently.

Learning Disabilities Experts believe that about one in eight children have *learning disabilities,* including difficulty with language development, ADHD, or **specific learning disabilities,** which include ongoing difficulty with reading, writing, or math (Danielson et al., 2018; Schaeffer, 2021; US Department of Education, 2020). Two common learning disabilities are *dyslexia,* an impaired abillity to connect speech sounds to written words, leading to difficulties reading and spelling, and *dyscalculia,* an impaired ability to understand and manipulate numbers. About 2 in 100 students experience broad challenges with learning that interfere with their everyday functioning (McKenzie et al., 2019). These children may have an **intellectual disability,** which means they not only have difficulty with academics but also with practical skills and social relationships (Tasse, 2016). Children with an intellectual disability or a specific learning disability may also be diagnosed with traumatic brain injury, autism spectrum disorder (ASD), ADHD, or a genetic condition such as fragile X or Down syndrome.

About five percent of students in the United States have been diagnosed with a specific learning disability, but some scholars suggest that the number should be much higher. Many children who have academic difficulties may never have been screened or diagnosed, preventing them from getting the extra help they need (Morgan et al., 2017, 2021). Children from low-income families who attend stressed and under-resourced schools are particularly likely to miss out on early-intervention services that address learning difficulties.

FIGURE 8.9 Types and Prevalence of Learning Differences in the United States About one in eight students has been diagnosed with some type of learning difference, from autism spectrum disorder (ASD) to visual impairment. Researchers suggest that the number who are diagnosed with a specific learning disability, like dyslexia or dyscalculia, is actually too low: More students could benefit from extra support to build their reading, writing, and math skills.

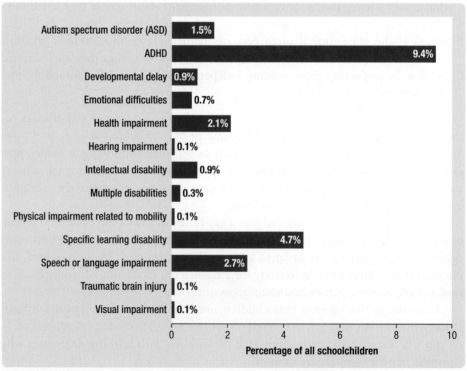

Data from U.S. Department of Education, 2020; Danielson et al., 2018.

Gifted Education Myra Brown is funny, loves cupcakes, and hopes to be a marine biologist when she grows up (Fleming, 2009). She is in gifted education because reading and math come easily to her, and her teachers felt she needed to be challenged. She flew through the material she was learning in class: She loved books and being creative.

Gifted education is an academic program for children who may need advanced or specialized education in order to meet their potential. Educators now prefer to refer to "gifted education" rather than "gifted children," focusing on the quality of education being provided rather than on a fixed description of children with special characteristics (Lo & Porath, 2017).

Historically, there has been a profoundly unequal distribution of children in gifted-and-talented programs in public schools (Peters et al., 2019). In the United States, gifted-and-talented slots at public schools are more likely to go to affluent White children than those from Black, Native American, or Latino backgrounds, like Myra (Peters, 2021).

One reason for this may be bias in the identification of children who would benefit from gifted programs. Most nominations for gifted programs come from teachers, and these teacher reports have been found to be susceptible to stereotypes. For instance, White teachers are likely to underestimate the talents of their Black students: Black children were four times less likely to be recommended for gifted education if their teacher was White than if their teacher was Black (Grissom & Redding, 2016).

As children grow, whether they are in gifted education or in the typical track, their advances in thinking, learning, and communicating also create opportunities for more complex emotions and relationships.

APPLY IT! **8.9** Logan has thrived in virtual school, which has given him the freedom to pursue his own interests. How has this contributed to his motivation?
8.10 A friend of Logan's is being evaluated for learning disabilities. How would you explain the value of identifying learning differences?

gifted education An academic program for children who may need enriched or specialized education in order to meet their potential.

Extra-Curiosity Education Gifted education provides extra support and stimulation—and sometimes more hands-on experimentation. These children in Montgomery County, Maryland, are receiving extra excitement and enrichment in science.

Wrapping It Up

LO 8.1 Describe variations in the pace of growth and motor development and maturation in the brain during middle childhood. (p. 225)

During middle childhood, children typically gain about 40 pounds (25 kilograms) and about a foot (35 centimeters). The hormonal changes of adrenarche trigger a growth spurt at about age 10 for girls and age 12 for boys. Children have a tremendous amount of energy for motor skill development, but which motor skills they learn depends on cultural and community values. Learning motor skills, particularly fine motor skills, can help children feel competent and adjust to the demands of school. During middle childhood, the cortex continues to mature, building more fast, myelinated connections and gradually pruning underused gray matter. Increasing connectivity between the subcortical region and the cortex help children develop emotion regulation. Children's experiences help shape how their brain matures.

LO 8.2 Identify common health challenges and protective habits in middle childhood. (p. 230)

Most children in affluent countries are healthy during middle childhood, but some have chronic conditions such as asthma or hypertension. Environmental pollution can trigger poor health. Rising rates of diabetes and hypertension may be linked to weight and weight-related stress. Getting enough sleep helps children stay healthy and learn. A healthy diet can help children grow: School lunch programs are one of the best ways of preventing malnutrition around the globe. Moving is one of the best ways to build resilience: Physical activity stimulates brain growth and builds stronger bones and muscles. For children, being active often comes through physical play. Many children are not able to stay active.

LO 8.3 Explain the key features of Piaget's concrete operational stage and why Vygotsky believed that learning comes from social interaction. (p. 236)

In middle childhood, children's thinking is flexible and curious. Piaget described this stage as concrete operations: Children can work through a problem logically and even reverse an action in their head. During this stage, children can pass typical conservation tasks and look at problems from multiple perspectives. They can perform tasks that require seriation or classification. Vygotsky observed that children learn in a rich cultural context: They learn what is valued in their communities, and how they learn and think is also influenced by where they live. Learning is best when it happens in your individual zone of proximal development and is scaffolded by a sensitive social partner.

LO 8.4 Describe the typical cognitive improvements during middle childhood. (p. 236)

Maturation involves dramatic improvements in children's executive function. Children's selective attention and memory also improve. Maturation in the brain, particularly in the hippocampus, helps make this possible, but so does practice. Metacognitive techniques enable students to manage their own learning. Intelligence testing is a way of comparing children's cognitive functioning, which may help identify children with learning or intellectual disabilities.

LO 8.5 Explain how advances in language help support children's learning. (p. 245)

Children's vocabulary, grammar, and pragmatics improve, allowing them to interact appropriately in a variety of contexts.

Children who are learning more than one language have a number of strengths, but many attend under-resourced schools and may have academic difficulties.

LO 8.6 Explain how schools influence achievement during middle childhood. (p. 247)

Children's achievement depends on where they go to school. Schools vary around the world, and children do not have equitable access to education. In the United States, schools are often segregated by family income: Higher-income neighborhoods have more highly resourced schools. Some children face discrimination from teachers and peers, making it more difficult to learn. Learning to read, write, and do math takes time and practice. Learning often benefits from strong relationships, growth mindset, grit, a sense of self-efficacy, and motivation. About one in eight students has learning difficulties that benefit from intervention. Some students have access to gifted education, which is designed to motivate capable students.

KEY TERMS

middle childhood (p. 225)
adrenarche (p. 229)
secondary sex characteristics (p. 229)
primary sex characteristics (p. 229)
concrete operations (p. 237)
classification (p. 238)

seriation (p. 238)
semantic memory (p. 241)
rehearsal (p. 242)
elaboration (p. 242)
metamemory (p. 242)
metacognition (p. 242)
intelligence (p. 243)
IQ (p. 243)

theory of multiple intelligences (p. 244)
theory of successful intelligence (p. 244)
pragmatics (p. 246)
literacy (p. 250)
numeracy (p. 250)
phonics-based instruction (p. 250)

whole-language approach (p. 250)
self-efficacy (p. 251)
grit (p. 251)
specific learning disabilities (p. 252)
intellectual disabilities (p. 252)
gifted education (p. 253)

CHECK YOUR LEARNING

1. The period of middle childhood ends with the onset of the physical changes of:
   a) infancy.
   b) myelination.
   c) puberty.
   d) dementia.

2. Children's ultimate height is primarily influenced by _____ if they are healthy and well-nourished.
   a) genes
   b) environment
   c) ethnicity
   d) parenting

3. Which of the following fine motor achievements is associated with higher success in elementary or primary school?
   a) Buttoning a shirt
   b) Writing by hand
   c) Typing on a keyboard
   d) Sewing

4. The coating of neurons with myelin creates brain tissue often described as:
   a) pruning.
   b) cortex.
   c) gray matter.
   d) white matter.

5. Cortical thinning in middle childhood is an indication of:
   a) child maltreatment.
   b) maturation.
   c) chromosomes.
   d) synaptic exuberance.

6. The hormonal changes during middle childhood that begin the first early changes of puberty are known as:
   a) menopause.
   b) amygdala.
   c) teratogens.
   d) adrenarche.

7. Which of the following statements about sleep in middle childhood is TRUE?
   a) Since children no longer need a nap, their sleep needs are the same as adults.
   b) Most children get much more sleep than they need.
   c) The recommended amount of sleep for healthy development is 9–12 hours per night.
   d) The recommended amount of sleep for healthy development is 12–14 hours per night.

8. During the concrete operations period of cognitive development, Jean Piaget noted that children's thinking is:

   a) more logical and flexible than in early childhood.

   b) constrained by logical errors, such as irreversibility.

   c) based purely on imagination and magical thinking.

   d) highly abstract and theoretical.

9. Improvements in executive function during middle childhood are NOT associated with the ability to:

   a) succeed at games like Simon Says.

   b) recover more quickly from emotional outbursts.

   c) do 10 sit-ups in a row.

   d) sit still for several minutes to practice writing.

10. Which of the following statements about Vygotsky's views of learning during middle childhood is TRUE?

    a) Children's learning follows a distinct set of stages.

    b) Children learn the same concepts in all cultures around the world.

    c) Children learn through independent exploration of the environment.

    d) Children learn the tools and skills of their culture through interacting with others.

11. Describe some of the cognitive and social benefits of free play.

12. Improvements in several forms of information processing during middle childhood make children much better at memorizing information than they were earlier. Explain the role of memory strategies like rehearsal, elaboration, and metamemory in supporting children's memorization.

Social and Emotional Development in Middle Childhood

9

Building Emotional Maturity

9.1 Explain the goals of emotion regulation during middle childhood.

Developing a Sense of Self

9.2 Describe advances in self-concept and the role of social comparison in self-esteem during middle childhood.

Family During Middle Childhood

9.3 Describe the importance of family relationships in middle childhood.

Getting Along with Other Children

9.4 Describe the role of friendships and peer relationships in middle childhood.

9.5 Define the role of popularity and other social status categories during middle childhood.

Moral Development

9.6 Describe the development of moral reasoning and moral behavior in middle childhood.

© Macmillan, Photo by Sidford House

Ten-year-old Amara loves TikTok, *Roblox*, and drawing. When she grows up, she wants to be a doctor, but before that she wants to be an activist, a singer, and maybe have a YouTube channel. She has some time before medical school but is already an activist, her mission since kindergarten. Her inspiration comes in equal parts from her mother, Martin Luther King Jr., and her teacher, Ms. Silver.

Many of us might feel awkward about making TikToks, dancing on camera, or rapping in front of a crowd. We might wish the world was different but never actually try to do something about it. Amara, on the other hand, can look into the camera and sing about police brutality, stereotyping, and the class bully.

Amara's mother says she has always been kind and outgoing, but the rest of the world didn't know it until Amara ended up in Ms. Silver's program. Now, thousands of people around the world have watched Amara's videos. She is coauthoring a book for children about the police and is writing a rap about Black history.

Schoolchildren can accomplish big things. For example, Amara has created dozens of videos, writes songs, and has helped write a book — all while getting through fourth grade on Zoom. Children everywhere know how to help their families and develop new talents, whether that means taking care of a younger sibling after school or performing in the school talent show. More mature emotions, bodies, and cognition help make this possible.

Nevertheless, children are not yet adults. Caregivers may not be as nearby as they once were, but relationships continue to be essential to healthy development.

Children benefit from increasingly diverse relationships, with friends, family, teachers, and even first crushes.

In this chapter, you will read about social and emotional development during middle childhood, which means many things around the world. Children may be hand-sewing masks to help support their families or practicing their TikTok dances, but from ages 6 to 12, all children are developing the emotion regulation and personality characteristics that will shape them as they move toward adulthood. They may not rap or advocate online as Amara does, but all children are trying to find their place in the world, supported by the people in their lives.

Scientific American Profile

© Macmillan, Photo by Sidford House

Meet Amara

Building Emotional Maturity

During middle childhood, children are expected to better control their feelings and impulses and manage their relationships without a lot of adult help. There is much variation in how they do this: Adversity requires some children to grow up more quickly than others. Children spend more of their waking hours with their friends and classmates than with their parents, and these relationships become critical to their happiness. But the emotional expectations and habits formed at home are still at the core of how they learn to manage feelings and relationships.

Learning Objective

9.1 Explain the goals of emotion regulation during middle childhood.

Growing Up Quickly

Despite the universal idea that children need special protections, millions of children around the world are forced to navigate adult situations. More than 14 million children worldwide live on their own, without parents or other adults in the home (Ntuli et al., 2020). For example, Sarita and Bipani (see photo) live with their siblings in the village of Puranguan, Nepal. They have raised themselves and their younger brother and sisters for the past five years since their parents left home to find work as migrant laborers (Aryal, 2016).

Researchers estimate that one in every eight young children around the globe is forced to take on adult roles, such as head of the family, soldier, or worker, before they are adolescents (ILO/UNICEF, 2021). Growing up quickly may be the only way children like Sarita and Bipani can survive in the short term, but taking on adult roles too early can have lasting effects on mental and physical health (Agorastos et al., 2019; McLaughlin et al., 2019). Children who have grown up on their own or endured significant adversity often have higher rates of emotional disorders and poor health in adulthood: Some scientists even see signs of accelerated aging in their cells (Colich et al., 2020; Marini et al., 2020).

In many communities, *who* is considered a child differs depending on their appearance and background (Priest et al., 2018). Adults often think of children as less innocent if they are from a group that is different from them, particularly if they are lower in social status. These discriminatory perceptions can affect immigrant children living in the Netherlands, Roma children living in Hungary, or children of color in the United States (Bruneau et al., 2020; D'hondt et al., 2021). In the United States, researchers have found that adults often rate young Black boys and girls as less innocent-looking than their White peers (Goff et al., 2014; Theim et al., 2019; Todd et al., 2016). In effect, prejudice forces some children to grow up before their time. Nevertheless, warm social relationships can help children build resilience and health despite their adult responsibilities or the stress induced by discrimination that might age them beyond their years.

©UNICEF Nepal/2016/NShrestha

On Their Own Sarita, age 13, Reema, age 6, Deepa, age 8, and Bipana, age 10, work on their homework at their home in the village of Puranguan, Nepal. The two older sisters, Sarita and Bipana, care for their younger siblings, the house, and their goats and cattle. Deepa and Reema are in school, and every day all four of them spend time on their studies.

Building Resilience

Most children can bounce back from acute stressors like sudden illness or a natural disaster, but not all navigate adversity and stress in the same way (Galatzer-Levy et al., 2018; Zhou & Wu, 2021). Remember from Chapter 1 that *resilience* refers to the ability to recover from stressors and challenges, even traumatic or chronic ones (Masten et al., 2021). It is a process that can be fostered as children grow (Garmezy & Rutter, 1983; Werner, 1989).

Resilience is built on social connections (Denckla et al., 2020; Luthar & Eisenberg, 2017). Positive early attachment, warm parenting, and strong friendships in middle childhood can help children heal from many traumas, including illness, loss, or disaster, and even maltreatment within their own families (Gach et al., 2018). Sometimes even just one loving, caring person can help a child who is experiencing adversity.

Children who develop strong early relationships are also more likely to build other skills like intelligence and emotion regulation that will also protect them over the long run (Luthar & Eisenberg, 2017; Rodman et al., 2019). Those who encounter adversity, such as childhood cancer or the loss of a parent, draw from positive relationships to find meaning in their experiences and respond to their trauma with a sense of purpose (Hamby et al., 2020). Researchers hope that these children not only are able to bounce back but also to find a way to thrive and feel optimistic about the future (Non et al., 2020).

Human beings have tremendous ability to be *plastic*, or to change, but nevertheless, chronic adversity, trauma, and stress can impair children's health and development. Cumulative stress inevitably takes a toll (Masten et al., 2021). One of the best ways to help a child who is experiencing adversity is early intervention to shield them from further trauma and stress. Lifting families out of poverty, reducing the everyday burden of getting by on a low income, can reduce overall stress. For instance, when a group of researchers monitored a group of at-risk families, they found that the rate of emotional problems dropped by more than half after their family incomes went up by about $6,000 (Costello et al., 2003). Simply having more money reduced family stress and allowed more children to recover. Nevertheless, no matter what their circumstances, disappointments, failures, and hardship allow children to practice their coping skills and build emotional maturity (Masten & Cicchetti, 2016).

Erikson's Stage of Industry Versus Inferiority

During middle childhood, children are typically expected to progress from playful preschoolers to more responsible schoolchildren who can get down to work. This could mean measuring ocean warming in a laboratory in the Great Barrier Reef, a long morning of achievement testing in Alabama, or keeping track of reindeer on the tundra in Norway.

Remember from Chapter 2 that Erik Erikson described eight stages of human development. He shared many ideas about middle childhood with Sigmund Freud. Freud described middle childhood as a period of *latency*, when major sensual and sexual drives are "sleeping" or only active in the background (Freud, 1905/2000). Both Freud and Erikson believed the task of middle childhood was for children to learn

TABLE 9.1 Erikson's Stages of Psychosocial Development: Middle Childhood

Stage	Age	Characteristics
Industry versus inferiority	5–12 years	Children need to resolve a conflict between a sense of competence and a sense of failure. If children feel that they are capable and can accomplish something, they will take that feeling of their own resourcefulness with them into adulthood.

how to tame their passions and imaginations to become more independent and dutiful learners (Erikson, 1993; Freud, 1905/2000).

Erikson called the crisis of the fourth stage of development **industry versus inferiority** (Erikson, 1950/1993). This conflict is successfully resolved when children develop a sense of their own *industriousness*, or their ability to be productive (see **Table 9.1**). Children can feel inferior if the pressure to learn new skills makes them feel inadequate or discouraged by a mismatch between their abilities and their community's expectations. Children who have academic difficulties might experience inferiority, as could children whose families have unrealistic expectations for their behavior (Trinidad, 2019).

Erikson was confident that encouraging children's interests during this stage is critical to developing a sense of identity as competent adults. Children who are not allowed to try something new, Erikson argued, may never learn that they can take the risks necessary to grow (Erikson, 1993).

Contemporary researchers have found that many of Erikson's observations still ring true today. Remember from Chapter 8 that researchers believe that children's commitment to learning new skills helps them grow into successful adults, although they rarely use Erikson's term *industry* to refer to this tendency. Instead, researchers use a variety of terms like *grit, conscientiousness*, or *achievement motivation* (Conger et al., 2021; Duckworth, 2016; Ponnock et al., 2020).

Regardless of the terminology, children who adopt these habits are more likely to use them in adulthood. The drive to work hard is a trait found in many successful children and adults (Blatný et al., 2015). As you will see, children who feel productive and successful when they learn new skills also are more likely to develop a positive self-concept and a sense of *self-efficacy*, or confidence in their own capabilities.

Ironically, as children enter school, it is typical for the buoyant self-confidence of preschool to falter. Their stronger social awareness forces them to become more realistic about their abilities (Wigfield & Eccles, 2020). Some declines in confidence may be inevitable, as Erikson predicted, but serious feelings of inadequacy or failure can lead to mental health problems (Ghandour et al., 2019). One way for children to feel competent is to give them a chance to help.

industry versus inferiority The fourth crisis of Erikson's theory in which children are challenged to build their sense of themselves as capable and avoid feeling inadequate.

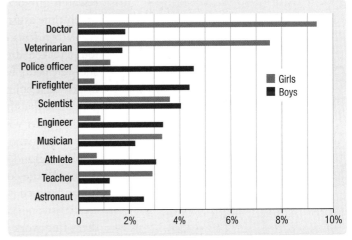

Age (years)	1st	2nd	3rd
1–2	Don't know	Doctor	Animal
2–3	Doctor	Parent	Firefighter
3–4	Super hero	Doctor	Parent
4–5	Veterinarian	Scientist	Doctor
5–6	Doctor	Firefighter	Athlete
6–7	Athlete	Doctor	Police Officer
7–8	Athlete	Engineer	Veterinarian
8–9	Video game designer	Teacher	Doctor
9–10	Athlete	Doctor	Video game designer
10+	Athlete	Chef/baker	Veterinarian

Data from Fatherly, 2015, 2017.

FIGURE 9.1 What Do You Want to Be When You Grow Up? As Erikson would have predicted, most children gradually abandon their fanciful plans to be superheroes and begin to think about careers that their community values. By elementary school, most children adopt slightly more realistic goals, such as becoming doctors or teachers, although many still have the optimistic goal of becoming a professional athlete.

Pitching In Whether they are watching the reindeer in Tsagaan Nuur, Mongolia, or bathing a baby sister in San Basilio de Palenque, Colombia, children who help out can build confidence in their own capabilities, or what Erikson called industriousness.

 MAKING A DIFFERENCE
The Benefits of Helping Out

Work outside of the classroom is the reality for many children around the globe (Lancy, 2020). More than 1 in 10 children worldwide works outside the home, selling things on the street or harvesting on a farm (ILO/UNICEF, 2021). Children help out at home, too, by watching younger siblings, cooking, or doing laundry (Lew-Levy et al., 2017). As Erikson may have predicted, developmental scientists suggest that work is beneficial for children's development. It makes them feel valued and connected to their families and builds their industriousness (Coppens et al., 2018; Gallois et al., 2015; Orellana, 2001).

In the United States, however, many families report that chores are too stressful to assign, since their children are unwilling to help. Only about 3 in 10 children under 11 have regular chores, and fewer than 1 in 100 have paid jobs, mostly on farms (Mercer, 2013; Wallace, 2015).

In the United States, higher-income parents often expect that their children will be too busy with schoolwork and activities to do chores. Helping is more common in lower-income households and immigrant families (Klein et al., 2009; Rende, 2015). One research group found that children in lower-income families spent nearly twice as much time assisting their families as children in wealthier ones (Coppens et al., 2018).

When researchers compared children who do chores with those who do not, they found that children who were expected to help had greater self-confidence and self-efficacy and were better behaved (White et al., 2019). One group of scientists compared children who helped their families by translating in the doctor's office or at parent–teacher conferences and found that the child-translators did better than their peers in school (Dorner et al., 2007).

Children who work with their parents outside of the home also show benefits. Researchers who have spent time with such children have found that work, whether helping a grandparent or pitching in at a family business, did not seem oppressive to them. On the contrary, working with their parents made them feel important, helpful, and valued (Grugel & Ferreira, 2012). Rather than shortening their childhood, working created stronger bonds with their families and built social relationships that helped them find work in adulthood (Estrada, 2019; Estrada & Hondagneu-Sotelo, 2011).

While some paid work may be risky to children, particularly if they are working with fertilizers or pesticides or operating heavy machinery, helping out has many benefits (Bourdillon et al., 2019; ILO/UNICEF, 2021). Researchers suggest we think of chores not as a distraction from school but as a way of caring for each other (Rende, 2015). The payoff will be children who feel capable and competent. 🌍

Emotion Regulation

Amara wants you to know that being a fourth-grader in the middle of a pandemic was not easy. Keeping her cool when the internet went down in the middle of a test and her mother had to drive to a place to log on was tough. She missed school, the friends she sang and danced with, Ms. Silver, and performing in front of live audiences. Nevertheless, she had much to look forward to. The California weather meant that she could meet her friends outside, and, when all else failed, she could have a game night with her mother.

Amara's efforts to keep her cool despite the stress of the pandemic are not unique: During middle childhood, all children take on the task of learning how to manage their feelings in a way that their community expects. Children in middle childhood still occasionally melt down, cry, and snap at their siblings, but it happens less often than in early childhood (National Survey of Children's Health, 2019). Families' strategies for managing emotions vary, but all children thrive when they can react to frustrations with some degree of calm and stay optimistic and motivated to do the hard work of learning that comes with middle childhood (Thompson, 2019).

The ability to manage emotions is critical to children's academic and social success alike (Distefano et al., 2021; Schlesier et al., 2019). Their developing cognitive skills help them with emotion regulation: Remember from Chapter 8 that children at this age have increased awareness of their own thinking, and this extends to their emotions (Raval & Walker, 2019). In many cultures, by middle childhood, children are adept at using words to describe how they are feeling, and many can understand how negative and positive thoughts affect their moods (Lagattuta et al., 2015; Raval & Green, 2018). They are also aware of how other people perceive them and how to manage their feelings in a complex social environment (Domitrovich et al., 2017; Saarni, 1999). These skills will help them throughout their lives.

Communities and families around the globe socialize emotional expression in different ways, as you may recall from Chapter 7 (Raval & Green, 2018). Children everywhere are expected to regulate their own feelings more independently as they grow, but what it means to be emotionally mature varies (Weis et al., 2016). Some communities value calmness and emotional restraint, and others value self-expression and outward displays of emotion (Raval & Walker, 2019). For instance, many families, including those from Mapuche communities in Chile, socialize their children to minimize fear, encouraging them to be "brave" and not overly anxious about thunder, wild animals, or other typical childhood worries (Halberstadt et al., 2020). Some communities, such as many in the United States, encourage pride when children are recognized for their accomplishments, but children from communities in Japan may be embarrassed by the attention (Furukawa et al., 2012).

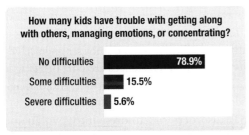

FIGURE 9.2 Emotional Development During Middle Childhood Most families report that their children can get along with others or manage their feelings, but that does not mean that they always stay calm when they experience frustration. During childhood, developing emotion regulation is an important skill, but maturity takes a long time.

CONNECTIONS

Remember that cultural values can be *collectivist* or *individualist*. Collectivist orientations mean that people value the group and interdependent relationships over individual desires and accomplishments (see Chapter 1). Individualistic orientations value the individual's autonomy and independence over the good of the larger group. Families and cultures often have a mix of these values.

Share It!

Reach out to a child: Children may need more support after the pandemic. The disruption in routines and access to counseling services were linked to a 25 percent increase in the number of U.S. children's visits to the emergency room for mental health crises.

(Leeb et al., 2020)

Scientific American: Lifespan Development

psychological disorder A pattern of feelings or behaviors that causes distress and makes it difficult to function.

internalizing disorders Psychological disorders in which children's emotions are focused inward, manifesting as overwhelming feelings of sadness (depression) or worry (anxiety).

Have you ever heard an adult remind a child to "use their words?" In North America and Europe, children are often encouraged to articulate and share their feelings, even those of anger or frustration (De Leersnyder et al., 2020). This emphasis on self-expression is far from universal (Ip et al., 2021; Jaramillo et al., 2017). For instance, researchers have found that children in some collectivist communities in India are discouraged from sharing feelings of sadness and anger, because doing so is considered impolite and damaging to interpersonal relationships (Raval & Green, 2018). More individualistic communities encourage children to freely express their feelings. In doing so, families may be sending the message that expressing your individual feelings is more important than making sure everyone is comfortable. Differences in emotional socialization reflect varying cultural values about the value of the individual versus the group.

Regardless of which culture they live in, children's emotion regulation is tied to their relationships. Parents who have strong emotion regulation skills and who have positive bonds with their children are more likely to have children who more easily manage their feelings. Relationship quality is the biggest predictor of children's emotional health, regardless of the specific practices that parents use to socialize their children (Cook et al., 2019; Raval & Walker, 2019).

The parenting practices that adults use to help children with their emotions are diverse. Some are common in the United States, such as asking children to name and talk about their feelings (Garrett-Peters et al., 2017). Other practices include offering comfort when children are upset; empathizing with their feelings; and coaching and problem solving through difficult situations (Eisenberg et al., 1998; Gottman et al., 1996; Morris et al., 2017). Some practices are clearly unhealthy: Dismissing or being contemptuous of children's feelings is problematic in every community (England-Mason et al., 2020).

Emotional Disorders

For many children, a trip to an amusement park is exciting, but for others it can be terrifying. One family shared the experience of their son, Erik, with researchers. He was afraid of the rides at the park, being left alone, and being kidnapped. Erik had a long list of worries: the dentist, asking for help in a store, walking to the bus stop alone (Lundkvist-Houndoumadi & Thastum, 2013). He had been anxious and shy as a toddler, and by the fifth grade, he often had stomach pains and panicked at the thought of going to school or running errands with his mother. Like about 1 in 20 children, Erik was diagnosed with an *anxiety disorder*, a state of constant worry that made it challenging for him to succeed in school, make friends, and live a full life (Ghandour et al., 2019).

Surveys have found that at least one in eight children around the world meets the criteria to be diagnosed with a **psychological disorder**, a pattern of feelings or behaviors that causes distress and makes it difficult to function (Danielson et al., 2021; Vasileva et al., 2021). Children with psychological disorders may have trouble learning, being understood and getting along with family members and friends (Baranne & Falissard, 2018). Diagnosing a psychological disorder in a child is often difficult. Children often do not see themselves as having any unusual difficulties (Lewis, 2014). Behavioral challenges are part of being a child and are typical as we grow, but when difficulties are severe, persistent, and damaging to the child's well-being, they are considered a disorder (Costello, 2016).

Researchers often organize emotional disorders in children into two major categories. In **internalizing disorders**, children's emotions are focused inward, and they experience overwhelming feelings of sadness (e.g., *depression*) or worry (e.g., *anxiety*). Since children often lack the vocabulary to talk about their feelings, their anxiety and depression frequently emerge as physical complaints, such as headaches, stomachaches, or difficulty sleeping (Mullen, 2018; Shanahan et al., 2015).

In contrast, **externalizing disorders** are characterized by problematic behaviors that affect others, such as acting out or severe aggression. Externalizing disorders include disruptive behavior disorders such as *oppositional defiant disorder (ODD)* and *conduct disorder (CD)* (Achenbach & McConaughy, 1992; Olson et al., 2017). Children with ODD are prone to unusual irritability and angry outbursts and have difficulty following rules and doing what they are told by authority figures (APA, 2022; Burke & Romano-Verthelyi, 2018). A diagnosis of CD or ODD indicates that a child's difficulty goes beyond bad moods and disrupts their daily life.

All children sometimes disobey a caregiver or teacher, but children with ODD exhibit a persistent and severe pattern of oppositional behavior at home and at school. Conduct disorder, a much more severe and uncommon behavioral disorder, is characterized by violence and disregard for other people. Children with CD might steal or fight with other children, hurt animals, or set fires, often without remorse (APA, 2022; Fairchild et al., 2019).

Some researchers point out that trauma often plays a role in diagnoses of CD and ODD: Children tend to be more reactive after they have experienced trauma and have difficulty managing their emotions (Beltrán et al., 2021). ODD and CD are often stigmatizing diagnoses: Evidence suggests that children with behavioral problems who are Black or Latino are more likely to be diagnosed with ODD than White children with similar behavior (Fadus et al., 2020). Many adults think that the behaviors associated with CD or ODD are best treated with strict discipline, but experts advise that harsh caregiving can make things worse: Children with these disorders often need intense professional help to help their families coach them toward more adaptive behavior with warmth, consistent limits, and acceptance (Booker et al., 2020).

Any psychological disorder results from a complicated mix of vulnerabilities, beginning with genetic risk, brain maturation, and prenatal development, coupled with environmental stress (Cicchetti, 2018; McQuillan et al., 2018). Trauma, stress, and adversity can all contribute to children's emotional problems (Koss & Gunnar, 2018). However, the environment can also be a source of resilience: Strong social relationships with family, friends, and community can help reduce children's risk for disorders like depression (Fritz et al., 2018).

For many children, difficulties can escalate as conflicts develop with friends and teachers at school (Costello et al., 2016). Fortunately, there are treatments that can help. Exposure therapy helped Erik, the boy who was afraid of the amusement park and leaving the house, to practice going into the situations that scared him with help of a supportive therapist. This helped him feel more confident in school and make new friends (Lundkvist-Houndoumadi & Thastum, 2013).

APPLY IT! 9.1 Erikson described middle childhood as a time when children should develop a sense of their own capabilities or industriousness. What are some ways that Amara is able to feel industrious?
9.2 Amara benefits from strong relationships with her mother and teacher. How else is she building resilience?

Developing a Sense of Self

During middle childhood, children develop a clearer sense of who they are. School and the world outside the family sometimes provide a harsh reality check for children: They may not do well in the spelling bee, they may get picked last for basketball, or they may feel that they do not fit in. Children's developing cognitive skills make much more sophisticated social comparisons possible (Lapan & Boseovski, 2017). As a result, children's self-concept, self-esteem, and feelings of general well-being dip in middle childhood, although most continue to feel good about themselves (Casas & González-Carrasco, 2019; Wigfield & Eccles, 2020).

externalizing disorders Psychological disorders characterized by difficult behaviors that affect others, such as acting out or severe aggression. Externalizing disorders include disruptive behavior disorders such as oppositional defiant disorder (ODD) and conduct disorder (CD).

Share It!

Does your tummy hurt? Stomach upset is often a way that children express their feelings of upset: Researchers suggest that may be because stress changes our intestinal microbiome.

(Callaghan et al., 2020)

Scientific American: Lifespan Development

Learning Objective

9.2 Describe advances in self-concept and the role of social comparison in self-esteem during middle childhood.

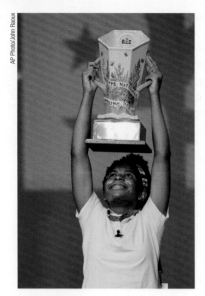

She Is Thrilled. Zaila Avant-Garde persevered through dozens of competitions to reach (and win) the championship in the Scripps National Spelling Bee. Middle childhood includes many opportunities for children to compare their skills—some with happy endings, like Zaila's.

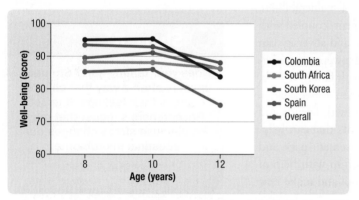

Data from Casas & González-Carrasco, 2019.

FIGURE 9.3 Life Gets Less Rosy over Time Maturity often means that children are better able to compare their lives with others'. For many, growing up provides a reality check. When researchers asked children from 18 nations whether they felt their lives were going well or if their lives were "just right," fewer were completely positive as they got older.

CONNECTIONS

Remember from Chapter 5 that researchers who measure personality in babies refer to differences in *temperament*. The Thomas and Chess model categorizes babies as *easy, slow-to-warm-up* and *difficult*. Other models measure babies' level of *effortful control, negative affect,* and *extraversion*.

Self-Understanding in a World of Peers

In school, children are constantly compared to each other. Sometimes this is subtle, as when reading comes easily to one friend and another has a hard time grasping long division. As children mature, their social comparison skills improve dramatically because of practice and cognitive abilities that make it easier to navigate complexity (Lapan & Boseovski, 2017).

Researchers seeking to measure self-esteem often ask children whether they like themselves (Harris et al., 2018). The answers to this question can have important consequences. For many, how they feel about themselves predicts how well they will do in school, how they get along with other children, and even how healthy and successful they will be as adults (Magnusson & Nermo, 2018; Zheng et al., 2020). Children with chronically low self-esteem are at risk for depression and other emotional disorders as they get older (Brummelman & Sedikides, 2020).

Self-esteem is built on a legacy of relating to others that began in early childhood. Children who have warm, securely attached relationships with their parents tend to have higher self-esteem (Harris et al., 2017). By the time children are in school, their friendships and their sense of how they compare to other children also begin to affect their self-esteem (Newland et al., 2019).

Self-concept also develops quickly once children start elementary school. Remember, self-concept refers to how children perceive themselves in various domains, such as how good they are at math, playing soccer, or even making friends (Harter, 2006; Shavelson et al., 1976). These distinctions will begin to form the basis for their identity or their sense of who they are (Oyserman et al., 2012).

When most children start elementary school, they have a positive self-concept and abundant enthusiasm for the new experience. They expect great things from themselves and are sure they will be great readers, doctors, or astronauts (Muenks et al., 2018). As mentioned, while children progress through school, reality sinks in, and often their beliefs in their abilities decline (Thomaes et al., 2017). Families and teachers can help children develop a healthy self-concept by giving them opportunities to improve their skills and by expressing positive beliefs about what they can accomplish (Koenka, 2020; Muenks et al., 2018).

Personality Development

Do you think Amara, outspoken and determined, will be the same kind of person as an adult as she is as a fourth-grader? Will her persistence help her in her journey to adulthood? These questions relate to the study of *personality*, or the individual differences that make each of us unique. As children move through middle childhood, their personalities tend to become more stable in ways that will stay with them through adulthood (Mõttus et al., 2019; Shiner, 2021).

Some of these individual patterns, like Amara's bravery and determination, will be an easy match to their communities' expectations and benefit children as they grow up, while others may cause difficulties (Conger et al., 2021; Stallings & Neppl, 2021).

Researchers measure personality in middle childhood using the same components as they do for adults, the *five-factor model*. These five parts of personality include *extraversion*, or how outgoing someone is; *agreeableness*, or how a child gets along with others; *conscientiousness*, or how diligent or hardworking a child is; *neuroticism*, or emotional stability; and *openness*, or imagination or curiosity about new experiences (Shiner, 2021). As children mature, researchers find that they typically become more conscientious and agreeable, and a little less curious and imaginative, as they prepare for the transition to adolescence (Brandes et al., 2021).

Culture affects how families react to children's emerging personalities. In the United States, many White and Black parents expect their children to be extraverted and outgoing rather than shy. Children are expected to show some initiative, such as being able to order by themselves at a restaurant. This preference for outgoing children is not universal; Latino and Asian American parents are more comfortable with shy children (Chen, 2018). The preference for extraverted children is common to many affluent countries around the world (Latham & Von Stumm, 2017). However, attitudes about what types of emotional displays are appropriate often change over time. For instance, over the past 20 years, as China has become more urban, some city parents are less accepting of shyness than they were in the past (Ding et al., 2020).

Warm parenting is closely associated with agreeable personalities, and parents who feel competent are more likely to raise children who are conscientious (Egberts et al., 2015). Other personality traits change because of experiences outside the home (Brandt et al., 2019). For instance, doing a lot of homework can make children more persistent and conscientious (Göllner et al., 2017). But some personality changes may be caused by random events that affect children differently, depending on their genetic makeup and personal history (Tucker-Drob, 2017). For instance, the success of Amara's online videos will probably expose her to more opportunities for public speaking and outreach, which may make her even more outgoing than she was before. Another child, with a different genome and set of life experiences, may respond to this type of notoriety differently.

Personality alone does not determine what will happen later in children's lives, but in many communities, some personality traits may make it easier for children to succeed (Kajonius & Carlander, 2017; Nave et al., 2017). Children who are conscientious and open to new things generally do well at school, and this success is likely to continue later in their lives (Israel et al., 2021; Soto & Tackett, 2015). On the other hand, children who have difficulty regulating their emotions, becoming conscientious and being understood by and understanding of others are more likely to break rules and act out (Tetzner et al., 2020).

A Little Shy to Meet You Personalities come in many different shapes and sizes. Some children are a bit nervous in new situations, while others may be bolder. Cultural expectations play a role in how accepting adults may be of the diversity in how children approach the world.

Gender Development

If you compare the colors of elementary schoolchildren's clothing with those of preschoolers' clothing, you will likely notice some stark differences, such as less pink on the older children (Martinez et al., 2019). One outcome of the new cognitive flexibility of middle childhood is that children's gender categories become less rigid as they learn to separate appearance from gender identity (Rogers, 2020). However, even as children become more flexible in their thinking, they are acquiring new stereotypes, attitudes, and ideas about what it means to identify as a boy or a girl, or as another gender identity. As you will learn, some of these are more serious than what colors you wear.

Although children in elementary school are willing to give up some of their very literal rules about gender, ideas about what is "for boys" and what is "for girls" are still limiting. About one in four girls tells researchers that she likes what are considered typical "boy" activities, such as robotics or football. Fewer boys admit to enjoying "girl" pursuits, and those who do may face more social consequences (Coyle et al., 2016; Rogers, 2020). Children who do not adhere to gender stereotypes, such as a boy who loves

CONNECTIONS

Remember from Chapter 7 that preschoolers tend to be very rigid about their ideas about gender, as they are with other categories, but that not all young children identify with stereotypes or binary gender categories. As children develop *concrete operational thought* and more flexibility in thinking, their ideas about gender become more flexible.

SDI Productions/E+/Getty Images

Just a Bunch of Children Playing Games in Austin, Texas
Whether you are trans (like some of these children) or not, growing up includes deciding how to express your gender identity, and how to make it to the next level on Mario.

Share It!

Stigma and bullying against children who are different is not inevitable: Adults can help. Encouraging children to be friends with children who are different can help all children feel that they belong.

(Halim et al., 2020)

Scientific American: Lifespan Development

sewing, are at higher risk for being harassed or bullied by their peers (Ioverno et al., 2021; Zosuls et al., 2016). Children who identify as gender nonconforming, transgender, or lesbian, gay, or bisexual are at even greater risk (Kwan et al., 2020; MacMullin et al., 2021; Martin-Storey & Fish, 2019).

As children mature, they become more aware of the stereotypes and attitudes about gender that surround them (Rogers & Meltzoff, 2017). Most children think that girls are more likely to be "good" or "nice" than boys. But, they also believe that boys have higher social status than girls (Hammond & Cimpian, 2021; Leaper & Brown, 2018). By the fourth grade, more than three in four boys and girls tell researchers that they are aware of gender discrimination (Brown et al., 2011). As one girl explained, "People say that boys can do more things than girls, I do not believe that at all" (Rogers, 2020, p. 188).

Children are even aware of complex stereotypes. For instance, most children are aware that girls are not "supposed" to be good at math or science (Bian et al., 2017). They also assume that boys are likely to be "trouble" (Chu, 2014). One fourth-grader explained that boys "always get into fights, always talking bad about other people, getting in trouble in class for talking back to the teacher . . . talking in class, being on their phones" (Rogers, 2020, p. 185).

Stereotypes about gender impact children's achievement in school. Girls tend to earn higher grades and test scores than boys, but stereotypes about girls' talent for math and science can make them feel that they do not belong in STEM fields (Bian et al., 2017; Leaper & Brown, 2018). Gender stereotypes likely have even more of an impact on boys than many realize. Boys often tell researchers that men are not supposed to talk about their feelings, ask for help, or work hard. These stereotypical attitudes about masculinity may be one reason boys begin to fall behind girls in achievement in school in many countries around the world (Leaper & Brown, 2018; O'Dea et al., 2018).

SCIENCE IN PRACTICE
Justine Ang Fonte, MPH, M.Ed., Health Educator

Most adults around the world agree that elementary schoolchildren are too young for romance. In fact, school districts around the United States have gone so far as to ban romantic relationships from elementary schools (Kobin, 2019). However, researchers point out that banning romance may be impossible, and that children should begin having comprehensive education about gender, sexuality, and romance in elementary school (Cacciatore et al., 2019; Fisher et al., 2015; Pound et al., 2017).

Justine Ang Fonte has been teaching for almost 20 years and educates elementary schoolchildren about gender identity, sexuality, stereotypes, and, yes, consent. She says that people sometimes freak out when they find out she talks to first-graders about sex (Safronova, 2021). But Fonte points out that hiding information from kids does not help them be healthy. Fonte talks to young children about stereotypes about gender, what makes people different biologically, what it is to have *agency*, or a sense of control, over your body, and what it means to be emotionally and physically ready for intimacy.

Developmental scientists have found that talking to children about biology, gender identity, sexuality, and relationships does not encourage children to have sex. In fact, it seems to decrease rates of sexual activity and may even reduce rates of bullying and discrimination (Hilliard & Liben, 2020; Robinson et al., 2017). This kind of education can also help children who are victims of sexual abuse find a safe place to heal (Tutty et al., 2020). Fonte comes prepared with two graduate degrees (in education and public health) and a career that started with teaching math.

What has changed the most in Fonte's work during the past several years? The internet. Many children in the United States have already learned about gender stereotypes and sex from images they have seen online or on their phones. More than 9 in 10 children have seen pornography online by the time they enter adolescence (Davis et al., 2019; Rothman et al., 2017).

Since teachers cannot always take students' phones away, Fonte takes another approach. It starts with talking about gender, agency, and sexuality to children who may be years away from puberty. She believes in educating children about media literacy—including what is real, what is fake, and how images stereotype and shock, along with what real relationships look like. She hopes that sitting down with kids, listening to what they have experienced and what they think, will make them more resilient to the power of the images and stereotypes they will inevitably encounter, either online or off. ◉

Ethnic and Racial Identity

Many children feel awkward talking about gender identity, but discussing ethnicity, race, or religious differences is sometimes even tougher (Pauker et al., 2015; Rogers & Meltzoff, 2017; Verkuyten, 2016). If researchers ask children to label pictures of other children, they are comfortable dividing them by gender, but children from many backgrounds have difficulty talking about the ethnic or racial differences between them (Pauker et al., 2015).

Researchers suspect this is because for many families, particularly those in privileged groups, talking about differences in cultural background, appearance, or ethnicity is considered impolite or unnecessary (Abaied & Perry, 2021; Pahlke et al., 2012; Zucker & Patterson, 2018). This "colorblindness" keeps children from understanding the impact of discrimination, privilege, and stereotypes (Yogeeswaran et al., 2018). Colorblindness does not make children more comfortable with peers who are from a different background (Scott et al., 2020). It also does not help children who are the target of negative stereotypes or discrimination counter bias and build healthy ethnic and racial identities (Umaña-Taylor & Hill, 2020).

Even if children are discouraged from talking about ethnic differences, they still pick up on stereotypes. By elementary school, children have already been exposed to stigmatizing stereotypes about ethnicity and race, among many others. Children who grow up in communities with histories of ethnic, religious, or racial discrimination are aware of stereotypes and bias earlier than those in other communities (Verkuyten, 2016). For instance, when researchers compared children who grew up in integrated, multiethnic Hawaii with those who lived in more segregated Massachusetts, they found that the children in Hawaii generally held fewer negative stereotypes about children who were not like them than those who grew up in Massachusetts (Pauker et al., 2016). The effects of negative stereotypes can be powerful; they can make children feel excluded and anxious. Children who report being the victims of discrimination and stigma often have lower grades and higher rates of mental health problems such as depression (Cave et al., 2020; Gillen-O'Neel et al., 2011; Shepherd et al., 2017).

Children from Latino, Black, Native American, and Asian American backgrounds in the United States experience discrimination in school and in the community (Delgado et al., 2019; Umaña-Taylor, 2016). When researchers interview adults,

Surfer, Tennis Player and Health Educator Justine Ang Fonte talks to children and adults about how to be healthy: not just physically, but also emotionally and socially. In middle childhood, children are ready to think about how to be empathetic and kind to each other in romantic relationships and how to talk about what they want.

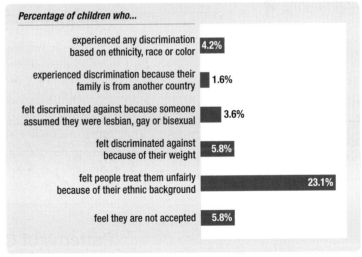

Percentage of children who...

experienced any discrimination based on ethnicity, race or color	4.2%
experienced discrimination because their family is from another country	1.6%
felt discriminated against because someone assumed they were lesbian, gay or bisexual	3.6%
felt discriminated against because of their weight	5.8%
felt people treat them unfairly because of their ethnic background	23.1%
feel they are not accepted	5.8%

Data from Argabright et al., 2021.

FIGURE 9.4 How Many Children Feel the Effects of Discrimination? Even elementary schoolchildren are not too young to experience discrimination. When researchers ask children whether they have ever experienced unfair treatment, name calling, or bullying based on their ethnicity or racial identity, children across the country report that this is part of their everyday lives. Discrimination can hurt children's sense of belonging and damage their self-esteem.

including those who work closely with children, such as pediatricians and teachers, they find that many harbor negative stereotypes about children of color, particularly about Black and Latino children (Johnson et al., 2017; Priest et al., 2018; Thiem et al., 2019).

What can boost children's resilience in the face of such stressors? Social connections, family ties, and pride in their identity can protect children from some of the corrosive effects of discrimination on their achievement and mental health (Barton & Brody, 2018; Marcelo & Yates, 2019; Umaña-Taylor & Hill, 2020). Remember from Chapter 7 that children who have a strong sense of their ethnic, religious, or racial identity are more likely to feel good about themselves (Huguley et al., 2019). Parents who encourage this are often trying to prepare children to experience and cope with discrimination. Families and communities can also reduce stigma and bias by encouraging friendships between children from diverse backgrounds and by openly talking about ethnicity, rather than pretending discrimination and bias do not exist (Gillen-O'Neel et al., 2021).

APPLY IT! **9.3** Amara's activism has helped her make friends and feel capable in a world filled with stereotypes and stigma. How would you explain the value of community pride to families who may not want their children involved in potentially divisive political conversations?

9.4 Amara is outspoken and energetic—characteristics her family and her community value. What are other personality traits that communities may admire?

Family During Middle Childhood

Learning Objective

9.3 Describe the importance of family relationships in middle childhood.

Children are more capable and self-reliant in middle childhood than they were in preschool, but they still need their families. Warm family relationships, between parents and children, between siblings, and across generations, protect children from adversity, help boost their achievement in school, and promote mental health (Collins & Masden, 2019). However, during middle childhood, families are often changing as parents separate, divorce, or begin new relationships (Raley & Sweeney, 2020). As you will see, this common experience can amplify children's stress.

Relationships

Children in many parts of the world spend about half as much time with their families as they did in preschool, but parents provide the same amount of emotional support and help as before; it is just compressed into less time (Collins & Masden, 2019). Further, the characteristics of this support change in middle childhood: Parents provide more homework help and fewer hugs. This does not mean that parents become impersonal when their children start elementary school. When they are responsive and attentive, they teach their children to cope with the effects of stress outside the home (Chen et al., 2017). During middle childhood, parents are still critically important in shaping children's success in school and giving them a strong foundation for their future (Rothenberg et al., 2021).

Patterns of Caregiving

Amara and her mother, Crystal, have a close relationship: Some of Amara's favorite times are when she and Crystal get a treat at Starbucks or play a board game together. Amara says her mother is her biggest role model, someone who has taught her to look out for other people. Despite their closeness, Amara does not take her mother's advice about everything, like what to wear to school or how much time to spend online. During middle childhood, relationships between parents and children inevitably change as children become more independent.

Healthy Relating As discussed, at this age, caregivers spend less time with their children and hug them less often. Nevertheless, researchers find that attachment, security, and authoritative parenting remain as critical to caregiving as they were in earlier stages of development.

In middle childhood, families are an emotional resource for children as they navigate peers and school. In securely attached families, children feel supported by their caregivers, and families provide a secure base for children to return to. Securely attached caregivers may be around less than they were when children were younger, but they need to be available when their children face stress, such as not getting invited to a birthday party, being cut from the soccer team, or failing a math test. Children begin to understand their parents' goals and values when their parents are not with them (Bosmans & Kerns, 2015). For most families, attachment patterns set in infancy and early childhood continue in middle childhood (Jewell et al., 2019; Waters et al., 2019). Not all children have secure attachments: Children with insecure patterns of attachment may feel rejected by their families or worry about whether their parents will be there for them (Bosmans & Kerns, 2015).

One way that families control their children's behavior is through **monitoring**, or keeping track of what children are doing (Dishion & McMahon, 1998). Monitoring is a form of caregiving that is focused on children's widening exploration of the world outside of home. Families are monitoring their children when they ask how the math test went, if there were try-outs for the soccer team, or who they are friends with on *Roblox* or another online game. Monitoring happens in real life and online. For instance, families that set limits on what children watch and play online tend to have healthier children who get more sleep and get along better with others (Collier et al., 2016; Gentile et al., 2014). Monitoring helps keep children safe; families know where their children are and what they are doing, and it also helps cement relationships.

Monitoring is a two-way interaction, because it requires that children be open and disclosing to their parents about what they are doing (Kerr et al., 2008). In strong relationships, adults and children share information so that families can figure out what happened at school, and children feel that their families care to hear the answer.

Setting boundaries and tracking children's activities can go too far. Researchers have found that parents who are too controlling of their children's behavior can negatively impact their mental health (Barber et al., 2005). Parents who are overly intrusive, or who try to control their children's feelings with guilt or shame, may put their children at risk for anxiety and depression (Chen-Bouck et al., 2019; Marusak et al., 2018; Pomerantz et al., 2014).

Relationships at Risk Children are better able to regulate themselves during middle childhood, but caregiving can still be difficult at times (Collins & Masden, 2019). Misbehavior may be harder to manage once children are too big to be physically removed from a challenging situation. Caregivers can develop harsh, rejecting, or disengaged relationship patterns that may damage children's mental and physical health. These cycles are particularly common for families under stress (Elder, 1998; Gard et al., 2020; Schenck-Fontaine et al., 2020; Suh & Luthar, 2020; Vreeland et al., 2019).

Harsh caregiving occurs when adults are consistently negative, angry, or disappointed in their children. This pattern may include screaming or using physical punishment. The adults' behavior often derives more from their inability to manage their own feelings than from their desire to harm the child (Hajal & Paley, 2020; Schofield et al., 2017). Harsh parenting is detrimental to physical and emotional development (Bauer et al., 2021).

Rejecting caregiving happens when adults demean their children or communicate that they disapprove of or dislike them (Rowe et al., 2015). Children who do not adhere to typical gender stereotypes or have an intellectual or physical disability are at particular

CONNECTIONS

Remember from Chapter 1 that developmental scientists use a variety of methods to assess what makes a relationship strong. Some scholars measure *attachment* (see Chapters 2 and 5). Secure attachment gives children a safe base to explore the world that they can return to for support and reassurance. Other scholars analyze *parenting styles* (see Chapter 7) and find that the key to a healthy, authoritative caregiving style is support that balances control and warmth.

Share It!

Love can fight colds: Researchers found that children who reported close bonds with their family had stronger immune systems and were better able to fight off the common cold, even if they had grown up with some disadvantages.

(Cohen et al., 2020)

Scientific American: Lifespan Development

monitoring When caregivers keep track of what their children are doing.

risk for parental rejection (Grossman et al., 2021; Mills-Koonce et al., 2018). If children grow up feeling that their families do not like or accept them, they risk depression, acting out, and profound social and academic difficulties (Putnick et al., 2015).

Disengaged parenting occurs when caregivers emotionally separate from their children, ignoring their requests for attention or responding in a perfunctory or hollow way. Families may disengage as a result of extreme stress, their own emotional problems, or a cycle of difficult interactions with their child (Lunkenheimer et al., 2016; Vreeland et al., 2019). Children whose caregivers have disengaged are more likely to act out and exhibit aggressive and oppositional behavior with friends and at school (Roskam, 2019).

Caregivers may disengage and reject their children, or they may escalate their discipline into progressively harsher punishments because they have fallen into what researchers call a *coercive cycle* (Patterson, 1982, 2016). A coercive cycle happens when children and parents behave in a harsh or unpleasant way but get what they want because the other person does not want to experience the unpleasantness anymore. For instance, an adult may ask a child to go to bed, and their child may react with a screaming fit. If the parent gives up, desperate to stop the yelling, and allows their child to stay up later, a coercive cycle may have begun.

Parents can also initiate the cycle. For instance, a child may seek attention, perhaps by asking for help with homework, and their parent reacts by saying they are too busy and telling them to "go away." If the child gives up because the rejection was too painful, the child may stop trying to receive help and a coercive cycle continues (Patterson, 1982, 2016). Families stuck in coercive cycles experience higher levels of violence than other families, and their children are at risk for developing externalizing disorders like CD or ODD and for engaging in criminal activity and substance abuse in adulthood (Chang & Shaw, 2016).

Unsupportive parenting has damaging effects on children's bodies and brains. Children with unsupportive families have higher rates of depression and externalizing disorders and also show signs of physical damage, such as high blood pressure and early signs of cardiovascular disease caused by the long-term effects of exposure to stress hormones (Brody et al., 2016). Family stress, like other forms of chronic adversity, including exposure to discrimination, creates epigenetic changes in children's DNA, causing what is called "weathering," or premature aging (Schofield et al., 2017).

Interventions to help boost supportive caregiving during middle childhood focus on boosting adults' mental health and teaching positive relationship skills (see **Table 9.2**). Programs such as the Family Check-Up offer skills training and one-on-one assessment to assist families (Berkel et al., 2021; Shelleby et al., 2018). The Family Check-Up focuses on families' strengths and helps them set their own goals, with positive impacts on family interactions and children's behavior. In the Strong African American Families Project (SAAF), a successful program that began in the rural Southeastern United States, families learn about being emotionally supportive, keeping a close eye on their children and the importance of having a sense of family and ethnic pride (Brody et al., 2004, 2019).

Families and Achievement

Many families have big dreams for their children. Parents' beliefs about their children's abilities can be a powerful predictor of children's success. If families do not believe their children are competent, even when teachers or the children themselves believe otherwise, the children are more likely to struggle (Putnick et al., 2020). However, just believing is not enough. When parents communicate to their children that achievement is a process and support their efforts, rather than telling them that success is based on an inborn ability, children have more academic success (Haimovitz & Dweck, 2016).

Parents' expectations also influence their children's success. Families who believe their children will score well in reading, or who expect their children to go to college, are likely to transmit those hopes to their children (Pinquart & Ebeling, 2020). However, parents who have overly high aspirations, such as expecting a child who has difficulties with math to become an engineer, or a shy child to become class president, may actually undermine their child's success (Murayama et al., 2016).

Parents' beliefs about their children's potential may not be as powerful as their ability to support their children's education. For example, there is an achievement gap between children of highly educated parents with high income and children whose parents lack these privileges (Egalite, 2016; see Chapter 8). This is due to variation in school quality (Darling-Hammond et al., 2017). Another factor is unequal access to often expensive enrichment activities and after-school programs that boost children's learning—an investment that often pays off with better grades (Knifsend et al., 2018). Well-educated and well-off families also have more time to spend with their children to help them with homework or drive them to after-school activities (Doepke & Zilibotti, 2019).

Family Transitions and Stress

Families change over time. In the United States, by age 12, most children experience a parent leaving the home, a formal separation, divorce, or a parental deployment, incarceration, or even death (Cavanagh & Fomby, 2019; Raley & Sweeney, 2020). Transition is common, but how children respond depends on how the changes fit into the bigger picture of their lives. Children and families can manage some adversity, but too much may lead to a cascade of difficulties.

Change Happens Family transitions are actually less common in the United States today than they were in the early 2000s (Finkelhor, 2020). However, in most communities, they are still a regular part of children's lives. Lower-income families, who are already managing the stress of poverty, are likely to experience more family transitions, and lower-income mothers are more likely to be parenting on their own (Amato et al., 2016). Similarly, lower-income children more commonly live in blended or complex families with half-siblings or stepsiblings (Fomby & Osborne, 2017).

What are the effects of family instability? Family transitions that involve adjusting to a new apartment or missing a loved parent or a close sibling can be hard for children, particularly in the short term. Their grades may suffer, or they may feel overwhelming loss or sadness (Bastaits & Mortelmans, 2016). Adults who are coping with relationship conflict or transition may parent with less patience and more harshness than usual (Amato, 2010; van Dijk et al., 2020). In the long term, however, most children adjust to their new circumstances (Härkönen et al., 2017; Lansford, 2009). For some children, like those from families struggling with substance abuse, violence, or constant conflict, transitions can even bring relief (Amato, 2010; Demo & Fine, 2010).

What helps children thrive during and after a family transition? Remember that the theory of resilience reminds us that people are our important asset. Positive, warm relationships with any caregivers, stepparents, extended family, or any combination help children recover from stress and avoid emotional hurt (Modecki et al., 2015; Nielsen, 2017). Helping families adjust often involves coaching adults to develop better strategies for co-parenting, addressing emotional challenges like depression, and training everyone to be positive and warm despite the increased challenges (Becher et al., 2019; Lamela et al., 2016; Weaver & Schofield, 2015).

Sandy Huffaker/AFP/Getty Images

Welcome Home! Family transitions and separations are part of childhood in many families. For Abigail and Declan, their separation ended when their father, a U.S. Marine, returned home to California from a deployment in the Middle East.

TABLE 9.2 Protective Parenting in Middle Childhood

Building resilience starts with getting along. Strong family relationships help children bounce back after adversity. Feeling understood and establishing secure attachments can help children weather everyday stresses and traumas. Acknowledging, naming, and problem-solving big feelings encourages children to calm down and be kinder in the heat of the moment.

Encourage strong friendships. Relationships with adults and children outside the home become important during middle childhood and can be a source of strength and, sometimes, stress. Social exclusion, discrimination, and rejection are part of life for many children: Relationships with teachers, extended family, and other children help buffer their effects.

Scaffold emotion regulation. Remember that children are more capable of managing their ups and downs during middle childhood, but that does not mean that they can always do it themselves. Everyone sometimes needs a shoulder to cry on or someone to celebrate the big win with. Children develop individual personality strengths and habits of coping.

Appreciate the new opportunities. Caregiving during middle childhood is not as time intensive as in earlier years, but it now requires families to manage education, play dates, and after-school activities. Understanding academic expectations and helping children find their way in more complex social groups has long-term benefits.

Get support. Parents and children can both benefit from extra help when there is too much stress or an emotional disorder.

Work to improve the context. Systems that are outside the family play an important role in how children develop, but caregivers sometimes need support to improve schools, neighborhoods or the environment.

Build pride and a sense of belonging. Connections to something outside of the family and to the greater community, whether that is a faith group, a cultural organization, or a shared commitment to a hobby, can help boost pride.

Information from National Academies of Sciences, Engineering, and Medicine, 2016.

Cumulative Stress For some children, however, a transition like a divorce, remarriage, or separation may be just one of many stresses that they face. The impact of the recent COVID-19 pandemic has been an added stressor, requiring children to adjust to remote school, grieve lost family members, and worry about family finances. These stressors were often experienced disproportionately by low-income children and families of color (Fraiman et al., 2021).

FAMILY INCLUDES MANY VARIETIES OF CAREGIVERS

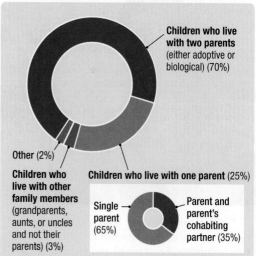

Data from U.S Census, 2021; Livingston, 2018.

CHILDREN'S HOUSEHOLDS

Data from Pilkauskas & Cross, 2018.

CHANGES IN FAMILIES

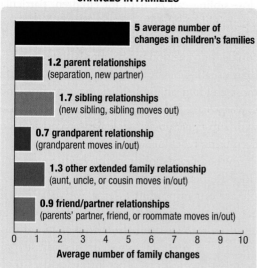

Data from Raley et al., 2019.

FIGURE 9.5 Family Structures and Transitions During Middle Childhood Children live in many types of family structures. Researchers studying U.S. families have found that change is common, with at least five changes in family structure during childhood.

As you have read, stress has a cumulative effect on children. For children already at risk, such as those living in poverty or who have emotional problems, the impact of family transition or other stressors is much greater (Härkönen et al., 2017). Repeated breakups and changes in living situations increase the likelihood that children will develop emotional difficulties that they express by acting out (Fomby & Osborne, 2017). Similarly, children from families with long histories of conflict prior to the transition tend to have higher rates of emotional disorders and report less satisfaction later in their lives (Amato & Anthony, 2014; Murphy et al., 2017; Wallerstein, 1987). The long-term consequences of stress and adversity before and after the transition, rather than the transition itself, is the likely cause of these challenges (Härkönen et al., 2017; Seijo et al., 2016).

The cumulative effect of stress means that family transitions, like other types of chronic stress, can take a toll on children's bodies and minds. For instance, scientists analyzed the chromosomes of children who had lost a parent to incarceration, separation, or death and found that this loss was reflected in their genes, particularly if families experienced additional adversity through loss of income. Children showed signs of epigenetic changes to their chromosomes. Their *telomeres*, or the endcaps on chromosomes that protect them, were dramatically shortened, as if the children had aged dramatically (see **Figure 9.6**) (Mitchell et al., 2017).

Stress may be damaging, but it does not have to be permanent. Just as the body can show signs of damage from chronic stress, it can also show signs of recovery (Raffington et al., 2021). Short telomeres can lengthen, and children can build resilience (Cowell et al., 2021).

Cultural Variations Families all around the world undergo transitions, but how communities experience them reflects their cultural values about family and gender roles.

Landscape of Loss There may be no silver lining when you lose your home to a fire, as these children did in Redding, California. But children can recover from stress: Strong relationships can help children bounce back. For many, however, the effects of cumulative stresses may add up, making it harder to heal.

CONNECTIONS

Remember from Chapter 3 that chromosomes are in the nucleus of every cell and direct cell replication throughout the lifespan. As telomeres degrade, errors in replication become more common, creating more risk for disease.

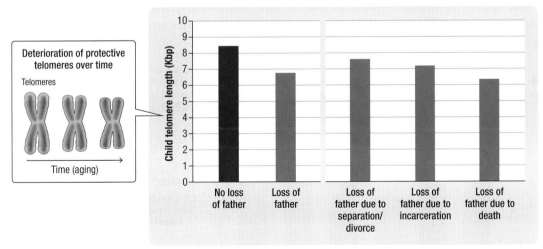

Data from Mitchell et al., 2017.

FIGURE 9.6 The Biological Impact of Stress Researchers measured changes in children's telomeres, the protective end-caps at the end of their chromosomes, over time. (Telomeres usually wear away as we age, but the pace of the change is often related to life experiences.) They found that the telomeres tended to be shorter (as measured in base pairs) in children who had experienced separation from one of their parents, including if they had lost their father to death, relationship transitions, or incarceration.

In middle childhood, resilience can be fostered through strong relationships at home, supportive friends and relationships with adults at school and in the community. The environment can make things difficult for some children: difficulties with health, finances, the environment, along with poorly-funded schools and stressed families make growing up harder.

STRESS

Difficulty in middle childhood may come from social stresses, financial and health concerns, or family difficulties.

1 in 5 8-year-olds around the globe were often worried about how much money they had.

1 in 10 said they did not always have enough to eat.

Social exclusion

An international survey of 10-year-old students asked whether they had experienced bullying or peer exclusion. ▼

12% Physically attacked by other children

18% Ridiculed by other students

16% Feel left out

THRIVING IN MIDDLE CHILDHOOD

Researchers studying children from 10 cities in Colombia, Finland, Portugal, Moscow, Turkey, Korea, China, Canada, and the U.S. found that most 10-year-olds felt good: Childhood is often a time for well-being and optimism. *Children report:* ▼

My life is interesting ✓ **61%**

I wake up feeling fresh and rested ✓ **52%**

I feel calm and relaxed ✓ **55%**

I feel cheerful ✓ **63%**

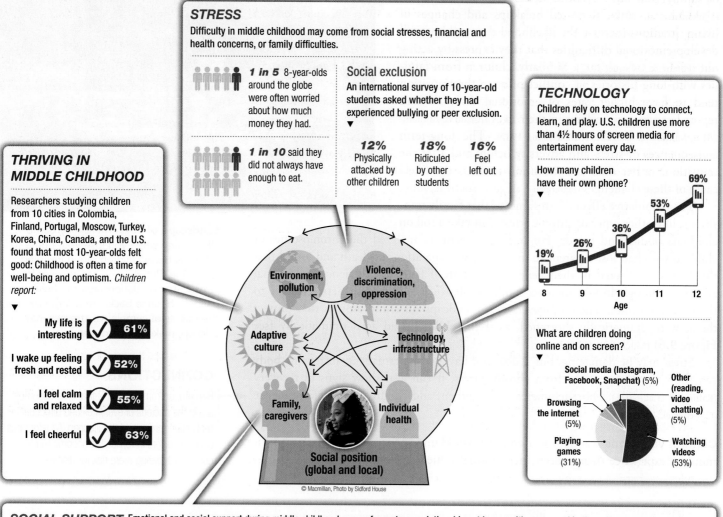

Environment, pollution

Violence, discrimination, oppression

Adaptive culture

Technology, infrastructure

Family, caregivers

Individual health

Social position (global and local)

© Macmillan, Photo by Sidford House

TECHNOLOGY

Children rely on technology to connect, learn, and play. U.S. children use more than 4½ hours of screen media for entertainment every day.

How many children have their own phone? ▼

8: 19%
9: 26%
10: 36%
11: 53%
12: 69%

Age

What are children doing online and on screen? ▼

Social media (Instagram, Facebook, Snapchat) (5%)

Other (reading, video chatting) (5%)

Browsing the internet (5%)

Playing games (31%)

Watching videos (53%)

SOCIAL SUPPORT
Emotional and social support during middle childhood comes from strong relationships at home, with peers, and in the school and community.

Family

What does it mean to have a strong family in middle childhood? Researchers measured U.S. families' strengths by looking at whether parents could manage the stresses of everyday life. ▼

55% are mostly or always able to work together to share problems and stay optimistic.

68% have a strong connection with their children.

66% cope with parenting very well.

School

Feeling like you belong in school is an important part of feeling supported and learning. Children around the world vary in terms of how well they do in school and how much they feel that they belong.

Percent of fourth-graders with a high sense of school belonging ▼

Global average: 58%
U.S.: 52%
Singapore: 45%
Finland: 60%
Canada: 53%
Chile: 57%

Friends

Friends are increasingly important in middle childhood, helping support children's emotional development and helping them learn how to get along with others. *10-year-olds around the world report:* ▼

61% say they have enough friends.

51% say friends are nice.

61% say friends are supportive.

For instance, in many European countries such as Norway and France, many parents never marry formally and cohabitation has long been accepted as the norm (Perelli-Harris, 2018). About 6 in 10 babies are born to parents in informal partnerships in France, compared to about 4 in 10 in the United States (McLanahan & Sawhill, 2015).

Culture also influences what happens after parents break up. In countries with strong traditions of gender equity, such as Sweden and Holland, parents typically share custody equally (Bergström et al., 2018). However, despite experts' recommendations that children share time with both parents, particularly in cases where conflict is low, joint custody is less common in the United States (Mahrer et al., 2018; Steinbach, 2019). Just because parents are separated does not mean that they are not invested in their children's lives: Some researchers have found that fathers who do not live with their children full time actually spend more hands-on time with their children than other dads (Jones & Mosher, 2013). Maintaining contact with a variety of caregivers provides children with an opportunity to experience a wide variety of relationships (Cabrera et al., 2018).

Extra Hands to Love Children thrive in all kinds of families, but having more than one parent to love you, like Sophia and Ava do, might mean you get extra attention and time for tickles.

APPLY IT! **9.5** Amara and her mother have abundant mutual admiration. What are three other signs of positive parenting in middle childhood?
9.6 What are ways that families can build resilience in the face of common stressors like financial strain, or family transition?

Getting Along with Other Children

In elementary school, children start spending most of their awake time away from home, in the company of other children. The friendships and the social skills that children build with their peers shape their academic success and their mental health for years to come (Bukowski & Raufelder, 2018; Rubin et al., 2015). Elementary schoolchildren practice social skills in larger groups than at home or in preschool. For some, friendship is a highlight of childhood, but for others, socializing comes less easily, and recess may be overwhelming. During the recent pandemic, friendships were often stressed by distance and physical separation, but positive bonds, whether fostered in "pandemic bubbles" or in friend groups, were a source of resilience (Cameron & Tenenbaum, 2021).

Learning Objectives

9.4 Describe the role of friendships and peer relationships in middle childhood.

9.5 Define the role of popularity and other social status categories during middle childhood.

Friendship

What makes someone a friend? By elementary school, children have the cognitive skills and emotion regulation to develop sophisticated ideas about maintaining friendships (Parker & Asher, 1993). Children in middle childhood can talk about their feelings, take other people's perspectives, and learn how to manage their emotions during conflicts. One young girl described her friend to researchers this way: "A best friend is somebody I can depend on. When I need you I can call you, and you come out here to see what's wrong. . . . You'll have my back." This girl describes her "true friend" as someone she really understands: "We got a real close connection. . . . I know what she's like. . . . It's so deep" (Chan Tack & Small, 2017, p. 240).

Friendships can be life-changing for children; they are a source of comfort in times of difficulty and teach habits of relating that will last into adulthood. Biologically, children's positive friendships protect their bodies by reducing stress hormone levels (Doom et al., 2017). Friendships can even reduce some of the risks from difficult early family relationships or personality traits (Buhs et al., 2018; Ladd, 1999). Perhaps most importantly, friends are fun: They do things with you, keep you company, and play with you at recess (Maunder & Monks, 2019).

Most studies find that between 60 and 80 percent of children have a friend (Rubin et al., 2015). Researchers test this not just by asking children if they have a friend, but by making sure that when children say someone is a friend that the feeling is truly

Learn It Together

Themes of Middle Childhood in Television

Plan What lessons do elementary-aged children obtain from television shows that target their age group? How do these messages correspond with what you have learned about social and emotional development? In this activity, you will watch a television show geared toward children aged 7–11 and give it a "grade" for how well it addresses a developmental concept for this age group.

Prepare Before class, identify a single episode of a show designed for the target age group (hint: look for shows that have a "family friendly" rating or description). Agree with your group members to all watch the same episode before class and take notes on the main storyline, messages, images, and themes that you notice. Some common themes may have to do with moral development (getting into trouble, doing the "right thing"), gender stereotypes (fitting in, not fitting in), social acceptance (bullying, popularity, being excluded from the group), or family themes (family conflicts, stresses).

Engage In class, meet with your group to share your insights. What connections can you make to topics from the chapter? Did you see examples of children displaying prosocial behavior or being challenged by social exclusion? Make note of specific developmental topics and terminology that relate to this episode.

Reflect As a team, write a summary of your observations in the form of an "evaluation" from the perspective of a developmental expert. Let the media executives know what important topics they portrayed or what they might have missed. Did the show do a good job of depicting important concepts for children of this age?

reciprocal (it is not always). Remember from Chapter 7 that, like adults, children tend to form friendships with people they perceive to be like them in fairly superficial ways. Children tend to follow the principle of *homophily*, or looking for friends who seem "like me." This means that most of the time, children end up with friends who mirror their age, gender identity, first language, ethnicity, behavior in school, and even athletic ability or academic achievement (Laninga-Wijnen et al., 2018; Mulvey et al., 2018).

Once children hit it off, the characteristics of a good relationship in elementary school are much the same as any good relationship across the lifespan. Friends care about each other and can manage the inevitable conflicts. Friends are there for help and even protection. They share secrets. And they have good times (Parker & Asher, 1993). Children's friendships are not fleeting: More than half of children's friendships last the entire school year (Rubin et al., 2015).

In their close relationships, children practice skills that they will use with friends and romantic partners over their lifetime. Those who start with secure, positive relationships with their parents and siblings are likely to establish warm friendships in elementary school (Furman & Rose, 2015). Children who do not learn at home how to be kind to other people or how to comfort someone who is upset will struggle with these skills in their friendships (Glick & Rose, 2011; Miller et al., 2020). Friendship gives these children a chance to develop new skills. Whether they are sharing a game of *Minecraft* or playing on the playground, friendships enable children to practice relationship skills such as managing conflict and asserting oneself without being mean (Rubin et al., 2015).

Children may struggle to make and keep friendships if they are very shy (Rubin et al., 2018). Shy or withdrawn children have difficulty speaking up in class or meeting someone new (Fredstrom et al., 2012). Their lack of experience with other children may also lead to trouble understanding others' points of view, such as what they need and want in a friendship (Penela et al., 2015). They may have a hard time understanding the social rules of friendships and opening up with their friends (Rubin et al., 2018). If they do not have an understanding friend, their social troubles may escalate, leading to more withdrawal, anxiety, and even depression (Penela et al., 2015).

Aggressive children, on the other hand, also have challenges navigating close relationships. They may be overreactive and misinterpret a harmless comment as threatening. If they are used to getting their way through physical or emotional aggression, many of their relationships may not be reciprocal and trusting (Rubin et al., 2015).

CAN YOU BELIEVE IT?
Can Online Games Be Play?

Play is at the core of children's relationships. Children squeeze in time for fun, whether it is in the lunch line, on the basketball court, or on the bus (Howard et al., 2017). In many communities around the world, play during middle childhood now often involves clicking and looking at screens. More than 97 percent of U.S. children ages 6 to 12 play online or video games (Adachi & Willoughby, 2017). During the COVID-19 pandemic, children's screen time more than doubled. More than half of children in the United States report having played *Roblox*, an interactive multiplayer game that, in one of its most popular versions, involves adopting virtual pets (Puleo, 2020; Richtel, 2021).

Despite the occasional headlines that warn that screen time is "digital heroin" that will "turn kids into psychotic junkies," many developmental scientists argue that playing video games is just play, and that it can help children build social skills and make friends (Granic et al., 2014; Kardaras, 2016; Richtel, 2021; Twenge & Campbell, 2018). Most of the video games children play are not solitary: The most popular games, like *Roblox* or *Minecraft*, require cooperation and social interaction (Adachi & Willoughby, 2017).

Even in war games, children collaborate on how to achieve victory. Researchers have found that in communities where most children play online games, the children who do not play may be socially isolated. When researchers compared a group of children in Norway who played online games with a group who did not, they found that playing video games did not hurt social skills such as the ability to share, listen to each other, and pick up on nonverbal cues (Hygen et al., 2020).

Children who struggle with social interaction may feel more comfortable playing online than in real life, but for those who have trouble making friends, online gaming is not a permanent solution. After the forced isolation of the pandemic, researchers worry that children who spend too much time online may remain isolated in real life (Hygen et al., 2020; Lobel et al., 2017). 🖐️

Spending Time in Groups

Pandemic restrictions notwithstanding, when children are at school, on the playground, or practicing sports, they spend most of their time in big groups. As they grow older, much of this time is away from the close supervision of adults who increasingly trust children to follow the rules and stay safe. This gives children the opportunity to develop their independence, but it also increases the likelihood that children will hurt each other or learn dangerous behaviors from other children.

Measuring Popularity In middle childhood, children use their stronger cognitive skills to compare and rank their popularity with their peers. In fact, if researchers ask children to rate whether they like or dislike the other children in a group, they find that children's descriptions of each other fall into predictable categories (Cillessen & Bukowski, 2018).

Most children are generally well-liked or **popular**, meaning that many in their class say they "like them" or that they are their friends (Newcomb et al., 1993). Some are **rejected**, or actively disliked by most children in the class. Another category of children is **neglected**, either forgotten altogether or not rated by children in their class. **Controversial** children receive mixed ratings, strongly disliked by some and strongly liked by others. Other children are just **average**, or fall around the middle of being liked and disliked, not quite making it into the other categories (Cillessen & Bukowski, 2018).

There are two types of popular children in any group. Likeable children have good social skills; they know how to show empathy, they can regulate their emotions to manage difficult situations, and they can assert themselves from time to time (Rubin et al., 2015; van den Berg et al., 2017). Children who have strong *perceived popularity* are dominant, whether that means they are captains of the kickball team or decide who sits where at lunch. These children may not be prosocial or kind. They may be socially aggressive or even bullying, and they may use manipulation, threats, and exclusion to gain social power (Laninga-Wijnen et al., 2019; Rubin et al., 2015).

Rejected children are described by their peers as unlikeable and actively excluded from the group. In some cases, they may be extremely shy or withdrawn. Others may be aggressive or mean. Researchers find that they tend to have trouble playing group games, are too shy to speak up, or are too volatile to play with (Rubin et al., 2015). Children often justify excluding them by explaining that they are too difficult, do not follow the rules, or are not fun (Rutland & Killen, 2015). Children are also rejected because they are different from their peers in some way: They may speak a different language, have a disability, or belong to a different racial or ethnic group (Killen & Smetana, 2015).

Imgorthand/E+/Getty Images

Playing with Friends At a time when children were staying at home and worried about transmitting COVID-19 to their siblings, online games gave them a way to be with each other, as was true for this child in Poland.

popular Children who are liked or perceived to be socially successful by many of their peers.

rejected Children who are actively disliked by most of their peers.

neglected Children who are unconsidered or forgotten altogether by their peers.

controversial Children who receive mixed ratings by their peers, strongly disliked by some and strongly liked by others.

average social acceptance Children who fall around the middle of being liked and disliked, not quite making it into the other categories.

Grins All Around Whether in Canada or in South Africa, fun with friends helps children learn how to get along with other people and learn to thrive in larger social groups.

Children who are controversial or neglected do not fit neatly into any other categories. They may receive mixed ratings from their peers or be forgotten altogether. Controversial children may include the class clown or bully, who displays more aggression or is prone to emotional outbursts. Neglected children are typically quiet, shy children who are forgotten by their peers. They are isolated from social activity, but their peers do not have a negative view of them (Kulawiak & Wilbert, 2020; Rytioja et al., 2019; van Der Wilt et al., 2019).

Tracking the Costs of Exclusion Being excluded in elementary school can hurt children in the short and long term. In the long term, repeated exclusion can damage children's sense of belonging and their emotional health (Schacter, 2021). Social neuroscientists scanning children's brains have found that being rejected or excluded really does hurt: Children who are excluded show signs of activity in cortical areas where the brain processes physical pain (Eisenberger et al., 2003; Lieberman & Eisenberger, 2015).

Repeated experiences of rejection affect the brain just like other repeated experiences. When children are consistently left out, excluded from play, or picked last for a team, negative emotional pathways in their brains are activated and strengthened, making them more readily available for processing future experiences. These networks influence how children process their social experiences for years to come (Guyer & Jarcho, 2018; Quinlan et al., 2020).

Children do not "get used to" being excluded. When researchers observe children over time, they find that for many the pain intensifies. They become likely to assume the worst, to overreact, and have more difficulty calming themselves down (Guyer & Jarcho, 2018; Will et al., 2016). This can lead to academic difficulties, not because the excluded children are cognitively incapable, but because they feel they just do not belong. They may experience depression or anxiety, or start acting out and behaving aggressively toward other children (Will et al., 2016). As they grow older, this emotional pain may increase their likelihood to experience bullying, emotional difficulties, substance abuse, and even criminal behavior.

Bullying

Bullying happens in all cultures around the world and has been documented since the earliest human civilizations (Nguyen et al., 2020; Richardson & Hiu, 2018; Savahl et al., 2019). Remember from Chapter 7 that *bullying* is any physical and/or social aggression between a child who is perceived as socially powerful and another with less social power (Olweus, 1978). Bullying can include physical violence or involve *relational aggression*, such as spreading rumors, social exclusion, and online attacks (*cyberbullying*).

In many communities, children who seem "different" or who do not "fit in" are targeted by bullies. Researchers call this *bias-related bullying*, and depending on the community, children who are from a different ethnic group or economic background, have a larger body size or a disability, or do not adhere to gender stereotypes may be targeted (Palmer & Abbott, 2018). Estimating just how many children are involved is challenging because victims do not always understand that what is happening to them is worth reporting. Only half of children who are bullied tell someone (Hawley, 2015). Researchers believe that about one in three children are involved in bullying during middle childhood, either as victims or as aggressors (Camerini et al., 2020; Zych et al., 2019).

Bullying typically happens in front of other children and adults, but the victims often feel invisible (Mazzone et al., 2021). Typically, recess monitors or teachers notice only 10 percent of playground bullying incidents and fewer than 20 percent of classroom incidents (Hawley, 2015). Other children may be passive bystanders, failing to intervene or, in some circumstances, even supporting the bully. But not all children are passive. Those who are both empathetic and socially confident are able to step in to defend a victim of bullying (Kärnä et al., 2013; Mazzone et al., 2016; van der Ploeg et al., 2020).

Children who are the victims of bullying and ostracism may carry the consequences with them into adulthood. Chronic exclusion is particularly harmful if it reinforces discrimination children face outside of school (Palmer & Abbott, 2018). Particularly if children lack the protection of a close friend or a nurturing family, the stress of social aggression can damage physical and mental health. Children may struggle in school and have higher rates of depression and anxiety (McDougall & Vaillancourt, 2015; Meter & Bauman, 2018). One child explained that victims take the effects of bullying "home with them at night. It lives inside them and eats away at them. It never ends. So neither should our struggle to end it" (Hymel & Swearer, 2015, p. 296).

Developmental scientists are working to end bullying. Interventions designed to combat social aggression try to turn children from passive bystanders into active defenders. Children who feel empowered to intervene can help change the school environment to make all children feel safer and more included (Herkama et al., 2017; Waasdorp et al., 2021).

APPLY IT! **9.7** Amara stood up for a friend who was targeted by other students at school for being taller than her peers. What are ways strong friendships can help children bounce back from social exclusion?

9.8 Social rankings happen outside of elementary school including on college campuses and in the workplace. How would you use the ways scientists measure popularity in the classroom to look at social dynamics in your community?

CONNECTIONS

Remember from Chapter 7 that peer victimization is not unique to middle childhood: Signs of social exclusion appear in preschool. Social aggression actually gets worse before it gets better (see Chapter 11) and reaches a peak in early adolescence.

Scientific American Profile

Standing Up to Bullying

Moral Development

Amara was bullied when she first started school. She does not like to talk about it, because she is sure that the children who made her cry didn't know what they were doing. "It wasn't anything," she says. "Kids hurt each other sometimes." Amara knows the importance of speaking up. Her friend was bullied because she is tall; Amara confronted her tormenters. Was she afraid? "No," she says. "You can't be afraid. Or even if you are, you still have to do it." That isn't the only nice thing that Amara has done lately. In fact, Her mother keeps a list of the kind things Amara likes to do for people: helping her grandmother by running an errand or washing the dishes. Amara wants to be a doctor when she grows up so she can continue to help those in need.

Learning Objective

9.6 Describe the development of moral reasoning and moral behavior in middle childhood.

CONNECTIONS

Remember that prosocial behavior is anything that helps other people, like helping someone in need, following the rules, or giving a hug to someone who is sad. Babies show signs of prosocial behavior before they can walk, for example, trying to comfort someone who is hurt (see Chapter 5). In early childhood, children are capable of empathy, sharing, and understanding the difference between who is nice and who is not (see Chapter 7).

How does Amara understand the importance of helping out? When do children know how to be nice? Most adults around the world do not think children are fully responsible for their actions during middle childhood (Lancy, 2018). However, most schools, families, and even other children expect that children will be able to treat each other *prosocially*, or kindly, during middle childhood. Children are expected to respect each other, to temper their outbursts, and to follow the rules. For many—but not all—children, this comes easily over time.

Thinking About Right and Wrong

When many people, including psychologists, think about right and wrong, they think about following rules (Haidt, 2009). Some scientists, beginning with Piaget, believed that children's development of moral behavior is a consequence of their improving ability to understand these rules (Piaget, 1965). Piaget believed that one way children learn to behave morally by playing increasingly complex rule-based games with other children. As children move from playing tag to playing kickball, they learn the consequences and the rewards of following directions. Like some other researchers, Piaget believed that children naturally learn to follow rules from their peers and do not need to be directly taught.

Psychologist Lawrence Kohlberg adapted Piaget's theories of cognitive development in his stage theory of children's moral reasoning (Kohlberg, 1978; Kohlberg & Kramer, 1969). For Kohlberg, moral decisions were not abstract, but deeply personal. Like so many others who served during World War II, Kohlberg wanted to understand why some people became killers, some sacrificed themselves, and others stood by (Snarey, 2012). To develop his stage theory, he posed moral dilemmas to children and observed how their moral reasoning became more complex as they grew older. He noted how children gradually moved from making decisions based on concrete factors, such as avoiding punishment, to thinking more abstractly about right and wrong (Kohlberg, 1981).

Kohlberg used a story called *Heinz's dilemma* to illustrate the development of moral reasoning. He asked children whether it would be okay for a sick woman's husband, named Heinz, to steal a medication that he could not afford in order to save her life. Did saving his partner's life justify the burglary? How children answered this dilemma depended on their level of cognitive development and moral reasoning. Kohlberg was interested in more than the children's answers: He wanted to know how children made sense of the moral problem. Could they understand that people might have different perspectives? Could they balance the man's desire to obey the law with the woman's desire to live? What about the perspective of the pharmacist who owned the medication? Or the police? Based on their answers to Heinz's dilemma, Kohlberg theorized there were three stages in children's moral development: *preconventional*, *conventional*, and *postconventional* moral reasoning.

Children in the **preconventional** stage of moral reasoning tend to use concrete and self-centered (*egocentric*) reasoning, as you might expect from children in Piaget's preoperational stage of cognitive development. Children at this stage are focused on the concrete effects of Heinz's choices. They say Heinz should not steal the medicine, because he will go to jail. Alternatively, they say that he should steal because if his wife dies, he will be sad and lonely.

In the next stage, **conventional** moral reasoning, children think more abstractly about what is right and wrong. They may talk about "rules" or "laws" that govern behavior, and they tend to have more sense of the consequences of breaking the law. Despite this, they will still show some empathy for Heinz and his family. A child in this stage might say something like, "Heinz may have been disappointed that the

preconventional stage of moral reasoning
Kohlberg's stage of moral reasoning in which children use concrete and self-centered (egocentric) reasoning.

conventional stage of moral reasoning
Kohlberg's stage of moral reasoning in which children think more abstractly about what is right and wrong.

drug was so expensive, but we need to have laws to make everything work." They might suggest that Heinz should have investigated other possibilities rather than breaking the law.

Many people remain in the conventional stage of moral reasoning, but Kohlberg believed that a small number of people, capable of deep perspective taking and empathy, move into the **postconventional** stage of moral reasoning. People who reach this stage can think abstractly and about right and wrong as something that supersedes rules and laws. Kohlberg viewed people such as Martin Luther King Jr. as a moral exemplar because they engaged in civil disobedience, breaking the law in pursuit of a higher, more just goal (Kohlberg, 1978).

In the many years since Kohlberg developed his theory of moral reasoning, its universality and relevance have been questioned by many critics (Goldschmidt et al., 2021; Haidt, 2009). Scholar Carol Gilligan pointed out that for many people, particularly women and girls in the United States, caring for other people is more important than following abstract rules, an orientation she called the *ethics of care*. Like others, she challenged Kohlberg's idea that being able to grapple with ideas like "justice" meant that people were more caring in real life (Brown & Gilligan, 1993; Gilligan, 1977, 1993). Many critics joined Gilligan in questioning whether Kohlberg's stages were actually as universal as Piaget's. Around the world, families believe that there is more to becoming a good person than being able to reason (Xu, 2019). In other cultures, many people value adherence to religious traditions or value the well-being of the group over being able to reason about what is best for one person, like Heinz's wife (Killen & Smetana, 2015).

The universality and relevance of Kohlberg's stages have also been questioned by researchers who discovered that children do not think that all moral choices are equivalent (Nucci & Turiel, 1978; Turiel, 1983; Turiel & Dahl, 2019). Even kindergarteners see that that not all rules are the same. They distinguish between *moral choices*, such as whether it is okay to hurt someone, *conventional rules*, such as not running in the hall, and *personal choices*, such as whether it is okay to dye your hair purple.

TABLE 9.3 Kohlberg's Stages of Moral Reasoning

Stage	Age	Characteristics
Preconventional	Typically at about the age of Piaget's preconventional reasoning, or until about ages 8–10.	Children are motivated by not getting in trouble. They follow rules so as not to get punished by a parent, teacher, or the police, not because of any internalized sense of right and wrong.
Conventional	Typically children reach this stage at around the same time as they gain the ability to reason abstractly and reach Piaget's concrete operational thought stage, or at around age 7. Many people spend the rest of their lives in this stage.	Children begin to think about the abstract values of being "good" or "bad" and want other people to think of them as "good." They may throw out their trash because "only bad kids litter." They begin to take on other people's perspectives when making moral decisions and to think about abstract values like "laws" or religious commandments that control their behavior.
Postconventional	Not all adults or children reach this stage, but those who do have acquired the ability for complex abstract thought, typically only possible in adolescence and beyond.	Individuals put moral actions above their own self-interest and the laws of their community. They stand up for what they believe is right, even if that means breaking the law. In this stage, individuals have internalized a sense that a community is bound together through a social contract, a commitment that humans are committed to work together for the good of the many.

postconventional stage of moral reasoning Kohlberg's stage of moral reasoning in which people can think abstractly and about right and wrong as something that supersedes rules and laws.

Sometimes a Doll Is Not Just a Doll.
Sometimes a doll inspires social action. Melissa Shang is a student, a writer, and an advocate for people with disabilities who has tried to convince manufacturers to create dolls that reflect the experiences of all children.

Doing Good

Children are capable of incredible acts of bravery and kindness. Ten-year-old Melissa Shang made herself internet famous by trying to convince the American Girl doll company to make a doll who had a visible disability. She started an online petition, pointing out that more than one in five Americans, including herself, has a disability. Melissa had more than 150,000 supporters, but the American Girl doll company was not convinced. Melissa is still working to accomplish big things: She is now writing a novel.

Scientists have found that many children, like Melissa, are good at thinking about the greater good. For instance, most adults tell scientists that they would spend lottery winnings on themselves, but children say they would spend their money on gifts and charity, particularly for their family (Kiang et al., 2016). Even if they are not spending weekends in social activism or handing out food at a food pantry, children act prosocially when doing everyday tasks and chores, like sharing with a friend or clearing the table. Children's maturing abilities to think about the world from other people's perspectives and control their behavior, help them do more for other people. There are individual and community variations in children's prosocial behavior, but the benefits of helping are profound (Aknin et al., 2018). Helping not only helps the receiver, but also gives the helper a sense of mission and meaning in their life.

Scientists have found that children are capable of extremely complex thinking when it comes to deciding how to share, including the consideration of who is worthy of sharing with and what is fair (House & Tomasello, 2018). For instance, around the world, most preschoolers would agree that the best way to share is to be precisely equal no matter what. For them, equal is fair, and each friend should get exactly the same number of coins (Huppert et al., 2019). But as children get older, their ideas about what is fair become more complex (Almas et al., 2015). Children's sharing reflects their developing ability to think abstractly and how well they have internalized the particular social rules of their community (Almas et al., 2015).

When researchers test children around the world to see how they share and with whom, they discover some surprising results. It turns out that U.S. children are actually very good at sharing compared to children from other communities, perhaps because being a "good sharer" is something that is emphasized in schools (Cowell et al., 2017; Rao & Stewart, 1999). U.S. children also tend to develop very complicated ideas about how to share fairly at earlier ages than children from other countries, perhaps because they are aware of more inequity than other children (Cowell et al., 2017; Huppert et al., 2019). If researchers compare how children share around the world, they find that all children gradually share more with peers who are hardworking, poor, or hurt, as they get older and break away from a strict idea of equality. But children from individualistic cultures, where inequity is more common, develop ideas about who deserves generosity at earlier ages. In contrast, those from more collectivist communities, hold on for longer to the idea that everyone deserves an equal share (Huppert et al., 2019).

Does Making Cards Build Gratitude?
Communities teach children about social relationships in different ways. These cards were made by children in Bangor, Northern Ireland, to thank frontline workers during the COVID-19 pandemic.

Whenever it happens, prosocial behavior, like sharing, gives children something more than the momentary rush of good feelings. Helping others benefits children in the long term by strengthening their relationships and connections with other people (Aknin et al., 2017; Miller & Hastings, 2019). Scientists have found that being prosocial even changes children's bodies, making them increasingly more flexible in their responses to stress and anxiety: Children who shared with others responded to stress more flexibly and were better able to manage their anxiety, a difference that remained when the researchers checked on the children again two years later (Miller, 2018). This suggests that children who can connect and respond to others in need with empathy and kindness will develop healthier reactions to anxiety and stress of their own. Helping others trains children's nervous system to manage anxiety in a healthier way (Miller, 2018; Miller et al., 2015).

As you will see in the next chapters, children's ability to help others only gets stronger as they get older. As children move into adolescence, they become even more industrious, and their prosocial behaviors become more visible and valued by their communities. Like Amara, they can think about how to solve problems in their community or advocate for something they believe in. Giving of themselves, which results in stronger social connections and a sense of their own competence, can continue to help children build resilience (Fuligni, 2019).

Scientific American Profile

Engaging with the World

APPLY IT! **9.9** Amara's mother has raised her to value being compassionate and helping other people in need. Her ethnotheories emphasize the value of kindness and advocacy. What ethnotheories about morality do you recognize in your own family? **9.10** Amara thinks abstractly about social issues. Where do you think she might fit in Kolhberg's stages of moral reasoning?

Wrapping It Up ⊂⊃

LO 9.1 Explain the goals of emotion regulation during middle childhood. (p. 257)

Children are expected to control their feelings more independently during middle childhood. Some are forced by adversity to grow up more quickly than others. In middle childhood, resilience is based on secure attachments, warm caregiving, and friendships. Erikson described middle childhood as a conflict between *industry versus inferiority*, a concept supported by contemporary researchers. Children learn how to manage their feelings in ways that are specific to their communities. Strong relationships help build strong emotion regulation. Some children develop psychological disorders, such as *internalizing disorders* like depression and anxiety and *externalizing disorders* like ADHD, oppositional defiant disorder, and conduct disorder. Disorders are caused by a complex mix of genes, brain development, and stress.

LO 9.2 Describe advances in self-concept and the role of social comparison in self-esteem during middle childhood. (p. 263)

Children develop a stronger sense of who they are and how they compare to other children in middle childhood. Scientists analyze personality in middle childhood (and beyond) using the *five-factor model*. Children tend to become more agreeable and conscientious as they get older. Culture affects children's personality development. Children continue to have stereotypes about gender and to develop a sense of their racial and ethnic identity. Many children experience discrimination; a sense of solidarity and pride can help buffer its effects.

LO 9.3 Describe the importance of family relationships in middle childhood. (p. 268)

Children are much more independent than in the preschool years but still benefit from strong, supportive family relationships. Warm caregiving supports secure attachments and includes monitoring children's behavior without being too controlling. Harsh, rejecting, and disengaged parenting can be harmful to children. Some families are caught in a coercive cycle of acting out. Families' beliefs and their resources can help children's school achievement. Many families are in transition and under stress. Cumulative stress can hurt children, but families can build resilience.

LO 9.4 Describe the role of friendships and peer relationships in middle childhood. (p. 275)

Friendships help children build social skills. Children have a better understanding of what makes a friend, and these patterns of relating will stick with children as they develop relationships later in life. Some children have difficulty finding and making friends, particularly if they are shy.

LO 9.5 Define the role of popularity and other social status categories during middle childhood. (p. 275)

Children spend much of their time in big groups. Scientists observe and categorize how children relate to each other and identify *popular, rejected, neglected, controversial,* and *average* children. Children in groups frequently exclude and bully others, which can lead to difficulties. Interventions are aimed at building a sense of belonging and empowering everyone in a community to intervene and stop exclusion and bullying.

LO 9.6 Describe the development of moral reasoning and moral behavior in middle childhood. (p. 279)

Children are capable of kindness and understand how to follow moral rules. Kolhberg described children's moral development as a series of increasingly complex stages modeled on Piaget's stages of cognitive development. He used a hypothetical scenario called *Heinz's dilemma* to evaluate children's moral reasoning. Kohlberg's critics have pointed out that morality is influenced by culture and that caring is often interpersonal, rather than based on abstract reasoning. Children are capable of very complex thinking about sharing and equality, which is also influenced by cultural values. Giving helps children build resilience, relationships, empathy, and a sense of competence.

KEY TERMS

industry versus inferiority (p. 259)

psychological disorder (p. 262)

internalizing disorders (p. 262)

externalizing disorders (p. 263)

monitoring (p. 269)

popular (p. 277)

rejected (p. 277)

neglected (p. 277)

controversial (p. 277)

average (p. 277)

preconventional (p. 280)

conventional (p. 280)

postconventional (p. 281)

CHECK YOUR LEARNING

1. According to Erikson, successful psychological development in middle childhood involves:
   a) tackling subconscious aggressive tendencies.
   b) developing a strict sense of gender identity.
   c) learning universal human concepts.
   d) navigating the expectations of school and social relationships.

2. Elementary-aged children who do not feel successful in school may experience what Erikson described as:
   a) inferiority.
   b) mistrust.
   c) shame.
   d) role confusion.

3. Which of the following statements is FALSE?
   a) Helping out is correlated with positive outcomes like self-confidence and self-efficacy.
   b) Most children resent having to do chores around the house.
   c) Children's participation in household chores or helping with other family work is more common among low-income U.S. families.
   d) Engaging in helpful activities at home is a form of industriousness.

4. The improving ability during middle childhood to control strong reactions like temper tantrums and to display responses appropriate in social settings is known as:
   a) cumulative stress.
   b) emotion regulation.
   c) latency.
   d) secure attachment.

5. Which of the following is an example of an internalizing disorder?
   a) Depression
   b) Oppositional defiant disorder
   c) Attention deficit/hyperactivity disorder
   d) Dyslexia

6. Boys' tendency to participate and persist more than girls in STEM activities during middle childhood is partially explained by:
   a) boys' higher achievement throughout school.
   b) stereotypes about the appropriateness of STEM for boys rather than girls.
   c) hormonal differences that make boys more interested in STEM.
   d) girls' poorer grades in math and science.

7. Supportive parenting includes all of the following EXCEPT:
   a) monitoring behavior when children are away from home.
   b) warm emotional interactions.
   c) coercive cycles.
   d) two-way communication.

8. Nine-year-old Dilan frequently leaves a mess in the kitchen when he makes his own after-school snack. When his father reprimands him and demands he clean it up, Dilan makes a dramatic show of his resentment and does a poor job cleaning. Despite wanting Dilan to take responsibility for his own mess, his father tends to finish the cleaning himself. This repeated pattern of family interaction is an example of:
   a) a coercive cycle.
   b) secure-base behavior.
   c) ADHD.
   d) neglectful parenting.

9. Which of the following statements about friendships during middle childhood is TRUE?
   a) Children form friendships with whomever they spend the most time with, regardless of individual characteristics.
   b) Children's stereotypes disappear in middle childhood and they tend to befriend children very different from them in gender, ethnicity, and interests.
   c) Children tend to form friendships with others who share their cultural experiences and interests.
   d) Most children's friendships last only a week or so.

10. Fourth-grader Cody has a goofy sense of humor and is somewhat of a "class clown." Some of his classmates admire him, but several others find him to be a little mean. Cody is likely:
    a) popular.
    b) rejected.
    c) neglected.
    d) controversial.

11. What approaches can adults use for supporting positive ethnic and racial identity among elementary-aged children?

12. What is cumulative stress and how does it impact development?

13. What is the difference between preconventional and conventional moral reasoning?

10 Physical and Cognitive Development in Adolescence

© Macmillan, Photo by Sidford House

Selected Resources from

Activities

Concept Practice: Puberty Changes Everything

Spotlight on Science: Does Online Media Make You Feel Bad?

Assessments

LearningCurve

Practice Quiz

Videos

Scientific American Profiles

The Timing of Puberty

Sleep: Why We Sleep

Sisters Ruby and Rosie spent a lot of time together in the last year, going back and forth between their mother's and father's houses each week. For most of the COVID-19 pandemic, they sat side-by-side in front of their laptops for remote school. Nevertheless, they still think the world of each other. Rosie admires her older sister for being talented and fun, and for making the best oatmeal cookies. Ruby admires her little sister for her energy and her creativity.

Having a sister at home meant they each had someone to turn to during the many isolated months of the pandemic. They worked hard to keep up with their friendships through occasional meetups in the front yard and on Zoom, all the while wondering what relationships would be left after the pandemic.

Both girls are in the middle of big transitions in their lives. Rosie is 11 and just starting middle school. Ruby is two years older and about to start high school. These changes scare them both a little: They love their teachers and have gotten used to the routines of Zoom school, despite the isolation. Their new schools are bigger and filled with unknowns, especially after a year at home.

The girls are a lot alike in many ways: They are responsible and can be trusted to keep up with their schoolwork without much of a hassle. They also help with dishwashing and cooking. They are not identical, though: Rosie is more active and would rather swing from a tree than read in a hammock like her sister. Ruby likes school, wants to learn about science, and maybe will be a psychologist when she grows up.

Scientific American Profile

Meet Ruby and Rosie

Their bodies have also changed during the past year: While Rosie still looks a lot like she did in fourth grade, Ruby has gone through a growth spurt and is taller than her friends. She looks more like a grown-up. She stays up later, sleeps later, and spends hours reading about science on the internet: Chromosomes, synapses, and dendrites are exciting to her (as are fancy cakes). Rosie would still rather have a dance party and play video games.

As you will learn, even when they are not navigating a global pandemic, adolescents are prepared to face and adapt to change, whether that is attending a new high school or learning how to multiply exponents. Developmental scientists have found that the biological and cognitive maturation of puberty helps adolescents like Rosie and Ruby prepare for new challenges with optimism as they begin the transition to adulthood.

What Is Adolescence?

Learning Objective

10.1 Define adolescence.

Changing the World One brushstroke at a time, Jessica helps to beautify her neighborhood in Milwaukee, Wisconsin, by participating in a community art project. Adolescents have the skills and independence to contribute more than younger children to their community.

adolescence The life stage that begins with the biological changes of puberty and ends when young people are recognized as adults.

puberty The process that transforms children into adults who are typically able to reproduce and have children of their own.

Most cultures over time and around the world recognize a special period between childhood and adulthood in which we are no longer children but are not quite adults (Kinney, 2004; Schlegel, 1995, 2015; Schlegel & Barry, 1991). Developmental scientists call this period of transition **adolescence**. This life stage begins with the biological changes of puberty and ends when young people are recognized as adults.

How long adolescence takes and what marks its end are determined by culture and history. For instance, in Classical China and among the Maya of ancient Mexico, some elite boys were considered adults at around 19 after years of learning laws, language, and religious beliefs, whereas girls were considered adults a few years earlier when they began to take on more household responsibilities (Kinney, 2004; Scherer, 2015). In England and the United States during the Industrial Revolution, children often took jobs in factories to support their families: For them, the period between childhood and adulthood was likely shorter (Modell & Goodman, 1990).

Today, adolescence in most affluent societies is generally considered to begin with the major biological milestones of puberty occurring as early as age 9 or 10 and end when teenagers reach the age of legal majority or adulthood, at about age 18. However, given the rising number of young people attending college and the fact that many privileges like drinking alcohol or renting a car are not granted until later, some experts argue that contemporary adolescence may last until age 25 (Patton et al., 2018)!

APPLY IT! **10.1** When did you first feel like an adolescent? Did you look forward to being a teenager with excitement or was it something you dreaded?
10.2 What markers of adulthood do you think signify the end of adolescence?

Changing Body

Learning Objectives

10.2 Identify the biological changes of puberty.

10.3 Explain healthy sexual development during adolescence.

Puberty is the process that transforms children into adults who are typically able to have children of their own. Puberty includes maturation of the reproductive organs, development of secondary sex characteristics, and a growth spurt (Witchel & Topaloglu, 2019). (See **Infographic 10.1**.) This process will also trigger social and emotional changes like sexual desire and increased sensitivity to stress (Sisk & Romeo, 2020).

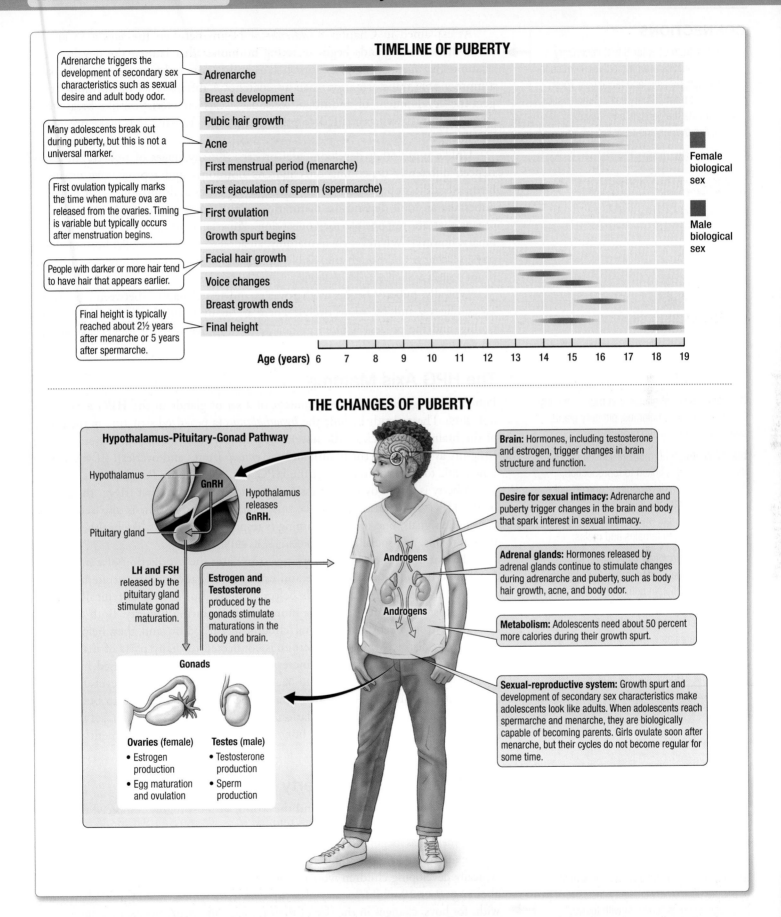

TIMELINE OF PUBERTY

Adrenarche triggers the development of secondary sex characteristics such as sexual desire and adult body odor.

Many adolescents break out during puberty, but this is not a universal marker.

First ovulation typically marks the time when mature ova are released from the ovaries. Timing is variable but typically occurs after menstruation begins.

People with darker or more hair tend to have hair that appears earlier.

Final height is typically reached about 2½ years after menarche or 5 years after spermarche.

Adrenarche
Breast development
Pubic hair growth
Acne
First menstrual period (menarche)
First ejaculation of sperm (spermarche)
First ovulation
Growth spurt begins
Facial hair growth
Voice changes
Breast growth ends
Final height

Age (years) 6 7 8 9 10 11 12 13 14 15 16 17 18 19

Female biological sex

Male biological sex

THE CHANGES OF PUBERTY

Hypothalamus-Pituitary-Gonad Pathway

Hypothalamus
GnRH
Pituitary gland

Hypothalamus releases GnRH.

LH and FSH released by the pituitary gland stimulate gonad maturation.

Estrogen and Testosterone produced by the gonads stimulate maturations in the body and brain.

Gonads

Ovaries (female)
- Estrogen production
- Egg maturation and ovulation

Testes (male)
- Testosterone production
- Sperm production

Androgens

Androgens

Brain: Hormones, including testosterone and estrogen, trigger changes in brain structure and function.

Desire for sexual intimacy: Adrenarche and puberty trigger changes in the brain and body that spark interest in sexual intimacy.

Adrenal glands: Hormones released by adrenal glands continue to stimulate changes during adrenarche and puberty, such as body hair growth, acne, and body odor.

Metabolism: Adolescents need about 50 percent more calories during their growth spurt.

Sexual-reproductive system: Growth spurt and development of secondary sex characteristics make adolescents look like adults. When adolescents reach spermarche and menarche, they are biologically capable of becoming parents. Girls ovulate soon after menarche, but their cycles do not become regular for some time.

HPG axis A set of glands that trigger puberty, including the hypothalamus, pituitary gland, and gonads (testes and ovaries).

testosterone A hormone produced by the gonads that is linked to reproduction, maturation, brain development, and sexual function. Testosterone levels are higher in biological males but are important to typical functioning in both females and males.

estrogen A hormone that is linked to reproduction, maturation, brain development, and sexual function in both males and females. Estrogen levels are higher in biological females but are important to typical functioning in both males and females.

growth spurt A very rapid increase in height and size that begins at about age 10 in girls and age 12 in boys.

As explained in Chapter 8, *adrenarche* begins between the ages of 5 and 9, when the adrenal glands begin secreting hormones that launch the development of some *secondary sex characteristics* such as body odor, and hair growth. Puberty is a more visible transformation than adrenarche: A different set of hormones triggers the development of additional secondary sex characteristics, like breasts and deeper voices, as well as changes to primary sex characteristics that make pregnancy possible.

Unlike some other developmental processes, many stages of puberty are experienced differently depending on children's hormones and reproductive organs at birth. Regardless of a child's gender identity, the genes and hormones that drive the pubertal transition depend on maturation of the *ovaries* or *testes*, the reproductive organs that are responsible for conception. Pubertal maturation is not completely binary, however: Whatever their anatomy, all adolescents have parallel hormonal and physical changes, although the visible signs of that maturation happen at different times (DuBois & Shattuck-Heidorn, 2020).

Typically, puberty begins as the ovaries and testes mature (between ages 8 and 13 and ages 9 and 14, respectively). There are many healthy variations in pubertal timing, and the process is often gradual, spanning five years or longer (Mendle et al., 2019; Wolf & Long, 2016).

The HPG Axis Matures

Puberty is triggered by the development of a set of glands in the **HPG axis** (Aylwin et al., 2019). These glands include the *hypothalamus* (a pea-sized structure in the center of the brain at the back of the nose); the *pituitary gland* (a tiny pencil-eraser-sized structure at the base of the brain); and the *gonads* (testes and ovaries). (If you need a mnemonic to help you remember the HPG axis, try Helping People Grow.)

Puberty is driven by the expression of hundreds of genes that trigger the activity in the HPG axis (Witchel & Topaloglu, 2019). This gene expression is also sensitive to epigenetic signals, one reason its timing is responsive to factors like health, environmental toxins, and social stress (Worthman et al., 2019).

Maturation of the testes and ovaries stimulates the production of a number of hormones, including **testosterone** and **estrogen**. All adolescents secrete both hormones at relatively the same levels before puberty, but the testes typically secrete more testosterone, and the ovaries more estrogen, during puberty. Both testosterone and estrogen reorganize neural circuits in the brain, and they help reshape the body in distinct ways. Testosterone is connected to many parts of maturation, including wider jaws, ovulation, increased sexual desire, and increased interest in risk-taking (Berli & Plemons, 2020; Jordan-Young & Karkazis, 2019). Estrogen levels fluctuate, making it difficult to study, but researchers believe it is connected to brain development that alters emotion regulation (Chung et al., 2019; Dai & Scherf, 2019; Goddings et al., 2019). Estrogen also triggers bone growth and breast development (DuBois & Shattuck-Heidorn, 2020).

The First Signs of Puberty

Although there are variations around the world, in most highly resourced countries, early signs of puberty begin before children are in middle school. By age 9, breast development has begun in many children (Eckert-Lind et al., 2020). Breasts begin to change and grow in most children who are biologically female and in nearly half of typically developing children who are biologically male (Lorek et al., 2019). Typically by about age 9 or 10, children may also experience the emergence of pubic hair along with, for boys, changes in the size of their testicles and penis (Wolf & Long, 2016).

The awakening of the glands in the HPG axis also triggers a **growth spurt**—a very rapid increase in height and size—that begins at about age 10 in children with ovaries and about age 12 in those with testes (Kozieł & Malina, 2018; Malina et al., 2020). The peak of growth for children with ovaries is about age 12, and for other children it is nearly two years later, making most children who are biological girls taller than their peers at about age 13 (Gardstedt et al., 2019; Kozieł & Malina, 2018). During the peak of growth, adolescents may grow more than 3 inches in a year, evident when a child grows two shoe sizes over a summer or needs a new pair of jeans before the first pair has worn out.

Menarche and Spermarche

The key biological event of puberty for most children is when the biological changes associated with reproduction occur. A first menstrual period, known as **menarche**, and a first ejaculation of sperm, or **spermarche**, signify young people's developing ability to have children of their own. These milestones typically occur several years after gonadal hormones have begun to flow through the body. There are variations around the world, but in the United States, as in many other highly resourced countries, menarche typically occurs at around age 12 and spermarche at around age 14 (Biro et al., 2018; Pyra & Schwarz, 2019; Tinggaard et al., 2012).

Adolescents experience menarche in different ways depending on their families' cultural beliefs (Marván & Alcalá-Herrera, 2019). In some communities, there is stigma attached to getting your period (Johnston-Robledo & Chrisler, 2013). But in many others, it is becoming less taboo. This major biological change is often described as an "annoying" but not traumatic part of growing up (Marván & Alcalá-Herrera, 2019; Ruble & Brooks-Gunn, 1982).

In some communities around the world, however, children lack basic understanding of menstruation, which can make them feel scared and embarrassed (Chandra-Mouli & Patel, 2020; Coast et al., 2019; Hebert-Beirne et al., 2017; Herbert et al., 2017). The cost of tampons or pads and the hassle of managing them can make it difficult for adolescents to attend school or participate in sports (Schmitt et al., 2021). Interventions include providing children with low-cost sanitary pads, washable menstrual underwear, and educational programs that battle menstruation-related discrimination (Chandra-Mouli et al., 2019; Hennegan et al., 2019; Plesons et al., 2021).

Maturation of the testes is formally marked by *spermarche*, the first ejaculation of sperm. This will probably not be an adolescent's first ejaculation, since children can ejaculate and orgasm prior to spermarche without expressing semen (Chad, 2020). Early ejaculation can take adolescents by surprise, with some reporting that they feel confused by what is happening to their bodies (Gaddis & Brooks-Gunn, 1985). Families and even pediatricians are often more uncomfortable talking about spermarche than they are about menstruation (Grubb et al., 2020; Marván & Alcalá-Herrera, 2019).

For children who identify as transgender or a nonbinary gender category, puberty can require them to confront the biological characteristics of a gender they may not identify with (Kimberly et al., 2018). This is a time when adolescents and their families may choose gender-confirmation or puberty-delaying hormone treatments (Panagiotakopoulos et al., 2020; Rafferty et al., 2018). Gender-diverse teenagers are frequently rejected by their communities and families and as a result have higher rates of emotional and mental health problems (Grossman et al., 2021). Allowing transgender and gender-questioning teenagers extra time to go through puberty, and hormonally transitioning them to their preferred gender, is

Puberty in the Real World Variations in the timing of puberty are common, as in this group practicing for a choir performance in New York City.

Share It!

Talk about it. Menstruation can be awkward to discuss, even for health professionals. This can keep young people from seeking help for its common complications, like menstrual cramps.

(Yücel et al., 2018)

Scientific American: Lifespan Development

Celebrating the Body Talking about menstruation can lesson the stigma. These campaigners are advocating for menstrual rights at a woman's equality rally in Berlin, Germany.

menarche The term for the first menstrual period.

spermarche The first ejaculation of sperm.

secular trend The term developmental scientists use to describe the gradual, long-term progression toward earlier puberty.

linked to positive mental health outcomes such as lower rates of depression (Rafferty et al., 2018; Turban et al., 2020).

Variations in Timing

Around the globe, puberty depends partly upon a population's health. For instance, in the late 1800s in the United States and much of Europe and in the early 2000s in less-resourced regions, most teenagers did not reach puberty until their mid- to late teens. However, because of widespread improvements in public health and nutrition, adolescents in most countries today reach menarche and spermarche at about age 12 or 13, five to six years earlier than their counterparts in the same places years ago (Kaplowitz et al., 2016; Moodie et al., 2020; Tijani et al., 2019). For instance, just 20 years ago, girls in Nepal did not reach puberty until about 16, but now they typically experience menarche at around 12½ (Chalise et al., 2018; Parent et al., 2003; Thomas et al., 2001). Other signs of maturation, like breast development, also occur earlier than they once did, although puberty often proceeds slowly, particularly in countries with limited resources (Campisi et al., 2020; Eckert-Lind et al., 2020).

Developmental scientists call this gradual, long-term progression toward earlier puberty a **secular trend**. Most experts believe that the tendency to reach puberty at younger ages is a result of improvements in health, since in the past, infectious diseases and malnutrition may have prevented young people from gaining enough weight and body fat necessary to trigger puberty (Papadimitriou, 2016). (See **Figure 10.1**.)

Common Variations in Pubertal Timing If you look at a line of middle school students waiting for the bus, you can see that puberty does not happen at the same time for everyone. Some adolescents reach puberty earlier or later than their peers: This diversity is typical since puberty is driven by a number of factors, including children's health, their environment, their genes, and their life experience (Worthman et al., 2019). While typically developing children could start puberty any time between ages 9 and 16, teenagers often are treated differently if they reach puberty at a different age than their communities expect (Seaton & Carter, 2019).

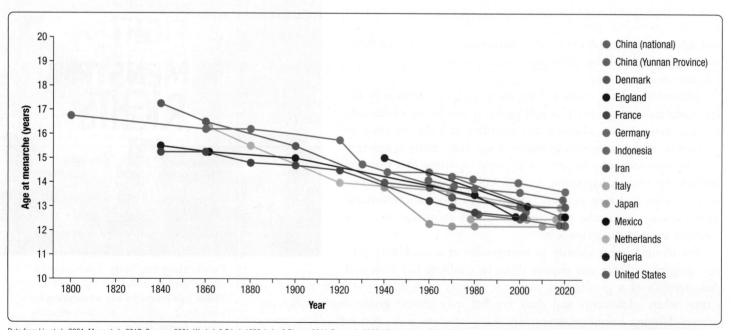

Data from Liu et al., 2021; Meng et al., 2017; Garenne, 2021; Wyshak & Frisch,1982; Lalys & Pineau, 2014; Bau et al., 2009; Whincup et al., 2001; Biro et al., 2018; Herman-Giddens, 2006; Helm & Grønlund, 1998; Talma et al., 2013; Wahab et al., 2020; Hosokawa et al., 2012; Piras et al., 2020.

FIGURE 10.1 The Secular Trend in Puberty In many nations, the age of puberty is stabilizing at around age 12 or 13 because of improvements in health.

Scientists have found that the HPG axis is tightly entangled with the hormones and chemicals that regulate metabolism. Hormones released in the gastrointestinal system and even the balance of bacteria in the microbiome help regulate the timing of puberty (Santoro et al., 2019; Worthman et al., 2019). As a result, children who do not get enough to eat or who do not have enough body fat may have delays in maturation (Richmond & Rogol, 2016).

In affluent communities, delays in puberty are particularly common for children who are extremely athletic (Logue et al., 2018). For instance, teenagers who participate in sports in which intensive exercise is combined with a preference for a thin frame, such as distance running, gymnastics, or wrestling, may have delayed menstruation or growth spurts (Huhmann, 2020; Roemmich & Sinning, 1997). Most will catch up when they slow down their training.

Teenagers who have a larger body size than their peers may also reach pubertal milestones at different times than their peers (Brix et al., 2020; O'Keeffe et al., 2020). For instance, breasts tend to develop earlier, at around age 7, in children with larger body sizes (Eckert-Lind et al., 2020). Researchers believe testicular development also is often accelerated in children who are slightly larger than their peers (Busch et al., 2020a; Herting et al., 2021; Pereira et al., 2021). At the same time, scientists have found that in significantly heavy adolescents, the pace of physical growth and testicular maturation is often slowed down compared to other adolescents (Bygdell et al., 2018; Lee et al., 2016).

Emerging evidence also links exposure to environmental pollution and some chemicals to accelerated puberty, including earlier menarche and breast development (Golestanzadeh et al., 2020; Harley et al., 2019). Children who are from Black or Latino communities, as well as those who live in low-income neighborhoods, are more likely to be exposed to these environmental toxins, which may contribute to a higher likelihood of early puberty (Attina et al., 2019; Galvez et al., 2018).

The Impact of Genetics and Life Stress If Rosie asked her pediatrician when she would start her growth spurt, her doctor would probably ask if she knew when her own parents reached puberty. This is because one of the strongest predictors of when children reach puberty is their genome (Busch et al., 2020b; Horvath et al., 2020; Wohlfahrt-Veje et al., 2016). Most children, if they are healthy, typically reach menarche or spermarche at about the same time as their parents, and in Rosie's case, she will probably reach her milestones at about the same time as her big sister, Ruby. So now is probably not the time to stock up on new clothes: A growth spurt is coming.

For some genetically susceptible children, *life stress* may trigger puberty to come a little early (Belsky, 2019; Sun et al., 2020). Researchers have found that children tend to reach puberty a bit sooner if they have felt threatened or experienced significant fear, as with family trauma, discrimination, or harsh parenting (Colich et al., 2020; Deardorff et al., 2019). These adverse experiences are thought to create chronic stress responses that can stimulate the biological changes associated with puberty (Deardorff et al., 2019).

Evolutionary or *life history theory* suggests that in the past, these biological responses to early life stress may have offered an advantage (Belsky, 2019). For instance, children who mature earlier tend to be able to have children earlier, which would have been beneficial at times during human evolution when there was a high risk of dying young (Ellis & Del Giudice, 2019).

The Consequences of Pubertal Timing In the past, many researchers believed that early puberty granted teenagers certain advantages, particularly for children who identified as boys. For instance, reaching puberty early may allow boys to excel in sports and be more dominant in groups because of their larger size (Deardorff et al., 2019; Huddleston & Ge, 2003). However, contemporary researchers often worry that early development may be less beneficial (Mendle et al., 2019). Children who look "older than their age" may be treated like adults before they are emotionally ready (Carter et al., 2018a).

 Share It!

Natural disasters may accelerate puberty. Some researchers found that living through an earthquake (and its frightening and chaotic aftermath) hurried puberty for young boys and girls, particularly those who were preschoolers at the time of the disaster.

(Lian et al., 2018)

 Scientific American: Lifespan Development

CONNECTIONS

Remember from Chapter 2 that *evolutionary*, or *life history*, *theory* focuses on how diversity in children's development may result from adaptations to the environment.

Learn It Together

Puberty Can Be Surprising

Plan Review the factors that influence when adolescents go through puberty.

Engage Choose two factors that are very surprising to you and that you did not know before. Pick a partner and share your surprises with one another, talking about why you were surprised and how this has changed how you think about puberty.

Reflect Does this make you think more about how biology and the environment interact to shape development? How would you explain the complexity of puberty to your family or friends?

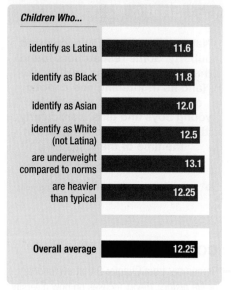

TIMING OF MENARCHE (AGE IN YEARS)

Children Who...

identify as Latina	11.6
identify as Black	11.8
identify as Asian	12.0
identify as White (not Latina)	12.5
are underweight compared to norms	13.1
are heavier than typical	12.25
Overall average	12.25

Data from Biro et al., 2018.

FIGURE 10.2 Variations in the Timing of Puberty In the United States, researchers have often linked group differences in the timing of puberty to ethnic differences, but puberty often varies depending on children's size and their family income. Many researchers study variations in the timing of menarche because it is easier to determine than the timing of spermarche.

Looking older also puts adolescents at risk for exclusion by their peers, particularly if they lack the social skills to navigate their new identities (Carter et al., 2018a). Perhaps as a result, some researchers have found that adolescents who develop early tend to join new friend groups, with teenagers who are older but not necessarily wiser.

There are different risks depending on adolescents' gender identity: Scientists have found that boys who are more physically mature than their peers are more likely to be victims of violent crime. They are also more likely to be diagnosed with behavioral or emotional disorders such as conduct disorder and depression than boys with more typical maturation (Dimler & Natsuaki, 2015; Hamlat et al., 2020; Mendle & Ferrero, 2012). However, late-developing boys also report some stresses: They often feel self-conscious about being smaller than their peers, and they, too, may be more likely to develop depression (Gaysina et al., 2015; Huddleston & Ge, 2003).

For adolescents who identify as girls, developing early often makes them more vulnerable to abuse by older partners (Chen et al., 2017; Javdani et al., 2019). They can feel isolated and are more likely to experience psychological disorders like depression, substance abuse, and eating disorders (Pfeifer & Allen, 2021; Wang et al., 2016). These difficulties may be exacerbated by the stereotypes adults, including teachers, hold about early developers. Some researchers have found that teachers expect young girls who are early developers, particularly if they are Black, to have more problems at school and with friends than other children, creating a cycle of low expectations that may be hard to break (Carter et al., 2018b).

Over the lifespan, research suggests that the health impact of early puberty can sometimes be significant. Being an early developer has been linked to increased risk of heart disease and diabetes and to the development of breast cancer (Bell et al., 2018; Magnus et al., 2020). However, it is difficult to conclude that early puberty truly *causes* these outcomes. The findings are *correlations*, and many of the worrisome health associations are connected to risk factors that predate puberty or the social stresses that result from it, rather than to pubertal timing itself (Bell et al., 2018).

Many of the challenges faced by early developers improve with time. For instance, the association of early puberty with acting out behavior seems to dissipate by the time adolescents reach their late 20s (Dimler & Natsuaki, 2021). As with so much else in development, social and family context makes an enormous difference. Supportive family and friends can buffer many of the challenges early developers may face (Deardorff et al., 2019).

CAN YOU BELIEVE IT?

Why Are There Group Differences in the Timing of Puberty?

In diverse countries like the United States, researchers, families, and pediatricians have noticed some common variations in the timing of puberty (see **Figure 10.2**). For instance, in the United States, many adolescents from Asian American backgrounds reach puberty later than those from other communities (Biro et al., 2018; Lee et al., 2016). In countries around the world, group differences often emerge as children mature. But these differences are not always aligned to ethnic identity.

The triggers for puberty are complex. In some contexts, extreme adversity leads to *later* puberty, when young people may lack adequate nutrition for puberty to start (Campisi et al., 2020). For instance, in China, high-income, urban children tend to reach puberty before rural children, who have more limited health care and access to nutrition (Sun et al., 2012).

In other situations, social stresses or chronic adversity may contribute to trigger *earlier* puberty. In Australia, as in the United States, where most children have enough to eat, family income makes a difference. Having low income often increases stress, and as a result, children who are low income are more likely to reach puberty early (Sun et al., 2017). In the United States, for instance, menarche happens nearly a year earlier in teenagers from low-income families than those from more privileged backgrounds (James-Todd et al., 2010). The everyday unfair treatment, hostility, and sense of threat associated with racism adds to stress, so adolescents from groups that experience discrimination are more likely to reach puberty early (Kelly et al., 2017; Suglia et al., 2020; Trent et al., 2019).

Because of the tremendous diversity in when adolescents reach puberty, scientists caution against assigning a genetic explanation for group differences (Deardorff et al., 2019). Remember from Chapter 2 that ethnic and racial labels do not accurately reflect differences in our genomes. Researchers suggest that group differences in the timing of puberty in the United States are linked to differences in environmental exposures to toxins, stress, birth size, poor health, and the stress of racism, not genetics (Herting et al., 2021; James-Todd et al., 2016).

These data remind us that ethnic labels are not an easy answer for differences between groups. The unequal circumstances children grow up in affect their development and biology. Puberty is yet another demonstration of how the social environment shapes children's development in complex ways. 🌀

Sexuality

Ruby and Rosie's mother, Jill, raises her eyebrows when we ask about dating. She says the pandemic changed all that. She does not think it is possible for anyone to even have a crush over Zoom, although she has talked to her girls about it. Maybe, she admits, she has not talked to them about it *much*, which may for her be a silver lining of the pandemic. Adults are not usually in a hurry to talk about adolescents and sex (Ashcraft & Murray, 2017; Astle et al., 2021).

Despite the awkwardness, changing brains and bodies spark a new interest in sexuality that starts before middle school (Suleiman et al., 2017). Sex also surrounds teenagers: They live in a world that is saturated with sexualized content, from billboard advertising to online pornography (Collins et al., 2017). Yet, despite their heightened interest in sex and the ubiquity of sexualized material, adolescents do not talk much with adults or each other about sexuality (Weissbourd et al., 2017).

Young people might be embarrassed to talk about it, but developmental scientists are not. As many researchers have discovered, sexual desire and behavior—at the right time, with the right person, and with the right protection—can be a healthy and positive part of adolescent life (Golden et al., 2016; Harden, 2014; Verbeek et al., 2020).

Despite the focus of many parents and the media on hookups and intercourse, sexuality emerges gradually and in many forms during the adolescent years. The hormonal changes of puberty help to create feelings of desire that adolescents—employing their increasingly mature cognitive and social abilities—explore by themselves and in their social relationships.

The Origins of Desire Many researchers believe that sexual desire begins with the first hormonal stirrings of adrenarche. Children as young as 9 or 10 have crushes and feel sexual attraction (McClintock & Herdt, 1996; Mustanski et al., 2014). By the time they are 14, most adolescents have fantasized about sex (Fortenberry, 2014).

Desire is triggered by the release of hormones, such as the adrenal hormone DHEA, estrogen, and testosterone during adrenarche and puberty. Interest in sex and romance are also set off by maturity in brain systems that help you feel pleasure and enjoy new experiences. Dopamine becomes prevalent in the subcortical structures involved in the *reward system* and adolescents' cortex is activated when they think about romantic relationships (Suleiman & Harden, 2016).

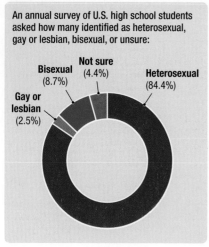

An annual survey of U.S. high school students asked how many identified as heterosexual, gay or lesbian, bisexual, or unsure:

Bisexual (8.7%)
Not sure (4.4%)
Gay or lesbian (2.5%)
Heterosexual (84.4%)

Data from YRBS, 2019.

FIGURE 10.3 Sexual Identity in Adolescence An increasing number of young people are comfortable saying that they are lesbian, gay, bisexual, or another category.

A Variety of Sexual Experiences In most places around the world, cultural ethno-theories make sexual activity taboo in early adolescence. As a result, very few teenagers have sex before they are 15, and the rate of sexual activity in young people is declining (Liang et al., 2019; Starrs et al., 2018). In the United States, only about half of teenagers have oral sex or penetrative intercourse before age 18 (Astle et al., 2021; Underwood et al., 2020). This is a significant change from the 1990s and 2000s: Fewer ninth- and tenth-graders are sexually active than young people were in their parents' generation (Lei & South, 2021). Many developmental scientists believe waiting may be protective: Older teenagers are more likely to make safer decisions about how and when to become intimate and usually have more positive experiences (Ethier et al., 2018; Janis et al., 2019; Lara & Abdo, 2016; Vasilenko et al., 2016).

Just because more teenagers are putting off intercourse does not mean that adolescents are not experimenting with their sexuality: Many adolescents participate in a variety of intimate activities, including solo masturbation and mutual touching. By the time they are 19, most have experimented with penetrative and oral sex (Astle et al., 2021). However, when young people become romantically involved, how they move from exchanging texts to physical intimacy, and what that entails, varies widely.

Around the world, teenagers' sexual identities and behaviors are more flexible than previous generations: For instance, about 4 in 100 identify as transgender or another nonbinary identity (Boyon & Silverstein, 2021). Young people are often nervous about answering questions about their sexual identity, but about 1 in 10 U.S. high school students polled in one survey indicated that they identified as gay, lesbian, or bisexual (see **Figure 10.3**) (YRBS, 2019). Adolescents' romantic partners and sexual identities do not always align or adhere to strict labels (Diamond, 2020; Watson et al., 2020). In addition, it is common for romantic and sexual preferences to change over time (Li & Davis, 2019; Stewart et al., 2019; Ybarra et al., 2019).

Researchers have found that nearly half of teenagers who identify as lesbian or gay are likely to have had an other-sex partner. Adolescents who are attracted to another sex may fall in love or become intimate with a same-sex partner (Ybarra et al., 2019). For some, these sexual experiences will form their sexual identity. For others, they are part of a continuum of sexual behavior that may include a variety of relationships (Diamond et al., 2015).

The Social Context of Sexuality

Although adolescents' hormonal and brain development may trigger their sexual interest, adolescent sexuality takes place within a larger social context of close relationships, families, and communities. Many adolescents tell researchers that they think sex should happen in serious relationships, after they have said "I love you" (Choukas-Bradley et al., 2015).

Families have a crucial influence on when adolescents begin to have sex and how healthy their relationships are (Nogueira Avelar e Silva et al., 2016). Teenagers from closer and supportive families tend to postpone sex until they are older, and they use protection more regularly (Astle et al., 2019; Cadely et al., 2020; Suleiman & Harden, 2016). Friends and peer groups also set expectations for adolescents' sexual activity (Van de Bongardt et al., 2015).

Cultural values about sex and relationships are an important factor in whether adolescents become sexually active. In Bhutan, for example, many young people do not have sex until they are in their 20s (GSSHS, 2016). In the United States, some young people delay sexual activity, but not always romance, if they have religious beliefs or cultural taboos about adolescent sexuality (Haglund & Fehring, 2010; Vasilenko & Espinosa-Hernández, 2019). Immigrant youth, particularly if they come from families with more conservative views on sexuality, also tend to have lower rates of sexual activity (Tsai et al., 2017). However, researchers caution that community values do not always reflect community practices. Adolescents from communities that value abstinence may not be abstinent themselves (Abboud et al., 2020; Munro-Kramer et al., 2016).

Healthy Sexual Practices

Many developmental researchers suggest that for many adolescents, sexual relationships can be positive, particularly for teenagers who put off sex until their late teens and have positive emotional bonds to their partner (Golden et al., 2016; Shulman et al., 2020). Researchers suggest that healthy sexual practices occur when sex is consensual, respectful, and enjoyable, and when teenagers are protected from risks of pregnancy or infection (Harden, 2014; UNESCO, 2018). Adolescents are better able to make safe sex choices if they are able to manage the romantic aspects of sexuality, know how to talk about sex with a partner, and know how to prevent sexually transmitted diseases and unplanned pregnancies (Widman et al., 2014).

Sex Education Around the world, teenagers learn about sex in a variety of ways: at home, in school, and on their own. For instance, schools in the Netherlands offer frank, relationship-oriented sexual education that involves discussions of desire, pleasure, and sexual diversity (Baams et al., 2017; van der Doef & Reinders, 2018).

Many developmental scientists have found that school-based, *comprehensive sexual education* can improve the sexual well-being of young people: promoting health, reducing stigma about sexual diversity, and fostering healthier relationships (Goldfarb & Lieberman, 2021). In the United States, families, educators, policy makers, and adolescents do not always share the same goals for sexual education or agree on where it should happen. As a result, school-based sexual education often focuses on abstinence and prevention of sexually transmitted infections and is ineffective at encouraging healthy sexual behaviors (Denford et al., 2017). In the United States, more than 90 percent of young people learn about sexually transmitted infections from their schools or their families, but much fewer learn about birth control, and even fewer feel prepared for the emotional and social aspects of sexuality (Garceau & Ronis, 2019; Kantor & Lindberg, 2020; Weissbourd et al., 2017). Adolescents often report to researchers that the message they receive about sex at school is that it is dangerous, risky, and even shameful (Stewart et al., 2021).

Most U.S. teenagers learn about sex from their friends and online (Nikkelen et al., 2020; Peter & Valkenburg, 2016). Some of the online resources used by young people contain factual information, and these resources and online communities may offer a needed and safe space for LGBTQIA+ youth to explore their sexuality (McInroy et al., 2019). Not many resources, however, provide much in terms of education about sexual feelings and communication (Simon & Daneback, 2013). For some youth, online pornography forms the basis of their sexual education and may contribute to poor body image and confusion about appropriate sexual gender roles (Bőthe et al., 2019; Coyne et al., 2019; Grubbs & Kraus, 2021; Rothman et al., 2021).

Sex education seems to be most effective if it starts at home (Guilamo-Ramos et al., 2020; Widman et al., 2019). Young people who can communicate with their partners and understand their own desire typically learn these skills from parents and friends with whom they have close relationships (Mastro & Zimmer-Gemebeck, 2015). It is perhaps not surprising, then, that young people who talk to their families about sex tend to have more positive experiences (Vasilenko et al., 2014; Widman et al., 2014; Wright et al., 2020).

Staying Protected Knowing about sex and how to talk about it increases the likelihood that young people will take measures that protect their physical health. Safer sex includes *barrier methods* that protect against sexually transmitted infections, like the internal or external condom, and, for partners who can get pregnant, *long-acting reversible contraception*, like implants, intrauterine devices (IUDs), or hormone shots (Francis & Gold, 2017).

Sexually transmitted infection, or **STI**, is the term health care providers use to describe diseases that can be passed from one person to another through intimate contact. STIs include viruses, bacterial infections, and parasites that can be harmful

Share It!

Do not assume adolescents know the basics about sexual anatomy. Most girls cannot identify the vagina on a diagram and do not know where urine leaves the body. Most boys think their penis is undersized. Sex education needs to start simple.

(Hebert-Beirne et al., 2017; Rothman et al., 2021)

Scientific American: Lifespan Development

sexually transmitted infection (STI) The term health care providers use to describe diseases that can be passed from one person to another through intimate contact.

C Flanigan/Getty Images

Speaking Up to Reduce Stigma
Canadian activist Ashley Rose Murphy
has been speaking up on behalf of
young people with HIV since she was 10.
She explains that HIV can be treated and
prevented and that all people, regardless
of their health conditions, should be
treated with kindness.

whether or not someone shows symptoms. Many providers use the term *STI* instead of *STD (sexually transmitted disease)* in order to reduce the stigma around these conditions, although the terms are often used interchangeably (Lederer & Laing, 2017).

Around the globe, *human immunodeficiency virus (HIV)* continues to be a leading cause of death in young people. HIV can be transmitted sexually but can also be acquired through blood transfusions and prenatally. It can lead to *acquired immune deficiency syndrome (AIDS)*, which can keep your body from fighting infection. Effective treatments, including preventative ones, exist for HIV, but not all adolescents know they carry the disease or have access to treatment. More than 34,000 teenagers worldwide died from complications of HIV in 2019 (UNAIDS, 2021). The virus continues to infect adolescents in the United States, who account for about one in five new infections (CDC, 2020).

In the United States, the rates of HIV are low, but nearly one in four adolescents has an STI (Shannon & Klausner, 2018). Common STIs among young people include *chlamydia, herpes simplex virus, trichomoniasis,* and *human papilloma virus (HPV)* (Kreisel et al., 2021). Developmental scientists believe that U.S. adolescents have high rates of STIs because they engage in unprotected sex in higher numbers than adults, particularly if they are very young or they drink or use substances (Kessler et al., 2020). Only about half of teenagers used barrier protection when they last had penetrative sexual contact (Szucs et al., 2020). In addition, young people are more prone to infections because their bodies are still biologically immature (Shannon & Klausner, 2018).

The biggest predictor of the use of barrier protection is whether young people feel comfortable talking about sex with their partners, which can be difficult for adolescents, especially when they are very young (Vasilenko et al., 2015; Widman et al., 2014). The ability to talk openly with their partners may also help young people identify and avoid coercive or abusive sexual relationships (Boislard et al., 2016). Some studies have shown that more than one in five young people have been in a relationship in which their partner used verbal or physical threats or abused them: Rates were higher in same-sex-attracted young people and transgender youth, who may be particularly isolated (Caputi et al., 2020; Miller et al., 2018).

Pregnancy Around the world, more than 16 million teenagers give birth every year, and many of these young parents and their babies experience some difficulties in their transition to parenthood. Babies born to adolescents are at high risk for complications, including being born early and too small. Pregnancy is a leading cause of death in young people around the globe (Chandra-Mouli et al., 2019; WHO, 2021).

In the United States, rates of teenage parenthood are at an all-time low, but they are still higher than in any other wealthy country (OECD, 2021a). Developmental scientists attribute this to widespread *economic inequality*, or the gap between financially well-off families and those who are poor, which has been linked to early pregnancy worldwide (Santelli et al., 2017). In the United States, rates of adolescent pregnancy are highest in rural counties and communities with pervasive inequality, and among low-income youth (Burrus, 2018; Kearney & Levine, 2015).

About 17 of every 1,000 teenage girls in the United States has had a baby (Maddow-Zimet & Kost, 2021; Martin et al., 2021). Researchers are unsure how many teenage boys become parents, but estimates are about 5 in every 1,000 (Bamishigbin et al., 2019; US DHHS, 2021). Income is typically not young parents' only hurdle: They are also likely to have a history of trauma (Flaviano & Harville, 2021; Ott et al., 2020). Being a young parent comes with stigma, as well. Adolescent parents often report feeling judged by adults, who question their ability to be competent caregivers (Conn et al., 2018).

Although the majority of adolescent pregnancies are unplanned, many are met with excitement (Finer & Zolna, 2016; Kost et al., 2017). Expectant young people often report feeling that their pregnancy was inevitable, or something that was "meant to be" (Borrero et al., 2015).

Many express ambivalence about what was likely a surprise, but they may also show some of the characteristic optimism of adolescents (Cashdollar, 2018; Lau et al., 2015). Nevertheless, balancing school, work, and an infant is challenging for parents of any age.

APPLY IT! **10.3** Ruby's mother, Jill, wonders whether her daughter's growth spurts came too early. How might you reassure her that there is a wide variety of natural variation in the timing of puberty?

10.4 If you had to teach a group of children Rosie's age about puberty, what would be the first three things you would tell them?

10.5 Communities vary in their ethnotheories about adolescent sexuality. How would the principles of *cultural humility* dictate how you might talk to adolescents and their families about sex?

10.6 Talking about sex is often the hardest part of positive sexual development. How might you explain to young adolescents how to put feelings into words?

Developing Healthy Habits

For many, adolescence is a time when teenagers begin to take control of their own health choices, whether they begin adolescence with chronic conditions or with the blessing of good health. Rosie and Ruby are starting to keep track of their physical activity and how much they sleep, and they both know how to find snacks when they are hungry.

Eating on Their Own

Unlike younger children, adolescents can make more of their own decisions about where, when, and what they eat. Rosie and Ruby, for instance, bake on their own, although even Ruby is a bit intimidated by the responsibility of making dinner. Mostly they like to make cake. All that cooking helps them get the calories they need to build bones and muscles: Teenagers need more food than they will at any other time of their lifespan. During the peak of the growth spurt, adolescents need between 2,200 and about 2,800 calories a day (Das et al., 2018).

Most U.S. adolescents are eating enough, but the vast majority are not following healthy dietary guidelines: Their diets are too high in sugar and too low in micronutrients, fruit, and vegetables. Adolescents tend to get too many of their calories from sweetened sports drinks instead of vegetables and fruit (Merlo et al., 2020). Researchers are not the only ones who understand that the habits adolescents are building may last a lifetime: Intensive food marketing efforts focused on teenagers are designed to foster loyalty to sweetened drinks and processed foods (Abarca-Gómez et al., 2017).

Developmental scientists have found that nagging adolescents to choose healthier habits does not work: Many teenagers do not want to be told what to do. Instead, one group of researchers educates young people about how food marketing aims to convince them that convenience foods are "cool." Adolescents told researchers that this awareness made them want to fight back and eat more healthily in the process (Bryan et al., 2019). The lesson? Adolescents want to be independent and respected: Intervention programs designed to harness their own decision-making powers may be more successful than those that do not recognize their capabilities.

Challenges of Body Size

Big picture social structures make it difficult for many teenagers around the world to maintain a healthy size. Physical activity is often something that gets squeezed into an already-busy day, instead of being integrated into everyday routines like

Learning Objective

10.4 Explain the best ways for adolescents to maintain positive health.

 **Share It!**

Micronutrients are not something to skip out on. Low iron levels can tire you out. Experts estimate that as many as 1 in 10 adolescents who menstruate have low iron levels.

(Sekhar et al., 2017; Sun & Weaver, 2021)

Scientific American: Lifespan Development

Taking the "Cool" Out of Junk Food
In one intervention program, teenagers were encouraged to mark up popular advertisements that encouraged them to eat unhealthily.

walking to school. Food that is high in sugars, fats, and refined carbohydrates is often inexpensive, convenient, and highly advertised (Shultz et al., 2020). Global stigma, particularly the belief that people with unhealthy weight lack self-control, also make it more difficult to maintain a healthy size (Puhl et al., 2021; Reinka et al., 2021).

While rates of unhealthy low weights are declining, rates of unhealthy heavier weights are increasing in families around the world because of globalization and the transition from traditional diets to processed foods high in fat and refined carbohydrates (Ameye & Swinnen, 2019; Popkin, 2021). In adolescence, there is scientific consensus on a correlation between what is termed *obesity* in research, which is defined as a high BMI (above 30) or weight that is higher than about 97.5 percent of the median on a growth chart, and cardiovascular health complications (Twig et al., 2019; Wühl, 2019). By these measures, about four in five adolescents in the United States has obesity, along with about 94 out of every 100 adolescents worldwide (Fryar et al., 2021; WHO, 2021).

Remember from Chapter 6 that BMI and growth charts are far from perfect. This is particularly true during adolescence, when puberty can change body size and BMI (Bomberg et al., 2021). However, despite the difficulty of measuring growth, having a very large body size in adolescence comes with an increased likelihood of adverse outcomes, including diabetes and high blood pressure (Abarca-Gómez et al., 2017; Havers et al., 2021).

Being larger has an increased stigma in adolescence, as teenagers become more focused on their social relationships, and continues to result in exclusion, particularly for those who identify as girls (Farhat, 2015; Koyanagi et al., 2020; Martin-Storey et al., 2015; Morrissey et al., 2020). As a result of this stigma and exclusion, adolescents of larger size may struggle with depression, stress, and even get less sleep than their peers (Lacroix et al., 2020; Rao et al., 2020).

If adolescents and their families are concerned that their size poses a health risk, one way to help adolescents build a healthy weight is to enlist the help of the entire family (Roberts et al., 2021). *Family-based treatment*, in which an entire family works together to increase activity and eat a healthier diet, can be an effective way for adolescents to reach a healthier size (Cardel et al., 2020; Spruijt-Metz, 2011). Pediatricians recommend adopting small, incremental changes and a positive approach to body image and overall health, rather than harmful alternatives like dieting, which are typically ineffective and damaging to body image (Golden et al., 2016). Regardless of their size, adolescents need support to protect against teasing and to build self-acceptance in a world that often stigmatizes people who do not match media ideals (Lacroix et al., 2020).

Unhealthy Eating

As children move toward adulthood, how they feel about their bodies, or their **body image**, is closely tied to how they feel about themselves (Andre et al., 2016). Teenagers often compare themselves to media images, whether they are images of their friends on Instagram or famous actors in movies (Marengo et al., 2018; Salomon & Brown, 2019). Particularly in early adolescence, and for those who identify as girls, as many as half of all teenagers are disappointed in how they look (Lacroix et al., 2020; Nelson et al., 2018). Adolescents' high standards for their appearance tend to appear across cultural communities. In affluent communities around the world, few adolescents are immune to poor body image or unhealthy eating habits (Espinoza et al., 2019; Hornberger et al., 2021).

In the United States, almost 40 percent of teenagers who identify as girls and 15 percent of those who identify as boys engage in *disordered eating*, a broad category of behaviors that could range from regularly skipping meals, to making themselves throw up, to extreme dietary restrictions (Solmi, Sharpe, et al., 2021; YRBS, 2019).

CONNECTIONS

Remember from Chapter 3 that some children are more likely to have difficulty with weight later in life because of low birthweight and rapid growth in infancy.

CONNECTIONS

Remember from Chapter 6 that the term *obesity* is stigmatizing even if it is the term used by scientists and health care providers. The term *unhealthy weight* is preferred when referring to people whose weight is in the high range, but is often imprecise.

 **Share It!**

Fighting body shame may begin with gratitude for the bodies we have. Researchers in Qatar found that writing thank-you notes to their bodies helped some young people build a healthier body image.

(O'Hara et al., 2021)

Scientific American: Lifespan Development

body image The feelings and ideas you have about your body.

Adolescents who are larger than their peers and those who are transgender have a higher likelihood for disordered eating, in part because of the stigma and exclusion they face (Hornberger et al., 2021).

While disordered eating is fairly common, eating disorders are more serious and unusual. **Eating disorders** are marked by long-term, unhealthy patterns of eating, obsessions with food, and poor body image that cause problems with teenagers' ability to function in everyday life (APA, 2022; Hornberger et al., 2021). The social stresses of adolescence and cultures that value thinness make young people susceptible to eating disorders (Ferguson et al., 2014). As with most psychological illnesses, both genetic and environmental factors contribute to eating disorders (Bakalar et al., 2015; Culbert et al., 2015; Munn-Chernoff et al., 2021).

The most commonly diagnosed eating disorders in adolescence are *binge-eating disorder*, *bulimia nervosa*, and *anorexia nervosa*. Around the world, **binge-eating disorder** is the most prevalent eating disorder in adolescents, affecting as many as 5 in every 100 teens (Marzilli et al., 2018). It is marked by episodes of compulsive, excessive eating that make you feel out of control, ashamed, or upset (APA, 2022).

Bulimia nervosa and **anorexia nervosa** occur in fewer than 1 percent of adolescents (Brodzki et al., 2018). Bulimia is a consistent pattern of disordered eating that involves behaviors like overeating compensated by throwing up, excessive exercise, or abusing laxatives (APA, 2022). Anorexia can involve similar extremes along with extreme calorie or food restriction and excessive exercise. Adolescents with anorexia diet to an unhealthy weight, yet still believe they are too heavy (APA, 2022). Those who have bulimia or anorexia are consumed with their weight and what they look like to the point that they can no longer function in their everyday lives in a healthy, productive way.

An eating disorder makes it difficult to enjoy and accomplish the important tasks of adolescence. The cost can be significant. Teenagers who have eating disorders are at higher risk for suicide and may continue to have difficulties with disordered eating as they grow up (Hornberger et al., 2021). Developmental researchers suggest that for most, family-based treatments are the most effective ways of building social support and treating eating disorders (Dalle Grave et al., 2021).

Keeping Active

One way to improve body image and eating habits is to stay active (Mulgrew, 2020). For many teenagers, this often means finding time to exercise. By the time they reach early adolescence, children no longer run around for the joy of it. Fifth-graders play tag, whereas eighth-graders stand in circles talking. By the time adolescents get to high school, they are unlikely to have any recess time at all, which means even less activity.

In most parts of the world, adolescents become less active when they hit puberty (Trang et al., 2012; Van Hecke et al., 2016). The time they used to spend playing tag is now increasingly spent doing homework, working, visiting with friends, and clicking on their phones. Ruby and Rosie provide a dramatic example of this: Rosie has trouble staying still during the hours of Zoom time and is ready to dash outside as soon as she gets a break. But her older sister is happy to stay sedentary, although not on Zoom, for hours reading and clicking online.

To stay healthy, pediatricians recommend that adolescents get about 60 minutes of exercise every day (WHO, 2020). However, fewer than 30 percent of adolescents in highly resourced countries, including the United States, are able to get enough activity (Guthold et al., 2020; Steene-Johannessen et al., 2020). High-income teenagers

CONNECTIONS

Psychological disorders often develop through an epigenetic process in which genetic vulnerabilities are triggered by environmental factors. Adolescents are particularly vulnerable to psychological disorders, as you will see in Chapter 11. Psychological disorders also emerge in childhood, as you may remember from Chapters 7 and 9.

eating disorders Psychological conditions that are marked by long-term, unhealthy patterns of eating, obsessions with food, and poor body image that cause problems with the ability to function.

binge-eating disorder The most prevalent eating disorder in adolescents marked by episodes of compulsive, excessive eating that make you feel out of control, ashamed, or upset.

bulimia nervosa A consistent pattern of disordered eating that involves overeating compensated by throwing up, excessive exercise, or abusing laxatives.

anorexia nervosa A consistent pattern of disordered eating that may involve extreme calorie restriction, purging, excessive exercise, and a distorted belief that one's body is overly heavy.

Swimming for Joy (and the Win) Paris (*center*) swims competitively near her home in Chicago and is even thinking of training for a triathlon. Working out with others on a team often helps young people stay active.

Sometimes a Dirt Road Is Enough for Recreation. These teenagers have the week off to help with the potato harvest near their home in Aroostock County, Maine. As you can see here, they get their physical activity from more than just digging.

Scientific American Profile

Sleep Changes

and boys are more likely to be getting their hour in every day, but lower-income girls are likely to be missing out, typically getting less than half the recommended time (Armstrong et al., 2018).

In adolescence, being active helps prevent depression and anxiety and boosts brain development (Belcher et al., 2021; Biddle et al., 2019). Exercise sharpens attention and focus and can even improve academic achievement (Belcher et al., 2021; Reigal et al., 2020). Staying active takes time and is easier if it is part of an everyday routine, whether that means biking to school or mowing lawns in the afternoon.

For many adolescents, regular activity comes in the form of organized exercise (UNICEF, 2019). Not all adolescents, however, have the opportunity to play. Some schools do not offer any athletic programs. Other schools may not have spots for all students or may charge fees that are unaffordable for some (NPAPA, 2018). For instance, one in three high schools located in high-poverty neighborhoods in the United States offers no sports at all, as compared to just one in six low-poverty neighborhood schools (Veliz et al., 2019).

Getting Enough Sleep

If you asked many adolescents what they could do to be happier, do better in school, and get along better at home, they would never guess that one thing is to simply get enough sleep. Most young people are trying to cram more things into their day, which prevents them from getting adequate sleep.

Adolescents function best with about 8 to 10 hours of sleep every night, but more than two in three high school students get fewer than 8 hours a night (Park et al., 2019; Wheaton et al., 2018). Lack of sleep is a problem around the world (Gariepy et al., 2020). Indeed, in affluent communities in East Asia, nearly 9 out of 10 adolescents do not get enough sleep (Ong et al., 2019; Yeo et al., 2019). Sleep-deprivation puts teenagers at risk: Sleep is important for the development of the adolescent brain and for overall physical and emotional health (Booth et al., 2021; Galván, 2020; Troxel & Wolfson, 2016). For many teenagers, the COVID-19 pandemic gave them a welcome opportunity to sleep later, but for others, the lack of a regular routine prevented them from getting enough rest (Bates et al., 2021; Becker et al., 2021; Gruber et al., 2020).

Developmental scientists have found that lack of sleep is associated with a long list of problems, including heightened anxiety, attention difficulties, and lower grades (Crowley et al., 2018; Gillen-O'Neel et al., 2013). Sleep deprivation is also linked to trouble with learning, higher levels of depression, trouble getting along with peers, emotion regulation problems, and even criminal behavior (Carskadon & Barker, 2020; McMakin et al., 2016; Telzer et al., 2013).

Adolescents have trouble with sleep because of what some researchers call a "perfect storm," in which their biology, which makes their sleep more flexible, collides with a culture that overloads, overschedules, and overstimulates them (Carskadon, 2011; Carskadon & Barker, 2020; Crowley et al., 2018; Leonard et al., 2021). At the beginning of puberty, adolescents' **circadian rhythm**, or their daily sleep-and-wake cycle, shifts so that they want to stay up later at night and sleep later in the morning. This is incompatible with school start times, which move earlier in the morning during middle and high school.

One solution would be for high schools to start later, after 8:30 A.M. (Troxel & Wolfson, 2016). Students in schools that have moved to later start times enjoy better academic performance, higher quality sleep, and greater well-being (Berry et al., 2021). However, few schools have adopted later start times, and for many teenagers, even starting school at 8:30 might not give them enough sleep.

circadian rhythm A person's daily sleep-and-wake cycle.

Experts recommend some simple interventions to help teenagers get more rest (Bonnar et al., 2015; Tarokh et al., 2016):

- Go to bed and wake up at a generally consistent time every day on weekdays and on weekends.
- Get some sunshine or bright light early in the morning to reset your internal clock.
- Avoid too much excitement, physical activity, bright light, and screen time an hour before bedtime.
- Leave electronic devices off to make sleeping through the night more likely.

APPLY IT! **10.7** Ruby and Rosie are becoming better sleepers: They try to get at least 9 hours of sleep a night. What are some of the benefits of this extra rest?

10.8 Some experts worry that an emphasis on appearance and the constant pressure of being connected on image-oriented social media makes it more likely for adolescents to feel badly about how they look. What are some solutions you might suggest to teenagers who want to feel better about themselves?

Up Too Early? Many young people still need to get on the school bus before dawn in order to get to class. Experts suggest that moving school start times later would improve their sleep, well-being, and grades.

Brain and Cognitive Development

From the outside, the changes in the brain during adolescence may not be very dramatic. For instance, if you could see the outside of Ruby's brain while she is studying biology, it would not look very different at 13 than when she was her sister's age. In fact, her brain might even be a little smaller if you could weigh it (Lenroot et al., 2007; Mills et al., 2016). Dramatic changes may not be visible from the outside, but on the microscopic level, Ruby's brain is in a major period of transition.

Three major changes characterize brain development during adolescence: maturation of the prefrontal cortex, heightened activation of subcortical regions and systems, and enhanced connectivity between these subcortical systems and the prefrontal cortex. Together, these changes make the adolescent brain more adaptable, or *plastic*, able to change as a function of life experience, than during adulthood (Guyer et al., 2018; Laube et al., 2020). This brain development helps make adolescence a sensitive period for learning, enabling adolescents like Ruby and Rosie to learn a tremendous amount as they prepare for what comes next (Fandakova & Hartley, 2020).

Developing Prefrontal Cortex

Adolescents can manage abstractions, solve chemical equations, and define the word "justice." Ruby can log on to Zoom, tell you how a synapse fires, and plan a presentation for her social studies class while waiting for her cookies to finish baking. Maturation in the cortex makes these cognitive skills easier to master in adolescence than they were in childhood (Dong et al., 2021; Knoll et al., 2015).

Remember that at the level of the neuron, brain maturation involves three interconnected processes. First, *synaptogenesis* involves the creation of synapses connecting neurons to each other. Second, *synaptic pruning* is the removal or pruning of underused synapses, or connections between neurons. Maturation also includes *myelination*, the growth of the fatty sheath that accelerates the signaling of neurons. Together, these processes allow for faster and more efficient signaling within the developing brain. In the teenage years, all three processes are supercharged as the adolescents' brain is reshaped, leading to teenagers' increased cognitive abilities of adolescents (Ismail et al., 2017).

Learning Objectives

10.5 Identify important elements of brain maturation during adolescence.

10.6 Describe the fundamental changes in cognition during adolescence.

Some of the most significant reshaping of the brain happens in the PFC (the *pre-frontal cortex*—the region linked to conscious control of our behavior and thinking) (Ando et al., 2021; Corrigan et al., 2021). Triggered by puberty, nearly half of an adolescents' synaptic connections will be replaced by millions of new, faster myelinated ones (Selemon, 2013; Vijayakumar et al., 2021). Faster connections mean quicker processing and learning and that the amount of *white matter*, or the myelinated axons of brain cells, increases dramatically. At the same time, the amount of *gray matter*, including brain cell bodies and synapses, decreases as unused connections are pruned away (Vijayakumar et al., 2018; see **Infographic 10.2**). Both pruning and myelination make the brain more efficient as communication becomes faster and more direct. These processes are one reason adolescents are able to develop such impressive memory, problem solving, abstract reasoning, and planning skills (Fuhrmann et al., 2015).

Active Subcortical Structures

Brain development is not just about the changes that allow Ruby to understand algebra or pick up nuances in *The Great Gatsby*. In adolescence, changes in the brain are also linked to how teenagers manage their emotions and develop social skills. The adolescent brain undergoes a massive restructuring in response to the hormones of puberty, including testosterone and estrogen. These hormones trigger new activity, growth, and increased responsiveness in the subcortical structures of the brain that are devoted to processing emotion, motivation, and rewards (Casey et al., 2019; Goddings et al., 2014; Shulman et al., 2016).

Changes in these structures help explain some of the characteristics of many adolescents: Teenagers have more intense emotions than younger children; their emotions are often linked to their social world; and they are intensely motivated to learn and try new things (McLaughlin et al., 2015; van Hoorn et al., 2019). Neuroscientists believe the maturation of adolescents' subcortical structures helps adolescents develop the social skills, motivation, and emotion regulation they need to for adulthood. In turn, these skills and the brain structures that support them are also shaped by teenagers' life experiences as they mature (Dahl et al., 2018).

What *Can't* an Adolescent Brain Do? Adolescents working together can be amazing. One team of girls from Afghanistan (*left*) won a silver medal in a robotics competition in 2017, defying gender stereotypes. A group of high school students from Carl Hayden Community High School in West Phoenix, Arizona (*right*), beat a team of college students in another competition—even though they had only $800 to build their project (as compared to more than $11,000 for the other team).

Three major changes characterize brain development during adolescence: maturation of the prefrontal cortex, heightened activation of the subcortical regions and systems, and enhanced connectivity between these subcortical systems and the prefrontal cortex. The brain is particularly flexible during adolescence, helping to power adolescents' ability to learn and adjust to the adult world.

SCULPTING THE CORTEX

During adolescence, myelination and growth continue in the prefrontal cortex (PFC), and thinning continues in the brain, particularly in the other sections of the cortex, such as the parietal lobe.

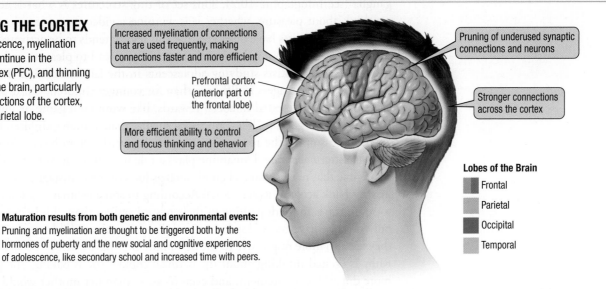

Increased myelination of connections that are used frequently, making connections faster and more efficient

Prefrontal cortex (anterior part of the frontal lobe)

More efficient ability to control and focus thinking and behavior

Pruning of underused synaptic connections and neurons

Stronger connections across the cortex

Lobes of the Brain
- Frontal
- Parietal
- Occipital
- Temporal

Maturation results from both genetic and environmental events: Pruning and myelination are thought to be triggered both by the hormones of puberty and the new social and cognitive experiences of adolescence, like secondary school and increased time with peers.

INCREASED ACTIVITY IN SUBCORTICAL SYSTEMS

During adolescence, maturation continues in the subcortical structures. The reward circuit matures and is particularly sensitive to and filled with higher levels of dopamine, the neurotransmitter associated with learning and reward. These developments allow young people to develop better emotion regulation, social skills, and an increased likelihood to be motivated by social experiences.

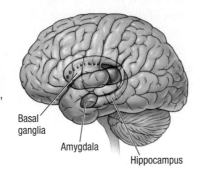

Basal ganglia
Amygdala
Hippocampus

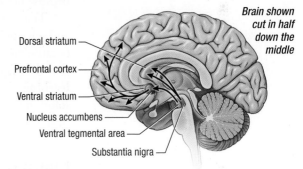

Brain shown cut in half down the middle

Dorsal striatum
Prefrontal cortex
Ventral striatum
Nucleus accumbens
Ventral tegmental area
Substantia nigra

The Reward Circuit (also known as the dopamine system) links many regions of the brain, including the dorsal and ventral striatum in the basal ganglia, with other regions, including the ventral tegmental area in the midbrain. The nucleus accumbens, a component of the ventral striatum, is linked to decision making about behaviors that tend to lead to pleasure and rewards.

MATURING CONNECTIONS ACROSS THE BRAIN

Connections continue to mature between the prefrontal cortex and subcortical structures of the social emotional brain, such as the amygdala. These stronger connections allow more control and regulation of emotions.

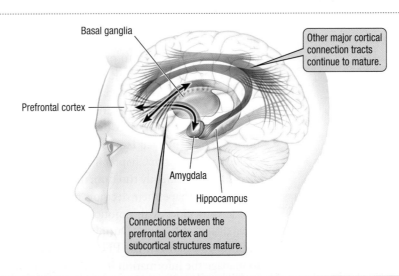

Basal ganglia

Prefrontal cortex

Other major cortical connection tracts continue to mature.

Amygdala
Hippocampus

Connections between the prefrontal cortex and subcortical structures mature.

One region in the subcortical brain activated during adolescence is the *reward system* or *circuit* (Galván, 2013; Schreuders et al., 2018). The reward system connects brain regions including the *dorsal* and *ventral striatum*, small structures inside the basal ganglia (see Infographic 10.2). This set of tiny structures is what is activated when we think about pleasure, whether it is winning a video game or enjoying ice cream afterwards. Scientists have observed that this region tends to be activated when we are making decisions about behaviors that are likely to lead to pleasure and other rewards (Floresco, 2015). Scientists studying adolescents in the laboratory find that what motivates or excites teenagers is different than for younger children. Unsurprisingly, teenagers are more interested in social rewards, like winning a game or impressing their friends, or even getting "likes" on social media, than younger children (Galván, 2013).

One reason for the responsiveness of the reward system has to do with the neurotransmitter *dopamine*. Dopamine plays a role in feeling pleasure as well as anything intangible that makes you feel good, such as likes on your Instagram post or a deposit in your bank account (Galván, 2017). According to some estimates, adolescents have up to seven times more dopamine in their reward system than children (Spear, 2013). Not only do they have more dopamine in their system than children (or adults) do, but they are also more responsive to the dopamine they have (Baker & Galván, 2020). So, when Ruby is excited thinking about the oatmeal cookies she is baking, she probably feels more dopamine, excitement, and even pleasure than her mother would (and not just because her mother might do the cleanup).

The maturation of the reward circuit helps power adolescents' motivation to learn and solve problems. Teenagers are motivated to try new things and explore alternatives because these activities bring them pleasure (Davidow et al., 2018). Studies have suggested that teenagers are better than both children and adults at what is called **exploratory learning**, or trying out different ways to solve a problem before deciding on the best solution (Davidow et al., 2016; Somerville et al., 2017). By trying different options and making mistakes early, teenagers can more easily find the best solution than adults.

Maturing Brain Networks

Although it is sometimes helpful to think about individual structures or circuits in the brain, such as the PFC or the reward system, separately, none of these function in isolation from one another. Remember from Chapter 6 that the brain is an interconnected system of networks called the *connectome*.

Scientists are particularly interested in the maturation of the connections between our subcortical structures and the prefrontal cortex during adolescence, because these connections are linked to our emotion regulation and decision making skills (Galván, 2017). These networks link the conscious, logical processing in the brain with the regions devoted to emotional processing. In essence, these connections shape how we react to emotional experiences and how our experiences trigger our emotional reactions. The maturation of these networks is a long process and is not complete until our mid- or even late-20s (Casey et al., 2019; Romer et al., 2017; Steinberg & Icenogle, 2019).

Remember from Chapter 8 that, as these networks mature during middle childhood, neural signals primarily run from the subcortical structures to the PFC, allowing children's emotions to shape their decision making while also contributing to some of children's typical difficulties with emotion regulation (Callaghan & Tottenham, 2016; Kopala-Sibley et al., 2020; Thijssen et al., 2017). During adolescence, the direction shifts: Neural connections begin to run between the PFC to the subcortical structures. In essence, the PFC starts to manage the information it is receiving from the subcortical structures (Casey et al., 2019; Gee et al., 2014; Tottenham & Gabard-Durnam, 2017). This allows the PFC to both respond to and guide how we process feelings, allowing adolescents to use cognitive strategies to reframe their emotions, control their motivation, and focus on long-term pleasures.

exploratory learning Trying out different ways to solve a problem before deciding on the best solution.

MAKING A DIFFERENCE
Protecting Adolescents from Brain Injury

Madeline Uretsky considered herself strong and capable. She played soccer, ice hockey, and *two* seasons of track, but all of this changed during one soccer game. Madeline cannot remember that day very well. Her friends told her she tumbled to the ground, and her head whiplashed, swinging back and forth hard. It soon became apparent that Madeline had suffered a severe concussion. For months she suffered from terrible headaches, dizziness, sensitivity to noise, bright lights hurt her eyes, and she couldn't keep track of what day it was. Ten years later, there are still times when she doesn't feel quite right; Madeline has to bring sunglasses wherever she goes to keep her headaches at bay, she has attention difficulties and changes in the weather cause extreme fatigue (Uretsky, 2021; Weintraub et al., 2013).

In the United States, nearly one in four adolescents like Madeline report that they have suffered a **concussion**, a form of *traumatic brain injury (TBI)* caused by a blow to the head (Veliz et al., 2021). A few decades ago, pediatricians and scientists believed that brain injuries during adolescence were not very serious and that concussions would not cause long-term challenges for most (Martini et al., 2018; Redelmeier & Raza, 2016). However, developmental scientists have helped demonstrate that concussions and other TBIs can cause lasting challenges for teenagers, including problems with executive function, emotion regulation, and attention (Christensen et al., 2021).

The rapid development of the adolescent brain makes it more vulnerable to trauma and injury. A TBI can derail development, since the brain has to spend energy on repair rather than on building new neural connections (Brett et al., 2020; Taylor et al., 2018). Adolescent concussions have been linked to greater risk for degenerative diseases like multiple sclerosis, amyotrophic lateral sclerosis (ALS), and *chronic traumatic encephalopathy (CTE)*, a debilitating disease that can result in significant mood changes and cognitive problems (Caffey & Daleck, 2021; Hornbeck et al., 2017; Povolo et al., 2021).

Concussions cause breakages in the cell walls of individual neurons as the entire brain is rocked, rotated, or rushed from side to side, and cause widespread inflammation (see **Figure 10.4**). For instance, Madeline's brain was injured both at the point of impact (when her head hit the ground) and also on its opposite side (when it was bruised as it banged against the back of her skull). The immediate effects of a concussion, like feeling spacey or dizzy, typically resolve within a few weeks, but about one in four teenagers does not get better right away (Lima Santos et al., 2021).

As was the case for Madeline, many head injuries come from sports, but concussions often also result from car accidents or assaults (Dufour et al., 2020; Haarbauer-Krupa et al., 2018). Some experts have suggested that young people avoid high-risk sports or change the rules to make them less dangerous (Hornbeck et al., 2017; Piedade et al., 2021). Particularly dangerous sports include football, hockey, martial arts, boxing, field

concussion A form of traumatic brain injury (TBI) caused by a blow to the head.

Passing the Help Along Madeline is still recovering from the effects of concussions she had as an adolescent, but is now working to help other young people recover from the impact of head injuries.

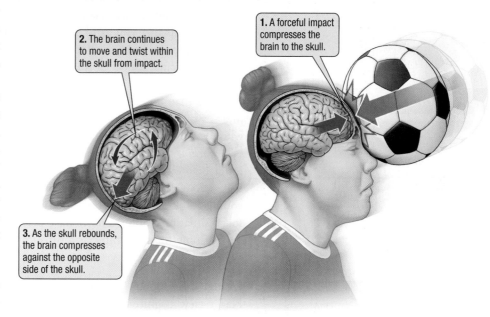

2. The brain continues to move and twist within the skull from impact.

1. A forceful impact compresses the brain to the skull.

3. As the skull rebounds, the brain compresses against the opposite side of the skull.

FIGURE 10.4 Brain Injury, Step By Step A concussion is the term for a mild brain injury caused by a blow to the head. Our brains may be able to recover, but injuries can cause long-term difficulties, particularly during a time of rapid development like adolescence.

hockey, and soccer (Halstead et al., 2018). Some evidence indicates that young women, like Madeline, may be particularly susceptible to brain injuries because of variations in neck strength or hormones (Sanderson, 2021).

Adolescents who experience a brain injury often face a long recovery. After months of rehab, Madeline was finally able to leave her darkened room, go back to school, and, step by step, start rebuilding her life. Her experience with concussions ignited her interest in neuroscience, and she wants to help prevent and treat head trauma in young athletes (Uretsky, 2021). 🏒

Cognitive Development

Maturation of the brain, as well as years of practice, brings dramatic enhancements to teenagers' cognitive abilities, including faster thinking and an improved ability to focus. Adolescents are now able to grasp abstractions and make wise decisions in everyday life, which is why they can be trusted to drive a car or babysit overnight. It is not just the components of thinking that improve: Reasoning ability becomes more logical. Adolescents can more easily work through a problem using formal operational thought and make decisions using analytic problem-solving skills. Early models of cognitive development suggested that adolescents are very egocentric and focused on their own selves (Elkind, 1967). However, little empirical research supported this. Research over the past two decades has revealed an increased sophistication to learning about the world that is driven in part by brain development, which motivates young people to explore.

Faster and More Focused Thought The ability to process information quickly increases throughout adolescence and into early adulthood (Kail & Ferrer, 2007; Luna et al., 2004). As you may remember from Chapter 2, researchers call this *processing speed*, or how rapidly you can respond to something, whether that is the sound of your name being called across the room or matching patterns in a cognitive test. In school or even in a dynamic conversation between friends, being able to process information quickly means that you can keep up when new material is presented.

Remember that in developmental science, *attention* refers to the ability to focus on one particular aspect of the environment. For many, this ability improves during adolescence (Fandakova & Hartley, 2020; Kuhn, 2009). Teenagers are better at ignoring distractions than younger children. It is easier for them to pay attention to one sound in a sea of noise, like a teacher's voice in a crowded auditorium filled with coughs, whispers, and cell phone vibrations (Karns et al., 2015).

Working memory, or the ability to keep track of what you can quickly hold in your mind before storing it long-term memory, improves throughout adolescence (Andre et al., 2016; Embury et al., 2019; Linares et al., 2016). Adolescents have better memory than younger children, although their sensitivity to social cues may sometimes interfere in social situations. Some studies have even shown that teenagers have trouble remembering something as simple as a three-digit number if they are stressed or excited by a social situation (Mills et al., 2015).

Formal Operational Thought Remember that developmental scientists like Jean Piaget view cognitive development as a series of discrete periods. In adolescence, Piaget focused on adolescents' ability to think abstractly about big, hard-to-define topics such as peace, love, or fate, and to go a step further and imagine not just a single abstraction, but what one abstraction could do to another. Piaget called the stage that begins in early adolescence and continues into adulthood **formal operational thought** (Inhelder & Piaget, 1958). The key characteristics of formal operational thinking are that it is both logical *and* abstract (see **Table 10.1**).

Scientific American Profile

Learning and Discovery

formal operational thought Piaget's stage of cognitive development that begins in early adolescence and lasts into adulthood and is both logical and abstract.

TABLE 10.1 Piaget's Stage of Formal Operational Thought

Stage	Age	Characteristics
formal operational thought	about 11 through adulthood	Children and adults can think abstractly and apply logical concepts to other logical concepts.

Piaget used a practical device to measure the changes in adolescents' thinking: a balance scale (see **Figure 10.5**). Before every grocery store had a scanner, post offices and fruit sellers used balance scales to measure the weight of packages or produce. With his colleague Bärbel Inhelder, Piaget used this balance scale to assess if adolescents could make hypotheses and logically test them out.

In order to balance a scale, the weights on both sides need to be equal. However, you can also balance the scale by adjusting the weights so that the heavier weights are farther away from the center of the scale, or the *fulcrum*, and the lighter weights are closer. Younger children are unable to systematically figure out how the scale works, but older children and adolescents begin to figure out how to solve the problem. Some, particularly those in the concrete operational stage, may use trial-and-error in their reasoning by randomly placing the weights at various points on the scale. But adolescents in the formal operational stage will be systematic in figuring out the balance scale: They can make predictions, test them out, and use words or symbols to explain their thinking. Piaget predicted that most children would be able to figure out how the balance scale works by age 12.

Despite Piaget's predictions, the math and physics skills of most of us are rusty. Many adults and teenagers do not use formal operational thought and have difficulty explaining how a balance scale works (Capon & Kuhn, 1982; Flynn & Shayer, 2018; Shayer & Ginsburg, 2009). Scientists now believe that achieving formal operational thought, or the ability to think abstractly *and* logically, and using it all the time requires significant motivation and a particular type of education (Commons & Davidson, 2015). Most adults make everyday decisions, like what kind of snack to buy or even who to vote for, by habit and impulse rather than using their logical thinking skills. As a result, many developmentalists believe that although reasoning ability *can* become more sophisticated in adolescence, people will not always use it consistently or think analytically or abstractly outside laboratory or classroom settings (Kokis et al., 2002; Siegler, 2016).

Analytical and Heuristic Thought Piaget was not the only developmental scientist who noticed adolescents' thinking becoming more logical. Other researchers noticed that there are multiple components to teenagers' reasoning abilities. For instance, adolescents working on an algebraic equation to solve the balance scale problem are using **analytic thinking**, a type of thinking that is logical, weighing evidence and making a decision that requires conscious thought. But researchers also identified an additional type of advanced reasoning that we use across the lifespan: **heuristic thinking**, which is the automatic thinking that you do outside of consciousness (Herbert, 2010). Heuristic thinking can be useful, as when you walk to your bus stop without consciously thinking about how to get there or driving to work without paying close attention to street names. In some ways, this represents the beginning of what may be called "wisdom" in adults much older: Adolescents' accumulation of experience helps them make quicker and more informed decisions (Romer et al., 2017).

When researchers ask adolescents to solve complex problems, older adolescents are more likely to use analytical thinking than younger ones, who are more likely to use more impulsive, heuristic thinking (Felmban & Klaczynski, 2019; Klaczynski, 2014; Kokis et al., 2002). These analytical skills will be useful in school. Students who are able to think

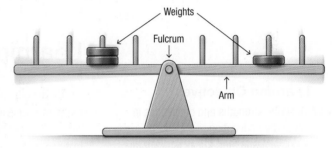

FIGURE 10.5 Can You Balance the Scale? A younger child might experiment randomly, but as children use formal operational thought, they are increasingly able to use abstract ideas to describe the relationship between distance and weight that is necessary to balance the scale.

analytic thinking A type of thinking that is logical, weighing evidence and making a decision that requires conscious thought.

heuristic thinking A type of advanced reasoning, which is automatic thinking that you do outside of consciousness.

analytically perform better on all the logical and abstract thinking tasks that school requires, from understanding all the reasons for the Civil War to completing biology.

But heuristic thinking is not without its benefits. Sometimes analytical thinking cannot help you with a problem, as when you are trying to figure out what advice to give a friend who is upset or decide what you want to do with your life. Adolescents, like adults, tend to switch to heuristic thinking particularly when they are in emotional or social situations, such as when they are upset or when they are with peers (Crone & Dahl, 2012; Somerville et al., 2010). As adolescents gain more experience in the world, they get better at finding the essence of real-life questions and getting to the "gist" of things (Reyna & Panagiotopoulos, 2020).

APPLY IT! **10.9** Scientists call adolescence a sensitive period for brain development. How does brain development help teenagers as they grow into adult roles?

10.10 How are teenagers' brains more sensitive to reward and emotional input than adults' brains?

10.11 Ruby is preparing a presentation for her science class about synaptic transmission and myelination. How does this abstract work represent her ability to do formal operational thought?

10.12 Ruby feels that she is faster at doing schoolwork than she used to be. How does this reflect her gains in information-processing skills?

Learning in and out of School

Learning Objectives

10.7 Describe strengths and challenges in secondary education.

10.8 Analyze group differences in academic achievement.

Brain development and cognitive maturation make adolescence a particularly sensitive time for learning: It is now easier and more efficient to learn new skills (Romer et al., 2017). What teenagers learn in adolescence, whether it is how to navigate friendships, how to concentrate, or how to write a five-paragraph essay, will shape them and provide a foundation for their development for years to come. You may think of learning as something that happens in school, but formal education is just one way that adolescents build their capabilities.

Secondary School Around the World

Secondary school is the formal name for middle and high schools designed for young people who have finished elementary or primary school at about age 11 or 12. For communities around the world, secondary schools help to create an educated workforce and are linked to economic growth (Goldin, 1998). But secondary schools are not just beneficial to communities: They are also good for the adolescents who attend them.

Secondary schools help to boost teenagers' cognitive skills, increase their likelihood to delay starting a family, and improve their financial potential (Rasmussen et al., 2019; Sheehan et al., 2017). School also helps build social connections: The longer adolescents stay in school, the more likely they are to have strong friendships as adults, someone to rely on in an emergency, and a place to volunteer in their communities (OECD, 2021b). Around the world, researchers suggest that encouraging more teenagers to stay in school may be the best investment in improving the well-being of all people (Patton et al., 2018; Sheehan et al., 2017).

Universal high schools are a relatively recent U.S. invention. It was not until the 1950s that more than half of all U.S. teenagers graduated from high school (Goldin, 1998). This idea soon took hold elsewhere (Goldin & Katz, 1997). After World War II,

Getting Ready for Space These students from Col. Nuestra Señora del Perpetuo Socorro High School in Puerto Rico created their own self-propelled rover, designed to use in space. They rode it and came in second, to another team from Puerto Rico, in an international competition in Huntsville, Alabama.

AP Photo/The Huntsville Times, Glenn Baeske

European countries and other affluent nations around the world also began to require that adolescents stay in school until they were in their late teens, a prospect designed to build workers who could thrive in a more challenging job environment. Today, high school education has become the norm worldwide. Low-income countries still lag behind wealthier countries in high school enrollment, but now more than three in four adolescents are enrolled in some kind of secondary school (UNESCO, 2020).

Schools around the world are commonly compared in terms of how their students perform on international or national tests. On international comparative tests, U.S. students typically score in the average or lower-average range, often behind other wealthy nations like Japan, the Netherlands, and Canada, although their scores seem to be improving (OECD, 2021c; Whitehurst, 2018). Many researchers have connected lagging U.S. scores to higher levels of poverty and inequality and unequal funding of schools (Carnoy & Rothstein, 2013; Rowley et al., 2020).

Secondary schools around the world have diverse curricula that reflect local values. Many focus on preparing adolescents for college. But, in addition to academic work, schools may include job training, religious training, such as in Saudi Arabia, or military training, such as in Eritrea (Human Rights Watch, 2019; Omar, 2020).

High schools in the United States are typically **comprehensive high schools**, a form of secondary education that serves a broad range of adolescents, regardless of their academic ability and future plans. Comprehensive high schools offer four years of broad-ranging education in math, history, English, and science. They are designed to help prepare adolescents for adult work that requires them to write clearly, read a technical manual, and know how diseases are transmitted. Mastering this wide range of skills will help teenagers succeed in a wide variety of careers in manufacturing, health care, and the service sector (Goldin & Katz, 2008; NASEM, 2019).

Career and Technical Education The U.S. commitment to comprehensive universal high school is relatively unique. In many other affluent countries in Europe and Asia, students are separated, or tracked, early in their academic careers by their interests and abilities and attend schools focused on either academic preparation for college or career training. Many of these schools offer high-quality *career and technical education (CTE)*, often called *vocational education* in the United States. In Europe and Asia, CTE is highly prized, and more than 4 in 10 students choose a vocational track because it often leads to earnings that are similar to those of an academic track (Musset, 2019).

Interest in career and technical education is having a resurgence in the United States (Jacob, 2017; Rosen et al., 2018). Policy makers agree that the idea that all adolescents should go to college and attend comprehensive high school has not served everyone well, particularly those who do not graduate from college, end up saddled with burdensome student loans, or have difficulties finding high-paying jobs (Jacob, 2017). The CTE high schools that are becoming more common in the United States are different from the vocational schools of the past. Their academic *and* technical standards are higher, giving students better preparation for a changing economy whether they choose to go to a four-year college, or get a two-year degree, or seek more technical training. These schools help students find meaningful work after they leave high school (Afranie & Clagett, 2020).

The Controversy over Tracking Even if most U.S. students attend a comprehensive secondary school, their experiences within the walls of that high school may be quite disparate. More than 80 percent of high school students in the United States and 75 percent of middle school students attend schools with some sort of **tracking**

comprehensive high schools High schools that serve all youth, regardless of their academic ability and future careers, helping to prepare them for adult work.

tracking The practice of grouping together students with similar achievement and test scores and offering them a more customized school curriculum.

Mark Peterson/Redux

CTE Works. Suriana Rodriguez graduated high school in Newburgh, New York, with a high school diploma, an associate's degree, and a full-time job at a technology company. Her CTE program allowed her to combine high school and technical education.

Share It!

Inequity persists in new CTE schools as it does in comprehensive high schools. Researchers suggest that students of color are underrepresented in CTE, particularly in the skilled trades.

(Anderson et al., 2021)

Scientific American: Lifespan Development

system (Loveless, 2016; Rui, 2009). Tracking involves grouping together students with similar achievement and test scores and offering them a school curriculum that matches both their interests and abilities.

Tracking is designed to give students with greater academic potential a more challenging curriculum. This enables promising young students to build the skills they will need to perform at the highest level in high school, whether that is in *International Baccalaureate* programs or *Advanced Placement* courses (Loveless, 2016). Tracking, however, does not seem beneficial for all students. Although grouping students by ability and achievement may sound sensible, tracking often segregates students by income and ethnicity (Rui, 2009). In many schools, students with low income, especially those whose parents have not finished college, are more likely to end up at the bottom track regardless of grades or test scores (Cullen et al., 2013; Parker et al., 2016). Such students also tend to be disproportionately Black, Latino, and English-language learners (Crosnoe & Muller, 2014; Kanno & Kangas, 2014). Adolescents who end up in lower tracks not only learn less, but may also feel inferior or shamed, and therefore are significantly more likely to leave school altogether (Francis et al., 2020; McGillicuddy & Devine, 2020).

Some call for "detracking" schools, but others would rather ensure that the more rigorous tracks are open to all striving teenagers (Card & Giuliano, 2016; Loveless, 2016). Accelerated coursework can have a larger impact on low-income Black and Latino children, raising their test scores substantially, particularly if it begins in middle school (Card & Giuliano, 2016; Cohodes, 2020).

Funding Inequalities The United States has a commitment to universal secondary education, but students' opportunities may be vastly different depending on where they attend school. Remember from Chapter 8 that, unlike many other high-income countries, public school funding in the United States is largely dependent on the wealth of the local community.

As a result of funding formulas in the United States, affluent communities spend more per pupil than do less affluent communities, resulting in inequitable quality of secondary education in the United States (NASEM, 2019; Schanzenbach et al., 2016). (See **Figure 10.6**). Secondary schools in lower-income communities tend to have teachers with fewer years of experience, more limited access to Advanced Placement courses, and more decayed physical environments (NASEM, 2019). Lower-income schools are more likely to have peeling paint, broken bathroom doors, and defective air conditioners (Cullen et al., 2013). These schools are disproportionately likely to serve students who are from rural and/or Black and Latino communities (NASEM, 2019). Regardless

STUDENTS DO NOT HAVE EQUITABLE ACCESS TO HIGH-QUALITY EDUCATION.

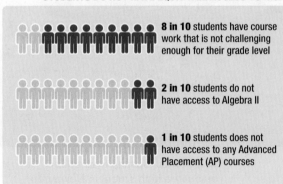

8 in 10 students have course work that is not challenging enough for their grade level

2 in 10 students do not have access to Algebra II

1 in 10 students does not have access to any Advanced Placement (AP) courses

Low-income districts receive only **9.3 dollars for every 10 dollars** received by high-income districts.

WHAT STUDENTS LEARN IN SCHOOL AFFECTS THEIR FUTURE.

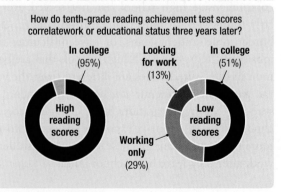

How do tenth-grade reading achievement test scores correlate to work or educational status three years later?

In college (95%) — Looking for work (13%) — In college (51%)

High reading scores

Low reading scores

Working only (29%)

Data from U.S. Department of Education, 2018; TNTP, 2018.

Data from Mamedova et al., 2021.

FIGURE 10.6 Inequity in High School Education Students do not always have equitable access to a high-quality education, which can affect their ability to find a well-paying job later in life. Inequity in education hurts communities by reducing the numbers of highly educated workers and taxpayers.

of cultural or ethnic background, being low-income and attending under-resourced schools increase adolescents' risk for academic difficulties: Students who go to under-resourced schools are more likely to leave high school early, less likely to complete college, and more likely to be underemployed as adults (Means et al., 2019; NASEM, 2019).

Inequity in Achievement

What leads to such disparities in school quality and student performance? One is an unequal starting point. Living in low-income neighborhoods brings a host of challenges for teenagers, not only under-resourced schools, but also exposure to neighborhood violence and discrimination (Gordon & Cui, 2018). Adolescents who are from marginalized groups face discriminatory behavior that can profoundly affect their academic performance, whether it is name-calling in the hallway, harassment by police on the way to school, or low expectations from teachers (Benner et al., 2018; Bryan et al., 2018; Schmader & Forbes, 2017; Spencer et al., 2016; Zeiders et al., 2021).

Stereotypes are shorthand assumptions we hold about other people based on characteristics such as appearance, ethnicity, body size, gender, sexual orientation, ability, or income level. **Stereotype threat** occurs when you feel judged in an area where there are common stereotypes about your group, and the resulting anxiety negatively affects your performance (Protzko & Aronson, 2016; Steele & Aronson, 1995). For instance, if children believe that they are from a group that "isn't good at math," and their membership to that group is pointed out, they perform poorly on tasks as basic as remembering a list of numbers. This finding has been replicated in groups ranging from children who have a larger body size than their peers, children of color, and girls and boys alike (Guardabassi & Tomasetto, 2020; Hartley & Sutton, 2013; McKowen & Strambler, 2009; Wasserberg, 2014).

Despite the opportunities for learning in adolescence, many students struggle to stay engaged in school (see **Figure 10.7**). In the United States, one in six ninth-graders will not graduate from high school in four years, although most will persevere and more than 95 percent will eventually earn a high school diploma or *General Education Diploma (GED)* by age 24 (NCES, 2021). However, students who do not graduate with a traditional high school diploma remain at a disadvantage, even with a GED. They are significantly less likely to find a well-paying job or finish college (Jepsen et al., 2017).

Improving Secondary Schools

Research suggests that secondary schools could be more effective and encourage more students to stay in school longer if they incorporated what is known about how adolescents learn best: strong relationships and opportunity for autonomy. This is what helped Ruby stay motivated at school throughout a pandemic: She loves the opportunity to work on her own. With no one looking over her shoulder or telling her to slow down, she finally has a chance to dive deep into things that interest her. On top of this, Ruby *loves* her teachers. She feels like they truly care about her: They take time to check in on her, and they appreciate her passion and her curiosity.

Teenagers' motivation to learn the skills that they will need to thrive in adulthood makes adolescence a perfect time for making changes in school performance. Researchers have found that teenagers are able to make major alterations to their academic trajectories in middle and high school, allowing them to catch up or move beyond what they had expected of themselves and set themselves up for more success in adulthood (Guryan et al., 2021).

Strengthening Relationships Developmental scientists have established that teenagers are highly motivated by positive relationships, with their peers and teachers alike. Establishing a feeling of trust, community, and belonging is an effective way to build a positive learning environment (Gray et al., 2018; Wang et al., 2020; Yeager et al., 2018).

stereotype threat The phenomenon that occurs when you feel judged in an area where there are common stereotypes about your group, and the resulting anxiety negatively affects your performance.

CONNECTIONS

Cultural exclusion and the effects of racism and sexism impact children throughout development. The stress of racism can even affect fetal development (see Chapter 3), and preschoolers already have stereotyped beliefs that shape their development (see Chapter 6).

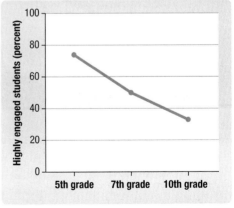

Data from Hodges, 2018.

FIGURE 10.7 Student Engagement Declines Young people spend hours a day on school work, but it becomes less interesting and inspiring as they get older. Researchers suggest that allowing students to make more choices about what they learn and strengthening their relationships with their peers and teachers could help reverse the trend.

Persevering for the Win Eleventh-graders India Skinner, Mikayla Sharrieff, and Bria Snell from Washington, D.C., created a plan for purifying lead-contaminated water for an online competition. They encountered discrimination and harassment, but they did not let it stop them. They are still determined to study science in college.

Staying Connected Using multiple devices, this high school student in Naples, Italy, tries to stay in the loop with her teachers and friends during the COVID-19 pandemic in 2020.

stage–environment fit The idea that we do better when the world matches our developmental needs.

Teenagers who feel closer to a teacher are more likely to perform better in school than children who lack that connection (Battistich et al., 2004; García-Moya et al., 2019). Programs like *looping*, in which students stay with one teacher for more than one year, are designed to promote teacher–student relationships (Rutledge et al., 2020). Strong connections may be one reason why smaller school size is linked to school success. Around the world, middle and high schools tend to be larger than grade schools, which often comes at a cost in terms of personal connections (NCES, 2020).

Relationships—with teachers as well as peers—generally suffered when students had to attend school remotely during the COVID-19 pandemic. Researchers suspect that social isolation was one reason many adolescents struggled both emotionally and academically during the pandemic (Duckworth et al., 2021; Orben et al., 2020). Many teenagers reported that they felt more distant from their teachers over Zoom than they did in real life (Lessard & Puhl, 2021). But, for some children who may have difficult social relationships or anxieties about friendships, the break from in-person socializing may have been a positive experience. For both Rosie and Ruby, there were silver linings about learning at home, including having a break from the social pressure that came with in-person school.

Increased Autonomy and Agency Although researchers have demonstrated that schools would be more effective if they fostered adolescents' needs for exploration, independence, and respect, many school environments put a premium on following the rules and limit students' independence and reward obedience rather than encouraging exploration (NASEM, 2019). Scientists call this a poor **stage–environment fit** (Eccles & Roeser, 2011).

Surprisingly, schoolwork can become *less* challenging for students in middle school than in elementary school. Increased use of worksheets and rote memorization at a time when adolescents are cognitively capable of quicker and more advanced learning leads to boredom, disengagement, and tuning out (Chase et al., 2014; Salmela-Aro et al., 2021). Perhaps as a result, student engagement declines dramatically as children reach middle school (Hodges, 2018). Strategies to avoid this slump include focusing on *project-based learning* in which students develop skills and mastery by working overtime to respond to a challenge or address a real-world problem (NASEM, 2019).

Adolescence is an ideal time to reinvigorate students' interest in learning: Teenagers are not too old to connect with school. Interventions to help improve students' engagement through mentoring, tutoring, and individualized projects can be effective in helping students connect with schools and catch up with their peers (Guryan et al., 2021).

Out-of-School Activities

What teenagers do outside of school, from after-school programs to mentorship opportunities, can make a difference in helping them stay in school and excel. Some teenagers may spend their time doing schoolwork or sports, learning new video games, or practicing a kickflip on a skateboard. Others do family chores and watch younger siblings. Many volunteer in their communities, feeding people at soup kitchens, cleaning harbors, or organizing for political work.

Extracurricular Activities Students who spend time in formal activities, such as sports, debate, or volunteering, tend to do better in school and have better mental health (Oberle et al., 2020; Vandell et al., 2019). Activities can give teenagers a sense of purpose, supervision, and skill development outside of school—and keep them from focusing too much on their social life (Tjaden et al., 2019).

Organized programs enable teenagers to develop closer relationships with adults outside the family, such as coaches or teachers. Organized activities and mentoring programs also help adolescents develop new skills that they can apply in future careers (Zarrett et al., 2020). The importance of relationships is underlined by the success of one-on-one mentoring programs, such as Big Brother/Big Sister, that have been shown to improve students' school performance and later success (Raposa et al., 2019; Tolan et al., 2020). It is also shown in an innovative program in New York City that puts teenagers on stage, and changes their lives.

SCIENCE IN PRACTICE
Alex Batres, Artistic Director, The Possibility Project

Alex Batres says that rapping saved his life (Batres, 2012). Before he started making music and finding himself as an artist, he had difficulty envisioning his future. But when he was in high school, he found his voice on stage and has been making music and performing poetry across New York City ever since. His goal is to be an entertainer, and he recently released his first EP. Currently, he coaches New York City teenagers, many of whom have been affected by the criminal justice system, on writing, producing, and performing their own musicals, videos, and podcasts. He works with a nonprofit community theater group called the Possibility Project that provides mentorship and *social and emotional learning (SEL)*. Batres's expertise is in music, but he is applying developmental science in his job every day.

Batres doesn't miss a thing. If a student is on their phone instead of paying attention, he finds a way to bring them back into focus. He is not just focused on relationships: He communicates high expectations and provides individualized instruction.

Batres is not only a creative coach; he is also training young people in skills that will help them succeed. Social and emotional skills, sometimes called *soft skills*, which include the ability to communicate, persevere, and work in a group, may matter as much as traditional ones that achievement tests measure (Gordon & Cui, 2018; NAP, 2019; Schanzenbach et al., 2016). Social and emotional soft skills have benefits that go beyond traditional measures: Students are not just likely to do better on tests and enroll in college, they are also more likely to finish college (Jackson et al., 2020).

Batres makes sure his participants feel safe, respected, and that they share control over what they are doing. Some of the students with whom he works do not have permanent housing. Most have long histories of trauma. They often face stigma and feel like outsiders in their high schools. At the Possibility Project, he holds them to high standards, but these standards come with a nod of understanding and the reassurance that Alex values them and believes they can succeed. He makes it possible for students to share their stories, to feel understood and part of something bigger than themselves.

Adults like Batres are able to build connections and trust with young people through high expectations and lots of warmth (Gregory & Weinstein, 2008; Lepper & Woolverton, 2002). These connections outside of school and their families help students achieve more, in addition to helping them feel good about themselves. At the Possibility Project, achieving more means finishing producing a movie and writing music. Researchers studying the Possibility Project have found that students in their program are more likely to stay in school, get higher grades, and continue on to college. They have built skills in empathy and conflict resolution, in part by the sense that they are a member of a new, shared community (Hanson, 2020). And, of course, the core belief

Jim West/Alamy

Serving More Than Casserole
Community service can help young people, like these teenagers from California serving a meal in Colorado, feel that they are contributing to others.

of the Possibility Project is "possibility": Developmental science that reminds us that all adolescents can build resilience and change. 🌐

Employment Adolescents may meet mentors not only in after-school programs but also at work. While teenage employment has been declining in recent years, about half of high school seniors has had a job over the summer months (U.S. Bureau of Labor Statistics, 2021). Most say they enjoy the independence of working, even though their jobs—most are working in food service or retail—are often dreary (Mortimer, 2020). The skills students learn in entry-level jobs may not be the most exciting, but they help prepare them for the transition to independence (Martin et al., 2014; Vuolo et al., 2014).

However, working too much can mean missing out on school. About 10 percent of teenagers put in more than 26 hours every week on the job (Staff et al., 2020). This intensive work may be too much: Some begin to struggle to keep up with their course work and may end up spending their money on social activities (Staff et al., 2020). However, other scientists have noted that teenagers from low-income families who work, particularly to save for college or help their families with everyday expenses do not seem to experience negative consequences from their jobs (McLoyd & Hallman, 2020). In fact, for these adolescents, working may even be a way of transitioning into the full-time workforce (Lee et al., 2018).

Community Service For the many teenagers who participate, community service and volunteering can be life changing (Sparks, 2018). Service seems to be effective in helping adolescents think beyond themselves, particularly if they are asked to reflect on what they have done by sharing the experience or writing about it (van Goethem et al., 2014). This ability to think beyond themselves helps adolescents excel in all aspects of their own lives, from doing better in school to finding happiness outside of it (Ballard et al., 2019, 2021). This ability will, as we will learn in the next chapter, help them tackle the social and emotional transitions of the teenage years.

APPLY IT! **10.13** Rosie has never been a big reader; she is more of an active person. Her mother, Jill, wonders whether it is too late for her to get excited about reading. How might you explain that adolescence is a time of opportunity for growth? **10.14** Virtual school was challenging for teenagers around the world, particularly those who did not have access to the internet or had limited opportunity for online classes. How did this reflect more general inequalities in secondary education around the world?

Wrapping It Up 🔗

LO 10.1 Define adolescence. (p. 286)

Adolescence is the transition that begins with the changes of puberty and ends when youth are recognized as adults. How long adolescence lasts is determined by the cultural context. In modern times, puberty often begins at age 9 and adolescence is said to end at around 18, but some argue that it may last until the mid-20s.

LO 10.2 Identify the biological changes of puberty. (p. 286)

Puberty is the biological process that transforms children into adults who can have children. It includes maturation of the reproductive organs, including the milestones of menarche and spermarche, development of secondary sex characteristics, and a growth spurt. Some secondary sex characteristics, like body odor, are among the changes of adrenarche, between the ages of 5 and 9. Puberty is triggered by maturation in the ovaries and testes between ages 8 and 13 in children with ovaries and ages 9 and 14 in children with testes. It is triggered by hormones released by the HPG axis. In what is known as the secular trend, the age of menarche has gradually stabilized at around age 12. Common variations in pubertal timing are linked to genetics, environmental stress, pollution, and health. Stigma and prejudice based on appearance mean that some children who reach puberty early or late may face exclusion or social stresses.

LO 10.3 Explain healthy sexual development during adolescence. (p. 286)

Sex can be a positive part of adolescent development. Sexual desire begins with adrenarche and grows during puberty. Positive sexual practices include knowing how to communicate about sex and how to manage the risk of pregnancy and STI. In the United States, many teenagers have limited sex education. Many participate in a variety of sexual activities. Adolescents have high rates of STIs in part because they have difficulty talking with their partners about sexual practices.

LO 10.4 Explain the best ways for adolescents to maintain positive health. (p. 297)

Adolescents are building the ability to maintain their own health independently. They need extra nutrition to power their growth spurt. Stigma about body size is on the rise in adolescence, and many teenagers struggle with body image. A few are diagnosed with eating disorders. Adolescents tend to be less active than younger children, but their physical and mental development benefits from getting about 60 minutes of exercise a day. Teenagers need 8 to 10 hours of sleep every night, but many are sleep-deprived, which can trigger a cascade of difficulties with growth, emotion regulation, and learning.

LO 10.5 Identify important elements of brain maturation during adolescence. (p. 301)

The brain is more plastic during adolescence as teenagers build the skills they will need to be independent in adulthood. Adolescence is a sensitive period for brain development. Highlights of brain development include: (1) maturation of the prefrontal cortex (PFC); (2) heightened activation of subcortical regions and systems; and (3) enhanced connectivity between these subcortical systems and the prefrontal cortex. Adolescents' subcortical regions and systems including the reward circuit are activated, contributing to adolescents' emotional intensity and their focus on social relationships. The connections between the PFC and the subcortical systems are strengthening, and the PFC increasingly shapes communication to the subcortical structures, allowing teenagers to have more emotional control.

LO 10.6 Describe the fundamental changes in cognition during adolescence. (p. 301)

Maturation in the brain helps contribute to adolescents' improving cognitive skills, including faster processing speed, stronger focus, and improved working memory. Jean Piaget described adolescence as the time of *formal operational thought*, or the ability to think logically about abstractions and even use logical reasoning about abstractions. Subsequent researchers have found that development of formal operational thought depends on education rather than just on simple maturation. Other researchers describe the development of heuristic and analytical thought during adolescence.

LO 10.7 Describe strengths and challenges in secondary education. (p. 308)

More students are enrolled in secondary schools than ever before. The quality of those schools is variable and often inequitable. Efforts to reform education in the United States often focus on incorporating more career and technical education and helping schools better match students' need for autonomy and strong personal relationships.

LO 10.8 Analyze group differences in academic achievement. (p. 308)

In the United States and around the world, there is inequity in access to high-resourced secondary education and inequality in students' achievement. Students who experience discrimination and those who do not have access to high-resourced schools are more likely to have difficulty finishing school and perform more poorly on achievement tests.

KEY TERMS

adolescence (p. 286)
puberty (p. 286)
HPG axis (p. 288)
testosterone (p. 288)
estrogen (p. 288)
growth spurt (p. 288)
menarche (p. 289)

spermarche (p. 289)
secular trend (p. 290)
sexually transmitted infection (STI) (p. 295)
body image (p. 298)
eating disorders (p. 299)
binge-eating disorder (p. 299)

bulimia nervosa (p. 299)
anorexia nervosa (p. 299)
circadian rhythm (p. 300)
exploratory learning (p. 304)
concussion (p. 305)
formal operational thought (p. 306)

analytic thinking (p. 307)
heuristic thinking (p. 307)
comprehensive high schools (p. 309)
tracking (p. 309)
stereotype threat (p. 311)
stage–environment fit (p. 312)

CHECK YOUR LEARNING

1. Which of the following is a marker for the end of adolescence?
   a) When teenagers get their drivers' license
   b) When adolescents move out of their parents' house
   c) When teenagers graduate high school
   d) When adolescents are recognized as adults by their community

2. What is the BEST way that families can prepare their children for puberty?
   a) Consider hormone treatments if puberty seems late.
   b) Ignore the signs of puberty in their child.
   c) Make sure their child is making friends and knows what to expect.
   d) Tell their child they are now ready for adult responsibilities.

3. Difficulties with sleep during adolescence are caused by:
   a) lack of self-control and emotion regulation.
   b) genetic differences.
   c) cultural expectations and biological flexibility.
   d) poor parenting practices.

4. Which skill BEST helps adolescents develop positive sexual health?
   a) Strong communication skills
   b) Knowing how to abstain from sexual activity
   c) Avoiding online media
   d) Awareness of the dangers of STIs

5. Adolescence is a time of maturation of the prefrontal cortex (PFC) and the:
   a) subcortical structures.
   b) hippocampus.
   c) cerebellum.
   d) spinal cord.

6. Why do scientists think adolescence is a sensitive period for brain development?
   a) The brain stops changing after adolescence.
   b) The brain grows larger and more quickly during adolescence than at any other point in the lifespan.
   c) The brain has heightened ability to change and is more plastic.
   d) Teenagers are self-centered and sensitive.

7. The type of reasoning that is more subconscious, intuitive, and more efficient at solving problems is called:
   a) heuristic thinking.
   b) formal operational thought.
   c) logical thinking.
   d) analytical thinking.

8. Piaget developed his theories of development based on close observation of young people in a highly resourced school in Switzerland. How might this group have influenced his idea that all children enter the stage of formal operational thought?

9. One challenge faced by secondary schools is that:
   a) adolescence is too late for school to make a difference.
   b) schools often stifle autonomy in an example of poor stage–environment fit.
   c) students learn more outside of school than in it.
   d) school does not make a difference in children's success.

Family Relationships

11.1 Explain the development of autonomy during adolescence.

11.2 Describe variations in parent–adolescent relationships.

Friends and Peers

11.3 Explain how adolescents make friends.

11.4 Analyze how peer groups influence adolescents.

Romantic Relationships

11.5 Identify the changes in romantic relationships during adolescence.

Finding Yourself: Identity Development

11.6 Explain how identity develops during adolescence.

Changing Feelings and Sense of Self

11.7 Describe how emotions and feelings change during adolescence.

11.8 Identify the psychological and behavioral challenges of adolescence.

Selected Resources from

 Achie√e

Activities

Concept Practice: The Search for Identity

Spotlight on Science: Do You Drive Like a Teenager?

Assessments

LearningCurve

Practice Quiz

Videos

Romantic Relationships in Adolescence

Could Smartphones Spot Teen Depression?

Jesús has things to do, and he is doing them. In the last year, he starred in his school's production of *Hamilton*, volunteered at his community center, painted murals, and planted a pollinator garden for monarch butterflies. He loves animals, acting, and art. He is immensely proud of his Mayan and Purépecha Indigenous Mexican heritage but also makes time to play handball and gossip over Instagram with his friends. Perhaps most impressively, Jesús is only 16.

Jesús wants to make a difference in the world, and now that his age affords him the skills to plan and follow through, he is doing just that. He leads classes about animal welfare and helps younger children with their homework. He harnesses his art skills to decorate his home and his neighborhood and draws pictures to make people happy (smiling dogs are always a hit). And, he shares his pride in his Indigenous heritage with anyone who will listen: posting drawings of traditional dancers online and helping to organize cultural festivals in real life.

Like many teenagers, Jesús is figuring out who he is as he grows up. That means asking his parents questions about who they were, where his family comes from (other than their bungalow in Los Angeles), and why they eat the food they eat and celebrate Mexican Independence Day. It also means looking different: not just getting taller, but also wearing the clothes that make him feel good.

What emboldens Jesús to speak out? Jesús's parents will tell you that he is a special teenager, and he certainly is, but as you will learn, his optimism, creativity, and energy is typical of adolescents. He is energized by his friends

Scientific American Profile

▶

Meet Jesús

and his family, including his parents, Jesús Senior and Martha, who are behind him 100 percent.

More than any other time during the lifespan, adolescence is when young people are motivated to take risks and to connect to the social world around them. Adolescents have enough brain maturation to learn things quickly, and enough flexibility to be profoundly changed by what they learn (Suleiman & Dahl, 2019). This may help them to take the risk of learning to drive, asking someone to prom, or starting a new school.

As is true for Jesús, having a sense of purpose and helping other people boosts resilience (Tashjian et al., 2021). As you will learn, whether they are starting a new school during a pandemic, trying to make a new friend, or deciding what kind of adult they want to become, adolescents benefit from support and resilience as they grow.

Family Relationships

Learning Objectives

11.1 Explain the development of autonomy during adolescence.

11.2 Describe variations in parent–adolescent relationships.

Many people have inaccurate ideas or mixed feelings about the relationship between teenagers and grown-ups. But Jesús, like most teenagers, gets along with his family. As he has gotten older, he has come to cherish them even more. He appreciates the hours his father spends driving him to a high school at the Los Angeles Zoo where he can study animals, and the way his mother has always championed his art and never disguised how proud she is of him. As he says, "they have always made me feel beloved."

Decades of research demonstrates that families remain important for adolescents as they create the foundation for their adult lives (Liu & Wang, 2021; Morris et al., 2013). Supportive families, like Jesús's, can help adolescents perform better in school and avoid antisocial and criminal behavior, depression, and substance abuse—all strengths that will help teenagers transition into their adult lives (Chen & Harris, 2019; Guan et al., 2016; Vagos et al., 2021).

Taking on Responsibility

One of the perks of growing up is being able to make your own decisions and having your own voice. Adolescents are eager to decide everything, from having that extra cookie to staying out later. They may also look forward to their ideas—about politics, dress codes, or even what phone to buy—having more impact. This is all a part of the adolescent quest for **autonomy**, or independence. Teenagers want to express their own *agency*, or control over their behavior. Having autonomy does not mean that teenagers are not connected to other people, but rather that they increasingly have more responsibility as they take on adult roles. Their growing sense of themselves, and of their own ideas and perspectives, plays a larger role in their lives than it did earlier in childhood (Benito-Gomez et al., 2020).

Teenagers often strive for more decision-making power, a type of autonomy sometimes called *behavioral autonomy* that refers to everyday choices, such as what kind of snack to pick up on the way home, which apps to download, or who to be friends with. Unsurprisingly, this type of agency can be a source of disagreement between caregivers and their children as they navigate what exactly can be a private decision (Chen-Gaddini et al., 2020; Smetana & Rote, 2019). Teenagers tend to be granted autonomy over their appearance, such as their hairstyle and clothing, before they are allowed to make choices about romantic partners or what high school courses to take. While it may seem superficial, choosing what to wear seems to be a universal first freedom (Romo et al., 2014). Jesús explains that he too

Share It!

Just don't do it. *Sharenting*, or posting online about teenagers, can be harmful to the parenting relationship. Experts advise asking first and posting later.

(Ouvrein & Verswijvel, 2019)

Scientific American: Lifespan Development

autonomy Taking responsibility, having greater agency, and making more decisions.

has made decisions about what to wear, heading out most days in the huarache sandals and guayabera pullover that he wears to represent his heritage. His parents have given him the space to make these decisions, as they trust him to become his own person in the world.

Adolescents often believe that who they are friends with, or who they date, is in their personal domain before their parents are ready to give up this control (Soenens & Vansteenkiste, 2020; Villalobos Solís et al., 2017). However, this does not mean that adolescents disagree with or disrespect their families' limits. As one teenager explained to a researcher: "they're your parents; you got to respect them. You got to do what they say" (qtd. in Villalobos Solís et al., 2017, p. 11). Autonomy development is a give-and-take process between adolescents and their parents. Teenagers who feel that they are respected and have a voice are less likely to *act out*, or have externalizing behavior, over time (Ravindran et al., 2020; Vrolijk et al., 2020).

Culture impacts how and when adolescents display their autonomy (Benito-Gomez et al., 2020; Tran & Raffaelli, 2020). Families differ in their expectations or ethno-theories about what timing is appropriate for various milestones, such as whether adolescents are old enough to commute home alone from school, go on a date, or get their own cell phone (Jensen & Dost-Gözkan, 2015; Silbereisen & Schmitt-Rodermund, 2020). Some families in the United States, such as those from some Latino or Asian American backgrounds or from immigrant communities, tend to have later timetables for certain markers of independence (Fuligni et al., 2009; Roche et al., 2014). In most cultures and communities around the world, however, there is a general trend toward increased behavioral autonomy as adolescence progresses (Lansford et al., 2021).

Getting Along Most of the Time

Contrary to some stereotypes, most teenagers and their parents get along. If you could peek into homes all around the world and watch families with teenagers preparing dinner, you would see mostly scenes of domestic tranquility. As Martha and Jesús Senior explain, they feel blessed to have Jesús in the house. They feel fortunate to have him as a son, and they are his biggest fans. At home, he makes them laugh, and they debate politics at dinner in the spirit of what Martha describes as "trust and openness."

Researchers who have surveyed or texted adolescents at different times of day, asked families to keep daily diaries, and interviewed caregivers and children together and apart have shown that most teenagers do get along with their parents as much as they did as children (Laursen et al., 1998). However, because they spend less time together, some parents feel that there is more conflict. When researchers ask families about their level of parenting stress, they often find it is highest during the adolescent years (Luthar & Ciciolla, 2016; Meier et al., 2018). Disagreements are often easily solved but are more irritating, as families and teenagers (who have become better arguers) try to navigate new responsibilities and routines. High-intensity conflict that involves screaming, for example, is *not* typical and may be a sign of deeper difficulties in the relationship (Fosco et al., 2021; LoBraico et al., 2020; Weymouth et al., 2016).

When it does occur, parent–adolescent conflict often reflects cultural values about arguing and family roles. For instance, families may interpret children's disagreement as disrespectful or "talking back," as in some Latino or Black families (Buehler, 2020; Juang & Cookston, 2009). In immigrant families, everyday conflicts may also reflect a generational disconnect (Juang et al., 2012). As one Latina mother explained, "Our son, who was born here, he has different customs; he is not like us . . . although we [my husband and I] have raised him. Americans do things differently . . .

Choosing What You Wear Around the world, young people express themselves by making choices about what they look like. In some cultures, being able to choose what you wear is an important part of becoming an adult; whereas, in others, children are expected to respect cultural expectations about what to wear. These young women in London are expressing their autonomy and their grownup looks.

Making It Work Like this mother–daughter duo in Norfolk, Virginia, most parents and children support and appreciate each other during adolescence.

Scientific American Profile

Family Relationships

This is part of the stress we face when our children become adolescents" (Roblyer et al., 2015, p. 13).

Close in a Different Way

Adolescents spend half as much time with, and feel less close to, their families than they did in elementary school (Fuligni, 1998). These changes have much to do with their involvement in things outside of the home and with the increased importance of peers. Adolescents hang out after school with friends, participate in afterschool programs, and have jobs (Lam et al., 2014; Larson et al., 1996). They increasingly turn to friends for advice or for fun (Allen & Tan, 2016; Rosenthal & Kobak, 2010).

Yet, teenagers still turn to their caregivers in a crisis, consider them the most important people in their lives, and feel loved by them on a daily basis (Coffey et al., 2020). Young people generally are closest to their mothers, but typically maintain good relationships with other family members, including their fathers and stepparents (King et al., 2018). Over time, a continuing feeling of closeness, support, and attachment with parents seems to protect teenagers: Adolescents who report this are more likely to say they are happy and are even more likely to attend college (Janssen et al., 2021; King et al., 2020). Young people who are not close with their family, or feel that they cannot trust their family, may need extra support. As a group, they are at increased risk for depression and for dangerous behavior such as substance abuse and criminal activity (Gault-Sherman, 2012; Mak et al., 2021).

Building Effective Relationships

Some parents tell researchers that they believe there is nothing they can do to help their children once they are teenagers (Lenhart, 2015). But scientific research consensus agrees that adolescents are not too old to benefit from their families' help: Adolescents are particularly *plastic* and able to change. Adolescence is a time when relationships have a great impact (Shirtcliff et al., 2017; Suleiman & Dahl, 2019).

Parenting practices adapt as children get older: Caregivers may stop checking homework and start to set curfews. Like Jesús's parents, older teenagers may be granted more space to make their own decisions and come and go as they wish. But,

FIGURE 11.1 What Are Adolescents Doing All Day? In the United States, adolescents spend less time at home with their families than they did in elementary school, but they still spend more time with their families as with their friends (at least in person). Much of adolescents' time online or on screens is spent communicating with their peers. These data are from before the pandemic: Many experts suggest that time online has increased since 2020.

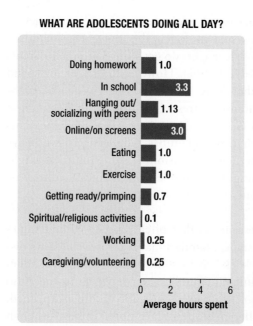

WHAT ARE ADOLESCENTS DOING ALL DAY?

Activity	Average hours spent
Doing homework	1.0
In school	3.3
Hanging out/socializing with peers	1.13
Online/on screens	3.0
Eating	1.0
Exercise	1.0
Getting ready/priming	0.7
Spiritual/religious activities	0.1
Working	0.25
Caregiving/volunteering	0.25

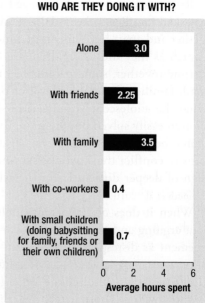

WHO ARE THEY DOING IT WITH?

With whom	Average hours spent
Alone	3.0
With friends	2.25
With family	3.5
With co-workers	0.4
With small children (doing babysitting for family, friends or their own children)	0.7

Data from Ortiz-Ospina, 2020; U.S. Bureau of Labor Statistics, 2021.

researchers have observed that the overall parenting style that works with teenagers is the same as the one that works with younger children (Baumrind, 2013; Horvath & Lee, 2015; Morris et al., 2013). *Authoritative* parenting, combining warmth with high expectations, continues to be associated with better outcomes for teenagers. Children with authoritative caregivers tend to have higher grades and test scores, better self-esteem, and closer friendships, and they are less likely to use substances or develop depression (Martinez et al., 2021; Meisel & Colder, 2021; Szkody et al., 2020).

Families with warm, close relationships encourage their children, help them feel better after talking over their problems, and enable them to more easily weather criticism and difficulty (Butterfield et al., 2021; Rodríguez et al., 2014). Emotional closeness does not mean emotional manipulation and control, however: Guilt and emotional threats are harmful, damaging both the relationship and children's sense of themselves (Meeus, 2016; Romm et al., 2020; Scharf & Goldner, 2018). Authoritative parents are not only close; they are also able to set limits for their children, whether on screen time or chores, in a mutually respectful way (Henry & Hubbs-Tait, 2013).

CONNECTIONS

Remember from Chapter 7 that the parenting styles framework measures the balance of warmth and expectations (also called *demandingness*) in the parent–child relationship. There are four parenting styles: *authoritative, authoritarian, neglectful,* and *permissive.*

MAKING A DIFFERENCE
Staying Close but Not Controlling

How do you improve the lives of teenagers and keep them out of trouble? For many years, the consensus of scientists, and of many policy makers, was that parents were the solution: If families would just keep a closer eye on their children, teenagers would stay out of harm's way. But, when a new generation of developmental scientists studied the data, they found that what sounded like good advice might actually be harmful.

What happened? For many years, researchers have noticed a strong *correlation* between **parental monitoring** and children's behavior (Boyd-Ball et al., 2014; Patterson & Dishion, 1985). In communities around the globe, parents who know what their teenagers are doing—who their friends are, what they are doing, and where they are—tend to have children who are more successful, with lower rates of emotional disorders, better grades, and less criminal behavior (Kapetanovic et al., 2020; Smetana & Rote, 2019). Increasing parental monitoring became a mantra for policy makers eager to improve the lives of adolescents, but this idea also fed into negative stereotypes: Parents, rather than schools or other institutions, were blamed when teenagers had difficulties. Adolescents were stereotyped as being dangerous troublemakers, which could foster even more unproductive behavior (Dishion & McMahon, 1998; Qu et al., 2016).

In addition, researchers found that telling parents to monitor their children simply did not work. Teenagers are open with parents who they trust and get along with, and who care about them and "get" them (Baudat et al., 2020; Kerr & Stattin, 2000; Liu et al., 2020). In the absence of such a relationship, prodding a teenager for information may result in blank stares or evasiveness. Overreaching may even backfire and encourage an authoritarian parenting style (Flanagan et al., 2019). Parents may damage their relationships by undermining trust, respect, and adolescents' sense of autonomy (Kobak et al., 2017; Lansford et al., 2014).

Parents who are too controlling and whose children feel disrespected may even be more likely to begin rule-breaking, using substances, lying, and getting into trouble with the law (Barber et al., 2012; Baudat et al., 2020; Tilton-Weaver et al., 2010). In one study of Swedish teenagers, children who felt their parents were too controlling were *more* likely to steal, drink alcohol, get into fights, or skip school (Tilton-Weaver et al., 2013).

When researchers observed that children whose parents knew a lot about them did not get into as much trouble as children whose parents were less aware, they mistook *correlation* for *causation.* They thought that monitoring led to better outcomes,

parental monitoring The process of caregivers observing and keeping track of what children are doing.

RELATIONSHIP OF PARENTAL MONITORING WITH PROBLEM BEHAVIOR

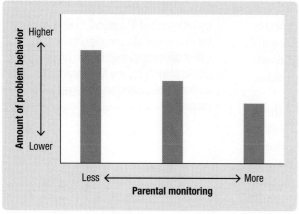

Information from Fosco et al., 2012.

FIGURE 11.2 Is This Correlation Faulty? In this study, children whose parents kept track of where they were in sixth grade and who they were with exhibited lower rates of problematic behavior than other children in eighth grade. But was there another variable in the mix? Just because parents who knew where their children were—and who they were with—had children who got into less trouble did not mean that asking was the key to raising safe children. There may have been other variables: the quality of the relationships in the family or the child's own level of functioning. The correlation between parental knowledge or monitoring and children's behavior did not mean that one variable led to the other. In fact, as other research demonstrated, too much parental monitoring might actually lead to the opposite effect.

cultural socialization The way children learn about their heritage or the community to which they belong, typically in their families.

familism The concept of responsibility of the family as a group.

but the critical factor was the quality of the relationship, not monitoring itself. With teenagers, the secret weapon is support, not only supervision (Mowen & Schroeder, 2018). Feeling understood, accepted, and respected, while still being subjected to high expectations, helps adolescents get along with their caregivers. 🌎

Learning About Culture in the Family For many young people, getting older means that they become more interested in their own heritage and cultural background (Hughes et al., 2016b). For Jesús, this means learning about traditional Indigenous dancing, reading about the history of colonialism, and painting murals of colorful flowers and lowriders.

Developmental scientists use the term **cultural socialization** to describe how families teach their children about their culture (Umaña-Taylor & Hill, 2020). As explained in Chapter 1, families may find a shared culture in cultural heritage, as in Jesús's Indigenous background, or in shared physical abilities, ethnicity, or race, or in any *intersectional* or *bicultural* combination (Safa & Umaña-Taylor, 2021). Remember that culture is not a genetic or a geographic link but a sense of togetherness in a community. In adolescence, families may encourage teenagers to celebrate their culture by learning a heritage language such as Chinese, cooking biryani, playing the bagpipes, or building a sweat lodge (Cross et al., 2020; Harding et al., 2017; Wang et al., 2020).

A sense of cultural pride is both powerful and protective. In many studies of families from various backgrounds, including Indigenous, Latino, Black, and Asian American, the children of parents who talked with them about their culture had lower rates of depression, better grades, and higher self-esteem than children from otherwise similar families (Hughes et al., 2016b; Pasco et al., 2021; Wheeler et al., 2017; Xie et al., 2021; Yasui et al., 2015). For instance, a study of Asian American teenagers in the southeastern United States found that teenagers whose families discussed their ethnic background and conveyed pride about their Asian roots were less likely to feel depressed and more likely to have high self-esteem years later (Gartner et al., 2014).

Families from European backgrounds also display a sense of cultural pride, often around religious or ethnic heritage communities, although White families often avoid talking directly about racial differences (Grossman & Charmaraman, 2009; Loyd & Gaither, 2018). As a young woman named Alysse explained, "I grew up understanding that my ethnicity was Italian and that was something I was extremely proud to be . . . all about talking with my hands, loving the hell out of my family, dressing gaudy and glamorous and never apologizing for who you are" (Dalessandro, 2015).

Remember from Chapter 2 that some cultures are said to hold *interdependent* or *collectivist* values, which emphasize a shared commitment to each other and respect for older members of the community. Many Latin American communities, for instance, value taking care of the family as a group, a concept often called **familism** (Fuligni et al., 1999; Knight et al., 2018; Padilla et al., 2020). In Muslim American communities, it is common for parents to share the value of respect for elders with their children (Carolan et al., 2000). In many families, cultural socialization includes a mix of values and cultural practices, like food. One young woman from Chicago explained to a researcher that her cultural identity combined the encouragement to succeed with cuisine: "Eating rice almost every single meal—that is Asian" (Yoon et al., 2017, p. 71).

Among the cultural values common in many communities is the belief that, as adolescents become more independent, they have an obligation to help their family (Elder & Conger, 2014; Fuligni & Tsai, 2015). This may involve working on a farm or at

Helping Out Whether they are harvesting lettuce in Palmer, Alaska, or selling crepes in Paris, France, adolescents are more capable of work that builds their skills, supports their families, and enables them to feel useful and capable.

a family restaurant, taking care of younger siblings, or doing laundry (Hernández & Bámaca-Colbert, 2016). Julio, who used his English skills as an interpreter for his Spanish-speaking family, reported: "I translated as I was asked. [It made me feel] empowered, proud, frustrated at times, [but] understanding of my parents' struggle" (Guan et al., 2014, p. 332). Too many family obligations can overburden teenagers and take time away from school and peer activities (Telzer & Fuligni, 2009). Still, there are benefits. In addition to sustaining close relationships with their families, helping out makes adolescents feel good about themselves, gives them a sense of accomplishment, and encourages family bonding and empathy (Armstrong-Carter et al., 2020; Estrada, 2019; Kiang & Fuligni, 2010).

Cultural socialization also prepares youth for the possibility that they will be mistreated by others because of their background (Priest et al., 2014). For many families like Jesús's, this may involve talking frankly to their children about the discrimination and abuse they may face from other children and institutions, including police officers and immigration officials (Cross et al., 2020; Whitaker & Snell, 2016). Martha and Jesús Senior needed to help Jesús prepare for the transition to a new school in a different part of their city where, as they recalled, "he would be one of only a few Brown-skinned students." Jesús would need to understand how to find the balance between being respectful and not backing down in the face of discrimination. This helped Jesús prepare for classmates who might make fun of his shoes and his outfits.

Many families worry about dangerous interactions with law enforcement officers: Black families, for instance, are more than four times as likely as White families to fear violence at the hands of police officers (Graham et al., 2020). This worry can have lasting consequences: Living in fear and distrusting the world around you, even when it is justified, can present challenges to adolescents' mental health (Cross et al., 2020).

APPLY IT! **11.1** Martha and Jesús Senior have a close relationship with their son. How do they illustrate the value of the support that families can give their growing children as they reach adolescence?

11.2 Some young people are not sure what their ethnic or cultural heritage might be. Perhaps they are adopted or from a multicultural family. How can family culture, whether it is a love of macaroni and cheese or the NBA, help build resilience in adolescence?

11.3 Not all adolescents are as fortunate as Jesús: Some teenagers are rejected or estranged from their families. Building on what you have learned, how can these teenagers be supported as they grow?

Friends and Peers

Learning Objectives

11.3 Explain how adolescents make friends.

11.4 Analyze how peer groups influence adolescents.

Adults try to prepare young people for the world, but teenagers are also learning life lessons from their friends. As children progress from middle school to high school, one constant is their new orientation toward classmates. Whether researchers are observing adolescents' brain activity or interviewing young people face-to-face, they find that friends and peers inspire more response and emotional intensity during adolescence than at any other time (Güroğlu, 2021; Somerville et al., 2013). This is a time for learning social skills, and adolescents learn many of them from friends (Ellis et al., 2012).

An eighth-grader might have friends they play video games with, TikTok followers, or YouTube subscribers, but if you ask them who their true friends are, they likely met them in real life and can count them on one hand (Lenhart, 2015). Researchers have found that adolescents typically have between one and about five close friends (Flynn et al., 2017; Hartl et al., 2015). These friendships often change, particularly as teenagers go through school transitions. While often painful, most adolescents can recover and build new, often deeper relationships (Nielson et al., 2020a). Young people begin to feel that their friends care about them and that they will "be there for them" in difficult times (Meeus, 2016). Adolescents with good friendships do better in school, feel better about themselves, and have fewer psychological challenges than other teens (Pinquar & Pfeiffer, 2020; Schwartz-Mette et al., 2020).

Making Friends

Who are middle and high school students making friends with? Many adolescents' friends are determined by social status, ethnicity, academic success, hobbies, or sports. Teenagers tend to befriend people who are similar to them, a tendency known as **homophily**, which is Greek for "love of the same" (Furman & Rose, 2015). Homophily can be powerful. Even when scientists put together a group of strangers in a laboratory, or when teenagers are thrown into a new group in a real-life school cafeteria, adolescents are motivated to befriend people who are like them. They find friends who like the same type of music, or enjoy the same activities, but do not necessarily have the same personalities (Hartl et al., 2015). Jesús, for instance, had an instant friendship with his bestie, Juan, because they both loved handball. Young people want friends who love what they love.

Adolescents with good social skills and good relationships with their families have more positive friendships (Furman & Rose, 2015; Staats et al., 2018). As one researcher described it, the "rich get richer" when it comes to friendship (Flynn et al., 2017, p. 21). Teenagers with healthy relationships keep developing healthy relationships. One reason may be that these young people are building on their existing social skills. Adolescents who can assert themselves, express their warmth, and back off in times of conflict tend to have better and closer relationships in the future (Allen et al., 2020; Flynn et al., 2018; Van Doorn et al., 2011).

Friendships give teenagers the chance to support each other and be supported in turn. Jesús and his friends will sacrifice and be there for each other, whether that means sharing money to buy a burger, or talking about their frustrations about school. They will spend a lot of time together, whether it is playing handball or making art. Caring for others through the ups and downs of teenage life can have benefits of its own, giving adolescents the opportunity to feel useful and competent as caregivers (Armstrong-Carter & Telzer, 2021).

Nick David/Getty Images

They Share More Than Friendship. What makes these two click? We don't know what it was on the phone that made these teenage friends in London, England, laugh, but we can guess that, like many adolescents, they have much in common.

homophily The tendency to like and associate with people we perceive as like us.

Gender Differences in Friendship

Most of the time, teenagers find friends who share their gender identity. This is particularly true early in middle school and seems common in communities around the globe (Al-Attar et al., 2017; Nielson et al., 2020b). By the end of high school, more diverse friendships are more common (Arndorfer & Stormshak, 2008).

Throughout adolescence, friendships and peer relationships serve as a way that adolescents practice the roles and communication styles that they have come to associate with their gender (Kågesten et al., 2016; Rose & Smith, 2018). For instance, teenagers who identify as girls often have more emotionally intense relationships earlier than do those who identify as boys (Borowski & Zeman, 2018; Costello et al., 2020). These relationships may dwell too much on feelings, which can exacerbate a cycle of stress and drama. Scientists use the term **rumination** to refer to this tendency to repetitively and obsessively focus on what is wrong (Rose et al., 2017).

Anyone can ruminate, and, in fact, relationships that include rumination tend to be more supportive, on average, than other friendships (Hruska et al., 2015). Sometimes, though, too much rumination can encourage negativity and catastrophizing rather than healthy problem solving. Some researchers connect ruminating in friendships to depression, which becomes more common during adolescence, particularly in people who identify as girls (Bastin et al., 2021; DiGiovanni et al., 2021; Stone & Gibb, 2015).

Teenagers who identify as boys may not ruminate as often as other teenagers, but this can be problematic as well. Many contemporary researchers worry that adolescents' beliefs about traditional masculinity can be damaging to young people who identify as male, preventing their friendships from being supportive. Male adolescents often explain that talking about their emotions with their friends will make them seem "effeminate" or "less of a man" (Way, 2019). As Kyle, a high school student, explained: "You're not supposed to be scared or you're not supposed to be worried about something. That I believe is kind of dumb, because emotions are normal" (Way et al., 2014, p. 245). Emerging research links these traditional ideas about masculinity, including admiring toughness and avoiding feelings, to mental health challenges and even externalizing behaviors (Amin et al., 2018; Exner-Cortens et al., 2021). However, not all adolescents who identify as male are reluctant to discuss their feelings and endorse the stereotypes about their gender: Many, like Jesús, are able to maintain close friendships (Rogers & Way, 2018).

Adolescents in Groups

In adolescence, friendships exist within larger social networks with less intimate relationships. Teenagers have friends, acquaintances, peers from the school bus, Instagram followers, and people they may only know from gaming. The overall number of people in social networks grows dramatically during adolescence, peaking in many groups in the beginning of high school (Felmlee et al., 2018; Wrzus et al., 2013).

Cliques and Crowds Typically, a **clique** is a small "friend group" who share interests and activities. Cliques may include the people with whom teenagers do things on a daily basis, such as having lunch together or hanging out after school. Cliques are subgroups of **crowds**, which are larger, looser collections of adolescents from the school or neighborhood. Crowds often have distinct identities, such as skaters, popular kids, athletes, music kids, nerds, rebels, and so on (Rubin et al., 2015). Crowd labels differ across schools and decades but tend to form along some predictable dimensions, such as academic success, athletic ability, economic status, popularity, substance use, and

Heather Ainsworth/The New York Times/Redux

Finding a Friend Jackie and Mason find some extra support at a transgender support group near their home in Syracuse, New York.

 Share It!

Break the stereotypes if you want to get along. Teenagers who believe in traditionally masculine gender roles are more likely to manage conflict in their relationships in unhealthy ways: They are more likely to be coercive and less likely to understand how to negotiate both partners' needs.

(Rogers et al., 2020)

🐾 **Scientific American: Lifespan Development**

rumination The tendency to repetitively and obsessively focus on what is wrong.

clique A small "friend group" that shares interests and activities.

crowds Larger, looser collections of adolescents within the school or neighborhood.

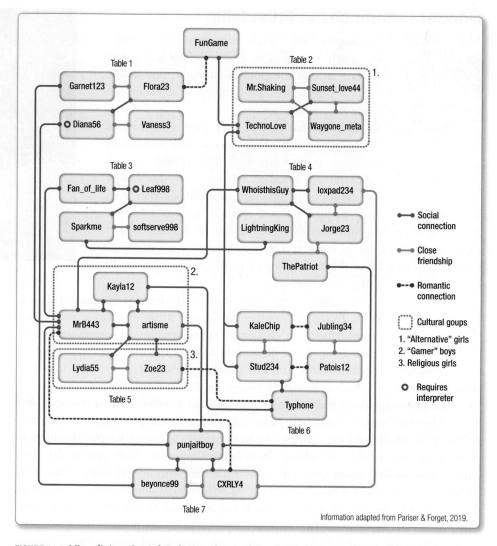

FIGURE 11.3 Visualizing Social Relationships This sociogram was adapted from the notes taken by an art teacher in Montreal, Quebec, who noted the groups of students in class and how they interacted online. Three major cliques emerged: "alternative" girls, "gamer" boys, and religious girls.

even aggression (Crabbe et al., 2019; Echols & Graham, 2013). These groups can be complex and overlapping, as you can see in **Figure 11.3** (McFarland et al., 2014).

Young people often are motivated to join a crowd to make friends and to feel like they belong to a group in the complicated social environment of middle and high school (Lachman et al., 2013). Adolescents, like adults, can also be assigned to a crowd by their peers even if they do not see themselves that way. Stereotyping and social reputations can pigeonhole people into groups without their even being aware of it.

The Role of Ethnicity in Crowds Much of the world is ethnically diverse, but peer groups on- and offline are often segregated (Leszczensky & Pink, 2019; Smith, 2018). In 1997, psychologist Beverly Tatum observed that adolescents ate at separate tables in the school cafeteria according to their ethnicity in her classic book, *Why Are All the Black Kids Sitting Together in the Cafeteria?* (Tatum, 1997/2017). Segregation is still evident in lunchrooms around the globe (Crosnoe, 2012; Leszczensky & Stark, 2019). In Vancouver, for instance, one reporter noticed that the Asian Canadian high school students spent their free time in the cafeteria, and the French-speaking students ate by their lockers (Lum, 2011). The adolescents themselves reported that these choices were not conscious. Sarah, a high school student in Vancouver, explained: "It's not

---

intentional . . . it's not like we're against each other. It just kinda happens" (Lum, 2011).

Exclusion is often invisible to students in the dominant or majority group (Cooley et al., 2019; Leszczensky & Stark, 2019). Young people like Sarah often say that they are not choosing friends on shared interests, not ethnicity. However, many assumptions teenagers have about each other are also influenced by stereotypes, negative beliefs about other groups, and acceptance of exclusion (Cooley et al., 2019; Rivas-Drake et al., 2019). Although adolescents often assume that young people of other backgrounds will not share their interests, research indicates that this is not the case and that relationships are more likely to thrive if teenagers share more important values and personality traits. Researchers suggest that multiethnic friendships reduce prejudice in school communities, help buffer the effects of discrimination, and create a greater sense of belonging for all students (Benner & Wang, 2016; Echols & Ivanich, 2021; Rivas-Drake et al., 2019).

Coming Together Researchers studied the Football United program in Sydney, Australia. Football United uses the magic of the world game (a.k.a. soccer) to promote social inclusion, bringing together refugee youth from places like Iraq and Sierra Leone with other Australians. One boy reported that the soccer program changed his life: "Everyone started playing and started talking and try and make a friend, which is good stuff" (Nathan et al., 2013). A shared passion launched new friendships and benefitted the entire community, with long-lasting positive impacts.

Do Peers Influence Behavior?

Years of scientific research reveal that peers have a surprising amount of influence over behavior in adolescence. Contrary to the notion that peer pressure is negative, peer pressure can also be a power for good (Andrews et al., 2021). Being with peers can encourage kindness and generosity (Busching & Krahé, 2020; van Hoorn et al., 2016). It can also influence what classes they sign up for: When high school students in Los Angeles were offered a free SAT prep course, who they were sitting next to in class was a major influence on whether they signed up (Bursztyn et al., 2019). Students who were given the offer in a classroom with honor-student peers were more likely to sign up for the prep course, whereas students in a classroom with less academically oriented friends were less likely. There are two major reasons peers are so important in adolescence: social structure and the developing teenage brain.

A Social Context that Magnifies the Power of Peers Several decades ago, Margaret Mead, a well-known anthropologist, suggested that peers become particularly important influences on children in societies that undergo rapid changes, like the transformations happening in our more technological, global world (Mead, 1975). Parents remain significant, but peers gain in importance because they know things about the changing world that parents do not. Additionally, adolescents in most affluent, industrialized societies spend a great deal of their time with other adolescents, whether in or out of school. Adolescents are more **age-segregated**—that is, grouped with other children of the same age—than they were as children (Schlegel, 2015). Researchers believe that when teenagers are separated from other age groups, they become more preoccupied with creating their own social structure and establishing **social status**, or their social rank within the larger group (Allen & Loeb, 2015). Peers become more influential, because adolescents are surrounded by them so much of the time and are anxious to fit into the group.

Margaret Mead did not anticipate the internet and social media, but these advances also serve to enhance the impact of peers. Within many technology-rich contemporary societies, online social networks amplify the power of peers in adolescence, allowing teenagers to superficially monitor and maintain connections with hundreds of people. They are efficient, if imperfect, vehicles for managing lots of complicated, intersecting relationships. This may explain why many young people spend hours every day checking updates, liking, and following others on social media (Davis et al., 2020; Sherman et al., 2018).

📱 Share It!

7½ hours a day. That is not how long teenagers sleep; it is how many hours some researchers have found that they consume screen media, when averaged year round, for entertainment and socialization (not counting schoolwork).

(Rideout & Robb, 2019)

Scientific American: Lifespan Development

age-segregated Grouped with other children of the same age.

social status A person's social rank within the larger group.

FIGURE 11.4 Adolescents' Social Brain When researchers told adolescents they were being observed over video by a peer while their brains were scanned in an fMRI, their brains reacted differently than those of children or adults. Adolescents said that they were embarrassed, and researchers believed that they were particularly sensitive to being observed. The key areas of activation were in the social brain networks in the cortex, including the medial prefrontal cortex (mPFC), particularly regions involved in thinking about other people's feelings, watching their faces, and interpreting their movements.

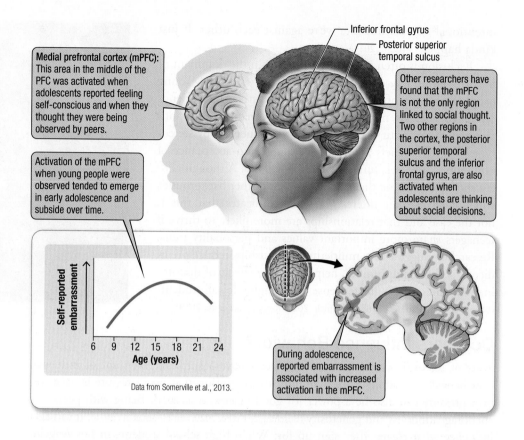

Inferior frontal gyrus

Posterior superior temporal sulcus

Medial prefrontal cortex (mPFC): This area in the middle of the PFC was activated when adolescents reported feeling self-conscious and when they thought they were being observed by peers.

Other researchers have found that the mPFC is not the only region linked to social thought. Two other regions in the cortex, the posterior superior temporal sulcus and the inferior frontal gyrus, are also activated when adolescents are thinking about social decisions.

Activation of the mPFC when young people were observed tended to emerge in early adolescence and subside over time.

During adolescence, reported embarrassment is associated with increased activation in the mPFC.

Data from Somerville et al., 2013.

A Brain that Magnifies the Power of Peers Along with social contexts, brain development shapes the power of peers. Remember from Chapter 10 that the reward system is active when teenagers are with their friends—more active than it is for children and adults (Andrews et al., 2021; Crone & Konijn, 2018; Shulman et al., 2016). At the same time, the **social brain**—neural networks associated with understanding the views and intentions of other people—undergoes significant development during adolescence (Andrews et al., 2021; Crone & Fuligni, 2020). Adolescents become more perceptive of the facial expressions, perspectives, and motivations of other people. Their perceptions are better coordinated with the reward system, making it more rewarding when they are accepted by their peers and more painful when they are excluded (Somerville et al., 2019; Tomova et al., 2021). Together, these developments appear to be linked with adolescents' tendency to pay more attention to the opinions and influence of their age-mates, particularly during early adolescence (Ahmed et al., 2020).

Researchers have examined the role of the brain in peer influence in a number of creative ways (van Hoorn et al., 2019). In one study, they scanned the brains of teenagers while they were viewing how many "likes" different posts received on Instagram. When adolescents see popular posts—those with more "likes" from other teenagers—there is greater activity in the brain's reward system than when they see posts with fewer "likes" (Sherman et al., 2018).

In another set of studies, scientists created a simulated driving game that required players to decide whether to go through yellow lights in order to reach their destination more quickly (Smith et al., 2014). They found that young people were more likely to drive through yellow lights when they thought that their peers were watching than when they thought that they were being observed by adults. This was not true of younger children or adults, who tended to play the same way regardless of whether peers were looking on (Albert et al., 2013; Smith et al., 2014). When the researchers imaged the youths' brains in an MRI machine, they found that the reward system was more active in teenagers than in children or adults when their friends were watching them play the game.

social brain Neural networks associated with understanding the views and intentions of other people.

Peer Victimization

Adolescents' sensitivity to their peers makes being with friends more exciting, but it can also make the feeling of exclusion even more painful, as when someone is kept off group chats, not invited to parties, or "ghosted." Social exclusion is most common during the middle school years. About 1 in 10 adolescents report having been harassed or victimized by another teen in any given year. Almost 30 percent report having been a victim of social aggression, and about 1 in 20 admits to having hurt someone on purpose (Juvonen & Graham, 2014; Lebrun-Harris et al., 2019).

Teenagers may be hurt, put down, or rejected by their peers but do not feel that the term *bullying* describes their experience. Being a victim is embarrassing and stigmatizing, and young people may not want to admit to it (Lai & Kao, 2018). Peer aggression in adolescence, as at other times in the lifespan, often targets people whose identity stands out: Young people are likely to experience peer aggression based on their gender expression, sexual orientation, size, physical abilities, or, in some schools, ethnicity or race (Jackman et al., 2020; Lessard & Juvonen, 2020).

Adolescents are particularly sensitive to social victimization: They want to be accepted by their peers and to feel that they are successful in their social world (Blakemore, 2018; Forbes et al., 2019). Teenagers who experience exclusion repeatedly may have long-term problems with depression and anxiety, which may be one reason they tend to miss school and see their grades slip (Juvonen & Schacter, 2018). Feeling excluded damages the body, boosting inflammation in ways that could impact later health (Schacter, 2021; Scott & Manczak, 2021).

The targets of peer aggression are not its only victims: Those who witness bullying also feel more anxious and negative about school (Midgett & Doumas, 2019; Werth et al., 2015). For the aggressors themselves, this behavior is not something that they grow out of. In adulthood, those who as children excluded or victimized others report having trouble in their relationships, using substances more frequently, and having higher rates of depression and criminal behavior than other adults do (Copeland et al., 2013; Hysing et al., 2019).

Social aggression is a global problem, but it occurs less frequently in some schools. Schools with more nurturing and positive social climates, where students and teachers feel content, tend to have lower rates of bullying whether researchers study them in Kenya or Peru or in the United States (Cornell et al., 2015; Miranda et al., 2019; Mucherah et al., 2018). Students in classrooms where bullies are confronted about their behavior show fewer of the negative effects of experiencing or witnessing victimization (Yun & Juvonen, 2020).

Fortunately, school climate can be changed. Intervention efforts have had some success in reducing bullying (Earnshaw et al., 2018; Fraguas et al., 2021). Many successful programs are based on the work of pioneering Norwegian psychologist Dan Olweus, which focus on increasing awareness, supervising students, and identifying aggressors and victims (Olweus, 1993; Olweus et al., 2019). Newer interventions designed to involve the entire school community include the KiVa program first established in Finland, whose success stems from encouraging peers to speak up when they witness victimization (Johander et al., 2021; Juvonen et al., 2016). In general, interventions that take a whole-school approach, provide information for parents, and include informal peer involvement tend to have the most success (Gaffney et al., 2021).

APPLY IT! 11.4 Jesús is close to his friends: They support and sacrifice for each other. How does this emotional closeness contrast with traditional gender roles researchers have found in some friendships in adolescence?

11.5 Boosting resilience for teenagers who have experienced exclusion or victimization can come from finding a friend, a mentor, or a support person. What kind of interventions could you imagine might support the resilience of adolescents who have experienced victimization?

Standing Up for Bravery Egypt Ify Ufele is a teenage fashion designer, entrepreneur, and the founder of the anti-bullying organization Bullychasers, all based in her family's home in Queens, New York.

Romantic Relationships

From first crushes to first dates, romantic relationships are one of the hallmarks of adolescence. In the United States, more than 8 in 10 middle-schoolers hope to be in a romantic relationship, and more than 7 in 10 have been in a relationship by the time they turn 18 (Suleiman & Deardorff, 2015). Adolescents with healthy romantic experiences benefit from the extra support and care: They are less likely to act out and to experience depression and have longer and happier relationships in adulthood (Beckmeyer & Weybright, 2020; Kansky & Allen, 2018). Romantic relationships can help adolescents practice social skills outside the family, often becoming a central and positive relationship in a teenager's life (Furman, 2018; Gómez-López et al., 2019). As 19-year-old Ty put it: "A girlfriend is something that you work on . . . You develop trust and different things. . . . You definitely gotta have responsibility. And just being there just to listen. Just to love" (Towner et al., 2015, p. 353).

In most places around the world, feelings of attraction transform into romantic relationships in mid to late adolescence, at about age 16, as the result of a combination of a changing social world, a changing brain, and hormonal activity. Neuroscientists even see that the reward circuit is activated when teenagers think about romance, much as it is when they might think about chocolate, a new car, or anything else that brings them pleasure (Telzer et al., 2015).

From Peers to Partners

Scientists observe that many teenagers progress through four stages of romantic development (Furman, 2018). In the first stage, socializing often happens in groups (Dunphy, 1963, 1969), evident in the large groups of 11- or 12-year-olds you see at a mall. In the second stage, adolescents develop crushes. They may trade anxious texts to find out if their crush even knows they exist or develop intense feelings about celebrities. In the third stage, romantic relationships are in their early phases; rather than spend a lot of time alone, couples go out in larger groups. In the fourth and final stage, older adolescents move to exclusive romantic relationships. These relationships last longer and exhibit some of the emotional intimacy of adult partnerships, such as sharing feelings and secrets, offering mutual support, and feeling loved and connected (Xia et al., 2018).

Although researchers often observe that the development of romantic relationships occurs in stages, this is not completely universal. Many adolescents, like Jesús, are happy without partners, believing that this is something that can wait until later, when they have more of their life figured out. In addition, cultural expectations and stigma against certain types of relationships may alter romantic development, particularly for young people who are gender nonbinary, gender fluid, lesbian, gay, bisexual, asexual, or another identity label (Araya et al., 2021; Savin-Williams & Cohen, 2015). Ongoing stigma often forces these teenagers to delay "coming out," affirming their gender identity, or starting a relationship (Araya et al., 2021; Bishop et al., 2021; Martos et al., 2015). Nevertheless, romantic relationships can provide many teenagers, particularly those who are gay, lesbian, or transgender, with a buffer against the stress around them (Araya et al., 2021; Whitton et al., 2018).

Variations in Romance

Cultures around the world have varying expectations for teenage romance. Most discourage dating. For instance, many families in India, Indonesia, and Mexico try to dissuade adolescents from starting romantic relationships

Will You Be Mine? This was Marie's fifth prom and the second time her boyfriend of three years, Caleb, was crowned prom king. This couple from Gorham, Maine, share a love of Pizza Hut, romantic movies, and, like many couples, kissing.

Ben McCanna/Portland Press Herald via Getty Images

until their 20s (van de Bongardt et al., 2015). However, in some rural communities in China, Niger, Georgia, and Pakistan, it is common for much younger adolescents, particularly those from low-income families, to get married as they advance quickly toward adulthood (Bremer, 2018; Efevbera & Bhabha, 2020; Nasrullah et al., 2017). For adolescents in affluent nations, cultural variations also dictate what kind of romance is acceptable. In some families, teenagers pledge to remain abstinent until marriage, but in others, young relationships are encouraged.

The dominant culture in North America and Europe allows and often encourages teenage relationships, with high school dances, movies, television series, and popular music that idealize romance (Sanchez et al., 2017). Parents and children may even see youthful relationships as a training ground for adult relationships. However, the acceptance of adolescent dating is far from universal (Connelly & McDonald, 2020). This may be true of a variety of cultural, religious, or ethnic backgrounds, from evangelical Christians and conservative Muslims to immigrant Catholic Mexican Americans (Raffaelli et al., 2012). Such parents are typically worried that romantic entanglements could derail their children's education, lead to unexpected pregnancy, or force teenagers to assume adult roles before they are ready (Yoon et al., 2017).

Some of these concerns are supported by research: Certain types of early intimate relationships can have risks (Kansky & Allen, 2018). For instance, some researchers have found that young people who have churning, short-term romantic relationships that start in the early teens may benefit from some extra support, because they are more likely to develop depression, use drugs, or do poorly in school. This may be because they have difficulty managing the stresses of romance, or because they had preexisting vulnerabilities (Kansky & Allen, 2018; Loeb et al., 2020).

Young people may also not know how to spot physical and emotional abuse in relationships—topics not often broached with families, peers, or in sex education programs (Francis & Pearson, 2019). Almost 1 in 10 U.S. teenagers reports having been physically hurt or emotionally abused in a relationship, the highest rate across the lifespan (Espelage et al., 2020). Other risks of adolescent relationships include excessive jealousy, harassment, or abuse, particularly online and by text (Cava et al., 2020; Francis & Pearson, 2019; Ha et al., 2019). Nevertheless, many adolescent relationships can help teenagers grow and find a source of emotional support as they discover what is important to them (Kansky & Allen, 2018).

APPLY IT! **11.6** Adolescent relationships may come, like all relationships, with heartbreak or happiness. What would you advise your younger self about what they might learn from romantic relationships?

11.7 What ethnotheories about romantic relationships do you see in the media or in your family community culture?

Crushes from Afar Sometimes adolescent romance involves crushes on celebrities. These young people are excited to see K-pop stars at a convention in New Jersey.

Finding Yourself: Identity Development

From posting a new picture to their Snapchat story to selecting classes, adolescents are surrounded by choices. Who are they? Who do they want to be? Do they want to be religious like their mothers or get into electronica like their friends? These choices help them define their **identity**, or their sense of who they are and how they fit into the social groups of the world.

Learning Objective

11.6 Explain how identity develops during adolescence.

identity A person's sense of who they are and how they fit into the social groups of the world.

Committing to their choices and creating an identity helps adolescents feel settled, mature, and happy (Beyers & Luyckx, 2016; Christiaens et al., 2021). For instance, Jesús feels that he has a strong sense of who he is as a person: He is an artist, is a proud Indigenous Mexican, and is committed to service. This commitment helps keeps him focused and connects him with opportunities to work with other people who appreciate him, whether he is sharing his art on Instagram or helping younger people draw a perfect giraffe.

Erikson's Identity Framework

As young people contemplate becoming adults, they discover that there are many roles open to them. Erik Erikson believed that the key task for adolescents is to resolve the **identity crisis**—the conflict in deciding between the possible roles they could play and the possible selves they could be—by creating a stable identity. He called this the stage of **identity versus role confusion** (Erikson, 1968; see **Table 11.1**). Erikson believed that exploration is necessary prior to establishing an adult identity (Erikson, 1950/1993, 1968).

Erikson's theories were not tested in the field until Canadian psychologist James Marcia gathered empirical data to establish four identity statuses: diffusion, moratorium, foreclosure, and achievement. These identity statuses, which were based on Erikson's theory, are determined according to adolescents' *exploration* of different identity options and their *commitment* to adopting specific identities.

- **Diffusion status** occurs when young people are not exploring or putting any effort toward creating an identity. This may be because they feel ambivalent about their choices or because they have difficulty making a plan (Becht et al., 2019; van Doeselaar et al., 2018). Diffusion is typical for young adolescents (and children), but remaining in this status can lead to long-term complications, such as academic underachievement, unemployment, mental illness, or substance abuse (Côté, 2018a).
- **Moratorium status** occurs when young people are actively exploring their options but have not committed to an identity quite yet. These adolescents are fully involved in the process of finding out who they are. They may be changing their profile photos, taking a broad range of college classes, or trying to decide whether to join the military or become a doctor (Côté, 2018b; Wood et al., 2016). Moratorium is a time of instability, and adolescents in this status tend to be more anxious than other young people (Meeus, 2011).
- **Foreclosure status** happens when young people have committed to an identity but have not done much exploration. For example, when someone quickly adopts their parents' political values without investigating the options, they are in foreclosure status. Many adolescents choose this path of early commitment, in part because making a choice, even if it may not be "perfect," leads to contentment (Crocetti, 2017).
- **Achievement status** occurs when young people have done a significant amount of exploration and have made a firm commitment. Because they have learned about themselves and discovered their path, as well as shown commitment to what they believe in, adolescents in this status tend to be more vocationally and personally successful than those in other identity statuses (Kroger & Marcia, 2011).

TABLE 11.1 Erikson's Stages of Psychosocial Development: Adolescence

Age	Stage	Characteristics
Adolescence	Identity versus Confusion	The key struggle of adolescence is finding something to be committed to as an adult and finding your role in the world.

CONNECTIONS

The identity crisis is the fifth of Erikson's eight stages of development. Remember that he observed that infants resolve the crisis of *trust versus mistrust*, and that toddlers navigate the crisis of *industry versus inferiority* (see Chapter 5). The preschool years are characterized by the crisis of *initiative versus guilt* (Chapter 7), and in elementary school, children strive to develop a sense of competence, or *industry*, rather than *inferiority* (Chapter 9).

identity crisis The conflict in deciding between the possible roles a person could play and the possible selves they could be.

identity versus role confusion In Erikson's theory of life span development, the crisis of adolescent development which is resolved when youth understand themselves and their role in the world.

diffusion status In Marcia's theory, this identity status occurs when adolescents are not exploring or committed to an identity.

moratorium status In Marcia's theory, this identity status occurs when adolescents have postponed committing to an identity and are exploring.

foreclosure status In Marcia's theory, this identity status occurs when adolescents have committed to a path or identity without exploration.

achievement status In Marcia's theory, this identity status occurs when adolescents have explored and committed to a path.

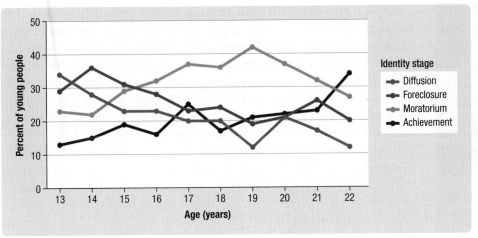

FIGURE 11.5 How Does Identity Status Change over Adolescence and the Transition to Adulthood? Researchers who tracked identity development longitudinally, over many years, found identity is not fixed by the time adolescents graduate from high school or even enter their 20s.

As you see in **Figure 11.5**, most young people tend to enter committed statuses in late adolescence and in their 20s (Kroger et al., 2010). Many do not go in a set order, say, from diffusion to moratorium to achievement (Meeus, 2011). Most adolescents (and adults) go through a period of exploration and identity experimentation before they develop a consistent sense of who they are (Crocetti, 2017). Some young people have a strong sense of who they are, but it is common and can be healthy for people to continue seeking their purpose into their 20s or later (Hatano & Sugimura, 2017; Schwartz et al., 2012).

Marcia's identity statuses do not apply to all cultures around the world. In many places, young people commonly do not experience moratorium or identity achievement at all (Schwartz et al., 2012). Moratorium, the prolonged and healthy period of exploration, may be somewhat unique to North America and Europe, particularly in affluent communities. In communities where young people lack the opportunity to explore in high school or college, they may need to quickly commit to an adult identity.

Multiple Identities

There are many pieces that make up your identity. Jesús, for instance, is not just an artist or an Indigenous Mexican. He is also man, a son, a Catholic, and a handball player. Having many facets to their identity means that adolescents must figure out who they are in a variety of arenas, which may include work, gender, ethnicity, sexuality, family, or religion. The term *intersectionality*, as you may remember from Chapter 1, refers to the fact that we all have multiple, intersecting identities (Moffitt et al., 2020).

Ethnic and Cultural Identity For many young people, developing a deeper **ethnic identity** becomes critical as they move outside of the family. In longitudinal studies, multiple scientists have surveyed and interviewed adolescents from a variety of backgrounds about their ethnic and cultural identities (Schwartz et al., 2012). They repeatedly found that when adolescents take pride in their heritage, they have higher self-esteem, face fewer challenges, such as depression or even criminal behavior, and perform better in school (Fuligni et al., 2005; Rivas-Drake et al., 2014). For instance, Mexican American boys perform better in high school if they report that they are proud of their Mexican roots (Umaña-Taylor et al., 2012).

For many young people, like Jesús, feeling positive about their ethnic or cultural identity can protect them from the effects of discrimination (Rivas-Drake et al., 2014; Wantchekon & Umaña-Taylor, 2021; Yip, 2014). Adolescents may encounter teasing from peers, experience unfair treatment from teachers, and even endure harassment from the police (Hughes et al., 2016a; Huynh & Fuligni, 2010). This increases the risk of many problems, from poor health to criminal behavior to academic difficulty (Gibbons et al., 2020; Zeiders et al., 2021).

Scientific American Profile

Cultural Identity

ethnic identity A sense of yourself as belonging to a particular ethnic group or community.

David Butow/The New York Times/Redux

What Is Your Identity? Like many adolescents, Sami, shown here with his younger brother, Juju, has more than one ethnic and cultural identity. His mother is from Mexico City. His father is from Dallas, Texas. So, like many adolescents, Sam can use many identity labels, as Mexican American, Jewish, and a little bit Texan, even though he now lives in Washington, D.C.

CONNECTIONS

Adolescence is not the first time that children recognize themselves as boys, girls, or another gender identity. Even young children begin to develop a sense of gender (see Chapters 7 and 9). Children who identify as *gender nonconforming* or *transgender* typically begin to explore alternate gender roles, expectations, and identities long before they reach puberty (see Chapter 7).

acculturation The process of adapting to some of the traditions and expectations of a cultural community.

The toll is even evident in teenagers' bodies. In a recent study, young people who reported more everyday discrimination had higher markers of stress such as higher levels of the hormone cortisol (Huynh et al., 2016).

Native American teenagers from a rural community in Oregon who learned about their nation and how to manage discrimination from their families reported lower levels of depression (Yasui et al., 2015). Feeling connected to something greater than themselves, such as tribe, culture, or community, can be a powerful source of resilience when adolescents face challenges.

More than one in five U.S. adolescents is an immigrant (Passel, 2011). Researchers use the term **acculturation** to describe the process of adapting to cultural change, which happens as immigrants move from one culture to another (Berry & Vedder, 2016). As they adapt to their new communities, immigrants may adopt aspects of their new culture while remaining linked (Yasui et al., 2015) to their heritage (Nguyen & Benet-Martínez, 2013).

For example, Sami speaks English fluently, participates in three afterschool clubs, and plays on a soccer team in his multiethnic school. But he has also maintained a connection to his family's culture of origin, speaks Spanish with his grandparents, eats traditional Mexican food, and celebrates Jewish holidays with his family's traditional Mexican silverware. Researchers call this a *bicultural*, or *multicultural*, identity (Nguyen & Benet-Martínez, 2013). Sami's flexibility and his ability to navigate multiple cultures may be an ideal way of adapting as an immigrant (Berry & Vedder, 2016). His ability to assimilate in some ways, such as with his mastery of English, makes it easier for him to be successful in his new country. But his continued embrace of his heritage helps him feel linked to his family.

Gender Identity Remember from Chapter 10 that, as adolescents begin to develop more adult bodies, their *gender identity*, and their gender expression, become more complex. For many adolescents, gender expression may intensify during early adolescence, which can bring new challenges and added discrimination (Johns et al., 2019; Lowry et al., 2018; Parker et al., 2018).

In a world that bombards young people with macho archetypes, those who identify as male may feel pressure to conform to a rigid idea of what it means to be a man (Nielson et al., 2020b; Perry & Pauletti, 2011). This rigidity is shared with their peers: Teenagers who identify as boys tend to be more popular if they conform to stereotypes of masculinity, particularly in middle school (Jewell & Brown, 2014). However, research suggests that in the long term, teenagers who resist these stereotypes and who are willing to show more emotion tend to be more successful academically and feel better about themselves in general (Exner-Cortens et al., 2021; McFadden et al., 2020).

Many communities are more flexible about feminine identity and gender expression. For instance, adolescents who identify as girls can be popular with their peers in high school even if they do not conform precisely to a gender stereotype, as with girls who are athletic or independent. However, adhering to traditional gender stereotypes tends to foster more peer popularity. And what traditional roles do people think are for girls? They tell researchers that girls are supposed to be easy to get along with and attractive (Jewell & Brown, 2014). However, adopting feminine stereotypes may only bring popularity in the short term. Preoccupation with traditionally feminine gender expression can be harmful, increasing risks for poor body image and depression (Calogero et al., 2017).

Remember that researchers estimate that about 2 percent of young people currently identify as transgender, but these numbers are increasing as public acceptance increases (Johns et al., 2019). Transgender teenagers still face peer aggression and discrimination (Norris & Orchowski, 2020). Communities and schools are finding ways to be welcoming and safe for all teenagers, whether they are transgender or identify as gender nonconforming, gender fluid, or questioning (Day et al., 2018).

Sexual Orientation During adolescence, adolescents often begin to express their *sexual orientation*, or their sense of themselves as being queer, straight, asexual, lesbian, gay, bisexual, or another label (Bishop et al., 2021). It is increasingly common for young people to report that they do not know or that their sexual orientation is fluid, in-between, or undefined by existing categories. Teenagers who feel their identity is accepted tend to feel more stable, particularly for those who are bisexual, who may feel in-between and less accepted (Diamond, 2016; Savin-Williams, 2016; Watson et al., 2020). Adolescents' sexual orientation identities are often multidimensional: One term may not always cover their romantic attraction, sexual behaviors, or outward identity (Calzo et al., 2017).

Many adolescents are able to "come out" and create a gay, lesbian, or bisexual identity in high school; for others, especially in communities unwelcoming to relationships that are not traditionally other-sex, this identity creation may be delayed until early adulthood (Martos et al., 2015). During this process, the reaction of families can be critical in helping support their children as they establish their adult identity (McConnell et al., 2016; Ryan et al., 2015). Family support also helps build adolescents' resilience in the face of exclusion and discrimination, reducing the chances that they will develop long-term emotional challenges or turn to substance abuse (Magette et al., 2018; McConnell et al., 2016). As you will read, learning to manage stress is important for all teenagers.

APPLY IT! **11.8** Not all adolescents know what they want to be. What questions might you ask a young person to better understand how they are exploring their identity?

11.9 What about you? How do you define yourself and your own journey to understand your own identity? If you had to put yourself in one of Marcia's statuses, which would you choose?

What Makes You Feel Grown Up? For Zarifeh, 17, it was finding the right glittery dress to celebrate being prom queen at Summit High School in Fontana, California. She found this dress in a family friend's closet, and the hijab belongs to her grandmother. Like many teenagers, Zarifeh is trying to figure out how to be a woman while balancing that with her other identities.

Changing Feelings and Sense of Self

Stereotypes suggest that teenagers are rife with drama and emotion or, in the words of an early psychologist, "storm and stress" (Hall, 1904). But the reality is more complicated. Adolescents generally feel good about themselves, but their emotions are changing. They are not as happy-go-lucky as they may have been in elementary school. They are more sensitive to stress and drawn to adventure. Like Jesús, they may be more aware of the realities and complexities of the world than when they were younger.

Despite the physical and social changes of early adolescence, most teenagers feel good about themselves, a trend that continues as they move into adulthood (see **Figure 11.6**) (Orth et al., 2018). Remember from Chapter 7 that *self-esteem* describes how you feel about yourself and includes the thoughts and beliefs you have about your capabilities in a variety of areas, from your body to your social relationships (Harter, 2012). As adolescents exercise more independence and take on adult roles, they experience an increase in self-esteem.

Changes in Emotion

Teenagers may feel good about themselves, but they are not always cheerful. Researchers note that while adolescents' self-esteem increases, they are actually less

Learning Objectives

11.7 Describe how emotions and feelings change during adolescence.

11.8 Identify the psychological and behavioral challenges of adolescence.

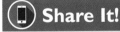 **Share It!**

Do not believe the hype: Stereotypes of adolescents can hurt them. Teenagers who believe that adolescence is filled with stress and that teenagers are irresponsible are themselves more likely to be irresponsible and stressed.

(Qu et al., 2020a, 2020b)

Scientific American: Lifespan Development

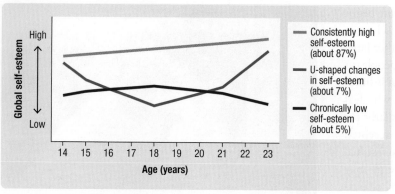

Data from Birkeland et al., 2012.

FIGURE 11.6 Life Keeps Getting Better
For many teenagers, self-esteem just keeps getting better. However, not everyone follows this trend. As you see, self-esteem stays low over time for about 5 percent of adolescents. For another 7 percent, self-esteem dips and then improves over time.

Adolescent Risk-Taking Can Be Heroic. For Lily, taking a risk meant intervening when she saw smoke coming out of a window when she was walking her dog, Isobel. She returned to the fire with a ladder from home (after calling the fire department) and helped the three people inside evacuate.

moodiness Emotional changeability, often leaning toward negative feelings like irritability.

happy than they were in childhood (Bailen et al., 2019; Larson et al., 2002; Weinstein et al., 2007). When researchers ask adolescents to report on their moods by logging them every night, responding to surveys, or replying to random alerts, they find that young adolescents experience more extremes of happiness and upset than they did in elementary school. This emotional changeability, often leaning toward negative feelings like irritability, is called **moodiness**. Moodiness tends to level off by the time adolescents adjust to high school, in about tenth grade (Maciejewski et al., 2015). Does this mean that adolescents are generally unhappy? Actually, they are mostly happy—just not as happy as they were in elementary school. On a scale from "very happy" to "very unhappy," they still rate themselves as "happy" almost all the time (Larson et al., 2002).

More Sensitive to Stress

One reason adolescents' emotions are changing is because their brains are more reactive to stress, which increases emotional intensity. Remember that the body secretes the hormone *cortisol* in response to stress. Teenagers produce more cortisol than children and adults in typical situations, and even higher levels when they are under stress (Doom et al., 2017). What triggers stress in adolescence is different than in childhood: Social situations, particularly with people their own age, are more likely to increase their levels of cortisol (Hostinar et al., 2014).

These short-term doses of cortisol can be helpful, supplying energy to push us to study harder, submit a job application, or muscle through a few more pull-ups in boot camp. Cortisol may also help teenagers react more quickly to challenging life transitions, like a new classroom, a new teacher, or glances from strangers at the bus stop. Unfortunately, this extra jolt of energy does not come without a cost. For some, this stress sensitivity may contribute to the higher levels of depression and other emotional problems during these years (Anniko et al., 2019; Spear, 2009).

More Excited to Take Risks

When you think about *risk-taking*, or any activity that may have a potential downside or loss, you may think about bungie jumping or drag racing. Teenagers all around the world tend to take risks—from drinking to driving too fast—and at higher rates than people in other life stages (Duell et al., 2018). But not all the risks teenagers take are harmful. Some risks help them mature and take on adult roles. For most adolescents, risk-taking is a positive experience that helps them explore what the world has to offer and transition from dependent children to young adults able to manage their own needs independently (Ellis et al., 2012; Romer et al., 2017). Even helping others—such as intervening when a classmate is being bullied—involves an element of risk-taking (Duell & Steinberg, 2020).

How does a 400-foot drop at 120 miles an hour sound to you? Not your thing? You will want to skip the Kingda Ka roller coaster at Six Flags Great Adventure in New Jersey, then, although the line is often hours long during the summer. Who is waiting in line? Lots of teenagers. Researchers are unsurprised: They agree that the drive to try something new and exciting increases during adolescence (Meeus et al., 2021).

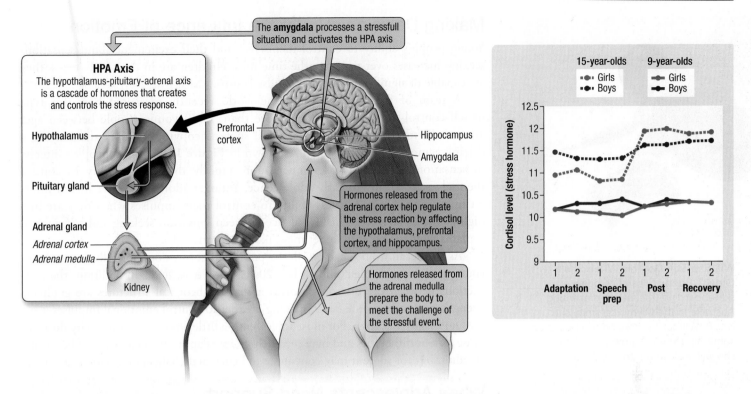

FIGURE 11.7 Stress in Adolescence When the brain detects threat, a coordinated physiological response is activated. The HPA axis involves regions of the hypothalamus, pituitary gland, and the adrenal glands. The hypothalamus releases hormones that trigger the pituitary gland to secrete hormones that in turn initiate the adrenal glands to release hormones, delivering a potent mix of hormones to the body. This allows it to react quickly in times of crisis, whether at the sight of a disturbing online update or a menacing python. This axis is often triggered by the amygdala, which processes fear and other strong emotional events. The prefrontal cortex can work to help reset the HPA axis and return it to normal levels. Scientists sometimes examine cortisol levels by asking people to give a speech, typically a stressful experience for most people. In this study, researchers observed that adolescents had higher levels of cortisol and were more sensitive to stress than children; their stress levels were slower to return to normal. All the children's cortisol levels rose as they were asked to speak, but the younger children's levels recovered after the task was over.

This is **sensation-seeking**, or the drive for excitement and the thrill of doing something a bit scary, like a 400-foot drop (Spielberg et al., 2014).

Teenagers' sensation-seeking increases after puberty and declines in late adolescence (Khurana et al., 2018; Quevedo et al., 2009; Romer, 2010; Steinberg, 2008). When researchers measure sensation-seeking, they ask adolescents how much they like excitement, such as whether they "like to do 'crazy' things for fun." They might also measure adolescents' heart rates or patterns of brain activation when they are in potentially exciting situations, such as playing a video game or looking at pictures of sharks or of threatening people (Quevedo et al., 2009; Steinberg, 2008).

Experimenters who studied adolescents longitudinally over the course of puberty found that children become more interested in excitement around the time their bodies are activating the HPG axis and the hormonal changes of puberty. Again, the reward circuit of the adolescent brain likely plays a role. As you read in Chapter 10, greater responsivity of the systems to rewards—perhaps due to higher levels of dopamine—is a key reason for young people's sensation-seeking (Galván, 2013). Researchers suspect that, as adolescents grow up, they gain more experiences with the world that help temper this sensation-seeking (Khurana et al., 2018). Brain development may also help limit the power of the reward circuit. Remember that, as teenagers grow, connections between the prefrontal cortex and the subcortical structures that process emotions tend to grow stronger, enabling better emotion regulation, including the desire for excitement (Casey, 2015; Shulman et al., 2016).

sensation-seeking The drive for excitement and the thrill of doing something a bit scary.

Will She Still Do This When She's Older? Poppy Olsen has been skateboarding (recently representing Australia in the Olympics) since she was 8. Will taking risks on the board be something she outgrows, or a profession she will stick with into middle age?

Making Decisions Under the Influence of Emotion

Young people's ability to control themselves and their excitement about sensation-seeking increases over time. By the time most children are in their early teens, they are capable of significantly better impulse control (Galván et al., 2007; Steinberg et al., 2017).

A team of researchers around the world recently measured how this type of self-control develops by asking more than 5,000 young people between ages 10 and 30 to engage in different tasks, such as copying pictures and playing a driving game (Steinberg et al., 2017). As shown in **Figure 11.8**, young people's interest in sensation-seeking increases much more rapidly than their ability to control themselves, especially in early adolescence. Younger adolescents have lots of interest in exciting things, but less ability to control their impulses when they are in a highly emotional state. This imbalance between sensation-seeking and self-control explains why adolescents sometimes take dangerous risks.

As you recall from Chapter 10, the prefrontal cortex does not fully mature until young people reach their mid to late 20s (Steinberg et al., 2017). In addition, the connections between the prefrontal cortex and the subcortical structures are gradually strengthened and become faster, making it easier to control emotional impulses (Casey et al., 2019; Liston et al., 2009). For most adolescents, a little emotional impulsivity does not cause serious difficulties and may even help them adapt to the challenges of becoming an adult, but for some it may contribute to behavioral challenges (Khurana et al., 2018).

When Adolescents Need Support

Most adolescents are able to gracefully navigate the transition from childhood to adulthood, but for some this can be a difficult time in a world that may not always give them the support they need. Rates of psychological disorders and adverse experiences increase in adolescence, approaching adult levels (see **Infographic 11.1**)

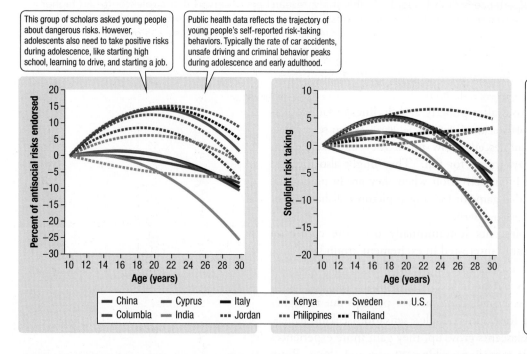

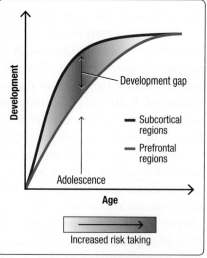

Adapted from Duell et al., 2018.

FIGURE 11.8 Risk-Taking During Adolescence A group of scholars asked more than 5,000 young people from over 11 countries in a study of risk-taking. As shown in the left panel, they observed that many young people were more willing to take some negative risks, like vandalism or fighting, in mid-adolescence. The middle panel shows the results of the researchers' experimental test of young people in a driving simulation. They found that in many countries, young people were more willing to take chances driving, such as running a red light or speeding, in mid-adolescence. The last panel shows a schematic of the relationship of brain development to risk-taking. The researchers suggest that differences in the timing of brain maturity contribute to risk taking. The subcortical brain regions connected to motivations for rewards and attention to social input mature more quickly than the prefrontal regions that help to logically control behavior.

BUILDING RESILIENCE IN ADOLESCENCE

CONNECTION AND CONTRIBUTION TO THE COMMUNITY

Helping others, whether it is coaching a sibling in basketball or volunteering at the food pantry, can help young people find new connections in the community, feel valued and build positive emotions.

How many young people volunteer in the US?

1 in 4
Volunteer

1 in 3
do favors for neighbors

1 in 5
regularly participate in civic organizations

Out of school activities can be a way of making new connections, discovering a passion or just having fun.

SDI Productions/E+/Getty Images

Percent of young people in extracurricular activities in the United States, by family income.

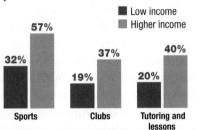

- ■ Low income
- ■ Higher income

Sports: 32% / 57%
Clubs: 19% / 37%
Tutoring and lessons: 20% / 40%

RELATIONSHIPS

Friendships are a crucial source of support in adolescence.

Maskot/Getty Images

How many adolescents in the U.S. report having strong friendships?

98% have one or more good friends

78% have 2 to 5 good friends

20% 6 or more good friends

2% have no close friends

Family continues to be a source of support and guidance as adolescents grow up: although relationships tend to change as young people develop their own autonomy and agency.

Boogich/E+/Getty Images

Most families in the U.S. report that they are able to share ideas and talk about meaningful subjects with their adolescent children.

60% say they are very good at talking about things that matter

33% say they are somewhat good at talking about things that matter

6% say they are not doing very well at talking about things that matter

TECHNOLOGY

gawravE+/Getty Images

Adolescents use technology to learn, create, make friends and entertain themselves. In the U.S., young people use screen-media for entertainment and socializing for about 7 hours a day.

Teenagers report that, on average they are spending that screen time:

- Watching videos (39%)
- Playing games (22%)
- Interacting on social media (16%)
- Browsing online (8%)
- Other (8%)
- Video calls (4%)
- Creating content (3%)

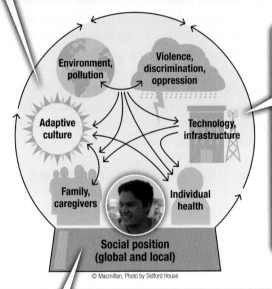

Environment, pollution

Violence, discrimination, oppression

Adaptive culture

Technology, infrastructure

Family, caregivers

Individual health

Social position (global and local)

© Macmillan, Photo by Sidford House

SOURCES OF STRESS

ADVERSE EXPERIENCES IN ADOLESCENCE
Adverse experiences in adolescence (per 100 children)

9.4 Witnessed family violence

4.8 Witnessed shooting

33 Witnessed assault in community

11.3 Injured in an assault

17 Experienced bias-related harassment

4.5 Harassed online or on the phone

8 Experienced parent's divorce or separation

7 Experienced physical abuse at home

7 Experienced neglect at home

15.7 Experienced emotional abuse at home

21 Experienced bullying

5.1 Boys

26 Girls
Sexually assaulted

ADOLESCENTS WHO NEED SUPPORT
Psychological disorders in adolescence (per 100 children)

18.7 Any psychological disorder

4.5 Substance use disorder

10.5 Anxiety disorder

6.1 Depression

7.5 Behavioral or conduct disorder

2.8 Eating disorders

2.4 Autism Spectrum Disorder

12 Attention Deficit Hyperactivity Disorder (ADHD)

2.5 Serious suicide attempt requiring medical treatment

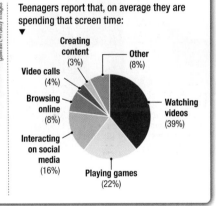

anxiety disorders A clinical diagnosis based on a pattern of excessive worry or fear that keeps children, adolescents or adults, from fully functioning in their lives.

depression A clinical diagnosis based on a pattern of sadness and lack of energy that impairs your ability to function.

📱 Share It!

Social isolation and the stress of a global pandemic deprived many teenagers of the support they needed to thrive. Rates of ER visits for mental health rose during the early months of COVID-19 pandemic.

(Leeb et al., 2020)

🔊 Scientific American: Lifespan Development

Finding Hope These teenagers are working with a coach to identify sources of social and emotional support in their community.

📱 Share It!

Help is out there. If you know someone who is at risk for suicide, seek out resources in your local community, call the National Suicide Prevention hotline at 1-800-273-TALK (833-456-4566 in Canada), or text "home" to the Crisis Text Line at 741741.

🔊 Scientific American: Lifespan Development

(SAMHSA, 2020). The combination of brain development, increases in hormones, and the realities of adjusting to a new social world with fewer supports poses risks. For some teenagers, an increase of stressors in the environment, such as family transition, violence, or economic instability, add to the mix (Guyer et al., 2016; Pfeifer & Allen, 2021; Shulman & Scharf, 2018). High rates of anxiety, depression, substance abuse, and externalizing behaviors in adolescence continue into young adulthood (Samek et al., 2017).

Emotional Disorders and Suicide Adolescents, like adults and children, may experience a cascade of brain, hormonal, and social stresses that may make them unable to function in their everyday life, and they may be diagnosed with a *psychological disorder*. For instance, the social sensitivity that makes spending time with peers particularly enjoyable can also make social rejection more painful and make going to school more anxiety provoking (Costello et al., 2011; Rapee et al., 2019). Because the developing adolescent brain leads to increased interest in risk-taking, teenagers may behave in impulsive ways that could end in self-harm or suicide (Ho et al., 2021).

Almost one in three adolescents has received an anxiety disorder or trauma-related diagnosis at some point (APA, 2022; SAMHSA, 2020). **Anxiety disorders** are characterized by excessive fear and worry that make it impossible to carry out everyday activities, whether that is making friends or going to school. Anxiety disorders include a broad range of psychological difficulties, from generalized anxiety to specific fears like that of public speaking, and are often related to *posttraumatic stress disorder (PTSD)* (Siegel & Dickstein, 2012). Teenagers who experience anxiety disorders or PTSD may have been exposed to abuse or trauma, or may have struggled with worry since childhood. Adolescents who are anxious may not even describe themselves as being anxious; instead, they may describe physical rather than emotional symptoms and complain about stomachaches or headaches. Their families may report that their children have become irritable, worried, or nervous.

Rates of depression also increase dramatically during the teenage years. Clinical **depression** is diagnosed when you feel unhappy and disconnected from your life so severely that you lose interest in things that once brought you joy and you can no longer function at home and at school (APA, 2022). Almost 1 in 10 adolescents in the United States has been diagnosed with depression, and many more report feeling sad or depressed (see Infographic Figure 11.1; Mojtabai et al., 2016). Such teenagers look fine on the outside but feel miserable inside. Or, they show more noticeable signs, such as spending a lot of time alone or being excessively tearful or touchy.

Thinking of suicide is uncomfortably common in adolescence, with almost one in five adolescents reporting suicidal thoughts, see Table 11.2 (Ivey-Stephenson et al., 2020). Although most do not hurt themselves, more than 2,500 die at their own hands in the United States every year (Miron et al., 2019; Nock et al., 2013). Around the world, more than 35,000 adolescents die from suicide every year, more than in terrorist attacks or war (WHO, 2021). Suicide is not the only way adolescents hurt themselves. Nearly one in six teenagers has injured themselves, a behavior formally called *nonsuicidal self-injury* (NSSI; Millner & Nock, 2020; Nock, 2009). (See **Table 11.2** for warning signs.)

Effective, empirically based treatments can help. Many of these treatments are distinct from those that work for children or adults (Kazdin, 2003; Weisz et al., 2013). Most teenagers who have emotional disorders are also helped by talk therapies that may involve their families and communities, building a sense of community and family support that aid recovery (Weisz et al., 2013). Some treatments for adolescents at risk for suicide, for instance, encourage a sense of ethnic pride that can protect young people from social stress, recognizing the importance of identity development to adolescents. One such treatment program, the Western Athabaskan Natural Helpers Program, reduced the rate of suicide attempts by more than half in high-risk communities in New Mexico and Canada (Goldston et al., 2008; May et al., 2005).

TABLE 11.2 Warning Signs of Suicide

— Always ask. Asking someone whether they are thinking of harming themselves may feel awkward or rude, but it also shows that you care.
— Worry when someone is talking about or threatening to hurt themselves, or looking for a means of hurting themselves, or writing or talking about dying in a way that is new to them.
— Be concerned if someone tells you they have no reason to keep going and feel hopeless and even withdraw from the people they care about.
— Check on someone if they are using substances more than usual.
— Look for help if someone is particularly anxious or depressed or if their mood seems different.
— Let them know that there is support out there if they are acting particularly angry, impulsive, or anxious for revenge. Sometimes people act out and hurt themselves.

CAN YOU BELIEVE IT?
Is Social Media to Blame for Adolescent Depression?

You have probably seen headlines about how much time teenagers spend on social media and their smartphones. Some developmental scientists have argued that new technologies are responsible for an epidemic of adolescent depression, loneliness, and retreat from the adult world (Twenge, 2017). This may ring true to anyone who has felt envious scrolling through the perfect-looking photos on someone's Instagram, disappointed about having someone ghost them, or hurt when a partner looked at their phone during an intimate conversation. New technology clearly has some downsides (Appel et al., 2016; Kross et al., 2013; McDaniel & Coyne, 2016). But, does social media harm adolescents? Is it truly "ruining a generation" (Twenge, 2017, 2019)? Let us look at the evidence.

• Large surveys of adolescents in the United States have consistently shown that rates of reported depression and other mental health challenges, as well as suicide, have risen by at least 10 percent in the past 10 to 20 years (Costello et al., 2005; Mojtabai et al., 2016; Twenge et al., 2018a; Weinberger et al., 2018).

• Over the same time period, adolescents (and adults) have embraced new technology, from smartphones to personal computers, for fun and schoolwork. Many teenagers now spend nearly 7½ hours a day on recreational technology (Rideout & Robb, 2019).

Is there a correlation between increased time spent online and the increase in mental health problems? Some researchers have found a connection between teenagers' media use and their rates of depression and observed that there is a correlation: Teenagers who use technology the most, particularly those who identify as girls, are indeed at greater risk of depression and other psychological disorders (Twenge et al., 2018a, 2018b). Others, however, have found somewhat different results (Daly, 2018). When researchers looked at the amount of time teenagers spend on their phones or social media, they found that moderate use is not correlated with depression at all. Only those who spent more than 40 hours a week are more likely to develop depression (Daly, 2018; Twenge, 2019; Twenge et al., 2018b).

In general, the findings are inconsistent and collectively do not point to social media as a critical factor in mental health (Kreski et al., 2021; Odgers et al., 2020). Why did these studies produce different results? First of all, they may have confused correlation with causation. They may have also forgotten about the theory of *differential susceptibility*: Not all children share the same risk factors, and it is unlikely that one element of the environment would affect all of them in exactly the same way (Ellis et al., 2011).

Social Media for Good Adolescents are often derided for spending too much time online. But 19-year-old Mohammad is using his phone to share the stories of people in his community, a camp for more than one million Rohingya refugees in Kutupalong, Bangaldesh, with followers all of the world, raising awareness and building community.

Munir Uz Zaman/AFP via Getty Images

The data showed that depression increased over the past 10 to 20 years, along with media use, but there was no proof that the media use *caused* depression. As some scholars pointed out, the causal factor may have been something completely different, such as the economic recession that occurred in 2008 (Daly, 2018). Or perhaps another third variable, such as economic inequality, discrimination, school performance anxiety, parent distraction with technology, or even not enough time spent being active, was the culprit (Daly, 2018; Goldman et al., 2018).

More recent studies that have examined smaller groups of teenagers over time have found that, in many cases, the relationship between media use and mental health is much more complex than the headlines indicate. For some teenagers, depression comes first and leads to more time spent online, perhaps exacerbating social isolation (Heffer et al., 2019). For adolescents at risk for depression or who are depressed, spending a lot of time online does not make them feel better (Boers et al., 2019). However, keep in mind that these associations are not universal and do not apply to all mental health challenges (George et al., 2018).

Does this mean that adolescents can click away on their phones without worry? Most experts do not go that far (Odgers, 2018). Too much time spent on your phone does seem to be problematic, particularly if it displaces healthy behaviors like getting enough sleep, completing homework, and exercising (Hawi & Samaha, 2016; Kenney & Gortmaker, 2017; Lemola et al., 2015; Toh et al., 2019). 😊

Using and Abusing Substances Although it is illegal for teenagers in the United States, experimenting with alcohol and marijuana is not uncommon. Before graduating from high school, more than 6 in 10 U.S. teenagers report that they have tried alcohol, and nearly half report having tried marijuana (Miech et al., 2021). U.S. teenagers have some of the highest rates of binge-drinking and marijuana use in the world, but adolescents around the globe experiment with, use, and abuse substances—typically alcohol, tobacco, and marijuana (Currie et al., 2012; Degenhardt et al., 2016). For many, it is a way to bond with friends and signals a new form of independence (Schulenberg et al., 2014). For others, alcohol and substances puts lives into disarray.

Rates of teenage substance use are lower than they have been for generations, but some adolescents use substances in an unhealthy and dangerous way (Miech et al., 2021). The risks of adolescent substance use range from brain damage after using MDMA to lung diseases from vaping marijuana (Dharmapuri et al., 2020; Mustafa et al., 2020). One study in the United States found that nearly one in six young people engaged in **binge drinking**, or consumed more than five drinks at one time, in the past month (Miech et al., 2021). Around 4 percent of adolescents develop a **substance use disorder (SUD)**, which is diagnosed when someone's use of substances prevents them from functioning or causes some kind of impairment in their life (SAMHSA, 2021). For teenagers, "impairment" means not keeping up with schoolwork, family obligations, or friendships. SUDs can lead to increasingly worse problems, such as lost friendships and failing grades, as well as criminal activity and death.

Family or individual therapy is the most effective treatment for substance use disorders. Family therapy involves the entire family to address the sources of stress and conflict that may contribute to the adolescent's substance use, to help the teenager get back to an active, productive life as quickly as possible (Fadus et al., 2019; Tanner-Smith et al., 2013).

Breaking Rules and Hurting Others Although many adolescents break the law in some way before they turn 18, most of these crimes are relatively minor: speeding, drinking alcohol, sneaking into a movie theater without paying for a ticket, or shoplifting a lipstick from a drugstore (NRC, 2013). Others are far more serious. Every year in the United States, teenagers are responsible for about 20 percent of violent crimes, which include assault, rape, and murder. About 1 in 10 teenagers has committed a violent

binge drinking Consuming more than five drinks at one time.

substance use disorder A clinical diagnosis based on a pattern of substance use that is causing someone functional difficulties in their everyday life.

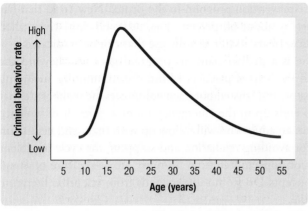

Information from U.S. Department of Justice, 2019.

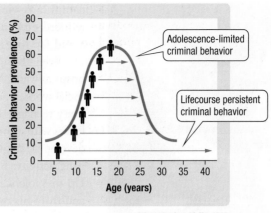

Information from Moffitt, 1993.

FIGURE 11.9 Criminal Behavior in Adolescence Many teenagers have broken the law in minor ways, whether by speeding or underage drinking. Most grow up and begin to follow the rules. A few have difficulties that continue, known as lifecourse persistent behavior.

crime, although not all of these crimes are reported (Oudekerk & Morgan, 2016). Only about 4 percent of all teenagers have ever been arrested, most for offenses such as fighting, robbery, or substance use (Puzzanchera, 2021). However, adolescents and young adults tend to break the law and get arrested more than older adults (see **Figure 11.9**).

Most teenagers who break the law become rule-abiding adults (NRC, 2013). Some have **adolescent-limited** criminal activity, only breaking the law during adolescence. Typically, adolescent-limited activity happens when adolescents break the law for social reasons, such as to gain their friends' approval or to prove their independence (Moffitt, 1993, 2006). However, about 10 percent of teenagers who are arrested become adults with lengthy histories of criminal behavior (Steinberg, 2014). **Lifecourse persistent** criminal activity often begins when people commit crimes such as petty theft or property destruction at young ages and continue into adulthood (Piquero & Moffitt, 2010).

Many adolescents with lifecourse persistent criminal activity have *conduct disorder*, which involves aggressive behaviors such as hurting people and animals and damaging property without remorse (Fairchild et al., 2019). In adolescence, these problems become more severe; children have more difficulty getting along with others, and their parents may even be afraid of them (Condry & Miles, 2014). Researchers suggest the best way to help children control their aggression and impulses is to intervene early. Intensive interventions can help at-risk young people develop the necessary skills to resist externalizing behaviors (Boisjoli et al., 2007; Conduct Problems Prevention Research Group, 2011; McMahon & Frick, 2019).

The vast majority of teenagers who run into trouble with the law, whether it is a violent offense or something less harmful, will grow out of that behavior and adapt to the adult world. Researchers suggest that the best approach for teenagers with adolescent-limited criminal behaviors is to help them make amends to their communities and ensure that their lives are not derailed by a criminal record (Steinberg, 2014). As one youth activist explained, "What changes people is relationships. Somebody willing to walk through the shadow of the valley of adolescence with them" (Bill Milliken qtd. Brooks, 2016, p. 23).

 SCIENCE IN PRACTICE
Noé Romo, M.D.

A busy emergency room at a major trauma center may be an unlikely place for developmental science in action, but this is where Dr. Noé Romo applies lessons learned from life and scientific research to stop gun violence (Romo, 2019). He developed a

adolescent-limited behavior A habit or behavior that is particular to the adolescent life stage.

lifecourse persistent behavior A habit or behavior that is consistent across the lifespan.

In Action in Front of the Cameras Whether he is in the emergency room or in front of the cameras, Dr. Noe Romo is trying to prevent young people from hurting themselves, and each other, by helping them find stronger, healthier relationships.

community violence prevention program in the Bronx, New York, that has reduced gun injuries by about 60 percent (Kim, 2021). His initiative, called Stand Up to Violence, treats assault as a disease that can be eradicated.

Even though he is a pediatrician, his program goes way beyond the hospital walls. With the help of partners within the community, including social workers, a pastor, and trusted outreach volunteers, he makes sure that every teenager who ends up in the emergency room as a result of violence leaves with a mentor: an adult who will follow up with them and help them develop strategies for avoiding retaliation and stopping the cycle of violent gang activity. Relationships and cultural humility are at the core of Stand Up to Violence, concepts Dr. Romo understands from scientific literature and from his own life.

Dr. Romo grew up in a low-income neighborhood in Los Angeles that was marked by community violence and discrimination. Many of his high school classmates ended up in jail. As a teenager, Dr. Romo was once told that medical school was not for him because children from his neighborhood were unlikely to become doctors. He proved them wrong, graduating from medical school and becoming a researcher, activist, and pediatrician. His work as a pediatrician was what inspired him to start his program. Dr. Romo explains that the hopeless grief from seeing a 16-year-old die from a gunshot wound spreads from the hospital staff to the child's families, friends, and neighbors and lasts for a long time (Romo, 2020).

Across the United States, gun violence is the second most common cause of death among teenagers (the first is car accidents). This is 35 times higher than in other affluent countries around the world, where guns are more restricted, and criminal violence is not as prevalent (Cunningham et al., 2018). Researchers like Dr. Romo suggest that young adolescents are particularly susceptible to gun violence because their peers are so important to them: Experiences of exclusion and a desire to be socially successful increase teenagers' likelihood to get involved with criminal groups and turn to violence (Estrada et al., 2018; Shelley & Peterson, 2019). These risks are especially potent in low-income neighborhoods where criminal activity is prevalent (Beardslee et al., 2019).

Dr. Romo has seen firsthand that relationships can determine whether a teenager ends up in jail or dead. One strength of his program is that he, and the other adults who work with the adolescents, understand the community they serve and respect the challenges these teenagers face. They are also motivated by their understanding that a bullet not only destroys a teenager's body; it also destroys communities. Stand Up to Violence helps adolescents build new relationships with adults who link them to activities that provide an alternative to dangerous peer groups: volunteering at a church, finding a part-time job, or buckling down with homework.

APPLY IT! **11.9** Jesús identifies as an artist, as Indigenous, and as a community activist. How would you define yourself in three words or less? How has your identity changed over time?

11.10 Connecting with a community and feeling like you belong can be sources of resilience in adolescence and across the lifespan. Jesús connects with his church, his heritage community, and his local neighborhood. How have communities supported your development?

11.11 We need support at any age, but development plays a role in what support we need and what types of interventions are effective. Which characteristics of adolescents may make them need extra support?

11.12 How might you design a program to boost the strengths of young people who were at risk for acting out in adolescence?

Wrapping It Up ⦾

LO 11.1 Explain the development of autonomy during adolescence. (p. 318)

As adolescents mature and prepare for adult roles, they take more responsibility. This includes taking on more autonomy. Autonomy does not mean you are completely independent; rather, it means that your own ideas play a larger role in your decisions. Teenagers often assert behavioral autonomy, or the ability to make decisions about things they consider personal, like what they wear and who they are friends with. Families and cultures often differ in the accepted milestones of autonomy, like when teenagers get their first phone or when they are ready to date.

LO 11.2 Describe variations in parent–adolescent relationships. (p. 318)

Most adolescents and their families get along. Conflicts arise between teenagers and their family as they do in any relationship, but they may seem more common because teenagers are better at articulating themselves and do not spend as much time with the family. Teenagers are still emotionally close to their families but are also developing stronger emotional attachments with their friends. Strong family support can help adolescents grow up healthier and do better in school. Researchers describe authoritative parenting, which includes lots of warmth and high expectations, as an ideal parenting style during adolescence. Adolescents benefit from building relationships with their family that are based on trust, understanding, and mutual respect, rather than control. Families teach their children about culture in adolescence: Cultural pride can help build resilience.

LO 11.3 Explain how adolescents make friends. (p. 324)

Adolescents learn social skills from their peers. Their peer groups often change as they move from middle to high school. Friendships are often based on homophily, or the idea that we befriend people we think are like us. Friends begin to provide support, and adolescents learn to support their friends. Friendships often include gendered communication styles: Teenagers who identify as girls are more likely to ruminate. Adolescents who identify as boys need to manage social norms that often suggest that men do not share their feelings.

LO 11.4 Analyze how peer groups influence adolescents. (p. 324)

Adolescents live inside complex social networks made up of cliques and crowds, which are based on identity characteristics and, in many schools, are ethnically and racially segregated. Diverse friendships and crowds help build a sense of belonging for all students. Age-segregated environments make peers more influential on adolescent behavior. Brain development makes teenagers more sensitive to their friends and makes it more rewarding to be accepted by them. These developments also make social exclusion and peer aggression more painful.

LO 11.5 Identify the changes in romantic relationships during adolescence. (p. 330)

Many adolescents begin romantic relationships, which can be a source of emotional support as well as instruction for social skills. Many adolescents move toward exclusive paired relationships through a series of stages: from socializing in nonromantic larger groups to smaller ones as they get older. Adolescents who are not gender binary, who are transgender, or who are attracted to the same sex may face discrimination as they become interested in romance. Cultures around the world differ in how accepting they are of adolescent romance. As it does across the lifespan, teenage romance comes with risks, including heartbreak and abuse.

LO 11.6 Explain how identity develops during adolescence. (p. 331)

Erikson described the crisis between identity and confusion, observing that adolescents need to explore possible options of who to be and what they believe in as they grow. Marcia described the process of identity development in terms of four identity statuses: diffusion, moratorium, foreclosure, and achievement. Most adolescents do not progress through these statuses as stages, but it is typical for teenagers to experiment with who they are. Developing a sense of purpose and identity helps boost mental health and well-being. Many young people have multiple, intersectional identities or identify as bicultural or multicultural. During adolescence, teenagers develop a sense of their ethnic or racial identity, their gender expression and identity, and their sexual orientation. A sense of community pride can boost resilience in teenagers who may be subject to discrimination.

LO 11.7 Describe how emotions and feelings change during adolescence. (p. 335)

Adolescents' emotions are more changeable than they were in childhood, but most teenagers are still generally content, and their self-esteem is rising as they become more capable. Teenagers are more sensitive to stress, particularly to social pressures. Adolescents are braver about risk-taking, which helps them take on adult roles and try new things in order to develop their adult capabilities. Teenagers are more interested in sensation-seeking after puberty. Younger teenagers may have limited ability to control their feelings in exciting situations and may be more impulsive, which helps them tackle their new roles and responsibilities.

LO 11.8 Identify the psychological and behavioral challenges of adolescence. (p. 335)

Rates of psychological disorders, including substance use disorder, externalizing disorders, and adverse experiences, increase during adolescence. This is a result of hormonal and brain development, a changing and often less supportive social world, and a stressful environment. Empirical treatments can support adolescents' resilience. Most teenagers in the United States experiment with marijuana and alcohol, but only a few are diagnosed with a substance use disorder. Many teenagers break the rules in minor ways, but some are involved in criminal activity, some of which is adolescent-limited.

KEY TERMS

autonomy (p. 318)
parental monitoring (p. 321)
cultural socialization (p. 322)
familism (p. 322)
homophily (p. 324)
rumination (p. 325)
clique (p. 325)

crowds (p. 325)
age-segregated (p. 327)
social status (p. 327)
social brain (p. 328)
identity (p. 331)
identity crisis (p. 332)
identity versus role confusion (p. 332)
diffusion status (p. 332)

moratorium status (p. 332)
foreclosure status (p. 332)
achievement status (p. 332)
ethnic identity (p. 333)
acculturation (p. 334)
moodiness (p. 336)
sensation-seeking (p. 337)
anxiety disorders (p. 340)

depression (p. 340)
binge drinking (p. 342)
substance use disorder (p. 342)
adolescent-limited (p. 343)
lifecourse-persistent (p. 343)

CHECK YOUR LEARNING

1. In adolescence, gaining more autonomy and agency typically includes all of the following EXCEPT:
   a) becoming more selfish and individualistic.
   b) expecting to take on more responsibility for chores.
   c) deciding what clothes to wear.
   d) having more of a say in everyday life.

2. Jesús has a friend who tells him that all he does with his parents is fight. What should Jesús tell him?
   a) This is just a typical relationship between teenagers and parents.
   b) He should seek some support from another adult, mentor, teacher, or health care provider.
   c) He is probably expecting too much from his parents.
   d) He does not need his parents anymore.

3. Jesús met his good friend, Juan, in their physical education class, and they had an instant friendship: They both loved handball and identified as Indigenous. This is an example of:
   a) adolescent sensation-seeking.
   b) homophily.
   c) adolescent stress sensitivity.
   d) puberty.

4. Is peer victimization an inevitable part of adolescence?
   a) Yes, because adolescents are always going to hurt each other
   b) No, because the rates of bullying vary between schools and nations
   c) Yes, because some people are always going to be victims
   d) Yes, because hormones drive adolescents to attack each other

5. How do scientists characterize romantic relationships in adolescents?
   a) Romantic relationships can allow teenagers to expand their network of support.
   b) Romantic relationships are mostly dangerous in adolescence.
   c) Romantic relationships are not important during adolescence.
   d) Romantic relationships should be avoided during adolescence.

6. Jesús's friend Paul is not sure what he wants to do with his life; he is taking advanced math in high school and trying out the drums and the guitar. What identity status BEST matches his experience?
   a) Identity achievement
   b) Identity moratorium
   c) Identity foreclosure
   d) Identity diffusion

7. Why do researchers think that developing your own identity may happen differently depending on your culture's ethnotheories and opportunities?

8. Which of the following is NOT a reason why researchers think adolescents are more susceptible to psychological disorders?
   a) A brain that is more sensitive to stress
   b) Increasing adversity in the environment
   c) Inadequate social support
   d) Lack of self-control and hard work

9. What unique strengths help make adolescence a time of positive risk-taking and opportunity?

10. Which of the following statements about adolescent emotional development is TRUE?
    a) Adolescents are usually unhappy.
    b) Adolescents usually feel poorly about themselves.
    c) Adolescents are likely to feel more deeply happy or sad than children or adults.
    d) Adolescents are capable of adult levels of emotional self-regulation.

12 Physical and Cognitive Development in Early Adulthood

© Macmillan, Photo by Sidford House

What Is Adulthood?

12.1 Identify the key historical markers and common variations in adulthood.

Brain and Cognitive Development

12.2 Describe the characteristics of brain development in early adulthood.

12.3 List four ways of describing the flexible thinking of young adults.

Building Healthy Habits

12.4 Discuss health risks and positive health practices in early adulthood.

Education after High School

12.5 Describe the benefits of college and challenges to success in college.

Succeeding on the Job

12.6 Analyze recent changes in employment and ways young people can identify their interests and employment strengths.

Selected Resources from

 Achieve

Activities

Concept Practice: The Peak of Physical Development and Health

Spotlight on Science: How Does Culture Change Your Thinking?

Assessments

LearningCurve

Practice Quiz

Videos

Scientific American Profiles

Physical Changes Animation

Decision Making

"What makes you feel adult?," we ask Haruki. Is it that she is a "dog momma" with a puppy of her own? Is it her age (she is 25)? Or that she has her own apartment, graduated college, or works full time as a school counselor? Or is it that she just married her partner, Marvin?

Haruki might be smiley and youthful looking, but she is clearly not a kid. Like many young people, it still surprises her to discover that *she* is the adult in the room — the one her students turn to when they want advice about where to go to college, where to find a good doctor, or how to get an oil change. Haruki cares for herself, pays her own bills, and chooses what to have for dinner and where to get health insurance. Although she has a lot of strengths — her close relationship with her mother, her Peruvian relatives, her partner, a satisfying job — she says being adult comes with a lot of pressure. Some days it is easier than others to be responsible.

Right now, Haruki's focus is on taking care of herself so she can care for her students and her family. She wants to make sure that she and Marvin are in good health so that they are ready for whatever comes next. Learning is at the top of her list: She wants to learn Pashtu so she can better connect with her immigrant students, and perhaps some Japanese to complement her Spanish so she can build stronger relationships with relatives in Peru and Japan.

Marvin is adjusting to his move to the United States from El Salvador: He and Haruki have a lot to learn about the immigration process as Marvin improves his English skills and considers training as an electrician. They are far from their adult dreams of having their own home and maybe having children. As Haruki says, everyone has their own timeline: There are inevitable bumps in the road and different ways to become the person you are meant to be.

At age 25, Haruki is in the life stage many developmental scientists refer to as **early adulthood**, or young adulthood. Early adulthood is a culturally defined period that typically ranges between ages 18 and 30 and is marked by tremendous individual flexibility and potential but less structure and assistance than many adolescents receive.

Although many young adults, like Haruki, have adult responsibilities and roles, they are not quite the same as older people and certainly differ from the teenagers they once were. Human bodies and brains are still maturing into the 20s. This enables young adults to adapt to their changing circumstances and acquire new skills, whether it is learning a third language or adjusting to full-time work.

In young adulthood, this impressive potential is combined with a decreasing amount of structure. The days of compulsory schooling are over, and although young people remain tied to their families and communities, there is no longer one path for everyone. Young adults are particularly sensitive to the long-term effects of social changes beyond their control, such as the impact of a global recession or the COVID-19 pandemic (Recksiedler & Settersten, 2020; Settersten et al., 2020). Social inequality means that young people do not begin adulthood on the same starting line. However, armed with cognitive flexibility and the ability to learn, they can develop the skills they need to thrive.

Scientific American Profile

▶

Meet Haruki

© Macmillan, Photo by Sidford House

What Is Adulthood?

Learning Objective

12.1 Identify the key historical markers and common variations in adulthood.

Like Haruki, many young people are unsure about what exactly makes you an adult and when, although they often feel adult responsibilities acutely. Unlike adolescence, which has a clear biological beginning in the unmistakable physical changes of puberty, the markers of adulthood are flexible to match the changing expectations of each culture, time, and place.

Most young adults are approaching biological maturity, but with much variation in timing due to genes and life experience. *Epigenetic aging*, or the signs of deterioration in your genome, began at birth in many of our cells and marks the passage of time. The pace of aging is highly influenced by how you live (Raj & Horvath, 2020). The signs of inequity in this aging process are apparent in the bodies of 20-year-olds. Young people who have grown up with poverty and discrimination are already more likely to experience systemic inflammation, increasing their risk for heart disease and for changes to their immune system that make fighting off infections more difficult (Cole et al., 2020).

Aging and maturation do not happen at the same time in all the body's systems. By age 25, most parts of your body have stopped growing, with a notable exception: Your brain continues to mature into your 20s or 30s. Bones continue to develop into your mid-30s (the last to mature is your collarbone) (Cameron, 2015; Milani & Benso, 2019). *Wisdom teeth*, or your third molars, may appear around age 20 (Cole, 2015). People who want to have a baby using their own ovaries and uterus are most likely to get pregnant in their mid-20s (Wesselink et al., 2017). People who want to use their own sperm to create a child are also most fertile in their mid-20s (Brandt et al., 2019).

early adulthood A culturally defined period typically ranging between ages 18 and 30 that is marked by tremendous individual flexibility and potential but less structure and assistance than adolescence.

In past centuries, people were considered adults at any time from about age 15 to 40. Historians note that although people in the past tended to have children earlier than many today, they were not necessarily considered ready for all responsibilities of adult life, like financial independence or political office, until they were older (Mintz, 2015). The legal markers of adulthood today remain highly variable. Anthropologists note that, in ancient human societies and among extremely rural communities today, most young adults are not independent: It often takes many years to become proficient at survival skills like hunting, foraging, or agriculture (Hochberg & Konner, 2020).

Despite these variations, researchers caution that it is always more respectful to treat someone as an adult. Young adults often feel discriminated against at work and in the community simply for being young (Bratt et al., 2020; Chasteen et al., 2020).

Markers of Adulthood

Scholars identify five aspirational *external* markers that mark adulthood in many communities today. These include: (1) finishing school; (2) establishing a household (which means taking responsibility to rent or buy a dwelling); (3) finding work; (4) committing to a long-term relationship; and (5) having children (Cepa & Furstenberg, 2021; Settersten et al., 2015). Other scholars point to *internal* markers, like the self-recognition of being emotionally mature or adult (Arnett & Mitra, 2020).

Scientific American Profile

Life Transitions

Even though many of us never reach all of these markers—many adults are happily single, in college in their 40s, and well-paying jobs are often hard to find—they continue to affect how adults judge themselves (Settersten et al., 2015). Adults who have achieved them, particularly those who have finished their education, found a job, and set up a household, are more likely to say they feel competent, accomplished, and satisfied with their lives (Cepa & Furstenberg, 2021; Culatta & Clay-Warner, 2021; Sharon, 2016). In some communities, particularly in the economic boom years of the 1950s and 1960s in the United States, these hallmarks were easier to reach than they are today. Many young people in that period graduated from high school, married, and found a well-paying job before age 22 (Mintz, 2015).

In most affluent countries today, fewer young people have jobs or have set up a home of their own (Gagné et al., 2021a). Researchers estimate that fewer than 25 percent of young adults in the United States meet even four of these markers before age 35 (Vespa, 2017; see **Infographic 12.1**). The reason? The economy, which has made it harder to find a stable, high-paying job in a globalized world where such jobs usually require a college education. As a result, it now takes longer for most young people to save the money to start a family and set up an independent household. If they seek a committed relationship and a family of their own, they often wait until their late 20s.

There is also more variety in how people start families: Adults may have children before they have finished their education or before they are married, or be happily partnerless or childless (Rybińska & Morgan, 2019; Tillman et al., 2019). Others may not maintain a separate household until their late 20s. Contemporary young adults are forced to be flexible, particularly those who do not have the resources to achieve their dreams right away or those who were transitioning into adulthood during the pandemic era (Dalessandro, 2019; McCue, 2021).

Some young people feel ambivalent about the label of adulthood. They may feel "adult" in some contexts, like at school or work, but still feel like teenagers at home with their families (Arnett, 2016). As Renato, a community college student, told a researcher, "You could be like 40, 35, but your mom could still be like '*mijito*'" (Katsiaficas et al., 2015, p. 106). One young woman told a researcher, "I think it may

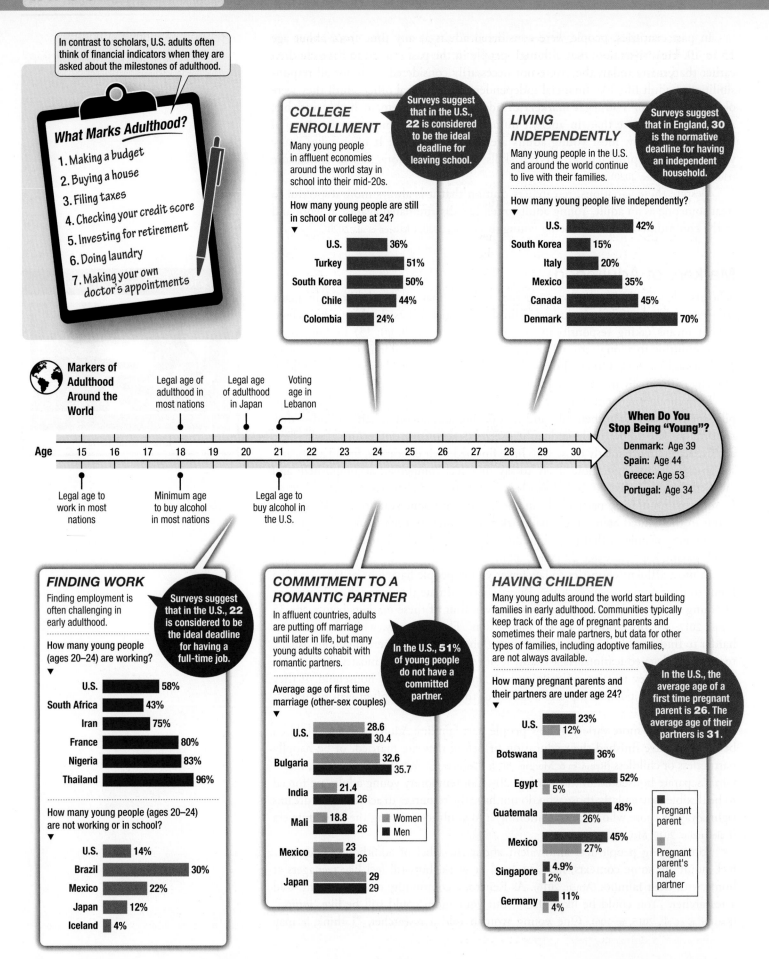

In contrast to scholars, U.S. adults often think of financial indicators when they are asked about the milestones of adulthood.

What Marks Adulthood?

1. Making a budget
2. Buying a house
3. Filing taxes
4. Checking your credit score
5. Investing for retirement
6. Doing laundry
7. Making your own doctor's appointments

COLLEGE ENROLLMENT

Many young people in affluent economies around the world stay in school into their mid-20s.

Surveys suggest that in the U.S., **22** is considered to be the ideal deadline for leaving school.

How many young people are still in school or college at 24?

- U.S. **36%**
- Turkey **51%**
- South Korea **50%**
- Chile **44%**
- Colombia **24%**

LIVING INDEPENDENTLY

Many young people in the U.S. and around the world continue to live with their families.

Surveys suggest that in England, **30** is the normative deadline for having an independent household.

How many young people live independently?

- U.S. **42%**
- South Korea **15%**
- Italy **20%**
- Mexico **35%**
- Canada **45%**
- Denmark **70%**

Markers of Adulthood Around the World

Legal age of adulthood in most nations	18
Legal age of adulthood in Japan	20
Voting age in Lebanon	21

Age 15 16 17 18 19 20 21 22 23 24 25 26 27 28 29 30

Legal age to work in most nations — 15

Minimum age to buy alcohol in most nations — 18

Legal age to buy alcohol in the U.S. — 21

When Do You Stop Being "Young"?

Denmark: Age 39
Spain: Age 44
Greece: Age 53
Portugal: Age 34

FINDING WORK

Finding employment is often challenging in early adulthood.

Surveys suggest that in the U.S., **22** is considered to be the ideal deadline for having a full-time job.

How many young people (ages 20–24) are working?

- U.S. **58%**
- South Africa **43%**
- Iran **75%**
- France **80%**
- Nigeria **83%**
- Thailand **96%**

How many young people (ages 20–24) are not working or in school?

- U.S. **14%**
- Brazil **30%**
- Mexico **22%**
- Japan **12%**
- Iceland **4%**

COMMITMENT TO A ROMANTIC PARTNER

In affluent countries, adults are putting off marriage until later in life, but many young adults cohabit with romantic partners.

In the U.S., **51%** of young people do not have a committed partner.

Average age of first time marriage (other-sex couples)

	Women	Men
U.S.	28.6	30.4
Bulgaria	32.6	35.7
India	21.4	26
Mali	18.8	26
Mexico	23	26
Japan	29	29

HAVING CHILDREN

Many young adults around the world start building families in early adulthood. Communities typically keep track of the age of pregnant parents and sometimes their male partners, but data for other types of families, including adoptive families, are not always available.

In the U.S., the average age of a first time pregnant parent is **26**. The average age of their partners is **31**.

How many pregnant parents and their partners are under age 24?

	Pregnant parent	Pregnant parent's male partner
U.S.	23%	12%
Botswana	36%	
Egypt	52%	5%
Guatemala	48%	26%
Mexico	45%	27%
Singapore	4.9%	2%
Germany	11%	4%

actually be a particularity of childhood to imagine that there will be a point when you feel completely adult, because . . . [that] may just be what it feels like to be grown up. You don't feel it" (Settersten, 2011, p. 257).

Is Emerging Adulthood for Everyone?

Some scholars use the term **emerging adulthood** to describe the period between ages 18 and about 29 (Arnett, 2000; Nelson, 2021). They suggest that a new label is needed to describe a period when young people are consciously postponing some of the milestones of adulthood, like committing to a partner or becoming responsible for children. These young adults are exploring their identity in an in-between stage rather than setting down roots (Arnett & Mitra, 2020).

The idea that emerging adulthood is a new and unique life stage is supported by the fact that nearly 6 in 10 young adults in the United States enter college, and fewer are married than in previous generations (U.S. Bureau of Labor Statistics, 2021a; Tillman et al., 2019). Scholars point out that many young people do not feel adult: They want more time to ask big questions about their future as they slowly take on more responsibility and control over their lives (Dallessandro, 2019; Nelson, 2021).

However, the idea that it is now universal, or even expected or beneficial, for young people to postpone adulthood has been criticized (Côté, 2014; Nelson, 2021). Many scholars suggest that emerging adulthood is not universal but rather a variation in a more general stage of young adulthood. Many young people do take on considerable responsibilities in their 20s. For instance, about half have a child of their own, and more than one in four cares for an older family member (D'Amen et al., 2021; Livingston, 2018). Additionally, while years of exploration may be valuable for those who can afford it, many young adults are constrained from adventure by limited finances or need to move more quickly into adult roles in order to fulfill their family and community responsibilities (Bowen et al., 2021).

Committing to a life path and having a sense of purpose leads to more satisfaction, stability, and contentment in young adulthood and throughout the lifespan (Côté, 2019). Being in between is often inevitable as young people search for work, partners, and a sense of what their future holds, but for some young adults, this is linked to mental health challenges and risky behavior (Nelson, 2021).

emerging adulthood A term used by some scholars to describe the period between about ages 18 and about 29 in which young people consciously postpone some of the milestones of adulthood to explore their identity.

Marking Adulthood with Rituals and Outfits Some communities ceremonially mark the transition to adulthood. In Seoul, South Korea, young men participate in a traditional ceremony to mark their twentieth birthdays. In Waterloo, Iowa, young women celebrate growing up at a debutante cotillion sponsored by a local club.

Learn It Together

How Do You Define Adulthood?

Plan Review the various markers that have been used to decide whether someone has reached adulthood.

Engage Find a partner, and each of you separately list the top three milestones that you think someone needs to achieve in order to be considered an adult. Share your list and your informal ethnotheories with one another, discuss why you chose them, and the ages at which you think someone should achieve them.

Reflect Do you think these markers are true for everyone around the world? How do you think they are similar or different from when your parents or grandparents were growing up?

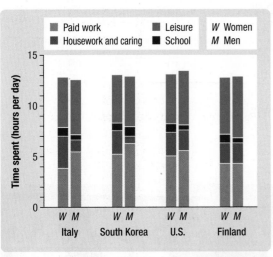

Data from Craig et al., 2019.

FIGURE 12.1 What Are Young Adults Doing? Community support affects how much time young adults have to spend in school, housework, or even leisure. One group of researchers compared how men and women in four different nations spent their everyday time. They found that, in nearly every country, women tend to spend more time than men in housework, caring tasks, and school. Young people in some nations with more community support for youth, such as Finland, had more leisure time than those in other countries.

Young adults who are already in a social structure that encourages exploration, like college, tend to thrive as they navigate this transition. Those who are not tend to have more difficulty unless they have a strong sense of where they want to be (Freelin & Staff, 2020).

Variable Paths to Adulthood

The pathways taken in early adulthood can limit the options available to young people in the years to come. Although life circumstances can always be altered, making changes becomes increasingly challenging. For instance, it can be difficult to go back to college after you have started a family, to move to a new city when you are laden with debt, or to change occupations without the right training (Nelson, 2021).

The journey to adulthood is shaped by young people's strengths, along with the environmental context in which they live (Shanahan et al., 2016). Inequities are starkly apparent: Young adults who have financial, emotional, and structural supports are more likely to thrive than those who do not (Nelson, 2021). Resilience can help ease the transition. One such source is strong family and social support: Relationships continue to provide young people with emotional and practical assistance, from a listening ear to help with the rent (Hartnett et al., 2018). This helps young people maintain their emotional health at a time when mental illnesses are more common than in any other period in the lifespan (Gagné et al., 2021b; SAMHSA, 2020).

Academic preparation is another source of strength. Young adults who have finished high school, particularly if they graduated with solid skills, are at much lower risk for unemployment and poverty (Torpey, 2021). A third source of stability comes from finances. Young adults who enter their 20s with economic resources—whether from their families or from good job opportunities—have an easier time becoming self-sufficient. Unfortunately, more young adults than ever are saddled with debt: American youth owe more money for student loans or on their credit cards than young people in previous generations (Houle & Warner, 2017; Wood et al., 2018).

Finally, structural and institutional supports can ease the transition into adulthood. Some nations, for instance, have ample social safety nets, including highly subsidized educational opportunities and school-to-work programs (Craig et al., 2020). In other countries, young adults may have to cobble together unstable part-time jobs in an increasingly unstable economy (Khatiwada & Sum, 2016; Macmillan & Shanahan, 2021). In recent years, about one in eight U.S. young adults was not in school or working (**Figure 12.1**). Young people have a higher rate of poverty or homelessness than any other group of adults (Morton et al., 2018; U.S. Census Bureau, 2020).

The COVID-19 pandemic affected people across the lifespan, but research suggests that it may have had a more significant impact on young people's long-term careers and economic well-being than on any other age group, since it disrupted many as they were just beginning their adult lives (Settersten et al., 2020).

APPLY IT!   **12.1** Haruki knows she is an adult because she feels responsible: for herself, for her partner, and for her students. When did you feel like an adult? What are the external markers that symbolize adulthood for you?

12.2 Researchers tell us that young adults can be shaped by external circumstances as they start their lives, more than other age groups. How did the historical circumstances that you grew up in shape how you have become an adult?

Brain and Cognitive Development

Haruki's adventures in young adulthood are supported by the development of her brain and cognitive abilities. As you may remember, dramatic changes occur in cognition and in the brain during adolescence, and development does not end at age 18 or even 25. Young adults' biology and thinking continues to allow the flexibility to learn and adapt to new adventures as they adjust to new responsibilities.

A Still-Maturing Brain

During early adulthood, the brain continues to be in a state of flux, enabling young adults to adapt to changing circumstances and new roles and powering them to learn new skills, from programming to parenting (Guyer et al., 2018). In younger adults, the parts of their brain that relate to social and emotional processing are still maturing, allowing them to take on and adapt to new roles as partners or school principals (Casey et al., 2019). Many neuroscientists suggest that the brain is not fully mature until adults are in their late 20s or 30s (see **Infographic 12.2**) (Somerville, 2016).

Three major events characterize brain development in early adulthood. First, the brain continues to become more efficient because of ongoing myelination and pruning, processes that continue across the lifespan but peak in childhood and adolescence. Myelination increases the amount of white matter in the brain and allows information to flow more quickly from neuron to neuron, leading to increased efficiency, particularly in the prefrontal cortex (PFC) — the area of the brain activated during logical thinking, self-control, and decision making (Mills et al., 2016; Vanes et al., 2020).

At around age 20, the areas of the brain that relate to social function experience their peak levels of myelination (Grydeland et al., 2019). Synaptic pruning continues during early adulthood, mostly in unmyelinated neurons, known as gray matter. The decline in the gray matter in early adulthood is so dramatic that scientists can observe the overall brain volume shrinking until it stabilizes in the mid-20s (Gennatas et al., 2017). Overall, this myelination and pruning help make early adulthood the prime of life for many types of thinking that involve fast processing.

Second, stronger regional connections continue to build across the regions of the brain (Faghiri et al., 2018). The PFC becomes more connected to the rest of the brain, which gives young adults more cognitive control over their behavior (Váša et al., 2020). The connections between the cortex and the regions of the brain that are devoted to social and emotional processing, like the subcortical structures, continue to be remodeled during early adulthood, helping young people embrace their new social roles: as caregivers, college students, and colleagues. These developing connections also may be why young people can make the brave decisions adulthood requires, such as starting a new job or going on a blind date.

Like adolescents, young adults still tend to make optimistic, emotional decisions, particularly in exciting situations (Rudoph et al., 2017). Researchers suggest that they are cognitively capable of making logical decisions but tend to value social and emotional rewards more than the long-term consequences in emotionally "hot" environments. One reason may be their still-immature brain connectivity (Casey et al., 2019; Icenogle et al., 2019).

Another reason for young adults' enthusiasm and ability to throw themselves into the adult world may be that the emotional and social regions of their brain, like their reward circuit, are still particularly reactive to social experiences. Young adults tend to be more deliberative in their emotional reactions than adolescents: They have learned better ways to manage their feelings but are still more sensitive than younger children or older adults to negative feelings, like fear or failure or

© Nathan Papes/Springfield News-Leader via Imagn Content Services, LLC

Learning Objectives

12.2 Describe the characteristics of brain development in early adulthood.

12.3 List four ways of describing the flexible thinking of young adults.

Finally Getting to Set the Thermostat For Boen, moving to his own apartment in Springfield, Missouri, after leaving foster care, meant setting the heat at a temperature he liked. Social supports meant that he also had someone to call in case of an emergency or for a little extra support, like when he wasn't quite sure how to make biscuits and gravy.

CONNECTIONS

Remember from Chapter 8 that white matter in the brain is mostly made up of axons covered in *myelin*, the white fatty substance that speeds the communication between neurons. Gray matter includes neurons and their dendrites that are not myelinated.

MATURATION OF THE BRAIN WITH CONTINUED INCREASE IN EFFICIENCY

Brain connections continue to increase in efficiency as young people enter adulthood, leveling off as they approach their mid-20s. Pruning continues, resulting in fewer, but more efficient connections in the frontal cortex.

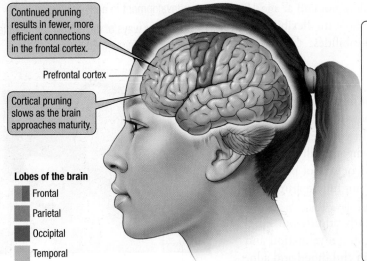

Continued pruning results in fewer, more efficient connections in the frontal cortex.

Prefrontal cortex

Cortical pruning slows as the brain approaches maturity.

Lobes of the brain
- Frontal
- Parietal
- Occipital
- Temporal

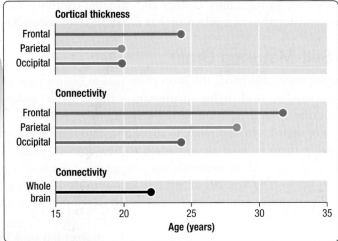

Approximate Ages At Which Brain Structures Mature

Cortical thickness
- Frontal
- Parietal
- Occipital

Connectivity
- Frontal
- Parietal
- Occipital

Connectivity
- Whole brain

Age (years) — 15, 20, 25, 30, 35

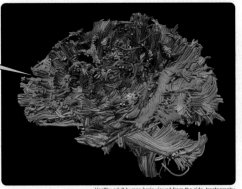

As the brain reaches the peak of speed and efficiency, the rate of myelination of slows.

Maturation of brain white matter tracts

This computer model shows the nerve tracts of a young adult. Neurons in different parts of the brain use these pathways to share information with each other. These pathways continue to increase in efficiency into early adulthood.

Healthy adult human brain viewed from the side, tractography.
Henrietta Howells, NatBrainLab. Attribution 4.0 International (CC BY 4.0)

MATURATION OF COGNITIVE CAPACITY

Cognitive capacity reaches levels of adult maturity by mid-adolescence.

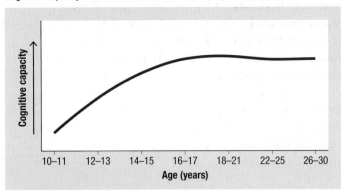

Cognitive capacity

Age (years) — 10–11, 12–13, 14–15, 16–17, 18–21, 22–25, 26–30

PSYCHOSOCIAL MATURITY

Psychosocial maturity continues through adolescence and early adulthood.

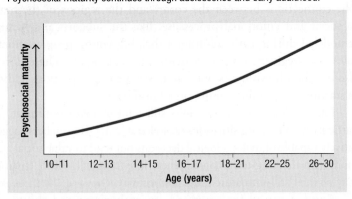

Psychosocial maturity

Age (years) — 10–11, 12–13, 14–15, 16–17, 18–21, 22–25, 26–30

social rejection (Bos et al., 2020; Rodman et al., 2021). Young adults are less optimistic than adolescents when taking chances and tend to be more thoughtful when taking risks, but they continue to be more hopeful than older adults (Bretzke et al., 2021; Rodman et al., 2020; Schreuders et al., 2018).

Everyone's brain is distinctive, and, as you may remember from Chapter 10, our connectomes are as unique as our thumbprints. These individual variations increase during adolescence and young adulthood. Some are marked by stressful experiences, which can lead to accelerated brain development (Cropley et al., 2021). Other variations, such as anomalies in brain maturation or increased sensitivity to stressors, are linked to conditions like schizophrenia and mood and personality disorders, which often emerge in early adulthood (Gur et al., 2019; Long & Corfas, 2014; Truelove-Hill et al., 2020).

So, when is the brain done growing? Neuroscientists do not agree on exactly when maturation ends, only that it does not happen at 18. Some argue that the brain is adult in the mid-20s (Scott et al., 2016). Others suggest that it is not fully mature until the mid-30s, when the connectivity within regions of the brain, like the late-maturing prefrontal cortex, is complete (Somerville, 2016). One challenge is that the brain never stops changing altogether, even though its genetically preprogrammed sequence of maturation may be complete. The brain remains plastic throughout the lifespan. As you learn and change—whether you immigrate to a new country, fall in love, or learn to juggle—your brain also changes, and new connections between neurons appear.

Cognitive Development

Memory, processing speed, executive function, and the ability to pay attention—the building blocks of thinking—reach adult levels by the end of adolescence. Young adults, however, put these skills to new uses in complex and amazing ways.

Relativistic Thinking For many young adults like Haruki, the world becomes more complex after high school. Decisions are not simple, and choices become less clear. Some of the decisions of adulthood are important, and some just *feel* important, as Haruki tells us. She describes overthinking many choices she has had to make: car insurance, her high-stress job, and even whether to get married. As she has learned, one part of adulthood is accepting that there is not just one right answer, and that you may have to ask for support in finding answers.

When Haruki says that there is no single right answer, she is embracing **relativistic thinking** (Sinnott et al., 2015). This way of thinking acknowledges that there is no absolute truth, but rather a collection of different perspectives. Instead of assuming there is one right answer to life's problems, relativistic thinkers are aware that their assumptions are biased and subjective. For example, Haruki has learned to accept that, for her, extra adult responsibility sometimes comes with a need for more support.

Relativistic thinking can be useful when you encounter different cultural, moral, or religious viewpoints. A relativistic point of view can help avoid conflict, say, about who you voted for in the last election, and help you realize that both sides may share similar beliefs and values. Relativism assumes that adults recognize that their point of view is just one of many possible ones (Vukman, 2005). Some scholars suggest that, with age, adults can employ more relativistic thinking (Vukman, 2005).

Dialectical Thinking Relativistic thinking is not the only new way young adults approach problems. **Dialectical thinking** is the ability to look at the opposing

Mark Peterson/Redux

Medical School Utilizes Your Cognitive Skills. These young medical students in Riverside, California, are learning new skills and vocabulary. They are taking advantage of their peak levels of processing speed, executive function, and attention.

relativistic thinking A type of thinking that acknowledges there is no absolute truth, but rather a collection of different perspectives. Instead of assuming there is one right answer to life's problems, relativistic thinkers understand that their assumptions are biased and subjective.

dialectical thinking The ability to look at the opposing sides to a problem, explore the contradictions between them, and accept that the solution may lie somewhere in between.

Scientific American Profile

Dialectical Reasoning and
Life Decisions

sides to a problem, explore the contradictions between them, and accept that the solution may lie somewhere in between. Dialectical thinkers know that "every coin has two sides," and that few problems have perfect solutions (Pang et al., 2017). Young adults who use dialectical thinking tend to be creative and flexible in determining solutions. For example, Haruki saw the complexity of her decision to get married, informed by her understanding of the complexity of relationships, especially long-distance romances, as well as by her bond with Marvin. Dialectical reasoning helps us understand that no choice is ever perfect or will ever satisfy all the people who give you advice.

Dialectical thinking is more common among adults who are comfortable with thinking abstractly and are capable of relativistic and flexible thinking (King & Kitchener, 2015). Cultures that describe the world as full of change and contradiction, like the complimentary and interrelated forces of yin and yang, are more likely to be comprised of dialectical thinkers (Pang et al., 2017). Some studies have found that young people from East Asian countries, including China, display more dialectical thinking than young people from the United States (Spencer-Rodgers et al., 2018).

For example, if college students in China and the United States are asked whether childhood enemies are likely to date in adulthood, Chinese college students are more likely to agree that love is possible. U.S. students are more likely to view the world as unchanging and believe that enemies could never be friends (Spencer-Rodgers et al., 2010). Chinese students' dialectical thinking may enable them to accept life's inevitable complexities and contradictions more easily (Chen et al., 2013). Some research shows that dialectical thinking can facilitate decision-making in a world overloaded with information, opinions, and choices. Recognizing that every choice has a potential downside can make complicated decisions easier, such as whether to move back home or which phone to buy (Pang et al., 2017).

CONNECTIONS

Remember from Chapter 10 that Jean Piaget believed that *formal operational thought*, the ability to think abstractly and systematically about the world, emerges in adolescence.

Postformal Thought Some researchers believe that flexible thinking marks a new stage of cognitive development that follows Piaget's adolescent stage of formal operational thought. This stage, called **postformal thought**, allows young adults to think through complex issues by reviewing different viewpoints and considering emotional, contextual, and interpersonal factors (Labouvie-Vief, 1980, 2015; Sinnott, 1998, 2002). Although Piaget did not include postformal thought in his core stages of cognitive development, researchers Gisela Labouvie-Vief and Jean Sinnott used some of his methods—observation and interviews—to investigate how young adults think. They found that young people who use postformal reasoning can see things from a variety of perspectives and understand that many challenges have multiple solutions (Galupo et al., 2009). Postformal thought can help adults be more flexible in their thinking and break beyond the binary choices that are commonplace in politics or in everyday life (Sinnott, 2021; Sinnott et al., 2020).

In one of their classic studies, Labouvie-Vief and her colleagues asked teenagers to comment on an imaginary scenario in which a woman vowed to leave her husband the next time he came home drunk. Adolescent participants were sure that the woman would leave her husband because "it said so" in the text that they read. But young adults, with more experience with empty threats and a better understanding of the long-term commitments of marriage, offered more complex answers. They went beyond the pure logic of the situation to understand what one participant called "the human dimension" (Labouvie-Vief, 1984, p. 191). These young adults were demonstrating postformal thought.

postformal thought A stage of thinking that allows young adults to think through complex issues by reviewing different viewpoints, considering emotional, contextual, and interpersonal factors.

Does Higher Education Change Your Thinking? Young adults *can* become more relativistic, balanced, and flexible, as well as display postformal reasoning with age, but not everyone does. Flexible thinking seems to rely on what people have experienced, particularly the kind of schooling they have received. It often results from higher education.

Does higher education actually change young people's thinking? In the past, researchers demonstrated that some students began to think relativistically while in college (King, 2009; Perry, 1999). More recent research has questioned whether attending college always helps young people think critically (Arum & Roksa, 2011; Mayhew et al., 2016; Pascarella & Terenzini, 2005).

Remember from Chapter 2 that critical thinking involves the ability to analyze a problem carefully, checking for bias and evaluating all the evidence. It requires you to not only make a decision, but also to reflect on how you are doing it (Halonen, 2008; Halpern & Butler, 2018). Critical thinking involves some of the same abilities as relativistic, dialectical, flexible, or postformal thought, but it also requires thinking about your own thinking and evaluating and weighing evidence. Students who can think critically tend to be more successful in their postcollege careers than others who get through college without these skills. Some scholars even suggest that scores on a critical-thinking test better predict future success than scores on a traditional test of intelligence do (Butler et al., 2012, 2017).

What scholars have found is that college does not inevitably help students develop critical-thinking skills: Many students leave college without them (Mayhew et al., 2016). In general, more academically rigorous college experiences tend to boost cognitive and critical-thinking skills (Evens et al., 2014; Mayhew et al., 2016). College courses that explicitly teach critical-thinking skills also are effective (Halpern & Butler, 2019). In sum, college attendance itself does not guarantee critical-thinking skills. What you do in college—courses, extracurricular activities, and other experiences—is what matters.

Share It!

Score one for first-generation students! They tend to have bigger gains in cognitive and critical-thinking skills than their peers whose parents had been to college.

(Kilgo et al., 2018)

 Scientific American: Lifespan Development

CAN YOU BELIEVE IT?
Can You Get Smarter in Young Adulthood?

Does your intellectual and cognitive maturation end in young adulthood? It may surprise you that research suggests that young adults are still flexible enough to boost their cognition in ways that will last a lifetime. One thing that will *not* boost their intelligence: stimulants. Stimulants like Adderall or Ritalin are among the most misused substances among young people around the world (Maier et al., 2018). They are used without a prescription by about 1 in every 12 young people in the United States to boost focus and thinking (McCabe et al., 2021; Schulenberg et al., 2021). But neuroscientists have found that stimulants do not improve memory or cognition and may actually *hurt* your focus, impairing your ability to make quick decisions if you do not have ADHD, the disorder these stimulants are intended to treat (Franke et al., 2017; Roberts et al., 2020).

Some scientists have found that the placebo effect may explain the popularity of these stimulants: Students simply expect to be able to focus better, so they do (Cropsey et al., 2017). Furthermore, misuse of stimulants can lead to addiction, anxiety, high blood pressure, and even paranoia (Lyon, 2017). Stimulant use is most common among students who are not doing well in school and who are also using other substances and binge-drinking (Kilmer et al., 2021).

Is there a nonprescription way to get smarter in adulthood? The answer may surprise you. Sleep is probably the most important thing you can do to improve your grades and work more efficiently (Chen & Chen, 2019; Ridner et al., 2016). A good night's sleep will help you retain what you study. One-on-one peer tutoring also helps boost motivation to learn difficult material (Pugatch & Wilson, 2018).

Beliefs and social support make a difference as well: Students who feel like they belong at school, who understand that setbacks are to be expected, and who know how to ask for help are more likely to succeed in college (Broda et al., 2018; Schwartz et al., 2018). In addition, spending time on schoolwork is important. That may seem obvious, but for students who are stressed by work, family, volunteer, and social commitments, finding the time to excel in college is challenging (Beattie et al., 2019).

APPLY IT!   **12.3** Haruki has learned to be more understanding of the complexity of adult decision-making. Choices are not always clear. Have you been able to appreciate the complexity of decisions in your own adult life?

12.4 Haruki is adapting to a new job as a high school counselor and a new role as a live-in partner. How does young-adult brain development help her adapt to these new roles?

12.5 Haruki is planning on studying a third language, Pashtu, and maybe also Japanese, in the coming year. What are strategies that can be applied to learning in or out of school during early adulthood?

Building Healthy Habits

Learning Objective

12.4 Discuss health risks and positive health practices in early adulthood.

Like many of us, Haruki grew more concerned about her health during the COVID-19 pandemic. Because of their strong immune systems, young people's lives were mostly spared the worst impacts of the virus (Ahmad et al., 2021; Leidman et al., 2021). However, even though younger adults are less likely to die from the disease, the pandemic has nevertheless impacted them: More than 8 million young adults had contracted the disease by November 2021 (CDC, 2021). Scientists estimate that more than 1 in 10 people who developed COVID-19 will have long-term effects, including cognitive fogginess and fatigue (Marshall, 2021). Young people are actually *more* likely than other age groups to contract the virus, because they are more likely to work in front-line occupations, to socialize in groups, and to be skeptical of public health guidance (Baum et al., 2021; Feldman et al., 2021; Wilson et al., 2020). Young people often accept stereotypes of themselves as healthy and invulnerable, but the reality is more complex.

Health Difficulties

Young adults' health risks are usually linked to behaviors rather than chronic or infectious illnesses. In the United States and around the globe, young people continue, like adolescents, to be at high risk for dying in car accidents, by suicide, or by homicide (WHO, 2020). More young people in the United States die from gun violence, whether at their own hand or in a violent attack, than they do in car accidents. However, the leading cause of death in people in their 20s is unintentional drug overdose (CDC, 2021).

While public health efforts have had great successes in improving the health of children and older adults, mortality among young adults in the United States has actually increased in recent decades, primarily as a result of suicide, gun violence, and drug overdose, with a death rate that is more than twice that of other affluent nations, such as the United Kingdom and France (Fox, 2021). Many scientists link the increase in young adult deaths to their increasingly vulnerable financial situation, limited access to mental health services and the increasing availability of powerful opiates, like fentanyl, which often cause accidental overdose (Cadigan et al., 2019; Gar et al., 2019; Silverstein et al., 2021).

Most young people in the United States, like Haruki, report that their physical health is good. However, as they move through their 20s, some begin to show signs of chronic illnesses like high blood pressure and diabetes (Magliano et al., 2021; Sokol et al., 2017). By age 32, only one in five young people is in ideal cardiovascular health, meaning that they are more likely to develop cardiovascular disease or already have high blood pressure, high cholesterol, or diabetes (Nagata et al., 2019). There are systemic reasons why it is difficult for young adults to stay healthy: Finding health care may be challenging as they transition from their childhood pediatrician to new medical practitioners. They are often stressed by competing priorities and trying to get by on a low income (Harris et al., 2017).

There are inequities in health in young adulthood just as there are across the lifespan. Experiences of adversity during childhood and adolescence, including financial strain, abuse, or a caregiver's serious illness, increase the likelihood that young adults have early signs of cardiovascular disease or epigenetic aging in their genome (McDade et al., 2019). But some experiences, like having a strong trusting relationship with your family, are protective of your health, regardless of your risk factors (Doom et al., 2017). To paraphrase one scientist: What happens in early adulthood does not always stay in early adulthood (Nelson, 2021). These risk factors will follow young adults as they age, making good health more elusive as they reach middle life.

SCIENCE IN PRACTICE
Susan Salcido, Community Outreach Worker

Susan puts in many hours on her feet every day: One of the most surprising things about her job as a community outreach worker in Los Angeles. The wear and tear on her shoes was unexpected, as was the gratitude she gets from people who are eager to have their questions answered about health care.

In the past year, Susan has been on the streets and in community centers trying to educate her community in Los Angeles about how they can protect themselves and their families from COVID-19. One of her missions is to fix the mistrust in health care she sees in young adults like herself. A few of her peers are completely opposed to the vaccine, but most others are simply nervous about it. These are the people who are often eager to talk.

Early on, developmental scientists found that about one in four young people was taking a wait-and-see approach to the vaccine (Adams et al., 2021). In fact, younger people tend to be more mistrustful than older people are of vaccines and of health care, whether for themselves or for their young children (Funk et al., 2019; Grant et al., 2021; Shih et al., 2021; Tram et al., 2021).

Is there something in young adults' cognition that makes them vulnerable to mistrust? Some researchers have pointed out that health care decisions, particularly in a stressful time like a global pandemic, tend to be more *heuristic* and intuitive than *analytical* (Jennings et al., 2021). People who are nervous about vaccines, for instance, tend to be making heuristic judgments: perhaps putting off the side effects or the uncertainty about the vaccine and mistrusting the risks of getting COVID-19 to their own health (Bronstein et al., 2019).

Young people often have personal reasons for why they are nervous about the COVID-19 vaccine. Compared to other age groups, young people are more likely to say that they have experienced discrimination in health care, and they are often more aware of historical discrimination within the health system (Benkert et al., 2019; Nong et al., 2020).

Building Relationships One Conversation at a Time Susan Salcido (*left*) is a community outreach worker in Los Angeles who educates her community about the importance of getting vaccinated for COVID-19 and, at the same time, tries to foster their confidence in the health care system.

Discrimination and mistrust go hand in hand: Both are at high levels in many groups of young people, including Black Americans, women, low-income adults, and those who identify as transgender, lesbian, gay, bisexual, or queer (Adams et al., 2021; Dean et al., 2021; Human Rights Campaign Foundation, 2018).

Susan is handing out masks and setting up vaccine appointments, but more than anything she is putting in her time and her empathy to help rebuild trust. Research supports what she is doing: Getting to know people and giving them time to get to know you is one way to build trust in the medical system (NORC, 2021). Susan is tackling that, one conversation at a time.

Building Resilience

Healthy habits, like getting balanced nutrition, maintaining a healthy body image, and getting enough sleep and activity, can help young adults build resilience. Every new beginning in young adulthood—from starting a new job to finding a romantic partner—offers a new opportunity to start fresh and adopt a healthy routine (Winpenny et al., 2017).

Managing Nutrition Across the lifespan, most adults fall short of what scientists recommend for an ideal diet. This is particularly true in young adulthood: Young adults tend to eat more high-carbohydrate foods and snacks than adolescents, particularly if they are no longer living at home (Baraldi et al., 2018; Winpenny, Smith, et al., 2020). Fewer than one in eight young adults meet the guidelines for fruit and vegetable intake (Moyer et al., 2020). Young adults who are food insecure, who are in college, and who are new parents are more likely to eat out more and skip out on the healthy meals. Stability seems to be linked to healthier nutrition: Finding a partner, moving in together, and working are all linked to eating better (Winpenny, Smith, et al., 2020; Winpenny, Winkler, et al., 2020).

Many people only think of eating healthy as a means of avoiding an unhealthy weight. Regardless of your size, what you eat affects your current and long-term health. High-fat, high-sugar diets can trigger inflammation that may damage brain health and increase the risk of infertility, cancer, and cardiovascular and liver disease (Harris et al., 2017; Panth et al., 2018; Spencer et al., 2017; Wegermann et al., 2021).

Diets that are filled with complex carbohydrates, fruits, and vegetables also make it easier to maintain a healthy weight, although adhering to such diets is challenging when convenience foods are heavily marketed and inexpensive (Harris & Fleming-Milici, 2019; Howse et al., 2018). As a result, unhealthy weight continues to be a concern during young adulthood: Many adults gain weight after high school. In the United States, more than one in four adults has an unhealthy weight, or what health providers call *obesity*, which is linked to higher rates of cardiovascular disease, cancer, arthritis, and diabetes (Dietz, 2017; Zheng et al., 2017).

Improving Body Image Many young adults tend to be critical of their bodies: Some experts find that nearly half of people who identify as women and one in four who identify as men feel disappointed in how they look (Wang et al., 2019). People might want to be skinnier, have prettier hair, or be more muscular, depending on the community standards they have adopted (Nagata et al., 2021). Social media and advertising often take the blame for young people's inability to appreciate themselves (Engeln et al., 2020; Rasmussen et al., 2020). However, there is more to healthy body image than avoiding Instagram: Researchers have found that poor body image is also triggered to stress, mental health, and a lack of social support (de Vries et al., 2019). In turn, poor body image can exacerbate depression and is linked to disordered eating and decreased quality of life (Nagata et al., 2018; Rounsefell et al., 2020).

Boosting Mood in Malaysia Staying active can help improve your body image, energy level, and emotions. Just a short walk in the park can be enough to improve your well being.

Social pressures and structural discrimination can also impact body image. People who have larger bodies face workplace discrimination and, as a result, have higher rates of unemployment and underemployment than people with smaller bodies (Harris, 2019; Lindeboom et al., 2010). People with visible physical limitations or who disclose a history of mental illness also face substantial discrimination in hiring (Namkung & Carr, 2019). It is illegal in many countries for employers to discriminate based on physical abilities, but researchers have found that they are less likely to seriously consider candidates who do not have smaller bodies or appear to be in typical health or ability (Bredgaard & Salado-Rasmussen, 2021). Nevertheless, some emerging research suggests that being mindful and compassionate may boost body pride and positivity (Moffitt et al., 2018; Rahimi-Ardabili et al., 2018). Staying active can also improve body image, although feeling badly about your body often makes that more difficult (Neumark-Sztainer et al., 2018; Sabiston et al., 2019).

Staying Active Physical activity benefits everyone, even those who may feel too busy to make time for it (Hogan et al., 2013). As young people transition out of high school, finding time to exercise becomes difficult. Young adults are less active than teenagers: They spend more time at work and school and on their phones (Winpenny, Winkler, et al., 2020). For Haruki and many other adults, leaving high school means no more gym class or soccer practice or a family to pester you to take a run before school. Young adults who continue getting enough exercise are those who developed strong exercise habits as teenagers, such as going for a run or participating in a pick-up team. Residential college students are the *least* likely to exercise, even though they have the most facilities for working out. This may be because they are in a new setting with many distractions (DeForche et al., 2015).

Cooper Neill/Bloomberg via Getty Images

Sometimes Being Sedentary Is a Job Skill. For many young people, work makes it difficult to be active. For this young woman making baseball gloves in a factory outside of Dallas, Texas, work means lots of focus and sitting down.

Experts recommend that young adults get at least 150 minutes of exercise a week, but only 50 percent are getting enough (Moyer et al., 2020; U.S. Department of Health and Human Services, 2018). Getting enough activity is a struggle if your job requires long periods of sitting or standing still—whether that is manning the checkout counter at Target or answering phones at a call desk. But young people who are working are the most likely to make time to exercise. Some researchers suggest that the feeling of being settled that comes with a job may help them make time to take care of their bodies.

Physical activity is beneficial in ways that go beyond just keeping muscles strong; it helps relieve depression, increases happiness, and continues to help boost brain growth and executive function, enabling faster learning (Ludyga et al., 2018; Paolucci et al., 2018; Slutsky-Ganesh et al., 2020). Moving can mean hitting the gym, walking, dancing, shoveling snow, or carrying your neighbor's groceries up the stairs: All these types of activity have a powerful effect on well-being (Edwards & Loprinzi, 2017; Pengpid & Peltzer, 2019).

Unhealthy Use of Substances While you might think of drinking and drug use as a personal choice, researchers suggest that many substance use habits are influenced by our community context. Around the world, many young adults begin to experiment with substances and alcohol in the late teen years, and in many cultures they tend to stop by their mid-20s. But rates of substance use vary depending on cohort, culture, and context: Young adults in the United States, for instance, are more likely than other young people to use marijuana. Young people in Italy are likely to use prescription medications. Young adults in Japan are unlikely to use any substances (Degenhardt et al., 2019). Youth in the United States tend to stop heavy drinking in their 20s, but adults in other parts of the world may continue into middle life (Taylor et al., 2017).

Despite these variations, more young people in general are binge drinking and using marijuana than they were in the previous decade. One possible reason is that

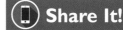

Share It!

Exercise helps keep anxiety away. Researchers found that adults who were able to maintain an exercise routine during the early months of the COVID-19 pandemic were also better able to keep their anxiety in check.

(López-Bueno et al., 2020)

Scientific American: Lifespan Development

stigma against alcohol and substance use is lessening. Marijuana is now legal in many communities, and the parents and grandparents of today's young people are more accepting of substances than previous generations were. In the United States and other affluent countries, young people are taking longer to "age out" of binge drinking and marijuana use (Schulenberg et al., 2021). In contrast, fewer young adults are smoking cigarettes than in previous generations, although some have shifted to vaping or using e-cigarettes (Al-Hamdani et al., 2020). For some young people, substance use seems to be relatively typical, but for others, heavy drinking and substance use are linked to overdoses, brain injury, and other risks, including car accidents and assault (Hall et al., 2020; Patrick et al., 2020).

Many young people think that the substances they use are safe and that heavy drinking and substance use is normative. However, not everyone is doing it: Substance use, like so much in young adulthood, is unequal. Whereas about one in three young people abstain, about one in eight are regular binge drinkers or users of marijuana (McCabe et al., 2021; Schulenberg et al., 2021). Experts caution that regular use of marijuana is linked with depression, suicide, and respiratory problems, and is unsafe during pregnancy (Gobbi et al., 2019; Hall et al., 2020). Nevertheless, young people increasingly believe that marijuana is safe (NASEM, 2017; Wen et al., 2019). Similarly, more young people are vaping nicotine, considering it to be a safe alternative to smoking. However, experts caution that vaping exposes young people to nicotine and potentially toxic pollutants and has long-term health consequences (Braymiller et al., 2020; Soneji et al., 2017).

The most common substance misused by young people is alcohol. Experts are most concerned about **binge drinking**, consuming a large number of alcoholic drinks in a short period of time. Precisely how much alcohol you need to consume to make it a binge depends on the size of the drinker and the size of the drink. For a 140-pound woman, for instance, this means about four standard-sized drinks—or about four 12-ounce beers or four 1.5-ounce shots of liquor (NIAAA, 2018). Rates of binge drinking are higher among residential college students than among other groups of young people (Schulenberg et al., 2021). For some, this seems to be an accepted part of college culture (Gates et al., 2016; Ven, 2011).

Binge drinking has higher costs than a morning hangover. It makes impulsive behavior—whether that is getting behind the wheel of a car, getting into fights, or hooking up without using protection—more likely (Kuntsche et al., 2017). Excessive drinking can create a vicious cycle. Young people say they drink to relieve stress and to relax, but drinking often increases feelings of anxiety and depression and difficulties with executive function (Harper et al., 2021; O'Connor & Kenny, 2015). Binge drinking may be particularly risky for young people, because they react differently to alcohol than older adults. Alcohol acts as a depressant for older people, but young people are more sensitive to the stimulating effects of alcohol and less likely to get sleepy, helping them drink more (Treloar et al., 2017).

During young adulthood, about 1 in 12 will be diagnosed with a *substance use disorder*, and one in four with *alcohol use disorder* (Grant et al., 2015, 2016). And, as you just read, accidental overdoses, often with opiates, are a leading cause of death among young adults (CDC, 2021). Treatment for young adults with substance use disorder is often complicated by the fact that many substances are still criminalized, people with substance use disorder face widespread discrimination and stigma, and mental health resources are often insufficient in many communities, discouraging many from seeking help (Hall et al., 2021; Stockings et al., 2016).

Although young people are developing independent lives, treatment for substance abuse disorders often involves close family and parents, who can help support a healthier lifestyle (Hamilton et al., 2021). Experts support a *harm-reduction*

binge drinking Consuming a large number of alcoholic drinks in a short period of time.

approach to treatment of substance abuse, reducing the stigma around substance use disorder and making sure that all young people have access to the help they need to improve their mental health and to keep them out of the criminal justice system (Silverstein et al., 2021).

APPLY IT! **12.6** One healthy practice that Haruki has figured out is getting enough sleep, particularly since she has to get up so early to make it to her job. What are your health practice "wins"?

12.7 Making time to prepare healthy meals and snacks is hard when you are working all day. Haruki says she is still trying to devise how to eat well. What practices could you recommend that might help her?

Education after High School

In earlier generations, a college degree was not necessary to find a well-paying job. High school graduates could find careers as machinists or as skilled auto workers in industrial plants. But over the past generation, many of these jobs have been automated or now require post–high school education (Rosenbaum et al., 2017; Yeung & Yang, 2020). Today, two in three jobs in the United States require at least some college education. This trend extends around the world: Well-paying jobs now require at least some post–high school coursework or certification (Marshall & Symonds, 2021; Symonds et al., 2011).

From Albania to Australia, more young people are in college than ever before (UNESCO, 2020). The United States is a world leader in college enrollment: More than 6 in 10 young people are enrolled in either community or four-year colleges (U.S. Bureau of Labor Statistics, 2021a). Less than a quarter of U.S. college students attend college full time and live on campus (Irwin et al., 2021). Most are juggling school, work, and family, which can be exhausting.

Benefits of College

For the almost 20 million college students in the United States, the investment may be worth it, particularly if they make it to graduation (Kim & Tamborini, 2019). Completing even a few college courses leads to income that is 13 percent higher than that of a high school diploma. By the time most college students reach age 30, those who finished with a B.A. degree in four years have more than paid off the cost of tuition (Ma et al., 2020).

The benefits of college can go beyond a higher paycheck. The children of college graduates have a much better chance at economic success than those whose parents did not graduate from college (OECD, 2021). A college education seems to benefit young adults in their personal lives, as well. College graduates tend to be more stable romantically: They are more likely to be married and stay with their partners: They are 60 percent less likely to get divorced (Trostel, 2015). After graduation, young people report more job satisfaction and more happiness. They are healthier—smoking less and exercising more—and typically live longer than adults who do not complete college (Hong et al., 2020; Ma et al., 2020; Trostel, 2015).

 Share It!

Hungry in class? College students may have higher salaries once they graduate, but while they are in school, they face high rates of food and housing insecurity: More than one in five are food insecure and about 1 in 10 is housing insecure.

(Broton & Goldrick-Rab, 2018; Freudenberg et al., 2019)

Scientific American: Lifespan Development

Challenges of College

Although graduating from college can help boost your earnings and even help you stay healthier, getting through college and paying for it can be complex and stressful. Millions of young people in United States optimistically enroll in college, but not all

Persevering for the Win Graduation is always sweet, but it may be even more so for young adults who are balancing many commitments, like Maricris. She is a parent and veteran who is celebrating her graduation from California State University, Los Angeles.

of them graduate. In fact, compared to other developed countries, the United States leads the pack in terms of students who leave college without a degree (Sarrico et al., 2017). Only about one in three students at two-year colleges graduates after three years (McFarland et al., 2017). While 9 in 10 college students think they will finish in four years, only half of them do (Marcus, 2021a). In other affluent countries, like Japan, fewer than one in five students leaves school without a degree (Sarrico et al., 2017).

Many students who leave school without a degree will not gain the full benefits of that diploma or certificate they had dreamed about, and they may end up paying the tuition bills for years. Students leave school for many reasons, including difficulties with finances and juggling college with work and family responsibilities, academic strain, and feeling a part of campus culture (Gopalan & Brady, 2020; NASEM, 2017; Sanchez & Kolodner, 2021).

Low-income students are much less likely to enroll in college and, if they do, are less likely to graduate in four years. In contrast, more than 90 percent of affluent college students who attend a private college full time and enroll right out of high school graduate in four years (Shapiro et al., 2014). Similarly, wealthy students are about eight times more likely to earn college degrees than low-income students (Kena et al., 2016).

Older students who attend school part time, who are more likely than younger students to juggle school, work, and family, also struggle to finish school. These students tend to come from less wealthy families, with parents who may not have attended college themselves, and they tend to be disproportionately Black, Latino, and Indigenous (Sanchez & Kolodner, 2021). They attend community colleges that offer fewer advising and support services, rather than highly resourced private or public four-year universities (Cahalan & Perna, 2015; Kena et al., 2016).

Students who are trying to finish college while changing diapers face obvious challenges. About one in three women and one in five men in college has a baby (GAO, 2019). Less than half of those parents complete their degrees in six years, because most colleges do not offer flexibility when babies get sick and even fewer have on-campus day care (Merisotis & Slaughter, 2016). As a result, parenting students often struggle just to get their basic needs met, let alone ace their classes (Goldrick-Rab et al., 2020).

Some policy makers suggest that colleges could offer more flexible schedules and more financial support to make it easier for students to graduate. They recommend making financial aid more comprehensive and transparent, so that it covers all the costs of college (including lab fees) and necessities like child care, and making sure that college students are not excluded from programs that provide food, housing, and income support (Balzer Carr & London, 2020; Chaplot et al., 2015). Research indicates that the more grants students receive, the more likely they are to stay in school: They spend more time studying and less time earning money for rent (Fries et al., 2014; Perna & Odle, 2014).

Finances also impact young people after they leave college. While most college students can manage their student loan burden, some are not so lucky. You may know someone like Jesse Suren, who is working 16-hour days to pay off her $90,000 student loan debt (Steele & Williams, 2016). However, Jesse's experience is not the norm. Most college students do not owe as much as Jesse. On average, four-year-college graduates leave school with about $30,000 in debt and have only about $13,000 of college debt by their 30s (Fry, 2014; Kerr & Wood, 2021; TICAS, 2020).

Waiting for Mommy to Finish Kristi is reading for her psychology class while her 3-year-old Kasiti watches a little television with friends. They all live on campus together at a college in Chambersburg, Pennsylvania, that offers housing and on-site day care for parents with young children.

Academic Strains If you asked campus administrators why most students leave college without a degree, many will tell you that they were not getting the help they needed to succeed academically: College does not always offer the support students need to get through tough courses (Millea et al., 2018). The United States is unique in that academically underprepared students (those in the bottom quarter of test scores) still hope to get a four-year degree but lack sufficient help to reach their dreams (Jerrim, 2014; Kalogrides & Grodsky, 2011). About one in four students enrolled in college needs to take developmental courses, such as algebra or English, in order to proceed in their programs (Sparks & Malkus, 2013). These courses are a block for many students, who may do better if they are given extra tutoring or advising (Dougherty et al., 2017).

Some programs try to remove testing requirements or integrate prerequisite courses material, such as algebra or English, with career-relevant skills training in major courses of study, such as nursing and mechanics. This type of applied learning tends to motivate students and make it more likely that they graduate (Martinson et al., 2018; Zeidenberg et al., 2010). However, revolutionizing how basic courses are taught requires a new way of teaching and a new curriculum that is unavailable on many campuses (Kosiewicz et al., 2016).

The Gender Gap in Education Haruki may not have felt like part of the majority on her college campus, but people who identify as women are indeed in the majority on many college campuses around the country. In the United States, where statistics do not track nonbinary adults, 6 in 10 undergraduate students identify as women (Belkin, 2021). In education programs like the one Haruki attended, the gender imbalance is even more significant: Women make up more than 75 percent of the graduate students in education in the United States (Okahana et al., 2020). Whereas 73 percent of young women who graduate from high school enroll in college, only 65 percent of men do (NCES, 2020; **Figure 12.2**). Women receive more than half of all associate's, bachelor's, and doctoral degrees (NCES, 2020). This is true not only in the United States, but also in dozens of other countries, from Iceland to Kazakhstan (Klevan et al., 2016; Marcus, 2019; UNECE, 2021).

Why is this happening? People who identify as men are not enrolling in college as frequently as women, and when they do, they are leaving without a degree in higher numbers (Huerta & Dizon, 2021). The origins of this phenomenon occurred long before

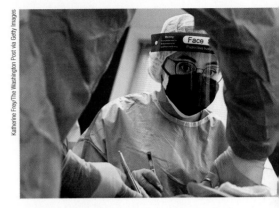

Hands-on Preparation Courses that feel relevant to your future career can boost motivation. Isabel is practicing in the mock operating room at Montgomery College in Maryland as she prepares for a career in surgical technology.

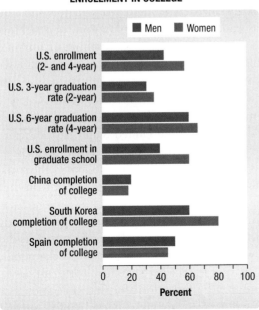

Data from OECD, 2019; U.S. Department of Education, 2019–2020.

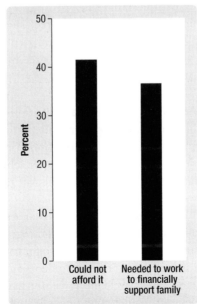

Data from Parker, 2021.

FIGURE 12.2 Gaps in Higher Education In the United States, people who identify as women are more likely to enroll in college and continue on to graduation. A lack of financial support often keeps students in the United States from attending college.

Matthew Staver/The New York Times/Redux

Drilling for More than Oil Shay, shown here at age 19, has been working full time in the oil industry in Montana since high school graduation and just bought this truck with his earnings. He says he would not trade places with his friends who are in college.

it was time to fill out college applications. Even before the fifth grade, children who identify as boys are more likely than girls to struggle in school, and they have more discipline troubles and lower test scores (Autor et al., 2019; Owens, 2016). These trends continue through high school, when boys leave without a diploma at a higher rate than girls (Reeves et al., 2021). Thus, U.S. college enrollments are part of an ongoing story about how boys fare in school.

- On average, young men are less academically prepared than young women are. More women take algebra II and chemistry in high school than boys do and their GPAs are higher (DiPrete & Buchman, 2013; Stoet & Geary, 2020).
- Men do not get the support they need once they are in school, a factor that makes them less likely to complete college once they enroll, compared to women (Reeves & Smith, 2021). Many men, particularly men of color, may not feel a sense of belonging on campus (Brooms, 2020).
- Young men have less social support for going to college. Remember from Chapter 7 that children are often the subject of gendered stereotypes about "masculine" and "feminine" behavior. Some parents and teachers assume that doing well in school is something "for girls" and do not always encourage it for boys (DiPrete & Buchman, 2013). Parents and teachers tend to talk to girls more about going to college than they do boys (Klevan et al., 2016).
- Men often feel that they need to postpone college and work to help their families (Lundberg, 2013). Asked one guidance counselor, "How do you go away to college and leave your family struggling when you know that if you just worked right now, you could help them with those everyday needs?" (qtd. in Marcus, 2021b). One option that pays the bills immediately is military service. Young women make up about 15 percent of today's U.S. military, but it is the largest employer of young men in the United States. About 1 in 10 young men serve a tour of duty (Teachman & Tedrow, 2014).

What are the consequences if men do not have the support they need to graduate from college? Researchers are not sure: The disproportionate rates of college enrollment do not always result in differences in the ability to find employment or earn a stable salary (Carnevale et al., 2018a). Men tend to work in jobs that do not require a college degree, such as construction, oil exploration, or trucking. Women, on the other hand, tend to cluster in jobs such as teaching or nursing, which require a college degree but have lower salaries (Barone & Assirelli, 2020; Dwyer, 2013; Yavorsky et al., 2021).

Adjusting to College Culture For many students, college is a new and imposing institution. Colleges around the world and within the United States have different cultures and social expectations. Some have lots of Greek life (fraternities and sororities), and others are commuter schools that are empty at night. No matter the social structure on campus, all colleges require students to be more independent than they were in high school.

Some scholars believe that the culture on some campuses can be particularly alienating to less affluent and *first-generation college students*, those whose parents did not attend college. When compared with peers from similar income backgrounds, first-generation college students are 60 percent less likely to graduate (Wilbur & Roscigno, 2016). An unwelcoming campus culture may be the culprit for first generation students and other young people, including those who are transgender, disabled, or from other marginalized backgrounds who may be less likely to feel at home on campus (Goldberg et al., 2019; Hernandez et al., 2021; Warnock & Hurst, 2016).

Haruki struggled with this herself: On a campus with seemingly countless options, she never quite figured out the ones that worked for her. An avid musician, she ended up playing in the marching band, but, even years later, worries that she might have been happier or found more friends with another activity. In big classes, she had difficulty finding an instructor who had time to talk to her or answer her questions. It wasn't until after she graduated and connected with an afterschool program for young students that Haruki found her path as a school counselor.

Students whose parents went to college benefit from their parents' experience and have an easier time navigating the new environment (Lareau, 2015). One first-generation college student reported, "Neither of my parents went to college. So they never told me what to do in college because they didn't really know how [help me] to interact with teachers, speak up in class, and develop my own opinions. These are the types of things I didn't know" (Stephens et al., 2012). While parents of first-generation college students may be committed to their children's success, they may not have the practical information to help their children navigate a new and unfamiliar institution (Nichols & Islas, 2016).

Less affluent and first-generation college students may also experience stereotype threat (Stephens et al., 2012). Perhaps you have experienced stereotyping yourself when people make assumptions about your ethnicity, income, religion, gender, or sexual orientation, or, as in this case, family income or experience with college. Whatever the stereotypes, they affect how you feel about yourself and interact with others. All people, including first-generation and low-income college students, are susceptible to the power of stereotype threat: When told that their university valued autonomy and independence, first-generation college students did worse on simple tests of reasoning (Stephens et al., 2012).

First-generation young adults can build on their own sense of pride and community to help boost their achievement: Students who recognize their own strengths and the grit they drew on to get them into college are more likely to succeed (Hernandez et al., 2021). Stereotypes affected Haruki, too: She says that she internalized the idea that she should be good at science because she "looked" Japanese, even though what she really loved was people and was much happier in education.

Campus culture that emphasizes social events rather than academic achievement can make it difficult for young people, particularly from low-income backgrounds, to succeed (Armstrong & Hamilton, 2013; Hamilton & Cheng, 2018). Campuses that emphasize parties, Greek life, and leisure activities have higher dropout rates for students from low-income backgrounds. As you just read, residential colleges often have high rates of binge drinking and substance use, and some may not be an ideal environment for all young people (Jozkowski & Wiersma-Mosley, 2017; Meda et al., 2017).

How to Succeed in College Some markers of whether young adults will do well in college are already in place before they set foot on campus. A major factor is what came before: Not surprisingly, the more academically rigorous their high school experience and the better their grades, the more successful the young adult will be in college (Allensworth & Clark, 2020). But many students have difficulty adjusting to the rigor and the pressures of college no matter their preparation. We have all been told what will help us succeed in college—showing up for class, doing the homework, and studying regularly (instead of cramming). What else matters? Building a support network, asking for help, spending time on assignments, and taking the right classes at the right time can all help you succeed. Here are some steps you can take:

- Build relationships and ask for help. Peers, parents, or mentors can advise about college majors or how to track down an advisor who is missing during office hours and not answering e-mails (Hamilton, 2016). A helpful instructor or administrator is a great resource for information about college majors, internships, or career paths

(Means & Pyne, 2017). Peers can help you find a network of support on campus. Feeling that you belong is an essential part of the college experience: Seek out community to help you feel that you fit in (Broda et al., 2018).

- Recognize your own strengths. Reflect on who you are and the strengths that got you there: persistence, dedication to a long-term goal, and hard work. Sometimes these can pick you up when things seem daunting (Hernandez et al., 2021). Feeling pride in your own identity and values can remind you of something greater than yourself that can ease the stress (Harackiewicz & Priniski, 2018).

- Befriend people who want to achieve. If your peers are studying, you are more likely to hit the books (Conley et al., 2015). And that time studying does pay off. Most students spend less than four hours a day, or less than 15 hours a week on classwork (and about the same time in leisure activities; Babcock & Marks, 2010). Balancing work, activities, and schoolwork can be challenging, but involvement in school activities seems to pay off and does not necessarily take time away from studying.

- Do not be intimidated by your instructors. Developing relationships with adults who can be role models and mentors is one of the transformative aspects of college, but you may need to persevere to make those relationships happen. Persistent students are often the ones who get attention from faculty (Means & Pyne, 2017; Schwartz et al., 2016).

- Make sure your school is the right fit for you. More than one in three students transfer to a different college during their college career (Shapiro et al., 2018). Some research indicates that students are more successful in schools with smaller classes, more motivated instructors, and engaging pedagogical methods (Brand et al., 2014; Kalogrides & Grodsky, 2011). A school-to-work or vocational trade program may be a better fit for those who want the financial benefits of college but are worn out by the academic demands that keep so many students from advancing (Jerrim, 2014).

School to Work

Some scholars point out that education is often more effective when it directly links to your future career. In fact, students enrolled in preprofessional tracks like health or pre-law are less likely to leave school without a degree than are those enrolled in general studies programs (Baum et al., 2013). For some students, school-to-work programs that link education more closely to employment, called *career and technical education (CTE) programs*, are valuable alternatives to traditional college programs.

Critics of the U.S. higher education system often suggest that college does not cultivate enough of the skills students need to succeed in their careers (Hanushek et al., 2020). They point to technical and school-to-work programs, often inspired by those in Europe, as models that should be more available to young people in the United States (Barnow et al., 2021; Bonvillian & Sarma, 2021). In many European countries, more than half of high school students enroll in work-related educational programs that lead to internships, apprenticeships, and job placement (Musset, 2019). These are not the trade or vocational schools you may be familiar with in the United States. European vocational schools are sophisticated, technically demanding programs that prepare students for the highly automated jobs of the current economy (Billett, 2014; Hanushek et al., 2017).

Remember from the discussion of high school tracks in Chapter 10 that how education is organized varies around the world. In Germany, 10-year-olds are evaluated to see if they belong on a vocational or academic track (Ozer & Perc, 2020). In other countries, such as Finland, students have a more comprehensive academic education until tenth grade, after which they test into academic or vocational programs

Recruiting Apprentices D.J. is explaining the benefits of apprenticeship and careers in the pipe trades to students in Oshkosh, Wisconsin.

(Bol & Van de Werfhorst, 2013). Some in the United States object to the early tracking of students, but the programs in Europe give less academically oriented young people an alternative path to high-paying careers (Darling-Hammond, 2011; Woessmann, 2016).

European work-training and apprenticeship programs are often more prestigious than vocational education programs in the United States. For starters, model programs such as those in Germany or Switzerland typically pay students around $1,000 a month (Westervelt, 2012). Students enroll in these programs in the final years of high school, attending school a few days a week and spending the rest of the time paired with a mentor at an apprenticeship (Hanushek et al., 2017). In many ways, these programs seem ideal for young people because they help them develop nurturing relationships, provide an opportunity to do meaningful work, and, since they are paid, afford independence.

In the United States, most CTE programs are more limited than those available in Europe. Some successful career-to-work programs often integrate academic material with vocational learning (Cullen et al., 2013; Symonds et al., 2011). Students in these programs have a higher completion rate compared to students in traditional general education tracks (Zeidenberg et al., 2010).

The United States offers a school-to-work program in Job Corps, a residential program serving about 60,000 young people every year. The program focuses on helping young people earn a GED and gain practical skills. Although about 7 in 10 Job Corps participants find work after participating in the program, their wages and long-term prospects are only modestly higher than those of young people who do not participate in the program (Blanco et al., 2013; Schochet, 2018). Unlike European apprenticeships programs, Job Corps is a small, relatively short-term intervention that may not always help graduates develop the technical skills they need for top-paying trades or careers (Fahrenthold, 2014).

Some do find success through the program: San Diego Job Corps graduate Travon Scaife was able to get a management job in security after attending Job Corps. He explained that his instructor inspired him to succeed and feel optimistic about the future ("San Diego Job Corps," 2013). So, while college may not be for everyone, alternatives can make all the difference for young adults who seek another path to success.

APPLY IT! 12.8 College is an investment of time and money that often takes much longer than young people plan. Haruki wishes she had been able to build more relationships in college. What has helped you identify your own college goals?
12.9 "College for all" is a mantra in many U.S. high schools. Based on what you have learned in this chapter, what do you see as the strengths and risks of this strategy?

Gaining Skills through Job Corps
Mandy is a student at the Job Corps program in Astoria, Oregon, where she had the opportunity to learn cooking techniques on a Coast Guard boat stationed nearby.

Succeeding on the Job

For many young adults, work is not only where they spend most of their time, it is also an important source of identity. Work is a way to support yourself and can also connect you to your community, and for those who are lucky enough, be a source of meaning. Haruki certainly finds meaning in going to work every day: building relationships and helping younger people find their way through high school. Whether young people join the workforce right out of high school or work while in college or after graduation, early job experiences will impact young people's development throughout the lifespan.

Learning Objective

12.6 Analyze recent changes in employment and ways young people can identify their interests and employment strengths.

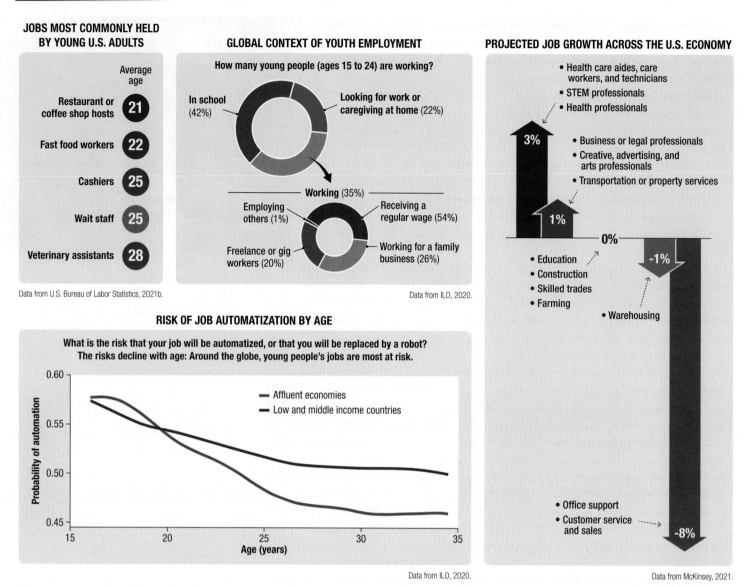

JOBS MOST COMMONLY HELD BY YOUNG U.S. ADULTS

Job	Average age
Restaurant or coffee shop hosts	21
Fast food workers	22
Cashiers	25
Wait staff	25
Veterinary assistants	28

Data from U.S. Bureau of Labor Statistics, 2021b.

GLOBAL CONTEXT OF YOUTH EMPLOYMENT

How many young people (ages 15 to 24) are working?

In school (42%)
Looking for work or caregiving at home (22%)
Working (35%)

Employing others (1%)
Receiving a regular wage (54%)
Freelance or gig workers (20%)
Working for a family business (26%)

Data from ILO, 2020.

PROJECTED JOB GROWTH ACROSS THE U.S. ECONOMY

- Health care aides, care workers, and technicians
- STEM professionals
- Health professionals

3%

- Business or legal professionals
- Creative, advertising, and arts professionals
- Transportation or property services

1%

0%
- Education
- Construction
- Skilled trades
- Farming

-1%
- Warehousing

- Office support
- Customer service and sales

-8%

Data from McKinsey, 2021.

RISK OF JOB AUTOMATIZATION BY AGE

What is the risk that your job will be automatized, or that you will be replaced by a robot? The risks decline with age: Around the globe, young people's jobs are most at risk.

— Affluent economies
— Low and middle income countries

Probability of automation (y-axis: 0.45, 0.50, 0.55, 0.60)
Age (years) (x-axis: 15, 20, 25, 30, 35)

Data from ILO, 2020.

FIGURE 12.3 How Many Young People Are Working? Young people are working in jobs across the economy, but careers in health care and technology are booming.

On the Job Training Senior Airman Christina Phillips, like many young adults, found a career in the military, the largest employer in the United States. Here she shows off her technical skills at Nellis Air Force Base in Nevada.

U.S. Air Force photo by Staff Sgt. Joshua Kleinholz

Who Is Working in Young Adulthood?

Haruki is like most college students and young adults: She has been working through college and plans to continue (Greene & Maggs, 2015). Like Haruki, about 60 percent of young adults in the United States are employed (U.S. Bureau of Labor Statistics, 2021b). (See **Figure 12.3**.) Others are able to focus on unpaid work, like internships or volunteering, during their college years. About one in eight young people is neither in the workforce or in college (NCES, 2021). In the United States and in most developed countries, youth unemployment has been high since the recession of 2008 and continues to stagnate because of the upheavals of the COVID-19 pandemic (ILO, 2021; Ross & Schowalter, 2020).In another reminder of the importance of college, the likelihood that young adults will be employed or in college or in some volunteer opportunity varies considerably depending on their level of education (see Figure 12.3). Young adults with some college are much more likely to be employed, or at least looking for work, than those with less education. Less educated young people are more likely to be unemployed or underemployed (Carnevale et al., 2013).

Some young people who are not working are excluded from these unemployment numbers because they are not looking for formal work. Economists and sociologists suspect that many of these people are working, but in informal gig work (Venkatesh, 2006). Researchers warn that these fragile work arrangements are more likely to be unstable and more stressful. It is often temporary, freelance, or part time (Staff et al., 2015). Young people, like many older people, increasingly find themselves cobbling together a living from various part-time and freelance jobs (Katz & Krueger, 2016). This unstable work may suit some people's independent spirit and allow them to find more work–family balance, but experts worry that it causes additional stress and can erode mental health (Macmillan & Shanahan, 2021).

There is significant inequality based on identity, family income, ethnicity, culture, and physical and cognitive disability in whether young people are in the workforce, what kinds of jobs they find, and how they succeed at work (Khatiwada & Sum, 2016). Discrimination in hiring is persistent and widespread around the globe. It can be based on appearance, ethnicity, and as for about 1 in every 100 young people, criminal history (Booker, 2016; Carnevale et al., 2019; Quillian et al., 2018; Wanberg et al., 2020). Inequality also impacts young people, as with those in rural areas, who may live too far from employment opportunities that meet their skills (Brooks, 2019).

Perhaps because so many jobs in our economy require more education, it is taking young people longer to find jobs with a good salary (Carnevale et al., 2013). In addition, work is unstable: Young people now tend to have about eight employers over the course of early adulthood (U.S. Bureau of Labor Statitics, 2021b). Only 1 in 10 of young adults says that their current job is their career job. And even for those with "career jobs" in industries previously considered stable, such as medicine or law, jobs can transform quickly, moving overseas or replacing people. Many jobs have moved outside of North America, with accountants, radiologists, or web developers elsewhere in the world responding to clients in the United States (Sako, 2014). Industrialization and advances in robotics mean that machines now do jobs that humans were once paid well to perform (Carnevale et al., 2018b).

How Do Young Adults Find Work?

Young people leave jobs four times more frequently than older people: staying in jobs for less than two years, on average (Gervais et al., 2016; Hairault et al., 2019). Part of this is because young people are looking for the "right fit," which may mean a more lucrative position or a career that better balances the needs of their young families (Marshall & Butler, 2015). Developmental science tells us that job transitions can be helpful. Job exploration, like identity exploration, can be critical to choosing the right career. The ideal is to find a job that matches your interests and values and gives you a sense of meaning.

Stages of Career Development The process of finding the right career extends over a lifetime. Some researchers break career development into a series of stages: *growth*, *career exploration*, *career establishment*, and *career maintenance*. These stages cycle over a lifetime and can restart as life demands (Super, 1953, 1992, 1994). The **growth stage** begins as big dreams in childhood and adolescence as children imagine themselves as race car drivers, basketball players, or movie stars. As individuals develop and become young adults, they enter a more practical stage, **career exploration**. In this stage, young people research various employment options. This stage is usually followed by **career establishment**, where a general interest is made a reality and becomes a job. Later in life, adults in the **maintenance stage** maintain their skills to keep up with a changing workplace, and they

growth stage The first stage of the process of career development that begins as ambitious dreams in childhood and adolescence.

career exploration The second stage of the process of career development in which young adults research employment options.

career establishment The third stage of the process of career development in which a general interest is made a reality and becomes a job.

maintenance stage The stage of the process of career development that occurs later in life in which people maintain their skills to keep up with a changing workplace, and may need to start all over again as the economy, their interests, or their life demand a change.

Joe Amon/The Denver Post via Getty Images

Hoping for a Better Opportunity
Michelle is protesting for paid sick leave and a higher minimum wage in Denver, Colorado. Like other young workers, she is looking for stable, well-paying work.

CONNECTIONS

This classic cycle of career development was influenced by Erikson and Marcia's ideas about identity development (see Chapter 11). Remember that in Marcia's theory of adolescent identity development, young people explore and commit to an identity in a process that is characterized by *diffusion*, *moratorium*, *foreclosure*, and *achievement*. The diffusion status is similar to the career growth stage. The moratorium status is much like career exploration, and the achievement status is analogous to career establishment.

may need to start all over again as the economy, their interests, or lives demands a change (Super, 1990).

Some young adults may end up in a job that does not reflect the outcome of career exploration. For example, David works in a meat-packing plant in the Midwest to support his family but dreams of a job in construction (Flores et al., 2011). For others, particularly those fortunate enough to get on a professional track or receive a college education, career development stages may be clearer and with easier transitions. No matter what type of job young people want, they will inevitably have to retool and cycle through these stages as they move through the lifespan. Haruki may be happy now working as a school counselor, but in the future, she may want to move to a new district or into an administrative position in another state, or perhaps to a new job at a nonprofit organization. She may have to adapt her skills and talents as her career shifts and grows.

Work Values and Interests No matter whether your job is designing computer games or marketing a sports team, researchers tell us that we will feel more satisfied and successful if we can find work that reflects our values, aligns with our interests, and meshes with our personality traits.

Just as people have values that guide their lives, they also hold values or beliefs about work. Developmentalists suggest that young people feel more satisfied and become more successful if they find work that reflects these values (Chow et al., 2017). **Work values** are the specific beliefs or core principles that we have that relate to work. They are in transition as young people begin to find jobs and begin careers (Jin & Rounds, 2012). Work values can include your ethnotheories or beliefs about the intrinsic value of work or whether you like your colleagues or feel satisfaction from helping people. Other work values may focus on the extrinsic benefits of work—the paycheck or generous vacation time.

Most adults want their work to be intrinsically satisfying, to do work for which they feel passion and find satisfying. Terry, who grew up in Baltimore, told a researcher that he kept looking and eventually found a job as an administrator for AmeriCorps, because "I just did that from following my heart, following my passion, which is doing something for other people" (DeLuca et al., 2016, p. 61). On the other hand, some people value a career based on prestige or financial stability.

In general, most adults value the intrinsic *and* extrinsic aspects of a job. Young people tend to hope for it all—ample vacation time, a good salary, a job they adore, and fun colleagues (Johnson & Monserud, 2012). Scientists are not sure whether finding a job that feels intrinsically rewarding, like Haruki's job, is more important than paying the bills, since both aspects of job satisfaction are important to well-being. But they do find that people who follow their hearts do tend to be a little happier in adulthood (Fukasawa et al., 2020).

Work values are one way to see if a job is a good fit; another way is to see if a career matches your interests. Not surprisingly, it is usually a better fit for both the employee and the employer if adults can find something that suits them (Nye et al., 2012; Rounds & Su, 2014). While children have countless interests, young adults tend to narrow down their areas of interest, becoming more interested than younger people in jobs that are social and involve generatively helping others as you can see in **Figure 12.4** (Hoff et al., 2018; Low & Rounds, 2007). Young adults who have jobs that are aligned with their interests are more likely to be successful at work and be more financially successful (Rounds & Su, 2014).

Sociologist John Holland (1997) has divided personalities and jobs into six categories: *realistic* (practical, concrete), *investigative* (research or problem-solving), *artistic, social, enterprising* (leadership), and *conventional* (order and structure). Understanding your own work personality can help you identify what types of career environments

work values The specific beliefs or core principles that relate to work.

might satisfy you. Most people may fit more than one of these categories and this fit may shift over time. Often, if young people find themselves in a career that matches their personality type, they stay in that line of work longer and feel more satisfied (Nauta, 2010).

Finding a Job with Meaning Many young people are unsure what they are interested in. Others may not have specific goals. As one young man explained to a researcher, "I don't really have goals for my future. What's the big deal about that?" (Damon, 2008, p. 28). The problem is that not having goals or a sense of purpose can make it difficult to become successful. Some adults even find life satisfaction by moving beyond following their interests to feeling like they have a purpose, a calling, or a meaning in life. About one in five young people reports having a strong sense of purpose, but about the same number lacks a clear sense of direction. Most young adults fall somewhere in the middle (Damon, 2008). But this sense of calling, like what inspires young firefighters to volunteer in Alaska or what led Eddie Ndopu to embark on a worldwide campaign for the rights of people with disabilities, can increase well-being (Sumner et al., 2018).

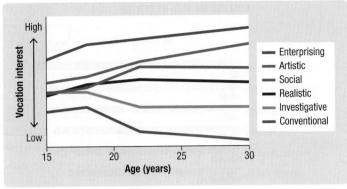

Data from Hoff et al., 2018.

FIGURE 12.4 Interests in Early Adulthood As young adults grow, their interests tend to change. People are more interested in careers that involve social interaction and less interested in more conventional jobs (like bookkeeping) or investigative jobs (like being a scientist). Careers in the arts or entrepreneurship remain popular.

Gender at Work

In more than 100 countries around the world, your gender assigned at birth impacts where you can work. For instance, people who identify as women are sometimes prohibited from even applying for certain jobs just because of their gender. In Russia, women are prohibited from being truck drivers on farms. In Argentina, women cannot be machinists (World Bank, 2015). Around the world, women earn about 60 percent of what men do (World Economic Forum, 2019). In the United States, people who identify as female have many more career choices than in many places in the world. However, the United States also has a gender-based wage gap that begins in young adulthood. Young people who identify as women in the United States earn just 90 percent of what men do, and this earning gap increases as young adults transition to parenthood (Brown & Patten, 2017; Sandler & Szembrot, 2019).

Work That Changes Lives Whether young people find a job as an emergency medical technician and volunteer firefighter, like these young people in Aniak, Alaska (*left*), or as an international human rights advocate, like Eddie Ndopu (*right*), finding work that aligns with your values can be inspiring and motivating.

COLLEGE MAJORS BY GENDER

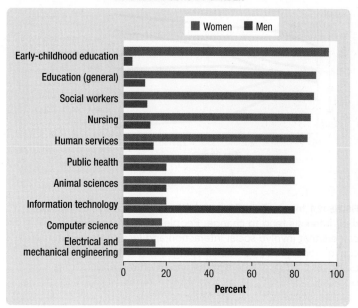

EARNING GROWTH BY EDUCATION AND COLLEGE MAJOR

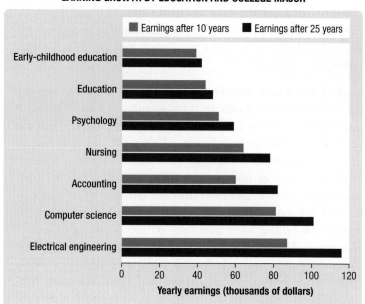

Data from Givens, 2021.

Data from Hamilton Project, n.d.

FIGURE 12.5 College Majors and Earnings When you chose your college major, did you think about the effects it might have on your future earnings? Men and women often choose different college majors. Some majors, particularly those in stereotypically male-dominated industries, are more likely to have significant earning growth after graduation.

U.S. Air National Guard photo by Tech. Sgt. Andrew Kleiser

Making a Job Transition While Still in Uniform As a member of the Illinois Air National Guard, Nick Hensley helped in vaccination campaigns during the COVID-19 pandemic but also found time to return to nursing school at Illinois State University. Career transitions like Nick's are common during young adulthood.

While many stereotypes have been dispelled, some jobs are still seen as typically "male" or "female" and most young people choose jobs and even college majors in line with gender stereotypes (see **Figure 12.5**). In an era when increasing numbers of adults identify as nonbinary or transgender, finding a fit in often-gendered markets can be difficult (Swenson et al., 2021). Some occupations, like construction and mining, tend to be overwhelmingly filled by people who identify as male. Others, like rehabilitation or nursing home care, tend to be overwhelmingly female (Cartwright et al., 2011). Not only do women end up segregated into lower-paid jobs, they also face increased discrimination when applying for jobs in male-dominated industries. Men do not face the same type of discrimination when applying for work in female-dominated industries, such as nursing or teaching (Koch et al., 2015; Yavorsky, 2019).

Over the past generation, the U.S. workforce has made major strides in becoming more inclusive. For instance, more than half of all medical school students are now women (Boyle, 2021). Health care has become a gender-integrated occupation. On the other hand, other high-status STEM careers, such as engineering, science, and computer science, are still overwhelmingly male (Corbett & Hill, 2015). Researchers point out that young women face discrimination, harassment, and bias even before they apply for a job in these industries and often avoid male-dominated college majors (Leaper & Starr, 2019; Sassler et al., 2017).

MAKING A DIFFERENCE
How to Land a Job That Works for You

For many young adults, finding a job is crucial to establishing an adult identity, a stepping stone similar to the other dreams, like finding a partner or having children (Mortimer, 2015). Some research suggests that taking time to find the right job—whether by trying different careers or staying true to your interests—may help you end up in a better paying and more satisfying career years later (Chow et al., 2015; Gervais et al., 2016). What do we know about finding the "right" job?

- Be ambitious. In the words of one researcher: Be "planful" and make finding the right job or career a priority (Clausen, 1991). One group of researchers found that young people who were not ambitious at 16 or 26 were more likely than their peers to struggle to find a job (Staff et al., 2010). No matter how challenging the world may be, young people who have higher expectations and stick to their dreams tend to end up with higher-paying and more satisfying jobs than their peers (Mortimer et al., 2014).

- Explore. Go to career days, volunteer, and ask for help. Young people who actively research careers are more likely to find jobs that are fulfilling and well-paying (Mortimer et al., 2014). College students may be able to access career centers for help in finding internships and learning about college majors and future careers. Young people who are ready for a job right out of high school are often at a disadvantage in finding job leads, because the pathway to work is often not clear. Be sure to ask questions about the long-term options for a career, not just the initial starting salary. Find out what kind of education is required and how people land jobs like these (Mortimer et al., 2002, 2014).

- Evaluate your own strengths. Your interests and personality are only two things that can contribute to your success at work, but they are a great place to start. Are you good at math? Do you love to write? Are you a musician? Thinking about what you are good at and enjoy may lead you to a vocational path.

- Consider your values. Even if you need to earn enough to pay student loans, focusing on the intrinsic values of work—that it is something you like and that feels meaningful—will pay off in the long run. If you enjoy your work, you will most likely be successful, which will lead to job satisfaction and more money. Even if you know that your goal is to be practical, dreaming a little may actually help you get there (Chow et al., 2015).

- Develop "soft" job skills. Employers look for communication skills, time management, punctuality, reliability, and creative problem solving (Chernyshenko et al., 2018; Lippman et al., 2015).

- Expect some transition pains. Work culture is different from the college environment, and the transition can be challenging. New workers are not evaluated regularly, they are often isolated and surrounded by colleagues who are different—many new employees do not feel that they belong (Wendlandt & Rochlen, 2008).

- Stick with it. Jobs are often routine, boring, and sometimes lonely. Young people are often disappointed with the lack of supervision and help from supervisors and by how little responsibility they are given (Wendlandt & Rochlen, 2008). Persistence in the face of such challenges can lead to greater success in the future (Duckworth & Gross, 2014; Rowan-Kenyon et al., 2017).

APPLY IT! **12.10** Haruki has found a job that makes her feel useful in a community where she feels that she belongs. She's been able to combine her interest in people and with a job that gives her purpose. Do you have a sense of purpose or meaning in your life that helps drive your career aspirations?

12.11 Employment structures are often unequitable, often segregated by family income, education, gender, and ethnicity (among other variables). How do scholars suggest that individuals can persevere to find meaningful work?

Wrapping It Up ⊙⊙

LO 12.1 Identify the key historical markers and common variations in adulthood. (p. 348)

The markers of adulthood are flexible to match the changing expectations of each culture, time, and place. Biological maturation is variable. There are five aspirational markers of adulthood: finishing school; establishing an independent household; finding work; finding a romantic partner; and having children. Most young adults do not reach these markers because of changing cultural expectations and economic strains. Some scholars suggest that there is a new life stage called *emerging adulthood*, in which young people explore who they are in their 20s. Other scholars suggest that this exploration may be a privilege. Young adults are more profoundly shaped by historical events, like the COVID-19 pandemic, than other age groups.

LO 12.2 Describe the characteristics of brain development in early adulthood. (p. 353)

The brain is not fully mature until adults are in their mid-20s or mid-30s. The brain is very plastic and easily shaped by the environment as adults adapt to new roles. The areas of the brain devoted to social and emotional processing mature during early adulthood. Connections between the subcortical structures that process emotion and the more logical prefrontal cortex are still not quite mature, allowing young adults to be more emotionally reactive and more optimistic about taking risks than adults, helping to power all the new adventures that young adulthood has in store.

LO 12.3 List four ways of describing the flexible thinking of young adults. (p. 353)

Scholars observe that young adults' thinking can become more relativistic as they grow, acknowledging that there is no absolute truth but different valuable perspectives. Dialectical thinking acknowledges that there are different viewpoints and that the ideal solution may be found from a hybrid position. A stage of thinking called *postformal thought* is inspired by Jean Piaget's stages and suggests that adult thought is flexible, nonbinary, and more aware of the human variability in real-life decisions. Higher education can help young adults build more flexible thinking skills. Sleep and social support are healthy ways to help boost learning.

LO 12.4 Discuss health risks and positive health practices in early adulthood. (p. 358)

Many young people feel that their health is good during early adulthood; however, young adults may die as a result of substance use and violence. Young people can build healthy habits by maximizing their nutrition, getting exercise, and maintaining a healthy body image. Some young adults have difficulties with binge drinking and substance use.

LO 12.5 Describe the benefits of college and challenges to success in college. (p. 363)

In affluent countries around the world, schooling often continues long into early adulthood. College has many benefits to health, social relationships, and employment but is not always an easy fit for young people. Many take a long time to graduate and may not complete their degree. Students who are low-income and who do not feel connected to campus community tend to be more likely to have difficulties in college. Scholars suggest that students need more support to succeed. There is a gender gap in education: More women than men are attending college, although because men tend to enter more high-income occupations, men continue to earn more than women. College programs that connect school to work can provide good opportunities.

LO 12.6 Analyze recent changes in employment and ways young people can identify their interests and employment strengths. (p. 369)

A globalized, technological economy means that work is often less permanent than it was in generations past. Many well-paying jobs require some college education or post-high school training. Young people often change jobs frequently. Some scholars break career development into four stages: growth, career exploration, career establishment, and career maintenance. Others examine our *work values*, or beliefs about whether work should fulfill our intrinsic or extrinsic needs or align with our interests. Finding a job that gives you a sense of purpose can boost well-being over the long term. Work often reflects gender stereotypes and pervasive gender-based discrimination.

KEY TERMS

early adulthood (p. 348)
emerging adulthood (p. 351)
relativistic thinking (p. 355)

dialectical thinking (p. 355)
postformal thought (p. 356)
binge drinking (p. 362)

growth stage (p. 371)
career exploration (p. 371)
career establishment (p. 371)

maintenance stage (p. 371)
work values (p. 372)

CHECK YOUR LEARNING

1. Which of the following is a marker for the beginning of adulthood?
   a) When your body has finished maturing
   b) When you stop going to school
   c) When you take on adult responsibilities
   d) When you are recognized as adults by your community

2. What are the possible advantages of a brain that is continuing to mature into early adulthood?
   a) It can be more easily damaged by head injuries.
   b) It is more susceptible to poor decision-making.
   c) It is more flexible as adults adapt to new roles.
   d) It drains more energy from physical growth.

3. Early adulthood is a time of rapid maturation of the brain structures related to:
   a) sensory processing.
   b) motor skill development.
   c) social relationships.
   d) language development.

4. What one health condition is NOT linked to having a positive body image during early adulthood?
   a) Likelihood of engaging in physical activity
   b) Resilience to feelings of depression
   c) Resilience to unhealthy eating habits
   d) Protection from developing plague

5. The type of reasoning that evaluates both sides of a problem is called:
   a) dialectical reasoning.
   b) formal operational thought.
   c) analytical thinking.
   d) heuristic thinking.

6. One challenge faced by students in college is that:
   a) young adults are too old to learn.
   b) college is no longer necessary for success.
   c) students often do not have the financial or social supports they need to succeed.
   d) students are not mature enough to take advantage of what college has to offer.

7. Why might be wrong with the notion of "college for all"?

8. Why have communities often looked down on career or technical education programs?

9. How has employment changed over the past 20 years?
   a) More automatization and use of robotics in many jobs
   b) Increased globalization of employment
   c) More short-term, gig work
   d) All of the above

10. Which is NOT a way that scholars have analyzed career development?
    a) Work values
    b) Career personality type
    c) Stages of career development
    d) Association with blood pressure

Changing Family Relationships

13.1 Explain how family relationships often become closer and more interdependent in young adulthood.

What Is This Thing Called Love?

13.2 Describe major theories of love in young adulthood.

13.3 Explain how culture and education shape partnering.

New Family Relationships

13.4 Describe common variations in family and parenting relationships during young adulthood.

When Young Adults Need More Support

13.5 Explain why some young adults experience mental health difficulties.

Community Engagement

13.6 Describe the patterns of civic engagement among young people.

Selected Resources from

 Achieve

Activities

Concept Practice: Attraction and Romantic Love

Spotlight on Science: Attachment Security and Romantic Relationships

Assessments

LearningCurve

Practice Quiz

Videos

Scientific American Profiles

How Online Dating is Affecting Society

COVID-19 and Mental Health in Young Adults

© Macmillan, Photo by Sidford House

Kevin is in his mid-20s, manages a team of nine in the banking industry, and lives on his own; he even helps his parents with their expenses. Even though Kevin now feels like an adult, making his mother proud still brings him joy.

Like many young people, Kevin did not have a predictable path through young adulthood. His mother wanted him to go to college. She and his stepfather moved to Atlanta, Georgia, from Mexico City so that Kevin and his two siblings would have an easier life. But college was not a good fit for Kevin.

Instead, after high school, Kevin went to work as a waiter until the constant routine of double shifts began to wear on him. He wanted to find something new and meaningful, so he began reading investment books and watching inspirational YouTube videos on his days off. His co-workers were not sure he was on the right path; his parents were worried.

Kevin found one mentor and then another who was willing to explain banking to a motivated young person. Kevin eagerly put in long hours and had a knack for working with other people and connecting with new clients. His efforts paid off: He became a manager and now crosses the country, giving presentations and even mentoring younger people himself.

Even though Kevin has been able to save money and has a girlfriend he adores as well as a steady career, the path forward is not always clear. Should he keep working long hours? Does he need to spend more time at home? When should he think about getting married and starting a family?

Kevin's story is exceptional, but it highlights the sometimes conflicting roles and paths toward adulthood. There is no typical order to life events such as childbearing, marriage, education, and work. Like many young people, Kevin first found a job and then eventually a place of his own. Even though he has a good job, is able to help his parents, and is saving for his first house, he does not feel quite settled.

Becoming an adult means navigating new relationships and roles, which may or may not include starting a family, graduating from college, or getting a house of your own. Relationships — whether with partners, friends, or children — can be one of the joys of life, but they also bring new challenges. Despite the inevitable challenges young adults face, there are also opportunities to build resilience as they take on new responsibilities. Like Kevin, many young adults strive to make a difference in the wider world by working or volunteering in their community.

Scientific American Profile

Meet Kevin

Changing Family Relationships

Young people's relationships with their families do not usually change dramatically after adolescence, although some families mark the transition with rituals or informal markers like being allowed to sit at the "adult table" for Thanksgiving dinner (Settersten, 2011, p. 262). Relationships tend to remain close, or get even closer, as both parents and children begin to respect each other's independence and relate more as equals (Padilla-Walker et al., 2021). But parents tend to remain parents: Kevin says that despite his independence, his mother still pesters him about getting enough sleep. Nevertheless, most young people maintain close family connections even as they build new lives of their own (Oliveira et al., 2020).

Learning Objective

13.1 Explain how family relationships often become closer and more interdependent in young adulthood.

Closer Ties

Now with their own independent lives, most young adults value their relationships with their families *more* than in adolescence. They find time spent with family more satisfying and less conflictual (Fang et al., 2021; Fuligni & Masten, 2010). Many young people feel more obligation and responsibility to their families than they did as teenagers (Tsai et al., 2013). Parents remain a critical source of advice and sometimes financial support, which becomes more reciprocal as young-adult children are able to contribute to their families in return. Kevin says he appeciates his mother's sacrifices for him even more now than he did as a teenager: He is still proud to wear the headphones she bought for him so he would fit in with his peers during high school.

Parents and children often stay in frequent contact if they live together, or they call, text, and visit if they are living apart. Half of all parents communicate with their adult children every day—and nearly all at least once a week (Fingerman et al., 2020; Fingerman & Suitor, 2017). These connections seem to benefit not only young people but also their parents (Fingerman et al., 2012).

Close and positive relationships are not universal: Young people may feel rejected or marginalized in their families or even be estranged (Scharp & Dorrance Hall, 2017). Some reports estimate that as many as 4 in 10 have been estranged at some point from a family member (Conti, 2015). Such young people are more likely to develop depression and have difficulties in college or finding a career (Doty & Mortimer, 2018; Hong et al., 2021; Steele & McKinney, 2020). Being unable to draw upon parents' advice, experience, and financial support often leads to more difficulty with the complexities of becoming a successful adult (Chainey & Burke, 2021; Hartnett et al., 2018).

Shared Support

The support provided by parents to adult children is not just emotional. Gifts of financial support, advice, and child care for young people who are parents themselves

In Young Adulthood, Family Support Comes in Different Forms. Sometimes supporting a young adult means supporting their children. Here Grandma shows her granddaughter some cooking techniques at home in Pennsylvania while her mother gets to enjoy some family time of her own.

Scientific American Profile

Changing Family Relationships

📱 **Share It!**

Young people around the world suffered more economic damage than did other age groups during the COVID-19 pandemic. They were more likely to be out of work.

(OECD, 2021)

ᴍ **Scientific American: Lifespan Development**

are typical across income levels (Napolitano et al., 2020; Swartz et al., 2017). In the United States, more than 7 in 10 young adults get some financial support from their families (Herron, 2019). That support is often freely given, but some families may disagree on how much support is needed for young adults to eventually reach financial independence (Lanz et al., 2020; Lowe & Arnett, 2020). Open communication is likely to reduce such conflict (LeBaron et al., 2020).

In many communities, young people begin to offer more support to their parents, either financially or in the form of help with household chores or younger siblings (Fuligni & Pedersen, 2002; Napolitano, 2015; Trieu, 2016). Many young adults around the world provide care to younger siblings and disabled or aging family members (D'Amen et al., 2021; Haugland et al., 2020). Although this sense of obligation is characteristic of all groups in the United States, it tends to be stronger in Latino American and Asian American families (Guan & Fuligni, 2016; Swartz, 2009). Remaining connected to family by helping and supporting each other becomes, for many young people, an enduring part of their adult self (Swartz & Busse, 2017).

Close relationships are beneficial, but parenting that violates young adults' autonomy is not. Overinvolved parenting, sometimes called *helicopter parenting*, is a form of control over young-adult children that is sometimes driven by the parents' own anxieties (Jiao & Segrin, 2021). Although researchers have found that helicopter parents are uncommon in real life, this type of parenting often appears in media portrayals of affluent U.S. families (Padilla-Walker et al., 2021). So-called helicopter parents might track their young-adult children online, call college presidents to complain about the cafeteria food, or challenge college instructors' grading (Fingerman & Suitor, 2017; Lythcott-Haims & Doyle, 2015; McKenna, 2017). Unsurprisingly, in early adulthood as in other times of the lifespan, families who are overly controlling and overinvolved tend to be harmful. Too much parental control is associated with frustration, depression, and even difficulties in school and work (Darlow et al., 2017; Schiffrin et al., 2019).

Staying or Returning Home

Today, most young adults in the United States and in many other affluent countries live at home with their families (OECD, 2021; U.S. Census, 2020a). Throughout history, this is quite typical (Goldscheider & Goldscheider, 1999; Mintz, 2015). The notion that young adults are supposed to live on their own and be independent by their early 20s was possible for only a few young people in the United States in the post–World War II era, when housing was inexpensive and well-paying jobs were plentiful.

Around the world, most young people live at home with their parents, even when an economic crisis has not forced them to make that choice, as you can see in **Figure 13.1** (Kleinepier et al., 2017). For instance, more than 6 in 10 young people in Japan live at home (Crocetti et al., 2015). In Algeria, Mexico, India, and Kenya, married couples expect to live with their parents while beginning their lives together, and most young people cannot afford to set out on their own (Juárez & Gayet, 2014; Kovacheva et al., 2018). Only in a few places with exceptional government supports, a strong job market, and affordable housing, like the northern European countries of Denmark and Finland, do most young people live independently in their 20s (Coulter et al., 2020; Flynn, 2020).

In the United States, sharing a home with family is particularly common for young people who are not earning high incomes and in some immigrant, Latino, and Asian American communities (Gillespie et al., 2020). Similarly, for young adults with cognitive or physical disabilities, living at home is typical, particularly for those who lack access to appropriate social supports (Eilenberg et al., 2019; Friedman, 2019; Gorter et al., 2014). It tends to be less common among Black and White families (Fry, 2016; Lei & South, 2016). For many, living with family is ideal, enabling them to save money and attend college

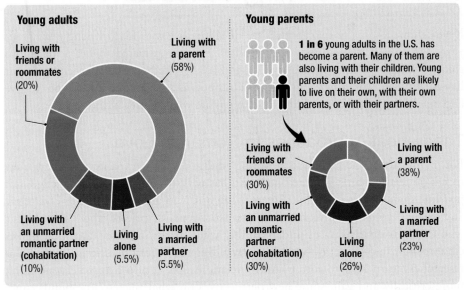

LIVING ARRANGEMENTS IN THE UNITED STATES

Young adults

Living with friends or roommates (20%)

Living with a parent (58%)

Living with an unmarried romantic partner (cohabitation) (10%)

Living alone (5.5%)

Living with a married partner (5.5%)

Young parents

1 in 6 young adults in the U.S. has become a parent. Many of them are also living with their children. Young parents and their children are likely to live on their own, with their own parents, or with their partners.

Living with friends or roommates (30%)

Living with a parent (38%)

Living with an unmarried romantic partner (cohabitation) (30%)

Living alone (26%)

Living with a married partner (23%)

Data from U.S. Census, 2021.   Data from Valerio, 2021.

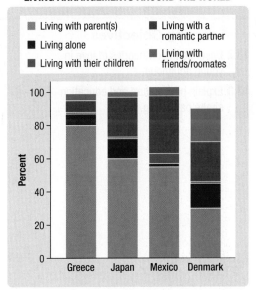

LIVING ARRANGEMENTS AROUND THE WORLD

Living with parent(s)   Living with a romantic partner

Living alone   Living with friends/roomates

Living with their children

Percent (y-axis: 0, 20, 40, 60, 80, 100)

Greece   Japan   Mexico   Denmark

Data from OECD, 2021.

FIGURE 13.1 Where Do Young Adults Live? Where young adults live tends to depend on the social supports that are available to them. In the United States, most young people live with their parents, although young parents are more likely to live on their own or with a romantic partner.

while maintaining close relationships with parents and siblings (Lei & South, 2016; Payne, 2019; Roberts et al., 2016).

Living at home is often the result of challenging economic times: High-paying jobs require more time in school, and housing is less affordable than it once was (Mawhorter, 2017). As a result, there are inequalities in the United States and in other affluent communities in whether young people can afford to live independently, particularly in expensive cities (Newman et al., 2018). This economic inequality builds: Young people with affluent parents are able to buy a home or live on their own, further boosting them above their less-affluent peers (Hochstenbach, 2018; Ronald & Lennartz, 2019).

At the other end of the economic spectrum, young people without college degrees are less likely to buy or rent their own home in their 20s (Mawhorter, 2017). About one in five young adults who do live independently falls under the poverty line (Hawkins, 2019). If young people have children, they are even more likely to have low income. Nearly 4 in 10 of all households with children headed by a young adult are poor (Annie E. Casey, 2018).

In the United States during the COVID-19 pandemic, more than 6 in 10 young adults lived with their parents (U.S. Census Bureau, 2020a). For some of them, moving back home was supposed to be temporary: Campus closures meant that college students needed to move back home and attend classes online. Others lost their jobs and moved in with their family because they no longer could afford their rent. Many families adjusted to this change, appreciating the opportunity to spend more time together. For other families, having extra adults at home created strain, particularly in communities already experiencing overcrowding because of the lack of affordable housing and the general uncertainty of a pandemic (Evandrou et al., 2021; Hall & Zygmunt, 2021).

APPLY IT! 13.1 Kevin lives on his own but still checks in with his parents (and younger brother) multiple times a week and helps them financially. How does this describe typical patterns found in many family relationships in young adulthood? **13.2** Many of us have our own ethnotheories about what young adults are "supposed to do." What expectations do you have about what young adulthood is supposed to be like? How do they align with your own lived experiences?

Living on Your Own Means Washing the Dishes. Chris lives on his own in an apartment in Atlanta, Georgia, with two other young people. Living independently often poses challenges for young adults with disabilities, but Chris and his roommates receive daily visits from professional support services, which make things easier.

What Is This Thing Called Love?

Learning Objectives

13.2 Describe major theories of love in young adulthood.

13.3 Explain how culture and education shape partnering.

Kevin knows a thing or two about love. He fell in love with his girlfriend nearly four years ago after searching apps and websites. He was attracted to her adventurous spirit: She loves to rock climb, skydive, and try new things. She is an entrepreneur like Kevin: She is building her own small business as a baker. She loves to be creative and helps him remember that the little things are what matter in life.

Theoretical Approaches to Romantic Love

For many, one of the hallmarks of young adulthood is the capability to create new romantic relationships like the one Kevin has with his girlfriend. A challenge, not just for Kevin but for all adults, is to figure out who and how to love. Over time and history, romantic love has been studied by poets, priests, and psychologists who each have their way of understanding what sparks intimacy and what makes close relationships function well. Understanding the theory behind intimacy helps researchers learn how to foster healthy relationships. It also helps everyone think more critically and gain some new perspectives on what makes close bonds function, giving us new vocabulary to describe the feelings and relationships that often shape adult life.

Intimacy Versus Isolation Erik Erikson's theory describes a key conflict of young adulthood as the struggle between **intimacy and isolation**. In his view, the successful resolution of this developmental stage is finding love, which entails not only physical intimacy but also a joint commitment to "significant sacrifices and compromises" and to making a new life together. To Erikson, who spent almost 65 years working, writing, and raising four children with his wife, Joan, the ideal life is built on the foundation of a close adult relationship. The antithesis of this *intimacy* was, in his mind, *isolation*, a life spent separate and uncommitted.

Erikson recognized that being in a relationship does not necessarily mean that one has achieved intimacy: He witnessed many young adults suffering in relationships that were merely joint isolation. The successful resolution of this stage, according to Erikson, requires companionship in which each partner creates a better life together: not because they are afraid of being alone, but because they have learned how to make a commitment (Erikson & Erikson, 1998).

In contrast with Erikson, many contemporary researchers point out that adults can be fulfilled without commitment or romance. Adults can build closeness in friendships, in family relationships, or in shared meaningful work (DePaulo, 2017). A committed partnership may have worked for the Eriksons, but increasingly among young adults around the world, closeness and love take different forms. Having a partner in early adulthood (or across the lifespan) does not mean that you are healthier or more "typical": In fact, most young adults are not partnered, and being partnered is no guarantee of psychological health (van den Berg & Verbakel, 2021). In addition, whereas Erikson optimistically assumed that development was linear, and that adults moved from establishing an identity to finding a partner as they grew, many contemporary scholars suggest that many young adults are still discovering who they are: a process of identity development and personality change that continues throughout early adulthood (Landberg et al., 2018).

The Attachment Approach Attachment theorists, as explained in Chapter 2, believe that adults' habits of relating—whether they trust their partners and want to be close—are formed over a lifetime by other relationships, including their relationships with their caregivers as infants and their friendships and caregiving experiences later

Scientific American Profile

Finding the Perfect Life Partner

CONNECTIONS

Intimacy versus isolation is the conflict described in Erikson's sixth stage, early adulthood. Chapter 11 reviewed the stage of identity versus role confusion: The quest for identity often continues into early adulthood.

intimacy and isolation Erikson's stage of human development that occurs in young adulthood. In his view, the successful resolution of the crisis is finding love.

in childhood and adolescence (Fraley & Roisman, 2019; Hazan & Shaver, 1987; Mikulincer & Shaver, 2021).

Recall from Chapter 5 that researchers measure infant–caregiver relationships in terms of attachment styles, categorized as *secure, anxious, avoidant,* and *disorganized.* Adult attachment researchers measure romantic relationships in a similar way: They look at how well romantic partners interact with their partners when they are stressed and how well they comfort each other (Fraley, 2019). Attachment researchers have also tested adults' attachments in a real-life version of the Strange Situation, watched how couples separate and reunite in airports, and observed how attachment styles are associated with neurotransmitters in the brain (Turtonen et al., 2021).

Many researchers use interviews and surveys to determine how young adults relate to their partners. Trained interviewers may talk to people about their current or past relationships or ask them to complete surveys about how they feel (Fraley, 2019; George et al., 1985; Main et al., 1985). As a result of this work, scientists have found that attachment continues to describe how adults relate. Some young adults have a *secure relationship style*: They are confident that their partners are available and supportive of them. Others are less so.

Researchers find that there are two key dimensions of attachment insecurity—*anxiety* and *avoidance.* They suggest we often take these habits of relating with us from childhood into new relationships (Chopik et al., 2021; Mikulincer & Shaver, 2021; Sandberg et al., 2017). People who have an *anxious relationship style* are unsure whether their partner will be there for them and need a lot of reassurance about their affection. People who have an *avoidant relationship style* believe that their partner will be unable to offer comfort and disengage as a result. They tend to be less open, intimate, and connected with their partners, believing it is safer to manage their feelings on their own.

How closely young people or their relationships fit these descriptions depends on the kind of relationship they are in, their level of stress, and what else is going on in their lives. These dimensions, like any way of categorizing people or relationships, are not absolute or permanent and often change over the history of a relationship and over the lifespan (Chopik et al., 2013; Fraley, 2019). Nevertheless, relationship styles impact how relationships develop, how happy the partners are, and even whether adults end up in a relationship at all. They have been found to be important regardless of the genders involved (Sommantico et al., 2021). Attachment styles impact not only romantic relationships but also the kind of friend or parent you become (Mikulincer & Shaver, 2019).

The Triangular Theory of Love You probably have a sense of what someone means when they say, "I completely fell for them." Psychologist Robert Sternberg made an abstraction like falling in love measurable: His **triangular theory of love** describes the different types of romantic relationships as varying degrees of three components that change over time (Sternberg, 1986).

- *Intimacy* is the feeling of closeness that comes from sharing emotions and moods with a partner. When someone says that their first weeks of romance were filled with time spent "talking about each other, talking about your stories from the past," they are talking about the development of intimacy in a relationship (Marie, 2014a).

- *Passion* is the rush of energy and sexual excitement that propels the feelings of desire and "falling in love." When one young woman explains that "Ruby is the most beautiful creature in the world, and I love her energy. She just glows," she is talking about passion (Out.com, 2015).

- *Commitment* is the decision to support, love, and form a long-term bond with someone. As one young woman, Sandhya, explained after she got married, "Marriage is for keeps. This is forever. It's not like buying a dress, not like, 'If it doesn't fit, I'll throw this [away] and get a new one'" (Marie, 2014b).

CONNECTIONS

Remember that attachment theory was developed by John Bowlby and others (see Chapter 2). Refer to Chapter 5 for a refresher on the theory of attachment in infancy, including the attachment styles based on the work of Mary Ainsworth, which classifies caregiving relationships as secure or insecure.

Welcome Home Sgt. Johnathan Link was welcomed home by his girlfriend, Christine, after he served nine months in Afghanistan. Scientists sometimes study couples reuniting to understand their attachment styles.

 Learn It Together

Understanding Attachment Styles During Young Adulthood

Plan Review the different adult attachment styles with their romantic partners.

Engage Find two partners, and each of you take one of the attachment styles. Each person should imagine a young adult in a romantic relationship, give them a name, and describe the type of relationship that they have with their partner. Contrast the different styles and talk about what each person would be like with one of the other styles.

Reflect Do you think the adult attachment styles are similar to those during infancy than you learned about earlier in class? Do you think this is a useful way to categorize romantic relationships during young adulthood?

triangular theory of love Sternberg's theory that there are different types of romantic relationships with varying degrees of intimacy, passion, and commitment.

Kind of love	Component		
	Intimacy	Passion	Commitment
Nonlove	♡	♡	♡
Liking	♥	♡	♡
Infatuated love	♡	♥	♡
Empty love	♡	♡	♥
Romantic love	♥	♥	♡
Companionate love	♥	♡	♥
Fatuous love	♡	♥	♥
Consummate love	♥	♥	♥

Most relationships fall somewhere within the spectrum of possibilities described by the discrete categories of Sternberg's triangular theory of love.

Liking

Romantic love — Companionate love

Consummate love

Infatuated love — Fatuous love — Empty love

FIGURE 13.2 What Makes Love? In Sternberg's triangular theory of love, relationships are theorized to be made up of a mix of intimacy, passion, and commitment.

Mixing Traditions Like many couples, Catherine and Max grew up in different faith communities. Catherine identifies as Roman Catholic and Max as Jewish. For their wedding in New York, they plan to blend religious traditions from both of their faiths.

These three components can be combined to produce seven different types of love relationships. *Liking*, in this case, is when you feel really close and open with someone but lack the spark of passion. *Infatuation* is a passionate crush, when you cannot get someone out of your mind even if you do not know them very well. *Empty love* is when you have made a commitment but do not feel anything for that person. *Fatuous love* is feeling attracted to and passionate about someone without sharing your feelings or your intimate self with them. For many, the ideal form of love is *consummate love*, which includes commitment, passion, and intimacy. *Companionate love* includes commitment and intimacy but no passion, and *passionate love* includes intimacy and sexual desire without commitment.

Culture and Love Anthropologists and other scholars remind us that romantic love exists across cultures and throughout human history (Fletcher et al., 2015; Hatfield et al., 2007; Jankowiak & Nelson, 2021). Romantic practices vary both within and across communities worldwide. Some young people are encouraged to date widely; others are encouraged to take a more conservative approach (Martinez et al., 2021). Some couples feel compelled to dress up on a first date; others keep it casual (Lamont, 2017). But universally, when they are surveyed, young people recognize love: Around the globe, they explain that falling in love makes both partners happy, confident, and even a little obsessed with each other (Jankowiak et al., 2015). Love makes you feel generous, emotionally understood, preoccupied with the other person (whom you idealize) and interested in sexual intimacy (Nelson & Yon, 2019).

What adults expect from relationships differs across cultures and time. For instance, some expect passion to be a part of committed love, but this is not universal. For instance, in the 1960s, 7 in 10 U.S. women said they would be happy to marry someone they did not love. Today, passionate love is a marriage prerequisite for more than 80 percent of young people in the United States (Reis & Aron, 2008; Simpson et al., 1986). This is not the case for everyone: In many communities, young people report that they prefer to have less fiery, companionate love. For instance, in a recent survey in Algeria, more than half of all married respondents reported that love was not a significant factor in their choice of a spouse (Friedland et al., 2016). Similarly, in India, anthropologists report that families value companionate love over passion in choosing a partner (Donner, 2016).

In many places, adults have intimate relationships that involve more than one person. Anthropologists have found that more than 85 percent of cultures have a history of formal partnerships with multiple people. However, most of these relationships were limited to a few relatively elite, mostly male, adults (Fletcher et al., 2015). Today, in some western African nations, about one in five families is *polygamous*, where one man has multiple wives (Pew Research Center, 2019). In a few places, particularly in the high peaks of the Himalayas, between India and China, some women have more than one husband, called *polyandry* (Rahimzadeh, 2020; Tiwari, 2008).

Whereas complex formal relationships are relatively uncommon, complex informal relationships are more prevalent. Sometimes these relationships are non-consensual. For instance, about one in five adults reports that they have had a lover during a committed relationship (Fletcher et al., 2015). In the United States, surveys typically report that about 1 in 12 adults is currently in a nonconsensual multipartner relationship (Levine et al., 2018). However, in many communities, infidelity violates many moral and religious expectations, so adults are frequently uncomfortable talking about those relationships, even with their health care providers (Chamie, 2018).

Another type of multipartner relationship is **polyamory**, the term for relationships that include romantic or sexual relationships between more than two consenting people. Some of these relationships may be committed and long-term, and others may be more fleeting (Balzarini et al., 2019). About 1 in every 25 people in the United States reports that they are in an "open" or polyamorous partnership (Levine et al., 2018). Some researchers suggest that polyamory may be even more prevalent (Andres, 2021; Olmstead, 2020). In many communities, monogamous relationships are seen as normative, and polyamorous partnerships face stigma, a challenge for such families (Klesse, 2019).

The Biology of Love If you have ever fallen in love, as have one in four college students, you likely remember the physical signs and signals: the racing heartbeat, the obsessive thoughts, and the rush of excitement (Aron et al., 1995). Researchers theorize that a number of biological factors come into play when we fall in love or experience long-term attachment, including changes in neurotransmitters, hormones, and brain activation. The biological factors that influence passionate love, companionate love, and sexual attraction are distinct but overlapping systems (Acevedo et al., 2020; Cacioppo, 2019).

Brain scans of people in love who are viewing images of their loved ones reveal activation in the reward system, including two subcortical structures: the *insula*, which is involved in emotion, and the *striatum*, which is involved in the reward circuit (Fisher et al., 2016; Kawamichi et al., 2016; Reis et al., 2013; Watanuki & Akama, 2020). Remember that the reward system is filled with dopamine, which increases when we feel passion (Barash, 2016; Cacioppo et al., 2012; Takahashi et al., 2015). So, it is unsurprising that some neuroscientists have compared being in love with being addicted to cocaine, although presumably it is better for you (Fisher et al., 2016; Wang et al., 2020). Even though who and how adults love differs according to individual preferences and cultures, researchers have observed activation in the same areas of the brain. For instance, the reward system is activated in fMRI scans in studies of couples in China and the United States regardless of their gender preferences (Reis et al., 2013).

Interestingly, the *anterior insula*, the part of the insula that is closest to the forehead, is activated when adults are experiencing romantic love, but the *posterior insula*, the part situated toward the back of the head, is activated when adults feel sexual attraction (Cacioppo, 2019). Just how important is the insula to love? For one couple, it

Share It!

France is for lovers. A [slim] majority of French adults think relationships outside of marriage are morally acceptable.

(Pew Research Center, 2014)

Scientific American: Lifespan Development

All You Need Is Love. Gabriel, May, Federico, and Deb, pictured in a park near their home in Buenos Aires, Argentina, are in a long-standing polyamorous relationship. Deb describes their bond as dynamic and open, based on meeting real needs rather than establishing ownership.

CONNECTIONS

Remember from Chapter 10 that the subcortical structures, including the reward system, play an important role in emotion and pleasure across the lifespan. Dopamine, the neurotransmitter responsible for pleasure in the reward system, triggers enjoyment of everything from gelato to good grades.

polyamory The practice or interest in romantic or sexual relationships between more than two consenting adults.

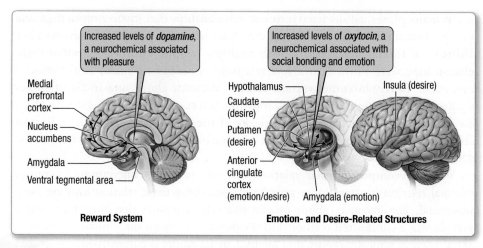

FIGURE 13.3 The Brain on Love Scientists have scanned the brains of young adults and found that distinctive regions of their brain were activated, including the reward system and emotion-related structures.

was critical. An Argentinian man whose insula was damaged from a stroke reported feeling sexual desire but could no longer love. Scientists could not find a cure, and his wife subsequently filed for divorce (Cacioppo et al., 2013; Heyman, 2017).

A different set of brain systems is involved in companionate love, or attachment, and is triggered not by dopamine (the pleasure hormone) but by oxytocin, the bonding hormone described in Chapter 3. Perhaps unsurprisingly, the brain systems involved in ongoing relationships are linked to brain systems that are involved in other social behaviors, such as empathy and parenting (see **Figure 13.3**; Feldman, 2019; Lieberwirth & Wang, 2016). Sexual attraction, passionate love, and companionate love are biologically distinguishable in both our brains and in lived experience.

Finding a Partner

Many young adults are not terribly interested in what we know about the theories of love. Many want to know how to find the right person (see **Figure 13.4**). Researchers are interested in how young adults find each other, not just necessarily because they want to help young people find the one (or ones), but because romance has an out-sized impact on our life. For instance, romance often leads to starting a family and sharing a home and finances, practices that shape communities and our life course. In addition, it is often shaped by the social structures and institutions around us.

FIGURE 13.4 What Are You Looking for in a Partner? Scientists have found that what you think you like does not always predict who you will end up with in real life: Most adults report they are looking for a partner who is funny and intelligent. But when scientists observe who is perceived as desirable by analyzing who clicks online, they find that contact is often driven by demographic factors like age, a bias that often favors older men.

Finding Romance There are 6 million people on Tinder, another 5 million on Grindr, and another 10 million on the Chinese dating app Jiayuan, but most will likely end up with people who live near them and who share similar backgrounds (Haandrikman, 2019; Huber & Malhotra, 2017; Iqbal, 2021; Thomala, 2021). Even when couples meet online, our tendency to like people who we think are similar to us, called *homophily*, plays an important role in finding a partner, just as it does in making a friend in fourth grade. People tend to match with people who share their politics and even use the same words in their dating profiles (Huber & Malhotra, 2017; Maldeniya et al., 2017). In this way, romance can perpetuate group differences and segregation (Mijs & Roe, 2021).

Young adults in the United States and in other afflu-ent countries are more accepting of some kinds of diverse

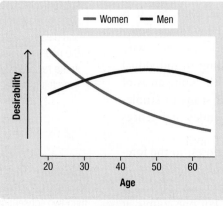

IDEAL CHARACTERISTICS	
1.	Funny
2.	Intelligent
3.	Honest
4.	Attractive
5.	Kind
6.	Understanding
7.	Ambitious
8.	Loyal
9.	Caring
10.	Trustworthy

Information from Sparks et al., 2020.

Information from Bruch & Newman, 2018.

partnerships than they were in the recent past (Choi & Goldberg, 2020). Same-sex, gender-diverse, interethnic, interreligious, and interracial relationships are at an all-time high in the United States. Today, one in six weddings occurs between people with different ethnic backgrounds (Livingston & Brown, 2017). Young same-sex couples tend to be even more open-minded about whom they live with or marry, with nearly one in five gay men living with someone from a different ethnic group (Ciscato et al., 2020; Lundquist & Lin, 2015).

However, young people today are less likely than previous generations to date people from different educational and occupational backgrounds. College-educated young adults in same- and other-sex partnerships tend to marry each other. People with high-status jobs tend to marry other people with high-status jobs: Doctors marry other doctors, and lawyers marry other lawyers (Schwartz et al., 2021). This trend is strongest for other-sex couples and for lesbian couples; men tend to be more open-minded about their partner's educational and job background when they seriously date or marry other men (Ciscato et al., 2020).

Researchers observe that this preference may come down to cultural homogamy: Wealthy people may be looking for other people who share their affinity for luxury (Lipset, 2015). People tend to assume that other people who share their educational or economic background will share their life values (Mijs & Roe, 2021). Others suggest economic segregation is to blame, which makes it increasingly unlikely that couples from different economic and educational backgrounds will meet (Luo, 2017).

Segregation in Dating More than 9 in 10 people in the United States support interethnic relationships (Curington et al., 2021; Livingston & Brown, 2017). But, in the United States and much of the world, who young people date is influenced by stereotypes and assumptions about cultural groups: People tend to date other people who are part of their cultural or ethnic group (Ranzini & Rosenbaum, 2020). Although many nations are culturally diverse, the romantic preferences among many daters are heavily influenced by culture and ethnicity, an example of what some researchers call *private* or *sexual racism* (Bedi, 2019a; Carlson, 2020).

Most daters claim to be open to almost anyone who matches their gender preferences, but their pattern of dating tends to be ethnically biased: They only click people from their same race. This is particularly true for White young adults. Some studies have found that Black young people, for instance, are 10 times as likely to swipe right on a White person than the reverse (Mendelsohn et al., 2014). However, some explain that their reluctance to date someone from a different background is simply a result of unconscious, rather than conscious, bias (Peck et al., 2021). As one White person explained to a researcher, "Just because you wouldn't want to date someone doesn't mean you're going to culturally oppress them" (qtd. in Curington et al., 2021, p. 3). Racial preferences are often perpetuated by online algorithms and continue after people meet: Online dating can be a venue for racist interactions and other demeaning experiences (Bedi, 2019b; Carlson, 2020). Similarly, online dating tends to emphasize superficial physical characteristics, making it sometimes unpleasant and unwelcoming for adults with disabilities and those who do not have an idealized size (Akers & Harding, 2021; Retznik et al., 2017).

Despite the continuing power of ethnicity and discriminatory categories in young people's dating preferences, romantic relationships are becoming more diverse. More U.S. young adults identify as multiethnic and multiracial than ever before (Jones et al., 2021). In many communities in the United States, more than half of all young people have dated someone from a different ethnic or cultural background (de Guzman & Nishina, 2017; Shenhav et al., 2017). Asian, Indigenous, and Latina adults are very likely to have a partner who does not share their background (Rico et al., 2018). Going to college also makes falling in love with someone from a different background more likely (Torche & Rich, 2016).

A Tinder Success Story At least that is how Wilmarie describes it: She is a graphic designer in Johannesburg, South Africa, who met her partner, Zakithi, an online analyst, on the app. They found that they "just had a connection."

Creating a Place to Play Stella Palikarova and her friend, Andrew Morrison-Gurza, have helped to organize sex-positive events for people with physical disabilities who are often perceived as lacking sexual desire.

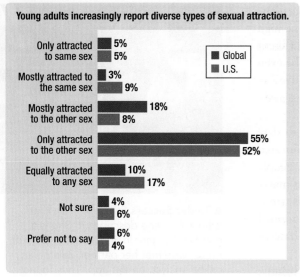

Data from Ipsos, 2021.

FIGURE 13.5 Increasing Diversity in Sexual Attraction Around the globe, researchers have found that nearly half of young people report being attracted to people of the same sex or of any sex.

Sexual Orientation One of the variables young people select when looking for a partner is gender. Increasingly, young adults are fluid in terms of their gender identity and to whom they are attracted, and their gender identity expression and their sexual attraction may continue to develop and change as they go through their 20s and beyond (Diamond, 2016; Kaestle, 2019; Kuper et al., 2018).

An increasing number of young adults now feel comfortable identifying as transgender or nonbinary. Recent surveys of young people in the United States and more than 27 other affluent countries found that about 3 in every 100 do not identity with gender-binary labels (Boyon & Silverstein, 2021; Harris Poll, 2017; Ipsos, 2021). Many young people in the United States, about 20 to 25 percent, depending on the survey, identify as having a sexual orientation other than "completely heterosexual," including bisexual, queer, pansexual, gay, or lesbian labels (Ipsos, 2021; Jones, 2021). This is similar to the estimate of about 30 percent of adults who identify as LGBTQIA+ in many other affluent countries (Boyon & Silverstein, 2021). (See **Figure 13.5**.) The language that younger adults use to describe their gender identity and sexual orientation often differs from that of older adults: They may prefer more modern terminology like queer, pansexual, or agender than older labels that reflect more fixed, exclusive, and binary identities (Bishop et al., 2020; McCormack & Savin-Williams, 2018).

As you read in Chapters 9 and 11, some people begin to identify as gay, lesbian, bisexual, or another label during adolescence, and some children express a gender-diverse identity in childhood. But, gender and sexual identity may not develop in a fixed series of stages (Pullen Sansfaçon et al., 2020). Expressing your identity often depends on family and community expectations. Many wait to come out or express a gender-diverse identity until they are more independent (Kuper et al., 2018; Medico et al., 2020). In general, young people come out earlier in more accepting communities and at younger ages than in previous generations, but many still face prejudice and rejection from their families (Bishop et al., 2020; van Bergen et al., 2021).

 CAN YOU BELIEVE IT?

Has Swiping Changed Dating?

Technology has changed how young people meet their romantic partners. Most U.S. couples now meet online (Rosenfeld et al., 2019). Online dating is popular worldwide: It is more popular in Russia, Brazil, and China than in the United States (Boxall, 2017).

The relationships young people begin online are not particularly different from those that start through blind dates or introductions from friends-of-friends. In general, they tend to have a similar chance of success and of breakup (Cacioppo et al., 2013; Rosenfeld, 2017). While some skeptics worried that the overabundance of choice available online might lead young people to break up more quickly than they might have without a cell phone to swipe, data do not appear to support that notion: In fact, some researchers have found that people who meet online tend to be more serious about relationships and more likely to become committed to each other (Rosenfeld, 2017; Schwartz & Velotta, 2018).

What about those clever algorithms that dating sites claim will guarantee you will find your soulmate? They are about as successful as your sister's best friend who claims to have an amazing reputation for matchmaking. In other words, they are not very accurate. However, they can be a self-fulfilling prophecy: If you believe in them, they may predispose you to be friendlier on that first interaction (Finkel et al., 2012). In fact,

Share It!

Who is losing out online? Some research suggests that as a group, men are likely to feel rejected online: They tend to get much less interest than they expect.

(Anderson et al., 2020)

 **Scientific American: Lifespan Development**

in one online experiment, a popular dating site told users, who were unaware they were part of an experiment, that they and a randomly selected partner were a "very good match." Their relationships turned out about as well as others that had been predicted by a proprietary formula (Rudder, 2014).

Online dating tends not to be very different from the world outside of it. For some, including people who were too shy to meet up in real life, identify as nonbinary, queer, or disabled, or belong to certain religious groups, online dating has opened up new possibilities for finding partners (Lundquist & Curington, 2019; Porter et al., 2017; Rochadiat et al., 2018; Rosenfeld & Thomas, 2012).

Unfortunately, toxic behavior is common online, with frequent reports of harassment and abuse (Anderson et al., 2020). Although many programs have removed race-based filters, exclusion based on race, size, and ability pervades interactions and even the apps' algorithms and filters (Wade & Harper, 2020). Users often feel that their particular preferences come down to uncontrollable impulses, justifying their attractions or rejections and, sometimes, their degrading or stereotypical comments (Anderson et al., 2020; Hutson et al., 2018). Social norms also often encourage online dating to be treated as a casual game when, for many, it is extensively curated and emotionally serious (Berkowitz et al., 2021).

One challenge is that many of us believe we know what we are looking for and what type of partner will work for us. But people are just not very good at predicting the spark of chemistry or the long-term compatibility that will make a relationship work (Sparks et al., 2020). Relationship success often comes down to how people get along, rather than the qualities that brought the two people together (Joel et al., 2017, 2020). 🌎

APPLY IT! **13.3** How would you explain the benefits of understanding the science behind romantic love?

13.4 Have you ever been in love? Can you analyze your experience using one of Erikson's crises, attachment theory, Sternberg's triangular theory, the cultural approach, or the biological approach?

13.5 If you've ever dated (or observed people who date), have your friends looked for potential partners? What are the cultural, economic and racial assumptions they make about finding a potential partner?

New Family Relationships

Like many young adults, Kevin is taking it slowly in terms of romance: He may be thinking about the future with his girlfriend, but he also wants to be more settled financially before he takes the next step. He wants to be able to take the time to be a good partner and father. Like Kevin, about 8 in 10 young people think they may want to be in a long-term relationship at some point, but that time is not now: Most are single (**Figure 13.6**) (Manning et al., 2019; Smock & Schwartz, 2020).

Learning Objective

13.4 Describe common variations in family and parenting relationships during young adulthood.

Happily Single

Singlehood is typical in young adulthood, even though it is often stigmatized in communities that see being paired off as normative (Zhang & Ang, 2020). But being single does not mean young adults are lonely, friendless, or not dating (Beckmeyer & Cromwell, 2019). Some young adults may identify as asexual or aromantic, but just because they are not dating does not mean that they have committed to one of these labels (Mitchell & Hunnicutt, 2019).

ROMANTIC PARTNERSHIPS IN YOUNG ADULTHOOD—UNITED STATES

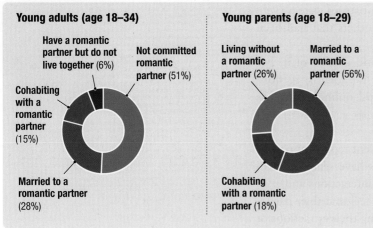

Young adults (age 18–34)

Have a romantic partner but do not live together (6%)

Not committed romantic partner (51%)

Cohabiting with a romantic partner (15%)

Married to a romantic partner (28%)

Young parents (age 18–29)

Living without a romantic partner (26%)

Married to a romantic partner (56%)

Cohabiting with a romantic partner (18%)

Data from General Social Survey, 2018.

Data from U.S. Census Bureau, 2020b.

FAMILY TRANSITIONS IN YOUNG ADULTHOOD—UNITED STATES

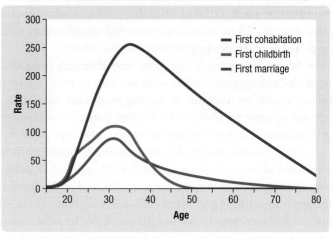

— First cohabitation
— First childbirth
— First marriage

Data from Manning, 2020.

FIGURE 13.6 Family Relationships in Early Adulthood Relationships and families are diverse in early adulthood in the United States. However, many young adults are cohabiting for the first time or are not currently commited.

Unabashedly Single Bollywood actress Sayani Gupta is not married and (when this picture was taken) not dating anyone. She has been outspoken in destigmatizing singlehood in India.

Researchers estimate that more than half of young people in the United States are not actively seeing anyone, which is broadly consistent with other affluent nations (Fry & Parker, 2021). Some young adults postpone relationships until they are married; others are waiting until they have accumulated the education and wealth that it takes to be independent (Shulman & Connolly, 2013). One young woman explained to an interviewer that she was not going to "date someone unless I really saw myself marrying them" and waited until she had graduated from college and lived on her own for a year before committing to her future husband (Armstrong & Hamilton, 2013). The COVID-19 pandemic complicated dating for many, forcing some young adults to be single, perhaps because they were temporarily in overcrowded homes or away from their social networks. This unplanned lull may have helped to trigger loneliness and a feeling of isolation for some (Lee et al., 2020).

Casual Relationships

Most romances during early adulthood do not lead to committed relationships. In the years after high school and in the early 20s, short-term, intimate relationships are common (Lyons et al., 2015). But it takes time to find a partner, even a casual one, which may explain why young adults who work full time have fewer of them, and why they are more common for traditional college students (Lyons et al., 2015; Olmstead, 2020). For many, short-term relationships are a way of beginning more emotionally intimate, long-term relationships (Eastwick et al., 2021; Watson et al., 2017). For others, casual relationships are mostly just about fun (Olmstead et al., 2021).

In young adulthood, casual sex may not be in the context of a committed relationship, but it does not necessarily mean "sex with strangers." In fact, people who have sex but do not consider themselves committed may actually have long-term, close relationships with their partners (Eastwick et al., 2021; Lyons et al., 2014). While some media portrayals may argue that "hookup culture" is pervasive, nearly 9 in 10 sexually active young adults had a stable, ongoing relationship with their last sexual partner, and many report having romance, rather than just intimacy on their minds (Tillman et al., 2019; Weitbrecht & Whitton, 2020).

Gender stereotypes often influence how adults experience casual relationships. In some communities, women are faced with the so-called double standard, which judges women who have casual sex negatively but sees men who have casual sex as successful "players" (Armstrong et al., 2014; Marks et al., 2018). A double standard also may apply to sex itself: Women in other-sex relationships often report less pleasure and fewer orgasms in casual relationships and explain that they are less likely to advocate or even be interested in their own pleasure in short-term relationships (Gusakova et al., 2020; Piemonte et al., 2019). Some men, on the other hand, say they use sex to prove their desirability and masculinity to other men (Kalish & Kimmel, 2011; Stinson et al., 2014). Others report feeling pressure to perform well in a culture where relationships may be fleeting or unattached (Epstein et al., 2009). This double standard also seems to prevail in same-sex relationships, where lesbian women tend to be less open to casual relationships than gay men are (Matsick et al., 2021).

Compared to previous generations, U.S. young people are having less sex and doing less casual dating than their parents were (Irfan et al., 2020; Twenge et al., 2017). Researchers suggest that less sexual activity may be one consequence of the economic instability of young adulthood: Those who are trying to build a career and finish school in a financially insecure environment may simply not have the time or money for close relationships (Lei & South, 2021; Tillman et al., 2019).

Committed Relationships

Throughout the lifespan, supportive, warm relationships are beneficial. Kevin explains that he and his girlfriend are a perfect match because they have a commitment to sharing experiences and handmade gifts rather than lavish spending. She appreciates him; Kevin feels that she enhances his well-being. Scientists agree: Good relationships are linked with well-being partly because people who are mentally healthy and who have strong attachments tend to be in couples. In addition, close relationships themselves can give people an emotional boost by reducing stress and making us more likely to take care of our health (Allen et al., 2020; Meeus et al., 2007).

Defining what constitutes a committed relationship is difficult, but most researchers consider it a relationship that lasts longer than a few months (Kansky & Allen, 2018). By age 25, most young people have been in a romantic relationship at some point (Rauer et al., 2013). However, there is not always a smooth path from a great first date to a long-term romance; relationships tend to be unstable (Boisvert & Poulin, 2017; Shulman et al., 2016). Breakups are common, and understanding how (and why) relationships begin and end is an awkward, uncomfortable task (Kansky & Allen, 2018).

Romantic relationships in early adulthood are more emotionally intimate than in adolescence: Young people are looking for someone who will provide emotional support as they transition from the safety and support of their parents to close emotional connections with other adults (Sassler, 2010). Attachments become deeper. Young people who develop secure attachments to a romantic partner, rather than to a friend or a parent, tend to be happier and less depressed than those without such relationships (Lehnart et al., 2010; Luciano & Orth, 2017; Wagner et al., 2015).

Living Together

At some point in a relationship — whether after a few weeks or years of dating — many couples move in together. There is no universal time frame, but it often happens within six months of the first date, regardless of gender (Orth & Rosenfeld, 2018; Sassler et al., 2018). Living together is an expression of closeness, symbolized by sharing a bed, a roof, and dirty dishes. As one young man told a reporter, "Living with a partner is easily the best thing I've ever done. It has made my life better in every possible way . . . But I . . . hate that she never refills the ice tray" (Sokol, 2015).

When romantic partners live together full time, they are *cohabiting*. **Cohabitation** is now more common than marriage among young adults (Manning et al., 2019). Other young adults choose to stay committed but *live apart together (LAT)*, living

Share It!

Casual sex may just be about fun for some people. But researchers have found that sex may be more enjoyable with emotional intimacy, where partners have the time to talk.

(van de Bongardt & de Graaf, 2020)

Scientific American: Lifespan Development

cohabitation Sharing a home with a romantic partner.

together on weekends or a few days a week but not sharing the rent or mortgage (Tillman et al., 2019). Most women have lived with someone before their 30th birthday, but LAT relationships tend to be more common among those who are college educated, who may have the financial means to maintain separate homes (Manning, 2020).

There are no universal reasons for why young people move in together. For some who cohabit, it is a short-term prelude to marriage or a way of "testing" the relationship (Tillman et al., 2019). For others, living together may be a way of saving money, helping out with a baby, or avoiding the risk of an expensive and painful divorce (Copen et al., 2013; Edin & Kefalas, 2005). However, without a formal ritual, like a wedding, to inaugurate living together, there is sometimes ambiguity between partners about what the goals and shared values are in a relationship. This does not always bode well for the future of a relationship—couples seem to do better when they agree about their level of commitment (Owen et al., 2013; Vennum et al., 2015).

For young U.S. couples who do not get married, or who never planned to, living together usually lasts a year or two (Lamidi et al., 2019). Generally, those who have financial resources, like a college degree or a well-paying job, are more likely to get married after living together than ones who are less financially stable (Zhang & Ang, 2020). Couples do not always live alone: They frequently share a home with their parents, roommates, or children (Rose-Greenland & Smock, 2012).

Cohabiting is common among same-sex and other-sex couples, although same-sex couples often report harassment or family disapproval. This may be one reason that same-sex relationships, particularly lesbian relationships, tend to be shorter lived than other-sex relationships, although lesbian women report that, in general, they get along better (Frost et al., 2015; Joyner et al., 2017). Cohabiting relationships in other parts of the world, such as Norway, France, or the Philippines, tend to be longer lasting, perhaps because they are more accepted as an alternative to marriage (Hiekel et al., 2014; Manning, 2020; Perelli-Harris et al., 2014; Schwanitz & Mulder, 2015).

Marriage

A generation ago, most young adults in the United States were married before age 25. Now, the median age for a first marriage is about 28 for women and 30 for men (U.S. Census, 2020b). Similar trends are happening around the world—couples are getting married later, and there is more diversity, including more cohabiting relationships, in relationships and in family forms (Zaidi & Morgan, 2017).

Researchers have observed that four major factors have shifted the timeline for marriage from the late teens to the late 20s. First, a changing and challenging economy makes it difficult for many young adults to gain financial stability before their late 20s (Zaidi & Morgan, 2017). Second, the roles of partners have changed. In many marriages, both partners now expect to establish independent identities and pursue careers, as well as share child care and domestic tasks (Mintz, 2015). Third, many adults no longer feel that marriage should come before children: Young adults who have children are much more likely to be unmarried (Annie E. Casey, 2018). Fourth, expectations of marriage have changed (Finkel, 2019). Many couples, like Kevin and his girlfriend, now believe that marriage is something that you enter into once you have your life together, rather than a journey that you embark on together (Coontz, 2016).

There is significant inequity in terms of who gets married in early adulthood: Marriage is something that many young people hope for, regardless of their background, but fewer are able to achieve (Schneider et al., 2018). Young people who are fortunate enough to have a college degree and families with financial resources are more likely to get married (Karney, 2021; Rosenfeld & Roestler, 2019). In the United States, where systems have long privileged lighter-skinned adults, White and Asian young people are more likely to get married than are people from other ethnic groups, who face more discrimination in education and in employment (Tillman et al., 2019).

Even though many young adults put off marriage, some U.S. couples do get married in their early 20s. This is more common in low-income families and in communities that are religiously or culturally conservative (Denton & Uecker, 2017; Uecker, 2014; Zhang & Ang, 2020). Nonetheless, early marriage comes with risks. The younger you are when you marry, the more likely you are to separate and divorce. In addition, couples who marry young are less likely to finish college (Sassler, 2010). Many young people today are aware of the risk and social stigma associated with early marriage, yet nearly one in four young adults decides to marry before age 30 (Tevington, 2018; Uecker, 2014).

Those who wait to marry often believe that marriage is about raising children and see it as the best way to provide for the next generation (Lundberg et al., 2016). Other young adults are not ready for a committed, long-term relationship. Some just do not want to be tied down. As one young professional from New York explained, "I feel like I'd rather be single. . . . I don't want to come home to a wife" (Kefalas et al., 2011, p. 865). Others are afraid of being hurt. One woman from San Antonio reported that "I try not to get my hopes up out of any relationship because it always seems to fail. . . . I'm scared. I'm scared to be in a relationship" (Cherlin et al., 2008, p. 930).

Challenges in Romantic Relationships

The quest for intimacy and love can lead to great satisfaction but also to pain. Happy, supportive relationships help create a new support system and a sense of belonging, and even inspire young people to be healthier (Whitton et al., 2016). Poor relationships can undermine all that: Unhappiness is contagious and undermines well-being in ways that may be difficult to reverse. Difficult relationships are linked to higher levels of body inflammation, depression, and even premature aging (Umberson & Thomeer, 2020).

Intimate Partner Violence Young adults are more likely than older adults to have relationship difficulties, perhaps because their relationships are often informal, in flux, and stressed by financial constraints (Halpern-Meekin et al., 2013). More than one in three young adults in the United States report that their arguments have turned violent, and one in four children around the world lives in a family whose parents have been physically harmed or feel unsafe (Smith et al., 2018; UNICEF, 2017).

Violence within relationships is called **intimate partner violence (IPV)**. Many partners, regardless of their gender identity, lash out at each other (Chen et al., 2020; Rollè et al., 2018; Smith et al., 2018). However, men who act out in anger are more likely to use dangerous levels of force, perhaps because of their greater physical size (Hamby, 2014). As a result, women are more likely to be murdered or severely injured by their partners, with more than half of female murder victims in the United States dying at the hands of their partners or former partners (Ertl et al., 2019; Petrosky et al., 2017). The consequences are significant: Chronic trauma and stress are linked to dozens of physical and mental health difficulties and lost job opportunities, for the couple as well as their families (McDonald et al., 2016; Miller & McCaw, 2019; Ouellet-Morin et al., 2015).

Violence occurs in all types of families but tends to be more severe in those with access to firearms and who are subject to multiple forms of isolation or discrimination and who may not feel like they have a place they belong (Messing et al., 2021; Peitzmeier et al., 2020). Financial stress, social stigma, and lack of social support make it difficult for people in such living situations to find help (Evans et al., 2020; Herrmann et al., 2019).

Social instability helps to explain part of why young adults are more likely to become violent than older ones, but inexperience may be another. Young adults often do not yet know how to manage relationship conflict: They may not have developed the problem-solving skills and assertiveness they need for managing breakups, jealousy, and, for many couples, raising young children (Wong et al., 2021; Xia et al., 2018). As in so many aspects of young adulthood, relationship difficulties are often linked to early life: Those who have secure, positive, and loving relationships with their families and friends

Share It!

Don't leave it hidden: There is help. If you or someone you know has experienced IPV or sexual violence, you can access the National Domestic Violence Hotline number (1-800-799-SAFE [7233] or the National Sexual Assault Hotline (1-800-656-HOPE [4673]).

Scientific American: Lifespan Development

CONNECTIONS

Family violence is one of the most common sources of trauma for young children. Almost one in four children has witnessed IPV. Recall from Chapter 8 that experiencing trauma can lead to increased rates of internalizing and externalizing disorders in children.

intimate partner violence (IPV) Violence within relationships.

TABLE 13.1 Best Practices for Stopping Family and Intimate Partner Violence

- Violence can happen to anyone: If you are worried about a family member, friend, coworker, or acquaintance, reach out and explain that violence and abuse happen to many people. This can help reduce the shame that survivors often face.
- Bystanders can help. Neighbors, coworkers, teachers, and friends can prevent violence by addressing it when it happens.
- Speaking up is hard. You may have to ask more than once. The goal is not just disclosure: It is to connect the affected person with resources in the community.
- Remind them that trauma and violence have consequences, for their health and their family's health and well-being.
- Reassure them that their families can be safe. Many people in abusive relationships worry about their children and even their pets. They worry that they may lose custody of their children or that their animals may be harmed.
- Find community resources that advocate in culturally appropriate ways, such as an LGBTQIA+ organization or support services in the affected person's home language.

are more likely to protect themselves, navigate stressful circumstances, and articulate their needs, all of which can help to prevent abuse (Allen et al., 2020; Shulman et al., 2019).

Regardless of why young people get into violent relationships, IPV can end (see **Table 13.1**). Recovery is not fast or easy: It takes intense, long-term interventions to treat trauma and find financial stability (Trabold et al., 2020). Many communities lack the resources and support that families and couples need, particularly as they navigate raising children with a partner who has been violent (Herbell et al., 2020; Snyder, 2019).

Sexual Violence Sexual violence is more prevalent for women during young adulthood than at any other point of the lifespan. Around the globe, sexual violence is sometimes a tool of political or criminal oppression or war, but it is most likely among two people who know each other. Many people do not even consider it rape or sexual assault, and few report what happened, making it difficult to estimate how common it truly is (Armstrong et al., 2018). Sexual violence is a devastating breach of a sense of safety and trust (Dworkin et al., 2017). Many recover, but trauma is linked to an increased likelihood of depression, posttraumatic stress disorder, and poor physical health in the years following the experience (Basile et al., 2020; Zinzow et al., 2012).

Worldwide, about one in three young women has been raped (WHO, 2021). Nearly one in five U.S. women is raped during her lifetime, and at least 40 percent of these attacks happen in young adulthood. Most are part of a dangerous constellation of IPV at the hands of boyfriends or husbands (Muehlenhard et al., 2017; Smith et al., 2018). Sexual violence is often part of a pattern of violent discrimination against marginalized groups. As a result, sexual violence rates are higher among disabled, transgender, lesbian, gay, and bisexual young people: More than one in four has been the victim of sexual assault (Armstrong et al., 2018; Edwards et al., 2015; Whitton et al., 2016). Men are also the victims of rape, but they are most in danger during childhood: Their abuse often goes unreported, particularly since it contradicts social expectations that men cannot be victims (Smith et al., 2018).

Sexual assault on college campuses often galvanizes public attention (Fedina et al., 2018). Rape happens about as frequently on campus as off (McMahon et al., 2019). In the United States, sexual assault is legally defined by individual states but is generally considered to be any type of physical violation without consent (Haugen et al., 2018). As in other cases of rape, college students are unlikely to report their assaults to authorities, and the perpetrators are unlikely to face consequences. Students are particularly less likely to report sexual assaults that happen while under the influence of alcohol or other substances (Fedina et al., 2016). On campus, there is often a tacit victim-blaming belief by people of all genders that alcohol can be a justification for sexual assault, and many cases of sexual assault are complicated by binge drinking (Fedina et al., 2018; Hayes et al., 2016). Campus-based interventions to prevent sexual assault focus on encouraging bystanders, and particularly men, to intervene in risky situations (McMahon et al., 2019). Interventions may also focus on educating young people about what it means to want to be intimate, how these desires often change during a sexual encounter, and what consent entails in close relationships (Brady et al., 2018).

Some surveys estimate that nearly one in five young men in the United States has sexually assaulted a woman (Thompson et al., 2013; Wegner et al., 2015). Some of these men may have expressed lifelong aggressive or antisocial behaviors (Jonason et al., 2017). Researchers believe that many lack empathy, enabling them to take advantage of others (Vachon et al., 2013; Zinzow & Thompson, 2015). As these people grow older, some may be limited-time offenders apt to hurt other people only in a specific context. Others may continue their abusive behavior, whether at work or at home, throughout their adult lives (McDermott et al., 2015). Interventions are designed both to prevent sexual assault and to help survivors get the support they need, including help to support their children (Brown et al., 2019).

Having Babies

Young adults may be postponing marriage, but they are not waiting quite as long to have children. Many begin raising a family before they have committed to a long-term relationship. In the United States, about 4 in 10 young adults have at least one child (U.S. Census, 2017, 2019). The average age of first-time U.S. pregnant parents is 27 and about 31 for their partners, which is similar to young people in other affluent countries (Khandwala et al., 2017; Martin et al., 2021). Around the world, about half of all pregnant parents have their first child before age 25, with families in low-income countries typically starting at earlier ages. For instance, in Bangladesh, parents typically have their first child before age 20, whereas first-time parents in Spain and Japan are nearly 31 (Ali et al., 2021; Eurostat, 2021; Statistics Japan, 2017). The partners of pregnant parents are often a few years older: In affluent countries like the Netherlands, first-time partners are about 33 (Statistica, 2020). In low-income countries, first-time partners are typically in their early 20s (Juárez & Gayet, 2014).

Brendan Bannon/The New York Times/Redux

Making a Family Joan and Paul have been a couple for many years but have not formally married. Many children in the United States, like their children Lucien and Rafael, grow up with parents who are committed and living together but not legally married.

While many adults look forward to starting a family, many college-educated adults put it off until they have more financial stability, typically in their 30s (Guzzo & Hayward, 2020). An increasing number of affluent young adults even undergo fertility treatments to freeze their ova in order to postpone having children until later (Brown & Patrick, 2018). Adults who have not finished college often do not wait: Many complete their families while they are still in their 20s (Guzzo & Hayward, 2020; Smock & Schwartz, 2020).

Experts suggest that the COVID-19 pandemic upended families' choices to have children: More than 4 in 10 young couples in the United States reported that they were putting off having children until the pandemic was under control (Levine & Kearney, 2021; Lindberg et al., 2020). Similar declines have been seen in other affluent nations, although a lack of access to health care services may mean families do not always have as much control over their reproductive choices (Bosley & Jarmisko, 2021).

Many young parents report that they had plans to have a baby at some point, but that the pregnancy was not quite planned. Some have mixed feelings about getting pregnant, have difficulty finding health care, or feel that having a child may be not entirely in their control (Finer & Zolna, 2016; Gómez et al., 2019; Higgins et al., 2012). As you will read in Chapter 15, parenthood is not easy at any age. The stress of having a child can be particularly challenging for young parents, whose incomes dip after their babies are born (Dill & Frech, 2019). Nevertheless, having children can be enormously

 **Share It!**

The COVID-19 pandemic was particularly hard on parents. During the early months of the crisis, parents took on nearly an additional 30 hours a week of child and home care.

(Krentz et al., 2020)

Scientific American: Lifespan Development

rewarding. As one parent explained to a researcher, having a baby is "the best thing that ever happened to me" (Edin & Kefalas, 2005, p. 195).

APPLY IT!   **13.6** Kevin worries about balancing the stress and long hours of his job with parenthood. How does this align with what you have read about why many adults postpone having children?

13.7 Most young adults are single, but there are many cultural expectations for being partnered. How would you explain the benefits and possible risks of commitment in early adulthood?

When Young Adults Need More Support

Learning Objective

13.5 Explain why some young adults experience mental health difficulties.

Elizabeth Conley/Houston Chronicle via AP

Resilience Can Come at Work.
Sometimes the right job can help build resilience, but finding careers can be more difficult for people who disclose that they have been diagnosed with a psychological disorder. Hannah, who was diagnosed with autism spectrum disorder, found the perfect job for a bibliophile at a nearby library in Houston, Texas, organizing books while planning for her dream job as a writer.

Share It!

Help is out there. National Suicide Prevention Lifeline: 800-273-8255. National Crisis Text Line: Text HOME to 774. National Substance Use Disorder and Mental Health National Hotline: 800-662-4357.

 Scientific American: Lifespan Development

During early adulthood, emotional difficulties can complicate the process of attaining a satisfying adult life (Newcomb-Anjo et al., 2017). Emotional or psychological conditions are a key reason young people leave college early, use substances, have trouble finding employment, become stagnant, and struggle in their relationships (Auerbach et al., 2018). At the same time, the transitions of early adulthood increase the likelihood of emotional stress.

In our modern era, there is limited social support and structure for young people, which may explain why nearly 3 in 10 U.S. young adults currently experience an emotional or psychological disorder, the highest rate at any point in the lifespan (SAMHSA, 2021). Indeed, many surveys in affluent countries show increases in depression and other emotional difficulties during young adulthood (Solmi et al., 2021; Weinberger et al., 2018). The number of young people thinking about suicide increased dramatically between 2009 and 2015, to more than 1 in 12. During the early months of the COVID-19 pandemic, nearly 3 in 10 U.S. young adults thought about ending their lives (Han et al., 2018; Harvard Kennedy School, 2021).

What is behind these numbers? Experts theorize that increased economic instability, high unemployment among young people, and difficulties establishing an adult identity may be triggers (Liu et al., 2019; Reeskens & Vandecasteele, 2017). The impact of discrimination, violence, and chronic stress takes a toll. Food and job insecurity, for instance, are chronic stressors that is linked to mental illness (Ganson et al., 2021; Nagata et al., 2019). Trauma also plays a part: The more trauma you experience as a child, the higher your risk for developing mental illness in adulthood (Copeland et al., 2018).

For many, encounters with the criminal justice system compound these stresses. More than 4 in 10 men have been arrested by age 23, but Black, Latino, and Indigenous men are disproportionately likely to spend time in jail, often as a result of unequal sentencing (Brame et al., 2014; Sentencing Project, 2018). The stigma associated with arrest and incarceration have long-term consequences, often making it difficult to find work and attend college (Johnson et al., 2021; Westrope, 2018). Arrest is stressful, particularly for marginalized groups, and is linked to an increase in depression and poor health, particularly for Black men (Bowleg et al., 2020; Sugie & Turney, 2017; Wildeman & Wang, 2017). Incarceration has an effect not only on those who are in prison, but in the families who support them while they are behind bars (Patterson et al., 2021).

Brain development may also play a role in young adults' vulnerability to mental health difficulties. Remember from Chapter 12 that the neural circuits that underlie emotional reactivity are still maturing in early adulthood. This may make young people particularly reactive to stress and difficulty, at a time when social and structural supports are waning (Bos et al., 2020; Casey et al., 2019).

The isolation, economic instability, and political turmoil surrounding the COVID-19 pandemic exacerbated stress for people of all ages, but particularly for young people around the world (Kowal et al., 2020). They took much of the brunt of the pandemic, as young parents and caregivers, front-line workers, and members of

SOURCES OF STRESS

Young people are more subject to certain stresses than older people. They are more likely to move, be incarcerated, and participate in the armed forces.

- - - Moving (across county lines)
— Men in armed forces
······ Male incarceration

Rate / Age (graph: 15%, 10%, 5%, 0%; Age 15, 20, 25, 30, 35, 40)

Young adults, particularly if they are women, are more likely to be low-income than other age groups. Women are particularly at risk because they are more likely to live on their own and to be supporting children.

Poverty ▶ rate (graph: 25%, 20%, 15%, 10%, 5%, 0%; Age <18, 18–24, 25–34, 35–44)

● Women
● Men

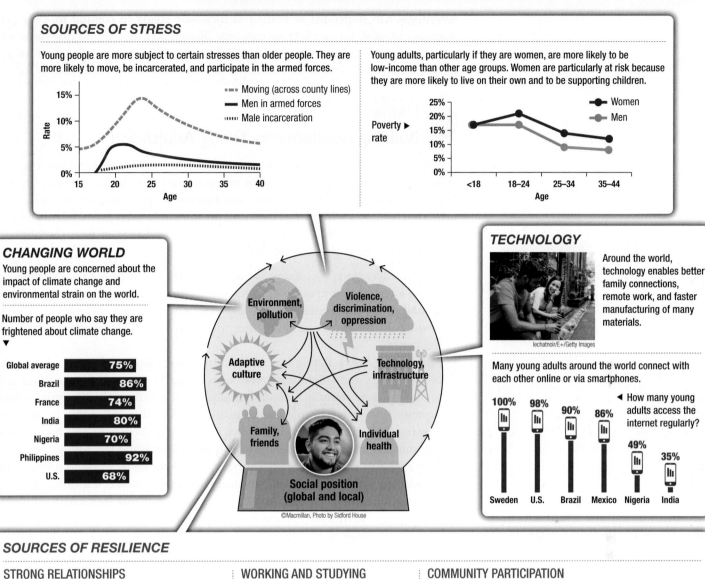

CHANGING WORLD

Young people are concerned about the impact of climate change and environmental strain on the world.

Number of people who say they are frightened about climate change.
▼

Global average	75%
Brazil	86%
France	74%
India	80%
Nigeria	70%
Philippines	92%
U.S.	68%

Environment, pollution

Violence, discrimination, oppression

Adaptive culture

Technology, infrastructure

Family, friends

Individual health

Social position (global and local)

©Macmillan, Photo by Sidford House

TECHNOLOGY

Around the world, technology enables better family connections, remote work, and faster manufacturing of many materials.

lechatnoir/E+/Getty Images

Many young adults around the world connect with each other online or via smartphones.

100% 98% 90% 86%   ◀ How many young adults access the internet regularly?
49% 35%

Sweden U.S. Brazil Mexico Nigeria India

SOURCES OF RESILIENCE

STRONG RELATIONSHIPS

hobo_018/E+/Getty Images

Young adults can rely on friends or family for support.

Friends
Romantic partner
Siblings
Parents
Other family

◀ Who do you rely on for emotional support?

■ Young men
■ Young women

0% 10% 20% 30% 40%

WORKING AND STUDYING

Around the world, most young people are able to stay in school or find work on their journey to adulthood. This is more common for those who have more education.

Percentage of young people in school or working
▼

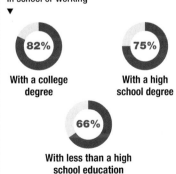

82% With a college degree

75% With a high school degree

66% With less than a high school education

COMMUNITY PARTICIPATION

Being active in the community, through service, work, political participation, or caregiving, can help change the world and boost our personal resilience across the lifespan. Young people tend to be less active in traditional politics but participate in emerging forms of involvement.

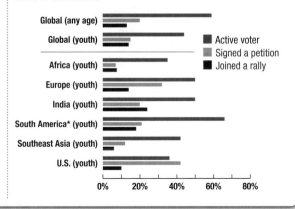

Global (any age)
Global (youth)
Africa (youth)
Europe (youth)
India (youth)
South America* (youth)
Southeast Asia (youth)
U.S. (youth)

■ Active voter
■ Signed a petition
■ Joined a rally

0% 20% 40% 60% 80%

*Voting is mandatory in Argentina, Bolivia, Brazil, and others.

cohort stuck in suspended animation as they were trying to commit to a life path (Settersten et al., 2020; Settersten & Thogmartin, 2018). Researchers have found that those who were parents or caregivers were particularly at risk for substance use disorder and mental health challenges as they managed new responsibilities (Czeisler et al., 2021).

MAKING A DIFFERENCE
Building Resilience in Young Adulthood

Young adults face many challenges in contemporary society. It is taking longer to establish an adult identity in an often uncertain and unwelcoming world. On college campuses, counselors report that more young people than ever are looking for help (Oswalt et al., 2020). Many feel increased pressure to be seen as successful and post about it on social media. What are the secrets to resilience in young adulthood? Some research offers practical advice:

- *Recognize that there is no shame in having a hard time.* Whether your challenge is failing a midterm or managing depression, staying quiet contributes to the stigma around failure and mental health (Gulliver et al., 2010; Spence et al., 2016; Stanley et al., 2018). Sharing your worries and difficulties with your friends or family can help you feel better.
- *Keep healthy habits.* Eating well and getting enough sleep and exercise helps your body manage stress (Bailey et al., 2018; Nagata et al., 2019; Palagini et al., 2019; Schuch et al., 2018). One large study in Canada found physical activity to be protective against depression in young people (Colman et al., 2014). Whether it is going to the gym, mowing the lawn, getting to bed earlier, or knowing where your next meal is coming from, healthy habits make it easier to bounce back and feel happy.
- *Find out where to get help.* Many young adults do not know where to turn or what affordable resources are available in their community (Gulliver et al., 2010). As many as one in four young people in the United States report that they have been unable to find mental health services (Cadigan et al., 2019). Remember that help may be available even if it is difficult to find.
- *Make time for the positive.* Even small steps like keeping a gratitude journal or practicing mindfulness can help you feel better. People who are grateful tend to have stronger relationships and be happier (Algoe et al., 2010; Lyubomirsky & Layous, 2013). Practicing self-compassion or meditation can help manage stress (Chi et al., 2018).
- *Be kind and connect with others.* Whether you are going out to brunch with your grandmother or meeting friends to organize a rally, relationships are the best source of support (Settersten & Thogmartin, 2018; Werner-Seidler et al., 2017). Remember from Chapter 11 that a sense of belonging and pride in a community enhances well-being, which continues in early adulthood (Meca et al., 2021). Social connections are often built on kindness: In one recently replicated study, young people who were required to do three nice things for someone else (or for the world) were happier and psychologically healthier than young people who did nice things for themselves (Curry et al., 2018; Nelson et al., 2016).

Psychological Disorders

Young adults in the United States experience some of the same psychological disorders as adolescents (see **Figure 13.7**). The most common is substance use disorder, particularly the unhealthy use of alcohol and marijuana, affecting almost one in seven young people (SAMHSA, 2021). Fewer young people are drinking than in the past, but more are binge-drinking (Bohm et al., 2021; McCabe et al.,

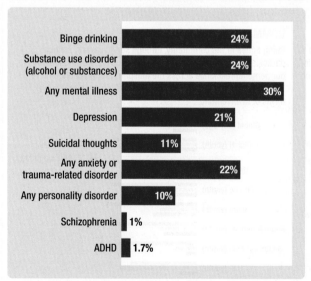

U.S. RATES OF MENTAL HEALTH DIAGNOSES IN EARLY ADULTHOOD

Binge drinking — 24%
Substance use disorder (alcohol or substances) — 24%
Any mental illness — 30%
Depression — 21%
Suicidal thoughts — 11%
Any anxiety or trauma-related disorder — 22%
Any personality disorder — 10%
Schizophrenia — 1%
ADHD — 1.7%

Data from Bohm et al., 2021; SAMHSA, 2021; Lenzenweger et al., 2007; NCS-R, 2005; Chung et al., 2019; He et al., 2020.

FIGURE 13.7 Rates of Psychological Disorders in Early Adulthood In many communities today, the highest rate of mental health diagnoses occurs in early adulthood.

2021). Substance use can both be a symptom and a trigger to further mental health difficulties: While young people may use marijuana, for instance, to relax or manage their sadness, researchers have found that it is linked to increases in depression later on (Glodosky & Cuttler, 2020; Gobbi et al., 2019). Depression, which becomes more common during adolescence (see Chapter 10), affects almost 1 in 10 young adults. Another one in eight has an anxiety disorder (Goodwin et al., 2020). Two conditions, *schizophrenia* and *personality disorder*, are often diagnosed for the first time in young adulthood.

Schizophrenia When one young man was diagnosed with **schizophrenia**, a disorder that can make everyday functioning difficult without treatment, he was afraid it was a "death sentence." Like many, he did not know what to expect. But with support, he learned to manage his condition, adjust to his medications, and manage his fear of being unwell (Smith, 2014). About 1 in 100 young people around the world has schizophrenia (McCutcheon et al., 2020). Those who are diagnosed with schizophrenia begin to have trouble distinguishing reality from *hallucinations* (seeing things that are not there or hearing voices), or they may have *delusions* (unusual beliefs), confused thinking and speech, emotional flatness, and difficulties in social interactions (APA, 2013).

Schizophrenia is a complex condition that involves genetic risks, environmental factors, and developmental timing. Schizophrenia, like other major psychological disorders, is more common in people whose parents or siblings have a history of major mental illness (Henriksen et al., 2017). Recall from Chapter 3 that many conditions and traits, including schizophrenia, are thought to be polygenetic: Although a shared series of genes underlie the risk of developing schizophrenia or another mental illness, there is no simple test that can predict whether you will develop this disorder (Gandal et al., 2018).

In addition, genetic risk alone is not enough to trigger the symptoms of schizophrenia. The disorder is more likely if you have experienced environmental stresses, including prenatal complications, traumatic stress, and adversity during childhood and substance abuse during young adulthood (Stilo & Murray, 2019). Developmental timing also contributes: The hormonal, structural, and brain connectivity changes during adolescence and young adulthood have all been implicated in its development (Keshavan et al., 2014).

Schizophrenia, like other mental illnesses, has long been stigmatized, but with early intervention and a variety of new therapies, people who have the condition can live rewarding lives (Fervaha et al., 2016; Rüsch et al., 2015). Intervention efforts now target young people who exhibit early symptoms before they have been formally diagnosed (Fusar-Poli et al., 2020; Millan et al., 2016).

Personality Disorders Remember that personality involves our unique approach to managing our emotions and ways of relating to others. **Personality disorders** are diagnosed when long-standing temperamental traits are particularly extreme or rigid and impair typical functioning (APA, 2022). For example, clinicians diagnose a personality disorder when an aspect of someone's personality, like a level of impulsiveness or moodiness, is so extreme that they can no longer get along with others or function. Experts estimate that around one in eight young adults in affluent countries has a personality disorder that may be diagnosed in addition to another disorder like depression, anxiety, or substance use (Volkert et al., 2018).

Borderline personality disorder (BPD) can cause significant disability during young adulthood. People with BPD have unstable and intense feelings, exhibit impulsive and often self-destructive behaviors, and have difficulty maintaining relationships (APA, 2022). These behaviors can include emotional outbursts of anger and violence, sometimes directed at themselves. Many young adults with BPD hurt themselves; according to some estimates, more than half have self-inflicted injuries (Reitz et al., 2015). People with this disorder desperately worry about being rejected by family members, friends, therapists, or partners (Shiner, 2009). They have trouble regulating intense

schizophrenia A condition whose symptoms include hallucinations, delusions, confused thinking, disorganized speech, emotional flatness, and difficulties in social interactions.

Schizophrenia Can't Stop Love. Brian and April were high school sweethearts and have been married for three years. Brian has been diagnosed with schizophrenia. He explains that he still has some bad days, but with his wife he is working to lessen the stigma around mental illness and help people understand that mental illness is not dangerous.

personality disorder A disorder that is diagnosed when long-standing traits are particularly extreme and impair typical functioning, as when someone's moodiness prevents them from getting along with others or functioning in life.

borderline personality disorder (BPD) A personality disorder that is characterized by unstable and intense feelings, impulsive and often self-destructive behaviors, and difficulty maintaining relationships.

emotions and sometimes turn to impulsive behaviors, such as constant texts and calls for reassurance or hurting themselves, to make themselves feel better (Videler et al., 2019).

Neuroscientists theorize that multiple biological markers contribute to why people with BPD respond so impulsively and emotionally to the world around them (Chapman, 2019). But researchers are still not sure whether brain structures or biology cause the condition, or if they are just symptoms of the stress that young people are going through.

As with schizophrenia and other psychological disorders, BPD involves environmental factors, genetic risks, and developmental timing. Most young people with BPD have a difficult history, including attachment challenges in infancy, maltreatment, neglect, and sexual abuse (Cattane et al., 2017). Some of the personality traits that put people at risk for BPD, like negative mood or impulsivity, may have genetic origins. But the complex genetics underlying BPD, as with other psychological disorders, involve multiple genes (Streit et al., 2020). Developmental timing also plays a role: Personality disorders including BPD often appear as young adults are establishing adult social relationships and identity, which may make them vulnerable (Sharp & Wall, 2018).

People with BPD and other personality disorders face particular stigma. Many friends or family members have labeled people with BPD as just immature or willful (Sheehan et al., 2016). In the past, many health care providers believed that personality disorders, including BPD, were untreatable (Klein et al., 2021). Evidence-based psychotherapies offer effective treatment for BPD (Choi-Kain et al., 2017; Gunderson et al., 2018). However, many young adults have difficulty locating and affording effective treatments for BPD and other conditions (Castro-Ramirez et al., 2021).

 SCIENCE IN PRACTICE
Ashley Wood, Occupational Therapist and Outreach Worker

Ashley Wood has a master's degree in occupational therapy and works with young adults in San Diego who are at risk for major mental illness, like schizophrenia. Occupational therapists are health care providers who work to help people across the lifespan stay active and productive. Unlike a psychologist or a social worker, they are primarily involved in figuring out the practical adjustments to the world—like designing activities to help an overactive first-grader focus in the classroom or an elder with arthritis continue to work as an illustrator.

Ashley delivers early interventions with young people who are at risk for or showing early symptoms of mental illness, like schizophrenia. Programs like Ashley's are aimed at prevention and helping people with early symptoms recover. She often spends time with clients out in the world, like at an arcade. One client, who Ashley worked with, was having difficulties and was not getting along with his mother. Some of this was typical, but her client was also starting to see things that were not there, which is where Ashley came in. Ashley focused on helping this young man build healthy habits, such as getting enough sleep and talking about his worries instead of acting out. To celebrate his achievements, she went with him to an arcade.

Programs like Ashley's are designed to help young people get through the challenging transition years of early adulthood with a bit less stress, to reduce the risk of developing a serious mental illness. These interventions have been shown to reduce the rates of psychological disorders by almost 40 percent (McFarlane et al., 2014). It seems to be working for her client, who is getting along better. And it is working for Ashley, too, who loves the satisfaction she gets from helping young people find their place in the world (Standen, 2014).

APPLY IT! **13.8** Young adults often do not have the supports they need, like a steady income, a supportive social network and meaningful work, as they are doing the important work of constructing an independent life. What are practices that can help build emotional resilience?

13.9 How does stigma about mental illness keep young people from getting the help they need when they need support?

Community Engagement

As young people move into adulthood, they take on new roles in the broader community. They may organize lunches in a soup kitchen, coach pee-wee soccer, or direct after-school programs. Whether it is volunteer work, organizing, or simply showing up in the voting booth, engagement with and service to the community is known as **civic engagement** (Delli Carpini, 2000).

As young people explore their identities, finding their place in the larger community helps them to understand who they are and connect more deeply with those who share their values (Flanagan, 2009; Marinica & Negru-Subtirica, 2020). Caring for and making a difference in the lives of others is an important developmental task that often begins in early adulthood (Lawford & Ramey, 2015; Veeh et al., 2019). Across the globe and through much of history, young adults have often been at the forefront of political movements (Harris et al., 2010). In recent decades, politically active young people, like those protesting in Tegucigalpa, Honduras, fighting in Afghanistan, or protesting in the United States, have helped make change around the world. Within the United States, many youth of color have a strong commitment to calling out and eradicating racism and structural inequalities that they see in U.S. society (Wray-Lake et al., 2020).

Around the world, many scholars report that today's generation of young people is less involved in formal aspects of politics and religious practice, like voting and attending worship services, than in the past (Flanagan, 2009; Pilkington & Pollock, 2015). However, some groups, particularly college students, report record levels of civic engagement, particularly online, and renewed interest in particular issues, from globalization to environmental activism (Grimm & Dietz, 2018a, 2018b). In recent surveys, more than 4 in 10 full-time college students reported that "becoming a leader in their community" was a very important goal (Stolzenberg et al., 2020). Young people who have historically been excluded from formal political activism, including many who are Black and Latino, often find their voice in less formal protests and community service (Wray-Lake et al., 2020). Civic engagement can also be boosted by a sense of group pride, as suggested by a recent study in which young people who were connected with their Black identity were more likely to be politically active (Chapman-Hilliard et al., 2020).

Whether they are protesting or volunteering, engagement not only benefits the community; it also adds meaning to young adults' lives (Fang et al., 2018; Zaff et al., 2010). Theorists link this to a building sense of belonging in the community and to a sense of being **generative**, or caring for people outside of yourself, central to Erikson's theories of adult development (Erikson, 1994). For instance, a recent study in Hong Kong and China revealed that the more young adults believe they have a role in social and political systems, the greater their civic engagement and, in turn, their social and psychological well-being (Chan & Mak, 2020). Similar findings were found among French-Canadian youth in Montreal, Quebec (Vézina & Poulin, 2020).

Researchers have found that young adults benefit when they feel like they have made a difference (Lawford & Ramey, 2015). Young people who are involved in their communities are happier, take better care of their health, and tend to stay in school longer (Ballard et al., 2019).

Learning Objective

13.6 Describe patterns of civic engagement among young people.

Not Too Young to Speak Out Jordan Steele-John is the youngest member of Australia's senate. He won his first election while he was still in college studying, fittingly, politics.

CONNECTIONS

Civic engagement is tied to two stages of Erikson's theory of personal development. Being involved in the community helps young people explore and commit to an identity, as explained in the discussion of identity versus role confusion in Chapter 11. You will learn in Chapter 13 that it is also important to the stage of generativity versus role confusion.

civic engagement Working to make a difference in the community in a variety of ways, including volunteering, organizing, and voting.

generative Caring and doing things for others beside yourself.

Civic Engagement

For many young people, community engagement comes from being involved with politics. This can take different forms: voting, attending rallies and marches, following political leaders, organizers, and movements on Twitter, or reading Instagram updates. Interest in politics, voting, and political action increases from age 18 to 24 (Wray-Lake et al., 2020). Young adults are more politically active than they were in the past, particularly online: Seven in ten young adults get political information online and 4 in 10 post, tag, or otherwise share political information on social media (Booth et al., 2020; Harvard Kennedy School, 2021).

For today's generation of young people, online political involvement often leads to offline participation, with high numbers of young people signing petitions, joining boycotts, and protesting. Nearly one in three young people participated in protests in the United States in 2020 (CIRCLE, 2018; Holbein et al., 2021). This participation can have individual as well as community benefits. For instance, young people who managed to stay politically active during the pandemic tended to report feeling more optimistic than their peers (Lundberg, 2021).

Young People with a Voice Early adulthood is often a time for political involvement, like the rally attended by these young people in Washington, D.C., in 2020.

However passionate they are, many young people are not participating in the formal political process by voting or running for political office. In the United States and around the world, many in their 20s feel unconnected to traditional political parties and even excluded from traditional political institutions (Deal, 2019; Weiss, 2020). In the United States, Europe and many nations in Africa, young adults have the lowest rates of voting of any age group (United Nations, 2016). Although more U.S. young people voted in the 2020 presidential election than in years past, only half of all young adults went to the polls (CIRCLE, 2021). Not all youth avoid the ballot box, however. In many countries in Latin America, more than 8 in 10 young people regularly vote (United Nations, 2016).

Some scholars point out that many young people around the world feel alienated and distrustful of politics (Dahl et al., 2018). Fiona, a young woman from Britain, explained that in her view, politics was just "boring . . . like all the old people . . . just doing nothing, just sitting there talking" (Pilkington & Pollock, 2015, p. 2). Other young people say that they are far from apathetic or alienated: They just do not have the time to make it to the polls or be active because they are trying to balance work, school, and family (Flanagan et al., 2017). As a young woman from Iowa explained apologetically, "I think voting is a fantastic privilege. . . . And I should, and I probably will once I am established somewhere. But I really think part [of it] is your 20s, you're not really established yet" (Flanagan et al., 2017, p. 197). Young adults' engagement in the formal political process often depends on their socioeconomic background. College students and those with degrees are more likely to vote and be politically active (Hirshorn & Settersten, 2013). (See **Infographic 13.1**.)

Making a Difference with Sticks Volunteer coach Jon Yip takes time to offer younger students some lacrosse tips. Scholars suggest that volunteering helps the volunteers as well as those they serve.

Although young people may not be in the voting booths in large numbers, many are making a difference in their community in a hands-on way. In college and high school, young people are connecting to their communities by teaching, serving food at soup kitchens, and coaching (Hill & den Dulk, 2013). One in four U.S. young adults frequently volunteers with schools or community organizations and one in three regularly does favors for their neighbors (CNCS, 2018). Outside of college, programs like AmeriCorps and City Year, funded by the U.S. federal government, offer stipends to help young people participate in public service when they may not be able to afford to do so on their own. One goal of intervention efforts is to make sure that all young people feel that they can give back to their communities.

Religious Participation

Many young people who volunteer do so through a religious organization, whether it is a food pantry at a local church or a tutoring program at a neighborhood synagogue. However, many do not attend services as regularly as they did in high school (Chan et al., 2015). For most young people, this seems to be more a reflection of their generally unsettled lifestyle than a rejection of the values or faith they grew up with. Kevin, for instance, still finds church and God a central part of his life, and an important reminder that there is more to life than work.

That is particularly true for young people who have not made their religion a central part of their identity, who describe themselves as "spiritual, but not religious" (Barry & Abo-Zena, 2014). But for some, young adulthood is a time to commit to their religion or to explore new spiritual practices, particularly if they have children (Denton & Euker, 2018; Negru-Subtirica et al., 2017). More than 7 in 10 U.S. young people report that their faith is an important part of their lives (Ryberg et al., 2018). For many, like Kevin, faith and connection to the broader community will continue to be a source of support as they navigate the transition to midlife.

Making Time for Faith The unsettled years of early adulthood often make attending services difficult, but young people often hold onto the faith that they grew up with.

APPLY IT! 13.10 Have you ever wanted to volunteer? Many students want to help others, but may not have the time or find an organization that feels like a good fit. What ideas do you have to design interventions to make service more accessible?

Wrapping It Up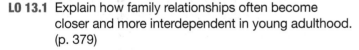

LO 13.1 Explain how family relationships often become closer and more interdependent in young adulthood. (p. 379)

Young adults' relationships with their parents tend to become closer and less conflictual as they become more independent. Relationships tend to become more reciprocal, as young people help their parents along with receiving help. Across the globe, most young adults continue to live with their parents, particularly if they live in communities or nations that do not provide young people with substantial financial support.

LO 13.2 Describe major theories of love in young adulthood. (p. 382)

Researchers have developed theories to describe love. Erikson's theory suggests that early adulthood involves the crisis between intimacy and isolation. Attachment theorists suggest that adult relationships are shaped based on habits of relating that began in childhood and can be described in terms of secure or insecure attachment styles. The triangular theory of love describes the essential components of love, intimacy, passion, and commitment, and describes consummate love as the one that balances all three. Cultural researchers point out that romantic practices differ: Love seems to be universal, but how romantic love is incorporated into

committed partnerships is often variable. Biological researchers have shown that the brain, and particularly the networks involved in the reward circuit, are activated when we are in love.

LO 13.3 Explain how culture and education shape partnering during young adulthood? (p. 382)

Researchers have revealed that finding a partner is not usually random: Social categories and segregation often play a role in who you end up with. People often are attracted to people they see as like them, following the principles of homophily. In the United States, people are more open minded than they used to be about dating people from different backgrounds, but couples are more likely than ever to share a similar educational and economic background. Many young adults discriminate on the basis of ethnicity and race when looking for a partner. More people describe themselves as gay, lesbian, queer or transgender, or another category, than in previous generations.

LO 13.4 Describe common variations in family and parenting relationships during young adulthood. (p. 389)

Most young adults are single, but some are also dating casually, cohabiting, or married. Increasingly, young adults put off getting married until they are in their late 20s. Cohabiting relationships tend to be more short-term in the United States. About 4 in 10 U.S. young adults have a child. Relationships can be a source of joy and support but also the context for IPV and sexual assault.

LO 13.5 Explain why some young adults experience mental health difficulties. (p. 396)

Emotional difficulties during young adulthood can make it harder to establish an independent life. Young people often have a lack of social support while they are transitioning to independent life: About 3 in 10 young adults has been diagnosed with an emotional disorder. Depression, anxiety and substance abuse disorder are the most common, but some conditions including schizophrenia and borderline personality disorder are also diagnosed for the first time in early adulthood.

Stigma and difficulty finding treatment often makes it difficult for youth to get help.

LO 13.6 Describe the patterns of civic engagement among young people. (p. 401)

Young people are more enthusiastic about making a difference in their community than they have been in many years. Volunteering and civic participation can help them connect and create a sense of generativity that benefits both young people and their communities. Young people are typically less connected to formal forms of civic participation, like voting, than older adults but are more active online and on the streets. Volunteer work and connections to faith communities continue to give young people a sense of belonging.

KEY TERMS

intimacy and isolation (p. 382)

triangular theory of love (p. 383)

polyamory (p. 385)

cohabitation (p. 391)

intimate partner violence (IPV) (p. 393)

schizophrenia (p. 399)

personality disorder (p. 399)

borderline personality disorder (BPD) (p. 399)

civic engagement (p. 401)

generative (p. 401)

CHECK YOUR LEARNING

1. In early adulthood, young adults are typically going to experience all of the following EXCEPT:
   a) closer to their parents and families.
   b) more likely to help their parents out.
   c) increased conflict with their parents.
   d) continuity in the patterns of relating that were established in adolescence.

2. Kevin has a friend whose partner frightens him, often "flies off the handle," and leaves him feeling afraid. What should Kevin tell him?
   a) Sometimes it is normal for couples to fight.
   b) He should seek help right away.
   c) He must have done something wrong to cause this.
   d) He should not tell anyone.

3. Kevin, like many young adults, has a girlfriend but has not made a formal commitment. How would you explain Erikson's stage of *intimacy versus isolation* to him?

4. Some relationships are passionate and intimate but not committed. Which of Sternberg's types of love does this seem to match?
   a) Consummate love
   b) Fatuous love
   c) Passionate love
   d) Liking

5. Why do scientists think that young people are less likely to have a romantic or sexual relationship than they were in the past?
   a) They are spending too much time on social media.
   b) They are less attractive than they were in the past.
   c) They are not economically stable yet.
   d) They are too worried about climate change.

6. How did the COVID-19 pandemic shape mental health in young adults?
   a) It was a time of improving mental health, since everything slowed down.
   b) Young adults' mental health tended to dip during the pandemic.
   c) Young adults could not manage the stress, and all young adults struggled.
   d) Young adults' mental health stayed about the same.

7. All the following are forms of civic engagement EXCEPT:
   a) sharing voting information with friends on Snapchat.
   b) volunteering as a poll worker.
   c) joining a rally.
   d) tutoring your younger brother.

8. Scholars note that volunteering and community service often helps build a sense of:
   a) generativity.
   b) excitement.
   c) affluence.
   d) contentment.

14 Physical and Cognitive Development in Middle Adulthood

©Macmillan, Photo by Sidford House

What Is Middle Adulthood?

14.1 What are the historical and contemporary markers of middle adulthood?

14.2 What factors trigger aging, and how do adults age during middle adulthood?

Challenges and Paths to Health in Adulthood

14.3 Describe disparities in chronic conditions and factors that can help boost resilience in adulthood.

Brain Development

14.4 Identify the areas of developmental change in the brain as adults reach midlife.

Cognitive Development

14.5 What are the cognitive strengths of midlife?

Work and Career

14.6 What are common challenges and ways of boosting work in midlife?

Selected Resources from

Activities

Spotlight on Science: Understanding the Data Behind Inequalities in Health

Concept Practice: Does Aging Influence Intelligence?

Assessments

LearningCurve

Practice Quiz

Videos

Scientific American Profiles

Physical Changes Animation

Sandra, in her mid-40s, knows that her running times are not what they were in her 20s. At her last marathon, she was lapped by a group of runners in their 80s who cheerfully encouraged her to keep going. "You can do it," she remembers, wryly. Sandra is not running to win; she has more important things to do nowadays. Nevertheless, running, biking, and hiking boost Sandra's confidence and strength, making her feel better than ever before. She still does cartwheels: She is proud to be the "cartwheeling counselor" at a suburban California middle school who challenges students' ideas about what it means to be a grownup.

Sandra was not always athletic. In fact, she remembers being clumsy in high school: tall enough that everyone wanted to pick her for their team but not good enough to compete. Now, 30 years after high school, she needs her strength to help all those who rely on her and so that she can keep on winning half-marathons. For Sandra, getting older offers some unknowns but also many opportunities: She feels unapologetically herself and comfortable in her own skin, despite the occasional ache in her shoulders and neck.

Sandra's life has included plenty of change. Most recently that meant inviting her father to live with her, as well as adjusting to the COVID-19 pandemic and meeting with students through masks. She loves to travel and once dreamed of making it to all seven continents. Now, she suspects that she will have to postpone Antarctica until after retirement. There have been difficulties, too, like the still-painful loss of her mother nine years ago.

Even though Sandra is stronger than when she was a teenager, she admits she no longer has the stamina to get through a school day on one cup of coffee

405

and four hours of sleep. She knows she looks different than she did 10 or 15 years ago. But, as Sandra explains, "you can't hold onto your youth like it was a life raft or a sinking ship. You have to let it go. It was great. But it is not now." Whereas she once assumed that adults had it all figured out, like the families shown on TV sitcoms, she now realizes that most adults just "wing it" every day.

For Sandra, things are looking up. She feels more confident and creative than ever: Her expertise and experience now give her the ability to think out of the box. As she says, "the color palette may be different, but now I can just use a whole new box of paint."

This chapter is a little like the health class on getting older that Sandra wished she had taken. It begins with a caveat: Just as in adolescence, there is great variability in physical and cognitive development. This is particularly true of middle adulthood, between about ages 35 to 65. Many, like Sandra, are still close to their athletic peak; many have babies for the first time; still others are now grandparents; and many are in their prime working years. Others have new or ongoing challenges with their bodies or their thinking. As Sandra tells us, she is living her dream. She has a meaningful job, she is able to take good care of her father, and she has a home she loves to come back to at the end of the day.

Scientific American Profile

▶

Meet Sandra

©Macmillan, Photo by Sidford House

What Is Middle Adulthood?

Learning Objectives

14.1 What are the historical and contemporary markers of middle adulthood?

14.2 What factors trigger aging, and how do adults age during middle adulthood?

As you may remember from Chapter 11, many of the markers of adulthood are flexible, changing to meet the goals of cultures and communities around the world. The milestones of middle adulthood are similarly variable, with key events determined more by culture and community than biology (Gire, 2019; Infurna et al., 2020). Both cognitive growth and aging characterize this life stage. We typically begin **middle adulthood** in our 30s as we establish independent lives, and we reach the end of middle adulthood as we recognize our own old age, often in our 60s or 70s (Dolberg & Ayalon, 2018; Toothman & Barrett, 2011).

How you define middle adulthood depends on your ethnotheories about aging, along with your age, health, and the place and time in which you live. Around the world, variations in the boundaries of adulthood are evident (Gire, 2019). (See **Infographic 14.1.**) Many people in less affluent nations (but not all) tell researchers that they think middle age ends at about age 55. This may be expected in countries where many adults die in their early 60s, about 20 years earlier than those in wealthier countries (WHO, 2020). In contrast, adults in most affluent nations today believe middle adulthood does not end until they reach their mid-60s (Ayalon et al., 2014). Improvements in health care mean that middle adulthood lasts longer and longer for many of us. As a result, middle adulthood in many nations is the longest stage in the lifespan: more than 30 years.

Developmental change in middle adulthood results from physical maturation and life events that are often unique and unpredictable. Adults are diverse because the critical events that change them, such as finding a job or a partner, do not happen in the same sequence for everyone. And for many, including Sandra, certain social events, like having a child or having a romantic partner, may not be part of adult life at all (Arnett et al., 2020). Nevertheless, the milestones of middle age often include exciting events like marriage, new jobs, or the birth of children or grandchildren, and more troubling ones like the death of a parent or divorce (Janssen & Haque, 2017; Shanahan & Busseri, 2019; Zaragoza Scherman et al., 2015).

Adults must often juggle the demands of work, family, and community responsibilities (Moen & Wethington, 1999). Thus, middle life can be rewarding but also difficult (Mehta et al., 2020). U.S. adults have more social ties with their children, friends, siblings,

Share It!

Are you established yet? Some researchers call middle age *established adulthood*, but many adults may never feel that they are ever really established.

(Mehta et al., 2020)

Scientific American: Lifespan Development

middle adulthood A flexible life stage that begins when adults establish independent lives and ends when they recognize themselves as old.

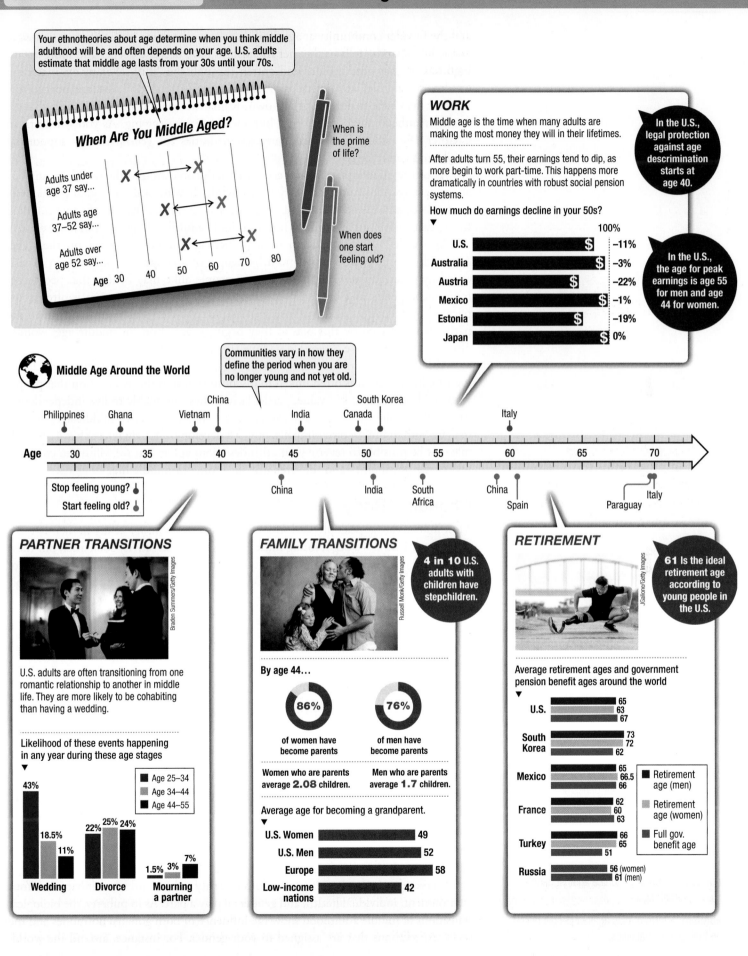

Your ethnotheories about age determine when you think middle adulthood will be and often depends on your age. U.S. adults estimate that middle age lasts from your 30s until your 70s.

When Are You Middle Aged?

Adults under age 37 say...

Adults age 37–52 say...

Adults over age 52 say...

Age 30 40 50 60 70 80

When is the prime of life?

When does one start feeling old?

WORK

Middle age is the time when many adults are making the most money they will in their lifetimes.

After adults turn 55, their earnings tend to dip, as more begin to work part-time. This happens more dramatically in countries with robust social pension systems.

How much do earnings decline in your 50s?

100%

U.S.	−11%
Australia	−3%
Austria	−22%
Mexico	−1%
Estonia	−19%
Japan	0%

In the U.S., legal protection against age discrimination starts at age 40.

In the U.S., the age for peak earnings is age 55 for men and age 44 for women.

🌐 Middle Age Around the World

Communities vary in how they define the period when you are no longer young and not yet old.

China   South Korea

Philippines   Ghana   Vietnam   India   Canada   Italy

Age   30   35   40   45   50   55   60   65   70

Stop feeling young?
Start feeling old?

China   India   South Africa   China   Spain   Paraguay   Italy

PARTNER TRANSITIONS

Braden Summers/Getty Images

U.S. adults are often transitioning from one romantic relationship to another in middle life. They are more likely to be cohabiting than having a wedding.

Likelihood of these events happening in any year during these age stages

■ Age 25–34
■ Age 34–44
■ Age 44–55

Wedding	Divorce	Mourning a partner
43%	22%	1.5%
18.5%	25%	3%
11%	24%	7%

FAMILY TRANSITIONS

Russell Monk/Getty Images

4 in 10 U.S. adults with children have stepchildren.

By age 44...

86% of women have become parents

76% of men have become parents

Women who are parents average **2.08** children.

Men who are parents average **1.7** children.

Average age for becoming a grandparent.

U.S. Women	49
U.S. Men	52
Europe	58
Low-income nations	42

RETIREMENT

JGalione/Getty Images

61 Is the ideal retirement age according to young people in the U.S.

Average retirement ages and government pension benefit ages around the world

U.S.	65 / 63 / 67
South Korea	73 / 72 / 62
Mexico	65 / 66.5 / 66
France	62 / 60 / 63
Turkey	66 / 65 / 51
Russia	56 (women) / 61 (men)

■ Retirement age (men)
■ Retirement age (women)
■ Full gov. benefit age

and the broader community at age 50 than at any other time in the lifespan (Dolberg & Ayalon, 2018). Sandra tells us that her friendships have become deeper and more meaningful as she has gotten older and gotten through the "fluff." For many, including Sandra, social roles are diverse and often in transition: Children are born, grow up, and may have children of their own. Romantic relationships begin and change; family members may offer support but also require caregiving. As you will learn in Chapter 15, middle life offers many opportunities for *generativity* by supporting family and community.

As is true of Sandra, scholars recognize that people around the world are anxious about getting older, and this worry begins while they are still quite young (Gire, 2019; North & Fiske, 2015; Sanchez Cabrero et al., 2019; Tomioka et al., 2019). The fear of aging is linked to the twin stigmas that begin to lurk in middle adulthood: *ageism* and *ableism*.

Ageism is a common form of prejudice against people based on their age. Although ageism can be experienced by people of any age, it is more often experienced by older adults. Older and younger people alike may believe that people get more incompetent and burdensome with age (Swift et al., 2018). Ageism is often complicated by prejudices against those seen as unattractive (Granleese, 2016). Women are particularly affected by this bias as they begin to age: Even in middle age, women often feel less attractive (Cameron et al., 2019; Hamermesh, 2011).

Ableism is discrimination or prejudice against people with disabilities, which can increase in midlife. It is often linked to discomfort and to the assumption that people who are disabled have less value, particularly if they are unable to live independently (Hehir, 2002; Martinson & Berridge, 2015; Rubinstein & de Medeiros, 2015). In middle age, the fear of aging and disability often impacts how we develop (Barber, 2017; Kornadt et al., 2018). It may not be possible to reverse your attitudes about aging, but we will try to convince you of the possibilities and the strengths that come in middle life.

Changing Body

Most humans are at peak physical strength, fertility, and sensory acuity in their late 20s (see **Figure 14.1**). We begin losing muscle strength and sensitivity soon after, but these changes are often subtle, unnoticeable, and easy to accommodate for adults who are not professional athletes (Cavazzana et al., 2018; Vaci et al., 2019). Sandra, for instance, is still able to adhere to a regimen of biking and running, keeping her more active than she was in her 20s. Maintaining this physical strength and sensory skill is tightly linked to longevity, cognitive health, and social relationships (Nyberg et al., 2020; Tari et al., 2019; Zotcheva et al., 2019). Health makes it easier to accommodate the commitments and joys of middle life.

The Mechanics of Aging

Aging, like maturation, is triggered by genetic changes in cells. Some changes are inevitable: Regardless of life experiences or environmental exposure, the telomeres at the end of each chromosome and the epigenetic marks at the edges of DNA will begin to wear away, although the pace of these changes may vary (Horvath & Raj, 2018; Jones et al., 2015; López-Otin et al., 2013). Even top athletes in peak physical condition have more inflammation, changes in immune function, and reduced ability to use the oxygen they breathe as they move through middle age (Minuzzi et al., 2019). What does not change, contrary to popular opinion, is metabolism. Adults' bodies continue to burn energy at about the same rate throughout adulthood, until about the age of 60, when adults begin to conserve their energy (Pontzer et al., 2021).

Everyone ages, yet there is tremendous diversity in how and when it happens. Your environment, individual health, and gender all play a part. As in puberty, the biological transitions of middle adulthood show the influence of both gonadal hormones and the social expectations that are assigned to your gender. For instance, around the world,

CONNECTIONS

Remember from Chapter 3 that DNA is a spiral of matched chemical bases. Hovering on the backbone of this spiral are epigenetic markers that help turn our genes on and off. Telomeres are the protective end caps at the end of our chromosomes that help ensure that chromosomes are copied correctly when cells replicate.

ageism A form of prejudice against people based on their age.

ableism A form of bias against people based on their physical abilities.

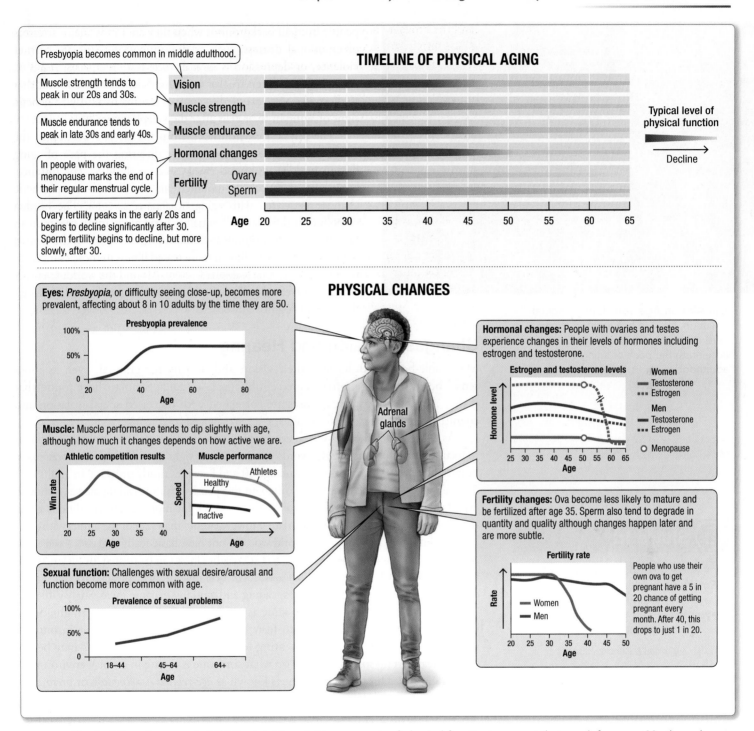

FIGURE 14.1 Physical Development in Middle Adulthood Many aspects of physical functioning are at their peak from our 20s through our 40s and begin to decline as we get older. The impact of life events can change how we experience and accommodate aging.

people who identify as men are more likely to experience disability and ill health in middle age, perhaps because they are less likely to seek early medical attention (Byhoff et al., 2019). Women experience more dramatic changes in their reproductive systems and more significant repercussions of ageism (Chrisler et al., 2016; Krekula et al., 2018).

Some adults are physically and genetically younger than others who are the same age (Jones et al., 2015). Whether scientists look at the epigenetic changes in their cells or at the strength in their muscles, adults in top condition age more slowly than their peers (Loprinzi & Loenneke, 2018). Adults with poor health tend to age more quickly (Hillary et al., 2020).

Adversity and life stress also take a toll on our bodies, which accelerates in middle age. Some researchers call this process *weathering* (Geronimus, 1992). Early aging happens to

paradoo/Shutterstock

The Air Can Age You. Environmental pollution, like the heavy smog shown here on a highway in Beijing, China, can accelerate the pace of aging in middle adulthood.

people from all backgrounds when they are hit by major stressors or emotional distress, such as discrimination, intimate partner violence, or depression (Chae et al., 2020; Foster et al., 2008; Han et al., 2019). It is also often true of veterans: Scientists have found that soldiers who were exposed to combat trauma had early epigenetic signs of aging in their cells after their deployment (Boks et al., 2015).

The physical environment, from the air you breathe to the water you drink, is a potent factor directing the pace of aging during middle adulthood (Ward-Caviness et al., 2016). For instance, hazardous chemicals in polluted air are linked to epigenetic changes associated with aging (Kaufman et al., 2016). The burden of pollution does not fall equally: Toxic air is more common in low-income communities and communities of color in the United States, which may be linked to increased illness in those communities (Ash & Boyce, 2018; Nadybal et al., 2020). Around the world, scientists correlate increased pollution with rapid increases in cardiovascular disease and cognitive disorders (Weuve et al., 2021; Zhang et al., 2018).

Changes to Vision and Hearing

Many able-bodied adults take their vision and hearing for granted, even as those senses begin to change, often imperceptibly (Andersen, 2012). Scholars have found that if they are not treated, these losses are correlated with increased social isolation and cognitive decline later in life (Varadaraj et al., 2021; Whitson et al., 2018).

As we get older, the lens of the eye gradually becomes less flexible, making it difficult to focus on small objects like the words you are reading right now. This is called *presbyopia,* or farsightedness, which begins around age 40 and becomes nearly universal in adults over 55 (Fricke et al., 2018). The treatment is often an inexpensive pair of reading glasses, although experts also recommend regular vision exams to check for more serious conditions and a more complex prescription if appropriate. However, more than half of the adults with presbyopia, about 800 million people worldwide, do not have basic reading glasses (Bourne et al., 2021; Frick et al., 2018). They may not know that farsightedness can be treated, or they may not be able to afford glasses (Wolffsohn & Davies, 2019). Left unaddressed, presbyopia can lead to eye strain, headaches, and isolation, as reading and working become increasingly difficult.

Our hearing does not stay the same as we age, nor do we lose it overnight. Some subtle degradation in our ability to hear high-pitched tones is apparent in our 20s (Roth, 2015). Typically, by age 40, hearing loss is more noticeable. Adults may be less able to hear certain sounds or pick up what someone is saying in a noisy environment (Davis et al., 2016). This gradual decline is known as *age-related hearing loss,* or *presbycusis.* It is caused by breakdown in the nerves and hair cells in the ears, and in the auditory nerves that connect to the brain (Wu, O'Malley, et al., 2020).

Adults should not be embarrassed by hearing loss, nor should they think it is an inevitable part of aging. By age 60, nearly half of adults in affluent countries report having hearing loss (WHO, 2018). Few are able to treat it: Three in four U.S. adults cannot afford the hearing aids that can be an effective treatment (Jilla et al., 2020). Making adjustments and seeking support can also facilitate communication with partners, children, and coworkers. Without intervention, hearing loss can increase the risk for isolation and even cognitive decline as we age (Davis et al., 2016; Whitson et al., 2018).

Changing on the Inside and Out

For people like Sandra, middle adulthood is a time when dreams of being an Olympic athlete are replaced with different athletic endeavors. In middle age, speed begins to decline, but sheer endurance and strength are at their peak.

📱 **Share It!**

An eye drop for eye aging? Emerging evidence suggests that eye drops may one day replace eye glasses for some people with presbyopia.

(Orman & Benozzi, 2021)

 **Scientific American: Lifespan Development**

Equestrians and golfers can continue to compete and win into their 50s, but that is not true for most swimmers or runners (Koeze, 2016). Even for the most elite athletes, the earliest physiological changes of aging begin to affect heart and lung efficiency, ability to recover from injury, and muscle strength as early as the late 20s (Haugen et al., 2017; Lavin et al., 2020; Lazarus & Harridge, 2018). And although compensating with their experience, wisdom, or skill may enable athletes to continue competing until their 40s, many have passed their peak by then (Haugen et al., 2018; Vaci et al., 2019).

This is not the case for everyone, however. Endurance persists longer than sheer strength: Ultramarathoners, like those who participate in 24-hour races and Ironman Triathlons, tend to be at their most competitive in their 40s (Knechtle & Nikolaidis, 2018). For typical adults, the decline in physical abilities is very subtle: Middle-aged parents may still be able to match their adolescent children in sprints (Fair & Kaplan, 2018; Goodpaster et al., 2006). As you will learn, regular exercise becomes even more important in middle adulthood for maintaining muscle mass and physical resilience (Lavin et al., 2020).

Many adults may not notice the slow decline in their strength, but superficial changes in hair and skin are harder to miss. As we age, the stem cells in our hair follicles that produce pigment gradually die off, and hair begins to turn gray. The precise timing of this depends on stress and genetics. And, yes, trauma really can turn hair gray: Traumatic stress can kill off the pigment-producing stem cells in the scalp, making it possible to go gray literally overnight (Rosenberg et al., 2021; Zhang et al., 2020). Gray hair is stigmatized, particularly for women: As a result, more than 8 in 10 U.S. women over 40 color their hair (Marshall, 2015).

Hair loss is another predictable sign of aging: By age 50, about half of men show some signs of hair loss as their hair follicles begin to produce miniature, rather than full-sized, hairs. There is a strong genetic component to this process (Hagenaars et al., 2017; Heilmann-Heimbach et al., 2017). Lighter-skinned men are more likely to lose their hair at earlier ages than men of color, who tend to keep their hair until they are in their mid-40s (Lulic et al., 2017; Tanaka et al., 2018). Hair loss can be a source of embarrassment. Scientific research and often pricey interventions, from topical medications to hair transplantation, have been developed to forestall and even reverse the process (Lulic et al., 2017; Tanaka et al., 2018).

As adults get older, skin begins to show wear and tear from the sun, pollution, and the pressures of gravity (Burke, 2018; Drakaki et al., 2014; Windhager et al., 2019). Skin itself begins to thin, the fat that supports facial features slowly fades, wrinkles appear, and color may become uneven (Vashi et al., 2016). Pollution and sun exposure take a faster toll on light skin, which typically shows early signs of aging at about age 30, long before adults with darker skin like Sandra (Windhager et al., 2019).

In the United States, middle-aged adults who identify as women are the largest market for plastic surgery, and more than 8 million surgical procedures are performed on them (The Aesthetic Society, 2019). This is partly because the demands of ageism tend to fall heavier on women, but researchers also suspect this may have to do with hormones: Changes in estrogen in people with ovaries trigger acceleration in the superficial markers of aging after menopause (Windhager et al., 2019).

Changes in Fertility and Sexuality

Aging has a profound effect on the reproductive system and imposes some constraints on fertility; however, as you will learn, it does not have the same effect on sexuality. While fertility has some limits, sexuality does not.

Impact of Age on Ova For many, a happy milestone of middle adulthood is starting a family. Remember from Chapter 13 that, in affluent countries around the world,

Tara Moore/Getty Images

Staying Active and Warm Swimming is an ideal form of exercise, even if you have to suit up against the cold to brave the waves, as these women in Tankerton, England, are doing.

Share It!

Gray hair may be reversible. Going gray is connected to psychological stress, and pigment sometimes returns.

(Rosenberg et al., 2021)

Scientific American: Lifespan Development

Share It!

The environment matters. Fertility is connected to air pollution: Toxins in the air seem to damage the delicate biology of early embryo and ova development. The more polluted air someone is exposed to, the more difficult it is to get pregnant.

(Gaskins et al., 2019)

Scientific American: Lifespan Development

CONNECTIONS

Remember from the discussion of the biology of conception in Chapter 3 that IVF involves the combination of an ovum and sperm out of the body. The resulting zygote (or zygotes) is then returned to a person's uterus to finish their development.

adults who choose to have a biological family typically have their first child in their late 20s or early 30s (Khandwala et al., 2017; Martin et al., 2020). However, in less-affluent countries, parents tend to start families at younger ages (Bongaarts et al., 2017). Although there are benefits to being an older parent, biological parenthood becomes more difficult, although far from impossible. People without children often face stigma in communities where having children is seen as a typical sign of adulthood and a form of fulfillment (Athan, 2020).

One challenge to fertility is that ova begin to show the signs of age as adults reach their 40s (Fitzpatrick et al., 1998). The process is slow: Ova are most healthy when adults are in their 20s, but it is not until after about age 35 that the decline becomes significant. By the time ova are 40, each ovum is less likely to be healthy, and adults have fewer chances of getting pregnant (Chua et al., 2020).

While many young people believe that fertility treatments such as IVF can preserve fertility indefinitely, these treatments are not failsafe: People who want to use their own ova when they are over 40 have only a 1 in 10 chance of getting pregnant using IVF and the rates for those over 45 are even lower (Boivin et al., 2019; Prior et al., 2019). However, if they use someone else's ovum, people can successfully carry a pregnancy even in their 60s (Maoz-Halevy et al., 2020). Pregnancy late in life is not without risks, but older parents have many strengths: They tend to be more emotionally and financially stable and to have more time and resources for their children (Fall et al., 2015).

Despite the expense, stress, and time associated with fertility treatments, they are an increasingly popular choice for adults who want to build biological families (see **Table 14.1**). In some European countries, including the Czech Republic and Denmark, more than 5 percent of new births are the result of IVF treatments (EIM et al., 2020). Some adults choose to freeze their ova, which can be an effective way to prolong fertility (Birenbaum-Carmeli et al., 2020; Dolmans & Donnez, 2021). Transgender or nonbinary adults may also choose to preserve ova, sperm, or reproductive tissues as part of their transition (Ainsworth et al., 2020). Fertility treatments and surrogacy are also options for single parents and for gay, lesbian, and transgender adults who want to build families (Fritz & Jindal, 2018). However, parenting does not always begin with the birth of a biological child: Every year, more than 2 in every 100 U.S. families begin with adoption (Kreider, 2020).

Menopause A decline in fertility is just one of the hormonal changes many people experience in midlife. The ovaries not only stop maturing ova, but they also stop releasing as many hormones, like estrogen and testosterone, into the bloodstream.

TABLE 14.1 Building a Family in Middle Life

Fertility is linked to age.	No matter how healthy you are, ova and sperm begin to deteriorate with age. Ova are particularly delicate: By age 40, they are about 90% less likely to be fertilized and implanted as they were at age 20. Sperm also age: Older sperm are linked to an increase in miscarriage.
There are more older parents today in the United States than there have been in 100 years.	Building a family is not just about biology: Families can be created from adoption. Older parents have many strengths including more financial and emotional stability.
Health is linked to fertility.	While good health cannot reverse aging, treating sexually transmitted infections, chronic health conditions and avoiding pollutants can improve fertility.
Fertility treatments do not always work.	Medical intervention can help adults build families. However, treatments have limitations and do not always work, particularly in older adults or those with chronic health conditions.

Information from Khandwala et al., 2017; Matthews & Hamilton, 2016; Nguyen et al., 2019.

As a result, menstrual periods become irregular and eventually end. This long process, known as **menopause**, typically lasts between 4 and 10 years (Greendale et al., 2020).

For most adults with ovaries, the early signs of menopause, known as *perimenopause*, begin in the mid-40s and last for two to five years (El Khoudary et al., 2019). The final menstrual period usually occurs at around age 51 in typical people living in affluent countries, and the symptoms and changes associated with the menopause transition typically end about two or three years later. The precise timing is a complex interplay of genetics and environment: Epigenetic mechanisms help regulate menopause. Accelerated aging, particularly in people who have experienced significant adversity, illness, or trauma, may be one reason some adults experience menopause earlier in lower-resourced countries (Bar-Sadeh et al., 2020).

These hormonal changes can be challenging. More than 80 percent of people who go through menopause experience *hot flashes* (El Khoudary et al., 2019). These are unpredictable moments of extreme sweat that might leave your sheets wet and your body overheated, as if you have just finished a run on a humid day. For the most part, hot flashes happen at night, but for some they may also occur during the day, and this natural process can even potentially cause embarrassment.

More than two out of three people going through menopause report some cognitive difficulties, such as forgetfulness (Greendale et al., 2020). When scientists investigate how menopausal people perform on formal tests of memory, they find that many do have some subtle difficulties that tend to pass after the menopause transition (Greendale et al., 2020). Researchers suspect that such difficulties are associated with sleep disruptions: Hot flashes cause interrupted sleep, and lack of sleep can cause memory problems (Thurston et al., 2019). Rates of depression also rise around the time of menopause, which some researchers connect to dropping estrogen levels and lack of sleep (Wariso et al., 2017).

The end of fertility does not mean the end of sexual desire, but it may lead to some challenges, like a lack of vaginal lubrication, that make intimacy more uncomfortable and even painful (El Khoudary et al., 2019). Couples around the world are often unprepared for this (Marlatt et al., 2018).

In many communities, menopause is stigmatized: As a result, people do not often talk about it or seek help (Chrisler, 2013). Culture affects how comfortable we are with discussing the symptoms and how upsetting we find them (Islam et al., 2017; Zhang et al., 2019). For instance, bisexual and lesbian adults often report fewer difficulties with menopause, perhaps because they are less susceptible to traditional stigma about traditional gender roles (Kruk et al., 2021). For many, physical symptoms overlap with other common stresses in midlife, like balancing families and work, raising children, and even caring for aging parents. This makes it hard to disentangle what can be blamed on menopause and what is due to life stress (Weidner et al., 2020).

Medical interventions for menopause have a controversial history. In the past, physicians suggested that menopause could be "cured" by taking supplemental doses of estrogen (McNeil, 2017). Studies showed, however, that long-term use of estrogen supplements can be risky and may lead to a higher likelihood of developing breast cancer, cognitive decline, and cardiovascular disease (Gartlehner et al., 2017; Grady, 2018). Researchers also found that transgender women who use these estrogen supplements to maintain their gender identity as they age face higher rates of heart disease (Gooren & T'Sjoen, 2018).

Nevertheless, safe and effective interventions can ease some of the symptoms of menopause. Short-term hormone therapy during the peak of the menopausal transition can help ease hot flashes, improving sleep (Shifren et al., 2019). For those who cannot take hormone therapy, some antidepressant medications have been shown to be effective in treating hot flashes (Cheng et al., 2021). Painful sex may be addressed by lubricants or topically applied hormones (Pitsouni et al., 2018). While there is no intervention that

menopause A hormonal change in midlife, in which the ovaries stop releasing hormones, causing menstrual periods to end.

can prevent menopause, there are ways to make this transition easier. Sleep can help, and for many, knowing that the cognitive, emotional, and physical responses to hormonal changes will not last forever can be reassuring.

Impact of Age on Testes and Sperm People with testes experience reproductive system changes as they age, but in a more gradual way than those with ovaries (Decaroli & Rochira, 2017). However, people who identify as men are also often distressed by the impact of age-related changes on their sexuality.

People with testes experience slight declines in their sex hormones of about 2 percent a year during middle adulthood (Walther et al., 2016). However, for most, these small changes do not seem to affect health or sexuality. While advertisements suggest that people should get their testosterone checked and perhaps supplemented in midlife, most experts advise a cautious approach (Decaroli & Rochira, 2017; Walther et al., 2016). Too much testosterone is linked to depression and a higher risk for cardiovascular disease (Decaroli & Rochira, 2016; Walther et al., 2016).

Fertility also dips as people with testes age. Although sperm are produced throughout the lifespan, some measures of sperm quality do not remain at peak due to age and environmental exposure (Ali & Parekh, 2020; Oluwayiose et al., 2021). Sperm counts are a barometer of health: People who are healthy tend to have healthier sperm, and those with chronic health conditions tend to have fewer sperm that can produce a baby (Del Giudice et al., 2020; Hanson et al., 2018). In modern times, the average sperm count has declined, which researchers blame on environmental contamination, lack of sleep, and unhealthy weight (Levine et al., 2017; Ma et al., 2019).

Sperm count and slowly declining hormone levels are often imperceptible, but **erectile dysfunction (ED)**, is often obvious. Formally defined as ongoing difficulty with maintaining an erection, ED is common (Yafi et al., 2016). As they reach 50, more than one in five of people with testes typically report erectile difficulties (Corona et al., 2010; Mitchell et al., 2013). As with low sperm count, ED is closely linked with health: Those who are inactive, and those who have cardiovascular disease or diabetes, are more likely to develop ED (Eisenberg & Meldrum, 2017).

Widely promoted medications like Viagra or Cialis can help by relaxing the muscles around the penis, allowing for extra blood flow to maintain an erection, but they are not a perfect solution (Shamloul & Ghanem, 2013). Addressing underlying health concerns can also address ED (Allen, 2019). Sexual concerns during midlife are rarely just biological: They have an impact on relationships and self-esteem that go beyond the bedroom.

Sexuality Scientists suggest that for many, sex is a critical component of good health. While some adults are happy and healthy without it, sex for most is a strong indicator of physical and emotional health (Robbins & Reissing, 2018; Stokes et al., 2020). As adults get older, their interest in sex and how often they have it tend to dip a bit, but most researchers suspect that social and cultural issues rather than biology are to blame (Graf & Patrick, 2014; Twenge et al., 2017). The good news is that sex tends to be more satisfying and happen most frequently in relationships, especially ones that are going well (Maxwell & McNulty, 2019).

During middle adulthood, sex tends to become less frequent for people who are new parents and for those going through menopause (Robbins & Reissing, 2018; Twenge et al., 2017). However, while frequency of sex may decrease, quality becomes more important. And during midlife, many adults report that quality is much improved (Forbes et al., 2017). Scientists suspect that with age, adults, particularly those who identify as women, become more skilled at navigating sexual relationships and, as a result, have more sexual desire (Easton et al., 2010; Gray et al., 2019).

erectile dysfunction (ED) The inability to maintain an erection.

In midlife, sexual experiences are deeply affected by gender roles and stereotypes (Leavitt et al., 2020). People who identify as women often harshly judge their bodies, deteriorating their sexual desire (Frederick et al., 2017; Lodge & Umberson, 2012; Robbins & Reissing, 2017). In other-sex relationships, sexual scripts often prioritize penis-to-vagina sex, which can put pressure on people with ED and result in less sexual satisfaction for their partners (Frederick et al., 2017). As measured by the rate of orgasms, women in other-sex relationships fare poorly. Whereas men in same- and other-sex relationships typically report having an orgasm in at least 9 out of 10 sexual encounters, as do women in lesbian relationships, women in other-sex relationships report having an orgasm about 6 out of 10 times they are intimate (Blair et al., 2017; Frederick et al., 2017). Women in same-sex relationships typically report more sexual satisfaction and desire than those in other-sex relationships (Henderson et al., 2009).

Over the course of the lifespan, it is typical for interest in sex to fluctuate in response to events in the outside world, such as raising children, work stress, or lack of free time (Mark & Lasslo, 2018; Robbins & Reissing, 2018). Scientists have some recipes for rekindling desire, such as focusing on the emotional, rather than the physical aspects of sex. Couples who talk more, who take more time, and who describe themselves as emotionally generous tend to be happier with their sex lives (Mallory et al., 2019; McNulty et al., 2019; Muise et al., 2016; Robbins & Reissing, 2018). Similarly, adults who reject stereotypes about getting old are more likely to be intimate (Syme & Cohn, 2021). These sexual relationships can be an important source of support and joy in middle life.

Body Image

Growing older is not just something that happens to your body: It also changes how you think of yourself. Remember from Chapter 10 that how you judge your body is referred to as your *body image*. Bombarded with stereotypes online and in the media, adults tend to have difficulties with their body image as they get older.

People who identify as women tend to develop harsh self-judgments about their bodies as they begin to show the inevitable signs of aging, particularly at around 50 (Berger, 2017; Hofmeier et al., 2017; Sanchez Cabrero et al., 2019; Sontag, 1972). As one 58-year-old explained: "I am ashamed of my aging body and ashamed that I am ashamed" (Hofmeier et al., 2017, p. 5). Remember that this dissatisfaction can lead to difficulties with sexual desire and is also linked to eating disorders and depression (Hofmeier et al., 2017; Sanchez Cabrero et al., 2019). One way of addressing dissatisfaction is to exercise, which, as you will learn, is a prescription for healing many of the complaints of middle adulthood (Stanton et al., 2018).

People who identify as men may also feel disappointment about their bodies, but they tend to focus on health rather than their appearance (Clarke & Mahal, 2017; Hurd & Mahal, 2019). This is in line with social expectations: People who identify as men are often perceived to be more valuable and attractive romantic partners as they grow older, but the opposite is true for women (Bruch & Newman, 2018). People who identify as men are often primarily concerned with maintaining their strength and their sexual function (Clarke & Mahal, 2017; Hurd & Mahal, 2019).

APPLY IT! **14.1** Sandra says she is in the best time of life. She feels strong and capable and knows she is contributing to her community. How does this compare with the stereotypes or ideas you have about life in middle age?

14.2 Sandra enjoys running, biking, and hiking as a 40-something woman. How does her positive attitude toward aging contrast with the research that reports that many middle-aged people have poor body image?

14.3 Sandra points out that many adults do not know what to expect as their bodies reach middle age. What are three lessons you would explain to a friend about what they may experience as they age?

Challenges and Paths to Health in Adulthood

Learning Objective

14.3 Describe disparities in chronic conditions and factors that can help boost resilience in adulthood.

Many adults are healthy in midlife, but at least 6 in 10 have a chronic condition that may keep them from feeling their best (Boersma et al., 2020; Buttorff et al., 2017). This does typically slow them down too much, however: Sandra has some chronic pain that does not keep her from being the "cartwheeling counselor."

The United States has a greater share of adults with chronic health concerns than many other affluent countries (OECD, 2021). Researchers blame an unequal distribution of social resources. Although the United States spends more on medical care than any other nation, it spends significantly less on social services like housing, education, and mental health care that can help prevent chronic conditions (Koh & Parkh, 2018; Mokdad et al., 2018). Research suggests that net worth at midlife is strongly correlated to health and longevity, even in siblings, who share many environmental and genetic risks (Finegood et al., 2021).

Chronic Conditions in Adulthood

Although most adults can expect to live into late adulthood, the United States has seen a surprising *increase* in midlife deaths over the past 10 years, as have a few other European nations, like Russia and Ukraine (Case & Deaton, 2015; Mokdad et al., 2018; Wang et al., 2012). Many of these deaths are the result of substance use and suicide (Koh & Parkh, 2018; Woolf et al., 2018). By midlife, the effects of trauma and adversity have made it difficult for many adults to be resilient (Baciu et al., 2017). (You will learn about emotional disorders and substance use disorder in Chapter 15.) The recent pandemic has also taken a toll: About 173,000 middle-aged adults in the United States died from COVID-19 in 2021, with substantially higher rates in adults who already had a chronic illness such as cardiovascular disease or cancer (National Center on Vital Statistics, 2021).

Chronic Pain In the United States, chronic pain is a leading cause of disability (Dahlhamer et al., 2018; Pitcher et al., 2019). For many, the pain is triggered by a lingering injury, typically in the back or the neck, that just never heals (Von Korff et al., 2016). Sandra, for all her athleticism, also has chronic pain in her back and shoulders that she tries to treat with massage, hot packs, positive self-talk, and the occasional visit to the chiropractor.

Levels of chronic pain, like other conditions, tend to be higher in lower-income adults than those who are more well off (Zajacova et al., 2021). Physicians are often at a loss for a reliable solution. For many years, the solution for chronic pain was opioid medications, which contributed to a dramatic increase in opioid use disorder (Murray et al., 2019).

Researchers have found that physical activity is another way to address chronic pain, but it is often very difficult to start moving when your body hurts. Other methods that have shown some success include mindfulness-based therapy, cognitive-behavioral therapy, and acupuncture (Garland et al., 2020; Tick et al., 2018). Like many other chronic conditions, chronic pain is often most effectively treated by a *biopsychosocial approach*, focusing not just on biological symptoms, but also on each adult's social and psychological needs. Unfortunately, many cannot easily access the full spectrum of help they need to address chronic pain, particularly Black and Latino adults who tend to have higher levels of undertreated discomfort (Gatchel & McGeary, 2020; Turk & Monarch, 2018; Yang et al., 2021).

Cardiovascular Disease While chronic pain, psychological disorders, and substance use cause more disability during middle adulthood than other conditions, a leading cause of death in middle adulthood (and later life) is **cardiovascular disease (CVD)**

Yoga for Healing This veteran was injured by a landmine during an armed conflict in Colombia. Now he works with a program designed to treat his pain through meditation and yoga.

cardiovascular disease (CVD) The leading cause of death in middle adulthood that includes a wide range of conditions affecting the heart and blood vessels, including heart attacks, stroke, abnormal heart rhythms, coronary artery disease, and heart failure.

(CDC, 2021). Cardiovascular disease includes a wide range of conditions that target the heart and blood vessels, including heart attacks, stroke, abnormal heart rhythms, coronary artery disease, and heart failure.

Early risk factors for cardiovascular disease include high blood pressure, formally called *hypertension*. A second key risk factor is *metabolic syndrome*, a cluster of conditions that include unregulated blood sugars or diabetes, high blood pressure, and high levels of cholesterol (Alberti et al., 2005; Moore et al., 2017). The third is tobacco use, which can double the risk of heart disease (Lubin et al., 2017). More than half of U.S. adults have high blood pressure, about one in four has metabolic syndrome, and one in five uses tobacco (Moore et al., 2017; National Center for Health Statistics, 2019).

All these factors are treatable: Blood pressure can often be managed by a combination of medication and lifestyle changes. Uncontrolled, it can lead to more than 60 percent increased likelihood of mortality (Zhou et al., 2018). Similarly, some aspects of metabolic syndrome can be treated by controlling blood sugar and cholesterol levels. Otherwise, metabolic syndrome can double the risk of heart attack (Tune et al., 2017). Tobacco use can be addressed, possibly with nicotine replacements, supportive therapy, or medication (Lindson-Hawley et al., 2016).

Worldwide and in the United States, the number of people with these risk factors peak in the busy years of middle life, when adults are often juggling family responsibilities and work (GBD Obesity Collaborators, 2017; Hirode & Wong, 2020). However, in one of public health's biggest success stories, tobacco use is slowly declining around the world. Worldwide, only about one in four adults still uses tobacco (WHO, 2021).

Remember from Chapter 12 that there is a strong *correlation* between larger size and cardiovascular disease. Adults who have a large body size, or what researchers call obesity, are five times as likely to develop diabetes, for instance (Haase et al., 2021). Losing weight in middle age is usually connected to improvements in health outcomes: One study found that people who lost weight as adults reduced their likelihood of early mortality by about half (Xie et al., 2020).

About half of all adults in the United States and about one in five adults around the globe weigh more than what experts recommend (Malik et al., 2020; National Center for Health Statistics, 2019). But many of these adults are still healthy, with healthy markers of inflammation, cholesterol, and insulin, which is what some refer to as *metabolically healthy obesity* (Zembic et al., 2021). People who are larger often face stigma in health care and in other parts of their lives, which may increase their risks and make it more difficult for them to get the help they need to stay healthy (Tomiyama et al., 2018).

Cancer Cancer is a disease caused by individual cells that will not stop reproducing. As you may remember from Chapter 3, DNA is at the heart of each cell in the body and regulates how often the cells reproduce, or go through *mitosis*. In cancer, mitosis continues unchecked as a result of mutations in individual genes that can no longer prevent them from endlessly copying themselves. These endlessly copied cells lead to tumors or blood diseases like leukemia (Mukherjee, 2010). In the United States, about one in seven adults develops cancer in middle age, typically in the breast, lungs, or prostate (Siegel et al., 2021).

In midlife, risk factors for cancer include the genes you inherited and the environment you live in (Turnbull et al., 2018). The environment can hasten the aging process, making it more likely that you develop disease. Like cardiovascular disease, cancer particularly preys on people whose bodies have been damaged by poor nutrition, lack of activity, alcohol abuse, and exposure to toxins in the environment (White et al., 2018; Wu et al., 2016). Although cardiovascular disease remains the leading cause of death around the world, as communities become more affluent and people live longer, cancer is taking its place as the leading killer of adults (Global Burden of Disease Cancer Collaboration, 2018; Hastings et al., 2018).

CONNECTIONS

Remember from Chapter 12 that as people around the world have become more affluent, they tend to eat more processed foods, a trend known as the *global nutrition transition*. This change in diet is linked to increasing rates of metabolic syndrome and diabetes.

Health Is Often Tied to Geography. Maxine lives in a beautiful area outside of Gallup, New Mexico. But, like many rural Americans, including residents of the nearby Navajo Nation, she has no access to safe drinking water at home. Climate change has only exacerbated drought conditions.

The United States leads the world in the effective treatment for cancer. More than 83 percent of women with breast cancer, and more than 98 percent of those with prostate cancer, survive their disease (Siegel et al., 2021). Intervention efforts in the United States focus on early detection: identifying the disease early through regular medical care and mammograms and prostate screening, and eliminating risk factors like tobacco use (a cause of more than 80 percent of cases of lung cancer), alcohol use disorder, and physical inactivity (Mueller et al., 2021; Siegel et al., 2021).

Disparities in Health Using large data sets, scientists compare the health outcomes from groups of people, giving them a bird's-eye view on health risks and patterns that may not be visible otherwise. Researchers have found that, around the world, the burden of poor health falls hardest on those who are marginalized and who are the targets of discrimination (Adler et al., 1994; Chetty et al., 2016; Leone, 2019). Social scientists call these differences *health gradients*, and they align to many facets of our identities including family income, social standing, education level, geography, and sometimes ethnicity and immigration status (Marmot et al., 1984; McLeod et al., 2012).

Although these differences can be found in most nations, the association between wealth and health is higher in the United States than in other affluent countries (Leone, 2019; Semyonov et al., 2013). For instance, among men in the United States, there is a gap of more than 14 years in life expectancy between those in the top 1 percent income bracket and those in the lowest 1 percent income bracket (there is a smaller gap of 10 years for women) (Chetty et al., 2016). A low-income 40-year-old man in the United States has a similar life expectancy to a man from a low-income country like Sudan or Pakistan. Such men are not likely to see their 75th birthday, but a wealthy man can expect to live well past 80 (WHO, 2020).

For many, these **health disparities** have been highlighted by the COVID-19 pandemic, which resulted in disproportionately more death and serious illness in low-income and marginalized communities around the world. For instance, in Hong Kong, the disease was more likely to strike lower-income communities (Chung et al., 2021). In England, men from immigrant Bangladeshi and Pakistani communities were twice as likely to die from the virus than White men (Booth & Barr, 2020).

Across the United States, Native American adults were nearly four times as likely to develop COVID-19, in part because they were not able to shelter in place (Hatcher et al., 2020; Hooper et al., 2020). In the New York City outbreak in the spring of 2020, Black Americans were nearly twice as likely as White Americans to be sick enough to be placed on ventilators, regardless of their income level (Yancy, 2020). However, these health disparities are not limited to rates of death: Family income, culture, geography, and other distinctions can create inequities in many facets of health, from rates of chronic disease to likelihood of recovering from cancer.

Developmental scientists have a number of theories to explain this complex issue.

1. *Unequal distribution of health care resources.* While the United States spends more on health care than any other wealthy country in the world, the care available to low-income people is not equivalent to that of higher-income adults (Cunningham et al., 2017; Khullar & Chokshi, 2018).

2. *Residential segregation.* Low-income adults and those who are from Latino, Native American, or Black communities are more likely to live in segregated, low-income communities (Bravo et al., 2019). Not only are these communities underserved, they are also more likely to be polluted (Dabass et al., 2018).

3. *Discrimination.* Experiencing prejudice contributes to ill health by hijacking the stress response system and prematurely aging chromosomes (Cuevas et al., 2020; Van Dyke et al., 2020). In addition, some health care providers may have negative biases that contribute to disparities in health care (Hall et al., 2015). Patients may feel more comfortable with health care providers who understand, empathize, and look like

health disparities Differences in the rate of health conditions based on social categories.

them. One study found that Black people were more likely to trust and follow the advice of a Black physician (Alsan et al., 2019).

4. *The impact of early life.* Developmental programming theorists point out that many of the health care concerns of middle age have their start in childhood, or even before birth (Duncan et al., 2018; Fleming et al., 2018; Ford et al., 2018; Prentice, 2018; Suglia et al., 2020). Remember from Chapter 3 that a baby's health in their first years of life can lead to lifelong changes in stress response, metabolism, immunity, and inflammatory processes (Duncan et al., 2019). Adolescence is another sensitive period: Teenagers who receive sensitive parenting or have strong friendships are more likely to be healthy later in life than other children who also experienced family conflict or financial adversity (Boylan et al., 2018; Cundiff & Matthews, 2018).

5. *Trauma and stress.* Experiencing trauma and chronic stress increases the likelihood that adults will have poor health (Jakubowski et al., 2018). Remember from Chapters 4 and 10 that researchers have linked *adverse experiences* with poorer health outcomes in adulthood. However, a history of trauma is often linked with poverty and discrimination, and for some, these concurrent factors may be more powerful than trauma history (Shaefer et al., 2018). Trauma in childhood can build a "chain of risk" that can lead an erosion of social relationships, poor coping skills, and difficulties with mental health. These factors can make it more difficult to practice protective behaviors that can keep you healthy (Monnat & Chandler, 2015; Roberts et al., 2020; Sheikh, 2018). Stress during adulthood, from difficult relationships to long work hours, also contributes to poor health (Constantino et al., 2019; Ervasti et al., 2020; Zhu et al., 2020).

Scientific American Profile

The Cartwheeling Counselor

Building Health in Adulthood

You can probably guess some of the behaviors that scientists recommend for maintaining health during adulthood: Maintain a healthy diet and stay active. Moderate your drinking and use of tobacco and marijuana (even if you are using a vape pen) (Dunton, 2018). Other recommendations might surprise you: Sleep and social relationships, as you will read in Chapter 15, can also be tools for building resilience and good health in your adult years (Hale et al., 2020; Zee & Weiss, 2019).

One set of researchers looked at the impact of just four of these factors (keeping a healthy weight, avoiding tobacco, limiting alcohol, and staying physically active) and found that adults with three healthy factors typically had nine more healthy years than those who did not, with lower likelihood of developing a vast array of health concerns, including cardiovascular disease, cancer, and cognitive decline (Nyberg et al., 2020).

Researchers have applied these theories to understand how to boost community health. One approach is inspired by Latino immigrants. When scientists compare Latino immigrants to U.S.-born Latino adults, they find that the immigrants are *half* as likely to have chronic health conditions in adulthood as those who were born in the United States (Cantu et al., 2013). Latino immigrants tend to be healthier than others who also had low income, like other Latinos and non-Latino White Americans (Alcántara et al., 2017).

In fact, researchers have found that even though Latino immigrants have higher rates of *disability*, in part because they often have jobs that are physically difficult and sometimes dangerous (Hayward et al., 2014), they are *still* less likely to develop chronic conditions. So, what is their secret? Lifestyle factors play a major role: Immigrants are less likely to smoke and drink alcohol excessively, which may reduce their risk (Alcantara et al., 2017).

Evidence-based interventions that have helped adults improve their health share a number of key features (Rotherman-Buros, 2021). First, they remove barriers to making good choices. For instance, some interventions encourage people to take the stairs by making the stairwells themselves more attractive and highlighting the benefits of walking (Bauman & Milton, 2020).

CONNECTIONS

Remember from Chapter 4 that evidence-based interventions are methods of improving health or well-being that have demonstrated effectiveness. For instance, the Nurse–Family Partnership designed to improve newborn health is one gold standard intervention.

Second, these interventions build motivation to change by reducing stigma, normalizing difficulties by focusing on strengths. One promising intervention that encourages adults to focus on their values and principles at the doctor's office helps mitigate the stigma and potential stereotype threat associated with having a chronic condition. After thinking of their strengths in the waiting room, they are more likely to follow up and treat their high blood pressure (Daugherty et al., 2019).

Finally, successful interventions build community support and pride around healthy practices. One intervention in Massachusetts enlisted Buddhist community leaders to encourage and build support for smoking cessation in the Cambodian community (Zhou et al., 2014).

The Impact of Nutrition and Activity What you eat is important to your health. There are a dizzying array of competing claims about what is healthy: blueberries or bacon, turmeric or tuna. Most scientists have found that diet is connected to cognitive and physical health, but the best evidence focuses on simple changes rather than on one miracle food. Avoiding sweets, fast food, and processed meat (like bacon), and eating more fruits, vegetables, beans, and whole grains are key (Kahan & Manson, 2017). Healthy foods are often more expensive than more calorie-filled carbohydrates, but researchers estimate that eating just one extra piece of fruit a day can reduce the risk of heart disease by 8 percent (Gehlich et al., 2019; Miller et al., 2017). Diet itself, regardless of other lifestyle choices, can slow the epigenetic signs of aging (Kim et al., 2021).

Starting small is how experts recommend beginning to exercise. No need to run a marathon: Just get some movement in your day. Exercise has a multitude of benefits. It reduces anxiety and depression, improves sleep, and lowers risks of cardiovascular disease and cancer (Harridge & Lazarus, 2017; King et al., 2019). Staying active has dramatic effects on the rate of cognitive decline, a worry for many as we get older. Some experts suggest that people who are active are 50 percent less likely to develop cognitive disorders like Alzheimer disease (Kennedy et al., 2017; Scarmeas et al., 2009). You do not have to have been a college athlete to benefit from this effect: It is enough to just improve your health in midlife (Tari et al., 2019; Zotcheva et al., 2019).

During adulthood, physical activity slows aging in the body (Lazarus & Harridge, 2018). Exercise reverses the inflammation and loss of muscle mass that are characteristic of aging, resulting in stronger and more resilient muscles (Lavin et al., 2020). Brisk walking four to five days a week is enough to change and lengthen the telomeres that mark aging on chromosomes (Werner et al., 2019). Running marathons, as Sandra does, also has benefits: When researchers studied a group of typical middle-aged adults training to run a marathon, they found that six months of training made the runners' hearts and coronary arteries look more than four years younger (Bhuva et al., 2020).

For adults in middle age, work is typically sedentary, commuting to and from work consists of driving, not walking or biking, and leisure time is spent in front of screens. Experts recommend getting at least 150 minutes of activity a week, but any activity, even just a few minutes, helps (Physical Activity Guidelines Advisory Committee, 2018). Around the world, only about half of adults get enough physical activity, and about one in four get no physical activity at all (King et al., 2019; Vancampfort et al., 2017).

Adults are more likely to be active if they live someplace that makes it easy to walk outside, hike, or bike regularly (King et al., 2019). Even small changes, such as taking the stairs instead of the elevator or parking in the back of the lot, are beneficial. Some people find it useful to use a smartphone to track their steps every day and build realistic goals. Eight thousand or more steps a day is a good start, and at more than 12,000 steps a day, researchers start to see significant improvements in health (Saint-Maurice et al., 2020).

Ricardo Rubio/Europa Press Via AP

Staying Active and Helping the Planet These adults in Madrid, Spain, are running and collecting litter in a public park: getting a boost for their heart rate and a sense of generativity from giving back to their community.

Sleep Do you wake up in the morning craving a coffee or an energy drink? It could be that you are not getting enough rest (Irwin, 2019; Mander et al., 2017). Your internal body clock shifts after adolescence, making it easier to go to bed earlier and get up in time for work while still getting the recommended seven hours of sleep a night (Fischer et al., 2017; Watson et al., 2016). Yet many are still waking up tired, either because of insufficient sleep or because they have a sleep disorder.

The benefits of sleep go beyond just being able to skip that Red Bull before work. Adults who get enough sleep tend to be more productive, better regulated, and more generous with their families (Barnes & Watson, 2019; da Estrela et al., 2018; Simon et al., 2020). Remember that sleep is when your brain processes memories and consolidates new skills, so it remains as important in adulthood as it was in earlier years (Walker, 2017). Sleep gives the body time to build immunity, lower inflammation, and recover from stress: People with healthy sleep habits tend to have lower rates of infectious disease, heart disease, and cancer (Irwin, 2019).

In adulthood, many sleep challenges arise from physical problems: It is difficult to sleep through the night if you are in pain or experiencing a hot flash from menopause (Baker et al., 2018; Haack et al., 2020). Some people have *sleep apnea*, a serious disorder in which breathing stops for short periods during the night. In the United States, more than one in five women and one in three men have been diagnosed with sleep apnea, which puts additional stress on the cardiovascular system and is linked to larger body size (Gottlieb & Punjabi, 2020; Jonas et al., 2017; Redline, 2017).

About one in four adults has periodic *insomnia*, which is difficulty getting to sleep, waking up too early, or being sleepless in the middle of the night (Irwin, 2019). The responsibilities of adulthood contribute to sleep problems: jobs that cause anxiety, shift work that keeps adults from sleeping at night, or children who wake up and need care (Buxton & Shea, 2020; Lee et al., 2017). Lack of sleep can create a vicious cycle — triggering anxiety and crankiness that may contribute to conflicts, making it even harder to get enough rest (Ben Simon et al., 2020).

Interventions to help improve sleep often begin with the basics: Keep a regular schedule; avoid screens, caffeine, and alcohol before bed; and make sure the room stays dark and cool (Walker, 2017). Other treatments to improve sleep can involve mindfulness or cognitive-behavioral therapy for insomnia and special breathing support machines, called *CPAPs*, for sleep apnea (Gottlieb & Punjabi, 2020; Qaseem et al., 2016; van Straten et al., 2018).

APPLY IT! **14.4** Sandra wisely reports that you should not just float through middle age: You have to take hold of the oars and make sure that you know where you are going. How has this attitude helped her physically and mentally?

14.5 Many adults with chronic conditions feel that they are blamed by others for their situation. How would you apply the lessons of cultural humility to encourage adults to adopt healthier behaviors?

Brain Development

As you have read thus far, the remarkable and rapid brain maturation of the first 30 years of life continues until myelination and synaptic pruning of the prefrontal cortex finishes in the mid- to late 20s. During middle adulthood, development is ongoing, but slower: Some parts of the brain slowly shrink, and the levels of some neurotransmitters gradually decline (Karrer et al., 2017; Mattson & Arumugam, 2018). Neuroscientists call the overall pattern of brain development in middle life "aging," not "maturation" (Mattson & Arumugam, 2018; Park & Festini, 2017). (See **Infographic 14.2**.) Not all adults age in the same way: Individual differences in health and life experience mean that there are vast differences in how and when the brain ages (Franke et al., 2018; Luo et al., 2020).

Learning Objective

14.4 Identify the areas of developmental change in the brain as adults reach midlife.

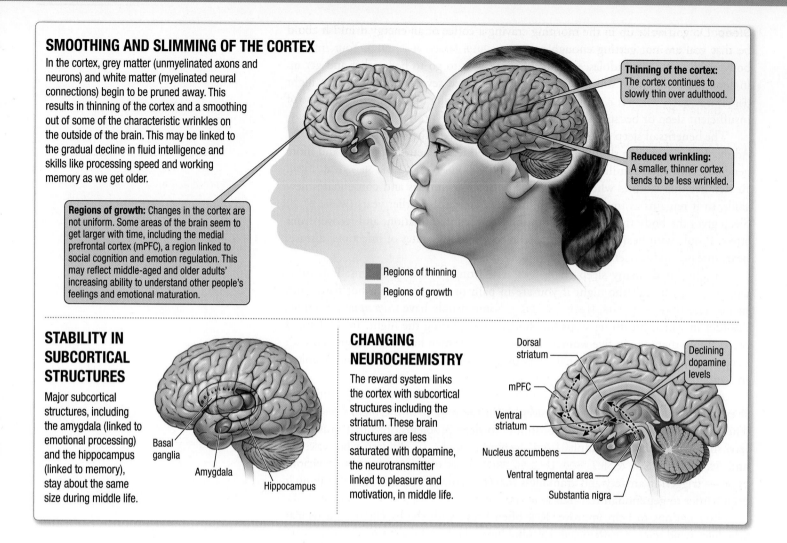

SMOOTHING AND SLIMMING OF THE CORTEX

In the cortex, grey matter (unmyelinated axons and neurons) and white matter (myelinated neural connections) begin to be pruned away. This results in thinning of the cortex and a smoothing out of some of the characteristic wrinkles on the outside of the brain. This may be linked to the gradual decline in fluid intelligence and skills like processing speed and working memory as we get older.

Regions of growth: Changes in the cortex are not uniform. Some areas of the brain seem to get larger with time, including the medial prefrontal cortex (mPFC), a region linked to social cognition and emotion regulation. This may reflect middle-aged and older adults' increasing ability to understand other people's feelings and emotional maturation.

Thinning of the cortex: The cortex continues to slowly thin over adulthood.

Reduced wrinkling: A smaller, thinner cortex tends to be less wrinkled.

Regions of thinning
Regions of growth

STABILITY IN SUBCORTICAL STRUCTURES

Major subcortical structures, including the amygdala (linked to emotional processing) and the hippocampus (linked to memory), stay about the same size during middle life.

Basal ganglia
Amygdala
Hippocampus

CHANGING NEUROCHEMISTRY

The reward system links the cortex with subcortical structures including the striatum. These brain structures are less saturated with dopamine, the neurotransmitter linked to pleasure and motivation, in middle life.

Dorsal striatum
mPFC
Ventral striatum
Nucleus accumbens
Ventral tegmental area
Substantia nigra
Declining dopamine levels

The Changing Cortex

The regions of the brain do not change at the same rate (Park & Festini, 2017). For most adults in midlife, brain development is characterized by slow shrinking in one region: the cortex, which is involved in the conscious control of thinking and behavior (Mattson & Arumugam, 2018). Much of it gradually loses volume, becomes thinner, and even flattens out some of its characteristic folds. However, this is not universal. Some areas of the prefrontal cortex actually seem to enlarge with age (Lamballais et al., 2020). In addition, the pace at which it sends information from one region to another also slows (Bennett & Madden, 2014; Grady, 2012; Hedden & Gabrieli, 2004).

Brain chemistry begins to change with age, as well: The amount of dopamine, the neurotransmitter involved in motivation and reward learning, declines (Karalija et al., 2018; Karrer et al., 2017). Overall, these brain changes may explain the slight declines in our ability to remember, pay attention, and process information that emerge during our late 40s and 50s (Storsve et al., 2014; Yuan et al., 2018).

The subcortical and limbic structures responsible for emotional processing and motivation, such as the striatum and amygdala, do not shrink as significantly during midlife. However, the amount of dopamine that powers the subcortical reward circuit decreases. Life is still rewarding and pleasurable, but this decrease in available dopamine may mean that adults are not as hungry to learn new things as teenagers and young adults are (Betts et al., 2019; Samanez-Larkin & Knutson, 2015). Instead, adults have different cognitive strengths: They have information and life experience that allow them to make wiser decisions (Romer et al., 2017).

Continued Plasticity

Even though aging has begun, the brain is still changing. It still responds with new synaptic connections and faster myelinated connections when we learn new things: whether we decide to learn how to play tennis or speak Italian (Lindenberger & Lövdén, 2019; May, 2011). According to some neuroscientists, our brain even produces new neurons that may help propel new learning and memories after 30, although the pace begins to slow (Takei, 2019).

Still, as we age, our brain becomes less flexible, so making wholesale changes is less likely. For instance, it is still possible to learn a new video-editing app or to master the guitar, but improving general cognitive characteristics like the speed of our thinking is more difficult. "Brain-training programs" or special supplements advertised to turn back the clock or make us a genius overnight are unlikely to help (Lindenberger & Lövdén, 2019; Lövdén et al., 2017; May, 2011). However, major life experiences, including parenting, create opportunities for plasticity in the brain.

 ## CAN YOU BELIEVE IT?
Does Parenting Change Your Brain?

New parents may not feel very smart. Most tell researchers that they are exhausted or overwhelmed, and more than half of all new parents have moments where they are tearful and depressed (Brown & Kathol, 2019). Despite the weariness, becoming a parent turns out to be a sensitive period for brain development (Feldman & Bakermans-Kranenburg, 2017; Lambert & Byrnes, 2019). Having a baby, whether you are a biological or an adoptive parent, grows the brain with changes that can last a lifetime (Kim, 2016; Swain & Ho, 2017).

During pregnancy and after the birth of a child, hormones are released that shape the creation of new synapses and enhanced connectivity in the brains of new parents (Pawluski et al., 2016). Remember from Chapter 3 that the hormone *oxytocin* is involved in attachment. During the period after childbirth, parents show an increase in their oxytocin levels, which helps to reshape their brains (Abraham et al., 2014; Feldman, 2019). Three brain circuits are particularly sensitive after the arrival of an infant: (1) the *emotion regulation networks* that may be connected to staying calm when a newborn cries in the middle of the night (Kim, 2016); (2) the *social information processing* network that helps us identify and understand other people's behavior, like why a baby is fussing (Abraham et al., 2014); and (3) the *reward processing circuits* that make these behaviors more pleasurable.

Evolutionary researchers point out that raising the next generation is one of the most important jobs an adult may have, so it seems obvious that the brain is designed to adapt. Researchers hope that understanding how this process unfolds can inform interventions that help families make positive adjustments to parenting, thus making this time an opportunity for long-term growth (Bakermans-Kranenburg et al., 2019; Feldman & Bakermans-Kranenburg, 2017).

Individual Differences

Although there are patterns in brain development, each brain is as distinct as your fingerprint. And just like the rest of the body, aging in the brain is unique to each individual. Challenging life circumstances, such as exposure to pollution, chronic illness, social stress, and malnutrition, can age the brain prematurely by more than 20 years (Babadjouni et al., 2017; Leone, 2019). In adulthood, neurological or emotional disorders such as schizophrenia, traumatic brain injury, and depression put adults at risk for accelerated brain aging (Cole & Franke, 2017; Franke & Gaser, 2019). Physical conditions,

such as cardiovascular disease, diabetes, and even chronic pain, can also stress the brain (Cruz-Almeida et al., 2019).

There are also ways the brain may be protected against aging, some of them more in our control than others. One of them is to have ovaries. Higher levels of estrogen mean that people with ovaries tend to have brains that age more slowly, particularly before menopause (Goyal et al., 2019; Zárate et al., 2017). Brain health builds on itself: Adults who had healthy brain development prenatally are particularly likely to stay healthy in midlife (Franke et al., 2018).

Neuroscientists have found that actively challenging your brain can help slow the pace of aging. A wide variety of adults, including those who are bilingual, who meditate, and who are amateur musicians, seem to have healthier brains than their peers (Franke & Gaser, 2019; Luders et al., 2016, 2021). Such challenge does not just come from thinking: Exercise is probably the most well-studied and potent way to maintain peak brain health (Tari et al., 2019; Zotcheva et al., 2019). Scientists suggest that exercise increases blood flow and may stimulate myelination and synaptogenesis. As you will learn, cognitive researchers also have ideas for how to maintain health during midlife, the peak years of cognition.

APPLY IT! **14.6** Sandra is thinking about starting a new career as a therapist in private practice or instructor at a community college. How will the strengths of her middle-aged brain help her take on a new challenge?
14.7 A friend asks you about an app that is supposed to make users smarter. What would you tell them about the evidence that computer programs can effectively improve your brain function?

Cognitive Development

Learning Objective

14.5 What are the cognitive strengths of midlife?

Seyllou/AFP via Getty Images

Still a Champion Mouhamed Niang is a champion Scrabble player in Senegal. Adults in midlife tend to excel at games like Scrabble that allow their accumulated crystallized reasoning to shine.

crystallized reasoning Knowledge of facts and processes that comes from past experience.

fluid reasoning The components of thinking including processing speed, memory, and the ability to think abstractly.

In midlife, adults are at their peak in many measures of cognitive ability. Many have developed skills that allow them to work and think with maximum efficiency. While many feel they are excelling intellectually, some basic components of their cognition, like memory, attention, and ability to multitask, may be slowly and often imperceptibly degrading (Salthouse, 2019). Most adults in midlife can use what they know to thrive intellectually: a skill that will help them preserve their abilities as they age. Sandra agrees: She is a more innovative problem solver, is more confident in her decisions, and has abundant energy to take on new tasks.

Types of Reasoning in Adulthood

Remember from Chapter 12 that psychologists have different ways of evaluating how we think. In adulthood, developmental scientists often analyze intellectual change by looking at two major component parts of our reasoning, or intelligence (Horn & Cattell, 1967; Weschler, 1958). **Crystallized reasoning** is our ability to use what we know to solve problems. It includes all that we know and all that we know how to do, from how to change a tire to the trivia we remember about our favorite band. Our **fluid reasoning** is the basic underpinning of our cognitive abilities, including attention, memory skills, and processing speed.

During middle adulthood, these two types of reasoning develop in opposite ways. Your crystallized reasoning keeps on improving as what you already know helps you to learn more. Meanwhile, your fluid reasoning begins to dip after about age 50 or 60, though the losses are mostly imperceptible until much later in life (see **Figure 14.2**) (Baltes, 1987; Hughes et al., 2018; Kaufman et al., 2016; Salthouse, 2019; Schaie, 2021).

This decline in fluid abilities has been documented across wide groups of people, regardless of their level of education. It happens to college professors in North America and to rural hunters in Bolivia (Gurven et al., 2017; Kaufman et al., 2016). Researchers suspect that universal, genetically driven processes of brain aging make it more difficult for adults to maintain the focus and attention they need to succeed at fluid reasoning tasks (Samanez-Larkin & Knutson, 2015).

In many large surveys, adults in good health maintain their thinking ability in a variety of areas much longer than those who have experienced more adversity. For instance, people with high blood pressure and who are malnourished tend to test more poorly, as do people who are anxious or who just "feel" old (Burmester et al., 2016; Stephan et al., 2020). Exercise seems to be protective against some of the cognitive effects of aging, as it slows other aspects of physical aging but does not completely prevent or delay the inevitable decline (Prakash et al., 2015).

Despite the changes in fluid reasoning that begin in late midlife, during their middle years, most adults' thinking is in its prime. Adults have developed **expertise**, or a deep level of skill, in many areas of their lives (Krampe & Charness, 2018). With practice, adults can maintain peak expertise into their 60s. Musicians and chess players continue to take on their younger rivals even as they approach retirement age (Pomarico, 2021; Wall, 2012).

So, even if adults show some slowness on laboratory tests, their everyday thinking and problem solving are stable, or even improving, as they go through midlife. Some experts suggest that adults' decision making is at its height: Older adults are not as impulsive or as motivated by immediate rewards as younger people, so they tend to make wiser decisions (Samanez-Larkin & Knutson, 2015). This may extend to their bank accounts: Some evidence suggests that financial reasoning peaks at middle age (Agarwal et al., 2007).

In the past, some have argued that certain jobs, like controlling air traffic, were too cognitively demanding to be held by people in their late 50s. Most evidence now questions those assumptions. Air traffic controllers outside of the United States now work into their 60s (Sedghi, 2015). Most adults do not need to be at peak cognition in everyday life: Many jobs and personal decisions are not as cognitively difficult as a laboratory intelligence test. So, in real life, you can use your accumulated knowledge and other skills, like motivation, experience, and adaptability, to make up for any declines in your processing. Being adaptable is a key component of resilient aging.

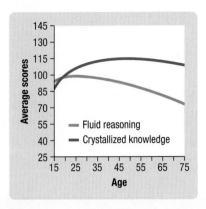

FIGURE 14.2 Changes in Fluid Versus Crystallized Reasoning

Still Keeping Track of Everything Being an air traffic controller, like Emil Watson, shown here working at Miami International Airport, requires keeping track of dozens of airplanes, runways, and conversations with pilots: skills that many adults continue to excel at.

SCIENCE IN PRACTICE
Maria Cristina Betancur, M.S., Progresso Latino

Maria Cristina Betancur is an expert. You can tell when you see her running a meeting or supporting someone who is applying for a job: She is animated, excited, and inspiring. She began as a parent organizer, inspired to volunteer to help improve her children's school, but then turned to organizing workers and parents and, along the way, earning her bachelor's and master's degrees (Geller & Betancur, 2016). Now she works with a local nonprofit and the local school system near her home in Rhode Island. Her goal now is to help parents and other adults find work and improve their academic skills.

Nearly half of all adults go back to school for at least one class every year (Brockett, 2015). Many of these courses are designed to help them in their careers. People may sign up to learn a new computer program, take a management training course, or, like many of adults Betancur connects with, find a fresh start in a new line of work. Adults can often benefit from a refresher in basic skills, particularly if, like many in Betancur's community, they are immigrants or speak English as a second language.

expertise Skill in a specific area.

More than one in five U.S. adults have weak reading skills and only basic math skills (OECD, 2019). Betancur tries to spark their enthusiasm by reminding them know how much they inspire their children with their own school work.

Betancur believes it is never too late to learn. She herself went back to school as an adult, motivated by her own children's success. She, too, made an honor society as an adult student and even authored an academic journal article. She is grateful for her work and the community: She knows that making people feel that they belong, whether it is at a job fair or volunteering at their children's school, can benefit them and their futures.

Still Learning, with Help Chad Nolan is working on his GED while serving time at the La Plata County Jail in Durango, Colorado. Mary Mullen is there to give him the hands-on support he needs to achieve his goal.

Building Expertise Innovation and creativity is a hallmark of thinking in middle adulthood. Genetic researcher Krystal Tsosie is working to understand the impact of the genome on high blood pressure during pregnancy, particularly in Indigenous populations.

Maximizing Cognition During Adulthood

Many adults are trying to juggle many responsibilities: families, jobs, making the rent. Cognitive scientists suggest that much of this can wear down the thinking needed to help them thrive. Sandra found this to be the case in her own life from time to time, when she felt that extra stress was gradually wearing away her ability to focus. Sandra is not alone: Many Americans reported high amounts of stress during recent years, leading to difficulties with attention (APA, 2021). To maximize cognition during adulthood, scientists suggest managing stress by avoiding multitasking and nurturing focus and creativity.

Many people *multitask*, or try to do more than one task at a time, like doing homework while also scanning Twitter and watching a movie. For many, this becomes a standard way of balancing work and home life, but it entails near constant interruptions. Some studies have shown that it is difficult for adults to spend more than 10 minutes on a computer without giving in to distraction (Baumgartner & Sumter, 2017). Scientists warn that the idea that we can "multitask" itself is an illusion: We cannot focus on more than one activity at a time, and rapid switching between projects decreases our productivity (Lui & Wong, 2019; Meijer & Krampe, 2017). As adults' fluid abilities decline, multitasking may become even less productive: The cognitive effort it requires may tax their attention systems. However, some research has found that older people have an easy workaround: They tend not to be as distracted as younger people, particularly by clickbait, advertising, and other online temptations (Baumgartner & Sumter, 2017).

The best advantage for middle-aged people may be their capacity for creative ideas. Sandra says that she is better at coming up with new solutions than ever before in her life, and she is more confident sharing them with other people. Scientists concur. Whether adults are 45 or 25, their thinking will never be as fast as that of the quickest supercomputer. Yet they excel at innovation, whether it is starting a new company, creating an app, or simply figuring out how to help a second-grader who is struggling with reading (Benedek et al., 2021). Researchers explain that creativity comes from curiosity, openness to new ideas, and the ability to recover from the inevitable setbacks that occur during the innovation process (Rietzchel et al., 2016). The relationship between age and creativity is complex: Many stereotypes assume that the young are more creative than the old, which may hold adults back from taking risks as they age (Rietzchel et al., 2016). Research indicates that scientists themselves are the most innovative in middle adulthood, in their 30s and early 40s, when measured by the popularity of their research over time (Gingaras et al., 2008; Stroebe, 2010).

Being able to counter the distractions of everyday life is essential to productivity, whether it is writing a report or welding a pipe (Csikszentmihalyi & LeFevre, 1989).

Researchers use the term *flow* to describe those times when we are so completely absorbed in a project that we forget how long we have been working. Flow can be playful and enjoyable, and it often entails feeling motivated, appropriately challenged, and fully attuned (Newport, 2016). This higher level of focus can be a secret to effective thinking and, as we will see, can also help with productivity at work.

APPLY IT! **14.8** One way scientists look at our thinking is to divide it into crystalized and fluid reasoning. How have you experienced changes in your crystalized and fluid skills as you have matured?
14.9 Sandra feels she is at her peak of creativity in middle life. What are some advantages that may be helping her maintain and improve her cognition?

Scientific American Profile

▶ Creative Thinking in Adulthood

Work and Career

For many adults, midlife is a time of continued work. For some, that means a successful skilled trade or career, and for others, just getting by paycheck to paycheck in a job that may not have been their dream. By middle adulthood, most U.S. adults have moved away from fast-paced entry-level jobs that require a lot of standing, and are not as likely to be restaurant workers or emergency medical technicians. Many have moved into more administrative, managerial jobs or are in the middle of their careers as teachers, nurses, or truck drivers (U.S. Bureau of Labor Statistics, 2021b). For most adults, this is a time of **peak career**, the highest income and status they will have at work. Expertise and experience on the job mean that adults have made their way up the workplace hierarchy and are more likely to be in positions of responsibility (Kearney, 2019).

Work enables adults to feel a sense of generativity and purpose. This sense that they are contributing to their community and family, whether through a paycheck that sustains their loved ones or through creative or compassionate work, is a crucial part of adult life and is protective of our health and well-being (Willroth et al., 2021). Sandra loves her job: It gives her countless opportunities to help people and to give them a feeling of warmth or goodness that she wants to be her legacy.

Peak Career for Some

Work does not happen at the same pace or on the same timetable for all adults. Even the timing and amount of peak earnings differ profoundly by gender and ethnicity. Most women reach their peak earnings at age 44, making $66,000 a year on average, but men reach their peak earnings more than 10 years later, at $101,000 a year. Black and Latino adults tend to have much lower peak earnings than their Asian American and White counterparts: There is a $50,000 difference between the peak earnings of Asian American men and those of Black men (Kearney, 2019).

Researchers suggest that diverging patterns of success in the workplace reflect an unequal starting line. There is a persistent pattern of job discrimination against Black and Latino adults: They are less likely to be hired than equivalent White applicants. If they are hired, they are 25 percent less likely to get a raise than their peers (Quillian et al., 2017).

For those who can find employment, what line of work they go into will affect their earnings over the long term. Women and people of color are often harmed by stereotypes and structural barriers when they are choosing a career (González et al., 2019; Quillian et al., 2017). Going further, Black Americans and Latinos encounter barriers to joining fields like the sciences and may experience discrimination at work once they do get hired (Flores et al., 2019). Similarly, gay, lesbian, and transgender adults and disabled and larger adults also often face discrimination in the hiring process (Ameri et al., 2018; Rich, 2014; Tilcsik et al., 2015; Wu, Roehling, et al., 2020).

Learning Objective
14.6 What are common challenges and ways of boosting work in midlife?

Inspiring Others Successful entrepreneurs, like these women at a convention for "Girlbosses," can be inspiring. Ramona Ortega (*left*) is known for developing a company designed to help young people from marginalized communities learn to manage their money. Yunah Lee (*right*) began an e-commerce company focused on luxury fashion.

peak career The time when earnings and prestige are at the high point.

Starting Fresh or Breaking Through in Midlife Aslihan Ozsahin (*left*) launched a new career as a beekeeper and now has more than 450 hives near her home in Izmir, Turkey. Meanwhile, Amy Sherald (*right*) has been a fine artist throughout her adult life, becoming famous at age 44 when she was chosen to paint a portrait of First Lady Michelle Obama.

Finding Joy in Expert Workmanship Adults have had time to develop precise skills, like those shown by this welder in Denmark.

Women face particular challenges to their promotion in the workplace once they become parents. Mothers are less likely to be hired than nonparents (Blau & Kahn, 2017). After women have children, their income plateaus or declines, particularly in the United States (Jee et al., 2019). Compared to other affluent countries, in the United States, fewer women continue to work after having children, which economists suspect is because child care in the United States is so expensive and out of reach, and because families tend to designate women to take care of the children. Cultural values also play a role: Some U.S. adults prefer women to be caregivers and to step back from work after they have children (Barroso & Horowitz, 2021). In other communities, and more frequently in people who are Black and Latino, women expect that they will continue to work without a break throughout their adult lives (Banks, 2019; U.S. Bureau of Labor Statistics, 2021a).

However, the global pandemic changed the plans of many families, and particularly those who are low income, forcing them to leave the workforce as they struggled to find child care for their young children. This was particularly severe for working mothers who did not have partners: They left the workforce at twice the rate of other families (Barroso & Kochhar, 2020). Even if these women return to the workforce, the long-term effects of a break from employment can be severe, which includes lower long-term earnings and less money saved for retirement. The global pandemic has also changed the value many adults place on work. Some researchers speculate that, as in the 2008 recession, economic stress will trigger adults to rethink their commitment to their careers and some may decide to spend more time away from the office (Recksiedler & Settersten, 2020; Settersten et al., 2020). Others may choose to take a leap and start a new job.

Ups and Downs of Work

Work can be more than a paycheck: Most U.S. adults report that they are learning at work and have opportunities to solve problems (Maestas et al., 2017a, 2017b). Sandra gushes about the meaning and the joy she finds at work, and the satisfaction of seeing her students, years later, some now with families of their own, who remember her and are grateful for her intervention in their lives. Jobs can also be a source of meaning and community. Even though many adults are juggling families and careers and may be rushing all the time, their busyness will pay off: These adults tend to be healthier and happier in the long run (Engels et al., 2021). Nevertheless, employment often comes with challenges. For instance, nearly half of all Americans report that their work is often unpleasant or hazardous.

One work-related challenge is scheduling (Federal Reserve Board, 2020). Many adults struggle to balance their time at home with their responsibilities at their job. This is more troublesome if day-to-day working hours are unpredictable, as is the case for nearly half of all U.S. adults (Maestas et al., 2017a, 2017b). Such workers may rely on seasonal work, or they may not know their weekly schedules in advance. As a result, they may lurch in and out of poverty as the months grind on (Morduch & Schneider, 2017). Workers of color are particularly vulnerable to erratic scheduling practices (Storer et al., 2020).

It is not just workers at the lower end of the income scale who are vulnerable to the challenges of work scheduling. Professionals and managers in many so-called "greedy" occupations, including medicine, law, and finance, are often expected to put in more than 80 hours a week, with promotions contingent on being always available. What keeps people going? For some, it is the hope that retirement will be easier, a time for fulfilling those dreams of travel or having enough time for family (Freund, 2020). However, burdensome work responsibilities take a toll on families, often contributing to parents' decline in wages and a culture of burnout (Cha, 2010; Gerstel & Clawson, 2018).

Burnout is one term researchers use to describe the emotional exhaustion caused by stressful working conditions that leads to a sense of detachment, bitterness, and ultimately a lack of confidence (Maslach & Leiter, 2017). Unlike depression or PTSD, which can also make us feel depleted, burnout is specifically tied to a job. It is a particular issue in jobs that are intense and focused on caregiving, like health care, education, disaster response, and community services (Maslach & Leiter, 2017; Skaalvik & Skaalvik, 2017). For many workers, the COVID-19 pandemic only exacerbated these stresses. As one nurse explained, "I have nightmares that I won't have my PPE [personal protective equipment]. I worry . . . I can't turn my brain off" (qtd. in Hoffman, 2020).

Zapped of compassion, workers experiencing burnout have a difficult time doing their jobs well. Addressing burnout can involve changing the workplace culture, giving workers frequent reminders that they are valued, encouraging resilience through the building of strong relationships, and granting workers more control over how work is done (West et al., 2020). It can also be addressed at the personal level: through exercise, individual therapy, and stress-reducing techniques such as meditation (Maslach & Leiter, 2017; Sun et al., 2017; West et al., 2016). Sandra, who listens to distressing stories from middle school students every day, is not immune to work frustration. Her school system, like other large organizations, can sometimes be rigid. She credits her middle-aged expertise, particularly in understanding the system itself, for helping her bounce back at work and step up to the challenges of the job, which gives back to her each day.

(left margin, rotated) Bonnie Jo Mount/The Washington Post via Getty Images

Thriving in Midlife Often Means Balancing. For Franny Tidwell, adulthood includes balancing her responsibilities to her twins, including talking them out of trees when necessary, with her own career aspirations.

Thriving in the Workplace

Work is changing worldwide. Adults may have hoped to reach midlife with a stable income but often find that work is not as reliable as they may have expected, and it comes with new challenges and stresses (Carnevale et al., 2019). Technology and the

burnout The term researchers use to describe the emotional exhaustion caused by stressful working conditions that leads to a sense of detachment, bitterness, and ultimately a lack of confidence in your skills.

ADULTS IN THE FORMAL WORK FORCE

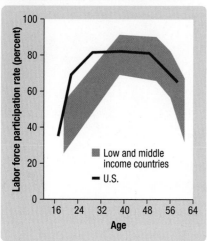

PEAK EARNINGS VARY

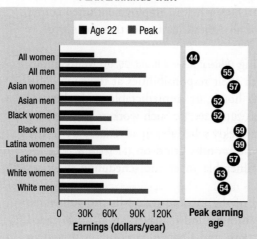

PEAK EXPERTISE

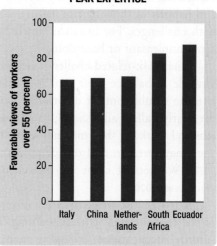

FIGURE 14.3 Changing Patterns of Work in Adulthood Adults in midlife are likely to be at the peak of their work lives, although they begin earlier in more affluent countries (see figure on the left). The timing of this peak, and how much adults earn, depends on their social identity (see middle figure). Stereotypes about older workers vary around the world, as you can see in the figure on the right.

Hugs Are Sometimes a Job Benefit. For this healthcare worker in New York, an appreciative embrace from a survivor of COVID-19 may be one of the rewards of difficult work. Finding meaning in a job can help all of us succeed at work.

increased interconnectedness of the global economy are both to blame. Over the past 20 years, the improving global economy has helped nations around the world improve their standards of living. As a result, more than a billion people around the globe are no longer living in extreme poverty (World Bank, 2020). Countries such as China and India now have a rising middle class (Shah, 2009). Yet economic change has made life more difficult for many. Stable, well-paying jobs with good benefits and long-term job security are not always available, particularly for people without higher education (see **Figure 14.3**) (Stiglitz, 2007, 2019). Growth in employment is often in the service sector.

In the United States, many manufacturing jobs have been lost to increasing automation, as robots replaced people in warehouses and on assembly lines (Manyika et al., 2017; Rowthorn & Ramaswamy, 1999; Smit et al., 2020). New technology has eliminated whole classes of workers: Data entry professionals, filing clerks, and secretaries have all seen their ranks decline. New jobs are often in the service sector: in sales, health care, or education (Pew Research Center, 2019). Well-paying careers in these industries often require higher education and the newest skill set, whether that is a new programming language or a new technique for welding (Acemoglu & Autor, 2011; Deming & Noray, 2018).

Experts suggest that thriving in this global marketplace takes flexibility. The typical worker will have more than 12 jobs before they retire (U.S. Bureau of Labor Statistics, 2021c). Many of these job changes will be involuntary: Recessions and widespread unemployment hit middle-aged workers the hardest (Glei et al., 2018). They often have more difficulty than younger workers getting rehired after layoffs, in part because their family responsibilities make it more difficult for them to be adaptable.

Some workforce-training programs, such as those provided by the U.S. federal government, have a positive impact on the earnings and economic fortunes of adults (Andersson et al., 2013; Barnow & Smith, 2015). Researchers suggest that learning new skills will be key to success in a world marked by change (Rudolph et al., 2017). Personal strengths can help adults succeed at work: Being conscientious and being able to control yourself continue to be key skills for helping adults succeed at work, as they were for teenagers in school (Allemand et al., 2019). Simply being able to focus on work itself is not all that helps us get ahead: Being generous can also help at work.

MAKING A DIFFERENCE
Helping Others Can Help You Get Ahead

In today's global world, with the pressures of adjusting to new technology, scheduling, and instability, do you have to be ruthless to get ahead? Researchers suggest that being persistent and hardworking are always valuable traits (Dale et al., 2018; Duckworth et al., 2018). One researcher, Adam Grant, has been part of a new generation of thinkers who challenge the idea that we need to be cunning and cruel to get ahead (Grant, 2019). In groundbreaking research, Grant has established that feeling your job is meaningful can make workers more productive and less likely to burn out, and that employees who are generous actually can get ahead in the long run (Bolino & Grant, 2016; Grant & Shandell, 2022; Sonnentag & Grant, 2012).

What is it about caring? Apparently, being generous is a powerful motivator: In experiments with lifeguards, nurses, and salespeople, workers who felt that they were helping people were more focused and worked harder (Grant & Gino, 2010; Sonnentag & Grant, 2012). Employees who were kind to each other at work—the people who took time to answer questions, to respond to an e-mail, to give career advice—also did well, most of the time (Grant, 2013). People who behave prosocially at work also need to have limits: They need to make sure they get their own work done and have some boundaries. In the long run, however, they tend to find support within organizations and rise to the top. Being selfish does not always mean success (Grant & Berry, 2011).

Sandra is excited about middle life: It has given her an opportunity to make a difference in the lives of the students she serves at school, and to take care of her father as he ages. She has developed expertise at work and on the trails and now feels confident both on the starting line and in picking up equipment at a sporting goods store. Her relationships are stronger, too: She describes them as more genuine and more supportive than they were earlier in her life, as she has grown into herself. As you will read in the next chapter, these strong relationships help adults build resilience in middle life.

APPLY IT! 14.10 Sandra is still excited to go to work, but she may move in a new direction as she gets older. What advice do you have for her about the strengths of midlife employees?

14.11 Systemic challenges like difficulties with work scheduling may contribute to professional challenges for many. What advice do you have to help adults thrive at work?

Wrapping It Up ⬭⬭

LO 14.1 What are the historical and contemporary markers of middle adulthood? (p. 406)

Middle adulthood begins as adults establish independent lives and ends as they recognize their own aging. Developmental events during middle adulthood are diverse: They may include parenthood, career, and/or caregiving.

LO 14.2 What factors trigger aging, and how do adults age during middle adulthood? (p. 406)

Many adults are anxious about getting older. They begin to show the outward signs of aging and may be faced with ageism and/or ableism. Aging is triggered by genetic and environmental changes, and the pace of aging reflects widespread social inequalities. Many adults develop changes in their vision and hearing. Fertility gradually declines, particularly as ova show the signs of age as adults reach their 40s. Menopause, typically around age 51, marks the end of ovulation and the hormonal changes that lead to menstruation. Hormones secreted by the testes also change with age, but the effects are less dramatic. Erectile dysfunction is a common condition in later life. For many adults, sexuality, however, continues to be a source of joy and support in middle life.

LO 14.3 Describe disparities in chronic conditions and factors that can help boost resilience in adulthood. (p. 416)

In many nations around the world, most adults have developed at least one chronic health condition by midlife. In some affluent countries, including the United States, many adults are less healthy and dying younger. Chronic pain is a leading cause of disability in the United States and other chronic conditions including cardiovascular disease and cancer affect many midlife adults. There continue to be significant disparities in health based on identity and economic categories including income, ethnicity, and race. These are exacerbated by unequal distribution of health care resources, residential segregation, discrimination, early life adversity, ongoing trauma, and health-related behaviors. Adults can build resilience through healthy nutrition, physical activity, and sleep.

LO 14.4 Identify the areas of developmental change in the brain as adults reach midlife. (p. 421)

The brain continues to change and develop as adults learn and change in middle life, but the overall pattern of maturation slows. Some parts of the brain shrink and levels of some neurotransmitters, such as dopamine, begin to decline. Most of these changes are not detectable outside of the laboratory. Life events, including parenting, continue to shape and change the brain. Individual differences continue to shape how the brain matures: Enriching experiences during early development and during middle life protect the brain and can slow aging.

LO 14.5 What are the cognitive strengths of midlife? (p. 424)

Adults often feel that they are at their peak cognition in middle adulthood. They have thinking skills and expertise that help them excel. On laboratory tests, adults' attention, memory, and ability to multitask are declining. Crystalized reasoning is what you know and how you can use it in the real world. Fluid reasoning includes the underpinning of your cognitive skills like your processing speed and memory skills. Adults' fluid reasoning declines as a result of brain aging. Good health, avoiding distractions, and multitasking can help adults' maintain their cognitive skills. Adults are not too old to learn new skills and be innovative, whether that is at work or at school.

LO 14.6 What are common challenges and ways of boosting work in midlife? (p. 427)

Middle adulthood is when many adults are at the peak of their career. Jobs can give adults a sense of generativity and purpose and the feeling that they are contributing. Work can have challenges: Not all adults have an equitable chance in the workforce. Parents, people of color, and other people with marginalized identities often face discrimination. Adults often have difficulty finding a work–family balance. Others may have difficulties with burn-out. Succeeding at work can come from feeling connected and prosocial.

KEY TERMS

middle adulthood (p. 406)
ageism (p. 408)
ableism (p. 408)
menopause (p. 413)

erectile dysfunction (ED) (p. 414)
cardiovascular disease (CVD) (p. 416)

health disparities (p. 418)
crystallized reasoning (p. 424)
fluid reasoning (p. 424)

expertise (p. 425)
peak career (p. 427)
burnout (p. 429)

CHECK YOUR LEARNING

1. Which of the following is a marker for the end of middle adulthood?
   a) When your hair turns gray
   b) When you stop going to school
   c) When you stop being carded buying alcohol
   d) When you recognize yourself as older

2. Middle adulthood is a flexible life stage marked by diversity in roles and health. How do you know if you are a middle-aged adult?
   a) When you recognize yourself as being no longer young but not yet older
   b) When you have children and a partner
   c) When you start watching network news
   d) When you bring a list to the grocery store

3. Sandra feels that she is at the peak of her health and strength in her forties. Despite her experience, without intervention, adults' bodies are beginning to:
   a) quickly deteriorate.
   b) slowly lose muscle strength.
   c) rapidly weaken.
   d) become stronger and more flexible.

4. Ableism is the prejudice based on the idea that people:
   a) have less value if they do not have typical abilities.
   b) should be able to do whatever they want.
   c) are able to thrive in adulthood.
   d) should be able to discriminate.

5. Which of the following characterizes the hormonal changes of menopause?

   a) Menopause is a traumatic event that always causes depression.

   b) Menopause is a gradual process and can take more than five years.

   c) Menopause is a natural process and you should not talk about it.

   d) Menopause marks the end of sexual life.

6. During adulthood, the brain:

   a) changes as people learn and react to life experiences.

   b) stays the same since nothing new happens after 30.

   c) grows rapidly in a pre-programmed process.

   d) rapidly and dramatically deteriorates.

7. Crystalized intelligence is building and often at a peak in middle adulthood. Sandra's crystalized intelligence includes:

   a) knowing how to help middle school children adapt to school.

   b) her abstract thinking skills.

   c) her working memory and processing speed.

   d) her strength in the last mile of a half-marathon.

8. In middle adulthood, some cognitive changes appear to be inevitable and genetically programmed, but what effect do the environment and life experience have?

   a) The environment has no impact on thinking skills in middle adulthood.

   b) With proper enrichment, adults can reverse all the cognitive aging that occurs during middle adulthood.

   c) Good health and environmental stimulation can build cognitive resilience but cannot completely forestall cognitive aging.

   d) Cognitive skills are completely genetic, and life experience has no effect on them.

9. Sandra has developed expertise in her job and has years of experience. Some experts would call this:

   a) peak career.

   b) midlife doldrums.

   c) burnout.

   d) the beginning of the end.

10. Which of the following is NOT a benefit of work in middle age?

    a) A sense of generativity and meaning

    b) Increased economic security

    c) Connections to others in the community

    d) Exhaustion and burnout

Emotional and Personality Development in Midlife

15.1 Describe the impact of life events and the social context on adult development.

15.2 Describe Erikson's crisis of generativity versus stagnation.

15.3 Explain the benefits of generativity in midlife.

Relationships in Midlife

15.4 Describe the diverse roles and relationships that characterize middle adulthood.

Emotional Risks and Resilience in Adulthood

15.5 Describe common emotional disorders that occur during middle adulthood.

Selected Resources from

 Achieve

Activities

Spotlight on Science: Understanding the Cohort Effect

Concept Practice: Adult Personality Development

Assessments

LearningCurve

Practice Quiz

Videos

Scientific American Profiles

Grandparents Raising Grandchildren

©Macmillan, Photo by Sidford House

Doug's life took a different turn in his 40s. He went back to school, got a degree in teaching, and started a new career in the classroom. His motivation? His daughter, Gwen. He wanted to be a parent who showed up, who was there in the morning and afternoon. That was impossible with his previous job, which required long weeks on the road.

Before Gwen, Doug loved that job. He and his wife, Stephanie, even had romantic weekend meetups and adventures in different cities. But once Gwen was born, Doug wanted to be close to home. He was so eager to see his daughter that he would run home and arrive at his apartment out of breath.

He came to love his new career. Teaching was a natural fit: Both his parents were teachers, and he wanted to do something that contributed to his community.

Gwen's early years were not easy, even though she was an adorable baby. Doug was gone more often than he ever was at his old job. This time, however, it was family that kept Doug away from his daughter. Doug and Stephanie were older parents, which meant that their parents were also older. There were perks to this: Stephanie's father, Bill, retired and moved close by to help with the baby. But Stephanie's mother was diagnosed with Alzheimer disease and could no longer live independently. Doug's parents, far away in Canada, also needed support.

Doug took the better part of a year off from working to help his parents stay in their own home. As Doug remembers, middle age "isn't for wimps." Doug and Stephanie have many strengths that keep them going: a 25-year marriage, the stability of two jobs they love (Stephanie is an actor), and the support of friends.

Like many people in midlife, Doug has been shaped by his past, unexpected life events, and his own personality. He has had his challenges, especially the years spent juggling the caregiving of a young child and older parents. Doug and Stephanie agree that their years of caregiving have made them better people: more patient, more thoughtful, and less self-centered. Doug admits that the most difficult times made him cherish Stephanie even more. As he remembers, he always loved her because she was "you know, smart and attractive and cool," but now he admires her even more after watching her care for Gwen and their parents.

Part of what makes Doug's life meaningful is caring for other people — whether as a parent, partner, son, or teacher. Indeed, developmental scientists have found that caring for other people is a critical source of resilience. Resilience is more important than ever in middle adulthood, when people experience joys and challenges alike. Particularly today, many adults must find a way to balance the responsibilities of family, work, and community, just as Doug does.

Remember from Chapter 14 that brain maturation offers us some advantages in midlife, such as improved emotion regulation. Developmental science and practical interventions can also help adults live more satisfying lives. At the basis of much of this work is the evidence that relationships, whether with family, friends, or romantic partners, can be a source of strength. Improving adults' ability to thrive is crucial because of their positions of responsibility at home and at work. Therefore, well-being has an exponential effect, because it also means helping the children and the elders for whom they care (Lachman et al., 2015).

Scientific American Profile

Meet Doug

Emotional and Personality Development in Midlife

Of all the stages of the lifespan, middle adulthood can be the longest, at more than 30 years for many adults who have established independent lives by their late 20s and do not consider themselves "older" until their 60s (Emling, 2017). Most developmental scientists agree that the emotional changes that happen during this time do not follow a universal pattern. Developmental change in middle adulthood results from life transitions that are often unique and unpredictable. Adults are diverse because the events that change them, like finding a job or a partner, do not happen to everyone and rarely occur in the same sequence.

During adulthood, context is critical. Remember from Bronfenbrenner's bioecological model that how, where, and when you live helps determine the events that shape you (Bronfenbrenner, 1979). By middle adulthood, outside forces have had many years to impact your identity, your emotion regulation, your ways of relating, and your personality. As a result, there is tremendous diversity in how adults develop (Bühler & Nikitin, 2020; Lachman et al., 2015). Doug, for instance, is shaped by his upbringing in Canada, his experience living in New York City as a young man, and his itinerant early adulthood, spent crisscrossing the continent for work. He is also shaped by his long-term commitment to his partner and his experiences in the classroom working with children.

Just as the cumulative effects of health behaviors begin to take a toll on your body in middle age, social, economic, and emotional factors impact your emotional and social development (Elder et al., 2015). Unemployment, poor health, intimate partner abuse, or chronic discrimination can all have lasting impacts. Privileged careers, loving partnerships, and years of exercise can make us stronger.

Learning Objectives

15.1 Describe the impact of life events and the social context on adult development.

15.2 Describe Erikson's crisis of generativity versus stagnation.

15.3 Explain the benefits of generativity in midlife.

Developmental science suggests there are ways adults can build resilience in midlife, no matter how they started out (Willis et al., 2019). If they are asked, many adults tell interviewers that being in midlife is a time of possibility, even if it can also be stressful (Arnett, 2018).

Transitions in Emotional and Social Development in Midlife

Although physical health begins to subtly decline during midlife, remember from Chapter 14 that middle-aged adults have many emotional and social advantages. For instance, while there is tremendous diversity in income and financial well-being, the peak earning years are in the 40s and 50s (Perez, 2019). Adults in the United States have more social ties with their children, friends, siblings, and the broader community at age 50 than at any other time in the lifespan (Dolberg & Ayalon, 2018).

Many adults report greater emotion regulation, or even a sense of emotional mellowing, in midlife (Dolberg & Ayalon, 2018; Livingstone & Isaacowitz, 2015; Zimmermann & Iwanski, 2014). This finding may, in part, reflect brain maturation: When compared to younger adults, researchers find that by midlife, the brain is less reactive to emotions (see **Figure 15.1**). Remember that in middle adulthood the reward system is not as flooded with the neurotransmitter dopamine as it was in early adulthood. In addition, strong connections have been built between the prefrontal cortex and the subcortical structures, making it easier to control emotional impulses (Cacioppo et al., 2011; Mather, 2016). As adults pass midlife, their nerve pathways begin to respond less quickly to intense experiences, resulting in more muted physical responses to strong emotions (MacCormack et al., 2020; Palve & Palve, 2018; Uchino et al., 2010).

Nevertheless, when researchers ask adults how happy or how satisfied they are with their lives, they find that adulthood is challenging for many. For people in affluent countries, midlife is at the bottom of a U-shaped curve: Most middle-aged adults report that life is harder than it was in early adulthood, even though they are generally happy (Blanchflower & Oswald, 2019; Cheng et al., 2017; Mehta et al., 2020; Steptoe et al., 2015). This is not the case in lower-income countries, where older adults are likely to have financial difficulties or feel like a burden on their families, and health care is not readily available. For them, midlife is much happier than what will come later (Gurven et al., 2017).

Nevertheless, most middle-aged adults still report being satisfied most of the time, just less frequently than they were in their younger years (Jebb et al., 2020). Most researchers do not see a drop in satisfaction as an inevitable part of being middle aged: They also do not see it as a dramatic midlife crisis. Rather, many psychologists, sociologists, and economists argue that difficulties with life satisfaction are tied to the complexity of adulthood today—the result of the stress of managing many roles and responsibilities in an uncertain world (Clark, 2018; Graham & Ruiz Pozuelo, 2017).

The burdens of midlife stress do not fall equally (Graham & Ruiz Pozuelo, 2017). (See **Figure 15.2**.) People who are in poor physical health, who are strained financially, and who are unemployed are particularly likely to have difficulties (Clark, 2018). But, people who have a sense of purpose, strong social support, and healthy emotion regulation fare better and may even live longer than those who do not (Jebb et al., 2020; O'Connor & Graham, 2019).

Share It!

The early months of the COVID-19 pandemic were hard on everyone. But midlife adults reported the greatest increase in stress and anxiety, mostly because they likely had to juggle the most daily hassles and caregiving.

(NORC, 2021)

Scientific American: Lifespan Development

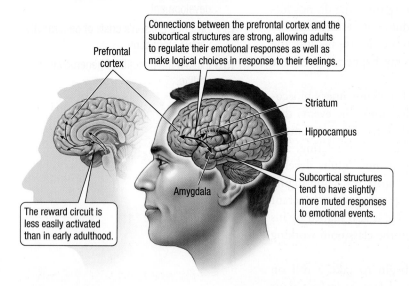

Connections between the prefrontal cortex and the subcortical structures are strong, allowing adults to regulate their emotional responses as well as make logical choices in response to their feelings.

Prefrontal cortex

Striatum

Hippocampus

Amygdala

Subcortical structures tend to have slightly more muted responses to emotional events.

The reward circuit is less easily activated than in early adulthood.

FIGURE 15.1 The Social and Emotional Brain in Middle Adulthood
During middle adulthood, adults often have greater ability to regulate their emotions and slightly more muted reaction to emotional events and the anticipation of rewards.

MIDLIFE DIP IN SATISFACTION IN THE UNITED STATES

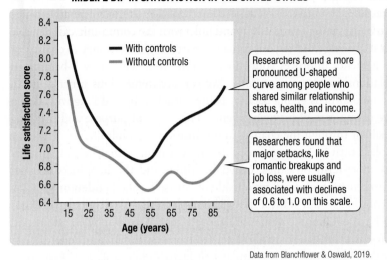

PEAK OF WORRY AND DECLINE OF HAPPINESS

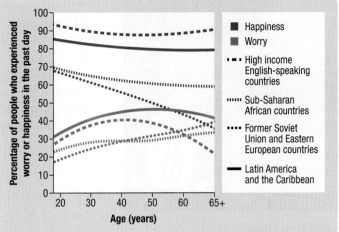

Data from Blanchflower & Oswald, 2019.

Data from Steptoe et al., 2015.

FIGURE 15.2 How Does Life Satisfaction Change over the Lifespan? Researchers have found that for many U.S. adults, there is a slight dip in life satisfaction during midlife (*left*). This dip is more temporary when scientists look at people who have not experienced major health problems or income loss. When researchers compared adults from many countries around the world (*right*), they found that life satisfaction was strongly linked to community supports. Countries with fewer supports tended to have more worry and less happiness with age.

Theories of Emotional and Social Development in Midlife

You probably have your own ideas about what it takes to thrive in adulthood. If you are like many college students today, you may aspire to travel abroad, buy a house, and make a difference in the world (Deloitte, 2019). Stephanie and Doug have dreams, too. They hope for more time with Gwen and Stephanie's father. More time playing games and make-believe. More trips to the corner bakery for an early-morning coffee and croissant.

Stephanie and Doug tell us that their own developmental ethnotheory is to be kind to other people and to be grateful for what they have: Life is always surprising. Stephanie likes to tell people what her father once told her, when she called him complaining that the life she had was not what she had imagined. "Oh sweetheart," he said to her, "I have never lived the life I have imagined, but I have never imagined the life I have lived." As you will see, researchers in fields ranging from developmental science to economics have tried to predict what will help adults live long, healthy, and happy lives.

Generativity Versus Stagnation In Erikson's view, middle adulthood is a time of conflict between **generativity versus stagnation** (Erikson, 1994; Erikson & Erikson, 1998). **Generativity** is the idea of making something or caring for something that has an impact upon the world. This means doing something for others, particularly for the next generation, leaving a legacy, or otherwise making the world a better place. *Stagnation* is generativity's opposite: being stuck in yourself, self-absorbed and self-centered, or feeling dissatisfied and having a lack of purpose.

Erikson believed that the goal of adulthood was to give back. He saw mulitple ways adults could accomplish this: by being parents, having a job that provides for others, or serving the community (Smelser & Erikson, 1980). In Erikson's view, adulthood was a "wonderful time to be alive, cared for and caring," a time of challenge and excitement (Erikson & Erikson, 1998, p. 116). For Erikson and his wife and collaborator, Joan, generativity meant a packed schedule of writing, community activism, and caring for their growing children (Elkind, 1970; Gardner, 1965).

The Benefits of Generativity In the years since Erikson proposed his classic theory, empirical research has supported his findings. Adults who are generative tend to be

CONNECTIONS

Remember from Chapter 13 Erikson's sixth stage, or crisis, of development: intimacy and isolation, when young adults address the development of close relationships.

generativity versus stagnation In Erikson's theory, the conflict in adulthood between making an impact on others and being stuck in your own needs.

generativity Caring or contributing to others in a way that has an impact on the world.

Enjoying a Moment of Rest For Erik Erikson and his wife, Joan, shown near their home in Tiburon, California, middle age was a time of generativity: continued learning, political activism, work, and parenthood.

CONNECTIONS

Remember from Chapter 2 that Maslow suggested that human beings have many needs that often compete for their attention. He pointed out that it is often difficult to move toward a point of generativity, self-improvement, and self-actualization if you have not addressed your own basic needs, like safety, food, and water.

Finding More Than Trash on the Beach These volunteers cleaning a beach near Naples, Italy, may be finding more than litter. Many adults who give back to their communities report feeling a sense of accomplishment and generativity.

hedonia The enjoyment you receive from short-term pleasures.

eudemonia The happiness you find from your commitment to higher values outside of yourself.

more successful and engaged parents, partners, and community members (Keyes & Ryff, 1999; McAdams & Guo, 2015; McAdams & Olson, 2010; Moen & Wethington, 1999). Generative adults take active steps to build strong relationships and links with the community. Generative behavior, whether it is being kind to your romantic partner, giving money to charity, or lending an ear to a friend, improves your mood, boosts your sense of well-being, and enhances your relationships (Nelson et al., 2018). We can see tremendous generativity in Doug's life: the sense that he is giving back by being a teacher, by cuddling with Gwen and a book, or by taking care of his own parents. This sense of purpose and meaning helps Doug be resilient through the changes and transitions of adult life.

Modern scholars turn to ancient Greek for the vocabulary that helps them distinguish between short-term pleasures, called **hedonia**, and the happiness you get from your commitment to higher values outside of yourself, called **eudemonia** (Yoo & Ryff, 2019). While no one would want a life without pleasure, researchers have found that people who have eudemonic values are more likely to be happy in adulthood (and beyond) (Ryff et al., 2021). They are also likely to have less inflammation and lower cholesterol levels than their peers with similar risk factors (Boyle et al., 2019; Radler et al., 2018; Steptoe et al., 2015).

Critiques of Erikson Despite the substantial body of research that supports the value of generativity and eudemonia, some researchers have nevertheless questioned Erikson's stage theory. They point out that generativity is not specific to middle adulthood: In fact, in some studies, younger adults have more of a generative drive than older adults (Lawford et al., 2021).

Other researchers have questioned whether Erikson's theory applies to everyone: Can you be generative if you must worry about everyday survival? Is being generative a privilege? These scholars, in line with the classic observations of Abraham Maslow described in Chapter 2, point out that many human beings need to have their basic needs met before they can try to be generative: It is difficult to feel like an accomplished caregiver if you are worrying about keeping food in the house or staying safe in a war-torn neighborhood (Maslow, 1943, 1970; Tay & Diener, 2011). Having a job and adequate income makes it easier to be generative (Andreoni et al., 2021; Jebb et al., 2020).

However, even in moments of extreme adversity, people can connect with others and with something greater than themselves (Goldy & Piff, 2020). Adults manage to take care of sick children, tend to ailing parents, and help their neighbors no matter what their income. So, despite scholarly disagreements about how much adversity impacts generativity, scientific consensus has established that generativity is an advantage.

Are There Stages in Adulthood? Another criticism of Erikson is that he lumped all adults into the same life stage. In his theory, for instance, a 35-year-old is about the same as a 55-year-old. In response, a number of theorists in the 1970s proposed that adult life proceeded in a series of steps: first the establishment of a romantic partnership, then a focus on a career, and then in later life, a turn to focusing on family and giving back (Gould, 1972, 1978; Levinson, 1978; Levinson & Levinson, 1996; Sheehy, 1976; Vaillant, 1998).

It may seem obvious that change happens during adulthood, but these stage theories have not withstood the test of time (Schmidt, 2020). Among their limitations: Many were based on research with small samples of affluent men. One researcher studied only men who were in the Harvard College classes of 1939 to 1941 (Vaillant, 1998). Another based his theory on just 40 people, all of whom identified as men, of whom 10 were biologists and another 10 were published writers (Levinson, 1978). As a result, most researchers today suggest that there are no universal stages in adulthood. However, these theorists helped to popularize another cultural idea about adulthood: the midlife crisis.

CAN YOU BELIEVE IT?
Is There a Midlife Crisis?

One of the first images of middle adulthood that may come to mind might be of a **midlife crisis**, a painful turning point when adults reevaluate their lives and make major changes (Abad-Santos, 2013). Actor Jake Gyllenhaal told a reporter that he had a midlife crisis, explaining: "I woke up one day and I wasn't in the right room . . . It was like a David Byrne song: 'That's not my beautiful house. That's not my beautiful wife'" (Gyllenhaal qtd. in Bhattacharya, 2015). Developmental science suggests that although Gyllenhaal may have had a moment of dramatic transition; a "crisis" does not happen to most people (Lachman, 2015; Wethington, 2000).

The idea of a midlife crisis originated in a renewed interest in self-fulfillment in the 1960s (Infurna et al., 2020; Jackson, 2020; Schmidt, 2020). Psychologists proposed that adults were destined to have a midlife crisis, which helped birth the stereotypical and heavily gendered image of a man who gets a younger girlfriend, a red sports car, and a "bachelor pad" (Levinson, 1978; Vaillant, 1998). Theorists also suggested that women went through a midlife transition after their children were grown and, like birds, were faced with an *empty nest* (Harkins, 1978; Raup & Myers, 1989).

When researchers studied the idea empirically, this midlife crisis turned out to be extremely uncommon (Wethington, 2000). Only about 15 percent of adults have a period of intense emotional turmoil in midlife, and most of them have chronic mental illness (Lachman, 2015). Many researchers now see the midlife crisis as something rooted in dated, stereotypical ideas about gender and careers that were popular in the 1970s. Current researchers agree that people do not need a fancy car to get through their 40s, and parents need not lose their identity after their children leave home (Jackson, 2020; Schmidt, 2020).

Although the idea that midlife can be difficult *does* line up with many research findings, the midlife slump in life satisfaction is not usually a dramatic moment or crisis that is quickly resolved. It is linked to stressful or traumatic experiences (Blanchflower & Oswald, 2019). Recognizing that the midlife crisis is a myth may help identify adults who are truly experiencing emotional and mental health challenges triggered by difficult life events, economic turmoil, and even genes, but not necessarily by milestones like children leaving home or turning 50 (Infurna et al., 2020; Mitchell, 2016).

The Power of Life Events   Scientists may have debunked the midlife crisis, but they still consider midlife to be a dynamic life stage, with life experiences often transforming who we are. What drives change in midlife? If adults do not inevitably mature in a consistent pattern of stages, why do some people at high school reunions seem so different and others so much the same? Scientists suggest that there are patterns in how life changes you, but these are driven by events, not stages (Bleidorn et al., 2018; Costa et al., 2019). Transitions such as finding a partner, getting a job, having a family, getting separated, losing a spouse, and caring for your aging parents all change who you are in ways that scientists find predictable. These major life events, not ages or even birthdays, are how adults describe and remember their lives (Köber et al., 2015).

Major events often require adults to relearn their daily habits in ways that create lasting changes. For instance, having to show up at work every day helps make adults more reliable, even outside of the office (Bleidorn et al., 2018; Borghuis et al., 2018). Becoming a parent often has the opposite effect: It tends to make parents moodier and less reliable as they juggle their new responsibilities (Denissen et al., 2019). Other major events, like losing a partner or experiencing a serious health problem, tend to change you in the short term. But most adults return to their usual patterns of relating after a period of potentially painful adjustment (Denissen et al., 2019).

Some events are more powerful than others. Losing your job, for instance, is particularly potent, challenging your sense of self, your value, and your ability to provide

midlife crisis A concept in popular culture without much empirical support, in which adults reevaluate their lives upon reaching a painful turning point and make major changes.

FIGURE 15.3 What Makes You Happy in Midlife? Researchers examined the impact of life events on well-being in midlife and found that some personality factors, like emotional stability and outgoingness, were often linked to positive feelings. Difficulties, including losing a job or a partner, often had a more negative impact.

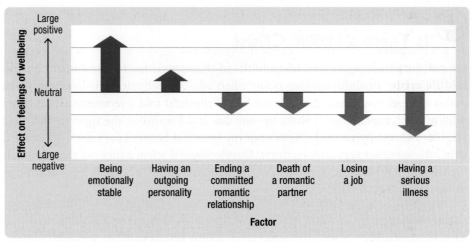

Data from Hentschel et al. 2017.

for others so much that its impact often cascades throughout your life. Difficult interpersonal relationships are another major stressor that can damage well-being in ways that are hard to rectify (Hentschel et al., 2017). (See **Figure 15.3**.)

Personality in Midlife

Doug admits that life has changed him, and Stephanie agrees. They both believe it is for the better. In particular, caregiving has made them more patient and more real. As Stephanie explains, "I had to love myself more because I was Gwen's mother." Researchers believe that what Doug and Stephanie report is not uncommon: Change is possible as adults go through midlife, although the changes are not typically drastic. Most adults still resemble who they were as teenagers. Getting older and settling into adult roles matures most people but does not usually lead to dramatic changes in personality (Borghuis et al., 2018; Mann et al., 2019).

CONNECTIONS

Remember from Chapter 9 that researchers often describe personality in terms of the discrete traits in the five-factor model: *openness* to new experiences (like curiosity); *conscientiousness* (like grit); *extraversion* (being outgoing); *agreeableness* (being easy to get along with); and *neuroticism* (moodiness or emotional sensitivity). They can be remembered with the acronym OCEAN.

Most adults become more emotionally stable over time. Researchers who study personality development under the lens of the *five-factor model* report that, in general, adults begin to settle down emotionally, becoming more conscientious, more agreeable, less neurotic, and a little less extraverted and open (Briley & Tucker-Drob, 2014; Costa et al., 2019; Mann et al., 2019). Neuroscientists suggest that brain development plays a role: As the reward system becomes less activated, you may feel less outgoing (DeYoung & Allen, 2019; Klimstra et al., 2013). Settling into adult roles, having a family, and being in a committed partnership also may make adults more reliable, easy to get along with, and emotionally stable (Roberts et al., 2005).

What Changes Over the Years? This couple got married at Tianjin University in northern China more than 30 years ago and returned to celebrate their reunion with other couples. Researchers who study personalty over time find that life events often change us. Being in a happy, committed relationship often makes us more emotionally stable, easier to get along with, and more conscientious.

Everyday experiences can add up to changes in overall personality: Supportive interactions that happen in a caring relationship tend to make people more agreeable, extraverted, and emotionally stable. But difficult, ongoing stresses, like those experienced in a challenging relationship, can actually make people less agreeable and more unstable (Borghuis et al., 2018).

There are cultural norms in terms of which personality traits are valued or discouraged, and some researchers even rank countries according to how conscientious or outgoing they claim to be (Ebert et al., 2019; Mõttus et al., 2012). These norms tend to be stereotypical. For instance, Americans are seen as being extraverted, outgoing, and brash. However, this does not mean that all Americans are outgoing (McCrae, 2017).

Around the world, people have a mix of personality types and forms (Kajonius & MacGiolla, 2017). Researchers estimate that less than 2 percent of your personality can be linked to your culture. Differences *between* people who share one culture are three times as large as those between any two cultures. This is a reminder of the importance of humility if you are tempted to base assumptions about someone's way of relating on their background.

While most adults are not dramatically different from their teenage selves, there are many exceptions (Masten & Wright, 2010). In one study, women who became parents as adolescents became more emotionally stable in their 30s (Werner & Smith, 1992). Some men who spent time in jail became exemplary citizens and leaders after they were released (Maruna, 2017). As noted by one researcher who followed a group of men over 60 years, people can change and grow, even after 40 (Vaillant, 2013). One constant in adults' lives is other people. Relationships can help make life happier and more meaningful.

APPLY IT! **15.1** Doug has changed a great deal in his middle-adult years: He has had a child, started a new career, and spent time caregiving for the older adults in his family. He says being middle-aged takes backbone. How might the theory of the U-shaped curve of life satisfaction give him hope for the future?
15.2 Research suggests that generativity helps give adults meaning and a sense of purpose in life. What are ways Doug shows his generativity?

Relationships in Midlife

Like many adults, Doug is attached to a team of people. First, there are the people with whom he lives: his partner of 25 years, Stephanie, and their daughter, Gwen. His team extends to Stephanie's father who lives down the street, to his brother and their parents in Canada, and to the broader community at the school where he teaches and the good friends they have made over the years.

While adults like Doug are more independent and may have children of their own, they are still tied to their own parents and their siblings, in a complex network of generations (Kim et al., 2022). In addition, adults are often embedded in a community that includes coworkers, acquaintances, and friends whom they see at the gym, at their house of worship, or at other local events. Quality social support from intimate partners, friends, or relatives has profound benefits for health and well-being. Relationships can help your body better regulate stress, reduce inflammation, and improve immune function. Scientists estimate that positive social relationships could be as important to your health as being active or maintaining a healthy weight (Kim et al., 2022; Woods et al., 2020).

Social relationships can provide you with *instrumental support*, as in hands-on assistance installing a new roof, sharing information about jobs at your workplace, or pestering you to take care of yourself (Wrzus et al., 2013). Friends and family can also give you *emotional support*: empathizing when you have had a bad day and helping you manage your feelings (Hilpert et al., 2016). Connections help maintain cognitive health by keeping you active and providing intellectual stimulation. They also help your body release feel-good hormones like oxytocin, which is involved in attachment and triggered by the touch of a loved one (as you read in Chapter 13), and endorphins (Holt-Lunstad, 2018). Endorphins are your body's "natural painkillers" and are often released when you share a laugh, a meal, or a glass of wine (Dunbar, 2018; Manninen et al., 2017). These hormones help you relax by soothing your stress response system (Antonucci et al., 2019).

During middle adulthood, adults' social roles are diverse and often in transition. Jobs begin and end, friendships start and fade, children are born and grow up, romantic relationships begin and change, family members may offer support and also require caregiving. As you can see in **Figure 15.4**, adults have diverse social connections in adulthood.

Learning Objective

15.4 Describe the diverse roles and relationships that characterize middle adulthood.

Hugs Help Build Resilience. Physical contact is one benefit of close relationships. Reunion was especially sweet for those who were able to see each other in real life, seen here in an airport in New Zealand, after being separated by restrictions tied to the COVID-19 pandemic.

PREVALENCE OF MULTIGENERATIONAL FAMILIES AROUND THE WORLD

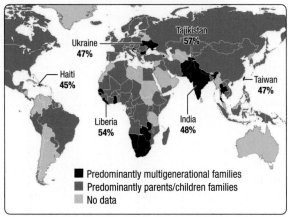

Ukraine 47%
Tajikistan 57%
Haiti 45%
Taiwan 47%
Liberia 54%
India 48%

■ Predominantly multigenerational families
■ Predominantly parents/children families
■ No data

Data from Pew Research Center, 2019.

STRUCTURE OF FAMILY LIFE IN MIDLIFE IN THE UNITED STATES

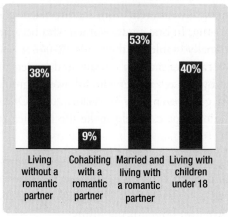

Living without a romantic partner: 38%
Cohabiting with a romantic partner: 9%
Married and living with a romantic partner: 53%
Living with children under 18: 40%

Data from Fry & Parker, 2021; U.S. Census, 2020.

LENGTH OF MARRIAGES IN THE UNITED STATES

Percentage of women still in their first marriage (y-axis: 0–100)
Years married (x-axis: 5, 15, 25, 35+)

Data from Mayol-Garcia et al., 2021.

FIGURE 15.4 Relationships in Midlife Diversity is the rule when it comes to family in midlife. Around the world, adults may live alone, in multigenerational families, or with their children. In the United States, families come in many forms. When researchers track how long marriages last, they find that more than 6 in 10 will last more than 30 years, but the major period of transition tends to be early in a relationship.

Scientific American Profile

Romantic Relationships in Midlife

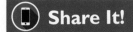
Romantic Relationships

Doug and Stephanie met more than 25 years ago and shared their first kiss on stage in a play. They were not sure at first whether their love was real or just stagecraft, but their relationship has lasted longer than that off-Broadway production. Like many couples in midlife, they have not had much time for themselves as they care for their daughter and their parents. Despite the infrequency of their date nights, they are grateful for their love and support of each other and the 90 minutes of Netflix they try to squeeze in after Gwen goes to sleep.

This is the case for many relationships in midlife: Adults' stronger emotion regulation and better impulse control makes many of the tasks of getting along easier. Relationships tend to be much less volatile, rates of intimate partner violence are much lower, and couples stay together longer (Smith et al., 2018). The rates of divorce in midlife are nearly one-third of what they are in early adulthood (Cohen, 2019). Despite these strengths, many relationships have seasons of strain.

Diversity of Close Relationships In the United States, many are moving into more committed, formal relationships as they reach midlife. These relationships take many forms. More than half of adults are married at 50; about 10 percent of middle-aged adults are cohabiting, far fewer than were in early adulthood (CPS, 2020). About another 10 percent are in long-term, committed relationships but not living with their partner, an arrangement known as *living apart together*, as you may remember from Chapter 13 (Benson & Coleman, 2016; Connidis & Barnett, 2018). About 3 in 10 are either casually dating, looking for a partner, or happily unpartnered (Kim et al., 2017). Relationship transitions like divorce still occur during midlife but at a much lower rate than earlier in adulthood (Wolfinger, 2015).

People who are not in a romantic relationship often encounter discrimination or stigma, including assumptions that they must be lonely or have something wrong with them (Fisher & Sakaluk, 2020; Gesselman et al., 2019). Unpartnered adults may even internalize these beliefs. Researchers have found that single people who believe that being married is superior to being single often feel particularly badly about themselves (Moss & Willoughby, 2018). Just because adults are not partnered does not mean they lack social support or are unhappy: Many are secure, content, and not at all lonely (Moore & Radtke, 2015; Pepping & MacDonald, 2019).

Marriage is more prevalent in the United States than in most other affluent countries around the globe, because many Americans believe that marriage is the ideal living situation (Horowitz et al., 2019). More children are born to married couples in the United States than in many other nations, including many in Europe and Latin America (OECD, 2020). Remember from Chapter 13 that many couples put off marriage until they are economically and emotionally settled. In the United States, marriage is increasingly a luxury: It is more common among college-educated and high-income couples, and less common among many groups who experience discrimination (Cherlin, 2020; Furstenberg, 2019). By midlife, about 7 in 10 U.S. adults have walked down the aisle (Mayol-Garcia et al., 2021).

Newlywed Bliss Many newlyweds, like this couple in Hong Kong, believe that marriage will lead to happiness. Scientists find that happy, committed relationships may give adults some advantages but that some of those may be due to correlation rather than causation.

Around the globe, marriage is tied to cultural beliefs about families and gender, and even demographics like the availability of prospective partners (Grossbard, 2018). Communities with strong social supports and traditions of gender equality, like in Sweden, tend to have lower rates of formal marriage but higher rates of committed cohabiting partnerships, which often are just as stable as marriages (Jalovaara & Kulu, 2018). There is even a Swedish word for these relationships: *sambo*. On the other hand, in communities with more conservative traditions about families and fewer supports for young families, traditional legal marriage is much more common (Grossbard, 2018; Zaidi & Morgan, 2017).

Is There Magic in Marriage? If you watch television shows like *The Bachelor* or *The Bachelorette*, or even just marvel at their popularity, you might believe that there is some magic to marriage. Does getting a ring or a rose really mean you will be happy? Are Doug and Stephanie happier because they are "official"? Developmental scientists tend to be cautious on this point. For many adults, getting married is a symbol of romance and commitment, but it is no guarantee that either will last (Horowitz et al., 2019).

In many surveys, people who are married tend to rank a bit higher in life satisfaction than those who are in less formal relationships or those who are single (Blieszner & Ogletree, 2018; Grover & Helliwell, 2019; Perelli-Harris et al., 2019). But these results are not universal. People who marry tend to have more economic, educational, and even emotional advantages than their single peers, which may have more to do with the boost in happiness than marriage itself (Coleman et al., 2018; Huntington et al., 2021).

Scientists also point out that not all marriages are the same. In about half, couples start out happy and stay that way. While you may have heard about the "seven-year itch," or a post-honeymoon dip in happiness, it turns out that these are myths (Amato & James, 2018; Anderson et al., 2010; Karney & Bradbury, 2020; Williamson & Lavner, 2020). Although a significant portion of marriages (probably about one in three) have difficulties, researchers believe that their problems were obvious from the very beginning (Caughlin et al., 2018; Lavner et al., 2014). And while many people end troubled relationships, more than one in eight chronically unhappy married couples do not seek divorce (Cervantes & Sherman, 2021).

A happy relationship can be a source of resilience, social support, and satisfaction in midlife, but an unhappy one damages well-being, hurts children, and can even shorten the lifespan (Carr et al., 2014; Lawrence et al., 2019). Healthy couples have a balance of giving and taking: Both partners feel supported by each other (Fincham & May, 2017). In a successful match, partners tend to spend time together and see each other in a forgiving light (Amato & James, 2018; Fincham, 2019). Affection and sex happen more frequently in a happy relationship, as does a more equitable division of household labor (Carlson et al., 2016). Some researchers have even found that couples' heartbeats are more aligned in highly satisfied relationships (Coutinho et al., 2021).

These bonds are not created magically. Healthy relationships are more likely when each individual comes equipped with personal strengths like a history of secure attachment, strong emotion regulation skills, and an even-tempered, conscientious personality (Shaver et al., 2019; Weidmann et al., 2017). Factors that signal a strong relationship are often

CONNECTIONS

Remember from Chapter 13 that finding a partner is a complicated mix of body and brain, involving your emotional history and attachment, your brain chemistry, your tendency to like people like yourself, and your cultural assumptions.

 Share It!

Be careful what you wish for. Many people have potentially harmful *ethnotheories*, or beliefs, about relationships. For instance, people who believe that the passion is destined to die are more likely to give up on their relationships than those who believe it can be rekindled.

(Carswell & Finkel, 2018)

Scientific American: Lifespan Development

practical, as in a couple's sense that both partners are committed, happy, and grateful to be together (Joel et al., 2020). But, as you will learn, often what makes relationships challenging is not partners' individual weaknesses, but outside stresses on their bond.

What Makes Relationships Hard? If you are struggling in a relationship, your pain may seem completely unique. Social scientists have searched for the patterns in these challenges, identifying poor communication, unfair division of household chores, disruptive use of technology, and unrealistically demanding expectations (Bühler & Nikitin, 2020). These problems are often exacerbated by systemic stresses like poverty and discrimination (Williamson & Lavner, 2020).

In popular media, much is often made of communication problems that can plague relationships (Gottman, 2014). Couples have spent millions of dollars on programs designed to help them communicate better (Bradbury & Bodenmann, 2020). Many of these interventions, targeted at teaching couples to talk to each other more kindly and empathetically, do not result in significant improvement to the relationship or reduce the rate of divorce (Karney & Bradbury, 2020; Schramm et al., 2017). In fact, scientists have found that the relationship between communication difficulties and couples' happiness is very slight (Kanter et al., 2021). Poor communication does not *cause* breakdowns in relationships: It is often the *symptom* of job-related stress, financial insecurity, or untreated mental health difficulties that eventually pushes couples to the breaking point (Fincham et al., 2018; Nguyen et al., 2020; Ross et al., 2019a).

One common strain for couples is the everyday stress of having children and managing household tasks (Gravningen et al., 2017). Developmental scientists suggest that a solution might come from outside the family: social policies that offer financial support for couples, helping them make time for their children and each other. Having a newborn, for instance, is a tremendous amount of work and nearly always stresses relationships, whether couples are wealthy or low-income, same-sex or other-sex (Don & Mickelson, 2014; Doss & Rhoades, 2017; O'Reilly Treter et al., 2021; Saxbe et al., 2018). (See **Figure 15.5**.) Social policies like paid family leave can help. For instance, paid leave eases the adjustment period of having a newborn, reducing caregivers' stress and improving relationship satisfaction for both members of the couple, particularly when both parents work (Petts & Knoester, 2020).

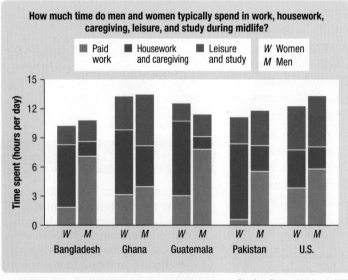

Data from Gimenez-Nadal et al., 2020.

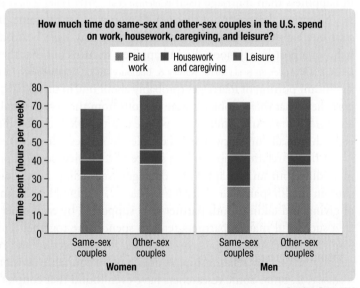

Data from Fettro, 2018.

FIGURE 15.5 Too Much Work to Go Around How much time adults spend in housework, paid work, and leisure often depends on their gender identity and the cultural assumptions and community supports where they live. On the left, researchers compared how adults in several nations spent their time, finding that in most nations, women took on more responsibility for housework and caregiving. On the right, a researcher examined how adults in same-sex and other-sex couples differed in how they spent their time.

Couples often disagree over how to share household tasks. While most partners say that they would rather split everything equally, in most other-sex couples, people who identify as women end up taking on most child care and do two or three times as much housework as their partners (Britt & Roy, 2014; Charbonneau et al., 2020; Evertsson et al., 2021; Hochschild & Machung, 2012; Lachance Grzela & Bouchard, 2010). Parents who identify as women in other-sex partnerships spend more time doing housework than most single parents (Pepin et al., 2018). In same-sex couples and in couples where one or both partners is transgender, the gender roles dictating who does what tend to be more fluid, and couples tend to be more egalitarian (Bauer, 2016; Evertsson et al., 2021; Tornello et al., 2020). However, in all couples, if one partner perceives the division of labor as unfair, they are very likely to feel unhappy (Britt & Roy, 2014; Chong & Mickelson, 2016; Lachance Grzela et al., 2019; Tornello et al., 2020).

Technology is another challenge for many relationships (Sbarra et al., 2019). Phones and screens take energy and attention, whether it is your boss contacting you on Slack, the allure of pornography or video games, or just an update from a friend. Nearly 7 in 10 of all midlife couples report that phones are a problem in their relationship (McDaniel & Coyne, 2016). Technology seems to require immediate responsiveness, which can often distract from people in real life. Although technology enables people to communicate across continents and in different languages, researchers have found that just the sight of a phone can keep people from focusing on each other (Aagaard, 2016; Wang et al., 2017).

The burden of difficult relationships does not fall equally: Lower-income adults break up at twice the rate as more affluent ones (Jackson et al., 2016). Adults who face discrimination or whose relationships are stigmatized—such as those in some multiethnic, same-sex, or transgender relationships—separate in higher numbers (Cooper & Pugh, 2020; Goldberg & Romero, 2019; Lavner et al., 2018). Childhood trauma and adversity increase the risk of depression, substance abuse, and other disorders, making a relationship even less sustainable (Merrick et al., 2017). The crisis of the COVID-19 pandemic highlighted this: The extra pressure of stay-at-home orders made things worse for couples who were already under strain, but it had less impact on couples who were getting along (Williamson, 2020). Effectively addressing systemic challenges requires much more than good communication skills: Couples must address adversity head on, together (Ross et al., 2019b).

MAKING A DIFFERENCE
Building Resilient Families

Have you ever come home in a foul mood, finding fault with everything and forgetting to thank your partner for making dinner, emptying the dishwasher, or listening to you complain? Researchers call this corrosive cascade of irritability, anger, and impatience that dumps onto relationships from the outside world *stress spillover* (Randall & Bodenmann, 2009). It comes from a variety of sources, such as the burnout from being a social worker or the anxiety from being a service member in combat (Finzi-Dottan & Berckovitch Kormosh, 2018; Schnittker, 2019). For many adults, it also comes from having to live with racism, discrimination, and poverty (Barton et al., 2018; Lavner et al., 2018; Nguyen et al., 2021).

While social relationships are critical for everyone, the benefits of a good relationship and the risks of a difficult one are even more pronounced for people who are living with adversity such as low income or chronic prejudice (Karney, 2021). Breaking up, divorcing, or enduring a painful relationship can have greater consequences for people who already accumulated stresses, perhaps accelerating a slide into poverty or making it more difficult to function as a parent (Coop Gordon et al., 2019).

One group of researchers decided to tackle the challenges faced by stressed families by focusing on causes rather than symptoms. In a program similar to the Nurse–Family

Share It!

Yes, things got worse for women during the COVID-19 pandemic. Early research suggests that gender gaps in child care and housework were exacerbated by the pandemic, with those who identify as women taking on more child care and housework than their other-sex partners.

(Collins et al., 2021)

Scientific American: Lifespan Development

Matt Carr/Getty Images

Do You See Any Mess? A division of household chores that seems fair often helps couples get along better. Some researchers have found that all adults see clutter and value neatness. But many feel that women are more responsible for picking up.

Partnership discussed in Chapter 3, one team went into the homes of low-income Black families in the rural south to help the families build resilience (Barton et al., 2018). Unlike other relationship education programs, the researchers focused not on communication skills, but on the external problems that were worrying these couples: money, extended family, parenting, and managing work (Barton et al., 2018; Jackson et al., 2016).

The program sought to build a sense of ethnic pride and family identity, encouraging couples to spend more time together and work as a team to solve problems. A randomized experiment (the gold standard for interventions, as you read in Chapter 1) found that the program was effective. Families were happier, and parenting skills improved (Barton et al., 2017, 2018; Lavner et al., 2020). Although researchers did not set out to improve communication skills, they found that helping families manage the external sources of stress in their relationships improved communication, too. Getting along is easier when you can tackle stress together. 🌎

Relationship Transitions in Midlife Breaking up is hard at any age. While separations are less common in midlife than they are in early adulthood, rates of divorce and separation have been increasing for middle-aged U.S. adults (Brown & Wright, 2017; Stepler, 2017). These adults have particular challenges: They are likely to have children, who can complicate and prolong transitions, and separation can often push one member of the former couple, typically a woman, into poverty (Lin et al., 2017).

The outcomes of relationship transitions, like relationships themselves, are not uniform (Bourassa et al., 2015). Some adults struggle during transitions; others, particularly if they experienced emotional or physical abuse, may see a boost in happiness and well-being after a breakup (Emery, 2012). Separation may cause a decline in health and an increase in stress, particularly for those who were already susceptible to depression (Sbarra & Manvelian, 2021; Sbarra & Whisman, 2022).

Transitions happen quickly. Typically, 7 out of 10 adults are in a new relationship within two years after a divorce (Anderson & Greene, 2011; Smock & Swartz, 2020). Many adults are happy to marry a second or even a third time: More than half of people who get divorced in midlife are remarried at least once (Horowitz et al., 2019; Mayol-Garcia et al., 2021).

Family in Midlife

Like Doug, many adults' emotional and social lives revolve around their family. Family roles are often changing: Many adults move from parenting their children to caring for their grandchildren and their own parents (Lachman et al., 2015). Adults' well-being is tied to this complex web of roles (Woods et al., 2020). Even in adulthood, these relationships, including those with grown children, are often complex and ambivalent (Pillemer et al., 2019). Maintaining family relationships, along with the challenges of demanding jobs, financial insecurity, and rapid technological change, can contribute to some of the strain that adults face in midlife.

Varieties of Families Around the world and within the United States, there is a diversity in how, when, and if adults become parents. Gender roles often affect the timing of parenthood, as you may recall from Chapter 13. Those who identify as women who have gone to college, particularly those with graduate degrees, tend to have children in their 30s, while those without college degrees tend to start their families much earlier. Those who identify as men tend to become fathers later, as it takes longer to get a financial footing and finish school: In the United States, most first-time fathers are 31 (Mayol-Garcia et al., 2021).

Similar patterns are found in affluent countries around the world (OECD, 2021). As a result of the diversity in when adults start families, they could be parenting a newborn or launching their children into adulthood at age 40. In the United States,

CONNECTIONS

Remember from Chapter 11 that relationship transitions, whether a formal divorce or a breakup, affect children, too. The conflict, stress, and financial strain that are typical of separation are often difficult to manage. However, most families are able to adapt.

kali9/E+/Getty Images

Hanging Out with the Baby Many adults, like this happy couple visiting their daughter's toddler in Florida, are grandparents. This couple is also raising their own teenage son (*right*), who gets to be uncle.

more than 6 out of 10 men and 8 out of 10 women are raising children during midlife (Geiger et al., 2019; Monte & Knop, 2019).

Scientists have wondered whether parents feel that the countless hours of changing dirty diapers, checking multiplication tables, and enforcing curfews are worth it. Do children make them happy? Children do typically bring more joy into adults' lives, along with a sense of purpose and generativity (Deaton & Stone, 2014; Nomaguchi & Milkie, 2020; Pollmann-Schult, 2014). This positive effect is particularly true for people who identify as men, who tend to experience fewer of the daily hassles and more of the emotional boosts from raising a family (Nelson-Coffey et al., 2019). However, many young families in the United States, particularly if they are struggling financially, tell researchers that children can cause extra stress. This can be even more true for single parents and for female parents, who tend to do more of the caregiving in other-sex relationships (Blanchflower & Clark, 2021; Nomaguchi & Milkie, 2020).

Blended families involving stepparents and stepchildren or half-siblings come with their own challenges (Ganong & Coleman, 2018). About 6 percent of men and about 8 percent of women are raising stepchildren (Kreider & Lofquist, 2014; Monte & Knop, 2019). Making a blended family function well is not always easy, particularly for stepmothers who often are tasked with the emotional work involved (Jensen & Sanner, 2021; Shapiro, 2014). Nevertheless, many adults report that being a stepparent can be a source of satisfaction and joy as their children grow (Ivanova, 2020).

Parenting Children and Adolescents Parenting is challenging because it takes time, which is often in short supply. Families are under increased pressure to be involved, intensive caregivers (Nomaguchi & Milkie, 2020). In comparison to earlier generations, parents—particularly those who are high income or who have finished college—often feel that they need to actively cultivate their children's development (Lareau, 2011). They believe that extra time in one-on-one play, or managing children's schoolwork, will give their children the needed edge for success in a highly competitive and insecure world (Doepke & Zilibotti, 2019; Kalil et al., 2012). This comes at a cost: Mothers in particular often feel overwhelmed (Geiger et al., 2019). But fathers, too, feel that they are failing. Most report that they do not feel that they are doing a very good job as parents (Parker & Horowitz, 2015).

The work of parenting changes as children grow. Babies require a lot of hands-on time, whereas older children need supervision with homework (Kalil & Mayer, 2016). Scientists have found that parenting also gets harder over time. The difficult stage? Adolescence. Parents often feel that what they are doing with their teenagers is not working, and that their input does not seem to matter. Children in elementary school also cause stress, particularly for parents who identify as women, who often feel tasked with making sure their children successfully adjust to school and the world of peers (Meier et al., 2018). (See **Figure 15.6**.)

Postresidential Parenting Even when children leave home, many parents remain attachment figures, and most parents report having close relationships with their children as they grow older (Fingerman et al., 2020). By the time they reach their late 50s, most parents in the United States no longer live with their children and are therefore in the **postresidential** phase of their family life (Monte, 2017).

Remember from Chapter 13 that two in three children live at home with their families throughout their early-adult years, and about 1 in 10 lives with their

postresidential A period in family life where parents may no longer live with their children.

FIGURE 15.6 How Is It to Be a Parent? While researchers found that happiness tends to dip (a bit) as children turn into adolescents, and parenting may feel slightly less meaningful during middle childhood, most parents report that they enjoy parenting and manage the stress.

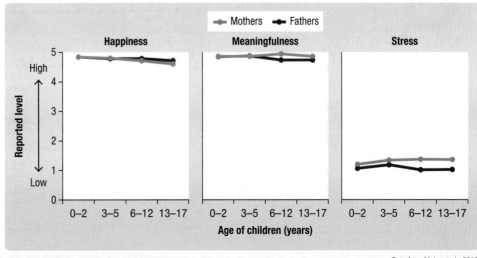

Data from Meier et al., 2018.

parents in midlife (Caputo, 2019; Fingerman et al., 2020). During the COVID-19 pandemic, families pulled together even more tightly and were more likely to live together and financially support each other than at any time since the Great Depression of the 1930s (Fry et al., 2020). More than 6 in 10 families financially support their children into their 30s (Barroso et al., 2019).

Economic pressures often make living together and sharing resources a sensible solution, but many communities value family togetherness even in a strong economy. Rates of intergenerational living tend to be higher in immigrant communities and families from Latino and Asian American backgrounds, even if financial strains are not a factor (Fuligni & Pedersen, 2002; Lei & South, 2016). (See **Figure 15.7**.)

While multigenerational living may keep families emotionally close, it is not always a smooth ride (Lüscher & Pillemer, 1998; Simon & Caputo, 2019). Many families, no matter their background, hope that young adults will be self-sufficient and may feel that their children are not successful if they are still dependent (Barroso et al., 2019; Pei & Cong, 2019). Parents often feel ambivalent about their young-adult children, particularly if they judge their children's decisions, like their romantic partners or school choices, or if their children have mental health challenges or substance abuse disorder (Kiecolt et al., 2011; Sloan et al., 2020).

For many parents, the transition to postresidential parenting is a milestone. The house is quiet; there are fewer errands to run and less food to buy at the store (Schmidt, 2020). Launching children into independence, as in moving them into their first apartment, can be tearful and include a loss of familiar routines. But more frequently, families report relief. Having their children grown makes parents feel successful and relieves them of some of the strain of managing a full house (Bouchard, 2014; Mitchell & Lovegreen, 2009).

Even when children are gone, parents and children still stay close: nearly 98 percent of adults are in touch with at least one parent (Hartnett et al., 2013). Phones, email, and texting have increased the frequency of communication between parents and adult children, and most are in touch nearly every day (Fingerman et al., 2016). The COVID-19 pandemic changed living arrangements. Many young adults moved back in with their parents, at least temporarily, a transition that often exacerbated stresses but also provided new opportunities for reconnection (Hall & Zygmunt, 2021).

Whether families live together or apart, the quality of relationships between adult children and their parents is linked to families' mental health, including the risk for

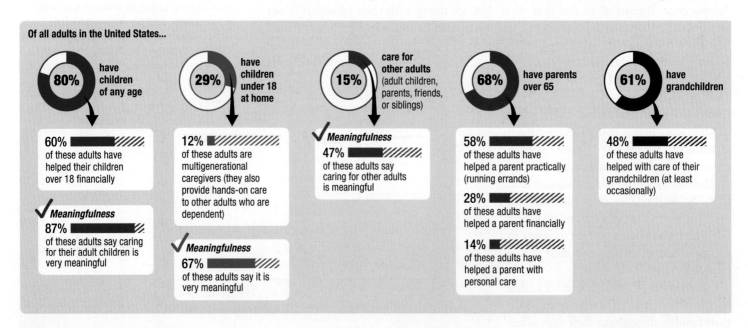

FIGURE 15.7 Caregiving in Midlife For many U.S. adults, caregiving for children, other adults, parents, and grandchildren is part of everyday life and can be a source of generativity (and sometimes stress).

depression and general satisfaction with life (Kim et al., 2020). In some surveys, families report that the easiest arrangement is when parents are only moderately engaged with their adult children. They may be helping out with the grandchildren but not fully responsible for their care, or giving gifts but not fully supporting their children. About 3 in 10 families fit into this category.

Families are more at risk if they have a lot of conflict, as is true of another 3 in 10 families, or if they are **estranged** (Silverstein et al., 2010). Intergenerational caregiving tends to fall on a U-shaped curve, like many types of stress: Too little caregiving does not seem to be enough to keep relationships close, but too much can be overtaxing (Archer et al., 2021; Kim et al., 2020). About one in four parents and two in three adults who were caring for both children and aging family members reported serious mental health symptoms during the pandemic. What helped build resilience? Quality relationships. Caregivers who had someone to rely on tended to do better (Czeisler et al., 2021).

Grandparenting For many, caregiving in midlife includes helping out with grandchildren. By their late 50s, two in three adults are grandparents (Monte, 2017). Active grandparents have become common around the world as parents' jobs become more intensive and grandparents step in to fill in the gaps (Dolbin-MacNab & Yancura, 2018; Sadruddin et al., 2019). About one in five U.S. grandparents provides some regular hands-on care to their grandchildren, and rates are nearly double that in many European countries and in China (AARP, 2019; Jianhui, 2017; Sanders & Burke, 2018). But most grandparents of young children are still working and may live too far away to see their grandchildren regularly.

Regardless of the frequency of contact, for many adults, becoming a grandparent is an opportunity to build a sense of family heritage and cultural pride (AARP, 2020). This shared sense of community can provide a sense of generativity and meaning for grandparents and bolster children's resilience (Mendoza et al., 2017). For instance, researchers found that in one Oklahoma community, children's warm relationships with their grandparents and their exposure to their Comanche heritage helped boost their resilience in later life (Ponce-Garcia et al., 2019).

Some grandparents take on the role of full-time or custodial grandparent to their grandchildren (Dolbin-MacNab & Yancura, 2018; Hayslip et al., 2019). In the United States, about 1 in 10 children lives with their grandparents and their parents, and an additional 2 out of 100 children are raised by their grandparents alone (ACS, 2020; Dunifon, 2018). It is difficult for researchers or for families themselves to pinpoint a precise number, however, since grandparents usually step in during times of crisis, when parents are moving away for work, are incarcerated, or have a substance use disorder. But many grandparents take on this role for a long time, often for more than five years (Generations United, 2015).

Adults in these **grandfamilies** are typically in their 50s, and many face major stresses (Pilkauskas & Dunifon, 2016). They are more likely than other people their age to be extremely low income, experience discrimination, and be unemployed. In addition, some are also dealing with their adult children's mental health problems or substance abuse (Hayslip et al., 2019). Even though grandchildren may be a bright spot, raising them can take a toll on adults' mental and physical health. Like other caregivers with complicated lives, they may benefit from interventions designed to help them manage the complex feelings and financial strain they are under. Helping grandparents find social support and advice on how to mitigate their grandchildren's trauma is a goal of many intervention programs (Meyer & Kandic, 2021; Sadruddin et al., 2019).

Children's successes and failures weigh heavily on parents throughout the lifespan. As one research team pointed out, parents are only as happy as their least happy child: Just one child who is struggling, whether it is with mental health, legal troubles,

estrangement A period of extreme strain in a relationship where family members no longer have contact.

grandfamilies Families headed by a grandparent.

Sharing with the Next Generation Grandparenting is often an opportunity to build cultural pride and generativity. Mark Soldier Wolf is helping to share his heritage language skills with his granddaughter, Blue Moccasin, who attends an Arapaho immersion preschool program near their home in Riverton, Wyoming.

Sometimes Grandparents Are Also Parents. Grandparents often step in as parents after trauma. Bentlee and Mercedes lost their father to a drug overdose, but their grandparents, Cindy and Michael, brought them into their home in Eliot, Maine. Cindy and Michael are now raising their grandchildren and advocating for more support for young people with substance use disorder, like the son they lost.

(⊕) Learn It Together

Caregiving in Midlife

Plan Read through the discussion of how middle adulthood often includes the need to care for one's aging parents.

Engage Pair-up with a classmate, and one of you play the role of someone in midlife and the other play the role of that person's aging parent. Pretend that you are having a discussion of the pros and cons of having the aging parent move in with the midlife child.

Reflect What is it like to talk about taking care of your aging parent? How would it change your life to have them live with you? What supports outside of the family could help with that transition?

or unemployment, is enough to increase the parents' risk of depression and feelings of dissatisfaction (Fingerman et al., 2012).

Caregiving in Midlife For Doug and Stephanie and many other adults, taking care of a parent in need is something they would do without question. Stephanie describes caring for her father as a "sacred" obligation. Doug, too, felt that caring for his parents after they became sick was important enough that he left his job and his preschooler for many weeks. When Stephanie's mother developed Alzheimer disease, Stephanie encouraged her to move into a care facility nearby but balanced caring for Gwen, who was just a toddler, with daily visits. She recalls feeling constantly torn between her daughter and her mother, who was miserable when left alone. She always felt she was not doing enough, but her doctor cautioned her to take better care of herself. She was so dehydrated the doctor could not even take a sample of her blood.

Stephanie laughed as she ruefully remembered the doctor's attempt to be helpful: She had no time for bubble baths or date night. She jokes about it, but it was a bitterly difficult time. Like many caregivers, she was overwhelmed by grief, guilt, and lack of sleep from trying to be in too many places at once, an experience that is not uncommon for middle-aged adults, particularly those who identify as women (Burke, 2017). Like many caregivers, even Stephanie's body took a toll, showing high levels of inflammation once they were able to draw her blood.

Family caregiving comes in a variety of forms (Parker & Patten, 2013). It may entail hands-on care, as with helping a family member get to the bathroom or driving them to a doctor's appointment. Caregiving can also be financial, as when you help your mother with an unexpected medical bill or your son with the rent. Emotional support is another form of caregiving: Being there on the phone when your child experiences their first breakup, or when your mother gets home from a funeral, is a critical part of giving care.

In all its forms, family caregiving is common everywhere. In Europe, where older adults benefit from a substantial social safety net, one in seven adults helps a parent with household chores. In China, with fewer supports, more than one in three adults is helping a parent (Burke, 2017). Different communities have different expectations when it comes to family obligation and how much intergenerational solidarity they may have. Black families often feel more strongly about the rewards and the obligation to care for aging parents (Fabius et al., 2020; Liu et al., 2021). Similarly, Latino and Asian American families often feel strong ties of filial responsibility and affection that inspire them to care for their parents (Maldonado, 2017; Miyawaki, 2020).

In the United States, where there are limited social supports for disabled and aging family members, about one in five of all adults spend time providing hands-on care for an older family member (Burke, 2017; Koumoutzis et al., 2021; Schulz et al., 2020). These caregivers estimate that they spend nearly 20 hours a week taking care of family members, often on top of full-time jobs (AARP & National Alliance for Caregiving, 2020).

Too much time spent caregiving and worrying about family members can overwhelm the body: Like Stephanie, caregivers under stress often have higher rates of hypertension, stress reactivity, and inflammation (Wetherell & Lovell, 2019). They also are more likely to experience depression and relationship strain (Roth et al., 2019; Schulz et al., 2020). The most difficult strain is often financial: Adults who worry about money and job security while caring for others have significant challenges (Koumoutzis et al., 2021). Effective interventions help caregivers understand the common pitfalls and benefits of caregiving and give them tools, like mindfulness training, to build their emotion regulation and resilience (Cheng et al., 2019; Tang & Chan, 2016).

Some researchers refer to the middle-aged adults who juggle caregiving responsibilities as a *sandwich generation*, lodged between the needs of the younger and the older generations (Miller, 1981). More than half of midlife adults provide multigenerational care. Most of this is financial and emotional care, but about one in eight provides hands-on care for both generations (Parker & Patten, 2013). Fortunately, there are benefits to caregiving, such as an opportunity to give back and a sense of being important, that help mitigate the challenges.

Social Networks

Family and children provide connection and generativity in midlife, but they are not the only sources of social contact. Adults are also surrounded by networks of friends, coworkers, and acquaintances that grow and change over the years (Birditt et al., 2020). Friendships and community relationships are important sources of support, providing empathy after a breakup, a ride home from the mechanic after your car has broken down, or even a job referral (Oesch & von Ow, 2017).

Some scientists describe the network of relationships that protects you and travels through time with you as a *social convoy*, like the line of cars in a motorcade (Fuller et al., 2020; Kahn & Antonucci, 1980). Typically, adults have their largest social group in late adolescence and early adulthood. These networks tend to shrink a bit as adults move from schools or colleges to workplaces. Frequently, the circle of close friends shrinks again as adults get married or move into stable relationships that take up a lot of social time in midlife (Birditt et al., 2020; Sharifian et al., 2022). Adults find new friends in midlife, particularly when they change jobs and have children (Wrzus et al., 2013). It is unusual for someone's social network to stay the same from year to year: Relationships change, and friends often grow apart, although family relationships tend to stay stable over time (Fischer & Offer, 2020).

Friendship Friends change over the course of adult life: Your friendships in adulthood are often less intimate than what you had with your high school BFF. Closeness takes time that is often in short supply in midlife (Sharifian et al., 2022). Maintaining friendships comes from sharing experiences and doing things together, whether that is taking an early-morning walk together, chatting while your children play soccer, or commiserating about work during a break. One notable advantage of the relationships adults build in midlife is that they are often more ethnically and culturally diverse than earlier in life (Thomas, 2019).

Many adults have friends who serve some of the functions of family: sharing holidays, obligations to look out for each other, and strong bonds of affection (Furstenberg et al., 2020). Scholars call these *kinships*, or **fictive kin**, but such ties are far from fictional, even if the relationships are not biological. This has been observed in many Black families, who may build networks of fictive kin, particularly through church (Chatters et al., 1994; Taylor et al., 2013). Similar bonds build *families of choice*, often in gay, lesbian, or transgender adults who may find support and community away from their biological families (Wardecker & Matsick, 2020).

Adults may have an enormous number of "friends" and connections on social media, but scientists think that it is the quality, rather than the quantity, that is important to your emotional health (Birditt et al., 2020). Younger adults often have enormous social networks, particularly if you count the people they are connected to on social media, but they also have very high levels of loneliness. Simply knowing people does not mean that you are actually close with them or that they are a source of support (Child & Lawton, 2019).

Culture has an impact. In communities that are characterized as more individualistic, like many in the United States, adults often have larger social networks. In contrast, in cultures that are more collectivist, adults' social networks are smaller and focused on family and close friends (Wrzus et al., 2013). In one survey, researchers

Scientific American Profile

Caregiving Between Generations

vgajic/E+/Getty Images

Friendships May Change in Midlife, but the Joy of Being Together Often Continues. These friends in Serbia, in southeastern Europe, enjoy dinner and wine under the string lights.

fictive kin Families that are bound by voluntary bonds of friendship and community, rather than biology.

Serving the Community and the Birds This woman is a trained volunteer who tags birds in England in order to track their migration patterns as they travel around the globe.

found that about 7 in 10 people in the social networks of people in Switzerland were family, as compared to more than 9 in 10 in more family-focused Lithuania (Wall et al., 2018).

Researchers suggest that human beings have a set point of the number of relationships they can actually manage (English & Carstensen, 2014; Sutcliffe et al., 2018). The magic number? Five. Most of these are family members and other people you see frequently in real life. In addition, adults may have about 15 less-intimate friends, or friends they see only a few times a year. Their total network of friends, including those who they might contact once a year or invite to a wedding or a funeral, is typically around 150. Some people, especially if they are more extraverted, might have larger social networks, but like everyone, they are limited in terms of the truly close friendships they can have (Wrzus et al., 2017). Scientists suggest that while you may want to have thousands of friends, you are limited by the number of hours in the day and your brain's ability to focus, to having just a handful of good ones (Dunbar et al., 2015).

Community Involvement Close relationships boost well-being in midlife, but less-intimate relationships also have benefits. Volunteering, serving on a neighborhood committee, or baking for coffee hour at temple helps to build social connections and can also give adults a sense of meaning and generativity (Cnaan & Heist, 2018; Dunbar, 2020). Being generous has immediate and long-term benefits to your emotional health: Giving activates your reward system and feels good. These eudemonic feelings, unlike the immediate rewards from hedonic pleasures such as eating a donut, can be long lasting (Fang et al., 2017). The relative stability of midlife means that middle-aged adults are more likely than younger adults to be active in their community, whether researchers measure how often they vote, volunteer for neighborhood committees, attend worship services, or join support organizations at their children's schools (Turner et al., 2020).

For many adults, it is difficult to find the time for community service. For instance, families with small children often have little time to volunteer: Finding a caregiver to watch your children while you work a phone bank is impractical. However, families with school-aged children are more likely to volunteer and often are the backbone of team sports, religious education, and other clubs (Fang et al., 2017). Service is often something adults learn while they are growing up and is a habit they maintain with their own families: whether this means taking their children to religious services or attending antiwar protests.

APPLY IT! **15.3** Doug and Stephanie have both done intensive caregiving during middle age. What sources of support might have helped them build resilience through these experiences?

15.4 What are your ethnotheories about romantic relationships in adulthood? How do they contrast with what researchers have found about the impact of external, rather than internal, factors on relationship satisfaction?

Emotional Risks and Resilience in Adulthood

Learning Objective

15.5 Describe common emotional disorders that occur during middle adulthood.

Many adults in midlife face enormous challenges, balancing the needs of their families and their jobs during a time of great social and economic change (Infurna et al., 2020). Their emotional health affects how well they can care for the many people who rely upon them and also their own well-being as they age.

Emotional and social health in midlife builds on the foundations built in early life (Baltes, 1987). For instance, adults who managed to be emotionally stable in their teens are likely to stay that way (Layard et al., 2014). However, this does not mean that what happens in midlife is predetermined by childhood experiences (Lee et al., 2019). For adults who experienced mental health conditions as children, the impact of discrimination, or other trauma or adversity is more likely to affect them emotionally in adulthood. Fortunately, their troubles do not have to be permanent (Covey et al., 2013; Lee et al., 2019). Most adults have experienced some traumatic events, either in childhood or in later life, and most are able to develop some resilience (Copeland et al., 2018).

The well-being of many adults has suffered in recent years because of broader economic factors (see **Infographic 15.1**). Adults have been shaken by the impact of two relatively recent global events: the Great Recession in 2008 and the social and economic challenges that accompanied the COVID-19 pandemic (Giuntella et al., 2021; Infurna et al., 2020). Middle-aged adults typically have more trouble than younger people finding a job and are particularly vulnerable to financial difficulties (Miller et al., 2020).

Although scientists have found that adults are usually able to bounce back from major life changes, such as divorce, having a baby, or even losing a partner, they do not quickly bounce back from long-term unemployment (Clark, 2021). Losing a job often means a loss of social connections, personal identity, and hope for the future. Indeed, adults have the most difficulty in situations where social stress is compounded by financial strain.

Many close relationships are often unstable and burdened by work demands and caregiving pressures. Social support can be hard to find (Sehmi et al., 2019). As a result of these broad social and economic forces, over the past decades, middle-aged adults are more likely to be depressed, declare bankruptcy, and have increasing rates of substance use disorders than they were in previous generations (Brody et al., 2018; Thorne et al., 2018).

Remember from Chapter 14 that health challenges are not evenly distributed. Similarly, rates of mental illness does not fall equitably. Researchers have found that midlife adults in the United States, particularly those without college degrees and those from rural communities where unemployment and social isolation are common, have experienced sharp increases in the rates of suicide and substance use disorders in recent years (Case & Deaton, 2015, 2021; Chetty et al., 2016). These communities have also seen a dramatic rise in the rates of midlife disability and chronic pain (Graham & Pinto, 2019).

A decline in optimism about the future has also hit many communities that have experienced increased unemployment. Many adults, particularly those who are not well off and have not been to college, are not hopeful about the future (O'Connor & Graham, 2019). Culture and gender play a role: White and Native American communities have seen faster declines in optimism and increases in mortality in midlife (Shiels et al., 2017). Black and Latino adults tend to be more optimistic about the future and have lower rates of some emotional disorders than White adults, perhaps because of stronger community ties or because they have more realistic views of the future (Assari & Lankarani, 2016; Cherlin, 2018; Graham & Pinto, 2019).

The often-intersectional impact of discrimination can worsen the physical and emotional symptoms of stress (Brody et al., 2018; Kim & Fredricksen-Goldsen, 2017; Vargas et al., 2020). Everyday discrimination has been linked to higher rates of depression, anxiety, and poor mental health in a variety of groups, from Indigineous Canadians to Black and Latino Americans (Kirsch et al., 2019; Siddiqi et al., 2017; Yoon et al., 2019). Anti-immigrant discrimination, including the threat of deportation, increases stress and anxiety (Morey, 2018). Gay, lesbian, bisexual, and transgender adults also are more likely to face prejudice, family rejection, and community isolation (Lyons et al., 2021). However, for many groups, being linked to community cultural institutions and sources of group pride can protect them from some of the effects of discrimination. For instance, living in a neighborhood with a community church or a food market is linked to lower rates of stress-related challenges among Asian American women (Morey et al., 2020).

SOURCES OF STRESS

ENVIRONMENT

The environment continues to be an important factor in health. Some research suggests that exposure to pollution is linked to accelerated aging and declines in cognitive function in midlife and beyond.

Researchers found that middle-aged adults who lived in areas with high air pollution experienced accelerated brain aging.

▼

Brain age of a 50-year-old not exposed to polluted air	Brain age of a 50-year-old exposed to polluted air
50 years	52.1 years

MENTAL HEALTH

Mental illness diagnoses peaks in midlife.

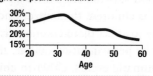

Mental illness diagnoses in the past year ▶ (graph: 30%, 25%, 20%, 15% vs Age 20 30 40 50 60)

TOO LITTLE TIME

Responsibilities at home and in the community during midlife make for very little free time.

Countries: U.S., China, Brazil, Indonesia, Germany, Kenya

◀ Proportion of work responsibilities to leisure time around the world

Legend: Housework/caring · Paid Work · Leisure/socializing

SUBSTANCE USE

Substance use can be a stressor and a symptom of mental health under strain. Around the world, binge drinking is common in many communities. About 1 in 8 adults reports heavy alcohol use, but alcohol use is often determined by a community's cultural traditions.

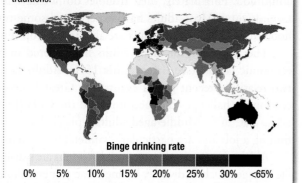

Binge drinking rate: 0% 5% 10% 15% 20% 25% 30% <65%

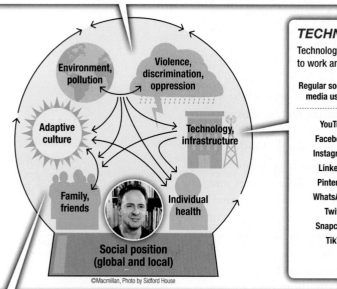

Environment, pollution · Violence, discrimination, oppression · Adaptive culture · Technology, infrastructure · Family, friends · Individual health · Social position (global and local)

©Macmillan, Photo by Sidford House

TECHNOLOGY

Technology can bring adults together, entertain them, and help them stay connected to work and learning over the lifespan.

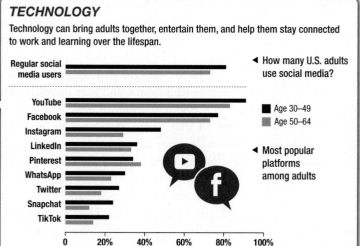

Regular social media users

◀ How many U.S. adults use social media?

Platforms: YouTube, Facebook, Instagram, LinkedIn, Pinterest, WhatsApp, Twitter, Snapchat, TikTok

Legend: Age 30–49 · Age 50–64

◀ Most popular platforms among adults

Scale: 0 20% 40% 60% 80% 100%

SOURCES OF RESILIENCE

OPTIMISM

Most adults feel optimistic about the future and believe that things are getting better, but adults in affluent countries tend to feel less optimistic.

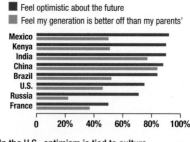

Legend: Feel optimistic about the future · Feel my generation is better off than my parents'

Countries: Mexico, Kenya, India, China, Brazil, U.S., Russia, France

Scale: 0 20% 40% 60% 80% 100%

In the U.S., optimism is tied to culture, racial identity, and income.

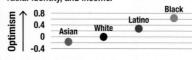

Optimism axis: 0.8, 0.4, 0, -0.4 — Asian, White, Latino, Black

GOOD WORK

Dream jobs from around the world.

▼

Countries: Kenya, U.S., China, India, France

Legend: Entrepreneur · Doctor · Teacher · Manager/businessperson · Does not want to work

Percent: 0 5 10 15 20 25 30

RELATIONSHIPS

Relationships continue to be a source of resilience and happiness in midlife.

What makes people in midlife happy?

▼

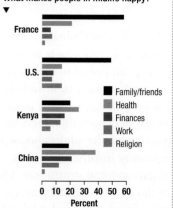

Countries: France, U.S., Kenya, China

Legend: Family/friends · Health · Finances · Work · Religion

Percent: 0 10 20 30 40 50 60

COMMUNITY PARTICIPATION

Midlife adults are particularly likely to know what is going on in their community and government.

Adults who say they are knowledgeable about what is going on in their community

▼

Country	Percent
India	62%
Germany	57%
China	55%
Brazil	53%
Russia	51%
Nigeria	50%
U.S.	47%
Mexico	40%

People who identify as women generally report higher levels of emotional disorders, depression, stress, and anxiety than men, a finding that researchers have tied to brain chemistry, experiences of violence and trauma, and the burden of caregiving (Kiely et al., 2019; Riecher-Rössler, 2017). In midlife, women are twice as likely as men to report a diagnosis of depression (Salk et al., 2017). But while they may not be formally diagnosed with psychological disorders as frequently as women, men also experience mental illness. Men are more likely to be diagnosed with a substance use disorder and are three times more likely to die by suicide (Hedegaard & Warner, 2021; SAMHSA, 2020). Men are also less likely to get the help they need. Men face pervasive stigma about mental health, particularly among communities of color (Agochukwu & Wittman, 2019; Eylem et al., 2020).

Depression and Anxiety

Many adults fear the stigma of mental illness, perhaps because they do not realize that having difficulties with functioning is common. In fact, psychological disorders are the leading cause of disability in adults worldwide (Rehm & Shield, 2019). Around the world, nearly 1 in 12 adults has depression, and slightly fewer have an anxiety disorder (Brody et al., 2018; Ruscio et al., 2017; WHO, 2017). Without support or intervention, these conditions can be debilitating or even trigger suicide, a leading cause of death in midlife (Hedegaard et al., 2021). Mental illness can also complicate other chronic health conditions: People with pain disorders or cardiovascular disease often also have depression or anxiety (van Hecke et al., 2017). In adulthood, as in other times of the lifespan, depression and anxiety are not caused by a failure of willpower: In fact, some scholars point out that adults who are managing mental illness may have more willpower than others, since they are trying to overcome additional bumps in their life journey (Vyncke & Van Gorp, 2020).

Many adults expect to be independent, well off, and at the peak of their health, family life, and career, even though these aspirations are often unreachable. Feeling depressed or worried often results when adults have trouble fulfilling these expectations and have to cope with the stress of instability: Rates of depression and anxiety are higher among adults who are unemployed, low-income, or in poor health (Brody et al., 2018; Ruscio et al., 2017). Although many adults understand that depression and anxiety are complex illnesses that are rooted in genetics, upbringing, and environment, they still tend to blame in-the-moment factors like people—and themselves—for their disorders (Eylem et al., 2020; NASEM, 2016). This may contribute to some adults' inability to find support, but another factor is that effective mental health services are often unavailable or unaffordable (Clement et al., 2015; Han et al., 2017a).

Effective treatments for depression and anxiety can come from a biological or behavioral approach. The former might focus on finding medications, while the latter might focus on psychotherapy (Cuijpers et al., 2020a). Typically, many scientists combine medications and psychotherapy to treat emotional disorders (Cuijpers et al., 2020b). Outside of therapy, adults can build resilience through healthy behaviors like sleep, exercise, and social relationships (Laird et al., 2019).

Substance Use In many communities around the world, substance use is often seen as an unavoidable part of life for the young. However, by midlife, adults are expected to stop using drugs and alcohol as they settle into jobs and build families and committed relationships. In the past decade, adults have shown that they are not giving up alcohol and substances as readily as they used to (SAMHSA, 2020). More than one in eight adults in the United States has difficulty managing their substance use (SAMHSA, 2020). Easily available, alcohol is the most misused substance in the United States and around the world, with rates increasing particularly for women (Grant et al., 2015; Hasin et al., 2019; McKetta & Keyes, 2020).

Changing social expectations about drug use and recent spikes in access to opioids mean that more adults are using substances than ever before (Gomes et al., 2018;

CONNECTIONS

Remember from Chapter 13 that treatment and interventions are available for people who are in crisis or thinking of suicide. The U.S. National Suicide Prevention Hotline is: (800) 273-8255. Referals for treatment are available at: (800) 662-4357.

CONNECTIONS

As you may recall from Chapter 11, substance and alcohol use disorders are diagnosed when an adult lacks control over their use of substances, and it is impairing their social relationships and ability to function.

Marijuana in Midlife Many adults believe marijuana use is safe, but experts are not sure it is a benefit to mental or physical health. As marjiunana becomes easier to find, as in this retail store in California, researchers expect use to increase.

CONNECTIONS

Remember from Chapter 13 that *binge drinking* is drinking heavily, which is defined by your physical size, metabolism, and the sex-linked hormones that help you process alcohol. As a result, definitions are typically linked to biological sex: four drinks (for women) or five drinks (for men) on one two-hour occasion. People who have *alcohol use disorder* may also binge-drink, but their drinking makes it difficult to function in their everyday life.

Hasin et al., 2019). Like other psychological disorders, substance use disorder can contribute to many other health conditions, such as cardiovascular disease and chronic pain. It can also increase the risk of violent behavior and negatively impact parenting, which can derail the lives of both adults and their loved ones (Tsai et al., 2019).

U.S. adults increasingly think marijuana is safe, and 15 percent of them regularly use it (Keyhani et al., 2018; SAMHSA, 2020). In fact, nearly half of adults tell researchers that they think marijuana benefits mental health (Ishida et al., 2020; Keyhani et al., 2018). Developmental scientists tend to disagree. While there is some evidence that marijuana can help treat some types of pain and occasional use may not be harmful, chronic marijuana use is actually a potent risk to mental health in the long run (Bigand et al., 2019). Particularly for younger adults, regular marijuana use increases the risk for serious mental illness, like psychosis (Marconi et al., 2016). In adults, marijuana can harm memory, and regular use increases the risk for depression (Gorfinkel et al., 2020). In addition, marijuana can induce harmful, long-term changes in brain function and chemistry: one reason it is linked to depression and cognitive challenges (Figueiredo et al., 2020; Keyhani et al., 2018; Leadbeater et al., 2019). Scholars are particularly concerned about an increase in marijuana use among pregnant people, because, as you may remember from Chapter 3, it is linked to fetal death and birth defects (Hurd et al., 2019; SAMHSA, 2020).

Whereas marijuana use, even in moderation, is often stigmatized, alcohol is often a way to celebrate a happy occasion, to soothe nerves on a first date, or even to share a religious experience. According to a few researchers, moderate use of alcohol (less than a serving a day) may be protective of cardiovascular health (Wood et al., 2018). However, many health experts recommend that the healthiest dosage of alcohol may be zero (Pallazola et al., 2019).

Excessive drinking is not healthy. Whether *binge drinking* or alcohol use disorder, excessive use of alcohol causes more than 1 in 10 deaths in the United States and is a leading cause of disability around the world (Degenhardt et al., 2018; Kanny et al., 2018). Excessive drinking is also linked to many physical problems, from liver cancer to cardiovascular disease, and to increased psychological disorders, violence, and car accidents (Kuntsche et al., 2017; Xi et al., 2017). It is the most common substance use disorder in the United States: About one in six adults binge-drinks once a week and about one in eight met the criteria for an alcohol-related disorder in the past year. Rates are increasing for adults in their early 30s (Grucza et al., 2018; Kanny et al., 2018).

One group binge drinking much more frequently is younger women (Hasin et al., 2019). The number of women who binge-drink in their 30s has nearly doubled in the past 15 years, although men still are more likely to drink excessively (McKetta & Keyes, 2020). Researchers are not sure what accounts for this increase: Many of these heavy drinkers are college educated and relatively affluent, and some experts suggest they may just have continued drinking at the same rate as they did in college (McKetta & Keyes, 2020). Others suggest that drinking is a symptom of the stress that many adults feel in today's economy (Rodriguez et al., 2020). Although traditional treatment for alcohol use disorder advocates complete abstinence, often achieved through group therapy, more contemporary treatments focus on limiting excessive drinking (Knox et al., 2019).

One type of substance abuse has had an outsized impact on the United States in the past 10 years: opioids. In the past few years, opioid use disorder has led to about 50,000 deaths per year, 100,000 children placed in foster care, and more than 10 million adults and their families coping with the fallout (Meinhofer & Angleró-Díaz, 2019; SAMHSA, 2020; Wilson et al., 2020). Recent attempts to better regulate prescription medications like fentanyl and OxyContin have resulted in substantial reductions in opioid use disorder (SAMHSA, 2020; Skolnick, 2018).

People who use opioids without a prescription tell researchers that they are trying to manage physical pain (Han et al., 2017b). But some scientists suggest that the misuse of opioids is also driven by widespread unemployment, a loss of a sense of community, and a feeling of purposelessness, as well as by irresponsible prescribers and drug manufacturers (Glei et al., 2020; Jalal et al., 2018). Empirically supported treatment for opioid use disorder is a complex combination of medication and interpersonal support, designed to help adults rebuild their lives (McCarty et al., 2018).

Loneliness Another challenge of mental health in midlife comes from *loneliness* (Jeste et al., 2020). It may be surprising that you can feel lonely even if you have a hundred friends or followers, and even if you live with other people. Scientists define loneliness as what you feel when your desired level of social interaction does not line up with the social contact you actually have (Peplau & Perlman, 1982). It is the feeling that you have no one to talk to or to care about you, regardless of how many social relationships or connections you actually have. Some experts believe that one in five adults in midlife experiences loneliness. Extreme loneliness can be dangerous, leading to depression and a deterioration in health that researchers have linked to a 20 percent increase in mortality, comparable to smoking (Holt-Lunstad et al., 2015; Wilson et al., 2019).

Feelings of isolation are more likely if you are not in a romantic relationship or if you develop serious health problems. As with other emotional and health conditions, rates are highest in adults who are financially stressed and who may be too anxious to connect with other people (Bruce et al., 2019; Luhmann & Hawkley, 2016; Qualter et al., 2015).

In many countries today, more adults choose to live alone than in the past, but, if you have adequate income and a partner, living in your own apartment is not linked to loneliness (Luhmann & Hawkley, 2016). Social media also does not seem to be linked with loneliness: Many adults spend hours every day online, but there is not a strong association between screen time and loneliness (Bruce et al., 2019). In fact, being online may give adults the opportunity to connect with family and friends who do not live close by or find a virtual community that shares a hobby or an identity. Using WhatsApp to check on a parent or a child who lives in a different time zone is a lifesaver for many adults (Antonucci et al., 2019).

Building Resilience

Although the stresses of midlife can damage your genes, shorten your life, and make you depressed, some of this damage can be repaired. Building strong emotional connections is often the best treatment for managing the ups and downs of adult life. But researchers have found, perhaps unsurprisingly, that just telling people to go out and make friends is not very effective (Masi et al., 2011).

Interventions that help adults recover from adversity and emotional difficulties work best when they are built *with*, not just *for*, the people they serve (Arevian et al., 2019). For instance, interventions that are designed around *community-based partnerships* are more effective in treating depression in low-income communities of color than standard treatment programs that do not involve a coalition from the neighborhoods they serve. Community-based partnership programs in mental health have been piloted in a number of cities, including Los Angeles, New Orleans, and New York. These programs bring together researchers who understand the latest science with community members such as clergy, hairdressers, and doctors who understand the neighborhood (Jones, 2018). These programs are not short term: Successful treatment for depression, for instance, often takes more than a year and a half but pays off over the long haul.

Addressing underlying mental health challenges makes it more likely that adults will find jobs and become more active parents (Arevian et al., 2019). Intervening in midlife, particularly with empirically based programs that are sensitive to the needs of middle-aged adults, can be effective. Some researchers are even hopeful that these

FIGURE 15.8 Midlife May Repair Your Telomeres. Researchers suggest that the stresses of early life do not need to lead to accelerated aging and shorter telomeres: Resilience in adulthood may stop the cascade of life stress that can be linked to accelerated aging.

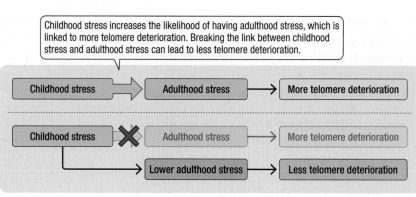

Childhood stress increases the likelihood of having adulthood stress, which is linked to more telomere deterioration. Breaking the link between childhood stress and adulthood stress can lead to less telomere deterioration.

| Childhood stress | ➡ | Adulthood stress | → | More telomere deterioration |

| Childhood stress | ✖ | Adulthood stress | → | More telomere deterioration |
| | | Lower adulthood stress | → | Less telomere deterioration |

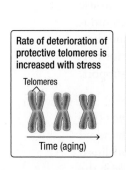

Rate of deterioration of protective telomeres is increased with stress

Telomeres

Time (aging) →

Experiencing the Benefits of More Than Just a Walk in the Park Emotional resilience in midlife often comes from relationships, along with exercise and some time in the natural world. These friends have found time to connect outdoors in Buenos Aires, Argentina.

treatments can begin to undo the damage that was done to telomeres as a result of adversity and, in effect, reverse the aging clock (Willis et al., 2019). (See **Figure 15.8**.)

Recovering from serious emotional disorders can often require years of committed work. Quick fixes that address the systemic and long-term challenges faced by many adults are not always possible. Scientists are always hunting for answers that will help adults improve their life satisfaction. There are a variety of interventions that are linked with increasing happiness including boosting creativity, taking time to sleep, being outdoors, and staying active. These may not cure underlying emotional problems, but they may help adults be more resilient to the challenges of midlife.

For instance, exercise can contribute to emotional as well as physical health in middle adulthood. Adults who are physically active in their free time are more likely to be happier and more satisfied than those who have more sedentary hobbies (Chen et al., 2021; White et al., 2017). While many adults are exhausted at the end of the day, sitting down with Netflix every night is not as helpful for our mental health as a walk in the park (Teychenne et al., 2020).

Similarly, leisure activities that are creative or generative can help adults bounce back from adversity. Just making something, even if it is an inexpert rendition of a song or a cake that slumps, can trigger feelings of competence and satisfaction (Conner et al., 2018). Generativity in the form of giving to other people, like donating to a food drive or volunteering at the school play, can also boost happiness (Hui et al., 2020; Lawton et al., 2021). Having life goals that include service can be protective and can help connect adults to the ideals that they share with a larger community (Zhang et al., 2018). These ideals have been crucial to Sister Norma Pimentel as she navigates midlife.

 SCIENCE IN PRACTICE
Sister Norma Pimentel, MJ

Like many adults, Sister Norma ended up in a very different place in midlife than she had planned. She went to school to be an architect. Then she became a licensed professional counselor. Now, she is not an artist but an administrator using developmental science every day. Sister Norma runs a charitable organization in the border city of McAllen, Texas, that helps more than 2,000 families a day as they seek asylum in the United States. Migrants arrive across the bridge from Matamoros, Mexico, often hungry, cold, and unsure of where to go, after months of sleeping in temporary facilities. Sister Norma knows the border well, because she was born in McAllen to parents who were also seeking asylum in the United States.

Her job is to help these traumatized families in the 24 hours before they get on buses to leave McAllen. Her priorities go back to the work of Maslow: People need to feel safe, to have their basic needs met, and to feel that they matter. Sister Norma and her volunteers make sure that everyone has food, a change of clothes, and a shower before they move on. Some also get a chance to sleep in small tents where they can find some privacy and rest.

But Sister Norma does not stop with basic needs. She wants to help people rebuild their dignity and their trust in other people, so she doles out smiles, welcomes them with hugs, and plays with their children. Sister Norma works with families who are scarred by what they have seen: children stuffed 100 to a cell, their voices echoing against concrete walls as they call out for help and their mothers.

Sister Norma is an example of the plasticity of life in middle age. Her life has been shaped by events that she could not have predicted when she graduated from college with her art degree. A migrant crisis and a calling to help transformed her life. As for many adults, midlife is not easy for Sister Norma. She tries to take care of her own needs by making time to pray. But she often feels that she is close to being overwhelmed. She is driven to continue, because she believes it is the right thing to do: Generativity gives her a sense of purpose. Her motto is, "There is always more to do" (Castro, 2020; Fuller, 2018; Lagunas, 2021).

A Welcoming Hand For Sister Norma Pimentel, generativity in midlife means being on hand to welcome new migrants as they arrive in Brownsville, Texas.

APPLY IT! **15.5** What factors do you think helped Doug boost his resilience and mental health during the stressful years of midlife? How did his financial stability, his bond with Stephanie, and the meaning he derives from work help him weather these years of strain?

15.6 How do external stressors contribute to mental health in midlife? What are common stresses that may make it difficult for adults to function?

Wrapping It Up

LO 15.1 Describe the impact of life events and the social context on adult development. (p. 435)

By middle adulthood, outside forces have had diverse and varied impacts on our personality, identity and emotion regulation. Midlife is a time of possibility, but many adults are under strain and at a low point of life satisfaction. Many report better emotion regulation, triggered by brain development and also often by financial well-being, in midlife. Life events like having a job and parenting change our personalities. Most people tend to become more emotionally stable over time, less extraverted, open, and neurotic and more conscientious and agreeable. Cultures differ in what personality traits they appreciate, but the differences within one culture are typically much greater than those between cultures.

LO 15.2 Describe Erikson's crisis of generativity versus stagnation. (p. 435)

Erikson described middle adulthood as a time of conflict between generativity versus stagnation. He suggested adults are happier if they can find a way to contribute to others or something greater than themselves. Some scholars argued that middle adulthood was divided into steps or stages and that adults commonly went through a midlife crisis as they grew, but there is limited empirical evidence for this.

LO 15.3 Explain the benefits of generativity in midlife. (p. 435)

Scholars believe that generativity is a benefit to health and well-being in adulthood and across the lifespan. Short-term pleasure, sometimes called hedonia, is not always linked to long-term satisfaction, but people who are committed to long-term joys and values outside of themselves, called eudemonia, tend to be more satisfied.

LO 15.4 Describe the diverse roles and relationships that characterize middle adulthood. (p. 441)

Adults often have diverse relationships in midlife: Some may be happily single, and others may have a partner or children. Social support is important for healthy development, but it can come from friends, family, or romantic partners. Around the world, some adults are in committed long-term relationships. Many difficulties in relationships come from stresses outside the relationship like overwork, poverty, or discrimination rather than from poor communication. Parenthood can be a source of joy but also strain throughout children's development. Parenting is often particularly challenging when children are infants and adolescents. Relationships change as children grow up, and support becomes more mutual. Adults often are often caring for other adult family members, which can be a source of strain.

LO 15.5 Describe common emotional disorders that occur during middle adulthood. (p. 452)

Emotional health is particularly important during midlife as adults care for others. Strains such as unemployment and poverty make it more difficult to maintain emotional health. Rates of suicide, substance use disorder, loneliness, and mental illness are rising among middle-aged adults in many affluent countries. Building resilience can come through formal therapies, social support, generativity, exercise, and better sleep.

KEY TERMS

generativity versus stagnation (p. 437)

generativity (p. 437)

hedonia (p. 438)

eudemonia (p. 438)

midlife crisis (p. 439)

postresidential (p. 447)

estrangement (p. 449)

grandfamilies (p. 449)

fictive kin (p. 451)

CHECK YOUR LEARNING

1. In middle adulthood, life experiences are diverse and have a major impact on adults' functioning. Adults can expect to have all of the following EXCEPT:
   a) stability in relationships, roles and responsibilities.
   b) predictable, universal development.
   c) universal milestones and stages.
   d) a midlife crisis.

2. What is a strength of emotional development in middle adulthood?
   a) Powerful sensation seeking
   b) Difficulties with impulse control
   c) Creative wisdom
   d) Increased emotion regulation

3. Doug contributes to his community through his parenting and his career as a teacher. His sense that he is giving back is known as:
   a) industriousness.
   c) cognitive dissonance.
   b) generativity.
   d) despair.

4. The midlife crisis is a myth for most adults. What better characterizes the well-being of most adults in affluent countries during midlife?
   a) A time of strain that will ease as they grow older
   b) The best of times
   c) A time of dramatic changes
   d) The top of a bellshaped curve of life satisfaction

5. Doug wonders whether he should have spent more time on simple hedonic pleasures, like bakery treats and sleeping in, rather than on creating meaning and giving back. Researchers have connected which type of focus to well-being in midlife?
   a) Hedonic pleasures: live for the present
   b) Both hedonic and eudemonic fulfillment
   c) Neither hedonic nor eudemonic fulfillment
   d) Eudemonic fulfillment: live for meaning

6. Doug is happily partnered and raising a child, but can adults find social support and comfort if they are not in family partnerships?
   a) Yes. Adults can find support in friendships and other community relationships.
   b) No. Committed partnerships are the only way adults can be happy.
   c) No. Adults without families cannot be fulfilled.
   d) No. Adults who are single are doomed to be lonely.

7. Which of the following is NOT a common stress in relationships?
   a) Stress from overwork
   b) Stress from financial insecurity
   c) Stress from pervasive discrimination
   d) Stress from communication difficulties

8. What is one thing that will NOT help adults boost their emotional health and resilience in midlife?
   a) Using marijuana
   b) Getting more sleep
   c) Boosting physical activity
   d) Doing something kind for someone else

9. Middle adulthood is a diverse life stage. Explain the impact of social context on adult's development.

10. Generativity is an important part of theories of resilience and well-being in middle adulthood. What are ways that adults may not have equitable access to opportunities for generativity?

16 Physical and Cognitive Development in Late Adulthood

©Macmillan, Photo by Sidford House

What Is Late Adulthood?

16.1 What are the markers of late adulthood?

16.2 What are the biological hallmarks of aging?

Changing Bodies in Late Adulthood

16.3 What changes in senses, strength, and sexuality may accompany aging?

Health in Late Adulthood

16.4 What are the common health conditions of later life?

The Changing Brain in Late Adulthood

16.5 How does the brain change in late adulthood?

Cognition in Late Adulthood

16.6 What are the typical cognitive changes in healthy aging?

Selected Resources from

Activities

Concept Practice: Aging, Memory, and Neurocognitive Disorders

Spotlight on Science: A Community Program to Promote Generativity

Assessments

LearningCurve

Practice Quiz

Videos

Scientific American Profiles

Brain Development Animation: Late Adulthood

Exercise and Happiness

Bart is no stranger to hard work. After a stint in the Army during the Vietnam War and 30 years in the auto industry, he was still crisscrossing the country in his late 60s as a corporate trainer. A couple of years ago, Bart decided to step back from his full-time job.

An accomplished public speaker who is always learning new things, Bart now spends more time on his houseboat with his partner, Darlene, and volunteers at a nearby nature center. Bart's presentations have become more personal: He speaks to audiences around the country about what it is like to be diagnosed with Alzheimer disease. Since his diagnosis, Bart has been working to break the stigma that surrounds his condition. His goal is to help people understand what they can expect if they or someone they love has been diagnosed with a major neurocognitive disorder.

Despite the age listed on his driver's license, Bart, like many adults, still considers himself middle aged. He always believed he could opt out of aging, but now everyone else seems to be getting younger. He once thought that he would never be too old to honky tonk, to ride a motorcycle, or to drive a stick-shift sports car. But now, he senses that those days may be coming to an end, ruefully remembering making fun of older men like a "damned fool." He still has moments when being older is embarrassing. He was embarrassed about his diagnosis, too: It took him a while to tell his children and his wide circle of friends and acquaintances.

Like Bart, many adults have misconceptions and worries about growing older, but simply acknowledging that aging is inevitable makes it less frightening (NORC, 2017). The changes of late adulthood often lead to losses: more fragile health, less reliable memory, and decreasing ability to do it all alone. Bart worries about giving

461

up his car keys, no longer being able to climb a 12-foot ladder, and needing someone else to help him with his boat. But late adulthood is a time of tremendous variability: Adults adapt differently to getting older, depending on their life experiences.

For instance, in the United States, older adults are more likely to qualify for Mensa (the organization for people who claim their IQs are over 150) than reside in a nursing home (Caffrey et al., 2021). Similarly, most U.S. adults over age 65 feel that they are in good health (Graham, 2019). They typically tell researchers that they feel better about aging the older they get—more comfortable with themselves, more respected by their community, and more purposeful than when they were younger (Solway et al., 2020).

Aging is not always so rosy: For many adults, particularly those who have already experienced a lifetime of disadvantage, getting older can be painful and involve cognitive losses (Peterson et al., 2020; Zahodne et al., 2020, 2021). For adults fortunate enough to live into their 70s and beyond, aging means acknowledging new limitations and adapting to new circumstances (Baltes & Baltes, 1990; Romo et al., 2013). For Bart, this means making short-term plans for his adventures. Late adulthood can nevertheless be a time for growth and building resilience.

Scientific American Profile

▶ Meet Bart

©Macmillan, Photo by Sidford House

What Is Late Adulthood?

Learning Objectives

16.1 What are the markers of late adulthood?

16.2 What are the biological hallmarks of aging?

Late adulthood, which traditionally begins when we consider ourselves "old" and ends in death, is the most diverse period of the lifespan. Aging is influenced by decades of life experience and, as a result, does not happen at the same rate for everyone. Adults in affluent countries like Switzerland are twice as likely to be healthy and independent in their 70s as those who live in less affluent countries like Mexico (WHO, 2015). Similar disparities can be seen within the United States. For instance, college-educated adults tend to be healthier in their 70s than their peers without a high school diploma who are in their 40s (Cantu et al., 2021; Zahodne et al., 2017). Adults who face discrimination tend to age more quickly than those from more privileged social groups, no matter their educational background (Jackson et al., 2019; Simons et al., 2020).

Many *gerontologists* (scientists who study aging) suggest that late adulthood begins at about age 65, but this date is not universal (Sanderson & Scherbov, 2020). In the past, late adulthood began when adults retired or stepped away from physically demanding work. In communities that rely on intensive physical labor and have limited health care, adults often age quickly, and late adulthood often begins in the 50s. But across human history, elites have continued to thrive and work long into late adulthood (Troyansky, 2015). In today's world, decades of life that were once reserved only for the wealthy are now available to more people (Sanderson & Scherbov, 2020). Even the traditional marker of late adulthood, retirement, has been pushed later in life in many nations (see **Figure 16.1**).

CONNECTIONS

Remember from Chapter 1 that the study of aging is known as *gerontology*. This field was established in the early twentieth century by scientists who wanted to prolong life and social reformers who were eager to improve the lives of vulnerable older people. *Gerontologists* include health care providers, psychologists, economists, anthropologists, and sociologists.

Categorizing Late Adulthood

Since late adulthood spans so many years, scholars often break the stage up into subcategories. The simplest way is to divide it by age. In this system, adults who are referred to as **young-old** are between 65 and 74. Adults who are **middle-old** are between 75 and 84. Adults who are 85 and older are known as the **oldest-old**. Thanks to improved public health, the fastest growing population group is the oldest-old category, particularly *centenarians* who are over 100 (Ortman et al., 2014; U.S. Census Bureau, 2020).

Another way to categorize late adulthood is to focus on an adult's capabilities, not their number of birthdays. Scales that measure an adults' **level of functioning** evaluate how much adults can manage in their daily life and help determine eligibility for

young-old The term for adults who are between ages 65 and 74.

middle-old The term for adults who are between ages 75 and 84.

oldest-old The term for adults who are 85 and older.

level of functioning A measure that evaluates how well adults can manage in their daily life.

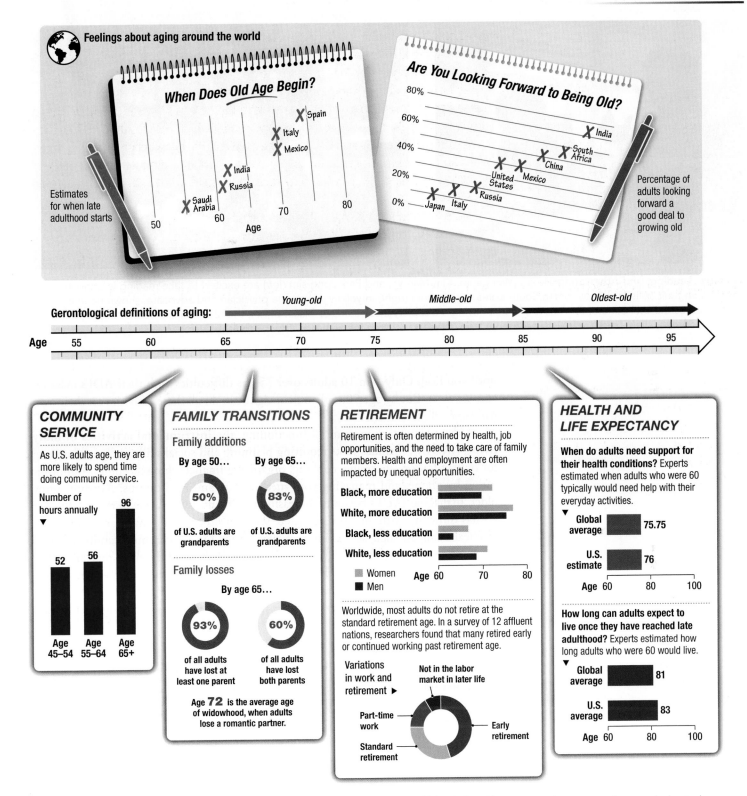

FIGURE 16.1 Markers of Late Adulthood Late adulthood is a diverse time of life, defined by community expectations and physical health. Retirement, bereavement, and more fragile health are hallmarks of this period for many.

U.S. government services (LaPlante, 2010). The basic skills known as **activities of daily living (ADLs)** include independently using the bathroom, getting dressed, bathing and feeding oneself, and moving short distances (Katz et al., 1963; Katz & Akpom, 1976). ADLs are tightly linked to physical health. If you break your right arm, for instance, your ADL score will be low, and you may need help with dishwashing and driving

activities of daily living (ADLs) Basic living skills that include independently using the bathroom, getting dressed, bathing and feeding oneself, and moving short distances.

Learning, Leading, and Advocating Hwang Woi-geum, Kim Mae-ye, and Park Jong-sim (*left*) are excited to take reading lessons to brush up on their skills in a classroom in South Korea. Lisa Iezzoni (*right*; in yellow jacket) is a physician and advocate, shown here as she addresses the U.S. Senate. She has found that having a disability often leads to bias. For her, the research is personal: As a result of multiple sclerosis, she's used a wheelchair for more than 30 years. You can follow her at #docswithdisabilities.

until you heal. Only 1 in 10 adults over 75 has difficulties with their ADLs (Adams & Martinez, 2016). But by age 90, only one in eight can do all these activities on their own (Freedman et al., 2014).

A complementary measure of functioning, the **instrumental activities of daily living (IADLs)**, includes tasks requiring planning and social skills, such as arranging for transportation, shopping, cooking, organizing finances, housekeeping, communicating by phone, and managing your medical care and medications. As adults grow older, managing IADLs becomes increasingly difficult. In fact, one in five adults over 75 has difficulty with an IADL (Adams & Martinez, 2016). Some limitations come from physical changes, such as hearing loss that might hinder communication (Lin et al., 2019). There also may be social or emotional reasons for difficulties that arise. For instance, some older men are reluctant to cook and clean, because they associate these tasks with women (Sheehan & Tucker-Drob, 2019). For others, inability to complete IADLs may be an early sign of cognitive declines linked to conditions like Alzheimer disease (Farias et al., 2018; Jutten et al., 2019).

Communicating About Age Without Ageism

No matter how researchers categorize late adulthood, these labels do not always line up with how older adults see themselves. As one woman explained to a researcher: "We really are 16 year olds trapped in older bodies. . . . We still feel young" (qtd. in Hofmeier et al., 2017, p. 7). Most 70-year-olds, including Bart, still think of themselves as being middle aged (Stephan et al., 2018).

One thing many older adults do not want to be called is "old" (Lamb, 2017). Remember from Chapter 14 that the twin prejudices of ageism and ableism can influence how adults feel about themselves and how they are treated by their families, neighbors, and health care providers (Levy et al., 2020; Nelson, 2017). Unfortunately, ridiculing older adults is nearly universal, even among older adults themselves (Burling, 2018; Calasanti & King, 2020; Levy et al., 2020; Malani et al., 2020). These prejudices also influence the words we use to talk about this age stage.

Researchers use terms for older adults that are not typically used outside of the laboratory, referring to people as "old-old" or "geriatric." In everyday life, these words, along with other terms like "senior citizen," "the elderly," and "mature adult" smack of ageism (Burling, 2018; Lamb, 2017; Pinsker, 2020). Using a people-first designation, such

instrumental activities of daily living (IADLs) A measure of functioning that includes tasks requiring planning and social skills, such as arranging for transportation, shopping, cooking, organizing finances, keeping your home clean, communicating by phone, and managing medical care and medications.

as "people who are older," is the most respectful policy. Other options, like the identity-first "older people" or "older adults," are also acceptable (Burling, 2018; Pinsker, 2020).

More Adults Reach Late Adulthood

Public health successes such as a reduction in cigarette smoking and better treatments for infectious diseases mean that more adults live into late adulthood than ever before, as you can see in **Figure 16.2**. In many nations, such health improvements combined with smaller families mean that there are now more older adults than children, causing a widespread population shift. More than one in four people in Japan is older, along with about one in five in most European countries and one in seven in the United States (Bauman et al., 2016; Goldman et al., 2018; He et al., 2016).

As the large cohort known as the baby boomers reaches later life, communities benefit from additional productive workers and caregivers (Harper, 2020; Pruchno, 2012). Older populations generally have a smaller ecological and environmental footprint than younger ones: Aging is good for the planet (Gotmark et al., 2018; Kluge et al., 2014).

Another Benefit of an Aging Population Longer lifespans and more older adults mean that more little ones will benefit from time with grandparents, like this doting grandfather in the coastal district of Kampot in Cambodia.

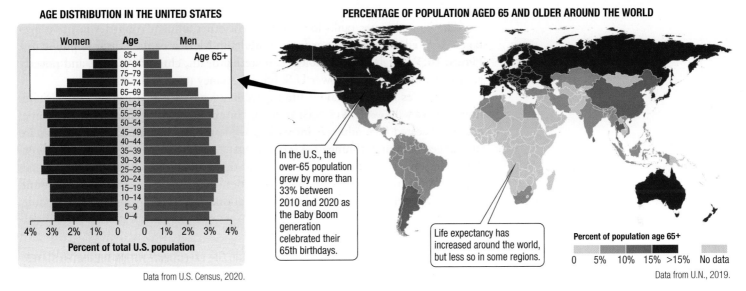

Data from U.S. Census, 2020.

Data from U.N., 2019.

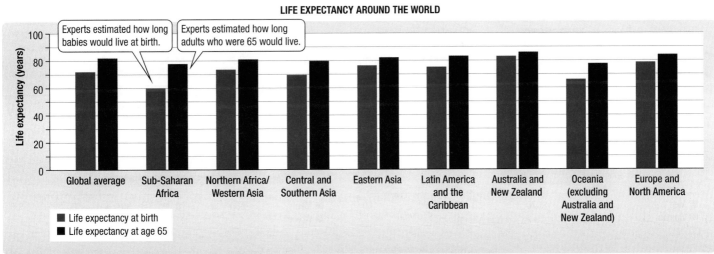

Data from U.N., 2019.

FIGURE 16.2 Aging Populations Around the World Around the globe, an aging population is common in affluent countries where good health makes it more likely that adults will live into late adulthood. Life expectancy can be measured at birth (see bottom figure) or at age 65, indicating how long adults would be expected to live, on average, once they reached their 65th birthday.

life expectancy A measurement of how long you can expect to live.

Variations in Life Expectancy

Around the world, adults are living longer, but not everyone gets a chance to blow out their 100th birthday candles (Kontis et al., 2017). Disparities in health affect how long adults live (Jordá & Niño-Zarazúa, 2017).

Life expectancy is a measurement of how long you can expect to live. Life expectancy can be measured at birth, or it can be measured from any other point in the lifespan. For instance, the *life expectancy measured at birth* for a girl born this year in the United States is over 80; for a boy, it is 75 (Arias et al., 2021). *Adult life expectancy* refers to how long an adult can expect to live, measured from the age they are now. In the United States, the adult life expectancy for someone turning 65 now is 85 (Medina et al., 2020).

Adult life expectancy is longest in nations with low poverty levels and strong social safety nets that guarantee access to necessities like medical care. Adults live the longest in affluent counties such as South Korea, France, and Iceland, where most will live to be over 85 (Foreman et al., 2018; Kontis et al., 2017). In countries with low adult life expectancy, adults too often endure the effects of HIV/AIDS and pregnancy complications, as well as poverty, violence, and lack of universal medical care. In countries with low life expectancy, someone turning 60 will have little chance of living past 75 (UN, 2017).

The United States ranks lower than most other affluent countries in life expectancy: U.S. adults live about as long as adults in Mexico or the Czech Republic (see **Figure 16.3**). High rates of violence, maternal death, chronic diseases, and poverty are frequently blamed for lower U.S. life expectancy (Kontis et al., 2017).

Disparities in average adult life expectancy have increased in the United States in recent years (Bosworth, 2018; NASEM, 2021). For example, the lifespan of high-income, college-educated U.S. adults is increasing, while for low-income adults, lifespans are unchanged or even declining (Case & Deaton, 2021; Chetty et al., 2016; Crimmins & Zhang, 2019). Adults in some rural communities are likely to die more than 20 years younger than those in more high-income, suburban counties (Dwyer-Lindgren et al., 2017). And around the world, people who experience discrimination, such as Indigenous or Black adults

GLOBAL DISPARITIES IN HEALTH AND LIFE EXPECTANCY

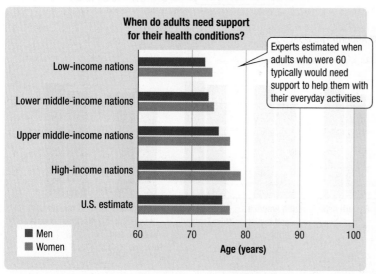

Data from WHO, Global Health Estimates, 2022.

DISPARITIES IN HEALTH AND LIFE EXPECTANCY WITHIN THE UNITED STATES

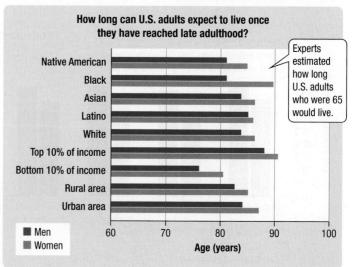

Data from Medina et al., 2020; Congressional Research Service, 2021; Vieboom & Preston, 2020.

FIGURE 16.3 Disparities in Life Expectancy Disparities in health and life expectancy are particularly pronounced in late adulthood. Health is often tied to income and to social exclusion and discrimination.

in the United States, Black adults in Brazil, or people of Pakistani origin in the United Kingdom, tend to have shorter lives (Medina et al., 2020).

Many scientists believe that improvements in health care mean that average life expectancy will continue to increase until most people live to be about 90 (Canudas-Romo et al., 2016; Dong et al., 2016; Marck et al., 2017). Some already live longer than average. The record for the *maximum lifespan* belongs to French woman Jeanne Calment, who lived to be 122, crediting her longevity to her love of chocolate (Rosenberg, 2019)! Scientists suggest that Calment may have survived to nearly the limit of human capability. Most believe that 125 is probably the maximum lifespan human beings can achieve (Dong et al., 2016; Marck et al., 2017).

The Biology of Aging

Scientists around the world are trying to unlock the secrets of aging to help adults live longer, healthier lives. Compared to other primates like gorillas or chimpanzees, who tend to die soon after their reproductive lives have ended, we human beings live well past middle age and care for our older community members (Bribiescas, 2020; Gomez-Olivencia & Ohman, 2018; Spikins et al., 2018). Scientists who take a *life history* or evolutionary perspective suggest that living to late adulthood helped our species thrive because in ancient times, older adults provided the extra help that enabled ancient families to hunt, gather, and keep their children safe (Loo et al., 2017; Nichols et al., 2016).

Still Lobstering at 101 Some of us are lucky to have a longer lifespan, like Virginia Oliver. She is over 100 but still working. She has been harvesting lobsters in Penboscot Bay, Maine since she was a teenager.

SCIENCE IN PRACTICE
Leslie Gordon, M.D., Ph.D.

Scientists are often inspired by personal passion. For instance, some mysteries of aging were discovered, in part, by one parent's work to save her son's life (Chen, 2004; Gordon et al., 2018).

Dr. Leslie Gordon always wanted to do research. She loved the idea of being part of a team. As she describes it, science is about being part of a community fueled by passion. Science is a beach, she explains: it "has a zillion grains of sand and . . . without all of those grains of sand, you can't have a beach. You can't find the answers" (qtd. in Chen, 2004). She became a doctor and specialized in research on visual processing.

When Leslie's son, Sam, was just a toddler, Leslie turned her attention from vision to a new area: saving Sam's life. Sam was adorable but was not developing like other children. His teeth were not coming in, and he did not have any hair. He was not growing as quickly as other babies. Sam was diagnosed with *Hutchinson-Gilford progeria syndrome (HGPS)*, a rare disease that causes premature aging. Without treatment, children with HGPS typically die of heart disease as teenagers (Gordon et al., 2018).

Leslie went into the laboratory to find a cure. Scientists around the world were also interested in the syndrome, not just because they wanted to help Sam and the other children who have this condition, but because they believed that HGPS might hold the key to understanding aging.

Unfortunately, like other children with HGPS, Sam died young, when he was just 17 (Botelho, 2014). But his mother's research helped to develop a treatment that slows the disease, giving children a few more years of life (Gordon et al., 2018).

Leslie's discovery also helped scientists better understand aging: Her work inspired the discovery of the gene that helps drive HGPS. One single gene causes the buildup of a malformed protein that leads to rapid aging in HGPS and contributes to heart disease in adults, a

Taking the Microphone for Science Sam Bems, shown here at 16, next to his parents, was active in trying to raise understanding about HGPS. His condition is often used as a model to understand aging in all people.

leading cause of death worldwide (Collins, 2016; Lowenstein & Bennett, 2018; Scaffidi & Mistelli, 2006). Leslie's work reminds us that the signs of aging you see in the hair loss and fragile skin of older adults, and in children like Sam, are driven by changes in your genes. (⊚)

You might think you will know aging when you see it: wrinkles, difficulty making it up the stairs, or forgetting where you parked the car. Bart pinpoints the time when even his doctor was younger than he was. Scientists have a more precise definition: *Aging* is a developmental process that leads to the gradual loss of physical functioning and makes you more vulnerable to death (Ferrucci et al., 2020; Lopez-Otin et al., 2013; Sierra, 2016). It happens as a result of changes in multiple areas of the body (see **Infographic 16.1**) (Bana & Cabreiro, 2019; Niedernhofer et al., 2018). We will focus on changes in five major areas: your genes, stem cells, immune system, inflammatory response, and hormones.

Can You Inherit a Long Life? How you age is related primarily to your life experience (Erikson et al., 2016; van Dijk, 2019). In fact, researchers estimate that less than 20 percent of the variation in how people age comes from genes they have inherited (Ash et al., 2015; Ruby et al., 2018a). Scientists have studied the historical records of long-lived families and have found that most of their longevity comes from social advantages, like affluence, rather than biology (Ash et al., 2015; Ruby et al., 2018a).

However, in a few cases, researchers have found that inherited genes are important to lifelong health. More than 500 different genes have been linked to longevity (Morris et al., 2019). Most research has focused on just two: *APOE* and *FOXO3*.

APOE is an acronym for *apolipoprotein E*, a protein that helps to maintain neurons and regulate metabolism and cholesterol. Like other genes, APOE comes in a variety of forms, or *alleles*. Although one APOE allele provides some protection against infectious diseases when you are young, in the long run, this allele increases the risk of cardiovascular disease by about one-third and increases the risk of Alzheimer disease by 3 to 15 times (Lowe et al., 2016; van Exel et al., 2017).

The tiny FOXO3 gene is linked to your metabolism, stem cells, and the regulation of cell death (Sanese et al., 2019; Stefanetti et al., 2018). Many people with exceptionally long lives have protective variations of the FOXO3 gene (Ahlenius et al., 2016). FOXO3 appears to help protect adults from heart disease, diabetes, and cancer, but it has less dramatic effects than APOE (Du et al., 2017).

Aging Genome Genes are not just something you are born with. Remember, genetic instructions are at work every day, creating the proteins that allow your body to function and triggering cell division to replace aging cells with new ones. Throughout your lifespan, however, the DNA you were born with is slowly damaged. As a result, your cells create toxic proteins instead of healthy ones, and rather than creating new cells, they allow old, damaged ones to linger (Bana & Cabreiro, 2019; Niedernhofer et al., 2018).

Genetic damage in one area of your cells, the **mitochondria**, is particularly important in aging (Son & Lee, 2019). Mitochondria are the energy center of your cells. As you age, errors in mitochondria build up. Scientists found 95 percent of the mitochondria in one 90-year-old man were damaged, as compared to the perfect mitochondria they found in a child (Linnane et al., 1998). The damaged mitochondria in older adults begin to flood their bodies with malformed and mistaken proteins, contributing to many diseases and conditions that are common in late adulthood (Yen et al., 2020).

Zhan Yan/Xinhua via Getty Images

Sometimes Longevity Runs in the Family. Sonam Drolma (*right*) is said to be 109 and still lives near her sister in their childhood village near Lhasa, in the Tibetan Autonomous Region of China.

mitochondria The energy center of your cells.

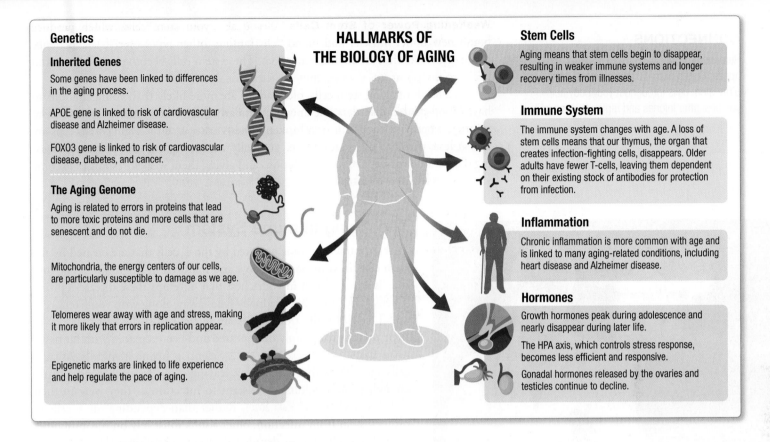

HALLMARKS OF THE BIOLOGY OF AGING

Genetics

Inherited Genes

Some genes have been linked to differences in the aging process.

APOE gene is linked to risk of cardiovascular disease and Alzheimer disease.

FOXO3 gene is linked to risk of cardiovascular disease, diabetes, and cancer.

The Aging Genome

Aging is related to errors in proteins that lead to more toxic proteins and more cells that are senescent and do not die.

Mitochondria, the energy centers of our cells, are particularly susceptible to damage as we age.

Telomeres wear away with age and stress, making it more likely that errors in replication appear.

Epigenetic marks are linked to life experience and help regulate the pace of aging.

Stem Cells

Aging means that stem cells begin to disappear, resulting in weaker immune systems and longer recovery times from illnesses.

Immune System

The immune system changes with age. A loss of stem cells means that our thymus, the organ that creates infection-fighting cells, disappears. Older adults have fewer T-cells, leaving them dependent on their existing stock of antibodies for protection from infection.

Inflammation

Chronic inflammation is more common with age and is linked to many aging-related conditions, including heart disease and Alzheimer disease.

Hormones

Growth hormones peak during adolescence and nearly disappear during later life.

The HPA axis, which controls stress response, becomes less efficient and responsive.

Gonadal hormones released by the ovaries and testicles continue to decline.

Remember from Chapters 9 and 14 that your *telomeres* are small areas on the end of your chromosomes that protect your DNA from making mistakes when it duplicates (Opresko & Shay, 2017). As you age, telomeres tend to shorten because of environmental stressors: Repeated experiences of discrimination, exposure to pollution, and chronic health conditions have all been linked to smaller telomeres (Chakravarti et al., 2021). Cells with shorter telomeres stop replicating themselves but remain in the body in a state of *senescence*. These senescent cells are not dead; rather, they have experienced so much damage that they can no longer replicate themselves. Cells may remain in senescence for many years, even as you get closer to death (Childs et al., 2017). Like damaged mitochondria, senescent cells produce malformed proteins that stress the body and cause inflammation (Martinez Cue & Rueda, 2020; Saez-Atienzar & Masliah, 2020).

Your *epigenetic marks* are also linked to aging. As discussed in Chapter 3, epigenetic changes direct how genes are expressed. Changes to your epigenetic marks accumulate as a result of a variety of lifetime experiences, from nurturing parenting to hearty nutrition, toxic stress to strength training (Gassen et al., 2017; Ryan et al., 2020). Some epigenetic alterations help people develop and adapt to their environments, but some can hasten the course of aging (Horvath & Raj, 2018).

Researchers are developing solutions that may one day reverse the genomic errors that are linked to aging (Horvath et al., 2019; Kulkarni et al., 2020). In the future, medications may help reverse genetic damage, but for now, behavioral changes are the most supported intervention. Social support, a healthy diet, meditation, and exercise all have been linked to reversing the epigenetic signs of aging (Brody et al., 2016; Kaliman, 2019; Rebelo-Marques et al., 2018).

Still Standing Up Aging may change stem cells, and time may be marked in the genome, but older adults still stand up for what is important to them. This woman in the Netherlands is advocating for the rights of the LGBTQIA+ community.

CONNECTIONS

Remember from Chapter 3 that *stem cells* appear during prenatal development. After birth, stem cells throughout your body help you heal after injuries and replenish worn-out cells.

Weakening Power of Stem Cells As you age, your stem cells, which produce brand-new bone, muscle, and blood cells (among other types of cells), experience damage just like the rest of your body does. These stem cells become less effective and begin to disappear (Chen & Kerr, 2019; Ermolaeva et al., 2018).

As a result of aging stem cells, older adults are more likely than younger adults to have blood-related disorders like anemia. Similarly, they take longer to recover from injuries, whether a paper cut or a broken bone (Vitale et al., 2017). Aging stem cells are also at least partly to blame for adults' gradually weakening immune system, increasing older adults' susceptibility to infections and giving them weaker responses to some vaccines (Hamazaki et al., 2016; Leins et al., 2018; Thomas et al., 2020).

Aging Does Not Stop Adults from Serving. More than one in eight physicians on the front lines of the COVID-19 pandemic were adults over age 65.

The Aging Immune System

Your immune system is powered by the T cells that are created by the stem cells in your bone marrow and matured in the *thymus*. The thymus is a little organ in your chest that develops these disease-fighting T cells early in life but gradually fades away, along with your stem cells and T cells. By the time adults are in their 60s, the vast majority of their thymus has simply disappeared and been replaced with fat tissue (Gui et al., 2012; Simanovsky et al., 2012). Scientists blame stem cells: As stem cells age, the thymus fades away, leaving some T cells behind but not enough to keep adults as resistant to infection as they were in their earlier years (Thomas et al., 2020). Rather than depending on T cells to protect them from infection, older adults must rely on the antibodies they have built up over decades of exposure to viruses.

As a result, when a new virus appears, such as COVID-19, older people are uniquely vulnerable to a disease from which their library of antibodies cannot protect them (Akbar & Gilroy, 2020). As one consequence, COVID-19 was a leading cause of death among older adults in 2020 and 2021 (Ahmad & Anderson, 2021).

Too Much Inflammation As a result of a waning immune system and a buildup of senescent cells, older adults' bodies are more likely to be stuck in a state of *inflammation* (Chung et al., 2019; Ferrucci & Fabbri, 2018). Inflammation is what happens when you get a cold or a bruise: Chemical messengers and immune cells swarm in to heal the area, resulting in pain, hotness, and swelling. The chronic inflammation that becomes more likely with age occurs throughout your body, sometimes attacking your tissues. Chronic inflammation is linked to the major conditions and diseases of aging: heart disease, diabetes, Alzheimer disease, and arthritis, along with depression, cognitive decline, and frailty (Ferrucci & Fabbri, 2018).

Time to Enjoy the Garden Adults with Down syndrome, like this woman in Bulgaria, tend to experience accelerated aging, partly as a result of inflammation in the body.

Most adults have some degree of inflammation, but certain factors make it more severe. Some evidence indicates that excess weight, for instance, triggers inflammation (Ferrucci & Fabbri, 2018). Social and behavioral factors are also strongly linked to inflammation: Everyday stress, social exclusion, and depression worsen inflammation (Cobb et al., 2020). Feelings of belonging and generativity, along with exercise and managing depression, can reduce inflammation (Moieni et al., 2020; Redwine et al., 2020). One program, in which older adults volunteered in elementary-school classrooms, reduced inflammation and increased volunteers' feelings of well-being (Seeman et al., 2020). Reducing chronic inflammation is a major goal for researchers: Less inflammation means longer and healthier lives (Arai et al., 2015).

Aging Hormones

Throughout the lifespan, hormones help direct the pace of your growth. Aging is no different: Hormones help regulate how you age.

In late adulthood, the hormones that once directed the rapid growth of childhood now affect the pace of aging (Colon et al., 2019). These growth hormones peak during adolescence and gradually decline until they nearly disappear in later life (Bartke, 2019). But growth hormones are not magical: Giving older adults supplemental growth hormones tends to make their bodies bulkier but not stronger and places them at higher risk for cancer, metabolic syndrome, and diabetes (Bartke, 2019; Clemmons et al., 2014).

Gonadal hormones released by the ovaries and testicles, like estrogen and testosterone, also decline during late adulthood and help explain some sex-linked differences in aging (Lejri et al., 2018; Sampathkumar et al., 2019). Throughout the lifespan, the ovaries produce more estrogen than the testes, and estrogen has protective effects on health. As the ovaries begin producing less estrogen during menopause, estrogen's protective effects begin to wane (Gubbels Bupp et al., 2018).

As you remember, the *HPA axis* helps you respond to stressors by releasing hormones such as cortisol (Epel & Lithgow, 2014). With age, the HPA axis gradually becomes less efficient, making it more difficult for adults to recover from stress (Gaffey et al., 2016; Yiallouris et al., 2019). Consequently, many older adults have chronically high levels of cortisol, which contribute to emotional disorders in late life. Like younger people, about one in four older adults experiences an emotional disorder like anxiety or depression (Faye et al., 2018; Gaffey et al., 2016).

APPLY IT! **16.1** Bart has continued to do some of the things he does well as he gets older, including public speaking, travel, and service work. How do these activities contradict stereotypes about age?

16.2 As Bart points out, getting older will happen to all of us, if we are fortunate enough. What are your own ethnotheories, or "bucket list" items, about your own late life?

16.3 Aging involves simultaneous changes in multiple body systems and parts of our cells. How do you explain the value of healthy behaviors like social support and addressing stress in changing the pace of aging?

16.4 Some scholars suggest that seeking a "cure for aging" is ageist and ableist. How might you explain the value of research into the biology of aging?

CONNECTIONS

Gonadal hormones begin to change during middle adulthood, as explained in Chapter 14. *Menopause* refers to the hormonal changes that people with ovaries experience in their early 50s that result in an end to ovulation and menstruation. People with testes also have hormonal changes in middle adulthood, but these are more gradual.

Natural Disasters Hit Everyone. But older adults' bodies are more sensitive to the effects of disasters, like the hurricane that hit these men's home in Cueto Bayamo, Cuba.

Changing Bodies in Late Adulthood

One of the realities of late adulthood is that a series of inescapable changes makes bones less resilient, muscles weaker, and bodies frailer. Although Bart stays active, he worries about being able to keep up with his boat and dreads the time when he will no longer be able to fix the engine himself. Aging changes all of the body's systems: Muscle strength, sexuality, and senses all adjust to the decades adults have lived, evident in the reading glasses littering Bart's desk.

Aging Senses

Many adults believe that variations in their sight, hearing, and even sense of smell are among the inevitable age-related changes that they must accept (Cacchione, 2014). However, these changes are *not* universal and may be treatable if that is desired. Sensory impairments are leading causes of disability: Many result from the stresses of the environment and exposure to sun and pollution (WHO, 2015).

Learning Objective

16.3 What changes in senses, strength, and sexuality may accompany aging?

Still in the Driver's Seat This taxi driver in Caracas, Venezuela, is still driving safely. While adults often have stereotypes about older drivers, many people who drive for a living around the world are older. About a quarter of Uber drivers in the United States, for instance, are older adults.

Vision Because of changes in the brain and the eye itself, vision becomes slower and less accurate as adults get older (see **Figure 16.4**) (Lin et al., 2016). Remember from Chapter 14 that the *lens* becomes less flexible with age, making it difficult to see objects up close. This is known as *presbyopia* and is what prompted Bart to invest in reading glasses.

With age, the lens itself clouds and yellows (Turner & Mainster, 2008). The *retina*, the part of the eye that converts light into signals that are read by your brain, begins to deteriorate. The nerve cells in the eye, like those in the brain, were present when you were born, and typically have begun to break down by your 70s, Sun damage, environmental pollution, and health conditions like diabetes and heart disease can take a toll on all the sensitive components of vision (Lin et al., 2016; Martin & Poche, 2019).

As a result, older adults may develop a number of visual conditions. They may have difficulty seeing contrasts between objects, which can make it hard to read or pick up a contact lens that has fallen on the floor (Owsley, 2016). Most people will begin to have difficulty seeing in low light, which can be frustrating when you are trying to read the menu at a candlelit restaurant. Night driving can become hazardous, because older adults are less able to adjust to changing light conditions (Owsley, 2016). Indeed, common vision problems are why adults over age 80 are at higher risk for car accidents than middle-aged adults (Owsley, 2016; Owsley et al., 2013; Tefft, 2017).

Older adults are also more susceptible to eye diseases that may cause blindness. For about 1 in 10 adults, conditions such as glaucoma, cataracts, and macular degeneration cause a loss of vision (Foreman et al., 2018; Jonas et al., 2017).

Older adults confront a world that is designed for perfect vision. Adaptations abound: taking a friend with you to help with paperwork when you vote, using a ride-share service instead of driving, and switching to large print or audiobooks (Zhang & Radhakrishnan, 2018). But compensation may never be a perfect substitute, and support may not always be easily available. Adults with visual loss, particularly if it is untreated, are at higher risk for depression and cognitive impairments (Whitson et al., 2018).

Hearing As you may recall from Chapter 14, both the environment and common diseases contribute to hearing loss. The tiny hair cells in your inner ear are damaged by

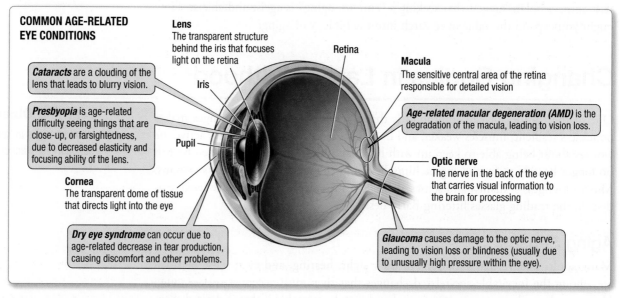

COMMON AGE-RELATED EYE CONDITIONS

Lens
The transparent structure behind the iris that focuses light on the retina

Retina

Macula
The sensitive central area of the retina responsible for detailed vision

Cataracts are a clouding of the lens that leads to blurry vision.

Iris

Presbyopia is age-related difficulty seeing things that are close-up, or farsightedness, due to decreased elasticity and focusing ability of the lens.

Pupil

Age-related macular degeneration (AMD) is the degradation of the macula, leading to vision loss.

Cornea
The transparent dome of tissue that directs light into the eye

Optic nerve
The nerve in the back of the eye that carries visual information to the brain for processing

Dry eye syndrome can occur due to age-related decrease in tear production, causing discomfort and other problems.

Glaucoma causes damage to the optic nerve, leading to vision loss or blindness (usually due to unusually high pressure within the eye).

FIGURE 16.4 The Aging Eye Older adults are more likely than younger adults to develop eye conditions such as age-related macular degeneration, cataracts, and glaucoma. Interventions can help support older adults' adaptation and in some cases can help treat the conditions.

loud noises, from music pounding out of your earbuds to the clanking of a subway train. Health conditions such as high blood pressure and diabetes also contribute to hearing loss (Whitson et al., 2018). More than half of all adults over 60 have some hearing loss, making it one of the leading causes of disability (Carroll et al., 2017). Adults often have particular difficulty following conversations that compete with background noise, such as a television or traffic (Henry et al., 2017).

Many adults are unaware that hearing aids or cochlear implants may effectively address hearing loss (CAAHHC, 2016; Buchman et al., 2020). Experts estimate that only one in five people with hearing loss has a hearing aid (Orji et al., 2020). Stigma and ableism play a role: Many adults are reluctant to wear hearing aids or implants, telling researchers that they do not want to "look disabled" (David & Werner, 2016; David et al., 2018). Hearing aids are often unaffordable, although modern technology now makes them smaller, more effective, and more comfortable to wear (Krabbe & Grodal, 2018).

Loss of hearing can lead to strained relationships (Barker et al., 2017). If it is not addressed, the lack of social interaction it can cause may result in brain changes: The regions that process language can shrink. People with hearing loss are 25 percent more likely to develop a neurocognitive disorder (Whitson et al., 2018). However, support, including helping families adopt new styles of communication or using hearing aids and cochlear implants, can lessen these risks, and cognitive losses may be reversed (Buchman et al., 2020).

Damage to the inner ear contributes to another common challenge in late adulthood: difficulties with balance. About 3 in 10 adults over 70 often feel tippy, dizzy, or unsteady (Jahn, 2019). The culprit is the **vestibular system**, which is located inside the inner ear and transmits information about where you are in space to the brain (Agrawal et al., 2020). If you have ever gotten carsick or seasick, you know how important this system is. As we get older, loss of hair cells in the inner ear and a reduction in the number of neurons that connect the vestibular system with the brain make it difficult to maintain balance. The resulting feeling of unsteadiness can cause older adults to feel less confident moving (Agrawal et al., 2020; Auais et al., 2017; Verma et al., 2016).

Smell and Taste Deteriorating senses can also make eating well difficult for older adults (Baugreet et al., 2017). About half of adults over 70 have diminished taste and smell, which can make food less appetizing (Correia et al., 2016; Doty & Kamath, 2014). With age, adults have fewer neurons in their mouth and in the *olfactory bulb* in their brain that help them process information about food (Moayedi et al., 2018; Riera & Dillin, 2016).

While all adults tend to have some loss of smell and taste as they get older, significant losses are not typical: They can be a marker of cognitive impairments (Devanand, 2016; Doty & Kamath, 2014). There are no treatments to improve taste or smell, so experts often advise older adults (and those cooking with them) to intensify flavor (Baugreet et al., 2017).

Changing Shape and Strength

Aging changes the bodies of even the most dedicated athletes (Marck et al., 2017). An accumulation of cellular damage leads to fewer muscle fibers and more porous bones (Corrado et al., 2020). However, strong health in middle age and some lifestyle choices can help some adults minimize these symptoms of aging (Peeters et al., 2019).

Losing Muscle All adults lose muscle strength and power as they get older (see **Figure 16.5**). Cellular changes mean that muscle neurons begin to disappear and muscle fibers become less resilient. Inflammation and lack of activity accelerate the process (Distefano & Goodpaster, 2018). Older people who exercise lose strength more slowly, and those who have fewer opportunities to move tend to lose it more quickly (Marck et al., 2017; Peeters et al., 2019).

Significant loss of muscle strength can mean older adults develop **sarcopenia**. Sarcopenia occurs when adults do not have the muscle mass and strength for

Greg Sorber/ZUMA Press/Newscom

Doing Well in His Side Hustle Nolan Shadeed won this 800-meter race, but he also excels at his day job as a jazz musician. Nolan is over 70 but runs faster than many high school racers. He is the world-record holder for his age group in more than a dozen events.

vestibular system Located inside the inner ear, this network transmits information to the brain about where you are in space.

sarcopenia Significant lack of muscle mass that limits adults' ability to perform everyday activities.

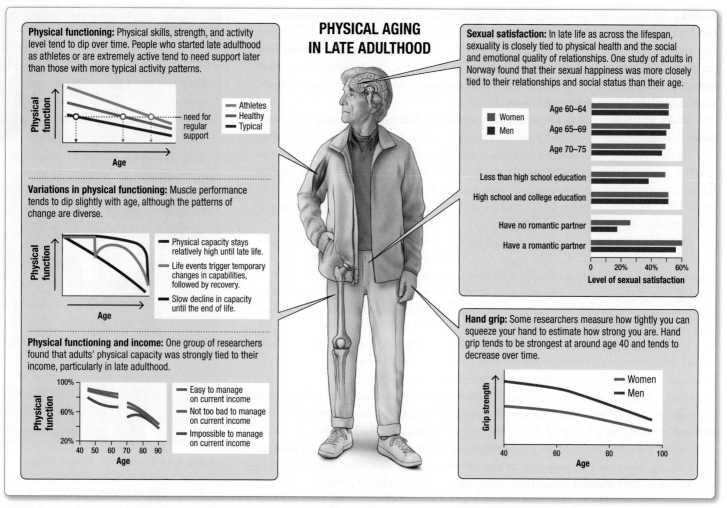

PHYSICAL AGING IN LATE ADULTHOOD

Physical functioning: Physical skills, strength, and activity level tend to dip over time. People who started late adulthood as athletes or are extremely active tend to need support later than those with more typical activity patterns.

Physical function / Age
— Athletes
— Healthy
— Typical
need for regular support

Variations in physical functioning: Muscle performance tends to dip slightly with age, although the patterns of change are diverse.

Physical function / Age
— Physical capacity stays relatively high until late life.
— Life events trigger temporary changes in capabilities, followed by recovery.
— Slow decline in capacity until the end of life.

Physical functioning and income: One group of researchers found that adults' physical capacity was strongly tied to their income, particularly in late adulthood.

Physical function / Age
— Easy to manage on current income
— Not too bad to manage on current income
— Impossible to manage on current income

Sexual satisfaction: In late life as across the lifespan, sexuality is closely tied to physical health and the social and emotional quality of relationships. One study of adults in Norway found that their sexual happiness was more closely tied to their relationships and social status than their age.

Women / Men
Age 60–64
Age 65–69
Age 70–75
Less than high school education
High school and college education
Have no romantic partner
Have a romantic partner
Level of sexual satisfaction

Hand grip: Some researchers measure how tightly you can squeeze your hand to estimate how strong you are. Hand grip tends to be strongest at around age 40 and tends to decrease over time.

Grip strength / Age
— Women
— Men

FIGURE 16.5 Changes in Physical Functioning There are wide variations in physical strength and functioning during late adulthood: many of them tied to life experience, income, and activity level.

frailty An age-linked condition including muscle weakness, exhaustion, physical inability to be active, and sometimes weight loss.

performing everyday activities like walking across a room or climbing stairs (Cruz-Jentoft et al., 2019; Rosenberg, 1989). Around the world, about one in five older adults have sarcopenia (Baugreet et al., 2017).

Losing muscle strength can increase the risk for hospitalization, falling, and inability to live independently. Weakening muscle function is also related to decreased mobility and *incontinence*, or loss of bladder or bowel control (Calasanti & King, 2020). By the time they are 80, about 6 in 10 women and 3 in 10 men worldwide have difficulties moving around on their own (Gomez-Olivencia & Ohman, 2018). About 4 in 10 have incontinence (Davis et al., 2020; Vaughan et al., 2018).

Sarcopenia and other forms of muscle weakness can be treated with a high-protein diet and exercise, particularly resistance or strength training (Morley, 2018; Ofori-Asenso et al., 2019). However, reversing sarcopenia is not always possible: Many adults do not have the good health, the time, or the support to take on an exercise regimen. Others may hurt too much to move (Rodrigues et al., 2017).

Sarcopenia and chronic illnesses also increase the risk that an adult may develop **frailty**, which occurs when an adult experiences muscle weakness, exhaustion, an inability to be active, and is often accompanied by weight loss (Fried et al., 2003; Howlett et al., 2021). For the one in six older adults who are frail, it may be difficult to live independently. But interventions can help address or reverse frailty (Ofori-Asenso et al., 2020). Exercise and nutrition will never help an older runner beat their previous racing times, but they typically give adults a better chance of avoiding frailty.

Fragile Bones Older people do not fall in greater numbers than younger people, but, as with other injuries and accidents in later adulthood, the consequences of falling are more serious (Lavedán et al., 2018; Meyer et al., 2019; Verma et al., 2016). Falling is the third leading cause of disability in older U.S. adults (Hartholt et al., 2019; Liu-Ambrose et al., 2019). Adults fall down because of bad luck, dizziness, or lack of muscle strength but develop a disability because of weakening bones. This increases anxiety about walking, which can actually increase the likelihood of a fall, thus causing older adults to limit their movement (Lavedán et al., 2018; Meyer et al., 2019).

During late adulthood, nearly half of all women and one-third of all men will fracture a bone (Cotts & Cifu, 2017; Sözen et al., 2018). The cause is a loss of bone mass, a process that may be imperceptible until a break happens, or you notice you have lost some height or developed a stoop. Adults may lose as much as an inch or two (or 2 or 5 cm) of height after they reach age 70 as a result of bone deterioration (Leslie et al., 2020; Mikula et al., 2017).

Extreme deterioration, when bones become so porous and fragile that they are vulnerable to breaks, is called **osteoporosis** (Curtis et al., 2018). Around the world, as adults become less active, rates of osteoporosis are rising: In the United States, about 1 in 10 older adults has osteoporosis (Wallace et al., 2015; Wu et al., 2019). Women are four times as likely as men to develop osteoporosis, partly because their bones are smaller and lighter and also because the rate of bone loss accelerates in women after menopause (Alswat, 2017).

In the United States, low bone density is often said to be more common in Asian American, White American, and Latino adults than it is among Black Americans (Looker et al., 2017; Xu & Wu, 2018). But scientists caution that such generalizations are not very useful. In fact, they demonstrate a shortcoming of racial labeling, that, these labels mask significant differences *within* groups. Adults whose origins are in East Africa, for instance, are at higher risk for osteoporosis, while those from West Africa tend to be at lower risk (Hilliard, 2016). In fact, experts believe that osteoporosis is underdiagnosed in the Black community in the United States (Noel et al., 2021). If it is caught in time, osteoporosis can be effectively treated, but many adults are not screened or cannot afford the medications (Khosla & Hofbauer, 2017; Tu et al., 2018).

Changes in bones and cartilage also lead to **arthritis**, the general term for pain in your joints. The most common form is *osteoarthritis*, which is caused by a degradation of cartilage and bone as a result of chronic inflammation (Tateiwa et al., 2019). In the United States, more than half of older adults have some form of osteoarthritis, which causes joints to be stiff, swollen, and painful, making it difficult to walk, open a jar, or lift groceries off the stoop (Frasca et al., 2017). Arthritis is linked to significant impairment and depression in late adulthood (Barbour et al., 2017).

Physical activity can reduce the limitations of arthritis (Geneen et al., 2017; Hootman et al., 2018). But starting an exercise regimen may be daunting, since movement can make pain worse in the short term. Many adults feel that arthritis and the accompanying chronic pain are inevitable, and they do not get the help they need to address it (Chen et al., 2020). Support can help ease some of the difficulties.

Sexual Activity

The idea of sex in late adulthood often makes people uncomfortable (Syme & Cohn, 2020). Even doctors are uncomfortable talking about sex with older people—one reason experts cite for the increasing rates of sexually transmitted infections among older adults (Braxton et al., 2018; Gewirtz-Meydan et al., 2018).

osteoporosis When bones become so porous and fragile that they are vulnerable to breaks.

arthritis A condition causing pain in the joints.

Keeping Their Connection Karsten Tüchsen Hansen and Inga Rasmussen live in separate countries. (She lives in Denmark and he lives over the border in Germany.) The couple were separated by COVID-19 restrictions in 2020. While their nights together ended as a result of the pandemic, they still met every day to have coffee on the border.

Emilie Ducke/The New York Times/Redux

There is great diversity in sexual expression in late life, just as there is across the lifespan (Srinivasan et al., 2019). As Stella, age 74, explained: "I know some people who are hot for sex and they're really old but they've been hot for sex their whole lives" (Bradway & Beard, 2015). However, ill health and lack of partners often keep older adults from being sexually active. While about half of adults in their 60s are having sex regularly, only about one in five continues after they reach age 80 (DeLamater & Koepsel, 2015). Cardiovascular disease, impaired mobility, depression, and diabetes can make intimate physical activity more difficult (Santos-Iglesias et al., 2016).

Adults often worry about their sexual functioning and lack of desire as they age (Lee et al., 2016; Srinivasan et al., 2019). There is an upside: Most sexually active older people tell researchers that the quality of their sexual activity is improving. Older people have more mastery over what they want and have a better understanding of their partners (Forbes et al., 2017; Syme et al., 2017).

Older people in long-term care facilities, like nursing homes, may face social limitations on sexual activity (Abellard et al., 2017; Srinivasan et al., 2019). About half of all care facilities expect families to give consent for their family member's sexual activity, even if the person has no cognitive impairment (Srinivasan et al., 2019). Model programs help ensure that adults can continue to be sexually active if that is what they wish: About half of all adults in nursing homes engage in some kind of romantic activity (Srinivasan et al., 2019).

Body Image

Some of the challenges adults report having with their sexuality relate to body image and the superficial changes of aging. Women, in particular, report insecurity about looking "old" (DeLameter et al., 2019). As one woman in her 70s explained to an interviewer, "We don't want to be checked off because of a few wrinkles or white hair. . . . when your hair turns white you become invisible" (Hofmeier et al., 2017). Throughout the lifespan, adults tend to have negative feelings about their *body image* (Sabik, 2017).

Age tends to show in our faces and skin as we reach 60. Bone and muscle wear away in the face as they do in the rest of the body, resulting in longer noses and less definition around the eyes and in the cheekbones (Cotofana et al., 2016; Mendelson & Wong, 2012). This process is accelerated in people who go through menopause (Tobin, 2017). By late adulthood, about half of all adults have some hair loss, and most have lost their hair color (Tobin, 2017). Much of skin aging results from sun damage and pollution, which helps accelerate wrinkles and skin discoloration (Wang & Dreesen, 2018).

Body dissatisfaction remains a constant for many across the lifespan (Hofmeier et al., 2017; Kilpela et al., 2015). People who identify as men are more likely to maintain a positive body image into late adulthood: Unlike people who identify as women, they tend to worry about how their bodies function rather than how they look (Hofmeier et al., 2017). Adults with a poor body image are more likely to put off physical activity such as exercise and sex (Kilpela et al., 2015). They are also more likely to be socially isolated (Sabik, 2017). Isolation and lack of physical activity are not just bad for your body image: They can also make you sick.

APPLY IT! **16.5** Aging is often accompanied by limitations that reduce the body's strength and resilience. As a result, adults need more support and benefit from new habits to help them bounce back. How can body image help change how adults' approach their changing bodies?

16.6 Myths about "typical aging" abound. We know that aging bodies are not the same as younger ones. How would you explain aging senses, muscles, bones, and sexual systems to someone who wants to know what to expect?

Health in Late Adulthood

Few adults reach late adulthood without some challenge to their mobility or an annoying ache or pain (WHO, 2015). Bart not only has Alzheimer disease; he has also recovered from cancer and a stroke. Like Bart, more than 8 in 10 adults over age 65 in most communities have more than one chronic condition, such as heart disease, diabetes, or depression (CDC, 2020; Perez, 2020; Vetrano et al., 2016). Aging bodies and chronic health conditions also make older adults more physically vulnerable, whether it is to infections like COVID-19 or to the effects of heat or natural disaster (WHO, 2015).

With age, chronic diseases, rather than violence or accidents, become the leading causes of death (Heron, 2019; WHO, 2015). Heart disease, stroke, COVID-19, cancer, and neurocognitive disorders like Alzheimer disease are linked to the highest mortality (Heron, 2019). Researchers believe that many of these deaths could be delayed if adults were able to be healthier earlier in life and able to avoid environmental challenges like chronic trauma, isolation, and pollution (Chang et al., 2019; James et al., 2018; Livingston et al., 2020; Nyberg et al., 2020).

Learning Objective

16.4 What are the common health conditions of later life?

Inequities in Health

The lasting effects of chronic stress from poverty, trauma, and discrimination continue to play a role in health during late adulthood (Brown et al., 2012, 2016). *Intersectionality* is an important contributor to health inequities in later years: Older adults face an overlapping set of vulnerabilities depending on their gender, ethnicity, race, income level, geographic location, and sexual orientation (see **Figure 16.6**) (Brown et al., 2016; Harris et al., 2020; Kim et al., 2017).

For affluent adults, 70 is the new 40. White men with a college degree report the same health at 70 as do 40-year-olds who only have a high school diploma (Zajacova et al., 2014). Around the world, low-income adults are much more likely to need help when they are older than are those with higher income (Freedman & Spillman, 2014; Stefler et al., 2021; Zaninotto et al., 2020). The health of Black men and women tends to decline more dramatically with age than those of their White male peers, perhaps because of the legacy of discrimination and social stress (Brown et al., 2016). Other groups, like lesbian and gay older adults, also tend to have higher rates of chronic illnesses than other adults: The more discrimination adults report experiencing throughout their lives, the more likely they are to have mental and physical health challenges as older adults (Fredriksen-Goldsen et al., 2017).

Around the world, women live longer than men but spend more of their lives coping with a chronic illness (Carmel, 2019; Rochelle et al., 2015). In the United States, for instance, two in three adults with a neurocognitive disorder are women (Nebel et al., 2018). Women are also nearly twice as likely to be frail (Clegg et al., 2013; Corbi et al., 2019). Some of their health risks and advantages may have a biological origin. Women have more active immune systems and are also protected by estrogen before menopause (Gubbels Bupp et al., 2018; Lejri et al., 2018; Zarate et al., 2017). Due to historical inequalities, older women today are much less likely to have gone to college or to have experienced intellectually challenging work, which could have helped them build resilience to neurocognitive disease (Carmel, 2019; Nebel et al., 2018).

Researchers suspect that sexism affects how older women are treated by health care providers: Women are often perceived as being less hardy than men and are less likely to receive invasive treatments than men (Chrisler, 2019). But culture also benefits women: They are less likely than men to die because of violence or suicide, particularly in late adulthood (CDC, 2020).

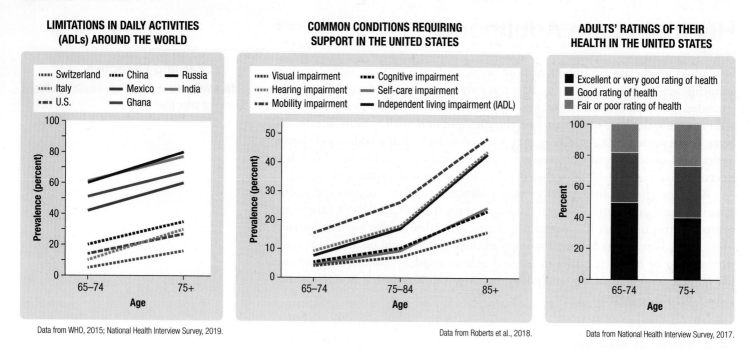

LIMITATIONS IN DAILY ACTIVITIES (ADLs) AROUND THE WORLD

Data from WHO, 2015; National Health Interview Survey, 2019.

COMMON CONDITIONS REQUIRING SUPPORT IN THE UNITED STATES

Data from Roberts et al., 2018.

ADULTS' RATINGS OF THEIR HEALTH IN THE UNITED STATES

Data from National Health Interview Survey, 2017.

FIGURE 16.6 Health in Late Adulthood Disparities in health abound around the world in late adulthood. In the United States, more adults need support as they get older, but many still have an optimistic view of their health.

Chronic Conditions

Some of the physical aspects of getting older are not deadly but may reduce life satisfaction and increase adults' likelihood of depression and cognitive decline (Senn & Monod, 2015; Vetrano et al., 2016). These conditions often compromise adults' ability to live independently, one of the biggest fears adults have about getting older (NORC, 2017). There is a long list of chronic conditions that are more common in late adulthood, including frailty, chronic pain, incontinence, and difficulty sleeping (Miner & Kryger, 2017; Senn & Monod, 2015). These are sometimes referred to as *geriatric syndromes* and are common worldwide (Liang et al., 2018; Liberman et al., 2018; Meyer et al., 2020).

Many adults, as well as their care providers, believe that chronic conditions are an inevitable part of the aging process, but they do not have to be silently endured (Makris et al., 2015; Veal et al., 2018). Interventions can address chronic conditions and support older adults who have them. While these programs may not be a cure, they can help adults adapt. For instance, pain management programs can help adults regain mobility and independence (Thielke et al., 2012). Addressing depression and isolation can boost resilience and the ability to cope (Livingston et al., 2020). However, as you will learn, experts suggest pressure to age "successfully" can make it harder for adults to manage in cultures that are disdainful of weakness.

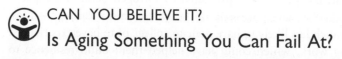

CAN YOU BELIEVE IT?

Is Aging Something You Can Fail At?

Who is to blame when people have health difficulties as they age? Some blame older adults, pointing out that healthy behaviors, like eating healthy food and staying active, are linked to longer lives and lower rates of chronic illness (Lourida et al., 2019; Nyberg et al., 2020). Even health care workers are prone to the assumption that poor health in older adults is a sign of personal failure (Wyman et al., 2018). Some scientists have suggested that to be a "successful" older person, you need to be healthy, independent, and intellectually engaged.

Older people themselves often hold these stereotypes and worry that by getting sick, they will no longer be treated as adults, or even as people (Buch, 2018). As one 88-year-old Latina woman explained: "What success is there when you are old? You are old. You continue to be old" (qtd. in Romo et al., 2013, p. 946). Expecting to age without any negative effects is an impossible standard for most, since only about 10 percent of adults make it to 70 without any health conditions (Havighurst, 1961; Martinson & Berridge, 2015; Rowe & Kahn, 1987, 2015; Rubinstein & de Medeiros, 2015).

So, are older adults failing if they have some health problems? No. Researchers have two major insights that counter this idea. First, the idea that sickness means failure places more value on the lives of healthy people than on others: It is both age-ist and ableist (Martinson & Berridge, 2015). There is more to being a human being than health. Adults who are not healthy still have value and can find satisfaction in their lives: They may still be able to give a hug, enjoy a coffee in the morning, or offer wisdom. Scientists and advocates point out that there should be no shame in needing help (Martinson & Berridge, 2015). Building empathy for aging, rather than contempt, is a goal for many scholars.

Second, the idea that everyone can control how they age is, at best, unrealistic. Some declines are inevitable (Lamb, 2017, 2019). Others are beyond individual control. For instance, being exposed to pollution and adversity before you are born is linked to accelerated aging in later life (Franke et al., 2017; Martens et al., 2017). Many of the core behaviors linked to healthy aging, including healthy eating, adequate physical activity, and social and intellectual engagement, are not equitably available (McLaughlin et al., 2012). Poverty, gender differences, discrimination, and geography change your health risks (Baum et al., 2020; Calasanti & King, 2020).

Some scholars suggest that older adults with disabilities should still feel successful. They point out that what disables people, at any age, is not their difficulties, but a mismatch between what they can do and what circumstances afford (Achenbaum, 2018). 🧠

Staying Healthy in Late Adulthood

Susie Paige is a Sunday school teacher in North Philadelphia, and, for the past three years, she has been a walking activist. She describes her commitment to daily walks as a rebellion (Cecil, 2018). Like Susie, many older Americans reached late adulthood with health concerns correlated with increased risk: extra weight, too much time sitting down, and some chronic conditions (Clare et al., 2017). Susie started walking 30 minutes every day, five days a week, with her neighbors. Her goals: to make new friends, to build community, and to make sure she would be there for her 93-year-old mother and her family for the long haul.

Susie's commitment to staying active is backed by research. Positive health practices, like exercise, healthy food, and restorative sleep, can delay disability and can improve cognitive functioning in later life (Chang et al., 2010; Jacob et al., 2016; Ngandu et al., 2015; Young & Williams, 2015).

Keeping Active Like Susie, many adults walk to stay healthy (WHO, 2015). Experts recommend at least 150 minutes a week of moderate activity, like walking, or 75 minutes a week of more vigorous activity, like jogging or salsa dancing. More is even better: 300 minutes of activity combined with three days of balance training and two days of muscle strengthening is ideal (Arem et al., 2015). Staying active means anything that keeps your body in motion and off the couch. Getting in about 2,000 steps (less than a mile) puttering around your house can help (Jacob et al., 2016).

Exercise is linked to many benefits in late adulthood, as it is across the lifespan. Older people who are active tend to be sturdier and healthier than their peers: Their risk of falling is lower, and they live as many as six years longer (Bauman et al., 2016; Marck et al., 2017).

Courtesy of Susie M. Paige

Racing with Family Susie Paige (*center*) shares the joy of staying active. She is shown here with her niece and sisters participating in a Thanksgiving day 5K race.

People who are physically active in late adulthood tend to have stronger ties to their community and report feeling less depressed and isolated (Arem et al., 2015).

Many older adults meet the minimum standards for physical exercise: Like Susie Paige, they are out walking, chasing after grandchildren, or working in physically demanding jobs. With age, however, adults have more difficulty getting enough exercise (Bauman et al., 2016; Watson et al., 2016). Most older adults spend more than two-thirds of their time sitting, much of that tied to screens (Harvey et al., 2015).

Adults are particularly likely to avoid activity when they are sick and in pain: The more chronic conditions you have, from arthritis to cognitive difficulties to poor vision, the more likely you are to stay still (Loprinzi, 2015; Vancampfort et al., 2017; Varma & Watts, 2017; Watson et al., 2016). Adults who do manage to remain active are usually lucky enough to be financially well off and in better health (Watson et al., 2016).

Interventions, whether they are medication prescribed by a doctor, or exercise, or nudges on a mobile device, are particularly effective in older adults, even those who already have complications with mobility (Pahor et al., 2014; Vancampfort et al., 2017).

Healthy Eating Getting older changes adults' nutritional needs, but about 6 in 10 adults are not eating well (Batsis & Zagaria, 2018; Baugreet et al., 2017). Older adults need more calcium, protein, and vitamin D to combat muscle and bone loss than they did when they were younger (Baugreet et al., 2017).

Nutrient deficiency often occurs because older adults just are not eating enough. A smaller appetite and diminished smell and taste make food less appetizing (Boesveldt et al., 2018). In addition, about 3 in 10 adults in affluent countries have dental problems, which can make eating difficult (WHO, 2015). Adults with neurocognitive disorders begin to have trouble swallowing and chewing: Many lose weight as they become sicker (Albanese et al., 2017; Batsis & Zagaria, 2018).

Some older adults may choose to lose weight in later life, which may make it easier to stay mobile. For older adults who worry that their size increases their risk for arthritis or other health concerns, researchers have found that losing 10 percent of their body weight can be enough to improve health (Jackson et al., 2019). Whatever their goal, older adults should stay active and get enough protein to meet their nutritional needs (Batsis & Zagaria, 2018).

Sleep for Resilience Aging puts new demands on the body: Sleep is one way that older people can recover. In late adulthood, as in earlier stages of the lifespan, the goal is to get about 7 to 8 hours of sleep a night (Hirshkowitz et al., 2015; Lo et al., 2016; Miner & Kryger, 2017).

Missing out on this rest hurts the brain. Remember from Chapter 4 that the brain does cellular maintenance during sleep: cleaning out malformed proteins and supporting the creation of new synapses (Fjell et al., 2020; Lo et al., 2016; Noble & Spires-Jones, 2019). Without enough sleep, the body is more likely to develop inflammation, making recovery from illnesses more difficult and increasing the likelihood of depression (Lo et al., 2016). Lack of sleep, because of chronic insomnia, shift work, or sleep apnea, is one of the most potent risk factors for developing a neurocognitive disorder and having trouble with executive function, memory, and processing speed (Lo et al., 2016; Noble & Spires-Jones, 2019).

Aging changes the brain, the light receptors in the eyes, and the amount of sleep-related hormones in the body, which explains the increasing number of older adults who do not get enough rest (Zhong et al., 2019). Circadian rhythms change: Adults tend to get sleepier earlier in the evening and to wake up earlier in the morning (Fischer et al., 2017; Tonetti et al., 2008). Adults do not get as tired at night as they used to, and they have difficulty staying asleep all night (Fjell et al., 2020; Li et al., 2018; Yiallouris et al., 2019).

Chronic pain, side effects from medication, and the stresses of taking care of others and of managing the grief of frequent losses often disrupt sleep (Miner & Kryger, 2017).

If older adults have stopped working or have become less mobile, they may overlook the triggers for healthy sleep habits, like exercise and bright light (Miner & Kryger, 2017).

Adults have more sleep difficulties in later life than at any other time during the lifespan: More than half experience insomnia, wake frequently at night, or wake up too early in the morning (Lo et al., 2016; Ohayon, 2002). Most adults do not recognize that they have a problem: As with so many aspects of aging, many think it is inevitable (Fjell et al., 2020; Miner & Kryger, 2017).

Sleep *can* be improved, benefiting mood, energy level, and even inflammation (Black et al., 2015; Rash et al., 2019). Healthy sleep routines, such as keeping a regular sleep schedule, avoiding naps, getting in the sunlight during the day, and minimizing stimulation before bed, help older adults get rest (Morin et al., 1994; Suzuki et al., 2017). Sleep medications are typically not recommended for older people. However, interventions such as cognitive-behavioral therapy, programs designed to improve work–life balance, and mindfulness-based practices have been shown to improve sleep (Black et al., 2015; Okajima et al., 2011; Robbins et al., 2019; Rusch et al., 2019; van Straten et al., 2018).

APPLY IT! **16.7** Bart says his doctor "yells at him" to stay healthy, reminding him to stay active and not drink too much. When he looks back at his life, he wishes that he had eaten less fast food when he was on the road and kept his gym membership. What health behaviors do you think you will want to stick with as you get older? **16.8** Building resilience can come from sleep, healthy nutrition, activity, and (as you will learn) social support and a feeling that you matter. What activities do you think help Bart maintain his equanimity as he ages?

A Little Samba in São Paulo This couple in Brazil is staying active through dance, but any kind of physical activity can be helpful for improving sleep and health during later life.

The Changing Brain in Late Adulthood

During late adulthood, the brain is more prone to instability and change than at any time since puberty. The brain gets smaller, connectivity slows, and injuries add up (Vinke et al., 2018). For some, like Bart, these injuries may lead to noticeable changes in thinking or behavior, but most adults compensate: learning, adjusting, and making up for what they are losing. They are able, as Bart is, to continue to work and thrive (Baltes & Baltes, 1990; Tucker-Drob, 2019). Age-related changes that may be seen on an MRI or laboratory test do not always indicate how an adult will be able to function or compensate: A lifetime of wisdom and experience can help adults as they manage their changing biology.

Learning Objective

16.5 How does the brain change in late adulthood?

A Smaller, Less Connected Brain

What happens to the brain during late adulthood is not always reassuring: Everyone's brain begins to shrink (Franke et al., 2017). Atrophy happens in *gray matter*, or the cell bodies of neurons, as well as in *white matter*, or the myelinated connections between neurons (Bennett & Madden, 2014; Grady, 2012; Hedden & Gabrieli, 2004; Storsve et al., 2014). As a result, the brains of people who are in their 90s usually weigh about 10 percent less than they did in midlife (Wyss-Coray, 2016).

Connectivity within the brain also changes: Less gray matter means that long-range connections within the brain are less efficient and slower (Wang et al., 2019). Aging is often associated with declines in the speed of neural networks linked to memory, executive function, and sensory systems (Sun et al., 2016). Levels of many neurotransmitters and hormones also decrease (Juarez et al., 2019; Karrer et al., 2019; Rieckmann et al., 2018).

Not all regions of the brain change at the same rate. Shrinking happens in the prefrontal cortex, which may impair planning ability (Fan et al., 2017; Pudas et al., 2018). The decreasing size of the *hippocampus* is closely linked to declines in memory functioning and in learning (Fan et al., 2017; Nyberg & Pudas, 2019). Deterioration in the *thalamus*, a small structure in the midbrain, is also connected to memory difficulties (Aggleton et al., 2016). In contrast, some regions of the brain, like the *subcortical structures* and the *amygdala*, seem to be relatively protected, which may be related to the strong emotional functioning in many older adults (Vinke et al., 2018).

Scientists are particularly interested in a tiny region in the brain stem known as the **locus coeruleus**. This structure is responsible for providing the neurotransmitter *norepinephrine* to neurons across the brain and, as a result, is a major hub of brain networks (Bari et al., 2020). Disruptions in the connections between the locus coeruleus and other regions of the brain are linked to impaired attention, executive function, and memory in older adults (Dahl et al., 2019, 2020). The locus coeruleus is one of the earliest areas of the brain to begin to degrade: Damaging proteins begin to build up in this region early in adulthood (Dahl et al., 2019). The locus coeruleus is linked to many neurocognitive disorders of late adulthood, including Alzheimer disease (Betts et al., 2019).

Aging Neurons and Accumulating Proteins

The shrinking and deterioration of the brain are caused by microscopic changes in your neurons and other brain cells. Remember that we are born with most of our neurons. With age, neurons lose some of their complexity. They begin to use energy less efficiently and dendrites and synapses are pruned (Camandola & Mattson, 2016; Dickstein et al., 2013; Zarate et al., 2017). The *myelin sheath* that helps to speed neural communication begins to degrade, slowing neural communication and leaving cluttered debris in its wake (Hill et al., 2018; Safaiyan et al., 2016).

One specific type of brain cell, called *glia*, is particularly linked to aging. **Glia** are the support cells of the brain, helping to clean out waste, regulate energy, build immunity, construct synapses and myelinated connections, and heal injured neurons (Vainchtein & Molofsky, 2020). Deteriorating glia are among the first signs of aging in the brain: Glia become more susceptible to inflammation and, as a result, less effective at building synapses and myelinated connections (Salas et al., 2020).

One result of aging glia is a buildup of destructive proteins. **Tau protein**, an essential building block of your neurons, helps move nutrients and energy from one part of the neuron to another. With age, more mistakes are made in the creation of tau proteins, and these faulty proteins accumulate (Katsumoto et al., 2019). Instead of seamlessly transporting energy from one part of your neurons to another, misshapen tau proteins bunch together like dust bunnies, creating **neurofibrillary tangles**. In typical aging, these tangles appear first in the brain stem and in the subcortical structures and finally move into the cortex. In neurocognitive diseases, tangles are more widespread and damage structures and connectivity throughout the brain (Sengoku, 2020).

Amyloid beta is another protein by-product implicated in brain aging. As you age, amyloid beta builds up as a result of inflammation and glial dysfunction, and it collects together into bundles known as *oligomers*, which begin to damage the body (Cline et al., 2018; Ries & Sastre, 2016). Too much amyloid beta can kill neurons, but more commonly it slows brain function by impeding the creation of new synapses, damaging glial cells, and disrupting metabolism (Cline et al., 2018).

Diversity in the Aging Brain

Researchers suspect that there may be more diversity in brain development during late adulthood than at any other point in the lifespan (Wyss-Coray, 2016). No one reaches their 70s without injury to their brain, but how much damage the brain experiences

locus coeruleus A region in the brainstem that is a hub of brain networks and provides some neurotransmitters to the brain.

glia Support cells located in the brain and nervous system.

tau protein An essential building block of neurons that helps move nutrients and energy from one part of the neuron to another. Misshapen tau protein can contribute to cognitive decline.

neurofibrillary tangles Misshapen tau proteins that bunch together, and can damage the brain and contribute to neurocognitive disorders.

amyloid beta A protein by-product implicated in brain aging that builds up as a result of inflammation and glial dysfunction.

OVERALL CHANGES IN THE BRAIN

The brain gradually shrinks with age, particularly the cortex. Both gray matter and white matter (myelinated connections) decline. Connectivity changes and becomes less efficient. Neurotransmitters and hormones in the brain also decrease. These changes are linked to declines in processing speed, skills, and memory.

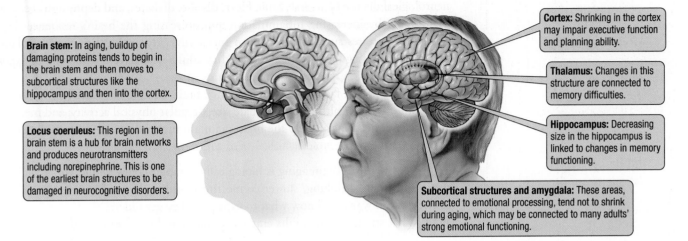

Brain stem: In aging, buildup of damaging proteins tends to begin in the brain stem and then moves to subcortical structures like the hippocampus and then into the cortex.

Locus coeruleus: This region in the brain stem is a hub for brain networks and produces neurotransmitters including norepinephrine. This is one of the earliest brain structures to be damaged in neurocognitive disorders.

Cortex: Shrinking in the cortex may impair executive function and planning ability.

Thalamus: Changes in this structure are connected to memory difficulties.

Hippocampus: Decreasing size in the hippocampus is linked to changes in memory functioning.

Subcortical structures and amygdala: These areas, connected to emotional processing, tend not to shrink during aging, which may be connected to many adults' strong emotional functioning.

MICROSCOPIC CHANGES IN THE BRAIN

Damage to neurons and glia and problems with protein creation in late life mean that destructive proteins tend to build up in the brain. Damaged glia are not as efficient at cleaning up these damaged proteins, which often build up into *neurofibrillary tangles*, *oligomers*, and *plaque*.

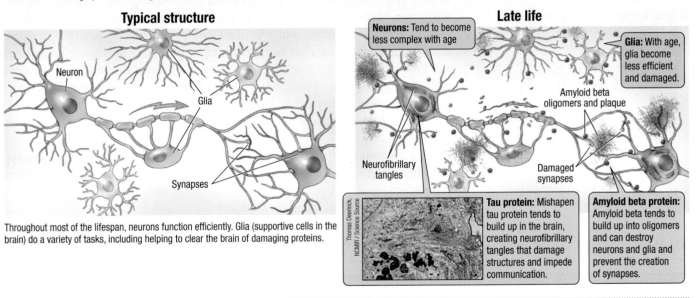

Typical structure

Neuron

Glia

Synapses

Throughout most of the lifespan, neurons function efficiently. Glia (supportive cells in the brain) do a variety of tasks, including helping to clear the brain of damaging proteins.

Late life

Neurons: Tend to become less complex with age

Glia: With age, glia become less efficient and damaged.

Amyloid beta oligomers and plaque

Neurofibrillary tangles

Damaged synapses

Thomas Deerinck, NCMIR / Science Source

Tau protein: Mishapen tau protein tends to build up in the brain, creating neurofibrillary tangles that damage structures and impede communication.

Amyloid beta protein: Amyloid beta tends to build up into oligomers and can destroy neurons and glia and prevent the creation of synapses.

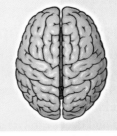

Risks to Brain Health

Health conditions including heart disease, diabetes, malnutrition, and depression ✗

Environmental stresses, including pollution ✗

Social stresses, including isolation, discrimination, or exclusion ✗

Resilience Factors for Brain Health

✓ Healthy nutrition

✓ Sleep

✓ Physical activity

✓ Social connections

and how well adults can compensate are highly variable. Bart, for instance, had a stroke that injured his brain, increasing his risk for a neurocognitive disorder.

Risk factors for brain dysfunction abound (Franke et al., 2017). Injuries from strokes, infections, or traumatic accidents become more common and increase the risk for neurological disease (Vinke et al., 2018). Heart disease, diabetes, and depression accelerate brain aging by increasing inflammation and decreasing the brain's resilience (Franke et al., 2017). Stresses such as exposure to social adversity, malnutrition, and isolation mean that brain aging is often accelerated in adults who have low income or experience discrimination or exclusion (Zahodne et al., 2022).

Environmental factors can also enhance brain health. For instance, researchers have found that a healthy diet, adequate sleep, regular physical activity, and meaningful social connections all help the brain maintain function (Anatürk et al., 2018; Ballesteros et al., 2015; Jackson et al., 2016; Liu-Ambrose et al., 2019; Sexton et al., 2016).

APPLY IT! **16.9** Brain aging is biologically complex. How would you explain the process of brain shrinking, slower connections, and buildup of harmful proteins to someone who wants to know what to expect as they get older?

16.10 What strengths can adults employ to maintain brain health as they get older?

Cognition in Late Adulthood

Learning Objective

16.6 What are the typical cognitive changes in healthy aging?

In later life, changes in the brain lead to inevitable changes in thinking. For many, this is one of the most feared parts of getting older (AARP, 2021). In late adulthood, older adults, their families, and even their care providers have powerful stereotypes about cognitive decline: They worry that they will become incompetent, ineffective, and unproductive (Barber, 2017; Levy & Banaji, 2002). Older adults tend to be even more worried about cognitive losses than younger people are. When a 20-year-old forgets where they put their keys, they assume it is because they were distracted. But when a 70-year-old does the same thing, they assume they are losing their memory (Laditka et al., 2011).

Understanding typical cognitive changes is a step toward breaking stereotypes and identifying real cognitive disorders when they do occur. Older adults typically experience cognitive losses, but that does not mean they have become incompetent. They often know more, based on a lifetime of experience, than younger adults (Shafto et al., 2019). Older adults also gain new cognitive skills (Jeste et al., 2019; Romer et al., 2017).

Most older adults compensate and adjust: At work, experts have found that their productivity does not decline (Börsch-Supan & Weiss, 2016). Older adults have even bested younger ones in competitive and fast-paced e-sports championships (Tuting, 2020). As Bart demonstrates, adults with neurocognitive disorders can nevertheless contribute, whether through work and volunteering, or through caregiving and relationships.

Changes in Thinking

Remember from Chapter 14 that researchers often divide thinking skills into what you know, or your *crystallized reasoning*, and how you think, or your *fluid reasoning* (Cattell, 1971; Wechsler, 1958). The core elements of fluid reasoning include processing speed, working memory, and the ability to multitask. These skills all peak in early adulthood and decline in late adulthood (Hartshorne & Germine, 2015; Salthouse, 2019). The pace of losses accelerates with time (Gerstorf et al., 2011; Salthouse, 2019; Singh-Manoux et al., 2012). Changes in fluid skills, like memory, attention, and processing speed, are closely tied to deterioration in higher-level abilities. For instance, executive function diminishes as you get older due to declines in fluid skills (DeLuca & Leventer, 2008).

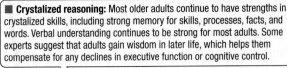

■ **Crystalized reasoning:** Most older adults continue to have strengths in crystalized skills, including strong memory for skills, processes, facts, and words. Verbal understanding continues to be strong for most adults. Some experts suggest that adults gain wisdom in later life, which helps them compensate for any declines in executive function or cognitive control.

How long can you remember 10 words?
Researchers asked adults from more than 36 low-, middle-, and high-income countries to remember 10 words. They found that older adults tended to recall fewer than younger adults.

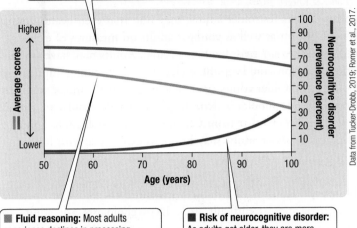

Data from Tucker-Drobb, 2019; Romer et al., 2017.

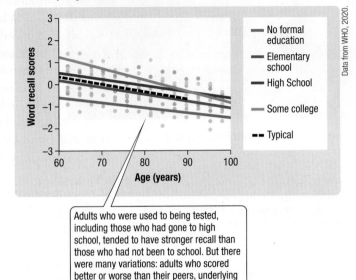

Data from WHO, 2020.

■ **Fluid reasoning:** Most adults experience declines in processing speed, working memory, and attention during late adulthood that are connected to changes in brain function. These are linked to declines in executive function and the ability to multitask.

■ **Risk of neurocognitive disorder:** As adults get older, they are more likely to develop a neurocognitive disorder. Signs that distinguish a neurocognitive disorder from typical aging include difficulty with executive function and planning for the future.

Adults who were used to being tested, including those who had gone to high school, tended to have stronger recall than those who had not been to school. But there were many variations: adults who scored better or worse than their peers, underlying the great diversity in cognitive aging.

Declines in Fluid Reasoning One of the most dramatic declines in cognitive skills is in processing speed, particularly after about age 70 (Habekost et al., 2013; Salthouse, 1996, 2019). Remember that processing speed is measured by how quickly you are able to register new information. It is fastest in early adulthood, when young people excel at video games or anything else requiring lightning-quick reaction times. But as you move from 70 to 85, your ability to quickly respond to new visual information declines by half (Habekost et al., 2013). This is thought to be caused by decreasing ability to pay attention to new visual information (Monge & Madden, 2016; Owsley, 2016; Whitson et al., 2018). Researchers believe slowing processing speed to be a contributor to some adults' difficulties with safe driving: Avoiding an accident requires a quick response (Owsley, 2016; Owsley et al., 2013).

Similarly, *working memory* also declines rapidly in later life (Brockmole & Logie, 2013; Hartshorne & Germine, 2015; Nissim et al., 2017). Remember that working memory is the temporary bank of information you are able to hold in short-term storage, like an e-mail address you remember just long enough to type it into your phone. By the time a typical adult is in their 70s, the number of items they can remember in working memory, such as a seven-digit phone number, has declined from its peak by more than two-thirds (Brockmole & Logie, 2013). Attention and planning ability are closely linked to your working memory: Losses in working memory make it difficult to multitask, to hold two things in mind at the same time, and to make quick decisions (Wasylyshyn et al., 2011).

Changes in Executive Function Remember, executive function involves your ability to plan, manage your behavior, and follow directions. It is also linked to *prospective memory*, or your ability to remember what you need to do in the future (Haines et al., 2019). Both prospective memory and executive function are involved in the tasks of everyday life. They help you keep track of a doctor's appointment or remember to pick up a gallon of milk. Adults who have difficulties with executive function may

Westend61/Getty Images

Declines in Processing Speed Don't Mean Everything. While many older adults experience a decline in processing speed, that does not prevent all older adults from being professional gamers and even winners in e-sports championships.

AP Photo/Firdia Lisnawati

Competing in the "Athletics of the Mind" The card game bridge was an official event in the Asian Games. This game tends to be dominated by older adults. Tetsuya Ueda of Japan, shown here, ultimately lost to a team from India with an average age of 58.

feel less competent and in control (Toh et al., 2020). As with executive function, losses in prospective memory make it difficult to live independently. However, many adults are able to compensate by making tasks detailed and specific, setting alarms and reminders, and making sure to keep to routines (Zuber & Kliegel, 2020).

When researchers test older adults, they find that even healthy older adults do not perform as well as younger adults on measures of executive function (DeLuca & Leventer, 2008; Janssen et al., 2014). Adults may have trouble remembering directions and keep themselves from responding impulsively (Maldonado et al., 2020). Older adults even take longer than younger adults to respond to the Head, Shoulders, Knees, and Toes task, similar to Simon Says, that you may remember from Chapter 6 (Cerino et al., 2019). Some of this may be a lack of practice: Older adults may have less experience with following directions and performing party games.

Challenges with Memory Adults have trouble with more than just prospective memory: Making new memories is difficult, too. If psychologists ask adults to remember a group of words and then quiz them to see how many they have remembered after a delay, older adults remember just 9 words, compared to a younger person who remembers 14 (Sun et al., 2016). The accuracy of *episodic memory* also gets weaker over time (Nyberg & Pudas, 2019). Episodic memory is your recollection of a specific event you have experienced, like your first date, your last birthday, or what you did last Friday. Older adults have difficulty piecing together what happened when and are more likely to confuse a birthday with the one that occurred the year before. While the ability to remember the basic gist of events remains intact, specific details may get muddled (Brainerd & Reyna, 2015).

Despite these challenges, older adults excel at some types of memory. They tend to be good at *semantic memory*, or remembering facts, language, and how to do things (Ward & Shanks, 2018). While these systems may not quite be at their peak in one's 70s and 80s, most researchers agree that they do not decline at the rate of other skills (Juhasz et al., 2019). Adults' *procedural memory*, or the memory for skills like riding a bicycle or changing a tire, continues to be strong.

In later life, as in other times across the lifespan, adults can continue to learn (Juhasz et al., 2019). For instance, your vocabulary continues to grow as you age, although you may have a hard time coming up with the right word from time to time (Hartshorne & Germine, 2015). Scientists believe that this bank of knowledge can help adults compensate for cognitive slowing and contributes to the development of *wisdom* (Goldberg, 2006).

Formal strategies also help adults learn to compensate for the fuzziness in their memory and difficulty with planning (Baltes & Baltes, 1990). Making lists, setting alarms, and using a GPS can all help adults stay independent (Farias et al., 2018; Weakley et al., 2019). While these strategies will not repair underlying cognitive impairment, they enable adults to maintain their everyday activities (Lindenberger & Mayr, 2014). Bart relies on his paper planner, the GPS in his truck, and a sticky note on his coffee pot to keep him on track every day.

The Advent of Wisdom Some of the traditional roles that older adults take on, such as community leader or insightful grandparent, utilize a new cognitive strength: **wisdom**. Wisdom is the ability to creatively reason about complex situations on the basis of deep insights about people (Reyna et al., 2011; Romer et al., 2017). It builds on older adults' emotion regulation and people skills (Oxman, 2018). If researchers ask adults to suggest solutions to complex interpersonal problems, older adults tend to reason more creatively and more insightfully than younger ones (Grossmann et al., 2012). Older people

wisdom The ability to reason creatively based on deep insights about people.

often explain that the core of wisdom comes from understanding your own limitations (Grossmann, 2017; Grossmann & Kross, 2014). As a hospice patient explained: "There is no way to know it all, that's the whole problem. . . . That's wisdom itself, realizing that you don't know anything" (qtd. in Montross-Thomas et al., 2018, p. 4).

Cognitive Reserve All older adults have some evidence of brain shrinkage, buildups of misshapen proteins, and alterations in connectivity (Nyberg & Pudas, 2019; Tucker-Drob, 2019; Wyss-Coray, 2016). These changes affect thinking in diverse ways: Some adults maintain their cognitive powers long after their 90th birthdays (Franke et al., 2017). Scientists theorize that there are two reasons for exceptional cognitive longevity: (1) some adults have much slower biological aging than others, or (2) they have developed what scholars call *cognitive reserve*, which helps them be more resilient to the stresses of aging (Nyberg & Pudas, 2019).

Cognitive reserve is the ability to maintain your thinking abilities despite getting older (Chapko et al., 2018). Cognitive reserve does not prevent adults from experiencing cognitive decline, but it helps delay it (Lövdén et al., 2020). Scientists have many explanations for what may give us a robust cognitive reserve, including good physical health, supportive social relationships, intellectual stimulation, and even playing a musical instrument (Fratiglioni et al., 2020; Lindenberger, 2014; Romeiser et al., 2021). However, most agree that education often correlates with cognitive health (Clouston et al., 2021; Kujawski et al., 2018; Lövdén et al., 2020).

In large population studies, adults who stayed in school and were fortunate enough to attend college have been shown to continue to experience cognitive benefits in later life. Did going to school make them smarter? Researchers are not sure. People who completed more years of education are more likely to have many other privileges: less stress, higher income, less discrimination, better health, and more enriching activities throughout their adult lives (Clouston et al., 2019; Livingston et al., 2020; Lövdén et al., 2020). Remember that across the lifespan, correlation does not equal causation.

Neurocognitive Disorders

When Bart learned that he had a *neurocognitive disorder*, he was not alone. More than one million Americans receive a similar diagnosis every year (Alzheimer's Association, 2021). **Neurocognitive disorders (NCDs)** include a spectrum of difficulties with thinking and independent functioning, ranging from mild to severe (Vermunt et al., 2019).

About one in every eight adults over 65 has some evidence of cognitive impairment, and as we age, our risk of developing a more serious neurocognitive disorder rises dramatically (Petersen et al., 2018). Only 5 percent of adults under 75 have been diagnosed with an NCD, but the rates increase over the next decade. By the time they are 80, more than three in ten have a NCD (Alzheimer's Association, 2021). And by the time adults reach 100, if they are that fortunate, the rate of NCDs is even greater: Experts suspect that nearly half of centenarians have significant cognitive decline (Corrada et al., 2010; Qiu & Fratiglioni, 2018).

In many wealthy countries, the rate of major neurocognitive disorders like Alzheimer disease has been dropping as a result of improving health (Wolters et al., 2020). In the United States and in other countries, major NCDs do not afflict all groups equally: Low-income groups and those with poorer health tend to be more at risk (Babulal et al., 2019; Matthews et al., 2019; Taylor et al., 2017).

Neurocognitive disorders, like other complex conditions, are caused by the interaction between genes and life experience. As you have learned, one allele of the gene APOE increases the likelihood of severe cognitive decline and increases the risk of Alzheimer disease, but this gene is not solely responsible for NCDs (Lourida et al., 2019; Reas et al., 2019; Tucker-Drob, 2019). Genes do not work alone: The degenerative process needs to be triggered by environmental factors (Livingston et al., 2020; Sims et al., 2020).

Anna Watson/Alamy Stock Photo

Discovered at 97 Venezuelan-born, U.S.-based artist Lucia Luchita Hurtado painted all her life but did not have her big break until she was 97. Did her decades of focused work help her build cognitive reserve that enabled her to maintain her productivity? Hurtaldo kept working until she passed away at 99.

 Learn It Together

Cognitive Challenges in Later Adulthood

Plan Review the various cognitive challenges that many people face in later adulthood.

Engage Gather with two other classmates and discuss how you could change features of the homes of older adults who experience cognitive challenges to enable them to function more easily in their daily lives.

Reflect Think about how even mundane features of typical homes may themselves make it more difficult for later adults experiencing cognitive challenges to fully enjoy their daily lives.

cognitive reserve The ability to maintain your thinking abilities in late adulthood.

TABLE 16.1 Telling the Difference Between a Neurocognitive Disorder and Typical Aging

Forgetting that makes it difficult to function. It is typical to forget things from time to time (like trying to find the phone that you are holding in your hand, or the glasses on your head). For people with cognitive impairments, forgetting is more frequent. People tend to have most difficulty with information they have learned recently, rather than things that are in their long-term memory. They may begin to rely on loved ones and on electronic devices to help them get through the day.
Difficulty following directions. We often forget why we went into the other room, but people who are developing difficulties with cognition have difficulty following multi-part directions and may be easily frustrated trying to learn a new game, remembering how to use the remote control, or opening an app on their phone.
Difficulty with judgment. Poor decisions, like trusting someone who turns out to be a criminal, can happen to everyone. People at risk for cognitive impairment may have increased difficulties making sensible decisions.
Increased isolation. Being social is cognitive work. Everyone may sometimes feel a little introverted, but people at risk for cognitive impairment may begin avoiding contact with friends and family. Cognitive issues can often be confused with other common challenges including depression, anxiety, or substance use disorder.

In general, ill health early in life, and particularly in middle age, increases the risk for a neurocognitive disorder in later life (Chi et al., 2017; McNeil et al., 2018). In middle age, heart disease, lack of exercise, and unhealthy weight are all linked to higher rates of NCDs, as are brain injuries, smoking, excessive alcohol use, and psychological conditions like major depressive disorder and schizophrenia (Jiménez-Pavón et al., 2019; Livingston et al., 2020). In later life, being socially isolated, breathing in polluted air, and having untreated sensory loss all substantially increase the risk of developing an NCD (Livingston et al., 2020; Whitson et al., 2018; Zheng et al., 2017).

Mild Cognitive Impairment Some adults are diagnosed with **mild cognitive impairment (MCI)**, which means they have more cognitive challenges than would be expected for a person of their age, but are still able to function in everyday life (APA, 2022; Petersen, 2016; Petersen et al., 1997, 2018). Mild cognitive impairment may be a very early stage of a major NCD, like Alzheimer disease or vascular cognitive disorder, but not everyone who is diagnosed with MCI develops a more severe condition. (See **Table 16.1**.) Some people can even recover, particularly if their MCI was due to a medical problem or to depression (Petersen, 2016).

There is no cure for MCI, nor are there medications that are empirically proven to consistently lessen its effects (Knopman et al., 2021; Schulman et al., 2021). However, experts have found that exercise can help improve memory in adults with MCI and slow its progression (Nagamatsu et al., 2012; Song et al., 2018). Although many adults are self-conscious about talking about their cognitive concerns, early intervention may help them avoid a more serious disorder (Grill et al., 2017).

Alzheimer Disease Bart was diagnosed with Alzheimer disease in the office of a friendly nurse practitioner who took nearly an hour to explain his diagnosis. He was with his life partner, Darlene, but neither of them remember much of the specifics about what the practitioner told them. They were both devastated.

Alzheimer disease (AD) is a degenerative neurocognitive disorder that is linked to difficulties with thinking and functioning. It is caused by the buildup of faulty tau and amyloid proteins, which occurs in hyperdrive for those with AD (see **Figure 16.7**). Poisonous tau protein forms tangles, while sticky bunches of amyloid simultaneously prevent neural communication, eventually destroying neurons altogether (Knopman et al., 2018). The brain is gradually damaged, beginning in the brain stem and in structures like the hippocampus, and finally in the connective links between

---

neurocognitive disorders (NCDs) A spectrum of age-linked difficulties with thinking and independent functioning.

mild cognitive impairment (MCI) When an adult has more cognitive challenges than would be expected for a person of their age but is still able to function in their everyday life. (Also called *mild neurocognitive disorder*.)

Alzheimer disease (AD) A degenerative neurocognitive disorder caused by the buildup of tau and amyloid proteins that is linked to difficulties with thinking and the ability to function.

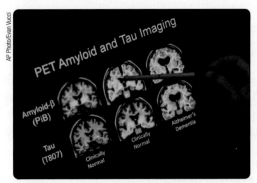
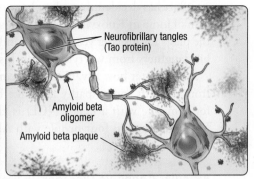
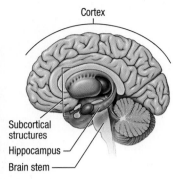

FIGURE 16.7 The Brain During Alzheimer Disease The brain injury caused by Alzheimer disease is often discovered on a PET scan (*left*). This condition is characterized by a buildup of faulty tau and amyloid proteins that form neurofobiliary tangles and plaques that hinder neural communication and destroy neurons. The damage caused by the disease typically begins in the brain stem, hippocampus, and other subcortical structures before moving toward the links between these regions and the cortex.

regions and the cortex, causing a breakdown in thinking and ultimately of functioning itself (Bejanin et al., 2017; Guzmán-Martinez et al., 2019).

Bart entered his health care provider's office with concerns and some misconceptions about AD. He had been having difficulties with executive function and memory. He was making more mistakes, particularly at work. He ended up at the wrong rental car counters and confused one hotel for another. One day, he arrived a day early for a corporate training. His providers arranged for him to have a PET scan, which measures the brain's metabolism.

Bart walked out of the PET scan looking like anyone else. As Bart explained to us, there were no outward signs that anything was wrong with him: No one "looks" like they have AD. But the PET scan revealed that some of his brain was no longer active, a sign of the damage inflicted by AD. Bart was devastated: He fell into a depression, aided by a spiral of fruitless internet searches for a cure. He had difficulty telling his three daughters and understanding how to plan for the future.

What Bart knew about AD was that it damages your memory and that it is fatal. But AD damages much more than the ability to remember. It often begins with memory lapses, feelings of disorientation, and difficulty making decisions, but as it progresses, it becomes more disruptive. People who are in advanced stages are often confused, may have delusions, and may become aggressive and fearful (McLachlan et al., 2018). Eventually, the shrunken brain makes it difficult to swallow, eat, and move. People with AD may die from pneumonia as a result of food or drink going into their lungs, malnutrition because they cannot swallow, or infections caused by their inability to move their own bodies (Faes et al., 2018).

Depending on how early the disorder is discovered, adults with AD typically live for three to six years after their initial diagnosis (Mayeda et al., 2017; Todd et al., 2013). Some medications are available that claim to boost neurotransmitters involved in brain communication and help prevent neurons from dying, but they are controversial and, at best, only modestly effective (Knopman et al., 2021; Schulman et al., 2021). Once someone has been diagnosed with AD, the focus turns to learning how to manage the symptoms and planning for the future.

Bart and Darlene adapted and adjusted to their lives. Whereas Bart used to plan for the next vacation, the next truck, or the next dog, he and Darlene are now working through his bucket list. His cognitive health is not improving: He has been known to put his medication in the refrigerator and recently fell apart because he could not find the off switch for a lamp he has owned for years. Other aspects of his memory are still intact: He jokes that he can tell you anything you need to know about rock bands from the 1970s. He uses a GPS in the car and a system of notes to get around, but he knows that one day he will need to give up his boat and the keys to his truck.

Scientific American Profile

Adjusting to Alzheimer Disease

Bart has decided that when he can no longer stay alone, he will move to the Veteran's Home in Knoxville, Tennessee, so Darlene can continue to work. He has made the plans for his later years himself and is glad he has been able to relieve Darlene and his daughters from worrying about his wishes and needs.

No matter how advanced their condition is, people with AD continue to benefit from warmth and empathy and, like Bart, can often continue to contribute. Caring for someone with a major NCD is challenging, although many families persevere: More than one in four people with AD are cared for at home until the end of their lives (Taylor et al., 2017).

Vascular Cognitive Disorder In nearly half of all cases of major neurocognitive disorders, adults have both AD and vascular cognitive disorder or another neurological condition (Bonnici-Mallia et al., 2018). **Vascular cognitive disorder** occurs when injuries to your cardiovascular system disrupt your brain and your cognitive functioning (see **Figure 16.8**). It is the second-most-common NCD of aging. In vascular cognitive disorder, the brain is crippled by the aftereffects of getting either too much or too little blood. In some cases, a stroke may flood the brain with too much blood, poisoning neurons in its wake, or it may block blood from getting to part of the brain, starving the brain of necessary nutrients (Kalaria, 2016).

It does not take a massive stroke to cause brain injury. Small, microscopic breaks in the tiniest blood vessels of the brain may also damage the brain, destroying neurons, removing myelin, and damaging the glia, the brain cells that are responsible for repair (Wolters & Ikram, 2019). Problems with blood flow in the brain may be so subtle that many adults may not even realize they have happened until long after neurons have been damaged and symptoms of cognitive decline appear. Damage to the tiny blood vessels of the brain is common in older adults, particularly those with heart disease, hypertension, diabetes, or depression (Diniz et al., 2013; ter Telgte et al., 2020). The severity of brain disease depends on where the brain injury occurs and how resilient older adults are: Good health, social contact, and education seem to make it more likely that adults can stave off the effects of cognitive impairment (ter Telgte et al., 2018).

Managing the Stigma As Bart reminds us, being diagnosed with a degenerative brain disorder is a terrible blow for adults and their families (Lee et al., 2013). As they progress, these conditions lead to dependence and disability that can end in years of struggle and death, prospects that adults and their families dread (Ashworth, 2020; Fletcher, 2021). It does not make things easier that many adults have faulty and stigmatizing ideas about neurocognitive disorders: They may blame themselves, consider NCDs a form of insanity, or believe they are an inevitable part of aging (Clare et al., 2021; Nguyen & Li, 2020). Like Bart, people who have been diagnosed often avoid telling their families, their friends, and even their health care providers (Werner & Heinik, 2008).

Many researchers and health care providers now use the term *neurocognitive disorder* to describe this group of conditions, because alternative terms like *dementia* are considered offensive and stigmatizing (Corner, 2017; Harris & Keady, 2008; Trachtenberg & Trojanowski, 2008). Experts note that families and older adults respond best when providers use specific terms and neutral language, like *neurocognitive disorder*, rather than vague euphemisms like *forgetfulness* or dated terminology like *senility* (O'Connor et al., 2018).

Adjusting to a diagnosis of a neurocognitive disorder is difficult, and there may be no graceful or positive way to manage the loss (Desai et al., 2016; Nowell et al., 2013). People with NCDs as well as their families benefit from early information, which helps them plan for managing their everyday needs and for their *end-of-life care* (Whitlatch & Orsulic-Jeras, 2018). Even while living with a debilitating disease, adults look to their relationships for strength and want to be useful and to be seen as individuals, rather than just as their diagnosis (Desai et al., 2016). In the early stages of their disease, some

Share It!

Do not ignore the five signs of a stroke: (1) sudden numbness; (2) difficulty with speech or confusion; (3) difficulty seeing; (4) sudden dizziness or difficulty walking; (5) sudden headache.

(Call 911 or go to the nearest emergency room)

Scientific American: Lifespan Development

Scientific American Profile

From Diagnosis to Advocacy

vascular cognitive disorder A disorder that occurs when injuries to the cardiovascular system disrupt the brain and cognitive functioning.

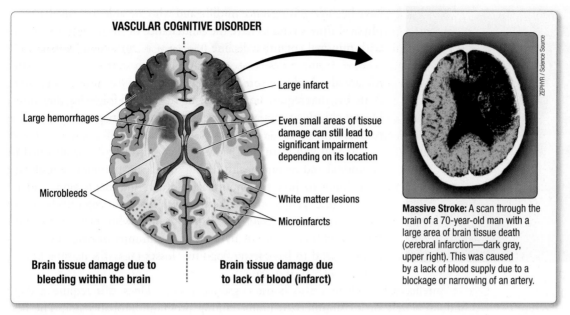

VASCULAR COGNITIVE DISORDER

Large hemorrhages

Large infarct

Even small areas of tissue damage can still lead to significant impairment depending on its location

Microbleeds

White matter lesions

Microinfarcts

Brain tissue damage due to bleeding within the brain

Brain tissue damage due to lack of blood (infarct)

Massive Stroke: A scan through the brain of a 70-year-old man with a large area of brain tissue death (cerebral infarction—dark gray, upper right). This was caused by a lack of blood supply due to a blockage or narrowing of an artery.

FIGURE 16.8 Vascular Cognitive Disorder Brain injuries that lead to vascular cognitive disorder may be caused by bleeding in the brain or by a lack of blood flow to the brain. Both large and small areas of damage can lead to difficulties with thinking and functioning.

are even able to find some positive aspects in their lives. As one man explained: "Maybe this was to slow me down to enjoy life and to enjoy my family. . . . I can say that I'm a better person for it . . . than I ever was when I was working that rat race back and forth day to day" (Post, 2004, p. 130).

Bart tells us that life has changed since his diagnosis with AD. He wants to use his experience to help other people by talking about the condition. He sees stigma about AD everywhere. The acquaintances he used to chat with about houseboats do not always feel comfortable visiting, as if they are afraid AD is something they might catch. But Bart is no longer in denial: He knows that he cannot plan too far ahead and that there is no cure. Sitting on his houseboat with his dog, he tells us that he is grateful that he has had a great life. "If this is all I've got," he says, "I have not done badly."

Building Cognitive Resilience

Cognitive health in later life is not caused by a single factor. Instead, cognitive health, like physical health, is built up over the entire lifespan: Risks and advantages add to and subtract from your overall bank of resilience (Fratiglioni et al., 2020). For instance, some dangers early in childhood, like poverty or malnourishment, may stress the body and brain (Whalley et al., 2016). However, there are ample opportunities in which brain health can recover from early stresses (Dekhtyar et al., 2015). Most interventions to boost cognitive health in later life focus on increasing physical activity, social relationships, and intellectual stimulation (Ballesteros et al., 2015; Jackson et al., 2016). None of these is a magic cure, but all show modest effects for preventing or slowing the progress of cognitive decline (Bamidis et al., 2015; Chang et al., 2010; Lindenberger, 2014).

During later life, physical and cognitive health are closely linked. So, it probably comes as no surprise that hundreds of scholars have found that staying physically active protects your brain and your thinking (Kramer & Colcombe, 2018). Adults who

Still in Love Kim and Robert Reid met in middle school near Atlanta, Georgia, and have been married for decades. Their devotion continues, through the years they spent raising two children and Kim's recent diagnosis of Alzheimer disease.

Alex Potemkin/Getty Images

Teaching the New Hire Working can help keep build cognitive resilience. Here, working includes explaining the computer system to the new person.

have been exercising since midlife and who are able to maintain their physical fitness tend to have the best chance of surviving into late life with minimal cognitive decline (Klaming et al., 2016; Nyberg & Pudas, 2019; Sexton et al., 2016; Stephen et al., 2017). Adults who start exercising in later life are also building some cognitive resilience (Liu-Ambrose et al., 2019). Activities that require not just staying fit but also following directions, like tai chi, show special promise in helping adults preserve executive function (Gomes-Osman et al., 2018; Sink et al., 2015).

As you will learn in Chapter 17, cognitive health is also tied to emotional and mental health. Being social boosts cognitive resilience by helping to prevent emotional disorders like depression, and by encouraging people to be both physically and cognitively active (Bourassa et al., 2017; Lindenberger, 2014). Adults who spend time with family and friends, or are involved in community or religious organizations, tend to have fewer cognitive losses (Anatürk et al., 2018; Klaming et al., 2016; Nyberg et al., 2020).

Intellectual challenges also boost cognitive health. Does this require a daily Sudoku puzzle or a computerized brain-training program? Probably not. The best evidence that using your brain intensively helps keep it stronger comes from people who have spent a lifetime in intellectually challenging activities, either at work or in their free time (Chan et al., 2018; Dekhtyar et al., 2015; Gow et al., 2017). People with work that requires them to learn new things are especially lucky (Yu et al., 2020). Having a hobby or volunteer activity that encourages you to keep learning, whether it is a chess club or a book group, is also protective (Anatürk et al., 2018; Gow et al., 2017; Guiney & Machado, 2018; Iizuka et al., 2019). More than 1 in 10 older U.S. adults has another intellectual advantage: They are multilingual (Blumenfeld et al., 2017). Remember from Chapter 7 that being bilingual can build executive function, and this advantage may add to adults' cognitive reserve as they age (Alladi et al., 2017; Antoniou & Wright, 2017; Bialystok et al., 2016).

One thing that may not build your cognitive resilience is formal training. Whether it is a one-week course in Scottish Gaelic or a computer program that promises to enhance your working memory, short-term interventions that are designed to train your brain do not work miracles (Bahar-Fuchs et al., 2019; Karbach & Verhaeghen, 2014). Most evidence indicates that adults get better at the games these programs offer, but the gains do not transfer into the real world (Gates et al., 2019; Hampshire et al., 2019; Simons et al., 2016; Staudinger, 2020).

For adults who are physically capable and who want to work, employment offers benefits beyond the paycheck, including a sense of purpose, social interaction, and stimulation for the brain (Azar et al., 2019; Schulte et al., 2018). Bart has found this the case in his life: He once wanted to be a rock star, but he found that being a corporate trainer and a public speaker brought out the performer in him in a way that reliably paid the bills and allows him to give back.

Adults whose jobs are cognitively challenging, creative, and encouraging of curiosity are most likely to thrive in later life (Dekhtyar et al., 2015; Fratiglioni et al., 2020; Sakaki et al., 2018; Yu et al., 2020). However, being able to keep these jobs has required advocacy from developmental scientists.

 MAKING A DIFFERENCE
Allowing Older Adults to Stay in the Workforce

The workplace can be ageist (Nelson, 2017). More than half of older workers report that they have been laid off, demoted, or forced into early retirement because of their age (Johnson & Gosslin, 2018). About three in five say that they have experienced active discrimination in the workforce (Terrell, 2018). Older adults who are eager to continue to work often find that they are pushed out before they want to leave. In the United States, older adults are legally protected from workplace discrimination, but in countries around the world, older adults are still legally forced out (Axelrad & Mahoney, 2017). In many countries in Europe, adults are encouraged to leave the workforce at 67, and in Japan, retirement begins at age 60 (Axelrad & Mahoney, 2017; Kajimoto, 2019). Developmental scientists have worked to identify ageism in the workforce, highlight the cognitive strengths of older workers, and advocate for retraining older workers to keep their skills sharp (Börsch-Supan & Weiss, 2016; Paccagnella, 2016; Staudinger et al., 2016).

Ageism hurts adults at work, but it does not just hurt older workers. As you might imagine, exposure to age stereotypes can make older adults feel less competent, and if older adults believe those stereotypes, their cognitive skills decline (Armstrong et al., 2017; Slebert et al., 2018). But younger workers also have difficulties: Any kind of prejudice makes all workers feel unsafe and keeps adults from working together as a team (Paleari et al., 2019).

Many employers believe that older adults should leave the workforce because they are not cognitively up to the job (Bersin & Chamorro-Premuzic, 2019). Mark Zuckerberg, the founder of the media giant Facebook, may have been one of the few to own up to his own biases when he is said to have explained that his company was filled with younger people because he believed that "young people are just smarter" (qtd. in Kotler, 2015). Developmental scientists have countered with studies that demonstrate that older workers can be just as productive as younger ones: Cognitive strengths mean that older adults often have more expertise and knowledge than younger adults, even if their processing speed may be slower (Bersin & Chamorro-Premuzic, 2019; Börsch-Supan & Weiss, 2016). 🌐

As you will read in the next chapter, work can benefit adults' social and emotional health: It often gives adults a purpose, encourages them to make new relationships, and can even help us through the inevitable personal losses of later life. But, as Bart reminds us, even painful losses do not negate life's great moments. There are times of bliss: For Bart, these sometimes come driving down the highway, listening to a great song on a beautiful day, feeling gratitude for his truck. In such moments, he may forget his exit and where he is supposed to be going until his GPS dings. But that happens to all of us, that moment of bliss on a beautiful day listening to a song we love.

APPLY IT! 16.11 Bart is an advocate for early detection so that people who may have a cognitive impairment can plan for their future, together with their loved ones. Bart has been exceptionally clearheaded as he plans for the future. How might you react to a diagnosis like his?

16.12 What stereotypes do you have about the cognitive decline that may happen in later life? How does Bart's experience contrast with these ideas?

Wrapping It Up ⭕⭕

LO 16.1 What are the markers of late adulthood? (p. 462)

Late adulthood begins when we consider ourselves "old" and ends in death. It is the most diverse period of the lifespan with variable markers. There are many disparities in health and well-being depending on older adults' life experiences and how much support they are offered by their communities. Adults' capabilities can be analyzed through their levels of functioning, including the activities of daily living (ADLs) and the instrumental activities of daily living (IADLs). Ageism and ableism affect the lives of older adults, impacting how they think of themselves and how others treat them. Life expectancy is increasing around the world, but inequity in health abounds.

LO 16.2 What are the biological hallmarks of aging? (p. 462)

Aging is a biological process that leads to the gradual loss of functioning and makes us more vulnerable to death. Genes, particularly APOE and FOX03, can help set the pace of aging. Life experiences can create epigenetic changes that age the genome and particularly effect telomeres, create new epigenetic marks, and damage mitochondria and force cells into senescence. Age leads to degradation of stem cells, a weakening of the immune system and a tendency for inflammation. Gonadal and growth hormones both tend to decline.

LO 16.3 What changes in senses, strength, and sexuality may accompany aging? (p. 471)

Many body systems become weaker and more vulnerable, but interventions can help support older adults' well-being and their ability to adjust. Changes in senses, particularly to hearing, vision, and the vestibular system that controls balance, can lead to challenges and isolation without adequate support. Adults lose muscle strength and power, but this can be slowed with activity. Some adults develop conditions such as sarcopenia, frailty, osteoporosis, and arthritis. There is great diversity in sexual expression in later life, but many adults report that sex becomes more enjoyable, particularly if they maintain a positive body image.

LO 16.4 What are the common health conditions of later life? (p. 477)

Many adults have chronic health conditions. Disparities in health align with income and gender identity. Women tend to live longer than men but tend to have more chronic conditions. Some conditions can make it difficult for adults to live independently. Health is not always in your control. Positive health practices like physical activity, healthy eating, and sleep can help boost resilience.

LO 16.5 How does the brain change in late adulthood? (p. 481)

The brain is unstable during late life and tends to shrink and be vulnerable to injury. The brain tends to be less connected and smaller. Areas of the brain connected to memory and executive function are likely to change more dramatically than regions connected to emotional functioning. Scientists link the locus coeruleus to the pace of aging. Across the brain, the myelin sheath tends to degrade over time; glia tend to be less effective; destructive proteins tend to build up. Some of these can form neurofibrillary tangles that damage connectivity. Healthy brain aging is linked to good physical health, social connections, physical activity, and sleep.

LO 16.6 What are the typical cognitive changes in healthy aging? (p. 484)

Typical aging involves some cognitive losses including declines in fluid reasoning skills like working memory, processing speed, and the ability to multitask. However, cognitive reasoning continues to be intact in most. Executive function diminishes with age as a result of declines in fluid skills. Older adults continue to have strong semantic and procedural memory but may be weaker in episodic memory. Some scientists suggest that cognitive reserve may help delay cognitive decline. Adults may be diagnosed with a neurocognitive disorder, including mild cognitive impairment, Alzheimer disease, or vascular cognitive disorder. Social support, work, or intellectual challenge can boost cognitive resilience.

KEY TERMS

young-old (p. 462)
middle-old (p. 462)
oldest-old (p. 462)
level of functioning (p. 462)
activities of daily living (ADLs) (p. 463)
instrumental activities of daily living (IADLs) (p. 464)

life expectancy (p. 466)
mitochondria (p. 468)
vestibular system (p. 473)
sarcopenia (p. 473)
frailty (p. 474)
osteoporosis (p. 475)
arthritis (p. 475)
locus coeruleus (p. 482)

glia (p. 482)
tau protein (p. 482)
neurofibrillary tangles (p. 482)
amyloid beta (p. 482)
wisdom (p. 486)
cognitive reserve (p. 487)

neurocognitive disorders (NCDs) (p. 487)
mild cognitive impairment (MCI) (p. 488)
Alzheimer disease (AD) (p. 488)
vascular cognitive disorder (p. 490)

CHECK YOUR LEARNING

1. Bart feels middle aged, but his drivers' license reveals him to be 72. How would a gerontologist classify him?
   a) Oldest-old
   b) Middle-old
   c) Young-old
   d) Middle aged

2. What is NOT a benefit of having an aging population?
   a) Lower environmental impact
   b) More workers
   c) More caregivers
   d) More pregnant parents

3. What organ disappears altogether as a result of aging?
   a) The thymus
   c) The thyroid gland
   b) The pancreas
   d) The adrenal gland

4. Body systems tend to become weaker and more vulnerable to injury in later life. Which of the following is an accurate statement about these body changes?
   a) With enough exercise, adults can stay the same at 80 as they were at 50.
   b) Adults who have health conditions are responsible for their own conditions and have failed to take care of themselves.
   c) Support and interventions may be able to address some of the symptoms of common conditions related to aging.
   d) Support and interventions can reverse health concerns related to aging if you can afford them.

5. Most older adults have at least one chronic health condition in later life. What are the goals of adapting and supporting health in later life?
   a) Reverse all signs of aging.
   b) Adapt to physical changes and support well-being.
   c) Conceal any signs of health difficulties.
   d) Regain the body of a 35-year-old.

6. The brain changes significantly in late life. Many of the changes are more dramatic in regions of the brain connected with:
   a) emotional functioning.
   b) motor skills.
   c) executive function and memory.
   d) language development.

7. Buildup of toxic proteins is linked to aging in the brain. Which of the following statements are accurate?
   a) Some toxic proteins are present in all aging brains.
   b) Toxic proteins inevitably lead to a diagnosis of a neurocognitive disorder.
   c) Good health and cognitive reserve can prevent buildup of toxic proteins.
   d) Toxic proteins can be vacuumed up by newly discovered medications.

8. Cognitive changes often occur in later life. Older adults' thinking skills are most likely to be resilience in which components of reasoning?
   a) Linguistic skills
   b) Working memory
   c) Executive function
   d) Processing speed

9. Cognitive reserve is the idea that:
   a) cognitive changes in later life can be avoided altogether.
   b) intellectual skills can help delay the onset of cognitive changes in later life.
   c) cognitive skills can reverse the cognitive changes related to aging.
   d) you have extra regions in your brain that are saved for later.

Social and Emotional Development in Late Adulthood

Selected Resources from

 Achieve

Activities

Concept Practice: Caring for Frail Older Adults

Spotlight on Science: Measuring the Power of Generativity

Assessments

LearningCurve

Practice Quiz

Videos

Scientific American Profiles

Grandparenting

Active and Healthy Aging: The Importance of Community

©Macmillan, Photo by Sidford House

Late adulthood is filled with changes, and Mamie~Louise has had her share. She has been a single parent, a writer and arts educator, an actress, and most recently, a jazz singer. She has experienced the deaths of both of her parents, many close friends, and one of her sisters. As she remembers, she grew up in the school of "hard knocks," and her early life was far from easy. Her son, his partner, and her grandchildren recently moved thousands of miles away, leaving her with a feeling of absence.

Nevertheless, Mamie~Louise believes that life keeps getting better now that she is 70. She feels a sense of serenity and credits her optimism both to the strength she inherited from her ancestors and to a feeling of gratitude that has only increased as she has aged. She realizes now more than ever how precious her relationships are, wishing she had more time with the people who are important to her and how often petty resentments kept her apart from her loved ones.

Being a parent and a grandparent has been one of the defining experiences of Mamie~Louise's life, whether that meant making sure her son got the best care when she was living in Boston as a college student, that he got into a good school when they moved to New York City, or that she got to spend as much time as she could with her granddaughters when they lived nearby in California.

That deep commitment to family does not preclude romance. Mamie~Louise has become more comfortable with her own company over the years, but she also enjoys the pleasures and joys of a night out. For Mamie~Louise, life after menopause has been wonderful. She is more self-sufficient and choosier about whom she forms relationships with while enjoying the surprise, the ritual, and the joy of being with someone.

Mamie~Louise says that getting older has made her calmer, more serene, more self-confident, and more aware of what is really important in life. She says she is a better friend and partner now than she was in her more people-pleasing years of middle adulthood. She is now eager to see what lies ahead.

In this chapter, you will be reminded of the diversity of later life: The experiences of older adults vary depending on their health, where they live, and what challenges and triumphs marked their earlier years (Zahodne et al., 2017). More than any other life stage, late adulthood is influenced profoundly by the cumulative effect of this *bioecological context* (Bronfenbrenner, 1979; Leone, 2019).

Fortunately, for Mamie~Louise and many others, later life is often the happiest life stage: Older adults are often better than younger ones at managing their feelings and maintaining their equilibrium (Carstensen et al., 2020). And although adults are inevitably shaped by an aging and more vulnerable body and brain, they are remarkably adaptable (Baltes & Baltes, 1993; Charles, 2010). Many opportunities remain for building resilience and maintaining health through stronger relationships, generative engagement, and a sense of purpose (Kiosses & Sachs-Ericsson, 2020).

Scientific American Profile

Meet Mamie~Louise

Perspectives on Late Adulthood

What makes us happy and satisfied during late adulthood? Mamie~Louise would say it is love. Young people in the United States often suggest that it is excitement and adventure (Tsai et al., 2018). And as they get older, many U.S. adults say they are looking forward to a "second chance" in later life: a new career, a new hobby, or a closer relationship with their grandchildren (Principi et al., 2018). Mamie~Louise is launching a career as a jazz vocalist.

Developmental theorists suggest that late adulthood is a time when adults benefit from feeling useful and engaged. Connectedness to others, whether through working, volunteering, or caregiving, helps both adults and their communities. People who have a sense of purpose and who feel generative tend to have longer and happier lives (Carr et al., 2018; Kim et al., 2013; Shiba et al., 2021). But staying active in late adulthood often requires adults to address the ageism that can keep them from thriving.

The Impact of Ageism

Some stresses in late adulthood come from having a more vulnerable body; others come from ageism. Remember from Chapter 16 that the dual challenges of *ageism* and *ableism* become more acute in later life (Ayalon & Tesch Römer, 2017; Butler, 1969; Radović-Marković, 2013). Older adults are beset by prejudice and also internalize misinformation about themselves (North & Fiske, 2017). Stereotypes about aging affect adults' health and cognition, but they also affect social relationships and emotions. The more older adults believe in ageist stereotypes about themselves, the more likely they are to worry, to feel old, and to experience loneliness, and even suicide (Emile et al., 2015; Kim & Lee, 2020; Levy et al., 2020; Li et al., 2017).

Ageism changes older adults' relationships. One way is that it enables people to generalize about older adults, negating the great diversity among them. It also explains why many older adults' basic need for dignity, respect, and common humanity are neglected, particularly when they need support (Butler, 1969; Iversen et al., 2009). Some ageist beliefs can seem well meaning, like the common idea that older people are friendlier than younger adults (North & Fiske, 2017). But even these seemingly positive generalizations tend to do more harm than good (Kornadt et al., 2019).

Learning Objective

17.1 Explain the major perspectives on social and emotional development in late life.

CONNECTIONS

Remember from Chapter 16 that late adulthood is the period between about age 65, or the time when adults traditionally retire from full-time work, and death. Grieving the passing of a loved one and accepting the finality of life is a constant in late adulthood. Death is so pivotal that we cover it in a dedicated chapter.

 Share It!

Even kids can be ageist. Some researchers found that ageism is high in early childhood and adolescence, when children tend to be susceptible to stereotypes. But good relationships with grandparents can break those stereotypes.

(Flamion et al., 2019)

Scientific American: Lifespan Development

What Is Possible in Late Life? Many of us admire adventure that is not possible for all older adults. Yuichiro Miura (*left*), a longtime athlete and mountain climber from Japan, is the oldest person to summit Mt. Everest, at age 80. Kauko Heikkinen (*right*) is a two-time Finnish Olympian and still kitesurfs in his 80s.

Scientific American Profile

Sense of Integrity in Late Adulthood

📱 **Share It!**

Reframe aging! Researchers found that adults had fewer biases about older people when they were exposed to a message that suggested that aging gave older adults the power, expertise, and momentum to make change in their communities.

(Busso et al., 2019)

📖 **Scientific American: Lifespan Development**

For many adults, age is *intersectional*, meaning that it overlaps with other identity markers, like ability, gender, income, culture, ethnicity, or sexual orientation (Ayalon & Tesch-Römer, 2017; Lu et al., 2020). Intersectional identities can be a source of strength in later life. For instance, a group of gay and lesbian older adults in South Africa reported that sharing an intersectional group identity as they aged helped support them in times of stress, particularly as they faced discrimination because of their romantic preferences, skin color, or medical conditions (Reygan & Henderson, 2019). Mamie~Louise finds that her pride in her ancestors and in her African American identity helps connect her to a wider community and heritage.

Variations in Ageism Age-based prejudices are common around the world and throughout history (Gire, 2019; Martin & North, 2021; Ng & Lim, 2021; Voss et al., 2018; Zhang et al., 2016). Mamie~Louise suggests that the entertainment industry in Los Angeles is particularly ageist: She thinks that older women, like herself, are often sidelined in the movie industry. Ageism is more prevalent in cultures and nations that encourage independence and self-reliance, such as the United Kingdom and the United States (Chopik et al., 2020; Ng & Lim, 2021). However, although affluent nations often rank high in ageism, they also tend to provide more governmental, social, and financial supports for their older people than less affluent nations (North & Fiske, 2017).

Stereotypes and expectations about late adulthood are also influenced by culture. For instance, older adults in Hong Kong are encouraged to be calm and restful, but older people in Europe and the United States are expected to be active and social (Albert & Tesch-Römer, 2021; Rothermund & dePaula Couto, 2018; Tsai et al., 2018). Americans tend to admire older adults who are adventurous, like Yuichiro Miura, who climbed Mount Everest at age 80 (Lieser, 2020). For those U.S. adults who admire outgoing parts of themselves, the physical limitations of late adulthood are often more disappointing than they are for those who prefer a quieter life (Kitayama et al., 2020; Tsai et al., 2018).

How to Fight Ageism Researchers and activists have been fighting ageism for millennia, pointing out that circumstances and discrimination, not poor health, are what keep older adults from living fulfilling lives (Achenbaum, 2018; Park, 2016; Troyansky, 2015). Reversing stereotypes is difficult: It is not enough to make people aware of their stereotypes or even require them to spend time with older people (Berger, 2017; Hehman & Bugenthal, 2015; Verhage et al., 2021). In fact, having contact with older people can make stereotypes *worse*. In one study, after medical students worked with older adults in a two-week internship, the students' attitudes became even more negative (Kusumastuti et al., 2017). Meaningful change comes from positive relationship building, which forces people to connect and understand the person behind the label (Drury et al., 2016; Flamion et al., 2019).

Erikson's Stage of Integrity Versus Despair

As you have read, Erik Erikson was one of the foremost theorists of lifespan development. Throughout his life, but particularly in his later years, he worked in close collaboration with his wife, Joan. The Eriksons believed that a satisfying late adulthood required that adults resolve an eighth stage of the life cycle, the crisis between **integrity and despair** (Erikson, 1994; Erikson & Erikson, 1998).

In the eighth life stage, adults review, or integrate, their past and make peace with themselves. The goal is to find a way to feel confident in your own wholeness, despite the inevitable missteps that have happened over a lifetime. For many older adults, the sense of satisfaction that comes from acknowledging their accomplishments and their generativity reassures them that they have made a positive mark on the world. This can help older people feel less intimidated by the inevitable end of their lives (Erikson, 1993; Major et al., 2016).

The Eriksons believed that reflecting on your life experiences helps build spiritual *wisdom*, or a sense of concern, understanding, and connection to the world. Many scholars agree: A shared belief among many cultures is that older adults should work to build spiritual knowledge as they approach the end of life (Janhsen et al., 2019). For instance, as described in Chapter 16, some scientists have found that older adults often have more insight about interpersonal relationships than younger adults (Greve & Bjorklund, 2009; Lind et al., 2020; Weststrate & Gluck, 2017). Contemporary research also finds that the process of reflecting on your life can boost your resilience. In fact, *reminiscence therapy* and *life review* can help adults find purpose, direction, and a new identity as they grow older (Butler, 1974; Friedman et al., 2019; Ko et al., 2019; Lind et al., 2020).

In the Eriksons' view, it is *generativity* that makes adulthood fulfilling (Erikson, 1950). Most older adults tell researchers that being generative is what they hope for in their later life (Reich et al., 2020). They often find new ways of being useful: transitioning from a nursing career to gardening for the local food pantry, or from teaching to looking after great-grandchildren. Throughout, feeling generative helps adults feel better about their lives (Moieni et al., 2020).

The Eriksons also recognized that old age is not always easy, and generativity may not always be possible. In her 90s, after watching her husband's final illness, Joan Erikson noted that even introspection may be too much to ask (Erikson et al., 1989; Friedman, 2000). Sometimes, she suggested, "remaining alive is the only goal" you can pursue (Erikson et al., 1994).

A Time to Act

Activity theory is the idea that communities and older people both benefit when older adults are engaged with the world (Cavan et al., 1949; Havighurst & Albrecht, 1953). The theory also suggests that older adults have the same needs for respect, dignity, and emotional connection as younger adults (Manalel et al., 2018). Although aging bodies may require adaptation, scientists agree that staying connected and involved helps adults live longer, happier, and healthier lives (Truxillo et al., 2015). This is in line with Maslow's theory of the hierarchy of human needs: Regardless of age or ability, people are more likely to feel satisfied if they feel creative and accomplished (Goebel & Brown, 1981; Maslow, 1943; Winston, 2016).

More than 60 years ago, in a perspective known as **disengagement theory**, some scholars suggested that severing social ties and increasing social isolation was a natural and inevitable part of aging (Cumming & Henry, 1961). The validity of this theory has

CONNECTIONS

Remember from Chapter 15 that Erikson believed that middle adulthood was the age stage in which adults needed to resolve the crisis of *generativity versus stagnation*, by being caring, giving, and productive.

📱 Share It!

Can you find spirituality in your later years? Older adults around the globe tend to be more likely than younger people to say that religious institutions are an important part of their lives. Six in ten U.S. older adults say religion is important to them.

(Kramer & Fahmy, 2018)

🐆 **Scientific American: Lifespan Development**

Commitment to Care. Neng Qing (on the right) has been a Buddhist nun for many years and now runs a facility for older adults at a temple in Fujian province, in Southeastern China.

integrity versus despair Erikson's eighth stage of cognitive development, in which adults review, or *integrate*, their past and make peace with themselves.

activity theory The idea that communities and older people both benefit when older adults are engaged with the world.

disengagement theory The discredited idea that severing social ties and increasing social isolation is a natural and inevitable part of aging.

Making Time for More Reps Lambert (*right*) is being trained by a volunteer coach, Eugene, to build his strength: an experience that may help both adults. They both benefit from a program in the Dixon Correctional Center that encourages volunteer caregiving for older adults.

been questioned based on the overwhelming evidence that loneliness and social isolation are destructive to older adults' mental and physical health. Indeed, according to some experts, isolation is even more dangerous to health than smoking (Conejero et al., 2018; Gale et al., 2018; Pantell et al., 2013).

You will learn throughout this chapter that older adults continue to develop as they age. But that does not mean that adults change abruptly when they get older. If you have been a quiet person throughout your life, you probably will not become outgoing after you turn 70. The **continuity perspective** points out that adults are happier in late adulthood if their identity stays relatively stable (Atchley, 1999; Cavan et al., 1949).

Adults may need and want to adapt: People often tell researchers they are happier working part time or cutting back on unpleasant social obligations (Baltes & Baltes, 1993; Hagestad & Settersten, 2017). Nevertheless, happier older adults are often those who stay busy.

APPLY IT!   17.1 Mamie-Louise explains that having a clear understanding of her strengths and weaknesses makes her stronger now than when she was younger. How is this in line with Erikson's notion that late adulthood is a time to find wholeness? **17.2** Mamie-Louise says she has more appreciation and understanding of how relationships work than she did when she was younger. This interpersonal wisdom is in line with which theories of development in later life?

Relationships in Late Life

Learning Objective

17.2 Describe the benefits and common challenges to relationships in later life.

In her 70s, Mamie-Louise still gets ready for a date: She does her nails, applies makeup, and perfects her eyeshadow. She has more of a sense of what pleases her in a relationship. She appreciates the more stable relationships of later life, with less drama and emotional turmoil.

In late life, relationships with family, friends, and romantic partners continue to be crucial to health and happiness. People with strong relationships have a lower risk of illness and a stronger sense of well-being (Dunkel Schetter, 2017). Healthy connections help people feel valued, give them a sense of purpose, and help support them through times of difficulty (Rook & Charles, 2017; Weston et al., 2021).

Late life comes with new stresses: Friendships, romances, and even bonds with acquaintances are nearly always in transition (Shin et al., 2018). At the same time, relationships are still subject to financial anxiety, mental health problems, discrimination, and isolation. Most older adults, drawing on a lifetime of experience, are able to adjust, whether through online dating, Facebook connections, or volunteer commitments (Carr & Utz, 2020).

Romantic Relationships

Around the world, older people with happy romantic relationships have better mental health and live longer and healthier lives (Han et al., 2019; Kulik, 2015; Umberson et al., 2015; Waldinger & Schultz, 2016). If researchers ask older people about their relationships, they are more likely than younger adults to say that they are content (Rook & Charles, 2017). Couples tend to have fewer conflicts in later life than they did in their earlier years: Older adults tend to step away from arguments (Hatch & Bulcroft, 2004; Luong et al., 2011). As Mamie-Louise explains, she knows herself well enough now and knows how to spot a petty disagreement, so she lets things go that may have become dramas in earlier years.

In later life, as in earlier stages of the lifespan, love comes in a variety of forms. Some older adults are in long-term, committed relationships. About half of all older adults in the United States are married to their first partner. Many older people, like

continuity perspective The idea that aspects of personality and identity stay the same as we age.

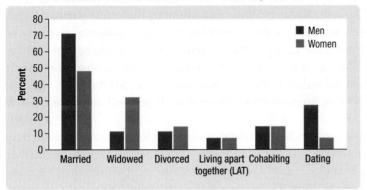

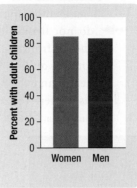

FIGURE 17.1 Relationships in Later Life Family and romantic relationships among older adults come in a variety of forms. For many in the United States, family often includes adult children, but many do not include a committed romantic partner.

younger ones, are in their second or third marriages or are dating like Mamie-Louise (see **Figure 17.1**) (Kreider & Ellis, 2011).

An increasing number of older adults in the United States and in other affluent countries cohabit with their romantic partner (Brown, Wright, et al., 2018; Reynolds & Brown, 2020). For instance, about 1 in 12 older U.S. adults is cohabiting. The numbers are even higher in Northern Europe, where cohabitation has been common for decades: There, about one in eight older adults are cohabiting (Carr & Utz, 2020). Remember from Chapters 13 and 15 that some adults also commit to a romantic partner but do not to live with them full-time. These *living apart together (LAT)* relationships are also common in later life (Benson & Coleman, 2016; Carr & Utz, 2020; Gierveld, 2004).

Less formal relationships often appeal to older adults because of the difficulties of merging finances and social networks (Benson & Coleman, 2016; Brown & Wright, 2017). In the United States, where older adults often worry about their health insurance coverage and pension benefits, cohabitation simplifies finances. It can protect adults from being responsible for each other's medical bills and maintain individual pension and Social Security benefits (Brown & Wright, 2017). LAT relationships offer an extra layer of independence, which is often particularly appealing to older women who are worried about being responsible for a partner's declining health (Carr & Utz, 2020).

Transitions in Close Relationships

During late adulthood, adults have more transitions in their relationships than they do in earlier times in the lifespan (Kreider & Ellis, 2011). More than half of all adults will lose a partner to death or divorce, and many will begin a new romance (Carr & Utz, 2020; Shin et al., 2018). Divorce is more likely for older adults than in previous generations, as social stigma about divorce began to lessen starting with the Baby Boomer cohort (Brown & Lin, 2012; Brown & Wright, 2017; Stepler, 2017).

In late life, as in other times in the lifespan, adults break up when they do not feel satisfied and when they have the economic security to live on their own (Lin et al., 2018). Marriages tend to be more strained if one person has already been through a divorce, or if couples are experiencing stresses like poverty, discrimination, mental illness, or substance abuse (Amato & Irving, 2013; Lin et al., 2018).

Widowed and divorced adults often adapt by finding a new partner. This is especially true for men, particularly if they are financially stable (Brown, Lin, et al., 2018; Schimmele & Wu, 2016). Nearly twice as many men as women end up living with or marrying someone

Scientific American Profile

Dating in Late Adulthood

Share It!

Is online romance forever young? Researchers have found that advertisements for online dating sites aimed at older adults tend to avoid signs of real-life aging, like wrinkles and gray hair.

(Gewirtz-Meydan & Ayalon, 2018)

Scientific American: Lifespan Development

CONNECTIONS

Remember from Chapter 16 that sexuality continues to be linked to well-being and health in later life. Intimacy is an important part of life for many older adults.

Together for Nearly 60 Years Peter Cott (*left*), and his husband, Ken Leedom, here in their apartment in New York, were only able to get married in 2013. They stayed together until the end of their lives.

new (Brown et al., 2019). Women who are interested in other-sex relationships often tell researchers that they are happy to stay on their own (Brown et al., 2019; Connidis et al., 2017).

Demographics can also make it harder for adults to find male partners: Men do not live as long as women, so there are fewer available potential partners to choose from (Rapp, 2018). Like younger people, older adults are dating and looking for love online (Anderson et al., 2020). Older adults are more likely to boast about their health and their financial stability than younger ones, but like everyone, they are also interested in looking attractive and finding both sex and romance (Davis & Fingerman, 2016).

Researchers have found that older adults are just as likely to have a supportive, positive relationship with a new cohabiting partner, or in a second marriage, as they are in a longer partnership (Carr & Utz, 2020; Wright, 2019). However, couples in less formal relationships and blended families are likely to struggle financially, since breakups often take an economic toll. They are also more likely to worry about not having partners to take care of them (Wright, 2017).

Long-time couples have some advantages: They tend to have more friends and more financial assets than those who have divorced (Carr & Mouzon, 2018). When researchers compare relationships that have lasted 30 years or longer with those of newlyweds, they find that couples who have stayed together over the years are much more likely to be happy, perhaps because many unhappy couples break up long before late adulthood (Amato & James, 2018; Anderson et al., 2010; Proulx, 2015; Wright et al., 2018).

Family Relationships

During late adulthood, extended families remain a major source of friendship, support, and responsibility for most older adults. In the United States and in other affluent nations, about three in four older adults have children and grandchildren, and about one in three in their 60s still has living parents (see **Figure 17.2**). By the time adults are in their 70s, about one in three is a great-grandparent (Margolis & Wright, 2017; Meyer & Kandic, 2017). Many of these relationships are built on more than just biology: More than half of older adults have a stepchild or step-grandchildren or have relationships with the children or grandchildren of their partners (Lin et al., 2018; Wright, 2017).

Older adults remain a vital source of support to their children, parents, and grandchildren, offering financial, emotional, and hands-on care to their family members (Margolis & Wright, 2017). As adults get older, their ability to give practical assistance to their families often becomes more limited, but they continue to provide emotional support until the end of their lives (Huo et al., 2019). As you approach your 80s, you may no longer be able to haul your grandchild's stroller up the front steps, but you can still provide comfort or a listening ear.

Close Together or Apart Around the globe, the vast majority of older adults live with their extended families: Only in affluent countries is it common for older adults to live alone (UN, 2019). As families become wealthier, it becomes less common for older adults to live with their children (Zueras et al., 2020). In the United States, particularly since the 2008 recession, an increasing number of older adults live with their adult children (Binette et al., 2021; Federal Reserve Board, 2021; Glaser et al., 2018). (See **Figure 17.3**.) But families live together not only to save money or to care for each other: Living together is often preferable for families who are emotionally close or share cultural beliefs (Cohn & Passel, 2018). Asian American and Latino families are more likely to have a stronger sense of cultural obligation and to want to live together (Muennig et al., 2018).

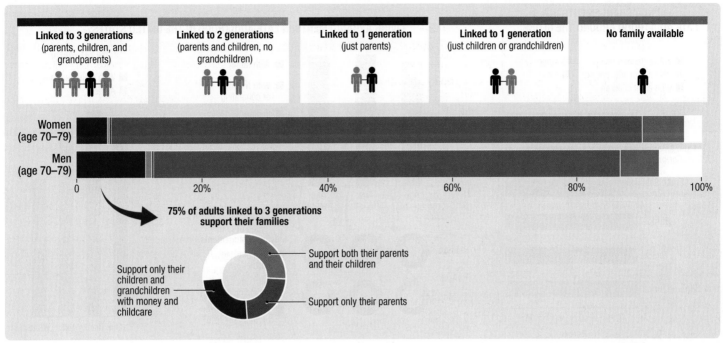

| Linked to 3 generations (parents, children, and grandchildren) | Linked to 2 generations (parents and children, no grandchildren) | Linked to 1 generation (just parents) | Linked to 1 generation (just children or grandchildren) | No family available |

75% of adults linked to 3 generations support their families

Support both their parents and their children

Support only their parents

Support only their children and grandchildren with money and childcare

Data from Margolis & Wright, 2017.

FIGURE 17.2 Connected to Family Across Generations One group of researchers found that many older adults were linked to family, either their own parents, children, or grandchildren. Many supported multiple generations, but older adults are diverse: Some were not connected to any family.

Even if families do not live together, many are close by (Raymo et al., 2019). In the United States, about three in four older adults live within 30 miles of one of their adult children or their own parents (Choi et al., 2019). Families tend to be more dispersed if they have immigrated: One in five aging adults in Mexico reports that they have a child who is now in the United States (Arenas et al., 2021). Families often become closer as adults age: Most parents eventually move closer to their children (Raymo et al., 2019).

Changing Parenting Relationships For many older adults, their closest relationships are with their now-adult children. Mamie-Louise reports that even though her son is now a continent away and has a family of his own, he is still the center of her life. In the United States, mothers tend to have close relationships with both their sons and daughters (Fingerman et al., 2020). Fathers are often not as close to their children as mothers, particularly if they did not live with their children when they were growing up (Fingerman et al., 2020).

Not all families get along. As many as 1 in 10 parents has no regular contact with their children (Becker & Hank, 2021; Gilligan et al., 2015). Families may be separated as a result of mental health or substance use disorders. Sometimes parents reject children because they do not share the same values, or because a child is lesbian, gay, or transgender (Thomeer et al., 2018). As adults age, they may expect another chance to rebuild their relationships, but that opportunity does not always come (Agllias, 2016; Scharp & Curran, 2018).

For many families, though, relationships get easier over time. Part of this comes from the tendency of older people and their families to avoid conflict (Birditt et al., 2019). Children also tend to be more forgiving of their parents' missteps (Luong et al., 2011). If parents become disabled, children often become even more accepting (Wang et al., 2019).

Sharing a Home and a Life Together Lynda Faye and her mother, Yetta Meise, share a home with their cat Hawthorne, in Amherst, Massachusetts (*top*). Christa and Brendan and their children share a home in Chicago with Christa's father, Joseph (*bottom*).

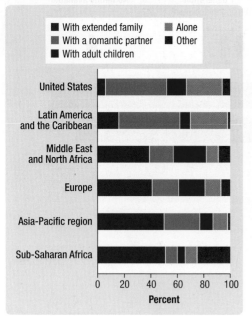

LIVING ARRANGEMENTS IN LATE ADULTHOOD AROUND THE GLOBE

Data from Pew Research Center, 2019.

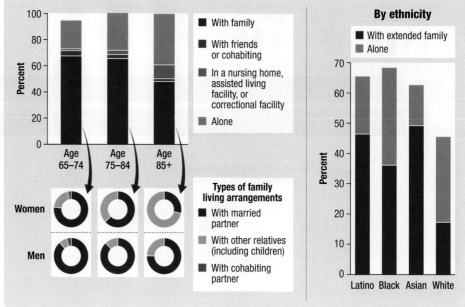

LIVING ARRANGEMENTS IN LATE ADULTHOOD IN THE UNITED STATES

Data from U.S. Census Bureau, 2016.   Data from Mutchler & Somerville, 2016.

FIGURE 17.3 Living Arrangements in Late Adulthood Culture, age, and ethnicity all play a role in where older adults live. Adults can thrive when they live alone, with romantic partners, or with extended family.

However, more than two in three older parents and three in four adult children tell researchers that they have frequent conflicts about older adults' autonomy. Grown children often describe their parents as "stubborn" for making their own decisions (Heid et al., 2017, 2018). Families fight about whether it is safe to drive, to walk, to take the train. Children worry about their parents' health and safety (Birditt et al., 2019; Wang et al., 2020). Adults want to maintain their independence. While common, these conflicts are not without consequence. These disagreements are linked to higher risk for depression.

Extended Family Bonds Many adults have close relationships with their siblings and grandchildren that deepen in later life. Mamie-Louise adores her two grand-daughters, or as she calls them, the "grand-ladies": new people to spoil, to adore, and to be the icing on the cake. About 8 in 10 older U.S. adults like Mamie-Louise have grandchildren, and by age 75, most have become great-grandparents (AARP, 2019; Even-Zohar, 2019; Meyer & Kandic, 2017).

In late adulthood, many grandparents continue to care for their grandchildren (Huo et al., 2019; Sadruddin et al., 2019). For instance, in Europe and the United States, about 4 in 10 older adults provide regular, hands-on care to their grandchildren (Di Gessa et al., 2016; Dunifon et al., 2018). In emergencies, grandparents step in as full-time caregivers, although such responsibility can take a toll, particularly on older grandparents, who are more vulnerable to physical and emotional strain (Harnett et al., 2014; Hayslip et al., 2019; Muthiah et al., 2019; Nadorff et al., 2019). In the United States, about half of all grandparents are close to their grandchildren (Meyer & Kandic, 2017). Relationships with great-grandchildren tend to be more distant (Even-Zohar, 2019).

With age, many adults become closer to their siblings, particularly if they are sharing caregiving responsibility for their parents (Hill et al., 2020; Jensen et al., 2020). Like all relationships, sibling bonds can be a resource or a strain (Gilligan et al., 2020). Even in late life, family relationships can be complicated by childhood rivalries and worries about parental favoritism (Stocker et al., 2020).

Continuing Bonds Whether adults are meeting a great-grandchild for the first time in Anhui Province, China (*left*), or playing with a grandson in Manawatu, New Zealand (*right*), relationships with younger family members can be a source of generativity and meaning in late adulthood.

Friendships

Having a variety of relationships in your social network is protective as you age: Interacting with people from a variety of backgrounds and experiences sharpens your cognition and offers you more opportunities to deepen your relationships (Fingerman et al., 2020). Scientists have found that all members of your social convoy are valuable, including the cashier who hands you a coffee in the morning and the pharmacist who asks after you when you pick up a prescription (Fingerman et al., 2020; Fuller et al., 2020).

Remember from Chapter 15 that for some older people, friends have become their closest contacts and their family—their *fictive kin* (Furstenberg et al., 2020; Jordan-Marsh & Harden, 2005). African American older adults sometimes have a close group of friends from church who have become their family (Chatters et al., 1994; Nelson, 2017; Taylor et al., 2013). Lesbian, gay, and transgender older adults, who are more likely to be estranged from their biological families, often establish "families of choice" with long-term friends (Tester & Wright, 2017).

Older adults invariably experience transitions in their friendships: losing touch with friends after retirement, a move, or a divorce. More than half of all adults experience the death of a partner or friend every year (Antonucci et al., 2019a; Litwin et al., 2020). In the United States, most people's social networks tend to shrink as they age, particularly if they have financial difficulties or cognitive decline, but this is not universal or inevitable (Ajrouch et al., 2018; Liao et al., 2019). Most older adults are remarkably resilient, expanding their social networks as they draw on a lifetime's experience in building connections (Cornwell et al., 2021; Litwin et al., 2020). More than two in three older adults have made a new friend in the past year (Badawy et al., 2019).

Older people are increasingly reliant on social media and texting to connect (Clark & Moloney, 2020; Szabo et al., 2019). As older adults begin to use social media more intensively, their networks of social acquaintances grow (Antonucci et al., 2019b). In fact, people in their 60s and 70s, the Baby Boomer generation, are among the most enthusiastic users of platforms like Facebook (Auxier & Anderson, 2021). Mamie-Louise boasts of more than 4,000 connections in her carefully curated Facebook account.

Older people who have close friendships tend to preserve their memory and their cognitive functioning longer than those who rely on family alone for companionship. Interaction keeps your brain active (Sharifian et al., 2019; Zahodne et al., 2019). Friends and acquaintances also provide another layer of social and emotional support. They can lend a sympathetic ear or offer a ride to the hospital during difficult times

CONNECTIONS

As explained in Chapter 15, researchers call the group of people you are connected to your *social convoy*. Think of the layers of closeness in your personal relationships as a series of concentric circles. Every person defines who is close to them in different ways.

Celebrations with Friends in Buenos Aires Social relationships in late adulthood often include long-term friend groups, like this one in Argentina.

(Fingerman et al., 2020; Han et al., 2019). Friends encourage each other to be physically as well as mentally active, inviting each other to take a walk, try salsa dancing, or help out in the garden (Sharifian et al., 2020). These connections protect physical, cognitive, and mental health (Ajrouch et al., 2018; Pantell et al., 2013).

Neighborhoods and Communities

With aging, adults tend to develop closer relationships with the people who live on their block or in the adjoining apartments. Neighborhoods often become an important part of older adults' social life (Ermer & Proulx, 2019). Older adults are more likely to stop and chat, trade favors, or check in on someone's cat. Neighbors often become friends (Bruine de Bruin et al., 2020). Indeed, feeling safe and connected to the people in the community—whether it is the person who cuts their hair or the laundromat attendant—boosts well-being (Cain et al., 2018; Choi & Matz-Costa, 2018).

Older adults can find community in a variety of places. Some live in *age-segregated neighborhoods*, such as retirement communities designed specifically for older people. Age-segregated communities often provide more opportunities for social engagement than other neighborhoods (Papke, 2021). About 7 in 10 adults prefer to **age in place**, or stay in their existing homes or neighborhoods (Binette & Vasold, 2019; Byrnes, 2016). Many believe that staying put will help them maintain connections to their friends and family (Wiles et al., 2020).

Homes that were comfortable and safe in the past may no longer work well for aging bodies: Stairs may be a challenge, front doors may not accommodate wheelchairs, and keeping a big space clean may be too difficult. Communities, policy makers, and inventors have experimented with solutions to make aging in place easier, from smart homes designed with responsive technology to contractors who can make apartments safer (Carnemolla & Bridge, 2019; Kim et al., 2017).

Towns and cities designated as *age-friendly* are designed to be easier for older people to navigate, particularly if they cannot drive or have trouble walking. Age-friendly communities are certified by entities such as the World Health Organization or the American Association for Retired People (AARP, 2020; WHO, 2018). These certifications help ensure that communities enable older people to thrive by providing safe, affordable housing, easy access to public transportation, and a variety of social opportunities.

 CAN YOU BELIEVE IT?

Do Deadlines Make You More Aware of What Really Matters?

If you had just a few hours left on Earth, with whom would you want to spend that time? Would it be someone famous, a blind date, or someone who could get you a job? Or might it be your best friend, your mother, or your son? Psychologist Laura Carstensen actually tested this. She and her team asked people of different ages who they would spend time with if they had no time constraints, or if their time was limited, perhaps because they were about to move across the country or because they were very old or very sick (Carstensen et al., 1999; Fredrickson & Carstensen, 1990; Liao & Carstensen, 2018). They found that time makes people more selective. Those who felt that they had years ahead of them were inclined to spend time with someone new. Those who imagined that their time was limited wanted to spend time with someone they cherished.

How does this apply to older adults? Carstensen has found that older people are more aware that the time they have left is short, that no one lives forever. Older adults tend to prefer to spend time with the people they care about *all* the time (unless they are asked to

age in place The idea that you would rather age in a community or a geographic location that is familiar to you, including your own home.

imagine a world where they will live forever). Many older adults would rather have dinner with their grandchildren than Beyoncé, or with their son than Barack Obama.

According to Carstensen, older people are not as motivated by acquiring knowledge, or by becoming rich or famous. Rather, they are interested in feeling good, close, and connected. In what is known as *social selectivity theory*, Carstensen proposes that when people are aware of the limits on their life, they prioritize social connections and their emotional well-being, rather than strive for long-term goals (Carstensen et al., 1999). Carstensen suggests that this helps explain why older adults tend to be more optimistic, more selective about who they spend time with, and more positive about their relationships (English & Carstensen, 2014). As you will read, these characteristics help some adults adapt to their changing social world.

APPLY IT! **17.3** Mamie-Louise says that her relationships have improved as she has gotten older and has more serenity and ability to focus on the big picture. She is growing into her role as the family matriarch. How does Mamie-Louise's sense of herself reflect the theories of social relationships in later life?

17.4 Do not assume later life does not include romance and passion: Mamie-Louise tells us that just because she has become less inclined to drama, she is still just as passionate as ever (and she is a great dancer). How does this reflect the continuing value many adults put on romance in later life?

Working and Civic Engagement

Mamie-Louise jokes that she failed at retirement. She has had many jobs over the decades: an arts administrator, actor, and, most recently, a cabaret singer.

Like Mamie-Louise, many adults remain active (Calvo et al., 2018). (See **Figure 17.4.**) But, as is so common across late adulthood, diversity is typical. Variations abound: About one in five U.S. adults over 65 is working, compared to 1 in 10 in Germany and nearly all men in Zambia (He et al., 2016; U.S. Bureau of Labor Statistics, 2021). About one in three older adults in the United States has formally volunteered for a community organization, compared to about 1 in every 50 adults in Spain (Hansen et al., 2018). Around the world, the most common type of civic engagement is informal, like bringing food

Learning Objective

17.3 Explain how work and civic engagement can benefit older adults and their communities.

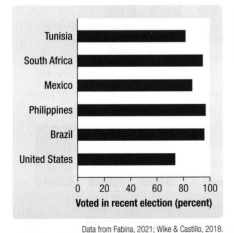

VOTING IN LATE ADULTHOOD AROUND THE WORLD

Data from Fabina, 2021; Wike & Castillo, 2018.

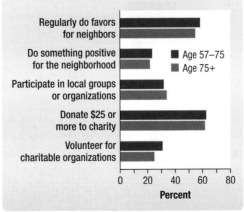

VOLUNTEERING AND HELPING AMONG OLDER ADULTS IN THE UNITED STATES

Data from Volunteering in America, 2018.

FIGURE 17.4 Community Engagement in Late Adulthood Around the world, older adults are often more likely to vote than younger ones. In the United States, older adults are often more likely to volunteer and participate in community organizations.

to a sick friend or giving a ride to a neighbor (Burr et al., 2018). No matter how they are involved in their community, civic engagement and work can help adults thrive.

Working in Late Life

Working has many benefits in late life, among them a sense of meaning and purpose and the cognitive and social stimulation of carrying out daily tasks (see **Figure 17.5**). Work keeps your mind and body busy by forcing you to interact with other people, to show up at a set time and place, and to follow directions. This often helps adults feel physically healthier, mentally sharp, and more satisfied and happier as they grow older (Weston et al., 2021). Another, more concrete benefit of work is income. Older adults often still need a paycheck to help cover expenses, rent, or medical bills (Hale et al., 2021). Working in late adulthood provides financial stability (Chen et al., 2019).

In the United States, older workers are legally protected and cannot be forced to retire if they do not want to, but this is not true worldwide. In Japan, for instance, workers are still expected to retire at 60 (Kajimoto, 2019). Similarly, in European countries, including Sweden and Slovenia, mandatory retirement encourages workers to leave the workforce in their 60s (OECD, 2018, 2021). But while workers in the United States have legal protections, that does not guarantee that they will find or keep jobs in later life.

A Passion or a Paycheck? Older adults who are working are usually doing so because they have a passion for something, like Mamie-Louise's love of jazz, or because they really need the paycheck. Around the world, only about half of all older people have any sort of savings or pension to help them financially (ILO, 2014). As a result, in low-income countries like Guatemala, more than three in four men over 65 are still working, because their communities do not offer robust pensions or social services for older adults. On the other hand, in more affluent countries like Italy, fewer than 1 in 10 adults is working after 65 (He et al., 2016).

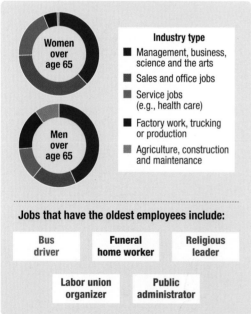

Still Up at Night Adrienne Kennedy says she writes in the middle of the night, on an iPad, in the house she shares with her children and grandchildren. She has been a playwright for more than 50 years.

Khue Bui/The New York Times/Redux

WHAT JOBS DO OLDER ADULTS HAVE IN THE UNITED STATES?

Women over age 65

Men over age 65

Industry type
- Management, business, science and the arts
- Sales and office jobs
- Service jobs (e.g., health care)
- Factory work, trucking or production
- Agriculture, construction and maintenance

Jobs that have the oldest employees include:

Bus driver	Funeral home worker	Religious leader

Labor union organizer	Public administrator

Data from (top) U.S. Census, 2016; (bottom) U.S. Census, 2020.

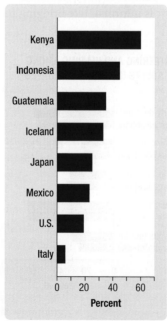

HOW MANY 65-YEAR-OLDS ARE WORKING AROUND THE WORLD?

Kenya
Indonesia
Guatemala
Iceland
Japan
Mexico
U.S.
Italy

Percent (0, 20, 40, 60)

Data from ILOStat Explorer, 2022.

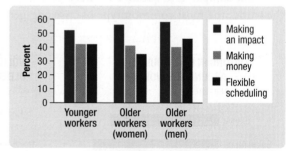

WHAT MOTIVATES OLDER U.S. WORKERS?

Percent (0, 10, 20, 30, 40, 50, 60)

Younger workers · Older workers (women) · Older workers (men)

- Making an impact
- Making money
- Flexible scheduling

Data from Deloitte insights, 2018.

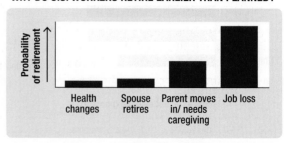

WHY DO U.S. WORKERS RETIRE EARLIER THAN PLANNED?

Probability of retirement

Health changes · Spouse retires · Parent moves in/ needs caregiving · Job loss

Data from Munnell, Rutledge, & Sazenbacher, 2019.

FIGURE 17.5 Work in Late Adulthood Many older U.S. adults are in the workforce in a variety of occupations. They are more likely to work in communities that offer limited social support to older adults. Older workers often have different motivations at work than younger ones. Retirement is often not a choice in the United States and is linked to unemployment.

In the United States, older people have access to social programs like Social Security and Medicaid to help them with their expenses and medical bills. Nevertheless, one in four older U.S. adults and about one in eight in other affluent countries around the world frequently have difficulty making ends meet (Li & Dalaker, 2019; OECD, 2021). Financial need is one reason why many U.S. adults say that they would like to work in later life (Calvo et al., 2018). Economists predict that in the next 20 years, one in three older Americans will be working (Schulte et al., 2018; U.S. Bureau of Labor Statistics, 2021).

In the United States, older adults tend to stay in jobs that either take advantage of their years of expertise or offer a steady paycheck (Pryor, 2017). Many workers who have stable, high-paying jobs continue to work until they are close to 70, and many who are passionate about what they do continue for the rest of their life. As then 93-year-old musician Pablo Casals explained: "I don't believe in retirement. . . . My work is my life" (Casals & Kahn, 1974).

However, for others, work is not about passion. Many adults without highly paid jobs do not have the savings or financial stability that will allow them to have a traditional retirement. Richard Dever is 74 and works cleaning campgrounds for $10 an hour. He explains, "I'm going to work until I die, if I can, because I need the money" (Jordan & Sullivan, 2017).

Adults such as Richard are also more likely to experience health problems and caregiving responsibilities that make it hard to keep full-time work. As a result, they are likely to transition in and out of part-time work for years. They are more likely to be women, adults without college degrees, and people of color (Calvo et al., 2018).

On the Road Richard and Jeannie Dever are doing laundry on their day off, but during the rest of the week they work full time in the tourism industry while living in their RV.

Barriers to Work Ageism, a mismatch in skills, inflexible schedules, unemployment, and growing health complaints keep older adults from finding the work they want (Schulte et al., 2018). Remember from Chapter 14, ageism begins to play a role in employment long before adults are eligible for Social Security: Older workers are less likely to be hired than younger ones (Clark & Ritter, 2020).

Ageism is not the only reason older workers have trouble finding work: They are also more likely to lack skills that employers are looking for, such as technical and computer skills. In many communities, older adults are less likely to have strong reading and writing abilities. Apprenticeships and training programs are designed to help older workers gain the skills they need to find well-paying jobs (OECD, 2018; Paccagnella, 2016).

Jobs also often do not offer the flexibility that adults need to accommodate their health needs and caregiving responsibilities (OECD, 2020; Park et al., 2017; WHO, 2015). Many do not offer part-time or flexible options. Older adults are then forced into less stable, lower-paying jobs, like food service, or even gig work, like driving for Uber.

Many older adults, particularly those without college degrees, had difficulty finding consistent work long before they reached later life (Hale et al., 2021). Workers now in their 60s were middle aged during the 2008 recession, and many had difficulties getting back to work. Older workers were also particularly vulnerable to job loss during the 2020 pandemic and subsequent economic turmoil (Miller, 2020; Settersten et al., 2020). Black and Latino workers are particularly likely to experience unemployment: Black men in their 60s are twice as likely as White men to be unemployed (Guzman & Gladden, 2015).

Many young people hope to retire early (Northwestern Mutual, 2020). However, in the United States and around the world, retiring early is often a sign of disadvantage (Allel et al., 2021). About half of all older adults report that they were forced to retire because of health problems, caregiving responsibilities, or lack of work (Federal Reserve Board, 2020). Early retirement disproportionately affects people who do not have a college education, those who grew up in low-income families, and those, particularly Black

Share It!

The stresses of the pandemic led many older workers to retire earlier than they had planned.

(Fry, 2020)

Scientific American: Lifespan Development

and Latino adults, who have experienced discrimination (Calvo et al., 2018; Gonzales et al., 2021; Lorenti et al., 2020).

Civic Engagement and Volunteering

In the United States and around the world, older adults are more involved in their communities than younger ones (Hansen et al., 2018). In later life, adults put in more hours as volunteers, are more likely to vote, and are more likely to help out informally in their communities than younger adults (Gronke et al., 2020; U.S. Bureau of Labor Statistics, 2021).

Older U.S. adults have great visibility in politics. Elected officials at all levels of government tend to be older than the average worker (U.S. Bureau of Labor Statistics, 2021). Older adults are also more likely to be interested in politics: They spend twice as much time talking about current events as young adults (Pew Research Center, 2018). Mamie-Louise actively keeps up with the news even though it often distresses her, connecting with people online to share her hopes and fears for the future. Before the COVID-19 pandemic, older people were more likely to volunteer for political campaigns and serve as poll workers (Gronke et al., 2020; Pew Research Center, 2018). However, older adults feel excluded from some political activity. For instance, they do not always feel as comfortable as younger people on the front lines of protest movements and are less likely to be involved online (Pew Research Center, 2018; Serrat et al., 2020).

Many volunteer organizations, particularly those run by faith communities, but also those that are connected to hobbies or social service agencies, consist primarily of older adults (Sandstrom & Alper, 2019). People often return to their religious roots in later life to do service and find new connections when they have experienced a major life change, such as retirement or the loss of a spouse (Lancee & Radl, 2014; Silverstein & Bengston, 2018).

The most common form of civic participation is something that most adults may not even think of as being service at all: the informal help that friends and neighbors give each other (Burr et al., 2018). When surveyed by researchers, older adults reported that they were helping someone on 9 out of the past 10 days (Chi et al., 2021). Even during the recent COVID-19 pandemic, older adults gave more of their time to others than younger adults (Sin et al., 2021).

Benefits of Prosocial Engagement Being kind and helping others tend to make people feel good in the moment (Sin et al., 2021). This is because being prosocial releases a pleasurable hormonal and emotional rush (Park et al., 2017). These benefits are not just momentary: Developmental scientists have found numerous long-term benefits for adults who are engaged in the community. Researchers have even suggested that volunteering slows physical aging, lowers risk of developing a neurocognitive disorder, and keeps cognitive functioning intact (Carr et al., 2018; Griep et al., 2017; Proulx et al., 2018). Volunteering also protects and builds mental health, reducing the risk of depression and loneliness (Carr et al., 2018; Creaven et al., 2018).

Until they did randomized studies, researchers were unsure if volunteering actually caused these improvements in health or if they had confused correlation with causation (Creaven et al., 2018). Volunteers are unlike other older adults in many ways: They are more likely to be wealthy, highly educated, and healthy before they start helping (Litwin & Shiovitz Ezra, 2011; Sandstrom & Alper, 2019). Likewise, those who are inclined to contribute their time and know how to find volunteer opportunities typically already have social connections. Volunteering is a habit that starts early: People who volunteered in adolescence and early adulthood are most likely to continue later in life (Lancee & Radl, 2014).

Community and Service over a Lifetime For some adults, like these members of the Alpha Kappa Alpha sorority from Knoxville College in Tennessee, service and community have been part of their lives for decades.

Catie McMekin/News Sentinel/USA TODAY NETWORK

There is some extra benefit to volunteering: The positive effects that come from social connection (Creaven et al., 2018). As with having a large friend group, a job, or a hobby, positive social relationships make volunteering powerful.

Other researchers were interested in some of the ways volunteering benefits aging people who are less advantaged. For low-income adults, volunteer opportunities are difficult to come by. Many are too busy trying to earn a living or caring for ailing family members (Park & Morrow Howell, 2020). But researchers have found that the boost of generativity that volunteers experience—the feeling of being a good person and of belonging—can dramatically improve the lives of older adults, no matter what their background (Seeman et al., 2020).

In one successful program, Experience Corps, older adults, many of them low income, tutor elementary school children two to three days a week for two years. One innovation of this program is that it pays participants a small stipend for helping, typically a few hundred dollars a month (McBride et al., 2011). The money is enough to cover transportation costs, and, according to many, is part of what enables them to participate. Experience Corps has opened the door to volunteering for many who would otherwise have been unable to benefit from it.

Randomized control trials have shown that participating in the program develops older adults' feelings of generativity along with their executive function skills and memory. As you can see in **Figure 17.6**, scientists even demonstrated that participation in the program led to brain growth in areas of the brain associated with executive function (Brydges et al., 2020; Carlson et al., 2009; Glass et al., 2004).

The program has been an admirable success for both children and their tutors. The children's academic skills get stronger, as does their ability to follow the rules in school. Volunteers also benefit. As one woman from the San Francisco area explained: "Experience Corps does more for me than anyone else. . . . My self-esteem soars. I'm doing something beneficial to the students which, in turn, benefits everyone" (Great Non Profits, 2013).

Finding Her Voice Like many adults, Paula experienced many transitions: ending her marriage, losing her parents, and moving away from longtime friends. She joined a church near her home in Los Angeles to find social connections and share her voice.

Gains All Around

Participating in volunteer work, like Experience Corps, has been shown to help adults build executive functioning skills and a sense of accomplishment. For Loretta Martin, who spent time tutoring first graders including Monae, near her home in Cleveland, Ohio, it gave her a sense that she was making a difference.

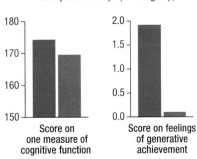

Gains in a Sense of Generativity and Executive Function

■ Adults who participated in Experience Corps

■ Adults who did not participate in Experience Corps (control group)

Score on one measure of cognitive function

Score on feelings of generative achievement

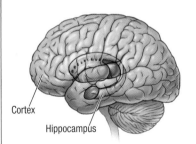

Boosting Brain Function

Cortex

Hippocampus

While older adults' brains tend to shrink over time, an experimental study of adults who participated in Experience Corps demonstrated that their cortex and their hippocampus, a region of the brain linked to memory, stopped shrinking during the program.

Data from Carlson et al., 2008; Gruenewald et al., 2015; New Jersey Herald, 2010.

FIGURE 17.6 The Benefits of Experience Corps Researchers studied Experience Corps to demonstrate that participants benefited from the program. Anecdotal reports often explained that adults (and children) appreciated the program, but large-scale studies over time also demonstrated that adults' scores on tests of cognitive function and generativity also increased. MRI scans showed that the rate of shrinkage in the brain, particularly in the cortex and the hippocampus, slowed in adults who participated in the program.

APPLY IT!   **17.5** Has serving others been part of your life experience or is it something you look forward to in later life? How does serving the broader community help older adults (and others) feel a sense of generativity?

Giving and Receiving Care

The longer you live, the more likely it is that you will need some help (Wolff & Jacobs, 2015). In late adulthood, older adults are often giving care to their own parents and to their partners, and as they get older, they frequently need caretaking themselves. By the time most U.S. adults are in their 80s, more than half need some assistance (Freedman & Spillman, 2014).

Many adults dread the idea of needing help: More than half of all Americans tell researchers they would rather die than be in a nursing home and do not want to live long enough to burden their families (Pew, 2013). At the same time, most avoid thinking about what will happen to them as they get older. The mindset for most is a mix of denial and optimism (Kahana et al., 2020). Most people tend to look on the bright side as they age, but when it comes to planning for the future, they prefer not to think about what they will do if they need help (Gould et al., 2017).

What Is Quality Caregiving?

Adult caregiving is often invisible and undervalued, both to those who need care and to those who are providing it (Zarit et al., 2019; Zwar et al., 2021). Caregivers often do not know how to talk about what they do: Many family caregivers are even unaware that what they are doing every day is called caregiving (Benton & Meyer, 2019). Professional caregivers often feel degraded and overlooked (Chung, 2013; Kusmaul & Bunting, 2017).

One part of caregiving is hands-on care. More than 9 in 10 adults who require caregiving need physical help, like assistance with their *IADLs (instrumental activities of daily living)*, which, as you may remember from Chapter 16, include getting to doctor's appointments or going grocery shopping. Nearly all adults who need help have complications with mobility: They have trouble getting out of bed and getting dressed (NAC & AARP, 2020). Nearly one in four also has a neurocognitive disorder or mental illness, like Alzheimer disease or severe depression (NAC & AARP, 2020).

High-quality caregiving involves much more than just ensuring that adults get the physical assistance they need. Caregiving should help older people compensate for their limitations *and* meet their physical, cognitive, social, and emotional needs (Tesch-Römer & Wahl, 2017). Quality care is often termed *person-centered*, meaning that it allows you to maintain your autonomy, make decisions about what you do every day and how you do it, and keep some purpose in your life (Fazio et al., 2018; Kogan et al., 2016).

Many older adults are afraid that needing help will strip them of their ability to make decisions and turn them into "children" (Buch, 2018). But with quality care, older adults who need support can maintain their relationships, continue to grow, and contribute and stay connected to their community (WHO, 2015). Culture is an essential part of care: Adults need to be helped in a way that respects their language, their traditions, and their customs (Feinberg, 2014).

Consider one research team's story of one man's successful adaptation to person-centered care. Frank spent his career playing music in nightclubs: He was used to staying up late and sleeping in. In later life, he developed a neurocognitive disorder and needed the extra support he found in a residential facility. In the facility, he played music until late in the night, just as he was used to, and he slept in every morning.

TABLE 17.1 What Does Quality Care Look Like in Later Life?

Understand individual needs.
People are more than their diagnoses or health conditions. Care should reflect the needs of a whole person with cultural values and history. Adults' social, emotional, cognitive, and spiritual needs should all be accounted for.
Build caring relationships.
Relationships need to be supportive and respectful: focused on "caring with" rather than "caring for." Care providers need to work as a team, including family, friends, and health care workers.
Support social engagement.
Adults benefit from interactions and experiences to participate in the community, create a sense of meaning and purpose from being with others. Building a community allows for a sense of belonging and connection.
Support autonomy.
Adults need opportunities for choice, independence, and self-direction, including the ability to choose the type of care that they receive.

When he wanted to, he entertained other residents by playing the piano in a common area. Frank had limitations. Yet he was able to retain meaning in his life and enjoyed his late nights and music until the end of his days (Fazio et al., 2018; Gaugler et al., 2014).

As Frank's experience demonstrates, quality caregiving is rooted in accepting, empathetic relationships between older adults and care providers. These positive relationships help adults feel happier and live longer: When care providers are too stressed, depressed, or are experiencing *burnout*, older adults are likely to become sick (see **Table 17.1**) (Lwi et al., 2017; Schulz et al., 2020; White et al., 2020).

A Facility That Feels Like Home Liz (*center*) is playing bingo with the director, Toni Davis (*right*), of the small caregiving facility in New Jersey, known as a Green Home, where she lives.

Varieties of Caregiving

Around the world, caregiving in late adulthood is often shared between informal caregivers, like family members, and formal caregivers, like *home health aides*, who are paid to look after older adults. But as with so much in late adulthood, diversity is standard (see **Figure 17.7**). In the United States, two in three older adults who need help rely solely on their close family or friends (Freedman & Spillman, 2014; Shiu et al., 2016). About one in four adults lives at home and receives some paid help. A small group (only about 2 in 10 adults who need help), receives caregiving outside their home in a **long-term-care facility** (CBO, 2013). Such facilities include a variety of residential care institutions, including nursing homes, skilled nursing facilities, assisted living facilities, and group homes.

Family Caregivers Most adults worldwide prefer to be cared for in their own homes (Kasper et al., 2019). This responsibility often falls first on romantic partners and next on children (Mendez-Luck et al., 2016; Wolff et al., 2016). For those without biological family members, particularly common among LGBTQIA+ older adults, friends often step in to provide care in later life (Shiu et al., 2016).

Around the world, the job of caring for aging adults traditionally fell on daughters (Nishi et al., 2010). However, as families become more affluent, multigenerational households are less common. As a result, older adults increasingly rely on their partners, rather than their children, for care (Jang et al., 2012). This has also led to a gender transition in who provides care in later life: While daughters still take on much of the care of their parents, men are increasingly likely to care for their partners. In the United States, 45 percent of those who take care of their partners are men (Wolff et al., 2016).

long-term-care facility Institutions including nursing homes, rehabilitation facilities that provide treatment and skilled nursing care.

CAREGIVING SITUATIONS IN THE UNITED STATES

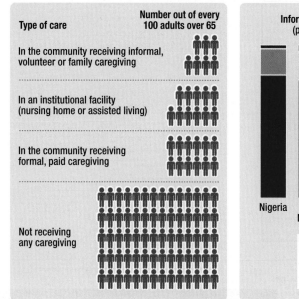

Type of care	Number out of every 100 adults over 65
In the community receiving informal, volunteer or family caregiving	
In an institutional facility (nursing home or assisted living)	
In the community receiving formal, paid caregiving	
Not receiving any caregiving	

Data from Wolff et al., 2018.

VARIATIONS IN CAREGIVING AROUND THE WORLD

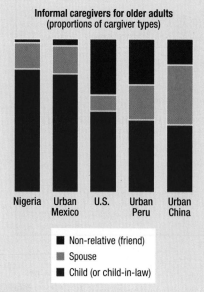

Informal caregivers for older adults
(proportions of cargiver types)

Nigeria   Urban Mexico   U.S.   Urban Peru   Urban China

- ■ Non-relative (friend)
- ■ Spouse
- ■ Child (or child-in-law)

Data from: China, Peru, Nigeria and Mexico from Mayston et al., 2017;
Data from Wolff et al., 2018.

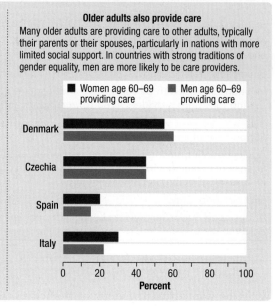

Older adults also provide care
Many older adults are providing care to other adults, typically their parents or their spouses, particularly in nations with more limited social support. In countries with strong traditions of gender equality, men are more likely to be care providers.

- ■ Women age 60–69 providing care
- ■ Men age 60–69 providing care

Denmark

Czechia

Spain

Italy

0   20   40   60   80   100
Percent

Data from WHO / Europe 2018 based on data from SHARE (wave 6).

WHAT IS THE IDEAL CAREGIVING SITUATION IN LATE ADULTHOOD?

Proportions of caregiving preference

Germany   Italy   U.S.

- ■ Stay in own home with help from family or paid help
- ■ Move into an institution (nursing home or assisted living)
- ■ Move in with family

Data from Germany & Italy Pew Research Center, 2015; U.S. from Kasper et al., 2019.

INFORMAL CAREGIVER LEVEL OF STRAIN

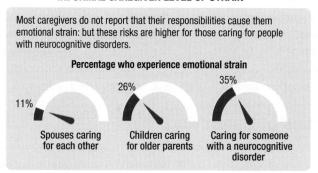

Most caregivers do not report that their responsibilities cause them emotional strain: but these risks are higher for those caring for people with neurocognitive disorders.

Percentage who experience emotional strain

11% — Spouses caring for each other
26% — Children caring for older parents
35% — Caring for someone with a neurocognitive disorder

Data from Wolff et al., 2018.

FIGURE 17.7 Caregiving in Late Adulthood Older adults are often receiving and giving support in late adulthood. Who gives and receives care often depends on the cultural traditions and financial supports available in a community.

Family caregiving takes many forms. For some, it is short term, such as needing an extra set of hands during chemotherapy or while recovering from a stroke. But many older adults need consistent, long-term care. On average, older people who need family caregiving require more than 20 hours a week for about four years (AARP, 2020; Schulz et al., 2020). Many older adults continue to be supported by their families even if they are living in a long-term-care facility (Wu et al., 2020). Restrictions during the COVID-19 pandemic made many of these visits impossible and are attributed by researchers to at least 23,000 additional deaths of older adults in 2020 (Cronin & Evans, 2020).

About one in five older adults takes care of another older person, typically a partner (Anderson et al., 2013). This transition from being life partners to caring for one another can be difficult (Meyer & Benton, 2018): Romantic partners must manage the grief that comes from watching their partner struggle and knowing they may never get better (Monin et al., 2017; Schulz et al., 2020). But over time, many couples learn to adjust to and cope with their new roles (Thai et al., 2016). For adults who are buoyed by a sense of purpose, and who are not financially or physically overburdened, caring for a partner in later life can be a positive experience (AARP, 2020; Grossman & Webb, 2016; Polenick et al., 2019).

As Allan, who retired to take care of his wife, explained "I'm quite happy doing it . . . she deserves it" (qtd in. Breheny et al., 2020).

Despite the commitment of many older adults to take care of their life partners in sickness and in health, many struggle with the demands, and the mental and physical health of both partners suffer (Pinquart & Sörensen, 2011). Caring for a partner who has a neurocognitive disorder is particularly hard (Wolff et al., 2016).

About one in three older adults must rely on their children for help. Children often feel responsible for taking care of their parents, even at the expense of their own finances, families, and health. Erika, for instance, quit her job to care for her mother, explaining she felt she had little choice because "family comes first" (qtd. in Mendez-Luck et al., 2016). Adults who rely on their children for care tend to be much sicker than those whose partners care for them. They are more likely to have a neurocognitive disorder, to be older, and to need more intensive help (Wolff et al., 2016).

Teaming Up with Friends One way of finding support in late adulthood is to get a roommate. Carolyn (*left*) and Marcia share the rent and some of the challenges of getting older in their two-bedroom apartment in Brooklyn, New York.

Cultural Variations in Family Caregiving Families around the world step in to help aging adults, but their motivations often depend on their culture (Fingerman et al., 2011). In the United States, families from a wide variety of cultural backgrounds, including Black, Latino, and Asian American families, share a belief that the younger generation should support and even sacrifice to take care of their older adults (Choi et al., 2018; Guo et al., 2019; Mendez-Luck et al., 2016; Richardson et al., 2019). Researchers sometimes attribute these strong ties to *familism*, or the sense that family is "in it together," or to *filial obligation*, the responsibility of the children for their aging parents and grandparents (Guo et al., 2019; Maldonado, 2017). Many of these children explain that they had little choice but to take care of their aging relatives: Allowing your parent to be placed in a nursing home, or to be cared for by a paid professional, often is unthinkable (Guo et al., 2019; Richardson et al., 2019).

Research suggests that White families tend to be more comfortable seeking professional help for their aging family members, and to see hands-on care as something you do if you cannot afford paid care, rather than as a moral imperative (Fingerman et al., 2011; Grossman & Webb, 2016; Miyawaki, 2016). Compared to Black and Latino caregivers, White family caregivers tend to have less social support, which may increase their level of stress and decrease the likelihood of a positive experience (Fabius et al., 2020; Moon et al., 2020).

A Space to Pray Culturally sensitive care can accommodate adults' spiritual needs. This residential facility in Germany includes a mosque so that residents like Dudu Erdogan (*right*) can worship.

Formal Caregiving Formal caregiving in later life can take many forms. In the United States, formal caregiving is not typically considered a health benefit and is not usually covered by health insurance or *Medicare*, the federal health insurance program that covers older and disabled Americans. Most health insurance plans, including Medicare, only cover short-term skilled nursing care, like time in a rehabilitation facility after a hospital stay. Some lower-income older adults may be eligible for financial help with formal caregiving through their states, or through federal Medicaid or Veterans Affairs programs.

Home health aides are also known as direct care workers, personal care attendants, or nurse's assistants (Reckrey et al., 2019). They are likely to be women, and more than half are people of color (D'astous et al., 2019; Travers et al., 2020). As is true for family caregivers, paid home care is challenging work: physically exhausting, emotionally draining, and often poorly paid (Kim, 2020). Like family caregivers, home health aides must manage and connect emotionally to clients in order to support them "like family" (Reckrey et al., 2019).

In some communities, families also have access to *adult day centers*, community-based organizations that provide social services and supervision, and sometimes access to skilled

Applying the Golden Rule Home health aide Barbara Ullman helps support Lillath, who has been diagnosed with Alzheimer disease, at her home. Lillath lives with her daughter, Ellen (*left*), but also benefits from Barbara's care five days a week. Barbara explains that she cares for Lillath as she would want to be cared for herself.

nursing and social work care (Harris-Kojetin et al., 2019). These centers can serve as a form of respite care for families who care for their loved ones at home, allowing them to work or get some rest. Adult day centers have shown some promise in reducing strain on caregivers as well as improving well-being for older adults (Zarit et al., 2019).

Residential long-term care provides hands-on care to older adults in an institution. In the United States, there are a variety of options. A *group home* typically provides meals and housekeeping assistance for those who may not be able to manage these tasks. *Assisted living communities* consist of private apartments and typically offer meals and community activities and, sometimes, nursing services or home care. *Nursing homes*, or skilled nursing facilities, offer more intensive hands-on care and, often, physical therapy or rehabilitation services. Retirement communities, public housing for older adults, and continuing care communities also usually provide various levels of care in one place.

Violence, Abuse, and Neglect

Around the world, experts believe that about 1 in 10 older adults has been mistreated (Pillemer et al., 2021). Experts still use the somewhat outdated term **elder abuse** to refer to any harmful actions that older adults experience within a close relationship (Bonnie et al., 2003; Pilemer et al., 2016). Elder abuse can take any of a number of forms: financial exploitation, psychological or emotional abuse, physical abuse, and sexual abuse.

The term **elder neglect** describes what happens when a caregiver fails to protect an older adult from harm (Bonnie et al., 2003). Neglect may occur when an older adult is not fed enough, or develops pressure ulcers from lying in one position for too long. Sometimes neglect is purposeful, but sometimes it arises when caregivers are overwhelmed or do not know what to do (DeLiema et al., 2016).

Abuse and neglect frequently happen when strains pile up (Weissberger et al., 2020). Older adults' risk is proportional to the severity of their disabilities: Adults with major neurocognitive disorders face two or three times the rate of abuse. People who hurt their family members likely have their own emotional challenges, from depression to substance abuse, and are often financially dependent on the person they are hurting (Pillemer et al., 2016).

Barriers to Quality Care

Caregiving is challenging, particularly when adults have more complex and demanding health conditions, such as Alzheimer disease. Providers are often tasked with meeting a wide variety of medical, social, and emotional needs, from catheter care and injections to ensuring that older adults have companionship and a way to pass the time (AARP, 2019; Reckrey et al., 2019). Older adults are not always easy to work with, particularly if they are experiencing cognitive or emotional difficulties: About one in three has physically or verbally attacked a family member (Isham et al., 2019). Professional care providers may also endure aggression, racist language, and verbal bullying: At least one in six has faced some sort of client abuse (Lachs et al., 2013; Ryosho, 2011; Travers et al., 2020).

Caregivers are often not given the support or training they need to do their jobs: As a result, many have difficulty providing the best care. There are disparities in risk, as well as empirically supported interventions that are designed to help improve the lives of older adults who need support.

Family Caregiving Stress Many older people assume that being helped at home means they will have the highest quality of care, but researchers have found that this is not always true. Family caregivers are often so stressed that they are unable to provide good care. In the United States, one in four older adults who is being cared for by

elder abuse When an older adult is harmed emotionally, physically, sexually or financially, by a loved one.

elder neglect When a caregiver fails to protect an older adult from harm.

their families has reported that they have been yelled at by their caregiver, and one in three older adults with complex needs, like those related to Alzheimer disease, has reported that they have been neglected (Beach et al., 2019; Schulz et al., 2020). This is not unique to the United States: Around the world, families are often unable to give older adults the care they need (Feng et al., 2020; Lwi et al., 2017).

Caregivers are often overwhelmed by their responsibilities. Providing care can lead to constant worry that is often unrecognized and unsupported (Breheny et al., 2020). As one caregiver explained: "We're taken advantage of, or we're part of the furniture" (qtd. in Mendez-Luck et al., 2016). It is unsurprising that many caregivers' emotional and physical health begin to show negative effects: Their immune systems and stress responses go on alert (Lovell & Wetherell, 2011). One in three caregivers has had a health setback as a result of helping out, and nearly half are clinically depressed (Gilhooly et al., 2016; Kohl et al., 2019). Caregivers who are unable to take care of themselves are less likely to give quality care to their families (Caceres et al., 2016; Lovell & Wetherell, 2011). The COVID-19 pandemic was a particular low point for caregivers: More than 7 in 10 reported having significant difficulties with their mental health, particularly if they felt they had no one to turn to for support (Czeisler et al., 2021).

The burdens of caregiving are frequently compounded by financial worry, causing time constraints and making it difficult to get help (AARP, 2019; Committee on Family Caregiving for Older Adults, 2016). Neurocognitive disorders, like Alzheimer disease, make caregiving harder (Cheng, 2017; Chiao et al., 2015).

Programs that help caregivers manage this strain often focus on boosting individual resilience. Interventions that emphasize exercise, support groups, mindfulness, or professional support services have all been shown to help improve the health of caregivers and of the people they care for (Cheng et al., 2019; Gilhooly et al., 2016; Liu et al., 2017; Puterman et al., 2018; Tang & Chan, 2016). For some families, particularly those who are Latino or African American, spiritual or religious support helps boost their ability to manage (AARP, 2019). As one woman who was taking care of her partner explained, "I don't know what people would do who don't have faith" (Richardson et al., 2019).

Structural solutions for alleviating caregiver strain include paying family members to care for family, providing paid family leave, and offering short-term respite care to give them a break. A patchwork of these policies has been implemented in some communities in the United States (Committee on Family Caregiving for Older Adults, 2016; Gkiouleka et al., 2018).

Challenges with Long-Term Care In the United States and around the globe, it is often difficult for long-term-care facilities to provide person-centered, high-quality care: Facilities are often understaffed, and the workers who provide direct care are often overburdened and underpaid (Feng et al., 2020; Song et al., 2020; Yuan et al., 2018). More than 8 in 10 facilities are actively trying to change their culture to provide higher-quality, more personalized care, but the process is challenging (Miller et al., 2018).

In long-term-care facilities, quality of care depends on people, and in such facilities, direct-care workers are often rushed and emotionally drained. Care providers may have to attend to as many as 15 adults on a shift: getting each one out of bed, dressed, and fed (Song et al., 2020; Travers et al., 2020). Rushing often means that aides are less sensitive than they might want to be: They avoid building social relationships, taking residents for walks, and talking (Song et al., 2020). Strapped for time and energy, aides often focus more on making sure that adults are clean and safe and less on the emotional connections that might benefit both the clients and aides alike (Chung, 2013).

Aides themselves often feel undervalued, enduring constant grief as they cope with their clients' deterioration and death (Chung, 2013; Kusmaul & Bunting, 2017; Ryosho, 2011). While many direct-care workers are driven to help others, they often cannot avoid experiencing burnout and emotional exhaustion (Cooper et al., 2016). To address these problems, developmental scientists are working to develop higher-quality, and often smaller, long-term-care systems. Emi Kiyota is one such scientist: She hopes that older adults, and those who care for them, will develop stronger relationships and feel valued and appreciated.

SCIENCE IN PRACTICE
Emi Kiyota, Environmental Gerontologist

Photo by Alex Kornhuber; Courtesy Emi Kiyota

As a young woman, Emi Kiyota visited her grandmother in the Japanese nursing home she had moved into after developing a neurocognitive disorder (Ibasho, 2021). The workers who cared for her grandmother were highly educated and had college degrees in caregiving, but they operated efficiently and coldly. Instead of seeing their clients as people, they seemed to see them as a job to be done. As Kiyota remembered, "I could see that my grandmother and most of the other patients were just existing there; they had no purpose, they were just waiting for release" (Miller, 2017). The visit changed her life: Kiyota dedicated herself to building better facilities for older adults.

Kiyota had trained in architecture and could see how the physical space of a nursing home was limiting. Nursing homes were not actually homes: They bore little resemblance to real life and afforded the residents little control over what they did each day. People felt marginalized and isolated even though they lived with hundreds of other people. Kiyota saw this for herself when she spent three weeks as a nursing home resident as part of her training. She still has not forgotten how difficult it is to have someone else brush her teeth (Miller, 2017).

Kiyota has now helped to build dozens of small, person-centered residential and social facilities in the United States, Nepal, the Philippines, and Japan (Galiana & Haseltine, 2019; Ibasho, 2021). She calls these facilities *Ibasho*, a Japanese word referring to a place where you feel comfortable and at home. Her programs are not just *for* older people; they are also *by* older people. These communities enable them to share their ideas and be part of the leadership of their community, rather than only being taken care of by others. Smaller programs like her Ibasho have shown promise in helping adults maintain their quality of life (Kok et al., 2018).

Working with Emi Kiyota (center) is working to design more inclusive and equitable communities that integrate older adults and make them active participants and leaders in their own lives.

Disparities in Care As with health care and education, there have long been disparities in the quality of care that older adults receive (Berridge & Mor, 2018; Cohen et al., 2017). How well older adults are cared for often depends on their income and their cultural identity (Chang et al., 2020; Kilaru & Gee, 2020). In the past, affluent U.S. adults hired private nurses to care for them at home as they aged (Buhler-Wilkerson, 2003). Lower-income adults did not have the same option: If there were no family members who could take care of them at home, they might be abandoned to unsanitary and crowded poor houses (Achenbaum, 1978; Denham, 2016).

Today, affluent adults are most likely to have access to the highest quality care. In the United States, for instance, high-income adults who have neurocognitive disorders are more likely to get professional caregiving at home and to live in a residential nursing facility (Mather & Scommegna, 2020). Researchers have suggested that expert care is one reason why these older adults have less depression, pain, and suffering in later life (McGiffin et al., 2019; Silveira et al., 2005; Smith et al., 2005).

In the United States, governmental supports are often not enough to help low-income families pay for professional home caregiving (Muir, 2017). Only a few nations, like Sweden, Iceland, and the Netherlands, provide a comprehensive system of caregiving for older people, making sure that all adults have the same access to professional care (OECD, 2017). The quality of care that older U.S. adults receive in long-term-care facilities often relates to where they live, what they can afford, and even what ethnicity they are (Miller et al., 2018; Yuan et al., 2018).

The quality of caregiving in the United States also varies by culture and gender identity. For instance, most U.S. nursing homes are informally segregated: Many serve primarily older adults of color, while the rest serve predominantly White adults. The care that is provided in institutions that serve older people of color are more likely to be underfunded and of poor quality: Residents in these institutions are more likely to endure untreated pain and bed sores (Chisholm et al., 2013; Li et al., 2015; Mor et al., 2004).

Quality residential caregiving is also often hard to find for older adults who do not speak English or who are lesbian, gay, or transgender. These adults may have trouble building new relationships in nursing homes and may face stigma (Caceres et al., 2020; Richardson et al., 2019).

While Black older adults may have difficulty finding quality institutional care, researchers have found that they benefit when they are cared for by family members at home (Berridge & Mor, 2018; Fabius et al., 2020; Liu et al., 2020). Black family caregivers are more likely to have training than other caregivers, more likely to appreciate their tasks, and less likely to be depressed (Burgdorf et al., 2019; Cohen et al., 2017; Fabius et al., 2020; Liu et al., 2020). Researchers suspect that this resilience protects older adults: Their caregivers are more likely to have a realistic idea of what caregiving entails, and to have more support from their family and their faith communities (Berridge & Mor, 2018; Fabius et al., 2020; Grossman & Webb, 2016).

APPLY IT! **17.6** Caregiving happens across the lifespan. What characteristics of high-quality care are shared by people providing care to infants or toddlers (see Chapters 5 or 7) or their own children (see Chapters 10 and 15)?

17.7 Mamie-Louise remarks that health becomes increasingly important as you grow older: often determining how you can do the hands-on work of caring for others. Caregiving is not always physical: What are the emotional and social aspects of caregiving in later life?

Emotional Resilience and Support

"Don't be afraid," Mamie-Louise says when we ask her for advice about getting older. "I have more opportunities to find out what really delights me, how to make myself happy and to understand how quickly things can change."

Mamie-Louise's experience of growth in emotional stability and self-awareness in later life is fortunate but not unusual. Late adulthood, like other times in the lifespan, can be a time of change and growth: Some researchers even find that there is more personality change during later life than at any other point since a person's 20s (Costa et al., 2019; Kandler et al., 2020; Staudinger & Kunzmann, 2005). This flexibility helps many older adults through the transitions and challenges that are common in later life. Many older adults have a reservoir of emotional strengths that can help them weather some of the inevitable stresses of late adulthood. For many, it is possible to be optimistic about life after 65 (Berglund et al., 2016; Puvill et al., 2016).

Learning Objective

17.5 Identify major risks to emotional health and three ways of building resilience.

Barriers to Emotional Health

With later life comes new vulnerabilities. An aging brain and social stresses like financial strain, grief, and social isolation often lead older adults to become less satisfied with their lives. An increasing number of older adults are diagnosed with emotional disorders (Gana et al., 2016; Puvill et al., 2016). Because physical health is closely tied to emotional health, older adults are more vulnerable to the effects of mental illness than younger people (see **Table 17.2**). Unfortunately, many older people die by suicide (Conejero et al., 2018; Faye et al., 2018).

The Impact of Brain Aging Biological developments may help to explain some of the strengths and the vulnerabilities of older adults' emotion regulation (Charles & Carstensen, 2010). Remember from Chapter 16, adults are *more* vulnerable to stress as

SOURCES OF STRESS

Financial insecurity

Many older U.S. adults have some financial support from Social Security and health care coverage under Medicare. This is not always enough to make ends meet, particularly for populations that have faced discrimination.

◄ Poverty rates

Men, age 85+
Women, age 85+
Black, age 65+
Native American, age 65+
Hmong, age 65+
Latino, age 65+
LGBT men, age 65+
LGBT women, age 65+

0 10 20 30
Percent

Around the world, how many adults are not at all confident that they have enough money to support themselves? ▼

China
Brazil
Nigeria
U.S.
South Korea
Italy
Russia

0 50 100
Percent

Worries about aging

Adults report having various worries and anxieties about aging. ▼

Not having enough money
Losing memory
Losing friends and family through death
Losing mobility
Being in pain

0 2 4 6 8 10
Percent

Worries about aging depend on cultural expectations.

How many adults are worried about aging around the world? ▼

South Korea
Saudi Arabia
South Africa
U.S.
Italy
Russia
China

0 20 40 60 80
Percent

Central diagram

Environment, pollution

Violence, discrimination, oppression

Adaptive culture

Technology, infrastructure

Family, friends

Individual health

Social position (global and local)

©Macmillan, Photo by Sidford House

TECHNOLOGY

How many U.S. adults ► (age 65+) have access to technology?

80% Computer access

73% Broadband internet access

62% Smartphone access

HEALTH

Most adults feel that they are in good health, even though more report chronic health conditions.

■ Report good health
■ Have some level of disability

100%
50%
0

Age 49–64   Age 65–74   Age 75+

Functioning means you have a good fit with your environment. With the support available in your community you can:

✓ Meet your basic needs (cook, wash, dress and pay for the support and the food and health care you need)

✓ Learn new things and make decisions about your life

✓ Get around on your own (being mobile, whether that is with mechanical or human support)

✓ Create and build relationships

✓ Contribute to your community, culture and those you care about

With age, more adults have difficulties functioning independently.

Disability rates ▼

Any disability — 19%
Communication difficulties — 8%
Difficulties with self-care — 9%
Visual impairment — 22%
Cognitive difficulties — 27%
Hearing impairment — 31%
Mobility impairment — 40%

SOURCES OF RESILIENCE

Time for leisure

Older adults tend to have more time for leisure: whether that includes socializing or time on screens. Free time tends to increase for U.S. adults as they grow older and spend less time at work.

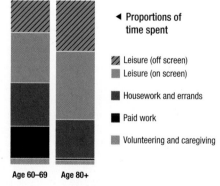

◄ Proportions of time spent

▨ Leisure (off screen)
▢ Leisure (on screen)
■ Housework and errands
■ Paid work
■ Volunteering and caregiving

Age 60–69   Age 80+

Service to others

Older adults are often caregivers, volunteers and give informal help to friends and neighbors. In one a representative sample of adults over age 65, many were involved in serving others.

38% Regularly volunteered

58% Helped neighbors or friends informally

10% Regular caregiver to a spouse or parent

Social connections

Grandparenting can be good for health and wellbeing

Percent of adults report that grandparenting helps with their: ▼

89% Mental wellbeing

67% Social wellbeing

66% Activity level

51% General health

Social support

Communities vary in how they expect older adults to care for themselves.

Who should support older adults? ▼

■ Support themselves
■ Family support
■ Government support

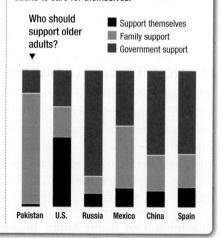

Pakistan   U.S.   Russia   Mexico   China   Spain

TABLE 17.2 Signs of Emotional Distress in Older Adults

Older adults may express emotional distress and depression in different ways than younger adults and may be more reticent about labeling their upset or getting professional support for their difficulties.
Concerning signs: – Thinking life is not worth living, feeling like a burden or feeling weary of living. – Expressing a lack of control over their daily lives and a lack of autonomy in everyday living. – Articulating a sense of uselessness or meaningfulness.
Common risks and stressors: – Grief and caregiver stress. – Social isolation – Chronic pain and other health concerns including cancer, stroke, and lack of sleep. – Substance use. Older adults tend to be more sensitive to alcohol and other substances and may be at higher risk for substance use disorder than younger adults.

they get older (Prenderville et al., 2015; Yiallouris et al., 2019). Changes in the HPA axis make it more difficult for older people to recover from episodes of acute stress that raise their cortisol levels. This might explain why older adults try to avoid stress and tamp down their emotional reactions (Almeida et al., 2020).

Brain development also plays a role in emotion regulation. Remember, the brain shrinks with age, becomes less interconnected, and tends to lose the myelin that makes communication efficient. The emotion-processing centers of the brain, like the amygdala, are largely spared from these changes and actually become *more* connected to the rest of the brain as you age (Mather, 2016).

When observed in an fMRI scanner, people seem to process emotion in the brain differently depending on their age: Younger people show more activation in the subcortical structures, like the amygdala, that are associated with emotion processing, and older people show more activation in their prefrontal cortex, which is associated with conscious thought, memory, and decision making. Some researchers suggest that this association means that older people are using more self-control and tapping into their lifetime of experience when encountering strong emotions, but this interpretation is not definitive (MacCormack et al., 2020).

Cognitive Vulnerability Remember from Chapter 16 that all adults experience some cognitive changes as they age, and many have less efficient executive function (Fjell et al., 2017). These changing cognitive abilities can make it difficult for some adults to manage their feelings and relationships. For instance, weakening cognitive skills may make it difficult for older adults to identify emotional expressions and even know when someone is lying or trying to trick them (Ceccato et al., 2019; Hayes et al., 2020).

Managing your feelings and your interactions with other people requires executive function that may be compromised in later life. This can lead to difficulties with regulating mood and relating to other people (Klimstra et al., 2013). Slowing processing speed, another side effect of cognitive aging, can also make it difficult to be socially engaged. Being outgoing with other people tends to sap cognitive energy, because following a conversation, remembering what someone else said, and knowing how to respond are not always easy (Sutin et al., 2019).

For some, cognitive challenges make it difficult to build and maintain relationships (Kanellopoulos et al., 2020). Adults with cognitive and sensory conditions and neurocognitive diseases are at higher risk for emotional and psychological disorders as they get older (Cerino et al., 2020; Chopik et al., 2020; Mueller et al., 2018; Simning et al., 2019). Nevertheless, the brain remains capable of plasticity and growth (Gheysen et al., 2018).

Social Risks Social and interpersonal factors can also make it difficult for adults to thrive in later life. While most older adults in North America tend to feel less

Looking for Respite Janetta, who lives in Springfield, Missouri, has had difficulty finding a home. More than 300,000 older U.S. adults do not have housing and may need to find a place to rest in the grass, as Janetta does, or in temporary shelters.

stress after 65, this is not universal: Many adults around the world face increased difficulties in later life (Bardo, 2017; Jebb et al., 2020; Lachman et al., 2015; Schwandt, 2016; Steptoe et al., 2015).

Discrimination, ageism, and poverty are leading contributors to poor mental health in later life, wearing older people down emotionally and cognitively (Settersten et al., 2016; Zahodne et al., 2020). Older adults with low income report spending twice as much time every month addressing their mental health as do people with high income, leading to missed opportunities for social interaction, increased anxiety, and problems with accessing treatment (Rehkopf et al., 2019). Older adults with low income or limited physical abilities are particularly likely to be isolated online, with limited opportunities or abilities to connect with other people via Zoom, social media, or e-mail (Seifert et al., 2021).

During late adulthood, difficult relationships and social isolation can also take a toll on emotional health. As adults get older and more physically vulnerable, negative social relationships do more damage (Birditt et al., 2020; Hakulinen et al., 2016). Persistent conflict or rejection damages the immune and cardiovascular systems (Holt-Lunstad & Steptoe, 2022; Liu & Waite, 2014; Rook, 2015). Difficult relationships can trigger depression, insomnia, anxiety, and a narrowing of social ties (Chen et al., 2015; Santini et al., 2015). In other-sex relationships, women tend to be more sensitive to strained relationships (Bulanda, 2011).

Over time, adults may become socially isolated, losing track of friends and family (Bruine de Bruin et al., 2020; Espirito Santo & Daniel, 2018; von Soest et al., 2020). Some researchers have estimated that as many as one in six older adults lacks a support system that can intervene if they need help (Carney et al., 2016; Valerio et al., 2021). Older adults are more likely to be isolated if they are also managing other stresses (Conejero et al., 2018; Litwin & Shiovitz-Ezra, 2011; Nagarajan et al., 2020).

Older adults who have immigrated to the United States are often at risk for social isolation, because they may face a language barrier or miss social connections and family that they left in their birthplace (Gierveld et al., 2015; Jang et al., 2021). Immigrants who connect with other people and find a shared sense of community have lower levels of loneliness and fewer health conditions (Gierveld et al., 2015; Plasencia, 2018).

Being alone and isolated is not always a risk factor, however. For many, like Mamie-Louise, "alone" is not synonymous with "lonely" (Mudrazija et al., 2020). Loneliness, or the feeling of dissatisfaction with your social bonds, tends to ease in later life (Mund et al., 2020). In fact, older adults were less lonely during the enforced social isolation of the pandemic of 2020 than younger adults were. For many older adults, a lifetime of emotional skills and experience allowed them to bounce back from stress (Carstensen et al., 2020). For others, the pandemic created a sense of community and togetherness that helped sustain their mental health (O'Connor et al., 2020).

But when older adults do get lonely, the consequences are more severe: Loneliness is linked to inflammation and hampered immune response (Creswell et al., 2012; Waldinger & Schultz, 2016). Older men are particularly likely to struggle with loneliness: They tend to have fewer social connections and to feel lonely even when they are partnered (Wright et al., 2019).

Psychological Disorders

Scientists estimate that in the last year at least one in six older adults around the world has been diagnosed with an emotional disorder, such as depression, anxiety, or substance use disorder (Faye et al., 2018; Reynolds et al., 2015). (See **Figure 17.8**.) Substance use disorder is an increasing diagnosis among older adults, even though they are less likely to see their use as a problem (Han & Moore, 2018; Lehmann & Fingerhood, 2018; Wu & Blazer, 2014). In many communities, the suicide rate among older adults is nearly twice

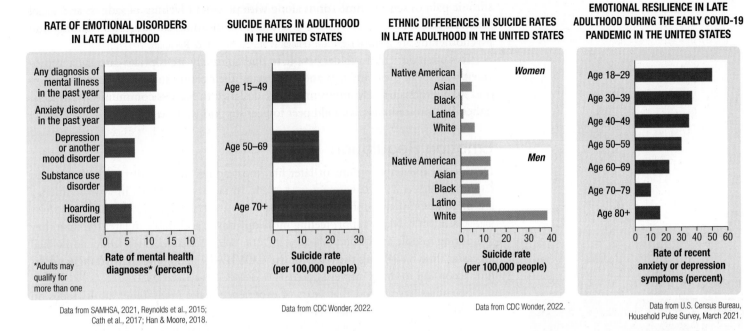

FIGURE 17.8 Mental Health in Late Life Adults of any age can be diagnosed with an emotional disorder. Older adults are less likely to be diagnosed than younger ones but are more likely to take their own lives. Older adults are also more likely to report being resilient in times of stress, like the COVID-19 pandemic.

what it is at other times in the lifespan (Cabello et al., 2020; Curtin et al., 2021). Mental health conditions increase the risk not only of suicide, but also of cardiovascular disease and other chronic conditions (Van Orden & Conwell, 2016; Wei et al., 2020).

These numbers may overlook many adults, whose difficulties may be underdiagnosed (Bor, 2015; Reynolds et al., 2015). Older adults are more likely than younger people to believe that feeling depressed or anxious is a sign of personal failure or an inevitable part of aging (Bor, 2015; Genesight, 2020). Indeed, older people tend to have more stigma about mental illness than younger people do, and to be more reluctant to seek help. This is even more likely for veterans and for Black, Latino, and Asian American older adults (Geller et al., 2017; Lavingia et al., 2020; Sirey et al., 2014).

The rate of suicide among older adults is the highest of the lifespan. Adults often contemplate suicide when they are in physical pain, have a serious illness, or feel socially isolated, particularly if they already experience emotional disorders (Choi et al., 2019; Nguyen et al., 2017; Santos et al., 2020). Older adults benefit from generativity, and feeling like a burden puts them at risk (Pedroso Chaparro et al., 2020; Stanley et al., 2016).

Rates of suicide vary dramatically by culture and by gender (Koo et al., 2017). For instance, White men have a higher risk of dying by suicide as men from other backgrounds, a trend that researchers connect to strong cultural beliefs that White men should be independent and strong (Ali et al., 2019; Conejero et al., 2018; Curtin et al., 2021). Native American older adults are less likely to attempt suicide in later life. Unlike many other groups in the United States, Indigenous communities tend to admire older adults, which may be protective against the discrimination and ageism that are linked to suicide (CDC, 2021; Danyluck et al., 2021).

Researchers have found that experiencing discrimination in everyday life is closely linked to experiencing suicidal thoughts, one reason older Asian American women have twice the rate of suicide as other women (Chu et al., 2020; Kim & Lee, 2020). In one study in Chicago, researchers found that older people who had experienced discrimination were twice as likely to think about suicide as other adults (Li et al., 2017).

Treatments are available that help older adults recover. Researchers recommend addressing physical and emotional disorders and conditions simultaneously, treating

CONNECTIONS

If you know someone who is at risk for suicide, seek out resources in your local community, call the National Suicide Prevention hotline at 1-800-273-TALK (**1-833-456-4566** in Canada), or text "home" to the Crisis Text Line at 741741 (**45645** in Canada).

chronic pain or sensory limitations along with persistent feelings of sadness and social isolation (Kok & Reynolds, 2017; Santos et al., 2020). Medication, mindfulness training, and psychotherapy are also beneficial (Haigh et al., 2018; Kok & Reynolds, 2017).

It is often difficult for older people to find culturally appropriate care, such as providers who speak their language and understand their community (Chu et al., 2019; Lavingia et al., 2020). Promising new interventions are designed to harness community volunteers, rather than professionals, to build peer to peer support (Geffen et al., 2019; Perissinotto, 2019).

Emotion Regulation

Despite the inevitable strains of later life, most adults manage to find meaning and happiness (Burr et al., 2020; Carstensen et al., 2020). In fact, many adults in North America are more emotionally upbeat after 65 (Bardo et al., 2017; Gana et al., 2013; Jebb et al., 2020; Jiménez et al., 2017). Many report feeling more optimistic and stable in later life than they did during middle adulthood (Mueller et al., 2018; Reitz & Staudinger, 2017). Older adults had an easier time navigating the stress of the COVID-19 pandemic than younger adults did, according to many surveys (American Psychological Association, 2021).

Scientists have found that years of experience make many older adults focus on the good things in life, rather than the bad (Burr et al., 2020; Carstensen et al., 2020; Eldesouky & English, 2018; Kennedy et al., 2020; Swirsky & Spaniol, 2019). Researchers call this the *positivity effect*, the finding that many older people tend to be better at remembering positive information than are younger adults, who tend to focus on the negative (Carstensen & DeLiema, 2018; Reed et al., 2014). For example, older adults will tend to remember the great food at a holiday dinner more than the after-dinner political arguments (Kalenzaga et al., 2016; Swirsky & Spaniol, 2019).

Interestingly, the benefits of the positivity effect are actually very slight when measured carefully in a controlled setting (Allard & Kensinger, 2018; Livingstone & Isaacowitz, 2019; Reed et al., 2014). Researchers also believe that being positive may not be culturally universal and that it may actually be unique to North America (Almeida et al., 2020; Gong & Fung, 2020).

Share It!

Is resilience a cohort effect? Some researchers suggest that living through stressful events of the past, like World War II or the Great Depression, might have changed older adults, making them value their social relationships and build their resilience.

(Bühler & Nikitin, 2020)

Scientific American: Lifespan Development

 MAKING A DIFFERENCE

Do You Get Nicer with Age?

Many people around the world assume that older folks are warmer and nicer than others (Burkley et al., 2017; Fiske, 2018). And as you have read, this stereotype does have some basis in fact: Psychologists have found that many older adults, particularly if they are healthy, are more easygoing than other adults (Chopik & Grimm, 2019; Götz et al., 2020; Reitz & Staudinger, 2017; Truxillo et al., 2015). But does being positive mean that older people are actually kinder?

Researchers have found that older people are significantly less likely than younger adults are to be selfish and hurtful. As we age, we tend to grow out of the extremes of selfishness or narcissism (Chopik & Grimm, 2019; Götz et al., 2020). Crime statistics bear this out: Older people are very unlikely to commit violent acts (Turanovic, 2019).

Not only do many researchers suggest that older people are easy to get along with, but also some scientists have found that many older adults do more prosocial activities than younger people do: They are more likely to give to charities and to spend more time volunteering, for instance (Mayr & Freund, 2020). Scientists suggest that older people, aware that their lives will not go on forever, are particularly eager to be generative and giving if they see someone in need (Bailey et al., 2021). In addition, older people get more of an emotional boost than younger people do from giving to others (Bjälkebring et al., 2020; Mayr & Freund, 2020; Sparrow et al., 2021).

But adults' cognitive and emotional development can also create limitations. Their positivity toward others often only includes people they see as like them. If their executive function declines, older adults are more likely to be biased against people they see as different, perhaps those of other ethnic groups or religious communities (Cassidy et al., 2016; Ceccato et al., 2019; Gonsalkorale et al., 2009). In one study, researchers found that older adults from non-Muslim backgrounds were more likely than younger people from non-Muslim backgrounds to be biased against Muslim people (Cassidy et al., 2020). 🌐

Strategies for Building Resilience

Aging comes with loss, requiring adjustments as you grieve for lost loved ones and learn to manage a changing body. Nevertheless, emotional resilience can help older people continue to feel satisfied with their lives (Berglund et al., 2016). Remember, resilience is what helps you bounce back from adversity and buffers the emotional and physical consequences of stress (Kiosses & Sachs-Ericsson, 2020).

Ten years ago, with his life marked by grief and change, Mark Graham did not think resilience was possible as he entered his eighth decade. He had retired from the army at 64 and lost two children much too soon, one to suicide and the other to the war in Iraq. Mark was able to recover by founding a peer-to-peer service organization that connects veterans with other veterans who are willing to share their experiences with mental illness. Now Mark has people with whom he likes to stay busy every day, and he feels that he has something important to live for.

Researchers suggest that Mark's advice exemplifies some of the best ways to build emotional health in later life. Scientists have found that there are three key ways to build resilience:

1. *Build relationships.* Whether you find social support from volunteering, a faith community, or family, late life is a journey best taken with company (Nguyen et al., 2017). Feeling connected to other people even helps the body become better regulated, reducing inflammation and calming the HPA system, which can help us live longer, healthier lives (Seeman et al., 2020; Waldinger & Schultz, 2016; Zueras et al., 2020).
2. *Stay generative.* Feeling useful and engaged in the world, whether that means reading aloud to a friend with vision loss or unloading the dishwasher for your son-in-law, helps keep you healthy (Moieni et al., 2020).
3. *Find something that matters to you.* Having a sense of purpose or meaning can help older adults feel stronger, maintain their memory, and even live longer (Boyle et al., 2021; Kim et al., 2017). No matter where they live in the world, older adults who say that they have a sense of meaning are more likely to feel satisfied and happy with the lives they have (Jebb et al., 2020). There is no right answer to what your life purpose needs to be: It may be a commitment to providing for your family, serving your community, or having an obsessive love of pinball machines (Kim et al., 2013, 2017; Weston et al., 2021).

No matter how hard we try to be resilient, the end of life is inevitable and is something older adults, including Mamie-Louise, cannot ignore. As you will learn, for some, even death itself can be an opportunity to find meaning and connection.

APPLY IT! 17.8 Older adults have many emotional strengths. Mamie-Louise boasts of her serenity, her meditation practice, and her trips to the gym. What practices can build emotional resilience across the lifespan?

Finding Strength Mark Graham (*top*), devoted his life to military service, but after losing his two sons, he began working to destigmatize mental illness. Archie Thompson (*bottom*), shown here at 93, was a welder and high school athlete who also worked to preserve the Yurok language spoken in his indigenous community in Northern California.

Wrapping It Up ⬭

LO 17.1 Explain the major perspectives on social and emotional development in late life. (p. 497)

Major theories of late adulthood observe that adults are happiest when they feel useful and connected. Ageism and stereotypes about disability and aging can make it more difficult for adults to feel they belong and build relationships. Erikson described older adulthood as a conflict between integrity and despair. Erikson's perspective continues to emphasize the importance of *generativity* throughout adulthood. Activity theory suggests that adults are likely to be happier if they stay involved. Disengagement theory which suggested that adults inevitably become withdrawn has been discredited by scholars. The continuity perspective observes that adults' identity remains stable as they age, although older people often need to adapt to changing circumstances.

LO 17.2 Describe the benefits and common challenges to relationships in later life. (p. 500)

In late adulthood, relationships are often in a stage of transition due to death, illness, and divorce. Supportive relationships continue to be a potent source of emotional resilience and health. Most romantic relationships in late adulthood tend to be happier and more emotionally stable. Partnerships can come in a variety of forms. Many older adults support extended families. Friends, neighbors, and acquaintances continue to give adults a sense of social support and belonging, and adults with strong friendships and social contacts tend to maintain their health. Researchers have observed that many adults become more optimistic and emotionally stable as they get older. Carstensen's social selectivity theory suggests that adults tend to prioritize social relationships and getting along as they are forced to confront the finiteness of life.

LO 17.3 Explain how work and civic engagement can benefit older adults and their communities. (p. 507)

Work and formal or informal volunteering and civic engagement helps adults stay connected. For many adults, paid work is a necessity but can become difficult as adults accumulate health conditions. Communities around the world vary in terms of the financial support, work opportunities, and health care they provide older adults. As a result, the timing of retirement is variable. Civic engagement and volunteering tend to be more common in older adults. Volunteering and civic engagement have many benefits to health and emotional well-being but opportunities are limited.

LO 17.4 Describe quality caregiving in later life and common challenges in finding it. (p. 512)

About half of older U.S. adults over age 80 need help with their instrumental activities of daily living (IADLs) and often have difficulties with mobility. Quality caregiving is person-centered and allows older adults the support they need to compensate for their limitations and meet their continuing social, emotional, cognitive, and physical needs. Caregiving is built on responsive, warm relationships and can be provided by family members, paid home health aides, or long-term-care facilities. Culture shapes the expectations and rewards family members bring to caregiving. Caregiving can be difficult for formal and family caregivers, and many do not receive the support or training they need. Disparities in caregiving based on the financial resources of older adults lead to disparities in health and well-being.

LO 17.5 Identify major risks to emotional health and three ways of building resilience. (p. 519)

Older adults tend to be more emotionally stable and emotionally optimistic than younger adults but this is not universal. Older adulthood can include many stresses including an aging brain, grief, and social isolation. Brain development may make it easier for some adults to control their strong feelings. Cognitive changes including reductions in executive function may make it more difficult for other adults to interact socially. Ageism, strained relationships and social isolation contribute to emotional disorders. Suicide is higher in late adulthood than in other life stages. Resilience can be created through stronger relationships, a feeling of generativity and purpose.

KEY TERMS

integrity and despair (p. 499)

activity theory (p. 499)

disengagement theory (p. 499)

continuity perspective (p. 500)

age in place (p. 506)

long-term-care facility (p. 513)

elder abuse (p. 516)

elder neglect (p. 516)

CHECK YOUR LEARNING

1. Which of the following reflects a positive adaptation to Erikson's stage of *integration versus despair*?
   a) Linda looks back on her life and sees only the mistakes: She did not take good enough care of herself and she is still disappointed that she remains estranged from her own mother.
   b) Charlie avoids thinking about the past: He is focused on moving forward.
   c) Tammy can see that there have been good times and bad in her past: She was never perfect and faced some unexpected misfortunes, but she can also remember that there were many times of joy.
   d) Gene can see nothing but sunshine as he thinks back over his life: He is just grateful that he has made it to 80.

2. What is one reason that scientists have rejected disengagement theory?
   a) Older adults are more likely than younger ones to break off engagements.
   b) Older adults are more likely to be happy and healthy if they are involved and connected with their community.
   c) Disengagement happens across the lifespan.
   d) Older adults who were disengaged turned out to be so happy they broke world records.

3. Mamie~Louise is not in a romantic relationship but is surrounded by many supportive friendships and family bonds. What are some characteristics of strong relationships in later life?
   a) Relationships boost resilience and physical health.
   b) Supportive relationships are draining in later life.
   c) Strong relationships are only available to the affluent.
   d) Strong relationships are only available to those with strong executive function skills.

4. Carstensen's social selectivity theory suggests that:
   a) older adults are pickier about who they are friends with as they get older.
   b) older adults would rather spend time with people they care about than form new relationships as they contemplate a finite life.
   c) older adults need to be more selective in who they date.
   d) people need to be more selective in how they classify older adults.

5. The timing of retirement often is linked to an adult's:
   a) health.
   b) desire to take more vacations.
   c) life plan.
   d) bucket list.

6. Quality caregiving is a skill that can be learned. What is NOT a necessary component of quality care?
   a) Empathy
   b) An outgoing personality
   c) Personalized treatment
   d) Cultural humility

7. What is NOT a common strength of emotional development in late adulthood?
   a) Stronger emotion regulation
   b) Wisdom about navigating conflict in relationships
   c) Optimism
   d) Strengthening executive function

8. What is NOT a common benefit of generativity in later life?
   a) Financial stability
   b) A feeling of connection to others
   c) A sense of meaning
   d) A sense of purpose

9. What demographic group has the highest rate of suicide in late adulthood?
   a) White men over 75
   b) Indigenous women over 75
   c) Black women over 75
   d) Latino men over 75

The End of Life

Death

EP.1 Describe common changes in the brain during death.

EP.2 List the medical and biological definitions of death.

Preparing for the End of Life

EP.3 Discuss common variations in preparing for the end of life.

Grief and Loss

EP.4 Review perspectives on grief and bereavement.

EP.5 Describe the social functions of mourning rituals.

Selected Resources from

 Achieve

Activities

Concept Practice: Attitudes toward Death and Dying

Spotlight on Science: The Impact of Technology on Traditional Mourning Practices

Assessments

LearningCurve

Practice Quiz

Videos

Scientific American Profiles

The End of Life: Interview with Laura Rothenberg

Bereavement and Grief: Late Adulthood

© Macmillan, Photo by Sidford House

Jane had not expected to become an expert in navigating the end of life. She did not anticipate spending years in a grief support group, or imagine that the hospice nurse and the end-of-life doula who supported her and her husband during his final months would become some of her closest friends.

Jane first met her husband John in high school: Their friendship began when they were just 15 and continued for more than 30 years before they became romantic in their 40s. They shared not only adventure, traveling, hiking, and trail building, but also a spiritual understanding, meditating and practicing yoga together. They often took time to reflect on how lucky they were to have such a beautiful life.

John had many careers, in technology, finance, energy healing, and massage therapy. But climbing was his true calling: He loved to scale rock faces and be in the woods. Much of his life was spent trying to protect and preserve land for public use, particularly in the gorges and mountains near his home in North Carolina. Yet, despite John's mental and physical stamina, he was diagnosed with *amyotrophic lateral sclerosis (ALS)*, a progressive and fatal neurological disease caused by the deterioration of the neurons that enable the muscles to move.

While no death can truly be said to be "good," Jane and John worked hard to make his passing the best it could be. John had all the legal paperwork in place as well as an impressive support network. Jane and John were fortunate enough to find a team that included hospice care and the help of an end-of-life physician and doula, Aditi Sethi. Nevertheless, dying was not easy: There was pain, and John was sometimes afraid of what was to come. As Jane remembers, the experience was heartbreaking, despite all their preparation and support.

Jane recalls thinking that she could not make it after he was gone: It was hard. At the same time, she says there were beautiful moments. Even after John had lost the ability to move, he could still feel the warmth of Jane next to him, and her touch would give him some peace. They were able to celebrate his life together in his last weeks and months: curating a playlist he could listen to at the end, writing down his hopes and dreams and visions for the future, and singing. In fact, music was one of Aditi's gifts to Jane and John, and to Jane after John was gone.

Aditi was among the people who watched over Jane and John in his last days of life. As a hospice physician with extensive medical training and expertise in palliative care, she is committed to helping people live as fully and comfortably as they can in the time they have. As an end-of-life doula, she provides a wider variety of support services to people who are dying. (Whereas a birth doula helps new families, a death doula provides nonmedicalized emotional and social support to families at the end of life.) Although Aditi worked for years as a conventional medical doctor, she felt called to do more with dying people and to integrate her interest in music and spirituality. As a doula, she connects with families through music, spiritual conversation, and rituals that are not typical of traditional hospice work.

Most deaths in the United States are, like John's, *expected*, occurring after long illnesses in later life. While the exact hour of death is often a surprise, families and caregivers have time to plan for their final days and, like John, even have the opportunity to make something beautiful from their passing. In more than 1 in 10 deaths, dying is sudden and *unexpected*: babies soon after birth, children in accidents, or adults lost to violence, substance use, or a sudden heart attack (Lewis et al., 2016).

No matter how it happens, death and grief are an inevitable part of human life. Yet there is remarkable diversity in how and when we experience these transitions: The challenge is, like many other stresses, distributed inequitably. Death is more common at the beginning and the end of the lifespan and, like poor health, is more common among those with disabilities, marginalized communities, and people with low income (Umberson et al., 2020). The overwhelming majority of people are resilient, like Jane, when they experience grief, even if they have lived through unimaginable traumas (Bonanno, 2019). But they nevertheless feel sad about their loss and think about those they have loved, even years later. Three years after John's death, Jane tells us that she is not yet over her loss: She still meets with her grief support group and misses John every day.

The study of death is known as **thanatology** (Fonseca & Testoni, 2012). It is an interdisciplinary field mixing academic researchers from the fields of psychology, sociology, and anthropology with practitioners in counseling, social work, death education, and the funeral industry (Chapple et al., 2017). Although thanatologists are a diverse group, they share a belief that understanding death and grieving can help us all die, grieve, and even live better (Corr, 2015).

thanatology The study of death, which combines insights from the fields of psychology, sociology, anthropology, counseling, social work, death education, and the funeral industry.

death The major social, biological, and spiritual transition that occurs when your body has experienced irreversible damage and can no longer recover.

Scientific American Profile
Meet Jane

Death

Death is a major social, biological, and spiritual transition that will happen to all of us and to those we love. In affluent societies around the world, death often occurs as part of a medical process that often involves unfamiliar milestones, jargon, and specialized technology, making many people and their families uncertain about what to expect.

Learning Objectives

EP.1 Describe common changes in the brain during death.

EP.2 List the medical and biological definitions of death.

terminal decline Changes in cognition, processing, and/or personality, which signify that a person is nearing death.

terminal agitation A condition in which a dying person becomes restless, upset, and/or delirious.

terminal lucidity An unexpected return to consciousness or cognitive clarity in people who are at the end of life.

The Biology of Death

The basic biology of death is universal and obvious: Death occurs when your body has experienced irreversible damage and can no longer recover (Burkle et al., 2014). For most of us, death happens when our heart stops beating and our lungs stop breathing (Kirschen et al., 2021). However, breakthroughs in biological science have revealed complexities in what it means to die. Scientists can now show more clearly how the body continues to change on the cellular level long after bodies are cold (Busl, 2019; Ferreira et al., 2018; Pozhitkov et al., 2017).

For those who will have expected, rather than sudden, deaths, dying is a process that can take days or weeks, as the body and brain slowly decline because of steadily accumulating damage. The first signs of death might be changes in your thinking. At the end of life, cognition and processing often slow, in a process known as **terminal decline**. Personality changes often accompany terminal decline: Many people become more emotional and less outgoing, less curious about learning new things, and less focused on getting things done, as their energy wanes (Mueller et al., 2019).

In the last days of life, your ability to feel and respond to sensations outside of your body begins to dull. People tend to lose interest in eating and drinking. For hours at a time, people may sleep or no longer have the energy to respond (Chu et al., 2020). Gradually, people lose the ability to communicate, typically followed by the ability to see, hear, and feel (Hallenbeck, 2005). Deterioration in the brain and nervous system make it hard to regulate temperature, to have a sense of day and night, and to even keep a steady heartbeat or blood pressure (Reid et al., 2017).

About one in four dying people experience an upsetting and disturbing condition known as **terminal agitation** in their final days (Hosker & Bennett, 2016). They may become restless or upset and are often delirious. They may cry out, moan, become aggressive, or hallucinate (Blaszczyk et al., 2021).

A few people are lucky enough to feel calmer as they get closer to death. In a rare condition known as **terminal lucidity** (sometimes called the *final rally*), dying people become unexpectedly articulate, often reversing weeks or even months of confusion (Mashour et al., 2019; Peterson et al., 2021). Some researchers suggest terminal lucidity is caused by a spontaneous release of steroids or reduction in inflammation that may allow the brain to function more effectively (Matloff, 2018; Peskin, 2017a, 2017b).

In the final hours of life, the body may become cooler, and breathing may slow. Sometimes people develop a *death rattle*, or a crackling when they breathe caused by buildup of saliva in their throat when they become too weak to swallow (van Esch et al., 2021). They may gasp for breath as they begin to struggle with lack of oxygen (Solis, 2021). For many, bodies become quiet and still as they approach their final moments. Some scientists suggest that the end of life may come with a burst of neurotransmitters, like serotonin, cortisol, and even pain-relieving endorphins, making the transition into death feel easier (Coyle, 2020; Wutzler et al., 2011).

People are remarkably resilient in their ability to regain lost functionality and adjust to injuries over the lifespan, but at the end of life, the brain experiences such intense trauma that it is no longer able to recover. Cardiac arrest may stop the heart from pumping blood to the brain, a difficult birth may starve the brain of energy, or lung damage may prevent oxygen from getting to the brain. Whatever the cause, the brain is so damaged that it can no longer repair itself (Burkle et al., 2014). (See **Figure E.1**.)

Damage to the *brain stem* often signals and triggers the end of life (Burkle et al., 2014). The brain stem is a ropelike region that links your brain to the spinal cord, running from the base of your skull to the deep interior of your brain. Key structures in the brain stem, like the *medulla* and the *pons*, help regulate basic functions such as breathing and heart rate. Without a functioning brain stem, you stop breathing and you are unable to feel pain or control your movements (Greer et al., 2020).

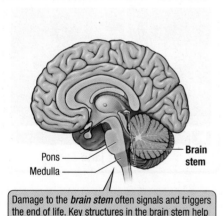

Pons
Medulla
Brain stem

Damage to the ***brain stem*** often signals and triggers the end of life. Key structures in the brain stem help regulate basic functions including breathing, sleep cycles, heart rate, and awareness of pain.

FIGURE E.1 The Brain at the End of Life At the end of life, the brain experiences irreversible damage. In many cases, damage to the *brain stem* triggers the end of life.

When people die from chronic illnesses like cancer or heart disease, the damage to the brain stem may lead to many of the final symptoms of the dying process: irregular blood pressure, breathing, and disrupted sleep cycles (Kadhim et al., 2012).

CAN YOU BELIEVE IT?
Is There Life After Death?

This is a science-based textbook, not a fictional one, so it should be unsurprising that many scientists uniformly agree that there is no evidence that we continue to live after death, at least with our physical bodies. However, this does not mean that all activity ceases at the moment the exhausted body expires. Researchers have found that activity continues on the microscopic level for hours (if not days). This does not mean that we are alive, but that our cells continue to develop. Consider the following:

- Some cells may *never* die. Sometimes, cells can live for decades in the laboratory, continually dividing long after their original owner has died (Skloot, 2010).
- When cells continue to divide after we are dead, they are directed to do so by genes. Researchers have found that genes are activated as we die and in the hours that follow (Ferreira et al., 2018; Pozhitkov et al., 2017). These genes have playfully been called "Zombie" genes, but they are doing basic biological housekeeping: They turn off our immune systems, stop our cells from responding to stress hormones, and slow the process of producing new proteins (Golembiewski, 2019).
- Animal studies suggest that after we die, there is a surge of connectivity, a release of neurotransmitters, and new electrical activity in the brain (Borjigin et al., 2013; Wutzler et al., 2011). Scientists studying pigs have found that neurons in their brain cells continue to fire, sometimes for hours or even days after death (Busl, 2019). One group of scientists was even able to restore some brain function in the heads of pigs after they were slaughtered by hooking them up to the "pig" version of a heart–lung machine after they had been killed (Vrselja et al., 2019). Nevertheless, there was no evidence that the pigs' heads were conscious, felt pain, or had any cross-brain electrical activity as measured by an EEG (Farahany et al., 2019).
- Some scientists suggest that the brain activity they have seen in animals at the end of life might also explain an unusual phenomenon known as the *near-death experience* (NDE) (Moody, 1975). They speculate that the continuing firing of neurons after death might explain the reports of seeing a bright light, having a feeling of joy, or connecting with a loved one or a religious figure that people have experienced after their hearts stopped (Parnia et al., 2014). About one in four people who have survived a cardiac arrest tell researchers that they had an out-of-body experience (Martial et al., 2019).

Despite the popularity of the idea that surviving death will make you nicer, more insightful, and spiritually blissful, a near-death experience does not improve most people's lives. If people survive a cardiac arrest, most experience profound traumatic brain injury and cognitive decline (Parnia et al., 2014). NDE might be more interesting to read about than to live through.

Defining Death

Since the beginning of written history, people have shared horror stories about those rare cases when death was declared too soon: people who woke up from their death beds or soldiers who miraculously revived on the battlefield (Angelone, 2016; Bondeson, 2002). People have worried about their ability to identify when death happens: The anxiety that living people would be declared dead too soon became more common in the 1800s and 1900s as researchers developed more effective technology to save lives.

Today, *life support* devices include *ventilators* to help you breathe, feeding tubes to give you nutrition, defibrillators to correct your heartbeat, and heart–lung machines to replace your heart and lungs through what is known as *extracorporeal membrane oxygenation (ECMO)* (Ross, 2018). In countries with modern medical systems, life support means that people can now survive for months, years, and sometimes even decades completely dependent on machines to keep their hearts beating and their blood full of oxygen (Truog et al., 2018). These devices have saved countless lives but have also inspired new questions about death (Lewis et al., 2017).

Medical Determination of Death Medical professionals, lawyers, and ethicists have tried to create standardized methods of defining death. Differences in resources and cultural and legal systems around the world mean there are many definitions of death, and one standard is still not in practice everywhere (Greer et al., 2020; Kirschen et al., 2021; Lewis et al., 2017).

Health care providers sometimes use the term **clinical death** to describe a stage in the dying process when your breathing and heart stop. Medical providers now use the term *cardiac arrest*, because it refers to the moment your heart stops beating (Parnia & Young, 2013). With the help of immediate and intensive medical intervention, such as *cardiopulmonary resuscitation (CPR)*, the use of a defibrillator, or even more cutting-edge technologies such as being cooled or placed on an ECMO, people can sometimes recover from clinical death. However, in practice, fewer than one in six people whose hearts stop leave their hospital rooms alive (Jacobsen et al., 2020; Mgbako et al., 2014).

Brain death occurs when someone is determined to have experienced *irreversible* brain damage that makes them unable to function and respond to any kind of stimulation (Greer et al., 2020). Brain death occurs in about 1 out of every 200 deaths of adults and more than 1 in every 5 deaths of children in the United States (Kirschen et al., 2021; Seifi et al., 2020). The bodies of people who are brain dead can occasionally continue to function for months or even years. These instances are very unusual: In most cases, the body begins to shut down and decay shortly after brain death occurs (Greer et al., 2020).

While brain death has been an accepted part of medical practice for more than 50 years, it remains controversial in some communities (Truog et al., 2018). In some low-income countries with limited medical systems, brain death does not usually signal the end of care. Instead, health care providers wait until someone's heartbeat has stopped (Wong et al., 2020). Families from some religious backgrounds, including some forms of orthodox Judaism, Sunni Islam, Buddhism, and some Native American traditions, are not comfortable with brain death. Other families, particularly those from marginalized communities, may distrust medical professionals' ability to accurately determine whether someone has died, perhaps because of experiences with bias and inadequate care (Williamson, 2021). As a result of these misgivings, families in some communities may reject the diagnosis of brain death and choose to keep their loved ones on life support.

For families, a diagnosis of brain death can be confusing, particularly because these deaths typically happen in younger people whose deaths are unexpected and who appear to be sleeping, with the help of life support. Families may have unrealistic expectations for how much medical providers can do to help people who have been injured (Jacobsen et al., 2020). Others may worry that their loved one is still alive and that they will be in pain if they are removed from life support (Timmermans, 2010).

Legal Issues in Dying In the United States and much of the world, the legal system steps in when there is conflict or confusion about the end of life. Around the world and even across the United States, there are a hodgepodge of official definitions and guidelines for the determination of death and for how people are allowed to end their

clinical death The stage in the dying process when breathing and heart stop. Medical providers use the term *cardiac arrest* rather than clinical death.

brain death When someone is determined to have experienced irreversible brain damage that makes them unable to function and respond to stimulation.

lives. This reflects a strong tradition of local control over health care that, in practice, does not affect many of us: Most deaths are not complex (Lewis et al., 2017; Ruiz et al., 2018).

In cases where families disagree with the diagnosis of brain death or feel that someone is still alive even if their brain is no longer functioning, they can choose to keep their loved ones on life support, in what is known as the *religious exemption* (Pope, 2018). In the United States, New Jersey allows families to choose to maintain life support indefinitely, a choice taken by only a few every year (Son & Setta, 2018). In some other states, including California, Illinois, and New York, doctors are legally bound to make some accommodations to family's religious or spiritual beliefs about the end of life (Lewis & Greer, 2017).

Legal Choices in Dying In nations around the world and in eight U.S. states, some people who are diagnosed with a terminal illness have the legal ability to receive medical assistance in planning their deaths (Death With Dignity, 2021). **Physician-assisted suicide** occurs when a medical professional helps a dying person end their life by providing either medication or information that will hasten the end of life. This can help when someone's suffering is unbearable and unremitting. Most Americans support the idea that doctors should be allowed to help people end their lives if they are in pain. Others, including some major medical organizations, worry that allowing doctors to help people die is unethical and could damage the doctor–patient relationship (Lipka, 2014; Sulmasy et al., 2018).

In the states where physician-assisted suicide, often termed *death with dignity*, has been legal for many years, researchers have found that most people who used the law had advanced stages of cancer with pain that was difficult to manage. While some advocates worried that assisted death would target low-income or marginalized communities, scientists have found that it is overwhelmingly used by White, college-educated adults over age 75 (Al Rabadi et al., 2019). Studies have found similar patterns in European countries where physician-assisted suicide has long been legalized (Dierickx et al., 2020).

In a few nations, physicians are permitted to actively help someone with a terminal illness die, in what is called **active euthanasia**. Active euthanasia is not legal anywhere in the United States, although more than 7 in 10 Americans support legalization (Brenan, 2018).

Some advocates argue for expanding the legal choices available in dying, particularly to allow people with neurocognitive disorders to receive help to end their lives (Cantor, 2018; Largent et al., 2019). However, critics caution that expanding legal aid in dying might sanction other types of assisted death and even more active measures for people who may be perceived as "burdens" on society, such as people with mental illnesses or disabilities (Cirpriani & Di Fiorino, 2019; Sulmasy, 2018).

physician-assisted suicide When a medical professional helps a dying person to end their life.

active euthanasia When a physician actively helps someone with a terminal illness die.

Trying to Help from Beyond Brittany Maynard was diagnosed with terminal brain cancer at 29. In order to have medical assistance to end her life, she moved to Oregon in her last months. After her death, her husband, Dan, played a video she had recorded to advocate for legislation in her home state of California that would support medical assistance in dying.

How Do You Talk About Death?

Jane remembers the meaningful conversations she had with John about the end of life before and after his ALS diagnosis, but many people avoid these conversations (Schoenborn et al., 2018; Zwakman et al., 2018). These conversations are also uncomfortable for health care professionals: More than half feel unprepared to have them (Isaacson & Minton, 2018; Jacobsen et al., 2020; Scholz et al., 2020). This reluctance to talk about death with medical providers is particularly acute for people with limited trust in their doctors (Schoenborn et al., 2018). Other patients may have traditions that make openly talking about death impolite, such as some from Taiwan, China, and Somalia (Cheng et al., 2015; Liu & Chi., 2021; Lien Foundation, 2010).

Building trust is an essential part of good communication about death. Many of us overestimate what science can do to prevent, forestall, or cure serious illnesses

 Share It!

Talk about the end of life but remember that care takes more than a single conversation. Talking and making plans is not enough to support quality of life in dying: It takes relationships.

(Jóhannesdóttir & Hjörleifsdóttir, 2018)

Scientific American: Lifespan Development

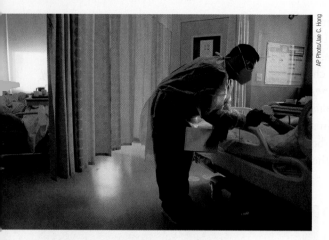

Comfort and Care at the End Chaplains often provide comfort and spiritual support at the end of life. During the COVID-19 pandemic, when families were often not able to visit the hospital, chaplains like Elias Mena were there to hold hands and pray.

(Jacobsen et al., 2020). Medicine can be imprecise. Even doctors and nurses cannot consistently provide an accurate prediction of when we will die (Detsky et al., 2017; Farinholt et al., 2018). Most doctors tend to be over optimistic: People do not live as long as they estimate (Chu et al., 2020; Mandelli et al., 2021).

Communication experts suggest that better conversations about end of life occur when medical professionals ask questions and take time to express empathy and to understand the individual needs of the family and the patient (Rosenberg et al., 2019). In situations where providers may not be familiar with a family's cultural traditions or expectations, the best practice is to employ cultural humility (Chi et al., 2018; Yamaguchi et al., 2021). At times, medical professionals benefit from the support of community members, social workers, hospital chaplains, or religious professionals to help people with terminal illnesses and their families understand the process of dying (Shinall et al., 2018).

Patterns in Dying Across the Lifespan

Many children and adults around the globe are living healthier and longer lives than ever before. The number of children who die before age 5 is less than half of what it was in 1990 (UNICEF, 2021). However, even in affluent countries like the United States, the first years of life and the years of older adulthood remain the most dangerous of the lifespan. In the United States, more than 40 percent of deaths are in older adults, but more than 20,000 babies died before age 1 and another 23,000 infants are *stillborn*, or die at birth or after the 20th week of fetal development (Hoyert & Gregory, 2020). You have about the same risk of dying as an infant as you do when you are 60 (Murphy et al., 2021).

Historical Changes in Mortality Better nutrition in the early years of life, more effective treatments for infectious diseases, and better prenatal care and support for birth itself have increased the likelihood that children around the world live into adulthood. During adulthood and later life, better public health and treatments

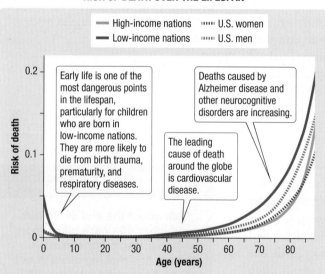

Data from Social Security Actuarial Life Tables, 2019.

Data from Dwyer-Lindgren et al., 2017.

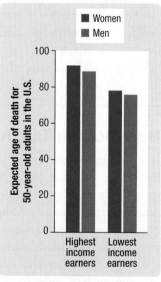

Data from National Academy of Sciences, 2015.

FIGURE E.2 Variations in Mortality Death will happen to all of us, but the patterns in when it happens are linked to where we live, our family income, and our gender identity.

for infectious diseases have made it more likely that some of us make it to our 80s and beyond (Christ & Latz, 2019). In high-income countries, more than 7 in 10 people die late in life from chronic conditions like neurocognitive disease, cardiovascular diseases, diabetes, and cancer (WHO, 2021).

The COVID-19 pandemic became a leading cause of death in the United States and one of the top five causes of death in dozens of countries around the world in 2020 and 2021 (Troeger, 2021). The pandemic took the lives of older adults, particularly those who were isolated in nursing homes and who were already frail or had neurocognitive conditions (Boucher, 2021; Cronin & Evans, 2020). The pandemic also preyed inequitably on low-income families and Black, Native American, and Latino adults (Xu et al., 2021).

The world has seen major health crises before: The largest was an epidemic of smallpox and measles that killed more than 8 in 10 people in North and South America in the 1600s (Nunn & Qian, 2010). These pandemics were closely rivaled by the plague that killed as many as one in three Europeans in the 1300s and the 1918–1919 influenza epidemic that killed more than 500 million people worldwide (Hagemann, 2020; Howard, 2020). In the past 40 years, more than 37 million people have died of HIV/AIDS, leading to major drops in life expectancy in African nations such as South Africa, Botswana, and Lesotho (Gona et al., 2020).

Inequity in Dying Even before the COVID-19 pandemic, the United States was experiencing a decrease in adult life expectancy for nearly a decade (Harris et al., 2021). Remember from Chapter 15 that increasing economic instability exacerbated by the recession of 2008 has been linked to an increase in deaths from substance use, suicide, and heart disease in middle-aged adults. Increases in mortality are particularly high in low-income groups, including White Americans in rural areas who did not attend college and people who have limited economic opportunities and lack a social safety net (Mullan et al., 2021). Increases are also occurring in urban areas and among other groups of low-income Americans, including Black, Latino, and Native Americans (Curtin & Arias, 2019; Elo et al., 2019).

This increase in mortality illustrates longstanding health inequalities across the United States: Low-income people from all ethnic groups and people who are Black, Latino, and Native American at all income levels are more likely to die early in life than more affluent and White Americans (Jones-Eversley & Rice, 2020; Singh et al., 2017). Structural factors such as discrimination, segregation, environmental pollution, and unequal economic opportunity are linked to many of these deaths (Bailey et al., 2017). White Americans live about four years longer than Black Americans and seven years longer than Native Americans, who have a life expectancy of just 72 (Arias et al., 2021). Americans with the highest incomes in all ethnic groups typically live over 10 years longer than those with the lowest incomes (Chetty et al., 2016).

Communities of color also have health advantages. Latino and Asian Americans tend to live longer than White European Americans (Borrell & Lancet, 2012). Native Americans and Black Americans who have reached late adulthood also tend to live longer than White Americans, a phenomenon attributable both to stronger traditions of caregiving and the sad fact that many adults at risk from those communities die before they reach later life (Jackson et al., 2011; Mayeda et al., 2019).

Sharing Loss and Sage Sisters Jessie Taken Alive-Rencountre and Nola Taken Alive tuck a bundle of sage next to the body of their mother, Cheryl, who lost her life during the COVID-19 pandemic. Their Lakota community in South Dakota lost many tribal members to the virus.

Growing Up with a Legacy Little Soleil has been raised by her grandmother, Wanda, since her mother's death shortly after her birth. As Soleil grows up, her family will keep alive her connection to her mother and her work. Her mother was Shalon Irving (in the photograph), a researcher. She had a PhD and a master's degree in public health: She studied the disparate impact of poor health on communities of color. Before she died, she declared on Twitter: "I see inequity wherever it exists, call it by name, and work to eliminate it."

APPLY IT! EP.1 Jane and John had long felt comfortable talking about their feelings about death, as well as their big goals for life. What are your own ethnotheories about death? How do they make it easier or harder to talk about it with the people you love?

EP.2 Death is a complex biological event with complex legal definitions. Do you think it makes it less intimidating to understand the biology of how death happens? How do your own ideas about when death happens align with the standards in your community?

Preparing for the End of Life

Learning Objective

EP.3 Discuss common variations in preparing for the end of life.

Most of us hesitate to talk about the end of life with our health care providers, but when it comes down to it, many of us also avoid talking about death with our families or planning for it (Schoenborn et al., 2018). For families like John's who know that the end was near, preparing for the end of life is unavoidable.

John and Jane fought his disease for as long as they could: traveling to experts, trying exotic treatments, searching for answers that would change his diagnosis or postpone his death. They were connected to a big support network of climbers and yoga practitioners near their home in North Carolina, but they also knew that they needed professional care. Hospice and Aditi's expertise helped make John and Jane's final months together easier. As Jane remembers, death is an inevitable process, but they were able to gain some richness from John's experience and to make sure that he felt complete and whole at the end of his life.

Theoretical Perspectives on Death

Around the world, communities have various ethnotheories for understanding how and when we die and cultural practices that help prepare us for death and, for many, the life beyond. Over the past hundred years, developmental scientists have also developed their own observations and models of how best to prepare for death.

Death Anxiety Many researchers point out that in the past, death was often part of our everyday lives. Losing a loved one was common, and family members died at home, cared for by people who knew them (Ariès, 1983; Kastenbaum, 2015). In contrast, death in many communities now often happens outside of the home: in a nursing home, hospice, or hospital where we are cared for by strangers. As a result, dying may be impersonal and filled with lost opportunities for connection (Toolis, 2018).

However, some theorists go farther than just criticizing how death is managed in modern institutions and argue that modern culture has made death itself taboo (Anderson et al., 2018; Gire, 2019; Kastenbaum, 2015; Tradii & Robert, 2019). These researchers draw from a long tradition in psychodynamic and sociological theories that suggests that modern, affluent European culture and many of us individually are driven by a fear of death, sometimes termed *death denial* or *death anxiety* (Becker, 1973; Cicirelli, 2002; Freud, 1915/1961). According to this line of thought, a tremendous amount of our generative energy and creativity is driven by our fear of death and our attempts to become immortal (Greenberg et al., 1986; Helm et al., 2020).

There is some intuitive appeal to the idea that we are afraid of death, since death is often difficult to talk about (Miller, 2020). However, scientists have found that there is only limited empirical support to the idea that death anxiety is universal (Chopik, 2017; Jong, 2021). Most people, including children, do not name death as one of their major fears if they are asked to list the things that scare them (Gutiérrez et al., 2020). For many, worries about death decline as they get older.

Erikson's Perspective on the End of Life Remember from Chapter 17 that Erik Erikson suggested that the final stage of psychosocial development was the achievement of a sense of wholeness, wisdom, and generativity (Erikson et al., 1994). In line with Erikson, many researchers have found that taking stock of what has come before and reminiscing about what has been lived through can make people at the end of life feel more content (Bluck & Mroz, 2018; Steinhauser et al., 2017). Even simple efforts can remind people of their generativity and improve well-being, like writing a last letter or recording a goodbye video on a cell phone (Miller, 2020).

Kübler-Ross's Stages of Dying One of the most popular perspectives on dying comes from Elisabeth Kübler-Ross, a psychiatrist who worked to improve the quality of care received by dying people in the United States and around the world. Inspired by other stage theories in developmental science, Kübler-Ross created a stage theory of dying that was later adapted to the grieving process (Kübler-Ross, 1969; Kübler-Ross & Kessler, 2005).

Kübler-Ross was trained as a psychodynamic therapist and believed in the importance of human relationships to mental health. Her theory of dying outlined five stages at the end of life: denial, anger, bargaining, depression, and acceptance. Her belief was that with support, people could achieve a sense of "closure" and a "peaceful" death (Kübler-Ross, 1969; Kübler-Ross, 1995).

While Kübler-Ross's theory continues to have popular appeal, empirical researchers have rejected many of its specifics. They point out that there is no evidence of a universal process of dying (or grieving) (Neimeyer, 2021). In fact, many caution that the idea of a stage theory can be harmful: People should not feel pressured to go through one "right" way of dying or grieving. Dying people have not failed if they still feel angry about dying and never accept the fact that they are near the end (Bonanno, 2019). In fact, many researchers point out that there is not one but many "good deaths" that are more often constrained by physical limitations and lack of support than by missed opportunities for introspection (Pollock & Seymour, 2018).

Common Ethnotheories of Dying Developmental scientists and anthropologists who specialize in the comparative study of culture remind us that death is a social process, and cultural practices help connect people to their community and provide comfort at the end of life (Engelke, 2019). While these ethnotheories, or lay theories, about the end of life are diverse and ever changing, they share some common features:

- *Saying goodbye:* Many cultural communities include rituals or religious services designed to ease the transition to the next life. In faith communities, this may include a pastoral visit or the administering of final sacraments or last rites (Choudry et al., 2018). It often includes an opportunity for close loved ones to gather with the person who is dying.
- *Mending relationships:* Many communities focus on the dying process as a time when we can mend relationships, forgive missteps, and come together (Graham et al., 2013). For instance, Xhosa families in South Africa, like many around the world, want everyone to be together in the last days of someone's life, so they have time to comfort each other. This is also part of establishing a continuing connection with the dead person's memory that will exist after their death.
- *Death as a special time:* In diverse communities around the globe, the dying person is seen to be in a heightened state of awareness, and even their last words are seen to

Joy at the Falls Twelve-Year-Old Lola Muñoz knew that she had a brain tumor that might take her life, but she found joy with her family on vacation at Niagara Falls. Lola accepted that she was not going to survive her illness, but wanted her death to have meaning: to inspire scientists to search for a cure. She explained, "I don't want them to remember me as the little girl who died."

Scientific American Profile

The Process of Death

be profound and meaningful (Graham et al., 2013). When last words are written down, some are more profound than others, such as poet Emily Dickinson's: "I must go in. The fog is rising." Others are more mundane, like actor Spike Milligan's quip "I told you I was ill" (Bluck & Mroz, 2018).

Cultures have diverse expectations for cultural practices at the end of life. For Jane and John, these included having company at the end of life. Jane was able to bathe him after he passed, and, with her friends, wrapped him in his meditation shawl and covered him in flowers, singing to him to say goodbye. They spent the evening with him after his death before taking his body to the crematorium, where it was burned along with some of the crystals he was holding at the end of his life.

John and Jane found comfort in rituals based around their meditation traditions and in music. But other end-of-life customs may vary, including:

- *Emotional displays at the end of life:* Are you supposed to be calm when you die? Or, are you allowed to express your feelings of regret, anger, or loss? At the end of life, some religious and cultural groups value a peaceful, mindful death, including many from Buddhist and Hindi faiths (Langford, 2013, 2016; Moale & Norvell, 2019). Others, including many from Native American communities, value a more straightforward expression of emotion (Colclough, 2017).
- *Decision making:* Are decisions made as a group or by one individual? Family cultures that are more collectivist, including Native American, Latin American, and Asian American communities may have decision-making practices that involve an entire group (He et al., 2021; Isaacson & Lynch, 2018; Lewis & McBride, 2004; Moale & Norvell, 2019).
- *Balancing modern and traditional medical care:* In many communities around the world, including in Native American and Chinese American cultures, traditional medicines are a comforting and supportive addition to modern medical care (He et al., 2021; Isaacson & Lynch, 2018).
- *Treatment of the body after death:* In Christian communities, most families believe that the spirit is separate from the body and leaves it immediately after death (Choudry et al., 2018). As a result, many Christians are comfortable with organ donation and autopsies done after death, but this is far from universal. In some communities, the body of the person who has died is revered and needs to be treated with respect, including remaining covered and being bathed (Langford, 2016). Many others believe that the spirit stays in the dead body for hours and even days after death. While Christianity, Buddhism, and Hinduism either permit or encourage cremation after death, other major religious traditions, including Islam, see cremation as a desecration of the body.
- *Cleanliness:* Dying can be messy. Many traditions, including Islam, Hinduism, and Judaism, believe that the body of the dying person needs to stay clean, out of respect and in order to ensure a peaceful emotional transition (Choudry et al., 2018).
- *Life after death:* Most people around the world report that they believe that life continues in a spiritual realm after death, although there are many variations in how this occurs (Watson-Jones et al., 2017). Some people, known as *atheists*, may not believe that there is any life after death: They see death as purely biological (Yancy, 2020).

Children's Understanding of Death Although adults wish to protect children from the reality of death, developmental scientists have found that young children are remarkably resilient and sophisticated in their understanding of the end of life — even when it is their own (Miller et al., 2014). Most children understand the finality of death, along with their communities' ethnotheories about it, by kindergarten (Gutiérrez et al., 2020; Menendez et al., 2020).

Many children and adults around the world believe that something continues to live on even though the body dies: that people will still, in some way, feel and observe the world around them, whether from heaven or from another spiritual place (Watson Jones et al., 2017). Sometimes, children mix their understanding of what happens in the next life: combining a spiritual understanding of life with a concrete, physical understanding of life after death. One little girl who lost her mother explained: "My mom's in heaven . . . but I think my mom is getting tired. If you were up in heaven all the time, wouldn't you want to sit down sometimes[?]" (Miller et al., 2014, p. 27).

In some families, adults try to shield children from emotional expressions of sadness and experiences of grief and loss. In others, such as some Mexican American communities, children grow up with rituals, like the Day of the Dead, that turn loss and death into a celebration (Gutiérrez et al., 2020; Longbottom & Slaughter, 2018). These types of celebrations are common around the world, such as the Gai Nai festival in Nepal, Famadihana in Madagascar, and U Juornu re Muorti in Sicily.

In the past, clinicians tried to shield terminally ill children from their own death. In-depth ethnographic work from developmental scientists revealed that this was confusing to children. Now, most experts suggest that children who are terminally ill be provided with honest information about their prognosis and palliative support as they die (Bluebond-Langner, 1978; Menendez et al., 2020). These children will understand that they will die biologically, but they also appreciate that they may live on in the memories and experiences of those who knew them (Harris, 2018).

Not Too Young to Dress Up Celerating the end of life is a part of many cultures, including this community in Mexico City, that includes children in parades for the Day of the Dead.

Legal Plans for the End of Life Medical providers and legal experts recommend making plans for the kind of care we want at the end of life. Many of us avoid planning for the end of life, hoping it will never come or that we will be able to deal with it later (Mignani et al., 2017; Yadav et al., 2017). Most of us, as Jane chides, avoid it until there is some emergency that forces it upon us.

Advance directives are formal documents that specify what kind of end-of-life care you would want if you are unable to convey your wishes directly, for instance if you are unconscious or too sick to communicate. **Living wills** are one form of advance directive that specifies care that you would want at the end of life. These documents might indicate whether you would want health care professionals to try and revive you if you stop breathing. For instance, if you do not want to be resuscitated if your heart stops, you can request that your directives specify *comfort care only* and include a *do not resuscitate (DNR) order*. Advanced directives also allow you to designate a friend or loved one to make medical decisions for you if you are not able to make them yourself. This designation may be formalized in a *health care proxy* or a *durable medical power of attorney* (Carr et al., 2021). (See **Figure E.3**.)

There is some limited evidence that people who complete advanced directives have end-of-life care that is closer to their stated goals or that they improve well-being at the end of life (Committee on Approaching Death, 2015; Jimenez et al., 2018; Korfage et al., 2020). However, researchers have found that advanced directives are not as effective as experts hope: People who have them do not necessarily get care that matches their expectations and their expectations often change over time. Most, in fact, have more medical interventions at the end of life than they have asked for (Hill et al., 2020; MacKenzie et al., 2018; Reuter et al., 2017).

Caregiving at the End of Life

The efforts of advocates for the dying have triggered improvements in end-of-life care around the world (Glaser & Strauss, 1965; Kübler-Ross, 1969; Strauss & Glaser, 1970). An international movement has begun to make dying less medicalized and less painful—more

advance directives Formal documents and instructions that specify end-of-life care.

living wills A form of advance directive that specifies care you would want at the end of life.

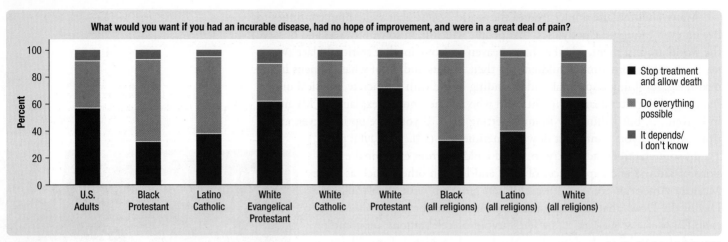

What would you want if you had an incurable disease, had no hope of improvement, and were in a great deal of pain?

Legend:
- Stop treatment and allow death
- Do everything possible
- It depends/ I don't know

Data from Pew Research Center, 2013.

FIGURE E.3 What Would You Want at the End of Life? When researchers asked adults what they would want if they were diagnosed with a terminal disease, they found that there were significant cultural, ethnic, and religious differences in how they felt about end-of-life care.

like the connected and meaningful death that John was able to experience (Gawande, 2014; Nuland, 1995).

End-of-life care, like other high-quality caregiving, needs to be customized around the individual needs of dying people and their families (Pillemer et al., 2020). At the end of life, that includes making sure you have the ability make your own decisions, participate in culturally appropriate rituals, find spiritual support, and receive care for your loved ones as they accompany you through this transition (Krikorian et al., 2020).

Two major movements have helped improve institutional care at the end of life: *hospice care* and *palliative care*. Both programs are designed to give all people the kind of high-quality, compassionate, pain-free caregiving that was once only available to the wealthy (Whelan, 2000).

Hospice is a program of end-of-life care that is focused not on curing a terminal disease but on making the last weeks as comfortable as possible. Hospice treats the emotional, physical, spiritual, and social needs of people and their families at the end of life. The international hospice movement was largely inspired by the work of one English doctor, Cicely Saunders (1918–2005). In the United States, more than 4 in 10 dying Americans have some hospice care like John, either at home, in free-standing hospice units, or in hospital-based hospice centers (Bhatnagar & Lagnese, 2021).

Palliative care is a type of medical treatment for seriously ill people focused on improving quality of life and eliminating suffering, rather than on curing the underlying disease. In the United States, palliative care has become more popular since the early 2000s, in part because it is less expensive to insurers than standard hospital-based care. It is now available for many in the hospital but is much less common outside of hospitals (Center to Advance Palliative Care, 2020). Some families supplement their own caregiving with additional end-of-life services provided by a home health aide, private nurse, or in some communities, a death doula like Aditi (Jones, 2019; Tugend, 2015).

By many measures, high-quality end-of-life care in the United States lags other affluent nations. Few people die with comprehensive care, particularly if they have low income or are people of color (Bhatnagar & Lagnese, 2021; Tulsky, 2015). Experts suggest that this is for two reasons: (1) financial support for end-of-life caregiving in the United States is much less comprehensive than that provided by other affluent countries, and (2) end-of-life caregiving is not sensitive to the needs of diverse families (Economist, 2010; Lien Foundation, 2015).

hospice A program of end-of-life care that focuses on eliminating suffering, by treating the emotional, physical, spiritual, and social needs of dying people and their families.

palliative care A type of medical treatment for seriously ill people that focuses on improving quality of life and eliminating discomfort.

How do you measure the quality of death? A team of researchers from around the world tried to measure how likely people were to receive high-quality end-of-life care and palliative care. Around the world, wealthy nations tend to rank higher than those with fewer resources, but some nations, including Mongolia and Costa Rica, have made investments in providing high-quality care for all.

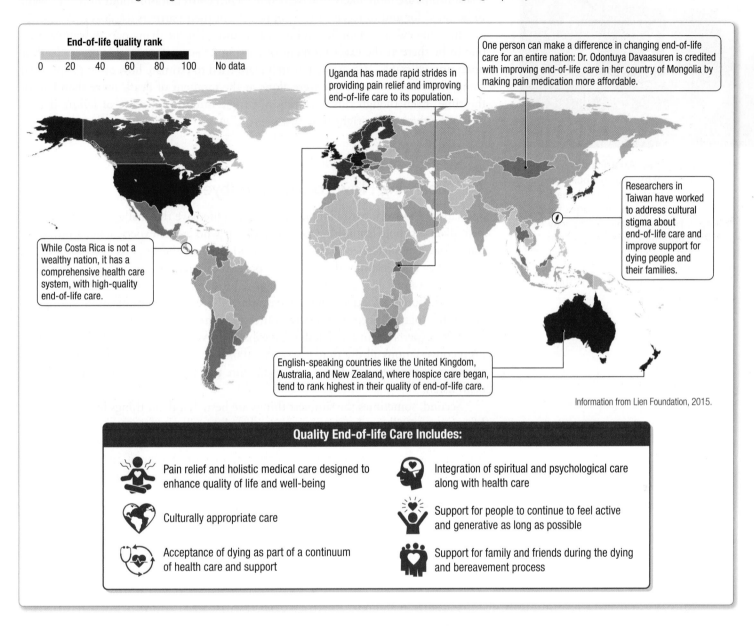

End-of-life quality rank

0   20   40   60   80   100   No data

Uganda has made rapid strides in providing pain relief and improving end-of-life care to its population.

One person can make a difference in changing end-of-life care for an entire nation: Dr. Odontuya Davaasuren is credited with improving end-of-life care in her country of Mongolia by making pain medication more affordable.

Researchers in Taiwan have worked to address cultural stigma about end-of-life care and improve support for dying people and their families.

While Costa Rica is not a wealthy nation, it has a comprehensive health care system, with high-quality end-of-life care.

English-speaking countries like the United Kingdom, Australia, and New Zealand, where hospice care began, tend to rank highest in their quality of end-of-life care.

Information from Lien Foundation, 2015.

Quality End-of-life Care Includes:

- Pain relief and holistic medical care designed to enhance quality of life and well-being
- Integration of spiritual and psychological care along with health care
- Culturally appropriate care
- Support for people to continue to feel active and generative as long as possible
- Acceptance of dying as part of a continuum of health care and support
- Support for family and friends during the dying and bereavement process

Family at the End of Life

Whether you die in hospice, in a nursing home or hospital, or at home, relationships are central to the end of life. Coming together, whether that is a family or a friend group, is often part of what people hope for at the end. One woman remembered her husband's last moments, as he died in a Veterans' Affairs hospital: "The whole family was there. . . . My daughter-in-law began to sing Amazing Grace. And I think most of us kinda joined in with her. And, of course, we saw him take his last breath and [at] that, she stopped singing" (qtd in Williams et al., 2013).

For many loved ones, the end of life is often a balance of providing comfort and hands-on care with managing their own grief (Lewis & McBride, 2004). Adults are often concerned about the impact of being cared for depending on their social roles and identities. For instance, women in other-sex relationships often worry about whether their partner will support them at the end of life and about being overwhelmed by

His Loss Changed America. Jim Obergefell (*left*) married his husband, John Arthur, shortly before his death. At that time, same-sex marriages were not legal, but Jim fought all the way to the U.S. Supreme Court for the right to be listed as John's spouse on his death certificate. The resulting decision legalized same-sex marriage in the United States.

caregiving responsibilities. People who identify as men tend to be more distrustful of the medical system and to avoid medical care (Vandello et al., 2019). People in same-sex relationships are more likely to have had in-depth conversations about how they want to be cared for and to receive more support from their partners (Donnelly et al., 2018).

In many cultures, families and friends assume that the dying person wants someone to be there at the exact moment of passing (Balmer et al., 2020). However, death is often unpredictable. When one research team tried to estimate how often people died alone, they found that people were alone at the moment of death more than half of the time. Even though this is common, people often feel a sense of failure if they cannot be there at the right time (Williams et al., 2013).

MAKING A DIFFERENCE
Learning How to Say Goodbye

Specialists who work with families at the end of life have the challenge of connecting with diverse people from different backgrounds who are all experiencing a profound transition. The challenge is daunting: Providers carry the responsibility of guiding people they have just met through an important moment in a way that respects their rituals and values. It is an experience that requires empathy and interpersonal skills. From this, some palliative experts have some advice for communication during the end of life that connects with many as they near the end (Byock, 2014).

First, experts remind us that dying is exhausting work: People may not want to have deep conversations all the time (Corr et al., 2018). Some people may not want to be too emotional or too deep. Ask first, and make sure that the dying person is ready to talk or to listen.

Second, sometimes the simplest things are best. Tell them things like, thank you; I forgive you; will you forgive me; you are loved; goodbye (Byock, 2014; Meier et al., 2016).

Third, remind them that they will be remembered after they are gone. As you will read, grief is one part of the process of creating memories. One of our gifts as human beings is that we are able to remember, learn, and take the past with us as we grow.

APPLY IT! **EP.3** Jane and John had the support of Aditi and hospice care during John's final days. What kind of care do you want for yourself or a loved one at the end of life? **EP.4** Communities often have different ethnotheories about how dying people are expected to behave and adjust to this major life transition. What ethnotheories about dying did you grow up with?

Grief and Loss

Learning Objectives

EP.4 Review perspectives on grief and bereavement.

EP.5 Describe the social functions of mourning rituals.

disenfranchised grief Grief that is not recognized by the greater community.

anticipatory grief The feeling of loss and sadness that begins before a death.

Grief and bereavement are a universal part of life. Loss is an experience we share with many other social mammals and even some birds (Anderson et al., 2018; Gonçalves & Carvalho, 2019). Grief is shaped by the culture that surrounds us. How we display the sadness over lost bonds and how we celebrate those lives depends on our community's expectations. The patterns of loss may also differ depending on whether a death is expected or unexpected, whether our community shares our grief, or whether it has to be hidden, as in so-called **disenfranchised grief** (Doka, 1999).

Some of this loss can begin before a death even occurs: **Anticipatory grief** is the feeling of sadness that begins before a death, as you contemplate the changes that have happened in your relationship and that are still to come. This form of grief is common in people who are losing their loved ones to a neurocognitive disorder or a long illness and are forced to acknowledge a changing relationship long before their loved one has died (Sweeting & Gilhooly, 1990).

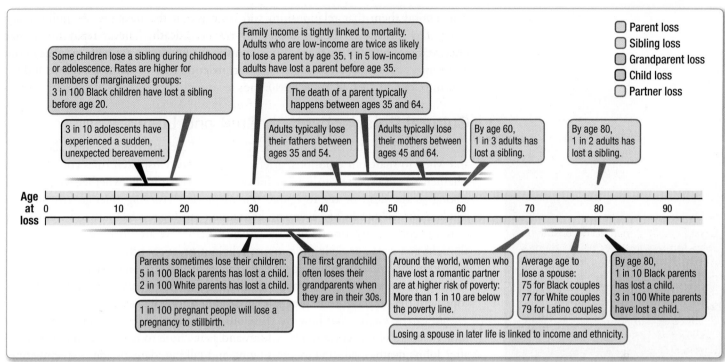

FIGURE E.4 Loss Happens over a Lifetime In the United States, researchers have found that there are patterns in when we lose loved ones. Disparities in health mean that these losses happen earlier for people who have experienced low income and discrimination.

After we experience a loss, whether we got the news over the phone or watched the breathing stop in the hospital, we often enter a period of *acute grief*. This is a time when our emotions are difficult to control: There is often terrible sadness or even anger, or we may feel nothing at all, just flatness and numbness. We may have trouble sleeping, eating, or even remembering what we need to do, in a cognitive fog for a period of time (O'Connor, 2019).

Most researchers have found that the sadness that comes with grief can be helpful and even help us bounce back, but cultures and communities often dictate how and when we can share these feelings (Cacciatore et al., 2008). As with other transitions across the lifespan, community support and strong social bonds can make the process easier. Scientists have found that, over time, most people are remarkably resilient in the face of loss: While some sadness remains, most will return to work and love again (Bonanno, 2019). Jane tells us that although she is still mourning John, she feels that she honored him in his last months.

Attachment and Loss

Attachment theorists like Bowlby point out that strong attachments help us thrive throughout the lifespan. When these bonds are broken by death, we must relearn how to be in the world and may feel emotionally overwhelmed, yearn for those we have lost, and even slip into depression, numbness, and despair (Bowlby, 1982). Contemporary psychodynamic and attachment researchers have reiterated these ideas. Even when we resolve acute feelings of grief, we may continue to be attached to those who are dead, in what some call *continuing bonds* (Fraley & Shaver, 2016; Kofod & Brinkman, 2017). Cultural practices around the world encourage links to our dead ancestors: We may leave them offerings on the day of the dead, leave flowers at a home altar, or just talk to them (Hidalgo et al., 2021; Steffen & Klass, 2018).

In a recent study, more than half of the children who had lost a parent still talked to their parents and most thought about them several times a week years after they were gone (Harris, 2018). For some, continuing bonds may be linked to religious beliefs that remind them that relationships will continue in the next life. As philosopher Karen Teel explained: "Before facing my mother's death, I never really knew that I believed that life continues. . . . But I know it as I know the sun will come up in the morning. . . . It's a gift and a mystery, this conviction that we come from love and we return to love" (K. Teel qtd. Yancy, 2020b).

Cultural Perspectives on Grief and Loss

Around the globe and throughout the lifespan, we are governed by rules about how and when to share our emotions; grief is no different. Unspoken rules communicate whether we are expected to wail at funerals or to sit stoically, whether we admit to talking to the dead or try to ignore our memories. *Grieving rules* govern how we regulate our feelings in bereavement, containing our biggest feelings and connecting us to the community around us (Doka, 2002). Whether we are sitting shiva, staying up all night at a wake, or saying the rosary, religious practices often give consolation by connecting us to something bigger than our own loss (Garcini et al., 2019; Klass, 2014). Cultural practices differ, but there are also many commonalities as human beings cope with the universal feeling of grief (Fernández-Basanta et al., 2020).

Researchers agree that how we share our expressions of loss is subject to the cultural practices of our communities. John and Jane chose to have a celebration of life after John's death, including lots of singing and talking, dancing, and remembering, with a song for John performed by Aditi. John and Jane's community valued expression and lots of talking about their feelings, but emotional expression at the end of life varies dramatically. In some communities, such as among Jewish families in Yemen, professional wailers are hired to amplify the feeling of sadness at funerals (Gamliel, 2010). But in Japan, many Buddhist families try to maintain their calm in times of public grief (Stearns, 2019).

One research team had a clever way of investigating cultural expectations for grieving: They looked at condolence cards (Koopmann-Holm & Tsai, 2014). They found that German sympathy cards were somber, sharing "deep sadness." In contrast, American sympathy cards were more likely to be happy, colorful, and focus on the positive. The researchers, along with others, suggest that many White European American and Latin American communities encourage upbeat, emotional expressions and repression of feelings of grief (Senft et al., 2020). U.S. culture is far from monolithic, however: Many communities have a less subdued grieving style, including some Native American and Chinese American communities (Colclough, 2017; Senft et al., 2020).

Some losses are more likely to be marginalized and shamed. Among them are deaths of newborns and stillborn infants: These are often deemed too painful or too awkward to discuss publicly (Kofod & Brinkman, 2017; Tseng et al., 2018). As a result, many families mourn their small children privately, although efforts are aimed to reverse the stigma and help them get the social support they need. Families of people who die from suicide or complications of substance use disorder are also often ashamed to talk about their loss publicly, which complicates their recovery (Erlangsen et al., 2017; Evans, & Abrahamson, 2020). People from the LGBTQIA+ community are more likely to experience disenfranchised grief if, for instance, they lose a partner and cannot mourn their loss at a job that does not accept their identity (Donnelly et al., 2018).

Coping and Resilience

When developmental scientists began studying how people react to grief, they found that most people were remarkably resilient (Bonanno et al., 2011). Some healthy people even reacted to death with a feeling of relief, particularly if they had been caregiving for a long time and the death was long expected (Boerner et al., 2017). However, most people experience a period of distress but can regain the ability to find

Saying Goodbye Away from Home This is a community of Karen refugees in Thailand who found refuge outside their ancestral villages in Myanmar. They have brought their funeral traditions with them, which include accompanying the body to its final resting place as a community (Bird, 2019).

pavlos christoforou/Alamy Stock Photo

TABLE E.1 Strategies for Managing Loss

Positive coping strategies	Maintain social connections or find support through service, support groups, or professional counseling.
	Search for a sense of meaning or purpose.
	If culturally appropriate, talk about feelings of loss and bereavement.
	Plan for the future and for restoring and creating a new life.
	Avoid ruminating on negative emotions.
	If culturally appropriate, find support from faith and spiritual communities.
Risky coping strategies	Avoiding grief, transition, and actively trying to forget.
	Managing pain with substances or alcohol use.
	Social isolation.

Information from Fernández-Basanta et al., 2020; Carr, 2020.

joy and meaning in their lives. As one woman explained to a researcher after losing her husband suddenly at 34, "I expected to collapse . . . But . . . I couldn't. Each day I got up and did what I had to. The days passed and somehow it was OK" (Bonanno, 2019, p. 11). These researchers suggest that for most people, grief is not something you need to consciously work at or something you can fail at, it is something that most human beings can manage. Coping with loss is part of how we live (Boerner et al., 2017).

Fewer than 1 in 10 of us will develop chronic feelings of grief or ongoing depression after a loss (Stroebe et al., 2017a). Effective coping, as researchers have found, includes focusing on the positive, rather than encouraging negative feelings (Bonanno, 2019). We must balance our feelings of loss, like the immediate feelings of grief that might keep us from moving forward. But we must also cope with the stress of restoring and creating a new life, a new identity, perhaps as a single person, or as a parent with a dead child, and learn new skills and adapt to a life without the one we love (Schut, 1999; Stroebe & Schut, 2010). (See **Table E.1**.)

Even if most people are able to bounce back from bereavement, grief is a physical stressor, increasing the wear and tear on the body for those left behind (O'Connor, 2019). The risk of having a heart attack is more than 28 times higher in the days after you have lost someone you love (Mostofsky et al., 2012). Bereavement tends to flood the body with the stress hormone cortisol, trigger an increase in inflammation, and lower resistance to disease (O'Connor, 2019).

Most people are resilient in the face of grief, but for some, losing a loved one becomes a chronic state of discontent that makes it hard to work and maintain relationships. Psychiatrists and psychologists often refer to this condition as *prolonged grief disorder* (APA, 2022; WHO, 2021). Interventions can help with prolonged grief. Established treatments include therapy, including exposure-based therapy for those who have experienced traumas, and sometimes antidepressant medications (Stroebe et al., 2017b). Emerging treatments include mindfulness meditation practices, efforts to find meaning in their experiences, and peer support (Papazoglou et al., 2020).

Losses over the Lifespan

Losses happen across the lifespan, not just in old age. Losing a child is more common than many people realize: A baby dies in 1 of every 160 births in the United States (Floyd et al., 2013). This is a major stressor, linked to increased rates of depression and PTSD (Donnelly et al., 2020; Floyd et al., 2013). In a global investigation of families who lost their infants in places such as urban South Africa, a Native American reservation in South Dakota, and urban communities in Great Britain, New Zealand, and Australia, researchers found that half of the mothers suffered prolonged grief years after the deaths of their babies (Goldstein et al., 2018).

From Loss to Service Maryanne O'Hara lost her daughter, Caitlin, to cystic fibrosis. Her grief inspired her to become an end-of-life doula, to help other families find meaning in this painful transition. Her most important recommendation? Talk to those who are dying, interview them about their legacies, and make the most of your time together.

Loss hits differently depending on how old we are. Children sometimes have more difficulty grieving than adults, particularly if death triggers a string of other transitions and stress in their lives (Pham et al., 2018). Bereavement is not uncommon in childhood: About 1 in 20 children lose a sibling, 1 in 14 lose a parent, and more than 3 in 10 teenagers have experienced a sudden death (Oosterhoff et al., 2018; Judi's House, 2021). Like adults, children are often temporarily emotionally upset by their loss, and have difficulty regulating their sadness and anger, but most are resilient (Menendez et al., 2020). Cultural ethnotheories vary about how children's grief and mourning should be recognized: Some communities keep children away from funerals and other end-of-life rituals, while others encourage children to participate (Hidalgo et al., 2021).

Losing a parent is an expected milestone of middle life that often marks the final transition into adulthood (Kim et al., 2019). For some, losing a parent is linked to family turmoil, division between siblings triggered by conflicts over caregiving and inheritance (Kim et al., 2013; Magai et al., 2016). For a few, these expected losses can lead to what some call *posttraumatic growth*, or an increase in awareness of the value of life and an appreciation for those around them (Quasim & Carson, 2020). Researchers have found that some adults experience an improvement in relationships with their own children after a loss, but this is not universal (Kim et al., 2019).

Older adults are remarkably resilient to loss, which researchers link to their stronger skills in emotion regulation and also to the reality that in later life, death is expected (Carstensen et al., 1999). Older adults experience the loss of a romantic partner as a common and painful milestone of late adulthood, a process known as *widowhood*. In late adulthood, losing a partner often forces partners to adjust to more than just the emotional longing for the person they loved. Adults need to adapt to new social roles and responsibilities and often new financial realities, which can add to strain (Carr, 2020; Liu et al., 2020). In the first few years after a loss, older adults tend to face the most difficulties, including increased risks for depression and heart disease (Becker et al., 2020; Shor et al., 2012).

Community Mourning

Mourning is the social activity that comes with bereavement, as we turn to others and the soothing power of ritual to connect our sadness and longing to something bigger than ourselves (Neimeyer et al., 2014). Rituals help make meanings from what we have lost. Mourning is a time to memorialize the dead and create continuing memories, whether in famous eulogies like the Gettysburg address, or in public vigils or demonstrations, or in John's celebration of life (Norton & Gino, 2014).

Rituals often include a ceremony, but they do not end with a funeral. For many families, mourning rituals continue for months and years (Mitima-Verloop et al., 2021). One group of families in New Orleans organizes yearly birthday parties for families who have lost their children to violence (Carter, 2018). Religious Islamic families may plan for a pilgrimage to Mecca in honor of the ones they have lost (Klass, 2014). Families may light candles on anniversaries, pay respects at yearly festivals, or remember their ancestors in home altars (Mitima-Verloop et al., 2021). Celebrations help us remember, come together, and keep those we love with us forever.

The global COVID-19 pandemic has forced families and communities to grapple with a scale of loss rarely seen. The losses have usually been unexpected and loved ones have often died alone, without the comfort of religious or cultural rituals. Researchers do not know yet how this will change how families grieve (Quasim & Carson, 2020).

Overwhelmed by Death Funeral directors, like the director of this home in Queens, New York, had to manage the comfort of grieving families and the logistics of enormous loss during the early waves of the COVID-19 pandemic.

Andrew Lichtenstein/Corbis via Getty Images

Cultural Perspectives on Mourning End-of-life rituals may be universal, but specific cultural practices vary around the world. Our families' cultural practices are often a specific blend of cultural and religious practices, such as hip-hop music and Christian hymns mixed with Jamaican food (Mitima-Verloop et al., 2021). In Haiti and New Orleans, funerals typically include live music, but in many communities, funerals are quiet and somber (Hidalgo et al., 2021). Some communities celebrate at home, and others incorporate religious ceremonies, funeral homes, or more informal get-togethers. Some groups value upbeat, joyous celebrations, as in some Irish wakes, Black American funerals, and Native American memorials (Burrell & Selman, 2020; Colclough, 2017; Moore et al., 2020).

Sociocultural theorists point out that culture never stays the same: It creatively adapts. For instance, families in Ethiopia now make their traditional graves from concrete, and eco-friendly, or "green," funerals are becoming popular in Italy (Boylston, 2015; Leland\ & Yalkin, 2018). Around the world, mourning happens online, with memorial webpages, "virtual tombs," and Facebook support groups (Dilmaç, 2018; Hamid et al., 2019).

Despite the universality of memorial services, not all scientists agree that they help with the process of grief (Burrell & Selman, 2020). Some have criticized the funeral industry for being exploitative, and they advocate for less expensive alternatives to corporatized funeral care (Mitford, 1996). Memorial experiences can be complex. For some, funerals do not feel meaningful: Speakers do not say the right things, the process feels artificial, and families may quarrel (Burrell & Selman, 2020; Mitima-Verloop et al., 2019). At other times, people report that funeral rituals have helped them gain control over their grief and are a lasting symbol of both social support and social status (Burrell & Selman, 2020; Norton & Gino, 2014).

Saying Goodbye over Zoom Rosemary Phillips passed away during the COVID-19 pandemic when restrictions in England prevented much of her family from attending her final service. Rosemary chose to be buried in a biodegradable willow coffin in a natural spot, in what is known as a "green burial."

Celebrating Lives

Death is a transition and, for many, an opportunity to celebrate and remember all the gifts of life. The power of loss can be a moment that triggers change (Holst-Warhalf, 2000; Walter, 2008). The pain of loss during the HIV epidemic of the 1980s spurred new research into the disease and accelerated the drive toward human rights for LGBTQIA+ Americans (Encarnación, 2014). The image of the body of 2-year-old Syrian refugee Alan Kurdi on a beach inspired many to intervene to help refugees struggling around the world (Berents, 2019). The countless bodies of Black people, including Breonna Taylor, George Floyd, and Ahmaud Arbery triggered a racial reckoning in 2020. And around the world, families have been forced to join together in a shared moment of grief wrought by COVID-19.

The end of life is a time to remember and to tell the stories of those who have come before, and to hold on to the opportunities we had to make connections and learn from one another. For Jane, that means holding in her hand the crystals she knew were with her partner at the end of his life, looking at the gorge that he loved to climb, and remembering his fulfilling life.

Change Can Come from Losses Aizada Kanatbekova was killed in Kyrgyzstan at age 27 after she was abducted in an attempted forced marriage. Hundreds of protesters gathered on the streets of Bishkek to remember her and call for justice.

APPLY IT! **EP.5** What are mourning rituals that are common in your community? How do they serve to create continuing bonds, remember those who are gone, and help mourning people access social support?

Wrapping It Up ⟨⟨⟩⟩

LO EP.1 Describe common changes in the brain during death. (p. 529)

Death occurs when the brain is damaged irreversibly. At the end of life, cognitive processes often slow. People may lose the ability to communicate, see, hear, and feel. Brain injury may make it difficult to regulate temperature and sleep cycles and to maintain heart rate and breathing. Damage to the brain stem often triggers death.

LO EP.2 List the medical and biological definitions of death. (p. 529)

Death is a biological process that happens when our bodies have experienced irreversible damage. Most people die when their heart stops and their lungs stop breathing. Dying can be expected or unexpected. Signs of the dying process may include terminal agitation, terminal lucidity, and cognitive decline. Medical processes and procedures, including life-support devices, can help people survive while being dependent on machines. Death can be defined both medically and legally, and communities around the world define death in different ways. Legal options available for some in the dying process include physician-assisted suicide and active euthanasia. Talking about death is a way people and their families can get more comfortable with the end of life. Death happens across the lifespan but is most common in young children and older adults. Over time, people have tended to live longer, but major pandemics, wars, and natural disasters have shortened life for many.

LO EP.3 Discuss common variations in preparing for the end of life. (p. 536)

Many people avoid talking about the end of life. Some theorists suggest that death has become stigmatized or taboo in modern cultures and that many adults have denial or anxiety about death. Erikson suggested that achieving a sense of wholeness at the end of life enhances well-being. Kübler-Ross developed a stage theory of dying focused on achieving a "good death." Her specific stages have been questioned, but her advocacy for improved end-of-life care remains influential. Many communities share ethnotheories that dying is a special time to say goodbye and mend relationships. Specific rituals and practices, including those regulating the expression of emotion, decision making, medical care, and treatment of the body after death, are often culturally specific. Adults can plan for their end-of-life care. Quality caregiving at the end of life can include hospice and palliative care.

LO EP.4 Review perspectives on grief and bereavement. (p. 542)

Grief and bereavement are shaped by culture. Cultures can make some forms of grief disenfranchised. Attachment theorists suggest that people can have continuing bonds with those they have lost after they are gone. Grieving rules are governed by cultural and community expectations. Many people are resilient in the face of grief: They may experience acute sadness but can return to their typical activities. In the short term, loss is a significant stressor. About 1 in 10 experience significant long-term grief. Losses are often more significant stressors if they trigger other transitions. Older adults tend to be more resilient to losses than younger ones.

LO EP.5 Describe the social functions of mourning rituals. (p. 542)

Community rituals can help individuals connect with the greater social community and find meaning. Many end-of-life rituals create a sense of continuing bonds with those we have lost. Cultural communities often have different rituals and expectations about end-of-life events, which often change over time. The end of life can be an opportunity to create memories of those we have lost and sometimes to advocate for changes inspired by their lives.

KEY TERMS

thanatology (p. 529)
death (p. 529)
terminal decline (p. 530)
terminal agitation (p. 530)

terminal lucidity (p. 530)
clinical death (p. 532)
brain death (p. 532)
physician-assisted suicide (p. 533)

active euthanasia (p. 533)
advance directives (p. 539)
living wills (p. 539)
hospice (p. 540)

palliative care (p. 540)
disenfranchised grief (p. 542)
anticipatory grief (p. 542)

CHECK YOUR LEARNING

1. When are people are MOST likely to lose their lives, even in affluent countries like the United States?
   a) Early infancy and late adulthood
   b) Adolescence and young adulthood
   c) Middle childhood and middle adulthood
   d) Early adulthood and late adulthood

2. Damage to which part of the brain often triggers and signals the end of life?
   a) Prefrontal cortex
   b) The brain stem
   c) The subcortical structures
   d) The cerebellum

3. Linda has been diagnosed with an incurable form of lung cancer. Her family culture discourages talking openly about death. How can her health care team apply the principle of cultural humility to advise Linda and her family about end-of-life care?
   a) Tell Linda and her family that a good death requires facing reality head on and talking about her condition frankly and openly.
   b) Ask Linda and her family how they want to talk about her condition and what would be appropriate within her cultural community.
   c) Avoid talking about Linda's death or end-of-life care.
   d) Tell Linda that you think she will probably be fine.

4. What is NOT a modern health care program that has been shown to improve end-of-life caregiving?
   a) Hospice care
   b) Palliative care
   c) Integrated team-based caregiving
   d) Centering the End, group-based end-of-life care

5. Which types of death are MOST likely to be disenfranchised?
   a) Stillborn death of an infant
   b) Loss of a partner in late adulthood
   c) Expected death of a parent in middle age
   d) Unexpected death of a grandparent

6. Julio lost his partner to a neurocognitive disorder after nearly a decade of caregiving. Julio had difficulty admitting to a sense of relief after his partner's death. How would you explain to Julio that grief and mourning take different expressions, depending on circumstance, and that a sense of relief is common when people die after years of discomfort?

7. Marta could not have a traditional funeral service for her partner, Kevin, because of pandemic restrictions. What are virtual ways that Marta could access the social support, sense of meaning and remember Kevin's generativity, in a time of limited in-person contacts?

GLOSSARY

ableism A form of bias against people based on their physical abilities. (p. 408)

abuse The legal term used to describe the most serious types of harm to children, which can be physical, emotional, sexual, or neglectful. (p. 213)

accommodation The process of reorganizing knowledge based on new experiences. (p. 45)

acculturation The process of adapting to some of the traditions and expectations of a cultural community. (p. 334)

achievement status In Marcia's theory, this identity status occurs when adolescents have explored and committed to a path. (p. 332)

active euthanasia When a physician actively helps someone with a terminal illness die. (p. 533)

activities of daily living (ADLs) Basic living skills that include independently using the bathroom, getting dressed, bathing and feeding oneself, and moving short distances. (p. 462)

activity theory The idea that communities and older people both benefit when older adults are engaged with the world. (p. 499)

adolescence The life stage that begins with the biological changes of puberty and ends when young people are recognized as adults. (p. 286)

adolescent-limited behavior A habit or behavior that is particular to the adolescent life stage. (p. 343)

adoption When parents become legal caregivers to a baby or child who is born to another biological parent. (p. 98)

adrenarche The first hormonal changes preparing the body for puberty, typically occurring between ages 5 and 9. (p. 229)

advance directives A variety of formal documents and instructions that specify what kind of end-of-life care you would want if you are unable to communicate your wishes directly. (p. 539)

affordance The term for what people can learn from objects in the world around them. (p. 118)

age in place The idea that you would rather age in a community or a geographic location that is familiar to you, including your own home. (p. 506)

ageism A form of prejudice against people based on their age. (p. 408)

age-segregated Grouped with other children of the same age. (p. 327)

alleles Genes that have different forms. (p. 68)

Alzheimer disease (AD) A degenerative neurocognitive disorder caused by the buildup of tau and amyloid proteins that is linked to difficulties with thinking and the ability to function. (p. 488)

amyloid beta A protein by-product implicated in brain aging that builds up as a result of inflammation and glial dysfunction. (p. 482)

analytic thinking A type of thinking that is logical, weighing evidence and making a decision that requires conscious thought. (p. 307)

animism The tendency to describe nonliving things as if they are alive and have human feelings or motives. (p. 174)

anorexia nervosa A consistent pattern of disordered eating that may involve extreme calorie restriction, purging, excessive exercise, and a distorted belief that one's body is overly heavy. (p. 299)

anticipatory grief The feeling of loss and sadness that begins before a death, as you contemplate the changes that have happened in your relationship and that are still to come. (p. 542)

anxiety disorders A clinical diagnosis based on a pattern of excessive worry or fear that keeps children, adolescents or adults, from fully functioning in their lives. (p. 340)

Apgar test A quick medical evaluation of breathing, activity, responsiveness, and heart rate that assesses which newborns need immediate medical care. (p. 96)

arthritis A condition causing pain in the joints. (p. 475)

assessment The use of a standardized tool or test. (p. 59)

assimilation The expansion of an existing schema with new knowledge or experience. (p. 45)

attachment An emotional bond in a close relationship. Attachment begins with the relationship between infants and their caregivers and may not always be positive. (p. 155)

attachment theory The theory pioneered that maintains that children's emotional bonds to their caregivers are an essential part of their development. (p. 40)

attention-deficit/hyperactivity disorder (ADHD) A disorder in which children have high energy levels and problems with focusing or controlling themselves, that interfere with school and/or home life. (p. 181)

authoritarian parenting A type of caregiving in which caregivers have high expectations for their children's behavior but very little warmth. Authoritarian parents make rules and expect their children to obey them. (p. 210)

authoritative parenting A type of caregiving associated with confident and successful children in which caregivers have high expectations for their children's behavior, but they also are warm and communicative. (p. 210)

autism spectrum disorder (ASD) A cognitive and communication disorder characterized by difficulties with communication and social interaction. (p. 122)

autonomy Taking responsibility, having greater agency, and making more decisions. (p. 318)

autonomy versus shame and doubt The second crisis in Erikson's stage theory of development in which toddlers learn to balance their desire to be independent with their limitations and frequent missteps. (p. 137)

average social acceptance Children who fall around the middle of being liked and disliked, not quite making it into the other categories. (p. 277)

axon The long, tail-like structure attached to the cell body that transmits a chemical signal to other neurons. (p. 112)

babbling Short, repetitive, syllable sounds, like ba-ba-ba or pa-pa-pa (in English), that begin at about 4 months and become more speechlike by 7 months. (p. 130)

behaviorism A branch of psychology that is focused on things that are measurable and suggests that we learn through pairing causes and effects. (p. 40)

binge drinking Consuming a large number of alcoholic drinks (more than five) in a short period of time. (pp. 342, 362)

binge-eating disorder The most prevalent eating disorder in adolescents marked by episodes of compulsive, excessive eating that make you feel out of control, ashamed, or upset. (p. 299)

biological perspective An emphasis on how psychological and behavioral development begins with roots in our brain, our genes, and innate or inborn instincts. (p. 35)

birth cohorts The categories that experts use to group people from different generations. (p. 16)

birth defects Major differences in the body or brain functioning present at birth. (p. 87)

blastocyst The ball of cells during the germinal stage of prenatal development that becomes larger and then separates into an outer layer and an inner mass, replicating until it is more than 150 cells. (p. 81)

body image The feelings and ideas you have about your body. (p. 298)

borderline personality disorder (BPD) A personality disorder that is characterized by unstable and intense feelings, impulsive and often self-destructive behaviors, and difficulty maintaining relationships. (p. 399)

brain death When someone is determined to have experienced irreversible brain damage that makes them unable to function and respond to any kind of stimulation. (p. 532)

bulimia nervosa A consistent pattern of disordered eating that involves overeating compensated by throwing up, excessive exercise, or abusing laxatives. (p. 299)

burnout The term researchers use to describe the emotional exhaustion caused by stressful working conditions that leads to a sense of detachment, bitterness, and ultimately a lack of confidence in your skills. (p. 429)

cardiovascular disease (CVD) The leading cause of death in middle adulthood that includes a wide range of conditions affecting the heart and blood vessels, including heart attacks, stroke, abnormal heart rhythms, coronary artery disease, and heart failure. (p. 416)

career establishment The third stage of the process of career development in which a general interest is made a reality and becomes a job. (p. 371)

career exploration The second stage of the process of career development in which young adults research employment options. (p. 371)

case study An in-depth analysis of one person, family, or institution's experience. (p. 56)

cephalocaudal Development that occurs in a head-downward pattern, beginning with a baby's ability to support their heavy head. (p. 117)

cesarean section A surgical procedure that involves making a small cut into the uterus and removing the baby. (Also called *c-section*.) (p. 94)

chromosomes The 23 pairs of long molecules of DNA containing genetic information and found in the nucleus of human cells. (p. 68)

circadian rhythm Your internal clock for the daily cycle of rest, wake, and sleep. (pp. 108, 300)

civic engagement Working to make a difference in the community in a variety of ways, including volunteering, organizing, and voting. (p. 401)

classical conditioning A model of learning in which a *stimulus* (or experience) is linked to a *response* (or behavior). (p. 41)

classification The categorization and grouping of objects according to multiple dimensions. (p. 238)

clinical death The stage in the dying process when your breathing and heart stop. Medical providers now use the term *cardiac arrest*, because it refers to the moment when your heart stops beating. (p. 532)

clique A small "friend group" that shares interests and activities. (p. 325)

cognitive development theory The theory that growth in thinking and understanding happens as a result of active exploration of the world. (p. 44)

cognitive reserve The ability to maintain your thinking abilities despite getting older. (p. 487)

cohabitation Sharing a home with a romantic partner. (p. 391)

collectivist Communities that place more value on relatedness and closeness and tend to value the family or the group over the individual. (p. 25)

Community Cultural Wealth The areas of strength and resilience identified by developmental scientists and educators that help people, particularly those who are marginalized or are people of color, succeed in a discriminatory world. (p. 18)

comprehensive high schools High schools that serve all youth, regardless of their academic ability and future careers, helping to prepare them for adult work. (p. 309)

concrete operations Piaget's stage of cognitive development occurring in middle childhood in which children's logical thinking abilities gradually improve as they begin to understand problems of greater complexity. (p. 237)

concussion A form of traumatic brain injury (TBI) caused by a blow to the head. (p. 305)

conservation tasks Piaget's hands-on tasks that measure how preschoolers' logical thinking develops. Each involves asking children what has happened to an object or a set of objects that is rearranged or manipulated in front of them to look different. Preschoolers struggle to logically complete the conservation tasks, but over time, their abilities improve. (p. 175)

context The term used by developmental scientists to describe the broad external factors that surround and influence each individual. (p. 14)

continuity perspective The idea that aspects of personality and identity stay the same as we age. (p. 500)

continuous A model of change that is relatively constant and stable. (p. 29)

controversial Children who receive mixed ratings by their peers, strongly disliked by some and strongly liked by others. (p. 277)

conventional stage of moral reasoning Kohlberg's stage of moral reasoning in which children think more abstractly about what is right and wrong. (p. 280)

cooperative play Playing together on a joint project. (p. 216)

correlational study A study in which a researcher gathers data and looks for relationships between variables but does not actually manipulate them. (p. 55)

critical thinking The ability to thoughtfully question what you believe or what other people believe. (p. 11)

cross-cultural research Research that compares people from two or more different cultural communities. (p. 61)

cross-sectional study A study that compares development in two or more groups of different ages at one point in time. (p. 57)

cross-sequential study A study that follows two or more different age groups over time in a combination of cross-sectional and longitudinal designs. (p. 57)

crowds Larger, looser collections of adolescents within the school or neighborhood. (p. 325)

crystallized reasoning Knowledge of facts and processes that comes from past experience. (p. 424)

cultural humility An openness to cultural diversity and a self-awareness of your own cultural background that helps to create respectful relationships in which everyone learns from each other and no one feels superior. (p. 20)

cultural perspective Explains how culture is integrated into all of development and how cultural variations and strengths can help everyone thrive. (p. 47)

cultural socialization The way children learn about their heritage or the community to which they belong, typically in their families. (p. 322)

culture The ideas, beliefs, and social practices that a group of people shares. (p. 14)

death The major social, biological, and spiritual transition that occurs when your body has experienced irreversible damage and can no longer recover. (p. 529)

dendrite A branch-like appendage that grows out of the cell body and receives communication from other neurons. (p. 112)

deoxyribonucleic acid (DNA) A spiral-, or helix-, shaped structure made up of paired chemicals that carries the genetic code. (p. 68)

dependent variable The factor that is measured during an experiment to determine the effect of the independent variable. (p. 53)

depression A clinical diagnosis based on a pattern of sadness and lack of energy that impairs your ability to function. (p. 340)

developmental niche A person's cultural environment, which is subject to the specific cultural practices, material setting, and beliefs of their family. (p. 25)

developmental science The systematic study of how humans grow and the underlying processes that create change and stability over time. (p. 4)

dialectical thinking The ability to look at the opposing sides to a problem, explore the contradictions between them, and accept that the solution may lie somewhere in between. (p. 355)

differential susceptibility Individual differences in how sensitive people are to environmental effects. (p. 141)

difficult In Thomas and Chess's dimensional approach to temperament, babies who are easily frustrated, are slow to adapt to change, and react intensely. This term is no longer preferred, outside of scholarly research. (p. 150)

diffusion status In Marcia's theory, this identity status occurs when adolescents are not exploring or committed to an identity. (p. 332)

discipline Caregiving practices or strategies used to teach children how to behave by setting rules, encouraging good behavior, and discouraging missteps. (p. 211)

discontinuous A model of change that is more irregular and unstable, happening in sprints and pauses. (p. 29)

disenfranchised grief Grief that is not recognized by the greater community as appropriate or legitimate, leading to a lack of social support. (p. 542)

disengagement theory The discredited idea that severing social ties and increasing social isolation is a natural and inevitable part of aging. (p. 599)

disorganized attachment In attachment theory, children who have unusual responses in the Strange Situation procedure and who may be afraid of their caregivers. (p. 156)

distal Caregiving practices that are physically distant but may include joint attention and face-to-face contact. (p. 138)

dizygotic Twins that develop when two (or more) ova are fertilized by separate sperm. (p. 76)

dominant inheritance pattern A type of genetic inheritance for single-gene disorders. A person with a dominant condition may have just one of the disease-carrying alleles. (p. 73)

Down syndrome A condition caused by an extra 21st chromosome that results in anomalies in brain development and may also impair muscle tone and cardiovascular development. (p. 75)

early adulthood A culturally defined period typically ranging between ages 18 and 30 that is marked by tremendous individual flexibility and potential but less structure and assistance than adolescence. (p. 348)

early childhood The period between ages 2½ and 6. It typically begins as toddlers develop language and movement skills and ends as they develop more abstract thinking and independent living skills and, in many communities, start formal schooling. (p. 164)

easy In Thomas and Chess's dimensional approach to temperament, babies who are flexible and usually content. (p. 150)

eating disorders Psychological conditions that are marked by long-term, unhealthy patterns of eating, obsessions with food, and poor body image that cause problems with the ability to function. (p. 299)

egocentrism In the Piagetian sense, children's inability to see the world from other people's point of view. (p. 176)

elaboration Adding information to the facts you need to remember so that they become more detailed and easier to recall. (p. 242)

elder abuse When an older adult is harmed emotionally, physically, sexually or financially, by a loved one. (p. 516)

elder neglect When a caregiver fails to protect an older adult from harm. (p. 516)

embryonic stage The second stage of prenatal development, in weeks 2 through 8, in which the embryo develops the major parts of its body—from legs to brain. (p. 79)

emergentist Scholars who argue that humans' drive to communicate and imitate and ability to recognize patterns, rather than brain processes specifically devoted to language, created the uniquely human ability to use language. (Also called *constructivist*.) (p. 132)

emerging adulthood A term used by some scholars to describe the period between about ages 18 and about 29 in which young people consciously postpone some of the milestones of adulthood to explore their identity. (p. 351)

emotion regulation The ability to manage your feelings in a way that is appropriate to your community circumstances. (p. 149)

emotional contagion The tendency to mimic feelings we observe in others. (p. 148)

emotions Reactions to your thoughts or your environment that involve your body, your thoughts, and your behaviors. (p. 144)

empathy The ability to identify with someone else's feelings. (p. 148)

epigenetics An area of study within the biological perspective that examines how physical and inborn characteristics, including gene activation, are changed by a person's environment. (pp. 10, 36)

epigenome The part of the genome that controls gene expression. (p. 70)

episodic memory Long-term memory for specific events. (p. 179)

erectile dysfunction (ED) The inability to maintain an erection. (p. 414)

estrangement A period of extreme strain in a relationship where family members no longer have contact. (p. 449)

estrogen A hormone that is linked to reproduction, maturation, brain development, and sexual function in both males and females. Estrogen levels are higher in biological females but are important to typical functioning in both males and females. (p. 288)

ethical standards Moral guidelines for protecting the interests of research participants and making sure scientific work is as honest as it can be. (p. 61)

ethnic identity A sense of yourself as belonging to a particular ethnic group or community. (p. 333)

ethnicity A way of referring to groups by their geographic origins and often their cultural heritage. (p. 21)

ethnography A longer, richly detailed investigation of everyday life. (p. 56)

ethnotheories Parents' ideas or beliefs about children's development. (p. 25)

ethology The theory that some human behaviors are universal and innate despite the wide diversity in human beings around the world. (p. 36)

eudemonia The happiness you find from your commitment to higher values outside of yourself. (p. 438)

evolution The idea that life on Earth develops and changes to adapt to the environment over successive generations. (p. 35)

executive function A group of thinking skills that allow you to control your behavior, suppress impulsive actions and implement long-term plans. (p. 180)

experience-dependent brain development Brain maturation that relies on the quantity or the quality of environmental input and, like all learning, continues throughout the lifespan. (p. 113)

experience-expectant brain development Brain maturation that relies on nearly universal environmental inputs. (p. 112)

experiment The act of testing a hypothesis that one factor is caused by another. (p. 53)

expertise Skill in a specific area. (p. 425)

explicit memory Memory of names, dates, and details. (p. 123)

exploratory learning Trying out different ways to solve a problem before deciding on the best solution. (p. 304)

externalizing disorders Psychological disorders characterized by difficult behaviors that affect others, such as acting out or severe aggression. Externalizing disorders include disruptive behavior disorders such as oppositional defiant disorder (ODD) and conduct disorder (CD). (p. 263)

extrinsic motivation The drive to do something because you are hoping for a reward. (p. 187)

familism The concept of responsibility of the family as a group. (p. 322)

fast-mapping A child's ability to quickly learn new words. (p. 130)

fetal stage The third stage of prenatal development, weeks 9 through birth, in which the fetus begins to look like a baby and adds pounds and the organs and brain structures that will allow it to survive on its own. (p. 79)

fictive kin Families that are bound by voluntary bonds of friendship and community, rather than biology. (p. 451)

fine motor development The development of small movements requiring precise coordination, like picking up little objects, swallowing, or pointing. (p. 116)

fluid reasoning The components of thinking including processing speed, memory, and the ability to think abstractly. (p. 424)

foreclosure status In Marcia's theory, this identity status occurs when adolescents have committed to a path or identity without exploration. (p. 332)

formal operational thought Piaget's stage of cognitive development that begins in early adolescence and lasts into adulthood and is both logical and abstract. (p. 306)

frailty An age-linked condition including muscle weakness, exhaustion, physical inability to be active, and sometimes weight loss. (p. 474)

functional play Play that has a goal or achievement orientation, such as art, puzzles, rule-based games, and physical skills such as hopping, climbing, etc. (p. 216)

gender The term for the social and cultural distinctions describing binary and less binary distinctions between men and women. (p. 71)

gender expression The term for how you express your gender in daily life, such as how you wear makeup, style your hair, or what clothing you like. (p. 71)

gender identity The term for your sense of yourself as a man, woman, or someone not as exclusively within the lines of these binary labels. (p. 71)

gender roles The social and cultural ideas a person holds about appropriate behaviors or roles of people based on their gender. (p. 203)

gender schema A framework for understanding the world in terms of cultural expectations related to gender identity. (p. 204)

generative Caring and doing things for others beside yourself. (p. 401)

generativity Caring or contributing to others in a way that has an impact on the world. (p. 437)

generativity versus stagnation In Erikson's theory, the conflict in adulthood between making an impact on others and being stuck in your own needs. (p. 437)

genes Sections of DNA that create particular proteins. (p. 68)

genome The unique set of instructions that includes everything a cell might need for creating your body parts and maintaining them over the lifespan. (p. 68)

genotype The genome that contributes your phenotype. (p. 70)

germinal stage The first stage of prenatal development, in which the single-celled zygote divides and implants into the uterus in the first week of development. (p. 79)

gerontology The study of aging. (p. 5)

gifted education An academic program for children who may need enriched or specialized education in order to meet their potential. (p. 253)

glia Support cells located in the brain and nervous system. (p. 482)

goodness of fit The idea that babies benefit from a good match between their personalities and their caregivers. (p. 151)

grandfamilies Families headed by a grandparent. (p. 449)

grit The ability to persevere in order to achieve a long-term goal. (p. 251)

gross motor development The development of bigger movements like walking, jumping, or skipping. (p. 116)

growth spurt A very rapid increase in height and size that begins at about age 10 in girls and age 12 in boys. (p. 288)

growth stage The first stage of the process of career development that begins as ambitious dreams in childhood and adolescence. (p. 371)

habituation A basic form of learning in which you become bored with something if you experience it repeatedly. (p. 123)

health disparities Differences in the rate of health conditions based on social categories. (p. 418)

hedonia The enjoyment you receive from short-term pleasures. (p. 438)

heuristic thinking A type of advanced reasoning, which is automatic thinking that you do outside of consciousness. (p. 307)

homophily The tendency to like and associate with people we perceive as like us. (p. 324)

hospice A program of end-of-life care that focuses on eliminating suffering, by treating the emotional, physical, spiritual, and social needs of dying people and their families, rather than focusing on curing terminal disease. (p. 540)

HPG axis A set of glands that trigger puberty, including the hypothalamus, pituitary gland, and gonads (testes and ovaries). (p. 288)

hypothesis A prediction about what a researcher expects to find from the data. (p. 51)

identity A person's sense of who they are and how they fit into the social groups of the world. (p. 331)

identity crisis The conflict in deciding between the possible roles a person could play and the possible selves they could be. (p. 332)

identity versus role confusion In Erikson's theory of life span development, the crisis of adolescent development which is resolved when youth understand themselves and their role in the world. (p. 332)

immunization A means of protection against diseases that introduces a tiny amount of an infectious virus into the body to teach it to defend itself against that virus. If the immunized person encounters the virus later, they are less likely to get sick, because their immune system is prepared. (p. 108)

implicit memory Memory of new skills and processes and ability to habituate. (p. 123)

in vitro fertilization (IVF) A procedure in which doctors combine egg and sperm outside the body in a hospital laboratory and then place the resulting zygotes in the uterus, where they can implant and develop into a baby (or babies). (p. 80)

independent Communities that value individual rights. (Also known as *autonomy*.) (p. 25)

independent variable A factor that is tested to see if it causes change in another variable. An independent variable is something that the researcher can change. (p. 53)

individualistic Communities that have strong traditions of valuing the individual over larger groups, communities, or families. (p. 25)

inductive reasoning A disciplinary approach that relies on motivating children to change their behavior through talk. (p. 212)

industry versus inferiority The fourth crisis of Erikson's theory in which children are challenged to build their sense of themselves as capable and avoid feeling inadequate. (p. 259)

infant-directed speech (IDS) Adults' use of high-pitched, sing-songy tones and simple sentences when they talk to infants. (p. 131)

information processing An approach that studies the development of thinking and understanding by describing how a person pays attention, remembers, and reacts to the world, similar to how a computer processes information. (p. 46)

initiative versus guilt Erikson's third stage of development, which occurs between ages 3 and 5 and involves the conflict between children's enthusiasm to try new things independently and their remorse when they get things wrong. (p. 195)

insecure attachment In attachment theory, children who have not established a sense of trust in their caregivers to soothe them when they are upset. (p. 156)

insecure-avoidant attachment In attachment theory, a form of insecure attachment characterized by babies' emotional distance from their caregivers who they perceive as being unable to soothe them. (p. 156)

insecure-resistant attachment In attachment theory, a form of insecure attachment characterized babies' angry and hostile responses to their caregiver who they perceive as inconsistent and unreliable. (p. 156)

Institutional Review Board (IRB) A committee that is designed to review scientific research and ensure that it is safe and adequately protects participants. (p. 61)

instrumental activities of daily living (IADLs) A measure of functioning that includes tasks requiring planning and social skills, such as arranging for transportation, shopping, cooking, organizing finances, keeping your home clean, communicating by phone, and managing medical care and medications. (p. 464)

integrity and despair Erikson's eighth stage of cognitive development, in which adults review, or *integrate*, their past and make peace with themselves. (p. 499)

intellectual disabilities Difficulties with academics, practical skills, or social relationships. (p. 252)

intelligence The ability to learn and apply what has been learned. (p. 243)

internal working model In attachment theory, the idea that our early habits of relating to our caregivers create a pattern of relating that we will use later on in our lives. (p. 155)

internalizing disorders Psychological disorders in which children's emotions are focused inward, manifesting as overwhelming feelings of sadness (depression) or worry (anxiety). (p. 262)

intersectionality A term that refers to the fact that we all have multiple, intersecting identities relating to age, gender, ability, ethnicity, nationality, romantic preferences, and so forth. (p. 20)

interventions Evidence-based programs or services designed to improve health, psychological well-being, or behavior. (p. 103)

intimacy and isolation Erikson's stage of human development that occurs in young adulthood. In his view, the successful resolution of the crisis is finding love. (p. 382)

intimate partner violence (IPV) Violence within relationships. (p. 393)

intrinsic motivation The drive to do something because it is its own reward and just doing it feels rewarding. (p. 187)

IQ A person's score on a standardized intelligence test which, for most people, is between 85 and 115. (p. 243)

kangaroo care A form of skin-to-skin contact that involves holding a lightly clothed newborn against a caregiver's chest. (p. 96)

level of functioning A measure that evaluates how well adults can manage in their daily life. (p. 462)

life expectancy A measurement of how long you can expect to live. (p. 466)

lifecourse persistent behavior A habit or behavior that is consistent across the lifespan. (p. 343)

lifespan development The pattern of changes and stability in individuals that happens between birth and death. It is also the study of what in the environment and in our genes make each of us unique. (p. 3)

literacy Reading and writing skills. (p. 250)

living wills A form of advance directive that specifies care that you would want at the end of life. (p. 539)

locus coeruleus A region in the brainstem that is a hub of brain networks and provides the neurotransmitters to the brain. (p. 482)

longitudinal research The study of the same group of people over time. (p. 56)

long-term-care facility Institutions including nursing homes, rehabilitation facilities that provide treatment and skilled nursing care. (p. 513)

low birthweight (LBW) Babies born weighing less than 2,500 grams (about 5½ pounds). (p. 94)

maintenance stage The stage of the process of career development that occurs later in life in which people maintain their skills to keep up with a changing workplace, and may need to start all over again as the economy, their interests, or their life demand a change. (p. 371)

malnutrition When someone does not have adequate nutrients to support their growth. (p. 102)

maltreatment The general term scholars use to describe the many types of abuse and neglect of children by adults who are responsible for them. (p. 213)

maturation The genetically programmed growth that drives many aspects of development. (p. 26)

meiosis A special form of cell division that creates the gametes, or sperm and ova cells. (p. 70)

menarche The term for the first menstrual period. (p. 289)

menopause A hormonal change in midlife, in which the ovaries stop releasing hormones, causing menstrual periods to end. (p. 413)

mental representation The ability to think things through using internal images rather than needing to act on the environment. (p. 121)

metacognition Awareness of how you are thinking and reflecting on it. (p. 242)

metamemory The awareness of the process of remembering. (p. 242)

microgenetic research Research that focuses on understanding how development happens by studying change as it happens. (p. 58)

middle adulthood A flexible life stage that begins when adults establish independent lives and ends when they recognize themselves as old. (p. 406)

middle childhood The period spanning ages 6 to 11 that begins as children develop the independence and self-regulation to take on new responsibilities. (p. 225)

middle-old The term for adults who are between ages 74 and 84. (p. 462)

midlife crisis A concept in popular culture without much empirical support, in which adults reevaluate their lives upon reaching a painful turning point and make major changes. (p. 439)

mild cognitive impairment (MCI) When an adult has more cognitive challenges than would be expected for a person of their age but is still able to function in their everyday life. (Also called *mild neurocognitive disorder*.) (p. 488)

mitochondria The energy center of your cells. (p. 468)

mitosis A type of cell division that creates two, new identical cells. (p. 68)

monitoring When caregivers keep track of what their children are doing. (p. 269)

monozygotic Twins with nearly identical DNA because they start off as a single zygote that separates into two in the first days after fertilization. (p. 76)

moodiness Emotional changeability, often leaning toward negative feelings like irritability. (p. 336)

moratorium status In Marcia's theory, this identity status occurs when adolescents have postponed committing to an identity and are exploring. (p. 332)

motor development The development of body coordination. (p. 116)

multifactorial Traits that are influenced by multiple variables. (p. 74)

myelin Layers of cholesterol-rich fat that insulate the axon, helping to speed up communication. (p. 112)

myelination The lifelong process of adding myelin to axons. (p. 112)

nativist approach A theoretical perspective that maintains that babies are born knowing a great deal about how the world works. (Also called the *core knowledge approach*.) (p. 124)

nature The influence of genetics on development. (p. 12)

neglected Children who are unconsidered or forgotten altogether by their peers. (p. 277)

neglectful parenting Caregiving without warmth or expectations. Children from neglectful families are at high risk for emotional and behavioral difficulties as they grow up. (p. 210)

neurocognitive disorders (NCDs) A spectrum of age-linked difficulties with thinking and independent functioning, ranging from mild to severe. (p. 487)

neurofibrillary tangles Misshapen tau proteins that bunch together, and can damage the brain and contribute to neurocognitive disorders. (p. 482)

neurons Nerve cells. (p. 82)

numeracy The ability to manipulate numbers and do arithmetic. (p. 250)

nurture The influence of experience on development. (p. 13)

object permanence Piaget's term for the understanding that objects continue to exist even when they are out of sight. (p. 121)

observation When scientists closely watch and record what people are doing—either in real life or in the laboratory. (p. 58)

oldest-old The term for adults who are ages 85 and older. (p. 462)

operant conditioning A process of learning in which rewards and punishments are used to shape behaviors. (p. 41)

osteoporosis When bones become so porous and fragile that they are vulnerable to breaks. (p. 475)

overextension An error in which a child assumes that a specific term relates to a larger category. (p. 131)

overweight When a child is heavier for their age and height than most other children, or above the 85th percentile. (p. 104)

ovum The egg cell. (p. 70)

palliative care A type of medical treatment for seriously ill people that focuses on improving quality of life and eliminating discomfort, rather than on curing the underlying disease. (p. 540)

parallel play When children play physically close together but are not working on a shared project. (p. 216)

parental monitoring The process of caregivers observing and keeping track of what children are doing. (p. 321)

parenting styles Dimensional descriptions of caregiving relationships during childhood. (p. 209)

peak career The time when earnings and prestige are at the high point. (p. 427)

people of color An inclusive term for people who identify as multiracial and for people who are Black, Latino, Asian American, or Native American and who have a feeling of solidarity and shared experience of marginalization. (p. 22)

percentile A way of statistically comparing an individual to a group. (p. 102)

perceptual narrowing The process by which infants become less sensitive to sensory input as they grow and begin to specialize in the sights and sounds to which they are exposed more often. (p. 115)

permissive parenting Caregiving without rules. Permissive parents have low expectations for children's behavior but a high degree of affection. (p. 210)

personality Habits of emotionally relating and responding to people and events in our lives. (p. 150)

personality disorder A disorder that is diagnosed when long-standing traits are particularly extreme and impair typical functioning, as when someone's moodiness prevents them from getting along with others or functioning in life. (p. 399)

phenotype Your individual observable characteristics. (p. 70)

phonics-based instruction Instruction that builds children's reading skills by reinforcing the links between letters and their sounds. (p. 250)

physician-assisted suicide When a medical professional helps a dying person to end their life, by providing either medication or information. (p. 533)

Piaget's stage theory of development The five periods of cognitive development described by Jean Piaget, in which children's thinking proceeds through qualitatively different ways of understanding the world. (p. 45)

placenta An organ that allows energy and waste to be transferred between the parent's body and the developing embryo through the umbilical cord. (p. 82)

plasticity The idea that human development is moldable, like plastic, by experiences. (p. 28)

polyamory The practice or interest in romantic or sexual relationships between more than two consenting adults. (p. 385)

polygenic Genetic characteristics that require a trigger or specific influence from the environment in order to be expressed. (p. 73)

popular Children who are liked or perceived to be socially successful by many of their peers. (p. 277)

postconventional stage of moral reasoning Kohlberg's stage of moral reasoning in which people can think abstractly and about right and wrong as something that supersedes rules and laws. (p. 281)

postformal thought A stage of thinking that allows young adults to think through complex issues by reviewing different viewpoints, considering emotional, contextual, and interpersonal factors. (p. 356)

postresidential A period in family life where parents may no longer live with their children. (p. 447)

power-assertive techniques Disciplinary strategies that rely on parents' control. (p. 211)

pragmatics Knowing how to talk with other people including, what is appropriate to talk about, and how to interpret tone of voice, gestures, and other cues. (p. 246)

preconventional stage of moral reasoning Kohlberg's stage of moral reasoning in which children use concrete and self-centered (egocentric) reasoning. (p. 280)

preferential looking technique A procedure that measures what babies perceive in which researchers harness babies' intrinsic interest in new things. (p. 115)

prefrontal cortex The area at the front of the brain beneath the forehead that is critical to logical thinking and controlling behavior. (p. 166)

premature Birth that occurs less than 35 weeks after fertilization. (p. 94)

preoperational thought The second stage in children's cognitive development spanning about ages 2 to 7, in which young children are capable of symbolic, but not quite logical, thought. (p. 174)

primary circular reactions The second stage of the sensorimotor period, from about 1 to 4 months, in which babies begin to adapt their reflexes to new uses and show more creative behavior. (p. 119)

primary sex characteristics The physical markers that babies are typically born with, like genitals. (p. 229)

private speech Vygotsky's term for the language children use when they talk to themselves. (p. 178)

proactive aggression Aggression that is planned and executed on purpose to gain personal advantage (sometimes called *instrumental aggression*). (p. 219)

prosocial Behaviors that are helpful or caring toward someone else. (p. 148)

proximal Caregiving practices that include physical closeness but not necessarily face-to-face contact. (p. 138)

proximity seeking The tendency for children (and adults) to seek comfort by being physically close to someone they are attached to. (p. 155)

proximodistal principle A pattern of physical development in which control of movement begins in the core and expands outward. (p. 117)

psychodynamic perspective An emphasis on how human behaviors are based on satisfying innate and often subconscious, biological needs for connection, protection, and love. (p. 37)

psychological disorder A pattern of feelings, thinking, or behaviors that causes distress and makes it difficult to function. (pp. 197, 262)

psychosexual stages The five stages of Freud's psychodynamic theory in which children learn how to manage different sensual and sexual energies. (p. 38)

puberty The process that transforms children into adults who are typically able to reproduce and have children of their own. (p. 286)

punishment Anything that weakens a behavior, making it less likely to happen. (p. 41)

qualitative research Research that involves in-depth analysis, observation, and investigation. (p. 58)

quantitative research Research that uses numbers to measure the topics being studied and to analyze the outcome of a study. (p. 58)

race A system of categorizing people based on their physical characteristics. These physical differences are often assumed to overlap with people's genes or geographical origins, but this is not accurate. (p. 21)

reactive aggression A hostile action out of frustration or anger in an immediate reaction to something that has just happened. (p. 219)

recessive inheritance pattern A type of genetic inheritance for single-gene conditions. In order to develop a recessive condition, you must have two of the disease-carrying alleles. (p. 72)

reflexes Automatic motor responses to stimuli that help babies adjust to the world. (p. 97)

rehearsal A memorization technique that involves repetition, either out loud, in your head, in front of someone else, or on paper. (p. 242)

reinforcement Anything that strengthens a behavior, making it more likely to happen. (p. 41)

rejected Children who are actively disliked by most of their peers. (p. 277)

relationally aggressive Using words and relationships to hurt another person socially or emotionally. (p. 219)

relativistic thinking A type of thinking that acknowledges there is no absolute truth, but rather a collection of different perspectives. Instead of assuming there is one right answer to life's problems, relativistic thinkers understand that their assumptions are biased and subjective. (p. 355)

resilience The ability to bounce back and recover despite difficult life circumstances. (p. 2)

responsiveness The idea that a caregiver should acknowledge and react to an infant's bids for attention. (p. 154)

rough-and-tumble play Physically active play where children chase, play fight, and wrestle. (p. 217)

rumination The tendency to repetitively and obsessively focus on what is wrong. (p. 325)

sarcopenia Significant lack of muscle mass that limits adults' ability to perform everyday activities. (p. 473)

scaffolding Vygotsky's term for teaching, whether by formal teachers, friends, peers, or family members, that engages children by considering their interests and individual abilities. (p. 177)

schema The word for each bit of knowledge a person develops. (p. 45)

schizophrenia A condition whose symptoms include hallucinations, delusions, confused thinking, disorganized speech, emotional flatness, and difficulties in social interactions. (p. 399)

science A process of gathering and organizing knowledge about the world in a way that is testable and reliable. (p. 2)

scientific method A multistep process in which scientists evaluate their ideas and find out if they are accurate by making observations, developing theories or hypotheses about those observations, and then testing them. (pp. 7, 51)

secondary circular reactions The third stage of the sensorimotor period, from about 4 to 8 months, in which babies learn to extend their activities to manipulate the world around them. (p. 121)

secondary sex characteristics The physical markers of what makes people look like adult males or females after puberty. Secondary sex characteristics include pubic hair, facial hair, the Adam's apple and breasts. (p. 229)

secular trend The term developmental scientists use to describe the gradual, long-term progression toward earlier puberty. (p. 290)

secure attachment In attachment theory, children who have a sense of trust in their caregivers that allows them to explore their environment. (p. 156)

secure base In attachment theory, a safe haven for children to return to when they may feel anxious. (p. 155)

self-awareness The understanding that you have a self that is separate from others. (p. 147)

self-efficacy The belief in one's ability to make a change or have an impact. (p. 251)

semantic memory The mental store for facts and information. (p. 241)

sensation-seeking The drive for excitement and the thrill of doing something a bit scary. (p. 337)

sensitive periods The times in the lifespan when growth is particularly responsive to input from the world. (p. 28)

sensorimotor Piaget's term for the cognitive stage that spans the first 18 months of a baby's life and focuses on learning through sensation and movement. (p. 119)

separation anxiety By about 6 months and continuing into toddlerhood, infants are upset and worried if their caregivers go away. This phenomenon is not universal but is influenced by cultural practices. (p. 146)

seriation The ordering of objects in a series according to an abstract rule. (p. 238)

sex The physical and genetic characteristics usually associated with being male, female, or a mixture. (p. 71)

sex chromosomes The 23rd pair of chromosomes. (p. 71)

sexually transmitted infection (STI) The term health care providers use to describe diseases that can be passed from one person to another through intimate contact. (p. 295)

slow-to-warm-up In Thomas and Chess's dimensional approach to temperament, these babies tend to be shy and slower to adjust to new circumstances, but not intense in their responses. (p. 150)

small for gestational age (SGA) Babies born smaller than expected for their level of development. (p. 94)

social brain Neural networks associated with understanding the views and intentions of other people. (p. 328)

social learning theory The theory that learning occurs through observing and imitating others. (p. 43)

social referencing The use of someone else's emotional response as a guide before expressing your own reaction to a new place, person, or object. (p. 147)

social smile A smile in reaction to the sight or sound of someone an infant is connected to. These smiles may appear as early as 6 weeks, but their development is influenced by caregiving practices. (p. 145)

social status A person's social rank within the larger group. (p. 327)

sociocultural theory The theory that culture plays a role in every part of human development. (p. 47)

sociodramatic play Play that involves pretending to be something you are not and requires symbolic thought and theory of mind. (p. 216)

socioeconomic status (SES) A key measure of a family or individual's income and social capital. (p. 18)

specific learning disabilities Difficulties with language development, reading, or arithmetic that lead to problems functioning in school or at home. (p. 252)

sperm The reproductive cell from a male. (p. 70)

spermarche The first ejaculation of sperm. (p. 289)

stage A period in which development changes dramatically. (p. 29)

stage–environment fit The idea that we do better when the world matches our developmental needs. (p. 312)

stages Distinct time periods when development changes dramatically. (p. 45)

stereotype threat The phenomenon that occurs when you feel judged in an area where there are common stereotypes about your group, and the resulting anxiety negatively affects your performance. (p. 311)

Strange Situation An empirical method for evaluating the attachment status of toddlers developed by Mary Ainsworth. (p. 156)

stranger anxiety Babies' demonstration of caution around new people, which emerges by about 8 months. This phenomenon is not culturally universal but is influenced by caregiving practices. (p. 146)

stress The feeling of being overwhelmed. (p. 91)

stunting When a child's growth has slowed so much that they are significantly shorter than they should be for their age. (p. 102)

substance use disorder A clinical diagnosis based on a pattern of substance use that is causing someone functional difficulties in their everyday life. (p. 342)

sudden unexpected infant deaths (SUID) When an otherwise healthy infant dies. SUIDs can include *sleep-related suffocation*. (p. 109)

synaptic pruning The process in which the brain cuts back on underused synapses. (p. 112)

synaptogenesis The process of creating new synapses between neurons, which begins before birth and continues throughout the lifespan. (p. 112)

tau protein An essential building block of neurons that helps move nutrients and energy from one part of the neuron to another. With age, misshapen tau protein can contribute to cognitive decline. (p. 482)

temperament An early pattern of personality in infants and toddlers. (p. 150)

teratogens Factors in a parent's body or the environment that damage the fetus. (p. 87)

terminal agitation An upsetting and disturbing condition in which a dying person becomes restless, upset, and/or delirious. (p. 530)

terminal decline Changes in cognition, processing, and/or personality, which signify that a person is nearing death. (p. 530)

terminal lucidity An unexpected return to consciousness or cognitive clarity in people who are at the end-of-life. (p. 530)

tertiary circular reactions Babies' ability to deliberately vary their actions to see the results. (p. 121)

testosterone A hormone produced by the gonads that is linked to reproduction, maturation, brain development, and sexual function. Testosterone levels are higher in biological males but are important to typical functioning in both females and males. (p. 288)

thanatology The study of death, which combines insights from the fields of psychology, sociology, anthropology, counseling, social work, death education, and the funeral industry. (p. 529)

theory An organized set of ideas that helps scientists think critically about what they observe. (p. 34)

theory of mind The ability to understand that other people have different beliefs, ideas, and desires. (p. 183)

theory of multiple intelligences Gardner's idea that intelligence is a broad set of discrete abilities and that all children have components of all these intelligences. (p. 244)

theory of successful intelligence Sternberg's idea that intelligence can best be measured by how you create a successful life through three types of intelligence. (p. 244)

three mountains task Piaget's test of how well children can imagine how someone else would see the world. (p. 176)

tracking The practice of grouping together students with similar achievement and test scores and offering them a more customized school curriculum. (p. 309)

transgender When a person consistently feels that their gender identity does not match the sex they were assigned at birth. (p. 205)

triangular theory of love Sternberg's theory that there are different types of romantic relationships with varying degrees of intimacy, passion, and commitment. (p. 383)

trust versus mistrust The first crisis in Erikson's stage theory of development in which infants learn that the world is reliable. (p. 137)

underextension An error in which a child insists that a word only applies to a specific member of the group, rather than the whole group itself. (p. 131)

universal grammar A child's inborn ability to recognize and use grammar. (p. 132)

variables The factors that are studied in an experiment. (p. 53)

vascular cognitive disorder A disorder that occurs when injuries to the cardiovascular system disrupt the brain and cognitive functioning. (p. 490)

vestibular system Located inside the inner ear, this network transmits information to the brain about where you are in space. (p. 473)

visual cliff A means of assessing what risks babies will take while crawling, in which a 2½-foot gap is covered with plexiglass that, if properly lit, appears to be an empty gap. (p. 119)

wasting When a child is so seriously malnourished that they are below the 5th percentile in the ratio of weight to height, or lighter for their height than 95 percent of children their age and height. (p. 102)

whole-language approach Instruction that is based on the idea that children will learn how to read more effectively in an environment that weaves literacy into everything they do. (p. 250)

wisdom The ability to reason creatively based on deep insights about people. (p. 486)

work values The specific beliefs or core principles that relate to work. (p. 372)

working memory A type of short-term memory that is essential to learning and to problem solving. (p. 179)

young-old The term for adults who are between ages 65 and 74. (p. 462)

zone of proximal development (ZPD) Vygotsky's term for the range of what students can learn with adult help. (p. 177)

zygote A new human cell with 46 chromosomes in 23 pairs. (p. 71)

REFERENCES

A San Diego Job Corps student success story. (2013, March 22). *Eagle & Times.* http://www.imperialbeachnewsca.com/news/article_00c8d98c-92eb-11e2-b538-0019bb2963f4.html

Aagaard, J. (2016). Mobile devices, interaction, and distraction: A qualitative exploration of absent presence. *AI & Society, 31*(2), 223–231. https://doi.org/10.1007/s00146-015-0638-z

AARP. (2019). *2018 Grandparents Today National Survey: General population report.* https://doi.org/10.26419/res.00289.001

AARP. (2020). *Who are today's grandparents? Hacking life shifts 2020.*

AARP, & National Alliance for Caregiving. (2020). *Caregiving in the United States, 2020.*

Abad-Santos, A. (2013, July 8). Men, no one is buying your "mid-life crisis." *The Atlantic.* https://www.theatlantic.com/national/archive/2013/07/men-no-one-buying-your-mid-life-crisis/313557/

Abaied, J. L., & Perry, S. P. (2021). Socialization of racial ideology by White parents. *Cultural Diversity and Ethnic Minority Psychology, 27*(3), 431–440. https://doi.org/10.1037/cdp0000454

Abarca-Gómez, L., Abdeen, Z. A., Hamid, Z. A., Abu-Rmeileh, N. M., Acosta-Cazares, B., Acuin, C., Adams, R. J., Aekplakorn, W., Afsana, K., Aguilar-Salinas, C. A., Agyemang, C., Ahmadvand, A., Ahrens, W., Ajlouni, K., Akhtaeva, N., Al-Hazzaa, H. M., Al-Othman, A. R., Al-Raddadi, R., Buhairan, F. A., ... Ezzati, M. (2017). Worldwide trends in body-mass index, underweight, overweight, and obesity from 1975 to 2016: A pooled analysis of 2416 population-based measurement studies in 128.9 million children, adolescents, and adults. *The Lancet, 390*(10113), 2627–2642. https://doi.org/10.1016/S0140-6736(17)32129-3

Abascal, F., Juan, D., Jungreis, I., Martinez, L., Rigau, M., Rodriguez, J. M., Vazquez, J., & Tress, M. L. (2018). Loose ends: Almost one in five human genes still have unresolved coding status. *Nucleic Acids Research, 46*(14), 7070–7084. https://doi.org/10.1093/nar/gky587

Abbott, D. M., Pelc, N., & Mercier, C. (2019). Cultural humility and the teaching of psychology. *Scholarship of Teaching and Learning in Psychology, 5*(2), 169–181. https://doi.org/10.1037/stl0000144

Abboud, S., Flores, D., Redmond, L., Brawner, B. M., & Sommers, M. S. (2020). Sexual attitudes and behaviours among Arab American young adults in the USA. *Culture, Health & Sexuality,* 1–17.

Abebe, T. (2018). *A plea for participatory ethics and knowledge production with children in Africa* (CODESIRA Policy Briefs No. 1). Council for the Development of Social Science Research in Africa.

Abellard, J., Rodgers, C., & Bales, A. L. (2017). Balancing sexual expression and risk of harm in elderly persons with dementia. *Journal of the American Academy of Psychiatry and the Law Online, 45*(4), 485–492.

Abney, D. H., Suanda, S. H., Smith, L. B., & Yu, C. (2020). What are the building blocks of parent–infant coordinated attention in free-flowing interaction? *Infancy, 25*(6), 871–887. https://doi.org/10.1111/infa.12365

Abraham, E., & Feldman, R. (2018). The neurobiology of human allomaternal care; Implications for fathering, coparenting, and children's social development. *Physiology & Behavior, 193,* 25–34. https://doi.org/10.1016/j.physbeh.2017.12.034

Abraham, E., Hendler, T., Shapira-Lichter, I., Kanat-Maymon, Y., Zagoory-Sharon, O., & Feldman, R. (2014). Father's brain is sensitive to childcare experiences. *Proceedings of the National Academy of Sciences, 111*(27), 9792–9797. https://doi.org/10.1073/pnas.1402569111

Aburto, J. M., Schöley, J., Zhang, L., Kashnitsky, I., Rahal, C., Missov, T. I., Mills, M. C., Dowd, J. B., & Kashyap, R. (2021). Quantifying impacts of the COVID-19 pandemic through life expectancy losses. *MedRxiv,* 2021.03.02.21252772. https://doi.org/10.1101/2021.03.02.21252772

Accavitti, M. R., & Williford, A. P. (2020). Teacher perceptions of externalizing behaviour subtypes in preschool: Considering racial factors. *Early Child Development and Care,* 1–15. https://doi.org/10.1080/03004430.2020.1825405

Acemoglu, D., & Autor, D. (2011). Skills, tasks and technologies: Implications for employment and earnings. In D. Card & O. Ashenfelter (Eds.), *Handbook of labor economics* (Vol. 4, pp. 1043–1171). Elsevier. https://doi.org/10.1016/S0169-7218(11)02410-5

Acevedo, B. P., Poulin, M. J., Collins, N. L., & Brown, L. L. (2020). After the honeymoon: Neural and genetic correlates of romantic love in newlywed marriages. *Frontiers in Psychology, 11,* 634. https://doi.org/10.3389/fpsyg.2020.00634

Achenbach, T. M., & McConaughy, S. H. (1992). Taxonomy of internalizing disorders of childhood and adolescence. In W. M. Reynolds (Ed.), *Internalizing disorders in children and adolescents* (pp. 19–60). Wiley.

Achenbaum, W. A. (1978). From womb through bloom to tomb: The birth of a new area of historical research. *Reviews in American History, 6*(2), 178–183. https://doi.org/10.2307/2701294

Achenbaum, W. A. (2018). Ever-emerging theories of aging. *Oxford Research Encyclopedia of Psychology.* https://doi.org/10.1093/acrefore/9780190236557.013.333

Ackerman, P. L., & Kanfer, R. (2020). Work in the 21st century: New directions for aging and adult development. *American Psychologist, 75*(4), 486–498. https://doi.org/10.1037/amp0000615

Adachi, P. J., & Willoughby, T. (2017). The link between playing video games and positive youth outcomes. *Child Development Perspectives, 11*(3), 202–206.

Adair, J. K., Colegrove, K. S.-S., & McManus, M. E. (2017). How the word gap argument negatively impacts young children of Latinx immigrants' conceptualizations of learning. *Harvard Educational Review, 87*(3), 309–334. https://doi.org/10.17763/1943-5045-87.3.309

Adams, E. L., Caccavale, L. J., Smith, D., & Bean, M. K. (2020). Food insecurity, the home food environment, and parent feeding practices in the era of COVID-19. *Obesity, 28*(11), 2056–2063. https://doi.org/10.1002/oby.22996

Adams, E. L., Master, L., Buxton, O. M., & Savage, J. S. (2020). Patterns of infant-only wake bouts and night feeds during early infancy: An exploratory study using actigraphy in mother-father-infant triads. *Pediatric Obesity, 15*(10), e12640. https://doi.org/10.1111/ijpo.12640

Adams, P. F., & Martinez, M. E. (2016). *Percentage of adults with activity limitations, by age group and type of limitation.* https://www.cdc.gov/mmwr/volumes/65/wr/mm6501a6.htm

Adams, S. H., Schaub, J. P., Nagata, J. M., Park, M. J., Brindis, C. D., & Irwin, C. E. (2021). Young adult perspectives on COVID-19 vaccinations. *The Journal of Adolescent Health, 69*(3), P511–P514. https://doi.org/10.1016/j.jadohealth.2021.06.003

Adelman, L. (2008). When the bough breaks. *Unnatural Causes* (Episode 2). https://unnaturalcauses.org/episode_descriptions.php?page=2

Adler, N. E., Boyce, T., Chesney, M. A., Cohen, S., Folkman, S., Kahn, R. L., & Syme, S. L. (1994). Socioeconomic status and health: The challenge of the gradient. *American Psychologist, 49*(1), 15.

Adolph, K. E. (2019). An ecological approach to learning in (not and) development. *Human Development, 63*(3–4), 180–201. https://doi.org/10.1159/000503823

Adolph, K. E., Cole, W. G., Komati, M., Garciaguirre, J. S., Badaly, D., Lingeman, J. M., Chan, G., & Sotsky, R. B. (2012). How do you learn to walk? Thousands of steps and dozens of falls per day. *Psychological Science, 23*(11), 1387–1394. https://doi.org/10.1177/0956797612446346

Adolph, K. E., & Franchak, J. M. (2017). The development of motor behavior. *Wiley Interdisciplinary Reviews. Cognitive Science, 8*(1–2), e1430. https://doi.org/10.1002/wcs.1430

Adolph, K. E., & Hoch, J. E. (2019). Motor development: Embodied, embedded, enculturated, and enabling. *Annual Review of Psychology, 70*(1), 141–164. https://doi.org/10.1146/annurev-psych-010418-102836

Adolph, K. E., & Hoch, J. E. (2020). The importance of motor skills for development. In M. M. Black, A. Singhal, & C. H. Hillman (Eds.), *Building future health and wellbeing of thriving toddlers and young children* (Nestlé Nutrition Institute Workshop Series, Vol. 95, pp. 136–144). Karger. https://doi.org/10.1159/000511511

Afranie, A., & Clagett, M. G. (2020). *Preparing opportunity youth for the future of work.* Jobs for the Future (JFF). https://www.jff.org/resources/preparing-opportunity-youth-future-work/

Agarwal, S., Driscoll, J. C., Gabaix, X., & Laibson, D. (2007). *The age of reason: Financial decisions over the lifecycle* (Working Paper No. 13191). National Bureau of Economic Research. https://doi.org/10.3386/w13191

Aggleton, J. P., Pralus, A., Nelson, A. J. D., & Hornberger, M. (2016). Thalamic pathology and memory loss in early Alzheimer's disease: Moving the focus from the medial temporal lobe to Papez circuit. *Brain, 139*(7), 1877–1890. https://doi.org/10.1093/brain/aww083

Agllias, K. (2016). *Family estrangement: A matter of perspective.* Routledge. https://doi.org/10.4324/9781315581910

Agochukwu, N. Q., & Wittmann, D. (2019). Chapter 3.2 — Stress, depression, mental illness, and men's health. In F. A. Yafi & N. R. Yafi (Eds.), *Effects of lifestyle on men's health* (pp. 207–221). Academic Press. https://doi.org/10.1016/B978-0-12-816665-9.00010-X

Agorastos, A., Pervanidou, P., Chrousos, G. P., & Baker, D. G. (2019). Developmental trajectories of early life stress and trauma: A narrative review on neurobiological aspects beyond stress system dysregulation. *Frontiers in Psychiatry, 10,* 118. https://doi.org/10.3389/fpsyt.2019.00118

Agrawal, Y., Merfeld, D. M., Horak, F. B., Redfern, M. S., Manor, B., Westlake, K. P., & Lipsitz, L. A. (2020). Aging, vestibular function, and balance: Proceedings of a National Institute on Aging/National Institute on Deafness and Other Communication Disorders workshop. *The Journals of Gerontology: Series A, 75*(12), 2471–2480.

Ahlenius, H., Chanda, S., Webb, A. E., Yousif, I., Karmazin, J., Prusiner, S. B., Brunet, A., Südhof, T. C., & Wernig, M. (2016). FoxO3 regulates neuronal reprogramming of cells from postnatal and aging mice. *Proceedings of the National Academy of Sciences, 113*(30), 8514–8519.

Ahlstrom, B., Dinh, T., Haselton, M. G., & Tomiyama, A. J. (2017). Understanding eating interventions through an evolutionary lens. *Health Psychology Review, 11*(1), 72–88. https://doi.org/10.1080/17437199.2016.1260489

Ahluwalia, N. (2020). Nutrition monitoring of children aged birth to 24 mo (B-24): Data collection and findings from the NHANES. *Advances in Nutrition, 11*(1), 113–127. https://doi.org/10.1093/advances/nmz077

Ahmad, F. B., & Anderson, R. N. (2021). The leading causes of death in the US for 2020. *JAMA, 325*(18), 1829–1830. https://doi.org/10.1001/jama.2021.5469

Ahmad, F. B., Cisewski, J. A., Miniño, A., & Anderson, R. N. (2021). Provisional mortality data — United States, 2020. *Morbidity and Mortality Weekly Report, 70*(14), 519–522. https://doi.org/10.15585/mmwr.mm7014e1

Ahmed, S., Foulkes, L., Leung, J. T., Griffin, C., Sakhardande, A., Bennett, M., Dunning, D. L., Griffiths, K., Parker, J., Kuyken, W., Williams, J. M. G., Dalgleish, T., & Blakemore, S. J. (2020). Susceptibility to prosocial and antisocial influence in adolescence. *Journal of Adolescence, 84,* 56–68. https://doi.org/10.1016/j.adolescence.2020.07.012

Ahmed, S. F., Tang, S., Waters, N. E., & Davis-Kean, P. (2019). Executive function and academic achievement: Longitudinal relations from early childhood to adolescence. *Journal of Educational Psychology, 111*(3), 446.

Ahn, R., Gonzalez, G. P., Anderson, B., Vladutiu, C. J., Fowler, E. R., & Manning, L. (2020). Initiatives to reduce maternal mortality and severe maternal morbidity in the United States. *Annals of Internal Medicine, 173*(11_Supplement), S3–S10. https://doi.org/10.7326/M19-3258

Ahnert, L. (2021). Attachment to child care providers. In R. A. Thompson, J. A. Simpson, L. J. Berlin, L. Ahnert, & T. Ai (Eds.), *Attachment: The fundamental questions* (pp. 31–38). Guilford.

Ahranjani, M. (2020). School "safety" measures jump constitutional guardrails. *Seattle University Law Review, 44*, 273.

Ainsworth, A. J., Allyse, M., & Khan, Z. (2020). Fertility preservation for transgender individuals: A review. *Mayo Clinic Proceedings, 95*(4), 784–792. https://doi.org/10.1016/j.mayocp.2019.10.040

Ainsworth, M. D. S., Blehar, M. C., Waters, E., & Wall, S. N. (2015). *Patterns of attachment: A psychological study of the strange situation*. Psychology Press. (Original work published 1978)

Ainsworth, M. D. S., & Bowlby, J. (1991). An ethological approach to personality development. *American Psychologist, 46*(4), 333–341. https://doi.org/10.1037/0003-066X.46.4.333

Ainsworth, M. D. S., & Marvin, R. S. (1995). On the shaping of attachment theory and research: An interview with Mary D. S. Ainsworth (Fall 1994). *Monographs of the Society for Research in Child Development, 60*(2–3), 3–21. https://doi.org/10.1111/j.1540-5834.1995.tb00200.x

Aizenman, N., & Warner, G. (2018). What can we learn from Ghana's obsession with preschool. *National Public Radio.*

Ajrouch, K. J., Fuller, H. R., Akiyama, H., & Antonucci, T. C. (2018). Convoys of social relations in cross-national context. *The Gerontologist, 58*(3), 488–499. https://doi.org/10.1093/geront/gnw204

Akbar, A. N., & Gilroy, D. W. (2020). Aging immunity may exacerbate COVID-19. *Science, 369*(6501), 256–257.

Akee, R., Copeland, W., Costello, E. J., & Simeonova, E. (2018). How does household income affect child personality traits and behaviors? *American Economic Review, 108*(3), 775–827. https://doi.org/10.1257/aer.20160133

Akers, A. Y., & Harding, J. (2021). The timing of obesity matters: Associations between current versus chronic obesity since adolescence and romantic relationship satisfaction among young adult women. *Women's Health Issues, 31*(5), 462–469.

Aknin, L. B., Van de Vondervoort, J. W., & Hamlin, J. K. (2018). Positive feelings reward and promote prosocial behavior. *Current Opinion in Psychology, 20*, 55–59.

Aktar, E., Mandell, D. J., de Vente, W., Majdandžić, M., Oort, F. J., van Renswoude, D. R., Raijmakers, M. E. J., & Bögels, S. M. (2018). Parental negative emotions are related to behavioral and pupillary correlates of infants' attention to facial expressions of emotion. *Infant Behavior and Development, 53*, 101–111. https://doi.org/10.1016/j.infbeh.2018.07.004

Alampay, L. P., Godwin, J., Lansford, J. E., Bombi, A. S., Bornstein, M. H., Chang, L., Deater-Deckard, K., Di Giunta, L., Dodge, K. A., Malone, P. S., Oburu, P., Pastorelli, C., Skinner, A. T., Sorbring, E., Tapanya, S., Uribe Tirado, L. M., Zelli, A., Al-Hassan, S., & Bacchini, D. (2017). Severity and justness do not moderate the relation between corporal punishment and negative child outcomes: A multicultural and longitudinal study. *International Journal of Behavioral Development, 41*(4), 491–502. https://doi.org/10.1177/0165025417697852

Al-Attar, G., De Meyer, S., El-Gibaly, O., Michielsen, K., Animosa, L. H., & Mmari, K. (2017). "A boy would be friends with boys … and a girl … with girls": Gender norms in early adolescent friendships in Egypt and Belgium. *Journal of Adolescent Health, 61*(4, Supplement), S30–S34. https://doi.org/10.1016/j.jadohealth.2017.03.013

Albanese, E., Launer, L. J., Egger, M., Prince, M. J., Giannakopoulos, P., Wolters, F. J., & Egan, K. (2017).

Body mass index in midlife and dementia: Systematic review and meta-regression analysis of 589,649 men and women followed in longitudinal studies. *Alzheimer's & Dementia: Diagnosis, Assessment & Disease Monitoring, 8*(1), 165–178. https://doi.org/10.1016/j.dadm.2017.05.007

Albert, D., Chein, J., & Steinberg, L. (2013). Peer influences on adolescent decision making. *Current Directions in Psychological Science, 22*(2), 114–120. https://doi.org/10.1177/0963721412471347

Albert, I., & Tesch-Römer, C. (2021). Cross-cultural psychogerontology. In D. Gu & M. E. Dupre (Eds.), *Encyclopedia of gerontology and population aging*. Springer. https://doi.org/10.1007/978-3-030-22009-9_95

Albert, M., & McCaig, L. F. (2014). *Injury-related emergency department visits by children and adolescents: United States, 2009–2010.* U.S. Department of Health and Human Services, Centers for Disease Control and Prevention, National Center for Health Statistics.

Alberti, K. G. M., Zimmet, P., & Shaw, J. (2005). The metabolic syndrome — A new worldwide definition. *The Lancet, 366*(9491), 1059–1062.

Alberts, B., Johnson, A., Lewis, J., Raff, M., Roberts, K., & Walter, P. (2002). Eggs. In B. Alberts, A. Johnson, & J. Lewis (Eds.), *Molecular biology of the cell* (4th ed.). Garland Science. https://www.ncbi.nlm.nih.gov/books/NBK26842/

Alcalá, L., Rogoff, B., & López Fraire, A. (2018). Sophisticated collaboration is common among Mexican-heritage US children. *Proceedings of the National Academy of Sciences, 115*(45), 11377–11384.

Alcántara, C., Estevez, C. D., & Alegría, M. (2017). Latino and Asian immigrant adult health: Paradoxes and explanations. In S. J. Schwartz & J. B. Unger (Eds.), *The Oxford handbook of acculturation and health* (pp. 197–220). Oxford University Press.

Algoe, S. B., Gable, S. L., & Maisel, N. C. (2010). It's the little things: Everyday gratitude as a booster shot for romantic relationships. *Personal Relationships, 17*(2), 217–233.

Al-Hamdani, M., Hopkins, D. B., & Park, T. (2020). Vaping among youth and young adults: A "red alert" state. *Journal of Public Health Policy, 41*(1), 63–69. https://doi.org/10.1057/s41271-019-00193-2

Ali, B., Rockett, I., & Miller, T. (2019). Variable circumstances of suicide among racial/ethnic groups by sex and age: A national violent-death reporting system analysis. *Archives of Suicide Research, 25*(1), 94–106. https://doi.org/10.1080/13811118.2019.1661894

Ali, M., Alauddin, S., Maniruzzaman, M., & Islam, S. M. S. (2021). Determinants of early age of mother at first birth in Bangladesh: A statistical analysis using a two-level multiple logistic regression model. *Journal of Public Health, 29*(5), 1081–1087.

Ali, M., & Parekh, N. (2020). Male age and andropause. In S. J. Parekattil, S. C. Esteves, & A. Agarwal (Eds.), *Male infertility: Contemporary clinical approaches, andrology, ART and antioxidants* (pp. 469–477). Springer International Publishing. https://doi.org/10.1007/978-3-030-32300-4_36

Alink, L. R. A., van Ijzendoorn, M. H., Bakermans-Kranenburg, M. J., Mesman, J., Juffer, R., & Koot, H. M. (2008). Cortisol and externalizing behavior in children and adolescents: Mixed meta-analytic evidence for the inverse relation of basal cortisol and cortisol reactivity with externalizing behavior. *Developmental Psychobiology, 50*, 427–450. https://doi.org/10.1002/dev.20300

Alladi, S., Bak, T. H., Shailaja, M., Gollahalli, D., Rajan, A., Surampudi, B., Hornberger, M., Duggirala, V., Chaudhuri, J. R., & Kaul, S. (2017). Bilingualism delays the onset of behavioral but not aphasic forms of frontotemporal dementia. *Neuropsychologia, 99*, 207–212. https://doi.org/10.1016/j.neuropsychologia.2017.03.021

Allard, E. S., & Kensinger, E. A. (2018). Cognitive emotion regulation in adulthood and old age: Positive gaze preferences across two strategies. *Aging, Neuropsychology, and Cognition, 25*(2), 213–230.

Allel, K., León, A. S., Staudinger, U. M., & Calvo, E. (2021). Healthy retirement begins at school: Educational differences in the health outcomes of early transitions into retirement. *Ageing & Society, 41*(1), 137–157.

Allemand, M., Job, V., & Mroczek, D. K. (2019). Self-control development in adolescence predicts love and work in adulthood. *Journal of Personality and Social Psychology, 117*(3), 621–634. https://doi.org/10.1037/pspp0000229

Allen, G. E. (2011). Eugenics and modern biology: Critiques of eugenics, 1910–1945. *Annals of Human Genetics, 75*(3), 314–325. https://doi.org/10.1111/j.1469-1809.2011.00649.x

Allen, J. P., & Loeb, E. L. (2015). The autonomy-connection challenge in adolescent peer relationships. *Child Development Perspectives, 9*(2), 101–105. https://doi.org/10.1111/cdep.12111

Allen, J. P., Narr, R. K., Kansky, J., & Szwedo, D. E. (2020). Adolescent peer relationship qualities as predictors of long-term romantic life satisfaction. *Child Development, 91*(1), 327–340. https://doi.org/10.1111/cdev.13193

Allen, J. P., & Tan, J. S. (2016). The multiple facets of attachment in adolescence. In J. Cassidy & P. R. Shaver (Eds.), *Handbook of attachment: Theory, research, and clinical applications* (pp. 399–415). Guilford.

Allen, M. S. (2019). Physical activity as an adjunct treatment for erectile dysfunction. *Nature Reviews Urology, 16*(9), 553–562. https://doi.org/10.1038/s41585-019-0210-6

Allen, R., Shapland, D. L., Neitzel, J., & Iruka, I. U. (2021). Viewpoint: Creating anti-racist early childhood spaces. *Young Children, 76*(2).

Allensworth, E. M., & Clark, K. (2020). High school GPAs and ACT scores as predictors of college completion: Examining assumptions about consistency across high schools. *Educational Researcher, 49*(3), 198–211. https://doi.org/10.3102/0013189X20902110

Allison, M. A., Attisha, E., & Council on School Health. (2019). The link between school attendance and good health. *Pediatrics, 143*(2), e20183648. https://doi.org/10.1542/peds.2018-3648

Almas, A. N., Degnan, K. A., Walker, O. L., Radulescu, A., Nelson, C. A., Zeanah, C. H., & Fox, N. A. (2015). The effects of early institutionalization and foster care intervention on children's social behaviors at the age of eight. *Social Development, 24*(2), 225–239.

Almeida, D. M., Charles, S. T., Mogle, J., Drewelies, J., Aldwin, C. M., Spiro, A., III., & Gerstorf, D. (2020). Charting adult development through (historically changing) daily stress processes. *American Psychologist, 75*(4), 511.

Alnæs, D., Kaufmann, T., Marquand, A. F., Smith, S. M., & Westlye, L. T. (2020). Patterns of sociocognitive stratification and perinatal risk in the child brain. *Proceedings of the National Academy of Sciences, 117*(22), 12419–12427.

Alper, R. M., Beiting, M., Luo, R., Jaen, J., Peel, M., Levi, O., Robinson, C., & Hirsh-Pasek, K. (2021). Change the things you can: Modifiable parent characteristics predict high-quality early language interaction within socioeconomic status. *Journal of Speech, Language, and Hearing Research, 64*(6), 1992–2004. https://doi.org/10.1044/2021_JSLHR-20-00412

Al Rabadi, L., LeBlanc, M., Bucy, T., Ellis, L. M., Hershman, D. L., Meyskens, F. L., Taylor, L., & Blanke, C. D. (2019). Trends in medical aid in dying in Oregon and Washington. *JAMA Network Open, 2*(8), e198648.

Alsan, M., Garrick, O., & Graziani, G. (2019). Does diversity matter for health? Experimental evidence from Oakland. *American Economic Review, 109*(12), 4071–4111. https://doi.org/10.1257/aer.20181446

Alswat, K. A. (2017). Gender disparities in osteoporosis. *Journal of Clinical Medicine Research, 9*(5), 382.

Alvarez, A. L., & Booth, A. E. (2014). Motivated by meaning: Testing the effect of knowledge-infused rewards on preschoolers' persistence. *Child Development, 85*(2), 783–791.

Álvarez-Bueno, C., Hillman, C. H., Cavero-Redondo, I., Sánchez-López, M., Pozuelo-Carrascosa, D. P., & Martínez-Vizcaíno, V. (2020). Aerobic fitness and academic achievement: A systematic review and meta-analysis. *Journal of Sports Sciences, 38*(5), 582–589. https://doi.org/10.1080/02640414.2020.1720496

Alzheimer's Association. (2021). Alzheimer's disease facts and figures. *Alzheimer's & Dementia, 17*(3), 327–406.

Amani, M. K., & Khalfaoui, A. (2019, March 28). Congolese warlord convicted of war crimes with the help of ABA ROLI. *ABA Journal*. https://www.abajournal.com/news/article/warlord-habarugira-drc-aba-abroad

Amato, P. R. (2010). Research on divorce: Continuing trends and new developments. *Journal of Marriage and Family, 72*(3), 650–666.

Amato, P. R., & Anthony, C. J. (2014). Estimating the effects of parental divorce and death with fixed effects models. *Journal of Marriage and Family, 76*(2), 370–386.

Amato, P. R., Booth, A., McHale, S. M., & Van Hook, J. (2016). *Families in an era of increasing inequality*. Springer International Publishing.

Amato, P. R., & Irving, S. (2013). Historical trends in divorce in the United States. In M. A. Fine & J. H. Harvey (Eds.), *Handbook of divorce and relationship dissolution* (pp. 57–74). Psychology Press.

Amato, P. R., & James, S. L. (2018). Changes in spousal relationships over the marital life course. In D. F. Alwin, D. H. Felmlee, & D. A. Kreager (Eds.), *Social networks and the life course: Integrating the development of human lives and social relational networks* (pp. 139–158). Springer International Publishing. https://doi.org/10.1007/978-3-319-71544-5_7

Ambridge, B., Kidd, E., Rowland, C. F., & Theakston, A. L. (2015). The ubiquity of frequency effects in first language acquisition. *Journal of Child Language, 42*(2), 239–273.

Ameri, M., Schur, L., Adya, M., Bentley, F. S., McKay, P., & Kruse, D. (2018). The disability employment puzzle: A field experiment on employer hiring behavior. *ILR Review, 71*(2), 329–364. https://doi.org/10.1177/0019793917717474

American Academy of Pediatrics, Council on Communications and Media (AAP). (2016). Media and young minds. *Pediatrics, 138*(5), e20162591. https://doi.org/10.1542/peds.2016-2591

American Association of Retired Persons (AARP). (2019). *2018 grandparents today national survey: General population report*. https://doi.org/10.26419/res.00289.001

American Association of Retired Persons (AARP). (2020). *AARP network of age-friendly states and communities*.

American Association of Retired Persons (AARP). (2021). *2021 AARP survey on the perceptions related to a dementia diagnosis: Adults age 40-plus*.

American Community Survey (ACS). (2015). *Detailed languages spoken at home and ability to speak English for the population 5 years and over: 2009–2013*. U.S. Census Bureau.

American Community Survey (ACS). (2020). *Population Reference Bureau, analysis of data from the U.S. Census Bureau, Census 2000 Supplementary Survey, 2001 Supplementary Survey, 2002 through 2019* (CS table B17001).

American Community Survey (ACS), U.S. Census Bureau. (2018). *Detailed languages spoken at home and ability to speak English for the population 5 years and over: 2009–2013 American Community Survey*. https://www.census.gov/data/tables/2018/demo/2009-2018-lang-tables.html

American Community Survey (ACS), U.S. Census Bureau. (2020, September 17). *2019 American Community Survey (ACS), 1-year estimates* (tables B10050 & S0201).

American Psychiatric Association (APA). (2013). *Diagnostic and statistical manual of mental disorders* (5th ed.) (*DSM-5*). American Psychiatric Association Publishing. https://doi.org/10.1176/appi.books.9780890425596

American Psychiatric Association (APA). (2022). *Diagnostic and statistical manual of mental disorders* (5th ed., text rev.) (*DSM-5-TR*). American Psychiatric Association Publishing.

American Psychological Association. (2020). *Publication manual of the American Psychological Association* (7th ed.).

American Psychological Association. (2021). *Stress in America 2021: Stress and decision-making during the pandemic*.

American Speech and Hearing Association (ASHA). (2017). *How does your child hear and talk?*

Ameye, H., & Swinnen, J. (2019). Obesity, income and gender: The changing global relationship. *Global Food Security, 23*, 267–281. https://doi.org/10.1016/j.gfs.2019.09.003

Ami, O., Maran, J. C., Gabor, P., Whitacre, E. B., Musset, D., Dubray, C., Mage, G., & Boyer, L. (2019). Three-dimensional magnetic resonance imaging of fetal head molding and brain shape changes during the second stage of labor. *PLOS ONE, 14*(5), e0215721. https://doi.org/10.1371/journal.pone.0215721

Amin, A., Kågesten, A., Adebayo, E., & Chandra-Mouli, V. (2018). Addressing gender socialization and masculinity norms among adolescent boys: Policy and programmatic implications. *Journal of Adolescent Health, 62*(3), S3–S5. https://doi.org/10.1016/j.jadohealth.2017.06.022

Amir, D., & McAuliffe, K. (2020). Cross-cultural, developmental psychology: Integrating approaches and key insights. *Evolution and Human Behavior, 41*(5), 430–444.

Amso, D., & Kirkham, N. (2021). A multiple-memory systems framework for examining attention and memory interactions in infancy. *Child Development Perspectives, 15*(2), 132–138. https://doi.org/10.1111/cdep.12410

Amso, D., & Lynn, A. (2017). Distinctive mechanisms of adversity and socioeconomic inequality in child development: A review and recommendations for evidence-based policy. *Policy Insights from the Behavioral and Brain Sciences, 4*(2), 139–146. https://doi.org/10.1177/2372732217721933

Amsterdam, B. (1972). Mirror self-image reactions before age two. *Developmental Psychobiology, 5*(4), 297–305. https://doi.org/10.1002/dev.420050403

Anatürk, M., Demnitz, N., Ebmeier, K. P., & Sexton, C. E. (2018). A systematic review and meta-analysis of structural magnetic resonance imaging studies investigating cognitive and social activity levels in older adults. *Neuroscience and Biobehavioral Reviews, 93*, 71–84. https://doi.org/10.1016/j.neubiorev.2018.06.012

Andersen, G. J. (2012). Aging and vision: Changes in function and performance from optics to perception. *Wiley Interdisciplinary Reviews: Cognitive Science, 3*(3), 403–410. https://doi.org/10.1002/wcs.1167

Anderson, C. A., Bushman, B. J., Bartholow, B. D., Cantor, J., Christakis, D., Coyne, S. M., Donnerstein, E., Brockmyer, J. F., Gentile, D. A., Green, C. S., Huesmann, R., Hummer, T., Krahé, B., Strasburger, V. C., Warburton, W., Wilson, B. J., & Ybarra, M. (2017). Screen violence and youth behavior. *Pediatrics, 140*(Suppl. 2), S142–S147. https://doi.org/10.1542/peds.2016-1758T

Anderson, D. I., Campos, J. J., Witherington, D. C., Dahl, A., Rivera, M., He, M., Uchiyama, I., & Barbu-Roth, M. (2013). The role of locomotion in psychological development. *Frontiers in Psychology, 4*, 440. https://doi.org/10.3389/fpsyg.2013.00440

Anderson, E. R., & Greene, S. M. (2011). "My child and I are a package deal": Balancing adult and child concerns in repartnering after divorce. *Journal of Family Psychology, 25*(5), 741.

Anderson, J. E. (1956). Child development: An historical perspective. *Child Development, 27*(2), 181–196. https://doi.org/10.2307/1126088

Anderson, J. R., Biro, D., & Pettitt, P. (2018). Evolutionary thanatology. *Philosophical Transactions of the Royal Society B: Biological Sciences, 373*(1754), 20170262. https://doi.org/10.1098/rstb.2017.0262

Anderson, J. R., Van Ryzin, M. J., & Doherty, W. J. (2010). Developmental trajectories of marital happiness in continuously married individuals: A group-based modeling approach. *Journal of Family Psychology, 24*(5), 587–596. https://doi.org/10.1037/a0020928

Anderson, M., Vogels, E. A., & Turner, E. (2020). *The virtues and downsides of online dating*. Pew Research Center.

Anderson, N. J., Graham, S. A., Prime, H., Jenkins, J. M., & Madigan, S. (2021). Linking quality and quantity of parental linguistic input to child language skills: A meta-analysis. *Child Development, 92*(2), 484–501. https://doi.org/10.1111/cdev.13508

Anderson, R., & Nagy, W. (1993). *The vocabulary conundrum* (No. 57). Center for the Study of Reading Technical Report.

Anderson, R. E. (2018). And still WE rise: Parent–child relationships, resilience, and school readiness in low-income urban Black families. *Journal of Family Psychology, 32*(1), 60–70.

Anderson, R. E., & Stevenson, H. C. (2019). RECASTing racial stress and trauma: Theorizing the healing potential of racial socialization in families. *American Psychologist, 74*(1), 63.

Anderson, T., Briggs, A., Spaulding, S., Zamani-Gallaher, E., & Lopez, D. (2021). *Racial and ethnic equity gaps in postsecondary career and technical education: Considerations for online learning (CTE COLAB)*. Urban Institute.

Anderson, T. M., Ferres, J. M. L., Ren, S. Y., Moon, R. Y., Goldstein, R. D., Ramirez, J.-M., & Mitchell, E. A. (2019). Maternal smoking before and during pregnancy and the risk of sudden unexpected infant death. *Pediatrics, 143*(4), e20183325. https://doi.org/10.1542/peds.2018-3325

Andersson, F., Holzer, H. J., Lane, J. I., Rosenblum, D., & Smith, J. (2013). *Does federally-funded job training work? Nonexperimental estimates of WIA training impacts using longitudinal data on workers and firms* (Working Paper No. 19446). National Bureau of Economic Research. https://doi.org/10.3386/w19446

Ando, A., Parzer, P., Kaess, M., Schell, S., Henze, R., Delorme, S., Stieltjes, B., Resch, F., Brunner, R., & Koenig, J. (2021). Calendar age and puberty-related development of regional gray matter volume and white matter tracts during adolescence. *Brain Structure & Function, 226*(3), 927–937. https://doi.org/10.1007/s00429-020-02208-1

Andre, J., Picchioni, M., Zhang, R., & Toulopoulou, T. (2016). Working memory circuit as a function of increasing age in healthy adolescence: A systematic review and meta-analyses. *NeuroImage: Clinical, 12*, 940–948.

Andreoni, J., Nikiforakis, N., & Stoop, J. (2021). Higher socioeconomic status does not predict decreased prosocial behavior in a field experiment. *Nature Communications, 12*(1), 4266. https://doi.org/10.1038/s41467-021-24519-5

Andres, M. (2021). What the heart wants: Polyamory, compersion and monogamish arrangements. In S. J. Dodd (Ed.), *The Routledge international handbook of social work and sexualities* (pp. 134–148). Routledge.

Andrews, J. L., Ahmed, S. P., & Blakemore, S.-J. (2021). Navigating the social environment in adolescence: The role of social brain development. *Biological Psychiatry, 89*(2), 109–118. https://doi.org/10.1016/j.biopsych.2020.09.012

Angelone, C. (2016). *To be buried alive is, beyond question, the most terrible of these extremes which has ever fallen to the lot of mere mortality*. https://histmed.collegeofphysicians.org/to-be-buried-alive-is-beyond-question/

Anim-Somuah, M., Smyth, R. M., Cyna, A. M., & Cuthbert, A. (2018). Epidural versus non-epidural or no analgesia for pain management in labour. *The Cochrane Database of Systematic Reviews, 5*, CD000331–CD000331. https://doi.org/10.1002/14651858.CD000331.pub4

Annie E. Casey Foundation. (2018). *Opening doors for young parents* (Policy Report: Kids Count).

Anniko, M. K., Boersma, K., & Tillfors, M. (2019). Sources of stress and worry in the development of stress-related mental health problems: A longitudinal investigation from early- to mid-adolescence. *Anxiety, Stress, & Coping, 32*(2), 155–167. https://doi.org/10.1080/10615806.2018.1549657

Ansari, A., & Crosnoe, R. (2018). The transition into kindergarten for English language learners. In A. J. Mashburn, J. LoCasale-Crouch, & K. C. Pears (Eds.), *Kindergarten transition and readiness: Promoting cognitive, social-emotional, and self-regulatory development* (pp. 185–204). Springer International Publishing. https://doi.org/10.1007/978-3-319-90200-5_8

Ansari, A., & Gottfried, M. A. (2020). Early childhood educational experiences and preschool absenteeism. *The Elementary School Journal, 121*(1), 34–51. https://doi.org/10.1086/709832

Ansari, A., & Gottfried, M. A. (2021). The grade-level and cumulative outcomes of absenteeism. *Child Development, 92*(4), e548–e564. https://doi.org/10.1111/cdev.13555

Anthony, E. R., Cho, Y., Fischer, R. L., & Matthews, L. (2021). Examining the causal impact of prenatal home visiting on birth outcomes: A propensity score analysis. *Maternal and Child Health Journal*. https://doi.org/10.1007/s10995-020-03054-7

Anton, M. T., Jones, D. J., & Youngstrom, E. A. (2015). Socioeconomic status, parenting, and externalizing problems in African American single-mother homes: A person-oriented approach. *Journal of Family Psychology, 29*(3), 405.

Antonarakis, S. E., Skotko, B. G., Rafii, M. S., Strydom, A., Pape, S. E., Bianchi, D. W., Sherman, S. L., & Reeves, R. H. (2020). Down syndrome. *Nature Reviews Disease Primers, 6*(1), 1–20.

Antoniou, M. (2019). The advantages of bilingualism debate. *Annual Review of Linguistics, 5*(1), 395–415. https://doi.org/10.1146/annurev-linguistics-011718-011820

Antoniou, M., & Wright, S. M. (2017). Uncovering the mechanisms responsible for why language learning may promote healthy cognitive aging. *Frontiers in Psychology, 8*, 2217. https://doi.org/10.3389/fpsyg.2017.02217

Antonucci, T. C., Ajrouch, K. J., & Webster, N. J. (2019a). Convoys of social relations: Cohort similarities and differences over 25 years. *Psychology and Aging, 34*(8), 1158–1169. https://doi.org/10.1037/pag0000375

Antonucci, T. C., Ajrouch, K. J., Webster, N. J., & Zahodne, L. B. (2019b). Social relations across the life span: Scientific advances, emerging issues, and future challenges. *Annual Review of Developmental Psychology, 1*(1), 313–336. https://doi.org/10.1146/annurev-devpsych-121318-085212

APA Ethics Committee Rules and Procedures. (2018). *Ethical principles of psychologists and code of conduct.* American Psychological Association. https://www.apa.org/ethics/code

Apergis, N., Bhattacharya, M., & Hadhri, W. (2020). Health care expenditure and environmental pollution: A cross-country comparison across different income groups. *Environmental Science and Pollution Research, 27*(8), 8142–8156. https://doi.org/10.1007/s11356-019-07457-0

Apostolou, M., O, J., & Esposito, G. (2020). Singles' reasons for being single: Empirical evidence from an evolutionary perspective. *Frontiers in Psychology, 11*, 746. https://doi.org/10.3389/fpsyg.2020.00746

Appel, H., Gerlach, A. L., & Crusius, J. (2016). The interplay between Facebook use, social comparison, envy, and depression. *Current Opinion in Psychology, 9*, 44–49.

Appleton, K. M., Hemingway, A., Rajska, J., & Hartwell, H. (2018). Repeated exposure and conditioning strategies for increasing vegetable liking and intake: Systematic review and meta-analyses of the published literature. *The American Journal of Clinical Nutrition, 108*(4), 842–856. https://doi.org/10.1093/ajcn/nqy143

Arai, Y., Martin-Ruiz, C. M., Takayama, M., Abe, Y., Takebayashi, T., Koyasu, S., Suematsu, M., Hirose, N., & von Zglinicki, T. (2015). Inflammation, but not telomere length, predicts successful ageing at extreme old age: A longitudinal study of semi-supercentenarians. *EBioMedicine, 2*(10), 1549–1558.

Arauz, R. M., Dexter, A. L., Rogoff, B., & Aceves-Azuara, I. (2019). Children's management of attention as cultural practice. In T. Tulviste, D. L. Best, & J. L. Gibbons (Eds.), *Children's social worlds in cultural context* (pp. 23–39). Springer International Publishing. https://doi.org/10.1007/978-3-030-27033-9_3

Araya, A. C., Warwick, R., Shumer, D., & Selkie, E. (2021). Romantic relationships in transgender adolescents: A qualitative study. *Pediatrics, 147*(2), e2020007906. https://doi.org/10.1542/peds.2020-007906

Arboleda, V. A., Sandberg, D. E., & Vilain, E. (2014). DSDs: Genetics, underlying pathologies and psychosexual differentiation. *Nature Reviews: Endocrinology, 10*(10), 603–615. https://doi.org/10.1038/nrendo.2014.130

Archer, J., Reiboldt, W., Claver, M., & Fay, J. (2021). Caregiving in quarantine: Evaluating the impact of the Covid-19 pandemic on adult child informal caregivers of a parent. *Gerontology and Geriatric Medicine, 7*. https://doi.org/10.1177/2333721421990150

Arem, H., Moore, S. C., Patel, A., Hartge, P., De Gonzalez, A. B., Visvanathan, K., & Matthews, C. E. (2015). Leisure time physical activity and mortality: A detailed pooled analysis of the dose-response relationship. *JAMA Internal Medicine, 175*(6), 959–967.

Arenas, E., Yahirun, J., Teruel, G., Rubalcava, L., & Gaitán-Rossi, P. (2021). Gender, family separation, and negative emotional well-being among recent Mexican migrants. *Journal of Marriage and Family, 83*(5), 1401–1419.

Arevian, A. C., Jones, F., Tang, L., Sherbourne, C. D., Jones, L., & Miranda, J. (2019). Depression remission from community coalitions versus individual program support for services: Findings from community partners in care, Los Angeles, California, 2010–2016. *American Journal of Public Health, 109*(S3), S205–S213. https://doi.org/10.2105/AJPH.2019.305082

Argabright, S. T., Visoki, E., Moore, T. M., Ryan, D. T., DiDomenico, G. E., Njoroge, W. F. M., Taylor, J. H., Guloksuz, S., Gur, R. C., Gur, R. E., Benton, T. D., & Barzilay, R. (2021). association between Discrimination Stress and Suicidality in Preadolescent Children. *Journal of the American Academy of Child & Adolescent Psychiatry.* https://doi.org/10.1016/j.jaac.2021.08.011

Arias, E., Tejada-Vera, B., & Ahmad, F. (2021). *Provisional life expectancy estimates for January through June, 2020* (Rapid Release No. 010). National Center for Vital Statistics.

Ariès, P. (1983). *Hour of our death.* Penguin Books.

Armstrong, B., Gallant, S. N., Li, L., Patel, K., & Wong, B. I. (2017). Stereotype threat effects on older adults' episodic and working memory: A meta-analysis. *The Gerontologist, 57*(suppl_2), S193–S205. https://doi.org/10.1093/geront/gnx056

Armstrong, E. A., Gleckman-Krut, M., & Johnson, L. (2018). Silence, power, and inequality: An intersectional approach to sexual violence. *Annual Review of Sociology, 44*, 99–122.

Armstrong, E. A., & Hamilton, L. T. (2013). *Paying for the party.* Harvard University Press.

Armstrong, E. A., Hamilton, L. T., Armstrong, E. M., & Seeley, J. L. (2014). "Good girls": Gender, social class, and slut discourse on campus. *Social Psychology Quarterly, 77*(2), 100–122. https://doi.org/10.1177/0190272514521220

Armstrong, S., Wong, C. A., Perrin, E., Page, S., Sibley, L., & Skinner, A. (2018). Association of physical activity with income, race/ethnicity, and sex among adolescents and young adults in the United States: Findings from the National Health and Nutrition Examination Survey, 2007–2016. *JAMA Pediatrics, 172*(8), 732–740.

Armstrong-Carter, E., Ivory, S., Lin, L. C., Muscatell, K. A., & Telzer, E. H. (2020). Role fulfillment mediates the association between daily family assistance and cortisol awakening response in adolescents. *Child Development, 91*(3), 754–768. https://doi.org/10.1111/cdev.13213

Armstrong-Carter, E., & Telzer, E. H. (2021). Daily provision of instrumental and emotional support to friends is associated with diurnal cortisol during adolescence. *Developmental Psychobiology, 63*(5), 1266–1278. https://doi.org/10.1002/dev.22101

Arndorfer, C. L., & Stormshak, E. A. (2008). Same-sex versus other-sex best friendship in early adolescence: Longitudinal predictors of antisocial behavior throughout adolescence. *Journal of Youth and Adolescence, 37*(9), 1059–1070. https://doi.org/10.1007/s10964-008-9311-x

Arnett, J. J. (2000). Emerging adulthood: A theory of development from the late teens through the twenties. *American Psychologist, 55*(5), 469–480. http://doi.org/10.1037/0003-066X.55.5.469

Arnett, J. J. (2006). G. Stanley Hall's *Adolescence*: Brilliance and nonsense. *History of Psychology, 9*(3), 186–197. https://doi.org/10.1037/1093-4510.9.3.186

Arnett, J. J. (2016). Does emerging adulthood theory apply across social classes? National data on a persistent question. *Emerging Adulthood, 4*(4), 227–235. https://doi.org/10.1177/2167696815613000

Arnett, J. J. (2018). Happily stressed: The complexity of well-being in midlife. *Journal of Adult Development, 25*(4), 270–278.

Arnett, J. J., & Mitra, D. (2020). Are the features of emerging adulthood developmentally distinctive? A comparison of ages 18–60 in the United States. *Emerging Adulthood, 8*(5), 412–419. https://doi.org/10.1177/2167696818810073

Arnett, J. J., Robinson, O., & Lachman, M. E. (2020). Rethinking adult development: Introduction to the special issue. *American Psychologist, 75*(4), 425. https://doi.org/10.1037/amp0000633

Aron, A., Paris, M., & Aron, E. N. (1995). Falling in love: Prospective studies of self-concept change. *Journal of Personality and Social Psychology, 69*(6), 1102.

Arsenio, W. (2014). Moral emotion attributions and aggression. In M. Killen & J. G. Smetana (Eds.), *Handbook of moral development* (pp. 235–255). Psychology Press.

Arshad, T., Paik, J. M., Biswas, R., Alqahtani, S. A., Henry, L., & Younossi, Z. M. (2021). Nonalcoholic fatty liver disease prevalence trends among adolescents and young adults in the United States, 2007–2016. *Hepatology Communications.* https://doi.org/10.1002/hep4.1760

Arum, R., & Roksa, J. (2011). Are undergraduates actually learning anything. *Chronicle of Higher Education, 57*(21), A30–A31.

Aryal, M. (2016, April 21). *A child-headed household perseveres a year after the Nepal earthquake.* https://www.unicef.org/stories/child-headed-household-perseveres-year-after-nepal-earthquake

Aschemeyer, F., Rosabal-Coto, M., Storm, S., & Keller, H. (2021). The role of culture and caregivers' formal education for babies' learning environments: The case of two Costa Rican Communities. *Journal of Cross-Cultural Psychology, 52*(2), 103–128. https://doi.org/10.1177/0022022120981715

Ash, A. S., Kroll-Desrosiers, A. R., Hoaglin, D. C., Christensen, K., Fang, H., & Perls, T. T. (2015). Are members of long-lived families healthier than their equally long-lived peers? Evidence from the long life family study. *The Journals of Gerontology: Series A, 70*(8), 971–976. https://doi.org/10.1093/gerona/glv015

Ash, M., & Boyce, J. K. (2018). Racial disparities in pollution exposure and employment at US industrial facilities. *Proceedings of the National Academy of Sciences, 115*(42), 10636–10641.

Ashcraft, A. M., & Murray, P. J. (2017). Talking to parents about adolescent sexuality. *Pediatric Clinics of North America, 64*(2), 305–320. https://doi.org/10.1016/j.pcl.2016.11.002

Ashworth, R. (2020). Perceptions of stigma among people affected by early- and late-onset Alzheimer's disease. *Journal of Health Psychology, 25*(4), 490–510. https://doi.org/10.1177/1359105317720818

Assari, S., & Lankarani, M. M. (2016). Association between stressful life events and depression; Intersection of race and gender. *Journal of Racial and Ethnic Health Disparities, 3*(2), 349–356. https://doi.org/10.1007/s40615-015-0160-5

Astington, J. W., & Gopnik, A. (1988). Knowing you've changed your mind: Children's understanding of representational change. In J. W. Astington, P. L. Harris, & D. R. Olson (Eds.), *Developing theories of mind* (pp. 193–206). Cambridge University Press.

Astington, J. W., Harris, P. L., & Olson, D. R. (1988). *Developing theories of mind.* Cambridge University Press.

Astle, S., Leonhardt, N., & Willoughby, B. (2019). Home base: Family of origin factors and the debut of vaginal sex, anal sex, oral sex, masturbation, and pornography use in a national sample of adolescents. *The Journal of Sex Research, 57*(9), 1089–1099. https://doi.org/10.1080/00224499.2019.1691140

Astle, S., Toews, M., Topham, G., & Vennum, A. (2021). To talk or not to talk: An analysis of parents' intentions to talk with children about different sexual topics using the theory of planned behavior. *Sexuality Research and Social Policy.* https://doi.org/10.1007/s13178-021-00587-6

Atchley, R. C. (1999). *Continuity and adaptation in aging: Creating positive experiences* (pp. xvi, 214). Johns Hopkins University Press.

Athan, A. M. (2020). Reproductive identity: An emerging concept. *American Psychologist, 75*(4), 445.

Attina, T. M., Malits, J., Naidu, M., & Trasande, L. (2019). Racial/ethnic disparities in disease burden and costs related to exposure to endocrine disrupting chemicals in the US: An exploratory analysis. *Journal of Clinical Epidemiology, 108*, 34–43. https://doi.org/10.1016/j.jclinepi.2018.11.024

Auais, M., Alvarado, B., Guerra, R., Curcio, C., Freeman, E. E., Ylli, A., & Deshpande, N. (2017). Fear of falling and its association with life-space mobility of older adults: A cross-sectional analysis using data from five international sites. *Age and Ageing, 46*(3), 459–465.

Auerbach, R. P., Mortier, P., Bruffaerts, R., Alonso, J., Benjet, C., Cuijpers, P., & Kessler, R. C. (2018). WHO world mental health surveys international college student project: Prevalence and distribution of mental disorders. *Journal of Abnormal Psychology, 127*(7), 623.

Augustine, M. E., & Stiller, C. A. (2019). Children's behavioral self-regulation and conscience: Roles of child temperament, parenting, and parenting context. *Journal of Applied Developmental Psychology, 63*, 54–64. https://doi.org/10.1016/j.appdev.2019.05.008

Ault, R., Morales, A., Ault, R., Spitale, A., & Martinez, G. A. (2019). Communication pitfalls in interpreted genetic counseling sessions. *Journal of Genetic Counseling, 28*(4), 897–907. https://doi.org/10.1002/jgc4.1132

Aumètre, F., & Poulin, F. (2018). Academic and behavioral outcomes associated with organized activity participation trajectories during childhood. *Journal of Applied Developmental Psychology, 54*, 33–41. https://doi.org/10.1016/j.appdev.2017.11.003

Aunio, P., & Räsänen, P. (2016). Core numerical skills for learning mathematics in children aged five to eight years—A working model for educators. *European Early Childhood Education Research Journal, 24*(5), 684–704. https://doi.org/10.1080/1350293X.2014.996424

Austerberry, C., & Fearon, P. (2021). Chapter 3—An overview of developmental behavioral genetics. In L. Provenzi & R. Montirosso (Eds.), *Developmental human behavioral epigenetics* (Vol. 23, pp. 59–80). Academic Press. https://doi.org/10.1016/B978-0-12-819262-7.00003-9

Austin, R. D., & Pisano, G. P. (2017, May–June). Neurodiversity as a competitive advantage. *Harvard Business Review*, 96– 103. https://hbr.org/2017/05/neurodiversity-as-a-competitive-advantage

Autor, D., Figlio, D., Karbownik, K., Roth, J., & Wasserman, M. (2019). Family disadvantage and the gender gap in behavioral and educational outcomes. *American Economic Journal: Applied Economics, 11*(3), 338–381. https://doi.org/10.1257/app.20170571

Auxier, B., & Anderson, M. (2021). *Social media use in 2021*. Pew Research Center.

Avagliano, L., Massa, V., George, T. M., Qureshy, S., Bulfamante, G., & Finnell, R. H. (2019). Overview on neural tube defects: From development to physical characteristics. *Birth Defects Research, 111*(19), 1455–1467. https://doi.org/10.1002/bdr2.1380

Axelrad, H., & Mahoney, K. J. (2017). Increasing the pensionable age: What changes are OECD countries making? What considerations are driving policy? *Open Journal of Social Sciences, 5*(7), 56–70. https://doi.org/10.4236/jss.2017.57005

Ayalon, L., Doron, I., Bodner, E., & Inbar, N. (2014). Macro- and micro-level predictors of age categorization: Results from the European Social Survey. *European Journal of Ageing, 11*(1), 5–18. https://doi.org/10.1007/s10433-013-0282-8

Ayalon, L., & Tesch-Römer, C. (2017). Taking a closer look at ageism: Self- and other-directed ageist attitudes and discrimination. *European Journal of Ageing, 14*(1), 1–4. https://doi.org/10.1007/s10433-016-0409-9

Aye, T., Oo, K. S., Khin, M. T., Kuramoto-Ahuja, T., & Maruyama, H. (2017). Gross motor skill development of 5-year-old kindergarten children in Myanmar. *Journal of Physical Therapy Science, 29*(10), 1772–1778. https://doi.org/10.1589/jpts.29.1772

Aylwin, C. F., Toro, C. A., Shirtcliff, E., & Lomniczi, A. (2019). Emerging genetic and epigenetic mechanisms underlying pubertal maturation in adolescence. *Journal of Research on Adolescence, 29*(1), 54–79. https://doi.org/10.1111/jora.12385

Ayoub, M., Briley, D. A., Grotzinger, A., Patterson, M. W., Engelhardt, L. E., Tackett, J. L., Harden, K. P., & Tucker-Drob, E. M. (2019). Genetic and environmental associations between child personality and parenting. *Social Psychological and Personality Science, 10*(6), 711–721. https://doi.org/10.1177/1948550618784890

Azad, M. B., Vehling, L., Chan, D., Klopp, A., Nickel, N. C., McGavock, J. M., Becker, A. B., Mandhane, P. J., Turvey, S. E., Moraes, T. J., Taylor, M. S., Lefebvre, D. L., Sears, M. R., Subbarao, P., & Investigators, on behalf of the CHILD Study Investigators. (2018). Infant feeding and weight gain: Separating breast milk from breastfeeding and formula from food. *Pediatrics, 142*(4), e20181092. https://doi.org/10.1542/peds.2018-1092

Azagba, S., Manzione, L., Shan, L., & King, J. (2020). Trends in smoking during pregnancy by socioeconomic characteristics in the United States, 2010–2017. *BMC Pregnancy and Childbirth, 20*(1), 52. https://doi.org/10.1186/s12884-020-2748-y

Azar, A., Staudinger, U. M., Slachevsky, A., Madero-Cabib, I., & Calvo, E. (2019). From snapshots to movies: The association between retirement sequences and aging trajectories in limitations to perform activities of daily living. *Journal of Aging and Health, 31*(2), 293–321. https://doi.org/10.1177/0898264318782096

Azhari, A., Leck, W. Q., Gabrieli, G., Bizzego, A., Rigo, P., Setoh, P., Bornstein, M. H., & Esposito, G. (2019). Parenting stress undermines mother-child brain-to-brain synchrony: A hyperscanning study. *Scientific Reports, 9*(1), 11407. https://doi.org/10.1038/s41598-019-47810-4

Baams, L., Dubas, J. S., & Van Aken, M. A. (2017). Comprehensive sexuality education as a longitudinal predictor of LGBTQ name-calling and perceived willingness to intervene in school. *Journal of Youth and Adolescence, 46*(5), 931–942.

Babadjouni, R. M., Hodis, D. M., Radwanski, R., Durazo, R., Patel, A., Liu, Q., & Mack, W. J. (2017). Clinical effects of air pollution on the central nervous system: A review. *Journal of Clinical Neuroscience, 43*, 16–24. https://doi.org/10.1016/j.jocn.2017.04.028

Babcock, P., & Marks, M. (2010). The falling time cost of college: Evidence from half a century of time use data. *The Review of Economics and Statistics, 93*(2), 468–478. https://doi.org/10.1162/REST_a_00093

Babulal, G. M., Quiroz, Y. T., Albensi, B. C., Arenaza-Urquijo, E., Astell, A. J., Babiloni, C., Bahar-Fuchs, A., Bell, J., Bowman, G. L., Brickman, A. M., Chételat, G., Ciro, C., Cohen, A. D., Dilworth-Anderson, P., Dodge, H. H., Dreux, S., Edland, S., Esbensen, A., Evered, L., … O'Bryant, S. E. (2019). Perspectives on ethnic and racial disparities in Alzheimer's disease and related dementias: Update and areas of immediate need. *Alzheimer's & Dementia, 15*(2), 292–312. https://doi.org/10.1016/j.jalz.2018.09.009

Baburamani, A. A., Patkee, P. A., Arichi, T., & Rutherford, M. A. (2019). New approaches to studying early brain development in Down syndrome. *Developmental Medicine & Child Neurology, 61*(8), 867–879. https://doi.org/10.1111/dmcn.14260

Baciu, A., Negussie, Y., Geller, A., Weinstein, J. N., & National Academies of Sciences, Engineering, and Medicine. (2017). The state of health disparities in the United States. In National Academies of Sciences, Engineering, and Medicine; Health and Medicine Division; Board on Population Health and Public Health Practice; Committee on Community-Based Solutions to Promote Health Equity in the United States; A. Baciu, Y. Negussie, A. Geller, & J. N. Weinstein (Eds.), *Communities in action: Pathways to health equity*. National Academies Press. https://www.ncbi.nlm.nih.gov/books/NBK425844/

Badawy, P. J., Schafer, M. H., & Sun, H. (2019). Relocation and network turnover in later life: How distance moved and functional health are linked to a changing social convoy. *Research on Aging, 41*(1), 54–84.

Bahar-Fuchs, A., Martyr, A., Goh, A. M., Sabates, J., & Clare, L. (2019). Cognitive training for people with mild to moderate dementia. *The Cochrane Database of Systematic Reviews, 2019*(3), CD013069. https://doi.org/10.1002/14651858.CD013069.pub2

Bai, L., Whitesell, C. J., & Teti, D. M. (2020). Maternal sleep patterns and parenting quality during infants' first 6 months. *Journal of Family Psychology, 34*(3), 291–300. https://doi.org/10.1037/fam0000608

Bailen, N. H., Green, L. M., & Thompson, R. J. (2019). Understanding emotion in adolescents: A review of emotional frequency, intensity, instability, and clarity. *Emotion Review, 11*(1), 63–73. https://doi.org/10.1177/1754073918768878

Bailey, A. P., Hetrick, S. E., Rosenbaum, S., Purcell, R., & Parker, A. G. (2018). Treating depression with physical activity in adolescents and young adults: A systematic review and meta-analysis of randomised controlled trials. *Psychological Medicine, 48*(7), 1068–1083.

Bailey, Z. D., Feldman, J. M., & Bassett, M. T. (2021). How structural racism works—racist policies as a root cause of U.S. racial health inequities. *New England Journal of Medicine, 384*(8), 768–773. https://doi.org/10.1056/NEJMms2025396

Bailey, Z. D., Krieger, N., Agénor, M., Graves, J., Linos, N., & Bassett, M. T. (2017). Structural racism and health inequities in the USA: Evidence and interventions. *The Lancet, 389*(10077), 1453–1463. https://doi.org/10.1016/S0140-6736(17)30569-X

Baillargeon, R. (1987). Young infants' reasoning about the physical and spatial properties of a hidden object. *Cognitive Development, 2*(3), 179–200. https://doi.org/10.1016/S0885-2014(87)90043-8

Baillargeon, R., Scott, R. M., & Bian, L. (2016). Psychological reasoning in infancy. *Annual Review of Psychology, 67*(1), 159–186. https://doi.org/10.1146/annurev-psych-010213-115033

Baird, D., Bybel, M., & Kowalski, A. W. (2019). Toilet training: Common questions and answers. *American Family Physician, 100*(8), 468–474.

Bakalar, J. L., Shank, L. M., Vannucci, A., Radin, R. M., & Tanofsky-Kraff, M. (2015). Recent advances in developmental and risk factor research on eating disorders. *Current Psychiatry Reports, 17*(6), 42. https://doi.org/10.1007/s11920-015-0585-x

Baker, A. E., & Galván, A. (2020). Threat or thrill? The neural mechanisms underlying the development of anxiety and risk taking in adolescence. *Developmental Cognitive Neuroscience, 45*, 100841.

Baker, F. C., De Zambotti, M., Colrain, I. M., & Bei, B. (2018). Sleep problems during the menopausal transition: Prevalence, impact, and management challenges. *Nature and Science of Sleep, 10*, 73.

Baker, K. E., & Harris, A. C. (2020). Terminology should accurately reflect complexities of sexual orientation and identity. *American Journal of Public Health, 110*(11), 1668–1669.

Bakermans-Kranenburg, M. J., Lotz, A., Dijk, K. A., & Van IJzendoorn, M. (2019). Birth of a father: Fathering in the first 1,000 days. *Child Development Perspectives, 13*(4), 247–253. https://doi.org/10.1111/cdep.12347

Bakermans-Kranenburg, M. J., & Van Ijzendoorn, M. H. (2015). The hidden efficacy of interventions: Gene × environment experiments from a differential susceptibility perspective. *Annual Review of Psychology, 66*, 381–409.

Baldacci, F., Mazzucchi, S., Della Vecchia, A., Giampietri, L., Giannini, N., Koronyo-Hamaoui, M., Ceravolo, R., Siciliano, G., Bonuccelli, U., Elahi, F. M., Vergallo, A., Lista, S., & Giorgi, F. S. (2020). The path to biomarker-based diagnostic criteria for the spectrum of neurodegenerative diseases. *Expert Review of Molecular Diagnostics, 20*(4), 421–441. https://doi.org/10.1080/14737159.2020.1731306

Baldwin, D., & Meyer, M. (2007). How inherently social is language? In E. Hoff & M. Shatz (Eds.), *Blackwell handbook of language development* (pp. 87–106). Blackwell Publishing.

Ballard, P. J., Daniel, S. S., Anderson, G., Nicolotti, L., Caballero Quinones, E., Lee, M., & Koehler, A. N. (2021). Incorporating volunteering into treatment for depression among adolescents: Developmental and clinical considerations. *Frontiers in Psychology, 12*, 1581.

Ballard, P. J., Hoyt, L. T., & Pachucki, M. C. (2019). Impacts of adolescent and young adult civic engagement on health and socioeconomic status in adulthood. *Child Development, 90*(4), 1138–1154.

Ballesteros, S., Kraft, E., Santana, S., & Tziraki, C. (2015). Maintaining older brain functionality: A targeted review. *Neuroscience and Biobehavioral Reviews, 55*, 453–477. https://doi.org/10.1016/j.neubiorev.2015.06.008

Balmer, D. G., Frey, R., Gott, M., Collier, A., & Boyd, M. (2020). A place to live and to die: A qualitative exploration of the social practices and rituals of death in residential aged care. *OMEGA—Journal of Death and Dying.* https://doi.org/10.1177/0030222820935217

Baltes, P. B. (1987). Theoretical propositions of life-span developmental psychology: On the dynamics between growth and decline. *Developmental Psychology, 23*(5), 611–626. https://doi.org/10.1037/0012-1649.23.5.611

Baltes, P. B., & Baltes, M. M. (1990). Psychological perspectives on successful aging: The model of selective optimization with compensation. In P. B. Baltes & M. M. Baltes (Eds.), *Successful aging: Perspectives from the behavioral sciences* (pp. 1–34). Cambridge University Press. https://doi.org/10.1017/CBO9780511665684.003

Baltes, P. B., & Baltes, M. M. (Eds.). (1993). *Successful aging: Perspectives from the behavioral sciences* (Vol. 4). Cambridge University Press.

Balzarini, R. N., Dharma, C., Kohut, T., Holmes, B. M., Campbell, L., Lehmiller, J. J., & Harman, J. J. (2019). Demographic comparison of American individuals in polyamorous and monogamous relationships. *The Journal of Sex Research, 56*(6), 681–694. https://doi.org/10.1080/00224499.2018.1474333

Balzer Carr, B., & London, R. A. (2020). Healthy, housed, and well-fed: Exploring basic needs support programming in the context of university student success. *AERA Open, 6*(4), 2332858420972619. https://doi.org/10.1177/2332858420972619

Bamidis, P. D., Fissler, P., Papageorgiou, S. G., Zilidou, V., Konstantinidis, E. I., Billis, A. S., & Kolassa, I. T. (2015). Gains in cognition through combined cognitive and physical training: The role of training dosage and severity of neurocognitive disorder. *Frontiers in Aging Neuroscience, 7*, 152.

Bamishigbin, O. N., Dunkel Schetter, C., & Stanton, A. L. (2019). The antecedents and consequences of adolescent fatherhood: A systematic review. *Social Science & Medicine, 232*, 106–119. https://doi.org/10.1016/j.socscimed.2019.04.031

Bana, B., & Cabreiro, F. (2019). The microbiome and aging. *Annual Review of Genetics, 53*, 239–261.

Bandura, A. (1999). *Self-efficacy: The exercise of control.* W. H. Freeman.

Bandura, A. (2018). Toward a psychology of human agency: Pathways and reflections. *Perspectives on Psychological Science, 13*(2), 130–136. https://doi.org/10.1177/1745691617699280

Bandura, A. (2019). Applying theory for human betterment. *Perspectives on Psychological Science, 14*(1), 12–15. https://doi.org/10.1177/1745691618815165

Banerjee, M., & Eccles, J. S. (2019). Perceived racial discrimination as a context for parenting in African American and European American youth. In H. E. Fitzgerald, D. J. Johnson, D. B. Qin, F. A. Villarruel, & J. Norder (Eds.), *Handbook of children and prejudice: Integrating research, practice, and policy* (pp. 233–247). Springer International Publishing. https://doi.org/10.1007/978-3-030-12228-7_13

Banghart, P., Halle, T., Bamdad, T., Cook, M., Redd, Z., Cox, A., Carlson, J., & Zaslow, M. (2020). *A review of the literature on access to high quality care for infants and toddlers.* Child Trends.

Banks, N. (2019, February 19). *Black women's labor market history reveals deep-seated race and gender discrimination.* Economic Policy Institute. https://www.epi.org/blog/black-womens-labor-market-history-reveals-deep-seated-race-and-gender-discrimination/

Barac, R., Bialystok, E., Castro, D. C., & Sanchez, M. (2014). The cognitive development of young dual language learners: A critical review. *Early Childhood Research Quarterly, 29*(4), 699–714. https://doi.org/10.1016/j.ecresq.2014.02.003

Baraldi, L. G., Steele, E. M., Canella, D. S., & Monteiro, C. A. (2018). Consumption of ultra-processed foods and associated sociodemographic factors in the USA between 2007 and 2012: Evidence from a nationally representative cross-sectional study. *BMJ Open, 8*(3), e020574. https://doi.org/10.1136/bmjopen-2017-020574

Baranne, M. L., & Falissard, B. (2018). Global burden of mental disorders among children aged 5–14 years. *Child and Adolescent Psychiatry and Mental Health, 12*(1), 19.

Barash, D. P. (2016). *Out of Eden: The surprising consequences of polygamy.* Oxford University Press.

Barata, M. C., & Yoshikawa, H. (2014). Mixed methods in research on child well-being. In A. Ben-Arieh, F. C. Frønes, & J. E. Korbin (Eds.), *Handbook of child well-being: Theories, methods and policies in global perspective* (pp. 2879–2893). Springer Netherlands. https://nyuscholars.nyu.edu/en/publications/mixed-methods-in-research-on-child-well-being

Barbara, V. (2019, January 16). Opinion | I put my baby daughter in dinosaur overalls. Am I an anarchist? *The New York Times.* https://www.nytimes.com/2019/01/16/opinion/brazil-gender-alves.html

Barber, B. K., Stolz, H. E., Olsen, J. A., Collins, W. A., & Burchinal, M. (2005). Parental support, psychological control, and behavioral control: Assessing relevance across time, culture, and method. *Monographs of the Society for Research in Child Development, 70*(4), i–147.

Barber, B. K., Xia, M., Olsen, J. A., McNeely, C. A., & Bose, K. (2012). Feeling disrespected by parents: Refining the measurement and understanding of psychological control. *Journal of Adolescence, 35*(2), 273–287. https://doi.org/10.1016/j.adolescence.2011.10.010

Barber, S. J. (2017). An examination of age-based stereotype threat about cognitive decline: Implications for stereotype-threat research and theory development. *Perspectives on Psychological Science, 12*(1), 62–90. https://doi.org/10.1177/1745691616656345

Barbot, B., Hein, S., Trentacosta, C., Beckmann, J. F., Bick, J., Crocetti, E., Liu, Y., Rao, S. F., Liew, J., Overbeek, G., Ponguta, L. A., Scheithauer, H., Super, C., Arnett, J., Bukowski, W., Cook, T. D., Côté, J., Eccles, J. S., Eid, M., … IJzendoorn, M. H. van. (2020). Manifesto for new directions in developmental science. *New Directions for Child and Adolescent Development, 2020*(172), 135–149. https://doi.org/10.1002/cad.20359

Barbour, K. E., Helmick, C. G., Boring, M., & Brady, T. J. (2017). Vital signs: Prevalence of doctor-diagnosed arthritis and arthritis-attributable activity limitation—United States, 2013–2015. *Morbidity and Mortality Weekly Report, 66*(9), 246–253. https://doi.org/10.15585/mmwr.mm6609e1

Barbuscia, A., Martikainen, P., Myrskylä, M., Remes, H., Somigliana, E., Klemetti, R., & Goisis, A. (2020). Maternal age and risk of low birth weight and premature birth in children conceived through medically assisted reproduction. Evidence from Finnish population registers. *Human Reproduction, 35*(1), 212–220. https://doi.org/10.1093/humrep/dez275

Bardanzellu, F., Fanos, V., & Reali, A. (2017). "Omics" in human colostrum and mature milk: Looking to old data with new eyes. *Nutrients, 9*(8), 843. https://doi.org/10.3390/nu9080843

Bardo, A. R. (2017). A life course model for a domains-of-life approach to happiness: Evidence from the United States. *Advances in Life Course Research, 33*, 11–22. https://doi.org/10.1016/j.alcr.2017.06.002

Bardo, A. R., Lynch, S. M., & Land, K. C. (2017). The importance of the baby boom cohort and the great recession in understanding age, period, and cohort patterns in happiness. *Social Psychological and Personality Science, 8*(3), 341–350. https://doi.org/10.1177/1948550616673874

Barendse, M., Flannery, J., Cavanagh, C., Aristizabal, M., Becker, S. P., Berger, E., Breaux, R., Campione-Barr, N., Church, J. A., Crone, E., Dahl, R., Dennis-Tiwary, T. A., Dvorsky, M., Dziura, S., Ho, T., Killoren, S. E., Langberg, J., Larguinho, T., Magis-Weinberg, L., … Pfeifer, J. (2021). Longitudinal change in adolescent depression and anxiety symptoms from before to during the COVID-19 pandemic: An international collaborative of 12 samples. *PsyArXiv.* https://doi.org/10.31234/osf.io/hn7us

Barfield, W. D. (2021). Social disadvantage and its effect on maternal and newborn health. *Seminars in Perinatology,* 151407. https://doi.org/10.1016/j.semperi.2021.151407

Bari, B. A., Chokshi, V., & Schmidt, K. (2020). Locus coeruleus-norepinephrine: Basic functions and insights into Parkinson's disease. *Neural Regeneration Research, 15*(6), 1006.

Barker, A. B., Leighton, P., & Ferguson, M. A. (2017). Coping together with hearing loss: A qualitative metasynthesis of the psychosocial experiences of people with hearing loss and their communication partners. *International Journal of Audiology, 56*(5), 297–305.

Barker, D. J. (1995). Fetal origins of coronary heart disease. *BMJ, 311*(6998), 171–174.

Barker, D. J. P. (2004). The developmental origins of chronic adult disease. *Acta Paediatrica, 93*(s446), 26–33. https://doi.org/10.1111/j.1651-2227.2004.tb00236.x

Barker, J. E., Semenov, A. D., Michaelson, L., Provan, L. S., Snyder, H. R., & Munakata, Y. (2014). Less-structured time in children's daily lives predicts self-directed executive functioning. *Frontiers in Psychology, 5*, 593. https://doi.org/10.3389/fpsyg.2014.00593

Barlow, J., Sembi, S., Parsons, H., Kim, S., Petrou, S., Harnett, P., & Dawe, S. (2019). A randomized controlled trial and economic evaluation of the parents under pressure program for parents in substance abuse treatment. *Drug and Alcohol Dependence, 194*, 184–194. https://doi.org/10.1016/j.drugalcdep.2018.08.044

Barlow, J., Smailagic, N., Huband, N., Roloff, V., & Bennett, C. (2014). Group-based parent training programmes for improving parental psychosocial health. *Cochrane Database of Systematic Reviews,* (5), CD002020. https://doi.org/10.1002/14651858.CD002020.pub4

Barnes, C. M., & Watson, N. F. (2019). Why healthy sleep is good for business. *Sleep Medicine Reviews, 47*, 112–118. https://doi.org/10.1016/j.smrv.2019.07.005

Barnett, L. M., Lai, S. K., Veldman, S. L. C., Hardy, L. L., Cliff, D. P., Morgan, P. J., Zask, A., Lubans, D. R., Shultz, S. P., Ridgers, N. D., Rush, E., Brown, H. L., & Okely, A. D. (2016). Correlates of gross motor competence in children and adolescents: A systematic review and meta-analysis. *Sports Medicine, 46*(11), 1663–1688.

Barnett, L. M., Stodden, D. F., Hulteen, R. M., & Sacko, R. S. (2020). Motor competence assessment. In T. Brusseau, S. Fairclough, & D. Lubans (Eds.), *The Routledge handbook of youth physical activity* (pp. 1–25). Routledge.

Barnow, B. S., Miller, L. M., & Smith, J. A. (2021). Workforce entry including career and technical education and training. *The Annals of the American Academy of Political and Social Science, 695*(1), 260–274. https://doi.org/10.1177/00027162211031811

Barnow, B. S., & Smith, J. (2015). Employment and training programs. In R. A. Moffitt (Ed.), *Economics of means-tested transfer programs in the United States* (Vol. 2, pp. 127–234). University of Chicago Press. https://www.nber.org/chapters/c13490

Baron, A. S., & Banaji, M. R. (2006). The development of implicit attitudes: Evidence of race evaluations from ages 6 and 10 and adulthood. *Psychological Science, 17*(1), 53–58.

Barone, C., & Assirelli, G. (2020). Gender segregation in higher education: An empirical test of seven explanations. *Higher Education, 79*(1), 55–78. https://doi.org/10.1007/s10734-019-00396-2

Barr, R. G., Kirkorian, H., Radesky, J., Coyne, S., Nichols, D., Blanchfield, O., Rusnak, S., Stockdale, L., Ribner, A., Durnez, J., Epstein, M., Heimann, M., Koch, F.-S., Sundqvist, A., Birberg-Thornberg, U., Konrad, C., Slussareff, M., Bus, A., Bellagamba, F., & Fitzpatrick, caroline on behalf of CAFE Consortium Key Investigators. (2020). Beyond screen time: A synergistic approach to a more comprehensive assessment of family media exposure during early childhood. *Frontiers in Psychology, 11*, 1283. https://doi.org/10.3389/fpsyg.2020.01283

Barr, R. G., Konner, M., Bakeman, R., & Adamson, L. (1991). Crying in !Kung San infants: A test of the cultural specificity hypothesis. *Developmental Medicine & Child Neurology, 33*(7), 601–610. https://doi.org/10.1111/j.1469-8749.1991.tb14930.x

Barrett, L. F., Adolphs, R., Marsella, S., Martinez, A. M., & Pollak, S. D. (2019). Emotional expressions reconsidered: Challenges to inferring emotion from human facial movements. *Psychological Science in the Public Interest, 20*(1), 1–68.

Barroso, A., & Horowitz, J. M. (2021, March 17). *The pandemic has highlighted many challenges for mothers, but they aren't necessarily new.* Pew Research Center.

Barroso, A., & Kochhar, R. (2020). *In the pandemic, the share of unpartnered moms at work fell more sharply than among other parents.* Pew Research Center.

Barroso, A., Parker, K., & Fry, R. (2019). *Majority of Americans say parents are doing too much for their young adult children: Young men are taking longer to reach financial independence, as young women have gained ground.* Pew Research Center.

Barrow, L., & Markman-Pithers, L. (2016). Supporting young English learners in the United States. *The Future of Children, 26*(2), 159–183.

Barry, C. M., & Abo-Zena, M. M. (2014). *Emerging adults' religiousness and spirituality: Meaning-making in an age of transition.* Oxford University Press.

Barry, E. S. (2021). What is "normal" infant sleep? Why we still do not know. *Psychological Reports, 124*(2), 651–692. https://doi.org/10.1177/0033294120909447

Barry-Anwar, R., Hadley, H., Conte, S., Keil, A., & Scott, L. S. (2018). The developmental time course and topographic distribution of individual-level monkey face discrimination in the infant brain. *Neuropsychologia, 108*, 25–31.

Bar-Sadeh, B., Rudnizky, S., Pnueli, L., Bentley, G. R., Stöger, R., Kaplan, A., & Melamed, P. (2020). Unravelling the role of epigenetics in reproductive adaptations to early-life environment. *Nature Reviews Endocrinology, 16*(9), 519–533. https://doi.org/10.1038/s41574-020-0370-8

Barshay, J. (2018, August 27). *A study finds promise in project-based learning for young low-income children.* The Hechinger Report. http://hechingerreport.org/a-study-finds-promise-in-project-based-learning-for-young-low-income-children/

Bartke, A. (2019). Growth hormone and aging: Updated review. *The World Journal of Men's Health, 37*(1), 19–30. https://doi.org/10.5534/wjmh.180018

Bartlett, J. D. (2021). Trauma-informed practices in early childhood education. *Zero to Three, 41*(3), 24–34.

Barton, A. W., Beach, S. R. H., Bryant, C. M., Lavner, J. A., & Brody, G. H. (2018). Stress spillover, African Americans' couple and health outcomes, and the stress-buffering effect of family-centered prevention. *Journal of Family Psychology: JFP: Journal of the Division of Family Psychology of the American Psychological Association (Division 43), 32*(2), 186–196. https://doi.org/10.1037/fam0000376

Barton, A. W., Beach, S. R. H., Lavner, J. A., Bryant, C. M., Kogan, S. M., & Brody, G. H. (2017). Is communication a mechanism of relationship education effects among rural African Americans? *Journal of Marriage and Family, 79*(5), 1450–1461. https://doi.org/10.1111/jomf.12416

Barton, A. W., & Brody, G. H. (2018). Parenting as a buffer that deters discrimination and race-related stressors from "getting under the skin": Theories, findings, and future directions. In B. Major, J. F. Dovidio, & B. G. Link (Eds.), *The Oxford handbook of stigma, discrimination, and health* (pp. 335–354). Oxford University Press.

Bashford, A., & Levine, P. (Eds.). (2010). *The Oxford handbook of the history of eugenics.* Oxford University Press.

Basile, K. C., Smith, S. G., Chen, J., & Zwald, M. (2020). Chronic diseases, health conditions, and other impacts associated with rape victimization of U.S. women. *Journal of Interpersonal Violence.* https://doi.org/10.1177/0886260519900335

Bassok, D., Finch, J. E., Lee, R., Reardon, S. F., & Waldfogel, J. (2016). Socioeconomic gaps in early childhood experiences: 1998 to 2010. *Aera Open, 2*(3), 2332858416653924.

Bastaits, K., & Mortelmans, D. (2016). Parenting as mediator between post-divorce family structure and children's well-being. *Journal of Child and Family Studies, 25*(7), 2178–2188.

Bastin, M., Luyckx, K., Raes, F., & Bijttebier, P. (2021). Co-rumination and depressive symptoms in adolescence: Prospective associations and the mediating role of brooding rumination. *Journal of Youth and Adolescence, 50*(5), 1003–1016. https://doi.org/10.1007/s10964-021-01412-4

Bates, L. C., Zieff, G., Stanford, K., Moore, J. B., Kerr, Z. Y., Hanson, E. D., Barone Gibbs, B., Kline, C. E., & Stoner, L. (2020). COVID-19 impact on behaviors across the 24-hour day in children and adolescents: Physical activity, sedentary behavior, and sleep. *Children, 7*(9), 138. https://doi.org/10.3390/children7090138

Bateson, P. (2015). Ethology and human development. In *Handbook of child psychology and developmental science*

(pp. 1–36). Wiley. https://doi.org/10.1002/9781118963418.childpsy106

Bateson, P. (2017). Adaptability and evolution. *Interface Focus, 7*(5), 20160126. https://doi.org/10.1098/rsfs.2016.0126

Bathelt, J., Gathercole, S. E., Butterfield, S., & Astle, D. E. (2018). Children's academic attainment is linked to the global organization of the white matter connectome. *Developmental Science, 21*(5), e12662. https://doi.org/10.1111/desc.12662

Bathelt, J., Gathercole, S. E., Johnson, A., & Astle, D. E. (2018). Differences in brain morphology and working memory capacity across childhood. *Developmental Science, 21*(3), e12579. https://doi.org/10.1111/desc.12579

Bathory, E., & Tomopoulos, S. (2017). Sleep regulation, physiology and development, sleep duration and patterns, and sleep hygiene in infants, toddlers, and preschool-age children. *Current Problems in Pediatric and Adolescent Health Care, 47*(2), 29–42. https://doi.org/10.1016/j.cppeds.2016.12.001

Batres, A. (2012, July 9). Alumni profile: Alejandro "Alex" Batres (Saturday cast, 2010–2012). *The Possibility Project Summer 2012 News.*

Batsis, J. A., & Zagaria, A. B. (2018). Addressing obesity in aging patients. *The Medical Clinics of North America, 102*(1), 65–85. https://doi.org/10.1016/j.mcna.2017.08.007

Battaglia, M., Garon-Carrier, G., Côté, S. M., Dionne, G., Touchette, E., Vitaro, F., Tremblay, R. E., & Boivin, M. (2017). Early childhood trajectories of separation anxiety: Bearing on mental health, academic achievement, and physical health from mid-childhood to preadolescence. *Depression and Anxiety, 34*(10), 918–927. https://doi.org/10.1002/da.22674

Battistich, V., Schaps, E., & Wilson, N. (2004). Effects of an elementary school intervention on students' "connectedness" to school and social adjustment during middle school. *Journal of Primary Prevention, 24*(3), 243–262.

Batty, P., & Lillicrap, D. (2019). Advances and challenges for hemophilia gene therapy. *Human Molecular Genetics, 28*(R1), R95–R101. https://doi.org/10.1093/hmg/ddz157

Bau, A. M., Ernert, A., Schenk, L., Wiegand, S., Martus, P., Grüters, A., & Krude, H. (2009). Is there a further acceleration in the age at onset of menarche? A cross-sectional study in 1840 school children focusing on age and bodyweight at the onset of menarche. *European Journal of Endocrinology, 160*(1), 107–113. https://doi.org/10.1530/EJE-08-0594

Baudat, S., Van Petegem, S., Antonietti, J.-P., Sznitman, G. A., & Zimmermann, G. (2020). Developmental changes in secrecy during middle adolescence: Links with alcohol use and perceived controlling parenting. *Journal of Youth and Adolescence, 49*(8), 1583–1600. https://doi.org/10.1007/s10964-020-01281-3

Bauer, A., Fairchild, G., Halligan, S. L., Hammerton, G., Murray, J., Santos, I. S., Munhoz, T. N., Barros, A. J. D., Barros, F. C., & Matijasevich, A. (2021). Harsh parenting and child conduct and emotional problems: Parent- and child-effects in the 2004 Pelotas Birth Cohort. *European Child & Adolescent Psychiatry*, 1–11.

Bauer, G. (2016). Gender roles, comparative advantages and the life course: The division of domestic labor in same-sex and different-sex couples. *European Journal of Population, 32*(1), 99–128.

Bauer, P. J. (2015). Development of episodic and autobiographical memory: The importance of remembering forgetting. *Developmental Review, 38*, 146–166. https://doi.org/10.1016/j.dr.2015.07.011

Bauer, P. J., & Larkina, M. (2014). The onset of childhood amnesia in childhood: A prospective investigation of the course and determinants of forgetting of early-life events. *Memory, 22*(8), 907–924. https://doi.org/10.1080/09658211.2013.854806

Bauer, P. J., & Larkina, M. (2019). Predictors of age-related and individual variability in autobiographical memory in childhood. *Memory, 27*(1), 63–78.

Baugreet, S., Hamill, R. M., Kerry, J. P., & McCarthy, S. N. (2017). Mitigating nutrition and health deficiencies in older adults: A role for food innovation? *Journal of Food Science, 82*(4), 848–855. https://doi.org/10.1111/1750-3841.13674

Baum, A., Wisnivesky, J., Basu, S., Siu, A. L., & Schwartz, M. D. (2020). Association of geographic differences in prevalence of uncontrolled chronic conditions with changes in individuals' likelihood of uncontrolled chronic conditions. *JAMA, 324*(14), 1429–1438.

Baum, M., Ognyanova, K., Chwe, H., Quintana, A., Perlis, R. H., Lazer, D., Druckman, J., Santillana, M., Lin, J., Volpe, J. D., Simonson, M. D., & Green, J. (2021). *The COVID States Project #14: Misinformation and vaccine acceptance.* OSF Preprints. https://doi.org/10.31219/osf.io/w974j

Baum, S., Ma, J., & Payea, K. (2013). *Education pays 2013.* The College Board. http://www.rilin.state.ri.us/Special/ses15/commdocs/Education%20Pays,%20The%20College%20Board.pdf

Bauman, A., Merom, D., Bull, F. C., Buchner, D. M., & Fiatarone Singh, M. A. (2016). Updating the evidence for physical activity: Summative reviews of the epidemiological evidence, prevalence, and interventions to promote "active aging." *The Gerontologist, 56*(Suppl_2), S268–S280. https://doi.org/10.1093/geront/gnw031

Bauman, A., & Milton, K. (2020). *Establishing the effectiveness of public health interventions using sequential meta-analysis: Case study using stair-promotion interventions.* SAGE Research Methods Cases.

Baumgartner, S. E., & Sumter, S. R. (2017). Dealing with media distractions: An observational study of computer-based multitasking among children and adults in the Netherlands. *Journal of Children and Media, 11*(3), 295–313.

Baumrind, D. (1971). Current patterns of parental authority. *Developmental Psychology, 4*(1, Pt. 2), 1–103. https://doi.org/10.1037/h0030372

Baumrind, D. (1972). An exploratory study of socialization effects on black children: Some black-white comparisons. *Child Development, 43*(1), 261–267.

Baumrind, D. (1989). Rearing competent children. In W. Damon (Ed.), *Child development today and tomorrow* (pp. 349–378). Jossey-Bass/Wiley.

Baumrind, D. (1991). The influence of parenting style on adolescent competence and substance use. *The Journal of Early Adolescence, 11*(1), 56–95. https://doi.org/10.1177/0272431691111004

Baumrind, D. (2012). Differentiating between confrontive and coercive kinds of parental power-assertive disciplinary practices. *Human Development, 55*(2), 35–51.

Baumrind, D. (2013). Authoritative parenting revisited: History and current status. In R. E. Larzelere, A. S. Morris, & A. W. Harrist (Eds.), *Authoritative parenting: Synthesizing nurturance and discipline for optimal child development* (pp. 11–34). American Psychological Association. https://doi.org/10.1037/13948-002

Baumrind, D., & Black, A. E. (1967). Socialization practices associated with dimensions of competence in preschool boys and girls. *Child Development, 38*(2), 291–327.

Baumrind, D., Larzelere, R. E., & Owens, E. B. (2010). Effects of preschool parents' power assertive patterns and practices on adolescent development. *Parenting: Science and Practice, 10*(3), 157–201.

Bayard, N. S., van Loon, M. H., Steiner, M., & Roebers, C. M. (2021). Developmental improvements and persisting difficulties in children's metacognitive monitoring and control skills: Cross-sectional and longitudinal perspectives. *Child Development, 92*(3), 1118–1136.

Bayley, N. (1956). Individual patterns of development. *Child Development, 27*(1), 45–74. https://doi.org/10.2307/1126330

Beach, S. R., Kinnee, E., & Schulz, R. (2019). Caregiving and place: Combining geographic information system (GIS) and survey methods to examine neighborhood context and caregiver outcomes. *Innovation in Aging, 3*(3), igz025.

Beam, C. R., & Turkheimer, E. (2017). Gene–environment correlation as a source of stability and diversity in development. In P. H. Tolan & B. L. Leventhal (Eds.), *Gene-environment transactions in developmental psychopathology: The role in intervention research* (pp. 111–130). Springer International Publishing. https://doi.org/10.1007/978-3-319-49227-8_6

Beardslee, J., Docherty, M., Mulvey, E., & Pardini, D. (2019). The direct and indirect associations between childhood socioeconomic disadvantage and adolescent gun violence. *Journal of Clinical Child & Adolescent Psychology, 50*(3), 326–336. https://doi.org/10.1080/15374416.2019.1644646

Beattie, G., Laliberté, J.-W. P., Michaud-Leclerc, C., & Oreopoulos, P. (2019). What sets college thrivers and divers apart? A contrast in study habits, attitudes, and mental health. *Economics Letters, 178*, 50–53. https://doi.org/10.1016/j.econlet.2018.12.026

Beauregard, J. L., Hamner, H. C., Chen, J., Avila-Rodriguez, W., Elam-Evans, L. D., & Perrine, C. G. (2019). Racial disparities in breastfeeding initiation and duration among U.S. infants born in 2015. *Morbidity and Mortality Weekly Report, 68*(34), 745–748. https://doi.org/10.15585/mmwr.mm6834a3

Beccaria, L., Kek, M. Y. C. A., & Huijser, H. (2018). Exploring nursing educators' use of theory and methods in search for evidence based credibility in nursing education. *Nurse Education Today, 65*, 60–66. https://doi.org/10.1016/j.nedt.2018.02.032

Becchetti, L., & Bellucci, D. (2020). Generativity, aging and subjective well-being. *International Review of Economics*. https://doi.org/10.1007/s12232-020-00358-6

Becher, E. H., Kim, H., Cronin, S. E., Deenanath, V., McGuire, J. K., McCann, E. M., & Powell, S. (2019). Positive parenting and parental conflict: Contributions to resilient coparenting during divorce. *Family Relations, 68*(1), 150–164.

Becht, A. I., Luyckx, K., Nelemans, S. A., Goossens, L., Branje, S. J. T., Vollebergh, W. A. M., & Meeus, W. H. J. (2019). Linking identity and depressive symptoms across adolescence: A multisample longitudinal study testing within-person effects. *Developmental Psychology, 55*(8), 1733–1742. https://doi.org/10.1037/dev0000742

Beck, A. F., Edwards, E. M., Horbar, J. D., Howell, E. A., McCormick, M. C., & Pursley, D. M. (2020). The color of health: How racism, segregation, and inequality affect the health and well-being of preterm infants and their families. *Pediatric Research, 87*(2), 227–234. https://doi.org/10.1038/s41390-019-0513-6

Becker, C. B., Taniyama, Y., Kondo-Arita, M., Yamada, S., & Yamamoto, K. (2020). How Grief, Funerals, and Poverty Affect Bereaved Health, Productivity, and Medical Dependence in Japan. OMEGA-Journal of Death and Dying, 0030222820947573. https://doi.org/10.1177/0030222820947573

Becker, E. (1973). *The denial of death*. Free Press.

Becker, O. A., & Hank, K. (2021). Adult children's estrangement from parents in Germany. *Journal of Marriage and Family*. https://doi.org/10.1111/jomf.12796

Becker, S. P., Dvorsky, M. R., Breaux, R., Cusick, C. N., Taylor, K. P., & Langberg, J. M. (2021). Prospective examination of adolescent sleep patterns and behaviors before and during COVID-19. *Sleep, 44*(8), zsab054.

Beckerman, J. P., Alike, Q., Lovin, E., Tamez, M., & Mattei, J. (2017). The development and public health implications of food preferences in children. *Frontiers in Nutrition, 4*, 66. https://doi.org/10.3389/fnut.2017.00066

Beckerman, M., van Berkel, S. R., Mesman, J., & Alink, L. R. A. (2018). Negative parental attributions mediate associations between risk factors and dysfunctional parenting: A replication and extension. *Child Abuse & Neglect, 81*, 249–258. https://doi.org/10.1016/j.chiabu.2018.05.001

Beckmeyer, J. J., & Cromwell, S. (2019). Romantic relationship status and emerging adult well-being: Accounting for romantic relationship interest. *Emerging Adulthood, 7*(4), 304–308.

Beckmeyer, J. J., & Weybright, E. H. (2020). Exploring the associations between middle adolescent romantic activity and positive youth development. *Journal of Adolescence, 80*, 214–219. https://doi.org/10.1016/j.adolescence.2020.03.002

Bedi, S. (2019a). *Private racism*. Cambridge University Press.

Bedi, S. (2019b). Online dating sites as public accommodations: Facilitating racial discrimination. In S. J. Brison & K. Gelber (Eds.), *Free speech in the digital age* (pp: 189–206). Oxford University Press. https://doi.org/10.1093/oso/9780190883591.003.0012

Beijers, R., Hartman, S., Shalev, I., Hastings, W., Mattern, B. C., de Weerth, C., & Belsky, J. (2020). Testing three hypotheses about effects of sensitive–insensitive parenting on telomeres. *Developmental Psychology, 56*(2), 237–250. https://doi.org/10.1037/dev0000879

Bejanin, A., Schonhaut, D. R., La Joie, R., Kramer, J. H., Baker, S. L., Sosa, N., & Rabinovici, G. D. (2017). Tau pathology and neurodegeneration contribute to cognitive impairment in Alzheimer's disease. *Brain, 140*(12), 3286–3300.

Belcher, B. R., Zink, J., Azad, A., Campbell, C. E., Chakravartti, S. P., & Herting, M. M. (2021). The roles of physical activity, exercise, and fitness in promoting resilience during adolescence: Effects on mental well-being and brain development. *Biological Psychiatry. Cognitive Neuroscience and Neuroimaging, 6*(2), 225–237. https://do.org/10.1016/j.bpsc.2020.08.005

Belkin, D. (2021, September 6). A generation of American men give up on college: 'I just feel lost.' *Wall Street Journal*.

Bell, A. D., Mello, C. J., Nemesh, J., Brumbaugh, S. A., Wysoker, A., & McCarroll, S. A. (2020). Insights into variation in meiosis from 31,228 human sperm genomes. *Nature, 583*(7815), 259–264. https://doi.org/10.1038/s41586-020-2347-0

Bell, C. N., Kerr, J., & Young, J. L. (2019). Associations between obesity, obesogenic environments, and structural racism vary by county-level racial composition. *International Journal of Environmental Research and Public Health, 16*(5), 861. https://doi.org/10.3390/ijerph16050861

Bell, J. A., Carslake, D., Wade, K. H., Richmond, R. C., Langdon, R. J., Vincent, E. E., Holmes, M. V., Timpson, N. J., & Smith, G. D. (2018). Influence of puberty timing on adiposity and cardiometabolic traits: A Mendelian randomisation study. *PLOS Medicine, 15*(8), e1002641. https://doi.org/10.1371/journal.pmed.1002641

Bell, L. (2018). Psychoanalytic theories of gender. In N. K. Dess, J. Marecek, & L. C. Bell (Eds.), *Gender, sex, and sexualities: Psychological perspectives* (pp. 195–217). Oxford University Press.

Beller, S., Bender, A., Chrisomalis, S., Jordan, F. M., Overmann, K. A., Saxe, G. B., & Schlimm, D. (2018). The cultural challenge in mathematical cognition. *Journal of Numerical Cognition, 4*(2), 448–463. https://doi.org/10.5964/jnc.v4i2.137

Belsky, J. (1984). The determinants of parenting: A process model. *Child Development*, 55(1), 83–96.

Belsky, J. (2019). Early-life adversity accelerates child and adolescent development. *Current Directions in Psychological Science, 28*(3), 241–246. https://doi.org/10.1177/0963721419837670

Belsky, J., Zhang, X., & Sayler, K. (2021). Differential susceptibility 2.0: Are the same children affected by different experiences and exposures? *Development and Psychopathology*, 1–9. https://doi.org/10.1017/S0954579420002205

Beltrán, S., Sit, L., & Ginsburg, K. R. (2021). A call to revise the diagnosis of oppositional defiant disorder—Diagnoses are for helping, not harming. *JAMA Psychiatry*. https://doi.org/10.1001/jamapsychiatry.2021.2127

Bem, S. L. (1981). Gender schema theory: A cognitive account of sex typing. *Psychological Review, 88*(4), 354–364. https://doi.org/10.1037/0033-295X.88.4.354

Bem, S. L. (1989). Genital knowledge and gender constancy in preschool children. *Child Development, 60*(3), 649–662. https://doi.org/10.2307/1130730

Ben Simon, E., Vallat, R., Barnes, C. M., & Walker, M. P. (2020). Sleep loss and the socio-emotional brain. *Trends in Cognitive Sciences, 24*(6), 435–450. https://doi.org/10.1016/j.tics.2020.02.003

Bender, J. M., & She, R. C. (2017). Elimination communication: Diaper-free in America. *Pediatrics, 140*(1), e20170398. https://doi.org/10.1542/peds.2017-0398

Benedek, M., Karstendiek, M., Ceh, S. M., Grabner, R. H., Krammer, G., Lebuda, I., Silvia, P. J., Cotter, K. N., Li, Y., Hu, W., Martskvishvili, K., & Kaufman, J. C. (2021). Creativity myths: Prevalence and correlates of misconceptions on creativity. *Personality and Individual Differences, 182*, 111068. https://doi.org/10.1016/j.paid.2021.111068

Benito-Gomez, M., Williams, K. N., McCurdy, A., & Fletcher, A. C. (2020). Autonomy-supportive parenting in adolescence: Cultural variability in the contemporary United States. *Journal of Family Theory & Review, 12*(1), 7–26. https://doi.org/10.1111/jftr.12362

Benkert, R., Cuevas, A., Thompson, H. S., Dove-Meadows, E., & Knuckles, D. (2019). Ubiquitous yet unclear: A systematic review of medical mistrust. *Behavioral Medicine, 45*(2), 86–101. https://doi.org/10.1080/08964289.2019.1588220

Benner, A. D., & Wang, Y. (2016). Racial/ethnic discrimination and adolescents' well-being: The role of cross-ethnic friendships and friends' experiences of discrimination. *Child Development, 88*(2), 493–504. https://doi.org/10.1111/cdev.12606

Benner, A. D., Wang, Y., Shen, Y., Boyle, A. E., Polk, R., & Cheng, Y. P. (2018). Racial/ethnic discrimination and well-being during adolescence: A meta-analytic review. *American Psychologist, 73*(7), 855.

Bennett, I. J., & Madden, D. J. (2014). Disconnected aging: Cerebral white matter integrity and age-related differences in cognition. *Neuroscience, 276*, 187–205. https://doi.org/10.1016/j.neuroscience.2013.11.026

Bennett, J., Fry, R., & Kochhar, R. (2020, July 23). *Are you in the American middle class? Find out with our income calculator*. Pew Research Center. https://www.pewresearch.org/fact-tank/2020/07/23/are-you-in-the-american-middle-class/

Benson, J. J., & Coleman, M. (2016). Older adults developing a preference for living apart together. *Journal of Marriage and Family, 78*(3), 797–812. https://doi.org/10.1111/jomf.12292

Benton, D., & Meyer, K. (2019). Healthcare providers can help to connect family caregivers to resources and supports: Services cannot truly "wrap around" care recipients unless caregivers are brought into the loop. *Generations*, 43–47.

Benza, S., & Liamputtong, P. (2014). Pregnancy, childbirth and motherhood: A meta-synthesis of the lived experiences of immigrant women. *Midwifery, 30*(6), 575–584. https://doi.org/10.1016/j.midw.2014.03.005

Berents, H. (2019). Apprehending the "telegenic dead": Considering images of dead children in global politics. *International Political Sociology, 13*(2), 145–160. https://doi.org/10.1093/ips/oly036

Bergelson, E., Casillas, M., Soderstrom, M., Seidl, A., Warlaumont, A. S., & Amatuni, A. (2019). What do North American babies hear? A large-scale cross-corpus analysis. *Developmental Science, 22*(1), e12724. https://doi.org/10.1111/desc.12724

Berger, R. (2017). Aging in America: Ageism and general attitudes toward growing old and the elderly. *Open Journal of Social Sciences, 5*(8), 183.

Berglund, H., Hasson, H., Wilhelmson, K., Dunér, A., & Dahlin-Ivanoff, S. (2016). The impact of socioeconomic conditions, social networks, and health on frail older people's life satisfaction: A cross-sectional study. *Health Psychology Research, 4*(1). https://doi.org/10.4081/hpr.2016.5578

Bergnehr, D., & Cekaite, A. (2018). Adult-initiated touch and its functions at a Swedish preschool: Controlling, affectionate, assisting and educative haptic conduct. *International Journal of Early Years Education, 26*(3), 312–331. https://doi.org/10.1080/09669760.2017.1414690

Bergström, M., Fransson, E., Fabian, H., Hjern, A., Sarkadi, A., & Salari, R. (2018). Preschool children living in joint physical custody arrangements show less psychological symptoms than those living mostly or only with one parent. *Acta Paediatrica, 107*(2), 294–300.

Berkel, C., Fu, E., Carroll, A. J., Wilson, C., Tovar-Huffman, A., Mauricio, A., Rudo-Stern, J., Grimm, K. J., Dishion, T. J., & Smith, J. D. (2021). Effects of the Family Check-Up 4 Health on Parenting and Child Behavioral Health: A Randomized Clinical Trial in Primary Care. *Prevention Science, 22*(4), 464–474.

Berkowitz, D., Tinkler, J., Peck, A., & Coto, L. (2021). Tinder: A game with gendered rules and consequences. *Social Currents, 8*(5), 491–509. https://doi.org/10.1177/23294965211019486

Berkowitz, T., Schaeffer, M. W., Maloney, E. A., Peterson, L., Gregor, C., Levine, S. C., & Beilock, S. L. (2015). Math at home adds up to achievement in school. *Science, 350*(6257), 196–198.

Berli, J. U., & Plemons, E. (2020). The importance of facial gender confirmation surgery. In L. S. Schechter (Ed.), *Gender confirmation surgery* (pp. 91–97). Springer.

Berman, G., Hart, J., O'Mathúna, D., Mattellone, E., Potts, A., O'Kane, C., Shusterman, J., & Tanner, T. (2016, June 30). *What we know about ethical research involving children in humanitarian settings: An overview of principles, the literature and case studies* (Innocenti Working Papers No. 2016/18). UNICEF Innocenti Research Centre. https://doi.org/10.18356/ce5b7789-en

Berridge, C., & Mor, V. (2018). Disparities in the prevalence of unmet needs and their consequences among Black and White older adults. *Journal of Aging and Health, 30*(9), 1427–1449. https://doi.org/10.1177/0898264317721347

Berry, J. W., & Vedder, P. (2016). Adaptation of immigrant children, adolescents, and their families. In U. P. Gielen & J. L. Roopnarine (Eds.), *Childhood and adolescence: Cross-cultural perspectives and applications* (pp. 321–346). Praeger /ABC-CLIO.

Berry, K. M., Erickson, D. J., Berger, A. T., Wahlstrom, K., Iber, C., Full, K. M., Redline, S., & Widome, R. (2021). Association of delaying school start time with sleep–wake behaviors among adolescents. *Journal of Adolescent Health*. https://doi.org/10.1016/j.jadohealth.2021.04.030

Bersin, J., & Chamorro-Premuzic, T. (2019, September 26). The case for hiring older workers. *Harvard Business Review*. https://hbr.org/2019/09/the-case-for-hiring-older-workers

Bertels, J., Bourguignon, M., de Heering, A., Chetail, F., De Tiège, X., Cleeremans, A., & Destrebecqz, A. (2020). Snakes elicit specific neural responses in the human infant brain. *Scientific Reports, 10*(1), 7443. https://doi.org/10.1038/s41598-020-63619-y

Berthelsen, C. B., & Kristensson, J. (2015). The content, dissemination and effects of case management interventions for informal caregivers of older adults: A systematic review. *International Journal of Nursing Studies, 52*(5), 988–1002. https://doi.org/10.1016/j.ijnurstu.2015.01.006

Berwick, R. C., & Chomsky, N. (2017). Why only us: Recent questions and answers. *Journal of Neurolinguistics, 43*, 166–177. https://doi.org/10.1016/j.jneuroling.2016.12.002

Besse, M., Lampe, N. M., & Mann, E. S. (2020). Experiences with achieving pregnancy and giving birth among transgender men: A narrative literature review. *The Yale Journal of Biology and Medicine, 93*(4), 517–528.

Betancourt, L. M., Avants, B., Farah, M. J., Brodsky, N. L., Wu, J., Ashtari, M., & Hurt, H. (2016). Effect of socioeconomic status (SES) disparity on neural development in female African-American infants at age 1 month. *Developmental Science, 19*(6), 947–956. https://doi.org/10.1111/desc.12344

Betts, M. J., Richter, A., de Boer, L., Tegelbeckers, J., Perosa, V., Chowdhury, R., Dolan, R. J., Seidenbecher, C., Schott, B. H., Düzel, E., Guitart-Masip, M., & Krauel, K. (2019). Learning in anticipation of reward and punishment: Perspectives across the human lifespan. *BioRxiv*. https://doi.org/10.1101/738211

Beyers, W., & Luyckx, K. (2016). Ruminative exploration and reconsideration of commitment as risk factors for suboptimal identity development in adolescence and emerging adulthood. *Journal of Adolescence, 47*, 169–178. https://doi.org/10.1016/j.adolescence.2015.10.018

Bhatnagar, M., & Lagnese, K. R. (2021). Hospice care. *StatPearls*.

Bhattacharya, S. (2015, May 28). Jake Gyllenhaal is *Esquire*'s July cover star. *Esquite (UK)*.

Bhopal, S. S., Bagaria, J., Olabi, B., & Bhopal, R. (2021). Children and young people remain at low risk of COVID-19 mortality. *The Lancet Child & Adolescent Health, 5*(5), e12–e13. https://doi.org/10.1016/S2352-4642(21)00066-3

Bhutta, Z. A., Akseer, N., Keats, E. C., Vaivada, T., Baker, S., Horton, S. E., Katz, J., Menon, P., Piwoz, E., Shekar, M., Victora, C., & Black, R. (2020). How countries can reduce child stunting at scale: Lessons from exemplar countries. *The American Journal of Clinical Nutrition, 112*(Supplement_2), 894S–904S. https://doi.org/10.1093/ajcn/nqaa153

Bhuva, A. N., D'Silva, A., Torlasco, C., Jones, S., Nadarajan, N., Zalen, J. V., Chaturvedi, N., Lloyd, G., Sharma, S., Moon, J. C., Hughes, A. D., & Manisty, C. H. (2020). Training for a first-time marathon reverses age-related aortic stiffening. *Journal of the American College of Cardiology, 75*(1), 60–71. https://doi.org/10.1016/j.jacc.2019.10.045

Bialystok, E. (2018). Bilingual education for young children: Review of the effects and consequences. *International Journal of Bilingual Education and Bilingualism, 21*(6), 666–679. https://doi.org/10.1080/13670050.2016.1203859

Bialystok, E. (2020). Bilingual effects on cognition in children. In *Oxford research encyclopedia of education*. https://doi.org/10.1093/acrefore/9780190264093.013.962

Bialystok, E., Abutalebi, J., Bak, T. H., Burke, D. M., & Kroll, J. F. (2016). Aging in two languages: Implications for public health. *Ageing Research Reviews, 27*, 56–60. https://doi.org/10.1016/j.arr.2016.03.003

Bialystok, E., & Barac, R. (2012). Emerging bilingualism: Dissociating advantages for metalinguistic awareness and executive control. *Cognition, 122*(1), 67–73.

Bian, L., Leslie, S.-J., & Cimpian, A. (2017). Gender stereotypes about intellectual ability emerge early and influence children's interests. *Science, 355*(6323), 389–391.

Biddle, S. J., Ciaccioni, S., Thomas, G., & Vergeer, I. (2019). Physical activity and mental health in children and adolescents: An updated review of reviews and an analysis of causality. *Psychology of Sport and Exercise, 42*, 146–155.

Bigand, T., Anderson, C. L., Roberts, M. L., Shaw, M. R., & Wilson, M. (2019). Benefits and adverse effects of cannabis use among adults with persistent pain. *Nursing Outlook, 67*(3), 223–231. https://doi.org/10.1016/j.outlook.2018.12.014

Biglan, A., Elfner, K., Garbacz, S. A., Komro, K., Prinz, R. J., Weist, M. D., Wilson, D. K., & Zarling, A. (2020). A strategic plan for strengthening America's families: A brief from the coalition of behavioral science organizations. *Clinical Child and Family Psychology Review, 23*(2), 153–175. https://doi.org/10.1007/s10567-020-00318-0

Billett, S. (2014). The standing of vocational education: Sources of its societal esteem and implications for its enactment. *Journal of Vocational Education & Training, 66*(1), 1–21.

Binette, J., Houghton, A., & Firestone, S. (2021). *Drivers & barriers to living in a multigenerational household: Pre-COVID–mid-COVID*. AARP Research. https://doi.org/10.26419/res.00414.001

Binette, J., & Vasold, K. (2019). Home and community preferences: A national survey of adults age 18-plus. AARP Research.

Binning, K. R., Kaufmann, N., McGreevy, E. M., Fotuhi, O., Chen, S., Marshman, E., Kalender, Z. Y., Limeri, L., Betancur, L., & Singh, C. (2020). Changing social contexts to foster equity in college science courses: An ecological-belonging intervention. *Psychological Science, 31*(9), 1059–1070.

Bird, J. N. (2019). Death and dying in a Karen refugee community: An overlooked challenge in the resettlement process. *Ethnography, 20*(4), 443–462. https://doi.org/10.1177/1466138118768624

Birditt, K. S., Polenick, C. A., Van Bolt, O., Kim, K., Zarit, S. H., & Fingerman, K. L. (2019). Conflict strategies in the parent–adult child tie: Generation differences and implications for well-being. *The Journals of Gerontology: Series B, 74*(2), 232–241. https://doi.org/10.1093/geronb/gbx057

Birditt, K. S., Sherman, C. W., Polenick, C. A., Becker, L., Webster, N. J., Ajrouch, K. J., & Antonucci, T. C. (2020). So close and yet so irritating: Negative relations and implications for well-being by age and closeness. *The Journals of Gerontology: Series B, 75*(2), 327–337. https://doi.org/10.1093/geronb/gby038

Birenbaum-Carmeli, D., Inhorn, M. C., & Patrizio, P. (2020). Transgender men's fertility preservation: Experiences, social support, and the quest for genetic parenthood. *Culture, Health & Sexuality*, 1–16.

Birkeland, M. S., Melkevik, O., Holsen, I., & Wold, B. (2012). Trajectories of global self-esteem development during adolescence. *Journal of Adolescence, 35*(1), 43–54.

Biro, F. M., Pajak, A., Wolff, M. S., Pinney, S. M., Windham, G. C., Galvez, M. P., Greenspan, L. C., Kushi, L. H., & Teitelbaum, S. L. (2018). Age of menarche in a longitudinal US cohort. *Journal of Pediatric and Adolescent Gynecology, 31*(4), 339–345. https://doi.org/10.1016/j.jpag.2018.05.002

Biros, M. (2018). Capacity, vulnerability, and informed consent for research. *The Journal of Law, Medicine & Ethics, 46*(1), 72–78. https://doi.org/10.1177/1073110518766021

Bishop, M. D., Fish, J. N., Hammack, P. L., & Russell, S. T. (2020). Sexual identity development milestones in three generations of sexual minority people: A national probability sample. *Developmental Psychology, 56*(11), 2177–2193. https://doi.org/10.1037/dev0001105

Bjälkebring, P., Henning, G., Västfjäll, D., Dickert, S., Brehmer, Y., Buratti, S., Hansson, I., & Johansson, B. (2020). Helping out or helping yourself? Volunteering and life satisfaction across the retirement transition. *Psychology and Aging, 36*(1), 119–130.

Bjorklund, D. F. (2020). *Child development in evolutionary perspective*. Cambridge University Press.

Bjorklund, D. F., Blasi, C. H., & Ellis, B. J. (2015). Evolutionary developmental psychology. In D. M. Buss (Ed.), *The handbook of evolutionary psychology* (pp. 1–21). American Cancer Society. https://doi.org/10.1002/9781119125563.evpsych238

Black, D. S., O'Reilly, G. A., Olmstead, R., Breen, E. C., & Irwin, M. R. (2015). Mindfulness meditation and improvement in sleep quality and daytime impairment among older adults with sleep disturbances: A randomized clinical trial. *JAMA Internal Medicine, 175*(4), 494–501.

Black, E. (2012). *War against the weak: Eugenics and America's campaign to create a master race*. Dialog Press.

Black, M. M., Trude, A. C. B., & Lutter, C. K. (2020). All children thrive: Integration of nutrition and early childhood development. *Annual Review of Nutrition, 40*(1), 375–406. https://doi.org/10.1146/annurev-nutr-120219-023757

Black, R., Mushtaq, F., Baddeley, A., & Kapur, N. (2020). Does learning the Qur'an improve memory capacity? Practical and theoretical implications. *Memory, 28*(8), 1014–1023.

Blackawton, P. S., Airzee, S., Allen, A., Baker, S., Berrow, A., Blair, C., & Lotto, R. B. (2011). Blackawton bees. *Biology Letters, 7*(2), 168-172.

Blackhorse, A. (2015, July 2). "Native American" 1 or "American Indian" 1? 5 more Native voices respond. *Indian Country Today*. https://indiancountrytoday.com/archive/blackhorse-native-american-or-american-indian-5-more-native-voices-respond?redir=1

Blackwell, C. K., Elliott, A. J., Ganiban, J., Herbstman, J., Hunt, K., Forrest, C. B., Camargo, C. A., & on behalf of program collaborators for Environmental influences on Child Health Outcomes. (2019). General health and life satisfaction in children with chronic illness. *Pediatrics, 143*(6), e20182988. https://doi.org/10.1542/peds.2018-2988

Blair, C., Zelazo, P. D., & Greenberg, M. T. (2016). *Measurement of executive function in early childhood: A special issue of developmental neuropsychology*. Psychology Press.

Blair, K. L., Cappell, J., & Pukall, C. F. (2017). Not all orgasms were created equal: Differences in frequency and satisfaction of orgasm experiences by sexual activity in same-sex versus mixed-sex relationships. *The Journal of Sex Research, 55*(6), 719–733. https://doi.org/10.1080/00224499.2017.1303437

Blakemore, S.-J. (2018). Avoiding social risk in adolescence. *Current Directions in Psychological Science, 27*(2), 116–122. https://doi.org/10.1177/0963721417738144

Blakemore, S.-J., & Mills, K. L. (2014). Is adolescence a sensitive period for sociocultural processing? *Annual Review of Psychology, 65*(1), 187–207. https://doi.org/10.1146/annurev-psych-010213-115202

Blanchflower, D. G., & Clark, A. E. (2021). Children, unhappiness and family finances. *Journal of Population Economics, 34*(2), 625–653. https://doi.org/10.1007/s00148-020-00798-y

Blanchflower, D. G., & Graham, C. L. (2020). *The mid-life dip in well-being: Economists (who find it) versus psychologists (who don't)!* (No. w26888). National Bureau of Economic Research. https://doi.org/10.3386/w26888

Blanchflower, D. G., & Oswald, A. J. (2019). Do humans suffer a psychological low in midlife? Two approaches (with and without controls) in seven data sets. In M. Rojas (Ed.), *The economics of happiness: How the Easterlin paradox*

transformed our understanding of well-being and progress (pp. 439–453). Springer International Publishing. https://doi.org/10.1007/978-3-030-15835-4_19

Blanco, G., Flores, C. A., & Flores-Lagunes, A. (2013). Bounds on average and quantile treatment effects of Job Corps training on wages. *Journal of Human Resources, 48*(3), 659–701.

Blanco, N. J., & Sloutsky, V. M. (2019). Adaptive flexibility in category learning? Young children exhibit smaller costs of selective attention than adults. *Developmental Psychology, 55*(10), 2060.

Bland, A. M., & DeRobertis, E. M. (2020). Maslow's unacknowledged contributions to developmental psychology. *Journal of Humanistic Psychology, 60*(6), 934–958. https://doi.org/10.1177/0022167817739732

Blankenship, T. L., Keith, K., Calkins, S. D., & Bell, M. A. (2018). Behavioral performance and neural areas associated with memory processes contribute to math and reading achievement in 6-year-old children. *Cognitive Development, 45,* 141–151.

Blankenship, T. L., Slough, M. A., Calkins, S. D., Deater-Deckard, K., Kim-Spoon, J., & Bell, M. A. (2019). Attention and executive functioning in infancy: Links to childhood executive function and reading achievement. *Developmental Science, 22*(6), e12824. https://doi.org/10.1111/desc.12824

Blasberg, A., Bromer, J., Nugent, C., Porter, T., Shivers, E. M., Tonyan, H., Tout, K., & Weber, B. (2019). A conceptual model for quality in home-based child care. *OPRE Report, 37.*

Blaszczyk, A. T., Bailey, T. A., & Tapia, S. (2021). ABH gel: Comforting cure or pricey placebo? *Journal of the American Medical Directors Association, 22*(1), 23–27. https://doi.org/10.1016/j.jamda.2020.10.005

Blatný, M., Millová, K., Jelínek, M., & Osecká, T. (2015). Personality predictors of successful development: Toddler temperament and adolescent personality traits predict well-being and career stability in middle adulthood. *PLOS ONE, 10*(4), e0126032.

Blau, F. D., & Kahn, L. M. (2017). The gender wage gap: Extent, trends, and explanations. *Journal of Economic Literature, 55*(3), 789–865. https://doi.org/10.1257/jel.20160995

Blau, F. D., Kahn, L. M., Brummund, P., Cook, J., & Larson-Koester, M. (2020). Is there still son preference in the United States? *Journal of Population Economics, 33*(2), 709–750. https://doi.org/10.1007/s00148-019-00760-7

Bleidorn, W., Hopwood, C. J., & Lucas, R. E. (2018). Life events and personality trait change. *Journal of Personality, 86*(1), 83–96.

Blell, M., & Hunter, M. A. (2019). Direct-to-consumer genetic testing's red herring: "Genetic ancestry" and personalized medicine. *Frontiers in Medicine, 6.* https://doi.org/10.3389/fmed.2019.00048

Blencowe, H., Kancherla, V., Moorthie, S., Darlison, M. W., & Modell, B. (2018). Estimates of global and regional prevalence of neural tube defects for 2015: A systematic analysis. *Annals of the New York Academy of Sciences, 1414*(1), 31–46.

Blieszner, R., & Ogletree, A. M. (2018). Close relationships in middle and late adulthood. In A. L. Vangelisti & D. Perlman (Eds.), *The Cambridge handbook of personal relationships* (pp. 148–160). Cambridge University Press. https://doi.org/10.1017/9781316417867.013

Blitvich, P. G.-C. (2018). Globalization, transnational identities, and conflict talk: The superdiversity and complexity of the Latino identity. *Journal of Pragmatics, 134,* 120–133. https://doi.org/10.1016/j.pragma.2018.02.001

Bluck, S., & Mroz, E. L. (2018). The end: Death as part of the life story. *The International Journal of Reminiscence and Life Review, 5*(1), 6–14.

Bluebond-Langner, M. (1978). *The private worlds of dying children.* Princeton University Press. https://doi.org/10.1515/9780691213088

Blumenfeld, H. K., Quinzon, S. J. R., Alsol, C., & Riera, S. A. (2017). Predictors of successful learning in multilingual older adults acquiring a majority language.

Frontiers in Communication, 2, 23. https://doi.org/10.3389/fcomm.2017.00023

Boddice, R. (2019). *A history of feelings.* Reaktion Books.

Boerner, K., Stroebe, M., Schut, H. A. W., & Wortman, C. B. (2017). Grief and bereavement: Theoretical perspectives. In N. A. Pachana (Ed.), *Encyclopedia of geropsychology* (pp. 979–986). Springer.

Boers, E., Afzali, M. H., Newton, N., & Conrod, P. (2019). Association of screen time and depression in adolescence. *JAMA Pediatrics, 173*(9), 853–859. https://doi.org/10.1001/jamapediatrics.2019.1759

Boersma, P., Black, L. I., & Ward, B. W. (2020). Prevalence of multiple chronic conditions among US adults, 2018. *Preventing Chronic Disease, 17,* 200130. https://doi.org/10.5888/pcd17.200130

Boesveldt, S., Bobowski, N., McCrickerd, K., Maître, I., Sulmont-Rossé, C., & Forde, C. G. (2018). The changing role of the senses in food choice and food intake across the lifespan. *Food Quality and Preference, 68,* 80–89. https://doi.org/10.1016/j.foodqual.2018.02.004

Bogin, B. (1997). Evolutionary hypotheses for human childhood. *American Journal of Physical Anthropology, 104*(S25), 63–89.

Bohm, M. K., Liu, Y., Esser, M. B., Mesnick, J. B., Lu, H., Pan, Y., & Greenlund, K. J. (2021). Binge drinking among adults, by select characteristics and state — United States, 2018. *MMWR. Morbidity and Mortality Weekly Report, 70*(41), 1441–1446.

Bohn, M., Kachel, G., & Tomasello, M. (2019). Young children spontaneously recreate core properties of language in a new modality. *Proceedings of the National Academy of Sciences, 116*(51), 26072–26077. https://doi.org/10.1073/pnas.1904871116

Bohren, M. A., Vogel, J. P., Hunter, E. C., Lutsiv, O., Makh, S. K., Souza, J. P., Aguiar, C., Coneglian, F. S., Diniz, A. L. A., Tunçalp, Ö., Javadi, D., Oladapo, O. T., Khosla, R., Hindin, M. J., & Gülmezoglu, A. M. (2015). The mistreatment of women during childbirth in health facilities globally: A mixed-methods systematic review. *PLOS Medicine, 12*(6), e1001847. https://doi.org/10.1371/journal.pmed.1001847

Boisjoli, R., Vitaro, F., Lacourse, É., Barker, E. D., & Tremblay, R. E. (2007). Impact and clinical significance of a preventive intervention for disruptive boys: 15-year follow-up. *The British Journal of Psychiatry, 191*(5), 415–419.

Boislard, M.-A., van de Bongardt, D., & Blais, M. (2016). Sexuality (and lack thereof) in adolescence and early adulthood: A review of the literature. *Behavioral Sciences, 6*(1). https://doi.org/10.3390/bs6010008

Boisvert, S., & Poulin, F. (2017). Navigating in and out of romantic relationships from adolescence to emerging adulthood: Distinct patterns and their correlates at age 25. *Emerging Adulthood, 5*(3), 216–223. https://doi.org/10.1177/2167696816675092

Boivin, J., Sandhu, A., Brian, K., & Harrison, C. (2019). Fertility-related knowledge and perceptions of fertility education among adolescents and emerging adults: A qualitative study. *Human Fertility, 22*(4), 291–299.

Boks, M. P., van Mierlo, H. C., Rutten, B. P. F., Radstake, T. R. D. J., De Witte, L., Geuze, E., Horvath, S., Schalkwyk, L. C., Vinkers, C. H., Broen, J. C. A., & Vermetten, E. (2015). Longitudinal changes of telomere length and epigenetic age related to traumatic stress and post-traumatic stress disorder. *Psychoneuroendocrinology, 51,* 506–512. https://doi.org/10.1016/j.psyneuen.2014.07.011

Bol, T., & Van de Werfhorst, H. G. (2013). Educational systems and the trade-off between labor market allocation and equality of educational opportunity. *Comparative Education Review, 57*(2), 285–308.

Bolino, M. C., & Grant, A. M. (2016). The bright side of being prosocial at work, and the dark side, too: A review and agenda for research on other-oriented motives, behavior, and impact in organizations. *Academy of Management Annals, 10*(1), 599–670.

Bombard, J. M., Kortsmit, K., Warner, L., Shapiro-Mendoza, C. K., Cox, S., Kroelinger, C. D., Parks, S. E., Dee, D. L., D'Angelo, D. V., Smith, R. A., Burley, K., Morrow, B., Olson, C. K., Shulman, H. B.,

Harrison, L., Cottengim, C., & Barfield, W. D. (2018). Vital signs: Trends and disparities in infant safe sleep practices — United States, 2009–2015. *Morbidity and Mortality Weekly Report, 67*(1), 39–46. https://doi.org/10.15585/mmwr.mm6701e1

Bomberg, E. M., Addo, O. Y., Sarafoglou, K., & Miller, B. S. (2021). Adjusting for pubertal status reduces overweight and obesity prevalence in the United States. *The Journal of Pediatrics, 231,* 200–206.e1. https://doi.org/10.1016/j.jpeds.2020.12.038

Bonanno, G. A. (2019). *The other side of sadness: What the new science of bereavement tells us about life after loss.* Basic Books.

Bonanno, G. A., & Malgaroli, M. (2020). Trajectories of grief: Comparing symptoms from the DSM-5 and ICD-11 diagnoses. *Depression and Anxiety, 37*(1), 17–25.

Bonanno, G. A., Westphal, M., & Mancini, A. D. (2011). Resilience to loss and potential trauma. *Annual Review of Clinical Psychology, 7,* 511–535.

Bondeson, J. (2002). *Buried alive: The terrifying history of our most primal fear.* W. W. Norton.

Bongaarts, J., Mensch, B. S., & Blanc, A. K. (2017). Trends in the age at reproductive transitions in the developing world: The role of education. *Population Studies, 71*(2), 139–154. https://doi.org/10.1080/00324728.2017.1291986

Bonnar, D., Gradisar, M., Moseley, L., Coughlin, A.-M., Cain, N., & Short, M. A. (2015). Evaluation of novel school-based interventions for adolescent sleep problems: Does parental involvement and bright light improve outcomes? *Sleep Health: Journal of the National Sleep Foundation, 1*(1), 66–74. https://doi.org/10.1016/j.sleh.2014.11.002

Bonnici-Mallia, A. M., Barbara, C., & Rao, R. (2018). Vascular cognitive impairment and vascular dementia. *InnovAiT, 11*(5), 249–255. https://doi.org/10.1177/1755738018760649

Bonnie, R. J., Wallace, R. B., & National Research Council. (2003). Concepts, definitions, and guidelines for measurement. In R. J. Bonnie & R. B. Wallace (Eds.), *Elder mistreatment: Abuse, neglect, and exploitation in an aging America* (pp. 34–59). National Academies Press.

Bontemps, B., Piponnier, E., Chalchat, E., Blazevich, A. J., Julian, V., Bocock, O., Duclos, M., Martin, V., & Ratel, S. (2019). Children exhibit a more comparable neuromuscular fatigue profile to endurance athletes than untrained adults. *Frontiers in Physiology, 10,* 119. https://doi.org/10.3389/fphys.2019.00119

Bonvillian, W. B., & Sarma, S. E. (2021). *Workforce education: A new roadmap.* MIT Press.

Booker, J. A., Capriola-Hall, N. N., Greene, R. W., & Ollendick, T. H. (2020). The parent-child relationship and post-treatment child outcomes across two treatments for oppositional defiant disorder. *Journal of Clinical Child & Adolescent Psychology, 49*(3), 405–419. https://doi.org/10.1080/15374416.2018.1555761

Booker, M. (2016). *BJS data shows graying of prisons.* Prison Policy Initiative.

Booth, R., & Barr, C. (2020). Black people four times more likely to die from Covid-19, ONS finds. *The Guardian, 7.*

Booth, R. B., Tombaugh, E., Kiesa, A., Lundberg, K., & Cohen, A. (2020). *Young people turn to online political engagement during COVID-19* (CIRCLE / Tisch College 2020 Pre-Election Youth Poll). Tufts University.

Booth, S. A., Carskadon, M. A., Young, R., & Short, M. A. (2021). Sleep duration and mood in adolescents: An experimental study. *Sleep, 44*(5), zsaa253. https://doi.org/10.1093/sleep/zsaa253

Boquien, C.-Y. (2018). Human milk: An ideal food for nutrition of preterm newborn. *Frontiers in Pediatrics, 6,* 295. https://doi.org/10.3389/fped.2018.00295

Bor, J. S. (2015). Among the elderly, many mental illnesses go undiagnosed. *Health Affairs, 34*(5), 727–731. https://doi.org/10.1377/hlthaff.2015.0314

Borchers, L. R., Dennis, E. L., King, L. S., Humphreys, K. L., & Gotlib, I. H. (2021). Prenatal and postnatal depressive symptoms, infant white matter, and toddler behavioral problems. *Journal of Affective Disorders, 282,* 465–471. https://doi.org/10.1016/j.jad.2020.12.075

Borghuis, J., Denissen, J. J., Sijtsma, K., Branje, S., Meeus, W. H., & Bleidorn, W. (2018). Positive daily experiences are associated with personality trait changes in middle-aged mothers. *European Journal of Personality, 32*(6), 672–689. https://doi.org/10.1002/per.2178

Borjigin, J., Lee, U., Liu, T., Pal, D., Huff, S., Klarr, D., Sloboda, J., Hernandez, J., Wang, M. M., & Mashour, G. A. (2013). Surge of neurophysiological coherence and connectivity in the dying brain. *Proceedings of the National Academy of Sciences, 110*(35), 14432–14437. https://doi .org/10.1073/pnas.1308285110

Bornstein, M. H. (1989). *Maternal responsiveness: Characteristics and consequences.* Jossey-Bass.

Bornstein, M. H. (2015). Culture, parenting, and zero-to-threes. *Zero to Three, 35*(4), 2–9.

Bornstein, M. H. (2019). Parenting infants. In M. H. Bornstein (Ed.), *Handbook of parenting* (pp. 3–55). Routledge.

Bornstein, M. H., Putnick, D. L., Deater-Deckard, K., Lansford, J. E., & Bradley, R. H. (2016). Gender in low- and middle-income countries: Reflections, limitations, directions, and implications. *Monographs of the Society for Research in Child Development, 81*(1), 123–144. https://doi .org/10.1111/mono.12229

Bornstein, M. H., Putnick, D. L., & Lansford, J. E. (2011). Parenting attributions and attitudes in cross-cultural perspective. *Parenting, Science and Practice, 11*(2–3), 214–237. https://doi.org/10.1080/15295192.2011.585568

Bornstein, M. H., Putnick, D. L., & Suwalsky, J. T. D. (2018). Parenting cognitions → parenting practices → child adjustment? The standard model. *Development and Psychopathology, 30*(2), 399–416. https://doi.org/10.1017 /S0954579417000931

Borowski, S. K., & Zeman, J. (2018). Emotional competencies relate to co-rumination: Implications for emotion socialization within adolescent friendships. *Social Development, 27*(4), 808–825. https://doi.org/10.1111 /sode.12293

Borrell, L. N., & Lancet, E. A. (2012). Race/ethnicity and all-cause mortality in US adults: Revisiting the Hispanic paradox. *American Journal of Public Health, 102*(5), 836–843. https://doi.org/10.2105/AJPH.2011.300345

Borrero, S., Nikolajski, C., Steinberg, J. R., Freedman, L., Akers, A. Y., Ibrahim, S., & Schwarz, E. B. (2015). "It just happens": A qualitative study exploring low-income women's perspectives on pregnancy intention and planning. *Contraception, 91*(2), 150–156.

Borsa, V. M., Perani, D., Della Rosa, P. A., Videsott, G., Guidi, L., Weekes, B. S., Franceschini, R., & Abutalebi, J. (2018). Bilingualism and healthy aging: Aging effects and neural maintenance. *Neuropsychologia, 111,* 51–61. https:// doi.org/10.1016/j.neuropsychologia.2018.01.012

Borsani, E., Della Vedova, A. M., Rezzani, R., Rodella, L. F., & Cristini, C. (2019). Correlation between human nervous system development and acquisition of fetal skills: An overview. *Brain and Development, 41*(3), 225–233. https:// doi.org/10.1016/j.braindev.2018.10.009

Börsch-Supan, A., & Weiss, M. (2016). Productivity and age: Evidence from work teams at the assembly line. *The Journal of the Economics of Ageing, 7,* 30–42. https://doi .org/10.1016/j.jeoa.2015.12.001

Bos, D. J., Dreyfuss, M., Tottenham, N., Hare, T. A., Galván, A., Casey, B. J., & Jones, R. M. (2020). Distinct and similar patterns of emotional development in adolescents and young adults. *Developmental Psychobiology, 62*(5), 591–599. https://doi.org/10.1002/dev.21942

Bošković, A., & Rando, O. J. (2018). Transgenerational epigenetic inheritance. *Annual Review of Genetics, 52*(1), 21–41. https://doi.org/10.1146/annurev-genet-120417-031404

Bosley, C., & Jarmisko, M. (2021, March 14). Global baby drought of Covid-19 crisis risks population crunch. *Bloomberg.* https://www.bloomberg.com/news/articles/2021-03-14/global-baby-drought-of-covid-19-crisis-risks-population-crunch

Bosmans, G., & Kerns, K. A. (2015). Attachment in middle childhood: Progress and prospects. *New Directions for Child and Adolescent Development, 2015*(148), 1–14.

Bosworth, B. (2018). Increasing disparities in mortality by socioeconomic status. *Annual Review of Public Health, 39*(1), 237–251. https://doi.org/10.1146/annurev-publhealth -040617-014615

Botelho, G. (2014, January 13). *Beloved teen Sam Berns dies at 17 after suffering from rare disease.* CNN.

Bőthe, B., Vaillancourt-Morel, M. P., Bergeron, S., & Demetrovics, Z. (2019). Problematic and non-problematic pornography use among LGBTQ adolescents: A systematic literature review. *Current Addiction Reports, 6*(4), 478–494.

Bottema-Beutel, K., Kapp, S. K., Lester, J. N., Sasson, N. J., & Hand, B. N. (2020). Avoiding ableist language: Suggestions for autism researchers. *Autism in Adulthood, 3*(1), 18–29. https://doi.org/10.1089/aut.2020.0014

Bouchard, G. (2014). How do parents react when their children leave home? An integrative review. *Journal of Adult Development, 21*(2), 69–79.

Boucher, N. A. (2021). No hugs allowed: Isolation and inequity in North Carolina long-term services and supports during COVID-19. *North Carolina Medical Journal, 82*(1), 57–61. https://doi.org/10.18043/ncm.82.1.57

Boundy, E. O., Dastjerdi, R., Spiegelman, D., Fawzi, W. W., Missmer, S. A., Lieberman, E., Kajeepeta, S., Wall, S., & Chan, G. J. (2016). Kangaroo mother care and neonatal outcomes: A meta-analysis. *Pediatrics, 137*(1). https://doi .org/10.1542/peds.2015-2238

Bourassa, K. J., Memel, M., Woolverton, C., & Sbarra, D. A. (2017). Social participation predicts cognitive functioning in aging adults over time: Comparisons with physical health, depression, and physical activity. *Aging & Mental Health, 21*(2), 133–146.

Bourassa, K. J., Sbarra, D. A., & Whisman, M. A. (2015). Women in very low quality marriages gain life satisfaction following divorce. *Journal of Family Psychology, 29*(3), 490.

Bourdillon, M. (2019). "Child labour" and children's lives. In A. T.-D. Imoh, M. Bourdillon, & S. Meichsner (Eds.), *Global childhoods beyond the North-South divide* (pp. 35–55). Palgrave Macmillan.

Bourne, R., Steinmetz, J. D., Flaxman, S., Briant, P. S., Taylor, H. R., Resnikoff, S., Casson, R. J., Abdoli, A., Abu-Gharbieh, E., Afshin, A., Ahmadieh, H., Akalu, Y., Alamneh, A. A., Alemayehu, W., Alfaar, A. S., Alipour, V., Anbesu, E. W., Androudi, S., Arabloo, J., ... Vos, T. (2021). Trends in prevalence of blindness and distance and near vision impairment over 30 years: An analysis for the Global Burden of Disease Study. *The Lancet Global Health, 9*(2), e130–e143. https://doi.org/10.1016/S2214-109X(20)30425-3

Bouza, J., Camacho-Thompson, D. E., Carlo, G., Franco, X., García Coll, C., Halgunseth, L. C., Marks, A., Livas Stein, G., Suarez-Orozco, C., & White, R. M. B. (2018). *The science is clear: Separating families has long-term damaging psychological and health consequences for children, families, and communities.* Society for Research in Child Development (SRCD). https://www.srcd.org/briefs-fact-sheets /the-science-is-clear

Bové, H., Bongaerts, E., Slenders, E., Bijnens, E. M., Saenen, N. D., Gyselaers, W., Van Eyken, P., Plusquin, M., Roeffaers, M. B. J., Ameloot, M., & Nawrot, T. S. (2019). Ambient black carbon particles reach the fetal side of human placenta. *Nature Communications, 10*(1), 3866. https://doi.org/10.1038/s41467-019-11654-3

Bowen, E., Ball, A., Jones, A. S., & Miller, B. (2021). Toward many emerging adulthoods: A theory-based examination of the features of emerging adulthood for cross-systems youth. *Emerging Adulthood, 9*(3), 189–201. https:// doi.org/10.1177/2167696821989123

Bowlby, J. (1951). *Maternal care and mental health* (Vol. 2). World Health Organization.

Bowlby, J. (1969). *Attachment.* Basic Books.

Bowlby, J. (1980). *Attachment and loss.* Basic Books.

Bowlby, J. (1982). Attachment and loss: Retrospect and prospect. *American Journal of Orthopsychiatry, 52*(4), 664.

Bowlby, J. (2008). *Attachment.* Basic Books.

Bowlby, J. (2012). *The making and breaking of affectional bonds.* Routledge.

Bowlby, J., Robertson, J., & Rosenbluth, D. (1952). A two-year-old goes to hospital. *The Psychoanalytic Study of the Child, 7*(1), 82–94.

Bowleg, L., Maria del Río-González, A., Mbaba, M., Boone, C. A., & Holt, S. L. (2020). Negative police encounters and police avoidance as pathways to depressive symptoms among US Black men, 2015–2016. *American Journal of Public Health, 110*(S1), S160–S166. https://doi .org/10.2105/AJPH.2019.305460

Boxall, A. (2017, February 16). *Russia loves its dating apps, tops the charts for download numbers.* Business of Apps. https://www.businessofapps.com/news/russia-loves-dating -apps-tops-charts-download-numbers/

Boyd-Ball, A. J., Véronneau, M.-H., Dishion, T. J., & Kavanagh, K. (2014). Monitoring and peer influences as predictors of increases in alcohol use among American Indian youth. *Prevention Science, 15*(4), 526–535. https:// doi.org/10.1007/s11121-013-0399-1

Boylan, J. M., Cundiff, J. M., Jakubowski, K. P., Pardini, D. A., & Matthews, K. A. (2018). Pathways linking childhood SES and adult health behaviors and psychological resources in Black and White men. *Annals of Behavioral Medicine, 52*(12), 1023–1035.

Boyle, C. C., Cole, S. W., Dutcher, J. M., Eisenberger, N. I., & Bower, J. E. (2019). Changes in eudaimonic well-being and the conserved transcriptional response to adversity in younger breast cancer survivors. *Psychoneuro-endocrinology, 103,* 173–179. https://doi.org/10.1016/j .psyneuen.2019.01.024

Boyle, P. (2021, February 2). *Nation's physician workforce evolves: More women, a bit older, and toward different specialties.* AAMC. https://www.aamc.org/news-insights/ nation-s-physician-workforce-evolves-more-women-bit-older-and-toward-different-specialties

Boyle, P. A., Wang, T., Yu, L., Barnes, L. L., Wilson, R. S., & Bennett, D. A. (2021). Purpose in life may delay adverse health outcomes in old age. *The American Journal of Geriatric Psychiatry.* https://doi.org/10.1016/j.jagp.2021.05.007

Boylston, T. (2015). "And unto dust shalt thou return": Death and the semiotics of remembrance in an Ethiopian Orthodox Christian village. *Material Religion, 11*(3), 281–302.

Boyon, N., & Silverstein, K. (2021). *LGBT+ Pride 2021 Global Survey points to a generation gap around gender identity and sexual attraction.* Ipsos. https://www.ipsos.com /en-us/news-polls/ipsos-lgbt-pride-2021-global-survey

Bozicevic, L., De Pascalis, L., Montirosso, R., Ferrari, P. F., Giusti, L., Cooper, P. J., & Murray, L. (2021). Sculpting culture: Early maternal responsiveness and child emotion regulation—A UK-Italy comparison. *Journal of Cross-Cultural Psychology, 52*(1), 22–42. https://doi .org/10.1177/0022022120971353

Braaten, E. B., & Norman, D. (2006). Intelligence (IQ) testing. *Pediatrics in Review, 27*(11), 403.

Brace, J. J., Morton, J. B., & Munakata, Y. (2006). When actions speak louder than words: Improving children's flexibility in a card-sorting task. *Psychological Science, 17*(8), 665–669.

Brace, S., Diekmann, Y., Booth, T. J., Faltyskova, Z., Rohland, N., Mallick, S., Ferry, M., Michel, M., Oppenheimer, J., Broomandkhoshbacht, N., Stewardson, K., Walsh, S., Kayser, M., Schulting, R., Craig, O. E., Sheridan, A., Pearson, M. P., Stringer, C., Reich, D., ... Barnes, I. (2018). Population replacement in Early Neolithic Britain. *BioRxiv,* 267443. https://doi.org/10.1101/267443

Bradbury, T. N., & Bodenmann, G. (2020). Interventions for couples. *Annual Review of Clinical Psychology, 16*(1), 99–123. https://doi.org/10.1146/annurev-clinpsy -071519-020546

Bradway, K. E., & Beard, R. L. (2015). "Don't be trying to box folks in": Older women's sexuality. *Affilia, 30*(4), 504–518.

Brady, G., Lowe, P., Brown, G., Osmond, J., & Newman, M. (2018). 'All in all it is just a judgement call': Issues surrounding sexual consent in young people's heterosexual encounters. *Journal of Youth Studies, 21*(1), 35–50.

Brainerd, C. J., & Reyna, V. F. (2015). Fuzzy-trace theory and lifespan cognitive development. *Developmental Review, 38*(Supplement C), 89–121. https://doi.org/10.1016/j .dr.2015.07.006

Brame, R., Bushway, S. D., Paternoster, R., & Turner, M. G. (2014). Demographic patterns of cumulative arrest prevalence by ages 18 and 23. *Crime and Delinquency, 60*(3), 471–486. https://doi.org/10.1177/0011128713514801

Brand, J. E., Pfeffer, F. T., & Goldrick-Rab, S. (2014). The community college effect revisited: The importance of attending to heterogeneity and complex counterfactuals. *Sociological Science, 1*, 448–465.

Brand, R. J., Escobar, K., & Patrick, A. M. (2020). Coincidence or cascade? The temporal relation between locomotor behaviors and the emergence of stranger anxiety. *Infant Behavior and Development, 58*. https://doi.org/10.1016/j.infbeh.2020.101423

Brandes, C. M., Kushner, S. C., Herzhoff, K., & Tackett, J. L. (2020). Facet-level personality development in the transition to adolescence: Maturity, disruption, and gender differences. *Journal of Personality and Social Psychology, 121*(5), 1095–1111. https://doi.org/10.1037/pspp0000367

Brandes-Aitken, A., Braren, S., Swingler, M., Voegtline, K., & Blair, C. (2019). Sustained attention in infancy: A foundation for the development of multiple aspects of self-regulation for children in poverty. *Journal of Experimental Child Psychology, 184*, 192–209. https://doi.org/10.1016/j.jecp.2019.04.006

Brandt, J. S., Ithier, M. A. C., Rosen, T., & Ashkinadze, E. (2019). Advanced paternal age, infertility, and reproductive risks: A review of the literature. *Prenatal Diagnosis, 39*(2), 81–87. https://doi.org/10.1002/pd.5402

Brandt, N. D., Mike, A., & Jackson, J. J. (2019). Do school-related experiences impact personality? Selection and socialization effects of impulse control. *Developmental Psychology, 55*(12), 2561–2574. https://doi.org/10.1037/dev0000817

Bratsberg, B., & Rogeberg, O. (2018). Flynn effect and its reversal are both environmentally caused. *Proceedings of the National Academy of Sciences, 115*(26), 6674–6678.

Bratsch-Hines, M. E., Zgourou, E., Vernon-Feagans, L., Carr, R., & Willoughby, M. (2020). Infant and toddler child-care quality and stability in relation to proximal and distal academic and social outcomes. *Child Development, 91*(6), 1854–1864. https://doi.org/10.1111/cdev.13389

Bratt, C., Abrams, D., & Swift, H. J. (2020). Supporting the old but neglecting the young? The two faces of ageism. *Developmental Psychology, 56*(5), 1029.

Bravo, M. A., Batch, B. C., & Miranda, M. L. (2019). Residential racial isolation and spatial patterning of hypertension in Durham, North Carolina. *Preventing Chronic Disease, 16*, E36. https://doi.org/10.5888/pcd16.18044

Braxton, J., Davis, D. W., Emerson, B., Flagg, E. W., Grey, J., Grier, L., & Womack, N. (2018). *Sexually transmitted disease surveillance 2017*. Centers for Disease Control & Prevention.

Braymiller, J. L., Barrington-Trimis, J. L., Leventhal, A. M., Islam, T., Kechter, A., Krueger, E. A., Cho, J., Lanza, I., Unger, J. B., & McConnell, R. (2020). Assessment of nicotine and cannabis vaping and respiratory symptoms in young adults. *JAMA Network Open, 3*(12), e2030189–e2030189. https://doi.org/10.1001/jamanetworkopen.2020.30189

Braza, P., Carreras, R., Muñoz, J. M., Braza, F., Azurmendi, A., Pascual-Sagastizábal, E., Cardas, J., & Sánchez-Martín, J. R. (2015). Negative maternal and paternal parenting styles as predictors of children's behavioral problems: Moderating effects of the child's sex. *Journal of Child and Family Studies, 24*(4), 847–856.

Bredekamp, S. (1992). What is "developmentally appropriate" and why is it important? *Journal of Physical Education, Recreation & Dance, 63*(6), 31–32. https://doi.org/10.1080/07303084.1992.10606612

Bredgaard, T., & Salado-Rasmussen, J. (2021). Attitudes and behaviour of employers to recruiting persons with disabilities. *Alter, 15*(1), 61–70.

Breheny, M., Horrell, B., & Stephens, C. (2020). Caring for older people: Relational narratives of attentiveness, commitment and acceptance. *International Journal of Care and Caring, 4*(2), 201–214. https://doi.org/10.1332/239788219X15730452705345

Breiding, M. J. (2014). Prevalence and characteristics of sexual violence, stalking, and intimate partner violence

victimization—National Intimate Partner and Sexual Violence Survey, United States, 2011. *Morbidity and Mortality Weekly Report. Surveillance Summaries, 63*(8), 1–18.

Bremer, G. (2018). Giving girls a chance: Ending child marriage and promoting education in Georgia and Niger. *Global Majority E-Journal, 9*(2), 59–70.

Brenan, M. (2018, May 31). *Americans' strong support for euthanasia persists*. Gallup.com. https://news.gallup.com/poll/235145/americans-strong-support-euthanasia-persists.aspx

Bretherton, I. (1992). The origins of attachment theory: John Bowlby and Mary Ainsworth. *Developmental Psychology, 28*(5), 759–775.

Bretherton, I. (2003). Mary Ainsworth: Insightful observer and courageous theoretician. In G. A. Kimble & M. Wertheimer (Eds.), *Portraits of pioneers in psychology* (Vol. 5, pp. 317–331). Erlbaum.

Bretherton, I., & Munholland, K. A. (2016). The internal working model construct in light of contemporary neuroimaging research. In J. Cassidy & P. R. Shaver (Eds.), *Handbook of attachment: Theory, research, and clinical application* (pp. 63–88). Guilford.

Brett, B. L., Savitz, J., Nitta, M., España, L., Teague, T. K., Nelson, L. D., McCrea, M. A., & Meier, T. B. (2020). Systemic inflammation moderates the association of prior concussion with hippocampal volume and episodic memory in high school and collegiate athletes. *Brain, Behavior, and Immunity, 89*, 380–388. https://doi.org/10.1016/j.bbi.2020.07.024

Bretzke, M., Wahl, H., Plichta, M. M., Wolff, N., Roessner, V., Vetter, N. C., & Buse, J. (2021). Ventral striatal activation during reward anticipation of different reward probabilities in adolescents and adults. *Frontiers in Human Neuroscience, 15*, 649724. https://doi.org/10.3389/fnhum.2021.649724

Bribiescas, R. G. (2020). Aging, life history, and human evolution. *Annual Review of Anthropology, 49*(1), 101–121. https://doi.org/10.1146/annurev-anthro-010220-074148

BrightFutures / American Academy of Pediatrics. (2021). *Recommendations for preventative pediatric health care*. American Academy of Pediatrics.

Briley, D. A., & Tucker-Drob, E. M. (2014). Genetic and environmental continuity in personality development: A meta-analysis. *Psychological Bulletin, 140*(5), 1303–1331. https://doi.org/10.1037/a0037091

Britt, S. L., & Roy, R. R. N. (2014). Relationship quality among young couples from an economic and gender perspective. *Journal of Family and Economic Issues, 35*(2), 241–250. https://doi.org/10.1007/s10834-013-9368-x

Brix, N., Ernst, A., Lauridsen, L. L. B., Parner, E. T., Arah, O. A., Olsen, J., Henriksen, T. B., & Ramlau-Hansen, C. H. (2020). Childhood overweight and obesity and timing of puberty in boys and girls: Cohort and sibling-matched analyses. *International Journal of Epidemiology, 49*(3), 834–844. https://doi.org/10.1093/ije/dyaa056

Brix, N., Ernst, A., Lauridsen, L. L. B., Parner, E., Støvring, H., Olsen, J., Henriksen, T. B., & Ramlau-Hansen, C. H. (2019). Timing of puberty in boys and girls: A population-based study. *Paediatric and Perinatal Epidemiology, 33*(1), 70–78. https://doi.org/10.1111/ppe.12507

Brockett, R. G. (2015). *Teaching adults: A practical guide for new teachers*. John Wiley & Sons.

Brockmole, J. R., & Logie, R. H. (2013). Age-related change in visual working memory: A study of 55,753 participants aged 8–75. *Frontiers in Psychology, 4*, 12. https://doi.org/10.3389/fpsyg.2013.00012

Brod, G., Bunge, S. A., & Shing, Y. L. (2017). Does one year of schooling improve children's cognitive control and alter associated brain activation? *Psychological Science, 28*(7), 967–978. https://doi.org/10.1177/0956797617699838

Broda, M., Yun, J., Schneider, B., Yeager, D. S., Walton, G. M., & Diemer, M. (2018). Reducing inequality in academic success for incoming college students: A randomized trial of growth mindset and belonging interventions. *Journal of Research on Educational Effectiveness, 11*(3), 317–338. https://doi.org/10.1080/19345747.2018.1429037

Brody, D. J., Pratt, L. A., & Hughes, J. P. (2018). *Prevalence of depression among adults aged 20 and over: United

States, 2013–2016* (NCHS Data Brief No. 303). National Center for Health Statistics.

Brody, G. H., & Flor, D. L. (1998). Maternal resources, parenting practices, and child competence in rural, single-parent African American families. *Child Development, 69*(3), 803–816.

Brody, G. H., Miller, G. E., Yu, T., Beach, S. R., & Chen, E. (2016). Supportive family environments ameliorate the link between racial discrimination and epigenetic aging: A replication across two longitudinal cohorts. *Psychological Science, 27*(4), 530–541.

Brody, G. H., Murry, V. M., Gerrard, M., Gibbons, F. X., Molgaard, V., McNair, L., Brown, A. C., Wills, T. A., Spoth, R. L., Luo, Z., Chen, Y.-F., & Neubaum-Carlan, E. (2004). The strong African American families program: Translating research into prevention programming. *Child Development, 75*(3), 900–917.

Brody, G. H., Yu, T., Chen, E., Beach, S. R. H., & Miller, G. E. (2016). Family-centered prevention ameliorates the longitudinal association between risky family processes and epigenetic aging. *Journal of Child Psychology and Psychiatry, and Allied Disciplines, 57*(5), 566–574. https://doi.org/10.1111/jcpp.12495

Brody, G. H., Yu, T., Miller, G. E., Ehrlich, K. B., & Chen, E. (2019). Preventive parenting intervention during childhood and young black adults' unhealthful behaviors: A randomized controlled trial. *Journal of Child Psychology and Psychiatry, 60*(1), 63–71.

Brodzki, I., Huryk, K. M., Casasnovas, A. F., Sanders, L., & Loeb, K. L. (2018). Eating disorders. In S. G. Forman & J. D. Shahidullah (Eds.), *Handbook of pediatric behavioral healthcare: An interdisciplinary collaborative approach* (pp. 229–241). Springer International Publishing. https://doi.org/10.1007/978-3-030-00791-1_17

Broesch, T., Crittenden, A. N., Beheim, B. A., Blackwell, A. D., Bunce, J. A., Colleran, H., Hagel, K., Kline, M., McElreath, R., Nelson, R. G., Pisor, A. C., Prall, S., Pretelli, I., Purzycki, B., Quinn, E. A., Ross, C., Scelza, B., Starkweather, K., Stieglitz, J., & Mulder, M. B. (2020). Navigating cross-cultural research: Methodological and ethical considerations. *Proceedings of the Royal Society B: Biological Sciences, 287*(1935), 20201245. https://doi.org/10.1098/rspb.2020.1245

Broesch, T., Rochat, P., Olah, K., Broesch, J., & Henrich, J. (2016). Similarities and differences in maternal responsiveness in three societies: Evidence from Fiji, Kenya, and the United States. *Child Development, 87*(3), 700–711.

Bronfenbrenner, U. (1977). Toward an experimental ecology of human development. *American Psychologist, 32*(7), 513–531. https://doi.org/10.1037/0003-066X.32.7.513

Bronfenbrenner, U. (1979). *The ecology of human development: Experiments by nature and design*. Harvard University Press.

Bronfenbrenner, U. (2005). *Making human beings human: Bioecological perspectives on human development*. Sage.

Bronstein, M. V., Pennycook, G., Bear, A., Rand, D. G., & Cannon, T. D. (2019). Belief in fake news is associated with delusionality, dogmatism, religious fundamentalism, and reduced analytic thinking. *Journal of Applied Research in Memory and Cognition, 8*(1), 108–117. https://doi.org/10.1016/j.jarmac.2018.09.005

Brooker, R. J., Kiel, E. J., MacNamara, A., Nyman, T., John-Henderson, N. A., Van Lieshout, R., & Schmidt, L. A. (2020). Maternal neural reactivity during pregnancy predicts infant temperament. *Infancy: The Official Journal of the International Society on Infant Studies, 25*(1), 46–66. https://doi.org/10.1111/infa.12316

Brooks, D. (2016, October 18). The power of a dinner table. *The New York Times*, p. 23.

Brooks, M. (2019). The uneven perils of unemployment and underemployment: The role of employment structure in explaining rural-urban poverty differences, 1970–2018 [Unpublished paper].

Brooks-Gunn, J., Fuligni, A. S., & Berlin, L. (2003). *Early child development in the 21st century: Profiles of current research initiatives*. Teachers College Press.

Brooks-Gunn, J., & Lewis, M. (1975). Mirror-image and self-recognition in infancy. In *Biennial Meeting of the Society for Research in Child Development, Denver, CO (ERIC Document Reproduction No. ED 114 193).

Brooms, D. R. (2020). Helping us think about ourselves: Black males' sense of belonging through connections and relationships with faculty in college. *International Journal of Qualitative Studies in Education, 33*(9), 921–938. https://doi.org/10.1080/09518398.2019.1687956

Broton, K. M., & Goldrick-Rab, S. (2018). Going without: An exploration of food and housing insecurity among undergraduates. *Educational Researcher, 47*(2), 121–133. https://doi.org/10.3102/0013189X17741303

Brown, A. (2020, February 25). *The changing categories the U.S. Census has used to measure race.* Pew Research Center. https://www.pewresearch.org/fact-tank/2020/02/25/the-changing-categories-the-u-s-has-used-to-measure-race/

Brown, A., & Patten, E. (2017, April 3). *The narrowing, but persistent, gender gap in pay.* Pew Research Center. http://www.pewresearch.org/fact-tank/2017/04/03/gender-pay-gap-facts/

Brown, C. L., Skinner, A. C., Yin, H. S., Rothman, R. L., Sanders, L. M., Delamater, A. M., Ravanbakht, S. N., & Perrin, E. M. (2016). Parental perceptions of weight during the first year of life. *Academic Pediatrics, 16*(6), 558–564. https://doi.org/10.1016/j.acap.2016.03.005

Brown, C. S., Alabi, B. O., Huynh, V. W., & Masten, C. L. (2011). Ethnicity and gender in late childhood and early adolescence: Group identity and awareness of bias. *Developmental Psychology, 47*(2), 463.

Brown, C. S., Mistry, R. S., & Yip, T. (2019). Moving from the margins to the mainstream: Equity and justice as key considerations for developmental science. *Child Development Perspectives, 13*(4), 235–240.

Brown, E., & Patrick, M. (2018). Time, anticipation, and the life course: Egg freezing as temporarily disentangling romance and reproduction. *American Sociological Review, 83*(5), 959–982.

Brown, K., & Kathol, D. (2019). Mood disorders in pregnancy. In M. A. O'Neal (Ed.), *Neurology and psychiatry of women: A guide to gender-based issues in evaluation, diagnosis, and treatment* (pp. 157–172). Springer.

Brown, L. M., & Gilligan, C. (1993). Meeting at the crossroads: Women's psychology and girls' development. *Feminism & Psychology, 3*(1), 11–35.

Brown, S. J., Khasteganan, N., Brown, K., Hegarty, K., Carter, G. J., Tarzia, L., Feder, G., & O'Doherty, L. (2019). Psychosocial interventions for survivors of rape and sexual assault experienced during adulthood. *The Cochrane Database of Systematic Reviews,* (11), CD013456. https://doi.org/10.1002/14651858.CD013456

Brown, S. L., & Lin, I.-F. (2012). The gray divorce revolution: Rising divorce among middle-aged and older adults, 1990–2010. *The Journals of Gerontology: Series B, 67*(6), 731–741. https://doi.org/10.1093/geronb/gbs089

Brown, S. L., Lin, I.-F., Hammersmith, A. M., & Wright, M. R. (2018). Later life marital dissolution and repartnership status: A national portrait. *The Journals of Gerontology: Series B, 73*(6), 1032–1042. https://doi.org/10.1093/geronb/gbw051

Brown, S. L., Lin, I.-F., Hammersmith, A. M., & Wright, M. R. (2019). Repartnering following gray divorce: The roles of resources and constraints for women and men. *Demography, 56*(2), 503–523. https://doi.org/10.1007/s13524-018-0752-x

Brown, S. L., & Wright, M. R. (2017). Marriage, cohabitation, and divorce in later life. *Innovation in Aging, 1*(2), igx015. https://doi.org/10.1093/geroni/igx015

Brown, S. L., Wright, M. R., & Howe-Huist, E. (2018). *The rise of cohabitation among older adults: A cross-national perspective.* PAA 2018 Annual Meeting, PAA.

Brown, S. S. (2014). *Transformation beyond greed: Native self-actualization.* Sidney Stone Brown.

Brown, T. H., O'Rand, A. M., & Adkins, D. E. (2012). Race-ethnicity and health trajectories: Tests of three hypotheses across multiple groups and health outcomes. *Journal of Health and Social Behavior, 53*(3), 359–377. https://doi.org/10.1177/0022146512455333

Brown, T. H., Richardson, L. J., Hargrove, T. W., & Thomas, C. S. (2016). Using multiple-hierarchy

stratification and life course approaches to understand health inequalities: The intersecting consequences of race, gender, SES, and age. *Journal of Health and Social Behavior, 57*(2), 200–222. https://doi.org/10.1177/0022146516645165

Brownell, C. A., & Drummond, J. (2020). Early childcare and family experiences predict development of prosocial behaviour in first grade. *Early Child Development and Care, 190*(5), 712–737. https://doi.org/10.1080/03004430.2018.1489382

Brownell, C. A., Lemerise, E. A., Pelphrey, K. A., & Roisman, G. I. (2015). Measuring socioemotional development. In M. E. Lamb & R. M. Lerner (Eds.), *Handbook of child psychology and developmental science: Socioemotional processes* (pp. 11–56). John Wiley & Sons. https://doi.org/10.1002/9781118963418.childpsy302

Brubacher, S. P., Peterson, C., La Rooy, D., Dickinson, J. J., & Poole, D. A. (2019). How children talk about events: Implications for eliciting and analyzing eyewitness reports. *Developmental Review, 51*, 70–89.

Brubaker, J. R., Hayes, G. R., & Dourish, P. (2013). Beyond the grave: Facebook as a site for the expansion of death and mourning. *The Information Society, 29*(3), 152–163. https://doi.org/10.1080/01972243.2013.777300

Bruce, L. D., Wu, J. S., Lustig, S. L., Russell, D. W., & Nemecek, D. A. (2019). Loneliness in the United States: A 2018 national panel survey of demographic, structural, cognitive, and behavioral characteristics. *American Journal of Health Promotion, 33*(8), 1123–1133.

Bruch, E. E., & Newman, M. E. J. (2018). Aspirational pursuit of mates in online dating markets. *Science Advances, 4*(8), eaap9815. https://doi.org/10.1126/sciadv.aap9815

Bruine de Bruin, W., Parker, A. M., & Strough, J. (2020). Age differences in reported social networks and well-being. *Psychology and Aging, 35*(2), 159–168. https://doi.org/10.1037/pag0000415

Bruininks, R. H. & Bruininks, B. D. (2005). *Bruininks-oseretsky test of motor proficiency: BOT-2.* NCS Pearson/AGS.

Brumbaugh, J. E., Hansen, N. I., Bell, E. F., Sridhar, A., Carlo, W. A., Hintz, S. R., Vohr, B. R., Colaizy, T. T., Duncan, A. F., & Wyckoff, M. H. (2019). Outcomes of extremely preterm infants with birth weight less than 400 g. *JAMA Pediatrics, 173*(5), 434–445.

Brumberg, H. L., Karr, C. J., & Council on Environmental Health. (2021). Ambient air pollution: Health hazards to children. *Pediatrics, 147*(6), e2021051484. https://doi.org/10.1542/peds.2021-051484

Brummelman, E., & Dweck, C. S. (2020). Paradoxical effects of praise: A transactional model. In E. Brummelman (Ed.), *Psychological perspectives on praise* (pp. 55–64). Routledge.

Brummelman, E., & Sedikides, C. (2020). Raising children with high self-esteem (but not narcissism). *Child Development Perspectives, 14*(2), 83–89. https://doi.org/10.1111/cdep.12362

Brummelman, E., Crocker, J., & Bushman, B. J. (2016). The praise paradox: When and why praise backfires in children with low self-esteem. *Child Development Perspectives, 10*(2), 111–115. https://doi.org/10.1111/cdep.12171

Bruneau, E., Szekeres, H., Kteily, N., Tropp, L. R., & Kende, A. (2020). Beyond dislike: Blatant dehumanization predicts teacher discrimination. *Group Processes & Intergroup Relations, 23*(4), 560–577. https://doi.org/10.1177/1368430219845462

Bruni, O., & Novelli, L. (2010). Sleep disorders in children. *BMJ Clinical Evidence, 2010*, 2304.

Bryan, C. J., Yeager, D. S., & Hinojosa, C. P. (2019). A values-alignment intervention protects adolescents from the effects of food marketing. *Nature Human Behaviour, 3*(6), 596–603. https://doi.org/10.1038/s41562-019-0586-6

Bryan, J., Williams, J. M., Kim, J., Morrison, S. S., & Caldwell, C. H. (2018). Perceived teacher discrimination and academic achievement among urban Caribbean Black and African American youth: School bonding and family support as protective factors. *Urban Education.* https://doi.org/10.1177/0042085918806959

Brydges, C. R., Carlson, M. C., Andrews, R. M., Rebok, G. W., & Bielak, A. A. M. (2020). Using cognitive

intraindividual variability to measure intervention effectiveness: Results from the Baltimore experience corps trial. *The Journals of Gerontology Series B: Psychological Sciences and Social Sciences, 76*(4), 661–670. https://doi.org/10.1093/geronb/gbaa009

Buch, E. D. (2018). *Inequalities of aging: Paradoxes of independence in American home care.* NYU Press.

Buchman, C. A., Gifford, R. H., Haynes, D. S., Lenarz, T., O'Donoghue, G., Adunka, O., Biever, A., Briggs, R. J., Carlson, M. L., Dai, P., Driscoll, C. L., Francis, H. W., Gantz, B. J., Gurgel, R. K., Hansen, M. R., Holcomb, M., Karltorp, E., Kirtane, M., Larky, J., … Zwolan, T. (2020). Unilateral cochlear implants for severe, profound, or moderate sloping to profound bilateral sensorineural hearing loss: A systematic review and consensus statements. *JAMA Otolaryngology — Head & Neck Surgery, 146*(10), 942–953. https://doi.org/10.1001/jamaoto.2020.0998

Buckley, K. W. (1989). *Mechanical man: John Broadus Watson and the beginnings of behaviorism.* Guilford.

Budd, C. J. (2015). Promoting maths to the general public. In R. C. Kadosh & A. Dowker (Eds.), *Oxford handbook of numerical cognition.* Oxford University Press.

Buehler, C. (2020). Family processes and children's and adolescents' well-being. *Journal of Marriage and Family, 82*(1), 145–174. https://doi.org/10.1111/jomf.12637

Bühler, J. L., & Nikitin, J. (2020). Sociohistorical context and adult social development: New directions for 21st century research. *American Psychologist, 75*(4), 457–469. https://doi.org/10.1037/amp0000611

Buhler-Wilkerson, K. (2003). *No place like home: A history of nursing and home care in the United States.* Johns Hopkins University Press.

Buhs, E. S., Koziol, N. A., Rudasill, K. M., & Crockett, L. J. (2018). Early temperament and middle school engagement: School social relationships as mediating processes. *Journal of Educational Psychology, 110*(3), 338.

Buiatti, M., Giorgio, E. D., Piazza, M., Polloni, C., Menna, G., Taddei, F., Baldo, E., & Vallortigara, G. (2019). Cortical route for facelike pattern processing in human newborns. *Proceedings of the National Academy of Sciences, 116*(10), 4625–4630. https://doi.org/10.1073/pnas.1812419116

Bukowski, W. M., & Raufelder, D. (2018). Peers and the self. In W. M. Bukowski, B. Laursen, & K. H. Rubin (Eds.), *Handbook of peer interactions, relationships, and groups* (pp. 141–156). Guilford.

Bulanda, J. R. (2011). Gender, marital power, and marital quality in later life. *Journal of Women & Aging, 23*(1), 3–22. https://doi.org/10.1080/08952841.2011.540481

Bull, M. J. (2020). Down sSyndrome. *New England Journal of Medicine, 382*(24), 2344–2352. https://doi.org/10.1056/NEJMra1706537

Bundy, D. A. P., de Silva, N., Horton, S., Patton, G. C., Schultz, L., & Jamison, D. T. (2017). Child and adolescent health and development: Realizing neglected potential. In D. A. P. Bundy, N. de Silva, S. Horton, D. T. Jamison, & G. C. Patton (Eds.), *Disease control priorities: Vol. 8. Child and adolescent health and development* (3rd ed., pp. 1–24). The World Bank. https://doi.org/10.1596/978-1-4648-0423-6_ch1

Bundy, D. A. P., de Silva, N., Horton, S., Patton, G. C., Schultz, L., Jamison, D. T., Abubakara, A., Ahuja, A., Alderman, H., Allen, N., Appleby, L., Aurino, E., Azzopardi, P., Baird, S., Banham, L., Behrman, J., Benzian, H., Bhalotra, S., Bhutta, Z., … Sawyer, S. M. (2018). Investment in child and adolescent health and development: Key messages from disease control priorities, 3rd Edition. *The Lancet, 391*(10121), 687–699. https://doi.org/10.1016/S0140-6736(17)32417-0

Burchinal, M. (2018). Measuring early care and education quality. *Child Development Perspectives, 12*(1), 3–9. https://doi.org/10.1111/cdep.12260

Burchinal, M. R., & Farran, D. C. (2020). What does research tell us about ECE programs? In *Getting it right: Using implementation research to improve outcomes in early care and education* (pp. 13–36). Foundation for Child Development.

Burgdorf, J., Roth, D. L., Riffin, C., & Wolff, J. L. (2019). Factors associated with receipt of training among caregivers of older adults. *JAMA Internal Medicine, 179*(6), 833–835. https://doi.org/10.1001/jamainternmed.2018.8694

Burghardt, G. M. (2010). Defining and recognizing play. In P. Nathan & A. D. Pellegrini (Eds.), *The Oxford handbook of the development of play.* https://doi.org/10.1093/oxfordhb/9780195393002.013.0002

Burke, J. D., & Romano-Verthelyi, A. M. (2018). Oppositional defiant disorder. In M. M. Martel (Ed.), *Developmental pathways to disruptive, impulse-control and conduct disorders* (pp. 21–52). Academic Press. https://doi.org/10.1016/B978-0-12-811323-3.00002-X

Burke, K. E. (2018). Mechanisms of aging and development—A new understanding of environmental damage to the skin and prevention with topical antioxidants. *Mechanisms of Ageing and Development, 172*, 123–130. https://doi.org/10.1016/j.mad.2017.12.003

Burke, R. J. (2017). *The sandwich generation: Individual, family, organizational and societal challenges and opportunities.* Elgar Publishing.

Burkle, C. M., Sharp, R. R., & Wijdicks, E. F. (2014). Why brain death is considered death and why there should be no confusion. *Neurology, 83*(16), 1464–1469. https://doi.org/10.1212/WNL.0000000000000883

Burkley, E., Durante, F., Fiske, S. T., Burkley, M., & Andrade, A. (2017). Structure and content of Native American stereotypic subgroups: Not just (ig)noble. *Cultural Diversity and Ethnic Minority Psychology, 23*(2), 209.

Burling, S. (2018, April 3). *Old and ageist: Why so many older people have prejudices about their peers—and themselves.* https://www.inquirer.com/philly/health/old-and-ageist-why-do-so-many-older-people-have-prejudices-about-their-peers-and-themselves-20180404.html

Burmester, B., Leathem, J., & Merrick, P. (2016). Subjective cognitive complaints and objective cognitive function in aging: A systematic review and meta-analysis of recent cross-sectional findings. *Neuropsychology Review, 26*(4), 376–393. https://doi.org/10.1007/s11065-016-9332-2

Burr, D. A., Castrellon, J. J., Zald, D. H., & Samanez-Larkin, G. R. (2020). Emotion dynamics across adulthood in everyday life: Older adults are more emotionally stable and better at regulating desires. *Emotion, 21*(3), 453–464. https://doi.org/10.1037/emo0000734

Burr, J. A., Han, S., Lee, H. J., Tavares, J. L., & Mutchler, J. E. (2018). Health benefits associated with three helping behaviors: Evidence for incident cardiovascular disease. *The Journals of Gerontology: Series B, 73*(3), 492–500. https://doi.org/10.1093/geronb/gbx082

Burrage, M. S., Ponitz, C. C., McCready, E. A., Shah, P., Sims, B. C., Jewkes, A. M., & Morrison, F. J. (2008). Age- and schooling-related effects on executive functions in young children: A natural experiment. *Child Neuropsychology, 14*(6), 510–524. https://doi.org/10.1080/09297040701756917

Burrell, A., & Selman, L. E. (2020). How do funeral practices impact bereaved relatives' mental health, grief and bereavement? A mixed methods review with implications for COVID-19. *OMEGA—Journal of Death and Dying.* https://doi.org/10.1177/0030222820941296

Burrus, B. B. (2018). Decline in adolescent pregnancy in the United States: A success not shared by all. *American Journal of Public Health, 108*(S1), S5–S6. https://doi.org/10.2105/AJPH.2017.304273

Bursztyn, L., Egorov, G., & Jensen, R. (2019). Cool to be smart or smart to be cool? Understanding peer pressure in education. *The Review of Economic Studies, 86*(4), 1487–1526. https://doi.org/10.1093/restud/rdy026

Burtless, G. (2019, August 15). *Despite scary headlines, America's elderly continue to prosper.* Brookings. https://www.brookings.edu/opinions/despite-scary-headlines-americas-elderly-continue-to-prosper/

Busch, A. S., Hagen, C. P., & Juul, A. (2020a). Heritability of pubertal timing: Detailed evaluation of specific milestones in healthy boys and girls. *European Journal of Endocrinology, 183*(1), 13–20. https://doi.org/10.1530/EJE-20-0023

Busch, A. S., Højgaard, B., Hagen, C. P., & Teilmann, G. (2020b). Obesity is associated with earlier pubertal onset in boys. *The Journal of Clinical Endocrinology and Metabolism, 105*(4), dgz222. https://doi.org/10.1210/clinem/dgz222

Busch, J. T. A., Watson-Jones, R. E., & Legare, C. H. (2020). Cultural variation in the development of beliefs about conservation. *Cognitive Science, 44*(10), e12909. https://doi.org/10.1111/cogs.12909

Busching, R., & Krahé, B. (2020). With a little help from their peers: The impact of classmates on adolescents' development of prosocial behavior. *Journal of Youth and Adolescence, 49*(9), 1849–1863. https://doi.org/10.1007/s10964-020-01260-8

Busl, K. M. (2019). When is dead really dead? Study on pig brains reinforces that death is a vast gray area. *The Conversation.* http://theconversation.com/when-is-dead-really-dead-study-on-pig-brains-reinforces-that-death-is-a-vast-gray-area-115750

Buss, A. T., & Spencer, J. P. (2018). Changes in frontal and posterior cortical activity underlie the early emergence of executive function. *Developmental Science, 21*(4), e12602. https://doi.org/10.1111/desc.12602

Buss, D. M., & von Hippel, W. (2018). Psychological barriers to evolutionary psychology: Ideological bias and coalitional adaptations. *Archives of Scientific Psychology, 6*(1), 148. https://doi.org/10.1037/arc0000049

Bussé, A. M. L., Hoeve, H. L. J., Nasserinejad, K., Mackey, A. R., Simonsz, H. J., & Goedegebure, A. (2020). Prevalence of permanent neonatal hearing impairment: Systematic review and Bayesian meta-analysis. *International Journal of Audiology, 59*(6), 475–485. https://doi.org/10.1080/14992027.2020.1716087

Bussey, K., & Bandura, A. (1999). Social cognitive theory of gender development and differentiation. *Psychological Review, 106*(4), 676.

Busso, D. S., Volmert, A., & Kendall-Taylor, N. (2019). Reframing aging: Effect of a short-term framing intervention on implicit measures of age bias. *The Journals of Gerontology: Series B, 74*(4), 559–564. https://doi.org/10.1093/geronb/gby080

Butler, G. H., Flood, K., Doyle, E., Geary, M. P., Betts, D. R., Foran, A., O'Marcaigh, A., & Cotter, M. (2016). Similar but different: Identical pathology with differing outcome in 'Not-so-identical' twins. *British Journal of Haematology, 178*(1), 152–153. https://doi.org/10.1111/bjh.14117

Butler, H. A., Dwyer, C. P., Hogan, M. J., Franco, A., Rivas, S. F., Saiz, C., & Almeida, L. S. (2012). The Halpern critical thinking assessment and real-world outcomes: Cross-national applications. *Thinking Skills and Creativity, 7*(2), 112–121. https://doi.org/10.1016/j.tsc.2012.04.001

Butler, H. A., Pentoney, C., & Bong, M. P. (2017). Predicting real-world outcomes: Critical thinking ability is a better predictor of life decisions than intelligence. *Thinking Skills and Creativity, 25*, 38–46. https://doi.org/10.1016/j.tsc.2017.06.005

Butler, R., & Katona, C. (2019). *Seminars in old age psychiatry.* Cambridge University Press.

Butler, R. N. (1969). Age-ism: Another form of bigotry. *The Gerontologist, 9*(4_Part_1), 243–246.

Butler, R. N. (1974). Successful aging and the role of the life review. *Journal of the American Geriatrics Society, 22*(12), 529–535.

Butterfield, R. D., Silk, J. S., Lee, K. H., Siegle, G. S., Dahl, R. E., Forbes, E. E., Ryan, N. D., Hooley, J. M., & Ladouceur, C. D. (2021). Parents still matter! Parental warmth predicts adolescent brain function and anxiety and depressive symptoms 2 years later. *Development and Psychopathology, 33*(1), 226–239. https://doi.org/10.1017/S0954579419001718

Butterworth, B., Gallistel, C. R., & Vallortigara, G. (2018). Introduction: The origins of numerical abilities. *Philosophical Transactions of the Royal Society B: Biological Sciences, 373*(1740). https://doi.org/10.1098/rstb.2016.0507

Butterworth, B., & Varma, S. (2013). Mathematical development. In D. Mareschal, B. Butterworth, & A. Tolmie (Eds.), *Educational neuroscience* (Chap. 8). John Wiley & Sons.

Butterworth, B., & Walsh, V. (2011). Neural basis of mathematical cognition. *Current Biology, 21*(16), R618–R621. https://doi.org/10.1016/j.cub.2011.07.005

Buttorff, C., Ruder, T., & Bauman, M. (2017). *Multiple chronic conditions in the United States.* RAND Corporation. https://www.rand.org/pubs/tools/TL221.html

Buultjens, M., Farouque, A., Karimi, L., Whitby, L., Milgrom, J., & Erbas, B. (2020). The contribution of group prenatal care to maternal psychological health outcomes: A systematic review. *Women and Birth.* https://doi.org/10.1016/j.wombi.2020.12.004

Buxton, O. M., Chang, A.-M., Spilsbury, J. C., Bos, T., Emsellem, H., & Knutson, K. L. (2015). Sleep in the modern family: Protective family routines for child and adolescent sleep. *Sleep Health, 1*(1), 15–27. https://doi.org/10.1016/j.sleh.2014.12.002

Byerley, B. M., & Haas, D. M. (2017). A systematic overview of the literature regarding group prenatal care for high-risk pregnant women. *BMC Pregnancy and Childbirth, 17*(1), 329. https://doi.org/10.1186/s12884-017-1522-2

Byers-Heinlein, K., & Lew-Williams, C. (2018). Language comprehension in monolingual and bilingual children. In E. M. Fernández & H. S. Cairns (Eds.), *The Handbook of Psycholinguistics* (pp. 516–535). Wiley.

Byers-Heinlein, K., Tsui, A. S. M., Bergmann, C., Black, A. K., Brown, A., Carbajal, M. J., Durrant, S., Fennell, C. T., Fiévet, A.-C., Frank, M. C., Gampe, A., Gervain, J., Gonzalez-Gomez, N., Hamlin, J. K., Havron, N., Hernik, M., Kerr, S., Killam, H., Klassen, K., ... Wermelinger, S. (2021). A multilab study of bilingual infants: Exploring the preference for infant-directed speech. *Advances in Methods and Practices in Psychological Science, 4*(1), 2515245920974622. https://doi.org/10.1177/2515245920974622

Bygdell, M., Kindblom, J. M., Celind, J., Nethander, M., & Ohlsson, C. (2018). Childhood BMI is inversely associated with pubertal timing in normal-weight but not overweight boys. *The American Journal of Clinical Nutrition, 108*(6), 1259–1263. https://doi.org/10.1093/ajcn/nqy201

Byhoff, E., Tripodis, Y., Freund, K. M., & Garg, A. (2019). Gender differences in social and behavioral determinants of health in aging adults. *Journal of General Internal Medicine, 34*(11), 2310–2312.

Byock, I. (2014). *The four things that matter most: A book about living.* Simon & Schuster.

Byrd, C. M. (2016). Does culturally relevant teaching work? An examination from student perspectives. *SAGE Open, 6*(3), 2158244016660744. https://doi.org/10.1177/2158244016660744

Byrnes, M. E. (2016). Grow old with me! Future directions of race, age, and place scholarship. *Sociology Compass, 10*(10), 906–917.

Cabell, S. Q., Justice, L. M., McGinty, A. S., DeCoster, J., & Forston, L. D. (2015). Teacher–child conversations in preschool classrooms: Contributions to children's vocabulary development. *Early Childhood Research Quarterly, 30*, 80–92.

Cabello, M., Miret, M., Ayuso-Mateos, J. L., Caballero, F. F., Chatterji, S., Tobiasz-Adamczyk, B., Haro, J. M., Koskinen, S., Leonardi, M., & Borges, G. (2020). Cross-national prevalence and factors associated with suicide ideation and attempts in older and young-and-middle age people. *Aging & Mental Health, 24*(9), 1533–1542. https://doi.org/10.1080/13607863.2019.1603284

Cabrera, N. J., & Tamis-LeMonda, C. S. (2013). *Handbook of father involvement: Multidisciplinary perspectives.* Routledge.

Cabrera, N. J., Volling, B. L., & Barr, R. (2018). Fathers are parents, too! Widening the lens on parenting for children's development. *Child Development Perspectives, 12*(3), 152–157. https://doi.org/10.1111/cdep.12275

Cacchione, P. Z. (2014). Sensory impairment: A new research imperative. *Journal of Gerontological Nursing, 40*(4), 3–5. https://doi.org/10.3928/00989134-20140306-01

Cacciatore, J., Rådestad, I., & Frederik Frøen, J. (2008). Effects of contact with stillborn babies on maternal anxiety and depression. *Birth, 35*(4), 313–320. https://doi.org/10.1111/j.1523-536X.2008.00258.x

Cacciatore, R., Korteniemi-Poikela, E., & Kaltiala, R. (2019). The steps of sexuality—A developmental, emotion-focused, child-centered model of sexual development and sexuality education from birth to adulthood. *International Journal of Sexual Health, 31*(3), 319–338. https://doi.org/10.1080/19317611.2019.1645783

Caceres, B. A., Frank, M. O., Jun, J., Martelly, M. T., Sadarangani, T., & de Sales, P. C. (2016). Family caregivers of patients with frontotemporal dementia: An integrative review. *International Journal of Nursing Studies, 55*, 71–84. https://doi.org/10.1016/j.ijnurstu.2015.10.016

Caceres, B. A., Travers, J., Primiano, J. E., Luscombe, R. E., & Dorsen, C. (2020). Provider and LGBT individuals' perspectives on LGBT issues in long-term care: A systematic review. *The Gerontologist, 60*(3), e169–e183. https://doi.org/10.1093/geront/gnz012

Cachero, P., Edgett, K., & Tsur, S. (2017, July 21). An untranslatable word for pure joy. *BBC.* https://www.bbc.com/culture/article/20170714-an-untranslatable-word-for-pure-joy

Cacioppo, J. T., Berntson, G. G., Bechara, A., Tranel, D., & Hawkley, L. C. (2011). *Could an aging brain contribute to subjective well-being? The value added by a social neuroscience perspective.* In A. Todorov, S. T. Fiske, & D. A. Prentice (Eds.), *Social neuroscience: Toward understanding the underpinnings of the social mind* (pp. 249–262). Oxford University Press. https://doi.org/10.1093/acprof:oso/9780195316872.003.0017

Cacioppo, S. (2019). Neuroimaging of love in the twenty-first century. In R. J. Sternberg & K. Sternberg (Eds.), *The new psychology of love* (pp. 64–83). Cambridge University Press.

Cacioppo, S., Bianchi-Demicheli, F., Hatfield, E., & Rapson, R. L. (2012). Social neuroscience of love. *Clinical Neuropsychiatry, 9*(1), 3–13.

Cacioppo, S., Couto, B., Bolmont, M., Sedeno, L., Frum, C., Lewis, J. W., Manes, F., Ibanez, A., & Cacioppo, J. T. (2013). Selective decision-making deficit in love following damage to the anterior insula. *Current Trends in Neurology, 7*, 15–19.

Cadely, H. S. E., Finnegan, V., Spears, E. C., & Kerpelman, J. L. (2020). Adolescents and sexual risk-taking: The interplay of constraining relationship beliefs, healthy sex attitudes, and romantic attachment insecurity. *Journal of Adolescence, 84*, 136–148.

Cadigan, J. M., Lee, C. M., & Larimer, M. E. (2019). Young adult mental health: A prospective examination of service utilization, perceived unmet service needs, attitudes, and barriers to service use. *Prevention Science, 20*(3), 366–376. https://doi.org/10.1007/s11121-018-0875-8

Cadoret, G., Bigras, N., Duval, S., Lemay, L., Tremblay, T., & Lemire, J. (2018). The mediating role of cognitive ability on the relationship between motor proficiency and early academic achievement in children. *Human Movement Science, 57*, 149–157. https://doi.org/10.1016/j.humov.2017.12.002

Caffey, A. L., & Dalecki, M. (2021). Evidence of residual cognitive deficits in young adults with a concussion history from adolescence. *Brain Research, 1768*, 147570.

Caffrey, C., Sengupta, M., & Melekin, A. (2021). *Residential care community resident characteristics: United States, 2018* (NCHS Data Brief No. 404). National Center for Health Statistics. https://doi.org/10.15620/cdc:103826.external icon

Cahalan, M., & Perna, L. (2015). *Indicators of higher education equity in the United States: 45 year trend report.* Pell Institute for the Study of Opportunity in Higher Education. https://eric.ed.gov/?id=ED555865

Cain, C. L., Wallace, S. P., & Ponce, N. A. (2018). Helpfulness, trust, and safety of neighborhoods: Social capital, household income, and self-reported health of older adults. *The Gerontologist, 58*(1), 4–14. https://doi.org/10.1093/geront/gnx145

Calasanti, T., & King, N. (2020). Beyond successful aging 2.0: Inequalities, ageism, and the case for normalizing old ages. *The Journals of Gerontology. Series B, Psychological Sciences and Social Sciences, 76*(9), 1817–1827. https://doi.org/10.1093/geronb/gbaa037

California Newsreel. (2008). News about people and communities appearing in the series. *Unnatural Causes.* https://unnaturalcauses.org/series_updates.php

Callaghan, B. L., Fields, A., Gee, D. G., Gabard-Durnam, L., Caldera, C., Humphreys, K. L., Goff, B., Flannery, J., Telzer, E. H., Shapiro, M., & Tottenham, N. (2020). Mind and gut: Associations between mood and gastrointestinal distress in children exposed to adversity. *Development and Psychopathology, 32*(1), 309–328. https://doi.org/10.1017/S0954579419000087

Callaghan, B. L., & Tottenham, N. (2016). The stress acceleration hypothesis: Effects of early-life adversity on emotion circuits and behavior. *Current Opinion in Behavioral Sciences, 7*(Supplement C), 76–81. https://doi.org/10.1016/j.cobeha.2015.11.018

Callaghan, T. (2020). The origins and development of a symbolic mind: The case of pictorial symbols. *Interchange, 51*(1), 53–64. https://doi.org/10.1007/s10780-020-09396-z

Callaghan, T., Moghtaderi, A., Lueck, J. A., Hotez, P., Strych, U., Dor, A., Fowler, E. F., & Motta, M. (2021). Correlates and disparities of intention to vaccinate against COVID-19. *Social Science & Medicine (1982), 272*, 113638. https://doi.org/10.1016/j.socscimed.2020.113638

Callaghan, T., Moll, H., Rakoczy, H., Warneken, F., Liszkowski, U., Behne, T., Tomasello, M., & Collins, W. A. (2011). *Early social cognition in three cultural contexts.* Wiley-Blackwell.

Callahan, M. (2018, July 12). "Autistic person" or "person with autism": Is there a right way to identify people? *News@Northeastern.* https://news.northeastern.edu/2018/07/12/unpacking-the-debate-over-person-first-vs-identity-first-language-in-the-autism-community/

Calogero, R. M., Tylka, T. L., Donnelly, L. C., McGetrick, A., & Leger, A. M. (2017). Trappings of femininity: A test of the "beauty as currency" hypothesis in shaping college women's gender activism. *Body Image, 21*, 66–70. http://www.sciencedirect.com/science/article/pii/S1740144516305034

Calvo, E., Madero-Cabib, I., & Staudinger, U. M. (2018). Retirement sequences of older Americans: Moderately destandardized and highly stratified across gender, class, and race. *The Gerontologist, 58*(6), 1166–1176. https://doi.org/10.1093/geront/gnx052

Calzo, J. P., Masyn, K. E., Austin, S. B., Jun, H.-J., & Corliss, H. L. (2017). Developmental latent patterns of identification as mostly heterosexual vs. lesbian, gay, and bisexual. *Journal of Research on Adolescence, 27*(1), 246–253. https://doi.org/10.1111/jora.12266

Camandola, S., & Mattson, M. P. (2017). Brain metabolism in health, aging, and neurodegeneration. *The EMBO Journal, 36*(11), 1474–1492

Camerini, A. L., Marciano, L., Carrara, A., & Schulz, P. J. (2020). Cyberbullying perpetration and victimization among children and adolescents: A systematic review of longitudinal studies. *Telematics and Informatics, 49*, 101362.

Cameron, C. E., Cottone, E. A., Murrah, W. M., & Grissmer, D. W. (2016). How are motor skills linked to children's school performance and academic achievement? *Child Development Perspectives, 10*(2), 93–98.

Cameron, E., Ward, P., Mandville-Anstey, S. A., & Coombs, A. (2019). The female aging body: A systematic review of female perspectives on aging, health, and body image. *Journal of Women & Aging, 31*(1), 3–17. https://doi.org/10.1080/08952841.2018.1449586

Cameron, L., & Tenenbaum, H. R. (2021). Lessons from developmental science to mitigate the effects of the COVID-19 restrictions on social development. *Group Processes & Intergroup Relations, 24*(2), 231–236. https://doi.org/10.1177/1368430220984236

Cameron, N. (2015). Can maturity indicators be used to estimate chronological age in children? *Annals of Human Biology, 42*(4), 302–307.

Camerota, M., & Willoughby, M. T. (2021). Applying interdisciplinary frameworks to study prenatal influences on child development. *Child Development Perspectives, 15*(1), 24–30.

Camodeca, M., & Coppola, G. (2016). Bullying, empathic concern, and internalization of rules among preschool children: The role of emotion understanding. *International Journal of Behavioral Development, 40*(5), 459–465.

Campbell, A., Shirley, L., & Caygill, L. (2002). Sex-typed preferences in three domains: Do two-year-olds need cognitive variables? *British Journal of Psychology, 93*(2), 203–217. https://doi.org/10.1348/000712602162544

Campisi, S. C., Humayun, K. N., Rizvi, A., Lou, W., Söder, O., & Bhutta, Z. A. (2020). Later puberty onset among chronically undernourished adolescents living in a Karachi slum, Pakistan. *Acta Paediatrica, 109*(5), 1019–1025. https://doi.org/10.1111/apa.15053

Camras, L. A. (2019). Facial expressions across the life span. In V. LoBue, K. Pérez-Edgar, & K. A. Buss (Eds.), *Handbook of emotional development* (pp. 83–103). Springer International Publishing. https://doi.org/10.1007/978-3-030-17332-6_5

Can Denmark's generous childcare system survive? (2016, December 30). *BBC News.* https://www.bbc.com/news/business-38254474

Cantlon, J. F. (2020). The balance of rigor and reality in developmental neuroscience. *NeuroImage, 216*, 116464. https://doi.org/10.1016/j.neuroimage.2019.116464

Cantor, N. L. (2018). On avoiding deep dementia. *Hastings Center Report, 48*(4), 15–24.

Cantu, P. A., Hayward, M. D., Hummer, R. A., & Chiu, C.-T. (2013). New estimates of racial/ethnic differences in life expectancy with chronic morbidity and functional loss: Evidence from the National Health Interview Survey. *Journal of Cross-Cultural Gerontology, 28*(3), 283–297. https://doi.org/10.1007/s10823-013-9206-5

Cantu, P. A., Sheehan, C. M., Sasson, I., & Hayward, M. D. (2021). Increasing education-based disparities in healthy life expectancy among U.S. Non-Hispanic Whites, 2000–2010. *The Journals of Gerontology Series B: Psychological Sciences and Social Sciences, 76*(2), 319–329. https://doi.org/10.1093/geronb/gbz145

Canudas-Romo, V., DuGoff, E., Wu, A. W., Ahmed, S., & Anderson, G. (2016). Life expectancy in 2040: What do clinical experts expect? *North American Actuarial Journal, 20*(3), 276–285. https://doi.org/10.1080/10920277.2016.1179123

Cao, M., Huang, H., & He, Y. (2017). Developmental connectomics from infancy through early childhood. *Trends in Neurosciences, 40*(8), 494–506. https://doi.org/10.1016/j.tins.2017.06.003

Capon, N., & Kuhn, D. (1982). Can consumers calculate best buys? *Journal of Consumer Research, 8*(4), 449–453. http://www.jstor.org/stable/2489032

Caprio, S., Santoro, N., & Weiss, R. (2020). Childhood obesity and the associated rise in cardiometabolic complications. *Nature Metabolism, 2*(3), 223–232. https://doi.org/10.1038/s42255-020-0183-z

Caputi, T. L., Shover, C. L., & Watson, R. J. (2020). Physical and sexual violence among gay, lesbian, bisexual, and questioning adolescents. *JAMA Pediatrics, 174*(8), 791–793. https://doi.org/10.1001/jamapediatrics.2019.6291

Caputo, J. (2019). Crowded nests: Parent–adult child coresidence transitions and parental mental health following the Great Recession. *Journal of Health and Social Behavior, 60*(2), 204–221. https://doi.org/10.1177/0022146519849113

Card, D., & Giuliano, L. (2016). Can tracking raise the test scores of high-ability minority students? *American Economic Review, 106*(10), 2783–2816. https://doi.org/10.1257/aer.20150484

Cardel, M. I., Atkinson, M. A., Taveras, E. M., Holm, J.-C., & Kelly, A. S. (2020). Obesity treatment among adolescents: A review of current evidence and future directions. *JAMA Pediatrics, 174*(6), 609–617. https://doi.org/10.1001/jamapediatrics.2020.0085

Cardenas, A., Rifas-Shiman, S. L., Agha, G., Hivert, M.-F., Litonjua, A. A., DeMeo, D. L., Lin, X., Amarasiriwardena, C. J., Oken, E., Gillman, M. W., & Baccarelli, A. A. (2017). Persistent DNA methylation changes associated with prenatal mercury exposure and cognitive performance during childhood. *Scientific Reports, 7*(1), 288. https://doi.org/10.1038/s41598-017-00384-5

Carey, S. (1978). The child as word learner. Linguistic theory and psychological reality In M. Halle, J. Bresnan, & G. A. Miller (Eds.), *Linguistic theory and psychological reality* (pp. 264–293). MIT Press.

Carey, S. (2010). Beyond fast mapping. *Language Learning and Development: The Official Journal of the Society for Language Development, 6*(3), 184–205. https://doi.org/10.1080/15475441.2010.484379

Carey, S., & Bartlett, E. (1978). Acquiring a single new word. *Papers and Reports on Child Language Development, 15*, 17–29.

Carey, S., Zaitchik, D., & Bascandziev, I. (2015). Theories of development: In dialog with Jean Piaget. *Developmental Review, 38*, 36–54. https://doi.org/10.1016/j.dr.2015.07.003

Carey, T. L. (2019, May 9). *DNA tests stand on shaky ground to define Native American identity.* National Human Genome Research Institute.

Carlson, B. (2020). Love and hate at the cultural interface: Indigenous Australians and dating apps. *Journal of Sociology, 56*(2), 133–150. https://doi.org/10.1177/1440783319833181

Carlson, D. L., Miller, A. J., Sassler, S., & Hanson, S. (2016). The gendered division of housework and couples' sexual relationships: A reexamination. *Journal of Marriage and Family, 78*(4), 975–995.

Carlson, F. M. (2011). Rough play: One of the most challenging behaviors. *Young Children, 66*(4), 18.

Carlson, M. C., Erickson, K. I., Kramer, A. F., Voss, M. W., Bolea, N., Mielke, M., McGill, S., Rebok, G. W., Seeman, T., & Fried, L. P. (2009). Evidence for neurocognitive plasticity in at-risk older adults: The experience corps program. *The Journals of Gerontology: Series A, 64A*(12), 1275–1282. https://doi.org/10.1093/gerona/glp117

Carlson, M. C., Saczynski, J. S., Rebok, G. W., Seeman, T., Glass, T. A., McGill, S., Tielsch, J., Frick, K. D., Hill, J., & Fried, L. P. (2008). Exploring the Effects of an "Everyday" Activity Program on Executive Function and Memory in Older Adults: Experience Corps®. *The Gerontologist, 48*(6), 793–801. https://doi.org/10.1093/geront/48.6.793

Carmel, S. (2019). Health and well-being in late life: Gender differences worldwide. *Frontiers in Medicine, 6*, 218. https://doi.org/10.3389/fmed.2019.00218

Carnemolla, P., & Bridge, C. (2019). Housing design and community care: How home modifications reduce care needs of older people and people with disability. *International Journal of Environmental Research and Public Health, 16*(11), 1951. https://doi.org/10.3390/ijerph16111951

Carnevale, A. P., Hanson, A. R., & Gulish, A. (2013). *Failure to launch: Structural shift and the new lost generation.* Georgetown University Center on Education and the Workforce. http://eric.ed.gov/?id=ED558185

Carnevale, A. P., Ridley, N., Cheah, B., Strohl, J., & Campbell, K. P. (2019). *Upskilling and downsizing in American manufacturing.* Georgetown University Center on Education and the Workforce.

Carnevale, A. P., Smith, N., & Gulish, A. (2018a). *Women can't win: Despite making educational gains and pursuing high wage majors, women still earn less than men.* Georgetown University Center on Education and the Workforce. https://cew.georgetown.edu/cew-reports/genderwagegap/

Carnevale, A. P., Strohl, J., Gulish, A., Van Der Werf, M., & Peltier Campbell, K. (2019). *The unequal race for good jobs: How Whites made outsized gains in education and good jobs compared to Blacks and Latinos.* Georgetown University Center on Education and the Workforce.

Carnevale, A. P., Strohl, J., Ridley, N., & Gulish, A. (2018b). *Three educational pathways to good jobs: High school, middle skills, and bachelor's degree.* Georgetown University Center on Education and the Workforce.

Carney, M. T., Fujiwara, J., Emmert, B. E., Liberman, T. A., & Paris, B. (2016). Elder orphans hiding in plain sight: A growing vulnerable population. *Current Gerontology and Geriatrics Research, 2016*, 4723250. https://doi.org/10.1155/2016/4723250

Carnoy, M., & Rothstein, R. (2013). *What do international tests really show about US student performance?* Economic Policy Institute.

Carolan, M. T., Bagherinia, G., Juhari, R., Himelright, J., & Mouton-Sanders, M. (2000). Contemporary Muslim families: Research and practice. *Contemporary Family Therapy, 22*(1), 67–79.

Carone, N., Lingiardi, V., Tanzilli, A., Bos, H. M. W., & Baiocco, R. (2020). Gender development in children with gay, lesbian, and heterosexual parents: Associations with family type and child gender. *Journal of Developmental & Behavioral Pediatrics, 41*(1), 38–47. https://doi.org/10.1097/DBP.0000000000000726

Carone, N., Rothblum, E. D., Bos, H. M., Gartrell, N. K., & Herman, J. L. (2020). Demographics and health outcomes in a US probability sample of transgender parents. *Journal of Family Psychology: JFP: Journal of the Division of Family Psychology of the American Psychological Association (Division 43), 35*(1), 57–68.

Carr, D. (2019). *Golden years? Social inequality in later life.* Russell Sage Foundation.

Carr, D. (2020). Mental health of older widows and widowers: Which coping strategies are most protective? *Aging & Mental Health, 24*(2), 291–299. https://doi.org/10.1080/13607863.2018.1531381

Carr, D., Freedman, V. A., Cornman, J. C., & Schwarz, N. (2014). Happy marriage, happy life? Marital quality and subjective well-being in later life. *Journal of Marriage and Family, 76*(5), 930–948.

Carr, D., Kalousova, L., Lin, K., & Burgard, S. (2021). Occupational differences in advance care planning: Are medical professionals more likely to plan? *Social Science & Medicine, 272*, 113730.

Carr, D., & Mouzon, D. M. (2018). Intimate partner relationships and health. In C. D. Ryff & R. F. Krueger (Eds.), *The Oxford handbook of integrative health science* (pp. 129–142). Oxford Library of Psychology.

Carr, D., & Utz, R. L. (2020). Families in later life: A decade in review. *Journal of Marriage and Family, 82*(1), 346–363. https://doi.org/10.1111/jomf.12609

Carr, D. C., Kail, B. L., Matz-Costa, C., & Shavit, Y. Z. (2018). Does becoming a volunteer attenuate loneliness among recently widowed older adults? *The Journals of Gerontology: Series B, 73*(3), 501–510. https://doi.org/10.1093/geronb/gbx092

Carroll, J. E., Mahrer, N. E., Shalowitz, M., Ramey, S., & Dunkel Schetter, C. (2020). Prenatal maternal stress prospectively relates to shorter child buccal cell telomere length. *Psychoneuroendocrinology, 121*, 104841. https://doi.org/10.1016/j.psyneuen.2020.104841

Carroll, J. M., Holliman, A. J., Weir, F., & Baroody, A. E. (2019). Literacy interest, home literacy environment and emergent literacy skills in preschoolers. *Journal of Research in Reading, 42*(1), 150–161.

Carroll, Y. I., Eichwald, J., Scinicariello, F., Hoffman, H. J., Deitchman, S., Radke, M. S., Themann, C. L., & Breysse, P. (2017). Vital signs: Noise-induced hearing loss among adults — United States 2011–2012. *Morbidity and Mortality Weekly Report, 66*(5), 139–144.

Carskadon, M. A. (2011). Sleep in adolescents: The perfect storm. *Pediatric Clinics of North America, 58*(3), 637.

Carskadon, M. A., & Barker, D. H. (2020). Editorial perspective: Adolescents' fragile sleep—shining light on a time of risk to mental health. *Journal of Child Psychology and Psychiatry, 61*(10), 1058–1060.

Carstensen, L. L., & DeLiema, M. (2018). The positivity effect: A negativity bias in youth fades with age. *Current Opinion in Behavioral Sciences, 19*, 7–12. https://doi.org/10.1016/j.cobeha.2017.07.009

Carstensen, L. L., Isaacowitz, D. M., & Charles, S. T. (1999). Taking time seriously: A theory of socioemotional selectivity. *American Psychologist, 54*(3), 165.

Carstensen, L. L., Shavit, Y. Z., & Barnes, J. T. (2020). Age advantages in emotional experience persist even under threat from the COVID-19 pandemic. *Psychological Science, 31*(11), 1374–1385. https://doi.org/10.1177/0956797620967261

Carswell, K. L., & Finkel, E. J. (2018). Can you get the magic back? The moderating effect of passion decay beliefs on relationship commitment. *Journal of Personality and Social Psychology, 115*(6), 1002–1033. https://doi.org/10.1037/pspi0000147

Carter, R., Halawah, A., & Trinh, S. L. (2018a). Peer exclusion during the pubertal transition: The role of social competence. *Journal of Youth and Adolescence, 47*(1), 121–134. https://doi.org/10.1007/s10964-017-0682-8

Carter, R., Mustafaa, F. N., & Leath, S. (2018b). Teachers' expectations of girls' classroom performance and behavior: Effects of girls' race and pubertal timing. *The Journal of Early Adolescence, 38*(7), 885–907. https://doi.org/10.1177/0272431617699947

Carter, R. L. (2018). Life-in-death: Raising dead sons in New Orleans. *Ethnos, 83*(4), 683–705. https://doi.org/10.1080/00141844.2017.1319874

Cartwright, B., Edwards, P. R., & Wang, Q. (2011). Jobs and industry gender segregation: NAICs categories and EEO-1 job groups. *Monthly Labor Review, 134*, 37.

Carvalho, M. E. S., de Miranda Justo, J. M. R., Gratier, M., & da Silva, H. M. F. R. (2019). The impact of maternal voice on the fetus: A systematic review. *Current Women's Health Reviews, 15*(3), 196–206. https://doi.org/10.2174/1573404814666181026094419

Casals, P., & Kahn, E. (1974). *Joys and sorrows.* Simon & Schuster.

Casas, F., & González-Carrasco, M. (2019). Subjective well-being decreasing with age: New research on children over 8. *Child Development, 90*(2), 375–394.

Case, A., & Deaton, A. (2015). Rising morbidity and mortality in midlife among white non-Hispanic Americans in the 21st century. *Proceedings of the National Academy of Sciences, 112*(49), 15078–15083.

Case, A., & Deaton, A. (2021). Life expectancy in adulthood is falling for those without a BA degree, but as educational gaps have widened, racial gaps have narrowed. *Proceedings of the National Academy of Sciences, 118*(11), e2024777118. https://doi.org/10.1073/pnas.2024777118

Casey, B. J. (2015). Beyond simple models of self-control to circuit-based accounts of adolescent behavior. *Annual Review of Psychology, 66*(1), 295–319. https://doi.org/10.1146/annurev-psych-010814-015156

Casey, B. J., Heller, A. S., Gee, D. G., & Cohen, A. O. (2019). Development of the emotional brain. *Neuroscience Letters, 693*, 29–34. https://doi.org/10.1016/j.neulet.2017.11.055

Cashdollar, S. E. (2018). Neither accidental nor intended: Pregnancy as an adolescent identity project among Hispanic teenage mothers in Doña Ana County, New Mexico. *Journal of Adolescent Research, 33*(5), 598–622. https://doi.org/10.1177/0743558417712014

Casillas, M., Bobb, S. C., & Clark, E. V. (2016). Turn taking, timing, and planning in early language acquisition. *Journal of Child Language, 43*, 1310–1337.

Caspari, R., & Lee, S.-H. (2004). Older age becomes common late in human evolution. *Proceedings of the National Academy of Sciences, 101*(30), 10895–10900. https://doi.org/10.1073/pnas.0402857101

Cassidy, B. S., Hughes, C., & Krendl, A. C. (2020). A stronger relationship between reward responsivity and trustworthiness evaluations emerges in healthy aging. *Aging, Neuropsychology, and Cognition, 28*(5), 669–686. https://doi.org/10.1080/13825585.2020.1809630

Cassidy, B. S., Lee, E. J., & Krendl, A. C. (2016). Age and executive ability impact the neural correlates of race perception. *Social Cognitive and Affective Neuroscience, 11*(11), 1752–1761. https://doi.org/10.1093/scan/nsw081

Castles, A., Rastle, K., & Nation, K. (2018). Ending the reading wars: Reading acquisition from novice to expert. *Psychological Science in the Public Interest, 19*(1), 5–51. https://doi.org/10.1177/1529100618772271

Castro, J. (2020). Sister Norma Pimentel is on the 2020 TIME 100 List. *Time Magazine.* https://time.com/collection/100-most-influential-people-2020/5888284/sister-norma-pimentel/

Castro-Ramirez, F., Al-Suwaidi, M., Garcia, P., Rankin, O., Ricard, J. R., & Nock, M. K. (2021). Racism and poverty are barriers to the treatment of youth mental health concerns. *Journal of Clinical Child & Adolescent Psychology, 50*(4), 534–546. https://doi.org/10.1080/15374416.2021.1941058

Catalano, P. M., & Shankar, K. (2017). Obesity and pregnancy: Mechanisms of short term and long term adverse consequences for mother and child. *BMJ, 356.* https://doi.org/10.1136/bmj.j1

Catillon, M., Cutler, D., & Getzen, T. (2018). *Two hundred years of health and medical care: The importance of medical care for life expectancy gains* (No. w25330). National Bureau of Economic Research. https://doi.org/10.3386/w25330

Cattane, N., Rossi, R., Lanfredi, M., & Cattaneo, A. (2017). Borderline personality disorder and childhood trauma: Exploring the affected biological systems and mechanisms. *BMC Psychiatry, 17*(1), 1–14.

Cattell, R. B. (1971). *Abilities: Their structure, growth, and action.* Houghton Mifflin.

Caughlin, J. P., Huston, T. L., & Wehrman, E. C. (2018). The affective structure of marriage over time. In A. L. Vangelisti & D. Perlman (Eds.), *The Cambridge handbook of personal relationships* (pp. 90–105). Cambridge University Press. https://doi.org/10.1017/9781316417867.009

Cava, M.-J., Martínez-Ferrer, B., Buelga, S., & Carrascosa, L. (2020). Sexist attitudes, romantic myths, and offline dating violence as predictors of cyber dating violence perpetration in adolescents. *Computers in Human Behavior, 111*, 106449. https://doi.org/10.1016/j.chb.2020.106449

Cavalli, G., & Heard, E. (2019). Advances in epigenetics link genetics to the environment and disease. *Nature, 571*(7766), 489–499. https://doi.org/10.1038/s41586-019-1411-0

Cavan, R. S., Burgess, E. W., Havighurst, R. J., & Goldhamer, H. (1949). *Personal adjustment in old age.* Science Research Associates.

Cavanagh, S. E., & Fomby, P. (2019). Family instability in the lives of American children. *Annual Review of Sociology, 45*(1), 493–513. https://doi.org/10.1146/annurev-soc-073018-022633

Cavanaugh, A. M., Stein, G. L., Supple, A. J., Gonzalez, L. M., & Kiang, L. (2018). Protective and promotive effects of Latino early adolescents' cultural assets against multiple types of discrimination. *Journal of Research on Adolescence, 28*(2), 310–326. https://doi.org/10.1111/jora.12331

Cavazzana, A., Röhrborn, A., Garthus-Niegel, S., Larsson, M., Hummel, T., & Croy, I. (2018). Sensory-specific impairment among older people. An investigation using both sensory thresholds and subjective measures across the five senses. *PLoS ONE, 13*(8), e0202969. https://doi.org/10.1371/journal.pone.0202969

Cave, L., Cooper, M. N., Zubrick, S. R., & Shepherd, C. C. (2020). Racial discrimination and child and adolescent health in longitudinal studies: A systematic review. *Social Science & Medicine, 250*, 112864.

Caye, A., Petresco, S., de Barros, A. J. D., Bressan, R. A., Gadelha, A., Gonçalves, H., & Rohde, L. A. (2020). Relative age and attention-deficit/hyperactivity disorder: Data from three epidemiological cohorts and a meta-analysis. *Journal of the American Academy of Child & Adolescent Psychiatry, 59*(8), 990–997.

Ceccato, I., Lecce, S., Cavallini, E., van Vugt, F. T., & Ruffman, T. (2019). Motivation and social-cognitive abilities in older adults: Convergent evidence from self-report measures and cardiovascular reactivity. *PLOS ONE, 14*(7), e0218785. https://doi.org/10.1371/journal.pone.0218785

Ceci, S. J., & Bruck, M. (1993). Suggestibility of the child witness: A historical review and synthesis. *Psychological Bulletin,* 113(3), 403.

Cecil, C. (2018, October 22). Take a walk. Join a movement. *Medium.* https://medium.com/it-starts-with-a-step-walking-for-a-better-world/take-a-walk-join-a-movement-62ee60f68336

Center to Advance Palliative Care. (2020). *The case for community-based palliative care: A new paradigm for improving serious illness care.*

Centers for Disease Control and Prevention (CDC). (2020). HIV surveillance report, 2018 (Updated; Vol. 31). http://www.cdc.gov/hiv/library/reports/hiv-surveillance.html

Centers for Disease Control and Prevention (CDC). (2020, July 28). *2018 sexually transmitted disease surveillance.* https://www.cdc.gov/std/stats18/default.htm

Centers for Disease Control and Prevention (CDC). (2021). *Demographic trends of Covid-19 cases and deaths in the US reported to CDC* (Covid Data Tracker).

Centers for Disease Control and Prevention (CDC). (2021). *Health United States, 2019* (table 9). https://www.cdc.gov/nchs/data/hus/2019/009-508.pdf

Centers for Disease Control and Prevention (CDC), National Center for Health Statistics. (2021). *Multiple cause of death 2018–2020 on CDC WONDER Online Database* [Data released in 2021 from the Multiple Cause of Death Files, 2018–2020, as compiled from data provided by the 57 vital statistics jurisdictions through the Vital Statistics Cooperative Program]. http://wonder.cdc.gov/mcd-icd10-expanded.html

Centers for Disease Control and Prevention (CDC), National Center for Health Statistics. (2021). *Underlying cause of death 1999–2020 on CDC WONDER Online Database, released in 2021.* http://wonder.cdc.gov/natality-expanded-current.html

Centers for Disease Control and Prevention (CDC), National Center for Health Statistics. (2021). *Underlying cause of death, 2019.* http://wonder.cdc.gov/ucd-icd10.html

Cepa, K., & Furstenberg, F. F. (2021). Reaching adulthood: Persistent beliefs about the importance and timing of adult milestones. *Journal of Family Issues, 42*(1), 27–57. https://doi.org/10.1177/0192513X20918612

Cerino, E. S., Hooker, K., Settersten, R. A., Jr., Odden, M. C., & Stawski, R. S. (2020). Daily linkages among high and low arousal affect and subjective cognitive complaints. *Aging & Mental Health, 25*(5), 844–855. https://doi.org/10.1080/13607863.2020.1711863

Cerino, E. S., Hooker, K., Stawski, R. S., & McClelland, M. (2019). A new brief measure of executive function: Adapting the head-toes-knees-shoulders task to older adults. *The Gerontologist, 59*(4), e258–e267.

Cervantes, M. V., & Sherman, J. (2021). Falling for the ones that were abusive: Cycles of violence in low-income women's intimate relationships. *Journal of Interpersonal Violence, 36*(13–14), NP7567–NP7595. https://doi.org/10.1177/0886260519829771

Cha, Y. (2010). Reinforcing separate spheres: The effect of spousal overwork on men's and women's employment in dual-earner households. *American Sociological Review, 75*(2), 303–329. https://doi.org/10.1177/0003122410365307

Chad, J. A. (2020). The first ejaculation: A male pubertal milestone comparable to menarche? *The Journal of Sex Research, 57*(2), 213–221. https://doi.org/10.1080/00224499.2018.1543643

Chad-Friedman, E., Botdorf, M., Riggins, T., & Dougherty, L. R. (2021). Early childhood cumulative risk is associated with decreased global brain measures, cortical thickness, and cognitive functioning in school-age children. *Developmental Psychobiology, 63*(2), 192–205. https://doi.org/10.1002/dev.21956

Chae, D. H., Wang, Y., Martz, C. D., Slopen, N., Yip, T., Adler, N. E., & Epel, E. S. (2020). Racial discrimination and telomere shortening among African Americans: The Coronary Artery Risk Development in Young Adults (CARDIA) Study. *Health Psychology, 39*(3), 209.

Chainey, C., & Burke, K. (2021). Emerging adult well-being: Associations with adverse childhood experiences, parenting practices and the parent-adolescent relationship. *Australian Psychologist, 56*(3), 217–232. https://doi.org/10.1080/00050067.2021.1893596

Chakravarti, D., LaBella, K. A., & DePinho, R. A. (2021). Telomeres: History, health, and hallmarks of aging. *Cell, 184*(2), 306–322. https://doi.org/10.1016/j.cell.2020.12.028

Chalise, U., Pradhan, A., Lama, C. P., Panta, P. P., & Dhungel, S. (2018). Age at menarche among the school going children of Jorpati, Kathmandu. *Journal of College of Medical Sciences-Nepal, 14*(3), 142–146. https://doi.org/10.3126/jcmsn.v14i3.19916

Chamie, J. (2018, April 12). World agrees: Adultery, while prevalent, is wrong—analysis. *Eurasia Review.* https://www.eurasiareview.com/12042018-world-agrees-adultery-while-prevalent-is-wrong-analysis/

Chan, D., Shafto, M., Kievit, R., Matthews, F., Spink, M., Valenzuela, M., & Henson, R. (2018). Lifestyle activities in mid-life contribute to cognitive reserve in late-life, independent of education, occupation and late-life activities. *Neurobiology of Aging, 70*, 180–183. https://doi.org/10.1016/j.neurobiolaging.2018.06.012

Chan, M., Tsai, K. M., & Fuligni, A. J. (2015). Changes in religiosity across the transition to young adulthood. *Journal of Youth and Adolescence, 44*(8), 1555–1566.

Chan, R. C., & Mak, W. W. (2020). Empowerment for civic engagement and well-being in emerging adulthood: Evidence from cross-regional and cross-lagged analyses. *Social Science & Medicine, 244*, 112703.

Chan Tack, A. M., & Small, M. L. (2017). Making friends in violent neighborhoods: Strategies among elementary school children. *Sociological Science, 4*, 224–248.

Chandra-Mouli, V., Ferguson, B. J., Plesons, M., Paul, M., Chalasani, S., Amin, A., Pallitto, C., Sommers, M., Avila, R., Eceéce Biaukula, K. V., Husain, S., Janušonytė, E., Mukherji, A., Nergiz, A. I., Phaladi, G., Porter, C., Sauvarin, J., Camacho-Huber, A. V., Mehra, S., … Engel, D. M. C. (2019). The political, research, programmatic, and social responses to adolescent sexual and reproductive health and rights in the 25 years since the international conference on population and development. *Journal of Adolescent Health, 65*(6, Supplement), S16–S40. https://doi.org/10.1016/j.jadohealth.2019.09.011

Chandra-Mouli, V., & Patel, S. V. (2020). Mapping the knowledge and understanding of menarche, menstrual hygiene and menstrual health among adolescent girls in low- and middle-income countries. In C. Bobel, I. T. Winkler, B. Fahs, K. A. Hasson, E. A. Kissling, & T.-A. Roberts (Eds.), *The Palgrave handbook of critical menstruation studies* (pp. 609–636). Palgrave.

Chang, A. Y., Skirbekk, V. F., Tyrovolas, S., Kassebaum, N. J., & Dieleman, J. L. (2019). Measuring population ageing: an analysis of the Global Burden of Disease Study 2017. *The Lancet Public Health, 4*(3), e159–e167.

Chang, C.-T., Shunmugam, P., Aziz, N. A. A., Razak, N. S. A., Johari, N., Mohamad, N., Ghazali, R., Rajagam, H., & Hss, A.-S. (2020). Exploring Malaysian mothers' plans on sleeping arrangement with their newborn. *Journal of Paediatrics and Child Health, 56*(3), 426–431. https://doi.org/10.1111/jpc.14646

Chang, H., & Shaw, D. S. (2016). The emergence of parent-child coercive processes in toddlerhood. Child Psychiatry and Human Development, 47(2), 226–235. https://doi.org/10.1007/s10578-015-0559-6

Chang, M., Jonsson, P. V., Snaedal, J., Bjornsson, S., Saczynski, J. S., Aspelund, T., Eiriksdottir, G., Jonsdottir, M. K., Lopez, O. L., Harris, T. B., Gudnason, V., & Launer, L. J. (2010). The effect of midlife physical activity on cognitive function among older adults: AGES—Reykjavik study. *The Journals of Gerontology: Series A, 65A*(12), 1369–1374. https://doi.org/10.1093/gerona/glq152

Chao, H.-C. (2018). Association of picky eating with growth, nutritional status, development, physical activity, and health in preschool children. *Frontiers in Pediatrics, 6*, 22. https://doi.org/10.3389/fped.2018.00022

Chapko, D., McCormack, R., Black, C., Staff, R., & Murray, A. (2018). Life-course determinants of cognitive reserve (CR) in cognitive aging and dementia—A systematic literature review. *Aging & Mental Health, 22*(8), 921–932. https://doi.org/10.1080/13607863.2017.1348471

Chaplot, P., Cooper, D., Johnstone, R., & Karandjeff, K. (2015). *Beyond financial aid: How colleges can strengthen the financial stability of low-income students and improve student outcomes.* http://www.luminafoundation.org/files/resources/beyond-financial-aid.pdf

Chapman, A. L. (2019). Borderline personality disorder and emotion dysregulation. *Development and Psychopathology, 31*(3), 1143–1156.

Chapman, T. W., & Hill, R. A. (2020). Myelin plasticity in adulthood and aging. *Neuroscience Letters, 715*, 134645. https://doi.org/10.1016/j.neulet.2019.134645

Chapman-Hilliard, C., Hunter, E., Adams-Bass, V., Mbilishaka, A., Jones, B., Holmes, E., & Holman, A. C. (2020). Racial identity and historical narratives in the civic engagement of Black emerging adults. *Journal of Diversity in Higher Education.*

Chapple, H. S., Bouton, B. L., Chow, A. Y. M., Gilbert, K. R., Kosminsky, P., Moore, J., & Whiting, P. P. (2017).

The body of knowledge in thanatology: An outline. *Death Studies, 41*(2), 118–125.

Charbonneau, A., Lachance-Grzela, M., & Bouchard, G. (2020). Threshold levels for disorder, inequity in household labor, and frustration with the partner among emerging adult couples: A dyadic examination. *Journal of Family Issues,* 0192513X20918616. https://doi.org/10.1177/0192513X20918616

Charles, S. T. (2010). Strength and vulnerability integration: A model of emotional well-being across adulthood. *Psychological Bulletin, 136*(6), 1068.

Charles, S., & Carstensen, L. L. (2010). Social and emotional aging. *Annual Review of Psychology, 61,* 383–409. https://doi.org/10.1146/annurev.psych.093008.100448

Charlesworth, T. E. S., & Banaji, M. R. (2021). Patterns of implicit and explicit stereotypes III: Long-term change in gender stereotypes. *Social Psychological and Personality Science,* 1948550620988425. https://doi.org/10.1177/1948550620988425

Charter, R., Ussher, J., Perz, J., & Robinson, K. (2021). Negotiating mental health amongst transgender parents in Australia. *International Journal of Transgender Health,* 1–13. https://doi.org/10.1080/26895269.2021.1875951

Chase, P. A., Hilliard, L. J., Geldhof, G. J., Warren, D. J., & Lerner, R. M. (2014). Academic achievement in the high school years: The changing role of school engagement. *Journal of Youth and Adolescence, 43*(6), 884–896.

Chasteen, A. L., Horhota, M., & Crumley-Branyon, J. J. (2020). Overlooked and underestimated: Experiences of ageism in young, middle-aged, and older adults. *The Journals of Gerontology: Series B, 76*(7), 1323–1328. https://doi.org/10.1093/geronb/gbaa043

Chater, N., McCauley, S. M., & Christiansen, M. H. (2016). Language as skill: Intertwining comprehension and production. *Journal of Memory and Language, 89,* 244–254.

Chatterjee, R., & Davis, R. (2017, December 20). How racism may cause black mothers to suffer the death of their infants. *Morning Edition.* National Public Radio.

Chatters, L. M., Taylor, R. J., & Jayakody, R. (1994). Fictive kinship relations in black extended families. *Journal of Comparative Family Studies, 25*(3), 297–312. https://doi.org/10.3138/jcfs.25.3.297

Chaudhuri, S. (2015). Excess female infant mortality and the gender gap in infant care in Bihar, India. *Feminist Economics, 21*(2), 131–161. https://doi.org/10.1080/13545701.2014.999007

Chawanpaiboon, S., Vogel, J. P., Moller, A.-B., Lumbiganon, P., Petzold, M., Hogan, D., Landoulsi, S., Jampathong, N., Kongwattanakul, K., Laopaiboon, M., Lewis, C., Rattanakanokchai, S., Teng, D. N., Thinkhamrop, J., Watananirun, K., Zhang, J., Zhou, W., & Gülmezoglu, A. M. (2019). Global, regional, and national estimates of levels of preterm birth in 2014: A systematic review and modelling analysis. *The Lancet Global Health, 7*(1), e37–e46. https://doi.org/10.1016/S2214-109X(18)30451-0

Chea, N., & Asefa, A. (2018). Prelacteal feeding and associated factors among newborns in rural Sidama, south Ethiopia: A community based cross-sectional survey. *International Breastfeeding Journal, 13*(1), 7. https://doi.org/10.1186/s13006-018-0149-x

Cheadle, A. C. D., Ramos, I. F., & Schetter, C. D. (2020). Stress and resilience in pregnancy. In *The Wiley encyclopedia of health psychology* (pp. 717–723). John Wiley & Sons. https://doi.org/10.1002/9781119057840.ch124

Cheadle, L., Rivera, S. A., Phelps, J. S., Ennis, K. A., Stevens, B., Burkly, L. C., Lee, W.-C. A., & Greenberg, M. E. (2020). Sensory experience engages microglia to shape neural connectivity through a non-phagocytic mechanism. *Neuron, 108*(3), 451–468.e9. https://doi.org/10.1016/j.neuron.2020.08.002

Chen, B., Vansteenkiste, M., Beyers, W., Soenens, B., & Van Petegem, S. (2013). Autonomy in family decision making for Chinese adolescents: Disentangling the dual meaning of autonomy. *Journal of Cross-Cultural Psychology, 44*(7), 1184–1209. https://doi.org/10.1177/0022022113480038

Chen, C., Chen, Q., Nie, B., Zhang, H., Zhai, H., Zhao, L., Xia, P., Lu, Y., & Wang, N. (2020). Trends in bone mineral density, osteoporosis, and osteopenia among U.S.

adults with prediabetes, 2005–2014. *Diabetes Care, 43*(5), 1008–1015. https://doi.org/10.2337/dc19-1807

Chen, C. R., & Lindo, E. J. (2018). Culturally responsive practices in special education evaluations: A review of literature. *Dialog: Journal of the Texas Educational Diagnosticians Association, 47*(2), 9–13.

Chen, D., & Kerr, C. (2019). The epigenetics of stem cell aging comes of age. *Trends in Cell Biology, 29*(7), 563–568.

Chen, E., Brody, G. H., & Miller, G. E. (2017). Childhood close family relationships and health. *American Psychologist, 72*(6), 555.

Chen, F. R., Rothman, E. F., & Jaffee, S. R. (2017). Early puberty, friendship group characteristics, and dating abuse in US girls. *Pediatrics, 139*(6), e20162847. https://doi.org/10.1542/peds.2016-2847

Chen, I. (2004, June 25). A race against time. *Science AAAS.* https://www.sciencemag.org/careers/2004/06/race-against-time

Chen, J., Walters, M. L., Gilbert, L. K., & Patel, N. (2020). Sexual violence, stalking, and intimate partner violence by sexual orientation, United States. *Psychology of Violence, 10*(1), 110–119.

Chen, J.-H., Waite, L. J., & Lauderdale, D. S. (2015). Marriage, relationship quality, and sleep among U.S. older adults. *Journal of Health and Social Behavior, 56*(3), 356–377. https://doi.org/10.1177/0022146515594631

Chen, P., & Harris, K. M. (2019). Association of positive family relationships with mental health trajectories from adolescence to midlife. *JAMA Pediatrics, 173*(12), e193336. https://doi.org/10.1001/jamapediatrics.2019.3336

Chen, W., & Adler, J. L. (2019). Assessment of screen exposure in young children, 1997 to 2014. *JAMA Pediatrics, 173*(4), 391–393. https://doi.org/10.1001/jamapediatrics.2018.5546

Chen, W.-L., & Chen, J.-H. (2019). Consequences of inadequate sleep during the college years: Sleep deprivation, grade point average, and college graduation. *Preventive Medicine, 124,* 23–28. https://doi.org/10.1016/j.ypmed.2019.04.017

Chen, X. (2018). Culture, temperament, and social and psychological adjustment. *Developmental Review, 50,* 42–53. https://doi.org/10.1016/j.dr.2018.03.004

Chen, X. (2019). Culture and shyness in childhood and adolescence. *New Ideas in Psychology, 53,* 58–66. https://doi.org/10.1016/j.newideapsych.2018.04.007

Chen, Y. C., Putnam, M., Lee, Y. S., & Morrow-Howell, N. (2019). Activity patterns and health outcomes in later life: The role of nature of engagement. *The Gerontologist, 59*(4), 698–708.

Chen, Y. T., Holahan, C. K., & Castelli, D. M. (2021). Sedentary behaviors, sleep, and health-related quality of life in middle-aged adults. *American Journal of Health Behavior, 45*(4), 785–797. https://doi.org/10.5993/AJHB.45.4.16

Chen-Bouck, L., Patterson, M. M., & Chen, J. (2019). Relations of collectivism socialization goals and training beliefs to Chinese parenting. *Journal of Cross-Cultural Psychology, 50*(3), 396–418.

Cheng, S.-T. (2017). Dementia caregiver burden: A research update and critical analysis. *Current Psychiatry Reports, 19*(9), 64. https://doi.org/10.1007/s11920-017-0818-2

Cheng, S.-T., Au, A., Losada, A., Thompson, L. W., & Gallagher-Thompson, D. (2019). Psychological interventions for dementia caregivers: What we have achieved, what we have learned. *Current Psychiatry Reports, 21*(7), 59. https://doi.org/10.1007/s11920-019-1045-9

Cheng, S.-Y., Suh, S.-Y., Morita, T., Oyama, Y., Chiu, T.-Y., Koh, S. J., Kim, H. S., Hwang, S.-J., Yoshie, T., & Tsuneto, S. (2015). A cross-cultural study on behaviors when death is approaching in East Asian countries: What are the physician-perceived common beliefs and practices? *Medicine, 94*(39), e1573. https://doi.org/10.1097/MD.0000000000001573

Cheng, T. C., Powdthavee, N., & Oswald, A. J. (2017). Longitudinal evidence for a midlife nadir in human well-being: Results from four data sets. *The Economic Journal, 127*(599), 126–142. https://doi.org/10.1111/ecoj.12256

Cheng, W., Rolls, E., Gong, W., Du, J., Zhang, J., Zhang, X.-Y., Li, F., & Feng, J. (2020). Sleep duration, brain

structure, and psychiatric and cognitive problems in children. *Molecular Psychiatry,* 1–12. https://doi.org/10.1038/s41380-020-0663-2

Cheng, Y.-S., Sun, C.-K., Yeh, P.-Y., Wu, M.-K., Hung, K.-C., & Chiu, H.-J. (2021). Serotonergic antidepressants for sleep disturbances in perimenopausal and postmenopausal women: A systematic review and meta-analysis. *Menopause, 28*(2), 207–216. https://doi.org/10.1097/GME.0000000000001647

Chen-Gaddini, M., Liu, J., & Nucci, L. (2020). "It's my own business!": Parental control over personal issues in the context of everyday adolescent–parent conflicts and internalizing disorders among urban Chinese adolescents. *Developmental Psychology, 56*(9), 1775–1786. https://doi.org/10.1037/dev0001053

Cherlin, A. J. (2018). Psychological health and socioeconomic status among non-Hispanic Whites. *Proceedings of the National Academy of Sciences, 115*(28), 7176–7178. https://doi.org/10.1073/pnas.1808753115

Cherlin, A. J. (2020). Degrees of change: An assessment of the deinstitutionalization of marriage thesis. *Journal of Marriage and Family, 82*(1), 62–80. https://doi.org/10.1111/jomf.12605

Cherlin, A., Cross-Barnet, C., Burton, L. M., & Garrett-Peters, R. (2008). Promises they can keep: Low-income women's attitudes toward motherhood, marriage, and divorce. *Journal of Marriage and the Family, 70*(4), 919–933. https://doi.org/10.1111/j.1741-3737.2008.00536.x

Chernyak, N., Turnbull, V., Gordon, R., Harris, P. L., & Cordes, S. (2020). Counting promotes proportional moral evaluation in preschool-aged children. *Cognitive Development, 56,* 100969.

Chernyshenko, O. S., Kankaraš, M., & Drasgow, F. (2018). *Social and emotional skills for student success and well-being: Conceptual framework for the OECD study on social and emotional skills.* OECD. https://doi.org/10.1787/db1d8e59-en

Chess, S., & Thomas, A. (1991). Temperament and the concept of goodness of fit. In J. Strelau & A. Angleitner (Eds.), *Explorations in temperament: International perspectives on theory and measurement* (pp. 15–28). Springer US. https://doi.org/10.1007/978-1-4899-0643-4_2

Chess, S., & Thomas, A. (1996). *Temperament: theory and practice.* Brunner/Mazel.

Chess, S., Thomas, A., Rutter, M., & Birch, H. G. (1963). Interaction of temperament and environment in the production of behavioral disturbances in children. *American Journal of Psychiatry, 120*(2), 142–148. https://doi.org/10.1176/ajp.120.2.142

Chetty, R. (2021). Improving equality of opportunity: New insights from big data. *Contemporary Economic Policy, 39*(1), 7–41. https://doi.org/10.1111/coep.12478

Chetty, R., Stepner, M., Abraham, S., Lin, S., Scuderi, B., Turner, N., Bergeron, A., & Cutler, D. (2016). The association between income and life expectancy in the United States, 2001–2014. *JAMA, 315*(16), 1750–1766. https://doi.org/10.1001/jama.2016.4226

Chevalier, N. (2018). Willing to think hard? The subjective value of cognitive effort in children. *Child Development, 89*(4), 1283–1295.

Chi, G. C., Fitzpatrick, A. L., Sharma, M., Jenny, N. S., Lopez, O. L., & DeKosky, S. T. (2017). Inflammatory biomarkers predict domain-specific cognitive decline in older adults. *The Journals of Gerontology: Series A, 72*(6), 796–803.

Chi, H. L., Cataldo, J., Ho, E. Y., & Rehm, R. S. (2018). Can we talk about it now? Recognizing the optimal time to initiate end-of-life care discussions with older Chinese Americans and their families. *Journal of Transcultural Nursing, 29*(6), 532–539.

Chi, K., Almeida, D. M., Charles, S. T., & Sin, N. L. (2021). Daily prosocial activities and well-being: Age moderation in two national studies. *Psychology and Aging, 36*(1), 83.

Chi, X., Bo, A., Liu, T., Zhang, P., & Chi, I. (2018). Effects of mindfulness-based stress reduction on depression in adolescents and young adults: A systematic review and meta-analysis. *Frontiers in Psychology, 9,* 1034. https://doi.org/10.3389/fpsyg.2018.01034

Chiao, C.-Y., Wu, H.-S., & Hsiao, C.-Y. (2015). Caregiver burden for informal caregivers of patients with dementia: A systematic review. *International Nursing Review, 62*(3), 340–350. https://doi.org/10.1111/inr.12194

Child, S. T., & Lawton, L. (2019). Loneliness and social isolation among young and late middle-age adults: Associations of personal networks and social participation. *Aging & Mental Health, 23*(2), 196–204. https://doi.org/10.1080/13607863.2017.1399345

Child Welfare Information Gateway. (2019). *Definitions of child abuse and neglect*. U.S. Department of Health and Human Services, Children's Bureau.

Children's Bureau. (2019). *What is child abuse and neglect? Recognizing the signs and symptoms* [Fact sheet].

Childs, B. G., Gluscevic, M., Baker, D. J., Laberge, R. M., Marquess, D., Dananberg, J., & Van Deursen, J. M. (2017). Senescent cells: An emerging target for diseases of ageing. *Nature Reviews: Drug Discovery, 16*(10), 718–735.

Chisholm, L., Weech-Maldonado, R., Laberge, A., Lin, F.-C., & Hyer, K. (2013). Nursing home quality and financial performance: Does the racial composition of residents matter? *Health Services Research, 48*(6 Pt 1), 2060–2080. https://doi.org/10.1111/1475-6773.12079

Chmielewska, B., Barratt, I., Townsend, R., Kalafat, E., Meulen, J. van der, Gurol-Urganci, I., O'Brien, P., Morris, E., Draycott, T., Thangaratinam, S., Doare, K. L., Ladhani, S., Dadelszen, P. von, Magee, L., & Khalil, A. (2021, March 31). Effects of the COVID-19 pandemic on maternal and perinatal outcomes: A systematic review and meta-analysis. *The Lancet Global Health, 9*(6), E759–E772. https://doi.org/10.1016/S2214-109X(21)00079-6

Choate, P. W., CrazyBull, B., Lindstrom, D., & Lindstrom, G. (2020). Where do we go from here? Ongoing colonialism from attachment theory. *Aotearoa New Zealand Social Work, 32*(1), 32–44.

Choate, P. W., Kohler, T., Cloete, F., CrazyBull, B., Lindstrom, D., & Tatoulis, P. (2019). Rethinking Racine v Woods from a decolonizing perspective: Challenging the applicability of attachment theory to indigenous families involved with child protection. *Canadian Journal of Law and Society/La Revue Canadienne Droit et Société, 34*(1), 55–78. https://doi.org/10.1017/cls.2019.8

Choe, D. E., Olson, S. L., & Sameroff, A. J. (2013). Effects of early maternal distress and parenting on the development of children's self-regulation and externalizing behavior. *Development and Psychopathology, 25*(2), 437–453.

Choi, K. H., & Goldberg, R. E. (2020). The social significance of interracial cohabitation: Inferences based on fertility behavior. *Demography, 57*(5), 1727–1751. https://doi.org/10.1007/s13524-020-00904-5

Choi, N. G., DiNitto, D. M., Marti, C. N., & Conwell, Y. (2019). Physical health problems as a late-life suicide precipitant: Examination of coroner/medical examiner and law enforcement reports. *The Gerontologist, 59*(2), 356–367. https://doi.org/10.1093/geront/gnx143

Choi, Y., Kim, T. Y., Noh, S., Lee, J., & Takeuchi, D. (2018). Culture and family process: Measures of familism for Filipino and Korean American parents. *Family Process, 57*(4), 1029–1048. https://doi.org/10.1111/famp.12322

Choi, Y. J., & Matz-Costa, C. (2018). Perceived neighborhood safety, social cohesion, and psychological health of older adults. *The Gerontologist, 58*(1), 196–206.

Choi-Kain, L. W., Finch, E. F., Masland, S. R., Jenkins, J. A., & Unruh, B. T. (2017). What works in the treatment of borderline personality disorder. *Current Behavioral Neuroscience Reports, 4*(1), 21–30.

Chomsky, N. (1957). Logical structures in language. *American Documentation, 8*(4), 284.

Chong, A., & Mickelson, K. D. (2016). Perceived fairness and relationship satisfaction during the transition to parenthood: The mediating role of spousal support. *Journal of Family Issues, 37*(1), 3–28. https://doi.org/10.1177/0192513X13516764

Chopik, W. J. (2017). Death across the lifespan: Age differences in death-related thoughts and anxiety. *Death Studies, 41*(2), 69–77. https://doi.org/10.1080/07481187.2016.1206997

Chopik, W. J., Edelstein, R. S., & Fraley, R. C. (2013). From the cradle to the grave: Age differences in attachment from early adulthood to old age. *Journal of Personality, 81*(2), 171–183. https://doi.org/10.1111/j.1467-6494.2012.00793.x

Chopik, W. J., & Grimm, K. J. (2019). Longitudinal changes and historic differences in narcissism from adolescence to older adulthood. *Psychology and Aging, 34*(8), 1109.

Chopik, W. J., Nuttall, A. K., & Oh, J. (2021). Relationship-specific satisfaction and adjustment in emerging adulthood: The moderating role of adult attachment orientation. *Journal of Adult Development*. https://doi.org/10.1007/s10804-021-09380-6

Chopik, W. J., Oh, J., Kim, E. S., Schwaba, T., Krämer, M. D., Richter, D., & Smith, J. (2020). Changes in optimism and pessimism in response to life events: Evidence from three large panel studies. *Journal of Research in Personality, 88*, 103985. https://doi.org/10.1016/j.jrp.2020.103985

Choudry, M., Latif, A., & Warburton, K. G. (2018). An overview of the spiritual importances of end-of-life care among the five major faiths of the United Kingdom. *Clinical Medicine, 18*(1), 23.

Choukas-Bradley, S., Goldberg, S. K., Widman, L., Reese, B. M., & Halpern, C. T. (2015). Demographic and developmental differences in the content and sequence of adolescents' ideal romantic relationship behaviors. *Journal of Adolescence, 45*, 112–126.

Chow, A., Galambos, N. L., & Krahn, H. J. (2017). Work values during the transition to adulthood and mid-life satisfaction: Cascading effects across 25 years. *International Journal of Behavioral Development, 41*(1), 105–114. https://doi.org/10.1177/0165025415608518

Chrisler, J. C. (2013). Teaching taboo topics: Menstruation, menopause, and the psychology of women. *Psychology of Women Quarterly, 37*(1), 128–132. https://doi.org/10.1177/0361684312471326

Chrisler, J. C. (2019). Sexism and ageism. In D. Gu & M. E. Dupre (Eds.), *Encyclopedia of gerontology and population aging* (pp. 1–7). Springer International Publishing. https://doi.org/10.1007/978-3-319-69892-2_603-1

Chrisler, J. C., Barney, A., & Palatino, B. (2016). Ageism can be hazardous to women's health: Ageism, sexism, and stereotypes of older women in the healthcare system. *Journal of Social Issues, 72*(1), 86–104.

Christensen, J., Eyolfson, E., Salberg, S., & Mychasiuk, R. (2021). Traumatic brain injury in adolescence: A review of the neurobiological and behavioural underpinnings and outcomes. *Developmental Review, 59*, 100943. https://doi.org/10.1016/j.dr.2020.100943

Christensen, N., Bruun, S., Søndergaard, J., Christesen, H. T., Fisker, N., Zachariassen, G., Sangild, P. T., & Husby, S. (2020). Breastfeeding and infections in early childhood: A cohort study. *Pediatrics, 146*(5), e20191892.

Christenson, A., Johansson, E., Reynisdottir, S., Torgerson, J., & Hemmingsson, E. (2019). "...Or else I close my ears": How women with obesity want to be approached and treated regarding gestational weight management: A qualitative interview study. *PLOS ONE, 14*(9), e0222543. https://doi.org/10.1371/journal.pone.0222543

Christiaens, A. H. T., Nelemans, S. A., Meeus, W. H. J., & Branje, S. (2021). Identity development across the transition from secondary to tertiary education: A 9-wave longitudinal study. *Journal of Adolescence*. https://doi.org/10.1016/j.adolescence.2021.03.007

Christian, C. W., & Committee on Child Abuse and Neglect. (2015). The evaluation of suspected child physical abuse. *Pediatrics, 135*(5), e1337–e1354. https://doi.org/10.1542/peds.2015-0356

Christopher, M. E., Hulslander, J., Byrne, B., Samuelsson, S., Keenan, J. M., Pennington, B., & Olson, R. K. (2015). Genetic and environmental etiologies of the longitudinal relations between prereading skills and reading. *Child Development, 86*(2), 342–361.

Chu, C., Anderson, R., White, N., & Stone, P. (2020). Prognosticating for adult patients with advanced incurable cancer: A needed oncologist skill. *Current Treatment Options in Oncology, 21*(1), 1–18.

Chu, J., Maruyama, B., Batchelder, H., Goldblum, P., Bongar, B., & Wickham, R. E. (2020). Cultural pathways for suicidal ideation and behaviors. *Cultural Diversity and Ethnic Minority Psychology, 26*(3), 367–377. https://doi.org/10.1037/cdp0000307

Chu, J., Robinett, E. N., Ma, J. K. L., Shadish, K. Y., Goldblum, P., & Bongar, B. (2019). Cultural versus classic risk and protective factors for suicide. *Death Studies, 43*(1), 56–61. https://doi.org/10.1080/07481187.2018.1430085

Chu, J. Y. (2014). *When boys become boys: Development, relationships, and masculinity*. New York University Press. https://www.degruyter.com/document/doi/10.18574/9780814724859/html

Chua, A. (2011). *Battle hymn of the tiger mother*. Penguin.

Chua, S. J., Danhof, N. A., Mochtar, M. H., van Wely, M., McLernon, D. J., Custers, I., Lee, E., Dreyer, K., Cahill, D. J., Gillett, W. R., Righarts, A., Strandell, A., Rantsi, T., Schmidt, L., Eijkemans, M. J. C., Mol, B. W. J., & van Eekelen, R. (2020). Age-related natural fertility outcomes in women over 35 years: A systematic review and individual participant data meta-analysis. *Human Reproduction, 35*(8), 1808–1820. https://doi.org/10.1093/humrep/deaa129

Chuang, S. S., Glozman, J., Green, D. S., & Rasmi, S. (2018). Parenting and family relationships in Chinese families: A critical ecological approach. *Journal of Family Theory & Review, 10*(2), 367–383. https://doi.org/10.1111/jftr.12257

Chung, G. (2013). Understanding nursing home worker conceptualizations about good care. *The Gerontologist, 53*(2), 246–254.

Chung, G. K., Chan, S. M., Chan, Y. H., Woo, J., Wong, H., Wong, S. Y., & Chung, R. Y. (2021). Socioeconomic patterns of COVID-19 clusters in low-incidence city, Hong Kong. *Emerging Infectious Diseases, 27*(11), 2874.

Chung, H. Y., Kim, D. H., Lee, E. K., Chung, K. W., Chung, S., Lee, B., Seo, A. Y., Chung, J. H., Jung, Y. S., Im, E., Lee, J., Kim, N. D., Choi, Y. J., Im, D. S., & Yu, B. P. (2019). Redefining chronic inflammation in aging and age-related diseases: Proposal of the senoinflammation concept. *Aging and Disease, 10*(2), 367–382. https://doi.org/10.14336/AD.2018.0324

Chung, W., Jiang, S.-F., Paksarian, D., Nikolaidis, A., Castellanos, F. X., Merikangas, K. R., & Milham, M. P. (2019). Trends in the prevalence and incidence of attention-deficit/hyperactivity disorder among adults and children of different racial and ethnic groups. *JAMA Network Open, 2*(11), e1914344. https://doi.org/10.1001/jamanetworkopen.2019.14344

Chyl, K., Fraga-González, G., Brem, S., & Jednoróg, K. (2021). Brain dynamics of (a)typical reading development—A review of longitudinal studies. *NPJ Science of Learning, 6*(1), 1–9. https://doi.org/10.1038/s41539-020-00081-5

Chzhen, Y., Rees, G., Gromada, A., Cuesta, J., & Bruckauf, Z. (2018). *An unfair start: Inequality in children's education in rich countries* (Innocenti Report Card No. 15). UNIECF Office of Research.

Ciarrusta, J., Christiaens, D., Fitzgibbon, S. P., Dimitrova, R., Hutter, J., Hughes, E., Duff, E., Price, A. N., Cordero-Grande, L., Tournier, J.-D., Rueckert, D., Hajnal, J. V., Arichi, T., McAlonan, G., Edwards, A. D., & Batalle, D. (2021). The developing brain structural and functional connectome fingerprint. *BioRxiv*, 2021.03.08.434357. https://doi.org/10.1101/2021.03.08.434357

Cicchetti, D. (2018). A multilevel developmental approach to the prevention of psychopathology in children and adolescents. In J. N. Butcher & P. C. Kendall (Eds.), *APA handbook of psychopathology: Child and adolescent psychopathology* (pp. 37–53). American Psychological Association. https://doi.org/10.1037/0000065-003

Cicirelli, V. G. (2002). Fear of death in older adults: Predictions from terror management theory. *The Journals of Gerontology: Series B, 57*(4), P358–P366. https://doi.org/10.1093/geronb/57.4.P358

Cillessen, A. H. N., & Bukowski, W. M. (2018). Sociometric perspectives. In W. M. Bukowski, B. Laursen, & K. H. Rubin (Eds.), *Handbook of peer interactions, relationships, and groups* (pp. 64–83). Guilford.

Cimpian, A. (2016). The privileged status of category representations in early development. *Child Development Perspectives, 10*(2), 99–104. https://doi.org/10.1111/cdep.12166

Cimpian, A. (2017). Early reasoning about competence is not irrationally optimistic, nor does it stem from inadequate cognitive representations. In A. J. Elliot, C. S. Dweck, & D. S. Yeager (Eds.), *Handbook of competence and motivation: Theory and application* (pp. 387–407). Guilford.

Cimpian, A., Arce, H.-M. C., Markman, E. M., & Dweck, C. S. (2007). Subtle linguistic cues affect children's motivation. *Psychological Science, 18*(4), 314–316. https://doi.org/10.1111/j.1467-9280.2007.01896.x

Cimpian, A., Hammond, M. D., Mazza, G., & Corry, G. (2017). Young children's self-concepts include representations of abstract traits and the global self. *Child Development, 88*(6), 1786–1798. https://doi.org/10.1111/cdev.12925

Cipriani, G., & Di Fiorino, M. (2019). Euthanasia and other end of life in patients suffering from dementia. *Legal Medicine, 40*, 54–59. https://doi.org/10.1016/j.legalmed.2019.07.007

CIRCLE. (2018). *So much for "slacktivism": Youth translate online engagement to offline political action* (CIRCLE / Tisch College 2018 Pre-Election Youth Poll). Tufts University.

CIRCLE. (2021, April 29). *Half of youth voted in 2020, an 11-point increase from 2016.* https://circle.tufts.edu/latest-research/half-youth-voted-2020-11-point-increase-2016

Ciscato, E., Galichon, A., & Goussé, M. (2020). Like attract like? A structural comparison of homogamy across same-sex and different-sex households. *Journal of Political Economy, 128*(2), 740–781. https://doi.org/10.1086/704611

Clare, L., Gamble, L. D., Martyr, A., Quinn, C., Litherland, R., Morris, R. G., & Matthews, F. E. (2021). Psychological processes in adapting to dementia: Illness representations among the IDEAL cohort. *Psychology and Aging*. Advance online publication. http://dx.doi.org/10.1037/pag0000650

Clare, L., Wu, Y. T., Teale, J. C., MacLeod, C., Matthews, F., Brayne, C., & CFAS-Wales Study Team. (2017). Potentially modifiable lifestyle factors, cognitive reserve, and cognitive function in later life: A cross-sectional study. *PLoS Medicine, 14*(3), e1002259.

Clark, A. E. (2018). Four decades of the economics of happiness: Where next? *Review of Income and Wealth, 64*(2), 245–269. https://doi.org/10.1111/roiw.12369.

Clark, C. A., Sheffield, T. D., Wiebe, S. A., & Espy, K. A. (2013). Longitudinal associations between executive control and developing mathematical competence in preschool boys and girls. *Child Development, 84*(2), 662–677.

Clark, H., Coll-Seck, A. M., Banerjee, A., Peterson, S., Dalglish, S. L., Ameratunga, S., Balabanova, D., Bhan, M. K., Bhutta, Z. A., Borrazzo, J., Claeson, M., Doherty, T., El-Jardali, F., George, A. S., Gichaga, A., Gram, L., Hipgrave, D. B., Kwamie, A., Meng, Q., ... Costello, A. (2020). A future for the world's children? A WHO–UNICEF–Lancet Commission. *The Lancet, 395*(10224), 605–658. https://doi.org/10.1016/S0140-6736(19)32540-1

Clark, K. A. (2021). Unemployed at midlife: Coping strategies that safeguard well-being. *Applied Research in Quality of Life, 16*(5), 1861–1879. https://doi.org/10.1007/s11482-020-09850-1

Clark, K. B., & Clark, M. K. (1939). The development of consciousness of self and the emergence of racial identification in Negro preschool children. *The Journal of Social Psychology, 10*(4), 591–599. https://doi.org/10.1080/00224545.1939.9713394

Clark, K. B., & Clark, M. K. (1940). Skin color as a factor in racial identification of Negro preschool children. *The Journal of Social Psychology, 11*(1), 159–169. https://doi.org/10.1080/00224545.1940.9918741

Clark, R., & Moloney, G. (2020). Facebook and older adults: Fulfilling psychological needs? *Journal of Aging Studies, 55*, 100897. https://doi.org/10.1016/j.jaging.2020.100897

Clark, R. L., & Ritter, B. M. (2020). How are employers responding to an aging workforce? *The Gerontologist, 60*(8), 1403–1410.

Clark-Gambelunghe, M. B., & Clark, D. A. (2015). Sensory development. *Pediatric Clinics, 62*(2), 367–384.

Clarke, A. J., & Wallgren-Pettersson, C. (2019). Ethics in genetic counselling. *Journal of Community Genetics, 10*(1), 3–33. https://doi.org/10.1007/s12687-018-0371-7

Clarke, L. H., & Mahal, R. (2017). I do like the way I look: Older men's perceptions and experiences of aging and body image. *Innovation in Aging, 1*(Suppl. 1), 1296.

Claro, S., Paunesku, D., & Dweck, C. S. (2016). Growth mindset tempers the effects of poverty on academic achievement. *Proceedings of the National Academy of Sciences, 113*(31), 8664–8668.

Clausen, J. S. (1991). Adolescent competence and the shaping of the life course. *American Journal of Sociology, 96*(4), 805–842.

Clearfield, M. W., & Jedd, K. E. (2013). The effects of socio-economic status on infant attention. *Infant and Child Development, 22*(1), 53–67. https://doi.org/10.1002/icd.1770

Clegg, A., Young, J., Iliffe, S., Rikkert, M. O., & Rockwood, K. (2013). Frailty in elderly people. *The Lancet, 381*(9868), 752–762.

Clemans-Cope, L., Lynch, V., Epstein, M., & Kenney, G. M. (2019). Opioid and substance use disorder and receipt of treatment among parents living with children in the United States, 2015–2017. *The Annals of Family Medicine, 17*(3), 207–211. https://doi.org/10.1370/afm.2389

Clement, S., Schauman, O., Graham, T., Maggioni, F., Evans-Lacko, S., Bezborodovs, N., & Thornicroft, G. (2015). What is the impact of mental health-related stigma on help-seeking? A systematic review of quantitative and qualitative studies. *Psychological Medicine, 45*(1), 11–27.

Clemmons, D. R., Molitch, M., Hoffman, A. R., Klibanski, A., Strasburger, C. J., Kleinberg, D. L., Ho, K., Webb, S. M., Bronstein, M. D., Bouillon, R., Ben-Shlomo, A., Hamrahian, A. H., Chanson, P., Barkan, A. L., Merriam, G. R., Blackman, M. R., & Salvatori, R. (2014). Growth hormone should be used only for approved indications. *The Journal of Clinical Endocrinology & Metabolism, 99*(2), 409–411.

Cline, E. N., Bicca, M. A., Viola, K. L., & Klein, W. L. (2018). The amyloid-β oligomer hypothesis: Beginning of the third decade. *Journal of Alzheimer's Disease, 64*(s1), S567–S610. https://doi.org/10.3233/JAD-179941

Cloninger, C. R., Cloninger, K. M., Zwir, I., & Keltikangas-Järvinen, L. (2019). The complex genetics and biology of human temperament: A review of traditional concepts in relation to new molecular findings. *Translational Psychiatry, 9*(1), 1–21. https://doi.org/10.1038/s41398-019-0621-4

Clouston, S. A. P., Terrera, G. M., Rodgers, J. L., O'Keefe, P., Mann, F. D., Lewis, N. A., Wänström, L., Kaye, J., & Hofer, S. M. (2021). Cohort and period effects as explanations for declining dementia trends and cognitive aging. *Population and Development Review, 47*(3), 611–637. https://doi.org/10.1111/padr.12409

Cnaan, R. A., & Heist, H. (2018). Religious congregations as community hubs and sources of social bonding. In R. A. Cnaan & C. Milofsky (Eds.), *Handbook of community movements and local organizations in the 21st century* (pp. 391–403). Springer International Publishing. https://doi.org/10.1007/978-3-319-77416-9_24

Coast, E., Lattof, S. R., & Strong, J. (2019). Puberty and menstruation knowledge among young adolescents in low- and middle-income countries: A scoping review. *International Journal of Public Health, 64*(2), 293–304. https://doi.org/10.1007/s00038-019-01209-0

Cobb, R. J., Parker, L. J., & Thorpe, R. J., Jr. (2020). Self-reported instances of major discrimination, race/ethnicity, and inflammation among older adults: Evidence from the health and retirement study. *The Journals of Gerontology: Series A, 75*(2), 291–296.

Cobbinah, S. S., & Lewis, J. (2018). Racism & health: A public health perspective on racial discrimination. *Journal of Evaluation in Clinical Practice, 24*(5), 995–998. https://doi.org/10.1111/jep.12894

Coe, C. (2019). *The new American servitude.* NYU Press. https://nyupress.org/9781479808830/the-new-american-servitude

Coe, C. (2020). Meaningful deaths: Home health workers' mediation of deaths at home. *Medical Anthropology, 39*(1), 96–108. https://doi.org/10.1080/01459740.2019.1693560

Coffey, J. K., Xia, M., & Fosco, G. M. (2020). When do adolescents feel loved? A daily within-person study of parent–adolescent relations. *Emotion.* https://doi.org/10.1037/emo0000767

Cohee, L. M., Halliday, K. E., Gelli, A., Mwenyango, I., Lavadenz, F., Burbano, C., Drake, L., & Bundy, D. A. P. (2021). The role of health in education and human capital: Why an integrated approach to school health could make a difference in the futures of schoolchildren in low-income countries. *The American Journal of Tropical Medicine and Hygiene, 104*(2), 424–428. https://doi.org/10.4269/ajtmh.20-0779

Cohen, J. S., Donnelly, K., Patel, S. J., Badolato, G. M., Boyle, M. D., McCarter, R., & Goyal, M. K. (2021). Firearms injuries involving young children in the United States during the COVID-19 pandemic. *Pediatrics, 148*(1), e2020042697. https://doi.org/10.1542/peds.2020-042697

Cohen, P. N. (2019). The coming divorce decline. *Socius, 5*, 2378023119873497.

Cohen, S., Chiang, J. J., Janicki-Deverts, D., & Miller, G. E. (2020). Good relationships with parents during childhood as buffers of the association between childhood disadvantage and adult susceptibility to the common cold. *Psychosomatic Medicine, 82*(6), 538–547. https://doi.org/10.1097/PSY.0000000000000818

Cohen, S. A., Cook, S. K., Sando, T. A., Brown, M. J., & Longo, D. R. (2017). Socioeconomic and demographic disparities in caregiving intensity and quality of life in informal caregivers: A first look at the national study of caregiving. *Journal of Gerontological Nursing, 43*(6), 17–24. https://doi.org/10.3928/00989134-20170224-01

Cohn, D., & Passel, J. S. (2018, April 5). *A record 64 million Americans live in multigenerational households.* Pew Research Center. http://www.pewresearch.org/fact-tank/2018/04/05/a-record-64-million-americans-live-in-multigenerational-households/

Cohodes, E. M., Kitt, E. R., Baskin-Sommers, A., & Gee, D. G. (2021). Influences of early-life stress on frontolimbic circuitry: Harnessing a dimensional approach to elucidate the effects of heterogeneity in stress exposure. *Developmental Psychobiology, 63*(2), 153–172. https://doi.org/10.1002/dev.21969

Cohodes, S. R. (2020). The long-run impacts of specialized programming for high-achieving students. *American Economic Journal: Economic Policy, 12*(1), 127–166. https://doi.org/10.1257/pol.20180315

Coker, D. L., Jr., & Kim, Y. S. G. (2018). Critical issues in the understanding of young elementary school students at risk for problems in written expression: Introduction to the special series. *Journal of Learning Disabilities, 51*(4), 315–319.

Colbert, D., Tyndall, I., Roche, B., & Cassidy, S. (2018). Can SMART training really increase intelligence? A replication study. *Journal of Behavioral Education, 27*(4), 509–531. https://doi.org/10.1007/s10864-018-9302-2

Colclough, Y. Y. (2017). Native American death taboo: Implications for health care providers. *American Journal of Hospice and Palliative Medicine, 34*(6), 584–591.

Cole, J. H., & Franke, K. (2017). Predicting age using neuroimaging: Innovative brain ageing biomarkers. *Trends in Neurosciences, 40*(12), 681–690.

Cole, M. (1990). Cognitive development and formal schooling: The evidence from cross-cultural research. In L. C. Moll (Ed.), *Vygotsky and education: Instructional implications and applications of sociohistorical psychology* (pp. 89–110). Cambridge University Press.

Cole, M. (2017). Idiocultural design as a tool of cultural psychology. *Perspectives on Psychological Science, 12*(5), 772–781. https://doi.org/10.1177/1745691617708623

Cole, M., & Packer, M. (2016). A bio-cultural-historical approach to the study of development. In M. J. Gelfand, C. Chiu, & Y. Hong (Eds.), *Handbook of advances in culture and psychology* (Vol. 6, pp. 1–76). Oxford University Press. https://doi.org/10.1093/acprof:oso/9780190458850.003.0001

Cole, P. M., & Jacobs, A. E. (2018). From children's expressive control to emotion regulation: Looking back, looking ahead. *The European Journal of Developmental Psychology, 15*(6), 658–677. https://doi.org/10.1080/1740562 9.2018.1438888

Cole, P. M., Tamang, B. L., & Shrestha, S. (2006). Cultural variations in the socialization of young children's anger and shame. *Child Development, 77*(5), 1237–1251.

Cole, S. W., Shanahan, M. J., Gaydosh, L., & Harris, K. M. (2020). Population-based RNA profiling in add health finds social disparities in inflammatory and antiviral gene regulation to emerge by young adulthood. *Proceedings of the National Academy of Sciences, 117*(9), 4601–4608. https://doi.org/10.1073/pnas.1821367117

Cole, T. J. (2012). The development of growth references and growth charts. *Annals of Human Biology, 39*(5), 382–394. https://doi.org/10.3109/03014460.2012.694475

Cole, T. J. (2015). The evidential value of developmental age imaging for assessing age of majority. *Annals of Human Biology, 42*(4), 379–388. https://doi.org/10.3109/0301446 0.2015.1031826

Coleman, M., Ganong, L., & Mitchell, S. (2018). Divorce and postdivorce relationships. In A. L. Vangelisti & D. Perlman (Eds.), *Cambridge handbook of personal relationships* (pp. 106–116). Cambridge University Press.

Coleman-Jensen, A., Rabbitt, M. P., Gregory, C. A., & Singh, A. (2019). *Household food security in the United States in 2018.* USDA. http://www.ers.usda.gov/publications /pub-details/?pubid=94848

Coleman-Jensen, A., Rabbitt, M. P., Gregory, C. A., & Singh, A. (2020). *Household food security in the United States in 2019.* http://www.ers.usda.gov/publications /pub-details/?pubid=99281

Colich, N. L., Rosen, M. L., Williams, E. S., & McLaughlin, K. A. (2020). Biological aging in childhood and adolescence following experiences of threat and deprivation: A systematic review and meta-analysis. *Psychological Bulletin, 146*(9), 721–764. https://doi.org/10.1037/bul0000270

Collier, K. M., Coyne, S. M., Rasmussen, E. E., Hawkins, A. J., Padilla-Walker, L. M., Erickson, S. E., & Memmott-Elison, M. K. (2016). Does parental mediation of media influence child outcomes? A meta-analysis on media time, aggression, substance use, and sexual behavior. *Developmental Psychology, 52*(5), 798.

Collier, V. P., & Thomas, W. P. (2017). Validating the power of bilingual schooling: Thirty-two years of large-scale, longitudinal research. *Annual Review of Applied Linguistics, 37*, 203–217.

Collins, C., Landivar, L. C., Ruppanner, L., & Scarborough, W. J. (2021). COVID-19 and the gender gap in work hours. *Gender, Work & Organization, 28*(S1), 101–112. https://doi.org/10.1111/gwao.12506

Collins, F. S. (2006). *The language of God: A scientist presents evidence for belief.* Simon & Schuster.

Collins, F. S. (2016). Seeking a cure for one of the rarest diseases: Progeria. *Circulation, 134*(2), 126–129. https:// doi.org/10.1161/CIRCULATIONAHA.116.022965

Collins, F. S., & Mansoura, M. K. (2001). The Human Genome Project. *Cancer, 91*(S1), 221–225. https://doi .org/10.1002/1097-0142(20010101)91:1+<221::AID-CNCR8>3.0.CO;2-9

Collins, N., & Roth, T. L. (2021). Chapter 7—Intergenerational transmission of stress-related epigenetic regulation. In L. Provenzi & R. Montirosso (Eds.), *Developmental human behavioral epigenetics* (Vol. 23, pp. 119–141). Academic Press. https://doi.org/10.1016/B978-0-12-819262-7.00007-6

Collins, R. L., Strasburger, V. C., Brown, J. D., Donnerstein, E., Lenhart, A., & Ward, L. M. (2017). Sexual media and childhood well-being and health. *Pediatrics, 140*(Supplement 2), S162–S166. https://doi.org/10.1542 /peds.2016-1758X

Collins, W. A., & Madsen, S. D. (2019). Parenting during middle childhood. In M. H. Bornstein (Ed.), *Handbook of parenting: Children and parenting* (3rd ed., Vol. 1, pp. 81–110). Routledge.

Collombet, S., Ranisavljevic, N., Nagano, T., Varnai, C., Shisode, T., Leung, W., Piolot, T., Galupa, R.,

Borensztein, M., Servant, N., Fraser, P., Ancelin, K., & Heard, E. (2020). Parental-to-embryo switch of chromosome organization in early embryogenesis. *Nature, 580*(7801), 142–146. https://doi.org/10.1038 /s41586-020-2125-z

Colman, I., Zeng, Y., McMartin, S. E., Naicker, K., Ataullahjan, A., Weeks, M., & Galambos, N. L. (2014). Protective factors against depression during the transition from adolescence to adulthood: Findings from a national Canadian cohort. *Preventive Medicine, 65*, 28–32.

Colon, G., Saccon, T., Schneider, A., Cavalcante, M. B., Huffman, D. M., Berryman, D., List, E., Ikeno, Y., Musi, N., Bartke, A., Kopchick, J., Kirkland, J. L., Tchkonia, T., & Masternak, M. M. (2019). The enigmatic role of growth hormone in age-related diseases, cognition, and longevity. *Geroscience, 41*(6), 759–774.

Colonnesi, C., Nikolić, M., & Bögels, S. M. (2020). Development and psychophysiological correlates of positive shyness from infancy to childhood. In L. A. Schmidt & K. L. Poole (Eds.), *Adaptive shyness: Multiple perspectives on behavior and development* (pp. 41–61). Springer International Publishing. https://doi.org/10.1007/978-3-030-38877-5_3

Committee on Accessible and Affordable Hearing Health Care for Adults (CAAHHC), National Academy of Science, Engineering, and Medicine. (2016). *Hearing health care for adults: Priorities for improving access and affordability* (D. G. Blazer, S. Domnitz, & C. T. Liverman, Eds.). National Academies Press.

Committee on Approaching Death: Addressing Key End of Life Issues & Institute of Medicine. (2015). *Dying in America: Improving quality and honoring individual preferences near the end of life.* National Academies Press. http://www .ncbi.nlm.nih.gov/books/NBK285681/

Committee on Family Caregiving for Older Adults, Board on Health Care Services, Health and Medicine Division, National Academies of Sciences, Engineering, and Medicine, Schulz, R., & Eden, J. (Eds.). (2016). *Families caring for an aging America.* National Academies Press. http://www.ncbi.nlm.nih.gov/books/NBK396401/

Committee on Fostering School Success for English Learners: Toward New Directions in Policy, Practice and Research (Committee on Fostering School Success) (2017). *Promoting the educational success of children and youth learning English: Promising futures* (R. Takanishi, S. Le Menestrel, and Board on Children, Youth and Families, & Board on Science Education, Eds.). National Academies Press.

Committee on Hospital Care and Child Life Council. (2014). Child life services. *Pediatrics, 133*(5), e1471–e1478. https://doi.org/10.1542/peds.2014-0556 (Reprinted February 2018).

Commons, M. L., & Davidson, M. N. (2015). The sufficiency of reinforcing problem solutions for transition to the formal stage. *Behavioral Development Bulletin, 20*(1), 114–130. https://doi.org/10.1037/h0101033

Compagnoni, M., & Losenno, K. M. (2020). "I'm the best! Or am I?": Academic self-concepts and self-regulation in kindergarten. *Frontline Learning Research, 8*(2), 131–152.

Condry, R., & Miles, C. (2014). Adolescent to parent violence: Framing and mapping a hidden problem. *Criminology & Criminal Justice, 14*(3), 257–275. https://doi .org/10.1177/1748895813500155

Conduct Problems Prevention Research Group. (2011). The effects of the Fast Track preventive intervention on the development of conduct disorder across childhood. *Child Development, 82*(1), 331–345.

Conejero, I., Olié, E., Courtet, P., & Calati, R. (2018). Suicide in older adults: Current perspectives. *Clinical Interventions in Aging, 13*, 691–699. https://doi.org/10.2147 /CIA.S130670

Conger, R. D., Martin, M. J., & Masarik, A. S. (2021). Dynamic associations among socioeconomic status (SES), parenting investments, and conscientiousness across time and generations. *Developmental Psychology, 57*(2), 147–163. https://doi.org/10.1037/dev0000463

Congressional Budget Office (CBO). (2013). *Rising demand for long-term services and supports for elderly people.* Congress of the United States.

Congressional Research Service. (2021). *The growing gap in life expectancy by income: Recent evidence and implications for the Social Security retirement age.*

Conley, M. I., Hindley, I., Baskin-Sommers, A., Gee, D. G., Casey, B. J., & Rosenberg, M. D. (2020). The importance of social factors in the association between physical activity and depression in children. *Child and Adolescent Psychiatry and Mental Health, 14*(1), 28. https://doi .org/10.1186/s13034-020-00335-5

Conley, T., Mehta, N., Stinebrickner, R., & Stinebrickner, T. (2015). *Social interactions, mechanisms, and equilibrium: Evidence from a model of study time and academic achievement* (No. w21418). National Bureau of Economic Research.

Conn, B. M., de Figueiredo, S., Sherer, S., Mankerian, M., & Iverson, E. (2018). "Our lives aren't over": A strengths-based perspective on stigma, discrimination, and coping among young parents. *Journal of Adolescence, 66*, 91–100. https://doi.org/10.1016/j.adolescence.2018.05.005

Conner, T. S., DeYoung, C. G., & Silvia, P. J. (2018). Everyday creative activity as a path to flourishing. *The Journal of Positive Psychology, 13*(2), 181–189.

Connidis, I. A., & Barnett, A. E. (2018). *Family ties and aging.* Sage.

Connidis, I. A., Borell, K., & Karlsson, S. G. (2017). Ambivalence and living apart together in later life: A critical research proposal. *Journal of Marriage and Family, 79*(5), 1404–1418.

Connolly, J., & McDonald, K. P. (2020). Cross-cultural perspectives on dating and marriage. In S. Hupp & J. D. Jewell (Eds.), *The encyclopedia of child and adolescent development* (pp. 1–13). American Cancer Society. https://doi .org/10.1002/9781119171492.wecad486

Connor, C. (2016). Using cognitive development research to inform literacy instruction and improve practice in the classroom. In C. M. Connor (Ed.), *The cognitive development of reading and reading comprehension* (pp. 166–185). Routledge.

Connor, C. M., Morrison, F. J., Fishman, B., Crowe, E. C., Al Otaiba, S., & Schatschneider, C. (2013). A longitudinal cluster-randomized controlled study on the accumulating effects of individualized literacy instruction on students' reading from first through third grade. *Psychological Science, 24*(8), 1408.

Conradt, E. (2017). Using principles of behavioral epigenetics to advance research on early-life stress. *Child Development Perspectives, 11*(2), 107–112. https://doi .org/10.1111/cdep.12219

Constantino, R. E., Angosta, A. D., Reyes, A. T., Kameg, B., Wu, L., Cobb, J., Hui, V., Palompon, D., Safadi, R., Daibes, M., & Schlenk, E. (2019). Is intimate partner violence a risk factor for cardiovascular disease in women? A review of the preponderance of the evidence. *Health, 11*(06), 841. https://doi.org/10.4236/health.2019.116067

Conte, E., Grazzani, I., & Pepe, A. (2018). Social cognition, language, and prosocial behaviors: A multitrait mixed-methods study in early childhood. *Early Education and Development, 29*(6), 814–830.

Conti, R. P. (2015). Family estrangement: Establishing a prevalence rate. *Journal of Psychology and Behavioral Science, 3*(2), 28–35.

Cook, C. J., Howard, S. J., Scerif, G., Twine, R., Kahn, K., Norris, S. A., & Draper, C. E. (2019). Associations of physical activity and gross motor skills with executive function in preschool children from low-income South African settings. *Developmental Science, 22*(5), e12820. https://doi .org/10.1111/desc.12820

Cooke, J. E., Kochendorfer, L. B., Stuart-Parrigon, K. L., Koehn, A. J., & Kerns, K. A. (2019). Parent–child attachment and children's experience and regulation of emotion: A meta-analytic review. *Emotion, 19*(6), 1103–1126. https:// doi.org/10.1037/emo0000504

Cooley, S., Burkholder, A. R., & Killen, M. (2019). Social inclusion and exclusion in same-race and interracial peer encounters. *Developmental Psychology, 55*(11), 2440–2450. https://doi.org/10.1037/dev0000810

Coontz, S. (2016). *The social origins of private life: A history of American families, 1600–1900.* Verso Books.

Coop Gordon, K., Cordova, J. V., Roberson, P. N. E., Miller, M., Gray, T., Lenger, K. A., Hawrilenko, M., & Martin, K. (2019). An implementation study of relationship checkups as home visitations for low-income at-risk couples. *Family Process, 58*(1), 247–265. https://doi.org/10.1111/famp.12396

Cooper, S. L., Carleton, H. L., Chamberlain, S. A., Cummings, G. G., Bambrick, W., & Estabrooks, C. A. (2016). Burnout in the nursing home health care aide: A systematic review. *Burnout Research, 3*(3), 76–87.

Copeland, W. E., Angold, A., Costello, E. J., & Egger, H. (2013). Prevalence, comorbidity, and correlates of DSM-5 proposed disruptive mood dysregulation disorder. *American Journal of Psychiatry, 170*(2), 173–179. https://doi.org/10.1176/appi.ajp.2012.12010132

Copeland, W. E., Shanahan, L., Hinesley, J., Chan, R. F., Aberg, K. A., Fairbank, J. A., van den Oord, E. J. C. G., & Costello, E. J. (2018). Association of childhood trauma exposure with adult psychiatric disorders and functional outcomes. *JAMA Network Open, 1*(7), e184493–e184493. https://doi.org/10.1001/jamanetworkopen.2018.4493

Copen, C. E., Daniels, K., & Mosher, W. D. (2013). First premarital cohabitation in the United States: 2006–2010 National Survey of Family Growth. *National Health Statistics Reports, 64*, 1–15.

Copen, C. E., Thoma, M. E., Kirmeyer, S. (2015). Interpregnancy intervals in the United States: Data from the birth certificate and the national survey of family growth. *National Vital Statistics Reports, 64*, 1–10.

Coplan, R. J., Rubin, K. H., & Findlay, L. C. (2006). Social and nonsocial play. In D. P. Fromberg & D. Bergen (Eds.), *Play from birth to twelve: Contexts, perspectives, and meanings* (pp. 75–86). Routledge.

Coppens, A. D., Alcalá, L., Rogoff, B., & Mejía-Arauz, R. (2018). Children's contributions in family work: Two cultural paradigms. In S. Punch & R. M. Vanderbeck (Eds.), *Families, intergenerationality, and peer group relations* (pp. 187–213). Springer Singapore. https://doi.org/10.1007/978-981-287-026-1_11

Coppinger, T., Milton, K., Murtagh, E., Harrington, D., Johansen, D., Seghers, J., Skovgaard, T., & Chalkley, A. (2020). Global Matrix 3.0 physical activity report card for children and youth: A comparison across Europe. *Public Health, 187*, 150–156. https://doi.org/10.1016/j.puhe.2020.07.025

Corapci, F., Friedlmeier, W., Benga, O., Strauss, C., Pitica, I., & Susa, G. (2018). Cultural socialization of toddlers in emotionally charged situations. *Social Development, 27*(2), 262–278. https://doi.org/10.1111/sode.12272

Corbett, C., & Hill, C. (2015). *Solving the equation: The variables for women's success in engineering and computing.* American Association of University Women (AAUW).

Corbi, G., Cacciatore, F., Komici, K., Rengo, G., Vitale, D. F., Furgi, G., & Ferrara, N. (2019). Inter-relationships between gender, frailty and 10-year survival in older Italian adults: An observational longitudinal study. *Scientific Reports, 9*(1), 1–7.

Cornell, D., Shukla, K., & Konold, T. (2015). Peer victimization and authoritative school climate: A multilevel approach. *Journal of Educational Psychology, 107*(4), 1186–1201. https://doi.org/10.1037/edu0000038

Corner, J. (2017, September 30). Dementia is a terrible word. Why do people still use it? *The Guardian.* https://www.theguardian.com/healthcare-network/2017/sep/30/dementia-terrible-word-impact-language

Cornwell, B., Goldman, A., & Laumann, E. O. (2021). Homeostasis revisited: Patterns of stability and rebalancing in older adults' social lives. *The Journals of Gerontology: Series B, 76*(4), 778–789. https://doi.org/10.1093/geronb/gbaa026

Cornwell, T. B., Setten, E., Paik, S.-H. W., & Pappu, R. (2020). Parents, products, and the development of preferences: Child palate and food choice in an obesogenic environment. *Journal of Public Policy & Marketing, 40*(3), 429–446. https://doi.org/10.1177/0743915620939581.

Corona, G., Lee, D. M., Forti, G., O'Connor, D. B., Maggi, M., O'Neill, T. W., & EMAS Study Group. (2010). Age-related changes in general and sexual health

in middle-aged and older men: Results from the European Male Ageing Study (EMAS). *The Journal of Sexual Medicine, 7*(4), 1362–1380.

Corporation for National and Community Service (CNCS). (2018). *Volunteering in America.*

Corr, C. A. (2015). Death education at the college and university level in North America. In J. Stillion & T. Attig (Eds.), *Death, dying and bereavement: Contemporary perspectives, institutions and practice* (pp. 207–219). Springer.

Corr, C. A., Corr, D. M., & Doka, K. J. (2018). *Death and dying, life and living.* Cengage Learning.

Corrada, M. M., Brookmeyer, R., Paganini-Hill, A., Berlau, D., & Kawas, C. H. (2010). Dementia incidence continues to increase with age in the oldest old. The 90+ study. *Annals of Neurology, 67*(1), 114–121. https://doi.org/10.1002/ana.21915

Corrado, A., Cici, D., Rotondo, C., Maruotti, N., & Cantatore, F. P. (2020). Molecular basis of bone aging. *International Journal of Molecular Sciences, 21*(10), 3679.

Correia, C., Lopez, K. J., Wroblewski, K. E., Huisingh-Scheetz, M., Kern, D. W., Chen, R. C., Schumm, L. P., Dale, W., McClintock, M. K., & Pinto, J. M. (2016). Global sensory impairment in older adults in the United States. *Journal of the American Geriatrics Society, 64*(2), 306–313. https://doi.org/10.1111/jgs.13955

Corrigan, N. M., Yarnykh, V. L., Hippe, D. S., Owen, J. P., Huber, E., Zhao, T. C., & Kuhl, P. K. (2021). Myelin development in cerebral gray and white matter during adolescence and late childhood. *NeuroImage, 227*, 117678. https://doi.org/10.1016/j.neuroimage.2020.117678

Corsaro, W. A. (2017). *The sociology of childhood.* Sage.

Corsi, D. J., Donelle, J., Sucha, E., Hawken, S., Hsu, H., El-Chaâr, D., Bisnaire, L., Fell, D., Wen, S. W., & Walker, M. (2020). Maternal cannabis use in pregnancy and child neurodevelopmental outcomes. *Nature Medicine, 26*(10), 1536–1540. https://doi.org/10.1038/s41591-020-1002-5

Costa, L. G., Cole, T. B., Dao, K., Chang, Y.-C., Coburn, J., & Garrick, J. M. (2020). Effects of air pollution on the nervous system and its possible role in neurodevelopmental and neurodegenerative disorders. *Pharmacology & Therapeutics, 210*, 107523. https://doi.org/10.1016/j.pharmthera.2020.107523

Costa, P. T., McCrae, R. R., & Löckenhoff, C. E. (2019). Personality across the life span. *Annual Review of Psychology, 70*(1), 423–448. https://doi.org/10.1146/annurev-psych-010418-103244

Costello, E. J. (2016). Early detection and prevention of mental health problems: Developmental epidemiology and systems of support. *Journal of Clinical Child & Adolescent Psychology, 45*(6), 710–717. https://doi.org/10.1080/15374416.2016.1236728

Costello, E. J., Compton, S. N., Keeler, G., & Angold, A. (2003). Relationships between poverty and psychopathology: A natural experiment. *JAMA, 290*(15), 2023–2029.

Costello, E. J., Copeland, W., & Angold, A. (2011). Trends in psychopathology across the adolescent years: What changes when children become adolescents, and when adolescents become adults? *Journal of Child Psychology and Psychiatry, and Allied Disciplines, 52*(10), 1015–1025. https://doi.org/10.1111/j.1469-7610.2011.02446.x

Costello, E. J., Egger, H., & Angold, A. (2005). 10-year research update review: The epidemiology of child and adolescent psychiatric disorders: I. Methods and public health burden. *Journal of the American Academy of Child and Adolescent Psychiatry, 44*(10), 972–986. https://doi.org/10.1097/01.chi.0000172552.41596.6f

Costello, M. A., Narr, R. K., Tan, J. S., & Allen, J. P. (2020). The intensity effect in adolescent close friendships: Implications for aggressive and depressive symptomatology. *Journal of Research on Adolescence, 30*(1), 158–169. https://doi.org/10.1111/jora.12508

Côté, J. E. (2014). The dangerous myth of emerging adulthood: An evidence-based critique of a flawed developmental theory. *Applied Developmental Science, 18*(4), 177–188. https://doi.org/10.1080/10888691.2014.954451

Côté, J. E. (2018a). The enduring usefulness of Erikson's concept of the identity crisis in the 21st century: An analysis of student mental health concerns. *Identity, 18*(4), 251–263.

Côté, J. E. (2018b). *Youth development in identity societies: Paradoxes of purpose.* Routledge. https://doi.org/10.4324/9780429433856

Côté, J. E. (2019). *Youth development in identity societies: Paradoxes of purpose.* Routledge.

Côté, S., Vaillancourt, T., LeBlanc, J. C., Nagin, D. S., & Tremblay, R. E. (2006). The development of physical aggression from toddlerhood to pre-adolescence: A nationwide longitudinal study of Canadian children. *Journal of Abnormal Child Psychology, 34*(1), 68–82. https://doi.org/10.1007/s10802-005-9001-z

Cotofana, S., Fratila, A. A. M., Schenck, T. L., Redka-Swoboda, W., Zilinsky, I., & Pavicic, T. (2016). The anatomy of the aging face: A review. *Facial Plastic Surgery, 32*(3), 253–260. https://doi.org/10.1055/s-0036-1582234

Cotts, K. G., & Cifu, A. S. (2018). Treatment of osteoporosis. *JAMA, 319*(10), 1040–1041.

Coulter, R., Bayrakdar, S., & Berrington, A. (2020). Longitudinal life course perspectives on housing inequality in young adulthood. *Geography Compass, 14*(5), e12488. https://doi.org/10.1111/gec3.12488

Coutinho, J., Pereira, A., Oliveira-Silva, P., Meier, D., Lourenço, V., & Tschacher, W. (2021). When our hearts beat together: Cardiac synchrony as an entry point to understand dyadic co-regulation in couples. *Psychophysiology, 58*(3), e13739. https://doi.org/10.1111/psyp.13739

Cover Jones, M. (1924). A laboratory study of fear: The case of Peter. *The Journal of Genetic Psychology, 31*, 308–315.

Covey, H. C., Menard, S., & Franzese, R. J. (2013). Effects of adolescent physical abuse, exposure to neighborhood violence, and witnessing parental violence on adult socioeconomic status. *Child Maltreatment, 18*(2), 85–97. https://doi.org/10.1177/1077559513477914

Covington, L. B., Rogers, V. E., Armstrong, B., Storr, C. L., & Black, M. M. (2019). Toddler bedtime routines and associations with nighttime sleep duration and maternal and household factors. *Journal of Clinical Sleep Medicine, 15*(6), 865–871. https://doi.org/10.5664/jcsm.7838

Cowell, J. M., & Decety, J. (2015). Precursors to morality in development as a complex interplay between neural, socioenvironmental, and behavioral facets. *Proceedings of the National Academy of Sciences, 112*(41), 12657–12662. https://doi.org/10.1073/pnas.1508832112

Cowell, J. M., Lee, K., Malcolm-Smith, S., Selcuk, B., Zhou, X., & Decety, J. (2017). The development of generosity and moral cognition across five cultures. *Developmental Science, 20*(4), e12403. https://doi.org/10.1111/desc.12403

Cowell, W., Tang, D., Yu, J., Guo, J., Wang, S., Baccarelli, A. A., Perera, F., & Herbstman, J. B. (2021). Telomere dynamics across the early life course: Findings from a longitudinal study in children. *Psychoneuroendocrinology, 129*, 105270. https://doi.org/10.1016/j.psyneuen.2021.105270

Coyle, E. F., Fulcher, M., & Trübutschek, D. (2016). Sissies, mama's boys, and tomboys: Is children's gender nonconformity more acceptable when nonconforming traits are positive? *Archives of Sexual Behavior, 45*(7), 1827–1838.

Coyle, S. (2020, February 6). *Death: Can our final moment be euphoric?* BBC.com. https://www.bbc.com/future/article/20200205-death-can-our-final-moment-be-euphoric

Coyne, S. M., Linder, J. R., Rasmussen, E. E., Nelson, D. A., & Birkbeck, V. (2016). Pretty as a princess: Longitudinal effects of engagement with Disney Princesses on gender stereotypes, body esteem, and prosocial behavior in children. *Child Development, 87*(6), 1909–1925. https://doi.org/10.1111/cdev.12569

Coyne, S. M., Linder, J. R., Rasmussen, E. E., Nelson, D. A., & Collier, K. M. (2014). It's a bird! It's a plane! It's a gender stereotype!: Longitudinal associations between superhero viewing and gender stereotyped play. *Sex Roles, 70*(9), 416–430. https://doi.org/10.1007/s11199-014-0374-8

Coyne, S. M., Ward, L. M., Kroff, S. L., Davis, E. J., Holmgren, H. G., Jensen, A. C., Erickson, S. E., & Essig, L. W. (2019). Contributions of mainstream sexual media exposure to sexual attitudes, perceived peer norms, and sexual behavior: A meta-analysis. *Journal of Adolescent Health, 64*(4), 430–436. https://doi.org/10.1016/j.jadohealth.2018.11.016

Crabbe, R., Pivnick, L. K., Bates, J., Gordon, R. A., & Crosnoe, R. (2019). Contemporary college students' reflections on their high school peer crowds. *Journal of Adolescent Research, 34*(5), 563–596. https://doi.org/10.1177/0743558418809537

Craig, A. T., Heywood, A. E., & Worth, H. (2020). Measles epidemic in Samoa and other Pacific islands. *The Lancet Infectious Diseases, 20*(3), 273-275.

Craig, L., Churchill, B., & van Tienoven, T. P. (2020). Young people's daily activity in a globalized world: A cross-national comparison using time use data. *Journal of Youth Studies, 23*(9), 1195–1216. https://doi.org/10.1080/13676261.2019.1659941

Crawford, S., Hadley, D., & Shepherd, G. (2018). *The Oxford handbook of the archaeology of childhood.* Oxford University Press.

Creaven, A.-M., Healy, A., & Howard, S. (2018). Social connectedness and depression: Is there added value in volunteering? *Journal of Social and Personal Relationships, 35*(10), 1400–1417. https://doi.org/10.1177/0265407517716786

Crenshaw, K. (1989). Demarginalizing the intersection of race and sex: A Black feminist critique of antidiscrimination doctrine, feminist theory and antiracist politics. *University of Chicago Legal Forum, 1989*, 139.

Creswell, J. D., Irwin, M. R., Burklund, L. J., Lieberman, M. D., Arevalo, J. M. G., Ma, J., Breen, E. C., & Cole, S. W. (2012). Mindfulness-based stress reduction training reduces loneliness and pro-inflammatory gene expression in older adults: A small randomized controlled trial. *Brain, Behavior, and Immunity, 26*(7), 1095–1101. https://doi.org/10.1016/j.bbi.2012.07.006

Crews, F. (2017). *Freud: The making of an illusion.* Metropolitan Books.

Crick, N. R., & Grotpeter, J. K. (1996). Children's treatment by peers: Victims of relational and overt aggression. *Development and Psychopathology, 8*(2), 367–380.

Crimmins, E. M., & Zhang, Y. S. (2019). Aging populations, mortality, and life expectancy. *Annual Review of Sociology, 45*(1), 69–89. https://doi.org/10.1146/annurev-soc-073117-041351

Crocetti, E. (2017). Identity formation in adolescence: The dynamic of forming and consolidating identity commitments. *Child Development Perspectives, 11*(2), 145–150. https://doi.org/10.1111/cdep.12226

Crocetti, E., Tagliabue, S., Sugimura, K., Nelson, L. J., Takahashi, A., Niwa, T., Sugiura, Y., & Jinno, M. (2015). Perceptions of emerging adulthood: A study with Italian and Japanese university students and young workers. *Emerging Adulthood, 3*(4), 229–243. https://doi.org/10.1177/2167696815569848

Crone, E. A., & Dahl, R. E. (2012). Understanding adolescence as a period of social–affective engagement and goal flexibility. *Nature Reviews Neuroscience, 13*(9), 636–650. https://doi.org/10.1038/nrn3313

Crone, E. A., & Fuligni, A. J. (2020). Self and others in adolescence. *Annual Review of Psychology, 71*(1), 447–469. https://doi.org/10.1146/annurev-psych-010419-050937

Crone, E. A., & Konijn, E. A. (2018). Media use and brain development during adolescence. *Nature Communications, 9*(1), 588. https://doi.org/10.1038/s41467-018-03126-x

Cronin, C. J., & Evans, W. N. (2020). *Nursing home quality, COVID-19 deaths, and excess mortality* (Working Paper No. 28012; Working Paper Series). National Bureau of Economic Research. https://doi.org/10.3386/w28012

Cropley, V. L., Tian, Y., Fernando, K., Mansour, L. S., Pantelis, C., Cocchi, L., & Zalesky, A. (2021). Brain-predicted age associates with psychopathology dimensions in youths. *Biological Psychiatry: Cognitive Neuroscience and Neuroimaging, 6*(4), 410–419. https://doi.org/10.1016/j.bpsc.2020.07.014

Cropsey, K. L., Schiavon, S., Hendricks, P. S., Froelich, M., Lentowicz, I., & Fargason, R. (2017). Mixed-amphetamine salts expectancies among college students: Is stimulant induced cognitive enhancement a placebo effect? *Drug and Alcohol Dependence, 178*, 302–309. https://doi.org/10.1016/j.drugalcdep.2017.05.024

Crosnoe, R. (2012). *Fitting in, standing out: Navigating the social challenges of high school to get an education.* Cambridge University Press.

Crosnoe, R., & Muller, C. (2014). Family socioeconomic status, peers, and the path to college. *Social Problems, 61*(4), 602–624. https://doi.org/10.1525/sp.2014.12255

Crosnoe, R., Purtell, K. M., Davis-Kean, P., Ansari, A., & Benner, A. D. (2016). The selection of children from low-income families into preschool. *Developmental Psychology, 52*(4), 599–612. https://doi.org/10.1037/dev0000101

Cross, F. L., Agi, A., Montoro, J. P., Medina, M. A., Miller-Tejada, S., Pinetta, B. J., Tran-Dubongco, M., & Rivas-Drake, D. (2020). Illuminating ethnic-racial socialization among undocumented Latinx parents and its implications for adolescent psychosocial functioning. *Developmental Psychology, 56*(8), 1458–1474. https://doi.org/10.1037/dev0000826

Crouch, E., Probst, J. C., Radcliff, E., Bennett, K. J., & McKinney, S. H. (2019). Prevalence of adverse childhood experiences (ACEs) among US children. *Child Abuse & Neglect, 92*, 209–218.

Crouch, J. L., Irwin, L. M., Milner, J. S., Skowronski, J. J., Rutledge, E., & Davila, A. L. (2017). Do hostile attributions and negative affect explain the association between authoritarian beliefs and harsh parenting? *Child Abuse & Neglect, 67*, 13–21. https://doi.org/10.1016/j.chiabu.2017.02.019

Crowley, S. J., Wolfson, A. R., Tarokh, L., & Carskadon, M. A. (2018). An update on adolescent sleep: New evidence informing the perfect storm model. *Journal of Adolescence, 67*, 55–65.

Crump, C., & Howell, E. A. (2020). Perinatal origins of cardiovascular health disparities across the life course. *JAMA Pediatrics, 174*(2), 113–114. https://doi.org/10.1001/jamapediatrics.2019.4616

Cruz-Almeida, Y., Fillingim, R. B., Riley, J. L. I., Woods, A. J., Porges, E., Cohen, R., & Cole, J. (2019). Chronic pain is associated with a brain aging biomarker in community-dwelling older adults. *Pain, 160*(5), 1119–1130. https://doi.org/10.1097/j.pain.0000000000001491

Cruz-Jentoft, A. J., Bahat, G., Bauer, J., Boirie, Y., Bruyère, O., Cederholm, T., Cooper, C., Landi, F., Rolland, Y., Sayer, A. A., Schneider, S. M., Sieber, C. C., Topinkova, E., Vandewoude, M., Visser, M., Zamboni, M., Writing Group for the European Working Group on Sarcopenia in Older People 2 (EWGSOP2), and the Extended Group for EWGSOP2. (2019). Sarcopenia: Revised European consensus on definition and diagnosis. *Age and Ageing, 48*(1), 16–31. https://doi.org/10.1093/ageing/afy169

CS Mott Children's Hospital. (2017). *Parents struggle with when to keep sick kids home from school* (National Poll on Children's Health, Vol. 28, Issue 3). https://mottpoll.org/reports-surveys/parents-struggle-when-keep-sick-kids-home-school

Csikszentmihalyi, M., & LeFevre, J. (1989). Optimal experience in work and leisure. *Journal of Personality and Social Psychology, 56*(5), 815.

Cuartas, J., Jeong, J., Rey-Guerra, C., McCoy, D. C., & Yoshikawa, H. (2020). Maternal, paternal, and other caregivers' stimulation in low- and middle-income countries. *PLOS One, 15*(7), e0236107. https://doi.org/10.1371/journal.pone.0236107

Cuevas, A. G., Ong, A. D., Carvalho, K., Ho, T., Chan, S. W. C., Allen, J., & Williams, D. R. (2020). Discrimination and systemic inflammation: A critical review and synthesis. *Brain, Behavior, and Immunity.*

Cuevas, K., & Sheya, A. (2019). Ontogenesis of learning and memory: Biopsychosocial and dynamical systems perspectives. *Developmental Psychobiology, 61*(3), 402–415. https://doi.org/10.1002/dev.21817

Cui, J., & Natzke, L. (2021). *Early childhood program participation: 2019 first look* (National Household Education Surveys Program NCES 2020-075REV). National Center for Education Statistics at the Institute of Education Sciences, U.S. Department of Education.

Cuijpers, P., Noma, H., Karyotaki, E., Vinkers, C. H., Cipriani, A., & Furukawa, T. A. (2020b). A network meta-analysis of the effects of psychotherapies, pharmacotherapies and their combination in the treatment of adult depression. *World Psychiatry, 19*(1), 92–107.

Cuijpers, P., Stringaris, A., & Wolpert, M. (2020a). Treatment outcomes for depression: Challenges and opportunities. *The Lancet Psychiatry, 7*(11), 925–927. https://doi.org/10.1016/S2215-0366(20)30036-5

Culatta, E., & Clay-Warner, J. (2021). Falling behind and feeling bad: Unmet expectations and mental health during the transition to adulthood. *Society and Mental Health.* https://doi.org/10.1177/2156869321991892

Culbert, K. M., Racine, S. E., & Klump, K. L. (2015). Research review: What we have learned about the causes of eating disorders – a synthesis of sociocultural, psychological, and biological research. *Journal of Child Psychology and Psychiatry, 56*(11), 1141–1164. https://doi.org/10.1111/jcpp.12441

Cullen, J. B., Levitt, S. D., Robertson, E., & Sadoff, S. (2013). What can be done to improve struggling high schools? *The Journal of Economic Perspectives, 27*(2), 133–152. http://www.ingentaconnect.com/contentone/aea/jep/2013/00000027/00000002/art00007

Cumming, E., & Henry, W. E. (1961). *Growing old, the process of disengagement.* Basic Books.

Cummings, K. J., & Leiter, J. C. (2019). Take a deep breath and wake up: The protean role of serotonin in preventing sudden death in infancy. *Experimental Neurology, 326*, 113165. https://doi.org/10.1016/j.expneurol.2019.113165

Cundiff, J. M., & Matthews, K. A. (2018). Friends with health benefits: The long-term benefits of early peer social integration for blood pressure and obesity in midlife. *Psychological Science, 29*(5), 814–823. https://doi.org/10.1177/0956797617746510

Cunningham, R. M., Walton, M. A., & Carter, P. M. (2018). The major causes of death in children and adolescents in the United States. *New England Journal of Medicine, 379*(25), 2468–2475. https://doi.org/10.1056/NEJMsr1804754

Cunningham, T. J., Croft, J. B., Liu, Y., Lu, H., Eke, P. I., & Giles, W. H. (2017). Vital signs: racial disparities in age-specific mortality among blacks or African Americans—United States, 1999–2015. *MMWR. Morbidity and Mortality Weekly Report, 66*(17), 444.

Curington, C. V., Lundquist, J. H., & Lin, K.-H. (2021). *The dating divide: Race and desire in the era of online romance.* University of California Press. https://doi.org/10.1525/9780520966703

Current Population Survey (CPS), U.S. Census Bureau. (2020). 2020 annual social and economic supplement. In *Families and households data tables.* U.S. Census Bureau.

Current Population Survey (CPS), U.S. Census Bureau. (2021). 2021 annual social and economic supplement. In *America's families and living arrangements: 2017* (table C1, "Household relationships and family status of children under 18 years, by age and sex: 2019"). U.S. Census Bureau.

Currie, C., Zanotti, C., Morgan, A., Currie, D., De Looze, M., Roberts, C., Samdal, O., Smith, O. R. F., & Barnekow, V. (2012). *Social determinants of health and well-being among young people. Health behaviour in school-aged children (HBSC) study: International report from the 2009/2010 survey* (Health Policy for Children and Adolescents). WHO Regional Office for Europe.

Curry, O. S., Rowland, L. A., Van Lissa, C. J., Zlotowitz, S., McAlaney, J., & Whitehouse, H. (2018). Happy to help? A systematic review and meta-analysis of the effects of performing acts of kindness on the well-being of the actor. *Journal of Experimental Social Psychology, 76*, 320–329.

Curtin, S. C., & Arias, E. (2019). *Mortality trends by race and ethnicity among adults aged 25 and over: United States, 2000–2017* (NCHS Data Brief No. 342). U.S. Department of Health and Human Services, Centers for Disease Control and Prevention, National Center for Health Statistics.

Curtin, S. C., Hedegaard, H., & Ahmad, F. B. (2021). *Provisional numbers and rates of suicide by month and demographic characteristics: United States, 2020* (NVSS-Vital Statistics Rapid Release). National Vital Statistics System.

Curtis, E. M., Harvey, N. C., & Cooper, C. (2018). The burden of osteoporosis. In N. C. Harvey & C. Cooper (Eds.), *Osteoporosis: A lifecourse epidemiology approach to skeletal health* (pp. 1–20). CRC Press.

Curtis, K., Zhou, Q., & Tao, A. (2020). Emotion talk in Chinese American immigrant families and longitudinal links to children's socioemotional competence.

Developmental Psychology, 56(3), 475–488. https://doi.org /10.1037/dev0000806

Cychosz, M., Cristia, A., Bergelson, E., Casillas, M., Baudet, G., Warlaumont, A. S., & Seidl, A. (2020). Canonical babble development in a large-scale crosslinguistic corpus. *PsyArXiv.*

Czeisler, M. É., Rohan, E. A., Melillo, S., Matjasko, J. L., DePadilla, L., Patel, C. G., Weaver, M. D., Drane, A., Winnay, S. S., Capodilupo, E. R., Robbins, R., Wiley, J. F., Facer-Childs, E. R., Barger, L. K., Czeisler, C. A., Howard, M. E., & Rajaratnam, S. M. W. (2021). Mental health among parents of children aged < 18 years and unpaid caregivers of adults during the COVID-19 pandemic— United States, December 2020 and February– March 2021. *Morbidity and Mortality Weekly Report, 70*(24), 879–887.

Dabass, A., Talbott, E. O., Rager, J. R., Marsh, G. M., Venkat, A., Holguin, F., & Sharma, R. K. (2018). Systemic inflammatory markers associated with cardiovascular disease and acute and chronic exposure to fine particulate matter air pollution (PM2.5) among US NHANES adults with metabolic syndrome. *Environmental Research, 161,* 485–491. https://doi.org/10.1016/j.envres.2017.11.042

Da Costa, D., Danieli, C., Abrahamowicz, M., Dasgupta, K., Sewitch, M., Lowensteyn, I., & Zelkowitz, P. (2019). A prospective study of postnatal depressive symptoms and associated risk factors in first-time fathers. *Journal of Affective Disorders, 249,* 371–377. https://doi.org/10.1016/j .jad.2019.02.033

da Estrela, C., Barker, E. T., Lantagne, S., & Gouin, J. P. (2018). Chronic parenting stress and mood reactivity: The role of sleep quality. *Stress and Health, 34*(2), 296–305.

Dagan, O., & Sagi-Schwartz, A. (2018). Early attachment network with mother and father: An unsettled issue. *Child Development Perspectives, 12*(2), 115–121. https://doi .org/10.1111/cdep.12272

Dahl, A. (2015). The developing social context of infant helping in two U.S. samples. *Child Development, 86*(4), 1080–1093. https://doi.org/10.1111/cdev.12361

Dahl, A. (2016). Infants' unprovoked acts of force toward others. *Developmental Science, 19*(6), 1049–1057.

Dahl, A. (2017). Ecological commitments: Why developmental science needs naturalistic methods. *Child Development Perspectives, 11*(2), 79–84. https://doi.org/10.1111 /cdep.12217

Dahl, A. (2019). The science of early moral development: On defining, constructing, and studying morality from birth. In J. B. Benson (Ed.), *Advances in child development and behavior* (Vol. 56, pp. 1–35). JAI. https://doi .org/10.1016/bs.acdb.2018.11.001

Dahl, A., & Brownell, C. A. (2019). The social origins of human prosociality. *Current Directions in Psychological Science, 28*(3), 274–279. https://doi .org/10.1177/0963721419830386

Dahl, A., & Killen, M. (2018). Moral reasoning: Theory and research in developmental science. In E. A. Phelps & L. Davachi (Vol. Eds.), *Stevens' handbook of experimental psychology and cognitive neuroscience* (Vol. 4, pp. 323–353). Wiley New York.

Dahl, A., & Kim, L. (2014). Why is it bad to make a mess? Preschoolers' conceptions of pragmatic norms. *Cognitive Development, 32,* 12–22.

Dahl, M. J., Mather, M., Düzel, S., Bodammer, N. C., Lindenberger, U., Kühn, S., & Werkle-Bergner, M. (2019). Rostral locus coeruleus integrity is associated with better memory performance in older adults. *Nature Human Behaviour, 3*(11), 1203–1214. https://doi.org/10.1038 /s41562-019-0715-2

Dahl, M. J., Mather, M., Sander, M. C., & Werkle-Bergner, M. (2020). Noradrenergic responsiveness supports selective attention across the adult lifespan. *Journal of Neuroscience, 40*(22), 4372–4390. https://doi .org/10.1523/JNEUROSCI.0398-19.2020

Dahl, R. E., Allen, N. B., Wilbrecht, L., & Suleiman, A. B. (2018). Importance of investing in adolescence from a developmental science perspective. *Nature, 554*(7693), 441–450.

Dahl, V., Amnå, E., Banaji, S., Landberg, M., Šerek, J., Ribeiro, N., Beilmann, M., Pavlopoulos, V., & Zani, B. (2018). Apathy or alienation? Political passivity among youths across eight European Union countries. *European Journal of Developmental Psychology, 15*(3), 284–301. https://doi .org/10.1080/17405629.2017.1404985

Dahlhamer, J., Lucas, J., Zelaya, C., Nahin, R., Mackey, S., DeBar, L., Kerns, R., Von Korff, M., Porter, L., & Helmick, C. (2018). Prevalence of chronic pain and high-impact chronic pain among adults — United States, 2016. *Morbidity and Mortality Weekly Report, 67*(36), 1001– 1006. https://doi.org/10.15585/mmwr.mm6736a2

Dai, J., & Scherf, K. S. (2019). Puberty and functional brain development in humans: Convergence in findings? *Developmental Cognitive Neuroscience, 39,* 100690.

Dai, X., Müller, H.-G., Wang, J.-L., & Deoni, S. C. (2019). Age-dynamic networks and functional correlation for early white matter myelination. *Brain Structure & Function, 224*(2), 535–551. https://doi.org/10.1007 /s00429-018-1785-z

Dale, G., Sampers, D., Loo, S., & Green, C. S. (2018). Individual differences in exploration and persistence: Grit and beliefs about ability and reward. *PLOS ONE, 13*(9), e0203131.

Dale, L. P., Vanderloo, L., Moore, S., & Faulkner, G. (2019). Physical activity and depression, anxiety, and self-esteem in children and youth: An umbrella systematic review. *Mental Health and Physical Activity, 16,* 66–79. https://doi .org/10.1016/j.mhpa.2018.12.001

Dalessandro, A. (2015, October 8). *I'm not your snooki.* Ready To Stare. https://www.readytostare.com/ im-not-your-snooki/

Dalessandro, C. (2019). "It's a lifestyle": Social class, flexibility, and young adults' stories about defining adulthood. *Sociological Spectrum, 39*(4), 250–263. https://doi.org/10.1 080/02732173.2019.1669239

Dalle Grave, R., Sartirana, M., Sermattei, S., & Calugi, S. (2021). Treatment of eating disorders in adults versus adolescents: Similarities and differences. *Clinical Therapeutics, 43*(1), 70–84. https://doi.org/10.1016/j.clinthera.2020.10.015

Daly, M. (2018). Social-media use may explain little of the recent rise in depressive symptoms among adolescent girls. *Clinical Psychological Science, 6*(3), 295.

Daly, M. B., Pilarski, R., Yurgelun, M. B., Berry, M. P., Buys, S. S., Dickson, P., Domchek, S. M., Elkhanany, A., Friedman, S., Garber, J. E., Goggins, M., Hutton, M. L., Khan, S., Klein, C., Kohlmann, W., Kurian, A. W., Laronga, C., Litton, J. K., Mak, J. S., ... Darlow, S. D. (2020). NCCN Guidelines insights: Genetic/familial high-risk assessment: Breast, ovarian, and pancreatic, Version 1.2020: Featured updates to the NCCN Guidelines. *Journal of the National Comprehensive Cancer Network, 18*(4), 380– 391. https://doi.org/10.6004/jnccn.2020.0017

Damashek, A., & Kuhn, J. (2014). Promise and challenges: Interventions for the prevention of unintentional injuries among young children. *Clinical Practice in Pediatric Psychology, 2*(3), 250–262.

D'Ambrosio, C., Jäntti, M., & Lepinteur, A. (2020). Money and happiness: Income, wealth and subjective well-being. *Social Indicators Research, 148*(1), 47–66. https://doi.org/10.1007/s11205-019-02186-w

D'Amen, B., Socci, M., & Santini, S. (2021). Intergenerational caring: A systematic literature review on young and young adult caregivers of older people. *BMC Geriatrics, 21*(1), 105. https:// doi.org/10.1186/s12877-020-01976-z

Damon, W. (2008). *The path to purpose: Helping our children find their calling in life.* Simon & Schuster.

Daneault, V., Dumont, M., Massé, É., Vandewalle, G., & Carrier, J. (2016). Light-sensitive brain pathways and aging. *Journal of Physiological Anthropology, 35*(1), 9. https:// doi.org/10.1186/s40101-016-0091-9

Daniele, M. A. S. (2021). Male partner participation in maternity care and social support for childbearing women: A discussion paper. *Philosophical Transactions of the Royal Society B: Biological Sciences, 376*(1827), 20200021. https:// doi.org/10.1098/rstb.2020.0021

Danielsen, V. M., Vidal-Piñeiro, D., Mowinckel, A. M., Sederevicius, D., Fjell, A. M., Walhovd, K. B., &

Westerhausen, R. (2020). Lifespan trajectories of relative corpus callosum thickness: Regional differences and cognitive relevance. *Cortex, 130,* 127–141. https://doi .org/10.1016/j.cortex.2020.05.020

Danielson, M. L., Bitsko, R. H., Ghandour, R. M., Holbrook, J. R., Kogan, M. D., & Blumberg, S. J. (2018). Prevalence of parent-reported ADHD diagnosis and associated treatment among U.S. children and adolescents, 2016. *Journal of Clinical Child & Adolescent Psychology, 47*(2), 199–212. https:// doi.org/10.1080/15374416.2017.1417860

Danielson, M. L., Bitsko, R. H., Holbrook, J. R., Charania, S. N., Claussen, A. H., McKeown, R. E., Cuffe, S. P., Owens, J. S., Evans, S. W., Kubicek, L., & Flory, K. (2021). Community-based prevalence of externalizing and internalizing disorders among school-aged children and adolescents in four geographically dispersed school districts in the United States. *Child Psychiatry & Human Development, 52*(3), 500–514. https://doi.org/10.1007 /s10578-020-01027-z

Dantchev, S., & Wolke, D. (2019). Trouble in the nest: Antecedents of sibling bullying victimization and perpetration. *Developmental Psychology, 55*(5), 1059.

Danyluck, C., Blair, I. V., Manson, S. M., Laudenslager, M. L., Daugherty, S. L., Jiang, L., & Brondolo, E. (2021). Older and wiser? Age moderates the association between discrimination and depressive symptoms in American Indians and Alaska Natives. *Journal of Aging and Health, 33*(7-8_suppl), 10S–17S. https://doi .org/10.1177/08982643211013699

Darling-Hammond, L. (2011). From "separate but equal" to "no child left behind": The collision of new standards and old inequalities. In E. B. Hilty (Ed.), *Thinking about schools* (pp. 419–438). Routledge.

Darling-Hammond, L., Burns, D., Campbell, C., Goodwin, A. L., & Low, E. L. (2017). International lessons in teacher education. In M. Akiba & G. K. LeTendre (Eds.), *International handbook of teacher quality and policy* (pp. 336–349). Routledge.

Darling-Hammond, L., & Hyler, M. E. (2020). Preparing educators for the time of COVID … and beyond. *European Journal of Teacher Education, 43*(4), 457–465. https://doi .org/10.1080/02619768.2020.1816961

Darling-Hammond, S., Fronius, T. A., Sutherland, H., Guckenburg, S., Petrosino, A., & Hurley, N. (2020). Effectiveness of restorative justice in US K-12 schools: A review of quantitative research. *Contemporary School Psychology, 24,* 295–308.

Darlow, V., Norvilitis, J. M., & Schuetze, P. (2017). The relationship between helicopter parenting and adjustment to college. *Journal of Child and Family Studies, 26*(8), 2291– 2298. https://doi.org/10.1007/s10826-017-0751-3

Darwin, C. (1856, March 9). *To Syms Covington* [Letter]. https://www.darwinproject.ac.uk/letter/DCP-LETT-1840 .xml

Darwin, C. (2009). *The origin of species by means of natural selection: Or, the preservation of favored races in the struggle for life.* A. L. Burt. (Original work published 1872)

Darwin, Z., Domoney, J., Iles, J., Bristow, F., Siew, J., & Sethna, V. (2021). Assessing the mental health of fathers, other co-parents, and partners in the perinatal period: Mixed methods evidence synthesis. *Frontiers in Psychiatry, 11.* https://doi.org/10.3389/fpsyt.2020.585479

Das, J. K., Lassi, Z. S., Hoodbhoy, Z., & Salam, R. A. (2018). Nutrition for the next generation: Older children and adolescents. *Annals of Nutrition and Metabolism, 72*(3), 56–64. https://doi.org/10.1159/000487385

Dasen, P. (1994). Culture and cognitive development from a Piagetian perspective. In W. J. Lonner & R. S. Malpass (Eds.), *Psychology and culture* (pp. 145–149). Allyn & Bacon.

D'astous, V., Abrams, R., Vandrevala, T., Samsi, K., & Manthorpe, J. (2019). Gaps in understanding the experiences of homecare workers providing care for people with dementia up to the end of life: A systematic review. *Dementia, 18*(3), 970–989.

Dato, S., Soerensen, M., Rango, F. D., Rose, G., Christensen, K., Christiansen, L., & Passarino, G. (2018). The genetic component of human longevity: New insights from the analysis of pathway-based SNP-SNP interactions. *Aging Cell, 17*(3), e12755. https://doi.org/10.1111/acel.12755

Daugherty, S. L., Vupputuri, S., Hanratty, R., Steiner, J. F., Maertens, J. A., Blair, I. V., Dickinson, L. M., Helmkamp, L., & Havranek, E. P. (2019). Using values affirmation to reduce the effects of stereotype threat on hypertension disparities: Protocol for the multicenter randomized Hypertension and Values (HYVALUE) trial. *JMIR Research Protocols, 8*(3), e12498. https://doi.org/10.2196/12498

David, D., & Werner, P. (2016). Stigma regarding hearing loss and hearing aids: A scoping review. *Stigma and Health, 1*(2), 59.

David, D., Zoizner, G., & Werner, P. (2018). Self-stigma and age-related hearing loss: A qualitative study of stigma formation and dimensions. *American Journal of Audiology, 27*(1), 126–136.

David, E., & Cruz, C. J. P. (2018). Big, *bakla*, and beautiful: Transformations on a Manila pageant stage. *Women's Studies Quarterly, 46*(1/2), 29–45.

Davidov, M., Paz, Y., Roth-Hanania, R., Uzefovsky, F., Orlitsky, T., Mankuta, D., & Zahn-Waxler, C. (2021). Caring babies: Concern for others in distress during infancy. *Developmental Science, 24*(2), e13016. https://doi.org/10.1111/desc.13016

Davidov, M., Vaish, A., Knafo-Noam, A., & Hastings, P. D. (2016). The motivational foundations of prosocial behavior from a developmental perspective–evolutionary roots and key psychological mechanisms: Introduction to the special section. *Child Development, 87*(6), 1655–1667.

Davidow, J. Y., Foerde, K., Galván, A., & Shohamy, D. (2016). An upside to reward sensitivity: The hippocampus supports enhanced reinforcement learning in adolescence. *Neuron, 92*(1), 93–99. https://doi.org/10.1016/j.neuron.2016.08.031

Davidow, J. Y., Insel, C., & Somerville, L. H. (2018). Adolescent development of value-guided goal pursuit. *Trends in Cognitive Sciences, 22*(8), 725–736.

Davies, B. (2010, October 29). Life in a snapshot: Amazing year-by-year sequence of the changing face of one British family. *Mail Online.* https://www.dailymail.co.uk/news/article-1325006/Year-year-changing-face-British-family.html

Davis, A., McMahon, C. M., Pichora-Fuller, K. M., Russ, S., Lin, F., Olusanya, B. O., & Tremblay, K. L. (2016). Aging and hearing health: The life-course approach. *The Gerontologist, 56*(Suppl_2), S256–S267.

Davis, A. C., Wright, C., Curtis, M., Hellard, M. E., Lim, M. S. C., & Temple-Smith, M. J. (2019). 'Not my child': Parenting, pornography, and views on education. *Journal of Family Studies,* 1–16. https://doi.org/10.1080/13229400.2019.1657929

Davis, D.-A. (2019). *Reproductive injustice: Racism, pregnancy, and premature birth.* New York University Press.

Davis, E. M., & Fingerman, K. L. (2016). Digital dating: Online profile content of older and younger adults. *The Journals of Gerontology: Series B, 71*(6), 959–967. https://doi.org/10.1093/geronb/gbv042

Davis, E. P., & Narayan, A. J. (2020). Pregnancy as a period of risk, adaptation, and resilience for mothers and infants. *Development and Psychopathology, 32*(5), 1625–1639. https://doi.org/10.1017/S0954579420001121

Davis, H. E., Crittenden, A. N., & Scalise Sugiyama, M. (2021). Ecological and developmental perspectives on social learning. *Human Nature.* https://doi.org/10.1007/s12110-021-09394-9

Davis, J., Redshaw, J., Suddendorf, T., Nielsen, M., Kennedy-Costantini, S., Oostenbroek, J., & Slaughter, V. (2021). Does neonatal imitation exist? Insights from a meta-analysis of 336 effect sizes. *Perspectives on Psychological Science.* https://doi.org/10.1177/1745691620959834

Davis, K. (2005). *A girl like me* [Short film].

Davis, K., Charmaraman, L., & Weinstein, E. (2020). Introduction to special issue: Adolescent and emerging adult development in an age of social media. *Journal of Adolescent Research, 35*(1), 3–15. https://doi.org/10.1177/0743558419886392

Davis, N. J., Wyman, J. F., Gubitosa, S., & Pretty, L. (2020). Urinary incontinence in older adults. *AJN: The American Journal of Nursing, 120*(1), 57–62. https://doi.org/10.1097/01.NAJ.0000652124.58511.24

Davis-Floyd, R., Gutschow, K., & Schwartz, D. A. (2020). Pregnancy, birth and the COVID-19 pandemic in the United States. *Medical Anthropology, 39*(5), 413–427. https://doi.org/10.1080/01459740.2020.1761804

Davydov, V. V. (1995). The influence of LS Vygotsky on education theory, research, and practice. *Educational Researcher, 24*(3), 12–21.

Dawood, F. S., Chung, J. R., Kim, S. S., Zimmerman, R. K., Nowalk, M. P., Jackson, M. L., Jackson, L. A., Monto, A. S., Martin, E. T., Belongia, E. A., McLean, H. Q., Gaglani, M., Dunnigan, K., Foust, A., Sessions, W., DaSilva, J., Le, S., Stark, T., Kondor, R. J., ... Flannery, B. (2020). Interim estimates of 2019–20 seasonal influenza vaccine effectiveness—United States, February 2020. *Morbidity and Mortality Weekly Report, 69*(7), 177–182. https://doi.org/10.15585/mmwr.mm6907a1

Dawson, A., Pike, A., & Bird, L. (2015). Parental division of household labour and sibling relationship quality: Family relationship mediators. *Infant and Child Development, 24*(4), 379–393. https://doi.org/10.1002/icd.1890

Day, J., Savani, S., Krempley, B. D., Nguyen, M., & Kitlinska, J. B. (2016). Influence of paternal preconception exposures on their offspring: Through epigenetics to phenotype. *American Journal of Stem Cells, 5*(1), 11–18.

Day, J. K., Perez-Brumer, A., & Russell, S. T. (2018). Safe schools? Transgender youth's school experiences and perceptions of school climate. *Journal of Youth and Adolescence, 47*(8), 1731–1742.

Deal, B. J., Huffman, M. D., Binns, H., & Stone, N. J. (2020). Perspective: Childhood obesity requires new strategies for prevention. *Advances in Nutrition, 11*(5), 1071–1078. https://doi.org/10.1093/advances/nmaa040

Deal, J. (2019, November 4). Youth political engagement and hope ahead of the 2020 election. *Harvard Political Review.* https://harvardpolitics.com/youth-political-engagement-and-hope-ahead-of-the-2020-election/

Dean, D. C., O'Muircheartaigh, J., Dirks, H., Waskiewicz, N., Walker, L., Doernberg, E., Piryatinsky, I., & Deoni, S. C. L. (2015). Characterizing longitudinal white matter development during early childhood. *Brain Structure and Function, 220*(4), 1921–1933. https://doi.org/10.1007/s00429-014-0763-3

Dean, L. T., Greene, N., Adams, M. A., Geffen, S. R., Malone, J., Tredway, K., & Poteat, T. (2021). Beyond Black and White: Race and sexual identity as contributors to healthcare system distrust after breast cancer screening among US women. *Psycho-Oncology, 30*(7), 1145–1150. https://doi.org/10.1002/pon.5670

Dear, P. (2008). *The intelligibility of nature: How science makes sense of the world.* University of Chicago Press.

Deardorff, J., Hoyt, L. T., Carter, R., & Shirtcliff, E. A. (2019). Next steps in puberty research: Broadening the lens toward understudied populations. *Journal of Research on Adolescence, 29*(1), 133–154. https://doi.org/10.1111/jora.12402

Death With Dignity. (2021). *Annual report: A year of online advocacy* [Annual report].

Deaton, A., & Stone, A. A. (2014). Evaluative and hedonic wellbeing among those with and without children at home. *Proceedings of the National Academy of Sciences, 111*(4), 1328–1333.

de Bont, J., Díaz, Y., Casas, M., García-Gil, M., Vrijheid, M., & Duarte-Salles, T. (2020). Time trends and sociodemographic factors associated with overweight and obesity in children and adolescents in Spain. *JAMA Network Open, 3*(3), e201171. https://doi.org/10.1001/jamanetworkopen.2020.1171

De Bruyckere, P., Kirschner, P. A., & Hulshof, C. (2020). *More urban myths about learning and education: Challenging eduquacks, extraordinary claims, and alternative facts.* Routledge.

DeCapua, A., & Wintergerst, A. C. (2016). *Crossing cultures in the language classroom.* University of Michigan Press.

Decaroli, M. C., & Rochira, V. (2017). Aging and sex hormones in males. *Virulence, 8*(5), 545–570. https://doi.org/10.1080/21505594.2016.1259053

de Carvalho Mrad, F. C., da Silva, M. E., de Oliveira Lima, E., Bessa, A. L., de Bessa Junior, J., Netto, J. M. B., & de Almeida Vasconcelos, M. M. (2021). Toilet training methods in children with normal neuropsychomotor development: A systematic review. *Journal of Pediatric Urology.* https://doi.org/10.1016/j.jpurol.2021.05.010

DeCasper, A. J., & Fifer, W. P. (1980). Of human bonding: Newborns prefer their mothers' voices. *Science, 208*(4448), 1174–1176. https://doi.org/10.1126/science.7375928

Decety, J. (2015). The neural pathways, development and functions of empathy. *Current Opinion in Behavioral Sciences, 3,* 1–6.

Decety, J., & Steinbeis, N. (2020). Multiple mechanisms of prosocial development. In J. Decety (Ed.), *The social brain: A developmental perspective* (pp. 219–246). MIT Press.

de Chambrier, A.-F., & Zesiger, P. (2018). Is a fact retrieval deficit the main characteristic of children with mathematical learning disabilities? *Acta Psychologica, 190,* 95–102.

Declercq, E. R., Sakala, C., Corry, M. P., Applebaum, S., & Herrlich, A. (2013). *Listening to mothers^SM III. New Mothers Speak Out.* Childbirth Connection.

De Coen, J., Verbeken, S., & Goossens, L. (2021). Media influence components as predictors of children's body image and eating problems: A longitudinal study of boys and girls during middle childhood. *Body Image, 37,* 204–213. https://doi.org/10.1016/j.bodyim.2021.03.001

Deer, B. (2011). How the case against the MMR vaccine was fixed. *BMJ, 342,* c5347. https://doi.org/10.1136/bmj.c5347

Deer, B. (2020). *The doctor who fooled the world: Science, deception, and the war on vaccines.* JHU Press.

DeForche, B., Van Dyck, D., Deliens, T., & De Bourdeaudhuij, I. (2015). Changes in weight, physical activity, sedentary behaviour and dietary intake during the transition to higher education: A prospective study. *International Journal of Behavioral Nutrition and Physical Activity, 12*(1), 16. https://doi.org/10.1186/s12966-015-0173-9

Degenhardt, L., Bharat, C., Glantz, M. D., Sampson, N. A., Al-Hamzawi, A., Alonso, J., Andrade, L. H., Bunting, B., Cia, A., de Girolamo, G., De Jonge, P., Demyttenaere, K., Gureje, O., Haro, J. M., Harris, M. G., He, Y., Hinkov, H., Karam, A. N., Karam, E. G., ... for the WHO World Mental Health Survey Collaborators. (2019). Association of cohort and individual substance use with risk of transitioning to drug use, drug use disorder, and remission from disorder: Findings from the World Mental Health Surveys. *JAMA Psychiatry, 76*(7), 708–720. https://doi.org/10.1001/jamapsychiatry.2019.0163

Degenhardt, L., Charlson, F., Ferrari, A., Santomauro, D., Erskine, H., Mantilla–Herrara, A., Whiteford, H., Leung, J., Naghavi, M., Griswold, M., Rehm, J., Hall, W., Sartorius, B., Scott, J., Vollset, S. E., Knudsen, A. K., Haro, J. M., Patton, G., Kopec, J., ... Vos, T. (2018). The global burden of disease attributable to alcohol and drug use in 195 countries and territories, 1990–2016: A systematic analysis for the Global Burden of Disease Study 2016. *The Lancet Psychiatry, 5*(12), 987–1012. https://doi.org/10.1016/S2215-0366(18)30337-7

Degenhardt, L., Stockings, E., Patton, G., Hall, W. D., & Lynskey, M. (2016). The increasing global health priority of substance use in young people. *The Lancet Psychiatry, 3*(3), 251–264. https://doi.org/10.1016/S2215-0366(15)00508-8

de Guzman, N. S., & Nishina, A. (2017). 50 years of loving: Interracial romantic relationships and recommendations for future research. *Journal of Family Theory & Review, 9*(4), 557–571. https://doi.org/10.1111/jftr.12215

De Haan, M. (2015). Neuroscientific methods in children. In W. Overton & P. Molenaar (Eds.), *Handbook of child psychology* (pp. 102–140). John Wiley & Sons.

Dehn, M. J. (2011). *Working memory and academic learning: Assessment and intervention.* Wiley.

De Houwer, A. (2020). Harmonious bilingualism: Well-being for families in bilingual settings. In A. C. Schalley &

S. A. Eisenchlas (Eds.), *Handbook of home language maintenance and development: Social and affective factors* (pp. 63–83). De Gruyter Mouton.

Deichmann, F., & Ahnert, L. (2021). The terrible twos: How children cope with frustration and tantrums and the effect of maternal and paternal behaviors. *Infancy, 26*(3), 469–493. https://doi.org/10.1111/infa.12389

Dekhtyar, S., Wang, H. X., Scott, K., Goodman, A., Koupil, I., & Herlitz, A. (2015). A life-course study of cognitive reserve in dementia—from childhood to old age. *The American Journal of Geriatric Psychiatry, 23*(9), 885–896.

de la Fontaine, N., Hahn, H., Stover, C. S., & Marans, S. (2021). Extending law enforcement reach to children exposed to violence: Police training evaluation. *Journal of Police and Criminal Psychology.* https://doi.org/10.1007/s11896-021-09448-9

DeLamater, J., & Koepsel, E. (2015). Relationships and sexual expression in later life: A biopsychosocial perspective. *Sexual and Relationship Therapy, 30*(1), 37–59. https://doi.org/10.1080/14681994.2014.939506

DeLamater, J., Koepsel, E. R., & Johnson, T. (2019). Changes, changes? Women's experience of sexuality in later life. *Sexual and Relationship Therapy, 34*(2), 211–227.

De Leersnyder, J., Mesquita, B., & Boiger, M. (2020). What has culture got to do with emotions? A lot. In M. J. Gelfand, C.-Y. Chiu, & Y.-Y. Hong (Eds.), *Handbook of advances in culture and psychology* (Vol. 8, pp. 62–119). Oxford University Press.

Delgado, M. Y., Nair, R. L., Zeiders, K. H., & Jones, S. K. (2019). Latino adolescents' experiences with ethnic discrimination: Moderating factors and mediating mechanisms. In H. E. Fitzgerald, D. J. Johnson, D. B. Qin, F. A. Villarruel, & J. Norder (Eds.), *Handbook of children and prejudice: Integrating research, practice, and policy* (pp. 515–531). Springer International Publishing. https://doi.org/10.1007/978-3-030-12228-7_29

Delgado, R. (1995). *Critical race theory.* Temple University Press.

Del Giudice, F., Kasman, A. M., Ferro, M., Sciarra, A., De Berardinis, E., Belladelli, F., Salonia, A., & Eisenberg, M. L. (2020). Clinical correlation among male infertility and overall male health: A systematic review of the literature. *Investigative and Clinical Urology, 61*(4), 355–371. https://doi.org/10.4111/icu.2020.61.4.355

DeLiema, M., Homeier, D. C., Anglin, D., Li, D., & Wilber, K. H. (2016). The forensic lens: Bringing elder neglect into focus in the emergency department. *Annals of Emergency Medicine, 68*(3), 371–377. https://doi.org/10.1016/j.annemergmed.2016.02.008

Delli Carpini, M. X. (2000). Gen.com: Youth, civic engagement, and the new information environment. *Political Communication, 17*(4), 341–349.

Deloitte. (2019). *The Deloitte Global Millennial Survey 2019: Societal discord and technological transformation create a "generation disrupted."*

DeLuca, C. R., & Leventer, R. J. (2008). Developmental trajectories of executive functions across the lifespan. In V. Anderson, R. Jacobs, & P. J. Anderson (Eds.), *Executive functions and the frontal lobes: A lifespan perspective* (pp. 23–56). Taylor & Francis.

DeLuca, S., Clampet-Lundquist, S., & Edin, K. (2016). *Coming of age in the other America.* Russell Sage Foundation.

Demedardi, M.-J., Brechet, C., Gentaz, E., & Monnier, C. (2021). Prosocial lying in children between 4 and 11 years of age: The role of emotional understanding and empathy. *Journal of Experimental Child Psychology, 203,* 105045. https://doi.org/10.1016/j.jecp.2020.105045

Deming, D. J., & Noray, K. L. (2018). *STEM careers and the changing skill requirements of work* (Working Paper No. 25065). National Bureau of Economic Research. https://doi.org/10.3386/w25065

Demo, D. H., & Fine, M. A. (2010). *Beyond the average divorce.* Sage.

Denckla, C. A., Cicchetti, D., Kubzansky, L. D., Seedat, S., Teicher, M. H., Williams, D. R., & Koenen, K. C. (2020). Psychological resilience: An update on definitions, a critical appraisal, and research recommendations. *European Journal of Psychotraumatology, 11*(1), 1822064.

Denford, S., Abraham, C., Campbell, R., & Busse, H. (2017). A comprehensive review of reviews of school-based interventions to improve sexual-health. *Health Psychology Review, 11*(1), 33–52. https://doi.org/10.1080/17437199.2016.1240625

Denham, M. (2016). *A brief history of the care of the elderly.* British Geriatric Society.

Denham, S. A. (2019). Emotional competence during childhood and adolescence. In V. LoBue, K. Pérez-Edgar, & K. A. Buss (Eds.), *Handbook of emotional development* (pp. 493–541). Springer International Publishing. https://doi.org/10.1007/978-3-030-17332-6_20

DeNicolo, C. P., Yu, M., Crowley, C. B., & Gabel, S. L. (2017). Reimagining critical care and problematizing sense of school belonging as a response to inequality for immigrants and children of immigrants. *Review of Research in Education, 41*(1), 500–530. https://doi.org/10.3102/0091732X17690498

Denissen, J. J. A., Luhmann, M., Chung, J. M., & Bleidorn, W. (2019). Transactions between life events and personality traits across the adult lifespan. *Journal of Personality and Social Psychology, 116*(4), 612–633. https://doi.org/10.1037/pspp0000196

Dennis, C.-L., Shiri, R., Brown, H. K., Santos, H. P., Schmied, V., & Falah-Hassani, K. (2019). Breastfeeding rates in immigrant and non-immigrant women: A systematic review and meta-analysis. *Maternal & Child Nutrition, 15*(3), e12809. https://doi.org/10.1111/mcn.12809

Denomme, M. M., Haywood, M. E., Parks, J. C., Schoolcraft, W. B., & Katz-Jaffe, M. G. (2020). The inherited methylome landscape is directly altered with paternal aging and associated with offspring neurodevelopmental disorders. *Aging Cell, 19*(8), e13178. https://doi.org/10.1111/acel.13178

Denton, M. L., & Uecker, J. E. (2018). What God has joined together: Family formation and religion among young adults. *Review of Religious Research, 60*(1), 1–22. https://doi.org/10.1007/s13644-017-0308-3

Deoni, S., Dean, D., Joelson, S., O'Regan, J., & Schneider, N. (2018). Early nutrition influences developmental myelination and cognition in infants and young children. *NeuroImage, 178,* 649–659. https://doi.org/10.1016/j.neuroimage.2017.12.056

de Onis, M. (2017). Child growth and development. In S. de Pee, D. Taren, & M. W. Bloem (Eds.), *Nutrition and health in a developing world* (pp. 119–141). Springer International Publishing. https://doi.org/10.1007/978-3-319-43739-2_6

de Onis, M., Borghi, E., Arimond, M., Webb, P., Croft, T., Saha, K., De-Regil, L. M., Thuita, F., Heidkamp, R., & Krasevec, J. (2019). Prevalence thresholds for wasting, overweight and stunting in children under 5 years. *Public Health Nutrition, 22*(1), 175–179. https://doi.org/10.1017/S1368980018002434

DePasquale, C. E. (2020). A systematic review of caregiver-child physiological synchrony across systems: Associations with behavior and child functioning. *Development and Psychopathology, 32*(5), 1754–1777. https://doi.org/10.1017/S0954579420001236

DePaulo, B. (2017). Toward a positive psychology of single life. In D. S. Dunn (Ed.), *Positive psychology: Established and emerging issues* (pp. 251–275). Routledge.

Derbyshire, S. W., & Bockmann, J. C. (2020). Reconsidering fetal pain. *Journal of Medical Ethics, 46*(1), 3–6. https://doi.org/10.1136/medethics-2019-105701

Desai, A. K., Desai, F. G., McFadden, S., & Grossberg, G. T. (2016). Experiences and perspectives of persons with dementia. In M. Boltz & J. E. Galvin (Eds.), *Dementia care: An evidence-based approach* (pp. 151–166). Springer International Publishing. https://doi.org/10.1007/978-3-319-18377-0_10

Desmond, C., Watt, K., Saha, A., Huang, J., & Lu, C. (2020). Prevalence and number of children living in institutional care: Global, regional, and country estimates. *The Lancet Child & Adolescent Health, 4*(5), 370–377. https://doi.org/10.1016/S2352-4642(20)30022-5

Detsky, M. E., Harhay, M. O., Bayard, D. F., Delman, A. M., Buehler, A. E., Kent, S. A., Ciuffetelli, I. V., Cooney, E., Gabler, N. B., Ratcliffe, S. J., Mikkelsen, M. E., &

Halpern, S. D. (2017). Discriminative accuracy of physician and nurse predictions for survival and functional outcomes 6 months after an ICU admission. *JAMA, 317*(21), 2187–2195. https://doi.org/10.1001/jama.2017.4078

Devanand, D. P. (2016). Olfactory identification deficits, cognitive decline, and dementia in older adults. *The American Journal of Geriatric Psychiatry, 24*(12), 1151–1157. https://doi.org/10.1016/j.jagp.2016.08.010

Devore, I., & Konner, M. J. (2019). 6. Infancy in hunter-gatherer life: An ethological perspective. In N. F. White (Ed.), *Ethology and psychiatry* (pp. 113–141). University of Toronto Press. https://www.degruyter.com/document/doi/10.3138/9781487575663-009/html

de Vries, D. A., Vossen, H. G. M., & van der Kolk – van der Boom, P. (2019). Social media and body dissatisfaction: Investigating the attenuating role of positive parent–adolescent relationships. *Journal of Youth and Adolescence, 48*(3), 527–536. https://doi.org/10.1007/s10964-018-0956-9

de Vries, R. (1969). Constancy of generic identity in the years three to six. *Monographs of the Society for Research in Child Development, 34*(3), iii–67. https://doi.org/10.2307/1165683

de Waal, F. (2019). *Mama's last hug: Animal emotions and what they tell us about ourselves.* W. W. Norton.

DeYoung, C. G., & Allen, T. A. (2019). Personality neuroscience: A developmental perspective. In D. P. McAdams, R. L. Shiner, & J. L. Tackett (Eds.), *Handbook of personality development* (pp. 79–105). Guilford.

Dharmapuri, S., Miller, K., & Klein, J. D. (2020). Marijuana and the pediatric population. *Pediatrics, 146*(2).

D'hondt, F., Maene, C., Vervaet, R., Van Houtte, M., & Stevens, P. A. (2021). Ethnic discrimination in secondary education: Does the solution lie in multicultural education and the ethnic school composition? *Social Psychology of Education,* 1–28.

Diamond, A. (1985). Development of the ability to use recall to guide action, as indicated by infants' performance on AB. *Child Development,* 868–883.

Diamond, A. (2013). Executive functions. *Annual Review of Psychology, 64*(1), 135–168. https://doi.org/10.1146/annurev-psych-113011-143750

Diamond, A., & Ling, D. S. (2016). Conclusions about interventions, programs, and approaches for improving executive functions that appear justified and those that, despite much hype, do not. *Developmental Cognitive Neuroscience, 18*(Supplement C), 34–48. https://doi.org/10.1016/j.dcn.2015.11.005

Diamond, L. M. (2016). Sexual fluidity in male and females. *Current Sexual Health Reports, 8*(4), 249–256. https://doi.org/10.1007/s11930-016-0092-z

Diamond, L. M. (2020). Gender fluidity and nonbinary gender identities among children and adolescents. *Child Development Perspectives, 14*(2), 110–115. https://doi.org/10.1111/cdep.12366

Diamond, L. M., Bonner, S. B., & Dickenson, J. (2015). The development of sexuality. In M. E. Lamb & R. M. Lerner (Eds.), *Handbook of child psychology and developmental science: Socioemotional processes* (pp. 888–931). Wiley.

Dias, N. M., & Seabra, A. G. (2015). Is it possible to promote executive functions in preschoolers? A case study in Brazil. *International Journal of Child Care and Education Policy, 9*(1), 6. https://doi.org/10.1186/s40723-015-0010-2

Diaz-Rojas, F., Matsunaga, M., Tanaka, Y., Kikusui, T., Mogi, K., Nagasawa, M., Asano, K., Abe, N., & Myowa, M. (2021). Development of the paternal brain in expectant fathers during early pregnancy. *NeuroImage, 225,* 117527. https://doi.org/10.1016/j.neuroimage.2020.117527

Dick, F., Krishnan, S., Leech, R., & Curtin, S. (2016). Language development. In G. Hickok & S. L. Small (Eds.), *Neurobiology of language* (pp. 373–388). Academic Press. https://doi.org/10.1016/B978-0-12-407794-2.00031-6

Dickstein, D. L., Weaver, C. M., Luebke, J. I., & Hof, P. R. (2013). Dendritic spine changes associated with normal aging. *Neuroscience, 251,* 21–32. https://doi.org/10.1016/j.neuroscience.2012.09.077

Dienel, G. A. (2019). Brain glucose metabolism: Integration of energetics with function. *Physiological Reviews, 99*(1), 949–1045.

Dierickx, S., Onwuteaka-Philipsen, B., Penders, Y., Cohen, J., van der Heide, A., Puhan, M. A., Ziegler, S.,

Bosshard, G., Deliens, L., & Chambaere, K. (2020). Commonalities and differences in legal euthanasia and physician-assisted suicide in three countries: A population-level comparison. *International Journal of Public Health, 65*(1), 65–73. https://doi.org/10.1007/s00038-019-01281-6

Dietz, W. H. (2017). Obesity and excessive weight gain in young adults: New targets for prevention. *JAMA, 318*(3), 241–242. https://doi.org/10.1001/jama.2017.6119

Dietz, W. H. (2019). We need a new approach to prevent obesity in low-income minority populations. *Pediatrics, 143*(6), e20190839. https://doi.org/10.1542/peds.2019-0839

Dietze, P., Gantman, A., Nam, H. H., Niemi, L., & Marginalia Science. (2019). Marginalised ideas are key to scientific progress. *Nature Human Behaviour, 3*(10), 1024–1024. https://doi.org/10.1038/s41562-019-0699-y

Digdon, N. (2020). The Little Albert controversy: Intuition, confirmation bias, and logic. *History of Psychology, 23*(2), 122.

Di Gessa, G., Glaser, K., & Tinker, A. (2016). The health impact of intensive and nonintensive grandchild care in Europe: New evidence from SHARE. *The Journals of Gerontology: Series B, 71*(5), 867–879. https://doi.org/10.1093/geronb/gbv055

DiGiovanni, A. M., Vannucci, A., Ohannessian, C. M., & Bolger, N. (2021). Modeling heterogeneity in the simultaneous emotional costs and social benefits of co-rumination. *PsyArXiv.* https://doi.org/10.31234/osf.io/gmjvk

Dijk, K. A., Thijssen, S., van 't Veer, A., Buisman, R. S. M., van IJzendoorn, M. H., & Bakermans-Kranenburg, M. (2020). Exploring the transition into fatherhood: Behavioral, hormonal, and neural underpinnings of responses to infant crying. *PsyArXiv.* https://doi.org/10.31234/osf.io/5bxk9

Dill, J., & Frech, A. (2019). Providing for a family in the working class: Gender and employment after the birth of a child. *Social Forces, 98*(1), 183–210. https://doi.org/10.1093/sf/soy106

Dillon, M. R., Kannan, H., Dean, J. T., Spelke, E. S., & Duflo, E. (2017). Cognitive science in the field: A preschool intervention durably enhances intuitive but not formal mathematics. *Science, 357*(6346), 47–55. https://doi.org/10.1126/science.aal4724

Dilmaç, J. A. (2018). The new forms of mourning: Loss and exhibition of the death on the internet. *OMEGA—Journal of Death and Dying, 77*(3), 280–295. https://doi.org/10.1177/0030222816633240

Dimler, L. M., & Natsuaki, M. N. (2015). The effects of pubertal timing on externalizing behaviors in adolescence and early adulthood: A meta-analytic review. *Journal of Adolescence, 45*, 160–170.

Dimler, L. M., & Natsuaki, M. N. (2021). Trajectories of violent and nonviolent behaviors from adolescence to early adulthood: Does early puberty matter, and, if so, how long? *Journal of Adolescent Health, 68*(3), 523–531. https://doi.org/10.1016/j.jadohealth.2020.06.034

Dimock, M. (2019, January 17). *Defining generations: Where Millennials end and Generation Z begins.* Pew Research Center. https://www.pewresearch.org/fact-tank/2019/01/17/where-millennials-end-and-generation-z-begins/

Ding, R., He, W., & Wang, Q. (2021). A comparative analysis of emotion-related cultural norms in popular American and Chinese storybooks. *Journal of Cross-Cultural Psychology, 52*(2), 209–226. https://doi.org/10.1177/0022022120988900

Ding, X., Chen, X., Fu, R., Li, D., & Liu, J. (2020). Relations of shyness and unsociability with adjustment in migrant and non-migrant children in urban China. *Journal of Abnormal Child Psychology, 48*(2), 289–300. https://doi.org/10.1007/s10802-019-00583-w

Ding, X. P., Heyman, G. D., Fu, G., Zhu, B., & Lee, K. (2018). Young children discover how to deceive in 10 days: A microgenetic study. *Developmental Science, 21*(3), e12566. https://doi.org/10.1111/desc.12566

Diniz, B. S., Butters, M. A., Albert, S. M., Dew, M. A., & Reynolds, C. F. (2013). Late-life depression and risk of vascular dementia and Alzheimer's disease: Systematic review and meta-analysis of community-based cohort studies. *The British Journal of Psychiatry, 202*(5), 329–335. https://doi.org/10.1192/bjp.bp.112.118307

DiPietro, J. A., Costigan, K. A., & Voegtline, K. M. (2015). Studies in fetal behavior: Revisited, renewed, and reimagined. *Monographs of the Society for Research in Child Development, 80*(3), vii, 1–151. https://doi.org/10.1111/mono.v80.3

DiPrete, T. A., & Buchmann, C. (2013). *The rise of women: The growing gender gap in education and what it means for American schools.* Russell Sage Foundation.

Dirix, C. E. H., Nijhuis, J. G., Jongsma, H. W., & Hornstra, G. (2009). Aspects of fetal learning and memory. *Child Development, 80*(4), 1251–1258.

Dirks, M. A., Persram, R., Recchia, H. E., & Howe, N. (2015). Sibling relationships as sources of risk and resilience in the development and maintenance of internalizing and externalizing problems during childhood and adolescence. *Clinical Psychology Review, 42*, 145–155. https://doi.org/10.1016/j.cpr.2015.07.003

Dirks, M. A., Recchia, H. E., Estabrook, R., Howe, N., Petitclerc, A., Burns, J. L., Briggs-Gowan, M. J., & Wakschlag, L. S. (2019). Differentiating typical from atypical perpetration of sibling-directed aggression during the preschool years. *Journal of Child Psychology and Psychiatry, 60*(3), 267–276. https://doi.org/10.1111/jcpp.12939

Dishion, T. J., & McMahon, R. J. (1998). Parental monitoring and the prevention of child and adolescent problem behavior: A conceptual and empirical formulation. *Clinical Child and Family Psychology Review, 1*(1), 61–75.

Distefano, G., & Goodpaster, B. H. (2018). Effects of exercise and aging on skeletal muscle. *Cold Spring Harbor Perspectives in Medicine, 8*(3), a029785.

Distefano, R., Grenell, A., Palmer, A. R., Houlihan, K., Masten, A. S., & Carlson, S. M. (2021). Self-regulation as promotive for academic achievement in young children across risk contexts. *Cognitive Development, 58*, 101050.

DiTomasso, D. (2019). Bearing the pain: A historic review exploring the impact of science and culture on pain management for childbirth in the United States. *The Journal of Perinatal & Neonatal Nursing, 33*(4), 322. https://doi.org/10.1097/JPN.0000000000000407

Di Ventra, M. (2018). *The scientific method: Reflections from a practitioner.* Oxford University Press.

Dixon, A. R., & Telles, E. E. (2017). Skin color and colorism: Global research, concepts, and measurement. *Annual Review of Sociology, 43*(1), 405–424. https://doi.org/10.1146/annurev-soc-060116-053315

Dixson, D. D., Worrell, F. C., Olszewski-Kubilius, P., & Subotnik, R. F. (2016). Beyond perceived ability: The contribution of psychosocial factors to academic performance. *Annals of the New York Academy of Sciences, 1377*(1), 67–77.

Dixson, H. G., Komugabe-Dixson, A. F., Dixson, B. J., & Low, J. (2018). Scaling theory of mind in a small-scale society: A case study from Vanuatu. *Child Development, 89*(6), 2157–2175.

Doan, S. N., Tardif, T., Miller, A., Olson, S., Kessler, D., Felt, B., & Wang, L. (2017). Consequences of 'tiger' parenting: A cross-cultural study of maternal psychological control and children's cortisol stress response. *Developmental Science, 20*(3), e12404.

Doebel, S. (2020). Rethinking executive function and its development. *Perspectives on Psychological Science, 15*(4), 942–956.

Doepke, M., & Zilibotti, F. (Eds.). (2019). *Love, money, and parenting: How economics explains the way we raise our kids.* Princeton University Press. https://doi.org/10.1515/9780691184210

Doering, J. J., Salm Ward, T. C., Strook, S., & Campbell, J. K. (2019). A comparison of infant sleep safety guidelines in nine industrialized countries. *Journal of Community Health, 44*(1), 81–87.

Doka, K. J. (1999). Disenfranchised grief. *Bereavement Care, 18*(3), 37–39.

Doka, K. J. (2002). Spirituality, loss and grief: The double-edged sword. *Bereavement Care, 21*(1), 3–5.

Dolberg, P., & Ayalon, L. (2018). Subjective meanings and identification with middle age. *The International Journal of Aging and Human Development, 87*(1), 52–76.

Dolbin-MacNab, M. L., & Yancura, L. A. (2018). International perspectives on grandparents raising grandchildren: Contextual considerations for advancing global discourse. *The International Journal of Aging and Human Development, 86*(1), 3–33. https://doi.org/10.1177/0091415016689565

Dolmans, M. M., & Donnez, J. (2021). Fertility preservation in women for medical and social reasons: Oocytes vs ovarian tissue. *Best Practice & Research Clinical Obstetrics & Gynaecology, 70*, 63–80.

Domitrovich, C. E., Durlak, J. A., Staley, K. C., & Weissberg, R. P. (2017). Social-emotional competence: An essential factor for promoting positive adjustment and reducing risk in school children. *Child Development, 88*(2), 408–416.

Don, B. P., & Mickelson, K. D. (2014). Relationship satisfaction trajectories across the transition to parenthood among low-risk parents. *Journal of Marriage and Family, 76*(3), 677–692. https://doi.org/10.1111/jomf.12111

Dong, H.-M., Margulies, D. S., Zuo, X.-N., & Holmes, A. J. (2021). Shifting gradients of macroscale cortical organization mark the transition from childhood to adolescence. *Proceedings of the National Academy of Sciences, 118*(28). https://doi.org/10.1073/pnas.2024448118

Dong, X., Milholland, B., & Vijg, J. (2016). Evidence for a limit to human lifespan. *Nature, 538*(7624), 257–259. https://doi.org/10.1038/nature19793

Donkin, I., & Barrès, R. (2018). Sperm epigenetics and influence of environmental factors. *Molecular Metabolism, 14*, 1–11. https://doi.org/10.1016/j.molmet.2018.02.006

Donkor, H. M., Toxe, H., Hurum, J., Bjerknes, R., Eide, G. E., Juliusson, P., & Markestad, T. (2021). Psychological health in preschool children with underweight, overweight or obesity: A regional cohort study. *BMJ Paediatrics Open, 5*(1), e000881. https://doi.org/10.1136/bmjpo-2020-000881

Donnelly, R., Reczek, C., & Umberson, D. (2018). What we know (and don't know) about the bereavement experiences of same-sex spouses. In A. E. Goldberg & A. Romero (Eds.), *LGBTQ divorce and relationship dissolution: Psychological and legal perspectives and implications for practice* (p. 109). Oxford University Press

Donnelly, R., Umberson, D., Hummer, R. A., & Garcia, M. A. (2020). Race, death of a child, and mortality risk among aging parents in the United States. *Social Science & Medicine, 249*, 112853. https://doi.org/10.1016/j.socscimed.2020.112853

Donner, H. (2016). Doing it our way: Love and marriage in Kolkata middle-class families. *Modern Asian Studies, 50*(4), 1147–1189.

Donoghue, E. A., & Council on Early Childhood, American Academy of Pediatrics. (2017). Quality early education and child care from birth to kindergarten. *Pediatrics, 140*(2), e20171488. https://doi.org/10.1542/peds.2017-1488

Donovan, B. M., Weindling, M., Salazar, B., Duncan, A., Stuhlsatz, M., & Keck, P. (2021). Genomics literacy matters: Supporting the development of genomics literacy through genetics education could reduce the prevalence of genetic essentialism. *Journal of Research in Science Teaching, 58*(4), 520–550. https://doi.org/10.1002/tea.21670

Doom, J. R., Doyle, C. M., & Gunnar, M. R. (2017). Social stress buffering by friends in childhood and adolescence: Effects on HPA and oxytocin activity. *Social Neuroscience, 12*(1), 8–21. https://doi.org/10.1080/17470919.2016.1149095

Doom, J. R., Mason, S. M., Suglia, S. F., & Clark, C. J. (2017). Pathways between childhood/adolescent adversity, adolescent socioeconomic status, and long-term cardiovascular disease risk in young adulthood. *Social Science & Medicine, 188*, 166–175.

Dorner, L. M., Orellana, M. F., & Li-Grining, C. P. (2007). "I helped my mom," and it helped me: Translating the skills of language brokers into improved standardized test scores. *American Journal of Education, 113*(3), 451–478.

Dorney, K., Dodington, J. M., Rees, C. A., Farrell, C. A., Hanson, H. R., Lyons, T. W., & Lee, L. K. (2020). Preventing injuries must be a priority to prevent disease in the twenty-first century. *Pediatric Research, 87*(2), 282–292. https://doi.org/10.1038/s41390-019-0549-7

Doss, B. D., & Rhoades, G. K. (2017). The transition to parenthood: Impact on couples' romantic relationships. *Current Opinion in Psychology, 13*, 25–28. https://doi.org/10.1016/j.copsyc.2016.04.003

Dotti Sani, G. M., & Scherer, S. (2018). Maternal employment: Enabling factors in context. *Work, Employment and Society, 32*(1), 75–92.

Doty, J. L., & Mortimer, J. T. (2018). Trajectories of mother-child relationships across the life course: Links with adult well-being. In D. F. Alwin, D. H. Felmlee, & D. A. Kreager (Eds.), *Social networks and the life course: Integrating the development of human lives and social relational networks* (pp. 391–413). Springer International Publishing. https://doi.org/10.1007/978-3-319-71544-5_18

Doty, R. L., & Kamath, V. (2014). The influences of age on olfaction: A review. *Frontiers in Psychology, 5*, 20. https://doi.org/10.3389/fpsyg.2014.00020

Douaud, G., Lee, S., Alfaro-Almagro, F., Arthofer, C., Wang, C., McCarthy, P., Lange, F., Andersson, J. L. R., Griffanti, L., Duff, E., Jbabdi, S., Taschler, B., Keating, P., Winkler, A. M., Collins, R., Matthews, P. M., Allen, N., Miller, K. L., Nichols, T. E., & Smith, S. M. (2022). SARS-CoV-2 is associated with changes in brain structure in UK Biobank. *Nature*, 1–17. https://doi.org/10.1038/s41586-022-04569-5

Dougherty, K. J., Lahr, H. E., & Morest, V. S. (2017). *Reforming the American community college: Promising changes and their challenges*. Community College Research Center, Columbia University.

Douthard, R. A., Martin, I. K., Chapple-McGruder, T., Langer, A., & Chang, S. (2021). U.S. maternal mortality within a global context: Historical trends, current state, and future directions. *Journal of Women's Health, 30*(2), 168–177. https://doi.org/10.1089/jwh.2020.8863

Downes, M., Bathelt, J., & Haan, M. D. (2017). Event-related potential measures of executive functioning from preschool to adolescence. *Developmental Medicine & Child Neurology, 59*(6), 581–590. https://doi.org/10.1111/dmcn.13395

Downes, S. M. (2015). Evolutionary psychology, adaptation and design. In T. Heams, P. Huneman, G. Lecointre, & M. Silberstein (Eds.), *Handbook of evolutionary thinking in the sciences* (pp. 659–673). Springer.

Downs, S., & Demmler, K. M. (2020). Food environment interventions targeting children and adolescents: A scoping review. *Global Food Security, 27*, 100403. https://doi.org/10.1016/j.gfs.2020.100403

Draganova, R., Schollbach, A., Schleger, F., Braendle, J., Brucker, S., Abele, H., Kagan, K. O., Wallwiener, D., Fritsche, A., Eswaran, H., & Preissl, H. (2018). Fetal auditory evoked responses to onset of amplitude modulated sounds: A fetal magnetoencephalography (fMEG) study. *Hearing Research, 363*, 70–77. https://doi.org/10.1016/j.heares.2018.03.005

Drakaki, E., Dessinioti, C., & Antoniou, C. V. (2014). Air pollution and the skin. *Frontiers in Environmental Science, 2*, 11. https://doi.org/10.3389/fenvs.2014.00011

Drake, G., & Walsh, K. (2020). *2020 Teacher prep review: Program performance in early reading instruction: Teacher preparation to teach reading: Summary of findings on NCTQ's Early Reading Standard.* National Center for Teacher Quality.

Druga, S., Williams, R., Breazeal, C., & Resnick, M. (2017). "Hey Google is it ok if I eat you?" Initial explorations in child-agent interaction. In *Proceedings of the 2017 Conference on Interaction Design and Children* (pp. 595–600).

Druga, S., Williams, R., Park, H. W., & Breazeal, C. (2018). How smart are the smart toys? Children and parents' agent interaction and intelligence attribution. In *Proceedings of the 17th ACM Conference on Interaction Design and Children* (pp. 231–240).

Drury, L., Hutchison, P., & Abrams, D. (2016). Direct and extended intergenerational contact and young people's attitudes towards older adults. *British Journal of Social Psychology, 55*(3), 522–543. https://doi.org/10.1111/bjso.12146

Du, W. W., Fang, L., Yang, W., Wu, N., Awan, F. M., Yang, Z., & Yang, B. B. (2017). Induction of tumor apoptosis through a circular RNA enhancing Foxo3 activity. *Cell Death & Differentiation, 24*(2), 357–370.

Dubé, È., Ward, J. K., Verger, P., & MacDonald, N. E. (2021). Vaccine hesitancy, acceptance, and anti-vaccination: Trends and future prospects for public health. *Annual Review of Public Health, 42*, 175–191.

DuBois, L. Z., & Shattuck-Heidorn, H. (2020). Challenging the binary: Gender/sex and the bio-logics of normalcy. *American Journal of Human Biology*, e23623. https://doi.org/10.1002/ajhb.23623

Duchesneau, N. (2020). *Social, emotional, and academic development through an equity lens.* Education Trust. https://eric.ed.gov/?id=ED607298

Duckett, L. J., & Ruud, M. (2019). Affirming language use when providing health care for and writing about childbearing families who identify as LGBTQI+. *Journal of Human Lactation, 35*(2), 227–232. https://doi.org/10.1177/0890334419830985

Duckworth, A. (2016). *Grit: The power of passion and perseverance.* Ebury Publishing.

Duckworth, A., & Gross, J. J. (2014). Self-control and grit: Related but separable determinants of success. *Current Directions in Psychological Science, 23*(5), 319–325. https://doi.org/10.1177/0963721414541462

Duckworth, A., Kautz, T., Defnet, A., Satlof-Bedrick, E., Talamas, S. N., Luttges, B. L., & Steinberg, L. (2021). Students attending school remotely suffer socially, emotionally, and academically. PsyArXiv. https://doi.org/10.31234/osf.io/rpz7h

Duckworth, A. L., Milkman, K. L., & Laibson, D. (2018). Beyond willpower: Strategies for reducing failures of self-control. *Psychological Science in the Public Interest, 19*(3), 102–129.

Duckworth, A. L., & Seligman, M. E. P. (2017). The science and practice of self-control. *Perspectives on Psychological Science, 12*(5), 715–718. https://doi.org/10.1177/1745691617690880

Duell, N., & Steinberg, L. (2020). Differential correlates of positive and negative risk taking in adolescence. *Journal of Youth and Adolescence, 49*(6), 1162–1178. https://doi.org/10.1007/s10964-020-01237-7

Duell, N., Steinberg, L., Icenogle, G., Chein, J., Chaudhary, N., Giunta, L. D., Dodge, K. A., Fanti, K. A., Lansford, J. E., Oburu, P., Pastorelli, C., Skinner, A. T., Sorbring, E., Tapanya, S., Tirado, L. M. U., Alampay, L. P., Al-Hassan, S. M., Takash, H. M. S., Bacchini, D., & Chang, L. (2018). Age patterns in risk taking across the world. *Journal of Youth and Adolescence, 47*(5), 1052–1072. https://doi.org/10.1007/s10964-017-0752-y

Dufour, S. C., Adams, R. S., Brody, D. L., Puente, A. N., & Gray, J. C. (2020). Prevalence and correlates of concussion in children: Data from the adolescent brain cognitive development study. *Cortex, 131*, 237–250.

Dunbar, A. S., Leerkes, E. M., Coard, S. I., Supple, A. J., & Calkins, S. (2017). An integrative conceptual model of parental racial/ethnic and emotion socialization and links to children's social-emotional development among African American families. *Child Development Perspectives, 11*(1), 16–22. https://doi.org/10.1111/cdep.12218

Dunbar, R. I. M. (2018). The anatomy of friendship. *Trends in Cognitive Sciences, 22*(1), 32–51. https://doi.org/10.1016/j.tics.2017.10.004

Dunbar, R. I. M. (2020). Structure and function in human and primate social networks: Implications for diffusion, network stability and health. *Proceedings of the Royal Society A, 476*(2240), 20200446.

Dunbar, R. I. M., Arnaboldi, V., Conti, M., & Passarella, A. (2015). The structure of online social networks mirrors those in the offline world. *Social Networks, 43*, 39–47. https://doi.org/10.1016/j.socnet.2015.04.005

Duncan, G. J., Kalil, A., & Ziol-Guest, K. M. (2018). Parental income and children's life course: Lessons from the Panel Study of Income Dynamics. *The Annals of the American Academy of Political and Social Science, 680*(1), 82–96. https://doi.org/10.1177/0002716218801534

Duncan, G., Magnuson, K., Murnane, R., & Votruba-Drzal, E. (2019). Income inequality and the well-being of American families. *Family Relations, 68*(3), 313–325.

Duncan, G. J., Magnuson, K., & Votruba-Drzal, E. (2015). Children and socioeconomic status. In *Handbook of child psychology and developmental science* (pp. 1–40). Wiley. https://doi.org/10.1002/9781118963418.childpsy414

Dunifon, R. E. (2018). *You've always been there for me: Understanding the lives of grandchildren raised by grandparents.* Rutgers University Press. https://doi.org/10.36019/9780813584027

Dunifon, R. E., Near, C. E., & Ziol-Guest, K. M. (2018). Backup parents, playmates, friends: Grandparents' time with grandchildren. *Journal of Marriage and Family, 80*(3), 752–767. https://doi.org/10.1111/jomf.12472

Dunk, R. D. P., Barnes, M. E., Reiss, M. J., Alters, B., Asghar, A., Carter, B. E., Cotner, S., Glaze, A. L., Hawley, P. H., Jensen, J. L., Mead, L. S., Nadelson, L. S., Nelson, C. E., Pobiner, B., Scott, E. C., Shtulman, A., Sinatra, G. M., Southerland, S. A., Walter, E. M., ... Wiles, J. R. (2019). Evolution education is a complex landscape. *Nature Ecology & Evolution, 3*(3), 327–329. https://doi.org/10.1038/s41559-019-0802-9

Dunkel Schetter, C. (2017). Moving research on health and close relationships forward—a challenge and an obligation: Introduction to the special issue. *American Psychologist, 72*(6), 511–516. https://doi.org/10.1037/amp0000158

Dunn, K., & Reid, V. (2020). Prenatal cognition. In *The encyclopedia of child and adolescent development* (pp. 1–9). Wiley. https://doi.org/10.1002/9781119171492.wecad137

Dunphy, D. C. (1963). The social structure of urban adolescent peer groups. *Sociometry*, 230–246.

Dunphy, D. C. (1969). *Cliques, crowds & gangs: Group life of Sydney adolescents.* Melbourne: Cheshire.

Dunst, C. J., & Espe-Sherwindt, M. (2017). Contemporary early intervention models, research, and practice for infants and toddlers with disabilities and delays. In J. M. Kauffman, D. P. Hallahan, & P. C. Pullen (Eds.), *Handbook of special education* (2nd ed., pp. 831–849). Routledge.

Dunton, G. F. (2018). Sustaining health-protective behaviors such as physical activity and healthy eating. *JAMA, 320*(7), 639–640.

Dunton, G. F., Do, B., & Wang, S. D. (2020). Early effects of the COVID-19 pandemic on physical activity and sedentary behavior in children living in the U.S. *BMC Public Health, 20*(1), 1351. https://doi.org/10.1186/s12889-020-09429-3

DuPaul, G. J., Fu, Q., Anastopoulos, A. D., Reid, R., & Power, T. J. (2020). ADHD parent and teacher symptom ratings: Differential item functioning across gender, age, race, and ethnicity. *Journal of Abnormal Child Psychology, 48*(5), 679–691. https://doi.org/10.1007/s10802-020-00618-7

Durrant, J., Plateau, D. P., Ateah, C. A., Holden, G. W., Barker, L. A., Stewart-Tufescu, A., Jones, A. D., Ly, G., & Ahmed, R. (2017). Parents' views of the relevance of a violence prevention program in high, medium, and low human development contexts. *International Journal of Behavioral Development, 41*(4), 523–531. https://doi.org/10.1177/0165025416687415

Dutil, S. (2020). Dismantling the school-to-prison pipeline: A trauma-informed, critical race perspective on school discipline. *Children & Schools, 42*(3), 171–178. https://doi.org/10.1093/cs/cdaa016

Dweck, C. S. (2002). The development of ability conceptions. In A. Wigfield & J. S. Eccles (Eds.), *Development of achievement motivation* (pp. 57–88). Academic Press. https://doi.org/10.1016/B978-012750053-9/50005-X

Dweck, C. S., & Yeager, D. S. (2019). Mindsets: A view from two eras. *Perspectives on Psychological Science, 14*(3), 481–496. https://doi.org/10.1177/1745691618804166

Dworkin, E. R., Menon, S. V., Bystrynski, J., & Allen, N. E. (2017). Sexual assault victimization and psychopathology: A review and meta-analysis. *Clinical Psychology Review, 56*, 65–81. https://doi.org/10.1016/j.cpr.2017.06.002

Dwyer, R. E., Hodson, R., & McCloud, L. (2013). Gender, debt, and dropping out of college. *Gender & Society, 27*(1), 30–55. https://doi.org/10.1177/0891243212464906

Dwyer-Lindgren, L., Bertozzi-Villa, A., Stubbs, R. W., Morozoff, C., Mackenbach, J. P., van Lenthe, F. J., Mokdad, A. H., & Murray, C. J. L. (2017). Inequalities in life expectancy among US counties, 1980 to 2014: Temporal trends and key drivers. *JAMA Internal Medicine, 177*(7), 1003–1011. https://doi.org/10.1001/jamainternmed.2017.0918

Earnshaw, V. A., Reisner, S. L., Menino, D. D., Poteat, V. P., Bogart, L. M., Barnes, T. N., & Schuster, M. A. (2018). Stigma-based bullying interventions: A systematic review. *Developmental Review, 48*, 178–200. https://doi.org/10.1016/j.dr.2018.02.001

Easton, J. A., Confer, J. C., Goetz, C. D., & Buss, D. M. (2010). Reproduction expediting: Sexual motivations, fantasies, and the ticking biological clock. *Personality and Individual Differences, 49*(5), 516–520. https://doi.org/10.1016/j.paid.2010.05.018

Eastwick, P. W., Joel, S., Molden, D. C., Finkel, E., & Carswell, K. L. (2021, March 8). Predicting romantic interest during early relationship development: A preregistered investigation using machine learning. *OSF Preprints.* https://doi.org/10.31219/osf.io/sh7ja

Ebert, T., Gebauer, J. E., Brenner, T., Bleidorn, W., Gosling, S., Potter, J., & Rentfrow, P. J. (2019). *Are regional differences in personality and their correlates robust? Applying spatial analysis techniques to examine regional variation in personality across the US and Germany* (Working Papers on Innovation and Space No. 05.19). Philipps University Marburg, Department of Geography.

Eccles, J. S., & Roeser, R. W. (2011). Schools as developmental contexts during adolescence. *Journal of Research on Adolescence, 21*(1), 225–241.

Eccles, J. S., & Wigfield, A. (2020). From expectancy-value theory to situated expectancy-value theory: A developmental, social cognitive, and sociocultural perspective on motivation. *Contemporary Educational Psychology, 61*, 101859.

Echegaray, C. (2017, December 7). From child life patient to child life specialist (Vanderbilt University Medical Center: VUMC Voice). *Employee Spotlight.* https://voice.vumc.org/child-life-patient-child-life-specialist/

Echevarria, J., Frey, N., & Fisher, D. (2015). *What it takes for English learners.* Educational Leadership.

Echols, L., & Graham, S. (2013). Birds of a different feather: How do cross-ethnic friends flock together? *Merrill-Palmer Quarterly, 59*(4), 461–488.

Echols, L., & Ivanich, J. (2021). From "fast friends" to true friends: Can a contact intervention promote friendships in middle school? *Journal of Research on Adolescence.* https://doi.org/10.1111/jora.12622

Eckert-Lind, C., Busch, A. S., Petersen, J. H., Biro, F. M., Butler, G., Bräuner, E. V., & Juul, A. (2020). Worldwide secular trends in age at pubertal onset assessed by breast development among girls: A systematic review and meta-analysis. *JAMA Pediatrics, 174*(4), e195881–e195881. https://doi.org/10.1001/jamapediatrics.2019.5881

Edde, M., Leroux, G., Altena, E., & Chanraud, S. (2021). Functional brain connectivity changes across the human life span: From fetal development to old age. *Journal of Neuroscience Research, 99*(1), 236–262.

Edin, K., & Kefalas, M. (2005). *Promises I can keep.* University of California Press. http://sites.dartmouth.edu/socyfamilyohp6/files/2014/03/Edin.pdf

Edwards, K. M., Sylaska, K. M., Barry, J. E., Moynihan, M. M., Banyard, V. L., Cohn, E. S., Walsh, W. A., & Ward, S. K. (2015). Physical dating violence, sexual violence, and unwanted pursuit victimization: A comparison of incidence rates among sexual-minority and heterosexual college students. *Journal of Interpersonal Violence, 30*(4), 580–600. https://doi.org/10.1177/0886260514535260

Edwards, M. K., & Loprinzi, P. D. (2017). Experimentally increasing sedentary behavior results in decreased life satisfaction. *Health Promotion Perspectives, 7*(2), 88–94. https://doi.org/10.15171/hpp.2017.16

Efevbera, Y., & Bhabha, J. (2020). Defining and deconstructing girl child marriage and applications to global public health. *BMC Public Health, 20*(1), 1547. https://doi.org/10.1186/s12889-020-09545-0

Egalite, A. J. (2016). How family background influences student achievement. *Education Next, 16*(2), 70–78.

Egalite, A. J., & Kisida, B. (2018). The effects of teacher match on students' academic perceptions and attitudes. *Educational Evaluation and Policy Analysis, 40*(1), 59–81.

Egberts, M. R., Prinzie, P., Deković, M., de Haan, A. D., & van den Akker, A. L. (2015). The prospective relationship between child personality and perceived parenting: Mediation by parental sense of competence. *Personality and Individual Differences, 77*, 193–198.

Eggum-Wilkens, N. D., Lemery-Chalfant, K., Aksan, N., & Goldsmith, H. H. (2015). Self-conscious shyness: Growth during toddlerhood, strong role of genetics, and no prediction from fearful shyness. *Infancy, 20*(2), 160–188. https://doi.org/10.1111/infa.12070

Ehrenthal, D. B., Kuo, H.-H. D., & Kirby, R. S. (2020). Infant mortality in rural and nonrural counties in the United States. *Pediatrics, 146*(5), e20200464. https://doi.org/10.1542/peds.2020-0464

Ehrlich, K. B., & Cassidy, J. (2021). Early attachment and later physical health. In R. A. Thompson, J. A. Simpson, & L. J. Berlin (Eds.), *Attachment: The fundamental questions.* Guilford.

Eid, A., Mhatre, I., & Richardson, J. R. (2019). Gene-environment interactions in Alzheimer's disease: A potential path to precision medicine. *Pharmacology & Therapeutics, 199*, 173–187. https://doi.org/10.1016/j.pharmthera.2019.03.005

Eilenberg, J. S., Paff, M., Harrison, A. J., & Long, K. A. (2019). Disparities based on race, ethnicity, and socioeconomic status over the transition to adulthood among adolescents and young adults on the autism spectrum: A systematic review. *Current Psychiatry Reports, 21*(5), 32. https://doi.org/10.1007/s11920-019-1016-1

Eisenberg, A. R. (1999). Emotion talk among Mexican American and Anglo American mothers and children from two social classes. *Merrill-Palmer Quarterly, 45*, 267–284.

Eisenberg, D. T. A., Lee, N. R., Rej, P. H., Hayes, M. G., & Kuzawa, C. W. (2019). Older paternal ages and grandpaternal ages at conception predict longer telomeres in human descendants. *Proceedings of the Royal Society B: Biological Sciences, 286*(1903), 20190800. https://doi.org/10.1098/rspb.2019.0800

Eisenberg, M. L., & Meldrum, D. (2017). Effects of age on fertility and sexual function. *Fertility and Sterility, 107*(2), 301–304. https://doi.org/10.1016/j.fertnstert.2016.12.018

Eisenberg, N. (2020). Findings, issues, and new directions for research on emotion socialization. *Developmental Psychology, 56*(3), 664–670. https://doi.org/10.1037/dev0000906

Eisenberg, N., Cumberland, A., & Spinrad, T. L. (1998). Parental socialization of emotion. *Psychological Inquiry, 9*(4), 241–273.

Eisenberg, N., Eggum-Wilkens, N. D., & Spinrad, T. L. (2015). The development of prosocial behavior. In D. A. Schroeder & W. G. Graziano (Eds.), *The Oxford handbook of prosocial behavior* (pp. 114–136). Oxford University Press.

Eisenberger, N. I., Lieberman, M. D., & Williams, K. D. (2003). Does rejection hurt? An fMRI study of social exclusion. *Science, 302*(5643), 290–292.

Ekas, N. V., Braungart Reiker, J. M., & Messinger, D. S. (2018). The development of infant emotion regulation: Time is of the essence. In P. M. Cole & T. Hollenstein (Eds.), *Emotion regulation: A matter of time* (pp. 49–69). Routledge.

El Khoudary, S. R., Greendale, G., Crawford, S. L., Avis, N. E., Brooks, M. M., Thurston, R. C., Karvonen-Gutierrez, C., Waetjen, L. E., & Matthews, K. (2019). The menopause transition and women's health at midlife: A progress report from the Study of Women's Health Across the Nation (SWAN). *Menopause, 26*(10), 1213–1227. https://doi.org/10.1097/GME.0000000000001424

Elder, G. H., Jr. (1998). The life course as developmental theory. *Child Development, 69*(1), 1–12.

Elder, G. H., Jr., & Conger, R. D. (2014). *Children of the land.* University of Chicago Press.

Elder, G. H., & George, L. K. (2016). Age, cohorts, and the life course. In M. J. Shanahan, J. T. Mortimer, & M. Kirkpatrick Johnson (Eds.), *Handbook of the life course* (Vol. 2, pp. 59–85). Springer International Publishing. https://doi.org/10.1007/978-3-319-20880-0_3

Elder, G. H., Shanahan, M. J., & Jennings, J. A. (2015). Human development in time and place. In R. M. Lerner (Ed.), *Handbook of child psychology and developmental science: Ecological settings and processes* (pp. 6–54). Wiley. https://doi.org/10.1002/9781118963418.childpsy402.

Eldesouky, L., & English, T. (2018). Another year older, another year wiser? Emotion regulation strategy selection and flexibility across adulthood. *Psychology and Aging, 33*(4), 572.

Elenbaas, L., Rizzo, M. T., & Killen, M. (2020). A developmental science perspective on social inequality. *Current Directions in Psychological Science, 29*(6), 610–616. https://doi.org/10.1177/0963721420964147

Eligon, J. (2020, June 26). A debate over identity and race asks, are African-Americans "Black" or "black"? *The New York Times.* https://www.nytimes.com/2020/06/26/us/black-african-american-style-debate.html

Eliot, L., Ahmed, A., Khan, H., & Patel, J. (2021). Dump the "dimorphism": Comprehensive synthesis of human brain studies reveals few male-female differences beyond size. *Neuroscience & Biobehavioral Reviews, 125*, 667–697. https://doi.org/10.1016/j.neubiorev.2021.02.026

Elkind, D. (1967). Egocentrism in adolescence. *Child Development, 38*(4), 1025–1034.

Elkind, D. (1970, April 5). One man in his time plays many psychosocial parts. *The New York Times.* https://www.nytimes.com/1970/04/05/archives/one-man-in-his-time-plays-many-psychosocial-parts-erik-eriksons.html

Elliott, A. M., & Evans, J. A. (2015). Derogatory nomenclature is still being used: The example of split hand/foot. *American Journal of Medical Genetics. Part A, 167A*(4), 928–929. https://doi.org/10.1002/ajmg.a.36952

Ellis, B. J., Abrams, L. S., Masten, A. S., Sternberg, R. J., Tottenham, N., & Frankenhuis, W. E. (2020). Hidden talents in harsh environments. *Development and Psychopathology, 1*, 19.

Ellis, B. J., Bianchi, J., Griskevicius, V., & Frankenhuis, W. E. (2017). Beyond risk and protective factors: An adaptation-based approach to resilience. *Perspectives on Psychological Science, 12*(4), 561–587. https://doi.org/10.1177/1745691617693054

Ellis, B. J., Boyce, W. T., Belsky, J., Bakermans-Kranenburg, M. J., & Ijzendoorn, M. H. van. (2011). Differential susceptibility to the environment: An evolutionary–neurodevelopmental theory. *Development and Psychopathology, 23*(1), 7–28. https://doi.org/10.1017/S0954579410000611

Ellis, B. J., & Del Giudice, M. (2019). Developmental adaptation to stress: An evolutionary perspective. *Annual Review of Psychology, 70*(1), 111–139. https://doi.org/10.1146/annurev-psych-122216-011732

Ellis, B. J., Del Giudice, M., Dishion, T. J., Figueredo, A. J., Gray, P., Griskevicius, V., Hawley, P. H., Jacobs, W. J., James, J., Volk, A. A., & Wilson, D. S. (2012). The evolutionary basis of risky adolescent behavior: Implications for science, policy, and practice. *Developmental Psychology, 48*(3), 598–623. https://doi.org/10.1037/a0026220

Ellis, B. J., Horn, A. J., Carter, C. S., van IJzendoorn, M. H., & Bakermans-Kranenburg, M. J. (2021). Developmental programming of oxytocin through variation in early-life stress: Four meta-analyses and a theoretical reinterpretation. *Clinical Psychology Review, 86*, 101985. https://doi.org/10.1016/j.cpr.2021.101985

Ellis, Y. G., Cliff, D. P., Janssen, X., Jones, R. A., Reilly, J. J., & Okely, A. D. (2017). Sedentary time, physical activity and compliance with IOM recommendations in young children at childcare. *Preventive Medicine Reports, 7*, 221–226. https://doi.org/10.1016/j.pmedr.2016.12.009

Elo, I. T., Hendi, A. S., Ho, J. Y., Vierboom, Y. C., & Preston, S. H. (2019). Trends in non-Hispanic white mortality in the United States by metropolitan-nonmetropolitan status and region, 1990–2016. *Population and Development Review, 45*(3), 549.

Elsner, C., & Wertz, A. E. (2019). The seeds of social learning: Infants exhibit more social looking for plants than other object types. *Cognition, 183*, 244–255. https://doi.org/10.1016/j.cognition.2018.09.016

Ely, D. M., & Driscoll, A. K. (2020). Infant mortality in the United States, 2018: Data from the period linked birth/infant death file. *National Vital Statistics Reports: From the Centers for Disease Control and Prevention, National Center*

for Health Statistics, National Vital Statistics System, 69(7), 1–18.

Embury, C. M., Wiesman, A. I., Proskovec, A. L., Mills, M. S., Heinrichs-Graham, E., Wang, Y.-P., Calhoun, V., & Wilson, T. W. (2019). Neural dynamics of verbal working memory processing in children and adolescents. *Neuroimage, 185*, 191–197.

Emery, R. E. (2012). *Renegotiating family relationships, second edition: Divorce, child custody, and mediation.* Guilford.

Emile, M., d'Arripe-Longueville, F., Cheval, B., Amato, M., & Chalabaev, A. (2015). An ego depletion account of aging stereotypes' effects on health-related variables. *Journals of Gerontology Series B: Psychological Sciences and Social Sciences, 70*(6), 876–885.

Emling, S. (2017, June 14). *The age at which you are officially old.* AARP. https://www.aarp.org/home-family/friends-family/info-2017/what-age-are-you-old-fd.html

Endendijk, J. J., Smit, A. K., van Baar, A. L., & Bos, P. A. (2019). Boys' toys, girls' toys: An fMRI study of mothers' neural responses to children violating gender expectations. *Biological Psychology, 148*, 107776. https://doi.org/10.1016/j.biopsycho.2019.107776

Engelke, M. (2019). The anthropology of death revisited. *Annual Review of Anthropology, 48*, 29–44.

Engeln, R., Loach, R., Imundo, M. N., & Zola, A. (2020). Compared to Facebook, Instagram use causes more appearance comparison and lower body satisfaction in college women. *Body Image, 34*, 38–45. https://doi.org/10.1016/j.bodyim.2020.04.007

Engels, M., Wahrendorf, M., Dragano, N., McMunn, A., & Deindl, C. (2021). Multiple social roles in early adulthood and later mental health in different labour market contexts. *Advances in Life Course Research, 100432.* https://doi.org/10.1016/j.alcr.2021.100432

England-Mason, G., & Gonzalez, A. (2020). Intervening to shape children's emotion regulation: A review of emotion socialization parenting programs for young children. *Emotion, 20*(1), 98.

English, D., Thompson, R., White, C. R., & Wilson, D. (2015). Why should child welfare pay more attention to emotional maltreatment? *Children and Youth Services Review, 50*, 53–63. https://doi.org/10.1016/j.childyouth.2015.01.010

English, T., & Carstensen, L. L. (2014). Selective narrowing of social networks across adulthood is associated with improved emotional experience in daily life. *International Journal of Behavioral Development, 38*(2), 195–202. https://doi.org/10.1177/0165025413515404

Enriquez, L. (2011). "Because we feel the pressure and we also feel the support": Examining the educational success of undocumented immigrant Latina/o students. *Harvard Educational Review, 81*(3), 476–500. https://doi.org/10.17763/haer.81.3.w7k703q050143762

Entringer, S. (2020). Prenatal stress exposure and fetal programming of complex phenotypes: Interactive effects with multiple risk factors. *Neuroscience & Biobehavioral Reviews, 117*, 3–4. https://doi.org/10.1016/j.neubiorev.2020.04.002

Entwisle, D. R., & Astone, N. M. (1994). Some practical guidelines for measuring youth's race/ethnicity and socioeconomic status. *Child Development, 65*(6), 1521–1540. https://doi.org/10.1111/j.1467-8624.1994.tb00833.x

Epel, E. S., & Lithgow, G. J. (2014). Stress biology and aging mechanisms: Toward understanding the deep connection between adaptation to stress and longevity. *The Journals of Gerontology: Series A, 69*(Suppl_1), S10–S16. https://doi.org/10.1093/gerona/glu055

Epstein, M., Calzo, J. P., Smiler, A. P., & Ward, L. M. (2009). "Anything from making out to having sex": Men's negotiations of hooking up and friends with benefits scripts. *Journal of Sex Research, 46*(5), 414–424. https://doi.org/10.1080/00224490902775801

Epstein, R., Blake, J., & González, T. (2017). *Girlhood interrupted: The erasure of black girls' childhood* (SSRN Scholarly Paper ID 3000695). Social Science Research Network. https://doi.org/10.2139/ssrn.3000695

Erck Lambert, A. B., Parks, S. E., Cottengim, C., Faulkner, M., Hauck, F. R., & Shapiro-Mendoza, C. K. (2019). Sleep-related infant suffocation deaths attributable to soft bedding, overlay, and wedging. *Pediatrics, 143*(5), e20183408. https://doi.org/10.1542/peds.2018-3408

Ereky-Stevens, K., Funder, A., Katschnig, T., Malmberg, L.-E., & Datler, W. (2018). Relationship building between toddlers and new caregivers in out-of-home childcare: Attachment security and caregiver sensitivity. *Early Childhood Research Quarterly, 42*, 270–279. https://doi.org/10.1016/j.ecresq.2017.10.007

Erik Erikson, 91, psychoanalyst who reshaped views of human growth, dies. (1994, May 13). *The New York Times*, B9.

Erikson, E. H. (1950). *Childhood and society.* W. W. Norton.

Erikson, E. H. (1959). Identity and the life cycle: Selected papers. *Psychological Issues, 1*, 1–171.

Erikson, E. H. (1968). *Identity: Youth and crisis.* W. W. Norton.

Erikson, E. H. (1969). *Gandhi's truth: On the origins of militant nonviolence.* W. W. Norton.

Erikson, E. H. (1993). *Childhood and society: The landmark work on the social significance of childhood.* W. W. Norton. (Original work published 1950)

Erikson, E. H. (1994). *Identity and the life cycle.* W. W. Norton.

Erikson, E. H. (1994). *Identity: Youth and crisis.* W. W. Norton.

Erikson, E. H., & Erikson, J. M. (1998). *The life cycle completed* (Extended version). W. W. Norton.

Erikson, E. H., Erikson, J. M., & Kivnick, H. Q. (1989). *Vital involvement in old age.* W. W. Norton.

Erikson, E. H., Erikson, J. M., & Kivnick, H. Q. (1994). *Vital involvement in old age* (Paperback ed.). W. W. Norton.

Erikson, G. A., Bodian, D. L., Rueda, M., Molparia, B., Scott, E. R., Scott-Van Zeeland, A. A., Topol, S. E., Wineinger, N. E., Niederhuber, J. E., Topol, E. J., & Torkamani, A. (2016). Whole-genome sequencing of a healthy aging cohort. *Cell, 165*(4), 1002–1011.

Erlangsen, A., Runeson, B., Bolton, J. M., Wilcox, H. C., Forman, J. L., Krogh, J., Shear, M. K., Nordentoft, M., & Conwell, Y. (2017). Association between spousal suicide and mental, physical, and social health outcomes: A longitudinal and nationwide register-based study. *JAMA Psychiatry, 74*(5), 456–464. https://doi.org/10.1001/jamapsychiatry.2017.0226

Ermer, A. E., & Proulx, C. M. (2019). Associations between social connectedness, emotional well-being, and self-rated health among older adults: Difference by relationship status. *Research on Aging, 41*(4), 336–361. https://doi.org/10.1177/0164027518815260

Ermolaeva, M., Neri, F., Ori, A., & Rudolph, K. L. (2018). Cellular and epigenetic drivers of stem cell ageing. *Nature Reviews Molecular Cell Biology, 19*(9), 594–610. https://doi.org/10.1038/s41580-018-0020-3

Ernst, M. M., Kogan, B. A., & Lee, P. A. (2020). Gender identity: A psychosocial primer for providing care to patients with a disorder/difference of sex development and their families [individualized care for patients with intersex (Disorders/differences of sex development): Part 2]. *Journal of Pediatric Urology, 16*(5), 606–611. https://doi.org/10.1016/j.jpurol.2020.06.026

Ernst, M. M., Liao, L.-M., Baratz, A. B., & Sandberg, D. E. (2018). Disorders of sex development/intersex: Gaps in psychosocial care for children. *Pediatrics, 142*(2). https://doi.org/10.1542/peds.2017-4045

Ertl, A., Sheats, K. J., Petrosky, E., Betz, C. J., Yuan, K., & Fowler, K. A. (2019). Surveillance for violent deaths—National Violent Death Reporting System, 32 states, 2016. *MMWR Surveillance Summaries, 68*(9), 1–36. https://doi.org/10.15585/mmwr.ss.6809a1

Ervasti, J., Pentti, J., Nyberg, S. T., Shipley, M. J., Leineweber, C., Sørensen, J. K., Alfredsson, L., Bjorner, J. B., Borritz, M., Burr, H., Knutsson, A., Madsen, I. E. H., Magnusson Hanson, L. L., Oksanen, T., Pejtersen, J. H., Rugulies, R., Suominen, S., Theorell, T., Westerlund, H., … Kivimäki, M. (2021). Long working hours and risk of 50 health conditions and mortality outcomes: A multicohort study in four European countries. *The Lancet Regional Health—Europe, 100212.* https://doi.org/10.1016/j.lanepe.2021.100212

Espelage, D. L., Leemis, R. W., Niolon, P. H., Kearns, M., Basile, K. C., & Davis, J. P. (2020). Teen dating violence perpetration: Protective factor trajectories from middle to high school among adolescents. *Journal of Research on Adolescence, 30*(1), 170–188. https://doi.org/10.1111/jora.12510

Espinoza, P., Penelo, E., Mora, M., Francisco, R., González, M. L., & Raich, R. M. (2019). Bidirectional relations between disordered eating, internalization of beauty ideals, and self-esteem: A longitudinal study with adolescents. *The Journal of Early Adolescence, 39*(9), 1244–1260. https://doi.org/10.1177/0272431618812734

Espirito Santo, H., & Daniel, F. (2018). Optimism and well-being among institutionalized older adults. *GeroPsych: The Journal of Gerontopsychology and Geriatric Psychiatry, 31*(1), 5–16. https://doi.org/10.1024/1662-9647/a000182

Esposito, G., Setoh, P., Shinohara, K., & Bornstein, M. H. (2017). The development of attachment: Integrating genes, brain, behavior, and environment. *Behavioural Brain Research, 325*(Pt. B), 87–89. https://doi.org/10.1016/j.bbr.2017.03.025

Estrada, E. (2019). *Kids at work.* NYU Press.

Estrada, E., Ferrer, E., Román, F. J., Karama, S., & Colom, R. (2019). Time-lagged associations between cognitive and cortical development from childhood to early adulthood. *Developmental Psychology, 55*(6), 1338–1352. https://doi.org/10.1037/dev0000716

Estrada, E., & Hondagneu-Sotelo, P. (2011). Intersectional dignities: Latino immigrant street vendor youth in Los Angeles. *Journal of Contemporary Ethnography, 40*(1), 102–131.

Estrada, J. N., Huerta, A. H., Hernandez, E., Hernandez, R., & Kim, S. (2018). Socio-ecological risk and protective factors for youth gang involvement. In H. Shapiro (Ed.), *The Wiley handbook on violence in education: Forms, factors, and preventions* (pp. 185–202). John Wiley & Sons.

Ethier, K. A., Kann, L., & McManus, T. (2018). Sexual intercourse among high school students — 29 states and United States overall, 2005–2015. *Morbidity and Mortality Weekly Report, 66*(5152), 1393–1397. https://doi.org/10.15585/mmwr.mm665152a1

Ethnologue. (2021). *How many languages are there in the world?* https://www.ethnologue.com/guides/how-many-languages

Eurostat. (2021). *Fertility statistics.* https://ec.europa.eu/eurostat/statistics-explained/index.php?title=Fertility_statistics

Evandrou, M., Falkingham, J., Qin, M., & Vlachantoni, A. (2021). Changing living arrangements and stress during Covid-19 lockdown: Evidence from four birth cohorts in the UK. *SSM—Population Health, 13,* 100761. https://doi.org/10.1016/j.ssmph.2021.100761

Evans, A., & Abrahamson, K. (2020). The influence of stigma on suicide bereavement: A systematic review. *Journal of Psychosocial Nursing and Mental Health Services, 58*(4), 21–27. https://doi.org/10.3928/02793695-20200127-02

Evans, M. L., Lindauer, M., & Farrell, M. E. (2020). A pandemic within a pandemic — intimate partner violence during Covid-19. *New England Journal of Medicine, 383*(24), 2302–2304. https://doi.org/10.1056/NEJMp2024046

Evens, M., Verburgh, A., & Elen, J. (2014). The development of critical thinking in professional and academic bachelor programmes. *Higher Education Studies, 4*(2), 42–51. https://doi.org/10.5539/hes.v4n2p42

Even-Zohar, A. (2019). Great-grandparenting in Israel. In B. Hayslip, Jr. & C. A. Fruhauf (Eds.), *Grandparenting: Influences on the dynamics of family relationships* (pp. 95–109). Springer Publishing Company. https://doi.org/10.1891/9780826149855.0006

Evers, K. S., & Wellmann, S. (2016). Arginine vasopressin and copeptin in perinatology. *Frontiers in Pediatrics, 4.* https://doi.org/10.3389/fped.2016.00075

Evertsson, M., Kirsch, M. E., & Geerts, A. (2021). Family sociological theories questioned: Same-sex parent families sharing work and care. In N. F. Schneider & M. Kreyenfeld (Eds.), *Research handbook on the sociology of the family* (pp. 373–385). Edward Elgar Publishing.

Ewald, P. W., & Swain Ewald, H. A. (2019). Genetics and epigenetics. In M. Brüne & W. Schiefenhövel (Eds.), *The Oxford handbook of evolutionary medicine* (pp. 77–130). Oxford University Press.

Exner-Cortens, D., Wright, A., Claussen, C., & Truscott, E. (2021). A systematic review of adolescent masculinities and associations with internalizing behavior problems and social support. *American Journal of Community Psychology.* https://doi.org/10.1002/ajcp.12492

Eylem, O., De Wit, L., Van Straten, A., Steubl, L., Melissourgaki, Z., Danışman, G. T., & Cuijpers, P. (2020). Stigma for common mental disorders in racial minorities and majorities: A systematic review and meta-analysis. *BMC Public Health, 20*, 1–20.

Fabina, J. (2021, April 29). *Despite Pandemic Challenges, 2020 Election Had Largest Increase in Voting Between Presidential Elections on Record.* Census.Gov. https://www.census.gov/library/stories/2021/04/record-high-turnout-in-2020-general-election.html

Fabius, C. D., Wolff, J. L., & Kasper, J. D. (2020). Race differences in characteristics and experiences of Black and White caregivers of older Americans. *The Gerontologist, 60*(7), 1244–1253. https://doi.org/10.1093/geront/gnaa042

Fadus, M. C., Ginsburg, K. R., Sobowale, K., Halliday-Boykins, C. A., Bryant, B. E., Gray, K. M., & Squeglia, L. M. (2020). Unconscious bias and the diagnosis of disruptive behavior disorders and ADHD in African American and Hispanic youth. *Academic Psychiatry, 44*(1), 95–102. https://doi.org/10.1007/s40596-019-01127-6

Fadus, M. C., Squeglia, L. M., Valadez, E. A., Tomko, R. L., Bryant, B. E., & Gray, K. M. (2019). Adolescent substance use disorder treatment: An update on evidence-based strategies. *Current Psychiatry Reports, 21*(10), 96. https://doi.org/10.1007/s11920-019-1086-0

Faes, K., Cohen, J., & Annemans, L. (2018). Resource use during the last 6 months of life of individuals dying with and of Alzheimer's disease. *Journal of the American Geriatrics Society, 66*(5), 879–885. https://doi.org/10.1111/jgs.15287

Faghiri, A., Stephen, J. M., Wang, Y.-P., Wilson, T. W., & Calhoun, V. D. (2018). Changing brain connectivity dynamics: From early childhood to adulthood. *Human Brain Mapping, 39*(3), 1108–1117.

Faherty, A. N., & Mitra, D. (2020). Emerging adulthoods: A microcultural approach to viewing the parent-child relationship. In B. K. Ashdown & A. N. Faherty (Eds.), *Parents and caregivers across cultures: Positive development from infancy through adulthood* (pp. 205–216). Springer International Publishing. https://doi.org/10.1007/978-3-030-35590-6_14

Fahrenthold, D. A. (2014, May 19). Great Society at 50: LBJ's Job Corps will cost taxpayers $1.7 billion this year. Does it work? *Washington Post.*

Fair, R. C., & Kaplan, E. H. (2018). Estimating aging effects in running events. *Review of Economics and Statistics, 100*(4), 704–711.

Fairchild, G., Hawes, D. J., Frick, P. J., Copeland, W. E., Odgers, C. L., Franke, B., Freitag, C. M., & De Brito, S. A. (2019). Conduct disorder. *Nature Reviews Disease Primers, 5*(1), 1–25. https://doi.org/10.1038/s41572-019-0095-y

Fall, C. H. D., & Kumaran, K. (2019). Metabolic programming in early life in humans. *Philosophical Transactions of the Royal Society B: Biological Sciences, 374*(1770), 20180123. https://doi.org/10.1098/rstb.2018.0123

Fall, C. H. D., Sachdev, H. S., Osmond, C., Restrepo-Mendez, M. C., Victora, C., Martorell, R., Stein, A. D., Sinha, S., Tandon, N., Adair, L., Bas, I., Norris, S., & Richter, L. M. (2015). Association between maternal age at childbirth and child and adult outcomes in the offspring: A prospective study in five low-income and middle-income countries (COHORTS collaboration). *The Lancet Global Health, 3*(7), e366–e377. https://doi.org/10.1016/S2214-109X(15)00038-8

Fan, H., Xu, J., Cai, Z., He, J., & Fan, X. (2017). Homework and students' achievement in math and science: A 30-year meta-analysis, 1986–2015. *Educational Research Review, 20*, 35–54. https://doi.org/10.1016/j.edurev.2016.11.003

Fan, X., Wheatley, E. G., & Villeda, S. A. (2017). Mechanisms of hippocampal aging and the potential for rejuvenation. *Annual Review of Neuroscience, 40*, 251–272. https://doi.org/10.1146/annurev-neuro-072116-031357

Fandakova, Y., Bunge, S. A., Wendelken, C., Desautels, P., Hunter, L., Lee, J. K., & Ghetti, S. (2018). The importance of knowing when you don't remember: Neural signaling of retrieval failure predicts memory improvement over time. *Cerebral Cortex, 28*(1), 90–102.

Fandakova, Y., & Hartley, C. A. (2020). Mechanisms of learning and plasticity in childhood and adolescence. *Developmental Cognitive Neuroscience, 42*(4), 100764. https://doi.org/10.1016/j.dcn.2020.100764

Fang, S., Galambos, N. L., & Johnson, M. D. (2021). Parent–child contact, closeness, and conflict across the transition to adulthood. *Journal of Marriage and Family, 83*(4), 1176–1193. https://doi.org/10.1111/jomf.12760

Fang, S., Galambos, N. L., Johnson, M. D., & Krahn, H. J. (2017). Happiness is the way: Paths to civic engagement between young adulthood and midlife. *International Journal of Behavioral Development,* 0165025417711056. https://doi.org/10.1177/0165025417711056

Fanger, S. M., Frankel, L. A., & Hazen, N. (2012). Peer exclusion in preschool children's play: Naturalistic observations in a playground setting. *Merrill-Palmer Quarterly (1982–)*, 224–254.

Farago, F., Davidson, K. L., & Byrd, C. M. (2019). Ethnic-racial socialization in early childhood: The implications of color-consciousness and colorblindness for prejudice development. In H. E. Fitzgerald, D. J. Johnson, D. B. Qin, F. A. Villarruel, & J. Norder (Eds.), *Handbook of children and prejudice: Integrating research, practice, and policy* (pp. 131–145). Springer International Publishing. https://doi.org/10.1007/978-3-030-12228-7_7

Farahany, N. A., Greely, H. T., & Giattino, C. M. (2019). Part-revived pig brains raise slew of ethical quandaries. *Nature, 568*(7752), 299–302. https://doi.org/10.1038/d41586-019-01168-9

Farhat, T. (2015). Stigma, obesity and adolescent risk behaviors: Current research and future directions. *Current Opinion in Psychology, 5*, 56–66. https://doi.org/10.1016/j.copsyc.2015.03.021

Farias, S. T., Giovannetti, T., Payne, B. R., Marsiske, M., Rebok, G. W., Schaie, K. W., Thomas, K. R., Willis, S. L., Dzierzewski, J. M., Unverzagt, F., & Gross, A. L. (2018). Self-perceived difficulties in everyday function precede cognitive decline among older adults in the ACTIVE study. *Journal of the International Neuropsychological Society, 24*(1), 104–112.

Farinholt, P., Park, M., Guo, Y., Bruera, E., & Hui, D. (2018). A comparison of the accuracy of clinician prediction of survival versus the palliative prognostic index. *Journal of Pain and Symptom Management, 55*(3), 792–797. https://doi.org/10.1016/j.jpainsymman.2017.11.028

Farmer, V. L., Williams, S. M., Mann, J. I., Schofield, G., McPhee, J. C., & Taylor, R. W. (2017). The effect of increasing risk and challenge in the school playground on physical activity and weight in children: A cluster randomised controlled trial (PLAY). *International Journal of Obesity, 41*(5), 793–800. https://doi.org/10.1038/ijo.2017.41

Farr, R. H., Bruun, S. T., Doss, K. M., & Patterson, C. J. (2018). Children's gender-typed behavior from early to middle childhood in adoptive families with lesbian, gay, and heterosexual parents. *Sex Roles, 78*(7), 528–541. https://doi.org/10.1007/s11199-017-0812-5

Fasoli, A. D., & Raeff, C. (2021). How does culture show up in development? Conclusion to the spotlight series on the concept of culture. *Applied Developmental Science, 25*(2), 106–113. https://doi.org/10.1080/10888691.2021.1876301

Fast, A. A., & Olson, K. R. (2018). Gender development in transgender preschool children. *Child Development, 89*(2), 620–637. https://doi.org/10.1111/cdev.12758

Fasteland, M. (2019). Reading the antimodern way: G. Stanley Hall's *Adolescence* and imperialist reading for White American boys. *The Journal of the History of Childhood and Youth, 12*(1), 7–25. https://doi.org/10.1353/hcy.2019.0001

Fatherly. (2015, November 19). *This is what kids in 2015 want to be when they grow up.* https://www.fatherly.com/news/what-kids-want-to-be-when-they-grow-up/

Fatherly. (2017, December 22). *The 2017 Imagination Report: What kids want to be when they grow up.* https://www.fatherly.com/love-money/the-2017-imagination-report-what-kids-want-to-be-when-they-grow-up/

Faye, C., McGowan, J. C., Denny, C. A., & David, D. J. (2018). Neurobiological mechanisms of stress resilience and implications for the aged population. *Current Neuropharmacology, 16*(3), 234–270. https://doi.org/10.2174/1570159X15666170818095105

Fazio, S., Pace, D., Flinner, J., & Kallmyer, B. (2018). The fundamentals of person-centered care for individuals with dementia. *The Gerontologist, 58*(suppl_1), S10–S19.

Federal Reserve Board. (2020). *Report on the economic well-being of U.S. households in 2018, May 2018.* Consumer and Community Research Section of the Federal Reserve Board, Division of Consumer and Community Affairs.

Federal Reserve Board. (2020). *Report on the economic well-being of U.S. households in 2019, featuring supplemental data from April 2020.* Consumer and Community Research Section of the Federal Reserve Board, Division of Consumer and Community Affairs.

Federal Reserve Board. (2021). *Report on the economic well-being of U.S. Households in 2020, housing.* Federal Reserve Board, Division of Consumer and Community Affairs.

Fedina, L., Holmes, J. L., & Backes, B. (2016). How prevalent is campus sexual assault in the United States. *National Institute of Justice, 277*, 26–30.

Fedina, L., Holmes, J. L., & Backes, B. L. (2018). Campus sexual assault: A systematic review of prevalence research from 2000 to 2015. *Trauma, Violence & Abuse, 19*(1), 76–93. https://doi.org/10.1177/1524838016631129

Feinberg, L. F. (2014). Moving toward person- and family-centered care. *Public Policy & Aging Report, 24*(3), 97–101. https://doi.org/10.1093/ppar/pru027

Feitoza, A. H. P., Henrique, R. S., Barnett, L. M., Ré, A. H. N., Lopes, V. P., Webster, E. K., Robinson, L. E., Cavalcante, W. A., & Cattuzzo, M. T. (2018). Perceived motor competence in childhood: Comparative study among countries. *Journal of Motor Learning and Development, 6*(2), S337–S350. https://doi.org/10.1123/jmld.2016-0079

Feldman, E. C. H., Balistreri, K. A., Lampert, S., Durkin, L. K., Bugno, L. T., Davies, W. H., & Greenley, R. N. (2021). Emerging adults' adherence to preventative health guidelines in response to COVID-19. *Journal of Pediatric Psychology, 46*(6), 635–644. https://doi.org/10.1093/jpepsy/jsab047

Feldman, R. (2019). The social neuroendocrinology of human parenting. In M. H. Bornstein (Ed.), *Handbook of parenting: Biology and ecology of parenting* (3rd ed., pp. 220–249). Routledge.

Feldman, R. (2020). What is resilience: Aan affiliative neuroscience approach. *World Psychiatry, 19*(2), 132–150. https://doi.org/10.1002/wps.20729

Feldman, R., & Bakermans-Kranenburg, M. J. (2017). Oxytocin: A parenting hormone. *Current Opinion in Psychology, 15*(Supplement C), 13–18. https://doi.org/10.1016/j.copsyc.2017.02.011

Felitti, V. J., Anda, R. F., Nordenberg, D., Williamson, D. F., Spitz, A. M., Edwards, V., Koss, M. P., & Marks, J. S. (1998). Relationship of childhood abuse and household dysfunction to many of the leading causes of death in adults: The Adverse Childhood Experiences (ACE) Study. *American Journal of Preventive Medicine, 14*(4), 245–258. https://doi.org/10.1016/S0749-3797(98)00017-8

Felmban, W. S., & Klaczynski, P. A. (2019). Adolescents' base rate judgments, metastrategic understanding, and stereotype endorsement. *Journal of Experimental Child Psychology, 178*, 60–85.

Felmlee, D. H., McMillan, C., Inara Rodis, P., & Osgood, D. W. (2018). The evolution of youth friendship networks from 6th to 12th grade: School transitions, popularity and centrality. In D. F. Alwin, D. H. Felmlee, & D. A. Kreager (Eds.), *Social networks and the life course: Integrating*

the development of human lives and social relational networks (pp. 161–184). Springer International Publishing. https://doi.org/10.1007/978-3-319-71544-5_8

Feng, X., Harkness, S., Super, C. M., Welles, B., Bermúdez, M. R., Bonichini, S., Moscardino, U., & Zylicz, P. O. (2020). Parents' concepts of the successful school child in seven western cultures. In S. Harkness & C. M. Super (Eds.), *Cross-cultural research on parents: Applications to the care and education of children* (pp. 143–170). Wiley.

Feng, Z., Glinskaya, E., Chen, H., Gong, S., Qiu, Y., Xu, J., & Yip, W. (2020). Long-term care system for older adults in China: Policy landscape, challenges, and future prospects. *The Lancet, 396*(10259), 1362–1372. https://doi.org/10.1016/S0140-6736(20)32136-X

Ferdinand, K. C. (2021). Overcoming barriers to COVID-19 vaccination in African Americans: The need for cultural humility. *American Journal of Public Health, 111*(4), 586–588. https://doi.org/10.2105/AJPH.2020.306135

Ferguson, C. A. (1964). Baby talk in six languages. *American Anthropologist, 66*(6_PART2), 103–114. https://doi.org/10.1525/aa.1964.66.suppl_3.02a00060

Ferguson, C. J., Muñoz, M. E., Garza, A., & Galindo, M. (2014). Concurrent and prospective analyses of peer, television and social media influences on body dissatisfaction, eating disorder symptoms and life satisfaction in adolescent girls. *Journal of Youth and Adolescence, 43*(1), 1–14. https://doi.org/10.1007/s10964-012-9898-9

Ferjan Ramírez, N., & Kuhl, P. K. (2016). *Bilingual language learning in children.* University of Washington, Institute for Learning and Brain Sciences.

Fernald, A., & Marchman, V. A. (2012). Individual differences in lexical processing at 18 months predict vocabulary growth in typically-developing and late-talking toddlers. *Child Development, 83*(1), 203–222. https://doi.org/10.1111/j.1467-8624.2011.01692.x

Fernandez, C., McCaffery, H., Miller, A. L., Kaciroti, N., Lumeng, J. C., & Pesch, M. H. (2020). Trajectories of picky eating in low-income US children. *Pediatrics, 145*(6), e20192018. https://doi.org/10.1542/peds.2019-2018

Fernández-Basanta, S., Coronado, C., & Movilla-Fernández, M.-J. (2020). Multicultural coping experiences of parents following perinatal loss: A meta-ethnographic synthesis. *Journal of Advanced Nursing, 76*(1), 9–21. https://doi.org/10.1111/jan.14211

Ferreira, P. G., Muñoz-Aguirre, M., Reverter, F., Sá Godinho, C. P., Sousa, A., Amadoz, A., Sodaei, R., Hidalgo, M. R., Pervouchine, D., Carbonell-Caballero, J., Nurtdinov, R., Breschi, A., Amador, R., Oliveira, P., Çubuk, C., Curado, J., Aguet, F., Oliveira, C., Dopazo, J., … Guigó, R. (2018). The effects of death and post-mortem cold ischemia on human tissue transcriptomes. *Nature Communications, 9*(1), 490. https://doi.org/10.1038/s41467-017-02772-x

Ferriss, S. (2015, April 10). How does your state rank on sending students to police? *Time.* https://time.com/3818075/student-police-ranking/

Ferrucci, L., & Fabbri, E. (2018). Inflammageing: Chronic inflammation in ageing, cardiovascular disease, and frailty. *Nature Reviews. Cardiology, 15*(9), 505–522. https://doi.org/10.1038/s41569-018-0064-2

Ferrucci, L., Gonzalez-Freire, M., Fabbri, E., Simonsick, E., Tanaka, T., Moore, Z., Salimi, S., Sierra, F., & de Cabo, R. (2020). Measuring biological aging in humans: A quest. *Aging Cell, 19*(2), e13080. https://doi.org/10.1111/acel.13080

Fervaha, G., Agid, O., Takeuchi, H., Foussias, G., & Remington, G. (2016). Life satisfaction and happiness among young adults with schizophrenia. *Psychiatry Research, 242,* 174–179.

Fettro, M. N. (2018). *Men's and women's time use: Comparing same-sex and different-sex couples* [Doctoral dissertation]. Bowling Green State University.

Figueiredo, P. R., Tolomeo, S., Steele, J. D., & Baldacchino, A. (2020). Neurocognitive consequences of chronic cannabis use: A systematic review and meta-analysis. *Neuroscience & Biobehavioral Reviews, 108,* 358–369. https://doi.org/10.1016/j.neubiorev.2019.10.014

Fiks, A. G., Ross, M. E., Mayne, S. L., Song, L., Liu, W., Steffes, J., McCarn, B., Grundmeier, R. W., Localio, A. R., & Wasserman, R. (2016). Preschool ADHD diagnosis and stimulant use before and after the 2011 AAP Practice Guideline. *Pediatrics, 138*(6), e20162025. https://doi.org/10.1542/peds.2016-2025

Filippa, M., Lordier, L., De Almeida, J. S., Monaci, M. G., Adam-Darque, A., Grandjean, D., Kuhn, P., & Hüppi, P. S. (2020). Early vocal contact and music in the NICU: New insights into preventive interventions. *Pediatric Research, 87*(2), 249–264. https://doi.org/10.1038/s41390-019-0490-9

Fincham, F. D. (2019). Forgiveness in marriage. In E. L. Worthington & N. G. Wade (Eds.), *Handbook of forgiveness* (2nd ed.). Routledge.

Fincham, F. D., & May, R. W. (2017). Infidelity in romantic relationships. *Current Opinion in Psychology, 13,* 70–74. https://doi.org/10.1016/j.copsyc.2016.03.008

Fincham, F. D., Rogge, R., & Beach, S. R. H. (2018). Relationship satisfaction. In A. L. Vangelisti & D. Perlman (Eds.), *The Cambridge handbook of personal relationships* (pp. 422–436). Cambridge University Press. https://doi.org/10.1017/9781316417867.033

Finegood, E. D., Briley, D. A., Turiano, N. A., Freedman, A., South, S. C., Krueger, R. F., Chen, E., Mroczek, D. K., & Miller, G. E. (2021). Association of wealth with longevity in US adults at midlife. *JAMA Health Forum, 2*(7), e211652–e211652. https://doi.org/10.1001/jamahealthforum.2021.1652

Finer, L. B., & Zolna, M. R. (2016). Declines in unintended pregnancy in the United States, 2008–2011. *New England Journal of Medicine, 374*(9), 843–852. https://doi.org/10.1056/NEJMsa1506575

Fingerman, K. L., Cheng, Y. P., Birditt, K., & Zarit, S. (2012). Only as happy as the least happy child: Multiple grown children's problems and successes and middle-aged parents' well-being. *Journals of Gerontology Series B: Psychological Sciences and Social Sciences, 67*(2), 184–193.

Fingerman, K. L., Huo, M., & Birditt, K. S. (2020). A decade of research on intergenerational ties: Technological, economic, political, and demographic changes. *Journal of Marriage and Family, 82*(1), 383–403. https://doi.org/10.1111/jomf.12604

Fingerman, K. L., Huo, M., & Birditt, K. S. (2020). Mothers, fathers, daughters, and sons: Gender differences in adults' intergenerational ties. *Journal of Family Issues, 41*(9), 1597–1625. https://doi.org/10.1177/0192513X19894369

Fingerman, K. L., Kim, K., Tennant, P. S., Birditt, K. S., & Zarit, S. H. (2016). Intergenerational support in a daily context. *The Gerontologist, 56*(5), 896–908.

Fingerman, K. L., Pillemer, K. A., Silverstein, M., & Suitor, J. J. (2012). The baby boomers' intergenerational relationships. *The Gerontologist, 52*(2), 199–209. https://doi.org/10.1093/geront/gnr139

Fingerman, K. L., Pitzer, L. M., Chan, W., Birditt, K., Franks, M. M., & Zarit, S. (2011). Who gets what and why? Help middle-aged adults provide to parents and grown children. *The Journals of Gerontology: Series B, 66B*(1), 87–98. https://doi.org/10.1093/geronb/gbq009

Fingerman, K. L., & Suitor, J. J. (2017). Millennials and their parents: Implications of the new young adulthood for midlife adults. *Innovation in Aging, 1*(3), igx026. https://doi.org/10.1093/geroni/igx026

Finkel, E. J. (2019). *The all-or-nothing marriage: How the best marriages work.* Penguin.

Finkel, E. J., Eastwick, P. W., Karney, B. R., Reis, H. T., & Sprecher, S. (2012). Online dating: A critical analysis from the perspective of psychological science. *Psychological Science in the Public Interest, 13*(1), 3–66.

Finkelhor, D. (2020). Trends in adverse childhood experiences (ACEs) in the United States. *Child Abuse & Neglect, 108,* 104641. https://doi.org/10.1016/j.chiabu.2020.104641

Finkelhor, D., Turner, H. A., Shattuck, A., & Hamby, S. L. (2013). Violence, crime, and abuse exposure in a national sample of children and youth: An update. *JAMA Pediatrics, 167*(7), 614–621. https://doi.org/10.1001/jamapediatrics.2013.42

Finkelhor, D., Turner, H., Wormuth, B. K., Vanderminden, J., & Hamby, S. (2019). Corporal punishment: Current rates from a national survey. *Journal of Child and Family Studies, 28*(7), 1991–1997. https://doi.org/10.1007/s10826-019-01426-4

Finkelstein, D. M., Petersen, D. M., & Schottenfeld, L. S. (2017). Promoting children's physical activity in low-income communities in Colorado: What are the barriers and opportunities? *Preventing Chronic Disease, 14,* 170111. https://doi.org/10.5888/pcd14.170111

Finken, M. J. J., van der Steen, M., Smeets, C. C. J., Walenkamp, M. J. E., de Bruin, C., Hokken-Koelega, A. C. S., & Wit, J. M. (2018). Children born small for gestational age: Differential diagnosis, molecular genetic evaluation, and implications. *Endocrine Reviews, 39*(6), 851–894. https://doi.org/10.1210/er.2018-00083

Finsaas, M. C., Kessel, E. M., Dougherty, L. R., Bufferd, S. J., Danzig, A. P., Davila, J., Carlson, G. A., & Klein, D. N. (2020). Early childhood psychopathology prospectively predicts social functioning in early adolescence. *Journal of Clinical Child and Adolescent Psychology, 49*(3), 353–364. https://doi.org/10.1080/15374416.2018.1504298

Finzi-Dottan, R., & Berckovitch Kormosh, M. (2018). The spillover of compassion fatigue into marital quality: A mediation model. *Traumatology, 24*(2), 113–122. https://doi.org/10.1037/trm0000137

Fischer, C. S., & Offer, S. (2020). Who is dropped and why? Methodological and substantive accounts for network loss. *Social Networks, 61,* 78–86.

Fischer, D., Lombardi, D. A., Marucci-Wellman, H., & Roenneberg, T. (2017). Chronotypes in the US—Influence of age and sex. *PLOS ONE, 12*(6), e0178782. https://doi.org/10.1371/journal.pone.0178782

Fischer, K. W., & Hencke, R. W. (1996). Infants' construction of actions in context: Piaget's contribution to research on early development. *Psychological Science, 7*(4), 204–210.

Fischer, N. M., Duffy, E. Y., & Michos, E. D. (2021). Protecting our youth: Support policy to combat health disparities fueled by targeted food advertising. *Journal of the American Heart Association, 10*(1), e018900. https://doi.org/10.1161/JAHA.120.018900

Fischhoff, B. (2013). The sciences of science communication. *Proceedings of the National Academy of Sciences, 110*(Suppl. 3), 14033–14039. https://doi.org/10.1073/pnas.1213273110

Fisher, A. N., & Sakaluk, J. K. (2020). Are single people a stigmatized "group"? Evidence from examinations of social identity, entitativity, and perceived responsibility. *Journal of Experimental Social Psychology, 86,* 103844. https://doi.org/10.1016/j.jesp.2019.103844

Fisher, A. V., Godwin, K. E., & Seltman, H. (2014). Visual environment, attention allocation, and learning in young children: When too much of a good thing may be bad. *Psychological Science, 25*(7), 1362–1370. https://doi.org/10.1177/0956797614533801

Fisher, C. B., Brunnquell, D. J., Hughes, D. L., Liben, L. S., Maholmes, V., Plattner, S., Russell, S. T., & Susman, E. J. (2013). *Preserving and enhancing the responsible conduct of research involving children and youth: A response to proposed changes in federal regulations* (Social Policy Report Vol. 27, No. 1). Society for Research in Child Development. https://eric.ed.gov/?id=ED540206

Fisher, C. M., Telljohann, S. K., Price, J. H., Dake, J. A., & Glassman, T. (2015). Perceptions of elementary school children's parents regarding sexuality education. *American Journal of Sexuality Education, 10*(1), 1–20.

Fisher, H. E., Xu, X., Aron, A., & Brown, L. L. (2016). Intense, passionate, romantic love: A natural addiction? How the fields that investigate romance and substance abuse can inform each other. *Frontiers in Psychology, 7,* 687. https://doi.org/10.3389/fpsyg.2016.00687

Fiske, A., & Holmboe, K. (2019). Neural substrates of early executive function development. *Developmental Review, 52,* 42–62. https://doi.org/10.1016/j.dr.2019.100866

Fiske, S. T. (2018). Stereotype content: Warmth and competence endure. *Current Directions in Psychological Science, 27*(2), 67–73.

Fitzgerald, C., Zimon, A. E., & Jones, E. E. (1998). Aging and reproductive potential in women. *The Yale Journal of Biology and Medicine, 71*(5), 367.

Fivush, R. (2014). Gendered narratives: Elaboration, structure, and emotion in parent-child reminiscing across the preschool years. In C. P. Thompson, D. J. Herrmann, D. Bruce, J. D. Read, D. G. Payne, & M. P. Toglia (Eds.), *Autobiographical memory: Theoretical and applied perspectives* (pp. 79–104). Psychology Press. https://doi.org/10.4324/9781315784250-6

Fivush, R. (2019). Sociocultural developmental approaches to autobiographical memory. *Applied Cognitive Psychology, 33*(4), 489–497. https://doi.org/10.1002/acp.3512

Fjell, A. M., Sneve, M. H., Grydeland, H., Storsve, A. B., & Walhovd, K. B. (2017). The disconnected brain and executive function decline in aging. *Cerebral Cortex, 27*(3), 2303–2317.

Fjell, A. M., Sørensen, Ø., Amlien, I. K., Bartrés-Faz, D., Bros, D. M., Buchmann, N., Demuth, I., Drevon, C. A., Düzel, S., Ebmeier, K. P., Idland, A.-V., Kietzmann, T. C., Kievit, R., Kühn, S., Lindenberger, U., Mowinckel, A. M., Nyberg, L., Price, D., Sexton, C. E., ... Walhovd, K. B. (2020). Self-reported sleep relates to hippocampal atrophy across the adult lifespan: Results from the Lifebrain consortium. *Sleep, 43*(5), zsz280. https://doi.org/10.1093/sleep/zsz280

Fjell, A. M., Westlye, L. T., Grydeland, H., Amlien, I., Espeseth, T., Reinvang, I., Raz, N., Holland, D., Dale, A. M., & Walhovd, K. B. (2013). Critical ages in the life course of the adult brain: Nonlinear subcortical aging. *Neurobiology of Aging, 34*(10), 2239–2247. https://doi.org/10.1016/j.neurobiolaging.2013.04.006

Flaherty, E. G., Stirling, J., & The Committee on Child Abuse and Neglect. (2010). The pediatrician's role in child maltreatment prevention. *Pediatrics, 126*(4), 833–841. https://doi.org/10.1542/peds.2010-2087

Flaherty, M., Hunsicker, D., & Goldin-Meadow, S. (2021). Structural biases that children bring to language learning: A cross-cultural look at gestural input to homesign. *Cognition, 211*, 104608. https://doi.org/10.1016/j.cognition.2021.104608

Flamion, A., Missotten, P., Marquet, M., & Adam, S. (2019). Impact of contact with grandparents on children's and adolescents' views on the elderly. *Child Development, 90*(4), 1155–1169. https://doi.org/10.1111/cdev.12992

Flanagan, C. (2009). Young people's civic engagement and political development. In A. Furlong (Ed.), *Handbook of youth and young adulthood* (pp. 309–316). Routledge.

Flanagan, C. A., Kefalas, M. J., & Carr, P. J. (2017). Connecting with the body politic: Civic engagement in young adulthood. In T. T. Swartz, D. Hartmann, & R. G. Rumbaut (Eds.), *Crossings to adulthood: How diverse young Americans understand and navigate their lives* (pp. 190–206). Brill.

Flanagan, I. M. L., Auty, K. M., & Farrington, D. P. (2019). Parental supervision and later offending: A systematic review of longitudinal studies. *Aggression and Violent Behavior, 47*, 215–229. https://doi.org/10.1016/j.avb.2019.06.003

Flavell, J. H. (1979). Metacognition and cognitive monitoring: A new area of cognitive–developmental inquiry. *American Psychologist, 34*(10), 906.

Flavell, J. H. (1996). Piaget's legacy. *Psychological Science, 7*(4), 200–203.

Flaviano, M., & Harville, E. W. (2021). Adverse childhood experiences on reproductive plans and adolescent pregnancy in the Gulf resilience on women's health cohort. *International Journal of Environmental Research and Public Health, 18*(1), 165.

Fleming, A. R. (2009, October 5). Can an intellectually disabled mom raise a gifted daughter? It's working so far for Bonnie and Myra Brown. *People*.

Fleming, K. C., Evans, J. M., & Chutka, D. S. (2003). A cultural and economic history of old age in America. *Mayo Clinic Proceedings, 78*(7), 914–921. https://doi.org/10.4065/78.7.914

Fleming, T. P., Watkins, A. J., Velazquez, M. A., Mathers, J. C., Prentice, A. M., Stephenson, J., & Godfrey, K. M. (2018). Origins of lifetime health around the time of conception: Causes and consequences. *The Lancet, 391*(10132), 1842–1852.

Fletcher, G. J. O., Simpson, J. A., Campbell, L., & Overall, N. C. (2015). Pair-bonding, romantic love, and evolution: The curious case of *Homo sapiens*. *Perspectives on Psychological Science, 10*(1), 20–36. https://doi.org/10.1177/1745691614561683

Fletcher, J. R. (2021). Destigmatising dementia: The dangers of felt stigma and benevolent othering. *Dementia, 20*(2), 417–426.

Flint, T. K. (2020). Responsive play: Creating transformative classroom spaces through play as a reader response. *Journal of Early Childhood Literacy, 20*(2), 385–410. https://doi.org/10.1177/1468798418763991

Flores, L. Y., Martinez, L. D., McGillen, G. G., & Milord, J. (2019). Something old and something new: Future directions in vocational research with people of color in the United States. *Journal of Career Assessment, 27*(2), 187–208. https://doi.org/10.1177/1069072718822461

Flores, L. Y., Mendoza, M. M., Ojeda, L., He, Y., Meza, R. R., Medina, V., ... & Jordan, S. (2011). A qualitative inquiry of Latino immigrants' work experiences in the Midwest. *Journal of Counseling Psychology, 58*(4), 522.

Floresco, S. B. (2015). The nucleus accumbens: An interface between cognition, emotion, and action. *Annual Review of Psychology, 66*, 25–52.

Floyd, F. J., Seltzer, M. M., Greenberg, J. S., & Song, J. (2013). Parental bereavement during mid-to-later life: Pre-to-post-bereavement functioning and intrapersonal resources for coping. *Psychology and Aging, 28*(2), 402–413. https://doi.org/10.1037/a0029986

Flynn, H. K., Felmlee, D. H., & Conger, R. D. (2017). The social context of adolescent friendships: Parents, peers, and romantic partners. *Youth & Society, 49*(5), 679–705. https://doi.org/10.1177/0044118X14559900

Flynn, H. K., Felmlee, D. H., Shu, X., & Conger, R. D. (2018). Mothers and fathers matter: The influence of parental support, hostility, and problem solving on adolescent friendships. *Journal of Family Issues, 39*(8), 2389–2412. https://doi.org/10.1177/0192513X18755423

Flynn, J. R. (2020). Secular changes in intelligence: The "Flynn effect." In R. J. Sternberg (Ed.), *The Cambridge handbook of intelligence* (pp. 940–963). Cambridge University Press.

Flynn, J. R., & Shayer, M. (2018). IQ decline and Piaget: Does the rot start at the top? *Intelligence, 66*, 112–121. https://doi.org/10.1016/j.intell.2017.11.010

Flynn, L. B. (2020). The young and the restless: Housing access in the critical years. *West European Politics, 43*(2), 321–343. https://doi.org/10.1080/01402382.2019.1603679

Fomby, P., & Osborne, C. (2017). Family instability, multipartner fertility, and behavior in middle childhood. *Journal of Marriage and Family, 79*(1), 75–93.

Fonagy, P., Luyten, P., Allison, E., & Campbell, C. (2016). Reconciling psychoanalytic ideas with attachment theory. In J. Cassidy & P. R. Shaver (Eds.), *Handbook of attachment: Theory, research, and clinical applications* (3rd ed., pp. 780–804). Guilford.

Fonseca, L. M., & Testoni, I. (2012). The emergence of thanatology and current practice in death education. *OMEGA—Journal of Death and Dying, 64*(2), 157–169.

Forbes, M. K., Eaton, N. R., & Krueger, R. F. (2017). Sexual quality of life and aging: A prospective study of a nationally representative sample. *Journal of Sex Research, 54*(2), 137–148. https://doi.org/10.1080/00224499.2016.1233315

Forbes, M. K., Fitzpatrick, S., Magson, N. R., & Rapee, R. M. (2019). Depression, anxiety, and peer victimization: Bidirectional relationships and associated outcomes transitioning from childhood to adolescence. *Journal of Youth and Adolescence, 48*(4), 692–702. https://doi.org/10.1007/s10964-018-0922-6

Ford, N. D., Behrman, J. R., Hoddinott, J. F., Maluccio, J. A., Martorell, R., Ramirez-Zea, M., & Stein, A. D. (2018). Exposure to improved nutrition from conception to age 2 years and adult cardiometabolic disease risk: A modelling study. *The Lancet Global Health, 6*(8), e875–e884. https://doi.org/10.1016/S2214-109X(18)30231-6

Foreman, J., Keel, S., van Wijngaarden, P., Bourne, R. A., Wormald, R., Crowston, J., Taylor, H. R., & Dirani, M. (2018). Prevalence and causes of visual loss among the indigenous peoples of the world: A systematic review. *JAMA Ophthalmology, 136*(5), 567–580. https://doi.org/10.1001/jamaophthalmol.2018.0597

Forger, N. G. (2018). Past, present and future of epigenetics in brain sexual differentiation. *Journal of Neuroendocrinology, 30*(2), e12492. https://doi.org/10.1111/jne.12492

Foronda, C., Baptiste, D. L., & Reinholdt, M. M. (2016). Cultural humility: A concept analysis. *Journal of Transcultural Nursing, 27*(3), 210–217.

Forry, N. (2015, September 21). Consumer education helps parents choose quality child care. *Child Trends*. https://www.childtrends.org/blog/consumer-education-helps-parents-choose-quality-child-care

Forry, N., Iruka, I., Tout, K., Torquati, J., Susman-Stillman, A., Bryant, D., & Daneri, M. P. (2013). *Predictors of quality and child outcomes in family child care settings*. Child Trends.

Forslund, T., Granqvist, P., van IJzendoorn, M. H., Sagi-Schwartz, A., Glaser, D., Steele, M., Hammarlund, M., Schuengel, C., Bakermans-Kranenburg, M. J., Steele, H., Shaver, P. R., Lux, U., Simmonds, J., Jacobvitz, D., Groh, A. M., Bernard, K., Cyr, C., Hazen, N. L., Foster, S., ... Duschinsky, R. (2021). Attachment goes to court: Child protection and custody issues. *Attachment & Human Development*, 1–52. https://doi.org/10.1080/14616734.2020.1840762

Fortenberry, J. D. (2014). Sexual learning, sexual experience, and healthy adolescent sex. In E. S. Lefkowitz & S. A. Vasilenko (Eds.), *Positive and negative outcomes of sexual behaviors* (pp. 71–86). Jossey-Bass/Wiley.

Fosco, G. M., McCauley, D. M., & Sloan, C. J. (2021). Distal and proximal family contextual effects on adolescents' interparental conflict appraisals: A daily diary study. *Journal of Family Psychology*. https://doi.org/10.1037/fam0000703

Fosco, G. M., Stormshak, E. A., Dishion, T. J., & Winter, C. E. (2012). Family relationships and parental monitoring during middle school as predictors of early adolescent problem behavior. *Journal of Clinical Child & Adolescent Psychology, 41*(2), 202–213.

Foster, H., Hagan, J., & Brooks-Gunn, J. (2008). Growing up fast: Stress exposure and subjective "weathering" in emerging adulthood. *Journal of Health and Social Behavior, 49*(2), 162–177. https://doi.org/10.1177/002214650804900204

Fox, J. (2021, June 18). Young American adults are dying—And not just from Covid. *Bloomberg*.

Fox, M. (2005, September 27). Urie Bronfenbrenner, 88, an authority on child development, dies. *The New York Times*. https://www.nytimes.com/2005/09/27/nyregion/urie-bronfenbrenner-88-an-authority-on-child-development-dies.html

Fraga, M. F., Ballestar, E., Paz, M. F., Ropero, S., Setien, F., Ballestar, M. L., Heine-Suñer, D., Cigudosa, J. C., Urioste, M., Benitez, J., Boix-Chornet, M., Sanchez-Aguilera, A., Ling, C., Carlsson, E., Poulsen, P., Vaag, A., Stephan, Z., Spector, T. D., Wu, Y.-Z., ... Esteller, M. (2005). Epigenetic differences arise during the lifetime of monozygotic twins. *Proceedings of the National Academy of Sciences of the United States, 102*(30), 10604–10609. https://doi.org/10.1073/pnas.0500398102

Fragile Families and Child Wellbeing Study (FFCWS). (2021). *About the Fragile Families and Child Wellbeing Study*. https://fragilefamilies.princeton.edu/about

Fraguas, D., Díaz-Caneja, C. M., Ayora, M., Durán-Cutilla, M., Abregú-Crespo, R., Ezquiaga-Bravo, I., Martín-Babarro, J., & Arango, C. (2021). Assessment of school antibullying interventions: A meta-analysis of randomized clinical trials. *JAMA Pediatrics, 175*(1), 44. https://doi.org/10.1001/jamapediatrics.2020.3541

Fraiman, Y. S., Litt, J. S., Davis, J. M., & Pursley, D. M. (2021). Racial and ethnic disparities in adult COVID-19 and the future impact on child health. *Pediatric Research, 89*(5), 1052–1054.

Fraley, R. C. (2019). Attachment in adulthood: Recent developments, emerging debates, and future directions. *Annual Review of Psychology, 70*(1), 401–422. https://doi.org/10.1146/annurev-psych-010418-102813

Fraley, R. C., & Roisman, G. I. (2019). The development of adult attachment styles: Four lessons. *Current Opinion in Psychology, 25*, 26–30.

Fraley, R. C., & Shaver, P. R. (2016). Attachment, loss, and grief: Bowlby's views, new developments, and current controversies. In J. Cassidy & P. R. Shaver (Eds.), *Handbook of attachment: Theory, research, and clinical applications* (3rd ed., pp. 40–62). Guilford Publications.

Franchak, J. M. (2019). Changing opportunities for learning in everyday life: Infant body position over the first year. *Infancy, 24*(2), 187–209.

Franchak, J. M. (2020). The ecology of infants' perceptual-motor exploration. *Current Opinion in Psychology, 32*, 110–114. https://doi.org/10.1016/j.copsyc.2019.06.035

Francis, B., Craig, N., Hodgen, J., Taylor, B., Tereshchenko, A., Connolly, P., & Archer, L. (2020). The impact of tracking by attainment on pupil self-confidence over time: Demonstrating the accumulative impact of self-fulfilling prophecy. *British Journal of Sociology of Education, 41*(5), 626–642. https://doi.org/10.1080/01425692.2020.1763162

Francis, J. K. R., & Gold, M. A. (2017). Long-acting reversible contraception for adolescents: A review. *JAMA Pediatrics, 171*(7), 694–701. https://doi.org/10.1001/jamapediatrics.2017.0598

Francis, L., & Pearson, D. (2019). The recognition of emotional abuse: Adolescents' responses to warning signs in romantic relationships. *Journal of Interpersonal Violence.* https://doi.org/10.1177/0886260519850537

Franck, L. S., & O'Brien, K. (2019). The evolution of family-centered care: From supporting parent-delivered interventions to a model of family integrated care. *Birth Defects Research, 111*(15), 1044–1059. https://doi.org/10.1002/bdr2.1521

Frank, L. (2020). *Out of milk: Infant food insecurity in a rich nation.* UBC Press.

Frank, L. D., Iroz-Elardo, N., MacLeod, K. E., & Hong, A. (2019). Pathways from built environment to health: A conceptual framework linking behavior and exposure-based impacts. *Journal of Transport & Health, 12*, 319–335. https://doi.org/10.1016/j.jth.2018.11.008

Frank, M. C., Braginsky, M., Yurovsky, D., & Marchman, V. A. (2021). *Variability and consistency in early language learning: The Wordbank Project.* MIT Press.

Franke, A. G., Gränsmark, P., Agricola, A., Schühle, K., Rommel, T., Sebastian, A., Balló, H. E., Gorbulev, S., Gerdes, C., Frank, B., Ruckes, C., Tüscher, O., & Lieb, K. (2017). Methylphenidate, modafinil, and caffeine for cognitive enhancement in chess: A double-blind, randomised controlled trial. *European Neuropsychopharmacology, 27*(3), 248–260. https://doi.org/10.1016/j.euroneuro.2017.01.006

Franke, K., & Gaser, C. (2019). Ten years of BrainAGE as a neuroimaging biomarker of brain aging: What insights have we gained? *Frontiers in Neurology, 10*, 789. https://doi.org/10.3389/fneur.2019.00789

Franke, K., Gaser, C., Roseboom, T. J., Schwab, M., & de Rooij, S. R. (2018). Premature brain aging in humans exposed to maternal nutrient restriction during early gestation. *NeuroImage, 173*, 460–471. https://doi.org/10.1016/j.neuroimage.2017.10.047

Franke, K., van den Bergh, B., de Rooij, S. R., Roseboom, T. J., Nathanielsz, P. W., Witte, O. W., & Schwab, M. (2017). Effects of prenatal stress on structural brain development and aging in humans. *BioRxiv.* https://doi.org/10.1101/148916

Frankenhuis, W. E. (2019). Modeling the evolution and development of emotions. *Developmental Psychology, 55*(9), 2002.

Frankenhuis, W. E., & Nettle, D. (2020). The strengths of people in poverty. *Current Directions in Psychological Science, 29*(1), 16–21. https://doi.org/10.1177/0963721419881154

Frankenhuis, W. E., & Walasek, N. (2019). Modeling the evolution of sensitive periods. *Developmental Cognitive Neuroscience, 41*. https://doi.org/10.1016/j.dcn.2019.100715

Frankenhuis, W. E., & Walasek, N. (2020). Modeling the evolution of sensitive periods. *Developmental Cognitive Neuroscience, 41*, 100715. https://doi.org/10.1016/j.dcn.2019.100715

Frasca, D., Blomberg, B. B., & Paganelli, R. (2017). Aging, obesity, and inflammation age-related diseases. *Frontiers in Immunology, 8*, 1745. https://doi.org/10.3389/fimmu.2017.01745

Fratiglioni, L., Marseglia, A., & Dekhtyar, S. (2020). Ageing without dementia: Can stimulating psychosocial and lifestyle experiences make a difference? *The Lancet Neurology, 19*(6), 533–543. https://doi.org/10.1016/S1474-4422(20)30039-9

Frazer, Z., McConnell, K., & Jansson, L. M. (2019). Treatment for substance use disorders in pregnant women: Motivators and barriers. *Drug and Alcohol Dependence, 205*, 107652. https://doi.org/10.1016/j.drugalcdep.2019.107652

Frederick, D. A., Lever, J., Gillespie, B. J., & Garcia, J. R. (2017). What keeps passion alive? Sexual satisfaction is associated with sexual communication, mood setting, sexual variety, oral sex, orgasm, and sex frequency in a national U.S. study. *The Journal of Sex Research, 54*(2), 186–201. https://doi.org/10.1080/00224499.2015.1137854

Fredrickson, B. L., & Carstensen, L. L. (1990). Choosing social partners: How old age and anticipated endings make people more selective. *Psychology and Aging, 5*(3), 335–347.

Fredriksen-Goldsen, K. I., Kim, H.-J., Bryan, A. E. B., Shiu, C., & Emlet, C. A. (2017). The cascading effects of marginalization and pathways of resilience in attaining good health among LGBT older adults. *The Gerontologist, 57*(suppl_1), S72–S83. https://doi.org/10.1093/geront/gnw170

Fredstrom, B. K., Rose-Krasnor, L., Campbell, K., Rubin, K. H., Booth-LaForce, C., & Burgess, K. B. (2012). Brief report: How anxiously withdrawn preadolescents think about friendship. *Journal of Adolescence, 35*(2), 451–454.

Freedman, V. A., Kasper, J. D., Spillman, B. C., Agree, E. M., Mor, V., Wallace, R. B., & Wolf, D. A. (2014). Behavioral adaptation and late-life disability: A new spectrum for assessing public health impacts. *American Journal of Public Health, 104*(2), e88–e94. https://doi.org/10.2105/AJPH.2013.301687

Freedman, V. A., & Spillman, B. C. (2014). Disability and care needs among older Americans. *The Milbank Quarterly, 92*(3), 509–541. https://doi.org/10.1111/1468-0009.12076

Freelin, B. N., & Staff, J. (2020). Uncertain adolescent educational expectations and college matriculation in the wake of the great recession. *The Sociological Quarterly*, 1–29. https://doi.org/10.1080/00380253.2020.1816862

French, B., Outhwaite, L. A., Langley-Evans, S. C., & Pitchford, N. J. (2020). Nutrition, growth, and other factors associated with early cognitive and motor development in Sub-Saharan Africa: A scoping review. *Journal of Human Nutrition and Dietetics, 33*(5), 644–669. https://doi.org/10.1111/jhn.12795

Freud, S. (1927). Some psychological consequences of the anatomical distinction between the sexes. *The International Journal of Psychoanalysis, 8*, 133–142.

Freud, S. (1953). On psychotherapy. In *The complete works of Sigmund Freud* (J. Strachey, Trans., Vol. 6, pp. 249–263). Hogarth. (Original work published 1905)

Freud, S. (1961). Thoughts for the times on war and death. In *The standard edition of the complete psychological works of Sigmund Freud* (Vol. 14; J. Strachey, Trans.). Hogarth Press. (Original work published 1915)

Freud, S. (1964). The interpretation of dreams. In The standard edition of the complete psychological works of Sigmund Freud (J. Strachey, Ed.). Macmillan. (Original work published 1899)

Freud, S. (1968a). Female sexuality (J. Strachey, Trans.). In *The standard edition of the complete psychological works of Sigmund Freud* (Vol. XXI, pp. 223–245). The Hogarth Press. (Original work published 1931)

Freud, S. (1968b). Femininity (J. Strachey, Trans.). In *The standard edition of the complete psychological works of Sigmund Freud* (Vol. XXII, pp. 112–135). The Hogarth Press. (Original work published 1933)

Freud, S. (1977). *A general introduction to psychoanalysis* (J. Strachey, Trans.). W. W. Norton.

Freud, S. (1989). Mourning and melancholia. In *The Freud Reader* (P. Gay, Ed.). New York: W. W. Norton. (Original work published 1917)

Freud, S. (2000). *Three essays on the theory of sexuality* (J. Strachey, Trans.). Basic Books. (Original work published 1905)

Freud, S. (2018). *The Sigmund Freud collection.* Charles River Editors.

Freudenberg, N., Goldrick-Rab, S., & Poppendieck, J. (2019). College students and SNAP: The new face of food insecurity in the United States. *American Journal of Public Health, 109*(12), 1652–1658. https://doi.org/10.2105/AJPH.2019.305332

Freund, A. M. (2020). The bucket list effect: Why leisure goals are often deferred until retirement. *American Psychologist, 75*(4), 499–510. https://doi.org/10.1037/amp0000617

Freund, J.-D., Linberg, A., & Weinert, S. (2019). Longitudinal interplay of young children's negative affectivity and maternal interaction quality in the context of unequal psychosocial resources. *Infant Behavior and Development, 55*, 123–132. https://doi.org/10.1016/j.infbeh.2019.01.003

Frick, K. D., Joy, S. M., Wilson, D. A., Naidoo, K. S., & Holden, B. A. (2015). The global burden of potential productivity loss from uncorrected presbyopia. *Ophthalmology, 122*(8), 1706–1710.

Fricke, T. R., Tahhan, N., Resnikoff, S., Papas, E., Burnett, A., Ho, S. M., Naduvilath, T., & Naidoo, K. S. (2018). Global prevalence of presbyopia and vision impairment from uncorrected presbyopia: Systematic review, meta-analysis, and modelling. *Ophthalmology, 125*(10), 1492–1499. https://doi.org/10.1016/j.ophtha.2018.04.013

Fried, L. P., Darer, J., & Walston, J. (2003). Frailty. In C. K. Cassel, R. Leipzig, H. J. Cohen, E. B. Larson, & D. E. Meier (Eds.), *Geriatric medicine: An evidence-based approach* (4th ed., pp. 1067–1076). Springer.

Friederici, A. D., Chomsky, N., Berwick, R. C., Moro, A., & Bolhuis, J. J. (2017). Language, mind and brain. *Nature Human Behaviour, 1*(10), 713–722. https://doi.org/10.1038/s41562-017-0184-4

Friedland, R., Afary, J., Gardinali, P., & Naslund, C. (2016). Love in the Middle East: The contradictions of romance in the Facebook world. *Critical Research on Religion, 4*(3), 229–258. https://doi.org/10.1177/2050303216676523

Friedman, C. (2019). The influence of residence type on personal outcomes. *Intellectual and Developmental Disabilities, 57*(2), 112–126. https://doi.org/10.1352/1934-9556-57.2.112

Friedman, E. M., Ruini, C., Foy, C. R., Jaros, L., Love, G., & Ryff, C. D. (2019). Lighten UP! A community-based group intervention to promote eudaimonic well-being in older adults: A multi-site replication with 6 month follow-up. *Clinical Gerontologist, 42*(4), 387–397. https://doi.org/10.1080/07317115.2019.1574944

Friedman, L. J. (2000). *Identity's architect: A biography of Erik H. Erikson.* Harvard University Press.

Fries, J., Göbel, C., & Maier, M. F. (2014). Do employment subsidies reduce early apprenticeship dropout? *Journal of Vocational Education & Training, 66*(4), 433–461. https://doi.org/10.1080/13636820.2014.948905

Friso-van den Bos, I., Kroesbergen, E. H., & Van Luit, J. E. H. (2018). Counting and number line trainings in kindergarten: Effects on arithmetic performance and number sense. *Frontiers in Psychology, 9*, 975. https://doi.org/10.3389/fpsyg.2018.00975

Frith, U. (2019). Flux of life. *Developmental Cognitive Neuroscience, 38*, 100669. https://doi.org/10.1016/j.dcn.2019.100669

Fritz, J., de Graaff, A. M., Caisley, H., van Harmelen, A.-L., & Wilkinson, P. O. (2018). A systematic review of amenable resilience factors that moderate and/or mediate the relationship between childhood adversity and mental health in young people. *Frontiers in Psychiatry, 9*, 230. https://doi.org/10.3389/fpsyt.2018.00230

Fritz, R., & Jindal, S. (2018). Reproductive aging and elective fertility preservation. *Journal of Ovarian Research, 11*(1), 66. https://doi.org/10.1186/s13048-018-0438-4

Frosh, S. (2013). Psychoanalysis, colonialism, racism. *Journal of Theoretical and Philosophical Psychology, 33*(3), 141–154. https://doi.org/10.1037/a0033398

Frost, D. M., Meyer, I. H., & Hammack, P. L. (2015). Health and well-being in emerging adults' same-sex relationships: Critical questions and directions for research in developmental science. *Emerging Adulthood, 3*(1), 3–13. https://doi.org/10.1177/2167696814535915

Fry, R. (2014, May 14). *Young adults, student debt and economic well-being.* Pew Research Center's Social & Demographic Trends Project. http://www.pewsocialtrends .org/2014/05/14/young-adults-student-debt-and-economic -well-being/

Fry, R. (2016, May 24). *For first time in modern era, living with parents edges out other living arrangements for 18- to 34-year-olds.* Pew Research Center's Social & Demographic Trends Project. http://www.pewsocialtrends .org/2016/05/24/for-first-time-in-modern-era-living-with-parents-edges-out-other-living-arrangements-for-18-to-34-year-olds/

Fry, R. (2020, November). *The pace of boomer retirements has accelerated in the past year.* Pew Research Center. https:// www.pewresearch.org/fact-tank/2020/11/09/the-pace-of-boomer-retirements-has-accelerated-in-the-past-year/

Fry, R., & Parker, K. (2021, October 5). Rising share of U.S. adults are living without a spouse or partner. *Social & Demographic Trends Project.* Pew Research Center. https:// www.pewresearch.org/social-trends/2021/10/05/rising-share-of-u-s-adults-are-living-without-a-spouse-or-partner/

Fry, R., Passel, J. S., & Cohn, D. (2020, September 4). *A majority of young adults in the U.S. live with their parents for the first time since the Great Depression.* Pew Research Center. https:// www.pewresearch.org/fact-tank/2020/09/04/a-majority-of-young-adults-in-the-u-s-live-with-their-parents-for-the-first-time-since-the-great-depression/

Fryar, C. D., Carroll, M. D., & Afful, J. (2020). *Prevalence of overweight and obesity among children and adolescents aged 2–19 years: United States, 1963–1965 through 2013–2014.* NCHS Health E-Stats 2020. https://www.cdc.gov/nchs/ data/hestat/obesity-child-17-18/obesity-child.htm

Fryar, C. D., Carroll, M. D., & Afful, J. (2020a). *Prevalence of low weight-for-recumbent length, recumbent length-for-age, and weight-for-age among infants and toddlers from birth to 24 months of age: United States, 1999–2000 through 2017–2018* [Health E Stats]. https://www.cdc.gov/nchs/ data/hestat/low-weight-recumbent-17-18/low-weight-recumbent.htm

Fryar, C. D., Carroll, M. D., & Afful, J. (2020b). *Prevalence of high weight-for-recumbent length among infants and toddlers from birth to 24 months of age: United States, 1971–1974 through 2017–2018* [Health E Stats]. https://www .cdc.gov/nchs/data/hestat/high-weight-recumbent-17-18 /high-weight-recumbent.htm

Fryar, C. D., Carroll, M. D., & Afful, J. (2021). *Prevalence of overweight, obesity, and severe obesity among children and adolescents aged 2–19 years: United States, 1963–1965 through 2017–2018* [Health E Stats]. Division of Health and Nutrition Examination Surveys. https://www.cdc.gov/ nchs/data/hestat/obesity-child-17-18/obesity-child.htm

Fuhrmann, D., Knoll, L. J., & Blakemore, S.-J. (2015). Adolescence as a sensitive period of brain development. *Trends in Cognitive Sciences, 19*(10), 558–566. https://doi .org/10.1016/j.tics.2015.07.008

Fujiki, M., & Brinton, B. (2017). Pragmatics and social communication in child language disorders. In R. G. Schwartz (Ed.), *Handbook of child language disorders* (2nd ed.). Psychology Press.

Fukasawa, M., Watanabe, K., Nishi, D., & Kawakami, N. (2020). Longitudinal association between adolescent work values and mental health and well-being in adulthood: A 23-year prospective cohort study. *Scientific Reports, 10*(1), 13547. https://doi.org/10.1038/s41598-020-70507-y

Fuligni, A. J. (1998). Authority, autonomy, and parent–adolescent conflict and cohesion: A study of adolescents from Mexican, Chinese, Filipino, and European backgrounds. *Developmental Psychology, 34*(4), 782.

Fuligni, A. J. (2019). The need to contribute during adolescence. *Perspectives on Psychological Science, 14*(3), 331–343.

Fuligni, A. J., Hughes, D. L., & Way, N. (2009). Ethnicity and immigration. In R. M. Lerner & L. Steinberg (Eds.), *Handbook of adolescent psychology: Contextual influences on adolescent development* (Vol. 2, 3rd ed., pp. 527–569). John Wiley & Sons. https://doi.org/10.1002/9780470479193 .adlpsy002016

Fuligni, A., & Masten, C. L. (2010). Daily family interactions among young adults in the United States from Latin American, Filipino, East Asian, and European backgrounds. *International Journal of Behavioral Development, 34*(6), 491–499. https://doi.org/10.1177/0165025409360303

Fuligni, A. J., & Pedersen, S. (2002). Family obligation and the transition to young adulthood. *Developmental Psychology, 38*(5), 856–868. http://dx.doi .org/10.1037/0012-1649.38.5.856

Fuligni, A. J., & Tsai, K. M. (2015). Developmental flexibility in the age of globalization: Autonomy and identity development among immigrant adolescents. *Annual Review of Psychology, 66*, 411–431.

Fuligni, A. J., Tseng, V., & Lam, M. (1999). Attitudes toward family obligations among American adolescents with Asian, Latin American, and European backgrounds. *Child Development, 70*(4), 1030–1044.

Fuligni, A. J., Witkow, M., & Garcia, C. (2005). Ethnic identity and the academic adjustment of adolescents from Mexican, Chinese, and European backgrounds. *Developmental Psychology, 41*(5), 799.

Fuligni, A. S., Howes, C., Huang, Y., Hong, S. S., & Lara-Cinisomo, S. (2012). Activity settings and daily routines in preschool classrooms: Diverse experiences in early learning settings for low-income children. *Early Childhood Research Quarterly, 27*(2), 198–209. https://doi.org/10.1016/j .ecresq.2011.10.001

Fullana, M. A., Dunsmoor, J. E., Schruers, K. R. J., Savage, H. S., Bach, D. R., & Harrison, B. J. (2020). Human fear conditioning: From neuroscience to the clinic. *Behaviour Research and Therapy, 124*, 103528. https://doi .org/10.1016/j.brat.2019.103528

Fuller, A. (2018). *A bridge among walls: 2018 Laetare Medalist Sister Norma Pimentel, M.J.* https://www.nd.edu /stories/laetare-2018-sister-norma/

Fuller, H. R., Ajrouch, K. J., & Antonucci, T. C. (2020). The convoy model and later-life family relationships. *Journal of Family Theory & Review, 12*(2), 126–146. https://doi .org/10.1111/jftr.12376

Fuller, S. C. (1912). Alzheimer's disease (senium praecox): The report of a case and review of published cases. *Journal of Nervous and Mental Disease, 39*(8), 536–557.

Fullerton, A. M. (1911). *A handbook of obstetric nursing for nurses, students and mothers.* P. Blakiston's Son. http:// archive.org/details/ahandbookobstet01fullgoog

Fullwiley, D. (2021, February 1). DNA and our twenty-first-century ancestors. *Boston Review.* http:// bostonreview.net/race/duana-fullwiley-dna-and-our-twenty -first-century-ancestors

Fung, H. H., Gong, X., Ngo, N., & Isaacowitz, D. M. (2019). Cultural differences in the age-related positivity effect: Distinguishing between preference and effectiveness. *Emotion, 19*(8), 1414–1424. https://doi.org/10.1037 /emo0000529

Funk, C., Hefferon, M., Kennedy, B., & Johnson, C. (2019). *Trust and mistrust in Americans' views of scientific experts.* Pew Research Center.

Furman, W. (2018). The romantic relationships of youth. In W. M. Bukowski, B. Laursen, & K. H. Rubin (Eds.), *Handbook of peer interactions, relationships, and groups* (2nd ed., pp. 410–428). Guilford.

Furman, W., & Rose, A. J. (2015). Friendships, romantic relationships, and peer relationships. In M. Lamb & R. M. Lerner (Eds.), *Handbook of child psychology and developmental science* (pp. 932–974). Wiley. https://doi .org/10.1002/9781118963418.childpsy322

Furstenberg, F. (2019). Family change in global perspective: How and why family systems change. Family Relations, 68(3), 326–341. https://doi.org/10.1111/fare.12361.

Furstenberg, F. F., Harris, L. E., Pesando, L. M., & Reed, M. N. (2020). Kinship practices among alternative family forms in Western industrialized societies. *Journal of Marriage and Family, 82*(5), 1403–1430.

Furth, C. (1988). Androgynous males and deficient females: Biology and gender boundaries in sixteenth- and seventeenth-century China. *Late Imperial China, 9*(2), 1–31. https://doi.org/10.1353/late.1988.0002

Furukawa, E., Tangney, J., & Higashibara, F. (2012). Cross-cultural continuities and discontinuities in shame, guilt, and pride: A study of children residing in Japan, Korea and the USA. *Self and Identity, 11*(1), 90–113.

Fusar-Poli, P., Salazar de Pablo, G., Correll, C. U., Meyer-Lindenberg, A., Millan, M. J., Borgwardt, S., Galderisi, S., Bechdolf, A., Pfennig, A., Kessing, L. V., van Amelsvoort, T., Nieman, D. H., Domschke, K., Krebs, M.-O., Koutsouleris, N., McGuire, P., Do, K. Q., & Arango, C. (2020). Prevention of Psychosis: Advances in Detection, Prognosis, and Intervention. *JAMA Psychiatry, 77*(7), 755–765. https://doi.org/10.1001 /jamapsychiatry.2019.4779

Futagi, Y., Toribe, Y., & Suzuki, Y. (2012). The grasp reflex and Moro reflex in infants: Hierarchy of primitive reflex responses. *International Journal of Pediatrics, 2012*, e191562. https://doi.org/10.1155/2012/191562

Gabard-Durnam, L., & McLaughlin, K. A. (2020). Sensitive periods in human development: Charting a course for the future. *Current Opinion in Behavioral Sciences, 36*, 120–128. https://doi.org/10.1016/j.cobeha.2020.09.003

Gabel, A. D., & Scheller, A. (2013). *Sensorimotor development and assessment.* Pearson Clinical Assessment.

Gach, E. J., Ip, K. I., Sameroff, A. J., & Olson, S. L. (2018). Early cumulative risk predicts externalizing behavior at age 10: The mediating role of adverse parenting. *Journal of Family Psychology, 32*(1), 92–102. https://doi .org/10.1037/fam0000360

Gaddis, A., & Brooks-Gunn, J. (1985). The male experience of pubertal change. *Journal of Youth and Adolescence, 14*(1), 61–69.

Gaffey, A. E., Bergeman, C. S., Clark, L. A., & Wirth, M. M. (2016). Aging and the HPA axis: Stress and resilience in older adults. *Neuroscience and Biobehavioral Reviews, 68*, 928–945. https://doi.org/10.1016/j.neubiorev.2016.05.036

Gaffney, H., Ttofi, M. M., & Farrington, D. P. (2021). What works in anti-bullying programs? Analysis of effective intervention components. *Journal of School Psychology, 85*, 37–56. https://doi.org/10.1016/j.jsp.2020.12.002

Gagné, T., Sacker, A., & Schoon, I. (2021a). Changes in patterns of social role combinations at ages 25–26 among those growing up in England between 1996 and 2015–16: Evidence from the 1970 British cohort and next steps studies. *Journal of Youth and Adolescence, 50*, 2052–2066. https://doi.org/10.1007/s10964-021-01477-1

Gagné, T., Schoon, I., & Sacker, A. (2021b). Trends in young adults' mental distress and its association with employment: Evidence from the behavioral risk factor surveillance system, 1993–2019. *Preventive Medicine, 150*, 106691. https://doi.org/10.1016/j.ypmed.2021.106691

Gago Galvagno, L. G., De Grandis, M. C., Clerici, G. D., Mustaca, A. E., Miller, S. E., & Elgier, A. M. (2019). Regulation during the second year: Executive function and emotion regulation links to joint attention, temperament, and social vulnerability in a Latin American sample. *Frontiers in Psychology, 10*, 1473. https://doi.org/10.3389/fpsyg.2019.01473

Gaias, L. M., Gal, D. E., Abry, T., Taylor, M., & Granger, K. L. (2018). Diversity exposure in preschool: Longitudinal implications for cross-race friendships and racial bias. *Journal of Applied Developmental Psychology, 59*, 5–15. https:// doi.org/10.1016/j.appdev.2018.02.005

Gaigbe-Togbe, V. (2015). *The impact of socio-economic inequalities on early childhood survival: Results from the demographic and health surveys* (Technical Paper No. 2015/1, p. 30). United Nations Population Division.

Galatzer-Levy, I. R., Huang, S. H., & Bonanno, G. A. (2018). Trajectories of resilience and dysfunction following potential trauma: A review and statistical evaluation. *Clinical Psychology Review, 63*, 41–55.

Gale, C. R., Westbury, L., & Cooper, C. (2018). Social isolation and loneliness as risk factors for the progression of frailty: The English longitudinal study of ageing. *Age and Ageing, 47*(3), 392–397.

Galiana, J., & Haseltine, W. A. (2019). *Aging well: Solutions to the most pressing global challenges of aging.* Palgrave Macmillan.

Gallagher, D., Andres, A., Fields, D. A., Evans, W. J., Kuczmarski, R., Lowe, W. L., Jr., Lumeng, J. C., Oken, E., Shepherd, J. A., & Sun, S. (2020). Body composition measurements from birth through 5 years: Challenges, gaps, and existing & emerging technologies—A National Institutes of Health Workshop. *Obesity Reviews, 21*(8), e13033.

Galler, J. R., Bringas-Vega, M. L., Tang, Q., Rabinowitz, A. G., Musa, K. I., Chai, W. J., Omar, H., Abdul Rahman, M. R., Abd Hamid, A. I., Abdullah, J. M., & Valdés-Sosa, P. A. (2021). Neurodevelopmental effects of childhood malnutrition: A neuroimaging perspective. *NeuroImage, 231*, 117828. https://doi.org/10.1016/j.neuroimage.2021.117828

Gallois, S., Duda, R., Hewlett, B., & Reyes-García, V. (2015). Children's daily activities and knowledge acquisition: A case study among the Baka from southeastern Cameroon. *Journal of Ethnobiology and Ethnomedicine, 11*(1), 86. https://doi.org/10.1186/s13002-015-0072-9

Gallup, G. G. (1970). Chimpanzees: Self-recognition. *Science, 167*(3914), 86–87. https://doi.org/10.1126/science.167.3914.86

Galton, F. (1883). *Inquiries into human faculty and its development.* Macmillan.

Galupa, R., & Heard, E. (2018). X-chromosome inactivation: A crossroads between chromosome architecture and gene regulation. *Annual Review of Genetics, 52*(1), 535–566. https://doi.org/10.1146/annurev-genet-120116-024611

Galupo, M. P., Cartwright, K. B., & Savage, L. S. (2009). Cross-category friendships and postformal thought among college students. *Journal of Adult Development, 17*(4), 208–214. https://doi.org/10.1007/s10804-009-9089-4

Galván, A. (2013). The teenage brain: Sensitivity to rewards. *Current Directions in Psychological Science, 22*(2), 88–93. https://doi.org/10.1177/0963721413480859

Galván, A. (2017). Adolescence, brain maturation and mental health. *Nature Neuroscience, 20*(4), 503–504.

Galván, A. (2020). The need for sleep in the adolescent brain. *Trends in Cognitive Sciences, 24*(1), 79–89. https://doi.org/10.1016/j.tics.2019.11.002

Galvan, A., Hare, T., Voss, H., Glover, G., & Casey, B. J. (2007). Risk-taking and the adolescent brain: Who is at risk? *Developmental Science, 10*(2), F8–F14.

Galvez, M. P., McGovern, K., Teitelbaum, S. L., Windham, G., & Wolff, M. S. (2018). Neighborhood factors and urinary metabolites of nicotine, phthalates, and dichlorobenzene. *Pediatrics, 141*(Supplement 1), S87–S95. https://doi.org/10.1542/peds.2017-1026L

Gamliel, T. (2010). "She who mourns will cry": Emotion and expertise in Yemeni-Israeli wailing. *Journal of Anthropological Research, 66*(4), 485–503.

Gana, K., Bailly, N., Saada, Y., Joulain, M., Trouillet, R., Hervé, C., & Alaphilippe, D. (2013). Relationship between life satisfaction and physical health in older adults: A longitudinal test of cross-lagged and simultaneous effects. *Health Psychology, 32*(8), 896–904. https://doi.org/10.1037/a0031656

Gana, K., Broc, G., Saada, Y., Amieva, H., & Quintard, B. (2016). Subjective wellbeing and longevity: Findings from a 22-year cohort study. *Journal of Psychosomatic Research, 85*, 28–34. https://doi.org/10.1016/j.jpsychores.2016.04.004

Gandal, M. J., Haney, J. R., Parikshak, N. N., Leppa, V., Ramaswami, G., Hartl, C., & Geschwind, D. H. (2018). Shared molecular neuropathology across major psychiatric disorders parallels polygenic overlap. *Science, 359*(6376), 693–697.

Gándara, P. (2017). The potential and promise of Latino students. *American Educator, 41*(1), 4.

Gándara, P. (2018). The economic value of bilingualism in the United States. *Bilingual Research Journal, 41*(4), 334–343. https://doi.org/10.1080/15235882.2018.1532469

Ganong, L., & Coleman, M. (2018). Studying stepfamilies: Four eras of family scholarship. *Family Process, 57*(1), 7–24. https://doi.org/10.1111/famp.12307

Ganson, K. T., Tsai, A. C., Weiser, S. D., Benabou, S. E., & Nagata, J. M. (2021). Job insecurity and symptoms of anxiety and depression among U.S. young adults during COVID-19. *Journal of Adolescent Health, 68*(1), 53–56. https://doi.org/10.1016/j.jadohealth.2020.10.008

Garbarino, J., & Bruyere, E. (2013). Resilience in the lives of children of war. In C. Fernando & M. Ferrari (Eds.), *Handbook of resilience in children of war* (pp. 253–266). Springer Science & Business Media.

Garceau, C., & Ronis, S. T. (2019). A qualitative investigation of expected versus actual initial sexual experiences before age 16. *Journal of Adolescence, 71*, 38–49.

García, D. G., & Yosso, T. J. (2020). Recovering our past: A methodological reflection. *History of Education Quarterly, 60*(1), 59–72. https://doi.org/10.1017/heq.2019.50

García, J. S. M., Oinonen, E., Merino, R., & Perosa, G. (2021). Education and inequality in Finland, Spain and Brazil. In P. López-Roldán & S. Fachelli (Eds.), *Towards a comparative analysis of social inequalities between Europe and Latin America* (pp. 105–140). Springer.

Garcia, K. E., Kroenke, C. D., & Bayly, P. V. (2018). Mechanics of cortical folding: Stress, growth and stability. *Philosophical Transactions of the Royal Society B: Biological Sciences, 373*(1759), 20170321. https://doi.org/10.1098/rstb.2017.0321

García Coll, C., Crnic, K., Lamberty, G., Wasik, B. H., Jenkins, R., García, H. V., & McAdoo, H. P. (1996). An integrative model for the study of developmental competencies in minority children. *Child Development, 67*(5), 1891–1914. https://doi.org/10.1111/j.1467-8624.1996.tb01834.x

García Coll, C., Miranda, A. G., Torres, I. B., & Bermúdez, J. N. (2018). On becoming cultural beings: A focus on race, gender, and language. *Research in Human Development, 15*(3–4), 332–344. https://doi.org/10.1080/15427609.2018.1491217

García-Moya, I., Bunn, F., Jiménez-Iglesias, A., Paniagua, C., & Brooks, F. M. (2019). The conceptualisation of school and teacher connectedness in adolescent research: A scoping review of literature. *Educational Review, 71*(4), 423–444.

Garcia-Sanchez, I. M. (2018). Children as interactional brokers of care. *Annual Review of Anthropology, 47*, 167–184.

Garcini, L. M., Brown, R. L., Chen, M. A., Saucedo, L., Fite, A. M., Ye, P., Ziauddin, K., & Fagundes, C. P. (2019). Bereavement among widowed Latinos in the United States: A systematic review of methodology and findings. *Death Studies, 45*(5), 342–353. https://doi.org/10.1080/07481187.2019.1648328

Gard, A. M., McLoyd, V. C., Mitchell, C., & Hyde, L. W. (2020). Evaluation of a longitudinal family stress model in a population-based cohort. *Social Development, 29*(4), 1155–1175. https://doi.org/10.1111/sode.12446

Gardner, H. (1965, July 15). Erik Erikson. *The New York Review of Books.* https://www.nybooks.com/articles/1965/07/15/erik-erikson/

Gardner, H. (1999). Are there additional intelligences? The case for naturalist, spiritual, and existential intelligences. In J. Kane (Ed.), *Education, information, and transformation* (pp. 111–131). Prentice Hall.

Gardner, H. (2011). *Frames of mind: The theory of multiple intelligences* (30-year ed.). Basic Books.

Gardstedt, J., Niklasson, A., Aronson, S., Albertsson-Wikland, K., & Holmgren, A. (2019). Menarche and its relation to the pubertal growth spurt. *ESPE Abstracts, 92*, P1–119. http://abstracts.eurospe.org/hrp/0092/hrp0092p1-119

Garenne, M. (2021). Age at menarche in Nigerian demographic surveys. *Journal of Biosocial Science, 53*(5), 745–757. http://dx.doi.org/10.1017/S0021932020000504

Gariepy, G., Danna, S., Gobiņa, I., Rasmussen, M., Gaspar de Matos, M., Tynjälä, J., Janssen, I., Kalman, M., Villeruša, A., Husarova, D., Brooks, F., Elgar, F. J., Klavina-Makrecka, S., Šmigelskas, K., Gaspar, T., & Schnohr, C. (2020). How are adolescents sleeping? Adolescent sleep patterns and sociodemographic differences in 24 European and North American countries. *Journal of Adolescent Health, 66*(6, Supplement), S81–S88. https://doi.org/10.1016/j.jadohealth.2020.03.013

Garland, E. L., Brintz, C. E., Hanley, A. W., Roseen, E. J., Atchley, R. M., Gaylord, S. A., Faurot, K. R., Yaffe, J., Fiander, M., & Keefe, F. J. (2020). Mind-body therapies for opioid-treated pain: A systematic review and meta-analysis. *JAMA Internal Medicine, 180*(1), 91–105. https://doi.org/10.1001/jamainternmed.2019.4917

Garmezy, N. E., & Rutter, M. E. (Eds.). (1983). *Stress, coping, and development in children.* Johns Hopkins University Press.

Garon, N. M., Longard, J., Bryson, S. E., & Moore, C. (2012). Making decisions about now and later: Development of future-oriented self-control. *Cognitive Development, 27*(3), 314–322. https://doi.org/10.1016/j.cogdev.2012.05.003

Garratt, R., Bamber, D., Powell, C., Long, J., Brown, J., Turney, N., Chessman, J., Dyson, S., & James-Roberts, I. S. (2019). Parents' experiences of having an excessively crying baby and implications for support services. *Journal of Health Visiting, 7*(3), 132–140. https://doi.org/10.12968/johv.2019.7.3.132

Garrett-Peters, P. T., Castro, V. L., & Halberstadt, A. G. (2017). Parents' beliefs about children's emotions, children's emotion understanding, and classroom adjustment in middle childhood. *Social Development, 26*(3), 575–590.

Gartlehner, G., Patel, S. V., Feltner, C., Weber, R. P., Long, R., Mullican, K., & Viswanathan, M. (2017). Hormone therapy for the primary prevention of chronic conditions in postmenopausal women: Evidence report and systematic review for the US Preventive Services Task Force. *JAMA, 318*(22), 2234–2249.

Gartner, M., Kiang, L., & Supple, A. (2014). Prospective links between ethnic socialization, ethnic and American identity, and well-being among Asian-American adolescents. *Journal of Youth and Adolescence, 43*(10), 1715–1727. https://doi.org/10.1007/s10964-013-0044-0

Gartstein, M. A., Hancock, G. R., & Iverson, S. L. (2018). Positive affectivity and fear trajectories in infancy: Contributions of mother–child interaction factors. *Child Development, 89*(5), 1519–1534. https://doi.org/10.1111/cdev.12843

Gartstein, M. A., & Putnam, S. P. (2018). *Toddlers, parents and culture: Findings from the joint effort toddler temperament consortium.* Routledge.

Gartstein, M. A., & Skinner, M. K. (2018). Prenatal influences on temperament development: The role of environmental epigenetics. *Development and Psychopathology, 30*(4), 1269–1303. https://doi.org/10.1017/S0954579417001730

Gaskins, A. J., Fong, K. C., Awad, Y. A., Di, Q., Mínguez-Alarcón, L., Chavarro, J. E., Ford, J. B., Coull, B. A., Schwartz, J., Kloog, I., Souter, I., Hauser, R., & Laden, F. (2019). Time-varying exposure to air pollution and outcomes of in vitro fertilization among couples from a fertility clinic. *Environmental Health Perspectives, 127*(7), 077002. https://doi.org/10.1289/EHP4601

Gassen, N. C., Chrousos, G. P., Binder, E. B., & Zannas, A. S. (2017). Life stress, glucocorticoid signaling, and the aging epigenome: Implications for aging-related diseases. *Neuroscience & Biobehavioral Reviews, 74*, 356–365. https://doi.org/10.1016/j.neubiorev.2016.06.003

Gatchel, R. J., & McGeary, D. (2020). Pain and health psychology. In K. Sweeny, M. L. Robbins, & L. M. Cohen (Eds), *The Wiley encyclopedia of health psychology* (pp. 183–191). John Wiley & Sons.

Gates, J. R., Corbin, W. R., & Fromme, K. (2016). Emerging adult identity development, alcohol use, and alcohol-related problems during the transition out of college. *Psychology of Addictive Behaviors, 30*(3), 345–355. https://doi.org/10.1037/adb0000179

Gates, N. J., Rutjes, A. W., Di Nisio, M., Karim, S., Chong, L.-Y., March, E., Martínez, G., & Vernooij, R. W. (2019). Computerised cognitive training for maintaining cognitive function in cognitively healthy people in midlife. *The Cochrane Database of Systematic Reviews, 3*(3), CD012278. https://doi.org/10.1002/14651858.CD012278.pub2

Gaugler, J. E., Yu, F., Davila, H. W., & Shippee, T. (2014). Alzheimer's disease and nursing homes. *Health Affairs (Project Hope), 33*(4), 650–657. https://doi.org/10.1377/hlthaff.2013.1268

Gaul, D., & Issartel, J. (2016). Fine motor skill proficiency in typically developing children: On or off the maturation track? *Human Movement Science, 46*, 78–85. https://doi.org/10.1016/j.humov.2015.12.011

Gault-Sherman, M. (2012). It's a two-way street: The bidirectional relationship between parenting and delinquency. *Journal of Youth and Adolescence, 41*(2), 121–145.

Gauvain, M. (2020). Vygotsky on learning and development. In A. Slater & P. C. Quinn (Eds.), *Developmental psychology: Revisiting the classic studies* (p. 89). Sage.

Gauvain, M., & Nicolaides, C. (2015). Cognition in childhood across cultures. In L. A. Jensen (Ed.), *The Oxford handbook of human development and culture: An interdisciplinary perspective* (pp. 198–213). Oxford University Press.

Gauvain, M., & Perez, S. (2015). Cognitive development and culture. In L. S. Liben, U. Müller, & R. M. Lerner (Eds.), *Handbook of child psychology and developmental science: Cognitive processes* (pp. 854–896). Wiley.

Gauvain, M., Perez, S. M., & Reisz, Z. (2018). Stability and change in mother–child planning over middle childhood. *Developmental Psychology, 54*(3), 571–585. https://doi.org/10.1037/dev0000456

Gavett, B. E., Zhao, R., John, S. E., Bussell, C. A., Roberts, J. R., & Yue, C. (2017). Phishing suspiciousness in older and younger adults: The role of executive functioning. *PLoS ONE, 12*(2), e0171620. https://doi.org/10.1371/journal.pone.0171620

Gavin, K. (2020, September 20). *Loneliness doubled for older adults in first months of COVID-19*. University of Michigan. https://labblog.uofmhealth.org/rounds/loneliness-doubled-for-older-adults-first-months-of-covid-19

Gawande, A. (2014). *Being mortal: Medicine and what matters in the end*. Metropolitan Books.

Gay, P. (1996). *The naked heart: The bourgeois experience Victoria to Freud* (Vol. 4). W. W. Norton.

Gay, P. (1998). *Freud: A life for our time*. W. W. Norton.

Gaysina, D., Richards, M., Kuh, D., & Hardy, R. (2015). Pubertal maturation and affective symptoms in adolescence and adulthood: Evidence from a prospective birth cohort. *Development and Psychopathology, 27*(4pt1), 1331–1340.

GBD 2015 Obesity Collaborators. (2017). Health effects of overweight and obesity in 195 countries over 25 years. *New England Journal of Medicine, 377*(1), 13–27.

Geangu, E., Hauf, P., Bhardwaj, R., & Bentz, W. (2011). Infant pupil diameter changes in response to others' positive and negative emotions. *PLOS ONE, 6*(11), e27132.

Gee, D. G. (2016). Sensitive periods of emotion regulation: Influences of parental care on frontoamygdala circuitry and plasticity. *New Directions for Child and Adolescent Development, 153*, 87–110.

Gee, D. G. (2020). Caregiving influences on emotional learning and regulation: Applying a sensitive period model. *Current Opinion in Behavioral Sciences, 36*, 177–184. https://doi.org/10.1016/j.cobeha.2020.11.003

Gee, D. G., Gabard-Durnam, L., Telzer, E. H., Humphreys, K. L., Goff, B., Shapiro, M., Flannery, J., Lumian, D. S., Fareri, D. S., Caldera, C., & Tottenham, N. (2014). Maternal buffering of human amygdala–prefrontal circuitry during childhood but not adolescence. *Psychological Science, 25*(11), 2067–2078. https://doi.org/10.1177/0956797614550878

Geffen, L. N., Kelly, G., Morris, J. N., & Howard, E. P. (2019). Peer-to-peer support model to improve quality of life among highly vulnerable, low-income older adults in Cape Town, South Africa. *BMC Geriatrics, 19*(1), 279.

Gehlbach, H., Brinkworth, M. E., King, A. M., Hsu, L. M., McIntyre, J., & Rogers, T. (2016). Creating birds of similar feathers: Leveraging similarity to improve teacher–student relationships and academic achievement. *Journal of Educational Psychology, 108*(3), 342.

Gehlich, K. H., Beller, J., Lange-Asschenfeldt, B., Köcher, W., Meinke, M. C., & Lademann, J. (2019). Fruit and vegetable consumption is associated with improved mental and cognitive health in older adults from non-Western developing countries. *Public Health Nutrition, 22*(4), 689–696. https://doi.org/10.1017/S1368980018002525

Geiger, A. W., Livingston, G., & Bialik, K. (2019, May 8). *6 Facts about U.S. moms*. Pew Research Center.

Geller, A., Baciu, A., Yang, S., Abudayyeh, H., Ahmed, J., Ali, K., Chou, J., David, J., Edmier, A., Hanfi, H., Harvey, M., Hayes, M., Hong, C., Hyman, B., Ismail, M., Ives, A., Kofman, D., Kropp, L., Kutscher, E., … Whittaker, L. (2017). Third annual DC public health case challenge: Supporting mental health in older veterans. *NAM Perspectives*. https://doi.org/10.31478/201710d

Geller, J., & Betancur, M. C. (2016). *Why families are engaged in early learning in Central Falls, Rhode Island*. Annenberg Institute for Education Reform.

Gelman, R. (1973). The nature and development of early number concepts. In H. W. Reese (Ed.), *Advances in child development and behavior* (Vol. 7, pp. 115–167). JAI. https://doi.org/10.1016/S0065-2407(08)60441-3

Geneen, L. J., Moore, R. A., Clarke, C., Martin, D., Colvin, L. A., & Smith, B. H. (2017). Physical activity and exercise for chronic pain in adults: An overview of Cochrane Reviews. *The Cochrane Database of Systematic Reviews, 4*, CD011279. https://doi.org/10.1002/14651858.CD011279.pub3

General Social Survey (GSS). (2018). *GSS Data Explorer*. https://gssdataexplorer.norc.org

Generations United. (2015). *The state of grandfamilies in America: 2015*. https://www.gu.org/resources/the-state-of-grandfamilies-in-america-2015/

Generett, G. G., & Olson, A. M. (2020). The stories we tell: How merit narratives undermine success for urban youth. *Urban Education, 55*(3), 394–423.

GeneSight Mental Health Monitor. (2020, November 17). *Suffering in silence: Two-thirds of older adults say they won't treat their depression*. https://genesight.com/news-and-press/suffering-in-silence-two-thirds-of-older-adults-say-they-wont-treat-their-depression/

Gennatas, E. D., Avants, B. B., Wolf, D. H., Satterthwaite, T. D., Ruparel, K., Ciric, R., Hakonarson, H., Gur, R. E., & Gur, R. C. (2017). Age-related effects and sex differences in gray matter density, volume, mass, and cortical thickness from childhood to young adulthood. *Journal of Neuroscience, 37*(20), 5065–5073. https://doi.org/10.1523/JNEUROSCI.3550-16.2017

Gentile, D. A., Reimer, R. A., Nathanson, A. I., Walsh, D. A., & Eisenmann, J. C. (2014). Protective effects of parental monitoring of children's media use: A prospective study. *JAMA Pediatrics, 168*(5), 479–484.

George, C., Kaplan, N., & Main, M. (1985). *Attachment interview for adults* [Unpublished manuscript]. University of California, Berkeley.

George, M. J., Russell, M. A., Piontak, J. R., & Odgers, C. L. (2018). Concurrent and subsequent associations between daily digital technology use and high-risk adolescents' mental health symptoms. *Child Development, 89*(1), 78–88. https://doi.org/10.1111/cdev.12819

Georgieff, M. K., Ramel, S. E., & Cusick, S. E. (2018). Nutritional influences on brain development. *Acta Paediatrica, 107*(8), 1310–1321. https://doi.org/10.1111/apa.14287

Geronimus, A. T. (1992). The weathering hypothesis and the health of African-American women and infants: Evidence and speculations. *Ethnicity & Disease, 2*(3), 207–221.

Gershenson, S., Hart, C. M. D., Hyman, J., Lindsay, C., & Papageorge, N. W. (2018). *The long-run impacts of same-race teachers* (No. w25254). National Bureau of Economic Research. https://doi.org/10.3386/w25254

Gershoff, E. T., & Font, S. A. (2016). Corporal punishment in U.S. public schools: Prevalence, disparities in use, and status in state and federal policy. *Social Policy Report, 30*, 1.

Gershoff, E. T., & Grogan-Kaylor, A. (2016). Spanking and child outcomes: Old controversies and new meta-analyses. *Journal of Family Psychology, 30*(4), 453.

Gershoff, E., Sattler, K. M. P., & Holden, G. W. (2019). School corporal punishment and its associations with achievement and adjustment. *Journal of Applied Developmental Psychology, 63*, 1–8. https://doi.org/10.1016/j.appdev.2019.05.004

Gerstel, N., & Clawson, D. (2018). Control over time: Employers, workers, and families shaping work schedules. *Annual Review of Sociology, 44*(1), 77–97. https://doi.org/10.1146/annurev-soc-073117-041400

Gerstorf, D., Ram, N., Hoppmann, C., Willis, S. L., & Schaie, K. W. (2011). Cohort differences in cognitive aging and terminal decline in the Seattle Longitudinal Study. *Developmental Psychology, 47*(4), 1026.

Gervais, M., Jaimovich, N., Siu, H. E., & Yedid-Levi, Y. (2016). What should I be when I grow up? Occupations and unemployment over the life cycle. *Journal of Monetary Economics, 83*, 54–70. https://doi.org/10.1016/j.jmoneco.2016.08.003

Gesell, A. (1928). *Infancy and human growth* (pp. xvii, 418). MacMillan. https://doi.org/10.1037/14664-000

Gesselman, A. N., Franco, C. Y., Brogdon, E. M., Gray, P. B., Garcia, J. R., & Fisher, H. E. (2019). Perceptions of married life among single never-married, single ever-married, and married adults. *Personal Relationships, 26*(4), 586–601. https://doi.org/10.1111/pere.12295

Gettler, L. T., Boyette, A. H., & Rosenbaum, S. (2020). Broadening perspectives on the evolution of human paternal care and fathers' effects on children. *Annual Review of Anthropology, 49*(1), 141–160. https://doi.org/10.1146/annurev-anthro-102218-011216

Gettler, L. T., Kuo, P. X., Sarma, M. S., Trumble, B. C., Burke Lefever, J. E., & Braungart-Rieker, J. M. (2021). Fathers' oxytocin responses to first holding their newborns: Interactions with testosterone reactivity to predict later parenting behavior and father-infant bonds. *Developmental Psychobiology, 63*(5), 1384–1398.

Gewirtz, J. L. (2001). J. B. Watson's approach to learning: Why Pavlov? Why not Thorndike? *Behavioral Development Bulletin, 10*(1), 23–25. http://dx.doi.org/10.1037/h0100478

Gewirtz-Meydan, A., & Ayalon, L. (2018). Forever young: Visual representations of gender and age in online dating sites for older adults. *Journal of Women & Aging, 30*(6), 484–502.

Gewirtz-Meydan, A., & Finkelhor, D. (2020). Sexual abuse and assault in a large national sample of children and adolescents. *Child Maltreatment, 25*(2), 203–214. https://doi.org/10.1177/1077559519873975

Gewirtz-Meydan, A., Mitchell, K. J., & Rothman, E. F. (2018). What do kids think about sexting? *Computers in Human Behavior, 86*, 256–265. https://doi.org/10.1016/j.chb.2018.04.007

Ghandour, R. M., Sherman, L. J., Vladutiu, C. J., Ali, M. M., Lynch, S. E., Bitsko, R. H., & Blumberg, S. J. (2019). Prevalence and treatment of depression, anxiety, and conduct problems in US children. *The Journal of Pediatrics, 206*, 256–267.e3. https://doi.org/10.1016/j.jpeds.2018.09.021

Ghavami, N., Katsiaficas, D., & Rogers, L. O. (2016). Toward an intersectional approach in developmental science: The role of race, gender, sexual orientation, and immigrant status. In S. S. Horn, M. D. Ruck, & L. S. Liben (Eds.), *Advances in child development and behavior* (Vol. 50, pp. 31–73). JAI. https://doi.org/10.1016/bs.acdb.2015.12.001

Gheysen, F., Poppe, L., DeSmet, A., Swinnen, S., Cardon, G., De Bourdeaudhuij, I., Chastin, S., & Fias, W. (2018). Physical activity to improve cognition in older adults: can physical activity programs enriched with cognitive challenges enhance the effects? A systematic review and meta-analysis. *International Journal of Behavioral Nutrition and Physical Activity, 15*(1), 63. https://doi.org/10.1186/s12966-018-0697-x

Ghimire, U., Papabathini, S. S., Kawuki, J., Obore, N., & Musa, T. H. (2021). Depression during pregnancy and the risk of low birth weight, preterm birth and intrauterine growth restriction — an updated meta-analysis. *Early Human Development, 152*, 105243. https://doi.org/10.1016/j.earlhumdev.2020.105243

Gibbons, F. X., Fleischli, M. E., Gerrard, M., Simons, R. L., Weng, C. Y., & Gibson, L. P. (2020). The impact of early racial discrimination on illegal behavior, arrest, and incarceration among African Americans. *American Psychologist, 75*(7), 952.

Gibson, E. J. (1988). Exploratory behavior in the development of perceiving, acting, and the acquiring of knowledge. *Annual Review of Psychology, 39*(1), 1–42.

Gibson, E. J., & Walk, R. D. (1960). The "visual cliff." *Scientific American, 202*(4), 64–71.

Gibson, E. L., Androutsos, O., Moreno, L., Flores-Barrantes, P., Socha, P., Iotova, V., Cardon, G., De Bourdeaudhuij, I., Koletzko, B., Skripkauskaite, S., Manios, Y., & on behalf of the Toybox-study Group. (2020). Influences of parental snacking-related attitudes, behaviours and nutritional knowledge on young children's healthy and unhealthy snacking: The ToyBox study. *Nutrients, 12*(2), 432. https://doi.org/10.3390/nu12020432

Gibson, J. J. (1979). *The ecological approach to visual perception: Classic edition.* Psychology Press.

Gibson, J. M., Fisher, M., Clonch, A., MacDonald, J. M., & Cook, P. J. (2020). Children drinking private well water have higher blood lead than those with city water. *Proceedings of the National Academy of Sciences, 117*(29), 16898–16907. https://doi.org/10.1073/pnas.2002729117

Gierveld, J. D. J. (2004). Remarriage, unmarried cohabitation, living apart together: Partner relationships following bereavement or divorce. *Journal of Marriage and Family, 66*(1), 236–243. https://doi.org/10.1111/j.0022-2445.2004.00015.x

Gierveld, J. D. J., Van der Pas, S., & Keating, N. (2015). Loneliness of older immigrant groups in Canada: Effects of ethnic-cultural background. *Journal of Cross-Cultural Gerontology, 30*(3), 251–268.

Gilhooly, K. J., Gilhooly, M. L. M., Sullivan, M. P., McIntyre, A., Wilson, L., Harding, E., Woodbridge, R., & Crutch, S. (2016). A meta-review of stress, coping and interventions in dementia and dementia caregiving. *BMC Geriatrics, 16*(1), 106. https://doi.org/10.1186/s12877-016-0280-8

Gilkerson, L., Burkhardt, T., Katch, L. E., & Hans, S. L. (2020). Increasing parenting self-efficacy: The Fussy Baby Network® intervention. *Infant Mental Health Journal, 41*(2), 232–245. https://doi.org/10.1002/imhj.21836

Gill, V. R., Liley, H. G., Erdei, C., Sen, S., Davidge, R., Wright, A. L., & Bora, S. (2021). Improving the uptake of Kangaroo Mother Care in neonatal units: A narrative review and conceptual framework. *Acta Paediatrica, 110*(5), 1407–1416. https://doi.org/10.1111/apa.15705

Gillam-Krakauer, M., & Gowen, C. W., Jr. (2020). Birth asphyxia. *StatPearls.*

Gillen-O'Neel, C., & Fuligni, A. (2013). A longitudinal study of school belonging and academic motivation across high school. *Child Development, 84*(2), 678–692.

Gillen-O'Neel, C., Huynh, V. W., & Fuligni, A. J. (2013). To study or to sleep? The academic costs of extra studying at the expense of sleep. *Child Development, 84*(1), 133–142.

Gillen-O'Neel, C., Huynh, V. W., Hazelbaker, T., & Harrison, A. (2021). From kindness and diversity to justice and action: White parents' ethnic–racial socialization goals. *Journal of Family Issues,* 0192513X21996392. https://doi.org/10.1177/0192513X21996392

Gillen-O'Neel, C., Ruble, D. N., & Fuligni, A. J. (2011). Ethnic stigma, academic anxiety, and intrinsic motivation in middle childhood. *Child Development, 82*(5), 1470–1485.

Gillespie, B. J., Bostean, G., & Malizia, S. (2020). Timing of departure from the parental home: Differences by immigrant generation and parents' region of origin. *Hispanic Journal of Behavioral Sciences, 42*(2), 165–190. https://doi.org/10.1177/0739986320916424

Gilliam, W. S. (2016). *Early childhood expulsions and suspensions undermine our nation's most promising agent of opportunity and social justice.* Robert Wood Johnson Foundation. https://scholar.google.com/citations?view_op=view_citation&hl=en&user=wJq1irQAAAAJ&sortby=pubdate&citation_for_view=wJq1irQAAAAJ:Zph67rFs4hoC

Gilliam, W. S., Malik, A. A., Shafiq, M., Klotz, M., Reyes, C., Humphries, J. E., Murray, T., Elharake, J. A., Wilkinson, D., & Omer, S. B. (2021). COVID-19 transmission in US child care programs. *Pediatrics, 147*(1), e2020031971. https://doi.org/10.1542/peds.2020-031971

Gilligan, C. (1977). In a different voice: Women's conceptions of self and of morality. *Harvard Educational Review, 47*(4), 481–517.

Gilligan, C. (1993). *In a different voice: Psychological theory and women's development.* Harvard University Press.

Gilligan, M., Stocker, C. M., & Conger, K. J. (2020). Sibling relationships in adulthood: Research findings and new frontiers. *Journal of Family Theory & Review, 12*(3), 305–320. https://doi.org/10.1111/jftr.12385

Gilligan, M., Suitor, J. J., & Pillemer, K. (2015). Estrangement between mothers and adult children: The role of norms and values. *Journal of Marriage and the Family, 77*(4), 908–920. https://doi.org/10.1111/jomf.12207

Gilmore, J. H., Langworthy, B., Girault, J. B., Fine, J., Jha, S. C., Kim, S. H., Cornea, E., & Styner, M. (2020). Individual variation of human cortical structure is established in the first year of life. *Biological Psychiatry: Cognitive Neuroscience and Neuroimaging, 5*(10), 971–980. https://doi.org/10.1016/j.bpsc.2020.05.012

Gilmore, J. H., Santelli, R. K., & Gao, W. (2018). Imaging structural and functional brain development in early childhood. *Nature Reviews Neuroscience, 19*(3), 123–137. https://doi.org/10.1038/nrn.2018.1

Gimenez-Nadal, J. I., & Molina, J. A. (2020). *The gender gap in time allocation in Europe* (No. 13461). IZA Discussion Papers.

Gindis, B. (1999). Vygotsky's vision: Reshaping the practice of special education for the 21st century. *Remedial and Special Education, 20*(6), 333–340. https://doi.org/10.1177/074193259902000606

Gingras, Y., Lariviere, V., Macaluso, B., & Robitaille, J. P. (2008). The effects of aging on researchers' publication and citation patterns. *PLoS ONE, 3*(12), e4048.

Giofrè, D., Toffalini, E., Altoè, G., & Cornoldi, C. (2017). Intelligence measures as diagnostic tools for children with specific learning disabilities. *Intelligence, 61,* 140–145.

Gire, J. T. (2019). Cultural variations in perceptions of aging. In K. D. Keith (Ed.), *Cross-cultural psychology: Contemporary themes and perspectives* (2nd ed., pp. 216–240). John Wiley & Sons. https://doi.org/10.1002/9781119519348.ch10

Giuntella, O., Hyde, K., Saccardo, S., & Sadoff, S. (2021). Lifestyle and mental health disruptions during COVID-19. *Proceedings of the National Academy of Sciences, 118*(9). https://doi.org/10.1073/pnas.2016632118

Givens, A. (2021, August 3). *College majors with the greatest gender disparities.* Chicagotribune.com. https://www.chicagotribune.com/business/careers-finance/sns-stacker-majors-gender-disparities-20210803-3rhi7s4vgvdhln4tjngcokmh2a-photogallery.html

Gkiouleka, A., Huijts, T., Beckfield, J., & Bambra, C. (2018). Understanding the micro and macro politics of health: Inequalities, intersectionality & institutions — A research agenda. *Social Science & Medicine, 200,* 92–98.

Glanz, K., Metcalfe, J. J., Folta, S. C., Brown, A., & Fiese, B. (2021). Diet and health benefits associated with in-home eating and sharing meals at home: A systematic review. *International Journal of Environmental Research and Public Health, 18*(4), 1577. https://doi.org/10.3390/ijerph18041577

Glaser, B. G., & Strauss, A. L. (1965). *Awareness of dying.* Aldine Transaction.

Glaser, K., Stuchbury, R., Price, D., Di Gessa, G., Ribe, E., & Tinker, A. (2018). Trends in the prevalence of grandparents living with grandchild(ren) in selected European countries and the United States. *European Journal of Ageing, 15*(3), 237–250. https://doi.org/10.1007/s10433-018-0474-3

Glass, T. A., Freedman, M., Carlson, M. C., Hill, J., Frick, K. D., Ialongo, N., McGill, S., Rebok, G. W., Seeman, T., Tielsch, J. M., Wasik, B. A., Zeger, S., & Fried, L. P. (2004). Experience corps: Design of an intergenerational program to boost social capital and promote the health of an aging society. *Journal of Urban Health: Bulletin of the New York Academy of Medicine, 81*(1), 94–105. https://doi.org/10.1093/jurban/jth096

Glei, D. A., Goldman, N., & Weinstein, M. (2018). Perception has its own reality: Subjective versus objective measures of economic distress. *Population and Development Review, 44*(4), 695.

Glei, D. A., Stokes, A., & Weinstein, M. (2020). Changes in mental health, pain, and drug misuse since the mid-1990s: Is there a link? *Social Science & Medicine (1982), 246,* 112789. https://doi.org/10.1016/j.socscimed.2020.112789

Glick, G. C., & Rose, A. J. (2011). Prospective associations between friendship adjustment and social strategies: Friendship as a context for building social skills. *Developmental Psychology, 47*(4), 1117.

Global Burden of Disease Cancer Collaboration. (2018). Global, regional, and national cancer incidence, mortality, years of life lost, years lived with disability, and disability-adjusted life-years for 29 cancer groups, 1990 to 2016: A systematic analysis for the Global Burden of Disease Study. *JAMA Oncology, 4*(11), 1553–1568. https://doi.org/10.1001/jamaoncol.2018.2706

Global School-based Student Health Survey (GSSHS). (2016). *Global School-based Student Health Survey, Bhutan, 2016 fact sheet.* World Health Organization.

Glodosky, N. C., & Cuttler, C. (2020). Motives matter: Cannabis use motives moderate the associations between stress and negative affect. *Addictive Behaviors, 102,* 106188. https://doi.org/10.1016/j.addbeh.2019.106188

Gobbi, G., Atkin, T., Zytynski, T., Wang, S., Askari, S., Boruff, J., Ware, M., Marmorstein, N., Cipriani, A., & Dendukuri, N. (2019). Association of cannabis use in adolescence and risk of depression, anxiety, and suicidality in young adulthood: A systematic review and meta-analysis. *JAMA Psychiatry, 76*(4), 426–434.

Goddings, A.-L., Beltz, A., Peper, J. S., Crone, E. A., & Braams, B. R. (2019). Understanding the role of puberty in structural and functional development of the adolescent brain. *Journal of Research on Adolescence, 29*(1), 32–53. https://doi.org/10.1111/jora.12408

Goddings, A.-L., Mills, K. L., Clasen, L. S., Giedd, J. N., Viner, R. M., & Blakemore, S.-J. (2014). The influence of puberty on subcortical brain development. *Neuroimage, 88,* 242–251. https://doi.org/10.1016/j.neuroimage.2013.09.073

Goddings, A.-L., Viner, R. M., Mundy, L., Romaniuk, H., Molesworth, C., Carlin, J. B., Allen, N. B., & Patton, G. C. (2021). Growth and adrenarche: Findings from the CATS observational study. *Archives of Disease in Childhood.* https://doi.org/10.1136/archdischild-2020-319341

Godleski, S. A., Kamper, K. E., Ostrov, J. M., Hart, E. J., & Blakely-McClure, S. J. (2015). Peer victimization and peer rejection during early childhood. *Journal of Clinical Child and Adolescent Psychology, 44*(3), 380–392. https://doi.org/10.1080/15374416.2014.940622

Godwin, K. E., Almeda, M. V., Seltman, H., Kai, S., Skerbetz, M. D., Baker, R. S., & Fisher, A. V. (2016). Off-task behavior in elementary school children. *Learning and Instruction, 44,* 128–143.

Godwin, K. E., Seltman, H., Almeda, M., Skerbetz, M. D., Kai, S., Baker, R. S., & Fisher, A. V. (2021). The elusive relationship between time on-task and learning: Not simply an issue of measurement. *Educational Psychology, 41*(4), 502–519. https://doi.org/10.1080/01443410.2021.1894324

Goebel, B. L., & Brown, D. R. (1981). Age differences in motivation related to Maslow's need hierarchy. *Developmental Psychology, 17*(6), 809–815. https://doi.org/10.1037/0012-1649.17.6.809

Goff, P. A., Jackson, M. C., Di Leone, B. A. L., Culotta, C. M., & DiTomasso, N. A. (2014). The essence of innocence: Consequences of dehumanizing Black children. *Journal of Personality and Social Psychology, 106*(4), 526.

Goldberg, A. E., Kuvalanka, K. A., & Black, K. (2019). Trans students who leave college: An exploratory study of their experiences of gender minority stress. *Journal of College Student Development, 60*(4), 381–400.

Goldberg, A. E., Moyer, A. M., & Kinkler, L. A. (2013). Lesbian, gay, and heterosexual adoptive parents' perceptions of parental bonding during early parenthood. *Couple and Family Psychology: Research and Practice, 2*(2), 146.

Goldberg, A. E., & Romero, A. P. (2019). Same-sex couples and relationship well-being, dissolution, and divorce. In A. E. Goldberg & A. P. Romero (Eds), *LGBTQ divorce and relationship dissolution: Psychological and legal perspectives and implications for practice* (Part I, pp. 31–144). Oxford University Press.

Goldberg, E. (2006). *The wisdom paradox: How your mind can grow stronger as your brain grows older*. Penguin.

Golden, C. R., & McHugh, M. C. (2017). The personal, political, and professional life of Sandra Bem. *Sex Roles, 76*(9), 529–543.

Golden, J. C., & Jacoby, J. W. (2018). Playing princess: Preschool girls' interpretations of gender stereotypes in Disney Princess media. *Sex Roles, 79*(5), 299–313. https://doi.org/10.1007/s11199-017-0773-8

Golden, R. L., Furman, W., & Collibee, C. (2016). The risks and rewards of sexual debut. *Developmental Psychology, 52*(11), 1913–1925. https://doi.org/10.1037/dev0000206

Goldfarb, E. S., & Lieberman, L. D. (2021). Three decades of research: The case for comprehensive sex education. *Journal of Adolescent Health, 68*(1), 13–27. https://doi.org/10.1016/j.jadohealth.2020.07.036

Goldin, C. (1998). America's graduation from high school: The evolution and spread of secondary schooling in the twentieth century. *The Journal of Economic History, 58*(2), 345–374. https://www.cambridge.org/core/journals/journal-of-economic-history/article/americas-graduation-from-high-school-the-evolution-and-spread-of-secondary-schooling-in-the-twentieth-century/6419955E40943932F792C9F26A3FA5AA

Goldin, C., & Katz, L. F. (1997). *Why the United States led in education: Lessons from secondary school expansion, 1910 to 1940*. National Bureau of Economic Research.

Goldin, C., & Katz, L. F. (2008). Transitions: Career and family life cycles of the educational elite. *American Economic Review, 98*(2), 363–369.

Goldin-Meadow, S. (2015). From action to abstraction: Gesture as a mechanism of change. *Developmental Review, 38*, 167–184.

Goldman, D. P., Chen, C., Zissimopoulos, J., Rowe, J. W., & the Research Network on an Aging Society. (2018). Opinion: Measuring how countries adapt to societal aging. *Proceedings of the National Academy of Sciences, 115*(3), 435–437. https://doi.org/10.1073/pnas.1720899115

Goldman, N., Glei, D. A., & Weinstein, M. (2018). Declining mental health among disadvantaged Americans. *Proceedings of the National Academy of Sciences, 115*(28), 7290–7295.

Goldrick-Rab, S., Welton, C. R., & Vanessa Coca. (2020). *Basic needs insecurity among students with children*. The Hope Center: For College, Community and Justice. https://hope4college.com/parenting-while-in-college-basic-needs-insecurity-among-students-with-children/

Goldscheider, F., & Goldscheider, C. (1999). *The changing transition to adulthood: Leaving and returning home*. SAGE.

Goldschmidt, L., Langa, M., Alexander, D., & Canham, H. (2021). A review of Kohlberg's theory and its applicability in the South African context through the lens of early childhood development and violence. *Early Child Development and Care, 191*(7–8), 1066–1078. https://doi.org/10.1080/03004430.2021.1897583

Goldstein, E. B., & Brockmole, J. (2017). *Sensation and perception*. Cengage Learning.

Goldstein, E. B., & Cacciamani, L. (2021). *Sensation and perception* (11th ed.). Cengage Learning.

Goldstein, R. D., Lederman, R. I., Lichtenthal, W. G., Morris, S. E., Human, M., Elliott, A. J., Tobacco, D., Angal, J., Odendaal, H., Kinney, H. C., Prigerson, H. G., for the PASS Network. (2018). The grief of mothers after the sudden unexpected death of their infants. *Pediatrics, 141*(5), e20173651. https://doi.org/10.1542/peds.2017-3651

Goldston, D. B., Molock, S. D., Whitbeck, L. B., Murakami, J. L., Zayas, L. H., & Hall, G. C. N. (2008). Cultural considerations in adolescent suicide prevention and psychosocial treatment. *American Psychologist, 63*(1), 14.

Goldy, S. P., & Piff, P. K. (2020). Toward a social ecology of prosociality: Why, when, and where nature enhances social connection. *Current Opinion in Psychology, 32*, 27–31. https://doi.org/10.1016/j.copsyc.2019.06.016

Golembiewski, K. (2019, August 2). After you die, these genes come to life. *Discover Magazine*. https://www.discovermagazine.com/health/after-you-die-these-genes-come-to-life

Golestanzadeh, M., Riahi, R., & Kelishadi, R. (2020). Association of phthalate exposure with precocious and delayed pubertal timing in girls and boys: A systematic review and meta-analysis. *Environmental Science: Processes & Impacts, 22*(4), 873–894. https://doi.org/10.1039/c9em00512a

Golinkoff, R. M., Hoff, E., Rowe, M. L., Tamis-LeMonda, C. S., & Hirsh-Pasek, K. (2019). Language matters: Denying the existence of the 30-million-word gap has serious consequences. *Child Development, 90*(3), 985–992. https://doi.org/10.1111/cdev.13128

Göllner, R., Damian, R. I., Rose, N., Spengler, M., Trautwein, U., Nagengast, B., & Roberts, B. W. (2017). Is doing your homework associated with becoming more conscientious? *Journal of Research in Personality, 71*, 1–12.

Golombok, S. (2017). Parenting in new family forms. *Current Opinion in Psychology, 15*, 76–80. https://doi.org/10.1016/j.copsyc.2017.02.004

Gomes, T., Tadrous, M., Mamdani, M. M., Paterson, J. M., & Juurlink, D. N. (2018). The burden of opioid-related mortality in the United States. *JAMA Network Open, 1*(2), e180217. https://doi.org/10.1001/jamanetworkopen.2018.0217

Gomes-Osman, J., Cabral, D. F., Morris, T. P., McInerney, K., Cahalin, L. P., Rundek, T., & Pascual-Leone, A. (2018). Exercise for cognitive brain health in aging: A systematic review for an evaluation of dose. *Neurology: Clinical Practice, 8*(3), 257–265.

Gómez, A., Arteaga, S., Villaseñor, E., Arcara, J., & Freihart, B. (2019). The misclassification of ambivalence in pregnancy intentions: A mixed-methods analysis. *Perspectives on Sexual and Reproductive Health, 51*(1), 7–15. https://doi.org/10.1363/psrh.12088

Gomez, J., Barnett, M., & Grill-Spector, K. (2019). Extensive childhood experience with Pokémon suggests eccentricity drives organization of visual cortex. *Nature Human Behaviour, 3*(6), 611–624. https://doi.org/10.1038/s41562-019-0592-8

Gómez-López, M., Viejo, C., & Ortega-Ruiz, R. (2019). Psychological well-being during adolescence: Stability and association with romantic relationships. *Frontiers in Psychology, 10*, 1772. https://doi.org/10.3389/fpsyg.2019.01772

Gomez-Olivencia, A., & Ohman, J. (2018). Neanderthals cared for each other and survived into old age—new research. *The Conversation*. http://theconversation.com/neanderthals-cared-for-each-other-and-survived-into-old-age-new-research-93110

Gómez-Roig, M. D., Pascal, R., Cahuana, M. J., García-Algar, O., Sebastiani, G., Andreu-Fernández, V., Martínez, L., Rodríguez, G., Iglesia, I., Ortiz-Arrabal, O., Mesa, M. D., Cabero, M. J., Guerra, L., Llurba, E., Domínguez, C., Zanini, M. J., Foraster, M., Larqué, E., Cabañas, F., … Vento, M. (2021). Environmental exposure during pregnancy: Influence on prenatal development and early life: A comprehensive review. *Fetal Diagnosis and Therapy, 48*(4), 245–257. https://doi.org/10.1159/000514884

Gona, P. N., Gona, C. M., Ballout, S., Rao, S. R., Kimokoti, R., Mapoma, C. C., & Mokdad, A. H. (2020). Burden and changes in HIV/AIDS morbidity and mortality in Southern Africa development community countries, 1990–2017. *BMC Public Health, 20*, 1–14.

Gong, X., & Fung, H. H. (2020). Remembering positive or relevant information? Cultural relevance may moderate the age-related positivity effect in memory. *Psychology and Aging, 35*(2), 267.

Gonsalkorale, K., Sherman, J. W., & Klauer, K. C. (2009). Aging and prejudice: Diminished regulation of automatic race bias among older adults. *Journal of Experimental Social Psychology, 45*(2), 410–414. https://doi.org/10.1016/j.jesp.2008.11.004

Gonzales, E., Lee, Y. J., & Marchiondo, L. A. (2021). Exploring the consequences of major lifetime discrimination, neighborhood conditions, chronic work, and everyday discrimination on health and retirement. *Journal of Applied Gerontology, 40*(2), 121–131.

Gonzalez, C. L. R., & Sacrey, L.-A. R. (2018). The development of the motor system. In R. Gibb & B. Kolb (Eds.), *The neurobiology of brain and behavioral development* (pp. 235–256). Academic Press. https://doi.org/10.1016/B978-0-12-804036-2.00009-1

González, M. J., Cortina, C., & Rodríguez, J. (2019). The role of gender stereotypes in hiring: A field experiment. *European Sociological Review, 35*(2), 187–204. https://doi.org/10.1093/esr/jcy055

Goodman, A. H., Moses, Y. T., & Jones, J. L. (2012). *Race: Are we so different?* John Wiley & Sons.

Goodman, W. B., Dodge, K. A., Bai, Y., Murphy, R. A., & O'Donnell, K. (2021). Effect of a universal postpartum nurse home visiting program on child maltreatment and emergency medical care at 5 years of age: A randomized clinical trial. *JAMA Network Open, 4*(7), e2116024–e2116024. https://doi.org/10.1001/jamanetworkopen.2021.16024

Goodnow, J. J., & Lawrence, J. A. (2015). Children and cultural context. In *Handbook of child psychology and developmental science* (pp. 1–41). American Cancer Society. https://doi.org/10.1002/9781118963418.childpsy419

Goodpaster, B. H., Park, S. W., Harris, T. B., Kritchevsky, S. B., Nevitt, M., Schwartz, A. V., & Newman, A. B. (2006). The loss of skeletal muscle strength, mass, and quality in older adults: The health, aging and body composition study. *The Journals of Gerontology Series A: Biological Sciences and Medical Sciences, 61*(10), 1059–1064.

Goodwin, R. D., Weinberger, A. H., Kim, J. H., Wu, M., & Galea, S. (2020). Trends in anxiety among adults in the United States, 2008–2018: Rapid increases among young adults. *Journal of Psychiatric Research, 130*, 441–446. https://doi.org/10.1016/j.jpsychires.2020.08.014

Gooren, L. J., & T'Sjoen, G. (2018). Endocrine treatment of aging transgender people. *Reviews in Endocrine and Metabolic Disorders, 19*(3), 253–262. https://doi.org/10.1007/s11154-018-9449-0

Gopalan, M., & Brady, S. T. (2020). College students' sense of belonging: A national perspective. *Educational Researcher, 49*(2), 134–137. https://doi.org/10.3102/0013189X19897622

Gopnik, A. (2020). Childhood as a solution to explore–exploit tensions. *Philosophical Transactions of the Royal Society B: Biological Sciences, 375*(1803), 20190502. https://doi.org/10.1098/rstb.2019.0502

Gopnik, A., Frankenhuis, W. E., & Tomasello, M. (2020). Introduction to special issue: 'Life history and learning: how childhood, caregiving and old age shape cognition and culture in humans and other animals.' *Philosophical Transactions of the Royal Society B: Biological Sciences, 375*(1803), 20190489. https://doi.org/10.1098/rstb.2019.0489

Gordon, L. B., Shappell, H., Massaro, J., D'Agostino, R. B., Brazier, J., Campbell, S. E., Kleinman, M. E., & Kieran, M. W. (2018). Association of lonafarnib treatment vs no treatment with mortality rate in patients with Hutchinson-Gilford progeria syndrome. *JAMA, 319*(16), 1687–1695. https://doi.org/10.1001/jama.2018.3264

Gordon, M. S., & Cui, M. (2018). The intersection of race and community poverty and its effects on adolescents' academic achievement. *Youth & Society, 50*(7), 947–965.

Gordon, R. A., Kaestner, R., & Korenman, S. (2008). Child care and work absences: Trade-offs by type of care. *Journal of Marriage and Family, 70*(1), 239–254. https://doi.org/10.1111/j.1741-3737.2007.00475.x

Gorfinkel, L. R., Stohl, M., & Hasin, D. (2020). Association of depression with past-month cannabis use among US adults aged 20 to 59 years, 2005 to 2016. *JAMA Network Open, 3*(8), e2013802. https://doi.org/10.1001/jamanetworkopen.2020.13802

Gorham, L. S., & Barch, D. M. (2020). White matter tract integrity, involvement in sports, and depressive symptoms in children. *Child Psychiatry & Human Development, 51*(3), 490–501. https://doi.org/10.1007/s10578-020-00960-3

Gorski, P. C. (2016). Poverty and the ideological imperative: A call to unhook from deficit and grit ideology and to strive for structural ideology in teacher education. *Journal of Education for Teaching, 42*(4), 378–386.

Gorter, J. W., Stewart, D., Smith, M. W., King, G., Wright, M., Nguyen, T., & Swinton, M. (2014). Pathways toward positive psychosocial outcomes and mental health for youth with disabilities: A knowledge synthesis of developmental trajectories. *Canadian Journal of Community Mental Health, 33*(1), 45–61.

Götmark, F., Cafaro, P., & O'Sullivan, J. (2018). Aging human populations: Good for us, good for the earth. *Trends in Ecology & Evolution, 33*(11), 851–862. https://doi.org/10.1016/j.tree.2018.08.015

Gottlieb, A. (2004). *The afterlife is where we come from.* University of Chicago Press.

Gottlieb, A. (2019). The new childhood studies: Reflections on some recent collaborations between anthropologists and psychologists. *AnthropoChildren.* https://doi.org/10.25518/2034-8517.3162

Gottlieb, D. J., & Punjabi, N. M. (2020). Diagnosis and management of obstructive sleep apnea: A review. *JAMA, 323*(14), 1389–1400. https://doi.org/10.1001/jama.2020.3514

Gottlieb, G. (2002). On the epigenetic evolution of species-specific perception: The developmental manifold concept. *Cognitive Development, 17*(3), 1287–1300. https://doi.org/10.1016/S0885-2014(02)00120-X

Gottlieb, G. (2007). Probabilistic epigenesis. *Developmental Science, 10*(1), 1–11. https://doi.org/10.1111/j.1467-7687.2007.00556.x

Gottman, J. (2011). *Raising an emotionally intelligent child.* Simon & Schuster.

Gottman, J. M. (2014). *What predicts divorce? The relationship between marital processes and marital outcomes.* Psychology Press.

Gottman, J. M., & Graziano, W. G. (1983). How children become friends. *Monographs of the Society for Research in Child Development, 48*(3), 1–86.

Gottman, J. M., Katz, L. F., & Hooven, C. (1996). Parental meta-emotion philosophy and the emotional life of families: Theoretical models and preliminary data. *Journal of Family Psychology, 10*(3), 243.

Götz, F. M., Bleidorn, W., & Rentfrow, P. J. (2020). Age differences in Machiavellianism across the life span: Evidence from a large-scale cross-sectional study. *Journal of Personality, 88*(5), 978–992. https://doi.org/10.1111/jopy.12545

Gould, O. N., Dupuis-Blanchard, S., Villalon, L., Simard, M., & Ethier, S. (2017). Hoping for the best or planning for the future: Decision making and future care needs. *Journal of Applied Gerontology, 36*(8), 953–970. https://doi.org/10.1177/0733464815591213

Gould, R. L. (1972). The phases of adult life: A study in developmental psychology. *American Journal of Psychiatry, 129*(5), 521–531.

Gould, R. L. (1978). *Transformations: Growth and change in adult life.* Simon & Schuster.

Government Accountability Office (GAO). (2019). *Higher education: More information could help student parents access additional federal student aid* (GAO-19-522).

Gow, A. J., Pattie, A., & Deary, I. J. (2017). Lifecourse activity participation from early, mid, and later adulthood as determinants of cognitive aging: The Lothian birth cohort 1921. *The Journals of Gerontology: Series B, 72*(1), 25–37. https://doi.org/10.1093/geronb/gbw124

Goyal, M. K., Johnson, T. J., Chamberlain, J. M., Cook, L., Webb, M., Drendel, A. L., Alessandrini, E., Bajaj, L., Lorch, S., Grundmeier, R. W., Alpern, E. R., & Pediatric Emergency Care Applied Research Network (PECARN). (2020). Racial and ethnic differences in emergency department pain management of children with fractures. *Pediatrics, 145*(5), e20193370. https://doi.org/10.1542/peds.2019-3370

Goyal, M. S., Blazey, T. M., Su, Y., Couture, L. E., Durbin, T. J., Bateman, R. J., & Vlassenko, A. G. (2019). Persistent metabolic youth in the aging female brain. *Proceedings of the National Academy of Sciences, 116*(8), 3251–3255.

Goyette, T. (2016, May 17). A letter to my husband as I go through postpartum depression. *Discovering Parenthood.* https://www.discoveringparenthood.com/about/

Grabell, A. S., Olson, S. L., Miller, A. L., Kessler, D. A., Felt, B., Kaciroti, N., Wang, L., & Tardif, T. (2015). The impact of culture on physiological processes of emotion regulation: A comparison of US and Chinese preschoolers. *Developmental Science, 18*(3), 420–435.

Grady, C. (2012). The cognitive neuroscience of ageing. *Nature Reviews Neuroscience, 13*(7), 491–505. https://doi.org/10.1038/nrn3256

Grady, D. (2018). Evidence for postmenopausal hormone therapy to prevent chronic conditions: Success, failure, and lessons learned. *JAMA Internal Medicine, 178*(2), 185–186. https://doi.org/10.1001/jamainternmed.2017.7861

Graf, A. S., & Patrick, J. H. (2014). The influence of sexual attitudes on mid-to late-life sexual well-being: Age, not gender, as a salient factor. *The International Journal of Aging and Human Development, 79*(1), 55–79.

Graham, A., Haner, M., Sloan, M. M., Cullen, F. T., Kulig, T. C., & Jonson, C. L. (2020). Race and worrying about police brutality: The hidden injuries of minority status in America. *Victims & Offenders, 15*(5), 549–573. https://doi.org/10.1080/15564886.2020.1767252

Graham, A., Powell, M. A., Anderson, D., Fitzgerald, R., & Taylor, N. J. (2013). *Ethical research involving children.* UNICEF Innocenti Research Centre.

Graham, C., & Pinto, S. (2019). Unequal hopes and lives in the USA: Optimism, race, place, and premature mortality. *Journal of Population Economics, 32*(2), 665–733. https://doi.org/10.1007/s00148-018-0687-y

Graham, C., & Ruiz Pozuelo, J. (2017). Happiness, stress, and age: How the U curve varies across people and places. *Journal of Population Economics, 30*(1), 225–264. https://doi.org/10.1007/s00148-016-0611-2.

Graham, J. (2019, June 13). Why so many older Americans rate their health as good or even excellent. *Kaiser Health News.* https://khn.org/news/why-so-many-older-americans-rate-their-health-as-good-or-even-excellent/

Granat, A., Gadassi, R., Gilboa-Schechtman, E., & Feldman, R. (2017). Maternal depression and anxiety, social synchrony, and infant regulation of negative and positive emotions. *Emotion, 17*(1), 11.

Granic, I., Lobel, A., & Engels, R. C. (2014). The benefits of playing video games. *American Psychologist, 69*(1), 66.

Granleese, J. (2016). Lookism. In R. C. Hoogland, M. Wickramasinghe, & W. C. A. Wong (Eds.), *The Wiley Blackwell encyclopedia of gender and sexuality studies* (pp. 1–3). John Wiley & Sons.

Granqvist, P., Sroufe, L. A., Dozier, M., Hesse, E., Steele, M., van Ijzendoorn, M. H., Solomon, J., Schuengel, C., Fearon, P., Bakermans-Kranenburg, M., Steele, H., Cassidy, J., Carlson, E., Madigan, S., Jacobvitz, D., Foster, S., Behrens, K., Rifkin-Graboi, A., Gribneau, N., … Duschinsky, R. (2017). Disorganized attachment in infancy: A review of the phenomenon and its implications for clinicians and policy-makers. *Attachment & Human Development, 19*(6), 534–558. https://doi.org/10.1080/14616734.2017.1354040

Grant, A. M. (2013). *Give and take: A revolutionary approach to success.* Penguin.

Grant, A. M. (2019). Writing a book for real people: On giving the psychology of giving away. *Perspectives on Psychological Science, 14*(1), 91–95. https://doi.org/10.1177/1745691618808514

Grant, A. M., & Berry, J. W. (2011). The necessity of others is the mother of invention: Intrinsic and prosocial motivations, perspective taking, and creativity. *Academy of Management Journal, 54*(1), 73–96.

Grant, A. M., & Gino, F. (2010). A little thanks goes a long way: Explaining why gratitude expressions motivate prosocial behavior. *Journal of Personality and Social Psychology, 98*(6), 946.

Grant, A. M., & Shandell, M. S. (2022). Social motivation at work: The organizational psychology of effort for, against, and with others. *Annual Review of Psychology, 73*(1), 301–326. https://doi.org/10.1146/annurev-psych-060321-033406

Grant, B. F., Goldstein, R. B., Saha, T. D., Chou, S. P., Jung, J., Zhang, H., Pickering, R. P., Ruan, W. J., Smith, S. M., Huang, B., & Hasin, D. S. (2015). Epidemiology of DSM-5 alcohol use disorder: Results from the National Epidemiologic Survey on Alcohol and Related Conditions III. *JAMA Psychiatry, 72*(8), 757–766. https://doi.org/10.1001/jamapsychiatry.2015.0584

Grant, B. F., Saha, T. D., Ruan, W. J., Goldstein, R. B., Chou, S. P., Jung, J., Zhang, H., Smith, S. M., Pickering, R. P., Huang, B., & Hasin, D. S. (2016). Epidemiology of DSM-5 drug use disorder: Results from the National Epidemiologic Survey on Alcohol and Related Conditions–III. *JAMA Psychiatry, 73*(1), 39–47. https://doi.org/10.1001/jamapsychiatry.2015.2132

Grant, S., Liao, K., Miller, C., Peterson, S., Elting, L., & Guadagnolo, B. A. (2021). Lower levels of trust in the medical profession among White, younger, and more-educated individuals with cancer. *American Journal of Clinical Oncology, 44*(4), 150–157. https://doi.org/10.1097/COC.0000000000000771

Gravholt, C. H., Viuff, M. H., Brun, S., Stochholm, K., & Andersen, N. H. (2019). Turner syndrome: Mechanisms and management. *Nature Reviews Endocrinology, 15*(10), 601–614. https://doi.org/10.1038/s41574-019-0224-4

Gravningen, K., Mitchell, K. R., Wellings, K., Johnson, A. M., Geary, R., Jones, K. G., Clifton, S., Erens, B., Lu, M., Chayachinda, C., Field, N., Sonnenberg, P., & Mercer, C. H. (2017). Reported reasons for breakdown of marriage and cohabitation in Britain: Findings from the third National Survey of Sexual Attitudes and Lifestyles (Natsal-3). *PLoS ONE, 12*(3). https://doi.org/10.1371/journal.pone.0174129

Gray, D. L., Hope, E. C., & Matthews, J. S. (2018). Black and belonging at school: A case for interpersonal, instructional, and institutional opportunity structures. *Educational Psychologist, 53*(2), 97–113. https://doi.org/10.1080/00461520.2017.1421466

Gray, P. (2017). What exactly is play, and why is it such a powerful vehicle for learning? *Topics in Language Disorders, 37*(3), 217–228.

Gray, P. (2020). Risky play: Why children love and need it. In S. Little, A. Cox, & P. E. Owens(Eds.), *The Routledge handbook of designing public spaces for young people: Processes, practices and policies for youth inclusion* (pp. 39–51). Routledge.

Gray, P. B., Garcia, J. R., & Gesselman, A. N. (2019). Age-related patterns in sexual behaviors and attitudes among single U.S. adults: An evolutionary approach. *Evolutionary Behavioral Sciences, 13*(2), 111–126. https://doi.org/10.1037/ebs0000126

Grayling, A. C. (2010). *Ideas that matter: The concepts that shape the 21st century.* Basic Books.

Gray-Lobe, G., Pathak, P. A., & Walters, C. R. (2021). *The long-term effects of universal preschool in Boston* (No. w28756). National Bureau of Economic Research. https://doi.org/10.3386/w28756

Grayson, G. (2018, January 22). My grandmother was Italian. Why aren't my genes Italian? *NPR.org.* https://www.npr.org/sections/health-shots/2018/01/22/578293890/my-grandmother-was-italian-why-arent-my-genes-italian

Great Non Profits. (2013, September 20). *Experience Corps Bay Area reviews and ratings | San Francisco, CA.* Experience Corps Bay Area. https://greatnonprofits.org/org/experience-corps-bay-area

Green, R. C., Berg, J. S., Grody, W. W., Kalia, S. S., Korf, B. R., Martin, C. L., McGuire, A. L., Nussbaum, R. L., O'Daniel, J. M., Ormond, K. E., Rehm, H. L., Watson, M. S., Williams, M. S., & Biesecker, L. G. (2013). ACMG recommendations for reporting of incidental findings in clinical exome and genome sequencing. *Genetics in Medicine, 15*(7), 565–574. https://doi.org/10.1038/gim.2013.73

Greenberg, J., Pyszczynski, T., & Solomon, S. (1986). The causes and consequences of a need for self-esteem: A terror management theory. In R. F. Baumeister (Ed.), *Public self and private self* (pp. 189–212). Springer.

Greendale, G. A., Karlamangla, A. S., & Maki, P. M. (2020). The menopause transition and cognition. *JAMA, 323*(15), 1495–1496. https://doi.org/10.1001/jama.2020.1757

Greene, D. J., Koller, J. M., Hampton, J. M., Wesevich, V., Van, A. N., Nguyen, A. L., Hoyt, C. R., McIntyre,

L., Earl, E. A., Klein, R. L., Shimony, J. S., Petersen, S. E., Schlaggar, B. L., Fair, D. A., & Dosenbach, N. U. F. (2018). Behavioral interventions for reducing head motion during MRI scans in children. *NeuroImage, 171*, 234–245. https://doi.org/10.1016/j.neuroimage.2018.01.023

Greene, K. M., & Maggs, J. L. (2015). Revisiting the time trade-off hypothesis: Work, organized activities, and academics during college. *Journal of Youth and Adolescence, 44*(8), 1623–1637. https://doi.org/10.1007/s10964-014-0215-7

Greenfield, P. M. (1997). You can't take it with you: Why ability assessments don't cross cultures. *American Psychologist, 52*(10), 1115–1124. https://doi.org/10.1037/0003-066X.52.10.1115

Greenfield, P. M. (1998). The cultural evolution of IQ. In U. Neisser (Ed.), *The rising curve: Long-term gains in IQ and related measures* (pp. 81–123). American Psychological Association. https://doi.org/10.1037/10270-003

Greenfield, P. M. (2012). Cultural change, human activity, and cognitive development. *Human Development, 55*(4), 229–232.

Greenfield, P. M. (2018). Studying social change, culture, and human development: A theoretical framework and methodological guidelines. *Developmental Review, 50*, 16–30. https://doi.org/10.1016/j.dr.2018.05.003

Greenfield, P. M., Keller, H., Fuligni, A., & Maynard, A. (2003). Cultural pathways through universal development. *Annual Review of Psychology, 54*(1), 461–490. https://doi.org/10.1146/annurev.psych.54.101601.145221

Greenough, W. T., Black, J. E., & Wallace, C. S. (1987). Experience and brain development. *Child Development, 58*(3), 539–559.

Greenspan, L. (2017, April 6). Why are girls starting puberty earlier? *US News & World Report.* https://health.usnews.com/wellness/for-parents/articles/2017-04-06/why-are-girls-starting-puberty-earlier

Greer, D. M., Shemie, S. D., Lewis, A., Torrance, S., Varelas, P., Goldenberg, F. D., Bernat, J. L., Souter, M., Topcuoglu, M. A., Alexandrov, A. W., Baldisseri, M., Bleck, T., Citerio, G., Dawson, R., Hoppe, A., Jacobe, S., Manara, A., Nakagawa, T. A., Pope, T. M., … Sung, G. (2020). Determination of brain death/death by neurologic criteria: The world brain death project. *JAMA, 324*(11), 1078–1097. https://doi.org/10.1001/jama.2020.11586

Gregory, A., & Fergus, E. (2017). Social and emotional learning and equity in school discipline. *The Future of Children, 27*(1), 117–136.

Gregory, A., & Weinstein, R. S. (2008). The discipline gap and African Americans: Defiance or cooperation in the high school classroom. *Journal of School Psychology, 46*(4), 455–475.

Greve, W., & Bjorklund, D. F. (2009). The Nestor effect: Extending evolutionary developmental psychology to a lifespan perspective. *Developmental Review, 29*(3), 163–179.

Griep, Y., Hanson, L. M., Vantilborgh, T., Janssens, L., Jones, S. K., & Hyde, M. (2017). Can volunteering in later life reduce the risk of dementia? A 5-year longitudinal study among volunteering and non-volunteering retired seniors. *PLOS ONE, 12*(3), e0173885. https://doi.org/10.1371/journal.pone.0173885

Grill, J. (2018). "In England, they don't call you black!" Migrating racialisations and the production of Roma difference across Europe. *Journal of Ethnic and Migration Studies, 44*(7), 1136–1155. https://doi.org/10.1080/1369183X.2017.1329007

Grill, J. D., Apostolova, L. G., Bullain, S., Burns, J. M., Cox, C. G., Dick, M., Hartley, D., Kawas, C., Kremen, S., Lingler, J., Lopez, O. L., Mapstone, M., Pierce, A., Rabinovici, G., Roberts, J. S., Sajjadi, S. A., Teng, E., & Karlawish, J. (2017). Communicating mild cognitive impairment diagnoses with and without amyloid imaging. *Alzheimer's Research & Therapy, 9*(1), 35. https://doi.org/10.1186/s13195-017-0261-y

Grimm, R. T., & Dietz, N. (2018a). *Good intentions, gap in action: The challenge of translating youth's high interest in doing good into civic engagement* [Research brief]. Do Good Institute, University of Maryland.

Grimm, R. T., & Dietz, N. (2018b). *Where are America's volunteers? A look at America's widespread decline in volunteering in cities and states* [Research brief]. Do Good Institute, University of Maryland.

Grissom, J. A., & Redding, C. (2016). Discretion and disproportionality: Explaining the underrepresentation of high-achieving students of color in gifted programs. *AERA Online, 2*(1), 1–15.

Groh, A. M., Fearon, R. M. P., van IJzendoorn, M. H., Bakermans-Kranenburg, M. J., & Roisman, G. I. (2017). Attachment in the early life course: Meta-analytic evidence for its role in socioemotional development. *Child Development Perspectives, 11*(1), 70–76. https://doi.org/10.1111/cdep.12213

Grohs, M. N., Reynolds, J. E., Liu, J., Martin, J. W., Pollock, T., Lebel, C., Dewey, D., & the APrON Study Team. (2019). Prenatal maternal and childhood bisphenol A exposure and brain structure and behavior of young children. *Environmental Health, 18*(1), 85. https://doi.org/10.1186/s12940-019-0528-9

Grolig, L., Cohrdes, C., Tiffin-Richards, S. P., & Schroeder, S. (2020). Narrative dialogic reading with wordless picture books: A cluster-randomized intervention study. *Early Childhood Research Quarterly, 51*, 191–203.

Gronke, P., Manson, P., Lee, J., & Foot, C. (2020). How elections under COVID-19 may change the political engagement of older voters. *The Public Policy and Aging Report, 30*(4), 147. https://doi.org/10.1093/ppar/praa030

Grossbard, S. (2018). Marriage and marriage markets. In S. L. Averett, L. M. Argys, & S. D. Hoffman (Eds.), *The Oxford handbook of women and the economy* (p. 55). Oxford University Press.

Grossman, A. H., Park, J. Y., Frank, J. A., & Russell, S. T. (2021). Parental responses to transgender and gender nonconforming youth: Associations with parent support, parental abuse, and youths' psychological adjustment. *Journal of Homosexuality, 68*(8), 1260–1277.

Grossman, B. R., & Webb, C. E. (2016). Family support in late life: A review of the literature on aging, disability, and family caregiving. *Journal of Family Social Work, 19*(4), 348–395.

Grossman, J. M., & Charmaraman, L. (2009). Race, context, and privilege: White adolescents' explanations of racial-ethnic centrality. *Journal of Youth and Adolescence, 38*(2), 139–152. https://doi.org/10.1007/s10964-008-9330-7

Grossmann, I. (2017). Wisdom in context. *Perspectives on Psychological Science, 12*(2), 233–257.

Grossmann, I., Karasawa, M., Izumi, S., Na, J., Varnum, M. E., Kitayama, S., & Nisbett, R. E. (2012). Aging and wisdom: Culture matters. *Psychological Science, 23*(10), 1059–1066.

Grossmann, I., & Kross, E. (2014). Exploring Solomon's paradox: Self-distancing eliminates the self-other asymmetry in wise reasoning about close relationships in younger and older adults. *Psychological Science, 25*(8), 1571–1580.

Grossmann, K., Grossmann, K. E., Spangler, G., Suess, G., & Unzner, L. (1985). Maternal sensitivity and newborns' orientation responses as related to quality of attachment in Northern Germany. *Monographs of the Society for Research in Child Development, 50*(1–2), 233–256. https://doi.org/10.2307/3333836

Grossmann, T. (2017). The eyes as windows into other minds: An integrative perspective. *Perspectives on Psychological Science, 12*(1), 107–121. https://doi.org/10.1177/1745691616654457

Grossmann, T. (2020). Early social cognition: Exploring the role of the medial prefrontal cortex. In J. Decety (Ed.), *The social brain: A developmental perspective* (pp. 67–88). MIT Press.

Grossmann, T., & Dela Cruz, K. L. (2021). Insights into the uniquely human origins of understanding other minds. *Behavioral and Brain Sciences.*

Grove, M. A., & Lancy, D. F. (2018). Cultural models of stages in the life course. In S. Crawford, D. M. Hadley, & G. Shepherd (Eds.), *The Oxford handbook of the archaeology of childhood* (pp. 90–103). Oxford University Press.

Grover, S., & Helliwell, J. F. (2019). How's life at home? New evidence on marriage and the set point for happiness. *Journal of Happiness Studies, 20*(2), 373–390. https://doi.org/10.1007/s10902-017-9941-3

Grubb, L. K., Powers, M., & Committee on Adolescence. (2020). Emerging issues in male adolescent sexual and reproductive health care. *Pediatrics, 145*(5), e20200627. https://doi.org/10.1542/peds.2020-0627

Grubbs, J. B., & Kraus, S. W. (2021). Pornography use and psychological science: A call for consideration. *Current Directions in Psychological Science, 30*(1), 68–75. https://doi.org/10.1177/0963721420979594

Gruber, R., Saha, S., Somerville, G., Boursier, J., & Wise, M. S. (2020). The impact of COVID-19 related school shutdown on sleep in adolescents: A natural experiment. *Sleep Medicine, 76*, 33–35. https://doi.org/10.1016/j.sleep.2020.09.015

Grubin, D. (2002). *Young Dr. Freud.* https://www.pbs.org/youngdrfreud/pages/family_parenthood.htm

Grucza, R. A., Sher, K. J., Kerr, W. C., Krauss, M. J., Lui, C. K., McDowell, Y. E., Hartz, S., Virdi, G., & Bierut, L. J. (2018). Trends in adult alcohol use and binge drinking in the early 21st-century United States: A meta-analysis of 6 national survey series. *Alcoholism: Clinical and Experimental Research, 42*(10), 1939–1950. https://doi.org/10.1111/acer.13859

Gruenewald, T. L., Tanner, E. K., Fried, L. P., Carlson, M. C., Xue, Q.-L., Parisi, J. M., Rebok, G. W., Yarnell, L. M., & Seeman, T. E. (2016). The Baltimore Experience Corps Trial: Enhancing Generativity via Intergenerational Activity Engagement in Later Life. *The Journals of Gerontology: Series B, 71*(4), 661–670. https://doi.org/10.1093/geronb/gbv005

Grugel, J., & Ferreira, F. P. M. (2012). Street working children, children's agency and the challenge of children's rights: Evidence from Minas Gerais, Brazil. *Journal of International Development, 24*(7), 828–840.

Grusec, J. E., Danyliuk, T., Kil, H., & O'Neill, D. (2017). Perspectives on parent discipline and child outcomes. *International Journal of Behavioral Development, 41*(4), 465–471.

Grydeland, H., Vértes, P. E., Váša, F., Romero-Garcia, R., Whitaker, K., Alexander-Bloch, A. F., Bjørnerud, A., Patel, A. X., Sederevičius, D., Tamnes, C. K., Westlye, L. T., White, S. R., Walhovd, K. B., Fjell, A. M., & Bullmore, E. T. (2019). Waves of maturation and senescence in micro-structural MRI markers of human cortical myelination over the lifespan. *Cerebral Cortex, 29*(3), 1369–1381. https://doi.org/10.1093/cercor/bhy330

Guan, S.-S. A., Bower, J. E., Almeida, D. M., Cole, S. W., Dahl, R. E., Irwin, M. R., Seeman, T. E., McDade, T., & Fuligni, A. J. (2016). Parental support buffers the association of depressive symptoms with cortisol and C-reactive protein during adolescence. *Brain, Behavior, and Immunity, 57*, 134–143. https://doi.org/10.1016/j.bbi.2016.03.007

Guan, S.-S. A., & Fuligni, A. J. (2016). Changes in parent, sibling, and peer support during the transition to young adulthood. *Journal of Research on Adolescence, 26*(2), 286–299. https://doi.org/10.1111/jora.12191

Guan, S.-S. A., Greenfield, P. M., & Orellana, M. F. (2014). Translating into understanding: Language brokering and prosocial development in emerging adults from immigrant families. *Journal of Adolescent Research, 29*(3), 331–355. https://doi.org/10.1177/0743558413520223

Guardabassi, V., & Tomasetto, C. (2020). Weight status or weight stigma? Obesity stereotypes — not excess weight — reduce working memory in school-aged children. *Journal of Experimental Child Psychology, 189*, 104706.

Gubbels Bupp, M. R., Potluri, T., Fink, A. L., & Klein, S. L. (2018). The confluence of sex hormones and aging on immunity. *Frontiers in Immunology, 9*, 1269.

Gui, J., Mustachio, L. M., Su, D.-M., & Craig, R. W. (2012). Thymus size and age-related thymic involution: Early programming, sexual dimorphism, progenitors and stroma. *Aging and Disease, 3*(3), 280–290. https://www.ncbi.nlm.nih.gov/pmc/articles/PMC3375084/

Guilamo-Ramos, V., Benzekri, A., Thimm-Kaiser, M., Dittus, P., Ruiz, Y., Cleland, C. M., & McCoy, W. (2020). A triadic intervention for adolescent sexual health: A randomized clinical trial. *Pediatrics, 145*(5), e20192808. https://doi.org/10.1542/peds.2019-2808

Guiney, H., & Machado, L. (2018). Volunteering in the community: Potential benefits for cognitive aging. *The Journals of Gerontology. Series B, Psychological Sciences and Social Sciences, 73*(3), 399–408. https://doi.org/10.1093/geronb/gbx134

Gülgöz, S., Alonso, D. J., Olson, K. R., & Gelman, S. A. (2021). Transgender and cisgender children's essentialist beliefs about sex and gender identity. *Developmental Science, 24*(6). https://doi.org/10.1111/desc.13115

Gülgöz, S., Glazier, J. J., Enright, E. A., Alonso, D. J., Durwood, L. J., Fast, A. A., Lowe, R., Ji, C., Heer, J., Martin, C. L., & Olson, K. R. (2019). Similarity in transgender and cisgender children's gender development. *Proceedings of the National Academy of Sciences, 116*(49), 24480–24485. https://doi.org/10.1073/pnas.1909367116

Gulliver, A., Griffiths, K. M., & Christensen, H. (2010). Perceived barriers and facilitators to mental health help-seeking in young people: A systematic review. *BMC Psychiatry, 10*(1), 1–9.

Gunderson, E. A., Donnellan, M. B., Robins, R. W., & Trzesniewski, K. H. (2018). The specificity of parenting effects: Differential relations of parent praise and criticism to children's theories of intelligence and learning goals. *Journal of Experimental Child Psychology, 173*, 116–135. https://doi.org/10.1016/j.jecp.2018.03.015

Gunderson, E. A., Sorhagen, N. S., Gripshover, S. J., Dweck, C. S., Goldin-Meadow, S., & Levine, S. C. (2018). Parent praise to toddlers predicts fourth grade academic achievement via children's incremental mindsets. *Developmental Psychology, 54*(3), 397.

Gunderson, J. G., Herpertz, S. C., Skodol, A. E., Torgersen, S., & Zanarini, M. C. (2018). Borderline personality disorder. *Nature Reviews Disease Primers, 4*(1), 1–20. https://doi.org/10.1038/nrdp.2018.29

Gunderson, L. (2013). Whole-language approaches to reading and writing. In *Instructional models in reading* (pp. 231–258). Routledge.

Güngör, D., Nadaud, P., LaPergola, C. C., Dreibelbis, C., Wong, Y. P., Terry, N., Abrams, S. A., Beker, L., Jacobovits, T., Järvinen, K. M., Nommsen-Rivers, L. A., O'Brien, K. O., Oken, E., Pérez-Escamilla, R., Ziegler, E. E., & Spahn, J. M. (2019). Infant milk-feeding practices and cardiovascular disease outcomes in offspring: A systematic review. *The American Journal of Clinical Nutrition, 109*(Suppl 1), 800S–816S. https://doi.org/10.1093/ajcn/nqy332

Gunnar, M. R. (2020). Early adversity, stress, and neurobehavioral development. *Development and Psychopathology, 32*(5), 1555–1562. https://doi.org/10.1017/S0954579420001649

Gunnar, M. R., DePasquale, C. E., Reid, B. M., Donzella, B., & Miller, B. S. (2019). Pubertal stress recalibration reverses the effects of early life stress in postinstitutionalized children. *Proceedings of the National Academy of Sciences, 116*(48), 23984–23988. https://doi.org/10.1073/pnas.1909699116

Guo, M., Kim, S., & Dong, X. (2019). Sense of filial obligation and caregiving burdens among Chinese immigrants in the United States. *Journal of the American Geriatrics Society, 67*(S3), S564–S570.

Gupta, N. D., & Simonsen, M. (2016). Academic performance and type of early childhood care. *Economics of Education Review, 53*, 217–229.

Gupta, P. (2015, October 12). This Navajo woman is planning the first Native American birthing center in the country. *Cosmopolitan.* https://www.cosmopolitan.com/politics/news/a47518/americas-first-native-american-birthing-center/

Gur, R. E., Moore, T. M., Rosen, A. F. G., Barzilay, R., Roalf, D. R., Calkins, M. E., Ruparel, K., Scott, J. C., Almasy, L., Satterthwaite, T. D., Shinohara, R. T., & Gur, R. C. (2019). Burden of environmental adversity associated with psychopathology, maturation, and brain behavior parameters in youths. *JAMA Psychiatry, 76*(9), 966–975. https://doi.org/10.1001/jamapsychiatry.2019.0943

Güroğlu, B. (2021). Adolescent brain in a social world: Unravelling the positive power of peers from a neurobehavioral perspective. *European Journal of Developmental Psychology, 18*(4), 471–493. https://doi.org/10.1080/17405629.2020.1813101

Gurven, M., Fuerstenberg, E., Trumble, B., Stieglitz, J., Beheim, B., Davis, H., & Kaplan, H. (2017). Cognitive performance across the life course of Bolivian forager-farmers with limited schooling. *Developmental Psychology, 53*(1), 160–176. https://doi.org/10.1037/dev0000175

Gurven, M., & Kaplan, H. (2008). Beyond the grandmother hypothesis: Evolutionary models of human longevity. *The Cultural Context of Aging: Worldwide Perspectives, 3*, 53–66. https://www.culturalcontextofaging.com/webbook-gurven/

Gurven, M., Stieglitz, J., Trumble, B., Blackwell, A. D., Beheim, B., Davis, H., Hooper, P., & Kaplan, H. (2017). The Tsimane Health and Life History Project: Integrating anthropology and biomedicine. *Evolutionary Anthropology: Issues, News, and Reviews, 26*(2), 54–73. https://doi.org/10.1002/evan.21515.

Guryan, J., Ludwig, J., Bhatt, M. P., Cook, P. J., Davis, J. M., Dodge, K., Farkas, G., Fryer, R. G., Jr., Mayer, S., Pollack, H., & Steinberg, L. (2021). *Not too late: Improving academic outcomes among adolescents.* National Bureau of Economic Research.

Gusakova, S., Conley, T. D., Piemonte, J. L., & Matsick, J. L. (2020). The role of women's orgasm goal pursuit in women's orgasm occurrence. *Personality and Individual Differences, 155*, 109628. https://doi.org/10.1016/j.paid.2019.109628

Guthold, R., Stevens, G. A., Riley, L. M., & Bull, F. C. (2020). Global trends in insufficient physical activity among adolescents: A pooled analysis of 298 population-based surveys with 1.6 million participants. *The Lancet Child & Adolescent Health, 4*(1), 23–35. https://doi.org/10.1016/S2352-4642(19)30323-2

Guthrie, J. T., Wigfield, A., Humenick, N. M., Perencevich, K. C., Taboada, A., & Barbosa, P. (2006). Influences of stimulating tasks on reading motivation and comprehension. *The Journal of Educational Research, 99*(4), 232–246. https://doi.org/10.3200/JOER.99.4.232-246

Gutiérrez, I. T., Menendez, D., Jiang, M. J., Hernandez, I. G., Miller, P., & Rosengren, K. S. (2020). Embracing death: Mexican parent and child perspectives on death. *Child Development, 91*(2), e491–e511.

Gutiérrez, K. D. (2016). 2011 AERA presidential address: Designing resilient ecologies: Social design experiments and a new social imagination. *Educational Researcher, 45*(3), 187–196.

Guyer, A. E., & Jarcho, J. M. (2018). Neuroscience and peer relations. In W. M. Bukowski, B. Laursen, & K. H. Rubin (Eds.), *Handbook of peer interactions, relationships, and groups* (pp. 177–199). Guilford.

Guyer, A. E., Pérez-Edgar, K., & Crone, E. A. (2018). Opportunities for neurodevelopmental plasticity from infancy through early adulthood. *Child Development, 89*(3), 687–697. https://doi.org/10.1111/cdev.13073

Guyer, A. E., Silk, J. S., & Nelson, E. E. (2016). The neurobiology of the emotional adolescent: From the inside out. *Neuroscience & Biobehavioral Reviews, 70*, 74–85.

Guzman, E., & Gladden, N. (2015). *Why raising the retirement age would hurt African Americans.* Center for Global Policy Solutions. Retrieved from http://globalpolicysolutions.org/wp-content/uploads/2015/07/Retirement-age.pdf.

Guzmán-Martinez, L., Maccioni, R. B., Farías, G. A., Fuentes, P., & Navarrete, L. P. (2019). Biomarkers for Alzheimer's disease. *Current Alzheimer Research, 16*(6), 518–528.

Guzzo, K. B., & Hayford, S. R. (2020). Pathways to parenthood in social and family context: Decade in review, 2020. *Journal of Marriage and the Family, 82*(1), 117–144. https://doi.org/10.1111/jomf.12618

Ha, T., Kim, H., & McGill, S. (2019). When conflict escalates into intimate partner violence: The delicate nature of observed coercion in adolescent romantic relationships. *Development and Psychopathology, 31*(5), 1729–1739. https://doi.org/10.1017/S0954579419001007

Haack, M., Simpson, N., Sethna, N., Kaur, S., & Mullington, J. (2020). Sleep deficiency and chronic pain: Potential underlying mechanisms and clinical implications. *Neuropsychopharmacology, 45*(1), 205–216.

Haandrikman, K. (2019). Partner choice in Sweden: How distance still matters. *Environment and Planning A: Economy and Space, 51*(2), 440–460. https://doi.org/10.1177/0308518X18786726

Haarbauer-Krupa, J., Lee, A. H., Bitsko, R. H., Zhang, X., & Kresnow-Sedacca, M. (2018). Prevalence of parent-reported traumatic brain injury in children and associated health conditions. *JAMA Pediatrics, 172*(11), 1078–1086. https://doi.org/10.1001/jamapediatrics.2018.2740

Haase, C. L., Eriksen, K. T., Lopes, S., Satylganova, A., Schnecke, V., & McEwan, P. (2021). Body mass index and risk of obesity-related conditions in a cohort of 2.9 million people: Evidence from a UK primary care database. *Obesity Science & Practice, 7*(2), 137–147. https://doi.org/10.1002/osp4.474

Habekost, T., Vogel, A., Rostrup, E., Bundesen, C., Kyllingsbæk, S., Garde, E., Ryberg, C., & Waldemar, G. (2013). Visual processing speed in old age. *Scandinavian Journal of Psychology, 54*(2), 89–94. https://doi.org/10.1111/sjop.12008

Hack, K. E. A., Vereycken, M. E. M. S., Torrance, H. L., Koopman-Esseboom, C., & Derks, J. B. (2018). Perinatal outcome of monochorionic and dichorionic twins after spontaneous and assisted conception: A retrospective cohort study. *Acta Obstetricia et Gynecologica Scandinavica, 97*(6), 717–726. https://doi.org/10.1111/aogs.13323

Hadders-Algra, M. (2018). Early human motor development: From variation to the ability to vary and adapt. *Neuroscience & Biobehavioral Reviews, 90*, 411–427. https://doi.org/10.1016/j.neubiorev.2018.05.009

Haga, M., Tortella, P., Asonitou, K., Charitou, S., Koutsouki, D., Fumagalli, G., & Sigmundsson, H. (2018). Cross-cultural aspects: Exploring motor competence among 7- to 8-year-old children from Greece, Italy, and Norway. *SAGE Open, 8*(2), 2158244018768381. https://doi.org/10.1177/2158244018768381

Hagemann, H. (2020, April 2). *The 1918 flu pandemic was brutal, killing more than 50 million people worldwide.* NPR. https://www.npr.org/2020/04/02/826358104/the-1918-flu-pandemic-was-brutal-killing-as-many-as-100-million-people-worldwide

Hagen, J. W., Lasagna, C. A., & Packett, S. E. (2020). A century of research in child development: The emergence of a new science. In N. Jones, M. Platt, K. D. Mize, & J. Hardin (Eds.), *Conducting research in developmental psychology: A topical guide for research methods utilized across the lifespan* (pp. 1–25). Routledge.

Hagenaars, S. P., Hill, W. D., Harris, S. E., Ritchie, S. J., Davies, G., Liewald, D. C., Gale, C. R., Porteous, D. J., Deary, I. J., & Marioni, R. E. (2017). Genetic prediction of male pattern baldness. *PLoS Genetics, 13*(2), e1006594. https://doi.org/10.1371/journal.pgen.1006594

Hagerman, C. J., Ferrer, R. A., Klein, W. M. P., & Persky, S. (2020). Association of parental guilt with harmful versus healthful eating and feeding from a virtual reality buffet. *Health Psychology: Official Journal of the Division of Health Psychology, American Psychological Association, 39*(3), 199–208. https://doi.org/10.1037/hea0000831

Hagestad, G. O., & Settersten, R. A., Jr. (2017). Aging: It's interpersonal! Reflections from two life course migrants. *The Gerontologist, 57*(1), 136–144.

Haglund, K. A., & Fehring, R. J. (2010). The association of religiosity, sexual education, and parental factors with risky sexual behaviors among adolescents and young adults. *Journal of Religion and Health, 49*(4), 460–472.

Haidt, J. (2009). Moral psychology and the misunderstanding of religion. In J. Schloss & M. Murray (Eds.), *The believing primate: Scientific, philosophical, and theological reflections on the origin of religion* (pp. 278–291). Oxford University Press.

Haigh, E. A., Bogucki, O. E., Sigmon, S. T., & Blazer, D. G. (2018). Depression among older adults: A 20-year update on five common myths and misconceptions. *The American Journal of Geriatric Psychiatry, 26*(1), 107–122.

Haight, W. (2006). A sociocultural perspective of parent–child play. In D. P. Fromberg & D. Bergen (Eds.), *Play from birth to twelve: Contexts, perspectives, and meanings* (pp. 309–314). Routledge.

Haimovitz, K., & Dweck, C. S. (2016). What predicts children's fixed and growth intelligence mind-sets? Not their parents' views of intelligence but their parents' views of failure. *Psychological Science, 27*(6), 859–869.

Haines, S. J., Shelton, J. T., Henry, J. D., Terrett, G., Vorwerk, T., & Rendell, P. G. (2019). Prospective memory and cognitive aging. In *Oxford research encyclopedia of psychology.* https://doi.org/10.1093/acrefore/9780190236557.013.381

Hairault, J. O., Langot, F., & Sopraseuth, T. (2019). Unemployment fluctuations over the life cycle. *Journal of Economic Dynamics and Control, 100*, 334–352.

Hairston, I. S., Handelzalts, J. E., Lehman-Inbar, T., & Kovo, M. (2019). Mother-infant bonding is not associated with feeding type: A community study sample.

BMC Pregnancy and Childbirth, 19(1), 125. https://doi.org/10.1186/s12884-019-2264-0

Hajal, N., Neiderhiser, J., Moore, G., Leve, L., Shaw, D., Harold, G., Scaramella, L., Ganiban, J., & Reiss, D. (2015). Angry responses to infant challenges: Parent, marital, and child genetic factors associated with harsh parenting. *Child Development, 86*(1), 80–93. https://doi.org/10.1111/cdev.12345

Hajal, N. J., & Paley, B. (2020). Parental emotion and emotion regulation: A critical target of study for research and intervention to promote child emotion socialization. *Developmental Psychology, 56*(3), 403–417. https://doi.org/10.1037/dev0000864

Hakulinen, C., Pulkki-Råback, L., Jokela, M., Ferrie, J. E., Aalto, A.-M., Virtanen, M., Kivimäki, M., Vahtera, J., & Elovainio, M. (2016). Structural and functional aspects of social support as predictors of mental and physical health trajectories: Whitehall II cohort study. *Journal of Epidemiology and Community Health, 70*(7), 710–715.

Halberstadt, A. G., Oertwig, D., & Riquelme, E. H. (2020). Beliefs about children's emotions in Chile. *Frontiers in Psychology, 11*, 34. https://doi.org/10.3389/fpsyg.2020.00034

Hale, J. M., Bijlsma, M. J., & Lorenti, A. (2021). Does postponing retirement affect cognitive function? A counterfactual experiment to disentangle life course risk factors. *SSM — Population Health, 15*, 100855. https://doi.org/10.1016/j.ssmph.2021.100855

Hale, L., Troxel, W., & Buysse, D. J. (2020). Sleep health: An opportunity for public health to address health equity. *Annual Review of Public Health, 41*, 81–99.

Hales, B., Scialli, A., & Tassinari, M. (Eds.). (2018). *Teratology primer* (3rd ed.). Society for Birth Defects Research & Prevention.

Halim, M. L. D. (2016). Princesses and superheroes: Social-cognitive influences on early gender rigidity. *Child Development Perspectives, 10*(3), 155–160.

Halim, M. L. D., Martin, C. L., Andrews, N. C., Zosuls, K. M., & Ruble, D. N. (2021). Enjoying each other's company: Gaining other-gender friendships promotes positive gender attitudes among ethnically diverse children. Personality and Social Psychology Bulletin, 0146167220984407.

Halim, M. L., Ruble, D., Tamis-LeMonda, C., & Shrout, P. E. (2013). Rigidity in gender-typed behaviors in early childhood: A longitudinal study of ethnic minority children. *Child Development, 84*(4), 1269–1284.

Halim, M. L. D., Ruble, D. N., Tamis-LeMonda, C. S., Shrout, P. E., & Amodio, D. M. (2017). Gender attitudes in early childhood: Behavioral consequences and cognitive antecedents. *Child Development, 88*(3), 882–899. https://doi.org/10.1111/cdev.12642

Halim, M. L. D., Walsh, A. S., Tamis-LeMonda, C. S., Zosuls, K. M., & Ruble, D. N. (2018). The roles of self-socialization and parent socialization in toddlers' gender-typed appearance. *Archives of Sexual Behavior, 47*(8), 2277–2285.

Hall, G. S. (1904). *Adolescence: Its psychology and its relations to physiology, anthropology, sociology, sex, crime, religion and education.* D. Appleton & Company. https://doi.org/10.1037/10616-006

Hall, O. T., Jordan, A., Teater, J., Dixon-Shambley, K., McKiever, M. E., Baek, M., Garcia, S., Rood, K. M., & Fielin, D. A. (2021). Experiences of racial discrimination in the medical setting and associations with medical mistrust and expectations of care among black patients seeking addiction treatment. *Journal of Substance Abuse Treatment,* 108551. https://doi.org/10.1016/j.jsat.2021.108551

Hall, S. S., & Zygmunt, E. (2021). Dislocated college students and the pandemic: Back home under extraordinary circumstances. *Family Relations, 70*(3), 689–704. https://doi.org/10.1111/fare.12544

Hall, S. S., & Zygmunt, E. (2021). "I hate it here": Mental health changes of college students living with parents during the COVID-19 quarantine. *Emerging Adulthood.* https://doi.org/10.1177/21676968211000494

Hall, W., Leung, J., & Lynskey, M. (2020). The effects of cannabis use on the development of adolescents and young adults. *Annual Review of Developmental Psychology, 2*(1), 461–483. https://doi.org/10.1146/annurev-devpsych-040320-084904

Hall, W. J., Chapman, M. V., Lee, K. M., Merino, Y. M., Thomas, T. W., Payne, B. K., Eng, E., Day, S. H., & Coyne-Beasley, T. (2015). Implicit racial/ethnic bias among health care professionals and its influence on health care outcomes: A systematic review. *American Journal of Public Health, 105*(12), e60–e76. https://doi.org/10.2105/AJPH.2015.302903

Hallenbeck, J. (2005). Palliative care in the final days of life "they were expecting it at any time." *JAMA, 293*(18), 2265–2271. https://doi.org/10.1001/jama.293.18.2265

Halonen, J. S. (2008). Measure for measure: The challenge of assessing critical thinking. In D. S. Dunn, J. S. Halonen, & R. A. Smith (Eds.), *Teaching critical thinking in psychology: A handbook of best practices* (pp. 59–75). John Wiley & Sons. https://doi.org/10.1002/9781444305173.ch6

Halpern, D. F., & Butler, H. A. (2018). Is critical thinking a better model of intelligence? In R. J. Sternber (Ed.), *The nature of human intelligence* (pp. 183–196). Cambridge University Press. https://doi.org/10.1017/9781316817049.013

Halpern, D. F., & Butler, H. A. (2019). Teaching critical thinking as if our future depends on it, because it does. In J. Dunlosky & K. A. Rawson (Eds.), *The Cambridge handbook of cognition and education* (pp. 51–66). Cambridge University Press. https://doi.org/10.1017/9781108235631.004

Halpern, H. P., & Perry-Jenkins, M. (2016). Parents' gender ideology and gendered behavior as predictors of children's gender-role attitudes: A longitudinal exploration. *Sex Roles, 74*(11), 527–542.

Halpern-Manners, A., Raymo, J. M., Warren, J. R., & Johnson, K. L. (2020). School performance and mortality: The mediating role of educational attainment and work and family trajectories across the life course. *Advances in Life Course Research, 46*, 100362.

Halpern-Meekin, S., Manning, W. D., Giordano, P. C., & Longmore, M. A. (2013). Relationship churning, physical violence, and verbal abuse in young adult relationships. *Journal of Marriage and the Family, 75*(1), 2–12. https://doi.org/10.1111/j.1741-3737.2012.01029.x

Halstead, M. E., Walter, K. D., Moffatt, K., & The Council on Sports Medicine and Fitness. (2018). Sport-related concussion in children and adolescents. *Pediatrics, 142*(6), e20183074. https://doi.org/10.1542/peds.2018-3074

Hamazaki, Y., Sekai, M., & Minato, N. (2016). Medullary thymic epithelial stem cells: Role in thymic epithelial cell maintenance and thymic involution. *Immunological Reviews, 271*(1), 38–55. https://doi.org/10.1111/imr.12412

Hamby, S. (2014). Intimate partner and sexual violence research: Scientific progress, scientific challenges, and gender. *Trauma, Violence, & Abuse, 15*(3), 149–158.

Hamby, S., Taylor, E., Mitchell, K., Jones, L., & Newlin, C. (2020). Poly-victimization, trauma, and resilience: Exploring strengths that promote thriving after adversity. *Journal of Trauma & Dissociation, 21*(3), 376–395. https://doi.org/10.1080/15299732.2020.1719261

Hamel, L. M., Penner, L. A., Albrecht, T. L., Heath, E., Gwede, C. K., & Eggly, S. (2016). Barriers to clinical trial enrollment in racial and ethnic minority patients with cancer. *Cancer Control: Journal of the Moffitt Cancer Center, 23*(4), 327–337.

Hamermesh, D. S. (2011). *Beauty pays: Why attractive people are more successful.* Princeton University Press. https://doi.org/10.1515/9781400839445

Hamid, W., Jahangir, M. S., Khan, T. A., & Maqbool, T. (2019). Role of technology in restructuring the traditional practices around death and mourning in Kashmir. *Death Studies,* 1–10. https://doi.org/10.1080/07481187.2019.1701146

Hamilton, H. R., Armeli, S., & Tennen, H. (2021). Meet the parents: Parental interactions, social influences, and college drinking. *Addictive Behaviors, 112*, 106624. https://doi.org/10.1016/j.addbeh.2020.106624

Hamilton, L. T. (2016). *Parenting to a degree: How family matters for college women's success.* University of Chicago Press.

Hamilton, L. T., & Cheng, S. (2018). Going Greek: The organization of campus life and class-based graduation gaps. *Social Forces, 96*(3), 977–1008. https://doi.org/10.1093/sf/sox089

Hamilton Project. (N.d.). *Career earnings by college major.* http://www.hamiltonproject.org/charts/career_earnings_by_college_major/

Hamlat, E. J., McCormick, K. C., Young, J. F., & Hankin, B. L. (2020). Early pubertal timing predicts onset and recurrence of depressive episodes in boys and girls. *Journal of Child Psychology and Psychiatry, and Allied Disciplines, 61*(11), 1266–1274. https://doi.org/10.1111/jcpp.13198

Hammer, P. J. (2019). The Flint Water Crisis, the Karegnondi Water Authority and strategic–structural racism. *Critical Sociology, 45*(1), 103–119. https://doi.org/10.1177/0896920517729193

Hammond, M. D., & Cimpian, A. (2021). "Wonderful but Weak": Children's ambivalent attitudes toward women. *Sex Roles, 84*(1), 76–90. https://doi.org/10.1007/s11199-020-01150-0

Hammond, S. I., Al-Jbouri, E., Edwards, V., & Feltham, L. E. (2017). Infant helping in the first year of life: Parents' recollection of infants' earliest prosocial behaviors. *Infant Behavior and Development, 47*, 54–57. https://doi.org/10.1016/j.infbeh.2017.02.004

Hammond, S. I., & Brownell, C. A. (2018). Happily unhelpful: Infants' everyday helping and its connections to early prosocial development. *Frontiers in Psychology, 9*, 1770. https://doi.org/10.3389/fpsyg.2018.01770

Hampshire, A., Sandrone, S., & Hellyer, P. J. (2019). A large-scale, cross-sectional investigation into the efficacy of brain training. *Frontiers in Human Neuroscience, 13*, 221. https://doi.org/10.3389/fnhum.2019.00221

Han, B., Compton, W. M., Blanco, C., & Colpe, L. J. (2017a). Prevalence, treatment, and unmet treatment needs of US adults with mental health and substance use disorders. *Health Affairs, 36*(10), 1739–1747. https://doi.org/10.1377/hlthaff.2017.0584

Han, B., Compton, W. M., Blanco, C., Colpe, L., Huang, L., & McKeon, R. (2018). National trends in the prevalence of suicidal ideation and behavior among young adults and receipt of mental health care among suicidal young adults. *Journal of the American Academy of Child & Adolescent Psychiatry, 57*(1), 20–27.

Han, B., Compton, W. M., Blanco, C., Crane, E., Lee, J., & Jones, C. M. (2017b). Prescription opioid use, misuse, and use disorders in US adults: 2015 National Survey on Drug Use and Health. *Annals of Internal Medicine, 167*(5), 293–301.

Han, B. H., & Moore, A. A. (2018). Prevention and screening of unhealthy substance use by older adults. *Clinics in Geriatric Medicine, 34*(1), 117–129. https://doi.org/10.1016/j.cger.2017.08.005

Han, D., & Adolph, K. E. (2020). The impact of errors in infant development: Falling like a baby. *Developmental Science, 24*(5), e13069. https://doi.org/10.1111/desc.13069

Han, L. K., Verhoeven, J. E., Tyrka, A. R., Penninx, B. W., Wolkowitz, O. M., Månsson, K. N., Lindqvist, D., Boks, M. P., Révész, D., Mellon, S. H., & Picard, M. (2019). Accelerating research on biological aging and mental health: Current challenges and future directions. *Psychoneuroendocrinology, 106*, 293–311. https://doi.org/10.1016/j.psyneuen.2019.04.004

Han, S. H., Kim, K., & Burr, J. A. (2019). Friendship and depression among couples in later life: The moderating effects of marital quality. *The Journals of Gerontology: Series B, 74*(2), 222–231. https://doi.org/10.1093/geronb/gbx046

Han, Y., Kebschull, J. M., Campbell, R. A. A., Cowan, D., Imhof, F., Zador, A. M., & Mrsic-Flogel, T. D. (2018). The logic of single-cell projections from visual cortex. *Nature, 556*(7699), 51–56. https://doi.org/10.1038/nature26159

Hanifan, L. J. (1916). The rural school community center. *The Annals of the American Academy of Political and Social Science, 67*(1), 130–138. https://doi.org/10.1177/000271621606700118

Hanna-Attisha, M. (2019). *What the eyes don't see: A story of crisis, resistance, and hope in an American city* (Reprint ed.). One World.

Hanna-Attisha, M., LaChance, J., Sadler, R. C., & Champney Schnepp, A. (2016). Elevated blood lead levels in children associated with the Flint drinking water crisis:

A spatial analysis of risk and public health response. *American Journal of Public Health, 106*(2), 283–290. https://doi.org/10.2105/AJPH.2015.303003

Hanner, E., Braham, E. J., Elliott, L., & Libertus, M. E. (2019). Promoting math talk in adult–child interactions through grocery store signs. *Mind, Brain, and Education, 13*(2), 110–118.

Hansen, N. S., Thayer, R. E., Feldstein Ewing, S. W., Sabbineni, A., & Bryan, A. D. (2018). Neural correlates of risky sex and response inhibition in high-risk adolescents. *Journal of Research on Adolescence, 28*(1), 56–69. https://doi.org/10.1111/jora.12344

Hanson, B. M., Eisenberg, M. L., & Hotaling, J. M. (2018). Male infertility: A biomarker of individual and familial cancer risk. *Fertility and Sterility, 109*(1), 6–19.

Hanson, M. H. (2020). Stories: Trauma, theatre, and theory. In K. Knutson, T. Okada, & K. Crowley (Eds.), *Multidisciplinary approaches to art learning and creativity* (pp. 64–85). Routledge.

Hanushek, E. (2020). Quality education and economic development. In B. Panth & R. Maclean (Eds.), *Anticipating and preparing for emerging skills and jobs* (pp. 25–32). Springer.

Hanushek, E. A., Peterson, P. E., Talpey, L. M., & Woessmann, L. (2019). *The unwavering SES achievement gap: Trends in U.S. student performance* (National Bureau of Economic Research No. 25648). National Bureau of Economic Research.

Hanushek, E. A., Schwerdt, G., Woessmann, L., & Zhang, L. (2017). General education, vocational education, and labor-market outcomes over the lifecycle. *Journal of Human Resources, 52*(1), 48–87. https://doi.org/10.3368/jhr.52.1.0415-7074R

Harackiewicz, J. M., & Priniski, S. J. (2018). Improving student outcomes in higher education: The science of targeted intervention. *Annual Review of Psychology, 69*(1), 409–435. https://doi.org/10.1146/annurev-psych-122216-011725

Harden, K. P. (2014). A sex-positive framework for research on adolescent sexuality. *Perspectives on Psychological Science, 9*(5), 455–469. https://doi.org/10.1177/1745691614535934

Harding, J. F., Hughes, D. L., & Way, N. (2017). Racial/ethnic differences in mothers' socialization goals for their adolescents. *Cultural Diversity and Ethnic Minority Psychology, 23*(2), 281–290. https://doi.org/10.1037/cdp0000116

Harel, Y., Zuk, L., Guindy, M., Nakar, O., Lotan, D., & Fattal-Valevski, A. (2017). The effect of subclinical infantile thiamine deficiency on motor function in preschool children. *Maternal & Child Nutrition, 13*(4), e12397.

Hargrove, T. W. (2019). Light privilege? Skin tone stratification in health among African Americans. *Sociology of Race and Ethnicity (Thousand Oaks, Calif.), 5*(3), 370–387. https://doi.org/10.1177/2332649218793670

Harkins, E. B. (1978). Effects of empty nest transition on self-report of psychological and physical well-being. *Journal of Marriage and the Family,* 549–556.

Harkness, S., & Super, C. M. (2021). Why understanding culture is essential for supporting children and families. *Applied Developmental Science, 25*(1), 14–25. https://doi.org/10.1080/10888691.2020.1789354

Harkness, S., Super, C. M., Mavridis, C. J., Barry, O., & Zeitlin, M. (2013). Culture and early childhood development. In P. R. Britto, P. L. Engle, & C. M. Super (Eds.), *Handbook of early childhood development research and its impact on global policy* (pp. 142–160). Oxford University Press.

Härkönen, J., Bernardi, F., & Boertien, D. (2017). Family dynamics and child outcomes: An overview of research and open questions. *European Journal of Population, 33*(2), 163–184.

Harley, K. G., Berger, K. P., Kogut, K., Parra, K., Lustig, R. H., Greenspan, L. C., Calafat, A. M., Ye, X., & Eskenazi, B. (2019). Association of phthalates, parabens and phenols found in personal care products with pubertal timing in girls and boys. *Human Reproduction, 34*(1), 109–117. https://doi.org/10.1093/humrep/dey337

Harlow, H. F. (1958). The nature of love. *American Psychologist, 13*(12), 673–685. https://doi.org/10.1037/h0047884

Harnett, P. H., Dawe, S., & Russell, M. (2014). An investigation of the needs of grandparents who are raising grandchildren. *Child & Family Social Work, 19*(4), 411–420. https://doi.org/10.1111/cfs.12036

Harper, J. (2013, July 6). Ice cream and crime: Where cold cuisine and hot disputes intersect. *Times-Picayune.* https://www.nola.com/news/crime_police/article_ca3c791c-d524-555f-9431-06dc69bcfbe1.html

Harper, J., Malone, S. M., Wilson, S., Hunt, R. H., Thomas, K. M., & Iacono, W. G. (2021). The effects of alcohol and cannabis use on the cortical thickness of cognitive control and salience brain networks in emerging adulthood: A co-twin control study. *Biological Psychiatry, 89*(10), 1012–1022. https://doi.org/10.1016/j.biopsych.2021.01.006

Harper, S. (2020, February 7). *The positive impacts of an ageing population.* Expert Voices: Age International. https://www.ageinternational.org.uk/policy-research/expert-voices/the-positive-impacts-of-an-ageing-population/

Harrell-Levy, M. K., & Kerpelman, J. L. (2015). The relationship between perceived transformative class experiences and subsequent prosocial intentions. *Education Research and Perspectives, 42,* 429–458.

Harridge, S. D., & Lazarus, N. R. (2017). Physical activity, aging, and physiological function. *Physiology, 32*(2), 152–161.

Harrington, E. M., Trevino, S. D., Lopez, S., & Giuliani, N. R. (2020). Emotion regulation in early childhood: Implications for socioemotional and academic components of school readiness. *Emotion, 20*(1), 48–53. https://doi.org/10.1037/emo0000667

Harris, A., Wyn, J., & Younes, S. (2010). Beyond apathetic or activist youth: 'Ordinary' young people and contemporary forms of participation. *Young, 18*(1), 9–32.

Harris, B. (2011). Arnold Gesell's progressive vision: Child hygiene, socialism and eugenics. *History of Psychology, 14*(3), 311–334.

Harris, H. R., Willett, W. C., Vaidya, R. L., & Michels, K. B. (2017). An adolescent and early adulthood dietary pattern associated with inflammation and the incidence of breast cancer. *Cancer Research, 77*(5), 1179–1187. https://doi.org/10.1158/0008-5472.CAN-16-2273

Harris, J. L., & Fleming-Milici, F. (2019). Food marketing to adolescents and young adults: Skeptical but still under the influence. In F. Folkvord (Ed.), *The psychology of food marketing and (over)eating* (pp. 25–43). Routledge.

Harris, J. L., & Pomeranz, J. L. (2020). Infant formula and toddler milk marketing: Opportunities to address harmful practices and improve young children's diets. *Nutrition Reviews, 78*(10), 866–883. https://doi.org/10.1093/nutrit/nuz095

Harris, K. M., Woolf, S. H., & Gaskin, D. J. (2021). High and rising working-age mortality in the US: A report from the national academies of sciences, engineering, and medicine. *JAMA, 325*(20), 2045–2046.

Harris, M. A., Donnellan, M. B., Guo, J., McAdams, D. P., Garnier-Villarreal, M., & Trzesniewski, K. H. (2017). Parental co-construction of 5-to 13-year-olds' global self-esteem through reminiscing about past events. *Child Development, 88*(6), 1810–1822.

Harris, M. A., Donnellan, M. B., & Trzesniewski, K. H. (2018). The lifespan self-esteem scale: Initial validation of a new measure of global self-esteem. *Journal of Personality Assessment, 100*(1), 84–95. https://doi.org/10.1080/00223891.2016.1278380

Harris, M. C. (2019). The impact of body weight on occupational mobility and career development. *International Economic Review, 60*(2), 631–660. https://doi.org/10.1111/iere.12364

Harris, P., Baum, F., Friel, S., Mackean, T., Schram, A., & Townsend, B. (2020). A glossary of theories for understanding power and policy for health equity. *Journal of Epidemiology and Community Health, 74*(6), 548–552. https://doi.org/10.1136/jech-2019-213692

Harris, P. B., & Keady, J. (2008). Wisdom, resilience and successful aging: Changing public discourses on living with dementia. *Sociology, 9.* http://collected.jcu.edu/soc-facpub/9

Harris, P. L. (2018). Children's understanding of death: From biology to religion. *Philosophical Transactions of the Royal Society B: Biological Sciences, 373*(1754), 20170266.

Harris Poll. (2017). *Accelerating acceptance, 2017.* GLAAD.

Harris-Kojetin, L., Sengupta, M., Lendon, J. P., Rome, V., Valverde, R., & Caffrey, C. (2019). Long-term care providers and services users in the United States, 2015–2016. National Center for Health Statistics. *Vital & Health Statistics, 3*(43), x–xii, 1–105.

Harrison, M., Brodribb, W., & Hepworth, J. (2017). A qualitative systematic review of maternal infant feeding practices in transitioning from milk feeds to family foods. *Maternal & Child Nutrition, 13*(2), e12360.

Harstad, E., Shults, J., Barbaresi, W., Bax, A., Cacia, J., Deavenport-Saman, A., Friedman, S., LaRosa, A., Loe, I. M., & Mittal, S. (2021). A2-Adrenergic agonists or stimulants for preschool-age children with attention-deficit/hyperactivity disorder. *JAMA, 325*(20), 2067–2075. https://doi.org/10.1001/jama.2021.6118

Hart, B., & Risley, T. R. (1995). *Meaningful differences in the everyday experience of young American children.* Paul H. Brookes Publishing.

Hart, J. L., & Tannock, M. T. (2019). Rough play: Past, present and potential. In P. K. Smith & J. L. Roopnarine (Eds.), *The Cambridge handbook of play: Developmental and disciplinary perspectives* (pp. 200–221). Cambridge University Press.

Hart, S. L. (2016). Proximal foundations of jealousy: Expectations of exclusivity in the infant's first year of life. *Emotion Review, 8*(4), 358–366. https://doi.org/10.1177/1754073915615431

Hart, S. L. (2020). Jealousy. In D. Güngör (Ed.), *The encyclopedia of child and adolescent development* (pp. 1–13). American Cancer Society. https://doi.org/10.1002/9781119171492.wecad162

Harter, S. (1993). Causes and consequences of low self-esteem in children and adolescents. In R. F. Baumeister (Ed.), *Self-esteem: The puzzle of low self-regard* (pp. 87–116). Springer US. https://doi.org/10.1007/978-1-4684-8956-9_5

Harter, S. (2006). Developmental and individual difference perspectives on self-esteem. In D. K. Mroczek & T. D. Little (Eds.), *Handbook of personality development* (pp. 311–334). Lawrence Erlbaum Associates.

Harter, S. (2012). Emerging self-processes during childhood and adolescence. In M. R. Leary & J. P. Tangney (Eds.), *Handbook of self and identity* (2nd ed., pp. 680–715). Guilford.

Harter, S. (2015). *The construction of the self: Developmental and sociocultural foundations.* Guilford.

Hartholt, K. A., Lee, R., Burns, E. R., & van Beeck, E. F. (2019). Mortality from falls among US adults aged 75 years or older, 2000-2016. *JAMA, 321*(21), 2131–2133. https://doi.org/10.1001/jama.2019.4185

Hartl, A. C., Laursen, B., & Cillessen, A. H. N. (2015). A survival analysis of adolescent friendships: The downside of dissimilarity. *Psychological Science, 26*(8), 1304–1315. https://doi.org/10.1177/0956797615588751

Hartley, B. L., & Sutton, R. M. (2013). A stereotype threat account of boys' academic underachievement. *Child Development, 84*(5), 1716–1733.

Hartnett, C. S., Fingerman, K. L., & Birditt, K. S. (2018). Without the ties that bind: U.S. young adults who lack active parental relationships. *Advances in Life Course Research, 35,* 103–113. https://doi.org/10.1016/j.alcr.2018.01.004

Hartnett, C. S., Furstenberg, F. F., Birditt, K. S., & Fingerman, K. L. (2013). Parental support during young adulthood: Why does assistance decline with age? *Journal of Family Issues, 34*(7), 975–1007.

Hartshorne, J. K., & Germine, L. T. (2015). When does cognitive functioning peak? The asynchronous rise and fall of different cognitive abilities across the lifespan. *Psychological Science, 26*(4), 433–443. https://doi.org/10.1177/0956797614567339

Hartup, W. W. (1996). The company they keep: Friendships and their developmental significance. *Child Development, 67*(1), 1–13.

Harvard Kennedy School Institute of Politics. (2021). *Harvard Youth Poll* (41st ed.). Harvard University.

Harvey, J. A., Chastin, S. F. M., & Skelton, D. A. (2015). How sedentary are older people? A systematic review of the amount of sedentary behavior. *Journal of Aging and Physical Activity, 23*(3), 471–487. https://doi.org/10.1123/japa.2014-0164

Hashikawa, A. N., Sells, J. M., DeJonge, P. M., Alkon, A., Martin, E. T., & Shope, T. R. (2020). Child care in the time of coronavirus disease-19: A period of challenge and opportunity. *The Journal of Pediatrics, 225*, 239–245. https://doi.org/10.1016/j.jpeds.2020.07.042

Hasin, D. S., Shmulewitz, D., & Keyes, K. (2019). Alcohol use and binge drinking among U.S. men, pregnant and non-pregnant women ages 18–44: 2002–2017. *Drug and Alcohol Dependence, 205*, 107590. https://doi.org/10.1016/j.drugalcdep.2019.107590

Hassan Toufaily, M. H., Westgate, M.-N., Lin, A. E., & Holmes, L. B. (2018). Causes of congenital malformations. *Birth Defects Research, 110*(2), 87–91. https://doi.org/10.1002/bdr2.1105

Hastings, K. G., Boothroyd, D. B., Kapphahn, K., Hu, J., Rehkopf, D. H., Cullen, M. R., & Palaniappan, L. (2018). Socioeconomic differences in the epidemiologic transition from heart disease to cancer as the leading cause of death in the United States, 2003 to 2015: An observational study. *Annals of Internal Medicine, 169*(12), 836–844.

Hatano, K., & Sugimura, K. (2017). Is adolescence a period of identity formation for all youth? Insights from a four-wave longitudinal study of identity dynamics in Japan. *Developmental Psychology, 53*(11), 2113.

Hatch, L. R., & Bulcroft, K. (2004). Does long-term marriage bring less frequent disagreements?: Five explanatory frameworks. *Journal of Family Issues, 25*(4), 465–495. https://doi.org/10.1177/0192513X03257766

Hatcher, S. M., Agnew-Brune, C., Anderson, M., Zambrano, L. D., Rose, C. E., Jim, M. A., & McCollum, J. (2020). COVID-19 among American Indian and Alaska native persons — 23 states, January 31–July 3, 2020. *Morbidity and Mortality Weekly Report, 69*(34), 1166.

Hatfield, E., Rapson, R. L., & Martel, L. D. (2007). Passionate love and sexual desire. In S. Kitayama & D. Cohen (Eds.), *Handbook of cultural psychology* (pp. 760–779). The Guilford Press.

Haugen, A. D., Rieck, S. M., Salter, P. S., & Phillips, N. L. (2018). What makes it rape? A lay theories approach to defining rape among college students. *Basic and Applied Social Psychology, 40*(1), 18–35.

Haugen, T. A., Solberg, P. A., Foster, C., Morán-Navarro, R., Breitschädel, F., & Hopkins, W. G. (2018). Peak age and performance progression in world-class track-and-field athletes. *International Journal of Sports Physiology and Performance, 13*(9), 1122–1129. https://doi.org/10.1123/ijspp.2017-0682

Haugland, B. S. M., Hysing, M., & Sivertsen, B. (2020). The burden of care: A national survey on the prevalence, demographic characteristics and health problems among young adult carers attending higher education in Norway. *Frontiers in Psychology, 10*, 2859. https://doi.org/10.3389/fpsyg.2019.02859

Haun, D. B. M., & Tomasello, M. (2011). Conformity to peer pressure in preschool children. *Child Development, 82*(6), 1759–1767. https://doi.org/10.1111/j.1467-8624.2011.01666.x

Havers, F. P. (2021). Hospitalization of adolescents aged 12–17 years with laboratory-confirmed COVID-19 — COVID-NET, 14 states, March 1, 2020–April 24, 2021. *Morbidity and Mortality Weekly Report, 70*(23), 851–857. https://doi.org/10.15585/mmwr.mm7023e1

Havighurst, R. J. (1961). Successful aging: Definition and measurement. *Journal of Gerontology, 16*(2), 134–143.

Havighurst, R. J., & Albrecht, R. (1953). *Older people.* Longmans, Green.

Hawi, N. S., & Samaha, M. (2016). To excel or not to excel: Strong evidence on the adverse effect of smartphone addiction on academic performance. *Computers & Education, 98*, 81–89. https://doi.org/10.1016/j.compedu.2016.03.007

Hawkes, K. (2020). The centrality of ancestral grandmothering in human evolution. *Integrative and Comparative Biology, 60*(3), 765–781. https://doi.org/10.1093/icb/icaa029

Hawkins, J. (2019). *The rise of young adult poverty in the U.S.* [Issue brief]. Berkeley Institute for the Future of Young Americans.

Hawley, P. H. (2015). Social dominance in childhood and its evolutionary underpinnings: Why it matters and what we can do. *Pediatrics, 135*(Supplement 2), S31–S38.

Hawley, P. H. (2016). Eight myths of child social development: An evolutionary approach to power, aggression, and social competence. In D. C. Geary & D. B. Berch (Eds.), *Evolutionary perspectives on child development and education* (pp. 145–166). Springer International Publishing. https://doi.org/10.1007/978-3-319-29986-0_6

Hawley, P. H., & Sinatra, G. M. (2019). Declawing the dinosaurs in the science classroom: Reducing Christian teachers' anxiety and increasing their efficacy for teaching evolution. *Journal of Research in Science Teaching, 56*(4), 375–401. https://doi.org/10.1002/tea.21479

Hay, D. F. (2017). The early development of human aggression. *Child Development Perspectives, 11*(2), 102–106. https://doi.org/10.1111/cdep.12220

Hay, D. F., Paine, A. L., Perra, O., Cook, K. V., Hashmi, S., Robinson, C., Kairis, V., & Slade, R. (2021). Prosocial and aggressive behavior: A longitudinal study. *Monographs of the Society for Research in Child Development, 86*(2), 7–103. https://doi.org/10.1111/mono.12427

Hayes, G. S., McLennan, S. N., Henry, J. D., Phillips, L. H., Terrett, G., Rendell, P. G., Pelly, R. M., & Labuschagne, I. (2020). Task characteristics influence facial emotion recognition age-effects: A meta-analytic review. *Psychology and Aging, 35*(2), 295–315. https://doi.org/10.1037/pag0000441

Hayes, R. M., Abbott, R. L., & Cook, S. (2016). It's her fault: Student acceptance of rape myths on two college campuses. *Violence Against Women, 22*(13), 1540–1555. https://doi.org/10.1177/1077801216630147

Hayne, H., Scarf, D., & Imuta, K. (2015). Childhood memories. *International Encyclopedia of the Social & Behavioral Sciences, 3*, 465–470.

Hays-Grudo, J., Morris, A. S., Beasley, L., Ciciolla, L., Shreffler, K., & Croff, J. (2021). Integrating and synthesizing adversity and resilience knowledge and action: The ICARE model. *American Psychologist, 76*(2), 203–215. https://doi.org/10.1037/amp0000766

Hayslip, B., Jr., Fruhauf, C. A., & Dolbin-MacNab, M. L. (2019). Grandparents raising grandchildren: What have we learned over the past decade? *The Gerontologist, 59*(3), e152–e163. https://doi.org/10.1093/geront/gnx106

Hayward, M. D., Hummer, R. A., Chiu, C. T., González-González, C., & Wong, R. (2014). Does the Hispanic paradox in US adult mortality extend to disability? *Population Research and Policy Review, 33*(1), 81–96.

Hazan, C., & Shaver, P. (1987). Romantic love conceptualized as an attachment process. *Journal of Personality and Social Psychology, 52*(3), 511–524.

He, F. X., Geng, X., & Johnson, A. (2021). The experience of palliative care among older Chinese people in nursing homes: A scoping review. *International Journal of Nursing Studies, 117*, 103878. https://doi.org/10.1016/j.ijnurstu.2021.103878

He, H., Liu, Q., Li, N., Guo, L., Gao, F., Bai, L., Gao, F., & Lyu, J. (2020). Trends in the incidence and DALYs of schizophrenia at the global, regional and national levels: Results from the Global Burden of Disease Study 2017. *Epidemiology and Psychiatric Sciences, 29*. https://doi.org/10.1017/S2045796019000891

He, W., Goodkind, D., & Kowal, P. (2016). *An aging world: 2015 international population reports* (U.S. Census Bureau International Population Reports, P95/16-16). National Institute on Aging, U.S. Census Bureau.

Headey, D. D., & Alderman, H. H. (2019). The relative caloric prices of healthy and unhealthy foods differ systematically across income levels and continents. *The Journal of Nutrition, 149*(11), 2020–2033. https://doi.org/10.1093/jn/nxz158

Headey, D., Heidkamp, R., Osendarp, S., Ruel, M., Scott, N., Black, R., Shekar, M., Bouis, H., Flory, A., Haddad, L., & Walker, N. (2020). Impacts of COVID-19 on childhood malnutrition and nutrition-related mortality. *The Lancet, 396*(10250), 519–521. https://doi.org/10.1016/S0140-6736(20)31647-0

Heal, G., & Park, J. (2015). *Goldilocks economies? Temperature stress and the direct impacts of climate change* (No. w21119). National Bureau of Economic Research.

Heavy Head, R. (2007). *Rediscovering Blackfoot science: How First Nations helped develop a keystone of modern psychology.* https://www.sshrc-crsh.gc.ca/society-societe/stories-histoires/story-histoire-eng.aspx?story_id=91

Hebert-Beirne, J. M., O'Conor, R., Ihm, J. D., Parlier, M. K., Lavender, M. D., & Brubaker, L. (2017). A pelvic health curriculum in school settings: The effect on adolescent females' knowledge. *Journal of Pediatric and Adolescent Gynecology, 30*(2), 188–192. https://doi.org/10.1016/j.jpag.2015.09.006

Heckman, J. J., Holland, M. L., Makino, K. K., Pinto, R., & Rosales-Rueda, M. (2017). *An analysis of the memphis nurse-family partnership program* (No. w23610). National Bureau of Economic Research. https://doi.org/10.3386/w23610

Hedden, T., & Gabrieli, J. D. E. (2004). Insights into the ageing mind: A view from cognitive neuroscience. *Nature Reviews Neuroscience, 5*(2), 87–96. https://doi.org/10.1038/nrn1323

Hedegaard, H., Curtin, S. C., & Warner, M. (2021). *Suicide mortality in the United States, 1999–2019* (NCHS Data Brief No. 398). National Center for Health Statistics. https://dx.doi.org/10.15620/cdc:101761

Hedegaard, H., & Warner, M. (2021). *Suicide mortality in the United States, 1999–2019* (NCHS Data Brief No. 398). National Center for Health Statistics. https://dx.doi.org/10.15620/cdc:101761

Heffer, T., Good, M., Daly, O., MacDonell, E., & Willoughby, T. (2019). The longitudinal association between social-media use and depressive symptoms among adolescents and young adults: An empirical reply to Twenge et al. (2018). *Clinical Psychological Science, 7*(3), 462–470. https://doi.org/10.1177/2167702618812727

Heft-Neal, S., Burney, J., Bendavid, E., Voss, K. K., & Burke, M. (2020). Dust pollution from the Sahara and African infant mortality. *Nature Sustainability, 3*(10), 863–871. https://doi.org/10.1038/s41893-020-0562-1

Hehir, T. (2002). Eliminating ableism in education. *Harvard Educational Review, 72*(1), 1–33.

Hehman, J. A., & Bugental, D. B. (2015). Responses to patronizing communication and factors that attenuate those responses. *Psychology and Aging, 30*(3), 552–560. https://doi.org/10.1037/pag0000041

Heid, A. R., Kim, K., Zarit, S. H., Birditt, K. S., & Fingerman, K. L. (2018). Relationship tensions and mood: Adult children's daily experience of aging parents' stubbornness. *Personal Relationships, 25*(1), 87–102. https://doi.org/10.1111/pere.12229

Heid, A. R., Zarit, S. H., & Fingerman, K. L. (2017). Adult children's responses to parent "stubbornness." *The Gerontologist, 57*(3), 429–440.

Heiligman, D. (2009). *Charles and Emma: The Darwins' leap of faith.* Henry Holt.

Heilmann-Heimbach, S., Herold, C., Hochfeld, L. M., Hillmer, A. M., Nyholt, D. R., Hecker, J., & Nöthen, M. M. (2017). Meta-analysis identifies novel risk loci and yields systematic insights into the biology of male-pattern baldness. *Nature Communications, 8*(1), 1–8.

Helldén, D., Andersson, C., Nilsson, M., Ebi, K. L., Friberg, P., & Alfvén, T. (2021). Climate change and child health: A scoping review and an expanded conceptual framework. *The Lancet Planetary Health, 5*(3), e164–e175. https://doi.org/10.1016/S2542-5196(20)30274-6

Helle, S. (2018). "Only in dress?" Methodological concerns regarding nonbinary gender. In S. L. Budin, M. Cifarelli, A. Garcia-Ventura, & A. Millet Albà (Eds.), *Gender and methodology in the ancient Near East: Approaches from Assyriology and beyond* (pp. 41–53). Edicions Universitat de Barcelona.

Helm, P., & Grønlund, L. (1998). A halt in the secular trend towards earlier menarche in Denmark. *Acta Obstetricia et Gynecologica Scandinavica, 77*(2), 198–200. https://doi.org/10.1080/j.1600-0412.1998.770213.x

Helm, P. J., Lifshin, U., & Greenberg, J. (2020). Terror management theory. In B. J. Carducci, C. S. Nave, & C. S. Nave (Eds.), *The Wiley encyclopedia of personality and individual differences* (pp. 407–411). Wiley. https://doi.org/10.1002/9781118970843.ch68

Henderson, A. W., Lehavot, K., & Simoni, J. M. (2009). Ecological models of sexual satisfaction among lesbian/bisexual and heterosexual women. *Archives of Sexual Behavior, 38*(1), 50–65.

Hendry, A., Johnson, M. H., & Holmboe, K. (2019). Early development of visual attention: Change, stability, and longitudinal associations. *Annual Review of Developmental Psychology, 1*, 251–275.

Hennegan, J., Shannon, A. K., Rubli, J., Schwab, K. J., & Melendez-Torres, G. J. (2019). Women's and girls' experiences of menstruation in low- and middle-income countries: A systematic review and qualitative metasynthesis. *PLoS Medicine, 16*(5), e1002803. https://doi.org/10.1371/journal.pmed.1002803

Henriksen, M. G., Nordgaard, J., & Jansson, L. B. (2017). Genetics of schizophrenia: Overview of methods, findings and limitations. *Frontiers in Human Neuroscience, 11*, 322. https://doi.org/10.3389/fnhum.2017.00322

Henrique, A. J., Gabrielloni, M. C., Rodney, P., & Barbieri, M. (2018). Non-pharmacological interventions during childbirth for pain relief, anxiety, and neuroendocrine stress parameters: A randomized controlled trial. *International Journal of Nursing Practice, 24*(3), e12642. https://doi.org/10.1111/ijn.12642

Henry, C. S., & Hubbs-Tait, L. (2013). New directions in authoritative parenting. In R. E. Larzelere, A. S. Morris, & A. W. Harrist (Eds.), *Authoritative parenting: Synthesizing nurturance and discipline for optimal child development* (pp. 237–264). American Psychological Association.

Henry, M. J., Herrmann, B., Kunke, D., & Obleser, J. (2017). Aging affects the balance of neural entrainment and top-down neural modulation in the listening brain. *Nature Communications, 8*(1), 15801. https://doi.org/10.1038/ncomms15801

Henselmans, I., Smets, E. M. A., Han, P. K. J., de Haes, H. C. J. C., & Van Laarhoven, H. W. M. (2017). How long do I have? Observational study on communication about life expectancy with advanced cancer patients. *Patient Education and Counseling, 100*(10), 1820–1827.

Hentschel, S., Eid, M., & Kutscher, T. (2017). The influence of major life events and personality traits on the stability of affective well-being. *Journal of Happiness Studies, 18*(3), 719–741.

Hepper, P. (2015). Behavior during the prenatal period: Adaptive for development and survival. *Child Development Perspectives, 9*(1), 38–43. https://doi.org/10.1111/cdep.12104

Herbell, K., Li, Y., Bloom, T., Sharps, P., & Bullock, L. F. C. (2020). Keeping it together for the kids: New mothers' descriptions of the impact of intimate partner violence on parenting. *Child Abuse & Neglect, 99*, 104268. https://doi.org/10.1016/j.chiabu.2019.104268

Herbert, A. C., Ramirez, A. M., Lee, G., North, S. J., Askari, M. S., West, R. L., & Sommer, M. (2017). Puberty experiences of low-income girls in the United States: A systematic review of qualitative literature from 2000 to 2014. *Journal of Adolescent Health, 60*(4), 363–379.

Herbert, W. (2010). Heuristics revealed. *APS Observer, 23*(8).

Herkama, S., Saarento, S., & Salmivalli, C. (2017). The KiVa antibullying program: Lessons learned and future directions. In P. Sturmey (Ed.), *The Wiley handbook of violence and aggression* (pp. 1–12). Wiley.

Herman-Giddens, M. E. (2006). Recent data on pubertal milestones in United States children: The secular trend toward earlier development. *International Journal of Andrology, 29*(1), 241–246.

Hernandez, I. A., Silverman, D. M., & Destin, M. (2021). From deficit to benefit: Highlighting lower-SES students' background-specific strengths reinforces their academic persistence. *Journal of Experimental Social Psychology, 92*, 104080. https://doi.org/10.1016/j.jesp.2020.104080

Hernández, M. M., & Bámaca-Colbert, M. Y. (2016). A behavioral process model of familism. *Journal of Family Theory & Review, 8*(4), 463–483. https://doi.org/10.1111/jftr.12166

Hernández, M. M., Robins, R. W., Widaman, K. F., & Conger, R. D. (2017). Ethnic pride, self-esteem, and school belonging: A reciprocal analysis over time. *Developmental Psychology, 53*(12), 2384–2396. https://doi.org/10.1037/dev0000434

Heron, M. P. (2019). *Deaths: leading causes for 2017*. Centers for Disease Control and Prevention.

Herrman, J. W., Palen, L.-A., Kan, M., Feinberg, M., Hill, J., Magee, E., & Haigh, K. M. (2019). Young mothers' and fathers' perceptions of relationship violence: A focus group study. *Violence Against Women, 25*(3), 274–296. https://doi.org/10.1177/1077801218780356

Herron, J. (2019, April 18). Millennials still lean on parents for money but want financial independence, survey says. *USA Today*. https://www.usatoday.com/story/money/2019/04/18/millennial-money-why-young-adults-still-need-support-parents/3500346002/

Herting, M. M., Uban, K. A., Gonzalez, M. R., Baker, F. C., Kan, E. C., Thompson, W. K., Granger, D. A., Albaugh, M. D., Anokhin, A. P., Bagot, K. S., Banich, M. T., Barch, D. M., Baskin-Sommers, A., Breslin, F. J., Casey, B. J., Chaarani, B., Chang, L., Clark, D. B., Cloak, C. C., … Sowell, E. R. (2021). Correspondence between perceived pubertal development and hormone levels in 9-10 year-olds from the adolescent brain cognitive development study. *Frontiers in Endocrinology, 11*, 549928. https://doi.org/10.3389/fendo.2020.549928

Hesselmar, B., Sjöberg, F., Saalman, R., Åberg, N., Adlerberth, I., & Wold, A. E. (2013). Pacifier cleaning practices and risk of allergy development. *Pediatrics, 131*(6), e1829–e1837.

Hesson, L. B., & Pritchard, A. L. (2019). Genetics and epigenetics: A historical overview. In L. B. Hesson & A. L. Pritchard (Eds.), *Clinical epigenetics* (pp. 1–46). Springer. https://doi.org/10.1007/978-981-13-8958-0_1

Hewitt, L., Benjamin-Neelon, S. E., Carson, V., Stanley, R. M., Janssen, I., & Okely, A. D. (2018). Child care centre adherence to infant physical activity and screen time recommendations in Australia, Canada and the United States: An observational study. *Infant Behavior & Development, 50*, 88–97. https://doi.org/10.1016/j.infbeh.2017.11.008

Heyman, S. (2017, November 8). Don't know what the angular gyrus is? Your heart does. *The New York Times*. https://www.nytimes.com/2017/11/08/style/modern-love-neuroscience.html

Hicken, M. T., Kravitz-Wirtz, N., Durkee, M., & Jackson, J. S. (2018). Racial inequalities in health: Framing future research. *Social Science & Medicine, 199*, 11–18. https://doi.org/10.1016/j.socscimed.2017.12.027

Hidalgo, I., Brooten, D., Youngblut, J. M., Roche, R., Li, J., & Hinds, A. M. (2021). Practices following the death of a loved one reported by adults from 14 countries or cultural/ethnic group. *Nursing Open, 8*(1), 453–462.

Hiekel, N., Liefbroer, A. C., & Poortman, A.-R. (2014). Understanding diversity in the meaning of cohabitation across Europe. *European Journal of Population, 30*(4), 391–410. https://doi.org/10.1007/s10680-014-9321-1

Higgins, J. A., Popkin, R. A., & Santelli, J. S. (2012). Pregnancy ambivalence and contraceptive use among young adults in the United States. *Perspectives on Sexual and Reproductive Health, 44*(4), 236–243. https://doi.org/10.1363/4423612

Higgins, L. T., & Xiang, G. (2009). The development and use of intelligence tests in China. *Psychology and Developing Societies, 21*(2), 257–275.

Higgitt, R. (2017). Challenging tropes: Genius, heroic invention, and the longitude problem in the museum. *Isis, 108*(2), 371–380. https://doi.org/10.1086/692691

Hilbrand, S., Coall, D. A., Gerstorf, D., & Hertwig, R. (2017). Caregiving within and beyond the family is associated with lower mortality for the caregiver: A prospective study. *Evolution and Human Behavior, 38*(3), 397–403. https://doi.org/10.1016/j.evolhumbehav.2016.11.010

Hill, B. (2021). Expanding our understanding and use of the ecological systems theory model for the prevention of maternal obesity: A new socioecological framework. *Obesity Reviews, 22*(3), e13147.

Hill, B., & Rodriguez, A. C. I. (2020). Weight stigma across the preconception, pregnancy, and postpartum periods: A narrative review and conceptual model. *Seminars in Reproductive Medicine, 38*(6), 414–422. https://doi.org/10.1055/s-0041-1723775

Hill, H. A., Yankey, D., Elam-Evans, L. D., Singleton, J. A., Pingali, S. C., & Santibanez, T. A. (2020). Vaccination coverage by age 24 months among children born in 2016 and 2017 — National Immunization Survey-Child, United States, 2017–2019. *Morbidity and Mortality Weekly Report, 69*(42), 1505–1511. https://doi.org/10.15585/mmwr.mm6942a1

Hill, J. P., & den Dulk, K. R. (2013). Religion, volunteering, and educational setting: The effect of youth schooling type on civic engagement. *Journal for the Scientific Study of Religion, 52*(1), 179–197. https://doi.org/10.1111/jssr.12011

Hill, M. S., Jensen, A. C., Coyne, S. M., & Yorgason, J. B. (2020). Look who's talking: Mediums of contact among mid-to later-life siblings. *The International Journal of Aging and Human Development, 92*(4), 450–471. https://doi.org/10.1177/0091415020912956

Hill, R. A., Li, A. M., & Grutzendler, J. (2018). Lifelong cortical myelin plasticity and age-related degeneration in the live mammalian brain. *Nature Neuroscience, 21*(5), 683–695. https://doi.org/10.1038/s41593-018-0120-6

Hill, R. E., Wakefield, C. E., Cohn, R. J., Fardell, J. E., Brierley, M.-E. E., Kothe, E., Jacobsen, P. B., Hetherington, K., & Mercieca-Bebber, R. (2020). Survivorship care plans in cancer: A meta-analysis and systematic review of care plan outcomes. *The Oncologist, 25*(2), e351–e372.

Hillary, R. F., Stevenson, A. J., McCartney, D. L., Campbell, A., Walker, R. M., Howard, D. M., & Marioni, R. E. (2020). Epigenetic measures of ageing predict the prevalence and incidence of leading causes of death and disease burden. *Clinical Epigenetics, 12*(1), 1–12.

Hilliard, C. B. (2016). High osteoporosis risk among East Africans linked to lactase persistence genotype. *BoneKEy Reports, 5*, 803. https://doi.org/10.1038/bonekey.2016.30

Hilliard, L. J., & Liben, L. S. (2020). Addressing sexism with children: Young adults' beliefs about bias socialization. *Child Development, 91*(2), 488–507. https://doi.org/10.1111/cdev.13230

Hilpert, P., Randall, A. K., Sorokowski, P., Atkins, D. C., Sorokowska, A., Ahmadi, K., Alghraibeh, A. M., Aryeetey, R., Bertoni, A., Bettache, K., Błażejewska, M., Bodenmann, G., Borders, J., Bortolini, T. S., Butovskaya, M., Castro, F. N., Cetinkaya, H., Cunha, D., David, O. A., … Yoo, G. (2016). The associations of dyadic coping and relationship satisfaction vary between and within nations: A 35-nation study. *Frontiers in Psychology, 7*, 1106. https://doi.org/10.3389/fpsyg.2016.01106

Hines, M. (2020). Human gender development. *Neuroscience & Biobehavioral Reviews, 118*, 89–96. https://doi.org/10.1016/j.neubiorev.2020.07.018

Hinshaw, S. P. (2018). Attention deficit hyperactivity disorder (ADHD): Controversy, developmental mechanisms, and multiple levels of analysis. *Annual Review of Clinical Psychology, 14*(1), 291–316. https://doi.org/10.1146/annurev-clinpsy-050817-084917

Hirode, G., & Wong, R. J. (2020). Trends in the prevalence of metabolic syndrome in the United States, 2011–2016. *JAMA, 323*(24), 2526–2528.

Hirshkowitz, M., Whiton, K., Albert, S. M., Alessi, C., Bruni, O., DonCarlos, L., & Ware, J. C. (2015). National Sleep Foundation's updated sleep duration recommendations. *Sleep Health, 1*(4), 233–243.

Hirshorn, B. A., & Settersten, R. A., Jr. (2013). Civic involvement across the life course: Moving beyond age-based assumptions. *Advances in Life Course Research, 18*(3), 199–211. https://doi.org/10.1016/j.alcr.2013.05.001

Hirsh-Pasek, K. (2021). *Play breeds better thinkers*. Science.

Ho, T. C., Gifuni, A. J., & Gotlib, I. H. (2021). Psychobiological risk factors for suicidal thoughts and behaviors in adolescence: A consideration of the role of puberty. *Molecular Psychiatry.* https://doi.org/10.1038/s41380-021-01171-5

Hochberg, Z., & Konner, M. (2020). Emerging adulthood, a pre-adult life-history stage. *Frontiers in Endocrinology, 10,* 918. https://doi.org/10.3389/fendo.2019.00918

Hochschild, A., & Machung, A. (2012). *The second shift: Working families and the revolution at home.* Penguin.

Hochstenbach, C. (2018). Spatializing the intergenerational transmission of inequalities: Parental wealth, residential segregation, and urban inequality. *Environment and Planning A: Economy and Space, 50*(3), 689–708. https://doi.org/10.1177/0308518X17749831

Hodel, A. S. (2018). Rapid infant prefrontal cortex development and sensitivity to early environmental experience. *Developmental Review, 48,* 113–144. https://doi.org/10.1016/j.dr.2018.02.003

Hodges, E. A., Propper, C. B., Estrem, H., & Schultz, M. B. (2020). Feeding during infancy: Interpersonal behavior, physiology, and obesity risk. *Child Development Perspectives, 14*(3), 185–191. https://doi.org/10.1111/cdep.12376

Hodges, T. (2018, October 25). *School engagement is more than just talk.* Gallup.com. https://www.gallup.com/education/244022/school-engagement-talk.aspx

Hoehl, S., Hellmer, K., Johansson, M., & Gredebäck, G. (2017). Itsy bitsy spider…: Infants react with increased arousal to spiders and snakes. *Frontiers in Psychology, 8,* 1710. https://doi.org/10.3389/fpsyg.2017.01710

Hoehl, S., Keupp, S., Schleihauf, H., McGuigan, N., Buttelmann, D., & Whiten, A. (2019). 'Over-imitation': A review and appraisal of a decade of research. *Developmental Review, 51,* 90–108. https://doi.org/10.1016/j.dr.2018.12.002

Hoff, E. (2018). Bilingual development in children of immigrant families. *Child Development Perspectives, 12*(2), 80–86. https://doi.org/10.1111/cdep.12262

Hoff, E., & Core, C. (2015). What clinicians need to know about bilingual development. *Seminars in Speech and Language, 36*(02), 089–099. https://doi.org/10.1055/s-0035-1549104

Hoff, K. A., Briley, D. A., Wee, C. J., & Rounds, J. (2018). Normative changes in interests from adolescence to adulthood: A meta-analysis of longitudinal studies. *Psychological Bulletin, 144*(4), 426.

Hofferth, S. L. (2009). Changes in American children's time—1997 to 2003. *Electronic International Journal of Time Use Research, 6*(1), 26.

Hoffman, J. (2020, September 1). Mistrust of a coronavirus vaccine could imperil widespread immunity. *The New York Times.* https://www.nytimes.com/2020/07/18/health/coronavirus-anti-vaccine.html

Hoffman, M. L. (1977). Personality and social development. *Annual Review of Psychology, 28*(1), 295–321. https://doi.org/10.1146/annurev.ps.28.020177.001455

Hoffmann, B., Kobel, S., Wartha, O., Kettner, S., Dreyhaupt, J., & Steinacker, J. M. (2019). High sedentary time in children is not only due to screen media use: A cross-sectional study. *BMC Pediatrics, 19*(1), 154. https://doi.org/10.1186/s12887-019-1521-8

Hofmeier, S. M., Runfola, C. D., Sala, M., Gagne, D. A., Brownley, K. A., & Bulik, C. M. (2017). Body image, aging, and identity in women over 50: The Gender and Body Image (GABI) study. *Journal of Women & Aging, 29*(1), 3–14. https://doi.org/10.1080/08952841.2015.1065140

Hogan, C. L., Mata, J., & Carstensen, L. L. (2013). Exercise holds immediate benefits for affect and cognition in younger and older adults. *Psychology and Aging, 28*(2), 587–594. https://doi.org/10.1037/a0032634

Höhle, B., Bijeljac-Babic, R., & Nazzi, T. (2020). Variability and stability in early language acquisition: Comparing monolingual and bilingual infants' speech perception and word recognition. *Bilingualism: Language and Cognition, 23*(1), 56–71. https://doi.org/10.1017/S1366728919000348

Høigaard, R., Kovač, V. B., Øverby, N. C., & Haugen, T. (2015). Academic self-efficacy mediates the effects of school psychological climate on academic achievement. *School Psychology Quarterly, 30*(1), 64–74. https://doi.org/10.1037/spq0000056

Holbein, J., Kawashima-Ginsberg, K., & Wang, T. (2021). *Quantifying the effects of protests on voter registration and turnout* (Study II of Protests, Politics, and Power: Exploring the Connections Between Youth Voting and Youth Movements). CIRCLE, Tufts University.

Holden, G. W., Williamson, P. A., & Holland, G. W. (2014). Eavesdropping on the family: A pilot investigation of corporal punishment in the home. *Journal of Family Psychology, 28*(3), 401.

Holland, D., Chang, L., Ernst, T. M., Curran, M., Buchthal, S. D., Alicata, D., Skranes, J., Johansen, H., Hernandez, A., Yamakawa, R., Kuperman, J. M., & Dale, A. M. (2014). Structural growth trajectories and rates of change in the first 3 months of infant brain development. *JAMA Neurology, 71*(10), 1266–1274. https://doi.org/10.1001/jamaneurol.2014.1638

Holland, J., Reynolds, T., & Weller, S. (2007). Transitions, networks and communities: The significance of social capital in the lives of children and young people. *Journal of Youth Studies, 10*(1), 97–116.

Holland, J. L. (1997). *Making vocational choices: A theory of vocational personalities and work environments* (3rd ed.). Psychological Assessment Resources.

Holodynski, M., & Seeger, D. (2019). Expressions as signs and their significance for emotional development. *Developmental Psychology, 55*(9), 1812.

Holst-Warhaft, G. (2000). *The cue for passion: Grief and its political uses.* Harvard University Press.

Holt-Lunstad, J. (2017). The potential public health relevance of social isolation and loneliness: Prevalence, epidemiology, and risk factors. *Public Policy & Aging Report, 27*(4), 127–130. https://doi.org/10.1093/ppar/prx030

Holt-Lunstad, J. (2018). Why social relationships are important for physical health: A systems approach to understanding and modifying risk and protection. *Annual Review of Psychology, 69,* 437–458.

Holt-Lunstad, J., Smith, T. B., Baker, M., Harris, T., & Stephenson, D. (2015). Loneliness and social isolation as risk factors for mortality: A meta-analytic review. *Perspectives on Psychological Science, 10*(2), 227–237.

Holt-Lunstad, J., & Steptoe, A. (2022). Social isolation: An underappreciated determinant of physical health. *Current Opinion in Psychology, 43,* 232–237. https://doi.org/10.1016/j.copsyc.2021.07.012

Holzen, K. V., & Nazzi, T. (2020). Emergence of a consonant bias during the first year of life: New evidence from own-name recognition. *Infancy, 25*(3), 319–346. https://doi.org/10.1111/infa.12331

Hong, K., Savelyev, P. A., & Tan, K. T. (2020). Understanding the mechanisms linking college education with longevity. *Journal of Human Capital, 14*(3), 371–400.

Hong, P., Cui, M., Ledermann, T., & Love, H. (2021). Parent-child relationship satisfaction and psychological distress of parents and emerging adult children. *Journal of Child and Family Studies, 30*(4), 921–931. https://doi.org/10.1007/s10826-021-01916-4

Hong, S.-J., Sisk, L. M., Caballero, C., Mekhanik, A., Roy, A. K., Milham, M. P., & Gee, D. G. (2021). Decomposing complex links between the childhood environment and brain structure in school-aged youth. *Developmental Cognitive Neuroscience, 48,* 100919. https://doi.org/10.1016/j.dcn.2021.100919

Hooper, E. G., Wu, Q., Ku, S., Gerhardt, M., & Feng, X. (2018). Maternal emotion socialization and child outcomes among African Americans and European Americans. *Journal of Child and Family Studies, 27*(6), 1870–1880. https://doi.org/10.1007/s10826-018-1020-9

Hooper, M. W., Nápoles, A. M., & Pérez-Stable, E. J. (2020). COVID-19 and racial/ethnic disparities. *JAMA, 323*(24), 2466. https://doi.org/10.1001/jama.2020.8598

Hootman, J. M., Murphy, L. B., Omura, J. D., Brady, T. J., Boring, M., Barbour, K. E., & Helmick, C. G. (2018). Health care provider counseling for physical activity or exercise among adults with arthritis—United States, 2002 and 2014. *Morbidity and Mortality Weekly Report, 66*(51–52), 1398–1401. https://doi.org/10.15585/mmwr.mm665152a2

Hopkins, A. A. (1921). Our latest science—eugenics. *Scientific American, 125*(16), 273–279.

Horbar, J. D., Edwards, E. M., Greenberg, L. T., Profit, J., Draper, D., Helkey, D., Lorch, S. A., Lee, H. C., Phibbs, C. S., Rogowski, J., Gould, J. B., & Firebaugh, G. (2019). Racial segregation and inequality in the neonatal intensive care unit for very low-birth-weight and very preterm infants. *JAMA Pediatrics, 173*(5), 455–461. https://doi.org/10.1001/jamapediatrics.2019.0241

Horn, J. L., & Cattell, R. B. (1967). Age differences in fluid and crystallized intelligence. *Acta Psychologica, 26,* 107–129. https://doi.org/10.1016/0001-6918(67)90011-X

Hornbeck, K., Walter, K., & Myrvik, M. (2017). Should potential risk of chronic traumatic encephalopathy be discussed with young athletes? *AMA Journal of Ethics, 19*(7), 686–692. https://doi.org/10.1001/journalofethics.2017.19.7.pfor1-1707.

Hornberger, L. L., Lane, M. A., & The Committee on Adolescence. (2021). Identification and management of eating disorders in children and adolescents. *Pediatrics, 147*(1), e2020040279. https://doi.org/10.1542/peds.2020-040279

Hornsey, M. J., Bain, P. G., Harris, E. A., Lebedeva, N., Kashima, E. S., Guan, Y., González, R., Chen, S. X., & Blumen, S. (2018). How much is enough in a perfect world? Cultural variation in ideal levels of happiness, pleasure, health, self-esteem, longevity, and intelligence. *Psychological Science, 29*(9), 1393–1404. https://doi.org/10.1177/0956797618768058

Horowitz, J. M., Graf, N., & Livingston, G. (2019, November 6). Views on marriage and cohabitation in the U.S. *Social & Demographic Trends Project* (blog). Pew Research Center. https://www.pewsocialtrends.org/2019/11/06/marriage-and-cohabitation-in-the-u-s/

Horta, B. L. (2019). Breastfeeding: Investing in the future. *Breastfeeding Medicine, 14*(S1), S-11–S-12.

Horta, B. L., de Sousa, B. A., & de Mola, C. L. (2018). Breastfeeding and neurodevelopmental outcomes. *Current Opinion in Clinical Nutrition and Metabolic Care, 21*(3), 174–178. https://doi.org/10.1097/MCO.0000000000000453

Horton, R., Crawford, G., Freeman, L., Fenwick, A., Wright, C. F., & Lucassen, A. (2019). Direct-to-consumer genetic testing. *BMJ, 367,* l5688. https://doi.org/10.1136/bmj.l5688

Horvath, C. A., & Lee, C. M. (2015). Parenting responses and parenting goals of mothers and fathers of adolescents. *Marriage & Family Review, 51*(4), 337–355. https://doi.org/10.1080/01494929.2014.955938

Horvath, G., Knopik, V. S., & Marceau, K. (2020). Polygenic influences on pubertal timing and tempo and depressive symptoms in boys and girls. *Journal of Research on Adolescence, 30*(1), 78–94. https://doi.org/10.1111/jora.12502

Horváth, K., & Plunkett, K. (2018). Spotlight on daytime napping during early childhood. *Nature and Science of Sleep, 10,* 97–104. https://doi.org/10.2147/NSS.S126252

Horvath, S. (2013). DNA methylation age of human tissues and cell types. *Genome Biology, 14*(10), 3156. https://doi.org/10.1186/gb-2013-14-10-r115

Horvath, S., Lu, A. T., Cohen, H., & Raj, K. (2019). Rapamycin retards epigenetic ageing of keratinocytes independently of its effects on replicative senescence, proliferation and differentiation. *Aging, 11*(10), 3238–3249. https://doi.org/10.18632/aging.101976

Horvath, S., & Raj, K. (2018). DNA methylation-based biomarkers and the epigenetic clock theory of ageing. *Nature Reviews Genetics, 19*(6), 371–384.

Hosker, C. M. G., & Bennett, M. I. (2016). Delirium and agitation at the end of life. *BMJ, 353,* i3085. https://doi.org/10.1136/bmj.i3085

Hosokawa, M., Imazeki, S., Mizunuma, H., Kubota, T., & Hayashi, K. (2012). Secular trends in age at menarche and time to establish regular menstrual cycling in Japanese women born between 1930 and 1985. *BMC Women's Health, 12,* 19. http://dx.doi.org/10.1186/1472-6874-12-19

Hostinar, C. E., Sullivan, R. M., & Gunnar, M. R. (2014). Psychobiological mechanisms underlying the social buffering of the hypothalamic–pituitary–adrenocortical axis: A review of animal models and human studies across development. *Psychological Bulletin, 140*(1), 256.

Houdé, O., Pineau, A., Leroux, G., Poirel, N., Perchey, G., Lanoë, C., Lubin, A., Turbelin, M., Rossi, S., Simon, G., Delcroix, N., Lamberton, F., Vigneau, M., Wisniewski, G., Vicet, J.-R., & Mazoyer, B. (2011). Functional magnetic resonance imaging study of Piaget's conservation-of-number task in preschool and school-age children: A neo-Piagetian approach. *Journal of Experimental Child Psychology, 110*(3), 332–346.

Houle, J. N., & Warner, C. (2017). Into the red and back to the nest? Student debt, college completion, and return to the parental home among young adults. *Sociology of Education, 90,* 89–108.

Hourigan, K. L. (2021). Girls try, boys aim high: Exposing difference in implied ability, activity, and agency of girls versus boys in language on McDonald's happy meal boxes. *Sex Roles, 84*(7), 377–391. https://doi.org/10.1007/s11199-020-01173-7

House, B. R. (2018). How do social norms influence prosocial development? *Current Opinion in Psychology, 20,* 87–91. https://doi.org/10.1016/j.copsyc.2017.08.011

House, B. R., & Tomasello, M. (2018). Modeling social norms increasingly influences costly sharing in middle childhood. *Journal of Experimental Child Psychology, 171,* 84–98.

Howard, J. (2020). Plague was one of history's deadliest diseases — then we found a cure. *National Geographic.* https://www.nationalgeographic.com/science/health-and-human-body/human-diseases/the-plague/

Howard, J., Miles, G. E., Rees-Davies, L., & Bertenshaw, E. J. (2017). Play in middle childhood: Everyday play behaviour and associated emotions. *Children & Society, 31*(5), 378–389.

Howard, L. M., & Khalifeh, H. (2020). Perinatal mental health: A review of progress and challenges. *World Psychiatry, 19*(3), 313–327. https://doi.org/10.1002/wps.20769

Howe, N., Della Porta, S., Recchia, H., & Ross, H. (2016). "Because if you don't put the top on, it will spill": A longitudinal study of sibling teaching in early childhood. *Developmental Psychology, 52*(11), 1832–1842. https://doi.org/10.1037/dev0000193

Howe, N., & Leach, J. (2018). Children's play and peer relations. In W. M. Bukowski, B. Laursen, & K. H. Rubin (Eds.), *Handbook of peer interactions, relationships, and groups* (2nd ed., pp. 222–242). Guilford.

Howell, B. R., Styner, M. A., Gao, W., Yap, P.-T., Wang, L., Baluyot, K., Yacoub, E., Chen, G., Potts, T., Salzwedel, A., Li, G., Gilmore, J. H., Piven, J., Smith, J. K., Shen, D., Ugurbil, K., Zhu, H., Lin, W., & Elison, J. T. (2019). The UNC/UMN Baby Connectome Project (BCP): An overview of the study design and protocol development. *NeuroImage, 185,* 891–905. https://doi.org/10.1016/j.neuroimage.2018.03.049

Howlett, S. E., Rutenberg, A. D., & Rockwood, K. (2021). The degree of frailty as a translational measure of health in aging. *Nature Aging, 1*(8), 651–665. https://doi.org/10.1038/s43587-021-00099-3

Howse, E., Hankey, C., Allman-Farinelli, M., Bauman, A., & Freeman, B. (2018). "Buying salad is a lot more expensive than going to McDonalds": Young adults' views about what influences their food choices. *Nutrients, 10*(8), 996. https://doi.org/10.3390/nu10080996

Hoy, M. K., Clemens, J., Martin, C., & Moshfegh, A. (2020). Fruit and vegetable intake among children by level of variety, what we eat in America, NHANES 2013–2016. *Current Developments in Nutrition, 4*(Supplement_2), 206. https://doi.org/10.1093/cdn/nzaa043_057

Hoyert, D. L., & Gregory, E. C. (2020). Cause-of-death data from the fetal death file, 2015–2017. *National Vital Statistics Reports, 69*(4), 1–20.

Hoyniak, C. P., Bates, J. E., Staples, A. D., Rudasill, K. M., Molfese, D. L., & Molfese, V. J. (2019). Child sleep and socioeconomic context in the development of cognitive abilities in early childhood. *Child Development, 90*(5), 1718–1737. https://doi.org/10.1111/cdev.13042

Hoyos-Quintero, A. M., & García-Perdomo, H. A. (2019). Factors related to physical activity in early childhood: A systematic review. *Journal of Physical Activity and Health, 16*(10), 925–936. https://doi.org/10.1123/jpah.2018-0715

Hraba, J., & Grant, G. (1970). Black is beautiful: A reexamination of racial preference and identification. *Journal of Personality and Social Psychology, 16*(3), 398.

Hrdy, S. B., & Burkart, J. M. (2020). The emergence of emotionally modern humans: Implications for language and learning. *Philosophical Transactions of the Royal Society B: Biological Sciences, 375*(1803), 20190499. https://doi.org/10.1098/rstb.2019.0499

Hruska, L. C., Zelic, K. J., Dickson, K. S., & Ciesla, J. A. (2015). Adolescents' co-rumination and stress predict affective changes in a daily-diary paradigm. *International Journal of Psychology, 52*(5), 372–380. https://doi.org/10.1002/ijop.12227

Huang, C.-Y., & Lamb, M. E. (2014). Are Chinese children more compliant? Examination of the cultural difference in observed maternal control and child compliance. *Journal of Cross-Cultural Psychology, 45*(4), 507–533.

Huber, G. A., & Malhotra, N. (2017). Political homophily in social relationships: Evidence from online dating behavior. *The Journal of Politics, 79*(1), 269–283. https://doi.org/10.1086/687533

Huddleston, J., & Ge, X. (2003). Boys at puberty: Psychosocial implications. In C. Hayward (Ed.), *Gender differences at puberty* (pp. 113–134). Cambridge University Press.

Hudson, K. N., Ballou, H. M., & Willoughby, M. T. (2020). Short report: Improving motor competence skills in early childhood has corollary benefits for executive function and numeracy skills. *Developmental Science, 24*(4), e13071. https://doi.org/10.1111/desc.13071

Huelke, D. F. (1998). An overview of anatomical considerations of infants and children in the adult world of automobile safety design. In *Annual Proceedings/Association for the Advancement of Automotive Medicine* (Vol. 42, pp. 93–113). Association for the Advancement of Automotive Medicine.

Huerta, A. H., & Dizon, J. P. M. (2021). Redistributing resources for men of color in higher education. *About Campus,* 10864822211038932.

Hughes, C., & Devine, R. T. (2015). Individual differences in theory of mind from preschool to adolescence: Achievements and directions. *Child Development Perspectives, 9*(3), 149–153. https://doi.org/10.1111/cdep.12124

Hughes, C., Devine, R. T., Ensor, R., Koyasu, M., Mizokawa, A., & Lecce, S. (2014). Lost in translation? Comparing British, Japanese, and Italian children's theory-of-mind performance. *Child Development Research, 2014,* 893492 .

Hughes, C., Devine, R. T., Mesman, J., & Blair, C. (2020). Understanding the terrible twos: A longitudinal investigation of the impact of early executive function and parent–child interactions. *Developmental Science, 23*(6), e12979. https://doi.org/10.1111/desc.12979

Hughes, C., Devine, R. T., & Wang, Z. (2018). Does parental mind-mindedness account for cross-cultural differences in preschoolers' theory of mind? *Child Development, 89*(4), 1296–1310.

Hughes, C., McHarg, G., & White, N. (2018). Sibling influences on prosocial behavior. *Current Opinion in Psychology, 20,* 96–101. https://doi.org/10.1016/j.copsyc.2017.08.015

Hughes, D., Del Toro, J., Harding, J. F., Way, N., & Rarick, J. R. D. (2016a). Trajectories of discrimination across adolescence: Associations with academic, psychological, and behavioral outcomes. *Child Development, 87*(5), 1337–1351. https://doi.org/10.1111/cdev.12591

Hughes, D. L., Watford, J. A., & Del Toro, J. (2016b). Chapter one — A transactional/ecological perspective on ethnic–racial identity, socialization, and discrimination. In S. S. Horn, M. D. Ruck, & L. S. Liben (Eds.), Advances in child development and behavior (Vol. 51, pp. 1–41). JAI. https://www.sciencedirect.com/science/article/abs/pii/S0065240716300209

Hughes, M. L., Agrigoroaei, S., Jeon, M., Bruzzese, M., & Lachman, M. E. (2018). Change in cognitive performance from midlife into old age: Findings from the Midlife in the United States (MIDUS) study. *Journal of the International Neuropsychological Society, 24*(8), 805–820.

Huguley, J. P., Wang, M. T., Vasquez, A. C., & Guo, J. (2019). Parental ethnic–racial socialization practices and the construction of children of color's ethnic–racial identity: A research synthesis and meta-analysis. *Psychological Bulletin, 145*(5), 437.

Huhmann, K. (2020). Menses requires energy: A review of how disordered eating, excessive exercise, and high stress lead to menstrual irregularities. *Clinical Therapeutics, 42*(3), 401–407. https://doi.org/10.1016/j.clinthera.2020.01.016

Hui, B. P., Ng, J. C., Berzaghi, E., Cunningham-Amos, L. A., & Kogan, A. (2020). Rewards of kindness? A meta-analysis of the link between prosociality and well-being. *Psychological Bulletin, 146*(12), 1084.

Huitsing, G., & Monks, C. P. (2018). Who victimizes whom and who defends whom? A multivariate social network analysis of victimization, aggression, and defending in early childhood. *Aggressive Behavior, 44*(4), 394–405.

Hulleman, C. S., Barron, K. E., Kosovich, J. J., & Lazowski, R. A. (2016). Student motivation: Current theories, constructs, and interventions within an expectancy-value framework. In A. A. Lipnevich, F. Preckel, & R. D. Roberts (Eds.), *Psychosocial skills and school systems in the 21st century: Theory, research, and practice* (pp. 241–278). Springer International Publishing. https://doi.org/10.1007/978-3-319-28606-8_10

Hulteen, R. M., Barnett, L. M., True, L., Lander, N. J., Cruz, B. del P., & Lonsdale, C. (2020). Validity and reliability evidence for motor competence assessments in children and adolescents: A systematic review. *Journal of Sports Sciences, 38*(15), 1717–1798. https://doi.org/10.1080/02640414.2020.1756674

Human Rights Campaign Foundation. (2018). *Healthcare Equality Index 2018: Rising to the new standard of promoting equitable and inclusive care for lesbian, gay, bisexual, transgender & queer patients and their families.*

Human Rights Watch. (2019). *"They are making us into slaves, not educating us": How indefinite conscription restricts young people's rights, access to education in Eritrea.* Human Rights Watch. https://www.hrw.org/report/2019/08/08/they-are-making-us-slaves-not-educating-us/how-indefinite-conscription-restricts

Humphreys, K., Guyon-Harris, K., Tibu, F., Nelson, C. A., Fox, N. A., & Zeanah, C. H. (2020). Causal effects of foster care on cognitive ability and adaptive functioning in young adulthood. *Biological Psychiatry, 87*(9), S43–S44. https://doi.org/10.1016/j.biopsych.2020.02.136

Humphreys, K. L., Miron, D., McLaughlin, K. A., Sheridan, M. A., Nelson, C. A., Fox, N. A., & Zeanah, C. H. (2018). Foster care promotes adaptive functioning in early adolescence among children who experienced severe, early deprivation. *Journal of Child Psychology and Psychiatry, and Allied Disciplines, 59*(7), 811–821. https://doi.org/10.1111/jcpp.12865

Hunley, K. L., Cabana, G. S., & Long, J. C. (2016). The apportionment of human diversity revisited. *American Journal of Physical Anthropology, 160*(4), 561–569. https://doi.org/10.1002/ajpa.22899

Hunt, D. M., & Carvalho, L. S. (2016). The genetics of color vision and congenital color deficiencies. In *Human color vision* (pp. 1–32). Springer. https://doi.org/10.1007/978-3-319-44978-4_1

Huntington, C., Stanley, S. M., Doss, B. D., & Rhoades, G. K. (2021). Happy, healthy, and wedded? How the transition to marriage affects mental and physical health. *Journal of Family Psychology.* https://doi.org/10.1037/fam0000913

Huo, M., Fuentecilla, J. L., Birditt, K. S., & Fingerman, K. L. (2019). Empathy and close social ties in late life. *The Journals of Gerontology Series B: Psychological Sciences and Social Sciences, 75*(8), 1648–1657. https://doi.org/10.1093/geronb/gbz044

Huppert, E., Cowell, J. M., Cheng, Y., Contreras-Ibáñez, C., Gomez-Sicard, N., Gonzalez-Gadea, M. L., Huepe, D., Ibanez, A., Lee, K., Mahasneh, R., Malcolm-Smith, S., Salas, N., Selcuk, B., Tungodden, B., Wong, A., Zhou, X., & Decety, J. (2019). The development of children's preferences for equality and equity across 13 individualistic and collectivist cultures. *Developmental Science, 22*(2), e12729.

Hurd, L., & Mahal, R. (2019). "I'm pleased with my body": Older men's perceptions and experiences of their aging bodies. *Men and Masculinities, 24*(2), 228–244. https://doi.org/10.1177/1097184X19879188

Hurd, Y. L., Manzoni, O. J., Pletnikov, M. V., Lee, F. S., Bhattacharyya, S., & Melis, M. (2019). Cannabis and the developing brain: Insights into its long-lasting effects. *Journal of Neuroscience, 39*(42), 8250–8258. https://doi.org/10.1523/JNEUROSCI.1165-19.2019

Hutson, J. A., Taft, J. G., Barocas, S., & Levy, K. (2018). Debiasing desire: Addressing bias & discrimination on intimate platforms. *Proceedings of the ACM on Human-Computer Interaction 2 (CSCW), 88*, 1–18.

Huttenlocher, P. R., & Dabholkar, A. S. (1997). Regional differences in synaptogenesis in human cerebral cortex. *The Journal of Comparative Neurology, 387*(2), 167–178. https://doi.org/10.1002/(SICI)1096-9861(19971020)387:2<167::AID-CNE1>3.0.CO;2-Z

Hutton, J. S., Dudley, J., Horowitz-Kraus, T., DeWitt, T., & Holland, S. K. (2020a). Associations between screen-based media use and brain white matter integrity in preschool-aged children. *JAMA Pediatrics, 174*(1), e193869.

Hutton, J. S., Dudley, J., Horowitz-Kraus, T., DeWitt, T., & Holland, S. K. (2020b). Associations between home literacy environment, brain white matter integrity and cognitive abilities in preschool-age children. *Acta Paediatrica, 109*(7), 1376–1386. https://doi.org/10.1111/apa.15124

Huynh, V. W., & Fuligni, A. J. (2010). Discrimination hurts: The academic, psychological, and physical well-being of adolescents. *Journal of Research on Adolescence, 20*(4), 916–941.

Huynh, V. W., Guan, S.-S. A., Almeida, D. M., McCreath, H., & Fuligni, A. J. (2016). Everyday discrimination and diurnal cortisol during adolescence. *Hormones and Behavior, 80*, 76–81. https://doi.org/10.1016/j.yhbeh.2016.01.009

Hviid, A., Hansen, J. V., Frisch, M., & Melbye, M. (2019). Measles, mumps, rubella vaccination and autism. *Annals of Internal Medicine, 170*(8), 513–520. https://doi.org/10.7326/M18-2101

Hyde, D. C. (2021). The emergence of a brain network for numerical thinking. *Child Development Perspectives.*

Hygen, B. W., Belsky, J., Stenseng, F., Skalicka, V., Kvande, M. N., Zahl-Thanem, T., & Wichstrøm, L. (2020). Time spent gaming and social competence in children: Reciprocal effects across childhood. *Child Development, 91*(3), 861–875.

Hym, C., Forma, V., Anderson, D. I., Provasi, J., Granjon, L., Huet, V., Carpe, E., Teulier, C., Durand, K., Schaal, B., & Barbu-Roth, M. (2021). Newborn crawling and rooting in response to maternal breast odor. *Developmental Science, 24*(3), e13061. https://doi.org/10.1111/desc.13061

Hyman, S. L., Levy, S. E., Myers, S. M., & Council on Children with Disabilities, Section on Developmental and Behavioral Pediatrics. (2020). Identification, evaluation, and management of children with autism spectrum disorder. *Pediatrics, 145*(1), e20193447. https://doi.org/10.1542/peds.2019-3447

Hymel, S., & Swearer, S. M. (2015). Four decades of research on school bullying: An introduction. *American Psychologist, 70*(4), 293.

Hysing, M., Askeland, K. G., La Greca, A. M., Solberg, M. E., Breivik, K., & Sivertsen, B. (2019). Bullying involvement in adolescence: Implications for sleep, mental health, and academic outcomes. *Journal of Interpersonal Violence.* https://doi.org/10.1177/0886260519853409

Ibasho. (2021). https://ibasho.org

Icenogle, G., Steinberg, L., Duell, N., Chein, J., Chang, L., Chaudhary, N., Di Giunta, L., Dodge, K. A., Fanti, K. A., Lansford, J. E., Oburu, P., Pastorelli, C., Skinner, A. T., Sorbring, E., Tapanya, S., Tirado, L. M. U., Alampay, L. P., Al-Hassan, S. M., Takash, H. M. S., & Bacchini, D. (2019). Adolescents' cognitive capacity reaches adult levels prior to their psychosocial maturity: Evidence for a "maturity gap" in a multinational, cross-sectional sample. *Law and*

Human Behavior, 43(1), 69–85. https://doi.org/10.1037/lhb0000315

Iizuka, A., Suzuki, H., Ogawa, S., Kobayashi-Cuya, K. E., Kobayashi, M., Takebayashi, T., & Fujiwara, Y. (2019). Can cognitive leisure activity prevent cognitive decline in older adults? A systematic review of intervention studies. *Geriatrics & Gerontology International, 19*(6), 469–482. https://doi.org/10.1111/ggi.13671

Incollingo Rodriguez, A. C., Tomiyama, A. J., Guardino, C. M., & Dunkel Schetter, C. (2019). Association of weight discrimination during pregnancy and postpartum with maternal postpartum health. *Health Psychology, 38*(3), 226–237. https://doi.org/10.1037/hea0000711

Infurna, F. J., Gerstorf, D., & Lachman, M. E. (2020). Midlife in the 2020s: Opportunities and challenges. *American Psychologist, 75*(4), 470–485. https://doi.org/10.1037/amp0000591

Inhelder, B., & Piaget, J. (1958). *The growth of logical thinking: From childhood to adolescence* (A. Parsons & S. Milgram, Trans.). Basic Books. https://doi.org/10.1037/10034-000

Inhelder, B., & Piaget, J. (1964). *The early growth of logic in the child.* Routledge.

Inselman, A. L., & Slikker, W. (2018). Is there a safe dose of a medication associated with birth defects? In B. Hales, A. Scialli, & M. Tassinari (Eds.), *Teratology primer* (3rd ed.). Society for Birth Defects Research & Prevention.

International Labour Organization (ILO). (2014). *Social protection policy papers: Social protection for older persons: Key policy trends and statistics.*

International Labour Organization (ILO). (2020). *Global employment trends for youth: Technology and the future of jobs.*

International Labour Organization (ILO). (2021). *An update on the youth labour market impact of the COVID-19 crisis* [Statistical brief].

International Labour Office & United Nations Children's Fund (ILO/UNICEF). (2021). *Child Labour: Global estimates 2020, trends and the road forward.*

Ioverno, S., DeLay, D., Martin, C. L., & Hanish, L. D. (2021). Who engages in gender bullying? The role of homophobic name-calling, gender pressure, and gender conformity. *Educational Researcher, 50*(4), 215–224. https://doi.org/10.3102/0013189X20968067

Ip, K. I., Miller, A. L., Karasawa, M., Hirabayashi, H., Kazama, M., Wang, L., Olson, S. L., Kessler, D., & Tardif, T. (2021). Emotion expression and regulation in three cultures: Chinese, Japanese, and American preschoolers' reactions to disappointment. *Journal of Experimental Child Psychology, 201*, 104972. https://doi.org/10.1016/j.jecp.2020.104972

Ipsos. (2021). *Gender identity and sexual orientation differences by generation.*

Iqbal, M. (2021, March). *Tinder revenue and usage statistics.* Business of Apps. https://www.businessofapps.com/data/tinder-statistics/

Irfan, M., Hussain, N. H. N., Noor, N. M., Mohamed, M., & Ismail, S. B. (2020). Sexual abstinence and associated factors among young and middle-aged men: A systematic review. *The Journal of Sexual Medicine, 17*(3), 412–430. https://doi.org/10.1016/j.jsxm.2019.12.003

Irwin, M. R. (2019). Sleep and inflammation: Partners in sickness and in health. *Nature Reviews Immunology, 19*(11), 702–715.

Irwin, V., Zhang, J., Wang, X., Hein, S., Wang, K., Roberts, A., York, C., Barmer, A., Bullock Mann, F., Dilig, R., Parker, S., Nachazel, T., Barnett, M., & Purcell, S. (2021). *Report on the condition of education 2021* (NCES 2021-144). National Center for Education Statistics. https://eric.ed.gov/?id=ED612942

Isaacson, M. J., & Lynch, A. R. (2018). Culturally relevant palliative and end-of-life care for U.S. indigenous populations: An integrative review. *Journal of Transcultural Nursing, 29*(2), 180–191. https://doi.org/10.1177/1043659617720980

Isaacson, M. J., & Minton, M. E. (2018). End-of-life communication. *Advances in Nursing Science, 41*(1), 2–17.

Isham, L., Hewison, A., & Bradbury-Jones, C. (2019). When older people are violent or abusive toward their

family caregiver: A review of mixed-methods research. *Trauma, Violence, & Abuse, 20*(5), 626–637.

Ishida, J. H., Zhang, A. J., Steigerwald, S., Cohen, B. E., Vali, M., & Keyhani, S. (2020). Sources of information and beliefs about the health effects of marijuana. *Journal of General Internal Medicine, 35*(1), 153–159. https://doi.org/10.1007/s11606-019-05335-6

Ishihara, T., Sugasawa, S., Matsuda, Y., & Mizuno, M. (2018). Relationship between sports experience and executive function in 6–12-year-old children: Independence from physical fitness and moderation by gender. *Developmental Science, 21*(3), e12555. https://doi.org/10.1111/desc.12555

Islam, R. M., Bell, R. J., Rizvi, F., & Davis, S. R. (2017). Vasomotor symptoms in women in Asia appear comparable with women in Western countries: A systematic review. *Menopause, 24*(11), 1313–1322.

Ismail, Z., Elbayoumi, H., Fischer, C. E., Hogan, D. B., Millikin, C. P., Schweizer, T., Mortby, M. E., Smith, E. E., Patten, S. B., & Fiest, K. M. (2017). Prevalence of depression in patients with mild cognitive impairment: A systematic review and meta-analysis. *JAMA Psychiatry, 74*(1), 58–67. https://doi.org/10.1001/jamapsychiatry.2016.3162

Israel, A., Brandt, N. D., Grund, S., Köller, O., Lüdtke, O., & Wagner, J. (2021). Personality and psychosocial functioning in early adolescence: Age-differential associations from the self- and parent perspective. *European Journal of Personality.* https://doi.org/10.1177/08902070211005636

Ivanova, K. (2020). My children, your children, our children, and my well-being: Life satisfaction of "empty nest" biological parents and stepparents. *Journal of Happiness Studies, 21*(2), 613–633. https://doi.org/10.1007/s10902-019-00097-8

Iversen, T. N., Larsen, L., & Solem, P. E. (2009). A conceptual analysis of ageism. *Nordic Psychology, 61*(3), 4–22.

Ivey-Stephenson, A. Z., Demissie, Z., Crosby, A. E., Stone, D. M., Gaylor, E., Wilkins, N., Lowry, R., & Brown, M. (2020). Suicidal ideation and behaviors among high school students—youth risk behavior survey, United States, 2019. *Morbidity and Mortality Weekly Report Supplements, 69*(1), 47–55. https://doi.org/10.15585/mmwr.su6901a6

Jaacks, L. M., Vandevijvere, S., Pan, A., McGowan, C. J., Wallace, C., Imamura, F., Mozaffarian, D., Swinburn, B., & Ezzati, M. (2019). The obesity transition: Stages of the global epidemic. *The Lancet. Diabetes & Endocrinology, 7*(3), 231–240. https://doi.org/10.1016/S2213-8587(19)30026-9

Jablonski, N. G. (2018). Eye color. In *The international encyclopedia of biological anthropology* (pp. 1–2). Wiley. https://doi.org/10.1002/9781118584538.ieba0541

Jackman, K., Kreuze, E. J., Caceres, B. A., & Schnall, R. (2020). Bullying and peer victimization of minority youth: Intersections of sexual identity and race/ethnicity. *Journal of School Health, 90*(5), 368–377. https://doi.org/10.1111/josh.12883

Jackson, C. K., Porter, S. C., Easton, J. Q., Blanchard, A., & Kiguel, S. (2020). School effects on socioemotional development, school-based arrests, and educational attainment. *American Economic Review: Insights, 2*(4), 491–508.

Jackson, F. M., Rashied-Henry, K., Braveman, P., Dominguez, T. P., Ramos, D., Maseru, N., Darity, W., Waddell, L., Warne, D., Legaz, G., Gupta, R., & James, A. (2020). A prematurity collaborative birth equity consensus statement for mothers and babies. *Maternal and Child Health Journal, 24*(10), 1231–1237. https://doi.org/10.1007/s10995-020-02960-0

Jackson, G. L., Trail, T. E., Kennedy, D. P., Williamson, H. C., Bradbury, T. N., & Karney, B. R. (2016). The salience and severity of relationship problems among low-income couples. *Journal of Family Psychology: JFP: Journal of the Division of Family Psychology of the American Psychological Association (Division 43), 30*(1), 2–11. https://doi.org/10.1037/fam0000158

Jackson, J. S., Hudson, D., Kershaw, K., Mezuk, B., Rafferty, J., & Tuttle, K. K. (2011). Discrimination, chronic stress, and mortality among black Americans: A life course framework. In R. G. Rogers & E. M.

Crimmins (Eds.), *International handbook of adult mortality* (pp. 311–328). Springer Netherlands. https://doi.org/10.1007/978-90-481-9996-9_15

Jackson, L., Pascalis, L. D., Harrold, J., & Fallon, V. (2021). Guilt, shame, and postpartum infant feeding outcomes: A systematic review. *Maternal & Child Nutrition, 17*(3), e13141. https://doi.org/10.1111/mcn.13141

Jackson, M. (2020). 2019 Wilkins–Bernal–Medawar lecture. Life begins at 40: The demographic and cultural roots of the midlife crisis. *Notes and Records: The Royal Society Journal of the History of Science, 74*(3), 345–364. https://doi.org/10.1098/rsnr.2020.0008

Jackson, M. L., Williams, W. L., Rafacz, S. D., & Friman, P. C. (2020). Encopresis and enuresis. In P. Sturmey (Ed.), *Functional analysis in clinical treatment* (2nd ed., pp. 199–225). Academic Press. https://doi.org/10.1016/B978-0-12-805469-7.00009-7

Jackson, P. A., Pialoux, V., Corbett, D., Drogos, L., Erickson, K. I., Eskes, G. A., & Poulin, M. J. (2016). Promoting brain health through exercise and diet in older adults: A physiological perspective. *The Journal of Physiology, 594*(16), 4485–4498. https://doi.org/10.1113/JP271270

Jackson, S. E., Hackett, R. A., Grabovac, I., Smith, L., & Steptoe, A. (2019). Perceived discrimination, health and wellbeing among middle-aged and older lesbian, gay and bisexual people: A prospective study. *PLOS ONE, 14*(5), e0216497. https://doi.org/10.1371/journal.pone.0216497

Jacob, B. A. (2017). *What we know about career and technical education in high school.* Brookings.

Jacob, M. E., Yee, L. M., Diehr, P. H., Arnold, A. M., Thielke, S. M., Chaves, P. H. M., Del Gobbo, L., Hirsch, C., Siscovick, D., & Newman, A. B. (2016). Can a healthy lifestyle compress the disabled period in older adults? *Journal of the American Geriatrics Society, 64*(10), 1952–1961. https://doi.org/10.1111/jgs.14314

Jacobsen, J. C., Tran, K. M., Jackson, V. A., & Rubin, E. B. (2020). Case 19-2020: A 74-year-old man with acute respiratory failure and unclear goals of care. *New England Journal of Medicine, 382*(25), 2450–2457. https://doi.org/10.1056/NEJMcpc2002419

Jacobson, L. A., Crocetti, D., Dirlikov, B., Slifer, K., Denckla, M. B., Mostofsky, S. H., & Mahone, E. M. (2018). Anomalous brain development is evident in preschoolers with attention-deficit/hyperactivity disorder. *Journal of the International Neuropsychological Society, 24*(6), 531–539. https://doi.org/10.1017/S1355617718000103

Jahn, K. (2019). The aging vestibular system: Dizziness and imbalance in the elderly. *Vestibular Disorders, 82*, 143–149. https://doi.org/10.1159/000490283

Jahoda, G. (2012). Critical reflections on some recent definitions of "culture." *Culture & Psychology, 18*(3), 289–303. https://doi.org/10.1177/1354067X12446229

Jakubowski, K. P., Cundiff, J. M., & Matthews, K. A. (2018). Cumulative childhood adversity and adult cardiometabolic disease: A meta-analysis. *Health Psychology, 37*(8), 701–715. https://doi.org/10.1037/hea0000637

Jalal, H., Buchanich, J. M., Roberts, M. S., Balmert, L. C., Zhang, K., & Burke, D. S. (2018). Changing dynamics of the drug overdose epidemic in the United States from 1979 through 2016. *Science, 361*(6408).

Jalovaara, M., & Kulu, H. (2018). Separation risk over union duration: An immediate itch? *European Sociological Review, 34*(5), 486–500.

James, C., Davis, K., Charmaraman, L., Konrath, S., Slovak, P., Weinstein, E., & Yarosh, L. (2017). Digital life and youth well-being, social connectedness, empathy, and narcissism. *Pediatrics, 140*(Supplement 2), S71–S75. https://doi.org/10.1542/peds.2016-1758F

James, S. L., Abate, D., Abate, K. H., Abay, S. M., Abbafati, C., Abbasi, N., & Briggs, A. M. (2018). Global, regional, and national incidence, prevalence, and years lived with disability for 354 diseases and injuries for 195 countries and territories, 1990–2017: A systematic analysis for the Global Burden of Disease Study 2017. *The Lancet, 392*(10159), 1789–1858.

James-Todd, T. M., Chiu, Y. H., & Zota, A. R. (2016). Racial/ethnic disparities in environmental endocrine disrupting chemicals and women's reproductive health outcomes: Epidemiological examples across the life course. *Current Epidemiology Reports, 3*(2), 161–180.

James-Todd, T., Tehranifar, P., Rich-Edwards, J., Titievsky, L., & Terry, M. B. (2010). The impact of socioeconomic status across early life on age at menarche among a racially diverse population of girls. *Annals of Epidemiology, 20*(11), 836–842. https://doi.org/10.1016/j.annepidem.2010.08.006

Janevic, T., Osypuk, T., Stojanovski, K., Jankovic, J., Gundersen, D., & Rogers, M. (2017). Associations between racial discrimination, smoking during pregnancy and low birthweight among Roma. *European Journal of Public Health, 27*(3), 410–415. https://doi.org/10.1093/eurpub/ckw214

Jang, H., & Reardon, S. F. (2019). States as sites of educational (in)equality: State contexts and the socioeconomic achievement gradient. *AERA Open, 5*(3), 2332858419872459. https://doi.org/10.1177/2332858419872459

Jang, S.-N., Avendano, M., & Kawachi, I. (2012). Informal caregiving patterns in Korea and European countries: A cross-national comparison. *Asian Nursing Research, 6*(1), 19–26. https://doi.org/10.1016/j.anr.2012.02.002

Jang, Y., Park, J., Choi, E. Y., Cho, Y. J., Park, N. S., & Chiriboga, D. A. (2021). Social isolation in Asian Americans: Risks associated with socio-demographic, health, and immigration factors. *Ethnicity & Health*, 1–14.

Janhsen, A., Golla, H., Mantell, P., & Woopen, C. (2019). Transforming spirituality through aging: Coping and distress in the search for meaning in very old age. *Journal of Religion, Spirituality & Aging, 33*(1), 38–53. https://doi.org/10.1080/15528030.2019.1676362

Janis, J. A., Ahrens, K. A., & Ziller, E. C. (2019). Female age at first sexual intercourse by rural–urban residence and birth cohort. *Women's Health Issues, 29*(6), 489–498. https://doi.org/10.1016/j.whi.2019.07.004

Jankowiak, W., & Nelson, A. J. (2021). The state of ethnological research on love: A critical review. In C.-H. Mayer & E. Vanderheiden (Eds.), *International handbook of love: Transcultural and transdisciplinary perspectives* (pp. 23–39). Springer Nature.

Jankowiak, W., Shen, Y., Yao, S., Wang, C., & Volsche, S. (2015). Investigating love's universal attributes: A research report from China. *Cross-Cultural Research, 49*(4), 422–436. https://doi.org/10.1177/1069397115594355

Janssen, G., van Aken, L., Mey, H. D., Witteman, C., & Egger, J. (2014). Decline of executive function in a clinical population: Age, psychopathology, and test performance on the Cambridge Neuropsychological Test Automated Battery (CANTAB). *Applied Neuropsychology: Adult, 21*(3), 210–219. https://doi.org/10.1080/09084282.2013.793191

Janssen, L. H. C., Elzinga, B. M., Verkuil, B., Hillegers, M. H. J., & Keijsers, L. (2021). The link between parental support and adolescent negative mood in daily life: Between-person heterogeneity in within-person processes. *Journal of Youth and Adolescence, 50*(2), 271–285. https://doi.org/10.1007/s10964-020-01323-w

Janssen, S. M., & Haque, S. (2018). The transmission and stability of cultural life scripts: A cross-cultural study. *Memory, 26*(1), 131–143.

Janssen, X., Martin, A., Hughes, A. R., Hill, C. M., Kotronoulas, G., & Hesketh, K. R. (2020). Associations of screen time, sedentary time and physical activity with sleep in under 5s: A systematic review and meta-analysis. *Sleep Medicine Reviews, 49*, 101226. https://doi.org/10.1016/j.smrv.2019.101226

Jaramillo, J. M., Rendón, M. I., Muñoz, L., Weis, M., & Trommsdorff, G. (2017). Children's self-regulation in cultural contexts: The role of parental socialization theories, goals, and practices. *Frontiers in Psychology, 8*, 923. https://doi.org/10.3389/fpsyg.2017.00923

Jarrett, O. (2016). Doll studies as racial assessments: A historical look at racial attitudes and school desegregation. In M. M. Patte & J. A. Sutterby (Eds.), *Celebrating 40 years of play research: Connecting our past, present, and future* (pp. 19–38). Hamilton Books. https://www.google.com/books/edition/Celebrating_40_Years_of_Play_Research/3VvnDAAAQBAJ?hl=en&gbpv=1&dq=Jarrett,+2016+doll&pg=PA19&printsec=frontcover

Javdani, S., Sadeh, N., White, H. I., Emerson, E., Houck, C., Brown, L. K., & Donenberg, G. R. (2019). Contextualizing pubertal development: The combination of sexual partners' age and girls' pubertal development confers risk for externalizing but not internalizing symptoms among girls in therapeutic day schools. *Journal of Adolescence, 71*, 84–90. https://doi.org/10.1016/j.adolescence.2019.01.001

Jebb, A. T., Morrison, M., Tay, L., & Diener, E. (2020). Subjective well-being around the world: Trends and predictors across the life span. *Psychological Science, 31*(3), 293–305. https://doi.org/10.1177/0956797619898826

Jebb, A. T., Tay, L., Diener, E., & Oishi, S. (2018). Happiness, income satiation and turning points around the world. *Nature Human Behaviour, 2*(1), 33–38. https://doi.org/10.1038/s41562-017-0277-0

Jee, E., Misra, J., & Murray-Close, M. (2019). Motherhood penalties in the U.S., 1986–2014. *Journal of Marriage and Family, 81*(2), 434–449. https://doi.org/10.1111/jomf.12543

Jelenkovic, A., Sund, R., Yokoyama, Y., Latvala, A., Sugawara, M., Tanaka, M., Matsumoto, S., Freitas, D. L., Maia, J. A., Knafo-Noam, A., Mankuta, D., Abramson, L., Ji, F., Ning, F., Pang, Z., Rebato, E., Saudino, K. J., Cutler, T. L., Hopper, J. L., … Silventoinen, K. (2020). Genetic and environmental influences on human height from infancy through adulthood at different levels of parental education. *Scientific Reports, 10*(1), 7974. https://doi.org/10.1038/s41598-020-64883-8

Jellison, S., Roberts, W., Bowers, A., Combs, T., Beaman, J., Wayant, C., & Vassar, M. (2020). Evaluation of spin in abstracts of papers in psychiatry and psychology journals. *BMJ Evidence-Based Medicine, 25*(5), 178–181. https://doi.org/10.1136/bmjebm-2019-111176

Jennings, M. K., & Zhang, N. (2005). Generations, political status, and collective memories in the Chinese countryside. *The Journal of Politics, 67*(4), 1164–1189. https://doi.org/10.1111/j.1468-2508.2005.00355.x

Jennings, W., Stoker, G., Willis, H., Valgardsson, V., Gaskell, J., Devine, D., McKay, L., & Mills, M. C. (2021). Lack of trust and social media echo chambers predict COVID-19 vaccine hesitancy. *MedRxiv*, 2021-01. https://doi.org/10.1101/2021.01.26.21250246

Jensen, A. C., Nielson, M. K., & Yorgason, J. B. (2020). The longest-lasting relationship: Patterns of contact and well-being among mid- to later-life siblings. *The Journals of Gerontology: Series B, 75*(10), 2240–2249. https://doi.org/10.1093/geronb/gbz083

Jensen, L. A., & Dost-Gözkan, A. (2015). Adolescent-parent relations in Asian Indian and Salvadoran immigrant families: A cultural-developmental analysis of autonomy, authority, conflict, and cohesion. *Journal of Research on Adolescence, 25*(2), 340–351. https://doi.org/10.1111/jora.12116

Jensen, T. M., & Sanner, C. (2021). A scoping review of research on well-being across diverse family structures: Rethinking approaches for understanding contemporary families. *Journal of Family Theory & Review, 13*(4), 463–495.

Jeon, M., Dimitriou, D., & Halstead, E. J. (2021). A systematic review on cross-cultural comparative studies of sleep in young populations: The roles of cultural factors. *International Journal of Environmental Research and Public Health, 18*(4), 2005.

Jepsen, C., Mueser, P., & Troske, K. (2017). Second chance for high school dropouts? A regression discontinuity analysis of postsecondary educational returns to the GED. *Journal of Labor Economics, 35*(S1), S273–S304.

Jerrim, J. (2014). The unrealistic educational expectations of high school pupils: Is America exceptional? Unrealistic educational expectations. *The Sociological Quarterly, 55*(1), 196–231. https://doi.org/10.1111/tsq.12049

Jeste, D. V., Lee, E. E., & Cacioppo, S. (2020). Battling the modern behavioral epidemic of loneliness: Suggestions for research and interventions. *JAMA Psychiatry, 77*(6), 553–554. https://doi.org/10.1001/jamapsychiatry.2020.0027

Jeste, D. V., Lee, E. E., Cassidy, C., Caspari, R., Gagneux, P., Glorioso, D., Miller, B. L., Semendeferi, K., Vogler, C., Nusbaum, H., & Blazer, D. (2019). The new science of practical wisdom. *Perspectives in Biology and Medicine, 62*(2), 216–236. https://doi.org/10.1353/pbm.2019.0011

Jewell, J. A., & Brown, C. S. (2014). Relations among gender typicality, peer relations, and mental health during early adolescence. *Social Development, 23*(1), 137–156.

Jewell, T., Gardner, T., Susi, K., Watchorn, K., Coopey, E., Simic, M., Fonagy, P., & Eisler, I. (2019). Attachment measures in middle childhood and adolescence: A systematic review of measurement properties. *Clinical Psychology Review, 68,* 71–82. https://doi.org/10.1016/j.cpr.2018.12.004

Jhang, Y., & Oller, D. K. (2017). Emergence of functional flexibility in infant vocalizations of the first 3 months. *Frontiers in Psychology, 8,* 300. https://doi.org/10.3389/fpsyg.2017.00300

Jiang, X., Dai, X., Goldblatt, S., Buescher, C., Cusack, T. M., Matson, D. O., & Pickering, L. K. (1998). Pathogen transmission in child care settings studied by using a cauliflower virus DNA as a surrogate marker. *The Journal of Infectious Diseases, 177*(4), 881–888. https://doi.org/10.1086/515253

Jiang, Y., Ekono, M., & Skinner, C. (2015). *Basic facts about low-income children: Children under 18 years, 2013.* National Center for Children in Poverty.

Jianhui, S. (2017, September 8). Raised by grandparents. *The World of Chinese.*

Jiao, J., & Segrin, C. (2021). Parent–emerging-adult-child attachment and overparenting. *Family Relations, 70*(3), 859–865. https://doi.org/10.1111/fare.12473

Jilla, A. M., Johnson, C. E., & Huntington-Klein, N. (2020). Hearing aid affordability in the United States. *Disability and Rehabilitation: Assistive Technology,* 1–7. https://doi.org/10.1080/17483107.2020.1822449

Jimenez, G., Tan, W. S., Virk, A. K., Low, C. K., Car, J., & Ho, A. H. Y. (2018). Overview of systematic reviews of advance care planning: Summary of evidence and global lessons. *Journal of Pain and Symptom Management, 56*(3), 436–459.

Jimenez, M. E., Wade, R., Lin, Y., Morrow, L. M., & Reichman, N. E. (2016). Adverse experiences in early childhood and kindergarten outcomes. *Pediatrics, 137*(2), e20151839.

Jiménez, M. G., Montorio, I., & Izal, M. (2017). The association of age, sense of control, optimism, and self-esteem with emotional distress. *Developmental Psychology, 53*(7), 1398.

Jiménez-Pavón, D., Carbonell-Baeza, A., & Lavie, C. J. (2019). Promoting the assessment of physical activity and cardiorespiratory fitness in assessing the role of vascular risk on cognitive decline in older adults. *Frontiers in Physiology, 10,* 670.

Jin, J., & Rounds, J. (2012). Stability and change in work values: A meta-analysis of longitudinal studies. *Journal of Vocational Behavior, 80*(2), 326–339. https://doi.org/10.1016/j.jvb.2011.10.007

Jin, M. K., Jacobvitz, D., Hazen, N., & Jung, S. H. (2011). Maternal sensitivity and infant attachment security in Korea: Cross-cultural validation of the strange situation. *Attachment & Human Development, 14*(1), 33–44. https://doi.org/10.1080/14616734.2012.636656

Joel, S., Eastwick, P. W., Allison, C. J., Arriaga, X. B., Baker, Z. G., Bar-Kalifa, E., Bergeron, S., Birnbaum, G. E., Brock, R. L., Brumbaugh, C. C., Carmichael, C. L., Chen, S., Clarke, J., Cobb, R. J., Coolsen, M. K., Davis, J., de Jong, D. C., Debrot, A., DeHaas, E. C., … Wolf, S. (2020). Machine learning uncovers the most robust self-report predictors of relationship quality across 43 longitudinal couples studies. *Proceedings of the National Academy of Sciences, 117*(32), 19061–19071. https://doi.org/10.1073/pnas.1917036117

Joel, S., Eastwick, P. W., & Finkel, E. J. (2017). Is romantic desire predictable? Machine learning applied to initial romantic attraction. *Psychological Science, 28*(10), 1478–1489. https://doi.org/10.1177/0956797617714580

Johander, E., Turunen, T., Garandeau, C. F., & Salmivalli, C. (2021). Different approaches to address bullying in KiVa schools: Adherence to guidelines, strategies implemented, and outcomes obtained. *Prevention Science, 22*(3), 299–310. https://doi.org/10.1007/s11121-020-01178-4

Jóhannesdóttir, S., & Hjörleifsdóttir, E. (2018). Communication is more than just a conversation: Family members' satisfaction with end-of-life care. *International Journal of Palliative Nursing, 24*(10), 483–491. https://doi.org/10.12968/ijpn.2018.24.10.483

Johns, M. M., Lowry, R., Andrzejewski, J., Barrios, L. C., Demissie, Z., McManus, T., Rasberry, C. N., Robin, L., & Underwood, J. M. (2019). Transgender identity and experiences of violence victimization, substance use, suicide risk, and sexual risk behaviors among high school students—19 states and large urban school districts, 2017. *Morbidity and Mortality Weekly Report, 68*(3), 67–71. https://doi.org/10.15585/mmwr.mm6803a3

Johnson, A., Kirk, R., Rosenblum, K. L., & Muzik, M. (2015). Enhancing breastfeeding rates among African American women: A systematic review of current psychosocial interventions. *Breastfeeding Medicine, 10*(1), 45–62. https://doi.org/10.1089/bfm.2014.0023

Johnson, J. D., Green, C. A., Vladutiu, C. J., & Manuck, T. A. (2020). Racial disparities in prematurity persist among women of high socioeconomic status. *American Journal of Obstetrics & Gynecology MFM, 2*(3), 100104.

Johnson, M. H., & de Haan, M. (2015). *Developmental cognitive neuroscience: An introduction.* John Wiley & Sons.

Johnson, M. K., & Monserud, M. A. (2012). Work value development from adolescence to adulthood. *Advances in Life Course Research, 17*(2), 45–58. https://doi.org/10.1016/j.alcr.2012.02.002

Johnson, R. M., Alvarado, R. E., & Rosinger, K. O. (2021). What's the "problem" of considering criminal history in college admissions? A critical analysis of "ban the box" policies in Louisiana and Maryland. *The Journal of Higher Education, 92*(5), 704–734. https://doi.org/10.1080/00221546.2020.1870849

Johnson, R. W., & Gosselin, P. (2018). *How secure is employment at older ages?* Urban Institute.

Johnson, S. B., Riis, J. L., & Noble, K. G. (2016). State of the art review: Poverty and the developing brain. *Pediatrics,* peds.2015-3075. https://doi.org/10.1542/peds.2015-3075

Johnson, T. J., Winger, D. G., Hickey, R. W., Switzer, G. E., Miller, E., Nguyen, M. B., Saladino, R. A., & Hausmann, L. R. M. (2017). Comparison of physician implicit racial bias toward adults versus children. *Academic Pediatrics, 17*(2), 120–126. https://doi.org/10.1016/j.acap.2016.08.010

Johnston-Goodstar, K., & VeLure Roholt, R. (2017). "Our kids aren't dropping out; they're being pushed out": Native American students and racial microaggressions in schools. *Journal of Ethnic & Cultural Diversity in Social Work, 26*(1–2), 30–47. https://doi.org/10.1080/15313204.2016.1263818

Johnston-Robledo, I., & Chrisler, J. C. (2013). The menstrual mark: Menstruation as social stigma. *Sex Roles, 68*(1), 9–18.

Joly, Y., Dalpé, G., Dupras, C., Bévière-Boyer, B., de Paor, A., Dove, E. S., Granados Moreno, P., Ho, C. W. L., Ho, C.-H., Ó Cathaoir, K., Kato, K., Kim, H., Song, L., Minssen, T., Nicolás, P., Otlowski, M., Prince, A. E. R., P. S. Nair, A. P. S., Van Hoyweghen, I., … Bombard, Y. (2020). Establishing the international Genetic Discrimination Observatory. *Nature Genetics, 52*(5), 466–468. https://doi.org/10.1038/s41588-020-0606-5

Jonas, D. E., Amick, H. R., Feltner, C., Weber, R. P., Arvanitis, M., Stine, A., Lux, L., & Harris, R. P. (2017). Screening for obstructive sleep apnea in adults: Evidence report and systematic review for the US preventive services task force. *JAMA, 317*(4), 415–433. https://doi.org/10.1001/jama.2016.19635

Jonas, J. B., Cheung, C. M. G., & Panda-Jonas, S. (2017). Updates on the epidemiology of age-related macular degeneration. *The Asia-Pacific Journal of Ophthalmology, 6*(6), 493–497. https://doi.org/10.22608/APO.2017251

Jonason, P. K., Girgis, M., & Milne-Home, J. (2017). The exploitive mating strategy of the dark triad traits: Tests of rape-enabling attitudes. *Archives of Sexual Behavior, 46*(3), 697–706. https://doi.org/10.1007/s10508-017-0937-1

Jones, C. R. G., Simonoff, E., Baird, G., Pickles, A., Marsden, A. J. S., Tregay, J., Happé, F., & Charman, T. (2018). The association between theory of mind, executive function, and the symptoms of autism spectrum disorder. *Autism Research, 11*(1), 95–109. https://doi.org/10.1002/aur.1873

Jones, D. E., Greenberg, M., & Crowley, M. (2015). Early social-emotional functioning and public health: The relationship between kindergarten social competence and future wellness. *American Journal of Public Health, 105*(11), 2283–2290. https://doi.org/10.2105/AJPH.2015.302630

Jones, J., & Mosher, W. D. (2013). *Fathers' involvement with their children: United States, 2006–2010* (National Health Statistics Reports No. 71). U.S. Department of Health and Human Services.

Jones, J. M. (2021, February 24). *LGBT identification rises to 5.6% in latest U.S. estimate.* Gallup.com. https://news.gallup.com/poll/329708/lgbt-identification-rises-latest-estimate.aspx

Jones, J. S., Milton, F., Mostazir, M., & Adlam, A. R. (2020). The academic outcomes of working memory and metacognitive strategy training in children: A double-blind randomized controlled trial. *Developmental Science, 23*(4), e12870. https://doi.org/10.1111/desc.12870

Jones, L. (2018). Commentary: 25 years of community partnered participatory research. *Ethnicity & Disease, 28*(Suppl 2), 291–294. https://doi.org/10.18865/ed.28.S2.291

Jones, M. (2019, December 19). The movement to bring death closer. *The New York Times.* https://www.nytimes.com/2019/12/19/magazine/home-funeral.html

Jones, M. J., Goodman, S. J., & Kobor, M. S. (2015). DNA methylation and healthy human aging. *Aging Cell, 14*(6), 924–932. https://doi.org/10.1111/acel.12349

Jones, N. A., & Sloan, A. (2018). Neurohormones and temperament interact during infant development. *Philosophical Transactions of the Royal Society B: Biological Sciences, 373*(1744), 20170159. https://doi.org/10.1098/rstb.2017.0159

Jones, S. L., Dufoix, R., Laplante, D. P., Elgbeili, G., Patel, R., Chakravarty, M. M., King, S., & Pruessner, J. C. (2019). Larger amygdala volume mediates the association between prenatal maternal stress and higher levels of externalizing behaviors: Sex specific effects in Project Ice Storm. *Frontiers in Human Neuroscience, 13.* https://doi.org/10.3389/fnhum.2019.00144

Jones-Eversley, S. D., & Rice, J. (2020). A call for epidemiology and thanatology to address the dying, death, and grief pipeline among Blacks in the United States. *Death Studies,* 1–8. https://doi.org/10.1080/07481187.2020.1721618

Jong, J. (2021). Death anxiety and religion. *Current Opinion in Psychology, 40,* 40–44. https://doi.org/10.1016/j.copsyc.2020.08.004

Jonsson, H., Magnusdottir, E., Eggertsson, H. P., Stefansson, O. A., Arnadottir, G. A., Eiriksson, O., Zink, F., Helgason, E. A., Jonsdottir, I., Gylfason, A., Jonasdottir, A., Jonasdottir, A., Beyter, D., Steingrimsdottir, T., Norddahl, G. L., Magnusson, O. T., Masson, G., Halldorsson, B. V., Thorsteinsdottir, U., … Stefansson, K. (2021). Differences between germline genomes of monozygotic twins. *Nature Genetics, 53*(1), 27–34. https://doi.org/10.1038/s41588-020-00755-1

Jordá, V., & Niño-Zarazúa, M. (2017). *Global inequality in length of life: 1950–2015* [Working paper]. United Nations University.

Jordan, K., & Tseris, E. (2018). Locating, understanding and celebrating disability: Revisiting Erikson's "stages." *Feminism & Psychology, 28*(3), 427–444. https://doi.org/10.1177/0959353517705400

Jordan, M., & Sullivan, K. (2017, September 30). The new reality of old age in America. *Washington Post.* https://www.washingtonpost.com/graphics/2017/national/seniors-financial-insecurity/

Jordan-Marsh, M., & Harden, J. T. (2005). Fictive kin: Friends as family supporting older adults as they age. *Journal of Gerontological Nursing, 31*(2), 24–31; quiz 58–59. https://doi.org/10.3928/0098-9134-20050201-07

Jordan-Young, R. M., & Karkazis, K. (2019). *Testosterone: An unauthorized biography.* Harvard University Press.

Jovanovic, T., Vance, L. A., Cross, D., Knight, A. K., Kilaru, V., Michopoulos, V., Klengel, T., & Smith, A. K. (2017). Exposure to violence accelerates epigenetic aging in children. *Scientific Reports, 7*(1), 8962. https://doi.org/10.1038/s41598-017-09235-9

Joyner, K., Manning, W., & Bogle, R. (2017). Gender and the stability of same-sex and different-sex relationships among young adults. *Demography, 54*(6), 2351–2374.

Jozkowski, K. N., & Wiersma-Mosley, J. D. (2017). The Greek system: How gender inequality and class privilege perpetuate rape culture. *Family Relations, 66*(1), 89–103.

Juang, L. P., & Cookston, J. T. (2009). A longitudinal study of family obligation and depressive symptoms among Chinese American adolescents. *Journal of Family Psychology, 23*(3), 396–404. https://doi.org/10.1037/a0015814

Juang, L. P., Syed, M., Cookston, J. T., Wang, Y., & Kim, S. Y. (2012). Acculturation-based and everyday family conflict in Chinese American families. *New Directions for Child and Adolescent Development, 2012*(135), 13–34. https://doi.org/10.1002/cd.20002

Juarez, E. J., Castrellon, J. J., Green, M. A., Crawford, J. L., Seaman, K. L., Smith, C. T., Dang, L. C., Matuskey, D., Morris, E. D., Cowan, R. L., Zald, D. H., & Samanez-Larkin, G. R. (2019). Reproducibility of the correlative triad among aging, dopamine receptor availability, and cognition. *Psychology and Aging, 34*(7), 921–932. https://doi.org/10.1037/pag0000403

Juárez, F., & Gayet, C. (2014). Transitions to adulthood in developing countries. *Annual Review of Sociology, 40*(1), 521–538. https://doi.org/10.1146/annurev-soc-052914-085540

Juhasz, D., Nemeth, D., & Janacsek, K. (2019). Is there more room to improve? The lifespan trajectory of procedural learning and its relationship to the between- and within-group differences in average response times. *PLOS ONE, 14*(7), e0215116. https://doi.org/10.1371/journal.pone.0215116

Jutten, R. J., Dicks, E., Vermaat, L., Barkhof, F., Scheltens, P., Tijms, B. M., & Sikkes, S. A. (2019). Impairment in complex activities of daily living is related to neurodegeneration in Alzheimer's disease–specific regions. *Neurobiology of Aging, 75*, 109–116.

Juvonen, J., & Graham, S. (2014). Bullying in schools: The power of bullies and the plight of victims. *Annual Review of Psychology, 65*(1), 159–185. https://doi.org/10.1146/annurev-psych-010213-115030

Juvonen, J., & Schacter, H. L. (2018). Bullying in school and online contexts: Social dominance, bystander compliance, and social pain of victims. In A. Rutland, D. Nesdale, & C. S. Brown (Eds.), *The Wiley-Blackwell handbook of group processes in children and adolescents* (pp. 317–332). Wiley-Blackwell.

Juvonen, J., Schacter, H. L., Sainio, M., & Salmivalli, C. (2016). Can a school-wide bullying prevention program improve the plight of victims? Evidence for risk × intervention effects. *Journal of Consulting and Clinical Psychology, 84*(4), 334–344. https://doi.org/10.1037/ccp0000078

Kabay, S., Wolf, S., & Yoshikawa, H. (2017). "So that his mind will open": Parental perceptions of early childhood education in urbanizing Ghana. *International Journal of Educational Development, 57*, 44–53.

Kadhim, H., Deltenre, P., Segers, V., & Sébire, G. (2012). Selective expression of a neuromodulatory cytokine (IL-2) in specific brainstem neurovegetative centers: A possible final common neuro-molecular pathway in dying patients. *Medical Hypotheses, 78*(6), 793–795.

Kaestle, C. E. (2019). Sexual orientation trajectories based on sexual attractions, partners, and identity: A longitudinal investigation from adolescence through young adulthood using a U.S. representative sample. *The Journal of Sex Research, 56*(7), 811–826. https://doi.org/10.1080/00224499.2019.1577351

Kaffenberger, M. (2019, May 17). *What have we learned about the learning crisis?* Brookings. https://www.brookings.edu/blog/education-plus-development/2019/05/17/what-have-we-learned-about-the-learning-crisis/

Kagan, J. (2018). Perspectives on two temperamental biases. *Philosophical Transactions of the Royal Society B: Biological Sciences, 373*(1744), 20170158. https://doi.org/10.1098/rstb.2017.0158

Kågesten, A., Gibbs, S., Blum, R. W., Moreau, C., Chandra-Mouli, V., Herbert, A., & Amin, A. (2016). Understanding factors that shape gender attitudes in early adolescence globally: A mixed-methods systematic review. *PLOS ONE, 11*(6), e0157805. https://doi.org/10.1371/journal.pone.0157805

Kagitcibasi, C. (2017). Doing psychology with a cultural lens: A half-century journey. *Perspectives on Psychological Science, 12*(5), 824–832.

Kahan, S., & Manson, J. E. (2017). Nutrition counseling in clinical practice: How clinicians can do better. *JAMA, 318*(12), 1101–1102. https://doi.org/10.1001/jama.2017.10434

Kahana, E., Kahana, B., Bhatta, T., Langendoerfer, K. B., Lee, J. E., & Lekhak, N. (2020). Racial differences in future care planning in late life. *Ethnicity & Health, 25*(4), 625–637. https://doi.org/10.1080/13557858.2019.1573974

Kahn, R. L., & Antonucci, T. C. (1980). Convoys over the life course: Attachment, roles, and social support. In P. B. Baltes & O. G. Brim (Eds.), *Life-span development and behavior* (pp. 253–267). Academic Press.

Kail, R. V., & Ferrer, E. (2007). Processing speed in childhood and adolescence: Longitudinal models for examining developmental change. *Child Development, 78*(6), 1760–1770. https://doi.org/10.1111/j.1467-8624.2007.01088.x

Kajimoto, T. (2019, April 10). Retiring late: As pensions underwhelm, more Japanese opt to prolong employment. *Reuters.* https://www.reuters.com/article/us-japan-economy-retirement/retiring-late-as-pensions-underwhelm-more-japanese-opt-to-prolong-employment-idUSKCN1RM0GP.

Kajonius, P. J., & Carlander, A. (2017). Who gets ahead in life? Personality traits and childhood background in economic success. *Journal of Economic Psychology, 59*, 164–170.

Kajonius, P., & Mac Giolla, E. (2017). Personality traits across countries: Support for similarities rather than differences. *PLoS ONE, 12*(6), e0179646. https://doi.org/10.1371/journal.pone.0179646

Kalaria, R. N. (2016). Neuropathological diagnosis of vascular cognitive impairment and vascular dementia with implications for Alzheimer's disease. *Acta Neuropathologica, 131*(5), 659–685.

Kalenzaga, S., Lamidey, V., Ergis, A. M., Clarys, D., & Piolino, P. (2016). The positivity bias in aging: Motivation or degradation? *Emotion, 16*(5), 602.

Kalil, A., & Mayer, S. E. (2016). Understanding the importance of parental time with children: Comment on Milkie, Nomaguchi, and Denny (2015). *Journal of Marriage and Family, 78*(1), 262–265. http://dx.doi.org/10.1111/jomf.12261

Kalil, A., Ryan, R., & Corey, M. (2012). Diverging destinies: Maternal education and the developmental gradient in time with children. *Demography, 49*(4), 1361–1383.

Kaliman, P. (2019). Epigenetics and meditation. *Current Opinion in Psychology, 28*, 76–80.

Kalish, R., & Kimmel, M. (2011). Hooking up: Hot hetero sex or the new numb normative? *Australian Feminist Studies, 26*(67), 137–151.

Kalogrides, D., & Grodsky, E. (2011). Something to fall back on: Community colleges as a safety net. *Social Forces, 89*(3), 853–877. https://doi.org/10.1353/sof.2011.0019

Kan, P. F. (2014). Novel word retention in sequential bilingual children. *Journal of Child Language, 41*(2), 416–438. https://doi.org/10.1017/S0305000912000761

Kanda, H., Ling, J., Tonomura, S., Noguchi, K., Matalon, S., & Gu, J. G. (2019). TREK-1 and TRAAK are principal K+ channels at the nodes of Ranvier for rapid action potential conduction on mammalian myelinated afferent nerves. *Neuron, 104*(5), 960–971.e7. https://doi.org/10.1016/j.neuron.2019.08.042

Kandel, E. R. (2012). *The age of insight: The quest to understand the unconscious in art, mind, and brain, from Vienna 1900 to the present.* Random House.

Kandler, C., Bratko, D., Butković, A., Hlupić, T. V., Tybur, J. M., Wesseldijk, L. W., de Vries, R. E., Jern, P., & Lewis, G. J. (2020). How genetic and environmental variance in personality traits shift across the life span: Evidence from a cross-national twin study. *Journal of Personality and Social Psychology, 121*(5), 1079–1094.

Kandler, C., Zapko-Willmes, A., Richter, J., & Riemann, R. (2021). Synergistic and dynamic genotype environment interplays in the development of personality differences. In J. F. Rauthmann (Ed.), *The handbook of personality dynamics and processes* (pp. 155–181). Academic Press. https://doi.org/10.1016/B978-0-12-813995-0.00007-8

Kanellopoulos, D., Rosenberg, P., Ravdin, L. D., Maldonado, D., Jamil, N., Quinn, C., & Kiosses, D. N. (2020). Depression, Cognitive, and functional outcomes of problem adaptation therapy (PATH) in older adults with major depression and mild cognitive deficits. *International Psychogeriatrics, 32*(4), 485–493. https://doi.org/10.1017/S1041610219001716

Kang, E., Klein, E. F., Lillard, A. S., & Lerner, M. D. (2016). Predictors and moderators of spontaneous pretend play in children with and without autism spectrum disorder. *Frontiers in Psychology, 7*, 1577.

Kang, S., & Harvey, E. A. (2020). Racial differences between black parents' and white teachers' perceptions of attention-deficit/hyperactivity disorder behavior. *Journal of Abnormal Child Psychology, 48*(5), 661–672. https://doi.org/10.1007/s10802-019-00600-y

Kanno, Y., & Kangas, S. E. (2014). "I'm not going to be, like, for the AP" English language learners' limited access to advanced college-preparatory courses in high school. *American Educational Research Journal, 51*(5), 848–878. http://journals.sagepub.com/doi/abs/10.3102/0002831214544716

Kanny, D., Naimi, T. S., Liu, Y., Lu, H., & Brewer, R. D. (2018). Annual total binge drinks consumed by U.S. adults, 2015. *American Journal of Preventive Medicine, 54*(4), 486–496. https://doi.org/10.1016/j.amepre.2017.12.021

Kansky, J., & Allen, J. P. (2018). Long-term risks and possible benefits associated with late adolescent romantic relationship quality. *Journal of Youth and Adolescence, 47*(7), 1531–1544. https://doi.org/10.1007/s10964-018-0813-x

Kansky, J., & Allen, J. P. (2018). Making sense and moving on: The potential for individual and interpersonal growth following emerging adult breakups. *Emerging Adulthood, 6*(3), 172–190. https://doi.org/10.1177/2167696817711766

Kansra, A. R., Lakkunarajah, S., & Jay, M. S. (2020). Childhood and adolescent obesity: A review. *Frontiers in Pediatrics, 8*, 866.

Kanter, J. B., Lavner, J. A., Lannin, D. G., Hilgard, J., & Monk, J. K. (2021). Does couple communication predict later relationship quality and dissolution? A meta-analysis. *Journal of Marriage and Family.* https://doi.org/10.1111/jomf.12804

Kantor, L. M., & Lindberg, L. (2020). Pleasure and sex education: The need for broadening both content and measurement. *American Journal of Public Health, 110*(2), 145–148. https://doi.org/10.2105/AJPH.2019.305320

Kapetanovic, S., Rothenberg, W. A., Lansford, J. E., Bornstein, M. H., Chang, L., Deater-Deckard, K., Di Giunta, L., Dodge, K. A., Gurdal, S., Malone, P. S., Oburu, P., Pastorelli, C., Skinner, A. T., Sorbring, E., Steinberg, L., Tapanya, S., Uribe Tirado, L. M., Yotanyamaneewong, S., Peña Alampay, L., … Bacchini, D. (2020). Cross-cultural examination of links between parent–adolescent communication and adolescent psychological problems in 12 cultural groups. *Journal of Youth and Adolescence, 49*(6), 1225–1244. https://doi.org/10.1007/s10964-020-01212-2

Kapitány, R., Nelson, N., Burdett, E. R., & Goldstein, T. R. (2020). The child's pantheon: Children's hierarchical belief structure in real and non-real figures. *PLOS ONE, 15*(6), e0234142.

Kaplowitz, P., Bloch, C., & the Section on Endocrinology of the American Academy of Pediatrics. (2016). Evaluation and referral of children with signs of early puberty. *Pediatrics, 137*(1), e20153732. https://doi.org/10.1542/peds.2015-3732

Kapp, S. K. (2020). *Autistic community and the neurodiversity movement: Stories from the frontline* (p. 330). Springer Nature.

Kar, P., Tomfohr-Madsen, L., Giesbrecht, G., Bagshawe, M., & Lebel, C. (2021). Alcohol and substance use in pregnancy during the COVID-19 pandemic. *Drug and Alcohol Dependence*, 108760. https://doi.org/10.1016/j.drugalcdep.2021.108760

Karably, K., & Zabrucky, K. M. (2009). Children's meta-memory: A review of the literature and implications for the classroom. *International Electronic Journal of Elementary Education*, 2(1), 32–52.

Karalija, N., Papenberg, G., Wåhlin, A., Johansson, J., Andersson, M., Axelsson, J., Riklund, K., Lövdén, M., Lindenberger, U., Bäckman, L., & Nyberg, L. (2018). C957T-mediated variation in ligand affinity affects the association between 11C-raclopride binding potential and cognition. *Journal of Cognitive Neuroscience*, 31(2), 314–325. https://doi.org/10.1162/jocn_a_01354

Karasik, L. B., Adolph, K. E., Tamis-LeMonda, C. S., & Bornstein, M. H. (2010). WEIRD walking: Cross-cultural research on motor development. *The Behavioral and Brain Sciences*, 33(2–3), 95–96. https://doi.org/10.1017/S0140525X10000117

Karasik, L. B., Tamis-LeMonda, C. S., Ossmy, O., & Adolph, K. E. (2018). The ties that bind: Cradling in Tajikistan. *PLoS One*, 13(1), e0204424. https://doi.org/10.1371/journal.pone.0204428

Karbach, J., & Verhaeghen, P. (2014). Making working memory work: A meta-analysis of executive-control and working memory training in older adults. *Psychological Science*, 25(11), 2027–2037.

Kardaras, N. (2016). *Glow kids: How screen addiction is hijacking our kids—and how to break the trance*. St. Martin's Press.

Kariuki, S. N., & Williams, T. N. (2020). Human genetics and malaria resistance. *Human Genetics*, 139(6), 801–811. https://doi.org/10.1007/s00439-020-02142-6

Karl, J. M., Slack, B. M., Wilson, A. M., Wilson, C. A., & Bertoli, M. E. (2019). Increasing task precision demands reveals that the reach and grasp remain subject to different perception-action constraints in 12-month-old human infants. *Infant Behavior and Development*, 57, 101382. https://doi.org/10.1016/j.infbeh.2019.101382

Karn, S., Yu, H., Karna, S., Chen, L., & Qiao, D. (2016). Women's awareness and attitudes towards labor analgesia influencing practice between developed and developing countries. *Advances in Reproductive Sciences*, 4(2), 46–52. https://doi.org/10.4236/arsci.2016.42007

Kärnä, A., Voeten, M., Little, T. D., Alanen, E., Poskiparta, E., & Salmivalli, C. (2013). Effectiveness of the KiVa antibullying program: grades 1–3 and 7–9. *Journal of Educational Psychology*, 105(2), 535.

Karney, B. R. (2021). Socioeconomic status and intimate relationships. *Annual Review of Psychology*, 72, 391–414. https://doi.org/10.1146/annurev-psych-051920-013658

Karney, B. R., & Bradbury, T. N. (2020). Research on marital satisfaction and stability in the 2010s: Challenging conventional wisdom. *Journal of Marriage and Family*, 82(1), 100–116. https://doi.org/10.1111/jomf.12635

Karns, C. M., Isbell, E., Giuliano, R. J., & Neville, H. J. (2015). Auditory attention in childhood and adolescence: An event-related potential study of spatial selective attention to one of two simultaneous stories. *Developmental Cognitive Neuroscience*, 13, 53–67. https://doi.org/10.1016/j.dcn.2015.03.001

Karra, M., Subramanian, S., & Fink, G. (2017). Height in healthy children in low- and middle-income countries: An assessment. *The American Journal of Clinical Nutrition*, 105(1), 121–126. https://doi.org/10.3945/ajcn.116.136705

Karrer, T. M., Josef, A. K., Mata, R., Morris, E. D., & Samanez-Larkin, G. R. (2017). Reduced dopamine receptors and transporters but not synthesis capacity in normal aging adults: A meta-analysis. *Neurobiology of Aging*, 57, 36–46. https://doi.org/10.1016/j.neurobiolaging.2017.05.006

Karrer, T. M., McLaughlin, C. L., Guaglianone, C. P., & Samanez-Larkin, G. R. (2019). Reduced serotonin receptors and transporters in normal aging adults: A meta-analysis of PET and SPECT imaging studies. *Neurobiology of Aging*, 80, 1–10. https://doi.org/10.1016/j.neurobiolaging.2019.03.021

Kärtner, J., Torréns, M. G., & Schuhmacher, N. (2021). Parental structuring during shared chores and the development of helping across the second year. *Social Development*, 30(2), 374–395. https://doi.org/10.1111/sode.12490

Kasper, J. D., Wolff, J. L., & Skehan, M. (2019). Care arrangements of older adults: What they prefer, what they have, and implications for quality of life. *The Gerontologist*, 59(5), 845–855. https://doi.org/10.1093/geront/gny127

Kastenbaum, R. (2015). *Death, society and human experience*. Routledge.

Kato, G. J., Piel, F. B., Reid, C. D., Gaston, M. H., Ohene-Frempong, K., Krishnamurti, L., Smith, W. R., Panepinto, J. A., Weatherall, D. J., Costa, F. F., & Vichinsky, E. P. (2018). Sickle cell disease. *Nature Reviews Disease Primers*, 4(1), 1–22. https://doi.org/10.1038/nrdp.2018.10

Katrinli, S., Stevens, J., Wani, A. H., Lori, A., Kilaru, V., van Rooij, S. J. H., Hinrichs, R., Powers, A., Gillespie, C. F., Michopoulos, V., Gautam, A., Jett, M., Hammamieh, R., Yang, R., Wildman, D., Qu, A., Koenen, K., Aiello, A. E., Jovanovic, T., … Smith, A. K. (2020). Evaluating the impact of trauma and PTSD on epigenetic prediction of lifespan and neural integrity. *Neuropsychopharmacology*, 45(10), 1609–1616. https://doi.org/10.1038/s41386-020-0700-5

Katsanis, N. (2016). The continuum of causality in human genetic disorders. *Genome Biology*, 17(1), 233. https://doi.org/10.1186/s13059-016-1107-9

Katsiaficas, D., Suárez-Orozco, C., & Dias, S. I. (2015). "When do I feel like an adult?" Latino and Afro-Caribbean immigrant-origin community college students' conceptualizations and experiences of (emerging) adulthood. *Emerging Adulthood*, 3(2), 98–112. https://doi.org/10.1177/2167696814548059

Katsumoto, A., Takeuchi, H., & Tanaka, F. (2019). Tau pathology in chronic traumatic encephalopathy and Alzheimer's disease: Similarities and differences. *Frontiers in Neurology*, 10, 980.

Katz, L. F., Gurtovenko, K., Maliken, A., Stettler, N., Kawamura, J., & Fladeboe, K. (2020). An emotion coaching parenting intervention for families exposed to intimate partner violence. *Developmental Psychology*, 56(3), 638–651. https://doi.org/10.1037/dev0000800

Katz, L. F., & Krueger, A. B. (2016). *The rise and nature of alternative work arrangements in the United States, 1995–2015*. NBER. http://scholar.harvard.edu/files/lkatz/files/katz_krueger_cws_v3. pdf, https://krueger.princeton.edu/sites/default/files/akrueger/files/katz_krueger_cws_-_march_29_20165.pdf

Katz, S., & Akpom, C. A. (1976). A measure of primary sociobiological functions. *International Journal of Health Services*, 6(3), 493–508.

Katz, S., Ford, A. B., Moskowitz, R. W., Jackson, B. A., & Jaffee, M. W. (1963) Studies of illness in the aged: The index of ADL: A standardized measure of biological and psychosocial function. *JAMA*, 185, 914–919.

Kaufman, A. S., Raiford, S. E., & Coalson, D. L. (2015). *Intelligent testing with the WISC-V*. Wiley.

Kaufman, J. D., Spalt, E. W., Curl, C. L., Hajat, A., Jones, M. R., Kim, S.-Y., Vedal, S., Szpiro, A. A., Gassett, A., Sheppard, L., Daviglus, M. L., & Adar, S. D. (2016). Advances in understanding air pollution and cardiovascular diseases: The multi-ethnic study of atherosclerosis and air pollution (MESA Air). *Global Heart*, 11(3), 343–352. https://doi.org/10.1016/j.gheart.2016.07.004

Kaufman, S. B. (2019, April 23). Who created Maslow's iconic pyramid? *Scientific American*. https://blogs.scientificamerican.com/beautiful-minds/who-created-maslows-iconic-pyramid/

Kavle, J. A., LaCroix, E., Dau, H., & Engmann, C. (2017). Addressing barriers to exclusive breast-feeding in low- and middle-income countries: A systematic review and programmatic implications. *Public Health Nutrition*, 20(17), 3120–3134. https://doi.org/10.1017/S1368980017002531

Kawakami, F., Tomonaga, M., & Suzuki, J. (2017). The first smile: Spontaneous smiles in newborn Japanese macaques (*Macaca fuscata*). *Primates*, 58(1), 93–101. https://doi.org/10.1007/s10329-016-0558-7

Kawamichi, H., Sugawara, S. K., Hamano, Y. H., Makita, K., Matsunaga, M., Tanabe, H. C., Ogino, Y., Saito, S., & Sadato, N. (2016). Being in a romantic relationship is associated with reduced gray matter density in striatum and increased subjective happiness. *Frontiers in Psychology*, 7, 1763. https://doi.org/10.3389/fpsyg.2016.01763

Kazda, L., Bell, K., Thomas, R., McGeechan, K., Sims, R., & Barratt, A. (2021). Overdiagnosis of attention-deficit/hyperactivity disorder in children and adolescents: A systematic scoping review. *JAMA Network Open*, 4(4), e215335–e215335. https://doi.org/10.1001/jamanetworkopen.2021.5335

Kazdin, A. E. (2003). Psychotherapy for children and adolescents. *Annual Review of Psychology*, 54(1), 253–276.

Kazdin, A. E., Glick, A., Pope, J., Kaptchuk, T. J., Lecza, B., Carrubba, E., McWhinney, E., & Hamilton, N. (2018). Parent management training for conduct problems in children: Enhancing treatment to improve therapeutic change. *International Journal of Clinical and Health Psychology*, 18(2), 91–101. https://doi.org/10.1016/j.ijchp.2017.12.002

Keane, L., & Loades, M. (2017). Low self-esteem and internalizing disorders in young people—a systematic review. *Child and Adolescent Mental Health*, 22(1), 4–15.

Kearins, J. M. (1981). Visual spatial memory in Australian aboriginal children of desert regions. *Cognitive Psychology*, 13(3), 434–460. https://doi.org/10.1016/0010-0285(81)90017-7

Kearney, C. (2019, June 4). *Earnings peak at different ages for different demographic groups data visualization*. Payscale—Salary Comparison, Salary Survey, Search Wages. https://www.payscale.com/research-and-insights/peak-earnings-data-visualization/

Kearney, M. S., & Levine, P. B. (2015). Investigating recent trends in the U.S. teen birth rate. *Journal of Health Economics*, 41, 15–29. https://doi.org/10.1016/j.jhealeco.2015.01.003

Keestra, S. M., Bentley, G. R., la Mora, A. N., Houghton, L. C., Wilson, H., Vázquez-Vázquez, A., Cooper, G. D., Dickinson, F., Griffiths, P., Bogin, B. A., & Varela-Silva, M. I. (2021). The timing of adrenarche in Maya girls, Merida, Mexico. *American Journal of Human Biology*, 33(2), e23465. https://doi.org/10.1002/ajhb.23465

Kefalas, M. J., Furstenberg, F. F., Carr, P. J., & Napolitano, L. (2011). "Marriage is more than being together": The meaning of marriage for young adults. *Journal of Family Issues*, 32(7), 845–875. https://doi.org/10.1177/0192513X10397277

Keller, H. (2017). Culture and development: A systematic relationship. *Perspectives on Psychological Science*, 12(5), 833–840. https://doi.org/10.1177/1745691617704097

Keller, H. (2018). Universality claim of attachment theory: Children's socioemotional development across cultures. *Proceedings of the National Academy of Sciences*, 115(45), 11414–11419. https://doi.org/10.1073/pnas.1720325115

Keller, H. (2019). The role of emotions in socialization processes across cultures: Implications for theory and practice. In D. Matsumoto & H. C. Hwang (Eds.), *The handbook of culture and psychology* (pp. 209–231). Oxford University Press.

Keller, H. (2020). Children's socioemotional development across cultures. *Annual Review of Developmental Psychology*, 2(1), 27–46. https://doi.org/10.1146/annurev-devpsych-033020-031552

Keller, H. (2021). Attachment theory: Fact or fancy? In R. A. Thompson, J. A. Simpson, & L. J. Berlin (Eds.), *Attachment: The fundamental questions* (pp. 229–236). Guilford.

Keller, H., & Otto, H. (2009). The cultural socialization of emotion regulation during infancy. *Journal of Cross-Cultural Psychology*, 40(6), 996–1011.

Kelley, A. S., Qin, Y., Marsh, E. E., & Dupree, J. M. (2019). Disparities in accessing infertility care in the United States: Results from the National Health and Nutrition Examination Survey, 2013–16. *Fertility and Sterility*, 112(3), 562–568. https://doi.org/10.1016/j.fertnstert.2019.04.044

Kelly, D. J., Duarte, S., Meary, D., Bindemann, M., & Pascalis, O. (2019). Infants rapidly detect human faces in complex naturalistic visual scenes. *Developmental Science, 22*(6), e12829. https://doi.org/10.1111/desc.12829

Kelly, M. G. (2020). The curious case of the missing tail: Trends among the top 1% of school districts in the United States, 2000–2015. *Educational Researcher, 49*(5), 312–320. https://doi.org/10.3102/0013189X20922999

Kelly, Y., Zilanawala, A., Sacker, A., Hiatt, R., & Viner, R. (2017). Early puberty in 11-year-old girls: Millennium Cohort Study findings. *Archives of Disease in Childhood, 102*(3), 232–237. https://doi.org/10.1136/archdischild-2016-310475

Kempe, A., Saville, A. W., Albertin, C., Zimet, G., Breck, A., Helmkamp, L., Vangala, S., Dickinson, L. M., Rand, C., & Humiston, S. (2020). Parental hesitancy about routine childhood and influenza vaccinations: A national survey. *Pediatrics, 146*(1), e20193852.

Kena, G., Hussar, W., McFarland, J., de Brey, C., Musu-Gillette, L., Wang, X., Zhang, J., Rathbun, A., Wilkinson-Flicker, S., Diliberti, M., Barmer, A., Bullock Mann, F., & Dunlop Velez, E. (2016). *The condition of education 2016* (NCES 2016-144). National Center for Education Statistics. https://eric.ed.gov/?id=ED565888

Kennedy, B. L., Huang, R., & Mather, M. (2020). Age differences in emotion-induced blindness: Positivity effects in early attention. *Emotion, 20*(7), 1266.

Kennedy, G., Hardman, R. J., Macpherson, H., Scholey, A. B., & Pipingas, A. (2017). How does exercise reduce the rate of age-associated cognitive decline? A review of potential mechanisms. *Journal of Alzheimer's Disease, 55*(1), 1–18.

Kenney, E. L., & Gortmaker, S. L. (2017). United States adolescents' television, computer, videogame, smartphone, and tablet use: Associations with sugary drinks, sleep, physical activity, and obesity. *The Journal of Pediatrics, 182*, 144–149. https://doi.org/10.1016/j.jpeds.2016.11.015

Kenrick, D. T., Cohen, A. B., Neuberg, S. L., & Cialdini, R. B. (2018). The science of antiscience thinking. *Scientific American, 319*(1), 36–41.

Keresztes, A., Bender, A. R., Bodammer, N. C., Lindenberger, U., Shing, Y. L., & Werkle-Bergner, M. (2017). Hippocampal maturity promotes memory distinctiveness in childhood and adolescence. *Proceedings of the National Academy of Sciences, 114*(34), 9212–9217.

Kerr, E., & Wood, S. (2021, September 14). See 10 years of average total student loan debt. *US News & World Report.* https://www.usnews.com/education/best-colleges/paying-for-college/articles/see-how-student-loan-borrowing-has-risen-in-10-years

Kerr, M., & Stattin, H. (2000). What parents know, how they know it, and several forms of adolescent adjustment: Further support for a reinterpretation of monitoring. *Developmental Psychology, 36*(3), 366. https://doi.org/10.1037/0012-1649.36.3.366

Kerr, M., Stattin, H., & Pakalniskiene, V. (2008). Parents react to adolescent problem behaviors by worrying more and monitoring less. In M. Kerr, H. Stattin, & R. Engels (Eds.), *What can parents do? New insights into the role of parents in adolescent problem behavior* (pp. 91–112). Wiley.

Keshavan, M. S., Giedd, J., Lau, J. Y., Lewis, D. A., & Paus, T. (2014). Changes in the adolescent brain and the pathophysiology of psychotic disorders. *The Lancet Psychiatry, 1*(7), 549–558.

Kessler, R., Hinkle, B. T., Moyers, A., & Silverberg, B. (2020). Adolescent sexual health: Identity, risk, and screening for sexually transmitted infections. *Primary Care: Clinics in Office Practice, 47*(2), 367–382. https://doi.org/10.1016/j.pop.2020.02.012

Kessler, S. E. (2020). Why care: Complex evolutionary history of human healthcare networks. *Frontiers in Psychology, 11.* https://doi.org/10.3389/fpsyg.2020.00199

Keyes, C. L. M., & Ryff, C. D. (1999). Psychological well-being in midlife. In S. L. Willis & J. D. Reid (Eds.), *Life in the middle* (pp. 161–180). Academic Press. https://doi.org/10.1016/B978-012757230-7/50028-6

Keyhani, S., Steigerwald, S., Ishida, J., Vali, M., Cerdá, M., Hasin, D., Dollinger, C., Yoo, S. R., & Cohen, B. E. (2018). Risks and benefits of marijuana use. *Annals of Internal Medicine, 169*(5), 282–290. https://doi.org/10.7326/M18-0810

Khandwala, Y. S., Zhang, C. A., Lu, Y., & Eisenberg, M. L. (2017). The age of fathers in the USA is rising: An analysis of 168 867 480 births from 1972 to 2015. *Human Reproduction, 32*(10), 2110–2116. https://doi.org/10.1093/humrep/dex267

Kharbanda, E. O., Vazquez-Benitez, G., Kunin-Batson, A., Nordin, J. D., Olsen, A., & Romitti, P. A. (2020). Birth and early developmental screening outcomes associated with cannabis exposure during pregnancy. *Journal of Perinatology, 40*(3), 473–480. https://doi.org/10.1038/s41372-019-0576-6

Khatiwada, I., & Sum, A. M. (2016). The widening socioeconomic divergence in the U.S. labor market. In I. Kirsch & H. Braun (Eds.), *The dynamics of opportunity in America* (pp. 197–252). Springer.

Khosla, S., & Hofbauer, L. C. (2017). Osteoporosis treatment: Recent developments and ongoing challenges. *The Lancet. Diabetes & Endocrinology, 5*(11), 898–907. https://doi.org/10.1016/S2213-8587(17)30188-2

Khullar, D., & Chokshi, D. A. (2018, October 4). *Health, income, & poverty: Where we are & what could help* (Health Affairs Brief). https://www.healthaffairs.org/do/10.1377/hpb20180817.901935/full/

Khurana, A., Romer, D., Betancourt, L. M., & Hurt, H. (2018). Modeling trajectories of sensation seeking and impulsivity dimensions from early to late adolescence: Universal trends or distinct sub-groups? *Journal of Youth and Adolescence, 47*(9), 1992–2005. https://doi.org/10.1007/s10964-018-0891-9

Kiang, L., & Fuligni, A. J. (2010). Meaning in life as a mediator of ethnic identity and adjustment among adolescents from Latin, Asian, and European American backgrounds. *Journal of Youth and Adolescence, 39*(11), 1253–1264. https://doi.org/10.1007/s10964-009-9475-z

Kiang, L., Mendonça, S., Liang, Y., Payir, A., O'Brien, L. T., Tudge, J. R. H., & Freitas, L. B. L. (2016). If children won lotteries: Materialism, gratitude and imaginary windfall spending. *Young Consumers, 17*(4), 404–418. https://doi.org/10.1108/YC-07-2016-00614

Kiecolt, K. J., Blieszner, R., & Savla, J. (2011). Long-term influences of intergenerational ambivalence on midlife parents' psychological well-being. *Journal of Marriage and Family, 73*(2), 369–382.

Kiely, K. M., Brady, B., & Byles, J. (2019). Gender, mental health and ageing. *Maturitas, 129*, 76–84. https://doi.org/10.1016/j.maturitas.2019.09.004

Kilaru, A. S., & Gee, R. E. (2020). Structural ageism and the health of older adults. *JAMA Health Forum, 1*(10), e201249. https://doi.org/10.1001/jamahealthforum.2020.1249

Kilgo, C. A., Phillips, C. W., Martin, G. L., Campbell, E., & Pascarella, E. T. (2018). Getting critical about critical thinking: The role of parental education on first-generation students' cognitive gains in college. *Journal of College Student Development, 59*(6), 756–761. https://doi.org/10.1353/csd.2018.0071

Killedar, A., Lung, T., Petrou, S., Teixeira-Pinto, A., Tan, E. J., & Hayes, A. (2020). Weight status and health-related quality of life during childhood and adolescence: Effects of age and socioeconomic position. *International Journal of Obesity, 44*(3), 637–645. https://doi.org/10.1038/s41366-020-0529-3

Killen, M. (2019). Developing inclusive youth: How to reduce social exclusion and foster equality and equity in childhood. *American Educator, 43*(3), 8.

Killen, M., Rutland, A., & Ruck, M. D. (2011). Promoting equity, tolerance, and justice in childhood. *Social Policy Report, 25*(4). https://srcd.onlinelibrary.wiley.com/doi/pdf/10.1002/j.2379-3988.2011.tb00069.x

Killen, M., & Smetana, J. G. (2015). Origins and development of morality. In R. M. Lerner (Ed.), *Handbook of child psychology and developmental science* (pp. 1–49). John Wiley & Sons. https://doi.org/10.1002/9781118963418.childpsy317

Kilmer, J. R., Fossos-Wong, N., Geisner, I. M., Yeh, J.-C., Larimer, M. E., Cimini, M. D., Vincent, K. B., Allen, H. K., Barrall, A. L., & Arria, A. M. (2021). Nonmedical use of prescription stimulants as a "red flag" for other substance use. *Substance Use & Misuse, 56*(7), 941–949.

Kilpela, L. S., Becker, C. B., Wesley, N., & Stewart, T. (2015). Body image in adult women: Moving beyond the younger years. *Advances in Eating Disorders: Theory, Research and Practice, 3*(2), 144–164.

Kim, C., McGee, S., Khuntia, S., Elnour, A., Johnson-Clarke, F., Mangla, A., Ivengar, P., & Nesbitt, L. (2021). Characteristics of COVID-19 cases and outbreaks at child care facilities — District of Columbia, July–December 2020. *Morbidity and Mortality Weekly Report, 70*(20), 744–748. https://doi.org/10.15585/mmwr.mm7020a3

Kim, C., & Tamborini, C. R. (2019). Are they still worth it? The long-run earnings benefits of an associate degree, vocational diploma or certificate, and some college. *RSF: The Russell Sage Foundation Journal of the Social Sciences, 5*(3), 64–85. https://doi.org/10.7758/RSF.2019.5.3.04

Kim, D.-J., Davis, E. P., Sandman, C. A., Glynn, L., Sporns, O., O'Donnell, B. F., & Hetrick, W. P. (2019). Childhood poverty and the organization of structural brain connectome. *NeuroImage, 184*, 409–416. https://doi.org/10.1016/j.neuroimage.2018.09.041

Kim, E. (2021, June 21). *How does treating gun violence as a public health crisis work? One Bronx program offers a potential flagship model.* Gothamist. https://gothamist.com

Kim, E. S., Kawachi, I., Chen, Y., & Kubzansky, L. D. (2017). Association between purpose in life and objective measures of physical function in older adults. *JAMA Psychiatry, 74*(10), 1039–1045. https://doi.org/10.1001/jamapsychiatry.2017.2145

Kim, E. T. (2020, June 30). Opinion | When you are paid 13 hours for a 24-hour shift. *The New York Times.* https://www.nytimes.com/2020/06/30/opinion/coronavirus-nursing-homes.html

Kim, G., & Lee, M.-A. (2020). Age discrimination and suicidal ideation among Korean older adults. *The American Journal of Geriatric Psychiatry, 28*(7), 748–754. https://doi.org/10.1016/j.jagp.2019.12.002

Kim, H., Duran, C. A. K., Cameron, C. E., & Grissmer, D. (2018). Developmental relations among motor and cognitive processes and mathematics skills. *Child Development, 89*(2), 476–494. https://doi.org/10.1111/cdev.12752

Kim, H.-J., & Fredriksen-Goldsen, K. I. (2017). Disparities in mental health quality of life between Hispanic and Non-Hispanic White LGB midlife and older adults and the influence of lifetime discrimination, social connectedness, socioeconomic status, and perceived stress. *Research on Aging, 39*(9), 991–1012. https://doi.org/10.1177/0164027516650003

Kim, H.-J., Jen, S., & Fredriksen-Goldsen, K. I. (2017). Race/ethnicity and health-related quality of life among LGBT older adults. *The Gerontologist, 57*(suppl_1), S30–S39. https://doi.org/10.1093/geront/gnw172

Kim, J. I., & Kim, G. (2018). Effects on inequality in life expectancy from a social ecology perspective. *BMC Public Health, 18*(1), 243. https://doi.org/10.1186/s12889-018-5134-1

Kim, K., Birditt, K. S., Zarit, S. H., & Fingerman, K. L. (2020). Typology of parent–child ties within families: Associations with psychological well-being. *Journal of Family Psychology, 34*(4), 448–458. https://doi.org/10.1037/fam0000595

Kim, K., Eggebeen, D. J., Zarit, S. H., Birditt, K. S., & Fingerman, K. L. (2013). Agreement between aging parent's bequest intention and middle-aged child's inheritance expectation. *The Gerontologist, 53*(6), 1020–1031. https://doi.org/10.1093/geront/gns147

Kim, K., Fingerman, K. L., & Nussbaum, J. F. (2022). Between younger and older generations: Family communication at midlife. In A. L. Vangelisti (Ed.), *The Routledge handbook of family communication* (3rd ed., pp. 85–98). Routledge.

Kim, M. H., Ahmed, S. F., & Morrison, F. J. (2021). The effects of kindergarten and first grade schooling on executive function and academic skill development: Evidence from a school cutoff design. *Frontiers in Psychology, 11*, 607973. https://doi.org/10.3389/fpsyg.2020.607973

Kim, P. (2016). Human maternal brain plasticity: Adaptation to parenting. *New Directions for Child and Adolescent Development, 2016*(153), 47–58. https://doi.org/10.1002/cad.20168

Kim, P., Evans, G. W., Angstadt, M., Ho, S. S., Sripada, C. S., Swain, J. E., Liberzon, I., & Phan, K. L. (2013). Effects of childhood poverty and chronic stress on emotion regulatory brain function in adulthood. *Proceedings of the National Academy of Sciences, 110*(46), 18442–18447. https://doi.org/10.1073/pnas.1308240110

Kim, S. A., Moore, L. V., Galuska, D., Wright, A. P., Harris, D., Grummer-Strawn, L. M., Merlo, C. L., Nihiser, A. J., & Rhodes, D. G. (2014). Vital signs: Fruit and vegetable intake among children—United States, 2003–2010. *Morbidity and Mortality Weekly Report, 63*(31), 671–676.

Kim, Y., Huan, T., Joehanes, R., McKeown, N. M., Horvath, S., Levy, D., & Ma, J. (2021). Higher diet quality relates to decelerated epigenetic aging. *The American Journal of Clinical Nutrition*, nqab201. https://doi.org/10.1093/ajcn/nqab201

Kim, Y. K., Kim, K., Boerner, K., Birditt, K. S., Zarit, S. H., & Fingerman, K. L. (2019). Recent parental death and relationship qualities between midlife adults and their grown children. *Journal of Marriage and Family, 81*(3), 616–630.

Kimberly, L. L., Folkers, K. M., Friesen, P., Sultan, D., Quinn, G. P., Bateman-House, A., Parent, B., Konnoth, C., Janssen, A., Shah, L. D., Bluebond-Langner, R., & Salas-Humara, C. (2018). Ethical issues in gender-affirming care for youth. *Pediatrics, 142*(6), e20181537. https://doi.org/10.1542/peds.2018-1537

King, A. C., Whitt-Glover, M. C., Marquez, D. X., Buman, M. P., Napolitano, M. A., Jakicic, J., Fulton, J. E., Tennant, B. L., for the 2018 Physical Activity Guidelines Advisory Committee*. (2019). Physical activity promotion: Highlights from the 2018 Physical Activity Guidelines Advisory Committee systematic review. *Medicine & Science in Sports & Exercise, 51*(6), 1340–1353. https://doi.org/10.1249/MSS.0000000000001945

King, C. (2019). *Gods of the upper air: How a circle of renegade anthropologists reinvented race, sex, and gender in the twentieth century.* Knopf Doubleday.

King, L. S., Humphreys, K. L., & Gotlib, I. H. (2019). The neglect–enrichment continuum: Characterizing variation in early caregiving environments. *Developmental Review, 51*, 109–122. https://doi.org/10.1016/j.dr.2019.01.001

King, P. M. (2009). Principles of development and developmental change underlying theories of cognitive and moral development. *Journal of College Student Development, 50*(6), 597–620.

King, P. M., & Kitchener, K. S. (2015). Cognitive development in the emerging adult: The emergence of complex cognitive skills. In J. J. Arnett (Ed.), *The Oxford handbook of emerging adulthood* (pp. 105–125). Oxford University Press.

King, V., Boyd, L. M., & Pragg, B. (2018). Parent-adolescent closeness, family belonging, and adolescent well-being across family structures. *Journal of Family Issues, 39*(7), 2007–2036. https://doi.org/10.1177/0192513X17739048

King, V., Pragg, B., & Lindstrom, R. (2020). Family relationships during adolescence and stepchilden's educational attainment in young adulthood. *Journal of Marriage and Family, 82*(2), 622–638. https://doi.org/10.1111/jomf.12642

Kingsbury, M. A., & Bilbo, S. D. (2019). The inflammatory event of birth: How oxytocin signaling may guide the development of the brain and gastrointestinal system. *Frontiers in Neuroendocrinology, 55*, 100794. https://doi.org/10.1016/j.yfrne.2019.100794

Kinney, A. B. (1995). *Chinese views of childhood.* University of Hawaii Press.

Kinney, A. B. (2004). *Representations of childhood and youth in early China.* Stanford University Press.

Kinney, H. C., Hefti, M. M., Goldstein, R. D., & Haynes, R. L. (2018). Sudden infant death syndrome. In H. Adle-Biassette, B. N. Harding, & J. Golden (Eds.), *Developmental neuropathology* (pp. 269–280). Wiley. https://doi.org/10.1002/9781119013112.ch25

Kiosses, D. N., & Sachs-Ericsson, N. (2020). Increasing resilience in older adults. *International Psychogeriatrics, 32*(2), 157–159.

Kirsch, J. A., Love, G. D., Radler, B. T., & Ryff, C. D. (2019). Scientific imperatives vis-à-vis growing inequality in America. *American Psychologist, 74*(7), 764–777. https://doi.org/10.1037/amp0000481

Kirschen, M. P., Lewis, A., Rubin, M., Kurtz, P., & Greer, D. M. (2021). New perspectives on brain death. *Journal of Neurology, Neurosurgery & Psychiatry, 92*(3), 255–262. https://doi.org/10.1136/jnnp-2020-323952

Kitayama, S., Berg, M. K., & Chopik, W. J. (2020). Culture and well-being in late adulthood: Theory and evidence. *American Psychologist, 75*(4), 567.

Kitayama, S., & Salvador, C. E. (2017). Culture embrained: Going beyond the nature-nurture dichotomy. *Perspectives on Psychological Science, 12*(5), 841–854. https://doi.org/10.1177/1745691617707317

Kitzman, H., Olds, D. L., Knudtson, M. D., Cole, R., Anson, E., Smith, J. A., Fishbein, D., DiClemente, R., Wingood, G., & Caliendo, A. M. (2019). Prenatal and infancy nurse home visiting and 18-year outcomes of a randomized trial. *Pediatrics, 144*(6), e20183876.

Klaczynski, P. A. (2014). Heuristics and biases: Interactions among numeracy, ability, and reflectiveness predict normative responding. *Frontiers in Psychology, 5*, 665.

Klaming, R., Annese, J., Veltman, D. J., & Comijs, H. C. (2017). Episodic memory function is affected by lifestyle factors: A 14-year follow-up study in an elderly population. *Aging, Neuropsychology, and Cognition, 24*(5), 528–542. https://doi.org/10.1080/13825585.2016.1226746

Klass, D. (2014). Grief, consolation, and religions: A conceptual framework. *OMEGA—Journal of Death and Dying, 69*(1), 1–18.

Klein, P., Fairweather, A. K., Lawn, S., Stallman, H. M., & Cammell, P. (2021). Structural stigma and its impact on healthcare for consumers with borderline personality disorder: Protocol for a scoping review. *Systematic Reviews, 10*(1), 1–7.

Klein, W., Graesch, A. P., & Izquierdo, C. (2009). Children and chores: A mixed-methods study of children's household work in Los Angeles families. *Anthropology of Work Review, 30*(3), 98–109.

Kleinepier, T., Berrington, A., & Stoeldraijer, L. (2017). Ethnic differences in returning home: Explanations from a life course perspective. *Journal of Marriage and Family, 79*(4), 1023–1040. https://doi.org/10.1111/jomf.12399

Klesse, C. (2019). Polyamorous parenting: Stigma, social regulation, and queer bonds of resistance. *Sociological Research Online, 24*(4), 625–643. https://doi.org/10.1177/1360780418806902

Klevan, S., Weinberg, S. L., & Middleton, J. A. (2016). Why the boys are missing: Using social capital to explain gender differences in college enrollment for public high school students. *Research in Higher Education, 57*(2), 223–257. https://doi.org/10.1007/s11162-015-9384-9

Klijs, B., Mendes de Leon, C. F., Kibele, E. U. B., & Smidt, N. (2017). Do social relations buffer the effect of neighborhood deprivation on health-related quality of life? Results from the LifeLines Cohort Study. *Health & Place, 44*, 43–51. https://doi.org/10.1016/j.healthplace.2017.01.001

Klimstra, T. A., Luyckx, K., Branje, S., Teppers, E., Goossens, L., & Meeus, W. H. J. (2013). Personality traits, interpersonal identity, and relationship stability: Longitudinal linkages in late adolescence and young adulthood. *Journal of Youth and Adolescence, 42*(11), 1661–1673. https://doi.org/10.1007/s10964-012-9862-8

Kluge, F., Zagheni, E., Loichinger, E., & Vogt, T. (2014). The advantages of demographic change after the wave: Fewer and older, but healthier, greener, and more productive? *PLOS ONE, 9*(9), e108501.

Kluger, R. (2011). *Simple justice: The history of* Brown v. Board of Education *and Black America's struggle for equality.* Knopf Doubleday.

Knechtle, B., & Nikolaidis, P. T. (2018). Physiology and pathophysiology in ultra-marathon running. *Frontiers in Physiology, 9*, 634. https://doi.org/10.3389/fphys.2018.00634

Knifsend, C. A., Camacho-Thompson, D. E., Juvonen, J., & Graham, S. (2018). Friends in activities, school-related affect, and academic outcomes in diverse middle schools. *Journal of Youth and Adolescence, 47*(6), 1208–1220.

Knight, G. P., Safa, M. D., & White, R. M. B. (2018). Advancing the assessment of cultural orientation: A developmental and contextual framework of multiple psychological dimensions and social identities. *Development and Psychopathology, 30*(5), 1867–1888. https://doi.org/10.1017/S095457941800113X

Knoll, L. J., Magis-Weinberg, L., Speekenbrink, M., & Blakemore, S.-J. (2015). Social influence on risk perception during adolescence. *Psychological Science, 26*(5), 583–592. https://doi.org/10.1177/0956797615569578

Knopman, D. S., Haeberlein, S. B., Carrillo, M. C., Hendrix, J. A., Kerchner, G., Margolin, R., Maruff, P., Miller, D. S., Tong, G., Tome, M. B., Murray, M. E., Nelson, P. T., Sano, M., Mattsson, N., Sultzer, D. L., Montine, T. J., Jack, C. R., Kolb, H., Petersen, R. C., ... Siemers, E. (2018). The National Institute on Aging and the Alzheimer's Association Research Framework for Alzheimer's disease: Perspectives from the research roundtable. *Alzheimer's & Dementia, 14*(4), 563–575. https://doi.org/10.1016/j.jalz.2018.03.002

Knopman, D. S., Jones, D. T., & Greicius, M. D. (2021). Failure to demonstrate efficacy of aducanumab: An analysis of the EMERGE and ENGAGE trials as reported by Biogen, December 2019. *Alzheimer's & Dementia, 17*(4), 696–701.

Knox, J., Hasin, D. S., Larson, F. R. R., & Kranzler, H. R. (2019). Prevention, screening, and treatment for heavy drinking and alcohol use disorder. *The Lancet Psychiatry, 6*(12), 1054–1067. https://doi.org/10.1016/S2215-0366(19)30213-5

Ko, H.-J., Hooker, K., Manoogian, M. M., & McAdams, D. P. (2019). Transitions to older adulthood: Exploring midlife women's narratives regarding purpose in life. *Journal of Positive School Psychology, 3*(2), 137–152.

Ko, J. Y., Coy, K. C., Haight, S. C., Haegerich, T. M., Williams, L., Cox, S., Njai, R., & Grant, A. M. (2020). Characteristics of marijuana use during pregnancy—Eight states, pregnancy risk assessment monitoring system, 2017. *Morbidity and Mortality Weekly Report, 69*(32), 1058–1063. https://doi.org/10.15585/mmwr.mm6932a2

Kobak, R., Abbott, C., Zisk, A., & Bounoua, N. (2017). Adapting to the changing needs of adolescents: Parenting practices and challenges to sensitive attunement. *Current Opinion in Psychology, 15*, 137–142. https://doi.org/10.1016/j.copsyc.2017.02.018

Köber, C., Schmiedek, F., & Habermas, T. (2015). Characterizing lifespan development of three aspects of coherence in life narratives: A cohort-sequential study. *Developmental Psychology, 51*(2), 260.

Kobin, B. (2019, September 26). Too many "broken hearts"? Elementary school tells fifth graders to stop dating. *The Courier Journal.* https://www.courier-journal.com/story/news/local/indiana/clark/2019/09/26/indiana-elementary-school-jeffersonville-riverside-no-dating-fifth-grade-students/3772740002/

Koch, A. J., D'Mello, S. D., & Sackett, P. R. (2015). A meta-analysis of gender stereotypes and bias in experimental simulations of employment decision making. *Journal of Applied Psychology, 100*(1), 128.

Kochanska, G. (2002). Mutually responsive orientation between mothers and their young children: A context for the early development of conscience. *Current Directions in Psychological Science, 11*(6), 191–195. https://doi.org/10.1111/1467-8721.00198

Kochanska, G., Boldt, L. J., & Goffin, K. C. (2019). Early relational experience: A foundation for the unfolding dynamics of parent–child socialization. *Child Development Perspectives, 13*(1), 41–47. https://doi.org/10.1111/cdep.12308

Kochanska, G., Boldt, L. J., Kim, S., Yoon, J. E., & Philibert, R. A. (2015). Developmental interplay between children's biobehavioral risk and the parenting environment from toddler to early school age: Prediction of socialization outcomes in preadolescence. *Development and Psychopathology, 27*(3), 775.

Kochhar, R. (2018, September 6). *The American middle class is stable in size, but losing ground financially to upper-income families.* Pew Research Center FactTank. https://www

.pewresearch.org/fact-tank/2018/09/06/the-american-middle-class-is-stable-in-size-but-losing-ground-financially-to-upper-income-families/

Koenka, A. C. (2020). Academic motivation theories revisited: An interactive dialog between motivation scholars on recent contributions, underexplored issues, and future directions. *Contemporary Educational Psychology, 61*, 101831.

Koeze, E. (2016, August 11). Old Olympians ride horses; young ones do flips. *FiveThirtyEight*. https://fivethirtyeight.com/features/old-olympians-ride-horses-young-ones-do-flips/

Kofod, E. H., & Brinkmann, S. (2017). Grief as a normative phenomenon: The diffuse and ambivalent normativity of infant loss and parental grieving in contemporary Western culture. *Culture & Psychology, 23*(4), 519–533.

Kogan, A. C., Wilber, K., & Mosqueda, L. (2016). Person-centered care for older adults with chronic conditions and functional impairment: A systematic literature review. *Journal of the American Geriatrics Society, 64*(1), e1–e7.

Koh, H. K., & Parekh, A. K. (2018). Toward a United States of health: Implications of understanding the US burden of disease. *JAMA, 319*(14), 1438–1440. https://doi.org/10.1001/jama.2018.0157

Kohl, N. M., Mossakowski, K. N., Sanidad, I. I., Bird, O. T., & Nitz, L. H. (2019). Does the health of adult child caregivers vary by employment status in the United States? *Journal of Aging and Health, 31*(9), 1631–1651.

Kohlberg, L. (1978). Revisions in the theory and practice of moral development. *New Directions for Child and Adolescent Development, 1978*(2), 83–87.

Kohlberg, L. (1981). *The philosophy of moral development: Moral stages and the idea of justice.* Harper & Row.

Kohlberg, L., & Kramer, R. (1969). Continuities and discontinuities in childhood and adult moral development. *Human Development, 12*(2), 93–120.

Kohler, R. (2014). *Jean Piaget.* Bloomsbury.

Kok, J. S., Nielen, M. M. A., & Scherder, E. J. A. (2018). Quality of life in small-scaled homelike nursing homes: An 8-month controlled trial. *Health and Quality of Life Outcomes, 16*(1), 38. https://doi.org/10.1186/s12955-018-0853-7

Kok, R. M., & Reynolds, C. F. (2017). Management of depression in older adults: A review. *JAMA, 317*(20), 2114–2122. https://doi.org/10.1001/jama.2017.5706

Kokis, J. V., Macpherson, R., Toplak, M. E., West, R. F., & Stanovich, K. E. (2002). Heuristic and analytic processing: Age trends and associations with cognitive ability and cognitive styles. *Journal of Experimental Child Psychology, 83*, 26–52.

Kollmayer, M., Schultes, M.-T., Schober, B., Hodosi, T., & Spiel, C. (2018). Parents' judgments about the desirability of toys for their children: Associations with gender role attitudes, gender-typing of toys, and demographics. *Sex Roles, 79*(5), 329–341. https://doi.org/10.1007/s11199-017-0882-4

Kommers, D., Oei, G., Chen, W., Feijs, L., & Oetomo, S. B. (2016). Suboptimal bonding impairs hormonal, epigenetic and neuronal development in preterm infants, but these impairments can be reversed. *Acta Paediatrica, 105*(7), 738–751. https://doi.org/10.1111/apa.13254

Kong, A., Thorleifsson, G., Frigge, M. L., Vilhjalmsson, B. J., Young, A. I., Thorgeirsson, T. E., Benonisdottir, S., Oddsson, A., Halldorsson, B. V., Masson, G., Gudbjartsson, D. F., Helgason, A., Bjornsdottir, G., Thorsteinsdottir, U., & Stefansson, K. (2018). The nature of nurture: Effects of parental genotypes. *Science, 359*(6374), 424–428.

Konrad, C., Hillmann, M., Rispler, J., Niehaus, L., Neuhoff, L., & Barr, R. (2021). Quality of mother-child interaction before, during, and after smartphone use. *Frontiers in Psychology, 12.* https://doi.org/10.3389/fpsyg.2021.616656

Konrad, C., & Seehagen, S. (2020). The effect of napping and nighttime sleep on memory in infants. *Advances in Child Development and Behavior, 60*, 31–56.

Kontis, V., Bennett, J. E., Mathers, C. D., Li, G., Foreman, K., & Ezzati, M. (2017). Future life expectancy in 35 industrialised countries: Projections with a Bayesian model

ensemble. *The Lancet, 389*(10076), 1323–1335. https://doi.org/10.1016/S0140-6736(16)32381-9

Koo, Y. W., Kõlves, K., & De Leo, D. (2017). Suicide in older adults: Differences between the young-old, middle-old, and oldest old. *International Psychogeriatrics, 29*(8), 1297–1306.

Koopmann-Holm, B., & Tsai, J. L. (2014). Focusing on the negative: Cultural differences in expressions of sympathy. *Journal of Personality and Social Psychology, 107*(6), 1092–1115. https://doi.org/10.1037/a0037684

Kopala-Sibley, D. C., Cyr, M., Finsaas, M. C., Orawe, J., Huang, A., Tottenham, N., & Klein, D. N. (2020). Early childhood parenting predicts late childhood brain functional connectivity during emotion perception and reward processing. *Child Development, 91*(1), 110–128. https://doi.org/10.1111/cdev.13126

Kopp, C. B. (1989). Regulation of distress and negative emotions: A developmental view. *Developmental Psychology, 25*(3), 343–354. https://doi.org/10.1037/0012-1649.25.3.343

Korfage, I. J., Carreras, G., Christensen, C. M. A., Billekens, P., Bramley, L., Briggs, L., Bulli, F., Caswell, G., Červ, B., van Delden, J. J. M., Deliens, L., Dunleavy, L., Eecloo, K., Gorini, G., Groenvold, M., Hammes, B., Ingravallo, F., Jabbarian, L. J., Kars, M. C., … Rietjens, J. A. C. (2020). Advance care planning in patients with advanced cancer: A 6-country, cluster-randomised clinical trial. *PLOS Medicine, 17*(11), e1003422. https://doi.org/10.1371/journal.pmed.1003422

Kornadt, A. E., Hess, T. M., Voss, P., & Rothermund, K. (2018). Subjective age across the life span: A differentiated, longitudinal approach. *The Journals of Gerontology: Series B, 73*(5), 767–777. https://doi.org/10.1093/geronb/gbw072

Kornadt, A. E., Siebert, J. S., & Wahl, H.-W. (2019). The interplay of personality and attitudes toward own aging across two decades of later life. *PLOS ONE, 14*(10), e0223622. https://doi.org/10.1371/journal.pone.0223622

Kosiewicz, H., Ngo, F., & Fong, K. (2016). Alternative models to deliver developmental math: Issues of use and student access. *Community College Review, 44*(3), 205–231. https://doi.org/10.1177/0091552116651490

Koss, K. J., & Gunnar, M. R. (2018). Annual research review: Early adversity, the hypothalamic–pituitary–adrenocortical axis, and child psychopathology. *Journal of Child Psychology and Psychiatry, 59*(4), 327–346.

Kost, K., Maddow-Zimet, I., & Arpaia, A. (2017). *Pregnancies, births and abortions among adolescents and young women in the United States, 2013: National and state trends by age, race and ethnicity.* Guttmacher Institute.

Köster, M., & Kärtner, J. (2019). Why do infants help? A simple action reveals a complex phenomenon. *Developmental Review, 51*, 175–187. https://doi.org/10.1016/j.dr.2018.11.004

Kotecki, P. (2018). 10 countries at risk of becoming demographic time bombs. *Business Insider*. https://www.businessinsider.com/10-countries-at-risk-of-becoming-demographic-time-bombs-2018-8

Kotler, S. (2015). Is Silicon Valley ageist or just smart? *Forbes*. https://www.forbes.com/sites/stevenkotler/2015/02/14/is-silicon-valley-ageist-or-just-smart/

Kotowski, J., Fowler, C., Hourigan, C., & Orr, F. (2020). Bottle-feeding an infant feeding modality: An integrative literature review. *Maternal & Child Nutrition, 16*(2), e12939. https://doi.org/10.1111/mcn.12939

Kotowski, J., Fowler, C., & Orr, F. (2021). Bottle-feeding, a neglected area of learning and support for nurses working in child health: An exploratory qualitative study. *Journal of Child Health Care.* https://doi.org/10.1177/13674935211007321

Koumoutzis, A., Cichy, K. E., Dellmann-Jenkins, M., & Blankemeyer, M. (2021). Age differences and similarities in associated stressors and outcomes among young, midlife, and older adult family caregivers. *The International Journal of Aging and Human Development, 92*(4), 431–449. https://doi.org/10.1177/0091415020905265

Kovacheva, S., Kabaivanov, S., & Roberts, K. (2018). Interrogating waithood: Family and housing life stage

transitions among young adults in North-West Africa countries. *International Journal of Adolescence and Youth, 23*(4), 441–456. https://doi.org/10.1080/02673843.2018.1430595

Kowal, M., Coll-Martín, T., Ikizer, G., Rasmussen, J., Eichel, K., Studzińska, A., Koszałkowska, K., Karwowski, M., Najmussaqib, A., Pankowski, D., Lieberoth, A., & Ahmed, O. (2020). Who is the most stressed during the COVID-19 pandemic? Data from 26 countries and areas. *Applied Psychology: Health and Well-Being, 12*(4), 946–966. https://doi.org/10.1111/aphw.12234

Koyanagi, A., Veronese, N., Vancampfort, D., Stickley, A., Jackson, S. E., Oh, H., Shin, J. I., Haro, J. M., Stubbs, B., & Smith, L. (2020). Association of bullying victimization with overweight and obesity among adolescents from 41 low- and middle-income countries. *Pediatric Obesity, 15*(1), e12571. https://doi.org/10.1111/ijpo.12571

Köymen, B., Lieven, E., Engemann, D. A., Rakoczy, H., Warneken, F., & Tomasello, M. (2014). Children's norm enforcement in their interactions with peers. *Child Development, 85*(3), 1108–1122. https://doi.org/10.1111/cdev.12178

Kozhimannil, K. B., Johnson, P. J., Attanasio, L. B., Gjerdingen, D. K., & McGovern, P. M. (2013). Use of non-medical methods of labor induction and pain management among U.S. women. *Birth (Berkeley, CA), 40*(4), 227–236. https://doi.org/10.1111/birt.12064

Kozhimannil, K. B., Vogelsang, C. A., Hardeman, R. R., & Prasad, S. (2016). Disrupting the pathways of social determinants of health: Doula support during pregnancy and childbirth. *The Journal of the American Board of Family Medicine, 29*(3), 308–317. https://doi.org/10.3122/jabfm.2016.03.150300

Kozieł, S. M., & Malina, R. M. (2018). Modified maturity offset prediction equations: Validation in independent longitudinal samples of boys and girls. *Sports Medicine, 48*(1), 221–236. https://doi.org/10.1007/s40279-017-0750-y

Krabbe, A. D., & Grodal, S. (2018). Big, beige and bulky: Aesthetic shifts in the hearing aid industry (1945–2015). *Academy of Management Proceedings, 2018*(1), 14487.

Kramer, A. F., & Colcombe, S. (2018). Fitness effects on the cognitive function of older adults: A meta-analytic study—revisited. *Perspectives on Psychological Science, 13*(2), 213–217. https://doi.org/10.1177/1745691617707316

Kramer, S., & Fahmy, D. (2018, June 13). *The age gap in religion around the world.* Pew Research Center. https://www.pewresearch.org/fact-tank/2018/06/13/younger-people-are-less-religious-than-older-ones-in-many-countries-especially-in-the-u-s-and-europe/

Krampe, R. T., & Charness, N. (2018). Aging and expertise. In K. A. Ericsson, R. R. Hoffman, A. Kozbelt, & A. M. Williams (Eds.), *The Cambridge handbook of expertise and expert performance* (2nd ed., pp. 835–856). Cambridge University Press. https://doi.org/10.1017/9781316480748.042

Krashen, S. D. (1999). *Three arguments against whole language and why they are wrong.* Heinemann.

Kreider, R. M. (2020). US adoption by the numbers. In G. M. Wrobel, E. Helder, & E. Marr (Eds.), *The Routledge handbook of adoption* (pp. 22–35). Routledge.

Kreider, R. M., & Ellis, R. (2011). *Number, timing, and duration of marriages and divorces, 2009.* US Department of Commerce, Economics and Statistics Administration, US Census Bureau.

Kreider, R. M., & Lofquist, D. A. (2014). *Adopted children and stepchildren: 2010* (No. P20-572). US Census Bureau. https://www.census.gov/library/publications/2014/demo/p20-572.html

Kreisel, K. M., Spicknall, I. H., Gargano, J. W., Lewis, F. M. T., Lewis, R. M., Markowitz, L. E., Roberts, H., Johnson, A. S., Song, R., St. Cyr, S. B., Weston, E. J., Torrone, E. A., & Weinstock, H. S. (2021). Sexually transmitted infections among US women and men: Prevalence and incidence estimates, 2018. *Sexually Transmitted Diseases, 48*(4), 208–214. https://doi.org/10.1097/OLQ.0000000000001355

Krekula, C., Nikander, P., & Wilińska, M. (2018). Multiple marginalizations based on age: Gendered ageism and beyond. In L. Ayalon & C. Tesch-Römer (Eds.), *Contemporary perspectives on ageism* (pp. 33–50). Springer.

Krentz, M., Kos, E., Green, A., & Garcia-Alonso, J. (2020, July 15). *Easing the COVID-19 burden on working parents.* BCG Global. https://www.bcg.com/publications/2020/helping-working-parents-ease-the-burden-of-covid-19

Kreski, N., Platt, J., Rutherford, C., Olfson, M., Odgers, C., Schulenberg, J., & Keyes, K. M. (2021). Social media use and depressive symptoms among United States adolescents. *Journal of Adolescent Health, 68*(3), 572–579. https://doi.org/10.1016/j.jadohealth.2020.07.006

Krikorian, A., Maldonado, C., & Pastrana, T. (2020). Patient's perspectives on the notion of a good death: A systematic review of the literature. *Journal of Pain and Symptom Management, 59*(1), 152–164. https://doi.org/10.1016/j.jpainsymman.2019.07.033

Kroger, J., & Marcia, J. E. (2011). The identity statuses: Origins, meanings, and interpretations. In S. J. Schwartz, K. Luyckx, & V. L. Vignoles (Eds.), *Handbook of identity theory and research* (pp. 31–53). Springer.

Kroger, J., Martinussen, M., & Marcia, J. E. (2010). Identity status change during adolescence and young adulthood: A meta-analysis. *Journal of Adolescence, 33*(5), 683–698. doi:10.1016/j.adolescence.2009.11.002

Krol, K. M., Moulder, R. G., Lillard, T. S., Grossmann, T., & Connelly, J. J. (2019a). Epigenetic dynamics in infancy and the impact of maternal engagement. *Science Advances, 5*(10), eaay0680. https://doi.org/10.1126/sciadv.aay0680

Krol, K. M., Puglia, M. H., Morris, J. P., Connelly, J. J., & Grossmann, T. (2019b). Epigenetic modification of the oxytocin receptor gene is associated with emotion processing in the infant brain. *Developmental Cognitive Neuroscience, 37*, 100648. https://doi.org/10.1016/j.dcn.2019.100648

Kross, E., Verduyn, P., Demiralp, E., Park, J., Lee, D. S., Lin, N., Shablack, H., Jonides, J., & Ybarra, O. (2013). Facebook use predicts declines in subjective well-being in young adults. *PLOS ONE, 8*(8), e69841. https://doi.org/10.1371/journal.pone.0069841

Kruk, M., Matsick, J. L., & Wardecker, B. M. (2021). Femininity concerns and feelings about menstruation cessation among lesbian, bisexual, and heterosexual women: Implications for menopause. *Journal of Women's Health.* https://doi.org/10.1089/jwh.2020.8757

Kübler-Ross, E. (1969). *On death and dying.* Macmillan.

Kübler-Ross, E. (1995). *Death is of vital importance: On life, death, and life after death.* Station Hill Press.

Kübler-Ross, E., & Kessler, D. (2005). *On grief and grieving: Finding the meaning of grief through the five stages of loss.* Simon & Schuster.

Kuczmarski, R. J., Ogden, C. L., Grummer-Strawn, L. M., Flegal, K. M., Guo, S. S., Wei, R., Mei, Z., Curtin, L. R., Roche, A. F., & Johnson, C. L. (2000). CDC growth charts: United States. *Advance Data, 314*, 1–27.

Kuhl, P. K., Ramírez, R. R., Bosseler, A., Lin, J. F. L., & Imada, T. (2014). Infants' brain responses to speech suggest analysis by synthesis. *Proceedings of the National Academy of Sciences, 111*(31), 11238–11245.

Kuhn, D. (2009). Adolescent thinking. In R. M. Lerner & L. Steinberg (Eds.), *Handbook of adolescent psychology: Individual bases of adolescent development* (pp. 152–186). John Wiley & Sons. https://doi.org/10.1002/9780470479193.adlpsy001007

Kujawski, S., Kujawska, A., Gajos, M., Topka, W., Perkowski, R., Androsiuk-Perkowska, J., & Kędziora-Kornatowska, K. (2018). Cognitive functioning in older people: Results of the first wave of Cognition of Older People, Education, Recreational Activities, Nutrition, Comorbidities, Functional Capacity Studies (COPERNICUS). *Frontiers in Aging Neuroscience, 10*, 421.

Kulawiak, P. R., & Wilbert, J. (2020). Introduction of a new method for representing the sociometric status within the peer group: The example of sociometrically neglected children. *International Journal of Research & Method in Education, 43*(2), 127–145.

Kulik, L. (2015). Long-term marriages. In S. K. Whitbourne (Ed.), *The encyclopedia of adulthood and aging*

(pp. 1–4). Wiley. https://doi.org/10.1002/9781118521373.wbeaa156

Kulkarni, A. S., Gubbi, S., & Barzilai, N. (2020). Benefits of metformin in attenuating the hallmarks of aging. *Cell Metabolism, 32*(1), 15–30.

Kuntsche, E., Kuntsche, S., Thrul, J., & Gmel, G. (2017). Binge drinking: Health impact, prevalence, correlates and interventions. *Psychology & Health, 32*(8), 976–1017.

Kuper, L. E., Wright, L., & Mustanski, B. (2018). Gender identity development among transgender and gender non-conforming emerging adults: An intersectional approach. *International Journal of Transgenderism, 19*(4), 436–455. https://doi.org/10.1080/15532739.2018.1443869

Kuppens, S., Moore, S. C., Gross, V., Lowthian, E., & Siddaway, A. P. (2020). The enduring effects of parental alcohol, tobacco, and drug use on child well-being: A multilevel meta-analysis. *Development and Psychopathology, 32*(2), 765–778. https://doi.org/10.1017/S0954579419000749

Kurtz-Costes, B., DeFreitas, S. C., Halle, T. G., & Kinlaw, C. R. (2011). Gender and racial favouritism in Black and White preschool girls. *British Journal of Developmental Psychology, 29*(2), 270–287. https://doi.org/10.1111/j.2044-835X.2010.02018.x

Kusmaul, N., & Bunting, M. (2017). Perspectives on caregiving: A qualitative evaluation of certified nursing assistants. *Geriatric Nursing, 38*(2), 146–151.

Kusumastuti, S., van Fenema, E., Polman-van Stratum, E. C., Achterberg, W., Lindenberg, J., & Westendorp, R. G. (2017). When contact is not enough: Affecting first year medical students' image towards older persons. *PLOS ONE, 12*(1), e0169977.

Kuzawa, C. W., & Blair, C. (2019). A hypothesis linking the energy demand of the brain to obesity risk. *Proceedings of the National Academy of Sciences, 116*(27), 13266–13275.

Kuzawa, C. W., Chugani, H. T., Grossman, L. I., Lipovich, L., Muzik, O., Hof, P. R., Wildman, D. E., Sherwood, C. C., Leonard, W. R., & Lange, N. (2014). Metabolic costs and evolutionary implications of human brain development. *Proceedings of the National Academy of Sciences, 111*(36), 13010–13015. https://doi.org/10.1073/pnas.1323099111

Kwan, K. M. W., Shi, S. Y., Nabbijohn, A. N., MacMullin, L. N., VanderLaan, D. P., & Wong, W. I. (2020). Children's appraisals of gender nonconformity: Developmental pattern and intervention. *Child Development, 91*(4), e780–e798.

Kwon, K.-A., Ford, T. G., Salvatore, A. L., Randall, K., Jeon, L., Malek-Lasater, A., Ellis, N., Kile, M. S., Horm, D. M., Kim, S. G., & Han, M. (2020). Neglected elements of a high-quality early childhood workforce: Whole teacher well-being and working conditions. *Early Childhood Education Journal.* https://doi.org/10.1007/s10643-020-01124-7

Kwon, K.-A., Jeon, S., Jeon, L., & Castle, S. (2019). The role of teachers' depressive symptoms in classroom quality and child developmental outcomes in early head start programs. *Learning and Individual Differences, 74*, 101748. https://doi.org/10.1016/j.lindif.2019.06.002

Kwon, S., & O'Neill, M. (2020). Socioeconomic and familial factors associated with gross motor skills among US children aged 3–5 years: The 2012 NHANES National Youth Fitness Survey. *International Journal of Environmental Research and Public Health, 17*(12), 4491. https://doi.org/10.3390/ijerph17124491

Labella, M. H. (2018). The sociocultural context of emotion socialization in African American families. *Clinical Psychology Review, 59*, 1–15. https://doi.org/10.1016/j.cpr.2017.10.006

Labouvie-Vief, G. (1980). Beyond formal operations: Uses and limits of pure logic in life-span development. *Human Development, 23*(3), 141–161. https://doi.org/10.1159/000272546

Labouvie-Vief, G. (1984). Culture, language and mature rationality. In K. A. McCluskey & H. W. Reese (Eds.), *Lifespan developmental psychology: Historical and generational effects* (pp. 109–128). Elsevier.

Labouvie-Vief, G. (1985). Intelligence and cognition. In J. E. Birren (Ed.), *Handbook of the psychology of aging* (2nd ed., pp. 500–530). Van Nostrand Reinhold.

Labouvie-Vief, G. (2015). Cognitive–emotional development from adolescence to adulthood. In G. Labouvie-Vief (Ed.), *Integrating emotions and cognition throughout the lifespan* (pp. 89–116). Springer International Publishing. https://doi.org/10.1007/978-3-319-09822-7_6

Lachance-Grzela, M., & Bouchard, G. (2010). Why do women do the lion's share of housework? A decade of research. *Sex Roles, 63*(11), 767–780. https://doi.org/10.1007/s11199-010-9797-z

Lachance-Grzela, M., McGee, S., & Ross-Plourde, M. (2019). Division of family labour and perceived unfairness among mothers: The role of mattering to family members. *Journal of Family Studies*, 1–15. https://doi.org/10.1080/13229400.2018.1564350

Lachman, M. E. (2015). Mind the gap in the middle: A call to study midlife. *Research in Human Development, 12*(3–4), 327–334.

Lachman, M. E., Teshale, S., & Agrigoroaei, S. (2015). Midlife as a pivotal period in the life course: Balancing growth and decline at the crossroads of youth and old age. *International Journal of Behavioral Development, 39*(1), 20–31.

Lachman, P., Roman, C. G., & Cahill, M. (2013). Assessing youth motivations for joining a peer group as risk factors for delinquent and gang behavior. *Youth Violence and Juvenile Justice, 11*(3), 212–229. https://doi.org/10.1177/1541204012461510

Lachman, R., Lachman, J. L., & Butterfield, E. C. (1979). *Cognitive psychology and information processing: An introduction.* Routledge.

Lachman, R., Lachman, J. L., & Butterfield, E. C. (2015). *Cognitive psychology and information processing: An introduction* (eBook ed.). Psychology Press. https://doi.org/10.4324/9781315798844

Lachs, M. S., Rosen, T., Teresi, J. A., Eimicke, J. P., Ramirez, M., Silver, S., & Pillemer, K. (2013). Verbal and physical aggression directed at nursing home staff by residents. *Journal of General Internal Medicine, 28*(5), 660–667. https://doi.org/10.1007/s11606-012-2284-1

Lacko, A. M., Maselko, J., Popkin, B., & Ng, S. W. (2021). Socio-economic and racial/ethnic disparities in the nutritional quality of packaged food purchases in the USA, 2008–2018. *Public Health Nutrition*, 1–13. https://doi.org/10.1017/S1368980021000367

Lacroix, E., Atkinson, M. J., Garbett, K. M., & Diedrichs, P. C. (2020). One size does not fit all: Trajectories of body image development and their predictors in early adolescence. *Development and Psychopathology*, 1–10. https://doi.org/10.1017/S0954579420000917

Ladd, G. W. (1999). Peer relationships and social competence during early and middle childhood. *Annual Review of Psychology, 50*(1), 333–359.

Laditka, J. N., Laditka, S. B., Liu, R., Price, A. E., Wu, B., Friedman, D. B., & Logsdon, R. G. (2011). Older adults' concerns about cognitive health: Commonalities and differences among six United States ethnic groups. *Ageing & Society, 31*(7), 1202–1228.

LaForett, D. R., & Mendez, J. L. (2017). Play beliefs and responsive parenting among low-income mothers of preschoolers in the United States. *Early Child Development and Care, 187*(8), 1359–1371.

Lagattuta, K. H., Kramer, H. J., Kennedy, K., Hjortsvang, K., Goldfarb, D., & Tashjian, S. (2015). Beyond Sally's missing marble: Further development in children's understanding of mind and emotion in middle childhood. *Advances in Child Development and Behavior, 48*, 185–217.

Lagunas, X. (2021, October 5). *Hispanic Heritage Month: Sister Norma, a beacon of hope.* KVEO-TV. https://www.valleycentral.com/news/local-news/hispanic-heritage-month-sister-norma-a-beacon-of-hope/

Lai, T., & Kao, G. (2018). Hit, robbed, and put down (but not bullied): Underreporting of bullying by minority and male students. *Journal of Youth and Adolescence, 47*(3), 619–635. https://doi.org/10.1007/s10964-017-0748-7

Laird, K. T., Krause, B., Funes, C., & Lavretsky, H. (2019). Psychobiological factors of resilience and depression in late life. *Translational Psychiatry, 9*(1), 1–18. https://doi .org/10.1038/s41398-019-0424-7

Lake, R., & Olson, L. (2020). *Learning as we go: Principles for effective assessment during the COVID-19 pandemic.* Center on Reinventing Public Education. https://eric .ed.gov/?id=ED606373

Lalys, L., & Pineau, J.-C. (2014). Age at menarche in a group of French schoolgirls. *Pediatrics International, 56*(4), 601–604. https://doi.org/10.1111/ped.12296

Lam, C. B., McHale, S. M., & Crouter, A. C. (2014). Time with peers from middle childhood to late adolescence: Developmental course and adjustment correlates. *Child Development, 85*(4), 1677–1693. https://doi.org/10.1111 /cdev.12235

Lam, J. R., Tyler, J., Scurrah, K. J., Reavley, N. J., & Dite, G. S. (2019). The association between socioeconomic status and psychological distress: A within and between twin study. *Twin Research and Human Genetics, 22*(5), 312–320. https://doi.org/10.1017/thg.2019.91

Lamb, S. (2017). *Successful aging as a contemporary obsession: Global perspectives.* Rutgers University Press.

Lamb, S. (2019). On being (not) old: Agency, self-care, and life-course aspirations in the United States. *Medical Anthropology Quarterly, 33*(2), 263–281. https://doi.org/10.1111 /maq.12498

Lamballais, S., Vinke, E. J., Vernooij, M. W., Ikram, M. A., & Muetzel, R. L. (2020). Cortical gyrification in relation to age and cognition in older adults. *NeuroImage, 212,* 116637. https://doi.org/10.1016/j .neuroimage.2020.116637

Lambert, G. H. (2016). Developmental toxicity. *Perspectives in Basic and Applied Toxicology, 242.*

Lambert, K. G., & Byrnes, E. M. (2019). Challenges to the parental brain: Neuroethological and translational considerations. *Frontiers in Neuroendocrinology, 53,* 100747.

Lamela, D., Figueiredo, B., Bastos, A., & Feinberg, M. (2016). Typologies of post-divorce coparenting and parental well-being, parenting quality and children's psychological adjustment. *Child Psychiatry & Human Development, 47*(5), 716–728.

Lamidi, E. O., Manning, W. D., & Brown, S. L. (2019). Change in the stability of first premarital cohabitation among women in the United States, 1983–2013. *Demography, 56*(2), 427–450.

Lamont, E. (2017). "We can write the scripts ourselves": Queer challenges to heteronormative courtship practices. *Gender & Society, 31*(5), 624–646. https://doi .org/10.1177/0891243217723883

Lampl, M., & Schoen, M. (2017). How long bones grow children: Mechanistic paths to variation in human height growth. *American Journal of Human Biology, 29*(2), e22983. https://doi.org/10.1002/ajhb.22983

Lancee, B., & Radl, J. (2014). Volunteering over the life course. *Social Forces, 93*(2), 833–862.

Lancy, D. F. (2018). Work in children's lives. In D. F. Lancy (Ed.), *Anthropological perspectives on children as helpers, workers, artisans, and laborers* (pp. 1–30). Palgrave Macmillan.

Lancy, D. F. (2020). *Child helpers: A multidisciplinary perspective.* Cambridge University Press.

Lancy, D. F. (2021). *Anthropological perspectives on children as helpers, workers, artisans, and laborers.* Palgrave Macmillan.

Landberg, M., Dimitrova, R., & Syed, M. (2018). International perspectives on identity and acculturation in emerging adulthood: Introduction to the special issue. *Emerging Adulthood, 6*(1), 3–6. https://doi .org/10.1177/2167696817748107

Landrigan, P. J., Fuller, R., Fisher, S., Suk, W. A., Sly, P., Chiles, T. C., & Bose-O'Reilly, S. (2019). Pollution and children's health. *Science of The Total Environment, 650,* 2389–2394. https://doi.org/10.1016/j .scitotenv.2018.09.375

Landrum, R. E., Brakke, K., & McCarthy, M. A. (2019). The pedagogical power of storytelling. *Scholarship of Teaching and Learning in Psychology, 5*(3), 247–253. https://doi .org/10.1037/stl0000152

Lange, E. M. S., Rao, S., & Toledo, P. (2017). Racial and ethnic disparities in obstetric anesthesia. *Seminars in Perinatology, 41*(5), 293–298. https://doi.org/10.1053/j .semperi.2017.04.006

Lange, S., Probst, C., Rehm, J., & Popova, S. (2018). National, regional, and global prevalence of smoking during pregnancy in the general population: A systematic review and meta-analysis. *The Lancet Global Health, 6*(7), e769–e776.

Langford, J. M. (2013). *Consoling ghosts: Stories of medicine and mourning from Southeast Asians in exile.* University of Minnesota Press.

Langford, J. M. (2016). Medical eschatologies: The Christian spirit of hospital protocol. *Medical Anthropology, 35*(3), 236–246. https://doi.org/10.1080/01459740.2015.1091820

Laninga-Wijnen, L., Harakeh, Z., Garandeau, C. F., Dijkstra, J. K., Veenstra, R., & Vollebergh, W. A. (2019). Classroom popularity hierarchy predicts prosocial and aggressive popularity norms across the school year. *Child Development, 90*(5), e637–e653.

Laninga-Wijnen, L., Ryan, A. M., Harakeh, Z., Shin, H., & Vollebergh, W. A. (2018). The moderating role of popular peers' achievement goals in 5th-and 6th-graders' achievement-related friendships: A social network analysis. *Journal of Educational Psychology, 110*(2), 289.

Lanphear, B. P., Rauch, S., Auinger, P., Allen, R. W., & Hornung, R. W. (2018). Low-level lead exposure and mortality in US adults: A population-based cohort study. *The Lancet Public Health, 3*(4), e177–e184. https://doi .org/10.1016/S2468-2667(18)30025-2

Lansford, J. E. (2009). Parental divorce and children's adjustment. *Perspectives on Psychological Science, 4*(2), 140–152.

Lansford, J. E. (2017). An international perspective on parenting and children's adjustment. In N. J. Cabrera & B. Leyendecker (Eds.), *Handbook on positive development of minority children and youth* (pp. 107–122). Springer International Publishing. https://doi .org/10.1007/978-3-319-43645-6_7

Lansford, J. E., & Bornstein, M. H. (2020). Parenting. In W. K. Halford & F. van de Vijver (Eds.), *Cross-cultural family research and practice* (pp. 565–602). Academic Press. https://doi.org/10.1016/B978-0-12-815493-9.00018-1

Lansford, J. E., Godwin, J., Al-Hassan, S. M., Bacchini, D., Bornstein, M. H., Chang, L., Chen, B.-B., Deater-Deckard, K., Di Giunta, L., Dodge, K. A., Malone, P. S., Oburu, P., Pastorelli, C., Skinner, A. T., Sorbring, E., Steinberg, L., Tapanya, S., Alampay, L. P., Uribe Tirado, L. M., & Zelli, A. (2018). Longitudinal associations between parenting and youth adjustment in twelve cultural groups: Cultural normativeness of parenting as a moderator. *Developmental Psychology, 54*(2), 362–377. https://doi.org/10.1037/dev0000416

Lansford, J. E., Godwin, J., McMahon, R. J., Crowley, M., Pettit, G. S., Bates, J. E., Coie, J. D., & Dodge, K. A. (2021). Early physical abuse and adult outcomes. *Pediatrics, 147*(1), e20200873. https://doi.org/10.1542 /peds.2020-0873

Lansford, J. E., Godwin, J., Uribe Tirado, L. M., Zelli, A., Al-Hassan, S. M., Bacchini, D., Bombi, A. S., Bornstein, M. H., Chang, L., Deater-Deckard, K., Di Giunta, L., Dodge, K. A., Malone, P. S., Oburu, P., Pastorelli, C., Skinner, A. T., Sorbring, E., Tapanya, S., & Alampay, L. P. (2015). Individual, family, and culture level contributions to child physical abuse and neglect: A longitudinal study in nine countries. *Development and Psychopathology, 27*(4 Pt. 2), 1417–1428. https://doi.org/10.1017 /S095457941500084X

Lansford, J. E., Laird, R. D., Pettit, G. S., Bates, J. E., & Dodge, K. A. (2014). Mothers' and fathers' autonomy-relevant parenting: Longitudinal links with adolescents' externalizing and internalizing behavior. *Journal of Youth and Adolescence, 43*(11), 1877–1889. https://doi.org/10.1007 /s10964-013-0079-2

Lansford, J. E., Rothenberg, W. A., & Bornstein, M. H. (2021). *Parenting across cultures from childhood to adolescence: Development in nine countries.* Routledge.

Lanz, M., Sorgente, A., & Danes, S. M. (2020). Implicit family financial socialization and emerging adults' financial well-being: A multi-informant approach. *Emerging Adulthood, 8*(6), 443–452. https://doi .org/10.1177/2167696819876752

Lapan, C., & Boseovski, J. J. (2017). When peer performance matters: Effects of expertise and traits on children's self-evaluations after social comparison. *Child Development, 88*(6), 1860–1872.

LaPlante, M. P. (2010). The classic measure of disability in activities of daily living is biased by age but an expanded IADL/ADL measure is not. *The Journals of Gerontology Series B: Psychological Sciences and Social Sciences, 65B*(6), 720–732. https://doi.org/10.1093/geronb/gbp129

Lara, L. A. S., & Abdo, C. H. N. (2016). Age at time of initial sexual intercourse and health of adolescent girls. *Journal of Pediatric and Adolescent Gynecology, 29*(5), 417–423. https://doi.org/10.1016/j.jpag.2015.11.012

Lareau, A. (2011). *Unequal childhoods: Class, race, and family life.* University of California Press.

Lareau, A. (2015). Cultural knowledge and social inequality. *American Sociological Review, 80*(1), 1–27. http://asr .sagepub.com/content/80/1/1.short

Largent, E. A., Terrasse, M., Harkins, K., Sisti, D. A., Sankar, P., & Karlawish, J. (2019). Attitudes toward physician-assisted death from individuals who learn they have an Alzheimer disease biomarker. *JAMA Neurology, 76*(7), 864. https://doi.org/10.1001/jamaneurol.2019.0797

Larson, R. W., Moneta, G., Richards, M. H., & Wilson, S. (2002). Continuity, stability, and change in daily emotional experience across adolescence. *Child Development, 73*(4), 1151–1165.

Larson, R. W., Richards, M. H., Moneta, G., Holmbeck, G., & Duckett, E. (1996). Changes in adolescents' daily interactions with their families from ages 10 to 18: Disengagement and transformation. *Developmental Psychology, 32*(4), 744–754. https://doi .org/10.1037/0012-1649.32.4.744

Lassi, M., & Teperino, R. (2020). Introduction to epigenetic inheritance: Definition, mechanisms, implications and relevance. In R. Teperino (Ed.), *Beyond our genes: Pathophysiology of gene and environment interaction and epigenetic inheritance* (pp. 159–173). Springer International Publishing. https://doi.org/10.1007/978-3-030-35213-4_9

Latham, R. M., & Von Stumm, S. (2017). Mothers want extraversion over conscientiousness or intelligence for their children. *Personality and Individual Differences, 119,* 262–265.

Lau, M., Lin, H., & Flores, G. (2015). Clusters of factors identify a high prevalence of pregnancy involvement among US adolescent males. *Maternal and Child Health Journal, 19*(8), 1713–1723.

Lau, Y.-F. C. (2020). Y chromosome in health and diseases. *Cell & Bioscience, 10*(1), 97. https://doi.org/10.1186/ s13578-020-00452-w

Laube, C., van den Bos, W., & Fandakova, Y. (2020). The relationship between pubertal hormones and brain plasticity: Implications for cognitive training in adolescence. *Developmental Cognitive Neuroscience, 42,* 100753. https:// doi.org/10.1016/j.dcn.2020.100753

Lauro, J., Core, C., & Hoff, E. (2020). Explaining individual differences in trajectories of simultaneous bilingual development: Contributions of child and environmental factors. *Child Development, 91*(6), 2063–2082. https://doi .org/10.1111/cdev.13409

Laursen, B., Coy, K. C., & Collins, W. A. (1998). Reconsidering changes in parent-child conflict across adolescence: A meta-analysis. *Child Development, 69*(3), 817–832.

Laursen, B., Little, T. D., & Card, N. A. (2012). *Handbook of developmental research methods.* Guilford.

Lavedán, A., Viladrosa, M., Jürschik, P., Botigué, T., Nuín, C., Masot, O., & Lavedán, R. (2018). Fear of falling in community-dwelling older adults: A cause of falls, a consequence, or both? *PLoS ONE, 13*(3), e0194967.

Lavelli, M., Carra, C., Rossi, G., & Keller, H. (2019). Culture-specific development of early mother–infant emotional co-regulation: Italian, Cameroonian, and West African immigrant dyads. *Developmental Psychology, 55*(9), 1850–1867. https://doi.org/10.1037/dev0000696

Lavigne, M., Birken, C. S., Maguire, J. L., Straus, S., & Laupacis, A. (2017). Priority setting in paediatric preventive care research. *Archives of Disease in Childhood, 102*(8), 748–753. https://doi.org/10.1136/archdischild-2016-312284

Lavin, K. M., Perkins, R. K., Jemiolo, B., Raue, U., Trappe, S. W., & Trappe, T. A. (2020). Effects of aging and lifelong aerobic exercise on basal and exercise-induced inflammation. *Journal of Applied Physiology, 128*(1): 87–99. https://doi.org/10.1152/japplphysiol.00495.2019

Lavingia, R., Jones, K., & Asghar-Ali, A. A. (2020). A systematic review of barriers faced by older adults in seeking and accessing mental health care. *Journal of Psychiatric Practice, 26*(5), 367–382. https://doi.org/10.1097/PRA.0000000000000491

Lavner, J. A., Barton, A. W., & Beach, S. R. (2020). Direct and indirect effects of a couple-focused preventive intervention on children's outcomes: A randomized controlled trial with African American families. *Journal of Consulting and Clinical Psychology, 88*(8), 696.

Lavner, J. A., Barton, A. W., Bryant, C. M., & Beach, S. R. H. (2018). Racial discrimination and relationship functioning among African American couples. *Journal of Family Psychology: JFP: Journal of the Division of Family Psychology of the American Psychological Association (Division 43), 32*(5), 686–691. https://doi.org/10.1037/fam0000415

Lavoie, J., Leduc, K., Arruda, C., Crossman, A. M., & Talwar, V. (2017a). Developmental profiles of children's spontaneous lie-telling behavior. *Cognitive Development, 41,* 33–45.

Lavoie, J., Nagar, P. M., & Talwar, V. (2017b). From Kantian to Machiavellian deceivers: Development of children's reasoning and self-reported use of secrets and lies. *Childhood, 24*(2), 197–211. https://doi.org/10.1177/0907568216671179

Law, E., Fisher, E., Eccleston, C., & Palermo, T. M. (2019). Psychological interventions for parents of children and adolescents with chronic illness. *Cochrane Database of Systematic Reviews, 3,* CD009660. https://doi.org/10.1002/14651858.CD009660.pub4

Lawford, H. L., & Ramey, H. L. (2015). "Now I know I can make a difference": Generativity and activity engagement as predictors of meaning making in adolescents and emerging adults. *Developmental Psychology, 51*(10), 1395.

Lawford, H. L., Ramey, H. L., & Hood, S. (2021). The associations between early generative concern, moral identity, and well-being in adolescence and early adulthood. *Journal of Moral Education,* 1–14. https://doi.org/10.1080/03057240.2021.1972948

Lawrence, E. M., Rogers, R. G., Zajacova, A., & Wadsworth, T. (2019). Marital happiness, marital status, health, and longevity. *Journal of Happiness Studies, 20*(5), 1539–1561. https://doi.org/10.1007/s10902-018-0009-9

Lawton, B. L., Foeman, A., & Surdel, N. (2018). Bridging discussions of human history: Ancestry DNA and new roles for Africana studies. *Genealogy, 2*(1), 5. https://doi.org/10.3390/genealogy2010005

Lawton, G., & Ifama, D. (2018). "It made me question my ancestry": Does DNA home testing really understand race? *The Guardian.*

Lawton, R. N., Gramatki, I., Watt, W., & Fujiwara, D. (2021). Does volunteering make us happier, or are happier people more likely to volunteer? Addressing the problem of reverse causality when estimating the wellbeing impacts of volunteering. *Journal of Happiness Studies, 22*(2), 599–624.

Layard, R., Clark, A. E., Cornaglia, F., Powdthavee, N., & Vernoit, J. (2014). What predicts a successful life? A life-course model of well-being. *Economic Journal (London, England), 124*(580), F720–F738. https://doi.org/10.1111/ecoj.12170

Lazarus, N. R., & Harridge, S. D. R. (2018). The inherent human aging process and the facilitating role of exercise. *Frontiers in Physiology, 9,* 1135. https://doi.org/10.3389/fphys.2018.01135

Leadbeater, B. J., Ames, M. E., & Linden-Carmichael, A. N. (2019). Age-varying effects of cannabis use frequency and disorder on symptoms of psychosis, depression and anxiety in adolescents and adults. *Addiction, 114*(2), 278–293. https://doi.org/10.1111/add.14459

Leaper, C., & Brown, C. S. (2018). Sexism in childhood and adolescence: Recent trends and advances in research.

Child Development Perspectives, 12(1), 10–15. https://doi.org/10.1111/cdep.12247

Leaper, C., & Starr, C. R. (2019). Helping and hindering undergraduate women's STEM motivation: Experiences with stem encouragement, STEM-related gender bias, and sexual harassment. *Psychology of Women Quarterly, 43*(2), 165–183. https://doi.org/10.1177/0361684318806302

Leavitt, C. E., Lefkowitz, E. S., Akyil, Y., & Serduk, K. (2020). A cross-cultural study of midlife relational and sexual health: Comparing Ukraine to the U.S. and Turkey. *Sexuality & Culture, 24*(3), 649–670. https://doi.org/10.1007/s12119-019-09654-y

LeBaron, A. B., Marks, L. D., Rosa, C. M., & Hill, E. J. (2020). Can we talk about money? Financial socialization through parent–child financial discussion. *Emerging Adulthood, 8*(6), 453–463. https://doi.org/10.1177/2167696820902673

Lebel, C., & Deoni, S. (2018). The development of brain white matter microstructure. *NeuroImage, 182,* 207–218. https://doi.org/10.1016/j.neuroimage.2017.12.097

LeBourgeois, M. K., Hale, L., Chang, A.-M., Akacem, L. D., Montgomery-Downs, H. E., & Buxton, O. M. (2017). Digital media and sleep in childhood and adolescence. *Pediatrics, 140*(Supplement 2), S92–S96. https://doi.org/10.1542/peds.2016-1758J

Lebrun-Harris, L. A., Sherman, L. J., Limber, S. P., Miller, B. D., & Edgerton, E. A. (2019). Bullying victimization and perpetration among U.S. children and adolescents: 2016 National Survey of Children's Health. *Journal of Child and Family Studies, 28*(9), 2543–2557. https://doi.org/10.1007/s10826-018-1170-9

Lederer, A. M., & Laing, E. E. (2017). What's in a name? Perceptions of the terms sexually transmitted disease and sexually transmitted infection among late adolescents. *Sexually Transmitted Diseases, 44*(11), 707–711. https://doi.org/10.1097/OLQ.0000000000000682

Lee, A. C., Blencowe, H., & Lawn, J. E. (2019). Small babies, big numbers: Global estimates of preterm birth. *The Lancet Global Health, 7*(1), e2–e3.

Lee, C. M., Cadigan, J. M., & Rhew, I. C. (2020). Increases in loneliness among young adults during the COVID-19 pandemic and association with increases in mental health problems. *Journal of Adolescent Health, 67*(5), 714–717. https://doi.org/10.1016/j.jadohealth.2020.08.009

Lee, D. R., McKeith, I., Mosimann, U., Ghosh-Nodyal, A., & Thomas, A. J. (2013). Examining carer stress in dementia: The role of subtype diagnosis and neuropsychiatric symptoms. *International Journal of Geriatric Psychiatry, 28*(2), 135–141.

Lee, E.-Y., Bains, A., Hunter, S., Ament, A., Brazo-Sayavera, J., Carson, V., Hakimi, S., Huang, W. Y., Janssen, I., Lee, M., Lim, H., Silva, D. A. S., & Tremblay, M. S. (2021). Systematic review of the correlates of outdoor play and time among children aged 3–12 years. *International Journal of Behavioral Nutrition and Physical Activity, 18*(1), 41. https://doi.org/10.1186/s12966-021-01097-9

Lee, G. Y., & Kisilevsky, B. S. (2014). Fetuses respond to father's voice but prefer mother's voice after birth. *Developmental Psychobiology, 56*(1), 1–11. https://doi.org/10.1002/dev.21084

Lee, J. M., Wasserman, R., Kaciroti, N., Gebremariam, A., Steffes, J., Dowshen, S., Harris, D., Serwint, J., Abney, D., Smitherman, L., Reiter, E., & Herman-Giddens, M. E. (2016). Timing of puberty in overweight versus obese boys. *Pediatrics, 137*(2), e20150164.

Lee, K. (2010). Developmental trajectories of Head Start children's reading and home environment scores: Across ethnicities. *Journal of Social Service Research.*

Lee, K., Quinn, P. C., & Heyman, G. D. (2017). Rethinking the emergence and development of implicit racial bias: A perceptual-social linkage hypothesis. In N. Budwig, E. Turiel, & P. D. Zelazo (Eds.), *New perspectives on human development* (pp. 27–46). Cambridge University Press.

Lee, K. T. H., Lewis, R. W., Kataoka, S., Schenke, K., & Vandell, D. L. (2018). Out-of-school time and behaviors during adolescence. Journal of Research on Adolescence, 28(2), 284–293. https://doi.org/10.1111/jora.12389

Lee, L. O., Aldwin, C. M., Kubzansky, L. D., Mroczek, D. K., & Spiro, A. (2019). The long arm of childhood

experiences on longevity: Testing midlife vulnerability and resilience pathways. *Psychology and Aging, 34*(7), 884–899. https://doi.org/10.1037/pag0000394

Lee, M. R., & Thai, C. J. (2015). Asian American phenotypicality and experiences of psychological distress: More than meets the eyes. *Asian American Journal of Psychology, 6*(3), 242–251. https://doi.org/10.1037/aap0000015

Lee, P. A., Nordenström, A., Houk, C. P., Ahmed, S. F., Auchus, R., Baratz, A., Dalke, K. B., Liao, L.-M., Lin-Su, K., Looijenga, L. H. J., 3rd, Mazur, T., Meyer-Bahlburg, H. F. L., Mouriquand, P., Quigley, C. A., Sandberg, D. E., Vilain, E., Witchel, S., & the Global DSD Update Consortium. (2016). Global disorders of sex development update since 2006: Perceptions, approach and care. *Hormone Research in Paediatrics, 85*(3), 158–180. https://doi.org/10.1159/000442975

Lee, S., Crain, T. L., McHale, S. M., Almeida, D. M., & Buxton, O. M. (2017). Daily antecedents and consequences of nightly sleep. *Journal of Sleep Research, 26*(4), 498–509. https://doi.org/10.1111/jsr.12488

Lee, S. J., Altschul, I., & Gershoff, E. T. (2013). Does warmth moderate longitudinal associations between maternal spanking and child aggression in early childhood? *Developmental Psychology, 49*(11), 2017–2028. https://doi.org/10.1037/a0031630

Leeb, R. T., Bitsko, R. H., Radhakrishnan, L., Martinez, P., Njai, R., & Holland, K. M. (2020). Mental health–related emergency department visits among children aged <18 years during the COVID-19 pandemic — United States, January 1–October 17, 2020. *Morbidity and Mortality Weekly Report, 69*(45), 1675–1680. https://doi.org/10.15585/mmwr.mm6945a3

Leerkes, E. M., & Zhou, N. (2018). Maternal sensitivity to distress and attachment outcomes: Interactions with sensitivity to non-distress and infant temperament. *Journal of Family Psychology, 32*(6), 753–761. https://doi.org/10.1037/fam0000420

Legare, C. H. (2019). The development of cumulative cultural learning. *Annual Review of Developmental Psychology, 1*(1), 119–147. https://doi.org/10.1146/annurev-devpsych-121318-084848

Legare, C. H., Clegg, J. M., & Wen, N. J. (2018). Evolutionary developmental psychology: 2017 redux. *Child Development, 89,* 2282–2287.

Lehmann, S. W., & Fingerhood, M. (2018). Substance-use disorders in later life. *New England Journal of Medicine, 379*(24), 2351–2360.

Lehnart, J., Neyer, F. J., & Eccles, J. (2010). Long-term effects of social investment: The case of partnering in young adulthood. *Journal of Personality, 78*(2), 639–670. https://doi.org/10.1111/j.1467-6494.2010.00629.x

Lei, L., & South, S. J. (2016). Racial and ethnic differences in leaving and returning to the parental home: The role of life course transitions, socioeconomic resources, and family connectivity. *Demographic Research, 34,* 109–142. https://doi.org/10.4054/DemRes.2016.34.4

Lei, L., & South, S. J. (2021). Explaining the decline in young adult sexual activity in the United States. *Journal of Marriage and Family, 83*(1), 280–295.

Leibold, L. J., & Buss, E. (2019). Masked speech recognition in school-age children. *Frontiers in Psychology, 10,* 1981. https://doi.org/10.3389/fpsyg.2019.01981

Leidman, E., Duca, L. M., Omura, J. D., Proia, K., Stephens, J. W., & Sauber-Schatz, E. K. (2021). COVID-19 trends among persons aged 0–24 years — United States, March 1–December 12, 2020. *Morbidity and Mortality Weekly Report, 70*(3), 88–94. https://doi.org/10.15585/mmwr.mm7003e1

Leins, H., Mulaw, M., Eiwen, K., Sakk, V., Liang, Y., Denkinger, M., Geiger, H., & Schirmbeck, R. (2018). Aged murine hematopoietic stem cells drive aging-associated immune remodeling. *Blood, 132*(6), 565–576. https://doi.org/10.1182/blood-2018-02-831065

Lejri, I., Grimm, A., & Eckert, A. (2018). Mitochondria, estrogen and female brain aging. *Frontiers in Aging Neuroscience, 10,* 124. https://doi.org/10.3389/fnagi.2018.00124

Leland, J., & Yalkin, D. (2018, June 22). The positive death movement comes to life. *The New York Times.* https://

www.nytimes.com/2018/06/22/nyregion/the-positive-death-movement-comes-to-life.html

Lemola, S., Perkinson-Gloor, N., Brand, S., Dewald-Kaufmann, J. F., & Grob, A. (2015). Adolescents' electronic media use at night, sleep disturbance, and depressive symptoms in the smartphone age. *Journal of Youth and Adolescence, 44*(2), 405–418.

Lenhart, A. (2015, August 6). *Teens, technology and friendships.* Pew Research Center: Internet, Science & Tech. http://www.pewinternet.org/2015/08/06/teens-technology-and-friendships/

Lennox, S. (2013). Interactive read-alouds—An avenue for enhancing children's language for thinking and understanding: A review of recent research. *Early Childhood Education Journal, 41*(5), 381–389. https://doi.org/10.1007/s10643-013-0578-5

Lenroot, R. K., Gogtay, N., Greenstein, D. K., Wells, E. M., Wallace, G. L., Clasen, L. S., Blumenthal, J. D., Lerch, J., Zijdenbos, A. P., Evans, A. C., Thompson, P. M., & Giedd, J. N. (2007). Sexual dimorphism of brain developmental trajectories during childhood and adolescence. *NeuroImage, 36*(4), 1065–1073. https://doi.org/10.1016/j.neuroimage.2007.03.053

Lenzenweger, M. F., Lane, M. C., Loranger, A. W., & Kessler, R. C. (2007). DSM-IV personality disorders in the National Comorbidity Survey Replication. *Biological Psychiatry, 62*(6), 553–564. https://doi.org/10.1016/j.biopsych.2006.09.019

Leonard, H., Khurana, A., & Hammond, M. (2021). Bedtime media use and sleep: Evidence for bidirectional effects and associations with attention control in adolescents. *Sleep Health, 7*(4), 491–499. https://doi.org/10.1016/j.sleh.2021.05.003

Leone, T. (2019). Women's mid-life health in low and middle income countries: A comparative analysis of the timing and speed of health deterioration in six countries. *SSM—Population Health, 7*, 100341. https://doi.org/10.1016/j.ssmph.2018.100341

Lepper, M. R., & Woolverton, M. (2002). The wisdom of practice: Lessons learned from the study of highly effective tutors. In J. Aronson (Ed.), *Improving academic achievement* (pp. 135–158). Academic Press.

Lerner, R. M. (2021). *Individuals as producers of their own development: The dynamics of person-context coactions.* Routledge.

Lerner, R. M., & Murray, E. D. (2016). Finally! A developmental science that privileges development. *Human Development, 59*(6), 377–385. https://doi.org/10.1159/000455030

le Roux, K. W., Almirol, E., Rezvan, P. H., Le Roux, I. M., Mbewu, N., Dippenaar, E., & Rotheram-Borus, M. J. (2020). Community health workers impact on maternal and child health outcomes in rural South Africa—A non-randomized two-group comparison study. *BMC Public Health, 20*(1), 1–14.

Leroy, J. L., Frongillo, E. A., Dewan, P., Black, M. M., & Waterland, R. A. (2020). Can children catch up from the consequences of undernourishment? Evidence from child linear growth, developmental epigenetics, and brain and neurocognitive development. *Advances in Nutrition, 11*(4), 1032–1041. https://doi.org/10.1093/advances/nmaa020

Leslie, W. D., Schousboe, J. T., Morin, S. N., Martineau, P., Lix, L. M., Johansson, H., & Kanis, J. A. (2020). Measured height loss predicts incident clinical fractures independently from FRAX: A registry-based cohort study. *Osteoporosis International, 31*(6), 1079–1087.

Lessard, L. M., & Juvonen, J. (2020). Weight stigma in the school setting: The role of inclusive weight climate—A commentary. *Journal of School Health, 90*(7), 507–510. https://doi.org/10.1111/josh.12898

Lessard, L. M., & Puhl, R. M. (2021). Adolescent academic worries amid COVID-19 and perspectives on pandemic-related changes in teacher and peer relations. *School Psychology.*

Leszczensky, L., & Pink, S. (2019). What drives ethnic homophily? A relational approach on how ethnic identification moderates preferences for same-ethnic friends. *American Sociological Review, 84*(3), 394–419. https://doi.org/10.1177/0003122419846849

Leszczensky, L., & Stark, T. (2019). Understanding the causes and consequences of segregation in youth's friendship networks: Opportunities and challenges for research. In P. F. Titzmann & P. Jugert (Eds.), *Youth in superdiverse societies* (pp. 233–248). Routledge.

Levin, D. E., & Carlsson-Paige, N. (2005). *The war play dilemma: What every parent and teacher needs to know.* Teachers College Press.

Levine, E. C., Herbenick, D., Martinez, O., Fu, T.-C., & Dodge, B. (2018). Open relationships, nonconsensual, nonmonogamy, and monogamy among U.S. adults: Findings from the 2012 national survey of sexual health and behavior. *Archives of Sexual Behavior, 47*(5), 1439–1450. https://doi.org/10.1007/s10508-018-1178-7

Levine, H., Jørgensen, N., Martino-Andrade, A., Mendiola, J., Weksler-Derri, D., Mindlis, I., Pinotti, R., & Swan, S. H. (2017). Temporal trends in sperm count: A systematic review and meta-regression analysis. *Human Reproduction Update, 23*(6), 646–659. https://doi.org/10.1093/humupd/dmx022

Levine, M. S. & Kearney, P. (2021, May 5). *The coming COVID-19 baby bust is here.* Brookings. https://www.brookings.edu/blog/up-front/2021/05/05/the-coming-covid-19-baby-bust-is-here/

LeVine, R. A., & LeVine, S. (2016). *Do parents matter? Why Japanese babies sleep soundly, Mexican siblings don't fight, and American families should just relax.* PublicAffairs.

Levinson, D. J. (1978). *The seasons of a man's life.* Ballantine Books.

Levinson, D. J., & Levinson, J. (1996). *The seasons of a woman's life: A fascinating exploration of the events, thoughts, and life experiences that all women share.* Random House.

Levy, B. R., & Banaji, M. R. (2002). Implicit ageism. In T. D. Nelson (Ed.), *Ageism: Stereotyping and prejudice against older persons, 2004* (pp. 49–75). MIT Press.

Levy, B. R., Slade, M. D., Chang, E.-S., Kannoth, S., & Wang, S.-Y. (2020). Ageism amplifies cost and prevalence of health conditions. *The Gerontologist, 60*(1), 174–181. https://doi.org/10.1093/geront/gny131

Levy, J., Lankinen, K., Hakonen, M., & Feldman, R. (2021). The integration of social and neural synchrony: A case for ecologically valid research using MEG neuroimaging. *Social Cognitive and Affective Neuroscience, 16*(1–2), 143–152. https://doi.org/10.1093/scan/nsaa061

Lewis, A., Cahn-Fuller, K., & Caplan, A. (2017). Shouldn't dead be dead? The search for a uniform definition of death. *Journal of Law, Medicine & Ethics, 45*(1), 112–128.

Lewis, A., & Greer, D. (2017). Current controversies in brain death determination. *Nature Reviews Neurology, 13*(8), 505–509. https://doi.org/10.1038/nrneurol.2017.72

Lewis, B. A., Billing, L., Schuver, K., Gjerdingen, D., Avery, M., & Marcus, B. H. (2017). The relationship between employment status and depression symptomatology among women at risk for postpartum depression. *Women's Health, 13*(1), 3–9.

Lewis, I. D., & McBride, M. (2004). Anticipatory grief and chronicity: Elders and families in racial/ethnic minority groups. *Geriatric Nursing, 25*(1), 44–47. https://doi.org/10.1016/j.gerinurse.2003.11.014

Lewis, K., Sandilos, L. E., Hammer, C. S., Sawyer, B. E., & Méndez, L. I. (2016). Relations among the home language and literacy environment and children's language abilities: A study of Head Start dual language learners and their mothers. *Early Education and Development, 27*(4), 478–494.

Lewis, M. (2014). Toward the development of the science of developmental psychopathology. In M. Lewis & K. D. Rudolph (Eds.), *Handbook of developmental psychopathology* (pp. 3–23). Springer Science & Business Media.

Lewis, M. (2017). The emergence of human emotions. In L. F. Barrett, M. Lewis, & J. M. Haviland-Jones (Eds.), *Handbook of emotions* (4th ed., pp. 271–291). Guilford.

Lewis, M., & Brooks-Gunn, J. (1979). Toward a theory of social cognition: The development of self. *New Directions for Child and Adolescent Development, 1979*(4), 1–20. https://doi.org/10.1002/cd.23219790403

Lewis, M., Takai-Kawakami, K., Kawakami, K., & Sullivan, M. W. (2010). Cultural differences in emotional responses to success and failure. *International Journal of Behavioral Development, 34*(1), 53–61. https://doi.org/10.1177/0165025409348559

Lewis, T. L., & Maurer, D. (2005). Multiple sensitive periods in human visual development: Evidence from visually deprived children. *Developmental Psychobiology, 46*(3), 163–183. https://doi.org/10.1002/dev.20055

Lew-Levy, S., Boyette, A. H., Crittenden, A. N., Hewlett, B. S., & Lamb, M. E. (2020). Gender-typed and gender-segregated play among Tanzanian Hadza and Congolese BaYaka hunter-gatherer children and adolescents. *Child Development, 91*(4), 1284–1301. https://doi.org/10.1111/cdev.13306

Lew-Levy, S., Reckin, R., Lavi, N., Cristóbal-Azkarate, J., & Ellis-Davies, K. (2017). How do hunter-gatherer children learn subsistence skills? *Human Nature, 28*(4), 367–394. https://doi.org/10.1007/s12110-017-9302-2

Li, C., Mendoza, M., & Milanaik, R. (2017). Touchscreen device usage in infants and toddlers and its correlations with cognitive development. *Pediatrics & Health Research, 2*(1). https://doi.org/10.21767/2574-2817.100013

Li, G., & Davis, J. T. M. (2019). Sexual experimentation in heterosexual, bisexual, lesbian/gay, and questioning adolescents from ages 11 to 15. *Journal of Research on Adolescence, 30*(2), 423–439. https://doi.org/10.1111/jora.12535

Li, J., Vitiello, M. V., & Gooneratne, N. (2018). Sleep in normal aging. *Sleep Medicine Clinics, 13*(1), 1–11. https://doi.org/10.1016/j.jsmc.2017.09.001

Li, K., Chan, W., Doody, R. S., Quinn, J., & Luo, S. (2017). Prediction of conversion to Alzheimer's disease with longitudinal measures and time-to-event data. *Journal of Alzheimer's Disease, 58*(2), 361–371. https://doi.org/10.3233/JAD-161201

Li, S., Nguyen, T. L., Wong, E. M., Dugué, P.-A., Dite, G. S., Armstrong, N. J., Craig, J. M., Mather, K. A., Sachdev, P. S., Saffery, R., Sung, J., Tan, Q., Thalamuthu, A., Milne, R. L., Giles, G. G., Southey, M. C., & Hopper, J. L. (2020). Genetic and environmental causes of variation in epigenetic aging across the lifespan. *Clinical Epigenetics, 12*(1), 158. https://doi.org/10.1186/s13148-020-00950-1

Li, T., Chen, X., Mascaro, J., Haroon, E., & Rilling, J. K. (2017). Intranasal oxytocin, but not vasopressin, augments neural responses to toddlers in human fathers. *Hormones and Behavior, 93*, 193–202. https://doi.org/10.1016/j.yhbeh.2017.01.006

Li, W., Wang, Z., Wang, G., Ip, P., Sun, X., Jiang, Y., & Jiang, F. (2021). Socioeconomic inequality in child mental health during the COVID-19 pandemic: First evidence from China. *Journal of Affective Disorders, 287*, 8–14. https://doi.org/10.1016/j.jad.2021.03.009

Li, Y., Harrington, C., Temkin-Greener, H., You, K., Cai, X., Cen, X., & Mukamel, D. B. (2015). Deficiencies in care at nursing homes and racial/ethnic disparities across homes fell, 2006–11. *Health Affairs, 34*(7), 1139–1146. https://doi.org/10.1377/hlthaff.2015.0094

Li, Y., Li, H., Decety, J., & Lee, K. (2013). Experiencing a natural disaster alters children's altruistic giving. *Psychological Science, 24*(9), 1686–1695. https://doi.org/10.1177/0956797613479975

Li, Y., Thompson, W. K., Reuter, C., Nillo, R., Jernigan, T., Dale, A., Sugrue, L. P., & ABCD Consortium. (2021). Rates of incidental findings in brain magnetic resonance imaging in children. *JAMA Neurology.* https://doi.org/10.1001/jamaneurol.2021.0306

Li, Z., & Dalaker, J. (2019). *Poverty among Americans aged 65 and older.* Congressional Research Service.

Lian, Q., Zuo, X., Mao, Y., Zhang, Y., Luo, S., Zhang, S., Lou, C., Tu, X., & Zhou, W. (2018). The impact of the Wenchuan earthquake on early puberty: A natural experiment. *PeerJ, 6*, e5085.

Liang, M., Simelane, S., Fillo, G. F., Chalasani, S., Weny, K., Canelos, P. S., Jenkins, L., Moller, A.-B., Chandra-Mouli, V., Say, L., Michielsen, K., Engel, D. M. C., & Snow, R. (2019). The state of adolescent sexual and reproductive health. *Journal of Adolescent Health, 65*(6), S3–S15.

Liang, Y., Rausch, C., Laflamme, L., & Möller, J. (2018). Prevalence, trend and contributing factors of geriatric syndromes among older Swedes: Results from the Stockholm County Council Public Health Surveys. *BMC Geriatrics, 18*(1), 1–9.

Liao, H. W., & Carstensen, L. L. (2018). Future time perspective: Time horizons and beyond. *GeroPsych: The Journal of Gerontopsychology and Geriatric Psychiatry, 31*(3), 163–167. http://dx.doi.org/10.1024/1662-9647/a000194

Liao, H.-W., Shavit, Y. Z., & Carstensen, L. L. (2019). Selective narrowing of peripheral social networks predicts poor long-term cognition in old age. *Innovation in Aging, 3*(Supplement_1), S174–S175. https://doi.org/10.1093/geroni/igz038.621

Liberman, O., Freud, T., Peleg, R., Keren, A., & Press, Y. (2018). Chronic pain and geriatric syndromes in community-dwelling patients aged ≥65 years. *Journal of Pain Research, 11*, 1171–1180. https://doi.org/10.2147/JPR.S160847

Liberman, Z., Kinzler, K. D., & Woodward, A. L. (2021). Origins of homophily: Infants expect people with shared preferences to affiliate. *Cognition, 212*, 104695. https://doi.org/10.1016/j.cognition.2021.104695

Lickliter, R., & Witherington, D. C. (2017). Towards a truly developmental epigenetics. *Human Development, 60*(2–3). https://www.karger.com/Article/Abstract/477996

Lieberman, A. (2019). *What if all children had access to a PreK4 SA?* New America Foundation.

Lieberman, M. D., & Eisenberger, N. I. (2015). The dorsal anterior cingulate cortex is selective for pain: Results from large-scale reverse inference. *Proceedings of the National Academy of Sciences, 112*(49), 15250–15255.

Lieberwirth, C., & Wang, Z. (2016). The neurobiology of pair bond formation, bond disruption, and social buffering. *Current Opinion in Neurobiology, 40*, 8–13. https://doi.org/10.1016/j.conb.2016.05.006, 10.1016/j.conb.2016.05.006

Lien Foundation. (2015). The 2015 quality of death index: Ranking palliative care across the world. *The Economist.*

Liepmann, H. (2018). The impact of a negative labor demand shock on fertility—evidence from the fall of the Berlin Wall. *Labour Economics, 54*, 210–224.

Lieser, E. K. (2020, August 22). "99% sure I would not survive": 50 years ago, Yuichiro Miura Skied down Mount Everest. *The National Interest.* The Center for the National Interest. https://nationalinterest.org/blog/buzz/%E2%80%9C99-sure-i-would-not-survive%E2%80%9D-50-years-ago-yuichiro-miura-skied-down-mount-everest-video

Lillard, A. S. (2016). *Montessori: The science behind the genius.* Oxford University Press.

Lillard, A. S. (2017). Why do the children (pretend) play? *Trends in Cognitive Sciences, 21*(11), 826–834. https://doi.org/10.1016/j.tics.2017.08.001

Lillard, A. S., Lerner, M. D., Hopkins, E. J., Dore, R. A., Smith, E. D., & Palmquist, C. M. (2013). The impact of pretend play on children's development: A review of the evidence. *Psychological Bulletin, 139*(1), 1.

Lim, N. (2016). Cultural differences in emotion: Differences in emotional arousal level between the East and the West. *Integrative Medicine Research, 5*(2), 105–109. https://doi.org/10.1016/j.imr.2016.03.004

Lima Santos, J. P., Kontos, A. P., Mailliard, S., Eagle, S. R., Holland, C. L., Suss, S. J., Abdul-waalee, H., Stiffler, R. S., Bitzer, H. B., Blaney, N. A., Colorito, A. T., Santucci, C. G., Brown, A., Kim, T., Iyengar, S., Skeba, A., Diler, R. S., Ladouceur, C. D., Phillips, M. L., … Versace, A. (2021). White matter abnormalities associated with prolonged recovery in adolescents following concussion. *Frontiers in Neurology, 12*, 681467. https://doi.org/10.3389/fneur.2021.681467

Limpo, T., & Graham, S. (2020). The role of handwriting instruction in writers' education. *British Journal of Educational Studies, 68*(3), 311–329. https://doi.org/10.1080/00071005.2019.1692127

Lin, H.-P., Chen, K.-L., Chou, W., Yuan, K.-S., Yen, S.-Y., Chen, Y.-S., & Chow, J. C. (2020). Prolonged touch screen device usage is associated with emotional and behavioral problems, but not language delay, in toddlers. *Infant Behavior and Development, 58*, 101424. https://doi.org/10.1016/j.infbeh.2020.101424

Lin, I.-F., Brown, S. L., & Hammersmith, A. M. (2017). Marital biography, social security receipt, and poverty. *Research on Aging, 39*(1), 86–110. https://doi.org/10.1177/0164027516656139

Lin, I.-F., Brown, S. L., Wright, M. R., & Hammersmith, A. M. (2018). Antecedents of gray divorce: A life course perspective. *The Journals of Gerontology. Series B, Psychological Sciences and Social Sciences, 73*(6), 1022–1031. https://doi.org/10.1093/geronb/gbw164

Lin, J. B., Tsubota, K., & Apte, R. S. (2016). A glimpse at the aging eye. *NPJ Aging and Mechanisms of Disease, 2*(1), 16003.

Lin, Q.-M., Spruyt, K., Leng, Y., Jiang, Y.-R., Wang, G.-H., Dong, S.-M., Mei, H., & Jiang, F. (2019). Cross-cultural disparities of subjective sleep parameters and their age-related trends over the first three years of human life: A systematic review and meta-analysis. *Sleep Medicine Reviews, 48*, 101203. https://doi.org/10.1016/j.smrv.2019.07.006

Lin, T. C., Yen, M., & Liao, Y. C. (2019). Hearing loss is a risk factor of disability in older adults: A systematic review. *Archives of Gerontology and Geriatrics, 85*, 103907.

Lin, Y., Stavans, M., & Baillargeon, R. (2021). Infants' physical reasoning and the cognitive architecture that supports it. In O. Houdé & G. Borst (Eds.), *Cambridge handbook of cognitive development.* Cambridge University Press.

Linares, R., Bajo, M. T., & Pelegrina, S. (2016). Age-related differences in working memory updating components. *Journal of Experimental Child Psychology, 147*, 39–52. https://doi.org/10.1016/j.jecp.2016.02.009

Lind, M., Bluck, S., & McAdams, D. P. (2020). More vulnerable? The life story approach highlights older people's potential for strength during the pandemic. *The Journals of Gerontology Series B: Psychological Sciences and Social Sciences, 76*(2), e45–e48. https://doi.org/10.1093/geronb/gbaa105

Lindberg, L. D., VandeVusse, A., Mueller, J., & Kirstein, M. (2020). *Early impacts of the COVID-19 pandemic: Findings from the 2020 Guttmacher survey of reproductive health experiences.* https://doi.org/10.1363/2020.31482

Lindeboom, M., Lundborg, P., & van der Klaauw, B. (2010). Assessing the impact of obesity on labor market outcomes. *Economics & Human Biology, 8*(3), 309–319. https://doi.org/10.1016/j.ehb.2010.08.004

Lindenberger, U. (2014). Human cognitive aging: *Corriger la fortune? Science, 346*(6209), 572–578.

Lindenberger, U., & Lövdén, M. (2019). Brain plasticity in human lifespan development: The exploration–selection–refinement model. *Annual Review of Developmental Psychology, 1*, 197–222.

Lindenberger, U., & Mayr, U. (2014). Cognitive aging: Is there a dark side to environmental support? *Trends in Cognitive Sciences, 18*(1), 7–15.

Lindson-Hawley, N., Hartmann-Boyce, J., Fanshawe, T. R., Begh, R., Farley, A., & Lancaster, T. (2016). Interventions to reduce harm from continued tobacco use. *Cochrane Database of Systematic Reviews, 10.* https://doi.org/10.1002/14651858.CD005231.pub3

Linnane, A. W., Kovalenko, S., & Gingold, E. B. (1998). The universality of bioenergetic disease: Age-associated cellular bioenergetic degradation and amelioration therapy. *Annals of the New York Academy of Sciences, 854*(1), 202–213.

Lin-Siegler, X., Ahn, J. N., Chen, J., Fang, F.-F. A., & Luna-Lucero, M. (2016). Even Einstein struggled: Effects of learning about great scientists' struggles on high school students' motivation to learn science. Journal of *Educational Psychology, 108*(3), 314–328. https://doi.org/10.1037/edu0000092

Lipina, S. J., Martelli, M. I., Vuelta, B., & Colombo, J. A. (2005). Performance on the A-not-B task of Argentinean infants from unsatisfied and satisfied basic needs homes. *Revista Interamericana de Psicología/Interamerican Journal of Psychology, 39*(1), 49–60.

Lipka, M. (2014, October 22). *Americans of all ages divided over doctor-assisted suicide laws.* Pew Research Center. https://www.pewresearch.org/fact-tank/2014/10/22/americans-of-all-ages-divided-over-doctor-assisted-suicide-laws/

Lipkin, P. H., Macias, M. M., Council on Children With Disabilities, S. O. D. A. B. P., Norwood, K. W., Jr., Brei, T. J., Davidson, L. F., Davis, B. E., Ellerbeck, K. A., Houtrow, A. J., Hyman, S. L., Kuo, D. Z., Noritz, G. H., Yin, L., Murphy, N. A., Levy, S. E., Weitzman, C. C., Bauer, N. S., Childers, D. O., Jr., Levine, J. M., … Voigt, R. G. (2020). Promoting optimal development: Identifying infants and young children with developmental disorders through developmental surveillance and screening. *Pediatrics, 145*(1), e20193449. https://doi.org/10.1542/peds.2019-3449

Lippman, L. H., Ryberg, R., Carney, R., & Moore, K. A. (2015). *Workforce connections: Key "soft skills" that foster youth workforce success: Toward a consensus across fields.* Child Trends.

Lipset, D. (2015). On the bridge: Class and the chronotope of modern romance in an American love story. *Anthropological Quarterly, 88*(1), 163–185.

Listman, J. D., & Dingus-Eason, J. (2018). How to be a deaf scientist: Building navigational capital. *Journal of Diversity in Higher Education, 11*(3), 279–294. https://doi.org/10.1037/dhe0000049

Liston, C., McEwen, B. S., & Casey, B. J. (2009). Psychosocial stress reversibly disrupts prefrontal processing and attentional control. *Proceedings of the National Academy of Sciences, 106*(3), 912–917. https://doi.org/10.1073/pnas.0807041106

Litovsky, R. (2015). Development of the auditory system. In M. J. Aminoff, F. Boller, D. F. Swaab (Eds.), *Handbook of clinical neurology* (Vol. 129, pp. 55–72). Elsevier. https://www.ncbi.nlm.nih.gov/pmc/articles/PMC4612629/

Little, E. E., Legare, C. H., & Carver, L. J. (2019). Culture, carrying, and communication: Beliefs and behavior associated with babywearing. *Infant Behavior and Development, 57*, 101320. https://doi.org/10.1016/j.infbeh.2019.04.002

Litwin, H., Levinsky, M., & Schwartz, E. (2020). Network type, transition patterns and well-being among older Europeans. *European Journal of Ageing, 17*(2), 241–250. https://doi.org/10.1007/s10433-019-00545-7

Litwin, H., & Shiovitz-Ezra, S. (2011). The association of background and network type among older Americans: Is "who you are" related to "who you are with"? *Research on Aging, 33*(6), 735–759. https://doi.org/10.1177/0164027511409441

Liu, B., Du, Y., Wu, Y., Sun, Y., Santillan, M. K., Santillan, D. A., & Bao, W. (2021). Prevalence and distribution of electronic cigarette use before and during pregnancy among women in 38 states of the United States. *Nicotine & Tobacco Research, ntab041.* https://doi.org/10.1093/ntr/ntab041

Liu, C., Badana, A. N. S., Burgdorf, J., Fabius, C. D., Roth, D. L., & Haley, W. E. (2021). Systematic review and meta-analysis of racial and ethnic differences in dementia caregivers' well-being. *The Gerontologist, 61*(5), e228–e243. https://doi.org/10.1093/geront/gnaa028

Liu, C., Moore, G. A., Beekman, C., Pérez-Edgar, K. E., Leve, L. D., Shaw, D. S., Ganiban, J. M., Natsuaki, M. N., Reiss, D., & Neiderhiser, J. M. (2018). Developmental patterns of anger from infancy to middle childhood predict problem behaviors at age 8. *Developmental Psychology, 54*(11), 2090–2100. https://doi.org/10.1037/dev0000589

Liu, C. H., Stevens, C., Wong, S. H. M., Yasui, M., & Chen, J. A. (2019). The prevalence and predictors of mental health diagnoses and suicide among U.S. college students: Implications for addressing disparities in service use. *Depression and Anxiety, 36*(1), 8–17.

Liu, D., Chen, D., & Brown, B. B. (2020). Do parenting practices and child disclosure predict parental knowledge? A meta-analysis. *Journal of Youth and Adolescence, 49*(1), 1–16. https://doi.org/10.1007/s10964-019-01154-4

Liu, H., Umberson, D., & Xu, M. (2020). Widowhood and mortality: Gender, race/ethnicity, and the role of economic resources. *Annals of Epidemiology, 45*, 69–75.e1. https://doi.org/10.1016/j.annepidem.2020.02.006

Liu, H., & Waite, L. (2014). Bad marriage, broken heart? Age and gender differences in the link between marital quality and cardiovascular risks among older adults. *Journal of*

Health and Social Behavior, 55(4), 403–423. https://doi.org/10.1177/0022146514556893

Liu, J. L., Harkness, S., & Super, C. M. (2020). Chinese mothers' cultural models of children's shyness: Ethnotheories and socialization strategies in the context of social change. *New Directions for Child and Adolescent Development, 2020*(170), 69–92. https://doi.org/10.1002/cad.20340

Liu, Q., & Wang, Z. (2021). Associations between parental emotional warmth, parental attachment, peer attachment, and adolescents' character strengths. *Children and Youth Services Review, 120*, 105765. https://doi.org/10.1016/j.childyouth.2020.105765

Liu, W., Yan, X., Li, C., Shu, Q., Chen, M., Cai, L., & You, D. (2021). A secular trend in age at menarche in Yunnan Province, China: A multiethnic population study of 1,275,000 women. *BMC Public Health, 21*, 1–10. http://dx.doi.org/10.1186/s12889-021-11951-x

Liu, X., Nie, Z., Chen, J., Guo, X., Ou, Y., Chen, G., Mai, J., Gong, W., Wu, Y., Gao, X., Qu, Y., Bell, E. M., Lin, S., & Zhuang, J. (2018). Does maternal environmental tobacco smoke interact with social-demographics and environmental factors on congenital heart defects? *Environmental Pollution, 234*, 214–222. https://doi.org/10.1016/j.envpol.2017.11.023

Liu, Y.-H., Chen, Y., Wang, Q.-H., Wang, L.-R., Jiang, L., Yang, Y., Chen, X., Li, Y., Cen, Y., Xu, C., Zhu, J., Li, W., Wang, Y.-R., Zhang, L.-L., Liu, J., Xu, Z.-Q., & Wang, Y.-J. (2022). One-Year Trajectory of Cognitive Changes in Older Survivors of COVID-19 in Wuhan, China: A Longitudinal Cohort Study. *JAMA Neurology.* https://doi.org/10.1001/jamaneurol.2022.0461

Liu, Z., Chen, Q., & Sun, Y. (2017). Mindfulness training for psychological stress in family caregivers of persons with dementia: A systematic review and meta-analysis of randomized controlled trials. *Clinical Interventions in Aging, 12*, 1521–1529. https://doi.org/10.2147/CIA.S146213

Liu-Ambrose, T., Barha, C., & Falck, R. S. (2019). Active body, healthy brain: Exercise for healthy cognitive aging. *International Review of Neurobiology, 147*, 95–120. https://doi.org/10.1016/bs.irn.2019.07.004

Livingston, G. (2018, January 18). *U.S. women more likely to have children than a decade ago.* Pew Research Center's Social & Demographic Trends Project. https://www.pewresearch.org/social-trends/2018/01/18/theyre-waiting-longer-but-u-s-women-today-more-likely-to-have-children-than-a-decade-ago/

Livingston, G. (2018, April 25). Facts on unmarried parents in the U.S. Pew Research Center's Social & Demographic Trends Project. https://www.pewresearch.org/social-trends/2018/04/25/the-changing-profile-of-unmarried-parents/

Livingston, G., & Brown, A. (2017, May 18). *Intermarriage in the U.S. 50 years after loving v. Virginia.* Pew Research Center's Social & Demographic Trends Project. http://www.pewsocialtrends.org/2017/05/18/intermarriage-in-the-u-s-50-years-after-loving-v-virginia/

Livingston, G., Huntley, J., Sommerlad, A., Ames, D., Ballard, C., Banerjee, S., Brayne, C., Burns, A., Cohen-Mansfield, J., Cooper, C., Costafreda, S. G., Dias, A., Fox, N., Gitlin, L. N., Howard, R., Kales, H. C., Kivimäki, M., Larson, E. B., Ogunniyi, A., … Mukadam, N. (2020). Dementia prevention, intervention, and care: 2020 report of the Lancet Commission. *The Lancet, 396*(10248), 413–446. https://doi.org/10.1016/S0140-6736(20)30367-6

Livingstone, K. M., & Isaacowitz, D. M. (2015). Situation selection and modification for emotion regulation in younger and older adults. *Social Psychological and Personality Science, 6*(8), 904–910. https://doi.org/10.1177/1948550615593148

Livingstone, K. M., & Isaacowitz, D. M. (2019). Age similarities and differences in spontaneous use of emotion regulation tactics across five laboratory tasks. *Journal of Experimental Psychology: General, 148*(11), 1972.

Lloyd-Fox, S., Begus, K., Halliday, D., Pirazzoli, L., Blasi, A., Papademetriou, M., Darboe, M. K., Prentice, A. M., Johnson, M. H., Moore, S. E., & Elwell, C. E. (2017). Cortical specialisation to social stimuli from the first days to the second year of life: A rural Gambian cohort. *Developmental Cognitive Neuroscience, 25*, 92–104. doi.org/10.1016/j.dcn.2016.11.005

Lo, C. O., & Porath, M. (2017). Paradigm shifts in gifted education: An examination vis-a-vis its historical situatedness and pedagogical sensibilities. *Gifted Child Quarterly, 61*(4), 343–360.

Lo, J. C., Groeger, J. A., Cheng, G. H., Dijk, D.-J., & Chee, M. W. L. (2016). Self-reported sleep duration and cognitive performance in older adults: A systematic review and meta-analysis. *Sleep Medicine, 17*, 87–98. https://doi.org/10.1016/j.sleep.2015.08.021

Lobel, A., Engels, R. C., Stone, L. L., Burk, W. J., & Granic, I. (2017). Video gaming and children's psychosocial wellbeing: A longitudinal study. *Journal of Youth and Adolescence, 46*(4), 884–897.

LoBraico, E. J., Brinberg, M., Ram, N., & Fosco, G. M. (2020). Exploring processes in day-to-day parent–adolescent conflict and angry mood: Evidence for circular causality. *Family Process, 59*(4), 1706–1721. https://doi.org/10.1111/famp.12506

LoBue, V., & Adolph, K. E. (2019). Fear in infancy: Lessons from snakes, spiders, heights, and strangers. *Developmental Psychology, 55*(9), 1889–1907. https://doi.org/10.1037/dev0000675

LoBue, V., Reider, L. B., Kim, E., Burris, J. L., Oleas, D. S., Buss, K. A., Pérez-Edgar, K., & Field, A. P. (2020). The importance of using multiple outcome measures in infant research. *Infancy, 25*(4), 420–437. https://doi.org/10.1111/infa.12339

Locke, J. (1847). *An essay concerning human understanding.* Kay & Troutman. (Original work published 1690)

Locke, J. L., & Bogin, B. (2006). Language and life history: A new perspective on the development and evolution of human language. *Behavioral and Brain Sciences, 29*(3), 259–280.

Lodge, A. C., & Umberson, D. (2012). All shook up: Sexuality of mid- to later life married couples. *Journal of Marriage and the Family, 74*(3), 428–443. https://doi.org/10.1111/j.1741-3737.2012.00969.x

Loeb, E. L., Kansky, J., Narr, R. K., Fowler, C., & Allen, J. P. (2020). Romantic relationship churn in early adolescence predicts hostility, abuse, and avoidance in relationships into early adulthood. *The Journal of Early Adolescence, 40*(8), 1195–1225. https://doi.org/10.1177/0272431619899477

Loeb, S. (2016). *Missing the target: We need to focus on informal care rather than preschool.* Brookings.

Loebach, J., & Gilliland, J. (2019). Examining the social and built environment factors influencing children's independent use of their neighborhoods and the experience of local settings as child-friendly. *Journal of Planning Education and Research,* 0739456X19828444. https://doi.org/10.1177/0739456X19828444

Logan, K., Cuff, S., & Council on Sports Medicine and Fitness. (2019). Organized sports for children, preadolescents, and adolescents. *Pediatrics, 143*(6), e20190997.

Logan, R. W., & McClung, C. A. (2019). Rhythms of life: Circadian disruption and brain disorders across the lifespan. *Nature Reviews Neuroscience, 20*(1), 49–65. https://doi.org/10.1038/s41583-018-0088-y

Logan, S. W., Kipling Webster, E., Getchell, N., Pfeiffer, K. A., & Robinson, L. E. (2015). Relationship between fundamental motor skill competence and physical activity during childhood and adolescence: A systematic review. *Kinesiology Review, 4*(4), 416–426. https://doi.org/10.1123/kr.2013-0012

Logue, D., Madigan, S. M., Delahunt, E., Heinen, M., Mc Donnell, S. J., & Corish, C. A. (2018). Low energy availability in athletes: A review of prevalence, dietary patterns, physiological health, and sports performance. *Sports Medicine, 48*(1), 73–96.

Lomawaima, K. T., Brayboy, B. M. J., & McCarty, T. L. (2018). Editors' introduction to the special issue: Native American boarding school stories. *Journal of American Indian Education, 57*(1), 1–10.

Long, P., & Corfas, G. (2014). Dynamic regulation of myelination in health and disease. *JAMA Psychiatry, 71*(11), 1296–1297. https://doi.org/10.1001/jamapsychiatry.2014.1049

Long, X., Benischek, A., Dewey, D., & Lebel, C. (2017). Age-related functional brain changes in young children. *NeuroImage, 155*, 322–330. https://doi.org/10.1016/j.neuroimage.2017.04.059

Longbottom, S., & Slaughter, V. (2018). Sources of children's knowledge about death and dying. *Philosophical Transactions of the Royal Society B: Biological Sciences, 373*(1754), 20170267. https://doi.org/10.1098/rstb.2017.0267

Loo, S. L., Hawkes, K., & Kim, P. S. (2017). Evolution of male strategies with sex-ratio–dependent pay-offs: Connecting pair bonds with grandmothering. *Philosophical Transactions of the Royal Society B: Biological Sciences, 372*(1729), 20170041.

Looker, A. C., Sarafrazi Isfahani, N., Fan, B., & Shepherd, J. A. (2017). Trends in osteoporosis and low bone mass in older US adults, 2005–2006 through 2013–2014. *Osteoporosis International, 28*(6), 1979–1988. https://doi.org/10.1007/s00198-017-3996-1

Loomis, A. M. (2018). The role of preschool as a point of intervention and prevention for trauma-exposed children: Recommendations for practice, policy, and research. *Topics in Early Childhood Special Education, 38*(3), 134–145. https://doi.org/10.1177/0271121418789254

López, B. G., Luque, A., & Piña-Watson, B. (2021). Context, intersectionality, and resilience: Moving toward a more holistic study of bilingualism in cognitive science. *Cultural Diversity and Ethnic Minority Psychology.* https://doi.org/10.1037/cdp0000472

Lopez, L. D., Walle, E. A., Pretzer, G. M., & Warlaumont, A. S. (2020). Adult responses to infant prelinguistic vocalizations are associated with infant vocabulary: A home observation study. *PLOS One, 15*(11), e0242232. https://doi.org/10.1371/journal.pone.0242232

López-Bueno, R., Calatayud, J., Ezzatvar, Y., Casajús, J. A., Smith, L., Andersen, L. L., & López-Sánchez, G. F. (2020). Association between current physical activity and current perceived anxiety and mood in the initial phase of COVID-19 confinement. *Frontiers in Psychiatry, 11*, 729. https://doi.org/10.3389/fpsyt.2020.00729

López-Otín, C., Blasco, M. A., Partridge, L., Serrano, M., & Kroemer, G. (2013). The hallmarks of aging. *Cell, 153*(6), 1194–1217. https://doi.org/10.1016/j.cell.2013.05.039

Loprinzi, P. D. (2015). Sedentary behavior and medical multimorbidity. *Physiology & Behavior, 151*, 395–397. https://doi.org/10.1016/j.physbeh.2015.08.016

Loprinzi, P. D., & Loenneke, J. P. (2018). Leukocyte telomere length and mortality among U.S. adults: Effect modification by physical activity behaviour. *Journal of Sports Sciences, 36*(2), 213–219. https://doi.org/10.1080/02640414.2017.1293280

Lorber, M. F., Del Vecchio, T., & Slep, A. M. S. (2018). The development of individual physically aggressive behaviors from infancy to toddlerhood. *Developmental Psychology, 54*(4), 601–612. https://doi.org/10.1037/dev0000450

LoRe, D., Ladner, P., & Suskind, D. (2018). Talk, read, sing: Early language exposure as an overlooked social determinant of health. *Pediatrics, 142*(3).

Lorek, M., Tobolska-Lorek, D., Kalina-Faska, B., Januszek-Trzciakowska, A., & Gawlik, A. (2019). Clinical and biochemical phenotype of adolescent males with gynecomastia. *Journal of Clinical Research in Pediatric Endocrinology, 11*(4), 388.

Lorenti, A., Dudel, C., Hale, J. M., & Myrskylä, M. (2020). Working and disability expectancies at older ages: The role of childhood circumstances and education. *Social Science Research, 91*, 102447.

Lorenz, K. (1981). *The foundations of ethology.* Springer Science & Business Media.

Lott, I. T., & Head, E. (2019). Dementia in Down syndrome: Unique insights for Alzheimer disease research. *Nature Reviews Neurology, 15*(3), 135–147. https://doi.org/10.1038/s41582-018-0132-6

Lou, H. C., Rømer Thomsen, K., & Changeux, J.-P. (2020). The molecular organization of self-awareness: Paralimbic dopamine-GABA interaction. *Frontiers in Systems Neuroscience, 14*, 3. https://doi.org/10.3389/fnsys.2020.00003

Lourida, I., Hannon, E., Littlejohns, T. J., Langa, K. M., Hyppönen, E., Kuźma, E., & Llewellyn, D. J. (2019). Association of lifestyle and genetic risk with incidence of dementia. *JAMA, 322*(5), 430–437. https://doi.org/10.1001/jama.2019.9879

Louv, R. (2008). *Last child in the woods: Saving our children from nature-deficit disorder.* Algonquin Books of Chapel Hill. https://www.google.com/books/edition/Last_Child_in_the_Woods/WnLBBwAAQBAJ?hl=en&gbpv=1&dq=louv+play+&pg=PP1&printsec=frontcover

Lovaas, O. I. (1987). Behavioral treatment and normal educational and intellectual functioning in young autistic children. *Journal of Consulting and Clinical Psychology, 55*(1), 3–9. https://doi.org/10.1037/0022-006X.55.1.3

Lövdén, M., Bäckman, L., & Lindenberger, U. (2017). The link of intellectual engagement to cognitive and brain aging. In R. Cabeza, L. Nyberg, & D. C. Park (Eds.), *Cognitive neuroscience of aging: Linking cognitive and cerebral aging* (pp. 461–484). Oxford University Press.

Lövdén, M., Fratiglioni, L., Glymour, M. M., Lindenberger, U., & Tucker-Drob, E. M. (2020). Education and cognitive functioning across the life span. *Psychological Science in the Public Interest, 21*(1), 6–41.

Loveless, T. (2016, March 24). *2016 Brown Center report on American education: How well are American students learning?* Brookings. https://www.brookings.edu/research/2016-brown-center-report-on-american-education-how-well-are-american-students-learning/

Lovell, B., & Wetherell, M. A. (2011). The cost of caregiving: Endocrine and immune implications in elderly and non elderly caregivers. *Neuroscience & Biobehavioral Reviews, 35*(6), 1342–1352. https://doi.org/10.1016/j.neubiorev.2011.02.007

Low, K. D., & Rounds, J. (2007). Interest change and continuity from early adolescence to middle adulthood. *International Journal for Educational and Vocational Guidance, 7*(1), 23–36.

Lowe, K., & Arnett, J. J. (2020). Failure to grow up, failure to pay? Parents' views of conflict over money with their emerging adults. *Journal of Family Issues, 41*(3), 359–382. https://doi.org/10.1177/0192513X19876061

Löwe, L. C., Gaser, C., Franke, K., & for the Alzheimer's Disease Neuroimaging Initiative. (2016). The effect of the APOE genotype on individual BrainAGE in normal aging, mild cognitive impairment, and Alzheimer's disease. *PLOS ONE, 11*(7), e0157514. https://doi.org/10.1371/journal.pone.0157514

Lowenstein, C. J., & Bennett, J. A. (2018). New vascular insights into premature aging. *The Journal of Clinical Investigation, 129*(2), 492–493. https://doi.org/10.1172/JCI125616

Lowry, R., Johns, M. M., Gordon, A. R., Austin, S. B., Robin, L. E., & Kann, L. K. (2018). Nonconforming gender expression and associated mental distress and substance use among high school students. *JAMA Pediatrics, 172*(11), 1020–1028. https://doi.org/10.1001/jamapediatrics.2018.2140

Loyd, A. B., & Gaither, S. E. (2018). Racial/ethnic socialization for White youth: What we know and future directions. *Journal of Applied Developmental Psychology, 59*, 54–64. https://doi.org/10.1016/j.appdev.2018.05.004

Lozada, M., & Carro, N. (2016). Embodied action improves cognition in children: Evidence from a study based on Piagetian conservation tasks. *Frontiers in Psychology, 7*, 393.

Lu, P., Kong, D., Shelley, M., & Davitt, J. (2020). Intersectional discrimination attributions and health outcome among American older adults. *Innovation in Aging, 4*(Supplement_1), 871.

Lubin, J. H., Couper, D., Lutsey, P. L., & Yatsuya, H. (2017). Synergistic and non-synergistic associations for cigarette smoking and non-tobacco risk factors for cardiovascular disease incidence in the Atherosclerosis Risk In Communities (ARIC) Study. *Nicotine & Tobacco Research, 19*(7), 826–835.

Luby, J. L., Baram, T. Z., Rogers, C. E., & Barch, D. M. (2020). Neurodevelopmental optimization after early-life adversity: Cross-species studies to elucidate sensitive periods and brain mechanisms to inform early intervention. *Trends in Neurosciences, 43*(10), 744–751. https://doi.org/10.1016/j.tins.2020.08.001

Lucas, R., Bernier, K., Perry, M., Evans, H., Ramesh, D., Young, E., Walsh, S., & Starkweather, A. (2019).

Promoting self-management of breast and nipple pain in breastfeeding women: Protocol of a pilot randomized controlled trial. *Research in Nursing & Health, 42*(3), 176–188. https://doi.org/10.1002/nur.21938

Luciano, E. C., & Orth, U. (2017). Transitions in romantic relationships and development of self-esteem. *Journal of Personality and Social Psychology, 112*(2), 307.

Luders, E., Cherbuin, N., & Gaser, C. (2016). Estimating brain age using high-resolution pattern recognition: Younger brains in long-term meditation practitioners. *Neuroimage, 134*, 508–513.

Luders, E., Jain, F. A., & Kurth, F. (2021). Diminished age-related decline of the amygdala in long-term meditation practitioners. *Psychosomatic Medicine, 83*(6), 650–654. https://doi.org/10.1097/PSY.0000000000000913

Ludwig, C. A., Callaway, N. F., Fredrick, D. R., Blumenkranz, M. S., & Moshfeghi, D. M. (2016). What colour are newborns' eyes? Prevalence of iris colour in the Newborn Eye Screening Test (NEST) study. *Acta Ophthalmologica, 94*(5), 485–488. https://doi.org/10.1111/aos.13006

Ludyga, S., Gerber, M., Brand, S., Pühse, U., & Colledge, F. (2018). Effects of aerobic exercise on cognitive performance among young adults in a higher education setting. *Research Quarterly for Exercise and Sport, 89*(2), 164–172. https://doi.org/10.1080/02701367.2018.1438575

Lugo-Candelas, C. I., Harvey, E. A., & Breaux, R. P. (2015). Emotion socialization practices in Latina and European-American mothers of preschoolers with behavior problems. *Journal of Family Studies, 21*(2), 144–162. https://doi-org.mimas.calstatela.edu/10.1080/13229400.2015.1020982

Luhmann, M., & Hawkley, L. C. (2016). Age differences in loneliness from late adolescence to oldest old age. *Developmental Psychology, 52*(6), 943–959. https://doi.org/10.1037/dev0000117

Luhmann, M., Orth, U., Specht, J., Kandler, C., & Lucas, R. E. (2014). Studying changes in life circumstances and personality: It's about time. *European Journal of Personality, 28*(3), 256–266.

Lui, K. F. H., & Wong, A. C.-N. (2019). Multiple processing limitations underlie multitasking costs. *Psychological Research, 84*, 1946–1964. https://doi.org/10.1007/s00426-019-01196-0

Luke, B., Brown, M. B., Wantman, E., Forestieri, N. E., Browne, M. L., Fisher, S. C., Yazdy, M. M., Ethen, M. K., Canfield, M. A., Watkins, S., Nichols, H. B., Farland, L. V., Oehninger, S., Doody, K. J., Eisenberg, M. L., & Baker, V. L. (2021). The risk of birth defects with conception by ART. *Human Reproduction, 36*(1), 116–129. https://doi.org/10.1093/humrep/deaa272

Lulic, Z., Inui, S., Sim, W.-Y., Kang, H., Choi, G. S., Hong, W., Hatanaka, T., Wilson, T., & Manyak, M. (2017). Understanding patient and physician perceptions of male androgenetic alopecia treatments in Asia–Pacific and Latin America. *The Journal of Dermatology, 44*(8), 892–902. https://doi.org/10.1111/1346-8138.13832

Lum, Z.-A. (2011, March). South Asian students on "Frenchies," ethnic cliques and the new cool. *The Vancouver Observer.*

Luna, B., Garver, K. E., Urban, T. A., Lazar, N. A., & Sweeney, J. A. (2004). Maturation of cognitive processes from late childhood to adulthood. *Child Development, 75*(5), 1357–1372. https://doi.org/10.1111/j.1467-8624.2004.00745.x

Lundberg, K. (2021). *Despite pandemic, civically engaged youth report higher well-being* (CIRCLE / Tisch College Post-Election Youth Poll). Tufts University. https://circle.tufts.edu/latest-research/despite-pandemic-civically-engaged-youth-report-higher-well-being

Lundberg, S. (2013). The college type: Personality and educational inequality. *Journal of Labor Economics, 31*(3), 421–441. http://www.jstor.org/stable/10.1086/671056

Lundberg, S., Pollak, R. A., & Stearns, J. (2016). Family inequality: Diverging patterns in marriage, cohabitation, and childbearing. *The Journal of Economic Perspectives, 30*(2), 79–102. https://doi.org/10.1257/jep.30.2.79

Lundkvist-Houndoumadi, I., & Thastum, M. (2013). A "Cool Kids" cognitive-behavioral therapy group for youth with anxiety disorders: Part 1, the case of Erik. *Pragmatic Case Studies in Psychotherapy, 9*(2), 122–178.

Lundquist, J. H., & Curington, C. V. (2019). Love me tinder, love me sweet. *Contexts, 18*(4), 22–27. https://doi.org/10.1177/1536504219883848

Lundquist, J. H., & Lin, K. H. (2015). Is love (color) blind? The economy of race among gay and straight daters. *Social Forces, 93*(4), 1423–1449.

Lunkenheimer, E., Lichtwarck-Aschoff, A., Hollenstein, T., Kemp, C. J., & Granic, I. (2016). Breaking down the coercive cycle: How parent and child risk factors influence real-time variability in parental responses to child misbehavior. *Parenting, 16*(4), 237–256.

Luo, J., Mills, K., le Cessie, S., Noordam, R., & van Heemst, D. (2020). Ageing, age-related diseases and oxidative stress: What to do next? *Ageing Research Reviews, 57*, 100982.

Luo, S. (2017). Assortative mating and couple similarity: Patterns, mechanisms, and consequences. *Social and Personality Psychology Compass, 11*(8), e12337. https://doi.org/10.1111/spc3.12337

Luong, G., Charles, S. T., & Fingerman, K. L. (2011). Better with age: Social relationships across adulthood. *Journal of Social and Personal Relationships, 28*(1), 9–23. https://doi.org/10.1177/0265407510391362

Lüscher, K., & Pillemer, K. (1998). Intergenerational ambivalence: A new approach to the study of parent-child relations in later life. *Journal of Marriage and the Family*, 413–425.

Luthar, S. S., & Ciciolla, L. (2016). What it feels like to be a mother: Variations by children's developmental stages. *Developmental Psychology, 52*(1), 143–154. https://doi.org/10.1037/dev0000062

Luthar, S. S., & Eisenberg, N. (2017). Resilient adaptation among at-risk children: Harnessing science toward maximizing salutary environments. *Child Development, 88*(2), 337–349.

Lwi, S. J., Ford, B. Q., Casey, J. J., Miller, B. L., & Levenson, R. W. (2017). Poor caregiver mental health predicts mortality of patients with neurodegenerative disease. *Proceedings of the National Academy of Sciences, 114*(28), 7319–7324. https://doi.org/10.1073/pnas.1701597114

Lynch, A. W. (2018). Identity and literacy practices in a bilingual classroom: An exploration of leveraging community cultural wealth. *Bilingual Research Journal, 41*(2), 117–132. https://doi.org/10.1080/15235882.2018.1452312

Lyon, J. (2017). Chess study revives debate over cognition-enhancing drugs. *JAMA, 318*(9), 784–786. https://doi.org/10.1001/jama.2017.8114

Lyons, A., Alba, B., Waling, A., Minichiello, V., Hughes, M., Barrett, C., Fredriksen-Goldsen, K., Edmonds, S., & Blanchard, M. (2021). Recent versus lifetime experiences of discrimination and the mental and physical health of older lesbian women and gay men. *Ageing & Society*, 1–22. https://doi.org/10.1017/S0144686X19001533

Lyons, H. A., Manning, W. D., Longmore, M. A., & Giordano, P. C. (2014). Young adult casual sexual behavior: Life course specific motivations and consequences. *Sociological Perspectives, 57*(1), 79–101. https://doi.org/10.1177/0731121413517557

Lyons, H. A., Manning, W. D., Longmore, M. A., & Giordano, P. C. (2015). Gender and casual sexual activity from adolescence to emerging adulthood: Social and life course correlates. *Journal of Sex Research, 52*(5), 543–557. https://doi.org/10.1080/00224499.2014.906032

Lythcott-Haims, J., & Doyle, L. (2015, July 5). Kids of helicopter parents are sputtering out. *Slate.* http://www.slate.com/articles/double_x/doublex/2015/07/helicopter_parenting_is_increasingly_correlated_with_college_age_depression.html

Lyubomirsky, S., & Layous, K. (2013). How do simple positive activities increase well-being? *Current Directions in Psychological Science, 22*(1), 57–62.

Ma, J., Pender, M., & Welch, M. (2016). *Education pays 2016: The benefits of higher education for individuals and society* (Trends in Higher Education Series). College Board. https://eric.ed.gov/?id=ED572548

Ma, J., Pender, M., & Welch, M. (2020). *Education pays 2019: The benefits of higher education for individuals and society* (Trends in Higher Education Series). College Board.

Ma, J., Wu, L., Zhou, Y., Zhang, H., Xiong, C., Peng, Z., Bao, W., Meng, T., & Liu, Y. (2019). Association between BMI and semen quality: An observational study of 3966 sperm donors. *Human Reproduction, 34*(1), 155–162. https://doi.org/10.1093/humrep/dey328

Määttä, S., Laakso, M.-L., Tolvanen, A., Ahonen, T., & Aro, T. (2014). Children with differing developmental trajectories of prelinguistic communication skills: Language and working memory at age 5. *Journal of Speech, Language, and Hearing Research, 57*(3), 1026–1039. https://doi.org/10.1044/2014_JSLHR-L-13-0012

Maccoby, E. E. (1992). The role of parents in the socialization of children: An historical overview. *Developmental Psychology, 28*(6), 1006–1017.

Maccoby, E. E., & Jacklin, C. N. (1987). Gender segregation in childhood. In H. W. Reese (Ed.), *Advances in child development and behavior* (Vol. 20, pp. 239–287). JAI. https://doi.org/10.1016/S0065-2407(08)60404-8

Maccoby, E. E., & Martin, J. A. (1983). Socialization in the context of the family: Parent-child interaction. In P. H. Mussen & E. M. Hetherington (Eds.), *Handbook of child psychology* (pp. 1–101). Wiley.

MacCormack, J. K., Stein, A. G., Kang, J., Giovanello, K. S., Satpute, A. B., & Lindquist, K. A. (2020). Affect in the aging brain: A neuroimaging meta-analysis of older vs. younger adult affective experience and perception. *Affective Science, 1*(3), 128–154.

Macdonald, K., Milne, N., Orr, R., & Pope, R. (2018). Relationships between motor proficiency and academic performance in mathematics and reading in school-aged children and adolescents: A systematic review. *International Journal of Environmental Research and Public Health, 15*(8), 1603. https://doi.org/10.3390/ijerph15081603

MacDonald, T. K. (2019). Lactation care for transgender and non-binary patients: Empowering clients and avoiding aversives. *Journal of Human Lactation, 35*(2), 223–226. https://doi.org/10.1177/0890334419830989

Maciejewski, D. F., van Lier, P. A., Branje, S. J., Meeus, W. H., & Koot, H. M. (2015). A 5-year longitudinal study on mood variability across adolescence using daily diaries. *Child Development, 86*(6), 1908–1921.

MacKenzie, M. A., Smith-Howell, E., Bomba, P. A., & Meghani, S. H. (2018). Respecting choices and related models of advance care planning: A systematic review of published evidence. *The American Journal of Hospice & Palliative Care, 35*(6), 897–907. https://doi.org/10.1177/1049909117745789

MacLeod, C. (2009). The invention of heroes. *Nature, 460*(7255), 572–573. https://doi.org/10.1038/460572a

Macmillan, R., & Shanahan, M. J. (2021). Why precarious work is bad for health: Social marginality as key mechanisms in a multi-national context. *Social Forces*, soab006. https://doi.org/10.1093/sf/soab006

MacMullin, L. N., Bokeloh, L. M., Nabbijohn, A. N., Santarossa, A., van der Miesen, A. I., Peragine, D. E., & VanderLaan, D. P. (2021). Examining the relation between gender nonconformity and psychological well-being in children: The roles of peers and parents. *Archives of Sexual Behavior, 50*(3), 823–841.

MacPhee, D., & Prendergast, S. (2019). Room for improvement: Girls' and boys' home environments are still gendered. *Sex Roles, 80*(5), 332–346. https://doi.org/10.1007/s11199-018-0936-2

MacPhee, D., Prendergast, S., Albrecht, E., Walker, A. K., & Miller-Heyl, J. (2018). The child-rearing environment and children's mastery motivation as contributors to school readiness. *Journal of Applied Developmental Psychology, 56*, 1–12.

MacSwan, J., Thompson, M. S., Rolstad, K., McAlister, K., & Lobo, G. (2017). Three theories of the effects of language education programs: An empirical evaluation of bilingual and English-only policies. *Annual Review of Applied Linguistics, 37*, 218–240.

MacWhinney, B. (2017). First language acquisition. In M. Aronoff & J. Ress-Miller (Eds.), *The handbook of linguistics* (2nd ed., pp. 397–413). Wiley. https://doi.org/10.1002/9781119072256.ch19

Maddow-Zimet, I., & Kost, K. (2021). *Pregnancies, births and abortions in the United States, 1973–2017: National and state trends by age.* Guttmacher Institute. https://www.guttmacher.org/report/pregnancies-births-abortions-in-united-states-1973-2017

Mader, J. (2020, February 8). How play is making a comeback in kindergarten. *The Hechinger Report.* http://hechinger-report.org/play-based-kindergarten-makes-a-comeback/

Madigan, S., Browne, D., Racine, N., Mori, C., & Tough, S. (2019). Association between screen time and children's performance on a developmental screening test. *JAMA Pediatrics, 173*(3), 244–250. https://doi.org/10.1001/jamapediatrics.2018.5056

Madigan, S., McArthur, B. A., Anhorn, C., Eirich, R., & Christakis, D. A. (2020). Associations between screen use and child language skills: A systematic review and meta-analysis. *JAMA Pediatrics, 174*(7), 665–675. https://doi.org/10.1001/jamapediatrics.2020.0327

Madigan, S., Racine, N., & Tough, S. (2020). Prevalence of preschoolers meeting vs exceeding screen time guidelines. *JAMA Pediatrics, 174*(1), 93–95. https://doi.org/10.1001/jamapediatrics.2019.4495

Madrigal, A. C. (2017, November 7). Should children form emotional bonds with robots? *The Atlantic.* https://www.theatlantic.com/magazine/archive/2017/12/my-sons-first-robot/544137/

Maenner, M. J., Shaw, K. A., Baio, J., Washington, A., Patrick, M., DiRienzo, M., Christensen, D. L., Wiggins, L. D., Pettygrove, S., Andrews, J. G., Lopez, M., Hudson, A., Baroud, T., Schwenk, Y., White, T., Rosenberg, C. R., Lee, L.-C., Harrington, R. A., Huston, M., ... Dietz, P. M. (2020). Prevalence of autism spectrum disorder among children aged 8 years—autism and developmental disabilities monitoring network, 11 sites, United States, 2016. *MMWR Surveillance Summaries, 69*(4), 1–12. https://doi.org/10.15585/mmwr.ss6904a1

Maestas, N., Mullen, K. J., Powell, D., von Wachter, T., & Wenger, J. B. (2017a). *Working conditions in the United States: Results of the 2015 American Working Conditions Survey.* RAND Corporation. https://www.rand.org/pubs/research_reports/RR2014.html

Maestas, N., Mullen, K. J., Powell, D., von Wachter, T., & Wenger, J. B. (2017b). *How Americans perceive the workplace: Results from the American Working Conditions Survey.* RAND Corporation. https://doi.org/10.7249/RB9972

Magai, C., Frias, M. T., & Shaver, P. R. (2016). Attachment in middle and later life. In J. Cassidy & P. Shaver (Eds.), *Handbook of attachment: Theory, research, and clinical applications* (pp. 534–552). Guilford.

Magai, C., & McFadden, S. H. (1995). *The role of emotions in social and personality development: History, theory and research.* Springer Science & Business Media.

Magallón, S., Narbona, J., & Crespo-Eguílaz, N. (2016). Acquisition of motor and cognitive skills through repetition in typically developing children. *PLOS ONE, 11*(7), e0158684. https://doi.org/10.1371/journal.pone.0158684

Magette, A. L., Durtschi, J. A., & Love, H. A. (2018). Lesbian, gay, and bisexual substance use in emerging adulthood moderated by parent-child relationships in adolescence. *The American Journal of Family Therapy, 46*(3), 272–286.

Magliano, D. J., Chen, L., Islam, R. M., Carstensen, B., Gregg, E. W., Pavkov, M. E., Andes, L. J., Balicer, R., Baviera, M., Boersma-van Dam, E., Booth, G. L., Chan, J. C. N., Chua, Y. X., Fosse-Edorh, S., Fuentes, S., Gulseth, H. L., Gurevicius, R., Ha, K. H., Hird, T. R., ... Shaw, J. E. (2021). Trends in the incidence of diagnosed diabetes: A multicountry analysis of aggregate data from 22 million diagnoses in high-income and middle-income settings. *The Lancet Diabetes & Endocrinology, 9*(4), 203–211. https://doi.org/10.1016/S2213-8587(20)30402-2

Magnus, M. C., Guyatt, A. L., Lawn, R. B., Wyss, A. B., Trajanoska, K., Küpers, L. K., Rivadeneira, F., Tobin, M. D., London, S. J., Lawlor, D. A., Millard, L. A. C., & Fraser, A. (2020). Identifying potential causal effects of age at menarche: A Mendelian randomization phenome-wide association study. *BMC Medicine, 18*(1), 71. https://doi.org/10.1186/s12916-020-01515-y

Magnusson, C., & Nermo, M. (2018). From childhood to young adulthood: the importance of self-esteem during childhood for occupational achievements among young men and women. *Journal of Youth Studies, 21*(10), 1392–1410.

Mahler, M. S. (1974). Symbiosis and individuation. *The Psychoanalytic Study of the Child, 29*(1), 89–106. https://doi.org/10.1080/00797308.1974.11822615

Mahrer, N. E., O'Hara, K. L., Sandler, I. N., & Wolchik, S. A. (2018). Does shared parenting help or hurt children in high-conflict divorced families? *Journal of Divorce & Remarriage, 59*(4), 324–347. https://doi.org/10.1080/10502556.2018.1454200

Maier, L. J., Ferris, J. A., & Winstock, A. R. (2018). Pharmacological cognitive enhancement among non-ADHD individuals—a cross-sectional study in 15 countries. *International Journal of Drug Policy, 58*, 104–112. https://doi.org/10.1016/j.drugpo.2018.05.009

Main, M., Kaplan, N., & Cassidy, J. (1985). Security in infancy, childhood, and adulthood: A move to the level of representation. *Monographs of the Society for Research in Child Development, 50*(1–2), 66–104.

Main, M., & Solomon, J. (1986). Discovery of an insecure-disorganized/disoriented attachment pattern. In T. Brazelton (Ed.), *Affective development in infancy* (pp. 95–124). Ablex.

Major, R. J., Whelton, W. J., Schimel, J., & Sharpe, D. (2016). Older adults and the fear of death: The protective function of generativity. *Canadian Journal on Aging/La Revue Canadienne du Vieillissement, 35*(2), 261–272.

Mak, H. W., Fosco, G. M., & Lanza, S. T. (2021). Dynamic associations of parent–adolescent closeness and friend support with adolescent depressive symptoms across ages 12–19. *Journal of Research on Adolescence, 31*(2), 299–316. https://doi.org/10.1111/jora.12597

Makris, U. E., Higashi, R. T., Marks, E. G., Fraenkel, L., Sale, J. E., Gill, T. M., & Reid, M. C. (2015). Ageism, negative attitudes, and competing co-morbidities—Why older adults may not seek care for restricting back pain: A qualitative study. *BMC Geriatrics, 15*(1), 1–9.

Malani, P., Kullgren, J., Solway, E., Allen, J. O., Singer, D., & Kirch, M. (2020). *Everyday ageism and health* (National Poll on Healthy Aging). University of Michigan.

Maldeniya, D., Varghese, A., Stuart, T., & Romero, D. M. (2017). The role of optimal distinctiveness and homophily in online dating. *Proceedings of the International AAAI Conference on Web and Social Media, 11*(1), 616–619.

Maldonado, L. (2017). Latinas and intergenerational caregiving: An integrative review of the literature. *Journal of Transcultural Nursing, 28*(2), 203–211. https://doi.org/10.1177/1043659615623329

Maldonado, T., Orr, J. M., Goen, J. R. M., & Bernard, J. A. (2020). Age differences in the subcomponents of executive functioning. *The Journals of Gerontology: Series B, 75*(6), e31–e55. https://doi.org/10.1093/geronb/gbaa005

Malik, R., Hamm, K., Lee, W. F., Davis, E. E., & Sojourner, A. (2020). *The coronavirus will make child care deserts worse and exacerbate inequality.* Center for American Progress.

Malik, V. S., Willet, W. C., & Hu, F. B. (2020). Nearly a decade on—trends, risk factors and policy implications in global obesity. *Nature Reviews Endocrinology, 16*(11), 615–616. https://doi.org/10.1038/s41574-020-00411-y

Malina, R. M., Kozieł, S. M., Králik, M., Chrzanowska, M., & Suder, A. (2020). Prediction of maturity offset and age at peak height velocity in a longitudinal series of boys and girls. *American Journal of Human Biology*, e23551.

Mallett, C. A. (2016). The school-to-prison pipeline: A critical review of the punitive paradigm shift. *Child and Adolescent Social Work Journal, 33*(1), 15–24.

Mallory, A. B., Stanton, A. M., & Handy, A. B. (2019). Couples' sexual communication and dimensions of sexual function: A meta-analysis. *The Journal of Sex Research.*

Malone, J. C. (2014). Did John B. Watson really "found" behaviorism? *The Behavior Analyst, 37*(1), 1–12. https://doi.org/10.1007/s40614-014-0004-3

Malone, J. C. (2017). John B. Watson. In J. Vonk & T. Shackelford (Eds.), *Encyclopedia of animal cognition and behavior* (pp. 978–983). Springer. https://doi.org/10.1007/978-3-319-47829-6

Malti, T., & Dys, S. P. (2018). From being nice to being kind: Development of prosocial behaviors. *Current Opinion in Psychology, 20*, 45-49.

Mamedova, S., Stephens, M., Liao, Y., Sennett, J., Sirma, P., & Burg, S. S. (2021). *2012–2016 Program for International Student Assessment Young Adult Follow-up Study (PISA YAFS): How reading and mathematics performance at age 15 relate to literacy and numeracy skills and education, workforce, and life outcomes at age 19* (NCES 2021-029). U.S. Department of Education.

Manalel, J. A., Morris, E., Ryan, L. H., & Smith, J. (2018). Social integration through activity engagement: Long-term effects on cognition. *Innovation in Aging, 2*(Suppl 1), 431. https://doi.org/10.1093/geroni/igy023.1615

Manczak, E. M., & Gotlib, I. H. (2019). Lipid profiles at birth predict teacher-rated child emotional and social development 5 years later. *Psychological Science, 30*(12), 1780–1789. https://doi.org/10.1177/0956797619885649

Mandelli, S., Riva, E., Tettamanti, M., Lucca, U., Lombardi, D., Miolo, G., Spazzapan, S., Marson, R., & on Behalf of the Via di Natale Hospice Investigators. (2021). How palliative care professionals deal with predicting life expectancy at the end of life: Predictors and accuracy. *Supportive Care in Cancer, 29*(4), 2093–2103. https://doi.org/10.1007/s00520-020-05720-6

Mander, B. A., Winer, J. R., & Walker, M. P. (2017). Sleep and human aging. *Neuron, 94*(1), 19–36. https://doi.org/10.1016/j.neuron.2017.02.004

Mandlik, N., & Kamat, D. (2020). Medical anthropology in pediatrics: Improving disparities by partnering with families. *Pediatric Annals, 49*(5), e222–e227. http://dx.doi.org/10.3928/19382359-20200421-02

Manfredi, C., Viellevoye, R., Orlandi, S., Torres-García, A., Pieraccini, G., & Reyes-García, C. A. (2019). Automated analysis of newborn cry: Relationships between melodic shapes and native language. *Biomedical Signal Processing and Control, 53*, 101561. https://doi.org/10.1016/j.bspc.2019.101561

Mann, F. D., DeYoung, C. G., & Krueger, R. F. (2019). Patterns of cumulative continuity and maturity in personality and well-being: Evidence from a large longitudinal sample of adults. *Personality and Individual Differences*, 109737.

Mannheim, K. (1970). The problem of generations. *Psychoanalytic Review, 57*(3), 378–404.

Manninen, S., Tuominen, L., Dunbar, R. I., Karjalainen, T., Hirvonen, J., Arponen, E., & Nummenmaa, L. (2017). Social laughter triggers endogenous opioid release in humans. *Journal of Neuroscience, 37*(25), 6125–6131.

Manning, B. L., Roberts, M. Y., Estabrook, R., Petitclerc, A., Burns, J. L., Briggs-Gowan, M., Wakschlag, L. S., & Norton, E. S. (2019). Relations between toddler expressive language and temper tantrums in a community sample. *Journal of Applied Developmental Psychology, 65*, 101070. https://doi.org/10.1016/j.appdev.2019.101070

Manning, W. D. (2020). Young adulthood relationships in an era of uncertainty: A case for cohabitation. *Demography, 57*(3), 799–819. https://doi.org/10.1007/s13524-020-00881-9

Manning, W. D., Smock, P. J., & Fettro, M. N. (2019). Cohabitation and marital expectations among single millennials in the U.S. *Population Research and Policy Review, 38*(3), 327–346. https://doi.org/10.1007/s11113-018-09509-8

Manyika, J., Lund, S., Chui, M., Bughin, J., Woetzel, J., Batra, P., & Sanghvi, S. (2017). *Jobs lost, jobs gained: Workforce transitions in a time of automation*. McKinsey Global Institute.

Maoz-Halevy, E., Pariente, G., Sheiner, E., & Wainstock, T. (2020). Perinatal outcomes of women aged 50 years and above. *American Journal of Perinatology, 37*(1), 79–85. https://doi.org/10.1055/s-0039-1700859

Marans, S., & Hahn, H. (2017). *Enhancing police responses to children exposed to violence: A toolkit for law enforcement*. International Association of Chiefs of Police and Yale Child Study Center, Office of Juvenile Justice and Delinquency Prevention, Office of Justice Programs, U.S. Department of Justice.

Marçal, K. E. (2021). Pathways to adolescent emotional and behavioral problems: An examination of maternal depression and harsh parenting. *Child Abuse & Neglect, 113*, 104917. https://doi.org/10.1016/j.chiabu.2020.104917

Marcelo, A. K., & Yates, T. M. (2019). Young children's ethnic–racial identity moderates the impact of early discrimination experiences on child behavior problems. *Cultural Diversity and Ethnic Minority Psychology, 25*(2), 253.

Marchi, J., Berg, M., Dencker, A., Olander, E. K., & Begley, C. (2015). Risks associated with obesity in pregnancy, for the mother and baby: A systematic review of reviews. *Obesity Reviews, 16*(8), 621–638. https://doi.org/10.1111/obr.12288

Marck, A., Antero, J., Berthelot, G., Saulière, G., Jancovici, J.-M., Masson-Delmotte, V., Boeuf, G., Spedding, M., Le Bourg, É., & Toussaint, J.-F. (2017). Are we reaching the limits of *Homo sapiens*? *Frontiers in Physiology, 8*, 812. https://doi.org/10.3389/fphys.2017.00812

Marconi, A., Di Forti, M., Lewis, C. M., Murray, R. M., & Vassos, E. (2016). Meta-analysis of the association between the level of cannabis use and risk of psychosis. *Schizophrenia Bulletin, 42*(5), 1262–1269.

Marcovitch, S., Clearfield, M. W., Swingler, M., Calkins, S. D., & Bell, M. A. (2016). Attentional predictors of 5-month-olds' performance on a looking A-not-B task. *Infant and Child Development, 25*(4), 233–246.

Marcovitch, S., & Zelazo, P. D. (1999). The A-not-B error: Results from a logistic meta-analysis. *Child Development, 70*(6), 1297–1313.

Marcus, J. (2019, October 27). In one country, women now outnumber men in college by two to one. *The Hechinger Report*. http://hechingerreport.org/in-one-country-women-now-outnumber-men-in-college-by-two-to-one/

Marcus, J. (2021a, January 19). The pandemic is speeding up the mass disappearance of men from college. *The Hechinger Report*. http://hechingerreport.org/the-pandemic-is-speeding-up-the-mass-disappearance-of-men-from-college/

Marcus, J. (2021b, October 10). Why college graduation rates are measured over six years instead of four. *The Hechinger Report*. http://hechingerreport.org/how-the-college-lobby-got-the-government-to-measure-graduation-rates-over-six-years-instead-of-four/

Marengo, D., Longobardi, C., Fabris, M. A., & Settanni, M. (2018). Highly-visual social media and internalizing symptoms in adolescence: The mediating role of body image concerns. *Computers in Human Behavior, 82*, 63–69. https://doi.org/10.1016/j.chb.2018.01.003

Marey-Sarwan, I., Keller, H., & Otto, H. (2016). Stay close to me: Stranger anxiety and maternal beliefs about children's socio-emotional development among Bedouins in the unrecognized villages in the Naqab. *Journal of Cross-Cultural Psychology, 47*(3), 319–332. https://doi.org/10.1177/0022022115619231

Margolis, R., & Wright, L. (2017). Healthy grandparenthood: How long is it, and how has it changed? *Demography, 54*(6), 2073–2099.

Margoni, F., & Surian, L. (2018). Infants' evaluation of prosocial and antisocial agents: A meta-analysis. *Developmental Psychology, 54*(8), 1445.

Marie, J. (2014a, August 12). The secret life of marrieds: A couple that keeps their sex life exciting. *Cosmopolitan*. http://www.cosmopolitan.com/sex-love/a30016/the-secret-life-of-marrieds-becki-kevin/

Marie, J. (2014b, November 25). What it's really like to have an arranged marriage. *Cosmopolitan*. http://www.cosmopolitan.com/sex-love/a33627/what-its-really-like-to-have-an-arranged-marriage/

Marini, S., Davis, K. A., Soare, T. W., Zhu, Y., Suderman, M. J., Simpkin, A. J., Smith, A. D. A. C., Wolf, E. J., Relton, C. L., & Dunn, E. C. (2020). Adversity exposure during sensitive periods predicts accelerated epigenetic aging in children. *Psychoneuroendocrinology, 113*, 104484. https://doi.org/10.1016/j.psyneuen.2019.104484

Marinica, B. V., & Negru-Subtirica, O. (2020). Relationships between volunteering functions and vocational identity in emerging adult volunteers. *International Journal for Educational and Vocational Guidance*, 1–21.

Marinović, V., & Träuble, B. (2021). Vicarious ostracism and control in young children. *Social Development, 30*(1), 225–238.

Marinović, V., Wahl, S., & Träuble, B. (2017). "Next to you"—Young children sit closer to a person following vicarious ostracism. *Journal of Experimental Child Psychology, 156*, 179–185. https://doi.org/10.1016/j.jecp.2016.11.011

Mark, K. P., & Lasslo, J. A. (2018). Maintaining sexual desire in long-term relationships: A systematic review and conceptual model. *The Journal of Sex Research, 55*(4–5), 563–581.

Marks, A. K., & García Coll, C. (2018). Education and developmental competencies of ethnic minority children: Recent theoretical and methodological advances. *Developmental Review, 50*, 90–98. https://doi.org/10.1016/j.dr.2018.05.004

Marks, M. J., Young, T. M., & Zaikman, Y. (2018). The sexual double standard in the real world: Evaluations of sexually active friends and acquaintances. *Social Psychology, 50*(2), 67–79.

Markus, H. R. (2017). American = independent? *Perspectives on Psychological Science, 12*(5), 855–866. https://doi.org/10.1177/1745691617718799

Marlatt, K. L., Beyl, R. A., & Redman, L. M. (2018). A qualitative assessment of health behaviors and experiences during menopause: A cross-sectional, observational study. *Maturitas, 116*, 36–42. https://doi.org/10.1016/j.maturitas.2018.07.014

Marmot, M. G., Shipley, M. J., & Rose, G. (1984). Inequalities in death—Specific explanations of a general pattern? *The Lancet, 323*(8384), 1003–1006.

Marrus, N., Eggebrecht, A. T., Todorov, A., Elison, J. T., Wolff, J. J., Cole, L., Gao, W., Pandey, J., Shen, M. D., Swanson, M. R., Emerson, R. W., Klohr, C. L., Adams, C. M., Estes, A. M., Zwaigenbaum, L., Botteron, K. N., McKinstry, R. C., Constantino, J. N., Evans, A. C., … Pruett, J. R., Jr. (2018). Walking, gross motor development, and brain functional connectivity in infants and toddlers. *Cerebral Cortex, 28*(2), 750–763. https://doi.org/10.1093/cercor/bhx313

Marsh, H., Seaton, M., Dicke, T., Parker, P., & Horwood, M. (2019). The centrality of academic self-concept to motivation and learning. In K. Renninger & S. Hidi (Eds.), *The Cambridge handbook of motivation and learning* (pp. 36–62). Cambridge University Press

Marshall, E. A., & Butler, K. (2015). School-to-work transitions in emerging adulthood. In J. J. Arnett (Ed.), *The Oxford handbook of emerging adulthood* (pp. 316–333). Oxford University Press. https://books.google.com/books?hl=en&lr=&id=ObuYCgAAQBAJ&oi=fnd&pg=PA316&dq=%22this+chapter,+we+look+at+the+changing+world+of+work+and+how+that+has+impacted%22+%22emerging+adults+in+North+America+are+in+the+workforce.+There+are+approximately%22+&ots=2Mgye4z5Du&sig=9NXgd8E4lGnBH8iTcSfKe_l1vSE

Marshall, E. A., & Symonds, J. E. (2021). Introduction and overview. In E. A. Marshall & J. E. Symonds (Eds.), *Young adult development at the school-to-work transition: International pathways and processes* (pp. xxi–xxxii). Oxford University Press.

Marshall, M. (2021). The four most urgent questions about long COVID. *Nature, 594*(7862), 168–170. https://doi.org/10.1038/d41586-021-01511-z

Marshall, S. (2015, September 18). When, and why, did women start dyeing their grays? *Elle*. https://www.elle.com/beauty/hair/news/a30556/when-and-why-did-women-start-dyeing-their-gray-hair/

Martens, D. S., Cox, B., Janssen, B. G., Clemente, D. B. P., Gasparrini, A., Vanpoucke, C., Lefebvre, W., Roels, H. A., Plusquin, M., & Nawrot, T. S. (2017). Prenatal air pollution and newborns' predisposition to accelerated biological aging. *JAMA Pediatrics, 171*(12), 1160–1167. https://doi.org/10.1001/jamapediatrics.2017.3024

Martial, C., Cassol, H., Charland-Verville, V., Pallavicini, C., Sanz, C., Zamberlan, F., Vivot, R. M., Erowid, F., Erowid, E., Laureys, S., Greyson, B., & Tagliazucchi, E. (2019). Neurochemical models of near-death experiences: A large-scale study based on the semantic similarity of written reports. *Consciousness and Cognition, 69*, 52–69.

Martin, A. E., & North, M. S. (2021). Equality for (almost) all: Egalitarian advocacy predicts lower endorsement of sexism and racism, but not ageism. *Journal of Personality and Social Psychology.*

Martin, C. L., Andrews, N. C. Z., England, D. E., Zosuls, K., & Ruble, D. N. (2017). A dual identity approach for conceptualizing and measuring children's gender identity. *Child Development, 88*(1), 167–182. https://doi.org/10.1111/cdev.12568

Martin, C. L., & Halverson, C. F. (1981). A schematic processing model of sex typing and stereotyping in children. *Child Development, 52*(4), 1119–1134. https://doi.org/10.2307/1129498

Martin, C. L., & Ruble, D. N. (2010). Patterns of gender development. *Annual Review of Psychology, 61*, 353–381. https://doi.org/10.1146/annurev.psych.093008.100511

Martin, J., Hamilton, B. E., & Osterman, M. J. K. (2020). *Births in the United States, 2019* (NCHS Data Brief No. 387). https://www.cdc.gov/nchs/products/databriefs/db387.htm

Martin, J. A., Hamilton, B. E., Osterman, M. J. K., & Driscoll, A. K. (2021). Births: Final data for 2019. *National Vital Statistics Reports: From the Centers for Disease Control and Prevention, National Center for Health Statistics, National Vital Statistics System, 70*(2), 1–51.

Martin, J. F., & Poché, R. A. (2019). Awakening the regenerative potential of the mammalian retina. *Development, 146*(23), dev18264

Martin, M. J., Blozis, S. A., Boeninger, D. K., Masarik, A. S., & Conger, R. D. (2014). The timing of entry into adult roles and changes in trajectories of problem behaviors during the transition to adulthood. *Developmental Psychology, 50*(11), 2473–2484. https://doi.org/10.1037/a0037950

Martínez, I., Murgui, S., Garcia, O. F., & Garcia, F. (2021). Parenting and adolescent adjustment: The mediational role of family self-esteem. *Journal of Child and Family Studies, 30*(5), 1184–1197. https://doi.org/10.1007/s10826-021-01937-z

Martinez, M. A., Gutierrez, B. C., Halim, M. L. D., & Leaper, C. (2021). Gender and ethnic variation in emerging adults' recalled dating socialization in relation to current romantic attitudes and relationship experiences. *Sexuality & Culture.* https://doi.org/10.1007/s12119-021-09873-2

Martinez, M. A., Osornio, A., Halim, M. L. D., & Zosuls, K. M. (2019). Gender: Awareness, identity, and stereotyping. In J. B. Benson (Ed.), *Encyclopedia of infant and early child development* (pp. 1–12). Elsevier Science.

Martínez-Cué, C., & Rueda, N. (2020). Cellular senescence in neurodegenerative diseases. *Frontiers in Cellular Neuroscience, 14*, 16. https://doi.org/10.3389/fncel.2020.00016

Martínez-Patiño, M. J. (2005). Personal account: A woman tried and tested. *The Lancet, 366*, S38. https://doi.org/10.1016/S0140-6736(05)67841-5

Martinez-Torteya, C., D'Amico, J., & Gilchrist, M. (2018). Trauma exposure: Consequences to maternal and offspring stress systems. In M. Muzik & K. L. Rosenblum (Eds.), *Motherhood in the face of trauma: Pathways towards healing and growth* (pp. 85–98). Springer.

Martini, D. N., & Broglio, S. P. (2018). Long-term effects of sport concussion on cognitive and motor performance: A review. *International Journal of Psychophysiology, 132*, 25–30.

Martinson, K., Cho, S. W., Gardiner, K., & Glosser, A. (2018). *Washington state's Integrated Basic Education and Skills Training (I-BEST) program in three colleges: Implementation and early impact report.* Office of Planning, Research, and Evaluation, Administration for Children and Families, U.S. Department of Health and Human Services.

Martinson, M., & Berridge, C. (2015). Successful aging and its discontents: A systematic review of the social gerontology literature. *The Gerontologist, 55*(1), 58–69. https://doi.org/10.1093/geront/gnu037

Martin-Storey, A., Cheadle, J. E., Skalamera, J., & Crosnoe, R. (2015). Exploring the social integration of sexual minority youth across high school contexts. *Child Development, 86*(3), 965–975. https://doi.org/10.1111/cdev.12352

Martin-Storey, A., & Fish, J. (2019). Victimization disparities between heterosexual and sexual minority youth from ages nine to fifteen. *Child Development, 90*(1), 71–81. https://doi.org/10.1111/cdev.13107

Martos, A. J., Nezhad, S., & Meyer, I. H. (2015). Variations in sexual identity milestones among lesbians, gay men, and bisexuals. *Sexuality Research and Social Policy, 12*(1), 24–33. https://doi.org/http://dx.doi.org/10.1007/s13178-014-0167-4

Marulis, L. M., & Neuman, S. B. (2010). The effects of vocabulary intervention on young children's word learning: A meta-analysis. *Review of Educational Research, 80*(3), 300–335.

Maruna, S. (2017). Desistance as a social movement. *Irish Probation Journal, 14*, 5–16.

Marusak, H. A., Thomason, M. E., Sala-Hamrick, K., Crespo, L., & Rabinak, C. A. (2018). What's parenting got to do with it: Emotional autonomy and brain and behavioral responses to emotional conflict in children and adolescents. *Developmental Science, 21*(4), e12605. https://doi.org/10.1111/desc.12605

Marván, M. L., & Alcalá-Herrera, V. (2019). Menarche: Psychosocial and cultural aspects. In J. M. Ussher, J. C. Chrisler, & J. Perz (Eds.), *Routledge international handbook of women's sexual and reproductive health* (pp. 28–38). Routledge.

Marx, V., & Nagy, E. (2017). Fetal behavioral responses to the touch of the mother's abdomen: A frame-by-frame analysis. *Infant Behavior and Development, 47*, 83–91. https://doi.org/10.1016/j.infbeh.2017.03.005

Marzilli, E., Cerniglia, L., & Cimino, S. (2018). A narrative review of binge eating disorder in adolescence: Prevalence, impact, and psychological treatment strategies. *Adolescent Health, Medicine and Therapeutics, 9*, 17–30. https://doi.org/10.2147/AHMT.S148050

Masek, L. R., McMillan, B. T. M., Paterson, S. J., Tamis-LeMonda, C. S., Golinkoff, R. M., & Hirsh-Pasek, K. (2021a). Where language meets attention: How contingent interactions promote learning. *Developmental Review, 60*, 100961. https://doi.org/10.1016/j.dr.2021.100961

Masek, L. R., Paterson, S. J., Golinkoff, R. M., Bakeman, R., Adamson, L. B., Owen, M. T., Pace, A., & Hirsh-Pasek, K. (2021b). Beyond talk: Contributions of quantity and quality of communication to language success across socioeconomic strata. *Infancy, 26*(1), 123–147.

Mashour, G. A., Frank, L., Batthyany, A., Kolanowski, A. M., Nahm, M., Schulman-Green, D., Greyson, B., Pakhomov, S., Karlawish, J., & Shah, R. C. (2019). Paradoxical lucidity: A potential paradigm shift for the neurobiology and treatment of severe dementias. *Alzheimer's & Dementia: The Journal of the Alzheimer's Association, 15*(8), 1107–1114.

Masi, C. M., Chen, H. Y., Hawkley, L. C., & Cacioppo, J. T. (2011). A meta-analysis of interventions to reduce loneliness. *Personality and Social Psychology Review, 15*(3), 219–266

Maslach, C., & Leiter, M. P. (2017). Understanding burnout: New models. In C. L. Cooper & J. C. Quick (Eds.), *The handbook of stress and health: A guide to research and practice* (pp. 36–56). Wiley-Blackwell. https://doi.org/10.1002/9781118993811.ch3

Maslow, A. H. (1943). A theory of human motivation. *Psychological Review, 50*(4), 370–396. https://doi.org/10.1037/h0054346

Maslow, A. H. (1970). New introduction: Religions, values, and peak-experiences. *Journal of Transpersonal Psychology, 2*(2), 83–90.

Masten, A. S. (2019). Resilience from a developmental systems perspective. *World Psychiatry, 18*(1), 101–102. https://doi.org/10.1002/wps.20591

Masten, A. S., & Cicchetti, D. (2016). Resilience in development: Progress and transformation. In D. Cicchetti (Ed.), *Developmental psychopathology: Risk, resilience, and intervention* (pp. 271–333). Wiley

Masten, A. S., Lucke, C. M., Nelson, K. M., & Stallworthy, I. C. (2021). Resilience in development and psychopathology: Multisystem perspectives. *Annual Review of Clinical Psychology, 17*, 521–549.

Masten, A. S., & Wright, M. O. D. (2010). Resilience over the lifespan: Developmental perspectives on resistance, recovery, and transformation. In J. W. Reich, A. J. Zautra, & J. S. Hall (Eds.), *Handbook of adult resilience* (pp. 213–237). Guilford.

Mastro, S., & Zimmer-Gembeck, M. J. (2015). Let's talk openly about sex: Sexual communication, self-esteem and efficacy as correlates of sexual well-being. *European Journal of Developmental Psychology, 12*(5), 579–598. https://doi.org/10.1080/17405629.2015.1054373

Matas, L., Arend, R. A., & Sroufe, L. A. (1978). Continuity of adaptation in the second year: The relationship between quality of attachment and later competence. *Child Development, 49*(3), 547–556. https://doi.org/10.2307/1128221

Mather, M. (2016). The affective neuroscience of aging. *Annual Review of Psychology, 67*(1), 213–238. https://doi.org/10.1146/annurev-psych-122414-033540

Mather, M., & Scommegna, P. (2020). *The demography of dementia and dementia caregiving.* Population Reference Bureau.

Matloff, J. (2018, July 24). The mystery of end-of-life rallies. *The New York Times.* https://www.nytimes.com/2018/07/24/well/the-mystery-of-end-of-life-rallies.html

Matsick, J. L., Kruk, M., Conley, T. D., Moors, A. C., & Ziegler, A. (2021). Gender similarities and differences in casual sex acceptance among lesbian women and gay men. *Archives of Sexual Behavior, 50*(3), 1151–1166. https://doi.org/10.1007/s10508-020-01864-y

Matthews, K. A., Xu, W., Gaglioti, A. H., Holt, J. B., Croft, J. B., Mack, D., & McGuire, L. C. (2019). Racial and ethnic estimates of Alzheimer's disease and related dementias in the United States (2015–2060) in adults aged ≥65 years. *Alzheimer's & Dementia, 15*(1), 17–24. https://doi.org/10.1016/j.jalz.2018.06.3063

Mattson, M. P., & Arumugam, T. V. (2018). Hallmarks of brain aging: Adaptive and pathological modification by metabolic states. *Cell Metabolism, 27*(6), 1176–1199. https://doi.org/10.1016/j.cmet.2018.05.011

Maunder, R., & Monks, C. P. (2019). Friendships in middle childhood: Links to peer and school identification, and general self-worth. *British Journal of Developmental Psychology, 37*(2), 211–229.

Maurer, D., & Werker, J. F. (2014). Perceptual narrowing during infancy: A comparison of language and faces. *Developmental Psychobiology, 56*(2), 154–178. https://doi.org/10.1002/dev.21177

Maware, M., Mubaya, T. R., van Reisen, M., & van Stant, G. (2016). Maslow's theory of human motivation and its deep roots in individualism: Interrogating Maslow's applicability in Africa. In *Theory, knowledge, development and politics: What role for the academy in the sustainability of Africa?* (pp. 55–72). Langaa RPCIG.

Mawhorter, S. L. (2017). Boomers and their boomerang kids: Comparing housing opportunities for baby boomers and millennials in the United States. In M. Moos, D. Pfeiffer, & T. Vinodrai (Eds.), *The millennial city* (pp. 143–152). Routledge.

Maxwell, J. A., & McNulty, J. K. (2019). No longer in a dry spell: The developing understanding of how sex influences romantic relationships. *Current Directions in Psychological Science, 28*(1), 102–107. https://doi.org/10.1177/0963721418806690

May, A. (2011). Experience-dependent structural plasticity in the adult human brain. *Trends in Cognitive Sciences, 15*(10), 475–482. https://doi.org/10.1016/j.tics.2011.08.002

May, P. A., Chambers, C. D., Kalberg, W. O., Zellner, J., Feldman, H., Buckley, D., Kopald, D., Hasken, J. M., Xu, R., Honerkamp-Smith, G., Taras, H., Manning, M. A., Robinson, L. K., Adam, M. P., Abdul-Rahman, O., Vaux, K., Jewett, T., Elliott, A. J., Kable, J. A., … Hoyme, H. E. (2018). Prevalence of fetal alcohol spectrum disorders in 4 US communities. *JAMA, 319*(5), 474–482. https://doi.org/10.1001/jama.2017.21896

May, P. A., Serna, P., Hurt, L., & DeBruyn, L. M. (2005). Outcome evaluation of a public health approach to suicide prevention in an American Indian Tribal Nation. *American Journal of Public Health, 95*(7), 1238–1244. https://doi.org/10.2105/AJPH.2004.040410

Mayeda, E. R., Glymour, M. M., Quesenberry, C. P., Johnson, J. K., Pérez-Stable, E. J., & Whitmer, R. A.

(2017). Survival after dementia diagnosis in five racial/ethnic groups. *Alzheimer's & Dementia, 13*(7), 761–769. https://doi.org/10.1016/j.jalz.2016.12.008

Mayers, A., Hambidge, S., Bryant, O., & Arden-Close, E. (2020). Supporting women who develop poor postnatal mental health: What support do fathers receive to support their partner and their own mental health? *BMC Pregnancy and Childbirth, 20*(1), 359. https://doi.org/10.1186/s12884-020-03043-2

Mayhew, M. J., Rockenbach, A. N., Bowman, N. A., Seifert, T. A. D., & Wolniak, G. C. (2016). *How college affects students: 21st century evidence that higher education works.* Wiley.

Mayol-Garcia, Y., Gurrentz, B., & Kreider, R. M. (2021). *Number, timing, and duration of marriages and divorces: 2016* (No. P70-167). U.S. Census Bureau. https://www.census.gov/library/publications/2021/demo/p70-167.html

Mayr, U., & Freund, A. M. (2020). Do we become more prosocial as we age, and if so, why? *Current Directions in Psychological Science, 29*(3), 248–254. https://doi.org/10.1177/0963721420910811

Mazzone, A., Camodeca, M., & Salmivalli, C. (2016). Interactive effects of guilt and moral disengagement on bullying, defending and outsider behavior. *Journal of Moral Education, 45*(4), 419–432.

Mazzone, A., Yanagida, T., Camodeca, M., & Strohmeier, D. (2021). Information processing of social exclusion: Links with bullying, moral disengagement and guilt. *Journal of Applied Developmental Psychology, 75*, 101292.

Mazzoni, S. E., & Carter, E. B. (2017). Group prenatal care. *American Journal of Obstetrics and Gynecology, 216*(6), 552–556. https://doi.org/10.1016/j.ajog.2017.02.006

McAdams, D. P., & Guo, J. (2015). Narrating the generative life. *Psychological Science, 26*(4), 475–483.

McAdams, D. P., & Olson, B. D. (2010). Personality development: Continuity and change over the life course. *Annual Review of Psychology, 61*(1), 517–542. https://doi.org/10.1146/annurev.psych.093008.100507

McAdams, D. P., & Zapata-Gietl, C. (2015). Three strands of identity development across the human life course: Reading Erik Erikson in full. In *The Oxford handbook of identity development* (pp. 81–94). Oxford University Press.

McArthur, B. A., Eirich, R., McDonald, S., Tough, S., & Madigan, S. (2021). Screen use relates to decreased offline enrichment activities. *Acta Paediatrica, 110*(3), 896–898. https://doi.org/10.1111/apa.15601

McBride, A. M., Gonzales, E., Morrow-Howell, N., & McCrary, S. (2011). Stipends in volunteer civic service: Inclusion, retention, and volunteer benefits. *Public Administration Review, 71*(6), 850–858.

McCabe, S. E., Arterberry, B. J., Dickinson, K., Evans-Polce, R. J., Ford, J. A., Ryan, J. E., & Schepis, T. S. (2021). Assessment of changes in alcohol and marijuana abstinence, co-use, and use disorders among US young adults from 2002 to 2018. *JAMA Pediatrics, 175*(1), 64–72. https://doi.org/10.1001/jamapediatrics.2020.3352

McCann, S., Amadó, M. P., & Moore, S. E. (2020). The role of iron in brain development: A systematic review. *Nutrients, 12*(7), 2001. https://doi.org/10.3390/nu12072001

McCarty, D., Priest, K. C., & Korthuis, P. T. (2018). Treatment and prevention of opioid use disorder: Challenges and opportunities. *Annual Review of Public Health, 39*, 525–541.

McClelland, M. M., & Cameron, C. E. (2019). Developing together: The role of executive function and motor skills in children's early academic lives. *Early Childhood Research Quarterly, 46*, 142–151. https://doi.org/10.1016/j.ecresq.2018.03.014

McClintock, M. K., & Herdt, G. (1996). Rethinking puberty: The development of sexual attraction. *Current Directions in Psychological Science, 5*(6), 178–183.

McConnell, E. A., Birkett, M., & Mustanski, B. (2016). Families matter: Social support and mental health trajectories among lesbian, gay, bisexual, and transgender youth. *Journal of Adolescent Health, 59*(6), 674–680.

McCormack, M., & Savin-Williams, R. (2018). Young men's rationales for non-exclusive gay sexualities. *Culture, Health & Sexuality, 20*(8), 929–944. https://doi.org/10.1080/13691058.2017.1398349

McCormick, B. J. J., Caulfield, L. E., Richard, S. A., Pendergast, L., Seidman, J. C., Maphula, A., Koshy, B., Blacy, L., Roshan, R., Nahar, B., Shrestha, R., Rasheed, M., Svensen, E., Rasmussen, Z., Scharf, R. J., Haque, S., Oria, R., Murray-Kolb, L. E., & MAL-ED Network Investigators. (2020). Early life experiences and trajectories of cognitive development. *Pediatrics, 146*(3), e20193660. https://doi.org/10.1542/peds.2019-3660

McCoy, D. C., & Wolf, S. (2018). Changes in classroom quality predict Ghanaian preschoolers' gains in academic and social-emotional skills. *Developmental Psychology, 54*(8), 1582.

McCrae, R. R. (2017). The Five-Factor Model across cultures. In A. T. Church (Ed.), *The Praeger handbook of personality across cultures: Trait psychology across cultures* (pp. 47–71). Praeger/ABC-CLIO.

McCue, D. (2021, March 8). *After a brief return, young adults quick to move out of parents homes as the pandemic continues.* Housing Perspectives: Joint Center for Housing Studies of Harvard University. https://www.jchs.harvard.edu/blog/after-brief-return-young-adults-quick-move-out-parents-homes-pandemic-continues

McCutcheon, R. A., Marques, T. R., & Howes, O. D. (2020). Schizophrenia—an overview. *JAMA Psychiatry, 77*(2), 201–210.

McDade, T. W., Ryan, C. P., Jones, M. J., Hoke, M. K., Borja, J., Miller, G. E., Kuzawa, C. W., & Kobor, M. S. (2019). Genome-wide analysis of DNA methylation in relation to socioeconomic status during development and early adulthood. *American Journal of Physical Anthropology, 169*(1), 3–11. https://doi.org/10.1002/ajpa.23800

McDaniel, B. T., & Coyne, S. M. (2016). "Technoference": The interference of technology in couple relationships and implications for women's personal and relational well-being. *Psychology of Popular Media Culture, 5*(1), 85.

McDaniel, B. T., & Coyne, S. M. (2016). Technology interference in the parenting of young children: Implications for mothers' perceptions of coparenting. *The Social Science Journal, 53*(4), 435–443. https://doi.org/10.1016/j.soscij.2016.04.010

McDaniel, B. T., & Radesky, J. S. (2018). Technoference: Parent distraction with technology and associations with child behavior problems. *Child Development, 89*(1), 100–109. https://doi.org/10.1111/cdev.12822

McDaniel, B. T., & Radesky, J. S. (2020). Longitudinal associations between early childhood externalizing behavior, parenting stress, and child media use. *Cyberpsychology, Behavior, and Social Networking, 23*(6), 384–391. https://doi.org/10.1089/cyber.2019.0478

McDermott, R. C., Kilmartin, C., McKelvey, D. K., & Kridel, M. M. (2015). College male sexual assault of women and the psychology of men: Past, present, and future directions for research. *Psychology of Men & Masculinity, 16*(4), 355–366.

McDonald, N. M., Perdue, K. L., Eilbott, J., Loyal, J., Shic, F., & Pelphrey, K. A. (2019). Infant brain responses to social sounds: A longitudinal functional near-infrared spectroscopy study. *Developmental Cognitive Neuroscience, 36*, 100638. https://doi.org/10.1016/j.dcn.2019.100638

McDonald, S. E., Shin, S., Corona, R., Maternick, A., Graham-Bermann, S. A., Ascione, F. R., & Herbert Williams, J. (2016). Children exposed to intimate partner violence: Identifying differential effects of family environment on children's trauma and psychopathology symptoms through regression mixture models. *Child Abuse & Neglect, 58*, 1–11. https://doi.org/10.1016/j.chiabu.2016.06.010

McDougall, P., & Vaillancourt, T. (2015). Long-term adult outcomes of peer victimization in childhood and adolescence: Pathways to adjustment and maladjustment. *American Psychologist, 70*(4), 300.

McEwen, B. S., & Bulloch, K. (2019). Epigenetic impact of the social and physical environment on brain and body. *Metabolism, 100*, 153941. https://doi.org/10.1016/j.metabol.2019.07.005

McFadden, K. E., Puzio, A., Way, N., & Hughes, D. (2020). Mothers' gender beliefs matter for adolescents' academic achievement and engagement: An examination of ethnically diverse US mothers and adolescents. *Sex Roles, 84*, 166–182.

McFarland, D. A., Moody, J., Diehl, D., Smith, J. A., & Thomas, R. J. (2014). Network ecology and adolescent social structure. *American Sociological Review, 79*(6), 1088–1121. https://doi.org/10.1177/0003122414554001

McFarland, J., Hussar, B., De Brey, C., Snyder, T., Wang, X., Wilkinson-Flicker, S., & Hinz, S. (2017). *The condition of education 2017* (NCES 2017-144). National Center for Education Statistics.

McFarlane, W. R., Susser, E., McCleary, R., Verdi, M., Lynch, S., Williams, D., & McKeague, I. W. (2014). Reduction in incidence of hospitalizations for psychotic episodes through early identification and intervention. *Psychiatric Services, 65*(10), 1194–1200.

McGiffin, J. N., Galatzer-Levy, I. R., & Bonanno, G. A. (2019). Socioeconomic resources predict trajectories of depression and resilience following disability. *Rehabilitation Psychology, 64*(1), 98.

McGillicuddy, D., & Devine, D. (2020). 'You feel ashamed that you are not in the higher group'—Children's psychosocial response to ability grouping in primary school. *British Educational Research Journal, 46*(3), 553–573. https://doi.org/10.1002/berj.3595

McGraw, M. B. (1943). *The neuromuscular maturation of the human infant* (p. 140). Columbia University Press.

McHarg, G., Ribner, A. D., Devine, R. T., & Hughes, C. (2020). Screen time and executive function in toddlerhood: A longitudinal study. *Frontiers in Psychology, 11*, 570392. https://doi.org/10.3389/fpsyg.2020.570392

McInroy, L. B., McCloskey, R. J., Craig, S. L., & Eaton, A. D. (2019). LGBTQ+ youths' community engagement and resource seeking online versus offline. *Journal of Technology in Human Services, 37*(4), 315–333.

McKenna, L. (2017, May 18). How (over)involved parents are changing college. *The Atlantic.* https://www.theatlantic.com/education/archive/2017/05/the-ethos-of-the-overinvolved-parent/527097/

McKenzie, K., Murray, G., Murray, A., Delahunty, L., Hutton, L., Murray, K., & O'Hare, A. (2019). Child and Adolescent Intellectual Disability Screening Questionnaire to identify children with intellectual disability. *Developmental Medicine & Child Neurology, 61*(4), 444–450. https://doi.org/10.1111/dmcn.13998

McKetta, S. C., & Keyes, K. M. (2020). Trends in U.S. women's binge drinking in middle adulthood by socioeconomic status, 2006–2018. *Drug and Alcohol Dependence, 108026.* https://doi.org/10.1016/j.drugalcdep.2020.108026

McKinsey Global Institute. (2021). *The future of work after COVID-19.*

McKowen, C., & Strambler, M. J. (2009). Developmental antecedents and social and academic consequences of stereotype-consciousness in middle childhood. *Child Development, 80*(6), 1643–1659.

McLachlan, E., Bousfield, J., Howard, R., & Reeves, S. (2018). Reduced parahippocampal volume and psychosis symptoms in Alzheimer's disease. *International Journal of Geriatric Psychiatry, 33*(2), 389–395.

McLanahan, S., & Sawhill, I. (2015). Marriage and child wellbeing revisited: Introducing the issue. *The Future of Children, 25*(2), 3–9.

McLaughlin, K. A., Colich, N. L., Rodman, A. M., & Weissman, D. G. (2020). Mechanisms linking childhood trauma exposure and psychopathology: A transdiagnostic model of risk and resilience. *BMC Medicine, 18*, 1–11.

McLaughlin, K. A., Garrad, M. C., & Somerville, L. H. (2015). What develops during emotional development? A component process approach to identifying sources of psychopathology risk in adolescence. *Dialogues in Clinical Neuroscience, 17*(4), 403–410. http://www.ncbi.nlm.nih.gov/pmc/articles/PMC4734878/

McLaughlin, K. A., Weissman, D., & Bitrán, D. (2019). Childhood adversity and neural development: A systematic review. *Annual Review of Developmental Psychology, 1*, 277–312.

McLaughlin, S. J., Jette, A. M., & Connell, C. M. (2012). An examination of healthy aging across a conceptual continuum: Prevalence estimates, demographic patterns, and validity. *The Journals of Gerontology: Series A, 67*(7), 783–789. https://doi.org/10.1093/gerona/glr234

McLeod, C. B., Hall, P. A., Siddiqi, A., & Hertzman, C. (2012). How society shapes the health gradient: Work-related health inequalities in a comparative perspective. *Annual Review of Public Health, 33*, 59–73.

McLoyd, V. C., & Hallman, S. K. (2020). Antecedents and correlates of adolescent employment: Race as a moderator of psychological predictors. *Youth & Society, 52*(6), 871–893.

McMahon, R. (2018). The history of transdisciplinary race classification: Methods, politics and institutions, 1840s–1940s. *The British Journal for the History of Science, 51*(1), 41–67. https://doi.org/10.1017/S0007087417001054

McMahon, R. J., & Frick, P. J. (2019). Conduct and oppositional disorders. In M. J. Prinstein, E. A. Youngstrom, E. J. Mash, & R. A. Barkley (Eds.), *Treatment of disorders in childhood and adolescence* (pp. 102–172). Guilford.

McMahon, S., Wood, L., Cusano, J., & Macri, L. M. (2019). Campus sexual assault: Future directions for research. *Sexual Abuse, 31*(3), 270–295. https://doi.org/10.1177/1079063217750864

McMakin, D. L., Dahl, R. E., Buysse, D. J., Cousins, J. C., Forbes, E. E., Silk, J. S., Siegle, G. J., & Franzen, P. L. (2016). The impact of experimental sleep restriction on affective functioning in social and nonsocial contexts among adolescents. *Journal of Child Psychology and Psychiatry, 57*(9), 1027–1037.

McMullen, M. B. (2018). The many benefits of continuity of care for infants, toddlers, families, and caregiving staff. *Young Children, 73*(3), 38–39. https://www.naeyc.org/resources/pubs/yc/jul2018/benefits-continuity-care

McNeel, B. (2018, July 17). Measuring success at the San Antonio public preschool program. *The Hechinger Report.* http://hechingerreport.org/measuring-success-at-san-antonios-public-preschool-program/

McNeil, C. J., Myint, P. K., Sandu, A.-L., Potter, J. F., Staff, R., Whalley, L. J., & Murray, A. D. (2018). Increased diastolic blood pressure is associated with MRI biomarkers of dementia-related brain pathology in normative ageing. *Age and Ageing, 47*(1), 95–100. https://doi.org/10.1093/ageing/afx102

McNeil, M. (2017). Menopausal hormone therapy: Understanding long-term risks and benefits. *JAMA, 318*(10), 911–913. https://doi.org/10.1001/jama.2017.11462

McNeill, J., Howard, S. J., Vella, S. A., Santos, R., & Cliff, D. P. (2018). Physical activity and modified organized sport among preschool children: Associations with cognitive and psychosocial health. *Mental Health and Physical Activity, 15*, 45–52. https://doi.org/10.1016/j.mhpa.2018.07.001

McNulty, J. K., Maxwell, J. A., Meltzer, A. L., & Baumeister, R. F. (2019). Sex-differentiated changes in sexual desire predict marital dissatisfaction. *Archives of Sexual Behavior, 48*(8), 2473–2489. https://doi.org/10.1007/s10508-019-01471-6

McQuillan, M. E., Kultur, E. C., Bates, J. E., O'Reilly, L. M., Dodge, K. A., Lansford, J. E., & Pettit, G. S. (2018). Dysregulation in children: Origins and implications from age 5 to age 28. *Development and Psychopathology, 30*(2), 695–713. https://doi.org/10.1017/S0954579417001572

McQuillan, M. E., Smith, L. B., Yu, C., & Bates, J. E. (2020). Parents influence the visual learning environment through children's manual actions. *Child Development, 91*(3), e701–e720. https://doi.org/10.1111/cdev.13274

McQuire, C., Daniel, R., Hurt, L., Kemp, A., & Paranjothy, S. (2020). The causal web of foetal alcohol spectrum disorders: A review and causal diagram. *European Child & Adolescent Psychiatry, 29*(5), 575–594. https://doi.org/10.1007/s00787-018-1264-3

Mead, M. (1975). Children's play style: Potentialities and limitations of its use as a cultural indicator. *Anthropological Quarterly, 48*(3), 157–181.

Means, D. R., Hudson, T. D., & Tish, E. (2019). A snapshot of college access and inequity: Using photography to illuminate the pathways to higher education for underserved youth. *The High School Journal, 102*(2), 139–158. https://doi.org/10.1353/hsj.2019.0003

Means, D. R., & Pyne, K. B. (2017). Finding my way: Perceptions of institutional support and belonging in low-income, first-generation, first-year college students. *Journal of College Student Development, 58*(6), 907–924. https://doi.org/10.1353/csd.2017.0071

Meca, A., Webb, T., Cowan, I., Moulder, A., Schwartz, S. J., Szabó, Á., & Ward, C. (2021). Effects of cultural stress on identity development and depression among Hispanic college students. *Identity*, 1–14. https://doi.org/10.1080/15283488.2021.1960838

Meda, S. A., Gueorguieva, R. V., Pittman, B., Rosen, R. R., Aslanzadeh, F., Tennen, H., Leen, S., Hawkins, K., Raskin, S., Wood, R. M., Austad, C. S., Dager, A., Fallahi, C., & Pearlson, G. D. (2017). Longitudinal influence of alcohol and marijuana use on academic performance in college students. *PLOS ONE, 12*(3), e0172213. https://doi.org/10.1371/journal.pone.0172213

Medico, D., Pullen Sansfaçon, A., Zufferey, A., Galantino, G., Bosom, M., & Suerich-Gulick, F. (2020). Pathways to gender affirmation in trans youth: A qualitative and participative study with youth and their parents. *Clinical Child Psychology and Psychiatry, 25*(4), 1002–1014. https://doi.org/10.1177/1359104520938427

Medina, L., Sabo, S., & Vespa, J. (2020). *Living longer: Historical and projected life expectancy in the United States, 1960 to 2060.* U.S. Department of Commerce, U.S. Census Bureau.

Meehan, C. L., & Crittenden, A. N. (2016). *Childhood: Origins, evolution, and implications.* University of New Mexico Press.

Meehan, C. L., & Hawks, S. (2013). Cooperative breeding and attachment among the Aka Foragers. In N. Quinn & J. M. Mageo (Eds.), *Attachment reconsidered: Cultural perspectives on a Western theory* (pp. 85–113). Palgrave Macmillan US. https://doi.org/10.1057/9781137386724_4

Meek, J. Y., Feldman-Winter, L., & Noble, L. (2020). Optimal duration of breastfeeding. *Pediatrics, 146*(5), e2020021063. https://doi.org/10.1542/peds.2020-021063

Meek, S., Smith, L., Allen, R., Catherine, E., Edyburn, K., Williams, C., Fabes, R., McIntosh, K., Garcia, E., Takanashi, R., Gordon, L., Jimenez-Castellanos, O., Hemmeter, M. L., Giliam, W., & Pontier, R. (2020). *Start with equity: From the early years to the early grades: Data, research and an actionable child equity policy agenda.* Children's Equity Project.

Meeus, W. (2011). The study of adolescent identity formation 2000–2010: A review of longitudinal research. *Journal of Research on Adolescence, 21*(1), 75–94.

Meeus, W. (2016). Adolescent psychosocial development: A review of longitudinal models and research. *Developmental Psychology, 52*(12), 1969–1993. https://doi.org/10.1037/dev0000243

Meeus, W. H. J., Branje, S. J. T., van der Valk, I., & de Wied, M. (2007). Relationships with intimate partner, best friend, and parents in adolescence and early adulthood: A study of the saliency of the intimate partnership. *International Journal of Behavioral Development, 31*(6), 569–580. https://doi.org/10.1177/0165025407080584

Meeus, W., Vollebergh, W., Branje, S., Crocetti, E., Ormel, J., van de Schoot, R., Crone, E. A., & Becht, A. (2021). On imbalance of impulse control and sensation seeking and adolescent risk: An intra-individual developmental test of the dual systems and maturational imbalance models. *Journal of Youth and Adolescence, 50*(5), 827–840. https://doi.org/10.1007/s10964-021-01419-x

Mehta, C. M., Arnett, J. J., Palmer, C. G., & Nelson, L. J. (2020). Established adulthood: A new conception of ages 30 to 45. *American Psychologist, 75*(4), 431–444. https://doi.org/10.1037/amp0000600

Meier, A., Musick, K., Fischer, J., & Flood, S. (2018). Mothers' and fathers' well-being in parenting across the arch of child development. *Journal of Marriage and Family, 80*(4), 992–1004. https://doi.org/10.1111/jomf.12491

Meier, E. A., Gallegos, J. V., Montross-Thomas, L. P., Depp, C. A., Irwin, S. A., & Jeste, D. V. (2016). Defining a good death (successful dying): Literature review and a call for research and public dialogue. *The American Journal of Geriatric Psychiatry: Official Journal of the American Association for Geriatric Psychiatry, 24*(4), 261–271. https://doi.org/10.1016/j.jagp.2016.01.135

Meijer, A., Königs, M., Vermeulen, G. T., Visscher, C., Bosker, R. J., Hartman, E., & Oosterlaan, J. (2020). The effects of physical activity on brain structure and neurophysiological functioning in children: A systematic review and meta-analysis. *Developmental Cognitive Neuroscience, 45*, 100828. https://doi.org/10.1016/j.dcn.2020.100828

Meijer, A. M., & Krampe, R. T. (2018). Movement timing and cognitive control: Adult-age differences in multitasking. *Psychological Research, 82*(1), 203–214.

Meinhofer, A., & Angleró-Díaz, Y. (2019). Trends in foster care entry among children removed from their homes because of parental drug use, 2000 to 2017. *JAMA Pediatrics, 173*(9), 881–883. https://doi.org/10.1001/jamapediatrics.2019.1738

Meisel, S. N., & Colder, C. R. (2021) An examination of the joint effects of adolescent interpersonal styles and parenting styles on substance use. *Development and Psychopathology*, 1–19. https://doi.org/10.1017/S0954579420001637

Melnitchouk, N., Scully, R. E., & Davids, J. S. (2018). Barriers to breastfeeding for US physicians who are mothers. *JAMA Internal Medicine, 178*(8), 1130–1132. https://doi.org/10.1001/jamainternmed.2018.0320

Meltzer, L. J., Williamson, A. A., & Mindell, J. A. (2021). Pediatric sleep health: It matters, and so does how we define it. *Sleep Medicine Reviews, 57*, 101425. https://doi.org/10.1016/j.smrv.2021.101425

Meltzoff, A. N. (2020). Imitation and modeling. In A. N. Meltzoff & R. A. Williamson (Eds.), *Encyclopedia of infant and early childhood development* (2nd ed., pp. 100–109). Elsevier.

Meltzoff, A. N., & Marshall, P. J. (2018). Human infant imitation as a social survival circuit. *Current Opinion in Behavioral Sciences, 24*, 130–136. https://doi.org/10.1016/j.cobeha.2018.09.006

Meltzoff, A. N., & Moore, M. K. (1977). Imitation of facial and manual gestures by human neonates. *Science, 198*(4312), 75–78.

Mendelsohn, G. A., Shaw Taylor, L., Fiore, A. T., & Cheshire, C. (2014). Black/White dating online: Interracial courtship in the 21st century. *Psychology of Popular Media Culture, 3*(1), 2.

Mendelson, B., & Wong, C.-H. (2012). Changes in the facial skeleton with aging: Implications and clinical applications in facial rejuvenation. *Aesthetic Plastic Surgery, 36*(4), 753–760. https://doi.org/10.1007/s00266-012-9904-3

Mendez-Luck, C. A., Applewhite, S. R., Lara, V. E., & Toyokawa, N. (2016). The concept of familism in the lived experiences of Mexican-origin caregivers. *Journal of Marriage and the Family, 78*(3), 813–829. https://doi.org/10.1111/jomf.12300

Mendle, J., Beltz, A. M., Carter, R., & Dorn, L. D. (2019). Understanding puberty and its measurement: Ideas for research in a new generation. *Journal of Research on Adolescence, 29*(1), 82–95. https://doi.org/10.1111/jora.12371

Mendle, J., & Ferrero, J. (2012). Detrimental psychological outcomes associated with pubertal timing in adolescent boys. *Developmental Review, 32*(1), 49–66.

Mendonça, B., Sargent, B., & Fetters, L. (2016). Cross-cultural validity of standardized motor development screening and assessment tools: A systematic review. *Developmental Medicine & Child Neurology, 58*(12), 1213–1222.

Mendoza, A. N., Fruhauf, C. A., Bundy-Fazioli, K., & Weil, J. (2017). Understanding Latino grandparents raising grandchildren through a bioecological lens. *The International Journal of Aging and Human Development.* https://doi.org/10.1177/0091415017702907

Menendez, D., Hernandez, I. G., & Rosengren, K. S. (2020). Children's emerging understanding of death. *Child Development Perspectives, 14*(1), 55–60. https://doi.org/10.1111/cdep.12357

Meng, X., Li, S., Duan, W., Sun, Y., & Jia, C. (2017). Secular trend of age at menarche in Chinese adolescents born from 1973 to 2004. *Pediatrics, 140*(2). https://doi.org/10.1542/peds.2017-0085

Mennella, J. A., Nolden, A. A., & Bobowski, N. (2018). Measuring sweet and bitter taste in children: Individual variation due to age and taste genetics. In J. C. Lumeng & J. O. Fisher (Eds.), *Pediatric food preferences and eating*

behaviors (pp. 1–34). Academic Press. https://doi.org/10.1016/B978-0-12-811716-3.00001-4

Menon, R. (2019). Initiation of human parturition: Signaling from senescent fetal tissues via extracellular vesicle mediated paracrine mechanism. *Obstetrics & Gynecology Science, 62*(4), 199. https://doi.org/10.5468/ogs.2019.62.4.199

Mercer, M. (2013, August 30). *Children as young as 10 can do farm work in some states.* Stateline. http://pew.org/2gMJaEb

Mercurio, M. R., & Carter, B. S. (2020). Resuscitation policies for extremely preterm newborns: Finally moving beyond gestational age. *Journal of Perinatology, 40*(12), 1731–1733. https://doi.org/10.1038/s41372-020-00843-4

Merisotis, J., & Slaughter, A. (2016, July 5). College kids, with kids. *The New York Times.* http://www.nytimes.com/2016/07/05/opinion/college-kids-with-kids.html

Merlo, C. L., Jones, S. E., Michael, S. L., Chen, T. J., Sliwa, S. A., Lee, S. H., Brener, N. D., Lee, S. M., & Park, S. (2020). Dietary and physical activity behaviors among high school students—Youth Risk Behavior Survey, United States, 2019. *MMWR Supplements, 69*(1), 64–76.

Merriam, A. P. (1971). Aspects of sexual behavior among the Bala (Basongye). In D. S. Marshall & R. C. Suggs (Eds.), *Human sexual behavior: Variations in the ethnographic spectrum* (pp. 71–102). Basic Books.

Merrick, M. T., Ports, K. A., Ford, D. C., Afifi, T. O., Gershoff, E. T., & Grogan-Kaylor, A. (2017). Unpacking the impact of adverse childhood experiences on adult mental health. *Child Abuse & Neglect, 69,* 10–19.

Merz, E. C., Wiltshire, C. A., & Noble, K. G. (2019). Socioeconomic inequality and the developing brain: Spotlight on language and executive function. *Child Development Perspectives, 13*(1), 15–20. https://doi.org/10.1111/cdep.12305

Mesman, J. (2021). Video observations of sensitive caregiving "off the beaten track": Introduction to the special issue. *Attachment & Human Development, 23*(2), 115–123. https://doi.org/10.1080/14616734.2020.1828511

Mesman, J., Minter, T., Angnged, A., Cissé, I. A. H., Salali, G. D., & Migliano, A. B. (2018). Universality without uniformity: A culturally inclusive approach to sensitive responsiveness in infant caregiving. *Child Development, 89*(3), 837–850. https://doi.org/10.1111/cdev.12795

Mesman, J., van Ijzendoorn, M. H., & Sagi-Schwartz, A. (2016). Cross-cultural patterns of attachment. In J. Cassidy & P. R. Shaver (Eds.), *Handbook of attachment: Theory, research, and clinical applications* (pp. 852–877). Guilford.

Messing, J. T., AbiNader, M. A., Pizarro, J. M., Campbell, J. C., Brown, M. L., & Pelletier, K. R. (2021). The Arizona Intimate Partner Homicide (AzIPH) study: A step toward updating and expanding risk factors for intimate partner homicide. *Journal of Family Violence, 36*(5), 563–572. https://doi.org/10.1007/s10896-021-00254-9

Meter, D. J., & Bauman, S. (2018). Moral disengagement about cyberbullying and parental monitoring: Effects on traditional bullying and victimization via cyberbullying involvement. *The Journal of Early Adolescence, 38*(3), 303–326.

Metzger, A. N., & Hamilton, L. T. (2021). The stigma of ADHD: Teacher ratings of labeled students. *Sociological Perspectives, 64*(2), 258–279.

Meyer, A. M., Becker, I., Siri, G., Brinkkötter, P. T., Benzing, T., Pilotto, A., & Polidori, M. C. (2020). The prognostic significance of geriatric syndromes and resources. *Aging Clinical and Experimental Research, 32*(1), 115–124. https://doi.org/10.1007/s40520-019-01168-9

Meyer, F., König, H.-H., & Hajek, A. (2019). Osteoporosis, fear of falling, and restrictions in daily living. Evidence from a nationally representative sample of community-dwelling older adults. *Frontiers in Endocrinology, 10,* 646. https://doi.org/10.3389/fendo.2019.00646

Meyer, H. M., & Kandic, A. (2017). Grandparenting in the United States. *Innovation in Ageing, 1*(2).

Meyer, K., & Benton, D. (2018). Caregivers' experiences of relationship tension with care recipients. *Innovation in Aging, 2*(Suppl 1), 764. https://doi.org/10.1093/geroni/igy023.2826

Meyer, M. H., & Kandic, A. (2021). How social policies affect grandparent care work. In J. M. Wilmoth & A. S. London (Eds.), *Life-course implications of US public policy* (pp. 114–123). Routledge.

Mgbako, O. U., Ha, Y. P., Ranard, B. L., Hypolite, K. A., Sellers, A. M., Nadkarni, L. D., Becker, L. B., Asch, D. A., & Merchant, R. M. (2014). Defibrillation in the movies: A missed opportunity for public health education. *Resuscitation, 85*(12), 1795–1798. https://doi.org/10.1016/j.resuscitation.2014.09.005

Mian, N. D., & Gray, S. A. O. (2019). Preschool anxiety: Risk and protective factors. In B. Fisak & P. Barrett (Eds.), *Anxiety in preschool children* (pp. 29–51). Routledge.

Michaelson, L. E., & Munakata, Y. (2020). Same data set, different conclusions: Preschool delay of gratification predicts later behavioral outcomes in a preregistered study. *Psychological Science, 31*(2), 193–201.

Midgett, A., & Doumas, D. M. (2019). Witnessing bullying at school: The association between being a bystander and anxiety and depressive symptoms. *School Mental Health, 11*(3), 454–463. https://doi.org/10.1007/s12310-019-09312-6

Midgley, N. (2007). Anna Freud: The Hampstead War Nurseries and the role of the direct observation of children for psychoanalysis. *The International Journal of Psychoanalysis, 88*(4), 939–959. https://doi.org/10.1516/V28R-J334-6182-524H

Miech, R. A., Johnston, L. D., O'Malley, P. M., Bachman, J. G., Schulenberg, J. E., & Patrick, M. E. (2021). *Monitoring the future: National Survey Results on Drug Use, 1975–2020. 2020 Volume I: Secondary school students.* University of Michigan Institute for Social Research.

Mignani, V., Ingravallo, F., Mariani, E., & Chattat, R. (2017). Perspectives of older people living in long-term care facilities and of their family members toward advance care planning discussions: A systematic review and thematic synthesis. *Clinical Interventions in Aging, 12,* 475–484. https://doi.org/10.2147/CIA.S128937

Miguel, P. M., Pereira, L. O., Silveira, P. P., & Meaney, M. J. (2019). Early environmental influences on the development of children's brain structure and function. *Developmental Medicine & Child Neurology, 61*(10), 1127–1133. https://doi.org/10.1111/dmcn.14182

Mijs, J. J. B., & Roe, E. L. (2021). Is America coming apart? Socioeconomic segregation in neighborhoods, schools, workplaces, and social networks, 1970–2020. *Sociology Compass, 15*(6), e12884. https://doi.org/10.1111/soc4.12884

Mikula, A. L., Hetzel, S. J., Binkley, N., & Anderson, P. A. (2017). Validity of height loss as a predictor for prevalent vertebral fractures, low bone mineral density, and vitamin D deficiency. *Osteoporosis International, 28*(5), 1659–1665. https://doi.org/10.1007/s00198-017-3937-z

Mikulincer, M., & Shaver, P. R. (2019). Attachment orientations and emotion regulation. *Current Opinion in Psychology, 25,* 6–10. https://doi.org/10.1016/j.copsyc.2018.02.006

Mikulincer, M., & Shaver, P. R. (2021). The continuing influence of early attachment orientations viewed from a personality-social perspective on adult attachment. In R. A. Thompson, J. A. Simpson, & L. J. Berlin (Eds.), *Attachment: The fundamental questions* (pp. 211–218). Guilford.

Mikwar, M., MacFarlane, A. J., & Marchetti, F. (2020). Mechanisms of oocyte aneuploidy associated with advanced maternal age. *Mutation Research/Reviews in Mutation Research, 785,* 108320. https://doi.org/10.1016/j.mrrev.2020.108320

Milani, S., & Benso, L. (2019). Why we can't determine reliably the age of a subject on the basis of his maturation degree. *Journal of Forensic and Legal Medicine, 61,* 97–101. https://doi.org/10.1016/j.jflm.2018.12.002

Millan, M. J., Andrieux, A., Bartzokis, G., Cadenhead, K., Dazzan, P., Fusar-Poli, P., & Weinberger, D. (2016). Altering the course of schizophrenia: Progress and perspectives. *Nature Reviews Drug Discovery, 15*(7), 485–515.

Millea, M., Wills, R., Elder, A., & Molina, D. (2018). What matters in college student success? Determinants of college retention and graduation rates. *Education, 138*(4), 309–322.

Miller, B. J. (2020, December 18). Opinion | What is death? *The New York Times.* https://www.nytimes.com/2020/12/18/opinion/coronavirus-death.html

Miller, C. E., & Meyers, S. A. (2015). Disparities in school discipline practices for students with emotional and learning disabilities and autism. *Journal of Education and Human Development, 4*(1), 255–267.

Miller, D. A. (1981). The "sandwich" generation: Adult children of the aging. *Social Work, 26*(5), 419–423.

Miller, E., Jones, K. A., & McCauley, H. L. (2018). Updates on adolescent dating and sexual violence prevention and intervention. *Current Opinion in Pediatrics, 30*(4), 466.

Miller, E., & McCaw, B. (2019). Intimate partner violence. *New England Journal of Medicine, 380*(9), 850–857.

Miller, J. G. (2018). Physiological mechanisms of prosociality. *Current Opinion in Psychology, 20,* 50–54. https://doi.org/10.1016/j.copsyc.2017.08.018

Miller, J. G., Goyal, N., & Wice, M. (2015). Ethical considerations in research on human development and culture. In *The Oxford handbook of human development and culture* (pp. 14–27). Oxford University Press.

Miller, J. G., & Hastings, P. D. (2019). Parenting, neurobiology, and prosocial development. In D. J. Laible, G. Carlo, & L. M. Padilla-Walker (Eds.), *The Oxford handbook of parenting and moral development* (pp. 129–144). Oxford University Press.

Miller, J. G., Kahle, S., & Hastings, P. D. (2015). Roots and benefits of costly giving: Children who are more altruistic have greater autonomic flexibility and less family wealth. *Psychological Science, 26*(7), 1038–1045.

Miller, K. (2017, April 4). *Emi Kiyota: Out to transform the rigid nursing-home culture.* Silver Century Foundation: Preparing for a Longer Life. https://www.silvercentury.org/2017/04/the-nursing-home-that-changed-peoples-lives/

Miller, L. M. S., Tancredi, D. J., Kaiser, L. L., & Tseng, J. T. (2020). Midlife vulnerability and food insecurity: Findings from low-income adults in the US National Health Interview Survey. *PLOS ONE, 15*(7), e0233029. https://doi.org/10.1371/journal.pone.0233029

Miller, M. (2020, August 14). America's retirement race gap, and ideas for closing it. *The New York Times.* https://www.nytimes.com/2020/08/14/business/retirement-inequality-racism.html

Miller, P. H. (2011). Piaget's theory: Past, present, and future. In U. Goswami (Ed.), *The Wiley-Blackwell handbook of childhood cognitive development* (pp. 649–672). Wiley-Blackwell.

Miller, P. J., Rosengren, K. S., & Gutiérrez, I. T. (2014). Children's understanding of death: Toward a contextualized and integrated account. *Monographs of the Society for Research in Child Development, 79*(1), 1–18. https://doi.org/10.1111/mono.12076

Miller, S. A. (2017). *Developmental research methods.* Sage.

Miller, S. C., Schwartz, M. L., Lima, J. C., Shield, R. R., Tyler, D. A., Berridge, C. W., Gozalo, P. L., Lepore, M. J., & Clark, M. A. (2018). The prevalence of culture change practice in US nursing homes: Findings from a 2016/17 nationwide survey. *Medical Care, 56*(12), 985–993. https://doi.org/10.1097/MLR.0000000000000993

Miller, S. E., Avila, B. N., & Reavis, R. D. (2020). Thoughtful friends: Executive function relates to social problem solving and friendship quality in middle childhood. *The Journal of Genetic Psychology, 181*(2–3), 78–94.

Miller, V., Mente, A., Dehghan, M., Rangarajan, S., Zhang, X., Swaminathan, S., Dagenais, G., Gupta, R., Mohan, V., Lear, S., Bangdiwala, S. I., Schutte, A. E., Wentzel-Viljoen, E., Avezum, A., Altuntas, Y., Yusoff, K., Ismail, N., Peer, N., Chifamba, J., ... Mapanga, R. (2017). Fruit, vegetable, and legume intake, and cardiovascular disease and deaths in 18 countries (PURE): A prospective cohort study. *The Lancet, 390*(10107), 2037–2049. https://doi.org/10.1016/S0140-6736(17)32253-5

Millner, A. J., & Nock, M. K. (2020). Self-injurious thoughts and behaviors. In E. A. Youngstrom, M. J. Prinstein, E. J. Mash, Y R. A. Barkley (Eds.), *Assessment of disorders in childhood and adolescence* (5th ed., pp. 245–267). Guilford.

Mills, K. L., Dumontheil, I., Speekenbrink, M., & Blakemore, S.-J. (2015). Multitasking during social interactions in adolescence and early adulthood.

Royal Society Open Science, 2(11), 150117. https://doi.org/10.1098/rsos.150117

Mills, K. L., Goddings, A.-L., Herting, M. M., Meuwese, R., Blakemore, S.-J., Crone, E. A., Dahl, R. E., Güroğlu, B., Raznahan, A., Sowell, E. R., & Tamnes, C. K. (2016). Structural brain development between childhood and adulthood: Convergence across four longitudinal samples. *NeuroImage, 141*, 273–281. https://doi.org/10.1016/j.neuroimage.2016.07.044

Mills-Koonce, W. R., Rehder, P. D., & McCurdy, A. L. (2018). The significance of parenting and parent–child relationships for sexual and gender minority adolescents. *Journal of Research on Adolescence, 28*(3), 637–649.

Milner, J. S., & Crouch, J. L. (2013). Assessment of maternal attributions of infant's hostile intent and its use in child maltreatment prevention/intervention efforts. *JAMA Pediatrics, 167*(6), 588–589.

Milojevich, H. M., Machlin, L., & Sheridan, M. A. (2020). Early adversity and children's emotion regulation: Differential roles of parent emotion regulation and adversity exposure. *Development and Psychopathology, 32*(5), 1788–1798. https://doi.org/10.1017/S0954579420001273

Mindell, J. A., Sadeh, A., Wiegand, B., How, T. H., & Goh, D. Y. (2010). Cross-cultural differences in infant and toddler sleep. *Sleep Medicine, 11*(3), 274–280.

Miner, B., & Kryger, M. H. (2017). Sleep in the aging population. *Sleep Medicine Clinics, 12*(1), 31–38. https://doi.org/10.1016/j.jsmc.2016.10.008

Mingebach, T., Kamp-Becker, I., Christiansen, H., & Weber, L. (2018). Meta-meta-analysis on the effectiveness of parent-based interventions for the treatment of child externalizing behavior problems. *PLOS ONE, 13*(9), e0202855. https://doi.org/10.1371/journal.pone.0202855

Mintz, S. (2004). *Huck's raft: A history of American childhood.* Harvard University Press.

Mintz, S. (2015). *The prime of life.* Harvard University Press.

Minuzzi, L. G., Chupel, M. U., Rama, L., Rosado, F., Muñoz, V. R., Gaspar, R. C., & Teixeira, A. M. (2019). Lifelong exercise practice and immunosenescence: Master athletes cytokine response to acute exercise. *Cytokine, 115*, 1–17.

Miranda, R., Oriol, X., & Amutio, A. (2019). Risk and protective factors at school: Reducing bullies and promoting positive bystanders' behaviors in adolescence. *Scandinavian Journal of Psychology, 60*(2), 106–115. https://doi.org/10.1111/sjop.12513

Mireault, G. C., Crockenberg, S. C., Heilman, K., Sparrow, J. E., Cousineau, K., & Rainville, B. (2018). Social, cognitive, and physiological aspects of humour perception from 4 to 8 months: Two longitudinal studies. *The British Journal of Developmental Psychology, 36*(1), 98–109. https://doi.org/10.1111/bjdp.12216

Miron, O., Yu, K.-H., Wilf-Miron, R., & Kohane, I. S. (2019). Suicide rates among adolescents and young adults in the United States, 2000–2017. *JAMA, 321*(23), 2362–2364. https://doi.org/10.1001/jama.2019.5054

Mischel, W. (1966). A social learning view of sex differences in behavior. In E. E. Maccoby (Ed.), *The development of sex differences* (pp. 56–81). Stanford University Press.

Mischel, W. (2014). *The marshmallow test: Mastering self-control.* Little, Brown.

Mischel, W. (2015). *The marshmallow test: Why self-control is the engine of success.* Little, Brown.

Mischel, W., & Ebbesen, E. B. (1970). Attention in delay of gratification. *Journal of Personality and Social Psychology, 16*(2), 329.

Mischel, W., Shoda, Y., & Rodriguez, M. I. (1989). Delay of gratification in children. *Science, 244*(4907), 933–938.

Mishra, S. (2020). Social networks, social capital, social support and academic success in higher education: A systematic review with a special focus on "underrepresented" students. *Educational Research Review, 29*, 100307. https://doi.org/10.1016/j.edurev.2019.100307

Mitchell, B. A. (2016). Empty nest. In *Encyclopedia of family studies.* John Wiley & Sons. https://doi.org/10.1002/9781119085621.wbefs008

Mitchell, B. A., & Lovegreen, L. D. (2009). The empty nest syndrome in midlife families: A multimethod exploration of parental gender differences and cultural dynamics. *Journal of Family Issues, 30*(12), 1651–1670.

Mitchell, C., McLanahan, S., Schneper, L., Garfinkel, I., Brooks-Gunn, J., & Notterman, D. (2017). Father loss and child telomere length. *Pediatrics, 140*(2), e20163245.

Mitchell, H., & Hunnicutt, G. (2019). Challenging accepted scripts of sexual "normality": Asexual narratives of non-normative identity and experience. *Sexuality & Culture, 23*(2), 507–524. https://doi.org/10.1007/s12119-018-9567-6

Mitchell, K. R., Mercer, C. H., Ploubidis, G. B., Jones, K. G., Datta, J., Field, N., Copas, A. J., Tanton, C., Erens, B., Sonnenberg, P., Clifton, S., Macdowall, W., Phelps, A., Johnson, A. M., & Wellings, K. (2013). Sexual function in Britain: Findings from the third National Survey of Sexual Attitudes and Lifestyles (Natsal-3). *The Lancet, 382*(9907), 1817–1829. https://doi.org/10.1016/S0140-6736(13)62366-1

Mitchell, L. M., Stephenson, P. H., Cadell, S., & Macdonald, M. E. (2012). Death and grief on-line: Virtual memorialization and changing concepts of childhood death and parental bereavement on the Internet. *Health Sociology Review, 21*(4), 413–431. https://doi.org/10.5172/hesr.2012.21.4.413

Mitford, J. (1996). *The American way of death.* Vintage.

Mitima-Verloop, H. B., Mooren, T. T. M., & Boelen, P. A. (2021). Facilitating grief: An exploration of the function of funerals and rituals in relation to grief reactions. *Death Studies, 45*(9), 735–745. https://doi.org/10.1080/07481187.2019.1686090

Miyamoto, Y., Yoo, J., Levine, C. S., Park, J., Boylan, J. M., Sims, T., Markus, H. R., Kitayama, S., Kawakami, N., Karasawa, M., Coe, C. L., Love, G. D., & Ryff, C. D. (2018). Culture and social hierarchy: Self- and other-oriented correlates of socioeconomic status across cultures. *Journal of Personality and Social Psychology, 115*(3), 427–445. https://doi.org/10.1037/pspi0000133

Miyawaki, C. E. (2016). Caregiving practice patterns of Asian, Hispanic, and non-Hispanic white American family caregivers of older adults across generations. *Journal of Cross-Cultural Gerontology, 31*(1), 35–55.

Miyawaki, C. E. (2020). Caregiving attitudes and needs of later-generation Chinese-American family caregivers of older adults. *Journal of Family Issues, 41*(12), 2377–2399. https://doi.org/10.1177/0192513X20930366

Moale, A., & Norvell, M. (2019). *Elder care: A resource for interprofessional providers.* Portal of Geriatrics Online Education.

Moayedi, Y., Duenas-Bianchi, L. F., & Lumpkin, E. A. (2018). Somatosensory innervation of the oral mucosa of adult and aging mice. *Scientific Reports, 8*(1), 9975. https://doi.org/10.1038/s41598-018-28195-2

Modecki, K. L., Hagan, M. J., Sandler, I., & Wolchik, S. A. (2015). Latent profiles of nonresidential father engagement six years after divorce predict long-term offspring outcomes. *Journal of Clinical Child & Adolescent Psychology, 44*(1), 123–136.

Modell, J., & Goodman, M. (1990). Historical perspectives. In S. S. Feldman & G. R. Elliott (Eds.), *At the threshold: The developing adolescent* (pp. 93–122). Harvard University Press.

Moen, P., & Wethington, E. (1999). Midlife development in a life course context. In S. L. Willis & J. D. Reid (Eds.), *Life in the middle* (pp. 3–23). Academic Press. https://doi.org/10.1016/B978-012757230-7/50020-1

Moffett, L., & Morrison, F. J. (2020). Off-task behavior in kindergarten: Relations to executive function and academic achievement. *Journal of Educational Psychology, 112*(5), 938–955. https://doi.org/10.1037/edu0000397

Moffitt, R. L., Neumann, D. L., & Williamson, S. P. (2018). Comparing the efficacy of a brief self-esteem and self-compassion intervention for state body dissatisfaction and self-improvement motivation. *Body Image, 27*, 67–76. https://doi.org/10.1016/j.bodyim.2018.08.008

Moffitt, T. E. (1993). Adolescence-limited and life-course-persistent antisocial behavior: A developmental taxonomy. *Psychological Review, 100*(4), 674. http://psycnet.apa.org/journals/rev/100/4/674/

Moffitt, T. E. (2006). Life-course-persistent versus adolescence-limited antisocial behavior. In D. Cicchetti & D. J. Cohen (Eds.), *Developmental psychopathology: Risk, disorder, and adaptation* (pp. 570–598). John Wiley & Sons.

Moffitt, U., Juang, L. P., & Syed, M. (2020). Intersectionality and youth identity development research in Europe. *Frontiers in Psychology, 11*, 78. https://doi.org/10.3389/fpsyg.2020.00078

Mohammed, H. (2021). Recognizing African-American contributions to neurology: The role of Solomon Carter Fuller (1872–1953) in Alzheimer's disease research. *Alzheimer's & Dementia, 17*(2), 246–250. https://doi.org/10.1002/alz.12183

Mohamoud, Y. A., Kirby, R. S., & Ehrenthal, D. B. (2021). County poverty, urban–rural classification, and the causes of term infant death: United States, 2012–2015. *Public Health Reports.* https://doi.org/10.1177/0033354921999169

Mohan, H., Verhoog, M. B., Doreswamy, K. K., Eyal, G., Aardse, R., Lodder, B. N., Goriounova, N. A., Asamoah, B., Brakspear, B., Clementine, A. B., Groot, C., van der Sluis, S., Testa-Silva, G., Obermayer, J., Boudewijns, Z. S. R. M., Narayanan, R. T., Baayen, J. C., Segev, I., Mansvelder, H. D., … P.j, C. (2015). Dendritic and axonal architecture of individual pyramidal neurons across layers of adult human neocortex. *Cerebral Cortex, 25*(12), 4839–4853. https://doi.org/10.1093/cercor/bhv188

Moieni, M., Irwin, M. R., Seeman, T. E., Robles, T. F., Lieberman, M. D., Breen, E. C., Okimoto, S., Lengacher, C., Arevalo, J. M. G., Olmstead, R., Cole, S. W., & Eisenberger, N. I. (2020). Feeling needed: Effects of a randomized generativity intervention on well-being and inflammation in older women. *Brain, Behavior, and Immunity, 84*, 97–105. https://doi.org/10.1016/j.bbi.2019.11.014

Mojtabai, R., Olfson, M., & Han, B. (2016). National trends in the prevalence and treatment of depression in adolescents and young adults. *Pediatrics, 138*(6), e20161878. https://doi.org/10.1542/peds.2016-1878

Mokdad, A. H., Ballestros, K., Echko, M., Glenn, S., Olsen, H. E., Mullany, E., Lee, A., Khan, A. R., Ahmadi, A., Ferrari, A. J., Kasaeian, A., Werdecker, A., Carter, A., Zipkin, B., Sartorius, B., Serdar, B., Sykes, B. L., Troeger, C., Fitzmaurice, C., … Murray, C. J. L. (2018). The state of US health, 1990–2016: Burden of diseases, injuries, and risk factors among US states. *JAMA, 319*(14), 1444–1472. https://doi.org/10.1001/jama.2018.0158

Molè, M. A., Weberling, A., & Zernicka-Goetz, M. (2020). Comparative analysis of human and mouse development: From zygote to pre-gastrulation. In L. Solnica-Krezel (Ed.), *Current topics in developmental biology* (Vol. 136, pp. 113–138). Academic Press. https://doi.org/10.1016/bs.ctdb.2019.10.002

Molina, G., Weiser, T. G., Lipsitz, S. R., Esquivel, M. M., Uribe-Leitz, T., Azad, T., Shah, N., Semrau, K., Berry, W. R., Gawande, A. A., & Haynes, A. B. (2015). Relationship between cesarean delivery rate and maternal and neonatal mortality. *JAMA, 314*(21), 2263–2270. https://doi.org/10.1001/jama.2015.15553

Moll, L. C. (2013). *LS Vygotsky and education.* Routledge.

Möllborg, P., Wennergren, G., Almqvist, P., & Alm, B. (2015). Bed sharing is more common in sudden infant death syndrome than in explained sudden unexpected deaths in infancy. *Acta Paediatrica, 104*(8), 777–783.

Molloy, C., Beatson, R., Harrop, C., Perini, N., & Goldfeld, S. (2021). Systematic review: Effects of sustained nurse home visiting programs for disadvantaged mothers and children. *Journal of Advanced Nursing, 77*(1), 147–161.

Monge, Z. A., & Madden, D. J. (2016). Linking cognitive and visual perceptual decline in healthy aging: The information degradation hypothesis. *Neuroscience and Biobehavioral Reviews, 69*, 166–173. https://doi.org/10.1016/j.neubiorev.2016.07.031

Monin, J. K., Levy, B. R., & Kane, H. S. (2017). To love is to suffer: Older adults' daily emotional contagion to perceived spousal suffering. *The Journals of Gerontology: Series B, 72*(3), 383–387. https://doi.org/10.1093/geronb/gbv070

Monnat, S. M., & Chandler, R. F. (2015). Long-term physical health consequences of adverse childhood experiences. *The Sociological Quarterly*, 56(4), 723–752.

Monsivais, P., Thompson, C., Astbury, C. C., & Penney, T. L. (2021). Environmental approaches to promote healthy eating: Is ensuring affordability and availability enough? *BMJ*, 372, n549. https://doi.org/10.1136/bmj.n549

Monte, L. M. (2017). *Fertility research brief: Household economic studies. current population reports* (No. P70BR-147). U.S. Census Bureau.

Monte, L. M., & Knop, B. (2019). *Men's fertility and fatherhood: 2014.* U.S. Department of Commerce, Economics and Statistics Administration, U.S. Census Bureau.

Monteiro, R., Rocha, N. B., & Fernandes, S. (2021). Are emotional and behavioral problems of infants and children aged younger than 7 years related to screen time exposure during the coronavirus disease 2019 confinement? An exploratory study in Portugal. *Frontiers in Psychology*, 12, 590279. https://doi.org/10.3389/fpsyg.2021.590279

Montirosso, R., Provenzi, L., & Mascheroni, E. (2021). The role of protective caregiving in epigenetic regulation in human infants. In L. Provenzi & R. Montirosso (Eds.), *Developmental human behavioral epigenetics* (Vol. 23, pp. 143–156). Academic Press. https://doi.org/10.1016/B978-0-12-819262-7.00008-8

Montross-Thomas, L. P., Joseph, J., Edmonds, E. C., Palinkas, L. A., & Jeste, D. V. (2018). Reflections on wisdom at the end of life: Qualitative study of hospice patients aged 58–97 years. *International Psychogeriatrics*, 30(12), 1759–1766. https://doi.org/10.1017/S1041610217003039

Moodie, J. L., Campisi, S. C., Salena, K., Wheatley, M., Vandermorris, A., & Bhutta, Z. A. (2020). Timing of pubertal milestones in low- and middle-income countries: A systematic review and meta-analysis. *Advances in Nutrition*, 11(4), 951–959. https://doi.org/10.1093/advances/nmaa007

Moody, R. A. (1975). *Life after life.* Bantam Doubleday Dell.

Moon, C. (2017). Prenatal experience with the maternal voice. In M. Filippa, P. Kuhn, & B. Westrup (Eds.), *Early vocal contact and preterm infant brain development: Bridging the gaps between research and practice* (pp. 25–37). Springer International Publishing. https://doi.org/10.1007/978-3-319-65077-7_2

Moon, H. E., Haley, W. E., Rote, S. M., & Sears, J. S. (2020). Caregiver well-being and burden: Variations by race/ethnicity and care recipient nativity status. *Innovation in Aging*, 4(6), igaa045. https://doi.org/10.1093/geroni/igaa045

Moon, R. Y., & Hauck, F. R. (2016). SIDS risk: It's more than just the sleep environment. *Pediatrics*, peds.2015-3665. https://doi.org/10.1542/peds.2015-3665

Moore, D. S. (2017). Behavioral epigenetics. *WIREs Systems Biology and Medicine*, 9(1), e1333. https://doi.org/10.1002/wsbm.1333

Moore, J. (2017). John B. Watson's classical S–R behaviorism. *The Journal of Mind and Behavior*, 38(1), 1–34.

Moore, J. A., & Radtke, H. L. (2015). Starting "real" life: Women negotiating a successful midlife single identity. *Psychology of Women Quarterly*, 39(3), 305–319.

Moore, J. X., Chaudhary, N., & Akinyemiju, T. (2017). Metabolic syndrome prevalence by race/ethnicity and sex in the United States, National Health and Nutrition Examination Survey, 1988–2012. *Preventing Chronic Disease*, 14.

Moore, K. A., Paschall, K., Pina, G., & Anderson, S. (2020). *Being healthy and ready to learn is linked with family and neighborhood characteristics for preschoolers.* Child Trends. https://www.childtrends.org/publications/being-healthy-and-ready-to-learn-is-linked-with-family-and-neighborhood-characteristics-for-preschoolers

Moore, K. L., Persaud, T. V. N., & Torchia, M. G. (2020). *The developing human—e-book: Clinically oriented embryology.* Elsevier Health Sciences.

Moore, S. E., Jones-Eversley, S. D., Tolliver, W. F., Wilson, B., & Harmon, D. K. (2020). Cultural responses to loss and grief among Black Americans: Theory and practice implications for clinicians. *Death Studies*, 1–11. https://doi.org/10.1080/07481187.2020.1725930

Mor, V., Zinn, J., Angelelli, J., Teno, J. M., & Miller, S. C. (2004). Driven to tiers: Socioeconomic and racial disparities in the quality of nursing home care. *The Milbank Quarterly*, 82(2), 227–256. https://doi.org/10.1111/j.0887-378X.2004.00309.x

Morales, D. X., Prieto, N., Grineski, S. E., & Collins, T. W. (2019). Race/ethnicity, obesity, and the risk of being verbally bullied: A national multilevel study. *Journal of Racial and Ethnic Health Disparities*, 6(2), 245–253. https://doi.org/10.1007/s40615-018-0519-5

Moran, A. J., Khandpur, N., Polacsek, M., & Rimm, E. B. (2019). What factors influence ultra-processed food purchases and consumption in households with children? A comparison between participants and non-participants in the Supplemental Nutrition Assistance Program (SNAP). *Appetite*, 134, 1–8. https://doi.org/10.1016/j.appet.2018.12.009

Morduch, J., & Schneider, R. (2017). *The financial diaries: How American families cope in a world of uncertainty.* Princeton University Press.

Morelli, G. A., Chaudhary, N., Gottlieb, A., Keller, H., Murray, M., Quinn, N., & Vicedo, M. (2017). A pluralistic approach to attachment. In H. Keller & K. A. Bard (Eds.), *The cultural nature of attachment: Contextualizing relationships and development* (pp. 140–169). MIT Press.

Morey, B. N. (2018). Mechanisms by which anti-immigrant stigma exacerbates racial/ethnic health disparities. *American Journal of Public Health*, 108(4), 460–463. https://doi.org/10.2105/AJPH.2017.304266

Morey, B. N., Gee, G. C., Shariff-Marco, S., Yang, J., Allen, L., & Gomez, S. L. (2020). Ethnic enclaves, discrimination, and stress among Asian American women: Differences by nativity and time in the United States. *Cultural Diversity and Ethnic Minority Psychology*, 26(4), 460–471. https://doi.org/10.1037/cdp0000322

Morgan, P. L. (2021). Unmeasured confounding and racial or ethnic disparities in disability identification. *Educational Evaluation and Policy Analysis*, 43(2), 351–361. https://doi.org/10.3102/0162373721991575

Morgan, P. L., Farkas, G., Cook, M., Strassfeld, N. M., Hillemeier, M. M., Pun, W. H., & Schussler, D. L. (2017). Are black children disproportionately overrepresented in special education? A best-evidence synthesis. *Exceptional Children*, 83(2), 181–198. https://doi.org/10.1177/0014402916664042

Morgenroth, T., Ryan, M. K., & Peters, K. (2015). The motivational theory of role modeling: How role models influence role aspirants' goals. *Review of General Psychology*, 19(4), 465–483. https://doi.org/10.1037/gpr0000059

Moriguchi, Y., Chevalier, N., & Zelazo, P. D. (2016). Development of executive function during childhood. *Frontiers in Psychology*, 7, 6.

Morin, C. M., Stone, J., McDonald, K., & Jones, S. (1994). Psychological management of insomnia: A clinical replication series with 100 patients. *Behavior Therapy*, 25(2), 291–309.

Morley, J. E. (2018). Treatment of sarcopenia: The road to the future. *Journal of Cachexia, Sarcopenia and Muscle*, 9(7), 1196–1199. https://doi.org/10.1002/jcsm.12386

Morning, A., Brückner, H., & Nelson, A. (2019). Socially desirable reporting and the expression of biological concepts of race. *Du Bois Review: Social Science Research on Race*, 16(2), 439–455. https://doi.org/10.1017/S1742058X19000195

Morris, A. S., Criss, M. M., Silk, J. S., & Houltberg, B. J. (2017). The impact of parenting on emotion regulation during childhood and adolescence. *Child Development Perspectives*, 11(4), 233–238. https://doi.org/10.1111/cdep.12238

Morris, A. S., Cui, L., & Steinberg, L. (2013). Parenting research and themes: What we have learned and where to go next. In R. E. Larzelere, A. S. Morris, & A. W. Harrist (Eds.), *Authoritative parenting: Synthesizing nurturance and discipline for optimal child development* (pp. 35–58). American Psychological Association.

Morris, A. S., Robinson, L. R., Hays-Grudo, J., Claussen, A. H., Hartwig, S. A., & Treat, A. E. (2017). Targeting parenting in early childhood: A public health approach to improve outcomes for children living in poverty. *Child Development*, 88(2), 388–397. https://doi.org/10.1111/cdev.12743

Morris, B. J., Willcox, B. J., & Donlon, T. A. (2019). Genetic and epigenetic regulation of human aging and longevity. *Biochimica et Biophysica Acta (BBA)—Molecular Basis of Disease*, 1865(7), 1718–1744. https://doi.org/10.1016/j.bbadis.2018.08.039

Morris, B. J., & Zentall, S. R. (2014). High fives motivate: The effects of gestural and ambiguous verbal praise on motivation. *Frontiers in Psychology*, 5, 928. https://doi.org/10.3389/fpsyg.2014.00928

Morrison, F. J., Kim, M. H., Connor, C. M., & Grammer, J. K. (2019). The causal impact of schooling on children's development: Lessons for developmental science. *Current Directions in Psychological Science*, 28(5), 441–449. https://doi.org/10.1177/0963721419855661

Morrison, M., Tay, L., & Diener, E. (2011). Subjective well-being and national satisfaction: Findings from a worldwide survey. *Psychological Science*, 22(2), 166–171. https://doi.org/10.1177/0956797610396224

Morrissey, B., Taveras, E., Allender, S., & Strugnell, C. (2020). Sleep and obesity among children: A systematic review of multiple sleep dimensions. *Pediatric Obesity*, 15(4), e12619. https://doi.org/10.1111/ijpo.12619

Morrongiello, B. A. (2018). Preventing unintentional injuries to young children in the home: Understanding and influencing parents' safety practices. *Child Development Perspectives*, 12(4), 217–222.

Mortimer, J. T. (2015). Social change and entry to adulthood. In *Emerging trends in the social and behavioral sciences* (pp. 1–17). American Cancer Society. https://doi.org/10.1002/9781118900772.etrds0305

Mortimer, J. T. (2019). A sociologist's perspective: The historic specificity of development and resilience in the face of increasingly ominous futures. In R. D. Parke & G. H. Elder Jr. (Eds.), *Children in changing worlds: Sociocultural and temporal perspectives* (pp. 287–298). Cambridge University Press. https://doi.org/10.1017/9781108264846.011

Mortimer, J. T. (2020). Youth, jobs, and the future: Problems and prospects. Contemporary Sociology, 49(2), 149–151. https://doi.org/10.1177/0094306120902418j

Mortimer, J. T., Vuolo, M., & Staff, J. (2014). Agentic pathways toward fulfillment in work. In A. C. Keller, R. Samuel, M. M. Bergman, & N. K. Semmer (Eds.), *Psychological, educational, and sociological perspectives on success and well-being in career development* (pp. 99–126). Springer Netherlands. https://doi.org/10.1007/978-94-017-8911-0_6

Mortimer, J. T., Zimmer-Gembeck, M. J., Holmes, M., & Shanahan, M. J. (2002). The process of occupational decision making: Patterns during the transition to adulthood. *Journal of Vocational Behavior*, 61(3), 439–465. https://doi.org/10.1006/jvbe.2002.1885

Morton, M. H., Dworsky, A., Matjasko, J. L., Curry, S. R., Schlueter, D., Chávez, R., & Farrell, A. F. (2018). Prevalence and correlates of youth homelessness in the United States. *Journal of Adolescent Health*, 62(1), 14–21.

Morton, S., & Brodsky, D. (2016). Fetal physiology and the transition to extrauterine life. *Clinics in Perinatology*, 43(3), 395–407. https://doi.org/10.1016/j.clp.2016.04.001

Moseson, H., Zazanis, N., Goldberg, E., Fix, L., Durden, M., Stoeffler, A., Hastings, J., Cudlitz, L., Lesser-Lee, B., Letcher, L., Reyes, A., & Obedin-Maliver, J. (2020). The imperative for transgender and gender nonbinary inclusion: Beyond women's health. *Obstetrics & Gynecology*, 135(5), 1059–1068. https://doi.org/10.1097/AOG.0000000000003816

Moss, E., & Willoughby, B. J. (2018). Associations between beliefs about marriage and life satisfaction: The moderating role of relationship status and gender. *Journal of Family Studies*, 24(3), 274–290. https://doi.org/10.1080/13229400.2016.1187658

Mostofsky, E., Maclure, M., Sherwood, J. B., Tofler, G. H., Muller, J. E., & Mittleman, M. A. (2012). Risk of acute myocardial infarction after the death of a significant person in one's life: The determinants of myocardial infarction onset study. *Circulation*, 125(3), 491–496.

Mõttus, R., Allik, J., Realo, A., Rossier, J., Zecca, G., Ah-Kion, J., & Johnson, W. (2012). The effect of response style on self-reported conscientiousness across 20 countries. *Personality and Social Psychology Bulletin, 38*(11), 1423–1436.

Mõttus, R., Briley, D. A., Zheng, A., Mann, F. D., Engelhardt, L. E., Tackett, J. L., Harden, K. P., & Tucker-Drob, E. M. (2019). Kids becoming less alike: A behavioral genetic analysis of developmental increases in personality variance from childhood to adolescence. *Journal of Personality and Social Psychology, 117*(3), 635.

Mousavi Khaneghah, A., Fakhri, Y., Nematollahi, A., & Pirhadi, M. (2020). Potentially toxic elements (PTEs) in cereal-based foods: A systematic review and meta-analysis. *Trends in Food Science & Technology, 96*, 30–44. https://doi .org/10.1016/j.tifs.2019.12.007

Mowen, T. J., & Schroeder, R. D. (2018). Maternal parenting style and delinquency by race and the moderating effect of structural disadvantage. *Youth & Society, 50*(2), 139–159. https://doi.org/10.1177/0044118X15598028

Moyer, S. M., Sharts-Hopko, N., & Oliver, T. (2020). Leisure-time physical activity and fruit and vegetable intake of young adult millennials. *Western Journal of Nursing Research, 42*(10), 795–804. https://doi .org/10.1177/0193945920907995

Mucherah, W., Finch, H., White, T., & Thomas, K. (2018). The relationship of school climate, teacher defending and friends on students' perceptions of bullying in high school. *Journal of Adolescence, 62*, 128–139. https://doi .org/10.1016/j.adolescence.2017.11.012

Mudrazija, S., Angel, J. L., Cipin, I., & Smolic, S. (2020). Living alone in the United States and Europe: The impact of public support on the independence of older adults. *Research on Aging, 42*(5–6), 150–162.

Muehlenhard, C. L., Peterson, Z. D., Humphreys, T. P., & Jozkowski, K. N. (2017). Evaluating the one-in-five statistic: Women's risk of sexual assault while in college. *The Journal of Sex Research, 54*(4–5), 549–576. https://doi.org/1 0.1080/00224499.2017.1295014

Muelbert, M., Galante, L., Alexander, T., Harding, J. E., Pook, C., & Bloomfield, F. H. (2021). Odor-active volatile compounds in preterm breastmilk. *Pediatric Research,* 1–12. https://doi.org/10.1038/s41390-021-01556-w

Mueller, J., Parry-Harries, E., Clough, G., & Verma, A. (2021). Feasibility of a community-based cancer awareness initiative: Views of those delivering and managing the intervention. *Journal of Public Health.* https://doi.org/10.1007 /s10389-021-01581-3

Mueller, S., Wagner, J., Smith, J., Voelkle, M. C., & Gerstorf, D. (2018). The interplay of personality and functional health in old and very old age: Dynamic within-person interrelations across up to 13 years. *Journal of Personality and Social Psychology, 115*(6), 1127–1147. https:// doi.org/10.1037/pspp0000173

Mueller, S., Wagner, J., Wagner, G. G., Ram, N., & Gerstorf, D. (2019). How far reaches the power of personality? Personality predictors of terminal decline in well-being. *Journal of Personality and Social Psychology, 116*(4), 634.

Muenks, K., Wigfield, A., & Eccles, J. S. (2018). I can do this! The development and calibration of children's expectations for success and competence beliefs. *Developmental Review, 48*, 24–39. https://doi.org/10.1016/j .dr.2018.04.001

Muennig, P., Jiao, B., & Singer, E. (2018). Living with parents or grandparents increases social capital and survival: 2014 General Social Survey-National Death Index. *SSM—Population Health, 4*, 71–75.

Muhlenkamp, K. (2012, April). Twin studies. *The University of Chicago Magazine.* https://mag.uchicago.edu /science-medicine/twin-studies

Muir, T. (2017). *Measuring social protection for long-term care* (OECD Health Working Papers). OECD.

Muise, A., Schimmack, U., & Impett, E. A. (2016). Sexual frequency predicts greater well-being, but more is not always better. *Social Psychological and Personality Science, 7*(4), 295–302. https://doi.org/10.1177/1948550615616462

Mukherjee, S. (2010). *The emperor of all maladies: A biography of cancer.* Simon & Schuster.

Mulgrew, K. (2020). Puberty and body image. In S. Hupp & J. Jewell (Eds.), *The encyclopedia of child and adolescent development* (pp. 1–9). Wiley. https://doi .org/10.1002/9781119171492.wecad355

Mullally, S. L., & Maguire, E. A. (2014). Learning to remember: The early ontogeny of episodic memory. *Developmental Cognitive Neuroscience, 9*, 12–29. https://doi .org/10.1016/j.dcn.2013.12.006

Mullan, K. (2019). A child's day: Trends in time use in the UK from 1975 to 2015. *The British Journal of Sociology, 70*(3), 997–1024. https://doi .org/10.1111/1468-4446.12369

Mullan, K., Woolf, S. H., & Gaskin, D. J. (2021). High and rising working-age mortality in the US: A report from the National Academy of Sciences, Engineering, and Medicine. *JAMA, 325*(20), 2045–2046.

Mullen, S. (2018). Major depressive disorder in children and adolescents. *Mental Health Clinician, 8*(6), 275–283. https://doi.org/10.9740/mhc.2018.11.275

Mulvey, K. L., Boswell, C., & Niehaus, K. (2018). You don't need to talk to throw a ball! Children's inclusion of language-outgroup members in behavioral and hypothetical scenarios. *Developmental Psychology, 54*(7), 1372.

Mund, M., Freuding, M. M., Möbius, K., Horn, N., & Neyer, F. J. (2020). The stability and change of loneliness across the life span: A meta-analysis of longitudinal studies. *Personality and Social Psychology Review, 24*(1), 24–52. https://doi.org/10.1177/1088868319850738

Munn-Chernoff, M. A., Johnson, E. C., Chou, Y.-L., Coleman, J. R. I., Thornton, L. M., Walters, R. K., Yilmaz, Z., Baker, J. H., Hübel, C., Gordon, S., Medland, S. E., Watson, H. J., Gaspar, H. A., Bryois, J., Hinney, A., Leppä, V. M., Mattheisen, M., Ripke, S., Yao, S., ... Agrawal, A. (2021). Shared genetic risk between eating disorder-and substance-use-related phenotypes: Evidence from genome-wide association studies. *Addiction Biology, 26*(1), e12880.

Munnell, A. H., Rutledge, M. S., & Sazenbacher, G. T. (2019). *Retiring Earlier than Planned: What Matters Most?* (Working Paper Number 19-3). Boston College Center for Retirement Research.

Munro-Kramer, M. L., Fava, N. M., Saftner, M. A., Darling-Fisher, C. S., Tate, N. H., Stoddard, S. A., & Martyn, K. K. (2016). What are we missing? Risk behaviors among Arab-American adolescents and emerging adults. *Journal of the American Association of Nurse Practitioners, 28*(9), 493–502. https://doi.org/10.1002/2327-6924.12352

Munzer, T. G., Miller, A. L., Peterson, K. E., Brophy-Herb, H. E., Horodynski, M. A., Contreras, D., Sturza, J., Lumeng, J. C., & Radesky, J. (2018). Media exposure in low-income preschool-aged children is associated with multiple measures of self-regulatory behavior. *Journal of Developmental and Behavioral Pediatrics, 39*(4), 303–309. https://doi.org/10.1097/DBP.0000000000000560

Murayama, K., Pekrun, R., Suzuki, M., Marsh, H. W., & Lichtenfeld, S. (2016). Don't aim too high for your kids: Parental overaspiration undermines students' learning in mathematics. *Journal of Personality and Social Psychology, 111*(5), 766–779. https://doi.org/10.1037/pspp0000079

Murphy, M. L., Cohen, S., Janicki-Deverts, D., & Doyle, W. J. (2017). Offspring of parents who were separated and not speaking to one another have reduced resistance to the common cold as adults. *Proceedings of the National Academy of Sciences, 114*(25), 6515–6520.

Murray, A., Hall, H., Speyer, L., Carter, L., Mirman, D., Caye, A., & Rohde, L. (2021). Developmental trajectories of ADHD symptoms in a large population-representative longitudinal study. *Psychological Medicine,* 1–7. https://doi .org/10.1017/S0033291721000349

Murray, M., Stone, A., Pearson, V., & Treisman, G. (2019). Clinical solutions to chronic pain and the opiate epidemic. *Preventive Medicine, 118*, 171–175. https://doi .org/10.1016/j.ypmed.2018.10.004

Musset, P. (2019). *Improving work-based learning in schools* (OECD Social, Employment and Migration Working Papers, No. 233). OECD Publishing. https://doi .org/10.1787/918caba5-en

Mustafa, N. S., Bakar, N. H. A., Mohamad, N., Adnan, L. H. M., Fauzi, N. F. A. M., Thoarlim, A., & Ahmad, R. (2020). MDMA and the brain: A short review on the role of neurotransmitters in neurotoxicity. *Basic and Clinical Neuroscience, 11*(4), 381.

Mustanski, B., Kuper, L., & Greene, G. J. (2014). Development of sexual orientation and identity. In D. L. Tolman & L. M. Diamond (Eds.), *APA handbook of sexuality and psychology* (Vol. 1. pp. 597–628). American Psychological Association.

Mutchler, J., Roldán, N. V., & Li, Y. (2020). *Living below the line: Racial and ethnic disparities in economic security among older Americans, 2020.* Center for Social and Demographic Research on Aging Publications. https:// scholarworks.umb.edu/demographyofaging/46

Muthiah, N., Adesman, A., & Keim, S. A. (2019). Grandparents raising grandchildren: Are they up to the job? *Pediatrics, 144*(2 MeetingAbstract), 77. https://doi.org/10.1542 /peds.144.2_MeetingAbstract.77

Myin-Germeys, I., Kasanova, Z., Vaessen, T., Vachon, H., Kirtley, O., Viechtbauer, W., & Reininghaus, U. (2018). Experience sampling methodology in mental health research: New insights and technical developments. *World Psychiatry, 17*(2), 123–132. https://doi.org/10.1002/wps.20513

Na, M., Jomaa, L., Eagleton, S. G., & Savage, J. S. (2021). Head start parents with or without food insecurity and with lower food resource management skills use less positive feeding practices in preschool-age children. *The Journal of Nutrition, 151*(5), 1294–1301. https://doi.org/10.1093/jn/nxab001

Nabors, L., Stough, C. O., Garr, K., & Merianos, A. (2019). Predictors of victimization among youth who are overweight in a national sample. *Pediatric Obesity, 14*(7), e12516. https://doi.org/10.1111/ijpo.12516

Nadorff, D. K., Williamson, E. A., & McKay, I. T. (2019). Could chasing grandkids keep us young? The association between custodial grandparent status and health. *Innovation in Aging, 3*(Suppl 1), S670. https://doi.org/10.1093/geroni /igz038.2477

Nadybal, S., Grineski, S., Collins, T., Castor, A., Flores, A., Griego, A., & Rubio, R. (2020). Environmental justice in the US and beyond: Frameworks, evidence, and social action. In K. M. Lersch & J. Chakraborty (Eds.), *Geographies of behavioural health, crime, and disorder* (pp. 187–209). Springer.

NAEYC Council on the Accreditation of Early Learning Programs (NAEYC). (2019). *NAEYC early learning program accreditation standards and assessment items.* National Association for the Education of Young Children. https://www.naeyc.org /defining-recognizing-high-quality-early-learning-programs

Nagamatsu, L. S., Handy, T. C., Hsu, C. L., Voss, M., & Liu-Ambrose, T. (2012). Resistance training promotes cognitive and functional brain plasticity in seniors with probable mild cognitive impairment. *Archives of Internal Medicine, 172*(8), 666–668.

Nagarajan, D., Lee, D.-C. A., Robins, L. M., & Haines, T. P. (2020). Risk factors for social isolation in post-hospitalized older adults. *Archives of Gerontology and Geriatrics, 88*, 104036. https://doi.org/10.1016/j.archger.2020.104036

Nagata, J. M., Compte, E. J., Cattle, C. J., Lavender, J. M., Brown, T. A., Murray, S. B., Flentje, A., Capriotti, M. R., Lubensky, M. E., Obedin-Maliver, J., & Lunn, M. R. (2021). Community norms of the Muscle Dysmorphic Disorder Inventory (MDDI) among cisgender sexual minority men and women. *BMC Psychiatry, 21*(1), 297. https://doi .org/10.1186/s12888-021-03302-2

Nagata, J. M., Garber, A. K., Tabler, J. L., Murray, S. B., & Bibbins-Domingo, K. (2018). Prevalence and correlates of disordered eating behaviors among young adults with overweight or obesity. *Journal of General Internal Medicine, 33*(8), 1337–1343. https://doi.org/10.1007 /s11606-018-4465-z

Nagata, J. M., Palar, K., Gooding, H. C., Garber, A. K., Whittle, H. J., Bibbins-Domingo, K., & Weiser, S. D. (2019). Food insecurity is associated with poorer mental health and sleep outcomes in young adults. *Journal of Adolescent Health, 65*(6), 805–811.

Nagy, E., Pilling, K., Blake, V., & Orvos, H. (2020). Positive evidence for neonatal imitation: A general response, adaptive engagement. *Developmental Science, 23*(2), e12894. https://doi.org/10.1111/desc.12894

Nakatsuka, N., Moorjani, P., Rai, N., Sarkar, B., Tandon, A., Patterson, N., Bhavani, G. S., Girisha, K. M., Mustak, M. S., Srinivasan, S., Kaushik, A., Vahab, S. A., Jagadeesh, S. M., Satyamoorthy, K., Singh, L., Reich, D., & Thangaraj, K. (2017). The promise of discovering population-specific disease-associated genes in South Asia. *Nature Genetics, 49*(9), 1403–1407. https://doi.org/10.1038/ng.3917

Namkung, E. H., & Carr, D. (2019). Perceived interpersonal and institutional discrimination among persons with disability in the U.S.: Do patterns differ by age? *Social Science & Medicine (1982), 239,* 112521. https://doi.org/10.1016/j.socscimed.2019.112521

Napolitano, L. (2015). "I'm not going to leave her high and dry": Young adult support to parents during the transition to adulthood. *The Sociological Quarterly, 56*(2), 329–354. https://doi.org/10.1111/tsq.12088

Napolitano, L., Furstenberg, F., & Fingerman, K. L. (2020). How families give and receive: A cross-class qualitative study of familial exchange. *Journal of Family Issues, 42*(9), 2159–2180. https://doi.org/10.1177/0192513X20968608

Nasrullah, M., Muazzam, S., Khosa, F., & Khan, M. M. H. (2017). Child marriage and women's attitude towards wife beating in a nationally representative sample of currently married adolescent and young women in Pakistan. *International Health, 9*(1), 20–28. https://doi.org/10.1093/inthealth/ihw047

Nathan, S., Kemp, L., Bunde-Birouste, A., MacKenzie, J., Evers, C., & Shwe, T. A. (2013). "We wouldn't of made friends if we didn't come to Football United": The impacts of a football program on young people's peer, prosocial and cross-cultural relationships. *BMC Public Health, 13*(1), 1–16.

National Academies of Sciences, Engineering, and Medicine (NASEM). (2016). *Ending discrimination against people with mental and substance use disorders: The evidence for stigma change.* National Academies Press.

National Academies of Sciences, Engineering, and Medicine (NASEM). (2016). *Parenting matters: Supporting parents of children ages 0–8.* National Academies Press. https://doi.org/10.17226/21868

National Academies of Sciences, Engineering, and Medicine (NASEM). (2017). *Supporting students' college success: The role of assessment of intrapersonal and interpersonal competencies.* National Academies Press. https://doi.org/10.17226/24697

National Academies of Sciences, Engineering, and Medicine (NASEM). (2018). *Transforming the financing of early care and education.* National Academies Press.

National Academies of Sciences, Engineering, and Medicine (NASEM). (2019). *Monitoring educational equity* (C. Edley, J. Koenig, N. Nielsen, & C. Citro, Eds.). National Academies Press. https://doi.org/10.17226/25389

National Academies of Sciences, Engineering, and Medicine (NASEM). (2020). *Feeding infants and children from birth to 24 months: Summarizing existing guidance.* National Academies Press. https://doi.org/10.17226/25747

National Academies of Sciences, Engineering, and Medicine (NASEM). (2020). *Social isolation and loneliness in older adults: Opportunities for the health care system.* National Academies Press. https://doi.org/10.17226/25663

National Academies of Sciences, Engineering, and Medicine (NASEM). (2021). *High and rising mortality rates among working-age adults.* The National Academies Press. https://doi.org/10.17226/25976

National Alliance for Caregiving and American Association for Retired People (NAC & AARP). (2020). *Caregiving in the U.S.*

National Association for the Education of Young Children (NAEYC). (2018). *Staff to child ratio and class size.* National Association for the Education of Young Children.

National Association for the Education of Young Children (NAEYC). (2020). *Developmentally appropriate practice: A position statement of the National Association for the Education of Young Children.*

National Center for Education Statistics (NCES). (2020). *Total number of 16- to 24-year-old high school dropouts (status dropouts) and percentage of dropouts among persons 16 to 24 years old (status dropout rate), by selected characteristics: 2007 through 2019* (Digest of Educational Statistics Table 219.80; U.S. Department of Commerce, Census Bureau, American Community Survey [ACS], 2007 through 2019).

National Center for Education Statistics (NCES). (2020, February). *Common Core of Data (CCD), "Public Elementary/Secondary School Universe Survey," 2017–18.*

National Center for Education Statistics (NCES). (2021). *Condition of education — Status dropout rates* and *public high school graduation rates.* https://nces.ed.gov/programs/coe/indicator/coj

National Center for Education Statistics (NCES). (2021). *Young adults neither enrolled in school nor working* (Population Characteristics and Economic Outcomes).

National Center for Health Statistics (NCHS). (2017). Table P-1a. Age-adjusted percent distribution (with standard errors) of respondent-assessed health status, by selected characteristics: United States, 2017. In *Summary health statistics: National Health Interview Survey, 2017.* National Health Interview Survey.

National Center for Health Statistics (NCHS). (2019). *Health, United States, 2019. At-a-glance table.* https://www.cdc.gov/nchs/hus/ataglance.htm.

National Center for Health Statistics (NCHS). (2019). *Percentage of disability for adults aged 18 and over, United States, 2019.* https://wwwn.cdc.gov/NHISDataQueryTool/SHS_2019_ADULT3/index.html

National Center for Health Statistics (NCHS). (2021, June 18). *Percentage of fair or poor health status for children under age 18 years, United States, 2019.* National Health Interview Survey. https://wwwn.cdc.gov/NHISDataQueryTool/SHS_2019_CHILD3/index.html

National Center for Health Statistics (NCHS), National Vital Statistics System (2021). *Leading causes of death reports, 1981–2019.* https://www.cdc.gov/injury/wisqars/LeadingCauses.html

National Center on Disability and Journalism (NCDJ). (n.d.). *Disability language style guide.* https://ncdj.org/style-guide/

National Center on Vital Statistics. (2021, September 1). *COVID-19 provisional counts — Weekly updates by select demographic and geographic characteristics.* https://www.cdc.gov/nchs/nvss/vsrr/covid_weekly/index.htm

National Comorbidity Survey, Replication. (2005). Table 2. Harvard Medical School.

National Council on Aging (NCOA). (2020, June 18). *NCOA statement: Inequities make aging well impossible.* https://www.ncoa.org/news/press-releases/ncoa-statement-inequities-make-aging-well-impossible/

National Health Interview Survey. (2015). *Public-use data file and documentation.* National Center for Health Statistics. http://www.cdc.gov/nchs/nhis/quest_data_related_1997_forward.htm. 2016

National Institute for Early Education Research (NIEER). (2019). *The state of preschool 2019.* Rutgers University.

National Institute on Alcohol Abuse and Alcoholism (NIAAA). (2018). *Drinking levels defined.*

National Physical Activity Plan Alliance (NPAPA). (2018). *The 2018 United States report card on physical activity for children and youth.*

National Research Council (NRC). (2013). *Reforming juvenile justice: A developmental approach.* National Academies Press.

National Society of Genetic Counselors (NSGC). (2019). *Prenatal testing for adult-onset conditions.* https://www.nsgc.org/Policy-Research-and-Publications/Position-Statements/Position-Statements/Post/prenatal-testing-for-adult-onset-conditions-1

National Survey of Children's Health (NSCH). (2011–2012). [Data query from the Child and Adolescent Health Measurement Initiative]. Data Resource Center for Child and Adolescent Health. www.childhealthdata.org

National Survey of Children's Health (NSCH). (2019). [2018–2019 data query, Child and Adolescent Health Measurement Initiative]. Data Resource Center for Child and Adolescent Health supported by the U.S. Department of Health and Human Services, Health Resources and Services Administration (HRSA), Maternal and Child Health Bureau (MCHB). https://mchb.hrsa.gov/data/national-surveys

National Survey of Children's Health (NSCH). (2021). *Child and adolescent health measurement initiative. 2018–2019 National Survey of Children's Health (NSCH) data query.* Data Resource Center for Child and Adolescent Health supported by the U.S. Department of Health and Human Services, Health Resources and Services Administration (HRSA), Maternal and Child Health Bureau (MCHB). www.childhealthdata.org

National Survey of Early Care and Education (NSECE). (2016). *National Survey of Early Care and Education, 2013. Number and characteristics of early care and education (ECE) teachers and caregivers: Initial findings.* National Survey of Early Care and Education. Research and Evaluation, Administration for Children and Families, U.S. Department of Health and Human Services.

Natu, V. S., Gomez, J., Barnett, M., Jeska, B., Kirilina, E., Jaeger, C., Zhen, Z., Cox, S., Weiner, K. S., Weiskopf, N., & Grill-Spector, K. (2019). Apparent thinning of human visual cortex during childhood is associated with myelination. *Proceedings of the National Academy of Sciences, 116*(41), 20750–20759.

Naumova, O. Y., Rychkov, S. Y., Kornilov, S. A., Odintsova, V. V., Anikina, V. O., Solodunova, M. Y., Arintcina, I. A., Zhukova, M. A., Ovchinnikova, I. V., Burenkova, O. V., Zhukova, O. V., Muhamedrahimov, R. J., & Grigorenko, E. L. (2019). Effects of early social deprivation on epigenetic statuses and adaptive behavior of young children: A study based on a cohort of institutionalized infants and toddlers. *PLOS ONE, 14*(3), e0214285. https://doi.org/10.1371/journal.pone.0214285

Nauta, M. M. (2010). The development, evolution, and status of Holland's theory of vocational personalities: Reflections and future directions for counseling psychology. *Journal of Counseling Psychology, 57*(1), 11–22. https://doi.org/10.1037/a0018213

Nave, C. S., Edmonds, G. W., Hampson, S. E., Murzyn, T., & Sauerberger, K. S. (2017). From elementary school to midlife: Childhood personality predicts behavior during cognitive testing over four decades later. *Journal of Research in Personality, 67,* 183–189. https://doi.org/10.1016/j.jrp.2016.10.001

Nebel, R. A., Aggarwal, N. T., Barnes, L. L., Gallagher, A., Goldstein, J. M., Kantarci, K., Mallampalli, M. P., Mormino, E. C., Scott, L., Yu, W. H., Maki, P. M., & Mielke, M. M. (2018). Understanding the impact of sex and gender in Alzheimer's disease: A call to action. *Alzheimer's & Dementia, 14*(9), 1171–1183. https://doi.org/10.1016/j.jalz.2018.04.008

Negru-Subtirica, O., Tiganasu, A., Dezutter, J., & Luyckx, K. (2017). A cultural take on the links between religiosity, identity, and meaning in life in religious emerging adults. *British Journal of Developmental Psychology, 35*(1), 106–126.

Neimeyer, R. A. (Ed.). (2021). *New techniques of grief therapy: Bereavement and beyond.* Routledge. https://doi.org/10.4324/9781351069120

Neimeyer, R. A., Klass, D., & Dennis, M. R. (2014). A social constructionist account of grief: Loss and the narration of meaning. *Death Studies, 38*(8), 485–498. https://doi.org/10.1080/07481187.2014.913454

Nelson, A. J., & Yon, K. J. (2019). Core and peripheral features of the cross-cultural model of romantic love. *Cross-Cultural Research, 53*(5), 447–482. https://doi.org/10.1177/1069397118813306

Nelson, C. A., Bhutta, Z. A., Harris, N. B., Danese, A., & Samara, M. (2020). Adversity in childhood is linked to mental and physical health throughout life. *BMJ, 371,* m3048. https://doi.org/10.1136/bmj.m3048

Nelson, C. A., Zeanah, C. H., & Fox, N. A. (2019). How early experience shapes human development: The case of psychosocial deprivation. *Neural Plasticity, 2019,* 1676285. https://doi.org/10.1155/2019/1676285

Nelson, K. (2018). Making memory: Meaning in development of the autobiographical self. In A. Rosa & J. Valsiner

(Eds.), *The Cambridge handbook of sociocultural psychology* (pp. 260–273). Cambridge University Press.

Nelson, L. J. (2021). The theory of emerging adulthood 20 years later: A look at where it has taken us, what we know now, and where we need to go. *Emerging Adulthood, 9*(3), 179–188. https://doi.org/10.1177/2167696820950884

Nelson, S. C., Kling, J., Wängqvist, M., Frisén, A., & Syed, M. (2018). Identity and the body: Trajectories of body esteem from adolescence to emerging adulthood. *Developmental Psychology, 54*(6), 1159–1171. https://doi.org/10.1037/dev0000435

Nelson, S. K., Layous, K., Cole, S. W., & Lyubomirsky, S. (2016). Do unto others or treat yourself? The effects of prosocial and self-focused behavior on psychological flourishing. *Emotion, 16*(6), 850.

Nelson, T. D. (2017). *Ageism: Stereotyping and prejudice against older persons* (2nd ed.). MIT Press.

Nelson-Coffey, S. K., Killingsworth, M., Layous, K., Cole, S. W., & Lyubomirsky, S. (2019). Parenthood is associated with greater well-being for fathers than mothers. *Personality and Social Psychology Bulletin, 45*(9), 1378–1390.

Netsi, E., Santos, I. S., Stein, A., Barros, F. C., Barros, A. J., & Matijasevich, A. (2017). A different rhythm of life: sleep patterns in the first 4 years of life and associated sociodemographic characteristics in a large Brazilian birth cohort. *Sleep Medicine, 37*, 77–87.

Neumark-Sztainer, D., MacLehose, R. F., Watts, A. W., Pacanowski, C. R., & Eisenberg, M. E. (2018). Yoga and body image: Findings from a large population-based study of young adults. *Body Image, 24*, 69–75. https://doi.org/10.1016/j.bodyim.2017.12.003

Newcomb, A. F., Bukowski, W. M., & Pattee, L. (1993). Children's peer relations: A meta-analytic review of popular, rejected, neglected, controversial, and average sociometric status. *Psychological Bulletin, 113*(1), 99.

Newcomb-Anjo, S. E., Barker, E. T., & Howard, A. L. (2017). A person-centered analysis of risk factors that compromise wellbeing in emerging adulthood. *Journal of Youth and Adolescence, 46*(4), 867–883.

Newheiser, A.-K., Dunham, Y., Merrill, A., Hoosain, L., & Olson, K. R. (2014). Preference for high status predicts implicit outgroup bias among children from low-status groups. *Developmental Psychology, 50*(4), 1081–1090. https://doi.org/10.1037/a0035054

Newland, L. A., Giger, J. T., Lawler, M. J., Roh, S., Brockevelt, B. L., & Schweinle, A. (2019). Multilevel analysis of child and adolescent subjective well-being across 14 countries: Child-and country-level predictors. *Child Development, 90*(2), 395–413.

Newman, R. S., Morini, G., & Chatterjee, M. (2013). Infants' name recognition in on- and off-channel noise. *The Journal of the Acoustical Society of America, 133*(5), EL377–EL383. https://doi.org/10.1121/1.4798269

Newman, S., Holupka, S., & Ross, S. L. (2018). There's no place like home: Racial disparities in household formation in the 2000s. *Journal of Housing Economics, 40*, 142–156. https://doi.org/10.1016/j.jhe.2018.04.002

Newport, C. (2016). *Deep work.* Grand Central Publishing.

Newton, A. T., Honaker, S. M., & Reid, G. J. (2020). Risk and protective factors and processes for behavioral sleep problems among preschool and early school-aged children: A systematic review. *Sleep Medicine Reviews, 52*, 101303. https://doi.org/10.1016/j.smrv.2020.101303

Ng, R., & Lim, W. J. (2021). Ageism linked to culture, not demographics: Evidence from an 8-billion-word corpus across 20 countries. *The Journals of Gerontology: Series B, 76*(9), 1791–1798. https://doi.org/10.1093/geronb/gbaa181

Ng'asike, J. T. (2011). Turkana children's sociocultural practices of pastoralist lifestyles and science curriculum and instruction in Kenyan early childhood education. In *Dissertation Abstracts International Section A: Humanities and social sciences* (Vol. 72, Issue 2–A, p. 546). ProQuest Information & Learning.

Ngandu, T., Lehtisalo, J., Solomon, A., Levälahti, E., Ahtiluoto, S., Antikainen, R., Bäckman, L., Hänninen, T., Jula, A., Laatikainen, T., Lindström, J., Mangialasche, F., Paajanen, T., Pajala, S., Peltonen, M., Rauramaa, R., Stigsdotter-Neely, A., Strandberg, T., Tuomilehto, J., ... Kivipelto, M. (2015). A 2 year multidomain intervention of diet, exercise, cognitive training, and vascular risk monitoring versus control to prevent cognitive decline in at-risk elderly people (FINGER): A randomised controlled trial. *The Lancet, 385*(9984), 2255–2263. https://doi.org/10.1016/S0140-6736(15)60461-5

Ngo, C. T., Alm, K. H., Metoki, A., Hampton, W., Riggins, T., Newcombe, N. S., & Olson, I. R. (2017). White matter structural connectivity and episodic memory in early childhood. *Developmental Cognitive Neuroscience, 28*, 41–53. https://doi.org/10.1016/j.dcn.2017.11.001

Nguyen, A. J., Bradshaw, C., Townsend, L., & Bass, J. (2020). Prevalence and correlates of bullying victimization in four low-resource countries. *Journal of Interpersonal Violence, 35*(19–20), 3767–3790.

Nguyen, A. M. D., & Benet-Martínez, V. (2013). Biculturalism and adjustment: A meta-analysis. *Journal of Cross-Cultural Psychology, 44*(1), 122–159.

Nguyen, A. W., Taylor, R. J., Chatters, L. M., Taylor, H. O., Lincoln, K. D., & Mitchell, U. A. (2017). Extended family and friendship support and suicidality among African Americans. *Social Psychiatry and Psychiatric Epidemiology, 52*(3), 299–309. https://doi.org/10.1007/s00127-016-1309-1

Nguyen, P. T., & Hinshaw, S. P. (2020). Understanding the stigma associated with ADHD: Hope for the future? *The ADHD Report, 28*(5), 1–10, 12. https://doi.org/10.1521/adhd.2020.28.5.1

Nguyen, T., & Li, X. (2020). Understanding public-stigma and self-stigma in the context of dementia: A systematic review of the global literature. *Dementia, 19*(2), 148–181. https://doi.org/10.1177/1471301218800122

Nguyen, T. P., Karney, B. R., & Bradbury, T. N. (2020). When poor communication does and does not matter: The moderating role of stress. *Journal of Family Psychology, 34*(6), 686–686.

Nguyen, T. P., Karney, B. R., Kennedy, D. P., & Bradbury, T. N. (2021). Couples' diminished social and financial capital exacerbate the association between maladaptive attributions and relationship satisfaction. *Cognitive Therapy and Research, 45*(3), 529–541. https://doi.org/10.1007/s10608-020-10161-w

NICHD Early Child Care Research Network. (2004). Trajectories of physical aggression from toddlerhood to middle childhood: Predictors, correlates, and outcomes. *Monographs of the Society for Research in Child Development, 69*(4), 1–129. https://doi.org/10.1111/j.0037-976x.2004.00312.x

Nichols, H. J., Zecherle, L., & Arbuckle, K. (2016). Patterns of philopatry and longevity contribute to the evolution of post-reproductive lifespan in mammals. *Biology Letters, 12*(2), 20150992. https://doi.org/10.1098/rsbl.2015.0992

Nichols, L., & Islas, Á. (2016). Pushing and pulling emerging adults through college: College generational status and the influence of parents and others in the first year. *Journal of Adolescent Research, 31*(1), 59–95. https://doi.org/10.1177/0743558415586255

Nicolopoulou, A., Cortina, K. S., Ilgaz, H., Cates, C. B., & de Sá, A. B. (2015). Using a narrative- and play-based activity to promote low-income preschoolers' oral language, emergent literacy, and social competence. *Early Childhood Research Quarterly, 31*, 147–162. https://doi.org/10.1016/j.ecresq.2015.01.006

Niedernhofer, L. J., Gurkar, A. U., Wang, Y., Vijg, J., Hoeijmakers, J. H., & Robbins, P. D. (2018). Nuclear genomic instability and aging. *Annual Review of Biochemistry, 87*, 295–322.

Nielsen, L. (2017). Re-examining the research on parental conflict, coparenting, and custody arrangements. *Psychology, Public Policy, and Law, 23*(2), 211.

Nielson, M. G., Delay, D., Flannery, K. M., Martin, C. L., & Hanish, L. D. (2020a). Does gender-bending help or hinder friending? The roles of gender and gender similarity in friendship dissolution. *Developmental Psychology, 56*(6), 1157.

Nielson, M. G., Schroeder, K. M., Martin, C. L., & Cook, R. E. (2020b). Investigating the relation between gender typicality and pressure to conform to gender norms. *Sex Roles, 83*, 523–535.

Nigra, A. E. (2020). Environmental racism and the need for private well protections. *Proceedings of the National Academy of Sciences, 117*(30), 17476–17478. https://doi.org/10.1073/pnas.2011547117

Nijhof, S. L., Vinkers, C. H., van Geelen, S. M., Duijff, S. N., Achterberg, E. J. M., van der Net, J., Veltkamp, R. C., Grootenhuis, M. A., van de Putte, E. M., Hillegers, M. H. J., van der Brug, A. W., Wierenga, C. J., Benders, M. J. N. L., Engels, R. C. M. E., van der Ent, C. K., Vanderschuren, L. J. M. J., & Lesscher, H. M. B. (2018). Healthy play, better coping: The importance of play for the development of children in health and disease. *Neuroscience & Biobehavioral Reviews, 95*, 421–429. https://doi.org/10.1016/j.neubiorev.2018.09.024

Nikkelen, S. W. C., van Oosten, J. M. F., & van den Borne, M. M. J. J. (2020). Sexuality education in the digital era: Intrinsic and extrinsic predictors of online sexual information seeking among youth. *The Journal of Sex Research, 57*(2), 189–199. https://doi.org/10.1080/00224499.2019.1612830

Nikolić, M., Brummelman, E., Colonnesi, C., de Vente, W., & Bögels, S. M. (2018). When gushing leads to blushing: Inflated praise leads socially anxious children to blush. *Behaviour Research and Therapy, 106*, 1–7. https://doi.org/10.1016/j.brat.2018.04.003

Nikolopoulos, H., Mayan, M., MacIsaac, J., Miller, T., & Bell, R. C. (2017). Women's perceptions of discussions about gestational weight gain with health care providers during pregnancy and postpartum: A qualitative study. *BMC Pregnancy and Childbirth, 17*(1), 97. https://doi.org/10.1186/s12884-017-1257-0

Nisbett, R. E., Aronson, J., Blair, C., Dickens, W., Flynn, J., Halpern, D. F., & Turkheimer, E. (2012). Intelligence: New findings and theoretical developments. *American Psychologist, 67*(2), 130–159. https://doi.org/10.1037/a0026699

Nishi, A., Tamiya, N., Kashiwagi, M., Takahashi, H., Sato, M., & Kawachi, I. (2010). Mothers and daughters-in-law: A prospective study of informal care-giving arrangements and survival in Japan. *BMC Geriatrics, 10*, 61. https://doi.org/10.1186/1471-2318-10-61

Nishijima, K., Yoneda, M., Hirai, T., Takakuwa, K., & Enomoto, T. (2019). Biology of the vernix caseosa: A review. *Journal of Obstetrics and Gynaecology Research, 45*(11), 2145–2149. https://doi.org/10.1111/jog.14103

Nissim, N. R., O'Shea, A. M., Bryant, V., Porges, E. C., Cohen, R., & Woods, A. J. (2017). Frontal structural neural correlates of working memory performance in older adults. *Frontiers in Aging Neuroscience, 8*, 328.

Nist, M. D., Harrison, T. M., & Steward, D. K. (2019). The biological embedding of neonatal stress exposure: A conceptual model describing the mechanisms of stress-induced neurodevelopmental impairment in preterm infants. *Research in Nursing & Health, 42*(1), 61–71. https://doi.org/10.1002/nur.21923

Niu, W. (2020). Intelligence in worldwide perspective: A twenty-first-century update. In R. J. Sternberg (Ed.), *The Cambridge handbook of intelligence* (pp. 893–915). Cambridge University Press.

Nix, R. L., Francis, L. A., Feinberg, M. E., Gill, S., Jones, D. E., Hostetler, M. L., & Stifter, C. A. (2021). Improving toddlers' healthy eating habits and self-regulation: A randomized controlled trial. *Pediatrics, 147*(1), e20193326. https://doi.org/10.1542/peds.2019-3326

Noble, K. G., & Giebler, M. A. (2020). The neuroscience of socioeconomic inequality. *Current Opinion in Behavioral Sciences, 36*, 23–28. https://doi.org/10.1016/j.cobeha.2020.05.007

Noble, W., & Spires-Jones, T. L. (2019). Sleep well to slow Alzheimer's progression? *Science, 363*(6429), 813–814.

Nock, M. K., Green, J. G., Hwang, I., McLaughlin, K. A., Sampson, N. A., Zaslavsky, A. M., & Kessler, R. C. (2013). Prevalence, correlates, and treatment of lifetime suicidal behavior among adolescents: Results from the National Comorbidity Survey Replication Adolescent Supplement. *JAMA Psychiatry, 70*(3), 300–310. https://doi.org/10.1001/2013.jamapsychiatry.55

Noel, S. E., Santos, M. P., & Wright, N. C. (2021). Racial and ethnic disparities in bone health and outcomes in the United States. *Journal of Bone and Mineral Research, 36*(10), 1881–1905. https://doi.org/10.1002/jbmr.4417

Nogueira Avelar e Silva, R., van de Bongardt, D., van de Looij-Jansen, P., Wijtzes, A., & Raat, H. (2016). Mother– and father–adolescent relationships and early sexual intercourse. *Pediatrics, 138*(6), e20160782. https://doi.org/10.1542/peds.2016-0782

Nomaguchi, K., & Milkie, M. A. (2020). Parenthood and well-being: A decade in review. *Journal of Marriage and the Family, 82*(1), 198–223. https://doi.org/10.1111/jomf.12646

Non, A. L., Román, J. C., Clausing, E. S., Gilman, S. E., Loucks, E. B., Buka, S. L., Appleton, A. A., & Kubzansky, L. D. (2020). Optimism and social support predict healthier adult behaviors despite socially disadvantaged childhoods. *International Journal of Behavioral Medicine, 27*(2), 200–212.

Nong, P., Raj, M., Creary, M., Kardia, S. L. R., & Platt, J. E. (2020). Patient-reported experiences of discrimination in the US health care system. *JAMA Network Open, 3*(12), e2029650. https://doi.org/10.1001/jamanetworkopen.2020.29650

Norbury, C. F., & Sonuga-Barke, E. (2017). Editorial: New frontiers in the scientific study of developmental language disorders. *Journal of Child Psychology and Psychiatry, 58*(10), 1065–1067. https://doi.org/10.1111/jcpp.12821

Norbury, C. F., Vamvakas, G., Gooch, D., Baird, G., Charman, T., Simonoff, E., & Pickles, A. (2017). Language growth in children with heterogeneous language disorders: A population study. *Journal of Child Psychology and Psychiatry, 58*(10), 1092–1105. https://doi.org/10.1111/jcpp.12793

NORC. (2017). *West Health Institute/NORC survey on aging in America.* https://www.norc.org/Research/Projects/Pages/WHI-NORC-Aging-Survey.aspx

NORC. (2021). *Needs assessment and environmental scan report: Maintaining physical and mental well-being of older adults and their caregivers during public health emergencies.* NORC at the University of Chicago.

NORC. (2021). *Surveys of trust in the U.S. health care system.* American Board of Internal Medicine Foundation.

Norris, A. L., & Orchowski, L. M. (2020). Peer victimization of sexual minority and transgender youth: A cross-sectional study of high school students. *Psychology of Violence, 10*(2), 201.

North, M. S., & Fiske, S. T. (2015). Modern attitudes toward older adults in the aging world: A cross-cultural meta-analysis. *Psychological Bulletin, 141*(5), 993.

North, M. S., & Fiske, S. T. (2017). Succession, consumption, and identity: Prescriptive ageism domains. In T. D. Nelson (Ed.), *Ageism: Stereotyping and prejudice against older persons* (pp. 77–103). Boston Review.

Northwestern Mutual. (2020). *30% of Americans say COVID-19 has changed the age at which they plan to retire.* https://news.northwesternmutual.com/2020-12-03-30-of-Americans-Say-COVID-19-Has-Changed-the-Age-at-Which-They-Plan-to-Retire

Norton, M. I., & Gino, F. (2014). Rituals alleviate grieving for loved ones, lovers, and lotteries. *Journal of Experimental Psychology: General, 143*(1), 266–272. https://doi.org/10.1037/a0031772

Nowell, Z. C., Thornton, A., & Simpson, J. (2013). The subjective experience of personhood in dementia care settings. *Dementia, 12*(4), 394–409.

Ntuli, B., Mokgatle, M., & Madiba, S. (2020). The psychosocial wellbeing of orphans: The case of early school leavers in socially depressed environment in Mpumalanga Province, South Africa. *PLOS ONE, 15*(2), e0229487. https://doi.org/10.1371/journal.pone.0229487

Nucci, L. P., & Turiel, E. (1978). Social interactions and the development of social concepts in preschool children. *Child Development, 49*(2), 400–407.

Nuland, S. B. (1995). *How we die: Reflections of life's final chapter, new edition.* Vintage.

Nunn, N., & Qian, N. (2010). The Columbian exchange: A history of disease, food, and ideas. *Journal of Economic Perspectives, 24*(2), 163–188.

Nutall, G. C. (1911, April 29). Eugenics and genetics. *Scientific American.* https://doi.org/10.1038/scientificamerican04291911-271supp

Nyberg, L., & Pudas, S. (2019). Successful memory aging. *Annual Review of Psychology, 70,* 219–243.

Nyberg, S. T., Singh-Manoux, A., Pentti, J., Madsen, I. E. H., Sabia, S., Alfredsson, L., Bjorner, J. B., Borritz, M., Burr, H., Goldberg, M., Heikkilä, K., Jokela, M., Knutsson, A., Lallukka, T., Lindbohm, J. V., Nielsen, M. L., Nordin, M., Oksanen, T., Pejtersen, J. H., ... Kivimäki, M. (2020). Association of healthy lifestyle with years lived without major chronic diseases. *JAMA Internal Medicine, 180*(5), 760–768. https://doi.org/10.1001/jamainternmed.2020.0618

Nye, C. D., Su, R., Rounds, J., & Drasgow, F. (2012). Vocational interests and performance: A quantitative summary of over 60 years of research. *Perspectives on Psychological Science, 7*(4), 384–403.

Nystrand, C., Feldman, I., Enebrink, P., & Sampaio, F. (2019). Cost-effectiveness analysis of parenting interventions for the prevention of behaviour problems in children. *PLOS ONE, 14*(12), e0225503. https://doi.org/10.1371/journal.pone.0225503

Oakley, A. (2018). *Women, peace and welfare: A suppressed history of social reform, 1880–1920.* Policy Press.

Oberle, E., Ji, X. R., Kerai, S., Guhn, M., Schonert-Reichl, K. A., & Gadermann, A. M. (2020). Screen time and extracurricular activities as risk and protective factors for mental health in adolescence: A population-level study. *Preventive Medicine, 141,* 106291. https://doi.org/10.1016/j.ypmed.2020.106291

Ochoa-Bernal, M. A., & Fazleabas, A. T. (2020). Physiologic events of embryo implantation and decidualization in human and non-human primates. *International Journal of Molecular Sciences, 21*(6), 1973. https://doi.org/10.3390/ijms21061973

O'Connor, D., Mann, J., & Wiersma, E. (2018). Stigma, discrimination and agency: Diagnostic disclosure as an everyday practice shaping social citizenship. *Journal of Aging Studies, 44,* 45–51. https://doi.org/10.1016/j.jaging.2018.01.010

O'Connor, D. B., Aggleton, J. P., Chakrabarti, B., Cooper, C. L., Creswell, C., Dunsmuir, S., Fiske, S. T., Gathercole, S., Gough, B., Ireland, J. L., Jones, M. V., Jowett, A., Kagan, C., Karanika-Murray, M., Kaye, L. K., Kumari, V., Lewandowsky, S., Lightman, S., Malpass, D., ... Armitage, C. J. (2020). Research priorities for the COVID-19 pandemic and beyond: A call to action for psychological science. *British Journal of Psychology, 111*(4), e12468. https://doi.org/10.1111/bjop.12468

O'Connor, K. J., & Graham, C. (2019). Longer, more optimistic, lives: Historic optimism and life expectancy in the United States. *Journal of Economic Behavior & Organization, 168,* 374–392. https://doi.org/10.1016/j.jebo.2019.10.018

O'Connor, M.-F. (2019). Grief: A brief history of research on how body, mind, and brain adapt. *Psychosomatic Medicine, 81*(8), 731–738. https://doi.org/10.1097/PSY.0000000000000717

O'Connor, R. M., & Kenny, P. J. (2015). Binge drinking and brain stress systems. *Nature, 520*(7546), 168–169.

O'Dea, R. E., Lagisz, M., Jennions, M. D., & Nakagawa, S. (2018). Gender differences in individual variation in academic grades fail to fit expected patterns for STEM. *Nature Communications, 9*(1), 3777. https://doi.org/10.1038/s41467-018-06292-0

Odgers, C. L. (2018). Smartphones are bad for some adolescents, not all. *Nature, 554*(7693), 432–434. https://doi.org/10.1038/d41586-018-02109-8

Odgers, C. L., Schueller, S. M., & Ito, M. (2020). Screen time, social media use, and adolescent development. *Annual Review of Developmental Psychology, 2*(1), 485–502. https://doi.org/10.1146/annurev-devpsych-121318-084815

O'Donnell, K. J., & Meaney, M. J. (2020). Epigenetics, development, and psychopathology. *Annual Review of*

Clinical Psychology, 16, 327–350. https://doi.org/10.1146/annurev-clinpsy-050718-095530

Oesch, D., & von Ow, A. (2017). Social networks and job access for the unemployed: Work ties for the upper-middle class, communal ties for the working class. *European Sociological Review, 33*(2), 275–291.

Ofori-Asenso, R., Chin, K. L., Mazidi, M., Zomer, E., Ilomaki, J., Ademi, Z., Bell, J. S., & Liew, D. (2020). Natural regression of frailty among community-dwelling older adults: A systematic review and meta-analysis. *The Gerontologist, 60*(4), e286–e298. https://doi.org/10.1093/geront/gnz064

Ofori-Asenso, R., Chin, K. L., Mazidi, M., Zomer, E., Ilomaki, J., Zullo, A. R., Gasevic, D., Ademi, Z., Korhonen, M. J., LoGiudice, D., Bell, J. S., & Liew, D. (2019). Global incidence of frailty and prefrailty among community-dwelling older adults: A systematic review and meta-analysis. *JAMA Network Open, 2*(8), e198398. https://doi.org/10.1001/jamanetworkopen.2019.8398

Oh, W., Volling, B. L., & Gonzalez, R. (2015). Trajectories of children's social interactions with their infant sibling in the first year: A multidimensional approach. *Journal of Family Psychology, 29*(1), 119.

O'Hara, L., Ahmed, H., & Elashie, S. (2021). Evaluating the impact of a brief health at Every Size®-informed health promotion activity on body positivity and internalized weight-based oppression. *Body Image, 37,* 225–237. https://doi.org/10.1016/j.bodyim.2021.02.006

O'Hara, M. W., & Engeldinger, J. (2018). Treatment of postpartum depression: Recommendations for the clinician. *Clinical Obstetrics and Gynecology, 61*(3), 604–614. https://doi.org/10.1097/GRF.0000000000000353

Ohayon, M. M. (2002). Epidemiology of insomnia: What we know and what we still need to learn. *Sleep Medicine Reviews, 6*(2), 97–111.

Ohtani, K., & Hisasaka, T. (2018). Beyond intelligence: A meta-analytic review of the relationship among metacognition, intelligence, and academic performance. *Metacognition and Learning, 13*(2), 179–212.

Okahana, H., Zhou, E., & Gao, J. (2020). *Graduate enrollment and degrees: 2009 to 2019.* Council of Graduate Schools and Educational Testing Service.

Okajima, I., Komada, Y., & Inoue, Y. (2011). A meta-analysis on the treatment effectiveness of cognitive behavioral therapy for primary insomnia. *Sleep and Biological Rhythms, 9*(1), 24–34.

O'Keeffe, C., & McNally, S. (2021). 'Uncharted territory': Teachers' perspectives on play in early childhood classrooms in Ireland during the pandemic. *European Early Childhood Education Research Journal, 29*(1), 79–95. https://doi.org/10.1080/1350293X.2021.1872668

O'Keeffe, L. M., Frysz, M., Bell, J. A., Howe, L. D., & Fraser, A. (2020). Puberty timing and adiposity change across childhood and adolescence: Disentangling cause and consequence. *Human Reproduction, 35*(12), 2784–2792. https://doi.org/10.1093/humrep/deaa213

Okonofua, J. A., & Eberhardt, J. L. (2015). Two strikes: Race and the disciplining of young students. *Psychological Science, 26*(5), 617–624. https://doi.org/10.1177/0956797615570365

Okonofua, J. A., Walton, G. M., & Eberhardt, J. L. (2016). A vicious cycle: A social–psychological account of extreme racial disparities in school discipline. *Perspectives on Psychological Science, 11*(3), 381–398. https://doi.org/10.1177/1745691616635592

Okowo-Bele, J.-M. (2015). *Together we can close the immunization gap.* World Health Organization. https://www.who.int/mediacentre/commentaries/vaccine-preventable-diseases/en/

Oladapo, O. T., Diaz, V., Bonet, M., Abalos, E., Thwin, S. S., Souza, H., Perdoná, G., Souza, J. P., & Gülmezoglu, A. M. (2018). Cervical dilatation patterns of 'low-risk' women with spontaneous labour and normal perinatal outcomes: A systematic review. *BJOG: An International Journal of Obstetrics & Gynaecology, 125*(8), 944–954. https://doi.org/10.1111/1471-0528.14930

Olds, D. L., Kitzman, H., Knudtson, M. D., Anson, E., Smith, J. A., & Cole, R. (2014). Effect of home visiting by nurses on maternal and child mortality: Results of a 2-decade follow-up of a randomized clinical trial. *JAMA Pediatrics, 168*(9), 800–806.

Oliveira, C., Fonseca, G., Sotero, L., Crespo, C., & Relvas, A. P. (2020). Family dynamics during emerging adulthood: Reviewing, integrating, and challenging the field. *Journal of Family Theory & Review, 12*(3), 350–367. https://doi.org/10.1111/jftr.12386

Oller, D. K., Caskey, M., Yoo, H., Bene, E. R., Jhang, Y., Lee, C.-C., Bowman, D. D., Long, H. L., Buder, E. H., & Vohr, B. (2019). Preterm and full term infant vocalization and the origin of language. *Scientific Reports, 9*(1), 14734. https://doi.org/10.1038/s41598-019-51352-0

Olmstead, S. B. (2020). A decade review of sex and partnering in adolescence and young adulthood. *Journal of Marriage and Family, 82*(2), 769–795. https://doi.org/10.1111/jomf.12670

Olmstead, S. B., McMahan, K. D., & Anders, K. M. (2021). Meanings ascribed to sex and commitment among college-attending and non-college emerging adults: A replication and extension. *Archives of Sexual Behavior, 50,* 2435–2446. https://doi.org/10.1007/s10508-021-02042-4

Olson, S. L., Choe, D. E., & Sameroff, A. J. (2017). Trajectories of child externalizing problems between ages 3 and 10 years: Contributions of children's early effortful control, theory of mind, and parenting experiences. *Development and Psychopathology, 29*(4), 1333–1351. https://doi.org/10.1017/S095457941700030X

Oluwayiose, O. A., Wu, H., Saddiki, H., Whitcomb, B. W., Balzer, L. B., Brandon, N., Suvorov, A., Tayyab, R., Sites, C. K., Hill, L., Marcho, C., & Pilsner, J. R. (2021). Sperm DNA methylation mediates the association of male age on reproductive outcomes among couples undergoing infertility treatment. *Scientific Reports, 11*(1), 3216. https://doi.org/10.1038/s41598-020-80857-2

Olweus, D. (1978). *Aggression in the schools: Bullies and whipping boys.* Hemisphere.

Olweus, D. (1993). Bully/victim problems among school-children: Long-term consequences and an effective intervention program. In S. Hodgins (Ed.), *Mental disorder and crime* (pp. 317–349). SAGE Publications.

Olweus, D., Limber, S. P., & Breivik, K. (2019). Addressing specific forms of bullying: A large-scale evaluation of the Olweus bullying prevention program. *International Journal of Bullying Prevention, 1*(1), 70–84. https://doi.org/10.1007/s42380-019-00009-7

Olza-Fernández, I., Gabriel, M. A. M., Gil-Sanchez, A., Garcia-Segura, L. M., & Arevalo, M. A. (2014). Neuroendocrinology of childbirth and mother–child attachment: The basis of an etiopathogenic model of perinatal neurobiological disorders. *Frontiers in Neuroendocrinology, 35*(4), 459–472.

Omar, M. T. M. (2020). Religious education in the Arab world: Saudi Arabia, Sudan and Egypt as models. *English Language Teaching, 13*(12), 27–36.

O'Neil, S., Clarke, E., & Peeters Grietens, K. (2017). How to protect your new-born from neonatal death: Infant feeding and medical practices in the Gambia. *Women's Studies International Forum, 60,* 136–143. https://doi.org/10.1016/j.wsif.2016.11.003

Ong, J. L., Tandi, J., Patanaik, A., Lo, J. C., & Chee, M. W. L. (2019). Large-scale data from wearables reveal regional disparities in sleep patterns that persist across age and sex. *Scientific Reports, 9*(1), 3415. https://doi.org/10.1038/s41598-019-40156-x

Ontai, L. L., Sutter, C., Sitnick, S., Shilts, M. K., & Townsend, M. S. (2019). Parent food-related behaviors and family-based dietary and activity environments: Associations with BMI z-scores in low-income preschoolers. *Childhood Obesity, 16*(S1), S-55–S-63. https://doi.org/10.1089/chi.2019.0105

Oosterhoff, B., Kaplow, J. B., & Layne, C. M. (2018). Links between bereavement due to sudden death and academic functioning: Results from a nationally representative sample of adolescents. *School Psychology Quarterly, 33*(3), 372.

Opresko, P. L., & Shay, J. W. (2017). Telomere-associated aging disorders. *Ageing Research Reviews, 33,* 52–66.

Orben, A., Tomova, L., & Blakemore, S. J. (2020). The effects of social deprivation on adolescent development and mental health. *The Lancet Child & Adolescent Health, 4*(8), 634–640.

Ordway, M. R., Sadler, L. S., Jeon, S., O'Connell, M., Banasiak, N., Fenick, A. M., Crowley, A. A., Canapari, C., & Redeker, N. S. (2020). Sleep health in young children living with socioeconomic adversity. *Research in Nursing & Health, 43*(4), 329–340. https://doi.org/10.1002/nur.22023

O'Reilly Treter, M., Rhoades, G. K., Scott, S. B., Markman, H. J., & Stanley, S. M. (2021). Having a baby: Impact on married and cohabiting parents' relationships. *Family Process, 60*(2), 477–492. https://doi.org/10.1111/famp.12567

Orellana, M. F. (2001). The work kids do: Mexican and Central American immigrant children's contributions to households and schools in California. *Harvard Educational Review, 71*(3), 366–390.

Orellana, M. F., & Phoenix, A. (2017). Re-interpreting: Narratives of childhood language brokering over time. *Childhood (Copenhagen, Denmark), 24*(2), 183–196. https://doi.org/10.1177/0907568216671178

Oreskes, N. (2019). *Why trust science?* Princeton University Press.

Organisation for Economic Co-operation and Development (OECD). (2017). *Preventing aging unequally.*

Organisation for Economic Co-operation and Development (OECD). (2017). *Starting strong 2017: Key OECD indicators on early childhood education and care.* OECD Publishing.

Organisation for Economic Co-operation and Development (OECD). (2018). *Average effective date of retirement in 1970–1918 in OECD countries (time series).*

Organisation for Economic Co-operation and Development (OECD). (2019). *CO3.1 educational attainment by gender.*

Organisation for Economic Co-operation and Development (OECD). (2019). *Skills matter: Additional results from the Survey of Adult Skills* (OECD Skills Studies). OECD Publishing. https://doi.org/10.1787/1f029d8f-en

Organisation for Economic Co-operation and Development (OECD). (2020). *Is childcare affordable?* (Policy brief on employment, labour and social affairs). OECD.

Organisation for Economic Co-operation and Development (OECD). (2020). *OECD Family Database. SF2.4: Share of births outside of marriage.*

Organisation for Economic Co-operation and Development (OECD). (2020). *Promoting an age-inclusive workforce: Living, learning and earning longer.* https://www.oecd.org/publications/promoting-an-age-inclusive-workforce-59752153-en.htm

Organisation for Economic Co-operation and Development (OECD). (2021a). *Age of mothers at childbirth and age-specific fertility* (SF2.3 OECD Family Database).

Organisation for Economic Co-operation and Development (OECD). (2021b). *Economic & social outcomes* (Education GPS).

Organisation for Economic Co-operation and Development (OECD). (2021c). *Education at a glance 2021: OECD indicators.* https://doi.org/10.1787/b35a14e5-en

Organisation for Economic Co-operation and Development (OECD). (2021). *Health at a glance, 2021.*

Organisation for Economic Co-operation and Development (OECD). (2021). *OECD Family Database: SF 2.3: Age of mothers at childbirth and age-specific fertility.*

Organisation for Economic Co-operation and Development (OECD). (2021). *Pensions at a glance 2021: OECD and G20 indicators.*

Organisation for Economic Co-operation and Development (OECD). (2021). *Young people's concerns during COVID-19: Results from Risks That Matter 2020.* https://read.oecd-ilibrary.org/view/?ref=1099_1099612-0juxn9tthe&title=Young-people-s-concerns-during-COVID-19-Results-from-Risks-That-Matter-2020

Orji, A., Kamenov, K., Dirac, M., Davis, A., Chadha, S., & Vos, T. (2020). Global and regional needs, unmet needs

and access to hearing aids. *International Journal of Audiology, 59*(3), 166–172. https://doi.org/10.1080/14992027.2020.1721577

Orman, B., & Benozzi, G. (2021). Pharmacological strategies for treating presbyopia. *Current Opinion in Ophthalmology, 32*(4), 319–323.

Oron, A. P., Chao, D. L., Ezeanolue, E. E., Ezenwa, L. N., Piel, F. B., Ojogun, O. T., Uyoga, S., Williams, T. N., & Nnodu, O. E. (2020). Caring for Africa's sickle cell children: Will we rise to the challenge? BMC Medicine, *18,* 1–8.

Orth, T., & Rosenfeld, M. (2018). Commitment timing in same-sex and different-sex relationships. *Population Review, 57*(1). https://doi.org/10.1353/prv.2018.0000

Orth, U., Erol, R. Y., & Luciano, E. C. (2018). Development of self-esteem from age 4 to 94 years: A meta-analysis of longitudinal studies. *Psychological Bulletin, 144*(10), 1045–1080. https://doi.org/10.1037/bul0000161

Ortiz-Ospina, E. (2020, December 11). *Who do we spend time with across our lifetime?* Our World in Data. https://ourworldindata.org/time-with-others-lifetime

Ortman, J. M., Velkoff, V. A., & Hogan, H. (2014). *An aging nation: The older population in the United States: Population estimates and projections* (No. P24-1140; Current Population Reports). U.S. Census Bureau.

Ose Askvik, E., van der Weel, F. R. (Ruud), & van der Meer, A. L. H. (2020). The importance of cursive handwriting over typewriting for learning in the classroom: A high-density EEG study of 12-year-old children and young adults. *Frontiers in Psychology, 11,* 1810. https://doi.org/10.3389/fpsyg.2020.01810

Oster, E. (2019). *Cribsheet: A data-driven guide to better, more relaxed parenting, from birth to preschool.* Penguin.

Oster, E. (2019, April 19). Opinion | The data all guilt-ridden parents need. *The New York Times.* https://www.nytimes.com/2019/04/19/opinion/sunday/baby-breast-feeding-sleep-training.html

Ostfeld, B. M., Schwartz-Soicher, O., Reichman, N. E., Teitler, J. O., & Hegyi, T. (2017). Prematurity and sudden unexpected infant deaths in the United States. *Pediatrics, 140*(1), e20163334. https://doi.org/10.1542/peds.2016-3334

Ostlund, B. D., Vlisides-Henry, R. D., Crowell, S. E., Raby, K. L., Terrell, S., Brown, M. A., Tinajero, R., Shakiba, N., Monk, C., Shakib, J. H., Buchi, K. F., & Conradt, E. (2019). Intergenerational transmission of emotion dysregulation: Part II. Developmental origins of newborn neurobehavior. *Development and Psychopathology, 31*(3), 833–846. https://doi.org/10.1017/S0954579419000440

O'Sullivan, A., & Monk, C. (2020). Maternal and environmental influences on perinatal and infant development. *Future of Children, 30*(2), 11–34.

Oswalt, S. B., Lederer, A. M., Chestnut-Steich, K., Day, C., Halbritter, A., & Ortiz, D. (2020). Trends in college students' mental health diagnoses and utilization of services, 2009–2015. *Journal of American College Health, 68*(1), 41–51.

Otgaar, H., Howe, M. L., Merckelbach, H., & Muris, P. (2018). Who is the better eyewitness? Sometimes adults but at other times children. *Current Directions in Psychological Science, 27*(5), 378–385.

Ott, M. A., Hunt, A. L., Katz, A. J., & Zaban, L. S. (2020). Tapping into community resiliency in rural adolescent pregnancy prevention: An implementation sciences approach. *Behavioral Medicine, 46*(3–4), 340–352. https://doi.org/10.1080/08964289.2020.1748863

Otto, H., Potinius, I., & Keller, H. (2014). Cultural differences in stranger–child interactions: A comparison between German middle-class and Cameroonian Nso stranger–infant dyads. *Journal of Cross-Cultural Psychology, 45*(2), 322–334. https://doi.org/10.1177/0022022113509133

Otto, H. W. R., Schuitmaker, N., Lamm, B., Abels, M., Serdtse, Y., Yovsi, R., & Tomlinson, M. (2017). Infants' social experiences in three African sociocultural contexts. *Child Development, 88*(4), 1235–1250. https://doi.org/10.1111/cdev.12661

Oudekerk, B., & Morgan, R. E. (2016). *Co-offending among adolescents in violent victimizations, 2004–13.* U.S. Department of Justice, Office of Justice Programs, Bureau of Justice Statistics.

Ouellet-Morin, I., Fisher, H. L., York-Smith, M., Fincham-Campbell, S., Moffitt, T. E., & Arseneault, L. (2015). Intimate partner violence and new-onset depression: A longitudinal study of women's childhood and adult histories of abuse. *Depression and Anxiety, 32*(5), 316–324. https://doi.org/10.1002/da.22347

Out.com. (2015, January 7). Not only fools rush in. *Out.*

Ouvrein, G., & Verswijvel, K. (2019). Sharenting: Parental adoration or public humiliation? A focus group study on adolescents' experiences with sharenting against the background of their own impression management. *Children and Youth Services Review, 99*, 319–327.

Ouwens, K. G., Jansen, R., Tolhuis, B., Slagboom, P. E., Penninx, B. W. J. H., & Boomsma, D. I. (2018). A characterization of postzygotic mutations identified in monozygotic twins. *Human Mutation, 39*(10), 1393–1401. https://doi.org/10.1002/humu.23586

Ou-Yang, M.-C., Sun, Y., Liebowitz, M., Chen, C.-C., Fang, M.-L., Dai, W., Chuang, T.-W., & Chen, J.-L. (2020). Accelerated weight gain, prematurity, and the risk of childhood obesity: A meta-analysis and systematic review. *PLOS ONE, 15*(5), e0232238. https://doi.org/10.1371/journal.pone.0232238

Overton, W. F. (2013). A new paradigm for developmental science: Relationism and relational-developmental systems. *Applied Developmental Science, 17*(2), 94–107. https://doi.org/10.1080/10888691.2013.778717

Overton, W. F. (2015). Processes, relations, and relational-developmental-systems. In *Handbook of child psychology and developmental science*. John Wiley & Sons. https://doi.org/10.1002/9781118963418.childpsy102

Owen, J., Rhoades, G. K., & Stanley, S. M. (2013). Sliding versus deciding in relationships: Associations with relationship quality, commitment, and infidelity. *Journal of Couple & Relationship Therapy, 12*(2), 135–149.

Owens, A. (2018). Income segregation between school districts and inequality in students' achievement. *Sociology of Education, 91*(1), 1–27.

Owens, J. (2016). Early childhood behavior problems and the gender gap in educational attainment in the United States. *Sociology of Education, 89*(3), 236–258. https://doi.org/10.1177/0038040716650926

Owens, J. (2021). Parental intervention in school, academic pressure, and childhood diagnoses of ADHD. *Social Science & Medicine, 272*, 113746. https://doi.org/10.1016/j.socscimed.2021.113746

Owens-Young, J., & Bell, C. N. (2020). Structural racial inequities in socioeconomic status, urban-rural classification, and infant mortality in US counties. *Ethnicity & Disease, 30*(3), 389–398. https://doi.org/10.18865/ed.30.3.389

Owsley, C. (2016). Vision and aging. *Annual Review of Vision Science, 2*, 255–271.

Owsley, C., McGwin, G., & Searcey, K. (2013). A population-based examination of the visual and ophthalmological characteristics of licensed drivers aged 70 and older. *The Journals of Gerontology: Series A, 68*(5), 567–573. https://doi.org/10.1093/gerona/gls185

Oxman, T. E. (2018). Reflections on aging and wisdom. *The American Journal of Geriatric Psychiatry, 26*(11), 1108–1118. https://doi.org/10.1016/j.jagp.2018.07.009

Oyserman, D. (2017). Culture three ways: Culture and subcultures within countries. *Annual Review of Psychology, 68*, 435–463.

Oyserman, D., Coon, H. M., & Kemmelmeier, M. (2002). Rethinking individualism and collectivism: Evaluation of theoretical assumptions and meta-analyses. *Psychological Bulletin, 128*(1), 3–72. https://doi.org/10.1037/0033-2909.128.1.3

Oyserman, D., Elmore, K., & Smith, G. (2012). Self, self-concept, and identity. In M. R. Leary & J. P. Tangney (Eds.), *Handbook of self and identity* (2nd ed., pp. 69–104). Guilford.

Özçalışkan, Ş., & Goldin-Meadow, S. (2005). Gesture is at the cutting edge of early language development. *Cognition, 96*(3), B101–B113.

Ozer, M., & Perc, M. (2020). Dreams and realities of school tracking and vocational education. *Palgrave Communications, 6*(1), 1–7. https://doi.org/10.1057/s41599-020-0409-4

Paavonen, E. J., Saarenpää-Heikkilä, O., Morales-Munoz, I., Virta, M., Häkälä, N., Pölkki, P., Kylliäinen, A., Karlsson, H., Paunio, T., & Karlsson, L. (2020). Normal sleep development in infants: Findings from two large birth cohorts. *Sleep Medicine, 69*, 145–154. https://doi.org/10.1016/j.sleep.2020.01.009

Paccagnella, M. (2016). *Age, ageing and skills: Results from the survey of adult skills* (OECD Education Working Papers, No. 132). OECD Publishing.

Packer, M. J., & Cole, M. (2020). Culture and human development. In *Oxford research encyclopedia of psychology*. https://doi.org/10.1093/acrefore/9780190236557.013.581

Padawer, R. (2016, June 28). The humiliating practice of sex-testing female athletes. *The New York Times.* https://www.nytimes.com/2016/07/03/magazine/the-humiliating-practice-of-sex-testing-female-athletes.html

Padilla, J., Jager, J., Updegraff, K. A., McHale, S. M., & Umanña-Taylor, A. J. (2020). Mexican-origin family members' unique and shared family perspectives of familism values and their links with parent-youth relationship quality. *Developmental Psychology, 56*(5), 993–1008. https://doi.org/10.1037/dev0000913

Padilla, N., & Lagercrantz, H. (2020). Making of the mind. *Acta Paediatrica, 109*(5), 883–892. https://doi.org/10.1111/apa.15167

Padilla-Walker, L. M., Son, D., & Nelson, L. J. (2021). Profiles of helicopter parenting, parental warmth, and psychological control during emerging adulthood. *Emerging Adulthood,* 9(2), 132–144. https://doi.org/10.1177/2167696818823626

Pahlke, E., Bigler, R. S., & Suizzo, M. A. (2012). Relations between colorblind socialization and children's racial bias: Evidence from European American mothers and their preschool children. *Child Development, 83*(4), 1164–1179.

Pahor, M., Guralnik, J. M., Ambrosius, W. T., Blair, S., Bonds, D. E., Church, T. S., Espeland, M. A., Fielding, R. A., Gill, T. M., Groessl, E. J., King, A. C., Kritchevsky, S. B., Manini, T. M., McDermott, M. M., Miller, M. E., Newman, A. B., Rejeski, W. J., Sink, K. M., Williamson, J. D., for the Life study Investigators. (2014). Effect of structured physical activity on prevention of major mobility disability in older adults: The LIFE study randomized clinical trial. *JAMA, 311*(23), 2387–2396. https://doi.org/10.1001/jama.2014.5616

Palagi, E., Celeghin, A., Tamietto, M., Winkielman, P., & Norscia, I. (2020). The neuroethology of spontaneous mimicry and emotional contagion in human and non-human animals. *Neuroscience & Biobehavioral Reviews, 111*, 149–165. https://doi.org/10.1016/j.neubiorev.2020.01.020

Palagini, L., Domschke, K., Benedetti, F., Foster, R. G., Wulff, K., & Riemann, D. (2019). Developmental pathways towards mood disorders in adult life: Is there a role for sleep disturbances? *Journal of Affective Disorders, 243*, 121–132. https://doi.org/10.1016/j.jad.2018.09.011

Paleari, F. G., Brambilla, M., & Fincham, F. D. (2019). When prejudice against you hurts others and me: The case of ageism at work. *Journal of Applied Social Psychology, 49*(11), 704–720.

Pallazola, V. A., Davis, D. M., Whelton, S. P., Cardoso, R., Latina, J. M., Michos, E. D., Sarkar, S., Blumenthal, R. S., Arnett, D. K., Stone, N. J., & Welty, F. K. (2019). A clinician's guide to healthy eating for cardiovascular disease prevention. *Mayo Clinic Proceedings: Innovations, Quality & Outcomes, 3*(3), 251–267. https://doi.org/10.1016/j.mayocpiqo.2019.05.001

Palmer, S. B., & Abbott, N. (2018). Bystander responses to bias-based bullying in schools: A developmental intergroup approach. *Child Development Perspectives, 12*(1), 39–44.

Palve, S. S., & Palve, S. B. (2018). Impact of aging on nerve conduction velocities and late responses in healthy individuals. *Journal of Neurosciences in Rural Practice, 9*(01), 112–116.

Panagiotakopoulos, L., Chulani, V., Koyama, A., Childress, K., Forcier, M., Grimsby, G., & Greenberg, K. (2020). The effect of early puberty suppression on treatment options and outcomes in transgender patients. *Nature Reviews Urology, 17*(11), 626–636. https://doi.org/10.1038/s41585-020-0372-2

Panchal, N., Kamal, R., Cox, C., Garfield, R., & Chidambaram, P. (2021). *Mental health and substance use considerations among children during the COVID-19 pandemic.* KFF. https://www.kff.org/coronavirus-covid-19/issue-brief/mental-health-and-substance-use-considerations-among-children-during-the-covid-19-pandemic/

Pang, J., Keh, H. T., Li, X., & Maheswaran, D. (2017). "Every coin has two sides": The effects of dialectical thinking and attitudinal ambivalence on psychological discomfort and consumer choice. *Journal of Consumer Psychology, 27*(2), 218–230.

Panikkar, R. (1994). *The Vedic experience: Mantramañjarī: An anthology of the Vedas for modern man and contemporary celebration.* Motilal Banarsidass.

Panofsky, A., & Bliss, C. (2017). Ambiguity and scientific authority: Population classification in genomic science. *American Sociological Review, 82*(1), 59–87. https://doi.org/10.1177/0003122416685812

Pant, R., Kanjlia, S., & Bedny, M. (2020). A sensitive period in the neural phenotype of language in blind individuals. *Developmental Cognitive Neuroscience, 41*, 100744. https://doi.org/10.1016/j.dcn.2019.100744

Pantell, M., Rehkopf, D., Jutte, D., Syme, S. L., Balmes, J., & Adler, N. (2013). Social isolation: A predictor of mortality comparable to traditional clinical risk factors. *American Journal of Public Health, 103*(11), 2056–2062. https://doi.org/10.2105/AJPH.2013.301261

Pantell, R. H., & Committee on Psychosocial Aspects of Child and Family Health. (2017). The child witness in the courtroom. *Pediatrics,* 139(3).

Panth, N., Gavarkovs, A., Tamez, M., & Mattei, J. (2018). The influence of diet on fertility and the implications for public health nutrition in the United States. *Frontiers in Public Health.* https://doi.org/10.3389/fpubh.2018.00211

Paoletti, J. B. (2012). *Pink and blue: Telling the boys from the girls in America.* Indiana University Press.

Paolucci, E. M., Loukov, D., Bowdish, D. M. E., & Heisz, J. J. (2018). Exercise reduces depression and inflammation but intensity matters. *Biological Psychology, 133*, 79–84. https://doi.org/10.1016/j.biopsycho.2018.01.015

Papadimitriou, A. (2016). Timing of puberty and secular trend in human maturation. In P. Kumanov & A. Agarwal (Eds.), *Puberty: Physiology and abnormalities* (pp. 121–136). Springer International Publishing. https://doi.org/10.1007/978-3-319-32122-6_9

Papageorgiou, K. A., Smith, T. J., Wu, R., Johnson, M. H., Kirkham, N. Z., & Ronald, A. (2014). Individual differences in infant fixation duration relate to attention and behavioral control in childhood. *Psychological Science, 25*(7), 1371–1379.

Papazoglou, K., Blumberg, D. M., Collins, P. I., Schlosser, M. D., & Bonanno, G. A. (2020). Inevitable loss and prolonged grief in police work: An unexplored topic. *Frontiers in Psychology, 11*, 1178. https://doi.org/10.3389/fpsyg.2020.01178

Papke, D. R. (2021). Segregation of a different sort: Age-segregation in the housing and accommodations of older Americans. *Elder Law Journal, 29*, 95.

Parade, S. H., Armstrong, L. M., Dickstein, S., & Seifer, R. (2018). Family context moderates the association of maternal postpartum depression and stability of infant temperament. *Child Development, 89*(6), 2118–2135. https://doi.org/10.1111/cdev.12895

Paradies, Y., Bastos, J. L., & Priest, N. (2017). Prejudice, stigma, bias, discrimination, and health. In *The Cambridge handbook of the psychology of prejudice* (pp. 559–581). Cambridge University Press. https://doi.org/10.1017/9781316161579.025

Paradise, R., Mejía-Arauz, R., Silva, K. G., Dexter, A. L., & Rogoff, B. (2014). One, two, three, eyes on me! Adults attempting control versus guiding in support of initiative. *Human Development, 57*(2/3), 131–149.

Parens, E., & Appelbaum, P. S. (2019). On what we have learned and still need to learn about the psychosocial impacts of genetic testing. *Hastings Center Report, 49*(S1), S2–S9. https://doi.org/10.1002/hast.1011

Parent, A. S., Teilmann, G., Juul, A., Skakkebaek, N. E., Toppari, J., & Bourguignon, J. P. (2003). The timing of normal puberty and the age limits of sexual precocity: Variations around the world, secular trends, and changes after migration. *Endocrine Reviews, 24*(5), 668–693.

Parents Together. (2020, April 23). Survey shows parents alarmed as kids' screen time skyrockets during COVID-19 crisis. *ParentsTogether.* https://parents-together.org/survey-shows-parents-alarmed-as-kids-screen-time-skyrockets-during-covid-19-crisis/

Pariser, D., & Forget, B. (2019). The social organization of students in class versus in an online social network: Freedom and constraint in two different settings. In J. C. Castro (Ed.), *Mobile media in and outside of the art classroom: Attending to identity, spatiality, and materiality* (pp. 47–76). Springer Nature.

Park, D. C., & Festini, S. B. (2017). The middle-aged brain: A cognitive neuroscience perspective. In R. Cabeza, L. Nyberg, & D. C. Park (Eds.), *Cognitive neuroscience of aging: Linking cognitive and cerebral aging* (pp. 363–388). Oxford University Press.

Park, H., Chiang, J. J., Irwin, M. R., Bower, J. E., McCreath, H., & Fuligni, A. J. (2019). Developmental trends in sleep during adolescents' transition to young adulthood. *Sleep Medicine, 60,* 202–210.

Park, H., & Lau, A. S. (2016). Socioeconomic status and parenting priorities: Child independence and obedience around the world: Socioeconomic status and child socialization. *Journal of Marriage and Family, 78*(1), 43–59. https://doi.org/10.1111/jomf.12247

Park, H. W. (2016). *Old age, new science: Gerontologists and their biosocial visions, 1900–1960.* University of Pittsburgh Press.

Park, I. J. K., Wang, L., Williams, D. R., & Alegría, M. (2018). Coping with racism: Moderators of the discrimination–adjustment link among Mexican-origin adolescents. *Child Development, 89*(3), e293–e310. https://doi.org/10.1111/cdev.12856

Park, M., O'Toole, A., & Katsiaficas, C. (2017). *Dual language learners: A national demographic and policy profile* (Fact sheet). Migration Policy Institute.

Park, S., & Morrow-Howell, N. (2020). Engaging older adults. In M. R. Rank (Ed.), *Toward a livable life: A 21st century agenda for social work* (pp. 253–275). Oxford University Press.

Park, S. Q., Kahnt, T., Dogan, A., Strang, S., Fehr, E., & Tobler, P. N. (2017). A neural link between generosity and happiness. *Nature Communications, 8*(1), 15964. https://doi.org/10.1038/ncomms15964

Parker, A. E., Halberstadt, A. G., Dunsmore, J. C., Townley, G., Bryant, A., Thompson, J. A., & Beale, K. S. (2012). "Emotions are a window into one's heart": A qualitative analysis of parental beliefs about children's emotions across three ethnic groups. Monographs of the Society for Research in Child Development, 77(3), i–144.

Parker, C. M., Hirsch, J. S., Philbin, M. M., & Parker, R. G. (2018). The urgent need for research and interventions to address family-based stigma and discrimination against lesbian, gay, bisexual, transgender, and queer youth. *Journal of Adolescent Health, 63*(4), 383–393. https://doi.org/10.1016/j.jadohealth.2018.05.018

Parker, J. G., & Asher, S. R. (1993). Friendship and friendship quality in middle childhood: Links with peer group acceptance and feelings of loneliness and social dissatisfaction. *Developmental Psychology, 29*(4), 611.

Parker, K. (2021, November 8). *What's behind the growing gap between men and women in college completion?* Pew Research Center. https://www.pewresearch.org/fact-tank/2021/11/08/whats-behind-the-growing-gap-between-men-and-women-in-college-completion/

Parker, K., & Horowitz, J. M. (2015). *Parenting in America: Outlook, worries, aspirations are strongly linked to financial situation.* Pew Research Center.

Parker, K., Horowitz, J. M., & Stepler, R. (2017). *On gender differences, no consensus on nature vs. nurture.* Pew Research Center.

Parker, K., & Patten, E. (2013, January 30). The sandwich generation. *Social and Demographic Trends Project.* Pew Research Center. https://www.pewresearch.org/social-trends/2013/01/30/the-sandwich-generation/

Parker, P. D., Jerrim, J., Schoon, I., & Marsh, H. W. (2016). A multination study of socioeconomic inequality in expectations for progression to higher education: The role

of between-school tracking and ability stratification. *American Educational Research Journal, 53*(1), 6–32. https://doi.org/10.3102/0002831215621786

Parks, S. E., Erck Lambert, A. B., Hauck, F. R., Cottengim, C. R., Faulkner, M., & Shapiro-Mendoza, C. K. (2021). Explaining sudden unexpected infant deaths, 2011–2017. *Pediatrics, 147*(5).

Parnia, S., Spearpoint, K., de Vos, G., Fenwick, P., Goldberg, D., Yang, J., Zhu, J., Baker, K., Killingback, H., McLean, P., Wood, M., Zafari, A. M., Dickert, N., Beisteiner, R., Sterz, F., Berger, M., Warlow, C., Bullock, S., Lovett, S., … Schoenfeld, E. R. (2014). AWARE—AWAreness during REsuscitation—A prospective study. *Resuscitation, 85*(12), 1799–1805. https://doi.org/10.1016/j.resuscitation.2014.09.004

Parnia, S., & Young, J. (2013). *Erasing death: The science that is rewriting the boundaries between life and death.* Harper Collins.

Parsons, A. W., Parsons, S. A., Malloy, J. A., Marinak, B. A., Reutzel, D. R., Applegate, M. D., Applegate, A. J., Fawson, P. C., & Gambrell, L. B. (2018). Upper elementary students' motivation to read fiction and nonfiction. *The Elementary School Journal, 118*(3), 505–523. https://doi.org/10.1086/696022

Partanen, E., & Virtala, P. (2017). Prenatal sensory development. In B. Hopkins, E. Geangu, & S. Linkenauger (Eds.), *The Cambridge encyclopedia of child development* (2nd ed., pp. 231–241). Cambridge University Press. https://doi.org/10.1017/9781316216491.041

Parten, M. B. (1932). Social participation among preschool children. *The Journal of Abnormal and Social Psychology, 27*(3), 243.

Paruthi, S., Brooks, L. J., D'Ambrosio, C., Hall, W. A., Kotagal, S., Lloyd, R. M., Malow, B. A., Maski, K., Nichols, C., Quan, S. F., Rosen, C. L., Troester, M. M., & Wise, M. S. (2016). Consensus statement of the American Academy of Sleep Medicine on the recommended amount of sleep for healthy children: Methodology and discussion. *Journal of Clinical Sleep Medicine, 12*(11), 1549–1561. https://doi.org/10.5664/jcsm.6288

Paruthi, S., Brooks, L. J., D'Ambrosio, C., Hall, W. A., Kotagal, S., Lloyd, R. M., Malow, B. A., Maski, K., Nichols, C., Quan, S. F., Rosen, C. L., Troester, M. M., & Wise, M. S. (2016). Recommended amount of sleep for pediatric populations: A consensus statement of the American Academy of Sleep Medicine. *Journal of Clinical Sleep Medicine, 12*(6), 785–786. https://doi.org/10.5664/jcsm.5866

Pascalis, O., De Haan, M., & Nelson, C. A. (2002). Is face processing species-specific during the first year of life? *Science, 296*(5571), 1321–1323.

Pascarella, E. T., & Terenzini, P. T. (2005). *How college affects students: A third decade of research* (Vol. 2). Jossey-Bass.

Paschall, K., Moore, K. A., Pina, G., & Anderson, S. (2020). *Comparing the national outcome measure of healthy and ready to learn with other well-being and school readiness measures.* Child Trends.

Paschall, K., & Tout, K. (2018, May 1). Most child care settings in the United States are homes, not centers. *Child Trends.* https://www.childtrends.org/blog/most-child-care-providers-in-the-united-states-are-based-in-homes-not-centers

Pasco, M. C., White, R., Iida, M., & Seaton, E. K. (2021). A prospective examination of neighborhood social and cultural cohesion and parenting processes on ethnic-racial identity among US Mexican adolescents. *Developmental Psychology, 57*(5), 783.

Passel, J. S. (2011). Demography of immigrant youth: Past, present, and future. *The Future of Children, 21*(1), 19–41. https://muse.jhu.edu/article/446008/summary

Pastorelli, C., Lansford, J. E., Luengo, B. K., Malone, P. S., Di, L. G., Bacchini, D., Bombi, A. S., Zelli, A., Miranda, M. C., Bornstein, M. H., Tapanya, S., Uribe, L. T., Alampay, L. P., Al-Hassan, S. M., Chang, L., Deater-Deckard, K., Dodge, K. A., Oburu, P., Skinner, A. T., & Sorbring, E. (2016). Positive parenting and children's prosocial behavior in eight countries. *Journal of Child Psychology and Psychiatry, and Allied Disciplines, 57*(7), 824–834. https://doi.org/10.1111/jcpp.12477

Patel, V., Saxena, S., Lund, C., Thornicroft, G., Baingana, F., Bolton, P., Chisholm, D., Collins, P. Y.,

Cooper, J. L., Eaton, J., Herrman, H., Herzallah, M. M., Huang, Y., Jordans, M. J. D., Kleinman, A., Medina-Mora, M. E., Morgan, E., Niaz, U., Omigbodun, O., … UnÜtzer, J. (2018). The Lancet commission on global mental health and sustainable development. *The Lancet, 392*(10157), 1553–1598. https://doi.org/10.1016/S0140-6736(18)31612-X

Patrick, M. E., Terry-McElrath, Y. M., Evans-Polce, R. J., & Schulenberg, J. E. (2020). Negative alcohol-related consequences experienced by young adults in the past 12 months: Differences by college attendance, living situation, binge drinking, and sex. *Addictive Behaviors, 105,* 106320. https://doi.org/10.1016/j.addbeh.2020.106320

Patterson, E. J., Talbert, R. D., & Brown, T. N. (2021). Familial incarceration, social role combinations, and mental health among African American women. *Journal of Marriage and Family, 83*(1), 86–101.

Patterson, G. R. (1982). *Coercive family process* (Vol. 3). Castalia Publishing.

Patterson, G. R. (2016). Coercion theory: The study of change. In T. J. Dishion & J. J. Snyder (Eds.), *The Oxford handbook of coercive relationship dynamics* (pp. 7–22). Oxford University Press.

Patterson, G. R., & Dishion, T. J. (1985). Contributions of families and peers to delinquency*. *Criminology, 23*(1), 63–79. https://doi.org/10.1111/j.1745-9125.1985.tb00326.x

Patton, G. C., Olsson, C. A., Skirbekk, V., Saffery, R., Wlodek, M. E., Azzopardi, P. S., Stonawski, M., Rasmussen, B., Spry, E., Francis, K., Bhutta, Z. A., Kassebaum, N. J., Mokdad, A. H., Murray, C. J. L., Prentice, A. M., Reavley, N., Sheehan, P., Sweeny, K., Viner, R. M., & Sawyer, S. M. (2018). Adolescence and the next generation. *Nature, 554*(7693), 458–466. https://doi.org/10.1038/nature25759

Pauker, K., Apfelbaum, E. P., & Spitzer, B. (2015). When societal norms and social identity collide: The race talk dilemma for racial minority children. *Social Psychological and Personality Science, 6*(8), 887–895. https://doi.org/10.1177/1948550615598379

Pauker, K., Xu, Y., Williams, A., & Biddle, A. M. (2016). Race essentialism and social contextual differences in children's racial stereotyping. *Child Development, 87*(5), 1409–1422.

Paul, S. E., Hatoum, A. S., Fine, J. D., Johnson, E. C., Hansen, I., Karcher, N. R., Moreau, A. L., Bondy, E., Qu, Y., Carter, E. B., Rogers, C. E., Agrawal, A., Barch, D. M., & Bogdan, R. (2021). Associations Between Prenatal Cannabis Exposure and Childhood Outcomes: Results From the ABCD Study. *JAMA Psychiatry, 78*(1), 64–76. https://doi.org/10.1001/jamapsychiatry.2020.2902

Paunesku, D., Walton, G. M., Romero, C., Smith, E. N., Yeager, D. S., & Dweck, C. S. (2015). Mind-set interventions are a scalable treatment for academic underachievement. *Psychological Science, 26*(6), 784–793.

Pawluski, J. L., Lambert, K. G., & Kinsley, C. H. (2016). Neuroplasticity in the maternal hippocampus: Relation to cognition and effects of repeated stress. *Hormones and Behavior, 77,* 86–97. https://doi.org/10.1016/j.yhbeh.2015.06.004

Payne, K. K. (2019). *Young adults in the parental home, 2007 & 2018* (Family Profiles, FP-19-04). National Center for Family & Marriage Research. https://doi.org/10.25035/ncfmr/fp-19-04

Paynter, M. J. (2019). Medication and facilitation of transgender women's lactation. *Journal of Human Lactation, 35*(2), 239–243. https://doi.org/10.1177/0890334419829729

Peahl, A. F., & Howell, J. D. (2021). The evolution of prenatal care delivery guidelines in the United States. *American Journal of Obstetrics and Gynecology, 224*(4), 339–347. https://doi.org/10.1016/j.ajog.2020.12.016

Pearl, M., & Pearl, D. (2015). *To train up a child: Child training for the 21st century.* No Greater Joy Ministries.

Peck, A. J., Berkowitz, D., & Tinkler, J. (2021). Left, right, Black, and White: How White college students talk about their inter- and intra- racial swiping preferences on Tinder. *Sociological Spectrum, 41*(4), 304–321. https://doi.org/10.1080/02732173.2021.1916663

Pedroso-Chaparro, M. S., Márquez-González, M., Vara-García, C., Cabrera, I., Romero-Moreno, R., Barrera-Caballero, S., & Losada, A. (2020). Guilt for perceiving oneself as a burden in healthy older adults. Associated factors. *Aging & Mental Health, 25*(12), 2330–2336. https://doi.org/10.1080/13607863.2020.1822291

Peeters, G., Beard, J. R., Deeg, D. J. H., Tooth, L. R., Brown, W. J., & Dobson, A. J. (2019). Longitudinal associations between lifestyle, socio-economic position and physical functioning in women at different life stages. *European Journal of Ageing, 16*(2), 167–179. https://doi.org/10.1007/s10433-018-0484-1

Pei, Y., & Cong, Z. (2019). Intergenerational ambivalence among Mexican American families. *Journal of Family Studies, 25*(3), 305–318.

Peitzmeier, S. M., Malik, M., Kattari, S. K., Marrow, E., Stephenson, R., Agénor, M., & Reisner, S. L. (2020). Intimate partner violence in transgender populations: Systematic review and meta-analysis of prevalence and correlates. *American Journal of Public Health, 110*(9), e1–e14. https://doi.org/10.2105/AJPH.2020.305774

Pellegrini, A. D., & Smith, P. K. (1998). The development of play during childhood: Forms and possible functions. *Child Psychology and Psychiatry Review, 3*(2), 51–57.

Pellizzoni, S., Apuzzo, G. M., Vita, C. D., Agostini, T., & Passolunghi, M. C. (2019). Evaluation and training of executive functions in genocide survivors: The case of Yazidi children. *Developmental Science, 22*(5), e12798. https://doi.org/10.1111/desc.12798

Penela, E. C., Walker, O. L., Degnan, K. A., Fox, N. A., & Henderson, H. A. (2015). Early behavioral inhibition and emotion regulation: Pathways toward social competence in middle childhood. *Child Development, 86*(4), 1227–1240.

Peng, P., & Kievit, R. A. (2020). The development of academic achievement and cognitive abilities: A bidirectional perspective. *Child Development Perspectives, 14*(1), 15–20.

Pengpid, S., & Peltzer, K. (2019). Sedentary behaviour, physical activity and life satisfaction, happiness and perceived health status in university students from 24 countries. *International Journal of Environmental Research and Public Health, 16*(12), 2084. https://doi.org/10.3390/ijerph16122084

Pennestri, M.-H., Burdayron, R., Kenny, S., Béliveau, M.-J., & Dubois-Comtois, K. (2020). Sleeping through the night or through the nights? *Sleep Medicine, 76*, 98–103. https://doi.org/10.1016/j.sleep.2020.10.005

Pennestri, M.-H., Laganière, C., Bouvette-Turcot, A.-A., Pokhvisneva, I., Steiner, M., Meaney, M. J., Gaudreau, H., & on behalf of the Mavan Research Team. (2018). Uninterrupted infant sleep, development, and maternal mood. *Pediatrics, 142*(6), e20174330.

Penniston, T., Reynolds, K., Pierce, S., Furer, P., & Lionberg, C. (2021). Challenges, supports, and postpartum mental health symptoms among non-breastfeeding mothers. *Archives of Women's Mental Health, 24*(2), 303–312. https://doi.org/10.1007/s00737-020-01059-3

Pepin, J. R., Sayer, L. C., & Casper, L. M. (2018). Marital status and mothers' time use: childcare, housework, leisure, and sleep. *Demography, 55*(1), 107–133. https://doi.org/10.1007/s13524-018-0647-x

Pepping, C. A., & MacDonald, G. (2019). Adult attachment and long-term singlehood. *Current Opinion in Psychology, 25*, 105–109. https://doi.org/10.1016/j.copsyc.2018.04.006

Pereira, A., Busch, A. S., Solares, F., Baier, I., Corvalan, C., & Mericq, V. (2021). Total and central adiposity are associated with age at gonadarche and incidence of precocious gonadarche in boys. *The Journal of Clinical Endocrinology & Metabolism, 106*(5), 1352–1361. https://doi.org/10.1210/clinem/dgab064

Perelli-Harris, B. (2018). Universal or unique? Understanding diversity in partnership experiences across Europe. In N. R. Cahn, J. Carbone, L. F. DeRose, & W. B. Wilcox (Eds.), *Unequal family lives* (pp. 83–104). Cambridge University Press.

Perelli-Harris, B., Hoherz, S., Lappegård, T., & Evans, A. (2019). Mind the "happiness" gap: The relationship between cohabitation, marriage, and subjective well-being in the United Kingdom, Australia, Germany, and Norway. *Demography, 56*(4), 1219–1246. https://doi.org/10.1007/s13524-019-00792-4

Perelli-Harris, B., Mynarska, M., Berghammer, C., Berrington, A., Evans, A., Isupova, O., Keizer, R.,

Klaerner, A., Lappegard, T., & Vignoli, D. (2014). Towards a deeper understanding of cohabitation: Insights from focus group research across Europe and Australia. *Demographic Research, 31*(34), 1043–1078. https://doi.org/10.4054/DemRes.2014.31.34

Perez, E. (2020, July 2). Black leaders started using the term "people of color" in the 1960s. Now it's a major identity. *Washington Post.* https://www.washingtonpost.com/politics/2020/07/02/people-color-are-protesting-heres-what-you-need-know-about-this-new-identity/

Perez, T. (2019, June 4). Earnings peak at different ages for different demographic groups. *Research & Insights.* Payscale. https://www.payscale.com/research-and-insights/peak-earnings/

Perez Rivera, M. B., & Dunsmore, J. C. (2011). Mothers' acculturation and beliefs about emotions, mother–child emotion discourse, and children's emotion understanding in Latino families. *Early Education and Development, 22*(2), 324–354. https://doi.org/10.1080/10409281003702000

Perissinotto, C., Holt-Lunstad, J., Periyakoil, V. S., & Covinsky, K. (2019). A practical approach to assessing and mitigating loneliness and isolation in older adults. *Journal of the American Geriatrics Society, 67*(4), 657–662. https://doi.org/10.1111/jgs.15746

Perlman, D., & Peplau, L. A. (1982). Theoretical approaches to loneliness. In L. A. Peplau & D. Perlman (Eds.), *Loneliness: A sourcebook of current theory, research and therapy* (pp. 123–134). John Wiley & Sons.

Perlman, S. B., Huppert, T. J., & Luna, B. (2016). Functional near-infrared spectroscopy evidence for development of prefrontal engagement in working memory in early through middle childhood. *Cerebral Cortex, 26*(6), 2790–2799. https://doi.org/10.1093/cercor/bhv139

Perna, L. W., & Odle, T. K. (2020, Winter). *Recognizing the reality of working college students.* AAUP. https://www.aaup.org/article/recognizing-reality-working-college-students

Perrin, E. M., Rothman, R. L., Sanders, L. M., Skinner, A. C., Eden, S. K., Shintani, A., Throop, E. M., & Yin, H. S. (2014). Racial and ethnic differences associated with feeding- and activity-related behaviors in infants. *Pediatrics*, peds.2013-1326. https://doi.org/10.1542/peds.2013-1326

Perrin, R., Miller-Perrin, C., & Song, J. (2017). Changing attitudes about spanking using alternative biblical interpretations. *International Journal of Behavioral Development, 41*(4), 514–522. https://doi.org/10.1177/0165025416673295

Perry, A. (2019, September 17). Black teachers matter, for students and communities. *The Hechinger Report.* https://hechingerreport.org/black-teachers-matter-for-students-and-communities/

Perry, D. G., & Pauletti, R. E. (2011). Gender and adolescent development. *Journal of Research on Adolescence, 21*(1), 61–74. https://doi.org/10.1111/j.1532-7795.2010.00715.x

Perry, M., Tan, Z., Chen, J., Weidig, T., Xu, W., & Cong, X. S. (2018). Neonatal pain: Perceptions and current practice. *Critical Care Nursing Clinics of North America, 30*(4), 549–561. https://doi.org/10.1016/j.cnc.2018.07.013

Perry, R. E., Blair, C., & Sullivan, R. M. (2017). Neurobiology of infant attachment: Attachment despite adversity and parental programming of emotionality. *Current Opinion in Psychology, 17*, 1–6. https://doi.org/10.1016/j.copsyc.2017.04.022

Perry, W. G. (1999). *Forms of intellectual and ethical development in the college years: A scheme* (Jossey-Bass Higher and Adult Education Series). Jossey-Bass. http://eric.ed.gov/?id=ED424494

Perszyk, D. R., Lei, R. F., Bodenhausen, G. V., Richeson, J. A., & Waxman, S. R. (2019). Bias at the intersection of race and gender: Evidence from preschool-aged children. *Developmental Science, 22*(3), e12788. https://doi.org/10.1111/desc.12788

Pertea, M., Shumate, A., Pertea, G., Varabyou, A., Breitwieser, F. P., Chang, Y.-C., Madugundu, A. K., Pandey, A., & Salzberg, S. L. (2018). CHESS: A new human gene catalog curated from thousands of large-scale RNA sequencing experiments reveals extensive transcriptional noise. *Genome Biology, 19*(1), 208. https://doi.org/10.1186/s13059-018-1590-2

Pesch, M. H., Levitt, K. J., Danziger, P., & Orringer, K. (2021). Pediatrician's beliefs and practices around rapid infant weight gain: A qualitative study. *Global Pediatric Health, 8*. https://doi.org/10.1177/2333794X21992164

Peskin, S. M. (2017a, July 11). The gentler symptoms of dying. *The New York Times.* https://www.nytimes.com/2017/07/11/well/live/the-gentler-symptoms-of-dying.html

Peskin, S. M. (2017b, June 20). The symptoms of dying. *The New York Times.* https://www.nytimes.com/2017/06/20/well/live/the-symptoms-of-dying.html

Pesu, L., Viljaranta, J., & Aunola, K. (2016). The role of parents' and teachers' beliefs in children's self-concept development. *Journal of Applied Developmental Psychology, 44*, 63–71. https://doi.org/10.1016/j.appdev.2016.03.001

Peter, J., & Valkenburg, P. M. (2016). Adolescents and pornography: A review of 20 years of research. *The Journal of Sex Research, 53*(4–5), 509–531. https://doi.org/10.1080/00224499.2016.1143441

Peters, S. J. (2021). The challenges of achieving equity within public school gifted and talented programs. *Gifted Child Quarterly,* 00169862211002535.

Peters, S. J., Gentry, M., Whiting, G. W., & McBee, M. T. (2019). Who gets served in gifted education? Demographic representation and a call for action. *Gifted Child Quarterly, 63*(4), 273–287.

Petersen, E. E. (2019). Racial/ethnic disparities in pregnancy-related deaths — United States, 2007–2016. *MMWR. Morbidity and Mortality Weekly Report, 68.* https://doi.org/10.15585/mmwr.mm6835a3

Petersen, R. C. (2016). Mild cognitive impairment. *Continuum: Lifelong Learning in Neurology, 22*(2 Dementia), 404–418. https://doi.org/10.1212/CON.0000000000000313

Petersen, R. C., Lopez, O., Armstrong, M. J., Getchius, T. S. D., Ganguli, M., Gloss, D., Gronseth, G. S., Marson, D., Pringsheim, T., Day, G. S., Sager, M., Stevens, J., & Rae-Grant, A. (2018). Practice guideline update summary: Mild cognitive impairment. *Neurology, 90*(3), 126–135. https://doi.org/10.1212/WNL.0000000000004826

Petersen, R. C., Smith, G. E., Waring, S. C., Ivnik, R. J., Kokmen, E., & Tangelos, E. G. (1997). Aging, memory, and mild cognitive impairment. *International Psychogeriatrics, 9*(S1), 65–69.

Peterson, A., Clapp, J., Largent, E. A., Harkins, K., Stites, S. D., & Karlawish, J. (2021). What is paradoxical lucidity? The answer begins with its definition. *Alzheimer's & Dementia.* https://doi.org/10.1002/alz.12424

Peterson, C., Slaughter, V., Moore, C., & Wellman, H. M. (2016). Peer social skills and theory of mind in children with autism, deafness, or typical development. *Developmental Psychology, 52*(1), 46.

Peterson, C. C., & Wellman, H. M. (2019). Longitudinal theory of mind (ToM) development from preschool to adolescence with and without ToM delay. *Child Development, 90*(6), 1917–1934. https://doi.org/10.1111/cdev.13064

Peterson, R. L., Butler, E. A., Ehiri, J. E., Fain, M. J., & Carvajal, S. C. (2020). Mechanisms of racial disparities in cognitive aging: An examination of material and psychosocial well-being. *The Journals of Gerontology: Series B,* gbaa003. https://doi.org/10.1093/geronb/gbaa003

Petitto, L. A., Katerelos, M., Levy, B. G., Gauna, K., Tétreault, K., & Ferraro, V. (2001). Bilingual signed and spoken language acquisition from birth: Implications for the mechanisms underlying early bilingual language acquisition. *Journal of Child Language, 28*(2), 453–496.

Petitto, L. A., Langdon, C., Stone, A., Andriola, D., Kartheiser, G., & Cochran, C. (2016). Visual sign phonology: Insights into human reading and language from a natural soundless phonology. *Wiley Interdisciplinary Reviews: Cognitive Science, 7*(6), 366–381. https://doi.org/10.1002/wcs.1404

Petitto, L. A., & Marentette, P. F. (1991). Babbling in the manual mode: Evidence for the ontogeny of language. *Science, 251*(5000), 1493–1496. https://doi.org/10.1126/science.2006424

Petrosky, E., Blair, J. M., Betz, C. J., Fowler, K. A., Jack, S. P., & Lyons, B. H. (2017). Racial and ethnic differences in homicides of adult women and the role of intimate partner violence — United States, 2003–2014. *Morbidity and Mortality Weekly Report, 66*(28), 741.

Petts, R. J., & Knoester, C. (2020). Are parental relationships improved if fathers take time off of work after the birth of a child? *Social Forces.* https://doi.org/10.1093/sf/soz014

Petts, R. J., Knoester, C., & Waldfogel, J. (2020). Fathers' paternity leave-taking and children's perceptions of father-child relationships in the United States. *Sex Roles, 82*(3), 173–188. https://doi.org/10.1007/s11199-019-01050-y

Peven, K., Day, L. T., Ruysen, H., Tahsina, T., KC, A., Shabani, J., Kong, S., Ameen, S., Basnet, O., Haider, R., Rahman, Q. S., Blencowe, H., Lawn, J. E., Rahman, Q. S., Rahman, A. E., Tahsina, T., Zaman, S. B., Ameen, S., Hossain, T., … EN-BIRTH Study Group. (2021). Stillbirths including intrapartum timing: EN-BIRTH multi-country validation study. *BMC Pregnancy and Childbirth, 21*(1), 226. https://doi.org/10.1186/s12884-020-03238-7

Pew Research Center. (2013). *Living to 120 and beyond: Americans' views on aging, medical advances and radical life extension* (Pew Research Center's Religion & Public Life).

Pew Research Center. (2014). *Global morality.* https://www.pewresearch.org/global/interactives/global-morality/

Pew Research Center. (2018). *The public, the political system and American democracy.*

Pew Research Center. (2019). *Religion and living arrangements around the world.*

Pew Research Center. (2019, November 6). *Views on marriage and cohabitation in the U.S.* Pew Research Center's Social & Demographic Trends Project. https://www.pewsocialtrends.org/2019/11/06/marriage-and-cohabitation-in-the-u-s/

Pezzin, L. E., Pollak, R. A., & Schone, B. S. (2013). Complex families and late-life outcomes among elderly persons: Disability, institutionalization, and longevity. *Journal of Marriage and the Family, 75*(5), 1084–1097.

Pfefferbaum, A., & Sullivan, E. V. (2015). Cross-sectional versus longitudinal estimates of age-related changes in the adult brain: Overlaps and discrepancies. *Neurobiology of Aging, 36*(9), 2563–2567. https://doi.org/10.1016/j.neurobiolaging.2015.05.005

Pfeifer, J. H., & Allen, N. B. (2021). Puberty initiates cascading relationships between neurodevelopmental, social, and internalizing processes across adolescence. *Biological Psychiatry, 89*(2), 99–108. https://doi.org/10.1016/j.biopsych.2020.09.002

Phadke, V. K., Bednarczyk, R. A., & Omer, S. B. (2020). Vaccine refusal and measles outbreaks in the US. *JAMA, 324*(13), 1344–1345. https://doi.org/10.1001/jama.2020.14828

Pham, S., Porta, G., Biernesser, C., Walker Payne, M., Iyengar, S., Melhem, N., & Brent, D. A. (2018). The burden of bereavement: Early-onset depression and impairment in youths bereaved by sudden parental death in a 7-year prospective study. *American Journal of Psychiatry, 175*(9), 887–896. https://doi.org/10.1176/appi.ajp.2018.17070792

Philpott, L. F., Savage, E., Leahy-Warren, P., & FitzGerald, S. (2020). Paternal perinatal depression: A narrative review. *International Journal of Men's Social and Community Health, 3*(1), e1–e15.

Physical Activity Guidelines Advisory Committee. (2018). *2018 physical activity guidelines advisory committee scientific report.* U.S. Department of Health and Human Services. https://health.gov/our-work/physical-activity/current-guidelines/scientific-report

Piaget, J. (1952). *The origins of intelligence in children* (M. Cook, Trans.). W. W. Norton. https://doi.org/10.1037/11494-000

Piaget, J. (1954). *The construction of reality in the child.* Basic Books. https://doi.org/10.1037/11168-000

Piaget, J. (1965). *The moral development.* Free Press.

Piaget, J. (1968). *Six psychological studies* (A. Tenzer, Trans.). Vintage Books.

Piaget, J. (1970). *Science of education and the psychology of the child* (D. Coltman, Trans.). Orion.

Piaget, J. (1971). The theory of stages in cognitive development. In D. R. Green, M. P. Ford, & G. B. Flamer (Eds.), *Measurement and Piaget* (pp. 1–11). McGraw-Hill.

Piaget, J. (2013). *Child's conception of the world: Selected works.* Routledge.

Piaget, J., & Inhelder, B. (1956). *The child's conception of space.* Routledge.

Piaget, J., & Inhelder, B. (1969). *The psychology of the child.* Basic Books.

Piaget, J., & Inhelder, B. (2019). *The psychology of the child* (Reprint ed.). Basic Books.

Piccolo, L. R., Merz, E. C., & Noble, K. G. (2019). School climate is associated with cortical thickness and executive function in children and adolescents. *Developmental Science, 22*(1), e12719. https://doi.org/10.1111/desc.12719

Piedade, S. R., Hutchinson, M. R., Ferreira, D. M., Cristante, A. F., & Maffulli, N. (2021). The management of concussion in sport is not standardized. A systematic review. *Journal of Safety Research, 76*, 262–268. https://doi.org/10.1016/j.jsr.2020.12.013

Piedra, L. M., Andrade, F. C. D., Hernandez, R., Trejo, L., Prohaska, T. R., & Sarkisian, C. A. (2018). Let's walk! Age reattribution and physical activity among older Hispanic/Latino adults: Results from the Caminemos! Randomized trial. *BMC Public Health, 18*(1), 964. https://doi.org/10.1186/s12889-018-5850-6

Piemonte, J. L., Conley, T. D., & Gusakova, S. (2019). Orgasm, gender, and responses to heterosexual casual sex. *Personality and Individual Differences, 151*, 109487. https://doi.org/10.1016/j.paid.2019.06.030

Pierce, C. A., Preston-Hurlburt, P., Dai, Y., Aschner, C. B., Cheshenko, N., Galen, B., Garforth, S. J., Herrera, N. G., Jangra, R. K., Morano, N. C., Orner, E., Sy, S., Chandran, K., Dziura, J., Almo, S. C., Ring, A., Keller, M. J., Herold, K. C., & Herold, B. C. (2020). Immune responses to SARS-CoV-2 infection in hospitalized pediatric and adult patients. *Science Translational Medicine, 12*(564), eabd5487. https://doi.org/10.1126/scitranslmed.abd5487

Pilkauskas, N. V., & Cross, C. (2018). Beyond the nuclear family: Trends in children living in shared households. *Demography, 55*(6), 2283–2297. https://doi.org/10.1007/s13524-018-0719-y

Pilkauskas, N. V., & Dunifon, R. E. (2016). Understanding grandfamilies: Characteristics of grandparents, nonresident parents, and children. *Journal of Marriage and the Family, 78*(3), 623–633. https://doi.org/10.1111/jomf.12291

Pilkington, H., & Pollock, G. (2015). 'Politics are bollocks': Youth, politics and activism in contemporary Europe. *The Sociological Review, 63*, 1–35.

Pillai, R. L. I. (2020). We all need a little TLC: An argument for an increased role of child life services in patient care and medical education. *Hospital Pediatrics, 10*(10), 913–917. https://doi.org/10.1542/hpeds.2020-0119

Pillemer, K., Burnes, D., & MacNeil, A. (2021). Investigating the connection between ageism and elder mistreatment. *Nature Aging, 1*(2), 159–164. https://doi.org/10.1038/s43587-021-00032-8

Pillemer, K., Burnes, D., Riffin, C., & Lachs, M. S. (2016). Elder abuse: Global situation, risk factors, and prevention strategies. *The Gerontologist, 56*(Suppl_2), S194–S205. https://doi.org/10.1093/geront/gnw004

Pillemer, K., Czaja, S. J., & Reid, M. C. (2020). Caring for chronically ill older adults: A view over the last 75 years. *The Journals of Gerontology Series B: Psychological Sciences and Social Sciences, 75*(10), 2165–2169. https://doi.org/10.1093/geronb/gbaa021

Pillemer, K., Suitor, J. J., & Baltar, A. L. (2019). Ambivalence, families and care. *International Journal of Care and Caring, 3*(1), 9–22.

Pinheiro, E. A., & Stika, C. S. (2020). Drugs in pregnancy: Pharmacologic and physiologic changes that affect clinical care. *Seminars in Perinatology, 44*(3), 151221. https://doi.org/10.1016/j.semperi.2020.151221

Pinker, S. (1984). *Language learnability and language development.* Harvard University Press.

Pinquart, M. (2017). Associations of parenting dimensions and styles with externalizing problems of children and adolescents: An updated meta-analysis. *Developmental Psychology, 53*(5), 873.

Pinquart, M., & Ebeling, M. (2020). Students' expected and actual academic achievement: A meta-analysis. *International Journal of Educational Research, 100*, 101524. https://doi.org/10.1016/j.ijer.2019.101524

Pinquart, M., & Kauser, R. (2018). Do the associations of parenting styles with behavior problems and academic achievement vary by culture? Results from a meta-analysis. *Cultural Diversity and Ethnic Minority Psychology, 24*(1), 75.

Pinquart, M., & Pfeiffer, J. P. (2020). Longitudinal associations of the attainment of developmental tasks with psychological symptoms in adolescence: A meta-analysis. *Journal of Research on Adolescence, 30*(S1), 4–14. https://doi.org/10.1111/jora.12462

Pinquart, M., & Sörensen, S. (2011). Spouses, adult children, and children-in-law as caregivers of older adults: A meta-analytic comparison. *Psychology and Aging, 26*(1), 1–14. https://doi.org/10.1037/a0021863

Pinsker, J. (2020, January 27). When does someone become 'old'? *The Atlantic.* https://www.theatlantic.com/family/archive/2020/01/old-people-older-elderly-middle-age/605590/

Pinto, T. M., Samorinha, C., Tendais, I., & Figueiredo, B. (2020). Depression and paternal adjustment and attitudes during the transition to parenthood. *Journal of Reproductive and Infant Psychology, 38*(3), 281–296. https://doi.org/10.1080/02646838.2019.1652256

Piquero, A. R., & Moffitt, T. E. (2010). Life-course persistent offending. In J. R. Adler (Ed.), *Forensic psychology* (pp. 233–254). Willan.

Piras, G. N., Bozzola, M., Bianchin, L., Bernasconi, S., Bona, G., Lorenzoni, G., Buzi, F., Rigon, F., Tonini, G., De Sanctis, V., & Perissinotto, E. (2020). The levelling-off of the secular trend of age at menarche among Italian girls. *Heliyon, 6*(6), e04222. https://doi.org/10.1016/j.heliyon.2020.e04222

Pitcher, M. H., Von Korff, M., Bushnell, M. C., & Porter, L. (2019). Prevalence and profile of high-impact chronic pain in the United States. *The Journal of Pain, 20*(2), 146–160.

Pitkin, W. B. (1932). *Life begins at forty.* Whittlesey House, McGraw-Hill.

Pitsouni, E., Grigoriadis, T., Douskos, A., Kyriakidou, M., Falagas, M. E., & Athanasiou, S. (2018). Efficacy of vaginal therapies alternative to vaginal estrogens on sexual function and orgasm of menopausal women: A systematic review and meta-analysis of randomized controlled trials. *European Journal of Obstetrics & Gynecology and Reproductive Biology, 229*, 45–56.

Pitula, C. E., DePasquale, C. E., Mliner, S. B., & Gunnar, M. R. (2019). Peer problems among postinstitutionalized, internationally adopted children: Relations to hypocortisolism, parenting quality, and ADHD symptoms. *Child Development, 90*(3), e339–e355. https://doi.org/10.1111/cdev.12986

Planalp, E. M., & Braungart-Rieker, J. M. (2015). Trajectories of regulatory behaviors in early infancy: Determinants of infant self-distraction and self-comforting. *Infancy, 20*(2), 129–159. https://doi.org/10.1111/infa.12068

Planalp, E. M., & Goldsmith, H. H. (2020). Observed profiles of infant temperament: Stability, heritability, and associations with parenting. *Child Development, 91*(3), e563–e580. https://doi.org/10.1111/cdev.13277

Planalp, E. M., van Hulle, C., Lemery-Chalfant, K., & Goldsmith, H. H. (2017). Genetic and environmental contributions to the development of positive affect in infancy. *Emotion, 17*(3), 412–420. https://doi.org/10.1037/emo0000238

Plasencia, M. (2018). How aging Latino immigrants cultivate community: The process of engaging, acquiring & reciprocating support. *Innovation in Aging, 2*(Suppl_1), 645–646.

Plesons, M., Patkar, A., Babb, J., Balapitiya, A., Carson, F., Caruso, B. A., Franco, M., Hansen, M. M., Haver, J., Jahangir, A., Kabiru, C. W., Kisangala, E., Phillips-Howard, P., Sharma, A., Sommer, M., & Chandra-Mouli, V. (2021). The state of adolescent menstrual health in low- and middle-income countries and suggestions for future action and research. *Reproductive Health, 18*, 31. https://doi.org/10.1186/s12978-021-01082-2

Plomin, R., & von Stumm, S. (2018). The new genetics of intelligence. *Nature Reviews Genetics, 19*(3), 148.

Poelker, K. E., & Gibbons, J. L. (2019). Sharing and caring: Prosocial behavior in young children around the world. In T. Tulviste, D. L. Best, & J. L. Gibbons (Eds.), *Children's social worlds in cultural context* (pp. 89–102). Springer.

Polenick, C. A., Sherman, C. W., Birditt, K. S., Zarit, S. H., & Kales, H. C. (2019). Purpose in life among family care partners managing dementia: Links to caregiving gains. *Gerontologist, 59*(5), e424–e432.

Pollak, S. D., Camras, L. A., & Cole, P. M. (2019). Progress in understanding the emergence of human emotion. *Developmental Psychology, 55*(9), 1801. https://doi.org/10.1037/dev0000789

Pollitt, A. M., Reczek, C., & Umberson, D. (2020). LGBTQ-parent families and health. In *LGBTQ-parent families: Innovations in research and implications for practice.* Springer Nature.

Pollmann-Schult, M. (2014). Parenthood and life satisfaction: Why don't children make people happy? *Journal of Marriage and Family, 76*(2), 319–336.

Pomarico, N. P. (2021, November 4). The oldest living musicians in 2021. *Best Life.* https://bestlifeonline.com/oldest-living-musicians-2021-news/

Pomerantz, E. M., Ng, F. F. Y., Cheung, C. S. S., & Qu, Y. (2014). Raising happy children who succeed in school: Lessons from China and the United States. *Child Development Perspectives, 8*(2), 71–76.

Pomerantz, E. M., & Wang, Q. (2009). The role of parental control in children's development in Western and East Asian countries. *Current Directions in Psychological Science, 18*(5), 285–289.

Ponce-Garcia, E., Calix, S., Madewell, A. N., Randell, J. A., Perales, L., Bread, D., & Turner, B. (2019). Through childhood relationship with grandparent, enculturation leads to resilience in Native American adults. *Journal of Intergenerational Relationships, 17*(3), 340–352.

Ponitz, C. E. C., McClelland, M. M., Jewkes, A. M., Connor, C. M., Farris, C. L., & Morrison, F. J. (2008). Touch your toes! Developing a direct measure of behavioral regulation in early childhood. *Early Childhood Research Quarterly, 23*(2), 141–158.

Ponnock, A., Muenks, K., Morell, M., Yang, J. S., Gladstone, J. R., & Wigfield, A. (2020). Grit and conscientiousness: Another jangle fallacy. *Journal of Research in Personality, 89*, 104021.

Pont, S. J., Puhl, R., Cook, S. R., Slusser, W., Section on Obesity, and The Obesity Society. (2017). Stigma experienced by children and adolescents with obesity. *Pediatrics, 140*(6), e20173034. https://doi.org/10.1542/peds.2017-3034

Ponticorvo, M., Sica, L. S., Rega, A., & Miglino, O. (2020). On the edge between digital and physical: Materials to enhance creativity in children. An application to atypical development. *Frontiers in Psychology, 11*, 755. https://doi.org/10.3389/fpsyg.2020.00755

Pontzer, H., Yamada, Y., Sagayama, H., Ainslie, P. N., Andersen, L. F., Anderson, L. J., Arab, L., Baddou, I., Bedu-Addo, K., Blaak, E. E., Blanc, S., Bonomi, A. G., Bouten, C. V. C., Bovet, P., Buchowski, M. S., Butte, N. F., Camps, S. G., Close, G. L., Cooper, J. A., ... IAEA DLW Database Consortium§. (2021). Daily energy expenditure through the human life course. *Science, 373*(6556), 808–812. https://www.science.org/doi/abs/10.1126/science.abe5017

Pope, T. (2018). Brain death and the law: Hard cases and legal challenges. *Hastings Center Report, 48*, S46–S48.

Popkin, B. M. (2021). Measuring the nutrition transition and its dynamics. *Public Health Nutrition, 24*(2), 318–320. https://doi.org/10.1017/S136898002000470X

Popova, S., Lange, S., Probst, C., Gmel, G., & Rehm, J. (2017). Estimation of national, regional, and global prevalence of alcohol use during pregnancy and fetal alcohol syndrome: A systematic review and meta-analysis. *The Lancet Global Health, 5*(3), e290–e299. https://doi.org/10.1016/S2214-109X(17)30021-9

Popple, P. R. (2018). *Social work practice and social welfare policy in the United States: A history.* Oxford University Press.

Porter, J. R., Sobel, K., Fox, S. E., Bennett, C. L., & Kientz, J. A. (2017). Filtered out: Disability disclosure practices in online dating communities. *Proceedings of the ACM on Human-Computer Interaction 1 (CSCW)*, 87, 1–13. https://doi.org/10.1145/3134722

Poskett, J. (2019). *Materials of the mind: Phrenology, race, and the global history of science, 1815–1920.* University of Chicago Press.

Posner, M. I., Rothbart, M. K., & Voelker, P. (2016). Developing brain networks of attention. *Current Opinion in Pediatrics, 28*(6), 720–724. https://doi.org/10.1097/MOP.0000000000000413

Post, S. G. (2004). Alzheimer's & grace. *First Things: A Monthly Journal of Religion and Public Life,* (142), 12–15.

Poulin-Dubois, D., Serbin, L. A., Eichstedt, J. A., Sen, M. G., & Beissel, C. F. (2002). Men don't put on make-up: Toddlers' knowledge of the gender stereotyping of household activities. *Social Development, 11*(2), 166–181. https://doi.org/10.1111/1467-9507.00193

Pound, P., Denford, S., Shucksmith, J., Tanton, C., Johnson, A. M., Owen, J., Hutten, R., Mohan, L., Bonell, C., Abraham, C., & Campbell, R. (2017). What is best practice in sex and relationship education? A synthesis of evidence, including stakeholders' views. *BMJ Open, 7*(5), e014791. https://doi.org/10.1136/bmjopen-2016-014791

Povolo, C. A., Reid, J. N., Shariff, S. Z., Welk, B., & Morrow, S. A. (2021). Concussion in adolescence and the risk of multiple sclerosis: A retrospective cohort study. *Multiple Sclerosis Journal, 27*(2), 180–187. https://doi.org/10.1177/1352458520908037

Powell, M. A., Fitzgerald, R. M., Taylor, N., & Graham, A. (2012). *International literature review: Ethical issues in undertaking research with children and young people.* Lismore, NSW: Childwatch International Research Network, Southern Cross University, Centre for Children and Young People, and University of Otago, Centre for Research on Children and Families.

Powell, R. A., Digdon, N., Harris, B., & Smithson, C. (2014). Correcting the record on Watson, Rayner, and Little Albert: Albert Barger as "psychology's lost boy." *American Psychologist, 69*(6), 600.

Powell, R. A., & Schmaltz, R. M. (2020). Did Little Albert actually acquire a conditioned fear of furry animals? What the film evidence tells us. *History of Psychology, 24*(2), 164–181. https://doi.org/10.1037/hop0000176

Pozhitkov, A. E., Neme, R., Domazet-Lošo, T., Leroux, B. G., Soni, S., Tautz, D., & Noble, P. A. (2017). Tracing the dynamics of gene transcripts after organismal death. *Open Biology, 7*(1), 160267.

Pradhan, E., Suzuki, E. M., Martínez, S., Schäferhoff, M., & Jamison, D. T. (2017). The effects of education quantity and quality on child and adult mortality: their magnitude and their value. In D. A. P. Bundy, N. D. Silva, S. Horton, D. T. Jamison, & G. C. Patton (Eds.), *Child and adolescent health and development* (3rd ed., Chap. 30). International Bank for Reconstruction and Development / World Bank.

Prakash, R. S., Voss, M. W., Erickson, K. I., & Kramer, A. F. (2015). Physical activity and cognitive vitality. *Annual Review of Psychology, 66*(1), 769–797. https://doi.org/10.1146/annurev-psych-010814-015249

Pramling Samuelsson, I., Wagner, J. T., & Eriksen Ødegaard, E. (2020). The coronavirus pandemic and lessons learned in preschools in Norway, Sweden and the United States: OMEP policy forum. *International Journal of Early Childhood, 52*(2), 129–144. https://doi.org/10.1007/s13158-020-00267-3

Pratt, M. E., McClelland, M. M., Swanson, J., & Lipscomb, S. T. (2016). Family risk profiles and school readiness: A person-centered approach. *Early Childhood Research Quarterly, 36*, 462–474.

Prenderville, J. A., Kennedy, P. J., Dinan, T. G., & Cryan, J. F. (2015). Adding fuel to the fire: The impact of stress on the ageing brain. *Trends in Neurosciences, 38*(1), 13–25.

Prentice, A. M. (2018). Early life nutritional supplements and later metabolic disease. *The Lancet Global Health, 6*(8), e816–e817. https://doi.org/10.1016/S2214-109X(18)30308-5

Pressman, S. (2017). *Rethinking antipoverty policy.* Edward Elgar Publishing. https://www.elgaronline.com/view/9781784717209.00032.xml

Price-Williams, D., Gordon, W., & Ramirez, M. (1969). Skill and conservation: A study of pottery-making children. *Developmental Psychology, 1*(6p1), 769.

Priest, N., Perry, R., Ferdinand, A., Paradies, Y., & Kelaher, M. (2014). Experiences of racism, racial/ethnic attitudes, motivated fairness and mental health outcomes among primary and secondary school students. *Journal of Youth and Adolescence, 43*(10), 1672–1687. https://doi.org/10.1007/s10964-014-0140-9

Priest, N., Slopen, N., Woolford, S., Philip, J. T., Singer, D., Kauffman, A. D., Mosely, K., Davis, M., Ransome, Y., & Williams, D. (2018). Stereotyping across intersections of race and age: Racial stereotyping among White adults working with children. *PLOS ONE, 13*(9), e0201696. https://doi.org/10.1371/journal.pone.0201696

Priest, N., Walton, J., White, F., Kowal, E., Baker, A., & Paradies, Y. (2014). Understanding the complexities of ethnic-racial socialization processes for both minority and majority groups: A 30-year systematic review. *International Journal of Intercultural Relations, 43*, 139–155. https://doi.org/10.1016/j.ijintrel.2014.08.003

Principi, A., Santini, S., Socci, M., Smeaton, D., Cahill, K. E., Vegeris, S., & Barnes, H. (2018). Retirement plans and active ageing: Perspectives in three countries. *Ageing & Society, 38*(1), 56–82. https://doi.org/10.1017/S0144686X16000866

Prior, E., Lew, R., Hammarberg, K., & Johnson, L. (2019). Fertility facts, figures and future plans: An online survey of university students. *Human Fertility, 22*(4), 283–290. https://doi.org/10.1080/14647273.2018.1482569

Pristavec, T. (2019). The burden and benefits of caregiving: A latent class analysis. *The Gerontologist, 59*(6), 1078–1091. https://doi.org/10.1093/geront/gny022

Profit, J., Gould, J. B., Bennett, M., Goldstein, B. A., Draper, D., Phibbs, C. S., & Lee, H. C. (2017). Racial/ethnic disparity in NICU quality of care delivery. *Pediatrics, 140*(3), e20170918. https://doi.org/10.1542/peds.2017-0918

Protzko, J. (2017). Raising IQ among school-aged children: Five meta-analyses and a review of randomized controlled trials. *Developmental Review, 46*, 81–101. https://doi.org/10.1016/j.dr.2017.05.001

Protzko, J., & Aronson, J. (2016). Context moderates affirmation effects on the ethnic achievement gap. *Social Psychological and Personality Science, 7*(6), 500–507.

Proulx, C. M. (2015). Marital trajectories. In S. K. Whitbourne (Ed.), *The encyclopedia of adulthood and aging* (pp. 1–4). Wiley. https://doi.org/10.1002/9781118521373.wbeaa194

Proulx, C. M., Curl, A. L., & Ermer, A. E. (2018). Longitudinal associations between formal volunteering and cognitive functioning. *The Journals of Gerontology: Series B, 73*(3), 522–531.

Pruchno, R. (2012). Not your mother's old age: Baby boomers at age 65. *The Gerontologist, 52*(2), 149–152. https://doi.org/10.1093/geront/gns038

Prüss-Üstün, A., Wolf, J., Corvalán, C., Bos, R., & Neira, M. (2016). *Preventing disease through healthy environments: A global assessment of the burden of disease from environmental risks.* World Health Organization.

Prüss-Üstün, A., World Health Organization, & Neira, M. (2016). *Preventing disease through healthy environments: A global assessment of the burden of disease from environmental risks.* World Health Organization.

Pryor, F. (2017). Occupational choices of the elderly. *Monthly Labor Review.* U.S. Bureau of Labor Statistics.

Przybylski, A. K. (2019). Digital screen time and pediatric sleep: Evidence from a preregistered cohort study. *The Journal of Pediatrics, 205*, 218–223.e1. https://doi.org/10.1016/j.jpeds.2018.09.054

Pudas, S., Josefsson, M., Rieckmann, A., & Nyberg, L. (2018). Longitudinal evidence for increased functional response in frontal cortex for older adults with hippocampal atrophy and memory decline. *Cerebral Cortex, 28*(3), 936–948. https://doi.org/10.1093/cercor/bhw418

Pugatch, T., & Wilson, N. (2018). Nudging study habits: A field experiment on peer tutoring in higher education. *Economics of Education Review, 62*, 151–161. https://doi.org/10.1016/j.econedurev.2017.11.003

Puhl, R. M., Lessard, L. M., Pearl, R. L., Himmelstein, M. S., & Foster, G. D. (2021). International comparisons of weight stigma: Addressing a void in the field. *International Journal of Obesity, 45*, 1976–1985. https://doi.org/10.1038/s41366-021-00860-z

Pulcini, C. D., Zima, B. T., Kelleher, K. J., Houtrow, A. J. (2017). Poverty and trends in 3 common chronic disorders. *Pediatrics, 139*(3), e20162539.

Puleo, A. (2020, July 22). *Roblox played by over half of kids in America.* Game Rant. https://gamerant.com/roblox-player-count-kids-america/

Pullen Sansfaçon, A., Medico, D., Suerich-Gulick, F., & Temple Newhook, J. (2020). "I knew that I wasn't cis, I knew that, but I didn't know exactly": Gender identity development, expression and affirmation in youth who access gender affirming medical care. *International Journal of Transgender Health, 21*(3), 307–320. https://doi.org/10.1080/26895269.2020.1756551

Puri, N., Coomes, E. A., Haghbayan, H., & Gunaratne, K. (2020). Social media and vaccine hesitancy: New updates for the era of COVID-19 and globalized infectious diseases. *Human Vaccines & Immunotherapeutics, 16*(11), 2586–2593. https://doi.org/10.1080/21645515.2020.1780846

Purpura, D. J., Schmitt, S. A., & Ganley, C. M. (2017). Foundations of mathematics and literacy: The role of executive functioning components. *Journal of Experimental Child Psychology, 153*, 15–34. https://doi.org/10.1016/j.jecp.2016.08.010

Puterman, E., Weiss, J., Hives, B. A., Gemmill, A., Karasek, D., Mendes, W. B., & Rehkopf, D. H. (2020). Predicting mortality from 57 economic, behavioral, social, and psychological factors. *Proceedings of the National Academy of Sciences, 117*(28), 16273–16282. https://doi.org/10.1073/pnas.1918455117

Puterman, E., Weiss, J., Lin, J., Schilf, S., Slusher, A. L., Johansen, K. L., & Epel, E. S. (2018). Aerobic exercise lengthens telomeres and reduces stress in family caregivers: A randomized controlled trial—Curt Richter Award Paper 2018. *Psychoneuroendocrinology, 98*, 245–252.

Putkinen, V., & Saarikivi, K. (2018). Neural correlates of enhanced executive functions: Is less more? *Annals of the New York Academy of Sciences.* https://doi.org/10.1111/nyas.13645

Putnam, H., & Walsh, K. (2021). *Knowledge of early reading—state teacher preparation and licensure requirements.* National Center for Teacher Quality. https://www.nctq.org/publications/Knowledge-of-Early-Reading----Excerpted-from-State-of-the-States-2021:-Teacher-Preparation-Policy

Putnam, R. D. (2000). Bowling alone: America's declining social capital. In L. Crothers & C. Lockhart (Eds.), *Culture and politics: A reader* (pp. 223–234). Palgrave Macmillan US. https://doi.org/10.1007/978-1-349-62965-7_12

Putnam, S. P., Garstein, M. A., & Rothbart, M. K. (2019). Historical background of the study of temperament and new perspectives on assessment. In R. DelCarmen-Wiggins & A. S. Carter (Eds.), *The Oxford handbook of infant, toddler, and preschool mental health assessment* (pp. 131–156). Oxford University Press.

Putnick, D. L., Bornstein, M. H., Lansford, J. E., Malone, P. S., Pastorelli, C., Skinner, A. T., Sorbring, E., Tapanya, S., Tirado, L. M. U., Zelli, A., Alampay, L. P., Al-Hassan, S. M., Bacchini, D., Bombi, A. S., Chang, L., Deater-Deckard, K., Di Giunta, L., Dodge, K. A., & Oburu, P. (2015). Perceived mother and father acceptance-rejection predict four unique aspects of child adjustment across nine countries. *Journal of Child Psychology and Psychiatry, 56*(8), 923–932.

Putnick, D. L., Hahn, C. S., Hendricks, C., Suwalsky, J. T., & Bornstein, M. H. (2020). Child, mother, father, and teacher beliefs about child academic competence: Predicting math and reading performance in European American adolescents. *Journal of Research on Adolescence, 30*, 298–314.

Puvill, T., Lindenberg, J., de Craen, A. J. M., Slaets, J. P. J., & Westendorp, R. G. J. (2016). Impact of physical and mental health on life satisfaction in old age: A population based observational study. *BMC Geriatrics, 16*(1), 194. https://doi.org/10.1186/s12877-016-0365-4

Puzzanchera, C. (2021). *Juvenile arrests, 2019* (Juvenile Justice Statistics, National Report Series Bulletin). U.S. Department of Justice.

Pynn, S. R., Neely, K. C., Ingstrup, M. S., Spence, J. C., Carson, V., Robinson, Z., & Holt, N. L. (2019). An intergenerational qualitative study of the good parenting ideal and active free play during middle childhood. *Children's Geographies, 17*(3), 266–277. https://doi.org/10.1080/14733285.2018.1492702

Pyra, E., & Schwarz, W. (2019). Puberty: Normal, delayed, and precocious. In S. Llahana, C. Follin, C. Yedinak, & A. Grossman (Eds.), *Advanced practice in endocrinology nursing* (pp. 63–84). Springer International Publishing. https://doi.org/10.1007/978-3-319-99817-6_4

Qaseem, A., Kansagara, D., Forciea, M. A., Cooke, M., & Denberg, T. D. (2016). Management of chronic insomnia disorder in adults: A clinical practice guideline from the American College of Physicians. *Annals of Internal Medicine, 165*(2), 125–133.

Qasim, K., & Carson, J. (2020). Does post-traumatic growth follow parental death in adulthood? An empirical investigation. *OMEGA—Journal of Death and Dying.*

Qi, H., & Roberts, K. P. (2019). Cultural influences on the development of children's memory and cognition. In J. B. Benson (Ed.), *Advances in child development and behavior* (Vol. 56, pp. 183–225). JAI. https://doi.org/10.1016/bs.acdb.2018.11.005

Qian, M., Heyman, G. D., Quinn, P. C., Messi, F. A., Fu, G., & Lee, K. (2021). Age-related differences in implicit and explicit racial biases in Cameroonians. *Developmental Psychology, 57*(3), 386–396. https://doi.org/10.1037/dev0001149

Qian, M. K., Quinn, P. C., Heyman, G. D., Pascalis, O., Fu, G., & Lee, K. (2017). Perceptual individuation training (but not mere exposure) reduces implicit racial bias in preschool children. *Developmental Psychology, 53*(5), 845–859. https://doi.org/10.1037/dev0000290

Qian, M. K., Quinn, P. C., Heyman, G. D., Pascalis, O., Fu, G., & Lee, K. (2019). A long-term effect of perceptual individuation training on reducing implicit racial bias in preschool children. *Child Development, 90*(3), e290–e305. https://doi.org/10.1111/cdev.12971

Qian, Y., Chen, W., & Guo, B. (2020). Zing-Yang Kuo and behavior epigenesis based on animal experiments. *Protein & Cell, 11*(6), 387–390. https://doi.org/10.1007/s13238-018-0516-9

Qiao, D. P., & Xie, Q. W. (2017). Public perceptions of child physical abuse in Beijing. *Child & Family Social Work, 22*(1), 213–225.

Qiu, C., & Fratiglioni, L. (2018). Aging without dementia is achievable: Current evidence from epidemiological research. *Journal of Alzheimer's Disease, 62*(3), 933–942.

Qu, Y., Pomerantz, E. M., Wang, M., Cheung, C., & Cimpian, A. (2016). Conceptions of adolescence: Implications for differences in engagement in school over early adolescence in the United States and China. *Journal of Youth and Adolescence, 45*(7), 1512–1526. https://doi.org/10.1007/s10964-016-0492-4

Qu, Y., Pomerantz, E. M., & Wu, G. (2020a). Countering youth's negative stereotypes of teens fosters constructive behavior. *Child Development, 91*(1), 197–213. https://doi.org/10.1111/cdev.13156

Qu, Y., Rompilla, D. B., Wang, Q., & Ng, F. F.-Y. (2020b). Youth's negative stereotypes of teen emotionality: Reciprocal relations with emotional functioning in Hong Kong and Mainland China. *Journal of Youth and Adolescence, 49*(10), 2003–2019. https://doi.org/10.1007/s10964-020-01303-0

Qualter, P., Vanhalst, J., Harris, R., Van Roekel, E., Lodder, G., Bangee, M., & Verhagen, M. (2015). Loneliness across the life span. *Perspectives on Psychological Science, 10*(2), 250–264.

Querido, J. G., Warner, T. D., & Eyberg, S. M. (2002). Parenting styles and child behavior in African American families of preschool children. *Journal of Clinical Child and Adolescent Psychology, 31*(2), 272–277.

Quevedo, K., Benning, S. D., Gunnar, M. R., & Dahl, R. E. (2009). The onset of puberty: Effects on the psychophysiology of defensive and appetitive motivation. *Development and Psychopathology, 21*(1), 27–45. https://doi.org/10.1017/S0954579409000030

Quillen, E. E., Norton, H. L., Parra, E. J., Lona-Durazo, F., Ang, K. C., Illiescu, F. M., Pearson, L. N., Shriver, M. D., Lasisi, T., Gokcumen, O., Starr, I., Lin, Y.-L., Martin, A. R., & Jablonski, N. G. (2019). Shades of complexity: New perspectives on the evolution and genetic architecture of human skin. *American Journal of Physical Anthropology, 168*(S67), 4–26. https://doi.org/10.1002/ajpa.23737

Quillian, L., Pager, D., Hexel, O., & Midtbøen, A. H. (2017). Meta-analysis of field experiments shows no change in racial discrimination in hiring over time. *Proceedings of the National Academy of Sciences, 114*(41), 10870–10875. https://doi.org/10.1073/pnas.1706255114

Quinlan, E. B., Barker, E. D., Luo, Q., Banaschewski, T., Bokde, A. L., Bromberg, U., Büchel, C., Desrivières, S., Flor, H., Frouin, V., Garavan, H., Chaarani, B., Gowland, P., Heinz, A., Brühl, R., Martinot, J.-L., Martinot, M.-L. P., Nees, F., Orfanos, D. P., Paus, T., … Schumann, G. (2020). Peer victimization and its impact on adolescent brain development and psychopathology. *Molecular Psychiatry, 25*(11), 3066–3076.

Quist, M., Kaciroti, N., Poehlmann-Tynan, J., Weeks, H. M., Asta, K., Singh, P., & Shah, P. E. (2019). Interactive effects of infant gestational age and infant fussiness on the risk of maternal depressive symptoms in a nationally representative sample. *Academic Pediatrics, 19*(8), 917–924. https://doi.org/10.1016/j.acap.2019.02.015

Rachwani, J., Herzberg, O., Golenia, L., & Adolph, K. E. (2019). Postural, visual, and manual coordination in the development of prehension. *Child Development, 90*(5), 1559–1568. https://doi.org/10.1111/cdev.13282

Rachwani, J., Tamis-LeMonda, C. S., Lockman, J. J., Karasik, L. B., & Adolph, K. E. (2020). Learning the designed actions of everyday objects. *Journal of Experimental Psychology. General, 149*(1), 67–78. https://doi.org/10.1037/xge0000631

Radesky, J. (2019). Mobile media and parent–child interaction. In C. Donohue (Ed.), *Exploring key issues in early childhood and technology: Evolving perspectives and innovative approaches* (pp. 85–90). Routledge.

Radler, B. T., Rigotti, A., & Ryff, C. (2018) Persistently high psychological well-being predicts better HDL cholesterol and triglyceride levels: Findings from the midlife in the U.S. (MIDUS) longitudinal study. *Lipids in Health and Disease, 17*(1), 1. https://doi.org/10.1186/s12944-017-0646-8

Radović-Marković, M. (2013). An aging workforce: Employment opportunities and obstacles. *Cadmus, 1*(6), 142–155.

Radwan, C. M. (2019). Toxic metals detected in nearly all baby foods. *Contemporary Pediatrics, 36*(12), 14.

Rae, J. R., Gülgöz, S., Durwood, L., DeMeules, M., Lowe, R., Lindquist, G., & Olson, K. R. (2019). Predicting early-childhood gender transitions. *Psychological Science, 30*(5), 669–681. https://doi.org/10.1177/0956797619830649

Raeff, C. (2016). *Exploring the dynamics of human development: An integrative approach.* Oxford University Press.

Raeff, C., Greenfield, P. M., & Quiroz, B. (2000). Conceptualizing interpersonal relationships in the cultural contexts of individualism and collectivism. *New Directions for Child and Adolescent Development, 2000*(87), 59–74. https://doi.org/10.1002/cd.23220008706

Raffaelli, M., Kang, H., & Guarini, T. (2012). Exploring the immigrant paradox in adolescent sexuality: An ecological perspective. In C. G. Coll & A. K. Marks (Eds.), *The immigrant paradox in children and adolescents: Is becoming American a developmental risk?* (pp. 109–134). American Psychological Association. https://doi.org/10.1037/13094-005

Rafferty, J., Committee on Psychosocial Aspects of Child and Family Health, Committee on Adolescence, & Section on Lesbian, Gay, Bisexual, and Transgender Health and Wellness. (2018). Ensuring comprehensive care and support for transgender and gender-diverse children and adolescents. *Pediatrics, 142*(4), e20182162. https://doi.org/10.1542/peds.2018-2162

Raffington, L., Belsky, D. W., Kothari, M., Malanchini, M., Tucker-Drob, E. M., & Harden, K. P. (2021). Socioeconomic disadvantage and the pace of biological aging in children. *Pediatrics, 147*(6). https://doi.org/10.1542/peds.2020-024406

Rahimi-Ardabili, H., Reynolds, R., Vartanian, L. R., McLeod, L. V. D., & Zwar, N. (2018). A systematic review of the efficacy of interventions that aim to increase self-compassion on nutrition habits, eating behaviours, body weight and body image. *Mindfulness, 9*(2), 388–400. https://doi.org/10.1007/s12671-017-0804-0

Rahimzadeh, A. (2020). Fraternal polyandry and land ownership in Kinnaur, Western Himalaya. *Human Ecology, 48*(5), 573–584. https://doi.org/10.1007/s10745-020-00181-1

Raj, K., & Horvath, S. (2020). Current perspectives on the cellular and molecular features of epigenetic ageing. *Experimental Biology and Medicine, 245*(17), 1532–1542. https://doi.org/10.1177/1535370220918329

Raley, R. K., & Sweeney, M. M. (2020). Divorce, repartnering, and stepfamilies: A decade in review. *Journal of Marriage and Family, 82*(1), 81–99.

Raley, R. K., Weiss, I., Reynolds, R., & Cavanagh, S. E. (2019). Estimating children's household instability between birth and age 18 using longitudinal household roster data. *Demography, 56*(5), 1957–1973. https://doi.org/10.1007/s13524-019-00806-1

Ramey, D. M. (2015). The social structure of criminalized and medicalized school discipline. *Sociology of Education, 88*(3), 181–201.

Ramírez, N. F., & Kuhl, P. K. (2016). *Bilingual language learning in children.* University of Washington, Institute for Learning and Brain Sciences.

Ramírez, N. F., Lytle, S. R., & Kuhl, P. K. (2020). Parent coaching increases conversational turns and advances infant language development. *Proceedings of the National Academy of Sciences, 117*(7), 3484–3491. https://doi.org/10.1073/pnas.1921653117

Randall, A. K., & Bodenmann, G. (2009). The role of stress on close relationships and marital satisfaction. *Clinical Psychology Review, 29*(2), 105–115.

Ranzini, G., & Rosenbaum, J. E. (2020). It's a match (?): Tinder usage and attitudes toward interracial dating. *Communication Research Reports, 37*(1–2), 44–54. https://doi.org/10.1080/08824096.2020.1748001

Rao, N., & Stewart, S. M. (1999). Cultural influences on sharer and recipient behavior: Sharing in Chinese and Indian preschool children. *Journal of Cross-Cultural Psychology, 30*(2), 219–241.

Rao, W.-W., Zong, Q.-Q., Zhang, J.-W., An, F.-R., Jackson, T., Ungvari, G. S., Xiang, Y., Su, Y.-Y., D'Arcy, C., & Xiang, Y.-T. (2020). Obesity increases the risk of depression in children and adolescents: Results from a systematic review and meta-analysis. *Journal of Affective Disorders, 267*, 78–85. https://doi.org/10.1016/j.jad.2020.01.154

Rapee, R. M., Oar, E. L., Johnco, C. J., Forbes, M. K., Fardouly, J., Magson, N. R., & Richardson, C. E. (2019). Adolescent development and risk for the onset of social-emotional disorders: A review and conceptual model. *Behaviour Research and Therapy, 123*, 103501. https://doi.org/10.1016/j.brat.2019.103501

Raposa, E. B., Rhodes, J., Stams, G. J. J., Card, N., Burton, S., Schwartz, S., Yovienne-Sykes, L. Y., Kanchewa, S., Kupersmidt, J., & Hussain, S. (2019). The effects of youth mentoring programs: A meta-analysis of outcome studies. *Journal of Youth and Adolescence, 48*(3), 423–443.

Rapp, I. (2018). Partnership formation in young and older age. *Journal of Family Issues, 39*(13), 3363–3390. https://doi.org/10.1177/0192513X18783469

Rash, J. A., Kavanagh, V. A., & Garland, S. N. (2019). A meta-analysis of mindfulness-based therapies for insomnia and sleep disturbance: Moving towards processes of change. *Sleep Medicine Clinics, 14*(2), 209–233.

Rasmussen, B., Maharaj, N., Sheehan, P., & Friedman, H. S. (2019). Evaluating the employment benefits of education and targeted interventions to reduce child marriage. *Journal of Adolescent Health, 65*(1), S16–S24.

Rasmussen, E. E., Punyanunt-Carter, N., LaFreniere, J. R., Norman, M. S., & Kimball, T. G. (2020). The serially mediated relationship between emerging adults' social media use and mental well-being. *Computers in Human Behavior, 102*, 206–213. https://doi.org/10.1016/j.chb.2019.08.019

Rasmussen, S. A., & Jamieson, D. J. (2021). Pregnancy, postpartum care, and COVID-19 vaccination in 2021. *JAMA, 325*(11), 1099–1100.

Raspa, M., Levis, D. M., Kish-Doto, J., Wallace, I., Rice, C., Barger, B., Green, K. K., & Wolf, R. B. (2015). Examining parents' experiences and information needs regarding early identification of developmental delays: Qualitative research to inform a public health campaign. *Journal of Developmental & Behavioral Pediatrics, 36*(8), 575–585. https://doi.org/10.1097/DBP.0000000000000205

Ratey, J. H., & Hagerman, E. (2013). *Spark: The revolutionary new science of exercise and the brain.* Little, Brown. https://www.amazon.com/Spark-Revolutionary-Science-Exercise-Brain/dp/0316113514

Rauer, A. J., Pettit, G. S., Lansford, J. E., Bates, J. E., & Dodge, K. A. (2013). Romantic relationship patterns in young adulthood and their developmental antecedents. *Developmental Psychology, 49*(11), 2159–2171. https://doi.org/10.1037/a0031845

Raup, J., & Myers, J. E. (1989). The empty nest syndrome: Myth or reality? *Journal of Counseling and Development, 68*(2), 180–183.

Raval, V. V., & Green, J. H. (2018). Children's developing emotional competence in a global context. In P. A. Kumar, S. T. George, & N. T. Sudhesh (Eds.) *Character strength development: Perspectives from positive psychology* (pp. 160–178). SAGE.

Ravindran, N., Berry, D., & McElwain, N. L. (2019). Dynamic bidirectional associations in negative behavior: Mother–toddler interaction during a snack delay. *Developmental Psychology, 55*(6), 1191–1198. https://doi.org/10.1037/dev0000703

Ravindran, N., Hu, Y., McElwain, N. L., & Telzer, E. H. (2020). Dynamics of mother–adolescent and father–adolescent autonomy and control during a conflict discussion task. *Journal of Family Psychology, 34*(3), 312–321. https://doi.org/10.1037/fam0000588

Raymo, J. M., Pike, I., & Liang, J. (2019). A new look at the living arrangements of older Americans using multistate life tables. *The Journals of Gerontology Series B: Psychological Sciences and Social Sciences, 74*(7), e84–e96. https://doi.org/10.1093/geronb/gby099

Reardon, S. F., & Portilla, X. A. (2016). Recent trends in income, racial, and ethnic school readiness gaps at kindergarten entry. *AERA Open, 2*(3), 2332858416657343.

Reardon, S., Weathers, E. S., Fahle, E. M., Jang, H., & Kalogrides, D. (2019). *Is separate still unequal? New evidence on school segregation and racial academic achievement gaps.* The Educational Opportunity Project at Stanford University. https://edopportunity.org

Reas, E. T., Laughlin, G. A., Bergstrom, J., Kritz-Silverstein, D., Barrett-Connor, E., & McEvoy, L. K. (2019). Effects of APOE on cognitive aging in community-dwelling older adults. *Neuropsychology, 33*(3), 406–416. https://doi.org/10.1037/neu0000501

Rebelo, M. A. B., Vieira, J. M. R., Pereira, J. V., Quadros, L. N., & Vettore, M. V. (2019). Does oral health influence school performance and school attendance? A systematic review and meta-analysis. *International Journal of Paediatric Dentistry, 29*(2), 138–148. https://doi.org/10.1111/ipd.12441

Rebelo-Marques, A., De Sousa Lages, A., Andrade, R., Ribeiro, C. F., Mota-Pinto, A., Carrilho, F., & Espregueira-Mendes, J. (2018). Aging hallmarks: The benefits of physical exercise. *Frontiers in Endocrinology, 9*, 258.

Reckrey, J. M., Tsui, E. K., Morrison, R. S., Geduldig, E. T., Stone, R. I., Ornstein, K. A., & Federman, A. D. (2019). Beyond functional support: The range of health-related tasks performed in the home by paid caregivers in New York. *Health Affairs, 38*(6), 927–933. https://doi.org/10.1377/hlthaff.2019.00004

Recksiedler, C., & Settersten, R. A. S., Jr. (2020). How young adults' appraisals of work and family goals changed over the Great Recession: An examination of gender and rural-urban differences. *Journal of Youth Studies, 23*(9), 1217–1233. https://doi.org/10.1080/13676261.2019.1663339

Reddy, A. (2007). The eugenic origins of IQ testing: Implications for post-Atkins litigation. *DePaul Law Review, 57*, 667.

Reddy, V. (2000). Coyness in early infancy. *Developmental Science, 3*(2), 186–192.

Reddy, V. (2019a). Humour as culture in infancy. In E. Loizou & S. L. Recchia (Eds.), *Research on young children's humor: Theoretical and practical implications for early childhood education* (pp. 187–201). Springer International Publishing. https://doi.org/10.1007/978-3-030-15202-4_11

Reddy, V. (2019b). Meeting infant affect. *Developmental Psychology, 55*(9), 2020–2024. https://doi.org/10.1037/dev0000773

Redelmeier, D. A., & Raza, S. (2016). Concussions and repercussions. *PLOS Medicine, 13*(8), e1002104. https://doi.org/10.1371/journal.pmed.1002104

Redline, S. (2017). Screening for obstructive sleep apnea: Implications for the sleep health of the population. *JAMA, 317*(4), 368–370. https://doi.org/10.1001/jama.2016.18630

Redwine, L. S., Pung, M. A., Wilson, K., Bangen, K. J., Delano-Wood, L., & Hurwitz, B. (2020). An exploratory randomized sub-study of light-to-moderate intensity exercise on cognitive function, depression symptoms and inflammation in older adults with heart failure. *Journal of Psychosomatic Research, 128*, 109883.

Reed, A. E., Chan, L., & Mikels, J. A. (2014). Meta-analysis of the age-related positivity effect: Age differences in preferences for positive over negative information. *Psychology and Aging, 29*(1), 1.

Reese, E., & Neha, T. (2015). Let's kōrero (talk): The practice and functions of reminiscing among mothers and children in Māori families. *Memory, 23*(1), 99–110. https://doi.org/10.1080/09658211.2014.929705

Reeskens, T., & Vandecasteele, L. (2017). Hard times and European youth: The effect of economic insecurity on human values, social attitudes and well-being. *International Journal of Psychology, 52*(1), 19–27.

Reetzke, R., Xie, Z., Llanos, F., & Chandrasekaran, B. (2018). Tracing the trajectory of sensory plasticity across different stages of speech learning in adulthood. *Current Biology, 28*(9), 1419–1427.e4. https://doi.org/10.1016/j.cub.2018.03.026

Reeves, R. V., Buckner, E., & Smith, E. (2021, January 12). *The unreported gender gap in high school graduation rates.* Brookings. https://www.brookings.edu/blog/up-front/2021/01/12/the-unreported-gender-gap-in-high-school-graduation-rates/

Reeves, R. V., & Smith, E. (2021). *The male college crisis is not just in enrollment, but completion.* Brookings Institution.

Regalado, A. (2018, February 12). 2017 was the year consumer DNA testing blew up. *Technology Review.* https://www.technologyreview.com/s/610233/2017-was-the-year-consumer-dna-testing-blew-up

Rehkopf, D. H., Furstenberg, F. F., & Rowe, J. W. (2019). Trends in mental and physical health-related quality of life in low-income older persons in the United States, 2003 to 2017. *JAMA Network Open, 2*(12), e1917868. https://doi.org/10.1001/jamanetworkopen.2019.17868

Rehm, J., & Shield, K. D. (2019). Global burden of disease and the impact of mental and addictive disorders. *Current Psychiatry Reports, 21*(2), 1–7. https://doi.org/10.1007/s11920-019-0997-0

Reich, A. J., Claunch, K. D., Verdeja, M. A., Dungan, M. T., Anderson, S., Clayton, C. K., Goates, M. C., & Thacker, E. L. (2020). What does "successful aging" mean to you?—Systematic review and cross-cultural comparison of lay perspectives of older adults in 13 countries, 2010–2020. *Journal of Cross-Cultural Gerontology, 35*(4), 455–478. https://doi.org/10.1007/s10823-020-09416-6

Reich, D. (2018, March 23). Opinion | How genetics is changing our understanding of "race." *The New York Times.* https://www.nytimes.com/2018/03/23/opinion/sunday/genetics-race.html

Reid, J. L., Lynn Kagan, S., Brooks-Gunn, J., & Melvin, S. A. (2021). Promoting quality in programs for infants and toddlers: Comparing the family child care and center-based teaching workforce. *Children and Youth Services Review, 122*, 105890. https://doi.org/10.1016/j.childyouth.2020.105890

Reid, V. L., McDonald, R., Nwosu, A. C., Mason, S. R., Probert, C., Ellershaw, J. E., & Coyle, S. (2017). A systematically structured review of biomarkers of dying in cancer patients in the last months of life: An exploration of the biology of dying. *PLOS ONE, 12*(4), e0175123. https://doi.org/10.1371/journal.pone.0175123

Reid, V. M., & Dunn, K. (2021). The fetal origins of human psychological development. *Current Directions in Psychological Science,* 0963721420984419. https://doi.org/10.1177/0963721420984419

Reid, V. M., Dunn, K., Young, R. J., Amu, J., Donovan, T., & Reissland, N. (2017). The human fetus preferentially engages with face-like visual stimuli. *Current Biology, 27*(12), 1825–1828.e3. https://doi.org/10.1016/j.cub.2017.05.044

Reigal, R. E., Moral-Campillo, L., Morillo-Baro, J. P., Juarez-Ruiz de Mier, R., Hernández-Mendo, A., & Morales-Sánchez, V. (2020). Physical exercise, fitness, cognitive functioning, and psychosocial variables in an adolescent sample. *International Journal of Environmental Research and Public Health, 17*(3), 1100.

Reinka, M. A., Quinn, D. M., & Puhl, R. M. (2021). Examining the relationship between weight controllability beliefs and eating behaviors: The role of internalized weight stigma and BMI. *Appetite, 164,* 105257. https://doi.org/10.1016/j.appet.2021.105257

Reis, H. T., & Aron, A. (2008). Love: What is it, why does it matter, and how does it operate? *Perspectives on Psychological Science, 3*(1), 80–86. https://doi.org/10.1111/j.1745-6916.2008.00065.x

Reis, H. T., Aron, A., Clark, M. S., & Finkel, E. J. (2013). Ellen Berscheid, Elaine Hatfield, and the emergence of relationship science. *Perspectives on Psychological Science, 8*(5), 558–572.

Reissland, N., Francis, B., & Buttanshaw, L. (2016). The Fetal Observable Movement System (FOMS). In N. Reissland & B. S. Kisilevsky (Eds.), *Fetal development: Research on brain and behavior, environmental influences, and emerging technologies* (pp. 153–176). Springer International Publishing. https://doi.org/10.1007/978-3-319-22023-9_9

Reissland, N., & Kisilevsky, B. S. (Eds.). (2016). *Fetal development: Research on brain and behavior, environmental influences, and emerging technologies.* Springer International Publishing.

Reitz, A. K., & Staudinger, U. M. (2017). Getting older, getting better? Toward understanding positive personality development across adulthood. In J. Specht (Ed.), *Personality development across the lifespan* (pp. 219–241). Academic Press. https://doi.org/10.1016/B978-0-12-804674-6.00014-4

Reitz, S., Kluetsch, R., Niedtfeld, I., Knorz, T., Lis, S., Paret, C., & Schmahl, C. (2015). Incision and stress regulation in borderline personality disorder: Neurobiological mechanisms of self-injurious behaviour. *The British Journal of Psychiatry, 207*(2), 165–172.

Rende, R. (2015). The developmental significance of chores: Then and now. *The Brown University Child and Adolescent Behavior Letter, 31*(1), 1–7.

Rentzou, K., Slutsky, R., Tuul, M., Gol-Guven, M., Kragh-Müller, G., Foerch, D. F., & Paz-Albo, J. (2019). Preschool teachers' conceptualizations and uses of play across eight countries. *Early Childhood Education Journal, 47*(1), 1–14.

Rescorla, L. A. (2019). Assessment of language in young children. In R. DelCarmen-Wiggins & A. S. Carter (Eds.), *The Oxford handbook of infant, toddler, and preschool mental health assessment* (2nd ed., p. 315). Oxford University Press.

Retznik, L., Wienholz, S., Seidel, A., Pantenburg, B., Conrad, I., Michel, M., & Riedel-Heller, S. (2017). Relationship status: Single? Young adults with visual, hearing, or physical disability and their experiences with partnership and sexuality. *Sexuality and Disability, 35.* https://doi.org/10.1007/s11195-017-9497-5

Reuter, P.-G., Agostinucci, J.-M., Bertrand, P., Gonzalez, G., De Stefano, C., Hennequin, B., Nadiras, P., Biens, D., Hubert, H., Gueugniaud, P.-Y., Adnet, F., & Lapostolle, F. (2017). Prevalence of advance directives and impact on advanced life support in out-of-hospital cardiac arrest victims. *Resuscitation, 116,* 105–108. https://doi.org/10.1016/j.resuscitation.2017.03.015

Rex, S. M., Kopetsky, A., Bodt, B., & Robson, S. M. (2021). Relationships among the physical and social home food environments, dietary intake, and diet quality in mothers and children. *Journal of the Academy of Nutrition and Dietetics.* https://doi.org/10.1016/j.jand.2021.03.008

Rex-Lear, M., Jensen-Campbell, L. A., & Lee, S. (2019). Young and biased: Children's perceptions of overweight peers. *Journal of Applied Biobehavioral Research, 24*(3), e12161. https://doi.org/10.1111/jabr.12161

Reygan, F., & Henderson, N. (2019). All bad? Experiences of aging among LGBT elders in South Africa. *The International Journal of Aging and Human Development, 88*(4), 405–421.

Reyna, V. F., Estrada, S. M., DeMarinis, J. A., Myers, R. M., Stanisz, J. M., & Mills, B. A. (2011). Neurobiological and memory models of risky decision making in adolescents versus young adults. *Journal of Experimental Psychology: Learning, Memory, and Cognition, 37*(5), 1125–1142. http://dx.doi.org/10.1037/a0023943

Reyna, V. F., & Panagiotopoulos, C. (2020). Morals, money, and risk taking from childhood to adulthood: The neurodevelopmental framework of fuzzy-trace theory. In J. Decety (Ed.), *The social brain: A developmental perspective.* MIT Press.

Reynolds, J. E., Grohs, M. N., Dewey, D., & Lebel, C. (2019). Global and regional white matter development in early childhood. *NeuroImage, 196,* 49–58. https://doi.org/10.1016/j.neuroimage.2019.04.004

Reynolds, K., Pietrzak, R. H., El-Gabalawy, R., Mackenzie, C. S., & Sareen, J. (2015). Prevalence of psychiatric disorders in U.S. older adults: Findings from a nationally representative survey. *World Psychiatry, 14*(1), 74–81. https://doi.org/10.1002/wps.20193

Reynolds, L., & Brown, S. L. (2020). *Age variation in cohabitation, 2018* (Family Profile FP-20-12). National Center for Family & Marriage Research @ Bowling Green State University.

Rhodes, M., & Baron, A. (2019). The development of social categorization. *Annual Review of Developmental Psychology, 1*(1), 359–386. https://doi.org/10.1146/annurev-devpsych-121318-084824

Ribot, K. M., Hoff, E., & Burridge, A. (2018). Language use contributes to expressive language growth: Evidence from bilingual children. *Child Development, 89*(3), 929–940. https://doi.org/10.1111/cdev.12770

Rich, J. (2014). *What do field experiments of discrimination in markets tell us? A meta-analysis of studies conducted since 2000* (SSRN Scholarly Paper ID 2517887). Social Science Research Network. https://papers.ssrn.com/abstract=2517887

Richardson, D., & Hiu, C. F. (2018). *Developing a global indicator on bullying of school-aged children* (Innocenti Working Papers). UNICEF. https://www.un-ilibrary.org/content/papers/25206796/160

Richardson, S. S., Daniels, C. R., Gillman, M. W., Golden, J., Kukla, R., Kuzawa, C., & Rich-Edwards, J. (2014). Society: Don't blame the mothers. *Nature News, 512*(7513), 131. https://doi.org/10.1038/512131a

Richardson, V. E., Fields, N., Won, S., Bradley, E., Gibson, A., Rivera, G., & Holmes, S. D. (2019). At the intersection of culture: Ethnically diverse dementia caregivers' service use. *Dementia, 18*(5), 1790–1809.

Richetto, J., & Meyer, U. (2021). Epigenetic modifications in schizophrenia and related disorders: Molecular scars of environmental exposures and source of phenotypic variability. *Biological Psychiatry, 89*(3), 215–226. https://doi.org/10.1016/j.biopsych.2020.03.008

Richmond, E., & Rogol, A. D. (2016). Endocrine responses to exercise in the developing child and adolescent. *Sports Endocrinology, 47,* 58–67.

Richmond, T. K., Thurston, I. B., & Sonneville, K. R. (2021). Weight-focused public health interventions — no benefit, some harm. *JAMA Pediatrics, 175*(3), 238–239. https://doi.org/10.1001/jamapediatrics.2020.4777

Richtel, M. (2021, January 16). Children's screen time has soared in the pandemic, alarming parents and researchers. *The New York Times.* https://www.nytimes.com/2021/01/16/health/covid-kids-tech-use.html

Richter, L. M., Daelmans, B., Lombardi, J., Heymann, J., Boo, F. L., Behrman, J. R., Lu, C., Lucas, J. E., Perez-Escamilla, R., Dua, T., Bhutta, Z. A., Stenberg, K., Gertler, P., & Darmstadt, G. L. (2017). Investing in the foundation of sustainable development: Pathways to scale up for early childhood development. *The Lancet, 389*(10064), 103–118. https://doi.org/10.1016/S0140-6736(16)31698-1

Rico, B., Krieder, R. M., & Anderson, L. (2018). *Growth in interracial and interethnic married-couple households.* U.S. Census Bureau. https://www.census.gov/library/stories/2018/07/interracial-marriages.html

Rideout, V. J. (2013). Zero to eight: Children's media use in America 2013. *Common Sense Media.*

Rideout, V., & Robb, M. B. (2019). *The common sense census: Media use by tweens and teens, 2019.* Common Sense Media.

Rideout, V., & Robb, M. B. (2020). *The common sense census: Media use by kids age zero to eight.* Common Sense Media.

Ridner, S. L., Newton, K. S., Staten, R. R., Crawford, T. N., & Hall, L. A. (2016). Predictors of well-being among college students. *Journal of American College Health, 64*(2), 116–124. https://doi.org/10.1080/07448481.2015.1085057

Riecher-Rössler, A. (2017). Sex and gender differences in mental disorders. *The Lancet Psychiatry, 4*(1), 8–9. https://doi.org/10.1016/S2215-0366(16)30348-0

Rieckmann, A., Johnson, K. A., Sperling, R. A., Buckner, R. L., & Hedden, T. (2018). Dedifferentiation of caudate functional connectivity and striatal dopamine transporter density predict memory change in normal aging. *Proceedings of the National Academy of Sciences, 115*(40), 10160–10165.

Rieffe, C., Broekhof, E., Kouwenberg, M., Faber, J., Tsutsui, M. M., & Güroğlu, B. (2016). Disentangling proactive and reactive aggression in children using self-report. *European Journal of Developmental Psychology, 13*(4), 439–451.

Riera, C. E., & Dillin, A. (2016). Emerging role of sensory perception in aging and metabolism. *Trends in Endocrinology & Metabolism, 27*(5), 294–303.

Ries, M., & Sastre, M. (2016). Mechanisms of Aβ clearance and degradation by glial cells. *Frontiers in Aging Neuroscience, 8,* 160. https://doi.org/10.3389/fnagi.2016.00160

Rietzschel, E. F., Zacher, H., & Stroebe, W. (2016). A lifespan perspective on creativity and innovation at work. *Work, Aging and Retirement, 2*(2), 105–129.

Riggins, T., Canada, K. L., & Botdorf, M. (2020). Empirical evidence supporting neural contributions to episodic memory development in early childhood: Implications for childhood amnesia. *Child Development Perspectives, 14*(1), 41–48. https://doi.org/10.1111/cdep.12353

Riggins, T., Geng, F., Botdorf, M., Canada, K., Cox, L., & Hancock, G. R. (2018). Protracted hippocampal development is associated with age-related improvements in memory during early childhood. *NeuroImage, 174,* 127–137. https://doi.org/10.1016/j.neuroimage.2018.03.009

Rinaldi, P., Caselli, M. C., Di Renzo, A., Gulli, T., & Volterra, V. (2014). Sign vocabulary in deaf toddlers exposed to sign language since birth. *The Journal of Deaf Studies and Deaf Education, 19*(3), 303–318. https://doi.org/10.1093/deafed/enu007

Rippon, G., Eliot, L., Genon, S., & Joel, D. (2021). How hype and hyperbole distort the neuroscience of sex differences. *PLOS Biology, 19*(5), e3001253. https://doi.org/10.1371/journal.pbio.3001253

Ristic, J., & Enns, J. T. (2015). The changing face of attentional development. *Current Directions in Psychological Science, 24*(1), 24–31.

Ritchie, S. J., & Bates, T. C. (2013). Enduring links from childhood mathematics and reading achievement to adult socioeconomic status. *Psychological Science, 24*(7), 1301–1308.

Rivas-Drake, D., Saleem, M., Schaefer, D. R., Medina, M., & Jagers, R. (2019). Intergroup contact attitudes across peer networks in school: Selection, influence, and implications for cross-group friendships. *Child Development, 90*(6), 1898–1916. https://doi.org/10.1111/cdev.13061

Rivas-Drake, D., Seaton, E. K., Markstrom, C., Quintana, S., Syed, M., Lee, R. M., Schwartz, S. J., Umaña-Taylor, A. J., French, S., Yip, T., & Ethnic and Racial Identity in the 21st Century Study Group. (2014). Ethnic and racial identity in adolescence: Implications for psychosocial, academic, and health outcomes. *Child Development, 85*(1), 40–57. https://doi.org/10.1111/cdev.12200

Rivas-Drake, D., & Umaña-Taylor, A. (2019). *Below the surface: Talking with teens about race, ethnicity, and identity.* Princeton University Press.

Rixon, A., Lomax, H., & O'Dell, L. (2019). Childhoods past and present: Anxiety and idyll in reminiscences of childhood outdoor play and contemporary parenting practices. *Children's Geographies, 17*(5), 618–629. https://doi.org/10.1080/14733285.2019.1605047

Robbins, A.-R., & Reissing, E. D. (2018). Out of "objectification limelight"? The contribution of body appreciation to sexual adjustment in midlife women. *The Journal of Sex Research, 55*(6), 758–771. https://doi.org/10.1080/00224499.2017.1372352

Robbins, R., Jackson, C. L., Underwood, P., Vieira, D., Jean-Louis, G., & Buxton, O. M. (2019). Employee sleep and workplace health promotion: A systematic review. *American Journal of Health Promotion, 33*(7), 1009–1019.

Roberton, T., Carter, E. D., Chou, V. B., Stegmuller, A. R., Jackson, B. D., Tam, Y., Sawadogo-Lewis, T., & Walker, N. (2020). Early estimates of the indirect effects of the COVID-19 pandemic on maternal and child mortality in low-income and middle-income countries: A modelling study. *The Lancet Global Health, 8*(7), e901–e908. https://doi.org/10.1016/S2214-109X(20)30229-1

Roberts, A. L., Sumner, J. A., Koenen, K. C., Kubzansky, L. D., Grodstein, F., Rich-Edwards, J., & Weisskopf, M. G. (2020). Childhood abuse and cognitive function in a large cohort of middle-aged women. *Child Maltreatment,* 1077559520970647. https://doi.org/10.1177/1077559520970647

Roberts, A. W., Ogunwole, S. U., Blakeslee, L., & Rabe, M. A. (2018). *The population 65 years and older in the United States: 2016* (American Community Survey Reports ACS-38). U.S. Census Bureau.

Roberts, B. W., Wood, D., & Smith, J. L. (2005). Evaluating five factor theory and social investment perspectives on personality trait development. *Journal of Research in Personality, 39*(1), 166–184.

Roberts, C. A., Jones, A., Sumnall, H., Gage, S. H., & Montgomery, C. (2020). How effective are pharmaceuticals for cognitive enhancement in healthy adults? A series of meta-analyses of cognitive performance during acute administration of modafinil, methylphenidate and D-amphetamine. *European Neuropsychopharmacology, 38,* 40–62. https://doi.org/10.1016/j.euroneuro.2020.07.002

Roberts, J., Noden, P., West, A., & Lewis, J. (2016). Living with the parents: The purpose of young graduates' return to the parental home in England. *Journal of Youth Studies, 19*(3), 319–337. https://doi.org/10.1080/13676261.2015.1072618

Roberts, K. J., Binns, H. J., Vincent, C., & Koenig, M. D. (2021). A scoping review: Family and child perspectives of clinic-based obesity treatment. *Journal of Pediatric Nursing, 57,* 56–72.

Robinson, K. H., Smith, E., & Davies, C. (2017). Responsibilities, tensions and ways forward: Parents' perspectives on children's sexuality education. *Sex Education, 17*(3), 333–347.

Robinson, L. E., Stodden, D. F., Barnett, L. M., Lopes, V. P., Logan, S. W., Rodrigues, L. P., & D'Hondt, E. (2015). Motor competence and its effect on positive developmental trajectories of health. *Sports Medicine, 45*(9), 1273–1284.

Roblyer, M. I. Z., Bámaca-Colbert, M. Y., Rojas, S. M., & Cervantes, R. C. (2015). "Our child is not like us": Understanding parent-child conflict among U.S. Latino families. *Family Science Review, 20*(2), 1–22.

Robson, D. A., Allen, M. S., & Howard, S. J. (2020). Self-regulation in childhood as a predictor of future outcomes: A meta-analytic review. *Psychological Bulletin, 146*(4), 324–354. https://doi.org/10.1037/bul0000227

Robson, E., & Evans, R. (2013). Dilemmas of dealing with distress in interviews with children. In M. A. Powell, N. Taylor, R. Fitzgerald, A. Graham, & D. Anderson (Eds.), *Ethical research involving children.* UNICEF Office of Research Innocenti.

Rochadiat, A. M., Tong, S. T., & Novak, J. M. (2018). Online dating and courtship among Muslim American women: Negotiating technology, religious identity, and culture. *New Media & Society, 20*(4), 1618–1639. https://doi.org/10.1177/1461444817702396

Rochat, P. (2018). The ontogeny of human self-consciousness. *Current Directions in Psychological Science, 27*(5), 345–350. https://doi.org/10.1177/0963721418760236

Rochat, P., Dias, M. D., Liping, G., Broesch, T., Passos-Ferreira, C., Winning, A., & Berg, B. (2009). Fairness in distributive justice by 3-and 5-year-olds across seven cultures. *Journal of Cross-Cultural Psychology, 40*(3), 416–442.

Roche, K. M., Caughy, M. O., Schuster, M. A., Bogart, L. M., Dittus, P. J., & Franzini, L. (2014). Cultural orientations, parental beliefs and practices, and Latino adolescents' autonomy and independence. *Journal of Youth and Adolescence, 43*(8), 1389–1403. https://doi.org/10.1007/s10964-013-9977-6

Rochelle, T. L., Yeung, D. K., Bond, M. H., & Li, L. M. W. (2015). Predictors of the gender gap in life expectancy across 54 nations. *Psychology, Health & Medicine, 20*(2), 129–138.

Rodgers, R. F., Damiano, S. R., Wertheim, E. H., & Paxton, S. J. (2017). Media exposure in very young girls: Prospective and cross-sectional relationships with BMIz, self-esteem and body size stereotypes. *Developmental Psychology, 53*(12), 2356–2363. https://doi.org/10.1037/dev0000407

Rodman, A. M., Jenness, J. L., Weissman, D. G., Pine, D. S., & McLaughlin, K. A. (2019). Neurobiological markers of resilience to depression and anxiety following childhood maltreatment: The role of neural circuits supporting the cognitive control of emotion. *Biological Psychiatry, 86*(6), 464–473. https://doi.org/10.1016/j.biopsych.2019.04.033

Rodman, A. M., Powers, K. E., Insel, C., Kastman, E. K., Kabotyanski, K. E., Stark, A. M., Worthington, S., & Somerville, L. H. (2021). How adolescents and adults translate motivational value to action: Age-related shifts in strategic physical effort exertion for monetary rewards. *Journal of Experimental Psychology: General, 150*(1), 103–113. https://doi.org/10.1037/xge0000769

Rodman, A. M., Powers, K., Kastman, E., Kabotyanski, K., Stark, A. M., Mair, P., & Somerville, L. (2020). Physical effort exertion for peer feedback reveals evolving social motivations from adolescence to young adulthood. *PsyArXiv.* https://doi.org/10.31234/osf.io/2gz6d

Rodrigues, I. B., Armstrong, J. J., Adachi, J. D., & MacDermid, J. C. (2017). Facilitators and barriers to exercise adherence in patients with osteopenia and osteoporosis: A systematic review. *Osteoporosis International, 28*(3), 735–745. https://doi.org/10.1007/s00198-016-3793-2

Rodriguez, L. M., Litt, D. M., & Stewart, S. H. (2020). Drinking to cope with the pandemic: The unique associations of COVID-19-related perceived threat and psychological distress to drinking behaviors in American men and women. *Addictive Behaviors, 110,* 106532.

Rodríguez, S. A., Perez-Brena, N. J., Updegraff, K. A., & Umaña-Taylor, A. J. (2014). Emotional closeness in Mexican-origin adolescents' relationships with mothers, fathers, and same-sex friends. *Journal of Youth and Adolescence, 43*(12), 1953–1968. https://doi.org/10.1007/s10964-013-0004-8

Roemmich, J. N., & Sinning, W. E. (1997). Weight loss and wrestling training: Effects on growth-related hormones. *Journal of Applied Physiology, 82*(6), 1760–1764. https://doi.org/10.1152/jappl.1997.82.6.1760

Roess, A. A., Jacquier, E. F., Catellier, D. J., Carvalho, R., Lutes, A. C., Anater, A. S., & Dietz, W. H. (2018). Food consumption patterns of infants and toddlers: Findings from the Feeding Infants and Toddlers Study (FITS) 2016. *The Journal of Nutrition, 148*(suppl_3), 1525S–1535S. https://doi.org/10.1093/jn/nxy171

Rogers, A. A., Ha, T., Byon, J., & Thomas, C. (2020). Masculine gender-role adherence indicates conflict resolution patterns in heterosexual adolescent couples: A dyadic, observational study. *Journal of Adolescence, 79,* 112–121. https://doi.org/10.1016/j.adolescence.2020.01.004

Rogers, L. O. (2020). "I'm kind of a feminist": Using master narratives to analyze gender identity in middle childhood. *Child Development, 91*(1), 179–196. https://doi.org/10.1111/cdev.13142

Rogers, L. O., & Meltzoff, A. N. (2017). Is gender more important and meaningful than race? An analysis of racial and gender identity among Black, White, and mixed-race children. *Cultural Diversity and Ethnic Minority Psychology, 23*(3), 323.

Rogers, L. O., & Way, N. (2018). Reimagining social and emotional development: Accommodation and resistance to dominant ideologies in the identities and friendships of boys of color. *Human Development, 61*(6), 311–331. https://doi.org/10.1159/000493378

Rogers, S. J., Estes, A., Lord, C., Munson, J., Rocha, M., Winter, J., Greenson, J., Colombi, C., Dawson, G., Vismara, L. A., Sugar, C. A., Hellemann, G., Whelan, F., & Talbott, M. (2019). A multisite randomized controlled two-phase trial of the Early Start Denver model compared to treatment as usual. *Journal of the American Academy of Child & Adolescent Psychiatry, 58*(9), 853–865. https://doi.org/10.1016/j.jaac.2019.01.004

Rogoff, B. (1990). *Apprenticeship in thinking: Cognitive development in social context.* Oxford University Press.

Rogoff, B. (2003). *The cultural nature of human development.* Oxford University Press.

Rogoff, B. (2016). Culture and participation: A paradigm shift. *Current Opinion in Psychology, 8,* 182–189. https://doi.org/10.1016/j.copsyc.2015.12.002

Rogoff, B., Callanan, M., Gutiérrez, K. D., & Erickson, F. (2016). The organization of informal learning. *Review of Research in Education, 40*(1), 356–401. https://doi.org/10.3102/0091732X16680994

Rogoff, B., Coppens, A. D., Alcalá, L., Aceves-Azuara, I., Ruvalcaba, O., López, A., & Dayton, A. (2017). Noticing learners' strengths through cultural research. *Perspectives on Psychological Science, 12*(5), 876–888. https://doi.org/10.1177/1745691617718355

Rogoff, B., Dahl, A., & Callanan, M. (2018). The importance of understanding children's lived experience. *Developmental Review, 50,* 5–15. https://doi.org/10.1016/j.dr.2018.05.006

Rogoff, B., & Mistry, J. (1985). Memory development in cultural context. In M. Pressley & C. J. Brainerd (Eds.), *Cognitive learning and memory in children* (pp. 117–142). Springer.

Rogoff, B., Sellers, M. J., Pirrotta, S., Fox, N., & White, S. H. (1975). Age of assignment of roles and responsibilities to children. *Human Development, 18*(5), 353–369.

Rogol, A. D., & Pieper, L. P. (2018). The interconnected histories of endocrinology and eligibility in women's sport. *Hormone Research in Paediatrics, 90*(4), 213–220. https://doi.org/10.1159/000493646

Roisman, G. I., & Groh, A. M. (2021). The legacy of early attachments: Past, present, future. In R. A. Thompson, J. A. Simpson, L. J. Berlin, L. Ahnert, & T. Ai (Eds.), *Attachment: The fundamental questions* (pp. 187–194). Guilford.

Rojas, N. M., Yoshikawa, H., Gennetian, L., Rangel, M. L., Melvin, S., Noble, K., Duncan, G., & Magunson, K. (2020). Exploring the experiences and dynamics of an unconditional cash transfer for low-income mothers: A mixed-methods study. *Journal of Children and Poverty, 26*(1), 64–84. https://doi.org/10.1080/10796126.2019.1704161

Rollè, L., Giardina, G., Caldarera, A. M., Gerino, E., & Brustia, P. (2018). When intimate partner violence meets same sex couples: A review of same sex intimate partner violence. *Frontiers in Psychology, 9,* 1506. https://doi.org/10.3389/fpsyg.2018.01506

Romeiser, J. L., Smith, D. M., & Clouston, S. A. P. (2021). Musical instrument engagement across the life course and episodic memory in late life: An analysis of 60 years of longitudinal data from the Wisconsin Longitudinal Study. *PLOS ONE, 16*(6), e0253053. https://doi.org/10.1371/journal.pone.0253053

Romer, D. (2010). Adolescent risk taking, impulsivity, and brain development: Implications for prevention. *Developmental Psychobiology, 52*(3), 263–276. https://doi.org/10.1002/dev.20442

Romer, D., Reyna, V. F., & Satterthwaite, T. D. (2017). Beyond stereotypes of adolescent risk taking: Placing the adolescent brain in developmental context. *Developmental Cognitive Neuroscience, 27,* 19–34. https://doi.org/10.1016/j.dcn.2017.07.007

Romero, R., Dey, S. K., & Fisher, S. J. (2014). Preterm labor: One syndrome, many causes. *Science (New York, NY), 345*(6198), 760–765. https://doi.org/10.1126/science.1251816

Romito, B., Jewell, J., Jackson, M., AAP Committee on Hospital Care, & Association of Child Life Professionals. (2021). Child life services. *Pediatrics, 147*(1). https://doi.org/10.1542/peds.2020-040261

Romm, K. F., Metzger, A., & Alvis, L. M. (2020). Parental psychological control and adolescent problematic outcomes: A multidimensional approach. *Journal of Child and Family Studies, 29*(1), 195–207. https://doi.org/10.1007/s10826-019-01545-y

Romo, L. F., Mireles-Rios, R., & Lopez-Tello, G. (2014). Latina mothers' and daughters' expectations for autonomy at age 15 (La Quinceanera). *Journal of Adolescent Research, 29*(2), 271–294. https://doi.org/10.1177/0743558413477199

Romo, N. D. (2019). Gone but not forgotten: Violent trauma victimization and the treatment of violence like a disease. *Hospital Pediatrics, 10*(1), 95–97. https://doi.org/10.1542/hpeds.2019-0196

Romo, R. D., Wallhagen, M. I., Yourman, L., Yeung, C. C., Eng, C., Micco, G., Pérez-Stable, E. J., & Smith, A. K. (2013). Perceptions of successful aging among diverse elders with late-life disability. *The Gerontologist, 53*(6), 939–949. https://doi.org/10.1093/geront/gns160

Ronald, R., & Lennartz, C. (2019). *Housing careers, intergenerational support and family relations.* Taylor & Francis.

Ronan, L., Alexander-Bloch, A., & Fletcher, P. C. (2020). Childhood obesity, cortical structure, and executive function in healthy children. *Cerebral Cortex, 30*(4), 2519–2528. https://doi.org/10.1093/cercor/bhz257

Ronkin, E. G., & Tone, E. B. (2020). Working with twin children and their families in mental health care settings. *Professional Psychology: Research and Practice, 51*(3), 237–246. https://doi.org/10.1037/pro0000288

Ronto, R., Wu, J. H., & Singh, G. M. (2018). The global nutrition transition: Trends, disease burdens and policy interventions. *Public Health Nutrition, 21*(12), 2267–2270. https://doi.org/10.1017/S1368980018000423

Rook, K. S. (2015). Social networks in later life: Weighing positive and negative effects on health and well-being. *Current Directions in Psychological Science, 24*(1), 45–51.

Rook, K. S., & Charles, S. T. (2017). Close social ties and health in later life: Strengths and vulnerabilities. *The American Psychologist, 72*(6), 567–577. https://doi.org/10.1037/amp0000104

Roopnarine, J. L., & Davidson, K. L. (2015). Parent–child play across cultures. In J. E. Johnson, S. G. Eberle, T. S. Henricks, & D. Kuschner (Eds.), *The handbook of the study of play* (Vol. 2, pp. 85–100). Rowman & Littlefield.

Rosado-May, F. J., Urrieta, L., Jr., Dayton, A., & Rogoff, B. (2020). Innovation as a key feature of indigenous ways of learning. In N. S. Nasir, C. D. Lee, R. Pea, & M. McKinney de Royston (Eds.) *Handbook of the cultural foundations of learning* (pp. 79–96). Routledge.

Rosander, K. (2020). Development of gaze control in early infancy. In *Oxford Research Encyclopedia of Psychology.* https://doi.org/10.1093/acrefore/9780190236557.013.825

Rose, A. J., Glick, G. C., Smith, R. L., Schwartz-Mette, R. A., & Borowski, S. K. (2017). Co-rumination exacerbates stress generation among adolescents with depressive symptoms. *Journal of Abnormal Child Psychology, 45*(5), 985–995. https://doi.org/10.1007/s10802-016-0205-1

Rose, A. J., & Smith, R. L. (2018). Gender and peer relationships. In W. M. Bukowski, B. Laursen, & K. H. Rubin (Eds.), *Handbook of peer interactions, relationships, and groups* (pp. 571–589). Guilford.

Rose-Greenland, F., & Smock, P. J. (2012). Living together unmarried: What do we know about cohabiting families? In G. W. Peterson & K. R. Bush (Eds.), *Handbook of marriage and the family* (pp. 255–273). Springer.

Rosen, M. L., Hagen, M. P., Lurie, L. A., Miles, Z. E., Sheridan, M. A., Meltzoff, A. N., & McLaughlin, K. A. (2020). Cognitive stimulation as a mechanism linking socioeconomic status with executive function: A longitudinal investigation. *Child Development, 91*(4), e762–e779. https://doi.org/10.1111/cdev.13315

Rosen, R., Visher, M., & Beal, K. (2018). *Career and technical education: Current policy, prominent programs, and evidence.* MDRC.

Rosenbaum, J. E. (2020). Educational and criminal justice outcomes 12 years after school suspension. *Youth & Society, 52*(4), 515–547. https://doi.org/10.1177/0044118X17752208

Rosenbaum, J. E., Ahearn, C. E., Rosenbaum, J. E., & Gamoran, A. (2017). *Bridging the gaps: College pathways to career success.* Russell Sage Foundation. https://muse.jhu.edu/book/52650

Rosenberg, A. M., Rausser, S., Ren, J., Mosharov, E. V., Sturm, G., Ogden, R. T., Patel, P., Kumar Soni, R., Lacefield, C., Tobin, D. J., Paus, R., & Picard, M. (2021). Quantitative mapping of human hair greying and reversal in relation to life stress. *eLife, 10*, e67437. https://doi.org/10.7554/eLife.67437

Rosenberg, A. R., Bona, K., Coker, T., Feudtner, C., Houston, K., Ibrahim, A., Macauley, R., Wolfe, J., & Hays, R. (2019). Pediatric palliative care in the multicultural context: Findings from a workshop conference. *Journal of Pain and Symptom Management, 57*(4), 846–855.e2. https://doi.org/10.1016/j.jpainsymman.2019.01.005

Rosenberg, I. H. (1989). Epidemiologic and methodologic problems in determining nutritional status of older persons [Summary comments]. *American Journal of Clinical Nutrition, 50*, 1231–1233.

Rosenberg, M. (1963). Parental interest and children's self-conceptions. *Sociometry, 26*(1), 35–49. https://doi.org/10.2307/2785723

Rosenblum, S. (2018). Inter-relationships between objective handwriting features and executive control among children with developmental dysgraphia. *PLOS ONE, 13*(4), e0196098. https://doi.org/10.1371/journal.pone.0196098

Rosenfeld, M. J. (2017). Marriage, choice, and couplehood in the age of the internet. *Sociological Science, 4*, 490–510.

Rosenfeld, M. J., & Roesler, K. (2019). Cohabitation experience and cohabitation's association with marital dissolution. *Journal of Marriage and Family, 81*(1), 42–58.

Rosenfeld, M. J., & Thomas, R. J. (2012). Searching for a mate: The rise of the internet as a social intermediary. *American Sociological Review, 77*(4), 523–547. https://doi.org/10.1177/0003122412448050

Rosenfeld, M. J., Thomas, R. J., & Hausen, S. (2019). Disintermediating your friends: How online dating in the United States displaces other ways of meeting. *Proceedings of the National Academy of Sciences, 116*(36), 17753–17758. https://doi.org/10.1073/pnas.1908630116

Rosenfield, R. L. (2021). Normal and premature adrenarche. *Endocrine Reviews*, bnab009. https://doi.org/10.1210/endrev/bnab009

Rosenke, M., Natu, V. S., Wu, H., Querdasi, F. R., Kular, H., Lopez-Alvarez, N., Grotheer, M., Berman, S., Mezer, A. A., & Grill-Spector, K. (2021). Myelin contributes to microstructural growth in human sensory cortex during early infancy. *BioRxiv*, 2021.03.16.435703. https://doi.org/10.1101/2021.03.16.435703

Rosenthal, N. L., & Kobak, R. (2010). Assessing adolescents' attachment hierarchies: Differences across developmental periods and associations with individual adaptation. *Journal of Research on Adolescence, 20*(3), 678–706. https://doi.org/10.1111/j.1532-7795.2010.00655.x

Rosenzweig, M. R., & Bennett, E. L. (1996). Psychobiology of plasticity: Effects of training and experience on brain and behavior. *Behavioural Brain Research, 78*(1), 57–65. https://doi.org/10.1016/0166-4328(95)00216-2

Roskam, I. (2019). Externalizing behavior from early childhood to adolescence: Prediction from inhibition, language, parenting, and attachment. *Development and Psychopathology, 31*(2), 587–599.

Ross, A., Wood, L., & Searle, M. (2020). The indirect influence of child play on the association between parent perceptions of the neighborhood environment and sense of community. *Health & Place, 65*, 102422. https://doi.org/10.1016/j.healthplace.2020.102422

Ross, D. B., Gale, J., Wickrama, K. K., Goetz, J., & Vowels, M. (2019a). The impact of family economic strain on work-family conflict, marital support, marital quality, and marital stability during the middle years. *Journal of Personal Finance, 18*(2).

Ross, J., Yilmaz, M., Dale, R., Cassidy, R., Yildirim, I., & Zeedyk, M. S. (2017). Cultural differences in self-recognition: The early development of autonomous and related selves? *Developmental Science, 20*(3), e12387. https://doi.org/10.1111/desc.12387

Ross, J. M., Karney, B. R., Nguyen, T. P., & Bradbury, T. N. (2019b). Communication that is maladaptive for middle-class couples is adaptive for socioeconomically disadvantaged couples. *Journal of Personality and Social Psychology, 116*(4), 582–597. https://doi.org/10.1037/pspi0000158

Ross, L. F. (2018). Respecting choice in definitions of death. *Hastings Center Report, 48*(S4), S53–S55. https://doi.org/10.1002/hast.956

Ross, M., & Showalter, T. (2020, December 18). *Millions of young adults are out of school or work. We need an education and employment promise.* Brookings.

Roth, D. L., Sheehan, O. C., Haley, W. E., Jenny, N. S., Cushman, M., & Walston, J. D. (2019). Is family caregiving associated with inflammation or compromised immunity? A meta-analysis. *The Gerontologist, 59*(5), e521–e534.

Roth, T. N. (2015). Aging of the auditory system. *Handbook of Clinical Neurology, 129*, 357–373.

Roth, W. D., & Ivemark, B. (2018). Genetic options: The impact of genetic ancestry testing on consumers' racial and ethnic identities. *American Journal of Sociology, 124*(1), 150–184. https://doi.org/10.1086/697487

Roth, W. D., Yaylacı, Ş., Jaffe, K., & Richardson, L. (2020). Do genetic ancestry tests increase racial essentialism? Findings from a randomized controlled trial. *PLOS ONE, 15*(1), e0227399. https://doi.org/10.1371/journal.pone.0227399

Rothenberg, W. A., Zeitz, S., Lansford, J. E., Bornstein, M. H., Deater-Deckard, K., Dodge, K. A., Malone, P. S., Skinner, A. T., & Steinberg, L. (2021). Four domains of parenting in three ethnic groups in the United States. In J. E. Lansford, W. A. Rothenberg, & M. H. Bornstein (Eds.), *Parenting across cultures from childhood to adolescence: Development in nine countries* (pp. 193–226). Routledge.

Rotheram-Borus, M. J. (2021). Designing evidence-based preventive interventions that reach more people, faster, and with more impact in global contexts. *Annual Review of Clinical Psychology, 17*, 551–575.

Rothermund, K., & de Paula Couto, M. C. P. (2018). Cultural differences in attitudes towards living in old age. *Innovation in Aging, 2*(Suppl 1), 413–414. https://doi.org/10.1093/geroni/igy023.1545

Rothman, E. F., Beckmeyer, J. J., Herbenick, D., Fu, T.-C., Dodge, B., & Fortenberry, J. D. (2021). The prevalence of using pornography for information about how to have sex: Findings from a nationally representative survey of U.S. adolescents and young adults. *Archives of Sexual Behavior, 50*(2), 629–646. https://doi.org/10.1007/s10508-020-01877-7

Rothman, E. F., Paruk, J., Espensen, A., Temple, J. R., & Adams, K. (2017). A qualitative study of what US parents say and do when their young children see pornography. *Academic Pediatrics, 17*(8), 844–849.

Rothman, J. (2018, February 3). The philosophy of the midlife crisis. *The New Yorker.* https://www.newyorker.com/books/page-turner/the-philosophy-of-the-midlife-crisis

Röttger-Rössler, B. (2020). Research across cultures and disciplines: Methodological challenges in an interdisciplinary and comparative research project on emotion socialization. In M. Schnegg & E. D. Lowe (Eds.), *Comparing cultures: Innovations in comparative ethnography* (pp. 180–200). Cambridge University Press.

Rounds, J., & Su, R. (2014). The nature and power of interests. *Current Directions in Psychological Science, 23*(2), 98–103. http://cdp.sagepub.com/content/23/2/98.short

Rounsefell, K., Gibson, S., McLean, S., Blair, M., Molenaar, A., Brennan, L., Truby, H., & McCaffrey, T. A. (2020). Social media, body image and food choices in healthy young adults: A mixed methods systematic review. *Nutrition & Dietetics, 77*(1), 19–40. https://doi.org/10.1111/1747-0080.12581

Rouse, M. L., Fishbein, L. B., Minshawi, N. F., & Fodstad, J. C. (2017). Historical development of toilet training.

In J. L. Matson (Ed.), *Clinical guide to toilet training children* (pp. 1–18). Springer International Publishing. https://doi.org/10.1007/978-3-319-62725-0_1

Rouse, M., & Hamilton, E. (2021). Rethinking sex and the brain: How to create an inclusive discourse in neuroscience. *Mind, Brain, and Education, 15*(2), 163–167. https://doi.org/10.1111/mbe.12285

Rousseau, J.-J. (2010). *Emile, or, On education: Includes Emile and Sophie, or, The solitaries.* UPNE.

Rousseau, P. V., Matton, F., Lecuyer, R., & Lahaye, W. (2017). The Moro reaction: More than a reflex, a ritualized behavior of nonverbal communication. *Infant Behavior and Development, 46,* 169–177. https://doi.org/10.1016/j.infbeh.2017.01.004

Rovee-Collier, C., & Cuevas, K. (2009). Multiple memory systems are unnecessary to account for infant memory development: An ecological model. *Developmental Psychology, 45*(1), 160–174. https://doi.org/10.1037/a0014538

Rovee-Collier, C., & Giles, A. (2010). Why a neuromaturational model of memory fails: Exuberant learning in early infancy. *Behavioural Processes, 83*(2), 197–206. https://doi.org/10.1016/j.beproc.2009.11.013

Rowan-Kenyon, H. T., Savitz-Romer, M., Ott, M. W., Swan, A. K., & Liu, P. P. (2017). Finding conceptual coherence: Trends and alignment in the scholarship on noncognitive skills and their role in college success and career readiness. In M. B. Paulsen (Ed.), *Higher education: Handbook of theory and research* (pp. 141–179). Springer.

Rowe, J. W., & Kahn, R. L. (1987). Human aging: Usual and successful. *Science, 237*(4811), 143–149.

Rowe, J. W., & Kahn, R. L. (2015). Successful aging 2.0: Conceptual expansions for the 21st century. *The Journals of Gerontology: Series B, 70*(4), 593–596. https://doi.org/10.1093/geronb/gbv025

Rowe, M. L., Leech, K. A., & Cabrera, N. (2017). Going beyond input quantity: Wh-questions matter for toddlers' language and cognitive development. *Cognitive Science, 41,* 162–179.

Rowe, S. L., Gembeck, M. J. Z., Rudolph, J., & Nesdale, D. (2015). A longitudinal study of rejecting and autonomy-restrictive parenting, rejection sensitivity, and socioemotional symptoms in early adolescents. *Journal of Abnormal Child Psychology, 43*(6), 1107–1118.

Rowley, K. J., Edmunds, C. C., Dufur, M. J., Jarvis, J. A., & Silveira, F. (2020). Contextualising the achievement gap: Assessing educational achievement, inequality, and disadvantage in high-income countries. *Comparative Education, 56*(4), 459–483.

Rowthorn, R., & Ramaswamy, R. (1999). Growth, trade, and deindustrialization. *IMF Staff Papers, 46*(1), 18–41. https://doi.org/10.2307/3867633

Rubin, K. H., Barstead, M. G., Smith, K. A., & Bowker, J. C. (2018). Peer relations and the behaviorally inhibited child. In K. Pérez-Edgar & N. A. Fox (Eds.), *Behavioral inhibition: Integrating theory, research, and clinical perspectives* (pp. 157–184). Springer.

Rubin, K. H., Bukowski, W. M., & Bowker, J. C. (2015). Children in peer groups. In M. H. Bornstein, T. Leventhal, & R. M. Lerner (Eds.), *Handbook of child psychology and developmental science: Ecological settings and processes* (pp. 175–222). Wiley. https://doi.org/10.1002/9781118963418.childpsy405

Rubino, F., Puhl, R. M., Cummings, D. E., Eckel, R. H., Ryan, D. H., Mechanick, J. I., Nadglowski, J., Ramos Salas, X., Schauer, P. R., Twenefour, D., Apovian, C. M., Aronne, L. J., Batterham, R. L., Berthoud, H.-R., Boza, C., Busetto, L., Dicker, D., De Groot, M., Eisenberg, D., … Dixon, J. B. (2020). Joint international consensus statement for ending stigma of obesity. *Nature Medicine, 26*(4), 485–497. https://doi.org/10.1038/s41591-020-0803-x

Rubinstein, R. L., & de Medeiros, K. (2015). "Successful aging," gerontological theory and neoliberalism: A qualitative critique. *The Gerontologist, 55*(1), 34–42. https://doi.org/10.1093/geront/gnu080

Ruble, D. N., & Brooks-Gunn, J. (1982). The experience of menarche. *Child Development, 53*(6), 1557–1566.

Ruble, D. N., Taylor, L. J., Cyphers, L., Greulich, F. K., Lurye, L. E., & Shrout, P. E. (2007). The role of gender constancy in early gender development. *Child Development, 78*(4), 1121–1136. https://doi.org/10.1111/j.1467-8624.2007.01056.x

Ruby, J. G., Wright, K. M., Rand, K. A., Kermany, A., Noto, K., Curtis, D., Varner, N., Garrigan, D., Slinkov, D., Dorfman, I, Granka, J. M., Byrnes, J., Myres, N., & Ball, C. (2018). Estimates of the heritability of human longevity are substantially inflated due to assortative mating. *Genetics, 210*(3), 1109–1124.

Rucinski, C. L., Brown, J. L., & Downer, J. T. (2018). Teacher–child relationships, classroom climate, and children's social-emotional and academic development. *Journal of Educational Psychology, 110*(7), 992–1004. https://doi.org/10.1037/edu0000240

Rudder, C. (2014). *We experiment on human beings.* OK Trends: Dating Research from OKCupid. http://blog.okcupid.com/index.php/we-experiment-on-human-beings.

Rüdiger, M., & Rozycki, H. J. (2020). It's time to reevaluate the Apgar score. *JAMA Pediatrics, 174*(4), 321–322.

Rudolph, C. W., Lavigne, K. N., & Zacher, H. (2017). Career adaptability: A meta-analysis of relationships with measures of adaptivity, adapting responses, and adaptation results. *Journal of Vocational Behavior, 98,* 17–34. https://doi.org/10.1016/j.jvb.2016.09.002

Rudolph, M. D., Miranda-Domínguez, O., Cohen, A. O., Breiner, K., Steinberg, L., Bonnie, R. J., & Fair, D. A. (2017). At risk of being risky: The relationship between "brain age" under emotional states and risk preference. *Developmental Cognitive Neuroscience, 24,* 93–106.

Rudzik, A. E. F., & Ball, H. L. (2021). Biologically normal sleep in the mother-infant dyad. *American Journal of Human Biology, 33*(5), e23589. https://doi.org/10.1002/ajhb.23589

Ruffman, T., Lorimer, B., & Scarf, D. (2017). Do infants really experience emotional contagion? *Child Development Perspectives, 11*(4), 270–274. https://doi.org/10.1111/cdep.12244

Rui, N. (2009). Four decades of research on the effects of detracking reform: Where do we stand?—A systematic review of the evidence. *Journal of Evidence-Based Medicine, 2*(3), 164–183. http://onlinelibrary.wiley.com/doi/10.1111/j.1756-5391.2009.01032.x/full

Ruiz, L., Posey, B. M., Neuilly, M. A., Stohr, M. K., & Hemmens, C. (2018). Certifying death in the United States. *Journal of Forensic Sciences, 63*(4), 1138–1145.

Ruprecht, K., Elicker, J., & Choi, J. Y. (2016). Continuity of care, caregiver–child interactions, and toddler social competence and problem behaviors. *Early Education and Development, 27*(2), 221–239. https://doi.org/10.1080/10409289.2016.1102034

Rusch, H. L., Rosario, M., Levison, L. M., Olivera, A., Livingston, W. S., Wu, T., & Gill, J. M. (2019). The effect of mindfulness meditation on sleep quality: A systematic review and meta-analysis of randomized controlled trials. *Annals of the New York Academy of Sciences, 1445*(1), 5.

Rüsch, N., Heekeren, K., Theodoridou, A., Müller, M., Corrigan, P. W., Mayer, B., & Rössler, W. (2015). Stigma as a stressor and transition to schizophrenia after one year among young people at risk of psychosis. *Schizophrenia Research, 166*(1–3), 43–48.

Ruscio, A. M., Hallion, L. S., Lim, C. C. W., Aguilar-Gaxiola, S., Al-Hamzawi, A., Alonso, J., Andrade, L. H., Borges, G., Bromet, E. J., Bunting, B., Caldas de Almeida, J. M., Demyttenaere, K., Florescu, S., de Girolamo, G., Gureje, O., Haro, J. M., He, Y., Hinkov, H., Hu, C., … Scott, K. M. (2017). Cross-sectional comparison of the epidemiology of DSM-5 generalized anxiety disorder across the globe. *JAMA Psychiatry, 74*(5), 465–475. https://doi.org/10.1001/jamapsychiatry.2017.0056

Rutherford, H. J. V., Potenza, M. N., Mayes, L. C., & Scheinost, D. (2020). The application of connectome-based predictive modeling to the maternal brain: Implications for mother–infant bonding. *Cerebral Cortex (New York, NY), 30*(3), 1538–1547. https://doi.org/10.1093/cercor/bhz185

Rutland, A., & Killen, M. (2015). A developmental science approach to reducing prejudice and social exclusion: Intergroup processes, social–cognitive development, and moral reasoning. *Social Issues and Policy Review, 9*(1), 121–154.

Rutledge, S. A., Cannata, M., Brown, S. L., & Traeger, D. G. (2020). *Steps to schoolwide success: Systemic practices for connecting social-emotional and academic learning.* Harvard Education Press.

Rutter, C., & Walker, S. (2021). Infant mortality inequities for Māori in New Zealand: A tale of three policies. *International Journal for Equity in Health, 20*(1), 10. https://doi.org/10.1186/s12939-020-01340-y

Ryan, J., Wrigglesworth, J., Loong, J., Fransquet, P. D., & Woods, R. L. (2020). A systematic review and meta-analysis of environmental, lifestyle, and health factors associated with DNA methylation age. *The Journals of Gerontology: Series A, 75*(3), 481–494. https://doi.org/10.1093/gerona/glz099

Ryan, W. S., Legate, N., & Weinstein, N. (2015). Coming out as lesbian, gay, or bisexual: The lasting impact of initial disclosure experiences. *Self and Identity, 14*(5), 549–569.

Ryberg, R., Harris, K. M., & Pearce, L. (2018). *Religiosity of young adults: The National Longitudinal Study of Adolescent to Adult Health* (Add Health Research Brief No. 4). Carolina Population Center, University of Carolina at Chapel Hill.

Rybińska, A., & Morgan, S. P. (2019). Childless expectations and childlessness over the life course. *Social Forces, 97*(4), 1571–1602. https://doi.org/10.1093/sf/soy098

Ryff, C. D., Boylan, J. M., & Kirsch, J. A. (2021). Eudaimonic and hedonic well-being: An integrative perspective with linkages to sociodemographic factors and health. In M. T. Lee, L. D. Kubzansky, & T. J. VanderWeele (Eds.), *Measuring well-being* (pp. 92–135). Oxford University Press. https://doi.org/10.1093/oso/9780197512531.003.0005

Ryosho, N. (2011). Experiences of racism by female minority and immigrant nursing assistants. *Affilia, 26*(1), 59–71. https://doi.org/10.1177/0886109910392519

Rysavy, M. A., Li, L., Bell, E. F., Das, A., Hintz, S. R., Stoll, B. J., Vohr, B. R., Carlo, W. A., Shankaran, S., Walsh, M. C., Tyson, J. E., Cotten, C. M., Smith, P. B., Murray, J. C., Colaizy, T. T., Brumbaugh, J. E., & Higgins, R. D. (2015). Between-hospital variation in treatment and outcomes in extremely preterm infants. *New England Journal of Medicine, 372*(19), 1801–1811. https://doi.org/10.1056/NEJMoa1410689

Rytioja, M., Lappalainen, K., & Savolainen, H. (2019). Behavioural and emotional strengths of sociometrically popular, rejected, controversial, neglected, and average children. *European Journal of Special Needs Education, 34*(5), 557–571.

Rzehak, P., Oddy, W. H., Mearin, M. L., Grote, V., Mori, T. A., Szajewska, H., Shamir, R., Koletzko, S., Weber, M., Beilin, L. J., Huang, R.-C., Koletzko, B., & for the WP10 working group of the Early Nutrition Project. (2017). Infant feeding and growth trajectory patterns in childhood and body composition in young adulthood. *The American Journal of Clinical Nutrition, 106*(2), 568–580. https://doi.org/10.3945/ajcn.116.140962

Saarni, C. (1984). An observational study of children's attempts to monitor their expressive behavior. *Child Development, 55*(4), 1504–1513. https://doi.org/10.2307/1130020

Saarni, C. (1999). *The development of emotional competence.* Guilford.

Sabik, N. J. (2017). Is social engagement linked to body image and depression among aging women? *Journal of Women & Aging, 29*(5), 405–416. https://doi.org/10.1080/08952841.2016.1213106

Sabiston, C. M., Pila, E., Vani, M., & Thogersen-Ntoumani, C. (2019). Body image, physical activity, and sport: A scoping review. *Psychology of Sport and Exercise, 42,* 48–57. https://doi.org/10.1016/j.psychsport.2018.12.010

Sacco, A., Thompson, D. N. P., Ushakov, F., David, A. L., & Deprest, J. (2020). Fetal surgery for spina bifida. *Obstetrics, Gynaecology & Reproductive Medicine, 30*(1), 26–30. https://doi.org/10.1016/j.ogrm.2019.10.005

Sadruddin, A. F. A., Ponguta, L. A., Zonderman, A. L., Wiley, K. S., Grimshaw, A., & Panter-Brick, C. (2019). How do grandparents influence child health and development? A systematic review. *Social Science & Medicine, 239,* 112476. https://doi.org/10.1016/j.socscimed.2019.112476

Saey, T. H. (2018, May 22). Consumer DNA testing promises more than it delivers. *Genetics.*

Saez-Atienzar, S., & Masliah, E. (2020). Cellular senescence and Alzheimer disease: The egg and the chicken scenario. *Nature Reviews Neuroscience, 21*(8), 433–444. https://doi.org/10.1038/s41583-020-0325-z

Safa, M. D., & Umaña-Taylor, A. J. (2021). Bicultural-ism and adjustment among US Latinos: A review of four decades of empirical findings. *Advances in Child Development and Behavior, 61*, 73–127.

Safaiyan, S., Kannaiyan, N., Snaidero, N., Brioschi, S., Biber, K., Yona, S., Edinger, A. L., Jung, S., Rossner, M. J., & Simons, M. (2016). Age-related myelin degradation burdens the clearance function of microglia during aging. *Nature Neuroscience, 19*(8), 995–998. https://doi.org/10.1038/nn.4325

Safar, K., & Moulson, M. C. (2020). Three-month-old infants show enhanced behavioral and neural sensitivity to fearful faces. *Developmental Cognitive Neuroscience, 42*, 100759.

Saffran, J. R. (2020). Statistical language learning in infancy. *Child Development Perspectives, 14*(1), 49–54. https://doi.org/10.1111/cdep.12355

Safronova, V. (2021, July 7). A private-school sex educator defends her methods. *The New York Times.* https://www.nytimes.com/2021/07/07/style/sex-educator-methods-defense.html

Saguy, T., Reifen-Tagar, M., & Joel, D. (2021). The gender-binary cycle: The perpetual relations between a biological-essentialist view of gender, gender ideology, and gender-labelling and sorting. *Philosophical Transactions of the Royal Society B: Biological Sciences, 376*(1822), 20200141. https://doi.org/10.1098/rstb.2020.0141

Sahota, A. K., Shapiro, W. L., Newton, K. P., Kim, S. T., Chung, J., & Schwimmer, J. B. (2020). Incidence of nonalcoholic fatty liver disease in children: 2009–2018. *Pediatrics, 146*(6). https://doi.org/10.1542/peds.2020-0771

Saint-Maurice, P. F., Troiano, R. P., Bassett, D. R., Graubard, B. I., Carlson, S. A., Shiroma, E. J., Fulton, J. E., & Matthews, C. E. (2020). Association of daily step count and step intensity with mortality among US adults. *JAMA, 323*(12), 1151–1160. https://doi.org/10.1001/jama.2020.1382

Sakai, J. (2020). Core concept: How synaptic pruning shapes neural wiring during development and, possibly, in disease. *Proceedings of the National Academy of Sciences of the United States of America, 117*(28), 16096–16099.

Sakaki, M., Yagi, A., & Murayama, K. (2018). Curiosity in old age: A possible key to achieving adaptive aging. *Neuroscience and Biobehavioral Reviews, 88*, 106–116. https://doi.org/10.1016/j.neubiorev.2018.03.007

Sako, M. (2014). Outsourcing and offshoring of professional services. In B. Hinings, D. Muzio, J. Broschak, & L. Empson (Eds.), *The Oxford handbook of professional service firms* (pp. 327–350). Oxford University Press. http://books.google.com/books?hl=en&lr=&id=JcdQCgAAQBAJ&oi=fnd&pg=PA327&dq=%22professional+services+and+non-professional+business+services.+It%22+%22firms.+We+focus+on+primary+activities+to+test+the+analytical%22+%22on+a+number+of+theories,+and+gauging+whether+different%22+&ots=0OxF26MaZ7&sig=zTUDY_gNhq-l_Evdm9rgre7vdHA

Salandy, S., Rai, R., Gutierrez, S., Ishak, B., & Tubbs, R. S. (2019). Neurological examination of the infant. *Clinical Anatomy, 32*(6), 770–777. https://doi.org/10.1002/ca.23352

Salas, I. H., Burgado, J., & Allen, N. J. (2020). Glia: Victims or villains of the aging brain? *Neurobiology of Disease, 143*, 105008. https://doi.org/10.1016/j.nbd.2020.105008

Salcedo-Arellano, M. J., Dufour, B., McLennan, Y., Martinez-Cerdeno, V., & Hagerman, R. (2020). Fragile X syndrome and associated disorders: Clinical aspects and pathology. *Neurobiology of Disease, 136*, 104740. https://doi.org/10.1016/j.nbd.2020.104740

Salinas, C. (2020). The complexity of the "x" in Latinx: How Latinx/a/o students relate to, identify with, and understand the term Latinx. *Journal of Hispanic Higher Education, 19*(2), 149–168. https://doi.org/10.1177/1538192719900382

Salk, R. H., Hyde, J. S., & Abramson, L. Y. (2017). Gender differences in depression in representative national samples: Meta-analyses of diagnoses and symptoms. *Psychological Bulletin, 143*(8), 783–822. https://doi.org/10.1037/bul0000102

Salmela-Aro, K., Tang, X., Symonds, J., & Upadyaya, K. (2021). Student engagement in adolescence: A scoping review of longitudinal studies 2010–2020. *Journal of Research on Adolescence, 31*(2), 256–272.

Salmon, D. A., Dudley, M. Z., Glanz, J. M., & Omer, S. B. (2015). Vaccine hesitancy. *American Journal of Preventive Medicine, 49*(6), S391–S398. https://doi.org/10.1016/j.amepre.2015.06.009

Salmon, K., & Reese, E. (2016). The benefits of reminiscing with young children. *Current Directions in Psychological Science, 25*(4), 233–238.

Salomon, I., & Brown, C. S. (2019). The selfie generation: Examining the relationship between social media use and early adolescent body image. *The Journal of Early Adolescence, 39*(4), 539–560. https://doi.org/10.1177/0272431618770809

Salthouse, T. A. (1996). The processing-speed theory of adult age differences in cognition. *Psychological Review, 103*(3), 403.

Salthouse, T. A. (2019). Trajectories of normal cognitive aging. *Psychology and Aging, 34*(1), 17–24. https://doi.org/10.1037/pag0000288

Salzmann, J. (1943). *Principles of orthodontics.* Lippincott.

Samanez-Larkin, G. R., & Knutson, B. (2015). Decision making in the ageing brain: Changes in affective and motivational circuits. *Nature Reviews Neuroscience, 16*, 278–289. https://doi.org/10.1038/nrn3917

Samek, D. R., Hicks, B. M., Keyes, M. A., Iacono, W. G., & McGue, M. (2017). Antisocial peer affiliation and externalizing disorders: Evidence for gene × environment × development interaction. *Development and Psychopathology, 29*(1), 155–172.

Sameroff, A. J. (2020). It's more complicated. *Annual Review of Developmental Psychology, 2*(1), 1–26. https://doi.org/10.1146/annurev-devpsych-061520-120738

Sameroff, A. J., & Haith, M. M. (1996). Interpreting developmental transitions. In A. Sameroff & M. Haith (Eds.), *The five to seven year shift: The age of reason and responsibility* (pp. 3–30). University of Chicago Press.

Sampathkumar, N. K., Bravo, J. I., Chen, Y., Danthi, P. S., Donahue, E. K., Lai, R. W., Lu, R., Randall, L. T., Vinson, N., & Benayoun, B. A. (2019). Widespread sex dimorphism in aging and age-related diseases. *Human Genetics, 139*(3), 333–356. https://doi.org/10.1007/s00439-019-02082-w

Sampedro-Piquero, P., Alvarez-Suarez, P., & Begega, A. (2018). Coping with stress during aging: The importance of a resilient brain. *Current Neuropharmacology, 16*(3), 284–296. https://doi.org/10.2174/1570159X15666170915141610

Sanchez, C. E., Barry, C., Sabhlok, A., Russell, K., Majors, A., Kollins, S. H., & Fuemmeler, B. F. (2018). Maternal pre-pregnancy obesity and child neurodevelopmental outcomes: A meta-analysis. *Obesity Reviews: An Official Journal of the International Association for the Study of Obesity, 19*(4), 464–484. https://doi.org/10.1111/obr.12643

Sanchez, D., Flannigan, A., Guevara, C., Arango, S., & Hamilton, E. (2017). Links among familial gender ideology, media portrayal of women, dating, and sexual behaviors in African American, and Mexican American adolescent young women: A qualitative study. *Sex Roles, 77*, 453–470. https://doi.org/10.1007/s11199-017-0739-x

Sanchez, O., & Kolodner, M. (2021, October 10). Why racial graduation gaps exist across the nation. *Hechinger Report.* http://hechingerreport.org/why-white-students-are-250-more-likely-to-graduate-than-black-students-at-public-universities/

Sánchez-Cabrero, R., León-Mejía, A. C., Arigita-García, A., & Maganto-Mateo, C. (2019). Improvement of body satisfaction in older people: An experimental study. *Frontiers in Psychology, 10*, 2823. https://doi.org/10.3389/fpsyg.2019.02823

Sánchez Romero, M. (2018). Care and socialization of children in the European Bronze Age. In S. Crawford, D. Hadley, & G. Shepherd (Eds.), *The Oxford handbook of the archaeology of childhood.* Oxford University Press. https://doi.org/10.1093/oxfordhb/9780199670697.013.18

Sandberg, J. G., Bradford, A. B., & Brown, A. P. (2017). Differentiating between attachment styles and behaviors and their association with marital quality. *Family Process, 56*(2), 518–531. https://doi.org/10.1111/famp.12186

Sanders, J. O., Qiu, X., Lu, X., Duren, D. L., Liu, R. W., Dang, D., Menendez, M. E., Hans, S. D., Weber, D. R., & Cooperman, D. R. (2017). The uniform pattern of growth and skeletal maturation during the human adolescent growth spurt. *Scientific Reports, 7*(1), 16705. https://doi.org/10.1038/s41598-017-16996-w

Sanders, M. R., & Burke, K. (2018). Towards a comprehensive, evidence-based system of parenting support over the lifespan. In M. R. Sanders & A. Morawska (Eds.), *Handbook of parenting and child development across the lifespan* (pp. 777–798). Springer.

Sanderson, K. (2021). Why sports concussions are worse for women. *Nature, 596*(7870), 26–28. https://doi.org/10.1038/d41586-021-02089-2

Sanderson, W. C., & Scherbov, S. (2020). Choosing between the UN's alternative views of population aging. *PLOS ONE, 15*(7), e0233602. https://doi.org/10.1371/journal.pone.0233602

Sandler, D., & Szembrot, N. (2019). *Maternal labor dynamics: Participation, earnings, and employer changes* (Working Paper No. 19-33). Center for Economic Studies, U.S. Census Bureau.

Sandseter, E. B. H., Kleppe, R., & Sando, O. J. (2021). The prevalence of risky play in young children's indoor and outdoor free play. *Early Childhood Education Journal, 49*(2), 303–312.

Sandstrom, A., & Alper, B. A. (2019, February 22). *Who's active in community groups? Often, those with more education or income.* Pew Research Center. https://www.pewresearch.org/fact-tank/2019/02/22/americans-with-higher-education-and-income-are-more-likely-to-be-involved-in-community-groups/

Sanese, P., Forte, G., Disciglio, V., Grossi, V., & Simone, C. (2019). FOXO3 on the road to longevity: Lessons from SNPs and chromatin hubs. *Computational and Structural Biotechnology Journal, 17*, 737–745. https://doi.org/10.1016/j.csbj.2019.06.011

Santelli, J. S., Song, X., Garbers, S., Sharma, V., & Viner, R. M. (2017). Global trends in adolescent fertility, 1990–2012, in relation to national wealth, income inequalities, and educational expenditures. *Journal of Adolescent Health, 60*(2), 161–168. https://doi.org/10.1016/j.jadohealth.2016.08.026

Santini, Z. I., Koyanagi, A., Tyrovolas, S., & Haro, J. M. (2015). The association of relationship quality and social networks with depression, anxiety, and suicidal ideation among older married adults: Findings from a cross-sectional analysis of the Irish Longitudinal Study on Ageing (TILDA). *Journal of Affective Disorders, 179*, 134–141. https://doi.org/10.1016/j.jad.2015.03.015

Santoro, N., Polotsky, A. J., Rieder, J., & Kondapalli, L. A. (2019). Nutrition and reproduction. In J. F. Strauss & R. L. Barbieri (Eds.), *Yen & Jaffe's reproductive endocrinology: Physiology, pathophysiology, and clinical management* (8th ed., 447–458.e6). Elsevier.

Santos, J., Martins, S., Azevedo, L. F., & Fernandes, L. (2020). Pain as a risk factor for suicidal behavior in older adults: A systematic review. *Archives of Gerontology and Geriatrics, 87*, 104000.

Santos-Iglesias, P., Byers, E. S., & Moglia, R. (2016). Sexual well-being of older men and women. *The Canadian Journal of Human Sexuality, 25*(2), 86–98. https://doi.org/10.3138/cjhs.252-A4

Sarrico, C., McQueen, A., & Samuel, S. (Eds.). (2017). *State of higher education, 2015–2016.* Organisation for Economic Co-operation and Development (OECD) Higher Education Programme (IMHE).

Sassler, S. (2010). Partnering across the life course: Sex, relationships, and mate selection. *Journal of Marriage and the Family, 72*(3), 557–575. https://doi.org/10.1111/j.1741-3737.2010.00718.x

Sassler, S., Glass, J., Levitte, Y., & Michelmore, K. M. (2017). The missing women in STEM? Assessing gender differentials in the factors associated with transition to first jobs. *Social Science Research, 63*, 192–208.

Sassler, S., Michelmore, K., & Qian, Z. (2018). Transitions from sexual relationships into cohabitation and beyond. *Demography, 55*(2), 511–534. https://doi.org/10.1007/s13524-018-0649-8

Sathyanesan, A., Zhou, J., Scafidi, J., Heck, D. H., Sillitoe, R. V., & Gallo, V. (2019). Emerging connections between cerebellar development, behavior, and complex brain disorders. *Nature Reviews Neuroscience, 20*(5), 298–313. https://doi.org/10.1038/s41583-019-0152-2

Sattari, M., Serwint, J. R., & Levine, D. M. (2019). Maternal implications of breastfeeding: A review for the internist. *The American Journal of Medicine, 132*(8), 912–920. https://doi.org/10.1016/j.amjmed.2019.02.021

Saucedo, M., Bouvier-Colle, M. H., Blondel, B., Bonnet, M. P., Deneux-Tharaux, C., & ENCMM Study Group. (2020). Delivery hospital characteristics and postpartum maternal mortality: A national case–control study in France. *Anesthesia & Analgesia, 130*(1), 52–62.

Saucedo, M., Esteves-Pereira, A. P., Pencolé, L., Rigouzzo, A., Proust, A., Bouvier-Colle, M.-H., & Deneux-Tharaux, C. (2021). Understanding maternal mortality in women with obesity and the role of care they receive: A national case-control study. *International Journal of Obesity, 45*(1), 258–265. https://doi.org/10.1038/s41366-020-00691-4

Sauerteig, L. D. H. (2012). Loss of innocence: Albert Moll, Sigmund Freud and the invention of childhood sexuality around 1900. *Medical History, 56*(2), 156–183. https://doi.org/10.1017/mdh.2011.31

Saulny, S. (2011, January 30). Black? White? Asian? More young Americans choose all of the above. *The New York Times.* https://www.nytimes.com/2011/01/30/us/30mixed.html

Savahl, S., Montserrat, C., Casas, F., Adams, S., Tiliouine, H., Benninger, E., & Jackson, K. (2019). Children's experiences of bullying victimization and the influence on their subjective well-being: A multinational comparison. *Child Development, 90*(2), 414–431.

Savin-Williams, R. C. (2016). Sexual orientation: Categories or continuum? Commentary on Bailey et al. (2016). *Psychological Science in the Public Interest, 17*(2), 37–44. https://doi.org/10.1177/1529100616637618

Savin-Williams, R. C., & Cohen, K. M. (2015). Developmental trajectories and milestones of lesbian, gay, and bisexual young people. *International Review of Psychiatry, 27*(5), 357–366. https://doi.org/10.3109/09540261.2015.1093465

Saxbe, D., Rossin-Slater, M., & Goldenberg, D. (2018). The transition to parenthood as a critical window for adult health. *American Psychologist, 73*(9), 1190.

Saxe, G. B. (1988). Candy selling and math learning. *Educational Researcher, 17*(6), 14–21.

Saxe, G. B., & de Kirby, K. (2014). Cultural context of cognitive development. *WIREs Cognitive Science, 5*(4), 447–461. https://doi.org/10.1002/wcs.1300

Sbarra, D. A., Briskin, J. L., & Slatcher, R. B. (2019). Smartphones and close relationships: The case for an evolutionary mismatch. *Perspectives on Psychological Science, 14*(4), 596–618.

Sbarra, D. A., & Manvelian, A. (2021). The psychological and biological correlates of separation and loss. In R. A. Thompson, J. A. Simpson, & L. J. Berlin (Eds.), *Attachment: The fundamental questions* (pp. 275–281). Guilford.

Sbarra, D. A., & Whisman, M. A. (2022). Divorce, health, and socioeconomic status: An agenda for psychological science. *Current Opinion in Psychology, 43*, 75–78. https://doi.org/10.1016/j.copsyc.2021.06.007

Scaffidi, P., & Misteli, T. (2006). Lamin A-dependent nuclear defects in human aging. *Science, 312*(5776), 1059–1063. https://doi.org/10.1126/science.1127168

Scarmeas, N., Luchsinger, J. A., Schupf, N., Brickman, A. M., Cosentino, S., Tang, M. X., & Stern, Y. (2009). Physical activity, diet, and risk of Alzheimer disease. *JAMA, 302*(6), 627–637.

Schacter, H. L. (2021). Effects of peer victimization on child and adolescent physical health. *Pediatrics, 147*(1), e2020003434. https://doi.org/10.1542/peds.2020-003434

Schaeffer, K. (2021). *As schools shift to online learning amid pandemic, here's what we know about disabled students in the U.S.* Pew Research Center. https://www.pewresearch.org/fact-tank/2020/04/23/as-schools-shift-to-online-learning-amid-pandemic-heres-what-we-know-about-disabled-students-in-the-u-s/

Schaie, K. W. (2021). History of adult cognitive aging research. In K. W. Schaie & S. L. Willis (Eds.), *Handbook of the psychology of aging* (9th ed., pp. 3–17). Academic Press. https://doi.org/10.1016/B978-0-12-816094-7.00017-9

Schanzenbach, D. W., Boddy, D., Mumford, M., & Nantz, G. (2016). *Fourteen economic facts on education and economic opportunity.* The Hamilton Project.

Scharf, M., & Goldner, L. (2018). "If you really love me, you will do/be…": Parental psychological control and its implications for children's adjustment. *Developmental Review, 49*, 16–30. https://doi.org/10.1016/j.dr.2018.07.002

Scharp, K. M., & Curran, T. (2018). Caregiving when there is family conflict and estrangement. *Generations, 42*(3), 51–56.

Scharp, K. M., & Dorrance Hall, E. (2017). Family marginalization, alienation, and estrangement: Questioning the nonvoluntary status of family relationships. *Annals of the International Communication Association, 41*(1), 28–45.

Schenck-Fontaine, A., Lansford, J. E., Skinner, A. T., Deater-Deckard, K., Di Giunta, L., Dodge, K. A., Oburu, P., Pastorelli, C., Sorbring, E., Steinberg, L., Malone, P. S., Tapanya, S., Uribe Tirado, L. M., Alampay, L. P., Al-Hassan, S. M., Bacchini, D., Bornstein, M. H., & Chang, L. (2020). Associations between perceived material deprivation, parents' discipline practices, and children's behavior problems: An international perspective. *Child Development, 91*(1), 307–326. https://doi.org/10.1111/cdev.13151

Scherer, A. K. (2015). *Mortuary landscapes of the classic maya: Rituals of body and soul.* University of Texas Press.

Scherrer, V., & Preckel, F. (2019). Development of motivational variables and self-esteem during the school career: A meta-analysis of longitudinal studies. *Review of Educational Research, 89*(2), 211–258. https://doi.org/10.3102/0034654318819127

Schiffrin, H. H., Erchull, M. J., Sendrick, E., Yost, J. C., Power, V., & Saldanha, E. R. (2019). The effects of maternal and paternal helicopter parenting on the self-determination and well-being of emerging adults. *Journal of Child and Family Studies, 28*(12), 3346–3359. https://doi.org/10.1007/s10826-019-01513-6

Schimmele, C. M., & Wu, Z. (2016). Repartnering after union dissolution in later life. *Journal of Marriage and Family, 78*(4), 1013–1031. https://doi.org/10.1111/jomf.12315

Schlegel, A. (1995). A cross-cultural approach to adolescence. *Ethos, 23*(1), 15–32.

Schlegel, A. (2015). The cultural context of adolescent self-regulation. In G. Oettingen & P. M. Gollwitzer (Eds.), *Self-regulation in adolescence* (pp. 288–307). Cambridge University Press.

Schlegel, A., & Barry, H. (1991). *Adolescence: An anthropological inquiry.* Free Press.

Schlesier, J., Roden, I., & Moschner, B. (2019). Emotion regulation in primary school children: A systematic review. *Children and Youth Services Review, 100*, 239–257. https://doi.org/10.1016/j.childyouth.2019.02.044

Schmader, T., & Forbes, C. (2017). Stereotypes and performance. In J. R. Smith & S. A. Haslam (Eds.), *Social psychology: Revisiting the classic studies* (p. 245). Sage.

Schmidt, S. (2020). *Midlife crisis: The feminist origins of a chauvinist cliché.* University of Chicago Press.

Schmitt, M. L., Hagstrom, C., Nowara, A., Gruer, C., Adenu-Mensah, N. E., Keeley, K., & Sommer, M. (2021). The intersection of menstruation, school and family: Experiences of girls growing up in urban areas in the U.S.A. *International Journal of Adolescence and Youth, 26*(1), 94–109. https://doi.org/10.1080/02673843.2020.1867207

Schneider, D., Harknett, K., & Stimpson, M. (2018). What explains the decline in first marriage in the United States? Evidence from the panel study of income dynamics, 1969 to 2013. *Journal of Marriage and Family, 80*(4), 791–811. https://doi.org/10.1111/jomf.12481

Schneider, M. (2020, June 25). Census shows white decline, nonwhite majority among youngest. *AP News.* https://apnews.com/article/a3600edf620ccf2759080d00f154c069

Schneider, W., & Ornstein, P. A. (2019). Determinants of memory development in childhood and adolescence.

International Journal of Psychology, 54(3), 307–315. https://doi.org/10.1002/ijop.12503

Schnittker, J. (2019). Health spillovers among military spouses: Evidence from active duty, veteran, and surviving spouses. *Journal of Veterans Studies, 4*(2), 64.

Schochet, P. Z. (2018). *National job corps study: 20-year follow-up study using tax data.* Princeton, NJ: Mathematica Policy Research.

Schoenborn, N. L., Janssen, E. M., Boyd, C., Bridges, J. F. P., Wolff, A. C., Xue, Q.-L., & Pollack, C. E. (2018). Older adults' preferences for discussing long-term life expectancy: Results from a national survey. *The Annals of Family Medicine, 16*(6), 530–537. https://doi.org/10.1370/afm.2309

Schofield, T. J., Conger, R. D., & Conger, K. J. (2017). Disrupting intergenerational continuity in harsh parenting: Self-control and a supportive partner. *Development and Psychopathology, 29*(4), 1279–1287.

Scholz, B., Goncharov, L., Emmerich, N., Lu, V. N., Chapman, M., Clark, S. J., Wilson, T., Slade, D., & Mitchell, I. (2020). Clinicians' accounts of communication with patients in end-of-life care contexts: A systematic review. *Patient Education and Counseling, 103*(10), 1913–1921. https://doi.org/10.1016/j.pec.2020.06.033

Schoppe-Sullivan, S. J., & Fagan, J. (2020). The evolution of fathering research in the 21st century: Persistent challenges, new directions. *Journal of Marriage and Family, 82*(1), 175–197. https://doi.org/10.1111/jomf.12645

Schramm, D. G., Galovan, A. M., & Goddard, H. W. (2017). What relationship researchers and relationship practitioners wished the other knew: Integrating discovery and practice in couple relationships. *Family Relations, 66*(4), 696–711. https://doi.org/10.1111/fare.12270

Schreiner, L. A. (2017). The privilege of grit. *About Campus, 22*(5), 11–20.

Schreuders, E., Braams, B. R., Blankenstein, N. E., Peper, J. S., Güroğlu, B., & Crone, E. A. (2018). Contributions of reward sensitivity to ventral striatum activity across adolescence and early adulthood. *Child Development, 89*(3), 797–810. https://doi.org/10.1111/cdev.13056

Schuch, F. B., Vancampfort, D., Firth, J., Rosenbaum, S., Ward, P. B., Silva, E. S., Hallgren, M., Leon, A. P. D., Dunn, A. L., Deslandes, A. C., Fleck, M. P., Carvalho, A. F., & Stubbs, B. (2018). Physical activity and incident depression: A meta-analysis of prospective cohort studies. *American Journal of Psychiatry.* https://doi.org/10.1176/appi.ajp.2018.17111194

Schuengel, C., Verhage, M. L., & Duschinsky, R. (2021). Prospecting the attachment research field: A move to the level of engagement. *Attachment & Human Development,* 1–21. https://doi.org/10.1080/14616734.2021.1918449

Schulenberg, J. E., Patrick, M. E., Johnston, L. D., O'Malley, P. M., Bachman, J. G., & Miech, R. A. (2021). *Monitoring the future national survey results on drug use, 1975–2020: Volume II. College students and adults ages 19–60.* Institute for Social Research, The University of Michigan. http://monitoringthefuture.org/pubs.html#monographs

Schulenberg, J., Patrick, M. E., Maslowsky, J., & Maggs, J. L. (2014). The epidemiology and etiology of adolescent substance use in developmental perspective. In M. Lewis & K. D. Rudolph (Eds.), *Handbook of developmental psychopathology* (pp. 601–620). Springer. https://doi.org/10.1007/978-1-4614-9608-3_30

Schulman, K. A., Greicius, M. D., & Richman, B. (2021). Will CMS find aducanumab reasonable and necessary for Alzheimer disease after FDA approval? *JAMA, 326*(5), 383–384. https://doi.org/10.1001/jama.2021.11768

Schulte, P. A., Grosch, J., Scholl, J. C., & Tamers, S. L. (2018). Framework for considering productive aging and work. *Journal of Occupational and Environmental Medicine, 60*(5), 440–448. https://doi.org/10.1097/JOM.0000000000001295

Schulz, E., Wu, C. M., Ruggeri, A., & Meder, B. (2019). Searching for rewards like a child means less generalization and more directed exploration. *Psychological Science, 30*(11), 1561–1572. https://doi.org/10.1177/0956797619863663

Schulz, J., Bahrami-Rad, D., Beauchamp, J., & Henrich, J. (2018). *The origins of WEIRD psychology* (SSRN Scholarly

Paper ID 3201031). Social Science Research Network. https://doi.org/10.2139/ssrn.3201031

Schulz, R., Beach, S. R., Czaja, S. J., Martire, L. M., & Monin, J. K. (2020). Family caregiving for older adults. *Annual Review of Psychology, 71*, 635–659. https://doi .org/10.1146/annurev-psych-010419-050754

Schunk, D. H., & Dibenedetto, M. K. (2016). Self-efficacy theory in education. *Handbook of Motivation at School, 2*, 34–54.

Schuster, R. C., Szpak, M., Klein, E., Sklar, K., & Dickin, K. L. (2019). "I try, I do": Child feeding practices of motivated, low-income parents reflect trade-offs between psychosocial- and nutrition-oriented goals. *Appetite, 136*, 114–123. https://doi .org/10.1016/j.appet.2019.01.005

Schut, M. S. H. (1999). The dual process model of coping with bereavement: Rationale and description. *Death Studies, 23*(3), 197–224.

Schwandt, H. (2016). Unmet aspirations as an explanation for the age U-shape in wellbeing. *Journal of Economic Behavior & Organization, 122*, 75–87.

Schwanitz, K., & Mulder, C. H. (2015). Living arrangements of young adults in Europe. *Comparative Population Studies, 40*(4). http://www.comparativepopulationstudies. de/index.php/CPoS/article/view/158

Schwartz, C. R., Wang, Y., & Mare, R. D. (2021). Opportunity and change in occupational assortative mating. *Social Science Research, 99*, 102600. https://doi.org/10.1016/j .ssresearch.2021.102600

Schwartz, P., & Velotta, N. (2018). Online dating: Changing intimacy one swipe at a time? In J. Van Hook, S. M. McHale, & V. King (Eds.), *Families and technology* (pp. 57–88). Springer.

Schwartz, S. E. O., Kanchewa, S. S., Rhodes, J. E., Cutler, E., & Cunningham, J. L. (2016). "I didn't know you could just ask": Empowering underrepresented college-bound students to recruit academic and career mentors. *Children and Youth Services Review, 64*, 51–59. https://doi.org/10.1016/j .childyouth.2016.03.001

Schwartz, S. E. O., Kanchewa, S. S., Rhodes, J. E., Gowdy, G., Stark, A. M., Horn, J. P., Parnes, M., & Spencer, R. (2018). "I'm having a little struggle with this, can you help me out?" Examining impacts and processes of a social capital intervention for first-generation college students. *American Journal of Community Psychology, 61*(1–2), 166–178. https:// doi.org/10.1002/ajcp.12206

Schwartz, S. J., Zamboanga, B. L., Meca, A., & Ritchie, R. A. (2012). Identity around the world: An overview. *New Directions for Child and Adolescent Development, 2012*(138), 1–18.

Schwartz-Mette, R. A., Shankman, J., Dueweke, A. R., Borowski, S., & Rose, A. J. (2020). Relations of friendship experiences with depressive symptoms and loneliness in childhood and adolescence: A meta-analytic review. *Psychological Bulletin, 146*(8), 664–700. https://doi.org/10.1037 /bul0000239

Scott, E. S., Bonnie, R. J., & Steinberg, L. (2016). Young adulthood as a transitional legal category: Science, social change, and justice policy. *Fordham Law Review, 85*, 641. https://heinonline.org/HOL/Page?handle=hein.journals /flr85&id=657&div=&collection=

Scott, K. A., Britton, L., & McLemore, M. R. (2019). The ethics of perinatal care for black women: Dismantling the structural racism in "mother blame" narratives. *The Journal of Perinatal & Neonatal Nursing, 33*(2), 108–115. https:// doi.org/10.1097/JPN.0000000000000394

Scott, K. E., Shutts, K., & Devine, P. G. (2020). Parents' expectations for and reactions to children's racial biases. *Child Development, 91*(3), 769–783.

Scott, S. R., & Manczak, E. M. (2021). Peripheral immune correlates of childhood and adolescent peer relationships: A systematic review. *Developmental Psychobiology, 63*(5), 985–996. https://doi.org/10.1002/dev.22119

Scrimgeour, M. B., Davis, E. L., & Buss, K. A. (2016). You get what you get and you don't throw a fit! Emotion socialization and child physiology jointly predict early prosocial development. *Developmental Psychology, 52*(1), 102.

Scrimshaw, S., Backes, E. P., & Committee on Assessing Health Outcomes by Birth Settings. (Eds.). (2020).

Birth settings in America: Outcomes, quality, access and choice. National Academies of Sciences, Engineering and Medicine.

Sear, R. (2021). The male breadwinner nuclear family is not the 'traditional' human family, and promotion of this myth may have adverse health consequences. *Philosophical Transactions of the Royal Society B: Biological Sciences, 376*(1827), 20200020. https://doi.org/10.1098/rstb.2020.0020

Seaton, E. K., & Carter, R. (2019). Perceptions of pubertal timing and discrimination among African American and Caribbean Black girls. *Child Development, 90*(2), 480–488.

Sebastián-Enesco, C., Hernández-Lloreda, M. V., & Colmenares, F. (2013). Two and a half-year-old children are prosocial even when their partners are not. *Journal of Experimental Child Psychology, 116*(2), 186–198. https://doi .org/10.1016/j.jecp.2013.05.007

Section on Endocrinology. (2014). *Physical development: What's normal? What's not? (Ages & Stages).* Healthy Children. https://www.healthychildren.org/English/ages-stages /gradeschool/puberty/Pages/Physical-Development-Whats-Normal-Whats-Not.aspx

Sedghi, A. (2015, April 9). Limits of control: The age debate behind the French air traffic controller strike. *The Guardian.* https://www.theguardian.com/news/datablog/2015/apr/09/ limits-of-control-the-age-debate-behind-the-french-air-traffic-controller-strike

Seeman, T., Merkin, S. S., Goldwater, D., & Cole, S. W. (2020). Intergenerational mentoring, eudaimonic well-being and gene regulation in older adults: A pilot study. *Psychoneuroendocrinology, 111*, 104468. https://doi.org/10.1016/j .psyneuen.2019.104468

Segal, N. L., Craig, J. M., & Umstad, M. P. (2020). Challenge to the assumed rarity of heteropaternal superfecundation: Findings from a case report. *Australian Journal of Forensic Sciences, 52*(5), 547–552. https://doi.org/10.1080 /00450618.2019.1616821

Sege, R. D., Siegel, B. S., Council on Child Abuse and Neglect, & Committee on Psychosocial Aspects of Child and Family Health. (2018). Effective discipline to raise healthy children | American Academy of Pediatrics. *Pediatrics, 142*(6). https://doi.org/10.1542/peds.2018-3112

Sehmi, R., Maughan, B., Matthews, T., & Arseneault, L. (2020). No man is an island: Social resources, stress and mental health at mid-life. *The British Journal of Psychiatry, 217*(5), 638–644. https://doi.org/10.1192/bjp.2019.25

Seidenberg, M. S., Cooper Borkenhagen, M., & Kearns, D. M. (2020). Lost in translation? Challenges in connecting reading science and educational practice. *Reading Research Quarterly, 55*, S119–S130.

Seifert, A., Cotten, S. R., & Xie, B. (2021). A double burden of exclusion? Digital and social exclusion of older adults in times of COVID-19. *The Journals of Gerontology. Series B, Psychological Sciences and Social Sciences, 76*(3), e99–e103. https://doi.org/10.1093/geronb/gbaa098

Seifi, A., Lacci, J. V., & Godoy, D. A. (2020). Incidence of brain death in the United States. *Clinical Neurology and Neurosurgery, 195*, 105885. https://doi.org/10.1016/j .clineuro.2020.105885

Seijo, D., Fariña, F., Corras, T., Novo, M., & Arce, R. (2016). Estimating the epidemiology and quantifying the damages of parental separation in children and adolescents. *Frontiers in Psychology, 7*, 1611.

Sekhar, D. L., Murray-Kolb, L. E., Kunselman, A. R., Weisman, C. S., & Paul, I. M. (2017). Association between menarche and iron deficiency in non-anemic young women. *PLOS ONE, 12*(5), e0177183.

Selemon, L. D. (2013). A role for synaptic plasticity in the adolescent development of executive function. *Translational Psychiatry, 3*(3), e238–e238.

Selman, R. L. (1980). *The growth of interpersonal understanding: Developmental and clinical analyses.* Academy Press.

Semega, J. U. C., Kollar, M., Shrider, E. A., & Creamer, J. (2020). *Income and poverty in the United States: 2019.* https://www.census.gov/library/publications/2020/demo /p60-270.html

Semenov, A. D., Kennedy, D., & Zelazo, P. D. (2020). Mindfulness and executive function: Implications for learning and early childhood education. In M. S. C. Thomas, D. Mareschal, & I. Dumontheil (Eds.), *Educational*

neuroscience: Development across the life span (pp. 298–331). Routledge.

Semyonov, M., Lewin-Epstein, N., & Maskileyson, D. (2013). Where wealth matters more for health: The wealth–health gradient in 16 countries. *Social Science & Medicine, 81*, 10–17. https://doi.org/10.1016/j.socscimed.2013.01.010

Senft, N., Campos, B., Shiota, M. N., & Chentsova-Dutton, Y. E. (2020). Who emphasizes positivity? An exploration of emotion values in people of Latino, Asian, and European heritage living in the United States. *Emotion, 21*(4), 707–719. https://doi.org/10.1037/emo0000737

Sengoku, R. (2020). Aging and Alzheimer's disease pathology. *Neuropathology, 40*(1), 22–29. https://doi.org/10.1111 /neup.12626

Senn, N., & Monod, S. (2015). Development of a comprehensive approach for the early diagnosis of geriatric syndromes in general practice. *Frontiers in Medicine, 2*, 78. https://doi.org/10.3389/fmed.2015.00078

Sentencing Project. (2018). *Report of the Sentencing Project to the United Nations Special Rapporteur on Contemporary Forms of Racism, Racial Discrimination, Xenophobia, and Related Intolerance: Regarding racial disparities in the United States criminal justice system.*

Serrat, R., Scharf, T., Villar, F., & Gómez, C. (2020). Fifty-five years of research into older people's civic participation: Recent trends, future directions. *The Gerontologist, 60*(1), e38–e51. https://doi.org/10.1093/geront/gnz021

Sesame Workshop. (2016). K is for kind: A national survey on kindness and kids. *Sesame Street.* http://kindness.sesame-street.org

Setoh, P., Lee, K. J. J., Zhang, L., Qian, M. K., Quinn, P. C., Heyman, G. D., & Lee, K. (2019). Racial categorization predicts implicit racial bias in preschool children. *Child Development, 90*(1), 162–179. https://doi.org/10.1111 /cdev.12851

Settersten, R. A. (2011). Becoming adult: Meanings and markers for young Americans. In M. C. Waters, P. J. Carr, M. Kefalas, & J. A. Holdaway (Eds.), *Coming of age in America: The transition to adulthood in the twenty-first century* (pp. 169–190). University of California Press. https://www.degruyter.com/document /doi/10.1525/9780520950184-008/html

Settersten, R. A., Bernardi, L., Härkönen, J., Antonucci, T. C., Dykstra, P. A., Heckhausen, J., Kuh, D., Mayer, K. U., Moen, P., Mortimer, J. T., Mulder, C. H., Smeeding, T. M., van der Lippe, T., Hagestad, G. O., Kohli, M., Levy, R., Schoon, I., & Thomson, E. (2020). Understanding the effects of Covid-19 through a life course lens. *Current Perspectives on Aging and the Life Cycle, 45*, 100360. https://doi.org/10.1016/j.alcr.2020.100360

Settersten, R. A., Godlewski, B., & Bengtson, V. L. (2016). Concepts and theories of age and aging. *Handbook of Theories of Aging, 3*, 9–25.

Settersten, R. A., Ottusch, T. M., & Schneider, B. (2015). Becoming adult: Meanings of markers to adulthood. In R. Scott & S. Koss (Eds.), *Emerging trends in the social and behavioral sciences: An interdisciplinary, searchable, and linkable resource* (pp. 1–16). Wiley.

Settersten, R. A., Jr., & Thogmartin, A. (2018). Flux: Insights into the social aspects of life transitions. *Research in Human Development, 15*(3–4), 360–373.

Sexton, C. E., Betts, J. F., Demnitz, N., Dawes, H., Ebmeier, K. P., & Johansen-Berg, H. (2016). A systematic review of MRI studies examining the relationship between physical fitness and activity and the white matter of the ageing brain. *NeuroImage, 131*, 81–90. https://doi .org/10.1016/j.neuroimage.2015.09.071

Shaefer, H. L., Lapidos, A., Wilson, R., & Danziger, S. (2018). Association of income and adversity in childhood with adult health and well-being. *Social Service Review, 92*(1), 69–92. https://doi.org/10.1086/696891

Shafto, M. A., Henson, R. N., Matthews, F. E., Taylor, J. R., Emery, T., Erzinclioglu, S., Hanley, C., Rowe, J. B., Cusack, R., Calder, A. J., Marslen-Wilson, W. D., Duncan, J., Dalgleish, T., Brayne, C., Cam-CAN, & Tyler, L. K. (2019). Cognitive diversity in a healthy aging cohort: Cross-domain cognition in the Cam-CAN project. *Journal of Aging and Health, 32*(9), 1029–1041. https://doi .org/10.1177/0898264319878095

Shah, G. (2009). The impact of economic globalization on work and family collectivism in India. *Journal of Indian Business Research, 1*(2/3), 95–118. https://doi.org/10.1108/17554190911005318

Shah, K., DeRemigis, A., Hageman, J. R., Sriram, S., & Waggoner, D. (2017). Unique characteristics of the X chromosome and related disorders. *NeoReviews, 18*(4), e209–e216. https://doi.org/10.1542/neo.18-4-e209

Shakiba, N., Ellis, B. J., Bush, N. R., & Boyce, W. T. (2020). Biological sensitivity to context: A test of the hypothesized U-shaped relation between early adversity and stress responsivity. *Development and Psychopathology, 32*(2), 641–660.

Shamloul, R., & Ghanem, H. (2013). Erectile dysfunction. *The Lancet, 381*(9861), 153–165. https://doi.org/10.1016/S0140-6736(12)60520-0

Shanahan, E., & Busseri, M. A. (2019). A systematic review of the relationship between perceived life script event age and valence across the life span. *Psychology and Aging, 34*(5), 698.

Shanahan, L., Zucker, N., Copeland, W. E., Bondy, C., Egger, H. L., & Costello, E. J. (2015). Childhood somatic complaints predict generalized anxiety and depressive disorders during adulthood in a community sample. *Psychological Medicine, 45*(8), 1721–1730. https://doi.org/10.1017/S0033291714002840

Shanahan, M. J., Mortimer, J. T., & Johnson, M. K. (2016). Introduction: Life course studies–trends, challenges, and future directions. In M. J. Shanahan, J. T. Mortimer, & M. K. Johnson (Eds.), *Handbook of the life course* (pp. 1–23). Springer.

Shanahan, T. (2020). What constitutes a science of reading instruction? *Reading Research Quarterly, 55*(S1), S235–S247. https://doi.org/10.1002/rrq.349

Shannon, C., & Klausner, J. (2018). The growing epidemic of sexually transmitted infections in adolescents: A neglected population. *Current Opinion in Pediatrics, 30*(1), 137–143. https://doi.org/10.1097/MOP.0000000000000578

Shapiro, D. (2014). Stepparents and parenting stress: The roles of gender, marital quality, and views about gender roles. *Family Process, 53*(1), 97–108.

Shapiro, D., Dundar, A., Huie, F., Wakhungu, P. K., Bhimdiwala, A., Nathan, A., & Hwang, Y. (2018). *Transfer and mobility: A national view of student movement in postsecondary institutions—Fall 2011 cohort* (Signature Report No. 15). National Student Clearinghouse Research Center.

Shapiro, D., Dundar, A., Yuan, X., Harrell, A. T., & Wakhungu, P. K. (2014). *Completing college: A national view of student attainment rates—Fall 2008 cohort* (Signature Report No. 8). National Student Clearinghouse. http://eric.ed.gov/?id=ED556471

Shapiro, G. D., Bushnik, T., Wilkins, R., Kramer, M. S., Kaufman, J. S., Sheppard, A. J., & Yang, S. (2018). Adverse birth outcomes in relation to maternal marital and cohabitation status in Canada. *Annals of Epidemiology, 28*(8), 503–509.e11. https://doi.org/10.1016/j.annepidem.2018.05.001

Sharifian, N., Kraal, A. Z., Zaheed, A. B., Sol, K., & Zahodne, L. B. (2020). Longitudinal associations between contact frequency with friends and with family, activity engagement, and cognitive functioning. *Journal of the International Neuropsychological Society, 26*(8), 815–824.

Sharifian, N., Manly, J. J., Brickman, A. M., & Zahodne, L. B. (2019). Social network characteristics and cognitive functioning in ethnically diverse older adults: The role of network size and composition. *Neuropsychology, 33*(7), 956–963. https://doi.org/10.1037/neu0000564

Sharifian, N., Sol, K., Zahodne, L. B., & Antonucci, T. C. (2022). Social relationships and adaptation in later life. In *Reference module in neuroscience and biobehavioral psychology*. Elsevier. https://doi.org/10.1016/B978-0-12-818697-8.00016-9

Sharma, S., van Teijlingen, E., Hundley, V., Angell, C., & Simkhada, P. (2016). Dirty and 40 days in the wilderness: Eliciting childbirth and postnatal cultural practices and beliefs in Nepal. *BMC Pregnancy and Childbirth, 16*, 147. https://doi.org/10.1186/s12884-016-0938-4

Sharma, S., Wong, D., Schomberg, J., Knudsen-Robbins, C., Gibbs, D., Berkowitz, C., & Heyming, T. (2021).

COVID-19: Differences in sentinel injury and child abuse reporting during a pandemic. *Child Abuse & Neglect, 116*, 104990. https://doi.org/10.1016/j.chiabu.2021.104990

Sharon, T. (2016). Constructing adulthood markers of adulthood and well-being among emerging adults. *Emerging Adulthood, 4*(3), 161–167. https://doi.org/10.1177/2167696815579826

Sharp, C., & Wall, K. (2018). Personality pathology grows up: Adolescence as a sensitive period. *Current Opinion in Psychology, 21*, 111–116. https://doi.org/10.1016/j.copsyc.2017.11.010

Shavelson, R. J., Hubner, J. J., & Stanton, G. C. (1976). Self-concept: Validation of construct interpretations. *Review of Educational Research, 46*(3), 407–441.

Shaver, P. R., Mikulincer, M., & Cassidy, J. (2019). Attachment, caregiving in couple relationships, and prosocial behavior in the wider world. *Current Opinion in Psychology, 25*, 16–20. https://doi.org/10.1016/j.copsyc.2018.02.009

Shayer, M., & Ginsburg, D. (2009). Thirty years on–a large anti-Flynn effect/(II): 13-and 14-year-olds. Piagetian tests of formal operations norms 1976–2006/7. *British Journal of Educational Psychology, 79*(3), 409–418.

Sheehan, C. M., & Tucker-Drob, E. M. (2019). Gendered expectations distort male–female differences in instrumental activities of daily living in later adulthood. *The Journals of Gerontology: Series B, 74*(4), 715–723.

Sheehan, L., Nieweglowski, K., & Corrigan, P. (2016). The stigma of personality disorders. *Current Psychiatry Reports, 18*(1), 11.

Sheehan, P., Sweeny, K., Rasmussen, B., Wils, A., Friedman, H. S., Mahon, J., & Laski, L. (2017). Building the foundations for sustainable development: A case for global investment in the capabilities of adolescents. *The Lancet, 390*(10104), 1792–1806.

Sheehy, G. (1976). *Passages: Predictable crises of adult life.* Dutton.

Sheikh, M. A. (2018). Childhood disadvantage, education, and psychological distress in adulthood: A three-wave population-based study. *Journal of Affective Disorders, 229*, 206–212. https://doi.org/10.1016/j.jad.2017.12.051

Shelleby, E. C., Shaw, D. S., Dishion, T. J., Wilson, M. N., & Gardner, F. (2018). Effects of the family check-up on reducing growth in conduct problems from toddlerhood through school age: An analysis of moderated mediation. *Journal of Consulting and Clinical Psychology, 86*(10), 856.

Shelley, W. W., & Peterson, D. (2019). "Sticks and stones may break my bones, but bullying will get me bangin'": Bullying involvement and adolescent gang joining. *Youth Violence and Juvenile Justice, 17*(4), 385–412.

Shenhav, S., Campos, B., & Goldberg, W. A. (2017). Dating out is intercultural: Experience and perceived parent disapproval by ethnicity and immigrant generation. *Journal of Social and Personal Relationships, 34*(3), 397–422.

Shepherd, C. C. J., Li, J., Cooper, M. N., Hopkins, K. D., & Farrant, B. M. (2017). The impact of racial discrimination on the health of Australian Indigenous children aged 5–10 years: Analysis of national longitudinal data. *International Journal for Equity in Health, 16*, 116.

Sherman, L. E., Greenfield, P. M., Hernandez, L. M., & Dapretto, M. (2018). Peer influence via Instagram: Effects on brain and behavior in adolescence and young adulthood. *Child Development, 89*(1), 37–47. https://doi.org/10.1111/cdev.12838

Shermer, M. (1990). Darwin, Freud, and the myth of the hero in science. *Science Communication, 11*(3), 280–301. https://doi.org/10.1177/107554709001100305

Shiba, K., Kubzansky, L. D., Williams, D. R., VanderWeele, T. J., & Kim, E. S. (2021). Associations between purpose in life and mortality by SES. *American Journal of Preventive Medicine, 61*(2), e53–e61. https://doi.org/10.1016/j.amepre.2021.02.011

Shiels, M. S., Chernyavskiy, P., Anderson, W. F., Best, A. F., Haozous, E. A., Hartge, P., Rosenberg, P. S., Thomas, D., Freedman, N. D., & de Gonzalez, A. B. (2017). Trends in premature mortality in the USA by sex, race, and ethnicity from 1999 to 2014: An analysis of death certificate data. *The Lancet, 389*(10073), 1043–1054. https://doi.org/10.1016/S0140-6736(17)30187-3

Shifren, J. L., Crandall, C. J., & Manson, J. E. (2019). Menopausal hormone therapy. *JAMA, 321*(24), 2458–2459.

Shih, S.-F., Wagner, A. L., Masters, N. B., Prosser, L. A., Lu, Y., & Zikmund-Fisher, B. J. (2021). Vaccine hesitancy and rejection of a vaccine for the novel coronavirus in the United States. *Frontiers in Immunology, 12*, 558270. https://doi.org/10.3389/fimmu.2021.558270

Shimon-Raz, O., Salomon, R., Bloch, M., Aisenberg Romano, G., Yeshurun, Y., Ulmer Yaniv, A., Zagoory-Sharon, O., & Feldman, R. (2021). Mother brain is wired for social moments. *ELife, 10*, e59436. https://doi.org/10.7554/eLife.59436

Shin, C.-N., Lee, Y.-S., & Belyea, M. (2018). Physical activity, benefits, and barriers across the aging continuum. *Applied Nursing Research, 44*, 107–112. https://doi.org/10.1016/j.apnr.2018.10.003

Shinall, M. C., Jr., Stahl, D., & Bibler, T. M. (2018). Addressing a patient's hope for a miracle. *Journal of Pain and Symptom Management, 55*(2), 535–539.

Shiner, R. L. (2009). The development of personality disorders: Perspectives from normal personality development in childhood and adolescence. *Development and Psychopathology, 21*(3), 715–734.

Shiner, R. L. (2017). Personality trait structure, processes, and development in childhood and adolescence. *European Journal of Personality, 31*, 567–568.

Shiner, R. L. (2021). Personality development in middle childhood. In O. P. John & R. W. Robins (Eds.), *Handbook of personality: Theory and research* (4th ed., pp. 284–302). Guilford.

Shirtcliff, E. A., Skinner, M. L., Obasi, E. M., & Haggerty, K. P. (2017). Positive parenting predicts cortisol functioning six years later in young adults. *Developmental Science, 20*(6), e12461. https://doi.org/10.1111/desc.12461

Shiu, C., Muraco, A., & Fredriksen-Goldsen, K. (2016). Invisible care: Friend and partner care among older lesbian, gay, bisexual, and transgender (LGBT) adults. *Journal of the Society for Social Work and Research, 7*(3), 527–546. https://doi.org/10.1086/687325

Shneidman, L., Gaskins, S., & Woodward, A. (2016a). Child-directed teaching and social learning at 18 months of age: Evidence from Yucatec Mayan and US infants. *Developmental Science, 19*(3), 372–381. https://doi.org/10.1111/desc.12318

Shneidman, L. A., & Goldin-Meadow, S. (2012). Language input and acquisition in a Mayan village: How important is directed speech? *Developmental Science, 15*(5), 659–673. https://doi.org/10.1111/j.1467-7687.2012.01168.x

Shneidman, L., Gweon, H., Schulz, L. E., & Woodward, A. L. (2016b). Learning from others and spontaneous exploration: A cross-cultural investigation. *Child Development, 87*(3), 723–735. https://doi.org/10.1111/cdev.12502

Shoaibi, A., Neelon, B., Østbye, T., & Benjamin-Neelon, S. E. (2019). Longitudinal associations of gross motor development, motor milestone achievement and weight-for-length z score in a racially diverse cohort of US infants. *BMJ Open, 9*(1), e024440. https://doi.org/10.1136/bmjopen-2018-024440

Shoda, Y., Mischel, W., & Peake, P. K. (1990). Predicting adolescent cognitive and self-regulatory competencies from preschool delay of gratification: Identifying diagnostic conditions. *Developmental Psychology, 26*(6), 978.

Shonkoff, J. P., Slopen, N., & Williams, D. R. (2021). Early childhood adversity, toxic stress, and the impacts of racism on the foundations of health. *Annual Review of Public Health, 42*(1), 115–134. https://doi.org/10.1146/annurev-publhealth-090419-101940

Shor, E., Roelfs, D. J., Bugyi, P., & Schwartz, J. E. (2012). Meta-analysis of marital dissolution and mortality: Reevaluating the intersection of gender and age. *Social Science & Medicine, 75*(1), 46–59.

Shulman, E. P., Smith, A. R., Silva, K., Icenogle, G., Duell, N., Chein, J., & Steinberg, L. (2016). The dual systems model: Review, reappraisal, and reaffirmation. *Developmental Cognitive Neuroscience, 17*, 103–117. https://doi.org/10.1016/j.dcn.2015.12.010

Shulman, S., & Connolly, J. (2015). The challenge of romantic relationships in emerging adulthood. In J. J.

Arnett (Ed.), *The Oxford handbook of emerging adulthood* (pp. 230–244). Oxford University Press.

Shulman, S., & Scharf, M. (2018). Adolescent psychopathology in times of change: The need for integrating a developmental psychopathology perspective. *Journal of Adolescence, 65*, 95–100.

Shulman, S., Scharf, M., Ziv, I., Norona, J., & Welsh, D. P. (2020). Adolescents' sexual encounters with either romantic or casual partners and the quality of their romantic relationships four years later. *The Journal of Sex Research, 57*(2), 155–165. https://doi.org/10.1080/00224499.2018.1560387

Shulman, S., Seiffge-Krenke, I., Scharf, M., Boiangiu, S. B., & Tregubenko, V. (2016). The diversity of romantic pathways during emerging adulthood and their developmental antecedents. *International Journal of Behavioral Development, 42*(2), 167–174. https://doi.org/10.1177/0165025416673474

Shulman, S., Seiffge-Krenke, I., Ziv, I., & Tuval-Mashiach, R. (2019). Patterns of romantic pathways among 23 year olds and their adolescent antecedents. *Journal of Youth and Adolescence, 48*(7), 1390–1402. https://doi.org/10.1007/s10964-018-0951-1

Shultz, J., Powers, M., Jewell, J., Taylor, G., & Djuhari, L. (2020). *Prevention of overweight and obesity in children and adolescents: UNICEF advocacy strategy and guidance.* UNICEF.

Shultz, S., Klin, A., & Jones, W. (2018). Neonatal transitions in social behavior and their implications for autism. *Trends in Cognitive Sciences, 22*(5), 452–469. https://doi.org/10.1016/j.tics.2018.02.012

Shumer, D. E., & Araya, A. (2019). Endocrine care of transgender children and adolescents. In L. Poretsky & W. C. Hembree (Eds.), *Transgender medicine: A multidisciplinary approach* (pp. 165–181). Springer International Publishing. https://doi.org/10.1007/978-3-030-05683-4_9

Shutts, K. (2015). Young children's preferences: Gender, race, and social status. *Child Development Perspectives, 9*(4), 262–266. https://doi.org/10.1111/cdep.12154

Shutts, K., Kenward, B., Falk, H., Ivegran, A., & Fawcett, C. (2017). Early preschool environments and gender: Effects of gender pedagogy in Sweden. *Journal of Experimental Child Psychology, 162*, 1–17.

Siddiqi, A., Shahidi, F. V., Ramraj, C., & Williams, D. R. (2017). Associations between race, discrimination and risk for chronic disease in a population-based sample from Canada. *Social Science & Medicine, 194*, 135–141. https://doi.org/10.1016/j.socscimed.2017.10.009

Siebert, J. S., Wahl, H. W., Degen, C., & Schröder, J. (2018). Attitude toward own aging as a risk factor for cognitive disorder in old age: 12-year evidence from the ILSE study. *Psychology and Aging, 33*(3), 461.

Siegel, R. L., Miller, K. D., Fuchs, H. E., & Jemal, A. (2021). Cancer statistics, 2021. *CA: A Cancer Journal for Clinicians, 71*(1), 7–33. https://doi.org/10.3322/caac.21654

Siegel, R. S., & Dickstein, D. P. (2012). Anxiety in adolescents: Update on its diagnosis and treatment for primary care providers. *Adolescent Health, Medicine and Therapeutics, 3*, 1.

Siegler, R. S. (1992). The other Alfred Binet. *Developmental Psychology, 28*(2), 179.

Siegler, R. S. (1999). Strategic development. *Trends in Cognitive Sciences, 3*(11), 430–435. https://doi.org/10.1016/S1364-6613(99)01372-8

Siegler, R. S. (2006). Microgenetic analyses of learning. In D. Kuhn, R. S. Siegler, W. Damon, & R. M. Lerner (Eds.), *Handbook of child psychology: Cognition, perception, and language* (pp. 464–510). John Wiley & Sons.

Siegler, R. S. (2016). Continuity and change in the field of cognitive development and in the perspectives of one cognitive developmentalist. *Child Development Perspectives, 10*(2), 128–133. https://doi.org/10.1111/cdep.12173

Siegler, R. S., & Braithwaite, D. W. (2017). Numerical development. *Annual Review of Psychology, 68*, 187–213.

Siegler, R. S., & Ellis, S. (1996). Piaget on childhood. *Psychological Science, 7*(4), 211–215. https://doi.org/10.1111/j.1467-9280.1996.tb00361.x

Siegler, R. S., Im, S.-H., & Braithwaite, D. (2020). Understanding development requires assessing the relevant environment: Examples from mathematics learning. *New Directions for Child and Adolescent Development, 2020*(173), 83–100. https://doi.org/10.1002/cad.20372

Sierra, F. (2016). The emergence of geroscience as an interdisciplinary approach to the enhancement of health span and life span. *Cold Spring Harbor Perspectives in Medicine, 6*(4), a025163. https://doi.org/10.1101/cshperspect.a025163

Signore, F., Gulìa, C., Votino, R., De Leo, V., Zaami, S., Putignani, L., Gigli, S., Santini, E., Bertacca, L., Porrello, A., & Piergentili, R. (2020). The role of number of copies, structure, behavior and copy number variations (CNV) of the Y chromosome in male infertility. *Genes, 11*(1), 40. https://doi.org/10.3390/genes11010040

Silbereisen, R. K., & Schmitt-Rodermund, E. (2020). German immigrants in Germany: Adaption of adolescents' timetables for autonomy. In P. Noack, M. Hofer, & J. Youniss (Eds.), *Psychological responses to social change: Human development in changing environments* (pp. 105–128). De Gruyter. https://www.degruyter.com/document/doi/10.1515/9783110877373-009/html

Silveira, M. J., Kabeto, M. U., & Langa, K. M. (2005). Net worth predicts symptom burden at the end of life. *Journal of Palliative Medicine, 8*(4), 827–837. https://doi.org/10.1089/jpm.2005.8.827

Silvers, J. A., & Guassi Moreira, J. F. (2019). Capacity and tendency: A neuroscientific framework for the study of emotion regulation. *Neuroscience Letters, 693*, 35–39. https://doi.org/10.1016/j.neulet.2017.09.017

Silverstein, M., & Bengtson, V. L. (2018). Return to religion? Predictors of religious change among baby-boomers in their transition to later life. *Journal of Population Ageing, 11*(1), 7–21.

Silverstein, M., Gans, D., Lowenstein, A., Giarrusso, R., & Bengtson, V. L. (2010). Older parent–child relationships in six developed nations: Comparisons at the intersection of affection and conflict. *Journal of Marriage and the Family, 72*(4), 1006–1021. https://doi.org/10.1111/j.1741-3737.2010.00745.x

Silverstein, M., Hadland, S. E., Hallett, E., & Botticelli, M. (2021). Principles of care for young adults with substance use disorders. *Pediatrics, 147*(Supplement 2), S195–S203. https://doi.org/10.1542/peds.2020-023523B

Simanovsky, N., Hiller, N., Loubashevsky, N., & Rozovsky, K. (2012). Normal CT characteristics of the thymus in adults. *European Journal of Radiology, 81*(11), 3581–3586. https://doi.org/10.1016/j.ejrad.2011.12.015

Simion, F., & Di Giorgio, E. (2015). Face perception and processing in early infancy: Inborn predispositions and developmental changes. *Frontiers in Psychology, 6*, 969.

Simning, A., Fox, M. L., Barnett, S. L., Sorensen, S., & Conwell, Y. (2019). Depressive and anxiety symptoms in older adults with auditory, vision, and dual sensory impairment. *Journal of Aging and Health, 31*(8), 1353–1375. https://doi.org/10.1177/0898264318781123

Simon, A., Pratt, M., Hutton, B., Skidmore, B., Fakhraei, R., Rybak, N., Corsi, D. J., Walker, M., Velez, M. P., Smith, G. N., & Gaudet, L. M. (2020). Guidelines for the management of pregnant women with obesity: A systematic review. *Obesity Reviews, 21*(3), e12972. https://doi.org/10.1111/obr.12972

Simon, E. B., Vallat, R., Barnes, C. M., & Walker, M. P. (2020). Sleep loss and the socio-emotional brain. *Trends in Cognitive Sciences, 24*(6), 435–450.

Simon, K. (2013, February 8). A life defined not by disability, but love (Story Corps). *Morning Edition.* National Public Radio.

Simon, L., & Daneback, K. (2013). Adolescents' use of the internet for sex education: A thematic and critical review of the literature. *International Journal of Sexual Health, 25*(4), 305–319. https://doi.org/10.1080/19317611.2013.823899

Simon, R. W., & Caputo, J. (2019). The costs and benefits of parenthood for mental and physical health in the United States: The importance of parenting stage. *Society and Mental Health, 9*(3), 296–315. https://doi.org/10.1177/2156869318786760

Simon, T. R., Shattuck, A., Kacha-Ochana, A., David-Ferdon, C. F., Hamby, S., Henly, M., Merrick, M. T., Turner, H. A., & Finkelhor, D. (2018). Injuries from physical abuse: National survey of children's exposure to violence I–III. *American Journal of Preventive Medicine, 54*(1), 129–132. https://doi.org/10.1016/j.amepre.2017.08.031

Simoni, Z. (2021). Social class, teachers, and medicalisation lag: A qualitative investigation of teachers' discussions of ADHD with parents and the effect of neighbourhood-level social class. *Health Sociology Review, 30*(2), 188–203. https://doi.org/10.1080/14461242.2020.1820364

Simons, C., Metzger, S. R., & Sonnenschein, S. (2020). Children's metacognitive knowledge of five key learning processes. *Translational Issues in Psychological Science, 6*(1), 32.

Simons, D. J., Boot, W. R., Charness, N., Gathercole, S. E., Chabris, C. F., Hambrick, D. Z., & Stine-Morrow, E. A. L. (2016). Do "brain-training" programs work? *Psychological Science in the Public Interest, 17*(3), 103–186. https://doi.org/10.1177/1529100616661983

Simons, R. L., Lei, M.-K., Klopack, E., Beach, S. R. H., Gibbons, F. X., & Philibert, R. A. (2020). The effects of social adversity, discrimination, and health risk behaviors on the accelerated aging of African Americans: Further support for the weathering hypothesis. *Social Science & Medicine, 282*, 113169. https://doi.org/10.1016/j.socscimed.2020.113169

Simpson, J. A., Campbell, B., & Berscheid, E. (1986). The association between romantic love and marriage: Kephart (1967) twice revisited. *Personality and Social Psychology Bulletin, 12*(3), 363–372. https://doi.org/10.1177/0146167286123011

Sims, R., Hill, M., & Williams, J. (2020). The multiplex model of the genetics of Alzheimer's disease. *Nature Neuroscience, 23*(3), 311–322. https://doi.org/10.1038/s41593-020-0599-5

Sin, N. L., Klaiber, P., Wen, J. H., & DeLongis, A. (2021). Helping amid the pandemic: Daily affective and social implications of COVID-19-related prosocial activities. *The Gerontologist, 61*(1), 59–70.

Singer, D. G., Singer, J. L., D'Agostino, H., & DeLong, R. (2009). Children's pastimes and play in sixteen nations: Is free-play declining? *American Journal of Play, 1*(3): 283–312.

Singh, G. K., Daus, G. P., Allender, M., Ramey, C. T., Martin, E. K., Perry, C., Reyes, A. A. D. L., & Vedamuthu, I. P. (2017). Social determinants of health in the United States: Addressing major health inequality trends for the nation, 1935–2016. *International Journal of MCH and AIDS, 6*(2), 139–164. https://doi.org/10.21106/ijma.236

Singh, G. K., & Siahpush, M. (2014). Widening rural-urban disparities in life expectancy, U.S., 1969–2009. *American Journal of Preventive Medicine, 46*(2), e19–29. https://doi.org/10.1016/j.amepre.2013.10.017

Singh, L., Tan, A., & Quinn, P. C. (2021). Infants recognize words spoken through opaque masks but not through clear masks. *Developmental Science, 24*(6), e13117. https://doi.org/10.1111/desc.13117

Singhal, A., Cole, T. J., Fewtrell, M., & Lucas, A. (2004). Breastmilk feeding and lipoprotein profile in adolescents born preterm: Follow-up of a prospective randomised study. *The Lancet, 363*(9421), 1571–1578.

Singh-Manoux, A., Kivimaki, M., Glymour, M. M., Elbaz, A., Berr, C., Ebmeier, K. P., Ferrie, J. E., & Dugravot, A. (2012). Timing of onset of cognitive decline: Results from Whitehall II prospective cohort study. *BMJ, 344*, d7622. https://doi.org/10.1136/bmj.d7622

Sink, K. M., Espeland, M. A., Castro, C. M., Church, T., Cohen, R., Dodson, J. A., Guralnik, J., Hendrie, H. C., Jennings, J., Katula, J., Lopez, O. L., McDermott, M. M., Pahor, M., Reid, K. F., Rushing, J., Verghese, J., Rapp, S., & Williamson, J. D. (2015). Effect of a 24-month physical activity intervention compared to health education on cognitive outcomes in sedentary older adults: The LIFE randomized trial. *JAMA, 314*(8), 781–790. https://doi.org/10.1001/jama.2015.9617

Sinno, S. M., Schuette, C. T., & Hellriegel, C. (2017). The impact of family and community on children's understanding of parental role negotiation.

Journal of Family Issues, 38(4), 435–456. https://doi.org/10.1177/0192513X15573867

Sinnott, J. (1998). *The development of logic in adulthood: Postformal thought and its applications.* Springer Science & Business Media.

Sinnott, J. D. (2002). Postformal thought and adult development. In J. Demick & C. Andreoletti (Eds.), *Handbook of adult development* (pp. 221–238). Springer.

Sinnott, J. D. (2021). Psychology, politics, and complex thought: A time for postformal thought in politics. In J. D. Sinnott & J. S. Rabin (Eds.), *The psychology of political behavior in a time of change* (pp. 147–176). Springer International Publishing. https://doi.org/10.1007/978-3-030-38270-4_5

Sinnott, J., Hilton, S., Wood, M., & Douglas, D. (2020). Relating flow, mindfulness, cognitive flexibility, and postformal thought: Two studies. *Journal of Adult Development, 27*(1), 1–11. https://doi.org/10.1007/s10804-018-9320-2

Sinnott, J., Hilton, S., Wood, M., Spanos, E., & Topel, R. (2015). Does motivation affect emerging adults' intelligence and complex postformal problem solving? *Journal of Adult Development, 23*(2), 69–78. https://doi.org/10.1007/s10804-015-9222-5

Sirey, J. A., Franklin, A. J., McKenzie, S. E., Ghosh, S., & Raue, P. J. (2014). Race, stigma, and mental health referrals among clients of aging services who screened positive for depression. *Psychiatric Services, 65*(4), 537–540. https://doi.org/10.1176/appi.ps.201200530

Sironi, M. (2018). Economic conditions of young adults before and after the Great Recession. *Journal of Family and Economic Issues, 39*(1), 103–116. https://doi.org/10.1007/s10834-017-9554-3

Sisk, C. L., & Romeo, R. D. (2020). *Coming of age: The neurobiology and psychobiology of puberty and adolescence.* Oxford University Press.

Skaalvik, E. M., & Skaalvik, S. (2017). Dimensions of teacher burnout: Relations with potential stressors at school. *Social Psychology of Education, 20*(4), 775–790.

Skelton, A. E., & Franklin, A. (2020). Infants look longer at colours that adults like when colours are highly saturated. *Psychonomic Bulletin & Review, 27*(1), 78–85. https://doi.org/10.3758/s13423-019-01688-5

Skinner, A. L., & Meltzoff, A. N. (2019). Childhood experiences and intergroup biases among children. *Social Issues and Policy Review, 13*(1), 211–240.

Skinner, B. F. (1938). *The behavior of organisms: An experimental analysis.* Appleton-Century.

Skinner, B. F. (1989). Teaching machines. *Science, 243*(4898), 1535–1535. https://doi.org/10.1126/science.243.4898.1535-b

Skinner, B. F. (2011). *About behaviorism.* Knopf Doubleday.

Skloot, R. (2010). *The immortal life of Henrietta Lacks.* Crown.

Skočajić, M. M., Radosavljević, J. G., Okičić, M. G., Janković, I. O., & Žeželj, I. L. (2020). Boys just don't! Gender stereotyping and sanctioning of counter-stereotypical behavior in preschoolers. *Sex Roles, 82*(3), 163–172.

Skolnick, P. (2018). The opioid epidemic: Crisis and solutions. *Annual Review of Pharmacology and Toxicology, 58,* 143–159.

Slaughter, V. (2021). Do newborns have the ability to imitate? *Trends in Cognitive Sciences, 25*(5), 377–387. https://doi.org/10.1016/j.tics.2021.02.006

Slaughter, V., Imuta, K., Peterson, C. C., & Henry, J. D. (2015). Meta-analysis of theory of mind and peer popularity in the preschool and early school years. *Child Development, 86*(4), 1159–1174. https://doi.org/10.1111/cdev.12372

Slaughter-Acey, J. C., Sneed, D., Parker, L., Keith, V. M., Lee, N. L., & Misra, D. P. (2019). Skin tone matters: Racial microaggressions and delayed prenatal care. *American Journal of Preventive Medicine, 57*(3), 321–329. https://doi.org/10.1016/j.amepre.2019.04.014

Slemaker, A., Espeleta, H. C., Heidari, Z., Bohora, S. B., & Silovsky, J. F. (2017). Childhood injury prevention: Predictors of home hazards in Latino families enrolled in SafeCare®+. *Journal of Pediatric Psychology, 42*(7), 738–747.

Sloan, C. J., Mailick, M. R., Hong, J., Ha, J.-H., Greenberg, J. S., & Almeida, D. M. (2020). Longitudinal changes in well-being of parents of individuals with developmental or mental health problems. *Social Science & Medicine, 264,* 113309. https://doi.org/10.1016/j.socscimed.2020.113309

Slobodskaya, H. R., Kozlova, E. A., Han, S. Y., Gartstein, M. A., & Putnam, S. P. (2018). Cross cultural differences in temperament. In M. A. Gartstein & S. P. Putnam (Eds.), *Toddlers, parents, and culture: Findings from the Joint Effort Toddler Temperament Consortium* (pp. 29–37). Routledge. https://doi.org/10.4324/9781315203713-3

Slot, P. L., Mulder, H., Verhagen, J., & Leseman, P. P. (2017). Preschoolers' cognitive and emotional self-regulation in pretend play: Relations with executive functions and quality of play. *Infant and Child Development, 26*(6), e2038.

Slutsky-Ganesh, A. B., Etnier, J. L., & Labban, J. D. (2020). Acute exercise, memory, and neural activation in young adults. *International Journal of Psychophysiology, 158,* 299–309. https://doi.org/10.1016/j.ijpsycho.2020.09.018

Smelser, N. J., & Erikson, E. H. (Eds.). (1980). *Themes of work and love in adulthood.* Harvard University Press.

Smetana, J. G. (2015). Talking the talk and walking the walk: Conversational pathways to moral development. *Human Development, 58*(4–5), 301–307. https://doi.org/10.1159/000439012

Smetana, J. G. (2017). Current research on parenting styles, dimensions, and beliefs. *Current Opinion in Psychology, 15,* 19–25. https://doi.org/10.1016/j.copsyc.2017.02.012

Smetana, J. G., & Rote, W. M. (2019). Adolescent–parent relationships: Progress, processes, and prospects. *Annual Review of Developmental Psychology, 1,* 41-68.

Smit, S., Tacke, T., Lund, S., Manyika, J., & Thiel, L. (2020). *The future of work in Europe.* McKinsey Global Institute.

Smith, A. R., Chein, J., & Steinberg, L. (2014). Peers increase adolescent risk taking even when the probabilities of negative outcomes are known. *Developmental Psychology, 50*(5), 1564–1568. https://doi.org/10.1037/a0035696

Smith, B., Rogers, S. L., Blissett, J., & Ludlow, A. K. (2020). The relationship between sensory sensitivity, food fussiness and food preferences in children with neurodevelopmental disorders. *Appetite, 150,* 104643. https://doi.org/10.1016/j.appet.2020.104643

Smith, C. E., Blake, P. R., & Harris, P. L. (2013). I should but I won't: Why young children endorse norms of fair sharing but do not follow them. *PLOS ONE, 8*(3), e59510.

Smith, C. E., Noh, J. Y., Rizzo, M. T., & Harris, P. L. (2017). When and why parents prompt their children to apologize: The roles of transgression type and parenting style. *Journal of Family Studies, 23*(1), 38–61. https://doi.org/10.1080/13229400.2016.1176588

Smith, D. (2014, October 15). This is what developing acute schizophrenia feels like. *VICE News.* https://www.vice.com/en/article/3b7yvv/this-is-what-developing-acute-schizophrenia-is-like-009

Smith, D. M., Langa, K. M., Kabeto, M. U., & Ubel, P. A. (2005). Health, wealth, and happiness: Financial resources buffer subjective well-being after the onset of a disability. *Psychological Science, 16*(9), 663–666. https://doi.org/10.1111/j.1467-9280.2005.01592.x

Smith, J. D., Dishion, T. J., Shaw, D. S., Wilson, M. N., Winter, C. C., & Patterson, G. R. (2014). Coercive family process and early-onset conduct problems from age 2 to school entry. *Development and Psychopathology, 26*(4 Pt. 1), 917–932. https://doi.org/10.1017/S0954579414000169

Smith, J. D., Fu, E., & Kobayashi, M. (2020). Prevention and management of childhood obesity and its psychological and health comorbidities. *Annual Review of Clinical Psychology, 16,* 351–378. https://doi.org/10.1146/annurev-clinpsy-100219-060201

Smith, K. A., Mei, L., Yao, S., Wu, J., Spelke, E., Tenenbaum, J. B., & Ullman, T. D. (2020). The fine structure of surprise in intuitive physics: When, why, and how much? In *Proceedings of the 42nd Annual Meeting of the Cognitive Science Society.*

Smith, K. E., & Pollak, S. E. (2021). Rethinking concepts and categories for understanding the neurodevelopmental effects of childhood adversity. *Perspectives on Psychological Science: A Journal of the Association for Psychological Science, 16*(1), 67–93. https://doi.org/10.1177/1745691620920725

Smith, L. B., Jayaraman, S., Clerkin, E., & Yu, C. (2018). The developing infant creates a curriculum for statistical learning. *Trends in Cognitive Sciences, 22*(4), 325–336. https://doi.org/10.1016/j.tics.2018.02.004

Smith, M. L., Bergeron, C. D., Goltz, H. H., Coffey, T., & Boolani, A. (2020). Sexually transmitted infection knowledge among older adults: Psychometrics and test–retest reliability. *International Journal of Environmental Research and Public Health, 17*(7). https://doi.org/10.3390/ijerph17072462

Smith, S. (2018). Befriending the same differently: Ethnic, socioeconomic status, and gender differences in same-ethnic friendship. *Journal of Ethnic and Migration Studies, 44*(11), 1858–1880. https://doi.org/10.1080/1369183X.2017.1374168

Smith, S. G., Zhang, X., Basile, K. C., Merrick, M. T., Wang, J., Kresnow, M., & Chen, J. (2018). *The National Intimate Partner and Sexual Violence Survey (NISVS): 2015 data brief— updated release.* National Center for Injury Prevention and Control, Centers for Disease Control and Prevention.

Smith, V. C., Wilson, C. R., & Committee on Substance Use and Prevention. (2016). Families affected by parental substance use. *Pediatrics, 138*(2), e20161575. https://doi.org/10.1542/peds.2016-1575

Smith-Bonahue, T., Smith-Adcock, S., & Harman Ehrentraut, J. (2015). "I won't be your friend if you don't!" Preventing and responding to relational aggression in preschool classrooms. *Young Children, 70*(1).

Smock, P. J., & Schwartz, C. R. (2020). The demography of families: A review of patterns and change. *Journal of Marriage and the Family, 82*(1), 9–34. https://doi.org/10.1111/jomf.12612

Snarey, J. R. (2012). Lawrence Kohlberg: His moral biography, moral psychology, and moral pedagogy. In W. E. Pickren, D. A. Dewsbury, & M. Wertheimer (Eds.), *Portraits of pioneers in developmental psychology* (pp. 277–296). Psychology Press.

Snow, C. E., & Matthews, T. J. (2016). Reading and language in the early grades. *The Future of Children, 26*(2), 57–74.

Snyder, R. L. (2019). *No visible bruises: What we don't know about domestic violence can kill us.* Bloomsbury.

Sobchuk, K., Connolly, S., & Sheehan, D. (2019). Exploring the literature on the benefits of nature and outdoor play and the role of play leaders. *The Journal of the Health and Physical Education Council of the Alberta Teachers Association, 50*(1), 36–45.

Söderström, F., Normann, E., Jonsson, M., & Ågren, J. (2021). Outcomes of a uniformly active approach to infants born at 22–24 weeks of gestation. *Archives of Disease in Childhood—Fetal and Neonatal Edition, 106,* 343. https://doi.org/10.1136/archdischild-2020-320486

Soenens, B., & Vansteenkiste, M. (2020). Taking adolescents' agency in socialization seriously: The role of appraisals and cognitive-behavioral responses in autonomy-relevant parenting. *New Directions for Child and Adolescent Development, 2020*(173), 7–26. https://doi.org/10.1002/cad.20370

Sokol, R., Ennett, S., Gottfredson, N., & Halpern, C. (2017). Variability in self-rated health trajectories from adolescence to young adulthood by demographic factors. *Preventive Medicine, 105,* 73–76. https://doi.org/10.1016/j.ypmed.2017.08.015

Sokol, Z. (2015, August 10). People in relationships remember what it was like to move in with someone for the first time. *VICE.* http://www.vice.com/read/couples-remember-what-it-was-like-to-first-move-in-together-111

Solarin, A. U., Olutekunbi, O. A., Madise-Wobo, A. D., & Senbanjo, I. (2017). Toilet training practices in Nigerian children. *South African Journal of Child Health, 11*(3), 122–128.

Solis, N. (2021). When death comes: An oncology nurse finds solace in Mary Oliver. *Literary Hub.* https://lithub.com/when-death-comes-an-oncology-nurse-finds-solace-in-mary-oliver/

Solmi, F., Sharpe, H., Gage, S. H., Maddock, J., Lewis, G., & Patalay, P. (2021). Changes in the prevalence and correlates of weight-control behaviors and weight perception in adolescents in the UK, 1986–2015. *JAMA Pediatrics, 175*(3), 267. https://doi.org/10.1001/jamapediatrics.2020.4746

Solmi, M., Radua, J., Olivola, M., Croce, E., Soardo, L., Salazar de Pablo, G., Il Shin, J., Kirkbride, J. B., Jones, P., Kim, J. H., Kim, J. Y., Carvalho, A. F., Seeman, M. V., Correll, C. U., & Fusar-Poli, P. (2021). Age at onset of mental disorders worldwide: Large-scale meta-analysis of 192 epidemiological studies. *Molecular Psychiatry,* 1–15. https://doi.org/10.1038/s41380-021-01161-7

Solway, E., Allen, J. O., Kirch, M., Singer, D., Kullgren, J., & Malani, P. (2020). Positive attributes of aging and connections to health: Evidence from the national poll on healthy aging. *Innovation in Aging, 4*(Suppl 1), 722–723. https://doi.org/10.1093/geroni/igaa057.2557

Somers, H. (2016, February 28). Genetically identical twins born with different eye and skin colour. *BioNews,* (841). https://www.bionews.org.uk/page_95408

Somerville, L. H. (2013). The teenage brain: Sensitivity to social evaluation. *Current Directions in Psychological Science, 22*(2), 121–127. https://doi.org/10.1177/0963721413476512

Somerville, L. H. (2016). Searching for signatures of brain maturity: What are we searching for? *Neuron, 92*(6), 1164–1167. https://doi.org/10.1016/j.neuron.2016.10.059

Somerville, L. H., Haddara, N., Sasse, S. F., Skwara, A. C., Moran, J. M., & Figner, B. (2019). Dissecting "peer presence" and "decisions" to deepen understanding of peer influence on adolescent risky choice. *Child Development, 90*(6), 2086–2103. https://doi.org/10.1111/cdev.13081

Somerville, L. H., Jones, R. M., & Casey, B. J. (2010). A time of change: Behavioral and neural correlates of adolescent sensitivity to appetitive and aversive environmental cues. *Brain and Cognition, 72*(1), 124–133. https://doi.org/10.1016/j.bandc.2009.07.003

Somerville, L. H., Jones, R. M., Ruberry, E. J., Dyke, J. P., Glover, G., & Casey, B. (2013). Medial prefrontal cortex and the emergence of self-conscious emotion in adolescence. *Psychological Science, 24*(8), 1554–1562. https://doi.org/10.1177/0956797613475633

Somerville, L. H., Sasse, S. F., Garrad, M. C., Drysdale, A. T., Abi Akar, N., Insel, C., & Wilson, R. C. (2017). Charting the expansion of strategic exploratory behavior during adolescence. *Journal of Experimental Psychology: General, 146*(2), 155.

Sommantico, M., Iorio, I., Lacatena, M., & Parrello, S. (2021). Adult attachment, differentiation of self, and relationship satisfaction in lesbians and gay men. *Contemporary Family Therapy, 43*(2), 154–164. https://doi.org/10.1007/s10591-020-09563-5

Son, J. M., & Lee, C. (2019). Mitochondria: Multifaceted regulators of aging. *BMB Reports, 52*(1), 13–23. https://doi.org/10.5483/BMBRep.2019.52.1.300

Son, R. G., & Setta, S. M. (2018). Frequency of use of the religious exemption in New Jersey cases of determination of brain death. *BMC Medical Ethics, 19*(1), 76. https://doi.org/10.1186/s12910-018-0315-0

Soneji, S., Barrington-Trimis, J. L., Wills, T. A., Leventhal, A. M., Unger, J. B., Gibson, L. A., Yang, J., Primack, B. A., Andrews, J. A., Miech, R. A., Spindle, T. R., Dick, D. M., Eissenberg, T., Hornik, R. C., Dang, R., & Sargent, J. D. (2017). Association between initial use of e-cigarettes and subsequent cigarette smoking among adolescents and young adults. *JAMA Pediatrics, 171*(8), 788–797. https://doi.org/10.1001/jamapediatrics.2017.1488

Song, D., Doris, S. F., Li, P. W., & Lei, Y. (2018). The effectiveness of physical exercise on cognitive and psychological outcomes in individuals with mild cognitive impairment: A systematic review and meta-analysis. *International Journal of Nursing Studies, 79,* 155–164.

Song, S., Su, M., Kang, C., Liu, H., Zhang, Y., McBride-Chang, C., Tardif, T., Li, H., Liang, W., Zhang, Z., & Shu, H. (2015). Tracing children's vocabulary development from preschool through the school-age years: An 8-year longitudinal study. *Developmental Science, 18*(1), 119–131. https://doi.org/10.1111/desc.12190

Song, Y., Broekhuizen, M. L., & Dubas, J. S. (2020). Happy little benefactor: Prosocial behaviors promote happiness in young children from two cultures. *Frontiers in Psychology, 11,* 1398. https://doi.org/10.3389/fpsyg.2020.01398

Song, Y., Hoben, M., Norton, P., & Estabrooks, C. A. (2020). Association of work environment with missed and rushed care tasks among care aides in nursing homes. *JAMA Network Open, 3*(1), e1920092. https://doi.org/10.1001/jamanetworkopen.2019.20092

Sonnentag, S., & Grant, A. M. (2012). Doing good at work feels good at home, but not right away: When and why perceived prosocial impact predicts positive affect. *Personnel Psychology, 65*(3), 495–530.

Sontag, S. (1972). The double standard of aging. *Saturday Review of Literature, 39,* 29–38.

Sonuga-Barke, E. J. S., Kennedy, M., Kumsta, R., Knights, N., Golm, D., Rutter, M., Maughan, B., Schlotz, W., & Kreppner, J. (2017). Child-to-adult neurodevelopmental and mental health trajectories after early life deprivation: The young adult follow-up of the longitudinal English and Romanian Adoptees study. *The Lancet, 389*(10078), 1539–1548. https://doi.org/10.1016/S0140-6736(17)30045-4

Sorenson Duncan, T., & Paradis, J. (2020). How does maternal education influence the linguistic environment supporting bilingual language development in child second language learners of English? *International Journal of Bilingualism, 24*(1), 46–61. https://doi.org/10.1177/1367006918768366

Sorkhabi, N., & Mandara, J. (2013). Are the effects of Baumrind's parenting styles culturally specific or culturally equivalent? In R. E. Larzelere, A. S. Morris, & A. W. Harrist (Eds.), *Authoritative parenting: Synthesizing nurturance and discipline for optimal child development* (pp. 113–135). American Psychological Association.

Soto, C. J., & Tackett, J. L. (2015). Personality traits in childhood and adolescence: Structure, development, and outcomes. *Current Directions in Psychological Science, 24*(5), 358–362.

Souto, P. H. S., Santos, J. N., Leite, H. R., Hadders-Algra, M., Guedes, S. C., Nobre, J. N. P., Santos, L. R., & Morais, R. L. de S. (2020). Tablet use in young children is associated with advanced fine motor skills. *Journal of Motor Behavior, 52*(2), 196–203.

Sözen, T., Özışık, L., & Başaran, N. Ç. (2017). An overview and management of osteoporosis. *European Journal of Rheumatology, 4*(1), 46.

Sparkes, A. C., Brighton, J., & Inckle, K. (2018). "'It's a part of me'": An ethnographic exploration of becoming a disabled sporting cyborg following spinal cord injury. *Qualitative Research in Sport, Exercise and Health, 10*(2), 151–166. https://doi.org/10.1080/2159676X.2017.1389768

Sparks, D., & Malkus, N. (2013). *First-year undergraduate remedial coursetaking: 1999–2000, 2003–04, 2007–08: Statistics in brief* (NCES 2013-013). National Center for Education Statistics. http://eric.ed.gov/?id=ED538339

Sparks, J., Daly, C., Wilkey, B. M., Molden, D. C., Finkel, E. J., & Eastwick, P. W. (2020). Negligible evidence that people desire partners who uniquely fit their ideals. *Journal of Experimental Social Psychology, 90,* 103968. https://doi.org/10.1016/j.jesp.2020.103968

Sparks, S. D. (2018, July 17). Volunteerism declined among young people. *Education Week.* https://www.edweek.org/leadership/volunteerism-declined-among-young-people/2018/07

Sparrow, E. P., Swirsky, L. T., Kudus, F., & Spaniol, J. (2021). Aging and altruism: A meta-analysis. *Psychology and Aging, 36*(1), 49.

Spear, L. P. (2009). Heightened stress responsivity and emotional reactivity during pubertal maturation: Implications for psychopathology. *Development and Psychopathology, 21*(1), 87–97. https://doi.org/10.1017/S0954579409000066

Spear, L. P. (2013). Adolescent neurodevelopment. *Journal of Adolescent Health, 52*(2), S7–S13.

Spelke, E. S. (2017). Core knowledge, language, and number. *Language Learning and Development, 13*(2), 147–170. https://doi.org/10.1080/15475441.2016.1263572

Spence, R., Owens-Solari, M., & Goodyer, I. (2016). Help-seeking in emerging adults with and without a history of mental health referral: A qualitative study. *BMC Research Notes, 9,* 415. https://doi.org/10.1186/s13104-016-2227-8

Spencer, B., Wambach, K., & Domain, E. W. (2015). African American women's breastfeeding experiences: Cultural, personal, and political voices. *Qualitative Health Research, 25*(7), 974–987. https://doi.org/10.1177/1049732314554097

Spencer, D., Pasterski, V., Neufeld, S. A., Glover, V., O'Connor, T. G., Hindmarsh, P. C., Hughes, I. A., Acerini, C. L., & Hines, M. (2021). Prenatal androgen exposure and children's gender-typed behavior and toy and playmate preferences. *Hormones and Behavior, 127,* 104889.

Spencer, M. B. (2010, April 28). CNN pilot demonstration. *CNN.* http://i2.cdn.turner.com/cnn/2010/images/05/13/expanded_results_methods

Spencer, M. B. (2017). *Privilege and critical race perspectives' intersectional contributions to a systems theory of human development.* Cambridge University Press.

Spencer, S. J., Korosi, A., Layé, S., Shukitt-Hale, B., & Barrientos, R. M. (2017). Food for thought: How nutrition impacts cognition and emotion. *npj Science of Food, 1*(1), 7. https://doi.org/10.1038/s41538-017-0008-y

Spencer, S. J., Logel, C., & Davies, P. G. (2016). Stereotype threat. *Annual Review of Psychology, 67*(1), 415–437. https://doi.org/10.1146/annurev-psych-073115-103235

Spencer-Rodgers, J., Anderson, E., Ma-Kellams, C., Wang, C., & Peng, K. (2018). What is dialectical thinking? Conceptualization and measurement. In J. Spencer-Rodgers & K. Peng (Eds.), *The psychological and cultural foundations of East Asian cognition: Contradiction, change, and holism* (pp. 1–34). Oxford University Press.

Spencer-Rodgers, J., Williams, M. J., & Peng, K. (2010). Cultural differences in expectations of change and tolerance for contradiction: A decade of empirical research. *Personality and Social Psychology Review, 14*(3), 296–312. https://doi.org/10.1177/1088868310362982

Spielberg, J. M., Olino, T. M., Forbes, E. E., & Dahl, R. E. (2014). Exciting fear in adolescence: Does pubertal development alter threat processing? *Developmental Cognitive Neuroscience, 8,* 86–95.

Spikins, P., Needham, A., Tilley, L., & Hitchens, G. (2018). Calculated or caring? Neanderthal healthcare in social context. *World Archaeology, 50*(3), 384–403.

Spitz, R. A. (1945). Hospitalism. *The Psychoanalytic Study of the Child, 1*(1), 53–74. https://doi.org/10.1080/00797308.1945.11823126

Spruijt-Metz, D. (2011). Etiology, treatment, and prevention of obesity in childhood and adolescence: A decade in review. *Journal of Research on Adolescence, 21*(1), 129–152.

Spyreli, E., McKinley, M. C., & Dean, M. (2021). Parental considerations during complementary feeding in higher income countries: A systematic review of qualitative evidence. *Public Health Nutrition,* 1–31. https://doi.org/10.1017/S1368980021001749

SRCD Governing Council. (2007). *Ethical standards for research with children.* Society for Research in Child Development (SRCD). https://www.srcd.org/about-us/ethical-standards-research-children

SRCD Governing Council. (2021). *Ethical principles and standards for developmental Scientists.* Society for Research on Child Development. https://www.srcd.org/about-us/ethical-principles-and-standards-developmental-scientist

Srinivasan, S., Glover, J., Tampi, R. R., Tampi, D. J., & Sewell, D. D. (2019). Sexuality and the older adult. *Current Psychiatry Reports, 21*(10), 1–9.

Sroufe, L. A. (2016). The place of attachment in development. In J. Cassidy & P. R. Shaver (Eds.), *Handbook of attachment: Theory, research, and clinical applications* (Vol. 3, pp. 997–1011). Guilford.

Sroufe, L. A. (2021). Then and now: The legacy and future of attachment research. *Attachment & Human Development, 23*(4), 396–403. https://doi.org/10.1080/14616734.2021.1918450

Staats, S., van der Valk, I. E., Meeus, W. H. J., & Branje, S. J. T. (2018). Longitudinal transmission of conflict management styles across inter-parental and adolescent relationships. *Journal of Research on Adolescence, 28*(1), 169–185. https://doi.org/10.1111/jora.12324

Staes, N., Smaers, J. B., Kunkle, A. E., Hopkins, W. D., Bradley, B. J., & Sherwood, C. C. (2019). Evolutionary divergence of neuroanatomical organization and related genes in chimpanzees and bonobos. Cortex: A Journal Devoted to the Study of the Nervous System and Behavior, 118, 154–164.

Staff, J., Harris, A., Sabates, R., & Briddell, L. (2010). Uncertainty in early occupational aspirations: Role exploration or aimlessness? *Social Forces, 89*(2), 659–683. https://doi.org/10.1353/sof.2010.0088

Staff, J., Mont'Alvao, A., & Mortimer, J. T. (2015). Children at work. In M. H. Bornstein, T. Leventhal, & R. M. Lerner (Eds.), *Handbook of child psychology and developmental science: Ecological settings and processes* (pp. 345–374). John Wiley & Sons. https://doi.org/10.1002/9781118963418.childpsy409

Staff, J., Yetter, A. M., Cundiff, K., Ramirez, N., Vuolo, M., & Mortimer, J. T. (2020). Is adolescent employment still a risk factor for high school dropout? *Journal of Research on Adolescence, 30*(2), 406–422. https://doi.org/10.1111/jora.12533

Stallings, M. C., & Neppl, T. (2021). An examination of genetic and environmental factors related to negative personality traits, educational attainment, and economic success. *Developmental Psychology, 57*(2), 191.

Stanberry, L. R., Thomson, M. C., & James, W. (2018). Prioritizing the needs of children in a changing climate. *PLOS Medicine, 15*(7), e1002627. https://doi.org/10.1371/journal.pmed.1002627

Standen, A. (2014, October 20). Halting schizophrenia before it starts. *KERA News.* https://www.keranews.org/2014-10-20/halting-schizophrenia-before-it-starts

Stanford, F. C., & Kyle, T. K. (2018). Respectful language and care in childhood obesity. *JAMA Pediatrics, 172*(11), 1001–1002. https://doi.org/10.1001/jamapediatrics.2018.1912

Stanley, C. T., Petscher, Y., & Catts, H. (2018). A longitudinal investigation of direct and indirect links between reading skills in kindergarten and reading comprehension in tenth grade. *Reading and Writing, 31*(1), 133–153.

Stanley, I. H., Hom, M. A., & Joiner, T. E. (2018). Modifying mental health help-seeking stigma among undergraduates with untreated psychiatric disorders: A pilot randomized trial of a novel cognitive bias modification intervention. *Behaviour Research and Therapy, 103*, 33–42.

Stanley, I. H., Hom, M. A., Rogers, M. L., Hagan, C. R., & Joiner, T. E. (2016). Understanding suicide among older adults: A review of psychological and sociological theories of suicide. *Aging & Mental Health, 20*(2), 113–122. https://doi.org/10.1080/13607863.2015.1012045

Stanton, A. M., Handy, A. B., & Meston, C. M. (2018). The effects of exercise on sexual function in women. *Sexual Medicine Reviews, 6*(4), 548–557. https://doi.org/10.1016/j.sxmr.2018.02.004

Starrs, A. M., Ezeh, A. C., Barker, G., Basu, A., Bertrand, J. T., Blum, R., Coll-Seck, A. M., Grover, A., Laski, L., Roa, M., Sathar, Z. A., Say, L., Serour, G. I., Singh, S., Stenberg, K., Temmerman, M., Biddlecom, A, Popinchalk, A., Summers, C., & Ashford, L. S. (2018). Accelerate progress — sexual and reproductive health and rights for all: Report of the Guttmacher–Lancet Commission. *The Lancet, 391*(10140), 2642–2692.

Statistica. (2020, September 22). *Netherlands: Age of father at birth of first child 2009–2019.* Statista. https://www.statista.com/statistics/521498/average-age-father-at-the-first-birth-in-the-netherlands/

Statistics Japan. (2017). *Mean age of mother at 1st child birth.* https://stats-japan.com/t/kiji/14299

Staton, S., Rankin, P. S., Harding, M., Smith, S. S., Westwood, E., LeBourgeois, M. K., & Thorpe, K. J. (2020). Many naps, one nap, none: A systematic review and meta-analysis of napping patterns in children 0–12 years. *Sleep Medicine Reviews, 50*, 101247. https://doi.org/10.1016/j.smrv.2019.101247

Staudinger, U. M. (2020). The positive plasticity of adult development: Potential for the 21st century. *American Psychologist, 75*(4), 540.

Staudinger, U. M., Finkelstein, R., Calvo, E., & Sivaramakrishnan, K. (2016). A global view on the effects of work on health in later life. *The Gerontologist, 56*(Suppl_2), S281–S292.

Staudinger, U. M., & Kunzmann, U. (2005). Positive adult personality development: Adjustment and/or growth? *European Psychologist, 10*(4), 320–329.

Stearns, P. N. (2016). *Childhood in world history.* Routledge.

Stearns, P. N. (2017). History of children's rights. In M. D. Ruck, M. Peterson-Badali, & M. Freeman (Eds.), *Handbook of children's rights: Global and multidisciplinary perspectives* (pp. 1–18). Taylor & Francis.

Steele, C. M., & Aronson, J. (1995). Stereotype threat and the intellectual test performance of African Americans. *Journal of Personality and Social Psychology, 69*(5), 797.

Steele, E. H., & McKinney, C. (2020). Relationships among emerging adult psychological problems, maltreatment, and parental psychopathology: Moderation by parent–child relationship quality. *Family Process, 59*(1), 257–272. https://doi.org/10.1111/famp.12407

Steele, J. B., & Williams, L. (2016, June 28). Who got rich off the student debt crisis? *Reveal.* http://revealnews.org/article/who-got-rich-off-the-student-debt-crisis/

Steene-Johannessen, J., Hansen, B. H., Dalene, K. E., Kolle, E., Northstone, K., Møller, N. C., Grøntved, A., Wedderkopp, N., Kriemler, S., Page, A. S., Puder, J. J., Reilly, J. J., Sardinha, L. B., van Sluijs, E. M. F., Andersen, L. B., van der Ploeg, H., Ahrens, W., Flexeder, C., Standl, M., ... On behalf of the Determinants of Diet and Physical Activity knowledge hub (DEDIPAC); International Children's Accelerometry Database (ICAD) Collaborators, I. C. and H. C. (2020). Variations in accelerometry measured physical activity and sedentary time across Europe — Harmonized analyses of 47,497 children and adolescents. *International Journal of Behavioral Nutrition and Physical Activity, 17*(1), 38. https://doi.org/10.1186/s12966-020-00930-x

Stefanetti, R. J., Voisin, S., Russell, A., & Lamon, S. (2018). Recent advances in understanding the role of FOXO3. *F1000Research, 7*, 1372. https://doi.org/10.12688/f1000research.15258.1

Stefano, L. D., Mills, C., Watkins, A., & Wilkinson, D. (2020). Ectogestation ethics: The implications of artificially extending gestation for viability, newborn resuscitation and abortion. *Bioethics, 34*(4), 371–384. https://doi.org/10.1111/bioe.12682

Steffen, E. M., & Klass, D. (2018). Culture, contexts and connections: A conversation with Dennis Klass about his life and work as a bereavement scholar. *Mortality, 23*(3), 203–214.

Stefler, D., Prina, M., Wu, Y.-T., Sánchez-Niubò, A., Lu, W., Haro, J. M., Marmot, M., & Bobak, M. (2021). Socioeconomic inequalities in physical and cognitive functioning: Cross-sectional evidence from 37 cohorts across 28 countries in the ATHLOS project. *Journal of Epidemiology and Community Health, 75*(10), 980–986. https://doi.org/10.1136/jech-2020-214714

Stein, R., Kempf, E., Gesing, J., Stanik, J., Kiess, W., & Körner, A. (2019). Pubertal milestones and related hormonal changes among children with obesity. *ESPE Abstracts, 92*, P2–110. https://abstracts.eurospe.org/hrp/0092/hrp0092p2-110

Steinbach, A. (2019). Children's and parents' well-being in joint physical custody: A literature review. *Family Process, 58*(2), 353–369.

Steinberg, L. (2008). A social neuroscience perspective on adolescent risk-taking. *Developmental Review, 28*(1), 78–106. https://doi.org/10.1016/j.dr.2007.08.002

Steinberg, L. (2014). Family structure, parenting practices, and adolescent adjustment: An ecological examination. In E. M. Hetherington (Ed.), *Coping with divorce, single parenting, and remarriage: A risk and resiliency perspective* (pp. 65). Lawrence Erlbaum Associates.

Steinberg, L., & Icenogle, G. (2019). Using developmental science to distinguish adolescents and adults under the law. *Annual Review of Developmental Psychology, 1*, 21–40.

Steinberg, L., Icenogle, G., Shulman, E. P., Breiner, K., Chein, J., Bacchini, D., Chang, L., Chaudhary, N., Giunta, L. D., Dodge, K. A., Fanti, K. A., Lansford, J.

E., Malone, P. S., Oburu, P., Pastorelli, C., Skinner, A. T., Sorbring, E., Tapanya, S., Tirado, L. M. U., ... Takash, H. M. S. (2017). Around the world, adolescence is a time of heightened sensation seeking and immature self-regulation. *Developmental Science, 21*(2), e12532. https://doi.org/10.1111/desc.12532

Steinberg, L., Lamborn, S. D., Darling, N., Mounts, N. S., & Dornbusch, S. M. (1994). Over-time changes in adjustment and competence among adolescents from authoritative, authoritarian, indulgent, and neglectful families. *Child Development, 65*(3), 754–770.

Steinhauser, K. E., Alexander, S., Olsen, M. K., Stechuchak, K. M., Zervakis, J., Ammarell, N., Byock, I., & Tulsky, J. A. (2017). Addressing patient emotional and existential needs during serious illness: Results of the outlook randomized controlled trial. *Journal of Pain and Symptom Management, 54*(6), 898–908. https://doi.org/10.1016/j.jpainsymman.2017.06.003

Stelzer, E.-M., Zhou, N., Maercker, A., O'Connor, M.-F., & Killikelly, C. (2020). Prolonged grief disorder and the cultural crisis. *Frontiers in Psychology, 10*, 2982. https://doi.org/10.3389/fpsyg.2019.02982

Stenson, A. F., Leventon, J. S., & Bauer, P. J. (2019). Emotion effects on memory from childhood through adulthood: Consistent enhancement and adult gender differences. *Journal of Experimental Child Psychology, 178*, 121–136. https://doi.org/10.1016/j.jecp.2018.09.016

Stephan, Y., Sutin, A. R., Luchetti, M., & Terracciano, A. (2020). Personality and memory performance over twenty years: Findings from three prospective studies. *Journal of Psychosomatic Research, 128*, 109885.

Stephan, Y., Sutin, A. R., & Terracciano, A. (2018). Subjective age and mortality in three longitudinal samples. *Psychosomatic Medicine, 80*(7), 659–664. https://doi.org/10.1097/PSY.0000000000000613

Stephen, R., Liu, Y., Ngandu, T., Rinne, J. O., Kemppainen, N., Parkkola, R., & Solomon, A. (2017). Associations of CAIDE Dementia Risk Score with MRI, PIB-PET measures, and cognition. *Journal of Alzheimer's Disease, 59*(2), 695–705.

Stephens, N. M., Fryberg, S. A., Markus, H. R., Johnson, C. S., & Covarrubias, R. (2012). Unseen disadvantage: How American universities' focus on independence undermines the academic performance of first-generation college students. *Journal of Personality and Social Psychology, 102*(6), 1178–1197. https://doi.org/10.1037/a0027143

Stepler, R. (2017). *Divorce rates up for Americans 50 and older, led by baby boomers.* Pew Research Center. https://www.pewresearch.org/fact-tank/2017/03/09/led-by-baby-boomers-divorce-rates-climb-for-americas-50-population/

Steptoe, A., Deaton, A., & Stone, A. A. (2015). Subjective wellbeing, health, and ageing. *The Lancet, 385*(9968), 640–648. https://doi.org/10.1016/S0140-6736(13)61489-0

Stern, A. M. (2015). Instituting eugenics in California. In A. M. Stern (Ed.), *Eugenic nation* (pp. 82–110). University of California Press.

Sternberg, R. J. (1985). *Beyond IQ: A triarchic theory of human intelligence.* Cambridge University Press.

Sternberg, R. J. (1986). A triangular theory of love. *Psychological Review, 93*(2), 119–135. https://doi.org/10.1037/0033-295X.93.2.119

Sternberg, R. J. (1997). The concept of intelligence and its role in lifelong learning and success. *American Psychologist, 52*(10), 1030.

Sternberg, R. J. (2015). Still searching for the Zipperumpazoo: A reflection after 40 years. *Child Development Perspectives, 9*(2), 106–110.

Sternberg, R. J. (2017). Some lessons from a symposium on cultural psychological science. *Perspectives on Psychological Science, 12*(5), 911–921. https://doi.org/10.1177/1745691617720477

Sternberg, R. J. (2018a). The triarchic theory of successful intelligence. In D. P. Flanagan & E. M. McDonough (Eds.), *Contemporary intellectual assessment: Theories, tests, and issues* (pp. 174–194). Guilford.

Sternberg, R. J. (2018b). Theories of intelligence. In S. I. Pfeiffer, E. Shaunessy-Dedrick, & M. Foley-Nicpon (Eds.), *APA handbook of giftedness and talent* (pp. 145–161).

American Psychological Association. https://doi.org/10.1037/0000038-010

Sternberg, R. J. (2021). *Adaptive intelligence: Surviving and thriving in times of uncertainty.* Cambridge University Press.

Stewart, J. L., Kamke, K., Widman, L., & Hope, E. C. (2021). "They see sex as something that's reproductive and not as something people do for fun": Shortcomings in adolescent girls' sexual socialization from adults. *Journal of Adolescent Research.* https://doi.org/10.1177/07435584211020299

Stewart, J. L., Spivey, L. A., Widman, L., Choukas-Bradley, S., & Prinstein, M. J. (2019). Developmental patterns of sexual identity, romantic attraction, and sexual behavior among adolescents over three years. *Journal of Adolescence, 77,* 90–97. https://doi.org/10.1016/j.adolescence.2019.10.006

Stiglitz, J. E. (2007). *Making globalization work.* W. W. Norton.

Stiglitz, J. (2019). *People, power, and profits: Progressive capitalism for an age of discontent.* Penguin UK.

Stiles, J., Brown, T. T., Haist, F., Jernigan, T. L., Liben, L., & Muller, U. (2015). Handbook of child psychology and developmental science. *Cognitive Processes,* 9–62.

Stilo, S. A., & Murray, R. M. (2019). Non-genetic factors in schizophrenia. *Current Psychiatry Reports, 21*(10), 100. https://doi.org/10.1007/s11920-019-1091-3

Stinson, R. D., Levy, L. B., & Alt, M. (2014). "They're just a good time and move on": Fraternity men reflect on their hookup experiences. *Journal of College Student Psychotherapy, 28*(1), 59–73.

St James-Roberts, I. (2012). *The origins, prevention and treatment of infant crying and sleeping problems: An evidence-based guide for healthcare professionals and the families they support.* Routledge.

St James-Roberts, I., Garratt, R., Powell, C., Bamber, D., Long, J., Brown, J., Morris, S., Dyson, S., Morris, T., Jaicim, N. B., James-Roberts, I. S., Garratt, R., Powell, C., Bamber, D., Long, J., Brown, J., Morris, S., Dyson, S., Morris, T., & Jaicim, N. B. (2019). *A support package for parents of excessively crying infants: Development and feasibility study.* NIHR Journals Library.

St James-Roberts, I., Roberts, M., Hovish, K., & Owen, C. (2015). Video evidence that London infants can resettle themselves back to sleep after waking in the night, as well as sleep for long periods, by 3 months of age. *Journal of Developmental and Behavioral Pediatrics, 36*(5), 324.

Stockdale, L. A., Porter, C. L., Coyne, S. M., Essig, L. W., Booth, M., Keenan-Kroff, S., & Schvaneveldt, E. (2020). Infants' response to a mobile phone modified still-face paradigm: Links to maternal behaviors and beliefs regarding technoference. *Infancy, 25*(5), 571–592. https://doi.org/10.1111/infa.12342

Stocker, C. M., Gilligan, M., Klopack, E. T., Conger, K. J., Lanthier, R. P., Neppl, T. K., & Wickrama, K. A. S. (2020). Sibling relationships in older adulthood: Links with loneliness and well-being. *Journal of Family Psychology, 34*(2), 175.

Stockings, E., Hall, W. D., Lynskey, M., Morley, K. I., Reavley, N., Strang, J., Patton, G., & Degenhardt, L. (2016). Prevention, early intervention, harm reduction, and treatment of substance use in young people. *The Lancet Psychiatry, 3*(3), 280–296. https://doi.org/10.1016/S2215-0366(16)00002-X

Stoet, G., & Geary, D. C. (2020). Gender differences in the pathways to higher education. *Proceedings of the National Academy of Sciences, 117*(25), 14073–14076.

Stokes, A., Lundberg, D. J., Sheridan, B., Hempstead, K., Morone, N. E., Lasser, K. E., Trinquart, L., & Neogi, T. (2020). Association of obesity with prescription opioids for painful conditions in patients seeking primary care in the US. *JAMA Network Open, 3*(4), e202012–e202012. https://doi.org/10.1001/jamanetworkopen.2020.2012

Stoll, S., & Lieven, E. (2014). Studying language acquisition cross linguistically. In H. Winskel & P. Pradakannaya (Eds.), *South and southeast Asian psycholinguistics* (pp. 19–35). Cambridge University Press.

Stoltenborgh, M., Bakermans-Kranenburg, M. J., Alink, L. R., & van IJzendoorn, M. H. (2015). The prevalence of child maltreatment across the globe: Review of a series of meta-analyses. *Child Abuse Review, 24*(1), 37–50.

Stolzenberg, B. E., Aragon, M. C., Romo, E., Couch, V., McLennan, D., Eagan, M. K., & Kang, N. (2020). *The American freshman: National norms Fall 2019.* Higher Education Research Institute, University of California, Los Angeles.

Stone, L. B., & Gibb, B. E. (2015). Brief report: Preliminary evidence that co-rumination fosters adolescents' depression risk by increasing rumination. *Journal of Adolescence, 38,* 1–4. https://doi.org/10.1016/j.adolescence.2014.10.008

Storer, A., Schneider, D., & Harknett, K. (2020). What explains racial/ethnic inequality in job quality in the service sector? *American Sociological Review, 85*(4), 537–572.

Storsve, A. B., Fjell, A. M., Tamnes, C. K., Westlye, L. T., Overbye, K., Aasland, H. W., & Walhovd, K. B. (2014). Differential longitudinal changes in cortical thickness, surface area and volume across the adult life span: Regions of accelerating and decelerating change. *Journal of Neuroscience, 34*(25), 8488–8498. https://doi.org/10.1523/JNEUROSCI.0391-14.2014

Stoskopf, A. (2012). Racism in the history of standardized testing: Legacies for today. In W. Au & M. B. Tempel (Eds.), *Pencils down: Rethinking high-stakes testing and accountability in public schools* (pp. 34–39). Rethinking Schools.

Stough, C. (2015, October 9). *Show us your smarts: A very brief history of intelligence testing.* The Conversation. http://theconversation.com/show-us-your-smarts-a-very-brief-history-of-intelligence-testing-45444

Stoute, B. J. (2020). Racism: A challenge for the therapeutic dyad. *American Journal of Psychotherapy, 73*(3), 69–71. https://doi.org/10.1176/appi.psychotherapy.20200043

Stover, C. S., Zhou, Y., Leve, L. D., Neiderhiser, J. M., Shaw, D. S., & Reiss, D. (2015). The relationship between genetic attributions, appraisals of birth mothers' health, and the parenting of adoptive mothers and fathers. *Journal of Applied Developmental Psychology, 41,* 19–27. https://doi.org/10.1016/j.appdev.2015.06.003

Strand, B. H., Knapskog, A.-B., Persson, K., Edwin, T. H., Amland, R., Mjørud, M., Bjertness, E., Engedal, K., & Selbæk, G. (2018). Survival and years of life lost in various aetiologies of dementia, mild cognitive impairment (MCI) and subjective cognitive decline (SCD) in Norway. *PLoS ONE, 13*(9), e0204436. https://doi.org/10.1371/journal.pone.0204436

Strauss, A. L., & Glaser, B. G. (1970). *Anguish: A case history of a dying trajectory.* Sociology Press.

Straussman, R., Nejman, D., Roberts, D., Steinfeld, I., Blum, B., Benvenisty, N., Simon, I., Yakhini, Z., & Cedar, H. (2009). Developmental programming of CpG island methylation profiles in the human genome. *Nature Structural & Molecular Biology, 16*(5), 564–571. https://doi.org/10.1038/nsmb.1594

Streit, F., Colodro-Conde, L., Hall, A. S., & Witt, S. H. (2020). Genomics of borderline personality disorder. In B. T. Baune (Ed.), *Personalized psychiatry* (pp. 227–237). Academic Press.

Strings, S. (2019). *Fearing the black body: The racial origins of fat phobia.* NYU Press.

Stroebe, M., & Schut, H. (2010). The dual process model of coping with bereavement: A decade on. *OMEGA—Journal of Death and Dying, 61*(4), 273–289.

Stroebe, M., Schut, H., & Boerner, K. (2017a). Cautioning health-care professionals: Bereaved persons are misguided through the stages of grief. *OMEGA—Journal of Death and Dying, 74*(4), 455–473.

Stroebe, M., Stroebe, W., Schut, H., & Boerner, K. (2017b). Grief is not a disease but bereavement merits medical awareness. *The Lancet, 389*(10067), 347–349. https://doi.org/10.1016/S0140-6736(17)30189-7

Stroebe, W. (2010). The graying of academia: Will it reduce scientific productivity? *American Psychologist, 65*(7), 660.

Strouse, G. A., Troseth, G. L., O'Doherty, K. D., & Saylor, M. M. (2018). Co-viewing supports toddlers' word learning from contingent and noncontingent video. *Journal of Experimental Child Psychology, 166,* 310–326. https://doi.org/10.1016/j.jecp.2017.09.005

Strum, P. (2014). We always tell our children they are Americans: *Mendez v. Westminster* and the beginning of the end of school segregation. *Journal of Supreme Court History, 39,* 307.

Stucke, N. J., Stoet, G., & Doebel, S. (2022). What are the kids doing? Exploring young children's activities at home and relations with externally cued executive function and child temperament. *Developmental Science,* e13226. https://doi.org/10.1111/desc.13226

Suarez-Rivera, C., Smith, L. B., & Yu, C. (2019). Multimodal parent behaviors within joint attention support sustained attention in infants. *Developmental Psychology, 55*(1), 96–109. https://doi.org/10.1037/dev0000628

Subbotsky, E. (2014). The belief in magic in the age of science. *SAGE Open, 4.* https://doi.org/10.1177/2158244014521433

Substance Abuse and Mental Health Services Administration (SAMHSA). (2020). *Key substance use and mental health indicators in the United States: Results from the 2019 National Survey on Drug Use and Health* (HHS Publication No. PEP20-07-01-001; NSDUH Series H-55). Center for Behavioral Health Statistics and Quality, SAMHSA.

Substance Abuse and Mental Health Services Administration (SAMHSA). (2021). *2020 National Survey on Drug Use and Health annual national report* [Annual report].

Substance Abuse and Mental Health Services Administration (SAMHSA). (2021). *Key substance use and mental health indicators in the United States: Results from the 2020 National Survey on Drug Use and Health.* Center for Behavioral Health Statistics and Quality, SAMHSA. https://www.samhsa.gov/data/

Substance Abuse and Mental Health Services Administration (SAMHSA), Center for Behavioral Health Statistics and Quality. (2020). *National Survey on Drug Use and Health, 2017 and 2018.*

Sudre, G., Mangalmurti, A., & Shaw, P. (2018). Growing out of attention deficit hyperactivity disorder: Insights from the 'remitted' brain. *Neuroscience & Biobehavioral Reviews, 94,* 198–209.

Suggate, S., Schaughency, E., McAnally, H., & Reese, E. (2018). From infancy to adolescence: The longitudinal links between vocabulary, early literacy skills, oral narrative, and reading comprehension. *Cognitive Development, 47,* 82–95. https://doi.org/10.1016/j.cogdev.2018.04.005

Sugie, N. F., & Turney, K. (2017). Beyond incarceration: Criminal justice contact and mental health. *American Sociological Review, 82*(4), 719–743. https://doi.org/10.1177/0003122417713188

Suglia, S. F., Campo, R. A., Brown, A. G., Stoney, C., Boyce, C. A., Appleton, A. A., & Watamura, S. E. (2020). Social determinants of cardiovascular health: Early life adversity as a contributor to disparities in cardiovascular diseases. *The Journal of Pediatrics, 219,* 267–273.

Suglia, S. F., Chen, C., Wang, S., Cammack, A. L., April-Sanders, A. K., McGlinchey, E. L., Kubo, A., Bird, H., Canino, G., & Duarte, C. S. (2020). Childhood adversity and pubertal development among Puerto Rican boys and girls. *Psychosomatic Medicine, 82*(5), 487–494. https://doi.org/10.1097/PSY.0000000000000817

Suh, B., & Luthar, S. S. (2020). Parental aggravation may tell more about a child's mental/behavioral health than adverse childhood experiences: Using the 2016 National Survey of Children's Health. *Child Abuse & Neglect, 101,* 104330.

Suizzo, M.-A. (2020). Parent–child relationships. In *The encyclopedia of child and adolescent development* (pp. 1–13). Wiley. https://doi.org/10.1002/9781119171492.wecad408

Suizzo, M.-A., Robinson, C., & Pahlke, E. (2008). African American mothers' socialization beliefs and goals with young children: Themes of history, education, and collective independence. *Journal of Family Issues, 29*(3), 287–316. https://doi.org/10.1177/0192513X07308368

Sukhodolsky, D. G., Smith, S. D., McCauley, S. A., Ibrahim, K., & Piasecka, J. B. (2016). Behavioral interventions for anger, irritability, and aggression in children and adolescents. *Journal of Child and Adolescent Psychopharmacology, 26*(1), 58–64. https://doi.org/10.1089/cap.2015.0120

Suleiman, A. B., & Dahl, R. (2019). Parent–child relationships in the puberty years: Insights from developmental neuroscience. *Family Relations, 68*(3), 279–287. http://dx .doi.org/10.1111/fare.12360

Suleiman, A. B., & Deardorff, J. (2015). Multiple dimensions of peer influence in adolescent romantic and sexual relationships: A descriptive, qualitative perspective. *Archives of Sexual Behavior, 44*(3), 765–775. https://doi .org/10.1007/s10508-014-0394-z

Suleiman, A. B., Galván, A., Harden, K. P., & Dahl, R. E. (2017). Becoming a sexual being: The 'elephant in the room' of adolescent brain development. *Developmental Cognitive Neuroscience, 25*, 209–220.

Suleiman, A. B., & Harden, K. P. (2016). The importance of sexual and romantic development in understanding the developmental neuroscience of adolescence. *Developmental Cognitive Neuroscience, 17*, 145–147. https://doi .org/10.1016/j.dcn.2015.12.007

Sullivan, A., & Brown, M. (2015). Reading for pleasure and progress in vocabulary and mathematics. *British Education Research Journal, 41*, 971–991. https://doi .org/10.1002/berj.3180

Sullivan, J., Moss-Racusin, C., Lopez, M., & Williams, K. (2018). Backlash against gender stereotype-violating preschool children. *PLOS ONE, 13*(4), e0195503. https://doi .org/10.1371/journal.pone.0195503

Sulmasy, D. P. (2018). An open letter to Norman Cantor regarding dementia and physician-assisted suicide. *Hastings Center Report, 48*(4), 28–30. https://doi.org/10.1002/ hast.868

Sulmasy, L. S., & Mueller, P. S. (2017). Ethics and the legalization of physician-assisted suicide: An American college of physicians position paper. *Annals of Internal Medicine, 167*(8), 576–578. https://doi.org/10.7326/M17-0938

Sumner, R., Burrow, A. L., & Hill, P. L. (2018). The development of purpose in life among adolescents who experience marginalization: Potential opportunities and obstacles. *American Psychologist, 73*(6), 740–752. https:// doi.org/10.1037/amp0000249

Sumontha, J., Farr, R. H., & Patterson, C. J. (2017). Children's gender development: Associations with parental sexual orientation, division of labor, and gender ideology. *Psychology of Sexual Orientation and Gender Diversity, 4*(4), 438–450. https://doi.org/10.1037/sgd0000242

Sun, F. W., Stepanovic, M. R., Andreano, J., Barrett, L. F., Touroutoglou, A., & Dickerson, B. C. (2016). Youthful brains in older adults: Preserved neuroanatomy in the default mode and salience networks contributes to youthful memory in superaging. *Journal of Neuroscience, 36*(37), 9659–9668.

Sun, H., Gong, T.-T., Jiang, Y.-T., Zhang, S., Zhao, Y.-H., & Wu, Q.-J. (2019). Global, regional, and national prevalence and disability-adjusted life-years for infertility in 195 countries and territories, 1990–2017: Results from a global burden of disease study, 2017. *Aging (Albany NY), 11*(23), 10952–10991. https://doi.org/10.18632/aging.102497

Sun, H., & Weaver, C. M. (2021). Decreased iron intake parallels rising iron deficiency anemia and related mortality rates in the US population. *The Journal of Nutrition, 151*(7), 1947–1955. https://doi.org/10.1093/jn/nxab064

Sun, H., & Yin, B. (2020). Multimedia input and bilingual children's language learning. *Frontiers in Psychology, 11*, 2023. https://doi.org/10.3389/fpsyg.2020.02023

Sun, J. W., Bai, H. Y., Li, J. H., Lin, P. Z., Zhang, H. H., & Cao, F. L. (2017). Predictors of occupational burnout among nurses: A dominance analysis of job stressors. *Journal of Clinical Nursing, 26*(23–24), 4286–4292.

Sun, Y., Fang, J., Wan, Y., Su, P., & Tao, F. (2020). Association of early-life adversity with measures of accelerated biological aging among children in China. *JAMA Network Open, 3*(9), e2013588–e2013588. https://doi.org/10.1001 /jamanetworkopen.2020.13588

Sun, Y., Tao, F., Su, P.-Y., & Collaboration, C. P. R. (2012). National estimates of pubertal milestones among urban and rural Chinese boys. *Annals of Human Biology, 39*(6), 461–467. https://doi.org/10.3109/03014460.2012.712156

Sunderam, S. (2020). Assisted reproductive technology surveillance—United States, 2017. *MMWR. Surveillance Summaries, 69*. https://doi.org/10.15585/mmwr.ss6909a1

Sung, J., Beijers, R., Gartstein, M. A., de Weerth, C., & Putnam, S. P. (2015). Exploring temperamental differences in infants from the United States of America (US) and the Netherlands. *The European Journal of Developmental Psychology, 12*(1), 15–28. https://doi.org/10.1080/17405629.2014 .937700

Supanitayanon, S., Trairatvorakul, P., & Chonchaiya, W. (2020). Screen media exposure in the first 2 years of life and preschool cognitive development: A longitudinal study. *Pediatric Research, 88*(6), 894–902. https://doi .org/10.1038/s41390-020-0831-8

Super, C. M., & Harkness, S. (1994). Temperament and the developmental niche. In W. B. Casey & S. C. McDevitt (Eds.), *Prevention and early intervention: Individual differences as risk factors for the mental health of children: A festschrift for Stella Chess and Alexander Thomas* (pp. 115–125). Brunner/Mazel.

Super, C. M., Harkness, S., Bonichini, S., Welles, B., Zylicz, P. O., Bermudez, M. R., & Palacios, J. (2020). Developmental continuity and change in the cultural construction of the "difficult child": A study in six Western cultures. In S. Harkness & C. M. Super (Eds.), *Cross cultural research on parents: Application to the care and education of children* (pp. 43–68). Wiley. https://doi.org/10.1002/cad.20338

Super, D. E. (1953). A theory of vocational development. *American Psychologist, 8*(5), 185–190. https://doi .org/10.1037/h0056046

Super, D. E. (1990). A life-span, life-space approach to career development. In D. Brown & L. Brooks (Eds.), *Career choice and development: Applying contemporary theories to practice* (pp. 197–261). Jossey-Bass.

Super, D. E. (1992). Toward a comprehensive theory of career development. In D. H. Montross & C. J. Shinkman (Eds.), *Career development: Theory and practice* (pp. 35–64). Charles C. Thomas.

Super, D. E. (1994). A life span, life space perspective on convergence. In M. L. Savikas & R. W. Lent (Eds.), *Convergence in career development theories: Implications for science and practice* (pp. 63–74). CPP Books.

Supplee, L. H., & Duggan, A. (2019). Innovative research methods to advance precision in home visiting for more efficient and effective programs. *Child Development Perspectives, 13*(3), 173–179. https://doi.org/10.1111/cdep.12334

Sutcliffe, A. G., Binder, J. F., & Dunbar, R. I. M. (2018). Activity in social media and intimacy in social relationships. *Computers in Human Behavior, 85*, 227–235. https://doi .org/10.1016/j.chb.2018.03.050

Sutin, A. R., Stephan, Y., Luchetti, M., & Terracciano, A. (2019). Five-factor model personality traits and cognitive function in five domains in older adulthood. *BMC Geriatrics, 19*(1), 343. https://doi.org/10.1186 /s12877-019-1362-1

Suwanwongse, K., & Shabarek, N. (2020). Epidemiology, clinical features, and outcomes of hospitalized infants with COVID-19 in the Bronx, New York. *Archives De Pediatrie, 27*(7), 400–401. https://doi.org/10.1016/j .arcped.2020.07.009

Suzuki, K., Miyamoto, M., & Hirata, K. (2017). Sleep disorders in the elderly: Diagnosis and management. *Journal of General and Family Medicine, 18*(2), 61–71. https://doi .org/10.1002/jgf2.27

Swain, J. E., & Ho, S.-H. S. (2017). Neuroendocrine mechanisms for parental sensitivity: Overview, recent advances and future directions. *Current Opinion in Psychology, 15*, 105–110. https://doi.org/10.1016/j.copsyc.2017.02.027

Swartz, T. T. (2009). Intergenerational family relations in adulthood: Patterns, variations, and implications in the contemporary United States. *Annual Review of Sociology, 35*(1), 191–212. https://doi.org/10.1146/annurev .soc.34.040507.134615

Swartz, T. T., & Busse, E. (2017). Family support in the transition to adulthood among diverse young adults in the United States. In D. Hartmann, R. G. Rumbaut, & T. T. Swartz (Eds.), *Crossings to adulthood: How diverse young Americans understand and navigate their lives (youth in a globalizing world)* (Vol. 4, pp. 17–41). Brill. https://doi .org/10.1163/9789004345874_003

Swartz, T. T., McLaughlin, H., & Mortimer, J. T. (2017). Parental assistance, negative life events, and attainment during the transition to adulthood. *The Sociological Quarterly, 58*(1), 91–110. https://doi.org/10.1080/00380253.2016.1246898

Sweeting, H. N., & Gilhooly, M. L. (1990). Anticipatory grief: A review. *Social Science & Medicine, 30*(10), 1073–1080.

Swenson, R., Alldred, P., & Nicholls, L. (2021). Doing gender and being gendered through occupation: Transgender and non-binary experiences. *British Journal of Occupational Therapy, 03080226211034422. https://doi .org/10.1177/03080226211034422

Swift, H. J., Abrams, D., Marques, S., Vauclair, C. M., Bratt, C., & Lima, M. L. (2018). Ageism in the European region: Finding from the European social survey. In L. Ayalon & C. Tesch-Römer (Eds.), *Contemporary perspectives on ageism* (pp. 441–459). Springer.

Swirsky, L. T., & Spaniol, J. (2019). Cognitive and motivational selectivity in healthy aging. *Wiley Interdisciplinary Reviews: Cognitive Science, 10*(6), e1512.

Swit, C. S., & Slater, N. M. (2021). Relational aggression during early childhood: A systematic review. *Aggression and Violent Behavior, 58*, 101556. https://doi.org/10.1016/j .avb.2021.101556

Switkowski, K. M., Gingras, V., Rifas-Shiman, S. L., & Oken, E. (2020). Patterns of complementary feeding behaviors predict diet quality in early childhood. *Nutrients, 12*(3), 810. https://doi.org/10.3390/nu12030810

Syed, M. (2021). The logic of microaggressions assumes a racist society. *Perspectives on Psychological Science, 16*(5), 926–931.

Syed, M., & Fish, J. (2018). Revisiting Erik Erikson's legacy on culture, race, and ethnicity. *Identity, 18*(4), 274–283. https://doi.org/10.1080/15283488.2018.1523729

Syed, M., Santos, C., Yoo, H. C., & Juang, L. P. (2018). Invisibility of racial/ethnic minorities in developmental science: Implications for research and institutional practices. *American Psychologist, 73*(6), 812–826. https://doi .org/10.1037/amp0000294

Syme, M. L., & Cohn, T. J. (2020). Aging sexual stereotypes and sexual expression in mid- and later life: Examining the stereotype matching effect. *Aging & Mental Health, 25*(8), 1507–1514. https://doi.org/10.1080/13607863.2020.1758909

Syme, M. L., Cohn, T. J., & Barnack-Tavlaris, J. (2017). A comparison of actual and perceived sexual risk among older adults. *Journal of Sex Research, 54*(2), 149–160. https://doi.org/10.1080/00224499.2015.1124379

Syme, M. L., Cohn, T. J., Stoffregen, S., Kaempfe, H., & Schippers, D. (2019). "At my age…": Defining sexual wellness in mid- and later life. *Journal of Sex Research, 56*(7), 832–842. https://doi.org/10.1080/00224499.2018.1456510

Symonds, W. C., Schwartz, R., & Ferguson, R. F. (2011). *Pathways to prosperity: Meeting the challenge of preparing young Americans.* Pathways to Prosperity Project, Harvard Graduate School of Education. http://globalpathwaysinstitute. org/wp-content/uploads/2015/03/Pathways_to_Prosperity_Feb2011-1.pdf

Szabo, A., Allen, J., Stephens, C., & Alpass, F. (2019). Longitudinal analysis of the relationship between purposes of internet use and well-being among older adults. *The Gerontologist, 59*(1), 58–68. https://doi.org/10.1093/geront/gny036

Szepsenwol, O., & Simpson, J. A. (2021). Early attachment from the perspective of life-history theory. In R. A. Thompson, J. A. Simpson, L. J. Berlin, L. Ahnert, & T. Ai (Eds.), *Attachment: The fundamental questions* (pp. 219–228). Guilford.

Szkody, E., Steele, E. H., & McKinney, C. (2020). Effects of parenting styles on psychological problems by self esteem and gender differences. *Journal of Family Issues, 42*(9), 1931–1954 0192513X20958445. https://doi.org/10.1177 /0192513X20958445

Szucs, L. E., Lowry, R., Fasula, A. M., Pampati, S., Copen, C. E., Hussaini, K. S., Kachur, R. E., Koumans, E. H., & Steiner, R. J. (2020). Condom and contraceptive use among sexually active high school students—youth risk behavior survey, United States, 2019. *Morbidity and Mortality Weekly Report, 69*(1), 11–18.

Tagi, V. M., & Chiarelli, F. (2020). Obesity and insulin resistance in children. *Current Opinion in Pediatrics, 32*(4), 582–588. https://doi.org/10.1097/MOP.0000000000000913

Takahashi, K., Mizuno, K., Sasaki, A. T., Wada, Y., Tanaka, M., Ishii, A., Tajima, K., Tsuyuguchi, N., Watanabe, K., Zeki, S., & Watanabe, Y. (2015). Imaging the passionate stage of romantic love by dopamine dynamics. *Frontiers in Human Neuroscience, 9,* 191. https://doi.org/10.3389/fnhum.2015.00191

Takanishi, R., & Le Menestrel, S. (2017). *Promoting the educational success of children and youth learning English: Promising futures.* National Academies Press.

Takei, Y. (2019). Age-dependent decline in neurogenesis of the hippocampus and extracellular nucleotides. *Human Cell, 32*(2), 88–94. https://doi.org/10.1007/s13577-019-00241-9

Talma, H., Schönbeck, Y., Dommelen, P. van, Bakker, B., Buuren, S. van, & HiraSing, R. A. (2013). Trends in menarcheal age between 1955 and 2009 in the Netherlands. *PLoS One, 8*(4), e60056. http://dx.doi.org/10.1371/journal.pone.0060056

Tamnes, C., & Mills, K. L. (2020). Imaging structural brain development in childhood and adolescence. In D. Poeppel, G. R. Mangun, & M. S. Gazzaniga (Eds.), *The cognitive neurosciences* (Vol. VI, pp. 17–25). MIT Press.

Tan, P. Z., Oppenheimer, C. W., Ladouceur, C. D., Butterfield, R. D., & Silk, J. S. (2020). A review of associations between parental emotion socialization behaviors and the neural substrates of emotional reactivity and regulation in youth. *Developmental Psychology, 56*(3), 516–527. https://doi.org/10.1037/dev0000893

Tanaka, T., Biancotto, A., Moaddel, R., Moore, A. Z., Gonzalez-Freire, M., Aon, M. A., Candia, J., Zhang, P., Cheung, F., Fantoni, G., CHI Consortium, Semba, R. D., & Ferrucci, L. (2018). Plasma proteomic signature of age in healthy humans. *Aging Cell, 17*(5), e12799. https://doi.org/10.1111/acel.12799

Tandon, P. S., Saelens, B. E., & Copeland, K. (2017). A comparison of parent and child-care provider's attitudes and perceptions about preschoolers' physical activity and outdoor time. *Child: Care, Health and Development, 43*(5), 679–686. https://doi.org/10.1111/cch.12429

Tang, H., & Barsh, G. S. (2017). Skin color variation in Africa. *Science, 358*(6365), 867–868. https://doi.org/10.1126/science.aaq1322

Tang, W. K., & Chan, C. Y. J. (2016). Effects of psychosocial interventions on self-efficacy of dementia caregivers: A literature review. *International Journal of Geriatric Psychiatry, 31*(5), 475–493. https://doi.org/10.1002/gps.4352

Tangherlini, T. R., Shahsavari, S., Shahbazi, B., Ebrahimzadeh, E., & Roychowdhury, V. (2020). An automated pipeline for the discovery of conspiracy and conspiracy theory narrative frameworks: Bridgegate, Pizzagate and storytelling on the web. *PLoS ONE, 15*(6), e0233879. https://doi.org/10.1371/journal.pone.0233879

Tanner-Smith, E. E., Wilson, S. J., & Lipsey, M. W. (2013). The comparative effectiveness of outpatient treatment for adolescent substance abuse: A meta-analysis. *Journal of Substance Abuse Treatment, 44*(2), 145–158. https://doi.org/10.1016/j.jsat.2012.05.006

Tardiff, N., Bascandziev, I., Carey, S., & Zaitchik, D. (2020). Specifying the domain-general resources that contribute to conceptual construction: Evidence from the child's acquisition of vitalist biology. *Cognition, 195,* 104090. https://doi.org/10.1016/j.cognition.2019.104090

Tari, A. R., Nauman, J., Zisko, N., Skjellegrind, H. K., Bosnes, I., Bergh, S., Stensvold, D., Selbæk, G., & Wisløff, U. (2019). Temporal changes in cardiorespiratory fitness and risk of dementia incidence and mortality: A population-based prospective cohort study. *The Lancet Public Health, 4*(11), e565–e574. https://doi.org/10.1016/S2468-2667(19)30183-5

Tarokh, L., Saletin, J. M., & Carskadon, M. A. (2016). Sleep in adolescence: Physiology, cognition and mental health. *Neuroscience & Biobehavioral Reviews, 70,* 182–188. https://doi.org/10.1016/j.neubiorev.2016.08.008

Taruscio, D., Baldi, F., Carbone, P., Neville, A. J., Rezza, G., Rizzo, C., & Mantovani, A. (2017). Primary prevention of congenital anomalies: Special focus on environmental chemicals and other toxicants, maternal health and health services and infectious diseases. In M. Posada de la Paz, D. Taruscio, & S. C. Groft (Eds.), *Rare diseases epidemiology: Update and overview* (pp. 301–322). Springer International Publishing. https://doi.org/10.1007/978-3-319-67144-4_18

Tashjian, S. M., Rahal, D., Karan, M., Eisenberger, N., Galván, A., Cole, S. W., & Fuligni, A. J. (2021). Evidence from a randomized controlled trial that altruism moderates the effect of prosocial acts on adolescent well-being. *Journal of Youth and Adolescence, 50*(1), 29–43. https://doi.org/10.1007/s10964-020-01362-3

Tasse, M. J. (2016). Defining intellectual disability: Finally we all agree … almost. *Spotlight on Disability Newsletter.* https://www.apa.org/pi/disability/resources/publications/newsletter/2016/09/intellectual-disability

Tate, C. (1996). Freud and his "Negro": Psychoanalysis as ally and enemy of African Americans. *Journal for the Psychoanalysis of Culture & Society, 1*(1), 53–62.

Tateiwa, D., Yoshikawa, H., & Kaito, T. (2019). Cartilage and bone destruction in arthritis: Pathogenesis and treatment strategy: A literature review. *Cells, 8*(8), 818. https://doi.org/10.3390/cells8080818

Tatum, B. D. (2017). *Why are all the black kids sitting together in the cafeteria? And other conversations about race.* Basic Books. (Original work published 1997)

Tay, L., & Diener, E. (2011). Needs and subjective well-being around the world. *Journal of Personality and Social Psychology, 101*(2), 354–365. https://doi.org/10.1037/a0023779

Tay, L., Morrison, M., & Diener, E. (2014). Living among the affluent: Boon or bane? *Psychological Science, 25*(6), 1235–1241. https://doi.org/10.1177/0956797614525786

Taylor, A. W., Bewick, B. M., Makanjuola, A. B., Qian, L., Kirzhanova, V. V., & Alterwain, P. (2017). Context and culture associated with alcohol use amongst youth in major urban cities: A cross-country population based survey. *PLOS ONE, 12*(11), e0187812. https://doi.org/10.1371/journal.pone.0187812

Taylor, C. A., Greenlund, S. F., McGuire, L. C., Lu, H., & Croft, J. B. (2017). Deaths from Alzheimer's Disease — United States, 1999–2014. *Morbidity and Mortality Weekly Report, 66*(20), 521–526. https://doi.org/10.15585/mmwr.mm6620a1

Taylor, C. M., & Emmett, P. M. (2019). Picky eating in children: Causes and consequences. *Proceedings of the Nutrition Society, 78*(2), 161–169. https://doi.org/10.1017/S0029665118002586

Taylor, J. L., McPheeters, M. L., Sathe, N. A., Dove, D., Veenstra-VanderWeele, J., & Warren, Z. (2012). A systematic review of vocational interventions for young adults with autism spectrum disorders. *Pediatrics, 130*(3), 531–538. https://doi.org/10.1542/peds.2012-0682

Taylor, K. M., Kioumourtzoglou, M.-A., Clover, J., Coull, B. A., Dennerlein, J. T., Bellinger, D. C., & Weisskopf, M. G. (2018). Concussion history and cognitive function in a large cohort of adolescent athletes. *The American Journal of Sports Medicine, 46*(13), 3262–3270. https://doi.org/10.1177/0363546518798801

Taylor, L., Claire, R., Campbell, K., Coleman-Haynes, T., Leonardi-Bee, J., Chamberlain, C., Berlin, I., Davey, M.-A., Cooper, S., & Coleman, T. (2021). Fetal safety of nicotine replacement therapy in pregnancy: Systematic review and meta-analysis. *Addiction, 116*(2), 239–277. https://doi.org/10.1111/add.15185

Taylor, R. J., Chatters, L. M., Woodward, A. T., & Brown, E. (2013). Racial and ethnic differences in extended family, friendship, fictive kin, and congregational informal support networks. *Family Relations, 62*(4), 609–624. https://doi.org/10.1111/fare.12030

Teachman, J., & Tedrow, L. (2014). Delinquent behavior, the transition to adulthood, and the likelihood of military enlistment. *Social Science Research, 45,* 46–55. https://doi.org/10.1016/j.ssresearch.2013.12.012

Tefft, B. C. (2017). *Rates of motor vehicle crashes, injuries and deaths in relation to driver age, United States, 2014–2015.* AAA Foundation for Traffic Safety.

Teicher, M. H., & Samson, J. A. (2016). Annual research review: Enduring neurobiological effects of childhood abuse and neglect. *Journal of Child Psychology and Psychiatry, 57*(3), 241–266.

Telzer, E. H., Flannery, J., Humphreys, K. L., Goff, B., Gabard-Durman, L., Gee, D. G., & Tottenham, N. (2015). "The cooties effect": Amygdala reactivity to opposite-versus same-sex faces declines from childhood to adolescence. *Journal of Cognitive Neuroscience, 27*(9), 1685–1696.

Telzer, E. H., & Fuligni, A. J. (2009). Daily family assistance and the psychological well-being of adolescents from Latin American, Asian, and European backgrounds. *Developmental Psychology, 45*(4), 1177.

Telzer, E. H., Fuligni, A. J., Lieberman, M. D., & Galván, A. (2013). The effects of poor quality sleep on brain function and risk taking in adolescence. *Neuroimage, 71,* 275–283.

Templin, M. C. (1957). *Certain language skills in children: Their development and interrelationships.* University of Minnesota Press.

Terman, L. M. (1916). The uses of intelligence tests. In L. M. Terman (Ed.), *The measurement of intelligence* (pp. 3–21). Houghton, Mifflin.

Terrell, K. (2018). *AARP survey finds age discrimination is common at work.* AARP. http://www.aarp.org/work/working-at-50-plus/info-2018/age-discrimination-common-at-work.html

ter Telgte, A., van Leijsen, E. M. C., Wiegertjes, K., Klijn, C. J. M., Tuladhar, A. M., & de Leeuw, F.-E. (2018). Cerebral small vessel disease: From a focal to a global perspective. *Nature Reviews Neurology, 14*(7), 387–398. https://doi.org/10.1038/s41582-018-0014-y

ter Telgte, A., Wiegertjes, K., Gesierich, B., Baskaran, B. S., Marques, J. P., Kuijf, H. J., & de Leeuw, F. E. (2020). Temporal dynamics of cortical microinfarcts in cerebral small vessel disease. *JAMA Neurology, 77*(5), 643–647.

Tervalon, M., & Murray-García, J. (1998). Cultural humility versus cultural competence: A critical distinction in defining physician training outcomes in multicultural education. *Journal of Health Care for the Poor and Underserved, 9*(2), 117–125. https://doi.org/10.1353/hpu.2010.0233

Tesch-Römer, C., & Wahl, H.-W. (2017). Toward a more comprehensive concept of successful aging: Disability and care needs. *The Journals of Gerontology: Series B, 72*(2), 310–318. https://doi.org/10.1093/geronb/gbw162

Tester, G., & Wright, E. R. (2017). Older gay men and their support convoys. *Journals of Gerontology Series B: Psychological Sciences and Social Sciences, 72*(3), 488–497.

Teti, D. M., Cole, P. M., Cabrera, N., Goodman, S. H., & McLoyd, V. C. (2017). Supporting parents: How six decades of parenting research can inform policy and best practice. *Social Policy Report, 30*(5), 1–34.

Tetzner, J., Becker, M., & Brandt, N. D. (2020). Personality-achievement associations in adolescence — examining associations across grade levels and learning environments. *Journal of Personality, 88*(2), 356–372. https://doi.org/10.1111/jopy.12495

Tevington, P. (2018). "You're throwing your life away": Sanctioning of early marital timelines by religion and social class. *Social Inclusion, 6*(2), 140–150.

Teychenne, M., White, R. L., Richards, J., Schuch, F. B., Rosenbaum, S., & Bennie, J. A. (2020). Do we need physical activity guidelines for mental health: What does the evidence tell us? *Mental Health and Physical Activity, 18,* 100315. https://doi.org/10.1016/j.mhpa.2019.100315

Thai, J. N., Barnhart, C. E., Cagle, J., & Smith, A. K. (2016). "It just consumes your life": Quality of life for informal caregivers of diverse older adults with late-life disability. *American Journal of Hospice and Palliative Medicine, 33*(7), 644–650. https://doi.org/10.1177/1049909115583044

Thakrar, A. P., Forrest, A. D., Maltenfort, M. G., & Forrest, C. B. (2018). Child mortality in the US and 19 OECD comparator nations: A 50-year time-trend analysis. *Health Affairs, 37*(1), 140–149. https://doi.org/10.1377/hlthaff.2017.0767

The Aesthetic Society. (2019). *Aesthetic plastic surgery national databank statistics.*

The Economist. (2010, July 15). Grim reapings. https://www.economist.com/international/2010/07/15/grim-reapings

The Editors of *The Lancet.* (2010). Retraction—Ileal-lymphoid-nodular hyperplasia, non-specific colitis, and pervasive developmental disorder in children. *The Lancet, 375*(9713), 445. https://doi.org/10.1016/S0140-6736(10)60175-4

The European IVF-monitoring Consortium (EIM) for the European Society of Human Reproduction and Embryology (ESHRE), Wyns, C., Bergh, C., Calhaz-Jorge, C., De Geyter, C., Kupka, M. S., Motrenko, T., Rugescu, I., Smeenk, J., Tandler-Schneider, A., Vidakovic, S., & Goossens, V. (2020). ART in Europe, 2016: Results generated from European registries by ESHRE. *Human Reproduction Open, 2020*(3). https://doi.org/10.1093/hropen/hoaa032

The Hanen Center (Hanen). (2017). *It takes two to talk: The Hanen program for parents of children with language delays.* The Hanen Center (Ontario).

The Institute for College Access & Success (TICAS). (2020). *Student debt and the class of 2019.*

Thelen, E., & Adolph, K. E. (1994). Arnold L. Gesell: The paradox of nature and nurture. In R. D. Parke, P. A. Ornstein, J. J. Rieser, & C. Zahn-Waxler (Eds.), *A century of developmental psychology* (pp. 357–387). American Psychological Association. https://doi.org/10.1037/10155-027

Thibodeau, R. B., Gilpin, A. T., Brown, M. M., & Meyer, B. A. (2016). The effects of fantastical pretend-play on the development of executive functions: An intervention study. *Journal of Experimental Child Psychology, 145,* 120–138.

Thiebaut de Schotten, M., Cohen, L., Amemiya, E., Braga, L. W., & Dehaene, S. (2014). Learning to read improves the structure of the arcuate fasciculus. *Cerebral Cortex, 24*(4), 989–995. https://doi.org/10.1093/cercor/bhs383

Thielke, S., Sale, J., & Reid, M. C. (2012). Aging: Are these 4 pain myths complicating care? *The Journal of Family Practice, 61*(11), 666–670.

Thiem, K. C., Neel, R., Simpson, A. J., & Todd, A. R. (2019). Are black women and girls associated with danger? Implicit racial bias at the intersection of target age and gender. *Personality and Social Psychology Bulletin, 45*(10), 1427–1439.

Thijssen, S., Muetzel, R. L., Bakermans-Kranenburg, M. J., Jaddoe, V. W. V., Tiemeier, H., Verhulst, F. C., White, T., & Ijzendoorn, M. H. V. (2017). Insensitive parenting may accelerate the development of the amygdala–medial prefrontal cortex circuit. *Development and Psychopathology, 29*(2), 505–518. https://doi.org/10.1017/S0954579417000141

Thomaes, S., Brummelman, E., & Sedikides, C. (2017). Why most children think well of themselves. *Child Development, 88*(6), 1873–1884.

Thomala, L. L. (2021). *China: MAUs of online dating and matchmaking apps 2020.* Statistica. https://www.statista.com/statistics/1130445/china-monthly-active-users-of-online-dating-and-matchmaking-apps/

Thomas, A., & Chess, S. (1957). An approach to the study of sources of individual differences in child behavior. *Journal of Clinical & Experimental Psychopathology, 18,* 347–357.

Thomas, A., & Chess, S. (1977). *Temperament and development.* Brunner/Mazel.

Thomas, A., Chess, S., & Birch, H. G. (1970). The origin of personality. *Scientific American, 223*(2), 102–109.

Thomas, E., Buss, C., Rasmussen, J. M., Entringer, S., Ramirez, J. S. B., Marr, M., Rudolph, M. D., Gilmore, J. H., Styner, M., Wadhwa, P. D., Fair, D. A., & Graham, A. M. (2019). Newborn amygdala connectivity and early emerging fear. *Developmental Cognitive Neuroscience, 37,* 100604. https://doi.org/10.1016/j.dcn.2018.12.002

Thomas, F., Renaud, F., Benefice, E., de Meeüs, T., & Guegan, J.-F. (2001). International variability of ages at menarche and menopause: Patterns and main determinants. *Human Biology, 73*(2), 271–290. JSTOR. https://www.jstor.org/stable/41465935

Thomas, M. C., Kamarck, T. W., Wright, A. G. C., Matthews, K. A., Muldoon, M. F., & Manuck, S. B. (2020). Hostility dimensions and metabolic syndrome in a healthy, midlife sample. *International Journal of Behavioral Medicine, 27,* 475–480. https://doi.org/10.1007/s12529-020-09855-y

Thomas, R. J. (2019). Sources of friendship and structurally induced homophily across the life course. *Sociological Perspectives, 62*(6), 822–843. https://doi.org/10.1177/0731121419828399

Thomason, M. E., Scheinost, D., Manning, J. H., Grove, L. E., Hect, J., Marshall, N., Hernandez-Andrade, E., Berman, S., Pappas, A., Yeo, L., Hassan, S. S., Constable, R. T., Ment, L. R., & Romero, R. (2017). Weak functional connectivity in the human fetal brain prior to preterm birth. *Scientific Reports, 7,* 39286. https://doi.org/10.1038/srep39286

Thomeer, M. B., LeBlanc, A. J., Frost, D. M., & Bowen, K. (2018). Anticipatory minority stressors among same-sex couples: A relationship timeline approach. *Social Psychology Quarterly, 81*(2), 126–148.

Thompson, D. K., Matthews, L. G., Alexander, B., Lee, K. J., Kelly, C. E., Adamson, C. L., Hunt, R. W., Cheong, J. L. Y., Spencer-Smith, M., Neil, J. J., Seal, M. L., Inder, T. E., Doyle, L. W., & Anderson, P. J. (2020). Tracking regional brain growth up to age 13 in children born term and very preterm. *Nature Communications, 11*(1), 696. https://doi.org/10.1038/s41467-020-14334-9

Thompson, D. L., & Thompson, S. (2018). Educational equity and quality in K–12 schools: Meeting the needs of all students. *Journal for the Advancement of Educational Research International, 12*(1), 34–46.

Thompson, J. A. (2019). Disentangling the roles of maternal and paternal age on birth prevalence of down syndrome and other chromosomal disorders using a Bayesian modeling approach. *BMC Medical Research Methodology, 19*(1), 1–8.

Thompson, M. P., Swartout, K. M., & Koss, M. P. (2013). Trajectories and predictors of sexually aggressive behaviors during emerging adulthood. *Psychology of Violence, 3*(3), 247–259. https://doi.org/10.1037/a0030624

Thompson, R., Kaczor, K., Lorenz, D. J., Bennett, B. L., Meyers, G., & Pierce, M. C. (2017). Is the use of physical discipline associated with aggressive behaviors in young children? *Academic Pediatrics, 17*(1), 34–44. https://doi.org/10.1016/j.acap.2016.02.014

Thompson, R. A. (2019). Emotion dysregulation: A theme in search of definition. *Development and Psychopathology, 31*(3), 805–815.

Thomsen, L. (2020). The developmental origins of social hierarchy: How infants and young children mentally represent and respond to power and status. *Current Opinion in Psychology, 33,* 201–208. https://doi.org/10.1016/j.copsyc.2019.07.044

Thorne, D., Foohey, P., Lawless, R. M., & Porter, K. M. (2018). *Graying of U.S. bankruptcy: Fallout from life in a risk society* (SSRN Scholarly Paper ID 3226574). Social Science Research Network. https://doi.org/10.2139/ssrn.3226574

Thorpe, K., Irvine, S., Pattinson, C., & Staton, S. (2020). Insider perspectives: The 'tricky business' of providing for children's sleep and rest needs in the context of early childhood education and care. *Early Years, 40*(2), 221–236.

Thurston, R. C., Chang, Y., Buysse, D. J., Hall, M. H., & Matthews, K. A. (2019). Hot flashes and awakenings among midlife women. *Sleep, 42*(9), zsz131. https://doi.org/10.1093/sleep/zsz131

Tice, P. (2020, August 2). *Growing old in Bloomingdale Part III.* Upper West Side History. http://www.upperwestsidehistory.org/1/post/2020/04/growing-old-in-bloomingdale-part-iii.html

Tick, H., Nielsen, A., Pelletier, K. R., Bonakdar, R., Simmons, S., Glick, R., & Zador, V. (2018). Evidence-based nonpharmacologic strategies for comprehensive pain care: The consortium pain task force white paper. *Explore, 14*(3), 177–211.

Tijani, A. M., Awowole, I. O., Badejoko, O. O., Badejoko, B. O., Ijarotimi, A. O., & Loto, O. M. (2019). Is menarche really occurring earlier? A study of secondary school girls in Ile-Ife, Nigeria. *Tropical Journal of Obstetrics and Gynaecology, 36*(1), 112–116. https://doi.org/10.4314/tjog.v36i1

Tilburg, W. C. (2017). Policy approaches to improving housing and health. *The Journal of Law, Medicine & Ethics, 45*(1_suppl), 90–93. https://doi.org/10.1177/1073110517703334

Tilcsik, A., Anteby, M., & Knight, C. R. (2015). Concealable stigma and occupational segregation: Toward a theory of gay and lesbian occupations. *Administrative Science Quarterly, 60*(3), 446–481. https://doi.org/10.1177/0001839215576401

Tillman, K. H., Brewster, K. L., & Holway, G. V. (2019). Sexual and romantic relationships in young adulthood. *Annual Review of Sociology, 45*(1), 133–153. https://doi.org/10.1146/annurev-soc-073018-022625

Tilton-Weaver, L. C., Burk, W. J., Kerr, M., & Stattin, H. (2013). Can parental monitoring and peer management reduce the selection or influence of delinquent peers? Testing the question using a dynamic social network approach. *Developmental Psychology, 49*(11), 2057–2070. https://doi.org/10.1037/a0031854

Tilton-Weaver, L., Kerr, M., Pakalniskeine, V., Tokic, A., Salihovic, S., & Stattin, H. (2010). Open up or close down: How do parental reactions affect youth information management? *Journal of Adolescence, 33*(2), 333–346. https://doi.org/10.1016/j.adolescence.2009.07.011

Timmermans, S. (2010). *Sudden death and the myth of CPR.* Temple University Press.

Timmons, K., Cooper, A., Bozek, E., & Braund, H. (2021). The impacts of COVID-19 on early childhood education: Capturing the unique challenges associated with remote teaching and learning in K-2. *Early Childhood Education Journal.* https://doi.org/10.1007/s10643-021-01207-z

Ting, F., Dawkins, M. B., Stavans, M., & Baillargeon, R. (2020). Principles and concepts in early moral cognition. In J. Decety (Ed.), *The social brain: A developmental perspective* (pp. 41–66). MIT Press.

Tinggaard, J., Mieritz, M. G., Sørensen, K., Mouritsen, A., Hagen, C. P., Aksglaede, L., Wohlfahrt-Veje, C., & Juul, A. (2012). The physiology and timing of male puberty. *Current Opinion in Endocrinology, Diabetes and Obesity, 19*(3), 197–203. https://doi.org/10.1097/MED.0b013e3283535614

Tipene-Leach, D., & Abel, S. (2019). Innovation to prevent sudden infant death: The wahakura as an indigenous vision for a safe sleep environment. *Australian Journal of Primary Health, 25*(5), 406–409. https://doi.org/10.1071/PY19033

Tiwari, G. (2008). Interplay of love, sex, and marriage in a polyandrous society in the High Himalayas of India. In W. R. Jankowiak (Ed.), *Intimacies: Love and sex across cultures* (pp. 122–147). Columbia University Press.

Tjaden, J., Rolando, D., Doty, J., & Mortimer, J. T. (2019). The long-term effects of time use during high school on positive development. Longitudinal and Life Course Studies, 10(1), 51–85. https://doi.org/10.1332/175795919X15468755933371

TNTP. (2018). *The opportunity myth: What students can show us about how school is letting them down—And how to fix it.* https://tntp.org/assets/documents/TNTP_The-Opportunity-Myth_Web.pdf

Tobin, D. J. (2017). Introduction to skin aging. *Journal of Tissue Viability, 26*(1), 37–46.

Todd, A. R., Thiem, K. C., & Neel, R. (2016). Does seeing faces of young black boys facilitate the identification of threatening stimuli? *Psychological Science, 27*(3), 384–393.

Todd, S., Barr, S., Roberts, M., & Passmore, A. P. (2013). Survival in dementia and predictors of mortality: A review. *International Journal of Geriatric Psychiatry, 28*(11), 1109–1124. https://doi.org/10.1002/gps.3946

Toe, D., Mood, D., Most, T., Walker, E., & Tucci, S. (2020). The assessment of pragmatic skills in young deaf and hard of hearing children. *Pediatrics, 146*(Supplement 3), S284–S291. https://doi.org/10.1542/peds.2020-0242H

Toh, S. H., Howie, E. K., Coenen, P., & Straker, L. M. (2019). "From the moment I wake up I will use it … every day, very hour": A qualitative study on the patterns of adolescents' mobile touch screen device use from adolescent and parent perspectives. *BMC Pediatrics, 19*(1), 1–16.

Toh, W. X., Yang, H., & Hartanto, A. (2020). Executive function and subjective well-being in middle and late adulthood. *The Journals of Gerontology: Series B, 75*(6), e69–e77. https://doi.org/10.1093/geronb/gbz006

Tolan, P. H., McDaniel, H. L., Richardson, M., Arkin, N., Augenstern, J., & DuBois, D. L. (2020). Improving understanding of how mentoring works: Measuring multiple intervention processes. *Journal of Community Psychology, 48*(6), 2086–2107.

Tomasello, M. (2016). Cultural learning redux. *Child Development, 87*(3), 643–653. https://doi.org/10.1111/cdev.12499

Tomasello, M. (2018). The normative turn in early moral development. *Human Development, 61*(4–5), 248–263. https://doi.org/10.1159/000492802

Tomasello, M. (2019). *Becoming human: A theory of ontogeny.* Harvard University Press.

Tomasello, M. (2020). The adaptive origins of uniquely human sociality. *Philosophical Transactions of the Royal Society B: Biological Sciences, 375*(1803), 20190493. https://doi.org/10.1098/rstb.2019.0493

Tomasello, M. (2021). *Becoming human: A theory of ontogeny.* Harvard University Press.

Tomaz, S. A., Jones, R. A., Hinkley, T., Bernstein, S. L., Twine, R., Kahn, K., Norris, S. A., & Draper, C. E. (2019). Gross motor skills of South African preschool-aged children across different income settings. *Journal of Science and Medicine in Sport, 22*(6), 689–694. https://doi.org/10.1016/j.jsams.2018.12.009

Tomioka, H., Zhan, G. Q., & Pearcey, S. M. (2019). A comparative study of college students' cultural orientation, aging attitude, and anxiety: Japan, China, and USA. *The Journal of Aging and Social Change, 9*(2), 15.

Tomiyama, A. J., Carr, D., Granberg, E. M., Major, B., Robinson, E., Sutin, A. R., & Brewis, A. (2018). How and why weight stigma drives the obesity "epidemic" and harms health. *BMC Medicine, 16*(1), 123. https://doi.org/10.1186/s12916-018-1116-5

Tomova, L., Andrews, J. L., & Blakemore, S.-J. (2021). The importance of belonging and the avoidance of social risk taking in adolescence. *Developmental Review, 61*, 100981. https://doi.org/10.1016/j.dr.2021.100981

Tonetti, L., Fabbri, M., & Natale, V. (2008). Sex difference in sleep-time preference and sleep need: A cross-sectional survey among Italian pre-adolescents, adolescents, and adults. *Chronobiology International, 25*(5), 745–759.

Tooley, U. A., Bassett, D. S., & Mackey, A. P. (2021). Environmental influences on the pace of brain development. *Nature Reviews Neuroscience, 22*(6), 372–384. https://doi.org/10.1038/s41583-021-00457-5

Toolis, K. (2018). *My father's wake: How the Irish teach us to live, love, and die.* Da Capo Press.

Toothman, E. L., & Barrett, A. E. (2011). Mapping midlife: An examination of social factors shaping conceptions of the timing of middle age. *Advances in Life Course Research, 16*(3), 99–111.

Toppe, T. (2020). Social inclusion increases over early childhood and is influenced by others' group membership. *Developmental Psychology, 56*(2), 324. https://doi.org/10.1037/dev0000873

Torche, F., & Rich, P. (2016). Declining racial stratification in marriage choices? Trends in Black/White status exchange in the United States, 1980 to 2010. *Sociology of Race and Ethnicity, 3*(1), 31–49. https://doi.org/10.1177/2332649216648464

Tornello, S. L. (2020). Division of labor among transgender and gender non-binary parents: Association with individual, couple, and children's behavioral outcomes. *Frontiers in Psychology, 11*, 15. https://doi.org/10.3389/fpsyg.2020.00015

Torpey, E. (2021). *Education pays, 2020* (Career Outlook: Data on Display). U.S. Bureau of Labor Statistics.

Torppa, M., Niemi, P., Vasalampi, K., Lerkkanen, M.-K., Tolvanen, A., & Poikkeus, A.-M. (2020). Leisure reading (but not any kind) and reading comprehension support each other—A longitudinal study across grades 1 and 9. *Child Development, 91*(3), 876–900. https://doi.org/10.1111/cdev.13241

Tottenham, N. (2020). Early adversity and the neotenous human brain. *Biological Psychiatry, 87*(4), 350–358. https://doi.org/10.1016/j.biopsych.2019.06.018

Tottenham, N., & Gabard-Durnam, L. J. (2017). The developing amygdala: A student of the world and a teacher of the cortex. *Current Opinion in Psychology, 17*, 55–60. https://doi.org/10.1016/j.copsyc.2017.06.012

Towner, S. L., Dolcini, M. M., & Harper, G. W. (2015). Romantic relationship dynamics of urban African American adolescents: Patterns of monogamy, commitment, and trust. *Youth & Society, 47*(3), 343–373. https://doi.org/10.1177/0044118X12462591

Trabold, N., McMahon, J., Alsobrooks, S., Whitney, S., & Mittal, M. (2020). A systematic review of intimate partner violence interventions: State of the field and implications for practitioners. *Trauma, Violence, & Abuse, 21*(2), 311–325. https://doi.org/10.1177/1524838018767934

Trachtenberg, D. I., & Trojanowski, J. Q. (2008). Dementia: A word to be forgotten. *Archives of Neurology, 65*(5), 593–595.

Tradii, L., & Robert, M. (2019). Do we deny death? II. Critiques of the death-denial thesis. *Mortality, 24*(4), 377–388. https://doi.org/10.1080/13576275.2017.1415319

Tram, K. H., Saeed, S., Bradley, C., Fox, B., Eshun-Wilson, I., Mody, A., & Geng, E. (2021). Deliberation, dissent, and distrust: Understanding distinct drivers of COVID-19 vaccine hesitancy in the United States. *Clinical Infectious Diseases,* ciab633. https://doi.org/10.1093/cid/ciab633

Tran, S. P., & Raffaelli, M. (2020). Configurations of autonomy and relatedness in a multiethnic U.S. sample of parent-adolescent dyads. *Journal of Research on Adolescence: The Official Journal of the Society for Research on Adolescence, 30*(1), 203–218. https://doi.org/10.1111/jora.12517

Trang, N. H. H. D., Hong, T. K., & Dibley, M. J. (2012). Cohort profile: Ho Chi Minh City youth cohort—changes in diet, physical activity, sedentary behaviour and relationship with overweight/obesity in adolescents. *BMJ Open, 2*(1), e000362.

Travers, J. L., Teitelman, A. M., Jenkins, K. A., & Castle, N. G. (2020). Exploring social-based discrimination among nursing home certified nursing assistants. *Nursing Inquiry, 27*(1), e12315. https://doi.org/10.1111/nin.12315

Treloar, H., Celio, M. A., Lisman, S. A., Miranda, R., & Spear, L. P. (2017). Subjective alcohol responses in a cross-sectional, field-based study of adolescents and young adults: Effects of age, drinking level, and dependence/consequences. *Drug and Alcohol Dependence, 170*, 156–163. https://doi.org/10.1016/j.drugalcdep.2016.11.009

Trends in International Mathematics and Science Study (TIMSS). (2019). International Association for the Evaluation of Educational Achievement (IEA).

Trent, M., Dooley, D. G., Dougé, J., Section on Adolescent Health, Council on Community Pediatrics, & Committee on Adolescence. (2019). The impact of racism on child and adolescent health. *Pediatrics, 144*(2), e20191765. https://doi.org/10.1542/peds.2019-1765

Trieu, M. M. (2016). Family obligation fulfillment among southeast Asian American young adults. *Journal of Family Issues, 37*(10), 1355–1383. https://doi.org/10.1177/0192513X14551174

Trinidad, J. E. (2019). Understanding when parental aspirations negatively affect student outcomes: The case of aspiration-expectation inconsistency. *Studies in Educational Evaluation, 60*, 179–188. https://doi.org/10.1016/j.stueduc.2019.01.004

Tronick, E., Als, H., Adamson, L., Wise, S., & Brazelton, T. B. (1978). The infant's response to entrapment between contradictory messages in face-to-face interaction. *Journal of the American Academy of Child Psychiatry, 17*(1), 1–13.

Trostel, P. A. (2015). *It's not just the money: The benefits of college education to individuals and to society.* Lumina Foundation.

Troude, P., Santin, G., Guibert, J., Bouyer, J., & de La Rochebrochard, E. (2016). Seven out of 10 couples treated by IVF achieve parenthood following either treatment, natural conception or adoption. *Reproductive BioMedicine Online, 33*(5), 560–567. https://doi.org/10.1016/j.rbmo.2016.08.010

Troxel, W., & Wolfson, A. (2016). Sleep science and policy: A focus on school start times. *Sleep Health, 2*(3), 186. https://doi.org/10.1016/j.sleh.2016.07.001

Troyansky, D. G. (2015). *Aging in world history.* Routledge.

Truelove-Hill, M., Erus, G., Bashyam, V., Varol, E., Sako, C., Gur, R. C., Gur, R. E., Koutsouleris, N., Zhuo, C., Fan, Y., Wolf, D. H., Satterthwaite, T. D., & Davatzikos, C. (2020). A multidimensional neural maturation index reveals reproducible developmental patterns in children and adolescents. *Journal of Neuroscience, 40*(6), 1265–1275. https://doi.org/10.1523/JNEUROSCI.2092-19.2019

Truog, R. D., Pope, T. M., & Jones, D. S. (2018). The 50-year legacy of the Harvard report on brain death. *JAMA, 320*(4), 335–336. https://doi.org/10.1001/jama.2018.6990

Truxillo, D. M., Cadiz, D. M., & Hammer, L. B. (2015). Supporting the aging workforce: A review and recommendations for workplace intervention research. *Annual Review of Organizational Psychology and Organizational Behavior, 2*(1), 351–381. https://doi.org/10.1146/annurev-orgpsych-032414-111435

Tsai, A. C., Alegría, M., & Strathdee, S. A. (2019). Addressing the context and consequences of substance use, misuse, and dependence: A global imperative. *PLOS Medicine, 16*(11), e1003000. https://doi.org/10.1371/journal.pmed.1003000

Tsai, J., Becker, D., Sussman, S., Bluthenthal, R., Unger, J. B., & Schwartz, S. J. (2017). Acculturation and risky sexual behavior among adolescents and emerging adults from immigrant families. In S. J. Schwartz & J. Unger (Eds.), *The Oxford handbook of acculturation and health* (p. 301). Oxford University Press.

Tsai, J. L., Louie, J. Y., Chen, E. E., & Uchida, Y. (2007). Learning what feelings to desire: Socialization of ideal affect through children's storybooks. *Personality and Social Psychology Bulletin, 33*(1), 17–30.

Tsai, J. L., Sims, T., Qu, Y., Thomas, E., Jiang, D., & Fung, H. H. (2018). Valuing excitement makes people look forward to old age less and dread it more. *Psychology and Aging, 33*(7), 975–992. https://doi.org/10.1037/pag0000295

Tsai, K. M., Telzer, E. H., & Fuligni, A. J. (2013). Continuity and discontinuity in perceptions of family relationships from adolescence to young adulthood. *Child Development, 84*(2), 471–484. https://doi.org/10.1111/j.1467-8624.2012.01858.x

Tseng, Y. F., Hsu, M. T., Hsieh, Y. T., & Cheng, H. R. (2018). The meaning of rituals after a stillbirth: A qualitative study of mothers with a stillborn baby. *Journal of Clinical Nursing, 27*(5–6), 1134–1142.

Tu, K. N., Lie, J. D., Wan, C. K. V., Cameron, M., Austel, A. G., Nguyen, J. K., Van, K., & Hyun, D. (2018). Osteoporosis: A review of treatment options. *Pharmacy and Therapeutics, 43*(2), 92–104.

Tucker-Drob, E. M. (2017). How do individual experiences aggregate to shape personality development. *European Journal of Personality, 31*(5), 570–571.

Tucker-Drob, E. M. (2019). Cognitive aging and dementia: A life-span perspective. *Annual Review of Developmental Psychology, 1*, 177–196.

Tudor-Locke, C., Craig, C. L., Beets, M. W., Belton, S., Cardon, G. M., Duncan, S., Hatano, Y., Lubans, D. R., Olds, T. S., Raustorp, A., Rowe, D. A., Spence, J. C., Tanaka, S., & Blair, S. N. (2011). How many steps/day are enough? For children and adolescents. *International Journal of Behavioral Nutrition and Physical Activity, 8*(1), 78. https://doi.org/10.1186/1479-5868-8-78

Tugend, A. (2015, January 23). Doulas, who usher in new life, find mission in support for the dying. *The New York Times.* https://www.nytimes.com/2015/01/24/your-money/death-doulas-help-the-terminally-ill-and-their-families-cope.html

Tulchin-Francis, K., Stevens, W., Gu, X., Zhang, T., Roberts, H., Keller, J., Dempsey, D., Borchard, J., Jeans, K., & VanPelt, J. (2021). The impact of the coronavirus disease 2019 pandemic on physical activity in U.S. children. *Journal of Sport and Health Science, 10*(3), 323–332. https://doi.org/10.1016/j.jshs.2021.02.005

Tulsky, J. A. (2015). Improving quality of care for serious illness: Findings and recommendations of the Institute of Medicine Report on Dying in America. *JAMA Internal Medicine, 175*(5), 840–841. https://doi.org/10.1001/jamainternmed.2014.8425

Tune, J. D., Goodwill, A. G., Sassoon, D. J., & Mather, K. J. (2017). Cardiovascular consequences of metabolic syndrome. *Translational Research, 183*, 57–70.

Turanovic, J. J. (2019). Victimization and desistance from crime. *Journal of Developmental and Life-Course Criminology*, 5(1), 86–106.

Turban, J. L., King, D., Carswell, J. M., & Keuroghlian, A. S. (2020). Pubertal suppression for transgender youth and risk of suicidal ideation. *Pediatrics*, 145(2), e20191725. https://doi.org/10.1542/peds.2019-1725

Turiel, E. (1983). *The development of social knowledge: Morality and convention.* Cambridge University Press.

Turiel, E., & Dahl, A. (2019). The development of domains of moral and conventional norms, coordination in decision-making, and the implications of social opposition. In N. Roughley & K. Bayertz (Eds.), *The normative animal? On the anthropological significance of social, moral, and linguistic norms* (pp. 195–213). Oxford University Press.

Turk, D. C., & Monarch, E. S. (2018). Biopsychosocial perspective on chronic pain. In D. C. Turk & R. J. Gatchel (Eds.), *Psychological approaches to pain management: A practitioner's handbook* (3rd ed, pp. 3–24). Guilford.

Turkheimer, E. (2019). Genetics and human agency: The philosophy of behavior genetics introduction to the special issue. *Behavior Genetics*, 49(2), 123–127. https://doi.org/10.1007/s10519-019-09952-z

Turkheimer, E., Pettersson, E., & Horn, E. E. (2014). A phenotypic null hypothesis for the genetics of personality. *Annual Review of Psychology*, 65(1), 515–540. https://doi.org/10.1146/annurev-psych-113011-143752

Turnbull, C., Sud, A., & Houlston, R. S. (2018). Cancer genetics, precision prevention and a call to action. *Nature Genetics*, 50(9), 1212–1218.

Turner, J. A., Klein, B. W., & Sorrentino, C. (2020, July). Making volunteer work visible: Supplementary measures of work in labor force statistics. *Monthly Labor Review.* U.S. Bureau of Labor Statistics. https://doi.org/10.21916/mlr.2020.15

Turner, J. D., D'Ambrosio, C., Vögele, C., & Diewald, M. (2020). Twin research in the post-genomic era: Dissecting the pathophysiological effects of adversity and the social environment. *International Journal of Molecular Sciences*, 21(9), 3142. https://doi.org/10.3390/ijms21093142

Turner, P. L., & Mainster, M. A. (2008). Circadian photoreception: Ageing and the eye's important role in systemic health. *British Journal of Ophthalmology*, 92(11), 1439–1444.

Turnwald, B. P., Goyer, J. P., Boles, D. Z., Silder, A., Delp, S. L., & Crum, A. J. (2019). Learning one's genetic risk changes physiology independent of actual genetic risk. *Nature Human Behaviour*, 3(1), 48–56. https://doi.org/10.1038/s41562-018-0483-4

Turoman, N., Tivadar, R. I., Retsa, C., Maillard, A. M., Scerif, G., & Matusz, P. J. (2021). The development of attentional control mechanisms in multisensory environments. *Developmental Cognitive Neuroscience*, 48, 100930. https://doi.org/10.1016/j.dcn.2021.100930

Turtonen, O., Saarinen, A., Nummenmaa, L., Tuominen, L., Tikka, M., Armio, R.-L., Hautamäki, A., Laurikainen, H., Raitakari, O., Keltikangas-Järvinen, L., & Hietala, J. (2021). Adult attachment system links with brain mu opioid receptor availability in vivo. *Biological Psychiatry: Cognitive Neuroscience and Neuroimaging*, 6(3), 360–369. https://doi.org/10.1016/j.bpsc.2020.10.013

Tuting, K. (2020, May 20). *Meet BirDie, the 78-year-old DreamHack CS:GO champion.* ONE Esports. https://www.oneesports.gg/culture/meet-birdie-the-78-year-old-dreamhack-csgo-champion/

Tutty, L. M., Aubry, D., & Velasquez, L. (2020). The "Who Do You Tell?" TM Child sexual abuse education program: Eight years of monitoring. *Journal of Child Sexual Abuse*, 29(1), 2–21. https://doi.org/10.1080/10538712.2019.1663969

Twenge, J. M. (2017, September). Have smartphones destroyed a generation? *The Atlantic.* https://www.theatlantic.com/magazine/archive/2017/09/has-the-smartphone-destroyed-a-generation/534198/

Twenge, J. M. (2019). More time on technology, less happiness? Associations between digital-media use and psychological well-being. *Current Directions in Psychological Science*, 28(4), 372–379. https://doi.org/10.1177/0963721419838244

Twenge, J. M. (2020). Why increases in adolescent depression may be linked to the technological environment. *Current Opinion in Psychology*, 32, 89–94. https://doi.org/10.1016/j.copsyc.2019.06.036

Twenge, J. M., & Campbell, W. K. (2018). Associations between screen time and lower psychological well-being among children and adolescents: Evidence from a population-based study. Preventive Medicine Reports, 12, 271–283. https://doi.org/10.1016/j.pmedr.2018.10.003

Twenge, J. M., Joiner, T. E., Rogers, M. L., & Martin, G. N. (2018a). Increases in depressive symptoms, suicide-related outcomes, and suicide rates among U.S. adolescents after 2010 and links to increased new media screen time. *Clinical Psychological Science*, 6(1), 3–17. https://doi.org/10.1177/2167702617723376

Twenge, J. M., Martin, G. N., & Campbell, W. K. (2018b). Decreases in psychological well-being among American adolescents after 2012 and links to screen time during the rise of smartphone technology. *Emotion*, 18(6), 765–780. https://doi.org/10.1037/emo0000403

Twenge, J. M., Sherman, R. A., & Wells, B. E. (2017). Declines in sexual frequency among American adults, 1989–2014. *Archives of Sexual Behavior*, 46(8), 2389–2401. https://doi.org/10.1007/s10508-017-0953-1

Twig, G., Reichman, B., Afek, A., Derazne, E., Hamiel, U., Furer, A., Gershovitz, L., Bader, T., Cukierman-Yaffe, T., Kark, J. D., & Pinhas-Hamiel, O. (2019). Severe obesity and cardio-metabolic comorbidities: A nationwide study of 2.8 million adolescents. *International Journal of Obesity*, 43(7), 1391–1399. https://doi.org/10.1038/s41366-018-0213-z

Uchino, B. N., Birmingham, W., & Berg, C. A. (2010). Are older adults less or more physiologically reactive? A meta-analysis of age-related differences in cardiovascular reactivity to laboratory tasks. *The Journals of Gerontology: Series B*, 65B(2), 154–162. https://doi.org/10.1093/geronb/gbp127.

Uecker, J. (2014). Religion and early marriage in the United States: Evidence from the add health study. *Journal for the Scientific Study of Religion*, 53(2), 392–415. https://doi.org/10.1111/jssr.12114

Ullah, F., & Kaelber, D. C. (2021). Using large aggregated de-identified electronic health record data to determine the prevalence of common chronic diseases in pediatric patients who visited primary care clinics. *Academic Pediatrics.* https://doi.org/10.1016/j.acap.2021.05.007

Umaña-Taylor, A. J. (2016). A post-racial society in which ethnic-racial discrimination still exists and has significant consequences for youths' adjustment. *Current Directions in Psychological Science*, 25(2), 111–118. https://doi.org/10.1177/0963721415627858

Umaña-Taylor, A. J., & Hill, N. E. (2020). Ethnic–racial socialization in the family: A decade's advance on precursors and outcomes. *Journal of Marriage and Family*, 82(1), 244–271. https://doi.org/10.1111/jomf.12622

Umaña-Taylor, A. J., Wong, J. J., Gonzales, N. A., & Dumka, L. E. (2012). Ethnic identity and gender as moderators of the association between discrimination and academic adjustment among Mexican-origin adolescents. *Journal of Adolescence*, 35(4), 773–786.

Umberson, D., Donnelly, R., Xu, M., Farina, M., & Garcia, M. A. (2020). Death of a child prior to midlife, dementia risk, and racial disparities. *The Journals of Gerontology: Series B*, 75(9), 1983–1995. https://doi.org/10.1093/geronb/gbz154

Umberson, D., & Thomeer, M. B. (2020). Family matters: Research on family ties and health, 2010–2020. *Journal of Marriage and the Family*, 82(1), 404–419. https://doi.org/10.1111/jomf.12640

Umberson, D., Thomeer, M. B., & Lodge, A. C. (2015). Intimacy and emotion work in lesbian, gay, and heterosexual relationships. *Journal of Marriage and the Family*, 77(2), 542–556. https://doi.org/10.1111/jomf.12178

UNAIDS. (2021). *AIDS-related deaths—adolescence (10–19).* https://aidsinfo.unaids.org

Underwood, J. M., Brener, N., Thornton, J., Harris, W. A., Bryan, L. N., Shanklin, S. L., Deputy, N., Roberts, A. M., Queen, B., Chyen, D., Whittle, L., Lim, C., Yamakawa, Y., Leon-Nguyen, M., Kilmer, G., Smith-Grant, J., Demissie, Z., Jones, S. E., Clayton, H., & Dittus, P. (2020). Overview and methods for the youth risk behavior surveillance system—United States, 2019. *Morbidity and Mortality Weekly Report Supplements*, 69, 1–10. https://doi.org/10.15585/mmwr.su6901a1

UNESCO. (2020). *School enrollment, tertiary (% gross) | Data.* UNESCO Institute of Statistics. https://data.worldbank.org/indicator/SE.TER.ENRR

UNESCO Institute for Statistics. (2020). *School enrollment, secondary (% gross)—Low & middle income | Data.* UNESCO. https://data.worldbank.org/indicator/SE.SEC.ENRR?locations=XO

UNESCO, UNICEF, and the World Bank (UNESCO). (2020). *What have we learnt? Overview of findings from a survey of ministries of education on national responses to COVID-19.* https://openknowledge.worldbank.org/bitstream/handle/10986/34700/National-Education-Responses-to-COVID-19-WEB-final_EN.pdf?sequence=10&isAllowed=y

UNICEF. (2017). *A familiar face: Violence in the lives of children and adolescents.* https://data.unicef.org/resources/a-familiar-face/

UNICEF. (2019). *Healthy mothers, healthy babies: Taking stock of maternal health.* UNICEF. https://data.unicef.org/resources/healthy-mothers-healthy-babies/

UNICEF. (2020). *Child protection advocacy briefing: Violence against children* [Advocacy brief].

UNICEF. (2021). *Data warehouse, global databases, 2021, based on MICS, DHS and other nationally representative household survey data.* https://data.unicef.org/resources/data_explorer/unicef_f/?ag=UNICEF&df=GLOBAL_DATAFLOW&ver=1.0&dq=.MNCH_ANC1+MNCH_ANC4..&startPeriod=2016&endPeriod=2021

UNICEF. (2021). *Primary education.* United Nations Children's Fund.

UNICEF. (2021). *Under-five mortality.* https://data.unicef.org/topic/child-survival/under-five-mortality/

UN Inter-agency Group for Child Mortality Estimation (UN IGME). (2020). *Child mortality estimates* (Prepared by the Data and Analytics Section; Division of Data, Analytics, Planning and Monitoring, UNICEF, Regional and global mortality rate, age 5–14). UNICEF. http://data.unicef.org

UN Inter-agency Group for Child Mortality Estimation (UN IGME). (2020). *Child mortality estimates, country-specific infant mortality rate, both sexes.* UNICEF. https://data.unicef.org/topic/child-survival/under-five-mortality/#status

UN Inter-agency Group for Child Mortality Estimation (UN IGME). (2020). *Levels & trends in child mortality: Report 2020.* United Nations Children's Fund.

United Nations (UN). (2017). *Population facts: Life expectancy at birth increasing in less developed regions.* United Nations Department of Economic and Social Affairs Population Division.

United Nations (UN). (2019). *World population ageing, 2019: Highlights.* United Nations Department of Economic and Social Affairs Population Division.

United Nations Children's Fund (UNICEF). (2019). *The state of the world's children 2019: Children, food and nutrition – growing well in a changing world.*

United Nations Children's Fund, Division of Data, Analysis, Planning and Monitoring (UNICEF). (2020). *Global UNICEF global databases: Infant and young child feeding: Exclusive breastfeeding, predominant breastfeeding* (UNICEF Global Database on infant and young child feeding) [Exclusive Breastfeeding]. United Nations. https://data.unicef.org/topic/nutrition/infant-and-young-child-feeding/

United Nations Children's Fund, World Health Organization, and World Bank Group. 2020. *UNICEF/WHO/World Bank joint child malnutrition estimates, March 2020 edition.*

United Nations, Department of Economic and Social Affairs. (2016). *Youth civic engagement* (UN World Youth Report). United Nations.

United Nations, Department of Economic and Social Affairs. (2019). *World population prospects 2019: Highlights.* Multimedia Library, United Nations Department of Economic and Social Affairs. https://www.un.org/development/desa/publications/world-population-prospects-2019-highlights.html

United Nations Economic Commission for Europe (UNECE). (2021). *Women outnumber men in higher education but gender stereotyped subject choices persist.* https://unece.org/statistics/news/women-outnumber-men-higher-education-gender-stereotyped-subject-choices-persist

United Nations Educational, Scientific and Cultural Organization (UNESCO). (2018). *International technical guidance on sexuality education: An evidence-informed approach.* https://www.unfpa.org/publications/international-technical-guidance-sexuality-education

Unsworth, S. (2016). Quantity and quality of language input in bilingual language development. In E. Nicoladis & S. Montanari (Eds.), *Bilingualism across the lifespan: Factors moderating language proficiency* (pp. 103–121). American Psychological Association.

Uretsky, M. (2021, August 25). *Photo of you as teen for textbook?* [Personal communication].

Urrila, A. S., Artiges, E., Massicotte, J., Miranda, R., Vulser, H., Bézivin-Frere, P., Lapidaire, W., Lemaître, H., Penttilä, J., Conrod, P. J., Garavan, H., Paillère Martinot, M.-L., & Martinot, J.-L. (2017). Sleep habits, academic performance, and the adolescent brain structure. *Scientific Reports, 7*(1), 41678. https://doi.org/10.1038/srep41678

U.S. Bureau of Labor Statistics. (2021). *American Time Use Survey: May to December 2019 and 2020 results.*

U.S. Bureau of Labor Statistics. (2021). *College enrollment and work activity of recent high school and college graduates summary* (USDL-21-0721). https://www.bls.gov/news.release/hsgec.nr0.htm

U.S. Bureau of Labor Statistics. (2021). *Employment and unemployment among youth — Summer 2021* (USDL-21-1515).

U.S. Bureau of Labor Statistics. (2021). *Labor force characteristics by race and ethnicity, 2020* (No. 1095; BLS Reports).

U.S. Bureau of Labor Statistics. (2021). *Labor force statistics from the current population survey* [Employment status of the civilian noninstitutional population by age, sex, and race, 2020]. U.S. Bureau of Labor Statistics.

U.S. Bureau of Labor Statistics. (2021). *Labor force statistics from the current population survey. Household data annual averages. 11b. Employed persons by detailed occupations and age.*

U.S. Bureau of Labor Statistics. (2021). *Labor force statistics from the current population survey, labor force participation rate — 65 yrs & over, 2019–2021* (No. LNU01300097Q).

U.S. Bureau of Labor Statistics. (2021). *Number of jobs, labor market experience, marital status and health: Results from a national longitudinal survey* (USDL-21-1567).

U.S. Census Bureau. (2017). *Becoming DAD: Father's age at birth of first child* (2014 Survey of Income and Program Participation, Wave 1).

U.S. Census Bureau. (2019, May 29). Table 2. Children ever born, number of mothers, and percent childless by age and marital status, and by nativity: June 2018.

U.S. Census Bureau. (2020). *65 and older population grows rapidly as baby boomers age* (Release No. CB20-99). https://www.census.gov/newsroom/press-releases/2020/65-older-population-grows.html

U.S. Census Bureau. (2020). *America's families and living arrangements: 2020.* https://www.census.gov/data/tables/2020/demo/families/cps-2020.html

U.S. Census Bureau. (2020). *Census Bureau releases new estimates on America's families and living arrangements.*

U.S. Census Bureau. (2020, December). *Current Population Survey, 2020 annual social and economic supplement, ages 18–29.*

U.S. Census Bureau. (2020). *Historical marital status tables.*

U.S. Census Bureau. (2021). *America's families and living arrangements.*

U.S. Census Bureau. (2021). *Current Population Survey: March and annual social and economic supplements.*

U.S. Census Bureau, American Community Survey. (2015). *Detailed languages spoken at home and ability to speak English.* https://www.census.gov/data/tables/2013/demo/2009-2013-lang-tables.html

U.S. Department of Commerce, Bureau of the Census. (2020). Digest of Education Statistics 2020, tables 218.85

and 218.90. In *Household Pulse Survey, collection period of September 2 to 14, 2020.*

U.S. Department of Education, National Center for Education Statistics. (2021). *Digest of education statistics, 2019* (NCES 2021-009).

U.S. Department of Education, National Center for Education Statistics, Integrated Postsecondary Education Data System (IPEDS). (2019–2020, Winter). Graduation rates component. In *Digest of education statistics 2020* (table 326.10).

U.S. Department of Education, Office for Civil Rights. (2018). *Civil rights data collection, 2017–18.* http://ocrdata.ed.gov

U.S. Department of Education, Office of Special Education Programs. (2020, February). National Center for Education Statistics, Statistics of Public Elementary and Secondary School Systems, 1977–78 and 1980–81; Common Core of Data (CCD), "State nonfiscal survey of public elementary/secondary education," 1990–91 through 2018–19; and National Elementary and Secondary Enrollment Projection Model, 1972 through 2029. In *Annual report to Congress on the implementation of the Individuals with Disabilities Education Act, selected years, 1979 through 2006; and Individuals with Disabilities Education Act (IDEA) database.* https://www2.ed.gov/programs/osepidea/618-data/state-level-data-files/index.html#bcc

U.S. Department of Education, Policy and Program Studies Service, Office of Planning, Evaluation and Policy Development. (2016). Prevalence of teachers without full state certification and variation across schools and states. U.S. Department of Education.

U.S. Department of Health and Human Services (USDHHS). (2018). *Physical activity guidelines for Americans* (2nd ed.).

U.S. Department of Health and Human Services (USDHHS). (2021). *Child maltreatment 2019.* Administration for Children and Families, Administration on Children, Youth and Families, Children's Bureau. https://www.acf.hhs.gov/cb/research-data-technology/statistics-research/child-maltreatment

U.S. Department of Health and Human Services (USDHHS), Administration for Health and Families, Administration on Children, Youth and Families, Children's Bureau. (2020). *The AFCARS report: Adoption and foster care analysis and reporting system FY 2019 data (as of June 23, 2020; No. 27).* Children's Bureau.

U.S. Department of Health and Human Services (USDHHS), Centers for Disease Control and Prevention (CDC), National Center for Health Statistics (NCHS), Division of Vital Statistics. (2021). *Natality public-use data 2016–2019.* CDC WONDER.

U.S. Department of Justice. (2019). *2019 crime in the United States.* Department of Justice, Federal Bureau of Investigation. https://ucr.fbi.gov/crime-in-the-u.s/2019/crime-in-the-u.s.-2019/tables/table-64/table-64.xls

Vachon, D. D., Lynam, D. R., Widiger, T. A., Miller, J. D., McCrae, R. R., & Costa, P. T. (2013). Basic traits predict the prevalence of personality disorder across the life span: The example of psychopathy. *Psychological Science, 24*(5), 698–705. https://doi.org/10.1177/0956797612460249

Vaci, N., Cocić, D., Gula, B., & Bilalić, M. (2019). Large data and Bayesian modeling — aging curves of NBA players. *Behavior Research Methods, 51*(4), 1544–1564. https://doi.org/10.3758/s13428-018-1183-8

Vagos, P., da Silva, D. R., & Macedo, S. (2021). The impact of attachment to parents and peers on the psychopathic traits of adolescents: A short longitudinal study. *European Journal of Developmental Psychology,* 1–16. https://doi.org/10.1080/17405629.2021.1890020

Vaillant, G. E. (1998). Adaptation to life. Harvard University Press.

Vaillant, G. E. (2013). *Triumphs of experience: The men of the Harvard Grant Study.* Harvard University Press. https://doi.org/10.4159/harvard.9780674067424

Vainchtein, I. D., & Molofsky, A. V. (2020). Astrocytes and microglia: In sickness and in health. *Trends in Neurosciences, 43*(3), 144–154. https://doi.org/10.1016/j.tins.2020.01.003

Vaish, A., & Hepach, R. (2020). The development of prosocial emotions. *Emotion Review, 12*(4), 259–273.

Vaivada, T., Akseer, N., Akseer, S., Somaskandan, A., Stefopulos, M., & Bhutta, Z. A. (2020). Stunting in childhood: An overview of global burden, trends, determinants, and drivers of decline. *The American Journal of Clinical Nutrition, 112*(Supplement_2), 777S–791S. https://doi.org/10.1093/ajcn/nqaa159

Valentine, C. J. (2020). Nutrition and the developing brain. *Pediatric Research, 87*(2), 190–191. https://doi.org/10.1038/s41390-019-0650-y

Valerio, T. (2021, June 14). *Half of U.S. parents ages 22 and younger lived with spouse or unmarried partner in 2018.* Census.gov. https://www.census.gov/library/stories/2021/06/living-arrangements-of-young-parents-solo-with-spouse-partner-or-parent.html

Valerio, T., Knop, B., Kreider, R. M., & He, W. (2021). *Childless older Americans: 2018* (Current Population Reports). U.S. Census Bureau.

Valkenborghs, S. R., Noetel, M., Hillman, C. H., Nilsson, M., Smith, J. J., Ortega, F. B., & Lubans, D. R. (2019). The impact of physical activity on brain structure and function in youth: A systematic review. *Pediatrics, 144*(4), e20184032. https://doi.org/10.1542/peds.2018-4032

Van Aggelpoel, T., Vermandel, A., Fraeyman, J., Massart, M., & Hal, G. V. (2019). Information as a crucial factor for toilet training by parents. *Child: Care, Health and Development, 45*(3), 457–462. https://doi.org/10.1111/cch.12653

van Beeck, A. E., Zomer, T. P., van Beeck, E. F., Richardus, J. H., Voeten, H. A., & Erasmus, V. (2016). Children's hand hygiene behaviour and available facilities: An observational study in Dutch day care centres. *The European Journal of Public Health, 26*(2), 297–300.

van Bergen, D. D., Wilson, B. D. M., Russell, S. T., Gordon, A. G., & Rothblum, E. D. (2021). Parental responses to coming out by lesbian, gay, bisexual, queer, pansexual, or two-spirited people across three age cohorts. *Journal of Marriage and Family, 83*(4), 1116–1133. https://doi.org/10.1111/jomf.12731

van Berkel, N., Goncalves, J., Lovén, L., Ferreira, D., Hosio, S., & Kostakos, V. (2019). Effect of experience sampling schedules on response rate and recall accuracy of objective self-reports. *International Journal of Human-Computer Studies, 125*, 118–128. https://doi.org/10.1016/j.ijhcs.2018.12.002

Vancampfort, D., Stubbs, B., & Koyanagi, A. (2017). Physical chronic conditions, multimorbidity and sedentary behavior amongst middle-aged and older adults in six low- and middle-income countries. *International Journal of Behavioral Nutrition and Physical Activity, 14*(1), 147. https://doi.org/10.1186/s12966-017-0602-z

van de Bongardt, D., & de Graaf, H. (2020). Youth's socio-sexual competences with romantic and casual sexual partners. *The Journal of Sex Research, 57*(9), 1166–1179. https://doi.org/10.1080/00224499.2020.1743226

van de Bongardt, D., Yu, R., Deković, M., & Meeus, W. H. J. (2015). Romantic relationships and sexuality in adolescence and young adulthood: The role of parents, peers, and partners. *European Journal of Developmental Psychology, 12*(5), 497–515. https://doi.org/10.1080/17405629.2015.1068689

Vandell, D. L., Simpkins, S. D., & Wegemer, C. M. (2019). Parenting and children's organized activities. In M. H. Bornstein (Ed.), *Handbook of parenting* (pp. 347–379). Routledge.

Vandello, J. A., Bosson, J. K., & Lawler, J. R. (2019). Precarious manhood and men's health disparities. In D. M. Griffith, M. A. Bruce, & R. J. Thorpe, Jr. (Eds.), *Men's health equity: A handbook* (pp. 27–41). Routledge/Taylor & Francis Group. https://doi.org/10.4324/9781315167428-3

van den Berg, L., & Verbakel, E. (2021). Trends in singlehood in young adulthood in Europe. *Advances in Life Course Research, 100449*. https://doi.org/10.1016/j.alcr.2021.100449

van den Berg, Y. H., Deutz, M. H., Smeekens, S., & Cillessen, A. H. (2017). Developmental pathways to preference and popularity in middle childhood. *Child Development, 88*(5), 1629–1641.

Van den Bergh, B. R., Dahnke, R., & Mennes, M. (2018). Prenatal stress and the developing brain: Risks for neurodevelopmental disorders. *Development and Psychopathology, 30*(3), 743–762. https://doi.org/10.1017/S0954579418000342

van den Noort, M., Struys, E., Bosch, P., Jaswetz, L., Perriard, B., Yeo, S., Barisch, P., Vermeire, K., Lee, S.-H., & Lim, S. (2019). Does the bilingual advantage in cognitive control exist and if so, what are its modulating factors? A systematic review. *Behavioral Sciences, 9*(3), 27. https://doi.org/10.3390/bs9030027

van der Doef, S., & Reinders, J. (2018). Stepwise sexual development of adolescents: The Dutch approach to sexuality education. *Nature Reviews Urology, 15*(3), 133–134. https://doi.org/10.1038/nrurol.2018.3

van der Horst, F. C. P., & van der Veer, R. (2010). The ontogeny of an idea: John Bowlby and contemporaries on mother–child separation. *History of Psychology, 13*(1), 25–45. https://doi.org/10.1037/a0017660

Van Der Horst, P. W. (1987). *Chaeremon, Egyptian priest and stoic philosopher: The fragments* (Vol. 101). Brill.

Vanderminden, J., Hamby, S., David-Ferdon, C., Kacha-Ochana, A., Merrick, M., Simon, T. R., Finkelhor, D., & Turner, H. (2019). Rates of neglect in a national sample: Child and family characteristics and psychological impact. *Child Abuse & Neglect, 88*, 256–265. https://doi.org/10.1016/j.chiabu.2018.11.014

van der Ploeg, R., Steglich, C., & Veenstra, R. (2020). The way bullying works: How new ties facilitate the mutual reinforcement of status and bullying in elementary schools. *Social Networks, 60*, 71–82.

Vanderwall, C., Eickhoff, J., Randall Clark, R., & Carrel, A. L. (2018). BMI z-score in obese children is a poor predictor of adiposity changes over time. *BMC Pediatrics, 18*(1), 187. https://doi.org/10.1186/s12887-018-1160-5

van der Wilt, F., van der Veen, C., van Kruistum, C., & van Oers, B. (2019). Why do children become rejected by their peers? A review of studies into the relationship between oral communicative competence and sociometric status in childhood. *Educational Psychology Review, 31*(3), 699–724.

van Dijk, I. K. (2019). Early-life mortality clustering in families: A literature review. *Population Studies, 73*(1), 79–99. https://doi.org/10.1080/00324728.2018.1448434

van Dijk, R., van der Valk, I. E., Deković, M., & Branje, S. (2020). A meta-analysis on interparental conflict, parenting, and child adjustment in divorced families: Examining mediation using meta-analytic structural equation models. *Clinical Psychology Review, 79*, 101861. https://doi.org/10.1016/j.cpr.2020.101861

van Doeselaar, L., Klimstra, T. A., Denissen, J. J., Branje, S., & Meeus, W. (2018). The role of identity commitments in depressive symptoms and stressful life events in adolescence and young adulthood. *Developmental Psychology, 54*(5), 950.

Van Doorn, M. D., Branje, S. J. T., VanderValk, I. E., De Goede, I. H. A., & Meeus, W. H. J. (2011). Longitudinal spillover effects of conflict resolution styles between adolescent-parent relationships and adolescent friendships. *Journal of Family Psychology, 25*(1), 157–161. https://doi.org/10.1037/a0022289

Van Dyke, M. E., Baumhofer, N. K., Slopen, N., Mujahid, M. S., Clark, C. R., Williams, D. R., & Lewis, T. T. (2020). Pervasive discrimination and allostatic load in African American and White Adults. *Psychosomatic Medicine, 82*(3), 316–323. https://doi.org/10.1097/PSY.0000000000000788

Vanes, L. D., Moutoussis, M., Ziegler, G., Goodyer, I. M., Fonagy, P., Jones, P. B., Bullmore, E. T., & Dolan, R. J. (2020). White matter tract myelin maturation and its association with general psychopathology in adolescence and early adulthood. *Human Brain Mapping, 41*(3), 827–839. https://doi.org/10.1002/hbm.24842

van Esch, H. J., van Zuylen, L., Geijteman, E. C. T., Oomen-de Hoop, E., Huisman, B. A. A., Noordzij-Nooteboom, H. S., Boogaard, R., van der Heide, A., & van der Rijt, C. C. D. (2021). Effect of prophylactic subcutaneous scopolamine butylbromide on death rattle in patients at the end of life: The SILENCE randomized clinical trial. *JAMA, 326*(13), 1268–1276. https://doi.org/10.1001/jama.2021.14785

van Exel, E., Koopman, J. J. E., van Bodegom, D., Meij, J. J., de Knijff, P., Ziem, J. B., Finch, C. E., & Westendorp, R. G. J. (2017). Effect of APOE ε4 allele on survival and fertility in an adverse environment. *PLOS ONE, 12*(7), e0179497. https://doi.org/10.1371/journal.pone.0179497

van Gelder, S. (2017, May 24). For new native mothers, a place for culture and comfort. *Yes! Magazine*.

Van Goethem, A., Van Hoof, A., Orobio de Castro, B., Van Aken, M., & Hart, D. (2014). The role of reflection in the effects of community service on adolescent development: A meta-analysis. *Child development, 85*(6), 2114–2130.

Van Groenou, M. B., & de Jong-Gierveld, J. (2014). Quality of marriage and social loneliness in later life. In A. C. Michalos (Ed.), *Encyclopedia of quality of life and well-being research* (pp. 5309–5312). Springer.

Van Hecke, L., Loyen, A., Verloigne, M., van der Ploeg, H. P., Lakerveld, J., Brug, J., De Bourdeaudhuij, I., Ekelund, U., Donnelly, A., Hendriksen, I., & Deforche, B. on Behalf of the DEDIPAC Consortium (2016). Variation in population levels of physical activity in European children and adolescents according to cross-European studies: A systematic literature review within DEDIPAC. *International Journal of Behavioral Nutrition and Physical Activity, 13*(1), 70–91.

van Hecke, O., Hocking, L. J., Torrance, N., Campbell, A., Padmanabhan, S., Porteous, D. J., McIntosh, A. M., Burri, A. V., Tanaka, H., Williams, F. M. K., & Smith, B. H. (2017). Chronic pain, depression and cardiovascular disease linked through a shared genetic predisposition: Analysis of a family-based cohort and twin study. *PLoS ONE, 12*(2). https://doi.org/10.1371/journal.pone.0170653

van Hoorn, J., Shablack, H., Lindquist, K. A., & Telzer, E. H. (2019). Incorporating the social context into neurocognitive models of adolescent decision-making: A neuroimaging meta-analysis. *Neuroscience & Biobehavioral Reviews, 101*, 129–142. https://doi.org/10.1016/j.neubiorev.2018.12.024

van Hoorn, J., van Dijk, E., Meuwese, R., Rieffe, C., & Crone, E. A. (2016). Peer influence on prosocial behavior in adolescence. *Journal of Research on Adolescence, 26*(1), 90–100. https://doi.org/10.1111/jora.12173

Van Hulle, C. A., Moore, M. N., Lemery-Chalfant, K., Goldsmith, H. H., & Brooker, R. J. (2017). Infant stranger fear trajectories predict anxious behaviors and diurnal cortisol rhythm during childhood. *Development and Psychopathology, 29*(3), 1119–1130. https://doi.org/10.1017/S0954579417000311

van IJzendoorn, M. H., & Bakermans-Kranenburg, M. J. (2021). Integrating temperament and attachment: The differential susceptibility paradigm. In *Attachment theory and research*. Wiley.

van IJzendoorn, M. H., Bakermans-Kranenburg, M. J., Coughlan, B., & Reijman, S. (2020). Annual research review: Umbrella synthesis of meta-analyses on child maltreatment antecedents and interventions: Differential susceptibility perspective on risk and resilience. *Journal of Child Psychology and Psychiatry, 61*(3), 272–290. https://doi.org/10.1111/jcpp.13147

van IJzendoorn, M. H., Bakermans-Kranenburg, M. J., & Juffer, F. (2007). Plasticity of growth in height, weight, and head circumference: Meta-analytic evidence of massive catch-up after international adoption. *Journal of Developmental and Behavioral Pediatrics: JDBP, 28*(4), 334–343. https://doi.org/10.1097/DBP.0b013e31811320aa

Van Orden, K. A., & Conwell, Y. (2016). Issues in research on aging and suicide. *Aging & Mental Health, 20*(2), 240–251. https://doi.org/10.1080/13607863.2015.1065791

van Raalte, A. A., Sasson, I., & Martikainen, P. (2018). The case for monitoring life-span inequality. *Science, 362*(6418), 1002–1004. https://doi.org/10.1126/science.aau5811

van Rosmalen, L., van der Horst, F. C. P., & van der Veer, R. (n.d.). From secure dependency to attachment: Mary Ainsworth's integration of Blatz's security theory into Bowlby's attachment theory. *History of Psychology, 19*(1), 22–39.

van Rosmalen, L., van der Veer, R. V. der, & van der Horst, F. V. der. (2015). Ainsworth's strange situation procedure: The origin of an instrument. *Journal of the History of the Behavioral Sciences, 51*(3), 261–284. https://doi.org/10.1002/jhbs.21729

Van Speybroeck, L. (2002). From epigenesis to epigenetics: The case of CH Waddington. *Annals of the New York Academy of Sciences, 981*(1), 61–81.

van Straten, A., van der Zweerde, T., Kleiboer, A., Cuijpers, P., Morin, C. M., & Lancee, J. (2018). Cognitive and behavioral therapies in the treatment of insomnia: A meta-analysis. *Sleep Medicine Reviews, 38*, 3–16.

VanTieghem, M., Korom, M., Flannery, J., Choy, T., Caldera, C., Humphreys, K. L., Gabard-Durnam, L., Goff, B., Gee, D. G., Telzer, E. H., Shapiro, M., Louie, J. Y., Fareri, D. S., Bolger, N., & Tottenham, N. (2021). Longitudinal changes in amygdala, hippocampus and cortisol development following early caregiving adversity. *Developmental Cognitive Neuroscience, 48*, 100916. https://doi.org/10.1016/j.dcn.2021.100916

Varadaraj, V., Munoz, B., Deal, J. A., An, Y., Albert, M. S., Resnick, S. M., & Swenor, B. K. (2021). Association of vision impairment with cognitive decline across multiple domains in older adults. *JAMA Network Open, 4*(7), e2117416–e2117416.

Vargas, C. M., Stines, E. M., & Granado, H. S. (2017). Health-equity issues related to childhood obesity: A scoping review. *Journal of Public Health Dentistry, 77*(S1), S32–S42. https://doi.org/10.1111/jphd.12233

Vargas, S. M., Huey, S. J., Jr., & Miranda, J. (2020). A critical review of current evidence on multiple types of discrimination and mental health. *American Journal of Orthopsychiatry, 90*(3), 374–390. https://doi.org/10.1037/ort0000441

Varma, V. R., & Watts, A. (2017). Daily physical activity patterns during the early stage of Alzheimer's disease. *Journal of Alzheimer's Disease, 55*(2), 659–667. https://doi.org/10.3233/JAD-160582

Váša, F., Romero-Garcia, R., Kitzbichler, M. G., Seidlitz, J., Whitaker, K. J., Vaghi, M. M., Kundu, P., Patel, A. X., Fonagy, P., Dolan, R. J., Jones, P. B., Goodyer, I. M., the NSPN Consortium, Vértes, P. E., & Bullmore, E. T. (2020). Conservative and disruptive modes of adolescent change in human brain functional connectivity. *Proceedings of the National Academy of Sciences, 117*(6), 3248–3253. https://doi.org/10.1073/pnas.1906144117

Vashi, N. A., de Castro Maymone, M. B., & Kundu, R. V. (2016). Aging differences in ethnic skin. *The Journal of Clinical and Aesthetic Dermatology, 9*(1), 31–38. https://www.ncbi.nlm.nih.gov/pmc/articles/PMC4756870/

Vasilenko, S. A., & Espinosa-Hernández, G. (2019). Multidimensional profiles of religiosity among adolescents: Associations with sexual behaviors and romantic relationships. *Journal of Research on Adolescence, 29*(2), 414–428. https://doi.org/10.1111/jora.12444

Vasilenko, S. A., Kreager, D. A., & Lefkowitz, E. S. (2015). Gender, contraceptive attitudes, and condom use in adolescent romantic relationships: A dyadic approach. *Journal of Research on Adolescence, 25*(1), 51–62.

Vasilenko, S. A., Kugler, K. C., & Rice, C. E. (2016). Timing of first sexual intercourse and young adult health outcomes. *The Journal of Adolescent Health, 59*(3), 291–297. https://doi.org/10.1016/j.jadohealth.2016.04.019

Vasilenko, S. A., Lefkowitz, E. S., & Welsh, D. P. (2014). Is sexual behavior healthy for adolescents? A conceptual framework for research on adolescent sexual behavior and physical, mental, and social health. *New Directions for Child and Adolescent Development, 2014*(144), 3–19.

Vasileva, M., Graf, R. K., Reinelt, T., Petermann, U., & Petermann, F. (2021). Research review: A meta-analysis of the international prevalence and comorbidity of mental disorders in children between 1 and 7 years. *Journal of Child Psychology and Psychiatry, 62*(4), 372–381.

Vasung, L., Abaci Turk, E., Ferradal, S. L., Sutin, J., Stout, J. N., Ahtam, B., Lin, P.-Y., & Ellen Grant, P. (2019). Exploring early human brain development with structural and physiological neuroimaging. *NeuroImage, 187*, 226–254. https://doi.org/10.1016/j.neuroimage.2018.07.041

Vaughan, C. P., Markland, A. D., Smith, P. P., Burgio, K. L., & Kuchel, G. A. (2018). Report and research agenda of the American Geriatrics Society and National Institute on

Aging Bedside-to-Bench Conference on urinary incontinence in older adults: A translational research agenda for a complex geriatric syndrome. *Journal of the American Geriatrics Society, 66*(4), 773–782. https://doi.org/10.1111/jgs.15157

Vaziri Flais, S., & American Academy of Pediatrics. (2018). *Caring for your school-age child: Ages 5 to 12* (3rd ed.). Penguin. https://www.penguinrandomhouse.com/books/162244/caring-for-your-school-age-child-3rd-edition-by-american-academy-of-pediatrics-shelly-vaziri-flais-md-faap-editor-in-chief/9780425286043

Veal, F., Williams, M., Bereznicki, L., Cummings, E., Thompson, A., Peterson, G., & Winzenberg, T. (2018). Barriers to optimal pain management in aged care facilities: An Australian qualitative study. *Pain Management Nursing, 19*(2), 177–185. https://doi.org/10.1016/j.pmn.2017.10.002

Veeh, C. A., Plassmeyer, M., Nicotera, N., & Brewer, S. E. (2019). A combined measure of civic engagement for use among emerging adults. *Journal of the Society for Social Work and Research, 10*(1), 13–34. https://doi.org/10.1086/701948

Veldman, S. L. C., Jones, R. A., Santos, R., Sousa-Sá, E., & Okely, A. D. (2018). Gross motor skills in toddlers: Prevalence and socio-demographic differences. *Journal of Science and Medicine in Sport, 21*(12), 1226–1231. https://doi.org/10.1016/j.jsams.2018.05.001

Velez, G., & Spencer, M. B. (2018). Phenomenology and intersectionality: Using PVEST as a frame for adolescent identity formation amid intersecting ecological systems of inequality. *New Directions for Child and Adolescent Development, 2018*(161), 75–90.

Vélez-Agosto, N. M., Soto-Crespo, J. G., Vizcarrondo-Oppenheimer, M., Vega-Molina, S., & García Coll, C. (2017). Bronfenbrenner's bioecological theory revision: Moving culture from the macro into the micro. *Perspectives on Psychological Science, 12*(5), 900–910. https://doi.org/10.1177/1745691617704397

Veliz, P., McCabe, S. E., Eckner, J. T., & Schulenberg, J. E. (2021). Trends in the prevalence of concussion reported by US adolescents, 2016–2020. *JAMA, 325*(17), 1789–1791. https://doi.org/10.1001/jama.2021.1538

Veliz, P., Snyder, M., & Sabo, D. (2019). *The state of high school sports in America: An evaluation of the nation's most popular extracurricular activity.* Women's Sports Foundation.

Ven, T. V. (2011). *Getting wasted: Why college students drink too much and party so hard.* NYU Press.

Venkatesh, S. A. (2006). *Off the books.* Harvard University Press.

Vennum, A., Hardy, N., Sibley, D. S., & Fincham, F. D. (2015). Dedication and sliding in emerging adult cyclical and non-cyclical romantic relationships. *Family Relations, 64*(3), 407–419. https://doi.org/10.1111/fare.12126

Ventura, A. K., Levy, J., & Sheeper, S. (2019). Maternal digital media use during infant feeding and the quality of feeding interactions. *Appetite, 143,* 104415. https://doi.org/10.1016/j.appet.2019.104415

Verbeek, M., van de Bongardt, D., Reitz, E., & Deković, M. (2020). A warm nest or 'the talk'? Exploring and explaining relations between general and sexuality-specific parenting and adolescent sexual emotions. *Journal of Adolescent Health, 66*(2), 210–216. https://doi.org/10.1016/j.jadohealth.2019.08.015

Verbruggen, S. W., Kainz, B., Shelmerdine, S. C., Hajnal, J. V., Rutherford, M. A., Arthurs, O. J., Phillips, A. T. M., & Nowlan, N. C. (2018). Stresses and strains on the human fetal skeleton during development. *Journal of the Royal Society Interface, 15*(138), 20170593. https://doi.org/10.1098/rsif.2017.0593

Verhage, M., Schuurman, B., & Lindenberg, J. (2021). How young adults view older people: Exploring the pathways of constructing a group image after participation in an intergenerational programme. *Journal of Aging Studies, 56,* 100912.

Verkuyten, M. (2016). Further conceptualizing ethnic and racial identity research: The social identity approach and its dynamic model. *Child Development, 87*(6), 1796–1812. https://doi.org/10.1111/cdev.12555

Verkuyten, M., Thijs, J., & Gharaei, N. (2019). Discrimination and academic (dis)engagement of ethnic-racial minority students: A social identity threat perspective. *Social Psychology of Education, 22*(2), 267–290. https://doi.org/10.1007/s11218-018-09476-0

Verma, S. K., Willetts, J. L., Corns, H. L., Marucci-Wellman, H. R., Lombardi, D. A., & Courtney, T. K. (2016). Falls and fall-related injuries among community-dwelling adults in the United States. *PLOS ONE, 11*(3), e0150939. https://doi.org/10.1371/journal.pone.0150939

Vermeir, I., & Van de Sompel, D. (2017). How advertising beauty influences children's self-perception and behavior. In Information Resources Management Association (Eds.), *Advertising and branding: Concepts, methodologies, tools, and applications* (pp. 1495–1511). IGI Global. https://doi.org/10.4018/978-1-5225-1793-1.ch069

Vermunt, L., Sikkes, S. A., Van Den Hout, A., Handels, R., Bos, I., Van Der Flier, W. M., & ICTUS/DSA study groups. (2019). Duration of preclinical, prodromal, and dementia stages of Alzheimer's disease in relation to age, sex, and APOE genotype. *Alzheimer's & Dementia, 15*(7), 888–898.

Vespa, J. (2017). *The changing economics and demographics of young adulthood: 1975-2016, population characteristics.* U.S. Census Bureau, U.S. Department of Commerce, Economics and Statistics Administration.

Vetrano, D. L., Foebel, A. D., Marengoni, A., Brandi, V., Collamati, A., Heckman, G. A., Hirdes, J., Bernabei, R., & Onder, G. (2016). Chronic diseases and geriatric syndromes: The different weight of comorbidity. *European Journal of Internal Medicine, 27,* 62–67. https://doi.org/10.1016/j.ejim.2015.10.025

Vézina, M. P., & Poulin, F. (2020). Civic participation profiles and predictors among French-Canadian youths transitioning into adulthood: A person-centered study. *Emerging Adulthood,* 2167696820970689.

Viarouge, A., Houdé, O., & Borst, G. (2019). The progressive 6-year-old conserver: Numerical saliency and sensitivity as core mechanisms of numerical abstraction in a Piaget-like estimation task. *Cognition, 190,* 137–142. https://doi.org/10.1016/j.cognition.2019.05.005

Vicedo, M. (2017). Putting attachment in its place: Disciplinary and cultural contexts. *European Journal of Developmental Psychology, 14*(6), 684–699.

Victora, C. G., Bahl, R., Barros, A. J., França, G. V., Horton, S., Krasevec, J., Murch, S., Sankar, M. J., Walker, N., & Rollins, N. C. (2016). Breastfeeding in the 21st century: Epidemiology, mechanisms, and lifelong effect. *The Lancet, 387*(10017), 475–490.

Videler, A. C., Hutsebaut, J., Schulkens, J. E. M., Sobczak, S., & van Alphen, S. P. J. (2019). A life span perspective on borderline personality disorder. *Current Psychiatry Reports, 21*(7), 51. https://doi.org/10.1007/s11920-019-1040-1

Vierboom, Y. C., & Preston, S. H. (2020). Life beyond 65: Changing spatial patterns of survival at older ages in the United States, 2000–2016. *The Journals of Gerontology: Series B, 75*(5), 1093–1103. https://doi.org/10.1093/geronb/gbz160

Vijayakumar, N., de Macks, Z. O., Shirtcliff, E. A., & Pfeifer, J. H. (2018). Puberty and the human brain: Insights into adolescent development. *Neuroscience & Biobehavioral Reviews, 92,* 417–436.

Vijayakumar, N., Youssef, G. J., Allen, N. B., Anderson, V., Efron, D., Hazell, P., Mundy, L., Nicholson, J. M., Patton, G., Seal, M. L., Simmons, J. G., Whittle, S., & Silk, T. (2021). A longitudinal analysis of puberty-related cortical development. *NeuroImage, 228,* 117684. https://doi.org/10.1016/j.neuroimage.2020.117684

Villalobos Solís, M., Smetana, J. G., & Tasopoulos-Chan, M. (2017). Evaluations of conflicts between Latino values and autonomy desires among Puerto Rican adolescents. *Child Development, 88*(5), 1581–1597.

Vinke, E. J., de Groot, M., Venkatraghavan, V., Klein, S., Niessen, W. J., Ikram, M. A., & Vernooij, M. W. (2018). Trajectories of imaging markers in brain aging: The Rotterdam study. *Neurobiology of Aging, 71,* 32–40. https://doi.org/10.1016/j.neurobiolaging.2018.07.001

Visser, B. A., Ashton, M. C., & Vernon, P. A. (2006). g and the measurement of multiple intelligences: A response to Gardner. *Intelligence, 34*(5), 507–510.

Vissing, N. H., Chawes, B. L., Rasmussen, M. A., & Bisgaard, H. (2018). Epidemiology and risk factors of infection in early childhood. *Pediatrics, 141*(6), e20170933. https://doi.org/10.1542/peds.2017-0933

Vitale, I., Manic, G., De Maria, R., Kroemer, G., & Galluzzi, L. (2017). DNA damage in stem cells. *Molecular Cell, 66*(3), 306–319. https://doi.org/10.1016/j.molcel.2017.04.006

Vittrup, B. (2018). Color blind or color conscious? White American mothers' approaches to racial socialization. *Journal of Family Issues, 39*(3), 668–692. https://doi.org/10.1177/0192513X16676858

Vivekanandarajah, A., Nelson, M. E., Kinney, H. C., Elliott, A. J., Folkerth, R. D., Tran, H., Cotton, J., Jacobs, P., Minter, M., McMillan, K., Duncan, J. R., Broadbelt, K. G., Schissler, K., Odendaal, H. J., Angal, J., Brink, L., Burger, E. H., Coldrey, J. A., Dempers, J., ... Network, P. (2021). Nicotinic receptors in the brainstem ascending arousal system in SIDS with analysis of pre-natal exposures to maternal smoking and alcohol in high-risk populations of the safe passage study. *Frontiers in Neurology, 12,* 636668. https://doi.org/10.3389/fneur.2021.636668

Vöhringer, I. A., Kolling, T., Graf, F., Poloczek, S., Fassbender, I., Freitag, C., Lamm, B., Suhrke, J., Teiser, J., Teubert, M., Keller, H., Lohaus, A., Schwarzer, G., & Knopf, M. (2018). The development of implicit memory from infancy to childhood: On average performance levels and interindividual differences. *Child Development, 89*(2), 370–382. https://doi.org/10.1111/cdev.12749

Volkert, J., Gablonski, T.-C., & Rabung, S. (2018). Prevalence of personality disorders in the general adult population in Western countries: Systematic review and meta-analysis. *The British Journal of Psychiatry, 213*(6), 709–715. https://doi.org/10.1192/bjp.2018.202

Volling, B. L. (2012). Family transitions following the birth of a sibling: An empirical review of changes in the firstborn's adjustment. *Psychological Bulletin, 138*(3), 497.

Volling, B. L., Yu, T., Gonzalez, R., Kennedy, D. E., Rosenberg, L., & Oh, W. (2014). Children's responses to mother-infant and father-infant interaction with a baby sibling: Jealousy or joy? *Journal of Family Psychology, 28*(5), 634–644. https://doi.org/10.1037/a0037811

Volpe, J. J. (2019). Dysmaturation of premature brain: Importance, cellular mechanisms, and potential interventions. *Pediatric Neurology, 95,* 42–66. https://doi.org/10.1016/j.pediatrneurol.2019.02.016

von Hofsten, C., & Rosander, K. (2018). The development of sensorimotor intelligence in infants. In J. M. Plumert (Ed.), *Studying the perception-action system as a model system for understanding development* (pp. 73–106). Elsevier Academic Press. https://doi.org/10.1016/bs.acdb.2018.04.003

Von Korff, M., Scher, A. I., Helmick, C., Carter-Pokras, O., Dodick, D. W., Goulet, J., Hamill-Ruth, R., LeResche, L., Porter, L., Tait, R., Terman, G., Veasley, C., & Mackey, S. (2016). United States National Pain Strategy for Population Research: Concepts, definitions, and pilot data. *The Journal of Pain, 17*(10), 1068–1080. https://doi.org/10.1016/j.jpain.2016.06.009

von Soest, T., Luhmann, M., Hansen, T., & Gerstorf, D. (2020). Development of loneliness in midlife and old age: Its nature and correlates. *Journal of Personality and Social Psychology, 118*(2), 388.

von Suchodoletz, A., Gestsdottir, S., Wanless, S. B., McClelland, M. M., Birgisdottir, F., Gunzenhauser, C., & Ragnarsdottir, H. (2013). Behavioral self-regulation and relations to emergent academic skills among children in Germany and Iceland. *Early Childhood Research Quarterly, 28*(1), 62–73.

Voss, P., Bodner, E., & Rothermund, K. (2018). Ageism: The relationship between age stereotypes and age discrimination. In L. Ayalon & C. Tesch-Römer (Eds.), *Contemporary perspectives on ageism* (pp. 11–31). Springer.

Vreeland, A., Gruhn, M. A., Watson, K. H., Bettis, A. H., Compas, B. E., Forehand, R., & Sullivan, A. D. (2019). Parenting in context: Associations of parental depression and socioeconomic factors with parenting behaviors. *Journal of Child and Family Studies, 28*(4), 1124–1133.

Vrolijk, P., Van Lissa, C. J., Branje, S. J. T., Meeus, W. H. J., & Keizer, R. (2020). Longitudinal linkages between father and mother autonomy support and adolescent problem behaviors: Between-family differences and within-family effects. *Journal of Youth and Adolescence, 49*(11), 2372–2387. https://doi.org/10.1007/s10964-020-01309-8

Vrselja, Z., Daniele, S. G., Silbereis, J., Talpo, F., Morozov, Y. M., Sousa, A. M. M., Tanaka, B. S., Skarica, M., Pletikos, M., Kaur, N., Zhuang, Z. W., Liu, Z., Alkawadri, R., Sinusas, A. J., Latham, S. R., Waxman, S. G., & Sestan, N. (2019). Restoration of brain circulation and cellular functions hours post-mortem. *Nature, 568*(7752), 336–343.

Vukman, K. B. (2005). Developmental differences in metacognition and their connections with cognitive development in adulthood. *Journal of Adult Development, 12*(4), 211–221. https://doi.org/10.1007/s10804-005-7089-6

Vuolo, M., Mortimer, J. T., & Staff, J. (2014). Adolescent precursors of pathways from school to work. *Journal of Research on Adolescence, 24*(1), 145–162.

Vygotsky, L. (1962). *Thought and language.* MIT Press. https://doi.org/10.1037/11193-000

Vygotsky, L. S. (2016). Play and its role in the mental development of the child (N. Veresov & M. Barrs, Trans.). *International Research in Early Childhood Education, 7*(2), 3–25. (Original work published in Russian in 1933)

Vygotsky, L. S., & Cole, M. (1978). *Mind in society: Development of higher psychological processes.* Harvard University Press.

Vyncke, B., & Van Gorp, B. (2020). Using counterframing strategies to enhance anti-stigma campaigns related to mental illness. *Social Science & Medicine, 258*, 113090.

Waasdorp, T. E., Fu, R., Perepezko, A. L., & Bradshaw, C. P. (2021). The role of bullying-related policies: Understanding how school staff respond to bullying situations. *European Journal of Developmental Psychology*, 1–16. https://doi.org/10.1080/17405629.2021.1889503

Waddington, C. H. (1952). Selection of the genetic basis for an acquired character. *Nature, 169*(4302), 625–626. https://doi.org/10.1038/169625b0

Wade, M., Fox, N. A., Zeanah, C. H., Nelson, C. A., & Drury, S. S. (2020). Telomere length and psychopathology: Specificity and direction of effects within the Bucharest Early Intervention Project. *Journal of the American Academy of Child & Adolescent Psychiatry, 59*(1), 140–148.e3. https://doi.org/10.1016/j.jaac.2019.02.013

Wade, M., Sheridan, M. A., Zeanah, C. H., Fox, N. A., Nelson, C. A., & McLaughlin, K. A. (2020). Environmental determinants of physiological reactivity to stress: The interacting effects of early life deprivation, caregiving quality, and stressful life events. *Development and Psychopathology, 32*(5), 1732–1742. https://doi.org/10.1017/S0954579420001327

Wade, M., Zeanah, C. H., Fox, N. A., Tibu, F., Ciolan, L. E., & Nelson, C. A. (2019). Stress sensitization among severely neglected children and protection by social enrichment. *Nature Communications, 10*(1), 1–8.

Wade, R. M., & Harper, G. W. (2020). Racialized sexual discrimination (RSD) in the age of online sexual networking: Are young Black gay/bisexual men (YBGBM) at elevated risk for adverse psychological health? *American Journal of Community Psychology, 65*(3–4), 504–523. https://doi.org/10.1002/ajcp.12401

Wadsworth, D. D., Johnson, J. L., Carroll, A. V., Pangelinan, M. M., Rudisill, M. E., & Sassi, J. (2020). Intervention strategies to elicit MVPA in preschoolers during outdoor play. *International Journal of Environmental Research and Public Health, 17*(2), 650. https://doi.org/10.3390/ijerph17020650

Wagner, D. (2005). *The poorhouse: America's forgotten institution.* Rowman & Littlefield.

Wagner, J., Becker, M., Lüdtke, O., & Trautwein, U. (2015). The first partnership experience and personality development: A propensity score matching study in young adulthood. *Social Psychological and Personality Science, 6*(4), 455–463. https://doi.org/10.1177/1948550614566092

Wahab, A., Wilopo, S. A., Hakimi, M., & Ismail, D. (2020). Declining age at menarche in Indonesia: A systematic review and meta-analysis. *International Journal of Adolescent Medicine and Health, 32*(6). http://dx.doi.org/10.1515/ijamh-2018-0021

Waite-Stupiansky, S. (2017). Jean Piaget's constructivist theory of learning. In L. E. Cohen & S. Waite-Stupiansky (Eds.), *Theories of early childhood education: Developmental, behaviorist, and critical* (pp. 3–17). Taylor & Francis.

Wakefield, A. J., Murch, S. H., Anthony, A., Linnell, J., Casson, D. M., Malik, M., Berelowitz, M., Dhillon, A. P., Thomson, M. A., & Harvey, P. (1998). *Retracted: Ileal-lymphoid-nodular hyperplasia, non-specific colitis, and pervasive developmental disorder in children.* Elsevier.

Wakschlag, L. S., Perlman, S. B., Blair, R. J., Leibenluft, E., Briggs-Gowan, M. J., & Pine, D. S. (2018). The neurodevelopmental basis of early childhood disruptive behavior: Irritable and callous phenotypes as exemplars. *American Journal of Psychiatry, 175*(2), 114–130. https://doi.org/10.1176/appi.ajp.2017.17010045

Walajahi, H., Wilson, D. R., & Hull, S. C. (2019). Constructing identities: The implications of DTC ancestry testing for tribal communities. *Genetics in Medicine, 21*(8), 1744–1750. https://doi.org/10.1038/s41436-018-0429-2

Waldinger, R. J., & Schulz, M. S. (2016). The long reach of nurturing family environments: Links with midlife emotion-regulatory styles and late-life security in intimate relationships. *Psychological Science, 27*(11), 1443–1450. https://doi.org/10.1177/0956797616661556

Walhovd, K. B., Fjell, A. M., Giedd, J., Dale, A. M., & Brown, T. T. (2017). Through thick and thin: A need to reconcile contradictory results on trajectories in human cortical development. *Cerebral Cortex, 27*(2), bhv301. https://doi.org/10.1093/cercor/bhv301

Walhovd, K. B., & Lövdén, M. (2020). A lifespan perspective on human neurocognitive plasticity. In D. Poeppel, G. Mangun, & M. S. Gazzaniga (Eds.), *The cognitive neurosciences* (pp. 47–60). MIT Press.

Walker, M. (2017). Sleep the good sleep. *New Scientist, 236*(3147), 30–33. https://doi.org/10.1016/S0262-4079(17)32022-5

Walker, S. M. (2019). Long-term effects of neonatal pain. *Seminars in Fetal and Neonatal Medicine, 24*(4), 101005. https://doi.org/10.1016/j.siny.2019.04.005

Wall, B. (2012, April 20). *Older chess players.* Chess.com. https://www.chess.com/article/view/older-chess-players

Wall, K., Widmer, E. D., Gauthier, J.-A., Česnuitytė, V., & Gouveia, R. (Eds.). (2018). *Families and personal networks: An international comparative perspective.* Springer.

Wallace, D. (2009). *This is water: Some thoughts, delivered on a significant occasion, about living a compassionate life.* Little, Brown.

Wallace, I. J., Rubin, C. T., & Lieberman, D. E. (2015). Osteoporosis: Evolution, Medicine, and Public Health, *2015*(1), 343. https://doi.org/10.1093/emph/eov032

Wallace, J. B. (2015, March 13). Why children need chores. *Wall Street Journal.* https://www.wsj.com/articles/why-children-need-chores-1426262655

Wallerstein, J. S. (1987). Children after divorce: Wounds that don't heal. *Perspectives in Psychiatric Care, 24*(3–4), 107–113.

Walsh, A., & Leaper, C. (2020). A content analysis of gender representations in preschool children's television. *Mass Communication and Society, 23*(3), 331–355. https://doi.org/10.1080/15205436.2019.1664593

Walter, T. (2008). The sociology of death. *Sociology Compass, 2*(1), 317–336. https://doi.org/10.1111/j.1751-9020.2007.00069.x

Walter, T. (2015). New mourners, old mourners: Online memorial culture as a chapter in the history of mourning. *New Review of Hypermedia and Multimedia, 21*(1–2), 10–24. https://doi.org/10.1080/13614568.2014.983555

Walter, T., Hourizi, R., Moncur, W., & Pitsillides, S. (2012). Does the internet change how we die and mourn? Overview and analysis. *OMEGA — Journal of Death and Dying, 64*(4), 275–302. https://doi.org/10.2190/OM.64.4.a

Walther, A., Philipp, M., Lozza, N., & Ehlert, U. (2016). The rate of change in declining steroid hormones: A new parameter of healthy aging in men? *Oncotarget, 7*(38), 60844–60857. https://doi.org/10.18632/oncotarget.11752

Walton, G. M., & Brady, S. T. (2020). The social-belonging intervention. In G. M. Walton & A. J. Crum (Eds.), *Handbook of wise interventions: How social-psychological insights can help solve problems* (pp. 36–62). Guilford.

Wan, M. W., Fitch-Bunce, C., Heron, K., & Lester, E. (2021). Infant screen media usage and social-emotional functioning. *Infant Behavior and Development, 62*, 101509. https://doi.org/10.1016/j.infbeh.2020.101509

Wanberg, C. R., Ali, A. A., & Csillag, B. (2020). Job seeking: The process and experience of looking for a job. *Annual Review of Organizational Psychology and Organizational Behavior, 7*, 315–337.

Wang, A. S., & Dreesen, O. (2018). Biomarkers of cellular senescence and skin aging. *Frontiers in Genetics, 9*, 247.

Wang, C., Song, S., d'Oleire Uquillas, F., Zilverstand, A., Song, H., Chen, H., & Zou, Z. (2020). Altered brain network organization in romantic love as measured with resting-state fMRI and graph theory. *Brain Imaging and Behavior, 14*(6), 2771–2784. https://doi.org/10.1007/s11682-019-00226-0

Wang, C.-H., Chang, W.-T., Huang, C.-H., Tsai, M.-S., Yu, P.-H., Wu, Y.-W., & Chen, W.-J. (2019). Factors associated with the decision to terminate resuscitation early for adult in-hospital cardiac arrest: Influence of family in an East Asian society. *PLOS ONE, 14*(3), e0213168. https://doi.org/10.1371/journal.pone.0213168

Wang, H., Dwyer-Lindgren, L., Lofgren, K. T., Rajaratnam, J. K., Marcus, J. R., Levin-Rector, A., Levitz, C. E., Lopez, A. D., & Murray, C. J. L. (2012). Age-specific and sex-specific mortality in 187 countries, 1970–2010: A systematic analysis for the Global Burden of Disease Study 2010. *The Lancet, 380*(9859), 2071–2094. https://doi.org/10.1016/S0140-6736(12)61719-X

Wang, H., Kim, K., Burr, J. A., Birditt, K. S., & Fingerman, K. L. (2020). Middle-aged adults' daily sleep and worries about aging parents and adult children. Journal of Family Psychology, 34(5), 621–629. https://doi.org/10.1037/fam0000642

Wang, H., Lin, S. L., Leung, G. M., & Schooling, C. M. (2016). Age at onset of puberty and adolescent depression: "Children of 1997" birth cohort. *Pediatrics, 137*(6), e20153231. https://doi.org/10.1542/peds.2015-3231

Wang, J., Knol, M. J., Tiulpin, A., Dubost, F., de Bruijne, M., Vernooij, M. W., & Roshchupkin, G. V. (2019). Gray matter age prediction as a biomarker for risk of dementia. *Proceedings of the National Academy of Sciences, 116*(42), 21213–21218.

Wang, M.-T., Degol, J. L., Amemiya, J., Parr, A., & Guo, J. (2020). Classroom climate and children's academic and psychological wellbeing: A systematic review and meta-analysis. Developmental Review, 57, 100912. https://doi.org/10.1016/j.dr.2020.100912

Wang, M.-T., Henry, D. A., Smith, L. V., Huguley, J. P., & Guo, J. (2020). Parental ethnic-racial socialization practices and children of color's psychosocial and behavioral adjustment: A systematic review and meta-analysis. *American Psychologist, 75*(1), 1–22. https://doi.org/10.1037/amp0000464

Wang, Q. (2016). Five myths about the role of culture in psychological research. *APS Observer, 30*(1). https://www.psychologicalscience.org/observer/five-myths-about-the-role-of-culture-in-psychological-research

Wang, S. B., Haynos, A. F., Wall, M. M., Chen, C., Eisenberg, M. E., & Neumark-Sztainer, D. (2019). Fifteen-year prevalence, trajectories, and predictors of body dissatisfaction from adolescence to middle adulthood. *Clinical Psychological Science, 7*(6), 1403–1415. https://doi.org/10.1177/2167702619859331

Wang, X., Xie, X., Wang, Y., Wang, P., & Lei, L. (2017). Partner phubbing and depression among married Chinese adults: The roles of relationship satisfaction and relationship length. *Personality and Individual Differences, 110*, 12–17. https://doi.org/10.1016/j.paid.2017.01.014

Wang, Y., Dong, W., Zhang, L., & Zhang, R. (2021). The effect of kangaroo mother care on aEEG activity and neurobehavior in preterm infants: A randomized controlled trial. *The Journal of Maternal-Fetal & Neonatal Medicine.* https://doi.org/10.1080/14767058.2021.1916460

Wang, Y., Liu, Q., Tang, F., Yan, L., & Qiao, J. (2019). Epigenetic regulation and risk factors during the development of human gametes and early embryos. *Annual Review of Genomics and Human Genetics, 20*(1), 21–40. https://doi.org/10.1146/annurev-genom-083118-015143

Wang, Z., Fong, F. T., & Meltzoff, A. N. (2021). Enhancing same-gender imitation by highlighting gender norms in Chinese pre-school children. *British Journal of Developmental Psychology, 39*(1), 133–152.

Wankoff, L. S. (2011). Warning signs in the development of speech, language, and communication: When to refer to a speech-language pathologist. *Journal of Child and Adolescent Psychiatric Nursing: Official Publication of the Association of Child and Adolescent Psychiatric Nurses, Inc., 24*(3), 175–184. https://doi.org/10.1111/j.1744-6171.2011.00292.x

Wantchekon, K. A., & Umaña-Taylor, A. J. (2021). Relating profiles of ethnic–racial identity process and content to the academic and psychological adjustment of Black and Latinx adolescents. *Journal of Youth and Adolescence, 50*(7), 1333–1352. https://doi.org/10.1007/s10964-021-01451-x

Ward, E. V., & Shanks, D. R. (2018, December 20). Implicit memory and cognitive aging. *In Oxford research encyclopedia of psychology.* https://doi.org/10.1093/acrefore/9780190236557.013.378

Ward, L. M., & Grower, P. (2020). Media and the development of gender role stereotypes. *Annual Review of Developmental Psychology, 2*(1), 177–199. https://doi.org/10.1146/annurev-devpsych-051120-010630

Ward-Caviness, C. K., Nwanaji-Enwerem, J. C., Wolf, K., Wahl, S., Colicino, E., Trevisi, L., & Peters, A. (2016). Long-term exposure to air pollution is associated with biological aging. *Oncotarget, 7*(46), 74510.

Wardecker, B. M., & Matsick, J. L. (2020). Families of choice and community connectedness: A brief guide to the social strengths of LGBTQ older adults. *Journal of Gerontological Nursing, 46*(2), 5–8. https://doi.org/10.3928/00989134-20200113-01

Wariso, B. A., Guerrieri, G. M., Thompson, K., Koziol, D. E., Haq, N., Martinez, P. E., Rubinow, D. R., & Schmidt, P. J. (2017). Depression during the menopause transition: Impact on quality of life, social adjustment, and disability. *Archives of Women's Mental Health, 20*(2), 273–282. https://doi.org/10.1007/s00737-016-0701-x

Warnock, D. M., & Hurst, A. L. (2016). "The poor kids' table": Organizing around an invisible and stigmatized identity in flux. *Journal of Diversity in Higher Education, 9*(3), 261.

Warren, A.-S., Goldsmith, K. A., & Rimes, K. A. (2019). Childhood gender-typed behavior and emotional or peer problems: A prospective birth-cohort study. *Journal of Child Psychology and Psychiatry, 60*(8), 888–896. https://doi.org/10.1111/jcpp.13051

Warren, M. (1948). The evolution of a geriatric unit from a public assistance institution, 1935–1947. *Proceedings of the Royal Society of Medicine, 41,* 337–338.

Warren, N. S. (2020). Cultural competency. In B. S. LeRoy, P. McCarthy Veach, & N. P. Callanan (Eds.), *Genetic counseling practice* (pp. 247–270). John Wiley & Sons. https://doi.org/10.1002/9781119529873.ch12

Wartosch, L., Schindler, K., Schuh, M., Gruhn, J. R., Hoffmann, E. R., McCoy, R. C., & Xing, J. (2021). Origins and mechanisms leading to aneuploidy in human eggs. *Prenatal Diagnosis, 41*(5), 620–630. https://doi.org/10.1002/pd.5927

Wass, S. V., Smith, C. G., Clackson, K., Gibb, C., Eitzenberger, J., & Mirza, F. U. (2019). Parents mimic and influence their infant's autonomic state through dynamic affective state matching. *Current Biology, 29*(14), 2415–2422.e4. https://doi.org/10.1016/j.cub.2019.06.016

Wasserberg, M. J. (2014). Stereotype threat effects on African American children in an urban elementary school. *The Journal of Experimental Education, 82*(4), 502–517.

Wasylyshyn, C., Verhaeghen, P., & Sliwinski, M. J. (2011). Aging and task switching: A meta-analysis. *Psychology and Aging, 26*(1), 15–20. https://doi.org/10.1037/a0020912

Watanuki, S., & Akama, H. (2020). Neural substrates of brand love: An activation likelihood estimation meta-analysis of functional neuroimaging studies. *Frontiers in Neuroscience, 14,* 534671. https://doi.org/10.3389/fnins.2020.534671

Waters, S. F., West, T. V., Karnilowicz, H. R., & Mendes, W. B. (2017). Affect contagion between mothers and infants: Examining valence and touch. *Journal of Experimental Psychology. General, 146*(7), 1043–1051. https://doi.org/10.1037/xge0000322

Waters, T. E. A., Facompré, C. R., Van de Walle, M., Dujardin, A., De Winter, S., Heylen, J., Santens, T., Verhees, M., Finet, C., & Bosmans, G. (2019). Stability and change in secure base script knowledge during middle childhood and early adolescence: A 3-year longitudinal study. *Developmental Psychology, 55*(11), 2379–2388.

Watson, C. (2020). Stillbirth rate rises dramatically during pandemic. *Nature, 585*(7826), 490–491. https://doi.org/10.1038/d41586-020-02618-5

Watson, J. B. (1913). Psychology as the behaviorist views it. *Psychological Review, 20*(2), 158–177. https://doi.org/10.1037/h0074428

Watson, J. B. (1928). *Psychological care of infant and child.* W. W. Norton.

Watson, K. B. (2016). Physical inactivity among adults aged 50 years and older — United States, 2014. *Morbidity and Mortality Weekly Report, 65*(36), 954–958. https://doi.org/10.15585/mmwr.mm6536a3

Watson, K. B., Carlson, S. A., Gunn, J. P., Galuska, D. A., O'Connor, A., Greenlund, K. J., & Fulton, J. E. (2016). Physical inactivity among adults aged 50 years and older — United States, 2014. *Morbidity and Mortality Weekly Report, 65*(36), 954–958. https://doi.org/10.15585/mmwr.mm6536a3

Watson, R. J., Snapp, S., & Wang, S. (2017). What we know and where we go from here: A review of lesbian, gay, and bisexual youth hookup literature. *Sex Roles, 77*(11–12), 801–811. https://doi.org/10.1007/s11199-017-0831-2

Watson, R. J., Wheldon, C. W., & Puhl, R. M. (2020). Evidence of diverse identities in a large national sample of sexual and gender minority adolescents. *Journal of Research on Adolescence, 30*(S2), 431–442. https://doi.org/10.1111/jora.12488

Watson-Jones, R. E., Busch, J. T. A., Harris, P. L., & Legare, C. H. (2017). Does the body survive death? Cultural variation in beliefs about life everlasting. *Cognitive Science, 41*(S3), 455–476. https://doi.org/10.1111/cogs.12430

Watts, N., Amann, M., Ayeb-Karlsson, S., Belesova, K., Bouley, T., Boykoff, M., Byass, P., Cai, W., Campbell-Lendrum, D., Chambers, J., Cox, P. M., Daly, M., Dasandi, N., Davies, M., Depledge, M., Depoux, A., Dominguez-Salas, P., Drummond, P., Ekins, P., … Costello, A. (2018). The Lancet Countdown on health and climate change: From 25 years of inaction to a global transformation for public health. *The Lancet, 391*(10120), 581–630. https://doi.org/10.1016/S0140-6736(17)32464-9

Watts, T. W., Duncan, G. J., & Quan, H. (2018). Revisiting the marshmallow test: A conceptual replication investigating links between early delay of gratification and later outcomes. *Psychological Science, 29*(7), 1159–1177. https://doi.org/10.1177/0956797618761661

Waugh, W. E., & Brownell, C. A. (2017). "Help yourself!" What can toddlers' helping failures tell us about the development of prosocial behavior? *Infancy, 22*(5), 665–680. https://doi.org/10.1111/infa.12189

Way, N. (2019). Reimagining boys in the 21st century. *Men and Masculinities, 22*(5), 926–929. https://doi.org/10.1177/1097184X19875170

Way, N., Cressen, J., Bodian, S., Preston, J., Nelson, J., & Hughes, D. (2014). "It might be nice to be a girl... Then you wouldn't have to be emotionless": Boys' resistance to norms of masculinity during adolescence. *Psychology of Men & Masculinity, 15*(3), 241–252. https://doi.org/10.1037/a0037262

Weakley, A., Weakley, A. T., & Schmitter-Edgecombe, M. (2019). Compensatory strategy use improves real-world functional performance in community dwelling older adults. *Neuropsychology, 33*(8), 1121–1135. https://doi.org/10.1037/neu0000591

Weatherhead, D., Arredondo, M. M., Nácar Garcia, L., & Werker, J. F. (2021). The role of audiovisual speech in fast-mapping and novel word retention in monolingual and bilingual 24-month-olds. *Brain Sciences, 11*(1), 114. https://doi.org/10.3390/brainsci11010114

Weaver, C. M., Shaw, D. S., Crossan, J. L., Dishion, T. J., & Wilson, M. N. (2015). Parent–child conflict and early childhood adjustment in two-parent low-income families: Parallel developmental processes. *Child Psychiatry and Human Development, 46*(1), 94–107. https://doi.org/10.1007/s10578-014-0455-5

Weaver, J., & Schofield, T. (2015). Mediation and moderation of divorce effects on children's behavior problems. *Journal of Family Psychology, 29*(1): 39–48. https://doi.org/10.1037/fam0000043

Weaver, J. M., Schofield, T. J., & Papp, L. M. (2018). Breastfeeding duration predicts greater maternal sensitivity over the next decade. *Developmental Psychology, 54*(2), 220.

Weaver, L. T. (2010). In the balance: Weighing babies and the birth of the infant welfare clinic. *Bulletin of the History of Medicine, 84*(1), 30–57. doi:10.1353/bhm.0.0315

Webster, E. K., Martin, C. K., & Staiano, A. E. (2019). Fundamental motor skills, screen-time, and physical activity in preschoolers. *Journal of Sport and Health Science, 8*(2), 114–121. https://doi.org/10.1016/j.jshs.2018.11.006

Wechsler, D. (1958). *The measurement and appraisal of adult intelligence* (4th ed.). Williams & Wilkins. https://doi.org/10.1037/11167-000

Wechsler, D. (2014). *WISC-V: Technical and interpretive manual.* Pearson.

Wegermann, K., Suzuki, A., Mavis, A. M., Abdelmalek, M. F., Diehl, A. M., & Moylan, C. A. (2021). Tackling nonalcoholic fatty liver disease: Three targeted populations. *Hepatology, 73*(3), 1199–1206. https://doi.org/10.1002/hep.31533

Wegner, R., Abbey, A., Pierce, J., Pegram, S. E., & Woerner, J. (2015). Sexual assault perpetrators' justifications for their actions: Relationships to rape supportive attitudes, incident characteristics, and future perpetration. *Violence Against Women, 21*(8), 1018–1037. https://doi.org/10.1177/1077801215589380

Wei, M.-C., Chou, Y.-H., Yang, Y.-S., Kornelius, E., Wang, Y.-H., & Huang, C.-N. (2020). Osteoporosis and stress urinary incontinence in women: A national health insurance database study. *International Journal of Environmental Research and Public Health, 17*(12), 4449. https://doi.org/10.3390/ijerph17124449

Weidmann, R., Ledermann, T., & Grob, A. (2017). The interdependence of personality and satisfaction in couples. *European Psychologist, 21*(4). https://doi.org/10.1027/1016-9040/a000261

Weidner, K., Bittner, A., Beutel, M., Goeckenjan, M., Brähler, E., & Garthus-Niegel, S. (2020). The role of stress and self-efficacy in somatic and psychological symptoms during the climacteric period — Is there a specific association? *Maturitas, 136,* 1–6. https://doi.org/10.1016/j.maturitas.2020.03.004

Weinberger, A. H., Gbedemah, M., Martinez, A. M., Nash, D., Galea, S., & Goodwin, R. D. (2018). Trends in depression prevalence in the USA from 2005 to 2015: Widening disparities in vulnerable groups. *Psychological Medicine, 48*(8), 1308–1315. https://doi.org/10.1017/S0033291717002781

Weininger, E. B., Lareau, A., & Conley, D. (2015). What money doesn't buy: Class resources and children's participation in organized extracurricular activities. *Social Forces, 94*(2), 479–503. https://doi.org/10.1093/sf/sov071

Weinstein, S. M., Mermelstein, R. J., Hankin, B. L., Hedeker, D., & Flay, B. R. (2007). Longitudinal patterns of daily affect and global mood during adolescence. *Journal of Research on Adolescence, 17*(3), 587–600.

Weintraub, S., Dikmen, S. S., Heaton, R. K., Tulsky, D. S., Zelazo, P. D., Bauer, P. J., Carlozzi, N. E., Slotkin, J., Blitz, D., Wallner-Allen, K., Fox, N. A., Beaumont, J. L., Mungas, D., Nowinski, C. J., Richler, J., Deocampo, J. A., Anderson, J. E., Manly, J. J., Borosh, B., ... Gershon, R. C. (2013). Cognition assessment using the NIH Toolbox. *Neurology, 80*(11 Suppl. 3), S54–S64. https://doi.org/10.1212/WNL.0b013e3182872ded

Weis, M., Trommsdorff, G., & Muñoz, L. (2016). Children's self-regulation and school achievement in cultural contexts: The role of maternal restrictive control. *Frontiers in Psychology, 7*, 722.

Weisberg, D. S. (2015). Pretend play. *WIREs Cognitive Science, 6*(3), 249–261. https://doi.org/10.1002/wcs.1341

Weisberg, D. S., Hirsh-Pasek, K., Golinkoff, R. M., Kittredge, A. K., & Klahr, D. (2016). Guided play: Principles and practices. *Current Directions in Psychological Science, 25*(3), 177–182.

Weisberg, S. P., Connors, T. J., Zhu, Y., Baldwin, M. R., Lin, W.-H., Wontakal, S., Szabo, P. A., Wells, S. B., Dogra, P., Gray, J., Idzikowski, E., Stelitano, D., Bovier, F. T., Davis-Porada, J., Matsumoto, R., Poon, M. M. L., Chait, M., Mathieu, C., Horvat, B., ... Farber, D. L. (2021). Distinct antibody responses to SARS-CoV-2 in children and adults across the COVID-19 clinical spectrum. *Nature Immunology, 22*(1), 25–31. https://doi.org/10.1038/s41590-020-00826-9

Weisner, T. S. (2020). Still the most important influence on human development: Culture, context, and methods pluralism. *Human Development, 64*(4–6), 238–244.

Weiss, J. (2020). What is youth political participation? Literature review on youth political participation and political attitudes. *Frontiers in Political Science, 2*, 1. https://doi.org/10.3389/fpos.2020.00001

Weiss, S. A., Wolchok, J. D., & Sznol, M. (2019). Immunotherapy of melanoma: Facts and hopes. *Clinical Cancer Research, 25*(17), 5191–5201. https://doi.org/10.1158/1078-0432.CCR-18-1550

Weissberger, G. H., Goodman, M. C., Mosqueda, L., Schoen, J., Nguyen, A. L., Wilber, K. H., Gassoumis, Z. D., Nguyen, C. P., & Han, S. D. (2020). Elder abuse characteristics based on calls to the national center on elder abuse resource line. *Journal of Applied Gerontology, 39*(10), 1078–1087. https://doi.org/10.1177/0733464819865685

Weissbourd, R., Anderson, T. R., Cashin, A., & McIntyre, J. (2017). The talk: How adults can promote young people's healthy relationships and prevent misogyny and sexual harassment. *Harvard Graduate School of Education, 16*(8), 1–46.

Weisz, J. R., Kuppens, S., Eckshtain, D., Ugueto, A. M., Hawley, K. M., & Jensen-Doss, A. (2013). Performance of evidence-based youth psychotherapies compared with usual clinical care: A multilevel meta-analysis. *JAMA Psychiatry, 70*(7), 750–761. https://doi.org/10.1001/jamapsychiatry.2013.1176

Weitbrecht, E. M., & Whitton, S. W. (2020). College students' motivations for "hooking up": Similarities and differences in motives by gender and partner type. *Couple and Family Psychology: Research and Practice, 9*(3), 123–143. https://doi.org/10.1037/cfp0000138

Wellesley College. (2013, November 11). *Wellesley salutes veterans on campus.* Wellesley College. http://www.wellesley.edu/news/2013/11/node/40223

Wellman, H. M. (2018). Theory of mind: The state of the art. *European Journal of Developmental Psychology, 15*(6), 728–755. https://doi.org/10.1080/17405629.2018.1435413

Welsh, R. O., & Little, S. (2018). The school discipline dilemma: A comprehensive review of disparities and alternative approaches. *Review of Educational Research, 88*(5), 752–794.

Wen, H., Hockenberry, J. M., & Druss, B. G. (2019). The effect of medical marijuana laws on marijuana-related attitude and perception among US adolescents and young adults. *Prevention Science, 20*(2), 215–223. https://doi.org/10.1007/s11121-018-0903-8

Wende, M. E., Stowe, E. W., Eberth, J. M., McLain, A. C., Liese, A. D., Breneman, C. B., Josey, M. J., Hughey, S. M., &

Kaczynski, A. T. (2020). Spatial clustering patterns and regional variations for food and physical activity environments across the United States. *International Journal of Environmental Health Research, 1*–15. https://doi.org/10.1080/09603123.2020.1713304

Wendlandt, N. M., & Rochlen, A. B. (2008). Addressing the college-to-work transition implications for university career counselors. *Journal of Career Development, 35*(2), 151–165. https://doi.org/10.1177/0894845308325646

Werchan, D. M., Kim, J.-S., & Gómez, R. L. (2021). A daytime nap combined with nighttime sleep promotes learning in toddlers. *Journal of Experimental Child Psychology, 202*, 105006. https://doi.org/10.1016/j.jecp.2020.105006

Werchan, D. M., Lynn, A., Kirkham, N. Z., & Amso, D. (2019). The emergence of object-based visual attention in infancy: A role for family socioeconomic status and competing visual features. *Infancy, 24*(5), 752–767. https://doi.org/10.1111/infa.12309

Werker, J. F. (2018). Speech perception, word learning, and language acquisition in infancy: The voyage continues. *Applied Psycholinguistics, 39*(4), 769–777. https://doi.org/10.1017/S0142716418000243

Werner, C. M., Hecksteden, A., Morsch, A., Zundler, J., Wegmann, M., Kratzsch, J., & Laufs, U. (2019). Differential effects of endurance, interval, and resistance training on telomerase activity and telomere length in a randomized, controlled study. *European Heart Journal, 40*(1), 34–46.

Werner, E. E. (1989). High-risk children in young adulthood: A longitudinal study from birth to 32 years. *American Journal of Orthopsychiatry, 59*(1), 72–81.

Werner, E. E. (1995). Resilience in development. *Current Directions in Psychological Science, 4*(3), 81–84.

Werner, E. E., & Smith, R. S. (1992). *Overcoming the odds: High risk children from birth to adulthood.* Cornell University Press.

Werner, L. A. (2017). Ontogeny of human auditory system function. In K. S. Cramer, A. B. Coffin, R. R. Fay, & A. N. Popper (Eds.), *Auditory development and plasticity: In honor of Edwin W Rubel* (pp. 161–192). Springer International Publishing. https://doi.org/10.1007/978-3-319-21530-3_7

Werner, P., & Heinik, J. (2008). Stigma by association and Alzheimer's disease. *Aging and Mental Health, 12*(1), 92–99.

Werner-Seidler, A., Afzali, M. H., Chapman, C., Sunderland, M., & Slade, T. (2017). The relationship between social support networks and depression in the 2007 National Survey of Mental Health and Well-being. *Social Psychiatry and Psychiatric Epidemiology, 52*(12), 1463–1473. https://doi.org/10.1007/s00127-017-1440-7

Werth, J. M., Nickerson, A. B., Aloe, A. M., & Swearer, S. M. (2015). Bullying victimization and the social and emotional maladjustment of bystanders: A propensity score analysis. *Journal of School Psychology, 53*(4), 295–308.

Wesselink, A. K., Rothman, K. J., Hatch, E. E., Mikkelsen, E. M., Sørensen, H. T., & Wise, L. A. (2017). Age and fecundability in a North American preconception cohort study. *American Journal of Obstetrics and Gynecology, 217*(6), 667-e1.

West, C. P., Dyrbye, L. N., Erwin, P. J., & Shanafelt, T. D. (2016). Interventions to prevent and reduce physician burnout: A systematic review and meta-analysis. *The Lancet, 388*(10057), 2272–2281. https://doi.org/10.1016/S0140-6736(16)31279-X

West, C. P., Dyrbye, L. N., Sinsky, C., Trockel, M., Tutty, M., Nedelec, L., Carlasare, L. E., & Shanafelt, T. D. (2020). Resilience and burnout among physicians and the general US working population. *JAMA Network Open, 3*(7), e209385. https://doi.org/10.1001/jamanetworkopen.2020.9385

Westervelt, E. (2012, April 4). The secret to Germany's low youth unemployment. *Morning Edition.* NPR. https://www.npr.org/2012/04/04/149927290/the-secret-to-germanys-low-youth-unemployment

Weston, S. J., Cardador, M. T., Hill, P. L., Schwaba, T., Lodi-Smith, J., & Whitbourne, S. K. (2021). The relationship between career success and sense of purpose: Examining linkages and changes. *The Journals of Gerontology: Series B, 76*(1), 78–87.

Westrope, E. (2018). Employment discrimination on the basis of criminal history: Why an anti-discrimination statute is a necessary remedy. *The Journal of Criminal Law and Criminology (1973–), 108*(2), 367–398.

Westrupp, E. M., Reilly, S., McKean, C., Law, J., Mensah, F., & Nicholson, J. M. (2020). Vocabulary development and trajectories of behavioral and emotional difficulties via academic ability and peer problems. *Child Development, 91*(2), e365–e382. https://doi.org/10.1111/cdev.13219

Weststrate, N., & Glück, J. (2017). Hard-earned wisdom: Exploratory processing of difficult life experience is positively associated with wisdom. *Developmental Psychology, 53*(4), 800–814. https://doi.org/10.1037/dev0000286

Wetherell, M., & Lovell, B. (2019). Lean on me: The psychobiological burden of caregiving. *Psychoneuroendocrinology, 107*, 55. https://doi.org/10.1016/j.psyneuen.2019.07.157

Wethington, E. (2000). Expecting stress: Americans and the "midlife crisis." *Motivation and Emotion, 24*(2), 85–103.

Weuve, J., Bennett, E. E., Ranker, L., Gianattasio, K. Z., Pedde, M., Adar, S. D., & Power, M. C. (2021). Exposure to air pollution in relation to risk of dementia and related outcomes: An updated systematic review of the epidemiological literature. *Environmental Health Perspectives, 129*(9), 096001.

Weymouth, B. B., Buehler, C., Zhou, N., & Henson, R. A. (2016). A meta-analysis of parent–adolescent conflict: Disagreement, hostility, and youth maladjustment. *Journal of Family Theory & Review, 8*(1), 95–112.

Whalen, D. J., Sylvester, C. M., & Luby, J. L. (2017). Depression and anxiety in preschoolers: A review of the past 7 years. *Child and Adolescent Psychiatric Clinics of North America, 26*(3), 503–522. https://doi.org/10.1016/j.chc.2017.02.006

Whalley, L. J., Staff, R. T., Fox, H. C., & Murray, A. D. (2016). Cerebral correlates of cognitive reserve. *Psychiatry Research: Neuroimaging, 247*, 65–70.

Wheaton, A. G., Jones, S. E., Cooper, A. C., & Croft, J. B. (2018). Short sleep duration among middle school and high school students—United States, 2015. *Morbidity and Mortality Weekly Report, 67*(3), 85.

Wheeler, L. A., Zeiders, K. H., Updegraff, K. A., Umaña-Taylor, A. J., Rodríguez de Jesús, S. A., & Perez-Brena, N. J. (2017). Mexican-origin youth's risk behavior from adolescence to young adulthood: The role of familism values. *Developmental Psychology, 53*(1), 126–137. https://doi.org/10.1037/dev0000251

Whelan, J. C. (2000). *Too many, too few: The supply, demand, and distribution of private duty nurses, 1910–1965.* University of Pennsylvania.

Whincup, P. H., Gilg, J. A., Odoki, K., Taylor, S. J. C., & Cook, D. G. (2001). Age of menarche in contemporary British teenagers: Survey of girls born between 1982 and 1986. *BMJ, 322*(7294), 1095–1096. https://doi.org/10.1136/bmj.322.7294.1095

Whitaker, A., & Losen, D. J. (2019). *The striking outlier: The persistent, painful and problematic practice of corporal punishment in schools.* https://escholarship.org/uc/item/9d19p8wt

Whitaker, R. T., & Snell, C. L. (2016). Parenting while powerless: Consequences of "the talk." *Journal of Human Behavior in the Social Environment, 26*(3–4), 303–309. https://doi.org/10.1080/10911359.2015.1127736

White, A. J., Bradshaw, P. T., & Hamra, G. B. (2018). Air pollution and breast cancer: A review. *Current Epidemiology Reports, 5*(2), 92–100. https://doi.org/10.1007/s40471-018-0143-2

White, E. M., Aiken, L. H., Sloane, D. M., & McHugh, M. D. (2020). Nursing home work environment, care quality, registered nurse burnout and job dissatisfaction. *Geriatric Nursing, 41*(2), 158–164. https://doi.org/10.1016/j.gerinurse.2019.08.007

White, E. M., DeBoer, M. D., & Scharf, R. J. (2019). Associations between household chores and childhood self-competency. *Journal of Developmental & Behavioral Pediatrics, 40*(3), 176–182. https://doi.org/10.1097/DBP.0000000000000637

White, E. S., & Mistry, R. S. (2016). Parent civic beliefs, civic participation, socialization practices, and child civic engagement. *Applied Developmental Science, 20*(1), 44–60. https://doi.org/10.1080/10888691.2015.1049346

White, J. (2006). *Intelligence, destiny and education: The ideological roots of intelligence testing.* Routledge.

White, R., Barreto, M., Harrington, J., Kapp, S. K., Hayes, J., & Russell, G. (2020). Is disclosing an autism spectrum disorder in school associated with reduced stigmatization? *Autism, 24*(3), 744–754.

White, R. E., & Carlson, S. M. (2016). What would Batman do? Self-distancing improves executive function in young children. *Developmental Science, 19*(3), 419–426. https://doi.org/10.1111/desc.12314

White, R. E., & Carlson, S. M. (2021). Pretending with realistic and fantastical stories facilitates executive function in 3-year-old children. *Journal of Experimental Child Psychology, 207,* 105090. https://doi.org/10.1016/j.jecp.2021.105090

White, R. L., Babic, M. J., Parker, P. D., Lubans, D. R., Astell-Burt, T., & Lonsdale, C. (2017). Domain-specific physical activity and mental health: A meta-analysis. *American Journal of Preventive Medicine, 52*(5), 653–666.

Whitehurst, G. J. "Russ." (2018, March 12). *Betsy DeVos is half-right on test scores, but test scores alone don't make the case for school choice.* Brookings. https://www.brookings.edu/blog/up-front/2018/03/12/betsy-devos-is-half-right-on-test-scores-but-test-scores-alone-dont-make-the-case-for-school-choice/

Whiten, A. (2017). Social learning and culture in child and chimpanzee. *Annual Review of Psychology, 68*(1), 129–154. https://doi.org/10.1146/annurev-psych-010416-044108

Whitlatch, C. J., & Orsulic-Jeras, S. (2018). Meeting the informational, educational, and psychosocial support needs of persons living with dementia and their family caregivers. *The Gerontologist, 58*(suppl_1), S58–S73.

Whitney, D. G., & Peterson, M. D. (2019). US national and state-level prevalence of mental health disorders and disparities of mental health care use in children. *JAMA Pediatrics, 173*(4), 389–391. https://doi.org/10.1001/jamapediatrics.2018.5399

Whitson, H. E., Cronin-Golomb, A., Cruickshanks, K. J., Gilmore, G. C., Owsley, C., Peelle, J. E., Recanzone, G., Sharma, A., Swenor, B., Yaffe, K., & Lin, F. R. (2018). American Geriatrics Society and National Institute on Aging Bench-to-Bedside Conference: Sensory impairment and cognitive decline in older adults. *Journal of the American Geriatrics Society, 66*(11), 2052–2058.

Whitton, S. W., Dyar, C., Newcomb, M. E., & Mustanski, B. (2018). Romantic involvement: A protective factor for psychological health in racially-diverse young sexual minorities. *Journal of Abnormal Psychology, 127*(3), 265–275. https://doi.org/10.1037/abn0000332

Whitton, S. W., Newcomb, M. E., Messinger, A. M., Byck, G., & Mustanski, B. (2016). A longitudinal study of IPV victimization among sexual minority youth. *Journal of Interpersonal Violence, 34*(5), 912–945. https://doi.org/10.1177/0886260516646093

Wick, K., Leeger-Aschmann, C. S., Monn, N. D., Radtke, T., Ott, L. V., Rebholz, C. E., Cruz, S., Gerber, N., Schmutz, E. A., Puder, J. J., Munsch, S., Kakebeeke, T. H., Jenni, O. G., Granacher, U., & Kriemler, S. (2017). Interventions to promote fundamental movement skills in childcare and kindergarten: A systematic review and meta-analysis. *Sports Medicine, 47*(10), 2045–2068. https://doi.org/10.1007/s40279-017-0723-1

Widman, L., Choukas-Bradley, S., Helms, S. W., Golin, C. E., & Prinstein, M. J. (2014). Sexual communication between early adolescents and their dating partners, parents, and best friends. *The Journal of Sex Research, 51*(7), 731–741. https://doi.org/10.1080/00224499.2013.843148

Widman, L., Evans, R., Javidi, H., & Choukas-Bradley, S. (2019). Assessment of parent-based interventions for adolescent sexual health: A systematic review and meta-analysis. *JAMA Pediatrics, 173*(9), 866–877. https://doi.org/10.1001/jamapediatrics.2019.2324

Wiersma, R., Haverkamp, B. F., van Beek, J. H., Riemersma, A. M. J., Boezen, H. M., Smidt, N., Corpeleijn, E., & Hartman, E. (2020). Unravelling the association between accelerometer-derived physical activity and adiposity among preschool children: A systematic review and meta-analyses. *Obesity Reviews, 21*(2), e12936. https://doi.org/10.1111/obr.12936

Wigfield, A., & Eccles, J. S. (2020). 35 years of research on students' subjective task values and motivation: A look back and a look forward. In A. J. Elliot (Ed.), *Advances in motivation science* (Vol. 7, pp. 161–198). Elsevier. https://doi.org/10.1016/bs.adms.2019.05.002

Wigfield, A., Eccles, J. S., Fredricks, J. A., Simpkins, S., Roeser, R. W., & Schiefele, U. (2015a). Development of achievement motivation and engagement. In R. M. Lerner (Ed.), *Handbook of child psychology and developmental science* (pp. 1–44). John Wiley & Sons. https://doi.org/10.1002/9781118963418.childpsy316

Wigfield, A., Gladstone, J. R., & Turci, L. (2016). Beyond cognition: Reading motivation and reading comprehension. *Child Development Perspectives, 10*(3), 190–195.

Wigfield, A., Muenks, K., & Rosenzweig, E. Q. (2015). Children's achievement motivation in school. In C. M. Rubie-Davies, J. M. Stephens, & P. Watson (Eds.), *Routledge international handbook of social psychology of the classroom* (pp. 9–20). Routledge.

Wike, R., & Castillo, A. (2018). *Many Around the World Are Disengaged from Politics.* Pew Research Center.

Wilbur, T. G., & Roscigno, V. J. (2016). First-generation disadvantage and college enrollment/completion. *Socius, 2.* https://doi.org/10.1177/2378023116664351

Wiles, J., Kearns, R., & Bates, L. (2020). Rural ageing in place and place attachment. In M. Skinner, R. Winterton, & K. Walsh (Eds.), *Rural gerontology* (pp. 175–187). Routledge.

Will, G. J., Crone, E. A., Van Lier, P. A., & Güroğlu, B. (2016). Neural correlates of retaliatory and prosocial reactions to social exclusion: Associations with chronic peer rejection. *Developmental Cognitive Neuroscience, 19,* 288–297.

Williams, B. R., Bailey, F. A., Woodby, L. L., Wittich, A. R., & Burgio, K. L. (2013). "A room full of chairs around his bed": Being present at the death of a loved one in veterans affairs medical centers. *OMEGA—Journal of Death and Dying, 66*(3), 231–263. https://doi.org/10.2190/OM.66.3.c

Williams, C. (2020). New research ignites debate on the '30 Million Word Gap.' *Edutopia.* https://www.edutopia.org/article/new-research-ignites-debate-30-million-word-gap

Williams, J. F., Smith, V. C., & the Committee on Substance Abuse. (2015). Fetal alcohol spectrum disorders. *Pediatrics, 136*(5), e1395–e1406. https://doi.org/10.1542/peds.2015-3113

Williams, R., Park, H. W., & Breazeal, C. (2019). A is for artificial intelligence: The impact of artificial intelligence activities on young children's perceptions of robots. In *Proceedings of the 2019 CHI Conference on Human Factors in Computing Systems* (pp. 1–11).

Williams, R. C., Biscaro, A., & Clinton, J. (2019). Relationships matter: How clinicians can support positive parenting in the early years. *Paediatrics & Child Health, 24*(5), 340–347. https://doi.org/10.1093/pch/pxz063

Williams, S. M., Sirugo, G., & Tishkoff, S. A. (2021). Embracing African genetic diversity. *Med, 2*(1), 19–20. https://doi.org/10.1016/j.medj.2020.12.019

Williamson, H. C. (2020). Early effects of the COVID-19 pandemic on relationship satisfaction and attributions. *Psychological Science, 31*(12), 1479–1487. https://doi.org/10.1177/0956797620972688

Williamson, H. C., & Lavner, J. A. (2020). Trajectories of marital satisfaction in diverse newlywed couples. *Social Psychological and Personality Science, 11*(5), 597–604. https://doi.org/10.1177/1948550619865056

Williamson, L. D. (2021). Beyond personal experiences: Examining mediated vicarious experiences as an antecedent of medical mistrust. *Health Communication,* 1–14. https://doi.org/10.1080/10410236.2020.1868744

Willis, M., Staudinger, U. M., Factor-Litvak, P., & Calvo, E. (2019). Stress and salivary telomere length in the second half of life: A comparison of life-course models. *Advances in Life Course Research, 39,* 34–41. https://doi.org/10.1016/j.alcr.2019.02.001.

Willroth, E. C., Mroczek, D. K., & Hill, P. L. (2021). Maintaining sense of purpose in midlife predicts better physical health. *Journal of Psychosomatic Research, 145,* 110485. https://doi.org/10.1016/j.jpsychores.2021.110485

Willumsen, J., & Bull, F. (2020). Development of WHO guidelines on physical activity, sedentary behavior, and sleep for children less than 5 years of age. *Journal of Physical Activity and Health, 17*(1), 96–100. https://doi.org/10.1123/jpah.2019-0457

Wilson, N., Kariisa, M., Seth, P., Smith, H., IV, & Davis, N. L. (2020). Drug and opioid-involved overdose deaths—United States, 2017–2018. *Morbidity and Mortality Weekly Report, 69*(11), 290.

Wilson, N., Lee, J. J., & Bei, B. (2019). Postpartum fatigue and depression: A systematic review and meta-analysis. *Journal of Affective Disorders, 246,* 224–233. https://doi.org/10.1016/j.jad.2018.12.032

Wilson, R. F., Sharma, A. J., Schluechtermann, S., Currie, D. W., Mangan, J., Kaplan, B., Goffard, K., Salomon, J., Casteel, S., Mukasa, A., Euhardy, N., Ruiz, A., Bautista, G., Bailey, E., Westergaard, R., & Gieryn, D. (2020). Factors influencing risk for COVID-19 exposure among young adults aged 18–23 years — Winnebago County, Wisconsin, March–July 2020. *Morbidity and Mortality Weekly Report, 69*(41), 1497–1502. https://doi.org/10.15585/mmwr.mm6941e2

Wilson, S. J., Woody, A., Padin, A. C., Lin, J., Malarkey, W. B., & Kiecolt-Glaser, J. K. (2019). Loneliness and telomere length: Immune and parasympathetic function in associations with accelerated aging. *Annals of Behavioral Medicine, 53*(6), 541–550.

Wimmer, H., & Perner, J. (1983). Beliefs about beliefs: Representation and constraining function of wrong beliefs in young children's understanding of deception. *Cognition, 13*(1), 103–128. https://doi.org/10.1016/0010-0277(83)90004-5

Windhager, S., Mitteroecker, P., Rupić, I., Lauc, T., Polašek, O., & Schaefer, K. (2019). Facial aging trajectories: A common shape pattern in male and female faces is disrupted after menopause. *American Journal of Physical Anthropology, 169*(4), 678–688. https://onlinelibrary.wiley.com/doi/full/10.1002/ajpa.23878

Winpenny, E. M., Penney, T. L., Corder, K., White, M., & van Sluijs, E. M. F. (2017). Change in diet in the period from adolescence to early adulthood: A systematic scoping review of longitudinal studies. *International Journal of Behavioral Nutrition and Physical Activity, 14*(1), 60. https://doi.org/10.1186/s12966-017-0518-7

Winpenny, E. M., Smith, M., Penney, T., Foubister, C., Guagliano, J. M., Love, R., Astbury, C. C., van Sluijs, E. M. F., & Corder, K. (2020). Changes in physical activity, diet, and body weight across the education and employment transitions of early adulthood: A systematic review and meta-analysis. *Obesity Reviews, 21*(4), e12962. https://doi.org/10.1111/obr.12962

Winpenny, E. M., Winkler, M. R., Stochl, J., van Sluijs, E. M. F., Larson, N., & Neumark-Sztainer, D. (2020). Associations of early adulthood life transitions with changes in fast food intake: A latent trajectory analysis. *International Journal of Behavioral Nutrition and Physical Activity, 17*(1), 130. https://doi.org/10.1186/s12966-020-01024-4

Winston, C. N. (2016). An existential-humanistic-positive theory of human motivation. *The Humanistic Psychologist, 44*(2), 142–163. https://doi.org/10.1037/hum0000028

Winthrop, R., & McGivney, E. (2015, June 10). *Why wait 100 years? Bridging the gap in global education.* Brookings. https://www.brookings.edu/research/why-wait-100-years-bridging-the-gap-in-global-education/

Witchel, S. F., & Topaloglu, A. K. (2019). Puberty: Gonadarche and adrenarche. In J. F. Strauss & R. L. Barbieri (Eds.), *Yen & Jaffe's reproductive endocrinology: Physiology, pathophysiology, and clinical management* (8th ed., pp. 394–446.e16). Elsevier. https://doi.org/10.1016/B978-0-323-47912-7.00017-2

Witherington, D. C., & Boom, J. (2019). Conceptualizing the dynamics of development in the 21st century: Process, (inter)action, and complexity. *Human Development, 63*(3–4), 147–152. https://doi.org/10.1159/000504097

Wittig, S. M. O., & Rodriguez, C. M. (2019). Emerging behavior problems: Bidirectional relations between maternal and paternal parenting styles with infant temperament. *Developmental Psychology, 55*(6), 1199–1210. https://doi.org/10.1037/dev0000707

Woessmann, L. (2016). The importance of school systems: Evidence from international differences in student achievement. *Journal of Economic Perspectives, 30*(3), 3–32. https://doi.org/10.1257/jep.30.3.3

Wohlfahrt-Veje, C., Mouritsen, A., Hagen, C. P., Tinggaard, J., Mieritz, M. G., Boas, M., Petersen, J. H., Skakkebæk, N. E., & Main, K. M. (2016). Pubertal onset in boys and girls is influenced by pubertal timing of both parents. *The Journal of Clinical Endocrinology & Metabolism, 101*(7), 2667–2674. https://doi.org/10.1210/jc.2016-1073

Wolf, R. M., & Long, D. (2016). Pubertal development. *Pediatrics in Review, 37*(7), 292–300. https://doi.org/10.1542/pir.2015-0065

Wolfe, V. V., & Kelly, B. M. (2019). Child maltreatment. In M. J. Prinstein, E. A. Youngstrom, E. J. Mash, & R. A. Barkley (Eds.), *Treatment of disorders in childhood and adolescence* (pp. 591–657). Guilford.

Wolff, J. L., Feder, J., & Schulz, R. (2016). Supporting family caregivers of older Americans. *New England Journal of Medicine, 375*(26), 2513–2515. https://doi.org/10.1056/NEJMp1612351

Wolff, J. L., & Jacobs, B. J. (2015). Chronic illness trends and the challenges to family caregivers: Organizational and health system barriers. In J. E. Gaugler & R. L. Kane (Eds.), *Family caregiving in the new normal* (pp. 79–103). Elsevier Academic Press.

Wolffsohn, J. S., & Davies, L. N. (2019). Presbyopia: Effectiveness of correction strategies. *Progress in Retinal and Eye Research, 68*, 124–143. https://doi.org/10.1016/j.preteyeres.2018.09.004

Wolfinger, N. H. (2015). Want to avoid divorce? Wait to get married, but not too long. *Institute for Family Studies, 16*, 2006–2010.

Wolke, D., Bilgin, A., & Samara, M. (2017). Systematic review and meta-analysis: Fussing and crying durations and prevalence of colic in infants. *The Journal of Pediatrics, 185*, 55–61.e4. https://doi.org/10.1016/j.jpeds.2017.02.020

Wolke, D., Johnson, S., & Mendonça, M. (2019). The life course consequences of very preterm birth. *Annual Review of Developmental Psychology, 1*(1), 69–92. https://doi.org/10.1146/annurev-devpsych-121318-084804

Wolraich, M., & American Academy of Pediatrics, (2016). *American Academy of Pediatrics guide to toilet training.* Bantam Books.

Wolraich, M. L., Hagan, J. F., Allan, C., Chan, E., Davison, D., Earls, M., & Zurhellen, W. (2019). Clinical practice guideline for the diagnosis, evaluation, and treatment of attention-deficit/hyperactivity disorder in children and adolescents. *Pediatrics, 144*(4).

Wolters, F. J., Chibnik, L. B., Waziry, R., Anderson, R., Berr, C., Beiser, A., Bis, J. C., Blacker, D., Bos, D., Brayne, C., Dartigues, J.-F., Darweesh, S. K. L., Davis-Plourde, K. L., Wolf, F. de, Debette, S., Dufouil, C., Fornage, M., Goudsmit, J., Grasset, L., ... Hofman, A. (2020). Twenty-seven-year time trends in dementia incidence in Europe and the United States: The Alzheimer Cohorts Consortium. *Neurology, 95*(5), e519–e531. https://doi.org/10.1212/WNL.0000000000010022

Wolters, F. J., & Ikram, M. A. (2019). Epidemiology of vascular dementia. *Arteriosclerosis, Thrombosis, and Vascular Biology, 39*(8), 1542–1549. https://doi.org/10.1161/ATVBAHA.119.311908

Wong, A., Prin, M., Purcell, L. N., Kadyaudzu, C., & Charles, A. (2020). Intensive care unit bed utilization and head injury burden in a resource-poor setting. *The American Surgeon, 86*(12), 1736–1740. https://doi.org/10.1177/0003134820950282

Wong, A. W., & Landes, S. D. (2021). Expanding understanding of racial-ethnic differences in ADHD prevalence rates among children to include Asians and Alaskan Natives/American Indians. *Journal of Attention Disorders,* 10870547211027932.

Wong, C. L., Ip, W. Y., Kwok, B. M. C., Choi, K. C., Ng, B. K. W., & Chan, C. W. H. (2018). Effects of therapeutic play on children undergoing cast-removal procedures: A randomised controlled trial. *BMJ Open, 8*(7), e021071. https://doi.org/10.1136/bmjopen-2017-021071

Wong, J. D., Marshall, A. D., & Feinberg, M. E. (2021). Intimate partner aggression during the early parenting years: The role of dissatisfaction with division of labor and childcare. *Couple and Family Psychology: Research and Practice, 10*(1), 1–16. https://doi.org/10.1037/cfp0000156

Wood, A. M., Kaptoge, S., Butterworth, A. S., Willeit, P., Warnakula, S., Bolton, T., Paige, E., Paul, D. S., Sweeting, M., Burgess, S., Bell, S., Astle, W., Stevens, D., Koulman, A., Selmer, R. M., Verschuren, W. M. M., Sato, S., Njølstad, I., Woodward, M., ... Danesh, J. (2018). Risk thresholds for alcohol consumption: Combined analysis of individual-participant data for 599 912 current drinkers in 83 prospective studies. *The Lancet, 391*(10129), 1513–1523. https://doi.org/10.1016/S0140-6736(18)30134-X

Wood, D., Bruner, J. S., & Ross, G. (1976). The role of tutoring in problem solving. *Journal of Child Psychology and Psychiatry, 17*(2), 89–100. https://doi.org/10.1111/j.1469-7610.1976.tb00381.x

Wood, D., Crapnell, T., Lau, L., Bennett, A., Lotstein, D., Ferris, M., & Kuo, A. (2018). Emerging adulthood as a critical stage in the life course. In N. Halfon, C. B. Forrest, R. M. Lerner, & E. M. Faustman (Eds.), *Handbook of life course health development* (pp. 123–143). Springer. https://doi.org/10.1007/978-3-319-47143-3_7

Wood, M. A., Bukowski, W. M., & Lis, E. (2016). The digital self: How social media serves as a setting that shapes youth's emotional experiences. *Adolescent Research Review, 1*(2), 163–173. https://doi.org/10.1007/s40894-015-0014-8

Woods, S. B., Priest, J. B., & Roberson, P. N. (2020). Family versus intimate partners: Estimating who matters more for health in a 20-year longitudinal study. *Journal of Family Psychology, 34*(2), 247.

Woodworth, K. R. (2020). Birth and infant outcomes following laboratory-confirmed SARS-CoV-2 infection in pregnancy—SET-NET, 16 jurisdictions, March 29–October 14, 2020. *MMWR. Morbidity and Mortality Weekly Report, 69.* https://doi.org/10.15585/mmwr.mm6944e2

Woolf, S. H., Chapman, D. A., Buchanich, J. M., Bobby, K. J., Zimmerman, E. B., & Blackburn, S. M. (2018). Changes in midlife death rates across racial and ethnic groups in the United States: Systematic analysis of vital statistics. *BMJ, 362.*

World Bank. (2015). *Women, business and the law 2016: Getting to equal.* https://doi.org/10.1596/978-1-4648-0677-3

World Bank. (2020). *Reversals of fortune: Poverty and shared prosperity 2020.*

World Economic Forum. (2019). *Global gender gap report 2020* [Insight report].

World Health Organization (WHO). (2006). *WHO child growth standards: Length/height-for-age, weight-for-age, weight-for-length, weight-for-height and body mass index-for-age: Methods and development.*

World Health Organization (WHO). (2015). *World report on ageing and health.*

World Health Organization (WHO). (2017). *Depression and other common mental disorders: Global health estimates* (No. WHO/MSD/MER/2017.2).

World Health Organization (WHO). (2018). *Addressing the rising prevalence of hearing loss.*

World Health Organization (WHO). (2018). *Air pollution and child health: Prescribing clean air.* https://www.who.int/publications-detail-redirect/air-pollution-and-child-health

World Health Organization (WHO). (2018). *The global network for age-friendly cities and communities: Looking back over the last decade, looking forward to the next* (No. WHO/FWC/ALC/18.4).

World Health Organization (WHO). (2019). *Guidelines on physical activity, sedentary behaviour and sleep for children under 5 years of age.*

World Health Organization (WHO). (2019). *Trends in maternal mortality 2000 to 2017: Estimates by WHO, UNICEF, UNFPA, World Bank Group and the United Nations Population Division.* https://apps.who.int/iris/handle/10665/327595

World Health Organization (WHO). (2020). *Children: Improving survival and well-being* [Fact sheet]. https://www.who.int/news-room/fact-sheets/detail/children-reducing-mortality

World Health Organization (WHO). (2020). *Companion of choice during labour and childbirth for improved quality of care. Evidence-to-action brief, 2020.*

World Health Organization (WHO). (2020, March 26). *Disability considerations during the COVID-19 outbreak* [Technical document].

World Health Organization (WHO). (2020). *Global health estimates 2019: Deaths by cause, age, sex, by country and by region, 2000–2019.*

World Health Organization (WHO). (2020). *Global health estimates 2020: Deaths by cause, age, sex, by country and by region, 2000–2019.*

World Health Organization (WHO). (2020). *Life expectancy and healthy life expectancy: Data by country* (World Health Statistics).

World Health Organization (WHO). (2020). *WHO guidelines on physical activity and sedentary behaviour.*

World Health Organization (WHO). (2021). *International classification of disease for mortality and morbidity statistics, eleventh revision (ICD-11).*

World Health Organization (WHO). (2021). *Obesity and overweight* [Fact sheet].

World Health Organization (WHO). (2021). *Suicide worldwide in 2019: Global health estimates.*

World Health Organization (WHO). (2021). *Violence against women* [Fact sheet].

World Health Organization (WHO). (2021). *WHO report on the global tobacco epidemic, 2021: Addressing new and emerging products.*

Wörmann, V., Holodynski, M., Kärtner, J., & Keller, H. (2014). The emergence of social smiling: The interplay of maternal and infant imitation during the first three months in cross-cultural comparison. *Journal of Cross-Cultural Psychology, 45*(3), 339–361. https://doi.org/10.1177/0022022113509134

Worthman, C. M., Dockray, S., & Marceau, K. (2019). Puberty and the evolution of developmental science. *Journal of Research on Adolescence, 29*(1), 9–31. https://doi.org/10.1111/jora.12411

Wray-Lake, L., Arruda, E. H., & Schulenberg, J. E. (2020). Civic development across the transition to adulthood in a national U.S. sample: Variations by race/ethnicity, parent education, and gender. *Developmental Psychology, 56*(10), 1948–1967. https://doi.org/10.1037/dev0001101

Wright, H., Jenks, R. A., & Demeyere, N. (2019). Frequent sexual activity predicts specific cognitive abilities in older adults. *The Journals of Gerontology: Series B, 74*(1), 47–51. https://doi.org/10.1093/geronb/gbx065

Wright, M. R. (2017). *Cohabitation among older adults: Well-being, relationships with adult children, and perceptions of care availability.* Bowling Green State University. https://etd.ohiolink.edu/apexprod/rws_olink/r/1501/10?clear=10&p10_accession_num=bgsu1497986334237288

Wright, M. R. (2019). Relationship quality among older cohabitors: A comparison to remarrieds. *The Journals of Gerontology: Series B, 75*(8), 1808–1817. https://doi.org/10.1093/geronb/gbz069

Wright, M. R., Brown, S. L., & Manning, W. D. (2018, April). *Midlife marital quality: Twenty-five years of change.* PAA 2018 Annual Meeting, PAA.

Wright, M. R., Hammersmith, A. M., Brown, S. L., & Lin, I.-F. (2019). The roles of marital dissolution and subsequent repartnering on loneliness in later life. *The Journals of Gerontology Series B: Psychological Sciences and Social Sciences, 75*(8), 1796–1807. https://doi.org/10.1093/geronb/gbz121

Wright, P. J., Herbenick, D., & Paul, B. (2020). Adolescent condom use, parent-adolescent sexual health communication, and pornography: Findings from a US probability sample. *Health Communication, 35*(13), 1576–1582.

Wrzus, C., Hänel, M., Wagner, J., & Neyer, F. J. (2013). Social network changes and life events across the life span: A meta-analysis. *Psychological Bulletin, 139*(1), 53–80. https://doi.org/10.1037/a0028601

Wrzus, C., Zimmermann, J., Mund, M., & Neyer, F. J. (2017). Friendships in young and middle adulthood: Normative patterns and personality differences. In M. Hojjat & A. Moyer (Eds), *The psychology of friendship* (pp. 21–38). Oxford University Press.

Wu, D., Roehling, M. V., & Dulebohn, J. (2020). The impact of obesity level on the relationship between weight bias and employment discrimination. *Academy of Management Proceedings, 2020*(1), 13585. https://doi.org/10.5465/AMBPP.2020.260

Wu, L., Feng, X., He, A., Ding, Y., Zhou, X., & Xu, Z. (2017). Prenatal exposure to the Great Chinese Famine and mid-age hypertension. *PLOS One, 12*(5), e0176413. https://doi.org/10.1371/journal.pone.0176413

Wu, L.-T., & Blazer, D. G. (2014). Substance use disorders and psychiatric comorbidity in mid and later life: A review. *International Journal of Epidemiology, 43*(2), 304–317. https://doi.org/10.1093/ije/dyt173

Wu, P. Z., O'Malley, J. T., de Gruttola, V., & Liberman, M. C. (2020). Age-related hearing loss is dominated by damage to inner ear sensory cells, not the cellular battery that powers them. *Journal of Neuroscience, 40*(33), 6357–6366.

Wu, Q., & Feng, X. (2020). Infant emotion regulation and cortisol response during the first 2 years of life: Association with maternal parenting profiles. *Developmental Psychobiology, 62*(8), 1076–1091. https://doi.org/10.1002/dev.21965

Wu, Q., Xu, Y., & Lin, G. (2019). Trends and disparities in self-reported and measured osteoporosis among US adults, 2007–2014. *Journal of Clinical Medicine, 8*(12), 2052. https://doi.org/10.3390/jcm8122052

Wu, S., Powers, S., Zhu, W., & Hannun, Y. A. (2016). Substantial contribution of extrinsic risk factors to cancer development. *Nature, 529*(7584), 43–47.

Wu, S. A., Morrison-Koechl, J., Slaughter, S. E., Middleton, L. E., Carrier, N., McAiney, C., Lengyel, C., & Keller, H. (2020). Family member eating assistance and food intake in long-term care: A secondary data analysis of the M3 Study. *Journal of Advanced Nursing, 76*(11), 2933–2944. https://doi.org/10.1111/jan.14480

Wühl, E. (2019). Hypertension in childhood obesity. *Acta Paediatrica, 108*(1), 37–43. https://doi.org/10.1111/apa.14551

Wutzler, A., Mavrogiorgou, P., Winter, C., & Juckel, G. (2011). Elevation of brain serotonin during dying. *Neuroscience Letters, 498*(1), 20–21. https://doi.org/10.1016/j.neulet.2011.04.051

Wyman, M. F., Shiovitz-Ezra, S., & Bengel, J. (2018). Ageism in the health care system: Providers, patients, and systems. In L. Ayalon & C. Tesch-Römer (Eds.), *Contemporary perspectives on ageism* (pp. 193–212). Springer.

Wyshak, G., & Frisch, R. (1982). Evidence for a secular trend in age of menarche. *The New England Journal of Medicine, 306*, 1033–1035. https://doi.org/10.1056/NEJM198204293061707

Wyss-Coray, T. (2016). Ageing, neurodegeneration and brain rejuvenation. *Nature, 539*(7628), 180–186. https://doi.org/10.1038/nature20411

Xi, B., Veeranki, S. P., Zhao, M., Ma, C., Yan, Y., & Mi, J. (2017). Relationship of alcohol consumption to all-cause, cardiovascular, and cancer-related mortality in U.S. adults. *Journal of the American College of Cardiology, 70*(8), 913–922. https://doi.org/10.1016/j.jacc.2017.06.054

Xia, M., Fosco, G. M., Lippold, M. A., & Feinberg, M. E. (2018). A developmental perspective on young adult romantic relationships: Examining family and individual factors in adolescence. *Journal of Youth and Adolescence, 47*(7), 1499–1516. https://doi.org/10.1007/s10964-018-0815-8

Xiao, S. X., Martin, C. L., DeLay, D., & Cook, R. E. (2021). A double-edged sword: Children's intergroup gender attitudes have social consequences for the beholder. *Developmental Psychology, 57*(9), 1510–1524. https://doi.org/10.1037/dev0001065

Xie, M., Fowle, J., Ip, P. S., Haskin, M., & Yip, T. (2021). Profiles of ethnic-racial identity, socialization, and model minority experiences: Associations with well-being among Asian American adolescents. *Journal of Youth and Adolescence, 50*(6), 1173–1188. https://doi.org/10.1007/s10964-021-01436-w

Xie, W., Lundberg, D. J., Collins, J. M., Johnston, S. S., Waggoner, J. R., Hsiao, C.-W., Preston, S. H., Manson, J. E., & Stokes, A. C. (2020). Association of weight loss between early adulthood and midlife with all-cause mortality risk in the US. *JAMA Network Open, 3*(8), e2013448–e2013448. https://doi.org/10.1001/jamanetworkopen.2020.13448

Xu, J. (2019). Learning "merit" in a Chinese preschool: Bringing the anthropological perspective to understanding moral development. *American Anthropologist, 121*(3), 655–666.

Xu, J. J., Chen, J. T., Belin, T. R., Brookmeyer, R. S., Suchard, M. A., & Ramirez, C. M. (2021). Racial and ethnic disparities in years of potential life lost attributable to COVID-19 in the United States: An analysis of 45 states and the District of Columbia. *International Journal of Environmental Research and Public Health, 18*(6), 2921. https://doi.org/10.3390/ijerph18062921

Xu, Y., & Wu, Q. (2018). Decreasing trend of bone mineral density in US multiethnic population: Analysis of continuous NHANES 2005–2014. *Osteoporosis International, 29*(11), 2437–2446.

Yadav, K. N., Gabler, N., Cooney, E., Kent, S., Kim, J., Herbst, N., Mante, A., Halpern, S. D., & Courtright, K. R. (2017). Prevalence of advance directives in the United States: A systematic review. B93. Updates in advanced care planning and end of life care in respiratory and critical illness. *American Journal of Respiratory and Critical Care Medicine, 195*, A4633. https://doi.org/10.1164/ajrccm-conference.2017.195.1_MeetingAbstracts.A4633

Yafi, F. A., Jenkins, L., Albersen, M., Corona, G., Isidori, A. M., Goldfarb, S., Maggi, M., Nelson, C. J., Parish, S., Salonia, A., Tan, R., Mulhall, J. P., & Hellstrom, W. J. G. (2016). Erectile dysfunction. *Nature Reviews. Disease Primers, 2*, 16003. https://doi.org/10.1038/nrdp.2016.3

Yakushko, O. (2019). Eugenics and its evolution in the history of western psychology: A critical archival review. *Psychotherapy and Politics International, 17*(2), e1495. https://doi.org/10.1002/ppi.1495

Yamaguchi, T., Maeda, I., Hatano, Y., Suh, S.-Y., Cheng, S.-Y., Kim, S. H., Chen, P.-J., Morita, T., Tsuneto, S., & Mori, M. (2021). Communication and behavior of palliative care physicians of patients with cancer near end of life in three east Asian countries. *Journal of Pain and Symptom Management, 61*(2), 315–322.e1. https://doi.org/10.1016/j.jpainsymman.2020.07.031

Yamamoto-Mitani, N., Aneshensel, C. S., & Levy-Storms, L. (2002). Patterns of family visiting with institutionalized elders: The case of dementia. *The Journals of Gerontology: Series B, 57*(4), S234–S246. https://doi.org/10.1093/geronb/57.4.S234

Yamato, T. P., Maher, C. G., Traeger, A. C., Wiliams, C. M., & Kamper, S. J. (2018). Do schoolbags cause back pain in children and adolescents? A systematic review. *British Journal of Sports Medicine, 52*(19), 1241–1245.

Yan, Y., Bazzano, L. A., Juonala, M., Raitakari, O. T., Viikari, J. S. A., Prineas, R., Dwyer, T., Sinaiko, A., Burns, T. L., Daniels, S. R., Woo, J. G., Khoury, P. R., Urbina, E. M., Jacobs, D. R., Hu, T., Steinberger, J., Venn, A., & Chen, W. (2019). Long-term burden of increased body mass index from childhood on adult dyslipidemia: The i3C consortium study. *Journal of Clinical Medicine, 8*(10), 1725. https://doi.org/10.3390/jcm8101725

Yancy, C. W. (2020). COVID-19 and african americans. *JAMA, 323*(19), 1891–1892.

Yancy, G. (2020a, May 20). Opinion | 'I believed that I would see her again.' *The New York Times.* https://www.nytimes.com/2020/05/20/opinion/christianity-death-afterlife.html

Yancy, G. (2020b, October 20). Opinion | How should an atheist think about death? *The New York Times.* https://www.nytimes.com/2020/10/20/opinion/philosophy-death-atheism.html

Yang, J. L., Anyon, Y., Pauline, M., Wiley, K. E., Cash, D., Downing, B. J., Greer, E., Kelty, E., Morgan, T. L., & Pisciotta, L. (2018). "We have to educate every single student, not just the ones that look like us": Support service providers' beliefs about the root causes of the school-to-prison pipeline for youth of color. *Equity & Excellence in Education, 51*(3–4), 316–331. https://doi.org/10.1080/10665684.2018.1539358

Yang, S., Martin, R. M., Oken, E., Hameza, M., Doniger, G., Amit, S., Patel, R., Thompson, J., Rifas-Shiman, S. L., Vilchuck, K., Bogdanovich, N., & Kramer, M. S. (2018). Breastfeeding during infancy and neurocognitive function in adolescence: 16-year follow-up of the PROBIT cluster-randomized trial. *PLoS Medicine, 15*(4), e1002554. https://doi.org/10.1371/journal.pmed.1002554

Yang, Y., Reid, M. C., Grol-Prokopczyk, H., & Pillemer, K. (2021). Racial-ethnic disparities in pain intensity and interference among middle-aged and older U.S. adults. *The Journals of Gerontology: Series A*, glab207. https://doi.org/10.1093/gerona/glab207

Yang, Y., & Wang, Q. (2019). Culture in emotional development. In V. LoBue, K. Pérez-Edgar, & K. A. Buss (Eds.), *Handbook of emotional development* (pp. 569–593). Springer International Publishing. https://doi.org/10.1007/978-3-030-17332-6_22

Yanık, B., & Yasar, M. (2018). An ethnographic approach to peer culture in a Turkish preschool classroom. *International Electronic Journal of Elementary Education, 10*(4), 489–496.

Yaniv, A. U., Salomon, R., Waidergoren, S., Shimon-Raz, O., Djalovski, A., & Feldman, R. (2021). Synchronous caregiving from birth to adulthood tunes humans' social brain. *Proceedings of the National Academy of Sciences, 118*(14). https://doi.org/10.1073/pnas.2012900118

Yap, C. X., Sidorenko, J., Wu, Y., Kemper, K. E., Yang, J., Wray, N. R., Robinson, M. R., & Visscher, P. M. (2018). Dissection of genetic variation and evidence for pleiotropy in male pattern baldness. *Nature Communications, 9*(1), 5407. https://doi.org/10.1038/s41467-018-07862-y

Yaremych, H. E., & Volling, B. L. (2020). Sibling relationships and mothers' and fathers' emotion socialization practices: A within-family perspective. *Early Child Development and Care, 190*(2), 195–209. https://doi.org/10.1080/03004430.2018.1461095

Yasnitsky, A. (2018). *Vygotsky: An intellectual biography.* Routledge.

Yasnitsky, A., & van der Veer, R. (2015). *Revisionist revolution in Vygotsky studies: The state of the art.* Routledge.

Yasui, M., Dishion, T. J., Stormshak, E., & Ball, A. (2015). Socialization of culture and coping with discrimination among American Indian families: Examining cultural correlates of youth outcomes. *Journal of the Society for Social Work and Research, 6*(3), 317–341. https://doi.org/10.1086/682575

Yates, J. (2018). Perspective: The long-term effects of light exposure on establishment of newborn circadian rhythm. *Journal of Clinical Sleep Medicine: Official Publication of the American Academy of Sleep Medicine, 14*(10), 1829–1830. https://doi.org/10.5664/jcsm.7426

Yavorsky, J. E. (2019). Uneven patterns of inequality: An audit analysis of hiring-related practices by gendered and classed contexts. *Social Forces, 98*(2), 461–492.

Yavorsky, J. E., Ruggs, E. N., & Dill, J. S. (2021). Gendered skills and unemployed men's resistance to "women's work." *Gender, Work & Organization, 28*(4), 1524–1545. https://doi.org/10.1111/gwao.12694

Yazejian, N., Bryant, D., Freel, K., & Burchinal, M. (2015). High-quality early education: Age of entry and time in care differences in student outcomes for English-only and dual language learners. *Early Childhood Research Quarterly, 32*(Supplement C), 23–39. https://doi.org/10.1016/j.ecresq.2015.02.002

Yazejian, N., Bryant, D. M., Hans, S., Horm, D., St. Clair, L., File, N., & Burchinal, M. (2017). Child and parenting outcomes after 1 year of Educare. *Child Development, 88*(5), 1671–1688. https://doi.org/10.1111/cdev.12688

Ybarra, M. L., Price-Feeney, M., & Mitchell, K. J. (2019). A cross-sectional study examining the (in) congruency of sexual identity, sexual behavior, and romantic attraction among adolescents in the US. *The Journal of Pediatrics, 214*, 201–208.

Ye, J., Betrán, A. P., Vela, M. G., Souza, J. P., & Zhang, J. (2014). Searching for the optimal rate of medically necessary cesarean delivery. *Birth, 41*(3), 237–244. https://doi.org/10.1111/birt.12104

Yeager, D. S., Dahl, R. E., & Dweck, C. S. (2018). Why interventions to influence adolescent behavior often fail but could succeed. *Perspectives on Psychological Science, 13*(1), 101–122.

Yen, K., Mehta, H. H., Kim, S.-J., Lue, Y., Hoang, J., Guerrero, N., Port, J., Bi, Q., Navarrete, G., Brandhorst, S., Lewis, K. N., Wan, J., Swerdloff, R., Mattison, J. A., Buffenstein, R., Breton, C. V., Wang, C., Longo, V., Atzmon, G., … Cohen, P. (2020). The mitochondrial derived peptide humanin is a regulator of lifespan and healthspan. *Aging, 12*(12), 11185–11199. https://doi.org/10.18632/aging.103534

Yeo, S. C., Jos, A. M., Erwin, C., Lee, S. M., Lee, X. K., Lo, J. C., Chee, M., & Gooley, J. J. (2019). Associations of sleep duration on school nights with self-rated health, overweight, and depression symptoms in adolescents: Problems and possible solutions. *Sleep Medicine, 60*, 96–108.

Yeung, W.-J. J., & Yang, Y. (2020). Labor market uncertainties for youth and young adults: An international perspective. *The Annals of the American Academy of Political and Social Science, 688*(1), 7–19. https://doi.org/10.1177/0002716220913487

Yiallouris, A., Tsioutis, C., Agapidaki, E., Zafeiri, M., Agouridis, A. P., Ntourakis, D., & Johnson, E. O. (2019). Adrenal aging and its implications on stress responsiveness in humans. *Frontiers in Endocrinology, 10*, 54.

Yip, T. (2014). Ethnic identity in everyday life: The influence of identity development status. *Child Development, 85*(1), 205–219.

Yip, T., Wang, Y., Mootoo, C., & Mirpuri, S. (2019). Moderating the association between discrimination and adjustment: A meta-analysis of ethnic/racial identity. *Developmental Psychology, 55*(6), 1274–1298. https://doi.org/10.1037/dev0000708

Yogeeswaran, K., Verkuyten, M., Osborne, D., & Sibley, C. G. (2018). "I have a dream" of a colorblind nation? Examining the relationship between racial colorblindness, system justification, and support for policies that redress inequalities. *Journal of Social Issues, 74*(2), 282–298. https://doi.org/10.1111/josi.12269

Yoo, J., & Ryff, C. D. (2019). Longitudinal profiles of psychological well-being and health: Findings from Japan. *Frontiers in Psychology, 10*, 2746. https://doi.org/10.3389/fpsyg.2019.02746

Yoon, E., Adams, K., Clawson, A., Chang, H., Surya, S., & Jérémie-Brink, G. (2017). East Asian adolescents' ethnic identity development and cultural integration: A qualitative investigation. *Journal of Counseling Psychology, 64*(1), 65–79. https://doi.org/10.1037/cou0000181

Yoon, E., Coburn, C., & Spence, S. A. (2019). Perceived discrimination and mental health among older African Americans: The role of psychological well-being. *Aging & Mental Health, 23*(4), 461–469. https://doi.org/10.1080/13607863.2017.1423034

Yoon, J., & Lee, C. (2019). Neighborhood outdoor play of White and Non-White Hispanic children: Cultural differences and environmental disparities. *Landscape and Urban Planning, 187*, 11–22. https://doi.org/10.1016/j.landurbplan.2019.01.010

York, B. N., Loeb, S., & Doss, C. (2019). One step at a time the effects of an early literacy text-messaging program for parents of preschoolers. *Journal of Human Resources, 54*(3), 537–566.

Yorke, L., Rose, P., Woldehanna, T., & Hagos, B. (2021). Primary school-level responses to the COVID-19 pandemic in Ethiopia: Evidence from phone surveys of school principals and teachers. *Perspectives in Education, 39*(1), 189–206. https://doi.org/10.18820/2519593X/pie.v39.i1.12

Yoshikawa, H., Weiland, C., & Brooks-Gunn, J. (2016). When does preschool matter? *The Future of Children, 26*(2), 21–35.

Yosso, T. J. (2005). Whose culture has capital? A critical race theory discussion of community cultural wealth. *Race Ethnicity and Education, 8*(1), 69–91. https://doi.org/10.1080/1361332052000341006

Yosso, T. J. (2006). Whose culture has capital? A critical race theory discussion of community cultural wealth. *Race Ethnicity and Education, 8*(1), 69–91. https://doi.org/10.1080/1361332052000341006

Yosso, T. J. (2020). Critical race media literacy for these urgent times. *International Journal of Multicultural Education, 22*(2), 5–13. https://doi.org/10.18251/ijme.v22i2.2685

Yosso, T. J., & Solórzano, D. G. (2005). Conceptualizing a critical race theory in sociology. In M. Romero & E. Margolis (Eds.), *The Blackwell companion to social inequalities* (pp. 117–146). John Wiley & Sons. https://doi.org/10.1002/9780470996973.ch7

Young, W. R., & Williams, A. M. (2015). How fear of falling can increase fall-risk in older adults: Applying psychological theory to practical observations. *Gait & Posture, 41*(1), 7–12. https://doi.org/10.1016/j.gaitpost.2014.09.006

YRBS. (2019). *Youth online: High school YRBS—2019 results.* Centers for Disease Control and Prevention. https://nccd.cdc.gov/youthonline/App/Results.aspx?

Yu, D., Caughy, M. O., Smith, E. P., Oshri, A., & Owen, M. T. (2020). Severe poverty and growth in behavioral self-regulation: The mediating role of parenting. *Journal of Applied Developmental Psychology, 68*, 101135. https://doi.org/10.1016/j.appdev.2020.101135

Yu, E., & Cantor, P. (2016, December 19). Putting PISA results to the test. *The 180 blog.* Turnaround For Children. https://turnaroundusa.org/2015-pisa-analysis/

Yu, K., Wu, S., Jang, Y., Chou, C.-P., Wilber, K. H., Aranda, M. P., & Chi, I. (2020). Longitudinal assessment of the relationships between geriatric conditions and loneliness. *Journal of the American Medical Directors Association, 22*(5), P1107–1113. https://doi.org/10.1016/j.jamda.2020.09.002

Yu, Y., & Kushnir, T. (2020). The ontogeny of cumulative culture: Individual toddlers vary in faithful imitation and goal emulation. *Developmental Science, 23*(1), e12862. https://doi.org/10.1111/desc.12862

Yuan, P., Voelkle, M. C., & Raz, N. (2018). Fluid intelligence and gross structural properties of the cerebral cortex in middle-aged and older adults: A multi-occasion longitudinal study. *NeuroImage, 172*, 21–30. https://doi.org/10.1016/j.neuroimage.2018.01.032

Yuan, Y., Louis, C., Cabral, H., Schneider, J. C., Ryan, C. M., & Kazis, L. E. (2018). Socioeconomic and geographic disparities in accessing nursing homes with high star ratings. *Journal of the American Medical Directors Association, 19*(10), 852–859.e2. https://doi.org/10.1016/j.jamda.2018.05.017

Yücel, G., Kendirci, M., & Gül, Ü. (2018). Menstrual characteristics and related problems in 9- to 18-year-old Turkish school girls. *Journal of Pediatric and Adolescent Gynecology, 31*(4), 350–355.

Yudell, M., Roberts, D., DeSalle, R., & Rishkoff, S. (2016). Taking race out of human genetics. *Science, 351*(6273), 564–565.

Yun, H.-Y., & Juvonen, J. (2020). Navigating the healthy context paradox: Identifying classroom characteristics that improve the psychological adjustment of bullying victims. *Journal of Youth and Adolescence, 49*(11), 2203–2213. https://doi.org/10.1007/s10964-020-01300-3

Zacharopoulos, G., Sella, F., & Kadosh, R. C. (2021). The impact of a lack of mathematical education on brain development and future attainment. *Proceedings of the National Academy of Sciences, 118*(24). https://doi.org/10.1073/pnas.2013155118

Zaff, J. F., Hart, D., Flanagan, C. A., Youniss, J., & Levine, P. (2010). Developing civic engagement within a civic context. In M. E. Lamb, A. M. Freund, & R. M. Lerner (Eds.), *The handbook of life-span development: Vol. 2. Social and emotional development* (pp. 590–630). John Wiley

& Sons, Inc. http://onlinelibrary.wiley.com/doi/10.1002/9780470880166.hlsd002015/full

Zahodne, L. B., Ajrouch, K. J., Sharifian, N., & Antonucci, T. C. (2019). Social relations and age-related change in memory. *Psychology and Aging, 34*(6), 751–765. https://doi.org/10.1037/pag0000369

Zahodne, L. B., Manly, J. J., Smith, J., Seeman, T., & Lachman, M. (2017). Socioeconomic, health, and psychosocial mediators of racial disparities in cognition in early, middle, and late adulthood. *Psychology and Aging, 32*(2), 118–130. https://doi.org/10.1037/pag0000154

Zahodne, L. B., Morris, E. P., Sharifian, N., Zaheed, A. B., Kraal, A. Z., & Sol, K. (2020). Everyday discrimination and subsequent cognitive abilities across five domains. *Neuropsychology, 34*(7), 783–790.

Zahodne, L. B., Sharifian, N., Kraal, A. Z., Morris, E. P., Sol, K., Zaheed, A. B., Meister, L., Mayeux, R., Schupf, N., Manly, J. J., & Brickman, A. M. (2022). Longitudinal associations between racial discrimination and hippocampal and white matter hyperintensity volumes among older Black adults. *Social Science & Medicine, 114789.* https://doi.org/10.1016/j.socscimed.2022.114789

Zahodne, L. B., Sharifian, N., Kraal, A. Z., Zaheed, A. B., Sol, K., Morris, E. P., Schupf, N., Manly, J. J., & Brickman, A. M. (2021). Socioeconomic and psychosocial mechanisms underlying racial/ethnic disparities in cognition among older adults. *Neuropsychology, 35*(3), 265–275.

Zaidi, B., & Morgan, S. P. (2017). The second demographic transition theory: A review and appraisal. *Annual Review of Sociology, 43*, 473–492. https://doi.org/10.1146/annurev-soc-060116-053442

Zajacova, A., Grol-Prokopczyk, H., & Zimmer, Z. (2021). Pain trends among American adults, 2002–2018: Patterns, disparities, and correlates. *Demography, 58*(2), 711–738. https://doi.org/10.1215/00703370-8977691

Zajacova, A., Montez, J. K., & Herd, P. (2014). Socioeconomic disparities in health among older adults and the implications for the retirement age debate: A brief report. *Journals of Gerontology Series B: Psychological Sciences and Social Sciences, 69*(6), 973–978.

Zakin, E. (2011). *Psychoanalytic feminism.* https://stanford.library.sydney.edu.au/entries/feminism-psychoanalysis/

Zamir, O., Gewirtz, A. H., Dekel, R., Lavi, T., & Tangir, G. (2020). Mothering under political violence: Posttraumatic symptoms, observed maternal parenting practices and child externalising behaviour. *International Journal of Psychology, 55*(1), 123–132. https://doi.org/10.1002/ijop.12557

Zaninotto, P., Batty, G. D., Stenholm, S., Kawachi, I., Hyde, M., Goldberg, M., Westerlund, H., Vahtera, J., & Head, J. (2020). Socioeconomic inequalities in disability-free life expectancy in older people from England and the United States: A cross-national population-based study. *The Journals of Gerontology: Series A, 75*(5), 906–913. https://doi.org/10.1093/gerona/glz266

Zaragoza Scherman, A., Salgado, S., Shao, Z., & Berntsen, D. (2015). Life span distribution and content of positive and negative autobiographical memories across cultures. *Psychology of Consciousness: Theory, Research, and Practice, 2*(4), 475–489. https://doi.org/10.1037/cns0000070

Zárate, S., Stevnsner, T., & Gredilla, R. (2017). Role of estrogen and other sex hormones in brain aging. Neuroprotection and DNA repair. *Frontiers in Aging Neuroscience, 9*, 430. https://doi.org/10.3389/fnagi.2017.00430

Zarit, S. H., Polenick, C. A., DePasquale, N., Liu, Y., & Bangerter, L. R. (2019). Family support and caregiving in middle and late life. In B. H. Fiese (Ed.), *APA handbook of contemporary family psychology: Applications and broad impact of family psychology* (Vol. 2, pp. 103–119). American Psychological Association.

Zarrett, N., Liu, Y., Vandell, D. L., & Simpkins, S. D. (2020). The role of organized activities in supporting youth moral and civic character development: A review of the literature. *Adolescent Research Review, 6*(2), 199–227.

Zeanah, C. H., Gunnar, M. R., McCall, R. B., Kreppner, J. M., & Fox, N. A. (2011). Sensitive periods. *Monographs of the Society for Research in Child Development,*

76(4), 147–162. https://doi.org/10.1111/j.1540-5834.2011.00631.x

Zee, K. S., & Weiss, D. (2019). High-quality relationships strengthen the benefits of a younger subjective age across adulthood. *Psychology and Aging, 34*(3), 374–388. https://doi.org/10.1037/pag0000349

Zeidenberg, M., Cho, S.-W., & Jenkins, D. (2010). *Washington State's integrated basic education and skills training program (I-BEST): New evidence of effectiveness* (CCRC Working Paper No. 20). Community College Research Center, Columbia University. http://eric.ed.gov/?id=ED512261

Zeiders, K. H., Umaña-Taylor, A. J., Carbajal, S., & Pech, A. (2021). Police discrimination among Black, Latina/x/o, and White adolescents: Examining frequency and relations to academic functioning. *Journal of Adolescence, 90*, 91–99. https://doi.org/10.1016/j.adolescence.2021.06.001

Zeifman, D. M., & St James-Roberts, I. (2017). Parenting the crying infant. *Current Opinion in Psychology, 15*, 149–154.

Zelazo, P. D. (2020). Executive function and psychopathology: A neurodevelopmental perspective. *Annual Review of Clinical Psychology, 16*(1), 431–454. https://doi.org/10.1146/annurev-clinpsy-072319-024242

Zelazo, P. D., & Carlson, S. M. (2020). The neurodevelopment of executive function skills: Implications for academic achievement gaps. *Psychology & Neuroscience, 13*(3), 273.

Zelazo, P. D., & Lee, W. S. C. (2010). Brain development. In *The handbook of life-span development*. Wiley. https://doi.org/10.1002/9780470880166.hlsd001004

Zembic, A., Eckel, N., Stefan, N., Baudry, J., & Schulze, M. B. (2021). An empirically derived definition of metabolically healthy obesity based on risk of cardiovascular and total mortality. *JAMA Network Open, 4*(5), e218505. https://doi.org/10.1001/jamanetworkopen.2021.8505

Zeng, S., Pereira, B., Larson, A., Corr, C. P., O'Grady, C., & Stone-MacDonald, A. (2021). Preschool suspension and expulsion for young children with disabilities. *Exceptional Children, 87*(2), 199–216. https://doi.org/10.1177/0014402920949832

Zentall, S. R., & Morris, B. J. (2010). "Good job, you're so smart": The effects of inconsistency of praise type on young children's motivation. *Journal of Experimental Child Psychology, 107*(2), 155–163. https://doi.org/10.1016/j.jecp.2010.04.015

Zero to Three. (2016a). *Celebrating all the moms out there. Hey moms—We hear you on Mother's Day and every day.*

Zero to Three. (2016b). *The discipline dilemma: Guiding principles for managing challenging behaviors.*

Zero to Three. (2016c). *Tuning in: Parents of young children tell us what they think, know and need.*

Zhang, B., Ma, S., Rachmin, I., He, M., Baral, P., Choi, S., & Hsu, Y. C. (2020). Hyperactivation of sympathetic nerves drives depletion of melanocyte stem cells. *Nature, 577*(7792), 676–681.

Zhang, D., Chan, D. C. C., Niu, L., Liu, H., Zou, D., Chan, A. T. Y., & Wong, S. Y. S. (2018). Meaning and its association with happiness, health and healthcare utilization: A cross-sectional study. *Journal of Affective Disorders, 227*, 795–802.

Zhang, D., Chen, Y., Hou, X., & Wu, Y. J. (2019). Near-infrared spectroscopy reveals neural perception of vocal emotions in human neonates. *Human Brain Mapping, 40*(8), 2434–2448.

Zhang, Q., Wang, C., Zhao, Q., Yang, L., Buschkuehl, M., & Jaeggi, S. M. (2019). The malleability of executive function in early childhood: Effects of schooling and targeted training. *Developmental Science, 22*(2), e12748. https://doi.org/10.1111/desc.12748

Zhang, W., & Radhakrishnan, K. (2018). Evidence on selection, optimization, and compensation strategies to optimize aging with multiple chronic conditions: A literature review. *Geriatric Nursing, 39*(5), 534–542. https://doi.org/10.1016/j.gerinurse.2018.02.013

Zhang, X., & Belsky, J. (2020). Three phases of gene × environment interaction research: Theoretical assumptions underlying gene selection. *Development and Psychopathology*, 1–12. https://doi.org/10.1017/S0954579420000966

Zhang, X., Chen, X., & Zhang, X. (2018). The impact of exposure to air pollution on cognitive performance. *Proceedings of the National Academy of Sciences, 115*(37), 9193–9197.

Zhang, X., Sayler, K., Hartman, S., & Belsky, J. (2021). Infant temperament, early-childhood parenting, and early-adolescent development: Testing alternative models of parenting × temperament interaction. *Development and Psychopathology*, 1–12. https://doi.org/10.1017/S0954579420002096

Zhang, X., Xing, C., Guan, Y., Song, X., Melloy, R., Wang, F., & Jin, X. (2016). Attitudes toward older adults: A matter of cultural values or personal values? *Psychology and Aging, 31*(1), 89.

Zhang, Y., & Ang, S. (2020). Trajectories of union transition in emerging adulthood: Socioeconomic status and race/ethnicity differences in the national longitudinal survey of youth 1997 cohort. *Journal of Marriage and Family, 82*(2), 713–732. https://doi.org/10.1111/jomf.12662

Zhang, Y., Luo, Q., Huang, C.-C., Lo, C.-Y. Z., Langley, C., Desrivières, S., Quinlan, E. B., Banaschewski, T., Millenet, S., Bokde, A. L. W., Flor, H., Garavan, H., Gowland, P., Heinz, A., Ittermann, B., Martinot, J.-L., Artiges, E., Paillère-Martinot, M.-L., Nees, F., ... for the IMAGEN consortium. (2021). The human brain is best described as being on a female/male continuum: Evidence from a neuroimaging connectivity study. *Cerebral Cortex, 31*(6), 3021–3033. https://doi.org/10.1093/cercor/bhaa408

Zhang, Y., Shi, J., Wei, H., Han, V., Zhu, W.-Z., & Liu, C. (2019). Neonate and infant brain development from birth to 2 years assessed using MRI-based quantitative susceptibility mapping. *NeuroImage, 185*, 349–360. https://doi.org/10.1016/j.neuroimage.2018.10.031

Zhang, Y., Zhao, X., Leonhart, R., Nadig, M., Wang, J., Zhao, Y., Wirsching, M., & Fritzsche, K. (2019). A cross-cultural comparison of climacteric symptoms, health-seeking behavior, and attitudes towards menopause among Mosuo women and Han Chinese women in Yunnan, China. *Transcultural Psychiatry, 56*(1), 287–301. https://doi.org/10.1177/1363461518804094

Zheng, L. R., Atherton, O. E., Trzesniewski, K., & Robins, R. W. (2020). Are self-esteem and academic achievement reciprocally related? Findings from a longitudinal study of Mexican-origin youth. *Journal of Personality, 88*(6), 1058–1074. https://doi.org/10.1111/jopy.12550

Zheng, M., Lamb, K. E., Grimes, C., Laws, R., Bolton, K., Ong, K. K., & Campbell, K. (2018). Rapid weight gain during infancy and subsequent adiposity: A systematic review and meta-analysis of evidence. *Obesity Reviews: An Official Journal of the International Association for the Study of Obesity, 19*(3), 321–332. https://doi.org/10.1111/obr.12632

Zheng, Y., Manson, J. E., Yuan, C., Liang, M. H., Grodstein, F., Stampfer, M. J., Willett, W. C., & Hu, F. B. (2017). Associations of weight gain from early to middle adulthood with major health outcomes later in life. *JAMA, 318*(3), 255–269. https://doi.org/10.1001/jama.2017.7092

Zhong, H.-H., Yu, B., Luo, D., Yang, L.-Y., Zhang, J., Jiang, H.-S., Hu, S.-J., Luo, Y.-Y., Yang, M., Hong, F., & Yang, S.-L. (2019). Roles of aging in sleep. *Neuroscience & Biobehavioral Reviews, 98*, 177–184. https://doi.org/10.1016/j.neubiorev.2019.01.013

Zhou, D., Xi, B., Zhao, M., Wang, L., & Veeranki, S. P. (2018). Uncontrolled hypertension increases risk of all-cause and cardiovascular disease mortality in US adults: The NHANES III Linked Mortality Study. *Scientific Reports, 8*(1), 9418. https://doi.org/10.1038/s41598-018-27377-2

Zhou, H., Tsoh, J. Y., Grigg-Saito, D., Tucker, P., & Liao, Y. (2014). Decreased smoking disparities among Vietnamese and Cambodian communities—Racial and Ethnic Approaches to Community Health (REACH) project, 2002–2006. *Strategies for Reducing Health Disparities—Selected CDC-Sponsored Interventions, United States, 63*(1), 37–45.

Zhou, N., Cao, H., & Leerkes, E. M. (2017). Interparental conflict and infants' behavior problems: The mediating role of maternal sensitivity. *Journal of Family Psychology, 31*(4), 464–474. https://doi.org/10.1037/fam0000288

Zhou, X., & Wu, X. (2021). Posttraumatic stress disorder and growth: Examination of joint trajectories in children and adolescents. *Development and Psychopathology*, 1–13.

Zhu, Y., Liu, J., Jiang, H., Brown, T. J., Tian, Q., Yang, Y., Wang, C., Xu, H., Liu, J., Gan, Y., & Lu, Z. (2020). Are long working hours associated with weight-related outcomes? A meta-analysis of observational studies. *Obesity Reviews, 21*(3), e12977. https://doi.org/10.1111/obr.12977

Zigler, E., & Gilman, E. (1991). The legacy of Jean Piaget. In G. A. Kimble & M. Wertheimer (Eds.), *Portraits of pioneers in psychology* (Vol. 3, Chap. 9). Psychology Press.

Zimmermann, P., & Iwanski, A. (2014). Emotion regulation from early adolescence to emerging adulthood and middle adulthood: Age differences, gender differences, and emotion-specific developmental variations. *International Journal of Behavioral Development, 38*(2), 182–194. https://doi.org/10.1177/0165025413515405.

Zinzow, H. M., Resnick, H. S., McCauley, J. L., Amstadter, A. B., Ruggiero, K. J., & Kilpatrick, D. G. (2012). Prevalence and risk of psychiatric disorders as a function of variant rape histories: Results from a national survey of women. *Social Psychiatry and Psychiatric Epidemiology, 47*(6), 893–902. https://doi.org/10.1007/s00127-011-0397-1

Zinzow, H. M., & Thompson, M. (2015). A longitudinal study of risk factors for repeated sexual coercion and assault in US college men. *Archives of Sexual Behavior, 44*(1), 213–222.

Ziv, Y., & Hotam, Y. (2015). Theory and measure in the psychological field: The case of attachment theory and the strange situation procedure. *Theory & Psychology, 25*(3), 274–291. https://doi.org/10.1177/0959354315577970

Zosuls, K. M., Andrews, N. C., Martin, C. L., England, D. E., & Field, R. D. (2016). Developmental changes in the link between gender typicality and peer victimization and exclusion. *Sex Roles, 75*(5), 243–256.

Zotcheva, E., Pintzka, C. W. S., Salvesen, Ø., Selbæk, G., Håberg, A. K., & Ernstsen, L. (2019). Associations of changes in cardiorespiratory fitness and symptoms of anxiety and depression with brain volumes: The HUNT study. *Frontiers in Behavioral Neuroscience, 13*, 53. https://doi.org/10.3389/fnbeh.2019.00053

Zreik, G., Oppenheim, D., & Sagi-Schwartz, A. (2017). Infant attachment and maternal sensitivity in the Arab minority in Israel. *Child Development, 88*(4), 1338–1349. https://doi.org/10.1111/cdev.12692

Zuber, S., & Kliegel, M. (2020). Prospective memory development across the lifespan. *European Psychologist, 25*(3). https://doi.org/10.1027/1016-9040/a000380

Zucker, J. K., & Patterson, M. M. (2018). Racial socialization practices among White American parents: Relations to racial attitudes, racial identity, and school diversity. *Journal of Family Issues, 39*(16), 3903–3930. https://doi.org/10.1177/0192513X18800766

Zueras, P., Rutigliano, R., & Trias-Llimós, S. (2020). Marital status, living arrangements, and mortality in middle and older age in Europe. *International Journal of Public Health, 65*(5), 627-636.

Zwaigenbaum, L., Bauman, M. L., Stone, W. L., Yirmiya, N., Estes, A., Hansen, R. L., McPartland, J. C., Natowicz, M. R., Choueiri, R., Fein, D., Kasari, C., Pierce, K., Buie, T., Carter, A., Davis, P. A., Granpeesheh, D., Mailloux, Z., Newschaffer, C., Robins, D., ... Wetherby, A. (2015). Early identification of autism spectrum disorder: Recommendations for practice and research. *Pediatrics, 136*(Supplement), S10–S40. https://doi.org/10.1542/peds.2014-3667C

Zwaigenbaum, L., Bryson, S. E., Brian, J., Smith, I. M., Sacrey, L., Armstrong, V., Roberts, W., Szatmari, P., Garon, N., Vaillancourt, T., & Roncadin, C. (2021). Assessment of autism symptoms from 6 to 18 months of age using the Autism Observation Scale for

Infants in a prospective high-risk cohort. *Child Development, 92*(3), 1187–1198. https://doi.org/10.1111/cdev.13485

Zwakman, M., Jabbarian, L. J., van Delden, J. J., van der Heide, A., Korfage, I. J., Pollock, K., Rietjens, J., Seymour, J., & Kars, M. C. (2018). Advance care planning: A systematic review about experiences of patients with a life-threatening or life-limiting illness. *Palliative Medicine, 32*(8), 1305–1321.

Zwar, L., Angermeyer, M. C., Matschinger, H., Riedel-Heller, S. G., König, H.-H., & Hajek, A. (2021). The importance of familiarity with caregiving for public caregiver stigma: Evidence from a cross-sectional study in Germany. *Archives of Gerontology and Geriatrics, 93*, 104301. https://doi.org/10.1016/j.archger.2020.104301

Zych, I., Baldry, A. C., Farrington, D. P., & Llorent, V. J. (2019). Are children involved in cyberbullying low on empathy? A systematic review and meta-analysis of research on empathy versus different cyberbullying roles. *Aggression and Violent Behavior, 45*, 83–97.

NAME INDEX

SUBJECT INDEX

Note: Page numbers followed by f indicate figures; those followed by t indicate tables. **Boldface** page numbers indicate key terms.